EMPLOYMENT, HOURS, AND EARNINGS

STATES AND AREAS

Fifth Edition
2010

EMPLOYMENT, HOURS, AND EARNINGS

STATES AND AREAS

Fifth Edition
2010

Edited by Sarah E. Baltic

Bernan Press

Lanham, MD

Published in the United States of America
by Bernan Press, a wholly owned subsidary of
The Rowman & Littlefield Publishing Group, Inc.
4501 Forbes Boulevard, Suite 200
Lanham, Maryland 20706

Bernan Press
800-865-3457
info@bernan.com
www.bernan.com

ISBN: 978-1-59888-419-7
eISBN: 978-1-59888-420-3

CONTENTS

PART B: METROPOLITAN STATISTICAL AREA DATA—*Continued*

PREFACE

Bernan Press is proud to present the fifth edition of *Employment, Hours, and Earnings: States and Areas, 2010.* This reference is a special edition of Bernan Press's *Handbook of U.S. Labor Statistics: Employment, Earnings, Prices, Productivity, and Other Labor Data.* It brings together a wealth of employment data compiled by the Bureau of Labor Statistics (BLS) and includes new data not presented in the previous editions.

Features of this publication include:

- Nearly 300 tables with data on employment for each state, the District of Columbia, and the nation's 75 largest metropolitan statistical areas (MSAs)

- Detailed industry data organized by month and on a non-seasonally adjusted basis

- Hours and earnings data are provided, where available, by industry for each state

- An introduction page for each state and the District of Columbia that emphasizes salient data and noteworthy trends, including data from the Local Area Unemployment Statistics (LAUS) program as well as an updated figure detailing employment by industry

- A ranking of the largest 75 MSAs that includes 2009 population estimates, 2009 unemployment rates, and the percent change in total nonfarm employment from 1990 to 2009.

- Concise technical notes that explain pertinent facts about the data, including sources, definitions, and significant changes; this section also provides references for further guidance on the subject

- An appendix that details the geographical components of the MSAs

The employment, hours, and earnings data in this publication provide a detailed and timely picture of the 50 states, the District of Columbia, and the nation's 75 largest MSAs. They can be used to analyze key factors affecting state and local economies and to compare national cyclical trends to local-level economic activity.

This reference is an excellent source of information for analysts in both the public and private sectors. Readers who are involved in public policy can use the data to determine the health of the economy, to clearly identify which sectors are growing and which are declining, and to determine the need for federal assistance. State and local jurisdictions can use the data to determine the need for services, including training and unemployment assistance, and for planning and budgetary purposes. In addition, the data can be used to forecast tax revenue. In private industry, the data can be used by business owners to compare their business to the economy as a whole. In particular, the data can be used to identify suitable locations when making decisions about plant locations and wholesale and retail trade outlets and for locating a particular sector base.

Sarah E. Baltic, associate editor with Bernan Press, received her bachelor's degree in magazine journalism from Syracuse University's S.I. Newhouse School of Public Communications and is a former magazine editor with *Voice of Youth Advocates.* Additionally, Ms. Baltic has worked in the publications field as a book acquisitions editor and a freelance magazine writer and editor. She has assisted with the *Social Security Handbook (Large Print Edition), County and City Extra,* and *The United States Government Internet Manual* and is currently working on *The Almanac of American Education;* all published by Bernan Press.

TECHNICAL NOTES

OVERVIEW

The fifth edition of *Employment, Hours, and Earnings: States and Areas* presents monthly and annual average data on employment for each state, the District of Columbia, and the nation's 75 largest metropolitan statistical areas (MSAs). In addition, hours and earnings data are provided, where available, for each state. The industry data are based on the North American Industry Classification System (NAICS), which is discussed in greater detail later in these notes. The employment data are presented on a monthly and annual basis for 1990 and 2000 through 2009. The hours and earnings data are available from 2007 through 2009.

The Bureau of Labor Statistics (BLS), the statistical agency within the U.S. Department of Labor, conducts the Current Employment Statistics (CES) survey to provide industry data on the employment, hours, and earnings of workers on nonfarm payrolls. The unemployment data and the civilian labor force estimates in this publication were obtained from the Local Area Unemployment Statistics (LAUS) program, which provides monthly employment and unemployment data for approximately 7,300 geographic areas including Census regions and divsions, states, counties, metropolitan areas, and many cities.

The data from both the CES and LAUS are derived from federal-state cooperative collection efforts in which state employment security agencies prepare data using concepts, definitions, and technical procedures prescribed by the BLS. Although the estimation of the two data sets are based on differing methodologies (described in more detail later in this section), their inclusion together in this reference is intended to provide a broad overview of state and local labor market conditions.

THE CURRENT EMPLOYMENT STATISTICS (CES) SURVEY–EMPLOYMENT, HOURS, AND EARNINGS DATA

The CES survey is a monthly survey commonly referred to as the establishment or payroll survey. Its estimates are derived from a sample of about 150,000 private nonfarm businesses and federal, state, and local government entities, which cover approximately 390,000 individual worksites in all 50 states, the District of Columbia, Puerto Rico, the U.S. Virgin Islands, and more than 300 metropolitan areas and divisions. These establishments are classified on the basis of their primary activity by major industry groupings in accordance with NAICS. For an establishment engaging in more than one activity, the entire establishment is included under the industry indicated as the principal activity.

All establishments with 1,000 employees or more are asked to participate in the survey, along with a representative sample of smaller businesses. Every month, the BLS Regional Data Collection Centers gather the data. Each firm is initially enrolled by telephone and the data is then collected for several months by a process called Computer Assisted Telephone Interviewing (CATI). Whenever possible, respondents are transferred to a self-reporting mode such as Touchtone Data Entry (TDE), fax, or Internet collection. Gathering data via the Internet is one of the fastest growing forms of data collection, but still remains a relatively small percentage of the total data collected each month. Electronic Data Interchange (EDI), in which each firm provides the BLS with an electronic file in a prescribed format, remains the most popular method for collecting data.

State estimation procedures are designed to produce accurate data for each individual state. The BLS independently develops the national series and does not force state estimates to sum to the national total. Because each state series is subject to larger sampling and nonsampling errors than the national series, summing them cumulates individual state level errors and can cause significant distortions at an aggregate level. As a result of these statistical limitations, the BLS does not compile a "sum of states" employment series, and cautions users that doing so may result in a series with a relatively large and volatile error structure.

More information on the exact methodology used to obtain data for employment, hours, and earnings was originally detailed in the *BLS Handbook of Methods*. The *Handbook* was updated in 2003 and can be found online at <http://www.bls.gov/opub/hom>. Information on the CES survey can also be found on the BLS Web site at <http://www.bls.gov/sae>.

CONCEPTS

Employment is the total number of persons employed either full or part-time in nonfarm business establishments during a specific payroll period. Temporary employees are included. Unpaid family members working in a family-owned business, domestic workers in private homes, and self-employed persons are all excluded from the CES. In addition, employees on layoff, on leave without pay, on strike for the entire pay period, or who had been hired but did not start work during the pay period are also excluded.

The reference period includes all persons who worked during, or received pay, for any part of the pay period that includes the 12th of the month, a standard for all federal agencies collecting employment data from business establishments. Workers who are on paid sick leave (when pay is received directly from the employer) or paid holiday or vacation, or who worked during only part of the specified pay period (because of unemployment or strike during the rest of the pay period) are counted as employed by the establishment survey. Employees on the payroll of more than one establishment during the pay period are counted in each establishment that reports them, whether the duplication is due to turnover or dual jobholding.

CES government employment statistics refer only to civilian government employees. Employees of the Central Intelligence Agency, the National Security Agency, the National Imagery and Mapping Agency, and the Defense Intelligence Agency are excluded.

Nonfarm employment includes employment in all goods-producing and service-providing industries. The goods-producing sector includes mining and logging, construction, and manufacturing, the last of which is made up of durable and non-durable goods (these breakdowns are not provided in this publication). The service-providing sector includes both private service-providing and government employment. Private service sector employment includes trade, transportation, and utilities (which is comprised of wholesale trade, retail trade, and transportation and utilities); information; financial activities; professional and business services; educational and health services; leisure and hospitality; and other services. Government employment encompasses federal-, state-, and local-level civilian employees. Subcategories of these industries are available on the BLS Web site at <http://www.bls.gov/sae>.

Unemployment consists of those who were not employed during the reference week but were available for work, except for temporary illness, and had made specific efforts to find employment some time during the 4-week period ending with the reference week. Persons who were waiting to be recalled to a job from which they had been laid off are classified as unemployed even if they have not been looking for another job.

The *unemployment rate* is the number of unemployed persons as a percent of the civilian labor force.

The *civilian labor force* consists of all persons classified as employed or unemployed as described above.

Hours and earnings data for each state are based on reports from industry payrolls and the corresponding hours paid for construction workers, production workers, and nonsupervisory workers. It includes workers who received pay for any part of the pay period that includes the 12th day of the month. Since not all sample respondents report production worker hours and earnings data, insufficient sample sizes preclude hours and earnings data from many sectors in many states. Therefore, the data available and thus published vary from state to state.

The payroll for these workers is reported before deductions of any kind including Social Security, unemployment insurance, group health insurance, withholding taxes, retirement plans, or union dues.

Included in the payroll report of earnings is pay for all hours worked, including overtime, shift premiums, vacations, holiday, and sick-leave pay. Bonuses and commissions are excluded unless they are earned and paid regularly each pay period. Benefits, such as health insurance and contribution to a retirement fund, are also excluded.

Hours include all hours worked (including overtime hours) and hours paid for holidays, vacations, and sick leave during the pay period that includes the 12th of the month. Average weekly hours differs from the concept of scheduled hours worked due to factors such as unpaid absenteeism, labor turnover, part-time work, and strikes, as well as fluctuations in work schedules. Average weekly hours are typically lower than scheduled hours of work.

Average hourly earnings are derived by dividing gross payrolls by total hours, reflecting the actual earnings of workers (including premium pay). They differ from wage rates, which are the amounts stipulated for a given unit of work or time. Average hourly earnings do not represent total labor costs per hour because they exclude retroactive payments and irregular bonuses, employee benefits, and the employer's share of payroll taxes. Earnings for employees not included in the production worker or nonsupervisory categories are not reflected in the estimates in this publication.

Average weekly earnings are derived by multiplying average weekly hours by average hourly earnings.

Users should note that in the context of historical data, long-term trends in hours and earnings data also reflect structural changes, such as the changing mixes of full-time and part-time employees and highly paid and lower-wage workers within businesses and across industries.

METROPOLITAN STATISTICAL AREAS (MSAS) AND NEW ENGLAND CITY AND TOWN AREAS (NECTAs)

A metropolitan statistical area (MSA) is a core area with a large population nucleus, combined with adjacent communities that have high degrees of economic and social integration with the core area. The standard definition of a MSA is determined by the Office of Management and Budget (OMB), which updates the definition based on the decennial census and updated information provided by the Census Bureau between the censuses.

New England city and town areas (NECTAs) are similar to MSAs, but are defined using cities and towns instead of counties in the six New England states. BLS only provides employment data on NECTAs in the New England region. Employment and Unemployment data are provided for the following NECTAs in this publication: Boston-Cambridge-Quincy, MA; Bridgeport-Stamford-Norwalk-CT; Hartford-West Hartford-East Hartford, CT; New Haven, CT; Providence-Fall River-Warwick, RI; Worcester, MA-CT; and Springfield, MA-CT. All other areas are MSAs.

The appendix that follows the tables details the geographic components for each MSA and NECTA.

REVISIONS TO THE DATA

North American Industry Classification System (NAICS)

The most far-reaching revision of the CES data occurred when the industrial classification system was changed from the 60-year-old Standard Industrial Classification (SIC) system to the North American Industry Classification System (NAICS) in January 2003. This changed how establishments were classified into industries in order to more accurately reflect the current composition of U.S. businesses. In March 2008, the CES state and area nonfarm payroll series was converted to the 2007 NAICS series. This resulted in relatively minor changes. NAICS was adopted as the standard measure of industry classification by statistical agencies in the United States, Canada, and Mexico in order to enhance the comparability of economic data across the North American Free Trade Association (NAFTA) trade area. These revisions were so profound as to preclude comparison between the present NAICS and the old SIC. BLS has thus not updated the SIC data nor (for the most part) linked the historical SIC data with the current NAICS data.

Benchmark Revisions

Employment estimates are adjusted annually to a complete count of jobs—called benchmarks—which are primarily derived from tax reports submitted by employers covered by state unemployment laws (which cover most establishments). In this re-anchoring of sample-based employment estimates to full population counts, the original sample-based estimates are replaced with the benchmark data from the previous year. The benchmark information is used to adjust monthly estimates between the new benchmark and the preceding benchmark, thereby preserving the continuity of the series and establishing the level of employment for the new benchmark month.

Seasonal Adjustment

Over the course of a year, the size of a state's employment level undergoes sharp fluctuations because of changes in the weather, reduced or expanded production, harvests, major holidays, and the like. Because these seasonal events follow a more or less regular pattern each year, adjusting the data on a month-to-month basis may eliminate their influence on data trends. These adjustments make it easier for users to observe the cyclical and other nonseasonal movements in the data series, but it must be noted that the seasonally adjusted series are only an approximation based on past experience. The seasonally adjusted data have a broader margin of error than the unadjusted data because they are subject to both sampling and other errors in the seasonal adjustment process. The data presented in this publication are not seasonally adjusted; therefore, the month-to-month variations in the data contain seasonal variations that may distort month-to-month comparisons. Data for the MSAs are also not seasonally adjusted, as the sample sizes do not allow for reliable estimates for seasonal adjustment factors.

THE LOCAL AREA UNEMPLOYMENT STATISTICS (LAUS) PROGRAM

The Local Area Unemployment Statistics (LAUS) program provides monthly and annual estimates on several labor force concepts including: employment, unemployment, labor force totals, and the employment-population ratio. As mentioned previously, the unemployment data as well as the civilian labor force estimates presented in this publication are from the LAUS program. The unemployment rate is shown for each state in 1990, 2000, and 2009 along with the rank for each state. The rankings are from lowest to highest. In 2009, unemployment ranged from a low of 4.3 percent in North Dakota to 13.6 percent in Michigan. Therefore, North Dakota is ranked first and Michigan is ranked 51st in 2009. Unemployment data are not available by industry.

The concepts and definitions underlying the LAUS program come from the Current Population Survey (CPS), the household survey conducted by the Census Bureau for the BLS. The LAUS models combine current and historical data from the CPS, the CES, and the State Unemployment Insurance (UI) Systems. There are numerous conceptual and technical differences between the household and establishment surveys, and estimates of monthly employment changes from these two surveys usually do not match in size or even direction. As a result, the unemployment data and the civilian labor force estimates on each state header page presented in this edition are not directly comparable to the employment data. However, this publication includes this information to provide complementary information on labor market conditions in each state and the District of Columbia. Monthly and annual data are available from the BLS on their Web site at <http://www.bls.gov/lau/>. More information on the differences between the surveys, as well as guidance on the complex methods used to obtain the LAUS data, is provided on the BLS Web site at <http://www.bls.gov/lau/laufaq.htm>.

PART A

STATE DATA

Population:
 1990 census: 4,040,389
 2000 census: 4,447,100
 2009 estimate: 4,708,708

Percent change in population:
 1990–2000: 10.1%
 2000–2009: 5.9%

Percent change in total nonfarm employment:
 1990–2009: 15.3%
 2008–2009: -5.3%

Industry with the largest growth in employment, 1990–2009 (thousands):
 Professional and Business Services, 87.5

Industry with the largest decline or smallest growth in employment, 1990–2009 (thousands):
 Manufacturing, -116.0

Civilian labor force:
 1990: 1,903,248
 2000: 2,154,545
 2009: 2,112,566

Unemployment rate and rank among states (lowest to highest):
 1990: 6.3%, 41st
 2000: 4.1%, 32nd
 2009: 10.1%, 37th

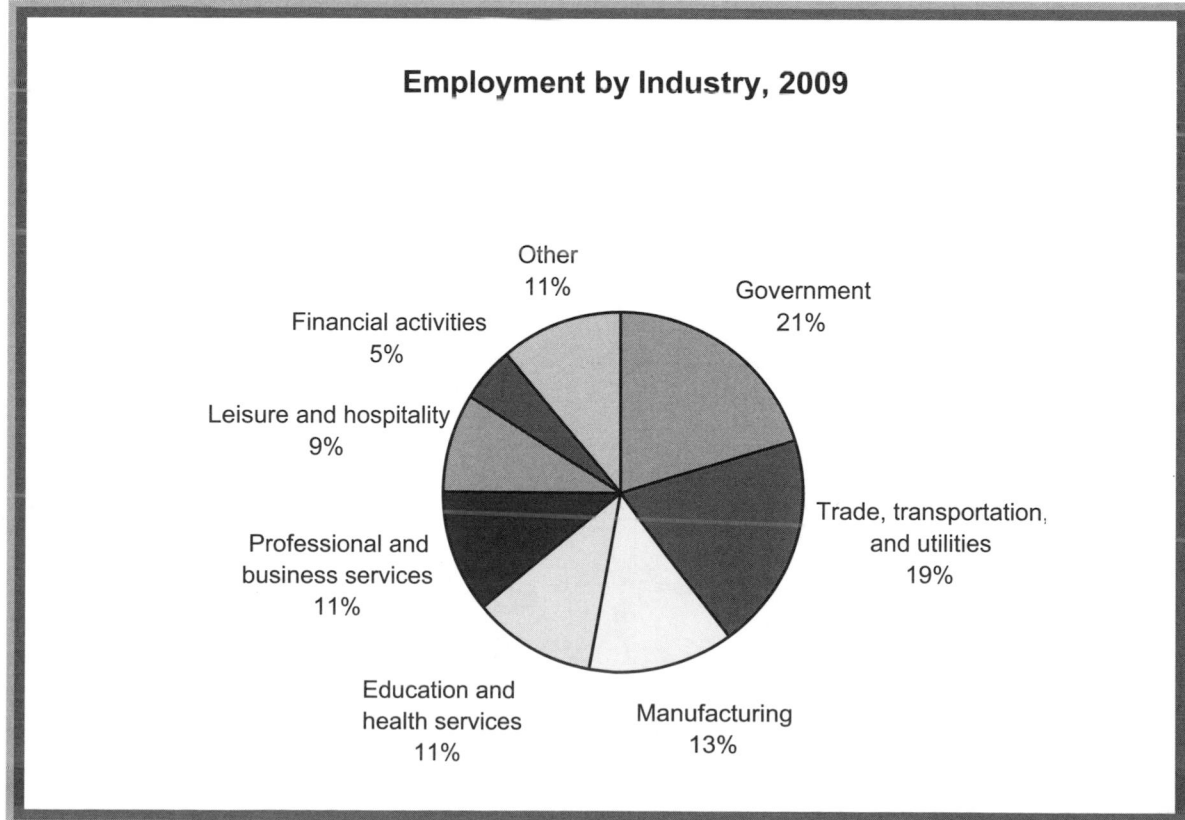

Employment by Industry, 2009

Other 11%
Financial activities 5%
Leisure and hospitality 9%
Professional and business services 11%
Education and health services 11%
Manufacturing 13%
Trade, transportation, and utilities 19%
Government 21%

Employment by Industry: Alabama, Selected Years, 1990–2009

(Numbers in thousands, not seasonally adjusted.)

Industry and year	January	February	March	April	May	June	July	August	September	October	November	December	Annual average
Total Nonfarm													
1990	1606.0	1608.0	1615.3	1635.3	1646.0	1647.8	1638.9	1632.8	1646.8	1648.7	1652.7	1651.0	1635.8
2000	1903.3	1910.4	1929.1	1931.3	1945.0	1941.0	1922.4	1928.7	1941.2	1936.3	1941.9	1943.7	1931.2
2001	1894.4	1903.9	1914.8	1919.6	1921.2	1918.6	1897.5	1905.2	1910.2	1903.5	1908.1	1907.9	1908.7
2002	1859.7	1868.4	1882.6	1888.3	1891.6	1886.1	1872.4	1879.8	1888.3	1889.9	1897.0	1894.8	1883.2
2003	1857.0	1864.0	1875.0	1879.1	1882.2	1875.8	1862.1	1869.3	1877.1	1883.7	1889.6	1891.8	1875.5
2004	1862.6	1872.4	1886.5	1899.3	1903.8	1908.8	1900.9	1903.9	1908.4	1915.6	1926.2	1932.4	1901.7
2005	1899.8	1910.5	1925.1	1943.1	1948.2	1951.4	1939.6	1947.9	1958.2	1961.9	1974.2	1979.2	1944.9
2006	1944.9	1956.1	1974.5	1978.5	1984.2	1994.6	1972.0	1981.0	1990.4	1984.2	1994.6	2000.1	1979.6
2007	1974.9	1987.3	2004.4	2000.9	2009.4	2018.4	1994.0	2004.4	2013.3	2012.4	2022.0	2026.7	2005.7
2008	1986.0	1994.5	2002.7	2008.7	2012.5	2012.1	1989.0	1991.1	1992.2	1981.3	1970.9	1964.4	1992.1
2009	1905.6	1899.9	1900.1	1900.7	1900.5	1894.5	1872.3	1870.4	1868.0	1872.2	1878.7	1866.0	1885.7
Total Private													
1990	1282.6	1282.3	1287.8	1304.6	1311.5	1326.3	1313.8	1322.8	1320.7	1317.8	1319.3	1320.0	1309.1
2000	1551.7	1556.0	1570.8	1574.7	1580.3	1592.6	1583.9	1592.0	1590.8	1583.0	1588.0	1589.8	1579.5
2001	1542.9	1548.5	1559.6	1564.4	1566.0	1570.1	1557.7	1563.8	1557.7	1547.8	1551.5	1551.3	1556.8
2002	1507.2	1512.5	1526.0	1530.0	1534.1	1534.8	1531.1	1537.2	1532.0	1529.7	1535.4	1533.4	1528.6
2003	1498.7	1502.0	1512.1	1515.7	1518.9	1521.4	1517.7	1522.9	1517.7	1521.1	1526.5	1530.3	1517.0
2004	1503.9	1510.7	1524.6	1536.5	1541.9	1550.0	1552.1	1553.3	1548.4	1553.9	1563.1	1569.2	1542.3
2005	1539.7	1547.5	1561.6	1578.3	1582.7	1587.2	1587.2	1592.8	1595.3	1594.5	1606.1	1611.4	1582.0
2006	1578.2	1587.1	1603.9	1606.4	1611.2	1622.4	1612.0	1618.4	1618.8	1610.3	1619.8	1624.8	1609.4
2007	1600.7	1610.7	1626.5	1622.5	1630.1	1639.3	1629.4	1635.8	1635.5	1632.0	1640.1	1644.9	1629.0
2008	1605.7	1610.4	1617.4	1622.1	1624.4	1624.2	1616.8	1616.1	1609.1	1593.7	1583.7	1576.6	1608.4
2009	1522.5	1514.7	1514.0	1512.3	1511.7	1506.8	1501.8	1497.5	1486.8	1487.1	1492.6	1480.6	1502.4
Goods-Producing													
1990	462.1	460.7	461.6	470.6	473.0	478.7	469.7	473.4	471.9	469.0	464.9	461.2	468.1
2000	469.5	469.5	472.3	472.2	472.5	476.7	471.9	475.0	473.3	467.6	465.7	464.6	470.9
2001	448.8	448.8	451.4	450.3	449.4	447.6	441.8	443.9	443.0	436.6	434.4	431.7	444.0
2002	420.1	419.9	422.5	422.3	423.5	422.2	418.9	421.9	421.4	420.1	418.3	415.7	420.6
2003	408.4	408.2	409.7	407.8	407.6	406.4	402.6	404.7	404.1	405.6	403.9	404.3	406.1
2004	398.3	400.1	402.7	404.5	405.9	407.0	409.0	408.3	409.2	412.1	412.1	412.4	406.8
2005	405.6	406.8	411.0	416.8	417.5	417.5	418.0	419.6	421.3	422.2	424.6	425.4	417.2
2006	421.6	423.7	427.6	427.9	428.0	430.5	427.7	427.2	426.6	423.3	422.3	422.6	425.8
2007	420.1	421.6	423.9	420.9	421.3	423.9	421.0	421.8	423.2	423.0	421.0	420.6	421.9
2008	413.2	412.5	412.1	411.1	411.2	411.1	409.0	406.0	404.6	397.1	389.8	386.1	405.3
2009	369.7	363.7	360.9	356.5	353.6	350.9	348.0	345.5	343.3	340.7	341.2	337.0	350.9
Mining and Logging													
1990	18.1	18.2	18.4	18.6	18.8	19.0	19.3	19.2	19.2	19.5	19.4	19.1	18.9
2000	14.6	14.4	14.4	13.8	13.7	13.8	13.7	13.7	13.7	13.7	13.7	13.6	13.9
2001	13.4	13.5	13.5	13.6	13.5	13.5	13.5	13.5	13.5	13.4	13.3	13.3	13.5
2002	13.2	13.1	13.2	13.0	13.0	13.0	12.9	13.0	12.9	12.6	12.5	12.5	12.9
2003	12.5	12.4	12.5	12.5	12.5	12.5	12.4	12.5	12.6	12.5	12.5	12.5	12.4
2004	12.2	12.2	12.2	12.2	12.3	12.4	12.4	12.5	12.6	12.7	12.6	12.7	12.4
2005	12.7	12.7	12.7	12.8	13.0	13.0	13.0	13.1	13.0	13.2	13.0	13.1	13.0
2006	13.0	13.1	13.1	13.0	13.0	13.2	13.1	13.1	13.2	12.9	13.0	13.1	13.1
2007	12.9	13.0	13.1	12.8	12.9	12.9	12.8	12.9	12.8	12.8	12.7	12.8	12.9
2008	12.5	12.6	12.6	12.6	12.4	12.5	12.6	12.6	12.7	12.6	12.5	12.5	12.6
2009	12.2	12.2	11.9	11.8	11.8	11.8	11.7	11.6	11.7	11.4	11.4	11.5	11.8
Construction													
1990	82.3	83.6	85.2	86.4	87.9	90.1	87.4	88.1	85.5	84.3	82.8	81.4	85.4
2000	101.1	101.7	103.6	104.6	105.0	106.8	107.3	108.3	109.4	107.2	106.6	105.9	105.6
2001	101.6	102.7	104.8	106.6	107.7	107.9	106.3	106.2	105.8	104.7	104.4	102.1	105.1
2002	96.8	98.3	100.5	99.7	100.9	100.0	100.3	101.4	102.1	102.7	101.1	99.2	100.3
2003	97.3	97.6	99.3	98.4	98.8	98.9	99.0	100.1	100.7	103.2	102.4	101.7	99.7
2004	99.6	101.2	103.0	102.4	102.6	102.6	104.1	103.1	103.2	104.9	104.0	103.3	102.8
2005	100.6	101.6	104.2	106.2	105.4	105.2	105.2	106.2	107.0	108.6	108.6	107.5	105.5
2006	105.1	106.2	109.5	110.2	110.2	111.1	110.4	111.0	111.7	111.1	111.0	110.2	109.8
2007	109.4	110.7	113.2	112.0	112.3	113.1	112.0	113.2	114.7	114.9	113.6	113.1	112.7
2008	109.5	110.0	110.4	110.3	110.9	110.7	110.1	109.0	108.8	105.9	103.8	102.3	108.5
2009	94.8	93.6	94.3	93.0	93.2	92.7	91.9	90.3	89.3	88.9	89.2	85.5	91.4
Manufacturing													
1990	361.7	358.9	358.0	365.6	366.3	369.6	363.0	366.1	367.2	365.2	362.7	360.7	363.8
2000	353.8	353.4	354.3	353.8	353.8	356.1	350.9	353.0	350.2	346.7	345.4	345.1	351.4
2001	333.8	332.6	333.1	330.1	328.2	326.2	322.0	324.2	323.7	318.5	316.7	316.3	325.5
2002	310.1	308.5	308.8	309.6	309.6	309.2	305.7	307.5	306.4	304.8	304.7	304.0	307.4
2003	298.6	298.2	297.9	296.9	296.3	295.0	291.2	292.1	290.8	289.9	289.0	290.1	293.8
2004	286.5	286.7	287.5	289.9	291.0	292.0	292.5	292.7	293.4	294.5	295.5	296.4	291.6
2005	292.3	292.5	294.1	297.8	299.1	299.3	299.7	300.4	301.1	300.6	302.9	304.8	298.7
2006	303.5	304.4	305.0	304.7	304.8	306.2	304.2	303.1	301.7	299.3	298.3	299.3	302.9
2007	297.8	297.9	297.6	296.1	296.1	297.9	296.2	295.7	295.7	295.3	294.7	294.7	296.3
2008	291.2	289.9	289.1	288.2	287.9	287.9	286.3	284.4	283.1	278.6	273.5	271.3	284.3
2009	262.7	257.9	254.7	251.7	248.6	246.4	244.4	243.6	242.3	240.4	240.6	240.0	247.8

Employment by Industry: Alabama, Selected Years, 1990–2009—*Continued*

(Numbers in thousands, not seasonally adjusted.)

Industry and year	January	February	March	April	May	June	July	August	September	October	November	December	Annual average
Service-Providing													
1990	1143.9	1147.3	1153.7	1164.7	1173.0	1169.1	1169.2	1159.4	1174.9	1179.7	1187.8	1189.8	1167.7
2000	1433.8	1440.9	1456.8	1459.1	1472.5	1464.3	1450.5	1453.7	1467.9	1468.7	1476.2	1479.1	1460.3
2001	1445.6	1455.1	1463.4	1469.3	1471.8	1471.0	1455.7	1461.3	1467.2	1466.9	1473.7	1476.2	1464.8
2002	1439.6	1448.5	1460.1	1466.0	1468.1	1463.9	1453.5	1457.9	1466.9	1469.8	1478.7	1479.1	1462.7
2003	1448.6	1455.8	1465.3	1471.3	1474.6	1469.4	1459.5	1464.6	1473.0	1478.1	1485.7	1487.5	1469.4
2004	1464.3	1472.3	1483.8	1494.8	1497.9	1501.8	1491.9	1495.6	1499.2	1503.5	1514.1	1520.0	1494.9
2005	1494.2	1503.7	1514.1	1526.3	1530.7	1533.9	1521.6	1528.3	1536.9	1539.7	1549.6	1553.8	1527.7
2006	1523.3	1532.4	1546.9	1550.6	1556.2	1564.1	1544.3	1553.8	1563.8	1560.9	1572.3	1577.5	1553.8
2007	1554.8	1565.7	1580.5	1580.0	1588.1	1594.5	1573.0	1582.6	1590.1	1589.4	1601.0	1606.1	1583.8
2008	1572.8	1582.0	1590.6	1597.6	1601.3	1601.0	1580.0	1585.1	1587.6	1584.2	1581.1	1578.3	1586.8
2009	1535.9	1536.2	1539.2	1544.2	1546.9	1543.6	1524.3	1524.9	1524.7	1531.5	1537.5	1529.0	1534.8
Trade, Transportation, and Utilities													
1990	314.6	311.6	312.4	313.2	315.0	319.0	317.8	319.8	319.3	318.5	323.7	327.7	317.7
2000	381.6	379.9	382.0	380.9	384.4	386.4	383.4	384.5	385.2	386.4	393.0	396.6	385.4
2001	379.9	377.7	379.9	379.4	380.8	382.3	378.5	379.0	377.3	378.3	384.8	387.6	380.5
2002	371.1	369.3	372.0	370.1	371.0	370.5	371.0	370.0	368.6	370.2	377.0	380.9	371.8
2003	366.0	364.2	367.1	368.1	369.2	370.7	372.2	372.9	371.9	374.4	379.5	383.5	371.6
2004	371.3	370.8	374.5	375.0	375.9	377.0	376.4	376.0	374.4	377.3	384.1	389.6	376.9
2005	376.6	376.0	378.3	380.5	381.6	382.9	382.4	382.8	382.5	383.3	391.2	396.3	382.9
2006	382.6	381.5	385.4	384.1	385.2	387.4	386.3	387.3	388.1	388.9	396.8	401.7	387.9
2007	387.8	387.5	391.8	390.8	394.4	396.2	395.2	394.8	395.1	394.9	402.6	406.0	394.8
2008	390.7	388.8	391.1	389.6	390.2	390.4	389.6	389.8	388.4	385.9	389.0	390.2	389.5
2009	371.3	367.5	366.8	364.7	365.7	365.3	363.5	362.4	361.6	364.1	367.3	366.9	365.6
Wholesale Trade													
1990	66.9	67.0	67.2	67.7	67.8	68.6	68.2	68.7	68.6	68.4	68.3	68.2	68.0
2000	83.4	83.6	84.1	83.6	84.1	84.5	84.3	84.6	84.6	84.7	84.9	85.1	84.3
2001	84.1	84.4	84.2	84.0	83.9	83.8	83.3	83.2	82.8	82.4	81.8	81.7	83.3
2002	79.9	79.5	79.5	78.7	78.6	78.6	78.5	78.5	78.4	78.0	78.2	78.4	78.7
2003	76.8	76.8	77.0	76.6	77.1	77.2	77.3	77.3	77.4	77.9	77.9	78.1	77.3
2004	76.9	77.0	77.6	78.1	78.3	78.6	78.7	78.7	78.5	79.0	78.8	79.1	78.3
2005	78.1	78.4	78.8	79.3	79.3	79.5	79.8	79.7	80.0	79.9	80.0	80.5	79.4
2006	79.9	80.3	81.0	81.0	81.5	81.9	81.9	82.0	82.1	81.9	82.1	82.5	81.5
2007	81.3	81.6	82.1	81.9	82.3	82.8	82.2	82.2	82.4	82.5	82.3	82.4	82.2
2008	80.8	80.8	81.0	81.0	81.3	81.3	80.9	80.8	80.7	80.4	79.5	79.1	80.6
2009	77.0	76.3	75.9	75.0	74.8	74.2	73.4	73.4	72.8	73.5	72.7	71.7	74.2
Retail Trade													
1990	190.0	186.9	187.3	187.8	189.0	191.2	191.0	192.6	192.4	191.7	197.4	201.3	191.6
2000	231.1	229.0	230.6	230.4	232.6	233.8	231.2	231.9	232.9	234.0	240.3	243.8	233.5
2001	229.2	226.0	227.9	227.4	228.6	229.7	227.0	227.4	226.5	228.1	235.5	238.2	229.3
2002	226.4	225.0	227.3	225.5	225.8	225.2	225.3	224.1	223.0	225.3	231.9	235.7	226.7
2003	223.5	222.2	224.8	226.6	226.6	227.7	228.7	229.6	228.7	230.7	236.0	239.7	228.7
2004	229.5	228.8	231.0	231.2	231.5	231.8	231.1	230.7	229.6	231.9	238.7	243.4	232.4
2005	232.7	231.5	233.1	234.3	234.9	235.4	234.6	235.2	234.3	234.7	242.4	246.3	235.8
2006	234.2	232.7	235.2	233.6	233.9	234.9	234.0	234.6	234.9	236.2	243.5	247.1	236.2
2007	236.4	235.7	238.9	238.5	240.8	241.7	241.5	241.0	240.7	240.7	248.0	250.5	241.2
2008	239.1	237.5	239.7	237.7	237.8	238.2	237.2	237.2	236.0	234.6	239.0	240.6	237.9
2009	227.5	224.7	224.7	224.3	225.1	225.4	224.7	223.4	223.4	224.2	228.6	229.5	225.5
Transportation and Utilities													
1990	57.7	57.7	57.9	57.7	58.2	59.2	58.6	58.5	58.3	58.4	58.0	58.2	58.2
2000	67.1	67.3	67.3	66.9	67.7	68.1	67.9	68.0	67.7	67.7	67.8	67.7	67.6
2001	66.6	67.3	67.8	68.0	68.3	68.8	68.2	68.4	68.0	67.8	67.5	67.7	67.9
2002	64.8	64.8	65.2	65.9	66.6	66.7	67.2	67.4	67.2	66.9	66.9	66.8	66.4
2003	65.7	65.2	65.3	64.9	65.5	65.8	66.2	66.0	65.8	65.8	65.6	65.7	65.6
2004	64.9	65.0	65.9	65.7	66.1	66.6	66.6	66.6	66.3	66.4	66.6	67.1	66.2
2005	65.8	66.1	66.4	66.9	67.4	68.0	68.0	67.9	68.2	68.7	68.8	69.5	67.6
2006	68.5	68.5	69.2	69.5	69.8	70.6	70.4	70.7	71.1	70.8	71.2	72.1	70.2
2007	70.1	70.2	70.8	70.4	71.3	71.7	71.5	71.6	72.0	71.7	72.3	73.1	71.4
2008	70.8	70.5	70.4	70.9	71.1	70.9	71.5	71.8	71.7	70.9	70.5	70.5	71.0
2009	66.8	66.5	66.2	65.4	65.8	65.7	65.4	65.6	65.4	66.4	66.0	65.7	65.9
Information													
1990	29.6	29.7	29.7	29.8	30.1	30.3	30.2	30.2	30.1	29.8	30.0	30.0	30.0
2000	32.4	32.5	33.0	32.9	33.2	33.7	34.2	34.5	34.4	34.6	34.8	35.2	33.8
2001	35.0	34.9	35.0	34.5	34.6	34.5	34.0	33.8	33.3	33.1	33.2	33.2	34.1
2002	32.9	32.6	32.8	32.5	32.4	32.4	32.3	31.9	31.4	31.4	31.4	31.3	32.1
2003	30.7	30.8	30.8	29.8	29.9	30.0	30.0	29.7	29.3	29.5	29.8	29.9	30.0
2004	29.5	29.4	29.5	29.6	29.6	29.7	29.7	29.5	29.3	29.3	29.5	29.6	29.5
2005	29.3	29.3	29.3	29.4	29.3	29.3	29.3	29.3	29.0	28.9	29.0	29.1	29.2
2006	28.7	28.7	28.8	28.7	28.8	28.8	28.5	28.4	28.2	28.1	28.2	28.3	28.5
2007	27.9	28.1	28.2	28.2	28.4	28.4	28.0	27.9	27.7	27.7	27.9	27.9	28.0
2008	27.4	27.3	27.3	27.3	27.3	27.1	26.9	26.8	26.4	26.2	26.2	26.3	26.9
2009	25.8	25.6	25.5	25.3	25.2	25.2	24.7	24.5	23.9	23.9	23.8	23.8	24.8

Employment by Industry: Alabama, Selected Years, 1990–2009—*Continued*

(Numbers in thousands, not seasonally adjusted.)

Industry and year	January	February	March	April	May	June	July	August	September	October	November	December	Annual average
Financial Activities													
1990	79.7	79.7	79.6	80.2	80.4	80.9	80.9	80.9	80.6	79.9	79.5	79.7	80.2
2000	97.3	97.3	98.0	98.5	98.7	99.3	100.0	100.0	99.4	99.4	99.4	99.8	98.9
2001	96.9	97.0	97.4	97.9	98.3	99.0	99.0	98.9	98.3	97.7	97.5	98.0	98.0
2002	96.8	96.4	96.7	97.3	97.6	97.8	97.9	97.8	97.0	97.0	96.8	97.2	97.2
2003	95.9	95.5	95.7	96.0	96.2	96.8	97.3	97.2	96.4	96.3	96.4	96.7	96.3
2004	95.6	95.9	96.2	96.5	96.8	97.7	97.7	97.8	97.2	97.7	97.7	97.9	97.1
2005	96.2	96.8	97.3	97.6	97.6	98.2	98.4	98.1	98.5	101.2	99.9	100.1	98.3
2006	97.1	98.3	98.5	98.4	98.8	99.4	99.1	99.1	98.9	98.8	99.1	99.7	98.8
2007	99.0	99.1	99.7	99.2	99.7	100.6	100.3	100.2	100.1	99.8	100.0	100.2	99.8
2008	98.8	99.2	99.2	99.2	99.2	99.6	99.8	99.7	99.2	99.0	98.4	98.2	99.1
2009	96.9	96.6	96.6	96.5	96.9	96.7	96.3	95.8	95.0	94.1	93.9	93.5	95.7
Professional and Business Services													
1990	111.3	112.3	113.9	116.1	116.1	118.7	117.6	118.9	119.2	120.7	120.5	120.8	117.2
2000	177.9	180.0	183.0	184.9	183.6	186.2	185.6	188.2	189.2	188.5	187.9	187.2	185.2
2001	183.2	185.3	187.7	187.7	186.6	188.3	187.5	190.0	189.0	187.4	185.4	184.8	186.9
2002	178.9	180.6	184.6	185.9	185.6	187.2	187.5	190.6	189.8	190.1	189.1	187.7	186.5
2003	184.1	185.8	187.4	188.2	188.2	188.7	187.9	189.5	189.3	189.5	190.3	190.3	188.3
2004	188.9	190.2	192.7	196.5	197.6	200.0	201.0	202.5	201.3	202.1	201.4	202.4	198.1
2005	200.1	202.9	204.2	206.8	206.3	207.8	209.7	212.0	213.5	214.7	215.4	214.9	209.0
2006	208.8	211.4	213.5	213.7	213.7	216.7	214.2	217.1	217.8	216.7	217.0	217.1	214.8
2007	215.4	218.1	221.1	219.8	219.9	221.7	218.8	221.8	222.4	222.2	223.7	224.8	220.8
2008	220.1	221.5	222.2	223.8	222.1	222.1	220.0	220.5	220.1	219.7	216.8	214.1	220.3
2009	205.6	205.3	204.7	205.8	203.8	203.1	205.3	205.4	202.9	204.2	206.7	204.0	204.7
Education and Health Services													
1990	125.2	126.4	126.9	127.4	127.2	126.8	126.5	127.6	129.8	131.6	132.9	133.4	128.5
2000	172.1	173.4	174.1	175.1	175.0	175.0	175.3	175.9	177.4	177.3	178.6	178.1	175.6
2001	171.8	174.8	174.9	176.9	176.3	175.8	175.9	176.8	179.1	179.8	182.5	182.4	177.3
2002	177.1	180.9	181.2	183.2	182.5	182.2	181.0	182.7	185.0	185.9	188.3	187.1	183.1
2003	184.4	186.2	186.5	187.7	187.4	185.7	185.6	185.8	186.6	188.1	190.0	189.3	186.9
2004	188.0	189.4	190.0	192.3	191.7	191.7	191.9	192.9	194.3	195.1	197.7	197.7	192.7
2005	196.0	197.3	198.2	199.4	200.1	199.1	199.2	200.3	202.6	200.7	202.2	201.8	199.7
2006	199.6	200.4	202.1	203.2	203.8	203.1	202.0	203.9	205.3	205.5	207.5	206.5	203.6
2007	204.8	206.6	207.5	207.8	208.3	207.8	207.3	209.8	210.1	210.5	211.4	212.1	208.7
2008	208.2	210.1	210.7	211.1	211.8	210.4	210.0	211.6	212.3	212.8	212.3	211.8	211.1
2009	209.2	209.8	209.9	210.8	211.4	209.2	208.8	210.4	210.2	212.0	213.8	212.1	210.6
Leisure and Hospitality													
1990	100.2	101.8	103.3	106.5	108.5	110.2	109.7	110.3	108.0	106.6	106.2	105.8	106.4
2000	141.8	143.5	147.3	149.1	151.7	153.6	151.8	152.4	150.5	147.8	147.3	146.7	148.6
2001	143.1	145.3	148.8	152.6	154.8	157.1	155.4	155.5	152.2	149.8	148.9	149.0	151.0
2002	144.3	146.2	149.2	151.9	154.6	155.9	156.3	156.2	153.5	150.3	150.1	149.6	151.5
2003	146.1	148.0	151.5	154.5	156.4	158.6	158.3	159.3	157.1	154.9	154.4	154.3	154.4
2004	151.2	153.5	157.2	160.2	162.2	164.1	164.1	164.2	161.3	159.1	159.4	158.4	159.6
2005	155.1	157.5	162.0	166.4	168.5	170.4	168.7	169.6	167.2	163.6	163.9	163.6	164.7
2006	160.3	163.3	167.6	170.1	172.6	174.9	173.5	174.8	173.4	169.0	168.8	168.7	169.8
2007	165.8	169.2	172.9	174.6	176.7	178.9	177.6	178.5	176.1	172.9	172.3	171.9	174.0
2008	166.3	169.2	172.7	177.8	180.3	181.2	179.3	179.9	176.6	171.8	170.3	169.3	174.6
2009	163.8	166.0	169.2	172.4	174.6	175.7	174.5	173.4	170.2	168.6	167.3	164.0	170.0
Other Services													
1990	59.9	60.1	60.4	60.8	61.2	61.7	61.4	61.7	61.8	61.7	61.6	61.4	61.1
2000	79.1	79.9	81.1	81.1	81.2	81.7	81.7	81.5	81.4	81.4	81.3	81.6	81.1
2001	84.2	84.7	84.5	85.1	85.2	85.5	85.6	85.9	85.5	85.1	84.8	84.6	85.1
2002	86.0	86.6	87.0	86.8	86.9	86.6	86.2	86.1	85.3	84.7	84.4	83.9	85.9
2003	83.1	83.3	83.4	83.6	84.0	84.5	83.8	83.8	83.0	82.8	82.2	82.0	83.2
2004	81.1	81.4	81.8	81.9	82.2	82.8	82.3	82.1	81.4	81.2	81.2	81.2	81.7
2005	80.8	80.9	81.3	81.4	81.8	82.0	81.5	81.1	80.7	79.9	79.9	80.2	81.0
2006	79.5	79.8	80.4	80.3	80.3	81.6	80.7	80.6	80.5	80.0	80.1	80.2	80.3
2007	79.9	80.5	81.4	81.2	81.4	81.8	81.2	81.0	80.8	81.0	81.2	81.4	81.1
2008	81.0	81.8	82.1	82.2	82.3	82.3	82.2	81.8	81.5	81.2	80.9	80.6	81.7
2009	80.2	80.2	80.4	80.3	80.5	80.7	80.7	80.1	79.7	79.5	78.6	79.3	80.0
Government													
1990	323.4	325.7	327.5	330.7	334.5	321.5	325.1	310.0	326.1	330.9	333.4	331.0	326.7
2000	351.6	354.4	358.3	356.6	364.7	348.4	338.5	336.7	350.4	353.3	353.9	353.9	351.7
2001	351.5	355.4	355.2	355.2	355.2	348.5	339.8	341.4	352.5	355.7	356.6	356.6	352.0
2002	352.5	355.9	356.6	358.3	357.5	351.3	341.3	342.6	356.3	360.2	361.6	361.4	354.6
2003	358.3	362.0	362.9	363.4	363.3	354.4	344.4	346.4	359.4	362.6	363.1	361.5	358.4
2004	358.7	361.7	361.9	362.8	361.9	358.8	348.8	350.6	360.0	361.7	363.1	363.2	359.4
2005	360.1	363.0	363.5	364.8	365.5	364.2	352.4	355.1	362.9	367.4	368.1	367.8	362.9
2006	366.7	369.0	370.6	372.1	373.0	372.2	360.0	362.6	371.6	373.9	374.8	375.3	370.2
2007	374.2	376.6	377.9	378.4	379.3	379.1	364.6	368.6	377.8	380.4	381.9	381.8	376.7
2008	380.3	384.1	385.3	386.6	388.1	387.9	372.2	375.0	383.1	387.6	387.2	387.8	383.8
2009	383.1	385.2	386.1	388.4	388.8	387.7	370.5	372.9	381.2	385.1	386.1	385.4	383.4

Average Weekly Hours by Selected Industry: Alabama, 2007–2009

(Not seasonally adjusted.)

Industry and year	January	February	March	April	May	June	July	August	September	October	November	December	Annual average
Total Private													
2007	36.2	36.2	36.6	36.9	36.8	36.7	36.7	36.7	36.8	36.5	36.6	36.8	36.6
2008	36.0	36.1	36.3	36.1	36.2	36.6	36.0	36.1	36.2	35.6	35.7	35.3	36.0
2009	34.8	35.2	35.1	34.8	34.7	35.1	34.6	35.1	34.6	34.6	34.9	34.7	34.9
Goods-Producing													
2007	41.1	40.4	41.3	41.3	41.5	41.4	41.1	41.7	41.7	41.4	41.6	41.9	41.4
2008	41.1	41.0	41.5	41.4	40.9	41.5	40.6	40.6	40.9	40.4	40.1	39.1	40.8
2009	38.4	39.0	39.1	38.9	38.8	39.2	38.7	39.3	38.6	38.9	39.2	39.3	39.0
Construction													
2007	41.7	41.6	41.7	41.6	41.6	41.8	41.8	41.7	41.7	41.8	41.7	41.6	41.7
2008	41.5	41.6	41.7	41.8	41.6	41.8	41.7	41.6	41.6	41.4	41.3	41.3	41.6
2009	41.2	41.4	41.2	41.1	41.0	41.1	41.0	41.1	41.0	41.0	40.9	40.8	41.1
Manufacturing													
2007	41.8	41.8	41.8	41.9	41.8	41.9	41.9	41.9	41.8	41.7	41.7	41.8	41.8
2008	41.7	41.6	41.7	41.8	41.6	41.7	41.6	41.6	41.5	41.4	41.3	41.4	41.6
2009	41.3	41.4	41.3	41.3	41.2	41.1	41.1	41.2	41.0	41.1	41.2	41.3	41.2
Trade, Transportation, and Utilities													
2007	36.0	36.0	36.1	36.1	36.0	36.0	36.1	35.9	36.1	36.0	36.0	36.1	36.0
2008	36.0	36.1	36.1	36.0	36.2	36.3	36.1	36.3	36.1	36.2	36.1	36.3	36.2
2009	36.1	36.3	36.4	36.2	36.3	36.5	36.3	36.5	36.3	36.2	36.2	36.4	36.3
Financial Activities													
2007	38.4	38.3	38.2	38.9	38.2	38.4	38.5	38.6	38.9	38.2	38.3	38.6	38.5
2008	37.2	37.2	37.8	37.7	37.5	37.9	37.4	37.2	37.5	37.1	37.3	36.5	37.4
2009	36.8	36.6	36.6	36.4	37.4	36.9	36.1	36.8	36.7	36.5	37.1	36.6	36.7
Professional and Business Services													
2007	35.1	35.0	35.4	35.4	35.3	35.4	35.5	35.6	35.6	35.4	35.3	35.4	35.4
2008	35.3	35.5	35.7	35.5	35.6	35.7	35.5	35.7	35.8	35.6	35.8	35.7	35.6
2009	35.8	35.9	36.0	36.2	36.1	36.3	36.1	36.2	36.0	36.0	36.1	36.0	36.1
Education and Health Services													
2007	36.7	37.0	36.5	36.7	36.3	36.2	36.1	36.0	36.1	35.9	36.2	36.4	36.3
2008	35.6	35.7	35.7	35.7	35.6	35.8	35.7	35.8	35.7	35.3	35.5	35.5	35.6
2009	35.3	35.5	35.0	34.7	34.4	34.3	34.4	34.8	34.4	34.5	34.8	34.5	34.7
Leisure and Hospitality													
2007	26.2	26.0	26.0	26.2	26.4	26.7	26.5	27.0	26.8	27.0	26.9	26.9	26.6
2008	25.9	26.0	26.1	26.2	26.2	26.5	26.3	25.7	25.9	25.6	25.8	25.7	26.0
2009	25.3	25.5	25.5	25.6	25.8	26.7	26.2	26.4	26.0	26.3	26.5	26.3	26.0
Other Services													
2007	31.4	31.8	31.4	31.7	31.6	31.9	31.7	32.6	32.8	32.4	32.4	32.5	32.0
2008	31.3	31.3	31.1	31.2	31.1	31.4	31.0	31.4	30.5	30.5	30.8	30.6	31.0
2009	30.0	30.3	30.7	30.9	31.7	30.9	31.0	31.3	30.2	30.4	30.3	28.9	30.6

Average Hourly Earnings by Selected Industry: Alabama, 2007–2009

(Dollars, not seasonally adjusted.)

Industry and year	January	February	March	April	May	June	July	August	September	October	November	December	Annual average
Total Private													
2007	19.25	19.29	19.40	19.53	19.42	19.36	19.35	19.29	19.37	19.25	19.34	19.56	19.37
2008	19.27	19.37	19.39	19.29	19.49	19.53	19.47	19.60	19.67	19.83	20.00	19.87	19.56
2009	19.82	19.87	19.57	19.69	19.64	19.42	19.44	19.59	19.66	19.70	19.86	19.87	19.68
Goods-Producing													
2007	19.59	19.56	19.83	19.87	19.81	19.88	19.63	19.75	19.84	19.80	19.88	20.14	19.80
2008	19.85	19.77	19.82	19.86	20.15	19.94	20.00	20.28	20.36	20.55	20.75	20.88	20.17
2009	20.84	21.01	20.94	21.07	20.87	20.91	21.09	20.92	21.20	21.20	21.32	21.22	21.05
Construction													
2007	18.05	18.08	18.04	18.03	18.05	18.12	18.16	18.04	18.08	18.11	18.03	18.00	18.07
2008	17.97	18.02	18.10	18.29	18.16	18.23	18.20	18.16	18.20	18.06	18.04	18.06	18.13
2009	17.97	18.20	18.13	18.04	17.94	18.04	18.04	18.07	18.03	18.08	18.05	18.00	18.05
Manufacturing													
2007	20.54	20.56	20.52	20.56	20.52	20.66	20.61	20.55	20.55	20.50	20.56	20.60	20.56
2008	20.52	20.49	20.52	20.55	20.50	20.59	20.55	20.50	20.46	20.40	20.38	20.40	20.49
2009	20.35	20.40	20.38	20.44	20.37	20.32	20.37	20.43	20.34	20.38	20.41	20.45	20.39
Trade, Transportation, and Utilities													
2007	16.65	16.58	16.68	16.67	16.62	16.60	16.64	16.58	16.61	16.55	16.61	16.65	16.62
2008	16.59	16.65	16.68	16.64	16.78	16.84	16.79	16.86	16.73	16.84	16.72	16.95	16.76
2009	16.80	16.93	16.97	16.86	16.96	17.12	17.03	17.14	17.05	17.00	17.06	17.12	17.00
Financial Activities													
2007	19.96	20.12	19.81	20.39	20.23	20.67	20.74	20.96	21.15	20.55	20.66	20.63	20.49
2008	20.11	20.02	20.24	20.26	20.32	20.34	20.27	20.32	20.41	20.36	20.31	20.34	20.28
2009	20.33	20.47	20.48	20.54	20.22	20.49	20.70	20.68	20.76	20.79	20.72	20.76	20.58
Professional and Business Services													
2007	23.11	23.18	23.28	23.34	23.24	23.29	23.32	23.36	23.42	23.36	23.34	23.38	23.30
2008	23.33	23.40	23.46	23.38	23.49	23.51	23.43	23.51	23.55	24.26	24.48	24.44	23.68
2009	24.48	24.52	24.55	24.67	24.56	24.65	24.54	24.59	24.50	24.51	24.59	24.53	24.56
Education and Health Services													
2007	20.02	20.28	20.21	20.20	20.18	20.19	20.14	19.94	20.02	20.03	20.16	20.18	20.13
2008	19.67	19.83	19.89	19.83	19.66	19.86	19.76	19.69	19.76	19.70	19.68	19.52	19.74
2009	19.40	19.42	19.26	19.39	19.60	19.52	19.51	19.79	19.80	19.82	19.81	19.85	19.60
Leisure and Hospitality													
2007	9.75	9.72	9.88	9.80	9.74	9.48	9.61	9.80	9.70	9.73	9.80	9.89	9.74
2008	9.91	9.97	10.04	10.04	9.97	10.03	10.08	10.03	10.04	10.12	10.05	10.10	10.03
2009	9.95	10.06	10.05	10.08	10.17	10.17	10.15	10.23	10.28	10.30	10.25	10.24	10.16
Other Services													
2007	17.29	17.67	17.76	17.86	17.86	17.86	17.19	17.30	17.40	17.29	17.29	17.24	17.50
2008	16.46	16.52	16.41	16.43	16.40	16.53	16.41	16.39	16.25	16.23	16.79	16.44	16.44
2009	16.20	16.28	16.09	16.09	15.58	15.40	15.65	15.58	15.77	15.77	15.89	15.84	15.84

Average Weekly Earnings by Selected Industry: Alabama, 2007–2009

(Dollars, not seasonally adjusted.)

Industry and year	January	February	March	April	May	June	July	August	September	October	November	December	Annual average
Total Private													
2007	696.85	698.30	710.04	720.66	714.66	710.51	710.15	707.94	712.82	702.63	707.84	719.81	708.94
2008	693.72	699.26	703.86	696.37	705.54	714.80	700.92	707.56	712.05	705.95	714.00	701.41	704.16
2009	689.74	699.42	686.91	685.21	681.51	681.64	672.62	687.61	680.24	681.62	693.11	689.49	686.83
Goods-Producing													
2007	805.15	790.22	818.98	820.63	822.12	823.03	806.79	823.58	827.33	819.72	827.01	843.87	819.72
2008	815.84	810.57	822.53	822.20	824.14	827.51	812.00	823.37	832.72	830.22	832.08	816.41	822.94
2009	800.26	819.39	818.75	819.62	809.76	819.67	816.18	822.16	818.32	824.68	835.74	833.95	820.95
Construction													
2007	752.69	752.13	752.27	750.05	750.88	757.42	759.09	752.27	753.94	757.00	751.85	748.80	753.52
2008	745.76	749.63	754.77	764.52	755.46	762.01	758.94	755.46	757.12	747.68	745.05	745.88	754.21
2009	740.36	753.48	746.96	741.44	735.54	741.44	739.64	742.68	739.23	741.28	738.25	734.40	741.86
Manufacturing													
2007	858.57	859.41	857.74	861.46	857.74	865.65	863.56	861.05	858.99	854.85	857.35	861.08	859.41
2008	855.68	852.38	855.68	858.99	852.80	858.60	854.88	852.80	849.09	844.56	841.69	844.56	852.38
2009	840.46	844.56	841.69	844.17	839.24	835.15	837.21	841.72	833.94	837.62	840.89	844.59	840.07
Trade, Transportation, and Utilities													
2007	599.40	596.88	602.15	601.79	598.32	597.60	600.70	595.22	599.62	595.80	597.96	601.07	598.32
2008	597.24	601.07	602.15	599.04	607.44	611.29	606.12	612.02	603.95	609.61	603.59	615.29	606.71
2009	606.48	614.56	617.71	610.33	615.65	624.88	618.19	625.61	618.92	615.40	617.57	623.17	617.10
Financial Activities													
2007	766.46	770.60	756.74	793.17	772.79	793.73	798.49	809.06	822.74	785.01	791.28	796.32	788.87
2008	748.09	744.74	765.07	763.80	762.00	770.89	758.10	755.90	765.38	755.36	757.56	742.41	758.47
2009	748.14	749.20	749.57	747.66	756.23	756.08	747.27	761.02	761.89	758.84	768.71	759.82	755.29
Professional and Business Services													
2007	811.16	811.30	824.11	826.24	820.37	824.47	827.86	831.62	833.75	826.94	823.90	827.65	824.82
2008	823.55	830.70	837.52	829.99	836.24	839.31	831.77	839.31	843.09	863.66	876.38	872.51	843.01
2009	876.38	880.27	883.80	893.05	886.62	894.80	885.89	890.16	882.00	882.36	887.70	883.08	886.62
Education and Health Services													
2007	734.73	750.36	737.67	741.34	732.53	730.88	727.05	717.84	722.72	719.08	729.79	734.55	730.72
2008	700.25	707.93	710.07	707.93	699.90	710.99	705.43	704.90	705.43	695.41	698.64	692.96	702.74
2009	684.82	689.41	674.10	672.83	674.24	669.54	671.14	688.69	681.12	683.79	689.39	684.83	680.12
Leisure and Hospitality													
2007	255.45	252.72	256.88	256.76	257.14	253.12	254.67	264.60	259.96	262.71	263.62	266.04	259.08
2008	256.67	259.22	262.04	263.05	261.21	265.80	265.10	257.77	260.04	259.07	259.29	259.57	260.78
2009	251.74	256.53	256.28	258.05	262.39	271.54	265.93	270.07	267.28	270.89	271.63	269.31	264.16
Other Services													
2007	542.91	561.91	557.66	566.16	564.38	569.73	544.92	563.98	570.72	560.20	560.20	560.30	560.00
2008	515.20	517.08	510.35	512.62	510.04	519.04	508.71	514.65	495.63	495.02	517.13	503.06	509.64
2009	486.00	493.28	493.96	497.18	493.89	475.86	485.15	487.65	476.25	479.41	481.47	457.78	484.70

ALASKA
At a Glance

Population:
    1990 census: 550,043
    2000 census: 626,932
    2009 estimate: 698,473

Percent change in population:
    1990–2000: 14.0%
    2000–2009: 11.4%

Percent change in total nonfarm employment:
    1990–2009: 35%
    2008–2009: -0.3%

Industry with the largest growth in employment, 1990–2009 (thousands):
    Education and Health Services, 22.5

Industry with the largest decline or smallest growth in employment, 1990–2009 (thousands):
    Manufacturing, -1.1

Civilian labor force:
    1990: 270,040
    2000: 319,002
    2009: 360,877

Unemployment rate and rank among states (lowest to highest):
    1990: 7.0%, 48th
    2000: 6.2%, 51st
    2009: 8.0%, 21st

Employment by Industry, 2009

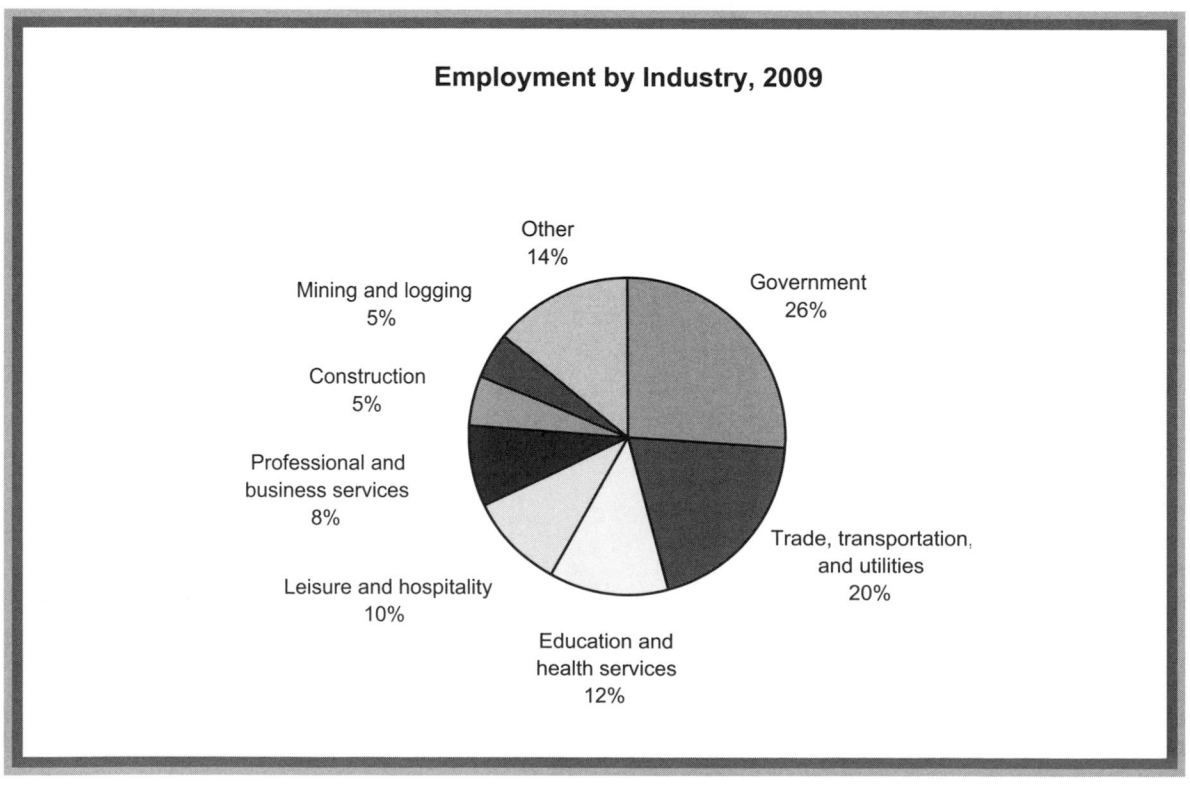

Other 14%
Mining and logging 5%
Construction 5%
Professional and business services 8%
Leisure and hospitality 10%
Education and health services 12%
Trade, transportation, and utilities 20%
Government 26%

Employment by Industry: Alaska, Selected Years, 1990–2009

(Numbers in thousands, not seasonally adjusted.)

Industry and year	January	February	March	April	May	June	July	August	September	October	November	December	Annual average
Total Nonfarm													
1990	213.9	220.5	225.4	232.8	240.6	252.7	257.2	256.6	249.4	240.0	234.7	233.1	238.0
2000	260.9	268.2	271.7	276.0	288.5	298.5	305.4	304.8	297.5	284.3	275.7	274.4	283.8
2001	264.8	274.2	276.8	281.9	293.4	303.8	311.7	312.4	305.1	290.4	280.2	277.3	289.3
2002	271.1	280.3	283.5	287.0	297.7	308.5	315.1	315.8	309.8	297.3	287.9	286.0	295.0
2003	278.2	284.5	287.5	290.2	303.8	314.7	319.9	320.5	314.7	299.6	290.5	288.5	299.4
2004	283.3	286.8	291.2	295.2	306.3	318.9	327.1	325.9	320.6	305.6	296.0	294.3	304.3
2005	288.6	293.0	296.3	301.3	313.5	325.4	333.4	333.1	325.5	308.7	301.2	297.1	309.8
2006	291.4	298.0	302.4	307.3	319.8	336.9	337.8	337.6	330.3	311.4	305.0	301.8	315.0
2007	296.3	303.0	305.8	309.9	322.1	336.6	339.8	340.4	332.2	315.5	308.2	304.9	317.9
2008	300.4	306.1	308.5	313.0	327.2	341.0	346.3	345.5	337.3	319.1	311.7	309.1	322.1
2009	302.7	307.7	309.0	313.6	322.9	338.2	343.7	342.6	334.4	320.0	311.8	307.2	321.2
Total Private													
1990	145.8	149.5	153.7	160.3	168.9	181.9	187.9	187.3	177.4	167.6	163.1	161.1	167.0
2000	188.2	193.7	195.8	200.0	210.9	225.0	234.0	233.4	223.1	208.7	200.3	198.9	209.3
2001	189.1	195.9	197.6	201.6	212.1	225.7	236.1	236.3	225.1	209.5	199.7	197.1	210.5
2002	193.4	199.8	202.2	204.9	215.6	228.2	239.3	238.4	227.8	215.1	205.7	202.9	214.4
2003	198.2	202.4	204.5	206.9	220.0	233.0	243.0	242.7	232.0	216.9	208.2	206.1	217.8
2004	202.4	205.0	208.2	212.1	223.6	238.5	250.4	248.6	239.0	223.0	213.7	211.6	223.0
2005	208.3	211.0	213.8	218.0	230.2	245.1	257.2	255.9	243.8	226.1	218.7	215.0	228.6
2006	212.4	215.9	219.6	223.7	236.1	254.5	261.4	259.9	247.8	228.8	222.7	219.7	233.5
2007	216.9	220.5	222.6	226.2	238.4	255.5	263.5	262.9	249.6	231.7	224.9	221.8	236.2
2008	219.4	223.1	225.2	228.4	243.7	258.3	268.4	266.2	253.2	234.5	227.3	225.2	239.4
2009	220.5	223.5	224.7	227.3	238.9	253.3	263.8	261.8	248.7	233.7	225.7	221.5	237.0
Goods-Producing													
1990	27.4	29.4	31.9	35.9	39.1	45.2	51.3	49.6	42.8	37.2	34.5	32.7	38.0
2000	28.5	32.1	32.5	34.2	36.5	41.4	49.0	48.2	43.4	37.7	32.5	30.2	37.1
2001	29.9	35.0	35.5	35.6	37.2	41.7	49.9	49.4	44.6	38.4	32.4	29.8	38.3
2002	30.9	35.0	35.3	34.5	36.2	40.9	48.9	47.9	43.6	39.2	33.8	31.0	38.1
2003	31.1	34.7	35.3	33.8	37.2	43.3	50.9	49.5	44.7	39.8	34.0	31.0	38.8
2004	33.7	35.0	35.6	35.6	38.3	44.8	53.2	50.8	46.0	40.6	35.2	32.3	40.1
2005	35.3	36.6	37.6	37.7	39.8	46.1	54.7	53.5	47.9	42.1	37.4	34.1	41.9
2006	36.3	38.2	39.3	40.0	41.7	50.6	56.6	54.9	49.3	43.6	39.2	35.8	43.8
2007	38.0	39.7	40.0	40.6	42.1	50.0	57.3	56.2	50.5	45.0	40.2	37.0	44.7
2008	38.6	40.7	41.2	41.1	43.8	51.2	58.5	57.1	51.3	45.1	40.1	37.7	45.5
2009	38.8	40.7	41.0	41.1	42.6	50.3	57.9	55.6	48.1	42.8	38.5	34.7	44.3
Mining and Logging													
1990	11.1	11.5	12.5	13.6	14.4	16.0	16.2	16.4	15.5	14.9	14.0	13.2	14.1
2000	8.9	10.1	10.3	10.4	10.9	11.2	11.7	12.1	12.8	11.8	11.4	11.5	11.0
2001	10.5	11.5	11.6	11.8	12.0	12.3	12.2	12.1	12.0	11.8	11.2	10.7	11.6
2002	10.5	10.7	10.8	11.1	10.9	11.1	11.6	11.5	11.2	11.1	10.8	10.5	11.0
2003	10.0	10.2	10.3	10.2	10.4	10.3	10.4	10.4	10.3	10.0	9.8	9.7	10.2
2004	9.4	9.7	9.9	10.2	10.3	10.4	10.5	10.6	10.3	10.1	10.0	10.1	10.1
2005	9.9	10.3	10.5	10.4	10.5	10.8	11.1	11.2	11.2	11.3	11.3	11.3	10.8
2006	11.0	11.4	11.5	12.1	12.4	12.8	12.7	12.9	12.9	12.8	12.8	12.9	12.4
2007	12.9	13.2	13.3	13.5	13.6	14.1	14.3	14.5	14.5	14.5	14.2	14.3	13.9
2008	14.2	14.5	14.7	14.8	15.1	15.5	15.7	16.0	16.0	15.9	15.7	16.1	15.4
2009	15.4	15.6	15.5	15.4	15.5	15.8	15.3	15.4	15.0	15.0	14.7	14.6	15.3
Construction													
1990	6.8	7.0	7.6	8.5	9.9	11.9	12.3	12.7	12.5	11.1	9.6	8.5	9.8
2000	11.1	11.5	11.8	12.5	14.3	16.6	17.0	17.7	16.6	15.8	13.3	12.5	14.2
2001	10.9	11.5	12.1	13.3	14.9	17.2	18.2	19.0	18.1	16.8	14.1	13.1	14.9
2002	12.2	12.4	12.8	13.4	15.8	18.1	19.0	19.6	18.9	17.7	15.5	14.3	15.8
2003	12.5	12.7	13.1	14.6	17.4	19.3	20.4	21.0	20.5	19.2	16.8	15.5	16.9
2004	13.7	13.8	14.1	15.3	17.7	20.1	21.4	21.7	21.0	19.6	17.5	16.2	17.7
2005	14.6	14.7	15.3	17.1	19.0	21.1	22.3	22.8	21.7	20.2	17.6	16.3	18.6
2006	14.5	14.7	15.3	16.6	18.8	21.0	21.4	21.5	21.0	19.8	17.4	16.1	18.2
2007	14.3	14.8	14.9	16.1	18.0	20.2	20.8	21.2	20.3	19.1	16.7	15.5	17.7
2008	13.7	14.1	14.5	15.7	17.8	19.9	20.7	21.2	20.1	18.7	15.7	14.7	17.2
2009	12.9	13.3	13.6	14.4	16.7	18.7	19.5	19.8	18.7	17.4	14.7	13.6	16.1
Manufacturing													
1990	9.5	10.9	11.8	13.8	14.8	17.3	22.8	20.5	14.8	11.2	10.9	11.0	14.1
2000	8.5	10.5	10.4	11.3	11.3	13.6	20.3	18.4	14.0	10.1	7.8	6.2	11.8
2001	8.5	12.0	11.8	10.5	10.3	12.2	19.5	18.3	14.5	9.8	7.1	6.0	11.7
2002	8.2	11.9	11.7	10.0	9.5	11.7	18.3	16.8	13.5	10.4	7.5	6.2	11.3
2003	8.6	11.8	11.9	9.0	9.4	13.7	20.1	18.1	13.9	10.6	7.4	5.8	11.7
2004	10.6	11.5	11.6	10.1	10.3	14.3	21.3	18.5	14.7	10.9	7.7	6.0	12.3
2005	10.8	11.6	11.8	10.2	10.3	14.2	21.3	19.5	15.0	10.6	8.5	6.5	12.5
2006	10.8	12.1	12.5	11.3	10.5	16.8	22.5	20.5	15.4	11.0	9.0	6.8	13.3
2007	10.8	11.7	11.8	11.0	10.5	15.7	22.2	20.5	15.7	11.4	9.3	7.2	13.2
2008	10.7	12.1	12.0	10.6	10.9	15.8	22.1	19.9	15.2	10.5	8.7	6.9	13.0
2009	10.5	11.8	11.9	11.3	10.4	15.8	23.1	20.4	14.4	10.4	9.1	6.5	13.0

Employment by Industry: Alaska, Selected Years, 1990–2009—*Continued*

(Numbers in thousands, not seasonally adjusted.)

Industry and year	January	February	March	April	May	June	July	August	September	October	November	December	Annual average
Service-Providing													
1990	186.5	191.1	193.5	196.9	201.5	207.5	205.9	207.0	206.6	202.8	200.2	200.4	199.9
2000	232.4	236.1	239.2	241.8	252.0	257.1	256.4	256.6	254.1	246.6	243.2	244.2	246.6
2001	234.9	239.2	241.3	246.3	256.2	262.1	261.8	263.0	260.5	252.0	247.8	247.5	251.1
2002	240.2	245.3	248.2	252.5	261.5	267.6	266.2	267.9	266.2	258.1	254.1	255.0	256.9
2003	247.1	249.8	252.2	256.4	266.6	271.4	269.0	271.0	270.0	259.8	256.5	257.5	260.6
2004	249.6	251.8	255.6	259.6	268.0	274.1	273.9	275.1	274.6	265.0	260.8	262.0	264.2
2005	253.3	256.4	258.7	263.6	273.7	279.3	278.7	279.6	277.6	266.6	263.8	263.0	267.9
2006	255.1	259.8	263.1	267.3	278.1	286.3	281.2	282.7	281.0	267.8	265.8	266.0	271.2
2007	258.3	263.3	265.8	269.3	280.0	286.6	282.5	284.2	281.7	270.5	268.0	267.9	273.2
2008	261.8	265.4	267.3	271.9	283.4	289.8	287.8	288.4	286.0	274.0	271.6	271.4	276.6
2009	263.9	267.0	268.0	272.5	280.3	287.9	285.8	287.0	286.3	277.2	273.3	272.5	276.8
Trade, Transportation, and Utilities													
1990	43.0	43.3	43.9	44.9	47.5	50.4	50.8	51.2	50.0	48.4	48.1	48.1	47.4
2000	56.5	56.6	57.1	57.8	61.3	63.9	64.7	65.2	63.3	60.1	59.0	59.1	60.3
2001	55.6	55.3	55.7	57.8	61.2	64.0	65.6	65.5	63.4	60.5	58.8	58.7	60.2
2002	56.6	57.0	57.9	58.8	62.4	64.9	66.3	66.4	64.1	61.2	59.4	59.3	61.2
2003	57.1	56.8	57.2	58.5	62.2	64.4	65.3	65.6	63.8	60.0	59.2	59.6	60.8
2004	57.0	57.0	58.0	59.5	63.6	65.8	67.5	67.4	65.7	62.0	60.7	60.7	62.1
2005	58.3	58.4	59.0	60.7	64.8	66.9	68.5	68.5	66.3	62.6	61.4	61.0	63.0
2006	59.4	58.9	60.0	61.6	65.8	68.6	69.0	69.0	66.5	62.2	61.8	61.9	63.7
2007	59.9	59.8	60.4	61.8	65.9	68.7	69.3	69.5	67.0	63.0	62.1	62.4	64.2
2008	60.8	60.6	61.3	62.5	66.9	69.0	69.8	69.5	67.2	63.0	62.3	62.5	64.6
2009	60.0	59.5	60.0	61.4	64.7	66.7	67.6	68.0	66.1	62.6	61.6	61.6	63.3
Wholesale Trade													
1990	5.1	5.3	5.4	5.4	5.7	5.9	6.1	6.0	5.7	5.6	5.5	5.5	5.6
2000	6.0	6.1	6.2	6.1	6.2	6.4	6.8	6.8	6.5	6.1	6.0	6.0	6.2
2001	5.9	5.9	5.9	6.0	6.2	6.4	7.0	6.9	6.4	6.0	5.9	5.9	6.2
2002	5.7	5.7	5.8	6.1	6.2	6.5	7.0	6.9	6.4	6.0	5.9	5.9	6.2
2003	5.9	5.8	5.8	5.9	6.1	6.4	6.5	6.5	6.4	6.1	6.0	6.0	6.1
2004	5.9	6.0	6.1	6.1	6.2	6.4	6.6	6.6	6.4	6.2	6.0	6.1	6.2
2005	5.9	6.0	6.0	6.1	6.4	6.5	6.8	6.7	6.5	6.3	6.2	6.2	6.3
2006	6.2	6.2	6.3	6.3	6.6	6.8	7.0	7.0	6.8	6.5	6.3	6.4	6.5
2007	6.3	6.3	6.4	6.5	6.6	6.9	6.9	7.0	6.7	6.5	6.4	6.4	6.6
2008	6.3	6.3	6.3	6.4	6.6	6.8	7.0	6.9	6.6	6.3	6.2	6.2	6.5
2009	6.2	6.1	6.2	6.2	6.4	6.6	6.6	6.6	6.4	6.1	6.1	6.0	6.3
Retail Trade													
1990	24.2	24.0	24.2	25.0	26.1	27.3	27.4	27.6	26.9	26.4	26.9	27.1	26.0
2000	32.1	31.7	32.0	32.4	33.9	35.1	35.2	35.1	34.4	33.5	33.6	33.8	33.5
2001	31.5	31.0	31.1	32.0	33.4	34.9	35.1	35.1	34.3	33.5	33.4	33.4	33.2
2002	32.0	31.9	32.2	32.6	34.2	35.4	35.8	35.6	34.9	34.3	34.0	34.2	33.9
2003	32.3	32.1	32.2	32.8	34.3	35.6	35.8	35.7	35.1	34.1	33.9	34.3	34.0
2004	32.4	32.2	32.8	33.7	35.4	36.9	37.3	37.2	36.3	35.3	35.4	35.5	35.0
2005	33.8	33.7	33.9	34.8	36.3	37.7	38.0	37.9	37.0	35.8	35.7	35.8	35.9
2006	34.3	33.6	34.0	34.9	36.5	37.9	37.8	37.5	36.5	35.4	35.5	35.7	35.8
2007	34.3	33.8	34.2	34.9	36.5	37.8	38.2	37.9	36.8	35.7	35.8	36.2	36.0
2008	35.0	34.3	34.6	35.3	36.7	37.9	38.1	37.6	36.8	36.0	35.9	36.0	36.2
2009	34.2	33.6	33.8	34.7	36.0	37.0	37.3	37.3	36.7	35.7	35.8	35.6	35.6
Transportation and Utilities													
1990	13.7	14.0	14.3	14.5	15.7	17.2	17.3	17.6	17.4	16.4	15.7	15.5	15.7
2000	18.4	18.8	18.9	19.3	21.2	22.4	22.7	23.3	22.4	20.5	19.4	19.3	20.5
2001	18.2	18.4	18.7	19.8	21.6	22.7	23.5	23.5	22.7	21.0	19.5	19.4	20.8
2002	18.9	19.4	19.9	20.1	22.0	23.0	23.5	23.9	22.8	20.9	19.5	19.2	21.1
2003	18.9	18.9	19.2	19.8	21.8	22.4	23.0	23.4	22.3	19.8	19.3	19.3	20.7
2004	18.7	18.8	19.1	19.7	22.0	22.5	23.6	23.6	23.0	20.5	19.3	19.1	20.8
2005	18.6	18.7	19.1	19.8	22.1	22.7	23.7	23.9	22.8	20.5	19.5	19.0	20.9
2006	18.9	19.1	19.7	20.4	22.7	23.9	24.2	24.5	23.2	20.3	20.0	19.8	21.4
2007	19.3	19.7	19.8	20.4	22.8	24.0	24.2	24.6	23.5	20.8	19.9	19.8	21.6
2008	19.5	20.0	20.4	20.8	23.6	24.3	24.7	25.0	23.8	20.7	20.2	20.3	21.9
2009	19.6	19.8	20.0	20.5	22.3	23.1	23.7	24.1	23.0	20.8	19.7	20.0	21.4
Information													
1990	5.2	5.2	5.3	5.3	5.5	5.6	5.5	5.5	5.6	5.6	5.6	5.6	5.4
2000	7.5	7.5	7.5	7.5	7.5	7.7	7.7	7.6	7.5	7.4	7.4	7.5	7.5
2001	7.3	7.4	7.4	7.2	7.4	7.5	7.5	7.5	7.3	7.3	7.3	7.2	7.4
2002	6.9	6.8	6.9	7.1	7.1	7.2	7.4	7.2	7.2	7.1	7.0	7.1	7.1
2003	6.8	6.8	6.8	6.9	7.0	7.1	7.1	7.0	7.0	6.9	6.9	6.9	6.9
2004	6.8	6.8	6.8	6.8	6.9	6.9	6.9	6.9	6.9	6.9	6.9	7.0	6.9
2005	6.8	6.9	6.9	6.9	7.0	7.0	7.0	7.0	7.0	6.9	7.0	7.0	7.0
2006	6.9	7.0	7.0	6.9	7.0	7.1	7.0	7.1	7.0	7.0	7.0	7.0	7.0
2007	6.9	6.9	6.9	6.8	6.9	7.0	7.0	7.0	7.0	6.9	6.9	6.9	6.9
2008	6.8	6.9	6.9	6.9	7.1	7.1	7.1	7.1	7.1	7.0	7.0	7.0	7.0
2009	6.7	6.8	6.7	6.6	6.6	6.6	6.6	6.6	6.5	6.5	6.5	6.4	6.6

Employment by Industry: Alaska, Selected Years, 1990–2009—*Continued*

(Numbers in thousands, not seasonally adjusted.)

Industry and year	January	February	March	April	May	June	July	August	September	October	November	December	Annual average
Financial Activities													
1990	10.0	10.0	10.2	10.3	10.8	11.1	10.9	11.0	10.9	11.0	10.8	10.8	10.6
2000	13.5	13.5	13.6	13.6	13.8	14.5	14.5	14.6	14.2	14.0	13.7	13.8	13.9
2001	13.4	13.4	13.4	13.6	14.0	14.5	14.3	14.5	14.0	13.7	13.5	13.5	13.8
2002	13.2	13.1	13.4	13.3	13.7	14.2	14.3	14.4	14.2	14.0	13.9	13.8	13.8
2003	13.6	13.6	13.9	14.0	14.4	14.8	15.0	15.1	14.8	14.6	14.3	14.4	14.4
2004	13.9	14.0	14.1	14.5	14.6	15.0	15.0	15.2	14.9	14.7	14.6	14.7	14.6
2005	14.3	14.2	14.2	14.4	14.7	15.1	15.3	15.3	15.2	15.1	14.9	14.8	14.8
2006	14.5	14.5	14.6	14.7	15.0	15.4	15.5	15.6	15.2	14.8	14.7	14.7	14.9
2007	14.4	14.6	14.7	14.8	15.2	15.6	15.5	15.7	15.2	15.0	14.8	14.8	15.0
2008	14.4	14.5	14.6	14.6	15.0	15.2	15.3	15.3	15.0	14.6	14.5	14.5	14.8
2009	14.3	14.3	14.2	14.4	14.6	15.0	15.3	15.3	14.9	15.0	14.3	14.4	14.7
Professional and Business Services													
1990	16.5	17.1	17.5	18.1	18.8	19.8	19.1	19.4	19.0	18.5	18.0	18.1	18.3
2000	22.2	22.7	23.0	23.6	24.6	26.1	26.1	26.0	25.3	24.7	23.8	24.0	24.3
2001	21.2	21.8	22.0	22.2	23.1	24.2	24.5	24.7	23.6	22.4	21.7	21.7	22.8
2002	21.2	21.8	22.0	22.2	23.1	24.0	23.9	24.2	23.2	22.6	22.0	21.9	22.7
2003	21.7	21.7	21.9	22.5	23.9	24.7	24.5	24.9	23.8	22.7	22.2	22.3	23.1
2004	21.7	21.9	22.4	22.6	23.2	24.4	24.9	25.0	24.7	23.4	22.8	22.9	23.3
2005	21.9	22.4	22.3	23.0	24.2	25.6	25.7	25.9	25.0	23.4	23.1	23.0	23.8
2006	22.2	22.9	23.3	23.8	25.0	26.1	25.9	25.9	25.6	24.1	23.6	23.8	24.4
2007	23.2	23.7	23.9	24.4	25.7	26.7	26.5	26.6	26.2	24.8	24.6	24.4	25.1
2008	24.1	24.6	24.7	25.6	27.0	27.9	28.2	28.1	27.5	26.3	25.8	25.9	26.3
2009	25.2	25.5	25.6	25.5	26.7	27.5	27.6	27.4	26.9	25.6	24.7	24.5	26.1
Education and Health Services													
1990	15.9	16.2	16.3	16.6	16.8	16.9	16.4	16.6	16.7	17.1	17.2	17.2	16.6
2000	25.2	25.8	25.8	25.7	26.0	26.0	25.6	25.8	26.0	26.0	26.1	26.4	25.8
2001	26.5	27.0	27.2	27.4	27.7	28.0	28.1	28.3	28.4	28.6	28.9	29.0	27.9
2002	29.0	29.4	29.7	30.1	30.5	30.8	30.8	31.0	30.8	31.2	31.5	31.9	30.6
2003	31.2	32.0	32.2	32.8	33.1	33.2	33.3	33.5	33.4	33.6	33.8	34.2	33.0
2004	33.8	34.2	34.5	34.8	35.0	34.9	34.6	34.4	34.7	34.9	35.1	35.5	34.7
2005	35.1	35.4	35.9	35.8	36.1	36.4	36.0	36.1	36.1	36.2	36.4	36.7	36.0
2006	36.4	36.9	37.0	37.2	37.5	37.6	37.2	37.2	37.1	36.7	36.9	37.0	37.1
2007	36.6	37.1	37.3	37.3	37.3	37.1	36.7	36.9	36.5	36.7	36.8	37.0	36.9
2008	36.8	37.3	37.5	37.5	37.7	37.5	37.7	37.7	37.5	37.8	38.0	38.3	37.6
2009	37.9	38.3	38.5	38.8	39.0	39.1	39.3	39.4	39.5	39.9	39.6	39.7	39.1
Leisure and Hospitality													
1990	18.1	18.4	18.7	19.6	21.2	23.6	24.5	24.5	23.0	20.6	19.5	19.3	20.9
2000	23.1	23.6	24.2	25.5	28.9	32.9	34.1	33.9	31.2	26.6	25.5	25.5	27.9
2001	23.8	24.5	24.7	26.0	29.3	33.5	34.1	34.2	31.7	26.7	25.3	25.4	28.3
2002	24.0	24.9	25.0	26.9	30.5	34.3	35.7	35.4	33.0	28.3	26.7	26.6	29.3
2003	25.7	25.7	26.0	27.1	30.8	34.1	35.6	35.8	33.4	28.1	26.7	26.6	29.6
2004	24.9	25.3	25.9	27.1	30.5	35.0	37.1	37.5	34.8	29.2	27.2	27.4	30.2
2005	25.8	26.1	26.8	28.3	32.4	36.7	38.6	38.3	35.1	28.6	27.3	27.3	30.9
2006	25.8	26.5	27.2	28.5	32.9	37.9	38.8	38.9	35.7	29.0	28.1	28.2	31.5
2007	26.8	27.3	27.9	29.3	33.8	39.0	39.8	39.6	35.9	29.1	28.3	28.1	32.1
2008	27.0	27.4	27.8	29.0	34.8	38.9	40.3	39.9	36.2	29.2	28.3	28.1	32.2
2009	26.5	27.1	27.5	28.1	33.1	36.5	37.8	37.8	35.2	29.7	29.1	28.7	31.4
Other Services													
1990	9.7	9.9	9.9	9.6	9.2	9.3	9.4	9.5	9.4	9.2	9.4	9.3	9.4
2000	11.7	11.9	12.1	12.1	12.3	12.5	12.3	12.1	12.2	12.2	12.3	12.4	12.1
2001	11.4	11.5	11.7	11.8	12.2	12.3	12.1	12.2	12.1	11.9	11.8	11.8	11.9
2002	11.6	11.8	12.0	12.0	12.1	11.9	12.0	11.9	11.7	11.5	11.4	11.3	11.8
2003	11.0	11.1	11.2	11.3	11.4	11.4	11.3	11.3	11.1	11.2	11.1	11.1	11.2
2004	10.6	10.8	10.9	11.2	11.5	11.7	11.2	11.4	11.3	11.3	11.2	11.1	11.2
2005	10.8	11.0	11.1	11.2	11.2	11.3	11.4	11.3	11.2	11.2	11.2	11.1	11.2
2006	10.9	11.0	11.2	11.0	11.2	11.2	11.4	11.3	11.4	11.4	11.4	11.3	11.2
2007	11.1	11.4	11.5	11.2	11.5	11.4	11.4	11.4	11.3	11.2	11.2	11.2	11.3
2008	10.9	11.1	11.2	11.2	11.4	11.5	11.5	11.5	11.4	11.5	11.3	11.2	11.3
2009	11.1	11.3	11.2	11.4	11.6	11.6	11.7	11.7	11.5	11.6	11.4	11.5	11.5
Government													
1990	68.1	71.0	71.7	72.5	71.7	70.8	69.3	69.3	72.0	72.4	71.6	72.0	71.0
2000	72.7	74.5	75.9	76.0	77.6	73.5	71.4	71.4	74.4	75.6	75.4	75.5	74.4
2001	75.7	78.3	79.2	80.3	81.3	78.1	75.6	76.1	80.0	80.9	80.5	80.2	78.9
2002	77.7	80.5	81.3	82.1	82.1	80.3	75.8	77.4	82.0	82.2	82.2	83.1	80.6
2003	80.0	82.1	83.0	83.3	83.8	81.7	76.9	77.8	82.7	82.7	82.3	82.4	81.6
2004	80.9	81.8	83.0	83.1	82.7	80.4	76.7	77.3	81.6	82.6	82.3	82.7	81.3
2005	80.3	82.0	82.5	83.3	83.3	80.3	76.2	77.2	81.7	82.6	82.5	82.1	81.2
2006	79.0	82.1	82.8	83.6	83.7	82.4	76.4	77.7	82.5	82.6	82.3	82.1	81.4
2007	79.4	82.5	83.2	83.7	83.7	81.1	76.3	77.5	82.6	83.8	83.3	83.1	81.7
2008	81.0	83.0	83.3	84.6	83.5	82.7	77.9	79.3	84.1	84.6	84.4	83.9	82.7
2009	82.2	84.2	84.3	86.3	84.0	84.9	79.9	80.8	85.7	86.3	86.1	85.7	84.2

Average Weekly Hours by Selected Industry: Alaska, 2007–2009

(Not seasonally adjusted.)

Industry and year	January	February	March	April	May	June	July	August	September	October	November	December	Annual average
Total Private													
2007	34.4	35.7	35.9	35.8	34.1	35.8	37.1	36.9	36.3	35.0	34.1	34.2	35.5
2008	33.8	35.3	35.7	34.5	34.8	36.2	36.4	36.8	35.7	34.8	34.9	34.2	35.3
2009	33.2	34.5	35.3	33.9	34.0	35.1	35.9	37.3	35.4	35.1	34.8	34.3	35.0
Goods-Producing													
2007	40.0	46.5	47.6	45.4	40.7	44.9	47.0	48.5	47.2	44.2	40.8	40.9	44.8
2008	39.2	47.3	46.5	42.3	42.5	45.1	47.7	48.8	45.5	43.4	43.0	42.6	44.8
2009	39.2	42.8	47.3	41.3	41.1	42.9	45.4	47.9	43.9	44.5	41.3	43.2	43.6
Construction													
2007	37.6	36.7	38.1	38.9	39.6	43.3	45.1	46.8	47.9	46.2	40.3	39.2	41.6
2008	38.7	39.3	40.8	40.2	40.9	43.2	41.9	44.7	42.1	40.7	38.4	39.1	41.1
2009	38.7	40.4	41.0	41.8	40.7	42.9	44.3	44.5	41.1	41.4	37.7	40.5	41.5
Manufacturing													
2007	34.8	55.5	56.8	51.3	42.1	48.5	49.8	51.7	46.0	40.4	40.1	36.3	46.1
2008	30.0	51.9	48.0	37.0	37.3	40.9	51.0	50.8	45.4	41.9	46.2	45.3	44.7
2009	35.5	40.5	52.1	31.5	31.5	36.6	41.3	49.5	42.6	44.1	41.4	42.1	41.3
Trade, Transportation, and Utilities													
2007	35.0	34.4	34.9	35.0	32.2	33.2	34.5	32.9	32.2	31.6	32.3	32.1	33.3
2008	31.7	31.9	32.9	31.8	32.6	33.6	32.5	33.2	32.8	31.9	32.9	31.4	32.5
2009	31.1	32.8	32.6	31.9	33.0	33.0	33.9	35.7	35.2	34.1	34.6	33.6	33.5
Professional and Business Services													
2007	35.7	38.5	38.3	38.8	37.4	38.3	38.7	39.5	38.4	37.5	35.4	35.8	37.7
2008	35.9	35.0	35.6	35.2	36.0	37.2	35.8	36.2	36.1	34.7	35.3	36.6	35.8
2009	34.8	35.0	35.2	35.7	35.2	37.0	36.2	38.4	36.0	36.8	37.0	36.1	36.1
Leisure and Hospitality													
2007	24.6	25.2	24.5	26.1	27.5	30.5	30.7	30.2	27.3	25.7	25.1	26.0	27.3
2008	26.2	26.4	27.7	26.7	26.1	28.9	29.6	28.9	27.9	27.4	26.9	27.2	27.6
2009	25.9	26.4	26.5	25.7	26.2	27.5	27.5	28.0	26.3	25.5	25.2	24.9	26.4

Average Hourly Earnings by Selected Industry: Alaska, 2007–2009

(Dollars, not seasonally adjusted.)

Industry and year	January	February	March	April	May	June	July	August	September	October	November	December	Annual average
Total Private													
2007	25.28	24.51	24.74	24.87	25.90	24.37	23.90	23.60	24.71	25.01	24.86	25.12	24.70
2008	24.74	24.11	24.69	25.27	25.23	25.35	24.78	24.97	25.60	25.21	25.16	24.87	25.01
2009	24.80	24.65	24.39	25.22	25.02	24.42	24.25	24.36	24.98	25.42	25.04	25.28	24.80
Goods-Producing													
2007	31.79	27.38	28.75	28.52	32.45	29.26	27.96	27.80	29.90	30.76	31.18	31.75	29.57
2008	30.43	26.87	28.73	31.86	33.65	31.68	28.80	29.56	31.37	30.05	29.43	30.12	30.16
2009	29.60	27.63	25.70	30.21	31.00	29.19	27.63	27.04	30.73	31.37	30.64	32.13	29.20
Construction													
2007	29.42	30.07	31.37	29.50	32.17	31.45	31.76	31.76	32.21	32.33	31.78	30.41	31.35
2008	29.18	30.06	31.76	32.38	34.07	34.95	34.22	34.78	34.41	32.78	32.05	31.45	33.00
2009	31.54	32.21	32.40	33.74	33.58	35.38	35.11	35.30	36.12	35.24	33.80	33.83	34.25
Manufacturing													
2007	23.38	19.47	19.02	22.24	22.75	18.35	16.93	16.88	17.89	19.35	22.96	24.69	20.33
2008	22.02	18.07	18.52	22.69	24.33	19.94	17.33	17.41	19.24	18.32	19.59	21.34	19.24
2009	17.89	16.26	14.54	17.88	21.77	17.41	15.30	14.64	18.59	20.66	20.79	24.12	17.40
Trade, Transportation, and Utilities													
2007	21.93	22.27	21.66	22.07	22.86	17.91	18.17	17.77	19.05	18.98	18.65	19.29	20.01
2008	19.28	19.50	19.74	19.63	19.40	18.56	18.81	18.87	19.62	19.98	20.45	19.82	19.45
2009	20.16	20.42	20.84	20.38	20.02	19.64	20.03	21.12	20.64	21.29	20.99	20.83	20.53
Professional and Business Services													
2007	29.98	28.73	28.56	30.45	28.17	30.60	28.32	28.13	28.65	29.28	29.86	33.35	29.46
2008	30.85	31.09	30.71	30.82	29.89	29.91	30.09	30.18	30.68	31.09	33.53	32.23	30.89
2009	32.13	32.69	32.77	32.30	31.89	30.41	29.51	29.93	29.81	31.05	32.19	31.55	31.30
Leisure and Hospitality													
2007	13.58	13.89	13.68	13.64	12.99	12.98	13.16	13.28	13.48	13.76	13.55	13.77	13.42
2008	13.43	13.50	13.64	13.36	13.50	13.41	13.51	13.52	13.57	13.47	13.31	13.45	13.48
2009	13.06	13.20	13.37	13.37	12.83	12.96	12.95	13.16	13.12	13.40	13.45	13.75	13.19

Average Weekly Earnings by Selected Industry: Alaska, 2007–2009

(Dollars, not seasonally adjusted.)

Industry and year	January	February	March	April	May	June	July	August	September	October	November	December	Annual average
Total Private													
2007	869.63	875.01	888.17	890.35	883.19	872.45	886.69	870.84	896.97	875.35	847.73	859.10	876.85
2008	836.21	851.08	881.43	871.82	878.00	917.67	901.99	918.90	913.92	877.31	878.08	850.55	882.85
2009	823.36	850.43	860.97	854.96	850.68	857.14	870.58	908.63	884.29	892.24	871.39	867.10	868.00
Goods-Producing													
2007	1271.60	1273.17	1368.50	1294.81	1320.72	1313.77	1314.12	1348.30	1411.28	1359.59	1272.14	1298.58	1324.74
2008	1192.86	1270.95	1335.95	1347.68	1430.13	1428.77	1373.76	1442.53	1427.34	1304.17	1265.49	1283.11	1351.17
2009	1160.32	1182.56	1215.61	1247.67	1274.10	1252.25	1254.40	1295.22	1349.05	1395.97	1265.43	1388.02	1273.12
Construction													
2007	1106.19	1103.57	1195.20	1147.55	1273.93	1361.79	1432.38	1486.37	1542.86	1493.65	1280.73	1192.07	1304.16
2008	1129.27	1181.36	1295.81	1301.68	1393.46	1509.84	1433.82	1554.67	1448.66	1334.15	1230.72	1229.70	1356.30
2009	1220.60	1301.28	1328.40	1410.33	1366.71	1517.80	1555.37	1570.85	1484.53	1458.94	1274.26	1370.12	1421.38
Manufacturing													
2007	813.62	1080.59	1080.34	1140.91	957.78	889.98	843.11	872.70	822.94	781.74	920.70	896.25	937.21
2008	660.60	937.83	888.96	839.53	907.51	815.55	883.83	884.43	873.50	767.61	905.06	966.70	860.03
2009	635.10	658.53	757.53	563.22	685.76	637.21	631.89	724.68	791.93	911.11	860.71	1015.45	718.62
Trade, Transportation, and Utilities													
2007	767.55	766.09	755.93	772.45	736.09	594.61	626.87	584.63	613.41	599.77	602.40	619.21	666.33
2008	611.18	622.05	649.45	624.23	632.44	623.62	611.33	626.48	643.54	637.36	672.81	622.35	632.13
2009	626.98	669.78	679.38	650.12	660.66	648.12	679.02	753.98	726.53	725.99	726.25	699.89	687.76
Professional and Business Services													
2007	1070.29	1106.11	1093.85	1181.46	1053.56	1171.98	1095.98	1111.14	1100.16	1098.00	1057.04	1193.93	1110.64
2008	1107.52	1088.15	1093.28	1084.86	1076.04	1112.65	1077.22	1092.52	1107.55	1078.82	1183.61	1179.62	1105.86
2009	1118.12	1144.15	1153.50	1153.11	1122.53	1125.17	1068.26	1149.31	1073.16	1142.64	1191.03	1138.96	1129.93
Leisure and Hospitality													
2007	334.07	350.03	335.16	356.00	357.23	395.89	404.01	401.06	368.00	353.63	340.11	358.02	366.37
2008	351.87	356.40	377.83	356.71	352.35	387.55	399.90	390.73	378.60	369.08	358.04	365.84	372.05
2009	338.25	348.48	354.31	343.61	336.15	356.40	356.13	368.48	345.06	341.70	338.94	342.38	348.22

ARIZONA

At a Glance

Population:
  1990 census: 3,665,339
  2000 census: 5,130,632
  2009 estimate: 6,595,778

Percent change in population:
  1990–2000: 40.0%
  2000–2009: 28.6%

Percent change in total nonfarm employment:
  1990–2009: 63.6%
  2008–2009: -7.3%

Industry with the largest growth in employment, 1990–2009 (thousands):
  Professional and Business Services, 203.4

Industry with the largest decline or smallest growth in employment, 1990–2009 (thousands):
  Manufacturing, -23.4

Civilian labor force:
  1990: 1,788,243
  2000: 2,505,306
  2009: 3,142,641

Unemployment rate and rank among states (lowest to highest):
  1990: 5.3%, 23rd
  2000: 4.0%, 28th
  2009: 9.1%, 32nd

Employment by Industry, 2009

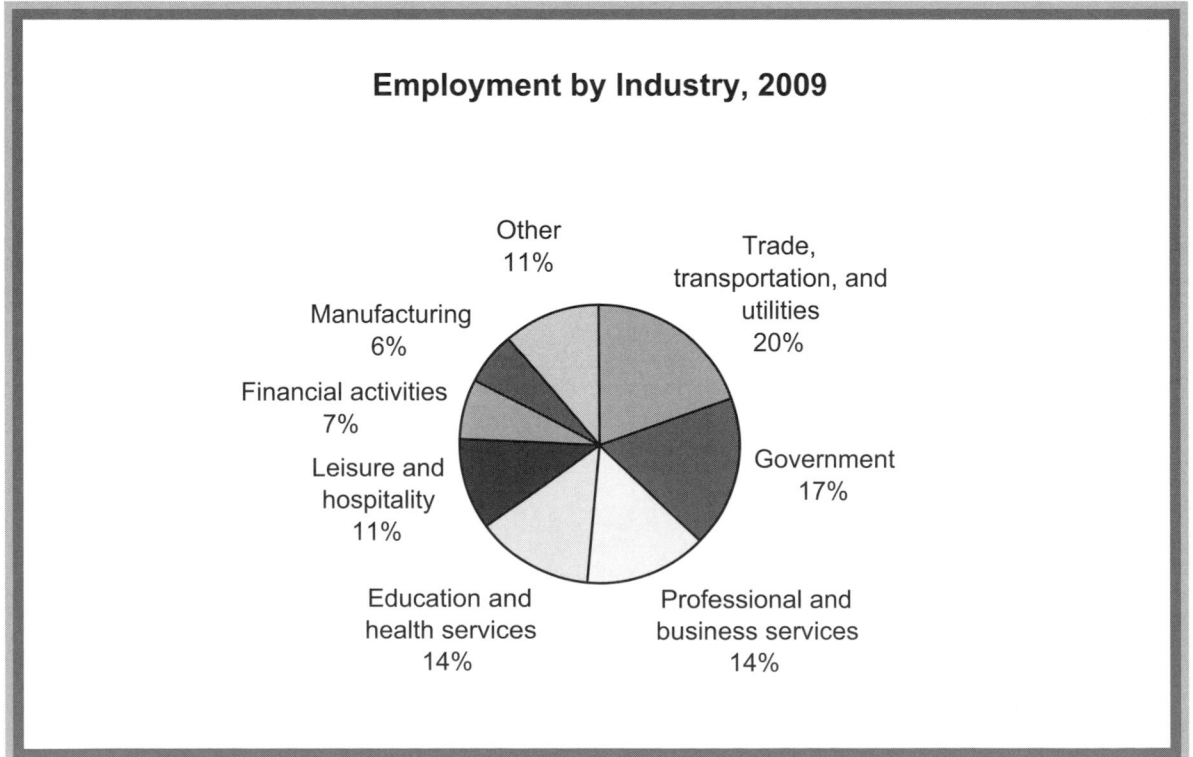

Other 11%
Trade, transportation, and utilities 20%
Manufacturing 6%
Financial activities 7%
Leisure and hospitality 11%
Government 17%
Education and health services 14%
Professional and business services 14%

Employment by Industry: Selected Years, Arizona, 1990–2009

(Numbers in thousands, not seasonally adjusted.)

Industry and year	January	February	March	April	May	June	July	August	September	October	November	December	Annual average
Total Nonfarm													
1990	1455.4	1476.6	1489.4	1494.8	1500.6	1470.6	1444.5	1454.6	1487.0	1499.2	1513.0	1511.4	1483.1
2000	2184.1	2220.3	2239.7	2240.3	2253.5	2224.9	2192.9	2218.5	2259.3	2274.6	2293.1	2311.5	2242.7
2001	2239.4	2275.4	2291.5	2287.0	2279.8	2251.8	2216.2	2243.8	2266.6	2269.7	2276.8	2281.5	2265.0
2002	2228.2	2251.8	2268.3	2279.9	2276.0	2250.9	2209.5	2245.4	2265.9	2282.2	2310.9	2311.9	2265.1
2003	2253.0	2279.4	2292.3	2297.7	2300.0	2271.3	2239.4	2279.5	2302.9	2330.7	2347.1	2363.2	2296.4
2004	2308.5	2339.1	2357.8	2375.8	2377.2	2352.9	2331.7	2368.3	2396.8	2435.9	2455.8	2475.8	2381.3
2005	2413.1	2454.6	2473.7	2506.0	2507.8	2481.1	2468.1	2507.4	2545.7	2558.1	2585.5	2604.6	2508.8
2006	2562.0	2606.5	2629.1	2634.7	2643.5	2615.9	2586.9	2624.2	2655.8	2669.2	2687.4	2698.6	2634.5
2007	2630.7	2668.5	2686.3	2676.8	2682.0	2649.8	2623.9	2662.6	2683.2	2695.1	2712.3	2713.6	2673.7
2008	2644.3	2666.9	2665.9	2655.9	2648.9	2599.4	2557.3	2595.4	2601.2	2594.2	2590.7	2575.4	2616.3
2009	2492.1	2487.0	2478.3	2458.0	2442.7	2382.2	2355.9	2380.6	2392.1	2408.0	2423.1	2416.5	2426.4
Total Private													
1990	1192.4	1200.5	1210.4	1212.6	1214.6	1218.3	1202.1	1206.3	1210.6	1212.6	1223.0	1221.5	1210.4
2000	1825.5	1848.7	1863.0	1862.1	1870.4	1880.7	1860.5	1876.2	1886.5	1895.6	1913.0	1930.5	1876.1
2001	1873.9	1891.5	1906.4	1900.3	1896.2	1898.2	1875.5	1882.9	1879.2	1876.1	1880.1	1886.0	1887.2
2002	1845.9	1856.5	1871.6	1879.4	1881.3	1879.7	1859.0	1871.4	1869.2	1877.2	1898.5	1906.2	1874.7
2003	1864.2	1875.4	1888.5	1894.4	1898.1	1896.6	1886.8	1901.4	1906.0	1924.8	1941.4	1956.9	1902.9
2004	1918.1	1933.0	1951.1	1967.7	1971.4	1975.9	1974.7	1983.9	1988.0	2020.1	2040.1	2059.1	1981.9
2005	2017.5	2040.0	2061.8	2093.5	2098.0	2102.5	2102.7	2118.4	2134.6	2143.2	2169.1	2189.3	2105.9
2006	2161.6	2190.2	2212.8	2218.5	2225.8	2233.4	2216.4	2230.1	2239.1	2244.3	2261.9	2277.5	2226.0
2007	2220.9	2242.9	2259.4	2250.3	2256.1	2258.2	2238.8	2250.6	2250.1	2258.3	2272.4	2274.4	2252.7
2008	2214.4	2224.3	2224.3	2213.1	2207.0	2193.0	2166.2	2173.2	2162.4	2151.5	2145.5	2137.8	2184.0
2009	2062.1	2047.4	2040.4	2017.9	2009.0	1990.4	1974.1	1975.4	1965.2	1979.5	1992.9	1991.2	2003.8
Goods-Producing													
1990	270.4	270.6	272.2	270.7	272.4	275.3	275.0	277.1	276.1	275.5	274.0	270.5	273.3
2000	375.6	378.6	380.7	382.1	384.5	391.2	390.5	393.6	394.4	393.7	393.6	395.5	387.8
2001	384.7	386.4	389.8	387.9	388.6	390.5	389.3	389.6	384.9	379.8	375.1	371.4	384.8
2002	363.5	363.5	365.1	364.8	365.6	367.4	367.0	368.4	365.1	362.7	361.2	359.4	364.5
2003	353.9	353.2	354.5	356.0	358.1	360.8	360.7	362.9	362.5	363.6	363.8	365.1	359.5
2004	360.6	363.7	366.6	368.9	371.6	377.1	380.5	381.7	383.2	388.4	389.9	393.1	377.1
2005	386.4	391.6	396.7	403.2	406.3	413.0	415.5	418.0	419.7	420.5	423.9	428.2	410.3
2006	423.7	430.4	435.0	437.9	440.4	445.0	443.5	442.6	439.8	434.6	430.1	428.5	436.0
2007	418.8	421.9	422.7	419.1	420.3	425.2	423.1	423.7	418.8	414.0	408.1	402.2	418.2
2008	391.5	388.9	386.8	383.1	381.6	380.2	376.2	373.5	367.1	357.8	347.3	338.6	372.7
2009	322.2	312.0	306.6	298.3	294.9	293.4	290.2	286.6	282.3	279.1	276.5	272.7	292.9
Mining and Logging													
1990	12.3	12.2	12.2	12.2	12.5	12.7	12.8	12.8	12.9	12.8	12.8	12.8	12.5
2000	9.6	9.7	9.7	9.7	9.8	10.0	9.9	9.9	9.8	9.7	9.6	9.7	9.7
2001	9.6	9.6	9.6	9.6	9.7	9.7	9.6	9.6	9.5	9.5	9.4	9.2	9.6
2002	8.9	8.9	8.9	9.0	8.8	8.9	8.7	8.7	8.7	8.6	8.4	8.4	8.7
2003	8.2	8.0	7.9	8.0	8.0	8.1	8.1	8.1	8.0	8.0	8.0	8.0	8.0
2004	7.8	7.9	7.9	8.1	8.3	8.4	8.4	8.5	8.5	8.7	8.7	8.7	8.3
2005	8.6	8.7	8.8	9.0	9.1	9.3	8.1	8.0	8.0	8.0	8.4	9.0	8.6
2006	9.0	9.1	9.2	9.5	9.7	10.1	10.2	10.3	10.4	10.4	10.5	10.5	9.9
2007	10.5	10.5	10.7	10.7	10.9	11.2	11.8	12.1	12.1	12.3	12.4	12.5	11.5
2008	12.7	12.7	12.9	13.0	13.3	13.7	14.0	14.2	14.4	14.0	13.8	13.8	13.5
2009	12.6	12.1	12.1	10.8	10.6	10.6	10.6	10.7	10.7	10.7	10.7	10.6	11.1
Construction													
1990	81.4	81.6	83.1	82.9	83.8	85.6	85.1	86.9	86.8	86.0	84.7	82.2	84.1
2000	159.6	161.2	162.9	164.3	166.7	170.3	169.9	171.9	172.5	172.9	172.1	173.4	168.1
2001	166.5	168.8	172.4	172.1	173.6	176.7	177.5	179.6	177.3	174.9	172.9	170.4	173.6
2002	167.0	167.4	169.7	170.1	172.0	174.0	174.1	176.6	174.8	174.3	173.9	172.4	172.2
2003	168.7	169.0	170.5	172.0	174.7	177.1	177.7	179.8	180.1	181.6	181.5	181.7	176.2
2004	178.3	180.6	183.0	185.8	187.9	191.4	194.3	195.7	197.1	201.0	201.8	203.8	191.7
2005	199.2	203.3	207.9	213.7	215.9	220.8	224.1	226.0	228.2	228.8	231.6	233.3	219.4
2006	229.7	234.4	238.7	241.1	244.0	247.5	246.1	245.6	243.8	240.0	237.8	235.4	240.3
2007	226.7	227.6	228.5	226.4	227.6	231.7	228.7	229.1	225.9	221.4	215.7	210.0	224.9
2008	200.7	198.8	198.2	195.1	193.6	192.0	188.6	186.3	181.1	173.9	165.8	158.8	186.1
2009	147.3	140.4	137.4	132.6	130.9	130.6	128.1	125.3	122.2	119.4	116.7	114.4	128.8
Manufacturing													
1990	176.7	176.8	176.9	175.6	176.1	177.0	177.1	177.4	176.4	176.7	176.5	175.5	176.5
2000	206.4	207.7	208.1	208.1	208.0	210.9	210.7	211.8	212.1	211.1	211.9	212.4	209.9
2001	208.6	208.0	207.8	206.2	205.3	204.1	202.2	200.4	198.1	195.4	192.8	191.8	201.7
2002	187.6	187.2	186.5	185.7	184.8	184.5	184.2	183.1	181.6	179.8	178.9	178.6	183.5
2003	177.0	176.2	176.1	176.0	175.4	175.6	174.9	175.0	174.4	174.0	174.3	175.4	175.3
2004	174.5	175.2	175.7	175.0	175.4	177.3	177.8	177.5	177.6	178.7	179.4	180.6	177.1
2005	178.6	179.6	180.0	180.5	181.3	182.9	183.3	184.0	183.5	183.7	183.9	185.9	182.3
2006	185.0	186.9	187.1	187.3	186.7	187.4	187.2	186.7	185.6	184.2	181.8	182.6	185.7
2007	181.6	183.8	183.5	182.0	181.8	182.3	182.6	182.5	180.8	180.3	180.0	179.7	181.7
2008	178.1	177.4	175.7	175.0	174.7	174.5	173.6	173.0	171.6	169.9	167.7	166.0	173.1
2009	162.3	159.5	157.1	154.9	153.4	152.2	151.5	150.6	149.4	149.0	149.1	147.7	153.1

Employment by Industry: Selected Years, Arizona, 1990–2009—*Continued*

(Numbers in thousands, not seasonally adjusted.)

Industry and year	January	February	March	April	May	June	July	August	September	October	November	December	Annual average
Service-Providing													
1990	1185.0	1206.0	1217.2	1224.1	1228.2	1195.3	1169.5	1177.5	1210.9	1223.7	1239.0	1240.9	1209.8
2000	1808.5	1841.7	1859.0	1858.2	1869.0	1833.7	1802.4	1824.9	1864.9	1880.9	1899.5	1916.0	1854.9
2001	1854.7	1889.0	1901.7	1899.1	1891.2	1861.3	1826.9	1854.2	1881.7	1889.9	1901.7	1910.1	1880.1
2002	1864.7	1888.3	1903.2	1915.1	1910.4	1883.5	1842.5	1877.0	1900.8	1919.5	1949.7	1952.5	1900.6
2003	1899.1	1926.2	1937.8	1941.7	1941.9	1910.5	1878.7	1916.6	1940.4	1967.1	1983.3	1998.1	1936.8
2004	1947.9	1975.4	1991.2	2006.9	2005.6	1975.8	1951.2	1986.6	2013.6	2047.5	2065.9	2082.7	2004.2
2005	2026.7	2063.0	2077.0	2102.8	2101.5	2068.1	2052.6	2089.4	2126.0	2137.6	2161.6	2176.4	2098.6
2006	2138.3	2176.1	2194.1	2196.8	2203.1	2170.9	2143.4	2181.6	2216.0	2234.6	2257.3	2270.1	2198.5
2007	2211.9	2246.6	2263.6	2257.7	2261.7	2224.6	2200.8	2238.9	2264.4	2281.1	2304.2	2311.4	2255.6
2008	2252.8	2278.0	2279.1	2272.8	2267.3	2219.2	2181.1	2221.9	2234.1	2236.4	2243.4	2236.8	2243.6
2009	2169.9	2175.0	2171.7	2159.7	2147.8	2088.8	2065.7	2094.0	2109.8	2128.9	2146.6	2143.8	2133.5
Trade, Transportation, and Utilities													
1990	310.4	309.3	311.0	309.0	310.5	310.6	305.2	306.3	308.9	309.5	317.4	319.9	310.7
2000	432.5	433.1	432.2	429.5	430.5	433.6	430.6	433.7	436.4	442.2	455.7	464.0	437.8
2001	444.1	441.9	440.9	439.7	438.4	438.5	434.8	434.9	434.7	439.1	447.2	452.5	440.6
2002	437.2	434.0	436.7	437.4	439.1	439.9	435.3	436.8	438.1	442.1	452.9	460.9	440.9
2003	442.6	441.7	442.7	440.7	441.1	440.5	439.5	441.4	441.9	450.3	461.3	469.0	446.0
2004	453.6	453.1	455.0	456.8	458.4	458.8	459.1	460.5	459.0	468.4	481.0	488.8	462.7
2005	476.8	477.8	479.9	481.8	482.3	482.3	485.8	487.2	490.1	494.4	507.7	516.8	488.6
2006	502.1	501.6	505.9	505.7	506.4	506.4	507.8	509.8	510.9	517.9	531.3	540.4	512.2
2007	522.0	520.8	523.2	522.7	524.0	523.8	524.2	525.2	526.0	528.8	542.4	549.2	527.7
2008	527.9	525.2	524.2	518.7	519.2	517.8	510.4	511.4	507.5	508.6	514.8	515.3	516.8
2009	495.5	487.2	484.8	479.0	477.9	474.6	472.6	472.3	469.8	474.8	482.2	487.8	479.9
Wholesale Trade													
1990	63.2	63.6	63.8	62.9	63.4	63.5	62.3	62.2	61.9	61.8	62.1	62.1	62.7
2000	94.4	95.3	95.8	93.6	93.7	94.3	93.9	93.9	94.4	95.4	97.1	98.7	95.0
2001	97.6	98.3	98.5	97.3	96.3	95.8	94.8	94.6	94.0	94.0	94.3	95.2	95.9
2002	94.2	94.4	95.0	93.5	94.3	94.0	93.4	93.4	93.3	94.0	94.6	95.4	94.1
2003	94.3	94.6	94.4	93.2	93.3	92.9	91.8	91.7	91.6	91.9	92.7	94.1	93.0
2004	94.3	94.5	94.8	94.5	94.9	95.3	95.8	95.8	94.5	96.4	97.0	98.5	95.5
2005	97.6	98.6	99.2	99.3	99.3	99.6	100.0	99.9	100.2	100.9	102.2	104.1	100.1
2006	103.5	104.3	104.8	104.6	104.7	105.3	105.6	105.8	106.2	106.8	107.9	109.4	105.7
2007	107.7	108.3	108.9	108.1	108.2	108.9	108.9	108.7	108.5	108.9	110.0	110.9	108.8
2008	109.3	109.7	109.6	108.3	108.4	107.9	107.0	107.1	106.9	107.2	107.1	106.8	107.9
2009	104.5	103.4	102.2	100.7	99.9	99.0	98.8	98.6	97.7	98.8	100.6	102.5	100.6
Retail Trade													
1990	196.4	194.6	195.5	195.2	195.9	195.9	192.2	193.2	195.5	196.0	203.5	206.0	196.6
2000	264.3	264.2	263.5	263.2	263.9	265.7	262.8	265.2	267.1	271.4	282.3	288.4	268.5
2001	270.0	266.8	265.7	265.6	264.7	265.1	262.9	263.3	264.2	269.0	277.4	282.4	268.1
2002	268.9	265.6	267.0	268.6	269.2	269.4	265.8	266.8	268.4	270.6	280.7	287.8	270.7
2003	271.5	270.3	271.4	270.9	271.2	271.3	271.7	273.5	273.9	281.1	291.2	297.0	276.2
2004	282.4	281.8	282.7	284.5	285.5	285.5	285.1	286.4	286.6	292.0	303.9	309.9	288.9
2005	299.5	299.1	300.6	302.7	302.3	302.0	305.0	305.8	307.8	311.5	322.4	328.1	307.2
2006	316.0	314.8	318.2	317.8	318.2	317.6	318.2	319.2	319.1	325.7	337.4	343.1	322.1
2007	328.5	326.6	328.5	328.4	329.0	327.7	328.6	329.3	330.0	332.8	344.7	348.4	331.9
2008	331.9	328.4	327.7	323.7	324.0	323.3	317.5	318.0	314.8	315.9	321.4	321.3	322.3
2009	306.3	299.8	298.8	296.7	296.5	294.5	293.2	292.9	292.3	296.1	301.9	304.3	297.8
Transportation and Utilities													
1990	50.8	51.1	51.7	50.9	51.2	51.2	50.7	50.9	51.5	51.7	51.8	51.8	51.3
2000	73.8	73.6	72.9	72.7	72.9	73.6	73.9	74.6	74.9	75.4	76.3	76.9	74.2
2001	76.5	76.8	76.7	76.8	77.4	77.6	77.1	77.0	76.5	76.1	75.5	74.9	76.6
2002	74.1	74.0	74.7	75.3	75.6	76.5	76.1	76.6	76.4	77.5	77.6	77.7	76.0
2003	76.8	76.8	76.9	76.6	76.6	76.3	76.0	76.2	76.4	77.3	77.4	77.9	76.7
2004	76.9	76.8	77.5	77.8	78.0	78.0	78.2	78.3	77.9	80.0	80.1	80.4	78.3
2005	79.7	80.1	80.1	79.8	80.7	80.7	80.8	81.5	82.1	82.0	83.1	84.6	81.3
2006	82.6	82.5	82.9	83.3	83.5	83.5	84.0	84.8	85.6	85.4	86.0	87.9	84.3
2007	85.8	85.9	85.8	86.2	86.8	87.2	86.7	87.2	87.5	87.1	87.7	89.9	87.0
2008	86.7	87.1	86.9	86.7	86.8	86.6	85.9	86.3	85.8	85.5	86.3	87.2	86.5
2009	84.7	84.0	83.8	81.6	81.5	81.1	80.6	80.8	79.8	79.9	79.7	81.0	81.5
Information													
1990	32.3	32.6	32.3	33.1	33.3	33.7	33.4	33.2	32.9	32.4	32.7	32.6	32.8
2000	51.6	52.6	54.8	55.1	55.6	55.6	55.1	55.1	54.5	53.6	54.1	54.6	54.3
2001	53.7	54.9	54.4	54.4	53.8	54.2	53.7	53.8	53.2	53.0	54.0	53.2	53.9
2002	53.2	53.2	52.7	52.7	52.3	51.7	51.6	51.4	50.6	49.9	50.7	50.8	51.7
2003	49.6	49.9	50.1	50.1	50.0	50.1	49.5	49.3	48.6	48.7	49.7	49.5	49.5
2004	48.5	48.5	48.8	48.7	48.0	47.7	46.8	45.9	44.6	44.8	45.3	44.9	46.9
2005	44.2	44.8	45.1	45.9	46.1	45.7	45.3	45.0	44.6	44.9	45.5	46.1	45.3
2006	45.4	45.5	45.5	44.5	44.7	44.6	43.8	43.7	42.9	42.5	43.1	43.3	44.1
2007	41.5	42.4	42.3	42.6	43.3	43.1	42.8	42.5	42.2	41.9	42.8	42.4	42.5
2008	41.7	42.6	43.0	42.1	43.2	42.8	41.6	41.3	41.7	40.8	41.3	41.5	42.0
2009	40.2	40.6	39.9	39.9	40.3	39.5	39.2	38.9	38.3	38.6	38.5	37.8	39.3

Employment by Industry: Selected Years, Arizona, 1990–2009—*Continued*

(Numbers in thousands, not seasonally adjusted.)

Industry and year	January	February	March	April	May	June	July	August	September	October	November	December	Annual average
Financial Activities													
1990	97.5	98.0	98.7	99.3	99.3	99.3	99.2	99.5	98.6	98.1	98.0	97.5	98.5
2000	147.2	149.9	149.9	149.2	150.1	151.6	150.5	151.4	152.0	152.7	153.0	154.4	150.9
2001	149.2	150.8	152.3	152.4	152.8	153.5	154.4	154.6	154.7	154.6	155.3	156.3	153.4
2002	153.2	154.7	154.2	155.2	154.6	154.5	154.2	154.4	154.5	155.7	157.7	158.6	155.1
2003	156.5	157.4	158.9	158.7	159.5	160.0	160.8	162.0	161.3	161.2	161.5	162.4	160.0
2004	160.3	161.2	162.2	164.3	164.0	164.2	165.1	165.5	165.2	167.4	168.0	169.2	164.7
2005	167.3	168.8	169.4	172.1	172.5	173.5	174.9	176.6	177.6	179.0	179.8	181.2	174.4
2006	178.5	179.9	180.9	181.4	182.2	182.7	182.8	183.5	184.0	185.1	185.3	187.2	182.8
2007	184.3	185.9	186.5	186.5	186.3	185.9	185.2	182.9	181.8	180.5	180.3	181.0	183.9
2008	176.4	177.7	177.6	177.1	177.0	176.5	175.1	174.8	174.0	173.3	172.2	172.1	175.3
2009	168.4	168.3	168.0	167.2	167.4	166.8	166.5	166.2	164.9	164.0	164.8	165.4	166.5
Professional and Business Services													
1990	138.4	139.8	142.6	143.3	142.2	144.2	144.3	144.7	144.0	142.4	142.3	142.9	142.5
2000	309.5	316.1	321.9	324.6	328.2	329.2	325.4	329.8	330.6	331.6	332.5	335.2	326.2
2001	319.1	324.5	328.7	326.4	324.1	324.7	318.1	318.4	317.3	314.5	310.6	312.2	319.9
2002	303.6	307.7	313.1	316.9	315.9	316.7	313.7	317.2	315.5	314.8	317.2	317.2	314.1
2003	308.8	313.2	317.3	319.7	320.6	321.6	318.2	321.1	322.7	326.0	326.3	329.3	320.4
2004	319.0	322.7	327.5	335.2	335.1	338.3	340.4	341.7	343.9	351.3	352.6	356.1	338.7
2005	346.0	351.5	356.1	363.6	363.2	366.5	367.7	371.5	374.8	374.2	377.2	379.7	366.0
2006	374.0	382.7	386.6	389.6	391.8	396.5	394.7	398.9	402.3	403.5	404.9	407.2	394.4
2007	394.5	399.3	403.9	401.8	401.9	404.5	401.8	405.4	404.0	407.4	408.7	406.5	403.3
2008	394.0	397.0	395.0	392.8	389.4	386.2	382.6	384.7	381.4	379.7	375.8	372.9	386.0
2009	358.1	354.9	352.1	348.0	343.8	341.3	340.1	338.7	337.6	343.9	345.9	346.2	345.9
Education and Health Services													
1990	132.1	133.8	134.8	135.5	135.6	135.9	133.3	133.3	135.4	137.1	138.3	138.4	135.2
2000	208.7	211.4	212.1	211.1	211.3	210.6	208.1	211.2	213.7	214.8	215.8	217.7	212.2
2001	214.5	216.8	218.6	218.5	218.2	218.5	215.3	220.1	221.8	223.5	225.3	227.6	219.9
2002	227.3	229.4	230.7	230.0	231.6	231.0	226.9	232.0	233.9	237.5	239.9	240.7	232.6
2003	239.8	242.5	243.1	245.7	246.2	245.1	243.2	247.9	250.3	251.3	252.8	254.2	246.8
2004	253.6	255.2	256.5	258.8	259.4	258.8	256.1	260.9	263.3	267.2	268.6	270.4	260.7
2005	266.2	268.4	271.4	275.6	276.7	273.7	271.5	277.0	279.6	281.0	282.9	284.3	275.7
2006	282.5	286.3	288.8	289.3	290.3	289.0	286.6	292.5	295.1	297.3	299.4	302.4	291.6
2007	296.6	301.1	302.8	301.5	303.2	302.0	299.7	305.2	307.9	312.1	313.1	314.9	305.0
2008	310.7	315.2	316.6	319.1	320.4	317.8	316.4	322.0	324.7	326.7	328.8	330.4	320.7
2009	324.7	327.0	327.8	327.1	328.0	324.8	323.0	328.8	330.4	334.8	338.2	337.7	329.4
Leisure and Hospitality													
1990	156.7	161.2	163.3	163.6	163.0	160.7	154.0	154.3	156.9	158.0	160.6	159.8	159.3
2000	224.1	229.3	233.2	233.2	232.4	230.1	222.6	224.1	227.6	229.4	230.3	230.6	228.9
2001	226.7	232.8	236.9	236.9	235.4	231.7	224.4	225.6	226.5	227.4	227.9	228.0	230.0
2002	223.0	228.4	232.5	235.7	235.2	230.8	224.3	225.1	225.3	228.3	232.6	232.2	229.5
2003	228.0	232.2	235.8	238.0	236.8	232.4	227.5	228.5	230.2	234.6	236.4	237.7	233.1
2004	234.7	239.5	244.9	246.2	246.0	241.8	237.2	238.1	239.4	242.4	244.5	246.0	241.7
2005	242.5	248.1	252.9	259.9	259.0	255.7	250.6	251.8	256.1	256.6	258.8	259.4	254.3
2006	258.1	264.2	268.9	271.6	270.1	267.6	261.3	262.6	266.6	267.5	271.0	271.1	266.7
2007	266.8	272.9	278.4	278.1	277.9	273.0	264.0	267.7	269.9	273.9	276.2	276.9	273.0
2008	272.0	276.3	279.1	279.2	275.1	270.3	263.2	265.3	266.0	265.6	266.2	263.8	270.2
2009	257.5	261.2	264.9	264.0	262.1	255.3	248.8	250.3	248.9	252.8	254.7	253.2	256.1
Other Services													
1990	54.6	55.2	55.5	58.1	58.3	58.6	57.7	57.9	57.8	59.6	59.7	59.9	57.7
2000	76.3	77.7	78.2	77.3	77.8	78.8	77.7	77.3	77.3	77.6	78.0	78.5	77.7
2001	81.9	83.4	84.8	84.1	84.9	86.6	85.5	85.9	86.1	84.2	84.7	84.8	84.7
2002	84.9	85.6	86.6	86.7	87.0	87.7	86.0	86.1	86.2	86.2	86.3	86.4	86.3
2003	85.0	85.3	86.1	85.5	85.8	86.1	87.4	88.3	88.5	89.1	89.6	89.7	87.2
2004	87.8	89.1	89.6	88.8	88.9	89.2	89.5	89.6	89.4	90.2	90.2	90.6	89.4
2005	88.1	89.0	90.3	91.4	91.9	92.1	91.4	91.3	92.1	92.6	93.3	93.6	91.4
2006	97.3	99.6	101.2	98.5	99.9	101.6	95.9	96.5	97.5	95.9	96.8	97.4	98.2
2007	96.4	98.6	99.6	98.0	99.2	100.7	98.0	98.0	99.5	99.7	100.8	101.3	99.2
2008	100.2	101.4	102.0	101.0	101.1	101.4	100.7	100.2	100.0	99.0	99.1	98.2	100.4
2009	95.5	96.2	96.3	94.4	94.6	94.7	93.7	93.6	93.0	91.5	92.1	90.4	93.8
Government													
1990	263.0	276.1	279.0	282.2	286.0	252.3	242.4	248.3	276.4	286.6	290.0	289.9	272.7
2000	358.6	371.6	376.7	378.2	383.1	344.2	332.4	342.3	372.8	379.0	380.1	381.0	366.6
2001	365.5	383.9	385.1	386.7	383.6	353.6	340.7	360.9	387.4	393.6	396.7	395.5	377.8
2002	382.3	395.3	396.7	400.5	394.7	371.2	350.5	374.0	396.7	405.0	412.4	405.7	390.4
2003	388.8	404.0	403.8	403.3	401.9	374.7	352.6	378.1	396.9	405.9	405.7	406.3	393.5
2004	390.4	406.1	406.7	408.1	405.8	377.0	357.0	384.4	408.8	415.8	415.7	416.7	399.4
2005	395.6	414.6	411.9	412.5	409.8	378.6	365.4	389.0	411.1	414.9	416.4	415.3	402.9
2006	400.4	416.3	416.3	416.2	417.7	382.5	370.5	394.1	416.7	424.9	425.5	421.1	408.5
2007	409.8	425.0	426.0	426.5	425.9	391.6	385.1	412.0	433.1	436.8	439.9	439.2	421.0
2008	429.9	442.6	441.6	442.8	441.9	406.4	391.1	422.2	438.8	442.7	445.2	442.6	432.3
2009	430.0	439.6	437.9	440.1	433.7	391.8	381.8	405.2	426.9	428.5	430.2	425.3	422.6

Average Weekly Hours by Selected Industry: Arizona, 2007–2009

(Not seasonally adjusted.)

Industry and year	January	February	March	April	May	June	July	August	September	October	November	December	Annual average
Total Private													
2007	35.4	35.5	35.5	35.7	35.2	35.4	35.5	35.2	35.0	34.7	34.6	35.1	35.2
2008	34.1	34.3	34.8	34.5	34.5	35.4	34.8	35.1	34.9	35.2	35.5	34.9	34.8
2009	34.8	35.0	35.1	34.5	34.4	34.5	34.6	35.1	34.6	34.8	35.3	34.7	34.8
Goods-Producing													
2007	38.9	38.8	38.7	38.6	38.8	38.6	38.3	38.4	38.3	38.4	38.2	37.7	38.5
2008	36.6	36.7	37.1	36.9	37.5	38.2	37.6	38.3	38.2	38.0	37.8	38.2	37.6
2009	37.6	36.5	37.1	36.4	36.5	37.4	37.2	37.8	37.1	37.6	37.8	37.3	37.2
Construction													
2007	38.9	38.7	38.6	38.0	38.5	38.3	37.9	38.2	37.7	37.9	37.7	37.1	38.1
2008	36.0	35.8	35.9	35.5	36.4	37.2	36.4	37.4	37.3	37.1	36.7	36.9	36.5
2009	36.5	35.5	36.2	35.7	36.0	37.0	36.8	37.1	36.4	37.0	36.9	35.9	36.4
Manufacturing													
2007	38.8	38.9	38.6	39.1	38.9	38.7	38.5	38.4	39.0	39.0	38.8	38.5	38.8
2008	37.6	38.0	38.6	38.6	38.5	39.0	38.7	38.3	38.3	38.3	38.4	39.1	38.5
2009	38.4	37.4	38.0	37.0	36.9	37.7	37.7	38.5	37.7	38.1	38.6	38.5	37.9
Trade, Transportation, and Utilities													
2007	35.7	36.1	36.2	36.2	35.9	36.4	36.1	36.1	36.5	35.5	35.4	36.4	36.0
2008	35.3	35.6	36.2	35.9	36.0	37.0	36.5	36.6	36.7	36.9	37.3	36.5	36.4
2009	36.1	36.3	36.0	35.5	35.6	35.6	35.2	35.6	35.5	35.1	35.9	35.2	35.6
Financial Activites													
2007	37.3	37.1	37.1	37.5	36.1	36.4	36.8	36.6	36.3	36.5	35.7	36.7	36.7
2008	36.4	36.1	36.7	36.5	36.3	37.3	36.8	36.5	36.3	37.0	37.5	37.0	36.7
2009	37.2	37.3	37.4	37.0	35.9	36.2	37.1	37.6	37.2	37.5	38.4	37.7	37.2
Professional and Business Services													
2007	35.8	36.0	36.1	36.3	35.7	36.3	36.5	35.8	35.7	35.5	35.5	35.9	35.9
2008	35.9	35.9	36.8	36.2	35.5	36.2	35.4	35.7	35.3	35.9	36.1	35.2	35.9
2009	35.7	35.5	35.7	35.4	35.5	34.7	34.3	35.3	34.5	35.1	35.4	34.6	35.2
Education and Health Services													
2007	35.0	34.7	34.7	34.8	34.5	34.7	34.8	34.6	34.7	34.1	34.1	34.0	34.6
2008	33.6	34.2	34.5	34.4	34.5	34.6	34.5	34.8	34.6	34.7	35.0	34.9	34.5
2009	35.0	35.5	35.5	35.0	35.1	35.0	35.6	35.6	35.2	35.1	35.5	35.6	35.3
Leisure and Hospitality													
2007	28.4	28.6	29.0	29.3	28.7	28.6	28.5	27.8	27.8	27.9	28.3	28.4	28.4
2008	27.7	28.3	28.7	28.1	28.0	28.0	27.2	27.6	27.4	28.0	27.8	27.0	27.8
2009	26.7	27.5	27.7	27.1	26.9	26.5	26.5	26.7	26.8	26.4	27.1	26.4	26.9
Other Services													
2007	34.3	34.9	35.1	35.8	35.6	34.8	34.7	35.7	35.1	35.3	34.6	34.3	35.0
2008	33.4	32.4	32.5	32.8	32.6	32.3	31.7	32.5	31.6	32.3	33.0	32.0	32.4
2009	31.7	31.7	32.6	31.9	32.1	32.5	32.8	33.1	32.2	32.8	33.2	34.0	32.5

Average Hourly Earnings by Selected Industry: Arizona, 2007–2009

(Dollars, not seasonally adjusted.)

Industry and year	January	February	March	April	May	June	July	August	September	October	November	December	Annual average
Total Private													
2007	19.98	20.03	19.93	20.05	19.97	19.98	19.61	19.58	19.86	19.61	19.51	19.91	19.84
2008	19.83	19.98	20.42	20.34	20.42	20.59	20.80	20.88	21.05	21.04	21.44	21.53	20.69
2009	21.71	21.93	21.78	21.86	21.90	21.87	22.13	22.08	22.17	22.27	22.20	22.55	22.03
Goods-Producing													
2007	20.68	20.66	20.59	20.95	20.79	20.74	21.00	20.60	20.71	21.19	20.97	21.52	20.86
2008	21.73	21.90	21.76	21.63	21.99	22.09	22.10	22.75	22.09	22.08	22.55	22.61	22.10
2009	22.61	22.92	23.01	23.13	23.11	23.16	23.21	22.92	23.27	23.24	23.29	23.69	23.12
Construction													
2007	19.61	19.44	19.37	19.87	19.53	19.53	19.68	19.57	19.84	19.85	20.37	20.86	19.78
2008	21.20	21.50	21.43	21.38	21.67	21.97	21.71	21.65	21.91	22.11	22.26	22.64	21.76
2009	22.23	22.46	22.20	22.38	22.41	22.63	22.53	22.40	23.00	22.86	22.91	23.25	22.59
Manufacturing													
2007	21.83	22.03	22.05	22.21	22.35	22.30	22.72	22.03	21.94	22.59	21.91	22.56	22.21
2008	22.63	22.49	22.33	22.05	22.45	22.28	22.64	23.31	22.61	22.31	22.97	22.67	22.56
2009	23.10	23.41	23.78	23.84	23.69	23.64	23.85	23.41	23.54	23.60	23.65	24.13	23.63
Trade, Transportation, and Utilities													
2007	19.15	18.98	19.37	19.39	19.31	19.25	18.36	18.58	18.85	18.33	18.52	18.09	18.84
2008	18.59	18.80	19.11	19.16	19.44	19.06	19.28	19.25	19.65	19.43	19.81	20.04	19.30
2009	20.64	20.86	20.33	20.32	20.28	20.60	21.06	20.55	20.61	20.88	20.69	20.64	20.62
Financial Activites													
2007	23.00	23.44	23.01	22.76	22.55	22.84	22.19	21.92	22.56	21.88	22.33	22.99	22.63
2008	22.36	22.56	23.22	22.60	22.60	22.11	21.97	21.95	22.24	22.34	22.90	22.49	22.45
2009	22.65	23.02	23.02	23.08	23.46	23.16	23.85	24.52	24.46	24.35	24.19	24.11	23.66
Professional and Business Services													
2007	21.46	21.83	21.28	21.60	21.80	21.94	22.23	22.28	22.94	22.25	22.11	22.66	22.03
2008	22.66	23.19	23.55	24.24	23.98	24.69	24.78	24.68	24.85	25.18	25.57	25.67	24.40
2009	25.59	26.04	26.49	26.52	26.50	26.47	26.94	26.71	26.42	26.26	26.70	26.43	26.42
Education and Health Services													
2007	21.66	21.65	21.81	21.91	22.09	21.61	21.38	21.45	22.01	22.20	22.18	22.84	21.90
2008	22.84	22.78	22.97	22.78	22.70	22.43	23.10	22.83	23.27	23.10	23.39	23.60	22.99
2009	23.53	23.50	23.56	23.60	23.63	23.37	23.31	23.45	23.60	23.77	23.51	23.43	23.52
Leisure and Hospitality													
2007	12.06	12.09	12.03	11.94	11.92	11.96	11.77	12.12	12.00	12.17	12.07	12.43	12.05
2008	12.06	12.30	12.51	12.76	12.63	12.54	12.64	12.62	12.99	12.85	13.09	13.28	12.68
2009	13.10	13.07	13.17	13.23	12.98	13.08	12.83	12.93	13.10	13.25	13.29	13.28	13.12
Other Services													
2007	16.92	16.73	16.81	16.88	16.45	16.40	16.73	16.23	16.14	15.66	16.12	16.60	16.47
2008	16.53	16.03	16.51	16.12	15.78	16.25	16.49	16.21	16.39	16.34	16.34	16.49	16.29
2009	16.42	16.61	16.19	16.54	16.20	16.13	16.05	16.24	16.49	16.13	16.16	15.85	16.25

Average Weekly Earnings by Selected Industry: Arizona, 2007–2009

(Dollars, not seasonally adjusted.)

Industry and year	January	February	March	April	May	June	July	August	September	October	November	December	Annual average
Total Private													
2007	707.29	711.07	707.52	715.79	702.94	707.29	696.16	689.22	695.10	680.47	675.05	698.84	698.37
2008	676.20	685.31	710.62	701.73	704.49	728.89	723.84	732.89	734.65	740.61	761.12	751.40	720.01
2009	755.51	767.55	764.48	754.17	753.36	754.52	765.70	775.01	767.08	775.00	783.66	782.49	766.64
Goods-Producing													
2007	804.45	801.61	796.83	808.67	806.65	800.56	804.30	791.04	793.19	813.70	801.05	811.30	803.11
2008	795.32	803.73	807.30	798.15	824.63	843.84	830.96	871.33	843.84	839.04	852.39	863.70	830.96
2009	850.14	836.58	853.67	841.93	843.52	866.18	863.41	866.38	863.32	873.82	880.36	883.64	860.06
Construction													
2007	762.83	752.33	747.68	755.06	751.91	748.00	745.87	747.57	747.97	752.32	767.95	773.91	753.62
2008	763.20	769.70	769.34	758.99	788.79	817.28	790.24	809.71	817.24	820.28	816.94	835.42	794.24
2009	811.40	797.33	803.64	798.97	806.76	837.31	829.10	831.04	837.20	845.82	845.38	834.68	822.28
Manufacturing													
2007	847.00	856.97	851.13	868.41	869.42	863.01	874.72	845.95	855.66	881.01	850.11	868.56	861.75
2008	850.89	854.62	861.94	851.13	864.33	868.92	876.17	892.77	865.96	854.47	882.05	886.40	868.56
2009	887.04	875.53	903.64	882.08	874.16	891.23	899.15	901.29	887.46	899.16	912.89	929.01	895.58
Trade, Transportation, and Utilities													
2007	683.66	685.18	701.19	701.92	693.23	700.70	662.80	670.74	688.03	650.72	655.61	658.48	678.24
2008	656.23	669.28	691.78	687.84	699.84	705.22	703.72	704.55	721.16	716.97	738.91	731.46	702.52
2009	745.10	757.22	731.88	721.36	721.97	733.36	741.31	731.58	731.66	732.89	742.77	726.53	734.07
Financial Activites													
2007	857.90	869.62	853.67	853.50	814.06	831.38	816.59	802.27	818.93	798.62	797.18	843.73	830.52
2008	813.90	814.42	852.17	824.90	820.38	824.70	808.50	801.18	807.31	826.58	858.75	832.13	823.92
2009	842.58	858.65	860.95	853.96	842.21	838.39	884.84	921.95	909.91	913.13	928.90	908.95	880.15
Professional and Business Services													
2007	768.27	785.88	768.21	784.08	778.26	796.42	811.40	797.62	818.96	789.88	784.91	813.49	790.88
2008	813.49	832.52	866.64	877.49	851.29	893.78	877.21	881.08	877.21	903.96	923.08	903.58	875.96
2009	913.56	924.42	945.69	938.81	940.75	918.51	924.04	942.86	911.49	921.73	945.18	914.48	929.98
Education and Health Services													
2007	758.10	751.26	756.81	762.47	762.11	749.87	744.02	742.17	763.75	757.02	756.34	776.56	757.74
2008	767.42	779.08	792.47	783.63	783.15	776.08	796.95	794.48	805.14	801.57	818.65	823.64	793.16
2009	823.55	834.25	836.38	826.00	829.41	817.95	829.84	834.82	830.72	834.33	834.61	834.11	830.26
Leisure and Hospitality													
2007	342.50	345.77	348.87	349.84	342.10	342.06	335.45	336.94	333.60	339.54	341.58	353.01	342.22
2008	334.06	348.09	359.04	358.56	353.64	351.12	343.81	348.31	355.93	359.80	363.90	358.56	352.50
2009	349.77	359.43	364.81	358.53	349.16	346.62	340.00	345.23	353.49	349.80	360.16	350.59	352.93
Other Services													
2007	580.36	583.88	590.03	604.30	585.62	570.72	580.53	579.41	566.51	552.80	557.75	569.38	576.45
2008	552.10	519.37	536.58	528.74	514.43	524.88	522.73	526.83	517.92	527.78	539.22	527.68	527.80
2009	520.51	526.54	527.79	527.63	520.02	524.23	526.44	537.54	530.98	529.06	536.51	538.90	528.13

ARKANSAS
At a Glance

Population:
    1990 census: 2,350,624
    2000 census: 2,673,400
    2009 estimate: 2,889,450

Percent change in population:
    1990–2000: 13.7%
    2000–2009: 8.1%

Percent change in total nonfarm employment:
    1990–2009: 26.1%
    2008–2009: -3.1%

Industry with the largest growth in employment, 1990–2009 (thousands):
    Education and Health Services, 71.5

Industry with the largest decline or smallest growth in employment, 1990–2009 (thousands):
    Manufacturing, -55.2

Civilian labor force:
    1990: 1,125,962
    2000: 1,260,256
    2009: 1,370,319

Unemployment rate and rank among states (lowest to highest):
    1990: 6.8%, 46th
    2000: 4.2%, 33rd
    2009: 7.3%, 17th

Employment by Industry, 2009

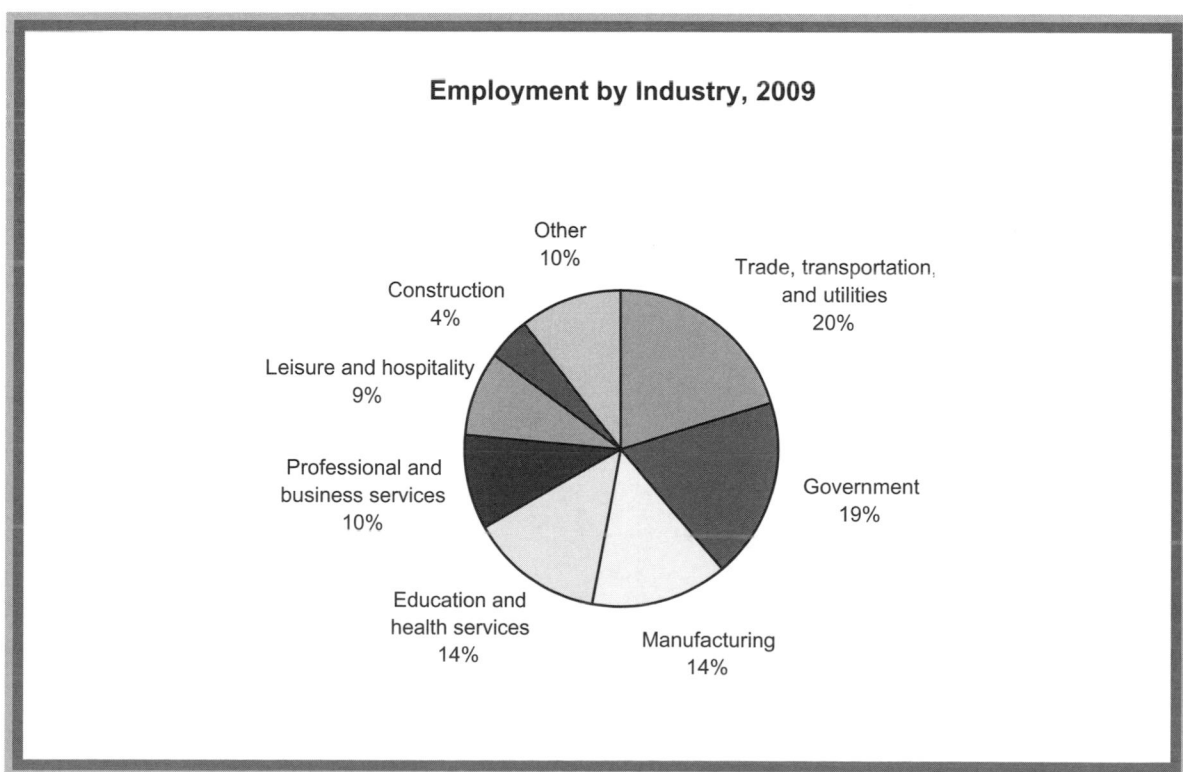

Other 10%

Trade, transportation, and utilities 20%

Construction 4%

Leisure and hospitality 9%

Government 19%

Professional and business services 10%

Education and health services 14%

Manufacturing 14%

Employment by Industry: Arkansas, Selected Years, 1990–2009

(Numbers in thousands, not seasonally adjusted.)

Industry and year	January	February	March	April	May	June	July	August	September	October	November	December	Annual average
Total Nonfarm													
1990	895.3	902.2	911.8	918.9	928.3	933.5	920.4	928.2	941.0	937.9	936.5	932.6	923.9
2000	1135.6	1143.8	1158.4	1158.7	1166.5	1168.3	1148.2	1156.6	1168.4	1168.1	1167.4	1163.1	1158.6
2001	1139.8	1147.3	1157.0	1160.8	1162.8	1161.3	1143.9	1151.5	1159.6	1155.5	1154.2	1151.0	1153.7
2002	1125.3	1132.8	1144.1	1148.4	1155.3	1155.0	1138.2	1143.2	1157.2	1151.7	1151.8	1152.4	1146.3
2003	1128.7	1133.1	1140.4	1142.6	1149.2	1146.0	1131.1	1141.2	1155.5	1159.1	1156.3	1158.4	1145.1
2004	1135.2	1142.5	1152.9	1157.7	1162.2	1161.1	1146.8	1155.4	1169.0	1168.7	1172.0	1173.6	1158.1
2005	1151.0	1162.1	1173.0	1178.4	1182.2	1180.9	1165.3	1172.0	1192.7	1189.1	1193.1	1194.7	1177.9
2006	1178.2	1186.6	1198.5	1203.8	1206.7	1205.3	1184.1	1193.2	1208.6	1205.5	1205.7	1207.3	1198.6
2007	1184.9	1193.3	1207.8	1207.4	1211.2	1209.7	1188.1	1200.1	1213.2	1211.2	1213.0	1214.2	1204.5
2008	1190.8	1200.0	1207.9	1207.9	1212.6	1208.4	1189.8	1198.4	1211.8	1205.4	1200.8	1195.9	1202.5
2009	1166.3	1169.2	1174.2	1174.4	1171.2	1163.9	1150.4	1153.5	1166.2	1167.3	1166.8	1158.7	1165.2
Total Private													
1990	738.8	741.9	749.2	757.5	764.1	776.1	774.1	780.0	778.6	774.4	771.9	768.8	764.6
2000	947.1	952.0	964.0	965.3	969.2	977.9	971.9	975.2	977.1	973.6	972.2	968.7	967.9
2001	948.5	951.8	960.5	963.7	966.4	970.3	965.1	969.1	963.8	956.5	954.0	951.2	960.1
2002	930.4	933.8	944.1	949.6	956.8	962.1	957.7	959.7	961.0	952.6	951.3	952.1	950.9
2003	932.0	932.8	939.0	941.7	948.7	950.3	945.8	952.7	954.7	955.4	951.8	954.6	946.6
2004	935.7	939.3	948.9	954.8	959.7	964.4	962.5	964.6	966.1	963.4	965.2	968.0	957.7
2005	950.1	956.1	966.6	970.5	975.6	979.5	976.9	979.4	985.2	980.2	983.7	986.3	974.2
2006	972.6	976.6	987.3	992.0	996.1	1001.2	992.3	996.2	997.8	993.2	992.1	995.0	991.0
2007	976.8	979.7	993.2	992.9	998.0	1001.1	994.4	1000.0	999.3	995.3	996.0	998.1	993.7
2008	979.8	983.6	990.6	990.5	995.0	996.6	992.3	996.0	995.3	986.8	981.4	977.3	988.8
2009	952.1	949.8	953.7	953.6	951.5	949.8	948.2	947.7	948.9	946.0	944.5	937.0	948.6
Goods-Producing													
1990	257.9	258.4	259.0	261.4	264.4	270.2	268.9	269.7	270.4	268.5	266.3	264.1	264.9
2000	297.2	297.7	301.0	300.0	301.3	303.5	302.5	302.4	302.1	299.8	298.1	297.0	300.2
2001	291.1	288.9	290.7	290.0	289.9	290.7	289.0	289.8	287.3	283.7	280.4	279.0	287.5
2002	273.3	273.4	274.6	274.9	276.7	278.9	277.8	277.3	276.7	273.1	270.9	270.1	274.8
2003	265.2	263.5	263.9	263.1	264.0	264.5	263.4	264.6	264.8	264.3	261.3	262.0	263.7
2004	257.8	257.7	259.8	262.3	263.8	265.3	264.7	265.0	264.8	262.5	261.5	260.8	262.2
2005	258.7	259.2	261.3	261.9	264.0	265.2	264.4	265.4	266.7	265.2	265.5	265.6	263.6
2006	262.8	263.7	263.6	265.4	266.3	268.7	266.1	266.9	265.9	262.5	259.2	259.9	264.3
2007	256.2	255.1	258.1	257.5	258.2	258.5	257.1	257.1	256.4	254.6	253.1	253.5	256.3
2008	249.7	249.5	251.2	251.0	252.2	253.2	253.1	253.4	253.1	250.5	246.4	243.8	250.6
2009	235.9	232.5	230.3	227.2	225.0	224.5	224.9	225.3	224.8	221.8	221.0	220.7	226.2
Mining and Logging													
1990	7.2	7.0	7.1	6.9	6.9	7.2	7.5	7.6	7.7	7.5	7.4	7.4	7.2
2000	6.7	6.6	6.6	6.5	6.7	6.9	6.9	7.0	7.0	6.9	6.7	6.8	6.7
2001	6.5	6.6	6.7	6.9	7.1	7.2	7.3	7.3	7.2	7.1	7.0	6.8	7.0
2002	6.5	6.5	6.6	6.6	6.8	6.9	6.9	7.0	7.0	6.9	6.9	6.8	6.8
2003	6.5	6.6	6.6	6.8	7.0	7.1	7.0	7.2	7.2	7.2	7.2	7.2	7.0
2004	7.0	6.9	6.9	6.9	7.0	7.0	7.0	7.2	7.2	7.0	6.8	6.8	7.0
2005	6.5	6.6	6.7	6.9	7.0	7.2	7.2	7.3	7.3	7.2	7.2	7.3	7.0
2006	6.8	6.8	6.9	7.4	7.6	7.8	7.7	7.8	8.1	8.0	8.1	8.2	7.6
2007	8.4	8.7	9.0	9.0	9.3	9.6	9.6	9.9	10.0	9.8	9.8	9.9	9.4
2008	9.9	9.8	10.0	10.2	10.6	10.8	11.0	11.0	11.1	11.3	11.4	11.2	10.7
2009	10.6	10.5	10.5	10.3	10.0	10.2	10.3	10.3	10.2	10.0	9.8	9.8	10.2
Construction													
1990	34.5	34.4	34.9	36.3	38.4	41.3	40.5	40.5	40.8	40.7	39.3	37.9	38.2
2000	50.3	50.7	53.0	52.5	53.4	54.5	54.1	54.5	55.0	53.9	52.8	52.0	53.0
2001	49.6	49.9	52.2	52.9	54.4	55.3	56.1	56.6	55.7	54.4	53.9	53.3	53.7
2002	51.3	51.7	53.2	54.0	55.2	56.6	57.1	57.1	56.0	54.2	53.0	52.2	54.3
2003	49.3	48.7	49.5	50.1	51.3	51.7	51.9	52.4	52.2	51.9	50.5	50.2	50.8
2004	47.8	47.8	49.7	51.3	52.4	53.3	53.3	53.4	53.3	52.1	51.6	51.2	51.4
2005	50.3	50.9	52.5	53.8	55.3	55.7	56.0	56.5	56.8	55.9	55.9	56.2	54.7
2006	54.0	55.0	54.8	56.6	57.9	58.9	57.8	58.4	59.0	57.3	56.1	56.4	56.9
2007	53.9	53.6	56.4	56.7	57.4	58.0	57.1	57.5	57.2	56.3	56.0	55.5	56.3
2008	53.4	53.8	55.1	55.7	56.6	57.3	57.8	58.5	58.2	57.4	56.0	55.0	56.2
2009	52.1	51.9	51.6	51.0	50.7	51.8	53.1	53.4	53.1	51.6	51.4	50.4	51.8
Manufacturing													
1990	216.2	217.0	217.0	218.2	219.1	221.7	220.9	221.6	221.9	220.3	219.6	218.8	219.3
2000	240.2	240.4	241.4	241.0	241.2	242.1	241.5	240.9	240.1	239.0	238.6	238.2	240.3
2001	235.0	232.4	231.8	230.2	228.4	228.2	225.6	225.9	224.4	222.2	219.5	218.9	226.9
2002	215.5	215.2	214.8	214.3	214.7	215.4	213.8	213.2	213.7	212.0	211.0	211.1	213.7
2003	209.4	208.2	207.8	206.2	205.7	205.7	204.5	205.0	205.4	205.2	203.6	204.6	205.9
2004	203.0	203.0	203.2	204.1	204.4	205.0	204.4	204.4	204.3	203.4	203.1	202.8	203.8
2005	201.9	201.7	202.1	201.2	201.7	202.3	201.2	201.6	202.6	202.1	202.4	202.1	201.9
2006	202.0	201.9	201.9	201.4	200.8	202.0	200.6	200.7	198.8	197.2	195.0	195.3	199.8
2007	193.9	192.8	192.7	191.8	191.5	190.9	190.4	189.7	189.2	188.5	187.3	188.1	190.6
2008	186.4	185.9	186.1	185.1	185.0	185.1	184.3	183.9	183.8	181.8	179.0	177.6	183.7
2009	173.2	170.1	168.2	165.9	164.3	162.5	161.5	161.6	161.5	160.2	159.8	160.5	164.1

Employment by Industry: Arkansas, Selected Years, 1990–2009—*Continued*

(Numbers in thousands, not seasonally adjusted.)

Industry and year	January	February	March	April	May	June	July	August	September	October	November	December	Annual average
Service-Providing													
1990	637.4	643.8	652.8	657.5	663.9	663.3	651.5	658.5	670.6	669.4	670.2	668.5	659.0
2000	838.4	846.1	857.4	858.7	865.2	864.8	845.7	854.2	866.3	868.3	869.3	866.1	858.4
2001	848.7	858.4	866.3	870.8	872.9	870.6	854.9	861.7	872.3	871.8	873.8	872.0	866.2
2002	852.0	859.4	869.5	873.5	878.6	876.1	860.4	865.9	880.5	878.6	880.9	882.3	871.5
2003	863.5	869.6	876.5	879.5	885.2	881.5	867.7	876.6	890.7	894.8	895.0	896.4	881.4
2004	877.4	884.8	893.1	895.4	898.4	895.8	882.1	890.4	904.2	906.2	910.5	912.8	895.9
2005	892.3	902.9	911.7	916.5	918.2	915.7	900.9	906.6	926.0	923.9	927.6	929.1	914.3
2006	915.4	922.9	934.9	938.4	940.4	936.6	918.0	926.3	942.7	943.0	946.5	947.4	934.4
2007	928.7	938.2	949.7	949.9	953.0	951.2	931.0	943.0	956.8	956.6	959.9	960.7	948.2
2008	941.1	950.5	956.7	956.9	960.4	955.2	936.7	945.0	958.7	954.9	954.4	952.1	951.9
2009	930.4	936.7	943.9	947.2	946.2	939.4	925.5	928.2	941.4	945.5	945.8	938.0	939.0
Trade, Transportation, and Utilities													
1990	191.1	190.5	191.3	192.1	193.6	195.8	195.4	196.9	196.1	196.2	197.6	198.4	194.5
2000	237.8	237.8	239.9	240.5	241.3	243.1	241.3	242.2	242.6	243.5	245.8	247.6	241.9
2001	238.6	237.5	240.4	241.5	242.5	243.2	241.4	241.7	240.9	241.2	243.7	244.6	241.4
2002	236.9	236.9	239.8	240.4	242.0	242.5	241.6	241.4	241.8	240.4	243.0	244.4	240.9
2003	236.2	235.3	236.7	237.3	238.2	238.7	238.5	239.7	240.9	242.4	244.1	246.3	239.5
2004	237.6	237.6	239.3	240.1	241.4	242.2	242.1	242.4	243.2	243.2	245.8	248.7	242.0
2005	241.1	240.6	242.7	244.2	244.9	246.0	245.7	245.4	247.2	246.4	249.7	252.0	245.5
2006	244.8	244.4	247.8	247.3	248.8	248.8	247.7	248.3	249.2	249.6	252.5	254.6	248.7
2007	246.2	245.9	250.3	248.2	250.2	250.8	249.7	250.4	250.4	249.8	253.5	255.2	250.1
2008	247.2	246.4	248.2	247.2	248.3	248.7	247.1	247.2	246.4	244.2	245.9	246.3	246.9
2009	237.3	235.2	236.8	236.3	235.8	235.1	234.5	233.7	234.0	232.2	234.8	233.2	234.9
Wholesale Trade													
1990	38.1	38.3	38.5	38.5	38.7	39.3	39.3	39.2	38.9	38.6	38.6	38.4	38.7
2000	44.6	44.9	45.6	45.6	45.9	46.7	46.4	46.2	46.2	45.9	45.6	45.6	45.7
2001	45.1	45.3	45.8	45.8	45.9	46.3	46.1	45.9	45.5	45.3	45.0	44.9	45.6
2002	44.2	44.2	44.8	44.9	45.1	45.6	45.3	45.2	45.3	44.9	44.6	44.6	44.9
2003	43.9	44.1	44.4	44.4	44.9	45.4	45.1	45.2	45.4	45.3	45.1	45.2	44.9
2004	44.6	44.8	45.4	46.0	46.5	46.8	46.9	46.5	46.6	46.5	46.6	47.1	46.2
2005	46.5	46.8	47.3	47.5	47.8	48.0	47.8	47.6	47.6	47.2	47.1	47.5	47.4
2006	46.9	47.1	47.5	47.9	48.2	48.5	48.1	48.1	48.2	47.9	47.9	48.2	47.9
2007	47.2	47.4	48.0	48.1	48.3	48.6	48.2	48.1	47.9	48.0	48.0	48.3	48.0
2008	47.8	48.1	48.4	48.6	48.9	49.0	48.9	48.8	48.8	48.4	48.2	48.1	48.5
2009	47.0	47.0	47.2	47.3	47.5	47.4	47.1	46.9	46.6	46.6	46.7	46.5	47.0
Retail Trade													
1990	102.6	101.8	101.9	102.6	103.5	104.3	103.9	105.0	104.5	104.2	106.0	107.3	103.9
2000	130.2	130.2	131.2	131.6	132.3	132.9	131.7	132.6	132.5	133.1	135.9	137.4	132.6
2001	130.5	129.0	130.9	131.5	132.4	132.5	130.9	130.8	130.3	130.3	133.5	134.6	131.4
2002	128.6	127.5	129.1	129.7	130.8	130.7	130.1	129.5	129.4	128.8	131.8	133.5	130.0
2003	127.1	126.0	126.8	127.3	127.8	127.9	127.9	128.7	129.3	130.2	132.4	134.6	128.8
2004	128.5	128.1	129.4	129.8	130.5	130.7	130.3	130.6	130.6	131.1	134.0	135.6	130.8
2005	129.9	128.8	130.2	131.3	131.5	132.1	131.6	131.4	131.9	132.2	135.5	136.9	131.9
2006	131.8	130.9	133.5	132.6	133.6	132.9	132.2	132.7	132.6	133.2	136.0	137.5	133.3
2007	132.3	131.4	134.6	132.9	134.2	134.3	134.0	134.1	134.3	133.9	137.7	139.4	134.4
2008	133.7	132.6	133.9	132.8	133.6	134.2	133.4	133.7	132.9	131.6	133.9	135.1	133.5
2009	129.2	128.0	129.6	129.6	130.0	129.6	129.2	129.2	129.3	129.0	131.0	130.4	129.5
Transportation and Utilities													
1990	50.4	50.4	50.9	51.0	51.4	52.2	52.2	52.7	52.7	53.4	53.0	52.7	51.9
2000	63.0	62.7	63.1	63.3	63.1	63.5	63.2	63.4	63.9	64.5	64.3	64.6	63.5
2001	63.0	63.2	63.7	64.2	64.2	64.4	64.4	65.0	65.1	65.6	65.2	65.1	64.4
2002	64.1	65.2	65.9	65.8	66.1	66.2	66.2	66.7	67.1	66.7	66.6	66.3	66.1
2003	65.2	65.2	65.5	65.6	65.5	65.4	65.5	65.8	66.2	66.9	66.6	66.5	65.8
2004	64.5	64.7	64.5	64.3	64.4	64.7	64.9	65.3	66.0	65.6	65.2	66.0	65.0
2005	64.7	65.0	65.2	65.4	65.6	65.9	66.3	66.4	67.7	67.0	67.1	67.6	66.2
2006	66.1	66.4	66.8	66.8	67.0	67.4	67.4	67.5	68.4	68.5	68.6	68.9	67.5
2007	66.7	67.1	67.7	67.2	67.7	67.9	67.5	68.2	68.2	67.9	67.8	67.5	67.6
2008	65.7	65.7	65.9	65.8	65.8	65.5	64.8	64.7	64.7	64.2	63.8	63.1	65.0
2009	61.1	60.2	60.0	59.4	58.3	58.1	58.2	57.6	58.1	56.6	57.1	56.3	58.4
Information													
1990	17.2	17.4	17.4	17.4	17.4	17.8	18.0	18.0	17.9	18.0	18.0	18.0	17.7
2000	19.9	19.9	20.1	19.8	20.1	20.4	20.6	21.0	21.1	21.2	21.4	21.5	20.5
2001	21.2	21.2	21.0	20.8	20.8	20.9	21.1	21.1	21.0	20.8	20.9	20.8	21.0
2002	20.8	20.5	20.2	20.2	20.2	20.5	20.4	20.3	20.2	20.2	20.4	20.3	20.4
2003	20.1	20.1	20.1	19.9	20.0	20.2	20.4	20.3	20.1	20.2	20.3	20.3	20.2
2004	20.1	20.0	20.0	19.8	19.8	19.9	19.7	19.7	19.6	19.5	19.7	19.7	19.8
2005	19.6	19.8	19.7	19.4	19.4	19.3	19.2	19.3	19.0	19.0	19.0	19.0	19.3
2006	18.8	18.8	18.8	18.8	18.7	18.6	18.6	18.7	18.6	18.3	18.3	18.3	18.6
2007	18.4	18.4	18.4	18.4	18.4	18.2	18.1	18.1	18.0	17.8	17.8	17.8	18.2
2008	17.6	17.7	17.6	17.8	17.5	17.6	17.5	17.5	17.2	17.0	16.9	16.9	17.4
2009	16.5	16.4	16.4	16.4	16.5	16.6	16.4	16.2	16.0	15.6	15.6	15.6	16.2

Employment by Industry: Arkansas, Selected Years, 1990–2009—*Continued*

(Numbers in thousands, not seasonally adjusted.)

Industry and year	January	February	March	April	May	June	July	August	September	October	November	December	Annual average
Financial Activities													
1990	39.6	39.5	39.7	40.0	40.2	40.8	40.6	40.7	39.9	40.1	40.1	40.1	40.1
2000	49.1	49.1	49.4	49.6	49.5	50.1	49.6	49.4	49.2	49.1	49.1	49.4	49.3
2001	48.7	48.9	49.0	49.1	49.4	49.8	49.8	49.7	49.6	49.2	49.4	49.9	49.4
2002	49.4	49.2	49.5	49.5	49.7	50.0	50.0	49.9	49.8	49.3	49.4	49.8	49.6
2003	49.4	49.4	49.6	49.9	50.2	50.7	50.9	50.9	50.7	50.6	50.8	51.3	50.4
2004	50.2	50.3	50.5	50.7	50.9	51.3	51.2	51.1	51.1	50.8	50.9	51.4	50.9
2005	50.8	50.7	50.9	50.7	51.0	51.6	51.8	51.8	51.8	51.7	51.8	52.5	51.4
2006	51.8	51.8	52.0	52.2	52.5	52.9	52.9	53.1	53.0	52.7	52.9	53.2	52.6
2007	52.4	52.4	52.6	53.1	53.3	53.7	53.7	53.6	53.4	53.2	53.1	53.3	53.2
2008	52.6	52.6	52.7	52.5	52.7	52.7	52.5	52.5	52.3	51.6	51.5	52.0	52.4
2009	51.0	50.7	50.8	50.8	50.9	51.0	50.7	50.5	50.2	50.2	50.3	51.0	50.7
Professional and Business Services													
1990	53.6	54.6	55.3	57.2	57.4	58.7	59.0	60.3	59.9	58.7	57.9	57.6	57.5
2000	98.3	99.4	101.4	100.2	100.9	102.4	101.9	103.9	104.2	103.2	102.6	100.5	101.6
2001	100.9	102.4	102.6	102.1	102.4	103.0	102.3	104.0	102.7	100.7	99.6	98.3	101.8
2002	96.4	96.9	99.1	100.4	101.2	102.4	102.3	103.3	104.5	103.7	102.6	102.9	101.3
2003	101.0	101.5	102.0	103.0	104.2	104.4	102.6	105.5	105.7	107.2	105.8	105.3	104.0
2004	105.2	105.2	106.5	107.1	107.1	107.9	109.0	109.7	109.3	110.4	110.7	110.7	108.2
2005	107.1	108.8	110.5	110.6	110.7	111.5	111.8	112.8	113.2	113.1	113.1	113.3	111.4
2006	111.5	112.9	115.1	114.5	114.9	115.6	114.0	114.6	115.6	115.1	114.7	114.6	114.4
2007	114.0	115.1	116.6	116.5	116.8	117.4	116.2	118.8	119.2	118.5	117.8	117.7	117.1
2008	115.0	117.2	117.3	117.0	117.8	117.2	116.4	117.9	118.1	117.9	116.3	115.5	117.0
2009	112.7	113.3	113.5	113.5	112.2	111.4	111.7	112.3	112.4	114.7	113.6	110.9	112.7
Education and Health Services													
1990	88.3	87.7	90.2	90.6	90.9	90.1	90.0	91.3	93.1	94.2	95.0	94.5	91.3
2000	125.5	126.9	127.7	127.7	127.0	126.0	124.9	125.4	128.9	129.3	129.6	129.1	127.3
2001	127.8	130.0	130.4	131.0	130.5	129.6	129.3	130.8	132.9	134.0	134.4	134.5	131.3
2002	133.0	133.8	135.0	135.4	135.3	134.1	133.2	134.9	137.4	137.9	138.6	138.7	135.6
2003	137.3	138.6	139.6	139.8	140.0	137.9	136.7	138.4	141.4	142.2	142.0	142.4	139.7
2004	140.1	141.4	142.3	142.7	142.3	141.2	140.2	141.1	143.9	144.9	145.3	145.2	142.6
2005	144.1	145.4	145.8	146.0	146.0	144.1	143.6	144.9	148.1	149.1	148.9	148.6	146.2
2006	148.4	149.7	150.7	151.2	150.9	150.0	148.2	149.8	152.5	152.7	152.8	153.0	150.8
2007	150.8	153.0	153.9	154.2	154.4	153.6	152.2	154.3	156.0	156.3	156.7	157.0	154.4
2008	156.8	157.7	158.5	157.5	157.6	156.3	155.3	156.9	159.3	160.0	160.0	159.7	158.0
2009	158.1	160.2	161.6	163.5	163.3	161.4	160.9	161.9	165.4	165.5	165.6	165.6	162.8
Leisure and Hospitality													
1990	58.8	61.3	63.6	66.0	67.1	68.8	68.3	69.2	67.5	64.9	63.1	62.1	65.0
2000	78.9	80.6	83.5	86.5	87.8	90.4	89.4	89.4	87.8	86.5	84.8	82.9	85.7
2001	79.7	82.3	85.3	88.3	89.8	91.3	90.7	90.6	88.5	86.4	85.2	83.7	86.8
2002	80.5	82.8	85.2	88.0	90.6	92.0	91.0	91.3	89.6	87.5	85.9	85.3	87.5
2003	82.6	84.3	86.6	88.0	91.0	92.2	92.0	92.1	90.2	87.7	86.7	86.1	88.3
2004	84.2	86.4	89.5	90.8	92.9	94.4	93.8	94.1	92.9	91.1	90.1	90.0	90.9
2005	87.5	90.1	93.5	94.9	96.6	98.3	97.1	96.8	96.2	93.4	93.3	92.7	94.2
2006	92.0	92.7	96.2	99.0	99.8	101.7	99.8	99.7	98.0	97.5	96.7	96.1	97.4
2007	94.0	94.9	97.8	99.7	101.3	102.8	101.8	102.1	100.6	99.9	98.8	98.2	99.3
2008	95.9	97.3	99.5	101.7	102.9	104.4	104.0	104.3	102.7	99.9	99.0	97.5	100.8
2009	95.6	96.5	99.1	100.9	102.6	104.2	103.6	102.6	101.2	101.1	99.1	96.3	100.2
Other Services													
1990	32.3	32.5	32.7	32.8	33.1	33.9	33.9	33.9	33.8	33.8	33.9	34.0	33.3
2000	40.4	40.6	41.0	41.0	41.3	42.0	41.7	41.5	41.2	41.0	40.8	40.7	41.1
2001	40.5	40.6	41.1	40.9	41.1	41.8	41.5	41.4	40.9	40.5	40.4	40.4	40.9
2002	40.1	40.3	40.7	40.8	41.1	41.7	41.4	41.3	41.0	40.5	40.5	40.6	40.8
2003	40.2	40.1	40.5	40.7	41.1	41.7	41.3	41.2	40.9	40.8	40.8	40.9	40.9
2004	40.5	40.7	41.0	41.3	41.5	42.2	41.8	41.5	41.3	41.0	41.2	41.5	41.3
2005	41.2	41.5	42.2	42.8	43.0	43.5	43.3	43.0	43.0	42.3	42.4	42.6	42.6
2006	42.5	42.6	43.1	43.6	44.2	44.9	45.0	45.1	45.0	44.8	45.0	45.3	44.3
2007	44.8	44.9	45.5	45.3	45.4	46.1	45.6	45.6	45.3	45.2	45.2	45.4	45.4
2008	45.0	45.2	45.6	45.8	46.0	46.5	46.4	46.3	46.2	45.7	45.4	45.6	45.8
2009	45.0	45.0	45.2	45.0	45.2	45.6	45.5	45.2	44.9	44.9	44.5	43.7	45.0
Government													
1990	156.5	160.3	162.6	161.4	164.2	157.4	146.3	148.2	162.4	163.5	164.6	163.8	159.2
2000	188.5	191.8	194.4	193.4	197.3	190.4	176.3	181.4	191.3	194.5	195.2	194.4	190.7
2001	191.3	195.5	196.5	197.1	196.4	191.0	178.8	182.4	195.8	199.0	200.2	199.8	193.7
2002	194.9	199.0	200.0	198.8	198.5	192.9	180.5	183.5	196.2	199.1	200.5	200.3	195.4
2003	196.7	200.3	201.4	200.9	200.5	195.7	185.3	188.5	200.8	203.7	204.5	203.8	198.5
2004	199.5	203.2	204.0	202.9	202.5	196.7	184.3	190.8	202.9	205.3	206.8	205.6	200.4
2005	200.9	206.0	206.4	207.9	206.6	201.4	188.4	192.6	207.5	208.9	209.4	208.4	203.7
2006	205.6	210.0	211.2	211.8	210.6	204.1	191.8	197.0	210.8	212.3	213.6	212.3	207.6
2007	208.1	213.6	214.6	214.5	213.2	208.6	193.7	200.1	213.9	215.9	217.0	216.1	210.8
2008	211.0	216.4	217.3	217.4	217.6	211.8	197.5	202.4	216.5	218.6	219.4	218.6	213.7
2009	214.2	219.4	220.5	220.8	219.7	214.1	202.2	205.8	217.3	221.3	222.3	221.7	216.6

Average Weekly Hours by Selected Industry: Arkansas, 2007–2009

(Not seasonally adjusted.)

Industry and year	January	February	March	April	May	June	July	August	September	October	November	December	Annual average
Total Private													
2007	33.7	34.2	34.2	35.4	35.5	36.3	35.5	35.3	35.3	34.9	34.9	35.5	35.0
2008	34.7	34.8	35.7	34.8	34.6	36.1	35.0	35.4	35.3	35.1	35.3	34.9	35.2
2009	34.6	35.3	34.0	33.8	34.3	34.7	34.4	35.3	34.3	34.5	35.1	34.8	34.6
Goods-Producing													
2007	37.3	39.0	39.5	39.6	40.0	40.8	39.8	40.2	40.7	40.5	39.9	40.8	39.8
2008	38.7	38.3	39.7	38.6	38.9	39.4	38.3	39.3	39.0	39.0	38.4	38.7	38.9
2009	37.6	37.9	36.4	36.1	37.7	38.2	37.3	39.2	37.3	38.4	39.6	39.2	37.9
Construction													
2007	36.5	35.5	37.8	37.4	39.2	40.7	37.8	40.2	38.3	39.1	39.0	36.6	38.2
2008	37.6	37.2	38.8	37.5	37.4	38.2	37.9	38.2	38.5	38.5	36.4	36.7	37.8
2009	37.9	36.6	34.7	36.5	36.7	38.5	37.0	38.7	36.9	36.5	38.4	36.5	37.1
Manufacturing													
2007	37.3	39.8	39.9	40.1	40.2	40.8	40.3	40.1	41.4	40.6	40.1	42.0	40.2
2008	38.6	38.3	39.6	38.6	39.1	39.5	38.0	39.6	39.0	39.0	38.9	39.2	39.0
2009	37.4	37.8	37.3	35.9	37.5	37.0	36.4	38.3	37.6	39.4	39.2	39.9	37.8
Trade, Transportation, and Utilities													
2007	37.4	36.3	36.2	37.0	36.2	37.2	37.1	36.8	37.1	36.6	36.5	37.2	36.8
2008	36.5	36.7	37.3	36.7	35.9	37.2	36.0	35.7	35.8	35.0	36.0	34.5	36.1
2009	35.0	36.4	35.0	35.7	35.5	36.5	36.1	36.6	36.6	36.1	36.1	35.6	35.9
Financial Activities													
2007	37.3	36.9	36.7	37.7	37.6	38.7	38.6	37.1	38.8	37.1	37.3	38.9	37.7
2008	38.5	38.6	39.7	37.4	36.8	39.4	37.2	38.0	38.1	38.0	37.9	37.3	38.1
2009	37.9	37.4	37.2	36.8	37.1	37.1	37.0	38.0	37.4	37.8	38.2	37.1	37.4
Professional and Business Services													
2007	32.8	37.3	36.9	37.2	36.7	35.4	36.2	36.4	36.2	35.7	35.2	35.2	35.9
2008	34.3	34.8	34.9	35.2	35.2	36.2	35.8	35.6	36.1	35.7	36.6	35.9	35.5
2009	34.9	35.9	34.5	33.7	33.0	33.5	33.0	34.4	32.6	32.0	33.7	34.5	33.8
Education and Health Services													
2007	30.0	29.2	29.0	32.6	32.6	33.6	31.4	31.3	31.3	31.2	31.5	31.7	31.3
2008	31.8	31.5	31.9	32.6	32.5	32.5	32.7	31.8	31.4	31.6	32.4	32.0	32.1
2009	32.1	32.7	32.2	32.0	32.3	32.6	32.8	33.0	32.8	32.7	33.0	32.8	32.6
Leisure and Hospitality													
2007	24.7	25.4	25.8	26.9	28.6	30.1	29.3	29.1	28.6	28.1	27.3	27.1	27.6
2008	26.2	26.6	26.6	26.7	26.7	28.7	27.4	27.7	26.4	27.0	26.4	26.5	26.9
2009	26.3	27.1	26.5	26.5	27.1	27.3	27.8	27.7	26.2	27.1	25.7	25.7	26.8

Average Hourly Earnings by Selected Industry: Arkansas, 2007–2009

(Dollars, not seasonally adjusted.)

Industry and year	January	February	March	April	May	June	July	August	September	October	November	December	Annual average
Total Private													
2007	15.88	15.96	15.91	16.19	15.94	15.88	16.40	16.31	16.52	16.68	16.62	16.93	16.27
2008	16.88	16.97	17.15	17.01	17.05	17.13	17.29	17.19	17.35	17.38	17.58	17.51	17.21
2009	17.73	17.85	17.91	18.01	18.05	17.82	17.79	17.90	17.99	18.10	18.27	18.27	17.97
Goods-Producing													
2007	16.24	15.98	15.92	16.03	16.19	16.47	16.31	16.43	16.85	17.22	17.17	17.12	16.50
2008	17.30	17.29	17.21	17.04	17.11	16.97	17.24	17.25	17.20	17.42	17.48	17.63	17.26
2009	17.47	17.74	17.69	17.54	17.38	17.16	17.10	17.08	17.15	17.15	17.15	17.39	17.33
Construction													
2007	16.67	16.55	16.58	16.99	17.04	16.58	17.07	16.77	17.56	17.50	17.72	17.68	17.06
2008	17.89	17.71	17.56	17.63	17.52	17.87	17.93	18.20	18.60	18.44	19.43	19.33	18.17
2009	18.90	19.08	19.20	19.18	19.06	18.32	18.15	18.00	18.11	18.40	18.03	19.01	18.61
Manufacturing													
2007	16.08	15.78	15.66	15.66	15.85	16.38	15.92	16.15	16.53	17.11	16.93	16.96	16.25
2008	17.12	17.13	17.08	16.83	16.92	16.59	16.95	16.88	16.56	16.91	16.71	16.86	16.88
2009	16.69	16.71	15.87	15.70	15.77	15.81	15.87	15.99	16.12	16.05	16.39	16.44	16.13
Trade, Transportation, and Utilities													
2007	15.35	15.05	15.21	15.60	15.51	15.28	16.52	15.70	16.26	15.65	15.66	16.35	15.68
2008	16.21	16.47	16.60	16.40	15.88	16.20	16.11	16.41	16.83	16.67	16.86	16.70	16.44
2009	16.99	16.98	17.10	17.15	17.20	17.03	17.17	17.44	17.29	17.32	17.59	17.65	17.24
Financial Activities													
2007	21.58	21.93	21.66	21.73	20.80	21.18	21.45	21.28	21.13	21.06	20.78	20.79	21.28
2008	21.23	20.95	21.43	21.13	21.00	21.14	21.11	20.43	20.32	20.73	21.46	21.30	21.02
2009	21.67	23.26	22.42	22.73	23.62	23.11	23.06	23.68	23.61	24.32	24.43	23.94	23.32
Professional and Business Services													
2007	16.16	16.52	17.53	18.85	18.23	17.96	19.22	18.70	18.99	18.77	19.39	20.31	18.40
2008	19.54	19.19	20.09	19.55	20.99	20.58	20.58	20.56	20.42	20.48	20.86	20.48	20.28
2009	20.23	20.16	20.23	20.28	20.32	20.75	20.65	20.49	20.46	20.27	20.65	20.41	20.41
Education and Health Services													
2007	15.61	16.16	15.75	15.84	15.57	15.20	15.96	15.83	15.99	16.10	16.08	16.44	15.87
2008	16.44	16.59	16.26	16.16	16.00	15.97	15.96	15.96	16.17	16.14	16.21	16.25	16.17
2009	16.31	16.16	16.40	16.32	16.44	16.39	16.51	16.66	16.83	17.10	16.91	16.95	16.59
Leisure and Hospitality													
2007	9.38	9.59	9.48	9.65	9.56	9.48	9.41	9.35	9.32	9.39	9.25	9.43	9.44
2008	9.26	9.43	9.67	9.49	9.36	9.19	9.31	9.36	9.57	9.79	9.84	9.81	9.50
2009	9.72	9.86	9.87	9.98	10.17	9.86	9.88	10.05	10.05	10.42	10.28	10.37	10.04

Average Weekly Earnings by Selected Industry: Arkansas, 2007–2009

(Dollars, not seasonally adjusted.)

Industry and year	January	February	March	April	May	June	July	August	September	October	November	December	Annual average
Total Private													
2007	535.16	545.83	544.12	573.13	565.87	576.44	582.20	575.74	583.16	582.13	580.04	601.02	569.45
2008	585.74	590.56	612.26	591.95	589.93	618.39	605.15	608.53	612.46	610.04	620.57	611.10	605.79
2009	613.46	630.11	608.94	608.74	619.12	618.35	611.98	631.87	617.06	624.45	641.28	635.80	621.76
Goods-Producing													
2007	605.75	623.22	628.84	634.79	647.60	671.98	649.14	660.49	685.80	697.41	685.08	698.50	656.70
2008	669.51	662.21	683.24	657.74	665.58	668.62	660.29	677.93	670.80	679.38	671.23	682.28	671.41
2009	656.87	672.35	643.92	633.19	655.23	655.51	637.83	669.54	639.70	658.56	679.14	681.69	656.81
Construction													
2007	608.46	587.53	626.72	635.43	667.97	674.81	645.25	674.15	672.55	684.25	691.08	647.09	651.69
2008	672.66	658.81	681.33	661.13	655.25	682.63	679.55	695.24	716.10	709.94	707.25	709.41	686.83
2009	716.31	698.33	666.24	700.07	699.50	705.32	671.55	696.60	668.26	671.60	692.35	693.87	690.43
Manufacturing													
2007	599.78	628.04	624.83	627.97	637.17	668.30	641.58	647.62	684.34	694.67	678.89	712.32	653.25
2008	660.83	656.08	676.37	649.64	661.57	655.31	644.10	668.45	645.84	659.49	650.02	660.91	658.32
2009	624.21	631.64	591.95	563.63	591.38	584.97	577.67	612.42	606.11	632.37	642.49	655.96	609.71
Trade, Transportation, and Utilities													
2007	574.09	546.32	550.60	577.20	561.46	568.42	612.89	577.76	603.25	572.79	571.59	608.22	577.02
2008	591.67	604.45	619.18	601.88	570.09	602.64	579.96	585.84	602.51	583.45	606.96	576.15	593.48
2009	594.65	618.07	598.50	612.26	610.60	621.60	619.84	638.30	632.81	625.25	635.00	628.34	618.92
Financial Activities													
2007	804.93	809.22	794.92	819.22	782.08	819.67	827.97	789.49	819.84	781.33	775.09	808.73	802.26
2008	817.36	808.67	850.77	790.26	772.80	832.92	785.29	776.34	774.19	787.74	813.33	794.49	800.86
2009	821.29	869.92	834.02	836.46	876.30	857.38	853.22	899.84	883.01	919.30	933.23	888.17	872.17
Professional and Business Services													
2007	530.05	616.20	646.86	701.22	669.04	635.78	695.76	680.68	687.44	670.09	682.53	714.91	660.56
2008	670.22	667.81	701.14	688.16	738.85	745.00	736.76	731.94	737.16	731.14	763.48	735.23	719.94
2009	706.03	723.74	697.94	683.44	670.56	695.13	681.45	704.86	667.00	648.64	695.91	704.15	689.86
Education and Health Services													
2007	468.30	471.87	456.75	516.38	507.58	510.72	501.14	495.48	500.49	502.32	506.52	521.15	496.73
2008	522.79	522.59	518.69	526.82	520.00	519.03	521.89	507.53	507.74	510.02	525.20	520.00	519.06
2009	523.55	528.43	528.08	522.24	531.01	534.31	541.53	549.78	552.02	559.17	558.03	555.96	540.83
Leisure and Hospitality													
2007	231.69	243.59	244.58	259.59	273.42	285.35	275.71	272.09	266.55	263.86	252.53	255.55	260.54
2008	242.61	250.84	257.22	253.38	249.91	263.75	255.09	259.27	252.65	264.33	259.78	259.97	255.55
2009	255.64	267.21	261.56	264.47	275.61	269.18	274.66	278.39	263.31	202.38	264.20	266.51	269.07

CALIFORNIA
At a Glance

Population:
    1990 census: 29,811,427
    2000 census: 33,871,648
    2009 estimate: 36,961,664

Percent change in population:
    1990–2000: 13.6%
    2000–2009: 9.1%

Percent change in total nonfarm employment:
    1990–2009: 12.6%
    2008–2009: -0.6%

Industry with the largest growth in employment, 1990–2009 (thousands):
    Education and Health Services, 621.7

Industry with the largest decline or smallest growth in employment, 1990–2009 (thousands):
    Manufacturing, -684.9

Civilian labor force:
    1990: 15,168,531
    2000: 16,857,578
    2009: 18,250,169

Unemployment rate and rank among states (lowest to highest):
    1990: 5.8%, 34th
    2000: 4.9%, 43rd
    2009: 11.4%, 48th

Employment by Industry, 2009

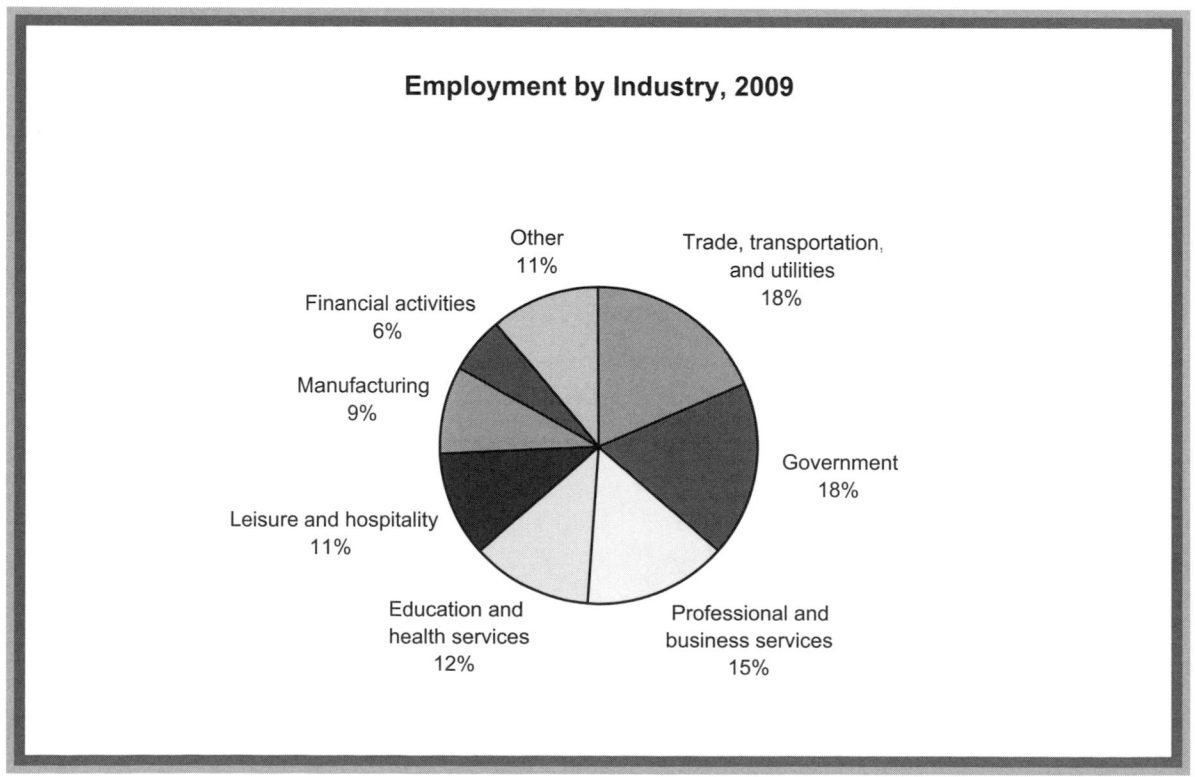

Other
11%

Trade, transportation,
and utilities
18%

Financial activities
6%

Manufacturing
9%

Government
18%

Leisure and hospitality
11%

Professional and
business services
15%

Education and
health services
12%

Employment by Industry: California, Selected Years, 1990–2009

(Numbers in thousands, not seasonally adjusted.)

Industry and year	January	February	March	April	May	June	July	August	September	October	November	December	Annual average
Total Nonfarm													
1990	12290.1	12360.0	12437.2	12463.4	12526.7	12583.9	12493.8	12471.2	12546.7	12580.9	12610.2	12633.5	12499.8
2000	14030.7	14170.1	14323.4	14354.0	14493.4	14599.8	14450.0	14521.9	14645.0	14649.8	14760.9	14859.0	14488.2
2001	14513.5	14598.0	14713.1	14650.1	14697.5	14752.3	14494.8	14534.8	14551.8	14549.5	14569.2	14598.9	14602.0
2002	14237.6	14328.0	14459.1	14448.7	14531.1	14581.6	14352.9	14404.4	14465.9	14505.6	14575.1	14604.0	14457.8
2003	14240.1	14302.1	14380.3	14379.4	14439.0	14493.8	14282.8	14328.7	14386.9	14452.7	14488.3	14539.7	14392.8
2004	14232.6	14328.5	14441.7	14462.2	14544.8	14605.6	14497.8	14504.4	14575.3	14670.2	14744.5	14783.3	14532.6
2005	14455.2	14571.6	14674.5	14729.3	14783.9	14852.2	14738.0	14794.5	14906.3	14952.4	15043.2	15114.9	14801.3
2006	14759.7	14885.2	14969.2	14971.6	15082.6	15170.5	14999.8	15052.2	15139.2	15173.8	15238.1	15281.6	15060.3
2007	14938.7	15047.9	15152.2	15102.7	15193.0	15265.5	15136.1	15145.2	15204.1	15241.4	15307.2	15348.2	15173.5
2008	14940.6	15031.4	15082.4	15091.2	15124.1	15147.0	14933.6	14917.5	14942.2	14911.4	14849.0	14806.8	14981.4
2009	14346.3	14281.4	14254.9	14177.6	14182.9	14153.0	13910.5	13898.4	13890.8	13963.0	13965.0	13928.3	14079.3
Total Private													
1990	10243.8	10292.3	10348.9	10361.5	10396.5	10459.0	10478.2	10505.3	10500.4	10485.8	10501.5	10526.9	10425.0
2000	11748.4	11859.0	11982.0	12004.4	12093.9	12239.6	12224.0	12312.7	12365.6	12313.6	12398.9	12499.4	12170.1
2001	12170.6	12231.5	12329.3	12242.4	12279.4	12332.9	12201.4	12249.8	12192.7	12128.7	12122.1	12158.0	12219.9
2002	11815.0	11878.2	11979.9	11958.2	12034.1	12089.5	11993.9	12062.3	12057.9	12038.7	12091.9	12129.3	12010.7
2003	11789.2	11839.2	11900.2	11904.7	11965.3	12023.5	11937.3	12012.6	12016.0	12033.8	12055.3	12123.9	11966.8
2004	11835.3	11916.2	12011.5	12026.7	12106.7	12167.1	12184.7	12215.5	12219.4	12258.3	12313.2	12363.8	12134.9
2005	12051.5	12141.8	12228.4	12277.4	12324.6	12398.5	12406.1	12467.7	12515.8	12512.6	12584.1	12665.5	12381.2
2006	12328.5	12428.3	12495.8	12494.7	12597.0	12686.4	12632.3	12698.5	12717.4	12692.5	12735.9	12789.2	12608.0
2007	12463.6	12549.1	12631.0	12577.8	12657.6	12731.0	12728.8	12752.1	12742.2	12727.0	12770.5	12816.7	12679.0
2008	12429.4	12494.2	12528.1	12529.0	12552.3	12573.6	12509.0	12503.7	12467.3	12382.0	12306.0	12275.7	12462.5
2009	11837.9	11751.0	11707.0	11616.2	11625.6	11610.9	11500.2	11499.2	11468.9	11466.9	11458.9	11441.3	11582.0
Goods-Producing													
1990	2604.9	2616.2	2631.5	2643.2	2655.6	2675.7	2682.2	2694.3	2683.4	2651.8	2622.5	2601.0	2646.9
2000	2513.7	2528.4	2555.5	2566.4	2590.6	2638.6	2649.7	2674.9	2682.0	2658.0	2658.3	2668.8	2615.4
2001	2603.1	2611.2	2631.8	2608.2	2615.7	2628.5	2604.9	2618.0	2588.1	2544.4	2505.3	2481.9	2586.8
2002	2402.2	2412.0	2429.4	2422.8	2441.3	2459.4	2443.3	2469.1	2459.7	2432.7	2410.8	2393.7	2431.4
2003	2334.6	2332.0	2345.2	2340.0	2357.6	2379.7	2370.9	2400.8	2399.8	2378.1	2362.0	2361.3	2363.5
2004	2318.4	2331.3	2353.2	2371.9	2392.2	2418.2	2442.0	2453.0	2449.8	2427.5	2405.0	2397.1	2396.6
2005	2336.3	2363.4	2384.6	2403.5	2419.6	2448.9	2472.7	2490.6	2493.5	2473.2	2460.3	2456.6	2433.6
2006	2404.9	2427.4	2430.7	2417.3	2456.7	2483.9	2479.6	2496.2	2494.2	2457.4	2428.8	2409.8	2448.9
2007	2356.3	2368.2	2385.2	2371.9	2390.0	2418.0	2424.7	2428.9	2410.2	2376.6	2347.5	2325.7	2383.6
2008	2261.2	2265.7	2264.8	2256.8	2265.7	2274.1	2274.2	2276.4	2257.7	2213.9	2163.5	2127.4	2241.8
2009	2042.2	1993.7	1977.7	1945.8	1944.4	1939.9	1919.4	1917.1	1899.8	1872.2	1848.7	1819.1	1926.7
Mining and Logging													
1990	33.2	33.1	33.3	34.8	36.3	37.8	38.6	38.3	38.8	38.2	37.1	35.6	36.3
2000	24.2	24.0	24.0	25.1	26.7	27.5	27.9	28.3	28.1	27.7	27.3	26.7	26.5
2001	24.6	24.1	24.2	25.1	26.4	26.8	26.4	26.7	26.6	26.2	25.8	24.2	25.5
2002	22.5	22.4	22.1	22.1	23.0	23.6	23.6	23.9	23.9	23.8	23.6	22.7	23.1
2003	20.8	21.0	21.0	21.0	21.8	22.7	23.2	23.2	22.9	23.5	23.0	22.7	22.2
2004	21.5	21.6	21.7	22.2	23.0	23.4	23.4	23.5	23.5	23.8	23.3	22.9	22.8
2005	21.7	21.9	22.0	22.4	23.0	23.8	24.5	24.7	24.8	24.9	24.6	24.3	23.6
2006	23.0	23.4	23.3	23.4	24.8	25.7	26.2	26.6	26.7	26.4	25.9	25.2	25.1
2007	24.6	24.8	24.6	25.3	26.3	27.0	27.7	28.0	28.0	28.2	28.0	27.5	26.7
2008	26.6	27.0	27.0	27.9	28.6	29.2	29.9	30.0	29.9	30.2	29.5	28.7	28.7
2009	27.1	26.5	26.0	25.4	25.5	26.0	26.0	25.7	25.6	25.2	24.9	24.0	25.7
Construction													
1990	617.2	617.8	628.4	636.6	646.1	659.3	661.1	666.5	666.8	656.9	646.9	634.6	644.9
2000	678.1	678.9	691.4	705.8	721.7	745.2	750.1	762.9	769.8	764.6	765.1	767.5	733.4
2001	738.7	742.9	760.1	766.7	783.0	798.1	800.2	814.7	804.7	797.1	785.0	773.4	780.4
2002	736.1	742.5	753.0	756.6	770.8	783.3	783.4	801.8	798.1	795.9	790.3	780.9	774.4
2003	755.0	752.3	764.9	770.1	788.6	805.9	810.9	827.0	826.6	825.4	819.3	815.7	796.8
2004	792.8	798.3	811.6	830.0	842.5	861.3	875.2	884.1	886.9	884.1	871.5	866.4	850.4
2005	823.8	844.8	862.3	880.4	895.0	915.7	931.5	942.8	947.4	944.2	940.1	935.6	905.3
2006	903.9	916.0	914.6	908.8	940.9	959.0	957.9	966.3	962.7	941.3	923.8	908.8	933.7
2007	874.6	879.9	894.0	890.6	903.5	917.8	918.7	919.8	905.3	886.9	868.9	850.8	892.6
2008	803.3	804.8	803.7	800.3	803.6	805.9	803.2	802.4	788.4	769.6	744.2	723.5	787.7
2009	674.4	644.7	644.1	630.2	632.0	631.8	619.5	616.9	605.1	594.2	583.4	564.5	620.1
Manufacturing													
1990	1954.5	1965.3	1969.8	1971.8	1973.2	1978.6	1982.5	1989.5	1977.8	1956.7	1938.5	1930.8	1965.8
2000	1811.4	1825.5	1840.1	1835.5	1842.2	1865.9	1871.7	1883.7	1884.1	1865.7	1865.9	1874.6	1855.5
2001	1839.8	1844.2	1847.5	1816.4	1806.3	1803.6	1778.3	1776.6	1756.8	1721.1	1694.7	1684.3	1780.8
2002	1643.6	1647.1	1654.3	1644.1	1647.5	1652.5	1636.3	1643.4	1637.7	1613.0	1596.9	1590.1	1633.9
2003	1558.8	1558.7	1559.3	1548.9	1547.2	1551.1	1536.8	1550.6	1550.3	1529.2	1519.7	1522.9	1544.5
2004	1504.1	1511.4	1519.9	1519.7	1526.7	1533.5	1543.4	1545.4	1539.4	1519.6	1510.2	1507.8	1523.4
2005	1490.8	1496.7	1500.3	1500.7	1501.6	1509.4	1516.7	1523.1	1521.3	1504.1	1495.6	1496.7	1504.8
2006	1478.0	1488.0	1492.8	1485.1	1491.0	1499.2	1495.5	1503.3	1504.8	1489.7	1479.1	1475.8	1490.2
2007	1457.1	1463.5	1466.6	1456.0	1460.2	1473.2	1478.3	1481.1	1476.9	1461.5	1450.6	1447.4	1464.4
2008	1431.3	1433.9	1434.1	1428.6	1433.5	1439.0	1441.1	1444.0	1439.4	1414.1	1389.8	1375.2	1425.3
2009	1340.7	1322.5	1307.6	1290.2	1286.9	1282.1	1273.9	1274.5	1269.1	1252.8	1240.4	1230.6	1280.9

Employment by Industry: California, Selected Years, 1990–2009—*Continued*

(Numbers in thousands, not seasonally adjusted.)

Industry and year	January	February	March	April	May	June	July	August	September	October	November	December	Annual average
Service-Providing													
1990	9685.2	9743.8	9805.7	9820.2	9871.1	9908.2	9811.6	9776.9	9863.3	9929.1	9987.7	10032.5	9852.9
2000	11517.0	11641.7	11767.9	11787.6	11902.8	11961.2	11800.3	11847.0	11963.0	11991.8	12102.6	12190.2	11872.8
2001	11910.4	11986.8	12081.3	12041.9	12081.8	12123.8	11889.9	11916.8	11963.7	12005.1	12063.9	12117.0	12015.2
2002	11835.4	11916.0	12029.7	12025.9	12089.8	12122.2	11909.6	11935.3	12006.2	12072.9	12164.3	12210.3	12026.5
2003	11905.5	11970.1	12035.1	12039.4	12081.4	12114.1	11911.9	11927.9	11987.1	12074.6	12126.3	12178.4	12029.3
2004	11914.2	11997.2	12088.5	12090.3	12152.6	12187.4	12055.8	12051.4	12125.5	12242.7	12339.5	12386.2	12135.9
2005	12118.9	12208.2	12289.9	12325.8	12364.3	12403.2	12265.3	12303.9	12412.8	12479.2	12582.9	12658.3	12367.7
2006	12354.8	12457.8	12538.5	12554.3	12625.9	12686.6	12520.2	12556.0	12645.0	12716.4	12809.3	12871.8	12611.4
2007	12582.4	12679.7	12767.0	12730.8	12803.0	12847.5	12711.4	12716.3	12793.9	12864.8	12959.7	13022.5	12789.9
2008	12679.4	12765.7	12817.6	12834.4	12858.4	12872.9	12659.4	12641.1	12684.5	12697.5	12685.5	12679.4	12739.7
2009	12304.1	12287.7	12277.2	12231.8	12238.5	12213.1	11991.1	11981.3	11991.0	12090.8	12116.3	12109.2	12152.7
Trade, Transportation, and Utilities													
1990	2407.0	2384.4	2386.0	2386.3	2392.9	2407.9	2415.4	2416.1	2415.5	2437.4	2477.2	2511.6	2419.8
2000	2671.8	2665.4	2676.9	2672.0	2690.0	2717.3	2719.1	2730.5	2737.9	2746.7	2807.5	2866.0	2725.1
2001	2753.9	2732.3	2743.2	2727.5	2733.5	2752.3	2733.7	2736.5	2736.7	2732.8	2770.4	2807.2	2746.7
2002	2695.9	2678.4	2692.8	2689.4	2705.2	2724.7	2710.5	2717.9	2726.0	2728.7	2780.2	2828.4	2723.2
2003	2698.1	2681.1	2684.9	2679.1	2692.1	2708.4	2693.5	2702.1	2712.0	2746.7	2776.0	2821.8	2716.3
2004	2700.5	2690.4	2705.2	2707.9	2727.1	2746.7	2744.8	2749.6	2755.9	2786.6	2846.1	2881.4	2753.5
2005	2776.8	2759.9	2766.9	2768.0	2782.9	2796.9	2807.9	2820.8	2835.4	2849.9	2909.7	2964.3	2820.0
2006	2829.8	2814.2	2827.2	2826.7	2846.4	2866.4	2866.2	2879.9	2888.5	2899.7	2964.8	3006.9	2876.4
2007	2895.7	2871.3	2878.1	2864.1	2881.1	2891.8	2906.9	2910.9	2912.3	2923.0	2986.9	3031.1	2912.8
2008	2894.0	2867.3	2862.9	2847.9	2851.7	2853.4	2842.8	2836.0	2827.5	2818.0	2837.1	2849.7	2849.0
2009	2712.8	2669.2	2647.4	2622.1	2629.9	2627.0	2605.5	2607.2	2613.0	2613.4	2638.7	2651.5	2636.5
Wholesale Trade													
1990	542.2	543.5	544.8	549.4	549.2	551.8	549.1	548.5	547.9	554.4	553.6	555.8	549.2
2000	627.7	633.5	637.9	637.7	641.1	647.6	646.0	648.2	649.8	647.8	648.9	654.4	643.4
2001	654.0	659.9	663.0	659.4	659.0	663.4	657.1	656.4	654.5	653.3	650.1	650.3	656.7
2002	641.9	645.3	649.4	649.3	651.7	654.3	650.6	652.7	652.9	649.8	650.3	651.8	650.0
2003	642.4	644.5	647.7	648.7	650.6	653.1	647.1	648.9	648.7	645.8	644.3	646.9	647.4
2004	639.5	643.0	646.3	648.4	651.9	657.2	655.9	656.0	655.9	659.7	660.8	661.6	653.0
2005	658.0	660.6	664.3	669.7	673.0	675.7	676.5	677.8	679.5	681.5	682.2	684.7	673.6
2006	681.4	688.0	692.2	695.0	699.1	704.9	704.2	705.7	708.3	706.6	707.4	710.2	700.3
2007	702.5	706.9	711.5	710.5	714.1	716.9	719.7	718.8	719.0	720.8	720.2	722.4	715.3
2008	710.6	711.8	713.7	710.4	710.0	709.1	705.4	703.1	699.5	696.0	688.9	684.0	703.5
2009	665.6	660.5	654.6	649.6	648.6	647.5	641.2	638.5	635.1	634.7	630.9	624.0	644.2
Retail Trade													
1990	1451.3	1426.3	1423.6	1417.6	1422.2	1430.4	1436.7	1437.7	1435.5	1450.4	1491.3	1519.1	1445.2
2000	1534.4	1522.4	1527.5	1520.4	1533.0	1549.4	1551.9	1560.1	1565.8	1577.1	1635.8	1683.5	1563.4
2001	1582.5	1558.7	1562.8	1550.7	1556.8	1570.1	1560.5	1564.0	1566.9	1566.0	1616.3	1655.7	1575.9
2002	1568.2	1545.6	1558.0	1551.9	1561.8	1575.8	1567.1	1570.8	1579.3	1585.7	1637.9	1684.2	1582.2
2003	1577.0	1558.5	1558.7	1553.4	1561.7	1572.3	1566.8	1573.7	1579.7	1615.9	1648.8	1693.7	1588.4
2004	1589.5	1575.6	1584.0	1584.3	1597.1	1607.9	1604.7	1609.3	1611.3	1631.1	1689.9	1728.3	1617.8
2005	1638.6	1618.0	1622.0	1615.6	1624.5	1634.8	1643.5	1654.7	1664.1	1676.5	1735.0	1783.8	1659.3
2006	1663.6	1640.6	1646.5	1644.3	1654.1	1663.5	1666.2	1676.0	1677.0	1690.6	1752.6	1785.9	1680.1
2007	1695.5	1666.1	1669.7	1653.8	1663.1	1668.0	1676.5	1682.2	1678.1	1687.9	1751.3	1787.1	1689.9
2008	1682.1	1649.1	1646.8	1635.1	1633.1	1635.7	1633.0	1627.6	1619.9	1618.7	1647.5	1662.5	1640.9
2009	1562.4	1528.8	1515.0	1499.9	1506.8	1505.3	1496.0	1499.4	1506.3	1505.2	1537.8	1554.4	1518.1
Transportation and Utilities													
1990	413.5	414.6	417.6	419.3	421.5	425.7	429.6	429.9	432.1	432.6	432.3	436.7	425.5
2000	509.7	509.5	511.5	513.9	515.9	520.3	521.2	522.2	522.3	521.8	522.8	528.1	518.3
2001	517.4	513.7	517.4	517.4	517.7	518.8	516.1	516.1	515.3	513.5	504.0	501.2	514.1
2002	485.8	487.5	485.4	488.2	491.7	494.6	492.8	494.4	493.8	493.2	492.0	492.4	491.0
2003	478.7	478.1	478.5	477.0	479.8	483.0	479.6	479.5	483.6	485.0	482.9	481.2	480.6
2004	471.5	471.8	474.9	475.2	478.1	481.6	484.2	484.3	488.7	495.8	495.4	491.5	482.8
2005	480.2	481.3	480.6	482.7	485.4	486.4	487.9	488.3	491.8	491.9	492.5	495.8	487.1
2006	484.8	485.6	488.5	487.4	493.2	498.0	495.8	498.2	503.2	502.5	504.8	510.8	496.1
2007	497.7	498.3	496.9	499.8	503.9	506.9	510.7	509.9	515.2	514.3	515.4	521.6	507.6
2008	501.3	506.4	502.4	502.4	508.6	508.6	504.4	505.3	508.1	503.3	500.7	503.2	504.6
2009	484.8	479.9	477.8	472.6	474.5	474.2	468.3	469.3	471.6	473.5	470.0	473.1	474.1
Information													
1990	385.8	391.0	385.8	387.2	388.0	389.6	393.1	393.4	393.7	397.6	400.0	399.0	392.0
2000	537.8	550.5	560.5	562.9	572.8	580.2	580.3	590.4	588.2	592.7	603.0	601.0	576.7
2001	587.3	588.8	590.2	571.4	557.8	554.8	537.6	534.7	529.4	524.2	523.7	522.8	551.9
2002	510.2	511.4	519.9	502.6	502.3	501.6	484.6	490.5	481.4	487.8	495.8	479.4	497.3
2003	480.3	487.1	481.7	470.7	475.2	467.9	467.1	478.4	466.3	476.9	483.7	477.8	476.1
2004	485.6	490.7	487.8	477.6	483.5	474.0	478.8	479.4	470.6	483.4	492.5	484.3	482.4
2005	473.1	477.0	480.7	470.3	469.9	470.3	466.9	473.2	472.5	471.4	480.2	477.9	473.6
2006	468.2	476.3	475.5	467.7	468.6	470.7	464.8	464.9	459.4	456.0	456.5	463.4	466.0
2007	463.3	471.2	473.5	464.6	470.1	473.5	471.4	475.7	474.4	464.1	470.3	477.9	470.8
2008	459.2	469.4	477.7	477.1	482.2	485.8	478.3	479.2	481.0	474.0	470.8	471.5	475.5
2009	450.2	451.3	453.5	442.4	441.6	444.9	442.4	444.6	445.6	446.3	448.7	449.5	446.8

Employment by Industry: California, Selected Years, 1990–2009—*Continued*

(Numbers in thousands, not seasonally adjusted.)

Industry and year	January	February	March	April	May	June	July	August	September	October	November	December	Annual average
Financial Activities													
1990	820.5	825.3	829.7	822.3	823.4	825.9	822.0	822.3	823.6	815.4	811.9	820.3	821.9
2000	797.0	802.5	806.5	800.5	803.8	810.8	805.1	809.7	809.0	808.5	809.8	819.5	806.9
2001	818.5	826.5	834.1	831.7	834.8	841.1	834.7	838.4	837.1	841.0	843.9	850.6	836.0
2002	835.1	840.7	844.0	845.0	848.7	853.7	852.5	857.8	858.1	860.2	866.5	873.9	853.0
2003	866.0	871.2	876.2	881.5	887.4	891.8	890.2	894.4	892.9	890.7	890.8	895.2	885.7
2004	886.9	890.5	894.9	896.4	899.0	902.1	907.3	908.7	907.2	907.7	910.2	915.2	902.2
2005	908.6	912.7	917.6	918.7	922.1	926.0	930.5	933.9	934.8	937.5	938.3	945.2	927.2
2006	934.3	937.1	940.2	939.3	943.1	942.3	935.7	935.3	932.6	927.8	926.1	928.5	935.2
2007	914.4	920.6	922.3	913.5	912.6	912.0	907.5	903.9	894.6	887.7	883.5	882.7	904.6
2008	865.0	866.0	864.4	857.7	856.1	854.3	851.9	848.5	841.3	836.6	831.4	830.7	850.3
2009	814.8	811.2	808.0	802.1	799.0	798.6	795.0	792.7	786.4	788.2	783.4	785.2	797.1
Professional and Business Services													
1990	1468.9	1487.6	1502.0	1495.1	1497.9	1505.8	1508.5	1512.2	1514.2	1513.3	1514.7	1523.2	1503.6
2000	2109.5	2140.0	2171.4	2193.6	2203.3	2240.6	2237.3	2264.3	2272.3	2264.0	2273.8	2291.2	2221.8
2001	2203.0	2216.0	2233.7	2202.9	2206.3	2212.5	2177.9	2183.6	2167.5	2149.3	2138.5	2144.5	2186.3
2002	2095.2	2108.4	2131.3	2114.0	2116.8	2124.5	2111.3	2126.6	2122.8	2120.0	2126.9	2129.9	2119.0
2003	2064.4	2077.8	2095.7	2090.7	2088.8	2096.1	2074.5	2089.0	2085.1	2079.8	2081.5	2089.9	2084.4
2004	2032.8	2054.6	2078.0	2078.0	2085.7	2101.7	2101.8	2115.1	2112.0	2125.4	2132.8	2144.8	2096.9
2005	2095.0	2121.7	2137.2	2142.8	2139.6	2156.7	2162.1	2178.6	2188.9	2187.1	2197.2	2210.1	2159.8
2006	2164.5	2192.2	2209.1	2215.2	2225.2	2250.8	2247.8	2267.0	2272.7	2279.9	2283.7	2289.5	2241.5
2007	2212.5	2240.2	2255.9	2243.6	2251.0	2269.2	2266.4	2276.5	2276.0	2291.3	2292.8	2296.6	2264.3
2008	2225.2	2246.9	2252.7	2255.3	2246.8	2253.4	2245.1	2250.5	2247.0	2229.5	2206.7	2192.4	2237.2
2009	2112.7	2096.6	2080.7	2058.2	2046.0	2042.4	2025.9	2030.7	2018.9	2032.1	2037.7	2037.1	2051.6
Education and Health Services													
1990	1086.3	1103.3	1109.7	1116.2	1114.4	1113.4	1102.9	1110.2	1120.9	1144.0	1152.7	1148.4	1118.5
2000	1378.2	1403.2	1413.1	1402.2	1404.6	1395.1	1375.0	1377.1	1414.5	1414.4	1421.2	1413.5	1401.0
2001	1406.7	1431.0	1444.8	1442.0	1451.1	1441.8	1414.6	1435.0	1454.4	1474.4	1487.1	1492.3	1447.9
2002	1465.6	1491.8	1503.1	1496.2	1504.4	1491.2	1474.3	1477.0	1500.2	1518.7	1531.0	1532.7	1498.9
2003	1502.3	1524.1	1534.5	1547.5	1550.6	1540.3	1513.8	1512.9	1536.8	1550.6	1557.7	1564.4	1536.3
2004	1535.8	1558.3	1569.7	1565.2	1565.0	1554.8	1532.6	1531.6	1556.1	1579.3	1585.4	1586.7	1560.0
2005	1557.4	1580.2	1588.1	1596.2	1597.1	1583.8	1556.2	1557.0	1586.8	1605.9	1614.7	1614.5	1586.5
2006	1582.8	1609.0	1618.8	1618.1	1620.2	1609.5	1582.8	1587.2	1617.4	1634.6	1642.4	1645.1	1614.0
2007	1626.1	1657.7	1672.0	1664.8	1672.2	1659.2	1644.0	1645.9	1677.4	1699.7	1710.3	1714.2	1670.3
2008	1689.4	1722.0	1727.5	1739.3	1738.2	1722.3	1689.7	1694.2	1722.0	1742.3	1749.9	1760.1	1724.7
2009	1727.8	1749.4	1756.6	1749.0	1749.4	1736.1	1703.0	1704.7	1725.1	1758.0	1760.1	1763.3	1740.2
Leisure and Hospitality													
1990	1063.2	1073.2	1088.7	1096.1	1107.4	1122.2	1132.9	1136.1	1127.5	1105.5	1103.0	1105.1	1105.1
2000	1267.1	1289.6	1311.7	1320.3	1339.6	1361.6	1368.3	1375.2	1368.3	1340.9	1336.4	1347.6	1335.6
2001	1313.8	1333.9	1352.8	1360.7	1378.0	1394.5	1396.9	1401.4	1377.3	1361.3	1352.7	1358.1	1365.1
2002	1310.3	1335.5	1355.6	1382.3	1403.3	1419.2	1410.0	1417.2	1402.9	1384.1	1375.0	1385.6	1382.4
2003	1345.9	1362.7	1376.5	1388.7	1404.4	1425.8	1425.3	1432.5	1418.7	1406.9	1401.8	1411.7	1400.1
2004	1380.9	1400.7	1418.0	1425.4	1447.2	1460.7	1471.1	1474.1	1461.4	1444.3	1438.5	1450.5	1439.4
2005	1408.5	1424.5	1446.1	1468.6	1483.0	1502.3	1504.9	1509.6	1497.4	1483.1	1480.9	1492.9	1475.2
2006	1451.1	1472.8	1491.8	1506.5	1526.6	1548.3	1548.4	1556.2	1540.4	1526.8	1523.6	1535.9	1519.0
2007	1496.8	1514.2	1534.7	1548.1	1569.4	1590.5	1593.5	1595.5	1580.0	1567.2	1562.8	1571.7	1560.4
2008	1529.7	1545.4	1563.1	1578.5	1593.0	1609.9	1611.7	1607.5	1585.8	1559.2	1543.7	1544.1	1572.6
2009	1489.9	1491.6	1494.3	1504.8	1522.4	1528.8	1523.5	1518.2	1500.0	1480.5	1466.4	1467.8	1499.0
Other Services													
1990	407.2	411.3	415.5	415.1	416.9	418.5	421.2	420.7	421.6	420.8	419.5	418.3	417.2
2000	473.3	479.4	486.4	486.5	489.2	495.4	489.2	490.6	493.4	488.4	488.9	491.8	487.7
2001	484.3	491.8	498.7	498.0	502.2	507.4	501.1	502.2	502.2	501.3	500.5	500.6	499.2
2002	492.5	500.0	503.8	505.9	512.1	515.2	507.4	506.2	506.8	506.5	505.7	505.7	505.7
2003	497.6	503.2	505.5	506.5	509.2	513.5	502.0	502.5	504.4	504.1	501.8	501.8	504.3
2004	494.4	499.7	504.7	504.3	507.0	508.9	506.3	504.0	506.4	504.1	502.7	503.8	503.9
2005	495.8	502.4	507.2	509.3	510.4	513.6	504.9	504.0	506.5	504.5	502.8	504.0	505.5
2006	492.9	499.3	502.5	503.9	510.2	514.5	507.0	511.8	512.2	510.3	510.0	510.1	507.1
2007	498.5	505.7	509.3	507.2	511.2	516.8	514.4	514.8	517.3	517.4	516.4	516.8	512.2
2008	505.7	511.5	515.0	516.4	518.6	520.4	515.3	511.4	510.0	508.5	502.9	499.8	511.3
2009	487.5	488.0	488.8	491.8	492.9	493.2	485.5	484.0	480.1	476.2	475.2	467.8	484.3
Government													
1990	2046.3	2067.7	2088.3	2101.9	2130.2	2124.9	2015.6	1965.9	2046.3	2095.1	2108.7	2106.6	2074.8
2000	2282.3	2311.1	2341.4	2349.6	2399.5	2360.2	2226.0	2209.2	2279.4	2336.2	2362.0	2359.7	2318.1
2001	2342.9	2366.5	2383.8	2407.7	2418.1	2419.4	2293.4	2285.0	2359.1	2420.8	2447.1	2440.9	2382.0
2002	2422.6	2449.8	2479.2	2490.5	2497.0	2492.1	2359.0	2342.1	2408.0	2466.9	2483.2	2474.7	2447.1
2003	2450.9	2462.9	2480.1	2474.7	2473.7	2470.3	2345.5	2316.1	2370.9	2418.9	2433.0	2415.8	2426.1
2004	2397.3	2412.3	2430.2	2435.5	2438.1	2438.5	2313.1	2288.9	2355.9	2411.9	2431.3	2419.5	2397.7
2005	2403.7	2429.8	2446.1	2451.9	2459.3	2484.1	2331.9	2326.8	2390.5	2439.8	2459.1	2449.4	2420.2
2006	2431.2	2456.9	2473.4	2476.9	2485.6	2484.1	2367.5	2353.7	2421.8	2481.3	2502.2	2492.4	2452.3
2007	2475.1	2498.8	2521.2	2524.9	2535.4	2534.5	2407.3	2393.1	2461.9	2514.4	2536.7	2531.5	2494.6
2008	2511.2	2537.2	2554.3	2562.2	2571.8	2573.4	2424.6	2413.8	2474.9	2529.4	2543.0	2531.1	2518.9
2009	2508.4	2530.4	2547.9	2561.4	2557.3	2542.1	2410.3	2399.2	2421.9	2496.1	2506.1	2487.0	2497.3

Average Weekly Hours by Selected Industry: California, 2007–2009

(Not seasonally adjusted.)

Industry and year	January	February	March	April	May	June	July	August	September	October	November	December	Annual average
Total Private													
2007	33.9	34.1	34.3	34.7	34.4	34.6	35.2	34.8	35.2	34.3	34.2	34.7	34.5
2008	33.4	33.7	34.5	33.9	34.1	34.9	34.1	34.4	34.3	34.3	34.8	34.1	34.2
2009	33.8	34.2	34.2	33.7	33.7	33.5	33.6	34.1	33.3	33.8	34.3	33.7	33.8
Goods-Producing													
2007	36.8	37.0	37.9	37.9	38.4	37.9	37.8	37.9	38.1	37.6	37.3	37.0	37.6
2008	35.9	36.6	37.4	37.4	37.3	37.8	37.5	37.8	38.0	37.9	37.7	38.0	37.4
2009	37.2	36.2	36.9	36.5	37.1	37.4	37.5	37.4	36.4	36.8	37.5	37.6	37.0
Construction													
2007	34.6	35.1	35.9	35.9	37.0	35.4	35.3	35.3	35.5	35.1	34.8	34.5	35.4
2008	33.1	33.8	35.2	35.4	35.5	36.0	35.7	36.2	35.8	35.7	34.7	35.9	35.3
2009	35.5	33.3	35.5	34.2	35.2	35.6	36.1	36.1	34.6	35.0	35.6	35.2	35.2
Manufacturing													
2007	38.2	38.3	39.2	39.3	39.4	39.6	39.4	39.5	39.7	39.2	38.9	39.0	39.1
2008	37.9	38.6	39.0	38.8	38.6	39.0	38.7	38.8	39.2	39.0	39.2	39.0	38.8
2009	38.0	37.6	37.5	37.5	37.9	38.2	37.0	37.8	37.4	37.8	38.5	39.0	37.8
Trade, Transportation, and Utilities													
2007	35.1	35.1	35.3	35.8	35.3	35.7	36.3	35.9	36.3	35.3	35.0	36.0	35.6
2008	34.6	34.5	35.3	34.6	35.4	36.0	35.3	35.6	35.3	35.2	35.3	34.9	35.2
2009	34.6	34.9	34.9	34.7	34.8	34.1	34.3	33.4	33.4	35.1	33.8	33.7	34.3
Information													
2007	33.8	34.2	34.5	35.5	34.0	35.3	36.7	36.2	36.5	36.3	36.2	35.5	35.4
2008	34.3	34.3	35.9	35.3	35.2	35.8	35.3	35.4	35.6	35.8	36.1	36.1	35.4
2009	35.2	36.4	35.4	34.9	35.0	35.6	35.6	36.3	35.7	36.1	36.7	35.8	35.7
Financial Activities													
2007	35.9	36.0	35.7	37.2	36.2	37.2	38.5	37.4	38.3	36.9	36.8	38.0	37.0
2008	36.4	36.5	37.9	36.5	36.4	37.9	36.4	36.9	36.3	36.6	37.9	36.1	36.8
2009	36.1	37.4	37.2	36.2	36.1	36.3	36.7	37.9	36.6	36.7	38.0	36.5	36.8
Professional and Business Services													
2007	35.7	36.4	36.3	36.3	36.0	36.3	36.9	36.4	37.0	35.9	35.9	36.0	36.3
2008	34.6	35.1	36.1	35.3	35.3	36.2	35.2	35.7	35.7	36.0	36.9	35.7	35.7
2009	35.4	36.2	36.0	35.5	35.2	34.3	33.8	35.2	34.6	34.7	36.1	34.9	35.2
Education and Health Services													
2007	32.1	32.1	32.1	32.9	32.5	32.3	33.4	32.9	33.5	32.7	32.8	33.8	32.8
2008	32.5	32.7	33.4	32.7	32.9	33.6	33.1	33.0	33.1	33.1	34.0	33.2	33.1
2009	33.2	34.0	34.0	33.3	33.4	33.3	33.4	34.1	33.1	33.2	34.2	33.9	33.6
Leisure and Hospitality													
2007	26.1	26.2	26.2	27.0	26.4	26.7	27.5	26.8	27.1	26.2	26.2	27.0	26.6
2008	25.8	26.2	27.0	26.3	26.3	27.3	26.4	26.7	26.2	26.2	26.6	25.7	26.4
2009	25.5	26.3	26.1	25.6	25.5	25.8	26.0	27.5	26.2	26.1	27.0	25.9	26.1
Other Services													
2007	30.9	30.5	30.9	31.5	30.5	31.0	31.6	30.8	31.5	31.2	30.0	31.0	31.0
2008	29.7	29.9	30.9	30.6	30.4	31.9	30.5	31.1	31.0	30.8	31.3	30.2	30.7
2009	30.6	30.6	31.0	30.9	30.6	30.7	31.2	31.7	30.3	29.7	30.5	29.3	30.6

Average Hourly Earnings by Selected Industry: California, 2007–2009

(Dollars, not seasonally adjusted.)

Industry and year	January	February	March	April	May	June	July	August	September	October	November	December	Annual average
Total Private													
2007	25.04	24.75	24.84	24.93	24.68	24.65	24.80	24.47	24.71	24.44	24.52	24.46	24.69
2008	24.20	24.17	24.49	24.61	24.55	24.65	24.67	24.62	24.80	24.88	25.23	25.55	24.70
2009	25.41	25.40	25.60	25.43	25.19	25.29	25.21	25.48	25.53	25.70	25.78	25.71	25.48
Goods-Producing													
2007	25.23	24.68	24.67	24.98	24.95	25.09	25.28	25.29	25.54	25.58	25.71	25.50	25.21
2008	25.03	24.65	24.99	25.12	25.40	25.79	26.05	26.19	26.45	26.64	27.33	28.64	26.02
2009	27.87	27.70	28.32	28.03	27.88	28.04	27.56	28.03	27.77	27.83	28.03	28.25	27.94
Construction													
2007	26.73	25.07	24.94	25.07	24.98	25.72	26.07	26.35	26.77	27.13	27.40	27.00	26.08
2008	24.83	25.01	25.21	25.40	25.70	26.44	26.07	26.67	26.20	26.75	28.26	30.25	26.37
2009	26.95	25.28	26.67	26.42	26.62	27.15	27.52	28.03	28.68	28.82	28.70	29.12	27.47
Manufacturing													
2007	24.32	24.38	24.43	24.85	24.85	24.66	24.76	24.64	24.75	24.65	24.72	24.75	24.65
2008	24.85	24.80	25.12	25.02	25.20	25.38	25.23	25.13	25.25	25.40	25.84	26.23	25.28
2009	26.97	26.70	27.08	26.71	26.72	26.55	26.68	26.64	26.68	26.76	27.16	27.37	26.84
Trade, Transportation, and Utilities													
2007	20.41	20.08	20.24	20.37	20.51	20.27	20.43	20.13	20.35	20.11	19.98	20.15	20.25
2008	20.05	20.17	20.60	20.46	20.31	20.40	20.24	20.29	20.40	20.58	20.70	20.49	20.39
2009	20.84	21.15	20.90	20.91	20.77	20.72	20.79	21.04	21.21	22.08	21.97	21.48	21.15
Information													
2007	35.64	34.63	35.63	35.38	34.19	34.25	35.08	34.52	35.34	34.75	35.36	35.45	35.02
2008	35.30	35.45	35.23	34.77	34.95	34.75	34.59	34.82	34.94	33.79	34.22	34.46	34.77
2009	34.40	33.38	33.38	34.04	34.54	34.37	33.77	33.37	33.75	34.04	32.80	33.27	33.75
Financial Activities													
2007	38.75	37.85	37.58	37.50	35.59	34.99	34.69	33.87	33.42	31.92	32.49	32.50	35.09
2008	31.87	32.03	31.50	31.51	30.98	31.12	30.86	30.30	30.22	30.16	29.88	29.93	30.87
2009	31.02	30.84	30.44	30.14	30.21	29.80	30.53	30.94	31.13	30.75	30.93	30.94	30.64
Professional and Business Services													
2007	30.19	30.06	30.38	30.41	30.21	30.31	30.40	29.59	30.14	29.76	29.54	29.50	30.04
2008	28.84	28.74	29.80	30.63	30.62	30.66	30.76	30.12	30.49	30.56	31.31	31.67	30.35
2009	30.95	31.00	32.19	31.67	30.79	31.46	31.78	32.00	31.91	31.66	31.83	31.62	31.57
Education and Health Services													
2007	24.53	24.54	24.55	24.44	24.31	24.52	24.76	24.63	24.73	24.68	25.01	25.02	24.65
2008	25.05	25.09	25.02	24.90	24.96	24.95	25.04	25.49	25.44	25.38	25.53	25.65	25.21
2009	25.60	25.65	25.35	25.46	25.28	25.35	25.08	25.30	25.49	25.53	25.47	25.39	25.41
Leisure and Hospitality													
2007	13.80	13.65	13.59	13.97	13.90	13.80	13.78	13.74	13.84	13.72	13.83	13.99	13.80
2008	14.15	14.05	14.11	14.31	14.20	14.09	14.08	14.08	14.06	14.16	14.28	14.57	14.18
2009	14.48	14.35	14.27	14.22	14.30	14.28	14.24	14.19	14.23	14.29	14.47	14.74	14.34
Other Services													
2007	18.23	18.41	18.53	18.89	18.73	18.55	19.06	18.78	19.07	19.02	19.35	19.20	18.82
2008	19.20	19.11	19.05	18.94	18.83	19.18	19.29	19.24	19.33	19.60	20.01	20.36	19.34
2009	20.36	20.64	20.89	20.94	20.90	20.87	20.50	20.84	20.86	21.16	21.41	22.07	20.94

Average Weekly Earnings by Selected Industry: California, 2007–2009

(Dollars, not seasonally adjusted.)

Industry and year	January	February	March	April	May	June	July	August	September	October	November	December	Annual average
Total Private													
2007	848.86	843.98	852.01	865.07	848.99	852.89	872.96	851.56	869.79	838.29	838.58	848.76	851.81
2008	808.28	814.53	844.91	834.28	837.16	860.29	841.25	846.93	850.64	853.38	878.00	871.26	844.74
2009	858.86	868.68	875.52	856.99	848.90	847.22	847.06	868.87	850.15	868.66	884.25	866.43	861.22
Goods-Producing													
2007	928.46	913.16	934.99	946.74	958.08	950.91	955.58	958.49	973.07	961.81	958.98	943.50	947.90
2008	898.58	902.19	934.63	939.49	947.42	974.86	976.88	989.98	1005.10	1009.66	1030.34	1088.32	973.15
2009	1036.76	1002.74	1045.01	1023.10	1034.35	1048.70	1033.50	1048.32	1010.83	1024.14	1051.13	1062.20	1033.78
Construction													
2007	924.86	879.96	895.35	900.01	924.26	910.49	920.27	930.16	950.34	952.26	953.52	931.50	923.23
2008	821.87	845.34	887.39	899.16	912.35	951.84	930.70	965.45	937.96	954.98	980.62	1085.98	930.86
2009	956.73	841.82	946.79	903.56	937.02	966.54	993.47	1011.88	992.33	1008.70	1021.72	1025.02	966.94
Manufacturing													
2007	929.02	933.75	957.66	976.61	979.09	976.54	975.54	973.28	982.58	966.28	961.61	965.25	963.82
2008	941.82	957.28	979.68	970.78	972.72	989.82	976.40	975.04	989.80	990.60	1012.93	1022.97	980.86
2009	1024.86	1003.92	1015.50	1001.63	1012.69	1014.21	987.16	1006.99	997.83	1011.53	1045.66	1067.43	1014.55
Trade, Transportation, and Utilities													
2007	716.39	704.81	714.47	729.25	724.00	723.64	741.61	722.67	738.71	709.88	699.30	725.40	720.90
2008	693.73	695.87	727.18	707.92	718.97	734.40	714.47	722.32	720.12	724.42	730.71	715.10	717.73
2009	721.06	738.14	729.41	725.58	722.80	706.55	713.10	702.74	708.41	775.01	742.59	723.88	725.45
Information													
2007	1204.63	1184.35	1229.24	1255.99	1162.46	1209.03	1287.44	1249.62	1289.91	1261.43	1280.03	1258.48	1239.71
2008	1210.79	1215.94	1264.76	1227.38	1230.24	1244.05	1221.03	1232.63	1243.86	1209.68	1235.34	1244.01	1230.86
2009	1210.88	1215.03	1181.65	1188.00	1208.90	1223.57	1202.21	1211.33	1204.88	1228.84	1203.76	1191.07	1204.88
Financial Activities													
2007	1391.13	1362.60	1341.61	1395.00	1288.36	1301.63	1335.57	1266.74	1279.99	1177.85	1195.63	1235.00	1298.33
2008	1160.07	1169.10	1193.85	1150.12	1127.67	1179.45	1123.30	1118.07	1096.99	1103.86	1132.45	1080.47	1136.02
2009	1119.82	1153.42	1132.37	1091.07	1090.58	1081.74	1120.45	1172.63	1139.36	1128.53	1175.34	1129.31	1127.55
Professional and Business Services													
2007	1077.78	1094.18	1102.79	1103.88	1087.56	1100.25	1121.76	1077.08	1115.18	1068.38	1060.49	1062.00	1090.45
2008	997.86	1008.77	1075.78	1081.24	1080.89	1109.89	1082.75	1075.28	1088.49	1100.16	1155.34	1130.62	1083.50
2009	1095.63	1122.20	1158.84	1124.29	1083.81	1079.08	1074.16	1126.40	1104.09	1098.60	1149.06	1103.54	1111.26
Education and Health Services													
2007	787.41	787.73	788.06	804.08	790.08	792.00	826.98	810.33	828.46	807.04	820.33	845.68	808.52
2008	814.13	820.44	835.67	814.23	821.18	838.32	828.82	841.17	842.06	840.08	868.02	851.58	834.45
2009	849.92	872.10	861.90	847.82	844.35	844.16	837.67	862.73	843.72	847.60	871.07	860.72	853.78
Leisure and Hospitality													
2007	360.18	357.63	356.06	377.19	366.96	368.46	378.95	368.23	375.06	359.46	362.35	377.73	367.08
2008	365.07	368.11	380.97	376.35	373.46	384.66	371.71	375.94	368.37	370.99	379.85	374.45	374.35
2009	369.24	377.41	372.45	364.03	364.65	368.42	370.24	390.23	372.83	372.97	390.69	381.77	374.27
Other Services													
2007	563.31	561.51	572.58	595.04	571.27	575.05	602.30	578.42	600.71	593.42	580.50	595.20	583.42
2008	570.24	571.39	588.65	579.56	572.43	611.84	588.35	598.36	599.23	603.68	626.31	614.87	593.74
2009	623.02	631.58	647.59	647.05	639.54	640.71	639.60	660.63	632.06	628.45	653.01	646.65	640.76

COLORADO
At a Glance

Population:
  1990 census: 3,294,473
  2000 census: 4,301,261
  2009 estimate: 5,024,748

Percent change in population:
  1990–2000: 30.6%
  2000–2009: 16.8%

Percent change in total nonfarm employment:
  1990–2009: 47.6%
  2008–2009: -4.5%

Industry with the largest growth in employment, 1990–2009 (thousands):
  Professional and Business Services, 150.8

Industry with the largest decline or smallest growth in employment, 1990–2009 (thousands):
  Manufacturing, -40.7

Civilian labor force:
  1990: 1,768,954
  2000: 2,364,990
  2009: 2,701,026

Unemployment rate and rank among states (lowest to highest):
  1990: 5.1%, 18th
  2000: 2.7%, 3rd
  2009: 7.7%, 19th

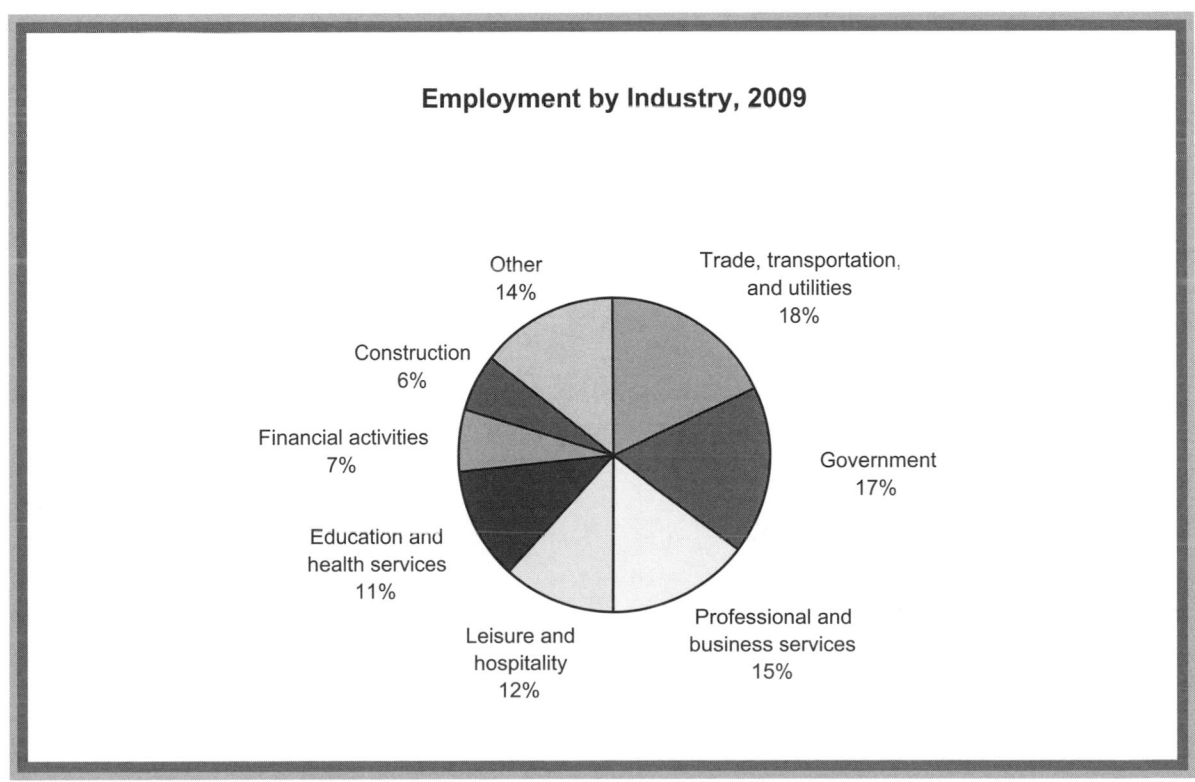

Employment by Industry, 2009

Other 14%
Trade, transportation, and utilities 18%
Construction 6%
Financial activities 7%
Education and health services 11%
Government 17%
Leisure and hospitality 12%
Professional and business services 15%

Employment by Industry: Colorado, Selected Years, 1990–2009

(Numbers in thousands, not seasonally adjusted.)

Industry and year	January	February	March	April	May	June	July	August	September	October	November	December	Annual average
Total Nonfarm													
1990	1478.0	1490.9	1502.7	1506.5	1517.0	1537.2	1521.6	1531.5	1535.2	1532.0	1544.5	1553.5	1520.8
2000	2134.4	2156.2	2181.4	2188.0	2202.3	2234.0	2227.4	2239.1	2239.6	2237.5	2251.4	2274.6	2213.8
2001	2210.5	2222.7	2236.5	2230.5	2232.1	2261.9	2240.1	2240.2	2225.5	2206.4	2203.7	2212.1	2226.9
2002	2148.8	2159.6	2172.9	2181.8	2191.1	2214.2	2193.6	2199.7	2189.0	2178.8	2183.0	2197.7	2184.2
2003	2131.3	2135.4	2139.3	2138.4	2147.2	2169.2	2156.1	2163.8	2158.1	2159.4	2158.0	2177.4	2152.8
2004	2123.5	2132.9	2151.7	2168.0	2174.1	2201.8	2190.0	2196.3	2197.2	2195.9	2199.6	2224.4	2179.6
2005	2163.5	2181.9	2199.1	2207.3	2215.8	2244.7	2238.4	2241.5	2247.8	2244.0	2251.3	2276.6	2226.0
2006	2220.1	2235.1	2254.9	2259.9	2274.4	2307.5	2286.3	2294.1	2295.1	2293.2	2302.9	2325.8	2279.1
2007	2262.6	2280.5	2306.3	2313.1	2327.7	2358.3	2342.0	2350.4	2352.2	2350.5	2359.1	2372.9	2331.3
2008	2314.6	2331.0	2343.6	2349.0	2359.8	2379.0	2363.3	2369.4	2361.0	2351.9	2341.0	2340.5	2350.3
2009	2271.2	2261.8	2257.9	2247.1	2249.4	2257.1	2237.3	2234.8	2232.0	2227.5	2227.3	2224.1	2244.0
Total Private													
1990	1210.2	1211.8	1221.5	1223.9	1231.0	1257.0	1261.9	1274.4	1259.7	1249.5	1258.0	1269.8	1244.0
2000	1810.6	1820.8	1840.7	1846.5	1853.2	1896.4	1906.2	1916.5	1901.8	1893.6	1906.1	1929.3	1876.8
2001	1878.4	1878.6	1891.5	1885.2	1883.5	1917.8	1911.9	1910.0	1878.0	1853.0	1847.9	1857.0	1882.7
2002	1804.7	1804.7	1814.7	1823.6	1828.8	1858.5	1854.9	1859.2	1832.5	1814.0	1817.1	1833.0	1828.8
2003	1780.8	1774.9	1776.8	1778.0	1781.0	1813.4	1818.1	1825.1	1801.9	1797.0	1795.7	1816.8	1796.6
2004	1773.9	1773.5	1789.5	1804.4	1807.8	1842.7	1851.4	1855.0	1836.8	1828.9	1831.8	1857.9	1821.1
2005	1810.7	1817.2	1833.2	1839.8	1845.1	1881.7	1893.2	1896.4	1882.8	1873.1	1880.6	1906.9	1863.4
2006	1863.3	1866.7	1883.3	1889.1	1899.9	1939.4	1937.5	1942.7	1925.3	1918.0	1926.9	1950.5	1911.9
2007	1902.3	1905.8	1928.3	1934.6	1945.7	1983.7	1986.5	1991.1	1972.7	1966.4	1973.5	1988.9	1956.6
2008	1943.9	1947.7	1957.3	1962.1	1967.2	1997.0	1998.7	1999.5	1972.5	1956.4	1945.0	1947.2	1966.2
2009	1888.7	1869.7	1863.2	1850.5	1847.9	1867.3	1867.2	1862.9	1838.6	1827.3	1827.1	1827.3	1853.1
Goods-Producing													
1990	241.2	239.7	241.1	244.7	249.3	255.5	257.2	259.2	257.0	256.6	255.1	252.5	250.8
2000	345.8	349.0	354.8	357.0	363.6	372.0	373.6	374.9	373.2	372.8	369.9	369.5	364.7
2001	356.8	356.6	360.4	360.7	365.0	370.5	369.2	367.9	362.6	356.7	350.5	344.1	360.1
2002	330.2	329.3	332.8	336.5	342.3	346.7	346.0	345.8	340.0	336.8	331.9	327.1	337.1
2003	314.4	311.6	311.0	313.1	317.8	323.3	323.2	323.0	319.2	319.4	315.4	312.6	317.0
2004	303.3	302.2	306.8	312.8	316.8	323.9	326.3	326.5	324.5	324.9	322.0	319.7	317.5
2005	309.5	312.1	316.4	319.4	324.2	332.6	337.4	338.7	337.0	335.9	335.0	333.3	327.6
2006	325.1	326.2	330.7	333.4	339.3	347.0	346.1	346.4	343.9	342.1	338.7	336.6	338.0
2007	323.1	323.6	330.5	334.2	341.5	349.2	350.2	350.2	346.3	347.0	344.4	338.8	339.9
2008	328.0	327.8	330.2	332.5	338.4	344.1	343.5	343.2	338.4	335.9	329.7	320.4	334.3
2009	302.6	295.5	291.6	286.4	286.4	288.3	286.5	283.8	279.7	274.0	272.3	264.3	284.3
Mining and Logging													
1990	16.7	16.7	16.7	16.8	17.0	17.4	17.6	17.5	17.1	17.1	17.2	17.0	17.0
2000	11.9	11.9	12.0	12.0	12.2	12.3	12.5	12.5	12.5	12.3	12.2	12.2	12.2
2001	11.9	12.1	12.4	12.5	12.8	13.2	13.5	13.4	13.4	13.3	13.4	13.3	12.9
2002	12.9	12.8	12.9	12.8	12.9	13.1	13.2	13.1	13.1	13.0	12.8	12.7	12.9
2003	12.5	12.6	12.7	12.8	13.1	13.3	13.4	13.5	13.4	13.6	13.6	13.5	13.2
2004	13.2	13.4	13.6	13.9	14.2	14.5	14.9	15.1	15.0	15.0	15.2	15.3	14.4
2005	15.4	15.8	16.1	16.2	16.5	17.2	17.7	18.1	18.1	18.2	18.5	18.7	17.2
2006	18.7	19.1	19.6	19.7	20.3	21.1	21.6	22.2	22.2	22.7	22.8	23.3	21.1
2007	23.1	23.6	23.9	24.5	25.2	25.9	25.9	26.2	25.8	25.9	26.2	26.2	25.2
2008	26.4	26.7	26.8	27.5	28.0	28.6	28.9	29.2	29.2	30.0	30.2	29.9	28.5
2009	28.4	27.0	26.0	24.2	23.8	23.5	23.0	22.9	22.8	22.8	23.3	23.2	24.2
Construction													
1990	55.8	54.7	55.8	58.5	62.8	66.9	68.1	70.1	69.0	68.7	67.2	64.4	63.5
2000	146.5	149.6	154.8	157.7	163.9	170.4	171.5	172.8	171.2	170.6	167.7	165.9	163.6
2001	159.1	159.4	163.1	165.3	169.7	175.2	175.7	176.1	172.9	169.6	165.4	160.3	167.7
2002	150.5	151.3	154.5	158.8	164.3	168.4	168.5	168.8	164.5	162.2	158.5	154.3	160.4
2003	145.2	143.1	143.4	145.6	150.3	155.3	156.1	155.9	153.4	153.7	149.8	147.2	149.9
2004	140.1	138.7	142.7	147.7	151.1	156.3	158.3	158.2	157.0	157.4	154.8	152.7	151.3
2005	144.7	146.3	150.1	153.3	157.7	164.6	168.1	169.3	168.3	167.2	166.0	164.2	160.0
2006	157.7	158.3	161.9	164.7	169.7	175.7	174.6	174.4	172.6	170.7	167.6	165.3	167.8
2007	154.0	154.4	160.5	164.1	169.8	175.7	176.9	176.7	173.1	173.1	170.1	164.7	167.8
2008	155.4	155.6	157.9	160.0	165.0	169.6	169.5	169.2	166.0	163.4	158.5	151.3	161.8
2009	138.4	134.8	133.3	131.3	132.5	135.3	134.6	132.7	129.6	125.5	123.3	114.7	130.5
Manufacturing													
1990	168.7	168.3	168.6	169.4	169.5	171.2	171.5	171.6	170.9	170.8	170.7	171.1	170.2
2000	187.4	187.5	188.0	187.3	187.5	189.3	189.6	189.6	189.5	189.9	190.0	191.4	188.9
2001	185.8	185.1	184.9	182.9	182.5	182.1	180.0	178.4	176.3	173.8	171.7	170.5	179.5
2002	166.8	165.2	165.4	164.9	165.1	165.2	164.3	163.9	162.4	161.6	160.6	160.1	163.8
2003	156.7	155.9	154.9	154.7	154.4	154.7	153.7	153.6	152.4	152.1	152.0	151.9	153.9
2004	150.0	150.1	150.5	151.2	151.5	153.1	153.1	153.2	152.5	152.5	152.0	151.7	151.8
2005	149.4	150.0	150.2	149.9	150.0	150.8	151.6	151.3	150.6	150.5	150.5	150.4	150.4
2006	148.7	148.8	149.2	149.0	149.3	150.2	149.9	149.8	149.1	148.7	148.3	148.0	149.1
2007	146.0	145.6	146.1	145.6	146.5	147.6	147.4	147.3	147.4	148.0	148.1	147.9	147.0
2008	146.2	145.5	145.5	145.0	145.4	145.9	145.1	144.8	143.2	142.5	141.0	139.2	144.1
2009	135.8	133.7	132.3	130.9	130.1	129.5	128.9	128.2	127.3	125.7	125.7	126.4	129.5

Employment by Industry: Colorado, Selected Years, 1990–2009—*Continued*

(Numbers in thousands, not seasonally adjusted.)

Industry and year	January	February	March	April	May	June	July	August	September	October	November	December	Annual average
Service-Providing													
1990	1236.8	1251.2	1261.6	1261.8	1267.7	1281.7	1264.4	1272.3	1278.2	1275.4	1289.4	1301.0	1270.1
2000	1788.6	1807.2	1826.6	1831.0	1838.7	1862.0	1853.8	1864.2	1866.4	1864.7	1881.5	1905.1	1849.2
2001	1853.7	1866.1	1876.1	1869.8	1867.1	1891.4	1870.9	1872.3	1862.9	1849.7	1853.2	1868.0	1866.8
2002	1818.6	1830.3	1840.1	1845.3	1848.8	1867.5	1847.6	1853.9	1849.0	1842.0	1851.1	1870.6	1847.1
2003	1816.9	1823.8	1828.3	1825.3	1829.4	1845.9	1832.9	1840.8	1838.9	1840.0	1842.6	1864.8	1835.8
2004	1820.2	1830.7	1844.9	1855.2	1857.3	1877.9	1863.7	1869.8	1872.7	1871.0	1877.6	1904.7	1862.1
2005	1854.0	1869.8	1882.7	1887.9	1891.6	1912.1	1901.0	1902.8	1910.8	1908.1	1916.3	1943.3	1898.4
2006	1895.0	1908.9	1924.2	1926.5	1935.1	1960.5	1940.2	1947.7	1951.2	1951.1	1964.2	1989.2	1941.2
2007	1939.5	1956.9	1975.8	1978.9	1986.2	2009.1	1991.8	2000.2	2005.9	2003.5	2014.7	2034.1	1991.4
2008	1986.6	2003.2	2013.4	2016.5	2021.4	2034.9	2019.8	2026.2	2022.6	2016.0	2011.3	2020.1	2016.0
2009	1968.6	1966.3	1966.3	1960.7	1963.0	1968.8	1950.8	1951.0	1952.3	1953.5	1955.0	1959.8	1959.7
Trade, Transportation, and Utilities													
1990	299.9	296.5	297.6	298.6	304.2	304.6	304.0	306.9	306.5	306.6	312.6	317.7	304.6
2000	410.1	409.1	409.3	411.2	412.1	416.8	416.5	420.6	419.7	423.7	435.1	443.0	418.9
2001	425.2	420.3	421.4	420.2	420.7	425.2	423.8	423.6	420.7	419.8	425.4	429.3	423.0
2002	409.0	405.3	406.4	408.1	410.3	415.0	413.7	413.6	410.6	409.8	418.3	424.6	412.1
2003	405.6	401.6	400.8	399.2	399.3	402.0	402.5	404.1	402.6	405.4	417.2	418.3	404.5
2004	401.7	397.7	399.3	401.5	403.2	406.9	407.9	408.6	406.3	408.2	415.6	422.8	406.6
2005	405.8	403.7	406.1	405.9	407.4	411.7	413.7	413.3	414.3	416.7	425.1	431.8	413.0
2006	414.2	409.5	411.9	413.3	414.8	419.6	418.9	419.6	418.7	421.9	431.2	438.3	419.3
2007	424.2	419.7	422.3	422.7	424.4	428.9	430.5	430.8	429.7	431.6	440.1	445.3	429.2
2008	430.9	426.6	428.2	427.7	427.8	431.5	431.8	431.7	427.8	426.1	428.8	432.1	429.3
2009	413.4	406.4	403.2	400.3	401.2	403.8	402.3	402.0	399.4	398.7	404.0	405.4	403.3
Wholesale Trade													
1990	71.4	71.6	72.0	72.3	72.8	73.5	72.9	73.3	73.5	73.8	73.9	73.6	72.9
2000	96.9	97.5	98.4	98.9	99.8	100.6	99.3	99.6	99.4	100.2	100.5	101.1	99.4
2001	100.0	100.8	101.0	100.5	100.4	100.7	100.1	100.0	99.2	98.5	98.1	98.0	99.8
2002	95.7	95.7	95.7	95.6	95.7	95.8	95.6	95.1	94.5	93.9	93.7	94.0	95.1
2003	92.8	92.3	92.4	92.2	92.2	92.5	92.2	91.9	91.5	91.9	91.5	91.8	92.1
2004	90.6	90.7	91.2	91.6	91.8	92.5	92.3	92.4	92.3	92.4	92.6	92.8	91.9
2005	91.7	92.1	92.6	92.9	93.2	93.7	94.2	94.4	94.4	94.2	94.3	94.7	93.5
2006	93.9	94.3	94.9	95.4	96.1	97.2	97.0	97.4	97.2	97.5	97.9	98.5	96.4
2007	97.2	97.7	98.4	98.7	99.2	100.0	99.9	100.0	99.6	100.2	100.3	100.5	99.3
2008	99.5	99.8	100.1	100.4	100.7	101.0	101.0	100.7	100.2	99.7	99.0	98.8	100.1
2009	96.7	95.7	94.7	93.8	93.6	93.4	92.8	92.4	91.7	91.1	90.6	90.3	93.1
Retail Trade													
1990	170.8	167.1	167.2	167.9	173.0	172.0	172.2	174.2	173.4	173.0	178.7	183.2	172.7
2000	240.5	238.6	238.1	238.6	239.1	242.6	242.7	246.1	245.6	248.5	257.9	264.6	245.2
2001	247.0	242.0	242.8	242.3	243.1	246.7	245.6	244.9	243.6	244.0	250.9	255.3	245.7
2002	240.2	236.4	237.6	239.1	240.8	244.9	243.5	243.5	241.3	241.3	249.1	254.5	242.7
2003	238.7	235.4	234.6	234.5	235.5	238.0	238.3	239.9	239.0	240.9	247.2	252.2	239.5
2004	238.8	234.7	235.6	236.9	238.3	240.7	241.4	242.2	240.4	242.4	249.5	254.7	241.3
2005	240.9	238.3	240.3	240.1	241.9	244.8	245.7	245.1	246.2	248.4	256.4	261.0	245.8
2006	246.3	241.4	243.0	244.2	245.0	247.4	247.3	247.5	246.8	250.0	258.4	262.5	248.3
2007	251.1	246.7	248.4	248.3	249.6	252.6	254.3	254.4	253.8	254.7	262.2	265.4	253.5
2008	254.0	250.3	251.4	250.7	250.6	253.5	253.7	254.1	251.7	251.3	254.3	256.1	252.6
2009	242.9	237.9	236.3	234.3	236.0	238.3	237.9	237.8	236.5	236.7	242.2	243.3	238.3
Transportation and Utilities													
1990	57.7	57.8	58.4	58.4	58.4	59.1	58.9	59.4	59.6	59.8	60.0	60.9	59.0
2000	72.7	73.0	72.8	73.7	73.2	73.6	74.5	74.9	74.7	75.0	76.7	77.3	74.3
2001	78.2	77.5	77.6	77.4	77.2	77.8	78.1	78.7	77.9	77.3	76.4	76.0	77.5
2002	73.1	73.2	73.1	73.4	73.8	74.3	74.6	75.0	74.8	74.6	75.5	76.1	74.3
2003	74.1	73.9	73.8	72.5	71.6	71.5	72.0	72.3	72.1	72.6	73.5	74.3	72.9
2004	72.3	72.3	72.5	73.0	73.1	73.7	74.2	74.0	73.6	73.4	73.5	75.3	73.4
2005	73.2	73.3	73.2	72.9	72.3	73.2	73.8	73.8	73.7	74.1	74.4	76.1	73.7
2006	74.0	73.8	74.0	73.7	73.7	75.0	74.6	74.7	74.7	74.4	74.9	77.3	74.6
2007	75.9	75.3	75.5	75.7	75.6	76.3	76.3	76.4	76.3	76.7	77.6	79.4	76.4
2008	77.4	76.5	76.7	76.6	76.5	77.0	77.1	76.9	75.9	75.1	75.5	77.2	76.5
2009	73.8	72.8	72.2	72.2	71.6	72.1	71.6	71.8	71.2	70.9	71.2	71.8	71.9
Information													
1990	51.8	52.2	51.7	51.3	51.5	52.1	52.5	52.6	52.3	52.4	52.7	53.1	52.2
2000	102.1	103.7	105.0	106.0	107.1	108.8	110.3	111.0	111.2	111.3	112.0	112.8	108.4
2001	113.2	112.8	112.0	110.3	109.3	109.3	106.6	105.5	103.8	102.2	101.7	100.5	107.3
2002	98.1	97.0	96.2	95.2	94.1	93.7	91.7	91.0	89.9	89.3	89.4	88.6	92.9
2003	86.5	86.1	85.7	84.9	84.8	84.8	84.5	84.2	83.3	83.1	83.6	83.7	84.6
2004	82.7	82.8	82.6	81.9	81.9	81.9	81.2	80.9	79.5	79.3	79.6	79.6	81.2
2005	78.3	77.9	77.8	77.1	77.1	77.1	76.8	76.4	76.0	75.8	76.0	76.2	76.9
2006	75.8	75.6	75.8	75.4	75.7	75.7	75.3	75.2	74.7	75.0	75.4	75.5	75.4
2007	74.9	75.0	75.0	75.8	76.2	77.0	76.7	76.8	76.3	77.3	77.6	77.9	76.4
2008	77.4	77.6	77.4	77.2	77.0	77.2	77.0	76.8	76.3	76.1	76.0	76.1	76.8
2009	76.7	76.2	76.0	75.4	75.0	74.8	74.5	74.0	73.5	73.7	73.9	73.5	74.8

Employment by Industry: Colorado, Selected Years, 1990–2009—*Continued*

(Numbers in thousands, not seasonally adjusted.)

Industry and year	January	February	March	April	May	June	July	August	September	October	November	December	Annual average
Financial Activities													
1990	104.8	105.5	106.7	104.8	103.7	104.7	104.6	105.0	103.8	103.1	103.6	104.7	104.6
2000	146.3	147.1	147.7	146.5	145.8	147.3	147.1	147.3	146.3	146.2	147.0	149.6	147.0
2001	147.0	147.7	149.0	148.7	148.1	149.7	149.4	148.9	147.4	147.3	147.5	149.2	148.3
2002	147.7	148.3	148.7	147.8	147.6	149.0	149.3	150.2	149.6	150.3	151.8	154.1	149.5
2003	152.4	152.8	153.2	153.3	153.2	154.6	155.5	156.0	154.6	154.2	153.8	155.9	154.1
2004	153.5	153.8	154.2	154.0	153.3	154.7	155.2	155.2	154.6	154.6	154.8	157.1	154.6
2005	155.2	156.0	157.0	157.2	157.1	158.7	159.6	160.0	159.9	159.3	159.9	162.4	158.5
2006	159.3	159.8	160.2	160.0	160.0	161.3	161.0	161.1	160.3	159.8	160.1	162.3	160.4
2007	159.6	160.1	160.4	159.9	159.2	160.5	160.3	160.0	158.7	157.8	157.9	159.2	159.5
2008	157.0	157.4	157.7	156.9	156.0	156.6	156.6	155.7	154.0	153.2	152.5	153.7	155.6
2009	150.5	149.8	149.1	148.0	147.0	147.4	147.2	146.9	145.4	144.2	143.6	145.6	147.1
Professional and Business Services													
1990	168.1	170.8	173.0	174.6	177.5	181.8	183.2	185.8	183.9	182.7	182.8	181.6	178.8
2000	302.2	303.1	308.2	313.1	316.6	322.8	325.9	328.2	327.9	326.6	325.1	325.8	318.8
2001	311.3	313.1	315.4	316.6	317.4	320.1	318.1	317.1	310.6	306.3	301.2	300.4	312.3
2002	288.6	291.0	292.8	297.4	300.0	301.7	299.6	302.7	298.7	295.8	293.4	293.0	296.2
2003	282.6	283.7	284.4	288.4	290.7	295.7	296.2	299.0	295.8	297.0	294.0	296.2	292.0
2004	287.2	289.8	293.7	301.9	303.8	309.2	311.7	312.5	310.4	310.0	308.2	310.9	304.1
2005	302.6	303.7	306.4	314.1	315.9	320.7	322.9	324.1	322.9	322.5	321.6	324.6	316.8
2006	314.7	318.4	321.6	327.4	331.9	338.6	337.8	340.0	338.1	337.5	337.0	339.1	331.8
2007	332.0	334.0	338.8	344.2	348.9	355.1	354.7	356.6	355.3	353.4	350.9	351.4	347.9
2008	342.5	345.3	346.6	352.9	354.4	358.6	358.1	359.5	355.8	354.0	348.8	346.5	351.9
2009	334.1	330.2	329.2	330.2	330.9	332.6	332.0	330.8	328.0	328.1	326.0	323.6	329.6
Education and Health Services													
1990	126.1	127.5	128.3	128.7	129.0	129.6	128.8	130.5	130.9	131.7	133.0	133.6	129.8
2000	187.4	189.3	190.1	191.3	191.8	193.0	192.1	193.4	194.6	195.2	196.9	198.0	192.8
2001	196.1	198.0	198.7	199.1	200.0	200.5	199.7	201.5	201.3	203.8	204.9	206.2	200.8
2002	204.2	205.7	206.4	208.0	208.7	208.4	207.7	209.1	209.7	210.2	211.4	212.0	208.5
2003	209.8	211.1	211.7	212.4	212.9	213.1	212.3	213.1	213.5	214.5	215.2	216.1	213.0
2004	214.7	216.0	217.1	217.6	218.2	218.3	217.0	218.1	219.5	220.5	221.6	223.1	218.5
2005	220.3	223.0	223.5	224.0	225.0	225.3	223.6	224.6	225.2	225.5	226.9	228.0	224.6
2006	225.9	228.5	229.3	230.0	231.1	231.2	229.4	230.8	232.1	233.9	235.3	236.5	231.2
2007	233.7	236.8	238.4	238.8	239.9	240.1	238.7	240.5	241.7	243.8	245.7	247.1	240.4
2008	244.5	247.6	248.0	248.8	250.2	249.3	248.9	250.6	251.6	254.2	256.1	256.1	250.5
2009	254.1	255.8	256.0	256.2	257.0	256.1	255.5	256.4	256.7	261.4	262.4	260.6	257.4
Leisure and Hospitality													
1990	163.7	164.5	167.7	165.8	160.2	171.9	174.7	177.2	169.2	160.3	162.0	170.3	167.3
2000	237.5	240.5	245.6	242.3	236.6	254.0	258.9	259.5	248.5	238.0	240.5	250.1	246.0
2001	246.2	247.4	251.2	246.3	239.4	257.0	259.9	260.3	247.9	233.8	233.7	243.6	247.2
2002	242.2	243.4	246.1	245.2	240.3	256.9	259.6	260.0	248.7	237.2	236.0	248.5	247.0
2003	243.8	242.8	244.8	241.2	236.6	252.5	256.6	258.8	247.6	238.2	236.1	247.9	245.6
2004	244.8	245.5	249.7	248.2	244.0	259.6	263.5	264.5	253.9	243.3	242.2	256.1	251.3
2005	250.8	252.7	257.5	253.7	250.0	266.0	269.7	270.0	259.1	249.5	248.6	262.5	257.5
2006	258.5	259.0	263.3	259.2	256.5	273.7	277.2	277.9	266.7	257.4	258.7	271.0	264.9
2007	263.4	264.7	270.0	266.5	263.0	278.6	281.9	282.6	271.7	262.5	264.1	275.7	270.4
2008	269.7	271.1	274.5	271.7	268.7	283.7	286.4	285.9	273.3	262.3	259.1	268.7	272.9
2009	262.2	261.3	263.5	260.2	256.5	269.3	274.4	274.6	262.4	253.9	251.6	260.0	262.5
Other Services													
1990	54.6	55.1	55.4	55.4	55.6	56.8	56.9	57.2	56.1	56.1	56.2	56.3	55.9
2000	79.2	79.0	80.0	79.1	79.6	81.7	81.8	81.6	80.4	79.8	79.6	80.5	80.2
2001	82.6	82.7	83.4	83.3	83.6	85.5	85.2	85.2	83.7	83.1	83.0	83.7	83.8
2002	84.7	84.7	85.3	85.4	85.5	87.1	87.3	86.8	85.3	84.6	84.9	85.1	85.6
2003	85.7	85.2	85.2	85.5	85.7	87.4	87.3	86.9	85.3	85.2	85.4	86.1	85.9
2004	86.0	85.7	86.1	86.5	86.6	88.2	88.6	88.7	88.1	88.1	87.8	88.6	87.4
2005	88.2	88.1	88.5	88.4	88.4	89.6	89.5	89.3	88.4	87.9	87.5	88.1	88.5
2006	89.8	89.7	90.5	90.4	90.6	92.3	91.8	91.7	90.8	90.4	90.5	91.2	90.8
2007	91.4	91.9	92.9	92.5	92.6	94.3	93.5	93.6	93.0	93.0	92.8	93.5	92.9
2008	93.9	94.3	94.7	94.4	94.7	96.0	96.4	96.1	95.3	94.6	94.0	93.6	94.8
2009	95.1	94.5	94.6	93.8	93.9	95.0	94.8	94.4	93.5	93.3	93.3	94.3	94.2
Government													
1990	267.8	279.1	281.2	282.6	286.0	280.2	259.7	257.1	275.5	282.5	286.5	283.7	276.8
2000	323.8	335.4	340.7	341.5	349.1	337.6	321.2	322.6	337.8	343.9	345.3	345.3	337.0
2001	332.1	344.1	345.0	345.3	348.6	344.1	328.2	330.2	347.5	353.4	355.8	355.1	344.1
2002	344.1	354.9	358.2	358.2	362.3	355.7	338.7	340.5	356.5	364.8	365.9	364.7	355.4
2003	350.5	360.5	362.5	360.4	366.2	355.8	338.0	338.7	356.2	362.4	362.3	360.6	356.2
2004	349.6	359.4	362.2	363.6	366.3	359.1	338.6	341.3	360.4	367.0	367.8	366.5	358.5
2005	352.8	364.7	365.9	367.5	370.7	363.0	345.2	345.1	365.0	370.9	370.7	369.7	362.6
2006	356.8	368.4	371.6	370.8	374.5	368.1	348.8	351.4	369.8	375.2	376.0	375.3	367.2
2007	360.3	374.7	378.0	378.5	382.0	374.6	355.5	359.3	379.5	384.1	385.6	384.0	374.7
2008	370.7	383.3	386.3	386.9	392.6	382.0	364.6	369.9	388.5	395.5	396.0	393.3	384.1
2009	382.5	392.1	394.7	396.6	401.5	389.8	370.1	371.9	393.4	400.2	400.2	396.8	390.8

Average Weekly Hours by Selected Industry: Colorado, 2007–2009

(Not seasonally adjusted.)

Industry and year	January	February	March	April	May	June	July	August	September	October	November	December	Annual average
Total Private													
2007	34.2	34.3	34.5	34.8	34.6	35.2	35.6	35.0	35.4	35.0	35.0	35.0	34.9
2008	34.3	34.4	35.0	34.5	34.7	35.6	35.1	34.9	34.7	35.3	35.3	34.1	34.8
2009	33.9	34.6	34.8	34.2	34.4	34.6	34.6	34.8	34.2	34.1	34.4	33.4	34.3
Goods-Producing													
2007	37.7	37.9	38.3	38.2	38.8	39.2	38.5	38.0	38.0	38.6	39.2	38.0	38.4
2008	37.2	37.6	38.0	37.6	37.9	39.7	38.8	38.9	38.8	38.9	39.6	37.9	38.4
2009	37.6	37.6	38.2	36.7	37.8	38.1	38.0	38.2	37.4	37.9	38.2	36.6	37.7
Construction													
2007	37.0	36.5	37.9	37.4	38.6	38.6	38.0	37.4	37.3	38.2	39.2	37.2	37.8
2008	36.6	37.4	38.2	37.4	38.7	40.4	39.4	39.3	38.9	38.8	38.9	37.0	38.5
2009	36.4	36.5	37.5	37.4	38.5	38.9	39.4	39.4	37.3	38.1	38.5	36.3	37.9
Manufacturing													
2007	37.7	38.5	38.2	38.6	38.5	39.0	38.5	38.1	38.3	38.7	38.7	38.5	38.4
2008	37.6	37.8	37.8	37.7	37.6	39.7	38.7	39.0	38.9	39.3	40.3	38.9	38.6
2009	38.7	38.4	38.5	37.8	38.1	38.2	38.0	38.3	37.6	37.8	38.4	36.7	38.1
Trade, Transportation, and Utilities													
2007	34.1	34.2	34.3	34.0	34.4	35.2	35.8	35.2	36.2	35.5	35.6	36.1	35.1
2008	34.7	35.0	35.4	34.6	34.9	35.8	35.4	35.1	35.0	34.7	35.5	34.8	35.1
2009	34.2	35.0	35.0	34.8	34.9	35.1	35.3	35.5	35.1	34.8	34.8	34.0	34.9
Financial Activities													
2007	36.3	35.8	35.6	36.3	34.9	35.7	36.8	35.4	35.8	35.6	35.0	37.2	35.9
2008	36.4	36.1	36.8	35.5	35.5	37.1	35.8	35.4	35.4	35.5	35.0	34.6	35.8
2009	34.9	35.4	35.7	35.4	35.3	35.3	35.2	35.2	34.6	34.8	36.1	35.3	35.3
Professional and Business Services													
2007	35.2	35.5	35.4	36.4	35.5	36.4	37.3	36.7	37.6	36.4	36.2	36.6	36.3
2008	35.7	35.8	36.1	36.1	36.0	36.7	36.1	36.3	36.2	36.5	37.2	35.8	36.2
2009	35.9	36.6	36.4	36.4	36.2	36.7	36.6	36.9	36.3	36.5	37.3	35.6	36.5
Education and Health Services													
2007	34.0	34.1	34.2	34.4	33.9	34.4	34.9	34.5	34.9	34.5	35.4	35.0	34.5
2008	34.5	34.7	35.1	34.7	34.4	34.5	34.8	34.6	34.5	34.5	34.5	35.0	34.7
2009	34.7	35.1	35.0	34.5	34.4	34.1	34.1	34.4	34.1	34.0	34.0	33.6	34.3
Leisure and Hospitality													
2007	24.6	24.6	25.3	25.1	24.9	25.7	26.0	25.7	24.8	23.9	23.0	23.3	24.8
2008	23.5	23.8	24.5	23.7	24.4	25.6	25.6	25.3	24.9	24.1	23.8	23.5	24.4
2009	23.9	24.3	24.7	24.3	24.6	25.2	25.5	26.3	25.1	24.3	24.1	24.0	24.8
Other Services													
2007	33.5	35.2	35.2	34.9	34.0	34.7	34.3	33.8	33.9	33.7	34.8	33.3	34.3
2008	33.3	33.3	33.8	33.5	32.8	33.8	33.8	33.7	33.5	33.5	34.8	32.9	33.6
2009	33.0	33.1	33.0	32.7	33.4	33.4	32.8	33.8	33.4	33.2	34.2	32.6	33.2

Average Hourly Earnings by Selected Industry: Colorado, 2007–2009

(Dollars, not seasonally adjusted.)

Industry and year	January	February	March	April	May	June	July	August	September	October	November	December	Annual average
Total Private													
2007	22.67	22.97	23.06	23.23	22.83	22.91	23.26	23.06	23.34	23.22	23.33	23.62	23.13
2008	23.68	23.92	24.07	23.84	23.59	23.46	23.61	23.57	23.71	23.74	24.18	24.23	23.80
2009	24.13	24.16	24.18	23.76	23.66	23.42	23.60	23.66	23.52	23.63	23.76	23.90	23.78
Goods-Producing													
2007	24.99	24.41	24.40	24.74	24.29	24.21	24.87	24.56	24.99	25.21	25.71	26.05	24.87
2008	26.16	26.12	25.98	26.23	26.07	25.53	26.06	25.84	25.59	25.47	26.06	26.35	25.95
2009	26.45	26.71	26.76	27.14	26.35	25.64	25.65	25.67	25.58	25.55	25.54	25.90	26.09
Construction													
2007	22.77	22.98	23.05	23.26	23.04	22.99	23.72	23.32	23.18	24.21	24.50	24.69	23.49
2008	24.78	24.67	24.53	24.54	24.61	24.09	24.20	24.18	24.23	24.23	24.76	24.88	24.46
2009	24.82	24.51	24.55	24.63	24.31	23.76	23.53	23.54	23.41	24.04	24.02	24.14	24.10
Manufacturing													
2007	26.59	25.19	25.22	25.69	25.06	24.88	25.61	25.61	26.68	25.96	26.92	27.12	25.88
2008	27.31	27.42	27.41	27.95	27.82	27.27	28.05	27.42	26.95	26.83	27.31	27.91	27.47
2009	27.69	27.75	27.77	27.72	27.59	27.39	27.20	27.09	27.06	27.29	27.23	27.33	27.43
Trade, Transportation, and Utilities													
2007	18.85	19.48	19.70	19.25	19.38	19.13	19.42	19.33	19.52	19.39	18.92	18.95	19.27
2008	19.50	19.20	19.53	19.21	19.20	19.26	19.20	19.24	19.45	19.41	19.57	19.27	19.34
2009	19.52	19.47	19.60	19.59	19.50	19.47	19.56	19.57	19.31	19.33	19.47	19.41	19.48
Financial Activities													
2007	23.09	22.69	22.27	22.94	22.76	23.81	23.88	22.97	23.74	22.64	22.62	22.10	22.96
2008	21.92	22.58	22.30	22.64	22.74	22.40	22.56	22.33	22.63	23.05	23.18	21.86	22.51
2009	21.88	21.91	21.96	21.76	22.21	22.27	22.20	22.04	21.75	21.82	22.07	21.90	21.98
Professional and Business Services													
2007	27.20	27.79	28.21	28.95	27.50	28.03	28.65	28.02	28.43	28.17	29.36	30.34	28.40
2008	30.39	30.79	31.00	30.27	28.95	28.86	29.05	29.18	29.53	29.53	30.34	30.76	29.87
2009	30.04	29.89	30.12	29.43	29.33	29.11	29.07	29.19	29.10	29.26	29.54	30.10	29.51
Education and Health Services													
2007	20.57	22.17	22.39	20.83	20.81	20.95	21.09	22.26	21.53	21.45	21.25	21.55	21.41
2008	21.31	22.11	22.25	21.72	21.75	22.04	22.18	22.17	22.00	22.14	22.46	23.03	22.10
2009	22.79	22.91	23.05	22.35	22.66	22.57	22.62	22.78	22.86	22.97	23.20	23.29	22.84
Leisure and Hospitality													
2007	12.70	13.02	13.22	12.89	12.98	13.42	13.55	13.27	13.32	13.19	13.14	13.54	13.19
2008	13.49	13.47	13.66	13.31	13.51	13.37	13.53	13.53	13.76	14.02	14.13	14.30	13.66
2009	14.31	14.44	14.49	14.32	14.09	13.99	14.11	14.20	14.13	14.13	14.07	14.26	14.21
Other Services													
2007	20.97	21.44	20.45	21.94	21.78	20.62	20.37	20.34	21.01	21.47	20.34	20.76	20.96
2008	20.87	20.72	20.67	20.86	21.32	20.95	20.87	20.68	20.58	20.48	21.02	20.50	20.79
2009	20.57	20.83	20.80	20.73	20.71	20.80	20.81	20.69	20.52	20.62	20.58	20.24	20.66

Average Weekly Earnings by Selected Industry: Colorado, 2007–2009

(Dollars, not seasonally adjusted.)

Industry and year	January	February	March	April	May	June	July	August	September	October	November	December	Annual average
Total Private													
2007	775.31	787.87	795.57	808.40	789.92	806.43	828.06	807.10	826.24	812.70	816.55	826.70	807.24
2008	812.22	822.85	842.45	822.48	818.57	835.18	828.71	822.59	822.74	838.02	853.55	826.24	828.24
2009	818.01	835.94	841.46	812.59	813.90	810.33	816.56	823.37	804.38	805.78	817.34	798.26	815.65
Goods-Producing													
2007	942.12	925.14	934.52	945.07	942.45	949.03	957.50	933.28	949.62	973.11	1007.83	989.90	955.01
2008	973.15	982.11	987.24	986.25	988.05	1013.54	1011.13	1005.18	992.89	990.78	1031.98	998.67	996.48
2009	994.52	1004.30	1022.23	996.04	996.03	976.88	974.70	980.59	956.69	968.35	975.63	947.94	983.59
Construction													
2007	842.49	838.77	873.60	869.92	889.34	887.41	901.36	872.17	864.61	924.82	960.40	918.47	887.92
2008	906.95	922.66	937.05	917.80	952.41	973.24	953.48	950.27	942.55	940.12	963.16	920.56	941.71
2009	903.45	894.62	920.63	921.16	935.94	924.26	927.08	927.48	873.19	915.92	924.77	876.28	913.39
Manufacturing													
2007	1002.44	969.82	963.40	991.63	964.81	970.32	985.99	975.74	1021.84	1004.65	1041.80	1044.12	993.79
2008	1026.86	1036.48	1036.10	1053.72	1046.03	1082.62	1085.54	1069.38	1048.36	1054.42	1100.59	1085.70	1060.34
2009	1071.60	1065.60	1069.15	1047.82	1051.18	1046.30	1033.60	1037.55	1017.46	1031.56	1045.63	1003.01	1045.08
Trade, Transportation, and Utilities													
2007	642.79	666.22	675.71	654.50	666.67	673.38	695.24	680.42	706.62	688.35	673.55	684.10	676.38
2008	676.65	672.00	691.36	664.67	670.08	689.51	679.68	675.32	680.75	673.53	694.74	670.60	678.83
2009	667.50	681.45	686.00	681.73	680.55	683.40	690.47	694.74	677.78	672.68	677.56	659.94	679.85
Financial Activities													
2007	838.17	812.30	792.81	832.72	794.32	850.02	878.78	813.14	849.89	805.98	791.70	822.12	824.26
2008	797.89	815.14	820.64	803.72	807.27	831.04	807.65	790.48	801.10	818.28	811.30	756.36	805.86
2009	763.61	775.61	783.97	770.30	784.01	786.13	781.44	775.81	752.55	759.34	796.73	773.07	775.89
Professional and Business Services													
2007	957.44	986.55	998.63	1053.78	976.25	1020.29	1068.65	1028.33	1068.97	1025.39	1062.83	1110.44	1030.92
2008	1084.92	1102.28	1119.10	1092.75	1042.20	1059.16	1048.71	1059.23	1068.99	1077.85	1128.65	1101.21	1081.29
2009	1078.44	1093.97	1096.37	1071.25	1061.75	1068.34	1063.96	1077.11	1056.33	1067.99	1101.84	1071.56	1077.12
Education and Health Services													
2007	699.38	756.00	765.74	716.55	705.46	720.68	736.04	767.97	751.40	740.03	752.25	754.25	738.65
2008	735.20	767.22	780.98	753.68	748.20	760.38	771.86	767.08	759.00	763.83	774.87	806.05	766.87
2009	790.81	804.14	806.75	771.08	779.50	769.64	771.34	783.63	779.53	780.98	788.80	782.54	783.41
Leisure and Hospitality													
2007	312.42	320.29	334.47	323.54	323.20	344.89	352.30	341.04	330.34	315.24	302.22	315.48	327.11
2008	317.02	320.59	334.67	315.45	320.64	342.27	346.37	342.31	342.62	337.88	336.29	336.05	333.30
2009	342.01	350.89	357.90	347.98	346.61	352.55	359.81	373.46	354.66	343.36	339.09	342.74	352.41
Other Services													
2007	702.50	754.69	719.84	765.71	740.52	715.51	698.69	687.49	712.24	723.54	707.83	691.31	718.93
2008	694.97	689.98	698.65	698.81	699.30	708.11	705.41	696.92	689.43	686.08	731.50	674.45	698.54
2009	678.81	689.47	686.40	677.87	691.71	694.72	682.57	699.32	685.37	684.58	703.84	659.82	685.91

CONNECTICUT
At a Glance

Population:
   1990 census: 3,287,116
   2000 census: 3,405,565
   2009 estimate: 3,518,288

Percent change in population:
   1990–2000: 3.6%
   2000–2009: 3.3%

Percent change in total nonfarm employment:
   1990–2009: 0.5%
   2008–2009: -4.2%

Industry with the largest growth in employment, 1990–2009 (thousands):
   Education and Health Services, 104.8

Industry with the largest decline or smallest growth in employment, 1990–2009 (thousands):
   Manufacturing, -129.0

Civilian labor force:
   1990: 1,814,924
   2000: 1,736,831
   2009: 1,889,929

Unemployment rate and rank among states (lowest to highest):
   1990: 4.9%, 14th
   2000: 2.3%, 1st
   2009: 8.2%, 27th

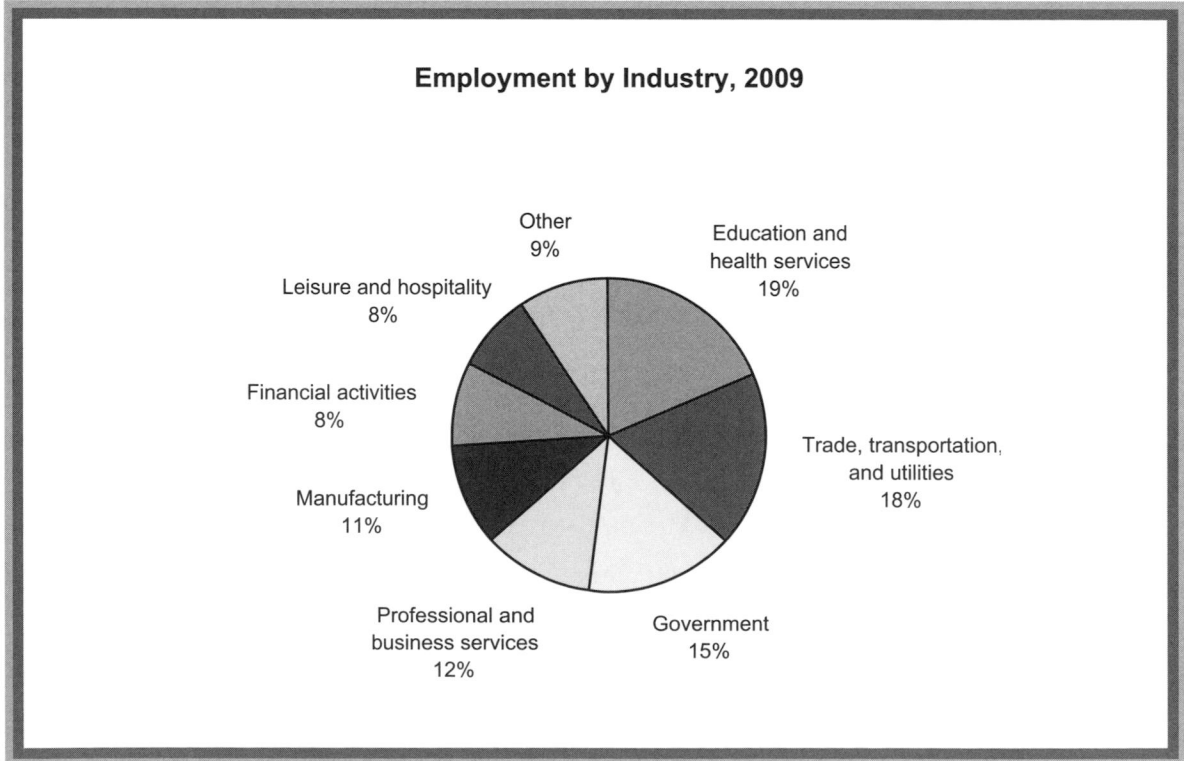

Employment by Industry, 2009

Other 9%
Education and health services 19%
Leisure and hospitality 8%
Trade, transportation, and utilities 18%
Financial activities 8%
Manufacturing 11%
Professional and business services 12%
Government 15%

Employment by Industry: Connecticut, Selected Years, 1990–2009

(Numbers in thousands, not seasonally adjusted.)

Industry and year	January	February	March	April	May	June	July	August	September	October	November	December	Annual average
Total Nonfarm													
1990	1621.6	1613.7	1624.8	1622.2	1633.9	1646.1	1612.6	1604.3	1620.9	1610.4	1611.7	1612.1	1619.5
2000	1655.0	1661.5	1675.9	1687.0	1700.9	1713.0	1695.5	1685.8	1703.4	1704.2	1712.1	1723.8	1693.2
2001	1665.2	1661.0	1667.3	1677.0	1690.4	1699.4	1676.5	1669.7	1683.4	1687.9	1694.2	1701.2	1681.1
2002	1648.1	1648.7	1657.5	1670.2	1679.9	1687.0	1655.0	1652.0	1663.3	1665.2	1673.1	1678.2	1664.9
2003	1630.9	1626.0	1630.8	1641.6	1653.8	1659.7	1633.2	1630.5	1642.6	1655.7	1663.3	1665.7	1644.5
2004	1616.6	1618.6	1627.7	1646.3	1658.3	1667.0	1644.2	1642.0	1655.7	1664.6	1675.4	1681.3	1649.8
2005	1630.3	1636.0	1639.6	1663.5	1670.4	1681.7	1653.9	1651.0	1668.0	1673.3	1683.9	1692.8	1662.0
2006	1648.5	1650.7	1656.0	1678.4	1687.3	1698.5	1672.5	1673.7	1685.3	1694.5	1704.9	1716.6	1680.6
2007	1666.5	1668.4	1671.9	1689.8	1705.6	1720.4	1691.4	1690.4	1704.3	1714.2	1724.2	1730.9	1698.2
2008	1685.3	1687.8	1692.5	1705.6	1717.7	1724.5	1690.4	1686.7	1697.2	1700.9	1701.4	1698.0	1699.0
2009	1639.3	1634.9	1626.9	1626.9	1639.4	1640.3	1609.1	1602.6	1617.0	1629.6	1630.0	1630.0	1627.2
Total Private													
1990	1412.2	1401.3	1410.7	1408.2	1417.1	1431.4	1415.6	1410.9	1413.0	1397.9	1395.1	1396.4	1409.2
2000	1417.6	1417.2	1428.6	1439.8	1450.2	1470.4	1466.4	1460.6	1463.3	1459.3	1465.5	1477.1	1451.3
2001	1423.4	1414.3	1420.0	1429.8	1443.3	1456.8	1449.0	1443.1	1438.9	1436.7	1438.7	1446.0	1436.7
2002	1399.4	1393.8	1401.7	1415.6	1425.7	1436.9	1423.9	1418.1	1416.5	1413.6	1417.8	1423.7	1415.6
2003	1380.6	1373.4	1377.6	1390.1	1402.6	1413.6	1405.0	1400.4	1400.4	1408.2	1413.0	1417.0	1398.5
2004	1374.3	1371.2	1378.9	1398.2	1411.4	1425.0	1419.2	1413.7	1416.3	1417.5	1425.3	1432.6	1407.0
2005	1388.8	1389.1	1393.2	1414.9	1422.6	1437.1	1428.8	1422.6	1424.8	1424.1	1432.1	1440.9	1418.3
2006	1402.9	1401.3	1406.8	1428.2	1437.5	1453.7	1444.4	1440.9	1441.4	1444.3	1451.8	1463.1	1434.7
2007	1419.0	1416.0	1420.1	1437.5	1453.6	1471.9	1460.5	1456.2	1456.1	1458.2	1465.5	1472.9	1449.0
2008	1432.7	1430.1	1435.8	1448.6	1460.1	1472.2	1456.6	1450.4	1447.1	1443.4	1441.6	1439.9	1446.5
2009	1387.5	1379.1	1371.8	1372.2	1384.5	1392.0	1380.2	1372.6	1373.2	1378.7	1375.6	1377.4	1378.7
Goods-Producing													
1990	368.6	365.3	366.3	367.8	368.3	369.8	365.8	363.8	364.8	359.0	356.0	352.0	364.0
2000	293.9	292.7	295.6	298.8	300.7	304.4	304.0	304.9	306.2	304.1	303.8	303.4	301.0
2001	293.5	291.3	292.5	295.4	296.7	298.5	295.1	294.7	292.8	289.6	287.3	285.8	292.8
2002	277.2	274.5	275.5	277.7	278.8	280.2	276.3	276.6	275.2	272.7	270.9	268.5	275.3
2003	261.0	257.3	257.9	261.5	264.1	266.2	264.3	265.1	264.4	264.2	264.0	262.4	262.7
2004	255.1	253.4	256.5	262.2	264.8	268.1	267.6	268.2	267.8	267.2	266.8	265.5	263.6
2005	258.0	255.9	257.1	261.7	263.8	267.0	265.6	265.2	263.6	262.4	261.9	260.2	261.9
2006	255.4	254.8	253.5	261.0	262.8	266.5	265.8	265.7	263.9	262.9	262.3	261.7	261.4
2007	255.1	253.0	254.8	258.4	261.0	265.1	264.2	264.5	262.7	261.8	261.4	259.3	260.1
2008	252.5	250.4	251.4	254.9	256.9	259.0	257.2	256.9	254.8	252.4	249.0	244.7	253.3
2009	233.9	229.3	227.5	227.5	228.5	229.7	226.7	225.7	224.9	226.2	223.9	223.0	227.2
Mining and Logging													
1990	0.9	0.9	0.9	1.0	1.0	1.0	1.0	1.0	0.9	1.0	0.9	0.9	0.9
2000	0.7	0.6	0.7	0.8	0.8	0.8	0.9	0.8	0.8	0.8	0.8	0.8	0.7
2001	0.7	0.6	0.7	0.7	0.8	0.8	0.8	0.8	0.8	0.7	0.7	0.7	0.7
2002	0.7	0.6	0.7	0.7	0.8	0.8	0.8	0.8	0.8	0.8	0.8	0.8	0.8
2003	0.7	0.6	0.6	0.7	0.8	0.8	0.8	0.8	0.8	0.8	0.8	0.7	0.7
2004	0.6	0.6	0.7	0.7	0.8	0.8	0.8	0.8	0.8	0.8	0.8	0.7	0.7
2005	0.7	0.6	0.6	0.7	0.8	0.8	0.8	0.8	0.8	0.8	0.8	0.7	0.7
2006	0.7	0.7	0.7	0.8	0.8	0.8	0.8	0.8	0.8	0.8	0.8	0.7	0.8
2007	0.7	0.6	0.6	0.7	0.7	0.8	0.8	0.8	0.8	0.8	0.8	0.7	0.7
2008	0.7	0.6	0.7	0.7	0.8	0.8	0.8	0.8	0.8	0.8	0.8	0.7	0.8
2009	0.6	0.6	0.6	0.6	0.7	0.7	0.7	0.7	0.7	0.6	0.6	0.6	0.6
Construction													
1990	61.1	59.2	59.9	61.5	63.8	65.3	65.9	65.9	65.3	62.1	59.9	56.6	62.2
2000	58.1	57.1	59.9	62.9	65.0	67.0	68.0	68.5	68.0	67.3	67.1	66.0	64.5
2001	59.1	58.3	59.6	64.2	66.7	68.5	69.8	70.0	68.8	67.6	66.6	65.1	65.4
2002	59.4	58.5	59.9	63.3	65.0	66.4	66.8	66.7	65.5	64.5	63.7	61.3	63.4
2003	56.2	54.3	55.2	59.1	62.4	64.0	65.9	66.4	65.6	65.5	65.3	63.3	61.9
2004	57.5	56.4	58.6	64.3	66.9	68.7	69.9	70.5	69.9	69.5	68.8	67.1	65.7
2005	60.9	59.6	60.5	65.2	67.1	69.0	70.0	70.1	68.9	67.7	67.2	65.1	65.9
2006	60.9	60.4	61.9	66.0	67.8	69.8	70.9	71.3	70.2	69.8	68.9	67.6	67.1
2007	62.6	60.7	62.4	67.1	69.7	71.9	72.7	72.9	71.9	71.7	71.0	68.8	68.6
2008	63.0	61.9	62.9	66.2	67.5	68.4	68.6	68.4	67.1	65.8	63.5	60.5	65.3
2009	53.8	52.0	51.8	53.7	55.5	56.7	56.7	56.5	56.0	56.7	55.1	53.1	54.8
Manufacturing													
1990	306.6	305.2	305.5	305.3	303.5	303.5	298.9	296.9	298.6	295.9	295.2	294.5	300.8
2000	235.1	235.0	235.0	235.1	234.9	236.6	235.1	235.6	237.4	236.0	235.9	236.6	235.7
2001	233.7	232.4	232.2	230.5	229.2	229.2	224.5	223.9	223.2	221.3	220.0	220.0	226.7
2002	217.1	215.4	214.9	213.7	213.0	213.0	208.7	209.1	208.9	207.4	206.4	206.4	211.2
2003	204.1	202.4	202.1	201.7	200.9	201.4	197.6	197.9	198.0	197.9	197.9	198.4	200.0
2004	197.0	196.4	197.2	197.2	197.1	198.6	196.9	196.9	197.1	196.9	197.2	197.7	197.2
2005	196.4	195.7	196.0	195.8	195.9	197.2	194.8	194.3	193.9	193.9	193.9	194.4	195.2
2006	193.8	193.7	190.9	194.2	194.2	195.9	194.1	193.6	192.9	192.3	192.6	193.4	193.5
2007	191.8	191.7	191.8	190.6	190.6	192.4	190.7	190.8	190.0	189.3	189.6	189.8	190.8
2008	188.8	187.9	187.8	188.0	188.6	189.8	187.8	187.7	186.9	185.8	184.7	183.5	187.3
2009	179.5	176.7	175.1	173.2	172.3	172.3	169.3	168.5	168.2	168.9	168.2	169.3	171.8

Employment by Industry: Connecticut, Selected Years, 1990–2009—*Continued*

(Numbers in thousands, not seasonally adjusted.)

Industry and year	January	February	March	April	May	June	July	August	September	October	November	December	Annual average
Service-Providing													
1990	1253.0	1248.4	1258.5	1254.4	1265.6	1276.3	1246.8	1240.5	1256.1	1251.4	1255.7	1260.1	1255.6
2000	1361.1	1368.8	1380.3	1388.2	1400.2	1408.6	1391.5	1380.9	1397.2	1400.1	1408.3	1420.4	1392.1
2001	1371.7	1369.7	1374.8	1381.6	1393.7	1400.9	1381.4	1375.0	1390.6	1398.3	1406.9	1415.4	1388.3
2002	1370.9	1374.2	1382.0	1392.5	1401.1	1406.8	1378.7	1375.4	1388.1	1392.5	1402.2	1409.7	1389.5
2003	1369.9	1368.7	1372.9	1380.1	1389.7	1393.5	1368.9	1365.4	1378.2	1391.5	1399.3	1403.3	1381.8
2004	1361.5	1365.2	1371.2	1384.1	1393.5	1398.9	1376.6	1373.8	1387.9	1397.4	1408.6	1415.8	1386.2
2005	1372.3	1380.1	1382.5	1401.8	1406.6	1414.7	1388.3	1385.8	1404.4	1410.9	1422.0	1432.6	1400.2
2006	1393.1	1395.9	1402.5	1417.4	1424.5	1432.0	1406.7	1408.0	1421.4	1431.6	1442.6	1454.9	1419.2
2007	1411.4	1415.4	1417.1	1431.4	1444.6	1455.3	1427.2	1425.9	1441.6	1452.4	1462.8	1471.6	1438.1
2008	1432.8	1437.4	1441.1	1450.7	1460.8	1465.5	1433.2	1429.8	1442.4	1448.5	1452.4	1453.3	1445.7
2009	1405.4	1405.6	1399.4	1399.4	1410.9	1410.6	1382.4	1376.9	1392.1	1403.4	1406.1	1407.0	1399.9
Trade, Transportation, and Utilities													
1990	327.5	318.8	319.8	316.3	317.9	320.3	313.1	312.4	315.0	313.8	317.4	321.8	317.8
2000	314.8	311.6	313.0	314.5	316.1	318.4	313.1	312.2	316.9	319.5	326.7	333.2	317.5
2001	314.2	306.4	307.0	308.8	311.5	313.6	309.5	307.8	310.0	313.6	318.9	324.7	312.2
2002	309.4	303.8	305.4	307.7	309.7	312.7	305.9	304.3	308.6	308.2	314.3	320.4	309.2
2003	306.3	300.9	302.5	301.4	304.0	306.9	300.5	299.4	303.9	308.5	313.6	318.1	305.5
2004	304.9	301.0	302.3	303.7	306.4	309.3	304.4	302.6	307.2	310.5	318.3	324.2	307.9
2005	310.2	306.3	306.6	308.4	310.0	312.4	306.2	304.9	309.2	310.2	317.5	324.5	310.5
2006	311.7	305.4	307.3	308.6	310.3	313.2	306.2	305.0	308.4	311.2	318.8	325.1	310.9
2007	311.2	305.3	306.6	306.3	311.4	314.9	308.2	306.7	310.4	312.7	320.3	327.0	311.8
2008	314.7	308.1	308.9	308.2	310.9	313.1	306.2	304.7	307.6	307.9	312.4	316.4	309.9
2009	300.4	294.3	292.3	287.9	293.3	295.7	288.4	287.2	290.7	291.1	295.9	299.6	293.1
Wholesale Trade													
1990	74.7	74.0	74.0	72.8	72.8	72.8	72.7	72.4	71.8	70.7	70.3	70.1	72.4
2000	66.9	67.0	67.3	68.1	68.5	68.7	68.4	68.2	68.5	68.4	68.9	69.3	68.1
2001	67.0	67.1	67.3	67.9	68.1	68.2	67.7	67.2	66.9	67.2	66.8	67.2	67.4
2002	65.9	65.5	65.7	66.1	66.3	66.4	66.3	66.2	66.0	65.8	65.8	66.2	66.0
2003	65.3	65.0	65.4	65.4	65.5	66.0	65.5	65.4	65.2	65.5	65.6	65.7	65.5
2004	64.8	64.9	65.4	65.9	66.2	66.7	66.0	66.0	65.8	65.4	65.8	66.2	65.8
2005	65.7	65.4	65.6	65.9	66.3	66.7	66.8	66.8	66.9	66.9	67.1	67.5	66.5
2006	66.9	66.8	67.1	67.5	67.7	68.1	67.7	67.6	67.3	67.7	67.7	67.9	67.5
2007	67.5	67.5	67.5	67.7	67.9	68.6	68.5	68.6	68.7	68.7	68.7	69.5	68.3
2008	69.2	69.1	69.5	69.4	69.8	70.0	69.4	69.1	68.9	68.7	68.6	68.4	69.2
2009	67.2	66.5	65.9	65.2	65.1	65.2	64.8	64.6	64.3	64.0	63.6	63.7	65.0
Retail Trade													
1990	203.7	196.6	196.6	194.5	195.7	197.5	193.5	193.2	193.7	193.9	198.0	202.0	196.6
2000	196.4	192.9	194.4	194.5	195.7	197.8	194.8	195.0	195.7	197.3	204.2	210.6	197.4
2001	195.6	188.6	189.4	190.0	192.3	194.6	193.6	193.8	193.0	195.3	201.4	206.8	194.5
2002	194.9	189.5	191.1	192.0	193.7	196.5	193.2	192.9	192.8	192.0	198.2	204.0	194.2
2003	192.1	187.3	188.2	187.5	189.6	191.6	189.3	189.3	189.3	192.2	197.3	201.7	191.3
2004	191.1	187.2	188.0	188.0	189.9	191.9	191.4	190.4	190.3	192.2	199.2	204.6	192.0
2005	193.0	189.3	189.1	190.1	191.0	192.4	190.2	189.8	189.2	190.4	196.7	202.2	192.0
2006	192.3	186.4	187.8	188.7	189.8	191.9	189.6	189.4	188.4	190.5	197.8	202.4	191.3
2007	191.1	185.5	186.7	186.4	190.6	192.9	190.4	190.0	188.7	190.7	198.0	202.7	191.1
2008	192.9	186.5	186.8	185.8	187.9	189.5	186.7	186.8	185.1	185.6	190.1	193.3	188.1
2009	181.2	176.3	175.2	174.0	177.2	179.6	176.7	177.0	176.2	177.6	182.2	185.0	178.2
Transportation and Utilities													
1990	49.1	48.2	49.2	49.0	49.4	50.0	46.9	46.8	49.5	49.2	49.1	49.7	48.8
2000	51.5	51.7	51.3	51.9	51.9	51.9	49.9	49.0	52.7	53.8	53.6	53.3	51.8
2001	51.6	50.7	50.3	50.9	51.1	50.8	48.2	46.8	50.1	51.1	50.7	50.7	50.3
2002	48.6	48.8	48.6	49.6	49.7	49.8	46.4	45.2	49.8	50.4	50.3	50.2	49.0
2003	48.9	48.6	48.9	48.5	48.9	49.3	45.7	44.7	49.4	50.8	50.7	50.7	48.8
2004	49.0	48.9	48.9	49.8	50.3	50.7	47.0	46.2	51.1	52.9	53.3	53.4	50.1
2005	51.5	51.6	51.9	52.4	52.7	53.3	49.2	48.3	53.1	52.9	53.7	54.8	52.1
2006	52.5	52.2	52.4	52.4	52.8	53.2	48.9	48.0	52.7	53.0	53.3	54.8	52.2
2007	52.6	52.3	52.4	52.2	52.9	53.4	49.3	48.1	53.0	53.3	53.6	54.8	52.3
2008	52.6	52.5	52.6	53.0	53.2	53.6	50.1	48.8	53.6	53.6	53.7	54.7	52.7
2009	52.0	51.5	51.2	48.7	51.0	50.9	46.9	45.6	50.2	49.5	50.1	50.9	49.9
Information													
1990	43.2	43.0	43.3	42.7	42.5	43.1	42.0	41.8	41.3	41.2	40.9	41.0	42.1
2000	45.2	45.4	45.7	45.5	45.8	46.5	46.9	47.0	47.0	47.1	47.4	47.6	46.4
2001	46.3	46.4	46.0	45.3	45.1	45.1	44.2	44.2	43.6	43.2	43.3	43.3	44.7
2002	42.2	41.9	41.8	41.5	41.4	41.5	41.0	40.7	40.2	40.0	39.9	40.0	41.0
2003	40.1	39.9	39.8	39.6	39.5	39.8	39.6	39.5	39.1	39.2	39.4	39.5	39.6
2004	39.2	38.8	38.9	38.9	39.0	39.4	39.3	39.3	38.8	38.6	38.9	38.8	39.0
2005	38.5	38.6	38.3	38.2	38.2	38.5	38.2	38.0	37.6	37.5	37.7	37.8	38.1
2006	37.9	37.9	37.9	37.7	37.8	37.9	38.0	38.0	37.7	37.8	38.1	38.3	37.9
2007	37.5	37.9	37.7	38.0	39.0	38.6	38.8	38.9	39.2	39.0	38.1	38.2	38.4
2008	37.9	38.2	37.9	38.5	38.6	38.6	37.9	38.1	37.1	36.9	36.9	37.0	37.8
2009	36.4	36.3	35.5	35.2	35.0	35.0	35.1	34.9	34.4	34.1	34.7	34.5	35.1

Employment by Industry: Connecticut, Selected Years, 1990–2009—*Continued*

(Numbers in thousands, not seasonally adjusted.)

Industry and year	January	February	March	April	May	June	July	August	September	October	November	December	Annual average
Financial Activities													
1990	153.5	153.7	154.1	153.2	154.0	155.3	155.7	155.4	153.3	151.6	150.2	151.1	153.4
2000	141.2	141.2	141.8	141.5	142.1	144.2	145.1	145.3	143.9	143.0	143.0	144.1	143.0
2001	142.1	141.8	142.1	142.0	142.5	144.1	144.8	144.9	143.1	142.3	142.4	143.2	142.9
2002	142.8	142.1	142.1	141.4	142.1	143.4	143.9	143.8	142.5	141.8	142.5	143.1	142.6
2003	142.4	141.7	141.7	142.6	143.3	144.7	144.3	144.0	142.4	141.5	141.4	142.0	142.7
2004	140.1	139.6	139.8	139.7	140.1	141.6	142.0	142.1	140.7	140.3	140.7	141.1	140.7
2005	140.5	140.5	140.5	141.6	141.5	143.4	144.2	144.0	142.7	142.4	142.6	143.5	142.3
2006	143.0	142.7	142.9	142.9	143.4	145.1	145.6	145.8	144.5	144.6	145.1	145.6	144.3
2007	144.9	144.4	144.1	144.1	144.4	146.3	146.2	145.7	144.0	143.6	143.5	144.1	144.6
2008	143.0	143.3	144.0	143.2	143.5	145.3	144.8	144.9	142.8	142.0	142.1	142.0	143.4
2009	139.8	139.4	139.3	137.7	137.4	138.4	138.3	137.7	135.7	136.0	136.4	136.1	137.7
Professional and Business Services													
1990	166.4	167.2	169.7	167.8	169.1	172.4	170.4	170.8	170.2	168.7	168.1	167.9	169.1
2000	207.7	208.9	211.6	214.4	216.1	220.9	219.7	219.5	219.4	217.6	217.2	218.0	215.9
2001	207.3	204.7	206.6	209.6	214.4	215.2	212.4	212.1	211.7	209.3	207.8	207.4	209.9
2002	197.7	197.7	200.7	203.2	203.9	206.2	203.3	204.1	203.4	201.6	201.2	201.0	202.0
2003	193.5	193.4	194.4	196.9	197.1	198.5	196.6	197.7	197.8	198.1	198.7	198.3	196.8
2004	191.2	191.3	193.4	196.7	197.7	200.7	199.3	199.6	199.4	197.2	198.5	199.6	197.1
2005	191.9	193.2	195.3	199.1	199.2	203.1	202.4	202.3	203.3	202.2	203.1	204.0	199.9
2006	196.0	198.5	200.8	204.6	204.7	208.8	205.0	206.2	206.8	205.7	206.3	208.3	204.3
2007	199.4	200.4	201.6	206.1	207.7	211.4	207.4	208.2	207.8	208.2	208.7	210.4	206.4
2008	203.6	203.3	205.0	207.9	207.6	210.2	206.9	206.2	204.8	202.6	200.9	199.8	204.9
2009	192.3	189.7	188.6	190.2	189.2	189.9	186.9	187.2	186.2	187.9	183.1	181.9	187.8
Education and Health Services													
1990	192.9	193.7	194.9	196.6	197.2	197.1	195.4	195.1	200.1	201.5	203.1	203.9	197.6
2000	243.4	245.6	246.7	246.3	245.7	244.5	244.2	240.6	244.6	245.7	247.0	248.8	245.2
2001	248.3	252.0	252.0	251.7	248.5	249.8	249.4	247.5	254.7	257.5	259.6	260.8	252.7
2002	255.1	258.9	258.9	260.3	259.6	257.1	255.9	253.7	259.4	264.4	266.5	266.9	259.7
2003	261.1	264.3	263.0	265.1	264.6	261.4	260.0	257.0	262.4	268.5	270.0	270.3	264.0
2004	264.4	268.2	267.0	270.3	270.3	266.6	264.3	261.3	268.3	274.0	275.0	274.8	268.7
2005	269.0	273.4	271.8	275.6	274.0	270.1	268.6	265.9	273.1	278.3	279.7	279.8	273.3
2006	274.7	278.4	277.2	280.9	279.5	276.1	275.8	273.7	280.6	284.8	286.4	287.2	279.6
2007	282.1	286.6	285.2	289.3	287.5	285.9	283.8	281.3	288.5	293.0	294.7	295.4	287.8
2008	290.7	295.8	295.3	297.9	296.2	294.4	292.2	289.8	296.8	302.2	304.6	304.7	296.7
2009	299.1	304.3	301.6	302.9	301.8	299.0	298.7	296.2	302.2	306.7	308.2	307.8	302.4
Leisure and Hospitality													
1990	102.3	101.7	104.1	106.2	110.5	114.7	114.3	113.3	111.4	106.6	104.3	104.2	107.8
2000	111.9	112.1	114.2	118.2	122.9	129.6	130.9	129.3	124.1	120.9	119.0	120.3	121.1
2001	111.0	111.0	112.7	115.8	122.9	127.7	129.7	128.6	121.2	118.9	116.9	118.0	119.5
2002	112.9	113.0	115.0	120.8	126.4	131.4	133.5	131.6	125.2	122.9	120.2	121.0	122.8
2003	114.7	114.6	116.4	121.3	127.8	132.9	136.1	134.7	128.7	126.2	123.9	124.1	125.1
2004	117.9	117.5	119.2	124.4	130.5	136.0	138.3	137.0	131.8	127.5	124.8	126.0	127.6
2005	119.1	119.5	121.5	127.6	133.0	138.5	139.5	138.8	132.8	128.6	126.9	127.7	129.5
2006	122.1	121.8	124.8	129.3	135.2	141.6	142.8	141.7	135.7	133.1	130.6	132.3	132.6
2007	125.4	125.2	126.5	131.4	138.5	144.4	146.4	146.0	139.5	136.1	135.0	134.5	135.7
2008	127.5	128.3	130.3	134.8	142.7	147.1	147.4	146.1	140.7	136.8	133.3	133.0	137.3
2009	124.2	124.9	125.9	129.8	138.0	142.1	144.0	142.0	137.9	134.9	131.5	132.8	134.0
Other Services													
1990	57.8	57.9	58.5	57.6	57.6	58.7	58.9	58.3	56.9	55.5	55.1	54.5	57.3
2000	59.5	59.7	60.0	60.6	60.8	61.9	62.5	61.8	61.2	61.4	61.4	61.7	61.0
2001	60.7	60.7	61.1	61.2	61.7	62.8	63.9	63.3	61.8	62.3	62.5	62.8	62.1
2002	62.1	61.9	62.3	63.0	63.8	64.4	64.1	63.3	62.0	62.0	62.3	62.8	62.8
2003	61.5	61.3	61.9	61.7	62.2	63.2	63.6	63.0	61.7	62.0	62.0	62.3	62.2
2004	61.5	61.4	61.8	62.3	62.6	63.3	64.0	63.6	62.3	62.2	62.3	62.6	62.5
2005	61.6	61.7	62.1	62.7	62.9	64.1	64.1	63.5	62.5	62.5	62.7	63.4	62.8
2006	62.1	61.8	62.4	63.2	63.8	64.5	65.2	64.8	63.8	64.2	64.2	64.6	63.7
2007	63.4	63.2	63.6	63.9	64.1	65.3	65.5	64.9	64.0	63.8	63.8	64.0	64.1
2008	62.8	62.7	63.0	63.2	63.7	64.5	64.0	63.7	62.5	62.6	62.4	62.3	63.1
2009	61.4	60.9	61.1	61.0	61.3	62.2	62.1	61.7	61.2	61.8	61.9	61.7	61.5
Government													
1990	209.4	212.4	214.1	214.0	216.8	214.7	197.0	193.4	207.9	212.5	216.6	215.7	210.4
2000	237.4	244.3	247.3	247.2	250.7	242.6	229.1	225.2	240.1	244.9	246.6	246.7	241.8
2001	241.8	246.7	247.3	247.2	247.1	242.6	227.5	226.6	244.5	251.2	255.5	255.2	244.4
2002	248.7	254.9	255.8	254.6	254.2	250.1	231.1	233.9	246.8	251.6	255.3	254.5	249.3
2003	250.3	252.6	253.2	251.5	251.2	246.1	228.2	230.1	242.2	247.5	250.3	248.7	246.0
2004	242.3	247.4	248.8	248.1	246.9	242.0	225.0	228.3	239.4	247.1	250.1	248.7	242.8
2005	241.5	246.9	246.4	248.6	247.8	244.6	225.1	228.4	243.2	249.2	251.8	251.9	243.8
2006	245.6	249.4	249.2	250.2	249.8	244.8	228.1	232.8	243.9	250.2	253.1	253.5	245.9
2007	247.5	252.4	251.8	252.3	252.0	248.5	230.0	231.2	248.2	256.0	258.7	258.0	249.7
2008	252.6	257.7	256.7	257.0	257.6	252.3	233.8	236.3	250.1	257.5	259.8	258.1	252.5
2009	251.8	255.8	255.1	254.7	254.9	248.3	228.9	230.0	243.8	250.9	254.4	252.6	248.4

Average Weekly Hours by Selected Industry: Connecticut, 2007–2009

(Not seasonally adjusted.)

Industry and year	January	February	March	April	May	June	July	August	September	October	November	December	Annual average
Total Private													
2007	34.0	33.6	33.9	34.3	34.5	34.6	34.6	34.6	34.5	34.3	34.5	34.2	34.3
2008	34.2	33.9	34.3	34.1	34.1	34.3	33.9	33.9	34.0	33.7	33.6	33.3	34.0
2009	33.3	33.4	33.1	32.7	33.1	32.9	33.0	33.1	33.0	32.5	33.0	32.7	33.0
Goods-Producing													
2007	39.4	39.2	40.0	40.3	40.8	40.0	40.6	41.0	41.1	41.1	41.1	40.5	40.4
2008	41.2	40.3	41.0	40.9	40.8	40.8	40.6	40.7	40.3	40.2	38.6	38.4	40.3
2009	38.0	37.7	37.8	37.0	37.9	38.0	38.6	38.3	38.4	38.3	38.8	38.5	38.1
Construction													
2007	35.8	35.0	35.3	36.4	38.4	37.5	39.2	39.3	38.9	39.5	38.7	37.6	37.7
2008	38.2	37.8	38.0	38.0	37.8	37.9	38.2	38.6	37.7	37.1	36.5	35.5	37.6
2009	34.3	35.0	35.5	35.4	36.6	36.5	37.2	37.4	36.4	36.8	36.5	35.5	36.1
Manufacturing													
2007	40.4	40.4	41.4	41.6	41.7	40.9	41.2	41.7	42.0	41.7	41.9	41.4	41.4
2008	41.5	40.5	41.5	41.6	41.6	41.6	41.2	41.3	41.0	41.2	40.2	40.1	41.1
2009	40.0	39.2	39.1	38.2	38.7	38.8	39.3	38.9	39.3	39.2	39.9	39.9	39.2
Trade, Transportation, and Utilities													
2007	34.0	33.5	33.7	34.5	34.6	35.3	35.2	34.9	34.8	34.3	34.3	33.8	34.4
2008	33.5	33.5	34.0	33.9	34.1	34.7	34.0	34.0	34.1	33.2	33.8	33.7	33.9
2009	33.7	33.4	33.4	33.0	33.5	33.3	33.2	33.3	33.6	33.0	33.3	33.8	33.4
Financial Activities													
2007	34.1	34.1	34.5	34.8	34.4	34.6	35.6	35.2	35.5	35.1	35.3	36.1	34.9
2008	35.4	35.7	36.5	35.6	35.7	36.0	35.3	35.2	35.1	34.7	35.8	35.6	35.6
2009	35.8	35.8	35.9	35.4	35.5	35.7	35.2	36.0	35.5	35.7	37.1	36.0	35.8
Professional and Business Services													
2007	34.0	33.4	34.1	34.6	34.8	35.1	34.4	34.5	34.1	33.8	33.7	34.1	34.2
2008	34.2	33.5	34.0	34.9	35.1	35.5	34.3	34.5	34.6	34.7	34.7	34.1	34.5
2009	33.0	33.6	33.2	33.2	33.5	33.1	33.1	33.5	32.7	33.2	34.1	33.0	33.3
Education and Health Services													
2007	32.3	31.5	31.5	31.8	31.5	31.8	31.1	31.3	31.1	30.9	31.6	31.0	31.4
2008	31.1	30.9	30.9	30.8	30.7	30.8	30.7	31.0	30.9	30.8	30.9	30.5	30.8
2009	30.7	31.0	30.5	30.0	30.1	30.1	30.3	30.3	30.8	30.7	30.7	30.5	30.5
Leisure and Hospitality													
2007	25.6	26.3	26.4	26.5	27.9	28.0	28.2	28.4	28.2	28.3	28.6	27.9	27.6
2008	27.4	27.8	28.0	26.2	26.5	26.0	27.1	26.2	26.3	26.4	26.3	26.1	26.7
2009	25.6	27.0	26.0	26.5	26.5	25.9	26.5	26.5	26.2	26.8	26.7	25.9	26.3
Other Services													
2007	33.4	32.6	32.7	33.3	32.4	32.6	32.3	31.5	31.9	31.8	32.9	31.7	32.4
2008	31.1	31.7	31.0	30.6	30.3	30.1	30.3	29.7	30.2	30.7	30.3	29.1	30.4
2009	29.2	28.8	28.8	28.7	29.5	29.7	29.6	29.7	29.5	29.8	29.7	29.2	29.4

Average Hourly Earnings by Selected Industry: Connecticut, 2007–2009

(Dollars, not seasonally adjusted.)

Industry and year	January	February	March	April	May	June	July	August	September	October	November	December	Annual average
Total Private													
2007	25.86	26.27	25.99	26.38	26.79	26.84	26.80	26.45	26.74	26.81	26.80	27.34	26.59
2008	27.36	27.45	27.66	27.79	27.51	27.97	27.74	27.43	27.73	27.89	27.95	28.09	27.71
2009	27.96	28.17	28.33	27.98	27.57	27.43	27.64	27.82	27.43	27.56	27.94	27.96	27.82
Goods-Producing													
2007	28.00	28.39	27.65	28.16	27.92	28.76	27.92	27.74	28.12	28.09	28.43	28.71	28.16
2008	28.42	28.81	28.78	28.89	28.92	29.05	29.26	29.08	29.19	29.11	29.08	29.80	29.03
2009	29.89	29.53	29.64	29.93	29.72	29.68	29.33	29.52	29.15	29.36	29.11	29.85	29.56
Construction													
2007	28.07	28.89	28.49	28.46	28.82	28.75	28.29	28.69	28.64	28.26	27.92	27.88	28.43
2008	28.80	29.17	29.49	29.11	28.79	28.85	28.89	28.72	28.60	28.91	28.82	28.86	28.91
2009	29.20	29.16	28.86	28.75	28.53	28.29	28.29	28.61	28.70	29.27	29.23	29.63	28.86
Manufacturing													
2007	28.02	28.30	27.46	28.11	27.70	28.83	27.85	27.44	27.96	28.03	28.57	28.92	28.10
2008	28.39	28.76	28.61	28.84	28.97	29.13	29.38	29.19	29.37	29.19	29.21	29.94	29.08
2009	29.93	29.31	29.55	30.02	29.85	29.90	29.57	29.76	29.19	29.20	28.90	29.77	29.58
Trade, Transportation, and Utilities													
2007	21.58	21.84	21.86	21.85	21.98	21.69	21.80	21.54	21.92	21.80	22.41	21.95	21.85
2008	22.24	22.58	22.22	23.00	22.65	22.55	22.37	22.30	22.60	22.22	21.95	21.71	22.37
2009	22.55	22.62	22.59	23.16	22.39	22.37	21.46	21.47	21.61	21.16	21.10	21.00	21.96
Financial Activities													
2007	38.70	40.40	38.23	40.59	40.75	41.84	40.96	40.13	39.70	41.03	40.29	42.66	40.45
2008	43.19	42.14	42.63	41.95	41.47	43.77	41.73	40.98	41.13	44.55	43.41	42.39	42.44
2009	40.42	42.19	43.26	41.48	41.41	40.49	40.92	41.82	39.72	41.15	41.98	41.57	41.37
Professional and Business Services													
2007	28.37	28.39	27.98	28.41	28.94	28.78	29.29	28.65	29.41	29.54	29.36	29.89	28.92
2008	30.28	31.20	31.53	30.99	30.62	31.63	31.81	30.97	30.96	30.38	30.89	31.78	31.09
2009	32.18	32.06	32.07	30.70	30.37	29.92	29.67	29.99	30.07	29.38	29.64	30.21	30.53
Education and Health Services													
2007	22.77	23.20	23.67	23.35	23.26	23.13	23.61	23.39	23.47	23.86	23.49	23.82	23.42
2008	24.00	23.93	24.56	24.65	24.45	24.23	24.66	24.37	24.61	24.63	25.28	25.86	24.61
2009	25.92	25.74	26.03	26.09	26.15	26.09	26.14	25.98	25.79	25.83	25.89	25.70	25.94
Leisure and Hospitality													
2007	14.85	14.68	15.13	15.15	15.23	14.89	15.14	15.24	15.47	15.57	15.63	16.37	15.29
2008	15.58	15.48	15.30	15.69	15.62	15.84	15.35	15.29	15.67	15.35	15.58	15.65	15.53
2009	15.55	15.40	15.17	15.16	15.02	15.40	15.26	15.53	15.71	15.34	15.22	15.45	15.35
Other Services													
2007	20.48	19.79	20.16	21.22	21.04	21.73	21.41	21.53	21.34	20.92	21.12	21.77	21.04
2008	21.58	22.03	22.36	22.58	22.24	22.72	22.98	22.72	23.78	23.08	23.03	22.98	22.67
2009	22.67	22.38	22.19	22.71	21.95	21.82	21.67	21.71	21.95	21.93	22.08	22.35	22.11

Average Weekly Earnings by Selected Industry: Connecticut, 2007–2009

(Dollars, not seasonally adjusted.)

Industry and year	January	February	March	April	May	June	July	August	September	October	November	December	Annual average
Total Private													
2007	879.24	882.67	881.06	904.83	924.26	928.66	927.28	915.17	922.53	919.58	924.60	935.03	912.04
2008	935.71	930.56	948.74	947.64	938.09	959.37	940.39	929.88	942.82	939.89	939.12	935.40	942.14
2009	931.07	940.88	937.72	914.95	912.57	902.45	912.12	920.84	905.19	895.70	922.02	914.29	918.06
Goods-Producing													
2007	1103.20	1112.89	1106.00	1134.85	1139.14	1150.40	1133.55	1137.34	1155.73	1154.50	1168.47	1162.76	1137.66
2008	1170.90	1161.04	1179.98	1181.60	1179.94	1185.24	1187.96	1183.56	1176.36	1170.22	1122.49	1144.32	1169.91
2009	1135.82	1113.28	1120.39	1107.41	1126.39	1127.84	1132.14	1130.62	1119.36	1124.49	1129.47	1149.23	1126.24
Construction													
2007	1004.91	1011.15	1005.70	1035.94	1106.69	1078.13	1108.97	1127.52	1114.10	1116.27	1080.50	1048.29	1071.81
2008	1100.16	1102.63	1120.62	1106.18	1088.26	1093.42	1103.60	1108.59	1078.22	1072.56	1051.93	1024.53	1087.02
2009	1001.56	1020.60	1024.53	1017.75	1044.20	1032.59	1052.39	1070.01	1044.68	1077.14	1066.90	1051.87	1041.85
Manufacturing													
2007	1132.01	1143.32	1136.84	1169.38	1155.09	1179.15	1147.42	1144.25	1174.32	1168.85	1197.08	1197.29	1163.34
2008	1178.19	1164.78	1187.32	1199.74	1205.15	1211.81	1210.46	1205.55	1204.17	1202.63	1174.24	1200.59	1195.19
2009	1197.20	1148.95	1155.41	1146.76	1155.20	1160.12	1162.10	1157.66	1147.17	1144.64	1153.11	1187.82	1159.54
Trade, Transportation, and Utilities													
2007	733.72	731.64	736.68	753.83	760.51	765.66	767.36	751.75	762.82	747.74	768.66	741.91	751.64
2008	745.04	756.43	755.48	779.70	772.37	782.49	760.58	758.20	770.66	737.70	741.91	731.63	758.34
2009	759.94	755.51	754.51	764.28	750.07	744.92	712.47	714.95	726.10	698.28	702.63	709.80	733.46
Financial Activities													
2007	1319.67	1377.64	1318.94	1412.53	1401.80	1447.66	1458.18	1412.58	1409.35	1440.15	1422.24	1540.03	1411.71
2008	1528.93	1504.40	1556.00	1493.42	1480.48	1575.72	1473.07	1442.50	1443.66	1545.89	1554.08	1509.08	1510.86
2009	1447.04	1510.40	1553.03	1468.39	1470.06	1445.49	1440.38	1505.52	1410.06	1469.06	1557.46	1496.52	1481.05
Professional and Business Services													
2007	964.58	948.23	954.12	982.99	1007.11	1010.18	1007.58	988.43	1002.88	998.45	989.43	1019.25	989.06
2008	1035.58	1045.20	1072.02	1081.55	1074.76	1122.87	1091.08	1068.47	1071.22	1054.19	1071.88	1083.70	1072.61
2009	1061.94	1077.22	1064.72	1019.24	1017.40	990.35	982.08	1004.67	983.29	975.42	1010.72	996.93	1016.65
Education and Health Services													
2007	735.47	730.80	745.61	742.53	732.69	735.53	734.27	732.11	729.92	737.27	742.28	738.42	735.39
2008	746.40	739.44	758.90	759.22	750.62	746.28	757.06	755.47	760.45	758.60	781.15	788.73	757.99
2009	795.74	797.94	793.92	782.70	787.12	785.31	792.04	787.19	794.33	792.98	794.82	783.85	791.17
Leisure and Hospitality													
2007	380.16	386.08	399.43	401.48	424.92	416.92	426.95	432.82	436.25	440.63	447.02	456.72	422.00
2008	426.89	430.34	428.40	411.08	413.93	411.84	415.99	400.60	412.12	405.24	409.75	408.47	414.65
2009	398.08	415.80	394.42	401.74	398.03	398.86	404.39	411.55	411.60	411.11	406.37	400.16	403.71
Other Services													
2007	684.03	645.15	659.23	706.63	681.70	708.40	691.54	678.20	680.75	665.26	694.85	690.11	681.70
2008	671.14	698.35	693.16	690.95	673.87	683.87	696.29	674.78	718.16	708.56	697.81	668.72	689.17
2009	661.96	644.54	639.07	651.78	647.53	648.05	641.43	644.79	647.53	653.51	655.78	652.62	650.03

DELAWARE

At a Glance

Population:
1990 census: 666,168
2000 census: 783,600
2009 estimate: 885,122

Percent change in population:
1990–2000: 17.6%
2000–2009: 13.0%

Percent change in total nonfarm employment:
1990–2009: 19.7%
2008–2009: -4.7%

Industry with the largest growth in employment, 1990–2009 (thousands):
Education and Health Services, 30.8

Industry with the largest decline or smallest growth in employment, 1990–2009 (thousands):
Manufacturing, -17.9

Civilian labor force:
1990: 362,098
2000: 416,503
2009: 434,704

Unemployment rate and rank among states (lowest to highest):
1990: 4.2%, 5th
2000: 3.3%, 14th
2009: 8.1%, 25th

Employment by Industry, 2009

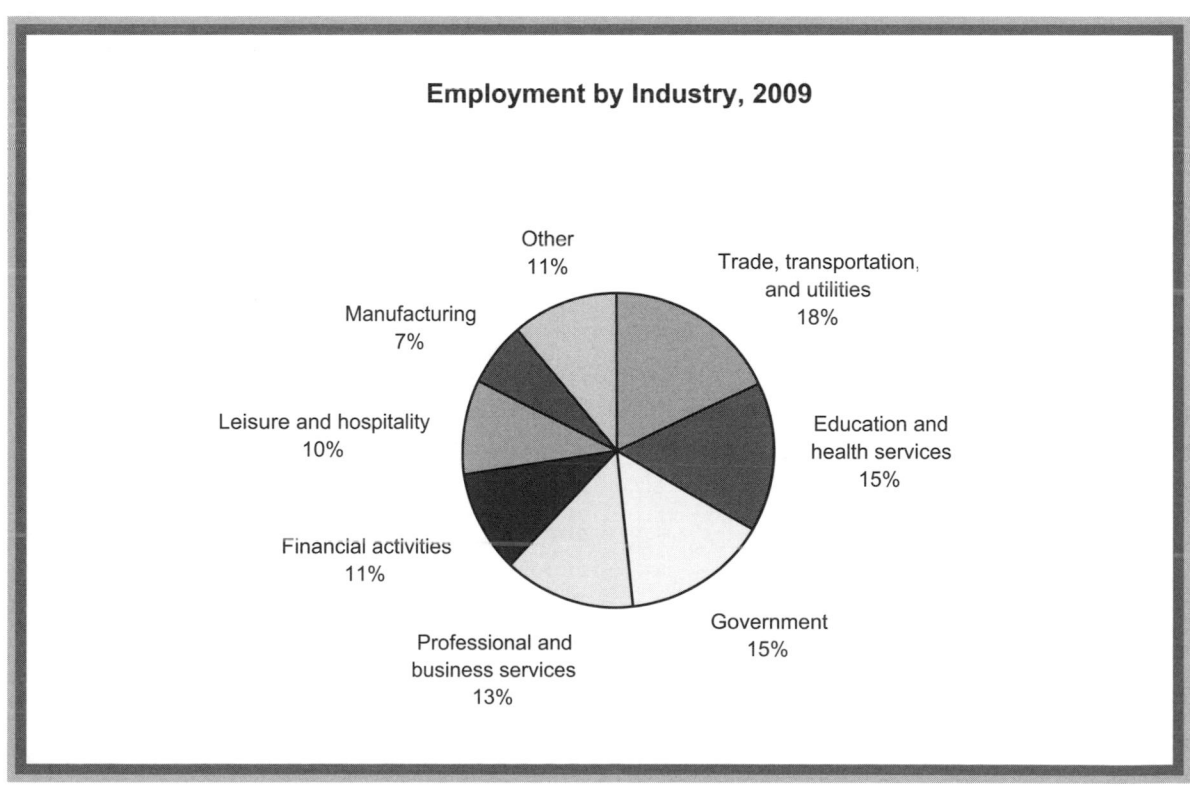

Other 11%
Trade, transportation, and utilities 18%
Manufacturing 7%
Leisure and hospitality 10%
Education and health services 15%
Financial activities 11%
Government 15%
Professional and business services 13%

Employment by Industry: Delaware, Selected Years, 1990–2009

(Numbers in thousands, not seasonally adjusted.)

Industry and year	January	February	March	April	May	June	July	August	September	October	November	December	Annual average
Total Nonfarm													
1990	335.2	341.4	345.4	346.8	351.7	355.0	350.7	352.7	351.0	348.3	345.4	346.2	347.4
2000	407.4	409.3	415.6	418.2	421.7	427.1	426.3	424.0	422.9	422.4	424.7	426.5	420.5
2001	411.5	412.9	420.3	420.5	423.6	427.9	423.6	422.2	418.7	418.6	420.7	420.6	420.1
2002	404.3	405.9	408.8	412.5	418.2	420.2	419.5	418.9	420.5	416.8	419.3	419.9	415.4
2003	404.1	401.5	405.7	411.0	417.2	422.5	419.2	419.2	420.2	420.9	422.4	424.1	415.7
2004	412.0	413.9	418.7	419.4	425.9	431.3	428.3	427.9	428.6	430.2	432.5	432.3	425.1
2005	418.3	419.4	424.3	430.2	434.7	436.1	435.9	436.0	437.1	437.3	442.1	440.9	432.7
2006	427.3	427.6	432.2	436.0	440.7	444.4	439.4	439.2	439.7	440.4	442.2	443.9	437.8
2007	427.8	427.0	432.4	436.0	441.6	446.4	442.0	441.1	439.7	438.8	442.5	443.9	438.3
2008	428.8	431.0	433.2	438.0	440.2	444.0	440.3	438.9	436.3	434.4	435.0	432.6	436.1
2009	414.1	413.6	413.4	415.7	420.4	422.2	417.0	416.1	414.8	413.4	414.7	413.9	415.8
Total Private													
1990	288.5	292.9	296.4	297.6	302.2	307.1	304.5	307.7	304.5	299.5	296.3	297.4	299.5
2000	353.1	353.6	358.1	360.4	363.4	369.9	369.4	369.3	367.7	365.9	367.0	368.7	363.9
2001	355.3	355.9	362.1	362.0	365.5	371.0	367.1	367.5	364.0	362.0	363.2	362.9	363.2
2002	348.6	348.9	351.1	354.6	360.5	364.0	364.7	365.5	363.0	358.2	360.0	360.9	358.3
2003	347.4	344.2	348.0	352.8	358.6	365.3	364.3	365.4	363.0	362.5	364.1	365.6	358.4
2004	354.9	356.1	359.9	361.3	367.3	374.0	373.1	373.2	370.4	371.7	373.8	373.5	367.4
2005	360.6	360.6	364.3	370.0	374.1	378.2	378.5	379.8	377.5	375.9	380.6	379.7	373.3
2006	367.6	366.9	370.1	373.8	378.3	384.7	381.2	382.1	379.5	378.8	380.3	382.3	377.1
2007	368.2	365.9	370.0	373.5	378.8	385.2	382.1	382.5	378.7	377.0	380.4	382.0	377.0
2008	368.6	369.0	370.9	375.2	377.2	382.2	379.4	378.6	373.6	371.2	371.9	369.6	374.0
2009	353.6	350.6	349.9	352.2	357.2	360.2	357.3	356.7	352.9	350.1	350.9	350.6	353.5
Goods-Producing													
1990	62.3	66.8	67.7	67.8	68.9	69.7	67.4	70.8	69.9	68.6	65.1	64.8	67.4
2000	64.3	64.8	66.1	66.3	67.0	68.3	66.5	66.7	66.4	66.8	65.8	65.4	66.2
2001	60.9	61.3	64.1	64.4	64.8	66.1	64.8	64.8	64.5	63.7	63.8	63.3	63.9
2002	60.5	61.1	61.2	59.7	61.8	62.2	62.3	62.2	61.9	61.1	60.8	60.8	61.3
2003	57.5	57.1	57.9	58.7	60.2	61.8	60.5	61.2	61.4	62.0	61.8	60.5	60.1
2004	58.7	59.1	60.1	60.8	61.2	62.2	62.2	62.1	61.2	61.7	61.6	61.0	61.0
2005	58.1	59.0	60.0	61.2	61.9	61.1	61.1	62.4	62.3	61.9	64.2	61.2	61.2
2006	61.7	61.3	62.0	62.7	63.1	64.1	63.0	63.7	63.8	63.7	63.2	62.8	62.9
2007	60.4	59.0	60.2	60.6	61.5	62.0	60.9	61.4	60.5	60.0	61.0	60.4	60.7
2008	57.3	58.1	58.0	58.6	57.6	58.6	56.9	56.8	55.5	54.7	55.4	53.9	56.8
2009	50.5	48.9	48.3	48.2	48.5	48.5	47.7	47.7	46.9	46.6	46.4	45.7	47.8
Mining, Logging, and Construction													
1990	20.2	20.5	21.3	21.8	22.4	22.7	22.8	22.8	22.1	21.5	21.1	20.4	21.6
2000	24.1	23.2	24.5	24.9	24.8	25.5	25.1	25.1	24.9	25.5	24.5	24.2	24.6
2001	23.0	23.1	23.6	23.9	24.4	25.4	24.8	25.2	25.1	25.0	25.5	24.9	24.5
2002	23.4	23.1	23.2	24.0	24.4	24.9	25.3	25.1	24.6	24.1	24.0	24.2	24.2
2003	23.0	21.6	22.2	23.4	24.3	24.9	25.5	25.5	25.2	25.7	25.8	25.6	24.4
2004	24.4	24.1	25.1	25.8	26.1	27.0	27.4	27.5	27.3	27.7	27.6	26.8	26.4
2005	25.9	25.5	26.3	27.5	27.9	28.5	28.7	28.5	28.4	29.6	30.4	28.9	28.0
2006	28.0	27.8	28.3	29.3	29.6	30.5	30.1	30.2	30.1	30.1	29.5	29.1	29.4
2007	27.2	26.0	26.8	27.4	28.0	28.2	28.1	28.0	28.0	27.3	27.5	26.9	27.5
2008	25.7	25.1	25.3	26.3	26.1	26.1	25.8	25.6	24.7	23.8	23.6	22.7	25.1
2009	20.7	19.9	20.1	20.0	20.4	20.6	20.4	20.3	19.6	19.1	19.1	18.4	19.9
Manufacturing													
1990	42.1	46.3	46.4	46.0	46.5	47.0	44.6	48.0	47.8	47.1	44.0	44.4	45.8
2000	40.2	41.6	41.6	41.4	42.2	42.8	41.4	41.6	41.5	41.3	41.3	41.2	41.5
2001	37.9	38.2	40.5	40.5	40.4	40.7	40.0	39.6	39.4	38.7	38.3	38.4	39.4
2002	37.1	38.0	38.0	35.7	37.4	37.3	37.0	37.1	37.3	37.0	36.8	36.6	37.1
2003	34.5	35.5	35.7	35.3	35.9	36.9	35.0	35.7	36.2	36.3	36.0	34.9	35.7
2004	34.3	35.0	35.0	35.0	35.1	35.2	34.8	34.6	33.9	34.0	34.0	34.2	34.6
2005	32.2	33.5	33.7	33.7	34.0	32.6	32.4	33.9	33.9	32.3	33.8	32.3	33.2
2006	33.7	33.5	33.7	33.4	33.5	33.6	32.9	33.5	33.7	33.6	33.7	33.7	33.5
2007	33.2	33.0	33.4	33.2	33.5	33.8	32.8	33.4	32.5	32.7	33.5	33.5	33.2
2008	31.6	33.0	32.7	32.3	31.5	32.5	31.1	31.2	30.8	30.9	31.8	31.2	31.7
2009	29.8	29.0	28.2	28.2	28.1	27.9	27.3	27.4	27.3	27.5	27.3	27.3	27.9
Service-Providing													
1990	272.9	274.6	277.7	279.0	282.8	285.3	283.3	281.9	281.1	279.7	280.3	281.4	280.0
2000	343.1	344.5	349.5	351.9	354.7	358.8	359.8	357.3	356.5	355.6	358.9	361.1	354.3
2001	350.6	351.6	356.2	356.1	358.8	361.8	358.8	357.4	354.2	354.9	356.9	357.3	356.2
2002	343.8	344.8	347.6	352.8	356.4	358.0	357.2	356.7	358.6	355.7	358.5	359.1	354.1
2003	346.6	344.4	347.8	352.3	357.0	360.7	358.7	358.0	358.8	358.9	360.6	363.6	355.6
2004	353.3	354.8	358.6	358.6	364.7	369.1	366.1	365.8	367.4	368.5	370.9	371.3	364.1
2005	360.2	360.4	364.3	369.0	372.8	375.0	374.8	373.6	374.8	375.4	377.9	379.7	371.5
2006	365.6	366.3	370.2	373.3	377.6	380.3	376.4	375.5	375.9	376.7	379.0	381.1	374.8
2007	367.4	368.0	372.2	375.4	380.1	384.4	381.1	379.7	379.2	378.8	381.5	383.5	377.6
2008	371.5	372.9	375.2	379.4	382.6	385.4	383.4	382.1	380.8	379.7	379.6	378.7	379.3

Employment by Industry: Delaware, Selected Years, 1990–2009—*Continued*

(Numbers in thousands, not seasonally adjusted.)

Industry and year	January	February	March	April	May	June	July	August	September	October	November	December	Annual average
Trade, Transportation, and Utilities													
1990	67.5	65.7	66.5	66.6	66.9	67.7	67.6	67.5	67.6	67.4	68.7	69.7	67.4
2000	77.4	76.6	76.7	77.9	78.5	79.7	79.6	79.4	79.5	79.4	80.9	83.0	79.0
2001	76.7	76.0	76.6	75.3	75.7	77.0	76.3	76.2	76.1	77.2	78.3	79.4	76.7
2002	74.9	74.2	75.1	75.4	76.9	77.8	77.8	77.7	77.9	77.3	79.0	80.4	77.0
2003	76.1	75.1	76.2	77.0	78.3	79.4	78.9	79.4	79.1	79.8	81.3	83.3	78.7
2004	78.6	78.1	78.7	79.4	80.2	81.8	81.3	81.0	80.8	81.5	83.6	84.5	80.8
2005	79.9	78.9	79.8	80.3	81.1	81.8	82.1	82.1	81.7	82.5	84.5	86.1	81.7
2006	81.1	80.1	80.9	81.7	82.8	83.5	83.0	82.4	81.9	82.5	84.7	85.6	82.5
2007	81.9	80.6	81.1	81.3	82.9	83.9	83.8	83.7	83.2	82.8	85.2	86.1	83.0
2008	81.5	80.4	80.9	80.4	81.3	81.9	81.3	80.9	80.3	80.7	81.7	82.6	81.2
2009	76.3	74.9	74.7	74.3	75.1	75.6	75.0	75.0	75.1	74.7	75.9	76.4	75.3
Wholesale Trade													
1990	11.7	11.5	11.6	11.6	11.7	11.7	11.9	11.8	11.9	11.7	11.7	11.7	11.7
2000	12.7	12.8	12.9	13.3	13.2	13.3	13.4	13.5	13.5	13.6	13.6	13.7	13.2
2001	13.4	13.5	13.6	13.3	13.3	13.4	13.3	13.3	13.3	13.4	13.3	13.4	13.4
2002	13.3	13.2	13.6	13.5	13.7	13.8	13.8	13.9	13.8	13.7	13.6	13.7	13.6
2003	13.6	13.6	13.9	14.0	14.3	14.2	14.4	14.5	14.4	14.3	14.3	14.4	14.2
2004	14.3	14.3	14.4	14.7	14.8	14.9	15.0	14.9	14.8	15.0	14.9	14.9	14.7
2005	14.8	14.8	14.9	14.9	14.9	14.8	14.8	14.9	14.8	15.0	15.1	15.3	14.9
2006	14.9	15.0	15.0	15.2	15.3	15.3	15.3	15.2	15.1	15.0	14.9	15.2	15.1
2007	14.8	14.7	14.7	14.9	15.0	15.1	15.2	15.2	15.0	14.8	14.9	14.9	14.9
2008	14.7	14.7	14.8	14.6	14.8	14.7	14.7	14.5	14.4	14.5	14.4	14.2	14.6
2009	13.7	13.6	13.5	13.5	13.4	13.2	13.2	13.1	13.0	12.7	12.7	12.7	13.2
Retail Trade													
1990	43.7	42.3	42.5	42.7	43.0	43.6	43.8	44.1	43.6	43.6	45.0	46.0	43.6
2000	50.3	49.4	49.4	50.2	50.9	52.2	52.2	51.9	51.7	51.5	53.1	55.0	51.4
2001	50.4	49.7	50.1	49.1	49.6	50.7	50.4	50.6	50.2	50.7	52.1	53.3	50.6
2002	49.6	48.7	49.3	49.7	50.7	51.7	51.9	51.9	51.6	51.0	52.8	54.2	51.1
2003	50.0	49.0	49.8	50.5	51.3	52.4	52.4	52.8	51.8	52.4	53.8	55.1	51.8
2004	51.0	50.3	50.7	51.1	51.9	53.2	53.1	53.2	52.4	52.8	54.9	55.7	52.5
2005	52.0	51.1	51.6	52.3	53.1	53.8	54.4	54.4	53.4	53.7	55.6	57.0	53.5
2006	52.9	51.7	52.4	52.9	53.6	54.2	54.3	53.9	52.8	53.2	55.7	56.1	53.6
2007	53.1	52.1	52.7	52.8	53.9	54.9	55.1	54.9	54.2	54.1	56.5	57.2	54.3
2008	53.4	52.2	52.5	52.2	52.8	53.6	53.2	53.1	52.2	52.4	53.5	54.3	53.0
2009	49.9	48.6	48.6	48.4	49.2	50.0	50.2	50.2	49.6	49.3	50.4	50.5	49.6
Transportation and Utilities													
1990	12.1	11.9	12.4	12.3	12.2	12.4	11.9	11.6	12.1	12.1	12.0	12.0	12.0
2000	14.4	14.4	14.4	14.4	14.4	14.2	14.0	14.0	14.3	14.3	14.2	14.3	14.2
2001	12.9	12.8	12.9	12.9	12.8	12.9	12.6	12.3	12.6	13.1	12.9	12.7	12.8
2002	12.0	12.3	12.2	12.2	12.5	12.3	12.1	11.9	12.5	12.6	12.6	12.5	12.3
2003	12.5	12.5	12.5	12.5	12.7	12.8	12.1	12.1	12.9	13.1	13.2	13.8	12.7
2004	13.3	13.5	13.6	13.6	13.5	13.7	13.2	12.9	13.6	13.7	13.8	13.9	13.5
2005	13.1	13.0	13.3	13.1	13.1	13.2	12.9	12.8	13.5	13.8	13.8	13.8	13.3
2006	13.3	13.4	13.5	13.6	13.9	14.0	13.4	13.3	14.0	14.3	14.1	14.3	13.8
2007	14.0	13.8	13.7	13.6	14.0	13.9	13.5	13.6	14.0	13.9	13.8	14.0	13.8
2008	13.4	13.5	13.6	13.6	13.7	13.6	13.4	13.3	13.7	13.8	13.8	14.1	13.6
2009	12.7	12.7	12.6	12.4	12.5	12.4	11.6	11.7	12.5	12.7	12.8	13.2	12.5
Information													
1990	4.9	5.0	5.0	5.0	5.0	5.1	5.1	5.1	5.0	4.9	4.9	4.9	4.9
2000	8.1	8.3	8.4	8.0	8.1	8.1	8.3	7.6	8.3	8.1	8.2	8.2	8.1
2001	8.0	8.0	8.1	8.1	8.1	8.2	8.2	8.2	8.1	7.9	8.0	8.0	8.1
2002	7.8	7.8	7.8	7.7	7.7	7.8	7.8	7.9	7.7	7.6	7.7	7.6	7.7
2003	7.5	7.5	7.5	7.4	7.4	7.4	7.4	7.4	7.3	7.1	7.2	7.2	7.4
2004	7.3	7.2	7.3	7.0	7.0	7.0	7.0	7.0	6.9	7.0	7.0	7.0	7.1
2005	6.4	6.4	6.5	6.7	6.8	6.8	6.8	6.7	6.7	6.8	6.8	6.8	6.7
2006	6.7	6.7	6.6	6.6	6.6	6.7	6.7	6.8	6.7	6.7	6.8	6.8	6.7
2007	6.8	6.8	6.8	6.8	6.8	6.9	7.0	7.0	7.0	7.1	7.1	7.1	6.9
2008	7.0	7.1	7.1	7.1	7.1	7.2	7.0	7.1	7.0	7.0	6.9	6.8	7.0
2009	6.8	6.7	6.7	6.6	6.6	6.5	6.5	6.4	6.3	6.3	6.5	6.7	6.6
Financial Activities													
1990	35.6	35.9	35.9	36.1	36.9	37.5	37.6	37.8	37.6	36.8	36.7	36.6	36.8
2000	46.2	46.4	46.3	46.0	46.1	46.6	46.7	46.9	46.4	46.2	46.5	46.8	46.4
2001	46.6	46.7	46.9	47.0	47.1	47.3	47.3	47.2	46.8	46.3	46.0	45.8	46.8
2002	46.7	46.6	46.6	46.3	46.5	46.7	47.1	46.9	46.2	45.8	45.8	45.8	46.4
2003	45.5	45.3	45.2	45.6	45.6	45.7	46.5	46.0	45.3	44.2	44.2	44.2	45.3
2004	44.1	44.1	44.3	44.3	44.6	45.0	45.6	45.7	45.0	44.4	44.6	44.5	44.7
2005	45.1	45.1	44.9	44.8	45.0	45.3	45.9	45.8	45.3	45.1	45.2	45.2	45.2
2006	44.5	44.4	44.2	44.5	44.4	44.6	44.7	45.3	45.0	44.9	45.0	45.2	44.7
2007	44.8	44.9	44.9	45.1	45.3	45.8	45.8	45.6	45.2	45.3	45.2	45.2	45.3
2008	45.0	45.0	45.2	45.5	45.7	46.3	46.5	46.2	45.5	45.3	45.0	44.6	45.5
2009	44.3	44.0	43.9	43.9	44.2	44.5	44.6	44.4	44.0	43.0	42.8	42.9	43.9

Employment by Industry: Delaware, Selected Years, 1990–2009—*Continued*

(Numbers in thousands, not seasonally adjusted.)

Industry and year	January	February	March	April	May	June	July	August	September	October	November	December	Annual average
Professional and Business Services													
1990	50.0	50.4	51.1	51.0	51.1	51.2	51.1	50.5	49.8	49.3	49.1	49.6	50.4
2000	64.9	64.8	65.9	65.6	65.2	66.2	66.7	67.0	67.0	66.7	67.2	67.3	66.2
2001	66.6	66.6	67.3	66.2	66.3	66.5	65.3	66.0	65.1	64.7	65.6	65.2	66.0
2002	61.0	60.6	60.3	61.2	61.0	60.1	60.5	60.9	60.9	60.5	60.8	61.3	60.8
2003	59.1	57.9	58.2	58.3	58.7	58.9	58.5	58.5	58.8	59.6	59.8	60.8	58.9
2004	59.8	61.2	61.8	60.1	61.5	62.2	61.4	61.7	61.5	62.4	63.0	63.5	61.7
2005	60.8	60.7	61.2	62.6	62.7	63.1	62.7	62.7	62.7	62.7	63.3	64.3	62.5
2006	60.8	61.0	61.5	61.3	61.4	61.2	60.7	61.0	60.7	60.7	60.9	62.6	61.2
2007	58.3	58.5	59.4	60.2	60.5	61.0	60.3	60.3	60.2	60.6	61.5	62.7	60.3
2008	59.6	59.4	59.4	60.3	59.9	60.0	59.6	59.4	59.0	59.0	59.5	59.5	59.6
2009	56.0	55.9	55.7	56.0	56.3	56.3	55.1	54.9	54.5	55.3	56.7	57.3	55.8
Education and Health Services													
1990	31.9	32.3	32.7	32.5	32.7	32.9	32.7	33.1	33.6	33.6	33.7	33.9	32.9
2000	44.9	45.3	45.7	45.8	45.7	45.8	45.9	46.1	46.6	46.6	47.0	47.2	46.1
2001	47.0	47.5	47.9	48.0	48.1	48.1	47.4	47.7	48.4	49.1	49.1	49.1	48.1
2002	48.4	48.8	49.1	49.5	49.7	49.5	49.0	49.7	50.2	50.3	50.6	50.7	49.6
2003	50.7	50.7	51.1	51.3	51.4	51.4	50.8	51.1	51.9	52.3	52.6	52.9	51.5
2004	52.3	52.4	52.7	52.9	53.2	53.2	52.6	52.7	53.6	54.9	54.8	55.1	53.4
2005	54.7	54.9	55.3	55.6	55.8	55.9	55.0	55.1	55.9	56.1	56.4	56.6	55.6
2006	56.5	56.7	57.0	57.4	57.7	57.9	58.0	57.9	58.3	58.6	59.1	59.2	57.9
2007	58.9	59.0	59.3	59.6	59.9	59.8	59.5	59.6	60.5	60.8	61.0	61.4	59.9
2008	61.4	62.0	61.9	62.6	62.8	62.7	62.1	62.4	62.9	63.0	63.4	63.4	62.6
2009	63.3	63.4	63.4	63.7	63.8	63.6	63.3	63.4	63.6	64.2	64.6	64.4	63.7
Leisure and Hospitality													
1990	24.8	25.2	25.9	27.0	28.9	30.8	31.0	30.9	29.4	27.1	26.4	26.1	27.7
2000	31.8	31.9	33.3	35.0	37.0	39.1	39.7	39.5	37.6	35.6	34.9	34.4	35.8
2001	32.4	32.7	33.9	35.8	38.1	39.9	40.4	40.0	37.8	35.8	35.1	34.7	36.4
2002	32.4	32.6	33.7	37.0	38.9	41.5	42.0	42.0	40.4	37.3	37.1	36.0	37.6
2003	33.3	33.0	34.2	36.6	38.9	42.1	43.1	43.1	40.8	38.9	38.4	37.9	38.4
2004	35.5	35.3	36.1	38.2	40.9	43.6	44.1	44.1	42.7	40.6	40.0	38.7	40.0
2005	36.3	36.3	37.2	39.2	41.2	44.4	45.0	45.0	43.1	40.7	40.0	39.2	40.6
2006	36.3	36.6	37.6	39.3	42.0	46.1	44.6	44.7	43.1	41.3	40.1	39.3	40.9
2007	36.8	37.0	38.0	39.7	41.7	45.3	44.6	44.9	42.2	40.3	39.3	38.9	40.7
2008	36.8	36.9	38.3	40.3	42.4	44.8	45.4	45.3	43.2	41.3	39.9	38.7	41.1
2009	36.6	37.0	37.5	39.7	42.6	44.8	45.0	44.9	42.8	40.2	38.4	37.5	40.6
Other Services													
1990	11.5	11.6	11.6	11.6	11.8	12.2	12.0	12.0	11.6	11.8	11.7	11.8	11.7
2000	15.5	15.5	15.7	15.8	15.8	16.1	16.0	16.1	15.9	16.5	16.5	16.4	15.9
2001	17.1	17.1	17.3	17.2	17.3	17.9	17.4	17.4	17.2	17.3	17.3	17.4	17.3
2002	16.9	17.2	17.3	17.8	18.0	18.4	18.2	18.2	17.8	18.3	18.2	18.3	17.9
2003	17.7	17.6	17.7	17.9	18.1	18.6	18.6	18.7	18.4	18.6	18.8	18.8	18.3
2004	18.6	18.7	18.9	18.6	18.7	19.0	18.9	18.9	18.7	19.2	19.2	19.2	18.9
2005	19.3	19.3	19.4	19.6	19.6	19.8	19.9	20.0	19.8	20.1	20.2	20.3	19.8
2006	20.0	20.1	20.3	20.3	20.3	20.6	20.5	20.3	20.0	20.4	20.5	20.8	20.3
2007	20.3	20.1	20.3	20.2	20.2	20.5	20.2	20.0	19.9	20.1	20.1	20.2	20.2
2008	20.0	20.1	20.1	20.4	20.4	20.7	20.6	20.5	20.2	20.2	20.1	20.1	20.3
2009	19.8	19.8	19.7	19.8	20.1	20.4	20.1	20.0	19.7	19.8	19.6	19.7	19.9
Government													
1990	46.7	48.5	49.0	49.2	49.5	47.9	46.2	45.0	46.5	48.8	49.1	48.8	47.9
2000	54.3	55.7	57.5	57.8	58.3	57.2	56.9	54.7	55.2	56.5	57.7	57.8	56.6
2001	56.2	57.0	58.2	58.5	58.1	56.9	56.5	54.7	54.7	56.6	57.5	57.7	56.9
2002	55.7	57.0	57.7	57.9	57.7	56.2	54.8	53.4	57.5	58.6	59.3	59.0	57.1
2003	56.7	57.3	57.7	58.2	58.6	57.2	54.9	53.8	57.2	58.4	58.3	58.5	57.2
2004	57.1	57.8	58.8	58.1	58.6	57.3	55.2	54.7	58.2	58.5	58.7	58.8	57.7
2005	57.7	58.8	60.0	60.2	60.6	57.9	57.4	56.2	59.6	61.4	61.5	61.2	59.4
2006	59.7	60.7	62.1	62.2	62.4	59.7	58.2	57.1	60.2	61.6	61.9	61.6	60.6
2007	59.6	61.1	62.4	62.5	62.8	61.2	59.9	58.6	61.0	61.8	62.1	61.9	61.2
2008	60.2	62.0	62.3	62.8	63.0	61.8	60.9	60.3	62.7	63.2	63.1	63.0	62.1
2009	60.5	63.0	63.5	63.5	63.2	62.0	59.7	59.4	61.9	63.3	63.8	63.3	62.3

Average Weekly Hours by Selected Industry: Delaware, 2007–2009

(Not seasonally adjusted.)

Industry and year	January	February	March	April	May	June	July	August	September	October	November	December	Annual average
Total Private													
2007	33.5	33.6	33.5	33.9	33.9	34.2	34.5	34.6	34.8	34.7	35.5	34.6	34.3
2008	34.0	34.0	34.6	34.3	33.7	34.4	34.1	33.9	33.4	33.3	33.1	33.0	33.8
2009	32.6	32.7	32.8	32.6	32.8	32.8	32.9	33.3	32.7	32.4	32.4	32.3	32.7
Goods-Producing													
2007	38.4	36.9	37.9	38.8	39.3	39.5	38.4	39.7	39.2	38.8	38.4	37.7	38.6
2008	37.0	36.3	37.6	37.7	36.6	37.8	37.4	37.6	37.8	37.0	35.8	37.8	37.2
2009	36.0	36.0	36.5	36.5	37.1	37.3	38.1	37.5	36.9	37.6	36.9	37.9	37.0
Mining, Logging, and Construction													
2007	37.6	35.1	36.6	37.4	39.1	38.7	38.7	38.4	38.0	37.4	37.1	36.1	37.5
2008	35.8	34.8	37.0	36.0	35.2	37.6	38.4	37.9	37.8	37.4	36.2	35.7	36.7
2009	35.7	36.2	36.1	34.9	36.0	35.5	37.3	36.2	35.4	35.8	35.8	36.6	36.0
Manufacturing													
2007	39.0	38.3	38.9	39.9	39.4	40.1	38.2	40.7	40.3	40.0	39.4	38.9	39.4
2008	37.9	37.4	37.9	39.1	37.8	37.9	36.6	.37.4	37.8	36.7	35.6	39.3	37.6
2009	36.2	35.7	36.6	37.5	37.9	38.7	38.6	38.4	38.0	38.7	37.8	38.8	37.7
Trade, Transportation, and Utilities													
2007	32.7	32.1	33.0	33.0	33.4	33.8	33.3	33.9	33.9	35.1	38.2	36.6	34.1
2008	34.9	34.6	35.8	35.5	34.6	34.2	33.7	33.2	33.2	33.0	33.1	33.2	34.1
2009	32.8	33.0	33.0	32.9	33.5	33.1	33.1	33.1	33.5	32.7	32.5	33.0	33.0
Financial Activities													
2007	38.1	38.4	38.4	38.5	38.3	38.0	39.2	38.8	39.5	39.1	39.4	39.6	38.8
2008	39.2	39.5	39.6	39.2	38.8	39.2	38.5	38.3	37.9	38.5	38.7	38.7	38.8
2009	38.2	37.5	37.5	36.5	36.9	36.8	36.1	35.8	35.3	35.2	34.6	35.0	36.3
Professional and Business Services													
2007	33.7	33.1	33.0	33.8	33.3	33.9	35.4	34.5	35.1	33.3	33.5	34.3	33.9
2008	33.3	33.1	33.8	33.9	33.7	34.6	33.7	33.9	33.3	33.3	33.4	33.2	33.6
2009	33.1	33.9	33.7	33.6	32.9	32.7	32.6	33.9	32.9	33.2	33.6	32.7	33.2
Education and Health Services													
2007	31.2	31.3	31.3	31.4	31.2	31.1	31.3	30.7	32.1	31.4	31.8	32.3	31.4
2008	32.2	32.2	33.1	32.4	32.0	33.0	33.3	32.5	32.3	33.1	32.7	31.9	32.6
2009	32.0	32.6	33.2	33.2	33.6	33.8	34.3	34.5	34.6	33.9	34.1	33.6	33.6
Leisure and Hospitality													
2007	24.9	24.4	24.4	25.7	25.9	27.4	28.1	27.8	26.7	25.9	25.9	25.9	26.2
2008	24.6	25.0	25.3	25.2	25.7	25.7	26.1	25.8	24.6	24.6	24.3	24.2	25.1
2009	23.9	24.6	24.3	24.5	24.3	25.2	25.7	25.9	24.5	23.8	23.6	23.8	24.6

Average Hourly Earnings by Selected Industry: Delaware, 2007–2009

(Dollars, not seasonally adjusted.)

Industry and year	January	February	March	April	May	June	July	August	September	October	November	December	Annual average
Total Private													
2007	22.05	22.24	22.10	22.57	21.58	21.38	21.79	21.70	22.21	21.79	21.72	22.64	21.98
2008	21.74	23.13	22.55	22.41	22.40	23.18	23.13	22.87	22.92	22.84	23.07	22.50	22.73
2009	22.49	22.53	22.43	22.04	21.69	21.46	22.96	22.63	22.64	22.55	22.70	22.40	22.38
Goods-Producing													
2007	22.25	22.71	22.47	22.42	23.25	22.88	23.34	23.55	23.69	23.64	23.35	24.35	23.16
2008	23.73	24.80	24.93	24.80	23.96	24.24	23.28	23.72	23.79	23.79	23.05	23.47	23.98
2009	22.60	22.87	22.89	22.68	22.53	22.36	22.59	22.86	23.12	22.46	23.01	22.85	22.73
Mining, Logging, and Construction													
2007	22.95	23.74	23.51	23.04	23.97	23.64	23.89	25.14	24.94	23.54	23.72	24.44	23.89
2008	25.63	26.25	25.80	25.94	26.29	25.78	25.58	26.25	26.29	26.09	25.78	26.56	26.01
2009	26.46	26.64	25.76	25.85	25.13	25.54	25.03	25.50	26.09	24.99	25.62	26.19	25.73
Manufacturing													
2007	21.70	21.97	21.69	21.94	22.65	22.27	22.87	22.30	22.68	23.72	23.07	24.28	22.59
2008	22.28	23.77	24.27	23.95	22.17	23.01	21.28	21.62	21.79	21.98	20.99	21.42	22.41
2009	19.94	20.25	20.88	20.59	20.73	20.21	20.83	21.01	21.14	20.83	21.28	20.73	20.70
Trade, Transportation, and Utilities													
2007	17.99	18.36	18.27	18.15	15.24	15.29	15.58	16.41	16.11	16.34	16.59	16.35	16.69
2008	16.77	17.11	16.97	17.43	16.94	16.94	17.35	17.38	17.20	17.54	18.21	17.88	17.30
2009	18.48	18.41	18.45	18.34	18.16	18.06	18.15	18.19	17.94	18.02	18.02	17.85	18.17
Financial Activities													
2007	28.08	28.34	27.89	29.63	28.21	28.12	29.07	27.93	29.67	27.95	27.55	29.49	28.50
2008	27.57	28.11	29.53	28.57	28.54	29.98	30.63	28.95	28.59	28.37	27.45	27.53	28.66
2009	27.16	27.62	27.71	26.59	26.13	25.91	26.65	26.30	26.31	26.80	26.74	26.32	26.69
Professional and Business Services													
2007	25.37	24.86	25.73	25.22	24.65	25.18	26.52	26.51	27.04	26.73	27.54	30.14	26.32
2008	27.97	27.90	28.68	28.58	28.88	29.02	29.23	29.24	29.33	29.35	30.00	29.18	28.95
2009	29.23	29.45	29.32	28.28	28.05	27.64	27.81	27.80	27.62	27.44	28.04	27.31	28.17
Education and Health Services													
2007	20.43	20.45	20.60	21.33	20.93	21.50	21.87	21.38	21.13	21.15	21.46	21.62	21.16
2008	20.72	22.02	20.52	20.37	20.65	20.58	20.96	20.89	21.41	21.16	23.15	21.20	21.14
2009	21.65	21.60	21.40	21.26	21.07	21.21	20.87	20.25	20.63	20.96	21.31	21.23	21.11
Leisure and Hospitality													
2007	12.96	13.19	12.90	13.16	13.70	12.95	11.47	11.93	12.19	12.38	12.06	12.12	12.55
2008	12.27	12.20	12.01	12.28	12.27	12.38	12.44	12.70	12.73	12.93	12.65	12.82	12.48
2009	12.83	12.87	12.86	12.61	12.77	12.63	12.36	12.39	12.79	12.88	12.94	12.97	12.72

Average Weekly Earnings by Selected Industry: Delaware, 2007–2009

(Dollars, not seasonally adjusted.)

Industry and year	January	February	March	April	May	June	July	August	September	October	November	December	Annual average
Total Private													
2007	738.68	747.26	740.35	765.12	731.56	731.20	751.76	750.82	772.91	756.11	771.06	783.34	753.91
2008	739.16	786.42	780.23	768.66	754.88	797.39	788.73	775.29	765.53	760.57	763.62	742.50	768.27
2009	733.17	736.73	735.70	718.50	711.43	703.89	755.38	753.58	740.33	730.62	735.48	723.52	731.83
Goods-Producing													
2007	854.40	838.00	851.61	869.90	913.73	903.76	896.26	934.94	928.65	917.23	896.64	918.00	893.98
2008	878.01	900.24	937.37	934.96	876.94	916.27	870.67	891.87	899.26	880.23	825.19	887.17	892.06
2009	813.60	823.32	835.49	827.82	835.86	834.03	860.68	857.25	853.13	844.50	849.07	866.02	841.01
Mining, Logging, and Construction													
2007	862.92	833.27	860.47	861.70	937.23	914.87	924.54	965.38	947.72	880.40	880.01	882.28	895.88
2008	917.55	913.50	954.60	933.84	925.41	969.33	982.27	994.88	993.76	975.77	933.24	948.19	954.57
2009	944.62	964.37	929.94	902.17	904.68	906.67	933.62	923.10	923.59	894.64	917.20	958.55	926.28
Manufacturing													
2007	846.30	841.45	843.74	875.41	892.41	893.03	873.63	907.61	914.00	948.80	908.96	944.49	890.05
2008	844.41	889.00	919.83	936.45	838.03	872.08	778.85	808.59	823.66	806.67	747.24	841.81	842.62
2009	721.83	722.93	764.21	772.13	785.67	782.13	804.04	806.78	803.32	806.12	804.38	804.32	780.39
Trade, Transportation, and Utilities													
2007	588.27	589.36	602.91	598.95	509.02	516.80	518.81	556.30	546.13	573.53	633.74	598.41	569.13
2008	585.27	592.01	607.53	618.77	586.12	579.35	584.70	577.02	571.04	578.82	602.75	593.62	589.93
2009	606.14	607.53	608.85	603.39	608.36	597.79	600.77	602.09	600.99	589.25	585.65	589.05	599.61
Financial Activities													
2007	1069.85	1088.26	1070.98	1140.76	1080.44	1068.56	1139.54	1083.68	1171.97	1092.85	1085.47	1167.80	1105.80
2008	1080.74	1110.35	1169.39	1119.94	1107.35	1175.22	1179.26	1108.79	1083.56	1092.25	1062.32	1051.65	1112.01
2009	1037.51	1035.75	1039.13	970.54	964.20	953.49	962.07	941.54	928.74	943.36	925.20	921.20	968.85
Professional and Business Services													
2007	854.97	822.87	849.09	852.44	820.85	853.60	938.81	914.60	949.10	890.11	922.59	1033.80	892.25
2008	931.40	923.49	969.38	968.86	973.26	1004.09	985.05	991.24	976.69	977.36	1002.00	968.78	972.72
2009	967.51	998.36	988.08	950.21	922.85	903.83	906.61	942.42	908.70	911.01	942.14	893.04	935.24
Education and Health Services													
2007	637.42	640.09	644.78	669.76	653.02	668.65	684.53	656.37	678.27	664.11	682.43	698.33	664.42
2008	667.18	709.04	679.21	659.99	660.80	679.14	697.97	678.93	691.54	700.40	757.01	676.28	689.16
2009	692.80	704.16	710.48	705.83	707.95	716.90	715.84	698.63	713.80	710.54	726.67	713.33	709.30
Leisure and Hospitality													
2007	322.70	321.84	314.76	338.21	354.83	354.83	322.31	331.65	325.47	320.64	312.35	313.91	328.81
2008	301.84	305.00	303.85	309.46	315.34	318.17	324.68	327.66	313.16	318.08	307.40	310.24	312.25
2009	306.64	316.60	312.50	308.95	310.31	318.28	317.65	320.90	313.36	306.54	305.38	308.69	312.91

DISTRICT OF COLUMBIA
At a Glance

Population:
  1990 census: 606,900
  2000 census: 572,059
  2009 estimate: 599,657

Percent change in population:
  1990–2000: -5.7%
  2000–2009: 4.8%

Percent change in total nonfarm employment:
  1990–2009: 2.5%
  2008–2009: -0.1%

Industry with the largest growth in employment, 1990–2009 (thousands):
  Professional and Business Services, 38.0

Industry with the largest decline or smallest growth in employment, 1990–2009 (thousands):
  Government, -35.2

Civilian labor force:
  1990: 331,700
  2000: 309,421
  2009: 331,952

Unemployment rate and rank among states (lowest to highest):
  1990: 6.0%, 37th
  2000: 5.7%, 49th
  2009: 10.2%, 40th

Employment by Industry, 2009

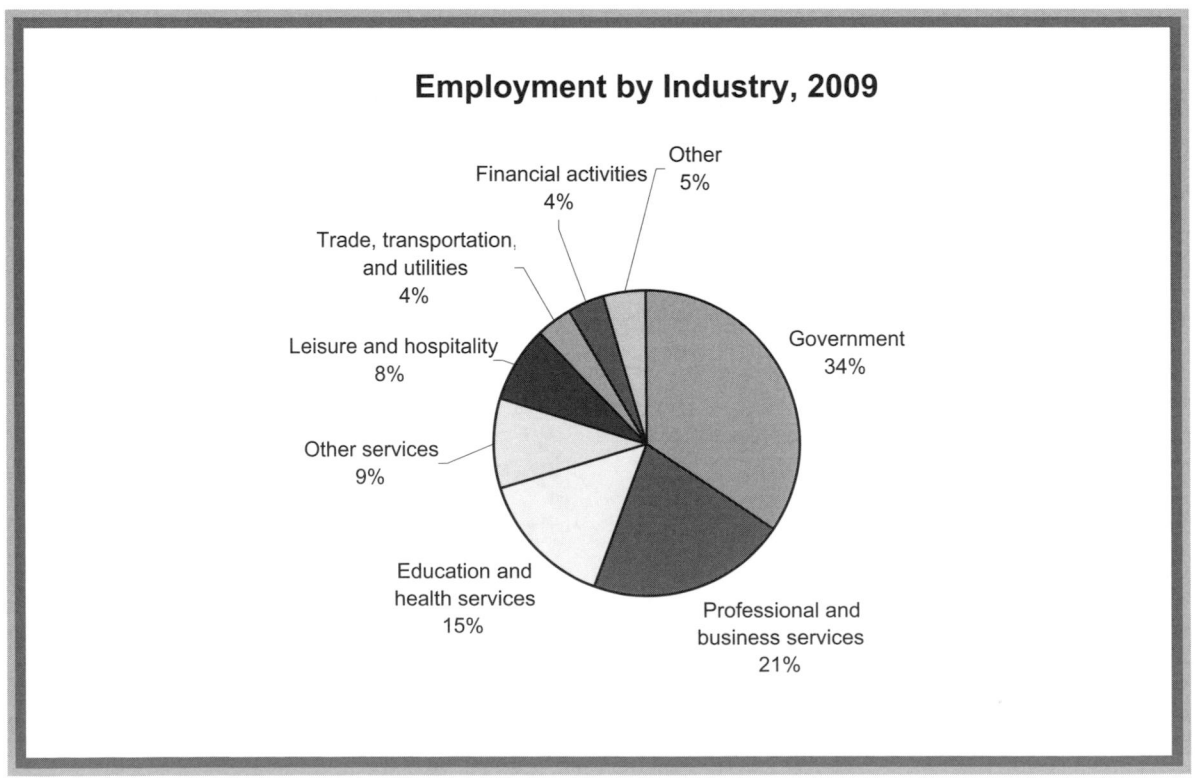

- Other 5%
- Financial activities 4%
- Trade, transportation, and utilities 4%
- Leisure and hospitality 8%
- Other services 9%
- Education and health services 15%
- Government 34%
- Professional and business services 21%

Employment by Industry: District of Columbia, Selected Years, 1990–2009

(Numbers in thousands, not seasonally adjusted.)

Industry and year	January	February	March	April	May	June	July	August	September	October	November	December	Annual average
Total Nonfarm													
1990	677.1	682.3	688.5	684.2	688.7	695.0	697.5	684.8	686.6	681.0	682.0	685.0	686.0
2000	628.8	634.5	638.9	643.9	644.0	652.1	661.5	656.6	654.0	659.0	662.9	667.2	650.2
2001	640.7	641.9	647.1	647.2	649.9	654.6	662.6	662.9	656.7	661.1	659.3	659.8	653.7
2002	648.3	653.3	660.3	662.6	660.9	664.8	674.4	669.9	666.9	667.4	670.9	671.1	664.2
2003	656.9	659.0	665.2	666.3	665.7	666.5	672.6	663.7	665.8	667.0	668.0	669.5	665.5
2004	657.9	665.1	670.7	673.8	673.9	676.6	680.0	679.0	675.0	678.8	680.8	678.6	674.2
2005	670.3	676.0	679.3	681.9	681.6	683.3	688.1	684.8	679.7	684.2	688.5	688.7	682.2
2006	675.4	681.8	686.2	685.3	684.6	689.4	695.5	689.8	685.3	691.4	693.6	693.4	687.6
2007	680.7	689.2	692.0	692.1	689.6	691.3	701.4	695.5	690.3	700.0	701.1	701.8	693.8
2008	689.0	693.6	698.2	701.3	702.8	704.2	720.1	716.0	705.2	706.0	706.1	704.6	703.9
2009	698.2	698.2	698.4	700.4	701.4	702.4	720.2	710.4	695.7	705.4	704.4	704.0	703.3
Total Private													
1990	401.2	407.0	411.9	409.3	411.7	413.4	407.8	409.1	410.7	406.7	407.7	408.4	408.7
2000	407.1	413.1	417.4	422.3	420.1	426.3	428.8	427.3	430.6	438.2	441.2	443.5	426.3
2001	419.7	423.3	427.2	427.2	428.6	428.8	427.8	428.1	427.4	431.4	430.8	429.9	427.5
2002	418.0	424.2	430.5	433.8	431.4	432.3	434.3	432.3	435.0	438.2	440.5	439.9	432.5
2003	427.3	429.4	434.2	435.9	435.2	434.3	435.5	432.2	435.6	438.1	439.8	441.0	434.9
2004	429.0	436.5	441.3	444.5	445.4	445.7	443.8	441.4	445.0	447.8	448.6	446.0	442.9
2005	438.6	444.8	448.1	450.1	449.7	448.6	446.1	443.4	448.8	452.0	455.5	456.1	448.5
2006	443.6	450.4	454.8	455.3	453.9	455.9	452.7	449.4	454.6	460.2	462.4	462.0	454.6
2007	453.8	461.4	464.9	465.2	462.3	461.3	459.8	456.9	461.6	467.3	469.0	469.5	462.8
2008	458.1	463.0	467.1	471.5	471.9	470.2	471.6	469.6	472.7	471.8	471.8	469.7	469.1
2009	463.8	463.5	463.4	464.6	464.6	461.6	458.1	454.7	454.9	462.7	461.5	460.4	461.2
Goods-Producing													
1990	21.7	21.9	22.3	21.3	21.1	21.2	21.3	21.1	21.2	20.7	20.7	20.5	21.3
2000	13.8	13.7	14.5	14.6	14.8	15.0	15.3	15.5	15.5	15.4	15.7	15.8	15.0
2001	14.9	14.7	14.8	15.0	15.4	15.6	15.2	15.4	15.0	14.8	14.6	14.4	15.0
2002	14.3	14.4	14.6	14.4	14.9	15.3	15.9	16.2	16.3	16.5	16.4	16.3	15.5
2003	15.6	15.4	15.8	15.4	15.2	15.4	15.7	15.7	15.7	15.4	15.2	14.9	15.5
2004	14.3	14.4	14.7	14.9	15.1	14.7	15.0	14.8	14.8	15.0	15.0	14.8	14.8
2005	14.5	14.8	14.8	15.1	15.2	15.2	14.8	14.9	14.5	14.3	14.4	14.4	14.7
2006	13.7	14.0	14.2	14.1	14.3	14.5	14.7	14.8	14.6	14.2	14.0	13.8	14.2
2007	13.9	13.7	13.8	13.9	14.3	14.5	14.6	15.0	14.9	14.8	14.7	14.2	14.4
2008	14.4	14.5	14.5	14.2	14.6	14.7	14.7	15.1	14.6	14.7	14.6	14.3	14.6
2009	14.1	14.1	13.6	13.5	13.5	13.3	12.8	12.7	12.5	12.5	12.4	12.1	13.1
Mining, Logging, and Construction													
1990	14.2	14.4	14.8	13.9	13.8	13.9	14.0	13.9	13.9	13.6	13.5	13.4	13.9
2000	10.1	10.1	10.8	10.9	11.1	11.3	11.6	11.8	11.8	11.7	12.0	12.0	11.3
2001	11.4	11.2	11.2	11.5	11.9	12.1	11.8	12.0	11.7	11.6	11.4	11.3	11.6
2002	11.1	11.3	11.4	11.5	12.0	12.4	12.8	13.1	13.2	13.4	13.3	13.3	12.4
2003	13.0	12.8	13.2	12.8	12.7	12.9	13.2	13.2	13.2	12.9	12.7	12.4	12.9
2004	11.9	11.9	12.2	12.5	12.7	12.3	12.5	12.3	12.3	12.6	12.6	12.5	12.4
2005	12.3	12.6	12.6	12.9	13.0	13.0	12.7	12.8	12.5	12.4	12.5	12.4	12.6
2006	11.9	12.2	12.4	12.3	12.5	12.7	13.0	13.1	12.9	12.5	12.3	12.1	12.5
2007	12.2	12.0	12.1	12.2	12.6	12.8	12.9	13.4	13.2	13.1	13.0	12.5	12.7
2008	12.7	12.8	12.8	12.6	12.9	13.0	13.1	13.5	13.1	13.2	13.1	12.8	13.0
2009	12.6	12.6	12.2	12.1	12.1	11.9	11.4	11.3	11.1	11.1	11.0	10.7	11.7
Manufacturing													
1990	7.5	7.5	7.5	7.4	7.3	7.3	7.3	7.2	7.3	7.1	7.2	7.1	7.3
2000	3.7	3.6	3.7	3.7	3.7	3.7	3.7	3.7	3.7	3.7	3.7	3.8	3.7
2001	3.5	3.5	3.6	3.5	3.5	3.5	3.4	3.4	3.3	3.2	3.2	3.1	3.4
2002	3.2	3.1	3.2	2.9	2.9	2.9	3.1	3.1	3.1	3.1	3.1	3.0	3.1
2003	2.6	2.6	2.6	2.6	2.5	2.5	2.5	2.5	2.5	2.5	2.5	2.5	2.5
2004	2.4	2.5	2.5	2.4	2.4	2.4	2.5	2.5	2.5	2.4	2.4	2.3	2.4
2005	2.2	2.2	2.2	2.2	2.2	2.2	2.1	2.1	2.0	1.9	1.9	2.0	2.1
2006	1.8	1.8	1.8	1.8	1.8	1.8	1.7	1.7	1.7	1.7	1.7	1.7	1.8
2007	1.7	1.7	1.7	1.7	1.7	1.7	1.7	1.6	1.7	1.7	1.7	1.7	1.7
2008	1.7	1.7	1.7	1.6	1.7	1.7	1.6	1.6	1.5	1.5	1.5	1.5	1.6
2009	1.5	1.5	1.4	1.4	1.4	1.4	1.4	1.4	1.4	1.4	1.4	1.4	1.4
Service-Providing													
1990	655.4	660.4	666.2	662.9	667.6	673.8	676.2	663.7	665.4	660.3	661.3	664.5	664.8
2000	615.0	620.8	624.4	629.3	629.2	637.1	646.2	641.1	638.5	643.6	647.2	651.4	635.3
2001	625.8	627.2	632.3	632.2	634.5	639.0	647.4	647.5	641.7	646.3	644.7	645.4	638.7
2002	634.0	638.9	645.7	648.2	646.0	649.5	658.5	653.7	650.6	650.9	654.5	654.8	648.8
2003	641.3	643.6	649.4	650.9	650.5	651.1	656.9	648.0	650.1	651.6	652.8	654.6	650.1
2004	643.6	650.7	656.0	658.9	658.8	661.9	665.0	664.2	660.2	663.8	665.8	663.8	659.4
2005	655.8	661.2	664.5	666.8	666.4	668.1	673.3	669.9	665.2	669.9	674.1	674.3	667.5
2006	661.7	667.8	672.0	671.2	670.3	674.9	680.8	675.0	670.7	677.2	679.6	679.6	673.4
2007	666.8	675.5	678.2	678.2	675.3	676.8	686.8	680.5	675.4	685.2	686.4	687.6	679.4
2008	674.6	679.1	683.7	687.1	688.2	689.5	705.4	700.9	690.6	691.3	691.5	690.3	689.4
2009	684.1	684.1	684.8	686.9	687.9	689.1	707.4	697.7	683.2	692.9	692.0	691.9	690.2

Employment by Industry: District of Columbia, Selected Years, 1990–2009—*Continued*

(Numbers in thousands, not seasonally adjusted.)

Industry and year	January	February	March	April	May	June	July	August	September	October	November	December	Annual average
Trade, Transportation, and Utilities													
1990	45.0	45.5	45.8	45.2	45.4	45.6	44.4	44.7	44.4	44.1	44.6	45.4	45.0
2000	29.3	29.4	29.4	29.2	29.2	29.8	29.1	29.0	29.4	29.7	30.5	31.3	29.6
2001	28.2	27.8	28.0	27.7	27.9	28.3	27.7	28.0	28.1	28.3	28.5	28.8	28.1
2002	27.5	27.7	27.4	27.6	27.7	28.0	27.9	27.6	27.7	27.9	28.4	29.0	27.9
2003	27.5	27.3	27.7	27.5	27.6	28.1	27.9	27.9	27.9	28.3	28.7	29.2	28.0
2004	27.8	27.7	28.1	27.9	28.1	28.3	27.8	27.4	27.6	27.6	28.0	28.4	27.9
2005	27.3	27.1	27.6	27.4	27.5	27.6	27.8	27.5	27.6	28.2	28.4	29.3	27.8
2006	28.1	27.9	27.8	27.5	27.6	27.9	27.7	27.6	27.8	27.9	28.2	28.6	27.9
2007	27.5	27.2	27.4	27.8	27.9	27.9	27.7	27.5	27.6	27.6	28.1	28.4	27.7
2008	27.4	27.5	27.4	27.9	27.9	28.2	28.3	27.9	28.0	27.6	28.3	28.5	27.9
2009	27.3	26.8	26.7	27.0	26.7	26.8	26.8	26.8	26.8	26.9	26.9	27.4	26.9
Wholesale Trade													
1990	6.5	6.6	6.6	6.6	6.7	6.6	6.6	6.6	6.5	6.4	6.3	6.4	6.5
2000	4.5	4.5	4.5	4.4	4.4	4.4	4.3	4.3	4.3	4.4	4.4	4.5	4.4
2001	4.3	4.3	4.3	4.3	4.3	4.4	4.5	4.5	4.5	4.4	4.3	4.4	4.4
2002	4.1	4.2	4.2	4.2	4.2	4.3	4.5	4.4	4.5	4.5	4.5	4.6	4.4
2003	4.5	4.5	4.5	4.4	4.5	4.5	4.6	4.5	4.5	4.6	4.6	4.6	4.5
2004	4.5	4.6	4.5	4.6	4.6	4.6	4.6	4.5	4.6	4.5	4.6	4.6	4.6
2005	4.6	4.6	4.6	4.6	4.6	4.7	4.6	4.6	4.6	4.6	4.5	4.6	4.6
2006	4.7	4.7	4.6	4.6	4.6	4.6	4.7	4.7	4.7	4.7	4.7	4.8	4.7
2007	4.8	4.8	4.8	4.8	4.8	4.8	4.8	4.8	4.8	4.8	4.8	4.8	4.8
2008	4.7	4.8	4.7	4.7	4.7	4.9	5.0	4.9	4.8	4.8	4.7	4.7	4.8
2009	4.7	4.6	4.6	4.6	4.6	4.6	4.6	4.5	4.4	4.4	4.4	4.4	4.5
Retail Trade													
1990	25.9	26.2	26.3	25.8	25.7	25.9	24.9	25.1	25.0	25.0	25.6	26.3	25.6
2000	17.1	17.0	17.2	16.9	17.0	17.4	17.1	17.1	17.6	17.8	18.5	18.9	17.5
2001	17.3	17.0	17.1	16.7	16.9	17.0	16.6	16.9	17.0	17.5	17.9	18.1	17.2
2002	17.3	17.2	17.0	17.0	17.1	17.2	17.0	16.8	16.9	17.0	17.5	18.0	17.2
2003	16.7	16.6	16.7	16.8	16.8	17.3	17.0	17.1	17.2	17.5	17.9	18.5	17.2
2004	17.2	17.1	17.3	17.4	17.6	17.9	17.6	17.4	17.5	17.6	17.9	18.4	17.6
2005	17.4	17.1	17.5	17.3	17.4	17.4	17.6	17.4	17.5	17.9	18.2	18.9	17.6
2006	18.0	17.9	17.8	17.5	17.5	17.9	17.8	17.7	18.0	18.2	18.5	18.8	18.0
2007	18.0	17.8	17.8	18.2	18.2	18.3	18.1	17.9	18.0	18.2	18.6	18.9	18.2
2008	18.1	18.2	18.2	18.6	18.5	18.6	18.5	18.3	18.5	18.1	18.9	19.0	18.5
2009	18.0	17.6	17.5	17.6	17.3	17.3	17.3	17.4	17.6	17.7	17.7	18.2	17.6
Transportation and Utilities													
1990	12.6	12.7	12.9	12.8	13.0	13.1	12.9	13.0	12.9	12.7	12.7	12.7	12.8
2000	7.7	7.9	7.7	7.9	7.8	8.0	7.7	7.6	7.5	7.5	7.6	7.9	7.7
2001	6.6	6.5	6.6	6.7	6.7	6.9	6.6	6.6	6.6	6.4	6.3	6.3	6.6
2002	6.1	6.3	6.2	6.4	6.4	6.5	6.4	6.4	6.3	6.4	6.4	6.4	6.4
2003	6.3	6.2	6.5	6.3	6.3	6.3	6.3	6.3	6.2	6.2	6.2	6.1	6.3
2004	6.1	6.0	6.3	5.9	5.9	5.8	5.6	5.5	5.5	5.5	5.5	5.4	5.8
2005	5.3	5.4	5.5	5.5	5.5	5.5	5.6	5.5	5.5	5.7	5.7	5.8	5.5
2006	5.4	5.3	5.4	5.4	5.5	5.4	5.2	5.2	5.1	5.0	5.0	5.0	5.2
2007	4.7	4.6	4.8	4.8	4.9	4.8	4.8	4.8	4.8	4.6	4.7	4.7	4.8
2008	4.6	4.5	4.5	4.6	4.7	4.7	4.8	4.7	4.7	4.7	4.7	4.8	4.7
2009	4.6	4.6	4.6	4.8	4.8	4.9	4.9	4.9	4.8	4.8	4.8	4.8	4.8
Information													
1990	25.7	25.8	25.9	25.9	26.0	26.4	26.2	26.4	26.3	25.8	25.9	26.1	26.0
2000	24.3	24.5	24.7	24.8	24.7	25.6	25.9	26.1	26.2	26.0	26.2	26.5	25.5
2001	25.3	25.5	25.5	25.8	25.8	25.8	25.5	26.3	26.0	26.0	26.0	26.1	25.8
2002	25.7	25.6	26.0	25.7	25.7	25.8	25.3	25.3	25.1	24.6	24.7	24.7	25.4
2003	25.0	25.3	25.4	24.5	24.6	24.4	24.5	24.4	24.4	23.9	24.0	23.8	24.5
2004	24.3	24.1	24.2	24.0	24.1	24.1	24.4	24.4	24.0	22.9	22.8	22.7	23.8
2005	22.8	23.0	22.8	22.6	22.4	22.6	22.7	22.5	22.4	22.2	22.3	22.3	22.6
2006	22.0	21.9	22.2	22.1	22.1	22.4	22.4	22.2	22.3	22.0	22.1	22.1	22.2
2007	22.4	22.5	22.4	21.8	21.8	22.2	22.5	22.3	21.4	21.3	21.3	21.3	21.9
2008	21.1	21.2	21.3	20.9	21.0	20.9	21.0	21.0	20.8	20.6	20.6	20.4	20.9
2009	19.8	19.7	19.0	19.4	19.4	19.4	19.0	18.8	18.7	18.6	18.4	18.3	19.0
Financial Activities													
1990	30.0	30.1	30.2	30.0	30.3	30.5	30.9	31.1	30.7	29.7	29.8	29.7	30.3
2000	29.4	29.6	29.9	29.5	29.2	29.6	30.1	30.3	30.3	30.5	30.7	31.4	30.0
2001	30.4	30.4	30.5	31.0	31.0	31.1	31.5	31.5	31.2	31.3	31.2	31.5	31.1
2002	30.4	30.6	30.9	30.3	30.3	30.6	31.0	31.2	31.0	31.2	31.3	31.3	30.8
2003	30.8	30.8	30.8	30.9	31.0	31.0	31.1	30.9	30.7	30.4	30.3	30.5	30.8
2004	30.0	30.1	30.2	30.8	31.0	31.2	30.6	30.5	30.5	30.6	30.7	30.7	30.6
2005	29.9	30.1	29.8	30.6	30.7	30.5	30.3	30.2	30.3	30.1	30.0	30.4	30.2
2006	29.5	29.7	29.9	29.2	29.3	29.4	29.6	29.6	29.5	29.3	29.1	29.2	29.4
2007	29.5	29.7	29.7	29.3	29.0	29.1	29.3	29.1	28.9	28.9	29.0	28.9	29.2
2008	28.3	28.4	28.3	28.4	28.3	28.4	28.2	28.2	28.2	27.8	27.8	27.6	28.2
2009	27.2	26.9	26.8	26.6	26.6	26.8	26.6	26.5	26.4	26.2	26.0	25.9	26.5

Employment by Industry: District of Columbia, Selected Years, 1990–2009—*Continued*

(Numbers in thousands, not seasonally adjusted.)

Industry and year	January	February	March	April	May	June	July	August	September	October	November	December	Annual average
Professional and Business Services													
1990	107.6	109.4	111.4	110.5	111.8	113.3	111.4	111.6	111.0	108.9	108.6	109.1	110.4
2000	126.4	128.5	128.8	130.5	131.0	133.9	135.6	134.8	135.1	139.3	140.1	141.4	133.8
2001	135.9	137.3	138.4	137.6	138.0	140.8	140.2	139.5	137.4	139.9	139.9	140.1	138.8
2002	135.2	136.2	137.5	139.3	139.1	141.1	141.2	140.2	139.5	139.6	140.0	140.5	139.1
2003	137.7	137.9	138.8	142.3	143.0	144.2	143.4	142.4	142.3	142.2	142.3	143.3	141.7
2004	137.7	139.5	140.9	142.9	144.0	146.8	146.2	145.5	145.1	146.0	145.5	146.1	143.9
2005	144.2	145.5	147.0	147.4	147.8	150.3	150.3	149.5	149.4	149.5	149.6	150.1	148.4
2006	147.4	149.2	150.5	151.4	152.1	155.8	153.7	152.5	152.3	153.4	153.5	153.5	152.1
2007	150.7	152.3	152.8	152.6	153.5	155.4	153.1	152.7	151.7	152.3	152.9	153.3	152.8
2008	150.5	152.0	153.3	153.6	153.6	155.0	153.6	152.9	151.9	151.8	150.6	150.1	152.4
2009	149.2	148.9	148.5	147.3	147.7	149.7	148.8	147.5	145.6	148.5	148.8	150.4	148.4
Education and Health Services													
1990	75.5	76.8	77.3	77.4	76.9	75.7	74.7	76.2	78.0	78.6	79.1	78.6	77.1
2000	84.2	86.0	86.7	87.9	85.3	85.5	86.6	86.7	87.6	89.9	91.0	90.8	87.4
2001	84.5	85.5	86.2	86.6	86.1	81.5	83.0	83.3	86.3	87.7	86.8	85.7	85.3
2002	86.9	89.7	92.1	92.1	88.5	85.6	86.3	86.5	89.5	92.7	93.5	92.4	89.6
2003	88.3	89.7	90.7	89.1	86.8	84.1	86.4	85.5	88.8	90.8	91.8	91.4	88.6
2004	89.7	94.2	94.9	94.7	92.2	89.0	88.8	88.2	92.1	94.5	95.1	93.5	92.2
2005	91.6	94.7	94.6	93.8	91.5	87.4	86.5	86.0	91.3	94.6	97.4	96.4	92.2
2006	92.6	96.0	96.4	96.6	93.1	88.8	88.3	87.5	92.6	97.1	99.4	98.8	93.9
2007	97.3	101.6	102.4	101.3	96.9	92.1	92.3	91.5	97.5	102.9	103.0	103.2	98.5
2008	99.4	100.8	101.5	102.6	102.2	97.8	99.7	99.7	103.8	104.8	105.9	106.2	102.0
2009	104.9	106.0	106.6	107.9	106.3	101.1	100.9	100.4	102.8	105.6	106.5	105.2	104.5
Leisure and Hospitality													
1990	45.6	47.1	48.1	47.8	48.8	48.8	47.2	46.7	47.5	47.6	47.3	47.2	47.5
2000	43.5	44.7	46.2	48.4	48.7	49.3	48.6	47.7	49.0	50.2	50.6	50.3	48.1
2001	45.9	47.6	48.6	48.0	48.6	49.1	48.9	48.3	47.7	46.7	47.0	46.2	47.7
2002	43.4	44.9	46.7	48.3	49.2	49.5	49.6	48.5	49.3	49.9	49.9	49.3	48.2
2003	47.4	47.7	49.2	50.3	50.8	50.5	49.6	48.9	49.4	50.5	50.6	50.4	49.6
2004	48.0	49.0	50.3	50.9	52.1	52.1	51.3	51.0	51.6	52.1	51.9	51.0	50.9
2005	50.5	51.5	52.8	54.2	55.4	55.1	54.1	53.4	54.4	54.4	54.3	53.8	53.7
2006	51.7	52.7	54.3	54.6	55.3	55.8	54.5	53.9	54.5	54.9	54.3	53.6	54.2
2007	51.5	52.8	54.5	56.3	56.3	56.4	56.4	55.7	56.5	56.4	56.6	56.3	55.5
2008	53.9	55.2	56.4	59.1	59.2	59.0	59.1	58.6	59.4	58.9	58.1	56.6	57.8
2009	56.0	56.0	57.4	58.4	59.7	59.0	58.2	57.4	57.9	59.3	58.5	57.6	58.0
Other services													
1990	50.1	50.4	50.9	51.2	51.4	51.9	51.7	51.3	51.6	51.3	51.7	51.8	51.3
2000	56.2	56.7	57.2	57.4	57.2	57.6	57.6	57.2	57.5	57.2	56.4	56.0	57.0
2001	54.6	54.5	55.2	55.5	55.8	56.6	55.8	55.8	55.7	56.7	56.8	57.1	55.8
2002	54.6	55.1	55.3	56.1	56.0	56.4	57.1	56.8	56.6	56.3	56.3	56.4	56.1
2003	55.0	55.3	55.8	55.9	56.2	56.6	56.9	56.5	56.4	56.6	56.9	57.5	56.3
2004	57.2	57.5	58.0	58.4	58.8	59.5	59.7	59.6	59.3	59.1	59.6	58.8	58.8
2005	57.8	58.1	58.7	59.0	59.2	59.9	59.6	59.4	58.9	58.7	59.1	59.4	59.0
2006	58.6	59.0	59.5	59.8	60.1	61.3	61.8	61.3	61.0	61.4	61.8	62.4	60.7
2007	61.0	61.6	61.9	62.2	62.6	63.7	63.9	63.1	63.1	63.1	63.4	63.9	62.8
2008	63.1	63.4	64.4	64.8	65.1	66.2	67.0	66.2	66.0	65.6	65.9	66.0	65.3
2009	65.3	65.1	64.8	64.5	64.7	65.5	65.0	64.6	64.2	65.1	64.0	63.5	64.7
Government													
1990	275.9	275.3	276.6	274.9	277.0	281.6	289.7	275.7	275.9	274.3	274.3	276.6	277.3
2000	221.7	221.4	221.5	221.6	223.9	225.8	232.7	229.3	223.4	220.8	221.7	223.7	223.9
2001	221.0	218.6	219.9	220.0	221.3	225.8	234.8	234.8	229.3	229.7	228.5	229.9	226.1
2002	230.3	229.1	229.8	228.8	229.5	232.5	240.1	237.6	231.9	229.2	230.4	231.2	231.7
2003	229.6	229.6	231.0	230.4	230.5	232.2	237.1	231.5	230.2	228.9	228.2	228.5	230.6
2004	228.9	228.6	229.4	229.3	228.5	230.9	236.2	237.6	230.0	231.0	232.2	232.6	231.3
2005	231.7	231.2	231.2	231.8	231.9	234.7	242.0	241.4	230.9	232.2	233.0	232.6	233.7
2006	231.8	231.4	231.4	230.0	230.7	233.5	242.8	240.4	230.7	231.2	231.2	231.4	233.0
2007	226.9	227.8	227.1	226.9	227.3	230.0	241.6	238.6	228.7	232.7	232.1	232.3	231.0
2008	230.9	230.6	231.1	229.8	230.9	234.0	248.5	246.4	232.5	234.2	234.3	234.9	234.8
2009	234.4	234.7	235.0	235.8	236.8	240.8	262.1	255.7	240.8	242.7	242.9	243.6	242.1

Average Weekly Hours by Selected Industry: District of Columbia, 2007–2009

(Not seasonally adjusted.)

Industry and year	January	February	March	April	May	June	July	August	September	October	November	December	Annual average
Total Private													
2007	35.7	35.5	36.1	37.4	36.7	36.5	36.9	36.1	36.6	36.1	35.9	36.4	36.3
2008	35.2	35.3	36.1	35.5	35.2	36.3	36.0	36.1	35.7	36.0	36.1	35.8	35.8
2009	36.7	36.8	36.5	36.2	35.9	36.1	36.0	36.6	36.2	36.0	36.4	35.6	36.3
Goods-Producing													
2007	32.1	31.5	32.4	32.9	32.4	31.9	30.7	30.5	30.2	29.3	30.1	31.3	31.2
2008	31.0	31.2	32.1	32.3	32.9	32.7	32.3	32.7	33.1	31.8	32.1	31.7	32.2
2009	32.1	32.4	32.6	32.4	32.7	32.8	33.0	33.0	32.7	33.0	32.5	32.6	32.6
Trade, Transportation, and Utilities													
2007	35.8	37.1	37.8	37.9	37.1	36.5	37.3	37.1	37.0	36.8	37.9	37.5	37.2
2008	37.2	37.0	37.1	37.0	36.2	36.7	36.3	36.4	36.6	37.0	36.5	36.4	36.7
2009	37.0	36.7	36.8	36.6	36.1	36.4	36.6	36.9	36.7	36.3	35.8	35.3	36.4
Professional and Business Services													
2007	38.1	37.9	37.5	38.9	37.8	37.7	38.8	37.7	38.1	37.4	37.6	38.0	38.0
2008	37.6	37.8	38.1	37.6	37.0	38.3	37.9	38.0	37.3	37.1	37.2	36.8	37.6
2009	37.1	37.3	37.0	36.7	36.4	36.8	36.8	37.7	37.1	36.6	37.5	36.2	36.9
Leisure and Hospitality													
2007	29.7	28.8	30.9	31.4	31.5	30.9	30.1	30.0	30.9	31.6	30.9	30.4	30.6
2008	29.1	30.3	31.7	32.0	31.6	32.9	32.4	31.7	32.4	33.1	32.8	33.1	32.0
2009	32.9	32.8	32.9	32.9	33.1	33.6	33.5	33.2	33.1	33.0	32.7	32.1	33.0
Other Services													
2007	34.0	33.3	33.6	34.4	33.7	34.1	34.2	34.4	34.6	35.0	34.6	34.4	34.2
2008	33.5	34.1	34.6	34.1	34.5	35.3	34.9	35.5	34.9	34.9	35.3	35.0	34.7
2009	35.1	35.3	35.8	35.7	35.8	35.7	36.0	36.3	35.9	36.1	36.3	35.9	35.8

Average Hourly Earnings by Selected Industry: District of Columbia, 2007–2009

(Dollars, not seasonally adjusted.)

Industry and year	January	February	March	April	May	June	July	August	September	October	November	December	Annual average
Total Private													
2007	32.94	33.83	33.38	34.03	33.69	33.93	33.84	33.34	33.57	33.26	33.19	33.41	33.54
2008	33.21	33.24	33.19	32.65	33.09	32.34	32.25	31.78	32.19	31.48	31.67	31.40	32.37
2009	30.90	31.50	31.38	31.17	30.94	31.07	30.70	31.43	31.11	31.46	32.33	32.41	31.37
Goods-Producing													
2007	34.90	35.89	36.17	36.80	37.16	36.90	37.73	36.44	35.46	35.41	34.76	33.71	35.96
2008	34.22	33.81	34.55	33.90	33.79	34.05	33.90	34.12	33.03	33.96	34.10	35.05	34.03
2009	32.91	32.97	33.23	33.09	33.62	33.92	33.52	33.41	33.58	33.63	34.04	34.30	33.50
Trade, Transportation, and Utilities													
2007	25.34	24.43	23.90	23.14	22.69	22.58	22.09	21.80	21.20	21.75	20.95	21.55	22.60
2008	21.81	21.56	21.55	21.54	22.24	22.55	22.63	23.04	23.15	23.41	24.00	23.75	22.60
2009	23.39	23.55	23.61	23.89	23.68	23.71	23.60	23.84	23.24	23.72	24.55	24.18	23.74
Professional and Business Services													
2007	37.62	38.39	37.77	38.05	38.63	38.79	38.00	37.50	38.05	38.01	37.99	38.50	38.11
2008	37.80	38.59	38.44	38.22	39.30	38.25	38.27	37.45	38.60	37.80	38.00	37.70	38.20
2009	37.00	37.96	38.33	38.23	37.59	37.95	37.33	37.71	37.25	37.57	38.00	38.22	37.76
Leisure and Hospitality													
2007	19.95	19.15	17.90	17.94	18.30	18.67	18.51	18.15	18.40	18.00	18.55	18.33	18.47
2008	18.10	17.83	17.28	17.48	17.41	16.75	16.73	16.98	17.20	17.13	17.06	17.25	17.25
2009	16.82	16.70	16.63	16.66	16.53	16.41	16.28	16.39	16.50	16.77	17.35	17.57	16.71
Other Services													
2007	37.69	37.92	38.50	37.37	37.28	37.80	38.20	39.35	39.60	39.85	39.50	39.28	38.54
2008	38.94	38.34	39.20	38.75	38.34	38.52	38.60	38.83	39.00	38.69	39.20	39.13	38.80
2009	38.88	39.08	38.75	38.71	38.44	38.77	38.81	39.12	39.35	39.14	39.33	39.06	38.95

Average Weekly Earnings by Selected Industry: District of Columbia, 2007–2009

(Dollars, not seasonally adjusted.)

Industry and year	January	February	March	April	May	June	July	August	September	October	November	December	Annual average
Total Private													
2007	1175.96	1200.97	1205.02	1272.72	1236.42	1238.45	1248.70	1203.57	1228.66	1200.69	1191.52	1216.12	1217.50
2008	1168.99	1173.37	1198.16	1159.08	1164.77	1173.94	1161.00	1147.26	1149.18	1133.28	1143.29	1124.12	1158.85
2009	1134.03	1159.20	1145.37	1128.35	1110.75	1121.63	1105.20	1150.34	1126.18	1132.56	1176.81	1153.80	1138.73
Goods-Producing													
2007	1120.29	1130.54	1171.91	1210.72	1203.98	1177.11	1158.31	1111.42	1070.89	1037.51	1046.28	1055.12	1121.95
2008	1060.82	1054.87	1109.06	1094.97	1111.69	1113.44	1094.97	1115.72	1093.29	1079.93	1094.61	1111.09	1095.77
2009	1056.41	1068.23	1083.30	1072.12	1099.37	1112.58	1106.16	1102.53	1098.07	1109.79	1106.30	1118.18	1092.10
Trade, Transportation, and Utilities													
2007	907.17	906.35	903.42	877.01	841.80	824.17	823.96	808.78	784.40	800.40	794.01	808.13	840.72
2008	811.33	797.72	799.51	796.98	805.09	827.59	821.47	838.66	847.29	866.17	876.00	864.50	829.42
2009	865.43	864.29	868.85	874.37	854.85	863.04	863.76	879.70	852.91	861.04	878.89	853.55	864.14
Professional and Business Services													
2007	1433.32	1454.98	1416.38	1480.15	1460.21	1462.38	1474.40	1413.75	1449.71	1421.57	1428.42	1463.00	1448.18
2008	1421.28	1458.70	1464.56	1437.07	1454.10	1464.98	1450.43	1423.10	1439.78	1402.38	1413.60	1387.36	1436.32
2009	1372.70	1415.91	1418.21	1403.04	1368.28	1396.56	1373.74	1421.67	1381.98	1375.06	1425.00	1383.56	1393.34
Leisure and Hospitality													
2007	592.52	551.52	553.11	563.32	576.45	576.90	557.15	544.50	568.56	568.80	573.20	557.23	565.18
2008	526.71	540.25	547.78	559.36	550.16	551.08	542.05	538.27	557.28	567.00	559.57	570.98	552.00
2009	553.38	547.76	547.13	548.11	547.14	551.38	545.38	544.15	546.15	553.41	567.05	564.00	551.43
Other Services													
2007	1281.46	1262.74	1293.60	1285.53	1256.34	1288.98	1306.44	1353.64	1370.16	1394.75	1366.70	1351.23	1318.07
2008	1304.49	1307.39	1356.32	1321.38	1322.73	1359.76	1347.14	1378.47	1361.10	1350.28	1383.76	1369.55	1346.36
2009	1364.69	1379.52	1387.25	1381.95	1376.15	1384.09	1397.16	1420.06	1412.67	1412.95	1427.68	1402.25	1394.41

FLORIDA
At a Glance

Population:
  1990 census: 12,938,071
  2000 census: 15,982,378
  2009 estimate: 18,537,969

Percent change in population:
  1990–2000: 23.5%
  2000–2009: 16.0%

Percent change in total nonfarm employment:
  1990–2009: 35.0%
  2008–2009: -6.1%

Industry with the largest growth in employment, 1990–2009 (thousands):
  Professional and Business Services, 698.4

Industry with the largest decline or smallest growth in employment, 1990–2009 (thousands):
  Manufacturing, -185.2

Civilian labor force:
  1990: 6,465,579
  2000: 7,869,690
  2009: 9,197,484

Unemployment rate and rank among states (lowest to highest):
  1990: 6.3%, 41st
  2000: 3.8%, 25th
  2009: 10.5%, 42nd

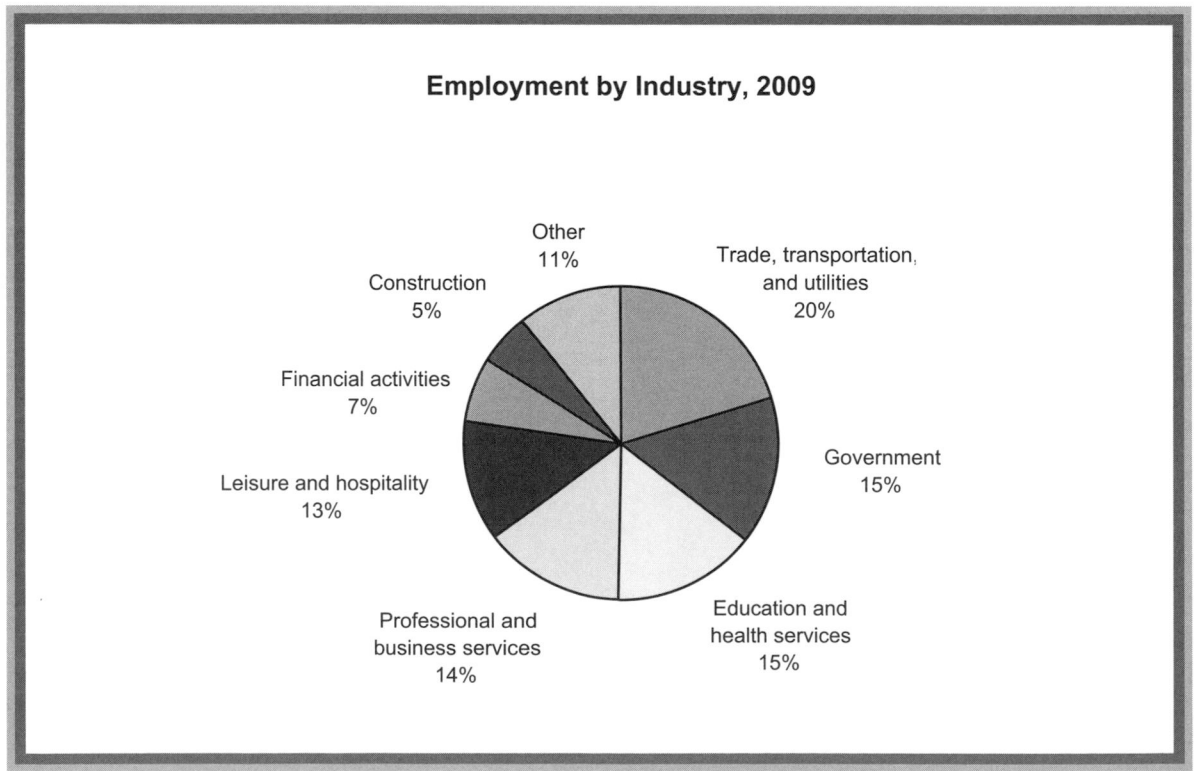

Employment by Industry, 2009

Other
11%

Trade, transportation,
and utilities
20%

Construction
5%

Financial activities
7%

Government
15%

Leisure and hospitality
13%

Professional and
business services
14%

Education and
health services
15%

Employment by Industry: Florida, Selected Years, 1990–2009

(Numbers in thousands, not seasonally adjusted.)

Industry and year	January	February	March	April	May	June	July	August	September	October	November	December	Annual average
Total Nonfarm													
1990	5323.7	5382.0	5437.0	5407.7	5419.4	5411.3	5293.1	5300.5	5351.9	5362.5	5403.0	5424.9	5376.4
2000	6919.5	6981.9	7061.4	7045.6	7079.3	7029.7	6963.8	7069.9	7104.9	7118.3	7197.1	7262.5	7069.5
2001	7096.7	7167.7	7229.5	7194.7	7198.5	7135.1	7046.0	7147.1	7147.8	7138.8	7187.0	7228.0	7159.7
2002	7089.1	7144.9	7206.4	7186.4	7198.3	7116.4	7037.0	7143.5	7154.3	7184.2	7253.2	7310.5	7168.7
2003	7176.8	7232.3	7287.6	7262.3	7266.8	7184.5	7116.9	7217.7	7238.0	7283.2	7331.2	7403.3	7250.1
2004	7332.7	7404.7	7470.8	7507.1	7511.6	7444.1	7405.6	7493.2	7471.0	7555.0	7657.0	7736.5	7499.1
2005	7621.9	7704.9	7751.6	7794.2	7812.4	7718.4	7698.1	7815.0	7860.0	7866.8	7941.2	8014.6	7799.9
2006	7882.6	7957.3	8037.8	8018.1	8035.9	7951.3	7878.1	7994.8	8011.0	8012.8	8096.3	8153.2	8002.4
2007	8011.9	8078.5	8142.9	8094.9	8089.6	7981.0	7872.1	7971.5	7958.2	7947.3	8020.1	8053.2	8018.4
2008	7871.8	7927.8	7949.4	7865.8	7834.3	7693.3	7583.2	7657.8	7629.2	7600.6	7607.9	7607.2	7735.7
2009	7404.0	7402.1	7398.8	7352.4	7313.4	7182.7	7099.9	7168.6	7162.0	7183.5	7216.9	7237.3	7260.1
Total Private													
1990	4494.2	4539.5	4583.4	4552.1	4549.7	4558.7	4495.5	4511.5	4497.5	4492.0	4528.0	4554.7	4529.7
2000	5927.9	5980.4	6051.7	6031.0	6045.2	6081.4	6031.1	6064.2	6095.0	6100.1	6171.7	6233.4	6067.8
2001	6082.0	6139.5	6195.2	6159.5	6161.9	6166.3	6093.1	6113.9	6108.6	6097.1	6139.2	6178.8	6136.3
2002	6055.2	6100.7	6157.6	6137.1	6144.6	6138.5	6073.0	6095.3	6097.7	6122.2	6188.4	6243.0	6129.4
2003	6124.1	6168.8	6220.5	6196.7	6194.8	6190.6	6135.9	6160.7	6175.1	6212.2	6257.6	6327.6	6197.0
2004	6268.1	6326.9	6390.2	6427.6	6432.1	6440.6	6413.4	6421.7	6394.9	6471.1	6565.1	6643.2	6432.9
2005	6540.8	6611.4	6655.8	6698.7	6713.7	6719.2	6697.4	6731.9	6762.1	6758.7	6830.3	6905.0	6718.8
2006	6782.3	6846.4	6923.1	6906.7	6928.0	6937.2	6863.3	6891.9	6895.9	6883.9	6959.6	7019.8	6903.2
2007	6888.1	6943.4	7002.3	6955.7	6954.0	6940.0	6831.0	6841.4	6820.0	6801.7	6868.8	6903.8	6895.9
2008	6731.5	6776.0	6800.7	6718.9	6693.4	6648.6	6539.4	6524.7	6487.0	6454.7	6463.1	6467.7	6608.8
2009	6270.3	6263.0	6262.0	6209.8	6183.0	6147.2	6062.8	6048.2	6031.1	6043.0	6076.3	6107.1	6142.0
Goods-Producing													
1990	947.5	949.3	952.1	938.5	939.5	941.0	929.1	929.0	922.2	911.4	904.0	894.9	929.9
2000	946.9	954.5	962.8	956.3	961.3	971.0	967.5	970.8	976.4	970.1	972.1	974.8	965.4
2001	960.4	962.5	965.3	958.0	959.0	963.1	955.1	958.0	955.0	953.1	952.3	951.9	957.8
2002	933.2	934.2	937.3	932.6	935.2	936.7	928.0	935.0	934.4	938.2	941.3	942.1	935.7
2003	928.1	931.7	934.9	927.4	932.9	937.6	931.6	937.7	940.6	942.5	943.2	951.0	936.6
2004	948.8	958.4	969.9	975.9	980.4	988.4	991.3	994.3	993.6	1003.2	1011.3	1020.1	986.3
2005	1009.5	1020.2	1028.2	1039.1	1047.9	1057.3	1061.8	1068.6	1077.2	1078.3	1085.4	1094.5	1055.7
2006	1081.4	1094.9	1107.3	1105.9	1113.0	1119.3	1105.9	1107.7	1105.2	1094.0	1089.4	1087.1	1100.9
2007	1059.0	1060.5	1064.3	1043.8	1042.9	1044.5	1018.4	1014.9	1005.2	986.5	979.3	972.8	1024.3
2008	940.9	939.7	934.5	911.2	907.6	904.5	882.3	875.8	868.4	848.5	833.8	819.2	888.9
2009	780.6	767.2	758.1	737.4	731.1	727.3	713.1	706.5	699.9	685.9	673.5	675.6	721.4
Mining and Logging													
2002	7.3	7.4	7.3	7.3	7.3	7.3	7.2	7.2	7.1	7.0	7.0	7.0	7.2
2003	7.1	7.0	7.0	6.9	7.1	7.1	7.1	7.2	7.2	7.2	7.2	7.2	7.1
2004	7.2	7.2	7.2	7.2	7.1	7.1	7.1	7.1	7.1	7.0	7.1	7.1	7.1
2005	7.1	7.1	7.1	7.2	7.2	7.2	7.2	7.2	7.0	6.8	6.8	6.9	7.1
2006	6.6	6.6	6.7	6.7	6.7	6.8	6.6	6.4	6.5	6.5	6.6	6.6	6.6
2007	6.7	6.8	6.7	6.8	6.8	6.9	6.6	6.7	6.6	6.6	6.7	6.7	6.7
2008	6.6	6.6	6.5	6.4	6.3	6.2	6.1	6.1	6.0	5.9	5.8	5.8	6.2
2009	5.7	5.6	5.5	5.5	5.5	5.4	5.4	5.4	5.4	5.4	5.4	5.4	5.5
Construction													
1990	418.9	420.4	423.0	415.6	415.0	417.0	412.4	411.9	407.8	402.6	395.6	387.6	410.7
2000	464.9	469.4	475.0	470.5	474.3	481.4	480.8	484.0	488.7	485.9	487.6	489.5	479.3
2001	484.2	487.0	490.4	487.7	490.4	496.5	496.5	500.2	500.2	502.4	503.3	502.7	495.1
2002	491.6	492.7	495.5	494.2	497.7	499.4	496.0	502.6	503.3	509.2	511.8	512.5	500.5
2003	503.3	507.7	511.1	509.0	514.8	519.9	519.7	524.9	527.2	529.9	531.3	537.2	519.7
2004	536.4	543.9	552.8	557.6	560.9	568.1	572.6	575.3	576.1	586.2	592.8	599.4	568.5
2005	593.0	601.5	608.0	617.6	624.8	632.6	638.9	644.8	652.5	654.7	661.4	668.0	633.2
2006	657.4	669.1	680.0	680.8	686.6	691.8	683.6	685.7	683.8	676.1	672.0	668.3	677.9
2007	645.7	646.7	650.8	633.0	632.6	634.7	614.7	611.9	604.3	588.9	582.9	576.9	618.6
2008	550.1	549.3	546.3	526.8	524.5	522.8	506.8	501.7	496.7	482.1	471.1	461.0	511.6
2009	429.8	421.9	417.1	403.3	399.4	397.6	389.1	383.9	379.4	370.0	360.7	362.6	392.9
Manufacturing													
1990	517.4	517.7	517.9	511.8	513.5	513.0	505.5	505.9	503.4	497.8	497.6	496.6	508.2
2000	473.2	476.3	478.9	477.2	478.3	480.8	478.1	478.2	479.0	475.4	475.9	476.7	477.3
2001	467.9	467.2	466.6	462.1	460.3	458.4	450.5	449.9	446.9	443.0	441.4	441.6	454.7
2002	434.3	434.1	434.5	431.1	430.2	430.0	424.8	425.2	424.0	422.0	422.5	422.6	427.9
2003	417.7	417.0	416.8	411.5	411.0	410.6	404.8	405.6	406.2	405.4	404.7	406.6	409.8
2004	405.2	407.3	409.9	411.1	412.4	413.2	411.6	411.9	410.4	410.0	411.4	413.6	410.7
2005	409.4	411.6	413.1	414.3	415.9	417.5	415.7	416.6	417.7	416.8	417.2	419.6	415.5
2006	417.4	419.2	420.6	418.4	419.7	420.7	415.7	415.6	414.9	411.4	410.8	412.2	416.4
2007	406.6	407.0	406.8	404.0	403.5	402.9	397.1	396.3	394.3	391.0	389.7	389.2	399.0
2008	384.2	383.8	381.7	378.0	376.8	375.5	369.4	368.0	365.7	360.5	356.9	352.4	371.1
2009	345.1	339.7	335.5	328.6	326.2	324.3	318.6	317.2	315.1	310.5	307.4	307.6	323.0

Employment by Industry: Florida, Selected Years, 1990–2009—*Continued*

(Numbers in thousands, not seasonally adjusted.)

Industry and year	January	February	March	April	May	June	July	August	September	October	November	December	Annual average
Service-Providing													
1990	4376.2	4432.7	4484.9	4469.2	4479.9	4470.3	4364.0	4371.5	4429.7	4451.1	4499.0	4530.0	4446.5
2000	5972.6	6027.4	6098.6	6089.3	6118.0	6058.7	5996.3	6099.1	6128.5	6148.2	6225.0	6287.7	6104.1
2001	6136.3	6205.2	6264.2	6236.7	6239.5	6172.0	6090.9	6189.1	6192.8	6185.7	6234.7	6276.1	6201.9
2002	6155.9	6210.7	6269.1	6253.8	6263.1	6179.7	6109.0	6208.5	6219.9	6246.0	6311.9	6368.4	6233.0
2003	6248.7	6300.6	6352.7	6334.9	6333.9	6246.9	6185.3	6280.0	6297.4	6340.7	6388.0	6452.3	6313.5
2004	6383.9	6446.3	6500.9	6531.2	6531.2	6455.7	6414.3	6498.9	6477.4	6551.8	6645.7	6716.4	6512.8
2005	6612.4	6684.7	6723.4	6755.1	6764.5	6661.1	6636.3	6746.4	6782.8	6788.5	6855.8	6920.1	6744.3
2006	6801.2	6862.4	6930.5	6912.2	6922.9	6832.0	6772.2	6887.1	6905.8	6918.8	7006.9	7066.1	6901.5
2007	6952.9	7018.0	7078.6	7051.1	7046.7	6936.5	6853.7	6956.6	6953.0	6960.8	7040.8	7080.4	6994.1
2008	6930.9	6988.1	7014.9	6954.6	6926.7	6788.8	6700.9	6782.0	6760.8	6752.1	6774.1	6788.0	6846.8
2009	6623.4	6634.9	6640.7	6615.0	6582.3	6455.4	6386.8	6462.1	6462.1	6497.6	6543.4	6561.7	6538.8
Trade, Transportation, and Utilities													
1990	1208.7	1206.0	1212.5	1207.3	1208.3	1210.6	1196.0	1201.2	1198.6	1207.7	1229.7	1254.2	1211.7
2000	1499.1	1498.0	1506.2	1498.4	1503.1	1510.1	1494.5	1505.2	1509.5	1515.1	1552.4	1583.5	1514.6
2001	1513.0	1508.6	1518.5	1507.8	1505.3	1501.5	1489.0	1494.0	1493.8	1496.4	1523.0	1545.8	1508.1
2002	1493.6	1484.5	1491.7	1484.4	1485.5	1480.0	1468.4	1474.7	1475.6	1482.6	1509.6	1538.5	1489.1
2003	1479.3	1471.7	1474.2	1469.6	1470.1	1465.8	1461.4	1467.0	1471.3	1485.0	1512.0	1542.3	1480.8
2004	1499.5	1497.3	1504.1	1508.7	1511.6	1509.9	1508.5	1510.2	1504.4	1526.5	1566.6	1597.8	1520.4
2005	1549.6	1552.8	1559.6	1570.2	1575.4	1574.0	1574.6	1580.3	1584.2	1591.7	1620.4	1651.9	1582.1
2006	1602.1	1601.3	1612.6	1608.8	1611.7	1609.6	1598.8	1603.3	1602.9	1610.1	1647.1	1676.7	1615.4
2007	1623.5	1620.2	1629.2	1623.3	1628.0	1622.8	1606.9	1608.6	1608.6	1611.8	1651.8	1672.6	1625.6
2008	1616.4	1611.7	1612.6	1593.8	1590.4	1578.8	1560.7	1558.4	1549.4	1546.6	1563.6	1578.0	1580.0
2009	1511.4	1498.2	1489.6	1474.3	1471.1	1462.9	1446.5	1444.7	1442.2	1446.3	1471.4	1485.4	1470.3
Wholesale Trade													
1990	244.0	245.7	246.7	246.6	247.1	247.5	245.4	246.8	247.2	246.4	246.9	247.1	246.5
2000	311.5	312.7	315.8	314.6	316.2	318.1	316.6	317.7	320.0	319.1	320.4	323.0	317.1
2001	315.5	317.3	319.1	318.2	318.2	317.2	314.5	314.9	315.1	314.8	314.9	316.4	316.3
2002	313.9	315.2	316.0	314.0	315.5	315.1	313.7	314.6	315.3	316.4	318.3	320.2	315.7
2003	315.4	316.3	316.8	316.3	316.4	316.1	315.8	316.6	317.6	318.1	319.6	322.7	317.3
2004	321.4	323.8	325.5	326.3	327.8	328.4	327.3	327.9	327.3	330.5	333.6	336.0	328.0
2005	333.7	336.0	336.8	339.9	341.9	341.9	341.6	342.4	343.6	343.9	345.5	349.1	341.4
2006	344.8	347.5	349.5	350.4	352.1	352.6	350.7	351.6	352.1	352.9	354.5	357.3	351.3
2007	355.7	358.2	359.3	357.9	358.8	358.6	354.7	354.6	354.4	354.9	355.9	357.5	356.7
2008	351.9	353.5	353.0	349.2	349.5	347.8	343.4	342.4	341.5	339.7	338.2	338.0	345.7
2009	329.0	327.8	324.8	321.5	320.7	318.0	313.4	312.3	310.9	310.9	313.5	313.6	318.0
Retail Trade													
1990	770.0	764.4	767.2	761.8	762.2	762.4	752.4	755.1	751.8	760.8	781.1	801.2	765.9
2000	938.2	935.6	939.8	933.5	936.5	941.6	927.9	937.0	937.7	944.8	978.4	1000.9	946.0
2001	948.6	942.3	949.4	938.8	937.3	935.0	925.6	929.9	929.8	934.1	961.1	977.8	942.5
2002	937.1	927.1	931.7	926.6	927.1	923.0	913.2	918.8	919.6	925.8	949.9	973.3	931.1
2003	926.6	919.2	921.1	916.8	918.7	916.8	913.5	917.7	921.0	933.9	958.8	981.8	928.8
2004	943.7	938.4	942.6	945.5	947.9	946.5	945.1	944.2	939.2	955.1	989.0	1012.4	954.1
2005	972.9	972.7	977.5	983.5	985.7	986.2	987.2	991.7	993.0	1000.4	1024.1	1046.5	993.5
2006	1007.8	1004.1	1011.8	1007.5	1008.5	1006.9	1000.7	1002.3	1000.6	1007.9	1040.8	1060.0	1013.2
2007	1018.2	1012.8	1019.4	1013.6	1018.1	1013.6	1003.8	1005.1	1004.6	1006.8	1042.2	1056.2	1017.9
2008	1014.4	1007.5	1008.5	995.8	992.8	985.9	974.9	973.5	967.3	966.0	983.3	992.1	988.5
2009	944.2	934.5	930.3	921.3	920.2	916.3	907.0	907.3	906.7	906.1	929.5	940.1	922.0
Transportation and Utilities													
1990	194.7	195.9	198.6	198.9	199.0	200.7	198.2	199.3	199.6	200.5	201.7	205.9	199.4
2000	249.4	249.7	250.6	250.3	250.4	250.4	250.0	250.5	251.8	251.2	253.6	259.6	251.5
2001	248.9	249.0	250.0	250.8	249.8	249.3	248.9	249.2	248.9	247.5	247.0	251.6	249.2
2002	242.6	242.2	244.0	243.8	242.9	241.9	241.5	241.3	240.7	240.4	241.4	245.0	242.3
2003	237.3	236.2	236.3	236.5	235.0	232.9	232.1	232.7	232.7	233.0	233.6	237.8	234.7
2004	234.4	235.1	236.0	236.9	235.9	235.0	236.1	238.1	237.9	240.9	244.0	249.4	238.3
2005	243.0	244.1	245.3	246.8	247.8	245.9	245.8	246.2	247.6	247.4	250.8	256.3	247.3
2006	249.5	249.7	251.3	250.9	251.1	250.1	247.4	249.4	250.2	249.3	251.8	259.4	250.8
2007	249.6	249.2	250.5	251.8	251.1	250.6	248.4	248.9	249.6	250.1	253.7	258.9	251.0
2008	250.1	250.7	251.1	248.8	248.1	245.1	242.4	242.5	240.6	240.9	242.1	247.9	245.9
2009	238.2	235.9	234.5	231.5	230.2	228.6	226.1	225.1	224.6	229.3	228.4	231.7	230.3
Information													
1990	126.7	127.0	126.8	126.9	127.1	127.8	127.7	127.7	127.5	128.2	129.0	129.9	127.7
2000	175.9	177.1	180.5	177.3	178.9	182.4	184.0	185.5	187.2	187.0	188.6	190.5	182.9
2001	186.1	187.1	187.7	185.9	185.8	185.5	183.3	182.2	180.3	178.4	178.4	179.1	183.3
2002	176.1	175.6	175.8	173.6	173.9	173.4	171.9	171.3	170.4	169.8	170.4	171.0	172.8
2003	167.3	167.6	168.0	165.7	166.7	166.3	166.1	166.1	165.1	164.9	165.6	166.3	166.3
2004	163.1	162.5	163.6	162.4	163.1	163.5	162.4	162.5	161.3	162.3	163.6	164.2	162.9
2005	161.9	162.7	162.9	162.1	163.8	163.9	163.5	163.5	164.0	162.6	163.6	164.0	163.2
2006	160.5	161.3	161.5	161.2	162.3	163.0	162.7	162.0	161.0	160.8	161.8	162.6	161.7
2007	160.2	161.2	161.8	162.4	163.1	163.4	161.7	161.4	160.0	159.8	159.8	160.3	161.3
2008	158.7	159.2	159.0	157.7	157.9	157.4	156.5	155.2	152.9	152.4	152.0	151.0	155.8
2009	147.9	147.5	146.5	145.1	144.5	144.2	141.9	140.8	138.9	141.4	140.0	137.3	143.0

Employment by Industry: Florida, Selected Years, 1990–2009—*Continued*

(Numbers in thousands, not seasonally adjusted.)

Industry and year	January	February	March	April	May	June	July	August	September	October	November	December	Annual average
Financial Activities													
1990	379.2	383.5	385.8	383.1	384.5	386.4	383.6	385.3	383.6	381.4	381.6	382.9	383.4
2000	460.2	461.9	466.3	465.8	468.0	474.1	469.9	471.1	471.8	471.6	473.1	476.3	469.2
2001	466.3	469.6	473.4	475.0	475.7	479.1	477.6	478.9	477.4	476.8	477.5	479.3	475.6
2002	475.7	477.9	479.5	478.0	478.9	481.1	481.7	483.0	481.7	482.7	485.5	487.9	481.1
2003	482.1	483.9	485.9	487.9	489.8	492.5	493.8	496.1	495.6	496.5	496.5	501.1	491.8
2004	496.7	499.7	503.1	507.4	508.7	510.7	513.0	513.8	512.0	516.8	518.8	523.8	510.4
2005	518.3	522.2	524.1	529.6	532.3	536.2	538.6	540.3	541.5	544.5	548.0	554.2	535.8
2006	544.3	548.5	552.0	552.7	554.7	556.2	552.9	553.6	551.6	552.9	553.9	558.3	552.6
2007	546.7	550.3	552.3	550.0	550.5	551.7	548.2	546.5	543.3	541.1	542.0	543.7	547.2
2008	533.4	534.2	534.2	528.5	527.8	525.7	520.9	518.4	513.9	509.9	507.6	508.1	521.9
2009	493.7	491.7	489.9	487.9	487.1	486.5	481.3	479.0	474.6	474.3	471.6	472.3	482.5
Professional and Business Services													
1990	327.0	337.5	345.9	344.6	345.3	351.0	343.4	348.1	348.1	350.9	354.4	352.2	345.7
2000	922.5	937.0	956.3	952.0	956.4	964.4	955.0	967.4	978.7	974.8	984.7	992.8	961.8
2001	972.9	996.6	1008.9	999.6	999.9	1001.6	986.3	991.8	990.3	987.0	988.5	989.1	992.7
2002	966.7	988.1	1002.3	1003.3	1004.4	1001.9	990.8	986.2	987.6	992.1	1004.1	1011.0	994.9
2003	992.8	1011.1	1027.9	1025.3	1016.0	1012.5	993.7	996.6	996.7	1014.7	1015.4	1021.2	1010.3
2004	1015.5	1035.1	1051.6	1071.0	1069.2	1074.5	1068.0	1069.1	1065.2	1088.7	1105.3	1122.1	1069.6
2005	1105.0	1126.4	1133.2	1142.8	1142.7	1144.2	1141.9	1151.8	1161.1	1153.5	1167.4	1177.9	1145.7
2006	1157.3	1172.4	1192.5	1189.1	1195.5	1202.2	1189.0	1198.7	1204.0	1195.9	1208.9	1220.1	1193.8
2007	1201.3	1216.7	1227.8	1216.1	1212.1	1209.9	1189.3	1192.9	1186.2	1185.5	1190.9	1194.7	1202.0
2008	1148.0	1163.1	1167.2	1149.9	1141.7	1134.5	1113.4	1112.3	1109.3	1105.5	1099.4	1098.3	1128.6
2009	1059.5	1060.6	1058.2	1049.4	1044.6	1042.6	1029.1	1028.9	1028.1	1032.7	1041.5	1054.5	1044.1
Education and Health Services													
1990	590.0	595.7	599.7	598.9	601.3	602.3	594.6	600.0	608.7	613.8	618.3	621.4	603.7
2000	818.6	826.3	833.2	829.9	832.1	832.9	828.4	835.2	844.6	847.9	853.2	858.4	836.7
2001	841.5	850.2	855.2	856.3	859.6	861.8	852.3	860.0	868.6	873.6	878.3	884.4	861.8
2002	867.6	875.4	883.0	879.9	883.2	881.9	872.0	881.4	889.7	896.0	902.1	906.4	884.9
2003	897.9	908.2	914.0	912.9	916.3	914.4	907.4	916.2	926.1	928.8	931.4	936.8	917.5
2004	930.3	938.4	942.6	945.5	948.2	944.2	936.2	941.6	943.0	950.4	956.3	959.3	944.7
2005	950.3	959.1	962.2	966.9	968.3	962.9	958.3	967.4	975.1	977.0	980.4	985.9	967.8
2006	974.6	983.0	989.6	989.8	993.7	991.1	982.1	992.9	1000.3	1002.2	1008.8	1014.6	993.6
2007	1004.5	1015.5	1020.8	1022.8	1025.2	1023.1	1009.9	1021.6	1029.5	1032.8	1039.3	1044.1	1024.1
2008	1034.3	1043.9	1048.4	1046.1	1048.8	1041.9	1030.3	1038.1	1044.4	1050.5	1057.5	1062.0	1045.5
2009	1045.0	1050.8	1055.9	1054.9	1057.6	1051.0	1042.7	1049.2	1056.5	1070.9	1079.2	1078.5	1057.7
Leisure and Hospitality													
1990	685.1	707.9	725.7	714.8	705.8	700.6	684.0	683.0	672.4	663.3	674.8	682.4	691.7
2000	812.9	831.4	849.0	853.8	846.2	845.1	831.8	829.9	826.3	831.7	845.7	854.3	838.2
2001	842.8	863.4	882.0	874.2	872.3	866.3	844.9	844.0	837.9	827.1	834.4	840.6	852.5
2002	833.0	853.1	872.4	872.8	869.5	867.8	846.5	848.9	843.2	842.8	855.0	864.5	855.8
2003	856.0	871.0	889.0	882.4	877.2	874.9	861.2	861.9	859.8	861.1	874.6	887.6	871.4
2004	890.3	909.1	927.7	927.6	920.5	915.9	903.3	900.2	886.0	894.8	911.6	924.1	909.3
2005	914.1	933.6	950.0	951.4	946.1	943.4	923.9	926.0	923.1	918.7	931.6	941.7	933.6
2006	931.5	950.8	970.0	962.8	958.5	954.3	935.3	936.7	932.1	928.8	947.9	956.6	947.1
2007	949.2	971.6	994.2	989.3	984.0	975.6	954.5	953.9	945.8	942.3	961.2	968.7	965.9
2008	956.3	978.1	996.1	987.9	976.3	964.9	941.4	934.2	921.2	916.9	927.5	931.4	952.7
2009	916.3	930.9	946.8	943.9	930.7	917.6	896.6	888.5	880.9	882.3	890.3	892.9	909.8
Other Services													
1990	228.5	231.1	233.4	232.0	231.9	233.0	231.1	231.2	230.4	229.3	230.2	230.8	231.1
2000	291.8	294.2	297.4	297.5	299.2	301.4	300.0	299.1	300.5	301.9	301.9	302.8	299.0
2001	299.0	301.5	304.2	302.7	304.3	307.4	304.6	305.0	305.3	304.7	306.8	308.6	304.5
2002	309.3	311.9	315.6	312.5	314.0	315.7	313.7	314.8	315.1	318.0	320.4	321.6	315.2
2003	320.6	323.6	326.6	325.5	325.8	326.6	320.7	319.1	319.9	318.7	318.7	321.3	322.3
2004	323.9	326.4	327.6	329.1	330.4	333.5	330.7	330.0	329.4	328.4	331.6	331.8	329.4
2005	332.1	334.4	335.6	336.6	337.2	337.3	334.8	334.0	335.9	332.4	333.5	334.9	334.9
2006	330.6	334.2	337.6	336.4	338.6	341.5	336.6	337.0	338.8	339.2	341.8	343.8	338.0
2007	343.7	347.4	351.9	348.0	348.2	349.0	342.1	341.6	341.4	341.9	344.5	346.9	345.6
2008	343.5	346.1	348.2	343.8	342.9	340.9	333.9	332.3	327.5	324.4	321.7	319.7	335.4
2009	315.9	316.1	317.0	316.9	316.3	315.1	311.6	310.6	310.0	309.2	308.8	310.6	313.2
Government													
1990	829.5	842.5	853.6	855.6	869.7	852.6	797.6	789.0	854.4	870.5	875.0	870.2	846.6
2000	991.6	1001.5	1009.7	1014.6	1034.1	948.3	932.7	1005.7	1009.9	1018.2	1025.4	1029.1	1001.7
2001	1014.7	1028.2	1034.3	1035.2	1036.6	968.8	952.9	1033.2	1039.2	1041.7	1047.8	1049.2	1023.4
2002	1033.9	1044.2	1048.8	1049.3	1053.7	977.9	964.0	1048.2	1056.6	1062.0	1064.8	1067.5	1039.2
2003	1052.7	1063.5	1067.1	1065.6	1072.0	993.9	981.0	1057.0	1062.9	1071.0	1073.8	1075.7	1053.0
2004	1064.6	1077.8	1080.6	1079.5	1079.5	1003.5	992.2	1071.5	1076.1	1083.9	1091.9	1093.3	1066.2
2005	1081.1	1093.5	1095.8	1095.5	1098.7	999.2	1000.7	1083.1	1097.9	1108.1	1110.9	1109.6	1081.2
2006	1100.3	1110.9	1114.7	1111.4	1107.9	1014.1	1014.8	1102.9	1115.1	1128.9	1136.7	1133.4	1099.3
2007	1123.8	1135.1	1140.6	1139.2	1135.6	1041.0	1041.1	1130.1	1138.2	1145.6	1151.3	1149.4	1122.6
2008	1140.3	1151.8	1149.2	1146.9	1140.9	1044.7	1043.8	1133.1	1142.2	1145.9	1144.8	1139.5	1126.9
2009	1133.7	1139.1	1136.8	1142.6	1130.4	1035.5	1037.1	1120.4	1130.9	1140.5	1140.6	1130.2	1118.2

Average Weekly Hours by Selected Industry: Florida, 2007–2009

(Not seasonally adjusted.)

Industry and year	January	February	March	April	May	June	July	August	September	October	November	December	Annual average
Total Private													
2007	35.2	35.7	35.2	35.9	35.1	35.4	35.6	35.2	35.4	35.0	35.2	35.7	35.4
2008	35.7	35.1	35.3	35.0	35.0	36.2	35.4	35.1	34.9	35.1	35.2	34.8	35.2
2009	34.6	35.0	34.9	34.8	34.7	34.8	35.0	35.2	35.1	34.9	35.4	35.4	35.0
Goods-Producing													
2007	40.9	40.5	40.9	41.3	40.3	39.5	40.2	39.9	39.9	39.6	40.5	41.9	40.4
2008	39.9	39.8	40.1	38.9	39.8	39.7	39.5	39.8	40.6	39.9	38.8	38.6	39.6
2009	37.8	38.7	38.5	38.0	38.1	38.4	38.9	39.1	40.2	41.0	41.7	41.8	39.3
Construction													
2007	39.5	39.2	40.3	40.9	39.1	37.8	38.8	38.6	38.6	38.2	39.8	40.1	39.2
2008	38.8	39.3	39.6	38.1	38.8	38.8	39.1	39.7	41.0	40.2	39.3	39.1	39.3
2009	38.3	39.4	39.1	38.3	38.4	38.8	38.4	38.4	38.9	41.0	41.0	40.9	39.2
Manufacturing													
2007	42.9	42.3	41.9	41.8	41.8	41.8	42.1	41.7	41.7	41.5	41.4	44.3	42.1
2008	41.1	40.3	40.6	39.7	40.8	40.7	39.7	39.7	40.1	39.7	38.3	38.0	39.9
2009	37.3	37.8	38.0	37.5	37.5	37.7	37.3	38.0	37.8	37.4	38.2	39.0	37.8
Trade, Transportation, and Utilities													
2007	34.2	34.7	33.5	33.8	34.0	34.1	34.4	34.3	34.4	33.7	33.5	34.6	34.1
2008	33.9	34.3	34.7	34.3	34.1	34.7	34.5	34.1	34.1	34.3	35.1	34.6	34.4
2009	34.6	35.1	35.0	34.8	34.9	34.7	34.8	35.0	34.7	34.6	35.0	35.1	34.9
Financial Activities													
2007	36.1	36.9	36.3	38.5	36.1	36.7	37.5	37.1	38.0	37.0	36.1	37.2	37.0
2008	36.4	36.5	36.9	36.4	36.2	37.0	36.6	37.0	37.0	37.0	37.4	37.5	36.8
2009	37.6	37.3	37.2	37.6	37.5	37.6	37.5	37.8	37.3	37.1	37.8	38.1	37.5
Professional and Business Services													
2007	34.9	36.5	36.2	37.4	37.5	37.8	37.9	37.8	38.2	37.8	37.6	37.9	37.3
2008	42.3	37.1	37.2	36.7	36.7	37.4	36.7	36.4	36.4	36.8	36.7	36.1	37.2
2009	35.7	36.3	36.1	36.3	36.2	36.9	36.9	37.1	37.2	36.8	37.2	36.6	36.6
Education and Health Services													
2007	35.3	36.0	35.8	36.1	34.8	36.0	35.7	34.8	35.3	34.9	36.1	35.1	35.5
2008	34.4	34.7	34.4	35.3	34.8	34.5	35.2	34.7	34.8	34.8	35.2	35.2	34.8
2009	35.4	35.7	35.7	35.7	35.7	35.3	35.6	35.2	35.2	35.1	35.3	35.3	35.4
Leisure and Hospitality													
2007	29.1	29.6	29.0	29.9	27.9	28.7	28.7	28.2	27.3	28.0	28.1	28.3	28.6
2008	26.9	29.1	29.4	29.1	29.2	28.9	28.8	28.4	27.4	28.4	28.6	27.9	28.5
2009	28.0	28.4	28.2	28.4	27.9	27.7	28.2	28.5	28.4	28.2	28.6	29.6	28.3
Other Services													
2007	34.3	34.4	34.0	34.0	34.0	33.6	33.7	33.8	34.4	33.4	34.4	35.3	34.1
2008	34.2	34.1	34.2	34.7	34.2	35.3	34.4	34.8	34.9	34.4	34.5	34.5	34.5
2009	34.0	33.8	34.2	33.8	33.9	33.8	33.6	34.0	34.3	34.4	34.9	34.7	34.1

Average Hourly Earnings by Selected Industry: Florida, 2007–2009

(Dollars, not seasonally adjusted.)

Industry and year	January	February	March	April	May	June	July	August	September	October	November	December	Annual average
Total Private													
2007	35.20	35.70	35.20	35.90	35.10	35.40	35.60	35.20	35.40	35.00	35.20	35.70	35.40
2008	35.70	35.10	35.30	35.00	35.00	36.20	35.40	35.10	34.90	35.10	35.20	34.80	35.20
2009	34.60	35.00	34.90	34.80	34.70	34.80	35.00	35.20	35.10	34.90	35.40	35.40	35.00
Goods-Producing													
2007	40.90	40.50	40.90	41.30	40.30	39.50	40.20	39.90	39.90	39.60	40.50	41.90	40.40
2008	39.90	39.80	40.10	38.90	39.80	39.70	39.50	39.80	40.60	39.90	38.80	38.60	39.60
2009	37.80	38.70	38.50	38.00	38.10	38.40	38.90	39.10	40.20	41.00	41.70	41.80	39.30
Construction													
2007	39.50	39.20	40.30	40.90	39.10	37.80	38.80	38.60	38.60	38.20	39.80	40.10	39.20
2008	38.80	39.30	39.60	38.10	38.80	38.80	39.10	39.70	41.00	40.20	39.30	39.10	39.30
2009	38.30	39.40	39.10	38.30	38.40	38.80	38.40	38.40	38.90	41.00	41.00	40.90	39.20
Manufacturing													
2007	42.90	42.30	41.90	41.80	41.80	41.80	42.10	41.70	41.70	41.50	41.40	44.30	42.10
2008	41.10	40.30	40.60	39.70	40.80	40.70	39.70	39.70	40.10	39.70	38.30	38.00	39.90
2009	37.30	37.80	38.00	37.50	37.50	37.70	37.30	38.00	37.80	37.40	38.20	39.00	37.80
Trade, Transportation, and Utilities													
2007	34.20	34.70	33.50	33.80	34.00	34.10	34.40	34.30	34.40	33.70	33.50	34.60	34.10
2008	33.90	34.30	34.70	34.30	34.10	34.70	34.50	34.10	34.10	34.30	35.10	34.60	34.40
2009	34.60	35.10	35.00	34.80	34.90	34.70	34.80	35.00	34.70	34.60	35.00	35.10	34.90
Financial Activities													
2007	36.10	36.90	36.30	38.50	36.10	36.70	37.50	37.10	38.00	37.00	36.10	37.20	37.00
2008	36.40	36.50	36.90	36.40	36.20	37.00	36.60	37.00	37.00	37.00	37.40	37.50	36.80
2009	37.60	37.30	37.20	37.60	37.50	37.60	37.50	37.80	37.30	37.10	37.80	38.10	37.50
Professional and Business Services													
2007	34.90	36.50	36.20	37.40	37.50	37.80	37.90	37.80	38.20	37.80	37.60	37.90	37.30
2008	42.30	37.10	37.20	36.70	36.70	37.40	36.70	36.40	36.40	36.80	36.70	36.10	37.20
2009	35.70	36.30	36.10	36.30	36.20	36.90	36.90	37.10	37.20	36.80	37.20	36.60	36.60
Education and Health Services													
2007	35.30	36.00	35.80	36.10	34.80	36.00	35.70	34.80	35.30	34.90	36.10	35.10	35.50
2008	34.40	34.70	34.40	35.30	34.80	34.50	35.20	34.70	34.80	34.80	35.20	35.20	34.80
2009	35.40	35.70	35.70	35.70	35.70	35.30	35.60	35.20	35.20	35.10	35.30	35.30	35.40
Leisure and Hospitality													
2007	29.10	29.60	29.00	29.90	27.90	28.70	28.70	28.20	27.30	28.00	28.10	28.30	28.60
2008	28.90	29.10	29.40	29.10	29.20	28.90	28.80	28.40	27.40	28.40	28.60	27.90	28.50
2009	28.00	28.40	28.20	28.40	27.90	27.70	28.20	28.50	28.40	28.20	28.60	29.60	28.30
Other Services													
2007	34.30	34.40	34.00	34.00	34.00	33.60	33.70	33.80	34.40	33.40	34.40	35.30	34.10
2008	34.20	34.10	34.20	34.70	34.20	35.30	34.40	34.80	34.90	34.40	34.50	34.50	34.50
2009	34.00	33.80	34.20	33.80	33.90	33.80	33.60	34.00	34.30	34.40	34.90	34.70	34.10

Average Weekly Earnings by Selected Industry: Florida, 2007–2009

(Dollars, not seasonally adjusted.)

Industry and year	January	February	March	April	May	June	July	August	September	October	November	December	Annual average
Total Private													
2007	711.39	721.50	709.98	719.80	714.29	727.12	741.19	732.51	741.28	722.40	730.05	765.77	728.53
2008	736.85	727.27	760.01	732.90	734.65	754.41	734.55	734.99	730.81	739.56	748.70	745.42	739.20
2009	744.25	758.80	753.49	743.68	749.52	744.02	757.05	767.36	758.86	755.93	771.37	766.06	756.35
Goods-Producing													
2007	829.86	824.18	834.77	828.89	810.43	792.77	810.43	831.52	816.75	810.61	845.64	870.26	824.16
2008	834.71	817.09	866.56	813.40	831.82	832.11	840.17	867.64	863.16	859.85	836.92	868.50	843.48
2009	867.13	879.26	894.74	862.22	872.11	864.77	894.31	903.99	906.91	931.52	942.84	981.05	898.79
Construction													
2007	795.14	780.86	821.72	814.32	778.48	743.53	765.14	766.60	765.82	763.24	800.38	823.65	783.61
2008	785.70	774.21	779.33	750.57	753.11	752.72	794.12	845.21	842.14	824.50	804.86	855.12	795.43
2009	842.22	850.25	853.16	836.86	835.58	843.12	857.86	861.70	872.14	910.61	880.68	898.98	860.83
Manufacturing													
2007	879.45	886.19	858.11	846.45	849.79	857.32	871.89	920.74	885.29	873.99	907.07	935.17	880.73
2008	894.75	870.08	906.60	879.36	895.97	903.54	892.85	892.85	874.98	875.78	864.43	872.48	885.38
2009	890.35	904.55	937.46	906.38	907.50	906.69	908.26	931.76	922.32	934.63	977.16	983.97	925.72
Trade, Transportation, and Utilities													
2007	632.02	657.57	640.86	646.93	656.20	663.93	671.14	654.79	672.86	645.69	642.87	650.83	653.02
2008	636.64	642.10	650.63	636.61	634.26	659.30	651.71	635.97	638.69	650.67	667.60	660.86	647.06
2009	658.09	669.71	671.30	651.80	658.56	647.85	660.85	672.70	670.06	662.94	684.25	674.97	665.89
Financial Activities													
2007	842.21	874.16	852.32	868.95	837.16	873.83	861.00	823.25	856.52	824.36	820.55	888.34	852.85
2008	829.56	830.74	870.47	839.02	830.79	879.86	849.85	862.84	865.43	866.91	914.06	933.38	863.70
2009	951.28	998.15	994.36	1015.20	1015.13	1007.68	1020.00	1053.86	1016.80	1012.83	1042.15	1014.22	1010.63
Professional and Business Services													
2007	764.66	797.16	790.61	849.73	841.13	870.16	896.71	896.24	916.42	879.61	895.63	921.35	859.77
2008	1002.93	886.32	896.15	889.98	889.98	851.97	876.03	857.22	842.30	854.86	856.58	819.47	877.18
2009	828.24	850.87	849.07	853.05	852.51	868.63	880.07	887.80	876.80	868.85	875.69	865.22	862.66
Education and Health Services													
2007	773.78	778.68	775.07	779.04	774.65	806.40	819.32	800.40	803.43	793.28	807.56	785.19	791.65
2008	640.18	791.16	798.42	768.48	796.57	795.57	804.67	787.69	793.09	811.54	821.22	839.87	786.83
2009	806.77	812.18	820.03	816.82	818.60	829.90	833.75	828.61	823.33	817.13	820.02	820.02	819.86
Leisure and Hospitality													
2007	389.07	405.82	399.04	397.97	390.32	393.76	410.70	399.03	386.30	384.72	379.07	390.54	394.39
2008	378.21	396.05	405.13	417.59	421.65	409.51	404.35	404.13	391.27	393.34	397.54	385.30	400.14
2009	386.68	392.20	394.24	412.37	405.39	392.51	397.62	397.29	395.04	398.75	411.27	419.73	399.60
Other Services													
2007	639.01	637.43	576.98	587.18	592.28	585.31	592.78	610.77	638.12	640.28	661.86	729.30	624.03
2008	715.81	707.58	733.59	766.52	744.53	768.48	713.11	723.49	715.45	690.06	682.76	693.80	721.40
2009	701.08	696.62	713.07	703.04	703.09	698.98	694.85	692.24	703.49	714.83	730.11	728.01	706.21

GEORGIA
At a Glance

Population:
  1990 census: 6,478,149
  2000 census: 8,186,453
  2009 estimate: 9,829,211

Percent change in population:
  1990–2000: 26.4%
  2000–2009: 20.1%

Percent change in total nonfarm employment:
  1990–2009: 29.6%
  2008–2009: -5.5%

Industry with the largest growth in employment, 1990–2009 (thousands):
  Education and Health Services, 231.1

Industry with the largest decline or smallest growth in employment, 1990–2009 (thousands):
  Manufacturing, -165.9

Civilian labor force:
  1990: 3,300,136
  2000: 4,242,889
  2009: 4,768,923

Unemployment rate and rank among states (lowest to highest):
  1990: 5.2%, 22nd
  2000: 3.5%, 19th
  2009: 9.6%, 35th

Employment by Industry, 2009

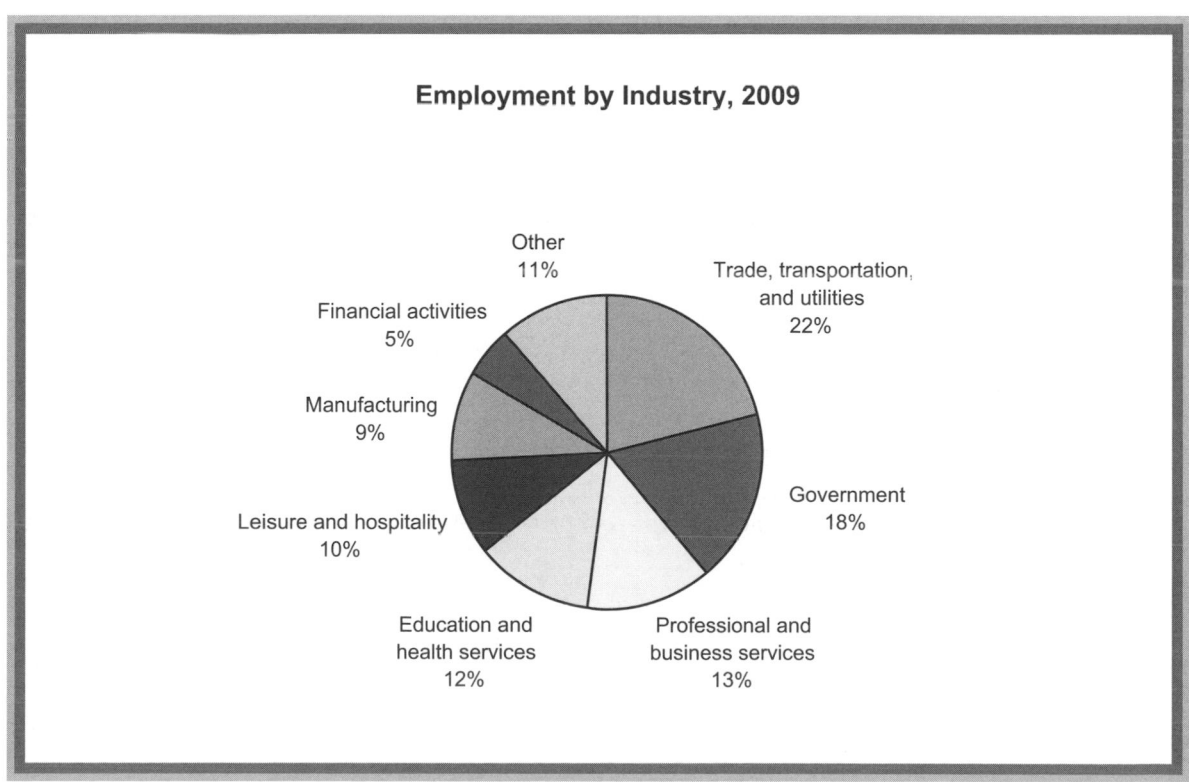

- Other 11%
- Trade, transportation, and utilities 22%
- Financial activities 5%
- Manufacturing 9%
- Government 18%
- Leisure and hospitality 10%
- Education and health services 12%
- Professional and business services 13%

Employment by Industry: Georgia, Selected Years, 1990–2009

(Numbers in thousands, not seasonally adjusted.)

Industry and year	January	February	March	April	May	June	July	August	September	October	November	December	Annual average
Total Nonfarm													
1990	2938.9	2951.1	2980.0	2979.7	3000.0	3024.6	2999.0	3010.7	3012.8	2994.8	3004.6	3005.2	2991.8
2000	3851.6	3880.3	3922.3	3925.6	3958.4	3971.6	3944.4	3970.6	3978.7	3982.0	3994.0	4012.1	3949.3
2001	3931.3	3945.2	3971.8	3951.7	3958.3	3962.4	3915.3	3947.1	3939.0	3929.7	3933.0	3934.7	3943.2
2002	3816.3	3833.3	3860.3	3870.6	3885.1	3895.3	3841.1	3875.6	3874.5	3881.8	3896.8	3903.3	3869.5
2003	3797.4	3809.7	3832.0	3836.4	3847.1	3842.0	3819.9	3858.1	3865.3	3861.1	3878.0	3892.1	3844.9
2004	3816.2	3836.1	3864.9	3888.9	3898.9	3892.0	3883.7	3920.8	3907.9	3943.5	3961.9	3967.3	3898.5
2005	3908.8	3929.5	3937.0	3993.3	4011.1	3996.2	3982.7	4032.3	4031.3	4044.6	4071.8	4076.0	4001.2
2006	4016.0	4037.5	4056.5	4082.6	4098.5	4091.0	4057.9	4099.9	4096.7	4128.1	4150.7	4153.6	4089.1
2007	4094.3	4114.8	4130.9	4140.2	4158.8	4147.3	4115.8	4160.0	4154.3	4164.0	4184.8	4181.1	4145.5
2008	4110.8	4130.7	4131.8	4137.5	4148.4	4120.4	4079.7	4107.4	4084.3	4074.6	4061.7	4039.3	4102.2
2009	3932.7	3922.7	3907.7	3912.7	3911.4	3878.6	3836.0	3847.0	3836.2	3844.9	3854.6	3835.0	3876.6
Total Private													
1990	2412.4	2421.5	2445.1	2446.8	2459.3	2485.2	2474.7	2489.0	2487.1	2459.4	2467.2	2470.9	2459.9
2000	3259.3	3283.4	3321.3	3324.6	3346.2	3374.5	3367.3	3385.6	3384.2	3381.8	3391.6	3408.3	3352.3
2001	3331.1	3339.2	3363.0	3342.8	3347.4	3356.2	3329.9	3340.8	3323.7	3308.9	3309.2	3312.3	3333.7
2002	3200.2	3214.7	3235.8	3245.1	3258.1	3277.2	3243.6	3255.3	3242.5	3248.3	3260.8	3270.4	3246.0
2003	3166.0	3173.4	3194.2	3199.4	3212.5	3220.4	3217.1	3237.0	3233.4	3224.1	3239.6	3255.1	3214.4
2004	3188.6	3201.5	3229.1	3246.9	3259.8	3267.9	3277.8	3289.1	3266.5	3299.7	3314.7	3323.6	3263.8
2005	3269.0	3282.3	3288.4	3344.6	3362.8	3360.8	3366.3	3385.1	3377.6	3387.6	3412.6	3417.7	3354.6
2006	3362.9	3376.8	3393.7	3421.8	3438.1	3439.4	3430.7	3444.8	3431.4	3457.7	3476.5	3480.3	3429.5
2007	3427.5	3439.1	3453.6	3464.9	3483.6	3483.6	3476.6	3494.4	3478.5	3480.8	3498.1	3495.4	3473.0
2008	3426.5	3436.4	3435.9	3443.2	3453.6	3437.8	3418.7	3422.2	3394.5	3374.7	3357.0	3337.9	3411.5
2009	3237.0	3221.1	3205.6	3210.9	3213.8	3196.4	3179.6	3174.8	3150.5	3150.6	3160.1	3145.7	3187.2
Goods-Producing													
1990	681.3	684.7	690.8	692.5	694.6	703.5	692.4	693.7	689.6	681.0	676.1	669.6	687.5
2000	752.0	755.8	762.8	761.5	764.2	769.3	762.0	764.7	762.5	755.7	751.8	752.4	759.6
2001	741.9	742.8	743.3	735.7	733.5	733.9	722.9	723.6	717.8	707.3	700.4	699.3	725.2
2002	678.4	684.1	686.8	685.7	686.3	687.6	684.3	684.0	680.5	675.5	672.7	670.2	681.3
2003	658.4	661.6	661.2	658.9	661.0	661.6	656.5	658.8	659.4	658.3	656.6	658.9	659.3
2004	648.2	651.5	655.3	656.1	656.7	661.5	664.8	666.3	662.7	667.2	666.5	666.7	660.3
2005	657.2	659.5	658.8	668.0	672.1	673.5	673.9	678.3	678.0	674.2	678.1	677.2	670.7
2006	672.0	674.8	676.1	679.0	681.9	685.0	681.7	684.7	682.0	678.8	674.4	671.7	678.5
2007	667.6	668.5	667.8	667.3	669.0	669.2	666.2	667.2	662.3	657.7	657.3	654.0	664.5
2008	643.8	642.3	638.7	634.4	633.7	631.0	626.0	623.5	617.0	608.9	596.9	586.9	623.6
2009	567.3	558.6	551.9	544.1	541.1	534.4	526.4	523.3	519.4	512.0	511.0	504.6	532.8
Mining and Logging													
1990	16.1	16.1	16.1	16.2	16.1	16.2	16.0	16.1	16.0	15.8	15.7	15.7	16.0
2000	14.0	14.2	14.2	13.8	13.9	13.9	14.0	14.0	13.9	13.8	13.8	13.8	13.9
2001	13.6	13.5	13.5	13.2	13.2	13.2	13.1	13.2	13.0	12.9	12.9	12.8	13.2
2002	12.7	12.7	12.8	12.6	12.6	12.6	12.1	12.3	12.2	11.9	11.8	12.0	12.4
2003	12.1	12.1	12.1	12.2	12.4	12.4	12.3	12.4	12.4	12.3	12.4	12.4	12.3
2004	12.3	12.2	12.2	12.1	12.1	12.2	12.3	12.3	12.2	12.1	12.1	12.2	12.2
2005	11.8	11.9	11.9	12.1	12.2	12.2	12.3	12.3	12.2	12.1	12.1	12.1	12.1
2006	12.4	12.1	12.1	12.3	12.3	12.3	12.3	12.3	12.1	12.2	12.1	12.1	12.2
2007	12.1	12.1	12.1	12.0	12.0	11.9	11.9	11.9	11.8	11.7	11.6	11.4	11.9
2008	10.8	10.6	10.5	10.5	10.4	10.3	10.3	10.3	10.3	10.3	10.2	10.1	10.4
2009	9.7	9.5	9.3	9.4	9.4	9.4	9.3	9.3	9.2	9.1	9.1	9.0	9.3
Construction													
1990	142.5	144.6	147.8	147.9	149.7	154.6	152.9	153.6	151.2	148.9	146.8	142.4	148.6
2000	198.1	200.6	205.8	205.5	207.5	211.8	211.2	211.4	211.4	209.9	207.6	207.9	207.4
2001	201.9	203.6	205.3	207.1	209.1	211.3	211.0	211.0	208.7	207.3	204.9	203.7	207.1
2002	195.2	197.8	199.1	198.3	199.0	200.0	199.3	199.5	198.2	196.5	195.8	194.3	197.8
2003	188.5	190.0	191.7	191.2	193.1	194.7	196.9	197.9	198.9	199.0	198.6	199.1	195.0
2004	193.7	193.3	196.0	196.8	197.2	200.4	203.7	203.6	200.9	204.4	204.0	203.7	199.8
2005	199.8	200.6	200.0	206.3	209.1	210.0	212.2	213.9	213.4	213.4	214.6	212.7	208.8
2006	209.2	211.0	212.5	215.4	217.9	220.6	223.0	224.5	223.7	223.6	222.9	221.4	218.8
2007	218.6	220.2	221.3	221.7	223.2	224.1	223.0	224.1	221.7	220.7	219.5	216.6	221.2
2008	211.1	211.4	209.9	208.7	209.5	208.1	206.9	204.5	201.2	197.4	193.0	187.7	204.1
2009	177.8	175.9	172.9	170.4	170.0	167.9	164.6	162.0	159.3	160.6	160.4	156.1	166.5
Manufacturing													
1990	522.7	524.0	526.9	528.4	528.8	532.7	523.5	524.0	522.4	516.3	513.6	511.5	522.9
2000	539.9	541.0	542.8	542.2	542.8	543.6	536.8	539.3	537.2	532.0	530.4	530.7	538.2
2001	526.4	525.7	524.5	515.4	511.2	509.4	498.8	499.4	496.1	487.1	482.6	482.8	505.0
2002	470.5	473.6	474.9	474.8	474.7	475.0	472.9	472.2	470.1	467.1	465.1	463.9	471.2
2003	457.8	459.5	457.4	455.5	455.5	454.5	447.3	448.5	448.1	447.0	445.6	447.4	452.0
2004	442.2	446.0	447.1	447.2	447.4	448.9	448.8	450.4	449.6	450.7	450.4	450.8	448.3
2005	445.6	447.0	446.9	449.6	450.8	451.3	449.4	452.1	452.4	448.7	451.4	452.4	449.8
2006	450.4	451.7	451.5	451.3	451.7	452.1	446.4	447.9	446.2	443.0	439.4	438.2	447.5
2007	436.9	436.2	434.4	433.6	433.8	433.2	431.3	431.2	428.8	425.3	426.2	426.0	431.4
2008	421.9	420.3	418.3	415.2	413.8	412.6	408.8	408.7	405.5	401.2	393.7	389.1	409.1
2009	379.8	373.2	369.7	364.3	361.7	357.1	352.5	352.0	350.9	342.3	341.5	339.5	357.0

Employment by Industry: Georgia, Selected Years, 1990–2009—*Continued*

(Numbers in thousands, not seasonally adjusted.)

Industry and year	January	February	March	April	May	June	July	August	September	October	November	December	Annual average
Service-Providing													
1990	2257.6	2266.4	2289.2	2287.2	2305.4	2321.1	2306.6	2317.0	2323.2	2313.8	2328.5	2335.6	2304.3
2000	3099.6	3124.5	3159.5	3164.1	3194.2	3202.3	3182.4	3205.9	3216.2	3226.3	3242.2	3259.7	3189.7
2001	3189.4	3202.4	3228.5	3216.0	3224.8	3228.5	3192.4	3223.5	3221.2	3222.4	3232.6	3235.4	3218.1
2002	3137.9	3149.2	3173.5	3184.9	3198.8	3207.7	3156.8	3191.6	3194.0	3206.3	3224.1	3233.1	3188.2
2003	3139.0	3148.1	3170.8	3177.5	3186.1	3180.4	3163.4	3199.3	3205.9	3202.8	3221.4	3233.2	3185.7
2004	3168.0	3184.6	3209.6	3232.8	3242.2	3230.5	3218.9	3254.5	3245.2	3276.3	3295.4	3300.6	3238.2
2005	3251.6	3270.0	3278.2	3325.3	3339.0	3322.7	3308.8	3354.0	3353.3	3370.4	3393.7	3398.8	3330.5
2006	3344.0	3362.7	3380.4	3403.6	3416.6	3406.0	3376.2	3415.2	3414.7	3449.3	3476.3	3481.9	3410.6
2007	3426.7	3446.3	3463.1	3472.9	3489.8	3478.1	3449.6	3492.8	3492.0	3506.3	3527.5	3527.1	3481.0
2008	3467.0	3488.4	3493.1	3503.1	3514.7	3489.4	3453.7	3483.9	3467.3	3465.7	3464.8	3452.4	3478.6
2009	3365.4	3364.1	3355.8	3368.6	3370.3	3344.2	3309.6	3323.7	3316.8	3332.9	3343.6	3330.4	3343.8
Trade, Transportation, and Utilities													
1990	655.2	653.4	657.0	656.3	659.9	665.8	669.0	673.6	675.3	672.3	681.8	691.5	667.6
2000	851.3	853.1	861.7	863.2	867.0	870.9	865.2	871.2	871.2	877.6	890.8	902.5	870.5
2001	872.0	866.0	870.9	856.2	857.6	858.9	858.5	859.1	858.1	857.0	867.5	873.7	863.0
2002	835.1	830.5	834.0	833.7	837.1	840.5	832.8	834.1	833.4	844.5	858.4	871.0	840.4
2003	819.0	814.2	818.2	814.4	818.6	819.5	820.2	823.9	824.7	828.5	842.1	851.4	824.6
2004	817.4	813.9	820.0	820.9	825.7	826.3	829.5	830.8	826.6	837.8	852.4	860.6	830.2
2005	832.8	831.4	833.1	846.2	850.1	848.4	856.3	855.2	853.3	861.4	878.8	887.7	852.9
2006	856.2	853.7	857.4	865.0	870.4	869.0	865.2	867.3	866.9	880.1	898.6	906.2	871.3
2007	880.7	874.8	877.1	878.5	884.2	884.7	885.1	885.7	884.9	889.9	906.6	910.7	886.9
2008	883.5	879.3	880.2	876.6	877.7	874.0	873.1	872.3	867.6	864.4	868.6	869.6	873.9
2009	834.9	824.0	819.8	816.9	819.1	815.6	814.4	814.3	809.3	808.9	818.5	823.1	818.2
Wholesale Trade													
1990	158.8	159.5	160.5	156.4	156.5	158.2	162.1	162.6	163.1	162.0	161.6	161.6	160.2
2000	209.2	210.7	212.5	213.2	214.1	215.4	214.3	215.1	214.8	215.5	214.8	215.0	213.7
2001	215.5	215.7	216.4	212.5	212.2	213.1	214.4	213.7	212.8	211.7	210.2	209.1	213.1
2002	206.0	206.1	207.4	207.2	207.2	207.7	206.3	205.9	205.0	207.6	206.7	206.7	206.7
2003	204.0	204.3	205.3	204.6	205.1	205.0	205.3	205.3	205.4	204.9	205.4	206.2	205.1
2004	202.8	202.9	204.2	205.7	206.8	207.2	207.7	208.3	207.2	209.1	209.2	209.6	206.7
2005	207.9	209.0	209.1	211.5	211.8	211.8	212.7	213.4	213.6	213.5	213.7	214.2	211.9
2006	211.8	212.6	213.0	214.2	215.8	215.4	216.2	216.3	216.5	219.2	218.2	218.4	215.6
2007	216.7	217.4	217.5	218.8	219.1	218.8	219.4	219.5	219.0	219.8	220.0	219.6	218.8
2008	218.0	218.8	218.2	219.0	219.0	218.0	217.7	217.9	217.0	216.2	213.8	211.6	217.1
2009	206.8	204.8	202.1	201.3	200.1	198.3	198.1	197.4	195.7	193.6	193.2	192.0	198.6
Retail Trade													
1990	358.0	354.0	355.4	355.9	358.7	361.4	359.5	361.5	362.7	361.8	371.7	380.0	361.7
2000	462.1	462.5	467.9	466.3	469.2	471.3	466.9	470.9	470.9	474.0	488.2	499.6	472.5
2001	473.0	467.3	471.6	461.4	462.7	463.0	459.7	461.4	462.0	460.4	475.0	482.3	466.7
2002	453.9	449.3	452.2	449.9	452.4	453.9	449.9	451.3	452.6	453.4	467.3	479.0	455.4
2003	440.7	436.1	438.6	437.6	440.5	441.1	440.8	443.7	443.9	446.9	459.2	467.8	444.7
2004	439.8	436.3	440.1	439.1	441.8	442.3	443.4	443.6	441.2	449.2	462.7	470.9	445.9
2005	447.5	443.6	444.8	454.9	457.7	456.6	460.8	459.5	456.4	464.3	479.3	486.1	459.3
2006	464.3	460.3	462.9	468.0	470.6	468.6	464.0	465.4	463.6	474.1	492.9	497.5	471.0
2007	479.3	472.3	474.0	473.4	476.5	474.7	475.9	475.2	473.9	477.9	494.2	496.3	478.6
2008	474.5	469.2	470.3	466.7	467.0	464.0	464.0	463.5	459.9	459.0	466.0	467.5	466.0
2009	443.3	436.3	435.2	435.5	438.3	436.3	435.7	436.7	433.8	435.5	444.8	448.6	438.3
Transportation and Utilities													
1990	138.4	139.9	141.1	144.0	144.7	146.2	147.4	149.5	149.5	148.5	148.5	149.9	145.6
2000	180.0	179.9	181.3	183.7	183.7	184.2	184.0	185.2	185.5	188.1	187.8	187.9	184.3
2001	183.5	183.0	182.9	182.3	182.7	182.8	184.4	184.0	183.3	184.9	182.3	182.3	183.2
2002	175.2	175.1	174.4	176.6	177.5	178.9	176.6	176.9	175.8	183.5	184.4	185.3	178.4
2003	174.3	173.8	174.3	172.2	173.0	173.4	174.1	174.9	175.4	176.7	177.5	177.4	174.8
2004	174.8	174.7	175.7	176.1	177.1	176.8	178.4	178.9	178.2	179.5	180.5	180.1	177.6
2005	177.4	178.8	179.2	179.8	180.6	180.0	182.8	182.3	183.3	183.6	185.8	187.4	181.8
2006	180.1	180.3	181.5	182.8	184.0	185.0	185.0	185.6	186.8	186.8	187.5	190.3	184.6
2007	184.7	185.1	185.6	186.3	188.6	191.2	189.8	191.0	192.0	192.2	192.4	194.3	189.4
2008	191.0	191.3	191.7	190.9	191.7	192.0	191.4	190.9	190.7	189.2	188.8	190.5	190.8
2009	184.8	182.9	182.5	180.1	180.7	181.0	180.6	180.2	179.8	179.8	180.5	182.5	181.3
Information													
1990	82.3	82.2	82.7	83.8	83.8	85.3	87.1	87.4	87.1	86.3	87.1	87.2	85.2
2000	138.7	139.1	138.8	137.8	139.0	141.6	142.0	143.3	143.2	144.4	145.3	146.7	141.7
2001	143.4	144.1	144.7	142.9	142.9	143.5	141.5	140.8	139.7	139.2	139.7	139.4	141.8
2002	132.5	132.3	130.9	130.2	129.9	129.4	129.0	128.5	127.7	128.2	126.2	126.2	129.2
2003	126.4	125.4	123.3	121.3	120.2	119.7	118.0	117.4	115.0	114.7	115.6	115.4	119.4
2004	114.3	113.9	114.2	115.3	115.0	115.5	114.8	114.3	113.4	112.1	113.0	112.9	114.1
2005	111.9	112.2	112.6	112.5	111.7	113.1	112.5	111.1	111.2	111.7	112.6	113.1	112.2
2006	111.5	111.8	112.5	111.5	112.0	111.6	110.1	110.2	110.2	110.8	111.8	112.3	111.4
2007	112.8	112.5	112.5	111.0	111.6	111.7	111.3	111.4	111.3	110.4	111.0	111.0	111.5
2008	108.7	109.6	109.7	109.5	110.0	110.4	109.3	109.1	108.4	107.3	107.8	107.8	109.0
2009	106.9	106.7	106.1	105.7	105.6	105.4	104.3	103.9	103.5	103.4	103.0	102.6	104.8

Employment by Industry: Georgia, Selected Years, 1990–2009—*Continued*

(Numbers in thousands, not seasonally adjusted.)

Industry and year	January	February	March	April	May	June	July	August	September	October	November	December	Annual average
Financial Activities													
1990	157.4	158.0	159.4	158.5	158.9	160.2	159.7	160.3	159.5	159.0	159.3	160.2	159.2
2000	208.9	209.6	210.3	213.1	213.8	215.6	213.9	213.9	212.3	211.7	211.9	213.5	212.4
2001	210.5	210.8	211.8	213.3	213.5	214.2	216.7	217.1	215.8	215.5	215.5	215.9	214.2
2002	214.4	213.7	213.5	213.6	214.4	215.2	214.8	215.5	214.1	215.8	216.0	217.3	214.9
2003	213.1	213.0	214.6	214.8	216.3	217.7	218.8	219.6	219.3	216.3	216.4	217.2	216.4
2004	214.9	215.9	216.4	217.7	218.0	218.0	219.5	219.7	218.5	221.9	221.8	222.7	218.8
2005	222.3	223.3	223.0	223.9	225.1	225.3	224.7	225.7	225.3	228.0	228.2	229.6	225.4
2006	226.0	227.4	227.8	229.6	230.7	230.6	231.2	232.3	231.7	233.5	233.5	234.1	230.7
2007	230.5	232.1	232.0	231.6	231.7	231.6	232.1	232.0	230.2	230.5	230.4	230.0	231.2
2008	226.3	227.1	226.1	226.3	226.6	225.5	225.6	224.5	222.0	222.5	219.8	219.0	224.3
2009	214.0	213.1	211.0	213.1	213.3	212.8	212.4	211.1	209.1	205.2	204.4	204.9	210.4
Professional and Business Services													
1990	278.1	283.1	286.1	281.0	282.4	286.0	286.6	288.5	288.3	281.4	282.0	281.1	283.7
2000	513.1	519.7	526.4	518.8	522.4	530.5	529.0	533.4	535.1	530.2	529.4	531.5	526.6
2001	517.7	519.3	522.5	517.9	516.4	517.0	515.3	520.3	515.9	513.7	509.4	509.5	516.2
2002	491.0	496.7	499.4	503.8	505.2	506.7	506.5	510.6	507.7	506.5	506.9	505.2	503.9
2003	482.5	487.2	490.0	491.3	489.4	492.2	495.7	501.1	500.6	499.5	500.2	502.6	494.4
2004	495.3	500.5	507.0	509.4	509.7	510.8	516.0	517.8	513.7	523.8	523.1	523.3	512.5
2005	519.1	524.2	524.5	531.0	532.4	533.7	536.4	544.5	545.7	547.5	548.3	546.4	536.1
2006	539.8	543.5	546.2	551.3	550.0	553.3	553.9	556.8	553.8	556.0	556.3	557.5	551.5
2007	549.9	555.1	560.6	558.9	561.8	563.6	562.4	569.7	567.7	569.2	569.7	574.7	563.6
2008	559.0	562.0	559.7	565.8	565.1	565.9	556.2	558.1	553.3	550.1	544.8	540.9	556.7
2009	516.2	514.3	509.6	507.9	505.0	506.9	503.8	501.6	498.4	505.0	506.3	505.1	506.7
Education and Health Services													
1990	241.1	240.2	242.3	243.1	243.4	242.6	241.1	243.1	247.4	248.5	250.2	251.4	244.5
2000	341.7	346.0	347.8	349.9	350.9	350.9	349.9	353.2	356.9	360.8	361.9	361.4	352.6
2001	356.2	359.4	362.6	362.2	362.7	363.4	360.6	364.9	368.7	371.5	373.1	373.4	364.9
2002	366.7	370.5	374.7	375.0	376.0	375.3	373.2	378.5	380.5	382.7	384.8	384.8	376.9
2003	385.1	387.4	392.1	396.0	398.3	396.5	394.4	399.6	401.7	401.9	403.9	405.0	396.8
2004	403.0	406.3	407.7	409.3	410.5	406.6	408.4	413.3	412.5	420.1	421.5	421.0	411.7
2005	418.5	420.5	417.6	426.3	427.8	422.5	424.6	429.1	430.5	434.7	436.1	435.5	427.0
2006	436.3	439.1	438.5	440.8	442.0	436.2	437.6	441.7	442.1	452.9	453.9	453.0	442.8
2007	449.7	453.8	453.0	457.3	458.1	453.4	453.8	460.7	463.0	467.1	468.5	465.9	458.7
2008	462.4	468.0	467.3	468.9	470.6	462.7	463.6	470.4	470.4	475.3	476.5	475.5	469.3
2009	473.3	475.9	473.6	476.4	478.3	470.2	470.7	476.4	474.8	479.2	480.6	477.5	475.6
Leisure and Hospitality													
1990	228.2	230.4	236.4	240.6	244.5	248.6	246.6	249.7	247.3	239.1	238.8	238.2	240.7
2000	319.6	323.1	333.2	336.0	341.4	344.9	348.4	347.9	343.1	338.9	337.1	334.3	337.3
2001	323.5	328.0	335.3	342.2	347.6	350.9	345.1	346.3	340.4	338.4	337.4	335.3	339.2
2002	321.3	325.5	334.4	343.0	348.4	361.0	346.8	347.7	343.0	338.5	338.3	339.1	340.6
2003	328.5	331.4	340.3	348.4	353.1	356.2	356.6	359.6	356.0	349.2	348.9	348.9	348.1
2004	340.6	344.6	352.0	361.2	366.9	370.7	366.9	369.5	363.6	361.8	361.2	361.6	360.1
2005	352.3	355.4	362.9	378.5	384.4	384.9	377.6	380.0	374.6	371.9	371.9	369.9	372.0
2006	364.2	369.6	377.7	385.3	390.6	392.6	389.7	391.3	385.6	386.3	388.5	387.0	384.0
2007	378.2	383.7	391.6	399.7	405.6	406.9	403.2	405.4	398.6	395.2	394.1	390.6	396.1
2008	383.3	387.2	393.4	400.2	407.2	405.1	402.4	402.3	395.4	386.6	383.3	379.9	393.9
2009	367.4	370.9	376.7	388.7	392.3	391.8	387.8	385.8	379.0	379.4	378.7	372.3	380.9
Other Services													
1990	88.8	89.5	90.4	91.0	91.8	93.2	92.2	92.7	92.6	91.8	91.9	91.7	91.5
2000	134.0	137.0	140.3	144.3	147.5	150.8	156.9	158.0	159.9	162.5	163.4	166.0	151.7
2001	165.9	168.8	171.9	172.4	173.2	174.4	169.3	168.7	167.3	166.3	166.2	165.8	169.2
2002	160.8	161.4	162.1	160.1	160.8	161.5	156.2	156.4	156.1	156.6	157.5	156.6	158.8
2003	153.0	153.2	154.5	154.3	155.6	157.0	156.9	157.0	156.7	155.7	155.9	155.7	155.5
2004	154.9	154.9	156.5	157.0	157.3	158.5	157.9	157.4	155.5	155.0	155.2	154.8	156.2
2005	154.9	155.8	155.9	158.2	159.2	159.4	160.3	161.2	159.0	158.2	158.6	158.3	158.3
2006	156.9	157.4	157.5	159.3	160.5	161.1	161.3	160.5	159.1	159.3	159.5	158.5	159.2
2007	158.1	158.6	159.0	160.6	161.6	162.5	162.5	162.3	160.5	160.8	160.5	159.0	160.5
2008	159.5	160.9	160.8	161.5	162.7	163.2	162.5	162.0	160.4	159.6	159.3	158.3	160.9
2009	157.0	157.6	156.9	158.1	159.1	159.3	159.8	158.4	157.0	157.5	157.6	155.6	157.8
Government													
1990	526.5	529.6	534.9	532.9	540.7	539.4	524.3	521.7	525.7	535.4	537.4	534.3	531.9
2000	592.3	596.9	601.0	601.0	612.2	597.1	577.1	585.0	594.5	600.2	602.4	603.8	597.0
2001	600.2	606.0	608.8	608.9	610.9	606.2	585.4	606.3	615.3	620.8	623.8	622.4	609.6
2002	616.1	618.6	624.5	625.5	627.0	618.1	597.5	620.3	632.0	633.5	636.0	632.9	623.5
2003	631.4	636.3	637.8	637.0	634.6	621.6	602.8	621.1	631.9	637.0	638.4	637.0	630.6
2004	627.6	634.6	635.8	642.0	639.1	624.1	605.9	631.7	641.4	643.8	647.2	643.7	634.7
2005	639.8	647.2	648.6	648.7	648.3	635.4	616.4	647.2	653.7	657.0	659.2	658.3	646.7
2006	653.1	660.7	662.8	660.8	660.4	651.6	627.2	655.1	665.3	670.4	674.2	673.3	659.6
2007	666.8	675.7	677.3	675.3	675.2	663.7	639.2	665.6	675.8	683.2	686.7	685.7	672.5
2008	684.3	694.3	695.9	694.3	694.8	682.6	661.0	685.2	689.8	699.9	704.7	701.4	690.7
2009	695.7	701.6	702.1	701.8	697.6	682.2	656.4	672.2	685.7	694.3	694.5	689.3	689.5

Average Weekly Hours by Selected Industry: Georgia, 2007–2009

(Not seasonally adjusted.)

Industry and year	January	February	March	April	May	June	July	August	September	October	November	December	Annual average
Total Private													
2007	35.1	34.9	34.8	35.7	35.4	35.7	36.0	35.6	36.4	35.8	35.8	35.9	35.6
2008	35.0	35.2	35.6	35.3	35.4	35.9	35.2	35.6	35.0	34.9	35.5	34.9	35.3
2009	34.6	35.1	35.1	34.4	34.6	34.3	34.6	34.7	34.1	34.3	35.0	34.6	34.6
Goods-Producing													
2007	39.8	39.2	39.7	39.8	39.8	39.8	39.6	41.0	40.2	39.7	40.1	40.3	39.9
2008	39.1	39.3	39.2	39.5	39.6	39.8	39.2	39.0	38.6	38.1	38.0	37.4	38.9
2009	36.9	37.2	37.5	36.9	37.8	37.4	38.1	37.6	37.4	37.9	38.4	38.5	37.6
Construction													
2007	38.8	37.6	38.5	38.5	39.6	39.7	39.0	40.5	39.9	40.0	39.8	39.6	39.3
2008	38.1	37.9	37.6	38.6	38.8	39.3	38.1	38.2	37.6	37.0	36.8	35.6	37.8
2009	36.2	36.4	36.9	35.6	36.5	35.8	36.5	36.3	37.0	37.4	38.0	37.6	36.7
Manufacturing													
2007	40.4	40.8	41.0	41.1	40.3	39.8	40.0	41.2	40.3	41.0	41.7	40.9	40.7
2008	39.9	39.6	39.8	39.6	39.8	39.9	39.7	39.5	39.1	38.8	38.7	38.6	39.4
2009	37.3	37.0	37.3	37.3	37.9	37.8	38.7	38.5	37.7	38.4	39.0	39.4	38.0
Trade, Transportation, and Utilities													
2007	34.6	34.1	34.5	35.4	34.9	35.5	35.3	33.9	35.8	35.2	35.8	35.7	35.1
2008	35.2	35.2	35.9	35.7	35.5	35.8	35.1	35.3	35.2	34.8	35.8	35.3	35.4
2009	34.3	35.0	35.2	34.8	35.2	34.8	34.6	34.9	34.3	34.8	34.9	34.7	34.8
Financial Activities													
2007	36.4	36.1	35.6	36.3	35.4	36.5	35.9	34.5	35.7	35.1	35.0	35.6	35.7
2008	34.3	34.7	36.0	35.3	35.4	36.7	35.9	35.8	35.7	36.5	37.8	37.0	35.9
2009	36.2	36.6	36.2	35.1	34.8	34.6	35.1	36.2	36.0	36.2	36.1	34.6	35.6
Professional and Business Services													
2007	33.4	34.4	34.0	35.0	34.9	34.5	35.0	34.6	36.5	35.3	35.0	34.9	34.8
2008	33.4	34.3	35.1	34.5	34.8	35.6	34.6	35.5	34.0	34.4	35.4	34.3	34.7
2009	34.3	35.4	35.0	34.7	35.0	34.6	34.9	35.3	34.5	34.5	35.6	35.1	34.9
Education and Health Services													
2007	37.5	37.7	36.9	38.6	38.5	39.2	39.3	38.0	38.2	37.9	38.1	38.2	38.2
2008	37.2	38.0	38.1	37.4	37.2	37.3	36.8	37.5	36.3	36.3	36.4	36.0	37.0
2009	37.1	35.8	36.1	35.5	35.7	35.4	35.5	35.5	35.0	34.9	35.6	35.1	35.6
Leisure and Hospitality													
2007	27.7	27.7	26.8	27.9	28.5	28.4	29.2	29.0	28.7	28.1	27.8	27.5	28.1
2008	26.9	27.5	28.0	27.9	27.7	28.5	27.9	27.7	27.2	27.1	27.3	27.6	27.6
2009	28.1	29.0	29.0	28.4	28.5	27.7	28.1	27.8	27.2	27.6	27.5	27.7	28.1
Other Services													
2007	30.5	30.3	30.4	31.9	33.0	32.7	32.0	32.8	33.0	32.3	32.0	32.1	31.9
2008	31.8	32.6	32.8	32.5	33.1	32.8	30.7	31.4	32.2	32.0	32.1	31.7	32.1
2009	31.6	32.2	31.8	31.2	30.9	31.9	31.2	31.1	31.0	30.9	31.7	31.9	31.5

Average Hourly Earnings by Selected Industry: Georgia, 2007–2009

(Dollars, not seasonally adjusted.)

Industry and year	January	February	March	April	May	June	July	August	September	October	November	December	Annual average
Total Private													
2007	20.07	20.13	20.83	20.05	19.79	21.03	20.34	20.96	20.58	20.74	20.62	20.08	20.43
2008	20.19	20.43	20.46	20.34	20.41	20.67	20.97	20.90	20.91	20.96	21.50	21.53	20.77
2009	21.10	21.49	21.32	21.07	20.53	20.70	20.82	21.05	21.00	20.99	21.46	21.37	21.08
Goods-Producing													
2007	18.47	18.37	18.57	18.21	18.02	18.75	18.50	18.52	19.45	19.78	19.89	19.02	18.79
2008	18.78	18.67	18.84	18.55	18.85	19.07	19.25	19.49	19.19	19.07	19.87	20.37	19.15
2009	20.31	20.06	20.10	20.30	20.05	20.69	20.54	20.80	21.03	21.05	21.53	21.36	20.64
Construction													
2007	18.61	16.99	17.68	17.61	17.10	17.27	17.83	18.11	18.81	18.37	18.57	18.75	17.98
2008	18.69	18.36	18.94	18.54	19.06	18.90	19.74	19.26	19.54	20.10	21.36	21.11	19.42
2009	20.90	20.58	20.71	20.53	20.39	21.08	21.28	21.62	21.94	21.98	21.75	21.61	21.19
Manufacturing													
2007	20.19	19.64	19.48	18.90	18.93	20.08	19.16	18.96	18.56	18.71	18.74	19.43	19.23
2008	19.03	19.05	18.95	18.66	18.80	19.25	19.00	19.66	18.99	18.35	18.83	19.89	19.04
2009	19.79	19.47	19.50	20.08	19.60	20.25	19.81	20.03	19.88	19.95	20.08	19.91	19.86
Trade, Transportation, and Utilities													
2007	19.31	19.77	20.05	19.11	18.76	19.52	19.37	19.07	19.34	19.64	19.00	18.81	19.31
2008	19.02	19.94	19.49	19.31	19.59	19.67	20.10	20.11	19.90	19.99	20.14	20.49	19.81
2009	19.94	20.25	20.26	20.11	19.70	19.73	19.75	19.96	19.69	19.16	19.63	19.44	19.80
Financial Activities													
2007	25.47	25.03	26.14	24.97	24.88	23.72	23.79	22.91	24.59	24.30	23.21	24.09	24.43
2008	23.76	24.01	24.83	25.00	25.11	25.49	25.30	24.98	25.02	24.52	25.57	25.73	24.95
2009	25.34	26.12	26.09	25.35	25.84	25.75	26.16	25.89	25.37	25.13	25.07	24.78	25.58
Professional and Business Services													
2007	25.98	25.69	25.62	25.69	25.17	26.38	24.88	24.61	25.66	25.09	24.86	25.60	25.43
2008	26.13	25.24	25.91	25.93	25.76	25.99	26.07	26.02	26.41	26.72	27.50	26.91	26.21
2009	27.20	27.32	27.16	26.35	26.11	26.15	25.74	26.15	26.31	26.39	27.00	27.00	26.58
Education and Health Services													
2007	20.14	20.29	20.72	20.34	19.97	19.41	19.75	19.72	20.52	20.41	20.77	20.18	20.18
2008	20.35	20.19	20.33	20.08	20.30	20.75	21.10	20.91	21.29	21.47	22.10	21.94	20.90
2009	21.28	21.88	21.74	22.10	21.65	21.89	22.02	21.97	21.85	22.40	22.49	22.16	21.95
Leisure and Hospitality													
2007	11.92	11.81	12.25	12.31	13.22	12.12	12.54	11.48	12.11	12.29	11.98	12.23	12.19
2008	12.43	12.22	12.14	12.27	12.14	11.90	11.90	11.78	11.91	11.87	11.92	11.83	12.02
2009	11.59	11.57	11.39	11.29	11.23	11.24	11.35	11.57	11.75	11.69	11.67	11.86	11.51
Other Services													
2007	16.06	15.88	16.21	15.66	14.73	14.95	14.79	14.53	14.40	14.29	15.18	16.01	15.20
2008	14.59	14.61	15.22	14.79	14.70	15.50	15.55	15.82	15.70	15.98	16.44	16.59	15.45
2009	16.67	16.91	17.01	16.93	16.74	16.89	16.91	17.19	17.40	17.69	17.63	17.90	17.15

Average Weekly Earnings by Selected Industry: Georgia, 2007–2009

(Dollars, not seasonally adjusted.)

Industry and year	January	February	March	April	May	June	July	August	September	October	November	December	Annual average
Total Private													
2007	704.46	702.54	724.88	715.79	700.57	750.77	732.24	746.18	749.11	742.49	738.20	720.87	727.31
2008	706.65	719.14	728.38	718.00	722.51	742.05	738.14	744.04	731.85	731.50	763.25	751.40	733.18
2009	730.06	754.30	748.33	724.81	710.34	710.01	720.37	730.44	716.10	719.96	751.10	739.40	729.37
Goods-Producing													
2007	735.11	720.10	737.23	724.76	717.20	746.25	732.60	759.32	781.89	785.27	797.59	766.51	749.72
2008	734.30	733.73	738.53	732.73	746.46	758.99	754.60	760.11	740.73	726.57	755.06	761.84	744.94
2009	749.44	746.23	753.75	749.07	757.89	773.81	782.57	782.08	786.52	797.80	826.75	822.36	776.06
Construction													
2007	722.07	638.82	680.68	677.99	677.16	685.62	695.37	733.46	750.52	734.80	739.09	742.50	706.61
2008	712.09	695.84	712.14	715.64	739.53	742.77	752.09	735.73	734.70	743.70	786.05	751.52	734.08
2009	756.58	749.11	764.20	730.87	744.24	754.66	776.72	784.81	811.78	822.05	826.50	812.54	777.67
Manufacturing													
2007	815.68	801.31	798.68	776.79	762.88	799.18	766.40	781.15	747.97	767.11	781.46	794.69	782.66
2008	759.30	754.38	754.21	738.94	748.24	768.08	754.30	776.57	742.51	711.98	728.72	767.75	750.18
2009	738.17	720.39	727.35	748.98	742.84	765.45	766.65	771.16	749.48	766.08	783.12	784.45	754.68
Trade, Transportation, and Utilities													
2007	668.13	674.16	691.73	676.49	654.72	692.96	683.76	646.47	692.37	691.33	680.20	671.52	677.78
2008	669.50	701.89	699.69	689.37	695.45	704.19	705.51	709.88	700.48	695.65	721.01	723.30	701.27
2009	683.94	708.75	713.15	699.83	603.44	686.60	683.35	696.60	675.37	666.77	685.09	674.57	689.04
Financial Activities													
2007	927.11	903.58	930.58	906.41	880.75	865.78	854.06	790.40	877.86	852.93	812.35	857.60	872.15
2008	814.97	833.15	893.88	882.50	888.89	935.48	908.27	894.28	893.21	894.98	966.55	952.01	895.71
2009	917.31	955.99	944.46	889.79	899.23	890.95	918.22	937.22	913.32	909.71	905.03	857.39	910.65
Professional and Business Services													
2007	867.73	883.74	871.08	899.15	878.43	910.11	870.80	851.51	936.59	885.68	870.10	893.44	884.96
2008	872.74	865.73	909.44	894.59	896.45	925.24	902.02	923.71	897.94	919.17	973.50	923.01	909.49
2009	932.96	967.13	950.60	914.35	913.85	904.79	898.33	923.10	907.70	910.46	961.20	947.70	927.64
Education and Health Services													
2007	755.25	764.93	764.57	785.12	768.85	760.87	776.18	749.36	783.86	773.54	791.34	770.88	770.88
2008	757.02	767.22	774.57	750.99	755.16	773.98	776.48	784.13	772.83	779.36	804.44	789.84	773.30
2009	789.49	783.30	784.81	784.55	772.91	774.91	781.71	779.94	764.75	781.76	800.64	777.82	781.42
Leisure and Hospitality													
2007	330.18	327.14	328.30	343.45	376.77	344.21	366.17	332.92	347.56	345.35	333.04	336.33	342.54
2008	334.37	336.05	339.92	342.33	336.78	339.15	332.01	326.31	323.95	321.68	325.42	326.51	331.75
2009	325.68	335.53	330.31	320.64	320.06	311.35	318.94	321.65	319.60	322.61	320.44	328.52	323.43
Other Services													
2007	489.83	481.16	492.78	499.55	486.09	488.87	473.28	476.58	475.20	461.57	485.76	513.92	484.88
2008	463.96	476.29	499.22	480.68	486.57	508.40	477.39	496.75	505.54	511.36	527.72	525.90	495.95
2009	526.77	544.50	540.92	528.22	517.27	538.79	527.59	534.61	539.40	546.62	558.87	571.01	540.23

HAWAII
At a Glance

Population:
    1990 census: 1,108,229
    2000 census: 1,211,537
    2009 estimate: 1,295,178

Percent change in population:
    1990–2000: 9.3%
    2000–2009: 6.9%

Percent change in total nonfarm employment:
    1990–2009: 11.9%
    2008–2009: -4.5%

Industry with the largest growth in employment, 1990–2009 (thousands):
    Education and Health Services, 27.9

Industry with the largest decline or smallest growth in employment, 1990–2009 (thousands):
    Manufacturing, -6.9

Civilian labor force:
    1990: 551,028
    2000: 609,018
    2009: 637,777

Unemployment rate and rank among states (lowest to highest):
    1990: 2.4%, 2nd
    2000: 4.0%, 28th
    2009: 6.8%, 12th

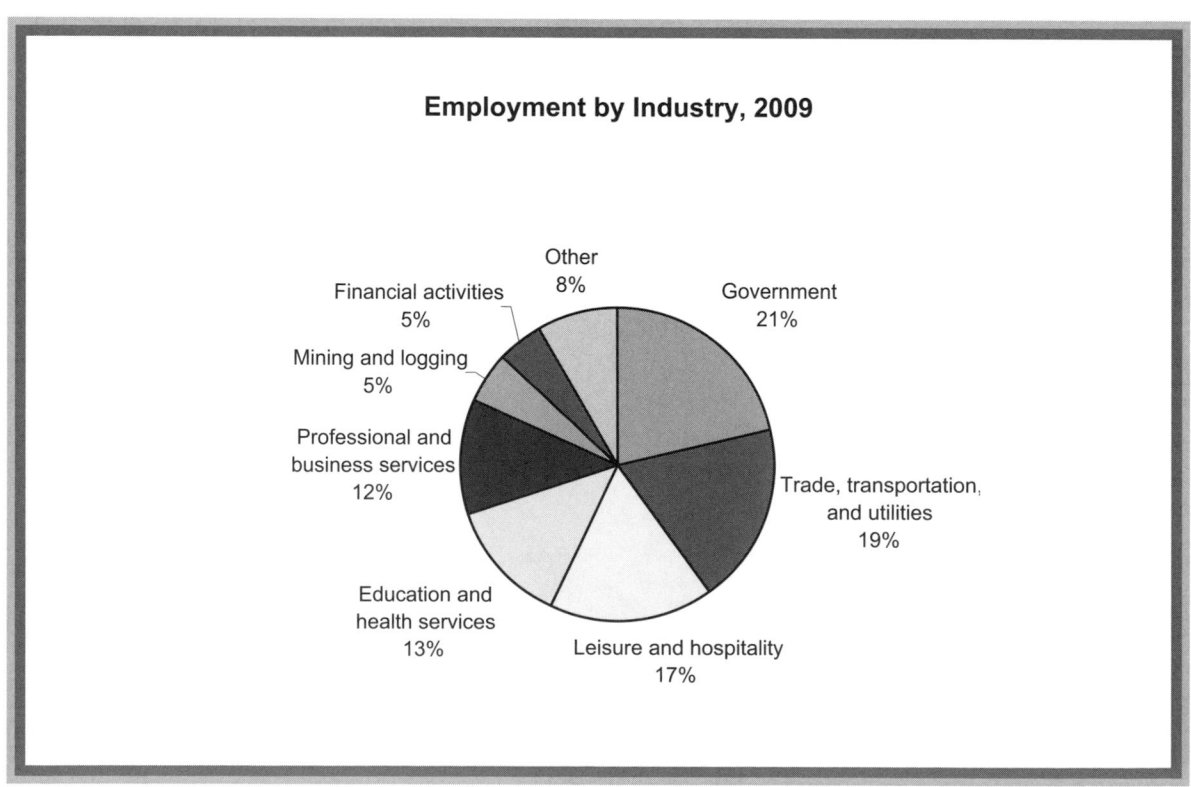

Employment by Industry, 2009

- Other 8%
- Financial activities 5%
- Mining and logging 5%
- Professional and business services 12%
- Education and health services 13%
- Leisure and hospitality 17%
- Trade, transportation, and utilities 19%
- Government 21%

Employment by Industry: Hawaii, Selected Years, 1990–2009

(Numbers in thousands, not seasonally adjusted.)

Industry and year	January	February	March	April	May	June	July	August	September	October	November	December	Annual average
Total Nonfarm													
1990	513.4	521.6	525.1	525.6	528.7	531.5	527.8	528.1	521.7	532.4	540.5	544.9	528.4
2000	535.1	542.9	548.8	548.3	552.2	556.3	547.6	548.2	552.3	555.3	561.9	567.4	551.4
2001	546.9	557.4	561.2	556.1	557.5	562.9	552.5	554.6	555.5	548.1	551.9	555.5	555.0
2002	541.9	549.4	554.0	547.9	558.0	564.7	553.2	554.2	557.3	560.7	566.9	573.4	556.8
2003	559.6	564.5	567.8	562.7	568.2	568.9	562.3	563.4	566.1	570.0	576.2	581.9	567.6
2004	568.9	574.5	578.0	578.6	582.4	584.2	578.9	580.5	584.1	589.8	599.2	601.8	583.4
2005	585.0	593.1	597.4	598.5	602.0	604.4	597.3	601.3	604.2	605.8	611.8	618.9	601.6
2006	600.2	611.0	615.2	612.5	617.9	621.0	610.6	615.7	620.4	618.2	630.3	632.3	617.1
2007	615.0	622.9	626.5	618.5	627.1	630.5	618.0	619.7	624.6	626.4	632.3	637.0	624.9
2008	619.9	626.6	629.4	620.5	626.6	624.4	612.6	613.4	613.0	611.5	618.1	614.8	619.2
2009	597.6	599.3	600.6	594.6	594.8	594.2	581.7	579.8	583.0	587.8	590.6	594.0	591.5
Total Private													
1990	412.2	416.7	417.2	416.8	418.2	423.9	425.4	426.0	424.3	427.3	431.3	434.6	422.8
2000	424.5	427.8	431.4	431.2	432.6	438.6	437.9	439.1	442.0	441.2	445.3	449.3	436.7
2001	438.8	441.3	444.1	440.9	442.7	445.6	443.7	444.8	443.5	432.6	432.8	435.5	440.5
2002	427.3	430.3	433.4	433.4	436.5	440.7	441.2	441.9	443.0	441.9	446.0	450.9	438.9
2003	440.7	442.9	445.4	443.7	445.8	447.8	448.4	450.3	451.8	450.3	454.9	460.0	448.5
2004	450.5	453.6	455.5	456.9	459.2	463.3	464.7	465.9	467.4	469.4	474.6	478.9	463.3
2005	468.8	472.1	475.2	477.1	479.3	482.9	483.3	485.6	487.7	485.7	490.0	496.3	482.0
2006	484.5	489.1	492.3	490.3	494.0	498.7	496.1	499.7	500.4	495.9	502.1	507.0	495.8
2007	495.1	498.7	501.6	498.6	501.8	507.0	502.6	504.3	503.7	502.7	506.8	510.4	502.8
2008	498.5	501.4	502.4	498.7	498.7	498.5	494.2	493.1	489.7	484.5	485.1	485.9	494.2
2009	472.5	472.2	471.6	465.6	464.5	466.2	461.5	461.0	460.5	462.5	464.5	467.1	465.8
Goods-Producing													
1990	54.6	55.4	55.7	54.8	55.1	56.2	56.5	56.7	56.6	57.4	57.4	57.6	56.2
2000	39.1	39.1	39.9	40.2	40.6	41.3	42.0	42.5	42.7	42.3	42.3	42.6	41.2
2001	41.4	41.3	41.4	40.9	41.2	41.2	41.3	41.6	41.5	40.5	40.6	40.7	41.1
2002	40.0	39.9	40.6	40.2	40.6	41.6	41.8	42.1	41.7	41.8	42.1	42.2	41.2
2003	41.4	41.5	41.8	42.4	42.8	43.1	43.4	43.7	43.8	43.9	43.9	43.8	43.0
2004	42.9	43.3	42.7	43.8	44.3	45.1	45.4	45.5	45.8	45.9	46.3	46.7	44.8
2005	45.9	46.3	47.0	47.5	48.1	48.7	49.1	49.7	50.2	49.9	50.1	50.6	48.6
2006	49.5	49.8	50.1	50.1	50.9	51.7	52.0	52.8	53.5	53.1	53.9	54.6	51.8
2007	52.8	53.2	53.4	53.5	54.0	54.9	54.7	55.1	55.3	55.1	55.3	55.2	54.4
2008	53.9	54.1	54.0	53.7	53.2	53.3	53.0	52.9	52.4	51.4	50.8	50.1	52.7
2009	48.0	47.1	46.6	45.5	45.2	45.3	44.8	44.1	43.7	44.0	43.5	43.7	45.1
Mining, Logging, and Construction													
1990	33.9	34.5	34.8	34.3	34.8	35.6	35.8	36.1	36.1	37.0	36.9	37.2	35.6
2000	23.0	23.1	23.7	24.0	24.4	24.8	25.5	25.8	26.0	25.6	25.6	25.9	24.8
2001	24.8	24.7	24.8	24.4	24.6	24.6	24.8	25.0	25.0	24.5	24.6	24.7	24.7
2002	24.4	24.3	24.9	25.1	25.4	26.2	26.6	27.0	26.8	26.9	27.1	27.2	26.0
2003	26.7	26.8	27.1	27.5	27.9	28.1	28.4	28.7	28.7	28.6	28.5	28.3	27.9
2004	27.6	27.9	27.4	28.4	28.9	29.5	30.0	30.1	30.4	30.6	30.9	31.3	29.4
2005	30.8	31.1	31.8	32.4	33.0	33.6	34.0	34.4	34.9	34.7	34.9	35.3	33.4
2006	34.5	34.7	34.9	35.0	35.7	36.4	36.7	37.3	37.9	37.8	38.4	39.0	36.5
2007	37.5	37.9	38.1	38.3	38.7	39.5	39.5	39.8	40.0	40.0	40.1	39.9	39.1
2008	38.9	39.0	38.9	38.6	38.1	38.2	38.1	37.9	37.7	37.0	36.3	35.6	37.9
2009	33.9	33.2	32.7	31.8	31.6	31.7	31.3	30.5	30.2	30.5	29.9	30.1	31.5
Manufacturing													
1990	20.7	20.9	20.9	20.5	20.3	20.6	20.7	20.6	20.5	20.4	20.5	20.4	20.6
2000	16.1	16.0	16.2	16.2	16.2	16.5	16.5	16.7	16.7	16.7	16.7	16.7	16.4
2001	16.6	16.6	16.6	16.5	16.6	16.6	16.5	16.6	16.5	16.0	16.0	16.0	16.4
2002	15.6	15.6	15.7	15.1	15.2	15.4	15.2	15.1	14.9	14.9	15.0	15.0	15.2
2003	14.7	14.7	14.7	14.9	14.9	15.0	15.0	15.0	15.1	15.3	15.4	15.5	15.0
2004	15.3	15.4	15.3	15.4	15.4	15.6	15.4	15.4	15.4	15.3	15.4	15.4	15.4
2005	15.1	15.2	15.2	15.1	15.1	15.1	15.1	15.3	15.3	15.2	15.2	15.3	15.2
2006	15.0	15.1	15.2	15.1	15.2	15.3	15.3	15.5	15.6	15.3	15.5	15.6	15.3
2007	15.3	15.3	15.3	15.2	15.3	15.4	15.2	15.3	15.3	15.1	15.2	15.3	15.3
2008	15.0	15.1	15.1	15.1	15.1	15.1	14.9	15.0	14.7	14.4	14.5	14.5	14.9
2009	14.1	13.9	13.9	13.7	13.6	13.6	13.5	13.6	13.5	13.5	13.6	13.6	13.7
Service-Providing													
1990	458.8	466.2	469.4	470.8	473.6	475.3	471.3	471.4	465.1	475.0	483.1	487.3	472.3
2000	496.0	503.8	508.9	508.1	511.6	515.0	505.6	505.7	509.6	513.0	519.6	524.8	510.1
2001	505.5	516.1	519.8	515.2	516.3	521.7	511.2	513.0	514.0	507.6	511.3	514.8	513.9
2002	501.9	509.5	513.4	507.7	517.4	523.1	511.4	512.1	515.6	518.9	524.8	531.2	515.6
2003	518.2	523.0	526.0	520.3	525.4	525.8	518.9	519.7	522.3	526.1	532.3	538.1	524.7
2004	526.0	531.2	535.3	534.8	538.1	539.1	533.5	535.0	538.3	543.9	552.9	555.1	538.6
2005	539.1	546.8	550.4	551.0	553.9	555.7	548.2	551.6	554.0	555.9	561.7	568.3	553.1
2006	550.7	561.2	565.1	562.4	567.0	569.3	558.6	562.9	566.9	565.1	576.4	577.7	565.3
2007	562.2	569.7	573.1	565.0	573.1	575.6	563.3	564.6	569.3	571.3	577.0	581.8	570.5
2008	566.0	572.5	575.4	566.8	573.4	571.1	559.6	560.5	560.6	560.1	567.3	564.7	566.5
2009	549.6	552.2	554.0	549.1	549.6	548.9	536.9	535.7	539.3	543.8	547.1	550.3	546.4

Employment by Industry: Hawaii, Selected Years, 1990–2009—*Continued*

(Numbers in thousands, not seasonally adjusted.)

Industry and year	January	February	March	April	May	June	July	August	September	October	November	December	Annual average
Trade, Transportation, and Utilities													
1990	111.3	112.0	112.0	111.4	111.8	113.4	114.2	113.8	113.5	114.2	116.0	117.6	113.4
2000	109.5	109.3	109.3	108.6	108.9	110.4	110.4	110.9	111.4	111.6	114.1	115.4	110.8
2001	112.3	111.7	111.9	111.2	111.5	112.2	111.8	112.0	111.6	108.9	107.6	109.2	111.0
2002	105.5	104.8	104.9	105.0	105.5	106.5	107.0	107.3	107.1	107.5	109.0	111.0	106.8
2003	107.4	107.0	106.8	106.2	106.4	106.9	107.6	107.9	108.0	108.2	110.1	112.2	107.9
2004	109.3	108.8	109.1	110.1	110.8	111.9	112.1	112.6	113.0	114.5	116.8	118.4	112.3
2005	114.9	114.9	115.2	115.5	116.4	117.3	118.2	118.7	119.1	118.9	120.7	122.9	117.7
2006	119.2	118.9	119.8	119.5	120.0	121.3	120.7	121.7	121.7	120.6	123.2	125.0	121.0
2007	121.6	120.3	121.4	120.3	120.8	121.6	121.3	121.4	121.2	121.5	124.5	126.4	121.9
2008	122.1	120.7	120.9	118.9	118.6	118.2	117.2	117.1	116.1	115.0	115.8	116.5	118.1
2009	113.4	112.3	111.7	110.3	110.0	110.4	110.0	109.8	109.7	109.5	111.0	112.8	110.9
Wholesale Trade													
1990	17.3	17.5	17.5	17.4	17.5	17.7	17.8	17.8	17.7	17.8	17.8	18.0	17.7
2000	16.0	16.0	16.1	16.0	16.0	16.3	16.3	16.4	16.4	16.4	16.5	16.5	16.2
2001	16.4	16.4	16.4	16.4	16.5	16.6	16.5	16.6	16.5	16.3	16.2	16.4	16.4
2002	16.1	16.1	16.2	16.2	16.3	16.4	16.5	16.5	16.5	16.6	16.7	16.9	16.4
2003	16.5	16.5	16.6	16.6	16.7	16.7	16.8	16.8	16.8	16.8	16.8	16.9	16.7
2004	16.7	16.8	16.8	16.9	17.0	17.1	17.1	17.1	17.1	17.2	17.3	17.4	17.0
2005	17.1	17.3	17.4	17.4	17.5	17.6	17.7	17.8	17.9	17.9	17.9	18.1	17.6
2006	17.7	17.7	17.7	17.8	17.9	18.1	18.0	18.2	18.2	18.2	18.4	18.5	18.0
2007	18.2	18.2	18.4	18.3	18.4	18.6	18.6	18.7	18.8	18.8	19.0	19.1	18.6
2008	18.7	18.8	18.9	18.8	18.9	18.9	18.9	18.8	18.8	18.7	18.6	18.6	18.8
2009	18.2	18.1	18.0	17.9	17.8	17.7	17.7	17.6	17.6	17.6	17.7	17.7	17.8
Retail Trade													
1990	66.6	66.5	66.5	66.1	66.4	67.3	67.9	67.4	67.1	67.5	69.0	70.2	67.4
2000	66.0	65.5	65.3	64.7	65.0	65.7	65.9	66.3	66.4	66.7	68.8	70.0	66.4
2001	67.2	66.5	66.5	65.9	65.9	66.3	66.1	66.3	66.0	64.9	65.3	66.7	66.1
2002	63.8	63.0	62.9	62.8	63.0	63.7	64.1	64.1	63.9	64.1	65.3	67.1	64.0
2003	64.0	63.4	63.1	62.8	63.0	63.7	64.3	64.4	64.3	64.6	66.4	68.4	64.4
2004	65.8	65.1	65.2	65.1	65.6	66.3	66.6	66.9	67.0	68.1	70.1	71.8	67.0
2005	68.5	68.1	68.2	67.8	68.0	68.3	69.1	69.3	69.3	69.7	71.3	73.3	69.2
2006	70.0	69.5	69.8	69.1	69.2	69.8	69.4	69.7	69.4	69.5	71.7	73.1	70.0
2007	70.4	69.4	70.1	69.3	69.6	70.1	69.9	69.8	69.6	69.8	72.4	73.8	70.4
2008	70.6	69.9	70.7	69.7	69.6	70.1	70.0	69.8	69.2	68.5	69.5	70.3	69.8
2009	67.9	67.0	66.6	65.6	65.3	65.8	65.6	65.4	65.7	65.3	66.6	68.4	66.3
Transportation and Utilities													
1990	27.4	28.0	28.0	27.9	27.9	28.4	28.5	28.6	28.7	28.9	29.2	29.4	28.4
2000	27.5	27.8	27.9	27.9	27.9	28.4	28.2	28.2	28.6	28.5	28.8	28.9	28.2
2001	28.7	28.8	29.0	28.9	29.1	29.3	29.2	29.1	29.1	27.7	26.1	26.1	28.4
2002	25.6	25.7	25.8	26.0	26.2	26.4	26.4	26.7	26.7	26.8	27.0	27.0	26.4
2003	26.9	27.1	27.1	26.8	26.7	26.5	26.5	26.7	26.9	26.8	26.9	26.9	26.8
2004	26.8	26.9	27.1	28.1	28.2	28.5	28.4	28.6	28.9	29.2	29.4	29.2	28.3
2005	29.3	29.5	29.6	30.3	30.9	31.4	31.4	31.6	31.9	31.3	31.5	31.5	30.9
2006	31.5	31.7	32.3	32.6	32.9	33.4	33.3	33.8	34.1	32.9	33.1	33.4	32.9
2007	33.0	32.7	32.9	32.7	32.8	32.9	32.8	32.9	32.8	32.9	33.1	33.5	32.9
2008	32.8	32.0	31.3	30.4	30.1	29.2	28.3	28.5	28.1	27.8	27.7	27.6	29.5
2009	27.3	27.2	27.1	26.8	26.9	26.9	26.7	26.8	26.4	26.6	26.7	26.7	26.8
Information													
1990	9.5	9.6	9.7	9.8	9.8	9.8	9.8	9.8	9.9	10.0	9.9	10.1	9.8
2000	11.5	11.5	11.7	12.4	12.3	12.7	12.0	12.5	13.3	12.9	12.4	12.1	12.3
2001	12.1	12.1	12.4	11.8	12.1	11.9	11.7	11.9	11.5	11.5	11.7	11.6	11.9
2002	11.7	11.7	11.6	11.5	11.5	11.3	11.2	11.3	12.0	11.1	11.1	11.7	11.5
2003	10.8	10.9	10.9	10.5	11.1	10.9	10.1	10.0	9.9	9.9	10.0	10.1	10.4
2004	10.2	10.1	10.4	10.2	10.5	10.6	11.1	11.0	11.1	11.1	11.6	11.5	10.8
2005	10.4	10.6	10.4	10.7	10.9	10.5	10.5	10.9	11.0	10.9	11.1	11.6	10.8
2006	10.8	11.1	10.9	10.2	11.0	10.8	10.3	10.5	11.0	10.3	10.8	10.9	10.7
2007	10.4	11.0	10.9	10.5	11.1	11.1	10.3	10.8	10.4	10.2	10.3	10.4	10.6
2008	9.6	10.1	10.4	10.4	10.7	11.1	9.9	9.6	9.6	9.4	9.8	10.0	10.1
2009	9.1	9.6	9.4	9.4	9.0	9.1	8.6	8.8	8.9	8.7	8.9	9.0	9.0
Financial Activities													
1990	30.5	30.7	31.0	30.8	31.1	31.6	31.8	32.0	31.8	31.9	31.9	32.1	31.4
2000	28.4	28.6	28.6	28.4	28.4	28.6	28.7	28.7	28.5	28.5	28.4	28.9	28.6
2001	28.1	28.2	28.4	28.2	28.2	28.3	28.1	28.1	28.0	27.6	27.6	27.7	28.0
2002	27.2	27.3	27.6	27.4	27.6	27.8	27.8	27.8	27.8	27.9	28.1	28.4	27.7
2003	27.7	27.9	28.1	28.0	28.2	28.5	28.6	28.8	28.6	28.6	28.5	28.8	28.4
2004	28.5	28.5	28.6	28.7	28.7	28.9	28.9	28.8	28.7	29.0	29.1	29.3	28.8
2005	28.7	29.0	29.0	28.9	29.1	29.2	29.4	29.5	29.5	29.5	29.7	29.9	29.3
2006	29.5	29.6	29.9	29.9	30.0	30.2	30.1	30.2	30.0	29.9	30.1	30.3	30.0
2007	29.9	30.0	30.2	29.9	30.0	30.2	30.2	30.1	29.9	30.0	29.9	30.1	30.0
2008	29.4	29.7	29.6	29.7	29.8	29.7	29.6	29.5	29.2	28.7	28.9	28.8	29.4
2009	27.9	27.9	27.8	27.9	27.9	27.9	27.6	27.6	27.5	27.9	27.8	28.1	27.8

Employment by Industry: Hawaii, Selected Years, 1990–2009—*Continued*

(Numbers in thousands, not seasonally adjusted.)

Industry and year	January	February	March	April	May	June	July	August	September	October	November	December	Annual average
Professional and Business Services													
1990	48.4	49.3	50.0	49.2	49.2	50.1	50.3	50.5	50.4	50.7	50.7	51.0	50.0
2000	59.3	59.8	60.6	60.7	60.7	61.4	61.6	61.7	62.4	62.5	63.0	63.7	61.5
2001	62.3	63.1	63.9	63.3	63.8	64.7	64.4	64.9	64.8	63.5	64.1	64.4	63.9
2002	63.5	64.9	65.4	65.9	66.5	67.5	67.8	68.6	68.8	68.8	68.6	70.6	67.2
2003	69.0	68.6	69.2	68.9	68.8	69.6	69.4	70.3	70.8	69.6	70.6	71.1	69.7
2004	69.4	70.1	70.6	70.2	69.5	70.2	70.6	71.4	71.2	71.3	71.7	72.7	70.7
2005	71.9	72.5	73.1	73.6	73.0	74.0	74.2	74.9	74.8	75.1	76.1	77.3	74.2
2006	75.3	76.8	77.2	76.7	76.6	77.6	77.5	77.7	77.2	75.6	76.1	77.2	76.8
2007	75.1	75.7	76.0	75.0	75.3	77.1	76.4	76.6	76.8	77.1	77.2	78.1	76.4
2008	75.8	76.1	76.3	76.1	75.8	75.5	75.4	75.6	75.1	74.7	74.5	75.4	75.5
2009	73.1	72.9	72.9	71.5	70.9	71.0	70.4	70.5	70.1	70.3	69.9	69.5	71.1
Education and Health Services													
1990	45.1	45.7	46.1	45.9	46.3	46.6	47.3	46.9	47.2	47.8	48.5	48.6	46.8
2000	58.2	59.4	59.9	59.4	59.7	60.7	60.0	59.1	60.0	60.0	60.9	61.5	59.9
2001	59.9	61.0	61.4	61.4	61.8	62.2	62.1	61.5	62.0	62.0	63.0	63.2	61.8
2002	61.5	62.6	62.9	63.0	63.4	63.5	63.5	62.5	63.7	63.8	65.0	64.4	63.3
2003	63.1	64.6	65.1	65.0	65.2	64.9	65.2	64.7	66.0	66.0	66.8	67.2	65.3
2004	65.5	66.6	67.1	66.9	67.7	67.7	67.4	67.0	68.3	68.5	69.4	69.9	67.7
2005	68.7	69.5	69.9	69.9	70.2	70.3	69.5	69.0	70.2	69.9	70.4	70.8	69.9
2006	68.9	70.1	70.7	70.7	71.4	71.8	70.6	71.2	71.7	71.8	72.6	73.0	71.2
2007	71.1	72.7	72.9	72.9	73.4	73.8	72.6	72.4	73.2	73.3	73.6	73.8	73.0
2008	72.5	73.7	73.9	73.8	74.2	74.7	74.0	73.8	74.4	74.7	75.2	75.5	74.2
2009	73.8	74.8	75.0	74.4	74.6	75.1	73.6	73.4	74.2	74.8	76.2	76.4	74.7
Leisure and Hospitality													
1990	93.6	94.7	93.0	95.3	95.3	96.0	95.5	96.3	95.2	95.3	97.0	97.6	95.4
2000	96.7	97.7	98.8	98.8	99.2	100.5	100.3	100.6	100.7	100.2	100.6	101.5	99.6
2001	99.5	100.5	101.0	100.4	100.5	101.1	100.4	101.1	100.4	95.3	94.9	95.3	99.2
2002	94.7	95.8	96.8	96.8	97.7	98.7	98.3	98.5	98.0	97.2	98.2	98.6	97.4
2003	97.8	98.5	99.5	98.5	99.0	99.5	99.9	100.6	100.4	99.9	100.5	102.2	99.7
2004	100.9	102.1	102.6	102.7	103.1	104.2	104.7	105.1	104.9	104.4	105.0	105.5	103.8
2005	103.8	104.7	105.9	105.9	106.2	107.5	107.2	107.5	107.4	106.1	106.4	107.4	106.3
2006	105.9	107.1	107.8	107.3	107.9	109.1	108.9	109.3	109.0	108.2	108.9	109.5	108.2
2007	108.4	109.6	110.4	110.2	110.7	111.7	110.5	111.1	110.0	108.5	108.9	109.4	110.0
2008	108.5	109.7	109.8	108.6	108.7	108.7	108.1	107.5	105.8	103.6	103.1	102.7	107.1
2009	101.2	101.4	101.8	100.8	101.0	101.5	100.9	101.0	100.4	100.4	100.8	101.1	101.0
Other Services													
1990	19.2	19.3	19.7	19.6	19.6	20.2	20.0	20.0	19.7	20.0	19.9	20.0	19.8
2000	21.8	22.4	22.6	22.7	22.8	23.0	22.9	23.1	23.0	23.2	23.6	23.6	22.9
2001	23.2	23.4	23.7	23.7	23.6	24.0	23.9	23.7	23.7	23.3	23.3	23.4	23.6
2002	23.2	23.3	23.6	23.6	23.7	23.8	23.8	23.8	23.9	23.8	23.9	24.0	23.7
2003	23.5	23.9	24.0	24.2	24.3	24.4	24.2	24.3	24.3	24.2	24.5	24.6	24.2
2004	23.8	24.1	24.4	24.3	24.6	24.7	24.5	24.5	24.4	24.7	24.7	24.9	24.5
2005	24.5	24.6	24.7	25.1	25.4	25.4	25.2	25.4	25.5	25.4	25.5	25.8	25.2
2006	25.4	25.7	25.9	25.9	26.2	26.2	26.0	26.3	26.3	26.4	26.5	26.5	26.1
2007	25.8	26.2	26.4	26.3	26.5	26.6	26.6	26.8	26.9	27.0	27.1	27.0	26.6
2008	26.7	27.3	27.5	27.5	27.7	27.3	27.0	27.1	27.1	27.0	27.0	26.9	27.2
2009	26.0	26.2	26.4	25.8	25.9	25.9	25.6	25.8	26.0	26.9	26.4	26.5	26.1
Government													
1990	101.2	104.9	107.9	108.8	110.5	107.6	102.4	102.1	97.4	105.1	109.2	110.3	105.6
2000	110.6	115.1	117.4	117.1	119.6	117.7	109.7	109.1	110.3	114.1	116.6	118.1	114.6
2001	108.1	116.1	117.1	115.2	114.8	117.3	108.8	109.8	112.0	115.5	119.1	120.0	114.5
2002	114.6	119.1	120.6	114.5	121.5	124.0	112.0	112.3	114.3	118.8	120.9	122.5	117.9
2003	118.9	121.6	122.4	119.0	122.4	121.1	113.9	113.1	114.3	119.7	121.3	121.9	119.1
2004	118.4	120.9	122.5	121.7	123.2	120.9	114.2	114.6	116.7	120.4	124.6	122.9	120.1
2005	116.2	121.0	122.2	121.4	122.7	121.5	114.0	115.7	116.5	120.1	121.8	122.6	119.6
2006	115.7	121.9	122.9	122.2	123.9	122.3	114.5	116.0	120.0	122.3	128.2	125.3	121.3
2007	119.9	124.2	124.9	119.9	125.3	123.5	115.4	115.4	120.9	123.7	125.5	126.6	122.1
2008	121.4	125.2	127.0	121.8	127.9	125.9	118.4	120.3	123.3	127.0	133.0	128.9	125.0
2009	125.1	127.1	129.0	129.0	130.3	128.0	120.2	118.8	122.5	125.3	126.1	126.9	125.7

Average Weekly Hours by Selected Industry: Hawaii, 2007–2009

(Not seasonally adjusted.)

Industry and year	January	February	March	April	May	June	July	August	September	October	November	December	Annual average
Total Private													
2007	32.5	32.5	32.0	33.2	32.0	32.4	33.4	32.6	33.4	32.1	32.2	32.9	32.6
2008	32.7	32.7	33.2	32.7	32.3	33.1	32.5	32.6	32.3	32.2	32.9	31.9	32.6
2009	32.3	33.4	33.0	32.5	32.3	32.5	32.3	32.6	32.1	32.2	32.7	32.2	32.5
Goods-Producing													
2007	36.1	36.1	35.4	36.1	35.6	33.4	34.3	33.4	34.9	33.6	34.2	34.7	34.8
2008	35.3	37.3	37.5	36.3	36.4	35.7	36.4	36.8	36.8	36.0	35.1	35.3	36.3
2009	36.1	36.6	37.0	36.4	36.5	35.4	36.1	35.5	34.4	34.4	34.6	36.1	35.8
Mining, Logging, and Construction													
2007	36.6	36.6	36.3	37.0	35.6	33.1	34.1	33.0	35.0	33.4	33.9	34.5	34.9
2008	35.5	37.9	37.8	36.6	36.9	35.3	36.6	36.4	36.4	35.5	34.0	35.5	36.2
2009	36.5	37.0	37.5	36.9	37.1	35.8	36.8	35.7	34.4	34.5	34.4	36.5	36.1
Manufacturing													
2007	34.7	34.9	33.2	33.8	35.6	34.3	34.9	34.4	34.7	34.3	35.1	35.2	34.6
2008	34.7	35.7	36.8	35.8	35.0	36.9	35.8	37.7	37.9	37.4	37.9	34.8	36.4
2009	35.2	35.7	35.7	35.4	35.1	34.4	34.7	35.1	34.2	34.1	35.2	35.3	35.0
Trade, Transportation, and Utilities													
2007	32.8	33.5	32.7	34.3	33.2	34.0	35.0	34.1	35.2	33.7	34.0	34.2	33.9
2008	33.7	33.5	34.1	34.0	32.8	34.1	32.5	32.9	32.8	32.1	32.5	31.6	33.1
2009	32.7	33.3	33.3	33.0	32.5	33.5	32.8	33.5	33.9	33.9	33.9	32.8	33.3
Professional and Business Services													
2007	33.2	32.9	31.3	33.1	31.5	31.4	32.7	31.8	32.4	31.2	30.7	31.6	32.0
2008	31.9	31.1	32.1	31.7	31.6	32.2	31.0	31.3	31.8	31.9	32.9	32.2	31.8
2009	31.8	33.0	33.0	32.6	32.4	32.7	32.3	32.6	32.1	32.6	33.3	33.0	32.6
Education and Health Services													
2007	32.0	31.6	31.1	32.4	31.0	32.8	33.2	32.8	32.9	32.1	32.3	33.5	32.3
2008	32.9	33.0	33.0	32.5	32.4	33.1	32.8	32.7	32.1	32.2	33.2	31.2	32.6
2009	30.8	32.5	31.7	30.9	30.8	30.2	30.9	31.2	30.8	30.2	31.0	30.7	31.0
Leisure and Hospitality													
2007	30.1	29.9	29.7	30.8	29.4	30.2	31.4	30.0	30.6	29.3	29.5	30.3	30.1
2008	30.2	29.7	30.3	29.9	29.8	30.8	30.9	30.7	29.7	29.9	30.7	29.3	30.2
2009	29.9	31.0	30.4	29.6	29.3	29.9	29.5	30.2	29.4	29.2	29.8	29.2	29.8

Average Hourly Earnings by Selected Industry: Hawaii, 2007–2009

(Dollars, not seasonally adjusted.)

Industry and year	January	February	March	April	May	June	July	August	September	October	November	December	Annual average
Total Private													
2007	20.63	20.38	20.62	20.65	20.65	20.62	20.64	20.61	20.78	20.66	20.67	21.17	20.68
2008	20.41	20.51	20.48	20.75	20.74	20.71	20.79	20.92	20.99	21.12	21.06	21.17	20.80
2009	21.01	21.12	21.07	20.94	20.84	20.93	21.03	21.10	21.29	21.19	21.38	21.47	21.11
Goods-Producing													
2007	27.13	28.07	27.92	27.87	28.33	28.44	28.17	28.33	28.50	27.83	28.90	29.63	28.26
2008	29.13	29.56	29.25	29.66	30.02	29.51	29.89	29.69	29.40	29.82	29.50	30.22	29.63
2009	29.60	29.62	29.82	30.07	29.85	29.93	29.85	29.70	30.06	29.94	29.97	30.12	29.87
Mining, Logging, and Construction													
2007	30.61	31.50	31.18	31.22	31.99	32.15	31.83	32.23	32.06	31.28	32.70	33.35	31.84
2008	32.50	32.91	32.66	33.31	33.73	33.17	33.43	33.35	32.87	33.49	33.07	33.34	33.15
2009	32.76	32.77	33.10	33.40	33.03	33.22	33.27	33.40	33.82	33.73	33.97	33.81	33.33
Manufacturing													
2007	18.13	19.16	19.06	18.62	19.05	19.23	18.85	18.60	19.11	18.93	19.23	20.13	19.01
2008	20.21	20.36	20.21	20.08	20.14	20.61	20.64	20.76	20.87	20.86	21.42	22.38	20.71
2009	21.72	21.86	21.74	22.01	22.07	21.96	21.42	21.21	21.65	21.31	21.34	21.67	21.67
Trade, Transportation, and Utilities													
2007	18.35	17.61	18.17	17.83	17.71	17.92	17.78	17.52	17.82	17.39	17.17	18.22	17.79
2008	17.75	17.57	17.67	17.52	17.65	17.88	17.96	18.43	18.21	18.55	18.25	18.34	17.97
2009	18.20	18.40	18.35	18.57	18.56	18.54	18.70	18.83	18.96	18.67	19.00	18.91	18.61
Professional and Business Services													
2007	22.82	22.34	22.97	23.04	23.49	23.14	23.44	22.79	22.78	22.65	22.51	22.64	22.88
2008	22.64	22.38	22.55	22.05	21.89	22.04	22.01	21.82	21.92	21.76	22.20	22.04	22.11
2009	22.03	22.35	21.86	21.56	21.44	21.59	21.57	21.75	21.71	21.55	21.62	21.44	21.71
Education and Health Services													
2007	22.96	22.82	23.24	23.06	23.19	22.63	22.77	22.66	22.79	23.12	23.05	23.29	22.96
2008	23.42	22.79	22.97	23.22	23.19	23.08	23.35	22.99	23.56	23.41	24.17	23.53	23.31
2009	22.76	22.71	23.05	22.86	22.56	22.40	22.13	21.98	22.01	22.17	22.19	22.05	22.41
Leisure and Hospitality													
2007	17.26	17.07	16.96	17.26	17.07	17.35	17.35	17.44	17.43	17.60	17.62	17.83	17.35
2008	17.51	17.89	17.72	17.71	17.37	17.16	17.16	17.35	17.29	17.48	17.08	17.07	17.40
2009	17.16	17.11	16.93	17.04	16.71	17.17	17.04	16.86	17.20	16.76	17.08	17.32	17.03

Average Weekly Earnings by Selected Industry: Hawaii, 2007–2009

(Dollars, not seasonally adjusted.)

Industry and year	January	February	March	April	May	June	July	August	September	October	November	December	Annual average
Total Private													
2007	670.48	662.35	659.84	685.58	660.80	668.09	689.38	671.89	694.05	663.19	665.57	696.49	674.17
2008	667.41	670.68	679.94	678.53	669.90	685.50	675.68	681.99	677.98	680.06	692.87	675.32	678.08
2009	678.62	705.41	695.31	680.55	673.13	680.23	679.27	687.86	683.41	682.32	699.13	691.33	686.08
Goods-Producing													
2007	979.39	1013.33	988.37	1006.11	1008.55	949.90	966.23	946.22	994.65	935.09	988.38	1028.16	983.45
2008	1028.29	1102.59	1096.88	1076.66	1092.73	1053.51	1088.00	1092.59	1081.92	1073.52	1035.45	1066.77	1075.57
2009	1068.56	1084.09	1103.34	1094.55	1089.53	1059.52	1077.59	1054.35	1034.06	1029.94	1036.96	1087.33	1069.35
Mining, Logging, and Construction													
2007	1120.33	1152.90	1131.83	1155.14	1138.84	1064.17	1085.40	1063.59	1122.10	1044.75	1108.53	1150.58	1111.22
2008	1153.75	1247.29	1234.55	1219.15	1244.64	1170.90	1223.54	1213.94	1196.47	1188.90	1124.38	1183.57	1200.03
2009	1195.74	1212.49	1241.25	1232.46	1225.41	1189.28	1224.34	1192.38	1163.41	1163.69	1168.57	1234.07	1203.21
Manufacturing													
2007	629.11	668.68	632.79	629.36	678.18	659.59	657.87	639.84	663.12	649.30	674.97	708.58	657.75
2008	701.29	726.85	743.73	718.86	704.90	760.51	738.91	782.65	790.97	780.16	811.82	778.82	753.84
2009	764.54	780.40	776.12	779.15	774.66	755.42	743.27	744.47	740.43	726.67	751.17	764.95	758.45
Trade, Transportation, and Utilities													
2007	601.88	589.94	594.16	611.57	587.97	609.28	622.30	597.43	627.26	586.04	583.78	623.12	603.08
2008	598.18	588.60	602.55	595.68	578.92	609.71	583.70	606.35	597.29	595.46	593.13	579.54	594.81
2009	595.14	612.72	611.06	612.81	603.20	621.09	613.36	630.81	642.74	632.91	644.10	621.23	620.71
Professional and Business Services													
2007	757.62	734.99	718.96	762.62	739.94	726.60	766.49	724.72	738.07	706.68	691.06	715.42	732.16
2008	722.22	696.02	723.86	698.99	691.72	709.69	682.31	682.97	697.06	694.14	730.38	709.69	703.10
2009	700.55	737.55	721.38	702.86	694.66	705.99	696.71	709.05	696.89	702.53	719.95	707.52	707.75
Education and Health Services													
2007	734.72	721.11	722.76	747.14	718.89	742.26	755.96	743.25	749.79	742.15	744.52	780.22	741.61
2008	770.52	752.07	758.01	754.65	751.36	763.95	765.88	751.77	756.28	753.80	802.44	734.14	759.91
2009	701.01	738.08	730.69	706.37	694.85	676.48	683.82	685.78	677.91	669.53	687.89	676.94	694.71
Leisure and Hospitality													
2007	519.53	510.39	503.71	531.61	501.86	523.97	544.79	523.20	533.36	515.68	519.79	540.25	522.24
2008	528.80	531.33	536.92	529.53	517.63	528.53	530.24	532.65	513.51	522.65	524.36	500.15	525.48
2009	513.08	530.41	514.67	504.38	489.60	513.38	502.68	509.17	505.68	489.39	508.98	505.74	507.49

IDAHO
At a Glance

Population:
   1990 census: 1,006,734
   2000 census: 1,293,953
   2009 estimate: 1,545,801

Percent change in population:
   1990–2000: 28.5%
   2000–2009: 19.5%

Percent change in total nonfarm employment:
   1990–2009: 58.3%
   2008–2009: -0.6%

Industry with the largest growth in employment, 1990–2009 (thousands):
   Education and Health Services, 48.8

Industry with the largest decline or smallest growth in employment, 1990–2009 (thousands):
   Mining and Logging, -3.6

Civilian labor force:
   1990: 494,121
   2000: 662,958
   2009: 749,660

Unemployment rate and rank among states (lowest to highest):
   1990: 5.5%, 29th
   2000: 4.6%, 41st
   2009: 8.0%, 21st

Employment by Industry, 2009

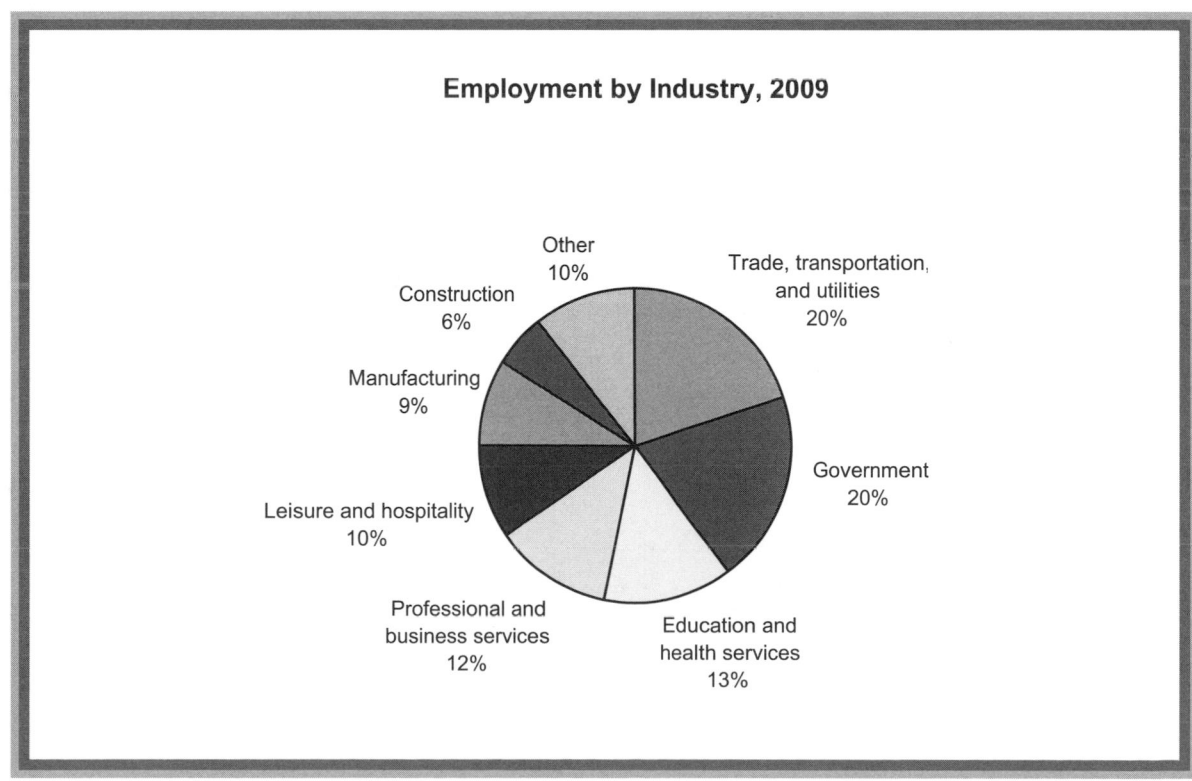

Other 10%
Construction 6%
Manufacturing 9%
Leisure and hospitality 10%
Professional and business services 12%
Education and health services 13%
Government 20%
Trade, transportation, and utilities 20%

Employment by Industry: Idaho, Selected Years, 1990–2009

(Numbers in thousands, not seasonally adjusted.)

Industry and year	January	February	March	April	May	June	July	August	September	October	November	December	Annual average
Total Nonfarm													
1990	364.1	367.9	373.2	378.9	384.1	391.1	387.0	392.4	399.8	398.5	394.7	392.8	385.4
2000	533.0	537.1	543.9	552.9	562.0	569.2	564.6	569.0	574.0	570.2	570.7	568.5	559.6
2001	549.3	553.7	561.0	565.2	571.1	578.9	572.3	576.3	578.0	572.5	568.7	565.6	567.7
2002	545.8	548.2	553.8	562.1	569.4	578.4	574.2	575.9	579.7	579.1	577.2	575.0	568.2
2003	555.3	556.5	561.2	564.8	571.5	580.4	574.9	578.2	583.1	581.0	578.6	578.2	572.0
2004	558.3	564.1	571.9	581.7	589.1	597.5	594.6	596.9	601.3	600.2	599.8	598.9	587.9
2005	581.5	588.5	594.4	603.2	609.5	617.9	617.5	621.1	628.4	624.0	624.6	625.0	611.3
2006	607.9	615.0	622.6	631.7	640.4	649.7	645.7	649.2	654.0	649.0	648.6	647.4	638.4
2007	628.2	635.5	642.3	649.8	659.6	668.7	661.6	665.3	666.9	661.6	661.3	658.3	654.9
2008	633.3	639.4	643.6	649.3	657.7	663.0	659.6	659.4	659.0	648.7	639.1	633.6	648.8
2009	606.7	605.5	604.3	607.7	612.9	617.9	611.3	611.3	615.1	614.0	609.7	603.8	610.0
Total Private													
1990	286.5	288.3	292.1	296.0	300.5	308.7	310.8	315.7	316.5	313.7	310.6	309.3	304.1
2000	428.0	429.3	435.2	441.8	447.0	458.3	460.5	465.8	465.8	459.4	460.1	458.6	450.8
2001	443.7	444.0	450.2	453.9	458.6	468.2	467.1	471.8	466.8	458.6	455.3	453.0	457.6
2002	436.4	436.2	440.6	448.8	454.9	464.1	467.4	470.3	467.7	464.6	462.5	461.1	456.2
2003	444.7	443.9	447.1	451.5	456.0	465.3	467.1	471.4	469.2	465.1	463.2	463.6	459.0
2004	447.9	450.0	457.0	465.6	472.3	482.9	485.7	488.3	485.8	482.8	482.6	483.0	473.7
2005	469.4	472.6	477.8	486.4	492.1	501.8	508.4	512.3	511.7	505.9	506.8	508.5	496.1
2006	493.9	497.6	504.8	513.1	521.1	532.4	535.7	539.6	537.6	530.6	530.8	530.9	522.3
2007	515.1	518.7	525.1	531.6	540.4	550.8	551.0	553.5	547.8	542.1	542.3	539.6	538.2
2008	517.9	519.9	523.5	528.9	536.0	542.8	545.8	545.2	538.4	527.2	517.6	512.5	529.6
2009	489.0	485.9	483.0	484.2	490.0	496.0	498.7	498.4	496.1	491.6	487.8	482.8	490.3
Goods-Producing													
1990	71.6	72.5	73.2	74.4	77.4	80.7	81.6	83.1	84.1	83.4	81.1	78.4	78.5
2000	105.0	104.8	106.0	107.9	110.5	114.5	115.3	116.3	115.8	114.4	114.0	111.7	111.4
2001	107.7	107.2	108.6	109.5	112.0	115.6	115.7	116.6	114.5	111.6	108.0	104.8	111.0
2002	100.0	98.8	99.6	101.8	105.5	108.8	110.5	111.0	110.0	109.2	107.8	105.7	105.7
2003	99.6	98.6	98.0	99.5	101.8	104.9	105.7	106.4	106.0	106.2	104.0	102.1	102.7
2004	97.9	97.9	99.8	103.1	105.5	108.8	110.4	111.4	110.4	110.6	109.1	107.7	106.1
2005	103.1	103.7	105.7	108.5	110.9	114.5	116.9	118.3	118.5	118.2	117.2	116.9	112.7
2006	112.4	113.5	115.9	118.8	122.4	127.1	128.1	128.4	127.8	126.0	124.5	122.6	123.3
2007	117.3	118.0	119.4	121.4	124.7	127.7	128.1	127.6	125.4	122.9	121.2	118.5	122.7
2008	111.6	110.2	110.7	112.0	114.6	116.7	117.2	116.5	114.8	111.8	106.5	102.9	112.1
2009	94.1	90.9	89.7	89.7	91.9	93.9	95.0	95.1	94.3	93.5	90.2	86.6	92.1
Mining and Logging													
1990	6.7	6.6	5.8	5.2	6.0	7.0	7.7	7.9	7.8	7.7	7.2	6.5	6.8
2000	4.6	4.5	3.9	3.7	4.2	4.9	5.2	5.2	5.2	5.0	4.8	4.6	4.7
2001	4.2	4.1	3.6	3.1	3.4	4.2	4.6	4.7	4.6	4.4	4.1	3.9	4.0
2002	3.7	3.6	3.2	2.7	3.1	4.0	4.3	4.3	4.3	4.2	4.0	3.7	3.7
2003	3.5	3.2	2.9	2.7	3.1	3.7	4.1	4.2	4.2	4.1	3.9	3.6	3.6
2004	3.6	3.5	3.2	3.1	3.7	4.2	4.5	4.5	4.6	4.4	4.2	4.0	4.0
2005	3.8	3.6	3.5	3.4	3.8	4.3	4.5	4.7	4.7	4.6	4.3	4.2	4.1
2006	3.8	3.7	3.7	3.5	4.0	4.6	4.7	4.7	4.8	4.5	4.3	4.3	4.2
2007	4.0	4.0	3.8	3.6	4.3	4.8	4.9	5.0	4.9	4.7	4.6	4.4	4.4
2008	4.1	4.1	3.7	3.5	4.0	4.5	4.8	4.8	4.6	4.4	4.1	3.9	4.2
2009	3.4	3.2	2.7	2.5	2.8	3.2	3.6	3.7	3.7	3.7	3.2	2.9	3.2
Construction													
1990	14.6	14.2	15.3	17.2	18.8	20.3	21.4	21.9	21.6	21.7	21.7	19.9	19.1
2000	31.4	31.2	32.6	34.9	36.5	38.7	39.3	40.1	39.7	38.5	37.6	36.0	36.4
2001	33.2	32.8	34.6	36.8	38.9	41.0	41.5	42.3	41.1	39.6	37.8	35.2	37.9
2002	31.5	31.0	31.9	34.4	37.3	38.6	40.0	40.1	39.4	39.0	38.0	36.8	36.5
2003	32.3	32.0	32.7	34.5	36.7	38.4	39.6	40.2	39.8	39.6	38.4	37.1	36.8
2004	33.6	33.5	35.4	38.3	40.1	41.8	43.0	43.7	43.0	42.8	42.1	41.1	39.9
2005	37.7	38.2	40.0	42.8	44.3	46.9	48.4	49.1	49.0	48.3	48.5	47.2	45.0
2006	44.4	45.4	47.4	50.1	52.8	55.9	56.2	56.5	55.6	54.3	53.5	51.4	52.0
2007	47.4	47.8	49.4	51.4	53.6	55.6	55.8	56.1	55.4	52.5	51.0	48.9	52.0
2008	43.3	42.1	43.2	44.8	46.9	48.2	48.5	48.2	47.1	45.0	42.2	39.8	44.9
2009	33.7	31.9	31.8	32.7	34.6	35.9	36.7	36.9	36.3	35.0	33.8	30.6	34.2
Manufacturing													
1990	50.3	51.7	52.1	52.0	52.6	53.4	52.5	53.3	54.7	54.0	52.2	52.0	52.6
2000	69.0	69.1	69.5	69.3	69.8	70.9	70.8	71.0	70.9	70.9	71.6	71.1	70.3
2001	70.3	70.3	70.4	69.6	69.7	70.4	69.6	69.6	68.8	67.6	66.1	65.7	69.0
2002	64.8	64.2	64.5	64.7	65.1	66.2	66.2	66.6	66.3	66.0	65.8	65.2	65.5
2003	63.8	63.4	62.4	62.3	62.0	62.8	62.0	62.0	62.0	62.5	61.7	61.4	62.4
2004	60.7	60.9	61.2	61.7	61.7	62.8	62.9	63.2	62.8	63.4	62.8	62.6	62.2
2005	61.6	61.9	62.2	62.3	62.8	63.3	64.0	64.5	64.8	65.3	64.4	65.5	63.6
2006	64.2	64.4	64.8	65.2	65.6	66.6	67.2	67.2	67.4	67.2	66.7	66.9	66.1
2007	65.9	66.2	66.2	66.4	66.8	67.3	67.4	66.5	66.1	65.7	65.6	65.2	66.3
2008	64.2	64.0	63.8	63.7	63.7	64.0	63.9	63.5	63.1	62.4	60.2	59.2	63.0
2009	57.0	55.8	55.2	54.5	54.5	54.8	54.7	54.5	54.3	54.8	53.2	53.1	54.7

Employment by Industry: Idaho, Selected Years, 1990–2009—*Continued*

(Numbers in thousands, not seasonally adjusted.)

Industry and year	January	February	March	April	May	June	July	August	September	October	November	December	Annual average
Service-Providing													
1990	292.5	295.4	300.0	304.5	306.7	310.4	305.4	309.3	315.7	315.1	313.6	314.4	306.9
2000	428.0	432.3	437.9	445.0	451.5	454.7	449.3	452.7	458.2	455.8	456.7	456.8	448.2
2001	441.6	446.5	452.4	455.7	459.1	463.3	456.6	459.7	463.5	460.9	460.7	460.8	456.7
2002	445.8	449.4	454.2	460.3	463.9	469.6	463.7	464.9	469.7	469.9	469.4	469.3	462.5
2003	455.7	457.9	463.2	465.3	469.7	475.5	469.2	471.8	477.1	474.8	474.6	476.1	469.2
2004	460.4	466.2	472.1	478.6	483.6	488.7	484.2	485.5	490.9	489.6	490.7	491.2	481.8
2005	478.4	484.8	488.7	494.7	498.6	503.4	500.6	502.8	509.9	505.8	507.4	508.1	498.6
2006	495.5	501.5	506.7	512.9	518.0	522.6	517.6	520.8	526.2	523.0	524.1	524.8	516.1
2007	510.9	517.5	522.9	528.4	534.9	541.0	533.5	537.7	541.5	538.7	540.1	539.8	532.2
2008	521.7	529.2	532.9	537.3	543.1	546.3	542.4	542.9	544.2	536.9	532.6	530.7	536.7
2009	512.6	514.6	514.6	518.0	521.0	524.0	516.3	516.2	520.8	520.5	519.5	517.2	517.9
Trade, Transportation, and Utilities													
1990	82.2	81.8	82.4	83.2	84.0	85.0	84.7	85.6	86.7	87.1	87.7	88.6	84.9
2000	116.3	115.6	116.8	118.4	119.7	121.5	121.9	123.8	123.8	123.5	124.8	124.6	120.9
2001	115.5	114.6	115.4	115.7	116.7	117.6	115.9	116.3	116.5	116.0	117.3	117.7	116.3
2002	113.0	112.1	112.8	114.1	115.3	116.1	115.9	116.4	116.5	116.2	117.9	118.4	115.4
2003	113.3	112.5	113.4	113.8	114.5	115.6	115.7	116.5	116.5	116.2	118.0	118.8	115.4
2004	113.4	113.0	114.2	115.9	117.4	118.4	118.8	118.8	118.6	119.2	121.1	122.2	117.6
2005	117.7	117.7	118.9	120.3	121.3	122.7	123.8	124.5	124.8	124.5	126.7	127.8	122.6
2006	122.9	122.6	123.7	125.3	126.6	128.3	128.1	129.1	129.5	129.6	131.9	132.9	127.5
2007	128.8	128.6	130.1	130.7	131.7	132.9	133.0	133.5	133.1	133.5	135.9	136.2	132.3
2008	130.7	129.9	130.4	130.9	131.9	132.6	133.2	133.0	131.6	130.9	131.3	131.1	131.5
2009	123.4	121.9	121.5	121.3	122.3	122.4	122.6	122.6	122.3	121.6	123.0	122.3	122.3
Wholesale Trade													
1990	18.5	18.4	18.5	18.5	18.4	18.4	18.4	18.3	19.0	19.1	18.9	18.9	18.6
2000	24.7	24.7	25.0	25.3	25.4	25.6	25.5	25.4	25.7	25.4	25.4	25.4	25.3
2001	24.8	24.8	25.1	25.1	25.2	25.2	24.6	24.3	24.6	24.6	24.6	24.4	24.8
2002	23.9	24.1	24.3	24.5	24.7	24.8	24.6	24.4	24.7	24.5	24.7	24.4	24.5
2003	23.8	23.9	23.9	24.4	24.5	24.5	24.6	24.4	24.6	24.0	24.2	24.3	24.3
2004	23.8	24.0	24.4	24.7	24.9	25.1	25.4	25.4	25.5	25.4	25.5	25.4	25.0
2005	25.7	25.9	26.4	26.6	26.6	26.6	26.8	26.7	27.0	26.7	26.8	26.8	26.6
2006	26.1	26.4	26.7	27.0	27.1	27.3	27.1	27.1	27.3	27.1	27.4	27.4	27.0
2007	27.2	27.5	27.7	27.8	28.0	28.3	28.3	28.3	28.4	28.1	28.1	28.1	28.0
2008	27.6	27.7	27.9	27.8	28.0	28.1	28.3	28.0	28.1	27.8	27.5	27.3	27.8
2009	26.4	26.3	26.3	26.2	26.1	26.1	26.3	25.8	25.9	25.5	25.1	24.9	25.9
Retail Trade													
1990	50.5	50.0	50.5	51.1	52.0	52.8	52.7	53.2	53.2	53.3	54.3	55.4	52.4
2000	73.4	72.7	73.7	74.9	76.1	77.1	77.6	79.1	78.9	78.8	80.3	79.6	76.9
2001	71.8	71.1	71.5	71.8	72.6	73.3	72.4	72.8	72.6	72.3	73.8	74.5	72.5
2002	70.9	69.7	70.3	71.3	72.2	72.7	72.9	73.1	72.8	72.5	74.2	75.0	72.3
2003	70.8	70.1	70.9	71.2	71.8	72.6	72.5	73.2	72.9	73.1	74.8	75.4	72.4
2004	71.0	70.5	71.1	72.5	73.7	74.2	74.4	74.4	74.0	74.6	76.4	77.4	73.7
2005	73.4	73.0	73.8	74.9	75.9	76.9	77.5	78.1	78.0	77.9	80.0	80.8	76.7
2006	77.3	76.6	77.5	78.5	79.7	80.7	80.9	81.6	81.7	82.0	83.9	84.5	80.4
2007	81.1	80.6	82.1	82.4	83.1	83.7	84.0	84.1	83.5	83.9	86.3	86.5	83.4
2008	82.4	81.5	82.0	82.4	83.1	83.4	83.8	83.6	82.2	81.7	82.6	82.4	82.6
2009	76.5	75.4	75.5	75.5	76.5	76.8	76.9	76.9	76.2	76.3	77.9	77.5	76.5
Transportation and Utilities													
1990	13.2	13.4	13.4	13.6	13.6	13.8	13.6	14.1	14.5	14.7	14.5	14.3	13.9
2000	18.2	18.2	18.1	18.2	18.2	18.8	18.8	19.3	19.2	19.3	19.1	19.6	18.8
2001	18.9	18.7	18.8	18.8	18.9	19.1	18.9	19.2	19.3	19.1	18.9	18.8	18.9
2002	18.2	18.3	18.2	18.3	18.4	18.6	18.4	18.9	19.0	19.2	19.0	19.0	18.6
2003	18.7	18.5	18.6	18.2	18.2	18.5	18.6	18.9	19.0	19.1	19.0	19.1	18.7
2004	18.6	18.5	18.7	18.7	18.8	19.1	19.0	19.0	19.1	19.2	19.2	19.4	18.9
2005	18.6	18.8	18.7	18.8	18.8	19.2	19.5	19.7	19.8	19.9	19.9	20.2	19.3
2006	19.5	19.6	19.5	19.8	19.8	20.3	20.1	20.4	20.5	20.5	20.6	21.0	20.1
2007	20.5	20.5	20.3	20.5	20.6	20.9	20.7	21.1	21.2	21.5	21.5	21.6	20.9
2008	20.7	20.7	20.5	20.7	20.8	21.1	21.1	21.4	21.3	21.4	21.2	21.4	21.0
2009	20.5	20.2	19.7	19.6	19.7	19.5	19.4	19.9	20.2	19.8	20.0	19.9	19.9
Information													
1990	7.4	7.4	7.4	7.5	7.6	7.7	7.6	8.1	7.7	7.5	7.5	7.5	7.6
2000	9.3	9.4	9.7	9.4	9.6	9.8	9.8	9.8	9.8	9.7	9.7	9.8	9.7
2001	9.6	9.7	9.7	9.6	9.6	9.8	9.7	9.8	9.5	9.4	9.4	9.4	9.6
2002	9.2	9.1	9.1	9.2	9.3	9.3	9.1	9.1	9.1	9.1	9.3	9.3	9.2
2003	9.1	9.1	9.1	9.2	9.2	9.2	9.1	9.1	9.1	9.1	9.3	9.3	9.2
2004	9.2	9.2	9.3	9.4	9.7	10.0	10.0	10.1	9.9	9.9	9.9	9.9	9.7
2005	10.0	10.1	10.1	10.3	10.4	10.4	10.5	10.3	10.3	10.5	10.4	10.6	10.3
2006	10.3	10.3	10.3	10.5	10.6	10.8	10.8	10.8	10.7	10.6	10.7	10.8	10.6
2007	10.6	10.6	10.7	10.8	10.9	11.0	10.9	11.0	10.8	10.9	11.0	11.0	10.9
2008	11.0	11.1	11.3	10.9	11.1	11.1	11.2	11.5	11.1	10.7	10.7	10.6	11.0
2009	10.4	10.5	10.3	10.0	10.1	10.1	10.0	9.9	9.7	9.7	9.7	9.7	10.0

Employment by Industry: Idaho, Selected Years, 1990–2009—*Continued*

(Numbers in thousands, not seasonally adjusted.)

Industry and year	January	February	March	April	May	June	July	August	September	October	November	December	Annual average
Financial Activities													
1990	18.9	18.8	19.0	19.0	19.1	19.3	19.3	19.6	19.5	19.3	19.3	19.2	19.2
2000	24.9	24.9	24.9	25.1	25.2	25.4	25.3	25.4	25.4	25.1	25.2	25.1	25.2
2001	24.2	24.2	24.5	24.8	24.9	25.2	25.4	25.7	25.2	25.1	25.1	25.4	25.0
2002	25.1	25.2	25.3	25.3	25.7	25.8	26.3	26.3	26.1	26.1	26.2	26.4	25.8
2003	26.1	26.1	26.3	26.5	26.8	27.2	27.5	27.6	27.4	27.4	27.3	27.6	27.0
2004	26.9	27.0	27.4	27.6	27.7	28.0	28.3	28.3	28.4	28.5	28.5	28.8	28.0
2005	28.3	28.5	28.4	28.8	29.1	29.6	30.2	30.4	30.5	30.5	30.7	30.8	29.7
2006	30.5	30.7	31.1	31.4	31.6	31.9	32.2	32.4	32.3	32.0	32.0	32.3	31.7
2007	31.8	31.9	32.0	32.3	32.7	32.7	33.0	32.8	32.4	32.3	32.5	32.4	32.4
2008	31.6	31.6	31.6	31.8	31.9	32.1	32.2	32.0	31.8	31.3	30.9	31.1	31.7
2009	30.1	30.0	29.8	29.8	29.6	29.6	29.8	29.5	29.2	29.3	29.3	29.2	29.6
Professional and Business Services													
1990	30.6	30.9	31.8	32.7	33.0	34.1	34.8	35.2	35.1	35.0	34.3	34.1	33.5
2000	55.6	56.2	57.9	58.9	60.3	62.1	61.7	62.7	63.4	63.1	63.4	62.6	60.7
2001	64.0	63.9	65.8	66.7	68.2	69.4	69.1	71.1	69.6	68.5	68.1	67.1	67.6
2002	63.7	64.5	65.5	68.5	69.1	70.8	70.8	71.9	71.2	71.7	70.8	69.9	69.0
2003	66.2	67.0	68.2	69.3	69.9	71.5	70.7	72.1	71.9	70.9	70.5	70.3	69.9
2004	67.1	68.1	69.8	72.0	73.5	75.4	75.3	76.1	75.7	75.1	74.9	74.8	73.2
2005	71.5	73.3	74.5	77.0	78.0	79.1	79.8	80.7	80.6	78.9	79.3	78.8	77.6
2006	76.0	77.3	78.8	80.9	82.6	83.9	83.3	84.3	83.8	81.9	81.9	81.0	81.3
2007	77.5	78.8	80.2	82.9	84.2	86.0	85.2	86.4	85.8	84.6	83.9	83.1	83.2
2008	77.1	78.7	79.5	82.4	83.4	84.0	84.0	84.7	83.2	81.1	79.0	78.0	81.3
2009	74.5	74.2	73.5	74.4	75.2	76.1	76.0	76.6	76.7	76.0	74.6	73.9	75.1
Education and Health Services													
1990	30.7	31.1	31.2	31.6	31.3	31.5	31.7	31.9	33.2	33.9	34.3	34.4	32.2
2000	51.3	51.9	52.2	52.3	51.4	51.8	51.7	52.3	53.9	54.3	54.7	55.3	52.8
2001	54.9	55.8	56.2	57.0	55.7	56.1	56.0	56.6	58.1	58.5	59.1	59.6	56.9
2002	58.6	58.9	59.4	59.8	58.9	59.1	59.0	59.1	60.4	60.8	61.3	61.6	59.7
2003	61.3	61.4	61.7	62.3	61.6	61.8	61.6	61.8	63.2	63.4	64.0	64.1	62.4
2004	63.2	64.0	64.6	65.2	64.4	65.0	64.4	64.6	66.3	67.0	67.6	67.3	65.3
2005	66.9	67.5	67.4	67.8	67.0	67.1	66.6	67.1	68.4	68.3	68.6	68.6	67.6
2006	67.8	68.5	69.2	69.2	68.8	68.8	69.9	70.4	71.8	72.1	72.7	72.7	70.2
2007	71.7	72.5	72.8	72.9	73.3	73.8	73.3	73.8	74.4	75.8	76.7	76.7	74.0
2008	75.9	77.0	77.5	77.5	77.3	77.5	77.6	76.3	78.0	79.2	79.3	79.6	77.7
2009	78.7	80.2	80.2	80.7	80.6	80.7	80.6	79.6	81.7	82.9	82.8	82.7	81.0
Leisure and Hospitality													
1990	33.8	34.5	35.6	36.0	36.6	38.7	39.3	40.3	38.8	36.2	35.0	35.7	36.7
2000	48.5	49.2	50.2	52.1	52.2	55.1	56.7	57.3	55.8	51.6	50.6	51.4	52.6
2001	50.0	50.6	51.7	52.3	53.2	55.9	56.8	57.2	55.3	51.7	50.6	51.3	53.0
2002	49.5	50.0	50.8	52.1	53.1	56.0	57.2	57.8	56.3	53.4	51.2	51.9	53.2
2003	51.4	51.4	52.4	52.8	54.1	56.8	58.3	59.2	56.9	53.9	52.1	53.4	54.4
2004	52.5	53.0	53.8	54.0	55.7	58.7	59.6	60.1	58.2	54.4	53.4	54.2	55.6
2005	54.0	53.7	54.7	55.4	57.0	59.8	61.5	62.0	60.1	56.5	55.4	56.6	57.2
2006	55.7	56.2	57.2	58.2	59.6	62.3	63.6	64.5	62.5	59.4	58.2	59.6	59.8
2007	58.7	59.4	60.7	61.3	63.4	66.9	67.6	68.3	66.3	62.7	61.8	62.3	63.3
2008	60.5	61.3	61.9	62.1	64.3	66.8	68.2	68.9	66.1	61.2	59.1	58.4	63.2
2009	56.7	56.9	56.8	57.1	58.9	61.5	63.0	63.3	61.0	58.2	57.9	58.0	59.1
Other Services													
1990	11.3	11.3	11.5	11.6	11.5	11.7	11.8	11.9	11.4	11.3	11.4	11.4	11.5
2000	17.1	17.3	17.5	17.7	18.1	18.1	18.1	18.2	17.9	17.7	17.7	18.1	17.8
2001	17.8	18.0	18.3	18.3	18.3	18.6	18.5	18.5	18.1	17.8	17.7	17.7	18.1
2002	17.3	17.6	18.1	18.0	18.0	18.2	18.6	18.7	18.1	18.1	18.0	17.9	18.1
2003	17.7	17.8	18.0	18.1	18.1	18.3	18.5	18.7	18.2	18.0	18.0	18.0	18.1
2004	17.7	17.8	18.1	18.4	18.4	18.6	18.9	18.9	18.3	18.1	18.1	18.1	18.3
2005	17.9	18.1	18.1	18.3	18.4	18.6	19.1	19.0	18.5	18.5	18.5	18.4	18.5
2006	18.3	18.5	18.6	18.8	18.9	19.3	19.7	19.7	19.2	19.0	18.9	19.0	19.0
2007	18.7	18.9	19.2	19.3	19.5	19.8	19.9	20.1	19.6	19.4	19.3	19.4	19.4
2008	19.5	20.1	20.6	21.3	21.5	22.0	22.2	22.3	21.8	21.0	20.8	20.8	21.2
2009	21.1	21.3	21.2	21.2	21.4	21.7	21.7	21.8	21.2	20.4	20.3	20.4	21.1
Government													
1990	77.6	79.6	81.1	82.9	83.6	82.4	76.2	76.7	83.3	84.8	84.1	83.5	81.3
2000	105.0	107.8	108.7	111.1	115.0	110.9	104.1	103.2	108.2	110.8	110.6	109.9	108.8
2001	105.6	109.7	110.8	111.3	112.5	110.7	105.2	104.5	111.2	113.9	113.4	112.6	110.1
2002	109.4	112.0	113.2	113.3	114.5	114.3	106.8	105.6	112.0	114.5	114.7	113.9	112.0
2003	110.6	112.6	114.1	113.3	115.5	115.1	107.8	106.8	113.9	115.9	115.4	114.6	113.0
2004	110.4	114.1	114.9	116.1	116.8	114.6	108.9	108.6	115.5	117.4	117.2	115.9	114.2
2005	112.1	115.9	116.6	116.8	117.4	116.1	109.1	108.8	116.7	118.1	117.8	116.5	115.2
2006	114.0	117.4	117.8	118.6	119.3	117.3	110.0	109.6	116.4	118.4	117.8	116.5	116.1
2007	113.1	116.8	117.2	118.2	119.2	117.9	110.6	111.8	119.1	119.5	119.0	118.7	116.8
2008	115.4	119.5	120.1	120.4	121.7	120.2	113.8	114.2	120.6	121.5	121.5	121.1	119.2
2009	117.7	119.6	121.3	123.5	122.9	121.9	112.6	112.9	119.0	122.4	121.9	121.0	119.7

Average Weekly Hours by Selected Industry: Idaho, 2007–2009

(Not seasonally adjusted.)

Industry and year	January	February	March	April	May	June	July	August	September	October	November	December	Annual average
Total Private													
2007	33.9	33.8	33.7	34.8	34.4	34.4	34.5	34.7	35.0	34.3	33.9	34.2	34.3
2008	33.5	33.3	34.0	33.6	33.7	34.9	34.5	34.3	34.4	33.7	33.4	33.0	33.9
2009	32.7	33.3	33.3	33.1	33.4	33.3	33.9	35.0	33.7	33.8	34.2	33.2	33.6
Goods-Producing													
2007	36.5	36.7	36.9	37.0	37.6	37.6	36.6	37.7	38.1	37.5	37.1	37.2	37.2
2008	35.9	36.3	36.1	36.4	36.8	37.4	36.9	36.9	38.0	37.2	34.9	35.3	36.5
2009	34.4	35.2	35.3	35.0	36.1	36.2	37.1	38.2	36.9	38.0	37.7	35.7	36.3
Construction													
2007	33.2	34.4	35.1	36.7	38.1	38.0	36.8	37.6	38.4	37.5	37.2	36.2	36.7
2008	34.0	35.0	32.3	33.7	35.4	36.4	36.0	34.9	36.1	34.3	32.7	32.1	34.4
2009	29.9	30.7	31.4	31.3	33.4	33.7	35.1	37.1	33.6	34.7	33.4	33.9	33.3
Manufacturing													
2007	37.7	37.4	37.5	36.8	37.0	37.0	35.9	37.1	37.4	37.0	37.1	37.3	37.1
2008	36.4	36.5	37.5	37.3	37.2	37.6	37.1	37.7	38.8	38.5	35.8	36.7	37.2
2009	36.3	37.3	37.0	36.7	37.0	37.2	37.6	38.1	38.0	39.1	39.7	38.2	37.7
Trade, Transportation, and Utilities													
2007	35.1	34.8	34.3	35.5	35.1	35.2	35.5	35.8	35.9	35.1	35.1	35.0	35.2
2008	34.2	34.2	34.9	34.6	34.7	35.5	35.7	36.0	35.2	34.5	34.5	34.6	34.9
2009	34.1	34.4	34.0	34.2	34.4	34.8	34.8	35.1	33.6	33.5	34.4	33.1	34.2
Financial Activities													
2007	37.3	35.8	35.6	37.5	35.1	34.8	37.1	34.7	36.2	35.4	35.7	37.5	36.1
2008	36.5	36.9	37.4	36.5	36.3	37.3	36.6	36.7	36.1	35.8	37.4	36.3	36.7
2009	37.2	37.4	37.2	36.5	36.1	35.9	36.7	38.1	37.0	37.0	38.0	36.5	37.0
Professional and Business Services													
2007	35.1	34.2	34.7	36.4	35.0	35.3	35.5	35.5	35.8	34.4	34.3	34.6	35.1
2008	34.0	33.9	34.6	34.7	34.5	36.0	35.7	35.0	35.7	34.4	34.3	33.6	34.7
2009	33.5	34.3	34.4	34.3	34.7	34.5	34.5	34.6	34.4	33.3	34.3	33.3	34.2
Education and Health Services													
2007	29.8	31.1	29.9	31.5	31.1	30.6	30.5	29.6	30.4	30.8	30.6	30.3	30.5
2008	29.9	30.0	30.8	30.0	30.4	31.6	31.3	31.1	31.4	31.4	32.4	30.6	30.9
2009	31.1	31.4	31.6	31.4	31.7	31.3	33.3	33.5	32.0	33.0	33.4	33.9	32.3
Leisure and Hospitality													
2007	23.9	24.0	24.7	26.4	26.2	26.6	27.7	27.4	27.5	26.0	25.9	26.5	26.1
2008	25.7	26.0	27.5	26.0	26.2	28.4	28.9	29.1	26.9	26.3	25.5	24.4	26.8
2009	23.8	25.7	25.0	24.2	25.2	23.9	24.5	25.4	23.2	22.8	21.5	21.5	24.0

Average Hourly Earnings by Selected Industry: Idaho, 2007–2009

(Dollars, not seasonally adjusted.)

Industry and year	January	February	March	April	May	June	July	August	September	October	November	December	Annual average
Total Private													
2007	15.93	15.94	16.05	16.05	16.10	16.35	16.35	16.42	17.19	17.22	17.25	17.22	16.51
2008	17.08	16.98	17.12	17.26	17.41	17.53	17.81	17.65	17.98	17.75	17.74	18.00	17.53
2009	18.38	18.88	19.04	19.02	19.03	19.07	19.23	19.26	19.52	19.69	19.95	19.95	19.26
Goods-Producing													
2007	19.43	19.70	19.62	19.80	19.94	20.02	20.50	20.79	20.82	20.97	21.03	21.08	20.32
2008	20.90	20.54	20.66	20.67	20.78	20.81	21.01	20.98	21.29	21.29	21.37	22.06	21.02
2009	22.34	22.65	22.90	23.07	22.44	22.29	22.59	22.54	22.88	22.75	22.90	22.98	22.69
Construction													
2007	16.09	16.42	16.39	16.64	16.87	17.06	16.80	16.95	17.71	17.87	17.83	17.87	17.07
2008	17.54	17.22	17.46	17.29	17.45	17.40	17.60	17.65	17.92	18.15	18.05	18.16	17.65
2009	18.36	19.13	19.56	19.25	18.47	18.64	18.68	19.08	19.28	19.46	19.44	19.81	19.09
Manufacturing													
2007	21.68	21.87	21.74	21.97	22.11	22.33	22.56	22.81	22.67	22.55	22.61	22.72	22.30
2008	22.48	22.06	22.25	22.41	22.46	22.45	22.64	22.50	22.70	22.73	22.81	22.94	22.53
2009	23.20	23.58	23.62	24.10	24.07	23.85	24.31	24.17	24.43	23.99	24.24	24.20	23.98
Trade, Transportation, and Utilities													
2007	14.72	14.85	14.97	14.84	14.93	15.16	15.04	15.16	16.07	15.76	15.76	15.87	15.27
2008	15.91	15.84	15.52	16.08	15.88	15.94	16.00	16.12	16.34	16.32	16.39	16.47	16.07
2009	17.05	17.25	17.44	17.03	17.40	17.34	17.50	17.55	17.70	17.58	17.61	17.53	17.41
Financial Activities													
2007	19.61	19.52	19.67	19.78	19.78	19.69	19.74	19.05	19.44	19.44	19.41	19.37	19.54
2008	20.02	19.84	19.77	19.99	20.12	19.80	20.09	19.87	19.84	20.15	20.24	20.26	20.00
2009	20.41	20.28	20.30	20.85	20.56	20.81	21.56	21.97	21.06	21.41	21.01	21.01	20.94
Professional and Business Services													
2007	19.07	19.22	19.90	19.85	20.22	20.62	20.68	21.75	22.12	23.11	23.07	23.01	21.07
2008	22.96	22.89	23.10	23.25	23.34	23.39	22.59	22.26	22.50	21.31	21.41	21.52	22.55
2009	22.10	22.93	23.32	23.64	23.77	24.22	24.40	25.19	25.28	25.85	26.48	26.53	24.48
Education and Health Services													
2007	15.49	15.42	15.68	15.73	15.77	15.99	16.06	16.30	16.35	16.44	16.54	16.54	16.03
2008	16.51	16.42	16.52	16.71	16.83	16.83	17.04	17.21	17.40	17.50	17.65	17.76	17.04
2009	17.48	18.45	18.58	18.62	18.39	17.67	17.15	16.48	17.10	17.36	17.94	17.78	17.74
Leisure and Hospitality													
2007	9.57	9.56	9.67	9.61	9.69	9.87	9.86	9.89	9.82	9.75	9.82	9.94	9.76
2008	9.86	9.89	10.01	10.06	10.25	10.49	9.98	9.89	10.05	10.02	10.07	10.12	10.06
2009	10.11	10.38	10.36	10.39	10.65	10.42	10.23	10.33	10.18	10.53	10.69	10.66	10.40

Average Weekly Earnings by Selected Industry: Idaho, 2007–2009

(Dollars, not seasonally adjusted.)

Industry and year	January	February	March	April	May	June	July	August	September	October	November	December	Annual average
Total Private													
2007	540.03	538.77	540.89	558.54	553.84	562.44	564.08	569.77	601.65	590.65	584.78	588.92	566.29
2008	572.18	565.43	582.08	579.94	586.72	611.80	614.45	605.40	618.51	598.18	592.52	594.00	594.27
2009	601.03	628.70	634.03	629.56	635.60	635.03	651.90	674.10	657.82	665.52	682.29	662.34	647.14
Goods-Producing													
2007	709.20	722.99	723.98	732.60	749.74	752.75	750.30	783.78	793.24	786.38	780.21	784.18	755.90
2008	750.31	745.60	745.83	752.39	764.70	778.29	775.27	774.16	809.02	791.99	745.81	778.72	767.23
2009	768.50	797.28	808.37	807.45	810.08	806.90	838.09	861.03	844.27	864.50	863.33	820.39	823.65
Construction													
2007	534.19	564.85	575.29	610.69	642.75	648.28	618.24	637.32	680.06	670.13	663.28	646.89	626.47
2008	596.36	602.70	563.96	582.67	617.73	633.36	633.60	615.99	646.91	622.55	590.24	582.94	607.16
2009	548.96	587.29	614.18	602.53	616.90	628.17	655.67	707.87	647.81	675.26	649.30	671.56	635.70
Manufacturing													
2007	817.34	817.94	815.25	808.50	818.07	826.21	809.90	846.25	847.86	834.35	838.83	847.46	827.33
2008	818.27	805.19	834.38	835.89	835.51	844.12	839.94	848.25	880.76	875.11	816.60	841.90	838.12
2009	842.16	879.53	873.94	884.47	890.59	887.22	914.06	920.88	928.34	938.01	962.33	924.44	904.05
Trade, Transportation, and Utilities													
2007	516.67	516.78	513.47	526.82	524.04	533.63	533.92	542.73	576.91	553.18	553.18	555.45	537.50
2008	544.12	541.73	541.65	556.37	551.04	565.87	571.20	580.32	575.17	563.04	565.46	569.86	560.84
2009	581.41	593.40	592.96	582.43	598.56	603.43	609.00	616.01	594.72	588.93	605.78	580.24	595.42
Financial Activities													
2007	731.45	698.82	700.25	741.75	694.28	685.21	732.35	661.04	703.73	688.18	692.94	726.38	705.39
2008	730.73	732.10	739.40	729.64	730.36	738.54	735.29	729.23	716.22	721.37	756.98	735.44	734.00
2009	759.25	758.47	755.16	761.03	742.22	747.08	791.25	837.06	779.22	792.17	798.38	766.87	774.78
Professional and Business Services													
2007	669.36	657.32	690.53	722.54	707.70	727.89	734.14	772.13	791.90	794.98	791.30	796.15	739.56
2008	780.64	775.97	799.26	806.78	805.23	842.04	806.46	779.10	803.25	733.06	734.36	723.07	782.49
2009	740.35	786.50	802.21	810.85	824.82	835.59	841.80	871.57	869.63	860.81	908.26	883.45	837.22
Education and Health Services													
2007	461.60	479.56	468.83	495.50	490.45	489.29	489.83	482.48	497.04	506.35	506.12	501.16	488.92
2008	493.65	492.60	508.82	501.30	511.63	531.83	533.35	535.23	546.36	549.50	571.86	543.46	526.54
2009	543.63	579.33	587.13	584.67	582.96	553.07	571.10	552.08	547.20	572.88	599.20	602.74	573.00
Leisure and Hospitality													
2007	228.72	229.44	238.85	253.70	253.88	262.54	273.12	270.99	270.05	253.50	254.34	263.41	254.74
2008	253.40	257.14	275.20	261.56	268.55	297.92	288.42	287.80	270.35	263.53	256.79	246.93	269.61
2009	240.62	266.77	265.22	251.44	268.38	249.04	250.64	262.38	236.18	240.08	229.84	229.19	249.60

ILLINOIS
At a Glance

Population:
　1990 census: 11,430,602
　2000 census: 12,419,293
　2009 estimate: 12,910,409

Percent change in population:
　1990–2000: 8.6%
　2000–2009: 4.0%

Percent change in total nonfarm employment:
　1990–2009: 7.0%
　2008–2009: -4.9%

Industry with the largest growth in employment, 1990–2009 (thousands):
　Education and Health Services, 279.6

Industry with the largest decline or smallest growth in employment, 1990–2009 (thousands):
　Manufacturing, -337.0

Civilian labor force:
　1990: 5,931,619
　2000: 6,467,692
　2009: 6,606,103

Unemployment rate and rank among states (lowest to highest):
　1990: 6.3%, 41st
　2000: 4.5%, 38th
　2009: 10.1%, 37th

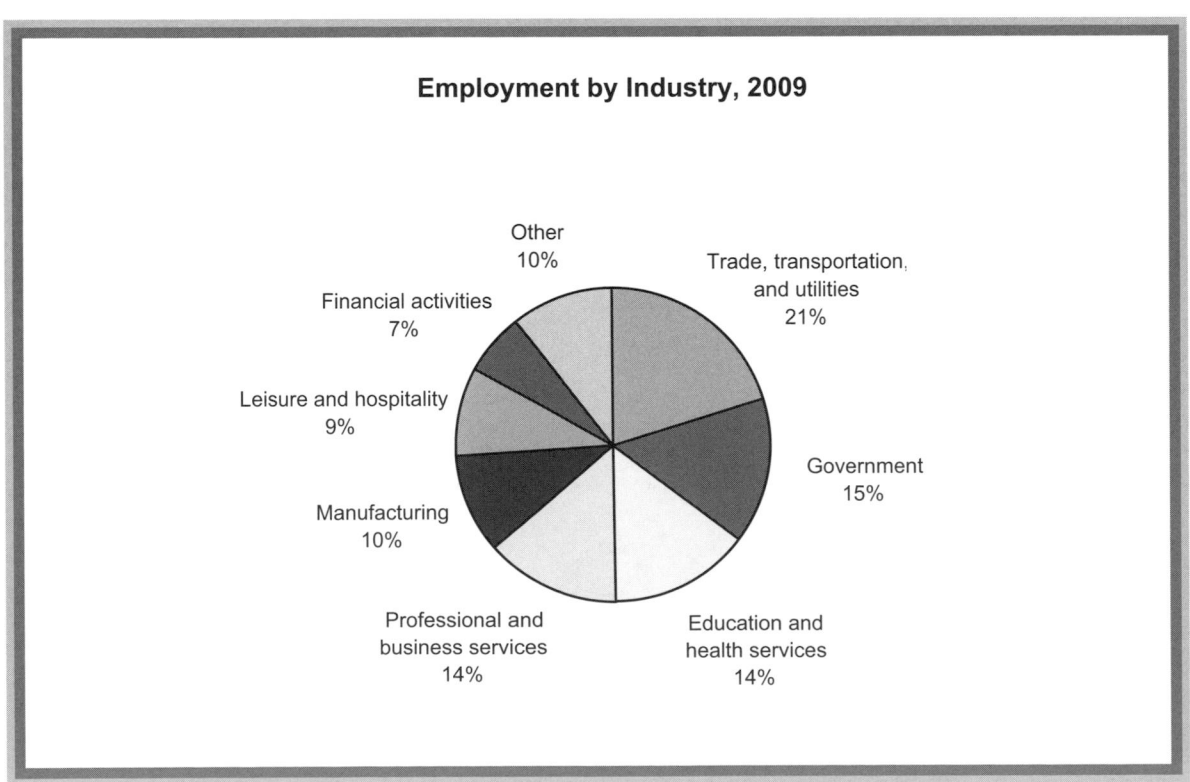

Employment by Industry, 2009

Other 10%

Trade, transportation, and utilities 21%

Financial activities 7%

Leisure and hospitality 9%

Government 15%

Manufacturing 10%

Professional and business services 14%

Education and health services 14%

Employment by Industry: Illinois, Selected Years, 1990–2009

(Numbers in thousands, not seasonally adjusted.)

Industry and year	January	February	March	April	May	June	July	August	September	October	November	December	Annual average
Total Nonfarm													
1990	5157.5	5176.7	5228.7	5252.5	5306.2	5351.7	5329.1	5336.2	5346.8	5320.5	5322.9	5322.8	5287.6
2000	5874.4	5906.8	5973.3	6025.9	6078.8	6124.8	6061.6	6080.5	6095.3	6092.5	6115.2	6108.5	6044.8
2001	5906.2	5930.3	5977.0	6016.0	6060.4	6093.1	6013.3	6012.8	6006.1	5976.1	5977.2	5974.4	5995.2
2002	5778.6	5781.4	5819.3	5875.3	5921.8	5948.7	5897.0	5910.8	5914.5	5914.1	5926.8	5918.3	5883.9
2003	5713.0	5712.1	5742.5	5797.6	5843.1	5869.6	5829.7	5839.2	5843.1	5845.7	5842.4	5851.7	5810.8
2004	5666.8	5673.3	5723.9	5789.2	5842.7	5877.9	5855.2	5855.0	5854.9	5872.1	5882.2	5897.6	5815.9
2005	5700.8	5716.3	5756.8	5844.9	5886.3	5904.9	5905.1	5907.1	5921.3	5922.6	5938.7	5938.4	5861.9
2006	5774.8	5798.4	5845.0	5904.9	5953.7	6003.7	5966.3	5972.5	5982.5	5987.1	6002.3	6001.7	5932.7
2007	5843.2	5845.5	5903.2	5958.4	6017.5	6049.1	6009.7	6011.7	6020.6	6024.2	6044.4	6036.5	5980.3
2008	5869.4	5874.8	5903.8	5962.1	6011.9	6023.3	5985.2	5982.8	5973.4	5968.1	5941.1	5900.6	5949.7
2009	5680.2	5660.1	5654.2	5676.3	5704.4	5700.2	5645.1	5631.3	5644.3	5654.2	5640.5	5599.9	5657.6
Total Private													
1990	4413.1	4413.7	4452.0	4474.1	4523.6	4580.8	4585.9	4603.0	4587.2	4543.6	4542.0	4541.0	4521.7
2000	5057.8	5065.8	5123.3	5178.3	5216.7	5278.9	5251.7	5274.2	5261.9	5243.1	5258.7	5251.9	5205.2
2001	5079.7	5077.5	5120.1	5159.7	5196.0	5242.0	5188.1	5194.2	5158.0	5111.7	5108.2	5103.3	5144.9
2002	4932.8	4915.3	4946.8	4999.5	5040.3	5083.5	5069.0	5088.1	5064.3	5042.3	5049.9	5043.0	5022.9
2003	4865.9	4846.5	4874.2	4927.0	4972.7	5013.4	5001.6	5019.4	5002.8	4988.6	4983.8	4995.5	4957.6
2004	4829.6	4821.1	4867.3	4934.3	4988.1	5036.6	5034.4	5039.2	5021.2	5016.1	5022.6	5044.8	4971.3
2005	4867.8	4865.2	4900.7	4990.7	5029.1	5067.8	5078.7	5085.9	5076.4	5067.1	5079.2	5084.0	5016.1
2006	4942.5	4945.0	4988.3	5050.2	5095.7	5158.7	5146.2	5157.4	5136.8	5133.3	5144.4	5148.9	5087.3
2007	5008.2	4988.7	5043.8	5096.4	5154.0	5204.2	5190.2	5197.1	5169.5	5163.2	5179.6	5177.9	5131.1
2008	5027.8	5010.5	5038.8	5094.4	5140.7	5172.6	5159.0	5164.2	5118.3	5098.1	5070.8	5034.1	5094.1
2009	4835.8	4795.6	4788.3	4800.1	4828.2	4847.1	4816.3	4815.3	4785.3	4783.1	4769.4	4737.7	4800.2
Goods-Producing													
1990	1128.4	1130.5	1139.6	1150.4	1167.3	1184.0	1178.6	1185.5	1176.8	1159.7	1149.7	1134.0	1157.0
2000	1112.9	1115.9	1132.6	1150.3	1160.8	1174.3	1169.7	1170.9	1166.6	1159.9	1154.2	1134.0	1150.1
2001	1091.1	1093.2	1102.0	1113.9	1122.0	1131.3	1114.4	1114.7	1106.3	1092.2	1082.5	1068.2	1102.7
2002	1020.9	1015.9	1023.0	1037.9	1047.3	1060.2	1055.9	1059.7	1055.8	1048.5	1041.8	1026.8	1041.1
2003	982.6	975.7	982.6	999.2	1009.1	1018.3	1013.7	1016.3	1010.5	999.8	990.7	981.5	998.3
2004	939.1	934.1	948.0	967.5	982.5	996.7	996.6	997.1	996.3	992.4	987.8	980.7	976.6
2005	931.9	931.2	940.0	963.7	974.0	984.9	984.1	985.2	984.0	980.1	976.5	963.5	966.6
2006	935.7	935.2	942.7	964.8	973.9	991.2	987.9	988.5	985.5	981.3	975.7	964.0	968.9
2007	931.2	918.6	936.6	953.0	967.3	980.6	975.6	975.8	970.8	963.8	961.1	947.5	956.8
2008	913.1	904.6	912.8	927.3	939.2	948.2	947.5	947.6	940.3	929.7	913.3	885.4	925.8
2009	832.9	819.1	814.5	809.6	808.6	812.4	807.8	808.0	805.1	802.5	788.8	763.6	806.1
Mining and Logging													
1990	18.2	18.0	18.2	18.1	18.3	18.7	18.8	19.0	18.9	18.7	18.6	18.6	18.5
2000	9.7	9.5	9.7	9.8	9.8	9.9	10.0	10.0	10.0	10.1	10.1	9.9	9.8
2001	9.4	9.4	9.8	10.0	10.1	10.2	10.4	10.2	10.2	10.1	10.1	10.0	10.0
2002	9.6	9.5	9.7	9.6	9.6	9.8	9.7	9.7	9.7	9.8	9.7	9.7	9.7
2003	9.1	9.1	9.3	9.6	9.6	9.8	9.4	9.5	9.5	9.5	9.5	9.3	9.4
2004	8.6	8.6	9.0	9.3	9.5	9.7	9.7	9.7	9.8	9.5	9.6	9.5	9.4
2005	8.8	8.9	9.2	9.6	9.8	10.1	10.2	10.2	10.3	10.4	10.4	10.4	9.9
2006	10.0	9.9	10.0	10.1	10.4	10.6	10.5	10.3	10.3	10.4	10.3	10.2	10.3
2007	9.7	9.7	10.0	10.2	10.5	10.7	10.5	10.3	10.0	10.1	10.1	9.7	10.1
2008	9.3	9.3	9.6	9.5	9.9	9.9	9.9	10.1	10.0	10.0	9.9	9.8	9.8
2009	9.2	9.3	9.4	9.6	9.5	9.7	9.5	9.4	9.5	9.5	9.6	9.3	9.5
Construction													
1990	197.9	197.9	203.8	215.9	227.6	236.2	242.2	244.6	240.7	233.9	229.1	216.4	223.8
2000	234.8	234.6	248.2	266.1	276.3	285.2	287.1	289.7	286.6	284.7	279.6	263.8	269.7
2001	239.0	241.5	252.3	272.0	284.5	293.0	295.5	297.6	292.8	291.1	289.4	278.9	277.3
2002	246.4	244.1	251.4	268.3	278.9	289.5	295.2	298.3	296.4	295.4	289.9	276.9	277.6
2003	246.8	240.8	248.2	268.1	280.1	289.4	295.1	297.7	294.0	287.4	280.1	270.1	274.8
2004	238.8	233.7	245.1	263.4	274.8	283.7	287.7	287.4	286.0	285.6	281.2	273.4	270.1
2005	236.7	235.7	243.1	263.5	273.8	281.6	285.0	285.8	285.6	284.8	280.5	266.4	268.5
2006	245.2	244.7	252.9	272.5	281.8	292.3	292.1	293.6	289.9	287.9	281.7	269.0	275.3
2007	244.5	233.6	249.8	266.5	279.8	288.9	289.4	290.1	287.2	284.3	278.9	263.8	271.4
2008	236.3	231.2	239.2	255.3	267.0	273.4	277.6	279.2	275.2	270.4	258.6	240.0	258.6
2009	206.8	203.0	207.3	216.0	223.8	230.0	233.5	233.4	230.5	230.5	217.6	196.3	219.1
Manufacturing													
1990	912.3	914.6	917.6	916.4	921.4	929.1	917.6	921.9	917.2	907.1	902.0	899.0	914.6
2000	868.4	871.8	874.7	874.4	874.7	879.2	872.6	871.2	870.0	865.1	864.5	860.3	870.5
2001	842.7	842.3	839.9	831.9	827.4	828.1	808.5	806.9	803.3	791.0	783.0	779.3	815.4
2002	764.9	762.3	761.9	760.0	758.8	760.9	751.0	751.7	749.7	743.3	742.2	740.2	753.9
2003	726.7	725.8	725.1	721.5	719.4	719.1	709.2	709.1	707.0	702.9	701.1	702.1	714.1
2004	691.7	691.8	693.9	694.8	698.2	703.3	699.2	700.0	700.5	697.3	697.0	697.8	697.1
2005	686.4	686.6	687.7	690.6	690.4	693.2	688.9	689.2	688.1	684.9	685.6	686.7	688.2
2006	680.5	680.6	679.8	682.2	681.7	688.3	685.3	684.6	685.3	683.0	683.7	684.8	683.3
2007	677.0	675.3	676.8	676.3	677.0	681.0	675.7	675.4	673.6	669.4	672.1	674.0	675.3
2008	667.5	664.1	664.0	662.5	662.3	664.9	660.0	658.3	655.1	649.3	644.8	635.6	657.4
2009	616.9	606.8	597.8	584.0	575.3	572.7	564.8	565.2	565.1	562.5	561.6	558.0	577.6

Employment by Industry: Illinois, Selected Years, 1990–2009—*Continued*

(Numbers in thousands, not seasonally adjusted.)

Industry and year	January	February	March	April	May	June	July	August	September	October	November	December	Annual average
Service-Providing													
1990	4029.1	4046.2	4089.1	4102.1	4138.9	4167.7	4150.5	4150.7	4170.0	4160.8	4173.2	4188.8	4130.6
2000	4761.5	4790.9	4840.7	4875.6	4918.0	4950.5	4891.9	4909.6	4928.7	4932.6	4961.0	4974.5	4894.6
2001	4815.1	4837.1	4875.0	4902.1	4938.4	4961.8	4898.9	4898.1	4899.8	4883.9	4894.7	4906.2	4892.6
2002	4757.7	4765.5	4796.3	4837.4	4874.5	4888.5	4841.1	4851.1	4858.7	4865.6	4885.0	4891.5	4842.7
2003	4730.4	4736.4	4759.9	4798.4	4834.0	4851.3	4816.0	4822.9	4832.6	4845.9	4851.7	4870.2	4812.5
2004	4727.7	4739.2	4775.9	4821.7	4860.2	4881.2	4858.6	4857.9	4858.6	4879.7	4894.4	4916.9	4839.3
2005	4768.9	4785.1	4816.8	4881.2	4912.3	4920.0	4921.0	4921.9	4937.3	4942.5	4962.2	4974.9	4895.3
2006	4839.1	4863.2	4902.3	4940.1	4979.8	5012.5	4978.4	4984.0	4997.0	5005.8	5026.6	5037.7	4963.9
2007	4912.0	4926.9	4966.6	5005.4	5050.2	5068.5	5034.1	5035.9	5049.8	5060.4	5083.3	5089.0	5023.5
2008	4956.3	4970.2	4991.0	5034.8	5072.7	5075.1	5037.7	5035.2	5033.1	5038.4	5027.8	5015.2	5024.0
2009	4847.3	4841.0	4839.7	4866.7	4895.8	4887.8	4837.3	4823.3	4839.2	4851.7	4851.7	4836.3	4851.5
Trade, Transportation, and Utilities													
1990	1142.7	1129.3	1134.7	1131.4	1140.2	1151.5	1148.4	1151.1	1146.6	1147.5	1160.3	1176.0	1146.6
2000	1232.7	1220.7	1226.6	1231.2	1238.7	1246.8	1242.8	1249.5	1249.3	1256.9	1280.0	1295.7	1247.6
2001	1241.9	1225.7	1230.2	1233.2	1236.7	1242.1	1225.1	1224.0	1221.6	1217.0	1234.9	1246.2	1231.6
2002	1194.2	1176.7	1182.1	1186.3	1193.8	1198.7	1192.2	1195.6	1196.6	1200.7	1221.0	1235.1	1197.8
2003	1180.2	1168.0	1171.1	1173.2	1181.7	1186.2	1173.0	1177.0	1178.7	1185.8	1201.8	1217.3	1182.8
2004	1164.7	1153.2	1159.7	1167.1	1179.1	1184.7	1176.7	1178.6	1180.0	1188.3	1206.5	1222.3	1180.1
2005	1170.9	1159.2	1166.4	1176.0	1184.5	1188.6	1184.2	1187.0	1188.4	1193.0	1213.1	1230.2	1186.8
2006	1182.0	1171.7	1179.7	1185.1	1195.2	1203.4	1195.6	1197.5	1197.8	1203.0	1226.4	1242.2	1198.3
2007	1201.3	1185.7	1196.3	1195.8	1209.8	1217.5	1210.4	1210.1	1211.1	1214.5	1240.7	1254.6	1212.3
2008	1210.4	1194.0	1199.0	1200.1	1209.1	1212.2	1203.4	1203.1	1198.4	1200.2	1210.9	1216.9	1204.8
2009	1161.9	1143.9	1138.2	1136.1	1142.9	1144.0	1129.5	1130.9	1128.1	1130.8	1144.9	1153.9	1140.4
Wholesale Trade													
1990	302.9	303.1	305.2	305.7	307.6	310.8	312.8	312.9	310.6	308.2	306.6	307.1	307.8
2000	315.9	316.3	318.2	319.5	321.0	323.6	322.9	322.5	321.9	322.6	322.2	323.2	320.8
2001	316.8	316.5	317.6	319.8	319.8	320.7	318.2	317.4	315.9	312.7	312.1	311.8	316.6
2002	305.7	305.0	305.9	307.0	307.9	310.4	308.1	307.8	307.3	307.3	307.7	307.7	307.3
2003	303.6	303.2	304.2	304.2	305.0	305.6	303.9	302.4	301.2	300.8	300.8	301.0	303.0
2004	296.0	295.4	297.1	298.9	301.0	302.6	301.6	301.0	300.3	301.5	301.6	302.4	300.0
2005	296.7	296.9	299.5	302.0	303.1	305.2	305.2	304.7	304.7	304.7	305.4	306.6	302.9
2006	303.2	303.3	305.2	306.7	308.4	311.2	309.7	308.9	308.3	308.8	308.8	310.0	307.7
2007	305.9	305.5	307.6	308.8	310.7	313.8	312.8	312.1	311.7	312.9	312.9	313.8	310.7
2008	309.0	308.2	309.5	310.7	312.8	314.1	312.3	311.4	309.7	309.9	308.8	307.4	310.3
2009	299.2	296.7	295.6	294.0	293.4	293.4	290.6	289.6	287.3	285.5	284.7	282.0	291.0
Retail Trade													
1990	613.3	598.6	599.2	596.5	601.2	608.5	606.5	608.9	604.2	607.1	620.9	635.6	608.3
2000	644.4	632.8	636.2	637.2	642.2	648.6	645.7	650.4	648.3	654.0	676.8	690.7	650.6
2001	650.5	636.2	638.6	638.1	640.9	647.5	637.0	637.4	633.9	634.2	655.4	669.4	643.3
2002	630.4	615.4	620.3	620.9	626.9	632.2	628.2	629.8	628.2	630.9	651.4	665.7	631.7
2003	621.0	611.1	613.4	614.7	621.0	626.4	620.3	623.5	622.1	627.5	643.7	658.8	625.3
2004	618.1	608.0	611.4	614.5	622.3	628.9	622.4	624.2	621.8	626.0	644.5	659.5	625.1
2005	619.9	608.1	611.4	617.0	623.2	626.6	625.8	627.4	624.1	627.3	645.4	659.3	626.3
2006	622.6	611.8	615.8	618.2	624.2	630.8	627.3	628.5	622.8	628.5	650.8	661.7	628.6
2007	632.8	618.0	624.5	623.3	632.6	638.2	635.6	634.1	630.3	632.4	657.1	667.1	635.5
2008	635.6	620.4	623.0	623.4	628.0	632.2	628.8	626.7	620.4	621.9	633.7	639.1	627.8
2009	604.1	590.7	587.6	590.3	596.7	600.0	594.0	594.0	589.7	592.2	607.3	616.8	597.0
Transportation and Utilities													
1990	226.5	227.6	230.3	229.2	231.4	232.2	229.1	229.3	231.8	232.2	232.8	233.3	230.4
2000	272.4	271.6	272.2	274.5	275.5	274.6	274.2	276.6	279.1	280.3	281.0	281.8	276.1
2001	274.6	273.0	274.0	275.3	276.0	273.9	269.9	269.2	271.8	270.1	267.4	265.0	271.7
2002	258.1	256.3	255.9	258.4	259.0	256.1	255.9	258.0	261.1	262.5	261.9	261.7	258.7
2003	255.6	253.7	253.5	254.3	255.7	254.2	248.8	251.1	255.4	257.5	257.3	257.5	254.6
2004	250.6	249.8	251.2	253.7	255.8	253.2	252.7	253.4	257.9	260.8	260.4	260.4	255.0
2005	254.3	254.2	255.5	257.0	258.2	256.8	253.2	254.9	259.6	261.0	262.3	264.3	257.6
2006	256.2	256.6	258.7	260.2	262.6	261.4	258.6	260.1	266.7	265.7	266.8	270.5	262.0
2007	262.6	262.2	264.2	263.7	266.5	265.5	262.0	263.9	269.1	269.2	270.7	273.7	266.1
2008	265.8	265.4	266.5	266.0	268.3	265.9	262.3	265.0	268.3	268.4	268.4	270.4	266.7
2009	258.6	256.5	255.0	251.8	252.8	250.6	244.9	247.3	251.1	253.1	252.9	255.1	252.5
Information													
1990	130.7	130.8	130.8	129.8	130.6	132.0	132.7	132.2	131.5	131.1	131.5	131.5	131.3
2000	143.9	144.4	145.8	145.8	147.0	148.5	148.9	149.5	147.8	148.7	150.0	150.8	147.6
2001	148.0	148.4	148.8	148.6	149.0	150.4	148.3	147.8	145.7	143.7	143.9	144.4	147.3
2002	141.3	140.6	140.4	140.3	140.0	139.6	136.7	136.2	133.5	133.0	132.5	132.0	137.2
2003	129.0	128.9	127.8	128.0	128.1	128.4	128.1	127.4	126.3	126.0	126.1	126.2	127.5
2004	122.2	122.1	121.8	121.6	121.7	121.8	121.1	120.4	118.9	119.2	119.3	120.0	120.8
2005	118.8	118.3	118.4	119.0	119.0	119.4	119.3	118.4	117.3	116.6	116.7	117.0	118.2
2006	116.4	116.0	116.2	116.9	117.1	117.4	117.1	116.3	115.1	115.3	115.3	115.9	116.3
2007	115.3	115.7	115.7	115.7	116.2	116.9	116.9	116.8	115.6	115.5	115.7	116.0	116.0
2008	115.4	115.4	115.9	115.6	115.9	115.8	115.5	115.0	113.0	112.1	111.7	111.6	114.4
2009	109.9	108.9	108.2	107.6	107.2	107.0	106.1	105.7	104.6	104.0	103.3	104.0	106.4

Employment by Industry: Illinois, Selected Years, 1990–2009—*Continued*

(Numbers in thousands, not seasonally adjusted.)

Industry and year	January	February	March	April	May	June	July	August	September	October	November	December	Annual average
Financial Activities													
1990	369.0	369.8	371.3	370.5	373.2	378.6	381.4	380.9	377.3	372.7	372.6	374.4	374.3
2000	403.0	402.8	402.6	402.1	402.7	407.4	406.2	406.8	402.1	402.8	403.1	407.6	404.1
2001	400.4	401.1	403.5	402.9	404.3	408.7	407.6	406.7	402.0	400.7	401.8	403.7	403.6
2002	398.7	398.3	399.1	398.2	399.4	403.3	402.7	402.9	400.1	400.2	401.3	403.7	400.7
2003	398.9	398.1	399.3	400.1	402.1	406.3	406.1	406.5	403.0	399.4	399.7	401.7	401.8
2004	396.7	396.2	398.0	397.0	398.6	402.5	403.0	403.0	399.1	398.7	398.8	401.7	399.4
2005	396.2	395.9	396.6	399.6	400.9	403.9	406.4	406.3	403.8	403.7	403.6	406.2	401.9
2006	401.0	401.1	402.4	403.2	404.5	408.1	408.6	408.7	405.6	406.0	405.7	407.3	405.2
2007	403.3	402.8	402.8	403.3	404.3	407.2	406.5	404.9	400.4	399.5	398.9	399.5	402.8
2008	393.6	393.5	393.7	393.4	394.1	396.0	394.3	393.7	388.6	387.6	385.7	385.7	391.7
2009	378.4	376.3	374.7	373.7	373.5	374.4	372.5	371.3	367.1	366.1	365.9	367.6	371.8
Professional and Business Services													
1990	551.4	555.5	564.8	567.6	571.7	580.6	588.1	591.7	589.4	576.9	573.4	568.6	573.3
2000	799.5	807.1	822.3	839.0	843.5	859.3	855.3	865.2	863.3	856.3	853.7	848.0	842.7
2001	812.2	810.9	816.3	823.7	828.2	837.2	828.8	832.7	824.4	818.0	807.9	804.0	820.4
2002	771.2	769.7	773.2	789.7	792.8	799.3	802.8	810.9	806.4	799.3	795.5	786.8	791.5
2003	754.9	753.7	757.2	769.9	774.7	779.2	781.8	789.9	793.4	795.3	789.2	789.2	777.4
2004	758.5	762.3	771.0	791.9	798.3	810.7	813.5	817.1	815.8	815.5	811.8	817.8	798.7
2005	786.6	790.8	797.8	820.0	821.6	832.1	838.5	843.2	845.1	850.4	848.7	844.4	826.6
2006	815.2	819.1	830.0	847.3	852.4	866.4	866.5	873.1	870.6	874.9	870.2	865.2	854.2
2007	835.2	837.5	847.2	866.4	872.5	882.9	884.9	889.7	884.6	886.3	882.2	878.8	870.7
2008	846.7	848.9	850.5	866.0	869.7	874.0	872.5	875.0	865.0	860.9	850.6	838.8	859.9
2009	797.3	788.0	780.1	785.4	787.0	788.3	785.8	786.6	780.1	785.6	780.7	773.9	784.9
Education and Health Services													
1990	525.5	529.1	533.7	531.8	534.6	532.3	531.0	532.7	544.0	549.5	552.7	554.1	537.5
2000	671.6	676.6	680.0	681.5	682.9	684.2	673.8	675.4	683.8	684.3	689.0	690.4	681.1
2001	682.2	688.5	694.9	696.8	698.0	697.7	692.0	695.5	702.4	703.2	706.7	707.9	697.2
2002	699.8	706.1	709.9	711.1	713.9	710.3	703.0	705.0	712.8	716.0	719.4	720.5	710.7
2003	709.0	712.2	716.0	715.6	717.9	716.7	712.7	715.1	720.5	724.8	727.2	728.7	718.0
2004	719.7	723.9	727.3	729.7	730.9	727.4	723.6	724.7	731.3	736.9	740.0	743.5	729.9
2005	734.6	738.3	740.1	745.5	746.9	741.7	740.8	740.8	748.8	752.4	755.1	757.2	745.2
2006	748.0	755.2	758.7	759.3	762.0	760.5	756.2	759.3	767.5	770.6	774.6	775.2	762.3
2007	765.9	773.8	777.4	777.6	779.2	777.3	772.7	774.1	782.4	788.6	793.0	795.2	779.8
2008	785.8	791.9	793.5	798.6	801.1	798.6	795.6	799.1	806.0	811.8	815.9	817.1	801.3
2009	806.5	812.4	816.1	815.0	817.8	815.6	810.7	810.7	817.5	825.9	830.5	825.9	817.1
Leisure and Hospitality													
1990	362.5	365.2	373.2	388.7	401.3	413.1	415.4	417.4	411.7	396.9	392.1	391.3	394.0
2000	454.1	457.1	469.7	483.6	496.1	509.4	506.9	508.6	501.5	489.5	483.5	479.5	486.6
2001	459.6	463.5	475.1	490.5	506.3	518.3	514.4	516.1	504.0	488.0	480.2	477.9	491.2
2002	459.7	460.6	469.9	486.1	502.6	515.0	515.6	517.6	508.1	494.9	488.0	486.7	492.1
2003	464.7	463.5	471.5	492.3	509.2	522.0	520.8	521.7	513.7	501.0	493.6	494.0	497.3
2004	473.9	473.3	483.5	501.5	518.3	528.8	531.4	531.4	522.4	507.8	501.5	499.5	506.1
2005	476.4	478.5	487.0	511.0	525.4	534.8	537.8	537.7	530.9	514.3	508.4	506.4	512.4
2006	487.5	491.0	500.7	517.9	533.4	548.1	547.9	547.4	537.1	524.3	518.6	518.9	522.7
2007	500.7	499.2	509.4	526.6	544.6	555.9	553.7	556.0	544.6	534.9	527.6	524.7	531.5
2008	504.7	503.5	513.1	532.8	548.8	559.7	556.7	557.6	543.9	533.3	521.1	517.0	532.7
2009	493.4	491.4	499.5	516.0	533.1	542.4	538.6	537.7	528.5	514.3	502.6	496.9	516.2
Other Services													
1990	203.1	203.5	203.9	204.4	204.7	208.7	210.3	211.5	209.9	209.3	209.7	211.1	207.5
2000	240.1	241.2	243.7	244.8	245.0	249.0	248.1	248.3	247.5	244.7	245.2	245.9	245.2
2001	244.3	246.2	249.3	250.1	251.5	256.3	257.5	256.7	251.6	248.9	250.3	251.0	251.1
2002	247.0	247.4	249.2	249.9	250.5	257.1	260.1	260.2	251.0	249.7	250.4	251.4	252.0
2003	246.6	246.4	248.7	248.7	249.9	256.3	265.4	265.5	256.7	256.5	255.5	256.9	254.4
2004	254.8	256.0	258.0	258.0	258.7	264.0	268.5	266.9	257.4	257.3	256.9	259.3	259.7
2005	252.4	253.0	254.4	255.9	256.8	262.4	267.6	267.3	258.1	256.6	257.1	259.1	258.4
2006	256.7	255.7	257.9	255.7	257.2	263.6	266.4	266.6	257.6	257.9	257.9	260.2	259.5
2007	255.3	255.4	258.4	258.0	260.1	265.9	269.5	269.7	260.0	260.1	260.4	261.6	261.2
2008	258.1	258.7	260.3	260.6	262.8	268.1	273.5	273.1	262.2	262.5	261.6	261.6	263.6
2009	255.5	255.6	257.0	256.7	258.1	263.0	265.3	264.4	254.3	253.9	252.7	251.9	257.4
Government													
1990	744.4	763.0	776.7	778.4	782.6	770.9	743.2	733.2	759.6	776.9	780.9	781.8	765.9
2000	816.6	841.0	850.0	847.6	862.1	845.9	809.9	806.3	833.4	849.4	856.5	856.6	839.6
2001	826.5	852.8	856.9	856.3	864.4	851.1	825.2	818.6	848.1	864.4	869.0	871.1	850.4
2002	845.8	866.1	872.5	875.8	881.5	865.2	828.0	822.7	850.2	871.8	876.9	875.3	861.0
2003	847.1	865.6	868.3	870.6	870.4	856.2	828.1	819.8	840.3	857.1	858.6	856.2	853.2
2004	837.2	852.2	856.6	854.9	854.6	841.3	820.8	815.8	833.7	856.0	859.6	852.8	844.6
2005	833.0	851.1	856.1	854.2	857.2	837.1	826.4	821.2	844.9	855.5	859.5	854.4	845.9
2006	832.3	853.4	856.7	854.7	858.0	845.0	820.1	815.1	845.7	853.8	857.9	852.8	845.5
2007	835.0	856.8	859.4	862.0	863.5	844.9	819.5	814.6	851.1	861.0	864.8	858.6	849.3
2008	841.6	864.3	865.0	867.7	871.2	850.7	826.2	818.6	855.1	870.0	870.3	866.5	855.6
2009	844.4	864.5	865.9	876.2	876.2	853.1	828.8	816.0	859.0	871.1	871.1	862.2	857.4

Average Weekly Hours by Selected Industry: Illinois, 2007–2009

(Not seasonally adjusted.)

Industry and year	January	February	March	April	May	June	July	August	September	October	November	December	Annual average
Total Private													
2007	33.9	33.9	34.3	34.4	34.3	34.5	34.7	34.3	35.0	34.3	34.2	34.7	34.4
2008	33.7	33.9	34.5	34.2	34.3	34.5	34.3	34.5	34.5	34.4	34.5	34.3	34.3
2009	34.1	34.5	34.5	34.4	34.4	34.4	34.4	34.5	34.5	34.4	34.5	34.5	34.4
Goods-Producing													
2007	39.0	38.8	39.7	39.3	40.0	40.1	39.3	39.7	40.3	39.8	39.6	39.6	39.6
2008	39.1	38.8	39.1	38.9	39.5	39.1	39.1	39.2	39.1	39.1	38.9	38.8	39.1
2009	38.8	38.8	39.2	39.1	39.3	39.4	39.3	39.5	39.4	39.6	39.7	39.6	39.3
Construction													
2007	36.0	34.0	36.9	36.3	38.3	38.7	37.7	37.8	38.5	38.3	37.3	36.1	37.2
2008	36.4	36.4	36.3	35.8	36.1	36.2	36.3	36.5	36.4	36.5	36.5	36.4	36.3
2009	36.3	37.5	37.6	37.6	37.7	37.9	37.8	38.0	37.9	38.1	38.1	38.2	37.7
Manufacturing													
2007	40.1	40.4	40.7	40.4	40.6	40.5	39.8	40.4	40.9	40.4	40.5	41.0	40.5
2008	40.2	39.9	40.2	39.9	40.1	39.7	39.6	39.7	39.6	39.5	39.5	39.4	39.8
2009	39.3	39.4	39.6	39.5	39.6	39.7	39.8	39.9	39.8	40.0	40.2	40.0	39.7
Trade, Transportation, and Utilites													
2007	33.6	33.7	34.0	34.3	34.3	34.6	34.6	34.2	35.2	34.5	34.3	34.9	34.4
2008	33.5	33.9	34.3	34.1	34.3	34.7	34.6	34.8	34.8	34.7	34.9	34.7	34.4
2009	33.6	33.9	33.9	33.9	33.9	33.7	33.8	33.9	33.9	33.8	34.0	34.2	33.9
Information													
2007	35.3	36.0	35.6	35.7	35.2	35.1	36.3	36.5	38.3	37.9	37.6	38.1	36.5
2008	36.8	36.9	37.7	37.4	37.0	37.3	37.0	37.3	37.3	37.4	37.5	37.3	37.2
2009	37.2	39.5	39.6	39.3	39.2	39.2	39.3	39.4	39.3	39.3	39.4	39.5	39.2
Financial Activities													
2007	37.4	37.8	37.0	37.9	36.4	36.6	37.9	36.7	37.4	35.9	36.0	36.6	37.0
2008	36.0	36.3	36.8	36.2	35.9	36.2	36.0	36.1	36.0	36.1	36.2	36.3	36.2
2009	36.4	37.0	37.0	36.9	36.8	36.8	37.0	37.1	37.0	36.8	36.8	36.7	36.9
Professional and Business Services													
2007	34.3	34.6	34.9	35.2	35.5	35.5	35.8	35.3	36.1	35.4	35.0	36.0	35.3
2008	34.9	35.1	36.4	35.8	36.0	36.3	36.1	36.3	36.2	36.3	36.3	36.3	36.0
2009	36.2	37.2	37.1	36.9	37.0	36.8	36.7	36.8	36.7	36.7	36.9	36.7	36.8
Education and Health Services													
2007	32.5	32.2	32.5	32.6	32.2	32.5	32.9	32.5	33.2	31.8	32.2	32.4	32.5
2008	32.1	32.1	32.4	32.2	31.9	32.2	32.0	32.2	32.3	32.3	32.4	32.3	32.2
2009	32.4	32.4	32.4	32.3	32.3	32.4	32.5	32.7	32.7	32.7	32.6	32.4	32.5
Leisure and Hospitality													
2007	25.3	25.4	25.8	25.5	25.4	25.7	25.8	25.5	25.4	25.3	25.0	25.4	25.5
2008	24.2	24.7	25.1	25.0	25.2	25.5	25.4	25.3	25.2	25.1	25.2	25.1	25.1
2009	25.0	26.1	26.1	26.0	26.1	26.2	26.0	25.8	25.7	25.5	25.7	25.6	25.8
Other Services													
2007	30.7	30.2	31.1	31.1	31.1	31.8	32.1	31.3	31.7	31.7	31.4	31.9	31.3
2008	31.0	32.2	32.5	32.7	32.7	32.9	32.7	32.8	32.7	32.3	32.7	31.8	32.4
2009	32.0	32.1	32.2	32.1	32.3	32.2	32.4	32.6	32.6	32.4	32.3	32.1	32.3

Average Hourly Earnings by Selected Industry: Illinois, 2007–2009

(Dollars, not seasonally adjusted.)

Industry and year	January	February	March	April	May	June	July	August	September	October	November	December	Annual average
Total Private													
2007	22.61	22.91	22.71	23.36	23.12	23.02	23.34	23.02	23.34	22.49	22.50	22.80	22.94
2008	22.81	22.50	22.63	22.63	22.54	22.63	22.66	22.67	22.74	22.75	22.74	22.77	22.67
2009	22.81	23.04	23.11	23.06	22.96	22.98	23.07	23.11	23.12	23.10	23.13	23.11	23.05
Goods-Producing													
2007	23.48	23.12	23.40	23.96	23.87	24.03	24.53	24.30	24.48	24.04	23.95	24.05	23.94
2008	23.63	23.73	24.04	24.21	24.19	24.49	24.63	24.72	24.74	24.83	24.71	24.77	24.39
2009	24.62	24.74	24.99	25.04	24.89	24.81	24.97	25.04	25.06	25.00	25.14	25.00	24.94
Construction													
2007	30.78	30.85	30.68	30.93	30.90	31.10	31.42	31.45	31.71	30.72	30.61	31.66	31.08
2008	30.22	30.90	31.17	31.32	31.46	31.59	31.59	31.58	31.48	31.45	31.32	31.53	31.32
2009	31.52	32.18	32.29	32.23	32.16	32.03	32.15	32.20	32.22	32.20	32.29	32.48	32.16
Manufacturing													
2007	22.54	22.25	22.13	22.57	22.06	22.05	22.52	22.15	22.20	21.54	21.67	21.76	22.12
2008	21.65	21.44	21.55	21.70	21.46	21.56	21.64	21.69	21.76	21.86	21.89	21.93	21.67
2009	21.92	22.05	22.13	22.12	22.08	22.14	22.05	22.11	22.13	22.00	22.20	22.22	22.09
Trade, Transportation, and Utilites													
2007	19.03	19.29	19.36	19.71	19.78	19.67	19.87	19.77	20.22	19.73	19.66	19.60	19.65
2008	19.95	19.43	19.32	19.29	19.27	19.42	19.50	19.42	19.56	19.43	19.54	19.46	19.47
2009	19.51	19.69	19.85	19.74	19.67	19.83	19.75	19.80	19.80	19.70	19.72	20.00	19.76
Information													
2007	26.97	26.80	26.60	26.60	27.32	26.63	27.21	27.70	27.70	26.20	26.05	26.90	26.89
2008	27.29	26.17	26.47	26.06	26.16	26.29	26.02	26.07	26.09	26.01	26.13	26.20	26.25
2009	26.30	26.19	26.22	26.39	26.39	26.47	26.62	26.74	26.76	26.77	26.61	26.57	26.50
Financial Activities													
2007	28.17	30.76	29.68	29.76	29.69	29.55	29.95	29.33	29.92	27.64	27.58	27.69	29.16
2008	27.41	27.70	27.81	28.11	27.77	27.89	27.69	27.80	27.71	27.80	27.78	27.87	27.78
2009	27.97	29.04	29.04	28.95	29.05	28.93	28.94	29.05	29.03	29.13	29.05	29.00	28.93
Professional and Business Services													
2007	29.06	29.23	28.82	29.36	28.11	28.16	28.49	27.68	28.18	26.65	26.90	28.30	28.23
2008	28.33	27.45	27.95	27.76	27.45	27.65	27.63	27.58	27.66	27.50	27.65	27.68	27.69
2009	27.78	28.15	28.19	28.09	28.00	28.08	28.24	28.16	28.15	28.00	28.17	28.00	28.08
Education and Health Services													
2007	21.12	21.00	21.05	21.57	21.20	21.11	21.22	20.91	21.04	21.72	21.79	21.94	21.31
2008	21.83	21.58	21.34	21.67	21.78	21.65	21.66	21.68	21.75	21.80	21.77	21.85	21.70
2009	21.90	22.07	22.11	22.19	22.07	22.10	22.19	22.17	22.10	22.26	22.74	22.30	22.15
Leisure and Hospitality													
2007	12.84	12.95	12.60	15.29	16.01	15.38	15.44	15.16	15.05	12.47	12.54	12.34	14.05
2008	12.27	12.44	12.39	12.29	12.27	12.23	12.33	12.37	12.48	12.48	12.37	12.53	12.37
2009	12.41	12.62	12.58	12.57	12.57	12.55	12.60	12.80	12.80	12.67	12.48	12.40	12.59
Other Services													
2007	21.10	21.79	20.87	21.67	21.49	21.27	21.65	21.76	22.20	21.26	21.38	21.74	21.52
2008	21.85	21.62	21.88	21.49	21.63	21.48	21.31	21.27	21.24	21.89	21.64	21.93	21.60
2009	21.99	21.53	21.59	21.64	21.76	21.81	21.99	22.04	22.02	22.13	22.18	22.04	21.89

Average Weekly Earnings by Selected Industry: Illinois, 2007–2009

(Dollars, not seasonally adjusted.)

Industry and year	January	February	March	April	May	June	July	August	September	October	November	December	Annual average
Total Private													
2007	766.48	776.65	778.95	803.58	793.02	794.19	809.90	789.59	816.90	771.41	769.50	791.16	789.14
2008	768.70	762.75	780.74	773.95	773.12	780.74	777.24	782.12	784.53	782.60	784.53	781.01	777.58
2009	777.82	794.88	797.30	793.26	789.82	790.51	793.61	797.30	797.64	794.64	797.99	797.30	792.92
Goods-Producing													
2007	915.72	897.06	928.98	941.63	954.80	963.60	964.03	964.71	986.54	956.79	948.42	952.38	948.02
2008	923.93	920.72	939.96	941.77	955.51	957.56	963.03	969.02	967.33	970.85	961.22	961.08	953.65
2009	955.26	959.91	979.61	979.06	978.18	977.51	981.32	989.08	987.36	990.00	998.06	990.00	980.14
Construction													
2007	1108.08	1048.90	1132.09	1122.76	1183.47	1203.57	1184.53	1188.81	1220.84	1176.58	1141.75	1142.93	1156.18
2008	1100.01	1124.76	1131.47	1121.26	1135.71	1143.56	1146.72	1152.67	1145.87	1147.93	1143.18	1147.69	1136.92
2009	1144.18	1206.75	1214.10	1211.85	1212.43	1213.94	1215.27	1223.60	1221.14	1226.82	1230.25	1240.74	1212.43
Manufacturing													
2007	903.85	898.90	900.69	911.83	895.64	893.03	896.30	894.86	907.98	870.22	877.64	892.16	895.86
2008	870.33	855.46	866.31	865.83	860.55	855.93	856.94	861.09	861.70	863.47	864.66	864.04	862.47
2009	861.46	868.77	876.35	873.74	874.37	878.96	877.59	882.19	880.77	880.00	892.44	888.80	876.97
Trade, Transportation, and Utilites													
2007	639.41	650.07	658.24	676.05	678.45	680.58	687.50	676.13	711.74	680.69	674.34	684.04	675.96
2008	668.33	658.68	662.68	657.79	660.96	673.87	674.70	675.82	680.69	674.22	681.95	675.26	669.77
2009	655.54	667.49	672.92	669.19	666.81	668.27	667.55	671.22	671.22	665.86	670.48	684.00	669.86
Information													
2007	952.04	964.80	946.96	949.62	961.66	934.71	987.72	1011.05	1060.91	992.98	979.48	1024.89	981.49
2008	1004.27	965.67	997.92	974.64	967.92	980.62	962.74	972.41	973.16	972.77	979.88	977.26	976.50
2009	978.36	1034.51	1038.31	1037.13	1034.49	1037.62	1046.17	1053.56	1051.67	1052.06	1048.43	1049.52	1038.80
Financial Activities													
2007	1053.56	1162.73	1098.16	1127.90	1080.72	1081.53	1135.11	1076.41	1119.01	992.28	992.88	1013.45	1078.92
2008	986.76	1005.51	1023.41	1017.58	996.94	1009.62	996.84	1003.58	997.56	1003.58	1005.64	1011.68	1005.64
2009	1018.11	1074.48	1074.48	1068.26	1069.04	1064.62	1070.78	1077.76	1074.11	1071.98	1069.04	1064.30	1067.52
Professional and Business Services													
2007	996.76	1011.36	1005.82	1033.47	997.91	999.68	1019.94	977.10	1017.30	943.41	941.50	1018.80	996.52
2008	988.72	963.50	1017.38	993.81	988.20	1003.70	997.44	1001.15	1001.29	998.25	1003.70	1004.78	996.84
2009	1005.64	1047.18	1045.85	1036.52	1036.00	1033.34	1036.41	1036.29	1033.11	1027.60	1039.47	1027.60	1033.34
Education and Health Services													
2007	686.40	676.20	684.13	703.18	682.64	686.08	698.14	679.58	698.53	690.70	701.64	710.86	692.58
2008	700.74	692.72	691.42	697.77	694.78	697.13	693.12	698.10	702.53	704.14	705.35	705.76	698.74
2009	709.56	715.07	716.36	716.74	712.86	716.04	721.18	724.96	725.61	727.90	725.02	722.52	719.88
Leisure and Hospitality													
2007	324.85	328.93	325.08	389.90	406.65	395.27	398.35	386.58	382.27	315.49	313.50	313.44	358.28
2008	296.93	307.27	310.99	307.25	309.20	311.87	313.18	312.96	314.50	313.25	311.72	314.50	310.49
2009	310.25	329.38	328.34	326.82	328.08	328.81	327.60	330.24	328.96	323.09	320.74	317.44	324.82
Other Services													
2007	647.77	658.06	649.06	673.94	668.34	676.39	694.97	681.09	703.74	673.94	671.33	693.51	673.58
2008	677.35	696.16	711.10	702.72	707.30	706.69	696.84	697.66	694.55	707.05	707.63	697.37	699.84
2009	703.68	691.11	695.20	694.64	702.85	702.28	712.48	718.50	717.85	717.01	716.41	707.48	707.05

INDIANA
At a Glance

Population:
    1990 census: 5,544,156
    2000 census: 6,080,485
    2009 estimate: 6,423,113

Percent change in population:
    1990–2000: 9.7%
    2000–2009: 5.6%

Percent change in total nonfarm employment:
    1990–2009: 10.5%
    2008–2009: -5.7%

Industry with the largest growth in employment, 1990–2009 (thousands):
    Education and Health Services, 165.5

Industry with the largest decline or smallest growth in employment, 1990–2009 (thousands):
    Manufacturing, -165.9

Civilian labor force:
    1990: 2,830,551
    2000: 3,144,379
    2009: 3,184,780

Unemployment rate and rank among states (lowest to highest):
    1990: 5.0%, 17th
    2000: 2.9%, 10th
    2009: 10.1%, 37th

Employment by Industry, 2009

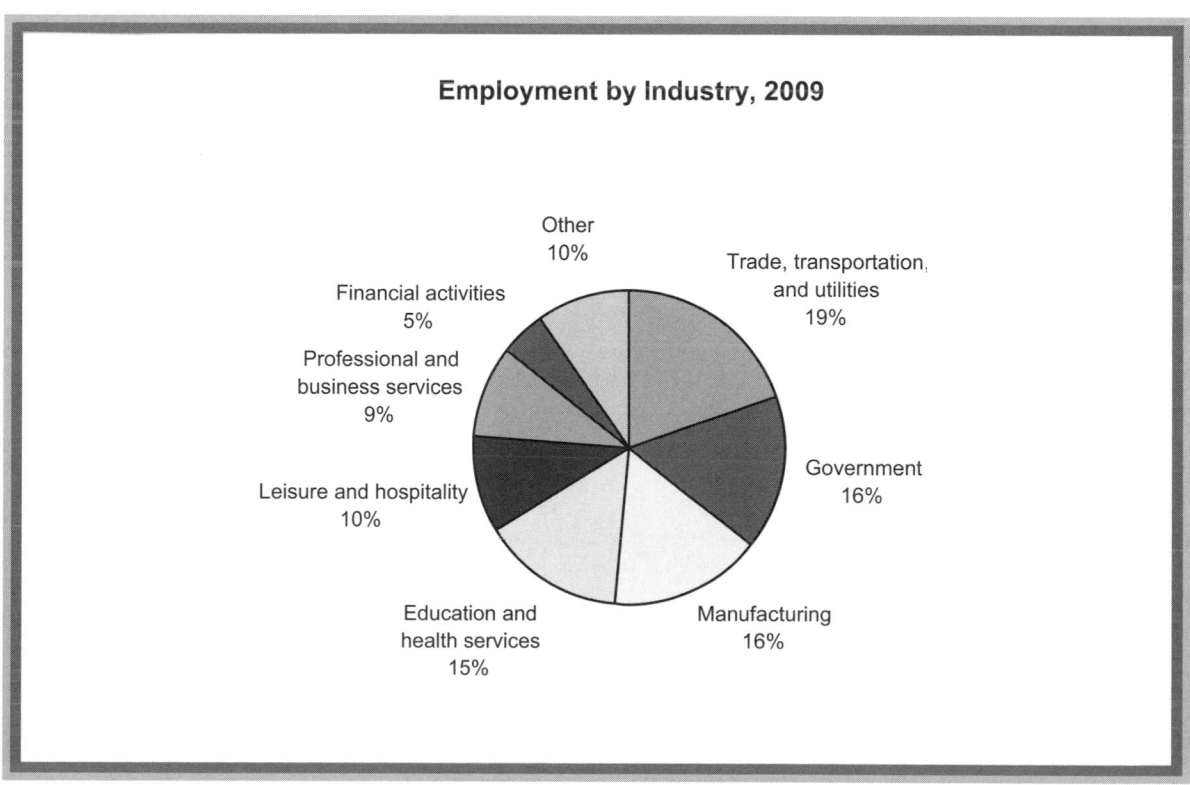

Other 10%
Trade, transportation, and utilities 19%
Financial activities 5%
Professional and business services 9%
Government 16%
Leisure and hospitality 10%
Education and health services 15%
Manufacturing 16%

Employment by Industry: Indiana, Selected Years, 1990–2009

(Numbers in thousands, not seasonally adjusted.)

Industry and year	January	February	March	April	May	June	July	August	September	October	November	December	Annual average
Total Nonfarm													
1990	2462.6	2469.7	2491.9	2501.2	2531.1	2537.0	2528.5	2543.7	2563.9	2551.9	2542.6	2538.8	2521.9
2000	2947.2	2957.5	2989.7	3016.3	3046.3	3024.0	2971.9	2986.0	3030.8	3014.3	3011.7	3005.0	3000.0
2001	2901.7	2915.7	2937.1	2959.2	2969.7	2949.5	2892.6	2918.5	2953.7	2938.8	2935.3	2928.8	2933.4
2002	2833.3	2847.0	2865.1	2893.0	2921.6	2907.8	2885.3	2912.7	2940.0	2932.8	2938.9	2933.2	2900.9
2003	2846.3	2849.6	2868.9	2894.4	2919.4	2896.1	2854.0	2887.2	2922.5	2936.4	2935.7	2933.2	2895.3
2004	2851.2	2857.3	2891.0	2934.1	2951.5	2935.8	2910.0	2923.1	2971.4	2974.5	2979.0	2967.9	2928.9
2005	2882.2	2900.6	2923.1	2963.7	2974.5	2956.2	2925.3	2940.6	2997.9	3000.0	3003.7	2994.0	2955.2
2006	2911.1	2927.8	2957.9	2979.2	2993.2	2984.2	2934.0	2958.2	3006.1	3009.4	3012.3	3011.3	2973.7
2007	2921.6	2924.6	2965.4	2989.3	3010.6	3000.7	2949.7	2984.7	3018.3	3021.9	3026.6	3015.7	2985.8
2008	2925.3	2936.2	2950.0	2975.7	3004.3	2980.6	2924.5	2961.6	2980.4	2972.3	2950.1	2918.8	2956.7
2009	2793.8	2785.9	2791.7	2801.2	2810.9	2779.0	2730.8	2762.1	2798.6	2806.3	2804.1	2781.5	2787.2
Total Private													
1990	2092.8	2092.4	2113.5	2119.6	2147.8	2166.3	2171.5	2185.0	2185.2	2169.8	2160.1	2157.4	2146.8
2000	2540.9	2544.1	2572.8	2598.0	2620.9	2633.1	2606.8	2618.1	2613.4	2602.1	2598.9	2593.9	2595.3
2001	2492.4	2492.9	2511.4	2534.7	2549.6	2559.3	2532.2	2543.9	2534.1	2514.2	2510.6	2505.3	2523.4
2002	2423.8	2423.0	2441.2	2466.4	2496.5	2514.7	2508.5	2521.3	2512.2	2498.3	2503.0	2498.0	2483.9
2003	2427.7	2418.6	2435.1	2462.9	2486.4	2493.0	2475.3	2495.2	2490.8	2497.4	2496.8	2493.7	2472.7
2004	2424.5	2422.7	2452.7	2496.9	2516.5	2530.5	2527.5	2533.8	2534.2	2532.9	2537.7	2530.9	2503.4
2005	2453.4	2461.4	2484.1	2524.7	2538.5	2553.3	2545.3	2553.8	2558.8	2557.1	2562.9	2556.3	2529.1
2006	2485.4	2490.3	2519.3	2542.1	2557.1	2580.0	2558.0	2567.5	2567.6	2566.7	2568.7	2567.4	2547.5
2007	2493.6	2484.0	2521.4	2548.1	2572.9	2590.7	2569.8	2576.3	2575.1	2575.2	2579.4	2569.1	2554.6
2008	2490.5	2487.2	2498.5	2525.8	2552.4	2557.8	2529.9	2538.6	2531.7	2518.1	2495.8	2468.0	2516.2
2009	2354.2	2338.0	2340.2	2348.8	2356.3	2360.7	2341.2	2346.5	2349.3	2350.5	2349.2	2330.0	2347.1
Goods-Producing													
1990	709.2	710.9	719.0	724.0	734.0	743.0	745.3	749.0	747.4	738.3	723.3	715.6	729.9
2000	810.7	811.4	818.8	825.7	831.5	838.2	831.8	834.3	827.6	817.1	809.6	800.3	821.4
2001	770.4	770.9	773.1	779.1	783.4	786.6	777.0	778.7	770.7	759.6	753.7	746.6	770.8
2002	723.6	724.0	729.0	735.7	744.1	754.3	753.2	757.8	752.9	745.6	742.7	734.6	741.5
2003	716.2	712.4	715.9	720.9	728.5	732.8	724.3	736.2	729.8	729.7	724.9	721.0	724.4
2004	703.2	701.6	710.5	723.6	732.6	740.0	735.2	741.7	738.8	734.2	730.4	726.6	726.5
2005	707.5	707.2	713.2	725.7	729.8	736.0	731.4	737.1	735.3	733.3	730.9	726.8	726.2
2006	710.2	707.8	715.8	723.6	728.1	738.2	729.9	734.1	727.9	724.3	718.9	716.1	722.9
2007	695.2	688.2	700.4	706.5	714.9	722.3	718.5	719.5	715.3	710.5	707.8	701.0	708.3
2008	679.2	676.7	675.7	681.2	689.2	692.8	676.7	682.0	673.0	663.1	649.0	628.8	672.3
2009	589.0	578.7	571.7	570.6	564.5	562.6	561.9	567.5	565.8	564.5	565.0	551.5	567.8
Mining and Logging													
1990	7.9	7.9	8.0	8.2	8.4	8.5	8.5	8.6	8.5	8.5	8.5	8.4	8.3
2000	6.5	6.5	6.6	6.8	6.9	6.9	6.9	6.9	6.9	6.8	6.8	6.7	6.7
2001	6.4	6.5	6.7	7.1	7.2	7.3	7.4	7.4	7.4	7.4	7.3	7.1	7.1
2002	6.8	6.9	7.0	7.2	7.2	7.3	7.2	7.2	7.2	7.1	7.0	7.0	7.1
2003	6.6	6.7	6.7	7.0	7.0	7.1	7.1	7.1	7.2	7.1	7.1	7.0	7.0
2004	6.8	6.7	7.0	7.3	7.4	7.4	7.3	7.3	7.2	6.9	6.9	6.8	7.1
2005	6.7	6.7	6.8	7.0	7.0	7.1	7.0	7.0	6.9	6.9	6.9	6.8	6.9
2006	6.5	6.5	6.6	7.0	7.1	7.2	7.2	7.1	7.1	7.1	7.0	7.0	7.0
2007	6.8	6.7	6.9	7.0	7.1	7.1	7.1	7.1	7.1	7.0	6.9	6.8	7.0
2008	6.4	6.4	6.5	6.7	6.8	6.9	6.8	6.9	6.9	6.9	6.8	6.7	6.7
2009	6.3	6.3	6.5	6.6	6.7	6.7	6.7	6.7	6.7	6.7	6.7	6.6	6.6
Construction													
1990	103.7	102.3	106.1	109.7	115.0	120.2	123.9	125.7	124.0	121.3	119.9	116.0	115.7
2000	138.0	136.8	144.3	151.1	155.3	159.1	159.2	159.3	156.4	151.7	148.5	142.7	150.2
2001	130.6	132.1	138.2	146.3	152.2	156.7	157.3	158.5	154.8	153.0	152.4	147.5	148.3
2002	134.4	133.5	137.0	142.9	147.9	152.3	155.2	155.1	152.6	149.5	148.1	143.6	146.0
2003	131.7	128.5	133.0	141.8	148.0	149.9	153.0	154.2	151.3	152.4	148.6	144.7	144.8
2004	131.4	129.6	136.5	146.7	152.6	155.6	158.9	156.8	155.0	153.5	151.1	146.5	147.9
2005	132.4	132.1	136.8	147.7	150.2	154.1	156.6	156.8	155.5	155.1	153.2	148.2	148.2
2006	136.9	136.1	140.9	148.0	153.4	157.1	157.3	157.8	156.2	156.4	154.3	152.0	150.5
2007	138.9	132.4	142.1	149.0	155.6	159.2	159.4	159.5	157.6	156.9	155.7	149.1	151.3
2008	135.5	133.2	137.6	143.6	148.7	151.8	153.2	152.0	150.0	149.2	143.3	133.7	144.3
2009	115.9	113.2	116.6	120.3	123.7	125.8	125.9	124.5	122.7	126.0	123.5	115.8	121.2
Manufacturing													
1990	597.6	600.7	604.9	606.1	610.6	614.3	612.9	614.7	614.9	608.5	594.9	591.2	605.9
2000	666.2	668.1	667.9	667.8	669.3	672.2	665.7	668.1	664.3	658.6	654.3	650.9	664.5
2001	633.4	632.3	628.2	625.7	624.0	622.6	612.3	612.8	608.5	599.2	594.0	592.0	615.4
2002	582.4	583.6	585.0	585.6	589.0	594.7	590.8	595.5	593.1	589.0	587.6	584.0	588.4
2003	577.9	577.2	576.2	572.1	573.5	575.8	564.2	574.9	571.3	570.2	569.2	569.3	572.7
2004	565.0	565.3	567.0	569.6	572.6	577.0	569.0	577.6	576.6	573.8	572.4	573.3	571.6
2005	568.4	568.4	569.6	571.0	572.6	574.8	567.8	573.3	572.9	571.3	570.8	571.8	571.1
2006	566.8	565.2	568.3	568.6	567.6	573.9	565.4	569.2	564.6	560.8	557.6	557.1	565.4
2007	549.5	549.1	551.4	550.5	552.2	556.0	552.0	552.9	550.6	546.6	545.2	545.1	550.1
2008	537.3	537.1	531.6	530.9	533.7	534.1	516.7	523.1	516.1	507.0	498.9	488.4	521.2
2009	466.8	459.2	448.6	443.7	434.1	430.1	429.3	436.3	436.4	431.8	434.8	429.1	440.0

Employment by Industry: Indiana, Selected Years, 1990–2009—*Continued*

(Numbers in thousands, not seasonally adjusted.)

Industry and year	January	February	March	April	May	June	July	August	September	October	November	December	Annual average
Service-Providing													
1990	1753.4	1758.8	1772.9	1777.2	1797.1	1794.0	1783.2	1794.7	1816.5	1813.6	1819.3	1823.2	1792.0
2000	2136.5	2146.1	2170.9	2190.6	2214.8	2185.8	2140.1	2151.7	2203.2	2197.2	2202.1	2204.7	2178.6
2001	2131.3	2144.8	2164.0	2180.1	2186.3	2162.9	2115.6	2139.8	2183.0	2179.2	2181.6	2182.2	2162.6
2002	2109.7	2123.0	2136.1	2157.3	2177.5	2153.5	2132.1	2154.9	2187.1	2187.2	2196.2	2198.6	2159.4
2003	2130.1	2137.2	2153.0	2173.5	2190.9	2163.3	2129.7	2151.0	2192.7	2206.7	2210.8	2212.2	2170.9
2004	2148.0	2155.7	2180.5	2210.5	2218.9	2195.8	2174.8	2181.4	2232.6	2240.3	2248.6	2241.3	2202.4
2005	2174.7	2193.4	2209.9	2238.0	2244.7	2220.2	2193.9	2203.5	2262.6	2266.7	2272.8	2267.2	2229.0
2006	2200.9	2220.0	2242.1	2255.6	2265.1	2246.0	2204.1	2224.1	2278.2	2285.1	2293.4	2295.2	2250.8
2007	2226.4	2236.4	2265.0	2282.8	2295.7	2278.4	2231.2	2265.2	2303.0	2311.4	2318.8	2314.7	2277.4
2008	2246.1	2259.5	2274.3	2294.5	2315.1	2287.8	2247.8	2279.6	2307.4	2309.2	2301.1	2290.0	2284.4
2009	2204.8	2207.2	2220.0	2230.6	2246.4	2216.4	2168.9	2194.6	2232.8	2241.8	2239.1	2230.0	2219.4
Trade, Transportation, and Utilities													
1990	525.9	520.4	522.5	521.0	526.7	528.9	531.2	535.5	534.9	534.6	543.7	548.4	531.1
2000	607.2	602.1	607.9	611.1	615.8	617.9	616.0	617.0	615.3	622.2	632.1	639.5	617.0
2001	602.0	594.3	596.1	599.2	602.4	604.6	599.0	599.4	596.2	595.6	604.0	608.0	600.1
2002	579.0	572.6	574.5	575.9	581.1	584.0	582.7	583.2	580.7	579.3	590.8	595.6	581.6
2003	568.8	561.7	564.6	570.2	573.7	575.1	572.5	574.0	572.7	576.9	586.4	591.1	574.0
2004	566.6	561.1	565.9	572.2	576.9	579.4	579.9	580.5	576.5	581.4	591.2	596.1	577.3
2005	570.1	567.6	571.7	578.4	583.6	584.0	585.2	585.4	585.0	588.0	597.7	600.9	583.1
2006	576.9	572.6	577.4	579.2	584.4	587.0	584.8	585.7	584.5	587.8	598.6	602.8	585.1
2007	578.8	572.5	579.9	582.0	588.3	592.1	588.3	587.1	585.4	587.1	599.6	602.7	587.0
2008	576.4	571.9	574.4	577.2	583.9	584.9	582.0	583.0	578.9	578.6	582.0	582.4	579.6
2009	553.1	545.7	544.5	545.9	550.5	552.0	548.1	547.4	544.8	548.4	556.2	558.1	549.6
Wholesale Trade													
1990	105.4	105.5	106.0	105.5	106.1	106.8	107.6	107.5	107.1	108.6	110.0	109.8	107.2
2000	123.8	124.2	125.5	125.7	126.4	127.2	126.9	126.8	126.2	126.2	126.0	125.8	125.9
2001	123.7	123.6	124.1	123.8	124.1	124.5	123.8	123.4	122.8	122.4	121.8	121.7	123.3
2002	119.7	119.3	119.3	120.0	120.6	121.1	120.5	119.9	119.2	118.5	118.3	118.3	119.6
2003	117.6	117.3	117.4	117.6	118.1	118.5	118.0	117.5	116.8	116.9	116.9	117.1	117.5
2004	116.1	116.3	117.5	118.9	119.8	120.6	121.2	120.8	119.8	120.5	120.5	120.6	119.4
2005	119.0	119.2	119.8	121.1	121.8	122.5	122.9	122.5	121.8	122.0	122.1	122.3	121.4
2006	121.1	121.2	122.0	122.8	123.8	125.0	124.4	123.8	123.4	123.6	123.5	123.9	123.2
2007	122.8	122.9	124.0	124.7	125.5	126.5	127.4	126.2	125.4	125.5	125.8	125.8	125.2
2008	124.0	124.1	124.6	125.3	126.2	126.4	125.9	125.2	124.2	123.7	122.6	121.7	124.5
2009	117.9	116.8	116.2	115.6	115.9	115.8	115.8	114.6	113.7	113.8	114.0	114.9	115.4
Retail Trade													
1990	310.5	304.4	305.3	304.3	308.1	308.6	310.1	313.4	313.0	311.9	319.8	324.4	311.2
2000	354.0	348.6	352.1	353.9	357.8	358.9	355.7	356.2	355.5	360.2	377.6	379.4	358.7
2001	351.8	344.9	345.4	346.5	349.4	350.8	346.0	345.8	344.6	346.1	355.7	358.8	348.8
2002	338.8	333.7	335.8	336.3	340.5	342.8	340.7	340.6	339.1	337.7	348.4	353.8	340.7
2003	331.1	325.4	327.8	331.0	334.3	335.8	333.0	334.4	333.4	335.2	345.0	349.5	334.7
2004	329.7	323.8	326.1	328.3	332.0	333.8	332.0	332.3	329.3	332.3	341.9	346.3	332.3
2005	325.4	321.8	324.5	328.1	332.0	331.5	332.5	331.9	331.3	333.7	342.4	345.7	331.7
2006	326.9	322.0	325.0	325.9	329.0	329.8	328.5	329.3	327.6	330.5	340.3	343.4	329.9
2007	325.6	319.5	324.0	324.7	329.1	330.7	327.7	326.9	325.4	327.1	338.0	340.5	328.3
2008	321.3	316.8	317.9	319.0	323.7	324.3	323.4	323.5	321.2	321.6	326.4	327.8	322.2
2009	308.4	303.0	303.1	305.6	309.4	311.1	308.3	307.8	305.7	307.1	313.7	315.8	308.3
Transportation and Utilities													
1990	110.0	110.5	111.2	111.2	112.5	113.5	113.5	114.6	114.8	114.1	113.9	114.2	112.8
2000	129.4	129.3	130.3	131.5	131.6	131.8	133.4	134.0	133.6	135.8	133.5	134.3	132.4
2001	126.5	125.8	126.6	128.9	128.9	129.3	129.2	130.2	128.8	127.1	126.5	127.5	127.9
2002	120.5	119.6	119.4	119.6	120.0	120.1	121.5	122.7	122.4	123.1	124.1	123.5	121.4
2003	120.1	119.0	119.4	121.6	121.3	120.8	121.5	122.1	122.5	124.8	124.5	124.5	121.8
2004	120.8	121.0	122.3	125.0	125.1	125.0	126.7	127.4	127.4	128.6	128.8	129.2	125.6
2005	125.7	126.6	127.4	129.2	129.8	130.0	129.8	131.0	131.9	132.3	133.2	132.9	130.0
2006	128.9	129.4	130.4	130.5	131.6	132.2	131.9	132.6	133.5	133.7	134.8	135.5	132.1
2007	130.4	130.1	131.9	132.6	133.7	134.9	133.2	134.0	134.6	134.8	135.8	136.4	133.5
2008	131.1	131.0	131.9	132.9	134.0	134.2	132.7	134.3	133.5	133.3	133.0	132.9	132.9
2009	126.8	125.9	125.2	124.7	125.2	125.1	124.0	125.0	125.4	127.5	128.5	127.4	125.9
Information													
1990	45.2	45.1	45.1	45.2	45.5	45.8	45.8	45.6	45.2	43.5	43.4	43.5	44.9
2000	45.7	45.9	46.4	45.4	46.0	46.7	46.1	46.4	46.1	45.7	46.2	46.3	46.1
2001	45.5	45.3	45.6	45.0	45.2	45.3	45.0	44.6	44.0	43.6	43.8	43.9	44.7
2002	42.9	42.6	42.9	42.5	42.8	43.1	42.8	42.8	42.1	41.7	41.9	41.8	42.5
2003	41.0	40.7	41.1	40.8	41.4	42.0	41.9	42.1	41.4	41.0	41.2	41.3	41.3
2004	40.8	40.4	40.9	40.8	41.3	41.8	41.4	41.1	40.3	40.5	40.6	40.8	40.9
2005	40.0	40.1	40.1	40.2	40.7	41.0	40.8	40.7	40.0	39.7	40.0	40.4	40.3
2006	39.5	39.8	39.8	39.9	40.2	40.6	40.3	40.1	39.5	39.3	39.6	39.8	39.9
2007	39.5	39.6	39.5	39.6	40.1	40.6	40.6	40.5	39.9	39.6	39.9	40.0	40.0
2008	39.6	39.6	39.7	39.8	40.3	40.5	40.4	40.2	39.5	39.1	39.1	39.3	39.8
2009	38.6	38.4	38.1	37.8	38.1	38.5	37.9	37.7	37.0	36.5	36.4	36.2	37.6

Employment by Industry: Indiana, Selected Years, 1990–2009—*Continued*

(Numbers in thousands, not seasonally adjusted.)

Industry and year	January	February	March	April	May	June	July	August	September	October	November	December	Annual average
Financial Activities													
1990	128.5	128.7	129.6	129.1	130.2	131.9	132.3	132.4	131.5	130.4	130.4	130.9	130.5
2000	144.4	144.1	144.5	144.7	145.7	147.1	146.3	146.0	144.7	143.9	143.9	144.9	145.0
2001	142.0	142.2	142.8	143.6	144.3	146.0	144.6	144.0	141.8	140.8	140.8	141.5	142.9
2002	139.2	138.9	138.9	138.8	139.8	141.1	141.5	141.6	140.3	139.8	140.1	140.8	140.1
2003	139.5	139.5	140.2	140.5	141.9	143.1	143.2	143.3	141.8	141.0	140.4	140.9	141.3
2004	138.6	138.6	138.9	139.2	140.3	141.6	141.7	141.6	139.8	139.5	139.3	140.0	139.9
2005	137.2	137.2	137.2	138.0	138.7	139.9	140.4	140.7	139.6	139.0	138.8	139.4	138.8
2006	138.4	138.6	138.8	139.1	139.9	141.2	140.6	140.5	139.2	138.8	138.5	139.3	139.4
2007	137.5	137.8	138.1	138.4	139.1	140.3	140.1	139.6	138.5	138.2	137.7	138.0	138.6
2008	135.6	135.8	136.0	136.1	136.6	137.6	137.8	137.1	135.5	134.9	134.0	134.0	135.9
2009	132.3	131.7	131.6	131.4	131.9	132.4	132.4	131.9	130.4	131.5	129.6	131.0	131.5
Professional and Business Services													
1990	149.3	150.3	153.0	153.8	155.2	157.0	158.0	159.1	160.0	161.4	158.5	157.5	156.1
2000	249.1	250.4	255.3	261.0	263.4	266.1	261.5	263.8	264.5	260.9	259.4	256.4	259.3
2001	241.6	242.2	246.1	250.3	251.7	253.8	252.1	256.2	252.7	251.9	249.6	247.6	249.7
2002	239.4	240.8	244.8	251.4	255.8	258.2	259.1	261.7	260.2	258.9	257.9	256.3	253.7
2003	246.5	246.5	248.2	251.2	254.4	255.4	254.4	257.8	257.8	259.7	260.1	257.4	254.1
2004	248.9	251.7	256.7	264.8	266.9	269.7	272.2	274.3	273.1	273.7	274.1	270.6	266.4
2005	260.5	264.1	266.8	273.1	274.2	276.2	276.2	279.8	280.4	281.2	280.5	278.2	274.3
2006	266.5	269.5	274.7	280.0	282.6	285.5	282.8	288.9	288.2	286.5	285.8	285.0	281.3
2007	275.8	276.8	283.5	289.6	292.3	294.0	290.1	295.7	295.5	295.1	293.7	292.0	289.5
2008	280.1	279.4	282.2	287.7	287.9	289.3	286.4	290.2	289.6	288.8	282.9	276.6	285.1
2009	259.4	257.7	258.3	259.2	258.0	259.6	256.5	261.7	263.8	267.8	267.4	263.5	261.1
Education and Health Services													
1990	243.3	244.3	245.7	247.2	247.9	247.7	246.3	248.0	253.2	255.5	256.5	256.9	249.4
2000	327.0	330.6	332.4	333.6	333.7	326.9	321.5	324.1	332.9	334.8	335.5	336.4	330.8
2001	335.6	338.4	340.0	341.8	337.0	330.0	327.7	330.2	346.3	346.7	348.3	349.1	339.3
2002	345.2	347.3	348.4	349.4	348.6	344.1	342.7	344.5	353.5	355.7	357.2	357.8	349.5
2003	357.5	359.6	360.8	362.7	359.2	351.5	350.3	349.0	362.0	367.7	367.6	367.8	359.6
2004	365.3	367.3	369.5	372.7	365.0	359.0	360.3	356.3	373.7	378.1	379.7	376.8	368.6
2005	371.6	375.7	377.5	380.6	373.1	371.3	369.8	366.6	382.9	388.5	390.1	387.0	377.9
2006	381.7	386.7	389.5	389.8	382.4	380.8	377.6	374.0	390.5	396.7	397.2	394.5	386.8
2007	389.2	391.4	393.6	396.5	392.2	389.8	387.3	385.5	400.2	407.5	408.7	406.5	395.7
2008	401.1	404.2	405.4	407.2	405.7	400.7	397.6	394.4	410.2	416.3	417.6	419.0	406.6
2009	409.6	412.9	416.4	416.6	416.5	415.2	408.3	404.5	418.4	422.7	420.1	417.7	414.9
Leisure and Hospitality													
1990	196.5	197.5	202.5	203.5	212.0	214.6	215.4	217.9	215.8	208.3	206.4	206.8	208.1
2000	250.0	251.9	258.4	266.8	274.6	279.2	274.2	276.9	273.0	269.1	264.0	261.7	266.7
2001	249.0	252.5	259.5	267.1	276.0	282.0	277.6	281.9	275.2	269.7	264.2	262.2	268.1
2002	250.5	252.1	257.1	266.2	276.3	280.9	278.7	282.1	276.1	271.2	266.5	265.0	268.6
2003	253.9	253.2	258.4	270.0	279.6	284.1	280.2	284.3	277.5	273.8	269.0	266.5	270.9
2004	255.0	255.3	262.5	274.4	283.6	287.7	285.6	287.2	281.8	275.1	272.4	269.9	274.2
2005	257.5	260.0	266.9	277.2	286.2	292.0	289.2	291.4	284.4	276.8	274.6	273.0	277.4
2006	263.2	266.0	272.6	279.2	287.2	293.3	289.8	292.2	286.4	282.5	279.9	279.1	281.0
2007	268.1	268.1	275.1	283.4	292.8	297.4	291.8	296.0	288.7	285.3	280.9	277.6	283.8
2008	267.9	268.8	273.8	284.0	294.9	297.8	295.5	298.8	293.2	285.3	280.1	277.2	284.8
2009	263.6	264.5	270.4	278.3	287.4	290.2	286.8	287.6	281.9	271.9	269.3	266.9	276.6
Other Services													
1990	94.9	95.2	96.1	95.8	96.3	97.4	97.2	97.5	97.2	97.8	97.9	97.8	96.8
2000	106.8	107.7	109.1	109.7	110.2	111.0	109.4	109.6	109.3	108.4	108.2	108.4	109.0
2001	106.3	107.1	108.2	108.6	109.6	111.0	109.2	108.9	107.2	106.3	106.2	106.4	107.9
2002	104.0	104.7	105.6	106.5	108.0	109.0	107.8	107.6	106.4	106.1	105.9	106.1	106.5
2003	104.3	105.0	105.9	106.6	107.7	109.0	108.5	108.5	107.8	107.6	107.2	107.7	107.2
2004	106.1	106.7	107.8	109.2	109.9	111.3	111.2	111.1	110.2	110.4	110.0	110.1	109.5
2005	109.0	109.5	110.7	111.5	112.2	112.9	112.3	112.1	111.2	110.6	110.3	110.6	111.1
2006	109.0	109.3	110.7	111.3	112.3	113.4	112.2	112.0	111.4	110.8	110.2	110.8	111.1
2007	109.5	109.6	111.3	112.1	113.2	114.2	113.1	112.4	111.6	111.6	111.1	111.3	111.8
2008	110.6	110.8	111.3	112.6	113.9	114.2	113.5	112.9	111.8	112.0	111.1	110.7	112.1
2009	108.6	108.4	109.2	109.0	109.4	110.2	109.3	108.2	107.2	107.2	105.2	105.1	108.1
Government													
1990	369.8	377.3	378.4	381.6	383.3	370.7	357.0	358.7	378.7	382.1	382.5	381.4	375.1
2000	406.3	413.4	416.9	418.3	425.4	390.9	365.1	367.9	417.4	412.2	412.8	411.1	404.8
2001	409.3	422.8	425.7	424.5	420.1	390.2	360.4	374.6	419.6	424.6	424.7	423.5	410.0
2002	409.5	424.0	423.9	426.6	425.1	393.1	376.8	391.4	427.8	434.5	435.9	435.2	417.0
2003	418.6	431.0	433.8	431.5	433.0	403.1	378.7	392.0	431.7	439.0	438.9	439.5	422.6
2004	426.7	434.6	438.3	437.2	435.0	405.3	382.5	389.3	437.2	441.6	441.3	437.0	425.5
2005	428.8	439.2	439.0	439.0	436.0	402.9	380.0	386.8	439.1	442.9	440.8	437.7	426.0
2006	425.7	437.5	438.6	437.1	436.1	404.2	376.0	390.7	438.5	442.7	443.6	443.9	426.2
2007	428.0	440.6	444.0	441.2	437.7	410.0	379.9	408.4	443.2	446.7	447.2	446.6	431.1
2008	434.8	449.0	451.5	449.9	451.9	422.8	394.6	423.0	448.7	454.2	454.3	450.8	440.5
2009	439.6	447.9	451.5	452.4	454.6	418.3	389.6	415.6	449.3	455.8	454.9	451.5	440.1

Average Weekly Hours by Selected Industry: Indiana, 2007–2009

(Not seasonally adjusted.)

Industry and year	January	February	March	April	May	June	July	August	September	October	November	December	Annual average
Total Private													
2007	35.3	34.3	35.5	35.7	36.0	35.8	35.6	35.6	35.9	35.4	35.4	35.7	35.5
2008	35.1	35.0	35.4	34.9	35.0	35.3	34.6	35.0	34.7	34.7	34.9	34.9	35.0
2009	34.4	34.9	34.7	34.1	34.1	34.3	34.7	35.0	34.4	34.5	35.2	35.1	34.6
Goods-Producing													
2007	40.5	38.3	40.7	40.4	40.3	40.6	40.2	40.7	41.5	40.5	40.8	41.0	40.5
2008	40.2	39.8	40.6	39.7	40.0	40.5	39.1	40.6	39.9	39.8	39.8	39.8	40.0
2009	37.9	38.7	38.6	38.0	38.3	39.2	39.2	39.9	39.3	39.7	41.0	41.0	39.2
Construction													
2007	38.7	34.6	38.6	37.7	39.8	39.7	39.7	39.2	39.4	39.5	38.6	38.7	38.7
2008	37.3	37.1	37.6	36.5	37.1	37.9	38.1	39.9	38.6	38.9	38.5	37.7	38.0
2009	36.4	37.7	38.3	37.3	38.2	38.3	40.1	40.6	38.6	38.3	40.2	37.8	38.5
Manufacturing													
2007	40.7	39.9	41.7	41.1	42.0	41.9	41.2	41.8	42.7	41.3	41.8	42.0	41.5
2008	41.2	40.7	41.2	40.4	40.3	40.5	39.6	40.1	40.0	39.9	40.3	39.3	40.3
2009	37.2	37.7	37.7	37.3	37.6	38.7	38.2	39.0	38.8	39.4	40.7	41.4	38.6
Trade, Transportation, and Utilites													
2007	36.5	36.4	36.6	37.5	38.2	37.7	37.6	37.5	37.4	37.3	37.0	37.3	37.3
2008	36.5	36.6	36.8	36.6	36.9	37.4	36.6	36.9	36.8	36.7	36.6	36.2	36.7
2009	36.1	36.1	35.7	35.5	35.7	35.9	36.4	36.3	36.1	36.1	36.4	36.1	36.0
Financial Activities													
2007	35.8	35.5	37.6	37.4	37.2	36.7	36.9	36.2	37.0	36.8	36.6	36.6	36.7
2008	36.3	37.1	36.7	36.7	37.3	36.9	36.6	36.6	36.8	36.7	37.0	36.8	36.8
2009	36.3	36.6	36.1	35.3	36.2	35.6	35.5	36.6	36.3	36.8	37.8	38.0	36.4
Professional and Business Services													
2007	33.7	32.7	33.7	34.4	35.0	34.4	34.3	34.4	34.9	34.8	34.8	34.9	34.3
2008	34.2	33.9	34.1	34.3	33.6	34.8	34.1	34.1	34.4	34.3	34.7	34.8	34.3
2009	34.9	35.5	35.7	35.2	34.4	34.9	35.3	35.7	34.7	34.5	35.0	35.1	35.1
Education and Health Services													
2007	32.7	32.4	32.9	33.2	33.5	32.7	32.8	32.7	32.9	32.3	32.8	32.9	32.8
2008	32.5	32.3	32.6	32.1	32.4	33.0	32.7	32.5	32.5	32.8	33.3	32.6	32.6
2009	33.0	33.0	33.0	32.8	32.7	32.5	33.5	33.6	32.5	32.1	33.0	32.7	32.9
Leisure and Hospitality													
2007	25.8	24.8	25.6	25.5	25.7	26.4	26.0	25.8	25.5	25.1	24.5	24.5	25.4
2008	24.1	24.5	24.6	24.1	24.6	25.2	25.4	25.1	24.7	24.6	24.9	24.4	24.7
2009	24.4	25.7	25.5	24.8	25.3	25.6	25.9	26.3	25.4	25.3	25.5	25.2	25.4
Other Services													
2007	28.2	27.8	29.4	28.4	28.6	29.2	29.0	28.5	28.0	27.5	28.4	28.8	28.5
2008	29.1	28.7	29.9	29.2	28.6	29.2	28.5	29.5	29.3	29.7	29.9	29.1	29.2
2009	29.1	29.3	29.7	28.8	28.5	30.0	29.7	29.6	29.7	29.5	31.0	30.1	29.5

Average Hourly Earnings by Selected Industry: Indiana, 2007–2009

(Dollars, not seasonally adjusted.)

Industry and year	January	February	March	April	May	June	July	August	September	October	November	December	Annual average
Total Private													
2007	19.76	20.01	19.83	19.97	19.61	19.71	19.93	19.96	20.17	19.86	20.06	20.37	19.94
2008	20.05	20.29	20.40	20.43	20.15	20.38	20.25	20.34	20.42	20.31	20.36	20.23	20.30
2009	20.50	21.00	20.74	20.67	20.55	20.51	20.41	20.36	20.51	20.34	20.53	20.58	20.56
Goods-Producing													
2007	22.22	22.69	22.64	23.06	22.68	22.65	23.23	23.31	23.32	22.90	23.10	23.45	22.94
2008	22.85	23.46	23.84	23.74	23.44	23.71	23.38	23.36	23.85	23.53	23.74	23.73	23.55
2009	23.54	24.18	23.87	24.00	23.86	23.71	23.83	23.45	23.66	23.51	23.92	23.30	23.73
Construction													
2007	23.06	23.65	23.45	22.72	22.85	22.63	22.96	22.71	23.34	23.05	23.42	23.62	23.11
2008	23.33	23.44	23.70	23.45	23.00	23.04	23.35	23.13	23.17	23.22	23.50	23.85	23.34
2009	23.83	24.04	24.30	24.59	24.31	24.49	24.56	24.47	24.60	24.38	24.40	24.56	24.39
Manufacturing													
2007	22.05	22.52	22.48	23.16	22.69	22.72	23.29	22.98	22.91	22.49	22.69	22.87	22.74
2008	22.25	23.01	22.70	22.76	22.59	22.68	22.44	22.46	22.53	22.40	22.77	22.79	22.61
2009	22.64	23.38	23.01	22.91	22.62	22.51	22.71	22.33	22.70	22.54	23.08	22.38	22.74
Trade, Transportation, and Utilites													
2007	17.68	17.79	17.51	17.32	16.99	17.29	17.37	17.20	17.51	17.02	17.15	17.33	17.34
2008	17.47	17.21	17.50	17.63	17.17	17.61	17.32	17.49	17.78	17.66	17.92	18.01	17.56
2009	18.31	18.34	18.53	18.24	18.20	18.60	18.30	18.66	18.78	18.65	18.80	19.07	18.54
Financial Activities													
2007	23.23	24.43	23.31	24.20	23.29	23.62	23.26	22.94	22.66	21.98	22.55	22.30	23.15
2008	21.69	21.91	21.99	22.01	21.24	21.48	21.45	21.46	21.86	21.77	21.62	21.90	21.70
2009	21.88	22.29	23.71	24.17	22.85	23.25	22.76	21.69	21.96	23.81	23.79	23.95	23.01
Professional and Business Services													
2007	19.23	19.94	19.66	19.65	19.14	19.37	19.36	19.64	19.64	19.36	19.30	19.64	19.49
2008	19.47	19.75	19.82	19.44	19.44	19.57	19.64	19.53	19.78	19.65	19.71	19.61	19.62
2009	21.21	21.64	21.05	20.83	21.31	21.22	21.19	21.05	20.83	19.22	19.48	19.65	20.72
Education and Health Services													
2007	21.24	20.80	20.81	20.96	21.23	21.40	21.54	21.30	21.53	21.81	22.01	21.96	21.39
2008	21.69	21.68	21.77	21.76	21.67	21.60	21.98	21.84	22.13	21.88	21.97	22.08	21.84
2009	21.64	21.56	21.50	21.50	21.62	21.58	21.56	21.40	21.54	21.48	21.42	21.85	21.55
Leisure and Hospitality													
2007	11.32	11.74	11.61	11.52	10.89	10.75	10.77	10.94	11.04	11.39	11.48	11.56	11.24
2008	11.15	11.27	11.13	11.18	11.19	11.28	11.19	11.49	11.53	11.64	11.61	11.95	11.38
2009	12.07	11.93	11.51	11.91	11.68	11.45	11.61	11.76	12.09	12.19	12.14	12.56	11.90
Other Services													
2007	17.07	17.22	16.24	17.23	16.16	16.48	16.69	16.44	16.54	16.09	16.40	16.85	16.61
2008	16.50	17.25	16.50	17.00	16.92	16.81	17.00	17.67	17.16	16.65	16.45	16.71	16.88
2009	17.95	18.32	18.14	17.89	18.14	17.11	17.44	18.23	18.41	18.75	19.00	19.23	18.21

Average Weekly Earnings by Selected Industry: Indiana, 2007–2009

(Dollars, not seasonally adjusted.)

Industry and year	January	February	March	April	May	June	July	August	September	October	November	December	Annual average
Total Private													
2007	697.53	686.34	703.97	712.93	705.96	705.62	709.51	710.58	724.10	703.04	710.12	727.21	707.87
2008	703.76	710.15	722.16	713.01	705.25	719.41	700.65	711.90	708.57	704.76	710.56	706.03	710.50
2009	705.20	732.90	719.68	704.85	700.76	703.49	708.23	712.60	705.54	701.73	722.66	722.36	711.38
Goods-Producing													
2007	899.91	869.03	921.45	931.62	914.00	919.59	933.85	948.72	967.78	927.45	942.48	961.45	929.07
2008	918.57	933.71	967.90	942.48	937.60	960.26	914.16	948.42	951.62	936.49	944.85	944.45	942.00
2009	892.17	935.77	921.38	912.00	913.84	929.43	934.14	935.66	929.84	933.35	980.72	955.30	930.22
Construction													
2007	892.42	818.29	905.17	856.54	909.43	898.41	911.51	890.23	919.60	910.48	904.01	914.09	894.36
2008	870.21	869.62	891.12	855.93	853.30	873.22	889.64	922.89	894.36	903.26	904.75	899.15	886.92
2009	867.41	906.31	930.69	917.21	928.64	937.97	984.86	993.48	949.56	933.75	980.88	928.37	939.02
Manufacturing													
2007	897.44	898.55	937.42	951.88	952.98	951.97	959.55	960.56	978.26	928.84	948.44	960.54	943.71
2008	916.70	936.51	935.24	919.50	910.38	918.54	888.62	900.65	901.20	893.76	917.63	895.65	911.18
2009	842.21	881.43	867.48	854.54	850.51	871.14	867.52	870.87	880.76	888.08	939.36	926.53	877.76
Trade, Transportation, and Utilites													
2007	645.32	647.56	640.87	649.50	649.02	651.83	653.11	645.00	654.87	634.85	634.55	646.41	646.78
2008	637.66	629.89	644.00	645.26	633.57	658.61	633.91	645.38	654.30	648.12	655.87	651.96	644.45
2009	660.99	662.07	661.52	647.52	649.74	667.74	666.12	677.36	677.96	673.27	684.32	688.43	667.44
Financial Activities													
2007	831.63	867.27	876.46	905.08	866.39	866.85	858.29	830.43	838.42	808.86	825.33	816.18	849.61
2008	787.35	812.86	807.03	807.77	792.25	792.61	785.07	785.44	804.45	798.96	799.94	805.92	798.56
2009	794.24	815.81	855.93	853.20	827.17	827.70	807.98	793.85	797.15	876.21	899.26	910.10	837.56
Professional and Business Services													
2007	648.05	652.04	662.54	675.96	669.90	666.33	664.05	675.62	685.44	673.73	671.64	685.44	668.51
2008	665.87	669.53	675.86	666.79	653.18	681.04	669.72	665.97	680.43	674.00	683.94	682.43	672.97
2009	740.23	768.22	751.49	733.22	733.06	740.58	748.01	751.49	722.80	663.09	681.80	689.72	727.27
Education and Health Services													
2007	694.55	673.92	684.65	695.87	711.21	699.78	706.51	696.51	708.34	704.46	721.93	722.48	701.59
2008	704.93	700.26	709.70	698.50	702.11	712.80	718.75	709.80	719.23	717.66	731.60	719.81	711.98
2009	714.12	711.48	709.50	705.20	706.97	701.35	722.26	719.04	700.05	689.51	706.86	714.50	709.00
Leisure and Hospitality													
2007	292.06	291.15	297.22	293.76	279.87	283.80	280.02	282.25	281.52	285.89	281.20	283.22	285.50
2008	268.72	276.12	273.80	269.44	275.27	284.26	284.23	288.40	284.79	286.34	289.09	291.58	281.09
2009	294.51	306.60	293.51	295.37	295.50	293.12	300.70	309.29	307.09	308.41	300.57	316.51	302.26
Other Services													
2007	481.37	478.72	477.46	489.33	462.18	481.22	484.01	468.54	463.12	442.48	465.76	485.28	473.39
2008	480.15	495.08	493.35	496.40	483.91	490.85	484.50	521.27	502.79	494.51	491.86	486.26	492.90
2009	522.35	536.78	538.76	515.23	516.99	513.30	517.97	539.61	546.78	553.13	589.00	578.82	537.20

IOWA
At a Glance

Population:
    1990 census: 2,776,831
    2000 census: 2,926,324
    2009 estimate: 3,007,856

Percent change in population:
    1990–2000: 5.4%
    2000–2009: 2.8%

Percent change in total nonfarm employment:
    1990–2009: 20.5%
    2008–2009: -3.0%

Industry with the largest growth in employment, 1990–2009 (thousands):
    Education and Health Services, 64.4

Industry with the largest decline or smallest growth in employment, 1990–2009 (thousands):
    Manufacturing, -15.2

Civilian labor force:
    1990: 1,458,858
    2000: 1,601,920
    2009: 1,673,806

Unemployment rate and rank among states (lowest to highest):
    1990: 4.5%, 11th
    2000: 2.8%, 8th
    2009: 6.0%, 4th

Employment by Industry, 2009

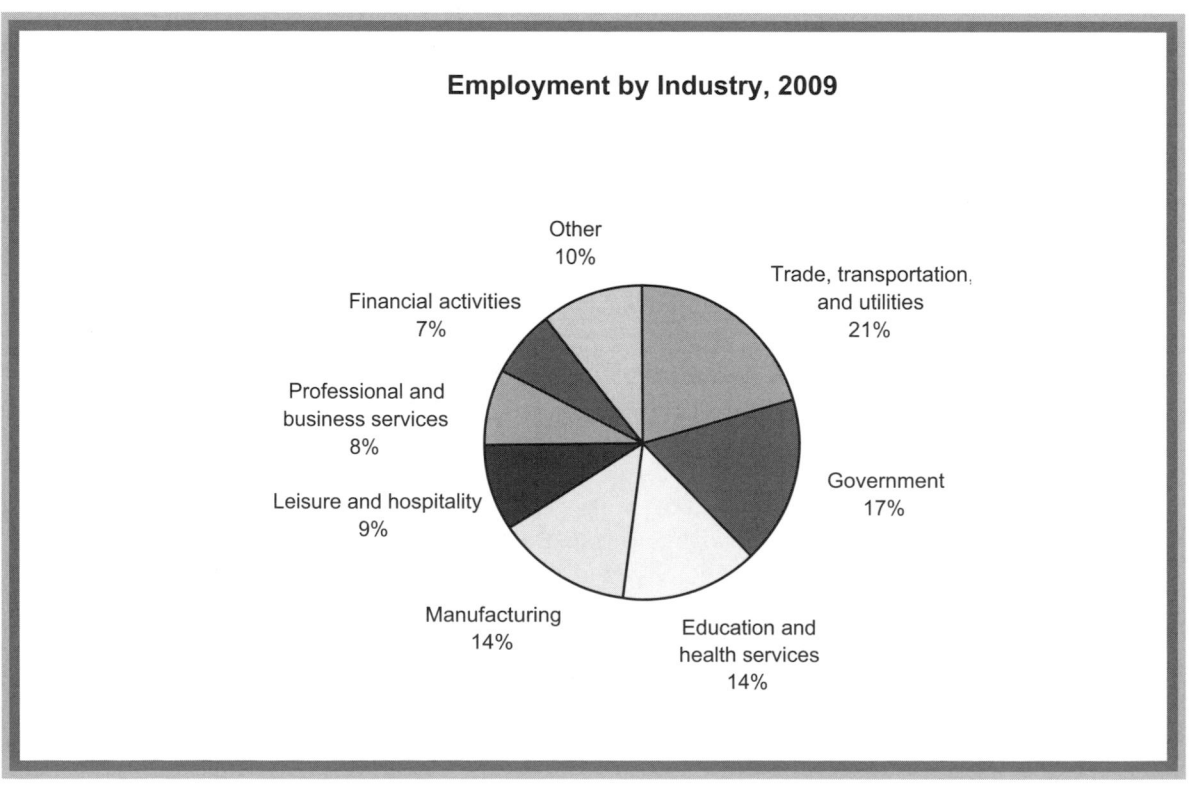

Other 10%

Trade, transportation, and utilities 21%

Financial activities 7%

Professional and business services 8%

Leisure and hospitality 9%

Government 17%

Manufacturing 14%

Education and health services 14%

Employment by Industry: Iowa, Selected Years, 1990–2009

(Numbers in thousands, not seasonally adjusted.)

Industry and year	January	February	March	April	May	June	July	August	September	October	November	December	Annual average
Total Nonfarm													
1990	1,188.1	1,195.3	1,203.4	1,222.6	1,237.1	1,239.9	1,224.2	1,223.8	1,244.5	1,245.8	1,248.2	1,243.5	1,226.3
2000	1,443.6	1,446.8	1,465.5	1,479.2	1,493.0	1,495.9	1,474.0	1,473.8	1,487.2	1,494.5	1,497.3	1,490.7	1,478.4
2001	1,446.7	1,444.5	1,455.0	1,475.3	1,488.0	1,490.3	1,457.6	1,458.1	1,469.9	1,468.0	1,468.7	1,464.8	1,465.6
2002	1,422.6	1,420.8	1,429.7	1,453.1	1,466.4	1,469.6	1,437.7	1,435.6	1,454.4	1,457.5	1,462.0	1,458.6	1,447.3
2003	1,411.9	1,411.4	1,420.5	1,440.2	1,453.7	1,455.2	1,427.0	1,430.3	1,450.8	1,460.6	1,462.4	1,461.3	1,440.4
2004	1,417.8	1,419.7	1,433.0	1,460.0	1,469.2	1,476.6	1,450.7	1,449.9	1,467.6	1,477.3	1,482.5	1,482.7	1,457.3
2005	1,434.2	1,442.3	1,459.1	1,483.4	1,494.3	1,499.3	1,473.1	1,472.6	1,496.0	1,501.7	1,505.7	1,504.3	1,480.5
2006	1,462.9	1,471.0	1,484.8	1,506.6	1,519.6	1,527.0	1,492.6	1,492.5	1,515.6	1,523.4	1,527.6	1,527.2	1,504.2
2007	1,482.6	1,485.7	1,496.4	1,517.8	1,534.1	1,542.2	1,508.5	1,508.8	1,529.3	1,538.6	1,545.9	1,538.9	1,519.1
2008	1,496.1	1,499.9	1,509.6	1,529.6	1,546.6	1,544.7	1,515.3	1,514.8	1,534.4	1,540.8	1,535.6	1,525.3	1,524.4
2009	1,471.7	1,472.0	1,473.0	1,486.8	1,496.4	1,492.7	1,458.5	1,459.3	1,476.5	1,487.5	1,491.2	1,473.0	1,478.2
Total Private													
1990	972.6	973.5	980.4	997.6	1009.4	1016.6	1017.5	1023.3	1028.8	1024.5	1024.5	1020.0	1007.3
2000	1202.1	1201.1	1217.5	1230.7	1240.2	1249.6	1248.4	1249.6	1245.9	1246.7	1248.1	1241.6	1235.1
2001	1202.1	1196.3	1205.9	1225.1	1236.7	1241.8	1230.7	1232.9	1225.4	1217.6	1216.4	1214.1	1220.4
2002	1177.4	1172.5	1180.5	1203.4	1214.7	1221.6	1214.3	1214.0	1212.7	1209.2	1211.7	1208.3	1203.4
2003	1168.9	1162.7	1170.7	1190.1	1201.7	1207.5	1203.1	1207.5	1206.7	1209.8	1210.1	1208.4	1195.6
2004	1174.5	1171.3	1184.0	1209.4	1217.7	1226.9	1227.1	1226.8	1224.3	1227.1	1230.7	1232.0	1212.7
2005	1191.8	1194.3	1209.7	1233.2	1241.8	1250.8	1248.9	1248.2	1250.5	1249.9	1252.6	1251.9	1235.3
2006	1219.1	1220.3	1233.5	1254.8	1265.9	1275.4	1266.9	1266.9	1267.8	1269.9	1272.7	1272.8	1257.2
2007	1235.0	1232.0	1242.8	1263.8	1277.6	1288.7	1279.9	1280.3	1279.0	1281.7	1287.8	1281.8	1269.2
2008	1246.2	1244.0	1252.6	1272.4	1286.1	1288.6	1284.0	1283.8	1279.7	1280.5	1274.3	1265.2	1271.5
2009	1218.6	1213.3	1213.3	1225.7	1233.3	1234.9	1224.2	1225.1	1222.0	1227.1	1230.5	1213.8	1223.5
Goods-Producing													
1990	254.6	253.8	253.2	261.3	266.8	272.3	273.5	274.8	274.8	271.0	269.4	262.8	265.7
2000	304.9	303.4	310.2	316.1	321.0	327.2	327.9	326.7	322.8	320.9	318.0	311.3	317.5
2001	300.6	298.7	300.7	307.8	312.8	317.1	316.0	314.9	309.7	302.6	299.9	296.7	306.5
2002	284.3	281.7	284.2	293.4	298.8	303.3	302.3	300.8	297.3	295.2	293.9	289.1	293.7
2003	277.2	273.3	275.7	283.0	288.2	292.9	292.7	294.3	292.5	293.4	292.1	288.6	287.0
2004	277.9	275.7	280.8	291.4	295.3	302.0	303.8	301.4	300.5	300.4	300.1	297.9	293.9
2005	285.5	284.9	290.8	300.0	304.3	311.0	312.6	312.0	309.7	308.6	307.9	303.6	302.6
2006	295.7	295.0	298.8	306.2	310.4	316.3	316.1	315.6	313.0	310.8	309.0	305.5	307.7
2007	293.6	289.3	292.9	299.5	305.2	311.5	313.1	313.3	310.8	310.2	309.9	304.7	304.5
2008	293.9	290.9	293.0	301.0	307.7	311.0	312.8	312.5	308.7	305.5	300.8	292.3	302.5
2009	274.3	268.5	266.4	270.2	272.0	274.1	271.9	273.0	271.2	271.9	270.8	262.3	270.6
Mining and Logging													
1990	1.6	1.6	1.8	2.0	2.1	2.1	2.1	2.2	2.1	2.1	2.1	1.9	1.9
2000	1.8	1.8	2.0	2.1	2.2	2.3	2.3	2.3	2.3	2.3	2.2	1.9	2.1
2001	1.6	1.7	1.8	2.1	2.2	2.2	2.2	2.2	2.1	2.0	2.0	2.0	2.0
2002	1.7	1.7	1.9	2.0	2.1	2.1	1.9	2.1	2.0	2.0	2.0	1.9	2.0
2003	1.5	1.5	1.6	1.9	2.0	2.1	2.0	2.2	2.2	2.1	2.1	2.0	1.9
2004	1.6	1.6	1.9	2.2	2.3	2.3	2.2	2.2	2.2	2.2	2.1	2.0	2.1
2005	1.7	1.7	2.0	2.1	2.2	2.3	2.3	2.3	2.2	2.2	2.2	2.0	2.1
2006	1.8	1.8	1.9	2.2	2.3	2.4	2.4	2.4	2.3	2.2	2.2	2.1	2.2
2007	1.8	1.7	2.0	2.1	2.2	2.3	2.3	2.3	2.3	2.3	2.3	2.1	2.1
2008	1.7	1.8	1.9	2.2	2.3	2.3	2.3	2.4	2.3	2.3	2.3	2.1	2.2
2009	1.6	1.8	2.0	2.3	2.4	2.4	2.4	2.4	2.4	2.4	2.3	2.1	2.2
Construction													
1990	35.1	34.8	36.5	42.4	46.0	49.0	50.6	51.9	50.8	49.6	48.1	43.9	44.8
2000	54.5	53.4	58.2	62.8	66.4	69.9	70.9	70.8	68.2	67.0	65.0	60.0	63.9
2001	53.4	52.6	54.1	61.0	66.6	70.4	71.5	71.9	69.4	68.5	67.4	63.7	64.2
2002	54.8	53.1	55.4	62.9	67.1	70.2	71.2	70.9	68.6	68.2	67.1	63.4	64.4
2003	55.2	52.5	54.6	62.0	66.9	69.8	71.2	72.2	70.7	70.9	69.2	66.0	65.1
2004	57.5	55.6	59.7	67.9	70.8	74.3	75.4	75.2	73.5	72.3	71.7	69.2	68.6
2005	59.0	58.4	62.3	69.9	72.7	76.6	78.5	78.8	77.0	76.4	75.9	71.3	71.4
2006	64.9	64.6	67.1	72.8	76.3	79.7	80.8	80.7	79.7	77.8	76.2	72.4	74.4
2007	64.0	60.7	63.4	69.5	74.6	78.4	79.0	79.4	77.9	77.7	76.6	71.4	72.7
2008	63.1	60.5	62.4	70.0	75.9	78.4	81.6	81.5	79.4	78.0	75.0	69.8	73.0
2009	58.7	57.2	58.2	64.5	67.4	69.4	70.4	69.9	68.6	67.0	65.5	59.4	64.7
Manufacturing													
1990	217.9	217.4	214.9	216.9	218.7	221.2	220.8	220.7	221.9	220.2	219.2	217.0	218.9
2000	248.6	248.2	250.0	251.2	252.4	255.0	254.7	253.6	252.3	251.6	250.8	249.4	251.4
2001	245.6	244.4	244.8	244.7	244.0	244.5	242.3	240.8	238.2	232.1	230.5	231.0	240.2
2002	227.8	226.9	226.9	228.5	229.6	231.0	229.2	227.8	226.7	225.0	224.8	223.8	227.3
2003	220.5	219.3	219.5	219.1	219.3	221.0	219.5	219.9	219.6	220.4	220.8	220.6	220.0
2004	218.8	218.5	219.2	221.3	222.2	225.4	226.2	224.0	224.8	225.9	226.3	226.7	223.3
2005	224.8	224.8	226.5	228.0	229.4	232.1	231.8	230.9	230.5	230.0	229.8	230.3	229.1
2006	229.0	228.6	229.8	231.2	231.8	234.2	232.9	232.5	231.0	230.8	230.6	231.0	231.1
2007	227.8	226.9	227.5	227.9	228.4	230.8	231.8	231.6	230.6	230.2	231.0	231.2	229.6
2008	229.1	228.6	228.7	228.8	229.5	230.3	228.9	228.6	227.0	225.2	223.5	220.4	227.4
2009	214.0	209.5	206.2	203.4	202.2	202.3	199.1	200.7	200.2	202.5	203.0	200.8	203.7

Employment by Industry: Iowa, Selected Years, 1990–2009—*Continued*
(Numbers in thousands, not seasonally adjusted.)

Industry and year	January	February	March	April	May	June	July	August	September	October	November	December	Annual average
Service-Providing													
1990	933.5	941.5	950.2	961.3	970.3	967.6	950.7	949.0	969.7	973.9	978.8	980.7	960.6
2000	1138.7	1143.4	1155.3	1163.1	1172.0	1168.7	1146.1	1147.1	1164.4	1173.6	1179.3	1179.4	1160.9
2001	1146.1	1145.8	1154.3	1167.5	1175.2	1173.2	1141.6	1143.2	1160.2	1165.4	1168.8	1168.1	1159.1
2002	1138.3	1139.1	1145.5	1159.7	1167.6	1166.3	1135.4	1134.8	1157.1	1162.3	1168.1	1169.5	1153.6
2003	1134.7	1138.1	1144.8	1157.2	1165.5	1162.3	1134.3	1136.0	1158.3	1167.2	1170.3	1172.7	1153.5
2004	1139.9	1144.0	1152.2	1168.6	1173.9	1174.6	1146.9	1148.5	1167.1	1176.9	1182.4	1184.8	1163.3
2005	1148.7	1157.4	1168.3	1183.4	1190.0	1188.3	1160.5	1160.6	1186.3	1193.1	1197.8	1200.7	1177.9
2006	1167.2	1176.0	1186.0	1200.4	1209.2	1210.7	1176.5	1176.9	1202.6	1212.6	1218.6	1221.7	1196.5
2007	1189.0	1196.4	1203.5	1218.3	1228.9	1230.7	1195.4	1195.5	1218.5	1228.4	1236.0	1234.2	1214.6
2008	1202.2	1209.0	1216.6	1228.6	1238.9	1233.7	1202.5	1202.3	1225.7	1235.3	1234.8	1233.0	1221.9
2009	1197.4	1203.5	1206.6	1216.6	1224.4	1218.6	1186.6	1186.3	1205.3	1215.6	1220.4	1210.7	1207.7
Trade, Transportation, and Utilities													
1990	261.9	259.1	261.6	266.4	268.9	270.9	271.0	272.9	273.2	274.0	276.4	278.2	269.5
2000	310.4	308.4	310.6	313.7	315.1	317.0	317.0	316.9	315.9	317.9	322.6	324.2	315.8
2001	310.8	306.3	306.9	310.3	312.6	313.2	311.9	312.8	310.5	309.7	314.7	315.4	311.3
2002	303.6	299.1	300.3	304.2	305.6	307.9	307.2	307.4	306.0	306.4	310.9	312.3	305.9
2003	299.5	295.7	297.6	301.1	304.0	304.1	304.6	304.5	303.1	304.9	308.8	310.0	303.2
2004	299.5	296.8	298.6	302.7	304.0	305.4	307.1	307.1	304.8	306.0	310.7	313.0	304.6
2005	300.1	298.2	301.1	305.4	306.9	307.8	308.3	307.5	306.7	307.5	312.3	314.9	306.4
2006	303.8	301.5	303.6	308.0	309.9	311.1	309.3	308.6	307.6	309.5	314.3	316.5	308.6
2007	305.5	302.5	304.1	306.9	310.6	312.2	310.1	308.8	307.7	309.0	314.7	315.9	309.0
2008	306.6	304.1	306.0	307.5	310.6	311.2	310.6	310.5	308.7	310.4	313.2	314.3	309.5
2009	301.9	299.3	299.7	301.7	304.0	304.8	303.5	303.3	300.0	298.9	304.3	301.6	301.9
Wholesale Trade													
1990	61.2	61.0	61.8	64.0	64.1	64.2	64.3	64.7	65.0	65.5	63.9	63.6	63.6
2000	66.4	66.3	67.5	68.8	68.7	69.2	70.6	69.2	68.8	68.5	67.7	67.4	68.2
2001	66.7	66.3	67.0	68.4	68.9	69.0	70.2	70.1	69.4	68.1	67.6	67.0	68.2
2002	65.8	65.4	65.5	66.9	66.8	67.3	68.8	68.0	67.3	67.0	66.5	66.0	66.8
2003	64.1	63.7	64.2	65.4	65.7	65.9	67.0	66.6	65.7	65.7	65.2	64.7	65.3
2004	63.9	63.7	64.4	66.2	66.1	66.6	67.8	67.4	66.6	67.0	67.0	66.8	66.1
2005	65.3	65.3	66.2	67.8	67.9	68.1	68.7	68.1	67.9	68.1	67.7	67.3	67.4
2006	66.6	66.3	66.8	68.0	68.1	68.3	68.4	67.9	67.7	67.5	67.7	67.1	67.5
2007	66.2	65.9	66.5	67.8	68.4	68.6	68.8	68.2	68.3	68.9	69.0	68.4	67.9
2008	67.3	67.2	67.8	68.7	69.8	69.6	69.8	69.2	68.5	69.4	68.7	68.2	68.7
2009	66.1	66.1	66.2	67.5	67.5	67.4	67.5	66.7	65.9	67.4	69.4	67.7	67.1
Retail Trade													
1990	156.8	154.3	155.3	158.1	160.1	161.6	161.7	162.9	162.8	163.3	167.1	169.2	161.1
2000	187.2	185.3	185.7	187.0	188.5	189.8	188.6	189.4	189.1	191.0	196.5	198.7	189.7
2001	187.7	183.6	183.3	185.1	186.6	186.8	185.0	185.6	184.4	184.8	190.1	191.5	186.2
2002	182.4	178.5	179.2	181.2	182.3	183.6	181.1	181.5	181.2	181.3	185.9	187.7	182.2
2003	179.0	175.8	176.6	178.7	180.8	181.0	180.1	180.0	179.7	180.9	185.3	186.9	180.4
2004	178.5	176.1	176.6	178.2	179.5	180.3	180.7	181.0	179.6	180.2	185.3	187.9	180.3
2005	177.6	175.6	176.8	179.0	180.2	180.8	180.4	180.1	179.1	179.5	184.3	186.7	180.0
2006	177.8	176.0	176.9	179.4	180.7	181.2	179.8	178.9	177.8	179.5	183.9	186.1	179.8
2007	178.0	175.3	175.7	177.1	179.6	180.6	179.4	178.3	177.0	177.6	182.7	184.3	178.8
2008	177.4	175.2	176.3	177.1	178.2	179.1	178.5	178.4	177.1	177.9	181.3	182.5	178.3
2009	174.7	172.5	172.8	173.9	176.0	177.5	176.4	176.6	174.3	173.0	176.2	175.0	174.9
Transportation and Utilities													
1990	43.9	43.8	44.5	44.3	44.7	45.1	45.0	45.3	45.4	45.2	45.4	45.4	44.8
2000	56.8	56.8	57.4	57.9	57.9	58.0	57.8	58.3	58.0	58.4	58.4	58.1	57.8
2001	56.4	56.4	56.6	56.8	57.1	57.4	56.7	57.1	56.7	56.8	57.0	56.9	56.8
2002	55.4	55.2	55.6	56.1	56.5	57.0	57.3	57.9	57.5	58.1	58.5	58.6	57.0
2003	56.4	56.2	56.8	57.0	57.5	57.2	57.5	57.9	57.7	58.3	58.3	58.4	57.4
2004	57.1	57.0	57.6	58.3	58.4	58.5	58.6	58.7	58.6	58.8	58.4	58.3	58.2
2005	57.2	57.3	58.1	58.6	58.8	58.9	59.2	59.3	59.7	59.9	60.3	60.9	59.0
2006	59.4	59.2	59.9	60.6	61.1	61.6	61.1	61.8	62.1	62.5	62.7	63.3	61.3
2007	61.3	61.3	61.9	62.0	62.6	63.0	61.9	62.3	62.4	62.5	63.0	63.2	62.3
2008	61.9	61.7	61.9	61.7	62.6	62.5	62.3	62.9	63.1	63.1	63.2	63.6	62.5
2009	61.1	60.7	60.7	60.3	60.5	59.9	59.6	60.0	59.8	58.5	58.7	58.9	59.9
Information													
1990	29.8	30.1	30.2	29.6	29.6	29.6	29.8	30.0	30.0	30.1	30.2	30.1	29.9
2000	39.8	39.7	40.2	40.6	40.8	41.3	40.5	40.0	39.7	39.9	40.6	41.2	40.3
2001	38.5	38.5	39.0	38.1	37.8	37.8	37.7	36.8	36.5	36.5	36.3	36.0	37.5
2002	35.6	35.6	35.4	35.5	35.6	35.6	34.8	34.7	34.4	34.4	34.7	34.5	35.1
2003	33.6	33.9	33.7	33.4	33.6	33.7	33.9	33.5	33.5	33.5	33.6	33.7	33.6
2004	33.3	33.3	33.4	33.6	33.6	33.7	34.0	34.0	33.7	33.7	33.9	34.0	33.7
2005	33.4	33.3	33.5	33.3	33.2	33.1	33.1	32.6	32.5	32.4	32.5	32.7	33.0
2006	32.2	32.4	32.6	32.9	33.0	33.2	33.1	33.0	33.0	33.1	33.4	33.7	33.0
2007	33.0	33.5	33.7	34.1	34.3	34.4	33.6	33.3	33.2	33.1	33.4	33.4	33.6
2008	33.2	33.5	33.5	33.8	33.9	33.6	33.0	32.6	32.3	32.3	31.9	31.7	32.9
2009	31.3	31.4	31.4	31.0	31.2	30.8	30.2	29.8	29.6	29.6	29.5	29.5	30.4

Employment by Industry: Iowa, Selected Years, 1990–2009—*Continued*

(Numbers in thousands, not seasonally adjusted.)

Industry and year	January	February	March	April	May	June	July	August	September	October	November	December	Annual average
Financial Activities													
1990	68.0	67.9	68.2	69.1	69.5	70.4	70.6	70.5	69.9	69.8	69.9	70.4	69.5
2000	88.8	88.7	88.5	89.1	89.5	90.6	90.5	90.7	90.0	89.6	89.8	90.3	89.6
2001	90.0	89.8	90.4	90.8	91.5	93.0	93.2	93.1	92.6	92.6	93.1	94.1	92.0
2002	93.0	93.0	93.3	93.7	93.7	94.7	95.0	94.7	93.8	93.8	93.7	94.2	93.9
2003	94.2	94.2	94.2	94.4	95.0	95.8	95.9	96.0	95.4	95.4	95.6	95.9	95.2
2004	95.3	95.4	95.4	96.3	96.7	97.6	98.1	98.3	97.3	97.3	97.3	98.1	96.9
2005	97.3	97.4	97.5	97.6	98.0	98.9	99.0	99.0	98.6	98.4	98.5	99.4	98.3
2006	98.8	99.0	99.7	99.8	100.4	101.6	101.5	101.3	101.2	101.1	100.9	101.8	100.6
2007	101.1	101.2	101.6	101.9	102.4	103.8	103.8	103.4	102.8	103.0	103.2	103.5	102.6
2008	102.6	102.7	102.8	102.6	102.8	103.6	103.6	103.2	102.0	101.8	101.9	102.4	102.7
2009	101.7	101.4	101.5	101.7	102.1	102.8	102.5	102.4	101.4	101.0	101.4	102.5	101.9
Professional and Business Services													
1990	66.6	67.1	67.9	67.6	67.6	69.1	70.5	70.8	70.7	70.2	69.9	70.1	69.0
2000	103.9	103.9	106.4	107.3	107.1	108.6	109.1	109.2	108.5	109.7	109.2	108.7	107.6
2001	107.3	106.2	106.7	108.8	109.1	109.1	106.9	108.3	106.8	107.4	105.6	105.4	107.3
2002	102.4	102.6	103.7	105.5	105.5	107.5	107.4	107.0	107.0	106.1	106.9	106.1	105.6
2003	102.3	102.2	102.5	105.6	104.8	106.2	106.6	107.9	107.2	107.8	107.0	107.1	105.6
2004	104.1	104.3	105.3	108.8	108.3	109.2	110.0	110.2	108.7	110.9	110.8	110.7	108.4
2005	107.0	108.4	109.8	112.6	112.5	113.9	114.6	115.1	116.1	116.7	116.3	116.2	113.3
2006	111.7	112.6	114.3	116.8	117.2	118.7	118.5	118.8	118.7	120.0	120.4	119.4	117.3
2007	116.1	117.1	117.7	121.4	120.9	123.2	123.1	124.0	122.9	123.0	123.0	123.2	121.4
2008	119.6	119.9	120.4	123.5	123.6	124.8	126.2	125.7	124.5	125.2	122.4	121.3	123.1
2009	117.1	117.3	116.0	117.3	117.0	117.7	117.3	118.1	117.3	118.7	119.3	118.1	117.6
Education and Health Services													
1990	144.5	146.9	147.5	147.0	146.7	140.8	139.5	140.6	149.2	151.5	152.7	152.4	146.6
2000	180.3	182.2	184.0	183.6	182.5	177.9	173.3	174.4	181.5	187.0	187.9	187.7	181.8
2001	183.8	185.5	187.9	188.9	187.3	182.0	176.4	177.5	184.9	190.0	190.4	190.7	185.4
2002	187.0	188.7	189.6	190.4	189.5	183.6	178.7	179.4	187.9	192.6	193.8	194.3	188.0
2003	189.9	191.9	193.1	191.9	190.4	185.3	180.3	180.6	188.7	193.7	194.6	194.5	189.6
2004	191.2	193.0	194.3	194.1	192.7	187.6	182.5	182.6	190.5	195.5	196.5	197.2	191.5
2005	193.1	195.5	196.7	197.2	196.0	191.1	186.7	186.8	195.5	199.9	200.9	201.5	195.1
2006	197.5	199.8	201.0	201.6	200.3	195.2	190.4	190.6	198.6	203.5	204.8	205.3	199.1
2007	201.2	204.1	205.5	205.7	204.1	199.2	193.7	194.7	203.1	208.2	210.1	209.8	203.3
2008	206.1	208.4	209.7	210.1	208.4	202.4	197.5	197.8	206.6	213.1	214.8	214.8	207.5
2009	210.5	212.9	213.9	213.4	211.5	205.8	200.9	201.4	209.9	216.7	217.6	216.9	211.0
Leisure and Hospitality													
1990	92.7	93.9	96.7	101.3	104.8	107.5	106.6	107.8	105.5	101.2	99.7	99.6	101.4
2000	118.0	118.7	121.2	123.7	127.4	129.6	132.6	134.5	130.7	124.9	123.0	121.5	125.4
2001	115.3	115.5	118.1	123.9	129.0	132.2	131.7	132.8	128.4	122.7	120.4	119.6	124.1
2002	115.7	115.9	117.7	123.9	129.1	131.6	131.7	132.9	129.8	124.0	121.2	121.5	124.0
2003	116.6	116.0	118.0	124.4	129.4	132.8	132.6	134.2	130.1	124.8	122.3	122.2	125.3
2004	117.3	117.3	120.3	126.2	130.7	134.3	134.5	136.5	132.4	126.8	125.1	124.7	127.2
2005	120.1	121.1	124.3	130.7	134.6	137.7	137.6	138.6	135.2	130.3	128.1	127.3	130.5
2006	123.5	124.3	127.3	132.9	137.8	141.5	140.6	141.9	138.9	135.1	132.9	133.3	134.2
2007	127.9	127.9	130.2	136.7	142.1	145.3	144.2	144.9	140.9	136.8	134.8	133.4	137.1
2008	127.1	127.7	130.0	136.2	140.9	143.3	141.9	143.4	139.1	134.0	131.2	130.4	135.4
2009	124.6	125.2	127.0	132.8	137.6	140.4	139.8	139.9	135.7	133.0	129.7	125.4	132.6
Other Services													
1990	54.5	54.7	55.1	55.3	55.5	56.0	56.0	55.9	55.5	55.8	56.3	56.4	55.5
2000	56.0	56.1	56.4	56.6	56.8	57.4	57.5	57.2	56.8	56.8	57.0	56.7	56.7
2001	55.8	55.8	56.2	56.5	56.6	57.4	56.9	56.7	56.0	56.1	56.0	56.2	56.4
2002	55.8	55.9	56.3	56.8	56.9	57.4	57.2	57.1	56.5	56.7	56.6	56.3	56.6
2003	55.6	55.5	55.9	56.3	56.3	56.7	56.5	56.5	56.2	56.3	56.1	56.4	56.2
2004	55.9	55.5	55.9	56.3	56.4	57.1	57.1	56.7	56.4	56.5	56.3	56.4	56.4
2005	55.3	55.5	56.0	56.4	56.3	57.3	57.0	56.6	56.2	56.1	56.1	56.3	56.3
2006	55.9	55.7	56.2	56.6	56.9	57.8	57.4	57.1	56.8	56.8	57.0	57.3	56.8
2007	56.6	56.4	57.1	57.6	58.0	59.1	58.3	57.9	57.6	57.8	57.8	57.9	57.7
2008	57.1	56.8	57.2	57.7	58.2	58.7	58.4	58.1	57.8	58.2	58.1	58.0	57.9
2009	57.2	57.3	57.4	57.6	57.9	58.5	58.1	57.2	56.9	57.3	57.9	57.5	57.6
Government													
1990	215.5	221.8	223.0	225.0	227.7	223.3	206.7	200.5	215.7	221.3	223.7	223.5	218.9
2000	241.5	245.7	248.0	248.5	252.8	246.3	225.6	224.2	241.3	247.8	249.2	249.1	243.3
2001	244.6	248.2	249.1	250.2	251.3	248.5	226.9	225.2	244.5	250.4	252.3	250.7	245.2
2002	245.2	248.3	249.2	249.7	251.7	248.0	223.4	221.6	241.7	248.3	250.3	250.3	244.0
2003	243.0	248.7	249.8	250.1	252.0	247.7	223.9	222.8	244.1	250.8	252.3	252.9	244.8
2004	243.3	248.4	249.0	250.6	251.5	249.7	223.6	223.1	243.3	250.2	251.8	250.7	244.6
2005	242.4	248.0	249.4	250.2	252.5	248.5	224.2	224.4	245.5	251.8	253.1	252.4	245.2
2006	243.8	250.7	251.3	251.8	253.7	251.6	225.7	225.6	247.8	253.5	254.9	254.4	247.1
2007	247.6	253.7	253.6	254.0	256.5	253.5	228.6	228.5	250.3	256.9	258.1	257.1	249.9
2008	249.9	255.9	257.0	257.2	260.5	256.1	231.3	231.0	254.7	260.3	261.3	260.1	252.9
2009	253.1	258.7	259.7	261.1	263.1	257.8	234.3	234.2	254.5	260.4	260.7	259.2	254.7

Average Weekly Hours by Selected Industry: Iowa, 2007–2009

(Not seasonally adjusted.)

Industry and year	January	February	March	April	May	June	July	August	September	October	November	December	Annual average
Total Private													
2007	33.6	33.8	33.9	34.0	34.3	34.7	34.6	34.3	34.6	34.2	34.3	34.2	34.2
2008	33.4	33.1	33.9	33.5	34.1	34.3	34.2	34.3	34.0	33.9	33.8	33.1	33.8
2009	32.8	33.3	32.8	32.8	32.8	33.1	33.4	34.0	33.8	33.9	34.2	33.3	33.4
Goods-Producing													
2007	39.4	38.9	39.6	39.2	40.8	41.0	40.8	40.9	41.3	41.2	41.5	40.3	40.4
2008	39.9	39.2	40.0	39.3	40.9	40.4	40.7	40.9	40.5	40.3	39.4	38.0	40.0
2009	36.8	37.3	36.7	36.5	37.2	38.2	38.1	39.0	39.7	40.2	40.0	38.0	38.1
Construction													
2007	37.5	37.4	38.7	37.9	41.0	42.2	42.0	40.9	40.8	41.3	41.4	40.6	40.3
2008	40.0	37.8	39.2	37.6	40.7	40.0	41.2	42.0	39.2	40.5	38.8	38.1	39.7
2009	37.1	38.0	37.4	38.5	38.1	41.8	42.4	42.2	42.0	41.6	41.5	38.5	40.1
Manufacturing													
2007	40.1	39.5	40.0	39.8	40.8	40.6	40.4	40.9	41.5	41.2	41.5	40.9	40.6
2008	40.5	40.2	40.7	40.3	40.6	40.2	40.2	40.2	40.8	40.1	39.6	38.0	40.1
2009	36.7	37.1	36.4	35.9	37.0	37.9	37.3	38.6	39.6	40.4	40.1	39.2	38.0
Trade, Transportation, and Utilities													
2007	31.8	32.0	31.9	31.6	31.7	32.2	32.0	31.7	31.6	31.7	32.1	32.2	31.9
2008	31.0	31.0	31.4	31.3	32.3	32.3	32.0	32.2	31.5	31.9	31.7	31.5	31.7
2009	31.3	31.6	31.8	32.1	31.6	31.7	32.1	32.4	32.3	32.3	33.1	31.5	32.0
Financial Activities													
2007	36.9	36.9	36.4	37.4	36.1	36.4	37.1	36.1	36.9	36.2	36.1	37.1	36.6
2008	35.3	34.7	35.8	35.2	35.2	36.5	35.3	35.9	35.5	35.4	36.5	35.5	35.6
2009	36.1	36.5	35.9	35.7	35.9	36.0	36.7	37.3	36.9	37.0	37.8	36.9	36.6
Professional and Business Services													
2007	33.1	33.7	34.3	35.2	34.8	34.8	34.7	33.9	34.6	34.0	33.3	33.5	34.2
2008	32.2	33.1	33.7	33.8	33.2	33.2	33.1	32.7	32.0	32.8	33.0	33.0	33.0
2009	32.6	33.8	32.5	32.3	32.2	32.9	33.5	33.4	32.6	33.4	33.8	33.2	33.0
Education and Health Services													
2007	31.7	32.5	32.1	32.6	32.3	33.2	32.8	32.3	32.9	32.5	32.7	32.9	32.5
2008	32.7	32.5	33.4	33.1	33.0	33.2	33.1	33.0	33.2	32.4	32.7	31.8	32.8
2009	32.6	32.7	31.4	31.7	31.3	31.2	31.7	32.1	31.4	31.2	31.5	31.0	31.7
Leisure and Hospitality													
2007	23.6	24.2	24.3	24.9	24.9	25.9	25.4	25.3	25.1	24.7	25.0	24.4	24.8
2008	23.9	23.2	24.3	23.6	24.0	24.9	25.1	25.1	24.8	24.7	24.6	23.3	24.3
2009	23.6	24.3	24.6	24.4	24.7	25.2	25.7	25.6	24.6	24.5	24.9	23.8	24.7
Other Services													
2007	26.3	27.6	26.6	27.6	27.8	27.9	28.3	28.2	28.2	27.0	26.6	26.2	27.4
2008	26.5	27.0	27.7	27.3	28.3	27.4	28.9	28.9	29.5	29.0	28.4	27.4	28.0
2009	27.2	27.9	27.9	27.8	27.8	28.4	27.8	29.1	28.2	28.1	27.7	27.1	27.9

Average Hourly Earnings by Selected Industry: Iowa, 2007–2009

(Dollars, not seasonally adjusted.)

Industry and year	January	February	March	April	May	June	July	August	September	October	November	December	Annual average
Total Private													
2007	18.15	18.39	18.09	17.84	17.61	17.86	17.98	17.89	18.22	18.10	17.97	18.11	18.01
2008	17.61	17.77	17.87	18.07	18.15	18.28	18.14	18.64	18.65	18.65	18.90	19.50	18.35
2009	19.78	19.94	19.77	19.77	19.93	19.86	20.05	20.04	19.94	20.09	20.30	20.62	20.01
Goods-Producing													
2007	19.13	19.92	19.18	19.57	19.18	19.40	19.55	19.28	19.77	19.44	19.47	19.61	19.46
2008	17.86	18.52	18.35	18.24	18.87	19.21	19.01	19.32	19.02	19.37	19.74	20.37	18.99
2009	20.39	20.55	20.90	20.36	20.45	20.73	20.61	20.92	20.63	20.55	20.88	21.03	20.67
Construction													
2007	20.00	20.40	20.96	20.69	20.62	20.58	20.46	20.61	21.03	20.74	21.03	21.19	20.70
2008	19.75	20.30	20.56	20.43	21.18	21.45	21.16	21.87	20.71	21.21	21.03	21.86	21.01
2009	22.01	21.72	21.85	21.85	21.77	22.49	22.30	22.36	22.27	22.38	22.54	22.48	22.19
Manufacturing													
2007	18.84	19.77	18.58	19.17	18.59	18.86	19.12	18.72	19.26	18.90	18.85	18.98	18.97
2008	17.15	17.90	17.62	17.53	17.97	18.36	18.13	18.30	18.37	18.66	19.27	19.84	18.24
2009	19.77	20.04	20.46	19.68	19.83	19.92	20.22	20.61	20.23	20.07	20.44	20.75	20.17
Trade, Transportation, and Utilities													
2007	16.15	16.39	16.26	16.22	15.70	15.58	15.75	15.90	15.94	16.02	15.77	15.97	15.97
2008	16.27	16.12	16.25	16.37	16.37	16.10	15.96	16.04	16.58	16.39	16.43	17.49	16.36
2009	18.12	18.42	18.21	18.55	18.16	17.90	18.02	17.95	17.12	17.24	17.18	16.44	17.77
Financial Activities													
2007	23.69	23.77	23.62	23.35	23.71	24.46	24.58	24.37	24.40	23.76	24.12	23.93	23.98
2008	23.96	23.92	24.28	25.17	25.09	24.88	25.11	25.31	25.49	25.46	25.38	25.35	24.95
2009	25.31	25.66	25.90	25.42	25.95	25.84	26.01	25.89	25.55	25.66	25.73	25.69	25.72
Professional and Business Services													
2007	21.49	21.19	20.93	20.84	20.36	21.72	20.29	20.13	20.15	20.04	19.52	20.04	20.55
2008	19.81	19.77	20.22	20.75	20.40	21.62	20.34	23.30	21.71	21.47	22.88	22.43	21.23
2009	23.48	23.71	21.73	21.23	22.49	21.62	21.72	22.07	21.67	21.42	21.45	21.62	22.02
Education and Health Services													
2007	15.98	15.98	15.54	15.87	15.70	15.77	16.31	16.13	16.57	16.64	16.93	16.98	16.21
2008	16.34	16.37	16.45	16.81	16.60	16.67	16.60	17.11	17.35	17.17	17.56	18.27	16.94
2009	18.37	18.25	18.21	19.48	18.73	18.97	19.10	19.01	19.37	20.27	19.26	20.21	19.10
Leisure and Hospitality													
2007	10.75	11.05	11.01	10.94	10.73	10.53	10.91	10.71	11.07	11.26	11.12	11.33	10.94
2008	11.44	11.45	11.31	11.19	11.13	10.92	11.07	11.23	11.40	11.47	11.49	11.84	11.32
2009	11.83	11.82	11.78	11.84	11.73	11.58	11.57	11.73	11.94	11.93	11.95	12.25	11.82
Other Services													
2007	15.97	14.52	14.61	14.47	14.00	14.31	14.05	14.27	14.63	14.65	14.31	14.32	14.50
2008	14.46	14.12	14.05	14.11	13.91	14.22	15.40	15.05	15.28	15.60	15.52	15.37	14.77
2009	15.61	15.66	15.80	15.67	15.85	15.53	15.48	15.56	16.27	15.98	16.39	16.56	15.86

Average Weekly Earnings by Selected Industry: Iowa, 2007–2009

(Dollars, not seasonally adjusted.)

Industry and year	January	February	March	April	May	June	July	August	September	October	November	December	Annual average
Total Private													
2007	609.84	621.58	613.25	606.56	604.02	619.74	622.11	613.63	630.41	619.02	616.37	619.36	615.94
2008	588.17	588.19	605.79	605.35	618.92	627.00	620.39	639.35	634.10	632.24	638.82	645.45	620.23
2009	648.78	664.00	648.46	648.46	653.70	657.37	669.67	681.36	673.97	681.05	694.26	686.65	668.33
Goods-Producing													
2007	753.72	774.89	759.53	767.14	782.54	795.40	797.64	788.55	816.50	800.93	808.01	790.28	786.18
2008	712.61	725.98	734.00	716.83	771.78	776.08	773.71	790.19	770.31	780.61	777.76	774.06	759.60
2009	750.35	766.52	767.03	743.14	760.74	791.89	785.24	815.88	819.01	826.11	835.20	799.14	787.53
Construction													
2007	750.00	762.96	811.15	784.15	845.42	868.48	859.32	842.95	858.02	856.56	870.64	860.31	834.21
2008	790.00	767.34	805.95	768.17	862.03	858.00	871.79	918.54	811.83	859.01	815.96	832.87	834.10
2009	816.57	825.36	817.19	841.23	829.44	940.08	945.52	943.59	935.34	931.01	935.41	865.48	889.82
Manufacturing													
2007	755.48	780.92	743.20	762.97	758.47	765.72	772.45	765.65	799.29	778.68	782.28	776.28	770.18
2008	694.58	719.58	717.13	706.46	729.58	738.07	728.83	735.66	749.50	748.27	763.09	753.92	731.42
2009	725.56	743.48	744.74	706.51	733.71	754.97	754.21	795.55	801.11	810.83	819.64	813.40	766.46
Trade, Transportation, and Utilities													
2007	513.57	524.48	518.69	512.55	497.69	501.68	504.00	504.03	503.70	507.83	506.22	514.23	509.44
2008	504.37	499.72	510.25	512.38	528.75	520.03	510.72	516.49	522.27	522.84	520.83	550.94	518.61
2009	567.16	582.07	579.08	595.46	573.86	567.43	578.44	581.58	552.98	556.85	568.66	517.86	568.64
Financial Activities													
2007	874.16	877.11	859.77	873.29	855.93	890.34	911.92	879.76	900.36	860.11	870.73	887.80	877.67
2008	845.79	830.02	869.22	885.98	883.17	908.12	886.38	908.63	904.90	901.28	926.37	899.93	888.22
2009	913.69	936.59	929.81	907.49	931.61	930.24	954.57	965.70	942.80	949.42	972.59	947.96	941.35
Professional and Business Services													
2007	711.32	714.10	717.90	733.57	708.53	755.86	704.06	682.41	697.19	681.36	650.02	671.34	702.81
2008	637.88	654.39	681.41	701.35	677.28	717.78	673.25	761.91	694.72	704.22	755.04	740.19	700.59
2009	765.45	801.40	706.23	685.73	724.18	711.30	727.62	737.14	706.44	715.43	725.01	717.78	726.66
Education and Health Services													
2007	506.57	519.35	498.83	517.36	507.11	523.56	534.97	521.00	545.15	540.80	553.61	558.64	526.83
2008	534.32	532.03	549.43	556.41	547.80	553.44	549.46	564.63	576.02	556.31	574.21	580.99	555.63
2009	598.86	596.78	571.79	617.52	586.25	591.86	605.47	610.22	608.22	632.42	606.69	626.51	605.47
Leisure and Hospitality													
2007	253.70	267.41	267.54	272.41	267.18	272.73	277.11	270.96	277.86	278.12	278.00	276.45	271.31
2008	273.42	265.64	274.83	264.08	267.12	271.91	277.86	281.87	282.72	283.31	282.65	275.87	275.08
2009	279.19	287.23	289.79	288.90	289.73	291.82	297.35	300.29	293.72	292.29	297.56	291.55	291.95
Other Services													
2007	420.01	400.75	388.63	399.37	389.20	399.25	397.62	402.41	412.57	395.55	380.65	375.18	397.30
2008	383.19	381.24	389.19	385.20	393.65	389.63	445.06	434.95	450.76	452.40	440.77	421.14	413.56
2009	424.59	436.91	440.82	435.63	440.63	441.05	430.34	452.80	458.81	449.04	454.00	448.78	442.49

KANSAS
At a Glance

Population:
  1990 census: 2,477,588
  2000 census: 2,688,418
  2009 estimate: 2,818,747

Percent change in population:
  1990–2000: 8.5%
  2000–2009: 4.8%

Percent change in total nonfarm employment:
  1990–2009: 23.1%
  2008–2009: -3.3%

Industry with the largest growth in employment, 1990–2009 (thousands):
  Education and Health Services, 75

Industry with the largest decline or smallest growth in employment, 1990–2009 (thousands):
  Manufacturing, -9.9

Civilian labor force:
  1990: 1,270,352
  2000: 1,405,104
  2009: 1,518,921

Unemployment rate and rank among states (lowest to highest):
  1990: 4.3%, 7th
  2000: 3.8%, 25th
  2009: 6.7%, 10th

Employment by Industry, 2009

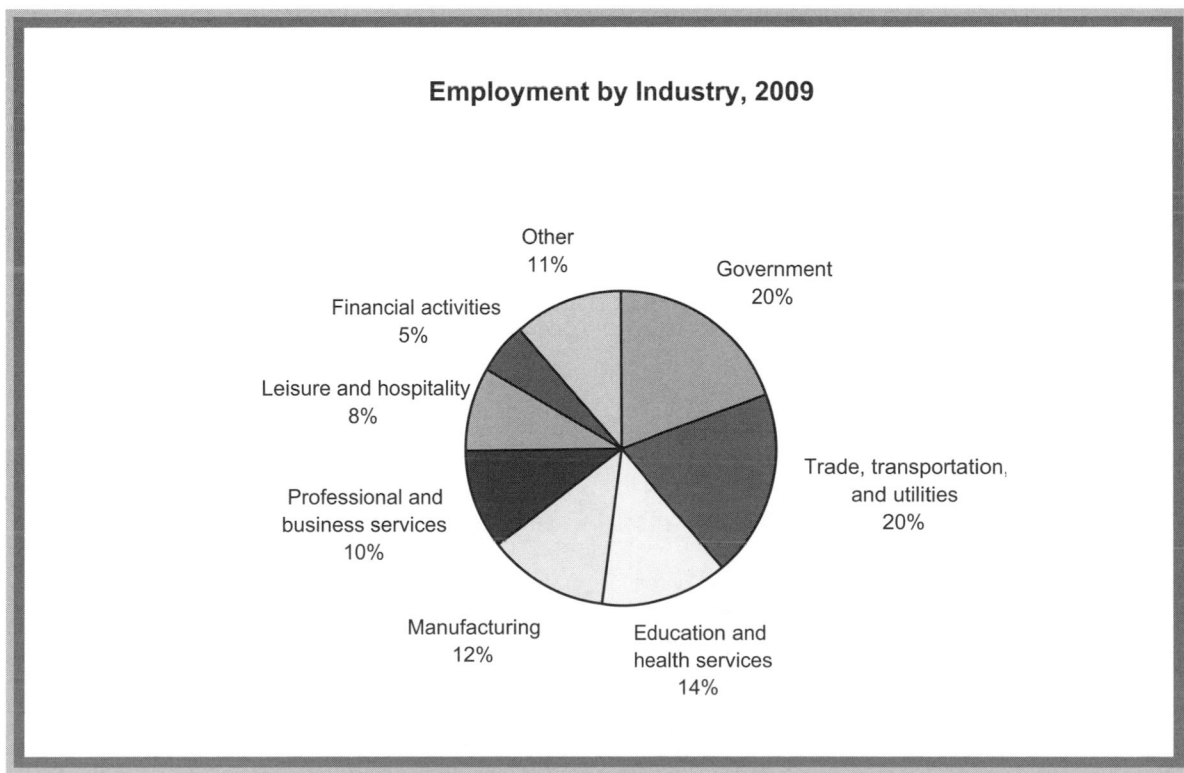

- Other 11%
- Government 20%
- Financial activities 5%
- Leisure and hospitality 8%
- Professional and business services 10%
- Trade, transportation, and utilities 20%
- Manufacturing 12%
- Education and health services 14%

Employment by Industry: Kansas, Selected Years, 1990–2009

(Numbers in thousands, not seasonally adjusted.)

Industry and year	January	February	March	April	May	June	July	August	September	October	November	December	Annual average
Total Nonfarm													
1990	1065.7	1073.4	1083.3	1095.0	1102.5	1105.2	1075.1	1081.6	1102.9	1101.8	1110.3	1106.2	1091.9
2000	1317.3	1320.0	1334.4	1350.8	1360.1	1365.4	1333.8	1332.6	1350.9	1359.4	1364.8	1363.7	1346.1
2001	1330.1	1333.1	1346.9	1356.7	1363.0	1365.5	1337.9	1333.7	1351.6	1355.2	1356.1	1356.2	1348.8
2002	1320.9	1319.7	1331.7	1345.5	1352.0	1354.7	1326.0	1324.7	1339.7	1335.9	1341.7	1340.7	1336.1
2003	1301.0	1301.9	1307.9	1316.4	1325.4	1324.7	1297.5	1295.8	1315.5	1320.7	1324.9	1326.2	1313.2
2004	1290.3	1291.1	1308.0	1327.9	1336.2	1339.9	1316.0	1312.8	1339.6	1342.1	1346.2	1349.3	1325.0
2005	1302.6	1315.3	1329.3	1338.2	1344.3	1349.4	1311.8	1312.2	1341.4	1344.7	1352.3	1355.9	1333.1
2006	1317.9	1333.2	1345.9	1351.5	1361.3	1369.7	1330.3	1335.8	1369.9	1371.8	1374.5	1384.0	1353.8
2007	1341.2	1351.9	1372.9	1377.7	1387.1	1397.5	1369.4	1368.1	1391.2	1396.8	1404.6	1402.1	1380.0
2008	1366.0	1377.0	1389.2	1399.4	1405.8	1404.9	1375.1	1370.0	1395.3	1403.4	1402.2	1398.7	1390.6
2009	1357.7	1355.2	1355.7	1357.9	1360.9	1353.2	1319.3	1314.6	1334.7	1343.1	1344.5	1337.8	1344.6
Total Private													
1990	853.2	855.2	863.8	874.3	881.5	891.7	887.9	888.0	887.4	882.1	881.1	884.0	877.5
2000	1078.0	1077.4	1086.7	1098.8	1103.8	1113.8	1107.7	1109.2	1110.5	1108.2	1110.7	1110.1	1101.2
2001	1085.0	1084.3	1094.2	1102.6	1108.1	1117.4	1108.9	1108.4	1103.8	1099.4	1098.7	1098.6	1100.8
2002	1070.4	1067.6	1075.7	1088.9	1093.1	1099.0	1093.4	1093.9	1090.7	1081.6	1085.3	1084.2	1085.3
2003	1050.4	1049.3	1052.2	1060.7	1066.9	1069.6	1066.0	1067.7	1068.0	1066.1	1068.1	1068.5	1062.8
2004	1040.9	1039.1	1053.0	1070.1	1076.5	1083.0	1085.9	1085.4	1087.9	1085.3	1087.7	1090.1	1073.7
2005	1057.2	1061.1	1071.3	1079.5	1084.7	1092.5	1089.7	1089.7	1089.8	1086.2	1091.9	1094.7	1082.4
2006	1069.8	1075.0	1084.7	1091.7	1097.8	1109.2	1104.6	1108.3	1112.4	1109.1	1110.4	1118.8	1099.3
2007	1090.0	1091.8	1109.5	1115.0	1121.9	1131.4	1132.8	1133.1	1131.4	1131.8	1137.7	1135.3	1121.8
2008	1111.7	1114.3	1122.6	1133.3	1135.6	1144.3	1140.2	1134.6	1134.6	1135.4	1132.3	1128.2	1130.6
2009	1095.5	1089.0	1087.8	1088.8	1087.2	1088.3	1083.7	1080.5	1074.3	1073.5	1073.1	1067.2	1082.4
Goods-Producing													
1990	220.6	222.5	225.8	229.4	231.5	236.4	235.5	232.9	233.5	232.2	229.5	229.9	229.9
2000	267.6	267.5	269.8	273.2	274.6	278.7	277.1	276.2	275.4	273.8	271.9	268.1	272.8
2001	262.1	260.4	264.3	268.3	269.5	272.5	271.5	270.9	268.1	265.8	264.3	260.5	266.5
2002	251.6	250.0	251.8	254.1	255.6	258.5	257.1	258.0	255.9	251.3	249.9	248.2	253.5
2003	239.9	241.1	242.2	242.6	245.6	245.2	245.9	246.5	245.4	245.2	244.1	242.2	243.8
2004	237.0	235.0	240.5	245.4	246.9	249.4	253.2	252.2	251.7	251.7	250.5	250.2	247.0
2005	240.4	241.7	245.9	248.5	251.0	254.8	255.7	255.3	253.2	252.6	252.6	251.5	250.3
2006	247.0	248.8	251.1	252.7	254.7	259.9	260.5	260.6	259.2	257.8	256.4	257.1	255.5
2007	251.9	250.2	256.2	256.7	258.7	263.5	265.5	265.8	264.8	263.9	264.7	262.5	260.4
2008	257.1	256.7	260.1	262.2	261.5	267.3	267.9	261.7	264.5	262.4	259.5	256.4	261.4
2009	245.6	241.9	239.7	237.2	233.6	234.3	232.8	231.7	228.2	228.2	228.6	222.2	233.7
Mining and Logging													
1990	8.9	8.9	8.9	9.1	9.1	9.5	9.6	9.5	9.6	9.8	9.9	10.1	9.4
2000	6.2	6.2	6.4	6.6	6.6	6.8	6.6	6.7	6.7	6.9	7.0	6.9	6.6
2001	6.6	6.6	6.7	6.8	7.0	7.1	7.1	7.3	7.3	7.1	7.0	7.0	7.0
2002	6.6	6.5	6.5	6.6	6.6	6.7	6.6	6.5	6.5	6.4	6.4	6.4	6.5
2003	6.2	6.2	6.3	6.4	6.5	6.6	6.6	6.7	6.7	6.7	6.8	6.8	6.5
2004	6.6	6.5	6.7	6.8	6.9	7.0	7.3	7.5	7.6	7.4	7.3	7.3	7.1
2005	7.2	7.3	7.3	7.4	7.5	7.6	7.6	7.7	7.7	7.9	7.9	8.0	7.6
2006	8.0	8.2	8.4	8.3	8.5	8.7	8.8	8.9	8.9	8.9	9.0	9.1	8.6
2007	8.9	8.9	9.0	9.2	9.1	9.1	9.3	9.3	9.2	9.3	9.3	9.4	9.2
2008	9.4	9.4	9.5	9.6	9.6	9.7	10.0	10.2	10.1	10.0	9.9	9.8	9.8
2009	8.7	8.3	8.1	7.8	7.7	7.8	8.0	8.0	8.0	7.8	8.1	8.2	8.0
Construction													
1990	37.9	37.5	39.4	42.2	44.0	46.8	46.6	46.5	45.1	44.5	43.6	41.9	43.0
2000	60.5	60.3	62.2	65.9	67.1	69.7	69.8	69.8	68.7	67.0	64.6	61.4	65.6
2001	57.9	57.5	60.7	64.9	66.6	68.9	68.3	68.0	65.9	65.1	64.5	62.2	64.2
2002	58.2	57.6	59.5	62.4	64.1	66.4	67.2	66.7	65.2	64.3	63.5	62.4	63.1
2003	58.0	58.1	59.7	62.4	63.9	65.6	65.8	65.8	64.7	64.3	63.1	60.7	62.7
2004	57.4	54.7	59.0	63.3	64.1	66.5	67.6	66.8	65.8	65.3	64.1	63.0	63.1
2005	55.1	56.0	59.3	61.7	63.3	65.6	66.7	66.6	65.3	64.5	63.6	61.6	62.4
2006	59.2	59.8	61.7	63.2	64.4	67.2	67.7	67.4	66.3	64.6	63.9	63.6	64.1
2007	60.6	57.8	62.5	63.6	64.8	67.8	68.5	68.6	67.8	67.3	67.0	64.4	65.1
2008	59.9	59.0	61.8	64.5	66.3	68.2	68.5	67.9	66.3	65.1	63.8	62.2	64.5
2009	56.1	55.5	56.2	57.3	58.9	60.3	61.4	60.1	58.4	58.7	59.1	54.8	58.1
Manufacturing													
1990	173.8	176.1	177.5	178.1	178.4	180.1	179.3	176.9	178.8	177.9	176.0	177.9	177.5
2000	200.9	201.0	201.2	200.7	200.9	202.2	200.7	199.7	200.0	199.9	200.3	199.8	200.6
2001	197.6	196.3	196.9	196.6	195.9	196.5	196.1	195.6	194.9	193.6	192.8	191.3	195.3
2002	186.8	185.9	185.8	185.1	184.9	185.4	183.3	184.8	184.2	180.6	180.0	179.4	183.9
2003	175.7	176.8	176.2	173.8	175.2	173.0	173.5	174.0	174.0	174.2	174.2	174.7	174.6
2004	173.0	173.8	174.8	175.3	175.9	175.9	178.3	177.9	178.3	179.0	179.1	179.9	176.8
2005	178.1	178.4	179.3	179.4	180.2	181.6	181.4	181.0	180.2	180.2	181.1	181.9	180.2
2006	179.8	180.8	181.0	181.2	181.8	184.0	184.0	184.3	184.0	184.3	183.5	184.4	182.8
2007	182.4	183.5	184.7	183.9	184.8	186.6	187.7	187.9	187.8	187.3	188.4	188.7	186.1
2008	187.8	188.3	188.8	188.1	185.6	189.4	189.4	183.6	188.1	187.3	185.8	184.4	187.2
2009	180.8	178.1	175.4	172.1	167.0	166.2	163.4	163.6	161.8	161.7	161.4	159.2	167.6

Employment by Industry: Kansas, Selected Years, 1990–2009—*Continued*

(Numbers in thousands, not seasonally adjusted.)

Industry and year	January	February	March	April	May	June	July	August	September	October	November	December	Annual average
Service-Providing													
1990	845.1	850.9	857.5	865.6	871.0	868.8	839.6	848.7	869.4	869.6	880.8	876.3	861.9
2000	1049.7	1052.5	1064.6	1077.6	1085.5	1086.7	1056.7	1056.4	1075.5	1085.6	1092.9	1095.6	1073.3
2001	1068.0	1072.7	1082.6	1088.4	1093.5	1093.0	1066.4	1062.8	1083.5	1089.4	1091.8	1095.7	1082.3
2002	1069.3	1069.7	1079.9	1091.4	1096.4	1096.2	1068.9	1066.7	1083.8	1084.6	1091.8	1092.5	1082.6
2003	1061.1	1060.8	1065.7	1073.8	1079.8	1079.5	1051.6	1049.3	1070.1	1075.5	1080.8	1084.0	1069.3
2004	1053.3	1056.1	1067.5	1082.5	1089.3	1090.5	1062.8	1060.6	1087.9	1090.4	1095.7	1099.1	1078.0
2005	1062.2	1073.6	1083.4	1089.7	1093.3	1094.6	1056.1	1056.9	1088.2	1092.1	1099.7	1104.4	1082.9
2006	1070.9	1084.4	1094.8	1098.8	1106.6	1109.8	1069.8	1075.2	1110.7	1114.0	1118.1	1126.9	1098.3
2007	1089.3	1101.7	1116.7	1121.0	1128.4	1134.0	1103.9	1102.3	1126.4	1132.9	1139.9	1139.6	1119.7
2008	1108.9	1120.3	1129.1	1137.2	1144.3	1137.6	1107.2	1108.3	1130.8	1141.0	1142.7	1142.3	1129.1
2009	1112.1	1113.3	1116.0	1120.7	1127.3	1118.9	1086.5	1082.9	1106.5	1114.9	1115.9	1115.6	1110.9
Trade, Transportation, and Utilities													
1990	237.3	235.1	237.0	237.1	239.0	241.4	240.7	241.0	240.9	239.5	241.7	243.5	239.5
2000	273.6	271.4	272.3	273.8	274.5	276.8	273.8	274.8	274.7	275.8	280.5	282.6	275.4
2001	272.5	269.2	269.2	270.4	271.9	272.5	271.3	271.8	270.5	271.6	274.1	276.5	271.8
2002	266.6	262.8	263.1	266.4	267.4	268.7	266.0	266.0	265.6	265.9	269.4	271.0	266.6
2003	260.2	258.0	258.3	260.0	261.2	261.3	260.9	261.8	262.5	263.0	266.5	268.7	261.9
2004	258.7	256.6	257.6	260.3	262.5	263.7	261.8	261.7	263.6	263.2	267.2	268.7	262.1
2005	258.6	257.5	258.5	259.7	261.0	261.7	260.4	260.8	260.4	260.4	264.8	267.4	260.9
2006	257.3	256.1	257.7	258.0	259.1	260.4	258.8	260.2	260.9	260.6	264.2	267.9	260.1
2007	258.9	257.7	261.5	261.2	262.8	263.9	263.4	263.5	262.9	264.1	268.5	269.7	263.2
2008	261.4	260.0	260.9	261.4	262.4	263.6	261.2	263.1	261.7	263.2	265.9	266.8	262.9
2009	258.1	255.9	255.6	255.8	256.3	257.1	255.9	255.1	254.2	254.8	258.2	259.9	256.4
Wholesale Trade													
1990	54.5	54.6	55.1	55.5	55.8	57.2	57.3	56.6	56.3	56.4	56.2	56.1	56.0
2000	61.6	61.6	61.9	61.6	61.9	63.2	62.6	62.0	61.7	61.6	61.3	61.4	61.9
2001	61.4	61.2	61.3	61.5	61.9	62.8	62.5	61.7	61.1	61.3	60.9	61.1	61.6
2002	60.6	60.5	60.7	61.2	61.1	61.9	61.9	61.3	60.8	60.3	60.1	60.1	60.9
2003	58.8	58.6	58.6	58.5	58.7	59.6	59.7	59.2	58.7	58.7	58.7	59.0	58.9
2004	57.5	57.5	57.9	58.3	58.8	60.1	60.2	59.7	59.3	59.3	59.2	59.0	58.9
2005	58.5	58.6	58.9	59.7	59.9	61.2	60.8	60.4	60.1	59.2	59.3	59.6	59.7
2006	58.9	59.1	59.3	58.3	58.7	60.2	60.1	59.8	59.7	59.3	59.2	59.8	59.4
2007	59.3	59.3	60.0	59.7	59.9	61.2	61.3	60.6	60.3	61.0	61.0	60.9	60.4
2008	61.1	60.9	60.8	61.1	61.4	62.3	63.0	62.0	61.5	61.7	61.6	61.3	61.6
2009	61.4	61.2	61.2	60.8	60.7	61.5	61.6	60.7	60.4	60.4	60.6	60.0	60.9
Retail Trade													
1990	136.6	134.3	134.8	134.9	136.1	136.8	136.2	137.3	137.2	137.2	139.5	140.7	136.8
2000	157.9	155.9	156.4	156.7	157.3	158.5	156.6	157.0	157.8	158.2	163.5	165.5	158.5
2001	156.7	154.0	154.1	155.0	156.0	156.6	155.8	156.3	155.4	155.7	159.2	161.8	156.4
2002	153.9	150.7	150.9	152.6	153.5	154.1	152.1	152.2	152.2	152.6	156.3	158.0	153.3
2003	149.5	147.5	147.9	148.8	149.7	150.0	149.7	150.7	151.0	151.4	155.0	157.0	150.7
2004	150.3	148.2	149.0	150.1	151.5	151.5	149.6	149.2	151.3	150.4	154.5	156.3	151.0
2005	148.1	146.8	147.3	147.9	148.9	148.8	147.7	147.3	147.1	148.2	152.1	153.7	148.7
2006	146.3	145.0	146.3	147.0	147.8	147.7	146.8	147.2	147.6	147.7	151.2	153.3	147.8
2007	146.3	145.3	147.8	147.3	148.5	148.1	148.2	148.1	147.4	148.3	152.3	153.3	148.4
2008	146.7	145.3	146.5	146.5	147.2	147.5	147.5	147.0	146.0	145.9	148.6	149.4	147.0
2009	142.2	140.5	140.7	141.7	142.5	142.5	141.5	141.4	141.2	141.7	144.1	145.1	142.1
Transportation and Utilities													
1990	46.2	46.2	47.1	46.7	47.1	47.4	47.2	47.1	47.4	45.9	46.0	46.7	46.8
2000	54.1	53.9	54.0	55.5	55.3	55.1	54.6	55.0	55.2	56.0	55.7	55.7	55.0
2001	54.4	54.0	53.8	53.9	54.0	53.1	53.0	53.8	54.0	54.6	54.0	53.6	53.9
2002	52.1	51.6	51.5	52.6	52.8	52.7	52.0	52.5	52.6	53.0	53.0	52.9	52.4
2003	51.9	51.9	51.8	52.7	52.8	51.7	51.5	51.9	52.8	52.9	52.8	52.7	52.3
2004	50.9	50.9	50.7	51.9	52.2	52.1	52.0	52.8	53.0	53.5	53.5	53.4	52.2
2005	52.0	52.1	52.3	52.1	52.2	51.7	51.9	53.1	53.2	53.0	53.4	54.1	52.6
2006	52.1	52.0	52.1	52.7	52.6	52.5	51.9	53.2	53.6	53.6	53.8	54.8	52.9
2007	53.3	53.1	53.7	54.2	54.4	54.6	53.9	54.8	55.2	54.8	55.2	55.5	54.4
2008	53.6	53.8	53.6	53.8	53.8	53.8	53.7	54.1	54.2	55.6	55.7	56.1	54.3
2009	54.5	54.2	53.7	53.3	53.1	53.1	52.8	53.0	52.6	52.7	53.5	54.8	53.4
Information													
1990	30.2	30.2	30.2	30.5	30.4	30.6	30.9	31.1	30.5	29.8	30.2	30.3	30.4
2000	44.7	44.7	45.1	46.8	46.9	47.6	48.5	48.5	48.8	47.8	48.7	48.9	47.3
2001	51.0	51.3	51.4	50.9	50.5	51.4	50.7	50.7	50.2	49.5	49.7	50.0	50.6
2002	50.0	49.8	49.9	50.0	49.5	49.3	48.9	48.4	47.6	46.8	47.2	47.2	48.7
2003	46.7	46.0	45.7	45.1	44.7	44.9	44.3	43.6	43.3	42.9	42.9	42.9	44.4
2004	42.9	42.7	42.5	42.5	42.6	42.6	42.3	41.8	41.2	40.0	40.1	40.5	41.8
2005	40.2	40.3	40.0	40.3	40.2	40.1	40.0	39.4	39.2	38.2	38.6	38.9	39.6
2006	38.6	38.6	39.0	40.1	40.1	40.5	40.4	40.2	40.1	40.5	40.7	40.9	40.0
2007	41.2	41.2	41.3	41.3	41.3	41.3	41.3	40.9	40.3	40.0	40.0	40.0	40.8
2008	39.8	39.8	39.7	39.7	39.2	39.2	39.1	38.6	37.8	38.0	37.4	37.3	38.8
2009	36.6	36.4	36.3	36.6	36.1	35.6	35.3	34.6	33.9	33.8	33.7	33.7	35.2

Employment by Industry: Kansas, Selected Years, 1990–2009—*Continued*

(Numbers in thousands, not seasonally adjusted.)

Industry and year	January	February	March	April	May	June	July	August	September	October	November	December	Annual average
Financial Activities													
1990	59.1	59.1	59.2	59.9	60.1	60.9	60.8	60.5	59.7	59.6	59.4	59.5	59.8
2000	64.7	64.7	64.5	65.0	65.5	66.1	66.3	66.4	65.9	65.8	65.6	66.6	65.6
2001	66.0	66.0	66.3	66.5	67.0	67.8	68.4	68.3	67.6	67.7	67.9	68.4	67.3
2002	68.2	68.4	68.8	68.4	68.7	69.0	69.5	69.3	68.8	69.0	69.3	69.6	68.9
2003	68.5	68.5	69.0	69.5	69.6	70.0	70.1	70.5	69.7	69.6	69.4	69.7	69.5
2004	68.8	69.0	69.6	69.9	70.0	70.6	71.0	70.8	70.0	69.8	69.7	70.3	70.0
2005	69.3	69.4	69.6	70.0	70.1	70.7	71.1	71.0	70.8	71.0	71.1	71.8	70.5
2006	70.9	70.8	71.0	71.6	72.1	72.5	73.3	73.2	73.0	72.9	73.3	74.2	72.4
2007	73.2	73.3	73.9	73.7	74.1	74.7	75.1	74.9	74.5	74.1	74.1	74.5	74.2
2008	73.0	73.1	72.9	73.3	73.4	73.7	73.6	73.5	72.7	72.9	72.7	73.0	73.2
2009	71.6	71.6	71.5	70.9	70.8	71.1	71.6	71.7	70.7	70.2	70.0	71.0	71.1
Professional and Business Services													
1990	81.2	81.7	82.8	83.9	84.3	84.8	84.5	85.3	84.8	84.6	84.5	84.3	83.9
2000	128.3	127.5	130.7	130.9	131.2	133.1	130.5	131.5	131.4	132.3	132.2	132.5	131.0
2001	128.8	130.3	132.3	131.2	131.2	133.6	131.1	130.6	130.7	129.1	127.6	127.5	130.3
2002	124.5	125.4	127.4	130.2	129.5	130.7	131.2	130.8	130.2	127.2	128.0	127.7	128.6
2003	123.5	123.1	122.9	126.0	125.5	127.7	124.9	125.3	124.6	124.6	124.7	126.2	124.9
2004	121.0	122.1	125.1	127.8	127.8	129.7	130.1	131.6	132.0	131.6	131.9	132.7	128.6
2005	127.8	128.7	130.5	131.8	131.3	133.0	133.9	135.2	135.3	135.8	136.8	137.7	133.2
2006	133.5	135.5	137.5	138.0	137.2	139.2	138.0	138.6	140.2	140.5	140.5	142.0	138.4
2007	138.1	139.5	141.3	143.5	144.0	145.0	146.6	147.7	148.0	147.8	149.2	148.4	144.9
2008	143.9	145.1	147.0	149.1	148.8	150.3	149.4	149.9	149.5	150.2	149.6	148.1	148.4
2009	142.8	141.2	140.8	141.5	140.7	140.5	140.4	139.6	138.6	137.3	136.3	134.1	139.5
Education and Health Services													
1990	102.3	103.3	103.7	105.0	105.6	104.8	104.2	105.1	106.6	106.6	107.1	107.3	105.1
2000	144.8	145.5	146.2	146.9	147.3	146.4	147.3	147.8	150.4	150.6	151.3	151.7	148.0
2001	150.0	151.6	152.3	153.4	153.8	153.4	151.7	152.2	154.3	153.3	154.2	155.4	153.0
2002	154.2	155.1	155.9	157.8	158.4	157.1	155.8	156.3	158.7	159.0	159.5	159.6	157.3
2003	156.0	156.2	155.9	158.2	157.8	155.6	155.4	155.7	158.2	158.5	158.8	158.8	157.1
2004	157.4	158.2	159.3	160.4	160.6	159.6	160.4	160.5	162.9	164.2	164.6	164.2	161.0
2005	163.3	163.9	164.2	165.1	165.1	164.4	161.7	161.8	164.6	163.8	164.4	165.0	163.9
2006	163.1	164.3	165.1	165.6	166.3	166.3	164.3	164.9	168.5	169.0	169.1	169.9	166.4
2007	167.6	168.8	170.1	170.7	171.0	171.3	170.0	170.4	173.0	174.3	174.5	174.8	171.4
2008	173.4	174.9	175.6	177.0	177.2	176.6	174.2	175.5	177.6	178.6	179.2	179.2	176.6
2009	178.2	178.9	179.1	179.9	180.4	179.6	178.3	178.6	180.2	182.8	182.8	182.4	180.1
Leisure and Hospitality													
1990	82.3	83.0	84.5	87.4	89.3	91.0	89.6	90.7	90.1	88.7	87.8	88.0	87.7
2000	103.1	104.5	106.4	110.8	112.1	113.3	112.2	112.0	111.6	109.8	108.4	107.5	109.3
2001	102.9	103.7	106.1	109.5	111.7	113.5	111.6	111.6	110.0	109.4	108.2	107.3	108.8
2002	103.0	103.7	106.0	108.9	110.9	111.8	111.8	112.3	110.6	109.5	109.2	108.0	108.8
2003	103.4	103.9	105.5	106.9	109.4	111.7	111.5	111.5	111.3	109.4	108.7	106.8	108.3
2004	103.0	103.2	105.7	110.2	112.8	113.9	114.0	113.9	113.1	111.6	110.6	110.3	110.2
2005	105.5	106.8	109.2	111.3	113.3	115.2	114.8	114.5	113.9	111.7	111.1	110.3	111.5
2006	107.6	108.7	110.7	114.1	116.4	118.4	117.9	118.9	118.2	116.2	114.7	114.9	114.7
2007	108.3	109.8	113.0	115.4	117.7	119.3	118.8	117.6	115.6	114.4	113.7	112.6	114.7
2008	110.7	111.5	113.0	116.9	119.2	120.3	118.3	118.9	117.5	116.5	114.6	114.4	116.0
2009	109.9	110.1	112.0	114.1	116.6	117.7	117.2	117.2	116.2	113.6	110.9	110.9	113.9
Other Services													
1990	40.2	40.3	40.6	41.1	41.3	41.8	41.7	41.4	41.3	41.1	40.9	41.2	41.0
2000	51.2	51.6	51.7	51.4	51.7	51.8	52.0	52.0	52.3	52.3	52.1	52.2	51.9
2001	51.7	51.8	52.3	52.4	52.5	52.7	52.6	52.3	52.4	53.0	52.7	53.0	52.5
2002	52.3	52.4	52.8	53.1	53.1	53.9	53.1	52.8	53.3	52.9	52.8	52.9	53.0
2003	52.2	52.5	52.7	52.4	53.1	53.2	53.0	52.8	53.0	52.9	53.0	53.2	52.8
2004	52.1	52.3	52.7	53.6	53.3	53.5	53.1	52.9	53.4	53.2	53.1	53.2	53.0
2005	52.1	52.8	53.4	52.8	52.7	52.6	52.1	51.7	52.4	52.7	52.5	52.1	52.5
2006	51.8	52.2	52.6	51.6	51.9	52.0	51.4	51.7	52.3	51.6	51.5	51.9	51.9
2007	50.8	51.3	52.2	52.5	52.3	52.4	52.1	52.3	52.3	53.2	53.0	52.8	52.3
2008	52.4	53.2	53.4	53.7	53.9	53.3	53.5	53.4	53.3	53.6	53.4	53.0	53.3
2009	52.7	53.0	52.8	52.8	52.7	52.4	52.2	52.0	52.3	52.8	52.6	53.0	52.6
Government													
1990	212.5	218.2	219.5	220.7	221.0	213.5	187.2	193.6	215.5	219.7	229.2	222.2	214.4
2000	239.3	242.6	247.7	252.0	256.3	251.6	226.1	223.4	240.4	251.2	254.1	253.6	244.9
2001	245.1	248.8	252.7	254.1	254.9	248.1	229.0	225.3	247.8	255.8	257.4	257.6	248.1
2002	250.5	252.1	256.0	256.6	258.9	255.7	232.6	230.8	249.0	254.3	256.4	256.5	250.8
2003	250.6	252.6	255.7	255.7	258.5	255.1	231.5	228.1	247.5	254.6	256.8	257.7	250.4
2004	249.4	252.0	255.0	257.8	259.7	256.9	230.1	227.4	251.7	256.8	258.5	259.2	251.2
2005	245.4	254.2	258.0	258.7	259.6	256.9	222.1	222.5	251.6	258.5	260.4	261.2	250.8
2006	248.1	258.2	261.2	259.8	263.5	260.5	225.7	227.5	257.5	262.7	264.1	265.2	254.5
2007	251.2	260.1	263.4	262.7	265.2	266.1	236.6	235.0	259.8	265.0	266.9	266.8	258.2
2008	254.3	262.7	266.6	266.1	270.2	260.6	234.9	235.4	260.7	268.0	269.9	270.5	260.0
2009	262.2	266.2	267.9	269.1	273.7	264.9	235.6	234.1	260.4	269.6	271.4	270.6	262.1

Average Weekly Hours by Selected Industry: Kansas, 2007–2009

(Not seasonally adjusted.)

Industry and year	January	February	March	April	May	June	July	August	September	October	November	December	Annual average
Total Private													
2007	33.4	33.8	34.1	34.3	34.4	35.5	35.8	35.2	35.5	34.7	34.7	34.9	34.7
2008	34.5	34.6	34.9	34.4	34.8	35.7	35.0	35.1	34.6	34.7	34.9	34.0	34.8
2009	33.8	34.2	34.1	33.5	33.4	34.1	34.2	35.4	34.3	34.2	35.0	33.8	34.2
Goods-Producing													
2007	37.9	38.3	39.3	38.5	39.3	40.0	40.4	39.9	40.6	40.0	39.9	40.4	39.6
2008	40.5	40.5	40.7	39.9	41.5	42.9	41.9	42.6	40.9	40.5	40.6	39.7	41.0
2009	39.0	39.1	39.6	38.7	39.1	39.6	39.7	43.9	42.1	43.0	43.7	41.9	40.8
Construction													
2007	34.6	33.0	37.5	35.1	38.4	38.5	39.4	38.9	38.0	37.3	38.5	33.1	36.9
2008	35.2	35.8	37.5	35.1	41.3	39.8	40.1	41.3	37.3	37.4	38.7	35.9	38.0
2009	35.6	36.5	37.3	36.2	38.5	37.8	39.9	41.2	36.3	39.2	40.5	36.6	38.0
Manufacturing													
2007	39.5	40.6	40.3	40.2	40.0	41.0	41.1	40.6	41.6	41.1	40.4	42.7	40.8
2008	42.2	42.0	41.7	41.5	41.4	44.1	42.3	42.8	41.9	41.2	40.9	40.6	41.9
2009	39.8	39.5	40.0	39.1	38.8	39.9	39.3	44.6	43.7	44.2	44.6	43.7	41.4
Trade, Transportation, and Utilities													
2007	33.9	34.2	34.9	35.0	35.0	35.3	35.9	35.5	35.3	34.7	34.8	35.5	35.0
2008	34.4	34.3	34.6	34.6	34.7	35.4	35.1	34.7	34.4	34.8	34.8	34.3	34.7
2009	34.1	34.4	34.3	33.8	34.0	34.5	35.0	35.3	34.3	34.0	34.4	34.4	34.4
Financial Activities													
2007	33.0	33.3	32.8	33.8	32.7	33.8	34.2	34.2	34.9	34.1	34.3	34.6	33.8
2008	34.0	34.2	35.1	33.7	34.4	35.4	35.2	34.6	34.4	34.9	36.6	35.2	34.8
2009	36.5	37.7	37.1	36.4	36.2	36.4	36.6	37.9	36.7	36.8	38.1	36.3	36.9
Professional and Business Services													
2007	32.5	33.2	33.7	33.7	33.1	34.3	34.4	33.4	34.5	33.4	34.1	33.3	33.6
2008	33.0	33.3	34.2	33.5	33.7	34.1	33.0	33.1	33.8	34.2	34.3	33.4	33.6
2009	32.9	34.1	34.2	32.7	33.0	33.4	33.0	33.0	32.4	32.4	33.5	31.9	33.1
Education and Health Services													
2007	32.1	32.3	32.1	32.7	33.1	36.0	35.8	34.8	34.9	33.9	34.0	34.2	33.8
2008	33.6	33.7	33.9	33.6	32.9	33.8	32.9	33.1	33.2	32.7	32.8	32.3	33.2
2009	32.1	31.5	31.5	32.6	31.0	33.1	33.1	33.2	32.7	31.2	32.2	31.3	32.1
Leisure and Hospitality													
2007	23.4	24.1	24.0	24.5	24.7	25.1	25.5	24.7	24.9	24.8	24.3	23.6	24.5
2008	23.1	23.4	23.6	23.5	23.3	24.3	24.2	24.7	24.0	24.2	24.4	23.4	23.9
2009	23.0	24.0	23.6	23.4	23.9	24.4	24.7	24.5	23.6	23.5	24.0	22.9	23.8
Other Services													
2007	30.9	31.1	32.6	33.2	34.3	35.2	34.9	34.6	33.3	30.6	30.0	33.2	32.8
2008	33.5	33.8	33.7	33.6	35.4	35.8	33.8	34.2	31.8	31.9	32.7	31.1	33.4
2009	31.4	32.8	32.0	31.3	30.0	29.6	31.5	32.8	30.0	30.4	31.2	30.1	31.1

Average Hourly Earnings by Selected Industry: Kansas, 2007–2009

(Dollars, not seasonally adjusted.)

Industry and year	January	February	March	April	May	June	July	August	September	October	November	December	Annual average
Total Private													
2007	19.56	19.81	19.13	19.76	19.69	19.57	19.42	19.33	19.50	19.63	19.78	20.48	19.64
2008	20.13	20.00	20.06	20.16	19.91	19.96	19.92	20.02	20.01	20.03	20.44	20.92	20.13
2009	20.40	20.54	20.40	20.27	20.46	20.07	20.22	19.57	19.82	20.12	20.14	20.16	20.18
Goods-Producing													
2007	21.12	21.11	21.11	21.26	22.49	21.01	20.84	21.09	21.27	21.07	21.24	23.01	21.39
2008	22.40	22.06	21.99	21.89	21.83	22.24	22.08	22.31	22.10	21.99	22.33	24.27	22.28
2009	22.56	22.28	22.38	22.64	22.80	22.34	22.34	20.03	20.60	21.26	21.31	22.68	21.91
Construction													
2007	17.51	17.99	18.00	18.09	19.80	18.91	19.13	19.25	20.17	19.79	19.65	21.74	19.20
2008	20.42	20.30	20.47	20.62	20.34	20.29	20.67	20.80	21.19	21.32	21.52	21.57	20.79
2009	21.82	21.46	21.99	22.43	22.65	22.04	21.89	21.70	22.38	22.59	23.09	23.66	22.30
Manufacturing													
2007	22.48	22.34	22.29	22.42	23.55	21.82	21.51	21.84	21.75	21.58	21.85	23.53	22.25
2008	23.05	22.65	22.40	22.26	22.23	22.84	22.50	22.76	22.33	22.25	22.61	25.19	22.75
2009	22.76	22.39	22.26	22.52	22.70	22.41	22.52	19.47	20.09	20.81	20.69	22.59	21.74
Trade, Transportation, and Utilities													
2007	18.37	18.16	17.67	18.19	17.88	17.79	17.83	17.95	18.21	17.62	17.83	18.10	17.96
2008	17.96	17.74	17.78	17.97	17.72	17.34	17.47	17.66	17.67	17.66	18.02	17.85	17.74
2009	17.99	18.10	18.31	18.02	18.08	17.77	17.95	18.28	18.34	18.70	18.66	17.95	18.18
Financial Activities													
2007	23.46	23.59	22.63	23.84	22.76	26.01	22.52	21.68	22.17	21.46	21.36	22.10	22.79
2008	21.83	21.94	22.24	21.84	21.45	22.03	20.61	20.85	20.79	21.17	22.26	21.67	21.56
2009	21.43	22.48	23.14	21.68	22.51	21.94	22.22	22.76	22.32	22.56	23.56	22.86	22.46
Professional and Business Services													
2007	22.46	25.77	22.09	24.13	22.59	21.59	22.70	22.77	23.22	23.94	24.89	25.02	23.43
2008	24.77	25.15	25.09	25.32	25.26	24.99	25.00	25.06	24.66	25.50	25.61	26.11	25.21
2009	26.23	26.27	25.52	25.53	25.86	25.46	25.92	24.93	25.59	25.24	25.35	24.60	25.55
Education and Health Services													
2007	16.85	16.66	16.55	17.13	17.33	17.44	18.17	17.41	16.94	18.91	18.64	18.90	17.60
2008	18.03	17.80	17.81	18.65	17.62	17.53	18.14	18.02	18.46	17.79	18.75	18.78	18.11
2009	17.90	18.35	17.76	18.08	18.40	18.14	18.40	17.77	17.90	18.34	17.43	17.90	18.03
Leisure and Hospitality													
2007	9.19	9.28	9.32	9.37	9.68	9.23	9.47	9.72	9.79	9.87	9.99	10.17	9.59
2008	10.52	10.56	10.56	10.51	10.79	10.69	10.71	10.65	10.74	10.82	10.75	10.76	10.67
2009	11.04	10.88	10.66	10.74	10.81	10.71	10.71	10.70	10.83	10.97	10.97	11.04	10.83
Other Services													
2007	18.11	17.45	17.05	16.56	16.14	16.22	17.76	17.69	17.40	17.82	17.73	18.38	17.34
2008	17.85	18.06	19.08	18.31	17.52	18.52	19.30	19.70	19.46	19.10	19.22	19.07	18.75
2009	20.32	20.45	20.68	20.85	21.05	21.31	21.56	21.34	21.09	21.02	21.27	20.87	20.98

Average Weekly Earnings by Selected Industry: Kansas, 2007–2009

(Dollars, not seasonally adjusted.)

Industry and year	January	February	March	April	May	June	July	August	September	October	November	December	Annual average
Total Private													
2007	653.30	669.58	652.33	677.77	677.34	694.74	695.24	680.42	692.25	681.16	686.37	714.75	681.51
2008	694.49	692.00	700.09	693.50	692.87	712.57	697.20	702.70	692.35	695.04	713.36	711.28	700.52
2009	689.52	702.47	695.64	679.05	683.36	684.39	691.52	692.78	679.83	688.10	704.90	681.41	690.16
Goods-Producing													
2007	800.45	808.51	829.62	818.51	883.86	840.40	841.94	841.49	863.56	842.80	847.48	929.60	847.04
2008	907.20	893.43	894.99	873.41	905.95	954.10	925.15	950.41	903.89	890.60	906.60	963.52	913.48
2009	879.84	871.15	886.25	876.17	891.48	884.66	886.90	879.32	867.26	914.18	931.25	950.29	893.93
Construction													
2007	605.85	593.67	675.00	634.96	760.32	728.04	753.72	748.83	766.46	738.17	756.53	719.59	708.48
2008	718.78	726.74	767.63	723.76	840.04	807.54	828.87	859.04	790.39	797.37	832.82	774.36	790.02
2009	776.79	783.29	820.23	811.97	872.03	833.11	873.41	894.04	812.39	885.53	935.15	865.96	847.40
Manufacturing													
2007	887.96	907.00	898.29	901.28	942.00	894.62	884.06	886.70	904.80	886.94	882.74	1004.73	907.80
2008	972.71	951.30	934.08	923.79	920.32	1007.24	951.75	974.13	935.63	916.70	924.75	1022.71	953.23
2009	905.85	884.41	890.40	880.53	880.76	894.16	885.04	868.36	877.93	919.80	922.77	987.18	900.04
Trade, Transportation, and Utilities													
2007	622.74	621.07	616.68	636.65	625.80	627.99	640.10	637.23	642.81	611.41	620.48	642.55	628.60
2008	617.82	608.48	615.19	621.76	614.88	613.84	613.20	612.80	607.85	614.57	627.10	612.26	615.58
2009	613.46	622.64	628.03	609.08	614.72	613.07	628.25	645.28	629.06	635.80	641.90	617.48	625.39
Financial Activities													
2007	774.18	785.55	742.26	805.79	744.25	879.14	770.18	741.46	773.73	731.79	732.65	764.66	770.30
2008	742.22	750.35	780.62	736.01	737.88	779.86	725.47	721.41	715.18	738.83	814.72	762.78	750.29
2009	782.20	847.50	858.49	789.15	814.86	798.62	813.25	862.60	819.14	830.21	897.64	829.82	828.77
Professional and Business Services													
2007	729.95	855.56	744.43	813.18	747.73	740.54	780.88	760.52	801.09	799.60	848.75	833.17	787.25
2008	817.41	837.50	858.08	848.22	851.26	852.16	825.00	829.49	833.51	872.10	878.42	872.07	847.06
2009	862.97	895.81	872.78	834.83	853.38	850.36	855.36	822.69	829.12	817.78	849.23	784.74	845.71
Education and Health Services													
2007	540.89	538.12	531.26	560.15	573.62	627.84	650.49	605.87	591.21	641.05	633.76	646.38	594.88
2008	605.81	599.86	603.76	626.64	579.70	592.51	596.81	596.46	612.87	581.73	615.00	606.59	601.25
2009	574.59	578.03	559.44	589.41	570.40	600.43	609.04	589.96	585.33	572.21	561.25	560.27	578.76
Leisure and Hospitality													
2007	215.05	223.65	223.68	229.57	239.10	231.67	241.49	240.08	243.77	244.78	242.76	240.01	234.96
2008	243.01	247.10	249.22	246.99	251.41	259.77	259.18	263.06	257.76	261.84	262.30	251.78	255.01
2009	253.92	261.12	251.58	251.32	258.36	261.32	259.18	262.15	255.59	257.80	263.28	252.02	257.75
Other Services													
2007	559.60	542.70	555.83	549.79	553.60	570.94	619.82	612.07	579.42	545.29	531.90	610.22	568.75
2008	597.98	610.43	643.00	615.22	620.21	663.02	652.34	673.74	618.83	609.29	628.49	593.08	626.25
2009	638.05	670.76	661.76	652.61	631.50	630.78	679.14	699.95	632.70	639.01	663.62	628.19	652.48

KENTUCKY
At a Glance

Population:
    1990 census: 3,686,892
    2000 census: 4,041,769
    2009 estimate: 4,314,113

Percent change in population:
    1990–2000: 9.6%
    2000–2009: 6.7%

Percent change in total nonfarm employment:
    1990–2009: 20.3%
    2008–2009: -4.4%

Industry with the largest growth in employment, 1990–2009 (thousands):
    Education and Health Services, 92.7

Industry with the largest decline or smallest growth in employment, 1990–2009 (thousands):
    Manufacturing, -59.5

Civilian labor force:
    1990: 1,747,605
    2000: 1,949,013
    2009: 2,080,409

Unemployment rate and rank among states (lowest to highest):
    1990: 6.1%, 39th
    2000: 4.2%, 33rd
    2009: 10.5%, 42nd

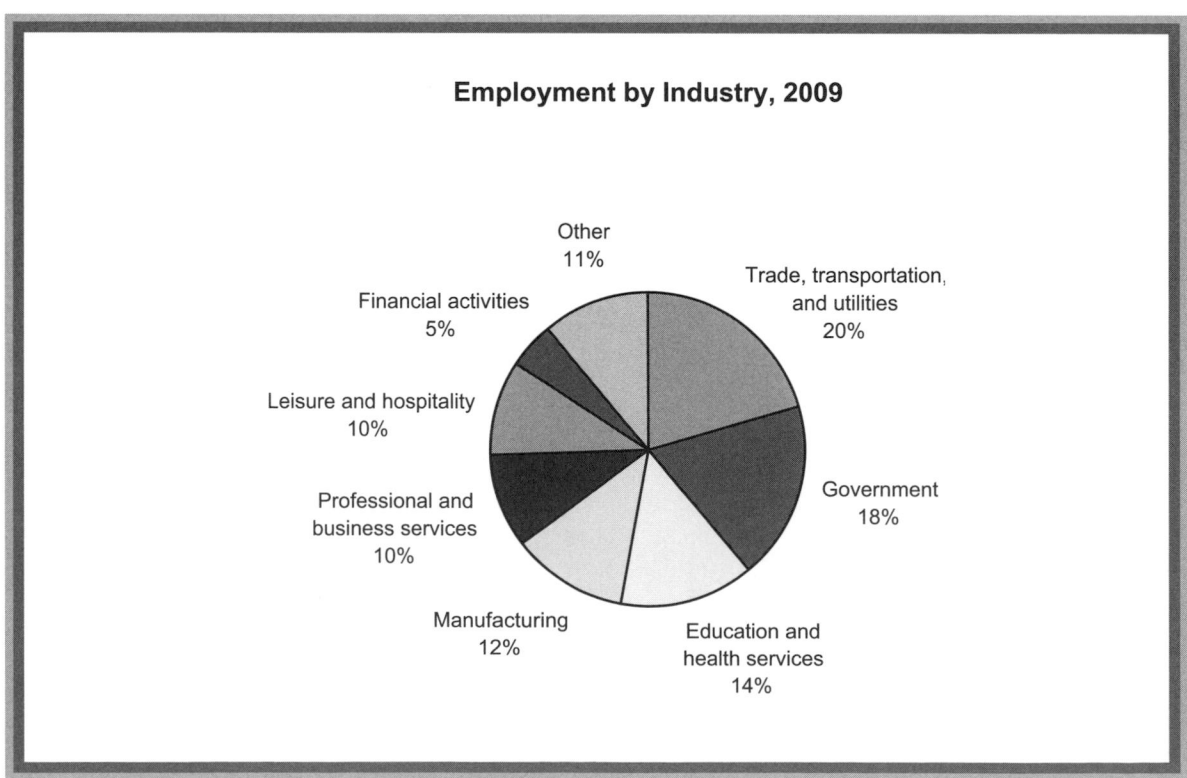

Employment by Industry, 2009

- Other 11%
- Trade, transportation, and utilities 20%
- Financial activities 5%
- Leisure and hospitality 10%
- Government 18%
- Professional and business services 10%
- Manufacturing 12%
- Education and health services 14%

Employment by Industry: Kentucky, Selected Years, 1990–2009

(Numbers in thousands, not seasonally adjusted.)

Industry and year	January	February	March	April	May	June	July	August	September	October	November	December	Annual average
Total Nonfarm													
1990	1430.6	1435.9	1455.0	1461.2	1480.4	1479.3	1469.3	1480.5	1489.9	1487.4	1488.0	1489.1	1470.5
2000	1781.5	1793.4	1817.0	1827.7	1842.9	1840.2	1821.5	1830.2	1837.8	1842.7	1844.7	1845.0	1827.1
2001	1791.5	1796.6	1800.6	1813.4	1821.5	1824.7	1800.3	1807.0	1803.6	1801.4	1804.6	1799.8	1805.4
2002	1759.5	1762.0	1774.7	1787.6	1800.6	1801.8	1783.5	1790.8	1796.1	1799.6	1806.6	1803.0	1788.8
2003	1754.8	1752.5	1767.8	1780.4	1793.8	1793.0	1770.4	1785.0	1794.8	1798.5	1802.5	1806.6	1783.3
2004	1760.8	1763.1	1779.0	1796.9	1803.7	1808.8	1789.1	1803.3	1811.9	1817.1	1824.1	1825.4	1798.6
2005	1778.9	1787.2	1801.4	1822.9	1833.2	1838.3	1818.2	1834.8	1841.5	1840.1	1849.5	1848.2	1824.5
2006	1810.2	1814.1	1836.0	1845.6	1857.1	1859.5	1833.9	1850.7	1856.4	1855.4	1865.8	1876.7	1846.8
2007	1830.8	1830.9	1849.8	1865.0	1881.9	1886.6	1860.5	1869.7	1874.7	1875.2	1887.6	1887.4	1866.7
2008	1839.1	1839.8	1848.2	1861.9	1878.4	1872.2	1849.6	1859.5	1847.8	1844.6	1844.3	1835.5	1851.7
2009	1765.1	1756.4	1762.1	1773.9	1779.0	1776.3	1758.6	1763.6	1767.3	1774.4	1780.0	1777.2	1769.5
Total Private													
1990	1171.6	1173.7	1187.8	1197.8	1211.7	1226.0	1224.3	1231.4	1229.0	1223.6	1223.0	1224.0	1210.3
2000	1484.1	1484.8	1503.6	1513.5	1525.5	1530.8	1526.2	1533.2	1532.3	1532.6	1533.1	1533.5	1519.4
2001	1482.9	1483.4	1486.5	1499.0	1505.4	1511.6	1498.9	1503.1	1489.9	1486.2	1488.4	1484.1	1493.3
2002	1447.2	1445.6	1456.5	1468.2	1480.9	1486.9	1480.8	1489.3	1480.3	1481.2	1486.9	1485.0	1474.1
2003	1442.1	1435.4	1450.0	1461.9	1473.5	1479.7	1471.2	1484.1	1482.7	1485.5	1489.0	1495.0	1470.8
2004	1451.5	1450.4	1464.7	1481.3	1489.9	1499.7	1490.7	1504.1	1501.4	1504.8	1510.8	1513.8	1488.6
2005	1469.3	1473.3	1486.2	1505.6	1514.9	1525.0	1515.3	1526.8	1525.9	1522.5	1530.7	1530.5	1510.5
2006	1496.3	1496.0	1516.4	1524.1	1534.5	1544.3	1527.2	1538.0	1535.9	1533.1	1542.5	1553.9	1528.5
2007	1513.0	1508.9	1526.2	1538.5	1553.7	1563.3	1546.6	1551.5	1549.6	1549.7	1560.4	1559.7	1543.4
2008	1516.5	1513.7	1521.0	1535.2	1550.5	1550.3	1528.8	1544.1	1528.0	1519.3	1518.3	1510.2	1528.8
2009	1447.3	1436.6	1439.4	1445.9	1450.0	1452.0	1444.6	1445.3	1441.9	1444.3	1449.6	1447.7	1445.4
Goods-Producing													
1990	360.9	363.1	368.1	369.8	374.6	379.9	378.6	380.4	379.0	376.1	373.5	370.7	372.8
2000	411.3	409.9	415.3	417.6	420.3	421.3	418.7	420.6	420.6	418.8	417.1	417.4	417.4
2001	400.6	401.1	400.1	404.0	405.4	407.3	401.1	402.0	398.8	395.1	393.5	390.2	399.9
2002	378.6	377.0	378.2	379.3	380.2	382.0	378.1	381.3	379.0	378.9	377.2	375.0	378.7
2003	364.4	360.6	363.4	365.1	367.5	369.1	367.7	370.3	370.7	371.1	369.4	370.4	367.5
2004	361.0	358.9	361.4	365.0	368.0	370.2	363.4	371.5	371.3	370.1	370.1	369.3	366.7
2005	358.9	359.1	362.2	366.8	369.4	372.3	365.4	372.0	372.3	371.8	372.5	370.6	367.8
2006	364.3	362.6	365.6	366.7	368.6	371.3	364.4	371.1	369.8	364.1	363.8	367.7	366.7
2007	358.7	356.1	358.5	363.5	366.1	369.8	362.7	364.6	367.2	362.6	365.9	361.8	363.1
2008	353.9	352.5	353.6	355.6	362.1	360.1	354.4	357.6	353.6	349.5	348.4	340.0	353.4
2009	321.4	317.5	314.6	313.6	311.5	310.7	307.2	308.1	308.0	305.1	304.2	301.8	310.3
Mining and Logging													
1990	34.1	34.4	34.9	35.0	35.3	35.5	34.8	35.2	35.3	34.0	33.7	33.5	34.6
2000	20.1	19.8	20.2	19.5	19.5	19.6	19.2	19.2	19.2	18.8	18.8	18.6	19.4
2001	18.7	19.0	19.2	19.8	20.2	20.6	20.8	21.2	21.3	21.5	21.8	21.8	20.5
2002	21.2	21.0	20.8	20.4	20.4	20.5	20.2	20.2	20.2	19.8	19.8	19.7	20.4
2003	19.4	19.3	19.3	18.7	18.6	18.8	18.7	18.9	19.1	19.0	19.0	19.5	19.0
2004	19.1	18.9	19.2	19.6	19.6	19.8	19.7	19.8	19.7	20.1	20.1	20.3	19.7
2005	20.1	20.1	20.5	20.9	21.2	21.5	21.6	21.8	22.2	22.3	22.6	22.7	21.5
2006	22.3	22.3	22.7	22.9	23.0	23.2	23.2	23.1	23.1	22.9	22.9	22.9	22.9
2007	22.2	22.2	22.4	22.1	22.0	22.2	22.0	22.1	22.1	22.1	22.1	22.2	22.1
2008	22.2	22.1	22.3	22.8	23.4	23.7	24.0	24.6	24.8	25.4	25.5	25.6	23.9
2009	25.1	25.0	25.2	24.9	24.3	24.0	23.0	22.9	22.9	23.0	22.8	23.2	23.9
Construction													
1990	58.7	58.7	61.2	63.8	66.1	68.7	69.2	70.0	68.8	68.2	67.8	64.7	65.4
2000	81.8	81.8	86.1	87.3	88.9	89.9	90.1	89.2	89.3	89.8	88.8	88.6	87.6
2001	79.9	81.4	82.3	87.9	89.8	92.2	92.5	92.0	90.8	89.2	88.4	85.4	87.7
2002	77.9	78.2	79.7	82.0	83.4	85.1	85.7	86.7	86.2	86.1	85.3	83.3	83.3
2003	76.6	74.2	78.4	82.4	84.4	85.5	86.5	86.3	86.0	87.1	85.4	83.8	83.1
2004	77.5	76.5	78.8	82.6	84.5	86.0	87.5	86.9	86.7	85.8	85.2	83.7	83.5
2005	76.2	77.4	79.5	83.2	85.6	87.6	89.1	88.0	87.2	87.0	86.0	84.0	84.2
2006	78.8	78.2	80.2	82.1	84.3	85.5	85.8	86.0	85.2	84.4	84.0	83.1	83.1
2007	77.4	75.5	80.9	84.3	86.5	88.3	88.7	89.1	88.9	89.3	88.4	85.8	85.3
2008	79.1	77.8	79.6	84.0	87.8	88.4	88.8	88.7	87.7	86.4	83.9	81.0	84.4
2009	72.7	71.1	71.9	73.3	74.3	75.2	75.8	75.1	74.8	73.8	72.2	69.2	73.3
Manufacturing													
1990	268.1	270.0	272.0	271.0	273.2	275.7	274.6	275.2	274.9	273.9	272.0	272.5	272.7
2000	309.4	308.3	309.0	310.8	311.9	311.8	309.4	312.2	312.1	310.2	309.5	310.2	310.4
2001	302.0	300.7	298.6	296.3	295.4	294.5	287.8	288.8	286.7	284.4	283.3	283.0	291.8
2002	279.5	277.8	277.7	276.9	276.4	276.4	272.2	274.4	272.6	273.0	272.1	272.0	275.1
2003	268.4	267.1	265.7	264.0	264.5	264.8	262.5	265.1	265.6	265.0	265.0	267.1	265.4
2004	264.4	263.5	263.4	262.8	263.9	264.4	256.2	264.8	264.9	264.2	264.8	265.3	263.6
2005	262.6	261.6	262.2	262.7	262.6	263.2	254.7	262.2	262.9	262.5	263.9	263.9	262.1
2006	263.2	262.1	262.7	261.7	261.3	262.6	255.4	262.0	261.5	256.8	256.9	261.7	260.7
2007	259.1	258.4	255.2	257.1	257.6	259.3	252.0	253.4	256.2	251.2	255.4	253.8	255.7
2008	252.6	252.6	251.7	248.8	250.9	248.0	241.6	244.3	241.1	237.7	239.0	233.4	245.1
2009	223.6	221.4	217.5	215.4	212.9	211.5	208.4	210.1	210.3	208.3	209.2	209.4	213.2

Employment by Industry: Kentucky, Selected Years, 1990–2009—*Continued*

(Numbers in thousands, not seasonally adjusted.)

Industry and year	January	February	March	April	May	June	July	August	September	October	November	December	Annual average
Service-Providing													
1990	1069.7	1072.8	1086.9	1091.4	1105.8	1099.4	1090.7	1100.1	1110.9	1111.3	1114.5	1118.4	1097.6
2000	1370.2	1383.5	1401.7	1410.1	1422.6	1418.9	1402.8	1409.6	1417.2	1423.9	1427.6	1427.6	1409.6
2001	1390.9	1395.5	1400.5	1409.4	1416.1	1417.4	1399.2	1405.0	1404.8	1406.3	1411.1	1409.6	1405.5
2002	1380.9	1385.0	1396.5	1408.3	1420.4	1419.8	1405.4	1409.5	1417.1	1420.7	1429.4	1428.0	1410.1
2003	1390.4	1391.9	1404.4	1415.3	1426.3	1423.9	1402.7	1414.7	1424.1	1427.4	1433.1	1436.2	1415.9
2004	1399.8	1404.2	1417.6	1431.9	1435.7	1438.6	1425.7	1431.8	1440.6	1447.0	1454.0	1456.1	1431.9
2005	1420.0	1428.1	1439.2	1456.1	1463.8	1466.0	1452.8	1462.8	1469.2	1468.3	1477.0	1477.6	1456.7
2006	1445.9	1451.5	1470.4	1478.9	1488.5	1488.2	1469.5	1479.6	1486.6	1491.3	1502.0	1509.0	1480.1
2007	1472.1	1474.8	1491.3	1501.5	1515.8	1516.8	1497.8	1505.1	1507.5	1512.6	1521.7	1525.6	1503.6
2008	1485.2	1487.3	1494.6	1506.3	1516.3	1512.1	1495.2	1501.9	1494.2	1495.1	1495.9	1495.5	1498.3
2009	1443.7	1438.9	1447.5	1460.3	1467.5	1465.6	1451.4	1455.5	1459.3	1469.3	1475.8	1475.4	1459.2
Trade, Transportation, and Utilities													
1990	304.0	300.2	301.4	302.1	304.6	307.1	308.5	310.9	309.5	309.8	313.9	317.5	307.5
2000	383.6	381.0	384.7	387.3	390.3	391.4	392.0	392.9	392.3	394.6	400.0	402.1	391.0
2001	383.0	379.4	378.9	379.5	379.8	380.0	377.9	378.2	375.8	378.2	383.2	384.3	379.9
2002	370.1	367.1	369.5	369.1	371.7	372.1	371.7	372.3	370.6	372.1	378.9	382.8	372.3
2003	366.0	362.9	365.9	366.8	369.7	370.2	369.0	372.2	371.5	373.9	379.2	383.5	370.9
2004	367.9	365.3	368.1	370.0	372.2	373.6	371.7	373.5	373.5	377.0	383.1	386.5	373.5
2005	372.4	370.1	372.7	375.1	377.5	378.5	378.3	379.0	377.8	377.9	385.5	388.7	377.8
2006	374.7	371.6	376.5	377.1	380.2	381.9	378.5	379.4	379.1	381.9	389.2	394.2	380.4
2007	381.1	378.2	383.2	382.9	386.4	388.3	384.9	384.9	385.2	387.6	394.4	396.6	386.1
2008	381.1	377.7	378.8	380.4	383.1	383.4	381.2	382.1	378.0	377.5	383.0	386.2	381.0
2009	366.0	360.0	360.2	360.6	362.6	363.6	361.1	361.0	360.4	361.7	365.4	365.4	362.3
Wholesale Trade													
1990	60.6	59.7	59.5	59.4	59.6	60.0	60.2	60.4	60.2	60.2	61.7	62.4	60.3
2000	72.7	72.6	73.1	73.3	73.5	73.5	73.0	73.1	73.1	74.5	75.3	75.1	73.6
2001	73.7	73.5	73.3	72.9	73.1	73.3	72.8	72.8	72.1	72.4	72.5	72.8	72.9
2002	72.2	72.1	71.5	71.8	72.3	72.2	71.9	72.1	71.8	72.3	72.8	73.2	72.2
2003	72.8	72.6	72.4	72.7	73.2	73.4	73.0	73.5	73.3	73.2	73.7	74.3	73.2
2004	73.7	73.5	73.6	73.9	73.9	74.1	74.3	74.2	73.9	74.2	74.8	75.2	74.1
2005	74.3	74.0	74.1	74.4	74.6	74.6	74.5	74.6	74.5	74.5	74.8	75.2	74.5
2006	74.7	74.7	75.4	75.8	76.2	76.5	75.9	76.0	75.9	76.5	76.7	77.3	76.0
2007	76.6	76.6	77.2	77.2	77.2	77.6	77.0	76.9	77.0	76.8	76.9	77.2	77.0
2008	76.5	76.6	76.6	76.4	76.6	76.9	76.5	76.4	75.8	75.9	75.9	75.7	76.3
2009	73.9	72.9	72.6	72.3	72.3	72.2	72.0	71.8	71.5	71.1	70.2	69.4	71.9
Retail Trade													
1990	184.4	181.7	182.8	183.2	184.9	186.0	186.6	188.4	188.0	188.2	191.4	194.4	186.6
2000	220.6	218.6	221.1	221.1	223.8	225.1	224.8	226.0	225.8	224.6	229.7	232.1	224.4
2001	217.0	214.1	214.6	214.8	216.4	216.6	213.5	214.1	213.0	214.0	219.3	220.6	215.7
2002	209.6	207.5	210.6	211.4	213.3	213.8	211.2	211.4	210.8	210.9	217.3	220.6	212.4
2003	207.3	204.3	206.4	207.5	209.8	210.2	209.7	211.3	211.2	212.3	217.6	221.0	210.7
2004	208.4	206.1	208.1	209.2	210.8	211.6	209.4	210.6	211.0	212.4	218.0	220.8	211.4
2005	210.0	207.7	209.5	210.6	212.5	212.7	212.2	212.0	210.9	211.1	217.5	220.3	212.3
2006	209.8	207.4	210.5	210.5	212.3	212.2	210.2	210.5	209.2	211.2	217.4	220.0	211.8
2007	211.0	208.5	212.3	212.0	214.8	214.8	213.6	212.8	212.2	212.7	219.0	220.4	213.7
2008	210.4	208.1	209.8	210.1	211.5	211.8	210.9	211.2	208.7	208.3	212.6	214.0	210.6
2009	202.2	198.4	199.0	200.8	202.5	203.1	201.6	200.8	200.3	201.2	206.1	205.9	201.8
Transportation and Utilities													
1990	59.0	58.8	59.1	59.5	60.1	61.1	61.7	62.1	61.3	61.4	60.8	60.7	60.5
2000	90.3	89.8	90.5	92.9	93.0	92.8	94.2	93.8	93.4	95.5	95.0	94.9	93.0
2001	92.3	91.8	91.0	91.8	90.3	90.1	91.6	91.3	90.7	91.8	91.4	90.9	91.3
2002	88.3	87.5	87.4	85.9	86.1	86.1	88.6	88.8	88.0	88.9	88.8	89.0	87.8
2003	85.9	86.0	87.1	86.6	86.7	86.6	86.3	87.4	87.0	88.4	87.9	88.2	87.0
2004	85.8	85.7	86.4	86.9	87.5	87.9	88.0	88.7	88.6	90.4	90.3	90.5	88.1
2005	88.1	88.4	89.1	90.1	90.4	91.2	91.6	92.4	92.4	92.3	93.2	93.2	91.0
2006	90.2	89.5	90.6	90.8	91.7	93.2	92.4	92.9	94.0	94.2	95.1	96.9	92.6
2007	93.5	93.1	93.7	93.7	94.4	95.9	94.3	95.2	96.0	98.1	98.5	99.0	95.5
2008	94.2	93.0	92.4	93.9	95.0	94.7	93.8	94.5	93.5	93.3	94.5	96.5	94.1
2009	89.9	88.7	88.6	87.5	87.8	88.3	87.5	88.4	88.6	89.4	89.1	90.1	88.7
Information													
1990	26.4	26.4	26.6	26.8	27.1	27.4	27.2	27.2	27.1	26.8	26.9	27.5	26.9
2000	31.9	32.2	32.8	32.8	33.2	33.4	33.5	33.7	33.7	33.4	33.4	33.5	33.1
2001	33.3	33.4	33.6	33.3	33.4	33.4	33.0	32.7	32.2	31.9	31.8	31.9	32.8
2002	32.3	32.2	32.2	31.6	31.5	31.6	31.3	31.2	30.9	30.5	30.7	30.8	31.4
2003	30.5	30.6	30.8	30.1	30.2	29.9	29.5	29.3	28.8	29.0	29.0	29.1	29.7
2004	28.9	29.0	29.0	29.0	29.1	29.4	29.3	29.1	28.7	28.9	29.1	29.4	29.1
2005	28.6	28.7	29.0	29.0	29.4	29.6	29.6	29.6	29.3	29.2	29.5	29.7	29.3
2006	29.4	29.5	29.5	29.4	29.6	29.7	29.5	29.4	29.2	29.5	29.6	29.7	29.5
2007	29.6	29.5	29.6	29.9	30.3	30.5	30.3	30.2	30.1	29.9	30.2	30.3	30.0
2008	29.8	29.7	29.7	29.6	29.8	30.1	29.7	29.6	29.1	28.5	28.6	28.3	29.4
2009	27.9	27.7	27.5	27.3	27.3	27.2	26.9	26.9	26.5	26.5	26.6	26.6	27.1

Employment by Industry: Kentucky, Selected Years, 1990–2009—*Continued*

(Numbers in thousands, not seasonally adjusted.)

Industry and year	January	February	March	April	May	June	July	August	September	October	November	December	Annual average
Financial Activities													
1990	63.2	63.3	63.7	64.4	64.9	65.6	65.8	65.9	65.0	64.9	64.8	65.1	64.7
2000	82.6	82.7	82.3	82.1	82.6	83.6	80.9	81.0	80.5	80.7	80.9	80.8	81.7
2001	81.2	81.0	81.4	82.0	82.4	83.2	83.0	83.2	82.5	81.9	82.1	82.8	82.2
2002	81.5	81.8	82.0	82.4	83.0	83.5	83.2	83.3	82.8	82.7	82.9	83.3	82.7
2003	82.7	82.6	83.1	83.7	84.3	85.0	84.9	85.7	85.3	85.3	85.4	85.8	84.5
2004	84.4	84.4	84.9	85.2	85.3	85.4	85.3	85.5	84.7	84.4	84.5	85.1	84.9
2005	84.3	84.4	84.5	85.2	85.4	86.3	86.1	86.3	86.1	86.3	86.5	87.1	85.7
2006	86.9	87.2	88.0	88.3	88.9	89.5	89.0	89.2	89.5	89.8	90.2	91.0	89.0
2007	90.2	90.2	90.3	90.8	91.1	91.8	91.9	91.8	91.2	91.4	91.5	92.1	91.2
2008	91.6	92.3	92.3	92.0	92.3	92.0	92.2	92.0	91.0	90.6	90.9	90.9	91.7
2009	89.5	88.9	88.7	88.8	89.0	88.7	88.6	88.0	87.3	86.6	86.4	87.0	88.1
Professional and Business Services													
1990	94.1	94.8	97.5	98.8	99.7	101.6	101.6	102.2	102.6	100.7	100.2	99.7	99.5
2000	154.5	154.9	158.7	157.7	158.5	159.3	160.9	163.0	163.9	164.9	165.1	163.9	160.4
2001	158.4	158.5	159.2	158.6	158.2	159.3	157.0	158.9	157.5	156.5	155.9	155.1	157.8
2002	151.3	151.3	153.2	154.8	156.7	158.4	157.9	161.6	160.2	160.1	160.8	159.6	157.2
2003	153.1	151.8	153.7	155.6	156.5	156.3	155.2	158.5	158.9	162.2	163.5	164.8	157.5
2004	155.8	156.9	158.6	161.4	162.0	163.4	164.9	167.7	169.0	171.8	172.8	173.2	164.8
2005	166.2	167.8	169.6	172.1	172.0	173.8	172.5	175.8	177.8	179.5	181.1	181.1	174.1
2006	174.2	174.5	179.1	179.2	179.5	181.7	180.1	183.0	183.5	184.7	187.1	189.5	181.3
2007	179.1	179.1	181.7	182.5	184.0	184.7	182.5	104.4	184.0	187.7	189.3	191.8	184.2
2008	182.4	181.7	182.2	184.3	184.4	185.9	183.5	184.1	182.3	181.3	179.9	180.1	182.7
2009	169.5	168.6	167.6	167.9	166.8	167.6	169.2	171.0	171.4	175.9	181.2	185.0	171.8
Education and Health Services													
1990	149.6	150.9	151.9	152.5	153.1	153.0	153.1	154.2	155.8	158.6	159.3	159.6	154.3
2000	204.7	206.8	207.7	208.0	208.4	208.1	207.8	209.4	209.9	210.4	210.6	210.4	208.5
2001	209.1	210.4	211.2	211.8	212.1	212.4	213.3	214.2	214.7	216.6	217.1	217.2	213.3
2002	217.3	218.2	218.7	221.5	222.0	222.2	222.3	223.4	224.6	226.1	227.3	227.5	222.6
2003	225.8	226.6	227.5	227.2	227.8	227.6	224.9	226.4	229.0	229.5	229.4	229.4	227.6
2004	227.7	229.2	230.1	230.3	230.1	230.2	230.4	231.2	232.0	233.4	234.0	234.3	231.1
2005	231.4	233.7	233.5	234.7	235.5	235.2	235.4	236.0	237.0	236.6	236.2	236.9	235.2
2006	235.1	236.3	237.3	237.7	237.6	238.1	236.7	236.8	238.0	239.3	239.3	240.1	237.7
2007	238.8	239.5	240.5	239.7	240.7	241.2	240.3	240.7	241.0	242.5	242.5	243.0	240.9
2008	241.1	241.4	242.3	244.2	244.6	244.0	243.8	244.9	245.2	246.9	247.0	247.1	244.4
2009	244.3	244.3	245.4	246.4	247.0	247.0	246.2	247.3	248.2	249.4	249.2	249.4	247.0
Leisure and Hospitality													
1990	111.6	112.8	115.9	120.8	124.7	127.9	126.1	127.2	126.8	124.2	122.0	121.6	121.8
2000	140.9	142.1	146.5	152.3	156.1	157.3	157.6	157.7	156.7	155.2	151.1	150.3	152.0
2001	143.2	145.2	147.4	155.0	159.0	160.0	159.0	159.3	154.6	152.3	151.1	148.3	152.9
2002	141.8	143.5	147.8	153.7	159.7	160.2	160.2	160.3	156.7	155.0	153.1	150.0	153.5
2003	144.1	144.7	149.4	156.7	160.3	163.6	162.6	163.7	160.8	156.7	155.6	154.2	156.0
2004	149.0	149.7	155.0	161.8	164.5	168.1	168.0	167.9	164.8	162.6	160.8	159.3	161.0
2005	152.1	153.6	158.4	166.5	169.1	172.6	171.9	172.0	169.6	165.4	163.5	160.4	164.6
2006	156.6	158.8	163.9	169.8	174.0	175.5	173.3	173.9	171.7	168.8	168.4	166.4	168.4
2007	160.9	161.7	166.9	173.5	178.8	180.2	178.3	179.1	175.2	172.8	171.1	168.5	172.3
2008	162.1	163.7	166.9	174.0	178.6	179.2	179.7	179.7	175.5	171.4	167.4	165.1	171.9
2009	158.3	158.9	164.4	170.8	175.2	176.1	175.0	172.7	170.4	170.5	168.9	164.5	168.8
Other Services													
1990	61.8	62.2	62.7	62.6	63.0	63.5	63.4	63.4	63.2	62.5	62.4	62.3	62.8
2000	74.6	75.2	75.6	75.7	76.1	76.4	74.8	74.9	74.7	74.6	74.9	75.1	75.2
2001	74.1	74.4	74.7	74.8	75.1	76.0	74.6	74.6	73.8	73.7	73.7	74.3	74.5
2002	74.3	74.5	74.9	75.8	76.1	76.9	76.1	75.9	75.5	75.8	76.0	76.0	75.7
2003	75.5	75.6	76.2	76.7	77.2	78.0	77.4	78.0	77.7	77.8	77.5	77.8	77.1
2004	76.8	77.0	77.6	78.6	78.7	79.4	77.7	77.7	77.4	76.6	76.4	76.7	77.6
2005	75.4	75.9	76.3	76.2	76.6	76.7	76.1	76.1	76.0	75.8	75.9	76.0	76.1
2006	75.1	75.5	76.5	75.9	76.1	76.6	75.7	75.2	75.1	75.0	74.9	75.3	75.6
2007	74.6	74.6	75.5	75.7	76.3	76.8	75.7	75.8	75.7	75.7	75.5	75.6	75.6
2008	74.5	74.7	75.2	75.1	75.6	75.6	74.3	74.1	73.3	73.6	73.1	72.5	74.3
2009	70.4	70.7	71.0	70.5	70.6	71.1	70.4	70.3	69.7	68.6	67.7	68.0	69.9
Government													
1990	259.0	262.2	267.2	263.4	268.7	253.3	245.0	249.1	260.9	263.8	265.0	265.1	260.2
2000	297.4	308.6	313.4	314.2	317.4	309.4	295.3	297.0	305.5	310.1	311.6	311.5	307.6
2001	308.6	313.2	314.1	314.4	316.1	313.1	301.4	303.9	313.7	315.2	316.2	315.7	312.1
2002	312.3	316.4	318.2	319.4	319.7	314.9	302.7	301.5	315.8	318.4	319.7	318.0	314.8
2003	312.7	317.1	317.8	318.5	320.3	313.3	299.2	300.9	312.1	313.0	313.5	311.6	312.5
2004	309.3	312.7	314.3	315.6	313.8	309.1	298.4	299.2	310.5	312.3	313.3	311.6	310.0
2005	309.6	313.9	315.2	317.3	318.3	313.3	302.9	308.0	315.6	317.6	318.8	317.7	314.0
2006	313.9	318.1	319.6	321.5	322.6	315.2	306.7	312.7	320.5	322.3	323.3	322.8	318.3
2007	317.8	322.0	323.6	326.5	328.2	323.3	313.9	318.2	325.1	325.5	327.2	327.7	323.3
2008	322.6	326.1	327.2	326.7	327.9	321.9	310.8	315.4	319.8	325.3	326.0	325.3	322.9
2009	317.8	319.8	322.7	328.0	329.0	324.3	314.0	318.3	325.4	330.1	330.4	329.5	324.1

Average Weekly Hours by Selected Industry: Kentucky, 2007–2009

(Not seasonally adjusted.)

Industry and year	January	February	March	April	May	June	July	August	September	October	November	December	Annual average
Total Private													
2007	36.8	36.7	37.0	37.1	36.9	37.1	37.3	37.0	36.9	36.3	36.5	36.6	36.8
2008	36.4	36.1	36.6	36.3	36.3	36.7	36.2	36.1	36.0	35.9	36.1	35.8	36.2
2009	35.6	35.9	35.7	35.2	35.2	35.3	35.2	35.5	35.1	35.1	35.8	35.5	35.4
Goods-Producing													
2007	39.4	39.2	39.6	39.8	39.7	40.4	40.7	40.5	40.6	40.4	41.2	40.4	40.2
2008	40.2	39.6	40.6	40.2	40.4	40.8	40.5	40.6	40.3	40.2	40.0	40.0	40.3
2009	40.1	40.2	39.8	39.3	39.4	39.5	38.9	39.5	39.3	39.7	41.0	40.9	39.8
Construction													
2007	36.7	36.2	37.4	37.8	37.9	38.7	39.4	39.7	39.6	39.3	40.2	37.5	38.4
2008	37.6	36.7	37.6	38.0	38.2	39.0	38.9	38.9	39.1	39.3	39.0	38.8	38.5
2009	38.8	40.0	39.5	39.1	39.1	40.3	40.8	40.8	39.7	38.3	41.9	38.5	39.7
Manufacturing													
2007	40.0	39.9	40.2	40.3	40.0	40.0	39.9	39.5	39.8	39.6	39.8	40.0	39.8
2008	39.7	39.2	40.2	39.5	39.4	39.8	39.6	39.7	39.2	39.0	38.9	38.8	39.4
2009	38.6	38.6	38.6	38.3	38.3	38.5	37.6	38.5	38.7	39.4	40.0	40.8	38.8
Trade, Transportation, and Utilities													
2007	35.7	35.6	35.7	35.5	35.7	36.0	35.7	35.8	35.9	35.1	35.0	35.6	35.6
2008	35.2	35.0	35.5	35.4	35.3	35.6	35.1	35.2	35.1	34.4	34.9	34.7	35.1
2009	34.6	34.9	34.6	34.1	34.2	34.7	34.6	34.3	34.6	34.4	34.4	34.5	34.5
Financial Activities													
2007	37.7	37.2	37.3	38.1	36.6	37.0	37.5	36.6	37.6	36.7	37.2	38.3	37.3
2008	37.8	38.2	38.7	38.3	37.5	38.4	37.3	37.7	37.3	37.8	38.7	38.0	38.0
2009	38.5	39.1	38.9	37.9	37.1	37.4	37.6	37.6	36.3	35.8	37.9	36.3	37.5
Professional and Business Services													
2007	35.8	35.6	35.6	36.1	36.1	35.7	36.2	35.6	35.9	35.5	35.6	35.5	35.8
2008	35.6	35.6	36.1	36.1	36.3	36.4	35.5	35.7	35.5	35.5	36.1	35.4	35.8
2009	35.0	35.3	35.4	35.5	35.6	35.4	35.9	36.4	36.0	36.5	36.6	36.7	35.9
Education and Health Services													
2007	35.6	35.4	36.0	36.0	36.2	36.7	37.4	36.9	36.6	36.0	35.8	36.1	36.2
2008	36.0	36.0	36.3	35.9	36.3	36.7	36.5	36.3	36.4	36.6	36.8	36.6	36.4
2009	36.1	36.2	36.1	35.6	35.7	35.8	35.7	36.0	35.4	35.5	36.0	35.7	35.8
Leisure and Hospitality													
2007	26.2	26.3	26.1	26.6	26.6	27.0	27.1	27.1	27.0	26.8	26.3	26.4	26.6
2008	26.0	26.1	26.5	26.7	27.4	27.9	27.9	27.5	27.3	27.6	27.6	26.9	27.1
2009	26.5	27.4	27.1	27.0	27.2	27.0	27.1	26.8	26.4	25.8	26.0	25.8	26.7

Average Hourly Earnings by Selected Industry: Kentucky, 2007–2009

(Dollars, not seasonally adjusted.)

Industry and year	January	February	March	April	May	June	July	August	September	October	November	December	Annual average
Total Private													
2007	17.73	17.91	17.68	17.73	17.50	17.54	17.87	17.70	17.92	17.82	17.64	17.72	17.73
2008	17.76	17.91	17.94	18.05	17.95	18.00	17.98	18.06	18.22	18.20	18.35	18.44	18.07
2009	18.63	18.77	18.62	18.50	18.75	18.67	18.69	18.71	18.95	19.04	19.24	19.22	18.82
Goods-Producing													
2007	18.78	18.82	18.64	18.70	18.78	19.05	19.24	19.26	19.36	19.31	19.34	19.64	19.08
2008	19.44	19.76	19.79	20.05	19.97	19.91	19.98	20.04	20.27	20.52	20.64	20.78	20.09
2009	21.01	21.13	21.15	21.18	21.35	21.45	21.24	21.22	21.73	22.01	22.18	22.54	21.51
Construction													
2007	19.15	19.07	19.01	19.34	19.25	19.77	20.64	20.04	20.00	20.37	20.34	20.92	19.86
2008	20.57	20.83	20.60	20.65	20.89	20.45	20.60	20.40	20.44	20.84	20.66	20.57	20.62
2009	20.11	20.43	20.12	20.15	20.37	20.80	20.93	21.01	21.14	21.91	21.54	22.03	20.88
Manufacturing													
2007	18.49	18.57	18.51	18.40	18.53	18.51	18.36	18.52	18.72	18.56	18.65	18.93	18.56
2008	18.74	19.20	19.30	19.59	19.46	19.50	19.50	19.66	19.88	20.06	20.16	20.17	19.59
2009	20.60	20.86	21.00	20.85	21.10	21.14	21.53	21.51	22.21	22.18	22.53	22.80	21.52
Trade, Transportation, and Utilities													
2007	15.38	15.57	15.43	15.44	15.12	15.39	15.70	15.54	15.70	15.67	15.26	15.25	15.45
2008	15.38	15.59	15.58	15.79	15.61	15.82	15.90	15.88	15.98	16.03	16.13	16.03	15.81
2009	16.35	16.35	16.36	16.37	16.50	16.09	16.36	16.44	16.64	16.37	16.64	16.44	16.41
Financial Activities													
2007	19.61	20.08	19.74	19.65	19.65	19.63	20.28	20.21	20.44	20.60	20.50	21.02	20.12
2008	20.88	21.20	21.06	21.17	21.46	21.79	21.78	21.85	21.76	21.40	21.69	21.68	21.47
2009	21.44	21.73	21.92	21.41	21.15	21.45	21.24	21.43	21.42	21.93	22.25	21.56	21.58
Professional and Business Services													
2007	19.95	20.09	20.11	20.17	19.95	19.51	19.98	19.30	19.51	18.95	18.66	18.53	19.55
2008	18.87	19.24	19.31	19.49	19.44	19.36	19.32	19.46	19.52	19.68	19.71	19.90	19.44
2009	20.27	20.48	20.13	20.01	20.31	20.21	19.80	20.09	20.29	20.60	21.02	20.84	20.35
Education and Health Services													
2007	18.30	18.58	18.14	18.18	18.26	18.21	18.21	18.40	19.13	19.19	19.11	18.96	18.56
2008	19.16	19.37	19.08	19.05	19.25	19.33	19.56	19.66	19.97	19.51	19.84	20.17	19.50
2009	20.44	20.28	19.55	19.80	19.81	19.72	19.76	19.62	19.55	19.64	19.62	20.22	19.83
Leisure and Hospitality													
2007	10.19	10.08	10.01	10.10	10.14	9.94	10.01	9.96	10.07	10.01	10.06	10.09	10.05
2008	10.11	10.14	10.03	9.97	10.14	10.11	9.99	10.07	9.99	10.15	10.04	10.28	10.08
2009	10.34	10.38	10.26	10.29	10.63	10.61	10.70	10.70	10.71	10.67	10.77	10.70	10.57

Average Hourly Earnings by Selected Industry: Kentucky, 2007–2009

(Dollars, not seasonally adjusted.)

Industry and year	January	February	March	April	May	June	July	August	September	October	November	December	Annual average
Total Private													
2007	17.73	17.91	17.68	17.73	17.50	17.54	17.87	17.70	17.92	17.82	17.64	17.72	17.73
2008	17.76	17.91	17.94	18.05	17.95	18.00	17.98	18.06	18.22	18.20	18.35	18.44	18.07
2009	18.63	18.77	18.62	18.50	18.75	18.67	18.69	18.71	18.95	19.04	19.24	19.22	18.82
Goods-Producing													
2007	18.78	18.82	18.64	18.70	18.78	19.05	19.24	19.26	19.36	19.31	19.34	19.64	19.08
2008	19.44	19.76	19.79	20.05	19.97	19.91	19.98	20.04	20.27	20.52	20.64	20.78	20.09
2009	21.01	21.13	21.15	21.18	21.35	21.45	21.24	21.22	21.73	22.01	22.18	22.54	21.51
Construction													
2007	19.15	19.07	19.01	19.34	19.25	19.77	20.64	20.04	20.00	20.37	20.34	20.92	19.86
2008	20.57	20.83	20.60	20.65	20.89	20.45	20.60	20.40	20.44	20.84	20.66	20.57	20.62
2009	20.11	20.43	20.12	20.15	20.37	20.80	20.93	21.01	21.14	21.91	21.54	22.03	20.88
Manufacturing													
2007	18.49	18.57	18.51	18.40	18.53	18.51	18.36	18.52	18.72	18.56	18.65	18.93	18.56
2008	18.74	19.20	19.30	19.59	19.46	19.50	19.50	19.66	19.88	20.06	20.16	20.17	19.59
2009	20.60	20.86	21.00	20.85	21.10	21.14	21.53	21.51	22.21	22.18	22.53	22.80	21.52
Trade, Transportation, and Utilities													
2007	15.38	15.57	15.43	15.44	15.12	15.39	15.70	15.54	15.70	15.67	15.26	15.25	15.45
2008	15.38	15.59	15.58	15.79	15.61	15.82	15.90	15.88	15.98	16.03	16.13	16.03	15.81
2009	16.35	16.35	16.36	16.37	16.50	16.09	16.36	16.44	16.64	16.37	16.64	16.44	16.41
Financial Activities													
2007	19.61	20.08	19.74	19.65	19.65	19.63	20.28	20.21	20.44	20.60	20.50	21.02	20.12
2008	20.88	21.20	21.06	21.17	21.46	21.79	21.78	21.85	21.76	21.40	21.69	21.68	21.47
2009	21.44	21.73	21.92	21.41	21.15	21.45	21.24	21.43	21.42	21.93	22.25	21.56	21.58
Professional and Business Services													
2007	19.95	20.09	20.11	20.17	19.95	19.51	19.98	19.30	19.51	18.95	18.66	18.53	19.55
2008	18.87	19.24	19.31	19.49	19.44	19.36	19.32	19.46	19.52	19.68	19.71	19.90	19.44
2009	20.27	20.48	20.13	20.01	20.31	20.21	19.80	20.09	20.29	20.60	21.02	20.84	20.35
Education and Health Services													
2007	18.30	18.58	18.14	18.18	18.26	18.21	18.21	18.40	19.13	19.19	19.11	18.96	18.56
2008	19.16	19.37	19.08	19.05	19.25	19.33	19.56	19.66	19.97	19.51	19.84	20.17	19.50
2009	20.44	20.28	19.55	19.80	19.81	19.72	19.76	19.62	19.55	19.64	19.62	20.22	19.83
Leisure and Hospitality													
2007	10.19	10.08	10.01	10.10	10.14	9.94	10.01	9.96	10.07	10.01	10.06	10.09	10.05
2008	10.11	10.14	10.03	9.97	10.14	10.11	9.99	10.07	9.99	10.15	10.04	10.28	10.08
2009	10.34	10.38	10.26	10.29	10.63	10.61	10.78	10.70	10.71	10.67	10.77	10.70	10.57

Average Weekly Earnings by Selected Industry: Kentucky, 2007–2009

(Dollars, not seasonally adjusted.)

Industry and year	January	February	March	April	May	June	July	August	September	October	November	December	Annual average
Total Private													
2007	652.46	657.30	654.16	657.78	645.75	650.73	666.55	654.90	661.25	646.87	643.86	648.55	652.46
2008	646.46	646.55	656.60	655.22	651.59	660.60	650.88	651.97	655.92	653.38	662.44	660.15	654.13
2009	663.23	673.84	664.73	651.20	660.00	659.05	657.89	664.21	665.15	668.30	688.79	682.31	666.23
Goods-Producing													
2007	739.93	737.74	738.14	744.26	745.57	769.62	783.07	780.03	786.02	780.12	796.81	793.46	767.02
2008	781.49	782.50	803.47	806.01	806.79	812.33	809.19	813.62	816.88	824.90	825.60	831.20	809.63
2009	842.50	849.43	841.77	832.37	841.19	847.28	826.24	838.19	853.99	873.80	909.38	921.89	856.10
Construction													
2007	702.81	690.33	710.97	731.05	729.58	765.10	813.22	795.59	792.00	800.54	817.67	784.50	762.62
2008	773.43	764.46	774.56	784.70	798.00	797.55	801.34	793.56	799.20	819.01	805.74	798.12	793.87
2009	780.27	817.20	794.74	787.87	796.47	838.24	853.94	857.21	839.26	839.15	902.53	848.16	828.94
Manufacturing													
2007	739.60	740.94	744.10	741.52	741.20	740.40	732.56	731.54	745.06	734.98	742.27	757.20	740.54
2008	743.98	752.64	775.86	773.81	766.72	776.10	772.20	780.50	779.30	782.34	784.22	782.60	771.85
2009	795.16	805.20	810.60	798.56	808.13	813.89	809.53	828.14	859.53	873.89	901.20	930.24	834.98
Trade, Transportation, and Utilities													
2007	549.07	554.29	550.85	548.12	539.78	554.04	560.49	556.33	563.63	550.02	534.10	542.90	550.02
2008	541.38	545.65	553.09	558.97	551.03	563.19	558.09	558.98	560.90	551.43	562.94	556.24	554.93
2009	565.71	570.62	566.06	558.22	564.30	558.32	566.06	563.89	575.74	563.13	572.42	567.18	566.15
Financial Activities													
2007	739.30	746.98	736.30	748.67	719.19	726.31	760.50	739.69	768.54	756.02	762.60	805.07	750.48
2008	789.26	809.84	815.02	810.81	804.75	836.74	812.39	823.75	811.65	808.92	839.40	823.84	815.86
2009	825.44	849.64	852.69	811.44	784.67	802.23	798.62	805.77	777.55	785.09	843.28	782.63	809.25
Professional and Business Services													
2007	714.21	715.20	715.92	728.14	720.20	696.51	723.28	687.08	700.41	672.73	664.30	657.82	699.89
2008	671.77	684.94	697.09	703.59	705.67	704.70	685.86	694.72	692.96	698.64	711.53	704.46	695.95
2009	709.45	722.94	712.60	710.36	723.04	715.43	710.82	731.28	730.44	751.90	769.33	764.83	730.57
Education and Health Services													
2007	651.48	657.73	653.04	654.48	661.01	668.31	681.05	678.96	700.16	690.84	684.14	684.46	671.87
2008	689.76	697.32	692.60	683.90	698.78	709.41	713.94	713.66	726.91	714.07	730.11	738.22	709.80
2009	737.88	734.14	705.76	704.88	707.22	705.98	705.43	706.32	692.07	697.22	706.32	721.85	709.91
Leisure and Hospitality													
2007	266.98	265.10	261.26	268.66	269.72	268.38	271.27	269.92	271.89	268.27	264.58	266.38	267.33
2008	262.86	264.65	265.80	266.20	277.84	282.07	278.72	276.93	272.73	280.14	277.10	276.53	273.17
2009	274.01	284.41	278.05	277.83	280.14	280.47	292.14	280.76	282.74	275.29	280.02	276.06	282.22

LOUISIANA
At a Glance

Population:
    1990 census: 4,221,826
    2000 census: 4,468,976
    2009 estimate: 4,492,076

Percent change in population:
    1990–2000: 5.9%
    2000–2009: 0.5%

Percent change in total nonfarm employment:
    1990–2009: 19.6%
    2008–2009: -2.0%

Industry with the largest growth in employment, 1990–2009 (thousands):
    Education and Health Services, 102.1

Industry with the largest decline or smallest growth in employment, 1990–2009 (thousands):
    Manufacturing, -34.2

Civilian labor force:
    1990: 1,877,388
    2000: 2,031,292
    2009: 2,067,886

Unemployment rate and rank among states (lowest to highest):
    1990: 5.9%, 36th
    2000: 5.0%, 44th
    2009: 6.8%, 12th

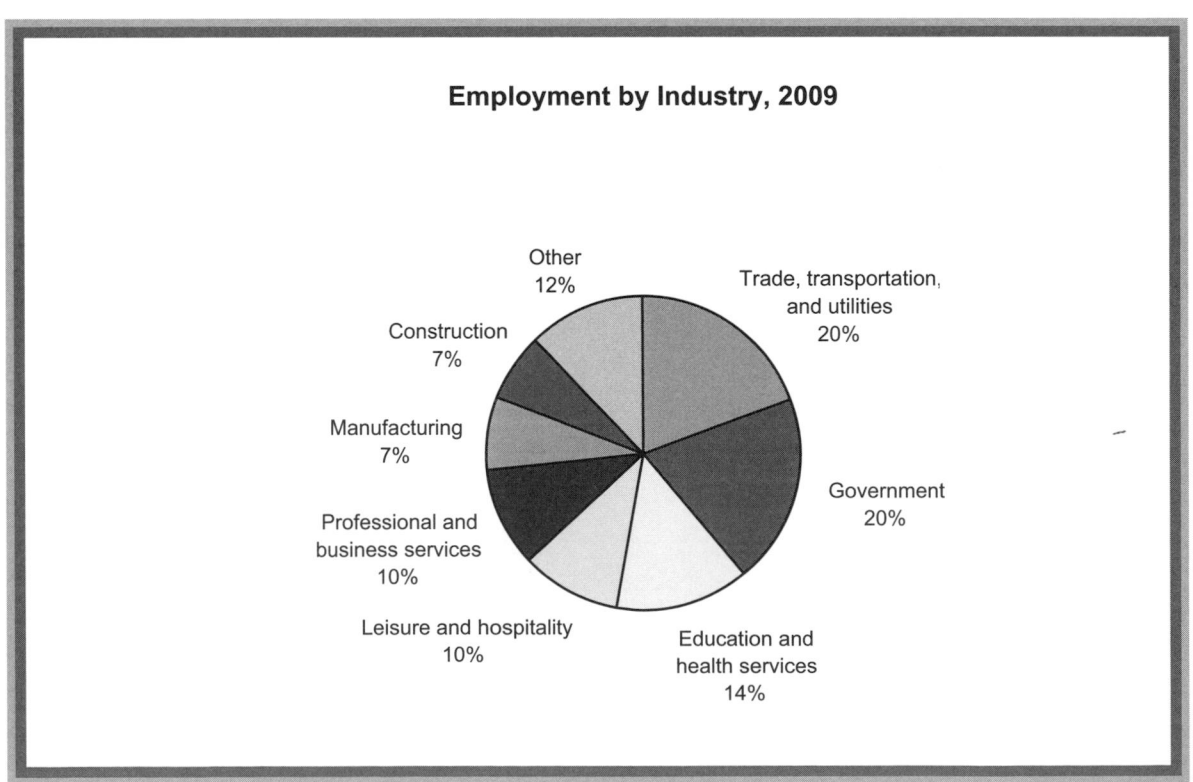

Employment by Industry, 2009

- Other 12%
- Construction 7%
- Manufacturing 7%
- Professional and business services 10%
- Leisure and hospitality 10%
- Education and health services 14%
- Government 20%
- Trade, transportation, and utilities 20%

Employment by Industry: Louisiana, Selected Years, 1990–2009

(Numbers in thousands, not seasonally adjusted.)

Industry and year	January	February	March	April	May	June	July	August	September	October	November	December	Annual average
Total Nonfarm													
1990	1541.4	1552.2	1565.8	1579.2	1598.1	1598.4	1587.0	1592.3	1603.7	1609.9	1612.6	1611.4	1587.7
2000	1887.8	1901.7	1916.5	1922.1	1938.3	1929.5	1904.4	1907.6	1922.4	1921.7	1925.8	1935.0	1917.7
2001	1897.3	1908.9	1923.1	1924.4	1930.8	1930.7	1900.6	1906.5	1918.5	1911.7	1915.8	1916.1	1915.4
2002	1872.2	1880.1	1890.9	1903.1	1907.1	1907.5	1883.9	1888.2	1899.8	1897.6	1908.7	1908.4	1895.6
2003	1882.8	1893.1	1899.4	1906.4	1913.2	1911.5	1890.8	1895.0	1908.7	1916.9	1923.4	1925.2	1905.5
2004	1891.4	1902.7	1919.7	1924.7	1923.0	1924.5	1905.9	1908.5	1913.3	1922.0	1935.8	1939.0	1917.5
2005	1904.9	1913.9	1930.8	1948.5	1951.8	1953.3	1937.6	1941.1	1823.8	1776.0	1801.9	1817.6	1891.8
2006	1789.8	1813.1	1839.8	1841.5	1854.3	1859.4	1835.0	1852.4	1874.9	1880.5	1892.9	1904.6	1853.2
2007	1876.5	1895.4	1915.5	1904.5	1911.6	1917.7	1894.0	1911.3	1922.0	1936.5	1947.1	1953.5	1915.5
2008	1910.6	1928.5	1937.6	1939.9	1945.5	1940.8	1919.8	1938.0	1922.5	1950.4	1957.5	1958.8	1937.5
2009	1910.3	1917.9	1918.1	1911.1	1913.8	1900.6	1877.1	1879.6	1882.0	1893.4	1893.7	1890.0	1899.0
Total Private													
1990	1223.5	1228.7	1241.2	1248.3	1261.1	1270.6	1264.1	1275.2	1282.2	1279.5	1282.0	1281.7	1261.5
2000	1517.2	1525.1	1537.0	1542.9	1553.3	1555.6	1539.6	1547.9	1550.8	1547.9	1552.1	1562.0	1544.3
2001	1525.2	1530.8	1544.0	1547.0	1553.8	1556.2	1537.9	1545.8	1545.5	1535.7	1538.2	1539.1	1541.6
2002	1502.2	1504.6	1513.8	1525.6	1529.5	1531.1	1517.2	1523.7	1524.7	1518.9	1527.5	1529.5	1520.7
2003	1508.3	1511.4	1516.3	1523.4	1531.1	1531.3	1519.4	1527.5	1529.5	1534.3	1539.0	1543.8	1526.3
2004	1514.1	1518.6	1533.8	1539.3	1539.2	1542.6	1532.2	1536.7	1530.3	1535.9	1548.9	1553.4	1535.4
2005	1528.4	1530.6	1547.7	1564.3	1569.6	1573.6	1567.8	1570.9	1445.7	1415.8	1441.1	1458.7	1517.9
2006	1446.8	1463.6	1488.7	1492.2	1504.4	1517.8	1501.0	1513.2	1522.0	1526.8	1536.9	1549.0	1505.2
2007	1527.8	1538.2	1556.0	1550.7	1558.0	1566.3	1553.8	1565.0	1561.8	1573.2	1581.2	1588.2	1560.0
2008	1553.4	1563.4	1573.2	1573.2	1578.7	1579.8	1566.5	1578.6	1557.5	1579.3	1583.9	1587.9	1573.0
2009	1545.6	1546.2	1546.6	1538.7	1542.2	1534.7	1520.1	1521.7	1512.7	1520.8	1520.4	1518.7	1530.7
Goods-Producing													
1990	313.8	316.1	320.6	323.0	327.6	329.7	329.2	334.5	336.5	337.6	336.3	332.0	328.1
2000	348.8	349.9	353.1	354.8	359.0	360.0	353.3	355.6	354.0	352.6	349.8	349.4	353.4
2001	343.7	345.5	350.7	350.2	354.6	355.6	351.2	352.4	350.0	345.2	341.3	337.2	348.1
2002	328.4	326.6	327.4	328.7	330.6	330.4	327.2	329.0	328.0	329.4	326.4	324.3	328.0
2003	321.1	320.1	320.4	319.3	324.8	325.6	321.6	322.8	322.9	324.5	320.9	319.1	321.9
2004	313.2	312.9	317.2	315.7	314.3	315.8	314.7	312.6	312.3	314.5	315.1	314.9	314.4
2005	308.9	310.5	314.4	319.9	321.9	323.5	321.6	323.0	307.5	311.6	315.1	317.7	316.3
2006	320.4	322.8	327.9	329.7	331.9	336.2	328.0	332.4	336.5	338.0	338.1	341.0	331.9
2007	332.2	335.5	338.7	340.2	342.7	344.9	342.3	344.3	343.6	345.9	345.2	344.0	341.6
2008	337.0	338.4	339.2	340.4	343.3	345.0	343.2	344.8	341.2	346.9	345.1	344.3	342.4
2009	335.5	332.6	330.4	326.4	326.6	324.7	322.7	320.5	317.4	317.7	313.0	308.8	323.0
Mining and Logging													
1990	54.0	54.2	54.7	54.8	54.9	55.6	55.9	56.4	55.9	56.7	57.1	57.0	55.6
2000	44.9	45.0	44.8	46.0	46.8	47.8	48.0	48.6	49.0	48.4	48.4	49.1	47.2
2001	50.0	51.1	51.0	52.1	52.0	52.7	53.0	53.4	53.1	51.8	50.2	50.2	52.0
2002	49.5	48.8	48.5	48.2	48.6	48.9	48.7	48.8	48.7	47.5	47.4	47.4	48.4
2003	47.3	47.3	47.4	47.2	47.4	48.2	47.3	47.5	47.0	46.8	46.5	45.8	47.1
2004	44.9	44.9	45.4	45.2	44.7	45.0	44.3	44.4	43.9	44.6	44.5	44.5	44.7
2005	44.0	44.2	44.8	45.2	45.5	46.0	45.8	46.0	45.7	45.4	45.1	45.3	45.3
2006	46.4	46.9	47.3	47.2	47.6	48.6	49.1	49.7	50.5	50.1	49.9	50.1	48.6
2007	49.6	49.8	50.0	51.2	51.7	52.1	52.0	53.0	52.4	52.6	53.0	52.9	51.7
2008	53.9	53.7	54.0	54.1	54.4	55.0	55.4	55.5	54.9	56.3	55.9	55.6	54.9
2009	55.0	54.1	53.3	51.1	51.2	51.0	50.1	49.9	49.5	48.1	47.2	47.3	50.7
Construction													
1990	89.9	90.8	93.7	94.6	97.2	95.9	96.0	98.9	100.2	100.6	98.6	94.9	95.9
2000	126.8	128.8	131.9	132.1	133.9	134.1	128.3	129.5	127.8	126.1	124.3	123.2	128.9
2001	118.9	120.5	124.5	124.6	127.3	127.2	126.4	127.6	126.5	125.3	124.4	121.7	124.6
2002	119.2	117.8	118.4	119.9	120.8	119.1	118.3	119.4	118.9	120.8	118.6	116.9	119.0
2003	117.2	117.3	117.0	118.1	120.9	120.3	119.6	119.9	120.1	121.5	118.7	117.6	119.0
2004	116.8	116.6	120.1	117.9	116.4	116.3	116.7	114.2	114.1	115.7	116.6	115.7	116.4
2005	112.2	113.9	116.2	120.7	121.4	121.6	120.9	121.2	114.5	118.5	121.8	122.8	118.8
2006	125.7	127.3	130.8	132.4	133.3	134.9	127.3	129.0	130.3	131.8	131.6	133.3	130.6
2007	129.1	130.5	132.7	132.2	133.8	134.3	132.3	133.8	133.5	134.7	133.6	132.8	132.8
2008	129.3	131.0	132.0	133.7	135.3	136.1	134.8	136.4	135.3	138.0	137.7	137.1	134.7
2009	132.7	132.9	132.6	131.0	131.8	131.4	131.7	130.0	127.6	128.1	126.0	124.6	130.0
Manufacturing													
1990	169.9	171.1	172.2	173.6	175.5	178.2	177.3	179.2	180.4	180.3	180.6	180.1	176.5
2000	177.1	176.1	176.4	176.7	178.3	178.1	177.0	177.5	177.2	178.1	177.1	177.1	177.2
2001	174.8	173.9	174.3	173.5	174.4	174.7	171.8	171.4	170.4	168.1	166.7	165.3	171.6
2002	159.7	160.0	160.5	160.6	161.2	162.4	160.2	160.8	160.4	161.1	160.4	160.0	160.6
2003	156.6	155.5	156.0	154.0	156.5	157.1	154.7	155.4	155.8	156.2	155.7	155.7	155.8
2004	151.5	151.4	151.7	152.6	153.2	154.5	153.7	154.0	154.3	154.2	154.0	154.7	153.3
2005	152.7	152.4	153.4	154.0	155.0	155.9	154.9	155.8	147.3	147.7	148.2	149.6	152.2
2006	148.3	148.6	149.8	150.1	151.0	152.7	151.6	153.7	155.7	156.1	156.6	157.6	152.7
2007	153.5	155.2	156.0	156.8	157.2	158.5	158.0	157.5	157.7	158.6	158.6	158.3	157.2
2008	153.8	153.7	153.2	152.6	153.6	153.9	153.0	152.9	151.0	152.6	151.5	151.6	152.8
2009	147.8	145.6	144.5	144.3	143.6	142.3	140.9	140.6	140.3	141.5	139.8	136.9	142.3

Employment by Industry: Louisiana, Selected Years, 1990–2009—*Continued*

(Numbers in thousands, not seasonally adjusted.)

Industry and year	January	February	March	April	May	June	July	August	September	October	November	December	Annual average
Service-Providing													
1990	1227.6	1236.1	1245.2	1256.2	1270.5	1268.7	1257.8	1257.8	1267.2	1272.3	1276.3	1279.4	1259.6
2000	1539.0	1551.8	1563.4	1567.3	1579.3	1569.5	1551.1	1552.0	1568.4	1569.1	1576.0	1585.6	1564.4
2001	1553.6	1563.4	1572.4	1574.2	1576.2	1575.1	1549.4	1554.1	1568.5	1566.5	1574.5	1578.9	1567.2
2002	1543.8	1553.5	1563.5	1574.4	1576.5	1577.1	1556.7	1559.2	1571.8	1568.2	1582.3	1584.1	1567.6
2003	1561.7	1573.0	1579.0	1587.1	1588.4	1585.9	1569.2	1572.2	1585.8	1592.4	1602.5	1606.1	1583.6
2004	1578.2	1589.8	1602.5	1609.0	1608.7	1608.7	1591.2	1595.9	1601.0	1607.5	1620.7	1624.1	1603.1
2005	1596.0	1603.4	1616.4	1628.6	1629.9	1629.8	1616.0	1618.1	1516.3	1464.4	1486.8	1499.9	1575.5
2006	1469.4	1490.3	1511.9	1511.8	1522.4	1523.2	1507.0	1520.0	1538.4	1542.5	1554.8	1563.6	1521.3
2007	1544.3	1559.9	1576.8	1564.3	1568.9	1572.8	1551.7	1567.0	1578.4	1590.6	1601.9	1609.5	1573.8
2008	1573.6	1590.1	1598.4	1599.5	1602.2	1595.8	1576.6	1593.2	1581.3	1603.5	1612.4	1614.5	1595.1
2009	1574.8	1585.3	1587.7	1584.7	1587.2	1575.9	1554.4	1559.1	1564.6	1575.7	1580.7	1581.2	1575.9
Trade, Transportation, and Utilities													
1990	350.5	349.0	350.7	352.1	354.6	357.3	354.7	356.2	356.9	355.8	359.5	362.6	355.0
2000	384.1	385.3	388.3	387.2	390.1	391.8	387.7	390.8	391.6	390.3	396.5	402.5	390.5
2001	386.0	384.9	387.9	387.8	388.3	389.8	386.8	389.2	388.2	386.5	391.9	395.3	388.6
2002	379.9	378.4	381.6	383.6	384.8	386.6	383.8	384.3	383.8	381.8	388.2	393.0	384.2
2003	379.1	377.9	379.4	379.5	379.8	380.8	378.0	379.6	378.9	380.7	386.1	390.2	380.8
2004	376.6	376.0	379.1	379.6	380.7	381.3	377.8	377.9	376.0	378.7	383.6	388.5	379.7
2005	375.8	375.1	378.2	381.3	382.9	384.2	385.1	385.1	353.2	348.5	361.8	369.9	373.4
2006	361.1	362.9	369.6	368.9	371.4	374.4	373.2	374.6	375.2	377.0	382.4	388.6	373.3
2007	378.9	377.9	382.4	378.8	380.3	381.3	380.6	382.3	382.7	385.8	391.9	396.2	383.3
2008	383.5	381.9	384.7	382.9	384.0	383.8	381.9	383.8	378.1	382.2	386.9	390.5	383.7
2009	375.5	373.0	373.0	369.4	369.8	370.3	367.0	366.1	364.7	363.3	368.4	370.4	369.2
Wholesale Trade													
1990	69.2	69.5	69.9	70.3	70.8	71.3	70.5	70.4	70.7	70.2	70.1	70.3	70.3
2000	76.2	76.4	77.2	77.8	78.4	78.6	78.4	78.6	78.4	77.3	77.3	77.8	77.7
2001	76.7	77.0	77.5	78.0	78.1	78.9	77.7	78.0	78.0	77.6	77.6	77.9	77.8
2002	76.5	76.6	76.9	77.6	78.0	78.2	77.4	77.4	77.2	76.6	76.7	76.7	77.2
2003	76.2	76.1	76.3	75.5	75.7	76.1	75.5	75.6	75.5	75.4	75.3	74.9	75.7
2004	75.1	75.1	75.6	75.9	75.9	75.7	75.3	75.4	75.3	74.3	74.4	74.4	75.2
2005	73.6	73.8	74.1	75.0	75.3	75.4	76.3	76.3	71.6	71.0	71.4	71.8	73.8
2006	70.5	71.1	71.8	72.1	72.7	73.5	73.2	73.5	73.5	73.4	73.7	74.1	72.8
2007	74.9	75.2	75.8	74.9	75.3	75.9	76.4	76.8	76.3	76.6	76.6	76.9	76.0
2008	75.6	75.9	76.3	75.9	76.1	76.1	75.8	76.0	75.5	75.4	75.0	75.2	75.7
2009	73.3	73.2	72.8	72.2	72.1	71.8	71.5	71.2	70.8	69.7	69.9	70.4	71.6
Retail Trade													
1990	199.0	196.7	197.6	198.8	200.3	201.5	200.0	200.9	200.6	200.5	204.4	207.4	200.6
2000	229.1	229.3	231.6	230.1	232.0	232.8	228.9	230.7	231.4	231.3	237.5	242.3	232.3
2001	228.6	226.3	228.2	226.8	227.2	227.3	226.1	227.7	226.7	224.9	231.4	234.5	228.0
2002	223.0	221.6	224.3	225.0	225.1	226.5	224.0	224.2	223.7	221.8	227.9	232.4	225.0
2003	221.6	220.5	222.2	222.1	221.9	222.5	221.0	222.3	221.9	223.4	228.3	232.7	223.4
2004	222.1	221.2	223.1	223.8	224.3	225.0	222.5	222.2	220.6	223.3	228.2	232.2	224.0
2005	222.1	220.9	223.1	224.9	225.8	226.7	226.5	226.6	204.2	201.7	213.4	219.6	219.6
2006	213.8	214.7	219.2	218.1	219.3	220.4	219.3	219.9	219.8	222.1	226.7	230.3	220.3
2007	222.3	221.2	224.8	222.6	223.6	223.6	223.2	223.4	224.3	226.6	232.6	236.1	225.4
2008	226.6	224.5	226.6	224.6	224.9	224.9	224.0	225.0	220.6	223.5	228.5	231.4	225.4
2009	220.7	219.7	220.3	219.6	220.6	221.4	218.9	218.2	217.6	217.7	222.3	222.2	219.9
Transportation and Utilities													
1990	82.3	82.8	83.2	83.0	83.5	84.5	84.2	84.9	85.6	85.1	85.0	84.9	84.0
2000	78.8	79.6	79.5	79.3	79.7	80.4	80.4	81.5	81.8	81.7	81.7	82.4	80.5
2001	80.7	81.6	82.2	83.0	83.0	83.6	83.0	83.5	83.5	84.0	82.9	82.9	82.8
2002	80.4	80.2	80.4	81.0	81.7	81.9	82.4	82.7	82.9	83.4	83.6	83.9	82.0
2003	81.3	81.3	80.9	81.9	82.2	82.2	81.5	81.7	81.5	81.9	82.5	82.6	81.8
2004	79.4	79.7	80.4	79.9	80.5	80.6	80.0	80.3	80.1	81.1	81.0	81.9	80.4
2005	80.1	80.4	81.0	81.4	81.8	82.1	82.3	82.2	77.4	75.8	77.0	78.5	80.0
2006	76.8	77.1	78.6	78.7	79.4	80.5	80.7	81.2	81.9	81.5	82.0	84.2	80.2
2007	81.7	81.5	81.8	81.3	81.4	81.8	81.0	82.1	82.1	82.6	82.7	83.2	81.9
2008	81.3	81.5	81.8	82.4	83.0	82.8	82.1	82.8	82.0	83.3	83.4	83.9	82.5
2009	81.5	80.1	79.9	77.6	77.1	77.1	76.6	76.7	76.3	75.9	76.2	77.8	77.7
Information													
1990	26.6	26.6	26.7	26.6	26.7	26.9	27.3	27.1	27.4	26.4	26.4	26.5	26.7
2000	28.9	28.5	28.8	29.1	29.2	29.9	30.7	30.9	30.5	30.3	30.5	31.0	29.8
2001	30.0	30.2	30.4	30.2	30.6	30.6	30.3	30.1	29.7	30.0	30.1	29.8	30.1
2002	29.3	29.3	29.5	29.0	28.9	29.3	29.0	29.0	28.9	28.5	28.8	28.9	29.0
2003	29.2	28.9	29.1	29.0	29.4	29.8	28.4	28.9	28.8	28.7	28.9	29.0	29.0
2004	29.1	29.4	29.3	30.3	30.0	30.7	29.6	31.1	29.9	30.9	33.0	31.5	30.4
2005	31.2	30.3	30.3	29.5	29.3	29.6	30.0	30.4	28.6	26.4	26.9	27.0	29.1
2006	27.2	27.3	29.2	28.2	28.3	27.6	25.9	25.8	25.7	25.8	26.4	26.6	27.0
2007	26.5	27.5	29.6	28.7	28.5	29.0	27.9	27.4	26.2	27.0	26.7	27.1	27.7
2008	26.7	28.5	30.2	30.1	30.8	31.7	26.6	28.0	27.9	26.2	27.1	27.8	28.5
2009	24.9	25.2	25.2	24.6	24.9	25.0	24.5	24.0	23.9	24.3	24.3	24.4	24.6

Employment by Industry: Louisiana, Selected Years, 1990–2009—*Continued*

(Numbers in thousands, not seasonally adjusted.)

Industry and year	January	February	March	April	May	June	July	August	September	October	November	December	Annual average
Financial Activities													
1990	85.4	85.7	86.4	86.5	86.7	87.7	86.7	87.2	87.2	87.0	87.2	88.8	86.9
2000	97.2	97.4	97.7	96.8	97.6	97.6	97.7	97.8	97.7	97.3	97.5	98.3	97.6
2001	96.6	97.2	97.0	97.1	97.0	97.6	97.7	97.8	97.1	96.8	96.8	96.9	97.1
2002	96.7	96.6	96.8	97.8	97.9	98.0	97.8	98.1	97.7	98.0	98.4	98.7	97.7
2003	98.6	98.8	98.6	98.8	98.9	99.2	99.5	99.8	99.5	99.8	99.5	100.2	99.3
2004	99.5	99.6	100.0	100.3	100.2	100.6	100.8	100.8	100.1	100.1	99.9	100.4	100.2
2005	98.6	98.9	99.1	98.8	98.9	99.6	100.5	100.7	95.3	96.2	96.8	97.0	98.4
2006	95.2	95.2	95.4	94.8	95.1	95.4	94.8	95.1	95.1	95.6	95.6	96.2	95.3
2007	97.7	98.0	97.1	96.3	96.2	96.4	96.3	96.0	95.4	95.7	95.7	95.8	96.4
2008	94.4	94.8	95.2	94.7	94.7	95.0	94.5	94.2	93.4	95.2	94.3	94.2	94.6
2009	92.1	91.9	92.1	91.7	91.6	91.7	91.0	90.5	89.8	89.7	89.2	88.5	90.8
Professional and Business Services													
1990	110.2	111.0	112.8	113.4	114.7	116.2	117.9	119.4	119.7	119.0	119.1	118.8	116.0
2000	178.4	179.3	181.1	184.7	184.1	183.4	182.5	184.1	185.3	184.6	185.1	186.6	183.3
2001	183.7	183.5	183.6	183.4	183.1	184.1	181.1	182.2	182.8	182.0	182.3	183.9	183.0
2002	181.7	182.1	183.3	183.7	182.0	182.3	179.3	180.2	179.3	177.7	177.4	177.3	180.5
2003	177.8	178.8	179.7	181.5	180.3	180.2	179.4	180.9	180.4	182.2	183.5	185.3	180.8
2004	181.8	182.9	185.0	186.5	184.8	185.9	183.2	184.2	182.9	184.1	186.1	187.1	184.5
2005	187.0	187.4	189.8	194.1	192.1	191.6	191.8	192.7	175.7	181.0	185.8	188.2	188.1
2006	185.7	188.5	191.4	192.4	193.8	195.6	193.3	195.5	196.8	197.1	197.1	198.1	193.8
2007	197.8	199.7	201.7	200.4	200.9	202.2	199.4	201.6	201.6	205.3	205.8	206.8	201.9
2008	201.7	204.2	204.1	204.5	204.8	204.1	202.6	204.7	203.6	205.9	206.5	206.3	204.4
2009	198.4	198.9	197.8	195.4	195.1	194.0	190.1	190.2	188.1	189.8	192.1	192.1	193.5
Education and Health Services													
1990	158.9	160.1	161.0	162.6	163.2	162.1	160.9	162.0	166.0	170.0	170.8	170.4	164.0
2000	220.6	223.4	223.9	224.6	223.6	220.6	219.5	220.0	224.4	227.9	227.9	228.4	223.7
2001	225.9	227.8	228.3	229.6	229.2	226.6	223.0	225.4	230.9	231.9	234.2	234.4	228.9
2002	230.1	232.5	232.8	235.5	234.8	232.3	230.7	233.8	240.1	240.5	243.5	242.6	235.8
2003	242.2	243.2	242.7	244.7	244.9	241.0	240.2	242.2	247.7	249.2	251.8	250.7	245.0
2004	248.7	249.8	250.5	252.3	251.7	247.6	247.9	251.4	252.7	253.0	254.7	253.5	251.2
2005	254.9	254.9	256.2	258.1	257.1	254.9	252.3	252.6	239.8	222.7	222.3	223.2	245.8
2006	225.1	226.8	228.8	232.0	233.6	233.0	232.2	234.9	238.4	240.0	242.1	241.2	234.0
2007	241.2	243.1	244.6	246.0	245.6	245.6	243.8	248.2	249.2	251.7	253.0	253.9	247.2
2008	251.2	254.2	255.2	255.9	254.9	253.8	254.4	259.1	257.3	260.7	261.8	262.1	256.7
2009	261.0	263.4	264.1	266.6	267.2	262.6	261.7	265.7	266.6	271.2	270.9	271.8	266.1
Leisure and Hospitality													
1990	121.3	123.2	125.6	126.2	129.6	132.2	128.8	130.3	129.9	125.5	124.6	124.5	126.8
2000	189.3	191.0	193.2	195.0	198.6	201.0	197.4	197.3	195.9	194.1	194.5	195.3	195.2
2001	190.4	192.5	196.3	197.4	199.4	200.1	197.1	197.6	195.7	192.7	191.3	191.6	195.2
2002	186.8	189.4	192.1	196.2	198.9	200.3	198.4	198.2	195.7	192.1	193.6	193.1	194.6
2003	190.0	193.3	195.5	199.5	201.5	202.9	202.1	203.0	200.9	198.3	197.6	198.6	198.6
2004	195.1	197.6	201.7	203.5	206.1	208.9	206.7	207.3	205.2	204.0	205.9	206.8	204.1
2005	202.0	203.3	208.3	211.0	215.6	218.0	214.3	214.3	180.4	167.3	169.8	171.9	198.0
2006	169.7	176.6	181.8	181.6	184.8	189.5	188.0	189.0	187.6	186.5	188.2	189.9	184.4
2007	186.4	188.7	193.2	192.5	195.5	198.2	195.3	196.2	193.7	192.3	193.4	194.7	193.3
2008	191.1	193.4	196.0	198.9	200.0	200.3	198.2	198.7	191.4	194.2	194.2	194.7	195.9
2009	190.7	193.4	196.1	196.8	198.9	198.6	195.4	196.1	193.2	196.0	193.3	194.9	195.3
Other Services													
1990	56.8	57.0	57.4	57.9	58.0	58.5	58.6	58.5	58.6	58.2	58.1	58.1	58.0
2000	69.9	70.3	70.9	70.7	71.1	71.3	70.8	71.4	71.4	70.8	70.3	70.5	70.8
2001	68.9	69.2	69.8	71.3	71.6	71.8	70.7	71.1	71.1	70.6	70.3	70.0	70.5
2002	69.3	69.7	70.3	71.1	71.6	71.9	71.0	71.1	71.2	70.9	71.2	71.6	70.9
2003	70.3	70.4	70.9	71.1	71.5	71.8	70.2	70.3	70.4	70.9	70.7	70.7	70.8
2004	70.1	70.4	71.0	71.1	71.4	71.8	71.5	71.4	71.2	70.6	70.6	70.7	71.0
2005	70.0	70.2	71.4	71.6	71.8	72.2	72.2	72.1	65.2	62.1	62.6	63.8	68.8
2006	62.4	63.5	64.6	64.6	65.5	66.1	65.6	65.9	66.7	66.8	67.0	67.4	65.5
2007	67.1	67.8	68.7	67.8	68.3	68.7	68.2	69.0	69.4	69.5	69.5	69.7	68.6
2008	67.8	68.0	68.6	65.8	66.2	66.1	65.1	65.3	64.6	68.0	68.0	68.0	66.8
2009	67.5	67.8	67.9	67.8	68.1	67.8	67.7	68.6	69.0	68.8	69.2	67.8	68.2
Government													
1990	317.9	323.5	324.6	330.9	337.0	327.8	322.9	317.1	321.5	330.4	330.6	329.7	326.1
2000	370.6	376.6	379.5	379.2	385.0	373.9	364.8	359.7	371.6	373.8	373.7	373.0	373.4
2001	372.1	378.1	379.1	377.4	377.0	374.5	362.7	360.7	373.0	376.0	377.6	377.0	373.7
2002	370.0	375.5	377.1	377.5	377.6	376.4	366.7	364.5	375.1	378.7	381.2	378.9	374.9
2003	374.5	381.7	383.1	383.0	382.1	380.2	371.4	367.5	379.2	382.6	384.4	381.4	379.3
2004	377.3	384.1	385.9	385.4	383.8	381.9	373.7	371.8	383.0	386.1	386.9	385.6	382.1
2005	376.5	383.3	383.1	384.2	382.2	379.7	369.8	370.2	378.1	360.2	360.8	358.9	373.9
2006	343.0	349.5	351.1	349.3	349.9	341.6	334.0	339.2	352.9	353.7	356.0	355.6	348.0
2007	348.7	357.2	359.5	353.8	353.6	351.4	340.2	346.3	360.2	363.3	365.9	365.3	355.5
2008	357.2	365.1	364.4	366.7	366.8	361.0	353.3	359.4	365.0	371.1	373.6	370.9	364.5
2009	364.7	371.7	371.5	372.4	371.6	365.9	357.0	357.9	369.3	372.6	373.3	371.3	368.3

Average Weekly Hours by Selected Industry: Louisiana, 2007–2009

(Not seasonally adjusted.)

Industry and year	January	February	March	April	May	June	July	August	September	October	November	December	Annual average
Total Private													
2007	34.5	35.3	35.1	35.7	35.8	35.9	36.1	36.0	36.3	35.8	36.1	36.5	35.8
2008	35.9	35.9	36.3	36.2	36.4	36.9	36.8	36.8	36.0	37.1	37.5	36.4	36.5
2009	36.2	36.6	36.5	35.7	36.1	36.2	35.9	36.6	35.1	35.6	36.7	35.7	36.1
Goods-Producing													
2007	37.6	39.4	39.0	39.3	41.1	40.5	39.7	39.7	39.3	39.5	40.8	40.2	39.7
2008	39.9	40.2	39.8	40.0	40.6	41.3	42.2	41.8	39.7	43.2	43.2	42.0	41.2
2009	41.1	40.8	40.3	39.3	40.9	41.5	40.4	41.1	39.7	41.3	43.3	41.7	40.9
Construction													
2007	38.2	40.7	41.5	41.6	43.3	40.8	39.5	39.3	38.1	40.0	41.3	41.9	40.5
2008	40.7	41.4	41.0	41.4	40.5	42.2	42.0	43.1	39.8	44.4	43.4	41.9	41.8
2009	43.4	42.4	41.7	39.7	40.6	40.4	39.5	40.6	38.0	40.8	43.9	40.9	41.0
Manufacturing													
2007	39.0	39.6	39.5	40.1	41.0	41.5	40.7	41.5	40.8	40.6	41.6	41.3	40.6
2008	39.4	40.9	40.7	40.5	41.9	42.0	43.5	42.0	41.0	43.3	43.3	42.8	41.8
2009	40.8	40.3	40.1	38.9	40.6	41.7	40.8	41.5	40.9	41.8	43.1	42.2	41.1
Trade, Transportation, and Utilities													
2007	34.2	35.0	35.5	36.2	36.7	36.7	37.1	36.9	36.6	36.0	36.0	36.1	36.1
2008	35.4	35.6	35.8	36.0	36.3	36.8	37.7	38.0	35.7	37.3	37.7	36.9	36.6
2009	37.2	37.6	37.6	36.9	37.8	37.6	37.1	37.8	36.2	36.8	37.6	36.7	37.2
Financial Activities													
2007	36.1	35.9	35.0	36.7	35.5	35.9	36.3	35.9	37.3	36.2	36.9	36.9	36.2
2008	36.0	35.5	36.6	36.1	37.6	37.9	35.9	36.5	35.5	35.4	37.1	35.8	36.3
2009	36.1	37.4	37.7	36.3	36.5	36.5	36.6	38.1	35.8	36.1	37.5	35.9	36.7
Professional and Business Services													
2007	36.6	37.0	36.0	37.5	36.5	37.0	37.0	37.3	37.9	37.5	37.6	38.2	37.2
2008	36.7	36.5	37.7	36.8	36.7	38.0	36.9	37.3	36.2	38.2	38.4	37.3	37.2
2009	37.7	38.8	39.3	37.9	38.0	37.6	37.3	38.7	36.9	37.7	39.0	38.0	38.1
Education and Health Services													
2007	32.1	32.5	32.2	32.9	32.5	33.0	33.6	33.2	33.7	32.9	32.8	33.9	32.9
2008	33.7	33.2	33.6	33.2	33.1	33.8	33.6	33.5	34.2	35.2	34.2	33.6	33.8
2009	33.2	33.4	33.3	33.1	32.3	32.3	32.4	32.6	32.0	31.6	32.5	32.3	32.6
Leisure and Hospitality													
2007	28.2	28.1	28.4	28.1	28.5	28.5	28.2	28.0	28.1	28.1	27.8	28.3	28.2
2008	27.9	27.8	28.3	28.2	27.8	28.0	27.9	27.6	27.2	27.5	28.4	27.8	27.9
2009	27.0	27.3	27.2	26.7	26.7	27.2	27.1	27.5	26.6	26.5	26.9	26.5	26.9

Average Hourly Earnings by Selected Industry: Louisiana, 2007–2009

(Dollars, not seasonally adjusted.)

Industry and year	January	February	March	April	May	June	July	August	September	October	November	December	Annual average
Total Private													
2007	18.01	17.93	18.30	18.76	18.56	18.61	18.66	19.08	19.34	19.14	19.08	19.24	18.73
2008	19.06	19.40	18.93	19.04	19.19	19.15	19.22	19.13	19.15	19.32	19.60	19.44	19.22
2009	19.45	19.57	19.42	19.44	19.44	19.42	19.34	19.45	19.53	19.39	19.49	19.56	19.46
Goods-Producing													
2007	22.05	21.95	22.42	22.13	21.82	22.25	22.70	22.84	23.10	22.83	23.01	22.99	22.51
2008	22.30	22.85	22.56	22.69	23.31	22.97	23.05	22.83	22.95	22.84	23.25	23.10	22.90
2009	22.89	22.94	22.84	22.81	22.82	22.33	22.45	23.02	23.21	23.04	22.96	23.27	22.88
Construction													
2007	20.38	20.66	20.31	20.98	20.38	20.87	20.52	20.19	20.87	20.18	20.52	20.71	20.55
2008	20.00	21.48	20.94	20.95	20.96	20.79	21.88	21.16	21.02	21.49	22.57	21.98	21.29
2009	21.54	21.08	21.31	21.46	21.32	20.63	19.97	20.59	20.70	21.08	21.09	21.17	21.00
Manufacturing													
2007	22.67	22.50	22.98	22.15	22.02	22.44	23.18	23.63	23.85	23.79	23.95	23.94	23.10
2008	23.32	23.63	23.88	24.05	24.18	23.71	23.28	23.33	23.60	23.20	23.28	23.21	23.55
2009	23.41	23.66	23.53	23.47	23.49	23.03	23.73	23.52	23.83	23.47	23.26	23.70	23.51
Trade, Transportation, and Utilities													
2007	15.52	15.60	16.05	16.13	16.18	16.05	15.88	15.88	15.80	15.66	15.28	15.27	15.77
2008	15.38	15.12	15.02	15.03	15.35	15.31	15.16	15.53	15.68	15.68	16.05	16.35	15.48
2009	16.36	16.68	16.77	16.62	16.89	16.85	16.74	17.01	16.64	16.50	16.96	16.74	16.73
Financial Activities													
2007	19.78	19.60	20.72	21.36	20.69	20.62	20.18	20.72	21.00	20.93	20.20	20.22	20.50
2008	19.80	19.50	19.76	19.96	19.14	18.82	18.91	19.06	18.37	19.48	20.46	19.12	19.37
2009	19.63	20.47	20.10	19.88	20.61	20.19	19.63	19.66	19.65	19.36	19.30	19.29	19.82
Professional and Business Services													
2007	22.47	22.40	22.41	23.53	22.86	23.03	23.29	23.11	23.60	22.97	23.05	23.08	22.99
2008	23.22	23.53	23.61	23.55	23.58	23.85	23.99	23.70	23.78	24.11	24.09	24.23	23.77
2009	23.86	23.72	23.84	23.80	23.20	23.43	23.55	22.90	23.52	23.24	23.28	23.67	23.50
Education and Health Services													
2007	15.50	15.57	15.73	15.53	15.72	15.58	15.60	15.33	15.34	15.45	15.61	15.51	15.54
2008	15.95	15.57	15.29	15.89	16.19	16.40	16.79	16.51	16.52	15.92	16.64	16.60	16.19
2009	16.84	16.71	16.69	17.14	17.17	17.23	17.40	17.48	17.68	17.45	17.31	17.15	17.18
Leisure and Hospitality													
2007	11.77	11.90	12.03	12.25	12.47	12.23	12.22	12.10	12.23	12.02	12.08	12.08	12.12
2008	12.19	12.01	11.88	11.90	11.70	11.67	11.67	11.70	12.01	12.14	11.74	11.58	11.85
2009	11.80	11.93	11.65	11.65	11.72	11.69	11.58	11.62	12.06	11.97	12.10	12.10	11.82

Average Weekly Earnings by Selected Industry: Louisiana, 2007–2009

(Dollars, not seasonally adjusted.)

Industry and year	January	February	March	April	May	June	July	August	September	October	November	December	Annual average
Total Private													
2007	621.35	632.93	642.33	669.73	664.45	668.10	673.63	686.88	702.04	685.21	688.79	702.26	670.53
2008	684.25	696.46	687.16	689.25	698.52	706.64	707.30	703.98	689.40	716.77	735.00	707.62	701.53
2009	704.09	716.26	708.83	694.01	701.78	703.00	694.31	711.87	685.50	690.28	715.28	698.29	702.51
Goods-Producing													
2007	829.08	864.83	874.38	869.71	896.80	901.13	901.19	906.75	907.83	901.79	938.81	924.20	893.65
2008	889.77	918.57	897.89	907.60	946.39	948.66	972.71	954.29	911.12	986.69	1004.40	970.20	943.48
2009	940.78	935.95	920.45	896.43	933.34	926.70	906.98	946.12	921.44	951.55	994.17	970.36	935.79
Construction													
2007	778.52	840.86	842.87	872.77	882.45	851.50	810.54	793.47	795.15	807.20	847.48	867.75	832.28
2008	814.00	889.27	858.54	867.33	848.88	877.34	918.96	912.00	836.60	954.16	979.54	920.96	889.92
2009	934.84	893.79	888.63	851.96	865.59	833.45	788.82	835.95	786.60	860.06	925.85	865.85	861.00
Manufacturing													
2007	884.13	891.00	907.71	888.22	902.82	931.26	943.43	980.65	973.08	965.87	996.32	988.72	937.86
2008	918.81	966.47	971.92	974.03	1013.14	995.82	1012.68	979.86	967.60	1004.56	1008.02	993.39	984.39
2009	955.13	953.50	943.55	912.98	953.69	960.35	968.18	976.08	974.65	981.05	1002.51	1000.14	966.26
Trade, Transportation, and Utilities													
2007	530.78	546.00	569.78	583.91	593.81	589.04	589.15	585.97	578.28	563.76	550.08	551.25	569.30
2008	544.45	538.27	537.72	541.08	557.21	563.41	571.53	590.14	559.78	584.86	605.09	603.32	566.57
2009	608.59	627.17	630.55	613.28	638.44	633.56	621.05	642.98	602.37	607.20	637.70	614.36	622.36
Financial Activities													
2007	714.06	703.64	725.20	783.91	734.50	740.26	732.53	743.85	783.30	757.67	745.38	746.12	742.10
2008	712.80	692.25	723.22	720.56	719.66	713.28	678.87	695.69	652.14	689.59	759.07	684.50	703.13
2009	708.64	765.58	757.77	721.64	752.27	736.94	718.46	749.05	703.47	698.90	723.75	692.51	727.39
Professional and Business Services													
2007	822.40	828.80	806.76	882.38	834.39	852.11	861.73	862.00	894.44	861.38	866.68	881.66	855.23
2008	852.17	858.85	890.10	866.64	865.39	906.30	885.23	884.01	860.84	921.00	925.06	903.78	884.24
2009	899.52	920.34	936.91	902.02	881.60	880.97	878.42	886.23	867.89	876.15	907.92	899.46	895.35
Education and Health Services													
2007	497.55	506.03	506.51	510.94	510.90	514.14	524.16	508.96	516.96	508.31	512.01	525.79	511.27
2008	537.52	516.92	513.74	527.55	535.89	554.32	564.14	553.09	564.98	560.38	569.09	557.76	547.22
2009	559.09	558.11	555.78	567.33	554.59	556.53	563.76	569.85	565.76	551.42	562.58	553.95	560.07
Leisure and Hospitality													
2007	331.91	334.39	341.65	344.23	355.40	348.56	344.60	338.80	343.66	337.76	335.82	341.86	341.78
2008	340.10	333.88	336.20	335.58	325.26	326.76	325.59	322.92	326.67	333.85	333.42	321.92	330.62
2009	318.60	325.69	316.88	311.06	312.92	317.97	313.82	319.55	320.80	317.21	325.49	320.65	317.96

MAINE
At a Glance

Population:
  1990 census: 1,227,928
  2000 census: 1,274,923
  2009 estimate: 1,318,301

Percent change in population:
  1990–2000: 3.8%
  2000–2009: 3.4%

Percent change in total nonfarm employment:
  1990–2009: 11.2%
  2008–2009: -3.6%

Industry with the largest growth in employment, 1990–2009 (thousands):
  Education and Health Services, 52.5

Industry with the largest decline or smallest growth in employment, 1990–2009 (thousands):
  Manufacturing, -40.5

Civilian labor force:
  1990: 631,147
  2000: 672,440
  2009: 704,134

Unemployment rate and rank among states (lowest to highest):
  1990: 5.3%, 23rd
  2000: 3.3%, 14th
  2009: 8.0%, 21st

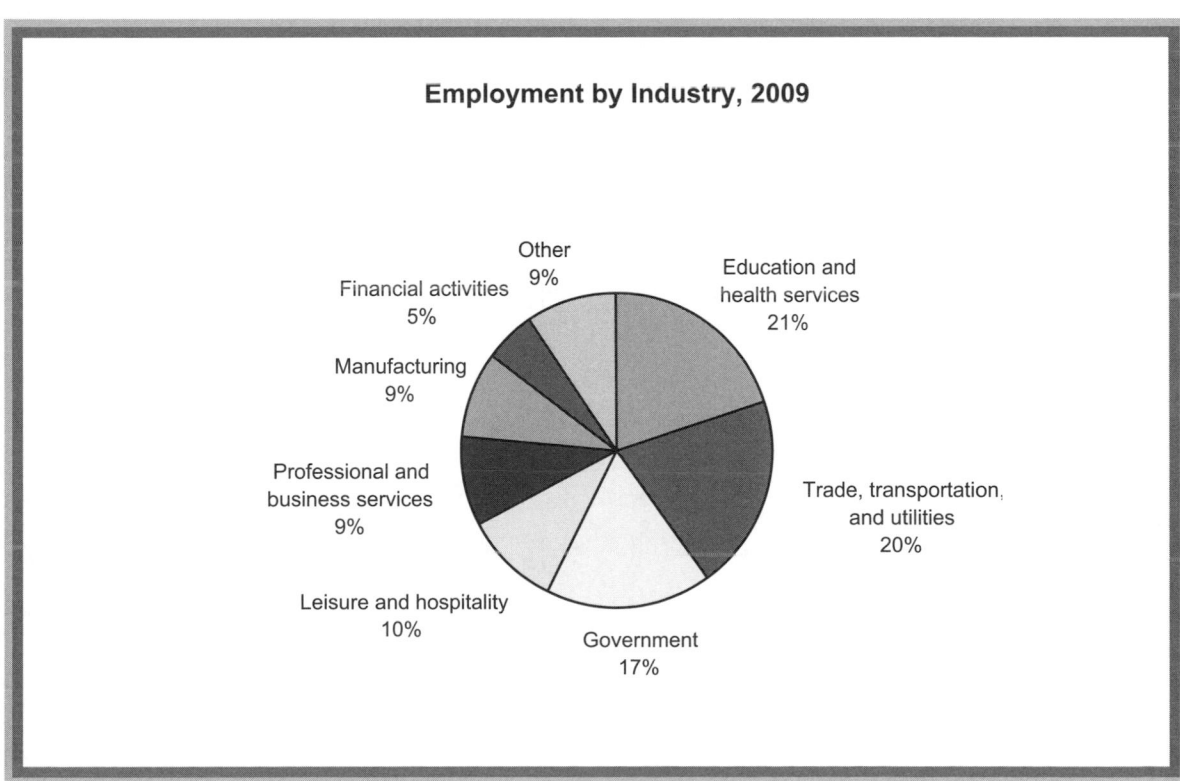

Employment by Industry, 2009

Other 9%
Financial activities 5%
Manufacturing 9%
Professional and business services 9%
Leisure and hospitality 10%
Government 17%
Education and health services 21%
Trade, transportation, and utilities 20%

Employment by Industry: Maine, Selected Years, 1990–2009

(Numbers in thousands, not seasonally adjusted.)

Industry and year	January	February	March	April	May	June	July	August	September	October	November	December	Annual average
Total Nonfarm													
1990	526.0	522.8	525.1	530.2	541.1	554.4	542.1	540.7	541.4	539.7	530.9	525.6	535.0
2000	576.1	580.2	586.0	593.8	606.9	617.8	615.8	614.4	614.7	611.5	612.8	611.7	603.5
2001	588.5	590.3	592.6	601.5	613.1	625.2	618.0	618.4	618.0	614.6	610.4	607.1	608.1
2002	583.7	585.5	588.9	598.3	610.4	622.3	618.5	618.2	617.1	614.2	610.5	609.9	606.5
2003	584.0	585.2	587.8	595.2	608.2	618.7	617.3	619.2	618.8	617.5	615.5	614.0	606.8
2004	588.4	591.6	594.0	601.9	614.0	625.4	622.8	623.5	622.8	620.0	619.6	616.7	611.7
2005	589.5	591.3	592.1	603.0	614.6	625.6	623.2	623.2	623.1	619.2	618.2	617.8	611.7
2006	592.1	592.6	596.1	606.5	617.4	629.9	624.1	626.6	625.1	622.9	621.1	621.4	614.7
2007	596.1	596.2	599.1	604.4	618.2	632.4	629.0	629.0	628.6	627.8	626.6	625.2	617.7
2008	599.7	600.1	601.8	609.6	623.0	633.6	630.0	628.1	625.8	625.0	617.6	612.6	617.2
2009	584.0	582.5	579.9	588.1	601.6	606.9	602.9	602.9	604.2	601.7	593.7	591.5	595.0
Total Private													
1990	429.4	425.4	426.9	431.0	441.8	456.9	456.8	456.9	446.5	441.6	430.9	426.5	439.2
2000	478.7	479.0	482.2	491.5	502.7	517.0	528.3	528.4	515.0	508.7	508.4	507.0	503.9
2001	488.0	486.4	488.3	496.8	508.0	522.1	528.1	528.7	515.5	508.4	503.5	499.4	506.1
2002	481.8	480.3	482.7	492.8	504.1	517.6	526.8	527.6	514.5	508.1	502.7	501.9	503.4
2003	481.1	478.7	480.8	488.5	501.5	514.2	525.6	527.8	515.5	510.4	507.1	505.3	503.0
2004	484.8	484.3	486.2	494.0	506.3	519.6	529.7	531.0	518.3	511.9	510.2	507.6	507.0
2005	485.5	483.7	484.5	495.4	506.7	519.3	530.2	530.6	518.0	511.5	509.2	508.9	507.0
2006	487.8	485.9	488.8	499.3	509.7	525.3	532.1	533.4	520.7	514.8	512.2	512.7	510.2
2007	492.4	489.9	492.1	497.9	510.5	527.3	536.8	537.6	523.9	519.5	517.8	516.5	513.5
2008	495.8	493.6	494.4	501.9	515.1	528.4	537.9	535.8	521.4	516.8	508.8	504.1	512.8
2009	480.5	476.3	473.3	480.7	494.1	502.3	512.4	512.3	500.7	495.1	486.8	484.2	491.6
Goods-Producing													
1990	124.0	122.3	122.3	123.0	126.9	130.6	128.0	131.6	128.0	125.5	121.2	118.0	125.1
2000	108.3	108.4	108.8	110.9	113.0	114.5	114.4	116.2	109.9	109.3	112.6	111.1	111.5
2001	106.7	105.3	105.8	106.2	108.7	110.9	109.1	110.1	108.3	106.0	105.4	102.8	107.1
2002	98.0	96.5	96.3	98.5	100.5	102.7	101.5	103.3	101.8	101.3	101.2	99.3	100.1
2003	93.9	92.1	92.6	94.0	97.2	99.2	99.2	100.9	99.8	99.4	99.5	97.6	97.1
2004	93.1	91.7	92.3	93.4	96.4	98.6	99.0	100.2	98.9	97.8	98.3	96.5	96.4
2005	91.3	90.5	90.5	92.8	95.0	97.2	97.6	98.1	96.6	95.6	96.3	94.8	94.7
2006	90.7	89.8	90.3	92.3	94.7	96.8	97.1	97.8	96.1	95.1	94.5	93.3	94.0
2007	89.3	87.7	88.5	89.7	92.3	95.7	96.1	96.5	95.1	95.2	95.2	93.5	92.9
2008	89.1	87.9	87.7	88.8	91.7	94.0	94.2	93.9	92.1	91.8	90.3	87.1	90.7
2009	80.9	78.6	76.8	77.5	80.0	81.1	82.0	82.1	80.9	80.5	80.5	78.1	79.9
Mining and Logging													
1990	3.8	3.7	3.3	2.0	2.3	3.1	3.6	3.7	3.7	3.6	3.6	3.7	3.3
2000	2.9	3.0	2.8	1.9	1.9	2.5	2.8	2.9	2.9	2.9	2.9	3.0	2.7
2001	2.9	2.9	2.8	2.0	1.9	2.5	2.8	2.8	2.9	2.8	2.8	2.8	2.7
2002	2.8	2.8	2.7	2.0	1.9	2.4	2.7	2.8	2.8	2.8	2.8	2.8	2.6
2003	2.7	2.7	2.6	2.0	1.8	2.4	2.7	2.8	2.7	2.7	2.7	2.7	2.5
2004	2.7	2.7	2.7	2.1	2.0	2.4	2.6	2.7	2.7	2.8	2.9	2.9	2.6
2005	2.9	2.9	2.8	2.2	2.0	2.5	2.8	2.8	2.8	2.8	2.9	2.9	2.7
2006	2.9	2.9	2.8	2.1	2.1	2.6	2.9	2.9	2.9	3.0	2.8	2.9	2.7
2007	2.9	2.9	2.9	2.0	1.8	2.5	2.8	2.8	2.8	2.8	2.9	2.8	2.7
2008	2.8	2.8	2.8	2.1	1.8	2.3	2.6	2.6	2.6	2.8	2.8	2.8	2.6
2009	2.8	2.8	2.6	1.5	1.5	1.9	2.4	2.6	2.6	2.6	2.7	2.7	2.4
Construction													
1990	27.0	26.0	26.3	27.7	30.7	31.8	32.4	32.2	30.6	29.7	27.0	24.3	28.8
2000	25.7	25.4	25.8	28.4	30.2	30.8	31.7	31.7	31.2	31.0	29.9	28.8	29.2
2001	26.6	26.1	26.7	28.3	30.8	32.0	32.5	32.2	31.7	31.3	30.6	29.0	29.8
2002	26.4	25.5	25.6	28.0	30.1	31.2	31.7	31.8	31.3	31.4	30.8	29.5	29.4
2003	27.0	26.0	26.5	28.5	31.3	32.5	33.2	33.2	32.8	32.8	31.8	30.3	30.5
2004	28.0	27.5	28.3	29.4	31.7	32.6	33.3	33.0	32.3	31.9	31.2	29.9	30.8
2005	27.0	26.5	26.7	29.2	31.4	32.8	33.6	33.2	32.7	32.4	31.9	30.4	30.7
2006	28.3	27.5	28.0	30.3	32.3	33.7	33.9	33.9	33.1	32.6	31.6	30.6	31.3
2007	28.1	26.9	27.4	29.1	31.4	33.0	33.2	33.3	32.8	32.7	31.9	30.3	30.8
2008	27.6	26.7	26.6	28.0	30.6	31.8	31.8	31.5	30.8	30.9	29.3	27.1	29.4
2009	24.0	22.8	22.3	23.8	26.0	26.7	27.1	26.9	26.4	25.4	25.2	23.3	25.0
Manufacturing													
1990	93.2	92.6	92.7	93.3	93.9	95.7	92.0	95.7	93.7	92.2	90.6	90.0	93.0
2000	79.7	80.0	80.2	80.6	80.9	81.2	79.9	81.6	75.8	75.4	79.8	79.3	79.5
2001	77.2	76.3	76.3	75.9	76.0	76.4	73.8	75.1	73.7	71.9	72.0	71.0	74.6
2002	68.8	68.2	68.0	68.5	68.5	69.1	67.1	68.7	67.7	67.1	67.6	67.0	68.0
2003	64.2	63.4	63.5	63.5	64.1	64.3	63.3	64.9	64.3	63.9	65.0	64.6	64.1
2004	62.4	61.5	61.3	61.9	62.7	63.6	63.1	64.5	63.9	63.1	64.2	63.7	63.0
2005	61.4	61.1	61.0	61.4	61.6	61.9	61.2	62.1	61.1	60.4	61.5	61.5	61.4
2006	59.5	59.4	59.5	59.9	60.3	60.5	60.3	61.0	60.1	59.5	60.1	59.8	60.0
2007	58.3	57.9	58.2	58.6	59.1	60.2	60.1	60.4	59.5	59.7	60.4	60.4	59.4
2008	58.7	58.4	58.3	58.7	59.3	59.9	59.8	59.8	58.7	58.1	58.2	57.2	58.8
2009	54.1	53.0	51.9	52.2	52.5	52.5	52.5	52.6	51.9	52.5	52.6	52.1	52.5

Employment by Industry: Maine, Selected Years, 1990–2009—*Continued*

(Numbers in thousands, not seasonally adjusted.)

Industry and year	January	February	March	April	May	June	July	August	September	October	November	December	Annual average
Service-Providing													
1990	402.0	400.5	402.8	407.2	414.2	423.8	414.1	409.1	413.4	414.2	409.7	407.6	409.9
2000	467.8	471.8	477.2	482.9	493.9	503.3	501.4	498.2	504.8	502.2	500.2	500.6	492.0
2001	481.8	485.0	486.8	495.3	504.4	514.3	508.9	508.3	509.7	508.6	505.0	504.3	501.0
2002	485.7	489.0	492.6	499.8	509.9	519.6	517.0	514.9	515.3	512.9	509.3	510.6	506.4
2003	490.1	493.1	495.2	501.2	511.0	519.5	518.1	518.3	519.0	518.1	516.0	516.4	509.7
2004	495.3	499.9	501.7	508.5	517.6	526.8	523.8	523.3	523.9	522.2	521.3	520.2	515.4
2005	498.2	500.8	501.6	510.2	519.6	528.4	525.6	525.1	526.5	523.6	521.9	523.0	517.0
2006	501.4	502.8	505.8	514.2	522.7	533.1	527.0	528.8	529.0	527.8	526.6	528.1	520.6
2007	506.8	508.5	510.6	514.7	525.9	536.7	532.9	532.5	533.5	532.6	531.4	531.7	524.8
2008	510.6	512.2	514.1	520.8	531.3	539.6	535.8	534.2	533.7	533.2	527.3	525.5	526.5
2009	503.1	503.9	503.1	510.6	521.6	525.8	520.9	520.8	523.3	521.2	513.2	513.4	515.1
Trade, Transportation, and Utilities													
1990	112.4	109.6	109.3	108.7	110.9	113.6	113.6	114.0	112.3	113.5	114.5	115.3	112.3
2000	118.4	116.1	116.3	117.4	119.4	123.8	126.1	126.1	125.2	126.1	128.8	128.7	122.7
2001	120.9	118.2	117.7	119.3	121.8	125.4	126.7	126.6	124.7	126.0	127.9	128.1	123.6
2002	120.3	118.1	118.1	119.6	121.7	125.2	127.1	127.0	124.5	124.0	125.7	127.4	123.2
2003	119.5	116.9	116.8	118.1	120.9	124.2	126.2	127.0	124.7	125.7	128.6	129.4	123.2
2004	121.3	119.8	119.7	120.8	123.4	126.4	128.2	128.3	126.0	127.2	130.0	131.5	125.7
2005	123.1	120.7	119.8	121.3	123.0	126.1	127.7	127.9	126.1	126.4	129.4	130.8	125.2
2006	123.4	119.9	120.3	121.7	123.3	126.7	127.7	128.0	126.2	127.2	131.1	132.2	125.6
2007	123.9	120.7	121.1	121.0	123.8	127.2	129.1	129.2	126.5	177.4	131.1	132.0	126.1
2008	124.7	121.1	120.8	121.7	123.9	126.4	127.7	127.6	124.8	125.3	126.9	127.0	124.8
2009	118.8	115.4	114.3	114.7	117.5	119.5	120.8	121.1	119.2	118.3	120.3	120.7	118.4
Wholesale Trade													
1990	18.3	18.2	18.2	18.1	18.3	18.5	18.4	18.6	18.2	18.1	18.0	17.9	18.2
2000	18.9	18.8	18.9	19.2	19.3	19.6	19.9	20.0	19.9	20.0	19.9	20.0	19.5
2001	20.0	19.8	19.8	20.1	20.1	20.5	20.7	20.6	20.3	20.4	20.2	20.3	20.2
2002	19.8	19.7	19.7	20.0	20.1	20.4	20.9	20.9	20.8	20.8	20.8	20.8	20.4
2003	20.4	20.2	20.3	20.6	20.9	21.3	21.5	21.6	21.5	21.4	21.5	21.5	21.1
2004	20.9	20.9	21.0	21.2	21.4	21.6	21.9	21.9	21.5	21.5	21.3	21.3	21.4
2005	20.9	20.9	20.9	21.1	21.4	21.7	21.9	21.9	21.7	21.6	21.5	21.6	21.4
2006	21.1	21.0	21.1	21.4	21.5	22.0	22.0	21.9	21.6	21.5	21.3	21.3	21.5
2007	20.8	20.7	20.9	20.9	21.2	21.4	21.6	21.5	21.2	21.1	20.9	21.0	21.1
2008	20.7	20.5	20.5	20.5	20.8	21.1	21.3	21.2	20.9	20.8	20.5	20.5	20.8
2009	19.7	19.4	19.3	19.3	19.5	19.6	20.0	19.9	19.6	19.3	18.9	18.9	19.5
Retail Trade													
1990	75.7	73.2	72.9	72.8	74.3	76.3	76.0	76.1	74.9	76.0	77.1	77.8	75.3
2000	80.8	79.0	79.1	80.1	81.8	84.7	86.3	86.7	85.7	86.2	88.3	88.8	83.9
2001	82.3	80.2	79.8	81.3	83.6	86.0	87.0	86.9	85.3	85.9	88.1	88.1	84.5
2002	82.4	80.5	80.7	81.8	83.5	86.3	87.5	87.4	84.9	84.4	86.2	87.4	84.4
2003	81.2	79.4	79.4	80.6	82.7	85.0	86.5	87.0	84.7	85.4	87.8	88.3	84.0
2004	82.5	81.5	81.4	82.3	84.3	86.4	87.8	87.7	85.9	86.5	88.7	89.7	85.4
2005	83.6	81.7	81.3	82.8	84.0	86.1	87.2	87.3	85.6	85.5	88.0	89.0	85.2
2006	83.8	80.9	81.4	82.7	83.9	86.1	87.0	87.5	85.8	86.4	89.6	90.2	85.4
2007	84.3	81.6	82.0	82.2	84.5	87.0	88.5	88.4	85.8	86.4	89.7	90.2	85.9
2008	85.4	82.5	82.3	83.4	85.1	86.9	87.9	87.9	85.4	85.8	87.2	87.1	85.6
2009	81.3	79.0	78.2	78.8	81.2	83.0	83.9	84.3	82.6	82.0	84.0	83.8	81.8
Transportation and Utilities													
1990	18.4	18.2	18.2	17.8	18.3	18.8	19.2	19.3	19.2	19.4	19.4	19.6	18.8
2000	18.7	18.3	18.3	18.1	18.5	19.5	19.9	19.4	19.6	19.9	20.6	19.9	19.2
2001	18.6	18.2	18.1	17.9	18.1	18.9	19.0	19.1	19.1	19.7	19.6	19.7	18.8
2002	18.1	17.9	17.7	17.8	18.1	18.5	18.7	18.7	18.8	18.8	18.7	19.2	18.4
2003	17.9	17.3	17.1	16.9	17.3	17.9	18.2	18.4	18.5	18.9	19.3	19.6	18.1
2004	17.9	17.4	17.3	17.3	17.7	18.4	18.5	18.7	18.6	19.2	20.0	20.5	18.5
2005	18.6	18.1	17.6	17.4	17.6	18.3	18.6	18.7	18.8	19.3	19.9	20.2	18.6
2006	18.5	18.0	17.8	17.6	17.9	18.6	18.7	18.6	18.8	19.3	20.2	20.7	18.7
2007	18.8	18.4	18.2	17.9	18.1	18.8	19.0	19.3	19.5	19.9	20.5	20.8	19.1
2008	18.6	18.1	18.0	17.8	18.0	18.4	18.5	18.5	18.5	18.7	19.2	19.4	18.5
2009	17.8	17.0	16.8	16.6	16.8	16.9	16.9	16.9	16.9	17.0	17.0	17.4	18.0	17.1
Information													
1990	10.5	10.4	10.4	10.4	10.3	10.4	10.3	10.2	10.1	10.0	9.9	9.9	10.2
2000	12.1	12.1	12.2	12.3	12.3	12.2	12.3	11.0	12.2	12.2	12.3	12.3	12.1
2001	12.3	12.4	12.3	12.3	12.3	12.3	12.2	12.1	12.0	11.8	11.9	11.9	12.2
2002	11.8	11.7	11.6	11.6	11.7	11.7	11.6	11.5	11.4	11.3	11.5	11.6	11.6
2003	11.3	11.4	11.3	11.3	11.2	11.3	11.3	11.3	11.2	11.5	11.5	11.6	11.4
2004	11.6	11.4	11.4	11.0	10.9	11.1	11.3	11.2	11.0	11.1	11.3	11.3	11.2
2005	11.2	11.1	11.2	11.1	11.2	11.1	11.2	11.2	11.1	11.1	11.1	11.3	11.2
2006	11.2	11.2	11.1	11.1	11.1	11.3	11.3	11.3	11.1	11.3	11.3	11.4	11.2
2007	11.2	11.4	11.4	11.4	11.3	11.3	11.3	11.2	11.0	11.1	11.1	11.1	11.2
2008	10.9	10.9	10.8	10.7	10.6	10.7	10.6	10.5	10.2	10.3	10.1	10.0	10.5
2009	9.6	9.4	9.2	9.3	9.4	9.2	9.2	9.1	9.0	9.1	9.1	9.1	9.2

Employment by Industry: Maine, Selected Years, 1990–2009—*Continued*

(Numbers in thousands, not seasonally adjusted.)

Industry and year	January	February	March	April	May	June	July	August	September	October	November	December	Annual average
Financial Activities													
1990	26.4	26.3	26.4	26.4	26.6	27.1	27.0	26.8	26.6	26.5	26.3	26.1	26.5
2000	33.4	33.3	33.5	33.7	33.8	34.3	34.9	34.9	34.4	34.2	34.1	34.6	34.1
2001	34.2	34.5	34.7	35.0	35.0	35.4	35.9	35.9	35.2	35.1	35.1	35.4	35.1
2002	34.6	34.6	34.8	34.7	34.9	35.5	35.7	35.6	35.2	35.2	35.2	35.4	35.1
2003	34.8	34.8	34.9	35.0	35.0	35.2	35.7	35.5	35.0	34.9	34.9	35.3	35.1
2004	34.9	35.0	34.9	34.8	35.0	35.3	35.5	35.4	34.6	34.5	34.3	34.4	34.9
2005	34.0	33.9	34.0	33.9	34.1	34.3	34.8	34.6	34.0	34.2	34.0	34.1	34.2
2006	33.7	33.6	33.5	33.5	33.5	34.1	34.0	34.1	33.4	33.5	33.2	33.5	33.6
2007	33.0	33.0	33.0	33.1	33.3	33.7	33.9	33.7	33.1	32.8	32.7	32.8	33.2
2008	32.4	32.5	32.5	32.7	33.0	33.3	33.5	33.4	32.5	32.3	32.2	32.0	32.7
2009	31.6	31.6	31.6	31.5	32.0	32.3	32.5	32.3	31.6	31.2	30.4	30.4	31.6
Professional and Business Services													
1990	33.1	32.9	33.2	34.2	34.6	35.4	34.4	34.3	33.3	33.1	32.6	32.5	33.6
2000	49.0	49.1	49.8	51.2	52.0	53.3	53.7	53.7	53.1	52.4	52.0	52.6	51.8
2001	50.8	51.0	51.4	52.7	53.2	53.8	52.8	52.5	51.4	51.1	50.6	50.4	51.8
2002	49.4	49.4	50.0	51.4	52.0	53.1	52.9	52.8	51.7	51.7	51.3	50.8	51.4
2003	49.2	49.1	49.3	50.1	50.5	51.1	51.4	51.8	51.1	50.5	49.9	49.5	50.3
2004	47.8	48.2	48.4	49.5	50.2	50.7	50.7	50.7	49.7	49.7	49.9	49.3	49.6
2005	47.8	47.8	48.2	49.7	50.6	51.2	51.9	52.1	51.3	51.2	50.9	51.0	50.3
2006	48.9	49.4	49.7	52.3	53.0	54.0	53.5	53.6	52.8	52.3	52.4	52.6	52.0
2007	51.1	51.0	51.3	53.0	54.0	55.4	55.5	55.7	54.8	55.1	55.3	55.2	54.0
2008	54.2	54.5	55.0	56.3	57.1	58.1	58.1	58.1	57.1	57.2	56.4	56.0	56.5
2009	54.2	53.9	53.6	54.7	55.7	56.0	55.8	56.0	55.1	55.1	53.7	53.3	54.8
Education and Health Services													
1990	64.7	66.0	66.2	67.1	66.6	66.9	65.5	65.1	66.8	67.3	67.1	67.1	66.4
2000	94.2	96.5	96.9	97.2	97.2	95.8	96.8	96.7	98.8	99.5	100.0	100.0	97.5
2001	97.7	100.1	100.5	100.5	100.5	99.7	99.7	99.9	101.3	102.8	102.9	103.2	100.7
2002	101.9	104.2	104.8	105.5	105.3	104.0	104.4	104.0	105.2	106.4	106.8	106.6	104.9
2003	104.3	106.3	107.0	107.2	106.9	106.0	106.7	106.3	108.0	109.5	109.6	109.9	107.3
2004	108.4	110.3	111.0	111.4	110.9	109.9	110.1	110.0	111.2	112.5	113.1	112.1	110.9
2005	110.0	111.6	111.9	112.7	112.8	111.5	111.5	111.3	112.3	113.6	114.1	113.5	112.2
2006	111.6	113.6	114.2	114.4	114.1	113.0	112.9	113.3	114.4	115.5	115.9	115.9	114.1
2007	114.2	116.5	116.6	116.4	116.2	115.1	114.7	115.0	115.9	117.1	117.5	117.7	116.1
2008	115.3	117.4	117.7	117.7	117.8	116.6	116.5	116.2	117.4	119.1	119.3	119.1	117.5
2009	117.2	119.0	119.1	119.8	119.8	117.8	117.6	117.5	118.3	120.1	120.2	120.0	118.9
Leisure and Hospitality													
1990	40.8	40.6	41.8	43.9	48.4	55.4	60.3	57.5	52.3	48.6	42.5	40.9	47.8
2000	45.5	45.7	46.8	50.6	56.6	64.4	71.1	70.9	62.9	56.7	50.4	49.4	55.9
2001	46.7	46.2	47.0	51.9	57.4	65.2	71.9	72.1	63.5	56.6	50.7	48.7	56.5
2002	46.7	46.7	47.9	51.9	58.2	65.4	73.0	72.8	64.6	58.5	51.3	51.1	57.3
2003	48.0	48.0	48.7	52.5	59.3	66.4	74.3	74.4	65.5	59.0	53.3	52.2	58.5
2004	48.1	48.3	48.9	53.2	59.4	67.4	74.2	74.5	66.6	59.1	53.4	52.6	58.8
2005	48.6	48.6	49.2	53.9	59.8	67.6	74.9	75.0	66.4	59.5	53.6	53.5	59.2
2006	48.9	49.0	50.2	54.5	60.3	69.4	75.3	75.2	67.1	60.2	54.1	54.0	59.9
2007	50.3	50.3	50.8	53.6	59.6	68.7	75.6	75.8	67.4	61.0	55.2	54.5	60.2
2008	49.8	49.8	50.3	54.3	61.0	69.0	76.8	76.0	67.5	60.8	53.7	53.1	60.2
2009	48.8	49.0	49.5	53.7	60.0	66.5	74.3	74.1	67.0	61.6	53.5	53.4	59.3
Other Services													
1990	17.5	17.3	17.3	17.3	17.5	17.5	17.7	17.4	17.1	17.1	16.8	16.7	17.3
2000	17.8	17.8	17.9	18.2	18.4	18.7	19.0	18.9	18.5	18.3	18.2	18.3	18.3
2001	18.7	18.7	18.9	18.9	19.1	19.4	19.8	19.5	19.1	19.0	19.0	18.9	19.1
2002	19.1	19.1	19.2	19.6	19.8	20.0	20.6	20.6	20.1	19.7	19.7	19.7	19.8
2003	20.1	20.1	20.2	20.3	20.5	20.8	20.8	20.6	20.2	19.9	19.8	19.8	20.3
2004	19.6	19.6	19.6	19.9	20.1	20.2	20.7	20.7	20.3	20.0	19.9	19.9	20.0
2005	19.5	19.5	19.7	20.0	20.2	20.3	20.6	20.4	20.2	19.9	19.8	19.9	20.0
2006	19.4	19.4	19.5	19.5	19.7	20.0	20.3	20.1	19.6	19.7	19.7	19.8	19.7
2007	19.4	19.3	19.4	19.7	20.0	20.2	20.6	20.5	20.1	19.8	19.7	19.7	19.9
2008	19.4	19.5	19.6	19.7	20.0	20.3	20.5	20.1	19.8	20.0	19.9	19.8	19.9
2009	19.4	19.4	19.2	19.5	19.7	19.9	20.2	20.1	19.6	19.2	19.1	19.2	19.5
Government													
1990	96.6	97.4	98.2	99.2	99.3	97.5	85.3	83.8	94.9	98.1	100.0	99.1	95.8
2000	97.4	101.2	103.8	102.3	104.2	100.8	87.5	86.0	99.7	102.8	104.4	104.7	99.6
2001	100.5	103.9	104.3	104.7	105.1	103.1	89.9	89.7	102.5	106.2	106.9	107.7	102.0
2002	101.9	105.2	106.2	105.5	106.3	104.7	91.7	90.6	102.6	106.1	107.8	108.0	103.1
2003	102.9	106.5	107.0	106.7	106.7	104.5	91.7	91.4	103.3	107.1	108.4	108.7	103.7
2004	103.6	107.3	107.8	107.9	107.7	105.8	93.1	92.5	104.5	108.1	109.4	109.1	104.7
2005	104.0	107.6	107.6	107.6	107.9	106.3	93.0	92.6	105.1	107.7	109.0	108.9	104.8
2006	104.3	106.7	107.3	107.2	107.7	104.6	92.0	93.2	104.4	108.1	108.9	108.7	104.4
2007	103.7	106.3	107.0	106.5	107.7	105.1	92.2	91.4	104.7	108.3	108.8	108.7	104.2
2008	103.9	106.5	107.4	107.7	107.9	105.2	92.1	92.3	104.4	108.2	108.8	108.5	104.4
2009	103.5	106.2	106.6	107.4	107.5	104.6	90.5	90.6	103.5	106.6	106.9	107.3	103.4

Average Weekly Hours by Selected Industry: Maine, 2007–2009

(Not seasonally adjusted.)

Industry and year	January	February	March	April	May	June	July	August	September	October	November	December	Annual average
Total Private													
2007	33.6	33.6	34.0	33.9	34.2	34.4	34.7	34.6	34.8	34.4	34.1	34.3	34.2
2008	34.0	34.5	34.4	34.4	34.5	34.7	34.8	34.8	34.4	34.1	33.5	33.2	34.3
2009	33.1	33.3	33.0	33.2	33.0	33.0	33.7	33.8	33.3	33.6	33.4	33.4	33.3
Goods-Producing													
2007	38.6	37.8	38.9	39.1	39.5	40.0	40.3	40.1	40.4	39.7	40.2	39.9	39.6
2008	40.5	39.5	40.2	40.5	41.8	42.1	41.5	41.3	41.4	40.9	39.9	39.0	40.7
2009	39.0	39.1	38.8	38.6	39.1	38.8	38.7	39.7	39.5	40.7	40.4	39.5	39.3
Construction													
2007	36.8	35.2	37.8	38.0	39.8	40.3	40.0	39.8	39.6	38.8	39.2	39.5	38.8
2008	40.0	37.3	39.9	40.3	41.7	41.2	41.0	40.2	40.7	40.2	38.2	36.6	39.8
2009	37.1	38.3	37.6	38.8	38.1	37.6	38.5	40.0	38.5	40.0	39.2	38.0	38.5
Manufacturing													
2007	39.4	38.7	39.3	39.7	39.2	39.5	40.1	39.9	40.7	40.0	40.7	40.4	39.8
2008	41.1	40.6	40.4	40.6	40.1	40.7	40.1	40.2	40.3	40.1	39.7	39.1	40.3
2009	39.5	39.0	39.0	38.2	39.0	38.7	38.3	39.1	39.5	40.3	41.0	40.3	39.3
Trade, Transportation, and Utilities													
2007	32.6	32.8	33.2	32.8	33.5	33.6	33.9	33.8	33.6	33.2	31.8	32.8	33.1
2008	31.6	33.2	32.7	32.8	32.4	33.2	33.5	33.5	32.7	32.3	31.1	32.1	32.6
2009	30.8	32.0	31.3	31.4	30.4	31.1	32.4	32.8	32.0	31.5	30.8	32.3	31.6
Professional and Business Services													
2007	36.1	36.9	36.9	36.8	37.2	37.0	37.0	36.8	36.5	36.2	36.1	35.9	36.6
2008	35.6	36.3	36.2	36.1	35.8	35.8	35.9	36.1	36.2	36.0	36.2	35.5	36.0
2009	36.4	36.2	36.1	35.6	35.5	35.3	35.4	35.4	34.7	35.3	35.0	34.9	35.5
Education and Health Services													
2007	31.9	31.9	31.8	31.6	31.6	31.9	32.0	31.9	31.9	31.9	32.5	32.1	31.9
2008	32.3	32.4	32.5	32.6	32.5	32.5	32.5	32.4	32.4	32.1	32.2	31.7	32.3
2009	31.8	31.9	31.7	32.0	31.9	32.0	32.0	31.9	32.1	32.5	32.7	32.6	32.1
Leisure and Hospitality													
2007	23.0	23.0	23.2	23.6	23.6	24.2	26.0	26.7	24.5	24.4	23.3	23.0	24.2
2008	23.0	23.8	23.2	23.2	24.3	24.6	26.5	27.1	24.5	24.2	23.2	21.9	24.3
2009	22.1	22.9	23.5	23.4	23.8	23.6	27.3	27.2	25.6	25.8	24.2	23.1	24.6

Average Hourly Earnings by Selected Industry: Maine, 2007–2009

(Dollars, not seasonally adjusted.)

Industry and year	January	February	March	April	May	June	July	August	September	October	November	December	Annual average
Total Private													
2007	18.81	18.83	18.91	19.13	18.90	18.64	18.56	18.45	18.74	18.64	18.69	18.63	18.74
2008	18.79	18.86	18.80	18.95	18.77	18.87	18.78	18.88	19.12	19.10	19.26	19.35	18.96
2009	19.30	19.39	19.27	19.25	19.09	19.00	18.76	18.96	19.23	19.05	19.39	19.25	19.16
Goods-Producing													
2007	20.58	20.65	20.56	20.87	20.66	20.40	20.45	20.51	20.63	20.49	20.70	20.54	20.58
2008	20.60	20.51	20.56	20.57	20.32	20.58	20.56	20.62	20.67	20.69	20.73	21.06	20.62
2009	20.90	21.13	21.05	21.07	21.15	21.26	21.14	21.27	21.63	21.11	21.33	21.45	21.21
Construction													
2007	18.85	19.06	19.33	19.38	19.26	18.95	18.79	18.71	18.74	18.68	18.77	18.93	18.94
2008	18.67	18.87	19.08	19.28	19.12	19.03	18.97	18.92	19.13	19.35	19.28	19.74	19.11
2009	19.71	19.94	19.72	19.95	19.79	19.83	19.71	19.98	19.99	19.82	19.89	19.92	19.86
Manufacturing													
2007	21.65	21.67	21.41	21.69	21.50	21.40	21.61	21.72	21.92	21.67	21.86	21.66	21.65
2008	21.81	21.51	21.52	21.48	21.29	21.61	21.66	21.84	21.81	21.68	21.74	21.95	21.66
2009	22.00	22.12	22.02	22.00	22.18	22.38	22.32	22.41	22.79	22.31	22.55	22.59	22.31
Trade, Transportation, and Utilities													
2007	16.78	17.15	17.27	17.23	16.97	16.71	16.77	16.69	16.85	16.60	16.52	16.41	16.82
2008	16.77	17.16	16.92	17.40	17.11	17.17	17.00	17.25	17.35	17.24	17.56	17.27	17.18
2009	17.72	17.95	17.77	17.62	17.59	17.30	17.25	17.54	17.65	17.71	17.89	17.37	17.61
Professional and Business Services													
2007	21.10	20.92	21.34	21.61	21.23	21.48	21.71	21.94	22.24	22.38	22.41	22.59	21.75
2008	22.53	22.86	22.57	22.48	22.44	22.46	22.59	22.57	22.69	22.48	22.36	22.57	22.55
2009	22.09	22.29	22.55	22.54	22.31	22.12	22.19	22.01	21.75	21.66	21.89	22.19	22.13
Education and Health Services													
2007	19.25	19.28	19.29	19.21	19.41	19.19	19.32	19.05	19.18	19.11	19.10	18.85	19.19
2008	19.17	18.93	18.98	18.70	18.90	19.15	19.40	19.29	19.50	19.40	19.31	19.57	19.19
2009	19.17	19.26	19.32	19.54	19.23	19.46	19.40	19.49	19.70	19.55	19.47	19.38	19.41
Leisure and Hospitality													
2007	11.91	11.92	12.06	12.17	11.89	11.57	11.37	11.53	12.01	12.17	12.19	12.28	11.88
2008	12.14	12.24	12.30	12.22	12.04	11.85	11.71	12.21	12.34	12.49	12.67	12.89	12.22
2009	12.61	12.87	12.73	12.62	12.45	12.36	11.74	12.05	12.41	12.45	12.56	12.87	12.42

Average Weekly Earnings by Selected Industry: Maine, 2007–2009

(Dollars, not seasonally adjusted.)

Industry and year	January	February	March	April	May	June	July	August	September	October	November	December	Annual average
Total Private													
2007	632.02	632.69	642.94	648.51	646.38	641.22	644.03	638.37	652.15	641.22	637.33	639.01	640.91
2008	638.86	650.67	646.72	651.88	647.57	654.79	653.54	657.02	657.73	651.31	645.21	642.42	650.33
2009	638.83	645.69	635.91	639.10	629.97	627.00	632.21	640.85	640.36	640.08	647.63	642.95	638.03
Goods-Producing													
2007	794.39	780.57	799.78	816.02	816.07	816.00	824.14	822.45	833.45	813.45	832.14	819.55	814.97
2008	834.30	810.15	826.51	833.09	849.38	866.42	853.24	851.61	855.74	846.22	827.13	821.34	839.23
2009	815.10	826.18	816.74	813.30	826.97	824.89	818.12	844.42	854.39	859.18	861.73	847.28	833.55
Construction													
2007	693.68	670.91	730.67	736.44	766.55	763.69	751.60	744.66	742.10	724.78	735.78	747.74	734.87
2008	746.80	703.85	761.29	776.98	797.30	784.04	777.77	760.58	778.59	777.87	736.50	722.48	760.58
2009	731.24	763.70	741.47	774.06	754.00	745.61	758.84	799.20	769.62	792.80	779.69	756.96	764.61
Manufacturing													
2007	853.01	838.63	841.41	861.09	842.80	845.30	866.56	866.63	892.14	866.80	889.70	875.06	861.67
2008	896.39	873.31	869.41	872.09	853.73	879.53	868.57	877.97	878.94	869.37	863.08	858.25	872.90
2009	869.00	862.68	858.78	840.40	865.02	866.11	854.86	876.23	900.21	899.09	924.55	910.38	876.78
Trade, Transportation, and Utilities													
2007	547.03	562.52	573.36	565.14	568.50	561.46	568.50	564.12	566.16	551.12	525.34	538.25	556.74
2008	529.93	569.71	553.28	570.72	554.36	570.04	569.50	577.88	567.35	556.85	546.12	554.37	560.07
2009	545.78	574.40	556.20	553.27	534.74	538.03	558.90	575.31	564.80	557.87	551.01	561.05	556.48
Professional and Business Services													
2007	761.71	771.95	787.45	795.25	789.76	794.76	803.27	807.39	811.76	810.16	809.00	810.98	796.05
2008	802.07	829.82	817.03	811.53	803.35	804.07	810.08	814.78	821.38	809.28	809.43	801.24	811.80
2009	804.08	806.90	814.06	802.42	792.01	780.84	785.53	779.15	754.73	764.60	766.15	774.43	785.62
Education and Health Services													
2007	614.08	615.03	613.42	607.04	613.36	612.16	618.24	607.70	611.84	609.61	620.75	605.09	612.16
2008	619.19	613.33	616.85	609.62	614.25	622.38	630.50	625.00	631.80	622.74	621.78	620.37	619.84
2009	609.61	614.39	612.44	625.28	613.44	622.72	620.80	621.73	632.37	635.38	636.67	631.79	623.06
Leisure and Hospitality													
2007	273.93	274.16	279.79	287.21	280.60	279.99	295.62	307.85	294.25	296.95	284.03	282.44	287.50
2008	279.22	291.31	285.36	283.50	292.57	291.51	310.32	330.89	302.33	302.26	293.94	282.29	296.95
2009	278.68	294.72	299.16	295.31	296.31	291.70	320.50	327.76	317.70	321.21	303.95	297.30	305.53

MARYLAND
At a Glance

Population:
    1990 census: 4,780,753
    2000 census: 5,296,486
    2009 estimate: 5,699,478

Percent change in population:
    1990–2000: 10.8%
    2000–2009: 7.6%

Percent change in total nonfarm employment:
    1990–2008: 16.0%
    2000–2008: -3.0%

Industry with the largest growth in employment, 2000–2009 (thousands):
    Education and Health Services, 167.3

Industry with the largest decline or smallest growth in employment, 1990–2009 (thousands):
    Manufacturing, -80.0

Civilian labor force:
    1990: 2,582,827
    2000: 2,811,657
    2009: 2,986,933

Unemployment rate and rank among states (lowest to highest):
    1990: 4.6%, 12th
    2000: 3.6%, 20th
    2009: 7.0%, 15th

Employment by Industry, 2009

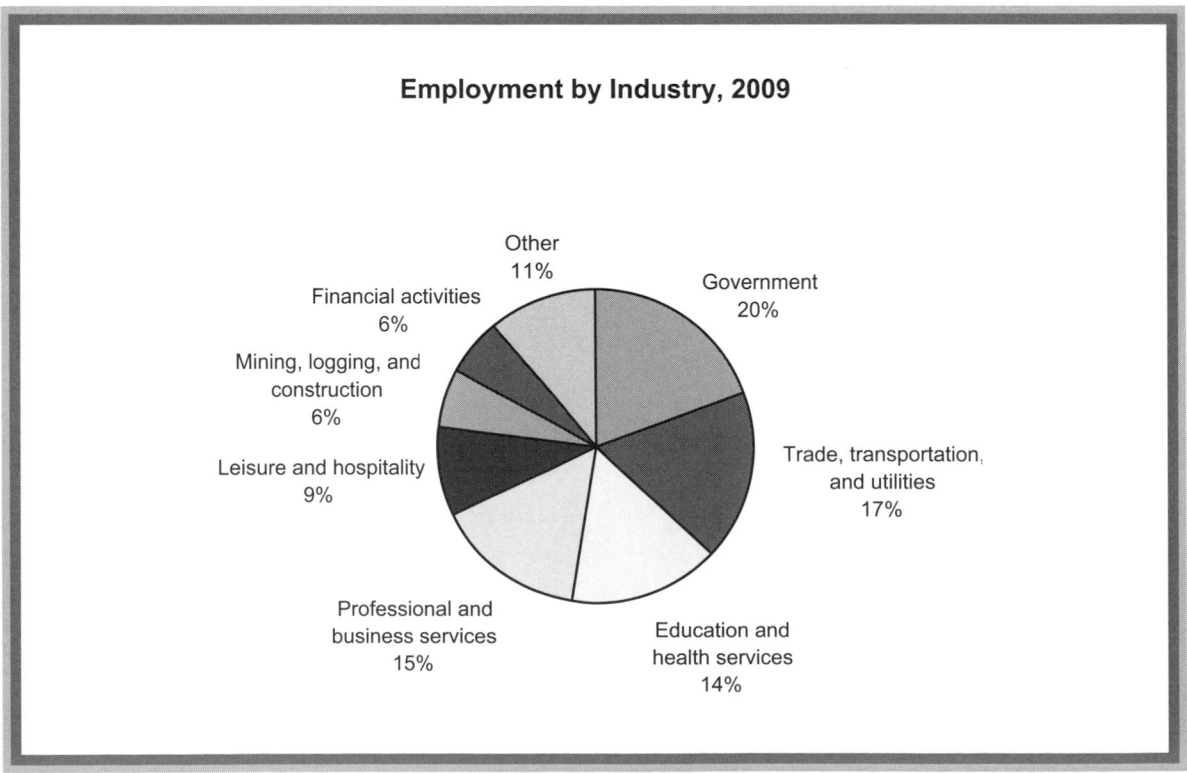

Other 11%
Financial activities 6%
Mining, logging, and construction 6%
Leisure and hospitality 9%
Professional and business services 15%
Government 20%
Trade, transportation, and utilities 17%
Education and health services 14%

Employment by Industry: Maryland, Selected Years, 1990–2009

(Numbers in thousands, not seasonally adjusted.)

Industry and year	January	February	March	April	May	June	July	August	September	October	November	December	Annual average
Total Nonfarm													
1990	2116.1	2135.5	2161.0	2172.1	2186.6	2215.2	2190.5	2191.6	2197.7	2170.2	2172.8	2170.7	2173.3
2000	2369.5	2377.8	2419.0	2439.9	2456.8	2485.8	2472.4	2468.9	2481.1	2483.8	2495.9	2509.8	2455.1
2001	2415.0	2429.3	2450.9	2462.7	2482.8	2506.4	2481.2	2481.6	2475.0	2481.9	2493.2	2500.7	2471.7
2002	2421.1	2436.6	2462.2	2472.8	2494.5	2513.4	2491.1	2490.3	2490.9	2490.0	2499.6	2501.6	2480.3
2003	2429.3	2426.9	2452.7	2477.4	2499.9	2519.4	2498.7	2495.5	2503.8	2505.8	2513.3	2519.8	2486.9
2004	2448.7	2451.5	2485.1	2501.8	2525.6	2547.0	2532.9	2532.2	2531.9	2543.7	2551.4	2560.6	2517.9
2005	2482.0	2494.1	2513.8	2544.2	2565.7	2581.1	2572.0	2571.0	2580.7	2577.4	2589.4	2597.1	2555.7
2006	2523.7	2535.9	2568.2	2583.6	2602.4	2619.4	2598.4	2596.4	2600.5	2604.4	2613.9	2626.2	2589.4
2007	2551.5	2553.4	2587.1	2599.4	2623.3	2637.4	2621.9	2620.2	2618.5	2620.4	2629.5	2637.5	2608.3
2008	2560.1	2569.4	2588.9	2609.9	2626.2	2629.6	2614.7	2608.9	2600.3	2602.6	2596.8	2592.0	2600.0
2009	2499.4	2498.5	2512.0	2527.8	2544.1	2552.9	2526.6	2519.8	2511.7	2521.2	2522.2	2513.9	2520.8
Total Private													
1990	1704.7	1715.5	1737.6	1746.7	1759.2	1788.6	1777.1	1781.5	1773.1	1745.3	1747.2	1746.1	1751.8
2000	1927.6	1931.0	1962.5	1984.5	2001.5	2034.9	2035.8	2036.5	2033.5	2027.0	2036.6	2050.2	2005.1
2001	1966.8	1971.7	1990.1	2000.9	2021.6	2052.1	2041.4	2042.4	2020.2	2017.1	2024.2	2031.7	2015.0
2002	1963.7	1969.2	1990.3	2004.4	2025.2	2049.6	2043.3	2043.2	2027.4	2017.5	2025.6	2028.9	2015.7
2003	1970.1	1958.5	1981.3	2007.1	2029.8	2056.6	2054.2	2057.6	2042.9	2038.5	2045.1	2052.4	2024.5
2004	1989.5	1986.9	2015.8	2033.9	2055.5	2086.6	2089.4	2089.1	2075.4	2073.3	2078.1	2089.1	2055.2
2005	2024.8	2027.9	2045.8	2074.5	2093.1	2119.8	2122.6	2122.0	2115.0	2102.2	2109.7	2119.2	2089.7
2006	2063.8	2064.0	2091.5	2106.0	2123.8	2153.3	2144.7	2144.2	2131.2	2123.5	2130.7	2142.4	2118.3
2007	2084.1	2074.9	2102.9	2116.3	2137.4	2163.8	2160.0	2158.8	2143.5	2133.2	2137.9	2146.2	2129.9
2008	2084.3	2080.5	2096.0	2116.2	2132.0	2147.0	2141.7	2136.6	2116.8	2105.9	2096.8	2092.7	2112.2
2009	2018.1	2004.6	2012.8	2025.4	2041.8	2062.6	2048.2	2042.6	2026.5	2019.9	2020.6	2014.6	2028.1
Goods-Producing													
1990	350.8	355.4	361.8	364.0	365.9	370.3	364.9	364.4	361.8	353.4	349.2	342.6	358.7
2000	320.4	318.4	326.6	329.7	332.3	338.1	339.4	340.4	339.8	338.3	336.9	336.1	333.0
2001	324.0	326.0	330.4	332.8	334.7	339.7	338.6	338.9	335.7	333.1	331.1	329.7	332.9
2002	316.6	317.4	320.9	323.2	325.1	328.6	326.4	326.9	324.1	320.2	319.6	316.8	322.2
2003	309.1	305.8	309.5	312.3	315.7	318.8	318.5	319.7	317.8	317.0	316.5	315.5	314.7
2004	306.5	305.1	311.3	315.9	319.2	323.7	325.9	326.3	324.9	323.6	322.7	323.2	319.0
2005	314.6	312.7	315.7	322.4	325.1	328.9	329.7	331.0	330.6	327.2	328.4	327.9	324.5
2006	318.6	317.9	323.1	325.0	326.5	331.2	330.9	331.0	329.2	326.5	325.2	324.9	325.8
2007	316.1	312.0	318.1	320.9	323.8	328.3	328.4	328.6	325.8	323.1	320.7	318.5	322.0
2008	310.3	308.7	310.1	310.9	311.1	313.5	313.1	312.5	309.3	304.8	300.0	294.5	308.2
2009	280.6	276.6	275.5	274.7	274.8	276.6	275.6	273.4	270.5	267.3	266.8	263.5	273.0
Mining, Logging, and Construction													
1990	154.1	155.9	161.7	165.1	166.2	168.9	164.7	164.8	162.3	157.1	152.8	147.4	160.1
2000	150.1	148.0	154.9	157.9	160.1	164.0	166.1	167.6	166.9	165.7	165.2	164.0	160.9
2001	155.5	157.2	161.7	164.7	167.6	171.6	171.6	172.7	170.4	169.5	168.6	167.3	166.5
2002	159.2	160.2	163.8	166.2	168.3	171.4	171.9	172.5	170.5	169.0	168.8	166.4	167.4
2003	160.8	158.3	161.7	165.1	168.8	171.7	173.8	175.5	174.5	174.5	174.0	173.3	169.3
2004	166.1	164.8	170.6	174.7	177.7	181.5	183.4	184.1	183.5	182.4	181.7	181.8	177.7
2005	174.7	173.0	175.8	182.5	185.4	189.0	190.5	191.5	191.7	189.4	190.3	189.7	185.3
2006	183.1	182.6	187.3	189.5	191.2	195.0	195.0	195.2	194.3	192.4	191.4	190.9	190.7
2007	183.9	180.2	186.0	188.9	191.5	195.2	195.6	195.9	194.0	191.5	189.4	187.0	189.9
2008	180.4	178.9	180.7	182.1	182.4	184.3	184.2	183.7	181.6	178.5	174.6	170.0	180.1
2009	158.8	156.3	155.8	155.9	156.3	157.9	158.0	156.2	153.7	150.1	148.6	145.6	154.4
Manufacturing													
1990	196.7	199.5	200.1	198.9	199.7	201.4	200.2	199.6	199.5	196.3	196.4	195.2	198.6
2000	170.3	170.4	171.7	171.8	172.2	174.1	173.3	172.8	172.9	172.6	171.7	172.1	172.2
2001	168.5	168.8	168.7	168.1	167.1	168.1	167.0	166.2	165.3	163.6	162.5	162.4	166.4
2002	157.4	157.2	157.1	157.0	156.8	157.2	154.5	154.4	153.6	151.2	150.8	150.4	154.8
2003	148.3	147.5	147.8	147.2	146.9	147.1	144.7	144.2	143.3	142.5	142.5	142.2	145.4
2004	140.4	140.3	140.7	141.2	141.5	142.2	142.5	142.2	141.4	141.2	141.0	141.4	141.3
2005	139.9	139.7	139.9	139.9	139.7	139.9	139.2	139.5	138.9	137.8	138.1	138.2	139.2
2006	135.5	135.3	135.8	135.5	135.3	136.2	135.9	135.8	134.9	134.1	133.8	134.0	135.2
2007	132.2	131.8	132.1	132.0	132.3	133.1	132.8	132.7	131.8	131.6	131.3	131.5	132.1
2008	129.9	129.8	129.4	128.8	128.7	129.2	128.9	128.8	127.7	126.3	125.4	124.5	128.1
2009	121.8	120.3	119.7	118.8	118.5	118.7	117.6	117.2	116.8	117.2	118.2	117.9	118.6
Service-Providing													
1990	1765.3	1780.1	1799.2	1808.1	1820.7	1844.9	1825.6	1827.2	1835.9	1816.8	1823.6	1828.1	1814.6
2000	2049.1	2059.4	2092.4	2110.2	2124.5	2147.7	2133.0	2128.5	2141.3	2145.5	2159.0	2173.7	2122.0
2001	2091.0	2103.3	2120.5	2129.9	2148.1	2166.7	2142.6	2142.7	2139.3	2148.8	2162.1	2171.0	2138.8
2002	2104.5	2119.2	2141.3	2149.6	2169.4	2184.8	2164.7	2163.4	2166.8	2169.8	2180.0	2184.8	2158.2
2003	2120.2	2121.1	2143.2	2165.1	2184.2	2200.6	2180.2	2175.8	2186.0	2188.8	2196.8	2204.3	2172.2
2004	2142.2	2146.4	2173.8	2185.9	2206.4	2223.3	2207.0	2205.9	2207.0	2220.1	2228.7	2237.4	2198.7
2005	2167.4	2181.4	2198.1	2221.8	2240.6	2252.2	2242.3	2240.0	2250.1	2250.2	2261.0	2269.2	2231.2
2006	2205.1	2218.0	2245.1	2258.6	2275.9	2288.2	2267.5	2265.4	2271.3	2277.9	2288.7	2301.3	2263.5
2007	2235.4	2241.4	2269.0	2278.5	2299.5	2309.1	2293.5	2291.6	2292.7	2297.3	2308.8	2319.0	2286.3
2008	2249.8	2260.7	2278.8	2299.0	2315.1	2316.1	2301.6	2296.4	2291.0	2297.8	2296.8	2297.5	2291.7
2009	2218.8	2221.9	2236.5	2253.1	2269.3	2276.3	2251.0	2246.4	2241.2	2253.9	2255.4	2250.4	2247.9

Employment by Industry: Maryland, Selected Years, 1990–2009—*Continued*

(Numbers in thousands, not seasonally adjusted.)

Industry and year	January	February	March	April	May	June	July	August	September	October	November	December	Annual average
Trade, Transportation, and Utilities													
1990	443.7	438.4	441.3	438.9	440.0	444.4	439.5	441.2	441.7	440.3	447.6	453.9	442.6
2000	459.9	456.5	460.1	463.1	466.3	471.9	469.3	471.8	472.7	477.1	488.2	498.5	471.3
2001	469.0	462.1	463.3	461.9	465.6	469.4	464.6	465.4	465.8	467.7	476.5	483.3	467.9
2002	460.5	455.0	459.4	460.4	463.9	468.6	463.7	463.1	463.4	465.3	472.7	480.0	464.7
2003	455.3	449.4	452.7	454.9	459.2	463.7	460.4	462.3	462.8	466.0	475.9	482.9	462.1
2004	459.8	455.2	459.0	460.4	464.4	471.4	466.3	466.5	466.6	470.6	479.4	487.6	467.3
2005	462.1	459.4	461.7	464.0	467.9	471.8	472.6	472.0	471.8	473.4	482.0	491.8	470.9
2006	470.6	465.1	468.9	469.8	473.5	477.6	473.9	473.7	472.6	476.4	487.5	496.0	475.5
2007	474.8	467.3	471.8	470.2	475.4	479.0	476.2	474.4	473.1	474.6	484.5	493.2	476.2
2008	469.3	462.5	464.2	463.0	465.4	468.6	465.0	464.3	461.5	461.2	465.4	470.0	465.0
2009	445.5	437.6	436.6	436.2	439.2	442.2	437.1	437.1	437.4	438.0	443.5	448.9	439.9
Wholesale Trade													
1990	92.5	92.6	93.2	93.2	93.0	93.7	93.2	93.2	93.2	91.8	91.8	91.6	92.8
2000	89.7	90.5	91.7	91.9	92.2	93.3	93.5	94.0	93.6	94.1	94.3	94.8	92.8
2001	93.3	93.7	94.4	94.8	94.9	95.0	94.5	94.5	94.3	94.1	94.1	94.2	94.3
2002	93.3	93.2	93.5	93.0	93.2	93.5	93.1	93.2	92.7	92.9	92.9	92.9	93.1
2003	91.1	90.7	91.3	91.0	91.5	91.8	91.4	91.3	91.1	91.1	91.3	91.4	91.3
2004	89.9	90.2	90.9	91.6	91.9	92.8	93.1	92.9	92.8	93.2	93.4	93.6	92.2
2005	92.6	92.9	93.1	93.8	94.4	95.0	95.2	95.1	94.6	94.4	94.4	95.0	94.2
2006	93.7	94.1	94.6	95.3	95.6	96.2	95.7	95.6	95.2	95.3	95.1	95.6	95.2
2007	94.0	94.3	94.7	95.1	95.4	95.7	95.3	95.2	94.9	94.3	94.3	94.7	94.8
2008	93.1	93.1	93.9	93.8	94.0	94.4	93.6	93.4	92.8	92.2	91.4	90.9	93.1
2009	89.2	88.7	88.2	88.3	88.3	88.3	87.7	87.7	87.4	88.7	87.5	88.2	88.2
Retail Trade													
1990	292.1	286.6	288.4	285.6	286.8	289.8	287.3	289.1	288.2	288.3	295.5	302.3	290.0
2000	291.5	287.7	289.7	292.3	295.1	299.0	297.6	299.0	298.7	300.7	312.0	321.0	298.7
2001	297.9	291.3	291.8	289.5	292.6	296.3	294.3	295.0	294.4	295.1	304.3	311.0	296.1
2002	292.1	287.0	290.8	290.3	292.7	297.2	295.0	294.2	294.0	294.5	302.4	309.6	295.0
2003	289.7	284.5	286.3	289.0	291.7	295.3	293.9	295.3	294.3	295.7	305.5	311.6	294.4
2004	292.1	287.6	289.9	290.2	293.2	298.3	295.4	296.1	294.8	298.4	306.9	313.8	296.4
2005	291.9	288.5	289.9	292.6	295.2	297.7	299.7	299.3	297.7	299.2	307.2	314.4	297.8
2006	298.2	291.8	294.5	294.8	297.5	300.1	298.8	298.5	296.2	299.9	310.7	316.2	299.8
2007	300.2	292.5	295.9	295.2	299.1	301.5	301.0	299.7	297.5	299.6	309.4	315.3	300.6
2008	297.6	290.7	292.1	291.3	292.9	294.9	293.5	292.8	289.7	289.9	294.1	297.2	293.1
2009	279.4	273.0	272.7	272.6	275.3	277.5	275.4	275.4	273.9	273.4	279.6	282.9	275.9
Transportation and Utilities													
1990	59.1	58.9	59.8	60.4	60.4	61.3	59.2	59.1	60.7	60.8	60.4	60.4	60.0
2000	78.4	78.0	78.4	78.8	78.8	79.4	78.1	78.8	80.4	82.3	81.9	82.5	79.7
2001	77.8	77.3	77.1	77.7	78.2	78.4	76.2	76.2	77.4	78.6	78.1	78.1	77.6
2002	75.2	74.8	75.1	77.2	78.1	78.0	75.6	75.7	76.7	77.9	77.4	77.5	76.6
2003	74.5	74.2	75.1	75.0	76.0	76.6	75.1	75.5	77.2	79.1	79.2	79.9	76.5
2004	77.7	77.5	78.2	78.5	79.2	80.1	77.6	77.3	78.8	78.9	79.0	80.2	78.6
2005	77.6	78.0	78.7	77.6	78.3	79.1	77.7	77.6	79.5	79.8	80.4	82.4	78.9
2006	78.7	79.2	79.8	79.7	80.4	81.3	79.4	79.6	81.2	81.2	81.7	84.2	80.5
2007	80.6	80.5	81.2	79.9	80.9	81.8	79.9	79.5	80.7	80.7	80.8	83.2	80.8
2008	78.6	78.7	78.2	77.9	78.5	79.3	77.9	78.1	79.0	79.1	79.9	81.9	78.9
2009	76.9	75.9	75.7	75.3	75.6	76.4	74.0	74.0	76.1	75.9	76.4	77.8	75.8
Information													
1990	46.7	47.3	47.5	47.3	47.1	47.2	47.8	47.7	47.0	47.6	47.5	47.4	47.3
2000	56.3	56.6	57.3	57.7	58.2	59.1	59.4	54.2	60.0	60.3	60.8	62.1	58.5
2001	59.7	60.1	60.1	59.3	59.4	59.5	58.4	58.1	57.0	56.8	56.7	56.6	58.5
2002	55.2	54.9	54.8	54.4	54.4	54.0	53.3	53.0	52.2	50.7	51.4	51.1	53.3
2003	50.4	50.5	50.6	51.1	51.7	51.6	51.4	51.1	50.7	50.7	51.4	51.5	51.1
2004	50.3	49.6	50.5	50.2	50.6	51.1	49.9	50.1	49.5	49.3	49.6	49.6	50.0
2005	48.8	49.0	49.1	49.3	49.8	50.1	51.3	51.7	51.6	51.9	51.8	51.9	50.5
2006	50.5	50.8	51.2	50.6	50.9	50.9	50.2	50.2	49.9	49.6	50.2	50.5	50.5
2007	49.3	49.7	50.5	50.5	51.0	51.8	51.4	52.1	51.5	50.0	50.8	51.4	50.8
2008	50.0	50.3	50.6	50.6	50.7	50.1	49.8	49.5	49.3	48.1	49.0	48.8	49.7
2009	46.4	46.6	47.5	46.2	46.1	46.9	45.7	46.2	45.1	45.0	45.3	45.5	46.0
Financial Activities													
1990	134.4	135.1	135.7	136.2	136.7	138.6	139.0	140.0	139.1	137.7	138.2	138.5	137.4
2000	144.0	144.2	145.2	145.4	146.1	148.4	148.7	148.7	147.8	147.1	147.9	149.2	146.9
2001	145.1	146.0	147.0	147.2	148.0	150.0	150.3	150.5	149.2	149.0	149.7	150.5	148.5
2002	148.7	149.2	149.3	149.8	150.6	152.2	152.5	152.8	152.1	152.0	152.6	153.7	151.3
2003	153.1	153.2	154.2	154.7	156.0	157.6	158.5	158.7	157.5	155.5	155.9	156.3	155.9
2004	153.6	153.7	154.7	154.8	155.4	156.1	157.4	157.7	156.4	157.2	157.1	157.8	156.0
2005	156.2	156.6	156.6	157.7	158.2	160.0	160.8	160.9	160.4	159.3	159.3	160.0	158.8
2006	158.5	159.0	159.6	159.6	159.9	161.6	161.2	161.0	159.8	159.1	159.1	160.1	159.9
2007	157.9	158.0	158.3	157.9	158.5	159.5	159.4	158.8	157.3	156.4	155.9	156.4	157.9
2008	153.5	153.9	154.1	153.8	153.9	154.6	154.1	153.6	151.8	151.5	150.4	150.7	153.0
2009	147.5	146.9	146.3	146.2	146.1	146.6	145.6	145.0	143.4	141.3	140.7	138.8	144.5

Employment by Industry: Maryland, Selected Years, 1990–2009—*Continued*

(Numbers in thousands, not seasonally adjusted.)

Industry and year	January	February	March	April	May	June	July	August	September	October	November	December	Annual average
Professional and Business Services													
1990	248.3	251.4	255.6	258.6	259.7	264.1	263.1	263.8	263.9	256.8	256.6	255.8	258.1
2000	352.8	357.4	365.4	367.5	369.5	374.6	373.9	377.9	375.4	372.8	373.0	373.1	369.4
2001	363.1	365.5	369.2	372.1	374.6	376.9	376.9	377.9	371.8	370.6	371.7	371.7	371.8
2002	357.3	360.1	364.2	367.2	370.0	372.5	371.9	374.4	371.0	369.4	369.9	369.8	368.1
2003	358.4	356.6	361.6	368.5	370.8	374.5	373.1	375.5	373.7	375.3	374.4	375.8	369.9
2004	364.5	366.6	373.7	375.2	378.4	382.7	383.8	384.3	382.5	384.4	383.3	384.8	378.7
2005	373.9	377.0	382.6	388.4	390.6	393.9	393.5	394.6	394.3	392.8	391.6	391.4	388.7
2006	383.4	386.3	392.7	396.3	397.4	400.9	400.2	400.9	398.5	396.7	395.5	396.1	395.4
2007	385.5	386.9	392.6	396.9	398.2	402.0	401.3	402.9	400.8	400.6	400.5	401.1	397.4
2008	390.3	391.1	394.3	400.4	400.7	402.2	402.6	403.2	399.9	398.2	395.2	392.6	397.6
2009	380.5	378.3	380.6	384.9	384.7	388.8	386.8	387.6	383.7	384.2	387.2	385.8	384.4
Education and Health Services													
1990	218.2	222.7	224.8	224.2	224.6	224.4	224.5	225.8	229.2	231.7	233.8	234.4	226.5
2000	299.1	302.0	303.9	308.5	308.2	308.2	308.7	308.0	311.9	313.9	315.8	317.6	308.8
2001	310.8	314.4	316.4	318.0	319.1	321.2	317.5	316.7	319.4	323.6	326.3	328.3	319.3
2002	324.1	329.0	330.0	328.9	330.0	329.5	327.9	326.8	329.6	334.2	337.0	337.6	330.4
2003	333.4	335.0	337.3	338.8	339.7	340.5	340.0	340.3	340.5	342.2	343.8	344.6	339.7
2004	342.9	343.4	345.5	345.4	346.5	347.6	349.6	348.2	347.8	350.2	351.9	352.1	347.6
2005	347.5	350.2	351.4	353.5	353.9	353.0	352.0	351.1	354.7	358.8	360.3	361.4	354.0
2006	356.7	359.5	362.4	362.7	363.8	363.7	360.9	360.2	364.5	368.1	370.0	371.7	363.7
2007	367.6	370.1	372.8	372.8	373.6	373.4	371.4	370.6	374.1	376.7	378.2	379.5	373.4
2008	376.1	378.8	380.7	382.8	383.9	382.9	382.2	381.5	385.7	389.9	391.4	392.9	384.1
2009	388.8	391.3	392.8	394.1	394.5	394.4	391.3	389.5	392.9	398.2	399.3	398.6	393.8
Leisure and Hospitality													
1990	168.6	170.6	174.9	181.9	188.5	200.9	201.0	200.6	192.8	182.1	178.6	177.5	184.8
2000	184.8	184.7	191.0	198.7	206.1	217.9	220.7	219.9	210.5	202.8	199.2	198.2	202.9
2001	186.2	187.6	192.8	199.3	208.3	221.3	221.9	222.1	210.7	205.6	201.5	200.1	204.8
2002	191.4	192.5	199.1	207.1	216.9	228.0	230.1	230.1	220.6	211.8	208.2	205.1	211.7
2003	197.5	194.7	200.3	210.7	220.1	230.9	233.2	233.1	224.6	216.8	212.7	210.5	215.4
2004	200.5	201.0	207.8	215.7	224.2	236.1	238.4	238.9	231.0	222.0	218.0	217.4	220.9
2005	206.8	207.3	212.1	222.6	230.6	244.0	245.5	243.8	235.4	223.6	220.7	218.8	225.9
2006	210.7	210.2	217.4	225.3	234.6	248.8	249.2	249.3	239.5	230.5	226.4	225.6	230.6
2007	216.7	214.7	221.4	229.5	238.6	249.9	252.0	252.5	242.5	233.5	228.7	227.3	233.9
2008	218.2	218.2	224.5	236.2	247.3	254.9	255.2	253.4	241.3	234.8	228.1	225.8	236.5
2009	213.3	212.5	218.1	227.2	239.9	249.3	249.2	247.9	238.3	230.3	222.2	217.9	230.5
Other Services													
1990	94.0	94.6	96.0	95.6	96.7	98.7	97.3	98.0	97.6	95.7	95.7	96.0	96.3
2000	110.3	111.2	113.0	113.9	114.8	116.7	115.7	115.6	115.4	114.7	114.8	115.4	114.3
2001	108.9	110.0	110.9	110.3	111.9	114.1	113.2	112.8	110.6	110.7	110.7	111.5	111.3
2002	109.9	111.1	112.6	113.4	114.3	116.2	117.5	116.1	114.4	113.9	114.2	114.8	114.0
2003	112.9	113.3	115.1	116.1	116.6	119.0	119.1	116.9	115.3	115.0	114.5	115.3	115.8
2004	111.4	112.3	113.3	116.3	116.8	117.9	118.1	117.1	116.7	116.0	116.1	116.6	115.7
2005	114.9	115.7	116.6	116.6	117.0	118.1	117.2	116.9	116.2	115.2	115.6	116.0	116.3
2006	114.8	115.2	116.2	116.7	117.2	118.6	118.2	117.9	117.2	116.6	116.8	117.5	116.9
2007	116.2	116.2	117.4	117.6	118.3	119.9	119.9	118.9	118.4	118.3	118.6	118.8	118.2
2008	116.6	117.0	117.5	118.5	119.0	120.2	119.7	118.6	118.0	117.4	117.3	117.4	118.1
2009	115.5	114.8	115.4	115.9	116.5	117.8	116.9	115.9	115.2	115.6	115.6	115.6	115.9
Government													
1990	411.4	420.0	423.4	425.4	427.4	426.6	413.4	410.1	424.6	424.9	425.6	424.6	421.5
2000	441.9	446.8	456.5	455.4	455.3	450.9	436.6	432.4	447.6	456.8	459.3	459.6	449.9
2001	448.2	457.6	460.8	461.8	461.2	454.3	439.8	439.2	454.8	464.8	469.0	469.0	456.7
2002	457.4	467.4	471.9	468.4	469.3	463.8	447.8	447.1	463.5	472.5	474.0	472.7	464.7
2003	459.2	468.4	471.4	470.3	470.1	462.8	444.5	437.9	460.9	467.3	468.2	467.4	462.4
2004	459.2	464.6	469.3	467.9	470.1	460.4	443.5	443.1	456.5	470.4	473.3	471.5	462.7
2005	457.2	466.2	468.0	469.7	472.6	461.3	449.4	449.0	465.7	475.2	479.7	477.9	466.0
2006	459.9	471.9	476.7	477.6	478.6	466.1	453.7	452.2	469.3	480.9	483.2	483.8	471.1
2007	467.4	478.5	484.2	483.1	485.9	473.6	461.9	461.4	475.0	487.2	491.6	491.3	478.4
2008	475.8	488.9	492.9	493.7	494.2	482.6	473.0	472.3	483.5	496.7	500.0	499.3	487.7
2009	481.3	493.9	499.2	502.4	502.3	490.3	478.4	477.2	485.2	501.3	501.6	499.3	492.7

Average Weekly Hours by Selected Industry: Maryland, 2007–2009

(Not seasonally adjusted.)

Industry and year	January	February	March	April	May	June	July	August	September	October	November	December	Annual average
Total Private													
2007	34.4	34.0	34.5	34.9	34.8	34.8	35.0	34.9	35.1	35.0	35.0	35.3	34.8
2008	34.8	34.7	35.0	34.8	34.7	34.9	34.7	34.6	34.6	34.7	34.5	34.1	34.7
2009	34.3	34.5	34.4	34.1	34.3	34.4	34.6	34.9	34.7	34.4	34.6	34.3	34.5
Goods-Producing													
2007	38.8	37.3	39.1	39.2	40.1	39.8	39.4	39.6	39.4	39.5	39.1	39.6	39.2
2008	39.2	38.7	39.7	39.7	39.3	39.5	39.3	39.5	39.1	39.3	39.0	38.5	39.2
2009	38.4	38.6	38.6	38.0	38.2	38.0	38.4	38.5	37.6	38.0	37.6	38.0	38.2
Mining, Logging, and Construction													
2007	38.9	37.0	39.4	39.9	41.0	40.4	40.1	40.2	39.7	40.2	39.4	40.0	39.7
2008	39.7	38.7	40.0	40.2	39.7	40.1	39.7	39.8	39.3	39.8	38.8	38.0	39.5
2009	37.9	38.0	38.1	37.6	37.8	37.3	37.5	38.0	36.1	36.6	36.1	36.6	37.3
Manufacturing													
2007	38.7	37.7	38.6	38.2	38.7	38.9	38.4	38.6	39.0	38.6	38.7	39.0	38.6
2008	38.5	38.7	39.2	39.0	38.8	38.7	38.7	39.0	38.9	38.6	39.2	39.1	38.9
2009	39.1	39.4	39.2	38.6	38.7	39.0	39.7	39.2	39.6	39.8	39.4	39.8	39.3
Trade, Transportation, and Utilities													
2007	33.9	33.4	33.7	34.1	34.3	34.3	34.4	34.5	34.3	34.9	34.9	35.3	34.3
2008	34.3	34.1	34.2	34.1	34.1	34.5	34.1	34.0	33.7	33.6	33.8	33.9	34.0
2009	33.4	33.4	33.7	33.5	33.8	33.8	34.2	34.3	35.2	34.6	34.5	33.9	34.0
Financial Activities													
2007	36.6	36.4	36.0	36.8	36.4	35.9	36.5	35.9	36.6	36.3	36.0	36.6	36.3
2008	36.2	35.9	36.1	35.9	35.9	36.1	36.0	36.0	36.0	36.3	36.4	35.9	36.1
2009	36.1	36.3	36.0	35.5	35.8	35.8	36.3	36.6	36.4	36.6	36.9	36.2	36.2
Professional and Business Services													
2007	36.3	36.2	36.8	37.6	37.2	37.4	37.7	37.4	37.6	36.8	37.1	37.6	37.1
2008	37.0	37.3	37.9	37.4	37.2	37.3	36.7	36.7	36.9	37.2	36.4	36.0	37.0
2009	35.9	36.2	36.0	36.4	36.7	36.8	36.9	37.4	36.4	36.5	36.8	36.4	36.5
Education and Health Services													
2007	32.7	32.4	32.9	32.7	32.3	32.7	33.1	32.7	33.1	32.9	33.1	33.3	32.8
2008	33.1	32.8	33.0	33.0	33.2	32.9	33.4	33.3	33.4	33.5	33.6	33.2	33.2
2009	33.5	33.2	33.2	32.8	32.8	33.1	33.1	33.3	33.3	33.3	33.8	33.3	33.2
Leisure and Hospitality													
2007	27.0	27.2	27.5	27.6	27.8	27.6	27.8	28.3	28.0	28.0	27.5	27.3	27.6
2008	26.7	27.4	27.3	27.2	26.9	27.2	27.3	27.0	26.9	26.5	25.8	25.7	26.8
2009	25.3	26.1	26.2	25.8	26.7	27.2	27.4	27.5	26.0	25.4	25.7	25.2	26.3
Other Services													
2007	30.7	30.1	30.4	31.3	31.3	31.7	31.7	31.4	31.9	31.3	31.2	31.2	31.2
2008	30.6	31.1	31.4	30.7	30.5	30.5	30.5	30.7	30.4	30.7	31.1	30.7	30.7
2009	30.0	30.7	30.9	30.5	30.4	30.9	30.3	31.7	31.9	31.3	31.4	31.3	30.9

Average Hourly Earnings by Selected Industry: Maryland, 2007–2009

(Dollars, not seasonally adjusted.)

Industry and year	January	February	March	April	May	June	July	August	September	October	November	December	Annual average
Total Private													
2007	24.00	24.31	24.14	24.12	23.79	23.76	23.89	23.68	24.09	24.18	24.14	24.45	24.04
2008	24.56	24.65	24.51	24.14	24.13	24.20	24.20	24.35	24.68	24.85	25.09	25.44	24.56
2009	25.23	25.82	25.24	25.32	24.83	25.00	24.99	25.46	25.49	25.57	25.99	26.05	25.42
Goods-Producing													
2007	24.27	24.17	23.75	23.95	23.91	23.75	23.74	23.42	23.80	23.74	23.80	24.06	23.86
2008	23.94	24.25	23.89	23.49	23.62	23.71	24.02	23.78	23.96	24.29	24.63	24.83	24.03
2009	24.52	24.27	24.32	24.26	23.98	24.04	23.89	24.21	24.39	24.66	24.80	24.72	24.33
Mining, Logging, and Construction													
2007	25.13	25.16	24.02	24.25	24.41	24.17	24.01	23.60	23.99	24.09	24.33	24.28	24.27
2008	24.29	24.96	24.49	24.01	24.12	24.22	24.62	24.31	24.66	24.77	25.19	25.84	24.61
2009	25.48	25.25	25.04	24.94	24.57	24.74	24.49	24.59	24.83	25.39	25.88	26.12	25.10
Manufacturing													
2007	23.07	22.85	23.36	23.50	23.14	23.10	23.32	23.14	23.52	23.22	23.01	23.73	23.25
2008	23.45	23.28	23.03	22.74	22.89	22.95	23.15	23.01	22.96	23.60	23.85	23.48	23.20
2009	23.30	23.04	23.41	23.40	23.22	23.16	23.13	23.72	23.86	23.81	23.55	23.14	23.39
Trade, Transportation, and Utilities													
2007	18.26	18.24	18.37	18.57	18.32	18.19	18.14	17.99	18.13	18.49	18.19	18.12	18.25
2008	18.41	18.72	18.47	18.31	18.15	17.99	17.97	18.16	18.45	18.57	18.52	18.94	18.39
2009	18.93	18.90	18.97	18.97	19.08	18.98	19.36	19.34	19.45	19.63	20.17	19.82	19.31
Financial Activities													
2007	30.61	30.94	30.25	29.80	29.52	29.66	29.25	29.03	29.71	29.23	29.22	29.89	29.76
2008	28.81	28.65	28.80	28.24	27.92	27.78	27.28	26.98	26.78	26.71	29.85	30.24	28.17
2009	28.97	29.12	28.68	28.03	28.12	27.57	28.69	30.10	29.02	28.86	29.52	28.83	28.79
Professional and Business Services													
2007	29.10	29.90	29.44	29.25	29.09	29.50	29.70	29.68	30.26	29.66	29.98	30.49	29.67
2008	30.61	30.83	30.59	30.11	30.52	31.02	31.03	31.38	31.94	32.13	32.27	33.00	31.28
2009	32.44	32.72	32.98	32.82	32.78	33.09	32.84	33.81	33.62	33.16	33.98	33.69	33.17
Education and Health Services													
2007	25.35	25.53	25.57	25.31	24.94	25.16	25.49	25.18	25.05	25.91	25.55	25.93	25.42
2008	26.14	25.84	25.84	25.63	25.33	25.74	25.93	26.35	26.54	26.36	26.18	26.57	26.04
2009	26.27	26.12	25.91	25.90	25.69	26.08	26.03	26.03	26.11	26.15	25.78	25.76	25.99
Leisure and Hospitality													
2007	17.13	17.53	17.44	17.53	17.19	16.89	16.87	16.73	17.33	17.41	17.62	17.61	17.26
2008	17.29	16.99	16.74	16.31	16.73	16.14	15.83	15.53	15.56	15.45	15.24	14.98	16.06
2009	14.62	14.71	14.43	14.95	14.49	14.10	14.22	13.96	14.34	14.66	14.98	15.37	14.54
Other Services													
2007	20.56	21.36	21.52	21.42	21.21	20.94	20.74	20.69	20.96	20.54	20.96	21.36	21.02
2008	20.76	20.35	20.05	20.17	19.84	19.89	19.80	20.25	20.33	20.43	20.73	21.00	20.30
2009	20.50	20.44	20.62	21.13	21.55	21.11	21.68	21.69	22.50	22.44	22.76	22.72	21.60

Average Weekly Earnings by Selected Industry: Maryland, 2007–2009

(Dollars, not seasonally adjusted.)

Industry and year	January	February	March	April	May	June	July	August	September	October	November	December	Annual average
Total Private													
2007	825.60	826.54	832.83	841.79	827.89	826.85	836.15	826.43	845.56	846.30	844.90	863.09	836.59
2008	854.69	855.36	857.85	840.07	837.31	844.58	839.74	842.51	853.93	862.30	865.61	867.50	852.23
2009	865.39	890.79	868.26	863.41	851.67	860.00	864.65	888.55	884.50	879.61	899.25	893.52	876.99
Goods-Producing													
2007	941.68	901.54	928.63	938.84	958.79	945.25	935.36	927.43	937.72	937.73	930.58	952.78	935.31
2008	938.45	938.48	948.43	932.55	928.27	936.55	943.99	939.31	936.84	954.60	960.57	955.96	941.98
2009	941.57	936.82	938.75	921.88	916.04	913.52	917.38	932.09	917.06	937.08	932.48	939.36	929.41
Mining, Logging, and Construction													
2007	977.56	930.92	946.39	967.58	1000.81	976.47	962.80	948.72	952.40	968.42	958.60	971.20	963.52
2008	964.31	965.95	979.60	965.20	957.56	971.22	977.41	967.54	969.14	985.85	977.37	981.92	972.10
2009	965.69	959.50	954.02	937.74	928.75	922.80	918.38	934.42	896.36	929.27	934.27	955.99	936.23
Manufacturing													
2007	892.81	861.45	901.70	897.70	895.52	898.59	895.49	893.20	917.28	896.29	890.49	925.47	897.45
2008	902.83	900.94	902.78	886.86	888.13	888.17	895.91	897.39	893.14	910.96	934.92	918.07	902.48
2009	911.03	907.78	917.67	903.24	898.61	903.24	918.26	929.82	944.86	947.64	927.87	920.97	919.23
Trade, Transportation, and Utilities													
2007	619.01	609.22	619.07	633.24	628.38	623.92	624.02	620.66	621.86	645.30	634.83	639.64	625.98
2008	631.46	638.35	631.67	624.37	618.92	620.66	612.78	617.44	621.77	623.95	625.98	642.07	625.26
2009	632.26	631.26	639.29	635.50	644.90	641.52	662.11	663.36	684.64	679.20	695.87	671.90	656.54
Financial Activities													
2007	1120.33	1126.22	1089.00	1096.64	1074.53	1064.79	1067.63	1042.18	1087.39	1061.05	1051.92	1093.97	1080.29
2008	1042.92	1028.54	1039.68	1013.82	1002.33	1002.86	982.08	971.28	964.08	969.57	1086.54	1085.62	1016.94
2009	1045.82	1057.06	1032.48	995.07	1006.70	987.01	1041.45	1101.66	1056.33	1056.28	1089.29	1043.65	1042.20
Professional and Business Services													
2007	1056.33	1082.38	1083.39	1099.80	1082.15	1103.30	1119.69	1110.03	1137.78	1091.49	1112.26	1146.42	1100.76
2008	1132.57	1149.96	1159.36	1126.11	1135.34	1157.05	1138.80	1151.65	1178.59	1195.24	1174.63	1188.00	1157.36
2009	1164.60	1184.46	1187.28	1194.65	1203.03	1217.71	1211.80	1264.49	1223.77	1210.34	1250.46	1226.32	1210.71
Education and Health Services													
2007	828.95	827.17	841.25	827.64	805.56	822.73	843.72	823.39	829.16	852.44	845.71	863.47	833.78
2008	865.23	847.55	852.72	845.79	840.96	846.85	866.06	877.46	886.44	883.06	879.65	882.12	864.53
2009	880.05	867.18	860.21	849.52	842.63	863.25	861.59	866.80	869.46	870.80	871.36	857.81	862.87
Leisure and Hospitality													
2007	462.51	476.82	479.60	483.83	477.88	466.16	468.99	473.46	485.24	487.48	484.55	480.75	476.38
2008	461.64	465.53	457.00	443.63	450.04	439.01	432.16	419.31	418.56	409.43	393.19	384.99	430.41
2009	369.89	383.93	378.07	385.71	386.88	383.52	389.63	383.90	372.84	372.36	384.99	387.32	382.40
Other Services													
2007	631.19	642.94	654.21	670.45	663.87	663.80	657.46	649.67	668.62	642.90	653.95	666.43	655.82
2008	635.26	632.89	629.57	619.22	605.12	606.65	603.90	621.68	618.03	627.20	644.70	644.70	623.21
2009	615.00	627.51	637.16	644.47	655.12	652.30	656.90	687.57	717.75	702.37	714.66	711.14	667.44

MASSACHUSETTS
At a Glance

Population:
    1990 census: 6,016,425
    2000 census: 6,349,097
    2009 estimate: 6,593,587

Percent change in population:
    1990–2000: 5.5%
    2000–2009: 3.9%

Percent change in total nonfarm employment:
    1990–2009: 6.2%
    2008–2009: -3.6%

Industry with the largest growth in employment, 1990–2009 (thousands):
    Education and Health Services, 191.2

Industry with the largest decline or smallest growth in employment, 1990–2009 (thousands):
    Manufacturing, -194.2

Civilian labor force:
    1990: 3,226,368
    2000: 3,365,573
    2009: 3,473,497

Unemployment rate and rank among states (lowest to highest):
    1990: 6.3%, 41st
    2000: 2.7%, 3rd
    2009: 8.4%, 28th

Employment by Industry, 2009

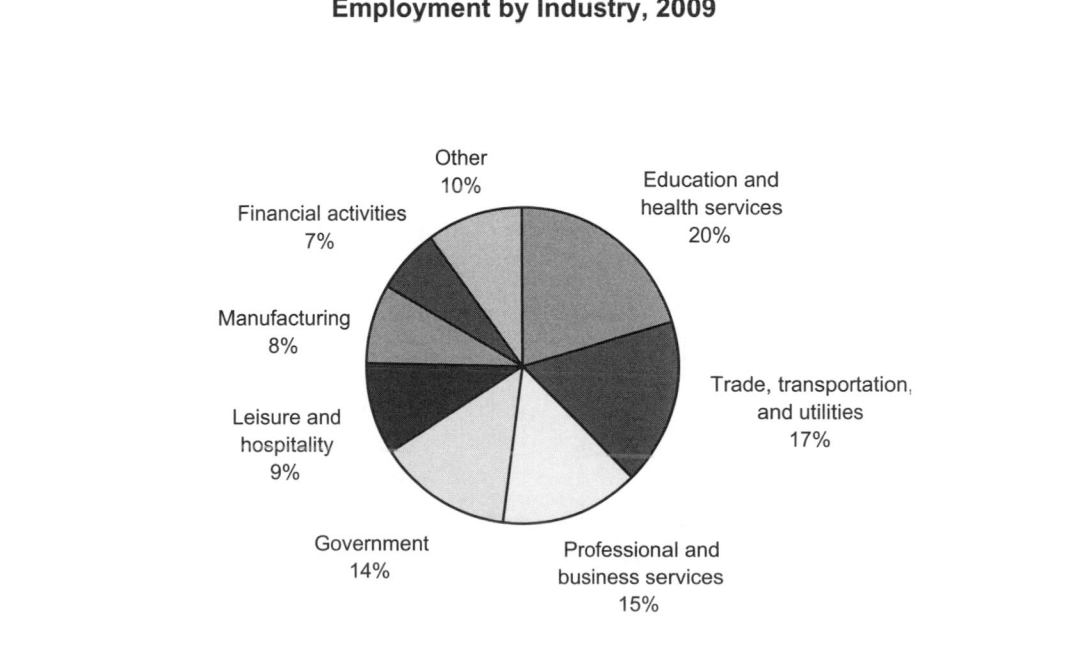

- Other 10%
- Education and health services 20%
- Financial activities 7%
- Manufacturing 8%
- Leisure and hospitality 9%
- Trade, transportation, and utilities 17%
- Government 14%
- Professional and business services 15%

Employment by Industry: Massachusetts, Selected Years, 1990–2009

(Numbers in thousands, not seasonally adjusted.)

Industry and year	January	February	March	April	May	June	July	August	September	October	November	December	Annual average
Total Nonfarm													
1990	2985.0	2989.2	3000.5	2998.9	3024.9	3040.3	2975.9	2969.8	2986.5	2966.6	2960.7	2953.9	2987.7
2000	3221.4	3240.7	3263.5	3308.1	3332.3	3362.9	3334.5	3325.1	3365.2	3385.2	3398.3	3413.9	3329.3
2001	3317.0	3326.5	3335.4	3356.2	3373.9	3390.0	3330.3	3322.3	3335.7	3331.8	3325.8	3326.2	3339.3
2002	3217.6	3216.2	3235.5	3261.5	3284.1	3298.0	3258.0	3249.2	3272.3	3272.6	3274.2	3272.1	3259.3
2003	3158.8	3148.5	3161.2	3195.7	3222.1	3233.5	3198.0	3188.4	3218.1	3219.2	3221.2	3215.9	3198.4
2004	3113.0	3123.0	3145.8	3188.7	3212.0	3232.6	3207.8	3194.9	3222.4	3230.3	3233.0	3235.8	3194.9
2005	3125.8	3142.6	3150.7	3204.9	3227.3	3248.4	3224.3	3214.9	3243.0	3243.9	3254.6	3258.3	3211.6
2006	3158.0	3169.0	3189.5	3233.2	3256.1	3286.0	3258.0	3249.7	3274.1	3285.3	3290.8	3295.8	3245.5
2007	3198.5	3206.1	3221.1	3262.9	3297.1	3327.3	3294.5	3287.5	3305.6	3318.4	3325.0	3322.3	3280.5
2008	3226.2	3238.7	3254.1	3293.4	3320.2	3336.5	3308.0	3296.0	3308.4	3317.8	3298.5	3282.4	3290.0
2009	3158.7	3157.8	3154.3	3182.5	3197.6	3203.3	3171.3	3155.0	3175.4	3183.5	3175.8	3160.2	3173.0
Total Private													
1990	2573.4	2568.8	2579.8	2577.7	2596.6	2622.2	2587.0	2589.5	2584.8	2557.6	2548.7	2542.3	2577.4
2000	2789.9	2799.9	2823.0	2863.3	2879.6	2923.9	2927.7	2925.9	2929.1	2942.6	2952.7	2969.4	2893.9
2001	2877.9	2878.5	2886.9	2906.5	2922.3	2949.1	2921.4	2917.8	2893.2	2883.0	2875.7	2875.3	2899.0
2002	2776.2	2767.3	2785.9	2814.2	2836.3	2860.5	2851.1	2847.4	2834.7	2835.9	2834.4	2834.2	2823.2
2003	2729.1	2712.0	2724.6	2759.1	2785.1	2805.4	2800.8	2797.3	2787.8	2790.6	2791.7	2786.9	2772.5
2004	2693.9	2694.0	2715.6	2756.9	2779.9	2808.4	2816.8	2811.1	2798.1	2800.9	2801.1	2804.8	2773.5
2005	2704.5	2709.2	2717.4	2770.4	2791.3	2821.4	2829.3	2827.1	2817.0	2809.9	2817.9	2823.6	2786.6
2006	2732.9	2733.2	2752.6	2795.2	2816.2	2853.7	2858.4	2857.9	2844.1	2847.3	2850.0	2856.6	2816.5
2007	2768.6	2766.4	2780.3	2820.9	2852.4	2891.4	2893.0	2892.6	2871.9	2876.6	2881.0	2879.1	2847.9
2008	2792.9	2793.8	2808.5	2846.1	2871.5	2897.8	2901.6	2896.5	2870.8	2870.7	2850.3	2835.6	2853.0
2009	2722.9	2709.5	2706.8	2730.6	2749.0	2766.2	2767.9	2759.8	2742.4	2741.4	2728.6	2712.3	2736.5
Goods-Producing													
1990	590.3	584.0	583.6	583.5	588.8	594.7	584.6	588.3	584.4	572.4	567.0	558.8	581.7
2000	512.6	510.6	517.4	527.6	532.5	543.0	541.1	545.4	541.3	544.8	545.0	543.7	533.8
2001	533.6	531.0	530.4	536.1	539.5	542.3	530.5	531.8	527.2	522.2	515.3	509.7	529.1
2002	490.0	483.7	485.9	491.6	497.4	501.2	494.2	496.1	493.4	491.5	488.7	481.3	491.3
2003	462.9	453.4	454.4	463.5	469.5	472.7	467.0	468.6	465.4	462.5	461.1	454.1	462.9
2004	436.7	433.5	439.5	450.5	457.8	464.3	462.6	465.0	461.9	457.9	456.7	452.4	453.2
2005	433.9	430.1	430.6	443.3	450.4	456.4	456.0	457.1	455.4	451.2	450.7	446.7	446.8
2006	431.1	428.3	430.8	441.4	446.1	452.5	451.1	451.9	449.0	445.9	442.7	439.8	442.6
2007	425.0	419.4	421.0	428.2	437.3	445.0	443.3	444.6	441.6	437.9	435.8	430.1	434.1
2008	414.3	410.0	412.4	420.0	426.3	431.1	430.7	430.6	425.8	421.6	414.6	405.1	420.2
2009	380.8	372.0	368.2	372.0	373.8	376.9	375.7	373.9	370.1	367.1	364.9	359.9	371.3
Mining and Logging													
1990	1.5	1.5	1.5	1.7	1.7	1.7	1.7	1.7	1.7	1.6	1.5	1.4	1.6
2000	1.2	1.2	1.3	1.5	1.5	1.5	1.5	1.5	1.5	1.5	1.5	1.4	1.4
2001	1.3	1.3	1.3	1.5	1.6	1.6	1.6	1.6	1.6	1.6	1.6	1.6	1.5
2002	1.3	1.3	1.4	1.6	1.7	1.7	1.7	1.7	1.8	1.8	1.8	1.7	1.6
2003	1.5	1.5	1.5	1.7	1.8	1.9	1.9	1.9	2.0	2.0	2.0	1.9	1.8
2004	1.7	1.6	1.6	1.9	2.0	2.0	2.1	2.1	2.0	2.0	2.0	2.0	1.9
2005	1.8	1.7	1.7	2.0	2.1	2.1	2.1	2.1	2.1	2.0	2.0	1.8	2.0
2006	1.6	1.6	1.7	1.8	1.9	1.9	2.0	1.9	1.9	1.9	1.9	1.7	1.8
2007	1.4	1.3	1.4	1.5	1.7	1.8	1.7	1.7	1.7	1.6	1.6	1.5	1.6
2008	1.2	1.2	1.2	1.4	1.5	1.5	1.5	1.4	1.4	1.4	1.4	1.3	1.4
2009	1.1	1.1	1.1	1.3	1.4	1.4	1.4	1.4	1.4	1.4	1.4	1.3	1.3
Construction													
1990	98.7	94.9	95.5	97.4	102.3	106.0	105.7	106.5	104.7	99.3	95.8	89.7	99.7
2000	112.5	110.1	115.6	124.5	129.0	134.6	138.3	139.4	137.7	137.6	136.9	134.0	129.1
2001	124.5	123.3	125.4	135.6	142.1	146.4	147.9	148.4	146.1	145.5	143.5	139.9	139.1
2002	128.4	125.8	128.8	137.8	144.3	147.0	148.6	149.4	146.6	147.5	145.9	139.3	140.8
2003	126.9	120.6	122.7	133.2	140.5	143.5	145.5	146.0	143.7	142.2	141.0	135.8	136.8
2004	122.5	120.1	124.8	134.6	141.8	146.3	148.6	148.8	146.5	144.6	143.4	139.2	138.4
2005	124.5	120.7	122.3	135.3	141.9	146.4	150.3	150.7	149.3	145.8	145.8	141.4	139.5
2006	129.2	126.6	129.3	140.1	144.4	148.3	150.2	150.4	147.7	145.4	142.5	138.7	141.1
2007	126.7	121.5	123.8	131.8	140.2	145.4	147.5	147.6	145.7	143.9	141.8	135.9	137.7
2008	123.4	120.4	123.1	130.7	136.7	139.9	142.4	141.6	138.7	136.1	131.7	124.8	132.5
2009	109.0	104.3	103.6	109.9	113.7	116.3	117.9	117.1	114.4	114.0	111.0	104.9	111.3
Manufacturing													
1990	490.1	487.6	486.6	484.4	484.8	487.0	477.2	480.1	478.0	471.5	469.7	467.7	480.4
2000	398.9	399.3	400.5	401.6	402.0	406.9	401.3	404.5	402.1	405.7	406.6	408.3	403.1
2001	407.8	406.4	403.7	399.0	395.8	394.3	381.0	381.8	379.5	375.1	370.2	368.2	388.6
2002	360.3	356.6	355.7	352.2	351.4	352.5	343.9	345.0	345.0	342.2	341.0	340.3	348.8
2003	334.5	331.3	330.2	328.6	327.2	327.3	319.6	320.7	319.7	318.3	318.1	316.4	324.3
2004	312.5	311.8	313.1	314.0	314.0	316.0	311.9	314.1	313.4	311.3	311.3	311.2	312.9
2005	307.6	307.7	306.6	306.0	306.4	307.9	303.6	304.3	304.0	303.4	302.9	303.5	305.3
2006	300.3	300.1	299.8	299.5	299.8	302.3	298.9	299.6	299.4	298.6	298.3	299.4	299.7
2007	296.9	296.6	295.8	294.9	295.4	297.8	294.1	295.3	294.2	292.4	292.4	292.7	294.9
2008	289.7	288.4	288.1	287.9	288.1	289.7	286.8	287.6	285.7	284.1	281.5	279.0	286.4
2009	270.7	266.6	263.5	260.8	258.7	259.2	256.4	255.4	254.3	251.7	252.5	253.7	258.6

Employment by Industry: Massachusetts, Selected Years, 1990–2009—*Continued*

(Numbers in thousands, not seasonally adjusted.)

Industry and year	January	February	March	April	May	June	July	August	September	October	November	December	Annual average
Service-Providing													
1990	2394.7	2405.2	2416.9	2415.4	2436.1	2445.6	2391.3	2381.5	2402.1	2394.2	2393.7	2395.1	2406.0
2000	2708.8	2730.1	2746.1	2780.5	2799.8	2819.9	2793.4	2779.7	2823.9	2840.4	2853.3	2870.2	2795.5
2001	2783.4	2795.5	2805.0	2820.1	2834.4	2847.7	2799.8	2790.5	2808.5	2809.6	2810.5	2816.5	2810.1
2002	2727.6	2732.5	2749.6	2769.9	2786.7	2796.8	2763.8	2753.1	2778.9	2781.1	2785.5	2790.8	2768.0
2003	2695.9	2695.1	2706.8	2732.2	2752.6	2760.8	2731.0	2719.8	2752.7	2756.7	2760.1	2761.8	2735.5
2004	2676.3	2689.5	2706.3	2738.2	2754.2	2768.3	2745.2	2729.9	2760.5	2772.4	2776.3	2783.4	2741.7
2005	2691.9	2712.5	2720.1	2761.6	2776.9	2792.0	2768.3	2757.8	2787.6	2792.7	2803.9	2811.6	2764.7
2006	2726.9	2740.7	2758.7	2791.8	2810.0	2833.5	2806.9	2797.8	2825.1	2839.4	2848.1	2856.0	2802.9
2007	2773.5	2786.7	2800.1	2834.7	2859.8	2882.3	2851.2	2842.9	2864.0	2880.5	2889.2	2892.2	2846.4
2008	2811.9	2828.7	2841.7	2873.4	2893.9	2905.4	2877.3	2865.4	2882.6	2896.2	2883.9	2877.3	2869.8
2009	2777.9	2785.8	2786.1	2810.5	2823.8	2826.4	2795.6	2781.1	2805.3	2816.4	2810.9	2800.3	2801.7
Trade, Transportation, and Utilities													
1990	586.7	572.9	573.7	567.3	571.7	581.7	565.4	565.5	567.8	561.0	567.1	573.2	571.1
2000	591.3	584.4	585.5	587.1	590.5	599.2	592.1	592.1	595.6	602.0	613.9	627.6	596.7
2001	595.1	584.9	585.4	587.4	591.1	600.3	589.7	588.3	588.2	589.7	599.9	607.0	592.3
2002	577.4	567.4	569.5	572.3	577.4	586.5	580.5	578.1	579.6	581.0	589.3	598.8	579.8
2003	568.8	560.2	562.2	566.2	571.6	579.6	572.6	571.7	574.2	578.2	587.2	593.5	573.8
2004	568.2	561.4	563.0	564.4	569.4	577.2	571.4	569.1	568.7	575.6	584.2	593.0	572.1
2005	565.2	559.8	559.0	563.7	568.2	575.4	569.6	569.4	568.5	570.9	579.9	590.5	570.0
2006	566.5	555.3	558.0	562.6	566.8	575.1	569.4	569.8	570.4	573.9	584.1	593.3	570.4
2007	567.3	557.2	558.8	560.7	568.5	577.5	571.1	569.3	568.9	574.1	585.7	592.2	570.9
2008	570.9	558.9	560.2	563.1	568.8	576.1	570.2	569.2	566.8	568.6	571.7	576.7	568.4
2009	547.4	536.7	533.1	532.6	538.9	547.0	539.9	538.8	539.6	538.5	542.2	545.2	540.0
Wholesale Trade													
1990	146.0	145.8	146.2	144.8	144.9	146.4	144.5	144.3	143.2	142.3	141.3	141.1	144.2
2000	137.1	137.1	137.9	138.4	138.9	140.7	139.6	139.6	139.7	140.7	141.3	143.0	139.5
2001	141.5	141.6	142.0	142.5	142.3	143.3	142.4	142.0	140.8	140.1	139.8	139.9	141.5
2002	136.4	135.7	136.2	136.0	136.5	137.7	136.9	136.6	135.8	135.4	135.5	136.3	136.3
2003	135.0	134.5	134.6	134.6	134.9	135.7	135.8	135.5	134.6	134.7	135.3	135.8	135.1
2004	133.6	133.6	134.7	134.3	134.1	135.0	134.4	133.9	132.7	132.6	132.5	132.7	133.7
2005	131.4	131.2	131.1	132.1	133.1	134.2	134.6	135.0	134.6	135.3	136.1	136.8	133.8
2006	134.9	134.5	135.0	136.2	136.6	138.1	138.3	138.7	137.9	138.1	138.2	138.8	137.1
2007	136.7	136.4	136.9	136.9	137.5	139.1	139.1	138.9	137.8	138.4	138.3	138.5	137.9
2008	137.0	135.9	136.3	136.8	137.1	138.1	137.6	136.8	135.6	134.9	134.0	133.6	136.1
2009	130.0	128.5	127.7	127.4	127.4	128.2	127.8	127.2	126.1	125.7	125.2	124.7	127.2
Retail Trade													
1990	360.9	347.0	346.6	343.1	346.1	353.7	343.2	342.8	342.1	338.3	345.7	351.8	346.7
2000	361.0	354.9	355.4	351.0	356.4	362.3	360.0	360.2	359.7	364.2	376.4	387.9	362.7
2001	360.9	350.7	351.0	351.7	354.9	361.9	357.2	357.2	354.1	357.2	369.7	378.0	358.7
2002	354.8	346.0	347.8	349.5	353.2	360.1	359.3	358.0	355.5	356.6	365.9	375.4	356.8
2003	348.4	341.1	342.7	346.5	350.7	357.3	354.9	355.1	353.3	357.4	366.2	372.4	353.8
2004	352.2	345.8	346.1	346.7	350.9	357.1	356.2	355.4	352.2	357.7	367.1	376.1	355.3
2005	352.3	347.2	346.5	349.5	352.2	357.3	355.1	355.4	351.0	353.4	361.7	370.3	354.3
2006	351.1	340.5	342.3	344.9	347.4	352.5	350.4	350.6	346.5	350.4	360.8	368.1	350.5
2007	347.3	338.1	338.8	340.3	346.2	352.0	350.2	349.3	344.8	349.5	361.7	366.8	348.8
2008	349.8	339.5	340.0	341.8	345.8	351.1	350.4	351.1	344.7	348.0	353.0	357.3	347.7
2009	335.7	327.3	324.6	325.0	330.3	336.8	334.8	335.5	331.9	332.3	336.8	340.0	332.6
Transportation and Utilities													
1990	79.8	80.1	80.9	79.4	80.7	81.6	77.7	78.4	82.5	80.4	80.1	80.3	80.1
2000	92.4	92.4	92.2	94.7	95.2	96.2	92.5	92.3	96.2	97.1	96.2	96.7	94.5
2001	92.7	92.6	92.4	93.2	93.9	95.1	90.1	89.1	93.3	92.4	90.4	89.1	92.0
2002	86.2	85.7	85.5	86.8	87.7	88.7	84.3	83.5	88.3	89.0	87.9	87.1	86.7
2003	85.4	84.6	84.9	85.1	86.0	86.6	81.9	81.1	86.3	86.1	85.7	85.3	84.9
2004	82.4	82.0	82.2	83.4	84.4	85.1	80.8	79.8	83.8	85.3	84.6	84.2	83.2
2005	81.5	81.4	81.4	82.1	82.9	83.9	79.9	79.0	82.9	82.2	82.1	83.4	81.9
2006	80.5	80.3	80.7	81.5	82.8	84.5	80.7	80.5	86.0	85.4	85.1	86.4	82.9
2007	83.3	82.7	83.1	83.5	84.8	86.4	81.8	81.1	86.3	86.2	85.7	86.9	84.3
2008	84.1	83.5	83.9	84.5	85.9	86.9	82.2	81.3	86.5	85.7	84.7	85.8	84.6
2009	81.7	80.9	80.8	80.2	81.2	82.0	77.3	76.1	81.6	80.5	80.2	80.5	80.3
Information													
1990	85.3	84.7	84.7	85.2	86.8	89.0	90.2	90.3	89.8	88.4	88.4	88.2	87.5
2000	104.1	105.2	106.8	108.6	110.4	112.7	115.4	107.3	115.1	115.0	115.9	116.7	111.1
2001	116.4	116.2	115.8	115.0	113.8	113.4	111.6	110.5	108.0	106.1	105.4	104.7	111.4
2002	103.5	102.7	102.5	100.4	100.0	99.9	99.5	98.8	96.9	96.9	96.7	96.9	99.6
2003	93.7	93.1	93.0	91.9	91.7	92.4	91.0	90.9	89.7	89.3	89.2	89.2	91.3
2004	87.4	86.8	87.5	86.8	87.2	87.8	87.8	87.7	86.9	87.0	87.6	87.7	87.4
2005	86.5	86.7	86.7	86.4	86.6	87.3	88.0	87.6	86.9	86.2	86.6	87.1	86.9
2006	86.5	86.5	86.5	85.9	86.4	87.3	87.1	87.5	86.5	87.0	87.4	88.0	86.9
2007	86.4	86.7	87.6	88.2	87.9	88.9	89.8	89.9	89.9	88.8	88.8	89.4	88.5
2008	87.7	88.7	89.4	90.7	90.6	90.5	89.7	89.5	88.8	87.7	87.6	87.8	89.1
2009	86.8	85.4	85.5	84.7	84.3	84.7	83.9	84.0	84.0	84.0	84.5	84.4	84.7

Employment by Industry: Massachusetts, Selected Years, 1990–2009—*Continued*

(Numbers in thousands, not seasonally adjusted.)

Industry and year	January	February	March	April	May	June	July	August	September	October	November	December	Annual average
Financial Activities													
1990	206.5	206.9	207.4	203.8	201.9	202.4	200.7	200.1	197.6	196.0	194.7	194.7	201.0
2000	224.7	224.0	224.6	225.7	226.0	230.0	230.3	230.6	229.0	229.5	230.0	232.4	228.0
2001	228.4	228.7	229.9	229.7	229.7	233.1	234.1	233.7	230.5	229.4	229.7	230.6	230.6
2002	230.2	228.9	228.3	226.8	227.2	229.7	230.8	230.3	226.9	226.4	225.6	226.4	228.1
2003	224.7	223.2	223.5	223.5	224.0	226.2	226.5	226.4	222.5	221.1	221.0	221.6	223.7
2004	218.8	218.6	218.9	219.3	219.6	222.2	223.3	222.6	219.8	217.9	217.4	218.5	219.7
2005	217.5	217.1	217.6	218.2	219.6	222.9	225.6	225.9	223.7	222.0	222.7	224.4	221.4
2006	220.6	220.4	220.8	221.5	222.8	225.8	227.9	227.4	225.0	224.2	224.3	225.9	223.9
2007	223.9	223.8	223.8	223.9	224.6	227.3	227.9	227.6	223.7	222.4	221.8	222.6	224.4
2008	220.5	220.2	220.5	220.7	221.2	223.7	224.8	224.3	221.1	220.2	219.2	219.3	221.3
2009	216.4	215.0	214.4	213.3	213.4	214.7	214.7	213.9	210.4	208.9	206.5	207.0	212.4
Professional and Business Services													
1990	339.7	342.4	345.2	344.3	345.2	349.2	345.8	347.1	343.4	337.4	335.7	333.7	342.4
2000	464.8	468.5	475.2	485.3	487.0	499.4	504.1	508.0	505.5	504.3	506.0	507.8	492.9
2001	494.3	492.1	493.3	493.1	493.4	496.5	487.0	485.9	479.5	472.3	468.0	466.6	485.2
2002	448.6	445.3	448.4	455.8	456.9	460.7	458.9	458.5	455.0	453.5	452.2	449.8	453.6
2003	433.5	428.3	429.5	438.9	441.0	444.8	446.3	446.0	443.4	444.6	445.5	445.4	440.6
2004	431.7	431.6	435.6	448.4	450.8	457.7	460.4	461.2	459.3	458.5	458.7	459.3	451.1
2005	443.1	443.3	445.4	459.5	460.8	467.9	468.8	469.5	468.3	466.5	468.5	467.8	460.8
2006	453.0	454.7	458.4	469.1	471.8	480.4	479.3	481.0	477.5	478.2	479.0	478.2	471.7
2007	461.9	463.8	467.2	480.2	484.7	492.4	490.4	492.5	487.5	488.3	489.8	489.5	482.4
2008	475.7	477.0	478.6	488.4	491.6	497.6	496.9	496.0	491.7	490.3	485.4	480.0	487.4
2009	461.5	457.1	455.1	461.9	461.2	464.3	463.6	463.3	459.8	462.7	463.9	456.4	460.9
Education and Health Services													
1990	448.0	459.7	461.6	464.6	460.9	450.7	445.7	443.8	457.5	470.2	473.1	474.2	459.1
2000	537.9	549.8	551.0	552.4	544.5	532.1	530.0	529.6	543.4	555.2	560.0	560.8	545.5
2001	543.4	556.3	557.2	560.0	553.5	541.5	541.6	541.5	553.0	566.9	571.1	572.5	554.9
2002	558.0	569.3	573.1	575.3	568.5	555.9	553.2	551.6	566.6	578.5	584.9	585.7	568.4
2003	568.3	578.1	581.5	583.3	575.5	561.9	560.8	558.1	573.9	585.3	589.9	589.4	575.5
2004	573.5	584.8	588.0	589.4	581.4	568.6	569.1	566.1	580.4	592.4	596.5	596.2	582.2
2005	578.9	591.7	593.4	596.8	589.2	576.4	576.8	574.6	588.8	601.5	606.9	606.7	590.1
2006	591.8	604.6	609.0	610.3	604.0	593.3	593.2	590.5	605.8	618.0	622.6	623.0	605.5
2007	612.0	623.1	624.7	630.3	623.8	610.7	612.9	611.1	623.9	637.8	641.7	642.4	624.5
2008	627.0	640.4	644.2	646.9	638.9	625.9	628.6	626.4	638.5	652.5	656.2	656.6	640.2
2009	641.3	653.3	656.8	658.4	650.1	635.2	638.2	635.6	647.3	659.8	663.5	663.5	650.3
Leisure and Hospitality													
1990	219.8	220.9	225.2	231.4	243.0	255.2	256.5	256.5	248.2	236.2	227.3	223.9	237.0
2000	246.9	249.0	253.4	266.8	277.8	294.8	301.1	299.6	287.6	280.1	270.1	267.8	274.5
2001	254.3	256.3	260.9	271.0	285.8	303.4	306.3	305.7	291.0	280.6	270.4	267.7	279.5
2002	254.1	255.4	262.0	275.6	291.3	306.8	312.4	312.7	299.5	291.1	279.9	278.0	284.9
2003	262.2	260.9	264.5	275.6	294.4	308.3	315.6	315.8	302.1	293.6	281.4	277.2	287.6
2004	263.4	262.8	267.5	282.2	296.8	311.6	321.4	319.1	305.1	295.4	283.9	280.9	290.8
2005	265.2	265.9	269.2	285.3	298.8	314.1	322.0	321.3	307.2	294.6	285.3	282.2	292.6
2006	267.6	267.9	272.1	286.7	299.7	317.2	326.8	326.6	311.3	302.0	292.1	289.9	296.7
2007	276.2	276.0	279.8	291.1	305.6	325.4	331.7	332.2	315.6	307.4	297.1	292.4	302.5
2008	279.5	280.7	284.5	297.1	313.8	329.0	334.6	335.2	318.1	310.2	296.4	291.2	305.9
2009	272.9	274.2	276.9	290.1	308.3	320.7	327.6	326.7	313.4	302.8	287.9	280.4	298.5
Other Services													
1990	97.1	97.3	98.4	97.6	98.3	99.3	98.1	97.9	96.1	96.0	95.4	95.6	97.2
2000	107.6	108.4	109.1	109.8	110.9	112.7	113.6	113.3	111.6	111.7	111.8	112.6	111.0
2001	112.4	113.0	114.0	114.2	115.5	118.6	120.6	120.4	115.8	115.8	115.9	116.5	116.1
2002	114.4	114.6	116.2	116.4	117.6	119.8	121.6	121.3	116.8	117.0	117.1	117.3	117.5
2003	115.0	114.8	116.0	116.2	117.4	119.5	121.0	119.8	116.6	116.0	116.4	116.5	117.1
2004	114.2	114.5	115.6	115.9	116.9	119.0	120.8	120.3	116.0	116.2	116.1	116.8	116.9
2005	114.2	114.6	115.5	117.2	117.7	121.0	122.5	121.7	118.2	117.0	117.3	118.2	117.9
2006	115.8	115.5	117.0	117.7	118.6	122.1	123.6	123.2	118.6	118.1	117.8	118.5	118.9
2007	115.9	116.4	117.4	118.3	120.0	124.2	125.9	125.4	120.8	119.9	120.3	120.5	120.4
2008	117.3	117.9	118.7	119.2	120.3	123.9	126.1	125.3	120.0	119.6	119.2	118.9	120.5
2009	115.8	115.8	116.8	117.6	119.0	122.7	124.3	123.6	117.8	117.6	115.2	115.5	118.5
Government													
1990	411.6	420.4	420.7	421.2	428.3	418.1	388.9	380.3	401.7	409.0	412.0	411.6	410.3
2000	431.5	440.8	440.5	444.8	452.7	439.0	406.8	399.2	436.1	442.6	445.6	444.5	435.3
2001	439.1	448.0	448.5	449.7	451.6	440.9	408.9	404.5	442.5	448.8	450.1	450.9	440.3
2002	441.4	448.9	449.6	447.3	447.8	437.5	406.9	401.8	437.6	436.7	439.8	437.9	436.1
2003	429.7	436.5	436.6	436.6	437.0	428.1	397.2	391.1	430.3	428.6	429.5	429.0	425.9
2004	419.1	429.0	430.2	431.8	432.1	424.2	391.0	383.8	424.3	429.4	431.9	431.0	421.5
2005	421.3	433.4	433.3	434.5	436.0	427.0	395.0	387.8	426.0	434.0	436.7	434.7	425.0
2006	425.1	435.8	436.9	438.0	439.9	432.3	399.6	391.8	430.0	438.0	440.8	439.2	429.0
2007	429.9	439.7	440.8	442.0	444.7	435.9	401.5	394.9	433.7	441.8	444.0	443.2	432.7
2008	433.3	444.9	445.6	447.3	448.7	438.7	406.4	399.5	437.6	447.1	448.2	446.8	437.0
2009	435.8	448.3	447.5	451.9	448.6	437.1	403.4	395.2	433.0	442.1	447.2	447.9	436.5

Average Weekly Hours by Selected Industry: Massachusetts, 2007–2009

(Not seasonally adjusted.)

Industry and year	January	February	March	April	May	June	July	August	September	October	November	December	Annual average
Total Private													
2007	32.80	33.20	33.20	33.60	33.50	33.80	33.80	33.90	33.90	33.50	33.60	33.80	33.50
2008	33.50	33.40	33.80	33.60	33.50	33.80	33.70	33.90	33.70	33.60	33.70	33.50	33.70
2009	33.50	33.60	33.60	33.40	33.40	33.50	33.60	33.70	33.50	33.50	33.90	33.70	33.60
Goods-Producing													
2007	38.60	38.80	39.20	39.00	39.20	40.40	38.60	38.50	38.90	38.30	38.70	38.90	38.90
2008	38.80	38.80	39.20	38.70	39.10	39.10	38.70	38.80	39.10	38.40	38.70	38.50	38.80
2009	38.80	38.70	38.80	38.70	38.50	39.10	38.50	39.00	38.40	39.10	40.00	40.00	39.00
Construction													
2007	36.40	36.10	36.40	36.80	37.70	37.70	37.10	36.20	36.30	35.20	35.90	36.60	36.50
2008	37.00	36.90	37.30	36.90	37.60	37.70	37.90	37.60	38.20	37.80	37.50	37.20	37.50
2009	37.60	37.30	37.00	38.00	38.40	38.20	38.80	39.10	37.70	36.80	37.50	37.60	37.90
Manufacturing													
2007	39.40	39.80	40.20	39.90	39.90	41.80	39.40	39.80	40.30	39.90	40.10	40.00	40.00
2008	39.70	39.70	40.20	39.60	39.80	39.70	39.00	39.30	39.50	38.70	39.40	39.20	39.50
2009	39.40	39.10	39.40	38.80	38.40	39.40	38.20	38.40	38.10	39.50	40.50	40.50	39.20
Trade, Transportation, and Utilities													
2007	31.70	32.20	32.50	32.50	32.70	32.80	33.30	33.50	33.60	32.80	32.70	33.30	32.80
2008	32.60	32.50	33.00	32.90	32.60	33.20	33.20	33.60	33.40	33.30	32.80	33.20	33.00
2009	32.60	32.90	33.10	32.80	33.00	33.00	33.20	33.00	33.10	32.70	33.20	33.40	33.00
Information													
2007	34.70	35.40	35.10	37.00	35.90	35.90	37.30	35.00	35.80	34.80	34.50	34.90	35.50
2008	35.20	35.00	35.80	34.10	33.50	35.00	35.20	35.10	35.10	34.90	35.80	36.50	35.10
2009	35.70	36.60	35.60	35.50	34.60	34.10	34.80	35.00	34.60	34.50	35.40	34.00	35.00
Financial Activities													
2007	35.20	35.70	35.50	35.60	35.00	35.60	36.40	36.30	36.10	35.50	36.20	37.20	35.90
2008	37.70	37.10	37.50	37.30	37.00	37.00	36.50	37.00	36.80	36.40	37.60	36.90	37.10
2009	37.30	37.00	37.10	36.70	35.80	36.60	36.80	37.60	37.40	36.80	37.40	37.00	37.00
Professional and Business Services													
2007	35.30	35.60	35.50	36.00	36.10	36.20	36.20	36.60	36.70	36.10	36.10	36.50	36.10
2008	35.90	35.80	36.80	36.60	36.20	36.80	35.80	35.80	35.50	35.60	36.00	35.40	36.00
2009	35.50	35.90	35.90	35.60	36.00	35.80	35.70	35.80	35.60	35.80	36.20	35.50	35.80
Education and Health Services													
2007	29.80	29.80	29.50	30.10	29.50	29.80	30.00	30.40	30.30	30.70	30.80	30.80	30.10
2008	30.70	30.70	30.70	30.60	30.60	31.00	31.40	31.50	31.20	31.40	31.50	31.20	31.00
2009	31.30	31.50	31.50	31.60	31.60	31.60	31.90	32.00	31.90	31.70	31.80	31.80	31.70
Leisure and Hospitality													
2007	26.90	27.90	28.10	29.20	29.60	29.40	30.00	29.80	29.10	28.70	28.30	27.50	28.80
2008	27.00	26.50	26.80	27.40	27.30	26.90	27.60	27.80	27.50	27.50	26.70	26.60	27.20
2009	25.80	25.40	25.50	25.50	26.00	26.00	26.70	26.90	26.60	26.20	25.90	25.80	26.10
Other Services													
2007	31.40	32.00	31.50	31.60	31.10	30.90	31.20	31.70	31.80	31.30	31.20	31.70	31.40
2008	31.30	31.70	32.10	31.50	32.10	31.70	32.30	32.80	31.80	31.50	32.00	31.80	31.90
2009	32.90	33.30	33.00	33.20	32.70	32.30	32.60	33.00	32.00	32.00	32.20	32.20	32.60

Average Hourly Earnings by Selected Industry: Massachusetts, 2007–2009

(Dollars, not seasonally adjusted.)

Industry and year	January	February	March	April	May	June	July	August	September	October	November	December	Annual average
Total Private													
2007	25.90	26.13	25.88	26.44	26.10	25.70	25.95	25.81	26.18	26.29	26.15	26.33	26.07
2008	26.17	26.31	26.41	26.27	26.16	26.16	26.06	26.25	26.55	26.53	26.85	26.78	26.38
2009	26.83	27.16	27.15	27.00	26.67	26.51	26.48	26.61	26.79	26.71	27.07	27.23	26.85
Goods-Producing													
2007	28.00	28.21	28.23	27.63	27.45	27.14	27.66	27.63	27.98	28.07	28.02	28.49	27.87
2008	28.11	28.20	28.22	28.22	28.13	27.84	28.26	28.39	28.52	28.67	28.79	28.84	28.35
2009	28.71	29.12	28.99	28.97	28.53	28.81	28.89	29.54	29.78	29.48	29.68	30.34	29.23
Construction													
2007	29.31	30.00	30.17	29.69	29.41	29.23	29.20	29.25	29.59	29.83	30.34	30.86	29.72
2008	30.46	30.88	30.86	30.57	29.89	29.64	30.10	30.82	31.06	31.21	31.51	31.76	30.72
2009	31.99	32.21	32.43	31.97	31.44	31.45	31.27	32.61	31.84	31.97	32.38	33.55	32.07
Manufacturing													
2007	27.58	27.65	27.61	26.82	26.57	26.20	26.89	26.82	27.21	27.29	26.90	27.38	27.07
2008	27.03	27.01	27.06	27.00	27.21	26.85	27.19	26.95	27.04	27.25	27.37	27.40	27.11
2009	27.19	27.19	26.89	27.05	26.65	27.10	27.25	27.61	28.39	28.02	28.18	28.66	27.51
Trade, Transportation, and Utilities													
2007	23.27	23.38	22.76	23.29	23.49	22.63	23.22	23.07	23.06	23.64	22.88	23.07	23.14
2008	23.35	23.94	23.91	23.51	23.44	23.31	23.52	23.66	23.39	23.25	22.93	22.55	23.39
2009	23.23	23.19	23.13	23.03	22.98	22.53	22.88	22.83	22.68	22.22	22.48	22.49	22.80
Information													
2007	38.06	37.04	37.20	36.89	35.78	36.68	37.03	37.14	37.56	37.20	36.80	37.03	37.03
2008	36.43	35.88	36.18	35.70	35.78	35.86	35.58	35.42	35.84	35.26	35.82	35.42	35.76
2009	34.71	35.22	35.06	34.53	34.74	34.63	34.18	34.68	34.22	33.94	34.57	35.41	34.66
Financial Activities													
2007	29.33	30.37	28.07	31.33	30.46	28.88	29.86	29.57	30.50	31.63	30.43	29.17	29.96
2008	28.41	28.88	29.14	28.91	28.93	29.45	28.71	29.44	29.71	30.27	30.75	30.54	29.42
2009	30.74	31.28	31.22	31.39	31.32	31.45	31.21	31.29	30.93	31.44	31.92	31.80	31.33
Professional and Business Services													
2007	31.94	32.44	32.55	33.83	32.92	32.32	32.40	32.12	32.49	31.87	32.12	32.97	32.50
2008	32.31	32.26	32.51	32.51	32.32	32.32	32.34	32.69	33.36	33.17	34.07	34.17	32.83
2009	34.21	34.75	35.17	34.83	34.35	33.87	33.93	33.96	34.42	34.11	34.73	34.87	34.43
Education and Health Services													
2007	22.84	22.94	23.16	23.61	23.44	24.12	24.11	23.83	24.01	24.05	24.25	24.24	23.72
2008	24.43	24.34	24.31	24.41	24.43	24.63	24.53	24.76	24.97	24.89	25.09	25.03	24.66
2009	24.68	25.20	25.19	25.16	24.75	24.84	24.80	24.76	24.96	24.99	25.19	25.32	24.99
Leisure and Hospitality													
2007	15.59	15.72	15.90	15.64	15.37	15.16	15.02	15.28	15.80	15.92	15.99	15.37	15.55
2008	15.32	15.53	15.59	15.75	15.59	15.36	15.15	15.25	15.53	15.57	15.70	16.31	15.54
2009	15.74	15.76	15.67	15.47	15.72	15.54	15.39	15.40	15.68	15.62	15.80	15.94	15.64
Other Services													
2007	21.37	21.65	21.45	21.69	22.56	21.32	21.09	21.16	21.11	21.14	21.09	21.54	21.43
2008	21.22	20.89	21.11	20.91	21.02	21.25	20.93	20.54	21.56	21.87	21.80	22.03	21.25
2009	21.71	21.80	21.66	21.63	21.44	21.07	20.94	21.00	21.99	22.35	22.20	22.34	21.66

Average Weekly Earnings by Selected Industry: Massachusetts, 2007–2009

(Dollars, not seasonally adjusted.)

Industry and year	January	February	March	April	May	June	July	August	September	October	November	December	Annual average
Total Private													
2007	849.52	867.52	859.22	888.38	874.35	868.66	877.11	874.96	887.50	880.72	878.64	889.95	873.35
2008	876.70	878.75	892.66	882.67	876.36	884.21	878.22	889.88	894.74	891.41	904.85	897.13	889.01
2009	898.81	912.58	912.24	901.80	890.78	888.09	889.73	896.76	897.47	894.79	917.67	917.65	902.16
Goods-Producing													
2007	1080.80	1094.55	1106.62	1077.57	1076.04	1096.46	1067.68	1063.76	1088.42	1075.08	1084.37	1108.26	1084.14
2008	1090.67	1094.16	1106.22	1092.11	1099.88	1088.54	1093.66	1101.53	1115.13	1100.93	1114.17	1110.34	1099.98
2009	1113.95	1126.94	1124.81	1121.14	1098.41	1126.47	1112.27	1152.06	1143.55	1152.67	1187.20	1213.60	1139.97
Construction													
2007	1066.88	1083.00	1098.19	1092.59	1108.76	1101.97	1083.32	1058.85	1074.12	1050.02	1089.21	1129.48	1084.78
2008	1127.02	1139.47	1151.08	1128.03	1123.86	1117.43	1140.79	1158.83	1186.49	1179.74	1181.63	1181.47	1152.00
2009	1202.82	1201.43	1199.91	1214.86	1207.30	1201.39	1213.28	1275.05	1200.37	1176.50	1214.25	1261.48	1215.45
Manufacturing													
2007	1086.65	1100.47	1109.92	1070.12	1060.14	1095.16	1059.47	1067.44	1096.56	1088.87	1078.69	1095.20	1082.80
2008	1073.09	1072.30	1087.81	1069.20	1082.96	1065.95	1060.41	1059.14	1068.08	1054.58	1078.38	1074.08	1070.85
2009	1071.29	1063.13	1059.47	1049.54	1023.36	1067.74	1040.95	1060.22	1081.66	1106.79	1141.29	1160.73	1078.39
Trade, Transportation, and Utilities													
2007	737.66	752.84	739.70	756.93	768.12	742.26	773.23	772.85	774.82	775.39	748.18	768.23	758.99
2008	761.21	778.05	789.03	773.48	764.14	773.89	780.86	794.98	781.23	774.23	752.10	748.66	771.87
2009	757.30	762.95	765.60	755.38	758.34	743.49	759.62	753.39	750.71	726.59	746.34	751.17	752.40
Information													
2007	1320.68	1311.22	1305.72	1364.93	1284.50	1316.81	1381.22	1299.90	1344.65	1294.56	1269.60	1292.35	1314.57
2008	1282.34	1255.80	1295.24	1217.37	1198.63	1255.10	1252.42	1243.24	1257.98	1230.57	1282.36	1292.83	1255.18
2009	1239.15	1289.05	1248.14	1225.82	1202.00	1180.88	1189.46	1213.80	1184.01	1170.93	1223.78	1203.94	1213.10
Financial Activities													
2007	1032.42	1084.21	996.49	1115.35	1066.10	1028.13	1086.90	1073.39	1101.05	1122.87	1101.57	1085.12	1075.56
2008	1071.06	1071.45	1092.75	1078.34	1070.41	1089.65	1047.92	1089.28	1093.33	1101.83	1156.20	1126.93	1091.48
2009	1146.60	1157.36	1158.26	1152.01	1121.26	1151.07	1148.53	1176.50	1156.78	1156.99	1193.81	1176.60	1159.21
Professional and Business Services													
2007	1127.48	1154.86	1155.53	1217.88	1188.41	1169.98	1172.88	1175.59	1192.38	1150.51	1159.53	1203.41	1173.25
2008	1159.93	1154.91	1196.37	1189.87	1169.98	1189.38	1157.77	1170.30	1184.28	1180.85	1226.52	1209.62	1181.88
2009	1214.46	1247.53	1262.60	1239.95	1236.60	1212.55	1211.30	1215.77	1225.35	1221.14	1257.23	1237.89	1232.59
Education and Health Services													
2007	680.63	683.61	683.22	710.66	691.48	718.78	723.30	724.43	727.50	738.34	746.90	746.59	713.97
2008	750.00	747.24	746.32	746.95	747.56	763.53	770.24	779.94	779.06	781.55	790.34	780.94	764.46
2009	772.48	793.80	793.49	795.06	782.10	784.94	791.12	792.32	796.22	792.18	801.04	805.18	792.18
Leisure and Hospitality													
2007	419.37	438.59	446.79	456.69	454.95	445.70	450.60	455.34	459.78	456.90	452.52	422.68	447.84
2008	413.64	411.55	417.81	431.55	425.61	413.18	418.14	423.95	427.08	428.18	419.19	433.85	422.69
2009	406.09	400.30	399.59	394.49	408.72	404.04	410.91	414.26	417.09	409.24	409.22	411.25	408.20
Other Services													
2007	671.02	692.80	675.68	685.40	701.62	658.79	658.01	670.77	671.30	661.68	658.01	682.82	672.90
2008	664.19	662.21	677.63	658.67	674.74	673.63	676.04	673.71	685.61	688.91	697.60	700.55	677.88
2009	714.26	725.94	714.78	718.12	701.09	680.56	682.64	693.00	703.68	715.20	714.84	719.35	706.12

MICHIGAN
At a Glance

Population:
  1990 census: 9,295,287
  2000 census: 9,938,444
  2009 estimate: 9,969,727

Percent change in population:
  1990–2000: 6.9%
  2000–2009: 0.3%

Percent change in total nonfarm employment:
  1990–2009: -1.8%
  2008–2009: -6.9%

Industry with the largest growth in employment, 1990–2009 (thousands):
  Education and Health Services, 201.5

Industry with the largest decline or smallest growth in employment, 1990–2009 (thousands):
  Manufacturing, -376.6

Civilian labor force:
  1990: 4,619,988
  2000: 5,143,916
  2009: 4,888,722

Unemployment rate and rank among states (lowest to highest):
  1990: 7.7%, 49th
  2000: 3.7%, 22nd
  2009: 13.6%, 51st

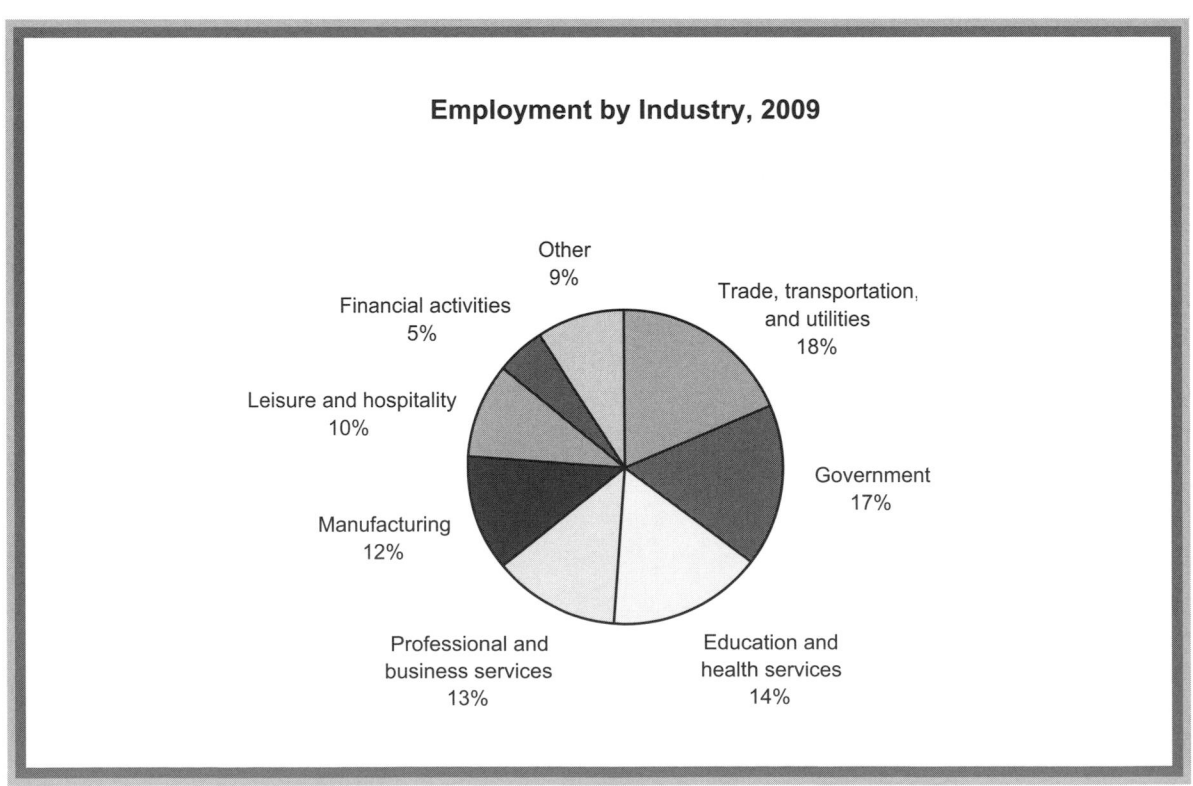

Employment by Industry, 2009

Other 9%

Financial activities 5%

Leisure and hospitality 10%

Manufacturing 12%

Professional and business services 13%

Education and health services 14%

Government 17%

Trade, transportation, and utilities 18%

Employment by Industry: Michigan, Selected Years, 1990–2009

(Numbers in thousands, not seasonally adjusted.)

Industry and year	January	February	March	April	May	June	July	August	September	October	November	December	Annual average
Total Nonfarm													
1990	3825.7	3876.8	3911.2	3929.6	3987.2	4006.7	3950.9	3963.8	3990.9	3990.5	3962.6	3961.3	3946.4
2000	4561.4	4584.5	4621.3	4672.6	4729.4	4744.9	4640.5	4667.8	4710.4	4728.9	4729.8	4723.2	4676.2
2001	4511.1	4535.0	4557.5	4583.9	4628.9	4640.5	4518.8	4548.1	4572.6	4561.5	4554.9	4549.1	4563.5
2002	4388.3	4409.2	4435.9	4468.9	4532.3	4547.1	4446.0	4484.4	4526.7	4536.3	4538.4	4526.9	4486.7
2003	4352.7	4356.0	4369.5	4395.3	4468.3	4475.4	4339.5	4392.6	4444.5	4467.5	4464.9	4461.4	4415.6
2004	4302.5	4312.6	4338.6	4397.1	4450.8	4449.4	4324.8	4381.8	4447.9	4459.3	4463.0	4456.2	4398.7
2005	4289.0	4322.7	4338.8	4397.5	4448.6	4440.0	4324.7	4365.7	4443.7	4432.8	4442.7	4426.3	4389.4
2006	4265.1	4279.5	4302.8	4340.6	4384.9	4393.7	4248.9	4294.4	4361.3	4344.1	4353.6	4344.7	4326.1
2007	4185.2	4211.9	4232.9	4261.3	4325.0	4329.6	4213.8	4255.9	4301.9	4293.5	4305.3	4292.4	4267.4
2008	4145.2	4158.3	4158.7	4172.5	4225.3	4243.4	4112.0	4147.1	4179.7	4168.1	4138.7	4091.7	4161.7
2009	3862.5	3879.9	3870.3	3895.6	3911.6	3886.1	3801.9	3826.9	3879.7	3925.4	3902.7	3871.1	3876.1
Total Private													
1990	3201.7	3232.5	3263.0	3283.0	3339.8	3386.5	3364.5	3381.4	3375.6	3342.5	3307.7	3311.7	3315.8
2000	3889.0	3889.1	3916.5	3972.4	4029.3	4072.1	4021.7	4055.8	4029.5	4025.5	4019.8	4017.5	3994.9
2001	3829.5	3834.4	3850.3	3880.1	3929.3	3959.7	3896.0	3927.4	3892.6	3856.4	3844.6	3841.9	3878.5
2002	3699.5	3703.4	3726.7	3771.8	3837.7	3872.3	3827.2	3864.7	3841.8	3821.5	3820.5	3814.2	3800.1
2003	3662.6	3646.8	3661.3	3691.2	3767.5	3801.9	3725.5	3782.0	3767.4	3752.6	3751.0	3752.9	3730.2
2004	3616.3	3611.4	3634.5	3695.9	3754.7	3780.8	3719.2	3778.5	3769.1	3756.0	3756.3	3754.7	3719.0
2005	3611.5	3625.3	3639.9	3699.9	3756.7	3776.7	3727.3	3766.7	3765.9	3737.5	3742.7	3733.4	3715.3
2006	3593.4	3589.1	3607.5	3652.9	3704.3	3739.8	3655.5	3704.5	3696.4	3659.2	3664.9	3662.3	3660.8
2007	3525.0	3534.0	3549.9	3587.0	3651.6	3682.8	3622.5	3661.8	3647.1	3622.2	3632.6	3624.0	3611.7
2008	3496.0	3492.8	3491.8	3504.3	3567.3	3601.5	3519.0	3548.5	3524.9	3497.4	3467.0	3429.7	3511.7
2009	3209.4	3215.6	3205.2	3226.9	3252.1	3248.1	3210.3	3238.9	3235.9	3259.4	3237.2	3216.0	3229.6
Goods-Producing													
1990	946.5	973.5	984.0	993.6	1008.9	1024.0	1009.3	1017.9	1020.8	1009.8	975.7	959.4	993.6
2000	1084.1	1084.3	1091.3	1116.4	1133.2	1146.9	1123.8	1139.7	1127.3	1126.5	1116.0	1104.4	1116.2
2001	1036.3	1041.7	1042.4	1046.4	1056.2	1062.4	1034.4	1048.0	1040.7	1022.6	1010.5	1004.6	1037.2
2002	948.1	954.8	957.1	964.0	980.7	992.3	973.9	990.1	981.6	975.5	968.8	957.6	970.4
2003	910.9	900.8	902.6	905.3	929.5	942.8	896.1	935.2	928.9	921.5	919.1	912.8	917.1
2004	875.0	869.8	877.8	895.9	911.1	917.9	876.4	921.0	918.7	913.0	909.6	901.6	899.0
2005	853.5	860.7	859.5	872.5	890.4	895.9	862.4	888.9	890.5	886.1	884.4	870.1	876.2
2006	829.2	824.9	827.4	844.4	855.0	863.7	814.8	848.7	843.6	829.4	828.0	817.5	835.6
2007	772.7	781.0	783.7	790.8	805.0	815.4	786.5	812.0	805.4	788.3	791.5	780.3	792.7
2008	745.8	743.3	732.2	730.3	744.3	769.6	723.8	747.9	740.5	728.2	715.7	691.7	734.4
2009	598.7	609.5	604.1	602.4	592.2	586.8	584.0	602.2	603.3	604.3	593.4	578.4	596.6
Mining and Logging													
1990	11.2	11.3	11.2	11.0	12.0	12.3	12.3	11.5	11.2	11.2	11.4	11.2	11.5
2000	8.8	8.6	8.7	9.2	9.4	9.7	10.1	10.1	9.8	10.1	10.0	9.6	9.5
2001	8.8	8.9	9.1	9.2	9.6	9.7	9.6	9.6	9.5	9.5	9.3	9.1	9.3
2002	8.0	8.0	8.1	8.4	8.9	9.0	9.0	8.8	8.9	8.9	8.8	8.5	8.6
2003	7.6	7.6	7.6	7.9	8.6	8.9	8.3	8.3	8.3	8.4	8.2	7.9	8.1
2004	7.4	7.4	7.6	8.0	8.4	8.4	8.6	8.7	8.7	8.5	8.3	7.9	8.2
2005	7.7	7.7	7.7	8.4	8.8	9.0	9.0	8.9	8.6	8.6	8.4	8.0	8.4
2006	7.4	7.5	7.5	7.9	8.2	8.5	8.5	8.5	8.3	8.3	8.1	7.6	8.0
2007	7.2	7.2	7.0	7.3	7.8	8.2	8.2	8.1	8.0	7.9	7.7	7.4	7.7
2008	7.1	7.1	7.1	7.5	8.0	8.2	8.4	8.4	8.3	8.2	8.1	7.8	7.9
2009	6.7	6.9	6.3	6.5	6.8	7.1	7.2	7.2	7.2	7.2	7.0	6.8	6.9
Construction													
1990	128.6	125.1	126.2	134.5	147.2	153.2	156.6	157.4	156.1	151.3	145.1	136.1	143.1
2000	182.3	180.4	188.3	205.6	216.6	224.8	227.7	227.1	224.2	220.6	213.9	203.2	209.6
2001	182.5	180.8	185.6	198.3	211.8	218.7	222.6	223.1	219.2	215.7	210.7	203.9	206.1
2002	182.3	177.8	180.4	192.3	206.9	213.0	216.0	215.8	210.7	207.6	201.5	190.6	199.6
2003	168.8	163.0	164.5	178.6	196.4	204.5	208.5	208.0	204.5	202.8	197.5	190.2	190.6
2004	166.8	163.4	167.4	183.2	195.7	203.9	208.6	207.8	205.2	203.9	200.5	191.2	191.5
2005	168.0	164.6	167.4	183.1	195.2	203.2	206.7	204.9	201.5	198.7	193.9	182.4	189.1
2006	162.5	158.7	161.7	174.5	185.4	192.5	192.5	191.2	187.7	183.5	177.0	168.7	178.0
2007	150.7	145.2	149.7	158.0	171.6	178.9	180.4	180.4	177.8	174.3	168.7	159.6	166.3
2008	142.8	137.8	139.3	146.4	160.1	166.0	166.1	166.1	163.2	159.3	150.6	138.4	153.0
2009	119.1	116.1	115.3	123.5	132.7	135.9	136.7	135.6	132.3	135.1	128.8	116.6	127.3
Manufacturing													
1990	806.7	837.1	846.6	848.1	849.7	858.5	840.4	849.0	853.5	847.3	819.2	812.1	839.0
2000	893.0	895.3	894.3	901.6	907.2	912.4	886.0	902.5	893.3	895.8	892.1	891.6	897.1
2001	845.0	852.0	847.7	838.9	834.8	834.0	802.2	815.3	812.0	797.4	790.5	791.6	821.8
2002	757.8	769.0	768.6	763.3	764.9	770.3	748.9	765.5	762.0	759.0	758.5	758.5	762.2
2003	734.5	730.2	730.5	718.8	724.5	729.4	679.3	718.9	716.1	710.3	713.4	714.7	718.4
2004	700.8	699.0	702.8	704.7	707.0	705.6	659.2	704.5	704.8	700.6	700.8	702.5	699.4
2005	677.8	688.4	684.4	681.0	686.4	683.7	646.7	675.1	680.4	678.8	682.1	679.7	678.7
2006	659.3	658.7	658.2	662.0	661.4	662.7	613.8	649.0	647.6	637.6	642.9	641.2	649.5
2007	614.8	628.6	627.0	625.5	625.6	628.3	597.9	623.5	619.6	606.1	615.1	613.3	618.8
2008	595.9	598.4	585.8	576.4	576.2	595.4	549.3	573.4	569.0	560.7	557.0	545.5	573.6
2009	472.9	486.5	482.5	472.4	452.7	443.8	440.1	459.4	463.8	462.0	457.6	455.0	462.4

Employment by Industry: Michigan, Selected Years, 1990–2009—*Continued*

(Numbers in thousands, not seasonally adjusted.)

Industry and year	January	February	March	April	May	June	July	August	September	October	November	December	Annual average
Service-Providing													
1990	2879.2	2903.3	2927.2	2936.0	2978.3	2982.7	2941.6	2945.9	2970.1	2980.7	2986.9	3001.9	2952.8
2000	3477.3	3500.2	3530.0	3556.2	3596.2	3598.0	3516.7	3528.1	3583.1	3602.4	3613.8	3618.8	3560.1
2001	3474.8	3493.3	3515.1	3537.5	3572.7	3578.1	3484.4	3500.1	3531.9	3538.9	3544.4	3544.5	3526.3
2002	3440.2	3454.4	3478.8	3504.9	3551.6	3554.8	3472.1	3494.3	3545.1	3560.8	3569.6	3569.3	3516.3
2003	3441.8	3455.2	3466.9	3490.0	3538.8	3532.6	3443.4	3457.4	3515.6	3546.0	3545.8	3548.6	3498.5
2004	3427.5	3442.8	3460.8	3501.2	3539.7	3531.5	3448.4	3460.8	3529.2	3546.3	3553.4	3554.6	3499.7
2005	3435.5	3462.0	3479.3	3525.0	3558.2	3544.1	3462.3	3476.8	3553.2	3546.7	3558.3	3556.2	3513.1
2006	3435.9	3454.6	3475.4	3496.2	3529.9	3530.0	3434.1	3445.7	3517.7	3514.7	3525.6	3527.2	3490.6
2007	3412.5	3430.9	3449.2	3470.5	3520.0	3514.2	3427.3	3443.9	3496.5	3505.2	3513.8	3512.1	3474.7
2008	3399.4	3415.0	3426.5	3442.2	3481.0	3473.8	3388.2	3399.2	3439.2	3439.9	3423.0	3400.0	3427.3
2009	3263.8	3270.4	3266.2	3293.2	3319.4	3299.3	3217.9	3224.7	3276.4	3321.1	3309.3	3292.7	3279.5
Trade, Transportation, and Utilities													
1990	763.5	756.6	759.6	762.1	774.2	782.1	781.4	782.8	773.1	777.0	786.2	803.1	775.1
2000	866.5	858.9	864.7	869.5	881.2	886.7	874.0	879.9	878.4	889.3	905.2	919.7	881.2
2001	865.3	854.8	855.5	859.5	867.4	870.6	857.1	860.2	853.7	853.6	865.3	871.7	861.2
2002	826.1	814.9	820.4	825.6	838.6	843.5	834.7	838.3	836.8	832.8	845.8	854.0	834.3
2003	807.8	798.8	800.7	803.8	816.9	822.8	814.9	820.3	819.5	823.8	833.4	841.8	817.0
2004	796.9	789.9	792.0	800.7	812.7	817.1	811.5	814.1	808.1	813.7	826.4	834.3	809.8
2005	791.0	785.3	788.1	796.9	807.8	811.9	811.0	811.7	806.8	806.1	818.8	825.7	805.1
2006	784.5	776.1	780.3	787.3	797.5	803.6	796.8	798.8	795.0	795.4	809.1	816.0	795.0
2007	779.2	770.1	772.1	777.1	789.4	794.4	789.6	791.1	787.3	787.0	800.6	806.5	787.0
2008	771.9	763.7	765.8	764.6	776.1	780.6	774.1	774.1	769.4	765.2	769.2	769.2	770.3
2009	723.6	714.0	709.8	712.0	720.9	723.1	714.1	717.4	712.4	714.1	719.6	722.7	717.0
Wholesale Trade													
1990	151.7	152.0	153.0	153.8	155.2	156.7	156.6	157.1	157.0	155.8	155.4	156.2	155.0
2000	184.0	184.8	185.8	185.8	187.1	188.0	187.0	186.7	185.2	185.8	185.3	186.4	186.0
2001	180.3	180.8	181.2	183.2	183.4	183.0	181.1	180.7	178.9	177.9	176.9	177.1	180.4
2002	173.0	173.0	173.6	175.0	177.1	177.8	176.5	176.7	175.4	175.3	175.5	175.9	175.4
2003	171.7	171.7	172.2	172.6	173.5	174.1	173.1	173.2	172.3	172.4	171.8	172.1	172.6
2004	167.2	167.4	168.8	170.2	171.6	172.6	172.3	172.0	171.0	171.1	171.0	171.3	170.5
2005	167.8	168.2	169.1	170.3	172.0	172.5	172.4	172.2	171.1	171.2	170.9	171.2	170.7
2006	167.9	168.1	169.0	171.1	172.2	173.7	172.8	172.0	170.7	170.0	169.5	169.8	170.6
2007	167.2	166.8	167.2	169.0	170.4	171.4	170.5	170.1	169.0	169.1	168.6	169.0	169.0
2008	167.0	167.1	167.7	168.5	170.0	170.6	169.1	169.0	168.1	166.9	165.3	163.8	167.8
2009	158.0	156.4	155.0	155.1	155.0	153.4	151.0	151.3	150.2	151.9	150.8	150.1	153.2
Retail Trade													
1990	498.3	490.1	491.2	492.5	500.8	504.8	506.2	506.5	496.8	504.2	514.3	528.4	502.8
2000	550.0	541.8	546.3	549.1	558.5	562.1	552.8	557.5	557.9	564.6	581.7	595.5	559.8
2001	553.8	544.2	544.9	544.2	550.8	553.0	543.8	546.0	542.5	542.4	556.8	563.5	548.8
2002	526.7	515.8	519.5	522.8	531.8	534.9	530.1	532.2	532.6	528.2	542.1	551.1	530.7
2003	511.0	503.1	503.9	505.8	516.4	521.0	517.0	520.8	521.2	524.5	535.6	543.7	518.7
2004	507.6	500.1	500.9	506.2	515.6	518.0	513.7	515.4	510.5	513.5	526.9	534.5	513.6
2005	499.0	492.2	493.5	500.1	507.5	509.7	510.5	508.8	505.5	504.9	517.4	523.3	506.0
2006	490.1	481.9	484.6	488.8	496.1	499.4	497.4	497.2	494.9	496.7	510.5	514.8	496.0
2007	486.6	476.7	478.6	481.1	490.0	492.4	492.3	490.9	488.5	489.3	503.2	507.1	489.7
2008	481.0	472.2	473.5	472.4	480.5	482.3	480.7	480.0	476.3	474.8	481.1	482.3	478.1
2009	452.6	443.3	441.4	444.7	453.5	457.4	451.7	453.6	449.0	450.7	457.4	460.3	451.3
Transportation and Utilities													
1990	113.5	114.5	115.4	115.8	118.2	120.6	118.6	119.2	119.3	117.0	116.5	118.5	117.3
2000	132.5	132.3	132.6	134.6	135.6	136.6	134.2	135.7	135.3	138.9	138.2	137.8	135.4
2001	131.2	129.8	129.4	132.1	133.2	134.6	132.2	133.5	132.3	133.3	131.6	131.1	132.0
2002	126.4	126.1	127.3	127.8	129.7	130.8	128.1	129.4	128.8	129.3	128.2	127.0	128.2
2003	125.1	124.0	124.6	125.4	127.0	127.7	124.8	126.3	126.0	126.9	126.0	126.0	125.8
2004	122.1	122.4	122.3	124.3	125.5	126.5	125.5	126.7	126.6	129.1	128.5	128.5	125.7
2005	124.2	124.9	125.5	126.5	128.3	129.7	128.1	130.7	130.2	130.0	130.5	131.2	128.3
2006	126.5	126.1	126.7	127.4	129.2	130.5	126.6	129.6	129.4	128.7	129.1	131.4	128.4
2007	125.4	126.6	126.3	127.0	129.0	130.6	126.8	130.1	129.8	128.6	128.8	130.4	128.3
2008	123.9	124.4	124.6	123.7	125.6	127.7	124.3	125.1	125.0	123.5	122.8	123.1	124.5
2009	113.0	114.3	113.4	112.2	112.4	112.3	111.4	112.5	113.2	111.5	111.4	112.3	112.5
Information													
1990	69.7	69.5	69.9	69.2	69.8	70.6	70.2	70.3	70.1	70.0	69.4	70.5	69.9
2000	72.3	72.0	72.7	71.9	72.6	73.0	72.9	73.0	73.7	71.8	72.6	73.3	72.7
2001	71.6	71.8	72.2	71.6	72.3	72.6	72.3	72.2	71.7	71.7	72.8	72.7	72.1
2002	72.5	72.3	72.2	70.8	71.3	71.3	69.9	69.5	68.5	68.5	69.1	69.4	70.4
2003	67.8	67.6	67.9	67.7	67.9	67.9	66.8	66.7	66.0	65.9	66.4	66.8	67.1
2004	65.7	65.3	65.5	65.4	65.8	66.2	66.2	66.0	65.2	65.4	65.9	66.3	65.7
2005	65.5	64.9	65.0	65.0	65.4	65.6	65.3	65.0	64.2	63.9	64.6	64.8	64.9
2006	64.4	64.5	64.1	64.2	64.7	65.1	63.8	63.6	62.8	62.9	63.2	63.3	63.9
2007	63.4	63.4	63.1	63.4	64.1	64.0	63.2	63.2	62.9	62.0	61.8	62.0	62.9
2008	61.2	61.2	60.5	60.0	60.6	60.9	59.9	60.2	60.2	59.0	59.5	59.1	60.2
2009	57.8	57.7	56.7	56.7	56.8	56.7	55.9	55.3	54.3	53.8	53.4	53.1	55.7

Employment by Industry: Michigan, Selected Years, 1990–2009—*Continued*

(Numbers in thousands, not seasonally adjusted.)

Industry and year	January	February	March	April	May	June	July	August	September	October	November	December	Annual average
Financial Activities													
1990	191.4	191.9	193.5	189.5	192.2	194.6	195.2	195.5	194.4	190.2	191.4	193.3	192.8
2000	205.5	205.2	205.2	207.5	208.7	211.0	210.9	210.1	208.0	208.0	208.0	209.6	208.1
2001	203.8	204.8	206.0	207.4	210.7	212.9	211.7	212.0	209.1	209.0	209.3	211.0	209.0
2002	210.6	210.7	210.7	212.2	214.1	215.1	215.3	216.1	213.7	213.3	213.8	214.9	213.4
2003	213.1	213.1	213.4	216.4	218.7	220.5	220.4	220.6	217.5	215.9	214.9	215.7	216.7
2004	212.8	212.3	213.4	215.4	217.0	218.7	219.0	218.4	216.1	214.4	214.6	216.0	215.7
2005	214.5	214.5	214.5	215.5	216.9	218.8	218.4	218.4	216.2	215.0	215.0	215.2	216.1
2006	213.4	213.3	213.0	213.5	215.2	217.3	216.0	215.9	213.2	211.6	211.2	212.0	213.8
2007	209.1	209.0	208.8	209.9	211.5	213.2	213.1	211.5	208.0	207.0	206.1	206.5	209.5
2008	204.4	204.4	203.6	203.0	205.0	205.3	203.7	203.0	199.8	198.2	196.8	196.5	202.0
2009	192.2	191.7	190.5	191.9	193.0	193.8	192.5	191.8	189.0	189.1	188.4	187.3	190.9
Professional and Business Services													
1990	379.2	381.8	387.3	394.3	401.0	407.7	406.5	408.7	410.7	402.9	398.4	396.9	398.0
2000	627.6	625.5	632.1	640.5	647.8	654.4	644.5	655.2	650.5	642.8	638.5	634.6	641.2
2001	607.7	608.0	609.9	616.0	618.9	623.4	610.5	620.3	613.4	602.6	596.6	592.7	610.0
2002	578.0	579.0	582.3	593.9	603.4	608.9	602.0	614.7	610.3	607.9	606.7	604.3	599.3
2003	578.6	577.0	579.2	589.3	597.6	600.6	585.4	596.0	592.4	587.9	588.6	585.9	588.2
2004	565.0	564.9	566.8	583.0	590.4	595.8	587.9	598.8	597.3	597.2	595.3	592.9	586.3
2005	573.7	574.7	576.2	592.1	596.8	599.7	594.7	604.4	606.8	601.1	600.1	597.2	593.1
2006	575.3	572.6	572.9	581.8	587.1	595.4	583.8	594.8	594.6	591.5	592.5	591.4	586.1
2007	565.0	567.7	568.1	577.5	584.5	588.3	575.5	586.3	585.8	589.8	592.1	588.4	580.8
2008	564.6	566.4	567.5	571.3	577.7	574.1	557.9	561.3	558.5	562.6	554.6	545.5	563.5
2009	510.1	509.4	505.2	508.8	508.2	501.8	490.0	497.0	506.3	523.6	524.5	519.2	508.7
Education and Health Services													
1990	404.7	408.5	411.5	408.4	408.4	410.0	406.6	408.7	415.9	417.2	418.9	421.9	411.7
2000	492.6	499.1	500.0	501.5	501.5	502.1	498.0	499.1	504.1	507.0	511.0	509.3	502.1
2001	504.0	509.1	512.2	516.0	518.0	520.3	515.1	516.6	520.2	524.7	528.9	529.0	517.8
2002	522.4	528.0	531.0	536.4	538.1	538.0	528.9	530.2	536.2	541.7	546.0	544.3	535.1
2003	538.5	544.1	544.8	544.7	546.5	544.7	540.0	540.8	547.9	554.2	558.3	558.2	546.9
2004	548.8	555.2	558.5	562.0	562.1	556.6	553.2	553.4	564.1	569.6	574.0	573.3	560.9
2005	564.1	572.8	576.0	576.1	577.1	570.1	566.4	566.9	579.7	583.8	588.6	588.1	575.8
2006	575.2	580.6	585.4	583.0	586.0	580.6	573.7	573.6	587.6	588.4	592.6	593.2	583.3
2007	584.9	591.3	594.2	596.0	598.4	594.8	588.6	589.3	599.4	605.2	608.6	609.2	596.7
2008	600.0	605.4	607.2	607.2	610.3	606.1	600.1	600.1	607.8	613.8	616.0	614.6	607.4
2009	602.6	609.9	611.8	611.7	614.4	610.4	602.4	603.1	608.9	625.5	627.4	629.9	613.2
Leisure and Hospitality													
1990	306.7	308.6	313.3	323.2	340.5	351.4	351.2	352.6	346.3	330.8	323.5	321.2	330.8
2000	369.7	371.5	376.2	389.7	408.4	420.6	420.5	421.4	411.8	404.7	393.1	390.7	398.2
2001	368.0	369.5	375.5	386.2	407.1	417.0	416.9	419.3	407.6	396.5	384.7	382.8	394.3
2002	367.2	367.8	375.6	390.1	411.0	421.1	421.3	424.0	414.3	402.1	391.1	389.3	397.9
2003	369.0	368.0	373.5	387.1	412.2	423.6	421.4	421.3	415.3	403.7	390.9	391.0	398.1
2004	375.3	375.9	381.3	395.1	415.5	426.7	424.8	426.3	419.1	402.6	391.3	390.5	402.0
2005	373.1	375.4	382.1	401.6	420.6	431.0	427.8	430.6	422.0	403.1	393.0	393.1	404.5
2006	376.6	381.2	386.9	401.1	419.8	433.0	428.2	430.3	421.7	403.8	392.2	391.9	405.6
2007	377.9	377.8	384.6	396.7	421.0	432.5	428.1	430.4	421.9	406.5	395.6	394.0	405.6
2008	374.8	374.2	379.8	391.9	415.2	425.3	422.0	424.5	412.6	395.5	382.5	381.2	398.3
2009	357.0	355.6	359.5	374.4	395.8	403.4	401.6	402.8	393.5	382.7	366.1	361.4	379.5
Other Services													
1990	140.0	142.1	143.9	142.7	144.8	146.1	144.1	144.9	144.3	144.6	144.2	145.4	143.9
2000	170.7	172.6	174.3	175.4	175.9	177.4	177.1	177.4	175.7	175.4	175.4	175.9	175.3
2001	172.8	174.7	176.6	177.0	178.7	180.5	178.0	178.8	176.2	175.7	176.5	177.4	176.9
2002	174.6	175.9	177.4	178.8	180.5	182.1	181.2	181.8	180.4	179.7	179.2	180.4	179.3
2003	176.9	177.4	179.2	176.9	178.2	179.0	180.5	181.1	179.9	179.7	179.4	180.7	179.1
2004	176.8	178.1	179.2	178.4	180.1	181.8	180.2	180.5	180.5	180.1	179.2	179.8	179.6
2005	176.1	177.0	178.5	180.2	181.7	183.7	181.3	180.8	179.7	178.4	178.2	179.2	179.6
2006	174.8	175.9	177.5	177.6	179.0	181.1	178.4	178.8	177.9	176.2	176.1	177.0	177.5
2007	172.8	173.7	175.3	175.6	177.7	180.2	177.9	178.3	177.3	176.6	176.1	177.1	176.6
2008	173.3	174.2	175.2	176.0	178.1	179.6	177.5	177.4	176.1	174.9	172.7	171.9	175.6
2009	167.4	167.8	167.6	169.0	170.8	172.1	169.8	169.3	168.2	166.3	164.4	164.0	168.1
Government													
1990	624.0	644.3	648.2	646.6	647.4	620.2	586.4	582.4	615.3	648.0	654.9	649.6	630.6
2000	672.4	695.4	704.8	700.2	700.1	672.8	618.8	612.0	680.9	703.4	710.0	705.7	681.4
2001	681.6	700.6	707.2	703.8	699.6	680.8	622.8	620.7	680.0	705.1	710.3	707.2	685.0
2002	688.8	705.8	709.2	697.1	694.6	674.8	618.8	619.7	684.9	714.8	717.9	712.7	686.6
2003	690.1	709.2	708.2	704.1	700.8	673.5	614.0	610.6	677.1	714.9	713.9	708.5	685.4
2004	686.2	701.2	704.1	701.2	696.1	668.6	605.6	603.3	678.8	703.3	706.7	701.5	679.7
2005	677.5	697.4	698.9	697.6	691.9	663.3	597.4	599.0	677.8	695.3	700.0	692.9	674.1
2006	671.7	690.4	695.3	687.7	680.6	653.9	593.4	589.9	664.9	684.9	688.7	682.4	665.3
2007	660.2	677.9	683.0	674.3	673.4	646.8	591.3	594.1	654.8	671.3	672.7	668.4	655.7
2008	649.2	665.5	666.9	668.2	658.0	641.9	593.0	598.6	654.8	670.7	671.7	662.0	650.0
2009	653.1	664.3	665.1	668.7	659.5	638.0	591.6	588.0	643.8	666.0	665.5	655.1	646.6

Average Weekly Hours by Selected Industry: Michigan, 2007–2009

(Not seasonally adjusted.)

Industry and year	January	February	March	April	May	June	July	August	September	October	November	December	Annual average
Total Private													
2007	34.60	34.60	34.70	34.80	34.90	35.10	35.00	35.30	35.30	34.90	34.70	35.10	34.90
2008	34.30	34.30	34.50	34.30	34.40	34.60	34.20	34.40	34.30	34.10	33.80	33.50	34.20
2009	32.60	33.50	33.40	33.00	33.10	33.40	33.50	34.00	33.30	33.40	33.50	33.20	33.30
Goods-Producing													
2007	40.40	39.80	40.30	40.50	40.60	40.80	39.80	41.20	41.40	41.10	40.10	41.50	40.60
2008	40.40	40.50	40.90	40.60	40.70	41.30	40.20	40.70	40.90	40.70	39.10	39.20	40.50
2009	36.30	38.10	38.30	38.00	37.50	39.20	39.20	40.00	38.30	39.30	39.00	40.00	38.60
Construction													
2007	38.00	36.50	37.40	37.40	38.40	39.10	39.10	38.50	38.70	39.00	37.10	38.10	38.20
2008	37.60	37.10	38.10	38.20	38.70	38.90	38.60	38.50	38.30	38.00	37.40	37.10	38.10
2009	36.10	36.80	35.80	35.70	37.50	36.90	38.10	38.40	36.30	38.50	37.40	37.20	37.10
Manufacturing													
2007	40.70	40.30	40.70	40.90	40.80	41.00	39.70	41.70	41.90	41.50	40.60	41.80	41.00
2008	41.10	41.30	41.50	41.20	41.20	42.60	41.00	41.60	41.90	41.40	40.00	40.30	41.30
2009	36.80	38.90	39.40	39.10	37.90	40.30	39.90	40.70	39.00	39.60	39.50	40.70	39.30
Trade, Transportation, and Utilities													
2007	33.50	33.60	33.40	33.50	33.70	34.30	34.70	34.80	34.60	34.20	34.40	34.60	34.10
2008	33.70	33.50	33.70	33.60	33.60	34.00	33.80	34.00	33.80	33.30	32.80	32.40	33.50
2009	32.20	32.50	32.30	32.10	32.70	32.60	33.00	33.10	33.10	32.60	32.70	32.40	32.60
Information													
2007	35.20	35.80	35.70	35.90	35.10	35.60	35.50	35.00	35.60	35.20	35.20	35.70	35.50
2008	34.80	35.90	35.90	35.40	35.60	35.90	35.30	35.30	34.90	34.80	35.90	36.40	35.50
2009	35.80	36.60	36.40	35.80	37.30	36.10	35.40	36.40	36.30	35.50	36.30	35.60	36.10
Financial Activities													
2007	35.60	35.40	35.30	35.60	35.40	35.90	36.30	35.80	36.00	35.80	35.90	36.40	35.80
2008	35.90	35.90	36.30	36.00	36.10	36.10	36.10	36.20	36.50	36.50	36.60	36.10	36.20
2009	35.30	36.00	36.10	36.20	36.00	36.00	36.20	36.60	35.80	36.00	36.70	36.20	36.10
Professional and Business Services													
2007	33.70	33.90	33.90	34.40	34.60	34.80	34.90	34.40	34.80	34.60	34.40	34.80	34.40
2008	33.80	33.90	34.50	34.30	34.50	34.70	34.10	34.10	33.80	34.00	34.50	34.20	34.20
2009	33.90	34.80	34.90	34.00	34.60	34.60	34.60	35.70	34.60	34.70	35.20	34.40	34.70
Education and Health Services													
2007	37.20	37.60	37.80	37.40	37.40	37.00	37.00	37.20	37.30	36.50	36.60	36.40	37.10
2008	35.70	35.60	35.60	35.20	35.30	34.90	34.80	34.50	34.70	34.10	34.40	34.00	34.90
2009	33.70	34.40	34.10	33.70	33.60	33.40	33.40	33.40	33.00	33.00	32.90	32.50	33.40
Leisure and Hospitality													
2007	23.20	23.30	23.40	23.40	23.70	24.40	24.80	24.80	23.90	23.20	23.00	23.00	23.70
2008	22.50	22.50	22.90	23.10	23.50	23.70	24.20	24.50	23.60	23.50	22.90	23.00	23.40
2009	22.30	22.90	22.80	22.70	23.50	23.90	24.50	24.70	23.90	23.70	23.40	23.40	23.50
Other Services													
2007	31.30	31.20	31.20	31.40	31.80	31.70	31.80	31.90	32.20	32.10	31.40	31.30	31.60
2008	31.10	31.00	30.90	30.70	30.30	31.00	31.60	31.60	31.00	31.20	31.60	31.30	31.10
2009	31.70	31.80	31.50	31.80	31.60	31.20	31.60	32.00	31.00	30.90	31.20	30.70	31.40

Average Hourly Earnings by Selected Industry: Michigan, 2007–2009

(Dollars, not seasonally adjusted.)

Industry and year	January	February	March	April	May	June	July	August	September	October	November	December	Annual average
Total Private													
2007	21.56	21.49	21.65	21.77	21.51	21.32	21.38	21.26	21.67	21.43	21.65	21.93	21.55
2008	21.93	21.90	21.97	21.73	21.30	21.43	21.09	21.17	21.45	21.54	22.00	21.93	21.62
2009	22.01	22.17	22.17	22.04	21.82	21.75	21.73	21.38	21.61	21.92	22.08	22.14	21.90
Goods-Producing													
2007	25.79	25.57	25.70	25.63	25.76	25.53	25.51	25.35	25.63	25.38	25.38	26.18	25.62
2008	25.64	25.64	25.78	25.34	24.99	25.07	24.50	24.40	24.76	24.71	25.16	25.37	25.11
2009	25.50	25.70	25.51	25.58	25.20	25.29	25.45	24.11	24.71	25.04	25.06	25.51	25.22
Construction													
2007	22.84	23.06	23.44	23.74	23.71	23.96	24.71	24.69	25.09	25.22	25.57	25.60	24.35
2008	26.29	26.45	26.50	26.76	25.96	25.84	26.17	26.11	26.54	26.05	26.22	27.06	26.31
2009	27.08	26.74	26.74	26.65	26.25	26.05	26.02	26.07	26.03	26.02	25.95	26.78	26.34
Manufacturing													
2007	23.12	23.14	23.79	23.97	24.07	23.94	23.93	23.92	24.34	24.15	24.20	25.11	23.98
2008	25.51	25.52	25.75	25.10	24.84	24.95	25.00	24.81	25.09	25.07	25.53	25.57	25.23
2009	25.70	24.80	24.66	24.82	24.52	24.72	24.97	23.15	24.09	24.48	24.56	24.73	24.59
Trade, Transportation, and Utilities													
2007	19.97	19.89	19.29	19.62	19.50	19.05	19.09	18.91	18.97	18.63	18.90	18.63	19.19
2008	19.21	19.15	18.96	19.05	18.67	18.85	18.85	18.69	18.50	18.54	18.95	18.39	18.82
2009	18.84	18.80	18.76	18.84	18.62	18.66	18.56	18.94	18.85	18.95	19.17	19.03	18.83
Information													
2007	22.09	21.79	21.99	22.24	22.69	22.24	22.64	22.15	22.98	22.34	22.16	22.42	22.31
2008	22.72	22.30	22.61	22.84	22.92	23.13	23.04	23.05	23.36	23.25	23.70	24.20	23.09
2009	24.78	25.27	25.29	25.27	26.12	26.25	27.51	27.18	27.11	27.83	28.74	29.16	26.67
Financial Activities													
2007	21.97	22.08	22.40	22.84	22.36	22.12	22.32	22.76	23.57	23.31	23.41	24.23	22.78
2008	23.60	23.27	23.69	24.08	23.45	23.97	23.59	23.39	23.21	23.20	23.80	22.90	23.51
2009	23.24	22.77	22.97	23.20	24.08	23.11	23.56	24.24	24.07	24.21	24.19	24.27	23.68
Professional and Business Services													
2007	24.92	25.21	25.64	25.80	25.29	25.22	25.48	25.22	25.86	24.96	25.81	26.08	25.46
2008	25.92	26.14	26.65	25.51	24.78	25.08	24.93	25.67	26.32	26.60	27.55	28.08	26.09
2009	28.08	28.99	29.03	28.44	28.13	27.80	27.66	25.96	25.98	26.21	27.05	27.01	27.52
Education and Health Services													
2007	18.97	18.86	19.69	19.67	19.08	19.26	19.65	19.30	19.73	19.75	19.84	20.06	19.49
2008	20.02	20.26	20.32	20.64	20.30	20.15	20.12	20.04	20.25	20.35	20.34	20.38	20.32
2009	20.59	20.45	20.51	20.53	20.54	20.80	20.86	21.08	21.49	21.86	21.24	21.27	20.93
Leisure and Hospitality													
2007	11.21	11.19	11.27	11.37	11.21	11.01	11.10	10.96	11.46	11.57	11.73	11.87	11.32
2008	11.56	11.53	11.60	11.48	11.45	11.28	11.23	11.20	11.50	11.38	11.55	11.60	11.44
2009	11.50	11.41	11.51	11.50	11.32	11.29	11.21	11.31	11.52	11.52	11.70	11.74	11.45
Other Services													
2007	19.54	19.22	19.37	19.44	19.16	19.29	19.31	19.11	19.04	19.65	19.74	19.03	19.32
2008	18.96	19.59	18.99	18.77	18.70	18.98	18.43	18.99	19.51	19.69	20.51	20.38	19.29
2009	20.42	20.02	20.32	19.64	19.64	19.44	19.06	18.78	19.05	19.20	19.03	19.43	19.50

Average Weekly Earnings by Selected Industry: Michigan, 2007–2009

(Dollars, not seasonally adjusted.)

Industry and year	January	February	March	April	May	June	July	August	September	October	November	December	Annual average
Total Private													
2007	745.98	743.55	751.26	757.60	750.70	748.33	748.30	750.48	764.95	747.91	751.26	769.74	752.10
2008	752.20	751.17	757.97	745.34	732.72	741.48	721.28	728.25	735.74	734.51	743.60	734.66	739.40
2009	717.53	742.70	740.48	727.32	722.24	726.45	727.96	726.92	719.61	732.13	739.68	735.05	729.27
Goods-Producing													
2007	1041.92	1017.69	1035.71	1038.02	1045.86	1041.62	1015.30	1044.42	1061.08	1043.12	1017.74	1086.47	1040.17
2008	1035.86	1038.42	1054.40	1028.80	1017.09	1035.39	984.90	993.08	1012.68	1005.70	983.76	994.50	1016.96
2009	925.65	979.17	977.03	972.04	945.00	991.37	997.64	964.40	946.39	984.07	977.34	1020.40	973.49
Construction													
2007	867.92	841.69	876.66	887.88	910.46	936.84	966.16	950.57	970.98	983.58	948.65	975.36	930.17
2008	988.50	981.30	1009.65	1022.23	1004.65	1005.18	1010.16	1005.24	1016.48	989.90	980.63	1003.93	1002.41
2009	977.59	984.03	957.29	951.41	984.38	961.25	991.36	1001.09	944.89	1001.77	970.53	996.22	977.21
Manufacturing													
2007	940.98	932.54	968.25	980.37	982.06	981.54	950.02	997.46	1019.85	1002.23	982.52	1049.60	983.18
2008	1048.46	1053.98	1068.63	1034.12	1023.41	1062.87	1025.00	1032.10	1051.27	1037.90	1021.20	1030.47	1042.00
2009	945.76	964.72	971.60	970.46	929.31	996.22	996.30	942.21	939.51	969.41	970.12	1006.51	966.39
Trade, Transportation, and Utilities													
2007	669.00	668.30	644.29	657.27	657.15	653.42	662.42	658.07	656.36	637.15	650.16	644.60	654.38
2008	647.38	641.53	638.95	640.08	627.31	640.90	637.13	635.46	625.30	617.38	621.56	595.84	630.47
2009	606.65	611.00	605.95	604.76	608.87	608.32	612.48	626.91	623.94	617.77	626.86	616.57	613.86
Information													
2007	777.57	780.08	785.04	798.42	796.42	791.74	803.72	775.25	818.09	786.37	780.03	800.39	792.01
2008	790.66	800.57	811.70	808.54	815.95	830.37	813.31	813.67	815.26	809.10	850.83	880.88	819.70
2009	887.12	924.88	920.56	904.67	974.28	947.63	973.85	989.35	984.09	987.97	1043.26	1038.10	962.79
Financial Activities													
2007	782.13	781.63	790.72	813.10	791.54	794.11	810.22	814.81	848.52	834.50	840.42	881.97	815.52
2008	847.24	835.39	859.95	866.88	846.55	865.32	851.60	846.72	847.17	846.80	871.08	826.69	851.06
2009	820.37	819.72	829.22	839.84	866.88	831.96	852.87	887.18	861.71	871.56	898.78	878.57	854.85
Professional and Business Services													
2007	839.80	854.62	869.20	887.52	875.03	877.66	889.25	867.57	899.93	863.62	887.86	907.58	875.82
2008	876.10	886.15	919.43	874.99	854.91	870.28	850.11	875.35	889.62	904.40	950.48	960.34	892.28
2009	951.91	1008.85	1013.15	966.96	973.30	961.88	957.04	926.77	898.91	909.49	952.16	929.14	954.94
Education and Health Services													
2007	705.68	709.14	744.28	735.66	713.59	712.62	727.05	717.96	735.93	720.88	726.14	730.18	723.08
2008	736.13	721.26	723.39	726.53	716.59	703.24	700.18	691.38	702.68	693.94	699.70	692.92	709.17
2009	693.88	703.48	699.39	691.86	690.14	694.72	696.72	704.07	709.17	721.38	698.80	691.28	699.06
Leisure and Hospitality													
2007	260.07	260.73	263.72	266.06	265.68	268.64	275.28	271.81	273.89	268.42	269.79	273.01	268.28
2008	260.10	259.43	265.64	265.19	269.08	267.34	271.77	274.40	271.40	267.43	264.50	266.80	267.70
2009	256.45	261.29	262.43	261.05	266.02	269.83	274.65	279.36	275.33	273.02	273.78	274.72	269.08
Other Services													
2007	611.60	599.66	604.34	610.42	609.29	611.49	614.06	609.61	613.09	630.77	619.84	595.64	610.51
2008	589.66	607.29	586.79	576.24	566.61	588.38	582.39	600.08	604.81	614.33	648.12	637.89	599.92
2009	647.31	636.64	640.08	624.55	620.62	606.53	602.30	600.96	590.55	593.28	593.74	596.50	612.30

MINNESOTA
At a Glance

Population:
    1990 census: 4,375,665
    2000 census: 4,919,479
    2009 estimate: 5,266,214

Percent change in population:
    1990–2000: 12.4%,
    2000–2009: 7.0%

Percent change in total nonfarm employment:
    1990–2009: 24.1%
    2008–2009: -4.1%

Industry with the largest growth in employment, 1990–2009 (thousands):
    Education and Health Services, 211.2

Industry with the largest decline or smallest growth in employment, 1990–2009 (thousands):
    Manufacturing, -41.4

Civilian labor force:
    1990: 2,390,010
    2000: 2,807,668
    2009: 2,967,967

Unemployment rate and rank among states (lowest to highest):
    2000: 3.1%, 12th
    2007: 4.6%, 31st
    2009: 8.0%, 21st

Employment by Industry, 2009

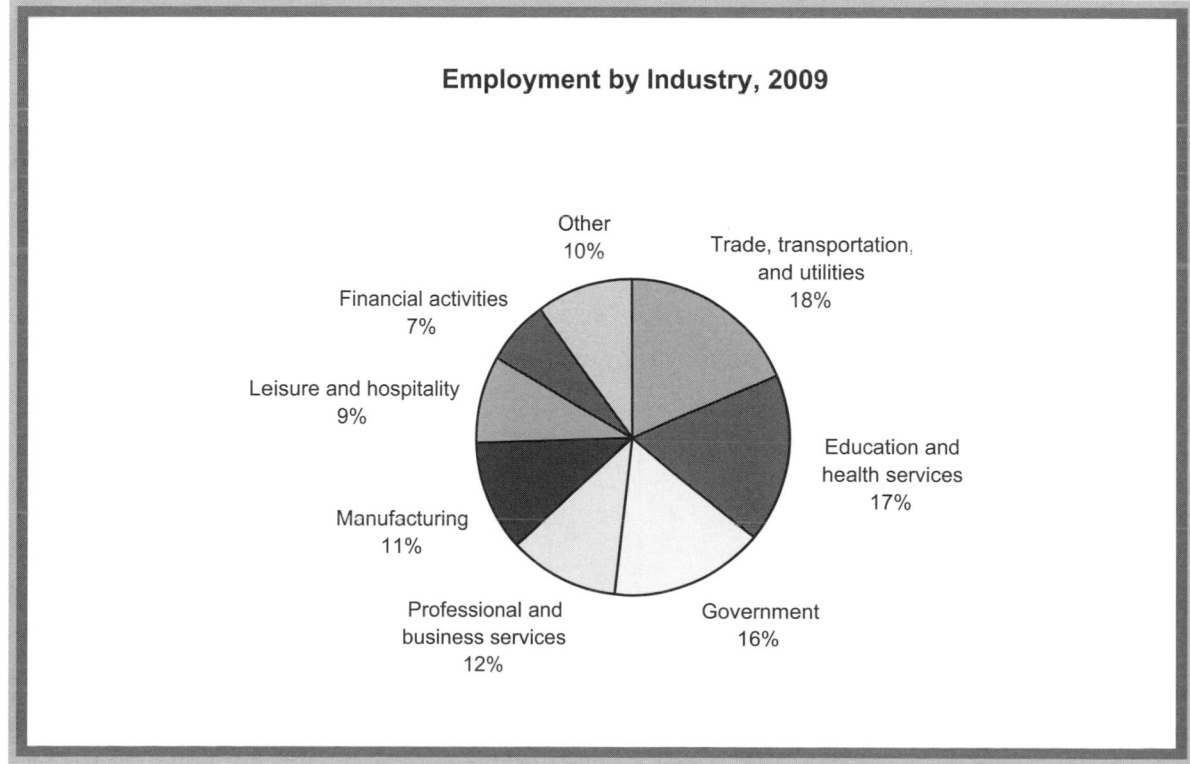

- Other 10%
- Trade, transportation, and utilities 18%
- Financial activities 7%
- Leisure and hospitality 9%
- Education and health services 17%
- Manufacturing 11%
- Professional and business services 12%
- Government 16%

Employment by Industry: Minnesota, Selected Years, 1990–2009

(Numbers in thousands, not seasonally adjusted.)

Industry and year	January	February	March	April	May	June	July	August	September	October	November	December	Annual average
Total Nonfarm													
1990	2079.1	2086.6	2095.4	2118.7	2150.3	2166.5	2138.7	2144.7	2157.5	2166.9	2167.5	2159.2	2135.9
2000	2600.1	2613.2	2633.4	2665.8	2700.3	2727.8	2690.8	2698.9	2713.0	2723.5	2727.4	2725.0	2684.9
2001	2648.8	2654.2	2664.9	2681.6	2716.0	2735.7	2690.0	2688.6	2699.3	2704.0	2700.8	2689.5	2689.5
2002	2612.2	2610.2	2617.1	2641.5	2681.6	2706.2	2673.8	2673.3	2690.0	2690.2	2693.5	2684.0	2664.5
2003	2605.4	2607.4	2613.4	2646.1	2685.6	2703.0	2663.6	2671.3	2681.5	2686.9	2680.3	2679.1	2660.2
2004	2598.2	2601.3	2612.8	2668.0	2705.2	2727.4	2690.3	2693.1	2707.5	2724.7	2720.9	2722.9	2681.0
2005	2629.3	2634.4	2648.3	2705.1	2746.5	2768.3	2737.9	2743.8	2757.5	2769.6	2769.8	2768.9	2723.3
2006	2701.9	2700.9	2715.7	2737.9	2775.2	2810.0	2766.1	2767.7	2775.9	2781.5	2783.9	2781.2	2758.2
2007	2711.5	2711.9	2722.2	2746.1	2793.9	2823.4	2784.3	2786.4	2788.4	2798.9	2799.7	2789.1	2771.3
2008	2719.1	2721.8	2729.4	2747.2	2792.1	2814.6	2775.1	2779.1	2777.4	2787.8	2768.4	2744.1	2763.0
2009	2654.2	2640.5	2632.0	2652.9	2683.3	2687.4	2646.9	2644.0	2633.7	2655.1	2644.4	2626.8	2650.1
Total Private													
1990	1732.3	1733.1	1743.7	1761.6	1789.2	1814.0	1814.3	1828.7	1821.7	1811.4	1805.6	1800.7	1788.0
2000	2198.8	2201.6	2218.7	2246.8	2276.2	2312.7	2311.0	2322.7	2312.5	2311.1	2308.3	2307.3	2277.3
2001	2243.9	2237.8	2247.7	2263.6	2295.9	2318.8	2308.5	2314.8	2295.1	2286.9	2280.4	2268.2	2280.1
2002	2197.9	2189.8	2197.1	2223.3	2261.5	2285.3	2282.4	2293.5	2279.6	2270.3	2266.1	2259.0	2250.5
2003	2192.6	2185.8	2192.0	2223.5	2263.4	2285.0	2278.8	2288.5	2277.0	2269.5	2260.6	2257.4	2247.8
2004	2186.6	2182.4	2193.9	2247.5	2282.8	2312.6	2306.6	2313.9	2300.4	2305.5	2297.5	2298.0	2269.0
2005	2212.9	2212.3	2225.4	2280.5	2321.6	2348.3	2346.8	2359.1	2348.8	2349.0	2349.6	2346.7	2308.4
2006	2286.7	2279.4	2293.2	2314.9	2351.7	2388.3	2374.9	2381.3	2365.0	2359.1	2358.1	2354.2	2342.2
2007	2297.3	2291.4	2302.6	2325.9	2369.9	2401.3	2394.8	2402.4	2380.8	2376.4	2373.8	2364.1	2356.7
2008	2302.0	2297.9	2305.0	2323.3	2363.9	2388.1	2383.0	2390.5	2363.5	2360.5	2337.8	2314.1	2344.1
2009	2236.8	2215.5	2206.8	2226.8	2255.3	2263.5	2254.4	2259.5	2229.6	2231.5	2218.0	2204.0	2233.5
Goods-Producing													
1990	408.9	407.2	409.5	415.8	426.5	440.0	444.4	450.1	445.2	438.5	429.9	418.0	427.8
2000	496.0	495.2	501.1	513.6	525.5	540.1	542.8	547.2	540.4	534.5	526.9	519.2	523.5
2001	500.5	496.7	497.3	501.3	511.8	520.9	523.2	524.8	519.5	511.1	502.3	490.7	508.3
2002	470.1	464.8	466.9	474.5	489.1	501.5	503.6	508.2	501.7	494.4	486.5	474.4	486.3
2003	455.7	450.3	451.6	461.9	477.3	489.6	491.1	494.8	489.1	485.2	477.3	467.4	474.3
2004	446.5	443.6	446.4	465.0	477.9	492.1	496.4	500.1	496.0	495.6	487.4	479.5	477.2
2005	454.7	452.5	455.7	470.7	487.2	499.4	502.9	506.4	500.7	494.2	488.6	477.6	482.6
2006	461.5	457.6	460.7	469.3	482.6	497.6	496.8	498.5	492.1	487.4	477.0	467.7	479.1
2007	452.0	446.6	449.4	454.9	471.9	485.5	485.0	486.9	479.0	474.8	468.0	456.5	467.5
2008	440.4	436.6	437.5	442.2	458.9	470.0	471.1	472.3	463.7	459.9	445.9	429.5	452.3
2009	406.2	395.5	389.5	392.5	401.0	407.6	408.0	408.1	403.4	396.8	388.9	376.4	397.8
Mining and Logging													
1990	7.6	7.5	7.8	7.9	8.4	8.8	9.1	9.1	9.1	9.0	8.7	8.1	8.4
2000	7.8	7.7	7.7	7.8	8.2	8.3	8.5	8.5	8.4	8.4	8.1	7.8	8.1
2001	7.5	6.9	6.6	6.3	6.7	6.9	6.3	7.0	6.9	6.9	6.3	6.2	6.7
2002	6.2	5.6	6.2	6.1	6.4	6.7	6.7	6.8	6.7	6.7	6.6	6.3	6.4
2003	6.1	6.0	6.0	5.9	6.3	6.4	6.5	6.1	5.9	6.0	5.8	5.6	6.0
2004	5.6	5.6	5.6	5.8	6.1	6.3	6.4	6.5	6.4	6.2	6.1	6.0	6.1
2005	5.6	5.7	5.7	5.8	6.1	6.3	6.3	6.3	6.2	6.1	6.0	5.7	6.0
2006	5.7	5.8	5.8	5.8	5.9	6.3	6.4	6.4	6.2	6.2	6.0	5.8	6.0
2007	5.6	5.6	5.6	5.6	5.9	6.1	6.3	6.4	6.2	6.2	6.2	6.0	6.0
2008	5.9	5.9	5.9	5.9	6.3	6.4	6.7	6.7	6.5	6.5	6.3	6.0	6.3
2009	5.8	5.6	5.3	5.1	4.6	4.4	5.2	5.0	4.6	4.6	4.4	4.4	4.9
Construction													
1990	64.5	63.1	63.9	71.4	79.6	86.2	88.9	90.7	88.6	86.0	81.0	71.3	77.9
2000	97.3	97.0	101.2	112.4	122.6	130.7	132.7	134.2	131.1	129.0	122.9	115.1	118.8
2001	104.0	102.6	104.9	112.5	123.9	134.0	138.1	139.3	135.0	133.6	129.2	120.0	123.1
2002	106.1	103.2	104.1	113.0	126.5	134.5	139.6	141.2	138.1	134.5	128.6	119.3	124.1
2003	106.0	102.6	103.6	113.3	127.2	136.1	140.2	141.9	138.9	137.1	130.7	121.4	124.9
2004	105.5	103.5	105.8	120.3	131.4	138.7	143.3	144.0	141.5	140.7	136.5	127.3	128.2
2005	108.3	106.5	108.5	120.6	132.7	140.9	145.5	146.1	143.2	139.0	135.1	126.4	129.4
2006	114.6	112.8	114.2	120.8	131.6	139.7	139.7	139.3	136.7	133.7	127.7	118.8	127.5
2007	108.0	104.0	106.5	110.3	124.9	132.6	132.7	133.4	129.2	126.7	121.6	111.3	120.1
2008	100.3	97.4	98.4	102.3	115.7	122.6	123.8	123.9	119.5	116.6	107.9	97.4	110.5
2009	82.1	79.6	79.6	86.6	98.0	102.5	103.7	103.8	102.5	99.2	93.5	82.5	92.8
Manufacturing													
1990	336.8	336.6	337.8	336.5	338.5	345.0	346.4	350.3	347.5	343.5	340.2	338.6	341.5
2000	390.9	390.5	392.2	393.4	394.7	401.1	401.6	404.5	400.9	397.1	395.9	396.3	396.6
2001	389.0	387.2	385.8	382.5	381.2	380.0	378.8	378.5	377.6	370.6	366.8	364.5	378.5
2002	357.8	356.0	356.6	355.4	356.2	360.3	357.3	360.2	356.9	353.2	351.3	348.8	355.8
2003	343.6	341.7	342.0	342.7	343.8	347.1	344.4	346.8	344.3	342.1	340.8	340.4	343.3
2004	335.4	334.5	335.0	338.9	340.4	347.1	346.7	349.6	348.1	348.7	344.8	346.2	343.0
2005	340.8	340.3	341.5	344.3	348.4	352.2	351.1	354.0	351.3	349.1	347.5	345.5	347.2
2006	341.2	339.0	340.7	342.7	345.1	351.6	350.7	352.8	349.2	347.5	343.3	343.1	345.6
2007	338.4	337.0	337.3	339.0	341.1	346.8	346.0	347.1	343.6	341.9	340.2	339.2	341.5
2008	334.2	333.3	333.2	334.0	336.9	341.0	340.6	341.7	337.7	336.8	331.7	326.1	335.6
2009	318.3	310.3	304.6	300.8	298.4	300.7	299.1	299.3	296.3	293.0	291.0	289.5	300.1

Employment by Industry: Minnesota, Selected Years, 1990–2009—*Continued*

(Numbers in thousands, not seasonally adjusted.)

Industry and year	January	February	March	April	May	June	July	August	September	October	November	December	Annual average
Service-Providing													
1990	1670.2	1679.4	1685.9	1702.9	1723.8	1726.5	1694.3	1694.6	1712.3	1728.4	1737.6	1741.2	1708.1
2000	2104.1	2118.0	2132.3	2152.2	2174.8	2187.7	2148.0	2151.7	2172.6	2189.0	2200.5	2205.8	2161.4
2001	2148.3	2157.5	2167.6	2180.3	2204.2	2214.8	2166.8	2163.8	2179.8	2192.9	2198.5	2198.8	2181.1
2002	2142.1	2145.4	2150.2	2167.0	2192.5	2204.7	2170.2	2165.1	2188.3	2195.8	2207.0	2209.6	2178.2
2003	2149.7	2157.1	2161.8	2184.2	2208.3	2213.4	2172.5	2176.5	2192.4	2201.7	2203.0	2211.7	2186.0
2004	2151.7	2157.7	2166.4	2203.0	2227.3	2235.3	2193.9	2193.0	2211.5	2229.1	2233.5	2243.4	2203.8
2005	2174.6	2181.9	2192.6	2234.4	2259.3	2268.9	2235.0	2237.4	2256.8	2275.4	2281.2	2291.3	2240.7
2006	2240.4	2243.3	2255.0	2268.6	2292.6	2312.4	2269.3	2269.2	2283.8	2294.1	2306.9	2313.5	2279.1
2007	2259.5	2265.3	2272.8	2291.2	2322.0	2337.9	2299.3	2299.5	2309.4	2324.1	2331.7	2332.6	2303.8
2008	2278.7	2285.2	2291.9	2305.0	2333.2	2344.6	2304.0	2306.8	2313.7	2327.9	2322.5	2314.6	2310.7
2009	2248.0	2245.0	2242.5	2260.4	2282.3	2279.8	2238.9	2235.9	2230.3	2258.3	2255.5	2250.4	2252.3
Trade, Transportation, and Utilities													
1990	442.0	437.1	438.2	442.3	447.6	451.7	447.6	451.5	450.8	450.8	458.5	462.1	448.4
2000	532.2	527.9	529.0	531.8	536.8	541.1	538.3	540.0	539.1	544.9	553.9	559.9	539.6
2001	540.6	533.4	534.3	536.0	542.4	544.2	540.1	539.3	534.9	538.4	544.9	547.1	539.6
2002	525.2	516.0	516.8	521.8	527.7	529.1	523.4	523.1	521.7	524.5	534.3	538.9	525.2
2003	518.6	511.2	511.4	517.4	523.9	524.8	518.4	520.2	518.9	522.9	528.9	532.2	520.7
2004	511.5	506.0	507.0	517.3	524.6	528.9	525.4	526.0	524.6	530.0	537.8	542.6	523.5
2005	517.6	512.7	514.4	522.6	528.3	531.1	527.6	528.7	526.9	531.9	540.0	545.0	527.2
2006	525.7	519.4	520.5	523.7	529.4	534.1	527.1	527.0	526.2	527.8	538.3	541.1	528.4
2007	523.7	518.8	519.3	523.2	530.7	534.4	529.4	529.8	528.2	531.7	539.6	543.0	529.3
2008	523.6	516.8	518.2	519.9	526.7	527.2	522.4	522.2	519.0	520.7	524.1	523.7	522.0
2009	502.9	495.2	492.5	494.2	500.0	501.4	494.7	494.9	490.9	491.8	499.1	497.5	496.3
Wholesale Trade													
1990	103.3	103.8	104.1	106.3	106.9	108.3	108.7	109.9	108.0	107.1	106.8	107.0	106.6
2000	126.6	126.5	127.3	128.2	129.0	131.2	130.0	130.5	129.0	129.6	130.0	130.4	129.0
2001	130.3	129.8	130.3	131.1	131.9	132.1	132.0	131.2	129.6	129.3	129.0	128.6	130.4
2002	126.6	126.4	126.2	127.4	128.1	128.6	128.7	128.1	126.5	127.0	126.6	126.3	127.2
2003	126.6	126.7	126.7	128.1	128.8	129.6	129.6	129.2	127.8	127.8	127.2	127.1	127.9
2004	125.0	125.0	125.5	129.1	130.0	131.3	131.3	131.1	129.3	129.8	129.8	129.9	128.9
2005	127.3	127.4	127.5	131.1	131.4	133.3	132.8	133.1	132.0	132.2	132.3	132.4	131.1
2006	131.3	131.4	132.2	133.1	134.0	135.1	134.6	134.5	133.1	133.0	133.0	132.7	133.2
2007	131.1	131.0	131.6	132.9	134.5	135.5	135.2	135.2	133.2	133.6	133.7	133.6	133.4
2008	131.7	131.5	132.1	132.8	134.3	134.9	135.0	134.9	132.9	132.6	132.1	131.2	133.0
2009	128.2	127.0	126.1	127.2	127.5	127.8	127.1	126.9	124.5	125.8	127.7	127.4	126.9
Retail Trade													
1990	255.3	249.8	249.8	250.8	254.0	256.4	254.2	256.0	254.5	256.4	264.2	267.9	255.8
2000	303.8	299.5	299.4	300.7	304.2	306.9	306.0	307.2	305.3	309.7	310.0	324.5	307.2
2001	307.6	301.6	301.6	301.7	306.5	309.0	306.8	307.7	303.2	307.4	316.2	319.9	307.4
2002	302.5	294.6	295.8	298.4	302.6	304.8	302.7	303.4	300.7	301.4	311.7	317.5	303.0
2003	299.0	292.2	292.5	296.7	302.1	303.7	299.5	302.0	299.2	301.4	308.4	312.3	300.8
2004	296.1	290.7	291.1	295.8	301.1	304.5	302.4	303.0	299.5	302.0	309.8	314.5	300.9
2005	296.0	290.7	291.9	296.0	300.7	303.2	300.3	301.8	299.8	303.8	311.9	316.5	301.1
2006	300.3	294.7	294.8	297.4	301.4	305.2	301.5	302.2	298.5	300.0	309.0	312.5	301.5
2007	299.2	293.7	294.4	296.3	301.5	304.9	302.3	302.7	299.2	301.2	309.2	311.6	301.4
2008	297.2	290.2	290.9	292.1	296.4	297.5	295.4	295.5	290.7	291.7	296.1	296.1	294.2
2009	282.8	276.8	274.8	276.2	281.4	283.9	280.6	281.8	276.2	276.2	282.9	281.4	279.6
Transportation and Utilities													
1990	83.4	83.5	84.3	85.2	86.7	87.0	84.7	85.6	88.3	87.3	87.5	87.2	85.8
2000	101.8	101.9	102.3	102.9	103.6	103.0	102.3	102.3	104.8	105.6	105.1	105.0	103.3
2001	102.7	102.0	102.4	103.2	104.0	103.1	101.3	100.4	102.1	101.7	99.7	98.6	101.8
2002	96.1	95.0	94.8	96.0	97.0	95.7	92.0	91.6	94.5	96.1	96.0	95.1	95.0
2003	93.0	92.3	92.2	92.6	93.0	91.5	89.3	89.0	91.9	93.7	93.3	92.8	92.1
2004	90.4	90.3	90.4	92.4	93.5	93.1	91.7	91.9	95.8	98.2	98.2	98.2	93.7
2005	94.3	94.6	95.0	95.5	96.2	94.6	94.5	93.8	95.1	95.9	95.8	96.1	95.1
2006	94.1	93.3	93.5	93.2	94.0	93.8	91.0	90.3	94.6	94.8	96.3	95.9	93.7
2007	93.4	94.1	93.3	94.0	94.7	94.0	91.9	91.9	95.8	96.9	96.7	97.8	94.5
2008	94.7	95.1	95.2	95.0	96.0	94.8	92.0	91.8	95.4	96.4	95.9	96.4	94.9
2009	91.9	91.4	91.6	90.8	91.1	89.7	87.0	86.2	90.2	89.8	88.5	88.7	89.7
Information													
1990	52.9	53.1	53.6	54.0	54.4	55.0	55.2	55.4	55.0	54.3	54.6	54.8	54.3
2000	66.7	67.3	67.5	68.2	68.7	70.3	70.7	70.8	69.8	70.0	70.5	70.6	69.2
2001	70.6	70.6	70.6	69.8	70.6	71.5	70.3	69.7	68.5	68.9	69.1	69.0	69.9
2002	67.5	67.2	67.2	67.4	67.3	67.7	67.2	66.1	64.9	64.4	64.5	64.3	66.3
2003	62.5	62.3	62.3	62.7	62.9	62.6	62.0	61.7	60.8	60.6	61.1	61.4	61.9
2004	60.6	60.5	60.7	61.1	61.3	61.0	60.1	59.5	58.8	58.6	59.2	59.2	60.1
2005	58.7	58.6	58.7	59.7	59.8	60.0	59.6	59.0	58.5	58.4	58.7	59.0	59.1
2006	58.3	58.1	58.4	57.8	58.3	58.7	58.2	58.3	57.5	57.3	57.7	57.8	58.0
2007	57.9	57.9	58.2	58.2	58.3	58.6	58.2	58.2	57.6	57.3	57.4	57.8	58.0
2008	57.6	57.4	57.6	57.8	57.7	57.9	58.0	58.0	57.6	57.0	57.1	56.4	57.5
2009	56.1	55.9	55.7	55.0	54.9	55.0	55.1	54.9	54.2	54.2	53.8	53.9	54.9

Employment by Industry: Minnesota, Selected Years, 1990–2009—*Continued*

(Numbers in thousands, not seasonally adjusted.)

Industry and year	January	February	March	April	May	June	July	August	September	October	November	December	Annual average
Financial Activities													
1990	127.1	127.5	128.2	127.9	128.2	129.5	131.7	131.9	130.7	130.1	129.2	129.8	129.3
2000	162.0	161.9	162.5	163.1	163.6	166.0	166.4	166.7	165.6	166.3	166.3	167.7	164.8
2001	166.2	166.9	167.6	168.0	168.7	170.7	170.6	170.7	168.8	168.2	168.7	169.4	168.7
2002	168.3	168.6	168.6	169.6	170.4	171.5	173.3	173.9	173.1	173.0	173.8	174.8	171.6
2003	172.0	172.6	173.2	174.9	176.1	178.1	178.3	178.7	177.3	175.3	175.1	175.9	175.6
2004	174.9	174.6	174.6	176.6	177.0	178.8	177.7	177.9	176.4	176.4	176.5	177.3	176.6
2005	175.2	175.1	175.7	179.9	180.6	182.5	181.5	182.1	180.8	180.0	180.2	181.2	179.6
2006	179.8	179.7	180.2	179.5	180.7	182.4	181.7	181.5	180.0	179.8	180.1	181.0	180.5
2007	178.6	179.2	179.3	178.9	178.9	181.1	180.8	180.6	178.9	178.8	178.9	179.4	179.5
2008	176.7	176.8	177.0	176.6	177.0	178.4	178.8	178.5	176.4	176.0	175.6	176.4	177.0
2009	173.7	173.2	172.6	172.3	172.9	173.6	173.4	172.9	171.0	171.1	170.8	170.2	172.3
Professional and Business Services													
1990	208.9	210.3	211.6	211.6	214.3	216.8	215.4	217.7	216.6	218.0	217.0	215.9	214.5
2000	308.6	307.9	311.6	316.3	317.8	325.0	323.6	325.5	323.7	325.0	324.0	322.1	319.2
2001	312.2	309.5	310.4	314.0	314.4	317.5	313.2	312.6	309.6	307.9	305.0	302.6	310.7
2002	290.1	289.8	290.4	292.7	295.5	299.7	301.3	304.4	302.2	302.9	300.3	297.7	297.3
2003	287.8	288.1	288.9	292.3	294.5	298.0	298.1	299.8	299.4	301.2	299.7	300.6	295.7
2004	288.7	290.6	292.8	299.7	302.2	306.6	306.2	307.3	304.7	306.9	305.4	304.1	301.3
2005	291.1	292.0	294.8	304.1	307.3	311.6	310.5	314.5	315.1	319.5	319.2	319.0	308.2
2006	313.2	313.6	315.3	319.8	322.9	329.0	327.0	329.5	328.1	329.6	329.5	328.6	323.8
2007	319.9	321.1	323.2	326.1	329.5	333.8	334.4	337.9	334.0	334.1	333.3	331.9	329.9
2008	322.7	323.5	323.3	326.3	329.5	332.9	333.8	336.2	332.5	332.7	328.3	324.3	328.8
2009	308.3	304.0	301.7	304.4	305.7	305.9	305.9	309.9	303.5	312.0	309.2	309.0	306.6
Education and Health Services													
1990	237.0	240.8	242.0	242.3	243.3	236.9	235.1	236.0	242.1	247.7	248.6	250.2	241.8
2000	315.7	321.3	323.5	324.6	324.7	320.4	318.5	317.4	325.8	332.3	334.5	335.6	324.5
2001	328.1	332.9	335.8	337.5	339.4	334.3	332.0	332.7	339.5	348.1	350.4	350.6	338.4
2002	346.3	353.1	355.2	357.1	359.4	352.9	349.9	351.0	356.7	363.2	365.5	365.9	356.4
2003	361.7	368.3	369.8	370.1	371.5	365.7	364.0	363.3	369.0	373.3	374.8	374.0	368.8
2004	369.6	374.1	375.7	377.9	379.0	374.4	372.3	371.8	375.6	381.9	383.3	385.7	376.8
2005	377.6	384.1	385.9	388.3	392.1	387.1	388.8	389.8	394.8	399.8	402.2	403.8	391.2
2006	399.2	402.1	404.4	407.0	408.3	406.3	407.7	407.9	411.4	415.2	419.0	420.6	409.1
2007	418.0	421.1	422.9	426.1	428.1	426.3	425.6	426.0	429.4	435.1	438.4	437.6	427.9
2008	433.0	437.8	439.8	442.9	442.4	439.6	438.6	439.8	443.2	450.5	452.7	452.9	442.8
2009	448.2	452.1	453.8	458.1	457.7	450.3	448.6	448.8	447.8	455.4	456.8	458.0	453.0
Leisure and Hospitality													
1990	166.7	167.8	171.0	176.8	183.7	191.1	192.7	193.9	189.6	180.2	175.7	177.2	180.5
2000	204.8	206.4	208.8	215.1	225.1	235.0	236.6	240.4	234.0	222.1	216.3	215.3	221.6
2001	209.7	211.5	214.2	219.2	230.4	241.0	242.4	248.0	237.9	226.5	220.5	220.0	226.8
2002	213.8	213.6	215.0	222.3	233.9	243.6	244.2	246.9	240.1	228.7	221.7	222.8	228.9
2003	216.6	215.1	216.4	225.8	238.5	246.5	246.4	249.4	242.4	232.0	224.6	226.1	231.7
2004	217.8	216.9	219.4	231.0	242.2	251.0	250.5	252.6	246.5	238.1	230.3	231.2	235.6
2005	223.0	222.3	224.6	237.0	247.3	256.9	256.8	259.0	252.7	246.0	241.7	241.3	242.4
2006	233.5	233.5	236.4	239.8	250.9	260.3	257.7	259.8	251.4	243.4	237.7	238.1	245.2
2007	232.1	231.9	234.0	241.6	254.8	263.3	263.6	265.1	257.0	248.1	241.3	240.5	247.8
2008	232.9	232.4	234.9	239.5	253.2	261.9	260.9	263.8	253.2	245.2	236.4	234.6	245.7
2009	226.7	224.9	225.8	234.2	246.6	252.3	252.2	253.5	243.4	235.6	226.4	225.9	237.3
Other Services													
1990	88.8	89.3	89.6	90.9	91.2	93.0	92.2	92.2	91.7	91.8	92.1	92.7	91.3
2000	112.8	113.7	114.7	114.1	114.0	114.8	114.1	114.7	114.1	116.0	115.9	116.9	114.6
2001	116.0	116.3	117.5	117.8	118.2	118.7	116.7	117.0	116.4	117.8	119.5	118.8	117.6
2002	116.6	116.7	117.0	117.9	118.2	119.3	119.5	119.9	119.2	119.2	119.5	120.2	118.6
2003	117.7	117.9	118.4	118.4	118.7	119.7	120.5	120.6	120.1	119.0	119.1	119.8	119.2
2004	117.0	116.1	117.3	118.9	118.6	119.8	118.0	118.7	117.8	118.0	117.6	118.4	118.0
2005	115.0	115.0	115.6	118.2	119.0	119.7	119.1	119.1	119.6	119.3	119.0	119.8	118.2
2006	115.5	115.4	117.3	118.0	118.6	119.9	118.7	118.8	118.3	118.6	118.8	119.3	118.1
2007	115.1	114.8	116.3	116.9	117.7	118.3	117.8	117.9	116.7	116.5	116.9	117.4	116.9
2008	115.1	116.6	116.7	118.1	118.5	120.2	119.4	119.7	117.9	118.5	117.7	116.3	117.9
2009	114.7	114.7	115.2	116.1	116.5	117.4	116.5	116.5	115.4	114.6	113.0	113.1	115.3
Government													
1990	346.8	353.5	351.7	357.1	361.1	352.5	324.4	316.0	335.8	355.5	361.9	358.5	347.9
2000	401.3	411.6	414.7	419.0	424.1	415.1	379.8	376.2	400.5	412.4	419.1	417.7	407.6
2001	404.9	416.4	417.2	418.0	420.1	416.9	381.5	373.8	404.2	417.1	420.4	421.3	409.3
2002	414.3	420.4	420.0	418.2	420.1	420.9	391.4	379.8	410.4	419.9	427.4	425.0	414.0
2003	412.8	421.6	421.4	422.6	422.2	418.0	384.8	382.8	404.5	417.4	419.7	421.7	412.5
2004	411.6	418.9	418.9	420.5	422.4	414.8	383.7	379.2	407.1	419.2	423.4	424.9	412.1
2005	416.4	422.1	422.9	424.6	424.9	420.0	391.1	384.7	408.7	420.6	420.2	422.2	414.9
2006	415.2	421.5	422.5	423.0	423.5	421.7	391.2	386.4	410.9	422.4	425.8	427.0	415.9
2007	414.2	420.5	419.6	420.2	424.0	422.1	389.5	384.0	407.6	422.5	425.9	425.0	414.6
2008	417.1	423.9	424.4	423.9	428.2	426.5	392.1	388.6	413.9	427.3	430.6	430.0	418.9
2009	417.4	425.0	425.2	426.1	428.0	423.9	392.5	384.5	404.1	423.6	426.4	422.8	416.6

Average Weekly Hours by Selected Industry: Minnesota, 2007–2009

(Not seasonally adjusted.)

Industry and year	January	February	March	April	May	June	July	August	September	October	November	December	Annual average
Total Private													
2007	33.5	33.6	33.6	34.0	33.6	34.0	34.0	34.2	34.2	33.7	33.6	34.0	33.8
2008	33.2	33.5	33.7	33.0	33.3	33.9	33.4	33.9	33.7	33.5	33.5	32.7	33.5
2009	32.5	32.8	32.7	32.7	32.3	32.3	32.5	33.1	32.2	32.6	33.1	32.6	32.6
Goods-Producing													
2007	39.4	39.5	39.7	39.9	40.1	41.2	39.7	41.3	41.1	40.6	40.9	40.9	40.4
2008	39.9	41.0	40.2	39.9	40.2	40.6	40.1	40.7	40.7	40.4	39.7	38.5	40.2
2009	37.6	38.0	37.8	37.7	38.7	38.1	38.3	38.8	37.7	38.0	38.2	38.0	38.1
Construction													
2007	35.9	35.8	36.0	36.5	37.4	40.8	39.8	39.5	39.7	38.4	38.5	37.9	38.2
2008	37.5	36.1	37.4	36.9	38.4	38.7	38.6	39.3	39.6	39.8	38.8	35.5	38.2
2009	33.3	34.9	34.2	36.1	38.1	37.8	38.3	38.4	35.5	35.8	36.2	33.0	36.1
Manufacturing													
2007	40.8	41.0	41.2	41.3	41.3	41.6	39.8	39.8	39.5	39.5	40.0	40.3	40.5
2008	39.2	41.3	39.9	39.8	39.7	40.3	39.8	40.4	40.2	39.7	39.4	39.0	39.9
2009	38.6	38.8	38.8	38.2	38.5	37.9	37.8	38.2	37.9	38.4	38.4	38.8	38.4
Trade, Transportation, and Utilities													
2007	32.4	33.4	32.9	32.8	33.5	33.3	33.2	33.4	33.5	33.1	33.3	33.7	33.2
2008	32.1	32.6	32.7	32.0	32.5	32.6	32.8	32.9	32.5	32.1	32.0	31.7	32.4
2009	31.0	31.4	31.5	31.3	31.2	31.2	31.4	32.1	31.5	31.8	32.5	32.2	31.6
Financial Activities													
2007	37.1	36.4	36.2	37.1	35.8	36.4	37.3	36.2	36.9	36.1	35.3	36.8	36.5
2008	36.6	36.1	37.2	36.2	36.3	37.3	36.0	36.0	35.9	35.9	36.7	35.7	36.3
2009	37.1	36.7	36.4	35.9	35.7	35.4	35.7	36.6	35.5	35.9	37.0	36.0	36.2
Professional and Business Services													
2007	34.5	34.9	35.0	35.8	34.3	34.9	35.2	34.4	35.3	35.1	35.4	35.5	35.0
2008	35.1	35.0	35.8	34.7	36.0	37.1	36.3	36.8	36.6	36.4	36.5	35.1	36.0
2009	35.2	36.2	36.4	36.1	35.9	36.2	35.7	36.6	35.4	35.6	36.2	35.3	35.9
Education and Health Services													
2007	32.7	32.4	32.1	32.4	32.2	32.4	32.9	32.9	32.2	31.9	31.7	32.0	32.3
2008	31.8	31.5	31.7	32.3	32.4	32.5	32.4	32.4	32.2	31.8	32.0	32.4	32.1
2009	32.2	31.9	31.5	31.2	31.2	31.2	31.2	31.5	30.7	30.8	31.1	30.8	31.3
Leisure and Hospitality													
2007	23.3	23.5	23.8	23.3	23.3	23.7	24.4	24.0	23.6	23.2	22.6	23.2	23.5
2008	22.5	23.4	23.8	22.6	22.4	23.0	22.3	23.5	23.3	23.3	23.1	22.4	23.0
2009	22.0	22.9	22.8	22.2	22.2	22.5	23.0	23.3	22.3	22.0	22.1	21.7	22.4
Other Services													
2007	23.0	23.8	23.7	24.1	23.9	24.4	24.7	25.5	26.1	25.5	25.0	25.7	24.6
2008	25.5	25.7	25.9	25.9	25.6	26.6	26.2	26.9	27.0	26.0	26.6	26.8	26.2
2009	26.4	27.5	26.2	25.8	26.9	27.5	27.8	28.5	27.3	27.9	28.4	27.2	27.3

Average Hourly Earnings by Selected Industry: Minnesota, 2007–2009

(Dollars, not seasonally adjusted.)

Industry and year	January	February	March	April	May	June	July	August	September	October	November	December	Annual average
Total Private													
2007	23.63	23.76	23.25	23.80	23.00	22.96	22.64	22.35	22.86	22.89	23.00	23.46	23.13
2008	22.89	23.20	23.27	23.46	23.27	22.97	23.13	22.88	23.08	23.44	23.55	23.66	23.23
2009	23.70	23.83	23.57	23.23	23.67	23.36	23.76	22.69	22.95	23.19	23.43	23.51	23.41
Goods-Producing													
2007	23.05	23.47	22.43	22.76	22.56	22.47	22.66	22.45	22.64	22.79	22.87	22.97	22.75
2008	23.03	22.82	23.01	22.94	22.77	22.92	23.15	23.09	23.64	23.85	24.19	23.82	23.26
2009	24.48	23.04	23.28	23.62	24.31	24.27	24.40	24.34	24.25	24.36	24.78	24.93	24.17
Construction													
2007	25.59	25.86	25.46	25.54	25.50	25.79	25.91	25.88	25.89	26.55	25.69	26.15	25.83
2008	26.18	26.23	26.86	26.75	26.63	26.36	27.16	26.94	27.12	27.06	27.09	25.46	26.69
2009	25.72	25.59	25.12	25.24	26.49	26.11	25.59	26.17	26.14	26.48	26.30	26.81	26.00
Manufacturing													
2007	22.24	22.72	21.46	21.80	21.48	21.12	21.27	21.07	21.29	21.39	21.81	22.27	21.66
2008	22.35	22.13	22.17	22.10	21.81	22.04	22.03	21.99	22.61	22.95	23.48	23.71	22.44
2009	24.47	24.24	24.00	24.18	24.30	24.02	24.47	24.60	24.34	24.57	25.16	25.09	24.45
Trade, Transportation, and Utilities													
2007	19.31	19.68	19.68	20.22	19.51	20.33	20.61	20.12	20.52	20.20	19.84	19.88	19.96
2008	20.44	20.74	20.24	20.78	20.77	20.40	20.06	19.67	20.05	19.96	19.86	20.06	20.25
2009	20.04	21.02	21.04	20.25	20.27	20.25	20.76	20.83	20.95	20.76	21.19	20.87	20.69
Financial Activities													
2007	28.23	28.64	27.71	27.85	27.89	27.48	27.94	27.67	27.92	27.22	27.62	27.83	27.83
2008	26.46	27.15	26.84	27.38	27.46	26.59	26.66	26.84	26.83	27.35	26.86	26.97	26.95
2009	26.71	28.45	27.01	26.61	27.07	25.93	26.26	27.35	26.94	27.27	27.60	27.74	27.08
Professional and Business Services													
2007	28.94	27.90	28.19	27.75	27.23	26.48	27.06	26.53	27.01	27.39	27.27	27.82	27.45
2008	26.99	27.64	28.26	27.90	27.51	27.30	27.63	27.39	27.41	27.74	28.45	29.49	27.80
2009	28.90	29.54	29.53	29.83	29.95	28.98	29.27	30.03	30.07	30.17	30.23	30.85	29.78
Education and Health Services													
2007	23.97	23.83	24.16	24.40	24.02	23.96	24.34	23.94	24.28	24.53	24.65	25.09	24.27
2008	24.11	24.40	24.58	24.93	24.54	24.05	24.57	24.41	24.74	25.04	24.90	24.46	24.56
2009	23.79	23.82	23.59	23.58	23.32	23.59	24.23	23.93	24.50	24.54	24.18	23.77	23.90
Leisure and Hospitality													
2007	12.03	12.11	11.95	11.93	11.84	11.75	11.68	11.74	12.04	12.25	12.27	12.54	12.00
2008	12.46	12.54	12.60	12.79	12.63	12.30	12.90	12.42	12.67	12.77	12.90	13.27	12.68
2009	13.41	13.27	13.26	13.03	12.97	12.68	12.33	12.77	13.12	13.38	13.50	13.58	13.09
Other Services													
2007	15.28	15.09	15.03	15.58	15.23	15.56	15.44	15.27	14.40	14.42	14.52	15.01	15.06
2008	15.28	15.66	15.61	15.18	15.24	15.66	15.83	15.96	15.53	15.58	16.10	16.50	15.68
2009	17.36	16.80	17.04	17.54	16.79	16.62	17.47	17.18	17.20	17.05	17.49	17.73	17.17

Average Weekly Earnings by Selected Industry: Minnesota, 2007–2009

(Dollars, not seasonally adjusted.)

Industry and year	January	February	March	April	May	June	July	August	September	October	November	December	Annual average
Total Private													
2007	791.61	798.34	781.20	809.20	772.80	780.64	769.76	764.37	781.81	771.39	772.80	797.64	781.79
2008	759.95	777.20	784.20	774.18	774.89	778.68	772.54	775.63	777.80	785.24	788.93	773.68	778.21
2009	770.25	781.62	770.74	759.62	764.54	754.53	772.20	751.04	738.99	755.99	775.53	766.43	763.17
Goods-Producing													
2007	908.17	927.07	890.47	908.12	904.66	925.76	899.60	927.19	930.50	925.27	935.38	939.47	919.10
2008	918.90	935.62	925.00	915.31	915.35	930.55	928.32	939.76	962.15	963.54	960.34	917.07	935.05
2009	920.45	875.52	879.98	890.47	940.80	924.69	934.52	944.39	914.23	925.68	946.60	947.34	920.88
Construction													
2007	918.68	925.79	916.56	932.21	953.70	1052.23	1031.22	1022.26	1027.83	1019.52	989.07	991.09	986.71
2008	981.75	946.90	1004.56	987.08	1022.59	1020.13	1048.38	1058.74	1073.95	1076.99	1051.09	903.83	1019.56
2009	856.48	893.09	859.10	911.16	1009.27	986.96	980.10	1004.93	927.97	947.98	952.06	884.73	938.60
Manufacturing													
2007	907.39	931.52	884.15	900.34	887.12	878.59	846.55	838.59	840.96	844.91	872.40	897.48	877.23
2008	876.12	913.97	884.58	879.58	865.86	888.21	876.79	888.40	908.92	911.12	925.11	924.69	895.36
2009	944.54	940.51	931.20	923.68	935.55	910.36	924.97	939.72	922.49	943.49	966.14	973.49	938.88
Trade, Transportation, and Utilities													
2007	625.64	657.31	647.47	663.22	653.59	676.99	684.25	672.01	687.42	668.62	660.67	669.96	662.67
2008	656.12	676.12	661.85	664.96	675.03	665.04	657.97	647.14	651.63	640.72	635.52	635.90	656.10
2009	621.24	660.03	662.76	633.83	632.42	631.80	651.86	668.64	659.93	660.17	688.68	672.01	653.80
Financial Activities													
2007	1047.33	1042.50	1003.10	1033.24	998.46	1000.27	1042.16	1001.65	1030.25	982.64	974.99	1024.14	1015.80
2008	968.44	980.12	998.45	991.16	996.80	991.81	959.76	966.24	963.20	981.87	985.76	962.83	978.29
2009	990.94	1044.12	983.16	955.30	966.40	917.92	937.48	1001.01	956.37	978.99	1021.20	998.64	980.30
Professional and Business Services													
2007	998.43	973.71	986.65	993.45	933.99	924.15	952.51	912.63	953.45	961.39	965.36	987.61	960.75
2008	947.35	967.40	1011.71	968.13	990.36	1012.83	1002.97	1007.95	1003.21	1009.74	1038.43	1035.10	1000.80
2009	1017.28	1069.35	1074.89	1076.86	1075.21	1049.08	1044.94	1099.10	1064.48	1074.05	1094.33	1089.01	1069.10
Education and Health Services													
2007	783.82	772.09	775.54	790.56	773.44	776.30	800.79	787.63	781.82	782.51	781.41	802.88	783.92
2008	766.70	768.60	779.19	805.24	795.10	781.63	796.07	790.88	796.63	796.27	796.80	792.50	788.38
2009	766.04	759.86	743.09	735.70	727.58	736.01	755.98	753.80	752.15	755.83	752.00	732.12	748.07
Leisure and Hospitality													
2007	280.30	284.59	284.41	277.97	275.87	278.48	284.99	281.76	284.14	284.20	277.30	290.93	282.00
2008	280.35	293.44	299.88	289.05	282.91	282.90	287.67	291.87	295.21	297.54	297.99	297.25	291.64
2009	295.02	303.88	302.33	289.27	287.93	285.30	283.59	297.54	292.58	294.36	298.35	294.09	293.22
Other Services													
2007	351.44	359.14	356.21	375.48	364.00	379.66	381.37	389.39	375.84	367.71	363.00	385.76	370.48
2008	389.64	402.46	404.30	393.16	390.14	416.56	414.75	429.32	419.31	405.08	428.26	442.20	410.82
2009	458.30	462.00	446.45	452.53	451.65	457.05	485.67	489.63	469.56	475.70	496.72	482.26	468.74

MISSISSIPPI
At a Glance

Population:
  1990 census: 2,575,475
  2000 census: 2,844,658
  2009 estimate: 2,951,996

Percent change in population:
  1990–2000: 10.5%
  2000–2009: 3.8%

Percent change in total nonfarm employment:
  1990–2009: 17.1%
  2008–2009: -4.4%

Industry with the largest growth in employment, 1990–2009 (thousands):
  Leisure and hospitality, 63.3

Industry with the largest decline or smallest growth in employment, 1990–2009 (thousands):
  Manufacturing, -88.4

Civilian labor force:
  1990: 1,175,744
  2000: 1,314,154
  2009: 1,291,949

Unemployment rate and rank among states (lowest to highest):
  1990: 7.7%, 50th
  2000: 5.7%, 49th
  2009: 9.6%, 35th

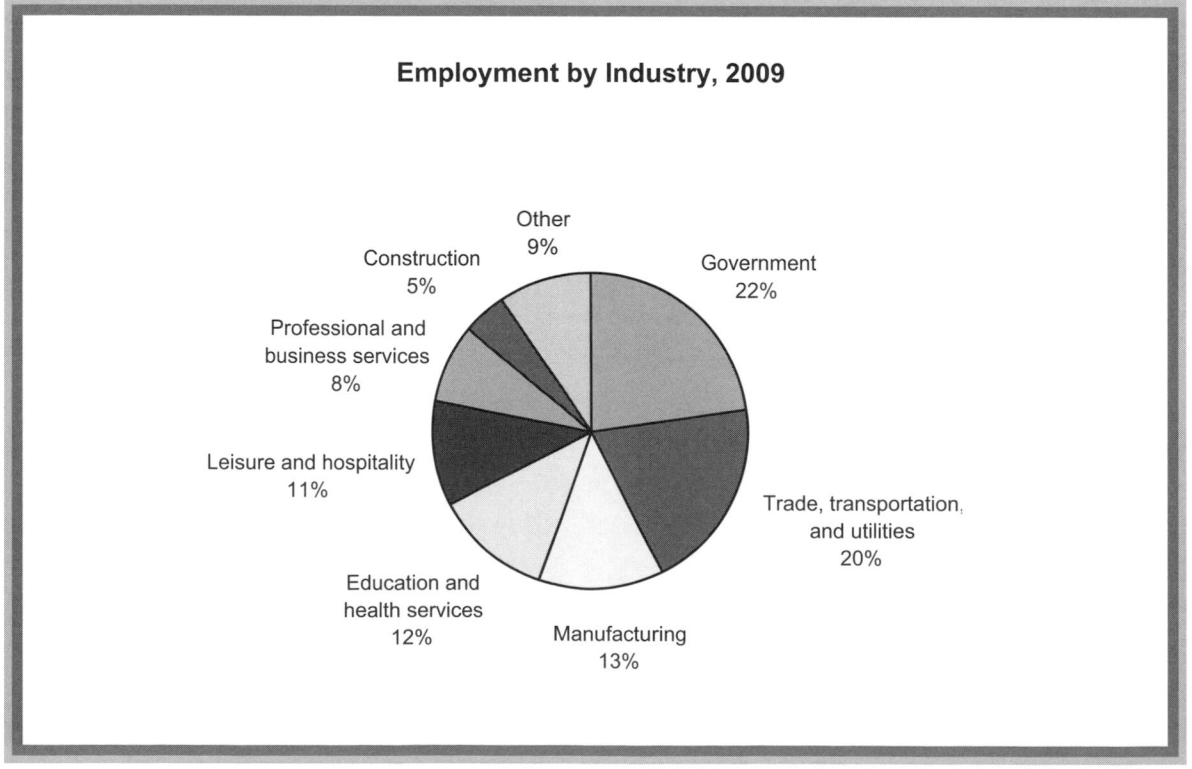

Employment by Industry, 2009

Other 9%
Construction 5%
Professional and business services 8%
Leisure and hospitality 11%
Education and health services 12%
Manufacturing 13%
Government 22%
Trade, transportation, and utilities 20%

Employment by Industry: Mississippi, Selected Years, 1990–2009

(Numbers in thousands, not seasonally adjusted.)

Industry and year	January	February	March	April	May	June	July	August	September	October	November	December	Annual average
Total Nonfarm													
1990	916.5	919.7	928.6	935.8	943.3	941.9	931.4	930.8	948.1	948.2	948.5	945.5	936.5
2000	1144.1	1145.0	1153.8	1158.3	1166.7	1164.0	1147.2	1157.0	1155.3	1149.8	1150.7	1150.7	1153.5
2001	1128.8	1128.8	1131.1	1136.3	1138.2	1135.1	1120.8	1131.7	1130.9	1124.9	1126.6	1126.1	1129.9
2002	1111.0	1113.8	1120.3	1127.8	1131.7	1133.2	1119.6	1128.3	1130.6	1122.1	1121.5	1123.2	1123.6
2003	1107.2	1108.7	1112.1	1116.4	1116.6	1110.8	1104.4	1111.7	1119.4	1123.1	1124.7	1123.2	1114.9
2004	1108.3	1113.3	1120.9	1129.8	1129.4	1125.6	1114.7	1124.1	1132.1	1130.3	1132.9	1133.1	1124.5
2005	1118.4	1126.1	1134.2	1139.0	1138.7	1133.6	1123.4	1134.3	1120.1	1125.0	1137.7	1132.0	1130.2
2006	1116.2	1126.0	1137.1	1141.0	1144.8	1143.9	1125.2	1143.8	1153.0	1149.0	1155.9	1156.0	1141.0
2007	1138.4	1144.6	1148.3	1153.8	1156.2	1152.9	1137.2	1153.8	1161.2	1158.3	1164.2	1164.3	1152.8
2008	1147.3	1153.5	1157.6	1161.6	1160.9	1152.6	1129.6	1143.7	1147.2	1143.5	1141.2	1131.7	1147.5
2009	1106.7	1106.1	1105.3	1103.9	1104.5	1097.1	1079.2	1087.7	1093.1	1094.3	1091.4	1091.1	1096.7
Total Private													
1990	712.4	714.3	721.7	728.8	733.2	744.7	739.5	739.7	741.9	740.7	741.1	739.7	733.1
2000	913.9	913.8	920.3	923.9	927.5	931.6	920.1	924.3	920.2	914.0	913.8	913.6	919.7
2001	891.6	890.5	892.6	897.2	899.0	898.8	890.4	895.5	892.3	885.9	887.8	887.3	892.4
2002	872.8	874.5	880.7	887.1	890.6	893.7	886.0	889.4	888.4	879.4	878.7	880.4	883.5
2003	865.9	866.5	869.0	873.0	875.3	873.7	871.9	875.9	876.3	878.8	880.3	882.4	874.1
2004	867.6	869.7	875.9	884.0	885.5	885.9	882.8	886.3	887.6	884.8	887.3	891.7	882.4
2005	878.0	881.9	889.6	894.4	895.2	893.6	891.6	896.8	878.8	883.6	895.6	893.9	889.4
2006	878.3	885.0	896.0	900.0	904.9	906.3	897.8	907.2	909.7	905.9	912.1	915.7	901.6
2007	897.6	900.0	903.5	907.8	910.9	910.9	904.2	912.6	914.0	909.7	915.6	918.8	908.8
2008	901.5	904.1	907.8	910.8	911.5	907.1	894.7	899.5	897.0	801.4	888.7	882.3	899.7
2009	858.2	854.8	853.0	851.2	851.7	847.8	839.4	842.3	841.2	839.8	837.6	838.0	846.3
Goods-Producing													
1990	268.1	269.8	272.3	274.7	277.8	281.1	277.7	281.0	282.0	282.5	281.3	277.5	277.2
2000	289.9	289.2	290.3	290.2	290.7	291.2	286.8	286.0	283.4	282.2	279.3	277.3	286.4
2001	269.0	266.8	264.3	265.9	265.0	264.9	260.1	260.9	259.8	258.3	257.6	255.1	262.3
2002	252.8	253.2	254.0	253.0	253.7	255.0	251.5	251.2	250.3	246.6	244.3	243.1	250.7
2003	239.8	239.6	239.3	239.2	239.1	238.2	236.6	236.4	237.2	238.6	237.9	237.5	238.3
2004	233.7	233.9	235.6	238.1	238.3	240.1	237.6	239.1	238.9	238.2	238.7	238.7	237.6
2005	235.9	235.8	238.0	239.7	240.2	240.7	239.4	239.8	236.0	239.8	241.9	243.7	239.2
2006	239.5	239.5	241.7	242.8	244.6	247.1	244.0	244.0	242.8	242.3	243.0	243.1	242.9
2007	239.0	238.2	235.0	239.3	238.9	238.7	236.5	237.5	238.0	236.5	236.9	237.8	237.7
2008	234.3	233.9	234.1	236.1	236.4	235.1	228.5	227.7	225.7	224.4	221.2	217.1	229.5
2009	209.3	206.5	204.8	202.8	202.7	202.3	199.8	198.7	197.5	195.0	194.3	194.8	200.7
Mining and Logging													
1990	9.9	9.9	10.0	10.3	10.4	10.5	10.5	10.6	10.5	10.6	10.6	10.5	10.3
2000	9.2	9.3	9.4	9.2	9.3	9.4	9.4	9.3	9.4	9.6	9.5	9.5	9.3
2001	9.3	9.3	9.6	9.7	9.6	9.7	9.7	9.8	9.8	9.6	9.6	9.6	9.6
2002	8.9	8.9	9.0	8.9	9.0	9.0	9.0	9.0	9.0	8.8	8.7	8.5	8.9
2003	8.3	8.3	8.5	8.7	8.8	8.8	8.9	9.0	9.1	8.9	8.9	8.9	8.8
2004	8.6	8.5	8.8	8.7	8.8	8.9	9.0	9.0	8.8	8.9	9.0	8.9	8.8
2005	8.5	8.4	8.6	8.8	8.8	8.8	8.8	8.9	8.8	8.9	8.9	8.9	8.8
2006	8.9	9.0	9.2	9.6	9.6	9.5	9.5	9.7	9.6	9.7	9.8	9.6	9.5
2007	9.2	9.3	9.4	9.6	9.7	9.5	9.5	9.6	9.6	9.5	9.7	9.6	9.5
2008	9.4	9.1	9.2	9.4	9.5	9.5	9.4	9.5	9.5	10.0	10.0	9.8	9.5
2009	9.2	9.0	8.8	8.5	8.4	8.4	8.2	8.2	8.1	8.0	8.2	8.1	8.4
Construction													
1990	34.5	34.5	35.7	36.3	37.4	38.1	37.6	38.3	38.5	39.0	39.1	37.2	37.2
2000	53.4	54.1	55.0	54.5	55.3	56.4	55.9	55.6	54.4	53.9	52.9	52.3	54.5
2001	48.6	49.6	49.9	51.3	51.7	52.4	52.2	53.2	53.0	53.4	54.2	53.7	51.9
2002	53.3	53.2	53.9	53.6	54.3	55.7	54.8	54.9	54.7	53.3	52.7	52.4	53.9
2003	51.0	51.1	50.8	51.1	50.9	50.9	50.6	50.6	50.7	50.4	49.6	49.2	50.6
2004	47.2	47.0	47.7	48.9	49.2	50.1	50.0	50.3	50.6	49.8	49.7	49.0	49.1
2005	47.4	47.5	49.0	50.5	51.5	52.1	52.3	52.6	54.5	55.6	56.4	57.3	52.2
2006	54.7	54.3	55.6	56.8	58.6	60.7	58.9	59.1	58.9	58.3	58.3	58.3	57.7
2007	56.9	56.6	58.4	58.0	58.2	58.7	58.5	59.0	59.4	59.5	60.2	61.2	58.7
2008	59.7	60.0	61.0	63.5	64.5	63.9	60.8	59.4	59.1	59.3	57.3	55.8	60.4
2009	52.5	52.1	52.1	52.0	53.1	53.9	52.3	51.3	49.8	48.5	47.9	47.7	51.1
Manufacturing													
1990	223.7	225.4	226.6	228.1	230.0	232.5	229.6	232.1	233.0	232.9	231.6	229.8	229.6
2000	227.3	225.8	225.9	226.5	226.1	225.4	221.5	221.1	219.6	218.7	216.9	215.5	222.5
2001	211.1	207.9	204.8	204.9	203.7	202.8	198.2	197.9	197.0	195.3	193.8	191.8	200.8
2002	190.6	191.1	191.1	190.5	190.4	190.3	187.7	187.3	186.6	184.5	182.9	182.2	187.9
2003	180.5	180.2	180.0	179.4	179.4	178.5	177.1	176.8	177.4	179.3	179.4	179.4	179.0
2004	177.9	178.4	179.1	180.5	180.3	181.1	178.6	179.8	179.5	179.5	180.0	180.8	179.6
2005	180.0	179.9	180.4	180.4	179.9	179.8	178.3	178.3	172.7	175.3	176.6	177.5	178.3
2006	175.9	176.2	176.9	176.4	176.4	176.9	175.6	175.2	174.3	174.3	174.9	175.2	175.7
2007	172.9	172.3	167.2	171.7	171.0	170.5	168.5	168.9	169.0	167.5	167.0	167.0	169.5
2008	165.2	164.8	163.9	163.2	162.4	161.7	158.3	158.8	157.1	155.1	153.9	151.5	159.7
2009	147.6	145.4	143.9	142.3	141.2	140.0	139.3	139.2	139.6	138.5	138.2	139.0	141.2

Employment by Industry: Mississippi, Selected Years, 1990–2009—*Continued*

(Numbers in thousands, not seasonally adjusted.)

Industry and year	January	February	March	April	May	June	July	August	September	October	November	December	Annual average
Service-Providing													
1990	648.4	649.9	656.3	661.1	665.5	660.8	653.7	649.8	666.1	665.7	667.2	668.0	659.4
2000	854.2	855.8	863.5	868.1	876.0	872.8	860.4	871.0	871.9	867.6	871.4	873.4	867.2
2001	859.8	862.0	866.8	870.4	873.2	870.2	860.7	870.8	871.1	866.6	869.0	871.0	867.6
2002	858.2	860.6	866.3	874.8	878.0	878.2	868.1	877.1	880.3	875.5	877.2	880.1	872.9
2003	867.4	869.1	872.8	877.2	877.5	872.6	867.8	875.3	882.2	884.5	886.8	885.7	876.6
2004	874.6	879.4	885.3	891.7	891.1	885.5	877.1	885.0	893.2	892.1	894.2	894.4	887.0
2005	882.5	890.3	896.2	899.3	898.5	892.9	884.0	894.5	884.1	885.2	895.8	888.3	891.0
2006	876.7	886.5	895.4	898.2	900.2	896.8	881.2	899.8	910.2	906.7	912.9	912.9	898.1
2007	899.4	906.4	913.3	914.5	917.3	914.2	900.7	916.3	923.2	921.8	927.3	926.5	915.1
2008	913.0	919.6	923.5	925.5	924.5	917.5	901.1	916.0	921.5	919.1	920.0	914.6	918.0
2009	897.4	899.6	900.5	901.1	901.8	894.8	879.4	889.0	895.6	899.3	897.1	896.3	896.0
Trade, Transportation, and Utilities													
1990	183.5	182.5	184.2	185.8	186.6	187.9	188.1	190.0	189.9	188.8	190.3	191.9	187.5
2000	225.1	224.5	225.7	226.1	227.8	228.5	226.1	227.4	227.3	226.5	229.1	231.4	227.1
2001	223.2	221.4	223.0	222.7	223.5	224.1	221.2	222.2	221.7	222.1	225.2	226.8	223.1
2002	217.9	217.1	218.1	219.7	220.9	222.6	221.2	221.6	221.7	220.6	223.1	225.6	220.8
2003	217.3	216.7	216.5	216.3	217.8	218.3	218.1	218.9	218.8	220.0	222.6	224.7	218.8
2004	217.2	216.4	218.0	218.7	219.9	220.2	219.2	219.7	219.4	220.6	223.1	226.4	219.9
2005	218.1	217.3	219.4	220.1	220.3	220.5	220.8	222.4	217.1	218.3	224.0	228.2	220.5
2006	221.3	221.5	224.7	224.7	225.8	226.1	224.8	226.1	226.2	225.7	228.7	231.8	225.6
2007	224.2	223.3	226.1	225.7	227.2	227.7	225.6	226.7	227.0	226.9	230.6	232.4	227.0
2008	225.1	224.4	226.1	224.5	224.4	224.0	222.9	224.2	223.2	221.7	224.1	225.3	224.2
2009	216.9	215.3	214.8	213.8	214.6	214.4	213.1	212.7	213.0	212.6	214.1	215.8	214.3
Wholesale Trade													
1990	31.9	31.9	32.1	32.2	32.3	32.8	32.8	33.2	32.9	32.4	32.3	32.2	32.4
2000	36.9	37.0	37.0	36.9	36.9	37.2	37.0	37.4	37.2	36.7	36.5	36.6	36.9
2001	35.9	35.4	35.5	35.2	35.1	35.4	35.4	35.7	35.5	35.0	34.8	35.2	35.3
2002	34.9	34.9	34.9	34.9	34.8	35.1	35.1	35.5	35.4	35.0	34.8	35.1	35.0
2003	34.7	34.6	34.5	34.6	34.8	35.2	34.9	35.1	35.0	34.9	34.9	35.1	34.9
2004	34.8	34.7	34.7	34.9	34.8	35.0	35.1	35.2	35.1	34.9	34.9	35.2	34.9
2005	34.6	34.7	34.9	35.2	35.4	35.5	35.6	35.9	35.3	35.2	35.3	35.8	35.3
2006	35.7	35.9	36.1	35.9	36.2	36.5	36.4	37.0	36.7	36.6	36.6	37.1	36.4
2007	36.6	36.6	36.6	36.6	36.7	36.8	36.8	37.2	37.0	36.7	36.5	37.2	36.8
2008	36.8	36.7	36.6	36.5	36.5	36.6	36.3	36.4	36.0	36.1	35.7	36.0	36.4
2009	35.5	35.4	35.1	34.8	34.7	34.7	34.6	34.7	34.4	34.6	34.0	35.2	34.8
Retail Trade													
1990	115.5	114.2	114.9	115.6	116.2	116.2	116.8	118.0	117.8	117.3	119.0	121.1	116.9
2000	143.7	142.9	144.0	144.2	145.5	145.8	143.9	144.6	144.7	144.6	147.6	150.0	145.1
2001	141.9	140.7	142.1	141.6	142.3	142.7	140.1	140.6	140.4	141.0	144.6	145.9	142.0
2002	138.3	137.5	138.7	139.8	140.4	141.5	140.3	139.7	139.9	139.0	141.8	144.3	140.1
2003	137.1	136.4	136.7	136.2	137.2	137.2	137.4	138.0	137.9	139.1	141.6	143.7	138.2
2004	136.8	136.0	137.2	137.5	138.2	138.3	137.6	137.4	137.2	138.3	140.9	143.3	138.2
2005	137.0	136.1	137.4	137.8	137.8	137.9	138.1	138.9	134.8	136.4	141.7	144.9	138.2
2006	139.1	138.8	141.5	141.5	142.0	142.0	141.2	141.4	141.3	141.0	143.9	145.9	141.6
2007	139.9	139.2	141.5	141.0	142.0	142.5	140.5	140.7	141.0	141.2	144.8	146.1	141.7
2008	140.2	139.5	141.2	140.0	139.7	139.1	138.3	138.7	138.1	137.0	139.6	140.8	139.4
2009	133.8	132.6	132.8	132.6	133.5	133.6	132.5	131.5	132.1	132.6	135.1	135.0	133.1
Transportation and Utilities													
1990	36.1	36.4	37.2	38.0	38.1	38.9	38.5	38.8	39.2	39.1	39.0	38.6	38.2
2000	44.5	44.6	44.7	45.0	45.4	45.5	45.2	45.4	45.4	45.2	45.0	44.8	45.1
2001	45.4	45.3	45.4	45.9	46.1	46.0	45.7	45.9	45.8	46.1	45.8	45.7	45.8
2002	44.7	44.7	44.5	45.0	45.7	46.0	45.8	46.4	46.4	46.6	46.5	46.2	45.7
2003	45.5	45.7	45.3	45.5	45.8	45.9	45.8	45.8	45.9	46.0	46.1	45.9	45.8
2004	45.6	45.7	46.1	46.3	46.9	46.9	46.5	47.1	47.1	47.4	47.3	47.9	46.7
2005	46.5	46.5	47.1	47.1	47.1	47.1	47.1	47.6	47.0	46.7	47.0	47.5	47.0
2006	46.5	46.8	47.1	47.3	47.6	47.6	47.2	47.7	48.2	48.1	48.2	48.8	47.6
2007	47.7	47.5	48.0	48.1	48.5	48.4	48.3	48.8	49.0	49.0	49.3	49.1	48.5
2008	48.1	48.2	48.3	48.0	48.2	48.3	48.3	49.1	49.1	48.6	48.8	48.5	48.5
2009	47.6	47.3	46.9	46.4	46.4	46.1	46.0	46.5	46.5	45.4	45.0	45.6	46.3
Information													
1990	12.5	12.5	12.8	12.9	13.0	13.1	13.2	13.4	13.2	13.2	13.2	13.2	13.0
2000	16.8	16.8	17.0	16.9	17.1	17.5	17.7	17.7	17.6	17.6	17.8	17.9	17.4
2001	17.6	17.5	17.4	17.1	17.1	17.3	17.0	16.7	16.5	16.4	16.5	16.5	17.0
2002	16.5	16.4	16.3	16.3	16.3	16.2	16.1	16.0	15.8	15.7	15.8	15.7	16.1
2003	15.5	15.3	15.3	15.1	15.1	15.0	15.0	15.0	15.0	14.9	14.9	15.0	15.1
2004	14.9	14.8	14.8	14.6	14.6	14.7	14.6	14.5	14.4	14.3	14.5	14.5	14.6
2005	14.5	14.5	14.5	14.4	14.4	14.6	14.3	14.3	14.0	14.0	14.0	14.1	14.3
2006	14.0	13.9	13.9	13.8	13.8	13.9	13.7	13.6	13.4	13.3	13.3	13.4	13.7
2007	13.2	13.3	13.3	13.3	13.3	13.5	13.6	13.5	13.4	13.3	13.5	13.5	13.4
2008	13.4	13.5	13.5	13.5	13.5	13.6	13.6	13.5	13.4	13.2	13.4	13.4	13.5
2009	13.3	13.2	13.1	13.0	12.9	12.9	12.7	12.6	12.6	12.6	12.5	12.5	12.8

Employment by Industry: Mississippi, Selected Years, 1990–2009—*Continued*

(Numbers in thousands, not seasonally adjusted.)

Industry and year	January	February	March	April	May	June	July	August	September	October	November	December	Annual average
Financial Activities													
1990	41.5	41.3	41.2	41.1	41.2	41.5	41.3	41.3	40.9	40.9	40.9	41.0	41.2
2000	45.8	45.8	45.9	45.9	46.0	46.5	46.1	45.9	46.0	45.6	45.7	46.0	45.9
2001	45.3	45.5	45.5	45.6	45.8	46.2	46.1	46.3	46.0	45.8	45.8	46.1	45.8
2002	45.6	45.4	45.5	45.7	45.7	46.1	45.8	45.8	45.6	45.7	46.0	46.0	45.7
2003	45.8	45.7	45.8	45.7	46.0	46.1	46.2	46.1	46.0	45.7	45.7	46.0	45.9
2004	45.5	45.4	45.6	45.9	45.9	46.3	46.3	46.3	46.1	46.1	46.1	46.5	46.0
2005	45.9	45.9	46.1	46.0	46.2	46.3	46.7	46.6	45.8	46.6	46.8	46.9	46.3
2006	45.6	46.3	46.3	46.2	46.3	46.7	46.8	46.8	46.7	46.5	46.8	47.1	46.5
2007	46.5	46.7	46.8	46.9	47.1	47.3	47.1	47.3	47.0	47.2	47.2	47.4	47.0
2008	47.0	47.0	47.2	47.0	47.1	47.1	47.0	46.9	46.7	47.0	46.8	47.0	47.0
2009	46.5	46.2	46.0	45.9	46.2	46.0	45.4	45.9	45.6	45.6	45.2	45.6	45.8
Professional and Business Services													
1990	49.4	50.0	50.7	51.3	51.1	52.0	51.6	52.0	52.0	51.9	51.6	51.8	51.3
2000	78.5	78.7	79.4	79.9	80.0	80.5	79.0	80.6	80.3	78.3	78.7	78.2	79.3
2001	76.2	77.1	76.9	77.2	76.9	76.8	77.1	77.7	77.2	76.1	76.0	76.6	76.8
2002	76.0	76.7	77.3	78.7	78.2	79.3	78.6	79.7	78.9	77.5	76.8	77.4	77.9
2003	77.3	75.5	77.4	79.1	78.7	78.8	79.0	79.9	80.2	81.0	81.1	81.8	79.3
2004	80.7	81.4	81.9	83.4	82.8	83.1	83.2	83.0	83.6	82.9	82.9	84.4	82.8
2005	84.6	86.7	87.0	87.1	85.7	85.8	86.2	87.1	87.5	89.9	91.6	91.3	87.5
2006	90.1	92.0	93.7	94.2	94.4	93.6	91.5	92.8	92.7	92.0	92.8	92.5	92.7
2007	91.0	92.3	93.4	92.4	92.2	92.3	91.9	93.2	93.9	94.0	95.0	95.8	93.1
2008	94.5	95.4	95.5	96.3	96.1	95.7	94.1	94.6	95.2	94.6	94.1	92.2	94.9
2009	89.8	89.5	89.0	87.8	87.1	86.7	85.1	86.2	85.9	86.5	85.7	83.6	86.9
Education and Health Services													
1990	73.1	73.3	73.7	74.4	74.3	78.4	77.6	71.7	74.5	76.0	76.3	76.6	75.0
2000	104.0	104.3	104.8	105.1	105.3	103.1	102.6	104.3	106.2	106.8	107.1	107.5	105.1
2001	108.0	108.7	109.3	109.8	110.2	107.6	107.6	110.0	111.4	111.8	112.2	112.6	109.9
2002	111.6	111.9	112.6	113.5	113.6	110.6	109.9	111.8	114.2	114.6	114.9	115.2	112.9
2003	114.3	114.7	115.2	116.1	116.2	113.6	112.9	115.2	116.7	118.0	118.4	118.3	115.8
2004	118.3	119.0	119.3	119.7	119.6	116.2	116.5	118.0	121.2	121.2	121.7	121.9	119.4
2005	121.3	122.0	122.3	122.6	122.4	118.9	118.6	120.9	122.1	122.0	122.3	123.1	121.5
2006	121.9	122.9	123.8	124.0	124.4	120.6	120.4	123.5	126.4	126.4	127.1	127.5	124.1
2007	126.5	127.2	127.9	127.9	128.3	125.5	124.5	128.5	129.9	129.9	129.9	129.9	128.0
2008	128.0	128.7	128.6	128.6	127.8	125.6	124.7	128.1	130.0	130.5	130.4	130.5	128.5
2009	129.1	129.4	129.7	130.1	129.6	126.8	126.9	129.7	132.1	134.6	133.9	134.0	130.5
Leisure and Hospitality													
1990	53.3	54.0	55.6	57.2	57.7	58.9	58.3	58.7	57.7	55.8	55.9	56.3	56.6
2000	118.9	119.3	121.6	124.1	124.8	127.9	125.8	126.6	123.6	121.6	120.7	119.8	122.9
2001	116.2	117.3	119.8	122.3	123.6	124.4	124.1	124.5	122.5	118.5	117.6	116.6	120.6
2002	115.6	116.9	119.6	122.7	124.6	125.9	125.4	126.0	124.6	121.6	120.7	120.3	122.0
2003	118.7	119.7	121.5	123.6	124.6	125.7	126.2	126.8	124.9	123.2	122.4	121.7	123.3
2004	119.8	121.0	123.0	125.6	126.5	127.2	127.8	128.3	126.6	124.4	123.3	122.3	124.7
2005	120.7	122.1	124.8	126.7	128.2	129.0	128.2	128.4	119.8	116.6	118.5	110.1	122.8
2006	109.6	111.9	114.9	117.3	118.6	120.8	119.4	123.3	124.6	123.1	123.9	123.8	119.3
2007	120.4	121.9	123.6	125.2	126.7	128.4	127.7	128.7	127.6	125.1	125.6	125.1	125.5
2008	122.4	124.0	125.3	127.3	128.4	128.4	126.7	127.4	125.6	123.2	122.4	120.8	125.2
2009	117.9	119.4	121.0	122.1	123.0	123.0	120.8	121.2	119.2	117.7	116.9	116.4	119.9
Other Services													
1990	31.0	30.9	31.2	31.4	31.5	31.8	31.7	31.6	31.7	31.6	31.6	31.4	31.5
2000	34.9	35.2	35.6	35.7	35.8	36.4	36.0	35.8	35.8	35.4	35.4	35.5	35.6
2001	36.1	36.2	36.4	36.6	36.9	37.5	37.2	37.2	37.2	36.9	36.9	37.0	36.8
2002	36.8	36.9	37.3	37.5	37.6	38.0	37.5	37.3	37.3	37.1	37.1	37.1	37.3
2003	37.2	37.3	38.0	37.9	37.8	38.0	37.9	37.6	37.5	37.4	37.3	37.4	37.6
2004	37.5	37.8	37.7	38.0	37.9	38.1	37.6	37.4	37.4	37.1	37.0	37.0	37.5
2005	37.0	37.6	37.5	37.8	37.8	37.8	37.4	37.3	36.5	36.4	36.5	36.5	37.2
2006	36.3	37.0	37.0	37.0	37.0	37.5	37.2	37.1	36.9	36.6	36.5	36.5	36.9
2007	36.8	37.1	37.4	37.1	37.2	37.5	37.3	37.2	37.2	36.8	36.9	36.9	37.1
2008	36.8	37.2	37.5	37.5	37.8	37.6	37.2	37.1	37.2	36.8	36.3	36.0	37.1
2009	35.4	35.3	35.4	35.7	35.6	35.7	35.6	35.3	35.3	35.2	35.0	35.3	35.4
Government													
1990	204.1	205.4	206.9	207.0	210.1	197.2	191.9	191.1	206.2	207.5	207.4	205.8	203.3
2000	230.2	231.2	233.5	234.4	239.2	232.4	227.1	232.7	235.1	235.8	236.9	237.1	233.8
2001	237.2	238.3	238.5	239.1	239.2	236.3	230.4	236.2	238.6	239.0	238.8	238.8	237.5
2002	238.2	239.3	239.6	240.7	241.1	239.5	233.6	238.9	242.2	242.7	242.8	242.8	240.1
2003	241.3	242.2	243.1	243.4	241.3	237.1	232.5	235.8	243.1	244.3	244.4	240.8	240.8
2004	240.7	243.6	245.0	245.8	243.9	239.7	231.9	237.8	244.5	245.5	245.6	241.4	242.1
2005	240.4	244.2	244.6	244.6	243.5	240.0	231.8	237.5	241.3	241.4	242.1	238.1	240.8
2006	237.9	241.0	241.1	241.0	239.9	237.6	227.4	236.6	243.3	243.1	243.8	240.3	239.4
2007	240.8	244.6	244.8	246.0	245.3	242.0	233.0	241.2	247.2	248.6	248.6	245.5	244.0
2008	245.8	249.4	249.8	250.8	249.4	245.5	234.9	244.2	250.2	252.1	252.5	249.4	247.8
2009	248.5	251.3	251.5	252.7	252.8	249.3	239.8	245.4	251.9	254.5	253.8	253.1	250.4

Average Weekly Hours by Selected Industry: Mississippi, 2007–2009

(Numbers in thousands, not seasonally adjusted.)

Industry and year	January	February	March	April	May	June	July	August	September	October	November	December	Annual average
Total Private													
2007	35.6	35.5	35.6	35.6	35.5	35.9	36.2	35.5	35.8	35.5	35.6	36.3	35.7
2008	35.6	35.7	35.8	35.5	35.4	36.1	35.6	35.6	35.6	35.5	35.8	35.4	35.6
2009	35.6	35.6	35.5	35.0	35.2	35.7	35.8	35.9	34.9	34.9	35.6	35.4	35.4
Goods-Producing													
2007	39.6	40.1	40.3	39.9	40.4	40.8	40.4	40.9	40.8	40.2	40.4	41.3	40.4
2008	39.5	39.2	39.7	39.4	39.5	40.4	40.9	40.2	40.8	40.2	40.1	39.9	40.0
2009	40.7	40.2	39.8	39.8	40.1	41.4	41.7	41.3	39.6	39.8	40.5	40.3	40.4
Construction													
2007	40.0	39.4	40.9	40.1	40.7	40.7	39.3	41.6	39.3	40.8	40.7	40.6	40.3
2008	37.9	38.9	39.9	39.8	39.4	40.7	39.6	39.0	41.4	39.7	38.6	36.9	39.3
2009	38.8	38.3	37.8	38.1	38.3	39.7	38.8	39.9	36.4	35.2	38.3	35.3	38.0
Manufacturing													
2007	39.7	40.2	39.9	39.5	40.0	40.5	40.4	40.5	41.1	40.0	40.3	41.6	40.3
2008	40.5	39.6	39.8	39.5	39.6	40.2	41.4	40.4	40.2	40.1	40.1	40.5	40.2
2009	40.8	40.4	40.1	39.1	39.3	40.6	40.4	40.4	39.8	40.3	40.5	40.9	40.2
Trade, Transportation, and Utilities													
2007	34.9	33.8	34.3	33.8	33.9	34.8	35.2	33.9	34.4	33.3	33.8	35.0	34.3
2008	35.2	35.7	35.8	35.6	35.7	36.3	35.6	35.8	35.1	35.0	35.0	35.1	35.5
2009	34.7	35.0	34.9	34.5	34.5	34.7	34.2	34.9	34.1	34.0	34.0	34.6	34.5
Financial Activities													
2007	35.7	36.5	35.7	38.4	35.9	36.0	39.2	36.8	38.6	37.0	36.7	38.3	37.1
2008	36.7	36.3	38.5	37.7	37.2	38.7	36.8	37.5	37.2	36.5	38.9	36.9	37.4
2009	37.9	39.2	38.9	37.5	37.1	37.7	36.2	38.8	35.8	35.8	37.8	35.4	37.4
Professional and Business Services													
2007	35.0	35.5	35.6	35.6	36.5	36.6	36.5	35.6	35.9	37.4	36.8	37.0	36.2
2008	36.5	35.8	36.7	37.1	35.7	36.6	35.4	36.5	36.1	36.3	36.0	34.9	36.1
2009	35.3	35.0	35.4	34.9	35.6	35.5	34.6	36.1	34.0	34.4	35.9	35.8	35.2
Education and Health Services													
2007	35.4	35.2	35.1	35.2	34.2	34.5	34.5	34.3	34.3	34.1	34.4	34.5	34.6
2008	33.9	34.8	33.6	34.0	33.4	34.1	34.0	33.5	33.8	33.7	34.1	34.0	33.9
2009	33.8	33.2	33.8	33.9	34.1	34.3	34.2	34.3	34.5	34.5	34.9	34.7	34.2
Leisure and Hospitality													
2007	26.5	25.8	25.9	26.3	26.2	26.0	26.7	25.3	26.1	26.7	26.5	26.7	26.2
2008	27.0	27.4	27.4	26.7	27.1	28.0	27.2	27.5	27.7	28.4	28.9	28.9	27.7
2009	28.7	29.3	29.0	28.7	29.3	29.7	32.3	31.9	30.8	30.8	31.4	30.8	30.2

Average Hourly Earnings by Selected Industry: Mississippi, 2007–2009

(Dollars, not seasonally adjusted.)

Industry and year	January	February	March	April	May	June	July	August	September	October	November	December	Annual average
Total Private													
2007	16.47	16.51	16.58	16.62	16.37	16.28	16.46	16.47	16.48	16.38	16.41	16.47	16.46
2008	16.53	16.78	16.81	16.75	16.69	16.85	16.92	17.04	17.04	17.10	17.22	16.99	16.89
2009	17.06	17.42	17.64	17.62	17.78	17.78	17.94	18.13	18.24	18.19	18.39	18.25	17.87
Goods-Producing													
2007	16.24	16.07	16.11	16.36	16.24	16.29	16.45	16.40	16.37	16.49	16.59	16.69	16.36
2008	16.76	17.15	17.19	17.10	17.14	17.25	17.32	17.33	17.29	17.36	17.57	17.03	17.21
2009	17.10	17.51	18.07	18.07	18.40	18.64	18.87	18.84	18.61	18.47	18.59	18.63	18.31
Construction													
2007	17.03	16.48	16.44	16.55	16.32	16.58	16.64	16.52	16.65	16.78	16.87	17.15	16.67
2008	17.30	17.89	17.81	17.79	17.95	17.67	17.93	17.98	18.04	18.10	18.29	18.06	17.90
2009	18.37	18.60	18.86	18.71	18.75	18.73	18.60	18.66	17.59	17.89	17.68	18.45	18.43
Manufacturing													
2007	15.99	15.92	15.89	16.23	16.17	16.14	16.33	16.32	16.20	16.26	16.39	16.36	16.18
2008	16.42	16.74	16.71	16.60	16.63	16.83	16.86	16.96	16.71	16.73	16.97	16.28	16.70
2009	16.32	16.83	17.37	17.26	17.46	17.65	17.49	17.57	17.69	17.48	17.78	17.62	17.37
Trade, Transportation, and Utilities													
2007	14.76	15.26	15.45	15.22	15.11	14.87	14.74	14.84	15.05	14.62	14.72	14.72	14.94
2008	14.92	14.87	14.88	15.01	14.92	14.84	14.58	15.78	15.73	15.48	15.30	14.81	15.09
2009	14.90	15.46	15.18	15.25	15.29	15.01	14.95	15.02	15.28	15.42	15.58	15.41	15.23
Financial Activities													
2007	19.12	18.88	20.06	18.69	17.14	17.60	18.07	18.57	18.04	17.97	18.57	18.45	18.42
2008	18.36	19.31	20.43	19.85	19.86	20.05	19.83	19.25	19.10	19.22	19.14	19.03	19.46
2009	19.06	18.99	20.16	19.29	19.23	19.39	19.56	19.60	19.58	19.64	19.82	20.06	19.53
Professional and Business Services													
2007	19.63	19.05	19.09	19.09	18.71	18.14	18.60	18.82	18.72	18.66	18.48	18.43	18.78
2008	18.63	18.03	18.13	17.94	17.74	17.89	18.27	18.13	18.39	18.97	18.79	18.98	18.32
2009	18.81	19.68	19.84	19.90	19.86	19.99	19.98	19.87	19.97	20.45	20.66	20.72	19.97
Education and Health Services													
2007	17.45	17.49	17.50	17.61	17.67	17.86	18.14	17.89	17.80	17.81	17.61	17.92	17.73
2008	18.00	18.40	18.43	18.45	18.36	18.54	19.02	19.02	18.80	18.69	18.60	18.84	18.60
2009	18.82	19.04	19.02	19.15	19.27	19.27	19.47	19.63	19.82	19.75	19.96	19.75	19.42
Leisure and Hospitality													
2007	10.26	10.23	10.20	10.38	10.26	10.02	10.07	10.23	10.45	10.12	10.42	10.79	10.29
2008	10.79	11.34	11.00	10.85	10.82	10.67	10.79	10.69	10.69	10.81	11.20	11.19	10.90
2009	11.23	11.75	11.59	11.57	11.50	11.42	11.42	11.56	11.69	11.70	11.74	11.90	11.59

Average Weekly Earnings by Selected Industry: Mississippi, 2007–2009

(Dollars, not seasonally adjusted.)

Industry and year	January	February	March	April	May	June	July	August	September	October	November	December	Annual average
Total Private													
2007	586.33	586.11	590.25	591.67	581.14	584.45	595.85	584.69	589.98	581.49	584.20	597.86	587.62
2008	588.47	599.05	601.80	594.63	590.83	608.29	602.35	606.62	606.62	607.05	616.48	601.45	601.28
2009	607.34	620.15	626.22	616.70	625.86	634.75	642.25	650.87	636.58	634.83	654.68	646.05	632.60
Goods-Producing													
2007	643.10	644.41	649.23	652.76	656.10	664.63	664.58	670.76	667.90	662.90	670.24	689.30	660.94
2008	662.02	672.28	682.44	673.74	677.03	696.90	708.39	696.67	705.43	697.87	704.56	679.50	688.40
2009	695.97	703.90	719.19	719.19	737.84	771.70	786.88	778.09	736.96	735.11	752.90	750.79	739.72
Construction													
2007	681.20	649.31	672.40	663.66	664.22	674.81	653.95	687.23	654.35	684.62	686.61	696.29	671.80
2008	655.67	695.92	710.62	708.04	707.23	719.17	710.03	701.22	746.86	718.57	705.99	666.41	703.47
2009	712.76	712.38	712.91	712.85	718.13	743.58	721.68	744.53	640.28	629.73	677.14	651.29	700.34
Manufacturing													
2007	634.80	639.98	634.01	641.09	646.80	653.67	659.73	660.96	665.82	650.40	660.52	680.58	652.05
2008	665.01	662.90	665.06	655.70	658.55	676.57	698.00	685.18	671.74	670.87	680.50	659.34	671.34
2009	665.86	679.93	696.54	674.87	686.18	716.59	706.60	709.83	704.06	704.44	720.09	720.66	698.27
Trade, Transportation, and Utilities													
2007	515.12	515.79	529.94	514.44	512.23	517.48	518.85	503.08	517.72	486.85	497.54	515.20	512.44
2008	525.18	530.86	532.70	534.36	532.64	538.69	519.05	564.92	552.12	541.80	535.50	519.83	535.70
2009	517.03	541.10	529.78	526.13	527.51	520.85	511.29	524.20	521.05	524.28	529.72	533.19	525.44
Financial Activities													
2007	682.58	689.12	716.14	717.70	615.33	633.60	708.34	683.38	696.34	664.89	681.52	706.64	683.38
2008	673.81	700.95	786.56	748.35	738.79	775.94	729.74	721.88	710.52	701.53	744.55	702.21	727.80
2009	722.37	744.41	784.22	723.38	713.43	731.00	708.07	760.48	700.96	703.11	749.20	710.12	730.42
Professional and Business Services													
2007	687.05	676.28	679.60	679.60	682.92	663.92	678.90	669.99	672.05	697.88	680.06	681.91	679.84
2008	680.00	645.47	665.37	665.57	633.32	654.77	646.76	661.75	663.88	688.61	676.44	662.40	661.35
2009	663.99	688.80	702.34	694.51	707.02	709.65	691.31	717.31	678.98	703.48	741.69	741.78	702.94
Education and Health Services													
2007	617.73	615.65	614.25	619.87	604.31	616.17	625.83	613.63	610.54	607.32	605.78	618.24	613.46
2008	610.20	640.32	619.25	627.30	613.22	632.21	646.68	637.17	635.44	629.85	634.26	640.56	630.54
2009	636.12	632.13	642.88	649.19	657.11	660.96	665.87	673.31	683.79	681.38	696.60	685.33	664.16
Leisure and Hospitality													
2007	271.89	263.93	264.18	272.99	268.81	260.52	268.87	258.82	272.75	270.20	276.13	288.09	269.60
2008	291.33	310.72	301.40	289.70	293.22	298.76	293.49	293.98	296.11	307.00	323.68	323.39	301.93
2009	322.30	344.28	336.11	332.06	336.95	339.17	368.87	368.76	360.05	360.36	368.64	368.37	350.02

MISSOURI
At a Glance

Population:
  1990 census: 5,116,901
  2000 census: 5,595,211
  2009 estimate: 5,987,580

Percent change in population:
  1990–2000: 9.3%
  2000–2009: 7.0%

Percent change in total nonfarm employment:
  1990–2009: 14.6%
  2008–2009: -3.6%

Industry with the largest growth in employment, 1990–2009 (thousands):
  Education and Health Services, 145.1

Industry with the largest decline or smallest growth in employment, 1990–2009 (thousands):
  Manufacturing, -136.4

Civilian labor force:
  1990: 2,607,584
  2000: 2,973,092
  2009: 3,036,622

Unemployment rate and rank among states (lowest to highest):
  1990: 5.8%, 34th
  2000: 3.3%, 14th
  2009: 9.3%, 34th

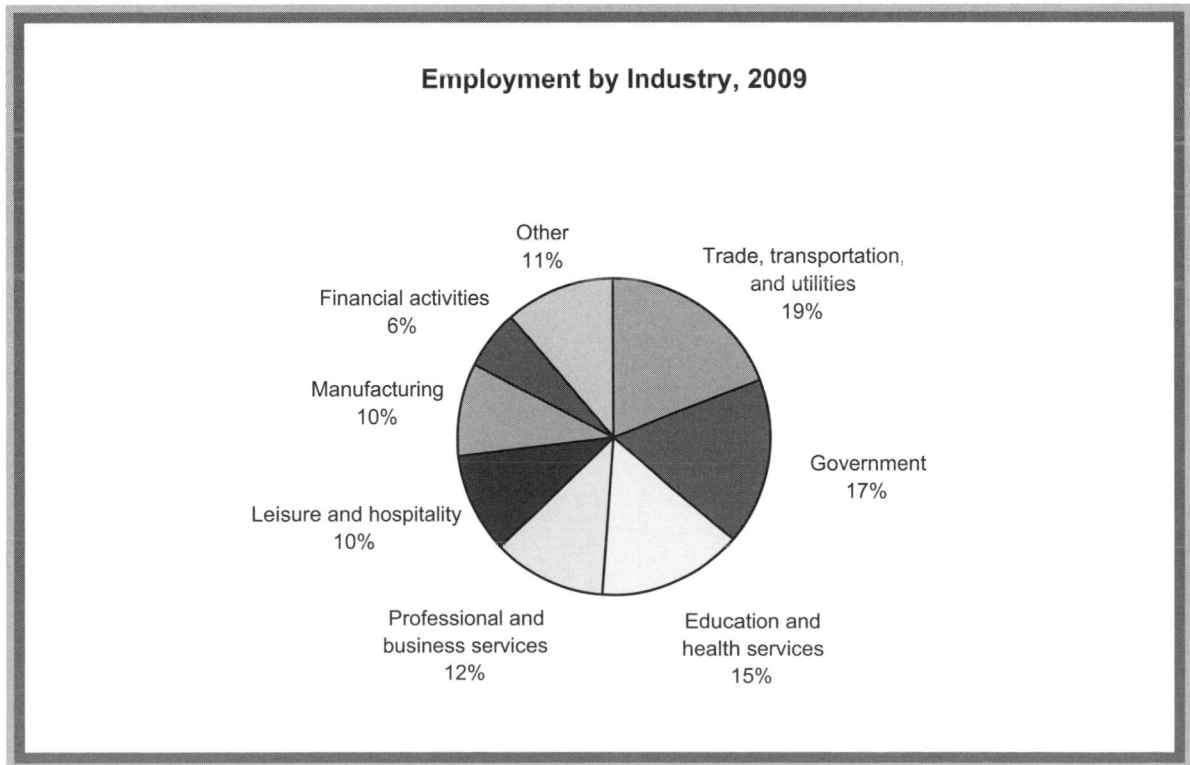

Employment by Industry, 2009

Other 11%
Financial activities 6%
Manufacturing 10%
Leisure and hospitality 10%
Professional and business services 12%
Trade, transportation, and utilities 19%
Government 17%
Education and health services 15%

Employment by Industry: Missouri, Selected Years, 1990–2009

(Numbers in thousands, not seasonally adjusted.)

Industry and year	January	February	March	April	May	June	July	August	September	October	November	December	Annual average
Total Nonfarm													
1990	2287.1	2301.9	2323.4	2341.7	2367.8	2371.4	2344.5	2353.8	2374.8	2362.2	2356.7	2355.1	2345.0
2000	2691.1	2701.1	2735.0	2758.5	2774.3	2786.0	2729.8	2733.4	2763.1	2771.8	2774.5	2766.2	2748.7
2001	2688.3	2700.8	2727.1	2751.7	2765.9	2775.1	2708.4	2717.0	2738.2	2730.3	2731.9	2730.4	2730.4
2002	2660.5	2667.2	2690.7	2705.7	2720.2	2727.9	2661.1	2677.6	2719.1	2716.1	2720.5	2720.0	2698.9
2003	2640.4	2643.1	2664.8	2690.0	2703.5	2709.6	2654.6	2662.6	2695.0	2704.2	2699.1	2698.5	2680.5
2004	2629.6	2630.8	2666.9	2702.5	2713.1	2724.1	2673.1	2684.3	2717.9	2730.2	2730.2	2730.9	2694.5
2005	2656.0	2671.5	2703.3	2749.3	2758.2	2764.0	2721.5	2735.7	2761.0	2763.2	2768.9	2771.5	2735.3
2006	2706.5	2722.9	2755.6	2784.7	2798.2	2804.6	2751.6	2760.9	2793.4	2797.3	2805.4	2809.4	2774.2
2007	2729.0	2741.7	2785.3	2803.5	2824.4	2825.6	2768.0	2785.8	2815.1	2815.3	2822.4	2818.7	2794.6
2008	2747.8	2761.1	2782.3	2809.9	2828.8	2828.5	2768.7	2780.1	2803.2	2800.7	2786.8	2771.7	2789.1
2009	2681.2	2679.1	2692.8	2706.7	2714.5	2708.7	2656.1	2663.4	2686.7	2695.1	2692.7	2680.2	2688.1
Total Private													
1990	1922.9	1927.5	1945.4	1962.5	1983.2	2007.6	1998.1	2010.6	2005.9	1986.4	1976.3	1977.4	1975.3
2000	2265.6	2267.4	2294.5	2325.0	2336.2	2355.5	2336.2	2340.1	2338.6	2342.4	2338.6	2330.9	2322.6
2001	2260.2	2265.4	2290.2	2314.3	2327.4	2341.0	2317.3	2324.5	2305.8	2293.7	2292.5	2287.9	2301.7
2002	2224.6	2228.1	2250.0	2264.7	2277.2	2294.2	2271.2	2287.0	2287.6	2275.9	2277.3	2275.9	2267.8
2003	2203.0	2200.5	2221.4	2242.8	2255.0	2269.0	2265.0	2273.0	2263.0	2266.2	2260.2	2260.4	2248.3
2004	2198.3	2193.4	2226.1	2260.4	2273.6	2294.8	2282.5	2291.6	2285.8	2292.4	2289.9	2292.0	2265.1
2005	2228.2	2235.0	2264.3	2309.0	2318.9	2335.1	2324.9	2335.0	2331.5	2327.3	2329.7	2331.9	2305.9
2006	2274.8	2281.4	2311.0	2339.8	2352.2	2373.7	2356.0	2361.9	2357.4	2353.9	2358.8	2363.2	2340.3
2007	2292.4	2295.3	2336.2	2353.0	2372.0	2387.5	2370.7	2381.6	2372.2	2363.4	2367.7	2365.3	2354.8
2008	2306.3	2307.9	2327.8	2352.9	2370.2	2381.6	2365.8	2367.9	2354.3	2341.5	2326.1	2311.7	2342.8
2009	2232.3	2221.5	2232.9	2242.9	2249.8	2255.7	2242.2	2243.9	2226.4	2228.0	2224.5	2213.6	2234.5
Goods-Producing													
1990	485.9	487.1	487.9	492.0	496.3	503.8	498.3	502.6	499.4	492.7	484.9	483.4	492.9
2000	501.8	500.9	505.3	509.6	513.7	520.5	510.0	511.4	508.3	512.7	509.6	503.9	509.0
2001	488.3	489.9	494.7	499.1	500.8	502.8	488.5	495.2	489.2	481.0	480.7	477.2	490.6
2002	461.9	462.5	465.8	464.5	465.6	470.8	458.1	471.2	469.8	465.5	462.9	461.2	465.0
2003	447.8	444.8	448.9	451.1	454.5	458.6	452.4	459.3	456.3	457.9	454.8	452.1	453.2
2004	439.9	435.9	445.7	453.2	456.0	462.4	453.6	462.8	460.3	458.0	455.6	454.4	453.2
2005	440.0	441.4	448.6	457.5	461.4	465.6	456.0	466.0	464.0	463.6	462.2	460.5	457.2
2006	449.7	451.0	457.6	462.0	463.4	470.3	464.1	465.4	462.5	459.8	458.8	457.4	460.2
2007	443.4	440.4	451.7	453.6	458.4	462.6	456.2	460.8	458.2	453.7	451.9	447.3	453.2
2008	433.9	432.5	434.5	438.4	443.3	446.3	441.8	439.9	437.0	431.0	422.9	413.6	434.6
2009	391.7	386.2	386.4	383.0	380.4	382.1	381.1	377.4	373.8	372.4	369.9	363.2	379.0
Mining and Logging													
1990	5.4	5.5	5.5	5.6	5.7	5.9	5.9	5.9	5.8	5.7	5.7	5.6	5.6
2000	5.5	5.5	5.6	6.0	6.0	6.0	5.5	5.5	5.4	5.4	5.3	5.1	5.6
2001	4.8	4.9	5.0	5.2	5.1	5.2	5.1	5.2	5.0	4.8	4.7	4.6	5.0
2002	4.5	4.5	4.5	4.5	4.6	4.7	4.7	4.7	4.7	4.6	4.6	4.5	4.6
2003	4.4	4.4	4.4	4.5	4.6	4.7	4.6	4.7	4.6	4.6	4.5	4.5	4.5
2004	4.6	4.5	4.6	4.8	4.8	4.9	5.0	5.0	5.0	4.9	4.8	4.7	4.8
2005	4.9	4.9	5.1	5.3	5.4	5.5	5.5	5.5	5.4	5.4	5.4	5.4	5.3
2006	5.3	5.3	5.4	5.4	5.5	5.6	5.6	5.5	5.5	5.4	5.3	5.2	5.4
2007	5.1	5.0	5.2	5.2	5.2	5.4	5.7	6.2	6.1	6.0	6.0	5.7	5.6
2008	5.4	5.2	5.1	5.0	4.9	5.0	5.1	5.3	5.4	5.4	4.9	4.7	5.1
2009	4.4	4.3	4.3	4.3	4.2	4.3	4.3	4.4	4.3	4.3	4.2	4.2	4.3
Construction													
1990	90.5	89.4	91.5	91.9	94.9	99.1	101.2	102.4	99.0	96.9	94.0	90.6	95.1
2000	129.0	128.6	133.0	136.8	139.7	144.2	143.7	144.9	144.1	142.9	140.1	135.1	138.5
2001	128.2	129.2	134.8	140.6	144.0	149.0	148.1	148.1	144.7	143.0	141.1	138.3	140.8
2002	129.8	129.0	132.1	131.8	134.0	138.9	141.7	141.0	138.8	137.4	135.1	133.8	135.3
2003	125.3	123.1	126.4	131.7	134.9	138.5	141.2	141.0	139.1	139.4	136.6	133.3	134.2
2004	126.2	122.3	130.3	136.5	139.0	142.7	145.2	144.2	142.3	141.3	139.1	137.7	137.2
2005	126.5	127.6	133.9	142.0	145.6	148.6	150.9	151.1	149.9	148.8	147.0	144.8	143.1
2006	139.1	139.5	143.6	147.8	149.2	153.9	153.6	153.4	151.1	149.3	146.9	145.1	147.7
2007	138.2	133.1	143.4	146.4	150.7	155.2	154.7	154.9	152.0	150.2	147.7	143.0	147.5
2008	136.0	132.5	137.4	140.4	144.3	146.6	147.3	147.2	143.9	141.0	136.8	130.7	140.3
2009	117.9	116.7	119.0	119.7	121.7	123.3	124.5	121.9	119.5	118.5	116.5	108.8	119.0
Manufacturing													
1990	390.0	392.2	390.9	394.5	395.7	398.8	391.2	394.3	394.6	390.1	385.2	387.2	392.1
2000	367.3	366.8	366.7	366.8	368.0	370.3	360.8	361.0	358.8	364.4	364.2	363.7	364.9
2001	355.3	355.8	354.9	353.3	351.7	348.6	335.3	341.9	339.5	333.2	334.3	334.3	344.9
2002	327.6	329.0	329.2	328.2	327.0	327.2	311.7	325.5	326.3	323.5	323.2	322.9	325.1
2003	318.1	317.3	318.1	314.9	315.0	315.4	306.6	313.6	312.6	313.9	313.7	314.3	314.5
2004	309.1	309.1	310.8	311.9	312.2	314.8	303.4	313.6	313.0	311.8	311.7	312.0	311.1
2005	308.6	308.9	309.6	310.2	310.4	311.5	299.6	309.4	308.7	309.4	309.8	310.3	308.9
2006	305.3	306.2	308.6	308.8	308.7	310.8	304.9	306.5	305.9	305.1	306.6	307.1	307.0
2007	300.1	302.3	303.1	302.0	302.5	302.0	295.8	299.7	300.1	297.5	298.2	298.6	300.2
2008	292.5	294.8	292.0	293.0	294.1	294.7	289.4	287.4	287.7	284.6	281.2	278.2	289.1
2009	269.4	265.2	263.1	259.0	254.5	254.5	252.3	251.1	250.0	249.6	249.2	250.2	255.7

Employment by Industry: Missouri, Selected Years, 1990–2009—*Continued*

(Numbers in thousands, not seasonally adjusted.)

Industry and year	January	February	March	April	May	June	July	August	September	October	November	December	Annual average
Service-Providing													
1990	1801.2	1814.8	1835.5	1849.7	1871.5	1867.6	1846.2	1851.2	1875.4	1869.5	1871.8	1871.7	1852.2
2000	2189.3	2200.2	2229.7	2248.9	2260.6	2265.5	2219.8	2222.0	2254.8	2259.1	2264.9	2262.3	2239.8
2001	2200.0	2210.9	2232.4	2252.6	2265.1	2272.3	2219.9	2221.8	2249.0	2249.3	2251.2	2253.2	2239.8
2002	2198.6	2204.7	2224.9	2241.2	2254.6	2257.1	2203.0	2206.4	2249.3	2250.6	2257.6	2258.8	2233.9
2003	2192.6	2198.3	2215.9	2238.9	2249.0	2251.0	2202.2	2203.3	2238.7	2246.3	2244.3	2246.4	2227.2
2004	2189.7	2194.9	2221.2	2249.3	2257.1	2261.7	2219.5	2221.5	2257.6	2272.2	2274.6	2276.5	2241.3
2005	2216.0	2230.1	2254.7	2291.8	2296.8	2298.4	2265.5	2269.7	2297.0	2299.6	2306.7	2311.0	2278.1
2006	2256.8	2271.9	2298.0	2322.7	2334.8	2334.3	2287.5	2295.5	2330.9	2337.5	2346.6	2352.0	2314.0
2007	2285.6	2301.3	2333.6	2349.9	2366.0	2363.0	2311.8	2325.0	2356.9	2361.6	2370.5	2371.4	2341.4
2008	2313.9	2328.6	2347.8	2371.5	2385.5	2382.2	2326.9	2340.2	2366.2	2369.7	2363.9	2358.1	2354.5
2009	2289.5	2292.9	2306.4	2323.7	2334.1	2326.6	2275.0	2286.0	2312.9	2322.7	2322.8	2317.0	2309.1
Trade, Transportation, and Utilities													
1990	500.6	495.6	499.9	499.8	504.4	507.1	504.2	506.3	508.1	507.7	512.1	515.8	505.1
2000	550.9	548.0	552.9	555.0	557.1	556.2	553.7	553.4	558.9	561.6	571.0	576.8	558.0
2001	544.1	538.8	541.3	542.4	544.6	545.7	541.8	541.5	542.7	544.8	553.4	556.2	544.8
2002	535.9	530.9	535.1	533.6	537.9	539.1	537.6	537.1	542.3	540.7	549.8	554.0	539.5
2003	529.4	524.8	527.6	528.8	530.7	530.4	529.1	530.1	530.4	538.0	543.8	547.3	532.5
2004	525.1	519.7	524.7	527.6	531.6	533.2	530.0	530.1	532.2	537.2	545.8	551.0	532.4
2005	530.4	526.0	531.2	538.0	540.8	541.5	540.4	541.2	541.0	542.8	551.9	556.3	540.1
2006	538.3	534.1	538.8	541.2	544.4	545.7	541.3	543.3	544.7	547.1	555.6	561.0	544.6
2007	542.1	538.4	546.0	546.5	550.2	549.9	545.7	546.0	547.3	548.8	559.4	562.1	548.5
2008	542.4	537.1	540.4	542.7	545.7	546.0	542.0	542.1	540.9	540.2	544.2	545.1	542.4
2009	522.7	516.9	516.8	518.2	520.5	520.2	516.4	517.7	517.2	515.9	521.1	522.6	518.9
Wholesale Trade													
1990	117.3	117.4	118.2	117.5	118.1	119.0	119.5	119.6	119.5	119.8	119.1	118.8	118.7
2000	120.5	121.1	122.1	121.6	121.6	122.2	121.6	121.3	122.1	122.1	122.6	123.2	121.8
2001	120.8	121.0	121.2	121.1	121.1	121.6	121.1	120.6	120.3	119.6	118.9	119.2	120.5
2002	119.3	119.2	119.8	119.4	119.5	120.2	120.4	119.4	119.5	118.8	118.8	118.7	119.4
2003	117.8	117.9	118.1	118.4	118.6	118.9	119.1	119.2	118.2	118.3	118.4	118.6	118.5
2004	117.7	117.6	118.6	119.6	119.8	121.2	120.9	120.1	121.0	120.4	120.4	121.1	119.9
2005	121.7	120.9	121.5	121.6	121.7	122.6	122.5	122.4	121.3	120.9	121.3	121.8	121.7
2006	120.7	120.5	121.5	122.3	123.0	124.0	123.1	123.4	123.3	123.5	123.8	124.8	122.8
2007	123.0	123.7	124.8	124.6	124.9	125.9	125.5	125.5	125.2	125.3	125.6	126.1	125.0
2008	124.7	124.6	125.2	125.6	125.7	126.3	125.9	125.7	125.0	124.5	123.6	123.4	125.0
2009	120.6	119.8	119.2	118.8	118.4	118.5	118.0	117.5	116.6	116.0	116.1	116.2	118.0
Retail Trade													
1990	273.0	267.3	269.7	269.6	272.7	275.0	273.5	274.4	273.3	273.9	279.0	283.2	273.7
2000	310.0	306.0	309.1	310.0	312.4	312.6	310.9	310.8	312.5	314.9	324.2	329.8	313.7
2001	310.6	305.1	306.7	308.0	310.0	311.9	308.9	308.4	309.3	312.3	321.5	325.0	311.5
2002	308.6	304.1	307.3	306.0	309.2	310.8	308.5	308.8	312.9	311.5	320.9	326.4	311.3
2003	305.3	300.7	303.7	305.3	307.3	308.0	307.2	308.6	309.1	315.8	322.6	326.1	310.0
2004	306.7	301.4	304.6	305.8	309.1	310.7	308.9	308.8	308.9	313.6	322.0	326.1	310.6
2005	309.2	305.7	309.5	313.8	316.0	316.3	316.8	316.4	315.3	317.5	325.8	328.7	315.9
2006	313.3	309.3	312.7	314.1	316.0	316.7	314.5	314.6	314.4	316.8	324.8	328.0	316.3
2007	312.9	308.6	314.0	315.4	317.9	318.2	315.4	314.4	314.3	315.9	325.5	327.2	316.6
2008	312.7	307.3	309.6	311.2	313.5	314.7	311.8	311.3	309.6	310.1	315.2	316.4	312.0
2009	300.5	296.3	297.4	299.0	301.6	303.0	300.9	301.5	301.1	301.7	307.3	307.6	301.5
Transportation and Utilities													
1990	110.3	110.9	112.0	112.7	113.6	113.1	111.2	112.3	115.3	114.0	114.0	113.8	112.8
2000	120.3	120.7	121.7	122.4	123.0	121.2	120.9	121.0	123.9	124.6	124.2	123.8	122.3
2001	112.7	112.7	113.4	113.3	113.5	112.2	111.8	112.5	113.1	112.9	113.0	112.0	112.8
2002	108.0	107.6	108.0	108.2	109.2	108.3	109.0	109.2	110.1	110.4	110.1	108.9	108.9
2003	106.3	106.2	105.8	105.1	104.8	103.5	102.8	102.3	103.1	103.9	102.8	102.6	104.1
2004	100.7	100.7	101.5	102.2	102.7	101.3	100.2	101.2	102.3	103.2	103.4	103.8	101.9
2005	99.5	99.4	100.2	102.6	103.1	102.6	101.1	102.4	104.4	104.4	104.8	105.8	102.5
2006	104.3	104.3	104.6	104.8	105.4	105.0	103.7	105.3	107.0	106.8	107.0	108.2	105.5
2007	106.2	106.1	107.2	106.5	107.4	105.8	104.8	106.1	107.8	107.6	108.3	108.8	106.9
2008	105.0	105.2	105.6	105.9	106.5	105.0	104.3	105.1	106.3	105.6	105.4	105.3	105.4
2009	101.6	100.8	100.2	100.4	100.5	98.7	97.5	98.7	99.5	98.2	97.7	98.8	99.4
Information													
1990	66.8	66.5	66.8	66.7	66.7	67.5	67.5	66.9	66.7	66.2	66.6	67.1	66.8
2000	77.0	76.9	76.8	76.8	76.6	76.6	76.3	76.2	76.0	75.9	75.9	75.7	76.4
2001	74.8	75.3	75.6	75.1	74.9	75.4	74.9	74.6	74.1	73.1	73.1	71.9	74.4
2002	72.8	72.8	72.4	70.9	71.1	71.1	69.2	69.1	68.7	66.9	67.4	67.6	70.0
2003	68.0	68.5	68.6	67.1	66.6	67.0	66.0	65.5	65.0	64.5	64.6	65.0	66.4
2004	65.1	65.2	65.3	64.8	64.6	64.7	63.9	63.2	62.8	63.6	64.1	63.6	64.2
2005	62.8	62.9	63.2	64.2	64.3	64.5	64.4	64.0	63.8	63.9	64.0	63.8	63.8
2006	63.0	63.0	63.2	62.9	63.0	63.4	62.9	62.8	62.8	62.7	63.1	63.5	63.0
2007	62.2	62.4	62.9	62.6	63.1	63.7	63.4	63.6	63.7	64.0	64.4	64.6	63.4
2008	64.3	64.0	64.2	63.8	64.4	64.9	64.6	64.5	64.1	64.2	64.0	64.5	64.3
2009	64.0	64.0	63.7	63.2	63.2	63.8	63.7	63.6	63.2	62.3	62.1	62.4	63.3

Employment by Industry: Missouri, Selected Years, 1990–2009—*Continued*

(Numbers in thousands, not seasonally adjusted.)

Industry and year	January	February	March	April	May	June	July	August	September	October	November	December	Annual average
Financial Activities													
1990	137.3	137.8	138.9	138.8	139.8	141.3	141.7	141.8	140.9	139.4	138.7	139.3	139.6
2000	155.3	155.6	156.4	157.8	158.0	159.9	160.2	159.8	158.8	159.3	159.7	160.6	158.5
2001	158.2	158.3	159.0	159.8	161.0	162.4	162.4	162.3	160.6	159.6	159.7	160.2	160.3
2002	158.5	158.4	160.7	160.3	160.8	161.5	161.3	161.6	160.8	160.8	161.1	162.0	160.7
2003	160.5	160.4	160.8	161.8	162.5	163.9	165.4	165.7	164.1	163.4	162.7	162.9	162.8
2004	160.1	159.8	160.4	161.8	162.2	164.1	164.5	164.8	163.1	163.2	162.7	163.1	162.5
2005	160.8	161.6	162.2	162.7	162.7	164.1	165.4	165.0	164.3	163.9	164.3	164.3	163.4
2006	162.1	162.5	163.3	164.5	165.6	167.0	166.9	167.2	166.4	165.1	165.0	165.6	165.1
2007	164.5	164.9	165.6	165.3	166.2	167.6	167.8	167.6	166.2	166.2	165.6	166.0	166.1
2008	165.3	165.6	165.3	165.3	166.2	166.8	167.3	167.3	165.8	165.7	165.3	165.1	165.9
2009	163.8	163.4	163.8	163.6	163.8	164.5	163.7	163.3	161.7	161.9	162.2	162.7	163.2
Professional and Business Services													
1990	211.4	213.9	215.6	215.8	216.7	219.1	219.0	220.2	220.5	218.0	216.4	217.1	217.0
2000	307.9	309.1	313.8	319.6	317.6	323.7	320.5	321.6	320.5	318.3	317.3	315.0	317.1
2001	312.8	314.8	318.3	318.9	317.1	318.7	313.7	315.1	311.8	310.1	307.8	308.7	314.0
2002	299.4	302.5	304.7	306.3	304.8	305.9	303.7	305.2	305.5	307.0	307.5	306.7	304.9
2003	296.5	297.0	299.7	301.2	299.9	302.4	301.4	303.2	303.2	303.2	301.4	302.8	301.0
2004	296.5	296.8	302.4	306.5	305.3	310.5	310.0	311.7	310.8	312.3	311.8	313.6	307.4
2005	309.4	311.9	316.0	321.8	319.2	322.8	323.2	323.1	324.7	323.5	324.1	325.4	320.4
2006	318.7	322.2	327.2	331.6	330.5	335.4	332.7	334.4	334.2	336.6	336.8	339.1	331.6
2007	327.6	328.9	334.8	337.4	337.2	340.8	339.9	342.0	340.2	339.7	340.0	341.1	337.5
2008	335.1	337.3	341.0	347.1	344.0	345.7	343.8	344.4	342.3	339.1	335.4	332.8	340.7
2009	321.6	319.9	319.3	319.9	317.0	317.5	314.7	315.1	312.3	313.4	311.4	312.0	316.2
Education and Health Services													
1990	247.7	251.1	252.3	253.3	254.2	253.9	254.3	257.0	259.5	262.4	263.3	264.5	256.1
2000	328.5	331.4	332.7	335.2	333.7	332.5	332.1	332.1	336.0	337.2	338.2	338.0	334.0
2001	336.4	339.1	340.8	342.8	342.9	342.7	342.8	343.0	345.2	346.7	348.3	348.4	343.3
2002	345.6	348.4	348.8	349.7	350.5	349.8	348.1	348.7	353.4	352.8	354.1	354.4	350.4
2003	349.7	352.0	353.1	353.2	352.3	351.3	352.2	352.1	354.8	355.5	356.1	356.7	353.3
2004	352.2	355.9	356.9	358.1	358.0	357.2	357.4	357.1	360.4	363.5	363.8	364.2	358.7
2005	359.6	363.1	364.4	368.7	368.1	367.2	367.2	367.4	371.7	374.6	375.4	376.2	368.6
2006	369.6	374.0	375.3	377.2	377.0	375.5	373.9	374.1	379.6	382.1	384.9	384.1	377.3
2007	376.3	381.2	383.2	384.5	384.4	382.7	382.4	383.4	387.5	389.3	390.6	391.5	384.8
2008	384.8	389.8	390.0	392.3	391.8	390.7	390.6	391.7	395.2	399.7	400.9	401.5	393.3
2009	395.1	398.2	399.0	400.0	400.0	397.4	397.2	398.6	401.9	408.0	410.2	408.5	401.2
Leisure and Hospitality													
1990	184.4	186.2	193.7	205.6	214.0	221.7	220.1	222.8	218.5	207.3	202.2	198.3	206.2
2000	231.3	232.1	242.1	256.0	264.1	270.1	267.8	269.7	263.9	261.0	250.6	244.2	254.4
2001	230.2	233.3	243.0	258.0	267.0	272.8	273.7	273.3	264.0	260.8	251.8	247.5	256.3
2002	234.9	236.5	245.6	261.8	268.6	276.8	274.9	276.0	269.4	264.6	257.2	252.7	259.9
2003	235.5	237.0	245.8	262.1	270.6	276.4	277.6	276.7	270.4	265.0	258.5	255.0	260.9
2004	242.6	243.0	252.5	268.7	276.1	281.7	282.1	281.3	276.0	274.2	266.3	262.6	267.3
2005	247.2	249.7	259.9	276.2	282.6	288.3	287.6	288.0	282.5	276.0	269.8	266.2	272.8
2006	254.3	256.5	266.6	280.2	288.0	294.6	292.9	293.8	286.9	280.4	274.4	272.2	278.4
2007	257.7	260.1	271.7	282.6	291.3	298.3	293.9	297.2	288.9	281.8	276.0	272.9	281.0
2008	260.5	261.3	271.4	282.1	293.0	298.5	293.3	295.8	287.4	280.0	273.2	269.6	280.5
2009	255.2	254.6	265.1	276.1	285.8	290.4	285.8	289.3	278.4	276.3	269.8	264.6	274.3
Other Services													
1990	88.8	89.3	90.3	90.5	91.1	93.2	93.0	93.0	92.3	92.7	92.1	91.9	91.5
2000	112.9	113.4	114.5	115.0	115.4	116.0	115.6	115.9	116.2	116.4	116.3	116.7	115.4
2001	115.4	115.9	117.5	118.2	119.1	120.5	119.5	119.5	118.2	117.6	117.7	117.8	118.1
2002	115.6	116.1	116.9	117.6	117.9	119.2	118.3	118.1	117.7	117.6	117.3	117.3	117.5
2003	115.6	116.0	116.9	117.5	117.9	119.0	120.9	120.4	118.8	118.7	118.3	118.6	118.2
2004	116.8	117.1	118.2	119.7	119.8	121.0	121.0	120.6	120.2	120.4	119.8	119.5	119.5
2005	118.0	118.4	118.8	119.9	119.8	121.1	120.7	120.3	119.5	119.0	118.5	119.0	119.4
2006	119.1	118.1	119.0	120.2	120.3	121.8	121.3	120.9	120.3	120.1	120.2	120.3	120.1
2007	118.6	119.0	120.3	120.5	121.2	121.9	121.4	121.0	120.2	119.9	119.8	119.8	120.3
2008	120.0	120.3	121.0	121.2	121.8	122.7	122.4	122.2	121.6	121.6	120.2	119.5	121.2
2009	118.2	118.3	118.8	118.9	119.1	119.8	119.6	118.9	117.9	117.8	117.8	117.6	118.6
Government													
1990	364.2	374.4	378.0	379.2	384.6	363.8	346.4	343.2	368.9	375.8	380.4	377.7	369.7
2000	425.5	433.7	440.5	433.5	438.1	430.5	393.6	393.3	424.5	429.4	435.9	435.3	426.2
2001	428.1	435.4	436.9	437.4	438.5	434.1	391.1	392.5	432.4	436.6	439.4	442.5	428.7
2002	435.9	439.1	440.7	441.0	443.0	433.7	389.9	390.6	431.5	440.2	443.2	441.1	431.1
2003	437.4	442.6	443.4	447.2	448.5	440.6	389.6	389.6	432.0	438.0	438.9	438.1	432.2
2004	431.3	437.4	440.8	442.1	439.5	429.3	390.6	392.7	432.1	437.8	440.3	438.9	429.4
2005	427.8	436.5	439.0	440.3	439.3	428.9	396.6	400.7	429.5	435.9	439.2	439.6	429.4
2006	431.7	441.5	444.6	444.9	446.0	430.9	395.6	399.0	436.0	443.4	446.6	446.2	433.9
2007	436.6	446.4	449.1	450.5	452.4	438.1	397.3	404.2	442.9	451.9	454.7	453.4	439.8
2008	441.5	453.2	454.5	457.0	458.6	446.9	402.9	412.2	448.9	459.2	460.7	460.0	446.3
2009	448.9	457.6	459.9	463.8	464.7	453.0	413.9	419.5	460.3	467.1	468.2	466.6	453.6

Average Weekly Hours by Selected Industry: Missouri, 2007–2009

(Not seasonally adjusted.)

Industry and year	January	February	March	April	May	June	July	August	September	October	November	December	Annual average
Total Private													
2007	33.9	33.8	34.4	34.6	34.1	34.6	34.9	34.4	34.9	34.5	34.1	34.6	34.4
2008	34.2	34.0	34.8	34.3	34.4	35.1	34.6	34.7	34.5	34.8	34.6	33.9	34.5
2009	33.7	34.4	33.9	33.4	33.6	33.3	33.8	34.4	33.9	33.7	34.5	33.8	33.9
Goods-Producing													
2007	37.5	37.0	38.8	38.8	38.6	39.5	39.4	39.4	39.5	39.4	38.8	38.7	38.8
2008	38.4	37.9	38.5	38.0	38.1	38.4	39.4	40.0	39.2	39.3	37.9	37.4	38.6
2009	36.7	37.7	37.5	36.9	37.9	37.9	38.9	39.7	38.7	38.8	39.4	38.7	38.2
Construction													
2007	36.0	34.9	37.7	35.2	37.0	38.2	38.5	38.4	38.1	38.1	37.7	37.1	37.3
2008	37.4	36.7	37.3	36.6	36.6	36.0	37.0	37.2	36.0	37.9	35.8	35.3	36.7
2009	35.6	35.8	35.3	35.2	37.0	37.9	39.0	38.5	36.5	37.1	37.1	35.3	36.7
Manufacturing													
2007	38.2	38.7	39.1	40.2	39.1	39.8	39.6	39.7	39.9	39.8	39.4	39.5	39.4
2008	39.0	39.0	39.7	39.2	39.3	39.8	40.2	40.4	40.5	39.8	38.8	38.3	39.5
2009	37.4	38.0	37.8	37.2	37.9	37.4	38.2	38.9	38.5	38.5	39.4	39.4	38.2
Trade, Transportation, and Utilities													
2007	33.3	33.4	34.1	33.9	34.3	34.1	34.5	33.9	34.5	34.1	33.8	34.3	34.0
2008	33.7	33.9	34.9	34.4	34.8	35.3	34.9	34.6	34.6	34.7	35.1	34.7	34.6
2009	33.7	34.8	34.4	34.4	34.9	34.0	34.6	34.8	34.7	34.1	34.5	33.9	34.4
Financial Activities													
2007	36.9	36.9	36.3	37.7	36.5	38.7	38.1	37.9	38.1	37.3	36.8	37.4	37.4
2008	36.5	36.1	37.7	36.9	36.3	38.1	36.2	36.8	36.5	36.8	38.1	36.6	36.9
2009	37.4	37.9	37.9	36.9	36.5	36.8	36.7	38.1	37.6	37.3	38.8	37.5	37.5
Professional and Business Services													
2007	34.7	35.6	35.7	35.9	34.3	34.8	35.9	35.6	36.5	35.6	35.5	36.1	35.5
2008	35.2	35.0	36.4	36.0	36.0	37.0	35.8	35.8	35.5	37.0	35.8	34.3	35.8
2009	34.7	35.4	35.1	34.8	34.5	34.2	34.4	35.7	34.3	35.0	35.9	34.9	34.9
Education and Health Services													
2007	33.3	32.9	33.2	33.7	33.0	33.2	33.7	32.9	33.3	32.7	32.4	32.9	33.1
2008	33.0	32.6	33.0	32.6	32.2	32.8	32.8	32.8	32.8	32.8	33.0	32.0	32.7
2009	32.3	32.7	32.4	32.0	31.9	32.3	32.2	32.2	32.3	31.8	32.5	31.9	32.2
Leisure and Hospitality													
2007	26.1	26.5	26.9	26.5	26.2	27.4	27.7	27.2	26.8	26.6	26.2	26.3	26.7
2008	25.8	26.1	26.0	25.7	26.4	27.2	26.2	25.6	24.9	25.1	25.1	24.6	25.7
2009	23.5	24.1	24.1	23.8	24.4	24.4	25.5	25.0	24.4	24.4	24.4	24.6	24.4

Average Hourly Earnings by Selected Industry: Missouri, 2007–2009

(Dollars, not seasonally adjusted.)

Industry and year	January	February	March	April	May	June	July	August	September	October	November	December	Annual average
Total Private													
2007	19.71	20.04	19.77	19.80	19.71	19.58	19.55	19.51	19.97	19.75	19.77	20.29	19.78
2008	19.84	20.38	20.47	20.29	20.46	20.34	20.33	20.61	20.58	20.90	21.32	21.28	20.57
2009	21.17	21.06	21.00	20.76	20.93	20.92	20.78	20.96	20.86	20.81	21.07	20.98	20.94
Goods-Producing													
2007	21.49	21.73	22.05	22.07	22.13	21.74	21.80	21.99	22.75	22.55	22.67	23.23	22.19
2008	22.87	23.09	23.48	23.59	23.99	23.46	23.84	24.19	23.72	24.20	24.60	25.27	23.85
2009	24.95	25.92	25.61	25.40	25.52	25.47	25.25	24.92	24.92	24.94	25.28	24.66	25.24
Construction													
2007	22.90	23.67	23.63	23.96	23.82	23.55	23.55	23.63	23.88	24.19	24.30	24.17	23.78
2008	24.57	25.14	25.11	25.26	26.16	24.96	25.96	26.38	26.06	26.63	26.86	27.30	25.86
2009	27.11	27.84	26.01	26.34	26.84	26.25	26.49	26.68	27.10	27.70	28.33	27.34	26.99
Manufacturing													
2007	20.93	21.09	21.42	21.37	21.41	20.92	21.01	21.26	22.32	21.91	22.12	22.96	21.56
2008	22.23	22.30	22.78	22.87	22.96	23.31	22.70	23.02	23.14	23.47	23.98	24.74	23.11
2009	24.30	25.05	25.48	24.99	24.80	25.04	24.63	24.46	24.36	24.11	24.41	24.05	24.64
Trade, Transportation, and Utilities													
2007	16.98	17.25	16.72	17.12	16.99	16.73	16.84	16.79	17.01	16.69	16.72	17.42	16.94
2008	16.90	17.91	17.64	17.61	17.80	17.71	17.47	17.75	17.94	17.97	18.37	18.81	17.83
2009	18.65	18.38	18.28	18.13	17.94	18.10	18.46	18.40	18.40	18.19	18.19	18.01	18.26
Financial Activities													
2007	23.01	24.92	24.06	24.24	23.03	24.10	23.24	22.83	22.51	22.30	22.17	23.18	23.30
2008	22.39	23.72	23.32	22.88	23.05	22.88	23.15	23.04	22.92	23.64	23.50	23.14	23.14
2009	22.91	23.15	22.20	21.92	22.56	22.08	22.21	22.58	22.26	22.17	22.38	22.37	22.40
Professional and Business Services													
2007	28.09	27.86	27.18	27.59	27.32	27.32	27.34	27.05	27.41	27.02	26.45	26.71	27.27
2008	26.63	26.54	27.16	26.26	26.67	26.45	26.14	26.37	25.92	26.43	27.11	26.04	26.48
2009	25.61	26.06	25.71	25.50	26.29	26.77	26.35	26.42	26.31	25.96	26.23	26.51	26.14
Education and Health Services													
2007	18.10	17.90	18.59	17.41	18.30	18.38	18.46	18.59	19.16	18.80	19.08	19.32	18.51
2008	19.15	19.55	19.69	19.73	19.60	19.80	19.20	19.59	19.66	19.68	20.38	20.05	19.68
2009	20.17	19.82	20.34	20.07	20.67	20.47	20.01	20.07	19.54	19.68	19.94	19.73	20.04
Leisure and Hospitality													
2007	11.55	11.58	11.31	11.43	11.40	11.31	11.51	11.47	11.56	11.62	11.68	12.11	11.54
2008	12.12	12.25	12.22	12.15	12.09	12.10	12.11	11.91	12.22	12.01	12.32	12.78	12.18
2009	12.92	12.82	12.86	12.47	12.53	12.59	12.59	12.51	12.64	12.57	12.76	13.05	12.69

Average Weekly Earnings by Selected Industry: Missouri, 2007–2009

(Dollars, not seasonally adjusted.)

Industry and year	January	February	March	April	May	June	July	August	September	October	November	December	Annual average
Total Private													
2007	668.17	677.35	680.09	685.08	672.11	677.47	682.30	671.14	696.95	681.38	674.16	702.03	680.43
2008	678.53	692.92	712.36	695.95	703.82	713.93	703.42	715.17	710.01	727.32	737.67	721.39	709.67
2009	713.43	724.46	711.90	693.38	703.25	696.64	702.36	721.02	707.15	701.30	726.92	709.12	709.87
Goods-Producing													
2007	805.88	804.01	855.54	856.32	854.22	858.73	858.92	866.41	898.63	888.47	879.60	899.00	860.97
2008	878.21	875.11	903.98	896.42	914.02	900.86	939.30	967.60	929.82	951.06	932.34	945.10	920.61
2009	915.67	977.18	960.38	937.26	967.21	965.31	982.23	989.32	964.40	967.67	996.03	954.34	964.17
Construction													
2007	824.40	826.08	890.85	843.39	881.34	899.61	906.68	907.39	909.83	921.64	916.11	896.71	886.99
2008	918.92	922.64	936.60	924.52	957.46	898.56	960.52	981.34	938.16	1009.28	961.59	963.69	949.06
2009	965.12	996.67	918.15	927.17	993.08	994.88	1033.11	1027.18	989.15	1027.67	1051.04	965.10	990.53
Manufacturing													
2007	799.53	816.18	837.52	859.07	837.13	832.62	832.00	844.02	890.57	872.02	871.53	906.92	849.46
2008	866.97	869.70	904.37	896.50	902.33	927.74	912.54	930.01	937.17	934.11	930.42	947.54	912.85
2009	908.82	951.90	963.14	929.63	939.92	936.50	940.87	951.49	937.86	928.24	961.75	947.57	941.25
Trade, Transportation, and Utilities													
2007	565.43	576.15	570.15	580.37	582.76	570.49	580.98	569.18	586.85	569.13	565.14	597.51	575.96
2008	569.53	607.15	615.64	605.78	619.44	625.16	609.70	614.15	620.72	623.56	644.79	652.71	616.92
2009	628.51	639.62	628.83	623.67	626.11	615.40	638.72	640.32	638.48	620.28	627.56	610.54	628.14
Financial Activities													
2007	849.07	919.55	873.38	913.85	840.60	932.67	885.44	865.26	857.63	831.79	815.86	866.93	871.42
2008	817.24	856.29	879.16	844.27	836.72	871.73	838.03	847.87	836.58	869.95	895.35	846.92	853.87
2009	856.83	877.39	841.38	808.85	823.44	812.54	815.11	860.30	836.98	826.94	868.34	838.88	840.00
Professional and Business Services													
2007	974.72	991.82	970.33	990.48	937.08	950.74	981.51	962.98	1000.47	961.91	938.98	964.23	968.09
2008	937.38	928.90	988.62	945.36	960.12	978.65	935.81	944.05	920.16	977.91	970.54	893.17	947.98
2009	888.67	922.52	902.42	887.40	907.01	915.53	906.44	943.19	902.43	908.60	941.66	925.20	912.29
Education and Health Services													
2007	602.73	588.91	617.19	586.72	603.90	610.22	622.10	611.61	638.03	614.76	618.19	635.63	612.68
2008	631.95	637.33	649.77	643.20	631.12	649.44	629.76	642.55	644.85	645.50	672.54	641.60	643.54
2009	651.49	648.11	659.02	642.24	659.37	661.18	644.32	646.25	631.14	625.82	648.05	629.39	645.29
Leisure and Hospitality													
2007	301.46	306.87	304.24	302.90	298.68	309.89	318.83	311.98	309.81	309.09	306.02	318.49	308.12
2008	312.70	319.73	317.72	312.26	319.18	329.12	317.28	304.90	304.28	301.45	309.23	314.39	313.03
2009	303.62	308.96	309.93	296.79	305.73	307.20	321.05	312.75	308.42	306.71	311.34	321.03	309.64

MONTANA
At a Glance

Population:
    1990 census: 799,065
    2000 census: 902,195
    2009 estimate: 974,989

Percent change in population:
    1990–2000: 12.9%
    2000–2009: 8.1%

Percent change in total nonfarm employment:
    1990–2009: 44.4%
    2008–2009: -3.7%

Industry with the largest growth in employment, 1990–2009 (thousands):
    Education and Health Services, 27.3

Industry with the largest decline or smallest growth in employment, 1990–2009 (thousands):
    Manufacturing, -2.1

Civilian labor force:
    1990: 408,301
    2000: 468,865
    2009: 498,907

Unemployment rate and rank among states (lowest to highest):
    1990: 6.0%, 37th
    2000: 4.8%, 42nd
    2009: 6.2%, 5th

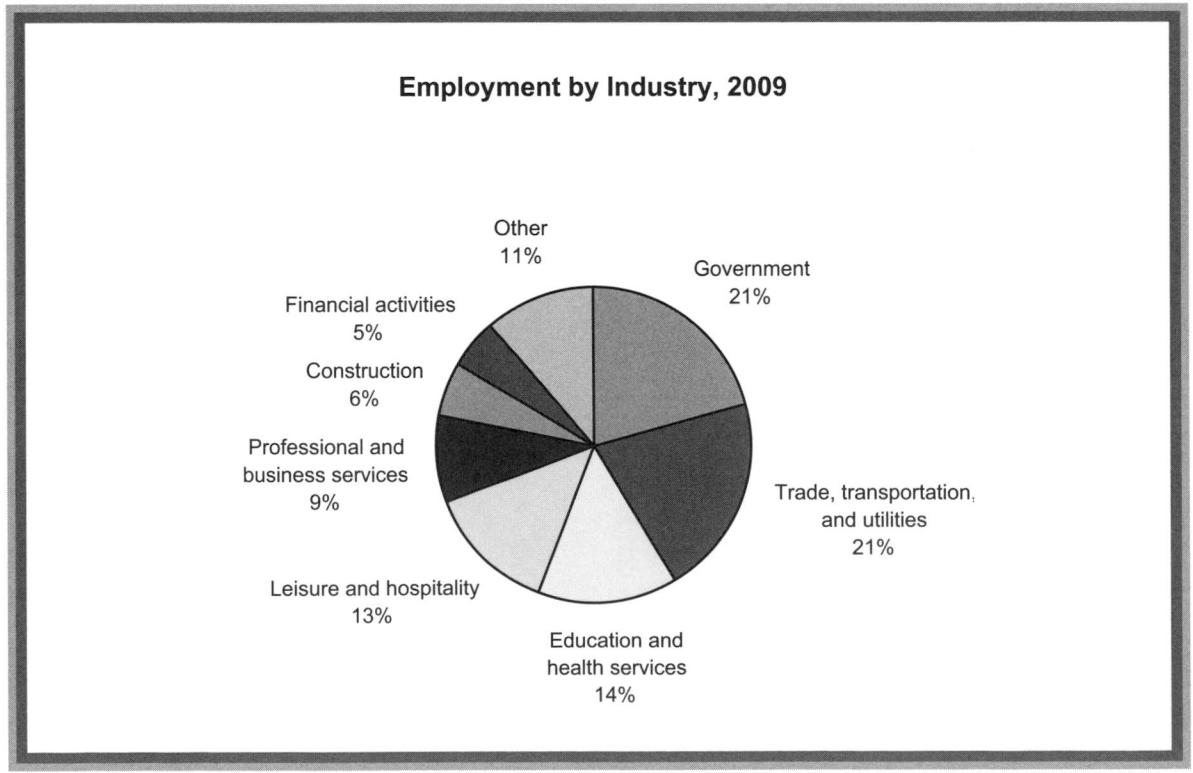

Employment by Industry, 2009

Other 11%
Government 21%
Financial activities 5%
Construction 6%
Professional and business services 9%
Trade, transportation, and utilities 21%
Leisure and hospitality 13%
Education and health services 14%

Employment by Industry: Montana, Selected Years, 1990–2009

(Numbers in thousands, not seasonally adjusted.)

Industry and year	January	February	March	April	May	June	July	August	September	October	November	December	Annual average
Total Nonfarm													
1990	283.9	284.1	288.5	294.2	299.9	306.0	298.3	301.1	304.3	305.1	302.1	299.6	297.3
2000	376.5	378.4	385.5	387.4	396.2	398.8	395.7	398.3	399.9	395.2	393.6	390.5	391.3
2001	379.8	381.1	385.1	388.0	396.1	400.6	395.3	397.3	397.4	395.3	392.7	391.1	391.7
2002	381.7	383.3	385.6	390.7	398.9	404.7	400.4	402.0	404.1	401.5	399.7	399.7	396.0
2003	386.4	388.7	390.4	397.1	404.1	407.1	404.5	407.7	408.3	407.1	403.6	403.9	400.7
2004	390.5	394.3	399.4	409.1	414.4	421.3	419.0	418.4	419.2	417.7	416.2	416.6	411.3
2005	400.7	405.9	410.6	414.7	421.3	428.4	428.2	428.5	429.7	428.8	427.6	426.8	420.9
2006	414.6	419.1	423.9	429.7	437.6	447.2	446.6	443.0	440.6	439.2	437.7	439.2	432.5
2007	427.0	430.1	436.5	439.9	447.7	454.1	452.9	453.7	450.3	450.5	448.0	448.0	444.9
2008	433.6	436.4	440.1	442.3	450.7	454.9	453.3	454.2	451.2	448.1	443.5	440.8	445.8
2009	421.1	421.0	420.7	426.1	432.2	439.0	436.2	436.0	434.2	433.0	429.3	422.2	429.3
Total Private													
1990	213.8	213.1	216.1	220.4	225.3	232.9	233.6	235.3	233.3	231.2	228.6	227.0	225.8
2000	294.0	294.3	298.8	301.5	308.0	316.8	318.0	319.4	314.9	308.5	307.1	305.5	307.2
2001	295.7	295.8	299.1	302.3	308.6	316.5	317.3	319.0	313.5	309.5	307.3	306.2	307.6
2002	298.1	298.2	299.9	304.9	311.3	319.6	321.1	322.9	318.6	315.2	312.3	312.0	311.2
2003	303.3	303.0	304.4	309.0	315.0	322.4	324.3	326.3	321.2	318.7	315.4	315.9	314.9
2004	306.4	307.3	311.8	320.5	325.0	333.6	337.0	337.3	332.2	329.1	326.8	328.0	324.6
2005	315.9	318.7	323.0	327.1	333.0	342.2	346.9	348.3	343.6	340.5	338.6	338.4	334.7
2006	329.8	331.5	335.5	340.9	347.3	358.1	358.3	359.7	354.1	350.4	348.0	350.7	347.0
2007	341.3	342.1	347.5	351.8	358.4	367.1	369.4	370.8	364.7	360.4	358.4	359.3	357.6
2008	348.2	348.5	351.6	354.2	359.9	366.8	369.6	370.2	363.2	356.9	351.7	350.7	357.6
2009	334.3	332.1	331.1	336.0	340.2	348.9	350.8	350.3	345.2	341.6	333.0	332.2	340.1
Goods-Producing													
1990	34.5	33.7	34.7	35.8	37.7	39.4	40.9	41.4	41.2	40.8	39.4	37.4	38.0
2000	45.1	44.9	46.1	47.7	49.4	51.3	51.5	52.0	51.2	51.4	49.9	47.9	49.0
2001	45.3	45.0	45.6	47.0	49.1	50.9	51.8	52.3	51.4	51.0	49.3	47.5	48.9
2002	44.0	43.5	43.4	45.3	47.8	50.1	50.9	51.6	50.6	50.5	49.0	47.5	47.9
2003	44.3	43.7	43.9	46.6	49.0	50.8	51.2	51.2	50.6	50.9	48.9	47.6	48.2
2004	45.0	45.0	46.4	50.0	51.2	53.4	54.7	54.8	53.9	54.3	53.2	52.2	51.2
2005	48.0	49.4	50.6	52.8	54.7	56.6	58.4	59.2	58.1	58.7	57.5	55.1	54.9
2006	52.7	52.8	53.8	55.8	58.9	62.0	62.4	62.5	61.5	61.4	60.1	59.2	58.6
2007	56.1	55.8	57.8	59.8	62.2	64.4	64.3	64.9	63.2	63.0	61.8	59.8	61.1
2008	55.6	55.1	56.0	57.0	59.1	60.5	61.4	61.2	59.5	58.8	56.5	53.8	57.9
2009	47.8	46.1	45.1	47.2	48.4	50.5	50.8	50.8	50.1	50.0	49.1	45.2	48.4
Mining and Logging													
1990	7.6	7.6	7.5	7.1	7.6	8.1	8.5	8.7	8.6	8.5	8.3	8.0	8.0
2000	5.9	5.8	5.8	5.6	5.9	6.3	6.1	6.2	6.0	6.3	6.3	6.1	6.0
2001	6.0	6.0	5.8	5.7	6.0	6.4	6.5	6.5	6.5	6.7	6.5	6.3	6.2
2002	5.9	5.9	5.8	5.8	6.0	6.3	6.4	6.5	6.4	6.5	6.3	6.2	6.2
2003	6.0	5.9	5.7	5.4	5.8	6.2	6.3	6.3	6.3	6.6	6.7	6.7	6.2
2004	6.6	6.5	6.6	6.8	7.0	7.3	7.6	7.5	7.4	7.4	7.5	7.4	7.1
2005	7.3	7.5	7.4	7.2	7.5	7.9	8.1	8.2	8.0	8.0	7.9	7.9	7.7
2006	7.8	7.8	7.9	7.8	8.2	8.6	8.7	8.6	8.4	8.4	8.4	8.3	8.2
2007	8.1	8.1	8.3	8.1	8.2	8.6	8.7	8.7	8.4	8.4	8.3	8.3	8.4
2008	7.9	7.9	7.9	7.8	8.0	8.4	8.6	8.8	8.8	8.8	8.8	8.4	8.3
2009	7.7	7.1	6.9	6.7	6.7	6.9	7.1	7.1	7.0	7.0	6.9	6.9	7.0
Construction													
1990	8.1	7.6	8.4	9.6	10.8	11.6	12.3	12.6	12.8	12.1	11.1	9.6	10.5
2000	17.0	16.9	18.0	19.9	21.1	22.4	22.7	23.0	22.3	22.2	20.7	19.4	20.4
2001	17.7	17.4	18.4	20.2	21.9	23.1	23.7	24.0	23.4	22.8	21.9	20.4	21.2
2002	18.2	18.0	18.1	19.9	21.9	23.5	24.1	24.5	24.0	23.7	22.7	21.5	21.7
2003	19.2	19.0	19.4	22.4	24.1	25.4	25.7	25.9	25.5	25.4	23.3	21.9	23.1
2004	19.8	19.9	21.1	24.4	25.2	26.8	27.6	27.8	27.1	27.4	26.2	25.2	24.9
2005	21.7	22.8	24.0	26.3	27.8	29.0	30.5	31.1	30.6	30.7	29.6	27.2	27.6
2006	25.3	25.3	26.2	28.2	30.6	32.9	33.2	33.5	32.8	32.5	31.1	30.2	30.2
2007	27.8	27.6	29.1	31.5	33.7	35.1	35.0	35.6	34.4	34.0	32.8	30.9	32.3
2008	27.6	27.2	28.1	29.1	30.8	31.7	32.5	32.2	31.0	30.1	28.3	26.3	29.6
2009	22.1	21.5	21.2	23.2	24.2	26.0	26.3	26.4	25.8	25.6	24.8	20.8	24.0
Manufacturing													
1990	18.8	18.5	18.8	19.1	19.3	19.7	20.1	20.1	19.8	20.2	20.0	19.8	19.5
2000	22.2	22.2	22.3	22.2	22.4	22.6	22.7	22.8	22.9	22.9	22.9	22.4	22.5
2001	21.6	21.6	21.4	21.1	21.2	21.4	21.6	21.8	21.5	21.5	20.9	20.8	21.4
2002	19.9	19.6	19.5	19.6	19.9	20.3	20.4	20.6	20.2	20.3	20.0	19.7	20.0
2003	19.1	18.8	18.8	18.8	19.1	19.2	19.2	19.0	18.8	18.9	18.9	19.0	19.0
2004	18.6	18.6	18.7	18.8	19.0	19.3	19.5	19.5	19.4	19.5	19.5	19.6	19.2
2005	19.0	19.1	19.2	19.3	19.4	19.7	19.8	19.9	19.5	20.0	20.0	20.0	19.6
2006	19.6	19.7	19.7	19.8	20.1	20.5	20.5	20.4	20.3	20.5	20.6	20.7	20.2
2007	20.2	20.1	20.4	20.2	20.3	20.7	20.6	20.6	20.4	20.6	20.7	20.6	20.5
2008	20.1	20.0	20.0	20.1	20.3	20.4	20.3	20.2	19.7	19.9	19.4	19.1	20.0
2009	18.0	17.5	17.0	17.3	17.5	17.6	17.4	17.3	17.3	17.4	17.4	17.5	17.4

Employment by Industry: Montana, Selected Years, 1990–2009—*Continued*

(Numbers in thousands, not seasonally adjusted.)

Industry and year	January	February	March	April	May	June	July	August	September	October	November	December	Annual average
Service-Providing													
1990	249.4	250.4	253.8	258.4	262.2	266.6	257.4	259.7	263.1	264.3	262.7	262.2	259.2
2000	331.4	333.5	339.4	339.7	346.8	347.5	344.2	346.3	348.7	343.8	343.7	342.6	342.3
2001	334.5	336.1	339.5	341.0	347.0	349.7	343.5	345.0	346.0	344.3	343.4	343.6	342.8
2002	337.7	339.8	342.2	345.4	351.1	354.6	349.5	350.4	353.5	351.0	350.7	352.2	348.2
2003	342.1	345.0	346.5	350.5	355.1	356.3	353.3	356.5	357.7	356.2	354.7	356.3	352.5
2004	345.5	349.3	353.0	359.1	363.2	367.9	364.3	363.6	365.3	363.4	363.0	364.4	360.2
2005	352.7	356.5	360.0	361.9	366.6	371.8	369.8	369.3	371.6	370.1	370.1	371.7	366.0
2006	361.9	366.3	370.1	373.9	378.7	385.2	384.2	380.5	379.1	377.8	377.6	380.0	373.9
2007	370.9	374.3	378.7	380.1	385.5	389.7	388.6	388.8	387.1	387.5	386.2	388.2	383.8
2008	378.0	381.3	384.1	385.3	391.6	394.4	391.9	393.0	391.7	389.3	387.0	387.0	387.9
2009	373.3	374.9	375.6	378.9	383.8	388.5	385.4	385.2	384.1	383.0	380.2	377.0	380.8
Trade, Transportation, and Utilities													
1990	67.9	67.5	68.1	69.1	70.4	71.7	71.3	72.0	71.6	71.8	72.1	72.6	70.5
2000	84.5	83.9	84.4	85.3	86.6	88.0	87.7	88.2	87.1	86.1	86.9	87.5	86.3
2001	83.9	83.0	83.5	84.6	85.9	86.5	86.2	86.3	85.2	85.0	85.6	85.9	85.1
2002	82.6	82.1	82.6	83.9	85.2	86.0	86.3	86.1	85.4	85.3	85.8	86.4	84.8
2003	82.5	81.8	82.2	82.8	84.4	85.2	85.0	85.5	85.3	85.6	86.5	87.0	84.5
2004	83.9	83.6	84.3	85.5	86.7	87.4	87.3	87.0	86.2	86.7	87.8	88.5	86.2
2005	85.0	84.6	85.5	86.3	87.4	88.5	88.9	88.9	88.2	88.3	89.0	90.2	87.6
2006	86.7	86.5	87.1	88.1	89.4	90.6	90.2	90.4	89.9	90.1	91.4	92.5	89.4
2007	89.6	89.4	90.2	90.6	92.2	92.8	93.7	93.3	93.1	93.4	94.8	95.5	92.4
2008	91.9	91.0	91.5	91.7	92.3	93.0	92.8	93.0	92.3	91.9	92.1	92.4	92.2
2009	87.9	86.7	86.1	87.2	88.2	89.2	88.9	89.0	88.2	89.3	90.6	89.9	88.4
Wholesale Trade													
1990	12.9	12.9	13.1	13.3	13.5	13.6	13.5	13.6	13.5	13.8	13.7	13.6	13.4
2000	15.5	15.5	15.6	15.9	16.0	16.1	15.9	15.8	15.7	15.4	15.3	15.4	15.6
2001	15.2	15.0	15.2	15.5	15.7	15.8	15.6	15.6	15.3	15.3	15.3	15.2	15.4
2002	14.9	14.8	14.9	15.3	15.5	15.6	15.7	15.6	15.4	15.4	15.4	15.5	15.3
2003	15.0	14.9	15.0	15.4	15.6	15.7	15.6	15.6	15.5	15.5	15.6	15.7	15.4
2004	15.5	15.5	15.7	16.0	16.1	16.3	16.5	16.4	16.2	16.1	16.3	16.3	16.1
2005	15.8	15.9	16.1	16.3	16.5	16.6	16.6	16.5	16.3	16.2	16.2	16.4	16.3
2006	16.0	16.1	16.3	16.3	16.6	16.8	16.8	16.8	16.7	16.7	16.8	16.8	16.6
2007	16.4	16.6	16.7	16.8	17.1	17.1	17.3	17.1	17.1	17.0	17.0	17.1	16.9
2008	16.5	16.5	16.7	16.8	16.9	17.0	16.9	16.9	16.7	16.6	16.5	16.5	16.7
2009	16.0	15.9	15.8	16.1	16.2	16.3	16.2	16.1	15.8	15.7	15.8	15.4	15.9
Retail Trade													
1990	39.6	39.2	39.5	40.2	41.1	42.0	42.1	42.5	42.0	41.7	42.0	42.6	41.2
2000	52.4	51.8	52.2	52.6	53.5	54.9	55.0	55.4	54.5	53.6	54.6	55.1	53.8
2001	52.6	51.9	52.0	52.6	53.5	54.2	54.6	54.8	53.9	53.5	54.3	54.6	53.5
2002	52.0	51.6	51.9	52.8	53.7	54.4	54.7	54.6	54.1	53.9	54.7	55.1	53.6
2003	52.2	51.7	52.0	52.3	53.4	54.1	54.3	54.6	54.1	54.3	55.2	55.7	53.7
2004	53.2	53.0	53.4	54.1	55.1	55.6	55.6	55.3	54.5	54.7	55.6	56.2	54.7
2005	53.6	53.1	53.7	54.3	55.1	56.0	56.4	56.4	55.7	55.8	56.5	57.2	55.3
2006	54.5	54.1	54.4	55.2	56.1	57.0	57.0	57.1	56.2	56.5	57.8	58.6	56.2
2007	56.5	56.0	56.7	56.9	58.0	58.8	59.5	59.4	58.9	59.1	60.5	60.9	58.4
2008	58.7	57.9	58.1	58.1	58.7	59.3	59.5	59.6	58.7	58.4	58.7	58.8	58.7
2009	55.5	54.5	54.1	54.7	55.5	56.4	56.6	56.7	55.8	56.5	58.1	57.6	56.0
Transportation and Utilities													
1990	15.4	15.4	15.5	15.6	15.8	16.1	15.7	15.9	16.1	16.3	16.4	16.4	15.8
2000	16.6	16.6	16.6	16.8	17.1	17.0	16.8	17.0	16.9	17.1	17.0	17.0	16.8
2001	16.1	16.1	16.3	16.5	16.7	16.5	16.0	15.9	16.0	16.2	16.0	16.1	16.2
2002	15.7	15.7	15.8	15.8	16.0	16.0	15.9	15.9	15.9	16.0	15.7	15.8	15.9
2003	15.3	15.2	15.2	15.1	15.4	15.4	15.1	15.3	15.7	15.8	15.7	15.6	15.4
2004	15.2	15.1	15.2	15.4	15.5	15.5	15.2	15.3	15.5	15.9	16.0	16.0	15.5
2005	15.6	15.6	15.7	15.7	15.8	15.9	15.9	16.0	16.2	16.3	16.3	16.6	16.0
2006	16.2	16.3	16.4	16.6	16.7	16.8	16.4	16.5	17.0	16.9	16.8	17.1	16.6
2007	16.7	16.8	16.8	16.9	17.1	16.9	16.9	16.8	17.1	17.3	17.3	17.5	17.0
2008	16.7	16.6	16.7	16.8	16.7	16.7	16.4	16.5	16.9	16.9	16.9	17.1	16.7
2009	16.4	16.3	16.2	16.4	16.5	16.5	16.1	16.2	16.6	17.1	16.7	16.9	16.5
Information													
1990	6.4	6.4	6.3	6.3	6.4	6.9	6.4	6.4	6.4	6.4	6.4	6.4	6.4
2000	7.9	7.9	8.0	8.0	8.1	8.1	7.8	7.8	7.8	8.0	8.0	8.0	7.9
2001	7.9	8.0	7.9	7.8	7.9	8.0	7.9	8.0	7.8	7.9	8.0	7.8	7.9
2002	7.8	7.8	7.8	7.8	7.9	7.9	8.0	7.9	7.8	7.7	7.8	7.8	7.8
2003	7.7	7.8	7.7	7.6	7.6	7.6	7.6	7.7	7.6	7.7	7.7	7.6	7.7
2004	7.6	7.6	7.7	7.7	7.8	7.9	8.0	8.1	7.8	7.7	7.8	7.8	7.8
2005	7.7	7.8	7.8	7.7	7.8	7.9	7.9	7.9	7.7	7.7	7.7	7.8	7.8
2006	7.7	7.8	7.7	7.7	7.8	7.9	7.8	7.8	7.7	7.6	7.6	7.7	7.7
2007	7.4	7.5	7.5	7.5	7.6	7.6	7.6	7.7	7.6	7.5	7.6	7.6	7.6
2008	7.6	7.6	7.6	7.7	7.7	7.8	7.7	7.7	7.8	7.7	7.7	7.8	7.7
2009	7.5	7.6	7.5	7.4	7.5	7.6	7.5	7.5	7.4	7.3	7.3	7.3	7.5

Employment by Industry: Montana, Selected Years, 1990–2009—*Continued*

(Numbers in thousands, not seasonally adjusted.)

Industry and year	January	February	March	April	May	June	July	August	September	October	November	December	Annual average
Financial Activities													
1990	13.5	13.5	13.7	13.8	13.8	14.0	14.0	14.0	14.0	13.7	13.9	14.0	13.8
2000	18.1	18.2	18.3	18.5	18.7	19.0	19.0	19.0	18.7	18.4	18.4	18.6	18.5
2001	18.4	18.3	18.4	18.5	18.8	19.1	19.3	19.2	19.1	18.8	18.8	19.0	18.8
2002	18.8	18.9	19.0	19.2	19.4	19.6	19.3	19.3	19.1	19.6	19.6	19.9	19.3
2003	19.9	19.9	20.0	19.9	20.0	20.4	20.6	20.8	20.5	20.5	20.5	20.7	20.3
2004	20.7	20.7	20.8	20.8	21.0	21.3	21.5	21.5	21.2	21.1	21.0	21.3	21.1
2005	20.8	20.8	20.8	21.0	21.2	21.5	21.8	21.8	21.7	21.8	21.9	22.2	21.4
2006	21.7	21.8	21.9	22.0	21.9	22.3	22.3	22.2	21.9	21.8	21.7	21.9	22.0
2007	21.4	21.4	21.6	21.5	21.7	21.9	22.0	22.1	21.8	21.9	21.8	22.2	21.8
2008	21.7	21.7	21.7	21.8	21.8	22.1	22.1	22.2	21.7	21.8	21.7	21.7	21.8
2009	21.1	21.0	21.0	21.0	21.1	21.3	21.4	21.5	21.1	20.7	20.6	21.2	21.1
Professional and Business Services													
1990	14.6	14.6	14.9	15.4	15.6	16.2	16.1	16.1	15.8	15.9	15.8	15.9	15.5
2000	28.6	29.1	29.9	30.2	30.7	31.7	31.9	31.9	31.6	31.6	31.8	31.3	30.8
2001	30.4	31.0	31.4	31.7	32.1	32.8	32.4	32.6	32.0	31.8	31.6	31.7	31.8
2002	31.3	31.6	31.7	31.9	32.0	32.8	33.0	33.4	33.3	32.9	32.3	31.7	32.3
2003	31.2	31.3	31.7	32.6	32.9	33.4	33.6	33.8	32.9	32.9	32.1	32.0	32.5
2004	30.4	31.0	31.6	33.2	33.8	34.7	34.9	34.9	34.3	34.2	33.9	33.3	33.4
2005	32.1	32.7	33.3	34.4	34.7	35.8	36.6	36.8	36.2	36.4	36.5	36.2	35.1
2006	35.5	35.9	36.6	37.5	38.2	39.6	39.4	40.2	39.2	39.0	38.5	38.6	38.2
2007	38.1	38.5	39.3	40.3	41.0	42.1	42.0	42.5	41.2	41.5	40.8	40.3	40.6
2008	39.1	39.6	39.7	40.8	41.6	41.8	42.2	42.2	40.9	40.4	39.5	39.3	40.6
2009	37.9	37.7	37.9	38.7	38.8	39.5	39.9	39.6	38.9	38.9	38.8	37.0	38.6
Education and Health Services													
1990	34.3	34.5	34.7	35.1	35.1	35.0	34.2	34.4	35.2	35.6	35.7	35.9	34.9
2000	48.6	49.0	49.2	48.9	49.2	48.9	48.2	48.6	49.2	49.1	49.5	49.6	49.0
2001	48.4	48.7	49.3	49.5	49.6	49.4	48.7	49.3	50.0	50.4	51.1	51.4	49.7
2002	51.4	51.6	51.9	52.2	52.4	51.9	50.6	50.9	51.8	52.8	53.3	53.3	52.0
2003	53.2	53.6	53.5	53.3	53.4	52.6	51.5	52.2	52.6	53.5	53.9	54.1	53.1
2004	53.5	53.7	54.3	54.5	54.4	54.0	53.1	53.3	54.6	55.1	55.7	56.1	54.4
2005	55.5	55.7	56.1	55.5	55.7	55.8	54.9	55.0	56.1	56.5	56.9	56.9	55.9
2006	56.4	56.9	57.3	57.7	57.6	57.2	56.4	56.8	57.9	58.0	58.4	58.7	57.4
2007	58.2	58.7	59.0	58.9	59.0	58.5	57.6	58.0	59.3	59.4	59.5	60.0	58.8
2008	60.0	60.6	60.9	60.9	61.0	60.3	59.6	60.2	61.3	61.7	62.0	62.5	60.9
2009	61.8	62.3	62.3	62.5	62.4	62.2	61.4	61.5	62.5	62.6	62.7	62.1	62.2
Leisure and Hospitality													
1990	31.4	31.6	32.3	33.4	34.7	37.9	38.9	39.2	37.4	35.4	33.7	33.2	34.9
2000	46.2	46.2	47.5	47.4	49.7	54.2	56.4	56.6	53.8	48.7	47.3	47.4	50.1
2001	45.9	46.2	47.1	47.1	48.9	53.3	54.9	55.3	51.9	48.7	47.0	46.9	49.4
2002	46.7	47.1	47.8	48.7	50.5	55.0	56.7	57.4	54.3	50.2	48.3	49.1	51.0
2003	48.6	49.0	49.4	49.8	51.3	56.0	58.4	58.8	55.2	51.0	49.3	50.2	52.3
2004	49.0	49.3	50.1	52.1	53.3	58.0	60.5	60.6	57.2	53.1	50.6	51.9	53.8
2005	50.4	51.1	52.2	52.7	54.7	59.1	61.7	61.9	58.8	54.5	52.5	53.2	55.2
2006	52.6	53.2	54.2	55.1	56.4	61.2	62.7	62.7	58.9	55.4	53.3	55.0	56.7
2007	53.7	54.0	54.9	55.9	57.5	62.3	65.0	65.2	61.4	56.5	54.9	56.7	58.2
2008	55.2	55.6	56.6	56.7	58.8	63.5	66.1	66.1	62.2	57.0	54.7	55.9	59.0
2009	53.5	53.7	54.2	55.0	56.7	61.3	63.6	63.4	60.0	56.1	52.8	53.7	57.0
Other Services													
1990	11.2	11.3	11.4	11.5	11.6	11.8	11.8	11.8	11.7	11.6	11.6	11.6	11.5
2000	15.0	15.1	15.4	15.5	15.6	15.6	15.5	15.3	15.5	15.2	15.3	15.2	15.3
2001	15.5	15.6	15.9	16.1	16.3	16.5	16.1	16.0	16.1	15.9	15.9	16.0	16.0
2002	15.5	15.6	15.7	15.9	16.1	16.3	16.3	16.3	16.3	16.2	16.2	16.3	16.1
2003	15.9	15.9	16.0	16.4	16.4	16.4	16.4	16.3	16.5	16.6	16.5	16.7	16.3
2004	16.3	16.4	16.6	16.7	16.8	16.9	17.0	17.1	17.0	16.9	16.8	16.9	16.8
2005	16.4	16.6	16.7	16.7	16.8	17.0	16.7	16.8	16.8	16.6	16.6	16.8	16.7
2006	16.5	16.6	16.9	17.0	17.1	17.3	17.1	17.1	17.1	17.1	17.0	17.1	17.0
2007	16.8	16.8	17.2	17.3	17.2	17.5	17.2	17.1	17.1	17.2	17.2	17.2	17.2
2008	17.1	17.3	17.6	17.6	17.6	17.8	17.7	17.6	17.5	17.6	17.5	17.3	17.5
2009	16.8	17.0	17.0	17.0	17.1	17.3	17.3	17.0	17.0	16.7	16.4	15.8	16.9
Government													
1990	70.1	71.0	72.4	73.8	74.6	73.1	64.7	65.8	71.0	73.9	73.5	72.6	71.4
2000	82.5	84.1	86.7	85.9	88.2	82.0	77.7	78.9	85.0	86.7	86.5	85.0	84.1
2001	84.1	85.3	86.0	85.7	87.5	84.1	78.0	78.3	83.9	85.8	85.4	84.9	84.1
2002	83.6	85.1	85.7	85.8	87.6	85.1	79.3	79.1	85.5	86.3	87.4	87.7	84.9
2003	83.1	85.7	86.0	88.1	89.1	84.7	80.2	81.4	87.1	88.4	88.2	88.0	85.8
2004	84.1	87.0	87.6	88.6	89.4	87.7	82.0	81.1	87.0	88.6	89.4	88.6	86.8
2005	84.8	87.2	87.6	87.6	88.3	86.2	81.3	80.2	86.1	88.3	89.0	88.4	86.3
2006	84.8	87.6	88.4	88.8	90.3	89.1	88.3	83.3	86.5	88.8	89.7	88.5	85.5
2007	85.7	88.0	89.0	88.1	89.3	87.0	83.5	82.9	85.6	90.1	89.6	88.7	87.3
2008	85.4	87.9	88.5	88.1	90.8	88.1	83.7	84.0	88.0	91.2	91.8	90.1	88.1
2009	86.8	88.9	89.6	90.1	92.0	90.1	85.4	85.7	89.0	91.4	91.0	90.0	89.2

Average Weekly Hours by Selected Industry: Montana, 2007–2009

(Not seasonally adjusted.)

Industry and year	January	February	March	April	May	June	July	August	September	October	November	December	Annual average
Total Private													
2007	31.8	32.0	31.9	32.9	43.0	42.4	42.2	41.0	33.0	32.2	31.8	32.5	35.6
2008	31.8	31.7	32.4	31.7	32.0	32.8	32.8	33.1	32.5	32.3	32.7	32.2	32.3
2009	30.0	30.7	30.5	30.4	30.9	31.0	31.3	32.1	31.6	31.7	32.2	31.4	31.2
Goods-Producing													
2007	37.2	38.5	38.1	38.5	39.6	39.8	39.6	39.7	36.8	37.3	36.0	35.8	38.1
2008	36.2	34.7	35.5	35.0	36.5	37.1	38.2	39.7	38.6	36.9	37.2	36.6	36.9
2009	36.1	36.1	35.4	36.4	36.3	38.1	38.1	39.4	37.2	38.1	37.9	35.5	37.1
Construction													
2007	36.6	39.3	39.1	39.1	41.2	38.8	39.0	38.9	33.8	35.2	32.7	33.0	37.2
2008	33.2	32.3	32.3	31.4	35.7	33.9	36.4	37.1	37.4	34.0	34.7	34.3	34.5
2009	33.1	33.1	32.0	32.8	33.6	35.5	35.0	38.3	33.4	34.6	34.7	29.6	34.0
Trade, Transportation, and Utilities													
2007	31.3	32.0	32.4	33.2	33.3	34.1	33.2	33.7	32.8	31.7	31.5	32.8	32.7
2008	31.2	32.2	32.5	30.9	32.3	33.3	33.2	33.9	32.7	32.5	32.8	33.2	32.6
2009	33.2	32.3	32.1	32.3	32.9	32.8	32.4	33.3	32.9	32.8	32.9	32.9	32.7
Financial Activities													
2007	37.4	37.0	38.6	38.7	37.2	37.4	37.7	37.2	36.2	36.6	36.2	38.8	37.4
2008	37.9	36.9	37.1	36.7	36.1	36.9	36.3	35.1	35.8	36.8	37.2	38.2	36.8
2009	37.0	38.2	38.4	38.5	37.7	37.6	36.6	36.8	36.5	36.5	37.2	35.8	37.2
Professional and Business Services													
2007	33.7	33.6	33.8	34.2	36.1	34.0	34.2	33.4	33.5	33.5	33.1	33.3	33.9
2008	33.4	33.8	35.2	35.0	33.0	34.5	34.6	33.9	33.9	34.4	33.9	33.1	34.1
2009	18.8	20.5	22.0	22.6	23.1	24.0	25.7	26.0	26.5	27.0	28.1	27.3	24.3
Education and Health Services													
2007	31.4	31.6	29.8	32.1	31.3	31.2	32.6	32.3	34.2	32.1	32.1	33.2	32.0
2008	32.3	32.0	32.9	32.4	32.1	33.0	32.2	32.3	31.9	32.3	33.0	32.8	32.4
2009	32.2	33.0	33.1	32.4	33.0	32.3	32.8	32.7	32.9	32.9	33.4	33.0	32.8
Leisure and Hospitality													
2007	24.0	23.6	25.0	25.7	43.0	43.8	44.8	42.4	25.4	24.1	24.0	24.8	31.4
2008	23.3	24.1	24.2	23.1	24.1	25.4	25.7	25.8	24.7	23.7	25.0	23.0	24.4
2009	23.4	24.4	24.0	22.9	24.4	24.1	25.2	27.0	25.3	25.0	25.7	24.5	24.7

Average Hourly Earnings by Selected Industry: Montana, 2007–2009

(Dollars, not seasonally adjusted.)

Industry and year	January	February	March	April	May	June	July	August	September	October	November	December	Annual average
Total Private													
2007	18.02	17.91	17.89	18.05	17.72	17.38	17.53	17.61	17.86	17.82	18.05	18.11	17.80
2008	18.19	18.27	18.16	18.26	18.55	18.23	18.05	18.33	18.77	18.54	18.91	18.94	18.43
2009	20.27	20.25	20.00	19.98	19.57	19.56	19.49	19.73	19.60	19.77	20.26	19.90	19.86
Goods-Producing													
2007	21.37	21.77	21.91	22.43	22.13	22.50	22.45	22.54	22.67	21.78	22.03	22.41	22.18
2008	22.22	23.02	22.78	22.52	23.00	22.59	21.77	22.16	22.64	21.83	22.42	22.47	22.44
2009	22.70	23.34	22.65	23.37	22.18	22.54	22.36	23.12	23.06	22.69	23.42	22.96	22.86
Construction													
2007	22.01	22.24	22.11	22.76	22.29	22.85	21.97	22.44	22.64	23.06	23.21	23.95	22.61
2008	24.19	23.72	23.54	23.22	23.67	22.43	22.80	22.43	24.06	22.42	22.30	23.36	23.15
2009	22.65	22.59	22.47	24.48	23.24	23.61	23.73	24.55	22.62	23.44	23.96	24.20	23.50
Trade, Transportation, and Utilities													
2007	14.91	14.66	15.56	14.86	14.50	14.04	14.89	15.23	14.68	14.52	15.05	14.85	14.81
2008	15.04	15.51	15.43	15.62	15.80	15.73	15.84	16.77	16.45	16.55	17.03	17.06	16.08
2009	17.68	17.54	17.53	17.47	17.78	17.88	17.48	18.44	17.93	18.33	17.97	18.02	17.84
Financial Activities													
2007	20.69	19.28	18.29	19.09	18.75	18.99	19.13	19.02	19.64	19.40	19.75	20.28	19.36
2008	20.24	19.04	19.55	19.49	19.98	20.17	19.34	19.67	19.87	19.97	19.19	19.66	19.68
2009	20.92	20.24	20.14	19.80	19.95	20.11	20.50	20.80	19.99	20.46	20.33	21.10	20.38
Professional and Business Services													
2007	21.03	20.47	20.30	20.63	21.15	19.42	19.03	19.22	19.53	19.15	19.54	20.21	19.96
2008	19.83	19.89	19.69	19.43	19.58	19.60	19.23	19.33	19.86	19.57	20.58	20.28	19.73
2009	26.15	26.21	25.65	24.73	24.27	23.28	23.05	23.15	22.73	22.58	22.63	22.39	23.74
Education and Health Services													
2007	18.70	18.74	18.98	19.16	19.00	19.00	19.33	19.19	17.88	18.64	18.74	18.54	18.82
2008	18.84	18.63	18.46	18.78	19.16	18.51	19.24	18.84	19.27	18.74	19.09	19.27	18.90
2009	20.01	19.61	19.76	19.81	19.54	19.82	20.13	20.18	19.99	20.15	20.06	18.75	19.82
Leisure and Hospitality													
2007	11.21	11.49	10.82	10.81	10.93	10.47	10.71	10.66	11.46	11.48	11.49	11.57	10.99
2008	11.46	11.68	11.59	11.63	11.55	11.43	11.12	11.49	12.92	13.09	13.23	13.27	12.01
2009	13.38	13.40	13.07	13.50	13.49	13.27	13.45	13.58	14.35	14.80	14.90	15.67	13.90

Average Weekly Earnings by Selected Industry: Montana, 2007–2009

(Dollars, not seasonally adjusted.)

Industry and year	January	February	March	April	May	June	July	August	September	October	November	December	Annual average
Total Private													
2007	573.04	573.12	570.69	593.85	761.96	736.91	739.77	722.01	589.38	573.80	573.99	588.58	633.68
2008	578.44	579.16	588.38	578.84	593.60	597.94	592.04	606.72	610.03	598.84	618.36	609.87	595.29
2009	608.10	621.68	610.00	607.39	604.71	606.36	610.04	633.33	619.36	626.71	652.37	624.86	619.63
Goods-Producing													
2007	794.96	838.15	834.77	863.56	876.35	895.50	889.02	894.84	834.26	812.39	793.08	802.28	845.06
2008	804.36	798.79	808.69	788.20	839.50	838.09	831.61	879.75	873.90	805.53	834.02	822.40	828.04
2009	819.47	842.57	801.81	850.67	805.13	858.77	851.92	910.93	857.83	864.49	887.62	815.08	848.11
Construction													
2007	805.57	874.03	864.50	889.92	918.35	886.58	856.83	872.92	765.23	811.71	758.97	790.35	841.09
2008	803.11	766.16	760.34	729.11	845.02	760.38	829.92	832.15	899.84	762.28	773.81	801.25	798.68
2009	749.72	747.73	719.04	802.94	780.86	838.16	830.55	940.27	755.51	811.02	831.41	716.32	799.00
Trade, Transportation, and Utilities													
2007	466.68	469.12	504.14	493.35	482.85	478.76	494.35	513.25	481.50	460.28	474.08	487.08	484.29
2008	469.25	499.42	501.48	482.66	510.34	523.81	525.89	568.50	537.92	537.88	558.58	566.39	524.21
2009	586.98	566.54	562.71	564.28	584.96	586.46	566.35	614.05	589.90	601.22	591.21	592.86	583.37
Financial Activities													
2007	773.81	713.36	705.99	738.78	697.50	710.23	721.20	707.54	710.97	710.04	714.95	786.86	724.06
2008	767.10	702.58	725.31	715.28	721.28	744.27	702.04	690.42	711.35	734.90	713.87	751.01	724.22
2009	774.04	773.17	784.90	762.30	752.12	756.14	750.30	765.44	729.64	746.79	756.28	755.38	758.14
Professional and Business Services													
2007	708.71	687.79	686.14	705.55	763.52	660.28	650.83	641.95	654.26	641.53	646.77	672.99	676.64
2008	662.32	672.28	693.09	680.05	646.14	676.20	665.36	655.29	673.25	673.21	697.66	671.27	672.79
2009	491.62	537.31	564.30	558.90	560.64	558.72	592.39	601.90	602.35	609.66	635.90	611.25	576.88
Education and Health Services													
2007	587.18	592.18	565.60	615.04	594.70	592.80	630.16	619.84	611.50	598.34	601.55	615.53	602.24
2008	608.53	596.16	607.33	608.47	615.04	610.83	619.53	608.53	614.71	605.30	629.97	632.06	612.36
2009	644.32	647.13	654.06	641.84	644.82	640.19	660.26	659.89	657.67	662.94	670.00	618.75	650.10
Leisure and Hospitality													
2007	269.04	271.16	270.50	277.82	469.99	458.59	479.81	451.98	291.08	276.67	275.76	286.94	345.09
2008	267.02	281.49	280.48	268.65	278.36	290.32	285.78	296.44	319.12	310.23	330.75	305.21	293.04
2009	313.09	326.96	313.68	309.15	329.16	319.81	338.94	366.66	363.06	370.00	382.93	383.92	343.33

NEBRASKA
At a Glance

Population:
  1990 census: 1,578,417
  2000 census: 1,711,263
  2009 estimate: 1,796,619

Percent change in population:
  1990–2000: 8.4%
  2000–2009: 5.0%

Percent change in total nonfarm employment:
  1990–2009: 29.2%
  2008–2009: -2.1%

Industry with the largest growth in employment, 1990–2009 (thousands):
  Education and Health Services, 59.4

Industry with the largest decline or smallest growth in employment, 1990–2009 (thousands):
  Information, -4.5

Civilian labor force:
  1990: 816,703
  2000: 949,762
  2009: 983,517

Unemployment rate and rank among states (lowest to highest):
  1990: 2.3%, 1st
  2000: 2.8%, 8th
  2009: 4.6%, 2nd

Employment by Industry, 2009

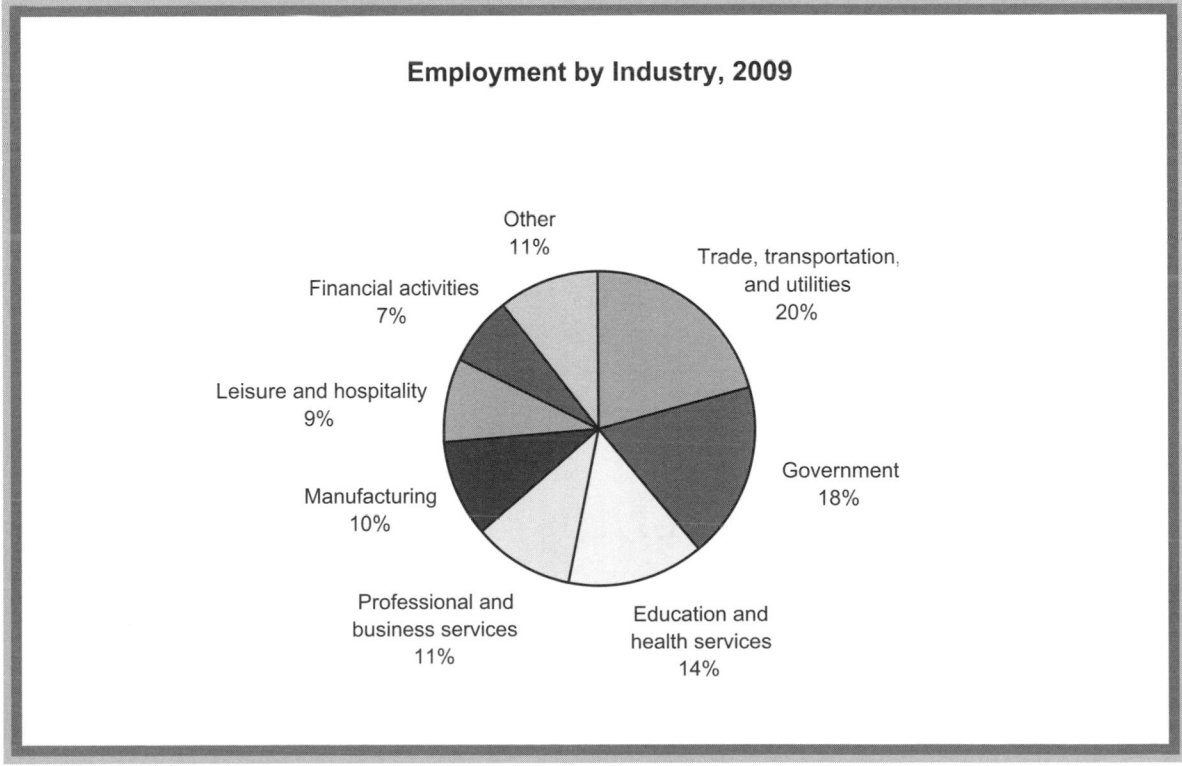

Other 11%

Financial activities 7%

Leisure and hospitality 9%

Manufacturing 10%

Professional and business services 11%

Trade, transportation, and utilities 20%

Government 18%

Education and health services 14%

Employment by Industry: Nebraska, Selected Years, 1990–2009

(Numbers in thousands, not seasonally adjusted.)

Industry and year	January	February	March	April	May	June	July	August	September	October	November	December	Annual average
Total Nonfarm													
1990	704.4	710.8	717.6	728.5	738.7	742.1	730.7	733.5	738.3	737.8	745.2	742.6	730.9
2000	888.7	892.0	901.4	907.1	917.9	926.5	911.1	912.2	914.9	915.9	920.8	919.8	910.7
2001	898.1	899.7	906.5	916.5	926.1	932.7	917.4	920.2	920.1	917.6	924.2	922.0	916.8
2002	889.7	893.4	899.1	909.3	917.1	922.3	907.3	907.9	911.7	911.3	913.7	914.3	908.1
2003	895.8	895.7	899.5	911.9	919.0	923.5	907.0	908.3	912.0	916.7	918.2	918.9	910.5
2004	896.0	894.0	903.0	915.9	925.0	930.2	918.7	919.7	924.6	926.2	929.3	929.9	917.7
2005	905.6	910.7	919.3	929.0	936.9	942.3	930.8	930.7	936.3	938.5	942.2	940.5	930.2
2006	918.9	924.1	930.8	937.5	947.2	954.2	939.7	940.7	947.4	949.0	954.2	953.7	941.5
2007	932.2	935.3	942.1	952.3	964.3	969.8	957.2	961.2	965.7	968.2	971.1	969.2	957.4
2008	949.1	950.6	956.8	965.2	975.4	975.0	962.1	964.9	968.0	973.7	971.4	967.3	965.0
2009	940.0	939.1	941.4	946.4	954.5	952.3	943.1	941.4	943.3	944.1	946.8	940.9	944.4
Total Private													
1990	565.1	568.2	573.3	582.7	588.1	595.2	595.4	598.6	595.8	593.8	596.2	596.7	587.4
2000	735.9	738.0	744.9	751.3	758.5	768.3	762.6	763.9	761.6	761.7	764.9	763.9	756.3
2001	745.3	744.4	749.9	758.8	765.4	772.5	767.3	768.9	762.9	759.1	763.2	761.9	760.0
2002	733.3	733.9	738.9	748.8	754.3	760.6	755.7	757.0	753.8	749.7	751.5	752.7	749.2
2003	736.1	735.0	738.8	748.4	754.0	759.7	755.7	758.7	755.6	755.2	756.7	757.6	751.0
2004	737.9	734.4	742.5	754.2	761.7	767.9	765.7	767.2	764.1	764.0	766.7	767.4	757.8
2005	746.6	749.7	757.4	766.4	772.3	779.0	777.1	777.6	774.5	774.6	778.0	777.2	769.2
2006	758.4	761.6	767.5	773.7	781.2	789.0	786.0	786.6	784.7	784.5	789.0	789.4	779.3
2007	770.5	772.0	778.4	788.1	797.3	804.1	804.3	807.1	803.5	803.4	805.8	805.1	795.0
2008	786.2	787.3	793.2	799.7	807.4	809.3	806.7	809.1	803.9	806.1	803.5	800.0	801.0
2009	774.3	771.1	772.7	775.7	782.0	782.4	779.6	779.1	775.2	773.0	774.9	770.8	775.9
Goods-Producing													
1990	119.3	119.7	121.2	124.7	126.3	129.4	130.3	131.0	129.4	129.3	129.1	127.1	126.4
2000	153.0	153.3	156.2	158.4	160.4	163.7	162.4	162.1	160.5	160.3	159.0	157.3	158.9
2001	152.8	152.1	152.9	156.2	158.5	160.5	159.8	159.4	156.9	156.3	155.3	153.9	156.2
2002	148.2	147.4	148.5	151.1	153.2	155.6	155.9	155.6	154.3	153.4	152.2	151.0	152.2
2003	145.7	144.5	145.1	148.4	150.8	152.9	153.2	153.4	151.6	151.8	150.7	149.8	149.8
2004	144.6	143.2	145.8	148.6	150.9	153.2	153.6	153.0	151.0	150.5	149.8	148.9	149.4
2005	142.7	143.2	145.7	148.3	150.0	152.7	153.3	152.8	151.5	150.9	150.3	148.3	149.1
2006	144.9	145.2	146.6	148.9	150.2	153.0	153.1	152.7	152.1	151.5	150.5	149.2	149.8
2007	144.7	144.4	146.6	149.7	152.1	155.0	156.7	156.9	155.8	155.0	153.9	151.7	151.9
2008	147.4	147.2	149.0	151.9	154.1	155.2	155.2	155.2	153.2	152.6	150.1	146.6	151.5
2009	140.2	138.7	138.9	140.3	142.4	143.4	143.6	143.0	141.9	140.5	141.0	138.1	141.0
Mining, Logging, and Construction													
1990	23.9	24.2	25.7	28.8	30.2	31.7	32.3	32.4	31.1	30.6	30.0	28.5	29.1
2000	40.5	40.4	42.3	44.7	46.4	48.4	48.0	48.2	47.0	46.4	44.7	42.9	45.0
2001	39.7	39.4	40.6	44.1	46.7	48.5	48.6	48.9	47.4	47.2	46.6	45.3	45.3
2002	41.2	40.8	42.4	45.3	47.2	48.8	49.3	49.1	48.3	47.9	46.9	45.8	46.1
2003	42.7	41.8	42.7	46.0	48.3	50.2	51.0	51.2	49.8	49.6	48.6	47.3	47.4
2004	43.6	42.4	44.9	48.3	50.1	51.8	52.2	51.7	50.2	49.7	48.7	47.3	48.4
2005	43.0	42.7	44.7	47.1	49.0	50.9	51.4	51.1	50.1	49.2	48.5	46.2	47.8
2006	43.4	43.5	44.9	47.4	49.2	51.2	51.3	51.1	50.8	50.1	49.4	48.0	48.4
2007	44.7	44.0	46.2	49.1	50.9	53.0	54.7	55.0	54.1	53.2	51.7	49.2	50.5
2008	45.5	45.0	46.7	49.9	51.9	53.1	53.5	53.4	52.3	51.7	49.9	48.0	50.1
2009	43.4	43.0	44.1	46.5	48.8	50.2	51.3	50.9	49.9	48.9	48.6	45.0	47.6
Manufacturing													
1990	95.4	95.5	95.5	95.9	96.1	97.7	98.0	98.6	98.3	98.7	99.1	98.6	97.3
2000	112.5	112.9	113.9	113.7	114.0	115.3	114.4	113.9	113.5	113.9	114.3	114.4	113.9
2001	113.1	112.7	112.3	112.1	111.8	112.0	111.2	110.5	109.5	109.1	108.7	108.6	111.0
2002	107.0	106.6	106.1	105.8	106.0	106.8	106.6	106.5	106.0	105.5	105.3	105.2	106.1
2003	103.0	102.7	102.4	102.4	102.5	102.7	102.2	102.2	101.8	102.2	102.1	102.5	102.4
2004	101.0	100.8	100.9	100.3	100.8	101.4	101.4	101.3	100.8	100.8	101.1	101.6	101.0
2005	99.7	100.5	101.0	101.2	101.0	101.8	101.9	101.7	101.4	101.7	101.8	102.1	101.3
2006	101.5	101.7	101.7	101.5	101.0	101.8	101.8	101.6	101.3	101.4	101.1	101.2	101.5
2007	100.0	100.4	100.4	100.6	101.2	102.0	102.0	101.9	101.7	101.8	102.2	102.5	101.4
2008	101.9	102.2	102.3	102.0	102.2	102.1	101.7	101.8	100.9	100.9	100.2	98.6	101.4
2009	96.8	95.7	94.8	93.8	93.6	93.2	92.3	92.1	92.0	91.6	92.4	93.1	93.5
Service-Providing													
1990	585.1	591.1	596.4	603.8	612.4	612.7	600.4	602.5	608.9	608.5	616.1	615.5	604.5
2000	735.7	738.7	745.2	748.7	757.5	762.8	748.7	750.1	754.4	755.6	761.8	762.5	751.8
2001	745.3	747.6	753.6	760.3	767.6	772.2	757.6	760.8	763.2	761.3	768.9	768.1	760.5
2002	741.5	746.0	750.6	758.2	763.9	766.7	751.4	752.3	757.4	757.9	761.5	763.3	755.9
2003	750.1	751.2	754.4	763.5	768.2	770.6	753.8	754.9	760.4	764.9	767.5	769.1	760.7
2004	751.4	750.8	757.2	767.3	774.1	777.0	765.1	766.7	773.6	775.7	779.5	781.0	768.3
2005	762.9	767.5	773.6	780.7	786.9	789.6	777.5	777.9	784.8	787.6	791.9	792.2	781.1
2006	774.0	778.9	784.2	788.6	797.0	801.2	786.6	788.0	795.3	797.5	803.7	804.5	791.6
2007	787.5	790.9	795.5	802.6	812.2	814.8	800.5	804.3	809.9	813.2	817.2	817.5	805.5
2008	801.7	803.4	807.8	813.3	821.3	819.8	806.9	809.7	814.8	821.1	821.3	820.7	813.5
2009	799.8	800.4	802.5	806.1	812.1	808.9	799.5	798.4	801.4	803.6	805.8	802.8	803.4

Employment by Industry: Nebraska, Selected Years, 1990–2009—*Continued*

(Numbers in thousands, not seasonally adjusted.)

Industry and year	January	February	March	April	May	June	July	August	September	October	November	December	Annual average
Trade, Transportation, and Utilities													
1990	164.5	163.1	164.3	166.2	167.7	169.0	169.4	169.6	169.3	169.3	171.2	172.8	168.0
2000	195.8	194.4	195.1	196.2	197.1	199.0	197.4	197.7	196.9	198.6	201.5	203.6	197.8
2001	197.0	195.0	195.6	197.2	199.2	199.4	198.0	198.0	197.4	197.7	201.2	202.7	198.2
2002	194.9	192.4	193.1	194.3	196.0	196.1	194.8	194.8	195.1	194.4	198.1	200.1	195.3
2003	193.0	191.5	192.5	193.6	194.8	195.2	193.4	194.1	194.1	195.4	197.9	199.9	194.6
2004	192.8	190.3	191.7	194.3	196.6	197.5	196.8	197.7	197.8	199.2	201.6	203.7	196.7
2005	197.1	196.5	198.1	198.6	200.9	201.0	200.1	200.1	199.7	200.4	203.4	205.1	200.1
2006	196.8	196.0	197.1	197.9	200.3	200.7	200.0	200.5	200.8	202.1	206.0	208.1	200.5
2007	200.9	199.9	201.1	202.4	205.0	205.4	204.9	205.3	205.1	205.9	209.5	211.1	204.7
2008	203.9	202.2	203.7	203.3	205.4	205.5	203.9	204.4	203.5	206.4	208.6	210.0	205.1
2009	200.6	198.1	198.1	197.5	198.8	198.0	196.6	196.4	195.6	194.9	197.5	199.6	197.6
Wholesale Trade													
1990	37.9	38.0	38.6	39.0	39.2	39.6	39.9	39.6	39.4	39.2	39.1	38.9	39.0
2000	41.7	41.8	41.9	41.6	41.7	42.0	42.1	42.1	41.6	41.4	41.3	41.2	41.7
2001	42.1	42.1	42.3	42.6	43.1	43.3	43.2	42.8	42.3	42.2	42.0	41.9	42.5
2002	41.1	40.9	41.3	41.6	42.0	42.2	42.5	42.0	41.6	41.0	41.0	41.1	41.5
2003	40.4	40.3	40.5	41.0	41.3	41.6	41.5	41.4	41.2	41.2	40.8	41.0	41.0
2004	40.0	39.9	40.3	41.0	41.2	41.3	41.6	41.1	40.8	40.9	40.7	40.7	40.8
2005	40.0	40.0	40.4	40.5	40.9	41.0	41.3	40.8	40.4	40.5	40.4	40.5	40.6
2006	40.2	40.2	40.4	40.8	41.2	41.4	41.3	40.9	40.7	40.6	40.6	40.9	40.8
2007	39.9	39.8	40.2	40.8	41.2	41.7	41.7	41.2	41.2	41.5	41.6	41.8	41.1
2008	41.2	41.2	41.5	41.9	42.5	42.8	42.5	42.1	41.9	42.3	42.1	42.1	42.0
2009	41.2	40.9	41.0	41.2	41.5	41.6	41.5	40.9	40.7	40.5	40.3	40.2	41.0
Retail Trade													
1990	93.0	91.4	91.9	93.4	94.3	95.0	95.4	95.3	95.1	94.9	97.2	98.8	94.6
2000	109.9	108.5	108.9	109.7	110.8	112.3	110.3	110.4	110.0	111.8	114.7	116.9	111.2
2001	110.1	108.0	108.2	109.1	110.6	110.8	109.5	110.0	109.8	110.4	113.9	115.3	110.5
2002	108.5	106.3	106.6	107.4	108.7	108.8	107.8	108.0	108.9	109.0	112.3	114.2	108.9
2003	106.7	104.9	105.6	106.2	106.8	106.9	105.9	106.2	106.3	107.7	110.7	112.3	107.2
2004	106.3	104.2	104.5	105.3	106.7	107.1	106.1	106.5	106.1	107.5	110.6	112.4	106.9
2005	106.0	105.0	105.9	106.5	107.7	107.4	106.8	106.8	106.3	107.2	109.8	111.1	107.2
2006	105.0	103.8	104.4	104.8	106.1	106.1	105.7	105.9	105.7	107.0	110.5	111.9	106.4
2007	105.6	104.5	105.2	106.1	107.9	107.7	107.2	107.5	106.9	107.7	110.9	112.4	107.5
2008	107.3	105.7	106.5	105.9	106.8	106.9	106.0	106.1	105.4	107.1	109.5	110.9	107.0
2009	105.0	103.2	103.3	103.6	104.6	104.4	103.7	104.0	103.3	102.6	105.9	107.8	104.3
Transportation and Utilities													
1990	33.6	33.7	33.8	33.8	34.2	34.4	34.1	34.7	34.8	35.2	34.9	35.1	34.4
2000	44.2	44.1	44.3	44.9	44.6	44.7	45.0	45.2	45.3	45.4	45.5	45.5	44.9
2001	44.8	44.9	45.1	45.5	45.5	45.3	45.3	45.2	45.3	45.1	45.3	45.5	45.2
2002	45.3	45.2	45.2	45.3	45.3	45.1	44.5	44.8	44.6	44.4	44.8	44.8	44.9
2003	45.9	46.3	46.4	46.4	46.7	46.7	46.0	46.5	46.6	46.5	46.4	46.6	46.4
2004	46.5	46.2	46.9	48.0	48.7	49.1	49.1	50.1	50.9	50.8	50.3	50.6	48.9
2005	51.1	51.5	51.8	51.6	52.3	52.6	52.0	52.5	53.0	52.7	53.2	53.5	52.3
2006	51.6	52.0	52.3	52.3	53.0	53.2	53.0	53.7	54.4	54.5	54.9	55.3	53.4
2007	55.4	55.6	55.7	55.5	55.9	56.0	56.0	56.6	57.0	56.7	57.0	56.9	56.2
2008	55.4	55.3	55.7	55.5	56.1	55.8	55.4	56.2	56.2	57.0	57.0	57.0	56.1
2009	54.4	54.0	53.8	52.7	52.7	52.0	51.4	51.5	51.6	51.8	51.3	51.6	52.4
Information													
1990	21.9	21.9	21.7	21.7	21.9	22.2	22.3	22.4	22.4	21.8	21.9	22.1	22.0
2000	27.5	27.1	26.7	27.2	26.8	27.0	27.0	26.7	26.4	26.4	26.6	26.6	26.8
2001	26.3	26.2	26.3	26.5	26.2	26.3	25.8	25.4	25.2	25.2	25.2	25.3	25.8
2002	24.5	24.3	24.0	23.8	23.5	23.3	23.0	22.8	22.5	22.3	22.0	21.8	23.2
2003	21.5	21.5	21.5	21.4	21.4	21.6	21.5	21.3	21.2	21.4	21.5	21.7	21.5
2004	21.3	21.3	21.3	21.2	21.1	21.2	21.2	21.0	20.9	20.8	20.9	20.7	21.1
2005	20.4	20.5	20.4	20.3	20.0	20.3	20.2	20.2	20.0	20.0	20.0	20.1	20.2
2006	19.7	19.6	19.6	19.6	19.5	19.7	19.6	19.5	19.3	19.1	19.2	19.3	19.5
2007	19.1	19.1	19.1	19.4	19.3	19.6	19.6	19.6	19.4	19.4	19.5	19.4	19.4
2008	19.2	19.2	19.1	19.1	18.8	18.8	18.7	18.5	18.2	18.2	18.2	18.1	18.7
2009	17.7	17.7	17.6	17.4	17.3	17.5	17.6	17.5	17.4	17.3	17.3	17.2	17.5
Financial Activities													
1990	48.1	48.4	48.4	48.5	48.9	49.3	49.2	49.1	48.8	48.5	48.6	49.1	48.7
2000	60.4	60.2	60.1	60.3	60.4	60.9	60.3	60.3	60.1	59.9	60.1	60.4	60.3
2001	59.1	59.2	59.3	59.7	60.1	61.0	60.8	60.8	60.5	60.3	60.5	61.0	60.2
2002	60.6	60.7	60.9	61.0	61.3	61.9	61.9	61.8	61.4	61.6	61.7	62.2	61.4
2003	61.8	61.9	62.0	62.0	62.3	62.9	63.0	62.9	62.3	62.3	62.3	62.8	62.4
2004	62.2	62.1	62.6	62.8	63.1	63.6	63.7	63.8	63.4	63.5	63.8	64.2	63.2
2005	63.5	63.8	63.9	64.1	64.5	64.9	64.9	65.0	64.7	64.8	64.7	65.0	64.5
2006	64.6	64.9	65.2	65.7	66.4	67.2	67.4	67.6	67.2	67.4	67.8	68.5	66.7
2007	67.7	68.2	68.4	68.4	69.1	69.4	69.4	69.1	68.7	68.6	68.6	68.8	68.7
2008	68.5	68.9	69.0	69.0	69.3	69.7	69.7	69.6	69.0	69.2	69.1	69.5	69.2
2009	68.6	68.8	68.8	68.4	68.4	68.5	68.1	68.0	67.6	67.7	67.3	67.6	68.2

Employment by Industry: Nebraska, Selected Years, 1990–2009—*Continued*

(Numbers in thousands, not seasonally adjusted.)

Industry and year	January	February	March	April	May	June	July	August	September	October	November	December	Annual average
Professional and Business Services													
1990	59.2	59.6	60.4	61.2	61.4	63.0	62.0	62.0	62.4	62.9	63.0	63.7	61.7
2000	92.0	92.5	93.6	95.4	95.7	97.8	97.5	97.7	97.3	97.9	98.4	98.8	96.2
2001	95.8	96.1	96.7	97.2	97.9	99.2	98.2	98.8	97.4	96.4	96.7	95.8	97.2
2002	89.0	89.8	91.4	92.9	92.7	93.1	91.3	91.2	90.8	90.9	90.9	90.5	91.2
2003	88.3	89.0	89.7	92.0	91.8	92.9	92.9	93.8	94.4	94.2	93.7	93.8	92.2
2004	91.1	91.1	92.3	94.7	94.8	96.0	95.2	95.7	94.7	95.3	95.4	95.1	94.3
2005	93.9	94.5	95.7	97.3	97.5	98.5	98.5	99.0	98.9	100.3	100.5	100.5	97.9
2006	97.9	98.7	100.4	101.2	102.3	104.4	103.8	103.4	102.9	102.5	102.5	102.1	101.8
2007	100.5	101.2	102.0	103.2	103.8	105.7	105.8	106.2	105.5	105.2	105.8	106.4	104.3
2008	103.8	104.4	105.2	106.6	106.8	107.2	106.7	106.7	106.5	106.6	105.3	104.2	105.8
2009	101.1	100.7	100.3	100.8	100.7	101.5	101.0	100.6	99.7	99.4	98.4	97.7	100.2
Education and Health Services													
1990	72.3	74.7	74.9	74.6	73.8	73.4	73.3	75.4	76.0	76.5	77.1	76.8	74.9
2000	104.2	106.3	106.9	104.8	106.8	106.9	106.0	106.7	109.3	109.5	111.4	110.2	107.4
2001	109.5	110.6	111.9	112.4	111.2	112.5	111.9	113.0	114.9	114.5	116.4	115.7	112.9
2002	112.1	114.2	114.7	115.4	115.4	116.2	114.9	115.8	117.1	116.9	117.6	118.0	115.7
2003	118.3	118.9	118.7	119.4	119.1	119.3	118.0	118.8	119.6	119.6	121.1	120.9	119.3
2004	119.6	120.2	120.6	121.7	121.2	121.1	120.1	120.7	122.1	122.3	123.6	123.3	121.4
2005	121.3	122.5	122.9	124.0	123.2	123.5	122.7	122.8	124.2	124.5	126.1	125.8	123.6
2006	123.7	125.2	125.4	125.3	125.5	125.6	124.3	125.3	126.5	126.4	128.5	127.4	125.8
2007	125.7	127.1	127.3	128.0	128.5	128.3	127.9	129.2	130.3	131.0	131.7	131.9	128.9
2008	130.3	132.1	132.1	132.2	132.8	131.5	131.6	133.1	133.9	134.2	135.2	135.0	132.8
2009	133.1	133.9	133.8	134.0	134.1	132.4	132.4	133.0	134.4	136.0	137.5	137.3	134.3
Leisure and Hospitality													
1990	54.8	55.6	57.1	59.9	62.2	62.8	62.7	63.2	61.6	59.6	59.7	59.5	59.9
2000	71.5	72.4	74.2	76.9	79.0	80.5	79.8	80.5	79.1	77.0	75.9	75.1	76.8
2001	72.6	72.8	74.5	77.0	79.4	80.6	79.7	80.5	78.0	75.9	75.1	74.8	76.7
2002	71.9	72.6	73.8	76.8	78.7	80.8	80.2	81.6	79.4	77.0	76.0	76.0	77.1
2003	73.9	74.0	75.3	77.5	79.7	80.6	79.7	80.6	78.7	76.9	75.9	75.2	77.3
2004	72.9	72.7	74.5	77.0	79.9	80.9	80.6	80.9	79.7	77.8	77.0	76.6	77.5
2005	73.9	74.4	76.3	79.3	81.5	83.2	82.5	83.1	81.1	79.4	78.8	78.2	79.3
2006	76.8	77.8	78.7	80.5	82.5	83.6	83.0	83.3	81.6	80.9	80.0	80.4	80.8
2007	77.7	77.8	79.2	82.1	84.4	85.6	85.1	86.1	84.1	83.3	81.8	80.8	82.3
2008	78.5	78.5	80.1	82.4	84.7	85.8	85.6	86.4	84.6	83.1	81.4	80.8	82.7
2009	77.8	77.9	79.9	81.8	84.5	85.1	84.4	84.9	83.1	81.6	79.6	77.9	81.5
Other Services													
1990	25.0	25.2	25.3	25.9	25.9	26.1	26.2	25.9	25.9	25.9	25.6	25.6	25.7
2000	31.5	31.8	32.1	32.1	32.3	32.5	32.2	32.2	32.0	32.1	32.0	31.9	32.1
2001	32.2	32.4	32.7	32.6	32.9	33.0	33.1	33.0	32.6	32.8	32.8	32.7	32.7
2002	32.1	32.5	32.5	33.5	33.5	33.6	33.7	33.4	33.2	33.2	33.0	33.1	33.1
2003	33.6	33.7	34.0	34.1	34.1	34.3	34.0	33.8	33.7	33.6	33.6	33.5	33.8
2004	33.4	33.5	33.7	33.9	34.1	34.4	34.5	34.4	34.5	34.6	34.6	34.9	34.2
2005	33.8	34.3	34.4	34.5	34.7	34.9	34.9	34.6	34.4	34.3	34.2	34.2	34.4
2006	34.0	34.2	34.5	34.6	34.5	34.8	34.8	34.3	34.3	34.6	34.5	34.4	34.5
2007	34.2	34.3	34.7	34.9	35.1	35.1	34.9	34.7	34.6	35.0	35.0	35.0	34.8
2008	34.6	34.8	35.0	35.2	35.5	35.6	35.3	35.2	35.0	35.8	35.6	35.8	35.3
2009	35.2	35.3	35.3	35.5	35.8	36.0	35.9	35.7	35.5	35.6	36.3	35.4	35.6
Government													
1990	139.3	142.6	144.3	145.8	150.6	146.9	135.3	134.9	142.5	144.0	149.0	145.9	143.4
2000	152.8	154.0	156.5	155.8	159.4	158.2	148.5	148.3	153.3	154.2	155.9	155.9	154.4
2001	152.8	155.3	156.6	157.7	160.7	160.2	150.1	151.3	157.2	158.5	161.0	160.1	156.8
2002	156.4	159.5	160.2	160.5	162.8	161.7	151.6	150.9	157.9	161.6	162.2	161.6	158.9
2003	159.7	160.7	160.7	163.5	165.0	163.8	151.3	149.6	156.4	161.5	161.5	161.3	159.6
2004	158.1	159.6	160.5	161.7	163.3	162.3	153.0	152.5	160.5	162.2	162.6	162.5	159.9
2005	159.0	161.0	161.9	162.6	164.6	163.3	153.7	153.1	161.8	163.9	164.2	163.3	161.0
2006	160.5	162.5	163.3	163.8	166.0	165.2	153.7	154.1	162.7	164.5	165.2	164.3	162.2
2007	161.7	163.3	163.7	164.2	167.0	165.7	152.9	154.1	162.2	164.8	165.3	164.1	162.4
2008	162.9	163.3	163.6	165.5	168.0	165.7	155.4	155.8	164.1	167.6	167.9	167.3	163.9
2009	165.7	168.0	168.7	170.7	172.5	169.9	163.5	162.3	168.1	171.1	171.9	170.1	168.5

Average Weekly Hours by Selected Industry: Nebraska, 2007–2009

(Not seasonally adjusted.)

Industry and year	January	February	March	April	May	June	July	August	September	October	November	December	Annual average
Total Private													
2007	33.1	33.0	33.2	33.6	33.4	33.9	34.2	33.7	33.9	33.5	33.4	33.6	33.5
2008	33.1	33.1	33.9	33.5	33.6	34.5	34.2	34.1	33.3	33.6	33.9	33.5	33.7
2009	33.3	33.7	33.8	33.4	33.7	33.9	33.9	34.3	33.3	33.7	34.1	33.1	33.7
Goods-Producing													
2007	40.7	39.7	41.5	40.9	41.4	41.6	42.4	42.2	41.8	41.8	41.6	39.8	41.3
2008	39.4	39.3	40.6	40.6	41.0	41.4	41.4	41.7	39.3	39.9	40.1	39.6	40.4
2009	38.5	38.4	38.7	38.5	39.5	39.5	40.4	40.6	39.6	40.6	40.6	38.7	39.5
Mining, Logging, and Construction													
2007	38.1	36.4	39.9	39.4	41.4	41.6	44.2	43.3	42.1	42.3	43.0	38.6	41.0
2008	39.0	38.7	39.9	38.3	40.4	42.3	42.1	41.9	38.7	39.6	40.0	41.1	40.2
2009	38.3	38.5	37.7	39.7	40.6	40.5	42.5	42.3	40.9	41.9	42.2	37.0	40.3
Manufacturing													
2007	41.9	41.2	42.2	41.6	41.4	41.6	41.4	41.6	41.7	41.5	40.9	40.4	41.4
2008	39.5	39.6	40.9	41.8	41.4	41.0	41.1	41.7	39.6	40.0	40.1	38.8	40.5
2009	38.6	38.3	39.2	37.9	39.0	39.0	39.2	39.7	38.9	40.0	39.8	39.5	39.1
Trade, Transportation, and Utilities													
2007	30.8	31.2	31.0	31.0	31.5	32.0	32.1	31.8	32.0	31.3	31.5	31.7	31.5
2008	31.9	31.5	32.0	31.7	32.0	32.5	32.6	32.4	31.8	32.1	31.7	32.1	32.0
2009	31.6	32.0	32.3	31.9	32.0	32.5	32.1	32.7	31.6	32.0	32.1	32.1	32.1
Financial Activities													
2007	36.9	36.9	36.7	38.0	36.6	36.6	37.8	35.8	37.0	36.2	35.7	38.0	36.8
2008	36.5	36.4	37.9	36.5	36.2	38.0	36.5	36.1	35.9	35.5	37.0	35.8	36.5
2009	36.8	38.3	38.0	36.2	36.1	36.4	36.4	37.7	36.2	36.4	38.1	36.5	36.9
Professional and Business Services													
2007	31.2	31.9	31.9	32.5	32.0	32.5	32.7	32.7	33.5	32.4	32.8	33.7	32.5
2008	33.1	33.0	34.2	33.5	33.3	34.5	34.6	34.6	34.2	34.3	34.9	34.4	34.1
2009	34.6	34.9	34.9	35.0	35.1	35.7	35.5	36.0	35.1	35.2	35.5	34.4	35.2
Education and Health Services													
2007	32.2	32.3	32.5	33.6	32.3	33.0	32.7	32.0	32.7	32.4	31.9	33.7	32.6
2008	32.9	33.0	33.5	33.1	33.3	34.2	33.8	33.6	33.3	33.5	33.7	32.9	33.4
2009	33.0	32.7	32.6	32.8	33.1	32.4	32.3	32.4	32.1	32.2	32.5	31.8	32.5
Leisure and Hospitality													
2007	20.1	20.9	20.1	20.7	20.9	21.7	22.0	21.6	20.9	20.7	20.8	20.7	20.9
2008	20.5	20.6	20.6	20.7	21.0	22.3	21.9	22.0	21.2	21.7	21.6	21.2	21.3
2009	21.3	22.4	22.1	21.1	21.5	22.4	22.4	22.6	20.4	21.1	21.4	20.6	21.6

Average Hourly Earnings by Selected Industry: Nebraska, 2007–2009

(Dollars, not seasonally adjusted.)

Industry and year	January	February	March	April	May	June	July	August	September	October	November	December	Annual average
Total Private													
2007	19.92	19.92	19.91	20.31	19.96	20.06	19.77	19.73	19.75	19.74	19.64	20.33	19.92
2008	19.97	20.11	20.02	19.58	19.71	19.49	19.25	19.50	19.84	19.89	20.09	20.12	19.79
2009	20.08	20.40	20.27	20.25	19.80	19.86	19.82	20.24	20.24	20.23	20.48	20.61	20.19
Goods-Producing													
2007	17.96	18.14	17.98	18.49	18.25	18.31	18.15	18.27	18.21	18.56	18.57	19.54	18.37
2008	18.69	18.62	18.80	18.30	18.15	18.49	18.32	18.73	19.17	19.19	19.46	19.94	18.81
2009	19.84	20.27	19.94	19.97	19.58	19.73	19.66	19.70	19.68	19.67	20.01	20.09	19.84
Mining, Logging, and Construction													
2007	18.69	18.83	18.41	18.48	18.10	18.67	18.11	18.09	18.05	18.72	18.71	19.31	18.49
2008	19.54	19.35	19.17	18.92	18.53	18.65	18.66	18.80	19.33	19.45	19.49	20.67	19.19
2009	20.49	21.14	20.58	19.50	19.29	19.40	19.19	19.37	19.43	19.59	19.84	20.37	19.79
Manufacturing													
2007	17.66	17.87	17.79	18.49	18.32	18.13	18.18	18.37	18.30	18.47	18.50	19.65	18.31
2008	18.31	18.31	18.63	18.02	17.96	18.40	18.13	18.70	19.09	19.06	19.45	19.57	18.62
2009	19.55	19.87	19.66	20.21	19.74	19.92	19.95	19.90	19.83	19.71	20.10	19.97	19.87
Trade, Transportation, and Utilities													
2007	16.61	16.45	16.45	16.92	16.67	17.81	16.57	16.36	16.57	16.20	16.39	17.97	16.75
2008	17.37	17.58	17.39	17.26	17.14	17.05	16.52	17.17	17.01	17.32	17.58	17.29	17.22
2009	17.31	17.26	17.18	17.44	17.34	17.15	17.26	17.86	17.75	17.71	17.90	18.10	17.52
Financial Activities													
2007	25.58	25.95	25.01	26.27	25.27	25.09	25.83	25.58	25.43	25.44	25.83	26.25	25.63
2008	26.43	27.74	26.81	26.32	26.63	26.81	26.08	25.60	25.94	26.10	26.42	25.93	26.40
2009	26.20	26.51	26.91	26.81	26.39	26.58	26.28	27.71	27.19	26.71	26.98	26.65	26.75
Professional and Business Services													
2007	24.10	23.77	24.40	24.37	24.60	24.55	24.44	25.09	24.61	24.54	24.01	24.14	24.39
2008	24.44	24.10	23.63	23.36	23.26	22.16	22.56	22.76	23.11	23.08	23.31	23.29	23.24
2009	22.65	24.11	23.81	23.45	22.15	22.10	22.06	22.42	22.57	22.93	23.36	23.43	22.91
Education and Health Services													
2007	21.98	21.99	22.40	22.28	22.26	21.63	21.69	21.36	21.29	21.69	21.22	20.73	21.71
2008	20.69	20.60	20.66	20.46	20.48	20.98	20.66	20.84	21.28	20.84	20.82	20.96	20.77
2009	20.79	20.48	20.25	20.19	19.90	20.20	20.10	20.32	20.30	20.00	20.01	20.16	20.22
Leisure and Hospitality													
2007	9.76	9.86	9.81	10.05	9.76	9.65	9.77	9.84	10.27	10.31	10.26	10.51	9.98
2008	10.42	10.51	10.49	10.56	10.34	10.43	10.49	10.62	10.58	10.67	10.70	10.86	10.56
2009	10.81	10.82	10.77	10.80	10.75	10.57	10.48	10.82	11.22	11.36	11.45	11.40	10.93

Average Weekly Earnings by Selected Industry: Nebraska, 2007–2009

(Dollars, not seasonally adjusted.)

Industry and year	January	February	March	April	May	June	July	August	September	October	November	December	Annual average
Total Private													
2007	659.35	657.36	661.01	682.42	666.66	680.03	676.13	664.90	669.53	661.29	655.98	683.09	667.32
2008	661.01	665.64	678.68	655.93	662.26	672.41	658.35	664.95	660.67	668.30	681.05	674.02	666.92
2009	668.66	687.48	685.13	676.35	667.26	673.25	671.90	694.23	673.99	681.75	698.37	682.19	680.40
Goods-Producing													
2007	730.97	720.16	746.17	756.24	755.55	761.70	769.56	770.99	761.18	775.81	772.51	777.69	758.68
2008	736.39	731.77	763.28	742.98	744.15	765.49	758.45	781.04	753.38	765.68	780.35	789.62	759.92
2009	763.84	778.37	771.68	768.85	773.41	779.34	794.26	799.82	779.33	798.60	812.41	777.48	783.68
Mining, Logging, and Construction													
2007	712.09	685.41	734.56	728.11	749.34	776.67	800.46	783.30	759.91	791.86	804.53	745.37	758.09
2008	762.06	748.85	764.88	724.64	748.61	788.90	785.59	787.72	748.07	770.22	779.60	849.54	771.44
2009	784.77	813.89	775.87	774.15	783.17	785.70	815.58	819.35	794.69	820.82	837.25	753.69	797.54
Manufacturing													
2007	739.95	736.24	750.74	769.18	758.45	754.21	752.65	764.19	763.11	766.51	756.65	793.86	758.03
2008	723.25	725.08	761.97	753.24	743.54	754.40	745.14	779.79	755.96	762.40	779.95	759.32	754.11
2009	754.63	761.02	770.67	765.96	769.86	776.88	782.04	790.03	771.39	788.40	799.98	788.82	776.92
Trade, Transportation, and Utilities													
2007	511.59	513.24	509.95	524.52	525.11	569.92	531.90	520.25	530.24	507.06	516.29	569.65	527.63
2008	554.10	553.77	556.48	547.14	548.48	554.13	538.55	556.31	540.92	555.97	557.29	555.01	551.04
2009	547.00	552.32	554.91	550.34	551.88	557.38	554.05	584.02	560.90	566.72	574.59	581.01	562.39
Financial Activities													
2007	943.90	957.56	917.87	998.26	924.88	918.29	976.37	915.76	940.91	920.93	922.13	997.50	943.18
2008	964.70	1009.74	1016.10	960.68	964.01	1018.78	951.92	924.16	931.25	926.55	977.54	928.29	963.60
2009	964.16	1015.33	1022.58	970.52	952.68	967.51	956.59	1044.67	984.28	972.24	1027.94	972.73	987.08
Professional and Business Services													
2007	751.92	758.20	778.36	792.03	787.20	797.88	799.19	820.44	824.44	795.10	787.53	813.52	792.68
2008	808.96	795.30	808.15	782.56	774.56	764.52	780.58	787.50	790.36	791.64	813.52	801.18	792.48
2009	783.69	841.44	830.97	820.75	777.47	788.97	783.13	807.12	792.21	807.14	829.28	805.99	806.43
Education and Health Services													
2007	707.76	710.28	728.00	748.61	719.00	713.79	709.26	683.52	696.18	702.76	676.92	698.60	707.75
2008	680.70	679.80	692.11	677.23	681.98	717.52	698.31	700.22	708.62	698.14	701.63	689.58	693.72
2009	686.07	669.70	660.15	662.23	658.69	654.48	649.23	658.37	651.63	644.00	650.33	641.09	657.15
Leisure and Hospitality													
2007	196.18	206.07	197.18	208.04	203.98	209.41	214.94	212.54	214.64	213.42	213.41	217.56	208.58
2008	213.61	216.51	216.09	218.59	217.14	232.59	229.73	233.64	224.30	231.54	231.12	230.23	224.93
2009	230.25	242.37	238.02	227.88	231.13	236.77	234.75	244.53	228.89	239.70	245.03	234.84	236.09

NEVADA
At a Glance

Population:
    1990 census: 1,201,675
    2000 census: 1,998,257
    2009 estimate: 2,643,085

Percent change in population:
    1990–2000: 66.3%
    2000–2009: 32.3%

Percent change in total nonfarm employment:
    1990–2009: 85.0%
    2008–2009: -9.1%

Industry with the largest growth in employment, 1990–2009 (thousands):
    Leisure and Hospitality, 115.0

Industry with the largest decline or smallest growth in employment, 1990–2009 (thousands):
    Mining and Logging, -2.1

Civilian labor force:
    1990: 655,896
    2000: 1,062,845
    2009: 1,369,891

Unemployment rate and rank among states (lowest to highest):
    1990: 5.1%, 18th
    2000: 4.5%, 38th
    2009:11.8%, 50th

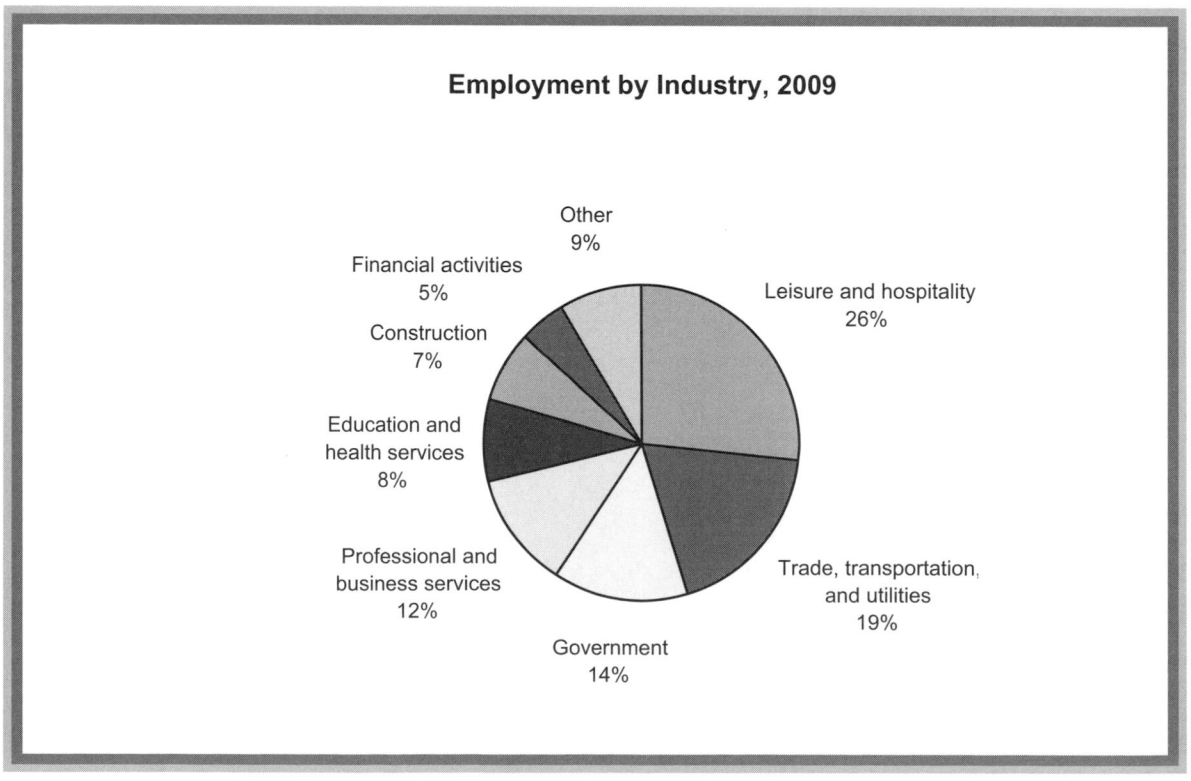

Employment by Industry, 2009

Other
9%

Financial activities
5%

Construction
7%

Education and
health services
8%

Professional and
business services
12%

Government
14%

Leisure and hospitality
26%

Trade, transportation,
and utilities
19%

Employment by Industry: Nevada, Selected Years, 1990–2009

(Numbers in thousands, not seasonally adjusted.)

Industry and year	January	February	March	April	May	June	July	August	September	October	November	December	Annual average
Total Nonfarm													
1990	595.9	598.2	606.4	612.0	619.5	625.1	627.1	631.9	634.5	633.9	636.4	630.9	620.9
2000	991.6	997.5	1007.4	1014.8	1028.0	1027.7	1024.8	1038.3	1043.6	1046.7	1051.1	1051.3	1026.9
2001	1033.8	1043.2	1051.7	1053.1	1060.2	1062.4	1052.3	1058.6	1063.1	1048.0	1047.0	1043.4	1051.4
2002	1019.1	1025.9	1037.4	1046.2	1055.6	1053.6	1049.2	1057.5	1063.6	1070.5	1072.2	1072.7	1052.0
2003	1053.5	1062.9	1071.8	1074.1	1084.1	1083.6	1083.2	1093.2	1103.9	1114.3	1115.2	1119.9	1088.3
2004	1101.5	1108.3	1122.0	1140.2	1148.3	1153.7	1153.6	1158.8	1174.0	1189.2	1189.4	1193.0	1152.7
2005	1166.7	1179.5	1195.0	1216.5	1221.8	1226.7	1225.7	1229.5	1246.4	1250.3	1256.3	1261.5	1223.0
2006	1239.8	1255.0	1268.3	1276.3	1286.3	1291.2	1279.8	1282.9	1292.6	1292.0	1294.8	1295.6	1279.6
2007	1268.2	1283.3	1290.9	1294.5	1303.8	1302.1	1287.2	1288.1	1292.3	1297.7	1301.0	1300.4	1292.5
2008	1269.1	1272.9	1275.8	1281.0	1286.2	1279.5	1265.2	1260.6	1261.6	1252.5	1238.1	1221.1	1263.6
2009	1180.8	1171.8	1163.4	1158.0	1155.6	1147.6	1133.4	1127.4	1134.6	1140.5	1136.1	1132.6	1148.5
Total Private													
1990	522.4	523.6	530.9	536.1	543.1	549.9	555.6	561.3	558.3	555.2	556.9	551.0	545.3
2000	874.0	876.6	884.7	891.7	900.8	910.5	910.2	920.1	922.2	920.9	925.1	925.4	905.1
2001	911.0	915.9	923.6	923.5	931.5	936.9	933.5	939.3	934.4	917.9	916.3	912.0	924.7
2002	893.2	895.0	905.4	914.4	922.9	924.3	926.5	934.5	932.5	934.3	935.4	935.5	921.2
2003	922.1	926.4	934.5	937.0	946.1	949.9	956.5	966.7	969.0	976.0	976.6	980.7	953.5
2004	967.8	970.3	981.7	999.9	1006.9	1017.2	1023.7	1029.4	1034.2	1045.0	1044.8	1048.1	1014.1
2005	1027.6	1035.3	1048.7	1070.3	1074.7	1084.2	1089.8	1094.7	1101.9	1101.1	1106.0	1110.9	1078.8
2006	1095.6	1104.9	1117.3	1124.0	1133.5	1143.0	1138.6	1142.2	1142.0	1135.9	1137.5	1138.2	1129.4
2007	1116.8	1125.4	1132.4	1134.4	1143.2	1146.4	1139.0	1141.1	1135.8	1136.0	1138.4	1137.1	1135.5
2008	1111.8	1109.6	1111.6	1115.7	1120.2	1118.7	1110.7	1107.3	1099.7	1085.8	1071.2	1054.6	1101.4
2009	1021.5	1008.5	1000.1	995.1	993.3	990.7	982.6	978.2	977.3	981.5	977.6	974.7	990.1
Goods-Producing													
1990	84.1	84.4	86.7	87.5	89.4	90.5	89.9	90.6	89.8	88.7	86.6	84.7	87.7
2000	137.3	137.9	140.4	141.1	142.9	145.9	145.8	146.7	145.1	144.2	144.0	143.9	142.9
2001	139.4	140.2	142.0	143.0	144.5	148.4	148.4	150.0	148.2	147.0	144.5	140.9	144.8
2002	136.1	136.6	139.0	141.9	144.1	144.7	147.1	149.6	148.2	148.2	147.0	145.6	144.0
2003	142.4	144.0	146.7	148.0	150.9	153.3	155.3	157.9	157.9	160.3	158.9	159.0	152.9
2004	155.8	158.8	161.6	168.2	170.8	174.7	178.5	180.6	182.5	185.4	183.8	183.9	173.7
2005	176.8	181.1	185.5	190.0	191.0	193.7	197.8	199.7	201.9	201.2	200.5	201.1	193.4
2006	196.3	200.1	202.5	205.6	208.7	211.5	210.0	210.5	208.5	204.4	201.3	198.9	204.9
2007	191.9	193.5	196.9	197.1	200.2	200.8	199.7	200.5	197.1	193.9	191.1	187.8	195.9
2008	179.8	179.9	179.3	179.7	181.6	182.5	182.8	181.2	177.6	173.1	165.6	158.5	176.8
2009	149.4	144.9	141.6	138.2	134.1	132.8	130.9	129.2	126.8	125.8	125.9	120.3	133.3
Mining and Logging													
1990	13.3	13.4	13.5	14.0	14.1	14.2	14.4	14.1	13.8	13.6	13.5	13.5	13.7
2000	10.9	11.2	11.2	10.6	10.7	10.8	10.8	10.7	10.6	10.6	10.5	10.4	10.7
2001	9.9	9.9	9.8	9.6	9.8	9.7	9.7	9.6	9.4	9.4	9.3	9.2	9.6
2002	9.0	8.9	8.8	8.8	8.8	8.9	8.9	8.9	8.8	8.8	8.8	8.7	8.8
2003	8.2	8.6	8.7	8.6	8.7	8.9	9.1	9.1	8.9	9.1	9.1	9.2	8.9
2004	9.0	9.1	9.2	9.2	9.3	9.5	9.9	10.0	10.0	9.9	9.8	9.8	9.6
2005	9.8	9.8	10.1	10.5	10.4	10.8	11.1	11.2	11.1	11.2	11.0	11.0	10.7
2006	11.0	10.9	11.1	11.3	11.5	11.7	11.9	12.0	11.9	11.8	11.8	11.8	11.6
2007	11.8	11.7	11.9	11.9	12.0	12.3	12.3	12.4	12.1	11.9	12.0	11.9	12.0
2008	11.9	11.9	11.9	11.9	12.0	12.2	12.5	12.6	12.5	12.2	12.2	12.0	12.2
2009	11.6	11.5	11.5	11.4	11.5	11.9	11.9	11.9	11.7	11.6	11.7	11.3	11.6
Construction													
1990	47.7	47.7	49.3	49.5	51.0	51.9	51.2	51.9	51.3	50.2	48.4	46.6	49.7
2000	84.7	84.8	87.0	88.4	89.9	92.3	92.1	93.0	91.5	90.1	89.8	89.5	89.4
2001	85.7	86.4	88.0	89.3	91.5	94.0	94.2	95.9	94.7	94.0	92.0	88.7	91.2
2002	85.0	85.6	88.1	90.8	92.6	92.9	94.8	97.3	96.1	95.7	94.7	93.3	92.2
2003	91.2	92.4	94.9	96.3	98.7	100.8	102.3	104.6	105.0	106.8	105.4	105.4	100.3
2004	102.8	105.2	107.5	113.6	115.6	118.9	122.2	123.9	126.1	128.8	127.1	127.3	118.3
2005	120.2	124.3	128.1	131.8	132.9	134.8	138.4	140.3	142.2	141.4	141.0	141.5	134.7
2006	136.9	140.2	141.9	144.2	146.7	148.8	146.9	147.3	145.3	141.9	138.8	136.3	142.9
2007	130.3	132.0	134.7	134.7	137.5	137.6	136.7	137.5	134.6	132.1	129.4	126.7	133.7
2008	118.9	119.2	118.7	119.0	120.6	121.2	121.3	119.8	117.0	113.3	107.1	101.3	116.5
2009	94.4	91.2	88.6	86.0	82.4	81.2	79.4	78.0	76.0	75.2	75.5	70.5	81.5
Manufacturing													
1990	23.1	23.3	23.9	24.0	24.3	24.4	24.3	24.6	24.7	24.9	24.7	24.6	24.2
2000	41.7	41.9	42.2	42.1	42.3	42.8	42.9	43.0	43.0	43.5	43.7	44.0	42.7
2001	43.8	43.9	44.2	44.1	44.2	44.7	44.5	44.5	44.1	43.6	43.2	43.0	44.0
2002	42.1	42.1	42.1	42.3	42.7	42.9	43.4	43.4	43.3	43.7	43.7	43.6	42.9
2003	43.0	43.0	43.1	43.1	43.5	43.6	43.9	44.2	44.0	44.4	44.4	44.4	43.7
2004	44.0	44.5	44.9	45.4	45.9	46.3	46.4	46.7	46.4	46.7	46.9	46.8	45.9
2005	46.8	47.0	47.3	47.7	47.7	48.1	48.3	48.2	48.6	48.6	48.5	48.6	48.0
2006	48.4	49.0	49.5	50.1	50.5	51.0	51.2	51.2	51.3	50.7	50.7	50.8	50.4
2007	49.8	49.8	50.3	50.5	50.7	50.9	50.7	50.6	50.4	49.9	49.7	49.2	50.2
2008	49.0	48.8	48.7	48.8	49.0	49.1	49.0	48.8	48.1	47.6	46.3	45.2	48.2
2009	43.4	42.2	41.5	40.8	40.2	39.7	39.6	39.3	39.1	39.0	38.7	38.5	40.2

NEW HAMPSHIRE
At a Glance

Population:
    1990 census: 1,109,252
    2000 census: 1,235,786
    2009 estimate: 1,324,575

Percent change in population:
    1990–2000: 11.4%
    2000–2009: 7.2%

Percent change in total nonfarm employment:
    1990–2009: 22.9%
    2008–2009: -3.4%

Industry with the largest growth in employment, 1990–2009 (thousands):
    Education and Health Services, 45.2

Industry with the largest decline or smallest growth in employment, 1990–2009 (thousands):
    Manufacturing, -30.9

Civilian labor force:
    1990: 620,037
    2000: 694,254
    2009: 742,132

Unemployment rate and rank among states (lowest to highest):
    1990: 5.6%, 31st
    2000: 2.7%, 3rd
    2009: 6.3%, 6th

Employment by Industry, 2009

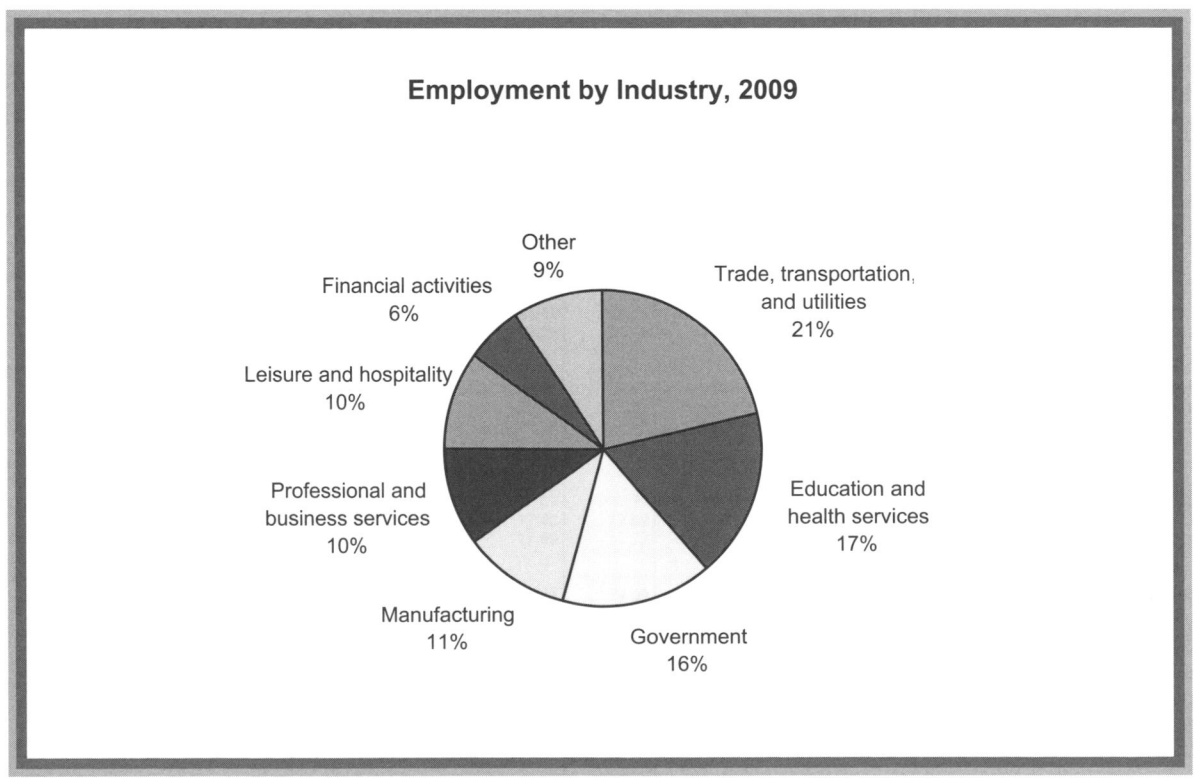

Other 9%
Financial activities 6%
Leisure and hospitality 10%
Professional and business services 10%
Manufacturing 11%
Government 16%
Education and health services 17%
Trade, transportation, and utilities 21%

Employment by Industry: New Hampshire, Selected Years, 1990–2009

(Numbers in thousands, not seasonally adjusted.)

Industry and year	January	February	March	April	May	June	July	August	September	October	November	December	Annual average
Total Nonfarm													
1990	508.4	505.8	507.3	505.7	511.2	517.0	506.4	509.9	514.5	506.6	502.1	501.8	508.0
2000	603.3	605.6	609.6	615.8	623.4	631.4	625.1	624.6	628.9	628.6	631.5	637.1	622.0
2001	622.1	622.8	623.6	625.3	633.4	638.4	627.4	627.4	628.3	626.0	624.6	627.4	627.2
2002	608.3	607.7	610.7	613.9	620.7	626.9	621.1	621.9	623.7	621.0	620.4	624.2	618.4
2003	603.5	602.7	605.1	608.9	617.4	625.4	621.1	624.3	624.6	625.8	626.0	629.4	617.9
2004	608.0	609.2	615.4	621.4	630.1	635.4	632.3	632.2	635.9	635.7	634.8	638.2	627.4
2005	621.4	620.2	622.0	630.7	638.1	643.9	640.8	639.5	645.1	642.2	643.2	648.2	636.3
2006	625.2	626.9	630.3	638.2	643.4	651.2	646.2	644.8	649.4	647.8	647.2	652.5	641.9
2007	632.0	633.8	635.7	638.4	648.5	656.4	650.2	649.3	651.7	650.2	651.0	654.9	646.0
2008	637.6	636.7	637.9	641.2	650.3	656.2	649.9	650.4	651.7	650.2	646.3	645.2	646.1
2009	624.3	621.0	617.7	619.9	628.7	632.1	620.3	620.7	624.4	626.9	622.6	630.4	624.1
Total Private													
1990	436.8	431.9	432.4	430.3	435.6	445.1	442.5	444.9	440.6	432.1	426.7	425.6	435.3
2000	520.7	519.7	522.9	529.4	536.2	549.3	550.7	551.7	544.9	542.6	544.3	550.5	538.5
2001	537.4	535.0	535.2	537.7	545.1	554.2	552.8	553.2	540.8	535.7	533.5	536.1	541.4
2002	521.4	517.4	519.6	523.9	531.6	540.2	541.9	543.7	535.1	528.7	526.8	530.5	530.1
2003	514.8	510.5	512.4	516.4	526.3	536.3	540.1	544.4	534.5	531.8	531.3	534.2	527.8
2004	518.9	517.4	521.8	528.3	536.9	547.6	552.4	553.6	545.0	541.1	539.9	543.1	537.2
2005	528.5	526.1	527.1	536.6	543.2	555.5	560.8	560.6	552.3	547.6	547.6	552.4	544.9
2006	535.0	532.1	534.9	542.8	548.1	562.2	564.7	565.1	554.8	551.4	550.7	555.2	549.8
2007	539.9	537.4	539.0	541.9	552.4	565.5	568.2	568.2	557.4	552.5	553.2	556.9	552.7
2008	543.9	539.6	539.6	543.4	552.6	563.0	566.7	566.4	554.1	550.5	545.2	544.2	550.8
2009	528.0	521.9	518.2	520.0	528.5	536.0	536.3	536.1	527.3	525.6	520.5	529.2	527.3
Goods-Producing													
1990	123.9	122.3	121.6	122.5	123.7	125.0	121.4	123.1	122.3	120.2	118.0	116.5	121.7
2000	124.8	124.2	125.2	127.1	128.4	130.0	129.3	130.8	129.9	130.4	131.0	131.3	128.5
2001	128.4	128.0	127.6	128.4	129.3	129.1	126.1	126.4	123.7	122.0	119.8	118.7	125.6
2002	114.5	113.2	113.2	114.4	115.5	115.5	114.4	114.9	113.7	112.8	111.6	112.2	113.8
2003	108.3	106.7	107.3	108.9	110.9	112.2	111.0	112.7	111.6	111.7	111.3	110.5	110.3
2004	106.7	105.8	106.7	109.6	111.3	112.9	113.2	113.4	112.6	111.7	110.8	110.3	110.4
2005	107.1	106.6	106.9	110.1	111.4	112.9	112.2	112.9	111.9	112.0	112.2	111.3	110.6
2006	106.5	105.4	106.2	108.8	109.8	111.0	110.0	111.1	110.2	109.8	108.6	107.4	108.7
2007	104.1	102.9	103.4	105.0	107.2	108.4	108.2	108.6	107.2	106.9	106.5	105.4	106.2
2008	102.2	101.3	101.6	102.6	104.0	105.2	105.2	105.5	103.8	103.2	101.6	99.2	103.0
2009	94.1	92.1	90.6	91.4	92.3	92.4	91.5	92.1	91.7	90.4	88.1	86.9	91.1
Mining and Logging													
1990	0.9	0.9	0.9	0.8	0.8	0.9	1.0	1.0	1.1	1.0	1.0	0.9	0.9
2000	1.0	1.0	1.0	0.9	1.0	1.1	1.1	1.1	1.1	1.1	1.1	1.1	1.0
2001	1.0	1.0	1.0	0.9	1.0	1.0	1.0	1.0	1.0	1.0	1.0	1.0	1.0
2002	0.9	0.9	0.9	0.9	0.9	1.0	1.0	1.0	1.0	1.0	0.9	0.9	0.9
2003	0.9	0.8	0.9	0.9	0.9	1.0	1.0	1.0	1.0	1.0	1.0	0.9	0.9
2004	0.8	0.9	0.9	0.9	1.0	1.0	1.0	1.0	1.1	1.1	1.0	1.0	1.0
2005	0.9	0.9	1.0	1.0	1.0	1.1	1.1	1.1	1.1	1.1	1.1	1.1	1.0
2006	0.9	0.9	1.0	1.0	1.1	1.1	1.2	1.2	1.2	1.2	1.1	1.1	1.1
2007	1.0	1.0	1.0	1.1	1.1	1.2	1.2	1.2	1.2	1.2	1.2	1.1	1.1
2008	1.0	1.0	1.0	1.0	1.0	1.1	1.1	1.1	1.1	1.1	1.0	0.9	1.0
2009	0.8	0.8	0.8	0.8	0.9	1.0	1.0	1.0	1.0	1.0	0.9	0.8	0.9
Construction													
1990	22.6	21.2	20.9	21.9	23.1	23.8	23.6	23.6	23.1	22.3	21.1	19.6	22.2
2000	22.4	21.8	22.5	24.0	25.1	26.3	26.7	26.8	26.2	26.1	26.0	25.5	24.9
2001	23.8	23.5	23.8	25.8	27.7	28.8	29.6	29.7	28.8	28.7	28.3	28.1	27.2
2002	26.2	25.4	25.7	27.4	28.9	29.0	28.8	29.4	28.8	28.9	28.2	28.0	27.9
2003	25.7	24.9	25.2	27.4	29.4	30.5	31.2	31.4	30.8	30.9	30.2	29.4	28.9
2004	26.4	25.7	26.2	28.8	30.3	31.2	31.8	31.6	31.0	30.5	29.7	29.0	29.4
2005	26.3	25.8	26.0	28.9	30.1	31.0	31.5	31.5	30.9	30.7	30.7	29.8	29.4
2006	27.2	26.5	27.1	29.2	30.2	31.3	31.3	31.3	30.9	30.3	29.2	28.0	29.4
2007	25.6	24.6	24.8	26.2	28.4	29.1	29.5	29.4	28.7	28.2	27.8	26.6	27.4
2008	24.2	23.6	23.9	25.5	26.7	27.3	28.2	28.0	27.2	27.0	26.0	24.5	26.0
2009	21.5	20.6	20.3	21.6	22.9	23.4	23.7	23.8	24.2	24.5	23.1	22.1	22.6
Manufacturing													
1990	100.4	100.2	99.8	99.8	99.8	100.3	96.8	98.5	98.1	96.9	95.9	96.0	98.5
2000	101.4	101.4	101.7	102.2	102.3	102.6	101.5	102.9	102.6	103.2	103.9	104.7	102.5
2001	103.6	103.5	102.8	101.7	100.6	99.3	95.5	95.7	93.9	92.3	90.5	89.6	97.4
2002	87.4	86.9	86.6	86.1	85.7	85.5	84.6	84.5	83.9	82.9	82.5	83.3	85.0
2003	81.7	81.0	81.2	80.6	80.6	80.7	78.8	80.3	79.8	79.8	80.1	80.2	80.4
2004	79.5	79.2	79.6	79.9	80.0	80.7	80.4	80.8	80.5	80.1	80.1	80.3	80.1
2005	79.9	79.9	79.9	80.2	80.3	80.8	79.6	80.3	79.9	80.2	80.4	80.4	80.2
2006	78.4	78.0	78.1	78.6	78.5	78.6	77.5	78.6	78.1	78.3	78.3	78.3	78.3
2007	77.5	77.3	77.6	77.7	77.7	78.1	77.5	78.0	77.3	77.5	77.5	77.7	77.6
2008	77.0	76.7	76.7	76.1	76.3	76.8	75.9	76.4	75.5	75.1	74.6	73.8	75.9
2009	71.8	70.7	69.5	69.0	68.5	68.0	66.8	67.3	66.5	64.9	64.1	64.0	67.6

Employment by Industry: New Hampshire, Selected Years, 1990–2009—*Continued*

(Numbers in thousands, not seasonally adjusted.)

Industry and year	January	February	March	April	May	June	July	August	September	October	November	December	Annual average
Service-Providing													
1990	384.5	383.5	385.7	383.2	387.5	392.0	385.0	386.8	392.2	386.4	384.1	385.3	386.3
2000	478.5	481.4	484.4	488.7	495.0	501.4	495.8	493.8	499.0	498.2	500.5	505.8	493.5
2001	493.7	494.8	496.0	496.9	504.1	509.3	501.3	501.0	504.6	504.0	504.8	508.7	501.6
2002	493.8	494.5	497.5	499.5	505.2	511.4	506.7	507.0	510.0	508.2	508.8	512.0	504.6
2003	495.2	496.0	497.8	500.0	506.5	513.2	510.1	511.6	513.0	514.1	514.7	518.9	507.6
2004	501.3	503.4	508.7	511.8	518.8	522.5	519.1	518.8	523.3	524.0	524.0	527.9	517.0
2005	514.3	513.6	515.1	520.6	526.7	531.0	528.6	526.6	533.2	530.2	531.0	536.9	525.7
2006	518.7	521.5	524.1	529.4	533.6	540.2	536.2	533.7	539.2	538.0	538.6	545.1	533.2
2007	527.9	530.9	532.3	533.4	541.3	548.0	542.0	540.7	544.5	543.3	544.5	549.5	539.9
2008	535.4	535.4	536.3	538.6	546.3	551.0	544.7	544.9	547.9	547.0	544.7	546.0	543.2
2009	530.2	528.9	527.1	528.5	536.4	539.7	528.8	528.6	532.7	536.5	534.5	543.5	533.0
Trade, Transportation, and Utilities													
1990	111.6	108.9	108.9	107.2	108.2	110.8	110.0	110.1	109.5	108.5	109.1	109.9	109.3
2000	135.6	133.0	133.3	134.8	136.3	138.6	137.0	137.1	136.3	137.4	141.0	144.8	137.1
2001	137.3	134.2	133.7	134.8	136.7	138.6	137.4	137.6	136.4	137.7	140.6	143.1	137.3
2002	137.1	133.6	134.3	135.9	137.3	139.5	138.6	139.2	138.9	138.7	141.0	144.6	138.2
2003	136.0	133.3	134.3	135.2	136.9	139.2	139.2	140.0	138.9	140.3	142.9	144.7	138.4
2004	137.1	135.2	136.3	137.5	139.2	140.9	140.5	140.1	139.5	140.6	143.0	145.7	139.6
2005	139.2	136.7	136.6	137.8	139.5	141.8	141.5	141.7	140.2	141.7	144.2	146.8	140.6
2006	140.2	137.5	138.3	140.1	141.1	143.0	142.2	142.3	140.7	141.5	144.9	147.7	141.6
2007	141.5	138.0	138.5	138.9	140.9	142.9	142.6	142.0	139.7	140.5	144.2	146.5	141.4
2008	140.9	137.6	137.4	137.2	139.4	141.4	141.0	140.8	138.6	139.8	141.4	142.7	139.9
2009	136.1	132.8	131.6	131.8	134.1	135.5	133.7	133.1	132.4	134.4	136.5	138.3	134.2
Wholesale Trade													
1990	20.2	20.2	20.2	20.1	20.2	20.4	20.1	20.1	20.0	20.0	19.7	19.5	20.0
2000	24.5	24.6	24.8	24.9	25.8	26.2	26.3	26.4	26.2	26.3	26.4	26.7	25.7
2001	26.3	26.3	26.3	26.5	26.6	26.9	27.0	26.9	26.7	26.9	26.6	26.8	26.7
2002	26.5	26.4	26.5	26.4	26.4	26.7	26.7	26.7	26.6	26.8	26.6	26.8	26.6
2003	26.2	26.1	26.0	26.4	26.6	27.0	27.2	27.3	26.9	26.9	26.9	26.9	26.7
2004	26.6	26.6	26.9	27.2	27.3	27.5	27.7	27.8	27.4	27.3	27.1	27.2	27.2
2005	27.1	26.9	27.0	27.4	27.6	27.7	27.8	27.7	27.4	27.8	27.7	27.7	27.5
2006	27.5	27.4	27.6	27.9	28.2	28.4	28.3	28.4	28.2	28.2	28.1	28.3	28.0
2007	28.2	28.0	28.2	28.3	28.4	28.5	28.5	28.4	28.2	28.1	28.1	28.1	28.3
2008	28.0	27.9	27.9	28.1	28.3	28.4	28.4	28.3	28.0	28.0	27.8	27.6	28.1
2009	27.1	26.7	26.5	26.6	26.7	26.6	26.4	26.4	26.1	26.5	27.1	27.0	26.6
Retail Trade													
1990	79.4	76.5	76.4	75.1	75.7	77.6	77.6	77.6	76.8	76.0	77.0	77.9	76.9
2000	94.2	91.7	91.9	93.1	93.7	95.2	94.6	94.6	93.3	94.0	97.8	101.2	94.6
2001	95.4	92.2	91.9	92.5	94.0	95.5	95.0	95.4	93.7	94.8	98.2	100.5	94.9
2002	95.3	92.0	92.5	93.7	94.9	96.6	96.2	96.9	96.3	95.8	98.4	101.6	95.9
2003	94.1	91.8	92.7	93.2	94.4	96.2	96.5	97.4	96.0	97.2	99.9	101.7	95.9
2004	95.1	93.4	94.2	95.0	96.3	97.6	97.8	97.6	96.4	97.3	100.2	102.8	97.0
2005	96.6	94.4	94.2	95.0	96.3	98.1	98.3	98.6	96.9	98.1	100.7	103.0	97.5
2006	97.5	94.9	95.4	96.7	97.2	98.6	98.5	98.6	96.6	97.6	101.1	103.2	98.0
2007	98.0	94.9	95.1	95.3	97.0	98.6	98.8	98.4	95.8	96.9	100.9	102.5	97.7
2008	97.9	95.0	94.8	94.3	95.8	97.6	97.7	97.6	95.3	96.6	98.6	99.6	96.7
2009	94.4	91.6	90.7	90.9	92.7	93.9	93.4	93.1	91.6	93.2	94.9	96.4	93.1
Transportation and Utilities													
1990	12.0	12.2	12.3	12.0	12.3	12.8	12.3	12.4	12.7	12.5	12.4	12.5	12.3
2000	16.9	16.7	16.6	16.8	16.8	17.2	16.1	16.1	16.8	17.1	16.8	16.9	16.7
2001	15.6	15.7	15.5	15.8	16.1	16.2	15.4	15.3	16.0	16.0	15.8	15.8	15.8
2002	15.3	15.2	15.3	15.8	16.0	16.2	15.7	15.6	16.0	16.1	16.0	16.2	15.8
2003	15.7	15.4	15.6	15.6	15.9	16.0	15.5	15.3	16.0	16.2	16.1	16.1	15.8
2004	15.4	15.2	15.2	15.3	15.6	15.8	15.0	14.7	15.7	16.0	15.7	15.7	15.4
2005	15.5	15.4	15.4	15.4	15.6	16.0	15.4	15.4	15.9	15.8	15.8	16.1	15.6
2006	15.2	15.2	15.3	15.5	15.7	16.0	15.4	15.3	15.9	15.7	15.7	16.2	15.6
2007	15.3	15.1	15.2	15.3	15.5	15.8	15.3	15.2	15.7	15.5	15.2	15.9	15.4
2008	15.0	14.7	14.7	14.8	15.3	15.4	14.9	14.9	15.3	15.2	15.0	15.5	15.1
2009	14.6	14.5	14.4	14.3	14.7	15.0	13.9	13.6	14.7	14.7	14.5	14.9	14.5
Information													
1990	10.7	10.5	10.5	10.5	10.5	10.5	10.6	10.6	10.4	10.4	10.4	10.4	10.5
2000	13.3	13.3	13.4	13.7	14.0	14.2	14.2	13.6	14.1	14.5	14.6	14.6	13.9
2001	14.3	14.2	14.1	13.8	13.7	13.8	13.7	13.6	13.5	13.4	13.4	13.4	13.7
2002	13.4	13.3	13.1	13.0	12.9	12.9	12.8	12.7	12.7	12.7	12.7	12.6	12.9
2003	12.4	12.2	12.2	12.1	12.1	12.2	12.2	12.1	11.9	12.0	12.2	12.3	12.2
2004	12.1	12.3	12.4	12.6	12.6	12.6	12.7	12.7	12.5	12.6	12.7	12.8	12.6
2005	12.5	12.5	12.5	12.7	12.8	12.8	12.9	12.9	12.7	12.7	12.9	12.9	12.7
2006	12.8	12.6	12.7	12.7	12.6	12.7	12.6	12.5	12.3	12.1	12.1	12.2	12.5
2007	12.3	12.2	12.1	12.3	12.3	12.5	12.6	12.8	12.4	12.4	12.5	12.5	12.4
2008	12.7	12.6	12.5	12.6	12.6	12.8	12.8	12.8	12.5	12.5	12.5	12.5	12.6
2009	12.5	12.4	12.3	12.7	12.7	12.7	12.6	12.5	12.4	12.5	12.5	12.5	12.5

Employment by Industry: New Hampshire, Selected Years, 1990–2009—*Continued*

(Numbers in thousands, not seasonally adjusted.)

Industry and year	January	February	March	April	May	June	July	August	September	October	November	December	Annual average
Financial Activities													
1990	33.2	32.9	32.9	33.1	33.4	33.7	33.5	33.4	32.8	32.3	32.1	32.2	32.9
2000	34.1	33.9	33.8	33.7	33.8	34.3	34.3	34.4	34.1	34.1	34.4	34.8	34.1
2001	34.9	35.1	35.3	35.4	35.7	36.1	36.1	36.3	35.8	35.6	35.8	36.3	35.7
2002	36.3	36.2	36.2	36.1	36.3	36.7	36.8	37.0	36.8	36.7	36.7	36.8	36.6
2003	36.8	36.8	36.7	37.1	37.3	37.5	37.5	37.5	36.8	36.6	36.6	36.8	37.0
2004	36.7	36.7	37.1	37.1	37.3	37.7	37.8	38.0	37.4	37.6	37.6	38.0	37.4
2005	38.2	38.1	38.3	38.9	39.1	39.8	40.3	40.4	40.0	39.7	39.6	40.0	39.4
2006	39.1	39.2	39.3	39.3	39.2	39.8	40.0	39.7	39.3	39.2	39.0	39.2	39.4
2007	38.1	38.1	38.2	38.1	38.4	38.8	39.1	39.1	38.4	38.1	38.2	38.4	38.4
2008	38.0	38.0	38.0	38.1	38.2	38.6	38.6	38.5	37.8	37.8	37.6	37.7	38.1
2009	37.3	36.9	36.7	36.7	36.8	37.2	36.8	36.5	35.9	35.3	35.3	35.2	36.4
Professional and Business Services													
1990	36.2	36.1	36.5	37.1	37.1	37.6	37.4	37.4	37.2	36.0	35.5	35.1	36.6
2000	55.4	56.1	57.1	58.1	58.4	59.8	59.4	60.0	59.3	59.5	60.0	60.3	58.6
2001	57.4	56.9	57.1	57.3	58.0	58.5	57.7	57.9	56.6	55.6	55.2	55.2	57.0
2002	53.0	52.8	53.1	53.9	54.7	55.0	55.4	55.7	55.0	54.5	54.6	53.9	54.3
2003	52.5	52.3	52.3	54.0	54.5	55.5	55.6	56.3	55.7	55.7	56.0	56.0	54.7
2004	54.3	54.6	55.6	57.2	57.6	58.0	58.2	59.2	58.0	58.3	58.5	58.5	57.3
2005	56.6	56.7	56.9	58.9	59.0	60.0	60.4	60.6	60.1	60.0	60.4	60.3	59.2
2006	58.3	58.8	58.8	61.6	61.7	63.4	63.2	63.4	63.0	63.2	63.1	63.4	61.8
2007	62.4	63.2	63.1	64.7	65.6	66.6	66.5	67.1	66.3	66.6	66.5	67.3	65.5
2008	65.4	65.0	64.8	67.3	67.7	67.9	67.3	67.5	67.0	66.4	65.8	64.6	66.4
2009	63.2	62.2	61.6	62.6	62.5	63.0	62.7	62.6	62.5	61.2	62.4	66.4	62.7
Education and Health Services													
1990	60.8	61.0	61.5	61.1	61.0	61.0	60.1	60.3	62.2	63.0	63.1	63.4	61.5
2000	81.8	82.8	83.3	84.3	84.1	84.2	83.2	83.4	85.1	84.8	85.4	85.5	83.9
2001	86.9	88.3	88.4	88.3	88.2	88.4	88.3	88.6	89.6	90.2	91.0	91.5	89.0
2002	90.4	91.5	92.2	92.1	92.4	92.1	91.0	91.0	92.4	91.8	92.4	92.3	91.8
2003	92.1	92.9	93.2	92.8	92.9	92.8	91.9	92.3	93.4	93.7	94.4	94.3	93.1
2004	93.6	94.5	94.9	95.1	95.0	94.8	94.0	94.0	95.4	96.0	96.5	96.2	95.0
2005	95.7	96.6	96.9	97.8	97.7	97.6	97.4	97.2	98.9	98.8	99.1	99.7	97.8
2006	98.7	99.4	99.8	99.9	99.9	100.2	99.6	99.5	100.7	101.2	101.8	102.5	100.3
2007	101.0	102.5	102.9	102.7	102.8	103.4	102.2	101.8	103.4	103.6	104.1	104.3	102.9
2008	103.3	103.8	104.5	104.7	105.0	104.9	104.9	104.4	105.7	106.3	106.8	107.2	105.1
2009	106.2	106.9	107.0	106.8	107.0	106.4	105.6	105.5	106.0	107.1	107.9	107.4	106.7
Leisure and Hospitality													
1990	42.7	42.6	42.8	41.2	44.1	48.7	51.6	52.1	48.5	44.1	41.0	40.7	45.0
2000	52.3	52.9	53.2	53.9	57.2	63.8	68.8	68.3	61.8	57.9	53.8	55.1	58.2
2001	54.4	54.6	54.5	55.4	59.1	65.4	69.5	69.4	62.3	58.7	55.1	55.6	59.5
2002	54.8	54.9	55.7	56.6	60.4	66.3	70.9	71.1	64.1	60.6	57.1	57.5	60.8
2003	56.3	56.0	55.9	55.9	61.1	66.2	71.4	72.2	65.4	61.3	57.3	58.9	61.5
2004	57.8	57.9	58.2	58.5	62.9	69.3	74.3	74.6	68.2	63.3	59.7	60.5	63.8
2005	58.5	58.2	58.1	59.0	62.3	69.0	74.3	73.1	67.0	61.6	58.1	60.1	63.3
2006	58.5	58.3	58.8	59.1	62.3	70.1	74.8	74.3	67.0	62.9	59.6	61.2	63.9
2007	59.2	59.1	59.2	58.7	63.3	70.3	74.2	74.1	67.9	62.3	59.2	60.4	64.0
2008	59.4	59.5	59.1	59.2	63.7	69.8	74.4	74.3	66.6	62.5	57.9	58.8	63.8
2009	57.5	57.5	57.3	56.9	61.6	67.1	71.7	71.9	65.2	63.1	56.4	60.2	62.2
Other Services													
1990	17.7	17.6	17.7	17.6	17.6	17.8	17.9	17.9	17.7	17.6	17.5	17.4	17.6
2000	23.4	23.5	23.6	23.8	24.0	24.4	24.5	24.1	24.3	24.0	24.1	24.1	23.9
2001	23.8	23.7	24.5	24.3	24.4	24.3	24.0	23.4	22.9	22.5	22.6	22.3	23.6
2002	21.9	21.9	21.8	21.9	22.1	22.2	22.0	22.1	21.5	20.9	20.7	20.6	21.6
2003	20.4	20.3	20.5	20.4	20.6	20.7	21.3	21.3	20.8	20.5	20.6	20.7	20.7
2004	20.6	20.4	20.6	20.7	21.0	21.4	21.7	21.6	21.4	21.0	21.1	21.1	21.1
2005	20.7	20.7	20.9	21.4	21.4	21.6	21.8	21.8	21.5	21.1	21.1	21.3	21.3
2006	20.9	20.9	21.0	21.3	21.5	22.0	22.3	22.3	21.6	21.5	21.6	21.6	21.5
2007	21.3	21.4	21.6	21.5	21.9	22.6	22.8	22.7	22.1	22.1	22.0	22.1	22.0
2008	22.0	21.8	21.7	21.7	22.0	22.4	22.5	22.6	22.1	22.0	21.6	21.5	22.0
2009	21.1	21.1	21.1	21.1	21.5	21.7	21.7	21.9	21.2	21.6	21.4	22.3	21.5
Government													
1990	71.6	73.9	74.9	75.4	75.6	71.9	63.9	65.0	73.9	74.5	75.4	76.2	72.6
2000	82.6	85.9	86.7	86.4	87.2	82.1	74.4	72.9	84.0	86.0	87.2	86.6	83.5
2001	84.7	87.8	88.4	87.6	88.3	84.2	74.6	74.2	87.5	90.3	91.1	91.3	85.8
2002	86.9	90.3	91.1	90.0	89.1	86.7	79.2	78.2	88.6	92.3	93.6	93.7	88.3
2003	88.7	92.2	92.7	92.5	91.1	89.1	81.0	79.9	90.1	94.0	94.7	95.2	90.1
2004	89.1	91.8	93.6	93.1	93.2	87.8	79.9	78.6	90.9	94.6	94.9	95.1	90.2
2005	92.9	94.1	94.9	94.1	94.9	88.4	80.0	78.9	92.8	94.6	95.6	95.8	91.4
2006	90.2	94.8	95.4	95.4	95.3	89.0	81.5	79.7	94.6	96.4	96.5	97.3	92.2
2007	92.1	96.4	96.7	96.5	96.1	90.9	82.0	81.1	94.3	97.7	97.8	98.0	93.3
2008	93.7	97.1	98.3	97.8	97.7	93.2	83.2	84.0	97.6	99.7	101.1	101.0	95.4
2009	96.3	99.1	99.5	99.9	100.2	96.1	84.0	84.6	97.1	101.3	102.1	101.2	96.8

Average Weekly Hours by Selected Industry: New Hampshire, 2007–2009

(Not seasonally adjusted.)

Industry and year	January	February	March	April	May	June	July	August	September	October	November	December	Annual average
Total Private													
2007	33.2	33.0	33.2	33.3	33.5	33.4	33.5	33.5	33.4	33.3	33.1	33.3	33.3
2008	32.6	32.8	32.9	32.8	32.7	32.7	32.7	32.7	33.1	33.0	32.8	32.3	32.8
2009	32.5	32.6	32.5	32.7	32.7	32.0	32.8	33.1	32.6	33.1	33.1	33.0	32.7
Goods-Producing													
2007	39.5	38.7	39.3	39.8	39.5	39.1	39.1	39.4	39.5	39.2	39.7	40.2	39.4
2008	39.7	39.3	39.5	39.4	39.3	39.5	38.9	39.2	40.4	39.0	39.3	38.5	39.3
2009	39.4	38.3	38.2	38.4	38.3	38.4	38.7	38.4	37.8	39.2	39.2	39.8	38.7
Manufacturing													
2007	41.0	40.3	40.5	41.0	40.7	40.3	40.0	40.3	40.7	40.3	40.7	41.2	40.6
2008	40.8	40.3	40.6	40.7	40.4	40.7	40.1	40.4	40.6	39.8	40.1	39.5	40.3
2009	40.6	39.0	39.2	39.2	38.9	39.1	39.1	38.8	38.1	39.4	39.6	40.4	39.3
Trade, Transportation, and Utilities													
2007	31.9	32.3	32.1	31.6	31.8	32.0	31.2	31.3	30.9	31.1	30.4	30.9	31.5
2008	30.1	30.6	30.8	30.4	30.1	29.9	29.8	29.6	30.0	29.8	30.4	30.0	30.1
2009	30.0	30.5	30.9	31.9	31.9	31.1	32.1	32.0	32.5	32.2	32.4	32.4	31.7
Professional and Business Services													
2007	36.2	35.1	36.3	37.1	37.8	36.9	37.5	36.6	36.6	36.4	36.4	36.8	36.6
2008	34.7	35.1	36.3	35.4	36.2	36.4	36.4	36.3	36.8	37.3	36.7	35.9	36.1
2009	35.7	36.4	36.0	36.5	35.6	34.9	34.5	35.4	34.9	35.3	35.0	35.1	35.4
Education and Health Services													
2007	31.7	31.6	31.8	31.8	32.1	31.8	32.1	32.2	32.2	32.0	31.9	31.5	31.9
2008	31.1	31.4	31.1	30.9	30.8	30.8	31.2	30.9	31.4	31.5	31.8	31.6	31.2
2009	31.7	31.6	31.7	31.5	31.5	31.1	32.0	32.2	31.8	32.2	32.3	32.3	31.8
Leisure and Hospitality													
2007	24.1	24.9	24.6	24.3	25.6	26.1	26.8	26.7	25.6	25.3	24.8	24.0	25.3
2008	24.3	24.3	24.0	24.3	24.6	24.7	25.4	25.6	23.6	24.0	23.0	22.1	24.2
2009	22.5	23.7	22.9	23.2	23.1	23.3	25.2	26.1	24.3	24.3	24.6	23.3	23.9

Average Hourly Earnings by Selected Industry: New Hampshire, 2007–2009

(Dollars, not seasonally adjusted.)

Industry and year	January	February	March	April	May	June	July	August	September	October	November	December	Annual average
Total Private													
2007	21.94	22.11	22.06	22.40	22.06	21.87	21.79	21.76	22.21	22.09	22.05	22.45	22.06
2008	22.42	22.44	22.62	22.54	22.45	22.29	22.27	22.51	23.14	23.00	23.05	23.22	22.66
2009	23.11	22.99	22.85	22.76	22.68	22.57	22.36	22.31	22.51	22.64	22.74	22.91	22.70
Goods-Producing													
2007	25.15	25.43	25.25	25.17	25.12	24.93	24.71	24.71	24.69	24.29	23.86	24.19	24.79
2008	24.23	24.36	24.73	24.70	24.02	24.12	24.52	24.69	25.18	25.01	25.26	25.63	24.70
2009	25.55	25.47	25.56	25.76	25.56	25.48	25.33	25.44	25.59	25.50	25.44	25.64	25.53
Manufacturing													
2007	26.23	26.34	26.16	25.95	25.81	25.62	25.40	25.29	25.22	24.69	24.17	24.50	25.45
2008	24.35	24.43	24.89	24.77	23.79	23.88	24.41	24.70	24.98	24.96	25.13	25.22	24.62
2009	25.26	25.21	25.22	25.08	25.01	25.08	25.12	25.32	25.50	25.53	25.73	25.83	25.32
Trade, Transportation, and Utilities													
2007	17.10	17.08	16.58	16.72	16.81	16.63	16.48	16.31	16.50	16.63	16.57	16.27	16.64
2008	16.56	17.22	17.51	17.57	17.58	17.49	17.35	17.34	17.99	17.96	17.92	18.86	17.61
2009	19.02	19.21	19.01	19.17	19.19	19.33	19.50	19.68	19.88	19.99	20.13	19.93	19.51
Professional and Business Services													
2007	30.30	31.18	31.29	31.73	30.25	30.65	30.50	29.97	30.25	29.94	29.68	29.91	30.46
2008	29.37	28.85	29.56	29.20	29.43	29.41	29.09	29.85	30.62	30.64	30.24	29.82	29.68
2009	29.99	29.65	29.82	29.62	29.47	29.66	29.66	28.84	29.04	28.93	28.84	28.79	29.36
Education and Health Services													
2007	20.25	20.28	20.44	20.84	20.70	20.98	21.05	20.92	21.39	21.38	21.66	21.79	20.98
2008	21.73	21.36	21.46	21.35	21.12	21.21	21.19	21.19	21.54	21.49	22.04	21.81	21.46
2009	21.78	21.76	21.81	21.87	21.99	22.00	21.95	21.87	22.02	22.17	22.01	22.21	21.95
Leisure and Hospitality													
2007	11.79	12.12	12.17	12.15	12.17	11.73	11.20	11.25	11.38	11.57	11.60	11.69	11.70
2008	11.71	11.99	12.08	11.92	12.46	12.29	12.41	12.39	12.92	12.93	12.92	13.40	12.44
2009	13.21	13.16	13.32	13.41	13.54	13.34	13.34	13.23	13.43	13.44	13.62	13.47	13.37

Average Weekly Earnings by Selected Industry: New Hampshire, 2007–2009

(Dollars, not seasonally adjusted.)

Industry and year	January	February	March	April	May	June	July	August	September	October	November	December	Annual average
Total Private													
2007	728.41	729.63	732.39	745.92	739.01	730.46	729.97	728.96	741.81	735.60	729.86	747.59	734.60
2008	730.89	736.03	744.20	739.31	734.12	728.88	728.23	736.08	765.93	759.00	756.04	750.01	743.25
2009	751.08	749.47	742.63	744.25	741.64	722.24	733.41	738.46	733.83	749.38	752.69	756.03	742.29
Goods-Producing													
2007	993.43	984.14	992.33	1001.77	992.24	974.76	966.16	973.57	975.26	952.17	947.24	972.44	976.73
2008	961.93	957.35	976.84	973.18	943.99	952.74	953.83	967.85	1017.27	975.39	992.72	986.76	970.71
2009	1006.67	975.50	976.39	989.18	978.95	978.43	980.27	976.90	967.30	999.60	997.25	1020.47	988.01
Manufacturing													
2007	1075.43	1061.50	1059.48	1063.95	1050.47	1032.49	1016.00	1019.19	1026.45	995.01	983.72	1009.40	1033.27
2008	993.48	984.53	1010.53	1008.14	961.12	971.92	978.84	997.88	1014.19	993.41	1007.71	996.19	992.19
2009	1025.56	983.19	988.62	983.14	972.89	980.63	982.19	982.42	971.55	1005.88	1018.91	1043.53	995.08
Trade, Transportation, and Utilities													
2007	545.49	551.68	532.22	528.35	534.56	532.16	514.18	510.50	509.85	517.19	503.73	502.74	524.16
2008	498.46	526.93	539.31	534.13	529.16	522.95	517.03	513.26	539.70	535.21	544.77	565.80	530.06
2009	570.60	585.91	587.41	611.52	612.16	601.16	625.95	629.76	646.10	643.68	652.21	645.73	618.47
Professional and Business Services													
2007	1096.86	1094.42	1135.83	1177.18	1143.45	1130.99	1143.75	1096.90	1107.15	1089.82	1080.35	1100.69	1114.84
2008	1019.14	1012.64	1073.03	1033.68	1065.37	1070.52	1058.88	1083.56	1126.82	1142.87	1109.81	1070.54	1071.45
2009	1070.04	1079.26	1073.52	1081.13	1049.13	1035.13	1023.27	1020.94	1013.50	1021.23	1009.40	1010.53	1039.34
Education and Health Services													
2007	641.93	640.85	649.99	662.71	664.47	667.16	675.71	673.62	688.76	684.16	690.95	686.39	669.26
2008	675.80	670.70	667.41	659.72	650.50	653.27	661.13	654.77	676.36	676.94	700.87	689.20	669.55
2009	690.43	687.62	691.38	688.91	692.69	684.20	702.40	704.21	700.24	713.87	710.92	717.38	698.01
Leisure and Hospitality													
2007	284.14	301.79	299.38	295.25	311.55	306.15	300.16	300.38	291.33	292.72	287.68	280.56	296.01
2008	284.55	291.36	289.92	289.66	306.52	303.56	315.21	317.18	304.91	310.32	297.16	296.14	301.05
2009	297.23	311.89	305.03	311.11	312.77	310.82	336.17	345.30	326.35	326.59	335.05	313.85	319.54

NEW JERSEY
At a Glance

Population:
    1990 census: 7,747,750
    2000 census: 8,414,350
    2009 estimate: 8,707,739

Percent change in population:
    1990–2000: 8.6%
    2000–2009: 3.5%

Percent change in total nonfarm employment:
    1990–2009: 9.9%
    2008–2009: 1.6%

Industry with the largest growth in employment, 1990–2009 (thousands):
    Education and Health Services, 236.1

Industry with the largest decline or smallest growth in employment, 1990–2009 (thousands):
    Manufacturing, -262.2

Civilian labor force:
    1990: 4,072,494
    2000: 4,287,783
    2009: 4,536,661

Unemployment rate and rank among states (lowest to highest):
    1990: 5.1%, 18th
    2000: 3.7%, 22nd
    2009: 9.2%, 33rd

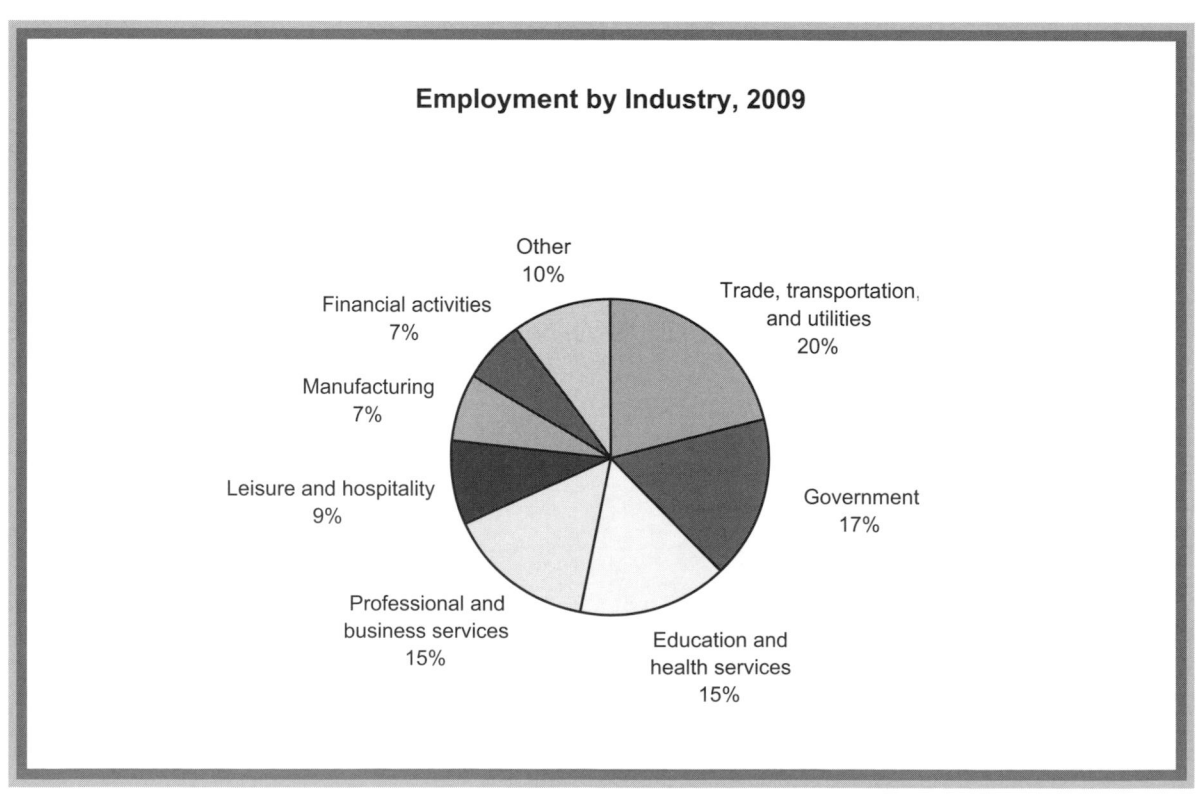

Employment by Industry, 2009

Employment by Industry: New Jersey, Selected Years, 1990–2009

(Numbers in thousands, not seasonally adjusted.)

Industry and year	January	February	March	April	May	June	July	August	September	October	November	December	Annual average
Total Nonfarm													
1990	3615.7	3620.2	3650.7	3642.7	3666.2	3711.3	3665.8	3653.1	3622.7	3599.2	3591.2	3582.4	3635.1
2000	3887.9	3896.4	3942.9	3975.9	4006.9	4060.6	4020.0	4002.5	4014.9	4017.6	4042.4	4066.5	3994.5
2001	3922.5	3931.9	3957.0	3994.2	4026.2	4073.3	4008.6	3990.9	3995.1	4010.2	4023.7	4032.5	3997.1
2002	3932.8	3940.2	3968.8	3982.7	4007.4	4042.7	3982.8	3970.8	3974.7	3983.2	4006.5	4014.6	3983.9
2003	3908.0	3898.5	3922.2	3956.5	3993.1	4032.1	4003.2	3986.4	3991.5	4006.7	4019.9	4027.9	3978.8
2004	3905.8	3907.6	3944.2	3969.9	4014.9	4063.0	4023.0	4005.1	4014.9	4026.9	4050.2	4064.0	3999.1
2005	3946.0	3951.3	3975.3	4024.8	4057.6	4111.9	4066.0	4048.7	4054.4	4059.1	4082.2	4091.9	4039.1
2006	3984.6	3992.5	4028.4	4050.8	4090.9	4143.4	4091.5	4076.5	4075.3	4088.1	4107.4	4122.3	4071.0
2007	3997.0	3993.2	4024.6	4053.9	4103.9	4159.6	4101.8	4086.0	4076.5	4103.4	4118.8	4128.4	4078.9
2008	4016.3	4017.0	4042.7	4062.7	4091.7	4133.8	4071.6	4042.1	4034.4	4033.5	4022.6	4012.6	4048.4
2009	3877.8	3862.1	3867.1	3884.4	3920.8	3958.0	3897.6	3876.1	3874.7	3894.5	3894.7	3892.6	3891.7
Total Private													
1990	3048.9	3043.9	3071.4	3057.8	3078.0	3119.7	3094.3	3090.8	3062.3	3023.6	3009.8	2999.8	3058.3
2000	3307.4	3306.1	3346.9	3379.8	3406.3	3463.7	3451.2	3444.9	3439.0	3421.2	3439.2	3462.4	3405.6
2001	3330.1	3326.5	3350.1	3385.9	3419.5	3465.1	3431.4	3421.9	3400.4	3394.7	3400.8	3408.4	3394.5
2002	3320.8	3317.8	3343.0	3358.9	3384.4	3421.7	3397.7	3395.3	3376.2	3362.9	3378.7	3387.5	3370.4
2003	3291.6	3271.1	3291.4	3325.1	3362.4	3402.2	3403.9	3401.0	3383.6	3375.9	3382.9	3391.8	3356.9
2004	3281.0	3271.3	3303.1	3329.6	3375.4	3422.0	3414.1	3406.7	3391.5	3381.9	3399.4	3412.6	3365.7
2005	3309.8	3302.7	3325.3	3373.0	3409.0	3461.0	3450.0	3443.0	3426.1	3409.3	3425.5	3435.4	3397.5
2006	3340.7	3336.1	3370.0	3392.0	3435.5	3486.1	3469.4	3465.5	3445.1	3433.0	3447.6	3462.8	3423.7
2007	3351.8	3336.6	3364.8	3394.6	3446.0	3499.1	3485.3	3476.3	3446.7	3447.8	3457.9	3467.6	3431.2
2008	3368.9	3358.3	3381.6	3401.8	3432.4	3475.5	3449.1	3434.9	3404.9	3380.9	3366.2	3357.8	3401.0
2009	3232.4	3207.9	3209.9	3224.2	3263.8	3300.4	3273.2	3263.2	3245.2	3235.6	3230.1	3229.7	3243.0
Goods-Producing													
1990	685.8	686.7	690.9	685.6	689.1	694.2	684.1	686.1	681.4	670.5	660.4	648.6	680.2
2000	556.8	555.3	565.1	573.8	577.5	583.6	574.7	577.5	578.0	578.5	578.6	577.6	573.1
2001	554.7	556.1	560.5	566.4	571.3	574.5	564.2	566.0	563.4	559.2	554.6	549.9	561.7
2002	527.3	526.6	529.5	534.1	537.7	540.0	532.7	535.9	533.9	530.2	528.0	523.7	531.6
2003	503.7	498.3	501.0	511.0	517.3	521.4	518.6	520.3	519.0	515.6	513.2	509.9	512.4
2004	490.6	487.4	495.3	501.6	508.7	514.5	513.9	514.9	514.8	511.2	509.0	506.9	505.7
2005	487.8	484.1	488.5	498.4	504.7	509.5	507.4	509.4	510.2	505.7	506.6	502.7	501.3
2006	489.5	488.7	494.8	501.9	505.9	509.2	506.5	507.0	505.3	501.1	498.7	495.9	500.4
2007	477.3	470.4	475.8	483.9	489.6	494.7	493.4	493.6	490.3	488.4	485.2	480.1	485.2
2008	463.7	460.3	464.3	469.8	472.4	475.6	472.3	471.4	467.6	462.0	454.8	445.0	464.9
2009	416.6	409.4	408.3	408.6	411.2	412.4	408.7	408.0	404.7	406.1	404.4	394.7	407.8
Mining and Logging													
1990	3.1	3.1	3.2	3.2	3.1	3.1	3.0	3.0	2.9	2.9	2.9	2.9	3.0
2000	1.9	1.7	1.8	2.0	2.0	2.0	2.0	2.0	2.1	2.0	2.0	1.9	1.9
2001	1.6	1.5	1.6	1.8	1.8	1.9	1.9	1.9	1.9	1.8	1.8	1.8	1.7
2002	1.6	1.6	1.7	1.5	1.5	1.6	1.5	1.5	1.5	1.6	1.7	1.7	1.6
2003	1.4	1.4	1.5	1.5	1.6	1.6	1.6	1.6	1.6	1.6	1.6	1.6	1.6
2004	1.5	1.4	1.5	1.6	1.7	1.7	1.7	1.7	1.7	1.7	1.7	1.7	1.6
2005	1.6	1.5	1.6	1.7	1.8	1.8	1.8	1.8	1.8	1.8	1.8	1.8	1.7
2006	1.6	1.6	1.7	1.8	1.8	1.8	1.8	1.7	1.7	1.7	1.7	1.6	1.7
2007	1.6	1.5	1.6	1.7	1.7	1.7	1.7	1.7	1.7	1.7	1.7	1.7	1.7
2008	1.6	1.5	1.6	1.6	1.7	1.7	1.7	1.7	1.7	1.7	1.7	1.6	1.7
2009	1.4	1.4	1.4	1.5	1.5	1.5	1.5	1.6	1.6	1.6	1.6	1.6	1.5
Construction													
1990	144.3	143.5	148.0	149.1	152.8	156.0	156.0	153.1	150.0	144.7	140.3	135.1	147.7
2000	138.2	135.3	143.2	148.7	151.6	154.7	153.9	155.1	154.8	153.6	153.6	152.0	149.5
2001	141.8	142.6	147.0	155.2	160.5	163.7	164.5	166.4	165.1	167.7	166.2	164.4	158.7
2002	153.0	152.2	155.2	160.7	164.1	166.9	167.5	169.2	167.5	166.9	165.7	161.8	162.6
2003	149.1	144.3	147.1	157.1	162.9	165.8	168.2	169.1	167.8	167.1	165.3	162.0	160.5
2004	151.0	148.0	154.9	162.4	167.8	171.4	173.4	174.7	173.9	173.0	171.2	169.0	165.9
2005	155.4	151.4	154.7	166.0	171.6	174.8	176.6	178.0	178.5	174.7	176.0	172.0	169.1
2006	161.5	161.2	166.5	175.4	178.8	180.9	181.0	182.2	181.1	178.3	176.7	175.2	174.9
2007	161.2	155.4	160.7	169.9	175.7	179.5	179.6	181.0	179.1	178.1	175.5	171.5	172.3
2008	158.7	156.7	160.1	165.4	168.8	171.1	171.1	170.8	168.5	166.2	161.4	154.9	164.5
2009	137.2	134.1	135.7	139.2	142.1	143.2	142.9	143.0	140.3	141.2	136.6	132.1	139.0
Manufacturing													
1990	538.4	540.1	539.7	533.3	533.2	535.1	525.1	530.0	528.5	522.9	517.2	510.6	529.5
2000	416.7	418.3	420.1	423.1	423.9	426.9	418.8	420.4	421.1	422.9	423.0	423.7	421.5
2001	411.3	412.0	411.9	409.4	409.0	408.9	397.8	397.7	396.4	389.7	386.6	383.7	401.2
2002	372.7	372.8	372.6	371.9	372.1	371.5	363.7	365.2	364.9	361.7	360.6	360.2	367.5
2003	353.2	352.6	352.4	352.4	352.8	354.0	348.8	349.6	349.6	346.9	346.3	346.3	350.4
2004	338.1	338.0	338.9	337.6	339.2	341.4	338.8	338.5	339.2	336.5	336.1	336.2	338.2
2005	330.8	331.2	332.2	330.7	331.3	332.9	329.0	329.6	329.9	329.2	328.8	328.9	330.4
2006	326.4	325.9	326.6	324.7	325.3	326.5	323.7	323.1	322.5	321.1	320.3	319.1	323.8
2007	314.5	313.5	313.5	312.3	312.2	313.5	312.1	310.9	309.5	308.6	308.0	306.9	311.3
2008	303.4	302.1	302.6	302.8	301.9	302.8	299.5	298.9	297.4	294.1	291.7	288.5	298.8
2009	278.0	273.9	271.2	267.9	267.6	267.7	264.3	263.4	262.8	263.3	266.2	261.0	267.3

Employment by Industry: New Jersey, Selected Years, 1990–2009—*Continued*
(Numbers in thousands, not seasonally adjusted.)

Industry and year	January	February	March	April	May	June	July	August	September	October	November	December	Annual average
Service-Providing													
1990	2929.9	2933.5	2959.8	2957.1	2977.1	3017.1	2981.7	2967.0	2941.3	2928.7	2930.8	2933.8	2954.8
2000	3331.1	3341.1	3377.8	3402.1	3429.4	3477.0	3445.3	3425.0	3436.9	3439.1	3463.8	3488.9	3421.4
2001	3367.8	3375.8	3396.5	3427.8	3454.9	3498.8	3444.4	3424.9	3431.7	3451.0	3469.1	3482.6	3435.4
2002	3405.5	3413.6	3439.3	3448.6	3469.7	3502.7	3450.1	3434.9	3440.8	3453.0	3478.5	3490.9	3452.3
2003	3404.3	3400.2	3421.2	3445.5	3475.8	3510.7	3484.6	3466.1	3472.5	3491.1	3506.7	3518.0	3466.4
2004	3415.2	3420.2	3448.9	3468.3	3506.2	3548.5	3509.1	3490.2	3500.1	3515.7	3541.2	3557.1	3493.4
2005	3458.2	3467.2	3486.8	3526.4	3552.9	3602.4	3558.6	3539.3	3544.2	3553.4	3575.6	3589.2	3537.9
2006	3495.1	3503.8	3533.6	3548.9	3585.0	3634.2	3585.0	3569.5	3570.0	3587.0	3608.7	3626.4	3570.6
2007	3519.7	3522.8	3548.8	3570.0	3614.3	3664.9	3608.4	3592.4	3586.2	3615.0	3633.6	3648.3	3593.7
2008	3552.6	3556.7	3578.4	3592.9	3619.3	3658.2	3599.3	3570.7	3566.8	3571.5	3567.8	3567.6	3583.5
2009	3461.2	3452.7	3458.8	3475.8	3509.6	3545.6	3488.9	3468.1	3470.0	3488.4	3490.3	3497.9	3483.9
Trade, Transportation, and Utilities													
1990	846.2	833.1	837.2	827.9	832.8	840.4	829.2	829.5	826.8	826.2	830.4	839.4	833.2
2000	885.2	876.5	882.5	887.9	892.7	899.8	896.9	896.5	900.5	905.8	922.7	941.1	899.0
2001	895.2	881.3	883.1	887.5	891.9	899.7	886.1	883.0	883.5	886.0	899.6	911.3	890.6
2002	879.3	869.5	874.8	873.0	877.3	887.4	875.0	873.2	877.8	882.3	896.1	910.7	881.4
2003	873.8	863.9	865.2	867.1	873.7	881.0	871.0	869.0	873.5	880.1	891.5	904.4	876.2
2004	866.8	859.3	863.2	860.7	872.4	882.2	871.0	869.5	872.0	879.7	893.2	906.5	874.7
2005	870.8	862.3	864.9	868.4	875.7	885.6	876.7	873.6	875.4	877.1	890.8	906.2	877.3
2006	870.9	858.6	863.1	862.4	871.8	880.5	871.5	868.9	870.8	877.4	894.0	908.8	874.9
2007	870.2	856.7	859.5	860.2	873.0	884.4	873.8	869.8	870.7	875.5	892.4	907.2	874.5
2008	870.5	856.8	859.5	856.9	864.4	872.5	860.9	856.9	856.2	856.2	862.3	869.2	861.9
2009	828.3	813.8	810.4	805.9	815.9	823.7	811.7	808.3	811.6	812.7	820.3	834.5	816.4
Wholesale Trade													
1990	231.5	231.1	232.5	230.7	230.3	231.3	228.5	228.8	227.1	225.7	224.5	223.4	228.7
2000	237.3	237.7	239.0	240.9	242.5	241.2	244.1	243.2	243.6	242.8	242.9	245.2	241.7
2001	241.7	242.1	242.7	243.5	243.3	244.1	242.7	242.1	241.7	239.5	239.4	239.5	241.8
2002	238.5	238.2	239.3	237.8	237.7	238.1	235.5	234.8	234.4	234.8	234.5	234.9	236.5
2003	232.3	232.0	232.1	233.5	233.6	234.4	234.0	232.6	232.1	231.6	231.6	232.1	232.7
2004	228.7	228.9	230.5	230.1	231.2	232.5	232.9	233.4	233.0	233.7	233.5	234.3	231.9
2005	232.7	233.2	233.2	233.8	234.3	236.0	234.7	234.9	234.1	232.9	232.9	233.3	233.8
2006	230.7	230.9	231.4	231.8	233.4	234.8	234.4	233.8	233.0	232.8	233.4	234.4	232.9
2007	230.8	230.3	230.8	231.3	232.6	234.9	234.3	234.1	233.2	233.8	233.8	234.6	232.9
2008	231.5	231.3	231.8	231.2	232.3	233.1	231.7	230.5	229.1	228.0	226.2	225.2	230.2
2009	221.5	219.5	218.1	217.7	217.7	218.2	215.9	214.9	213.8	214.7	214.6	214.4	216.8
Retail Trade													
1990	449.8	437.2	437.9	431.7	435.3	440.8	437.8	437.4	433.4	433.1	439.0	448.2	438.4
2000	457.9	448.7	452.7	453.8	457.5	464.8	463.2	465.2	462.0	463.8	479.9	495.4	463.7
2001	465.5	451.0	452.4	453.3	459.3	466.9	460.2	460.2	454.9	459.1	475.2	487.5	462.2
2002	461.2	451.7	455.7	455.1	459.4	468.1	464.3	464.4	461.9	462.8	477.1	491.9	464.5
2003	461.9	453.3	454.1	456.5	462.3	468.5	465.3	466.1	462.7	467.9	479.6	491.1	465.8
2004	461.5	453.8	455.3	455.1	463.3	471.1	468.5	468.2	463.0	468.7	481.9	494.2	467.1
2005	466.1	457.3	457.7	460.8	466.7	473.3	472.5	470.7	465.1	467.2	479.7	492.3	469.1
2006	465.7	452.9	456.7	456.3	462.1	469.1	466.7	465.7	459.9	466.0	481.0	491.9	466.2
2007	464.8	452.7	454.2	455.5	463.4	470.9	469.1	466.6	459.7	463.3	479.3	489.9	465.8
2008	463.7	450.0	451.3	449.7	455.3	462.5	460.5	458.3	452.2	454.5	462.4	469.5	457.5
2009	439.4	427.9	426.7	425.2	433.2	439.8	437.4	436.8	433.9	432.6	439.7	449.4	435.2
Transportation and Utilities													
1990	164.9	164.8	166.8	165.5	167.2	168.3	162.9	163.3	166.3	167.4	166.9	167.8	166.0
2000	190.0	190.1	190.8	193.2	192.7	193.8	189.6	188.1	194.9	199.2	199.9	200.5	193.5
2001	188.0	188.2	188.0	188.7	189.3	188.7	183.2	180.7	186.9	187.4	185.0	184.3	186.5
2002	179.6	179.6	179.8	180.1	180.2	181.2	175.2	174.0	181.5	184.7	184.5	183.9	180.4
2003	179.6	178.6	179.0	177.1	177.8	178.1	171.7	170.3	178.7	180.6	180.3	181.2	177.8
2004	176.6	176.6	177.4	175.5	177.9	178.6	169.6	167.9	176.0	177.3	177.8	178.0	175.8
2005	172.0	171.8	174.0	173.8	174.7	176.3	169.5	168.0	176.2	177.0	178.2	180.6	174.3
2006	174.5	174.8	175.0	174.3	176.3	176.6	170.4	169.4	177.9	178.6	179.6	182.5	175.8
2007	174.6	173.7	174.5	173.4	177.0	178.6	170.4	169.1	177.8	178.4	179.3	182.7	175.8
2008	175.3	175.5	176.4	176.0	176.8	176.9	168.7	168.1	174.9	173.7	173.7	174.5	174.2
2009	167.4	166.4	165.6	163.0	165.0	165.7	158.4	156.6	163.9	165.4	166.0	170.7	164.5
Information													
1990	124.1	122.3	122.7	120.2	119.2	120.6	122.3	121.4	120.7	117.2	117.7	117.6	120.5
2000	126.6	126.3	127.4	126.2	126.8	128.5	128.0	123.7	127.4	126.2	127.4	128.6	126.9
2001	127.2	127.8	128.4	127.0	127.3	128.1	126.1	123.5	126.3	124.5	125.3	125.3	126.4
2002	121.0	120.3	120.3	116.3	116.5	115.7	111.4	111.0	109.4	104.6	106.1	105.6	113.2
2003	102.8	102.4	102.8	102.0	102.1	102.5	102.3	102.9	101.0	101.1	101.4	101.2	102.0
2004	100.1	98.7	99.6	98.2	98.0	97.9	97.3	97.1	96.2	96.9	97.5	97.9	98.0
2005	96.7	96.4	97.0	96.2	96.6	97.8	97.4	97.2	96.7	96.9	97.8	98.3	97.1
2006	97.4	98.1	98.2	97.0	97.4	98.3	97.6	98.0	97.8	96.3	96.1	96.4	97.4
2007	96.3	97.1	97.5	96.7	96.5	96.7	96.5	97.2	95.4	94.0	94.3	93.9	96.0
2008	93.7	94.2	94.2	92.8	92.2	92.7	91.0	90.8	89.7	88.4	88.3	87.8	91.3
2009	86.5	85.9	86.1	84.7	85.0	85.0	83.9	84.4	82.7	81.9	81.3	82.5	84.2

Employment by Industry: New Jersey, Selected Years, 1990–2009—*Continued*

(Numbers in thousands, not seasonally adjusted.)

Industry and year	January	February	March	April	May	June	July	August	September	October	November	December	Annual average
Financial Activities													
1990	237.9	237.7	238.3	236.3	236.0	238.3	237.8	236.1	231.5	228.3	226.6	226.6	234.2
2000	262.5	263.0	264.1	264.9	266.1	271.1	272.4	271.6	268.8	265.8	265.4	266.7	266.8
2001	262.0	261.9	262.2	265.5	267.1	271.1	270.0	269.1	266.8	280.9	279.9	281.3	269.8
2002	277.3	276.2	275.1	275.7	276.1	277.7	279.4	278.9	276.6	275.1	275.8	276.4	276.7
2003	274.5	273.8	274.3	274.0	275.0	278.2	279.5	279.6	276.9	276.3	276.1	275.8	276.2
2004	273.1	272.7	273.6	275.6	276.9	279.5	280.9	280.4	277.0	277.2	277.7	278.1	276.9
2005	275.8	275.1	275.9	277.5	278.7	281.8	284.0	284.4	281.7	279.6	280.8	281.0	279.7
2006	276.8	276.5	277.3	278.3	279.6	281.9	283.6	283.0	279.1	278.4	278.1	278.3	279.2
2007	274.9	274.3	274.3	274.8	276.1	278.7	279.9	279.0	274.7	274.0	274.0	273.9	275.7
2008	272.0	271.9	272.3	271.7	272.4	274.2	273.5	272.7	268.4	265.7	264.6	264.0	270.3
2009	258.6	257.7	256.8	257.2	257.4	258.4	257.5	256.3	253.8	250.6	250.0	249.0	255.3
Professional and Business Services													
1990	435.7	437.6	441.4	438.8	439.3	445.0	444.5	444.9	440.2	432.9	430.1	428.3	438.2
2000	575.8	579.3	591.6	595.6	597.6	610.9	608.7	610.3	608.5	598.7	601.0	604.3	598.5
2001	580.7	582.0	590.9	597.3	599.8	607.5	599.2	599.6	595.0	588.9	586.3	582.4	592.4
2002	569.0	570.8	581.0	584.2	583.6	588.2	584.9	587.8	582.2	580.1	581.9	579.9	581.1
2003	562.2	559.0	565.2	572.0	575.1	581.0	585.4	589.1	587.6	586.8	586.8	587.6	578.2
2004	564.0	562.7	572.1	582.0	585.3	592.1	592.1	593.0	591.5	592.3	593.9	592.8	584.5
2005	570.0	571.5	577.0	593.0	594.2	604.3	600.3	601.6	599.8	600.7	600.3	597.4	592.5
2006	577.8	583.3	592.3	598.2	603.9	613.7	611.9	616.0	613.1	614.2	615.6	615.1	604.6
2007	588.8	590.1	599.1	610.3	616.5	626.5	628.0	630.7	626.3	627.6	628.9	626.9	616.6
2008	605.5	606.8	612.7	618.9	620.0	626.5	625.5	626.2	620.4	615.0	611.1	605.5	616.2
2009	583.3	578.3	578.1	585.7	586.9	593.0	589.2	589.9	587.2	583.1	576.4	573.7	583.7
Education and Health Services													
1990	355.6	359.6	362.6	362.2	361.2	362.5	356.3	355.4	362.6	366.9	370.3	370.3	362.1
2000	484.3	488.2	490.7	494.2	494.7	496.8	493.3	491.0	497.9	503.1	506.2	509.2	495.8
2001	492.6	496.4	499.3	504.4	507.8	511.1	503.6	501.6	505.8	510.3	514.3	517.1	505.3
2002	517.6	522.9	524.4	526.2	528.8	529.4	524.7	522.0	526.6	531.3	535.6	536.2	527.1
2003	532.3	532.5	536.2	537.3	540.9	540.2	536.5	531.8	537.3	541.6	544.1	544.8	538.0
2004	537.4	539.9	543.6	544.5	548.9	549.6	543.2	540.1	545.6	552.5	554.7	556.4	546.4
2005	549.3	552.9	555.3	556.9	561.3	561.0	555.3	551.2	557.1	565.0	567.6	568.1	558.4
2006	560.8	563.2	567.1	566.1	571.1	571.3	563.7	562.0	567.3	572.7	575.9	579.1	568.4
2007	571.6	575.6	580.1	577.4	583.8	582.0	575.1	571.4	577.2	586.7	586.1	589.6	579.7
2008	583.7	587.7	590.5	590.3	592.2	593.2	584.9	581.7	587.8	593.1	595.3	599.8	590.0
2009	590.5	594.5	597.0	597.7	600.2	601.3	592.1	588.5	594.8	605.9	608.1	608.3	598.2
Leisure and Hospitality													
1990	244.0	247.5	257.9	266.6	279.5	296.5	297.6	295.6	279.7	263.8	257.5	252.6	269.9
2000	278.0	278.5	285.1	295.4	308.3	328.1	330.8	329.3	315.5	301.5	296.3	292.6	303.7
2001	278.9	281.6	285.4	296.0	310.6	327.2	334.2	332.4	315.6	299.1	294.6	294.2	304.1
2002	283.3	285.0	290.8	302.2	316.0	333.2	338.8	336.5	322.4	310.8	306.8	306.0	311.0
2003	293.7	292.7	297.3	310.3	325.8	342.8	354.8	352.9	334.9	321.0	316.2	314.0	321.4
2004	298.1	299.2	303.5	314.0	330.3	349.5	358.5	355.3	340.5	318.1	319.3	319.5	325.5
2005	305.1	305.3	311.3	324.2	338.8	359.8	367.5	364.9	348.2	327.7	324.5	323.9	333.4
2006	310.7	310.8	319.0	327.5	343.7	366.5	371.5	368.7	352.7	333.2	329.2	328.1	338.5
2007	313.2	312.8	318.2	328.0	345.6	367.9	371.9	369.2	349.7	337.9	333.4	332.1	340.0
2008	317.3	317.9	325.0	336.2	352.2	371.7	373.4	368.9	351.7	337.7	327.5	324.4	342.0
2009	309.1	308.3	313.0	323.9	344.8	361.7	365.7	364.0	349.8	334.3	328.7	326.3	335.8
Other Services													
1990	119.6	119.4	120.4	120.2	120.9	122.2	122.5	121.8	119.4	117.8	116.8	116.4	119.7
2000	138.2	139.0	140.4	141.8	142.6	144.9	146.4	145.0	142.4	141.6	141.6	142.3	142.1
2001	138.8	139.4	140.3	141.8	143.7	145.9	148.0	146.7	144.0	145.8	146.2	146.9	143.9
2002	146.0	146.5	147.1	147.2	148.4	150.1	150.8	150.0	147.3	148.5	148.4	149.0	148.3
2003	148.6	148.5	149.4	151.4	152.5	155.1	155.8	155.4	153.4	153.4	153.6	154.1	152.6
2004	150.9	151.4	152.2	153.0	154.9	156.7	157.2	156.4	153.9	154.0	154.1	154.5	154.1
2005	154.3	155.1	155.4	158.4	159.0	161.2	161.4	160.7	157.0	156.6	157.1	157.8	157.8
2006	156.8	156.9	158.2	160.6	162.1	164.7	163.1	161.9	159.0	159.7	160.0	161.1	160.3
2007	159.5	159.6	160.3	163.3	164.9	168.2	166.7	165.4	162.4	163.7	163.6	163.9	163.5
2008	162.5	162.7	163.1	165.2	166.6	169.1	167.6	166.3	163.1	162.8	162.3	162.1	164.5
2009	159.5	160.0	160.2	160.5	162.4	164.9	164.4	163.8	160.6	161.0	160.9	160.7	161.6
Government													
1990	566.8	576.3	579.3	584.9	588.2	591.6	571.5	562.3	560.4	575.6	581.4	582.6	576.7
2000	580.5	590.3	596.0	596.1	600.6	596.9	568.8	557.6	575.9	596.4	603.2	604.1	588.8
2001	592.4	605.4	606.9	608.3	606.7	608.2	577.2	569.0	594.7	615.5	622.9	624.1	602.6
2002	612.0	622.4	625.8	623.8	623.0	621.0	585.1	575.5	598.5	620.3	627.8	627.1	613.5
2003	616.4	627.4	630.8	631.4	630.7	629.9	599.3	585.4	607.9	630.8	637.0	636.1	621.9
2004	624.8	636.3	641.1	640.3	639.5	641.0	608.9	598.4	623.4	645.0	650.8	651.4	633.4
2005	636.2	648.6	650.0	651.8	648.6	650.9	616.0	605.7	628.3	649.8	656.7	656.5	641.6
2006	643.9	656.4	658.4	658.8	655.4	657.3	622.1	611.0	630.2	655.1	659.8	659.5	647.3
2007	645.2	656.6	659.8	659.3	657.9	660.5	616.5	609.7	629.8	655.6	660.9	660.8	647.7
2008	647.4	658.7	661.1	660.9	659.3	658.3	622.5	607.2	629.5	652.6	656.4	654.8	647.4
2009	645.4	654.2	657.2	660.2	657.0	657.6	624.4	612.9	629.5	658.9	664.6	662.9	648.7

Average Weekly Hours by Selected Industry: New Jersey, 2007–2009

(Not seasonally adjusted.)

Industry and year	January	February	March	April	May	June	July	August	September	October	November	December	Annual average
Total Private													
2007	33.8	33.7	33.8	34.0	34.2	34.2	34.3	34.1	34.2	33.9	33.9	34.3	34.0
2008	33.3	33.3	33.8	33.9	33.8	34.0	33.8	33.7	33.4	33.4	33.7	33.3	33.6
2009	33.0	33.4	33.3	33.1	33.5	33.5	33.7	33.9	33.7	33.9	33.9	33.9	33.6
Goods-Producing													
2007	39.1	39.0	39.4	38.9	39.3	39.6	39.5	38.9	39.0	39.0	38.8	39.6	39.2
2008	39.6	38.8	39.5	39.7	39.2	40.0	39.2	39.4	39.1	38.9	38.5	38.6	39.2
2009	38.3	38.1	38.4	37.6	38.6	38.2	38.3	36.9	36.5	36.8	37.4	37.9	37.8
Construction													
2007	38.2	36.2	37.5	37.2	38.6	38.5	38.3	37.9	38.3	38.1	37.1	37.4	37.8
2008	37.9	36.4	37.1	37.2	35.8	37.4	36.8	37.4	37.4	37.1	36.1	35.8	36.9
2009	35.8	36.3	36.7	35.6	37.5	36.1	37.1	36.5	35.3	35.3	35.6	36.2	36.2
Manufacturing													
2007	39.4	40.0	40.1	39.6	39.5	40.1	40.1	39.6	39.4	39.6	39.9	40.5	39.8
2008	38.6	39.9	40.3	40.6	40.7	41.1	40.2	40.3	39.9	39.8	39.8	40.0	40.1
2009	39.6	39.1	39.4	38.8	39.3	39.5	39.0	39.4	39.3	39.5	39.7	40.0	39.4
Trade, Transportation, and Utilities													
2007	34.2	34.0	34.4	34.7	35.0	35.2	35.5	35.2	35.1	34.5	34.5	34.7	34.8
2008	33.3	33.3	34.0	33.8	33.5	34.2	33.1	33.0	32.6	32.6	33.0	33.4	33.3
2009	32.5	32.9	33.0	32.3	32.8	33.3	33.7	33.8	33.3	33.7	33.8	34.0	33.3
Financial Activities													
2007	36.2	35.9	37.1	37.6	36.5	36.2	36.4	36.4	36.7	36.5	36.7	37.2	36.6
2008	36.4	36.2	36.9	36.9	37.8	37.7	37.8	37.3	37.1	37.0	36.8	36.6	37.0
2009	36.9	37.1	37.0	37.3	36.5	36.3	36.2	36.5	36.4	36.0	36.9	36.4	36.6
Professional and Business Services													
2007	34.7	35.1	34.5	35.0	34.9	35.2	35.0	34.8	34.9	35.2	35.1	35.6	35.0
2008	33.5	33.8	34.2	34.5	34.4	35.2	33.8	33.9	34.0	34.6	34.5	34.4	34.2
2009	33.9	34.9	34.9	34.8	36.3	35.7	35.0	36.2	36.0	36.3	36.5	35.7	35.5
Education and Health Services													
2007	30.6	30.6	30.7	30.7	31.0	30.9	30.9	30.6	31.3	31.0	30.8	31.2	30.9
2008	30.2	30.3	30.6	30.5	30.4	30.6	30.5	30.4	30.6	30.6	30.8	31.1	30.6
2009	31.1	31.3	30.9	31.1	31.1	31.1	31.7	31.8	31.3	32.5	32.7	32.3	31.6
Leisure and Hospitality													
2007	28.8	28.8	28.7	29.3	29.5	29.2	29.9	29.8	29.1	28.6	28.8	28.5	29.1
2008	28.1	28.2	28.3	28.2	28.2	28.9	29.8	29.4	28.1	27.9	26.6	26.0	28.2
2009	26.3	26.7	26.1	26.0	26.7	26.8	28.2	28.3	27.9	26.7	26.5	25.9	26.9
Other Services													
2007	30.5	30.6	29.6	30.5	31.2	30.8	32.0	32.4	31.3	31.0	31.5	31.9	31.1
2008	32.5	32.1	32.4	32.0	32.0	33.0	32.4	33.2	32.7	32.3	33.7	33.1	32.6
2009	32.8	33.0	32.9	32.4	32.4	32.3	32.5	33.8	33.9	33.2	33.4	33.3	33.0

Average Hourly Earnings by Selected Industry: New Jersey, 2007–2009

(Dollars, not seasonally adjusted.)

Industry and year	January	February	March	April	May	June	July	August	September	October	November	December	Annual average
Total Private													
2007	25.90	25.46	25.03	25.14	24.63	24.51	24.47	24.29	24.64	24.73	24.68	24.69	24.84
2008	25.58	25.47	25.51	25.51	25.15	25.19	24.98	25.27	25.47	25.26	24.77	25.71	25.32
2009	25.56	25.71	26.05	25.83	25.64	25.49	25.53	25.63	26.09	26.05	26.84	26.66	25.92
Goods-Producing													
2007	27.04	26.60	26.08	26.62	27.39	27.14	27.48	27.61	27.85	27.84	27.58	27.30	27.22
2008	27.30	27.03	27.37	27.45	27.28	27.32	27.21	27.30	27.69	27.44	27.66	28.09	27.42
2009	27.42	28.16	28.22	27.63	27.61	27.66	27.18	28.06	28.04	27.84	27.86	28.64	27.85
Construction													
2007	31.94	32.42	31.48	31.98	34.72	34.68	35.25	35.37	35.35	35.35	35.38	34.20	34.09
2008	33.26	33.43	33.46	34.01	33.84	33.87	33.70	34.04	35.08	34.45	34.33	34.84	34.03
2009	33.62	34.51	34.19	33.62	33.25	33.83	33.34	33.19	33.28	33.18	33.73	33.96	33.63
Manufacturing													
2007	24.95	24.46	23.93	24.39	24.05	23.72	23.86	23.86	24.18	24.15	24.07	24.25	24.16
2008	23.74	24.07	24.22	24.12	23.99	24.02	23.85	23.73	23.99	23.66	24.39	24.84	24.05
2009	24.53	25.19	25.25	24.63	24.79	24.60	23.85	23.87	23.82	23.67	23.69	24.03	24.33
Trade, Transportation, and Utilities													
2007	24.33	24.00	22.97	23.61	22.80	22.71	22.86	22.50	22.95	23.00	22.72	22.55	23.07
2008	25.16	24.51	24.59	24.27	23.82	23.80	24.11	24.58	24.69	24.53	24.53	24.27	24.40
2009	24.52	24.01	24.35	23.93	23.98	23.44	23.69	23.57	23.59	23.35	24.11	23.26	23.81
Financial Activities													
2007	30.93	28.53	28.37	20.67	27.48	29.82	29.43	29.27	28.85	28.79	29.08	29.12	29.03
2008	28.74	28.48	28.60	28.91	28.48	28.70	27.61	28.02	27.99	27.99	28.43	28.40	28.36
2009	28.21	28.57	30.80	32.35	31.43	31.35	33.03	34.30	33.08	32.99	33.00	32.55	31.78
Professional and Business Services													
2007	28.73	28.79	29.36	28.06	27.28	26.87	27.02	26.95	27.13	26.81	27.31	27.70	27.64
2008	28.19	28.91	29.32	28.56	28.36	28.60	28.79	28.89	28.51	28.23	29.19	30.04	28.80
2009	29.66	30.50	30.41	29.79	28.79	28.72	29.09	28.77	28.78	29.03	30.36	30.46	29.52
Education and Health Services													
2007	25.50	25.52	24.85	25.42	24.93	24.89	25.09	24.97	24.88	25.37	25.36	25.25	25.17
2008	25.55	25.15	25.37	25.35	25.11	25.11	25.33	25.46	25.48	25.29	25.43	25.44	25.34
2009	25.25	25.17	25.55	25.46	25.51	25.37	25.31	25.50	25.61	25.27	25.70	25.93	25.47
Leisure and Hospitality													
2007	20.44	19.60	19.13	18.64	18.18	17.59	16.97	16.64	16.95	16.93	16.83	17.08	17.86
2008	16.69	16.74	17.06	16.81	16.49	16.17	15.54	15.57	15.82	15.49	15.30	15.59	16.10
2009	15.33	15.52	15.29	15.68	16.84	17.97	17.35	16.96	16.65	16.42	16.63	16.33	16.47
Other Services													
2007	19.08	19.85	20.29	19.45	18.77	18.51	17.91	17.82	18.41	18.57	18.68	18.89	18.83
2008	18.75	18.70	18.84	18.49	18.48	18.88	18.43	18.20	18.55	19.28	19.42	19.48	18.79
2009	20.33	21.02	21.16	21.63	21.63	21.97	21.59	22.27	22.67	23.43	23.61	23.13	22.05

Average Weekly Earnings by Selected Industry: New Jersey, 2007–2009

(Dollars, not seasonally adjusted.)

Industry and year	January	February	March	April	May	June	July	August	September	October	November	December	Annual average
Total Private													
2007	875.42	858.00	846.01	854.76	842.35	838.24	839.32	828.29	842.69	838.35	836.65	846.87	844.56
2008	851.81	848.15	862.24	864.79	850.07	856.46	844.32	851.60	850.70	843.68	834.75	856.14	850.75
2009	843.48	858.71	867.47	854.97	858.94	853.92	860.36	868.86	879.23	883.10	909.88	903.77	870.91
Goods-Producing													
2007	1057.26	1037.40	1027.55	1035.52	1076.43	1074.74	1085.46	1074.03	1086.15	1085.76	1070.10	1081.08	1067.02
2008	1081.08	1048.76	1081.12	1089.77	1069.38	1092.80	1066.63	1075.62	1082.68	1067.42	1064.91	1084.27	1074.86
2009	1050.19	1072.90	1083.65	1038.89	1065.75	1056.61	1040.99	1035.41	1023.46	1024.51	1041.96	1085.46	1052.73
Construction													
2007	1220.11	1173.60	1180.50	1189.66	1340.19	1335.18	1350.08	1340.52	1353.91	1346.84	1312.60	1279.08	1288.60
2008	1260.55	1216.85	1241.37	1265.17	1211.47	1266.74	1240.16	1273.10	1311.99	1278.10	1239.31	1247.27	1255.71
2009	1203.60	1252.71	1254.77	1196.87	1246.88	1221.26	1236.91	1211.44	1174.78	1171.25	1200.79	1229.35	1217.41
Manufacturing													
2007	983.03	978.40	959.59	965.84	949.98	951.17	956.79	944.86	952.69	956.34	960.39	982.13	961.57
2008	916.36	960.39	976.07	979.27	976.39	987.22	958.77	956.32	957.20	941.67	970.72	993.60	964.41
2009	971.39	984.93	994.85	955.64	974.25	971.70	930.15	940.48	936.13	934.97	940.49	961.20	958.60
Trade, Transportation, and Utilities													
2007	832.09	816.00	790.17	819.27	798.00	799.39	811.53	792.00	805.55	793.50	783.84	782.49	802.84
2008	837.83	816.18	836.06	820.33	797.97	813.96	798.04	811.14	804.89	799.68	809.49	810.62	812.52
2009	796.90	789.93	803.55	772.94	786.54	780.55	798.35	796.67	785.55	786.90	814.92	790.84	792.87
Financial Activities													
2007	1119.67	1024.23	1052.53	1077.99	1003.02	1079.48	1071.25	1065.43	1058.80	1050.84	1067.24	1083.26	1062.50
2008	1046.14	1030.98	1055.34	1066.78	1076.54	1081.99	1043.66	1045.15	1038.43	1035.63	1046.22	1039.44	1049.32
2009	1040.95	1059.95	1139.60	1206.66	1147.20	1138.01	1195.69	1251.95	1204.11	1187.64	1217.70	1184.82	1163.15
Professional and Business Services													
2007	996.93	1010.53	1012.92	982.10	952.07	945.82	945.70	937.86	946.84	943.71	958.58	986.12	967.40
2008	944.37	977.16	1002.74	985.32	975.58	1006.72	973.10	979.37	969.34	976.76	1007.06	1033.38	984.96
2009	1005.47	1064.45	1061.31	1036.69	1045.08	1025.30	1018.15	1041.47	1036.08	1053.79	1108.14	1087.42	1047.96
Education and Health Services													
2007	780.30	780.91	762.90	780.39	772.83	769.10	775.28	764.08	778.74	786.47	781.09	787.80	777.75
2008	771.61	762.05	776.32	773.18	763.34	768.37	772.57	773.98	779.69	773.87	783.24	791.18	775.40
2009	785.28	787.82	789.50	791.81	793.36	789.01	802.33	810.90	801.59	821.28	840.39	837.54	804.85
Leisure and Hospitality													
2007	588.67	564.48	549.03	546.15	536.31	513.63	507.40	495.87	493.25	484.20	484.70	486.78	519.73
2008	468.99	472.07	482.80	474.04	465.02	467.31	463.09	457.76	444.54	432.17	406.98	405.34	454.02
2009	403.18	414.38	399.07	407.68	449.63	481.60	489.27	479.97	464.54	438.41	440.70	422.95	443.04
Other Services													
2007	581.94	607.41	600.58	593.23	585.62	570.11	573.12	577.37	576.23	575.67	588.42	602.59	585.61
2008	609.38	600.27	610.42	591.68	591.36	623.04	597.13	604.24	606.59	622.74	654.45	644.79	612.55
2009	666.82	693.66	696.16	700.81	700.81	709.63	701.68	752.73	768.51	777.88	788.57	770.23	727.65

NEW MEXICO
At a Glance

Population:
  1990 census: 1,515,069
  2000 census: 1,819,046
  2009 estimate: 2,009,671

Percent change in population:
  1990–2000: 20.1%
  2000–2009: 10.5%

Percent change in total nonfarm employment:
  1990–2009: 40.0%
  2008–2009: -4.1%

Industry with the largest growth in employment, 1990–2009 (thousands):
  Education and Health Services, 67.8

Industry with the largest decline or smallest growth in employment, 1990–2009 (thousands):
  Manufacturing, -7.9

Civilian labor force:
  1990: 711,891
  2000: 852,293
  2009: 955,904

Unemployment rate and rank among states (lowest to highest):
  1990: 6.8%, 46th
  2000: 5.0%, 44th
  2009: 7.2%, 16th

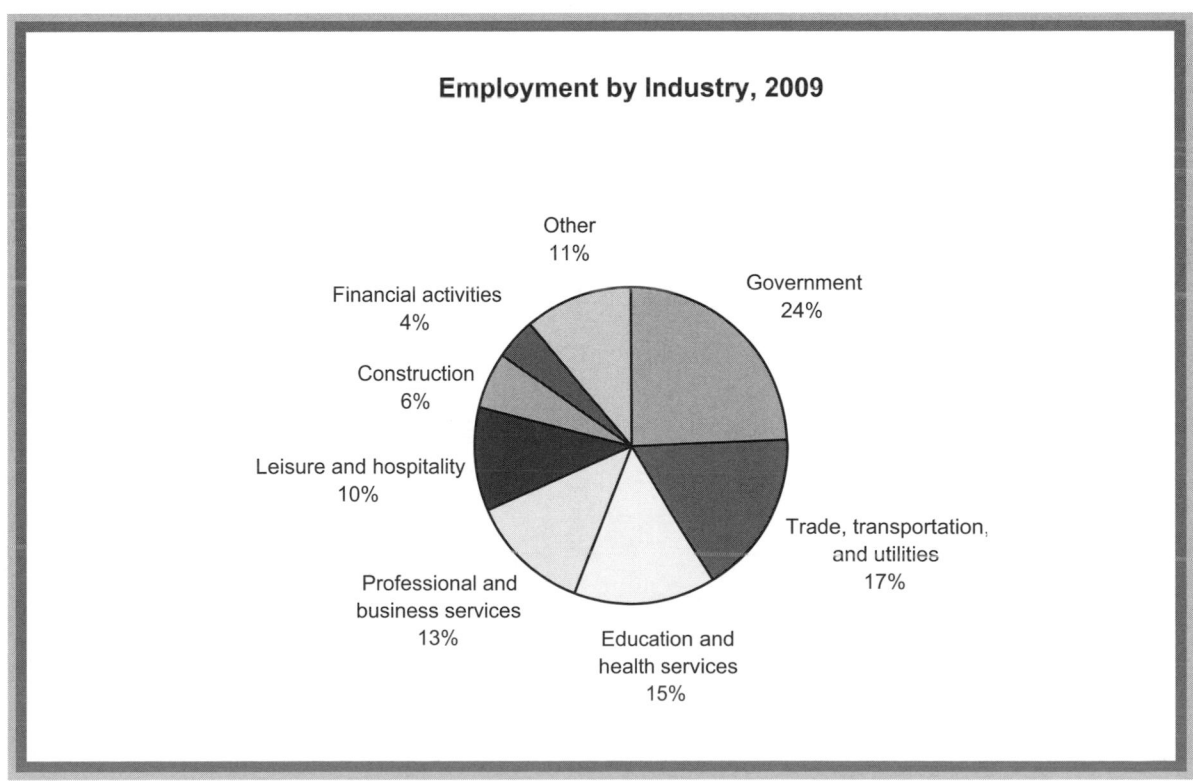

Employment by Industry, 2009

Other 11%
Government 24%
Financial activities 4%
Construction 6%
Leisure and hospitality 10%
Trade, transportation, and utilities 17%
Professional and business services 13%
Education and health services 15%

Employment by Industry: New Mexico, Selected Years, 1990–2009

(Numbers in thousands, not seasonally adjusted.)

Industry and year	January	February	March	April	May	June	July	August	September	October	November	December	Annual average
Total Nonfarm													
1990	561.2	565.9	572.0	578.8	586.1	587.7	579.0	582.8	587.6	587.1	590.4	586.2	580.4
2000	722.5	730.2	738.0	741.0	747.3	746.2	742.3	748.3	754.9	752.3	755.5	759.1	744.8
2001	739.8	748.1	755.1	756.4	762.3	762.5	754.7	759.6	763.9	759.9	761.1	762.6	757.2
2002	748.5	754.1	760.9	764.2	770.0	769.4	763.7	768.3	774.1	770.6	773.7	776.2	766.1
2003	759.5	765.2	769.9	772.6	777.2	776.5	772.1	776.7	781.4	783.8	784.8	787.4	775.6
2004	769.8	778.0	783.8	788.7	792.6	791.1	787.0	789.5	795.3	801.5	802.5	805.2	790.4
2005	786.5	793.6	799.1	806.9	810.1	808.6	805.2	809.7	818.8	818.5	822.3	824.5	808.7
2006	809.2	819.7	827.1	828.6	835.2	837.3	828.0	832.0	842.5	839.5	842.9	844.3	832.2
2007	824.4	833.9	842.3	840.2	845.6	845.9	837.8	843.2	850.2	851.9	853.9	855.3	843.7
2008	834.0	843.3	847.5	848.8	852.8	850.2	841.7	846.8	854.7	852.2	847.2	842.4	846.8
2009	816.9	818.2	816.7	815.4	816.5	811.2	802.7	807.4	812.5	810.4	812.6	809.4	812.5
Total Private													
1990	416.9	415.3	420.3	425.6	432.7	439.3	436.2	440.3	437.1	434.5	434.8	435.4	430.7
2000	543.8	546.3	551.4	554.5	559.3	566.9	565.1	570.8	570.8	567.6	570.8	573.5	561.7
2001	560.5	562.5	567.7	568.8	574.2	578.4	576.2	579.6	574.6	571.6	572.6	573.8	571.7
2002	563.4	563.4	568.8	572.1	576.9	579.1	579.2	582.5	580.3	576.7	579.0	581.0	575.2
2003	569.0	569.9	573.4	575.3	580.6	582.8	583.8	587.4	584.6	584.6	585.8	588.3	580.5
2004	576.8	578.5	583.1	587.9	592.3	594.5	596.3	597.5	595.9	599.3	599.7	602.8	592.1
2005	590.3	591.5	595.7	603.2	606.0	609.1	611.4	614.9	615.4	613.9	617.3	620.1	607.4
2006	610.4	614.1	620.8	623.2	629.3	645.7	642.5	645.1	647.0	642.8	645.9	647.4	634.5
2007	633.8	637.9	644.6	643.4	648.9	653.2	651.3	655.5	653.9	653.7	654.7	655.9	648.9
2008	640.8	644.6	647.8	649.3	652.4	654.5	652.4	656.3	654.9	650.8	645.3	640.8	649.2
2009	621.2	617.3	615.0	612.8	614.3	613.8	611.7	615.4	613.4	608.7	609.0	607.1	613.3
Goods-Producing													
1990	81.2	80.3	81.6	82.8	85.0	86.3	86.1	87.5	87.1	87.0	86.3	85.1	84.6
2000	95.4	96.2	97.6	98.7	100.4	102.4	103.4	105.9	105.7	104.7	104.0	103.9	101.5
2001	101.6	101.7	103.3	103.8	105.2	106.4	105.9	107.1	105.3	103.6	102.3	100.9	103.9
2002	97.6	96.6	97.5	98.0	98.8	99.2	99.4	100.5	98.9	98.5	97.2	96.3	98.2
2003	94.4	94.1	94.9	95.9	97.4	99.0	99.7	100.9	99.6	100.1	99.2	98.4	97.8
2004	96.1	96.0	97.2	99.0	100.6	102.1	104.2	104.4	103.9	104.8	103.6	104.1	101.3
2005	101.4	101.4	103.0	104.5	105.7	107.4	109.8	110.7	111.2	111.3	111.6	111.4	107.5
2006	110.1	111.7	113.1	113.8	115.3	117.2	117.5	118.3	118.4	118.3	116.5	115.7	115.5
2007	112.5	113.1	114.4	114.5	115.9	117.6	117.2	118.1	117.0	117.1	115.8	114.9	115.7
2008	112.0	112.5	113.1	114.2	114.9	115.9	115.1	116.6	115.9	114.3	111.6	108.3	113.7
2009	102.2	99.6	97.4	95.7	95.2	95.4	94.8	95.4	93.9	92.5	92.1	90.2	95.4
Mining and Logging													
1990	14.8	14.4	14.4	14.5	14.7	15.0	15.1	15.1	15.1	15.6	16.0	16.0	15.0
2000	13.9	14.2	14.3	14.6	14.8	14.8	14.9	15.3	15.4	15.2	15.3	15.6	14.8
2001	15.6	15.7	15.8	15.8	16.0	15.8	16.0	16.1	15.8	15.3	14.9	14.9	15.6
2002	14.6	14.4	14.3	14.0	14.0	13.9	13.8	13.9	13.7	13.9	13.8	13.8	14.0
2003	13.8	13.9	14.0	14.1	14.3	14.4	14.4	14.4	14.4	14.6	14.7	14.8	14.3
2004	14.4	14.3	14.5	14.7	14.8	15.0	15.1	15.4	15.4	15.6	15.7	16.1	15.1
2005	15.9	15.9	16.1	16.2	16.4	16.6	17.2	17.4	17.8	17.8	17.7	17.7	16.9
2006	17.8	18.0	18.1	18.3	18.5	18.8	18.8	19.1	19.1	19.2	19.1	19.2	18.7
2007	19.3	19.0	19.1	19.2	19.4	19.7	19.9	20.0	19.6	19.7	19.9	19.9	19.6
2008	19.8	19.8	20.0	20.6	21.0	21.3	21.5	22.1	22.1	22.1	21.9	21.3	21.1
2009	19.9	19.1	18.3	17.7	17.4	17.3	17.2	17.2	16.8	16.8	16.6	16.2	17.5
Construction													
1990	29.8	29.5	30.4	31.1	32.4	33.1	32.9	33.0	32.1	32.1	31.8	31.0	31.6
2000	41.1	41.4	42.5	43.4	44.4	45.7	46.4	47.2	47.0	46.7	46.5	46.3	44.8
2001	44.5	44.7	45.9	46.7	47.9	49.4	49.1	49.4	48.2	47.6	48.0	46.9	47.4
2002	44.7	44.3	45.1	45.8	46.3	46.5	46.1	46.8	45.8	46.2	46.0	45.6	45.8
2003	44.4	44.2	44.9	46.0	47.1	48.0	48.4	48.9	47.8	48.4	48.0	47.7	47.0
2004	46.7	46.8	47.7	48.9	50.0	50.9	52.6	52.1	51.5	52.3	51.7	51.9	50.3
2005	50.2	50.3	51.6	52.8	53.7	55.0	56.5	56.6	56.5	56.4	56.9	56.8	54.4
2006	55.9	56.8	58.1	58.5	59.8	60.9	60.4	60.4	60.4	60.4	59.4	58.7	59.1
2007	56.0	56.8	58.1	58.6	59.6	60.8	60.2	60.5	59.9	60.6	59.7	59.0	59.2
2008	57.0	57.5	58.1	58.5	58.6	59.1	58.0	58.3	57.6	57.2	55.7	53.6	57.4
2009	50.7	49.6	48.9	48.1	48.1	48.2	47.8	48.1	47.2	46.0	45.8	44.7	47.8
Manufacturing													
1990	36.6	36.4	36.8	37.2	37.9	38.2	38.1	39.4	39.9	39.3	38.5	38.1	38.0
2000	40.4	40.6	40.8	40.7	41.2	41.9	42.1	43.4	43.3	42.8	42.2	42.0	41.7
2001	41.5	41.3	41.6	41.3	41.3	41.2	40.8	41.6	41.3	40.7	39.4	39.1	40.9
2002	38.3	37.9	38.1	38.2	38.5	38.8	39.5	39.8	39.4	38.4	37.4	36.9	38.4
2003	36.2	36.0	36.0	35.8	36.0	36.6	36.9	37.6	37.4	37.1	36.5	35.9	36.5
2004	35.0	34.9	35.0	35.4	35.8	36.2	36.5	36.9	37.0	36.9	36.2	36.1	36.0
2005	35.3	35.2	35.3	35.5	35.6	35.8	36.1	36.7	36.9	37.1	37.0	36.9	36.1
2006	36.4	36.9	36.9	37.0	37.0	37.5	38.3	38.8	38.9	38.7	38.0	37.8	37.7
2007	37.2	37.3	37.2	36.7	36.9	37.1	37.1	37.6	37.5	36.8	36.2	36.0	37.0
2008	35.2	35.2	35.0	35.1	35.3	35.5	35.6	36.2	36.2	35.0	34.0	33.4	35.1
2009	31.6	30.9	30.2	29.9	29.7	29.9	29.8	30.1	29.9	29.7	29.7	29.3	30.1

Employment by Industry: New Mexico, Selected Years, 1990–2009—*Continued*

(Numbers in thousands, not seasonally adjusted.)

Industry and year	January	February	March	April	May	June	July	August	September	October	November	December	Annual average
Service-Providing													
1990	480.0	485.6	490.4	496.0	501.1	501.4	492.9	495.3	500.5	500.1	504.1	501.1	495.7
2000	627.1	634.0	640.4	642.3	646.9	643.8	638.9	642.4	649.2	647.6	651.5	655.2	643.2
2001	638.2	646.4	651.8	652.6	657.1	656.1	648.8	652.5	658.6	656.3	658.8	661.7	653.2
2002	650.9	657.5	663.4	666.2	671.2	670.2	664.3	667.8	675.2	672.1	676.5	679.9	667.9
2003	665.1	671.1	675.0	676.7	679.8	677.5	672.4	675.8	681.8	683.7	685.6	689.0	677.8
2004	673.7	682.0	686.6	689.7	692.0	689.0	682.8	685.1	691.4	696.7	698.9	701.1	689.1
2005	685.1	692.2	696.1	702.4	704.4	701.2	695.4	699.0	707.6	707.2	710.7	713.1	701.2
2006	699.1	708.0	714.0	714.8	719.9	720.1	710.5	713.7	724.1	721.2	726.4	728.6	716.7
2007	711.9	720.8	727.9	725.7	729.7	728.3	720.6	725.1	733.2	734.8	738.1	740.4	728.0
2008	722.0	730.8	734.4	734.6	737.9	734.3	726.6	730.2	738.8	737.9	735.6	734.1	733.1
2009	714.7	718.6	719.3	719.7	721.3	715.8	707.9	712.0	718.6	717.9	720.5	719.2	717.1
Trade, Transportation, and Utilities													
1990	116.2	115.1	115.6	116.0	117.8	118.1	117.0	118.0	118.1	118.1	119.7	120.8	117.5
2000	134.8	134.0	134.4	135.5	137.1	137.7	136.3	137.6	137.8	138.4	141.2	142.3	137.2
2001	136.4	134.4	134.7	134.3	135.5	135.4	135.0	135.8	134.8	134.7	137.0	138.5	135.5
2002	133.9	132.7	133.1	133.7	135.3	135.7	135.0	136.0	135.8	135.9	138.2	139.9	135.4
2003	134.1	133.3	134.1	134.1	135.2	134.8	134.7	135.9	135.8	136.9	139.0	140.6	135.7
2004	135.9	135.4	136.2	136.5	137.4	137.2	137.1	137.3	136.9	138.5	140.7	142.2	137.6
2005	137.5	136.9	137.4	138.0	139.2	138.9	139.5	140.4	140.0	140.5	143.0	144.5	139.7
2006	139.6	138.5	139.8	140.0	141.3	141.4	141.6	142.3	142.0	142.0	144.9	146.3	141.6
2007	142.3	141.8	143.2	142.4	144.1	143.8	144.3	145.2	145.0	146.3	149.1	150.5	144.8
2008	145.8	145.1	145.8	144.9	145.0	144.3	144.1	144.5	143.7	143.3	143.7	144.2	144.5
2009	138.7	136.5	136.3	134.9	135.4	135.2	134.7	135.2	135.1	134.2	134.7	134.6	135.5
Wholesale Trade													
1990	21.7	21.7	21.8	22.0	22.2	22.3	21.8	22.0	21.8	22.0	22.0	22.0	21.9
2000	21.9	22.0	22.3	22.6	22.9	23.0	22.8	22.9	22.9	22.9	22.8	22.8	22.6
2001	22.7	22.7	22.8	22.7	22.9	23.1	23.0	23.0	23.0	22.7	22.7	22.7	22.8
2002	22.5	22.5	22.5	22.5	22.6	22.8	22.9	22.8	22.5	22.5	22.5	22.5	22.6
2003	21.9	21.9	22.2	22.2	22.1	22.2	22.2	22.2	22.0	22.0	21.9	22.0	22.1
2004	21.7	21.8	22.1	22.3	22.3	22.4	22.5	22.3	22.2	22.3	22.2	22.4	22.2
2005	22.2	22.4	22.5	22.6	22.8	22.9	23.0	22.9	22.8	22.8	22.9	23.0	22.7
2006	22.6	22.7	22.9	23.1	23.3	23.6	23.7	23.7	23.6	23.5	23.5	23.5	23.3
2007	23.4	23.4	23.4	23.5	23.6	23.9	24.1	24.0	23.9	24.1	24.1	24.2	23.8
2008	23.9	23.8	23.8	23.9	23.9	23.9	23.9	23.8	23.4	23.3	23.0	22.7	23.6
2009	22.3	22.1	22.0	21.7	21.7	21.8	21.6	21.4	21.3	21.3	21.5	21.1	21.7
Retail Trade													
1990	72.3	71.2	71.5	72.1	73.7	74.5	73.8	74.3	73.9	73.7	75.2	76.2	73.5
2000	89.7	88.7	88.9	89.2	90.2	91.2	90.0	91.1	90.7	91.2	94.1	95.2	90.9
2001	90.2	88.7	88.8	88.7	89.6	90.1	90.0	90.1	88.7	88.8	91.3	92.7	89.8
2002	88.7	87.6	88.2	88.5	89.9	90.8	90.1	90.4	90.2	90.1	92.4	94.1	90.1
2003	89.5	88.7	89.2	89.2	90.3	90.4	90.4	91.1	90.7	91.6	93.9	95.3	90.9
2004	90.9	90.4	90.8	91.1	91.9	92.2	92.1	92.0	91.4	92.7	95.1	96.3	92.2
2005	92.3	91.5	91.6	92.2	93.1	93.4	93.9	94.2	93.6	94.1	96.4	97.3	93.6
2006	93.1	91.9	93.1	93.1	94.0	94.2	94.3	94.6	94.1	94.3	97.0	97.8	94.3
2007	94.2	93.6	95.0	94.2	95.6	95.7	96.2	96.3	95.8	96.6	99.3	100.2	96.1
2008	96.5	96.1	96.7	96.1	96.0	96.5	96.6	96.5	96.0	95.9	96.7	97.3	96.4
2009	92.7	90.9	91.1	90.5	90.9	91.5	91.5	91.9	91.8	91.5	92.0	91.9	91.5
Transportation and Utilities													
1990	22.2	22.2	22.3	21.9	21.9	21.3	21.4	21.7	22.4	22.4	22.5	22.6	22.0
2000	23.2	23.3	23.2	23.7	24.0	23.5	22.9	23.6	24.2	24.3	24.3	24.3	23.7
2001	23.5	23.0	23.1	22.9	23.0	22.2	22.0	22.7	23.1	23.2	23.0	23.1	22.9
2002	22.7	22.6	22.4	22.7	22.8	22.1	22.0	22.8	23.1	23.3	23.3	23.3	22.8
2003	22.7	22.7	22.7	22.7	22.8	22.2	22.1	22.6	23.1	23.3	23.2	23.3	22.8
2004	23.3	23.2	23.3	23.1	23.2	22.6	22.5	23.0	23.3	23.5	23.4	23.5	23.2
2005	23.0	23.0	23.3	23.2	23.3	22.6	22.6	23.3	23.6	23.6	23.7	24.2	23.3
2006	23.9	23.9	23.8	23.8	24.0	23.6	23.6	24.0	24.3	24.2	24.4	25.0	24.0
2007	24.7	24.8	24.8	24.7	24.9	24.2	24.0	24.9	25.3	25.6	25.7	26.1	25.0
2008	25.4	25.2	25.3	24.9	25.1	23.9	23.6	24.2	24.3	24.1	24.0	24.2	24.5
2009	23.7	23.5	23.2	22.7	22.8	21.9	21.6	21.9	22.0	21.4	21.2	21.6	22.3
Information													
1990	10.7	10.7	10.6	10.6	10.7	10.7	10.9	10.9	10.8	10.4	10.4	10.5	10.6
2000	16.3	16.3	16.4	16.3	16.4	16.7	16.9	17.2	17.3	16.7	16.7	17.2	16.7
2001	17.3	17.6	17.5	16.9	17.1	17.0	16.8	16.9	17.0	16.9	17.0	17.0	17.1
2002	16.8	17.1	17.2	17.0	17.0	16.8	17.0	16.8	16.6	16.4	16.8	16.8	16.9
2003	16.3	16.1	16.3	15.8	16.0	16.0	15.7	15.5	15.5	15.2	15.3	15.3	15.8
2004	14.9	15.2	15.0	14.7	15.0	14.9	14.7	14.7	14.3	14.9	15.1	15.0	14.9
2005	13.9	14.1	14.1	15.3	15.1	14.7	14.8	14.8	14.5	14.9	15.0	15.4	14.7
2006	14.5	15.4	15.9	15.0	15.6	17.4	15.1	15.9	17.1	14.9	15.9	16.9	15.8
2007	14.5	15.5	15.8	14.4	14.8	16.3	15.3	16.5	17.4	16.8	17.1	17.1	16.0
2008	15.6	16.3	16.1	15.1	15.4	16.2	16.0	15.8	16.5	16.3	16.3	15.6	15.9
2009	14.0	14.4	14.3	14.5	14.8	15.1	14.6	15.0	15.6	15.5	15.6	15.4	14.9

Employment by Industry: New Mexico, Selected Years, 1990–2009—*Continued*

(Numbers in thousands, not seasonally adjusted.)

Industry and year	January	February	March	April	May	June	July	August	September	October	November	December	Annual average
Financial Activities													
1990	27.5	27.2	27.4	27.3	27.5	27.9	27.8	27.8	27.6	27.9	27.8	27.9	27.6
2000	33.5	33.5	33.6	33.3	33.4	33.5	33.4	33.3	33.2	33.3	33.5	33.8	33.4
2001	33.1	33.3	33.4	33.3	33.3	33.5	33.5	33.4	33.1	33.1	33.1	33.5	33.3
2002	33.4	33.3	33.4	33.3	33.4	33.4	33.7	33.9	33.6	33.4	33.5	33.8	33.5
2003	33.3	33.4	33.4	33.5	33.8	34.0	34.2	34.5	34.2	34.1	34.0	34.4	33.9
2004	34.3	34.1	34.4	34.1	34.1	34.4	34.5	34.4	34.4	34.5	34.5	34.9	34.4
2005	34.7	34.6	34.6	34.7	34.8	35.1	35.2	35.1	35.0	34.9	35.0	35.6	34.9
2006	35.2	35.2	35.2	35.1	35.2	35.3	35.2	35.1	35.0	34.9	34.9	35.3	35.1
2007	34.9	35.0	35.3	35.1	35.2	35.4	35.5	35.5	35.2	35.2	35.1	35.3	35.2
2008	34.7	34.8	34.8	34.7	34.7	34.8	34.9	34.8	34.7	34.4	34.1	34.3	34.6
2009	33.7	33.5	33.2	33.7	33.8	33.5	33.4	33.3	33.1	32.9	33.8	33.4	33.4
Professional and Business Services													
1990	54.5	54.4	55.4	57.3	57.7	59.2	57.9	58.0	58.0	57.8	57.4	58.4	57.1
2000	82.7	83.4	84.1	85.4	85.3	86.7	86.5	87.0	87.7	87.6	88.6	89.0	86.1
2001	86.4	87.4	88.4	88.7	88.9	89.7	89.3	89.4	88.3	89.1	88.4	88.6	88.6
2002	87.7	87.8	88.9	88.6	89.0	89.2	90.1	90.0	89.9	89.3	89.7	90.2	89.2
2003	87.7	88.6	88.8	88.6	88.6	88.4	88.5	88.8	88.2	88.6	88.2	88.7	88.5
2004	87.0	87.6	88.6	89.6	90.0	90.2	90.5	90.8	91.0	92.1	91.3	91.7	90.0
2005	90.2	90.5	90.7	92.8	92.4	93.3	93.2	93.6	94.0	93.5	94.3	94.3	92.7
2006	93.6	94.5	95.2	96.0	96.6	108.1	107.3	107.6	107.5	107.7	107.6	107.9	102.5
2007	106.3	107.6	108.3	108.3	108.7	109.3	109.5	110.3	109.2	108.6	108.4	108.2	108.6
2008	106.5	107.5	107.4	108.1	108.5	109.0	109.2	110.3	109.7	109.1	107.5	107.0	108.3
2009	104.1	103.4	102.4	101.8	101.4	101.9	102.2	103.1	102.3	100.7	100.8	100.6	102.1
Education and Health Services													
1990	49.2	49.7	50.4	50.3	50.6	49.8	49.7	50.4	51.8	52.3	52.7	52.8	50.8
2000	81.2	82.3	82.8	82.4	82.2	80.5	78.8	79.7	83.1	83.5	84.4	84.6	82.1
2001	85.1	86.6	87.2	87.5	88.0	85.3	84.9	86.1	89.5	89.8	91.0	91.2	87.7
2002	91.7	92.6	93.5	94.6	94.6	91.3	90.4	91.7	95.9	96.4	97.6	97.3	94.0
2003	97.7	98.5	98.6	99.2	99.2	95.8	95.9	96.7	100.5	100.8	101.9	102.0	98.9
2004	101.6	102.4	102.4	103.1	103.0	99.7	99.0	100.0	103.5	104.1	105.4	104.8	102.4
2005	104.0	104.6	105.1	105.4	105.6	102.0	101.5	102.7	106.7	107.1	107.6	107.6	105.0
2006	106.9	107.4	108.4	108.3	108.7	105.6	104.5	105.2	109.4	109.7	110.8	110.6	108.0
2007	110.1	110.9	111.8	112.4	112.8	109.2	107.9	108.6	112.0	113.2	113.8	114.2	111.4
2008	112.6	114.1	114.8	115.8	116.3	113.0	111.9	113.2	116.9	117.8	118.3	118.7	115.3
2009	117.8	118.9	119.4	119.4	119.8	115.8	114.9	116.3	119.8	120.2	121.0	120.3	118.6
Leisure and Hospitality													
1990	56.8	57.0	58.2	60.2	61.9	64.0	63.5	64.3	61.9	59.3	58.9	58.3	60.3
2000	73.4	73.8	75.7	76.1	77.3	80.2	80.6	81.1	79.4	77.0	75.9	76.2	77.2
2001	74.8	75.3	76.8	77.9	79.5	81.9	81.5	82.1	79.7	77.8	77.1	77.3	78.5
2002	75.7	76.3	78.0	79.6	81.3	83.6	83.6	83.9	81.9	79.1	78.4	79.1	80.0
2003	78.0	78.3	79.6	80.7	82.5	84.6	84.7	85.0	82.6	80.8	80.1	80.7	81.5
2004	79.1	79.7	81.1	82.8	83.8	85.3	85.4	85.3	83.4	82.0	80.8	81.8	82.5
2005	80.6	81.1	82.5	84.1	84.6	86.7	86.3	86.7	85.2	83.3	82.3	82.7	83.8
2006	82.6	83.0	84.6	86.3	87.6	89.3	89.9	89.7	88.4	86.3	86.3	86.0	86.7
2007	84.9	85.3	86.9	87.6	88.4	90.2	90.3	90.6	89.2	87.5	86.5	86.7	87.8
2008	84.9	85.1	86.5	87.2	87.9	89.0	89.1	89.4	87.8	85.7	84.3	83.9	86.7
2009	82.4	82.5	83.5	84.5	85.4	86.2	86.5	86.9	85.3	85.0	83.3	84.9	84.7
Other Services													
1990	20.8	20.9	21.1	21.1	21.5	23.3	23.3	23.4	21.8	21.7	21.6	21.6	21.8
2000	26.5	26.8	26.8	26.8	27.2	29.2	29.2	29.0	26.6	26.4	26.5	26.5	27.2
2001	25.8	26.2	26.4	26.4	26.7	29.2	29.3	28.8	26.9	26.6	26.7	26.8	27.2
2002	26.6	27.0	27.2	27.3	27.6	29.9	30.0	29.7	27.7	27.7	27.6	27.6	28.0
2003	27.5	27.6	27.7	27.5	27.9	30.2	30.4	30.1	28.2	28.1	28.1	28.2	28.5
2004	27.9	28.1	28.2	28.1	28.4	30.7	30.9	30.6	28.5	28.4	28.3	28.3	28.9
2005	28.0	28.3	28.3	28.4	28.6	31.0	31.1	30.9	28.8	28.4	28.5	28.6	29.1
2006	27.9	28.4	28.6	28.7	29.0	31.4	31.4	31.0	29.2	29.0	29.0	28.7	29.4
2007	28.3	28.7	28.9	28.7	29.0	31.4	31.3	30.7	28.9	29.0	28.9	29.0	29.4
2008	28.7	29.2	29.3	29.3	29.7	32.3	32.1	31.7	29.7	29.9	29.5	28.8	30.0
2009	28.3	28.5	28.5	28.3	28.5	30.7	30.6	30.2	28.3	27.7	27.7	27.7	28.8
Government													
1990	144.3	150.6	151.7	153.2	153.4	148.4	142.8	142.5	150.5	152.6	155.6	150.8	149.7
2000	178.7	183.9	186.6	186.5	188.0	179.3	177.2	177.5	184.1	184.7	184.7	185.6	183.0
2001	179.3	185.6	187.4	187.6	188.1	184.1	178.5	180.0	189.3	188.3	188.5	188.8	185.5
2002	185.1	190.7	192.1	192.1	193.1	190.3	184.5	185.8	193.8	193.9	194.7	195.2	190.9
2003	190.5	195.3	196.5	197.3	196.6	193.7	188.3	189.3	196.8	199.2	199.0	199.1	195.1
2004	193.0	199.5	200.7	200.8	200.3	196.6	190.7	192.0	199.4	202.2	202.8	202.4	198.4
2005	196.2	202.1	203.4	203.7	204.1	199.5	193.8	194.8	203.4	204.6	205.0	204.4	201.3
2006	198.8	205.6	206.3	205.4	205.9	191.6	185.5	186.9	195.5	196.7	197.0	196.9	197.7
2007	190.6	196.0	197.7	196.8	196.7	192.7	186.5	187.7	196.3	198.2	199.2	199.4	194.8
2008	193.2	198.7	199.7	199.5	200.4	195.7	189.3	190.5	199.8	201.4	201.9	201.6	197.6
2009	195.7	200.9	201.7	202.6	202.2	197.4	191.0	192.0	199.1	201.7	203.6	202.3	199.2

Average Weekly Hours by Selected Industry: New Mexico, 2007–2009

(Not seasonally adjusted.)

Industry and year	January	February	March	April	May	June	July	August	September	October	November	December	Annual average
Total Private													
2007	34.4	34.2	34.1	34.8	34.4	34.5	35.0	34.7	34.8	34.5	34.3	35.2	34.6
2008	34.6	34.6	34.8	35.1	35.3	35.6	35.7	35.6	35.6	35.9	36.2	35.4	35.4
2009	35.7	35.5	35.0	34.8	34.9	35.2	35.2	35.4	34.7	34.9	35.4	34.7	35.1
Goods-Producing													
2007	38.7	38.5	38.2	38.7	39.2	38.8	38.9	38.9	38.6	39.8	39.0	39.8	38.9
2008	38.5	37.7	37.5	38.8	39.8	39.4	39.4	40.1	39.7	40.7	39.2	39.0	39.2
2009	42.5	39.8	38.3	38.4	39.6	39.2	39.3	39.8	38.0	39.2	39.7	39.2	39.4
Construction													
2007	38.1	38.3	37.9	39.1	40.6	40.4	40.4	40.2	39.5	41.4	40.5	39.7	39.7
2008	39.5	39.0	38.0	39.4	41.1	42.6	42.3	43.1	40.1	40.6	40.4	39.1	40.5
2009	39.5	39.0	38.3	38.4	39.2	39.1	39.2	39.6	36.9	39.2	40.1	38.8	38.9
Trade, Transportation, and Utilities													
2007	35.4	35.9	36.2	36.4	36.1	36.8	36.8	36.9	36.3	36.0	34.4	35.0	36.0
2008	34.6	34.9	35.2	35.2	35.4	35.7	35.1	35.6	35.7	36.1	36.7	35.9	35.5
2009	35.8	35.2	34.2	34.1	34.0	35.3	34.8	35.4	34.5	34.8	35.1	34.8	34.8
Professional and Business Services													
2007	36.6	35.4	35.7	36.6	35.5	36.2	36.5	36.4	36.6	35.5	36.0	36.5	36.1
2008	36.7	36.3	36.6	35.9	35.8	37.0	36.7	36.0	36.2	35.8	37.5	37.2	36.5
2009	35.9	36.5	35.8	36.1	36.0	36.7	35.6	35.9	35.7	36.0	36.8	36.0	36.1
Education and Health Services													
2007	33.5	33.2	32.9	34.0	33.7	33.4	34.0	33.5	33.9	33.6	33.7	34.6	33.7
2008	35.2	35.5	35.4	35.6	35.1	35.0	36.1	35.0	35.2	35.7	36.1	35.5	35.5
2009	36.0	37.1	36.5	35.7	35.7	36.2	36.5	36.2	36.0	35.7	36.3	35.7	36.1
Leisure and Hospitality													
2007	25.2	26.3	26.4	26.5	26.7	26.4	28.5	28.2	27.2	26.7	26.5	24.9	26.6
2008	25.6	26.1	27.5	27.8	29.0	29.6	29.1	29.4	27.7	27.8	27.9	26.0	27.8
2009	26.2	27.0	26.7	25.8	26.8	26.3	27.1	27.2	26.6	26.2	26.5	25.9	26.5

Average Hourly Earnings by Selected Industry: New Mexico, 2007–2009

(Dollars, not seasonally adjusted.)

Industry and year	January	February	March	April	May	June	July	August	September	October	November	December	Annual average
Total Private													
2007	18.34	18.64	18.43	18.75	18.67	18.58	18.72	18.37	18.69	18.61	18.53	18.50	18.57
2008	18.54	18.58	18.87	18.75	18.74	18.83	18.73	18.72	18.36	18.76	18.92	19.00	18.73
2009	18.77	18.80	18.73	18.66	18.83	18.69	18.83	18.90	19.19	19.11	19.32	19.19	18.92
Goods-Producing													
2007	19.66	19.58	19.77	19.74	19.65	19.41	19.75	19.21	19.36	19.31	19.45	19.97	19.57
2008	20.38	20.80	20.95	20.77	20.56	20.29	20.63	21.06	20.86	20.95	21.68	22.43	20.94
2009	21.73	21.90	21.53	21.02	21.59	21.21	21.40	21.30	21.16	21.54	21.80	21.52	21.48
Construction													
2007	18.93	18.37	19.41	18.45	18.29	18.03	18.43	18.35	18.90	18.82	18.92	19.06	18.66
2008	18.70	18.44	19.17	18.79	19.07	18.96	19.48	19.58	19.92	20.05	20.30	22.03	19.52
2009	20.94	21.00	21.07	20.71	20.98	20.72	21.41	21.22	21.09	21.52	21.58	21.61	21.15
Trade, Transportation, and Utilities													
2007	15.86	16.22	16.24	16.58	16.84	17.07	16.75	16.31	16.45	16.84	16.67	16.33	16.52
2008	16.30	16.46	16.80	17.45	16.89	16.91	17.15	17.14	17.03	16.77	16.92	16.72	16.88
2009	17.22	17.85	17.24	17.10	17.31	17.46	17.93	18.07	18.46	17.70	18.07	17.75	17.68
Professional and Business Services													
2007	24.58	27.55	25.40	26.44	26.36	26.01	26.28	25.68	25.48	25.02	24.63	25.26	25.72
2008	25.11	24.46	24.95	24.81	24.68	25.80	25.12	23.08	22.89	23.89	23.72	23.21	24.31
2009	23.28	23.05	22.74	22.96	22.52	21.95	21.93	22.12	22.35	22.14	22.03	21.84	22.41
Education and Health Services													
2007	15.94	15.54	16.47	16.70	16.66	16.60	16.27	16.54	17.08	17.37	16.93	16.64	16.57
2008	16.47	16.48	17.17	16.87	17.02	16.99	17.18	18.14	17.91	17.90	17.89	18.01	17.34
2009	16.79	16.60	17.03	17.50	17.22	17.72	18.00	18.05	18.61	18.97	18.90	19.18	17.88
Leisure and Hospitality													
2007	10.38	10.25	10.42	10.48	10.59	10.51	10.72	10.76	11.17	11.20	11.00	11.58	10.81
2008	10.98	10.94	11.00	11.02	11.19	11.04	10.96	11.03	11.11	11.63	11.05	11.17	11.09
2009	11.53	11.55	11.60	11.19	11.75	11.61	11.62	11.48	12.19	11.98	12.24	12.00	11.73

Average Weekly Earnings by Selected Industry: New Mexico, 2007–2009

(Dollars, not seasonally adjusted.)

Industry and year	January	February	March	April	May	June	July	August	September	October	November	December	Annual average
Total Private													
2007	630.90	637.49	628.46	652.50	642.25	641.01	655.20	635.70	650.41	642.05	635.58	651.20	642.52
2008	641.48	642.87	656.68	658.13	661.52	670.35	668.66	666.43	653.62	673.48	684.90	672.60	663.04
2009	670.09	667.40	655.55	649.37	657.17	657.89	662.82	669.06	665.89	666.94	683.93	665.89	664.09
Goods-Producing													
2007	760.84	753.83	755.21	763.94	770.28	753.11	768.28	747.27	747.30	768.54	758.55	794.81	761.27
2008	784.63	784.16	785.63	805.88	818.29	799.43	812.82	844.51	828.14	852.67	849.86	874.77	820.85
2009	923.53	871.62	824.60	807.17	854.96	831.43	841.02	847.74	804.08	844.37	865.46	843.58	846.31
Construction													
2007	721.23	703.57	735.64	721.40	742.57	728.41	744.57	737.67	746.55	779.15	766.26	756.68	740.80
2008	738.65	719.16	728.46	740.33	783.78	807.70	824.00	843.90	798.79	814.03	820.12	861.37	790.56
2009	827.13	819.00	806.98	795.26	822.42	810.15	839.27	840.31	778.22	843.58	865.36	838.47	822.74
Trade, Transportation, and Utilities													
2007	561.44	582.30	587.89	603.51	607.92	628.18	616.40	601.84	597.14	606.24	573.45	571.55	594.72
2008	563.98	574.45	591.36	614.24	597.91	603.69	601.97	610.18	607.97	605.40	620.96	600.25	599.24
2009	616.48	628.32	589.61	583.11	588.54	616.34	623.96	639.68	636.87	615.96	634.26	617.70	615.26
Professional and Business Services													
2007	899.63	975.27	906.78	967.70	935.78	941.56	959.22	934.75	932.57	888.21	886.68	921.99	928.49
2008	921.54	887.90	913.17	890.68	883.54	954.60	921.90	830.88	828.62	855.26	889.50	863.41	887.32
2009	835.75	841.33	814.09	828.86	810.72	805.57	780.71	794.11	797.90	797.04	810.70	786.24	809.00
Education and Health Services													
2007	533.99	515.93	541.86	567.80	561.44	554.44	553.18	554.09	579.01	583.63	570.54	575.74	558.41
2008	579.74	585.04	607.82	600.57	597.40	594.65	620.20	634.90	630.43	639.03	645.83	639.36	615.57
2009	604.44	615.86	621.60	624.75	614.75	641.46	657.00	653.41	669.96	677.23	686.07	684.73	645.47
Leisure and Hospitality													
2007	261.58	269.58	275.09	277.72	282.75	277.46	305.52	303.43	303.82	301.18	307.40	288.34	287.55
2008	281.09	285.53	302.50	306.36	324.51	326.78	318.94	324.28	307.75	323.31	308.30	290.42	308.30
2009	302.09	311.85	309.72	288.70	314.90	305.34	314.90	312.26	324.25	313.88	324.36	310.80	310.85

NEW YORK
At a Glance

Population:
  1990 census: 17,990,778
  2000 census: 18,976,457
  2009 estimate: 19,541,453

Percent change in population:
  1990–2000: 5.5%
  2000–2009: 3.0%

Percent change in total nonfarm employment:
  1990–2009: 4.2%
  2008–2009: -2.7%

Industry with the largest growth in employment, 1990–2009 (thousands):
  Education and Health Services, 586.5

Industry with the largest decline or smallest growth in employment, 1990–2009 (thousands):
  Manufacturing, -504.5

Civilian labor force:
  1990: 8,808,856
  2000: 9,166,972
  2009: 9,699,492

Unemployment rate and rank among states (lowest to highest):
  1990: 5.3%, 23rd
  2000: 4.5%, 38th
  2009: 8.4%, 28th

Employment by Industry, 2009

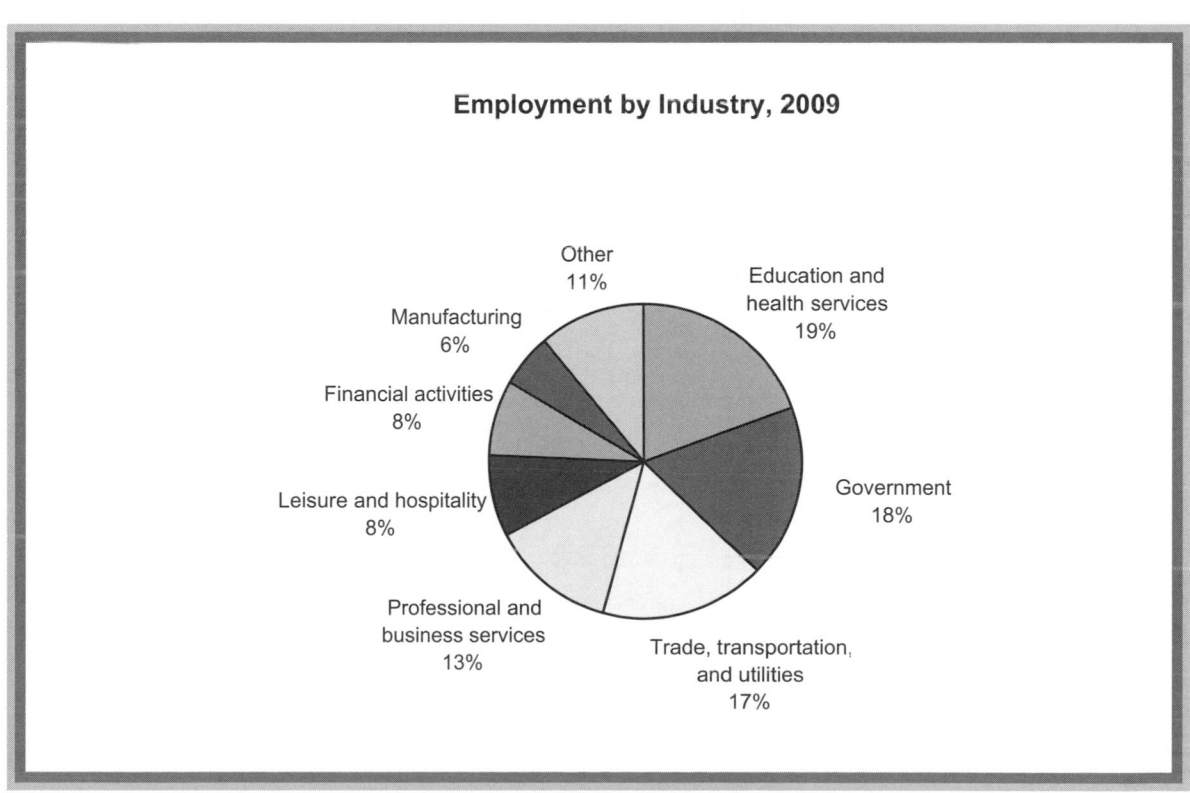

- Other 11%
- Education and health services 19%
- Manufacturing 6%
- Financial activities 8%
- Leisure and hospitality 8%
- Government 18%
- Professional and business services 13%
- Trade, transportation, and utilities 17%

Employment by Industry: New York, Selected Years, 1990–2009

(Numbers in thousands, not seasonally adjusted.)

Industry and year	January	February	March	April	May	June	July	August	September	October	November	December	Annual average
Total Nonfarm													
1990	8103.1	8131.4	8190.9	8197.8	8293.2	8343.5	8212.5	8215.8	8223.4	8221.1	8220.8	8211.6	8213.8
2000	8394.2	8445.8	8520.4	8590.7	8676.0	8719.3	8648.0	8606.0	8666.4	8754.0	8800.8	8834.2	8638.0
2001	8523.9	8560.4	8605.4	8608.1	8688.5	8721.0	8587.8	8552.3	8553.8	8550.6	8584.9	8598.2	8594.6
2002	8294.4	8342.2	8395.4	8430.6	8510.7	8540.2	8459.2	8444.1	8446.3	8528.7	8563.4	8585.9	8461.8
2003	8267.2	8300.3	8344.0	8368.0	8446.9	8479.4	8387.4	8365.5	8399.8	8483.8	8523.8	8550.9	8409.8
2004	8235.7	8292.2	8365.7	8401.1	8499.6	8543.8	8480.9	8453.2	8485.1	8572.2	8607.0	8642.3	8464.9
2005	8332.2	8372.1	8417.2	8512.2	8567.0	8617.3	8540.9	8526.5	8568.6	8614.1	8666.5	8709.8	8537.0
2006	8405.3	8446.7	8511.7	8568.6	8647.4	8704.7	8608.4	8584.9	8634.2	8715.0	8771.8	8821.9	8618.4
2007	8532.9	8571.5	8627.9	8663.6	8760.8	8825.7	8732.4	8702.3	8739.2	8842.5	8888.2	8921.5	8734.0
2008	8636.0	8679.9	8720.3	8786.1	8849.5	8891.8	8819.4	8780.9	8795.6	8856.3	8852.1	8845.9	8792.8
2009	8506.0	8522.9	8525.1	8545.5	8609.1	8614.3	8574.0	8526.9	8507.5	8577.6	8590.7	8570.6	8555.9
Total Private													
1990	6647.0	6657.8	6704.4	6705.4	6781.4	6838.5	6768.5	6788.4	6791.0	6746.9	6734.5	6726.9	6740.9
2000	6949.1	6981.6	7041.7	7098.9	7162.7	7239.5	7194.3	7195.3	7239.9	7277.2	7315.5	7353.6	7170.8
2001	7071.4	7088.0	7127.1	7120.4	7204.2	7246.1	7161.1	7149.4	7113.7	7064.3	7082.2	7099.2	7127.3
2002	6817.8	6840.5	6885.5	6929.5	7001.3	7034.8	6989.0	6996.0	6993.0	7031.5	7049.3	7067.7	6969.7
2003	6788.4	6797.9	6837.4	6866.1	6941.9	6976.1	6934.2	6933.2	6948.7	6991.7	7016.2	7037.9	6922.5
2004	6764.8	6799.2	6865.8	6904.8	6991.3	7040.2	7026.6	7020.8	7036.6	7081.0	7103.3	7137.6	6981.0
2005	6853.0	6874.6	6918.1	7007.1	7057.8	7108.7	7079.3	7085.3	7107.4	7121.3	7161.6	7199.2	7047.8
2006	6930.0	6953.5	7016.1	7069.8	7143.4	7203.6	7156.5	7154.5	7176.6	7220.2	7265.4	7307.4	7133.1
2007	7043.4	7062.5	7116.8	7154.3	7243.1	7308.7	7265.8	7252.0	7264.3	7329.7	7365.4	7390.3	7233.0
2008	7140.6	7164.0	7200.5	7256.3	7315.9	7358.4	7320.1	7309.8	7307.9	7330.1	7317.0	7306.8	7277.3
2009	6998.9	6991.4	6990.7	7007.5	7065.7	7082.2	7038.1	7018.8	7030.7	7054.2	7057.6	7047.3	7031.9
Goods-Producing													
1990	1290.7	1293.2	1306.9	1308.4	1329.9	1348.0	1326.7	1334.5	1334.8	1313.8	1287.8	1259.2	1311.2
2000	1044.9	1043.2	1056.8	1068.0	1084.5	1102.1	1093.2	1103.4	1106.0	1103.3	1095.9	1084.1	1082.1
2001	1034.1	1032.3	1038.3	1044.9	1060.3	1072.4	1055.1	1056.3	1045.8	1036.3	1024.7	1010.4	1042.6
2002	954.6	951.1	959.0	970.9	986.0	995.9	989.6	998.5	992.4	988.7	980.3	965.3	977.7
2003	917.3	910.3	919.6	926.6	943.6	954.1	946.7	954.1	951.7	945.8	939.9	926.8	936.4
2004	882.3	881.6	896.3	908.1	927.3	941.5	940.3	948.4	946.0	942.9	938.3	927.4	923.4
2005	879.8	873.7	881.3	900.1	914.8	928.2	926.5	934.2	931.1	923.5	922.8	910.6	910.6
2006	874.0	870.5	879.6	899.1	915.6	930.9	925.6	932.8	929.1	927.5	921.7	913.3	910.0
2007	877.1	867.8	877.5	894.1	915.9	931.2	928.8	933.1	928.8	929.1	924.1	912.2	910.0
2008	876.4	869.9	876.3	891.0	908.4	919.2	920.7	924.7	916.4	910.0	892.8	868.0	897.8
2009	815.3	801.0	798.6	805.7	815.3	819.4	820.0	820.2	811.6	803.8	791.6	775.1	806.5
Mining and Logging													
1990	6.0	6.0	6.2	6.6	6.9	7.1	7.2	7.2	7.1	7.1	6.9	6.5	6.7
2000	4.7	4.6	5.1	5.4	5.7	5.9	5.9	6.0	6.0	5.8	5.7	5.2	5.5
2001	4.6	4.7	5.0	5.2	5.6	5.6	5.7	5.7	5.5	5.7	5.5	5.2	5.3
2002	4.4	4.4	4.6	5.0	5.4	5.4	5.5	5.5	5.4	5.4	5.3	4.9	5.1
2003	4.4	4.4	4.6	5.0	5.5	5.6	5.7	5.8	5.8	5.7	5.6	5.4	5.3
2004	4.7	4.6	5.0	5.4	5.8	6.0	6.1	6.2	6.2	6.1	6.0	5.7	5.7
2005	4.9	4.8	5.0	5.7	6.0	6.3	6.4	6.5	6.4	6.4	6.2	5.9	5.9
2006	5.0	5.1	5.4	6.1	6.4	6.6	6.7	6.7	6.7	6.8	6.6	6.1	6.2
2007	5.2	5.3	5.5	5.9	6.4	6.7	6.8	6.7	6.7	6.7	6.6	6.2	6.2
2008	5.3	5.2	5.5	6.0	6.6	6.9	7.1	7.0	6.9	6.8	6.3	5.8	6.3
2009	4.8	4.8	4.9	5.2	5.6	5.8	5.9	5.8	5.8	5.8	5.5	5.1	5.4
Construction													
1990	300.2	297.4	305.1	313.9	330.3	340.1	341.3	345.3	342.3	331.2	321.2	305.5	322.8
2000	289.5	286.9	299.6	312.3	327.4	338.5	343.3	348.1	349.3	349.0	346.3	337.6	327.3
2001	302.2	300.3	306.4	322.0	339.2	348.0	347.7	349.3	342.8	341.9	337.6	328.8	330.5
2002	293.8	291.5	297.1	311.3	323.9	332.0	338.4	342.7	338.5	337.4	332.7	323.2	321.9
2003	291.4	286.3	293.2	307.3	323.0	331.2	337.9	340.1	336.9	333.9	328.9	319.6	319.1
2004	285.6	283.7	293.6	309.8	325.3	334.6	341.6	344.5	342.4	340.4	336.9	327.9	322.2
2005	295.0	290.1	294.8	314.6	328.6	337.8	341.7	346.8	345.1	339.4	340.0	329.1	325.3
2006	303.3	300.3	308.0	326.3	340.6	350.8	353.1	358.6	356.2	356.0	351.1	344.9	337.4
2007	318.8	310.5	318.8	336.9	355.9	367.7	370.5	374.2	371.7	373.1	369.5	358.8	352.2
2008	334.9	330.1	335.9	351.3	366.3	373.1	379.8	383.3	377.3	374.5	363.6	345.8	359.7
2009	310.9	305.3	307.8	319.1	330.9	336.1	341.5	342.3	334.5	329.5	321.3	308.0	323.9
Manufacturing													
1990	984.5	989.8	995.6	987.9	992.7	1000.8	978.2	982.0	985.4	975.5	959.7	947.2	981.6
2000	750.7	751.7	752.1	750.3	751.4	757.7	744.0	749.3	750.7	748.5	743.9	741.3	749.3
2001	727.3	727.3	726.9	717.7	715.5	718.8	701.7	701.3	697.5	688.7	681.6	676.4	706.7
2002	656.4	655.2	657.3	654.6	656.7	658.5	645.7	650.3	648.5	645.9	642.3	637.2	650.7
2003	621.5	619.6	621.8	614.3	615.1	617.3	603.1	608.2	609.0	606.2	605.4	601.8	611.9
2004	592.0	593.3	597.7	592.9	596.2	600.9	592.6	597.7	597.4	596.4	595.4	593.8	595.5
2005	579.9	578.8	581.5	579.8	580.2	584.1	578.4	580.9	579.6	577.7	576.6	575.6	579.4
2006	565.7	565.1	566.2	566.7	568.6	573.5	565.8	567.5	566.2	564.7	564.0	562.3	566.4
2007	553.1	552.0	553.2	551.3	553.6	556.8	551.5	552.2	550.4	549.3	548.0	547.2	551.6
2008	536.2	534.6	534.9	533.7	535.5	539.2	533.8	534.4	532.2	528.7	522.9	516.4	531.9
2009	499.6	490.9	485.9	481.4	478.8	477.5	472.6	472.1	471.3	468.5	464.8	462.0	477.1

Employment by Industry: New York, Selected Years, 1990–2009—*Continued*

(Numbers in thousands, not seasonally adjusted.)

Industry and year	January	February	March	April	May	June	July	August	September	October	November	December	Annual average
Service-Providing													
1990	6812.4	6838.2	6884.0	6889.4	6963.3	6995.5	6885.8	6881.3	6888.6	6907.3	6933.0	6952.4	6902.6
2000	7349.3	7402.6	7463.6	7522.7	7591.5	7617.2	7554.8	7502.6	7560.4	7650.7	7704.9	7750.1	7555.9
2001	7489.8	7528.1	7567.1	7563.2	7628.2	7648.6	7532.7	7496.0	7508.0	7514.3	7560.2	7587.8	7552.0
2002	7339.8	7391.1	7436.4	7459.7	7524.7	7544.3	7469.6	7445.6	7453.9	7540.0	7583.1	7620.6	7484.1
2003	7349.9	7390.0	7424.4	7441.4	7503.3	7525.3	7440.7	7411.4	7448.1	7538.0	7583.9	7624.1	7473.4
2004	7353.4	7410.6	7469.4	7493.0	7572.3	7602.3	7540.6	7504.8	7539.1	7629.3	7668.7	7714.9	7541.5
2005	7452.4	7498.4	7535.9	7612.1	7652.2	7689.1	7614.4	7592.3	7637.5	7690.6	7743.7	7799.2	7626.5
2006	7531.3	7576.2	7632.1	7669.5	7731.8	7773.8	7682.8	7652.1	7705.1	7787.5	7850.1	7908.6	7708.4
2007	7655.8	7703.7	7750.4	7769.5	7844.9	7894.5	7803.6	7769.2	7810.4	7913.4	7964.1	8009.3	7824.1
2008	7759.6	7810.0	7844.0	7895.1	7941.1	7972.6	7898.7	7856.2	7879.2	7946.3	7959.3	7977.9	7895.0
2009	7690.7	7721.9	7726.5	7739.8	7793.8	7794.9	7754.0	7706.7	7695.9	7773.8	7799.1	7795.5	7749.4
Trade, Transportation, and Utilities													
1990	1581.3	1560.9	1565.1	1553.9	1568.7	1581.6	1556.4	1561.2	1569.2	1571.4	1587.1	1604.4	1571.8
2000	1524.8	1508.2	1514.6	1515.2	1528.8	1548.6	1527.7	1534.8	1547.9	1559.1	1588.7	1618.7	1543.1
2001	1533.9	1511.8	1513.8	1502.5	1519.2	1533.3	1501.0	1497.9	1498.6	1499.1	1522.3	1543.6	1514.8
2002	1467.3	1447.0	1455.7	1457.0	1471.9	1489.0	1466.1	1467.2	1481.0	1491.1	1514.8	1541.6	1479.1
2003	1464.5	1445.7	1449.5	1449.1	1465.4	1480.5	1460.0	1462.4	1474.4	1491.4	1515.2	1538.7	1474.7
2004	1457.1	1443.2	1451.3	1453.1	1476.2	1494.2	1481.3	1481.5	1493.2	1512.2	1536.1	1562.0	1486.8
2005	1480.5	1463.3	1468.3	1479.3	1492.8	1509.4	1492.5	1494.3	1503.6	1510.7	1537.6	1568.9	1500.1
2006	1493.2	1469.8	1477.9	1480.4	1499.0	1519.9	1498.1	1496.5	1506.6	1524.1	1556.5	1583.2	1509.0
2007	1513.3	1489.6	1496.6	1494.7	1517.8	1538.4	1517.5	1510.2	1521.9	1535.7	1569.7	1593.5	1524.9
2008	1526.1	1502.1	1507.4	1508.7	1520.7	1536.7	1515.0	1512.2	1521.1	1525.8	1541.1	1556.7	1522.8
2009	1471.3	1447.7	1441.3	1435.4	1453.3	1467.7	1445.2	1444.4	1452.3	1453.2	1473.7	1486.9	1456.0
Wholesale Trade													
1990	410.9	411.3	413.3	411.9	413.6	415.8	412.0	412.0	410.7	407.7	406.5	405.5	410.9
2000	369.7	370.9	373.4	370.5	372.3	375.3	372.8	374.0	374.7	375.0	375.3	377.3	373.4
2001	369.5	370.3	370.7	367.3	368.5	370.4	366.7	366.1	364.1	362.9	362.2	362.7	366.8
2002	352.8	353.0	354.0	353.5	355.2	356.7	353.6	355.4	354.9	357.2	357.9	358.8	355.3
2003	350.5	350.3	351.7	350.5	353.4	355.3	354.1	354.3	353.8	354.5	356.0	357.4	353.5
2004	347.8	348.2	350.3	351.2	353.4	355.8	355.9	355.4	354.2	356.6	357.2	359.0	353.8
2005	348.2	349.0	350.0	351.4	352.8	354.5	354.5	355.4	355.0	355.2	356.3	358.7	353.4
2006	348.9	348.8	350.9	352.2	354.0	357.0	355.5	356.2	355.1	356.2	356.6	359.9	354.3
2007	353.2	353.0	354.4	354.1	356.1	359.1	358.0	357.0	356.0	358.5	358.2	359.8	356.5
2008	352.4	352.1	352.5	352.4	353.1	354.9	353.3	352.2	351.0	349.9	348.2	347.0	351.6
2009	338.4	335.2	333.3	331.1	331.2	331.8	328.9	328.7	327.0	327.5	327.5	325.5	330.5
Retail Trade													
1990	874.5	853.2	854.0	844.4	853.7	861.3	850.7	854.2	853.7	859.8	877.5	894.9	861.0
2000	877.9	860.3	863.1	866.3	875.6	890.2	881.2	887.6	887.5	894.6	924.5	950.7	888.3
2001	880.9	858.6	859.6	854.1	863.3	874.6	859.1	861.2	853.2	856.9	885.7	907.7	867.9
2002	850.1	830.7	837.7	837.8	847.9	862.1	854.2	856.8	857.1	862.0	886.5	912.0	857.9
2003	848.6	830.9	832.1	836.0	846.6	859.1	851.2	854.4	854.0	867.1	890.4	911.4	856.8
2004	849.0	835.3	840.0	841.0	856.8	870.7	867.6	869.1	870.1	881.6	905.6	928.9	868.0
2005	868.4	850.7	853.8	862.2	870.8	882.8	878.3	880.3	876.0	883.8	907.7	932.0	878.9
2006	875.6	853.2	857.8	862.4	871.5	886.0	881.3	880.5	875.8	891.8	922.1	940.4	883.2
2007	889.1	866.1	870.7	869.9	885.2	899.7	894.9	891.6	887.9	897.6	930.6	948.7	894.3
2008	899.6	876.8	880.4	879.7	888.2	899.9	896.0	895.4	891.0	897.7	914.2	926.3	895.4
2009	865.2	846.3	843.2	840.4	855.2	868.4	862.1	863.2	861.2	860.3	877.7	891.4	861.2
Transportation and Utilities													
1990	295.9	296.4	297.8	297.6	301.4	304.5	293.7	295.0	304.8	303.9	303.1	304.0	299.8
2000	277.2	277.0	278.1	278.4	280.9	283.1	273.7	273.2	285.7	289.5	288.9	290.7	281.4
2001	283.5	282.9	283.5	281.1	287.4	288.3	275.2	270.6	281.3	279.3	274.4	273.2	280.1
2002	264.4	263.3	264.0	265.7	268.8	270.2	258.3	255.0	269.0	271.9	270.4	270.8	266.0
2003	265.4	264.5	265.7	262.6	265.4	266.1	254.7	253.7	266.6	269.8	269.1	269.9	264.5
2004	260.3	259.7	261.0	260.9	266.0	267.7	257.8	257.0	268.9	274.0	273.3	274.1	265.1
2005	263.9	263.6	264.5	265.7	269.2	272.1	259.7	258.6	272.6	271.7	273.6	278.2	267.8
2006	268.7	267.8	269.2	268.8	273.5	276.9	261.3	259.8	275.7	276.1	277.8	282.9	271.5
2007	271.0	270.5	271.5	270.7	276.5	279.6	264.6	261.6	278.0	279.6	280.9	285.0	274.1
2008	274.1	273.2	274.5	276.6	279.4	281.9	265.7	264.6	279.1	278.2	278.7	283.4	275.8
2009	267.7	266.2	264.8	263.9	266.9	267.5	254.2	252.5	264.1	265.4	268.5	270.0	264.3
Information													
1990	284.1	284.2	283.3	284.7	287.8	287.5	288.1	288.4	288.0	284.0	284.4	286.9	286.0
2000	303.2	307.8	311.0	314.0	318.1	322.7	322.0	300.6	325.9	328.4	331.1	332.5	318.1
2001	325.6	328.5	329.0	326.4	329.2	329.3	325.1	322.9	317.2	315.4	318.5	316.3	323.6
2002	298.1	302.0	297.7	297.1	303.9	301.4	290.9	293.1	287.6	288.7	290.9	289.3	295.1
2003	275.7	279.7	276.8	273.8	279.1	275.4	270.9	274.7	271.1	273.5	277.4	276.1	275.4
2004	266.4	267.9	269.4	268.2	268.7	268.2	267.8	269.4	269.5	268.8	271.5	269.6	268.8
2005	263.2	265.4	266.2	266.5	268.3	272.4	269.7	270.6	270.3	271.1	272.3	275.5	269.3
2006	266.7	266.8	268.1	265.3	267.3	269.9	267.5	267.9	265.7	263.7	265.7	267.3	266.8
2007	260.4	261.9	262.3	261.9	264.5	267.1	265.6	266.2	264.7	263.2	265.4	266.7	264.2
2008	259.9	261.7	262.2	260.7	263.5	266.7	264.6	265.3	264.8	263.5	264.3	265.6	263.6
2009	256.7	254.6	255.1	254.0	254.6	254.7	254.0	253.3	252.7	251.4	250.8	252.9	253.7

Employment by Industry: New York, Selected Years, 1990–2009—*Continued*

(Numbers in thousands, not seasonally adjusted.)

Industry and year	January	February	March	April	May	June	July	August	September	October	November	December	Annual average
Financial Activities													
1990	782.5	783.3	783.7	779.0	779.9	785.7	784.1	784.4	777.9	771.2	770.2	771.4	779.4
2000	738.9	740.9	742.4	740.7	742.8	754.6	752.4	752.9	748.2	747.4	748.4	753.6	746.9
2001	739.9	740.2	742.4	737.7	738.0	747.2	745.4	742.4	733.3	704.1	701.7	707.8	731.7
2002	705.5	705.5	705.4	703.4	703.7	710.2	710.5	709.5	699.6	700.3	700.7	703.4	704.8
2003	692.2	690.1	689.7	689.9	693.5	701.6	704.7	704.0	696.7	695.6	696.8	702.8	696.5
2004	692.0	692.7	695.5	694.2	695.8	705.1	711.5	710.5	702.5	705.0	705.6	712.5	701.9
2005	701.0	701.2	703.4	707.1	707.2	717.6	723.6	723.6	716.3	716.4	718.2	723.8	713.3
2006	712.8	714.7	717.8	719.4	722.6	732.5	736.7	737.3	728.6	727.7	729.8	735.1	726.3
2007	723.0	724.4	726.4	725.2	726.0	737.9	741.3	739.0	729.3	731.9	733.3	735.8	731.1
2008	723.3	723.0	723.6	720.9	720.9	728.5	730.6	729.6	715.6	711.5	708.5	708.7	720.4
2009	692.9	687.5	683.9	679.7	678.2	680.6	680.9	678.1	670.1	669.2	666.3	667.6	677.9
Professional and Business Services													
1990	845.0	849.3	856.8	862.6	865.9	873.7	868.0	870.4	865.6	858.2	856.6	854.8	860.6
2000	1066.8	1078.3	1090.6	1103.4	1114.1	1131.4	1133.7	1141.4	1139.5	1145.1	1146.8	1150.6	1120.1
2001	1102.3	1106.4	1109.7	1104.6	1110.5	1118.3	1110.8	1108.3	1097.5	1078.0	1076.2	1076.9	1100.0
2002	1033.8	1037.7	1043.4	1052.9	1057.1	1067.4	1064.3	1064.7	1059.1	1062.8	1064.0	1064.6	1056.0
2003	1020.8	1020.5	1030.1	1040.2	1043.2	1054.4	1050.8	1050.8	1048.1	1054.2	1056.7	1061.3	1044.3
2004	1018.7	1026.7	1039.1	1053.4	1059.3	1074.6	1072.3	1072.3	1067.3	1071.7	1076.1	1083.8	1059.6
2005	1046.3	1047.9	1054.0	1077.3	1078.5	1093.4	1096.5	1098.9	1097.8	1097.3	1104.3	1111.1	1083.6
2006	1071.5	1076.0	1089.3	1100.7	1104.4	1122.5	1120.1	1123.6	1117.5	1122.0	1130.6	1138.3	1109.7
2007	1100.3	1105.7	1117.3	1125.7	1132.8	1153.1	1153.2	1156.0	1143.6	1156.0	1160.4	1166.0	1139.2
2008	1130.9	1137.6	1144.2	1159.1	1160.0	1174.9	1176.2	1173.9	1160.9	1159.3	1154.1	1149.6	1156.7
2009	1101.3	1096.9	1096.3	1099.5	1097.7	1107.1	1103.3	1098.1	1089.3	1087.9	1090.2	1088.3	1096.3
Education and Health Services													
1990	1054.0	1071.6	1081.2	1077.8	1080.8	1072.6	1056.4	1056.6	1082.0	1096.9	1105.3	1108.8	1078.7
2000	1359.7	1379.7	1390.4	1398.8	1390.2	1368.7	1348.5	1342.0	1373.6	1402.3	1420.3	1426.4	1383.4
2001	1401.2	1425.6	1438.9	1441.3	1443.2	1417.3	1395.7	1391.0	1429.5	1461.7	1471.7	1475.7	1432.7
2002	1433.3	1461.4	1474.8	1477.4	1475.8	1446.1	1434.8	1428.9	1470.0	1503.2	1511.4	1512.9	1469.2
2003	1474.0	1501.9	1512.8	1511.5	1507.9	1478.7	1457.2	1447.8	1492.4	1525.9	1534.6	1535.0	1498.3
2004	1494.0	1526.4	1539.2	1536.0	1536.0	1501.5	1483.5	1472.7	1514.7	1553.6	1561.2	1564.1	1523.6
2005	1514.9	1548.2	1557.2	1562.5	1553.4	1518.0	1497.3	1490.9	1540.3	1573.6	1584.0	1585.7	1543.8
2006	1541.0	1576.0	1586.8	1589.2	1584.4	1549.0	1521.4	1513.0	1571.2	1608.1	1618.2	1623.9	1573.5
2007	1571.8	1605.0	1616.0	1613.4	1606.0	1572.8	1545.2	1537.6	1594.8	1637.0	1643.7	1647.3	1599.2
2008	1600.0	1637.2	1644.0	1647.4	1638.6	1606.7	1576.0	1571.0	1627.1	1665.3	1677.7	1683.9	1631.2
2009	1637.5	1674.8	1680.2	1680.8	1671.9	1638.7	1610.8	1604.9	1655.2	1703.2	1714.2	1710.5	1665.2
Leisure and Hospitality													
1990	536.7	540.1	549.9	561.1	587.2	606.5	607.8	611.5	594.0	571.7	563.6	561.8	574.3
2000	581.7	591.1	600.2	621.4	644.5	670.4	676.6	680.4	658.0	647.6	639.7	641.5	637.8
2001	594.8	601.1	610.4	619.2	656.8	679.0	681.8	685.2	650.1	625.9	621.0	621.3	637.2
2002	584.3	592.8	603.8	624.0	653.4	674.0	683.3	686.0	656.9	646.2	635.2	638.0	639.8
2003	598.7	603.4	610.1	625.7	657.0	678.0	692.4	690.0	666.4	654.7	644.4	644.8	647.1
2004	608.7	613.3	624.3	640.0	672.5	697.8	714.6	712.7	690.3	670.5	657.8	659.5	663.5
2005	617.5	623.5	634.1	656.3	683.3	708.6	714.9	716.8	692.0	671.8	664.0	663.3	670.5
2006	620.7	628.4	641.7	656.6	690.7	717.5	728.6	727.1	700.3	686.7	681.6	682.4	680.2
2007	640.9	649.8	659.8	677.3	713.5	739.7	750.3	748.2	719.4	711.0	702.0	700.9	701.1
2008	662.3	669.8	678.2	701.8	733.7	754.4	767.4	765.0	734.9	724.7	708.8	704.8	717.2
2009	662.2	666.1	671.2	687.5	726.4	745.1	757.1	755.0	737.5	720.6	704.7	700.6	711.2
Other Services													
1990	272.1	274.6	276.9	277.3	280.6	282.3	280.4	280.8	278.9	279.1	278.9	279.0	278.4
2000	328.5	331.8	335.1	336.8	339.1	340.4	339.6	339.2	340.2	343.4	344.0	345.6	338.6
2001	339.0	341.5	344.0	343.2	346.4	348.7	345.6	344.8	341.1	343.2	345.5	346.6	344.1
2002	340.3	342.4	345.1	346.2	348.9	350.2	348.9	347.5	345.8	349.9	351.4	352.0	347.4
2003	344.6	345.7	348.2	348.7	351.6	352.8	350.9	348.8	347.3	350.0	350.6	351.8	349.3
2004	345.0	346.8	350.1	351.2	354.9	356.7	354.7	352.7	352.5	355.7	356.1	358.1	352.9
2005	349.2	350.8	353.0	357.4	358.9	360.5	357.7	355.4	355.4	356.3	357.8	359.7	356.0
2006	349.5	350.7	354.3	355.5	358.8	360.8	357.9	355.7	357.0	359.8	360.7	363.3	357.0
2007	356.0	357.7	360.3	361.4	366.0	367.9	363.3	361.1	361.2	365.2	366.2	367.3	362.8
2008	361.7	362.7	364.6	366.7	370.1	371.3	369.6	368.1	367.1	370.0	369.7	369.5	367.6
2009	361.7	362.8	364.1	364.9	368.3	368.9	366.8	364.8	362.0	364.9	366.1	365.4	365.1
Government													
1990	1456.1	1473.6	1486.5	1492.4	1511.8	1505.0	1444.0	1427.4	1432.4	1474.2	1486.3	1484.7	1472.9
2000	1445.1	1464.2	1478.7	1491.8	1513.3	1479.8	1453.7	1410.7	1426.5	1476.8	1485.3	1480.6	1467.2
2001	1452.5	1472.4	1478.3	1487.7	1484.3	1474.9	1426.7	1402.9	1440.1	1486.3	1502.7	1499.0	1467.3
2002	1476.6	1501.7	1509.9	1501.1	1509.4	1505.4	1470.2	1448.1	1453.3	1497.2	1514.1	1518.2	1492.1
2003	1478.8	1502.4	1506.6	1501.9	1505.0	1503.3	1453.2	1432.3	1451.1	1492.1	1507.6	1513.0	1487.3
2004	1470.9	1493.0	1499.9	1496.3	1508.3	1503.6	1454.3	1432.4	1448.5	1490.2	1503.7	1504.7	1483.8
2005	1479.2	1497.5	1499.1	1505.1	1509.2	1508.6	1461.6	1441.2	1461.2	1492.8	1504.9	1510.6	1489.3
2006	1475.3	1493.2	1495.6	1498.8	1504.0	1501.1	1451.9	1430.4	1457.6	1494.8	1506.4	1514.5	1485.3
2007	1489.5	1509.0	1511.1	1509.3	1517.7	1517.0	1466.6	1450.3	1474.9	1512.8	1522.8	1531.2	1501.0
2008	1495.4	1515.9	1519.8	1529.8	1533.6	1533.4	1499.3	1471.1	1487.7	1526.2	1535.1	1539.1	1515.5
2009	1507.1	1531.5	1534.4	1538.0	1543.4	1532.1	1535.9	1508.1	1476.8	1523.4	1533.1	1523.3	1523.9

Average Weekly Hours by Selected Industry: New York, 2007–2009

(Not seasonally adjusted.)

Industry and year	January	February	March	April	May	June	July	August	September	October	November	December	Annual average
Total Private													
2007	33.7	33.6	33.8	34.1	33.9	34.2	34.3	34.1	34.5	34.2	34.3	34.6	34.1
2008	34.0	34.1	34.3	34.1	34.2	34.5	34.2	34.4	34.1	33.9	34.2	33.7	34.1
2009	33.6	34.0	33.8	33.5	33.7	33.6	33.7	34.1	33.7	33.7	34.0	33.7	33.8
Goods-Producing													
2007	38.1	37.0	37.5	37.8	38.1	38.2	37.8	37.8	38.2	37.7	37.8	38.1	37.8
2008	37.5	37.5	37.9	37.5	37.6	37.9	37.4	37.8	37.6	37.3	37.5	37.3	37.6
2009	36.8	36.9	37.0	36.3	37.2	37.5	37.3	37.8	37.2	37.7	38.1	37.9	37.3
Construction													
2007	36.1	34.7	35.7	35.7	36.6	36.9	36.5	36.4	36.8	36.3	36.1	35.9	36.2
2008	35.9	35.7	35.9	35.6	36.0	36.4	36.5	36.4	36.5	36.2	36.4	36.1	36.2
2009	36.1	36.0	36.3	35.7	36.4	36.2	36.6	36.7	35.3	36.0	36.8	36.1	36.2
Manufacturing													
2007	39.1	38.1	38.5	39.0	39.1	39.1	38.8	38.7	39.2	38.7	38.9	39.4	38.9
2008	38.4	38.5	39.1	38.7	38.6	38.8	38.0	38.6	38.3	37.9	38.1	37.9	38.4
2009	37.1	37.3	37.3	36.8	37.7	38.3	37.6	38.3	38.3	38.5	38.6	39.0	37.9
Trade, Transportation, and Utilities													
2007	34.6	34.5	35.0	34.9	35.1	35.4	35.0	34.7	35.3	35.0	34.9	35.4	35.0
2008	34.3	34.5	34.7	34.3	34.4	34.8	34.3	34.2	34.1	33.9	34.1	33.9	34.3
2009	33.4	33.7	33.7	33.6	33.9	33.8	34.0	34.2	34.1	33.9	34.3	34.3	33.9
Information													
2007	32.0	32.3	32.7	32.7	32.5	32.7	33.8	33.2	34.1	33.5	33.7	34.4	33.1
2008	33.7	33.9	34.5	33.9	34.1	34.5	34.6	34.6	34.6	34.6	35.0	33.9	34.3
2009	33.7	34.8	34.2	33.9	33.9	33.9	33.8	34.7	33.9	33.8	34.8	32.7	34.0
Financial Activities													
2007	36.4	36.3	36.2	37.1	36.2	36.5	37.2	37.0	37.6	37.1	37.3	37.3	36.9
2008	36.8	36.9	37.0	36.8	37.1	37.2	36.9	37.0	36.8	36.8	37.3	36.4	36.9
2009	36.7	37.7	37.0	36.5	36.4	36.6	36.6	37.2	36.8	36.9	36.9	36.4	36.8
Professional and Business Services													
2007	34.7	35.1	34.9	35.5	34.9	35.2	35.5	34.8	35.7	35.0	35.1	35.9	35.2
2008	35.1	35.1	35.8	35.3	35.4	36.0	35.3	35.8	35.7	35.1	35.8	34.9	35.4
2009	35.0	35.7	35.4	34.6	34.8	34.7	34.3	34.9	34.3	34.5	35.2	34.6	34.8
Education and Health Services													
2007	32.0	32.2	32.7	32.7	32.6	33.1	33.1	33.2	33.4	33.1	33.4	33.3	32.9
2008	33.4	33.3	33.3	33.2	33.4	33.6	33.4	33.7	33.4	33.3	33.6	33.3	33.4
2009	33.4	33.4	33.2	33.1	33.1	33.0	33.2	33.1	33.1	32.9	32.9	32.7	33.1
Leisure and Hospitality													
2007	27.4	27.4	27.5	27.3	28.0	28.2	28.5	28.7	28.2	28.3	28.4	28.0	28.0
2008	27.8	28.0	28.1	28.3	28.4	28.6	28.8	28.7	27.9	27.9	27.8	27.0	28.2
2009	26.9	27.4	27.2	27.5	28.1	27.5	28.3	28.6	27.9	28.1	28.1	28.0	27.8
Other Services													
2007	29.8	29.8	29.3	30.3	29.7	29.7	30.3	30.4	30.1	29.8	29.9	30.5	30.0
2008	30.4	30.5	30.7	30.7	30.6	30.8	30.8	30.9	30.2	29.9	30.0	29.7	30.4
2009	29.9	30.2	30.2	30.3	30.6	30.9	31.5	31.8	30.6	30.8	30.9	31.0	30.7

Average Hourly Earnings by Selected Industry: New York, 2007–2009

(Dollars, not seasonally adjusted.)

Industry and year	January	February	March	April	May	June	July	August	September	October	November	December	Annual average
Total Private													
2007	25.42	25.54	25.34	25.58	25.12	25.09	25.27	25.15	25.22	25.08	25.08	25.25	25.26
2008	25.33	25.44	25.67	25.50	25.39	25.37	25.33	25.42	25.51	25.46	25.65	25.66	25.48
2009	25.66	25.79	25.72	25.52	25.35	25.60	25.56	25.72	25.80	25.76	25.98	25.97	25.70
Goods-Producing													
2007	24.69	24.94	25.16	25.09	25.13	24.91	25.06	25.08	25.22	24.90	25.16	25.23	25.05
2008	25.23	25.20	25.20	25.31	25.23	25.20	25.09	25.03	25.06	25.28	25.56	25.68	25.25
2009	25.48	25.52	25.84	26.00	25.91	25.81	26.37	26.31	26.61	26.36	26.40	26.45	26.09
Construction													
2007	29.66	30.65	30.29	29.85	29.74	29.09	29.35	29.47	29.66	29.73	29.99	30.27	29.79
2008	30.33	30.40	30.28	29.97	29.97	29.86	29.88	30.09	30.05	30.01	30.45	30.46	30.14
2009	30.60	30.45	30.54	30.42	30.31	30.42	31.08	31.02	31.69	31.27	31.23	31.80	30.90
Manufacturing													
2007	22.30	22.37	22.70	22.77	22.66	22.67	22.75	22.73	22.80	22.34	22.69	22.81	22.63
2008	22.85	22.88	22.92	23.03	22.78	22.73	22.60	22.49	22.56	22.88	23.02	23.32	22.84
2009	23.00	23.07	23.24	23.46	23.23	22.96	23.27	23.20	23.48	23.32	23.39	23.36	23.25
Trade, Transportation, and Utilities													
2007	21.34	21.59	21.39	21.56	21.11	21.30	21.30	21.46	21.34	21.27	21.26	21.17	21.34
2008	21.57	21.48	21.72	21.53	21.60	21.43	21.53	21.61	21.54	21.27	21.34	21.26	21.49
2009	21.57	21.57	21.53	21.53	21.26	21.40	21.29	21.59	21.50	21.55	21.45	21.55	21.48
Information													
2007	34.14	33.65	32.38	32.63	32.36	33.12	32.53	32.65	32.64	32.75	32.80	32.87	32.87
2008	33.06	32.86	33.16	33.89	33.30	33.40	33.27	33.51	33.93	33.79	34.18	35.36	33.64
2009	34.87	35.05	34.67	34.07	34.76	35.47	35.81	35.38	35.66	35.80	35.86	36.02	35.28
Financial Activities													
2007	35.50	35.47	35.46	35.90	35.26	35.28	35.55	35.21	35.09	34.48	34.35	35.15	35.22
2008	35.01	35.55	35.78	35.24	34.80	34.99	34.50	34.84	34.62	34.53	34.74	34.28	34.91
2009	34.13	34.33	34.79	34.59	34.53	34.56	34.47	34.98	34.71	34.78	35.85	35.49	34.76
Professional and Business Services													
2007	30.43	31.17	30.52	31.32	30.90	30.65	31.12	30.88	31.15	31.44	31.36	31.65	31.06
2008	31.78	32.40	32.56	32.21	32.18	32.28	32.37	32.34	32.48	33.00	33.18	33.34	32.51
2009	33.30	33.86	33.50	33.07	32.59	33.17	33.43	33.59	33.42	33.75	33.94	34.04	33.47
Education and Health Services													
2007	23.24	22.99	22.86	22.71	22.35	22.13	22.03	22.04	21.87	21.70	21.69	21.73	22.27
2008	21.66	21.52	21.94	21.94	21.91	21.77	22.00	21.81	22.00	21.88	22.01	22.10	21.88
2009	22.11	22.10	21.95	22.00	22.05	22.09	22.09	21.99	22.23	22.10	22.28	22.28	22.11
Leisure and Hospitality													
2007	16.76	16.50	16.71	16.96	16.49	16.76	17.36	16.65	17.20	17.38	17.42	17.64	16.99
2008	17.39	17.58	17.67	17.57	17.41	17.40	16.88	17.63	18.10	17.71	17.93	18.32	17.62
2009	17.53	17.54	17.38	16.95	16.96	18.00	17.39	17.38	18.03	17.43	17.76	18.15	17.55
Other Services													
2007	22.73	22.41	22.64	22.72	22.62	22.45	22.14	22.10	22.56	22.18	22.11	22.08	22.39
2008	21.82	21.83	21.87	21.67	21.74	21.50	21.45	21.40	21.81	21.70	21.79	21.70	21.69
2009	21.66	21.44	21.39	21.08	21.20	21.07	20.19	20.86	21.75	21.60	21.84	21.74	21.31

Average Weekly Earnings by Selected Industry: New York, 2007–2009

(Dollars, not seasonally adjusted.)

Industry and year	January	February	March	April	May	June	July	August	September	October	November	December	Annual average
Total Private													
2007	856.65	858.14	856.49	872.28	851.57	858.08	866.76	857.62	870.09	857.74	860.24	873.65	861.37
2008	861.22	867.50	880.48	869.55	868.34	875.27	866.29	874.45	869.89	863.09	877.23	864.74	868.87
2009	862.18	876.86	869.34	854.92	854.30	860.16	861.37	877.05	869.46	868.11	883.32	875.19	868.66
Goods-Producing													
2007	940.69	922.78	943.50	948.40	957.45	951.56	947.27	948.02	963.40	938.73	951.05	961.26	946.89
2008	946.13	945.00	955.08	949.13	948.65	955.08	938.37	946.13	942.26	942.94	958.50	957.86	949.40
2009	937.66	941.69	956.08	943.80	963.85	967.88	983.60	994.52	989.89	993.77	1005.84	1002.46	973.16
Construction													
2007	1070.73	1063.56	1081.35	1065.65	1088.48	1073.42	1071.28	1072.71	1091.49	1079.20	1082.64	1086.69	1078.40
2008	1088.85	1085.28	1087.05	1066.93	1078.92	1086.90	1090.62	1095.28	1096.83	1086.36	1108.38	1099.61	1091.07
2009	1104.66	1096.20	1108.60	1085.99	1103.28	1101.20	1137.53	1138.43	1118.66	1125.72	1149.26	1147.98	1118.58
Manufacturing													
2007	871.93	852.30	873.95	888.03	886.01	886.40	882.70	879.65	893.76	864.56	882.64	898.71	880.31
2008	877.44	880.88	896.17	891.26	879.31	881.92	858.80	868.11	864.05	867.15	877.06	883.83	877.06
2009	853.30	860.51	866.85	863.33	875.77	879.37	874.95	888.56	899.28	897.82	902.85	911.04	881.18
Trade, Transportation, and Utilities													
2007	738.36	744.86	748.65	752.44	740.96	754.02	745.50	744.66	753.30	744.45	741.97	749.42	746.90
2008	739.85	741.06	753.68	738.48	743.04	745.76	738.48	739.06	734.51	721.05	727.69	720.71	737.11
2009	720.44	726.91	725.56	723.41	720.71	723.32	723.86	738.38	733.15	730.55	735.74	739.17	728.17
Information													
2007	1092.48	1086.90	1058.83	1067.00	1051.70	1083.02	1099.51	1083.98	1113.02	1097.13	1105.36	1130.73	1088.00
2008	1114.12	1113.95	1144.02	1148.87	1135.53	1152.30	1151.14	1159.45	1173.98	1169.13	1196.30	1198.70	1153.85
2009	1175.12	1219.74	1185.71	1154.97	1178.36	1202.43	1210.38	1227.69	1208.87	1210.04	1247.93	1177.85	1199.52
Financial Activities													
2007	1292.20	1287.56	1283.65	1331.89	1276.41	1287.72	1322.46	1302.77	1319.38	1279.21	1281.26	1311.10	1299.62
2008	1288.37	1311.80	1323.86	1296.83	1291.08	1301.63	1273.05	1289.08	1274.02	1270.70	1295.80	1247.79	1288.18
2009	1252.57	1294.24	1287.23	1262.54	1256.89	1264.90	1261.60	1301.26	1277.33	1283.38	1322.87	1291.84	1279.17
Professional and Business Services													
2007	1055.92	1094.07	1065.15	1111.86	1078.41	1078.88	1104.76	1074.62	1112.06	1100.40	1100.74	1136.24	1093.31
2008	1115.48	1137.24	1165.65	1137.01	1139.17	1162.08	1142.66	1157.77	1159.54	1158.30	1187.84	1163.57	1150.85
2009	1165.50	1208.80	1185.90	1144.22	1134.13	1151.00	1146.65	1172.29	1146.31	1164.38	1194.69	1177.78	1164.76
Education and Health Services													
2007	743.68	740.28	747.52	742.62	728.61	732.50	729.19	731.73	730.46	718.27	724.45	723.61	732.08
2008	723.44	716.62	730.60	728.41	731.79	731.47	734.80	735.00	734.80	728.60	739.54	735.93	730.79
2009	738.47	738.14	720.74	728.20	729.86	728.97	733.39	727.87	735.81	727.09	733.01	728.56	731.84
Leisure and Hospitality													
2007	459.22	452.10	459.53	463.01	461.72	472.63	494.76	477.86	485.04	491.85	494.73	493.92	475.72
2008	483.44	492.24	496.53	497.23	494.44	497.64	486.14	505.98	504.99	494.11	498.45	505.63	496.88
2009	471.56	480.60	472.74	466.13	476.58	495.00	492.14	497.07	503.04	489.78	499.06	508.20	487.89
Other Services													
2007	677.35	667.82	663.35	688.42	671.81	666.77	670.84	671.84	679.06	660.96	661.09	673.44	671.70
2008	663.33	665.82	671.41	665.27	665.24	662.20	660.66	661.26	658.66	648.83	653.70	644.49	659.38
2009	647.63	647.49	645.98	638.72	648.72	651.06	635.99	663.35	665.55	665.28	674.86	673.94	654.22

NORTH CAROLINA
At a Glance

Population:
  1990 census: 6,632,448
  2000 census: 8,049,313
  2009 estimate: 9,380,884

Percent change in population:
  1990–2000: 21.4%
  2000–2009: 16.5%

Percent change in total nonfarm employment:
  1990–2009: 25.4%
  2008–2009: -5.3%

Industry with the largest growth in employment, 1990–2009 (thousands):
  Education and Health Services, 309.7

Industry with the largest decline or smallest growth in employment, 1990–2009 (thousands):
  Manufacturing, -376.2

Civilian labor force:
  1990: 3,497,568
  2000: 4,123,812
  2009: 4,544,622

Unemployment rate and rank among states (lowest to highest):
  1990: 4.2%, 5th
  2000: 3.7%, 22nd
  2009: 10.6%, 45th

Employment by Industry, 2009

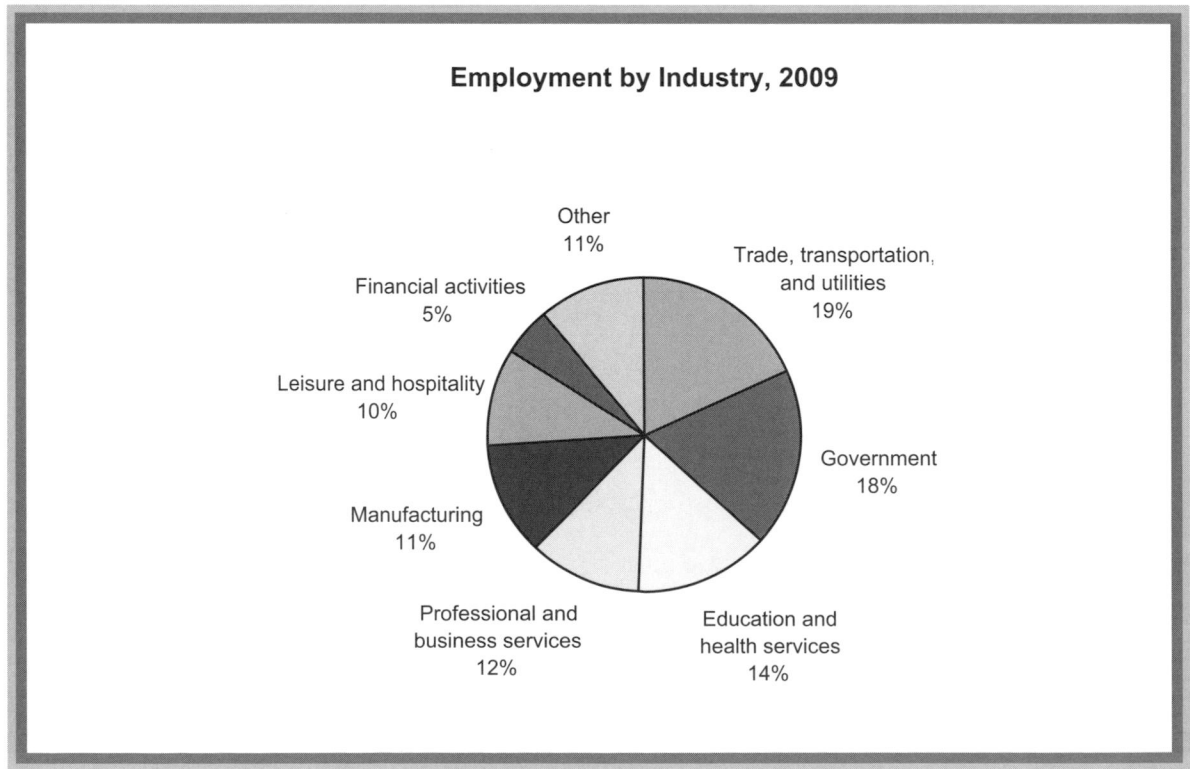

Employment by Industry: North Carolina, Selected Years, 1990–2009

(Numbers in thousands, not seasonally adjusted.)

Industry and year	January	February	March	April	May	June	July	August	September	October	November	December	Annual average
Total Nonfarm													
1990	3070.9	3091.6	3114.4	3124.8	3142.7	3160.7	3095.5	3116.1	3140.4	3132.5	3141.3	3127.3	3121.5
2000	3822.0	3842.8	3888.6	3911.2	3940.9	3960.0	3882.7	3932.6	3949.9	3945.2	3954.8	3950.5	3915.1
2001	3884.8	3896.7	3914.4	3917.5	3932.3	3924.0	3845.4	3887.5	3890.4	3885.6	3877.5	3866.7	3893.6
2002	3782.2	3798.7	3827.4	3852.0	3874.3	3857.2	3791.8	3842.1	3852.1	3857.4	3852.8	3845.7	3836.1
2003	3749.6	3752.5	3775.9	3796.5	3823.9	3808.3	3716.6	3776.6	3800.9	3821.9	3817.6	3821.9	3788.5
2004	3738.7	3748.9	3785.5	3818.6	3851.0	3844.3	3797.3	3858.6	3887.2	3891.3	3900.7	3910.1	3836.0
2005	3831.7	3848.0	3878.8	3905.3	3925.2	3909.4	3853.7	3925.5	3961.4	3968.8	3983.5	3986.1	3914.8
2006	3921.8	3936.6	3972.7	4019.5	4051.6	4048.6	3991.3	4063.7	4089.1	4111.2	4137.9	4143.3	4040.6
2007	4053.7	4076.9	4117.2	4126.7	4164.3	4167.9	4081.1	4159.8	4186.3	4189.2	4207.4	4210.5	4145.1
2008	4113.5	4133.2	4154.0	4156.5	4182.2	4163.9	4071.8	4139.8	4159.3	4135.6	4117.0	4094.2	4135.1
2009	3952.2	3940.7	3933.9	3926.4	3942.8	3917.0	3817.9	3879.1	3911.0	3926.7	3929.6	3910.7	3915.7
Total Private													
1990	2591.2	2604.2	2620.8	2630.8	2643.2	2665.7	2651.6	2669.1	2659.9	2637.2	2637.1	2629.2	2636.7
2000	3218.1	3231.7	3268.2	3288.3	3311.9	3345.4	3327.7	3331.6	3325.6	3313.2	3319.9	3318.4	3300.0
2001	3257.3	3262.4	3276.8	3283.9	3296.1	3313.7	3277.3	3279.4	3254.2	3234.3	3223.7	3217.3	3264.7
2002	3143.7	3153.2	3177.5	3204.3	3225.1	3241.0	3221.2	3233.0	3215.6	3204.2	3202.4	3199.8	3201.8
2003	3114.7	3112.2	3131.2	3153.5	3177.7	3192.6	3154.0	3169.5	3158.6	3157.9	3161.2	3167.8	3154.2
2004	3095.3	3100.5	3132.4	3166.5	3196.2	3221.2	3226.2	3236.2	3224.5	3224.4	3231.6	3242.0	3191.4
2005	3172.7	3182.6	3209.3	3236.3	3254.0	3274.9	3281.7	3294.9	3291.4	3294.5	3306.1	3310.7	3259.1
2006	3251.6	3260.1	3290.9	3335.3	3363.7	3390.1	3404.4	3417.1	3406.6	3420.2	3436.4	3443.6	3368.3
2007	3367.0	3383.5	3418.6	3428.2	3461.7	3493.4	3480.0	3494.0	3482.2	3484.3	3495.1	3499.5	3457.3
2008	3411.4	3423.4	3439.0	3439.8	3460.9	3470.5	3457.1	3459.3	3433.7	3408.3	3384.8	3364.0	3429.4
2009	3234.7	3219.3	3207.3	3196.0	3213.0	3218.3	3198.6	3197.6	3182.7	3183.0	3182.0	3167.4	3200.0
Goods-Producing													
1990	997.9	1005.3	1007.4	1005.5	1005.0	1011.0	1000.9	1004.8	999.9	986.8	984.6	975.6	998.7
2000	989.4	990.3	998.7	997.4	1001.2	1008.2	1002.1	998.8	1001.5	989.5	991.6	987.8	996.3
2001	972.9	968.5	965.4	959.8	953.4	953.0	938.3	934.8	927.3	916.2	905.6	898.4	941.1
2002	879.4	878.8	879.3	876.8	877.6	875.7	870.2	871.8	866.5	860.9	855.0	850.1	870.2
2003	834.6	829.2	830.0	829.1	828.9	827.9	810.4	810.5	808.0	806.2	802.4	799.9	818.1
2004	787.7	786.4	792.9	798.9	803.3	809.3	810.6	810.1	809.3	808.3	806.8	806.8	802.5
2005	794.6	795.6	798.5	800.7	803.8	807.7	805.9	807.7	808.2	802.8	802.6	800.8	802.4
2006	789.2	788.7	793.6	805.2	807.8	812.8	813.0	815.0	812.8	810.7	808.9	809.8	805.6
2007	797.6	797.8	801.5	796.8	799.6	807.4	801.9	804.1	802.5	799.0	797.5	795.7	800.1
2008	776.2	775.2	775.0	767.5	768.3	766.8	762.7	759.4	755.0	743.9	732.4	720.8	758.6
2009	685.1	673.9	662.2	652.6	647.6	645.6	638.0	635.3	632.9	624.5	621.7	615.9	644.6
Mining and Logging													
1990	7.8	7.9	8.0	8.1	8.1	8.1	7.8	7.9	7.8	7.7	7.8	7.8	7.9
2000	8.4	8.3	8.5	8.4	8.5	8.5	8.5	8.5	8.5	8.4	8.4	8.4	8.4
2001	8.2	8.1	8.1	8.2	8.7	8.2	8.1	8.1	8.1	8.0	8.0	8.0	8.1
2002	8.0	8.0	8.1	8.0	8.0	7.9	7.8	7.8	7.8	7.8	7.7	7.7	7.9
2003	7.6	7.5	7.6	7.6	7.6	7.6	7.1	7.2	7.1	7.2	7.0	7.0	7.3
2004	6.8	6.8	6.9	6.9	6.9	7.0	6.9	7.0	7.1	6.9	6.9	6.9	6.9
2005	6.8	6.8	6.8	6.7	6.6	6.7	6.6	6.6	6.6	6.7	6.7	6.6	6.7
2006	6.6	6.6	6.7	6.7	6.7	6.8	6.9	7.0	7.0	6.9	6.9	6.9	6.8
2007	6.9	6.9	7.0	7.1	7.1	7.1	7.0	7.1	7.0	6.9	6.9	6.9	7.0
2008	6.8	6.8	6.7	6.6	6.6	6.6	6.6	6.6	6.6	6.5	6.5	6.4	6.6
2009	6.1	6.0	6.0	5.9	5.9	6.0	6.0	6.0	6.0	6.0	6.0	6.0	6.0
Construction													
1990	161.5	164.3	167.9	167.2	169.3	172.6	171.6	171.2	167.8	165.1	163.9	160.5	166.9
2000	220.0	219.3	227.4	228.1	231.2	235.2	233.8	235.2	235.0	232.4	232.0	230.7	230.0
2001	223.6	224.7	230.0	230.3	233.1	235.8	233.1	232.6	230.0	227.4	224.9	222.3	229.0
2002	214.4	214.4	216.9	221.0	223.3	224.1	222.7	223.3	220.1	217.2	214.5	213.7	218.8
2003	206.1	204.6	206.8	209.7	214.2	215.4	212.5	212.8	212.2	215.3	214.0	213.3	211.4
2004	206.0	205.0	210.1	214.9	218.2	221.0	223.7	223.9	222.9	224.3	223.9	224.6	218.2
2005	219.3	220.2	223.4	227.2	230.4	233.5	237.2	238.0	238.5	235.6	235.5	234.5	231.1
2006	230.2	231.2	236.4	242.1	244.7	248.7	251.5	253.5	252.5	251.9	252.5	252.7	245.7
2007	246.5	247.0	252.0	253.7	256.0	259.8	258.6	259.2	258.4	256.6	255.0	253.0	254.7
2008	242.1	241.6	242.3	239.9	241.0	240.6	240.2	237.3	234.7	229.9	223.9	218.4	236.0
2009	202.2	199.6	197.5	193.5	193.6	194.0	192.3	190.6	188.3	181.3	180.7	177.0	190.9
Manufacturing													
1990	828.6	833.1	831.5	830.2	827.6	830.3	821.5	825.7	824.3	814.0	812.9	807.3	823.9
2000	761.0	762.7	762.8	760.9	761.5	764.5	759.8	755.1	758.0	748.7	751.2	748.7	757.9
2001	741.1	735.7	727.3	721.3	712.1	709.0	697.1	694.1	689.2	680.8	672.7	668.1	704.0
2002	657.0	656.4	654.3	647.8	646.3	643.7	639.7	640.7	638.6	635.9	632.8	628.7	643.5
2003	620.9	617.1	615.6	611.8	607.1	604.9	590.8	590.5	588.7	583.7	581.4	579.6	599.3
2004	574.9	574.6	575.9	577.1	578.2	581.3	580.0	579.2	579.3	577.1	576.0	575.3	577.4
2005	568.5	568.6	568.3	566.8	566.8	567.5	562.1	563.1	563.1	560.5	560.4	559.7	564.6
2006	552.4	550.9	550.5	556.4	556.4	557.3	554.6	554.5	553.3	551.9	549.5	550.2	553.2
2007	544.2	543.9	542.5	536.0	536.5	540.5	536.3	537.8	537.1	535.5	535.6	535.8	538.5
2008	527.3	526.8	526.0	521.0	520.7	519.6	515.9	515.5	513.7	507.5	502.0	496.0	516.0
2009	476.8	468.3	458.7	453.2	448.1	445.6	439.7	438.7	438.6	437.2	435.0	432.9	447.7

Employment by Industry: North Carolina, Selected Years, 1990–2009—*Continued*

(Numbers in thousands, not seasonally adjusted.)

Industry and year	January	February	March	April	May	June	July	August	September	October	November	December	Annual average
Service-Providing													
1990	2073.0	2086.3	2107.0	2119.3	2137.7	2149.7	2094.6	2111.3	2140.5	2145.7	2156.7	2151.7	2122.8
2000	2832.6	2852.5	2889.9	2913.8	2939.7	2951.8	2880.6	2933.8	2948.4	2955.7	2963.2	2962.7	2918.7
2001	2911.9	2928.2	2949.0	2957.7	2978.9	2971.0	2907.1	2952.7	2963.1	2969.4	2971.9	2968.3	2952.4
2002	2902.8	2919.9	2948.1	2975.2	2996.7	2981.5	2921.6	2970.3	2985.6	2996.5	2997.8	2995.6	2966.0
2003	2915.0	2923.3	2945.9	2967.4	2995.0	2980.4	2906.2	2966.1	2992.9	3015.7	3015.2	3022.0	2970.4
2004	2951.0	2962.5	2992.6	3019.7	3047.7	3035.0	2986.7	3048.5	3077.9	3083.0	3093.9	3103.3	3033.5
2005	3037.1	3052.4	3080.3	3104.6	3121.4	3101.7	3047.8	3117.8	3153.2	3166.0	3180.9	3185.3	3112.4
2006	3132.6	3147.9	3179.1	3214.3	3243.8	3235.8	3178.3	3248.7	3276.3	3300.5	3329.0	3333.5	3235.0
2007	3256.1	3279.1	3315.7	3329.9	3364.7	3360.5	3279.2	3355.7	3383.8	3390.2	3409.9	3414.8	3345.0
2008	3337.3	3358.0	3379.0	3389.0	3413.9	3397.1	3309.1	3380.4	3404.3	3391.7	3384.6	3373.4	3376.5
2009	3267.1	3266.8	3271.7	3273.8	3295.2	3271.4	3179.9	3243.8	3278.1	3302.2	3307.9	3294.8	3271.1
Trade, Transportation, and Utilities													
1990	628.8	629.0	632.1	628.2	630.5	633.4	629.4	634.3	635.4	635.0	641.5	646.9	633.7
2000	735.4	734.6	741.8	746.9	753.2	759.2	751.1	753.8	752.6	755.6	765.1	772.7	751.8
2001	746.2	740.9	745.0	742.6	745.6	748.4	739.8	738.9	737.3	735.4	742.0	746.3	742.4
2002	715.3	710.2	716.6	720.1	723.8	728.4	725.0	727.4	724.9	725.2	738.2	745.0	725.0
2003	710.8	707.9	710.5	712.0	716.0	720.6	714.4	717.4	716.3	721.2	731.9	739.0	718.2
2004	710.2	706.9	712.6	718.7	724.7	728.4	727.7	729.9	728.5	731.5	743.2	751.9	726.2
2005	723.0	722.9	727.7	733.2	736.5	738.6	741.2	741.7	739.5	748.4	761.2	769.2	740.3
2006	739.5	734.4	740.4	749.8	755.0	756.1	761.6	763.4	761.4	767.9	784.5	791.4	758.8
2007	765.6	761.8	770.5	770.4	777.3	779.9	779.0	779.1	776.4	780.0	795.1	802.1	778.1
2008	771.0	768.0	772.6	769.1	771.7	773.3	770.6	768.9	763.0	763.3	767.5	768.9	769.0
2009	729.5	721.0	720.1	715.1	720.0	722.1	717.1	715.8	712.2	713.5	724.0	725.7	719.7
Wholesale Trade													
1990	137.8	139.0	140.5	139.0	138.5	140.3	140.0	141.4	141.5	141.0	140.1	139.4	139.8
2000	160.7	161.6	162.9	163.9	164.6	165.7	165.2	165.8	165.6	166.1	165.3	166.1	164.4
2001	162.1	162.1	162.8	161.6	162.0	162.8	163.0	162.8	162.8	162.6	161.9	162.0	162.4
2002	160.1	160.1	160.7	162.3	162.7	163.6	163.4	163.4	163.6	164.0	164.2	164.2	162.7
2003	162.0	161.9	162.8	163.2	163.6	164.6	163.8	164.3	163.8	165.1	165.5	166.1	163.9
2004	164.5	164.2	165.3	165.6	166.2	167.0	167.0	167.6	167.7	167.9	168.0	168.8	166.7
2005	166.3	166.9	166.8	168.9	169.9	170.2	171.2	171.6	171.8	173.4	174.3	174.8	170.5
2006	171.7	172.1	172.9	175.5	176.3	176.7	177.7	177.7	177.7	177.7	178.6	179.1	176.1
2007	179.1	180.0	181.3	181.7	182.4	183.7	183.6	183.1	182.8	183.0	183.2	183.6	182.3
2008	181.3	182.1	182.8	180.8	181.4	181.3	180.4	179.8	178.4	178.3	176.7	175.2	179.9
2009	170.6	169.9	168.8	167.0	166.7	166.3	164.8	164.5	163.6	164.1	165.3	163.5	166.3
Retail Trade													
1990	374.9	372.5	373.5	371.7	374.2	375.6	373.4	375.4	374.8	374.7	382.7	387.9	375.9
2000	442.4	440.1	445.1	448.3	453.5	457.5	450.2	451.9	450.7	451.6	463.0	470.3	452.0
2001	448.9	442.8	446.1	444.5	447.1	449.4	442.5	443.0	442.3	441.5	451.0	455.6	446.2
2002	431.0	426.5	431.8	433.6	436.2	438.6	434.9	436.5	434.7	433.7	446.4	453.4	436.4
2003	424.7	421.2	423.6	425.0	428.2	431.5	427.0	428.7	427.0	430.6	441.5	446.9	429.7
2004	423.3	419.4	423.4	427.4	432.1	434.2	432.6	434.2	432.5	435.4	446.6	453.5	432.9
2005	430.7	429.7	434.0	437.0	438.9	439.9	442.6	442.3	439.5	445.6	456.5	462.9	441.6
2006	440.1	434.5	438.6	445.3	448.9	448.9	452.3	453.4	450.9	457.0	472.3	478.1	451.7
2007	456.3	452.3	458.7	458.7	464.4	465.7	465.8	466.3	464.1	468.2	482.7	488.0	465.9
2008	463.4	459.7	463.6	462.1	463.4	465.0	464.0	462.7	459.0	459.4	465.3	467.0	462.9
2009	438.4	432.4	433.2	431.7	437.0	438.9	436.8	436.3	433.3	434.6	442.6	446.1	436.8
Transportation and Utilities													
1990	116.1	117.5	118.1	117.5	117.8	117.5	116.0	117.5	119.1	119.3	118.7	119.6	117.9
2000	132.3	132.9	133.8	134.7	135.1	136.0	135.7	136.1	136.3	137.9	136.8	136.3	135.3
2001	135.2	136.0	136.1	136.5	136.5	136.2	134.3	133.1	132.2	131.3	129.1	128.7	133.8
2002	124.2	123.6	124.1	124.2	124.9	126.2	126.7	127.5	126.6	127.5	127.6	127.4	125.9
2003	124.1	124.8	124.1	123.8	124.2	124.5	123.6	124.4	125.5	125.5	124.9	126.0	124.6
2004	122.4	123.3	123.9	125.7	126.4	127.2	128.1	128.1	128.3	128.2	128.6	129.6	126.7
2005	126.0	126.3	126.9	127.3	127.7	128.5	127.4	127.8	128.2	129.4	130.4	131.5	128.1
2006	127.7	127.8	128.9	129.0	129.8	130.5	131.6	132.3	132.8	133.2	133.6	134.2	131.0
2007	130.2	129.5	130.5	130.0	130.5	130.5	129.6	129.7	129.5	128.8	129.2	130.5	129.9
2008	126.3	126.2	126.2	126.2	126.9	127.0	126.2	126.4	125.6	125.6	125.5	126.7	126.2
2009	120.5	118.7	118.1	116.4	116.3	116.9	115.5	115.0	115.3	114.8	116.1	116.1	116.6
Information													
1990	50.0	50.6	51.0	51.6	51.8	52.4	52.5	52.4	52.8	52.1	52.4	52.7	51.9
2000	72.3	72.7	73.5	75.0	75.4	76.6	77.1	77.6	77.6	78.0	78.6	78.5	76.1
2001	76.9	78.2	78.0	76.5	76.9	76.6	75.6	75.7	74.0	73.8	74.3	73.1	75.8
2002	73.8	73.6	73.8	73.5	73.7	73.6	72.8	72.4	71.7	71.9	71.9	72.1	72.9
2003	70.4	70.3	70.0	68.6	69.0	69.4	68.9	68.9	67.8	67.7	67.8	67.9	68.9
2004	67.2	66.7	67.0	66.4	66.3	67.1	67.1	67.2	66.7	68.1	69.3	69.7	67.4
2005	69.6	69.4	69.6	70.1	70.4	71.0	71.4	72.1	72.5	72.8	73.2	74.5	71.4
2006	74.1	74.0	73.9	72.7	72.9	73.5	72.6	72.7	72.3	72.5	72.5	72.9	73.1
2007	72.2	72.6	72.4	72.5	72.7	73.1	73.0	72.7	72.4	72.7	72.9	72.8	72.7
2008	72.0	72.3	72.2	72.2	72.4	72.6	72.2	72.2	71.5	72.2	72.5	72.4	72.2
2009	71.3	71.1	70.6	70.4	70.2	69.9	69.5	69.0	68.3	68.8	69.2	69.3	69.8

Employment by Industry: North Carolina, Selected Years, 1990–2009—*Continued*

(Numbers in thousands, not seasonally adjusted.)

Industry and year	January	February	March	April	May	June	July	August	September	October	November	December	Annual average
Financial Activities													
1990	134.0	135.4	136.1	136.7	137.1	138.7	138.6	138.8	138.4	137.1	136.8	136.9	137.0
2000	181.8	182.6	183.8	183.8	185.2	187.6	187.8	188.1	187.0	187.7	187.0	188.4	185.9
2001	184.5	185.1	186.0	186.3	187.1	189.1	189.2	189.4	187.9	187.3	187.2	187.4	187.2
2002	185.3	185.9	187.1	186.5	187.2	189.5	190.5	191.0	190.1	190.4	189.6	190.1	188.6
2003	187.1	187.7	188.9	190.0	191.3	193.1	190.8	192.0	191.3	191.9	189.9	191.3	190.4
2004	189.4	189.8	190.5	191.7	192.0	194.2	195.9	196.2	195.5	193.6	193.2	193.8	193.0
2005	191.4	192.2	192.9	195.8	196.6	198.9	200.6	200.8	199.9	199.6	199.0	199.8	197.3
2006	196.6	198.0	199.4	203.5	204.7	206.9	210.6	211.0	209.2	209.4	208.8	209.1	205.6
2007	206.6	207.7	209.1	211.1	212.2	214.5	214.1	214.2	212.5	212.3	211.3	211.8	211.5
2008	209.1	210.3	210.9	212.6	212.7	214.6	213.6	213.6	211.1	210.3	208.5	208.6	211.3
2009	204.2	203.6	202.8	202.1	202.8	203.3	202.6	201.9	199.4	200.6	199.9	199.9	201.9
Professional and Business Services													
1990	237.7	232.2	235.4	239.2	241.0	242.9	242.6	245.3	244.5	245.3	243.9	241.5	241.0
2000	406.2	410.8	417.7	421.7	421.9	426.7	425.0	428.3	427.4	427.8	426.9	422.2	421.9
2001	413.3	418.1	419.6	424.6	426.8	428.9	419.5	422.4	419.0	419.6	415.7	416.1	420.3
2002	405.6	411.9	416.4	421.7	425.6	428.8	422.9	429.6	429.5	427.1	424.4	423.8	422.3
2003	412.6	414.2	419.4	424.6	427.9	428.9	418.3	423.7	423.4	427.6	427.9	427.1	423.0
2004	417.8	421.7	426.5	429.6	432.8	435.8	437.0	441.3	440.0	444.7	442.6	442.7	434.4
2005	435.6	437.4	441.4	446.8	443.5	445.4	450.1	454.4	457.2	460.9	460.0	458.9	449.3
2006	455.4	458.7	463.4	470.3	473.7	479.8	483.4	488.7	489.8	493.9	493.9	492.6	478.6
2007	477.4	484.4	490.1	495.1	400.6	505.6	502.4	507.1	508.7	510.9	508.7	508.7	499.8
2008	497.3	501.1	502.8	505.7	506.8	508.9	504.2	508.4	504.2	502.2	492.4	486.0	501.7
2009	470.5	467.8	463.5	460.8	459.3	459.6	457.8	460.5	462.2	469.2	467.5	463.6	463.5
Education and Health Services													
1990	224.1	227.5	228.9	230.0	230.3	230.8	231.3	234.5	237.1	238.2	239.6	240.5	232.7
2000	375.1	379.0	381.2	382.0	382.9	384.1	384.3	386.1	388.2	389.5	391.1	391.9	384.6
2001	394.6	398.2	401.1	403.7	405.2	405.9	405.8	409.4	411.0	413.2	415.2	416.6	406.7
2002	414.6	418.5	420.2	425.3	426.0	424.6	421.6	425.1	427.0	430.4	431.6	431.7	424.7
2003	427.4	430.5	432.5	434.0	435.1	434.3	433.9	438.3	440.8	442.4	443.6	445.4	436.5
2004	439.8	442.7	445.9	450.3	451.9	451.3	451.6	455.5	458.7	460.1	462.4	463.9	452.8
2005	460.2	463.7	467.3	468.4	469.9	468.4	469.9	474.8	479.1	479.8	482.6	482.4	472.2
2006	482.4	486.5	489.2	490.8	492.9	493.0	493.4	498.1	501.7	506.0	509.5	511.1	496.2
2007	506.1	512.5	516.2	518.9	521.7	521.4	518.7	524.5	527.7	532.3	535.1	536.2	522.6
2008	528.2	533.3	533.8	533.5	536.0	533.8	530.9	534.6	538.0	538.8	542.6	542.7	535.5
2009	537.1	541.5	541.5	540.9	542.9	540.6	535.9	539.2	541.1	547.7	549.9	550.1	542.4
Leisure and Hospitality													
1990	220.0	224.3	229.2	238.1	245.5	253.4	253.0	255.4	249.3	241.4	236.6	233.6	240.0
2000	306.2	308.3	316.6	326.0	335.6	344.3	341.7	341.2	334.2	328.4	323.0	320.2	327.1
2001	312.4	315.7	322.9	331.9	340.8	349.0	345.9	346.4	336.3	327.8	322.3	318.1	330.8
2002	311.4	315.1	324.0	338.2	348.3	356.1	356.3	356.4	348.8	340.1	334.8	332.7	338.5
2003	319.0	319.3	326.6	339.0	351.3	357.9	356.5	358.5	350.8	344.9	342.2	340.6	342.2
2004	326.0	328.0	336.7	350.8	362.2	369.1	372.7	373.7	365.4	357.2	353.1	351.8	353.9
2005	337.9	339.8	349.4	358.9	368.7	377.4	377.7	378.4	371.3	365.1	362.0	359.3	362.2
2006	349.3	353.1	362.3	377.0	388.3	396.3	401.2	400.9	394.2	390.7	388.8	386.9	382.4
2007	372.8	376.6	386.8	394.6	408.4	417.2	415.6	417.6	409.3	402.6	400.0	397.5	399.9
2008	384.7	389.2	397.6	403.3	415.3	420.7	422.6	423.0	414.3	402.8	395.0	391.7	405.0
2009	374.3	376.8	382.9	390.3	404.4	409.7	408.8	407.4	399.8	396.0	387.9	383.0	393.4
Other Services													
1990	98.7	99.9	100.7	101.5	102.0	103.1	103.3	103.6	102.5	101.3	101.7	101.5	101.7
2000	151.7	153.4	154.9	155.5	156.5	158.7	158.6	157.7	157.1	156.7	156.6	156.7	156.2
2001	156.5	157.7	158.8	158.5	160.3	162.8	163.2	162.4	161.4	161.0	161.4	161.3	160.4
2002	158.3	159.2	160.1	162.2	162.9	164.3	161.9	159.3	157.1	158.2	156.9	154.3	159.6
2003	152.8	153.1	153.3	156.2	158.2	160.5	160.8	160.2	160.2	156.0	155.5	156.6	157.0
2004	157.2	158.3	160.3	160.1	163.0	166.0	163.6	162.3	160.4	160.9	161.0	161.4	161.2
2005	160.4	161.6	162.5	162.4	164.6	167.5	164.9	165.0	163.7	165.1	165.5	165.8	164.1
2006	165.1	166.7	168.7	166.0	168.4	171.7	168.6	167.3	165.2	169.1	169.5	169.8	168.0
2007	168.7	170.1	172.0	168.8	171.2	174.3	175.3	174.7	172.7	174.5	174.5	174.7	172.6
2008	172.9	174.0	174.1	175.9	177.7	179.8	180.3	179.2	176.6	174.8	173.9	172.9	176.0
2009	162.7	163.6	163.7	163.8	165.8	167.5	168.9	168.5	166.8	162.7	161.9	159.9	164.7
Government													
1990	479.7	487.4	493.6	494.0	499.5	495.0	443.9	447.0	480.5	495.3	504.2	498.1	484.9
2000	603.9	611.1	620.4	622.9	629.0	614.6	555.0	601.0	624.3	632.0	634.9	632.1	615.1
2001	627.5	634.3	637.6	633.6	636.2	610.3	568.1	608.1	636.2	651.3	653.8	649.4	628.9
2002	638.5	645.5	649.9	647.7	649.2	616.2	570.6	609.1	636.5	653.2	650.4	645.9	634.4
2003	634.9	640.3	644.7	643.0	646.2	615.7	562.6	607.1	642.3	664.0	656.4	654.1	634.3
2004	643.4	648.4	653.1	652.1	654.8	623.1	571.1	622.4	662.7	666.9	669.1	668.1	644.6
2005	659.0	665.4	669.5	669.0	671.2	634.5	572.0	630.6	670.0	674.3	677.4	675.4	655.7
2006	670.2	676.5	681.8	684.2	687.9	658.5	586.9	646.6	682.5	691.0	701.5	699.7	672.3
2007	686.7	693.4	698.6	698.5	702.6	674.5	601.1	665.8	704.1	704.9	712.3	711.0	687.8
2008	702.1	709.8	715.0	716.7	721.3	693.4	614.7	680.5	725.6	727.3	732.2	730.2	705.7
2009	717.5	721.4	726.6	730.4	729.8	698.7	619.3	681.5	728.3	743.7	747.6	743.3	715.7

Average Weekly Hours by Selected Industry: North Carolina, 2007–2009

(Not seasonally adjusted.)

Industry and year	January	February	March	April	May	June	July	August	September	October	November	December	Annual average
Total Private													
2007	34.4	34.5	34.8	35.0	34.9	35.1	35.2	34.9	35.1	34.6	34.3	34.8	34.8
2008	33.8	33.9	34.6	34.3	34.1	34.7	34.4	34.1	34.1	34.5	34.5	34.1	34.3
2009	33.6	34.0	33.7	33.5	33.8	33.8	33.8	34.0	33.9	34.0	34.0	33.8	33.8
Goods-Producing													
2007	39.7	39.5	40.0	40.3	40.3	40.5	40.5	40.6	40.6	40.2	40.1	40.4	40.2
2008	39.6	38.7	40.3	39.4	39.0	39.8	38.8	39.6	38.8	39.3	38.4	38.1	39.2
2009	37.5	37.6	37.5	37.1	38.0	38.4	38.7	38.7	38.6	38.6	38.5	38.5	38.1
Construction													
2007	38.2	37.1	38.7	38.6	39.1	38.9	39.5	40.4	40.0	39.8	39.2	40.0	39.1
2008	39.3	37.5	40.4	39.0	38.8	38.9	38.6	39.2	37.9	38.7	37.3	37.3	38.6
2009	36.9	37.6	37.3	37.2	37.8	38.4	38.5	38.0	37.7	37.1	36.1	36.1	37.4
Manufacturing													
2007	40.3	40.6	40.6	41.0	40.8	41.1	40.8	40.6	40.8	40.3	40.5	40.5	40.7
2008	39.8	39.4	40.2	39.7	39.1	40.3	38.8	39.8	39.2	39.6	39.0	38.6	39.5
2009	37.9	37.8	37.7	37.2	38.2	38.5	38.6	38.9	39.1	39.3	39.7	40.0	38.6
Trade, Transportation, and Utilities													
2007	34.0	34.0	34.2	34.5	34.4	34.7	34.7	34.1	34.8	34.0	34.3	34.4	34.3
2008	33.7	34.8	35.6	34.9	35.1	35.4	35.7	34.2	35.0	35.5	35.3	35.9	35.1
2009	34.6	34.5	34.3	33.9	34.4	34.7	34.8	35.1	35.0	35.3	34.7	34.8	34.7
Information													
2007	36.1	35.5	35.8	36.2	35.3	35.4	35.9	35.2	35.3	35.1	35.3	35.6	35.6
2008	35.9	35.7	36.9	36.1	37.0	37.4	37.3	37.6	37.9	36.4	36.5	35.9	36.7
2009	35.6	34.8	35.3	35.0	34.7	34.7	35.0	35.1	35.0	35.2	35.8	35.8	35.1
Financial Activities													
2007	35.8	35.9	35.8	37.1	35.4	35.8	36.7	36.4	37.7	38.3	35.3	37.0	36.4
2008	34.8	35.8	36.3	36.1	35.4	37.4	35.9	35.7	35.6	36.7	39.3	38.2	36.4
2009	38.0	38.4	37.9	37.2	36.8	36.7	36.0	36.1	35.8	35.8	36.5	35.6	36.7
Professional and Business Services													
2007	34.3	34.7	35.2	35.1	34.7	35.5	36.0	35.4	36.0	35.2	35.1	35.9	35.3
2008	34.1	34.6	35.3	35.5	35.3	36.2	34.4	35.5	35.3	35.5	36.0	34.8	35.2
2009	34.8	35.8	35.5	35.6	35.4	35.0	34.7	35.0	34.9	35.3	35.7	35.1	35.2
Education and Health Services													
2007	33.1	33.1	33.5	33.7	34.0	33.1	33.0	33.3	33.2	32.6	32.4	33.0	33.2
2008	31.9	31.7	31.6	31.6	32.2	32.4	32.8	32.7	32.4	32.3	32.8	32.0	32.2
2009	31.8	32.2	31.9	31.9	32.3	31.9	31.9	32.0	31.9	32.1	32.1	31.6	32.0
Leisure and Hospitality													
2007	25.4	25.7	25.9	26.2	26.6	27.0	26.9	26.6	25.7	25.5	25.1	25.2	26.0
2008	24.4	26.0	25.7	25.6	25.6	26.0	26.4	25.8	25.8	25.7	25.4	25.4	25.7
2009	24.5	26.2	25.7	26.3	26.3	26.6	26.6	26.7	26.4	26.3	26.1	26.0	26.2
Other Services													
2007	33.1	33.1	33.7	33.2	34.0	34.5	34.2	32.4	32.0	31.3	31.4	31.1	32.8
2008	31.0	28.1	30.2	30.4	28.2	29.2	30.6	27.7	28.9	30.0	29.3	28.7	29.4
2009	29.1	29.6	29.1	29.3	29.0	28.9	29.3	29.5	29.5	29.5	29.6	29.5	29.3

Average Hourly Earnings by Selected Industry: North Carolina, 2007–2009

(Dollars, not seasonally adjusted.)

Industry and year	January	February	March	April	May	June	July	August	September	October	November	December	Annual average
Total Private													
2007	19.25	19.43	19.49	19.39	19.08	19.01	19.08	18.81	19.44	19.21	19.30	19.49	19.25
2008	19.50	19.46	19.43	20.04	19.61	19.82	19.64	19.84	19.68	20.34	20.87	20.66	19.90
2009	20.85	20.70	20.70	20.59	20.36	20.44	20.38	20.44	20.50	20.52	20.79	20.63	20.57
Goods-Producing													
2007	18.35	18.47	18.92	18.34	18.50	18.43	18.49	18.45	18.63	18.49	18.43	18.70	18.52
2008	18.48	18.64	18.48	18.82	18.67	19.17	18.44	18.71	18.59	18.97	19.45	19.74	18.84
2009	19.76	19.83	19.95	20.09	19.90	19.89	19.83	19.90	19.89	19.77	19.93	19.90	19.89
Construction													
2007	18.09	18.98	18.55	18.27	18.27	18.30	18.50	18.35	18.59	18.40	18.39	18.96	18.47
2008	17.97	19.36	19.41	19.39	19.48	21.04	18.85	18.82	19.30	19.42	19.80	20.48	19.43
2009	20.42	20.34	20.48	20.64	20.51	20.25	19.99	20.12	20.22	20.23	20.56	20.66	20.36
Manufacturing													
2007	18.54	18.33	19.15	18.43	18.65	18.54	18.53	18.54	18.68	18.55	18.48	18.62	18.59
2008	18.74	18.35	18.08	18.61	18.36	18.33	18.32	18.72	18.30	18.79	19.33	19.43	18.61
2009	19.50	19.62	19.75	19.75	19.55	19.54	19.56	19.62	19.60	19.42	19.53	19.49	19.58
Trade, Transportation, and Utilities													
2007	17.60	17.50	17.29	16.99	16.85	17.05	17.17	16.87	17.78	17.59	17.65	17.45	17.32
2008	17.78	17.56	17.55	18.87	17.95	18.05	19.47	18.38	18.33	19.91	19.98	19.61	18.63
2009	20.16	19.90	20.04	19.39	19.03	19.44	19.17	19.32	19.42	19.42	19.49	19.13	19.49
Information													
2007	29.47	29.36	29.46	30.30	29.24	29.49	29.59	28.41	30.30	28.75	29.90	30.57	29.57
2008	29.53	29.25	30.17	29.69	30.17	29.76	30.29	30.87	29.32	27.73	29.38	27.74	29.50
2009	28.16	28.00	28.16	27.36	27.78	27.54	27.55	27.66	27.48	28.35	29.07	28.12	27.94
Financial Activities													
2007	27.85	29.54	31.51	30.48	28.64	27.81	28.01	27.11	28.01	26.53	25.98	26.27	28.13
2008	25.69	27.72	28.06	27.64	28.01	27.90	26.27	27.27	27.23	26.51	27.20	25.81	27.11
2009	25.50	25.07	25.00	24.97	25.29	25.42	25.93	25.99	25.88	25.66	26.36	25.51	25.54
Professional and Business Services													
2007	24.50	24.63	23.98	24.99	23.93	23.92	24.40	24.03	24.59	24.08	24.62	24.86	24.38
2008	25.23	23.96	23.99	24.22	23.79	24.05	23.59	23.77	24.02	25.47	26.83	26.63	24.62
2009	26.65	26.41	26.57	26.91	26.59	26.85	26.88	26.89	26.90	26.80	27.38	27.43	26.85
Education and Health Services													
2007	18.30	18.42	18.43	18.36	18.40	18.72	18.09	17.61	18.28	18.47	18.81	18.99	18.41
2008	19.25	19.92	19.79	21.01	20.56	20.62	20.48	21.31	20.24	20.59	20.57	20.69	20.42
2009	20.73	20.74	20.69	20.50	20.32	20.42	20.39	20.29	20.37	20.39	20.47	20.56	20.49
Leisure and Hospitality													
2007	11.35	11.39	11.39	11.43	12.06	11.16	11.18	11.16	11.46	11.62	11.53	11.80	11.46
2008	11.58	11.44	11.48	11.84	11.20	11.18	10.66	11.50	11.77	11.72	12.01	11.95	11.52
2009	11.90	11.98	11.30	11.84	11.71	11.57	11.58	11.66	11.77	11.87	11.89	11.84	11.74
Other Services													
2007	16.68	16.93	16.38	16.70	16.30	15.92	16.03	16.23	16.63	16.49	16.76	17.18	16.51
2008	16.90	15.97	15.81	15.88	15.69	15.79	15.56	15.74	16.31	16.06	16.57	16.72	16.08
2009	16.50	16.43	16.30	16.33	16.38	15.94	15.92	15.99	16.01	16.05	16.16	16.37	16.20

Average Weekly Earnings by Selected Industry: North Carolina, 2007–2009

(Dollars, not seasonally adjusted.)

Industry and year	January	February	March	April	May	June	July	August	September	October	November	December	Annual average
Total Private													
2007	662.20	670.34	678.25	678.65	665.89	667.25	671.62	656.47	682.34	664.67	661.99	678.25	669.90
2008	659.10	659.69	672.28	687.37	668.70	687.75	675.62	676.54	671.09	701.73	720.02	704.51	682.57
2009	700.56	703.80	697.59	689.77	688.17	690.87	688.84	694.96	694.95	697.68	706.86	697.29	695.27
Goods-Producing													
2007	728.50	729.57	756.80	739.10	745.55	746.42	748.85	749.07	756.38	743.30	739.04	755.48	744.50
2008	731.81	721.37	744.74	741.51	728.13	762.97	715.47	740.92	721.29	745.52	746.88	752.09	738.53
2009	741.00	745.61	748.13	745.34	756.20	763.78	767.42	770.13	767.75	763.12	767.31	766.15	757.81
Construction													
2007	691.04	704.16	717.89	705.22	714.36	711.87	730.75	741.34	743.60	732.32	720.89	758.40	722.18
2008	706.22	726.00	784.16	756.21	755.82	818.46	727.61	737.74	731.47	751.55	738.54	763.90	750.00
2009	753.50	764.78	763.90	767.81	775.28	777.60	769.62	764.56	762.29	750.53	742.22	745.83	761.46
Manufacturing													
2007	747.16	744.20	777.49	755.63	760.92	761.99	756.02	752.72	762.14	747.57	748.44	754.11	756.61
2008	745.85	722.99	726.82	738.82	717.88	738.70	710.82	745.06	717.36	744.08	753.87	750.00	735.10
2009	739.05	741.64	744.58	734.70	746.81	752.29	755.02	763.22	766.36	763.21	775.34	779.60	755.79
Trade, Transportation, and Utilities													
2007	598.40	595.00	591.32	586.16	579.64	591.64	595.80	575.27	618.74	598.06	605.40	600.28	594.08
2008	599.19	611.09	624.78	658.56	630.05	638.97	695.08	628.60	641.55	706.81	705.29	704.00	653.91
2009	697.54	686.55	687.37	657.32	654.63	674.57	667.12	678.13	679.70	685.53	676.30	665.72	676.30
Information													
2007	1063.87	1042.28	1054.67	1096.86	1032.17	1043.95	1062.28	1000.03	1069.59	1009.13	1055.47	1088.29	1052.69
2008	1060.13	1044.23	1113.27	1071.81	1116.29	1113.02	1129.82	1160.71	1111.23	1009.37	1072.37	995.87	1082.65
2009	1002.50	974.40	994.05	957.60	963.97	955.64	964.25	970.87	961.80	997.92	1040.71	1006.70	980.69
Financial Activities													
2007	997.03	1060.49	1128.06	1130.81	1013.86	995.60	1027.97	986.80	1055.98	1016.10	917.09	971.99	1023.93
2008	894.01	992.38	1018.58	997.80	991.55	1043.46	943.09	973.54	969.39	972.92	1068.96	985.94	986.80
2009	969.00	962.69	947.50	928.88	930.67	932.91	933.48	938.24	926.50	918.63	962.14	908.16	937.32
Professional and Business Services													
2007	840.35	854.66	844.10	877.15	830.37	849.16	878.40	850.66	885.24	847.62	864.16	892.47	860.61
2008	860.34	829.02	846.85	859.81	839.79	870.61	811.50	843.84	847.91	904.19	965.88	926.72	866.62
2009	927.42	945.48	943.24	958.00	941.29	939.75	932.74	941.15	938.81	946.04	977.47	962.79	945.12
Education and Health Services													
2007	605.73	609.70	617.41	618.73	625.60	619.63	596.97	586.41	606.90	602.12	609.44	626.67	611.21
2008	614.08	631.46	625.36	663.92	662.03	668.09	671.74	696.84	655.78	665.06	674.70	662.08	657.52
2009	659.21	667.83	660.01	653.95	656.34	651.40	650.44	649.28	649.80	654.52	657.09	649.70	655.68
Leisure and Hospitality													
2007	288.29	292.72	295.00	299.47	320.80	301.32	300.74	296.86	294.52	296.31	289.40	297.36	297.96
2008	282.55	297.44	295.04	303.10	286.72	290.68	281.42	296.70	303.67	301.20	305.05	303.53	296.06
2009	291.55	313.88	290.41	311.39	307.97	307.76	308.03	311.32	310.73	312.18	310.33	307.84	307.59
Other Services													
2007	552.11	560.38	552.01	554.44	554.20	549.24	548.23	525.85	532.16	516.14	526.26	534.30	541.53
2008	523.90	448.76	477.46	482.75	442.46	461.07	476.14	436.00	471.36	481.80	485.50	479.86	472.75
2009	480.15	486.33	474.33	478.47	475.02	460.67	466.46	471.71	472.30	473.48	478.34	482.92	474.66

NORTH DAKOTA
At a Glance

Population:
  1990 census: 638,800
  2000 census: 642,200
  2009 estimate: 646,844

Percent change in population:
  1990–2000: 0.5%
  2000–2009: 0.7%

Percent change in total nonfarm employment:
  1990–2009: 37.8%
  2008–2009: -0.3%

Industry with the largest growth in employment, 1990–2009 (thousands):
  Education and Health Services, 17.3

Industry with the largest decline or smallest growth in employment, 1990–2009 (thousands):
  Transportation and utilities, 1.0

Civilian labor force:
  1990: 318,795
  2000: 345,881
  2009: 364,970

Unemployment rate and rank among states (lowest to highest):
  1990: 4.0%, 4th
  2000: 2.9%, 10th
  2009: 4.3%, 1st

Employment by Industry, 2009

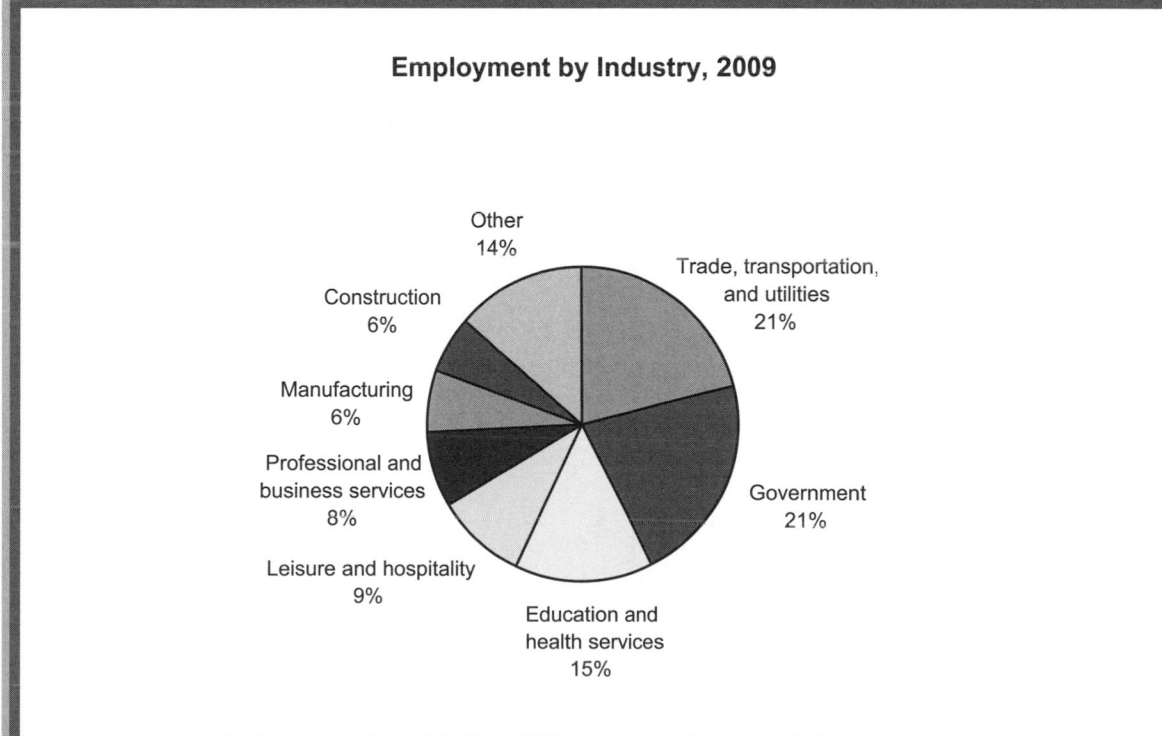

Other 14%

Trade, transportation, and utilities 21%

Construction 6%

Manufacturing 6%

Professional and business services 8%

Government 21%

Leisure and hospitality 9%

Education and health services 15%

Employment by Industry: North Dakota, Selected Years, 1990–2009

(Numbers in thousands, not seasonally adjusted.)

Industry and year	January	February	March	April	May	June	July	August	September	October	November	December	Annual average
Total Nonfarm													
1990	256.7	257.6	259.5	264.2	269.5	269.8	266.1	265.7	268.5	271.5	270.6	270.3	265.8
2000	319.2	320.4	323.2	327.1	332.8	329.0	327.6	327.2	331.5	332.9	330.9	330.9	327.7
2001	322.5	324.2	326.3	330.1	335.3	333.6	324.9	325.5	333.9	335.0	333.2	332.1	329.7
2002	322.6	323.9	323.9	328.6	333.8	333.4	325.1	327.0	334.2	335.5	334.5	334.5	329.8
2003	323.9	325.3	327.2	331.7	336.9	335.4	326.7	330.9	338.7	340.1	337.7	337.2	332.6
2004	326.5	328.2	330.6	337.1	342.0	341.2	334.9	336.2	343.7	346.1	344.8	343.9	337.9
2005	333.4	336.1	338.3	345.7	349.7	348.3	339.5	342.3	351.4	350.7	350.5	350.8	344.7
2006	341.1	343.7	347.0	352.2	357.0	356.2	345.6	349.1	358.6	358.8	358.3	359.0	352.2
2007	348.5	349.6	352.6	356.2	362.7	362.7	352.9	354.2	364.2	365.8	365.8	365.6	358.4
2008	356.9	359.0	361.6	365.9	371.8	371.2	363.0	364.0	373.7	374.9	373.6	372.1	367.3
2009	358.6	359.9	360.6	362.8	370.4	371.5	362.1	363.0	372.2	373.1	372.3	369.4	366.3
Total Private													
1990	188.5	188.5	190.3	194.2	198.9	201.2	201.3	202.5	202.7	203.3	202.3	201.8	198.0
1991	194.3	194.6	195.9	199.2	202.2	205.3	205.8	207.2	207.4	207.2	205.2	204.6	202.4
2000	246.4	246.0	248.3	252.5	257.4	260.1	261.1	260.8	258.5	258.5	256.7	256.1	255.2
2001	248.5	249.1	251.1	254.9	260.4	263.0	261.8	261.5	259.7	259.4	257.8	256.3	257.0
2002	247.5	247.8	247.9	252.3	257.3	261.3	260.7	261.0	258.6	258.3	257.2	256.2	255.5
2003	248.5	247.8	249.3	253.4	258.4	262.5	262.0	263.9	261.8	261.8	259.8	259.0	257.4
2004	251.0	251.6	253.8	259.9	265.0	268.9	270.6	270.2	267.5	268.3	267.2	266.0	263.3
2005	257.8	258.4	260.4	267.3	271.6	275.2	275.5	276.2	274.7	273.1	272.8	272.8	269.7
2006	264.9	266.0	268.8	273.7	278.6	282.5	281.4	282.8	281.7	280.3	279.8	280.1	276.7
2007	272.0	271.8	274.6	277.8	284.2	288.0	287.7	287.9	287.2	287.5	287.1	286.8	282.7
2008	279.9	280.6	283.4	287.4	292.5	296.4	296.9	297.0	296.0	295.6	294.3	292.5	291.0
Goods-Producing													
1990	25.2	25.2	25.8	27.0	29.8	30.9	31.4	31.7	31.6	32.5	30.9	29.2	29.3
2000	38.9	38.7	39.3	41.3	44.3	46.3	46.8	46.5	45.5	44.8	42.2	40.7	42.9
2001	38.9	38.5	39.6	41.0	43.7	45.4	46.3	46.1	46.2	45.2	43.1	41.1	42.9
2002	38.4	38.2	38.4	40.2	42.7	44.4	45.0	45.3	44.2	43.7	42.4	40.9	42.0
2003	38.5	38.0	38.4	40.2	43.2	45.4	45.9	46.7	46.2	45.7	43.6	42.1	42.8
2004	39.5	39.5	40.5	43.6	46.1	48.6	49.5	49.4	48.6	48.1	46.6	44.6	45.4
2005	42.0	42.3	43.2	45.8	48.2	50.1	51.1	51.2	50.4	49.6	48.8	47.3	47.5
2006	44.4	44.4	45.1	48.0	50.1	52.0	52.4	52.7	52.0	50.9	50.1	49.0	49.3
2007	45.9	45.3	46.4	48.2	50.9	52.9	53.7	53.6	53.2	53.1	52.1	50.4	50.5
2008	48.1	48.3	49.6	51.4	54.3	57.0	58.0	58.0	57.7	57.1	55.3	53.0	54.0
2009	47.6	47.7	47.7	48.4	51.1	53.5	54.5	55.0	54.7	54.1	52.6	48.4	51.3
Mining and Logging													
1990	3.3	3.4	3.4	3.5	3.7	3.8	3.8	3.8	3.8	3.9	3.8	3.7	3.7
2000	3.0	3.0	3.0	3.1	3.4	3.4	3.6	3.7	3.7	3.5	3.3	3.2	3.3
2001	3.1	3.1	3.3	3.3	3.5	3.7	3.8	3.7	3.7	3.7	3.5	3.3	3.5
2002	2.9	2.8	2.9	3.1	3.3	3.4	3.4	3.4	3.3	3.4	3.3	3.1	3.2
2003	2.9	2.9	3.0	3.2	3.5	3.6	3.6	3.6	3.5	3.6	3.4	3.3	3.3
2004	3.2	3.2	3.3	3.4	3.5	3.6	3.7	3.8	3.8	3.7	3.7	3.6	3.5
2005	3.6	3.7	3.7	3.9	4.1	4.2	4.3	4.5	4.4	4.3	4.4	4.4	4.1
2006	4.1	4.3	4.3	4.6	4.8	4.7	4.7	4.9	5.0	5.1	5.1	5.0	4.7
2007	4.8	4.7	4.8	4.9	5.1	5.2	5.3	5.3	5.3	5.3	5.3	5.5	5.1
2008	5.4	5.6	5.9	6.2	6.5	6.8	6.9	7.3	7.5	7.8	8.0	7.9	6.8
2009	7.4	7.2	7.1	6.7	6.8	6.8	6.7	6.7	6.8	6.8	6.9	7.0	6.9
Construction													
1990	7.3	7.1	7.3	8.6	10.9	11.5	12.1	12.4	11.8	11.9	10.6	9.2	10.1
2000	13.2	12.9	13.3	14.9	17.1	18.5	18.9	18.6	17.3	16.9	14.8	13.5	15.8
2001	12.1	11.8	12.5	13.8	16.0	17.3	18.1	18.4	17.8	17.4	15.8	14.1	15.4
2002	12.4	12.2	12.2	13.6	15.7	16.9	17.6	17.8	17.1	16.4	15.3	14.2	15.1
2003	12.4	12.2	12.4	13.9	16.3	17.9	18.4	19.1	18.9	18.2	16.6	15.1	16.0
2004	13.1	13.0	13.7	16.3	18.2	19.8	20.4	20.1	19.5	19.0	17.6	15.9	17.2
2005	13.6	13.6	14.1	16.3	18.2	19.5	20.4	20.3	19.7	19.0	18.1	16.6	17.5
2006	14.8	14.7	15.2	17.6	19.4	20.9	21.0	21.2	20.6	20.2	18.8	17.6	18.5
2007	15.6	15.3	16.1	17.7	19.9	21.2	21.8	22.0	21.6	21.4	20.4	18.6	19.3
2008	16.7	16.6	17.5	18.9	21.4	23.3	24.3	24.2	23.7	22.7	21.0	19.3	20.8
2009	16.7	16.3	16.5	17.9	20.7	23.0	24.3	24.8	24.5	23.6	22.2	18.2	20.7
Manufacturing													
1990	14.6	14.7	15.1	14.9	15.2	15.6	15.5	15.5	16.0	16.7	16.5	16.3	15.6
2000	22.7	22.8	23.0	23.3	23.8	24.4	24.3	24.2	24.5	24.4	24.1	24.0	23.8
2001	23.7	23.6	23.8	23.9	24.2	24.4	24.4	24.0	24.7	24.1	23.8	23.7	24.0
2002	23.1	23.2	23.3	23.5	23.7	24.1	24.0	24.1	23.8	23.9	23.8	23.6	23.7
2003	23.2	22.9	23.0	23.1	23.4	23.9	23.9	24.0	23.8	23.9	23.6	23.7	23.5
2004	23.2	23.3	23.5	23.9	24.4	25.2	25.4	25.5	25.3	25.4	25.3	25.1	24.6
2005	24.8	25.0	25.4	25.6	25.9	26.4	26.4	26.4	26.3	26.3	26.3	26.3	25.9
2006	25.5	25.4	25.6	25.8	25.9	26.4	26.7	26.6	26.4	25.6	26.2	26.4	26.0
2007	25.5	25.3	25.5	25.6	25.9	26.5	26.6	26.3	26.3	26.4	26.4	26.3	26.1
2008	26.0	26.1	26.2	26.3	26.4	26.9	26.8	26.5	26.5	26.6	26.3	25.8	26.4
2009	23.5	24.2	24.1	23.8	23.6	23.7	23.5	23.5	23.4	23.7	23.5	23.2	23.6

Employment by Industry: North Dakota, Selected Years, 1990–2009—*Continued*

(Numbers in thousands, not seasonally adjusted.)

Industry and year	January	February	March	April	May	June	July	August	September	October	November	December	Annual average
Service-Providing													
1990	231.5	232.4	233.7	237.2	239.7	238.9	234.7	234.0	236.9	239.0	239.7	241.1	236.6
2000	280.3	281.7	283.9	285.8	288.5	282.7	280.8	280.7	286.0	288.1	288.7	290.2	284.8
2001	283.6	285.7	286.7	289.1	291.6	288.2	278.6	279.4	287.7	289.8	290.1	291.0	286.8
2002	284.2	285.7	285.5	288.4	291.1	289.0	280.1	281.7	290.0	291.8	292.1	293.6	287.8
2003	285.4	287.3	288.8	291.5	293.7	290.0	280.8	284.2	292.5	294.4	294.1	295.1	289.8
2004	287.0	288.7	290.1	293.5	295.9	292.6	285.4	286.8	295.1	298.0	298.2	299.3	292.6
2005	291.4	293.8	295.1	299.9	301.5	298.2	288.4	291.1	301.0	301.1	301.7	303.5	297.2
2006	296.7	299.3	301.9	304.2	306.9	304.2	293.2	296.4	306.6	307.9	308.2	310.0	303.0
2007	302.6	304.3	306.2	308.0	311.8	309.8	299.2	300.6	311.0	312.7	313.7	315.2	307.9
2008	308.8	310.7	312.0	314.5	317.5	314.2	305.0	306.0	316.0	317.8	318.3	319.1	313.3
2009	311.0	312.2	312.9	314.4	319.3	318.0	307.6	308.0	317.5	319.0	319.7	321.0	315.1
Trade, Transportation, and Utilities													
1990	63.2	62.6	62.8	63.9	64.8	65.0	64.6	65.0	65.0	65.4	66.6	67.4	64.7
2000	71.5	70.7	70.8	71.9	72.6	72.2	71.9	72.1	71.8	72.7	73.6	74.3	72.2
2001	71.3	70.7	71.0	71.9	73.1	72.7	72.0	71.9	71.3	71.7	72.8	73.1	72.0
2002	71.0	70.3	70.3	70.9	72.2	72.4	71.7	71.5	71.2	71.8	72.9	73.6	71.7
2003	70.9	70.2	70.4	71.5	72.3	72.3	71.5	72.0	71.6	72.6	73.5	74.1	71.9
2004	71.3	71.0	71.3	72.4	73.5	73.4	73.0	72.9	72.5	73.5	74.8	75.6	72.9
2005	72.3	72.3	72.8	74.3	75.0	74.9	74.4	74.2	74.4	74.8	75.7	76.5	74.3
2006	74.0	73.9	74.6	76.0	76.9	76.9	76.1	76.3	76.2	76.4	77.4	78.0	76.1
2007	75.4	75.0	75.1	75.9	77.0	76.8	76.7	76.4	76.2	77.1	78.3	78.9	76.6
2008	76.6	76.3	76.7	77.4	78.1	78.0	78.1	77.9	77.9	78.4	79.3	79.7	77.9
2009	77.0	76.5	76.6	76.9	78.5	78.4	78.2	77.8	77.8	77.9	78.3	78.9	77.7
Wholesale Trade													
1990	15.3	15.2	15.4	15.7	16.0	16.0	15.9	15.9	15.7	15.9	15.8	15.7	15.7
2000	18.1	17.9	18.0	18.5	18.7	18.6	18.3	18.3	18.1	18.2	18.2	18.2	18.3
2001	18.0	18.0	18.2	18.4	19.1	18.9	18.6	18.5	18.1	18.2	18.1	18.0	18.3
2002	17.8	17.7	17.7	18.0	18.4	18.6	18.2	18.1	17.8	18.0	17.9	17.8	18.0
2003	17.5	17.3	17.4	18.1	18.4	18.4	18.2	18.1	17.8	18.1	18.0	18.0	17.9
2004	17.8	17.8	18.0	18.6	18.8	18.8	18.7	18.6	18.2	18.4	18.5	18.6	18.4
2005	18.1	18.1	18.3	19.0	19.3	19.3	19.1	19.0	18.8	19.0	18.9	19.0	18.8
2006	18.6	18.6	18.8	19.3	19.6	19.6	19.2	19.2	19.0	19.1	19.0	19.0	19.1
2007	18.8	18.7	18.9	19.4	19.8	19.8	19.5	19.4	19.2	19.5	19.5	19.4	19.3
2008	19.1	19.2	19.4	19.9	20.3	20.2	20.2	20.1	19.9	20.0	20.0	20.0	19.9
2009	19.7	19.7	19.8	20.0	20.7	20.7	20.5	20.3	20.0	19.9	19.8	19.8	20.1
Retail Trade													
1990	34.2	33.6	33.6	34.3	34.9	35.0	34.8	35.2	35.0	35.1	36.5	37.2	35.0
2000	40.6	40.1	40.0	40.5	40.9	40.8	40.9	40.9	40.6	41.1	42.1	42.8	40.9
2001	40.3	39.8	40.0	40.4	41.0	40.7	40.4	40.4	40.2	40.5	41.6	42.0	40.6
2002	40.3	39.8	39.8	40.0	40.8	40.8	40.5	40.5	40.4	40.7	41.9	42.6	40.7
2003	40.3	39.9	39.9	40.3	40.9	41.0	40.5	41.0	40.7	41.2	42.2	42.8	40.9
2004	40.6	40.2	40.4	40.8	41.5	41.5	41.2	41.2	41.0	41.5	42.7	43.3	41.3
2005	41.1	41.0	41.2	41.9	42.3	42.3	42.1	42.0	42.1	42.3	43.3	43.8	42.1
2006	41.9	41.7	42.1	43.0	43.6	43.6	43.3	43.3	43.3	43.4	44.5	44.9	43.2
2007	42.9	42.5	42.4	42.6	43.1	43.1	43.2	42.9	42.7	43.1	44.2	44.8	43.1
2008	43.0	42.5	42.6	42.8	43.0	43.0	43.2	42.9	42.9	43.1	44.0	44.3	43.1
2009	42.4	41.9	41.9	42.0	42.7	42.7	42.8	42.6	42.7	42.9	43.4	43.7	42.6
Transportation and Utilities													
1990	13.7	13.8	13.8	13.9	13.9	14.0	13.9	13.9	14.3	14.4	14.3	14.5	14.0
2000	12.8	12.7	12.8	12.9	13.0	12.8	12.7	12.9	13.1	13.4	13.3	13.3	13.0
2001	13.0	12.9	12.8	13.1	13.0	13.1	13.0	13.0	13.0	13.0	13.1	13.1	13.0
2002	12.9	12.8	12.8	12.9	13.0	13.0	13.0	12.9	13.0	13.1	13.1	13.2	13.0
2003	13.1	13.0	13.1	13.1	13.0	12.9	12.8	12.9	13.1	13.3	13.3	13.3	13.1
2004	12.9	13.0	12.9	13.0	13.2	13.1	13.1	13.1	13.3	13.6	13.6	13.7	13.2
2005	13.1	13.2	13.3	13.4	13.4	13.3	13.2	13.2	13.5	13.5	13.5	13.7	13.4
2006	13.5	13.6	13.7	13.7	13.7	13.7	13.6	13.8	13.9	13.9	13.9	14.1	13.8
2007	13.7	13.8	13.8	13.9	14.1	13.9	14.0	14.1	14.3	14.5	14.6	14.7	14.1
2008	14.5	14.6	14.7	14.7	14.8	14.8	14.7	14.9	15.1	15.3	15.3	15.4	14.9
2009	14.9	14.9	14.9	14.9	15.1	15.0	14.9	14.9	15.1	15.1	15.1	15.4	15.0
Information													
1990	6.0	6.1	6.0	6.0	6.0	6.1	6.0	6.0	6.0	5.9	5.9	5.9	6.0
2000	8.4	8.4	8.5	8.5	8.5	8.5	8.5	8.3	8.4	8.4	8.4	8.5	8.4
2001	8.4	8.4	8.4	8.4	8.5	8.6	8.5	8.5	8.5	8.6	8.5	8.4	8.5
2002	8.0	8.0	7.9	7.9	8.0	8.0	8.0	7.9	7.8	7.8	7.8	7.9	7.9
2003	7.7	7.6	7.7	7.7	7.7	7.7	7.7	7.7	7.7	7.7	7.7	7.7	7.7
2004	7.6	7.6	7.6	7.6	7.7	7.7	7.8	7.8	7.7	7.8	7.8	7.7	7.7
2005	7.6	7.6	7.5	7.6	7.6	7.6	7.6	7.6	7.6	7.4	7.4	7.5	7.6
2006	7.4	7.4	7.4	7.4	7.4	7.5	7.5	7.6	7.5	7.5	7.6	7.6	7.5
2007	7.6	7.6	7.6	7.6	7.7	7.6	7.6	7.7	7.5	7.5	7.5	7.5	7.6
2008	7.4	7.4	7.4	7.4	7.5	7.6	7.6	7.6	7.6	7.6	7.6	7.6	7.5
2009	7.7	7.7	7.6	7.5	7.5	7.5	7.5	7.5	7.4	7.4	7.4	7.4	7.5

Employment by Industry: North Dakota, Selected Years, 1990–2009—*Continued*

(Numbers in thousands, not seasonally adjusted.)

Industry and year	January	February	March	April	May	June	July	August	September	October	November	December	Annual average
Financial Activities													
1990	12.5	12.5	12.6	12.6	12.8	13.0	12.9	12.9	12.8	12.8	12.7	12.8	12.7
2000	16.9	16.9	16.9	16.7	17.0	17.0	17.1	17.2	17.2	17.2	17.3	17.5	17.1
2001	17.4	17.4	17.4	17.5	17.6	17.7	17.7	17.8	17.8	17.9	17.8	18.0	17.7
2002	17.7	17.8	17.8	17.8	17.9	18.1	18.1	18.3	18.1	18.3	18.3	18.4	18.1
2003	18.2	18.1	18.3	18.2	18.3	18.4	18.5	18.6	18.5	18.4	18.4	18.5	18.4
2004	18.5	18.6	18.7	18.5	18.6	18.7	18.7	18.6	18.6	18.6	18.7	18.8	18.6
2005	18.6	18.6	18.7	18.7	18.8	18.8	18.9	19.1	18.8	18.9	18.8	19.1	18.8
2006	18.9	19.0	19.1	19.0	19.1	19.3	19.4	19.4	19.3	19.2	19.3	19.6	19.2
2007	19.3	19.4	19.5	19.5	19.8	19.9	20.0	20.0	19.9	20.0	19.9	20.2	19.8
2008	19.9	20.0	20.1	20.1	20.2	20.4	20.5	20.5	20.4	20.5	20.5	20.7	20.3
2009	20.2	20.1	20.1	20.1	20.1	20.2	20.4	20.3	20.2	20.0	20.1	20.6	20.2
Professional and Business Services													
1990	11.5	11.4	11.5	11.8	11.8	12.1	12.2	12.3	12.5	12.4	12.1	11.9	12.0
2000	23.2	23.7	24.2	24.5	24.7	25.2	25.6	25.3	25.0	25.2	25.1	25.2	24.7
2001	24.5	25.5	25.1	25.5	25.6	26.1	25.4	25.3	25.0	25.2	25.1	25.0	25.3
2002	23.1	23.5	23.6	24.1	24.1	25.0	24.6	24.7	24.7	24.4	24.0	23.8	24.1
2003	23.2	23.5	23.3	23.5	23.5	24.1	23.8	24.3	24.1	23.9	23.8	23.6	23.7
2004	22.9	23.3	23.4	24.2	24.5	25.0	25.0	25.1	24.7	25.6	25.1	25.2	24.5
2005	24.5	24.7	24.7	26.4	26.6	27.1	27.4	27.7	27.4	27.3	27.2	27.3	26.5
2006	26.8	27.1	27.5	27.8	28.4	29.1	28.9	28.9	29.1	29.0	28.7	28.6	28.3
2007	28.1	28.3	28.8	29.0	29.5	29.9	29.7	29.9	30.0	29.9	29.7	29.8	29.4
2008	29.3	29.5	29.8	30.3	30.6	31.0	30.8	30.9	30.7	30.4	30.0	29.7	30.3
2009	28.8	28.8	28.7	28.7	29.1	29.7	29.3	29.4	29.8	29.2	29.2	29.0	29.1
Education and Health Services													
1990	34.8	35.1	35.2	35.7	35.8	35.9	36.0	36.1	36.4	36.5	36.6	37.0	35.9
2000	44.7	44.7	45.0	44.9	45.0	45.3	45.4	45.5	45.3	45.8	46.0	46.1	45.3
2001	45.5	45.8	45.9	45.8	46.0	46.2	46.3	46.2	45.8	46.1	46.4	46.6	46.1
2002	46.2	46.3	46.0	46.4	46.6	46.9	46.9	46.9	46.7	47.0	47.1	47.2	46.7
2003	46.9	47.0	47.1	47.4	47.5	48.1	48.1	47.9	47.7	47.8	48.0	48.3	47.7
2004	47.9	47.9	48.1	48.5	48.5	48.7	48.8	48.7	48.3	48.3	48.4	48.5	48.4
2005	48.2	48.2	48.2	48.5	48.4	49.1	48.9	49.0	49.0	49.0	49.1	49.4	48.8
2006	49.1	49.3	49.7	49.6	49.4	50.0	49.8	49.9	49.8	50.0	50.0	50.3	49.7
2007	50.0	50.1	50.3	50.3	50.6	51.2	51.0	51.2	51.3	51.4	51.4	51.7	50.9
2008	51.3	51.6	51.6	52.1	52.1	52.2	52.2	52.1	52.2	52.6	52.5	52.8	52.1
2009	52.2	52.8	52.7	52.7	53.2	53.4	53.2	53.1	53.4	53.9	54.0	54.1	53.2
Leisure and Hospitality													
1990	22.6	22.9	23.6	24.2	24.9	25.3	25.4	25.6	25.3	24.6	24.3	24.3	24.4
2000	27.7	27.7	28.3	29.3	30.0	30.4	30.6	30.7	30.1	29.1	28.8	28.5	29.3
2001	27.5	27.7	28.5	29.4	30.5	31.0	30.5	30.5	29.8	29.4	28.8	28.7	29.4
2002	28.0	28.4	28.6	29.6	30.4	31.1	31.2	31.2	30.7	30.1	29.4	29.2	29.8
2003	28.1	28.2	28.9	29.6	30.6	31.3	31.4	31.5	30.6	30.4	29.6	29.4	30.0
2004	28.5	28.7	29.2	30.0	31.0	31.6	32.7	32.6	32.1	31.3	30.7	30.5	30.7
2005	29.7	29.7	30.1	30.8	31.8	32.5	32.3	32.5	32.2	31.2	30.9	30.7	31.2
2006	29.5	30.0	30.4	30.9	32.2	32.8	32.4	32.9	32.8	32.2	31.4	31.6	31.6
2007	30.7	31.1	31.7	32.1	33.5	34.4	33.9	34.1	33.9	33.3	32.9	33.0	32.9
2008	32.1	32.2	32.7	33.2	34.1	34.7	34.4	34.7	34.2	33.7	33.7	33.6	33.6
2009	32.4	32.4	32.8	33.3	34.7	35.4	35.0	35.2	34.8	34.3	34.3	34.1	34.1
Other Services													
1990	12.7	12.7	12.8	13.0	13.0	12.9	12.8	12.9	13.1	13.2	13.2	13.3	13.0
2000	15.1	15.2	15.3	15.4	15.3	15.2	15.2	15.2	15.2	15.3	15.3	15.3	15.3
2001	15.0	15.1	15.2	15.4	15.4	15.3	15.1	15.2	15.3	15.3	15.3	15.4	15.3
2002	15.1	15.3	15.3	15.4	15.4	15.4	15.2	15.2	15.2	15.2	15.3	15.2	15.3
2003	15.0	15.2	15.2	15.3	15.3	15.2	15.1	15.2	15.4	15.3	15.2	15.3	15.2
2004	14.8	15.0	15.0	15.1	15.1	15.2	15.1	15.1	15.0	15.1	15.1	15.1	15.1
2005	14.9	15.0	15.2	15.2	15.2	15.1	14.9	14.9	14.9	14.9	14.9	15.0	15.0
2006	14.8	14.9	15.0	15.0	15.1	14.9	14.9	15.1	15.0	15.1	15.3	15.4	15.0
2007	15.0	15.0	15.2	15.2	15.2	15.3	15.1	15.0	15.2	15.2	15.3	15.3	15.2
2008	15.2	15.3	15.5	15.5	15.6	15.5	15.3	15.3	15.3	15.3	15.4	15.4	15.4
2009	15.2	15.2	15.3	15.5	15.5	15.4	15.4	15.3	15.3	15.6	15.8	15.8	15.4
Government													
1990	68.2	69.1	69.2	70.0	70.6	68.6	64.8	63.2	65.8	68.2	68.3	68.5	67.9
2000	72.8	74.4	74.9	74.6	75.4	68.9	66.5	66.4	73.0	74.4	74.2	74.8	72.5
2001	74.0	75.1	75.2	75.2	74.9	70.6	63.1	64.0	74.2	75.6	75.4	75.8	72.8
2002	75.1	76.1	76.0	76.3	76.5	72.1	64.4	66.0	75.6	77.2	77.3	78.3	74.2
2003	75.4	77.5	77.9	78.3	78.5	72.9	64.7	67.0	76.9	78.3	77.9	78.2	75.3
2004	75.5	76.6	76.8	77.2	77.0	72.3	64.3	66.0	76.2	77.8	77.6	77.9	74.6
2005	75.6	77.7	77.9	78.4	78.1	73.1	64.0	66.1	76.7	77.6	77.7	78.0	75.1
2006	76.2	77.7	78.2	78.5	78.4	73.7	64.2	66.3	76.9	78.5	78.5	78.9	75.5
2007	76.5	77.8	78.0	78.4	78.5	74.7	65.2	66.3	77.0	78.3	78.7	78.8	75.7
2008	77.0	78.4	78.2	78.5	79.3	74.8	66.1	67.0	77.7	79.3	79.3	79.6	76.3
2009	77.5	78.7	79.1	79.7	80.7	78.0	68.6	69.4	78.8	80.7	80.6	81.1	77.7

Average Weekly Hours by Selected Industry: North Dakota, 2007–2009

(Not seasonally adjusted.)

Industry and year	January	February	March	April	May	June	July	August	September	October	November	December	Annual average
Total Private													
2007	32.3	32.4	32.4	32.8	33.1	33.8	34.0	33.4	34.1	32.7	32.5	32.6	33.0
2008	31.8	31.7	32.4	32.1	32.7	33.2	33.0	32.9	32.7	32.3	32.2	31.7	32.4
2009	31.4	31.9	31.3	31.3	31.9	32.5	32.5	33.1	32.0	31.9	32.4	31.6	32.0
Goods-Producing													
2007	38.7	38.7	39.8	39.7	41.6	40.9	41.6	41.4	40.9	40.7	39.5	38.0	40.2
2008	36.6	36.1	37.3	37.1	39.0	38.1	39.6	40.0	40.0	39.9	37.5	37.1	38.3
2009	35.4	35.8	35.1	36.7	38.5	39.9	39.3	40.4	38.9	38.9	39.3	38.0	38.1
Construction													
2007	35.6	35.3	34.5	35.9	42.0	41.5	44.0	43.7	43.9	42.6	40.7	37.6	40.2
2008	35.0	33.4	35.2	36.0	41.9	38.5	42.6	42.5	42.9	41.8	37.2	36.4	39.0
2009	32.4	32.7	32.2	34.7	38.8	41.6	41.2	42.6	40.6	40.7	42.0	37.6	38.1
Manufacturing													
2007	39.6	39.7	41.8	40.9	40.8	39.8	39.7	39.4	38.3	38.8	37.8	37.0	39.5
2008	36.3	36.4	37.2	36.9	37.4	38.1	38.0	38.7	38.4	38.7	37.4	37.1	37.6
2009	35.8	36.0	35.0	36.4	37.4	37.8	37.4	38.3	37.7	37.8	37.5	37.8	37.1
Trade, Transportation, and Utilities													
2007	34.3	33.9	33.8	33.5	34.3	35.4	35.5	34.0	33.2	32.6	32.8	34.2	34.0
2008	32.9	32.8	33.4	33.2	33.6	34.5	33.6	33.3	32.6	32.6	33.5	33.2	33.3
2009	32.7	33.3	33.1	32.8	33.7	34.9	34.3	35.2	34.5	34.1	34.8	33.9	34.0
Financial Activities													
2007	35.3	35.4	34.7	37.3	35.9	36.4	36.9	36.0	36.8	35.9	35.6	36.9	36.1
2008	36.0	36.1	37.0	36.5	35.8	37.7	36.6	36.5	36.0	36.5	36.1	36.9	36.5
2009	39.3	39.6	37.4	36.4	35.8	35.9	35.7	37.6	35.2	34.9	36.7	35.1	36.6
Professional and Business Services													
2007	34.3	34.6	34.5	34.4	34.4	35.2	34.7	35.6	35.5	34.5	34.4	35.2	34.8
2008	34.3	33.0	34.8	34.5	35.4	34.7	34.8	35.1	34.2	33.6	33.0	33.6	34.3
2009	32.2	33.0	33.3	32.5	31.7	32.8	33.6	33.3	31.5	32.0	32.7	31.9	32.5
Education and Health Services													
2007	30.6	31.0	30.8	31.0	30.5	31.4	31.4	30.6	33.9	30.9	31.2	30.8	31.2
2008	31.0	31.0	31.1	30.9	31.2	31.3	30.3	30.1	30.5	30.1	30.5	30.4	30.7
2009	30.6	30.9	30.5	30.4	30.5	30.9	30.8	30.9	30.7	30.8	31.3	31.3	30.8
Leisure and Hospitality													
2007	20.2	20.4	20.9	21.2	21.3	22.8	23.7	23.3	22.9	22.1	21.9	22.5	22.0
2008	21.0	21.2	22.0	21.9	22.1	23.5	23.0	22.8	21.8	21.4	21.5	20.1	21.9
2009	20.5	20.8	20.5	20.5	21.2	21.5	21.9	22.0	20.8	20.3	20.5	20.0	21.0
Other Services													
2007	25.5	25.0	24.0	25.2	26.2	27.0	26.3	26.9	25.5	24.8	23.9	24.8	25.4
2008	23.9	24.4	25.1	24.5	24.9	25.7	26.5	25.6	24.5	23.4	23.8	23.3	24.6
2009	22.7	23.3	22.8	23.2	24.1	25.0	24.5	24.4	23.8	23.5	23.9	23.1	23.7

Average Hourly Earnings by Selected Industry: North Dakota, 2007–2009

(Dollars, not seasonally adjusted.)

Industry and year	January	February	March	April	May	June	July	August	September	October	November	December	Annual average
Total Private													
2007	18.54	18.32	18.29	18.55	18.20	17.95	18.31	18.15	18.17	18.34	18.41	18.90	18.34
2008	18.50	18.59	18.54	18.58	18.30	18.43	18.65	18.84	19.32	19.08	19.09	19.14	18.75
2009	19.21	19.11	19.18	19.11	19.02	18.89	19.08	19.32	19.47	19.40	19.42	19.27	19.21
Goods-Producing													
2007	19.71	19.71	19.69	19.79	19.49	19.59	19.47	19.83	20.12	19.95	20.10	20.01	19.79
2008	19.83	20.13	20.51	19.99	19.97	19.75	20.33	20.88	21.29	21.07	20.82	21.05	20.49
2009	21.41	21.45	21.91	21.70	21.39	21.24	21.18	21.24	20.89	21.27	21.42	21.24	21.34
Construction													
2007	22.06	22.61	22.07	21.90	21.33	20.90	21.02	20.66	20.60	20.20	20.19	20.29	21.02
2008	19.96	20.05	20.31	19.28	19.12	18.82	19.26	19.56	19.63	19.43	19.52	20.32	19.55
2009	20.59	20.29	20.70	19.98	20.01	19.91	20.27	20.34	19.29	19.94	20.41	20.41	20.13
Manufacturing													
2007	17.36	17.36	17.45	17.69	17.43	17.74	17.46	18.23	18.56	18.71	18.57	18.26	17.89
2008	18.26	18.67	18.80	18.78	18.66	18.35	18.50	19.16	19.69	19.71	19.42	19.44	18.96
2009	19.44	19.46	20.06	20.07	19.54	19.43	19.31	19.36	19.70	19.66	19.59	19.61	19.60
Trade, Transportation, and Utilities													
2007	18.68	18.56	18.29	19.21	18.98	18.06	18.52	18.72	19.17	18.84	18.76	19.09	18.74
2008	18.91	18.70	18.71	19.12	18.97	18.90	18.97	18.94	19.24	19.57	19.35	18.99	19.03
2009	19.08	19.10	18.81	18.76	18.86	19.01	19.15	20.12	20.42	20.67	20.33	19.89	19.53
Financial Activities													
2007	19.58	17.92	17.93	18.35	17.99	18.36	20.14	18.54	19.12	18.97	19.14	19.09	18.77
2008	15.69	16.65	16.45	16.60	17.12	17.12	16.95	17.48	17.99	17.65	17.65	17.41	17.07
2009	17.07	17.26	17.34	17.41	17.82	17.82	18.22	18.82	18.46	18.58	18.89	18.78	18.03
Professional and Business Services													
2007	19.57	19.49	19.32	19.99	19.22	19.28	20.25	18.65	19.44	19.14	19.32	24.52	19.86
2008	22.88	23.49	22.79	22.19	21.54	21.63	21.01	21.08	20.97	20.83	21.82	21.06	21.76
2009	21.81	21.85	22.23	22.70	22.60	21.92	21.78	22.80	23.10	22.48	23.15	23.10	22.46
Education and Health Services													
2007	19.19	18.99	18.98	18.80	18.26	18.07	18.24	18.33	17.37	18.46	18.60	18.95	18.51
2008	18.92	18.85	18.75	18.93	17.92	18.62	19.06	19.02	19.92	19.10	19.26	19.53	18.99
2009	19.44	19.08	19.23	19.32	19.05	19.02	19.54	19.48	19.89	19.62	19.49	19.54	19.39
Leisure and Hospitality													
2007	9.70	9.59	9.54	9.86	9.69	9.51	9.49	9.66	9.74	10.04	10.00	10.04	9.74
2008	10.16	10.12	10.09	10.10	10.19	9.92	10.07	10.32	10.39	10.36	10.42	10.47	10.21
2009	10.44	10.47	10.66	10.63	10.57	10.43	10.68	10.72	10.88	11.01	11.02	11.24	10.73
Other Services													
2007	15.24	15.11	16.53	15.00	15.73	14.70	14.40	11.83	12.06	12.31	12.40	12.45	13.98
2008	12.46	12.38	12.54	12.66	12.99	13.11	12.85	13.24	13.40	13.42	13.52	14.04	13.04
2009	14.04	13.95	14.69	14.66	15.11	15.56	15.72	16.18	16.00	15.98	16.00	16.18	15.36

Average Weekly Earnings by Selected Industry: North Dakota, 2007–2009

(Dollars, not seasonally adjusted.)

Industry and year	January	February	March	April	May	June	July	August	September	October	November	December	Annual average
Total Private													
2007	598.84	593.57	592.60	608.44	602.42	606.71	622.54	606.21	619.60	599.72	598.33	616.14	605.22
2008	588.30	589.30	600.70	596.42	598.41	611.88	615.45	619.84	631.76	616.28	614.70	606.74	607.50
2009	603.19	609.61	600.33	598.14	606.74	613.93	620.10	639.49	623.04	618.86	629.21	608.93	614.72
Goods-Producing													
2007	762.78	762.78	783.66	785.66	810.78	801.23	809.95	820.96	822.91	811.97	793.95	760.38	795.56
2008	725.78	726.69	765.02	741.63	778.83	752.48	805.07	835.20	851.60	840.69	780.75	780.96	784.77
2009	757.91	767.91	769.04	796.39	823.52	847.48	832.37	858.10	812.62	827.40	841.81	807.12	813.05
Construction													
2007	785.34	798.13	761.42	786.21	895.86	867.35	924.88	902.84	904.34	860.52	821.73	762.90	845.00
2008	698.60	669.67	714.91	694.08	801.13	724.57	820.48	831.30	842.13	812.17	726.14	739.65	762.45
2009	667.12	663.48	666.54	693.31	776.39	828.26	835.12	866.48	783.17	811.56	857.22	767.42	766.95
Manufacturing													
2007	687.46	689.19	729.41	723.52	711.14	706.05	693.16	718.26	710.85	725.95	701.95	675.62	706.66
2008	662.84	679.59	699.36	692.98	697.88	699.14	703.00	741.49	756.10	762.78	726.31	721.22	712.90
2009	695.95	700.56	702.10	730.55	730.80	734.45	722.19	741.49	742.69	743.15	734.63	741.26	727.16
Trade, Transportation, and Utilities													
2007	640.72	629.18	618.20	643.54	651.01	639.32	657.46	636.48	636.44	614.18	615.33	652.88	637.16
2008	622.14	613.36	624.91	634.78	637.39	652.05	637.39	630.70	627.22	637.98	648.23	630.47	633.70
2009	623.92	636.03	622.61	615.33	635.58	663.45	656.85	708.22	704.49	704.85	707.48	674.27	664.02
Financial Activities													
2007	691.17	634.37	622.17	684.46	645.84	668.30	743.17	667.44	703.62	681.02	681.38	704.42	677.60
2008	564.84	601.07	608.65	605.90	612.90	645.42	620.37	638.02	647.64	644.23	637.17	642.43	623.06
2009	670.85	683.50	648.52	633.72	637.96	639.74	650.45	707.63	649.79	648.44	693.26	659.18	659.90
Professional and Business Services													
2007	671.25	674.35	666.54	687.66	661.17	678.66	702.68	663.94	690.12	660.33	664.61	863.10	691.13
2008	784.78	775.17	793.09	765.56	762.52	750.56	731.15	739.91	717.17	699.89	720.06	707.62	746.37
2009	702.28	721.05	740.26	737.75	716.42	718.98	731.81	759.24	727.65	719.36	757.01	736.89	729.95
Education and Health Services													
2007	587.21	588.69	584.58	582.80	556.93	567.40	572.74	560.90	588.84	570.41	580.32	583.66	577.51
2008	586.52	584.35	583.13	584.94	559.10	582.81	577.52	572.50	607.56	574.91	587.43	593.71	582.99
2009	594.86	589.57	586.52	587.33	581.03	587.72	601.83	601.93	610.62	604.30	610.04	611.60	597.21
Leisure and Hospitality													
2007	195.94	195.64	199.39	209.03	206.40	216.83	224.91	225.08	223.05	221.88	219.00	225.90	214.28
2008	213.36	214.54	221.98	221.19	225.20	233.12	231.61	235.30	226.50	221.70	224.03	210.45	223.60
2009	214.02	217.70	218.53	217.47	224.08	224.25	233.89	245.49	226.30	223.50	225.91	224.80	225.33
Other Services													
2007	388.62	377.75	396.72	378.00	412.13	396.90	378.72	318.23	307.53	305.29	296.36	308.76	355.09
2008	297.79	302.07	314.75	310.17	323.45	336.93	340.53	338.94	328.30	314.03	321.78	327.13	320.78
2009	318.71	325.04	334.93	340.11	364.15	389.00	385.14	394.79	380.80	375.53	382.40	373.76	364.03

OHIO
At a Glance

Population:
  1990 census: 10,847,115
  2000 census: 11,353,140
  2009 estimate: 11,542,645

Percent change in population:
  1990–2000: 4.7%
  2000–2009: 1.7%

Percent change in total nonfarm employment:
  1990–2009: 3.9%
  2008–2009: -5.4%

Industry with the largest growth in employment, 1990–2009 (thousands):
  Education and Health Services, 285.9

Industry with the largest decline or smallest growth in employment, 1990–2009 (thousands):
  Manufacturing, -430.3

Civilian labor force:
  1990: 5,389,113
  2000: 5,807,036
  2009: 5,970,188

Unemployment rate and rank among states (lowest to highest):
  1990: 5.7%, 32nd
  2000: 4.0%, 28th
  2009: 10.2, 40th

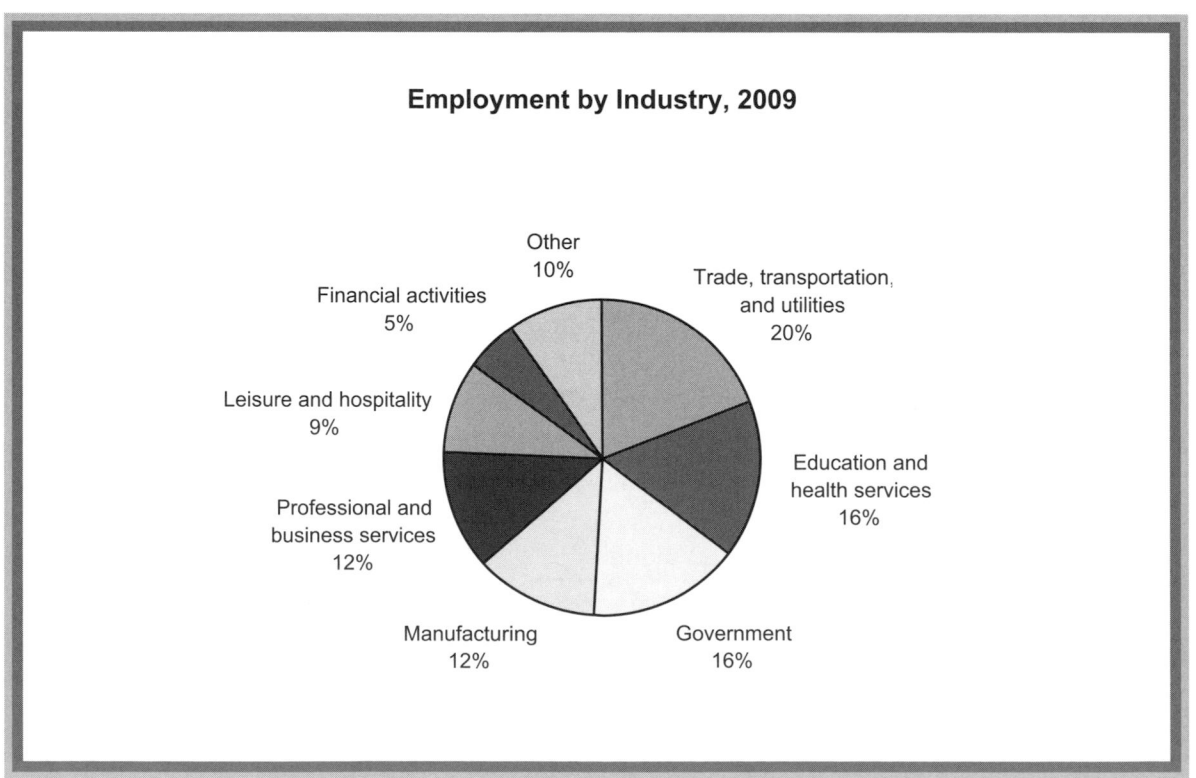

Employment by Industry, 2009

Other 10%

Trade, transportation, and utilities 20%

Financial activities 5%

Leisure and hospitality 9%

Education and health services 16%

Professional and business services 12%

Manufacturing 12%

Government 16%

Employment by Industry: Ohio, Selected Years, 1990–2009

(Numbers in thousands, not seasonally adjusted.)

Industry and year	January	February	March	April	May	June	July	August	September	October	November	December	Annual average
Total Nonfarm													
1990	4738.4	4770.3	4819.8	4859.0	4925.8	4955.7	4895.7	4904.3	4940.4	4933.5	4926.2	4918.5	4882.3
2000	5503.9	5524.9	5573.4	5610.8	5668.2	5690.3	5624.0	5629.5	5643.3	5661.2	5680.4	5686.0	5624.6
2001	5488.3	5501.1	5532.2	5560.1	5596.3	5612.1	5529.5	5533.5	5530.6	5539.3	5546.9	5541.5	5542.6
2002	5348.7	5363.6	5398.0	5429.2	5480.1	5492.5	5443.4	5456.6	5469.5	5479.1	5492.6	5486.2	5445.0
2003	5309.8	5307.0	5338.5	5390.0	5439.9	5440.2	5389.2	5405.0	5414.5	5441.1	5446.5	5450.7	5397.7
2004	5277.0	5292.7	5342.6	5395.2	5438.4	5454.9	5417.2	5423.5	5439.9	5466.1	5476.4	5476.5	5408.4
2005	5287.2	5313.9	5354.0	5424.3	5465.4	5472.4	5431.2	5440.1	5469.1	5476.8	5494.6	5491.3	5426.7
2006	5326.3	5347.0	5389.7	5434.8	5478.6	5494.3	5428.9	5441.3	5461.6	5466.4	5480.0	5480.9	5435.8
2007	5324.2	5321.0	5369.0	5417.4	5474.8	5493.7	5424.3	5438.6	5452.2	5465.3	5482.7	5472.4	5428.0
2008	5316.7	5325.9	5325.7	5384.6	5435.2	5428.4	5368.7	5372.4	5376.2	5370.7	5341.3	5303.2	5362.4
2009	5099.9	5084.7	5078.5	5095.3	5119.5	5092.4	5037.8	5034.8	5053.5	5071.6	5069.6	5045.4	5073.6
Total Private													
1990	4022.6	4040.3	4081.5	4123.9	4175.8	4230.9	4215.7	4237.4	4232.1	4198.6	4183.8	4178.2	4160.0
2000	4728.7	4734.3	4778.0	4814.6	4856.1	4906.7	4879.5	4892.8	4865.9	4861.7	4875.2	4881.8	4839.6
2001	4702.0	4697.6	4724.2	4754.3	4788.2	4822.7	4781.2	4788.2	4742.2	4728.3	4729.7	4724.3	4748.6
2002	4553.9	4550.4	4580.5	4615.3	4663.4	4697.5	4684.8	4704.0	4677.7	4667.0	4673.4	4668.8	4644.7
2003	4511.5	4493.9	4520.9	4573.2	4619.6	4642.1	4625.4	4648.1	4621.8	4627.1	4627.3	4630.3	4595.1
2004	4481.7	4477.4	4522.3	4577.3	4618.2	4654.6	4654.9	4666.9	4650.1	4653.7	4660.3	4662.2	4606.6
2005	4494.9	4501.5	4539.6	4611.7	4646.7	4677.6	4672.1	4683.9	4677.7	4664.1	4676.8	4678.1	4627.1
2006	4530.8	4536.0	4575.6	4622.7	4659.8	4697.9	4669.9	4684.4	4668.9	4653.5	4663.0	4666.6	4635.8
2007	4530.4	4513.3	4557.7	4607.7	4660.4	4697.6	4667.4	4683.5	4662.9	4656.0	4669.4	4665.7	4630.9
2008	4523.9	4515.2	4516.7	4574.7	4620.5	4636.2	4614.4	4619.4	4588.7	4560.8	4526.6	4497.3	4566.2
2009	4309.7	4279.6	4273.1	4286.3	4309.4	4306.0	4291.1	4291.0	4273.1	4269.4	4264.0	4245.5	4283.2
Goods-Producing													
1990	1222.5	1238.7	1252.2	1263.1	1279.0	1296.8	1290.0	1298.4	1297.9	1284.7	1264.5	1247.6	1269.6
2000	1258.9	1259.4	1273.0	1281.2	1292.7	1307.1	1290.3	1294.2	1285.7	1280.7	1276.0	1261.8	1280.0
2001	1216.9	1211.9	1215.5	1216.5	1219.6	1227.9	1214.5	1216.8	1200.1	1190.3	1180.5	1166.9	1206.5
2002	1117.8	1113.3	1118.0	1125.1	1137.5	1150.8	1143.4	1155.9	1147.0	1138.8	1131.9	1119.6	1133.3
2003	1080.0	1069.0	1073.5	1082.7	1096.8	1103.5	1089.1	1099.7	1092.0	1088.9	1081.9	1075.1	1086.0
2004	1037.2	1034.8	1047.9	1063.5	1074.5	1086.1	1083.6	1089.1	1083.2	1079.8	1073.5	1066.3	1068.3
2005	1025.7	1024.2	1032.4	1052.7	1062.5	1074.1	1071.5	1075.6	1071.7	1066.2	1062.3	1050.5	1055.8
2006	1018.1	1016.0	1024.1	1039.4	1046.3	1059.4	1049.0	1054.1	1048.8	1039.3	1032.4	1024.5	1037.6
2007	990.4	982.2	993.7	1003.5	1017.5	1028.9	1016.4	1027.0	1019.7	1009.6	1007.2	996.9	1007.8
2008	962.1	957.8	952.7	964.4	976.3	986.1	978.0	978.8	971.5	960.6	940.5	915.9	962.1
2009	855.4	842.4	832.9	826.3	823.5	819.3	815.8	821.2	817.2	816.9	804.7	792.2	822.3
Mining and Logging													
1990	17.2	16.9	17.2	17.7	17.9	18.3	18.4	18.3	18.2	18.0	17.9	17.4	17.8
2000	12.5	12.5	12.8	12.9	13.1	13.3	13.0	13.0	13.0	13.0	13.0	12.8	12.9
2001	12.2	12.4	12.7	12.8	13.0	13.3	13.3	13.3	13.3	13.0	12.9	12.7	12.9
2002	12.0	12.0	12.1	12.4	12.0	12.3	12.2	12.3	12.2	12.2	12.0	11.9	12.1
2003	11.5	11.3	11.4	11.6	11.7	11.8	11.8	11.9	11.8	11.8	11.8	11.6	11.7
2004	11.3	11.3	11.5	11.6	11.8	11.9	11.9	11.9	11.9	11.7	11.6	11.6	11.7
2005	10.8	10.8	10.9	11.3	11.4	11.5	11.7	11.6	11.6	11.7	11.7	11.5	11.4
2006	11.0	11.0	11.2	11.6	11.6	11.8	11.8	11.9	11.7	11.7	11.7	11.6	11.6
2007	11.3	11.0	11.2	11.6	11.8	11.9	12.0	12.1	11.9	11.8	11.9	11.7	11.7
2008	11.3	11.2	11.1	11.5	11.9	12.0	12.4	12.5	12.4	12.5	12.5	12.1	12.0
2009	11.6	11.4	11.5	11.8	12.0	12.0	12.2	12.0	11.8	11.7	11.5	11.2	11.7
Construction													
1990	169.2	168.5	176.4	185.2	195.8	204.0	207.8	209.7	207.3	202.5	197.4	184.7	192.4
2000	220.7	219.5	232.7	242.8	253.6	263.6	264.3	263.2	257.0	252.8	247.6	235.8	246.1
2001	212.5	213.1	221.4	232.6	243.1	252.8	258.7	260.3	253.8	252.3	247.8	238.1	240.5
2002	212.2	210.4	216.8	226.3	236.9	246.5	253.8	255.7	250.8	249.0	243.4	232.2	236.2
2003	207.5	200.8	207.5	224.0	234.2	242.6	246.0	248.7	245.2	245.5	240.1	232.8	231.2
2004	208.5	205.6	216.0	229.0	238.3	246.8	252.0	250.7	247.6	246.4	241.1	232.8	234.6
2005	204.9	203.9	209.5	228.3	237.6	246.0	250.4	250.3	247.3	244.9	241.4	230.0	232.9
2006	208.1	207.5	215.2	227.2	234.9	241.5	243.4	244.0	240.5	237.2	232.4	225.0	229.7
2007	204.3	195.6	206.1	219.2	231.3	238.7	239.7	240.2	237.2	235.9	230.7	218.6	224.8
2008	196.4	192.2	194.6	208.3	218.3	223.7	226.0	225.9	221.3	219.6	210.8	196.8	211.2
2009	173.5	168.9	172.0	175.8	185.8	190.7	193.4	191.7	186.6	185.9	183.9	168.7	181.4
Manufacturing													
1990	1036.1	1053.3	1058.6	1060.2	1065.3	1074.5	1063.8	1070.4	1072.4	1064.2	1049.2	1045.5	1059.5
2000	1025.7	1027.4	1027.5	1025.5	1026.0	1030.2	1013.0	1018.0	1015.7	1014.9	1015.4	1013.2	1021.0
2001	992.2	986.4	981.4	971.1	963.5	961.8	942.5	943.2	933.0	925.0	919.8	916.1	953.0
2002	893.6	890.9	889.1	886.4	888.6	892.0	877.4	887.9	884.0	877.6	876.5	875.5	885.0
2003	861.0	856.9	854.6	847.1	850.9	849.1	831.3	839.1	835.0	831.6	830.0	830.7	843.1
2004	817.4	817.9	820.4	822.9	824.4	827.4	819.7	826.5	823.7	821.7	820.8	821.9	822.1
2005	810.0	809.5	812.0	813.1	813.5	816.6	809.4	813.7	812.8	809.6	809.2	809.0	811.5
2006	799.0	797.5	797.7	800.6	799.8	806.1	793.8	798.2	796.6	790.4	788.3	787.9	796.3
2007	774.8	775.6	776.4	772.7	774.4	778.3	764.7	774.7	770.6	761.9	764.6	766.6	771.3
2008	754.4	754.4	747.0	744.6	746.1	750.4	739.6	740.4	737.8	728.5	717.2	707.0	739.0
2009	670.3	662.1	649.4	638.7	625.7	616.6	610.2	617.5	618.8	619.3	609.3	612.3	629.2

Employment by Industry: Ohio, Selected Years, 1990–2009—*Continued*

(Numbers in thousands, not seasonally adjusted.)

Industry and year	January	February	March	April	May	June	July	August	September	October	November	December	Annual average
Service-Providing													
1990	3515.9	3531.6	3567.6	3595.9	3646.8	3658.9	3605.7	3605.9	3642.5	3648.8	3661.7	3670.9	3612.7
2000	4245.0	4265.5	4300.4	4329.6	4375.5	4383.2	4333.7	4335.3	4357.6	4380.5	4404.4	4424.2	4344.5
2001	4271.4	4289.2	4316.7	4343.6	4376.7	4384.2	4315.0	4316.7	4330.5	4349.0	4366.4	4374.6	4336.2
2002	4230.9	4250.3	4280.0	4304.1	4342.6	4341.7	4300.0	4300.7	4322.5	4340.3	4360.7	4366.6	4311.7
2003	4229.8	4238.0	4265.0	4307.3	4343.1	4336.7	4300.1	4305.3	4322.5	4352.2	4364.6	4375.6	4311.7
2004	4239.8	4257.9	4294.7	4331.7	4363.9	4368.8	4333.6	4334.4	4356.7	4386.3	4402.9	4410.2	4340.1
2005	4261.5	4289.7	4321.6	4371.6	4402.9	4398.3	4359.7	4364.5	4397.4	4410.6	4432.3	4440.8	4370.9
2006	4308.2	4331.0	4365.6	4395.4	4432.3	4434.9	4379.9	4387.2	4412.8	4427.1	4447.6	4456.4	4398.2
2007	4333.8	4338.8	4375.3	4413.9	4457.3	4464.8	4407.9	4411.6	4432.5	4455.7	4475.5	4475.5	4420.2
2008	4354.6	4368.1	4373.0	4420.2	4458.9	4442.3	4390.7	4393.6	4404.7	4410.1	4400.8	4387.3	4400.4
2009	4244.5	4242.3	4245.6	4269.0	4296.0	4273.1	4222.0	4213.6	4236.3	4254.7	4264.9	4253.2	4251.3
Trade, Transportation, and Utilities													
1990	951.3	942.0	947.4	952.8	961.0	968.5	964.0	968.5	966.0	964.3	977.1	991.1	962.8
2000	1107.9	1097.0	1100.2	1101.8	1107.7	1113.5	1107.4	1108.6	1103.9	1123.9	1145.8	1165.8	1115.2
2001	1105.8	1089.5	1091.8	1094.0	1098.7	1102.3	1088.2	1086.3	1081.2	1087.4	1107.2	1117.0	1095.8
2002	1058.2	1045.3	1050.2	1053.2	1060.1	1064.7	1061.5	1061.5	1053.5	1057.7	1077.5	1089.2	1061.1
2003	1034.7	1023.7	1026.8	1035.9	1042.4	1044.6	1040.2	1042.7	1039.2	1051.1	1067.2	1078.6	1043.9
2004	1026.0	1015.1	1021.0	1025.4	1033.0	1039.8	1039.7	1041.7	1036.1	1049.2	1068.6	1080.9	1039.7
2005	1028.2	1020.4	1027.2	1035.0	1041.3	1043.1	1042.8	1042.2	1038.5	1044.5	1066.3	1082.4	1042.7
2006	1034.4	1024.5	1029.7	1034.6	1043.6	1047.5	1043.7	1044.9	1041.5	1047.3	1071.5	1085.1	1045.7
2007	1038.6	1024.8	1033.8	1038.8	1050.5	1054.8	1052.5	1051.1	1047.2	1053.2	1076.6	1088.0	1050.8
2008	1038.7	1024.4	1025.5	1032.1	1039.9	1040.2	1036.6	1037.2	1028.3	1028.0	1035.5	1041.0	1034.0
2009	985.6	970.0	966.3	964.5	969.9	969.2	964.5	962.2	955.7	959.0	973.0	980.0	968.3
Wholesale Trade													
1990	208.9	210.2	211.7	212.6	213.3	214.7	214.9	215.0	214.4	213.8	213.0	213.6	213.0
2000	244.2	244.9	246.1	246.4	247.6	249.2	248.0	247.8	247.2	248.5	248.7	250.0	247.4
2001	247.6	247.6	248.4	248.2	248.8	249.3	247.9	247.1	244.6	243.8	242.8	243.1	246.6
2002	238.4	237.7	238.6	239.3	240.2	240.9	240.7	240.2	238.3	237.7	237.6	238.3	239.0
2003	233.7	233.5	234.1	234.4	235.1	235.3	235.1	234.7	232.5	232.9	232.4	232.4	233.8
2004	228.1	228.0	229.0	229.9	231.5	233.1	234.5	234.7	233.0	234.8	235.4	236.4	232.4
2005	232.0	232.1	232.9	234.9	235.7	237.0	238.1	237.6	236.2	235.9	236.6	237.4	235.5
2006	234.7	235.1	235.7	237.0	238.2	239.9	239.5	239.3	237.6	237.5	237.9	238.8	237.6
2007	236.5	236.1	237.1	237.7	239.1	240.3	240.2	239.6	237.8	238.0	237.9	238.5	238.2
2008	235.5	235.2	235.2	236.8	238.2	238.8	238.5	238.0	235.7	235.1	233.1	231.7	236.0
2009	226.8	224.6	223.3	221.7	221.1	220.7	220.2	219.0	217.0	214.6	214.9	215.6	220.0
Retail Trade													
1990	593.7	583.1	586.3	589.8	595.4	600.5	596.5	600.5	598.9	597.7	611.6	625.9	598.3
2000	669.8	658.8	661.1	660.0	664.2	668.5	663.5	664.9	660.4	675.2	697.0	715.9	671.6
2001	665.9	651.0	652.6	652.8	656.8	660.4	648.7	647.5	645.4	651.5	673.3	684.4	657.5
2002	637.4	626.1	630.3	631.1	635.8	639.8	635.8	634.9	629.4	631.3	650.7	662.9	637.1
2003	618.8	609.4	612.3	619.4	623.8	626.1	622.5	624.4	622.5	629.8	646.2	657.5	626.1
2004	616.4	607.0	611.2	612.4	616.9	621.1	617.8	618.5	613.7	619.1	637.0	647.6	619.9
2005	607.0	598.8	603.4	608.7	613.0	613.0	609.7	608.7	604.3	607.2	624.6	637.6	611.3
2006	599.9	589.8	593.6	596.1	602.0	603.4	600.6	600.4	595.9	601.1	621.4	630.8	602.9
2007	594.7	583.3	590.4	592.8	601.0	602.6	601.2	598.7	595.2	599.2	619.1	627.5	600.5
2008	592.2	579.7	581.1	585.5	590.8	592.2	591.2	591.0	584.9	586.0	595.8	603.5	589.5
2009	563.3	552.4	552.2	555.7	562.2	563.1	560.3	559.5	555.9	559.5	573.0	582.7	561.7
Transportation and Utilities													
1990	148.7	148.7	149.4	150.4	152.3	153.3	152.6	153.0	152.7	152.8	152.5	151.6	151.5
2000	193.9	193.3	193.0	195.4	195.9	195.8	195.9	195.9	196.3	200.2	200.1	199.9	196.3
2001	192.3	190.9	190.8	193.0	193.1	192.6	191.6	191.7	191.2	192.1	191.1	189.5	191.7
2002	182.4	181.5	181.3	182.8	184.1	184.0	185.0	186.4	185.8	188.7	189.2	188.0	184.9
2003	182.2	180.8	180.4	182.1	183.5	183.2	182.6	183.6	184.2	188.4	188.6	188.7	184.0
2004	181.5	180.1	180.8	183.1	184.6	185.6	187.4	188.5	189.4	195.3	196.2	196.9	187.5
2005	189.2	189.5	190.9	191.4	192.6	193.1	195.0	195.9	198.0	201.4	205.1	207.4	195.8
2006	199.8	199.6	200.4	201.5	203.4	204.2	203.6	205.2	208.0	207.7	212.2	215.5	205.2
2007	207.4	205.4	206.3	208.3	210.4	211.9	211.1	212.8	214.2	216.0	219.6	222.0	212.1
2008	211.0	209.5	209.2	209.8	210.9	209.2	206.9	208.2	207.7	206.9	206.6	205.8	208.5
2009	195.5	193.0	190.8	187.1	186.6	185.4	184.0	183.7	182.8	184.9	185.1	181.7	186.7
Information													
1990	99.4	99.4	99.7	100.5	100.9	102.1	102.3	102.4	102.1	101.9	102.2	102.4	101.3
2000	106.7	106.8	107.6	106.4	106.6	107.7	107.1	107.6	106.8	107.2	107.8	108.5	107.2
2001	108.4	108.3	108.0	106.1	106.4	107.3	106.8	106.3	104.8	104.3	104.4	104.6	106.3
2002	103.5	102.5	102.2	101.9	101.7	101.9	101.3	100.8	99.5	98.4	99.1	99.2	101.0
2003	98.2	97.7	97.7	97.4	97.6	97.4	97.0	96.5	94.8	94.4	94.5	94.6	96.5
2004	93.4	93.0	92.9	92.4	92.6	93.3	92.9	92.3	90.8	90.5	91.5	91.1	92.2
2005	89.9	89.5	89.5	90.0	90.6	90.8	90.6	90.3	89.7	89.0	89.4	89.8	89.9
2006	88.8	88.6	88.7	88.3	88.6	88.9	88.8	88.6	87.8	87.5	87.8	88.0	88.4
2007	87.3	87.4	87.0	87.8	88.4	88.9	88.8	88.5	87.3	86.9	87.1	87.4	87.7
2008	86.3	86.2	86.1	86.4	86.4	86.4	86.5	86.4	84.8	84.5	84.9	84.8	85.8
2009	83.6	83.1	82.2	81.4	81.4	81.2	81.0	80.4	79.2	77.5	77.6	78.4	80.6

Employment by Industry: Ohio, Selected Years, 1990–2009—*Continued*

(Numbers in thousands, not seasonally adjusted.)

Industry and year	January	February	March	April	May	June	July	August	September	October	November	December	Annual average
Financial Activities													
1990	250.0	251.5	253.0	253.0	254.5	258.0	258.1	258.6	256.9	254.4	254.1	254.5	254.7
2000	304.2	304.1	304.5	304.7	305.2	307.4	305.9	305.9	304.6	303.2	305.3	307.7	305.2
2001	302.6	303.8	304.9	305.5	306.9	310.8	310.4	310.7	307.7	306.5	308.3	309.4	307.3
2002	305.6	306.9	307.5	306.4	307.5	309.6	310.7	310.3	307.9	308.0	309.6	311.1	308.4
2003	307.9	308.7	309.6	309.4	311.5	314.1	314.3	315.2	312.8	311.9	311.9	313.8	311.8
2004	309.8	310.5	311.3	310.4	311.1	313.5	313.5	313.3	309.6	308.8	308.8	309.9	310.9
2005	305.7	305.8	305.9	306.8	308.0	310.6	310.9	311.2	309.2	309.0	309.1	309.8	308.5
2006	305.6	305.5	306.3	306.1	306.5	307.9	307.3	306.1	304.2	304.5	304.1	303.5	305.6
2007	301.5	301.2	300.0	301.8	302.3	301.7	301.5	301.0	297.9	297.1	295.5	295.8	299.8
2008	292.1	291.6	291.3	291.4	292.1	292.5	291.7	291.2	288.3	287.4	286.9	286.8	290.3
2009	282.9	281.5	280.8	280.3	280.8	281.3	281.1	279.7	277.3	273.9	272.0	272.1	278.6
Professional and Business Services													
1990	429.3	432.8	439.5	449.3	455.2	461.6	463.1	466.7	465.7	466.0	462.8	457.8	454.2
2000	618.5	622.4	630.9	642.7	645.4	655.2	653.3	657.6	656.0	654.1	653.0	649.5	644.9
2001	621.3	622.0	628.0	633.5	635.3	640.2	636.0	636.6	629.8	625.9	620.8	618.7	629.0
2002	596.8	597.0	603.2	610.5	613.8	618.9	621.4	626.3	625.4	627.1	625.2	621.5	615.6
2003	597.8	597.4	602.2	609.5	611.2	614.1	615.2	620.7	616.6	619.9	619.9	615.8	611.7
2004	600.5	601.1	608.6	620.0	622.0	631.1	634.0	639.7	640.2	641.9	640.4	638.8	626.5
2005	615.1	619.0	625.2	639.8	640.5	646.4	649.6	656.4	658.5	659.4	657.1	657.2	643.7
2006	633.4	636.0	644.2	653.4	654.9	663.6	661.2	668.9	666.4	666.0	664.3	664.4	656.4
2007	645.1	646.7	653.4	664.2	667.3	676.8	674.1	677.7	676.0	680.2	680.6	678.8	668.4
2008	660.5	662.1	661.9	673.3	674.0	677.2	678.2	680.1	674.1	668.9	660.4	652.6	668.6
2009	625.7	619.0	614.1	617.1	615.7	614.8	613.1	615.3	612.6	620.6	620.2	610.0	616.5
Education and Health Services													
1990	529.9	533.2	535.7	536.4	536.2	537.1	534.9	537.4	545.5	550.5	553.1	554.7	540.4
2000	666.9	674.9	677.9	677.8	677.3	677.5	676.0	679.3	685.6	687.0	690.4	693.4	680.3
2001	680.1	690.2	691.7	696.2	693.5	688.6	680.3	683.6	695.4	706.7	710.5	711.2	694.0
2002	698.2	708.9	709.8	711.8	710.6	703.2	697.2	700.2	714.0	724.7	728.7	728.9	711.4
2003	719.1	725.2	727.2	730.1	726.9	719.6	717.7	719.9	734.4	743.8	746.9	747.2	729.8
2004	734.7	741.5	744.1	748.3	744.0	736.3	734.6	732.9	749.7	760.0	763.2	766.2	746.3
2005	748.6	757.1	760.2	763.3	759.8	753.3	748.7	750.2	768.6	775.8	780.0	781.4	762.3
2006	766.8	777.6	781.0	782.0	778.5	769.8	763.5	765.6	783.1	789.3	792.3	792.1	778.5
2007	779.9	785.2	789.5	792.5	791.6	785.0	780.7	783.9	801.7	809.2	814.0	814.1	793.9
2008	803.9	811.5	812.6	815.1	813.3	803.7	799.2	802.1	818.9	826.5	829.9	829.9	813.9
2009	818.6	825.7	827.3	828.8	825.8	815.8	814.0	815.0	829.6	836.3	838.5	839.9	826.3
Leisure and Hospitality													
1990	369.5	370.7	380.1	393.7	412.2	426.9	424.9	425.9	417.6	396.9	388.7	388.0	399.6
2000	446.7	448.7	460.8	476.8	496.8	512.9	515.2	515.4	499.6	482.1	473.4	471.3	483.3
2001	443.8	447.6	458.5	474.7	498.0	514.6	515.4	516.6	495.2	478.5	469.0	467.3	481.6
2002	448.2	449.9	461.1	477.9	502.0	516.7	519.4	518.4	502.5	484.5	473.9	471.2	485.5
2003	449.1	447.1	456.7	480.5	504.2	519.3	523.1	524.7	506.0	490.3	479.5	479.3	488.3
2004	457.4	457.8	470.1	489.8	512.1	524.4	527.0	529.2	513.9	496.3	487.9	484.0	495.8
2005	460.6	463.2	475.1	498.4	517.5	531.8	531.7	532.0	517.8	496.6	488.7	483.7	499.8
2006	463.8	467.4	479.5	496.2	517.2	533.9	531.9	532.6	514.9	497.6	489.1	486.8	500.9
2007	468.3	466.4	478.4	495.9	519.4	535.5	529.3	530.9	512.5	498.5	487.6	483.9	500.6
2008	462.6	463.3	467.8	491.8	516.6	527.1	522.3	522.2	503.7	485.8	471.1	469.6	492.0
2009	445.5	445.2	455.9	474.2	497.4	509.1	506.9	504.1	490.5	474.1	465.4	461.4	477.5
Other Services													
1990	170.7	172.0	173.9	175.1	176.8	179.9	178.4	179.5	180.4	179.9	181.3	182.1	177.5
2000	218.9	221.0	223.1	223.2	224.4	225.4	224.3	224.2	223.7	223.5	223.5	223.8	223.3
2001	223.1	224.3	225.8	227.8	229.8	231.0	229.6	231.3	228.0	228.7	229.0	229.2	228.1
2002	225.6	226.6	228.5	228.5	230.2	231.7	229.9	230.6	227.9	227.8	227.5	228.1	228.6
2003	224.7	225.1	227.2	227.7	229.0	229.5	228.8	228.7	226.0	226.8	225.5	225.9	227.1
2004	222.7	223.6	226.4	227.5	228.9	230.1	229.6	228.7	226.6	227.2	226.4	225.0	226.9
2005	221.1	222.3	224.1	225.7	226.5	227.5	226.3	226.0	223.7	223.6	223.9	223.3	224.5
2006	219.9	220.4	222.1	222.7	224.2	226.9	224.5	223.6	222.2	222.0	221.5	222.2	222.7
2007	219.3	219.4	221.9	222.2	223.4	226.0	224.1	223.4	220.6	221.3	220.8	220.8	221.9
2008	217.7	218.3	218.8	220.2	221.9	223.0	221.9	221.4	219.1	219.1	217.4	216.7	219.6
2009	212.4	212.7	213.6	213.7	214.9	215.3	214.7	213.1	211.0	211.1	212.6	211.5	213.1
Government													
1990	715.8	730.0	738.3	735.1	750.0	724.8	680.0	666.9	708.3	734.9	742.4	740.3	722.2
2000	775.2	790.6	795.4	796.2	812.1	783.6	744.5	736.7	777.4	799.5	805.2	804.2	785.0
2001	786.3	803.5	808.0	805.8	808.1	789.4	748.3	745.3	788.4	811.0	817.2	817.2	794.0
2002	794.8	813.2	817.5	813.9	816.7	795.0	758.6	752.6	791.8	812.1	819.2	817.4	800.2
2003	798.3	813.1	817.6	816.8	820.3	798.1	763.8	756.9	792.7	814.0	819.2	820.4	802.6
2004	795.3	815.3	820.3	817.9	820.2	800.3	762.3	756.6	789.8	812.4	816.1	814.3	801.7
2005	792.3	812.4	814.4	812.6	818.7	794.8	759.1	756.2	791.4	812.7	817.8	813.2	799.6
2006	795.5	811.0	814.1	812.1	818.8	796.4	759.0	756.9	792.7	812.9	817.0	814.3	800.1
2007	793.8	807.7	811.3	810.7	814.4	796.1	756.9	755.1	789.3	809.3	813.3	806.7	797.1
2008	792.8	810.7	809.0	809.9	814.7	792.2	754.3	753.0	787.5	809.9	814.7	805.9	796.2
2009	790.2	805.1	805.4	809.0	810.1	786.4	746.7	743.8	780.4	802.2	805.6	799.9	790.4

Average Weekly Hours by Selected Industry: Ohio, 2007–2009

(Not seasonally adjusted.)

Industry and year	January	February	March	April	May	June	July	August	September	October	November	December	Annual average
Total Private													
2007	33.5	32.9	33.9	34.2	34.0	34.2	34.3	34.2	34.4	34.1	33.9	33.9	33.9
2008	33.6	33.7	34.0	34.0	34.0	34.3	34.0	34.2	34.0	34.0	34.0	33.4	33.9
2009	32.5	33.0	32.9	32.5	32.8	32.9	32.9	33.3	33.0	33.0	33.5	33.2	33.0
Goods-Producing													
2007	38.6	36.7	39.3	39.0	39.4	39.7	39.1	39.3	39.9	39.8	39.7	39.6	39.2
2008	38.8	39.1	39.7	39.6	39.7	39.8	39.0	40.2	40.1	39.7	39.3	38.9	39.5
2009	36.2	36.7	36.5	36.5	37.2	37.7	37.5	38.2	37.6	37.9	38.5	38.8	37.4
Construction													
2007	36.8	35.3	37.5	37.1	38.8	39.5	38.9	39.0	39.0	38.5	37.8	36.5	38.0
2008	36.9	36.8	36.5	36.1	36.1	37.1	37.1	37.6	37.7	38.3	37.3	36.8	37.0
2009	35.3	36.3	35.8	35.1	36.5	37.3	38.0	38.8	38.3	37.7	38.1	37.5	37.1
Manufacturing													
2007	39.1	37.0	39.8	39.6	39.7	39.8	39.2	39.0	40.7	40.5	40.4	40.5	39.6
2008	39.4	39.7	40.3	40.5	40.6	40.5	39.4	40.5	40.4	40.1	39.9	39.5	40.1
2009	37.6	37.7	37.8	37.9	38.1	38.4	37.9	38.9	38.5	38.8	39.2	39.6	38.4
Trade, Transportation, and Utilities													
2007	33.1	32.7	33.3	34.1	34.0	34.1	34.0	33.7	34.1	34.1	33.7	32.8	33.6
2008	33.2	33.1	33.1	33.3	33.4	33.8	33.6	33.8	33.7	34.0	33.7	33.4	33.5
2009	33.1	33.5	33.3	33.1	33.6	33.7	33.6	33.9	33.9	33.6	33.6	33.6	33.5
Financial Activities													
2007	36.6	36.2	36.4	36.8	36.0	36.3	37.6	37.2	37.8	36.9	36.8	37.7	36.9
2008	36.8	36.9	37.6	37.0	36.6	36.9	36.1	36.6	35.9	36.6	37.6	36.8	36.8
2009	36.8	37.3	36.7	36.1	36.4	36.5	36.1	36.7	36.4	36.1	36.9	36.5	36.5
Professional and Business Services													
2007	34.9	35.1	35.6	36.3	36.2	35.9	36.1	35.6	35.8	35.6	35.4	35.4	35.7
2008	35.1	35.1	35.9	35.8	35.6	35.9	35.7	35.6	35.6	35.8	35.9	34.8	35.6
2009	34.7	34.8	34.7	34.7	34.5	34.4	34.2	34.6	34.2	34.0	34.6	34.2	34.5
Education and Health Services													
2007	32.5	32.1	32.7	32.7	32.4	32.6	32.2	32.2	32.5	32.0	32.1	32.0	32.3
2008	31.8	32.4	32.4	32.3	32.4	32.6	32.6	32.6	32.6	32.5	32.8	32.7	32.5
2009	32.2	32.7	32.8	32.1	32.9	32.6	32.7	33.0	32.9	32.8	33.2	32.8	32.7
Leisure and Hospitality													
2007	22.8	22.5	23.3	23.5	23.4	24.5	24.7	24.6	24.3	24.3	23.5	23.3	23.8
2008	23.0	23.3	23.2	23.8	23.9	24.4	24.6	24.5	23.8	24.0	23.9	23.3	23.8
2009	22.3	22.4	22.5	22.2	22.8	23.3	23.6	23.6	23.3	23.2	23.4	23.6	23.0
Other Services													
2007	32.6	31.3	31.4	31.5	32.0	31.7	32.2	32.5	31.5	31.4	31.4	31.1	31.7
2008	31.6	31.9	31.8	31.7	32.0	31.5	31.8	31.6	31.5	31.6	32.1	31.7	31.7
2009	31.2	30.6	30.4	29.7	29.9	29.7	29.9	30.3	29.9	30.3	30.3	30.2	30.2

Average Hourly Earnings by Selected Industry: Ohio, 2007–2009

(Dollars, not seasonally adjusted.)

Industry and year	January	February	March	April	May	June	July	August	September	October	November	December	Annual average
Total Private													
2007	20.08	20.51	20.24	20.39	19.96	19.99	20.06	20.07	20.30	20.29	20.35	20.39	20.22
2008	19.95	20.03	20.19	20.08	19.83	19.96	19.94	20.02	20.31	20.22	20.31	20.52	20.11
2009	20.02	20.01	19.95	19.98	19.85	19.76	19.73	19.74	19.95	20.03	20.11	20.24	19.95
Goods-Producing													
2007	22.50	23.39	23.32	22.94	22.81	22.72	22.94	22.64	22.79	22.84	22.87	22.90	22.88
2008	22.22	22.26	22.26	21.99	21.57	21.95	22.04	22.22	22.49	22.19	22.12	22.61	22.16
2009	21.80	22.11	21.92	21.93	21.86	21.82	21.80	21.47	21.65	21.54	21.67	21.56	21.76
Construction													
2007	23.23	23.87	23.13	23.29	23.52	23.53	23.49	23.57	23.92	24.23	24.40	24.56	23.73
2008	23.67	23.88	24.36	24.30	24.46	24.83	24.54	25.07	25.38	25.00	24.81	24.92	24.62
2009	24.64	24.88	24.93	24.78	25.19	24.91	24.70	24.68	24.79	24.90	25.00	25.12	24.87
Manufacturing													
2007	22.33	23.22	23.39	22.89	22.61	22.48	22.78	23.66	22.61	22.42	22.37	22.47	22.77
2008	21.84	21.85	21.74	21.95	21.44	21.74	21.83	22.17	22.36	22.31	22.23	22.31	21.98
2009	21.89	21.93	21.86	21.85	21.63	21.56	21.54	21.13	21.28	21.17	21.36	21.22	21.54
Trade, Transportation, and Utilities													
2007	17.37	17.80	17.48	17.81	17.43	17.67	17.66	17.77	17.88	17.93	17.81	17.97	17.72
2008	17.92	18.08	18.29	18.19	18.12	18.35	18.15	18.04	18.17	18.15	18.20	17.89	18.13
2009	18.30	18.46	18.49	18.40	18.41	18.34	18.48	18.56	18.50	18.44	18.46	18.29	18.43
Financial Activities													
2007	24.08	23.76	23.65	23.68	23.75	23.82	24.01	24.17	24.16	24.20	24.05	23.89	23.94
2008	24.27	24.14	24.40	24.62	24.62	24.30	24.04	24.10	24.00	23.77	23.72	23.84	24.15
2009	23.50	23.75	23.55	23.71	23.54	23.31	23.49	23.42	23.42	23.35	23.27	23.35	23.47
Professional and Business Services													
2007	23.90	23.96	23.55	24.06	24.07	24.23	24.35	23.78	24.04	23.66	23.79	23.89	23.94
2008	23.61	24.07	23.97	23.62	23.88	23.99	23.94	23.92	24.04	24.11	24.07	24.26	23.96
2009	24.42	24.07	24.08	23.92	23.60	23.67	23.61	23.72	23.56	23.78	23.89	24.00	23.86
Education and Health Services													
2007	18.91	18.67	18.48	18.69	18.77	18.89	18.69	18.50	18.73	18.83	18.78	18.83	18.73
2008	19.26	19.10	19.42	19.35	18.87	18.88	19.14	19.18	19.36	19.24	19.44	19.54	19.23
2009	19.47	19.41	19.67	19.89	20.19	20.25	20.06	20.03	20.23	20.34	20.29	20.44	20.03
Leisure and Hospitality													
2007	10.91	11.26	11.16	11.16	10.86	11.20	11.11	11.02	10.99	11.02	11.10	11.12	11.07
2008	11.21	11.12	11.09	11.01	11.12	10.97	10.85	10.92	11.11	11.01	11.03	10.99	11.03
2009	11.12	11.10	11.05	10.99	10.90	10.84	10.86	10.88	10.99	11.13	11.28	11.26	11.03
Other Services													
2007	15.37	15.31	15.30	15.40	15.62	16.04	16.15	16.28	16.16	16.23	16.33	16.38	15.88
2008	15.95	16.14	16.08	15.87	15.82	16.17	16.19	16.33	16.30	16.33	16.48	16.30	16.16
2009	16.32	16.39	16.19	15.86	15.72	15.79	15.63	16.29	16.35	16.17	16.19	16.22	16.09

Average Weekly Earnings by Selected Industry: Ohio, 2007–2009

(Dollars, not seasonally adjusted.)

Industry and year	January	February	March	April	May	June	July	August	September	October	November	December	Annual average
Total Private													
2007	672.68	674.78	686.14	697.34	678.64	683.66	688.06	686.39	698.32	691.89	689.87	691.22	685.46
2008	670.32	675.01	686.46	682.72	674.22	684.63	677.96	684.68	690.54	687.48	690.54	685.37	681.73
2009	650.65	660.33	656.36	649.35	651.08	650.10	649.12	657.34	658.35	660.99	673.69	671.97	658.35
Goods-Producing													
2007	868.50	858.41	916.48	894.66	898.71	901.98	896.95	889.75	909.32	909.03	907.94	906.84	896.90
2008	862.14	870.37	883.72	870.80	856.33	873.61	859.56	893.24	901.85	880.94	869.32	879.53	875.32
2009	789.16	811.44	800.08	800.45	813.19	822.61	817.50	820.15	814.04	816.37	834.30	836.53	813.82
Construction													
2007	854.86	842.61	867.38	864.06	912.58	929.44	913.76	919.23	932.88	932.86	922.32	896.44	901.74
2008	873.42	878.78	889.14	877.23	883.01	921.19	910.43	942.63	956.83	957.50	925.41	917.06	910.94
2009	869.79	903.14	892.49	869.78	919.44	929.14	938.60	957.58	949.46	938.73	952.50	942.00	922.68
Manufacturing													
2007	873.10	859.14	930.92	906.44	897.62	894.70	892.98	922.74	920.23	908.01	903.75	910.04	901.69
2008	860.50	867.45	876.12	888.98	870.46	880.47	860.10	897.89	903.34	894.63	886.98	881.25	881.40
2009	823.06	826.76	826.31	828.12	824.10	827.90	816.37	821.96	819.28	821.40	837.31	840.31	827.14
Trade, Transportation, and Utilities													
2007	574.95	582.06	582.08	607.32	592.62	602.55	600.44	598.85	609.71	611.41	600.20	589.42	595.39
2008	594.94	598.45	605.40	605.73	605.21	620.23	609.84	609.75	612.33	617.10	613.34	597.53	607.36
2009	605.73	618.41	615.72	609.04	618.58	618.06	620.93	629.18	627.15	619.58	620.26	614.54	617.41
Financial Activities													
2007	881.33	860.11	860.86	871.42	855.00	864.67	902.78	899.12	913.25	892.98	885.04	900.65	883.39
2008	893.14	890.77	917.44	910.94	901.09	896.67	867.84	882.06	861.60	869.98	891.87	877.31	888.72
2009	864.80	885.88	864.29	855.93	856.86	850.82	847.99	859.51	852.49	842.94	858.66	852.28	856.66
Professional and Business Services													
2007	834.11	841.00	838.38	873.38	871.33	869.86	879.04	846.57	860.63	842.30	842.17	845.71	854.66
2008	828.71	844.86	860.52	845.60	850.13	861.24	854.66	851.55	855.82	863.14	864.11	844.25	852.98
2009	847.37	837.64	835.58	830.02	814.20	814.25	807.46	820.71	805.75	808.52	826.59	820.80	823.17
Education and Health Services													
2007	614.58	599.31	604.30	611.16	608.15	615.81	601.82	595.70	608.73	602.56	602.84	602.56	604.98
2008	612.47	618.84	629.21	625.01	611.39	615.49	623.96	625.27	631.14	625.30	637.63	638.96	624.98
2009	626.93	634.71	645.18	638.47	664.25	660.15	655.96	660.99	665.57	667.15	673.63	670.43	654.98
Leisure and Hospitality													
2007	248.75	253.35	260.03	262.26	254.12	274.40	274.42	271.09	267.06	267.79	260.85	259.10	263.47
2008	257.83	259.10	257.29	262.04	265.77	267.67	266.91	267.54	264.42	264.24	263.62	256.07	262.51
2009	247.98	248.64	248.63	243.98	248.52	252.57	256.30	256.77	256.07	258.22	263.95	265.74	253.69
Other Services													
2007	501.06	479.20	480.42	485.10	499.84	508.47	520.03	529.10	509.04	509.62	512.76	509.42	503.40
2008	504.02	514.87	511.34	503.08	506.24	509.36	514.84	516.03	513.45	516.03	529.01	516.71	512.27
2009	509.18	501.53	492.18	471.04	470.03	468.96	467.34	493.59	488.87	489.95	490.56	489.84	485.92

OKLAHOMA
At a Glance

Population:
  1990 census: 3,145,576
  2000 census: 3,450,654
  2009 estimate: 3,687,050

Percent change in population:
  1990–2000: 9.7%
  2000–2009: 6.9%

Percent change in total nonfarm employment:
  1990–2009: 29.4%
  2008–2009: -3.4%

Industry with the largest growth in employment, 1990–2009 (thousands):
  Education and Health Services, 85.4

Industry with the largest decline or smallest growth in employment, 1990–2009 (thousands):
  Manufacturing, -26.1

Civilian labor force:
  1990: 1,520,852
  2000: 1,661,045
  2009: 1,773,186

Unemployment rate and rank among states (lowest to highest):
  1990: 5.7%, 32nd
  2000: 3.1%, 12th
  2009: 6.4%, 7th

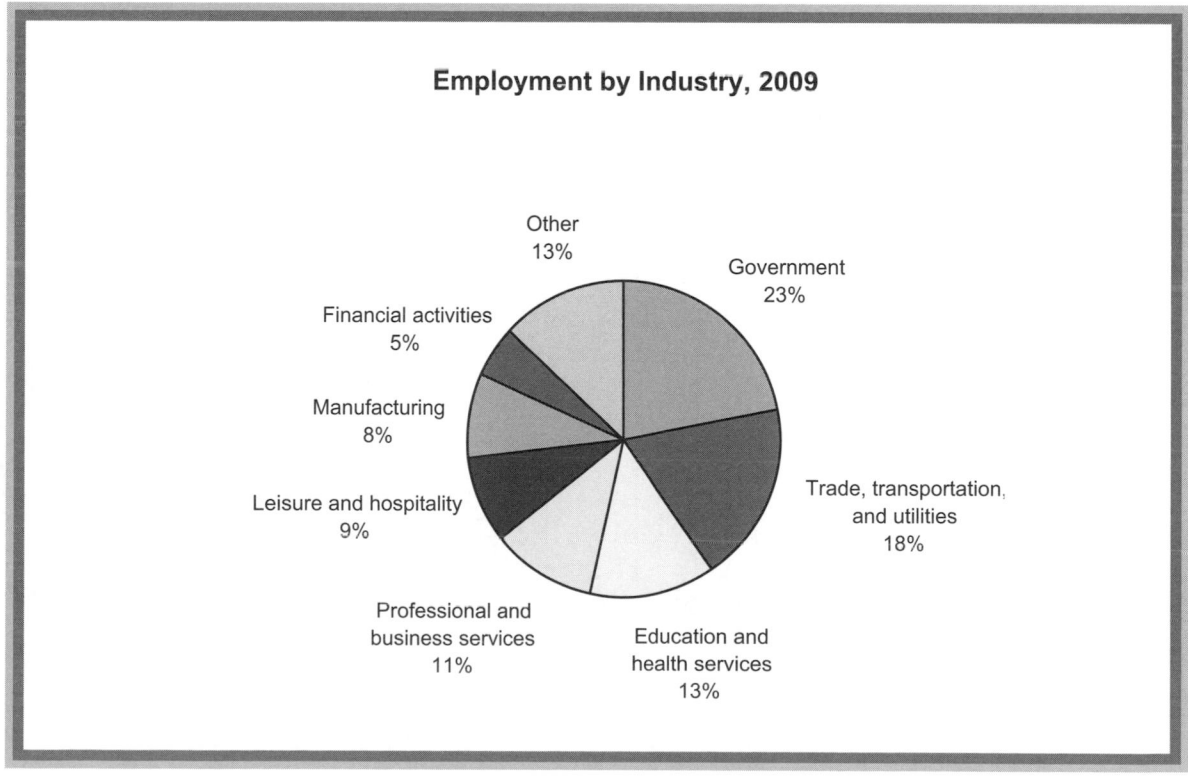

Employment by Industry, 2009

- Other 13%
- Government 23%
- Financial activities 5%
- Manufacturing 8%
- Leisure and hospitality 9%
- Trade, transportation, and utilities 18%
- Professional and business services 11%
- Education and health services 13%

Employment by Industry: Oklahoma, Selected Years, 1990–2009

(Numbers in thousands, not seasonally adjusted.)

Industry and year	January	February	March	April	May	June	July	August	September	October	November	December	Annual average
Total Nonfarm													
1990	1156.3	1166.9	1176.6	1183.2	1193.0	1197.2	1182.4	1190.3	1206.2	1201.7	1204.2	1206.1	1188.7
2000	1438.3	1447.5	1464.0	1474.4	1490.7	1489.0	1471.0	1479.9	1495.7	1498.8	1507.9	1508.0	1480.4
2001	1467.5	1480.1	1493.8	1503.2	1512.3	1507.0	1481.0	1488.9	1499.2	1492.9	1501.9	1498.5	1493.9
2002	1455.6	1463.9	1474.7	1483.8	1495.9	1480.8	1461.2	1469.9	1475.5	1471.6	1476.4	1473.8	1473.6
2003	1435.2	1439.2	1442.6	1448.2	1457.5	1440.4	1429.2	1435.7	1448.0	1453.3	1456.4	1457.7	1445.3
2004	1426.8	1435.4	1450.3	1460.1	1467.4	1458.9	1450.7	1458.1	1472.6	1480.9	1485.3	1490.6	1461.4
2005	1452.6	1467.0	1483.9	1497.8	1506.5	1500.3	1486.3	1497.6	1514.3	1520.0	1531.1	1536.5	1499.5
2006	1503.3	1517.5	1534.0	1533.8	1547.5	1545.4	1525.4	1539.5	1554.2	1554.0	1559.9	1565.6	1540.0
2007	1528.8	1543.8	1565.3	1563.0	1573.6	1572.3	1552.4	1568.3	1581.0	1586.7	1594.9	1590.1	1568.4
2008	1566.3	1581.2	1592.5	1596.5	1606.5	1592.3	1578.0	1589.5	1601.3	1603.6	1603.4	1601.5	1592.7
2009	1555.0	1555.8	1558.4	1551.1	1551.6	1539.5	1512.0	1513.6	1523.7	1534.7	1534.1	1532.5	1538.7
Total Private													
1990	894.9	899.4	909.0	918.2	926.5	941.6	937.9	944.1	944.0	933.5	935.9	936.5	926.8
2000	1155.4	1158.7	1171.5	1183.1	1192.8	1204.0	1201.0	1208.8	1208.9	1204.3	1211.7	1212.4	1192.7
2001	1175.5	1181.6	1193.4	1203.1	1209.4	1217.4	1203.2	1208.3	1201.3	1188.5	1194.8	1192.6	1197.4
2002	1157.3	1159.9	1169.0	1177.9	1186.4	1185.3	1176.9	1183.1	1175.7	1165.0	1169.1	1166.6	1172.7
2003	1140.1	1138.1	1141.8	1148.0	1155.3	1151.3	1150.7	1156.1	1152.4	1151.7	1153.9	1154.5	1149.5
2004	1132.3	1133.6	1146.7	1156.1	1161.3	1164.1	1166.3	1167.5	1166.1	1169.5	1173.8	1177.6	1159.6
2005	1147.4	1154.4	1169.1	1181.3	1187.5	1193.5	1193.5	1199.0	1199.9	1198.1	1207.8	1213.2	1187.1
2006	1188.5	1194.6	1209.6	1210.1	1220.8	1230.8	1223.3	1230.4	1229.7	1224.0	1229.4	1235.5	1218.9
2007	1206.8	1215.1	1234.8	1233.9	1242.5	1253.0	1248.5	1257.0	1252.4	1253.6	1260.7	1257.7	1243.0
2008	1245.2	1252.6	1262.2	1263.4	1270.1	1272.6	1269.6	1273.7	1269.6	1264.3	1263.1	1261.1	1264.0
2009	1223.3	1217.2	1216.8	1207.6	1205.9	1207.4	1192.2	1188.7	1183.4	1188.0	1187.7	1188.2	1200.5
Goods-Producing													
1990	226.1	227.6	230.2	232.7	234.9	239.3	239.4	238.6	238.5	238.1	236.7	235.4	234.8
2000	260.4	260.7	263.2	262.6	264.7	267.6	267.7	269.1	267.9	266.0	266.7	268.5	265.4
2001	263.0	264.7	266.8	267.1	269.0	272.5	268.2	267.1	265.7	259.2	259.2	257.7	265.0
2002	246.6	246.3	246.7	245.8	248.1	248.7	247.1	246.8	243.7	241.2	240.1	239.6	245.1
2003	237.2	235.6	236.0	236.0	236.6	235.6	238.0	239.2	237.8	236.8	235.0	235.2	236.6
2004	231.8	230.9	233.9	234.8	236.9	237.5	241.0	240.8	240.2	241.3	240.5	242.2	237.7
2005	236.8	238.3	241.7	243.9	244.7	246.3	249.6	250.4	250.5	251.7	252.8	255.9	246.9
2006	253.8	255.4	258.7	256.7	259.7	263.8	263.3	265.6	265.0	264.5	264.4	266.0	261.4
2007	260.7	261.2	265.4	264.6	266.3	270.5	271.1	273.0	270.6	271.9	273.3	272.5	268.4
2008	272.3	273.7	275.6	276.8	279.0	280.9	281.5	281.7	280.2	278.0	275.3	273.3	277.4
2009	263.8	258.3	253.7	246.6	243.5	242.0	237.2	234.5	231.8	231.5	229.3	229.1	241.8
Mining and Logging													
1990	37.4	37.2	37.2	37.8	37.8	38.9	38.6	38.9	38.3	38.6	38.5	39.2	38.2
2000	26.5	26.6	26.6	25.5	26.0	26.3	27.2	27.4	27.5	27.3	27.6	28.6	26.9
2001	27.9	28.6	28.9	28.7	29.2	30.2	29.8	29.8	29.2	29.0	29.0	28.8	29.1
2002	28.1	28.1	28.1	28.2	28.7	29.0	28.9	28.9	28.3	27.9	27.8	27.9	28.3
2003	28.7	28.8	28.9	28.9	29.3	29.9	30.0	30.4	30.5	30.5	30.5	30.8	29.8
2004	30.8	30.9	31.3	31.6	32.1	32.8	32.9	33.0	32.9	33.5	33.9	34.4	32.5
2005	34.4	34.5	34.8	34.8	35.3	35.8	36.1	36.5	36.8	37.2	37.5	37.9	36.0
2006	38.4	39.2	40.0	40.7	41.3	42.4	42.5	43.5	43.6	43.4	43.9	44.5	42.0
2007	44.3	44.2	44.8	44.9	45.3	46.4	47.2	47.9	47.6	48.6	49.2	49.3	46.6
2008	49.6	49.9	50.2	50.5	51.4	52.5	52.9	53.5	53.3	53.8	53.3	52.7	52.0
2009	50.4	48.9	47.3	44.8	43.6	43.1	42.1	41.7	40.8	39.6	39.9	38.9	43.4
Construction													
1990	38.1	37.6	38.0	39.3	40.3	42.2	43.3	44.0	42.3	42.3	42.2	40.7	40.9
2000	58.1	58.1	59.7	61.1	62.2	63.2	62.8	63.6	62.9	63.1	62.5	62.2	61.6
2001	60.6	62.5	65.0	66.3	67.6	69.4	68.9	69.5	67.6	66.3	65.1	64.4	66.1
2002	63.1	63.3	63.7	63.6	65.2	65.9	66.5	66.4	64.8	64.0	63.3	63.1	64.4
2003	62.0	61.3	61.8	63.7	64.6	65.9	65.9	65.7	64.3	63.6	62.1	62.3	63.6
2004	59.7	59.2	61.3	61.7	62.6	64.0	65.2	64.8	64.5	64.3	63.1	63.4	62.8
2005	61.1	61.4	63.6	65.5	65.3	66.9	68.1	68.1	68.0	68.1	68.0	68.8	66.1
2006	67.7	68.1	69.7	69.6	70.1	72.1	71.1	71.5	71.3	71.0	70.4	70.5	70.3
2007	67.5	67.7	70.2	70.0	70.7	73.0	72.4	73.5	72.4	72.8	73.3	72.2	71.3
2008	71.6	72.3	73.8	74.8	76.2	77.0	78.0	78.0	77.7	76.8	75.7	74.7	75.6
2009	71.4	70.7	70.7	69.4	69.3	70.3	68.7	68.0	67.1	67.6	66.3	65.7	68.8
Manufacturing													
1990	150.6	152.8	155.0	155.6	156.8	158.2	157.5	155.7	157.9	157.2	156.0	155.5	155.7
2000	175.8	176.0	176.9	176.0	176.5	178.1	177.7	178.1	177.5	175.6	176.6	177.7	176.9
2001	174.5	173.6	172.9	172.1	172.2	172.9	169.5	167.8	168.9	163.9	165.1	164.5	169.8
2002	155.4	154.9	154.9	154.0	154.2	153.8	151.7	151.5	150.6	149.3	149.0	148.6	152.3
2003	146.5	145.5	145.3	143.4	142.7	139.8	142.1	143.1	143.0	142.7	142.4	142.1	143.2
2004	141.3	140.8	141.3	141.5	142.2	140.7	142.9	143.0	142.8	143.5	143.5	144.4	142.3
2005	141.3	142.4	143.3	143.6	144.1	143.6	145.4	145.8	145.7	146.4	147.3	149.2	144.8
2006	147.7	148.1	149.0	146.4	148.3	149.3	149.7	150.6	150.1	150.1	150.1	151.0	149.2
2007	148.9	149.3	150.4	149.7	150.3	151.1	151.5	151.6	150.6	150.5	150.8	151.0	150.5
2008	151.1	151.5	151.6	151.5	151.4	151.4	150.6	150.2	149.2	147.4	146.3	145.9	149.8
2009	142.0	138.7	135.7	132.4	130.6	128.6	126.4	124.8	123.9	124.3	123.1	124.5	129.6

Employment by Industry: Oklahoma, Selected Years, 1990–2009—*Continued*

(Numbers in thousands, not seasonally adjusted.)

Industry and year	January	February	March	April	May	June	July	August	September	October	November	December	Annual average
Service-Providing													
1990	928.7	937.8	944.9	949.0	956.6	956.4	941.5	950.2	966.2	962.1	966.0	969.2	952.4
2000	1177.0	1185.9	1199.9	1210.9	1225.1	1220.5	1202.4	1209.9	1226.9	1231.9	1240.3	1238.6	1214.1
2001	1204.5	1215.4	1227.0	1236.1	1243.3	1234.5	1212.8	1221.8	1233.5	1233.7	1242.7	1240.8	1228.8
2002	1209.0	1217.6	1228.0	1238.0	1247.8	1232.1	1214.1	1223.1	1231.8	1230.4	1236.3	1234.2	1228.5
2003	1198.0	1203.6	1206.6	1212.2	1220.9	1204.8	1191.2	1196.5	1210.2	1216.5	1221.4	1222.5	1208.7
2004	1195.0	1204.5	1216.4	1225.3	1230.5	1221.4	1209.7	1217.3	1232.4	1239.6	1244.8	1248.4	1223.8
2005	1215.8	1228.7	1242.2	1253.9	1261.8	1254.0	1236.7	1247.2	1263.8	1268.3	1278.3	1280.6	1252.6
2006	1249.5	1262.1	1275.3	1277.1	1287.8	1281.6	1262.1	1273.9	1289.2	1289.5	1295.5	1299.6	1278.6
2007	1268.1	1282.6	1299.9	1298.4	1307.3	1301.8	1281.3	1295.3	1310.4	1314.8	1321.6	1317.6	1299.9
2008	1294.0	1307.5	1316.9	1319.7	1327.5	1311.4	1296.5	1307.8	1321.1	1325.6	1328.1	1328.2	1315.4
2009	1291.2	1297.5	1304.7	1304.5	1308.1	1297.5	1274.8	1279.1	1291.9	1303.2	1304.8	1303.4	1296.7
Trade, Transportation, and Utilities													
1990	242.8	241.0	242.1	242.9	245.2	249.2	247.8	250.0	248.7	247.7	251.3	253.8	246.9
2000	287.0	285.0	286.3	288.9	291.6	294.1	292.2	294.7	294.7	295.7	302.0	304.2	293.0
2001	290.7	287.7	289.2	289.8	291.1	292.2	287.9	288.5	286.5	286.7	291.2	293.0	289.5
2002	283.5	281.3	283.9	283.9	285.1	284.9	282.5	283.1	281.8	280.7	285.5	287.3	283.6
2003	275.9	273.8	274.9	275.4	277.0	276.1	274.6	276.0	275.2	277.0	281.5	284.5	276.8
2004	273.3	271.1	274.0	274.1	275.7	276.0	273.6	273.4	272.1	274.1	279.1	282.4	274.9
2005	272.1	271.8	274.3	276.7	278.1	278.5	279.0	280.3	280.5	282.3	287.6	290.6	279.3
2006	278.1	278.1	280.3	281.8	284.4	284.9	282.8	283.8	283.7	284.0	288.8	292.8	283.6
2007	282.8	282.6	288.3	285.2	287.3	288.2	286.7	287.3	286.4	287.8	293.1	294.1	287.5
2008	285.9	285.4	288.1	288.1	289.3	289.9	289.8	290.5	289.7	290.4	294.0	295.6	289.7
2009	284.6	282.5	283.0	281.9	282.5	282.4	279.0	278.5	277.8	276.6	279.9	280.3	280.8
Wholesale Trade													
1990	48.5	48.5	48.9	49.4	49.8	51.1	51.2	51.5	51.1	50.6	50.7	50.4	50.1
2000	55.7	55.8	56.2	56.2	56.5	58.1	57.0	57.5	57.4	57.3	57.3	57.4	56.9
2001	56.0	55.9	56.4	56.6	56.9	57.7	57.0	57.1	56.9	56.8	56.7	57.0	56.7
2002	56.4	56.1	56.5	56.2	56.6	57.0	56.8	56.9	56.6	56.0	56.1	56.1	56.4
2003	54.9	54.5	54.9	54.6	55.0	55.3	54.6	54.5	54.6	54.9	54.6	54.7	54.8
2004	54.1	53.7	53.9	54.0	54.7	55.3	55.1	55.1	54.8	55.2	55.4	55.7	54.8
2005	54.9	55.1	55.5	56.0	56.3	56.9	57.1	57.2	57.0	57.3	57.4	57.7	56.5
2006	57.2	57.6	58.0	57.8	58.4	58.9	58.7	58.8	58.8	58.6	58.7	58.9	58.4
2007	58.4	58.6	59.4	59.3	59.5	60.3	59.5	59.2	59.0	59.6	59.7	59.7	59.4
2008	59.2	59.1	59.3	59.2	59.5	59.9	59.6	59.3	59.1	59.1	59.1	58.9	59.3
2009	58.0	57.8	57.5	57.1	56.7	56.7	56.2	55.7	55.5	55.5	55.7	56.1	56.5
Retail Trade													
1990	143.6	141.5	142.1	142.0	143.2	144.7	143.6	145.6	144.9	144.2	147.4	149.8	144.4
2000	174.8	172.9	173.8	175.4	177.5	177.9	177.3	179.1	174.5	180.3	186.6	188.7	178.7
2001	176.2	173.6	174.5	174.6	175.5	175.9	172.8	173.4	172.5	173.2	177.9	179.8	174.9
2002	172.0	170.2	172.2	172.5	173.2	172.5	170.2	170.9	170.1	169.7	174.7	176.9	172.1
2003	167.6	165.8	166.6	167.9	169.1	168.5	167.8	169.1	168.7	170.0	174.8	177.6	169.5
2004	167.6	165.9	168.2	168.7	169.4	168.8	166.5	166.3	165.3	166.7	171.5	173.9	168.2
2005	165.5	164.9	166.7	168.1	169.0	168.5	168.6	169.5	170.0	171.6	176.4	178.5	169.8
2006	167.6	167.2	168.7	169.7	171.1	170.8	168.9	169.3	168.8	169.1	173.5	176.3	170.1
2007	167.8	167.1	171.7	169.5	171.0	170.7	169.9	170.9	170.5	171.6	176.7	177.3	171.2
2008	170.8	170.5	172.8	172.4	172.9	172.8	172.8	173.6	172.9	173.4	177.0	178.3	173.4
2009	170.2	168.7	169.7	169.3	170.5	170.4	168.1	168.5	168.3	167.1	170.6	169.7	169.3
Transportation and Utilities													
1990	50.7	51.0	51.1	51.5	52.2	53.4	53.0	52.9	52.7	52.9	53.2	53.6	52.4
2000	56.5	56.3	56.3	57.3	57.6	58.1	57.9	58.1	57.8	58.1	58.1	58.1	57.5
2001	58.5	58.2	58.3	58.6	58.7	58.6	58.1	58.0	57.1	56.7	56.6	56.2	57.8
2002	55.1	55.0	55.2	55.2	55.3	55.4	55.5	55.3	55.1	55.0	54.7	54.3	55.1
2003	53.4	53.5	53.4	52.9	52.9	52.3	52.2	52.4	51.9	52.1	52.1	52.2	52.6
2004	51.6	51.5	51.9	51.4	51.6	51.9	52.0	52.0	52.0	52.2	52.2	52.8	51.9
2005	51.7	51.8	52.1	52.6	52.8	53.1	53.3	53.6	53.5	53.4	53.8	54.4	53.0
2006	53.3	53.3	53.6	54.3	54.9	55.2	55.2	55.7	56.1	56.3	56.6	57.6	55.2
2007	56.6	56.9	57.2	56.4	56.8	57.2	57.3	57.2	56.9	56.6	56.7	57.1	56.9
2008	55.9	55.8	56.0	56.5	56.9	57.2	57.4	57.6	57.7	57.9	57.9	58.4	57.1
2009	56.4	56.0	55.8	55.5	55.3	55.3	54.7	54.3	54.0	54.0	53.6	54.5	55.0
Information													
1990	22.5	22.4	22.4	22.6	22.8	23.1	23.0	23.1	23.0	22.9	22.9	22.9	22.8
2000	33.9	34.4	34.5	34.8	35.0	35.6	36.0	36.2	36.6	36.1	36.5	36.7	35.5
2001	36.7	37.0	36.5	36.9	36.7	36.4	36.6	37.4	37.5	37.5	38.0	37.8	37.0
2002	36.8	36.9	36.4	35.6	35.4	35.1	35.0	34.9	34.5	34.3	34.4	34.0	35.3
2003	33.5	33.2	32.9	32.7	32.8	32.4	32.0	31.6	31.3	31.7	31.9	32.2	32.4
2004	31.6	31.6	31.4	31.2	31.1	31.4	31.4	30.9	30.1	30.5	30.4	30.5	31.0
2005	30.2	30.4	30.1	30.4	30.4	30.4	30.5	30.2	29.9	29.8	30.0	30.3	30.2
2006	30.0	30.0	30.0	29.7	29.8	29.8	29.9	29.8	29.6	29.3	29.3	30.2	29.8
2007	29.2	29.0	28.6	28.6	28.8	28.8	28.8	28.8	28.6	28.8	28.9	29.0	28.8
2008	28.7	28.9	28.8	29.0	29.1	29.0	29.1	28.8	28.4	28.2	28.2	28.2	28.7
2009	27.8	27.8	27.7	27.7	27.7	27.7	27.6	27.4	27.0	27.1	27.0	26.9	27.5

Employment by Industry: Oklahoma, Selected Years, 1990–2009—*Continued*

(Numbers in thousands, not seasonally adjusted.)

Industry and year	January	February	March	April	May	June	July	August	September	October	November	December	Annual average
Financial Activities													
1990	66.4	66.5	66.8	67.6	68.1	68.8	68.4	68.8	68.1	66.8	67.1	67.3	67.6
2000	80.1	80.3	80.4	81.0	81.6	82.7	81.8	82.2	81.9	81.6	81.5	82.0	81.4
2001	80.8	81.2	81.7	82.3	82.8	83.6	83.3	83.7	83.1	82.7	82.6	82.6	82.5
2002	82.9	82.6	82.6	82.7	83.3	84.0	83.8	83.8	82.9	82.4	82.5	82.5	83.0
2003	81.6	81.7	82.0	82.7	83.2	83.8	83.7	84.0	83.6	83.8	83.8	84.0	83.2
2004	83.1	83.3	83.9	84.1	84.1	84.7	84.2	84.2	83.6	83.7	83.7	84.0	83.9
2005	82.3	82.4	82.8	82.4	83.0	83.7	83.8	83.8	83.4	82.8	83.0	84.0	83.1
2006	83.5	83.5	84.0	83.0	83.5	84.0	83.4	83.5	83.1	82.9	82.9	83.0	83.4
2007	82.8	83.3	83.5	82.4	82.6	83.1	83.0	83.1	82.7	82.9	82.9	83.0	82.9
2008	83.0	83.0	83.1	83.1	83.4	83.5	83.8	83.3	83.0	82.8	82.8	83.2	83.2
2009	81.7	81.4	81.5	80.9	81.3	81.6	81.3	81.1	80.5	81.3	81.2	80.9	81.2
Professional and Business Services													
1990	92.4	93.5	95.2	96.1	96.5	98.9	98.8	99.9	101.0	96.5	97.2	97.3	96.9
2000	154.9	156.0	159.6	162.8	164.3	166.3	167.0	168.7	168.3	168.2	168.3	167.1	164.3
2001	160.8	163.1	166.0	168.7	169.1	171.1	168.2	168.9	167.1	163.9	164.0	163.6	166.2
2002	156.5	158.3	160.7	163.9	165.6	165.1	162.2	164.2	163.5	161.4	160.7	160.5	161.9
2003	154.3	154.8	154.8	156.6	158.1	157.9	158.3	158.8	159.0	158.5	158.3	157.7	157.3
2004	154.2	155.8	157.0	161.3	161.3	162.5	165.0	165.8	166.3	167.9	168.4	168.1	162.8
2005	162.2	164.9	166.9	169.7	170.1	171.6	171.2	173.2	174.4	172.7	174.6	173.8	170.4
2006	170.1	172.1	174.8	174.7	175.8	178.0	176.5	178.4	178.9	176.5	177.3	176.6	175.8
2007	173.6	176.4	179.7	180.3	181.3	182.9	182.0	184.9	184.6	184.2	184.6	184.2	181.6
2008	181.5	183.7	184.6	184.7	184.4	184.4	182.7	184.2	183.6	182.0	180.6	178.5	182.9
2009	170.0	170.1	168.8	166.4	164.8	165.5	162.6	162.3	162.0	165.9	164.2	164.3	165.6
Education and Health Services													
1990	112.8	114.2	115.2	114.6	114.6	115.0	115.2	116.7	118.3	118.9	119.4	119.3	116.2
2000	157.2	159.2	160.1	162.2	162.6	162.2	162.2	163.0	165.0	164.2	166.2	165.4	162.5
2001	163.2	164.8	165.9	167.1	166.9	165.4	164.8	167.2	169.1	169.1	171.1	170.9	167.1
2002	169.2	170.8	171.1	173.1	172.6	171.2	171.6	174.8	176.3	175.3	178.4	177.3	173.5
2003	175.2	175.9	175.7	176.3	175.9	173.6	173.3	174.7	176.4	175.8	177.4	175.7	175.5
2004	176.7	177.9	178.8	180.2	179.1	177.1	177.6	178.3	180.5	180.9	181.8	181.4	179.2
2005	178.6	179.4	181.1	183.0	183.5	183.4	182.6	184.2	186.0	185.7	187.4	187.7	183.6
2006	184.0	184.7	186.3	186.8	187.7	188.3	186.4	187.7	189.6	189.3	190.6	190.3	187.6
2007	186.8	188.6	190.0	192.5	193.0	193.7	192.3	194.0	195.2	196.3	196.4	195.9	192.9
2008	194.4	196.6	197.2	197.7	198.3	196.5	195.8	197.5	198.4	198.9	199.7	199.7	197.6
2009	198.2	198.5	199.4	199.6	200.1	200.8	200.6	201.5	202.7	205.0	206.3	206.2	201.6
Leisure and Hospitality													
1990	86.6	89.0	91.1	95.4	97.7	99.5	98.1	99.2	99.2	95.9	94.7	93.4	95.0
2000	119.1	120.2	123.7	126.2	128.0	129.4	128.8	129.6	128.8	127.4	125.4	122.8	125.8
2001	119.2	121.4	124.6	129.3	131.3	132.6	131.0	132.0	129.3	126.5	125.9	124.3	127.2
2002	120.2	121.8	125.2	128.1	131.3	131.1	130.2	131.3	129.4	127.4	125.4	123.5	127.1
2003	120.9	121.4	123.8	127.6	130.5	130.1	129.4	130.6	128.3	127.6	125.7	124.5	126.7
2004	121.5	122.6	126.5	129.1	131.5	132.6	131.9	132.8	132.5	130.6	129.4	128.3	129.1
2005	124.9	126.5	130.9	134.2	136.5	138.0	135.1	135.6	134.1	132.1	131.4	129.9	132.4
2006	128.7	130.2	134.3	136.2	138.0	139.2	138.7	139.4	137.8	135.6	134.1	134.4	135.6
2007	129.4	131.9	136.6	137.2	139.8	141.3	140.8	142.1	140.6	138.7	138.5	136.3	137.8
2008	136.8	138.2	141.3	140.2	142.7	144.2	142.9	143.7	142.8	140.4	139.5	139.8	141.0
2009	135.3	136.7	140.5	142.4	143.7	144.7	141.9	141.9	140.2	138.8	138.2	137.7	140.2
Other Services													
1990	40.8	40.7	41.3	41.7	42.1	43.1	42.5	43.0	42.5	42.0	41.9	42.4	42.0
2000	59.2	59.3	60.0	60.9	61.3	62.3	61.6	61.6	61.9	61.4	61.4	61.9	61.1
2001	61.1	61.7	62.7	61.9	62.5	63.6	63.2	63.5	63.0	62.9	62.8	62.7	62.6
2002	61.6	61.9	62.4	64.8	65.0	65.2	64.5	64.2	63.6	62.3	62.1	61.9	63.3
2003	61.5	61.7	61.7	60.7	61.2	61.8	61.4	61.2	60.8	60.5	60.3	60.7	61.1
2004	60.1	60.4	61.2	61.3	61.6	62.3	61.6	61.3	60.8	60.5	60.5	60.7	61.0
2005	60.3	60.7	61.3	61.0	61.2	61.6	61.7	61.3	61.1	61.0	61.0	61.0	61.1
2006	60.3	60.6	61.2	61.2	61.9	62.8	62.3	62.2	62.0	61.9	62.0	62.2	61.7
2007	61.5	62.1	62.7	63.1	63.4	64.5	63.8	63.8	63.7	63.0	63.0	62.7	63.1
2008	62.6	63.1	63.5	63.8	63.9	64.2	64.0	64.0	63.5	63.6	63.0	62.8	63.5
2009	61.9	61.9	62.2	62.1	62.3	62.7	62.0	61.5	61.4	61.8	61.6	62.8	62.0
Government													
1990	261.4	267.5	267.6	265.0	266.5	255.6	244.5	246.2	262.2	268.2	268.3	269.6	261.8
2000	282.9	288.8	292.5	291.3	297.9	285.0	270.0	271.1	286.8	294.5	296.2	295.6	287.7
2001	292.0	298.5	300.4	300.1	302.9	289.6	277.8	280.6	297.9	304.4	307.1	305.9	296.4
2002	298.3	304.0	305.7	305.9	309.5	295.5	284.3	286.8	299.8	306.6	307.3	307.2	300.9
2003	295.1	301.1	300.8	300.2	302.2	289.1	278.5	279.6	295.6	301.6	302.5	303.2	295.8
2004	294.5	301.8	303.6	304.0	306.1	294.8	284.4	290.6	306.5	311.4	311.5	313.0	301.9
2005	305.2	312.6	314.8	316.5	319.0	306.8	292.8	298.6	314.4	321.9	323.3	323.3	312.4
2006	314.8	322.9	324.4	323.7	326.7	314.6	302.1	309.1	324.5	330.0	330.5	330.1	321.1
2007	322.0	328.7	330.5	329.1	331.1	319.3	303.9	311.3	328.6	333.1	334.2	332.4	325.4
2008	321.1	328.6	330.3	333.1	336.4	319.7	308.4	315.8	331.7	339.3	340.3	340.4	328.8
2009	331.7	338.6	341.6	343.5	345.7	332.1	319.8	324.9	340.3	346.7	346.4	344.3	338.0

Average Weekly Hours by Selected Industry: Oklahoma, 2007–2009

(Not seasonally adjusted.)

Industry and year	January	February	March	April	May	June	July	August	September	October	November	December	Annual average
Total Private													
2007	34.7	34.9	34.8	35.4	34.1	35.1	35.3	35.1	35.2	35.3	35.1	35.2	35.0
2008	34.9	35.0	35.9	35.4	35.7	36.6	35.6	36.0	35.3	35.0	35.6	35.2	35.5
2009	34.8	35.3	35.0	34.3	34.2	35.0	35.3	36.0	35.1	34.9	36.1	35.4	35.1
Goods-Producing													
2007	40.9	41.7	41.0	43.1	40.6	42.5	42.2	43.7	42.1	43.1	43.3	40.9	42.1
2008	42.2	41.8	42.2	42.7	43.0	43.5	43.5	42.5	41.7	41.6	41.4	41.7	42.3
2009	40.1	40.6	40.0	40.4	39.4	41.5	42.3	41.9	40.9	40.4	42.2	41.8	40.9
Construction													
2007	39.1	39.5	38.2	41.7	36.0	39.0	42.1	46.0	43.5	43.8	45.0	40.3	41.2
2008	42.6	41.5	41.7	41.3	42.1	41.5	42.1	41.3	40.0	39.8	40.5	40.4	41.2
2009	39.0	39.2	39.0	39.9	39.3	40.7	40.8	41.5	39.5	39.7	41.6	40.0	40.0
Manufacturing													
2007	42.4	43.3	42.9	44.4	43.5	44.8	41.8	42.2	40.3	41.7	41.8	40.1	42.4
2008	41.6	40.7	41.1	42.8	42.8	44.2	44.0	42.0	41.7	42.0	40.8	41.9	42.1
2009	39.8	40.6	40.2	40.5	38.8	40.6	41.8	39.8	40.6	40.2	41.5	42.6	40.6
Trade, Transportation, and Utilities													
2007	31.5	31.9	32.9	32.5	31.7	33.6	33.0	32.6	33.0	33.2	32.5	33.3	32.6
2008	32.8	32.8	34.0	33.6	34.0	36.0	34.5	34.0	34.5	34.2	35.1	34.6	34.2
2009	34.7	34.8	34.4	34.2	34.6	34.9	35.0	35.8	35.9	35.8	35.7	35.9	35.1
Financial Activities													
2007	37.1	34.8	36.5	36.8	35.2	36.0	37.3	35.3	37.3	36.4	34.7	37.0	36.2
2008	34.5	34.2	35.9	35.5	34.7	37.0	35.3	37.3	37.5	37.9	38.4	37.3	36.3
2009	36.4	38.1	38.1	36.4	36.6	37.6	37.1	38.1	37.0	35.6	37.1	35.7	37.0
Professional and Business Services													
2007	36.5	36.8	35.2	37.2	36.4	36.9	37.4	35.7	35.4	35.2	35.7	35.2	36.1
2008	35.7	36.1	36.5	36.9	36.4	36.9	37.3	37.4	35.9	36.5	37.7	36.7	36.7
2009	36.7	38.8	38.3	36.6	37.2	38.4	37.0	38.4	36.8	37.4	38.4	37.1	37.6
Education and Health Services													
2007	36.2	35.9	35.0	34.9	33.2	33.4	34.3	33.3	34.2	33.4	32.8	33.8	34.2
2008	32.7	33.7	34.7	32.9	33.9	34.0	32.2	34.4	33.7	32.8	33.2	32.9	33.4
2009	32.5	32.5	32.6	31.6	31.6	31.8	32.6	33.9	32.4	32.2	33.8	32.2	32.5
Leisure and Hospitality													
2007	23.5	24.3	24.8	24.7	24.8	25.7	26.2	26.1	25.2	25.3	27.2	27.0	25.4
2008	25.9	26.8	27.5	27.2	27.5	28.0	26.5	26.0	25.6	25.1	26.7	25.9	26.6
2009	26.5	27.3	27.1	26.3	26.1	26.7	26.7	26.7	25.6	25.8	26.4	25.8	26.4

Average Hourly Earnings by Selected Industry: Oklahoma, 2007–2009

(Dollars, not seasonally adjusted.)

Industry and year	January	February	March	April	May	June	July	August	September	October	November	December	Annual average
Total Private													
2007	17.39	17.25	16.98	17.18	17.43	17.15	17.49	17.40	17.46	17.29	17.41	17.57	17.33
2008	17.34	17.24	17.21	17.17	17.34	17.39	17.38	17.34	17.63	17.59	17.95	17.64	17.43
2009	17.80	17.94	17.87	17.89	18.05	17.88	18.03	18.19	18.25	18.29	18.40	18.34	18.08
Goods-Producing													
2007	19.57	19.05	18.77	18.51	18.96	18.66	18.94	19.20	19.34	19.08	19.33	19.87	19.11
2008	19.13	19.29	19.58	19.25	19.71	19.33	19.35	20.01	20.62	20.42	21.17	20.46	19.85
2009	20.66	20.77	20.57	20.43	21.32	20.70	20.78	21.34	20.92	21.02	21.15	20.88	20.87
Construction													
2007	18.60	18.71	17.26	17.21	18.05	17.50	17.77	17.24	17.55	17.60	17.70	19.58	17.87
2008	17.98	18.32	18.58	18.64	18.39	18.72	18.64	19.04	18.79	18.81	18.92	19.26	18.67
2009	19.63	20.11	19.78	19.91	20.47	19.64	19.87	19.93	20.06	20.37	19.72	20.03	19.96
Manufacturing													
2007	19.70	18.62	19.02	18.44	18.50	18.18	18.39	19.33	19.68	18.96	19.30	18.56	18.88
2008	18.39	18.64	18.73	18.35	19.27	18.02	18.26	19.17	20.32	20.03	20.40	19.58	19.08
2009	19.25	18.85	18.52	18.30	19.35	18.60	18.49	19.36	18.74	18.74	19.67	18.93	18.90
Trade, Transportation, and Utilities													
2007	15.91	15.72	15.06	15.52	15.28	15.83	16.69	16.35	16.80	16.43	16.40	16.40	16.04
2008	16.43	16.09	15.94	16.33	16.32	16.87	16.94	16.56	16.86	17.00	17.03	17.18	16.64
2009	17.47	17.58	17.60	17.74	17.55	17.68	17.79	17.99	17.93	17.98	18.21	17.89	17.79
Financial Activities													
2007	19.63	19.87	19.70	20.08	19.55	17.67	17.71	17.56	17.38	17.43	18.34	17.87	18.56
2008	18.48	17.94	17.94	17.93	17.61	17.47	16.66	16.85	17.05	17.23	17.85	16.97	17.49
2009	17.55	17.93	17.83	17.61	18.03	18.33	18.26	18.70	18.79	18.57	18.98	18.78	18.28
Professional and Business Services													
2007	19.65	19.72	19.63	19.90	22.03	20.15	20.31	19.79	19.76	19.44	19.38	20.29	20.01
2008	19.43	19.54	19.29	19.54	19.82	19.08	19.36	19.69	19.06	19.53	19.89	19.68	19.49
2009	19.91	20.50	20.60	20.85	20.42	19.84	20.01	20.29	20.01	19.72	20.12	20.12	20.20
Education and Health Services													
2007	17.07	17.20	17.42	17.65	17.45	17.84	17.77	17.76	17.53	17.65	17.49	17.63	17.54
2008	17.35	17.00	16.88	16.77	17.00	17.11	17.44	16.57	17.09	16.69	16.94	16.64	16.95
2009	16.71	16.97	17.07	17.24	17.49	17.45	17.87	17.09	17.87	17.93	17.54	17.83	17.42
Leisure and Hospitality													
2007	8.94	9.25	9.00	8.97	8.85	9.06	9.24	9.42	9.48	9.44	9.88	9.93	9.30
2008	9.92	9.77	9.72	9.62	10.06	10.26	9.76	10.01	10.16	10.30	10.54	10.53	10.05
2009	10.56	10.41	10.42	10.53	10.52	10.39	10.28	10.53	10.53	11.07	10.69	10.78	10.56

Average Weekly Earnings by Selected Industry: Oklahoma, 2007–2009

(Dollars, not seasonally adjusted.)

Industry and year	January	February	March	April	May	June	July	August	September	October	November	December	Annual average
Total Private													
2007	603.43	602.03	590.90	608.17	594.36	601.97	617.40	610.74	614.59	610.34	611.09	618.46	606.55
2008	605.17	603.40	617.84	607.82	619.04	636.47	618.73	624.24	622.34	615.65	639.02	620.93	618.77
2009	619.44	633.28	625.45	613.63	617.31	625.80	636.46	654.84	640.58	638.32	664.24	649.24	634.61
Goods-Producing													
2007	800.41	794.39	769.57	797.78	769.78	793.05	799.27	839.04	814.21	822.35	836.99	812.68	804.53
2008	807.29	806.32	826.28	821.98	847.53	840.86	841.73	850.43	859.85	849.47	876.44	853.18	839.66
2009	828.47	843.26	822.80	825.37	840.01	859.05	878.99	894.15	855.63	849.21	892.53	872.78	853.58
Construction													
2007	727.26	739.05	659.33	717.66	649.80	682.50	748.12	793.04	763.43	770.88	796.50	789.07	736.24
2008	765.95	760.28	774.79	769.83	774.22	776.88	784.74	786.35	751.60	748.64	766.26	778.10	769.20
2009	765.57	788.31	771.42	794.41	804.47	799.35	810.70	827.10	792.37	808.69	820.35	801.20	798.40
Manufacturing													
2007	835.28	806.25	815.96	818.74	804.75	814.46	768.70	815.73	793.10	790.63	806.74	744.26	800.51
2008	765.02	758.65	769.80	785.38	824.76	796.48	803.44	805.14	847.34	841.26	832.32	820.40	803.27
2009	766.15	765.31	744.50	741.15	750.78	755.16	772.88	770.53	760.84	753.35	816.31	806.42	767.34
Trade, Transportation, and Utilities													
2007	501.17	501.47	495.47	504.40	484.38	531.89	550.77	533.01	554.40	545.48	533.00	546.12	522.90
2008	538.90	527.75	541.96	548.69	554.88	607.32	584.43	563.04	581.67	581.40	597.75	594.43	569.09
2009	606.21	611.78	605.44	606.71	607.23	617.03	622.65	644.04	643.69	643.68	650.10	642.25	624.43
Financial Activities													
2007	728.27	691.48	719.05	738.94	688.16	636.12	660.58	619.87	648.27	634.45	636.40	661.19	671.07
2008	637.56	613.55	644.05	636.52	611.07	646.39	588.10	628.51	639.38	653.02	685.44	632.98	634.89
2009	638.82	683.13	679.32	641.00	659.90	689.21	677.45	712.47	695.23	661.09	704.16	670.45	676.36
Professional and Business Services													
2007	717.23	725.70	690.98	740.28	801.89	743.54	759.59	706.50	699.50	684.29	691.87	714.21	722.36
2008	693.65	705.39	704.09	721.03	721.45	704.05	722.13	736.41	684.25	712.85	749.85	722.26	715.28
2009	730.70	795.40	788.98	763.11	759.62	761.86	740.37	779.14	736.37	737.53	772.61	746.45	759.52
Education and Health Services													
2007	617.93	617.48	609.70	615.99	579.34	595.86	609.51	591.41	599.53	589.51	573.67	595.89	599.87
2008	567.35	572.90	585.74	551.73	576.30	581.74	561.57	570.01	575.93	547.43	562.41	547.46	566.13
2009	543.08	551.53	556.48	544.78	552.68	554.91	582.56	579.35	578.99	577.35	592.85	574.13	566.15
Leisure and Hospitality													
2007	210.09	224.78	223.20	221.56	219.48	232.84	242.09	245.86	238.90	238.83	268.74	268.11	236.22
2008	256.93	261.84	267.30	261.66	276.65	287.28	258.64	260.26	260.10	258.53	281.42	272.73	267.33
2009	279.84	284.19	282.38	276.94	274.57	277.41	274.48	281.15	269.57	285.61	282.22	278.12	278.78

OREGON
At a Glance

Population:
　1990 census: 2,842,337
　2000 census: 3,421,399
　2009 estimate: 3,825,657

Percent change in population:
　1990–2000: 20.4%
　2000–2009: 11.8%

Percent change in total nonfarm employment:
　1990–2009: 28.4%
　2008–2009: -6.2%

Industry with the largest growth in employment, 1990–2009 (thousands):
　Education and Health Services, 93.4

Industry with the largest decline or smallest growth in employment, 1990–2009 (thousands):
　Manufacturing, -36.9

Civilian labor force:
　1990: 1,506,240
　2000: 1,810,150
　2009: 1,963,567

Unemployment rate and rank among states (lowest to highest):
　1990: 5.4%, 27th
　2000: 5.1%, 47th
　2009: 11.1%, 46th

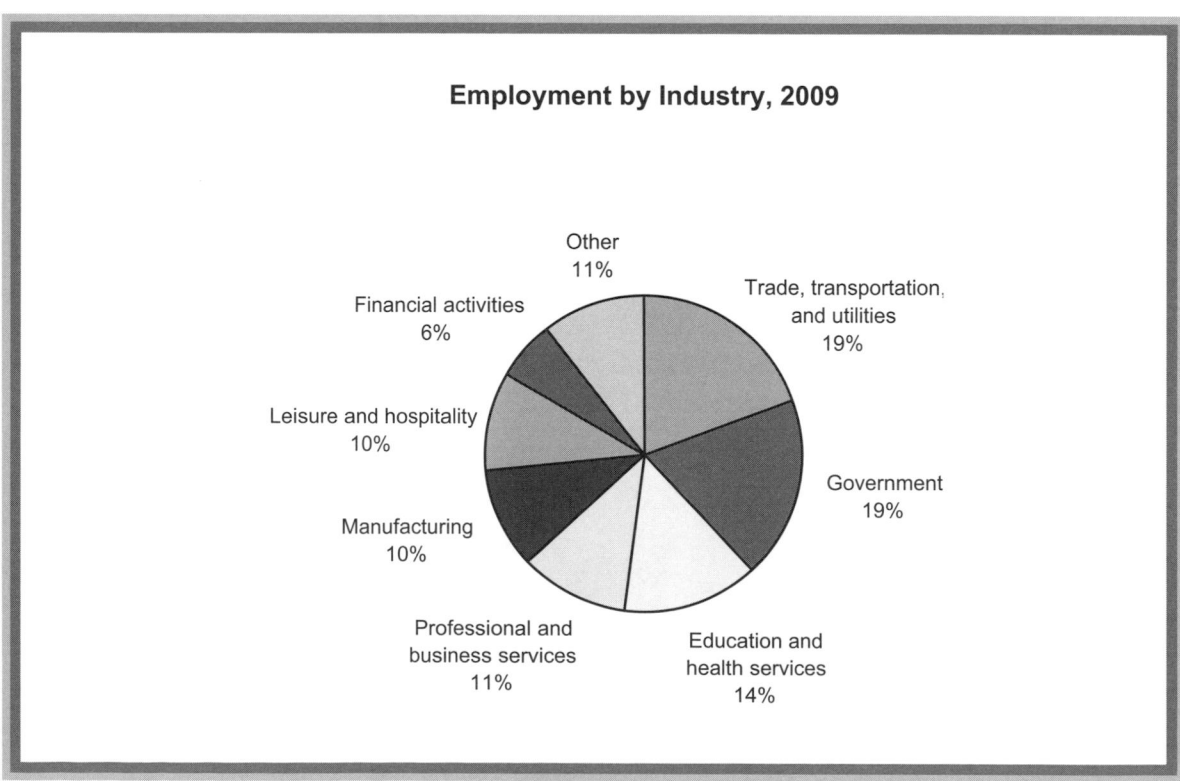

Employment by Industry, 2009

Other 11%

Financial activities 6%

Leisure and hospitality 10%

Manufacturing 10%

Professional and business services 11%

Education and health services 14%

Government 19%

Trade, transportation, and utilities 19%

Employment by Industry: Oregon, Selected Years, 1990–2009

(Numbers in thousands, not seasonally adjusted.)

Industry and year	January	February	March	April	May	June	July	August	September	October	November	December	Annual average
Total Nonfarm													
1990	1212.0	1214.2	1229.0	1245.3	1260.1	1275.3	1257.9	1275.0	1276.8	1279.0	1276.5	1266.5	1255.6
2000	1567.9	1581.4	1591.8	1603.5	1621.6	1638.0	1614.6	1620.9	1635.1	1644.0	1650.2	1645.1	1617.8
2001	1593.1	1600.9	1606.0	1607.5	1616.3	1629.4	1597.3	1600.1	1606.0	1610.0	1603.1	1596.3	1605.5
2002	1548.1	1558.8	1567.2	1575.9	1589.5	1602.4	1584.7	1591.6	1599.8	1607.0	1603.6	1595.2	1585.3
2003	1552.9	1557.7	1561.6	1561.2	1572.4	1582.6	1561.4	1570.9	1582.1	1597.8	1595.8	1595.5	1574.3
2004	1542.4	1558.7	1574.6	1591.5	1604.9	1622.4	1610.1	1615.9	1628.5	1642.6	1643.7	1644.5	1606.7
2005	1598.9	1613.8	1628.4	1640.2	1651.2	1668.0	1651.3	1658.6	1673.0	1683.6	1691.7	1694.7	1654.5
2006	1648.2	1665.2	1678.0	1690.6	1707.3	1722.7	1700.4	1707.1	1720.7	1732.3	1735.5	1734.4	1703.5
2007	1688.3	1704.5	1717.7	1721.0	1736.3	1748.9	1723.2	1732.5	1740.8	1755.0	1755.9	1751.7	1731.3
2008	1702.9	1714.8	1721.7	1728.3	1735.6	1740.5	1718.2	1718.9	1724.6	1724.6	1706.1	1684.5	1718.4
2009	1626.0	1621.3	1613.0	1615.4	1620.6	1624.2	1601.6	1596.0	1603.9	1611.5	1608.7	1601.7	1612.0
Total Private													
1990	984.0	982.9	995.8	1009.0	1018.5	1033.3	1041.5	1061.2	1052.5	1039.6	1035.3	1028.7	1023.5
2000	1291.1	1299.5	1308.5	1319.5	1330.4	1348.5	1355.2	1364.1	1367.9	1360.5	1364.7	1361.3	1339.3
2001	1314.7	1315.9	1318.7	1320.8	1325.7	1338.2	1336.8	1340.7	1333.7	1320.2	1311.6	1307.1	1323.7
2002	1262.7	1267.8	1274.3	1284.4	1295.1	1307.1	1318.0	1326.8	1323.6	1317.2	1311.9	1306.6	1299.6
2003	1267.3	1269.3	1273.4	1274.6	1284.0	1295.4	1305.3	1314.2	1314.7	1313.8	1309.9	1312.0	1294.5
2004	1263.4	1273.7	1286.7	1304.6	1315.4	1330.1	1346.4	1353.1	1354.7	1354.6	1353.1	1356.0	1324.3
2005	1312.8	1323.4	1337.0	1348.3	1357.7	1372.6	1387.1	1394.9	1398.7	1395.1	1399.5	1405.5	1369.4
2006	1363.7	1374.6	1385.9	1399.4	1412.2	1426.2	1435.1	1442.4	1444.6	1440.9	1440.2	1443.6	1417.4
2007	1401.7	1412.4	1423.5	1426.7	1437.1	1448.4	1454.4	1464.4	1462.3	1458.4	1455.9	1453.6	1441.6
2008	1408.1	1414.7	1419.7	1425.9	1429.9	1433.7	1438.4	1440.6	1436.3	1420.3	1398.1	1379.3	1420.4
2009	1325.0	1315.4	1306.3	1307.5	1310.1	1314.9	1320.4	1317.7	1318.4	1308.2	1303.2	1298.7	1312.2
Goods-Producing													
1990	258.9	257.2	262.3	266.2	270.2	276.9	282.1	289.7	283.5	275.3	269.6	263.0	271.2
2000	306.6	308.0	309.7	311.1	314.5	323.1	327.4	329.5	329.9	323.1	320.3	317.3	318.4
2001	307.7	306.7	305.0	304.4	304.8	310.5	314.8	314.3	309.4	304.0	294.3	290.1	305.5
2002	280.5	280.5	281.6	283.7	287.0	292.7	299.6	301.3	298.3	294.0	287.7	283.5	289.2
2003	276.2	275.7	275.0	272.9	275.7	281.5	286.2	290.0	288.7	287.8	283.4	281.4	281.2
2004	272.1	275.4	278.4	284.2	288.3	295.0	304.0	306.2	304.9	303.4	298.4	296.3	292.2
2005	289.2	291.4	294.4	296.8	300.1	309.9	313.4	315.9	314.8	313.2	309.2	307.9	304.4
2006	302.3	305.4	308.0	311.1	315.0	321.4	328.6	330.2	328.3	325.1	319.5	316.8	317.6
2007	309.7	311.2	312.9	312.1	315.4	319.9	325.6	328.9	325.5	322.1	316.0	311.3	317.6
2008	301.1	300.7	299.7	299.6	300.5	302.4	306.0	306.4	302.2	296.3	284.7	274.7	297.9
2009	259.8	252.2	247.3	245.2	245.0	247.9	252.9	251.9	250.7	246.2	241.7	236.6	248.1
Mining and Logging													
1990	12.4	11.7	11.6	12.0	12.7	13.5	14.0	14.6	14.4	13.9	12.8	11.5	12.9
2000	9.2	9.3	9.1	9.3	9.7	10.2	10.3	10.4	10.3	10.4	10.0	9.7	9.8
2001	9.2	9.1	8.8	8.6	9.0	9.6	9.9	10.1	9.8	9.7	9.2	8.8	9.3
2002	8.7	8.7	8.7	8.6	9.0	9.5	9.9	9.9	9.8	9.8	9.7	9.5	9.3
2003	8.9	8.9	8.8	8.9	9.1	9.6	9.9	9.9	9.8	9.8	9.5	9.3	9.4
2004	8.8	9.0	9.2	9.4	9.6	10.0	10.2	10.2	10.1	10.0	9.7	9.7	9.7
2005	9.2	9.4	9.3	9.1	9.2	9.6	10.1	10.1	9.9	9.8	9.6	9.4	9.6
2006	8.8	9.0	8.9	9.0	9.3	9.7	9.9	10.0	9.9	9.8	9.4	9.2	9.4
2007	8.7	8.9	8.9	9.1	9.3	9.6	9.7	9.7	9.6	9.4	9.2	8.8	9.2
2008	8.4	8.4	8.3	8.3	8.5	8.8	9.1	9.3	9.2	9.0	8.7	8.1	8.7
2009	7.1	7.0	6.7	6.7	6.7	7.0	7.2	7.3	7.4	7.3	7.2	6.8	7.0
Construction													
1990	47.1	46.7	50.1	53.1	54.8	56.3	57.5	59.6	59.0	57.3	55.3	53.0	54.2
2000	77.9	78.4	79.2	80.3	82.0	85.5	86.8	88.9	89.3	86.7	84.8	83.3	83.6
2001	78.6	78.4	78.9	78.6	79.7	82.2	83.6	85.0	83.2	81.7	78.8	76.8	80.5
2002	72.6	72.9	73.9	75.0	77.2	79.9	82.6	84.9	83.3	81.8	79.1	76.5	78.3
2003	72.1	72.0	72.1	72.6	74.6	76.9	79.9	82.4	81.7	81.6	79.5	78.1	77.0
2004	72.4	74.2	76.2	79.2	81.4	84.2	87.9	89.0	88.9	88.1	85.9	85.2	82.7
2005	80.8	82.0	84.0	86.1	88.5	91.4	95.2	97.3	98.0	96.9	95.3	95.1	90.9
2006	91.3	93.3	94.7	97.2	100.2	103.2	105.7	107.2	106.9	105.7	103.5	101.9	100.9
2007	97.4	98.9	100.5	101.5	104.2	105.8	109.4	110.8	109.2	107.4	104.5	101.3	104.2
2008	94.4	94.3	94.2	94.7	95.8	96.9	98.7	98.6	96.9	93.1	87.9	83.4	94.1
2009	76.9	74.2	72.6	72.5	73.1	75.0	77.0	77.1	76.1	73.2	70.8	66.9	73.8
Manufacturing													
1990	199.4	198.8	200.6	201.1	202.7	207.1	210.6	215.5	210.1	204.1	201.5	198.5	204.2
2000	219.5	220.3	221.4	221.5	222.8	227.4	230.3	230.2	230.3	226.0	225.5	224.3	225.0
2001	219.9	219.2	217.3	217.2	216.1	218.7	221.3	219.2	216.4	212.6	206.3	204.5	215.7
2002	199.2	198.9	199.0	200.1	200.8	203.3	207.1	206.5	205.2	202.4	198.9	197.5	201.6
2003	195.2	194.8	194.1	191.4	192.0	195.0	196.4	197.7	197.2	196.4	194.4	194.0	194.9
2004	190.9	192.2	193.0	195.6	197.3	200.8	205.9	207.0	205.9	205.3	202.8	201.4	199.8
2005	199.2	200.0	201.1	201.6	202.4	204.9	208.1	208.5	206.9	206.5	204.3	203.4	203.9
2006	202.2	203.1	204.4	204.9	205.5	208.5	213.0	213.0	211.5	209.6	206.6	205.7	207.3
2007	203.6	203.4	203.5	201.5	201.9	204.5	206.5	208.4	206.7	205.3	202.3	201.2	204.1
2008	198.3	198.0	197.2	196.6	196.2	196.7	198.2	198.5	196.1	194.2	188.1	183.2	195.1
2009	175.8	171.0	168.0	166.0	165.2	165.9	168.7	167.5	167.2	165.7	163.7	162.9	167.3

Employment by Industry: Oregon, Selected Years, 1990–2009—*Continued*

(Numbers in thousands, not seasonally adjusted.)

Industry and year	January	February	March	April	May	June	July	August	September	October	November	December	Annual average
Service-Providing													
1990	953.1	957.0	966.7	979.1	989.9	998.4	975.8	985.3	993.3	1003.7	1006.9	1003.5	984.4
2000	1261.3	1273.4	1282.1	1292.4	1307.1	1314.9	1287.2	1291.4	1305.2	1320.9	1329.9	1327.8	1299.5
2001	1285.4	1294.2	1301.0	1303.1	1311.5	1318.9	1282.5	1285.8	1296.6	1306.0	1308.8	1306.2	1300.0
2002	1267.6	1278.3	1285.6	1292.2	1302.5	1309.7	1285.1	1290.3	1301.5	1313.0	1315.9	1311.7	1296.1
2003	1276.7	1282.0	1286.6	1288.3	1296.7	1301.1	1275.2	1280.9	1293.4	1310.0	1312.4	1314.1	1293.1
2004	1270.3	1283.3	1296.2	1307.3	1316.6	1327.4	1306.1	1309.7	1323.6	1339.2	1345.3	1348.2	1314.4
2005	1309.7	1322.4	1334.0	1343.4	1351.1	1362.1	1337.9	1342.7	1358.2	1370.4	1382.5	1386.8	1350.1
2006	1345.9	1359.8	1370.0	1379.5	1392.3	1401.3	1371.8	1376.9	1392.4	1407.2	1416.0	1417.6	1385.9
2007	1378.6	1393.3	1404.8	1408.9	1420.9	1429.0	1397.6	1403.6	1415.3	1432.9	1439.9	1440.4	1413.8
2008	1401.8	1414.1	1422.0	1428.7	1435.1	1438.1	1412.2	1412.5	1422.4	1428.3	1421.4	1409.8	1420.5
2009	1366.2	1369.1	1365.7	1370.2	1375.6	1376.3	1348.7	1344.1	1353.2	1365.3	1367.0	1365.1	1363.9
Trade, Transportation, and Utilities													
1990	258.1	255.1	257.1	259.0	260.7	263.9	265.6	269.9	269.0	268.0	271.8	273.9	264.3
2000	318.9	317.7	318.2	320.5	322.4	326.0	325.9	327.6	328.0	331.2	339.8	340.4	326.4
2001	320.7	316.9	317.6	317.6	318.9	321.4	321.2	321.7	321.0	320.5	325.4	326.7	320.8
2002	309.7	307.4	308.6	310.5	312.5	314.9	316.8	317.2	317.8	318.4	323.2	326.3	315.3
2003	310.4	308.3	308.4	308.6	310.9	312.9	314.8	315.9	316.5	319.4	324.7	326.5	314.8
2004	311.7	309.1	310.9	313.7	316.3	319.2	322.4	323.2	323.9	325.9	331.9	335.1	320.3
2005	319.1	317.8	320.5	321.6	323.1	327.0	329.2	331.3	332.9	334.1	341.2	345.5	328.6
2006	328.4	326.9	328.3	329.5	332.7	335.0	335.9	337.3	338.4	339.3	345.6	349.7	335.6
2007	334.4	332.3	333.8	334.4	336.3	339.2	340.3	342.2	343.5	344.0	350.7	352.9	340.3
2008	336.9	334.6	335.0	335.3	335.4	336.1	337.2	337.6	337.2	335.4	335.3	334.6	335.9
2009	317.7	312.9	309.9	309.0	310.4	310.5	310.9	311.0	312.1	312.8	317.1	319.4	312.8
Wholesale Trade													
1990	64.0	64.3	65.2	65.0	64.9	65.6	66.0	67.0	66.8	66.7	66.5	66.3	65.7
2000	75.5	75.8	76.0	75.9	76.0	76.6	77.3	77.3	77.2	77.5	77.4	77.2	76.6
2001	74.7	74.8	75.2	75.0	74.8	75.3	75.7	75.4	75.2	74.1	73.6	73.2	74.8
2002	72.7	72.8	72.8	73.1	73.2	73.7	74.7	74.7	74.6	75.0	74.7	74.7	73.9
2003	73.7	74.0	74.0	74.0	74.2	74.4	75.6	75.1	75.4	75.2	75.1	74.9	74.6
2004	73.7	74.1	74.3	74.6	75.0	75.5	76.7	76.7	76.7	76.5	76.7	76.9	75.6
2005	76.1	76.6	76.9	77.1	76.9	77.7	78.5	78.6	79.1	78.7	78.9	78.9	77.8
2006	78.1	78.9	79.0	79.2	79.8	80.1	80.4	80.4	80.4	80.8	80.8	80.7	79.9
2007	80.1	80.6	80.5	80.4	80.5	80.8	81.4	81.2	81.0	81.3	81.2	81.0	80.8
2008	80.0	80.6	80.7	80.5	80.7	80.7	81.3	81.0	80.9	80.8	79.9	79.1	80.5
2009	77.4	76.9	76.1	75.8	75.7	75.5	75.4	75.0	74.5	74.7	74.1	74.8	75.5
Retail Trade													
1990	148.5	145.2	145.8	147.5	148.8	151.0	153.0	154.8	154.4	154.3	158.4	160.3	151.8
2000	186.8	185.2	185.4	187.6	189.5	191.6	191.6	192.7	192.5	195.2	203.6	204.9	192.2
2001	189.5	185.7	186.2	186.6	187.4	189.5	189.2	189.0	188.4	188.5	194.3	196.2	189.2
2002	181.7	179.3	180.5	181.7	183.3	184.9	186.3	186.1	186.6	186.8	192.2	195.4	185.4
2003	181.2	179.0	179.4	179.7	181.6	183.1	184.1	184.8	184.7	187.3	192.9	195.0	184.4
2004	182.4	179.6	180.9	183.0	185.0	187.3	189.1	189.6	189.2	190.7	196.8	199.9	187.8
2005	186.8	184.8	186.7	187.9	189.6	192.3	194.2	195.7	195.7	197.5	204.3	207.4	193.6
2006	193.2	190.5	191.7	192.7	194.9	196.1	197.7	198.8	198.8	199.3	205.6	208.8	197.3
2007	196.6	193.9	195.3	195.9	197.5	199.3	201.0	202.6	202.9	202.9	209.3	210.9	200.7
2008	198.3	195.2	195.6	195.6	195.4	196.2	197.7	197.9	197.1	195.8	197.9	197.9	196.7
2009	185.1	181.6	180.0	179.9	181.2	181.8	183.1	183.4	183.8	184.4	188.9	190.0	183.6
Transportation and Utilities													
1990	46.0	45.8	46.3	46.5	47.0	47.3	46.8	47.7	47.7	47.3	47.3	47.4	46.9
2000	56.7	56.8	56.8	57.1	57.3	57.8	56.9	57.6	58.6	58.5	58.9	58.3	57.6
2001	56.5	56.4	56.2	56.0	56.7	56.6	56.3	57.3	57.4	57.9	57.5	57.3	56.8
2002	55.3	55.3	55.3	55.7	56.0	56.3	55.8	56.4	56.6	56.6	56.3	56.2	56.0
2003	55.5	55.3	55.0	54.9	55.1	55.4	55.1	56.0	56.4	56.9	56.7	56.6	55.7
2004	55.6	55.4	55.7	56.1	56.3	56.4	56.6	56.9	58.0	58.7	58.4	58.3	56.9
2005	56.2	56.4	56.9	56.6	56.6	57.0	56.5	57.0	58.1	57.9	58.0	59.2	57.2
2006	57.1	57.5	57.6	57.6	58.0	58.8	57.8	58.1	59.2	59.2	59.2	60.2	58.4
2007	57.7	57.8	58.0	58.1	58.3	59.1	57.9	58.4	59.6	59.8	60.2	61.0	58.8
2008	58.6	58.8	58.7	59.2	59.3	59.2	58.2	58.7	59.2	58.8	57.5	57.6	58.7
2009	55.2	54.4	53.8	53.3	53.5	53.2	52.4	52.6	53.8	53.7	54.1	54.6	53.7
Information													
1990	26.8	26.9	26.9	27.0	27.2	27.5	26.9	27.2	27.1	26.9	27.0	27.1	27.0
2000	38.1	38.2	38.6	38.6	39.2	39.6	40.4	40.4	40.5	41.1	41.2	41.8	39.8
2001	41.1	40.9	40.8	41.2	41.1	41.8	39.3	39.1	38.5	38.4	38.5	38.5	39.9
2002	38.1	38.2	37.5	36.0	36.0	35.9	35.7	35.7	35.4	35.4	35.3	36.0	36.3
2003	35.0	34.7	34.5	33.7	33.9	33.4	32.9	33.1	32.7	32.9	33.3	33.1	33.6
2004	32.7	32.8	32.6	32.8	33.1	33.2	33.1	33.2	32.9	32.8	33.2	33.1	33.0
2005	32.6	33.0	32.9	33.2	33.5	33.6	33.7	33.6	33.8	34.1	34.4	35.1	33.6
2006	34.1	34.5	34.5	34.2	34.5	34.8	35.0	35.1	35.1	35.3	35.3	35.9	34.9
2007	34.9	35.3	35.8	35.9	36.2	36.5	36.0	36.2	36.0	35.8	36.2	37.2	36.0
2008	36.1	36.3	36.3	35.9	36.1	36.3	35.6	35.7	35.4	34.8	34.5	34.2	35.6
2009	33.4	33.5	33.3	32.9	33.2	34.2	33.0	32.9	32.3	32.5	32.7	33.2	33.1

Employment by Industry: Oregon, Selected Years, 1990–2009—*Continued*

(Numbers in thousands, not seasonally adjusted.)

Industry and year	January	February	March	April	May	June	July	August	September	October	November	December	Annual average
Financial Activities													
1990	70.1	70.4	71.0	72.0	72.7	73.2	73.0	73.8	73.6	74.2	73.8	74.0	72.7
2000	94.2	94.1	94.4	95.3	95.9	96.4	96.4	96.5	95.8	94.8	94.7	95.4	95.3
2001	93.2	93.7	94.2	94.5	95.0	95.8	96.5	96.3	95.8	95.7	95.7	95.8	95.2
2002	93.7	94.1	93.9	93.6	94.1	94.5	96.5	96.9	96.5	96.4	96.3	97.1	95.3
2003	95.2	95.5	96.2	96.9	97.1	98.0	98.8	99.1	98.1	97.0	96.3	96.4	97.1
2004	94.1	94.4	94.9	95.9	96.9	98.0	98.7	99.2	98.8	99.1	99.1	99.9	97.4
2005	98.0	98.8	99.5	100.4	101.1	102.0	103.9	104.3	103.9	103.8	104.3	105.1	102.1
2006	103.2	103.8	104.3	105.1	105.8	106.8	107.4	107.9	107.6	107.0	106.9	107.6	106.1
2007	105.8	106.5	107.1	106.4	106.8	107.4	107.9	107.5	105.8	105.6	105.1	105.3	106.4
2008	102.5	102.8	102.6	102.9	102.8	102.5	102.5	102.4	101.2	100.7	99.7	99.5	101.8
2009	96.4	96.2	95.7	95.7	95.7	95.4	96.0	95.8	95.2	95.6	94.5	94.6	95.6
Professional and Business Services													
1990	97.9	98.9	100.8	102.8	102.8	103.7	104.2	106.5	105.9	105.1	104.2	103.3	103.0
2000	172.9	175.4	178.1	180.8	182.0	185.0	187.2	189.4	190.1	188.6	187.9	186.2	183.6
2001	180.1	179.4	179.5	178.0	177.9	179.7	178.2	179.4	177.5	173.5	172.2	170.3	177.1
2002	164.6	166.7	168.4	170.4	171.7	174.0	176.1	179.4	177.5	176.4	174.1	171.0	172.5
2003	164.5	165.7	166.7	167.8	169.5	170.8	173.3	175.2	175.6	174.6	172.2	173.7	170.8
2004	165.5	168.1	171.0	173.9	174.5	177.0	179.8	181.2	180.5	181.2	180.4	181.7	176.2
2005	174.8	177.9	180.0	182.7	183.1	186.1	188.9	190.5	190.6	190.0	190.3	191.9	185.6
2006	184.2	187.0	188.8	191.6	193.0	196.2	197.8	199.5	199.7	199.5	198.0	197.4	194.4
2007	190.6	193.0	195.3	196.1	196.6	198.9	199.2	201.3	200.2	200.5	198.0	197.1	197.2
2008	191.4	193.9	195.3	197.5	197.8	198.5	200.6	201.6	199.6	196.7	191.9	188.5	196.1
2009	182.1	180.8	179.1	180.1	179.1	179.9	181.3	179.9	179.5	176.1	174.3	172.8	178.8
Education and Health Services													
1990	126.8	128.4	129.1	129.4	129.2	128.2	128.1	129.4	131.1	132.9	132.8	132.2	129.8
2000	167.9	171.4	172.2	172.6	172.4	169.5	166.8	168.5	173.9	176.8	177.8	177.9	172.3
2001	174.4	178.7	179.4	179.7	179.3	176.6	173.2	174.3	179.1	182.4	183.9	184.5	178.8
2002	180.5	184.0	185.1	186.6	186.4	183.4	180.4	180.9	185.2	189.5	190.7	190.1	185.2
2003	186.7	189.4	190.1	189.9	189.7	186.1	183.3	183.3	188.2	192.3	193.0	193.6	188.8
2004	187.0	191.8	193.1	193.8	193.0	190.2	187.5	187.7	193.9	197.5	198.9	199.1	192.8
2005	193.9	197.8	199.0	199.7	199.8	196.1	194.0	193.8	199.8	202.7	204.4	204.0	198.8
2006	200.1	204.1	205.5	206.8	206.7	202.7	198.5	199.0	205.2	208.9	210.9	211.0	205.0
2007	206.3	211.3	212.4	212.8	212.7	209.3	205.2	206.2	212.3	217.1	218.0	218.0	211.8
2008	213.7	218.8	219.8	220.8	220.1	217.3	213.8	214.2	220.7	224.7	225.3	225.4	219.6
2009	219.7	223.8	224.1	225.3	224.5	221.6	218.3	218.2	223.3	226.4	226.0	227.1	223.2
Leisure and Hospitality													
1990	102.0	102.1	104.1	106.9	109.7	113.0	114.3	116.8	114.9	109.8	108.6	107.8	109.2
2000	138.8	140.2	142.2	145.3	148.3	153.2	156.2	156.8	153.7	148.9	147.1	146.7	148.1
2001	141.4	142.6	145.0	148.3	151.4	154.9	156.9	158.9	155.6	149.2	145.6	145.5	149.6
2002	140.8	141.6	143.6	147.4	150.8	155.1	156.6	159.0	156.3	150.5	148.1	146.4	149.7
2003	143.7	144.1	146.2	148.4	150.3	156.0	159.2	160.6	157.3	152.7	150.2	150.4	151.6
2004	144.9	145.9	148.8	153.1	156.0	159.5	162.9	164.6	161.6	156.0	154.0	154.0	155.1
2005	149.4	150.1	153.9	156.7	159.5	164.1	166.4	167.9	165.2	159.6	158.2	158.4	159.1
2006	154.6	155.5	158.4	162.5	165.2	169.4	172.6	173.9	170.8	166.2	164.6	165.6	164.9
2007	161.5	163.2	166.2	169.0	172.4	176.1	179.8	181.4	178.4	172.5	171.2	171.1	171.9
2008	166.6	167.2	170.2	172.8	175.5	178.9	181.6	181.7	178.6	171.1	167.0	163.3	172.9
2009	158.1	158.1	159.2	161.4	164.2	167.5	170.1	170.1	167.8	162.1	160.1	158.4	163.1
Other Services													
1990	43.4	43.9	44.5	45.7	46.0	46.9	47.3	47.9	47.4	47.4	47.5	47.4	46.3
2000	53.7	54.5	55.1	55.3	55.7	55.7	54.9	55.4	56.0	56.0	55.9	55.6	55.3
2001	56.1	57.0	57.2	57.1	57.3	57.5	56.7	56.7	56.8	56.5	56.0	55.7	56.7
2002	54.8	55.3	55.6	56.2	56.6	56.6	56.3	56.4	56.6	56.6	56.5	56.2	56.1
2003	55.6	55.9	56.3	56.4	56.9	56.7	56.8	57.0	57.6	57.1	56.8	56.9	56.7
2004	55.4	56.2	57.0	57.2	57.3	58.0	58.0	57.8	58.2	58.7	57.2	56.8	57.3
2005	55.8	56.6	56.8	57.2	57.5	57.8	57.6	57.6	57.7	57.6	57.5	57.6	57.3
2006	56.8	57.4	58.1	58.6	59.3	59.9	59.3	59.5	59.5	59.6	59.4	59.6	58.9
2007	58.5	59.6	60.0	60.0	60.7	61.1	60.4	60.7	60.6	60.8	60.7	60.7	60.3
2008	59.8	60.4	60.8	61.1	61.7	61.7	61.1	61.0	61.4	60.6	59.7	59.1	60.7
2009	57.8	57.9	57.7	57.9	58.0	57.9	57.9	57.9	57.5	56.5	56.8	56.6	57.5
Government													
1990	228.0	231.3	233.2	236.3	241.6	242.0	216.4	213.8	224.3	239.4	241.2	237.8	232.1
2000	276.8	281.9	283.3	284.0	291.2	289.5	259.4	256.8	267.2	283.5	285.5	283.8	278.6
2001	278.4	285.0	287.3	286.7	290.6	291.2	260.5	259.4	272.3	289.8	291.5	289.2	281.8
2002	285.4	291.0	292.9	291.5	294.4	295.3	266.7	264.8	276.2	289.8	291.7	288.6	285.7
2003	285.6	288.4	288.2	286.6	288.4	287.2	256.1	256.7	267.4	284.0	285.9	283.5	279.8
2004	279.0	285.0	287.9	286.9	289.5	292.3	263.7	262.8	273.8	288.0	290.6	288.5	282.3
2005	286.1	290.4	291.4	291.9	293.5	295.4	264.2	263.7	274.3	288.5	292.2	289.2	285.1
2006	284.5	290.6	292.1	291.2	295.1	296.5	265.3	264.7	276.1	291.4	295.3	290.8	286.1
2007	286.6	292.1	294.2	294.3	299.2	300.5	268.8	268.1	278.5	296.6	300.0	298.1	289.8
2008	294.8	300.1	302.0	302.4	305.7	306.8	279.8	278.3	288.3	304.3	300.0	305.2	298.0
2009	301.0	305.9	306.7	307.9	310.5	309.3	281.2	278.3	285.5	303.3	305.5	303.0	299.8

Average Weekly Hours by Selected Industry: Oregon, 2007–2009

(Not seasonally adjusted.)

Industry and year	January	February	March	April	May	June	July	August	September	October	November	December	Annual average
Total Private													
2007	33.1	34.0	33.8	34.8	33.9	34.4	35.0	34.3	35.1	33.8	33.4	34.6	34.2
2008	32.9	33.6	34.4	33.7	33.8	34.9	33.8	34.2	33.7	33.5	34.2	32.7	33.8
2009	32.8	33.7	33.4	32.9	32.7	33.0	32.9	34.1	33.3	33.3	34.0	33.0	33.2
Goods-Producing													
2007	37.0	38.8	38.8	39.5	39.5	39.7	39.6	39.5	39.5	39.1	38.3	39.2	39.0
2008	37.0	37.6	38.0	37.7	38.4	38.9	37.9	38.5	38.0	37.7	38.0	37.0	37.9
2009	36.7	36.9	37.1	37.0	37.4	38.0	37.4	38.0	37.0	37.5	37.3	37.2	37.3
Construction													
2007	34.9	36.9	36.8	37.0	37.7	38.3	37.7	38.1	38.0	37.7	36.2	36.8	37.2
2008	34.1	35.4	35.5	35.8	37.3	37.7	36.9	38.0	37.7	37.1	36.5	36.2	36.5
2009	36.4	35.8	35.0	35.0	34.9	35.5	35.9	36.3	34.8	35.3	35.3	34.6	35.4
Manufacturing													
2007	38.1	39.8	39.9	40.8	40.5	40.4	40.6	40.2	40.2	40.0	39.5	40.6	40.1
2008	38.7	38.9	39.5	39.0	39.2	39.7	38.7	38.8	38.3	38.1	38.8	37.6	38.8
2009	37.2	37.4	38.1	38.0	38.5	39.1	38.3	38.9	38.0	38.6	38.4	38.3	38.2
Trade, Transportation, and Utilities													
2007	33.3	34.3	33.7	35.0	34.1	34.6	35.3	34.7	35.8	34.2	34.0	34.8	34.5
2008	33.5	34.0	34.8	34.2	34.2	35.3	34.8	35.2	34.9	34.5	34.8	34.0	34.5
2009	33.8	34.5	34.1	33.7	33.5	34.0	34.2	35.1	34.7	33.9	34.1	33.8	34.1
Financial Activities													
2007	36.2	36.6	35.7	37.0	35.2	35.8	37.0	35.6	37.3	35.2	35.4	37.1	36.2
2008	34.7	36.0	37.7	36.0	36.0	37.6	35.6	36.6	35.8	36.1	38.3	36.1	36.4
2009	36.7	37.9	37.2	35.8	35.5	35.3	35.1	37.4	35.7	35.8	37.9	35.7	36.3
Professional and Business Services													
2007	33.3	34.4	34.5	35.3	34.2	34.8	35.6	34.4	35.8	34.4	34.1	35.7	34.7
2008	33.9	34.5	35.5	34.6	34.7	36.1	34.5	34.8	34.6	34.5	35.2	33.7	34.7
2009	33.9	35.2	35.0	34.3	33.8	34.0	34.1	35.2	33.1	33.6	34.9	34.2	34.3
Education and Health Services													
2007	31.2	31.7	31.3	32.4	31.3	31.6	32.4	31.1	32.7	31.5	31.2	32.5	31.7
2008	31.9	32.3	33.0	32.5	32.1	33.2	32.0	32.0	31.9	31.4	32.2	30.3	32.1
2009	30.4	31.3	30.9	30.4	30.0	30.0	29.7	30.8	30.2	30.1	31.2	29.8	30.4
Leisure and Hospitality													
2007	24.5	24.5	24.8	25.6	24.2	24.9	26.2	25.5	26.0	24.0	23.7	24.6	24.9
2008	23.1	23.8	24.8	24.4	24.6	26.2	25.4	26.1	24.7	24.2	24.7	22.9	24.6
2009	23.6	25.1	25.0	24.5	24.7	25.0	25.3	27.2	24.9	24.7	25.1	23.9	24.9
Other Services													
2007	28.3	29.4	28.9	30.5	28.5	30.4	29.2	29.3	29.3	27.7	27.3	27.9	28.9
2008	25.7	27.7	28.4	27.3	27.9	28.4	27.0	28.3	27.8	27.9	29.2	27.1	27.7
2009	27.2	28.7	28.3	27.7	28.0	28.3	28.4	30.4	34.1	34.6	35.1	33.3	30.3

Average Hourly Earnings by Selected Industry: Oregon, 2007–2009

(Dollars, not seasonally adjusted.)

Industry and year	January	February	March	April	May	June	July	August	September	October	November	December	Annual average
Total Private													
2007	20.92	20.70	20.67	20.77	20.44	20.45	20.57	20.28	20.60	20.55	20.48	20.87	20.61
2008	20.85	20.86	20.82	20.88	20.81	20.79	20.84	20.94	20.93	21.04	21.17	21.34	20.93
2009	21.42	21.68	21.63	21.31	21.27	21.06	20.95	21.21	21.25	21.21	21.39	21.52	21.33
Goods-Producing													
2007	21.23	20.84	20.93	21.04	20.89	21.22	20.91	20.98	21.33	20.95	20.77	21.42	21.04
2008	21.32	21.18	21.20	21.25	21.38	21.67	21.76	21.95	21.56	21.77	21.84	22.12	21.58
2009	22.32	22.40	22.55	22.43	22.53	22.23	22.44	22.47	22.26	22.37	22.50	22.42	22.41
Construction													
2007	23.03	22.62	22.98	23.05	23.30	23.39	22.92	23.56	23.59	23.42	23.07	23.74	23.23
2008	24.04	23.72	23.82	23.89	23.94	24.12	25.03	24.83	24.61	24.76	25.01	25.19	24.41
2009	25.24	25.33	25.71	25.62	25.92	25.54	25.70	25.84	26.01	25.95	26.04	26.40	25.76
Manufacturing													
2007	20.39	20.00	19.94	20.08	19.64	20.12	19.87	19.59	20.18	19.66	19.67	20.37	19.96
2008	20.21	20.07	20.04	20.07	20.15	20.48	20.14	20.52	20.06	20.34	20.48	20.85	20.28
2009	21.02	21.17	21.13	21.09	21.15	20.80	20.96	21.01	20.71	20.90	21.11	21.07	21.01
Trade, Transportation, and Utilities													
2007	17.23	17.32	17.57	17.40	17.05	17.34	17.58	17.24	17.73	17.65	17.77	18.07	17.50
2008	18.10	18.48	18.62	18.31	18.33	18.21	18.32	18.43	18.37	18.66	19.00	19.03	18.49
2009	19.34	19.51	20.32	19.51	19.57	19.24	19.36	19.50	19.22	19.11	19.24	19.49	19.45
Financial Activities													
2007	26.82	27.26	25.78	26.16	25.23	24.32	24.70	24.37	24.04	25.12	24.39	25.27	25.29
2008	25.02	24.53	23.48	25.21	24.72	23.71	23.93	24.40	23.88	24.25	24.13	23.74	24.24
2009	23.93	25.51	24.41	24.37	24.82	24.64	25.46	25.60	25.42	25.35	25.66	26.38	25.13
Professional and Business Services													
2007	25.07	23.27	24.05	23.80	23.62	23.33	23.39	23.12	23.62	23.44	23.38	23.95	23.66
2008	24.03	24.16	24.28	24.06	24.01	24.70	24.95	24.92	24.89	25.02	24.85	25.19	24.59
2009	25.29	25.33	24.62	24.55	24.04	23.94	23.92	24.08	24.18	24.05	24.45	24.44	24.41
Education and Health Services													
2007	22.66	22.99	22.50	23.24	22.72	23.33	23.90	22.97	22.95	22.79	23.11	22.70	22.99
2008	22.27	22.04	22.28	22.23	22.06	21.99	22.01	22.21	22.20	21.95	21.93	22.17	22.11
2009	21.87	21.62	21.61	21.47	21.61	21.67	21.77	21.74	22.09	21.93	21.63	21.78	21.73
Leisure and Hospitality													
2007	14.31	14.04	14.12	13.82	14.04	13.42	13.49	13.17	13.00	12.94	12.75	12.83	13.48
2008	12.81	12.97	12.66	12.71	12.59	12.50	12.52	12.55	12.64	12.70	12.79	13.07	12.70
2009	13.08	13.10	13.06	12.84	12.84	12.62	12.59	12.57	12.78	13.04	13.10	13.17	12.89
Other Services													
2007	18.18	18.03	18.12	18.18	17.82	17.17	17.03	16.86	17.60	17.60	17.20	17.29	17.59
2008	17.40	17.41	17.25	17.37	17.37	17.01	16.70	16.97	17.51	17.58	17.64	17.99	17.35
2009	17.99	18.08	18.02	17.84	17.78	17.89	17.72	17.76	17.95	17.63	18.13	18.19	17.92

Average Weekly Earnings by Selected Industry: Oregon, 2007–2009

(Dollars, not seasonally adjusted.)

Industry and year	January	February	March	April	May	June	July	August	September	October	November	December	Annual average
Total Private													
2007	692.45	703.80	698.65	722.80	692.92	703.48	719.95	695.60	723.06	694.59	684.03	722.10	704.86
2008	685.97	700.90	716.21	703.66	703.38	725.57	704.39	716.15	705.34	704.84	724.01	697.82	707.43
2009	702.58	730.62	722.44	701.10	695.53	694.98	689.26	723.26	707.63	706.29	727.26	710.16	708.16
Goods-Producing													
2007	785.51	808.59	812.08	831.08	825.16	842.43	828.04	828.71	842.54	819.15	795.49	839.66	820.56
2008	788.84	796.37	805.60	801.13	820.99	842.96	824.70	845.08	819.28	820.73	829.92	818.44	817.88
2009	819.14	826.56	836.61	829.91	842.62	844.74	839.26	853.86	823.62	838.88	839.25	834.02	835.89
Construction													
2007	803.75	834.68	845.66	852.85	878.41	895.84	864.08	897.64	896.42	882.93	835.13	873.63	864.16
2008	819.76	839.69	845.61	855.26	892.96	909.32	923.61	943.54	927.80	918.60	912.87	911.88	890.97
2009	918.74	906.81	899.85	896.70	904.61	906.67	922.63	937.99	905.15	916.04	919.21	913.44	911.90
Manufacturing													
2007	776.86	796.00	795.61	819.26	795.42	812.85	806.72	787.52	811.24	786.40	776.97	827.02	800.40
2008	782.13	780.72	791.58	782.73	789.88	813.06	779.42	796.18	768.30	774.95	794.62	783.96	786.86
2009	781.94	791.76	805.05	801.42	814.28	813.28	802.77	817.29	786.98	806.74	810.62	806.98	802.58
Trade, Transportation, and Utilities													
2007	573.76	594.08	592.11	609.00	581.41	599.96	620.57	598.23	634.73	603.63	604.18	628.84	603.75
2008	606.35	628.32	647.98	626.20	626.89	642.81	637.54	648.74	641.11	643.77	661.20	647.02	637.91
2009	653.69	673.10	692.91	657.49	655.60	654.16	662.11	684.45	666.93	647.83	656.08	658.76	663.25
Financial Activities													
2007	970.88	997.72	920.35	967.92	888.10	870.66	913.90	867.57	896.69	884.22	863.41	937.52	915.50
2008	868.19	883.08	885.20	907.56	889.92	891.50	851.91	893.04	854.90	875.43	924.18	857.01	882.34
2009	878.23	966.83	908.05	872.45	881.11	869.79	893.65	957.44	907.49	907.53	972.51	941.77	912.22
Professional and Business Services													
2007	834.83	800.49	829.73	840.14	807.80	811.88	832.68	795.33	845.60	806.34	797.26	855.02	821.00
2008	814.62	833.52	861.94	832.48	833.15	891.67	860.78	867.22	861.19	863.19	874.72	848.90	853.27
2009	857.33	891.62	861.70	842.07	812.55	813.96	815.67	847.62	800.36	808.08	853.31	835.85	837.26
Education and Health Services													
2007	706.99	728.78	704.25	752.98	711.14	737.23	774.36	714.37	750.47	717.89	721.03	737.75	728.78
2008	710.41	711.89	735.24	722.48	708.13	730.07	704.32	710.72	708.18	689.23	706.15	671.75	709.73
2009	664.85	676.71	667.75	652.69	648.30	650.10	646.57	669.59	667.12	660.09	674.86	649.04	660.59
Leisure and Hospitality													
2007	350.60	343.98	350.18	353.79	339.77	334.16	353.44	335.84	338.00	310.56	302.18	315.62	335.65
2008	295.91	308.69	313.97	310.12	309.71	327.50	318.01	327.56	312.21	307.34	315.91	299.30	312.42
2009	308.69	328.81	326.50	314.58	317.15	315.50	318.53	341.90	318.22	322.09	328.81	314.76	320.96
Other Services													
2007	514.49	530.08	523.67	554.49	507.87	521.97	497.28	494.00	515.68	487.52	469.56	482.39	508.35
2008	447.18	482.26	489.90	474.20	484.62	483.08	450.90	480.25	486.78	490.48	515.09	487.53	480.60
2009	489.33	518.90	509.97	494.17	497.84	506.29	503.25	539.90	612.10	610.00	636.36	605.73	542.98

PENNSYLVANIA

At a Glance

Population:
    1990 census: 11,882,842
    2000 census: 12,281,054
    2009 estimate: 12,604,767

Percent change in population:
    1990–2000: 3.4%
    2000–2009: 2.6%

Percent change in total nonfarm employment:
    1990–2009: 8.5%
    2008–2009: -3.3%

Industry with the largest growth in employment, 1990–2009 (thousands):
    Education and health services, 361.8

Industry with the largest decline or smallest growth in employment, 1990–2009 (thousands):
    Manufacturing, -305.6

Civilian labor force:
    1990: 5,826,666
    2000: 6,085,833
    2009: 6,414,162

Unemployment rate and rank among states (lowest to highest):
    1990: 5.4%, 27th
    2000: 4.2%, 33rd
    2009: 8.1%, 25th

Employment by Industry, 2009

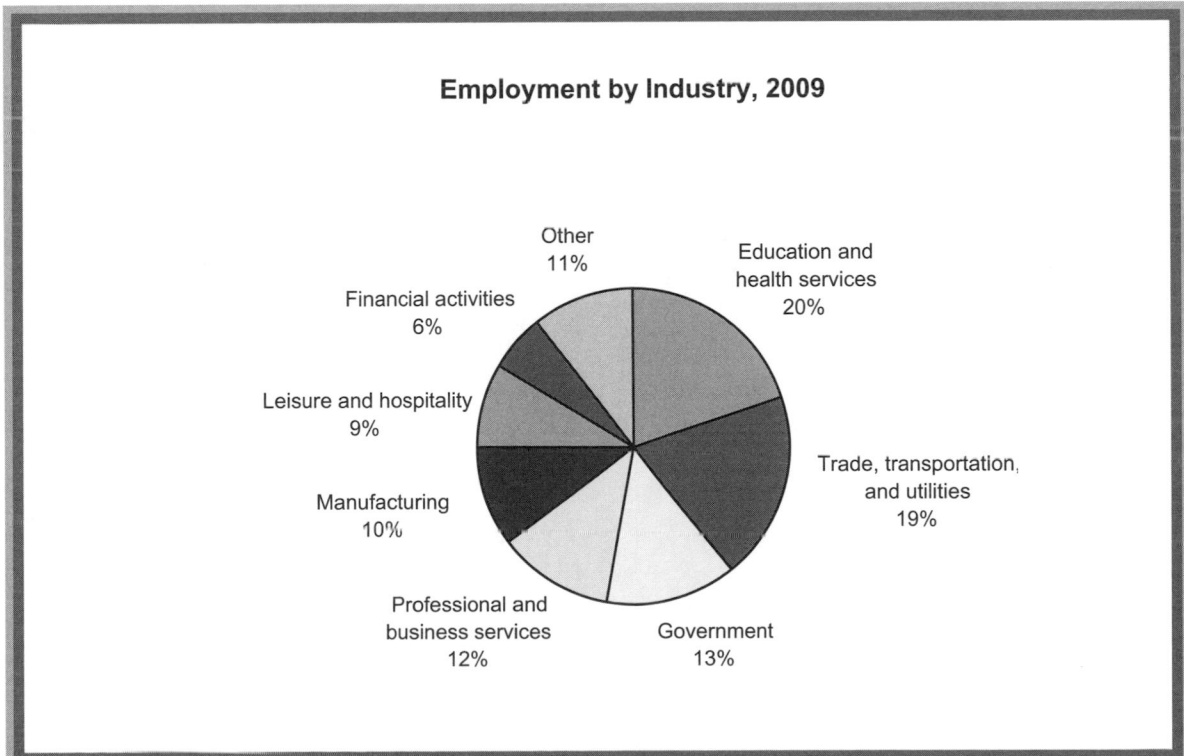

Other 11%
Financial activities 6%
Leisure and hospitality 9%
Manufacturing 10%
Professional and business services 12%
Government 13%
Trade, transportation, and utilities 19%
Education and health services 20%

Employment by Industry: Pennsylvania, Selected Years, 1990–2009

(Numbers in thousands, not seasonally adjusted.)

Industry and year	January	February	March	April	May	June	July	August	September	October	November	December	Annual average
Total Nonfarm													
1990	5088.1	5106.9	5145.0	5167.2	5202.7	5214.9	5166.2	5164.6	5196.4	5200.1	5201.9	5187.8	5170.2
2000	5547.2	5577.0	5635.7	5690.1	5730.3	5740.2	5688.3	5673.7	5734.4	5744.8	5766.6	5767.1	5691.3
2001	5613.1	5641.0	5676.5	5702.3	5729.1	5738.7	5652.4	5654.8	5690.9	5692.9	5703.4	5694.9	5682.5
2002	5549.6	5575.0	5613.8	5647.0	5680.8	5692.4	5614.3	5614.2	5661.8	5681.0	5689.2	5670.0	5640.8
2003	5522.5	5530.4	5569.3	5609.3	5648.2	5656.9	5575.9	5579.5	5628.3	5668.6	5676.0	5671.2	5611.3
2004	5507.1	5530.4	5582.2	5633.9	5674.8	5691.9	5628.4	5622.1	5679.2	5719.0	5732.4	5728.7	5644.2
2005	5568.3	5598.2	5628.8	5708.2	5739.8	5747.6	5692.1	5684.6	5741.7	5764.3	5781.6	5771.5	5702.2
2006	5621.9	5656.0	5700.7	5760.2	5795.2	5800.3	5731.5	5729.6	5787.3	5821.1	5835.1	5834.2	5756.1
2007	5678.9	5690.3	5741.5	5792.7	5837.6	5853.3	5784.8	5776.7	5818.5	5860.7	5875.3	5865.0	5797.9
2008	5711.9	5732.1	5760.5	5826.8	5862.1	5855.8	5783.4	5777.3	5819.4	5845.3	5822.9	5794.7	5799.4
2009	5600.8	5604.7	5604.0	5634.5	5660.6	5637.0	5567.2	5544.4	5591.6	5627.1	5627.1	5603.5	5608.5
Total Private													
1990	4397.1	4398.8	4431.8	4449.4	4484.0	4514.3	4498.0	4509.9	4509.3	4493.1	4489.5	4478.1	4471.1
2000	4828.7	4840.6	4891.3	4943.4	4973.9	5020.4	5010.1	5005.5	5014.5	5009.2	5025.2	5031.7	4966.2
2001	4892.5	4901.0	4933.6	4955.3	4986.1	5020.2	4978.1	4981.6	4962.0	4945.9	4950.1	4944.6	4954.3
2002	4814.1	4819.6	4856.6	4887.4	4926.4	4960.3	4932.1	4938.9	4925.2	4924.7	4925.0	4912.3	4901.9
2003	4783.0	4768.3	4803.1	4842.9	4886.3	4910.5	4885.3	4893.6	4888.6	4906.3	4909.6	4911.0	4865.7
2004	4766.0	4770.3	4817.1	4866.1	4911.1	4947.5	4942.8	4942.1	4938.5	4959.5	4965.8	4970.5	4899.8
2005	4824.9	4835.7	4862.5	4938.7	4979.1	5005.1	5003.0	5002.1	5000.7	5005.0	5016.6	5012.7	4957.2
2006	4882.1	4894.6	4936.4	4994.2	5031.1	5058.0	5044.2	5044.1	5043.9	5060.1	5066.3	5071.5	5010.5
2007	4936.9	4929.0	4976.9	5027.4	5076.3	5111.0	5095.7	5090.4	5078.5	5100.9	5110.1	5104.3	5053.1
2008	4968.9	4970.5	4995.5	5059.0	5101.3	5110.6	5095.3	5086.7	5067.3	5073.6	5046.9	5025.2	5050.1
2009	4851.2	4834.4	4831.5	4854.7	4889.4	4886.6	4864.0	4849.4	4837.6	4853.3	4848.3	4830.9	4852.6
Goods-Producing													
1990	1188.9	1182.7	1193.3	1200.3	1213.1	1226.8	1219.9	1225.8	1218.9	1205.7	1192.5	1174.5	1203.5
2000	1099.9	1092.8	1112.0	1126.0	1135.2	1153.7	1153.5	1155.8	1150.1	1140.3	1132.3	1122.0	1131.1
2001	1096.3	1090.4	1095.9	1101.6	1105.7	1114.7	1105.2	1105.1	1093.7	1077.5	1063.6	1051.0	1091.7
2002	1017.1	1012.9	1019.0	1027.7	1036.0	1048.0	1043.2	1045.1	1035.1	1027.3	1014.5	999.1	1027.1
2003	972.6	959.4	965.5	975.1	985.1	992.8	989.3	989.0	982.4	977.7	969.0	957.8	976.3
2004	928.9	922.5	935.8	950.6	963.6	977.5	981.6	981.1	976.3	972.4	965.9	958.2	959.5
2005	928.9	921.9	928.3	948.9	961.6	973.7	975.6	976.2	969.3	964.4	961.4	947.7	954.8
2006	924.4	921.9	934.4	948.8	958.0	969.8	969.5	971.8	965.6	959.8	952.1	944.1	951.7
2007	921.4	906.3	922.2	936.3	948.8	962.6	962.4	961.9	955.3	953.4	945.7	932.9	942.4
2008	910.1	901.9	909.4	923.2	934.9	943.3	941.0	939.6	930.2	922.3	905.7	885.8	920.6
2009	844.8	828.2	822.9	825.1	826.0	828.8	825.2	823.0	818.2	813.0	806.3	791.6	821.1
Mining and Logging													
1990	27.1	27.0	27.5	27.8	28.1	28.5	28.0	28.2	28.2	27.8	27.3	26.9	27.7
2000	18.9	18.8	19.2	19.2	19.3	19.7	19.9	19.9	19.9	19.6	19.4	19.0	19.4
2001	18.6	18.6	18.9	19.2	19.7	20.0	20.1	20.2	20.0	19.9	19.7	19.3	19.5
2002	18.7	18.7	18.8	18.9	19.2	19.4	18.9	19.3	18.9	18.8	18.4	17.8	18.8
2003	17.2	17.1	17.3	17.5	17.8	18.1	18.3	18.3	18.4	18.4	18.3	17.9	17.9
2004	17.2	17.2	17.7	18.4	18.7	19.2	19.5	19.5	19.3	19.3	19.3	19.1	18.7
2005	18.6	18.6	18.6	19.6	19.8	20.3	20.5	20.4	20.4	20.2	20.1	19.6	19.7
2006	19.2	19.3	19.7	20.3	20.6	20.9	21.0	20.9	20.8	20.7	20.7	20.3	20.4
2007	19.9	19.8	20.2	20.8	21.2	21.7	21.9	21.9	21.6	21.5	21.4	21.0	21.1
2008	20.6	20.5	20.9	21.6	22.2	22.8	22.9	23.1	23.1	23.4	23.3	22.5	22.2
2009	21.8	21.5	21.2	21.7	21.8	22.3	22.4	22.5	22.5	23.0	23.1	22.3	22.2
Construction													
1990	206.3	204.3	212.6	221.1	232.4	239.9	242.0	243.2	239.1	233.7	225.5	211.9	226.0
2000	220.5	215.9	230.3	245.0	254.5	261.7	263.9	265.3	262.3	258.6	252.8	241.6	247.7
2001	226.2	225.4	232.7	244.7	255.7	263.9	266.3	267.8	263.1	259.4	253.2	245.1	250.3
2002	225.3	224.8	231.9	243.9	253.4	260.8	264.0	265.8	260.4	258.6	252.2	240.7	248.5
2003	224.1	218.6	226.4	239.4	250.6	256.5	261.7	263.1	259.2	258.0	252.7	242.2	246.0
2004	223.8	219.9	231.3	243.7	254.1	262.0	266.7	266.5	264.9	262.4	257.1	249.5	250.2
2005	229.3	225.4	230.6	250.9	260.8	268.2	272.7	273.7	270.8	267.8	265.3	253.4	255.7
2006	237.2	236.4	245.3	258.1	265.9	272.3	274.8	276.6	274.2	270.4	263.7	256.6	261.0
2007	241.8	232.9	244.0	257.3	267.9	275.9	278.1	278.7	276.0	274.3	266.5	253.9	262.3
2008	239.1	234.0	240.3	255.2	264.3	269.3	270.2	269.8	264.7	260.9	250.5	236.9	254.6
2009	215.4	211.8	215.9	224.7	230.6	234.4	235.7	234.4	231.1	230.3	226.0	213.6	225.3
Manufacturing													
1990	955.5	951.4	953.2	951.4	952.6	958.4	949.9	954.4	951.6	944.2	939.7	935.7	949.8
2000	860.5	858.1	862.5	861.8	861.4	872.3	869.7	870.6	867.9	862.1	860.1	861.4	864.0
2001	851.5	846.4	844.3	837.7	830.3	830.8	818.8	817.1	810.6	798.2	790.7	786.6	821.9
2002	773.1	769.4	768.3	764.9	763.4	767.8	760.3	760.0	755.8	749.9	743.9	740.6	759.8
2003	731.3	723.7	721.8	718.2	716.7	718.2	709.3	707.6	704.8	701.3	698.0	697.7	712.4
2004	687.9	685.4	686.8	688.5	690.8	696.3	695.4	695.1	692.1	690.7	689.5	689.6	690.7
2005	681.0	677.9	679.1	678.4	681.0	685.2	682.4	682.1	678.1	676.4	676.0	674.7	679.4
2006	668.0	666.2	669.4	670.4	671.5	676.6	673.7	674.3	670.6	668.7	667.7	667.2	670.4
2007	659.7	653.6	658.0	658.2	659.7	665.0	662.4	661.3	657.7	657.6	657.8	658.0	659.1
2008	650.4	647.4	648.2	646.4	648.4	651.2	647.9	646.7	642.4	638.0	631.9	626.4	643.8
2009	607.6	594.9	585.8	578.7	573.6	572.1	567.1	566.1	564.6	559.7	557.2	555.7	573.6

Employment by Industry: Pennsylvania, Selected Years, 1990–2009—*Continued*

(Numbers in thousands, not seasonally adjusted.)

Industry and year	January	February	March	April	May	June	July	August	September	October	November	December	Annual average
Service-Providing													
1990	3899.2	3924.2	3951.7	3966.9	3989.6	3988.1	3946.3	3938.8	3977.5	3994.4	4009.4	4013.3	3966.6
2000	4447.3	4484.2	4523.7	4564.1	4595.1	4586.5	4534.8	4517.9	4584.3	4604.5	4634.3	4645.1	4560.2
2001	4516.8	4550.6	4580.6	4600.7	4623.4	4624.0	4547.2	4549.7	4597.2	4615.4	4639.8	4643.9	4590.8
2002	4532.5	4562.1	4594.8	4619.3	4644.8	4644.4	4571.1	4569.1	4626.7	4653.7	4674.7	4670.9	4613.7
2003	4549.9	4571.0	4603.8	4634.2	4663.1	4664.1	4586.6	4590.5	4645.9	4690.9	4707.0	4713.4	4635.0
2004	4578.2	4607.9	4646.4	4683.3	4711.2	4714.4	4646.8	4641.0	4702.9	4746.6	4766.5	4770.5	4684.6
2005	4639.4	4676.3	4700.5	4759.3	4778.2	4773.9	4716.5	4708.4	4772.4	4799.9	4820.2	4823.8	4747.4
2006	4697.5	4734.1	4766.3	4811.4	4837.2	4830.5	4762.0	4757.8	4821.7	4861.3	4883.0	4890.1	4804.4
2007	4757.5	4784.0	4819.3	4856.4	4888.8	4890.7	4822.4	4814.8	4863.2	4907.3	4929.6	4932.1	4855.5
2008	4801.8	4830.2	4851.1	4903.6	4927.2	4912.5	4842.4	4837.7	4889.2	4923.0	4917.2	4908.9	4878.7
2009	4756.0	4776.5	4781.1	4809.4	4834.6	4808.2	4742.0	4721.4	4773.4	4814.1	4820.8	4811.9	4787.5
Trade, Transportation, and Utilities													
1990	1043.9	1033.1	1036.1	1038.5	1044.8	1048.1	1036.0	1038.7	1041.5	1046.1	1060.5	1068.4	1044.6
2000	1112.0	1101.1	1106.2	1119.0	1125.0	1131.0	1119.1	1123.4	1131.5	1142.5	1164.7	1179.3	1129.6
2001	1129.5	1112.2	1116.1	1115.9	1121.7	1125.5	1108.4	1110.1	1116.2	1123.7	1143.8	1155.0	1123.2
2002	1111.4	1094.5	1101.1	1101.7	1111.9	1115.5	1102.3	1104.8	1109.1	1117.9	1135.7	1148.5	1112.9
2003	1101.4	1085.7	1090.7	1096.8	1105.6	1110.6	1095.6	1098.9	1105.5	1120.6	1137.1	1150.4	1108.2
2004	1102.3	1091.8	1097.7	1101.9	1111.3	1115.4	1104.6	1105.2	1110.1	1123.9	1142.2	1157.3	1113.6
2005	1108.9	1097.7	1102.0	1110.1	1119.2	1121.5	1113.6	1113.9	1118.5	1127.7	1147.6	1162.9	1120.3
2006	1119.6	1103.2	1110.5	1115.7	1122.7	1123.7	1113.6	1115.2	1122.2	1135.0	1156.5	1172.3	1125.8
2007	1130.6	1110.6	1119.1	1122.9	1134.2	1137.3	1126.6	1123.9	1127.6	1137.1	1162.1	1174.4	1133.9
2008	1133.4	1114.2	1118.3	1121.9	1130.8	1130.3	1117.6	1115.4	1119.4	1126.7	1136.3	1146.5	1125.9
2009	1093.5	1077.3	1072.5	1071.7	1082.3	1081.5	1065.5	1063.9	1070.1	1076.7	1091.8	1099.9	1078.9
Wholesale Trade													
1990	225.3	224.8	226.2	225.9	226.5	228.0	226.6	226.0	224.2	222.1	222.4	221.6	225.0
2000	221.0	221.3	223.0	227.6	227.6	229.4	228.5	228.7	227.7	228.4	228.6	228.9	226.7
2001	227.0	226.7	227.4	227.8	228.1	229.8	229.8	229.5	228.1	226.6	226.6	227.7	227.9
2002	225.4	224.3	225.2	225.3	226.8	228.3	227.9	227.3	225.9	226.5	226.8	227.5	226.4
2003	225.4	225.2	226.7	226.9	228.2	228.7	228.2	228.1	227.0	227.3	227.7	228.6	227.3
2004	225.7	225.4	227.1	227.9	229.0	231.1	231.8	231.8	230.5	231.1	231.3	232.4	229.6
2005	229.9	230.0	231.2	233.2	234.6	235.7	236.2	236.2	235.2	235.3	235.5	236.5	234.1
2006	233.3	233.8	235.0	236.7	238.2	239.9	239.7	239.9	238.6	239.0	239.0	239.3	237.7
2007	236.5	235.6	237.2	238.3	239.3	241.2	241.5	240.7	239.2	239.7	240.6	240.8	239.2
2008	237.8	237.7	238.4	239.3	240.5	241.2	241.2	240.3	238.1	237.7	235.6	234.5	238.5
2009	230.0	228.0	227.1	226.4	226.8	226.8	225.9	225.0	223.7	222.4	222.2	221.3	225.5
Retail Trade													
1990	640.8	630.4	630.7	627.2	631.1	633.5	629.8	632.2	630.6	636.7	651.6	660.6	636.3
2000	671.6	661.0	663.0	670.3	675.2	680.7	675.8	680.3	679.8	684.9	707.2	722.3	681.0
2001	679.7	663.3	666.5	663.8	668.0	672.5	664.3	667.3	664.7	668.9	689.9	701.6	672.5
2002	666.2	651.2	656.1	655.1	662.5	666.8	661.7	664.4	659.9	663.1	682.0	695.3	665.4
2003	657.1	642.8	646.4	650.7	656.7	662.4	657.3	660.4	657.8	667.2	683.7	697.0	661.6
2004	657.9	647.9	650.8	652.7	659.8	663.0	660.9	661.6	656.4	666.6	684.3	696.8	663.2
2005	658.2	647.0	648.6	652.9	658.7	661.2	661.3	660.9	653.5	661.0	678.4	690.0	661.0
2006	655.8	639.6	643.9	646.6	650.0	652.6	649.8	650.3	645.6	656.0	676.7	688.2	654.6
2007	655.7	637.7	642.8	644.6	653.1	655.7	655.1	653.3	646.6	655.6	678.2	687.9	655.5
2008	656.7	638.4	641.7	642.6	648.8	650.1	647.2	645.8	639.5	646.6	658.1	667.6	648.6
2009	628.5	616.0	613.4	613.9	623.5	625.9	622.5	622.4	617.1	623.3	636.9	643.6	623.9
Transportation and Utilities													
1990	177.8	177.9	179.2	185.4	187.2	186.6	179.6	180.5	186.7	187.3	186.5	186.2	183.4
2000	219.4	218.8	220.2	221.1	222.2	220.9	214.8	214.4	224.0	229.2	228.9	228.1	221.8
2001	222.8	222.2	222.2	224.3	225.6	223.2	214.3	213.3	223.4	228.2	227.3	225.7	222.7
2002	219.8	219.0	219.8	221.3	222.6	220.4	212.7	213.1	223.3	228.3	226.9	225.7	221.1
2003	218.9	217.7	217.6	219.2	220.7	219.5	210.1	210.4	220.7	226.1	225.7	224.8	219.3
2004	218.7	218.5	219.8	221.3	222.5	221.3	211.9	211.8	223.2	226.2	226.6	228.1	220.8
2005	220.8	220.7	222.2	224.0	225.9	224.6	216.1	216.8	229.8	231.4	233.7	236.4	225.2
2006	230.5	229.8	231.6	231.9	234.5	231.7	224.1	225.0	238.0	240.0	240.8	244.8	233.5
2007	238.4	237.3	239.1	240.0	241.8	240.4	230.0	229.9	241.8	241.8	243.3	245.7	239.1
2008	238.9	238.1	238.2	240.0	241.5	239.0	229.2	229.3	241.8	242.4	242.6	244.4	238.8
2009	235.0	233.3	232.0	231.4	232.0	228.8	217.1	216.5	229.3	231.0	232.7	235.0	229.5
Information													
1990	108.0	108.2	108.5	108.4	109.2	109.9	109.8	109.9	109.5	109.3	109.6	110.2	109.2
2000	132.5	133.2	133.8	133.3	134.7	136.8	138.6	129.4	138.9	138.6	140.2	141.3	135.9
2001	138.2	138.1	138.1	136.4	136.5	136.8	136.5	135.4	133.2	132.6	132.8	132.9	135.6
2002	130.6	130.2	130.9	129.3	129.9	129.6	128.3	127.9	126.3	125.7	126.0	125.9	128.4
2003	124.3	123.7	124.5	122.8	122.4	122.1	120.6	119.8	118.1	116.7	116.6	115.6	120.6
2004	114.1	113.4	113.4	112.7	112.8	113.2	113.1	112.2	110.8	110.4	110.3	110.2	112.2
2005	109.1	108.8	109.0	109.4	110.0	110.5	109.6	109.4	111.6	108.1	108.8	109.1	109.5
2006	107.6	108.0	107.7	108.1	108.7	108.9	108.6	108.4	108.3	108.0	107.5	108.3	108.2
2007	106.8	106.5	106.4	106.6	107.3	109.0	108.1	108.0	108.1	107.0	107.6	108.9	107.5
2008	107.2	106.8	106.5	108.1	108.3	107.8	106.2	105.3	103.9	103.7	103.4	103.2	105.9
2009	101.6	101.0	100.8	100.6	100.4	100.6	100.0	99.0	98.3	98.4	98.3	99.3	99.9

Employment by Industry: Pennsylvania, Selected Years, 1990–2009—*Continued*

(Numbers in thousands, not seasonally adjusted.)

Industry and year	January	February	March	April	May	June	July	August	September	October	November	December	Annual average
Financial Activities													
1990	324.1	324.0	324.8	323.0	325.6	327.4	328.3	328.0	325.3	322.7	322.2	323.4	324.9
2000	335.9	335.4	335.9	337.0	338.0	342.2	342.1	341.4	338.4	337.8	338.8	341.1	338.7
2001	339.4	339.3	340.6	338.9	339.3	342.1	341.3	340.8	337.0	335.8	335.4	336.8	338.9
2002	334.7	334.5	335.5	335.1	336.3	339.7	340.1	340.6	337.4	335.4	335.7	337.1	336.8
2003	335.9	335.8	336.7	336.9	338.9	341.4	342.2	342.2	338.6	337.5	337.5	338.5	338.5
2004	336.5	335.4	336.4	335.4	337.0	339.0	339.8	338.6	334.3	333.4	333.2	335.2	336.2
2005	332.3	332.4	332.9	333.9	335.5	338.2	339.4	339.9	336.0	335.0	335.6	337.1	335.7
2006	333.9	333.7	334.1	334.9	335.9	339.3	338.9	337.4	333.6	332.7	332.6	333.2	335.0
2007	330.4	330.4	330.6	331.0	332.3	335.9	337.2	336.4	332.5	331.8	332.3	332.3	332.8
2008	328.2	328.7	329.3	329.9	331.1	333.7	334.2	333.6	328.5	327.0	326.5	326.6	329.8
2009	321.5	320.4	319.9	319.4	320.3	321.8	321.8	319.8	316.4	315.8	314.6	315.2	318.9
Professional and Business Services													
1990	443.8	446.8	452.6	455.2	457.9	464.0	462.4	464.0	462.8	458.0	456.2	453.7	456.5
2000	589.1	592.4	603.4	611.1	611.4	619.9	623.4	625.3	621.9	616.9	616.9	616.4	612.3
2001	603.7	606.9	612.2	618.1	619.2	625.0	615.7	620.4	616.0	611.9	608.5	603.5	613.4
2002	589.0	589.9	596.7	604.8	607.0	613.3	611.6	615.5	611.1	610.6	610.4	608.4	605.7
2003	589.6	587.3	592.9	603.1	607.3	611.7	612.7	620.1	621.2	624.8	627.1	627.7	610.5
2004	610.1	611.8	620.1	631.1	634.9	644.3	645.4	649.1	647.9	654.0	654.3	653.6	638.1
2005	634.3	638.1	642.4	657.9	659.1	666.6	668.6	671.3	669.9	672.9	673.0	671.3	660.5
2006	653.8	658.9	666.9	679.1	682.6	692.3	693.0	697.3	696.1	701.4	701.8	700.4	685.3
2007	679.9	681.6	688.1	701.8	706.3	716.3	715.2	717.4	713.7	715.8	716.8	715.8	705.7
2008	695.7	695.5	699.7	713.3	714.8	719.0	720.0	721.0	713.8	713.1	706.8	699.5	709.4
2009	675.9	671.1	669.7	673.7	672.3	674.0	670.4	671.4	666.6	668.9	667.1	664.3	670.5
Education and Health Services													
1990	720.2	735.6	739.6	740.1	732.8	722.5	721.1	720.7	743.3	759.6	762.9	763.5	738.5
2000	902.4	925.8	924.8	924.3	916.3	903.7	897.5	895.7	919.4	933.6	940.4	938.8	918.6
2001	917.5	941.2	946.0	944.9	937.2	928.4	923.7	922.6	944.2	956.0	963.8	962.7	940.7
2002	948.9	971.2	974.9	971.6	963.3	953.0	945.4	942.8	965.3	980.6	985.7	976.8	965.0
2003	965.6	985.5	989.7	988.8	979.6	967.6	957.9	954.2	977.9	998.2	1002.1	998.7	980.5
2004	975.1	997.4	1003.4	1005.0	996.7	983.7	980.8	975.5	1000.7	1021.3	1026.9	1024.1	999.2
2005	1005.1	1029.6	1030.2	1037.9	1027.7	1010.3	1010.4	1006.5	1034.4	1055.3	1058.7	1054.4	1030.0
2006	1032.7	1057.6	1058.7	1064.2	1056.1	1036.7	1033.0	1029.4	1057.2	1074.8	1078.3	1073.8	1054.4
2007	1052.3	1076.0	1081.2	1082.6	1074.8	1056.6	1053.5	1050.9	1075.9	1100.0	1101.3	1096.3	1075.1
2008	1074.5	1103.0	1102.9	1110.2	1099.9	1080.5	1078.7	1077.8	1103.2	1125.1	1129.3	1126.4	1101.0
2009	1104.6	1128.2	1127.0	1130.1	1120.6	1100.6	1099.4	1092.2	1114.4	1140.3	1145.2	1136.2	1119.9
Leisure and Hospitality													
1990	361.6	361.2	367.7	374.5	389.9	402.2	407.3	409.5	397.2	381.8	375.9	374.8	383.6
2000	413.2	415.2	426.7	442.4	462.2	478.8	481.1	481.0	463.7	448.9	440.8	440.9	449.6
2001	420.3	424.2	431.7	445.8	470.1	487.9	488.1	488.7	466.5	452.7	445.6	444.9	455.5
2002	428.0	430.6	440.8	458.6	481.8	497.6	497.9	499.8	482.0	468.3	458.3	457.0	466.7
2003	437.4	435.1	444.7	460.4	486.3	500.4	502.9	506.4	485.2	470.9	460.7	461.8	471.0
2004	441.1	440.1	449.1	467.6	491.1	506.5	508.9	512.9	493.9	479.6	469.0	467.6	477.3
2005	446.1	446.5	455.6	477.9	502.4	518.3	519.6	521.4	501.6	483.0	473.1	472.5	484.8
2006	454.4	455.5	466.8	485.0	506.9	524.6	525.0	524.0	503.4	491.4	481.2	483.1	491.8
2007	463.0	464.8	474.9	490.6	515.5	533.5	532.3	533.6	510.5	501.2	489.6	489.4	499.9
2008	468.5	469.5	478.2	498.6	525.8	537.7	538.8	536.7	513.5	501.7	485.9	485.0	503.3
2009	461.4	460.2	469.5	485.0	515.8	525.3	527.6	528.0	505.7	492.0	478.0	476.8	493.8
Other Services													
1990	206.6	207.2	209.2	209.4	210.7	213.4	213.2	213.3	210.8	209.9	209.7	209.6	210.3
2000	243.7	244.7	248.5	250.3	251.1	254.3	254.8	253.5	250.6	250.6	251.1	251.9	250.4
2001	247.6	248.7	253.0	253.7	256.4	259.8	259.2	258.5	255.2	255.7	256.6	257.8	255.2
2002	254.4	255.8	257.7	258.6	260.2	263.6	263.3	262.4	258.9	258.9	258.7	259.5	259.3
2003	256.2	255.8	258.4	259.0	261.1	263.9	264.1	263.0	259.7	259.9	259.5	260.5	260.1
2004	257.9	257.9	261.2	261.8	263.7	267.9	268.6	267.5	264.5	264.5	264.0	264.3	263.7
2005	260.2	260.7	262.1	262.7	263.6	266.0	266.2	263.5	259.4	258.6	258.4	257.7	261.6
2006	255.7	255.8	257.3	258.9	260.2	262.7	262.6	260.6	257.5	257.0	256.3	256.3	258.4
2007	252.5	252.8	254.4	255.6	257.1	259.8	260.4	258.3	254.9	254.6	254.7	254.3	255.8
2008	251.3	250.9	251.2	253.8	255.7	258.3	258.8	257.3	254.8	254.0	253.0	252.2	254.3
2009	247.9	248.0	249.2	249.1	251.7	254.0	254.1	252.1	247.9	248.2	247.0	247.6	249.7
Government													
1990	691.0	708.1	713.2	717.8	718.7	700.6	668.2	654.7	687.1	707.0	712.4	709.7	699.0
2000	718.5	736.4	744.4	746.7	756.4	719.8	678.2	668.2	719.9	735.6	741.4	735.4	725.1
2001	720.6	740.0	742.9	747.0	743.0	718.5	674.3	673.2	728.9	747.0	753.3	750.3	728.3
2002	735.5	755.4	757.2	759.6	754.4	732.1	682.2	675.3	736.6	756.3	764.2	757.7	738.9
2003	739.5	762.1	766.2	766.4	761.9	746.4	690.6	685.9	739.7	762.3	766.4	760.2	745.6
2004	741.1	760.1	765.1	767.8	763.7	744.4	685.6	680.0	740.7	759.5	766.6	758.2	744.4
2005	743.4	762.5	766.3	769.5	760.7	742.5	689.1	682.5	741.0	759.3	765.0	758.8	745.1
2006	739.8	761.4	764.3	766.0	764.1	742.3	687.3	685.5	743.4	761.0	768.8	762.7	745.6
2007	742.0	761.3	764.6	765.3	761.3	742.3	689.1	686.3	740.0	759.8	765.2	760.7	744.8
2008	743.0	761.6	765.0	767.8	760.8	745.2	688.1	690.6	752.1	771.7	776.0	769.5	749.3
2009	749.6	770.3	772.5	779.8	771.2	750.4	703.2	695.0	754.0	773.8	778.8	772.6	755.9

Average Weekly Hours by Selected Industry: Pennsylvania, 2007–2009

(Not seasonally adjusted.)

Industry and year	January	February	March	April	May	June	July	August	September	October	November	December	Annual average
Total Private													
2007	33.3	33.0	33.4	33.9	33.9	34.0	34.2	34.0	34.1	33.8	33.9	34.2	33.8
2008	33.6	33.5	34.0	33.9	33.7	34.0	33.8	33.8	33.7	33.7	33.8	33.3	33.7
2009	33.0	33.4	33.1	32.9	33.0	32.9	33.0	33.2	32.9	32.9	33.3	33.1	33.1
Goods-Producing													
2007	38.6	37.4	38.3	38.8	39.2	39.4	39.4	39.4	39.7	39.6	39.7	40.0	39.1
2008	39.7	39.2	40.1	40.2	39.4	39.8	39.4	39.4	38.4	38.8	38.6	38.1	39.3
2009	37.7	37.8	37.8	37.1	37.6	38.0	37.9	38.5	37.8	38.2	38.6	38.4	38.0
Construction													
2007	37.1	34.8	36.4	37.6	39.0	39.0	38.8	38.2	38.9	38.5	38.2	38.0	37.9
2008	38.5	36.8	38.6	39.1	38.0	39.2	39.1	39.1	38.1	38.7	37.8	36.7	38.3
2009	36.1	36.5	37.4	36.8	37.6	37.3	37.9	37.9	36.5	36.9	36.8	36.6	37.0
Manufacturing													
2007	39.0	38.1	38.8	39.1	39.1	39.4	39.6	39.8	40.1	40.0	40.3	40.5	39.5
2008	40.1	40.0	40.6	40.6	40.0	40.2	39.7	40.0	40.2	40.4	40.3	39.7	40.2
2009	39.2	39.0	38.7	38.0	38.5	39.0	38.6	39.3	38.7	39.0	39.5	39.3	38.9
Trade, Transportation, and Utilities													
2007	33.3	32.6	33.3	33.8	33.8	34.2	34.3	34.0	33.9	33.5	33.7	34.0	33.7
2008	32.9	32.8	33.7	33.3	33.6	33.9	33.9	34.1	34.1	33.8	33.7	33.7	33.6
2009	33.2	33.4	33.1	33.3	33.7	33.6	33.5	33.6	33.9	33.5	33.6	33.7	33.5
Information													
2007	34.8	34.5	33.5	34.8	33.5	33.7	34.5	33.3	34.1	33.6	33.7	34.8	34.1
2008	33.5	33.9	35.3	34.6	33.7	33.8	32.6	32.6	32.1	32.2	32.2	32.1	33.2
2009	32.1	32.0	32.1	31.6	31.4	31.9	31.9	32.2	31.4	31.1	31.9	31.5	31.8
Financial Activities													
2007	34.6	34.6	35.3	35.6	35.0	35.0	35.8	35.7	36.1	35.9	36.4	37.2	35.6
2008	37.0	36.9	36.6	36.0	35.8	35.3	34.6	34.7	35.1	35.4	36.1	35.7	35.8
2009	36.0	36.3	36.3	35.3	35.8	35.4	35.3	35.5	35.0	35.2	36.0	35.6	35.6
Professional and Business Services													
2007	34.5	34.5	34.3	35.4	35.1	35.1	35.5	35.2	35.7	34.8	34.8	35.5	35.0
2008	34.3	34.6	35.0	35.1	35.0	35.3	35.1	35.3	35.2	35.2	35.6	34.3	35.0
2009	34.0	34.8	34.5	34.0	34.3	34.0	34.1	34.6	33.7	34.1	34.6	34.2	34.2
Education and Health Services													
2007	32.3	32.6	32.7	33.0	32.7	33.1	33.2	32.8	32.9	32.5	32.7	32.9	32.8
2008	32.7	32.8	33.0	32.6	32.5	32.8	32.6	32.5	32.6	32.5	32.9	32.3	32.7
2009	32.0	32.4	32.4	32.4	32.0	31.7	32.1	32.2	31.8	31.8	32.1	32.0	32.1
Leisure and Hospitality													
2007	24.0	24.5	25.1	25.8	26.3	26.0	25.8	26.1	25.4	25.4	25.2	25.4	25.4
2008	24.3	24.4	24.2	24.8	25.1	25.5	25.5	25.3	25.0	25.4	24.5	24.4	24.9
2009	23.6	24.8	24.0	24.1	24.3	24.0	24.2	24.3	23.8	23.7	23.7	23.6	24.0
Other Services													
2007	29.2	29.3	29.6	30.0	29.6	29.6	29.9	29.9	29.8	29.7	29.4	29.2	29.6
2008	29.3	29.3	30.2	30.3	30.1	30.7	31.3	31.3	31.8	31.3	31.7	31.7	30.8
2009	31.6	31.3	30.7	30.5	30.4	30.5	30.9	31.4	30.9	31.4	31.8	31.3	31.1

Average Hourly Earnings by Selected Industry: Pennsylvania, 2007–2009

(Dollars, not seasonally adjusted.)

Industry and year	January	February	March	April	May	June	July	August	September	October	November	December	Annual average
Total Private													
2007	20.15	20.12	20.01	20.10	19.94	19.92	19.98	20.00	20.14	20.11	20.14	20.28	20.07
2008	20.30	20.34	20.37	20.37	20.32	20.35	20.40	20.39	20.51	20.55	20.68	20.58	20.43
2009	20.65	20.65	20.70	20.68	20.64	20.62	20.64	20.76	20.82	20.87	20.94	20.94	20.74
Goods-Producing													
2007	21.34	21.27	21.21	21.41	21.26	21.32	21.24	21.32	21.41	21.46	21.56	21.64	21.37
2008	21.71	21.69	21.82	21.85	21.90	21.92	21.95	22.06	22.18	22.29	22.32	22.13	21.98
2009	22.15	22.25	22.37	22.42	22.38	22.39	22.49	22.60	22.62	22.74	22.79	22.91	22.51
Construction													
2007	24.23	23.96	23.82	23.86	23.70	23.72	23.56	23.80	23.65	23.80	24.06	23.96	23.83
2008	24.04	23.81	23.96	23.97	24.08	24.04	23.82	23.93	23.84	23.98	23.92	24.21	23.96
2009	24.18	24.32	24.28	24.26	24.43	24.51	24.53	24.79	24.75	24.89	24.89	24.99	24.57
Manufacturing													
2007	20.52	20.57	20.47	20.67	20.54	20.60	20.54	20.57	20.73	20.73	20.70	20.81	20.62
2008	20.88	20.91	21.05	21.10	21.04	21.07	21.17	21.19	21.24	21.32	21.41	21.32	21.14
2009	21.42	21.49	21.62	21.70	21.64	21.64	21.77	21.74	21.80	21.81	21.90	22.06	21.71
Trade, Transportation, and Utilities													
2007	17.56	17.70	17.57	17.67	17.47	17.56	17.58	17.75	17.84	17.81	17.60	17.76	17.66
2008	17.74	17.84	17.87	17.91	17.79	17.85	17.94	17.82	17.97	18.06	18.26	18.20	17.94
2009	18.34	18.39	18.46	18.46	18.50	18.39	18.39	18.58	18.69	18.61	18.67	18.59	18.51
Information													
2007	24.24	23.93	23.80	23.61	23.45	23.20	23.00	22.88	22.87	23.01	22.91	22.97	23.32
2008	23.07	23.20	23.22	23.23	23.02	23.26	23.32	23.51	23.31	23.14	22.93	22.91	23.18
2009	22.79	22.58	22.51	22.61	22.26	22.45	22.35	22.25	22.14	22.23	22.18	22.16	22.38
Financial Activities													
2007	25.28	25.24	25.36	25.55	25.61	25.58	25.59	25.53	25.64	25.66	25.65	25.76	25.54
2008	25.50	25.74	25.83	25.70	25.80	26.01	26.03	26.12	26.23	26.30	26.45	26.47	26.01
2009	26.62	26.78	26.74	26.88	26.68	26.69	26.78	26.87	26.88	26.89	27.04	27.11	26.83
Professional and Business Services													
2007	25.01	25.21	25.04	25.07	24.84	24.68	24.71	24.62	24.72	24.61	24.72	24.95	24.84
2008	24.92	24.98	25.06	24.92	24.95	24.95	24.78	24.94	24.99	25.12	25.34	25.41	25.03
2009	25.50	25.69	25.73	25.76	25.94	25.89	25.89	26.10	26.15	26.24	26.35	26.42	25.97
Education and Health Services													
2007	19.13	18.92	18.86	18.94	18.97	18.92	19.11	19.12	19.25	19.13	19.23	19.34	19.08
2008	19.37	19.24	19.21	19.35	19.34	19.44	19.63	19.42	19.53	19.49	19.51	19.42	19.41
2009	19.31	19.14	19.16	19.16	19.17	19.23	19.31	19.36	19.47	19.43	19.40	19.43	19.30
Leisure and Hospitality													
2007	12.67	12.71	12.61	12.62	12.52	12.45	12.44	12.41	12.52	12.59	12.68	12.80	12.58
2008	12.67	12.78	12.86	12.74	12.82	12.67	12.72	12.66	12.88	12.84	12.83	12.84	12.77
2009	12.75	12.60	12.55	12.53	12.40	12.33	12.25	12.23	12.39	12.51	12.53	12.54	12.46
Other Services													
2007	18.04	17.81	17.80	17.56	17.31	17.17	17.29	17.14	17.25	17.30	17.45	17.56	17.47
2008	17.67	17.91	17.70	17.83	17.88	17.96	18.13	18.26	18.29	18.09	18.09	18.28	18.01
2009	18.39	18.39	18.49	18.62	18.48	18.39	18.32	18.21	18.24	18.28	18.32	18.38	18.37

Average Weekly Earnings by Selected Industry: Pennsylvania, 2007–2009

(Dollars, not seasonally adjusted.)

Industry and year	January	February	March	April	May	June	July	August	September	October	November	December	Annual average
Total Private													
2007	671.00	663.96	668.33	681.39	675.97	677.28	683.32	680.00	686.77	679.72	682.75	693.58	678.37
2008	682.08	681.39	692.58	690.54	684.78	691.90	689.52	689.18	691.19	692.54	698.98	685.31	688.49
2009	681.45	689.71	685.17	680.37	681.12	678.40	681.12	689.23	684.98	686.62	697.30	693.11	686.49
Goods-Producing													
2007	823.72	795.50	812.34	830.71	833.39	840.01	836.86	840.01	849.98	849.82	855.93	865.60	835.57
2008	861.89	850.25	874.98	878.37	862.86	872.42	864.83	869.16	851.71	864.85	861.55	843.15	863.81
2009	835.06	841.05	845.59	831.78	841.49	850.82	852.37	870.10	855.04	868.67	879.69	879.74	855.38
Construction													
2007	898.93	833.81	867.05	897.14	924.30	925.08	914.13	909.16	919.99	916.30	919.09	910.48	903.16
2008	925.54	876.21	924.86	937.23	915.04	942.37	931.36	935.66	908.30	928.03	904.18	888.51	917.67
2009	872.90	887.68	908.07	892.77	918.57	914.22	929.69	939.54	903.38	918.44	915.95	914.63	909.09
Manufacturing													
2007	800.28	783.72	794.24	808.20	803.11	811.64	813.38	818.69	831.27	829.20	834.21	842.81	814.49
2008	837.29	836.40	854.63	856.66	841.60	847.01	840.45	847.60	853.85	861.33	862.82	846.40	849.83
2009	839.66	838.11	836.69	824.60	833.14	843.96	840.32	854.38	843.66	850.59	865.05	866.96	844.52
Trade, Transportation, and Utilities													
2007	584.75	577.02	585.08	597.25	590.49	600.55	602.99	603.50	604.78	596.64	593.12	603.84	595.14
2008	583.65	585.15	602.22	596.40	597.74	605.12	608.17	607.66	612.78	610.43	615.36	613.34	602.78
2009	608.89	614.23	611.03	614.72	623.45	617.90	616.07	624.29	633.59	623.44	627.31	626.48	620.09
Information													
2007	843.55	825.59	797.30	821.63	785.58	781.84	793.50	761.90	779.87	773.14	772.07	799.36	795.21
2008	772.85	786.48	819.67	803.76	775.77	786.19	760.23	766.43	748.25	745.11	738.35	735.41	769.58
2009	731.56	722.56	722.57	714.48	698.96	716.16	712.97	716.45	695.20	691.35	707.54	698.04	711.68
Financial Activities													
2007	874.69	873.30	895.21	909.58	896.35	895.30	916.12	911.42	925.60	921.19	933.66	958.27	909.22
2008	943.50	949.81	945.38	925.20	923.64	918.15	900.64	906.36	920.67	931.02	954.85	944.98	931.16
2009	958.32	972.11	970.66	948.86	955.14	944.83	945.33	953.89	940.80	946.53	973.44	965.12	955.15
Professional and Business Services													
2007	862.85	869.75	858.87	887.48	871.88	866.27	877.21	866.62	882.50	856.43	860.26	885.73	869.40
2008	854.76	864.31	877.10	874.69	873.25	880.74	869.78	880.38	879.65	884.22	902.10	871.56	876.05
2009	867.00	894.01	887.69	875.84	889.74	880.26	882.85	903.06	881.26	894.78	911.71	903.56	888.17
Education and Health Services													
2007	617.90	616.79	616.72	625.02	620.32	626.25	634.45	627.14	633.33	621.73	628.82	636.29	625.82
2008	633.40	631.07	633.93	630.81	628.55	637.63	639.94	631.15	636.68	633.43	641.88	627.27	634.71
2009	617.92	620.14	620.78	620.78	613.44	609.59	619.85	623.39	619.15	617.87	622.74	621.76	619.53
Leisure and Hospitality													
2007	304.08	311.40	316.51	325.60	329.28	323.70	320.95	323.90	318.01	319.79	319.54	325.12	319.53
2008	307.88	311.83	311.21	315.95	321.78	323.09	324.36	320.30	322.00	326.14	314.34	313.30	317.97
2009	300.90	312.48	301.20	301.97	301.32	295.92	296.45	297.19	294.88	296.49	296.96	295.94	299.04
Other Services													
2007	526.77	521.83	526.88	526.80	512.38	508.23	516.97	512.49	514.05	513.81	513.03	512.75	517.11
2008	517.73	524.76	534.54	540.25	538.19	551.37	567.47	571.54	581.62	566.22	573.45	579.48	554.71
2009	581.12	575.61	567.64	567.91	561.79	560.90	566.09	571.79	563.62	573.99	582.58	575.29	571.31

RHODE ISLAND
At a Glance

Population:
    1990 census: 1,003,464
    2000 census: 1,048,319
    2009 estimate: 1,053,209

Percent change in population:
    1990–2000: 4.5%
    2000–2009: 0.5%

Percent change in total nonfarm employment:
    1990–2009: 1.1%
    2008–2009: -4.8%

Industry with the largest growth in employment, 1990–2009 (thousands):
    Education and health services, 31.0

Industry with the largest decline or smallest growth in employment, 1990–2009 (thousands):
    Manufacturing, -47.1

Civilian labor force:
    1990: 521,633
    2000: 543,404
    2009: 567,093

Unemployment rate and rank among states (lowest to highest):
    1990: 6.1%, 39th
    2000: 4.2%, 33rd
    2009: 11.2%, 47th

Employment by Industry, 2009

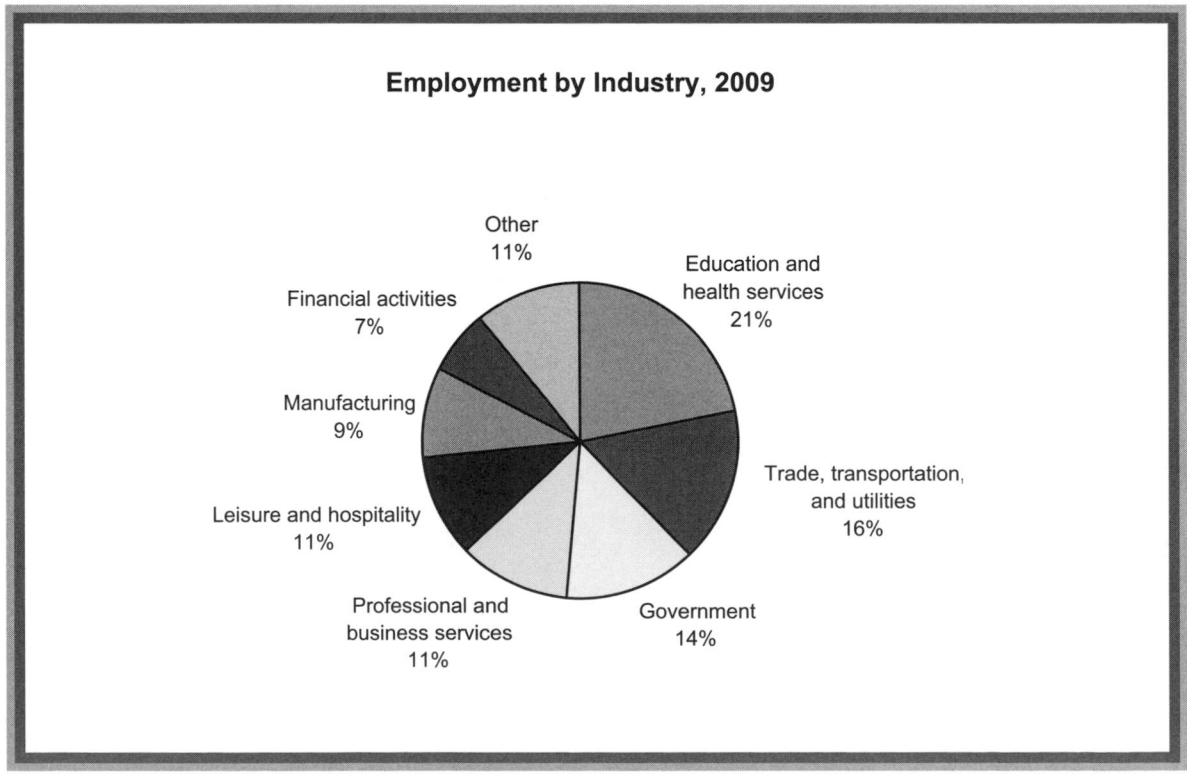

- Other 11%
- Financial activities 7%
- Manufacturing 9%
- Leisure and hospitality 11%
- Professional and business services 11%
- Education and health services 21%
- Trade, transportation, and utilities 16%
- Government 14%

Employment by Industry: Rhode Island, Selected Years, 1990–2009

(Numbers in thousands, not seasonally adjusted.)

Industry and year	January	February	March	April	May	June	July	August	September	October	November	December	Annual average
Total Nonfarm													
1990	449.6	449.9	453.1	453.6	459.0	460.9	447.4	451.5	458.2	456.8	455.7	452.4	454.0
2000	460.2	462.3	467.3	475.0	482.0	481.8	474.1	476.1	482.2	485.3	486.7	487.6	476.7
2001	468.4	471.0	472.8	479.1	483.2	484.2	474.1	478.5	481.8	482.6	482.1	483.1	478.4
2002	466.0	467.1	471.4	478.6	484.3	485.3	475.4	479.5	484.7	486.0	487.1	487.2	479.4
2003	469.9	469.9	473.5	482.0	489.4	490.7	482.7	485.1	490.5	492.1	492.8	492.4	484.3
2004	473.2	475.5	478.5	486.0	494.4	494.7	487.7	489.3	494.7	496.4	496.5	495.3	488.5
2005	475.8	478.6	481.0	491.0	495.7	498.1	491.2	492.8	497.5	496.7	497.8	496.1	491.0
2006	475.5	478.5	482.9	494.0	497.3	500.6	491.4	493.8	500.6	501.5	501.9	501.3	493.3
2007	481.9	483.5	485.9	493.2	499.5	501.3	492.9	492.7	495.9	496.0	495.0	493.4	492.6
2008	474.3	476.4	478.2	484.9	489.9	490.5	480.3	481.2	485.3	483.8	480.9	477.2	481.9
2009	455.3	456.5	455.9	459.8	466.0	466.2	455.9	455.6	460.8	461.2	459.0	455.7	459.0
Total Private													
1990	386.5	386.6	389.9	389.6	393.7	396.4	389.7	394.7	396.7	393.8	392.1	388.9	391.6
2000	395.8	397.9	402.1	409.8	414.5	417.7	412.7	415.9	418.8	420.0	420.9	421.8	412.3
2001	403.0	405.4	407.0	413.2	416.8	418.6	412.4	417.3	417.3	416.4	415.1	415.9	413.2
2002	399.3	400.3	404.3	411.4	416.6	418.6	413.5	417.8	419.4	419.1	419.7	419.6	413.3
2003	402.8	402.8	406.1	414.8	421.7	422.9	420.7	423.0	424.8	425.4	426.0	425.5	418.0
2004	407.1	409.2	411.6	419.8	427.4	428.0	425.7	427.5	429.5	430.5	430.0	429.5	423.0
2005	410.3	412.8	415.1	425.2	429.6	432.2	429.7	432.1	433.4	430.9	431.7	430.2	426.1
2006	410.1	412.6	417.0	428.4	431.5	435.0	430.1	432.8	435.9	435.8	435.5	435.3	428.3
2007	416.7	418.1	420.6	427.9	433.5	436.4	431.4	431.5	432.0	431.3	430.2	428.4	428.2
2008	409.7	411.9	413.3	420.1	424.4	426.0	420.1	421.7	422.9	420.7	416.9	413.5	418.4
2009	392.2	393.2	392.7	396.3	402.4	403.2	398.0	398.1	399.5	398.9	396.5	393.3	397.0
Goods-Producing													
1990	113.5	113.2	113.5	113.6	114.3	115.9	110.8	115.5	115.4	115.1	113.6	111.3	113.8
2000	87.1	87.2	88.2	88.6	90.0	91.5	86.6	90.8	91.3	91.6	91.1	90.7	89.5
2001	87.8	87.7	87.8	88.5	88.3	88.4	83.8	87.3	87.3	86.8	85.4	85.0	87.0
2002	81.1	81.0	81.9	82.1	83.0	83.6	79.4	82.8	82.7	82.2	82.0	80.9	81.9
2003	77.5	76.3	77.0	79.2	80.3	81.0	78.5	81.3	81.8	81.3	81.1	79.9	79.6
2004	75.5	75.0	75.4	77.5	78.5	79.5	77.8	79.8	79.9	80.3	79.9	79.1	78.2
2005	74.8	74.2	74.5	77.1	78.0	79.1	76.4	78.7	78.6	77.6	77.8	76.8	77.0
2006	73.1	72.8	73.4	76.0	76.7	77.8	75.5	77.5	77.3	76.9	76.4	76.0	75.8
2007	72.6	71.6	71.9	73.0	74.2	74.8	72.7	74.3	74.1	73.8	73.1	71.7	73.2
2008	68.4	67.4	67.9	69.3	70.2	70.8	68.4	70.0	69.8	68.5	67.2	65.5	68.6
2009	60.9	59.0	58.5	59.3	59.7	59.9	58.4	59.2	58.8	58.9	58.7	57.5	59.1
Mining and Logging													
1990	0.2	0.2	0.2	0.2	0.2	0.2	0.2	0.2	0.2	0.2	0.2	0.2	0.2
2000	0.2	0.2	0.2	0.2	0.2	0.2	0.2	0.2	0.2	0.3	0.3	0.2	0.2
2001	0.2	0.2	0.2	0.2	0.3	0.3	0.3	0.3	0.2	0.3	0.2	0.2	0.2
2002	0.2	0.2	0.2	0.2	0.2	0.2	0.3	0.2	0.2	0.2	0.2	0.2	0.2
2003	0.2	0.1	0.2	0.2	0.2	0.2	0.2	0.2	0.2	0.2	0.2	0.2	0.2
2004	0.2	0.2	0.2	0.2	0.2	0.2	0.2	0.2	0.3	0.3	0.3	0.3	0.2
2005	0.2	0.2	0.2	0.3	0.3	0.3	0.3	0.3	0.3	0.3	0.3	0.3	0.3
2006	0.2	0.2	0.2	0.3	0.3	0.3	0.3	0.3	0.3	0.3	0.3	0.3	0.3
2007	0.2	0.2	0.2	0.3	0.3	0.3	0.3	0.3	0.3	0.3	0.3	0.2	0.3
2008	0.2	0.2	0.2	0.2	0.3	0.3	0.3	0.3	0.3	0.3	0.3	0.2	0.3
2009	0.2	0.1	0.2	0.2	0.2	0.2	0.2	0.2	0.2	0.2	0.2	0.2	0.2
Construction													
1990	16.6	16.4	16.9	18.3	19.1	19.9	20.2	20.1	19.7	19.0	18.3	17.2	18.4
2000	16.4	15.8	17.0	17.8	18.3	18.9	19.1	19.1	19.1	19.0	18.9	18.4	18.1
2001	16.6	16.5	16.9	18.6	19.2	19.8	20.3	20.5	20.3	20.0	19.8	19.5	19.0
2002	17.4	17.3	18.0	19.1	19.9	20.4	20.4	20.6	20.5	20.1	19.9	19.4	19.4
2003	17.2	16.6	17.3	19.6	21.1	21.8	22.8	23.0	23.0	22.7	22.4	21.5	20.8
2004	18.6	18.0	18.4	20.3	21.1	21.8	22.5	22.4	22.3	22.4	22.2	21.6	21.0
2005	18.8	18.3	18.6	21.3	22.3	23.4	23.5	23.6	23.5	22.8	23.1	22.2	21.8
2006	19.8	19.4	20.0	22.5	23.3	24.3	24.4	24.7	24.4	24.0	23.7	23.3	22.8
2007	21.0	19.9	20.4	21.6	22.8	23.4	23.6	23.4	23.0	22.8	22.5	21.4	22.2
2008	18.8	18.3	18.7	20.3	21.3	21.9	22.0	21.9	21.7	20.9	20.2	19.0	20.4
2009	16.4	15.9	15.9	17.1	17.8	18.0	18.0	18.0	17.5	17.6	17.3	17.0	17.2
Manufacturing													
1990	96.7	96.6	96.4	95.1	95.0	95.8	90.4	95.2	95.5	95.9	95.1	93.9	95.1
2000	70.5	71.2	71.0	70.6	71.5	72.4	67.3	71.5	72.0	72.3	71.9	72.1	71.1
2001	71.0	71.0	70.7	69.7	68.8	68.3	63.2	66.5	66.8	66.5	65.4	65.3	67.8
2002	63.5	63.5	63.7	62.8	62.9	63.0	58.7	62.0	62.0	61.9	61.9	61.3	62.3
2003	60.1	59.6	59.5	59.4	59.0	59.0	55.5	58.1	58.6	58.4	58.5	58.2	58.7
2004	56.7	56.8	56.8	57.0	57.2	57.5	55.1	57.2	57.3	57.6	57.4	57.2	57.0
2005	55.8	55.7	55.7	55.5	55.4	55.4	52.6	54.8	54.8	54.5	54.4	54.3	54.9
2006	53.1	53.2	53.2	53.2	53.1	53.2	50.8	52.5	52.6	52.6	52.4	52.4	52.7
2007	51.4	51.5	51.3	51.1	51.1	51.1	48.8	50.6	50.8	50.7	50.3	50.1	50.7
2008	49.4	48.9	49.0	48.8	48.6	48.6	46.1	47.8	47.8	47.3	46.7	46.3	47.9
2009	44.3	43.0	42.4	42.0	41.7	41.7	40.2	41.0	41.1	41.1	41.2	40.3	41.7

Employment by Industry: Rhode Island, Selected Years, 1990–2009—*Continued*

(Numbers in thousands, not seasonally adjusted.)

Industry and year	January	February	March	April	May	June	July	August	September	October	November	December	Annual average
Service-Providing													
1990	336.1	336.7	339.6	340.0	344.7	345.0	336.6	336.0	342.8	341.7	342.1	341.1	340.2
2000	373.1	375.1	379.1	386.4	392.0	390.3	387.5	385.3	390.9	393.7	395.6	396.9	387.2
2001	380.6	383.3	385.0	390.6	394.9	395.8	390.3	391.2	394.5	395.8	396.7	398.1	391.4
2002	384.9	386.1	389.5	396.5	401.3	401.7	396.0	396.7	402.0	403.8	405.1	406.3	397.5
2003	392.4	393.6	396.5	402.8	409.1	409.7	404.2	403.8	408.7	410.8	411.7	412.5	404.7
2004	397.7	400.5	403.1	408.5	415.9	415.2	409.9	409.5	414.8	416.1	416.6	416.2	410.3
2005	401.0	404.4	406.5	413.9	417.7	419.0	414.8	414.1	418.9	419.1	420.0	419.3	414.1
2006	402.4	405.7	409.5	418.0	420.6	422.8	415.9	416.3	423.3	424.6	425.5	425.3	417.5
2007	409.3	411.9	414.0	420.2	425.3	426.5	420.2	418.4	421.8	422.2	421.9	421.7	419.5
2008	405.9	409.0	410.3	415.6	419.7	419.7	411.9	411.2	415.5	415.3	413.7	411.7	413.3
2009	394.4	397.5	397.4	400.5	406.3	406.3	397.5	396.4	402.0	402.3	400.3	398.2	399.9
Trade, Transportation, and Utilities													
1990	79.4	78.0	78.6	76.8	77.3	78.0	75.2	76.3	77.2	77.4	77.5	78.2	77.5
2000	77.5	76.9	77.1	79.0	79.1	79.3	78.3	79.2	80.3	81.3	83.0	84.2	79.6
2001	78.9	77.9	77.7	78.5	78.6	79.7	78.7	78.8	79.2	79.8	81.4	82.4	79.3
2002	79.0	77.7	77.9	79.1	79.9	81.0	80.0	80.1	81.2	82.0	83.3	84.5	80.5
2003	79.6	78.5	78.6	79.3	80.4	81.3	80.2	80.4	81.3	81.9	83.4	84.3	80.8
2004	79.7	78.9	78.8	78.3	80.2	80.8	79.8	79.6	80.2	81.1	82.2	83.1	80.2
2005	78.9	78.3	78.3	79.3	79.9	80.7	79.8	80.0	80.1	80.7	82.1	83.1	80.1
2006	78.6	77.7	78.0	79.2	79.5	80.2	79.0	79.0	79.9	80.6	82.1	83.2	79.8
2007	79.1	78.0	78.2	78.9	79.8	80.7	79.8	79.6	79.7	79.8	81.2	82.2	79.8
2008	77.8	76.7	76.6	77.0	77.4	78.3	77.2	77.3	77.3	77.4	77.6	78.0	77.4
2009	73.8	72.8	72.4	71.8	73.2	73.8	72.5	72.5	73.2	72.6	73.2	73.6	73.0
Wholesale Trade													
1990	17.4	17.2	17.3	17.4	16.8	17.1	16.5	17.0	17.1	16.9	16.8	16.7	17.0
2000	15.7	15.9	16.0	16.5	16.5	16.7	16.5	16.7	16.8	17.0	17.1	17.2	16.5
2001	16.0	16.2	16.3	16.5	16.5	16.6	16.6	16.7	16.6	16.7	16.7	16.8	16.5
2002	16.5	16.3	16.4	16.5	16.6	16.7	16.4	16.4	16.3	16.4	16.5	16.4	16.5
2003	16.4	16.2	16.3	16.4	16.6	16.7	16.5	16.4	16.4	16.4	16.4	16.3	16.4
2004	16.1	16.0	16.1	16.3	16.4	16.6	16.6	16.6	16.5	16.6	16.6	16.7	16.4
2005	16.3	16.4	16.5	16.8	16.9	17.0	16.9	17.0	16.9	16.9	16.9	17.0	16.8
2006	16.7	16.7	16.8	17.0	17.0	17.1	17.1	17.1	17.1	17.2	17.2	17.2	17.0
2007	17.0	16.9	16.9	17.2	17.3	17.4	17.4	17.3	17.1	17.2	17.3	17.4	17.2
2008	16.9	16.9	16.9	16.9	17.0	17.1	17.0	16.9	16.9	16.9	16.8	16.7	16.9
2009	16.3	16.2	16.1	16.0	16.1	16.2	15.9	15.9	16.0	15.9	16.0	15.9	16.0
Retail Trade													
1990	52.5	51.3	51.8	49.8	50.8	51.0	49.6	50.2	50.2	50.7	51.0	51.6	50.9
2000	51.1	50.4	50.4	51.5	51.5	51.5	51.2	51.7	52.3	53.0	54.7	55.8	52.1
2001	52.0	50.7	50.4	50.7	50.9	51.8	51.3	51.4	51.3	51.7	53.3	54.4	51.7
2002	51.7	50.9	51.0	51.8	52.4	53.1	53.1	53.3	53.7	54.2	55.5	56.8	53.1
2003	52.4	51.5	51.3	51.8	52.4	53.1	52.9	53.3	53.3	54.0	55.5	56.5	53.2
2004	52.6	52.0	51.8	51.7	52.5	53.0	52.9	52.8	52.5	53.5	54.7	55.4	53.0
2005	52.1	51.4	51.3	51.7	52.0	52.5	52.2	52.2	51.9	52.6	54.0	54.8	52.4
2006	51.3	50.4	50.6	51.3	51.4	51.8	51.4	51.3	51.4	52.1	53.6	54.6	51.8
2007	51.3	50.5	50.7	50.7	51.3	51.9	51.7	51.6	51.1	51.2	52.5	53.2	51.5
2008	50.1	49.1	49.0	49.1	49.3	49.9	49.6	49.6	49.1	49.5	50.0	50.2	49.5
2009	47.3	46.5	46.3	45.9	46.9	47.3	47.0	46.9	46.7	46.4	47.0	47.3	46.8
Transportation and Utilities													
1990	9.5	9.5	9.5	9.6	9.7	9.9	9.1	9.1	9.9	9.8	9.7	9.9	9.6
2000	10.7	10.6	10.7	11.0	11.1	11.1	10.6	10.8	11.2	11.3	11.2	11.2	10.9
2001	10.9	11.0	11.0	11.3	11.2	11.3	10.8	10.7	11.3	11.4	11.4	11.2	11.1
2002	10.8	10.5	10.5	10.8	10.9	11.2	10.5	10.4	11.2	11.4	11.3	11.3	10.9
2003	10.8	10.8	11.0	11.1	11.4	11.5	10.8	10.7	11.6	11.5	11.5	11.5	11.2
2004	11.0	10.9	10.9	10.3	11.3	11.2	10.3	10.2	11.2	11.0	10.9	11.0	10.9
2005	10.5	10.5	10.5	10.8	11.0	11.2	10.7	10.8	11.3	11.2	11.2	11.3	10.9
2006	10.6	10.6	10.6	10.9	11.1	11.3	10.5	10.6	11.4	11.3	11.3	11.4	11.0
2007	10.8	10.6	10.6	11.0	11.2	11.4	10.7	10.7	11.5	11.4	11.4	11.6	11.1
2008	10.8	10.7	10.7	11.0	11.1	11.3	10.6	10.8	11.3	11.0	10.8	11.1	10.9
2009	10.2	10.1	10.0	9.9	10.2	10.3	9.6	9.7	10.5	10.3	10.2	10.4	10.1
Information													
1990	10.3	10.2	10.1	10.0	10.0	10.1	10.2	10.1	10.1	9.8	9.9	10.0	10.0
2000	10.8	10.9	10.8	10.9	11.0	11.2	11.2	10.0	11.1	11.1	11.1	11.1	10.9
2001	11.1	11.1	11.1	11.2	11.4	11.4	11.4	11.3	11.3	11.2	11.2	11.3	11.3
2002	11.3	11.2	11.3	11.2	11.2	11.3	11.3	11.2	11.2	10.9	11.1	11.2	11.2
2003	11.1	11.1	11.0	11.0	11.0	11.2	11.0	11.0	10.8	11.0	11.0	10.9	11.0
2004	11.1	11.0	11.1	11.1	11.0	10.9	10.7	10.7	10.6	10.6	10.6	10.6	10.8
2005	10.8	10.8	10.7	10.7	10.7	10.7	10.8	10.8	10.7	10.8	10.9	11.0	10.8
2006	11.0	10.9	11.0	11.3	11.3	11.4	10.8	10.7	10.7	10.6	10.8	10.9	11.0
2007	10.5	10.4	10.5	10.5	10.6	10.6	10.6	10.7	10.6	10.5	10.8	10.8	10.6
2008	10.6	10.9	10.9	10.8	10.6	10.9	10.6	11.0	10.8	10.8	10.5	10.4	10.7
2009	10.4	10.3	10.2	10.4	10.4	10.4	10.0	10.0	9.9	9.9	9.9	9.9	10.1

Employment by Industry: Rhode Island, Selected Years, 1990–2009—*Continued*

(Numbers in thousands, not seasonally adjusted.)

Industry and year	January	February	March	April	May	June	July	August	September	October	November	December	Annual average
Financial Activities													
1990	26.7	26.7	26.9	26.5	26.7	27.1	27.1	26.9	26.8	26.9	26.8	26.5	26.8
2000	30.0	30.0	30.2	30.7	30.5	31.4	32.0	31.7	31.6	31.5	31.7	32.0	31.1
2001	32.0	32.1	32.3	32.0	32.0	32.5	32.5	32.3	32.2	32.2	32.2	32.4	32.2
2002	32.3	32.3	32.2	32.6	32.6	32.9	33.3	33.2	33.1	33.2	33.3	33.6	32.9
2003	33.1	33.2	33.5	33.2	33.5	33.9	34.0	34.0	33.8	33.8	33.9	34.1	33.7
2004	33.8	33.8	33.8	33.9	34.2	34.3	34.2	34.2	34.0	34.1	34.1	34.1	34.0
2005	33.7	33.8	33.8	34.3	34.3	34.5	34.7	34.7	34.5	34.2	34.3	34.6	34.3
2006	34.2	34.1	34.4	34.5	34.8	34.9	35.2	35.6	35.7	35.6	35.7	36.1	35.1
2007	35.2	35.3	35.2	35.3	35.4	35.3	35.0	34.7	34.6	34.1	34.1	34.0	34.9
2008	33.6	33.7	33.5	33.4	33.5	33.5	33.3	33.2	33.3	32.4	32.3	32.3	33.2
2009	31.9	31.9	31.6	31.2	31.3	31.5	31.3	30.9	30.6	30.3	30.2	30.8	31.1
Professional and Business Services													
1990	39.5	39.9	40.7	41.8	42.3	43.1	44.2	44.3	44.7	43.8	43.8	43.4	42.6
2000	48.2	48.4	49.5	50.9	51.5	52.2	51.0	51.4	51.8	51.9	51.7	51.9	50.8
2001	48.4	48.9	49.0	50.6	50.7	51.1	50.7	51.5	51.6	51.8	50.9	50.6	50.5
2002	47.2	47.0	47.7	49.4	49.4	50.1	48.9	49.3	49.7	49.7	49.4	48.8	48.9
2003	46.4	46.5	47.0	49.2	49.8	50.9	50.9	51.5	51.4	52.2	52.0	52.0	50.0
2004	49.9	50.3	50.9	53.2	53.7	54.5	54.3	55.0	55.4	55.6	55.2	54.7	53.6
2005	51.8	52.2	52.7	55.2	55.3	55.9	56.2	56.9	57.2	56.2	56.2	55.8	55.1
2006	52.6	53.0	53.6	56.6	56.8	57.9	56.9	57.8	58.7	58.4	57.8	57.3	56.5
2007	54.3	54.0	54.3	56.4	56.9	58.0	56.8	56.8	56.6	56.2	56.0	55.7	56.0
2008	53.2	52.9	53.1	55.2	55.3	56.2	55.4	55.5	55.9	55.5	54.8	53.6	54.7
2009	51.1	51.0	51.1	52.5	52.7	53.5	52.5	52.8	53.0	54.0	52.7	50.9	52.3
Education and Health Services													
1990	68.7	70.2	70.9	70.8	71.0	67.4	65.2	65.2	67.6	69.5	70.3	70.4	68.9
2000	81.1	83.2	84.0	84.8	84.8	80.2	80.3	80.0	83.2	85.0	86.1	86.1	83.2
2001	83.0	85.4	86.2	86.1	86.3	82.0	81.2	82.1	84.8	86.5	87.5	88.0	84.9
2002	85.6	87.7	88.7	88.9	89.1	84.6	84.0	85.1	88.4	90.3	91.5	92.2	88.0
2003	89.6	91.6	92.6	93.0	93.2	88.0	87.1	86.6	90.3	92.6	93.4	93.7	91.0
2004	90.8	93.3	94.4	95.0	95.2	89.9	89.1	88.9	92.7	94.6	95.4	95.9	92.9
2005	92.7	95.2	96.2	96.7	96.6	92.5	92.0	91.7	96.0	97.9	98.5	97.8	95.3
2006	94.0	97.4	98.6	99.2	98.2	94.4	93.4	93.1	96.8	99.7	100.5	100.0	97.1
2007	96.9	100.1	101.0	101.2	100.9	96.7	95.6	95.1	98.8	101.2	101.9	101.3	99.2
2008	97.8	101.4	102.1	102.0	101.5	97.3	95.9	96.0	99.4	102.2	102.5	102.5	100.1
2009	98.7	102.2	102.6	102.2	101.9	98.0	96.9	96.4	99.8	103.4	104.3	103.6	100.8
Leisure and Hospitality													
1990	32.5	32.5	33.2	34.3	36.2	38.8	40.5	40.1	38.7	35.1	34.1	33.1	35.7
2000	41.1	41.2	41.9	44.3	47.0	50.8	52.0	51.4	48.6	46.6	45.4	44.8	46.2
2001	41.1	41.7	42.2	45.4	48.4	51.8	52.4	52.2	49.8	47.0	45.2	44.8	46.8
2002	41.7	42.3	43.4	46.6	49.6	52.7	53.9	53.5	51.0	48.5	46.8	45.8	48.0
2003	43.3	43.4	44.0	47.1	50.4	53.1	55.2	54.6	52.3	49.6	47.9	47.2	49.0
2004	43.6	44.1	44.3	47.7	51.2	54.4	55.8	55.5	53.4	50.7	49.0	48.5	49.9
2005	44.7	45.4	45.8	48.8	51.4	55.1	55.8	55.3	53.2	50.5	48.8	48.1	50.2
2006	44.4	44.5	45.6	48.7	51.1	54.8	55.6	55.5	53.7	50.7	48.9	48.6	50.2
2007	45.5	46.0	46.7	49.6	52.4	56.4	57.1	56.7	54.6	52.6	50.0	49.5	51.4
2008	45.9	46.4	46.7	49.7	53.0	55.8	55.9	55.5	53.7	51.2	49.4	48.7	51.0
2009	43.6	44.1	44.4	46.8	51.0	53.6	53.7	53.9	52.4	48.4	45.9	45.0	48.6
Other Services													
1990	15.9	15.9	16.0	15.8	15.9	16.0	16.5	16.3	16.2	16.2	16.1	16.0	16.1
2000	20.0	20.1	20.4	20.6	20.6	21.1	21.3	21.4	20.9	21.0	20.8	21.0	20.8
2001	20.7	20.6	20.7	20.9	21.1	21.7	21.7	21.8	21.1	21.1	21.3	21.4	21.2
2002	21.1	21.1	21.2	21.5	21.8	22.4	22.7	22.6	22.1	22.3	22.3	22.6	22.0
2003	22.2	22.2	22.4	22.8	23.1	23.5	23.8	23.6	23.1	23.0	23.3	23.4	23.0
2004	22.7	22.8	22.9	23.1	23.4	23.7	24.0	23.8	23.3	23.5	23.6	23.5	23.4
2005	22.9	22.9	23.1	23.1	23.4	23.7	24.0	24.0	23.1	23.0	23.1	23.0	23.3
2006	22.2	22.2	22.4	22.9	23.1	23.6	23.7	23.6	23.1	23.3	23.3	23.2	23.1
2007	22.6	22.7	22.8	23.0	23.3	23.9	23.8	23.6	23.0	23.1	23.1	23.2	23.2
2008	22.4	22.5	22.5	22.7	22.9	23.2	23.4	23.2	22.7	22.7	22.6	22.5	22.8
2009	21.8	21.9	21.9	22.1	22.2	22.5	22.7	22.4	21.8	21.4	21.6	22.0	22.0
Government													
1990	63.1	63.3	63.2	64.0	65.3	64.5	57.7	56.8	61.5	63.0	63.6	63.5	62.4
2000	64.4	64.4	65.2	65.2	67.5	64.1	61.4	60.2	63.4	65.3	65.8	65.8	64.3
2001	65.4	65.6	65.8	65.9	66.4	65.6	61.7	61.2	64.5	66.2	67.0	67.2	65.2
2002	66.7	66.8	67.1	67.2	67.7	66.7	61.9	61.7	65.3	66.9	67.4	67.6	66.1
2003	67.1	67.1	67.4	67.2	67.7	67.8	62.0	62.1	65.7	66.7	66.8	66.9	66.2
2004	66.1	66.3	66.9	66.2	67.0	66.7	62.0	61.8	65.2	65.9	66.5	65.8	65.5
2005	65.5	65.8	65.9	65.8	66.1	65.9	61.5	60.7	64.1	65.8	66.1	65.9	64.9
2006	65.4	65.9	65.9	65.6	65.8	65.6	61.3	61.0	64.7	65.7	66.4	66.0	64.9
2007	65.2	65.4	65.3	65.3	66.0	64.9	61.5	61.2	63.9	64.7	64.8	65.0	64.4
2008	64.6	64.5	64.9	64.8	65.5	64.5	60.2	59.5	62.4	63.1	64.0	63.7	63.5
2009	63.1	63.3	63.2	63.5	63.6	63.0	57.9	57.5	61.3	62.3	62.5	62.4	62.0

Average Weekly Hours by Selected Industry: Rhode Island, 2007–2009

(Numbers in thousands, not seasonally adjusted.)

Industry and year	January	February	March	April	May	June	July	August	September	October	November	December	Annual average
Total Private													
2007	33.3	33.6	33.8	33.4	33.4	33.8	33.5	33.7	33.4	33.1	33.9	33.7	33.5
2008	33.7	33.8	34.2	33.9	34.2	34.5	34.3	34.3	34.0	34.0	34.0	33.8	34.1
2009	33.5	33.8	33.6	33.8	33.7	33.6	33.9	34.0	34.0	34.1	34.2	34.1	33.9
Goods-Producing													
2007	37.8	38.0	38.4	37.8	38.9	38.2	37.3	38.0	38.3	37.7	38.2	38.0	38.1
2008	38.5	37.7	38.5	37.6	39.4	39.7	38.9	38.8	38.8	38.3	37.9	37.4	38.5
2009	36.4	36.3	36.0	35.9	35.7	35.6	36.0	35.9	35.8	36.1	35.7	36.7	36.0
Construction													
2007	36.2	36.0	36.9	36.4	38.1	37.4	37.2	36.9	36.6	35.5	35.7	35.3	36.5
2008	34.1	34.3	35.4	34.9	37.5	38.0	38.1	37.4	36.8	37.8	36.2	36.1	36.5
2009	33.9	34.0	34.3	35.1	35.9	34.8	36.8	36.4	36.2	35.6	35.5	36.0	35.4
Manufacturing													
2007	38.5	38.7	39.0	38.4	39.4	38.7	37.6	38.6	39.1	38.7	39.3	38.9	38.7
2008	39.8	38.7	39.4	39.1	40.3	40.6	38.9	39.3	39.7	39.0	39.3	38.8	39.4
2009	38.7	38.3	38.0	37.3	36.9	37.4	37.4	38.4	38.2	38.5	37.9	38.6	38.0
Trade, Transportation, and Utilities													
2007	33.7	33.7	33.4	33.5	34.0	34.8	34.1	34.7	34.4	33.5	34.0	34.1	34.0
2008	34.1	34.4	35.5	34.7	35.1	34.8	35.0	35.0	34.7	34.1	33.8	34.8	34.7
2009	34.2	34.6	34.0	34.2	34.5	34.5	34.9	35.6	34.6	35.1	35.7	35.2	34.8
Professional and Business Services													
2007	34.6	36.3	36.4	36.5	37.1	36.0	35.6	34.4	35.0	35.1	35.7	35.5	35.7
2008	36.7	36.9	37.4	36.8	36.1	36.7	36.1	35.2	35.3	35.8	35.0	35.2	36.1
2009	36.1	36.1	35.7	36.4	36.5	36.7	37.1	37.2	37.2	37.3	36.9	36.0	36.6
Education and Health Services													
2007	32.3	32.4	32.4	31.7	31.4	32.4	31.9	31.8	31.7	31.8	32.9	31.9	32.1
2008	32.1	31.8	32.2	32.5	32.3	32.1	32.3	32.3	32.2	32.5	33.3	32.2	32.3
2009	32.2	32.8	33.2	33.4	33.8	34.2	34.1	33.9	33.9	33.7	34.1	32.9	33.5
Leisure and Hospitality													
2007	22.0	23.2	23.8	23.8	24.0	25.4	26.0	25.3	24.6	24.3	23.8	24.5	24.3
2008	24.0	24.5	24.4	23.9	24.3	25.0	25.6	24.9	24.3	24.9	24.8	24.0	24.6
2009	24.4	24.7	24.9	26.0	26.1	25.9	26.8	27.3	26.6	26.1	26.2	26.3	26.0

Average Hourly Earnings by Selected Industry: Rhode Island, 2007–2009

(Dollars, not seasonally adjusted.)

Industry and year	January	February	March	April	May	June	July	August	September	October	November	December	Annual average
Total Private													
2007	22.14	22.37	22.20	22.19	21.97	22.00	22.29	21.92	22.43	22.05	22.08	22.39	22.17
2008	22.75	22.61	22.47	22.58	22.15	22.29	22.47	22.15	22.37	22.59	22.73	22.86	22.50
2009	22.81	22.63	22.98	22.64	22.49	22.34	22.19	22.31	22.36	22.44	22.59	22.53	22.52
Goods-Producing													
2007	21.65	21.85	21.79	22.20	22.27	22.98	23.06	22.45	22.42	22.01	22.19	22.37	22.27
2008	22.56	22.28	22.19	22.33	22.34	22.34	22.40	22.13	22.14	23.09	22.94	23.14	22.48
2009	22.74	22.51	22.54	23.19	23.33	23.28	23.79	24.04	23.75	23.80	23.93	23.74	23.38
Construction													
2007	25.82	27.26	26.98	27.62	27.23	27.96	27.09	26.54	27.05	26.41	26.13	26.24	26.87
2008	26.09	26.63	26.77	26.73	26.95	27.49	27.70	27.09	27.51	27.06	27.50	27.15	27.09
2009	26.06	26.54	27.05	27.29	27.38	26.95	27.27	27.63	27.56	27.54	27.40	27.42	27.20
Manufacturing													
2007	20.14	20.28	20.26	20.58	20.60	21.23	21.59	21.00	20.86	20.78	20.89	21.20	20.78
2008	21.32	21.27	21.33	21.40	21.41	21.39	21.63	21.36	21.10	21.30	20.94	21.29	21.31
2009	20.96	21.15	21.00	21.56	21.80	21.63	22.13	22.19	22.20	22.28	22.36	22.04	21.76
Trade, Transportation, and Utilities													
2007	18.99	19.58	19.19	19.49	19.10	19.34	19.65	19.45	19.74	19.41	19.69	20.04	19.48
2008	20.15	20.35	20.34	20.24	20.29	20.40	20.46	20.15	20.38	19.89	20.18	20.03	20.24
2009	19.51	19.81	20.24	19.68	19.51	19.46	19.19	19.70	20.04	20.07	20.26	20.04	19.79
Professional and Business Services													
2007	28.52	28.75	27.94	28.14	28.66	28.01	28.96	28.84	28.77	28.67	28.63	28.48	28.53
2008	28.73	28.79	28.87	28.46	28.57	28.49	28.55	28.47	28.58	28.40	28.92	28.99	28.65
2009	29.10	29.13	28.50	27.88	27.72	27.56	27.00	26.88	26.79	26.83	26.86	27.03	27.59
Education and Health Services													
2007	23.04	23.37	23.14	22.91	22.87	23.05	23.07	22.89	22.92	22.95	22.89	22.74	22.99
2008	23.15	23.05	23.12	23.18	23.03	23.09	23.19	22.91	22.61	22.96	23.05	23.46	23.07
2009	23.41	23.91	23.73	23.69	23.70	23.24	23.04	23.17	23.26	23.34	23.40	24.08	23.50
Leisure and Hospitality													
2007	13.83	14.38	14.66	14.24	14.62	13.57	13.68	14.01	14.73	14.60	14.89	15.68	14.39
2008	14.97	14.72	14.77	14.67	14.58	14.60	14.47	14.32	15.00	14.80	14.88	15.31	14.74
2009	15.39	15.49	15.63	15.23	15.25	15.06	14.59	14.42	14.49	14.42	14.47	14.57	14.89

Average Weekly Earnings by Selected Industry: Rhode Island, 2007–2009

(Dollars, not seasonally adjusted.)

Industry and year	January	February	March	April	May	June	July	August	September	October	November	December	Annual average
Total Private													
2007	737.26	751.63	750.36	741.15	733.80	743.60	746.72	738.70	749.16	729.86	748.51	754.54	742.70
2008	766.68	764.22	768.47	765.46	757.53	769.01	770.72	759.75	760.58	768.06	772.82	772.67	767.25
2009	764.14	764.89	772.13	765.23	757.91	750.62	752.24	758.54	760.24	765.20	772.58	768.27	763.43
Goods-Producing													
2007	818.37	830.30	836.74	839.16	866.30	877.84	860.14	853.10	858.69	829.78	847.66	850.06	848.49
2008	868.56	839.96	854.32	839.61	880.20	886.90	871.36	858.64	859.03	884.35	869.43	865.44	865.48
2009	827.74	817.11	811.44	832.52	832.88	828.77	856.44	863.04	850.25	859.18	854.30	871.26	841.68
Construction													
2007	934.68	981.36	995.56	1005.37	1037.46	1045.70	1007.75	979.33	990.03	937.56	932.84	926.27	980.76
2008	889.67	913.41	947.66	932.88	1010.63	1044.62	1055.37	1013.17	1012.37	1022.87	995.50	980.12	988.79
2009	883.43	902.36	927.82	957.88	982.94	937.86	1003.54	1005.73	997.67	980.42	972.70	987.12	962.88
Manufacturing													
2007	775.39	784.84	790.14	790.27	811.64	821.60	811.78	810.60	815.63	804.19	820.98	824.68	804.19
2008	848.54	823.15	840.40	836.74	862.82	868.43	841.41	839.45	837.67	830.70	822.94	826.05	839.61
2009	811.15	810.05	798.00	804.19	804.42	808.96	827.66	852.10	848.04	857.78	847.44	850.74	826.88
Trade, Transportation, and Utilities													
2007	639.96	659.85	640.95	652.92	649.40	673.03	670.07	674.92	679.06	650.24	669.46	683.36	662.32
2008	687.12	700.04	722.07	702.33	712.18	709.92	716.10	705.25	707.19	678.25	682.08	697.04	702.33
2009	667.24	685.43	688.16	673.06	673.10	671.37	669.73	701.32	693.38	704.46	723.28	705.41	688.69
Professional and Business Services													
2007	986.79	1043.63	1017.02	1027.11	1063.29	1008.36	1030.98	992.10	1006.95	1006.32	1022.09	1011.04	1018.52
2008	1054.39	1062.35	1079.74	1047.33	1031.38	1045.58	1030.66	1002.14	1008.87	1016.72	1012.20	1020.45	1034.27
2009	1050.51	1051.59	1017.45	1014.83	1011.78	1011.45	1001.70	999.94	996.59	1000.76	991.13	973.08	1009.79
Education and Health Services													
2007	744.19	757.19	749.74	726.25	718.12	746.82	735.93	727.90	726.56	729.81	753.08	725.41	737.98
2008	743.12	732.99	744.46	753.35	743.87	741.19	749.04	739.99	728.04	746.20	767.57	755.41	745.16
2009	753.80	784.25	787.84	791.25	801.06	794.81	785.66	785.46	788.51	786.56	797.94	792.23	787.25
Leisure and Hospitality													
2007	304.26	333.62	348.91	338.91	350.88	344.68	355.68	354.45	362.36	354.78	354.38	384.16	349.68
2008	359.28	360.64	360.39	350.61	354.29	365.00	370.43	356.57	364.50	368.52	369.02	367.44	362.60
2009	375.52	382.60	389.19	395.98	398.03	390.05	391.01	393.67	385.43	376.36	379.11	383.19	387.14

SOUTH CAROLINA
At a Glance

Population:
    1990 census: 3,486,310
    2000 census: 4,012,012
    2009 estimate: 4,561,242

Percent change in population:
    1990–2000: 15.1%
    2000–2009: 13.7%

Percent change in total nonfarm employment:
    1990–2009: 18.3%
    2008–2009: -5.5%

Industry with the largest growth in employment, 1990–2009 (thousands):
    Education and Health Services, 109.3

Industry with the largest decline or smallest growth in employment, 1990–2009 (thousands):
    Manufacturing, -134.0

Civilian labor force:
    1990: 1,722,150
    2000: 1,988,159
    2009: 2,179,366

Unemployment rate and rank among states (lowest to highest):
    1990: 4.9%, 14th
    2000: 3.6%, 20th
    2009: 11.7%, 49th

Employment by Industry, 2009

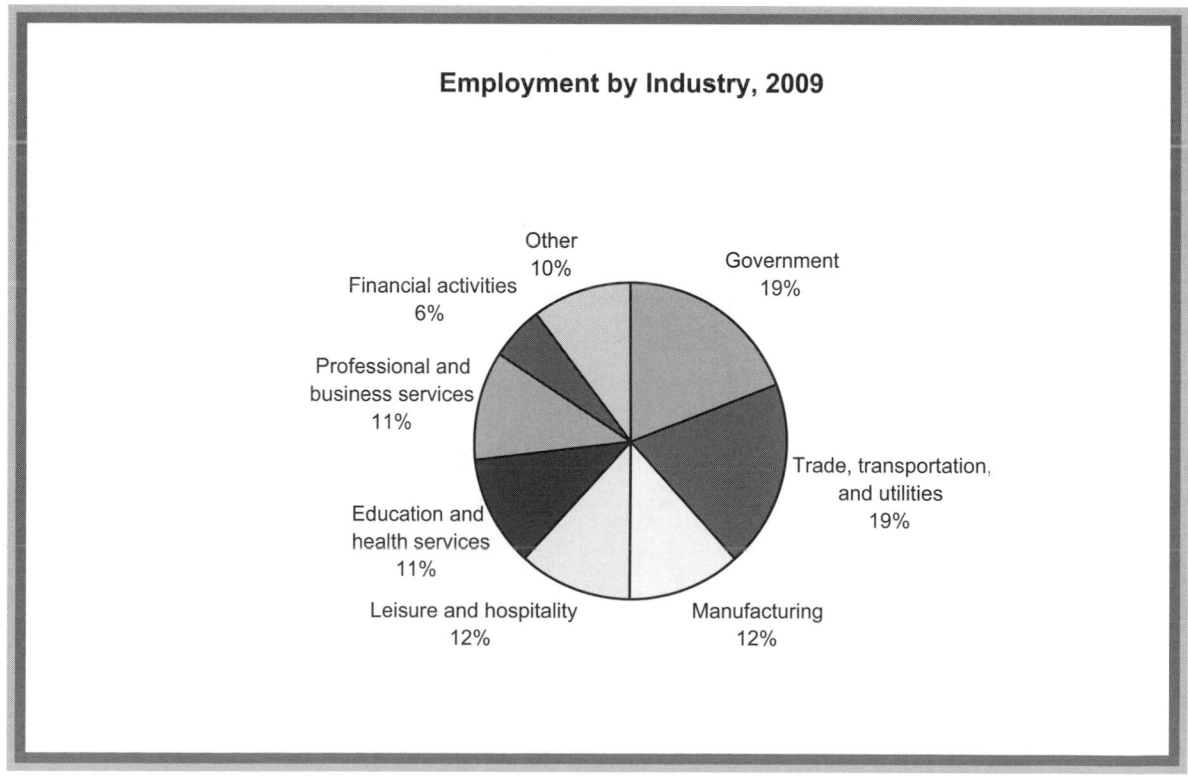

Employment by Industry: South Carolina, Selected Years, 1990–2009

(Numbers in thousands, not seasonally adjusted.)

Industry and year	January	February	March	April	May	June	July	August	September	October	November	December	Annual average
Total Nonfarm													
1990	1497.1	1512.3	1528.2	1541.4	1558.5	1563.8	1534.4	1540.4	1558.9	1550.6	1549.5	1544.4	1540.0
2000	1824.0	1836.7	1862.4	1868.4	1887.1	1900.5	1834.5	1851.9	1851.5	1861.2	1864.4	1866.3	1859.1
2001	1808.5	1816.8	1832.8	1837.1	1842.7	1842.1	1804.9	1827.1	1826.2	1812.0	1814.2	1811.4	1823.0
2002	1761.6	1773.0	1794.3	1812.5	1823.8	1829.5	1784.5	1813.9	1813.9	1814.3	1813.8	1813.7	1804.1
2003	1776.7	1789.6	1806.2	1812.7	1822.3	1821.5	1785.1	1812.0	1814.5	1814.1	1814.1	1817.3	1807.2
2004	1781.0	1790.7	1815.8	1835.6	1848.0	1851.3	1816.7	1842.7	1846.2	1852.5	1857.7	1857.4	1833.0
2005	1820.5	1833.9	1845.9	1869.5	1880.0	1869.3	1852.2	1880.9	1879.0	1886.6	1895.3	1884.7	1866.5
2006	1859.4	1877.8	1898.7	1916.0	1925.1	1905.7	1875.8	1902.7	1910.1	1931.8	1935.7	1943.0	1906.8
2007	1904.3	1916.2	1939.6	1947.4	1960.7	1968.8	1925.1	1943.2	1956.6	1954.6	1959.4	1957.4	1944.4
2008	1918.9	1929.4	1944.5	1947.7	1961.3	1955.8	1903.5	1922.6	1924.3	1913.1	1905.2	1889.4	1926.3
2009	1827.8	1822.8	1826.7	1832.8	1837.9	1830.2	1793.0	1815.9	1816.1	1818.6	1820.8	1812.7	1821.3
Total Private													
1990	1220.7	1229.1	1242.9	1255.4	1268.3	1282.2	1274.3	1278.7	1275.0	1259.3	1256.5	1251.1	1257.8
2000	1502.4	1512.1	1533.9	1541.3	1554.1	1570.4	1539.7	1540.0	1530.6	1535.2	1536.6	1538.1	1536.2
2001	1485.8	1490.0	1504.9	1510.2	1516.1	1520.1	1515.2	1513.5	1500.2	1483.2	1483.5	1479.4	1500.2
2002	1436.2	1444.2	1464.3	1482.4	1493.2	1505.1	1493.5	1494.7	1485.4	1483.4	1480.4	1480.1	1478.6
2003	1448.5	1456.6	1472.6	1479.3	1489.9	1496.9	1491.8	1495.7	1486.7	1485.0	1483.6	1485.8	1481.0
2004	1454.6	1462.6	1486.0	1505.0	1517.7	1528.2	1527.2	1526.7	1518.9	1522.2	1526.0	1525.5	1508.4
2005	1493.5	1503.6	1514.3	1537.4	1548.0	1542.9	1558.7	1563.2	1546.4	1551.3	1557.5	1546.7	1538.6
2006	1528.5	1542.6	1559.6	1577.2	1586.2	1579.3	1581.2	1584.3	1578.5	1593.5	1596.8	1602.9	1575.9
2007	1568.3	1577.0	1598.1	1607.4	1619.8	1632.0	1621.8	1623.0	1614.8	1608.6	1610.3	1609.0	1607.5
2008	1573.2	1580.4	1594.4	1596.8	1608.3	1607.5	1592.8	1591.9	1574.7	1559.1	1549.0	1533.9	1580.2
2009	1478.6	1472.0	1475.3	1478.6	1483.9	1482.4	1478.9	1477.4	1461.9	1460.4	1460.9	1453.9	1472.0
Goods-Producing													
1990	449.6	451.1	452.4	452.5	453.7	457.2	452.5	452.0	449.5	443.7	440.5	436.8	449.2
2000	453.4	455.9	458.6	458.3	460.0	463.9	454.7	455.0	454.0	454.6	453.9	454.0	456.3
2001	444.1	442.5	442.6	440.4	439.3	436.8	431.3	428.5	425.0	419.2	418.6	415.9	432.0
2002	406.9	406.7	407.8	409.4	410.6	411.6	407.8	408.0	405.6	404.1	400.8	399.4	406.6
2003	397.4	397.9	398.6	396.3	395.1	393.7	392.5	391.7	391.0	390.4	388.0	387.2	393.3
2004	383.0	382.7	386.6	387.9	389.1	390.8	390.6	389.8	389.1	387.5	386.4	385.9	387.5
2005	382.6	383.2	384.3	384.6	385.3	383.3	383.1	383.5	380.6	381.2	381.2	378.2	382.6
2006	377.7	379.0	381.0	383.4	385.1	383.3	382.1	381.8	380.4	383.3	382.8	384.6	382.0
2007	378.9	379.8	382.8	381.2	382.5	384.7	381.1	380.4	379.3	375.9	374.9	374.4	379.7
2008	368.3	366.7	367.0	362.1	362.6	361.3	357.2	355.1	352.3	346.8	342.7	337.3	356.6
2009	326.6	321.0	317.0	310.3	307.2	305.8	300.7	298.5	296.1	293.7	294.4	294.1	305.5
Mining and Logging													
1990	6.0	6.2	6.3	6.2	6.2	6.2	6.1	6.1	6.1	5.9	5.8	5.8	6.0
2000	5.6	5.7	5.7	5.6	5.7	5.5	5.6	5.4	5.3	5.4	5.4	5.4	5.5
2001	5.2	5.2	5.2	5.2	5.2	5.2	5.2	5.2	5.2	5.2	5.2	5.2	5.1
2002	5.1	5.1	5.1	5.1	5.1	5.1	5.0	5.0	5.0	5.0	5.0	5.0	5.1
2003	5.1	5.1	5.1	5.0	5.0	5.0	5.0	5.0	5.0	5.0	5.0	5.0	5.0
2004	5.1	5.1	5.1	5.1	5.1	5.1	5.1	5.1	5.1	5.0	5.0	5.0	5.1
2005	4.9	4.9	4.9	4.9	4.9	4.9	4.8	4.8	4.7	4.7	4.7	4.7	4.8
2006	4.7	4.7	4.7	4.7	4.7	4.7	4.7	4.7	4.7	4.7	4.7	4.8	4.7
2007	4.7	4.7	4.7	4.6	4.6	4.7	4.6	4.6	4.6	4.6	4.6	4.6	4.6
2008	4.5	4.5	4.5	4.4	4.4	4.3	4.3	4.3	4.3	4.3	4.3	4.3	4.4
2009	4.2	4.1	4.1	4.1	4.1	4.1	4.1	4.2	4.2	4.1	4.1	4.1	4.1
Construction													
1990	92.0	93.9	95.6	95.9	97.1	99.3	98.5	98.5	96.9	93.8	92.7	90.6	95.4
2000	112.7	113.4	116.1	115.4	116.7	118.9	113.3	113.3	112.4	114.4	114.0	114.1	114.5
2001	111.2	111.1	112.9	114.2	115.4	116.0	114.3	114.2	113.0	112.4	112.2	110.9	113.1
2002	107.5	108.8	110.4	112.0	113.4	114.2	113.9	113.8	112.8	112.5	111.8	111.0	111.8
2003	110.7	111.1	112.3	110.9	111.7	112.6	112.5	113.0	113.3	114.5	113.4	113.0	112.4
2004	110.8	110.9	113.2	114.4	115.3	115.7	116.4	116.0	115.6	115.5	114.7	113.8	114.4
2005	112.5	112.9	114.0	115.1	117.4	116.8	118.7	119.4	118.2	119.5	120.4	118.2	116.9
2006	119.3	120.8	122.5	123.8	125.4	123.9	125.7	126.2	125.8	128.1	127.7	127.6	124.7
2007	124.2	124.4	126.7	125.8	126.6	127.7	126.7	126.7	125.6	122.9	121.8	120.8	125.0
2008	116.3	115.7	116.0	112.5	112.6	112.5	109.9	109.0	107.3	104.4	102.1	99.4	109.8
2009	94.6	92.4	92.5	89.7	89.3	89.0	86.2	84.7	84.2	83.1	81.9	82.5	87.5
Manufacturing													
1990	351.6	351.0	350.5	350.4	350.4	351.7	347.9	347.4	346.5	344.0	342.0	340.4	347.8
2000	335.1	336.8	336.8	337.3	337.6	339.5	335.8	336.3	336.3	334.8	334.5	334.5	336.2
2001	327.7	326.2	324.5	321.0	318.7	315.6	311.8	309.1	306.8	301.6	301.2	299.8	313.6
2002	294.3	292.8	292.3	292.3	292.1	292.3	288.9	289.2	287.8	286.6	284.0	283.4	289.7
2003	281.6	281.7	281.2	280.4	278.4	276.1	275.0	273.7	272.7	270.9	269.6	269.2	275.9
2004	267.1	266.7	268.3	268.4	268.7	270.0	269.1	268.7	268.4	267.0	266.7	267.1	268.0
2005	265.2	265.4	265.4	264.6	263.0	261.6	259.6	259.3	257.7	257.0	256.1	255.3	260.9
2006	253.7	253.5	253.8	254.9	255.0	254.7	251.7	250.9	249.9	250.5	250.4	252.2	252.6
2007	250.0	250.7	251.4	250.8	251.3	252.3	249.8	249.1	249.1	248.4	248.5	249.0	250.0
2008	247.5	246.5	246.5	245.2	245.6	244.5	243.0	241.8	240.7	238.1	236.3	233.6	242.4
2009	227.8	224.5	220.4	216.5	213.8	212.7	210.4	209.6	207.7	206.5	208.4	207.5	213.8

Employment by Industry: South Carolina, Selected Years, 1990–2009—*Continued*

(Numbers in thousands, not seasonally adjusted.)

Industry and year	January	February	March	April	May	June	July	August	September	October	November	December	Annual average
Service-Providing													
1990	1047.5	1061.2	1075.8	1088.9	1104.8	1106.6	1081.9	1088.4	1109.4	1106.9	1109.0	1107.6	1090.7
2000	1370.6	1380.8	1403.8	1410.1	1427.1	1436.6	1379.8	1396.9	1397.5	1406.6	1410.5	1412.3	1402.7
2001	1364.4	1374.3	1390.2	1396.7	1403.4	1405.3	1373.6	1398.6	1401.2	1392.8	1395.6	1395.5	1391.0
2002	1354.7	1366.3	1386.5	1403.1	1413.2	1417.9	1376.7	1405.9	1408.3	1410.2	1413.0	1414.3	1397.5
2003	1379.3	1391.7	1407.6	1416.4	1427.2	1427.8	1392.6	1420.3	1423.5	1423.7	1426.1	1430.1	1413.9
2004	1398.0	1408.0	1429.2	1447.7	1458.9	1460.5	1426.1	1452.9	1457.1	1465.0	1471.3	1471.5	1445.5
2005	1437.9	1450.7	1461.6	1484.9	1494.7	1486.0	1469.1	1497.4	1498.4	1505.4	1514.1	1506.5	1483.9
2006	1481.7	1498.8	1517.7	1532.6	1540.0	1522.4	1493.7	1520.9	1529.7	1548.5	1552.9	1558.4	1524.8
2007	1525.4	1536.4	1556.8	1566.2	1578.2	1584.1	1544.0	1562.8	1577.3	1578.7	1584.5	1583.0	1564.8
2008	1550.6	1562.7	1577.5	1585.6	1598.7	1594.5	1546.3	1567.5	1572.0	1566.3	1562.5	1552.1	1569.7
2009	1501.2	1501.8	1509.7	1522.5	1530.7	1524.4	1492.3	1517.4	1520.0	1524.9	1526.4	1518.6	1515.8
Trade, Transportation, and Utilities													
1990	294.3	293.5	296.4	299.4	302.2	306.3	306.4	307.8	306.5	303.9	306.7	310.2	302.8
2000	359.1	359.0	363.7	362.3	365.7	368.2	362.2	363.0	361.6	363.9	370.1	372.7	364.3
2001	352.6	349.7	352.9	352.0	354.3	355.2	354.3	353.8	351.5	349.7	353.9	355.7	353.0
2002	339.9	339.0	343.3	345.8	347.6	349.5	346.8	346.5	345.3	346.1	351.5	355.1	346.4
2003	341.7	340.9	343.5	343.5	346.2	348.9	347.3	348.2	346.8	347.6	352.2	356.5	346.9
2004	345.1	344.4	348.8	350.0	353.2	353.8	356.0	356.2	354.7	357.2	363.0	366.7	354.1
2005	354.2	354.0	355.5	358.7	362.4	360.1	363.5	364.2	359.7	363.9	369.7	372.1	361.5
2006	360.4	363.7	367.7	367.8	367.9	366.5	366.5	368.0	367.6	373.1	381.0	384.0	369.5
2007	369.1	368.4	373.9	373.8	376.8	379.0	378.5	378.0	377.2	378.5	384.9	387.9	377.2
2008	374.5	373.4	376.1	374.9	374.8	375.0	373.0	372.2	369.5	367.5	369.5	370.2	372.6
2009	352.0	347.6	347.6	348.8	350.5	350.8	349.8	349.2	347.4	347.6	348.5	350.0	349.2
Wholesale Trade													
1990	48.5	48.8	49.2	48.8	49.0	49.3	49.6	49.7	49.8	49.4	49.0	48.9	49.2
2000	61.9	62.1	63.0	62.6	63.0	63.3	62.6	62.5	62.6	62.9	63.0	63.3	62.7
2001	62.6	62.8	63.1	63.1	63.1	63.5	63.4	63.1	62.9	62.3	62.2	61.8	62.8
2002	60.8	61.5	62.2	62.4	62.4	63.1	62.6	62.2	61.9	62.6	62.7	62.5	62.2
2003	61.8	62.2	62.4	62.4	62.8	63.0	62.7	62.7	62.5	62.6	62.6	63.0	62.6
2004	62.6	62.8	63.5	63.9	64.4	64.7	65.3	65.6	65.5	65.7	66.1	66.1	64.7
2005	66.7	67.1	67.1	66.8	67.8	67.0	67.4	67.6	67.3	67.9	68.0	67.7	67.4
2006	68.1	68.6	68.8	69.7	69.8	69.6	68.5	68.9	69.3	70.5	70.7	70.8	69.4
2007	69.8	70.2	70.9	71.0	71.0	71.5	71.2	71.0	71.0	71.3	71.2	71.6	71.0
2008	71.0	71.5	71.7	71.4	71.5	71.6	71.4	71.3	71.0	71.1	70.6	69.9	71.2
2009	67.6	66.9	66.3	66.1	65.8	65.2	65.3	64.9	65.9	65.5	65.1	64.7	65.8
Retail Trade													
1990	194.3	192.8	194.9	197.3	199.5	202.6	203.2	203.7	202.5	201.1	204.7	207.9	200.3
2000	234.2	233.1	236.3	235.9	238.4	240.2	234.0	235.5	234.7	235.9	241.8	244.0	237.0
2001	229.2	226.2	228.7	228.3	230.0	230.7	229.4	228.9	227.1	225.9	230.3	232.9	228.9
2002	220.0	217.8	221.4	223.0	224.6	226.3	224.6	224.2	223.3	222.7	227.5	231.6	223.9
2003	219.8	218.3	220.5	221.0	222.9	225.2	224.3	224.9	223.8	224.0	228.4	232.0	223.8
2004	222.5	221.3	224.7	226.1	228.0	228.1	228.8	228.1	227.0	229.0	234.2	238.0	228.0
2005	226.7	225.9	227.2	230.0	231.8	230.7	232.9	233.1	229.0	232.6	238.0	240.2	231.5
2006	229.4	231.6	235.3	234.6	234.3	232.7	234.2	234.9	234.0	237.7	245.2	247.3	235.9
2007	235.4	233.7	238.2	237.8	240.3	241.6	241.9	241.2	240.4	241.0	246.9	248.9	240.6
2008	238.6	236.7	239.5	238.4	238.4	238.7	237.5	236.6	235.0	232.5	235.2	236.3	237.0
2009	223.3	220.2	221.1	223.0	224.8	225.6	224.9	224.0	221.9	223.3	224.2	225.0	223.4
Transportation and Utilities													
1990	51.5	51.9	52.3	53.3	53.7	54.4	53.6	54.4	54.2	53.4	53.0	53.4	53.2
2000	63.0	63.8	64.4	63.8	64.3	64.7	64.7	65.0	64.3	65.1	65.3	65.4	64.4
2001	60.8	60.7	61.1	60.6	61.2	61.0	61.5	61.8	61.5	61.5	61.4	61.0	61.1
2002	59.1	59.7	59.7	60.4	60.6	60.1	59.6	60.1	60.1	60.8	61.3	61.0	60.2
2003	60.1	60.4	60.6	60.1	60.5	60.7	60.3	60.6	60.5	61.0	61.2	61.5	60.6
2004	60.0	60.3	60.6	60.0	60.8	61.0	61.9	62.5	62.2	62.5	62.7	62.6	61.4
2005	60.8	61.0	61.2	61.9	62.8	62.4	63.2	63.5	63.4	63.4	63.7	64.2	62.6
2006	62.9	63.5	63.6	63.5	63.8	64.2	63.8	64.2	64.3	64.9	65.1	65.9	64.1
2007	63.9	64.5	64.8	65.0	65.5	65.9	65.4	65.8	65.8	66.2	66.8	67.4	65.6
2008	64.9	65.2	64.9	65.1	64.9	64.7	64.1	64.3	63.5	63.9	63.7	64.0	64.4
2009	61.1	60.5	60.2	59.7	59.9	60.0	59.6	60.3	59.6	58.8	59.2	60.3	59.9
Information													
1990	22.2	22.4	22.4	22.6	22.8	23.1	23.9	24.1	24.0	23.9	23.5	23.3	23.1
2000	30.0	30.0	30.4	29.9	30.2	31.0	30.5	30.8	30.7	30.6	30.8	31.2	30.5
2001	29.7	29.8	29.8	29.1	29.1	29.2	28.7	28.7	28.4	27.9	28.1	28.0	28.8
2002	27.7	27.6	27.8	27.5	28.0	28.1	27.8	27.9	27.4	27.9	28.3	28.3	27.9
2003	27.5	27.6	27.5	26.7	26.9	26.9	27.1	27.1	26.9	26.7	26.8	26.9	27.1
2004	26.8	26.5	26.5	26.5	26.9	27.0	27.0	26.9	26.6	26.8	26.7	27.2	26.8
2005	26.6	26.7	26.6	27.0	27.3	27.2	27.2	27.1	26.9	26.9	27.1	27.4	27.0
2006	27.2	27.6	27.4	27.5	27.6	27.7	27.5	27.4	27.1	27.3	27.8	27.9	27.5
2007	27.1	27.2	27.4	27.6	27.9	28.5	28.7	28.5	28.0	28.1	28.2	28.4	28.0
2008	28.1	28.2	28.2	28.6	28.8	29.0	29.1	28.9	28.4	28.2	28.2	28.4	28.5
2009	27.9	27.7	27.9	27.7	27.5	27.5	27.7	27.6	27.6	27.6	27.7	27.9	27.7

Employment by Industry: South Carolina, Selected Years, 1990–2009—*Continued*

(Numbers in thousands, not seasonally adjusted.)

Industry and year	January	February	March	April	May	June	July	August	September	October	November	December	Annual average
Financial Activities													
1990	71.2	71.0	70.8	70.8	71.4	72.3	72.3	73.0	71.9	70.7	70.4	69.5	71.2
2000	85.9	86.4	87.0	87.6	88.3	89.7	87.9	88.1	86.7	87.4	87.1	87.3	87.4
2001	85.9	86.5	87.0	87.8	88.1	89.3	90.4	89.9	88.5	87.8	88.2	87.8	88.1
2002	86.4	86.7	87.5	88.9	89.7	90.8	90.4	90.0	89.3	89.2	89.2	89.6	89.0
2003	88.8	88.8	89.5	91.1	92.3	93.4	92.8	93.6	91.9	91.9	91.5	91.9	91.5
2004	90.3	91.0	92.0	93.1	93.8	95.4	95.0	95.2	94.9	95.2	95.3	95.9	93.9
2005	95.4	95.7	95.9	96.9	98.1	98.4	99.7	99.8	99.1	98.4	98.5	99.0	97.9
2006	99.4	100.0	100.3	102.0	102.6	103.2	104.0	104.5	104.0	104.5	104.3	104.8	102.8
2007	104.1	104.1	105.0	105.4	106.2	107.2	106.9	106.9	106.2	106.2	106.2	106.6	105.9
2008	105.2	106.0	106.3	106.2	106.7	107.6	106.9	106.7	105.2	104.7	104.1	104.0	105.8
2009	101.7	101.6	101.6	101.6	102.1	102.5	102.4	102.6	101.7	100.9	100.7	100.1	101.6
Professional and Business Services													
1990	124.5	126.3	128.3	130.8	133.6	135.1	132.0	133.8	135.3	135.8	136.6	135.4	132.2
2000	186.9	188.2	192.1	195.9	197.8	200.9	197.1	198.1	197.8	197.2	195.9	195.7	195.3
2001	185.3	187.3	188.8	189.6	188.9	188.8	187.7	189.4	187.9	185.0	183.1	182.1	186.9
2002	174.4	176.7	179.4	183.7	184.4	186.6	184.3	187.2	186.5	187.8	185.9	185.4	183.5
2003	180.4	183.0	186.7	187.2	187.6	187.7	186.2	188.4	187.5	190.8	191.1	191.2	187.3
2004	185.1	187.4	191.8	195.5	195.3	197.8	197.9	199.3	198.2	200.9	200.8	199.4	195.8
2005	195.5	197.6	197.7	203.3	204.1	203.4	205.8	209.3	209.4	212.3	213.6	210.6	205.2
2006	211.6	213.6	215.1	217.9	219.2	217.0	216.3	218.3	219.7	222.7	220.7	223.3	218.0
2007	219.9	222.6	224.2	226.0	227.5	229.0	225.7	228.2	228.2	226.9	226.5	225.5	225.9
2008	219.7	222.3	223.6	224.3	226.5	224.5	220.2	222.5	219.7	217.6	215.6	209.6	220.5
2009	200.1	198.9	199.2	199.0	198.7	198.1	198.6	201.7	201.0	205.1	211.5	208.7	201.7
Education and Health Services													
1990	95.6	97.3	97.7	98.1	98.4	95.8	94.6	95.4	100.0	101.2	102.0	102.7	98.2
2000	154.6	155.5	156.5	156.4	156.7	156.8	153.2	154.1	156.0	157.7	158.4	159.2	156.2
2001	158.7	160.1	161.3	161.4	162.4	163.3	163.7	165.3	167.9	168.0	169.4	170.4	164.3
2002	168.9	170.2	172.1	171.8	172.4	171.6	171.6	172.5	174.1	174.1	175.2	174.9	172.5
2003	173.2	174.5	175.4	176.4	176.9	176.2	175.6	177.4	179.6	179.0	179.2	179.6	176.9
2004	178.3	179.5	180.2	181.1	181.8	180.5	179.8	181.0	182.2	183.0	184.1	184.3	181.3
2005	182.6	184.3	184.7	187.5	187.8	184.7	187.2	187.8	189.2	190.5	191.0	189.9	187.3
2006	189.2	191.4	191.8	192.7	193.0	189.6	189.9	191.5	193.8	197.9	198.2	199.0	193.2
2007	196.0	198.1	199.1	199.7	200.2	199.7	199.6	200.6	202.6	203.4	204.1	204.0	200.6
2008	204.1	206.2	207.2	205.8	207.2	206.1	205.2	206.5	208.1	209.1	209.5	209.1	207.0
2009	205.9	207.5	207.4	207.8	208.4	206.6	204.1	206.5	208.2	208.2	209.2	210.5	207.5
Leisure and Hospitality													
1990	117.5	121.3	128.0	134.4	138.8	144.4	143.9	144.4	139.5	132.1	128.9	126.0	133.2
2000	175.1	179.0	186.5	191.2	195.3	199.9	195.8	192.8	185.8	184.6	181.6	179.5	187.2
2001	169.1	173.2	180.4	187.6	191.3	194.8	196.7	195.2	188.4	183.0	179.2	176.5	184.6
2002	169.4	173.9	181.7	191.1	195.6	201.3	200.6	197.9	191.9	190.5	185.7	183.4	188.6
2003	176.1	180.0	186.7	194.0	200.1	204.8	205.4	204.1	197.7	193.3	189.2	186.5	193.2
2004	181.0	185.5	193.6	202.0	207.6	211.4	211.8	209.0	203.5	201.0	197.9	194.1	199.9
2005	185.5	189.7	196.5	206.7	209.7	212.9	217.3	215.9	206.1	202.7	200.7	194.6	203.2
2006	191.1	194.7	200.1	209.8	214.5	216.1	218.7	217.0	210.6	210.0	207.7	205.0	207.9
2007	199.8	203.0	211.3	219.4	224.1	229.3	227.9	227.4	220.9	217.9	214.0	210.6	217.1
2008	203.1	207.2	214.7	223.2	229.3	231.5	229.0	228.0	219.9	214.0	208.5	204.8	217.8
2009	195.0	198.1	204.8	213.6	219.2	220.9	224.7	221.8	211.7	208.4	200.5	194.7	209.5
Other Services													
1990	45.8	46.2	46.9	46.8	47.4	48.0	48.7	48.2	48.3	48.0	47.9	47.2	47.4
2000	57.4	58.1	59.1	59.7	60.1	60.0	58.3	58.1	58.0	59.2	58.8	58.5	58.7
2001	60.4	60.9	62.1	62.3	62.7	62.7	62.4	62.7	62.6	62.6	63.0	63.0	62.2
2002	62.6	63.4	64.7	64.2	64.9	65.6	64.2	64.7	65.3	63.7	63.8	64.0	64.3
2003	63.4	63.9	64.7	64.1	64.8	65.3	64.9	65.2	65.3	65.3	65.6	66.0	64.9
2004	65.0	65.6	66.5	68.9	70.0	71.5	69.1	69.3	69.7	70.6	71.8	72.0	69.2
2005	71.1	72.4	73.1	72.7	73.3	72.9	74.9	75.6	75.4	75.4	75.7	74.9	74.0
2006	71.9	72.6	76.2	76.1	76.3	75.9	76.2	75.8	75.3	74.7	74.3	74.3	75.0
2007	73.4	73.8	74.4	74.3	74.6	74.6	73.4	73.0	72.4	71.7	71.5	71.6	73.2
2008	70.2	70.4	71.3	71.7	72.4	72.5	72.2	72.0	71.6	71.2	70.9	70.5	71.4
2009	69.4	69.6	69.8	69.8	70.3	70.2	70.9	69.5	68.2	68.9	68.4	67.9	69.4
Government													
1990	276.4	283.2	285.3	286.0	290.2	281.6	260.1	261.7	283.9	291.3	293.0	293.3	282.1
2000	321.6	324.6	328.5	327.1	333.0	330.1	294.8	311.9	320.9	326.0	327.8	328.2	322.8
2001	322.7	326.8	327.9	326.9	326.6	322.0	289.7	313.6	326.0	328.8	330.7	332.0	322.8
2002	325.4	328.8	330.0	330.1	330.6	324.4	291.0	319.2	328.5	330.9	333.4	333.6	325.5
2003	328.2	333.0	333.6	333.4	332.4	324.6	293.3	316.3	327.8	329.1	330.5	331.5	326.1
2004	326.4	328.1	329.8	330.6	330.3	323.1	289.5	316.0	327.3	330.3	331.7	331.9	324.6
2005	327.0	330.3	331.6	332.1	332.0	326.4	293.5	317.7	332.6	335.3	337.8	338.0	327.9
2006	330.9	335.2	339.1	338.8	338.9	326.4	294.6	318.4	331.6	338.3	338.9	340.1	330.9
2007	336.0	339.2	341.5	340.0	340.9	336.8	303.3	320.2	341.8	346.0	349.1	348.4	336.9
2008	345.7	349.0	350.1	350.9	353.0	348.3	310.7	330.7	349.6	354.0	356.2	355.5	346.1
2009	349.2	350.8	351.4	354.2	354.0	347.8	314.1	338.5	354.2	358.2	359.9	358.8	349.3

Average Weekly Hours by Selected Industry: South Carolina, 2007–2009

(Not seasonally adjusted.)

Industry and year	January	February	March	April	May	June	July	August	September	October	November	December	Annual average
Total Private													
2007	36.2	36.0	36.4	36.1	35.9	36.2	36.2	36.2	35.9	35.6	35.8	36.1	36.0
2008	35.3	35.3	36.1	35.6	35.9	37.0	35.8	35.6	34.8	35.1	35.5	35.3	35.6
2009	34.8	34.9	35.0	34.6	34.8	34.8	34.6	34.9	34.2	34.4	34.7	35.0	34.7
Goods-Producing													
2007	39.5	39.7	40.2	39.6	40.6	41.0	39.9	40.6	41.0	41.3	42.0	42.1	40.6
2008	41.0	41.1	41.0	40.3	42.1	43.2	40.3	40.4	39.1	40.2	40.5	40.7	40.8
2009	39.9	40.0	40.2	39.4	40.9	40.9	40.7	41.0	40.3	40.2	40.5	41.1	40.4
Construction													
2007	36.9	36.6	37.4	36.9	37.9	38.8	37.9	38.8	38.6	39.4	38.7	38.9	38.1
2008	38.7	37.9	38.4	37.5	37.6	39.5	39.2	38.6	35.0	37.9	38.8	37.1	38.0
2009	37.3	37.4	36.6	36.0	36.5	37.5	37.7	37.6	36.3	35.9	36.6	37.3	36.9
Manufacturing													
2007	41.1	41.9	42.1	41.5	42.4	42.5	41.3	41.9	42.7	42.6	44.3	44.3	42.4
2008	42.7	43.1	43.0	42.2	44.7	45.3	41.1	41.5	41.7	41.7	41.6	42.8	42.6
2009	41.6	41.6	41.9	40.6	42.7	42.1	42.0	42.5	42.1	42.2	42.5	42.8	42.1
Trade, Transportation, and Utilities													
2007	35.0	35.1	35.4	35.4	34.9	35.6	35.2	34.6	34.7	34.3	34.1	34.7	34.9
2008	34.6	34.3	34.8	35.3	34.9	35.1	34.9	34.4	34.0	33.7	34.4	34.1	34.5
2009	34.1	34.2	34.4	34.4	34.8	34.7	34.4	34.5	34.2	34.5	34.5	34.8	34.5
Financial Activities													
2007	36.0	36.9	37.0	37.7	37.2	37.9	38.0	37.5	38.2	37.5	37.3	38.3	37.5
2008	36.6	37.4	38.4	36.7	36.4	37.1	36.4	36.4	36.0	36.0	37.3	35.7	36.7
2009	35.8	36.7	36.5	36.4	36.9	36.6	36.9	37.6	35.7	36.7	37.5	36.7	36.7
Professional and Business Services													
2007	42.7	41.7	43.1	43.3	42.1	41.9	42.9	43.4	41.1	39.9	39.9	40.0	41.8
2008	37.8	37.8	41.0	41.5	42.2	41.2	40.8	39.8	39.4	39.7	40.4	40.8	40.2
2009	38.3	37.5	38.4	37.1	36.7	37.6	37.1	37.4	37.0	36.3	36.2	37.4	37.2
Education and Health Services													
2007	37.0	34.8	35.4	33.9	33.7	35.2	35.2	34.5	35.0	34.0	35.6	35.6	35.0
2008	34.7	35.1	34.7	32.7	32.7	34.1	32.8	32.4	32.4	32.9	33.1	32.8	33.4
2009	32.4	33.1	32.9	32.6	31.8	31.9	32.0	32.1	31.7	31.7	32.8	33.0	32.3
Leisure and Hospitality													
2007	24.6	24.9	25.7	25.9	25.4	26.2	26.8	26.7	24.7	24.8	24.5	24.4	25.4
2008	24.0	24.9	26.0	25.9	25.9	26.9	26.6	26.7	24.6	25.1	24.8	24.5	25.5
2009	24.7	25.4	25.9	26.4	26.4	26.9	27.0	27.0	25.2	25.4	25.3	25.0	25.9
Other Services													
2007	37.2	36.5	36.3	35.7	35.5	34.7	35.8	36.5	35.9	36.3	35.7	37.1	36.1
2008	35.8	35.4	36.4	35.0	34.5	35.1	32.2	34.3	33.1	32.4	32.5	32.4	34.1
2009	31.9	31.8	31.9	32.3	31.2	30.2	30.6	30.8	30.9	30.8	30.8	31.2	31.2

Average Hourly Earnings by Selected Industry: South Carolina, 2007–2009

(Dollars, not seasonally adjusted.)

Industry and year	January	February	March	April	May	June	July	August	September	October	November	December	Annual average
Total Private													
2007	18.77	19.12	18.77	19.01	18.82	18.63	18.65	18.38	18.77	18.59	18.62	19.03	18.76
2008	19.00	19.04	19.42	18.54	18.37	18.36	18.62	18.60	18.74	18.70	18.99	19.25	18.80
2009	19.16	19.33	18.75	18.74	18.70	18.67	18.78	19.40	19.70	19.41	19.72	19.77	19.17
Goods-Producing													
2007	17.69	17.95	17.76	18.48	18.27	18.33	18.64	18.25	18.35	18.28	18.31	19.06	18.28
2008	18.55	19.10	19.38	19.41	18.91	18.87	19.33	19.35	19.14	19.56	19.63	20.19	19.27
2009	20.26	20.07	20.29	20.43	20.22	20.09	20.16	20.06	20.08	20.13	20.81	20.70	20.27
Construction													
2007	18.21	18.24	18.14	17.46	17.72	17.77	17.95	17.44	17.64	17.97	18.48	19.30	18.02
2008	18.17	19.24	18.65	18.86	19.05	18.86	19.53	19.75	19.13	20.24	19.69	21.35	19.34
2009	20.98	20.15	20.24	20.35	21.42	21.46	21.29	21.20	21.18	21.19	21.56	21.39	21.02
Manufacturing													
2007	17.40	17.80	17.58	19.76	19.28	19.32	19.64	19.26	19.28	18.96	18.65	19.33	18.86
2008	19.10	18.92	19.04	19.14	18.43	18.49	18.89	18.85	18.88	19.00	19.41	19.50	18.96
2009	19.67	19.67	19.98	20.18	19.89	19.68	19.88	19.70	19.73	19.77	20.26	20.21	19.88
Trade, Transportation, and Utilities													
2007	17.82	17.96	18.09	17.86	18.40	18.29	18.68	18.20	18.95	18.70	18.21	18.64	18.32
2008	18.17	18.99	19.02	16.72	16.91	17.06	17.36	17.34	17.67	17.32	17.57	17.46	17.63
2009	17.57	17.66	18.01	17.28	17.17	17.30	17.34	17.70	17.65	17.71	17.90	17.76	17.59
Financial Activities													
2007	21.59	21.94	19.93	20.48	20.88	20.35	20.98	20.43	20.36	20.05	20.56	20.30	20.65
2008	22.24	20.59	20.93	21.03	21.61	22.70	22.88	22.46	22.76	22.99	22.82	22.44	22.11
2009	22.26	22.37	20.55	20.56	20.70	20.98	21.34	21.62	21.96	22.03	22.49	22.26	21.59
Professional and Business Services													
2007	26.05	27.00	26.32	26.85	25.56	24.65	23.95	23.31	24.16	23.62	23.85	25.06	25.04
2008	24.99	24.25	25.88	23.77	23.05	23.00	22.82	22.51	22.55	21.80	22.64	23.20	23.37
2009	23.27	24.46	23.56	23.94	23.88	23.37	23.01	25.41	25.64	23.62	23.65	23.49	23.94
Education and Health Services													
2007	17.32	18.34	19.00	18.71	17.60	18.84	18.89	19.36	19.08	19.17	19.19	19.16	18.72
2008	19.73	19.64	19.46	19.66	19.40	18.79	19.44	19.74	19.44	19.34	19.91	20.42	19.58
2009	19.75	20.48	20.80	20.77	21.22	21.22	21.87	21.79	22.19	22.16	22.03	22.90	21.43
Leisure and Hospitality													
2007	10.51	10.49	10.10	10.46	10.25	10.21	10.26	10.18	10.39	10.40	10.62	10.64	10.37
2008	10.70	10.57	10.60	10.59	10.54	10.39	10.63	10.80	10.64	10.64	10.82	10.90	10.65
2009	10.79	10.96	10.87	10.90	10.80	10.76	10.90	11.05	11.16	11.00	11.09	11.11	10.95
Other Services													
2007	15.72	16.44	16.01	16.08	16.51	16.04	16.24	17.08	16.57	16.35	17.29	16.45	16.39
2008	16.78	16.57	16.72	16.92	16.63	16.32	16.61	16.28	17.43	17.17	17.13	16.89	16.78
2009	16.63	17.03	16.44	16.14	15.91	15.90	15.68	16.00	16.08	15.74	16.04	16.04	16.14

Average Weekly Earnings by Selected Industry: South Carolina, 2007–2009

(Dollars, not seasonally adjusted.)

Industry and year	January	February	March	April	May	June	July	August	September	October	November	December	Annual average
Total Private													
2007	679.47	688.32	683.23	686.26	675.64	674.41	675.13	665.36	673.84	661.80	666.60	686.98	675.36
2008	670.70	672.11	701.06	660.02	659.48	679.32	666.60	662.16	652.15	656.37	674.15	679.53	669.28
2009	666.77	674.62	656.25	648.40	650.76	649.72	649.79	677.06	673.74	667.70	684.28	691.95	665.20
Goods-Producing													
2007	698.76	712.62	713.95	731.81	741.76	751.53	743.74	740.95	752.35	754.96	769.02	802.43	742.17
2008	760.55	785.01	794.58	782.22	796.11	815.18	779.00	781.74	748.37	786.31	795.02	821.73	786.22
2009	808.37	802.80	815.66	804.94	827.00	821.68	820.51	822.46	809.22	809.23	842.81	850.77	818.91
Construction													
2007	671.95	667.58	678.44	644.27	671.59	689.48	680.31	676.67	680.90	708.02	715.18	750.77	686.56
2008	703.18	729.20	716.16	707.25	716.28	744.97	765.58	762.35	669.55	767.10	763.97	792.09	734.92
2009	782.55	753.61	740.78	732.60	781.83	804.75	802.63	797.12	768.83	760.72	789.10	797.85	775.64
Manufacturing													
2007	715.14	745.82	740.12	820.04	817.47	821.10	811.13	806.99	823.26	807.70	826.20	856.32	799.66
2008	815.57	815.45	818.72	807.71	823.82	837.60	776.38	782.28	787.30	792.30	807.46	834.60	807.70
2009	818.27	818.27	837.16	819.31	849.30	828.53	834.96	837.25	830.63	834.29	861.05	864.99	836.95
Trade, Transportation, and Utilities													
2007	623.70	630.40	640.39	632.24	642.16	651.12	657.54	629.72	657.57	641.41	620.96	646.81	639.37
2008	628.68	651.36	661.90	590.22	590.16	598.81	605.86	596.50	600.78	583.68	604.41	595.39	608.24
2009	599.14	603.97	619.54	594.43	597.52	600.31	596.50	610.65	603.63	611.00	617.55	618.05	606.86
Financial Activities													
2007	777.24	809.59	737.41	772.10	776.74	771.27	797.24	766.13	777.75	751.88	766.89	777.49	774.38
2008	813.98	770.07	803.71	771.80	786.60	842.17	832.83	817.54	819.36	827.64	851.19	801.11	811.44
2009	796.91	820.98	750.08	748.38	763.83	767.87	787.45	812.91	783.97	808.50	843.38	816.94	792.35
Professional and Business Services													
2007	1112.34	1125.90	1134.39	1162.61	1076.08	1032.84	1027.46	1011.65	992.98	942.44	951.62	1002.40	1046.67
2008	944.62	916.65	1061.08	986.46	972.71	947.60	931.06	895.90	888.47	865.46	914.66	946.56	939.47
2009	891.24	917.25	904.70	888.17	876.40	878.71	853.67	950.33	948.68	857.41	856.13	878.53	890.57
Education and Health Services													
2007	640.84	638.23	672.60	634.27	593.12	663.17	664.93	667.92	667.80	651.78	683.16	682.10	655.20
2008	684.63	689.36	675.26	642.88	634.38	640.74	637.63	639.58	629.86	636.29	659.02	669.78	653.97
2009	639.90	677.89	684.32	677.10	674.80	676.92	699.84	699.46	703.42	702.47	722.58	755.70	692.19
Leisure and Hospitality													
2007	258.55	261.20	259.57	270.91	260.35	267.50	274.97	271.81	256.63	257.92	260.19	259.62	263.40
2008	256.80	263.19	275.60	274.28	272.99	279.49	282.76	288.36	261.74	267.06	268.34	267.05	271.58
2009	266.51	278.38	281.53	287.76	285.12	289.44	294.30	298.35	281.23	279.40	280.58	277.75	283.61
Other Services													
2007	584.78	600.06	581.16	574.06	586.11	556.59	581.39	623.42	594.86	593.51	617.25	610.30	591.68
2008	600.72	586.58	608.61	592.20	573.74	572.83	534.84	558.40	576.93	556.31	556.73	547.24	572.20
2009	530.50	541.55	524.44	521.32	496.39	480.18	479.81	492.80	496.87	484.79	494.03	500.45	503.57

SOUTH DAKOTA
At a Glance

Population:
    1990 census: 696,004
    2000 census: 754,844
    2009 estimate: 812,383

Percent change in population:
    1990–2000: 8.5%
    2000–2009: 7.6%

Percent change in total nonfarm employment:
    1990–2009: 39.9%
    2008–2009: -1.9%

Industry with the largest growth in employment, 1990–2009 (thousands):
    Education and Health Services, 26.4

Industry with the largest decline or smallest growth in employment, 1990–2009 (thousands):
    Information, 1.25

Civilian labor force:
    1990: 350,642
    2000: 408,685
    2009: 446,351

Unemployment rate and rank among states (lowest to highest):
    1990: 3.7% 3rd
    2000: 2.7%, 3rd
    2009: 4.8%, 3rd

Employment by Industry, 2009

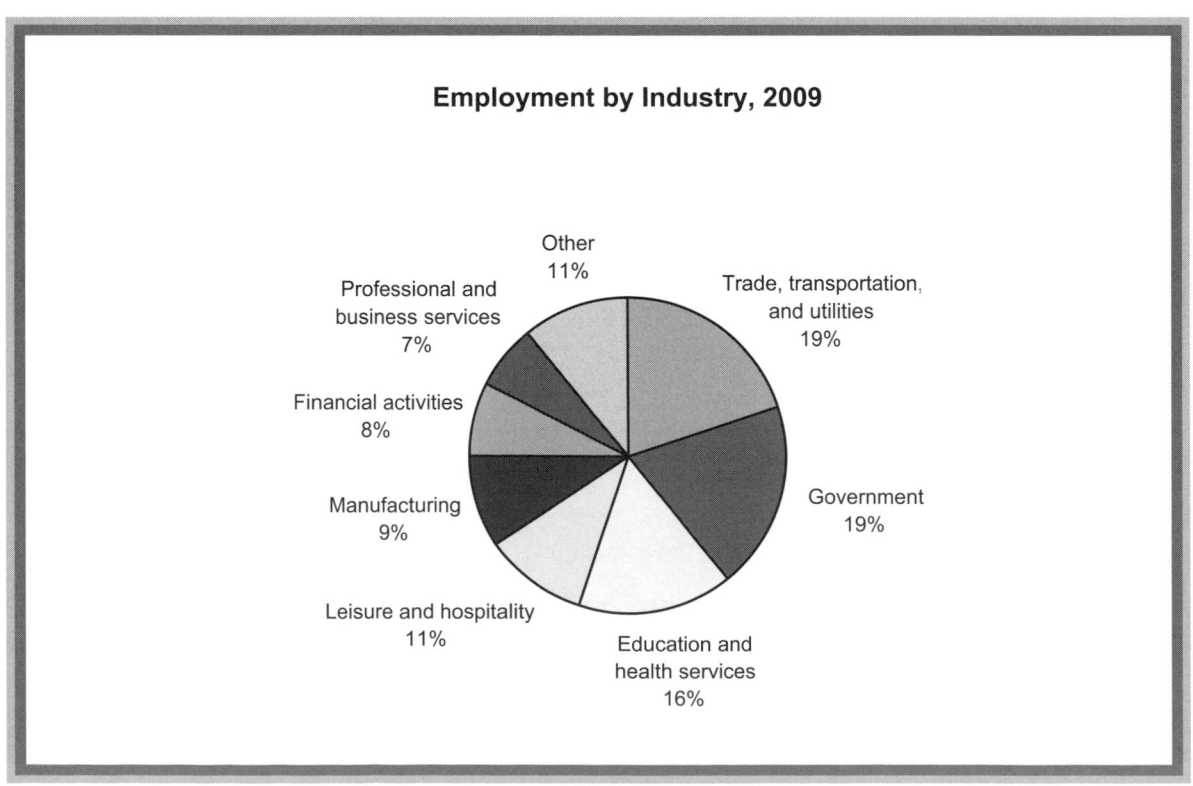

Other
11%

Professional and
business services
7%

Trade, transportation,
and utilities
19%

Financial activities
8%

Manufacturing
9%

Government
19%

Leisure and hospitality
11%

Education and
health services
16%

Employment by Industry: South Dakota, Selected Years, 1990–2009

(Numbers in thousands, not seasonally adjusted.)

Industry and year	January	February	March	April	May	June	July	August	September	October	November	December	Annual average
Total Nonfarm													
1990	275.6	276.3	279.9	284.5	291.7	296.6	293.2	293.6	292.4	293.4	292.7	292.2	288.5
2000	367.1	367.7	371.8	376.7	383.5	388.3	381.8	382.2	380.3	379.9	377.6	377.3	377.9
2001	369.2	369.5	371.4	376.3	385.1	389.6	383.8	384.5	380.5	379.4	378.1	376.8	378.7
2002	365.7	365.7	367.3	373.6	382.9	388.1	383.2	384.7	381.1	380.9	378.7	378.6	377.5
2003	367.9	367.2	368.9	375.0	383.0	387.8	383.4	386.0	381.2	381.1	380.2	379.5	378.4
2004	369.7	370.0	372.1	381.0	388.9	394.1	388.4	391.2	388.9	388.0	386.3	385.4	383.7
2005	375.3	376.3	379.6	386.8	393.9	399.8	395.6	398.2	395.7	393.7	393.2	393.5	390.1
2006	384.0	385.0	388.1	393.3	402.7	408.8	404.0	407.4	403.4	402.6	401.8	401.9	398.6
2007	391.9	392.8	396.4	401.5	411.6	416.7	413.3	415.8	411.0	410.4	409.1	407.8	406.5
2008	399.6	401.1	403.5	407.1	416.5	420.9	416.6	420.1	415.3	414.8	411.6	409.7	411.4
2009	397.5	396.9	397.2	399.1	409.3	412.8	408.8	409.2	406.2	406.0	403.9	398.0	403.7
Total Private													
1990	213.2	213.2	216.2	219.8	226.1	231.4	233.9	235.7	231.1	229.5	227.9	227.4	225.5
2000	296.8	296.5	299.3	304.1	309.6	315.4	314.6	314.7	309.5	308.1	305.8	305.2	306.6
2001	296.9	296.5	298.9	302.8	309.7	313.7	313.8	314.0	307.2	305.1	303.5	301.9	305.3
2002	292.4	291.6	293.1	299.3	306.8	311.8	312.0	313.2	307.1	305.9	303.5	303.0	303.3
2003	294.0	292.4	293.8	299.7	306.5	311.6	312.4	314.2	306.9	305.7	304.9	304.0	303.8
2004	295.4	295.1	297.0	304.9	311.7	317.3	317.2	320.1	313.8	312.1	310.1	309.1	308.7
2005	300.4	300.9	303.7	310.7	316.6	322.8	323.8	326.7	320.4	317.7	317.0	317.5	314.9
2006	309.6	309.5	312.3	317.4	325.2	331.5	332.1	335.4	328.5	326.5	325.4	325.8	323.3
2007	317.7	317.0	320.6	325.7	334.0	339.9	340.7	343.0	335.7	334.0	332.5	331.5	331.0
2008	324.9	324.6	327.0	330.5	338.1	344.0	344.5	346.8	339.3	337.2	333.9	332.1	335.2
2009	321.4	319.6	319.4	320.5	328.9	334.0	331.0	334.5	328.1	327.2	325.1	319.9	326.1
Goods-Producing													
1990	43.4	43.5	44.4	45.6	47.5	49.6	51.1	50.9	49.7	49.5	48.5	47.2	47.6
2000	59.8	59.5	60.4	62.1	63.4	65.8	66.7	66.2	64.9	64.5	62.7	60.9	63.1
2001	59.1	58.3	58.5	60.1	61.6	63.7	63.7	63.3	61.4	60.7	59.3	57.7	60.6
2002	55.0	54.0	54.2	56.3	58.8	60.6	61.3	60.9	59.6	59.3	58.0	56.9	57.9
2003	54.3	53.6	54.2	56.7	59.1	60.6	61.0	61.0	59.5	59.3	58.4	56.9	57.9
2004	54.7	54.4	55.3	58.7	60.6	62.4	63.1	62.8	61.7	61.5	60.7	59.5	59.6
2005	56.9	56.8	57.7	60.5	62.3	64.3	64.9	64.7	63.7	63.7	63.0	61.5	61.7
2006	59.9	59.6	60.5	62.8	65.1	67.1	67.8	67.6	66.4	65.9	64.9	64.1	64.3
2007	61.5	60.6	61.9	63.6	65.9	67.8	68.4	68.1	67.2	66.9	66.1	64.6	65.2
2008	62.7	62.3	63.2	64.8	67.4	68.8	69.1	68.7	67.7	67.3	65.9	63.4	65.9
2009	59.6	58.4	57.8	57.7	60.3	62.1	62.2	61.3	60.1	59.9	59.2	56.4	59.6
Mining, Logging, and Construction													
1990	11.4	11.2	11.8	13.0	14.3	15.7	16.4	16.3	15.6	15.3	14.5	13.4	14.1
2000	16.1	15.8	16.7	18.6	20.1	21.7	22.3	22.1	21.2	20.5	18.8	17.7	19.3
2001	16.2	15.9	16.4	18.2	20.3	22.2	22.6	22.6	21.6	21.0	19.9	18.6	19.5
2002	16.4	16.1	16.3	18.1	20.5	21.9	22.2	22.1	21.2	20.9	19.9	19.0	19.6
2003	16.8	16.4	16.8	19.1	21.4	22.7	23.1	23.0	22.0	21.6	20.5	19.3	20.2
2004	17.1	16.7	17.4	20.0	21.7	22.9	23.5	23.4	22.4	22.2	21.4	20.5	20.7
2005	18.1	17.9	18.6	21.0	22.7	24.2	24.7	24.7	23.7	23.5	22.7	21.2	21.9
2006	19.5	19.3	19.8	21.8	23.7	25.1	25.7	25.5	24.4	23.7	22.7	21.8	22.8
2007	19.7	19.0	20.0	21.5	23.9	25.4	26.1	26.0	25.2	24.6	23.9	22.5	23.2
2008	20.6	20.0	20.5	22.2	24.5	25.6	25.9	25.7	24.9	24.4	23.3	21.6	23.3
2009	19.0	18.7	18.9	19.9	22.6	24.4	25.3	24.3	23.2	22.5	21.8	19.2	21.7
Manufacturing													
1990	32.0	32.3	32.6	32.6	33.2	33.9	34.7	34.6	34.1	34.2	34.0	33.8	33.5
2000	43.7	43.7	43.7	43.5	43.3	44.1	44.4	44.1	43.7	44.0	43.9	43.2	43.8
2001	42.9	42.4	42.1	41.9	41.3	41.5	41.1	40.7	39.8	39.7	39.4	39.1	40.9
2002	38.6	37.9	37.9	38.2	38.3	38.7	39.1	38.8	38.4	38.4	38.1	37.9	38.4
2003	37.5	37.2	37.4	37.6	37.7	37.9	37.9	38.0	37.5	37.7	37.9	37.6	37.7
2004	37.6	37.7	37.9	38.7	38.9	39.5	39.6	39.4	39.3	39.3	39.3	39.0	38.9
2005	38.8	38.9	39.1	39.5	39.6	40.1	40.2	40.0	40.0	40.2	40.3	40.3	39.8
2006	40.4	40.3	40.7	41.0	41.4	42.0	42.1	42.1	42.0	42.2	42.2	42.3	41.6
2007	41.8	41.6	41.9	42.1	42.0	42.4	42.3	42.1	42.0	42.3	42.2	42.1	42.1
2008	42.1	42.3	42.7	42.6	42.9	43.2	43.2	43.0	42.8	42.9	42.6	41.8	42.7
2009	40.6	39.7	38.9	37.8	37.7	37.7	36.9	37.0	36.9	37.4	37.4	37.2	37.9
Service-Providing													
1990	232.2	232.8	235.5	238.9	244.2	247.0	242.1	242.7	242.7	243.9	244.2	245.0	240.9
2000	307.3	308.2	311.4	314.6	320.1	322.5	315.1	316.0	315.4	315.4	314.9	316.4	314.8
2001	310.1	311.2	312.9	316.2	323.5	325.9	320.1	321.2	319.1	318.7	318.8	319.1	318.1
2002	310.7	311.7	313.1	317.3	324.1	327.5	321.9	323.8	321.5	321.6	320.7	321.7	319.6
2003	313.6	313.6	314.7	318.3	323.9	327.2	322.4	325.0	321.7	321.8	321.8	322.6	320.6
2004	315.0	315.6	316.8	322.3	328.3	331.7	325.3	328.4	327.2	326.5	325.6	325.9	324.1
2005	318.4	319.5	321.9	326.3	331.6	335.5	330.7	333.5	332.0	330.0	330.2	332.0	328.5
2006	324.1	325.4	327.6	330.5	337.6	341.7	336.2	339.8	337.0	336.7	336.9	337.8	334.3
2007	330.4	332.2	334.5	337.9	345.7	348.9	344.9	347.7	343.8	343.5	343.0	343.2	341.3
2008	336.9	338.8	340.3	342.3	349.1	352.1	347.5	351.4	347.6	347.5	345.7	346.3	345.5
2009	337.9	338.5	339.4	341.4	349.0	350.7	346.6	347.9	346.1	346.1	344.7	341.6	344.2

Employment by Industry: South Dakota, Selected Years, 1990–2009—*Continued*

(Numbers in thousands, not seasonally adjusted.)

Industry and year	January	February	March	April	May	June	July	August	September	October	November	December	Annual average
Trade, Transportation, and Utilities													
1990	61.8	61.4	61.9	62.8	63.9	64.5	65.3	65.5	64.9	65.6	66.1	66.8	64.2
2000	75.1	74.7	75.0	76.9	77.7	78.0	77.3	77.4	76.5	77.2	78.1	78.4	76.9
2001	75.7	75.7	76.3	76.5	77.9	78.0	77.4	77.4	76.2	77.0	77.9	78.4	77.0
2002	75.0	74.3	74.3	75.9	77.2	77.8	77.0	77.4	76.4	77.1	77.7	78.2	76.5
2003	75.1	74.3	74.5	76.0	77.0	77.4	77.0	77.2	75.9	76.5	77.3	78.0	76.4
2004	75.2	74.4	74.7	76.2	77.7	78.2	77.8	78.7	77.1	77.8	78.7	79.3	77.2
2005	76.4	76.4	76.9	78.3	79.4	79.6	79.6	80.5	79.2	79.2	80.2	81.0	78.9
2006	78.3	77.7	78.3	79.0	80.4	81.2	80.7	81.6	80.1	80.5	81.4	82.2	80.1
2007	79.5	78.7	79.5	80.2	81.7	82.3	82.3	82.6	81.2	81.6	82.4	82.9	81.2
2008	81.0	80.3	80.6	81.1	82.3	83.0	83.3	83.7	82.2	82.6	82.6	83.1	82.2
2009	80.0	79.2	79.1	79.4	81.2	81.6	81.5	81.9	80.7	81.1	81.8	81.8	80.8
Wholesale Trade													
1990	14.7	14.6	14.8	14.9	14.9	14.9	15.5	14.9	14.7	14.7	14.5	14.5	14.8
2000	16.3	16.4	16.5	16.7	16.7	16.7	16.5	16.5	16.4	16.5	16.5	16.5	16.5
2001	16.5	16.5	16.6	16.8	17.0	16.9	16.7	16.6	16.4	16.7	16.7	16.7	16.6
2002	16.6	16.6	16.6	16.9	16.9	17.0	16.7	16.6	16.3	16.6	16.6	16.6	16.7
2003	16.4	16.3	16.4	16.8	16.9	16.8	16.7	16.6	16.6	16.9	16.9	16.9	16.7
2004	16.6	16.6	16.9	17.2	17.3	17.3	17.1	17.1	16.9	17.4	17.3	17.4	17.1
2005	17.1	17.1	17.1	17.5	17.7	17.7	17.6	17.8	17.6	17.8	17.8	17.8	17.6
2006	18.0	18.0	18.1	18.3	18.6	18.6	18.3	18.3	18.0	18.2	18.1	18.1	18.2
2007	18.0	17.9	18.1	18.3	18.6	18.6	18.5	18.6	18.4	18.5	18.6	18.6	18.4
2008	18.6	18.6	18.7	18.8	19.0	19.0	18.9	18.9	18.6	18.8	18.4	18.6	18.7
2009	18.1	18.1	18.1	18.2	18.6	18.5	18.5	18.4	18.1	18.2	18.3	18.3	18.3
Retail Trade													
1990	37.6	37.2	37.5	38.3	39.0	39.8	40.0	40.7	40.2	40.8	41.5	42.1	39.6
2000	46.9	46.5	46.8	48.3	48.9	49.4	49.0	49.0	47.9	48.4	49.3	49.6	48.3
2001	47.3	47.3	47.7	47.6	48.7	49.0	48.8	49.0	47.7	48.0	49.0	49.5	48.2
2002	46.8	46.1	46.1	47.2	48.3	48.9	48.7	49.1	48.2	48.7	49.4	49.8	48.1
2003	47.2	46.6	46.7	47.8	48.5	49.0	48.8	49.1	47.8	48.1	48.9	49.6	48.2
2004	47.4	46.7	46.7	47.7	48.9	49.3	49.2	50.0	48.4	48.5	49.5	50.1	48.5
2005	47.7	47.7	48.2	49.0	49.7	49.9	49.9	50.5	49.2	49.0	50.0	50.6	49.3
2006	48.0	47.4	47.8	48.2	49.0	49.8	49.7	50.3	49.1	49.3	50.4	51.0	49.2
2007	48.8	48.2	48.8	49.1	50.1	50.7	50.9	51.0	49.6	49.9	50.7	51.2	49.9
2008	49.4	48.7	48.9	49.2	50.0	50.7	51.1	51.5	50.2	50.4	50.9	51.2	50.2
2009	48.9	48.2	48.2	48.5	49.6	50.2	50.3	50.6	49.6	49.9	50.7	50.7	49.6
Transportation and Utilities													
1990	9.5	9.6	9.6	9.6	10.0	9.8	9.8	9.9	10.0	10.1	10.1	10.2	9.9
2000	11.9	11.8	11.7	11.9	12.1	11.9	11.8	11.9	12.2	12.3	12.3	12.3	12.0
2001	11.9	11.9	12.0	12.1	12.2	12.1	11.9	11.8	12.1	12.3	12.2	12.2	12.0
2002	11.6	11.6	11.6	11.8	12.0	11.9	11.6	11.7	11.9	11.8	11.7	11.8	11.8
2003	11.5	11.4	11.4	11.4	11.6	11.6	11.5	11.5	11.5	11.5	11.5	11.5	11.5
2004	11.2	11.1	11.1	11.3	11.5	11.6	11.5	11.6	11.8	11.9	11.9	11.8	11.5
2005	11.6	11.6	11.6	11.8	12.0	12.0	12.1	12.2	12.4	12.4	12.4	12.6	12.1
2006	12.3	12.3	12.4	12.5	12.8	12.8	12.7	13.0	13.0	13.0	12.9	13.1	12.7
2007	12.7	12.6	12.6	12.8	13.0	13.0	12.9	13.0	13.2	13.2	13.1	13.1	12.9
2008	13.0	13.0	13.0	13.1	13.3	13.3	13.3	13.3	13.4	13.4	13.3	13.3	13.2
2009	13.0	12.9	12.8	12.7	13.0	12.9	12.7	12.9	13.0	13.0	12.8	12.8	12.9
Information													
1990	5.7	5.6	5.5	5.4	5.5	5.5	5.5	5.5	5.5	5.4	5.4	5.4	5.5
2000	6.8	6.7	6.8	6.9	7.0	7.0	7.0	6.9	6.9	6.8	6.9	6.9	6.9
2001	6.8	6.8	6.8	6.7	6.9	6.9	6.9	6.8	6.8	6.8	6.8	6.8	6.8
2002	6.8	6.7	6.8	6.7	6.8	6.9	6.9	6.8	6.7	6.9	6.9	6.9	6.8
2003	6.8	6.7	6.7	6.6	6.7	6.8	6.7	6.8	6.7	6.8	6.9	6.9	6.8
2004	6.8	6.8	6.8	6.7	6.8	6.7	6.8	6.8	6.7	6.6	6.6	6.6	6.7
2005	6.6	6.6	6.5	6.5	6.7	6.8	6.9	6.9	6.9	6.9	6.9	6.9	6.8
2006	6.8	6.9	6.9	6.8	6.9	7.0	7.1	7.1	7.0	6.9	6.9	7.0	6.9
2007	7.0	7.1	7.0	7.3	7.4	7.5	7.1	7.2	7.0	7.0	7.0	7.0	7.1
2008	7.0	7.0	6.9	6.8	6.9	7.0	7.0	7.1	6.9	6.9	6.9	6.9	6.9
2009	6.8	6.8	6.7	6.6	6.8	6.7	6.7	6.7	6.7	6.7	6.7	6.7	6.7
Financial Activities													
1990	16.8	16.8	17.0	16.9	17.0	17.2	17.1	17.3	17.1	17.0	17.2	17.4	17.1
2000	25.6	25.6	25.7	25.9	26.0	26.4	26.5	26.4	26.3	26.5	26.7	27.2	26.2
2001	27.5	27.7	27.8	27.8	28.0	28.3	28.4	28.2	28.1	27.9	28.0	28.1	28.0
2002	28.0	28.0	27.9	27.9	27.9	28.1	28.0	28.0	27.7	27.6	27.7	28.0	27.9
2003	27.6	27.6	27.8	27.5	27.4	27.6	27.8	27.8	27.6	27.7	27.7	28.0	27.7
2004	27.7	27.6	27.8	27.5	27.7	28.0	27.9	28.0	27.9	27.8	27.8	28.1	27.8
2005	28.2	28.0	28.2	27.9	28.2	28.8	28.6	28.6	28.7	28.5	28.6	29.2	28.5
2006	29.0	29.0	29.1	29.0	29.2	29.5	29.7	29.9	29.8	29.8	29.9	30.2	29.5
2007	30.2	30.4	30.7	30.6	30.8	31.3	31.3	31.2	31.1	31.2	31.2	31.2	30.9
2008	31.0	31.0	31.3	30.9	31.2	31.5	31.4	31.1	31.0	30.6	30.6	30.7	31.0
2009	30.7	30.8	30.9	30.7	30.7	30.9	30.6	30.4	30.0	30.2	29.9	29.6	30.5

Employment by Industry: South Dakota, Selected Years, 1990–2009—*Continued*

(Numbers in thousands, not seasonally adjusted.)

Industry and year	January	February	March	April	May	June	July	August	September	October	November	December	Annual average
Professional and Business Services													
1990	10.5	10.6	10.7	10.9	11.0	11.5	11.5	11.7	11.4	11.4	11.3	11.3	11.2
2000	26.8	27.1	27.2	27.4	27.4	28.0	27.9	27.7	27.3	27.3	26.7	27.0	27.3
2001	26.1	25.9	25.9	26.4	26.5	26.6	26.4	26.3	25.6	25.5	25.1	24.9	25.9
2002	24.2	24.6	24.7	25.1	25.1	25.5	25.1	25.4	24.7	24.9	25.0	24.9	24.9
2003	24.2	24.4	24.2	24.2	24.3	24.5	24.5	24.6	24.0	24.2	24.5	24.2	24.3
2004	23.2	23.8	23.4	24.3	24.5	24.5	24.5	25.2	24.7	24.5	24.1	24.0	24.2
2005	23.2	23.7	23.9	24.6	24.4	24.7	25.0	25.2	24.6	24.6	24.8	25.3	24.5
2006	24.6	25.0	25.0	25.5	25.7	26.0	26.1	26.1	25.8	26.1	26.1	26.4	25.7
2007	26.0	26.4	26.6	27.4	28.0	28.5	28.5	28.6	27.9	27.6	27.5	27.8	27.6
2008	27.4	27.6	27.8	28.2	28.2	28.6	28.5	28.8	28.1	27.8	27.7	27.8	28.0
2009	27.1	27.0	26.7	26.7	26.9	27.1	27.0	26.8	26.3	25.6	25.4	25.3	26.5
Education and Health Services													
1990	36.4	36.7	36.9	36.9	37.2	36.5	35.9	36.1	37.3	37.5	37.7	37.7	36.9
2000	50.8	51.1	51.3	51.5	51.5	51.0	50.3	50.4	51.2	51.9	52.0	52.4	51.3
2001	51.7	52.3	52.7	52.8	52.9	52.1	51.9	52.0	52.5	53.1	53.7	53.6	52.6
2002	53.1	53.5	53.8	54.2	54.1	53.7	53.2	53.4	54.1	54.7	54.9	55.0	54.0
2003	54.9	54.8	54.9	55.2	55.3	54.9	55.0	55.2	55.4	56.2	56.4	56.5	55.4
2004	55.8	56.2	56.4	56.6	56.5	56.4	55.8	55.7	56.4	57.0	57.3	57.5	56.5
2005	56.8	57.0	57.3	57.5	57.3	57.2	56.6	57.0	57.6	57.9	58.2	58.4	57.4
2006	57.8	58.0	58.3	58.4	58.4	58.2	57.9	58.2	58.9	59.0	59.5	59.6	58.5
2007	58.9	59.1	59.5	59.8	60.1	59.8	59.6	59.9	60.5	60.9	61.2	61.3	60.1
2008	61.2	61.5	61.7	61.6	62.0	61.9	61.4	61.9	62.2	62.7	63.0	63.4	62.0
2009	62.6	62.7	62.9	63.0	63.2	63.1	62.7	62.6	63.1	64.3	64.7	64.6	63.3
Leisure and Hospitality													
1990	24.8	24.8	25.8	27.6	30.1	32.6	33.5	34.5	31.7	29.1	27.8	27.5	29.2
2000	34.9	35.1	35.8	36.8	39.8	42.5	42.7	43.6	40.6	37.8	36.6	36.3	38.5
2001	34.5	34.3	35.3	36.9	40.1	42.2	43.1	44.0	40.8	38.2	36.9	36.6	38.6
2002	34.7	34.9	35.7	37.4	40.8	43.1	44.3	45.2	41.9	39.4	37.5	37.4	39.4
2003	35.6	35.5	36.0	37.8	40.9	43.9	44.5	45.7	42.0	39.3	38.0	37.7	39.7
2004	36.4	36.3	36.9	39.0	41.8	45.0	45.2	46.8	43.3	40.7	38.8	38.5	40.7
2005	37.0	37.0	37.8	39.9	42.7	45.7	46.5	48.1	44.1	41.5	39.8	39.7	41.7
2006	37.9	38.0	38.8	40.4	43.8	46.7	46.9	49.0	44.7	42.6	41.0	40.6	42.5
2007	39.0	39.1	39.7	41.1	44.2	46.7	47.5	49.5	45.0	43.1	41.5	41.0	43.1
2008	39.1	39.3	39.9	41.3	44.1	47.1	47.6	49.3	45.2	43.3	41.4	41.0	43.2
2009	39.0	39.1	39.8	40.7	44.0	46.6	47.4	48.9	45.5	43.6	41.8	39.9	43.0
Other Services													
1990	13.8	13.8	14.0	13.7	13.9	14.0	14.0	14.2	13.5	14.0	13.9	14.1	13.9
2000	17.0	16.7	17.1	16.6	16.8	16.7	16.2	16.1	15.8	16.1	16.1	16.1	16.4
2001	15.5	15.5	15.6	15.6	15.8	15.9	16.0	16.0	15.8	15.9	15.8	15.8	15.8
2002	15.6	15.6	15.7	15.8	16.1	16.1	16.2	16.1	16.0	16.0	15.8	15.7	15.9
2003	15.5	15.5	15.5	15.7	15.8	15.9	15.9	15.9	15.8	15.7	15.7	15.8	15.7
2004	15.6	15.6	15.7	15.9	16.1	16.1	16.1	16.1	16.0	16.2	16.1	15.6	15.9
2005	15.3	15.4	15.4	15.5	15.6	15.7	15.7	15.7	15.6	15.4	15.5	15.5	15.5
2006	15.3	15.3	15.4	15.5	15.7	15.8	15.9	15.9	15.8	15.7	15.7	15.7	15.6
2007	15.6	15.6	15.7	15.7	15.9	16.0	16.0	15.9	15.8	15.7	15.6	15.7	15.8
2008	15.5	15.6	15.6	15.8	16.0	16.1	16.2	16.2	16.0	16.0	15.8	15.8	15.9
2009	15.6	15.6	15.5	15.7	15.8	15.9	15.9	15.9	15.7	15.8	15.6	15.6	15.7
Government													
1990	62.4	63.1	63.7	64.7	65.6	65.2	59.3	57.9	61.3	63.9	64.8	64.8	63.1
2000	70.3	71.2	72.5	72.6	73.9	72.9	67.2	67.5	70.8	71.8	71.8	72.1	71.2
2001	72.3	73.0	72.5	73.5	75.4	75.9	70.0	70.5	73.3	74.3	74.6	74.9	73.4
2002	73.3	74.1	74.2	74.3	76.1	76.3	71.2	71.5	74.0	75.0	75.2	75.6	74.2
2003	73.9	74.8	75.1	75.3	76.5	76.2	71.0	71.8	74.3	75.4	75.3	75.5	74.6
2004	74.3	74.9	75.1	76.1	77.2	76.8	71.2	71.1	75.1	75.9	76.2	76.3	75.0
2005	74.9	75.4	75.9	76.1	77.3	77.0	71.8	71.5	75.3	76.0	76.2	76.0	75.3
2006	74.4	75.5	75.8	75.9	77.5	77.3	71.9	72.0	74.9	76.1	76.4	76.1	75.3
2007	74.2	75.8	75.8	75.8	77.6	76.8	72.6	72.8	75.3	76.4	76.6	76.3	75.5
2008	74.7	76.5	76.5	76.6	78.4	76.9	72.1	73.3	76.0	77.6	77.7	77.6	76.2
2009	76.1	77.3	77.8	78.6	80.4	78.8	74.8	74.7	78.1	78.8	78.8	78.1	77.7

Average Weekly Hours by Selected Industry: South Dakota, 2007–2009

(Not seasonally adjusted.)

Industry and year	January	February	March	April	May	June	July	August	September	October	November	December	Annual average
Total Private													
2007	31.9	32.4	33.4	32.7	32.5	33.6	34.0	33.2	33.4	32.8	32.4	33.0	33.0
2008	32.3	32.5	32.7	32.6	32.8	33.7	33.2	33.2	32.9	32.8	32.8	32.7	32.9
2009	32.4	32.8	32.9	32.3	33.2	33.1	34.0	34.5	34.1	33.1	33.9	33.6	33.3
Goods-Producing													
2007	36.7	38.7	39.9	39.3	39.6	40.8	41.0	38.9	39.9	39.8	39.4	38.9	39.4
2008	38.4	38.8	38.3	38.7	39.6	39.6	39.6	40.1	40.9	40.4	39.5	38.8	39.4
2009	36.3	36.6	35.6	34.8	37.3	36.3	37.7	38.5	37.7	37.5	38.6	37.7	37.1
Mining, Logging, and Construction													
2007	36.9	39.2	42.1	40.8	43.0	44.0	44.8	43.1	43.0	42.5	41.4	39.1	41.8
2008	38.0	38.1	38.7	39.1	42.0	41.7	41.5	41.4	43.1	41.5	38.0	38.1	40.2
2009	36.6	37.2	37.6	37.9	40.4	39.1	41.6	41.8	40.3	38.6	39.9	37.0	39.2
Manufacturing													
2007	36.6	38.4	38.9	38.5	37.7	38.9	38.7	36.3	38.0	38.2	38.2	38.8	38.1
2008	38.7	39.1	38.1	38.4	38.2	38.4	38.5	39.3	39.6	39.7	40.4	39.2	39.0
2009	36.1	36.3	34.6	33.2	35.5	34.5	35.1	36.4	36.0	36.9	37.9	38.0	35.9
Trade, Transportation, and Utilities													
2007	29.8	30.1	30.5	29.4	31.2	32.3	33.5	33.4	33.3	31.8	31.9	32.5	31.7
2008	30.9	31.2	31.7	31.1	31.5	31.9	31.4	31.7	31.3	31.2	31.5	32.4	31.5
2009	31.5	32.3	32.2	31.6	33.3	33.0	33.1	33.1	32.9	32.7	33.5	33.4	32.7
Professional and Business Services													
2007	32.1	31.1	31.7	32.4	28.1	28.4	28.4	27.5	29.0	30.8	30.8	30.9	30.1
2008	32.0	31.8	32.4	32.2	31.7	33.4	33.6	32.9	32.1	32.1	32.4	32.2	32.4
2009	32.8	33.4	34.5	33.1	32.2	33.1	33.5	34.3	33.5	33.7	34.4	34.1	33.5
Education and Health Services													
2007	36.3	36.2	39.9	37.1	36.1	37.0	35.3	34.9	35.7	33.9	33.7	34.5	35.9
2008	33.7	33.9	33.5	33.4	32.8	34.0	32.5	32.8	31.8	31.6	31.7	31.6	32.8
2009	33.8	33.0	35.4	35.2	34.9	35.2	37.1	37.0	37.2	33.5	34.0	34.5	35.1
Leisure and Hospitality													
2007	21.8	22.8	22.9	23.8	23.4	25.8	27.1	26.4	25.0	24.1	22.4	23.1	24.2
2008	22.4	22.5	23.3	22.9	23.5	25.9	24.8	24.1	23.1	22.5	22.5	21.7	23.3
2009	21.9	23.5	22.9	22.2	23.1	24.1	25.0	25.5	23.9	22.7	23.2	22.3	23.4

Average Hourly Earnings by Selected Industry: South Dakota, 2007–2009

(Dollars, not seasonally adjusted.)

Industry and year	January	February	March	April	May	June	July	August	September	October	November	December	Annual average
Total Private													
2007	16.81	16.90	16.56	17.76	16.59	16.24	15.96	16.02	16.47	16.12	16.22	16.12	16.47
2008	16.31	16.46	16.36	16.42	16.47	16.31	16.13	16.37	16.51	16.61	17.11	17.39	16.53
2009	17.72	17.78	17.89	17.69	17.80	17.60	18.10	17.78	18.10	18.12	18.30	18.42	17.94
Goods-Producing													
2007	18.18	18.40	17.36	17.59	18.05	17.29	17.06	16.76	16.83	17.21	16.80	16.83	17.34
2008	17.47	17.30	17.20	17.30	17.14	17.08	17.07	17.10	16.98	17.10	17.13	17.75	17.21
2009	17.73	18.31	18.35	18.28	17.86	18.13	18.16	17.95	18.09	18.13	17.79	17.84	18.05
Mining, Logging, and Construction													
2007	18.66	20.22	19.71	19.25	19.89	18.48	18.00	18.04	18.35	18.76	18.18	18.37	18.76
2008	19.13	19.17	18.70	18.82	18.34	18.51	18.28	18.54	18.53	18.68	19.14	19.76	18.76
2009	20.40	21.09	20.43	19.88	19.56	19.25	19.32	19.31	19.05	19.28	19.64	19.63	19.67
Manufacturing													
2007	17.95	17.56	16.14	16.69	16.85	16.49	16.39	15.82	15.80	16.20	15.96	16.00	16.48
2008	16.68	16.44	16.46	16.50	16.39	16.16	16.29	16.19	15.99	16.16	16.10	16.74	16.34
2009	16.47	16.96	17.25	17.32	16.70	17.31	17.22	16.93	17.42	17.41	16.66	16.94	17.04
Trade, Transportation, and Utilities													
2007	13.78	13.46	14.00	13.60	13.65	13.46	13.68	13.77	14.81	13.74	14.35	14.22	13.88
2008	14.61	14.70	14.66	14.90	14.86	14.96	14.76	15.08	15.04	15.22	16.20	16.84	15.16
2009	17.50	17.71	18.13	17.98	18.41	18.25	18.50	18.51	19.37	19.60	20.34	20.13	18.72
Professional and Business Services													
2007	22.40	22.07	21.95	21.78	22.23	22.50	21.23	21.75	21.58	21.10	22.04	21.38	21.83
2008	21.28	21.49	21.98	21.60	22.38	21.35	21.13	21.87	21.99	21.60	23.37	22.16	21.85
2009	22.42	21.94	21.32	20.68	21.38	20.63	20.78	21.46	20.81	21.02	21.13	21.23	21.23
Education and Health Services													
2007	16.36	16.25	16.71	17.11	16.62	16.80	16.41	16.09	16.13	16.05	15.81	15.75	16.35
2008	15.68	15.91	15.81	15.72	16.19	16.59	16.32	16.37	16.80	17.04	17.42	16.95	16.39
2009	17.25	17.03	17.78	17.98	17.67	18.01	19.02	18.58	18.67	18.21	18.22	18.38	18.08
Leisure and Hospitality													
2007	11.16	10.88	10.93	10.72	10.64	10.14	10.54	10.96	11.13	11.27	11.06	11.17	10.86
2008	11.16	11.20	11.05	11.36	11.21	10.85	10.86	10.83	11.05	11.22	11.28	11.69	11.12
2009	11.58	11.56	11.30	11.43	11.29	10.94	10.78	11.26	10.00	10.23	10.47	10.83	10.95

Average Weekly Earnings by Selected Industry: South Dakota, 2007–2009

(Dollars, not seasonally adjusted.)

Industry and year	January	February	March	April	May	June	July	August	September	October	November	December	Annual average
Total Private													
2007	536.24	547.56	553.10	580.75	539.18	545.66	542.64	531.86	550.10	528.74	525.53	531.96	543.51
2008	526.81	534.95	534.97	535.29	540.22	549.65	535.52	543.48	543.18	544.81	561.21	568.65	543.84
2009	574.13	583.18	588.58	571.39	590.96	582.56	615.40	613.41	617.21	599.77	620.37	618.91	597.40
Goods-Producing													
2007	667.21	712.08	692.66	691.29	714.78	705.43	699.46	651.96	671.52	684.96	661.92	654.69	683.20
2008	670.85	671.24	658.76	669.51	678.74	676.37	675.97	685.71	694.48	690.84	676.64	688.70	678.07
2009	643.60	670.15	653.26	636.14	666.18	658.12	684.63	691.08	681.99	679.88	686.69	672.57	669.66
Mining, Logging, and Construction													
2007	688.55	792.62	829.79	785.40	855.27	813.12	806.40	777.52	789.05	797.30	752.65	718.27	784.17
2008	726.94	730.38	723.69	735.86	770.28	771.87	758.62	767.56	798.64	775.22	727.32	752.86	754.15
2009	746.64	784.55	768.17	753.45	790.22	752.68	803.71	807.16	767.72	744.21	783.64	726.31	771.06
Manufacturing													
2007	656.97	674.30	627.85	642.57	635.25	641.46	634.29	574.27	600.40	618.84	609.67	620.80	627.89
2008	645.52	642.80	627.13	633.60	626.10	620.54	627.17	636.27	633.20	641.55	650.44	656.21	637.26
2009	594.57	615.65	596.85	575.02	592.85	597.20	604.42	616.25	627.12	642.43	631.41	643.72	611.74
Trade, Transportation, and Utilities													
2007	410.64	405.15	427.00	399.84	425.88	434.76	458.28	459.92	493.17	436.93	457.77	462.15	440.00
2008	451.45	458.64	464.72	463.39	468.09	477.22	463.46	478.04	470.75	474.86	510.30	545.62	477.54
2009	551.25	572.03	583.79	568.17	613.05	602.25	612.35	612.68	637.27	640.92	681.39	672.34	612.14
Professional and Business Services													
2007	719.04	686.38	695.82	705.67	624.66	639.00	602.93	598.13	625.82	649.88	678.83	660.64	657.08
2008	680.96	683.38	712.15	695.52	709.45	713.09	709.97	719.52	705.88	693.36	757.19	713.55	707.94
2009	735.38	732.80	735.54	684.51	688.44	682.85	696.13	736.08	697.14	708.37	726.87	723.94	711.21
Education and Health Services													
2007	593.87	588.25	666.73	634.78	599.98	621.60	579.27	561.54	575.84	544.10	532.80	543.38	586.97
2008	528.42	539.35	529.64	525.05	531.03	564.06	530.40	536.94	534.24	538.46	552.21	535.62	537.59
2009	583.05	561.99	629.41	632.90	616.68	633.95	705.64	687.46	694.52	610.04	619.48	634.11	634.61
Leisure and Hospitality													
2007	243.29	248.06	250.30	255.14	248.98	261.61	285.63	289.34	278.25	271.61	247.74	258.03	262.81
2008	249.98	252.00	257.47	260.14	263.44	281.02	269.33	261.00	255.26	252.45	253.80	253.67	259.10
2009	253.60	271.66	258.77	253.75	260.80	263.65	269.50	287.13	239.00	232.22	242.90	241.51	256.23

TENNESSEE
At a Glance

Population:
    1990 census: 4,877,203
    2000 census: 5,689,283
    2009 estimate: 6,296,254

Percent change in population:
    1990–2000: 16.7%
    2000–2009: 10.7%

Percent change in total nonfarm employment:
    1990–2009: 19.4%
    2008–2009: -5.6%

Industry with the largest growth in employment, 1990–2009 (thousands):
    Education and Health Services, 156.8

Industry with the largest decline or smallest growth in employment, 1990–2009 (thousands):
    Manufacturing, -187.8

Civilian labor force:
    1990: 2,401,093
    2000: 2,871,539
    2009: 3,020,016

Unemployment rate and rank among states (lowest to highest):
    1990: 5.5%, 29th
    2000: 4.0%, 28th
    2009: 10.5%, 42nd

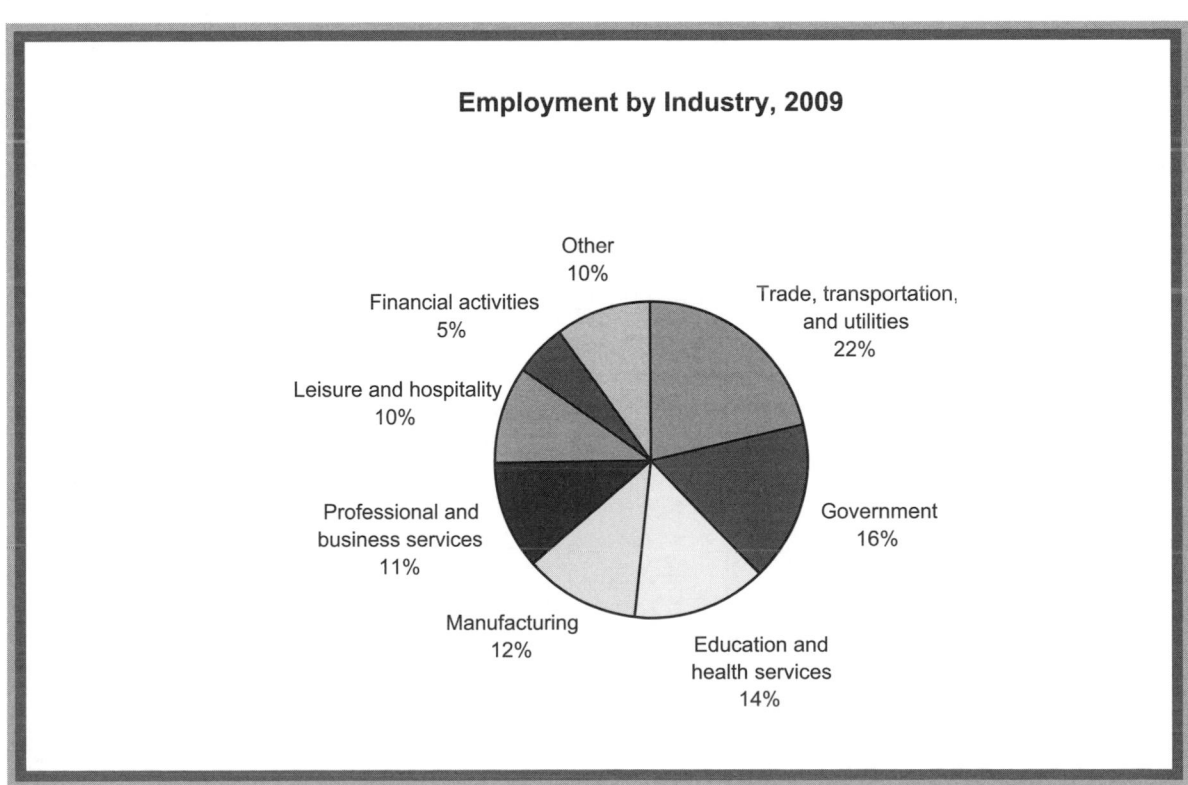

Employment by Industry, 2009

Other 10%
Financial activities 5%
Leisure and hospitality 10%
Professional and business services 11%
Manufacturing 12%
Education and health services 14%
Government 16%
Trade, transportation, and utilities 22%

Employment by Industry: Tennessee, Selected Years, 1990–2009

(Numbers in thousands, not seasonally adjusted.)

Industry and year	January	February	March	April	May	June	July	August	September	October	November	December	Annual average
Total Nonfarm													
1990	2144.0	2154.3	2175.4	2192.2	2209.7	2215.7	2184.4	2206.4	2219.5	2207.1	2207.1	2202.7	2193.2
2000	2665.1	2683.9	2727.5	2725.7	2740.8	2745.2	2719.4	2737.3	2748.5	2745.9	2753.1	2754.7	2728.9
2001	2673.4	2683.1	2701.2	2705.5	2708.1	2703.2	2666.2	2684.1	2691.2	2676.8	2683.3	2683.0	2688.3
2002	2611.9	2622.8	2643.7	2660.0	2670.2	2672.0	2657.2	2674.7	2684.2	2684.6	2693.5	2698.1	2664.4
2003	2619.8	2627.9	2646.0	2662.8	2671.8	2668.1	2637.3	2661.8	2675.7	2683.5	2694.7	2702.4	2662.7
2004	2637.4	2668.4	2678.9	2700.4	2706.7	2710.6	2693.6	2716.3	2725.5	2732.6	2746.2	2756.2	2706.1
2005	2671.3	2696.1	2718.4	2739.5	2746.5	2743.7	2731.8	2753.6	2776.3	2767.1	2784.7	2788.3	2743.1
2006	2727.1	2734.8	2765.3	2781.4	2791.6	2791.4	2769.8	2796.8	2810.2	2793.8	2811.4	2818.6	2782.7
2007	2744.9	2753.7	2784.0	2787.9	2799.3	2798.0	2782.4	2811.2	2821.7	2815.9	2833.6	2836.4	2797.4
2008	2762.4	2771.9	2790.1	2797.1	2805.4	2784.3	2758.6	2779.0	2779.4	2766.1	2758.6	2745.1	2774.8
2009	2647.6	2636.8	2634.6	2628.8	2629.9	2601.3	2584.4	2603.5	2613.5	2613.1	2621.6	2611.8	2618.9
Total Private													
1990	1796.9	1802.1	1820.2	1835.2	1851.6	1869.1	1849.8	1866.8	1863.4	1850.2	1849.5	1846.5	1841.7
2000	2275.0	2285.7	2308.6	2322.4	2332.8	2352.7	2341.2	2349.3	2352.3	2342.3	2347.8	2348.9	2329.9
2001	2275.2	2276.0	2292.1	2295.6	2300.6	2309.2	2285.7	2292.7	2286.5	2266.7	2269.9	2270.9	2285.1
2002	2205.5	2208.0	2226.9	2240.8	2255.1	2266.4	2271.0	2278.9	2275.1	2268.9	2274.5	2278.7	2254.2
2003	2211.4	2212.6	2228.4	2242.6	2254.1	2263.6	2248.4	2263.4	2264.1	2267.5	2277.7	2284.7	2251.5
2004	2226.3	2235.3	2257.8	2279.7	2289.2	2303.1	2301.8	2313.8	2310.2	2313.6	2325.0	2334.3	2290.8
2005	2261.1	2278.4	2299.4	2322.9	2331.4	2343.9	2339.8	2352.1	2358.0	2347.1	2363.1	2367.6	2330.4
2006	2315.1	2317.2	2345.0	2359.3	2371.0	2387.0	2371.8	2386.7	2387.4	2370.0	2385.1	2393.4	2365.8
2007	2326.8	2331.2	2358.7	2365.2	2376.0	2392.8	2382.1	2396.7	2394.0	2384.5	2400.3	2405.3	2376.1
2008	2337.7	2341.8	2357.7	2363.8	2371.5	2378.6	2352.7	2360.0	2348.8	2327.3	2318.6	2306.5	2347.1
2009	2219.7	2204.1	2200.1	2193.8	2195.3	2196.3	2179.2	2185.4	2180.5	2175.2	2183.9	2175.9	2190.8
Goods-Producing													
1990	594.8	594.7	598.6	601.2	605.7	609.3	600.1	602.9	602.5	596.4	592.7	588.8	599.0
2000	624.4	625.4	630.1	628.8	631.7	636.3	628.2	628.5	626.3	618.0	613.6	611.1	625.2
2001	593.0	588.5	591.4	588.8	586.8	587.6	579.3	578.8	574.3	565.2	561.8	558.5	579.5
2002	544.6	543.1	544.3	546.3	551.1	554.0	552.0	554.1	552.4	547.8	543.1	543.2	548.0
2003	530.3	528.2	530.3	532.4	534.7	537.0	532.0	534.9	534.5	533.6	532.3	533.5	532.8
2004	522.0	522.8	526.7	531.8	536.5	539.8	537.3	539.1	538.9	534.1	533.2	533.0	532.9
2005	526.0	527.4	531.2	532.4	535.0	538.4	534.3	538.1	539.7	535.6	536.5	533.3	534.0
2006	530.3	529.7	535.0	536.7	538.4	541.8	535.4	538.5	537.7	529.6	527.4	525.2	533.8
2007	517.8	517.4	522.1	520.0	518.2	522.0	517.1	519.4	518.5	515.5	513.6	512.2	517.8
2008	502.0	502.2	503.6	501.9	502.8	503.9	494.7	496.3	491.5	482.8	473.2	464.9	493.3
2009	443.7	435.5	430.9	423.1	418.6	415.2	413.6	414.2	413.7	410.9	409.0	401.7	419.2
Mining, Logging, and Construction													
1990	97.9	96.7	98.8	99.8	101.6	103.7	104.1	104.3	102.7	100.6	99.8	97.4	100.6
2000	125.6	126.6	131.2	130.5	133.1	135.1	133.1	133.6	133.9	130.7	129.1	127.6	130.8
2001	120.0	120.9	124.8	125.8	127.4	129.3	128.7	128.4	126.6	124.5	124.6	122.4	125.3
2002	114.5	114.3	115.9	117.9	120.5	122.5	122.4	122.7	122.3	121.1	119.9	120.1	119.5
2003	113.6	112.4	115.0	118.5	120.9	122.5	122.5	123.3	123.2	121.8	120.7	120.8	119.6
2004	115.3	115.2	117.8	120.2	122.8	124.8	124.8	124.4	123.8	122.0	121.8	120.9	121.2
2005	117.0	117.6	120.3	121.4	124.2	127.0	128.1	129.4	130.1	129.4	129.2	129.1	125.2
2006	126.4	126.9	131.6	133.3	135.2	138.3	137.4	138.4	138.6	136.5	135.5	134.8	134.4
2007	129.9	130.1	135.0	136.5	138.6	141.5	140.3	141.6	141.5	141.0	139.9	138.5	137.9
2008	132.7	132.6	134.0	134.3	135.6	136.3	134.7	134.7	133.0	130.2	127.1	123.2	132.4
2009	113.2	111.1	111.4	110.3	110.0	111.0	110.8	110.1	110.1	107.5	106.3	101.7	109.5
Manufacturing													
1990	496.0	497.2	498.9	500.5	503.2	504.7	495.1	497.7	498.9	494.9	492.0	490.7	497.5
2000	497.7	497.6	497.7	497.1	497.3	499.8	493.8	493.5	491.0	485.9	483.1	482.1	493.1
2001	473.0	467.6	466.6	463.0	459.4	458.3	450.6	450.4	447.7	440.7	437.2	436.1	454.2
2002	430.1	428.8	428.4	428.4	430.6	431.5	429.6	431.4	430.1	426.7	423.2	423.1	428.5
2003	416.7	415.8	415.3	413.9	413.8	414.5	409.5	411.6	411.3	411.8	411.6	412.7	413.2
2004	406.7	407.6	408.9	411.6	413.7	415.0	412.5	414.7	415.1	412.1	411.4	412.1	411.8
2005	409.0	409.8	410.9	411.0	410.8	411.4	406.2	408.7	409.6	406.2	407.3	404.2	408.8
2006	403.9	402.8	403.4	403.4	403.2	403.5	398.0	400.1	399.1	393.1	391.9	390.4	399.4
2007	387.9	387.3	387.1	383.5	379.6	380.5	376.8	377.8	377.0	374.5	373.7	373.7	380.0
2008	369.3	369.6	369.6	367.6	367.2	367.6	360.0	361.6	358.5	352.6	346.1	341.7	361.0
2009	330.5	324.4	319.5	312.8	308.6	304.2	302.8	304.1	303.6	303.4	302.7	300.0	309.7
Service-Providing													
1990	1549.2	1559.6	1576.8	1591.0	1604.0	1606.4	1584.3	1603.5	1617.0	1610.7	1614.4	1613.9	1594.2
2000	2040.7	2058.5	2097.4	2096.9	2109.1	2108.9	2091.2	2108.8	2122.2	2127.9	2139.5	2143.6	2103.7
2001	2080.4	2094.6	2109.8	2116.7	2121.3	2115.6	2086.9	2105.3	2116.9	2111.6	2121.5	2124.5	2108.8
2002	2067.3	2079.7	2099.4	2113.7	2119.1	2118.0	2105.2	2120.6	2131.8	2136.8	2150.4	2154.9	2116.4
2003	2089.5	2099.7	2115.7	2130.4	2137.1	2131.1	2105.3	2126.9	2141.2	2149.9	2162.4	2168.9	2129.8
2004	2115.4	2145.6	2152.2	2168.6	2170.2	2170.8	2156.3	2177.2	2186.6	2198.5	2213.0	2223.2	2173.1
2005	2145.3	2168.7	2187.2	2207.1	2211.5	2205.3	2197.5	2215.5	2236.6	2231.5	2248.2	2255.0	2209.1
2006	2196.8	2205.1	2230.3	2244.7	2253.2	2249.6	2234.4	2258.3	2272.5	2264.2	2284.0	2293.4	2248.9
2007	2227.1	2236.3	2261.9	2267.9	2281.1	2276.0	2265.3	2291.8	2303.2	2300.4	2320.0	2324.2	2279.6
2008	2260.4	2269.7	2286.5	2295.2	2302.6	2280.4	2263.9	2282.7	2287.9	2283.3	2285.4	2280.2	2281.5
2009	2203.9	2201.3	2203.7	2205.7	2211.3	2186.1	2170.8	2189.3	2199.8	2202.2	2212.6	2210.1	2199.7

Employment by Industry: Tennessee, Selected Years, 1990–2009—*Continued*

(Numbers in thousands, not seasonally adjusted.)

Industry and year	January	February	March	April	May	June	July	August	September	October	November	December	Annual average
Trade, Transportation, and Utilities													
1990	476.1	473.0	476.3	478.8	482.3	486.5	482.9	487.9	488.1	486.4	492.4	496.2	483.9
2000	580.5	582.0	586.8	590.1	590.8	596.0	593.9	592.1	592.7	596.4	604.9	608.2	592.9
2001	593.1	589.1	591.6	590.6	592.3	592.2	584.8	586.5	586.2	585.5	593.4	596.6	590.2
2002	569.4	566.1	570.1	570.3	572.3	573.6	576.6	576.6	577.5	581.3	590.2	597.1	576.8
2003	571.2	569.0	572.1	573.4	574.5	576.4	574.4	578.0	579.5	584.7	593.3	598.1	578.7
2004	575.9	574.8	580.0	582.0	583.1	586.0	584.9	587.3	587.6	594.5	604.9	613.0	587.8
2005	578.4	585.4	590.5	593.6	595.8	595.8	599.5	600.2	601.7	602.0	613.5	620.0	598.0
2006	598.3	596.2	602.2	603.5	606.1	607.0	604.2	607.7	608.6	607.4	619.4	626.6	607.3
2007	603.8	600.6	607.1	606.3	609.1	609.6	606.8	609.5	610.3	611.2	623.5	628.4	610.5
2008	605.4	602.4	606.1	602.9	602.5	601.5	598.3	599.3	596.7	591.7	596.4	598.1	600.1
2009	571.7	564.4	561.8	557.0	557.5	556.8	554.5	556.0	554.2	552.0	559.6	561.0	558.9
Wholesale Trade													
1990	114.0	113.8	115.0	114.9	115.5	116.3	116.5	116.5	116.2	115.4	115.9	115.9	115.5
2000	133.3	134.0	134.9	133.7	133.2	133.4	132.8	132.5	132.4	131.5	131.4	131.5	132.9
2001	128.0	128.1	128.6	128.2	128.1	128.0	126.5	126.9	127.4	126.8	126.9	126.7	127.5
2002	124.7	125.0	125.2	125.4	125.8	126.1	127.0	127.2	127.0	127.8	128.1	128.9	126.5
2003	126.7	127.0	127.2	127.2	127.4	127.2	125.9	126.0	125.9	125.8	126.2	126.1	126.6
2004	124.9	125.4	126.6	127.2	127.5	128.4	128.7	129.1	129.0	129.5	129.9	130.2	128.0
2005	128.4	128.8	129.7	130.1	130.7	130.4	130.5	130.6	131.0	130.7	131.1	131.4	130.3
2006	130.0	130.6	131.4	131.7	132.3	132.5	132.6	132.9	133.0	132.4	132.5	132.5	132.0
2007	131.0	131.4	132.3	132.7	133.0	133.4	133.1	133.3	133.8	134.0	133.7	133.9	133.0
2008	132.5	132.9	133.1	132.8	133.1	132.5	131.8	131.9	131.7	130.5	129.3	128.2	131.7
2009	124.9	123.9	123.0	122.1	121.5	121.2	120.0	119.8	119.2	118.1	118.9	118.7	120.9
Retail Trade													
1990	263.6	260.1	261.1	263.9	265.2	267.0	266.1	269.0	268.4	268.3	273.4	276.7	266.9
2000	311.1	310.6	313.3	315.8	316.7	320.5	319.4	319.6	320.6	323.6	332.2	335.8	319.9
2001	322.1	318.4	320.5	319.4	320.0	319.8	314.7	314.8	314.1	314.7	323.7	327.5	319.1
2002	307.8	304.8	307.5	307.7	309.0	310.0	311.2	310.6	312.4	313.9	322.3	328.9	312.2
2003	307.3	304.9	307.0	308.1	308.7	310.2	309.5	312.0	313.5	318.6	326.5	331.9	313.2
2004	313.7	312.2	314.8	315.5	316.3	317.9	316.3	317.4	317.5	322.7	332.4	337.0	319.5
2005	311.7	318.1	321.0	322.2	323.5	323.7	324.1	323.7	324.1	324.8	334.9	339.7	324.3
2006	323.2	320.8	324.7	325.9	327.0	327.4	325.7	327.1	326.7	327.6	338.6	343.7	328.2
2007	327.1	323.5	328.3	327.1	329.0	329.1	327.3	328.0	328.3	330.0	342.3	346.5	330.5
2008	328.7	325.9	329.6	326.5	325.5	325.2	323.6	323.6	321.3	320.4	325.9	327.6	325.3
2009	310.6	305.9	305.1	303.6	304.9	305.1	305.6	306.6	305.3	306.3	312.9	314.7	307.2
Transportation and Utilities													
1990	98.5	99.1	100.2	100.0	101.6	103.2	100.3	102.4	103.5	102.7	103.1	103.6	101.5
2000	136.1	137.4	138.6	140.6	140.9	142.1	141.7	140.0	139.7	141.3	141.3	140.9	140.1
2001	143.0	142.6	142.5	143.0	144.2	144.4	143.6	144.8	144.7	144.0	142.8	142.4	143.5
2002	136.9	136.3	137.4	137.2	137.5	137.5	138.4	138.8	138.1	139.6	139.8	139.3	138.1
2003	137.2	137.1	137.9	138.1	138.4	139.0	139.0	140.0	140.1	140.3	140.6	140.1	139.0
2004	137.3	137.2	138.6	139.3	139.3	139.7	139.9	140.8	141.1	142.3	142.6	145.8	140.3
2005	138.3	138.5	139.8	141.3	141.6	141.7	144.9	145.9	146.6	146.5	147.5	148.9	143.5
2006	145.1	144.8	146.1	145.9	146.8	147.1	145.9	147.7	148.9	147.4	148.3	150.4	147.0
2007	145.7	145.7	146.5	146.5	147.1	147.1	146.4	148.2	148.2	147.2	147.5	148.0	147.0
2008	144.2	143.6	143.4	143.6	143.9	143.8	142.9	143.8	143.7	140.8	141.2	142.3	143.1
2009	136.2	134.6	133.7	131.3	131.1	130.5	128.9	129.6	129.7	127.6	127.8	127.6	130.7
Information													
1990	44.5	44.7	45.0	44.6	44.6	44.6	45.3	45.2	45.0	44.5	44.7	45.0	44.8
2000	55.1	55.2	55.6	54.6	54.7	55.2	54.6	54.9	55.0	55.2	56.4	56.8	55.3
2001	56.0	56.3	56.5	55.2	55.2	55.7	55.3	55.3	54.5	54.6	55.1	55.4	55.4
2002	54.1	53.9	54.4	53.6	53.8	53.3	52.9	53.0	52.4	52.7	53.1	52.9	53.3
2003	52.1	51.9	51.8	51.7	51.4	51.1	50.5	50.4	49.9	50.6	51.3	51.4	51.2
2004	50.1	49.9	49.7	49.7	49.4	49.6	49.5	49.5	48.3	49.0	49.3	50.0	49.5
2005	49.7	49.7	49.6	49.5	49.7	49.9	49.4	49.2	48.8	48.8	49.3	49.3	49.4
2006	49.1	49.2	49.4	49.9	50.1	50.2	49.3	49.2	49.4	49.4	49.8	50.0	49.6
2007	49.1	49.3	49.2	49.6	50.1	50.4	50.7	50.6	50.6	50.6	51.2	51.8	50.3
2008	51.0	51.0	51.2	50.9	51.1	51.2	50.7	50.3	49.9	49.7	49.5	49.7	50.5
2009	49.1	48.8	48.3	47.7	47.5	47.1	46.7	46.7	46.6	46.0	46.3	46.1	47.2
Financial Activities													
1990	111.5	111.9	112.4	112.9	113.9	114.9	114.4	114.9	114.2	113.5	113.2	113.6	113.4
2000	140.2	140.2	140.4	140.3	140.8	141.9	141.3	141.0	140.7	139.9	140.0	140.7	140.6
2001	137.7	138.0	138.6	138.6	138.8	139.9	139.4	139.3	138.3	137.7	137.8	137.6	138.5
2002	137.2	137.6	137.9	137.7	138.2	138.9	138.2	138.5	137.6	138.0	138.8	139.1	138.1
2003	137.9	137.9	138.5	138.8	139.4	140.1	140.5	140.9	140.2	140.4	141.2	142.0	139.8
2004	140.6	140.4	140.8	141.0	141.5	142.0	142.3	142.5	142.1	142.8	143.1	144.0	141.9
2005	141.3	141.7	142.4	142.9	143.4	144.3	143.9	144.1	144.0	143.5	143.7	144.1	143.3
2006	142.5	142.8	143.5	143.1	143.6	144.3	143.7	144.2	143.7	143.2	143.5	144.2	143.5
2007	142.0	142.8	143.8	143.8	145.0	146.1	145.8	146.0	145.5	145.2	145.6	146.3	144.8
2008	144.5	144.9	145.2	145.1	145.6	146.3	145.8	145.7	144.9	144.3	144.1	144.0	145.0
2009	141.8	141.6	141.1	140.8	140.9	140.7	140.0	140.3	139.2	139.2	139.5	139.6	140.4

Employment by Industry: Tennessee, Selected Years, 1990–2009—*Continued*

(Numbers in thousands, not seasonally adjusted.)

Industry and year	January	February	March	April	May	June	July	August	September	October	November	December	Annual average
Professional and Business Services													
1990	159.2	161.6	164.4	165.5	166.5	168.9	167.6	169.4	169.9	170.5	170.4	169.7	167.0
2000	295.4	298.7	302.7	302.2	302.5	304.8	304.2	308.4	310.4	307.2	305.7	305.6	304.0
2001	299.2	300.5	301.0	299.8	298.3	298.7	296.2	299.4	301.2	297.9	297.4	299.8	299.1
2002	292.3	293.4	297.3	297.4	297.4	297.6	297.8	300.4	298.6	296.2	295.8	293.4	296.5
2003	281.3	282.2	284.0	284.0	286.0	286.7	282.8	288.9	290.9	292.6	294.8	295.5	287.5
2004	288.5	291.8	294.5	299.2	298.9	301.7	301.5	306.5	307.4	312.4	313.6	314.4	302.5
2005	300.6	304.4	306.5	309.9	308.7	310.6	308.3	315.1	319.6	319.8	322.6	325.6	312.6
2006	310.9	311.3	314.9	316.2	316.0	319.6	315.4	321.6	324.3	321.9	327.2	329.1	319.0
2007	310.8	312.6	316.0	318.0	319.3	322.6	321.9	326.5	328.6	328.2	332.7	333.7	322.6
2008	318.1	319.3	321.2	325.0	324.1	327.4	317.8	321.2	322.1	321.3	319.4	316.2	321.1
2009	297.9	296.8	294.1	291.2	291.2	291.1	284.5	289.6	291.7	295.3	297.0	295.7	293.0
Education and Health Services													
1990	203.1	206.4	207.4	208.4	208.9	207.3	207.5	211.2	213.8	214.4	215.1	215.3	209.9
2000	274.2	276.9	279.5	280.9	279.8	278.8	279.1	280.2	285.4	287.3	288.5	288.8	281.6
2001	278.0	281.7	283.6	284.7	285.0	284.0	284.4	286.0	289.5	289.9	291.0	291.9	285.8
2002	288.7	291.2	293.8	296.3	297.8	297.6	299.7	301.8	306.3	307.7	309.6	310.5	300.1
2003	307.2	310.5	311.3	312.7	312.3	311.3	310.1	311.6	314.8	316.9	316.9	317.5	312.8
2004	313.6	316.5	318.6	319.4	318.8	318.5	320.7	322.2	323.5	324.9	326.0	326.6	320.8
2005	323.1	325.2	325.9	329.6	329.5	329.1	330.0	331.7	334.0	334.3	335.2	335.8	330.3
2006	332.6	334.3	336.5	338.9	339.6	339.9	340.1	341.9	344.7	345.5	346.6	347.2	340.7
2007	342.7	345.7	347.4	347.4	348.0	347.6	349.4	352.1	354.9	353.9	354.3	355.0	349.9
2008	351.1	353.3	354.4	356.6	357.2	356.8	357.2	360.0	362.4	364.3	365.5	366.2	358.8
2009	361.0	362.3	362.3	365.4	365.1	365.7	364.7	365.5	368.4	371.8	373.4	374.6	366.7
Leisure and Hospitality													
1990	160.2	162.5	168.4	177.0	182.9	189.2	187.1	188.4	183.2	179.0	175.5	173.3	177.0
2000	218.3	219.4	224.1	233.9	240.2	247.0	247.1	247.4	243.7	237.4	235.9	234.1	235.7
2001	219.0	220.8	228.0	236.5	242.1	247.6	245.4	246.3	240.9	235.4	232.9	231.3	235.5
2002	220.6	223.1	228.9	239.0	243.1	248.7	250.8	252.3	247.4	242.3	241.2	239.7	239.8
2003	229.9	231.6	238.2	247.0	252.6	257.6	255.6	256.6	252.2	247.0	246.2	245.0	246.6
2004	234.8	237.6	244.7	254.6	259.0	262.7	263.2	264.7	261.0	254.9	253.9	252.7	253.7
2005	243.0	244.8	252.0	263.6	268.0	273.4	272.9	272.9	269.3	263.1	261.8	259.6	262.0
2006	252.7	254.3	262.7	270.2	275.3	280.2	280.8	280.8	276.1	270.9	269.0	268.6	270.1
2007	258.9	260.5	268.9	276.2	281.2	288.3	285.9	288.2	281.7	276.0	275.5	274.1	276.3
2008	262.4	264.3	270.7	276.6	282.2	285.1	283.1	282.5	277.4	269.3	267.2	264.4	273.8
2009	253.2	253.0	259.1	265.9	271.7	275.4	271.8	270.6	265.0	258.8	258.1	256.2	263.2
Other Services													
1990	47.5	47.3	47.7	46.8	46.8	48.4	44.9	46.9	46.7	45.5	45.5	44.6	46.6
2000	86.9	87.9	89.4	91.6	92.3	92.7	92.8	96.8	98.1	100.9	102.8	103.6	94.7
2001	99.2	101.1	101.4	101.4	102.1	103.5	100.9	101.1	101.6	100.5	100.5	99.8	101.1
2002	98.6	99.6	100.2	100.2	101.4	102.7	103.0	102.2	102.9	102.9	102.7	102.8	101.6
2003	101.5	101.3	102.2	102.6	103.2	103.4	102.5	102.1	102.1	101.7	101.7	101.7	102.2
2004	100.8	101.5	102.8	102.0	102.0	102.8	102.4	102.0	101.4	101.0	101.0	100.6	101.7
2005	99.0	99.8	101.3	101.4	101.3	102.4	101.5	100.8	100.9	100.0	100.5	99.9	100.7
2006	98.7	99.4	100.8	100.8	101.9	104.0	102.9	102.8	102.9	102.1	102.2	102.5	101.8
2007	101.7	102.3	104.2	103.9	105.1	106.2	104.5	104.4	103.9	103.9	103.9	103.8	104.0
2008	103.2	104.4	105.3	104.8	106.0	106.4	105.1	104.7	103.9	103.9	103.3	103.0	104.5
2009	101.3	101.7	102.5	102.7	102.8	104.3	103.4	102.5	101.7	101.2	101.0	101.0	102.2
Government													
1990	347.1	352.2	355.2	357.0	358.1	346.6	334.6	339.6	356.1	356.9	357.6	356.2	351.4
2000	390.1	398.2	418.9	403.3	408.0	392.5	378.2	388.0	396.2	403.6	405.3	405.8	399.0
2001	398.2	407.1	409.1	409.9	407.5	394.0	380.5	391.4	404.7	410.1	413.4	412.1	403.2
2002	406.4	414.8	416.8	419.2	415.1	405.6	386.2	395.8	409.1	415.7	419.0	419.4	410.3
2003	408.4	415.3	417.6	420.2	417.7	404.5	388.9	398.4	411.6	416.0	417.0	417.7	411.1
2004	411.1	433.1	421.1	420.7	417.5	407.5	391.8	402.5	415.3	419.0	421.2	421.9	415.2
2005	410.2	417.7	419.0	416.6	415.1	399.8	392.0	401.5	418.3	420.0	421.6	420.7	412.7
2006	412.0	417.6	420.3	422.1	420.6	404.4	398.0	410.1	422.8	423.8	426.3	425.2	416.9
2007	418.1	422.5	425.3	422.7	423.3	405.2	400.3	414.5	427.7	431.4	433.3	431.1	421.3
2008	424.7	430.1	432.4	433.3	433.9	405.7	405.9	419.0	430.6	438.8	440.0	438.6	427.8
2009	427.9	432.7	434.5	435.0	434.6	405.0	405.2	418.1	433.0	437.9	437.7	435.9	428.1

Average Weekly Hours by Selected Industry: Tennessee, 2007–2009

(Not seasonally adjusted.)

Industry and year	January	February	March	April	May	June	July	August	September	October	November	December	Annual average
Total Private													
2007	34.8	35.2	35.3	35.2	35.2	35.4	35.3	35.2	35.6	35.3	35.1	35.5	35.3
2008	34.8	34.8	35.2	35.0	35.2	35.8	35.1	35.4	35.1	35.3	35.5	35.0	35.2
2009	34.6	35.2	34.9	34.7	35.0	35.3	35.1	35.7	35.1	35.5	35.8	35.4	35.2
Goods-Producing													
2007	38.1	39.1	39.3	39.2	39.9	39.4	38.8	40.2	39.9	39.6	39.7	38.9	39.3
2008	38.5	38.5	38.8	39.0	39.3	40.1	39.1	39.8	39.5	39.3	39.4	38.8	39.2
2009	37.9	38.6	38.4	38.7	38.9	40.0	39.9	40.6	40.0	40.5	41.0	40.7	39.6
Mining, Logging, and Construction													
2007	35.9	36.4	37.6	37.2	37.9	38.0	37.6	38.2	38.8	38.9	38.5	37.1	37.7
2008	36.4	37.5	37.3	37.8	37.5	38.6	37.9	38.4	38.1	38.0	37.6	36.1	37.6
2009	36.3	36.4	36.6	36.4	36.4	37.4	37.5	38.0	36.3	35.9	36.8	36.4	36.7
Manufacturing													
2007	38.8	40.0	39.9	39.9	40.6	39.9	39.2	41.0	40.3	39.9	40.1	39.5	39.9
2008	39.2	38.8	39.3	39.5	39.9	40.7	39.5	40.3	40.0	39.8	40.1	39.8	39.7
2009	38.5	39.3	39.0	39.5	39.8	41.0	40.7	41.6	41.3	42.1	42.5	42.2	40.6
Trade, Transportation, and Utilities													
2007	35.4	35.5	35.8	34.9	34.8	35.2	34.9	34.7	35.0	34.7	34.3	34.9	35.0
2008	34.6	34.3	34.7	34.2	34.7	35.2	34.6	34.7	34.8	35.1	35.7	35.5	34.8
2009	34.9	35.7	35.3	34.7	35.0	34.9	34.5	35.0	35.4	36.2	35.9	36.0	35.3
Information													
2007	34.9	36.9	35.8	35.4	35.5	35.7	36.4	34.9	35.5	35.6	37.2	36.4	35.9
2008	35.5	35.9	35.8	36.1	36.3	36.3	35.8	36.1	36.0	37.3	36.9	35.6	36.1
2009	35.9	37.2	37.0	36.4	36.6	36.6	36.8	37.8	36.8	36.5	37.1	36.7	36.8
Financial Activities													
2007	37.3	37.6	38.1	38.4	37.5	38.1	38.8	37.8	39.0	37.6	37.2	38.5	38.0
2008	37.6	37.2	37.6	37.2	36.7	37.4	36.8	37.1	36.6	36.7	37.4	37.1	37.1
2009	37.1	37.5	37.3	36.5	36.9	37.0	37.1	38.1	36.8	37.0	37.4	36.7	37.1
Professional and Business Services													
2007	35.1	35.0	35.9	36.1	36.0	36.3	36.5	36.2	36.8	36.5	35.9	37.8	36.2
2008	36.5	36.6	37.3	36.6	37.4	37.3	37.0	37.6	36.7	37.1	37.4	36.6	37.0
2009	36.2	36.9	36.3	35.9	37.6	37.8	36.9	37.9	36.7	36.7	37.5	36.6	36.9
Education and Health Services													
2007	33.4	34.2	33.5	33.8	34.0	34.4	34.3	33.9	34.5	33.9	34.1	34.7	34.1
2008	33.6	34.2	34.4	34.2	34.1	34.7	34.5	34.5	34.2	34.0	34.3	33.4	34.2
2009	34.3	34.3	34.4	34.2	34.0	34.2	34.6	35.0	34.4	34.6	34.6	33.8	34.4
Leisure and Hospitality													
2007	27.4	27.4	27.4	27.9	27.3	28.3	28.3	27.3	27.2	27.5	27.3	26.9	27.5
2008	26.7	26.5	26.5	27.1	26.8	27.8	26.7	26.7	26.2	26.9	26.5	26.2	26.7
2009	25.7	26.8	26.7	26.6	26.7	27.4	27.2	27.1	26.4	26.6	26.6	26.3	26.7
Other Services													
2007	33.0	33.3	33.5	33.5	33.0	33.6	34.1	32.6	35.7	34.6	34.6	35.5	33.9
2008	35.4	34.6	35.7	35.1	35.8	36.4	35.5	35.9	35.3	35.5	35.7	34.9	35.5
2009	33.5	33.5	33.4	33.6	33.1	33.2	32.8	34.2	32.1	32.5	33.4	33.0	33.2

Average Hourly Earnings by Selected Industry: Tennessee, 2007–2009

(Dollars, not seasonally adjusted.)

Industry and year	January	February	March	April	May	June	July	August	September	October	November	December	Annual average
Total Private													
2007	18.98	19.04	19.03	19.14	18.78	18.92	19.09	18.88	19.15	18.85	18.91	19.33	19.01
2008	19.35	19.43	19.23	19.11	19.34	19.36	19.47	19.39	19.48	19.46	19.62	19.60	19.40
2009	19.41	19.65	19.59	19.50	19.39	19.39	19.47	19.60	19.65	19.53	19.59	19.50	19.52
Goods-Producing													
2007	19.64	19.07	19.42	19.38	18.98	19.03	19.52	19.41	19.59	19.68	19.59	20.19	19.46
2008	20.21	20.44	20.28	19.75	20.04	19.77	19.81	19.91	19.98	19.96	20.10	20.06	20.02
2009	20.04	20.51	20.51	20.69	20.56	20.87	20.98	21.24	21.42	21.30	21.25	21.02	20.87
Mining, Logging, and Construction													
2007	18.49	18.32	18.14	17.92	18.04	18.25	18.65	18.91	19.27	19.95	19.08	19.39	18.72
2008	19.19	19.50	19.48	19.32	19.45	19.31	19.21	19.01	19.29	19.27	19.15	19.42	19.30
2009	19.71	19.78	20.00	20.12	20.18	20.01	19.95	20.29	20.24	20.49	20.07	20.37	20.10
Manufacturing													
2007	20.00	19.30	19.84	19.87	19.30	19.30	19.83	19.58	19.70	19.58	19.78	20.47	19.71
2008	20.55	20.77	20.56	19.90	20.24	19.93	20.02	20.23	20.22	20.21	20.43	20.27	20.28
2009	20.15	20.74	20.68	20.87	20.69	21.15	21.33	21.55	21.79	21.55	21.61	21.21	21.11
Trade, Transportation, and Utilities													
2007	17.90	18.21	18.82	18.84	18.32	19.09	18.79	18.09	18.27	17.84	17.83	17.97	18.33
2008	18.00	18.36	18.12	18.14	18.71	18.92	19.32	19.00	19.14	18.97	19.13	19.46	18.77
2009	19.01	19.10	19.06	19.01	18.67	18.54	18.60	18.60	18.35	17.99	18.05	17.96	18.58
Information													
2007	19.94	20.26	20.10	20.98	20.65	20.09	20.18	21.07	21.40	21.01	21.32	20.93	20.67
2008	20.73	20.51	20.75	20.60	20.47	20.94	21.01	21.20	21.43	21.67	22.06	22.17	21.12
2009	22.46	23.05	22.82	22.35	22.86	22.70	22.43	23.53	23.18	23.36	23.51	23.24	22.96
Financial Activities													
2007	21.11	21.77	20.61	21.57	20.79	20.55	21.82	21.52	21.36	21.49	21.11	21.59	21.28
2008	21.11	20.78	20.90	20.89	20.63	20.72	20.67	20.72	20.83	21.20	21.47	21.11	20.92
2009	21.35	21.89	21.63	21.24	21.26	21.24	21.20	21.25	21.17	21.39	21.43	21.33	21.37
Professional and Business Services													
2007	22.38	22.71	21.91	22.16	22.12	21.87	22.56	22.38	23.01	22.37	23.01	23.40	22.50
2008	23.90	23.06	22.92	23.05	22.91	23.07	23.18	22.94	22.97	22.61	22.69	22.24	22.96
2009	22.39	22.92	22.79	22.52	22.33	22.29	22.63	22.26	22.47	22.28	22.35	22.55	22.48
Education and Health Services													
2007	21.08	20.87	20.58	20.53	20.25	20.57	19.94	20.08	20.27	19.92	19.97	20.40	20.37
2008	20.42	20.63	20.21	20.17	20.38	20.58	20.34	20.33	20.45	20.72	20.82	20.91	20.50
2009	20.38	20.48	20.67	20.59	20.65	20.69	20.58	20.77	21.06	20.98	21.03	21.00	20.74
Leisure and Hospitality													
2007	10.74	11.19	11.02	11.32	11.22	11.14	11.55	11.24	11.73	10.80	10.77	11.22	11.17
2008	10.98	11.17	11.00	11.32	11.52	11.72	11.72	11.60	11.60	11.62	11.75	11.88	11.49
2009	11.27	11.33	11.27	11.22	11.42	11.35	11.46	11.95	11.87	11.89	11.98	11.87	11.57
Other Services													
2007	17.31	17.42	17.38	17.45	16.97	16.67	16.37	16.54	16.25	16.62	16.70	17.31	16.91
2008	17.10	17.87	17.59	17.45	17.58	17.08	17.18	17.18	16.94	16.93	17.16	16.44	17.21
2009	16.61	16.49	16.25	16.41	16.27	16.19	16.38	16.26	16.16	16.34	16.46	16.51	16.36

Average Weekly Earnings by Selected Industry: Tennessee, 2007–2009

(Dollars, not seasonally adjusted.)

Industry and year	January	February	March	April	May	June	July	August	September	October	November	December	Annual average
Total Private													
2007	660.50	670.21	671.76	673.73	661.06	669.77	673.88	664.58	681.74	665.41	663.74	686.22	671.05
2008	673.38	676.16	676.90	668.85	680.77	693.09	683.40	686.41	683.75	686.94	696.51	686.00	682.88
2009	671.59	691.68	683.69	676.65	678.65	684.47	683.40	699.72	689.72	693.32	701.32	690.30	687.10
Goods-Producing													
2007	748.28	745.64	763.21	759.70	757.30	749.78	757.38	780.28	781.64	779.33	777.72	785.39	764.78
2008	778.09	786.94	786.86	770.25	787.57	792.78	774.57	792.42	789.21	784.43	791.94	778.33	784.78
2009	759.52	791.69	787.58	800.70	799.78	834.80	837.10	862.34	856.80	862.65	871.25	855.51	826.45
Mining, Logging, and Construction													
2007	663.79	666.85	682.06	666.62	683.72	693.50	701.24	722.36	747.68	776.06	734.58	719.37	705.74
2008	698.52	731.25	726.60	730.30	729.38	745.37	728.06	729.98	734.95	732.26	720.04	701.06	725.68
2009	715.47	719.99	732.00	732.37	734.55	748.37	748.13	771.02	734.71	735.59	738.58	741.47	737.67
Manufacturing													
2007	776.00	772.00	791.62	792.81	783.58	770.07	777.34	802.78	793.91	781.24	793.18	808.57	786.43
2008	805.56	805.88	808.01	786.05	807.58	811.15	790.79	815.27	808.80	804.36	819.24	806.75	805.12
2009	775.78	815.08	806.52	824.37	823.46	867.15	868.13	896.48	899.93	907.26	918.43	895.06	857.07
Trade, Transportation, and Utilities													
2007	633.66	646.46	673.76	657.52	637.54	671.97	655.77	627.72	639.45	619.05	611.57	627.15	641.55
2008	622.80	629.75	628.76	620.39	649.24	665.98	668.47	659.30	666.07	665.85	682.94	690.83	653.20
2009	663.45	681.87	672.82	659.65	653.45	647.05	641.70	651.00	649.59	651.24	648.00	646.56	655.87
Information													
2007	695.91	747.59	719.58	742.69	733.08	717.21	734.55	735.34	759.70	747.96	793.10	761.85	742.05
2008	735.92	736.31	742.85	743.66	743.06	760.12	752.16	765.32	771.48	808.29	814.01	789.25	762.43
2009	806.31	857.46	844.34	813.54	836.68	830.82	825.42	889.43	853.02	852.64	872.22	852.91	844.93
Financial Activities													
2007	787.40	818.55	785.24	828.29	779.63	782.96	846.62	813.46	833.04	808.02	785.29	831.22	808.64
2008	793.74	773.02	785.84	777.11	757.12	774.93	760.66	768.71	762.38	778.04	802.98	783.18	776.13
2009	792.09	820.88	806.80	775.26	784.49	785.88	786.52	809.63	779.06	791.43	801.48	782.81	792.83
Professional and Business Services													
2007	785.54	794.85	786.57	799.98	796.32	793.88	823.44	810.16	846.77	816.51	826.06	884.52	814.50
2008	872.35	844.00	854.92	843.63	856.83	860.51	857.66	862.54	843.00	838.83	848.61	813.98	849.52
2009	810.52	845.75	827.28	808.47	839.61	842.56	835.05	843.65	824.65	817.68	838.13	825.33	829.51
Education and Health Services													
2007	704.07	713.75	689.43	693.91	688.50	707.61	683.94	680.71	699.32	675.29	680.98	707.88	694.62
2008	686.11	705.55	695.22	689.81	694.96	714.13	701.73	701.39	699.39	704.48	714.13	698.39	701.10
2009	699.03	702.46	711.05	704.18	702.10	707.60	712.07	726.95	724.46	725.91	727.64	709.80	713.46
Leisure and Hospitality													
2007	294.28	306.61	301.95	315.83	306.31	315.26	326.87	306.85	319.06	297.00	294.02	301.82	307.18
2008	287.68	296.01	291.50	306.77	308.74	325.82	312.92	309.72	303.92	312.58	311.38	311.26	306.78
2009	289.64	303.64	300.91	298.45	304.91	310.99	311.71	323.85	313.37	316.27	318.67	312.18	308.92
Other Services													
2007	571.23	580.09	582.23	584.58	560.01	560.11	558.22	539.20	580.13	575.05	577.82	614.51	573.25
2008	605.34	618.30	627.96	612.50	629.36	621.71	609.89	616.76	597.98	601.02	612.61	573.76	610.96
2009	556.44	552.42	542.75	551.38	538.54	537.51	537.26	556.09	518.74	531.05	549.76	544.83	543.15

TEXAS
At a Glance

Population:
 1990 census: 16,986,335
 2000 census: 20,851,820
 2009 estimate: 24,782,302

Percent change in population:
 1990–2000: 22.8%
 2000–2009: 18.8%

Percent change in total nonfarm employment:
 1990–2009: 45.2%
 2008–2009: -2.8%

Industry with the largest growth in employment, 1990–2009 (thousands):
 Education and Health Services, 659.1

Industry with the largest decline or smallest growth in employment, 1990–2009 (thousands):
 Manufacturing, -106.9

Civilian labor force:
 1990: 8,593,724
 2000: 10,347,847
 2009: 11,930,847

Unemployment rate and rank among states (lowest to highest):
 1990: 6.4%, 45th
 2000: 4.4%, 37th
 2009: 7.6%, 18th

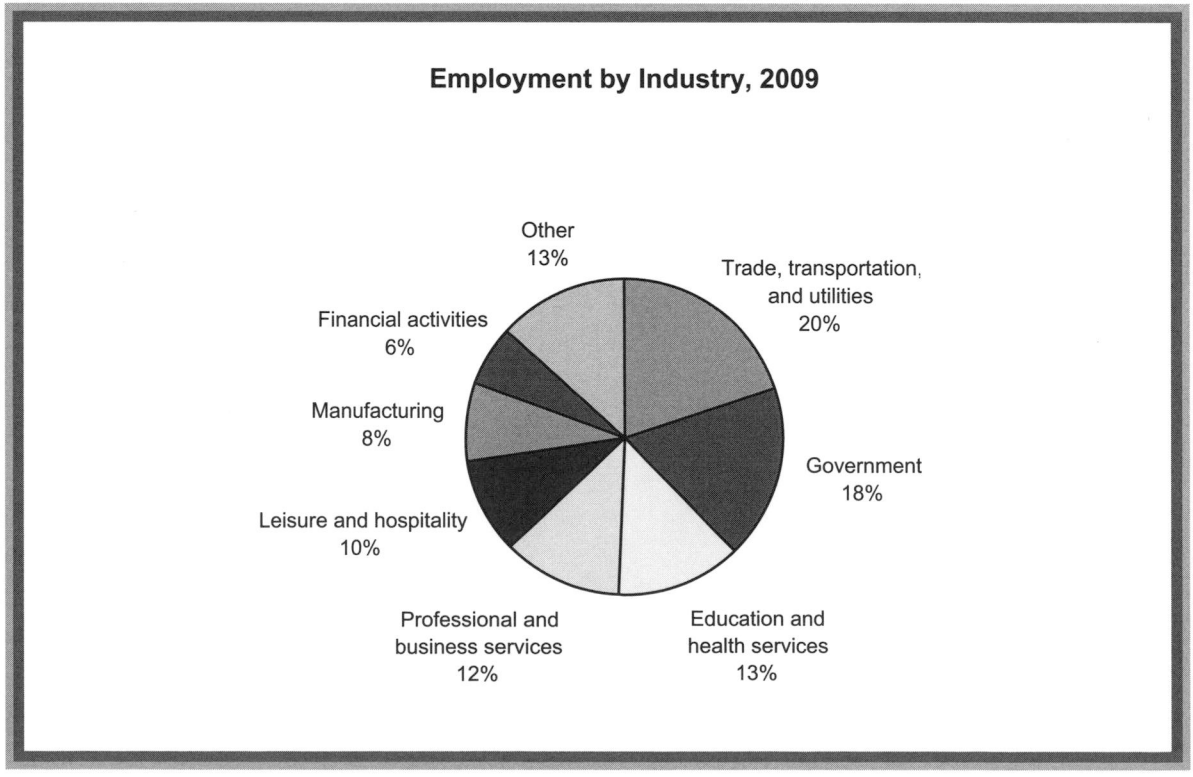

Employment by Industry, 2009

Other 13%

Trade, transportation, and utilities 20%

Financial activities 6%

Manufacturing 8%

Leisure and hospitality 10%

Professional and business services 12%

Education and health services 13%

Government 18%

Employment by Industry: Texas, Selected Years, 1990–2009

(Numbers in thousands, not seasonally adjusted.)

Industry and year	January	February	March	April	May	June	July	August	September	October	November	December	Annual average
Total Nonfarm													
1990	6895.2	6943.3	6995.7	7049.8	7119.7	7153.9	7108.0	7132.6	7178.7	7199.0	7218.7	7220.4	7101.3
2000	9195.5	9275.1	9357.0	9369.7	9444.6	9472.3	9387.9	9455.5	9521.4	9522.1	9564.4	9614.1	9431.6
2001	9423.3	9493.1	9549.9	9547.4	9574.5	9583.3	9460.7	9511.1	9532.0	9488.6	9498.4	9502.6	9513.7
2002	9306.0	9360.0	9417.2	9423.0	9469.0	9451.9	9347.7	9400.8	9450.5	9428.7	9461.3	9472.9	9415.8
2003	9280.6	9326.8	9360.9	9374.3	9402.1	9379.8	9281.2	9336.8	9394.5	9403.8	9432.2	9465.1	9369.8
2004	9306.7	9371.4	9433.7	9480.1	9506.6	9507.0	9450.5	9496.2	9545.5	9585.0	9621.4	9658.6	9496.9
2005	9492.8	9563.6	9633.8	9700.6	9730.7	9736.4	9697.7	9751.3	9833.9	9846.9	9926.7	9968.6	9740.3
2006	9809.7	9892.4	9981.0	10005.3	10060.9	10090.1	9994.3	10073.6	10158.5	10177.9	10249.5	10299.2	10066.0
2007	10111.7	10212.3	10307.7	10338.9	10397.9	10435.9	10352.5	10404.9	10459.1	10514.2	10584.6	10619.2	10394.9
2008	10439.7	10535.2	10579.7	10609.6	10656.7	10657.0	10573.5	10612.1	10609.3	10660.4	10681.2	10669.6	10607.0
2009	10403.4	10399.1	10394.7	10352.9	10352.3	10321.4	10201.2	10192.3	10215.0	10281.0	10322.7	10297.5	10311.1
Total Private													
1990	5646.1	5674.1	5719.2	5767.4	5816.0	5903.1	5904.6	5937.9	5920.1	5914.8	5924.4	5926.7	5837.9
2000	7648.4	7698.9	7773.1	7785.4	7837.1	7935.3	7912.7	7955.8	7957.0	7938.4	7972.0	8022.3	7869.7
2001	7857.6	7898.4	7949.9	7946.2	7972.5	8023.6	7966.5	7988.3	7928.9	7864.5	7862.1	7871.8	7927.5
2002	7700.6	7722.0	7772.1	7778.3	7821.6	7852.3	7817.4	7850.0	7818.0	7760.6	7783.4	7801.3	7789.8
2003	7637.8	7649.0	7684.8	7696.9	7724.9	7747.7	7725.8	7766.3	7752.3	7739.7	7758.9	7801.4	7723.8
2004	7666.5	7697.0	7757.6	7803.4	7827.9	7870.3	7882.5	7910.0	7883.6	7900.2	7927.5	7970.1	7841.4
2005	7826.3	7862.9	7930.7	7995.4	8023.7	8076.0	8100.2	8132.9	8143.6	8131.0	8198.9	8253.2	8056.2
2006	8113.3	8163.5	8251.0	8278.8	8333.7	8406.2	8385.3	8438.8	8447.2	8436.7	8499.5	8556.7	8359.2
2007	8395.4	8464.2	8553.2	8585.2	8641.2	8718.5	8706.0	8749.3	8727.6	8743.2	8798.6	8837.6	8660.0
2008	8677.9	8741.5	8777.8	8814.4	8857.5	8893.1	8879.4	8910.6	8835.5	8850.9	8852.6	8846.5	8828.1
2009	8599.3	8566.7	8555.5	8507.9	8509.2	8512.3	8469.3	8463.0	8408.2	8419.0	8449.0	8436.0	8491.3
Goods-Producing													
1990	1414.6	1421.8	1431.5	1437.6	1448.9	1470.1	1472.6	1480.8	1476.7	1478.3	1472.8	1461.5	1455.6
2000	1737.3	1753.3	1771.5	1763.4	1774.2	1796.9	1789.9	1794.1	1794.6	1785.0	1782.0	1785.3	1777.3
2001	1765.5	1778.4	1787.2	1775.8	1777.0	1784.5	1767.0	1768.5	1751.9	1731.2	1718.3	1705.7	1759.3
2002	1672.4	1673.1	1679.6	1668.8	1673.4	1680.3	1667.4	1670.0	1657.8	1639.3	1630.0	1621.5	1661.1
2003	1600.5	1600.7	1600.3	1600.0	1605.3	1609.0	1600.1	1603.2	1600.0	1589.5	1580.5	1582.1	1597.6
2004	1565.5	1568.7	1577.3	1580.6	1583.1	1593.7	1596.5	1598.8	1596.1	1597.9	1596.6	1599.7	1587.9
2005	1583.7	1591.8	1605.5	1615.9	1620.9	1635.0	1642.4	1645.4	1650.9	1648.1	1655.0	1664.2	1629.9
2006	1654.1	1670.3	1690.4	1690.8	1706.9	1731.2	1725.9	1735.3	1742.7	1739.6	1745.6	1751.9	1715.4
2007	1733.0	1750.5	1766.9	1772.3	1783.5	1807.1	1799.9	1808.6	1807.0	1812.6	1818.0	1819.0	1789.9
2008	1799.2	1817.5	1822.6	1825.6	1834.8	1843.6	1840.7	1845.7	1836.1	1838.1	1825.0	1805.9	1827.9
2009	1750.5	1726.6	1700.0	1663.0	1647.7	1636.2	1620.2	1612.4	1599.3	1583.5	1584.4	1573.4	1641.4
Mining and Logging													
1990	158.0	157.9	158.5	159.6	160.9	163.2	163.8	164.2	164.4	167.6	168.1	169.2	163.0
2000	140.6	140.5	141.5	139.5	140.6	142.2	143.3	144.1	144.6	146.1	146.3	149.4	143.2
2001	146.9	148.7	150.4	151.2	152.3	155.2	155.9	156.8	155.7	155.1	154.1	153.6	153.0
2002	147.7	146.8	146.0	144.5	145.3	146.2	144.9	145.5	145.5	143.7	143.8	144.1	145.3
2003	142.6	143.3	144.4	144.6	145.9	147.3	148.2	149.3	148.8	147.8	147.8	149.5	146.6
2004	149.2	149.3	150.6	150.2	151.2	152.9	153.8	154.6	154.6	155.6	156.3	157.5	153.0
2005	158.4	159.1	160.1	161.6	163.1	165.9	168.1	169.1	169.7	170.9	172.0	174.0	166.0
2006	173.2	175.6	177.5	179.3	181.4	185.9	188.0	190.3	192.5	194.3	195.5	197.1	185.9
2007	197.6	199.3	201.4	202.6	204.3	208.2	209.9	211.9	211.2	213.3	215.1	216.9	207.6
2008	218.6	221.6	222.9	224.4	226.5	230.7	233.6	235.9	236.0	238.8	237.8	235.8	230.2
2009	227.7	221.5	215.4	206.7	202.5	200.6	200.0	199.1	198.0	197.6	200.6	201.6	205.9
Construction													
1990	325.0	330.0	336.2	338.0	347.1	356.0	353.8	357.9	356.3	353.1	350.9	345.3	345.8
2000	539.4	550.4	562.9	561.1	567.3	579.6	577.1	579.9	578.2	571.2	567.6	567.3	566.8
2001	564.2	575.5	584.4	581.4	586.5	591.5	586.2	590.4	583.7	576.5	574.1	568.5	580.2
2002	556.3	562.9	572.5	569.4	575.2	579.5	574.0	577.4	571.0	563.7	558.7	552.8	567.8
2003	545.5	547.1	549.7	551.0	557.9	559.4	555.5	558.5	556.3	551.9	543.5	543.4	551.6
2004	534.1	535.4	541.8	543.6	543.1	548.1	548.9	549.5	548.5	548.9	545.9	546.6	544.5
2005	540.1	545.5	555.3	564.6	565.9	570.6	573.6	574.8	579.3	576.6	577.9	581.1	567.1
2006	575.8	586.0	599.5	594.7	602.9	614.8	609.3	613.4	617.4	615.6	617.5	619.8	605.6
2007	609.2	622.2	635.2	637.7	644.9	657.9	652.2	658.7	659.4	665.3	668.5	666.3	648.1
2008	653.8	667.0	672.5	675.3	679.8	681.8	678.0	681.4	676.6	680.2	671.7	661.4	673.3
2009	634.0	627.8	620.5	607.0	603.9	602.1	596.5	590.0	581.0	565.7	563.7	553.2	595.5
Manufacturing													
1990	931.6	933.9	936.8	940.0	940.9	950.9	955.0	958.7	956.0	957.6	953.8	947.0	946.9
2000	1057.3	1062.4	1067.1	1062.8	1066.3	1075.1	1069.5	1070.1	1071.8	1067.7	1068.1	1068.6	1067.2
2001	1054.4	1054.2	1052.4	1043.2	1038.2	1037.8	1024.9	1021.3	1012.5	999.6	990.1	983.6	1026.0
2002	968.4	963.4	961.1	954.9	952.9	954.6	948.5	947.1	941.3	931.9	927.5	924.6	948.0
2003	912.4	910.3	906.2	904.4	901.5	902.3	896.4	895.4	894.9	889.8	889.2	889.2	899.3
2004	882.2	884.0	884.9	886.8	888.8	892.7	893.8	894.7	893.0	893.4	894.4	895.6	890.4
2005	885.2	887.2	890.1	889.7	891.9	898.5	900.7	901.5	901.9	900.6	905.1	909.1	896.8
2006	905.1	908.7	913.4	916.8	922.6	930.5	928.6	931.6	932.8	929.7	932.6	935.0	924.0
2007	926.2	929.0	930.3	932.0	934.3	941.0	937.8	938.0	936.4	934.0	934.4	935.8	934.1
2008	926.8	928.9	927.2	925.9	928.5	931.1	929.1	928.4	923.5	919.1	915.5	908.7	924.4
2009	888.8	877.3	864.1	849.3	841.3	833.5	823.7	823.3	820.3	820.2	820.1	818.6	840.0

Employment by Industry: Texas, Selected Years, 1990–2009—*Continued*

(Numbers in thousands, not seasonally adjusted.)

Industry and year	January	February	March	April	May	June	July	August	September	October	November	December	Annual average
Service-Providing													
1990	5480.6	5521.5	5564.2	5612.2	5670.8	5683.8	5635.4	5651.8	5702.0	5720.7	5745.9	5758.9	5645.7
2000	7458.2	7521.8	7585.5	7606.3	7670.4	7675.4	7598.0	7661.4	7726.8	7737.1	7782.4	7828.8	7654.3
2001	7657.8	7714.7	7762.7	7771.6	7797.5	7798.8	7693.7	7742.6	7780.1	7757.4	7780.1	7796.9	7754.5
2002	7633.6	7686.9	7737.6	7754.2	7795.6	7771.6	7680.3	7730.8	7792.7	7789.4	7831.3	7851.4	7754.6
2003	7680.1	7726.1	7760.6	7774.3	7796.8	7770.8	7681.1	7733.6	7794.5	7814.3	7851.7	7883.0	7772.2
2004	7741.2	7802.7	7856.4	7899.5	7923.5	7913.3	7854.0	7897.4	7949.4	7987.1	8024.8	8058.9	7909.0
2005	7909.1	7971.8	8028.3	8084.7	8109.8	8101.4	8055.3	8105.9	8183.0	8198.8	8271.7	8304.4	8110.4
2006	8155.6	8222.1	8290.6	8314.5	8354.0	8358.9	8268.4	8338.3	8415.8	8438.3	8503.9	8547.3	8350.6
2007	8378.7	8461.8	8540.8	8566.6	8614.4	8628.8	8552.6	8596.3	8652.1	8701.6	8766.6	8800.2	8605.0
2008	8640.5	8717.7	8757.1	8784.0	8821.9	8813.4	8732.8	8766.4	8773.2	8822.3	8856.2	8863.7	8779.1
2009	8652.9	8672.5	8694.7	8689.9	8704.6	8685.2	8581.0	8579.9	8615.7	8697.5	8738.3	8724.1	8669.7
Trade, Transportation, and Utilities													
1990	1558.1	1545.7	1552.5	1552.9	1561.3	1577.7	1575.5	1582.0	1582.0	1585.3	1604.8	1621.9	1575.0
2000	1942.2	1938.4	1945.0	1942.9	1954.0	1974.7	1967.7	1986.4	1980.9	1992.0	2029.3	2064.0	1976.5
2001	1986.1	1974.2	1981.3	1977.6	1982.7	1991.1	1982.3	1990.1	1978.9	1975.6	1993.1	2014.0	1985.6
2002	1944.8	1932.4	1939.5	1937.8	1945.6	1950.2	1945.3	1950.0	1942.4	1937.5	1964.9	1989.7	1948.3
2003	1910.7	1896.0	1898.8	1896.9	1897.7	1903.4	1900.7	1915.7	1914.0	1922.6	1951.5	1978.6	1915.6
2004	1913.6	1907.7	1917.9	1925.5	1931.9	1935.8	1941.6	1956.1	1945.8	1956.9	1990.0	2018.0	1945.1
2005	1954.1	1942.7	1954.5	1964.7	1973.4	1983.5	1992.8	2007.1	2004.3	2006.5	2055.0	2086.1	1993.7
2006	2013.7	2004.8	2022.0	2022.9	2031.7	2040.4	2039.5	2056.4	2054.2	2062.6	2104.0	2135.6	2049.0
2007	2071.9	2064.4	2084.8	2084.7	2095.3	2107.8	2111.1	2121.9	2118.8	2130.9	2171.2	2198.5	2113.4
2008	2129.7	2124.1	2132.0	2127.5	2133.2	2142.1	2143.8	2157.0	2136.7	2142.2	2166.1	2182.6	2143.1
2009	2098.3	2072.7	2070.5	2055.0	2052.8	2051.1	2045.1	2050.4	2041.0	2051.1	2080.6	2096.4	2063.8
Wholesale Trade													
1990	363.9	365.0	367.2	367.9	369.2	374.0	375.5	376.3	375.1	375.0	375.6	374.9	371.6
2000	459.4	461.5	462.9	463.6	465.5	470.2	470.6	471.3	472.2	471.3	472.6	475.1	468.0
2001	472.6	474.2	476.4	475.5	475.5	476.8	475.7	475.3	472.6	469.7	467.2	467.8	473.3
2002	460.6	460.4	463.0	461.4	463.0	465.1	465.0	465.6	464.7	462.6	463.5	464.4	463.3
2003	456.9	456.5	457.7	456.9	457.9	460.1	459.0	459.5	459.4	458.0	458.5	460.2	458.4
2004	454.7	455.4	457.9	460.1	461.6	463.9	466.1	466.5	466.1	467.7	468.3	469.7	463.2
2005	465.1	466.1	468.7	472.7	474.9	477.7	480.9	481.8	483.8	482.9	485.1	488.8	477.4
2006	485.4	488.2	492.1	492.6	495.5	499.9	499.1	501.3	503.1	503.1	505.9	509.2	498.0
2007	504.7	508.1	511.4	513.1	516.2	521.7	521.8	523.5	523.3	526.4	527.0	530.2	519.0
2008	525.0	527.4	527.6	529.0	530.4	532.6	531.6	532.2	529.2	529.1	527.2	526.2	529.0
2009	515.7	510.5	507.1	501.6	499.8	498.4	496.1	495.0	492.3	498.4	499.1	494.3	500.7
Retail Trade													
1990	898.1	883.6	886.8	888.4	893.7	901.4	896.8	901.7	900.9	905.4	924.3	939.2	901.7
2000	1086.0	1078.2	1083.3	1080.6	1088.0	1100.1	1093.4	1108.0	1100.7	1111.1	1145.1	1171.7	1103.9
2001	1107.6	1095.2	1100.3	1099.0	1102.1	1107.8	1100.7	1107.1	1099.9	1099.8	1125.6	1147.0	1107.7
2002	1093.7	1082.7	1087.6	1087.9	1092.0	1093.5	1087.3	1089.3	1084.8	1080.1	1107.4	1130.7	1093.1
2003	1065.8	1053.0	1055.0	1054.5	1055.7	1058.6	1056.9	1067.8	1066.2	1073.3	1101.1	1122.2	1069.2
2004	1068.7	1060.4	1067.1	1070.6	1074.4	1075.5	1076.1	1089.6	1079.9	1087.0	1118.0	1139.1	1083.9
2005	1088.2	1077.6	1085.3	1090.2	1094.9	1102.1	1106.1	1115.9	1109.7	1111.9	1154.2	1176.0	1109.3
2006	1118.6	1106.5	1117.1	1116.8	1120.5	1122.5	1122.5	1134.1	1127.9	1135.3	1172.0	1191.0	1132.1
2007	1142.8	1130.4	1144.0	1142.9	1148.3	1152.4	1156.9	1162.8	1158.4	1167.5	1206.5	1224.5	1161.5
2008	1171.3	1161.4	1169.0	1162.1	1163.4	1168.7	1171.2	1180.6	1164.8	1171.7	1197.3	1210.6	1174.3
2009	1152.4	1136.8	1138.1	1133.1	1134.3	1135.1	1133.5	1141.2	1134.7	1140.2	1166.3	1177.5	1143.6
Transportation and Utilities													
1990	296.1	297.1	298.5	296.6	298.4	302.3	303.2	304.0	306.0	304.9	304.9	307.8	301.7
2000	396.8	398.7	398.8	398.7	400.5	404.4	403.7	407.1	408.0	409.6	411.6	417.2	404.6
2001	405.9	404.8	404.6	403.1	405.1	406.5	405.9	407.7	406.4	406.1	400.3	399.2	404.6
2002	390.5	389.3	388.9	388.5	390.6	391.6	393.0	395.1	392.9	394.8	394.0	394.6	392.0
2003	388.0	386.5	386.1	385.5	384.1	384.7	384.8	388.4	388.4	391.3	391.9	396.2	388.0
2004	390.2	391.9	392.9	394.8	395.9	396.4	399.4	400.0	399.8	402.2	403.7	409.2	398.0
2005	400.8	399.0	400.5	401.8	403.6	403.7	405.8	409.4	410.8	411.7	415.7	421.3	407.0
2006	409.7	410.1	412.8	413.5	415.7	418.0	417.9	421.0	423.2	424.2	426.1	435.4	419.0
2007	424.4	425.9	429.4	428.7	430.8	433.7	432.4	435.6	437.1	437.0	437.7	443.8	433.0
2008	433.4	435.3	435.4	436.4	439.4	440.8	441.0	444.2	442.7	441.4	441.6	445.8	439.8
2009	430.2	425.4	425.3	420.3	418.7	417.6	415.5	414.2	414.0	412.5	415.2	424.6	419.5
Information													
1990	173.4	173.6	174.4	174.9	175.6	177.6	180.5	179.8	178.3	177.2	178.1	178.2	176.8
2000	258.0	259.5	262.1	266.3	269.6	275.3	276.5	278.5	279.7	278.1	280.4	280.5	272.0
2001	273.2	274.4	274.7	273.5	273.1	273.4	269.5	268.5	266.3	264.6	263.9	261.7	269.7
2002	258.1	256.1	255.0	251.7	251.6	251.3	247.7	246.5	244.2	243.6	243.0	242.4	249.3
2003	238.4	237.7	237.3	235.2	235.1	235.1	234.1	232.9	230.3	229.2	229.6	229.2	233.7
2004	227.4	225.5	227.2	225.8	226.1	226.8	225.2	224.2	222.3	222.4	222.6	223.2	224.9
2005	221.8	222.1	222.5	222.8	223.1	224.6	224.1	223.9	223.9	222.0	223.1	223.7	223.1
2006	221.2	222.1	222.3	221.9	222.7	223.9	221.7	221.4	221.0	219.9	220.6	221.3	221.7
2007	219.4	220.7	220.7	220.0	221.9	222.4	221.9	222.2	220.4	220.0	221.1	221.0	221.0
2008	219.0	219.2	219.2	218.3	219.3	219.3	218.2	217.3	214.4	213.8	214.3	214.3	217.2
2009	211.2	210.2	209.2	207.4	206.8	206.2	204.5	203.1	200.8	201.4	200.8	201.3	205.2

Employment by Industry: Texas, Selected Years, 1990–2009—*Continued*

(Numbers in thousands, not seasonally adjusted.)

Industry and year	January	February	March	April	May	June	July	August	September	October	November	December	Annual average
Financial Activities													
1990	450.1	453.0	454.5	458.7	461.0	465.9	463.1	463.7	461.9	457.1	455.5	458.0	458.5
2000	558.4	560.1	563.0	563.9	565.2	570.0	571.2	571.3	570.2	570.3	571.2	575.2	567.5
2001	569.1	572.1	574.5	575.7	577.5	582.3	582.2	582.2	579.1	577.9	577.0	579.9	577.5
2002	574.8	575.5	576.8	576.2	579.6	582.4	582.7	583.3	580.4	579.9	581.5	582.7	579.7
2003	577.4	579.4	580.8	582.2	584.8	587.5	589.0	590.9	587.8	587.8	587.6	590.2	585.5
2004	586.1	587.0	588.5	591.2	592.0	596.1	599.4	600.4	599.1	600.2	600.1	604.3	595.4
2005	597.0	598.7	600.2	602.4	603.7	608.2	613.9	616.1	616.8	617.1	618.7	621.6	609.5
2006	614.2	616.8	620.7	624.0	626.6	631.9	630.5	633.4	633.2	633.5	634.4	638.9	628.2
2007	633.7	636.8	639.8	640.1	643.6	648.1	648.3	649.7	646.4	645.6	646.7	648.4	643.9
2008	641.7	645.2	644.7	647.8	650.6	652.9	652.4	651.7	646.9	644.3	642.4	643.2	647.0
2009	632.9	632.4	630.9	629.1	629.6	630.4	629.5	627.9	624.5	626.3	627.8	628.4	629.1
Professional and Business Services													
1990	591.4	599.7	612.4	626.1	633.9	653.4	652.2	658.6	660.3	662.7	663.9	664.0	639.9
2000	1058.6	1069.4	1085.2	1091.2	1097.2	1119.8	1120.9	1129.4	1134.0	1130.2	1129.1	1134.3	1108.3
2001	1107.3	1113.1	1119.1	1115.5	1113.3	1120.6	1110.0	1112.7	1101.2	1084.8	1081.0	1079.5	1104.8
2002	1048.5	1053.4	1061.0	1066.7	1068.5	1072.8	1070.7	1080.7	1075.2	1067.2	1066.7	1064.5	1066.3
2003	1039.3	1043.6	1049.9	1055.6	1056.0	1057.0	1056.1	1064.9	1065.5	1067.2	1070.3	1078.9	1058.7
2004	1060.7	1069.5	1078.1	1094.1	1095.1	1104.2	1110.4	1116.0	1112.3	1120.1	1122.0	1125.4	1100.7
2005	1108.5	1122.3	1131.7	1150.6	1148.1	1157.8	1163.1	1172.9	1183.6	1193.1	1200.3	1208.5	1161.7
2006	1189.0	1204.1	1219.6	1225.8	1231.8	1244.4	1245.8	1257.2	1261.9	1261.7	1272.2	1279.6	1241.1
2007	1250.9	1269.0	1283.0	1287.8	1292.6	1307.3	1307.0	1319.3	1319.4	1326.1	1330.0	1335.8	1302.4
2008	1313.4	1327.2	1330.8	1338.7	1339.8	1345.3	1341.7	1351.3	1338.9	1345.3	1336.4	1327.3	1336.3
2009	1280.1	1272.3	1266.4	1254.3	1248.8	1250.2	1240.1	1239.4	1231.2	1242.3	1237.7	1228.5	1249.3
Education and Health Services													
1990	651.1	660.2	664.1	667.9	670.7	672.2	673.8	682.7	688.8	691.8	694.2	692.7	675.9
2000	980.2	988.3	993.8	995.3	999.3	998.9	996.0	1005.3	1018.0	1015.6	1019.1	1021.4	1002.6
2001	1013.0	1023.7	1029.5	1031.2	1036.2	1040.7	1038.3	1047.3	1053.6	1055.6	1059.9	1062.5	1041.0
2002	1054.0	1065.4	1070.2	1073.7	1079.6	1076.3	1076.8	1089.3	1100.4	1096.2	1102.2	1104.9	1082.4
2003	1098.0	1107.0	1111.6	1113.1	1116.3	1108.7	1110.5	1120.8	1132.9	1134.8	1136.4	1136.2	1118.9
2004	1124.0	1135.0	1140.3	1143.7	1145.3	1141.1	1143.0	1150.0	1159.1	1169.1	1170.8	1173.8	1149.6
2005	1156.8	1167.1	1173.4	1176.6	1178.8	1175.9	1180.3	1188.5	1200.0	1198.3	1203.3	1206.3	1183.8
2006	1192.5	1201.1	1205.3	1205.9	1209.3	1209.4	1207.2	1220.5	1230.4	1231.8	1235.8	1239.6	1215.7
2007	1221.9	1237.0	1245.2	1246.1	1251.4	1251.1	1250.7	1259.9	1267.1	1268.4	1273.3	1274.8	1253.9
2008	1258.1	1272.6	1273.2	1278.9	1286.2	1282.0	1281.9	1291.0	1295.7	1304.0	1308.6	1314.4	1287.2
2009	1296.5	1307.0	1313.6	1322.5	1329.9	1329.9	1335.7	1341.3	1347.6	1363.6	1365.6	1367.0	1335.0
Leisure and Hospitality													
1990	553.9	565.0	573.0	590.0	602.6	618.5	618.1	621.2	606.0	596.9	590.6	587.1	593.6
2000	775.4	789.0	808.1	817.1	830.4	847.3	839.3	840.2	829.2	818.6	813.1	813.2	818.4
2001	793.1	809.7	827.1	840.1	854.0	867.5	860.5	862.4	844.7	825.5	819.3	819.1	835.3
2002	800.6	815.4	834.4	847.4	864.2	876.2	868.4	871.4	859.7	847.4	839.2	839.8	846.6
2003	820.9	830.9	847.7	857.4	872.2	885.0	877.0	880.4	867.0	858.2	852.7	854.4	858.7
2004	838.3	850.4	869.8	884.3	897.3	912.2	908.8	909.7	897.7	886.1	880.1	880.4	884.6
2005	861.4	874.1	893.6	912.2	925.0	936.6	930.7	928.6	916.1	902.1	899.7	898.7	906.6
2006	887.8	901.8	923.9	938.3	954.4	970.3	964.3	965.5	955.8	940.7	939.2	942.0	940.3
2007	919.8	937.3	960.9	980.6	996.6	1013.0	1007.7	1008.7	991.8	982.7	980.8	982.6	980.2
2008	961.6	977.8	995.7	1014.8	1028.8	1039.2	1032.4	1028.8	1004.9	999.4	996.4	996.3	1006.3
2009	971.2	984.8	1003.7	1014.8	1029.6	1040.4	1028.0	1024.7	1004.0	993.3	994.7	987.4	1006.4
Other Services													
1990	253.5	255.1	256.8	259.3	262.0	267.7	268.8	269.1	266.1	265.5	264.5	263.3	262.6
2000	338.3	340.9	344.4	345.3	347.2	352.4	351.2	350.6	350.4	348.6	347.8	348.4	347.1
2001	350.3	352.7	356.5	356.7	358.7	363.4	356.7	356.6	353.2	349.3	349.6	349.4	354.4
2002	347.4	350.8	355.6	356.0	359.2	362.9	358.4	358.8	357.9	354.4	355.9	355.8	356.1
2003	352.6	353.7	358.4	356.5	357.5	362.0	358.3	357.5	354.8	350.4	350.3	351.8	355.3
2004	350.9	353.2	358.5	358.2	357.1	360.4	357.6	354.8	351.2	347.5	345.3	345.3	353.3
2005	343.0	344.1	349.3	350.2	350.7	354.4	352.9	350.4	348.0	343.8	343.8	344.1	347.9
2006	340.8	342.5	346.8	349.2	350.3	354.7	350.4	349.1	348.0	346.9	347.7	347.8	347.9
2007	344.8	348.5	351.9	353.6	356.3	361.7	359.4	359.0	356.7	356.9	357.5	357.5	355.3
2008	355.2	357.9	359.6	362.8	364.8	368.7	368.3	367.8	361.9	363.8	363.4	362.5	363.1
Government													
1990	1249.1	1269.2	1276.5	1282.4	1303.7	1250.8	1203.4	1194.7	1258.6	1284.2	1294.3	1293.7	1263.4
2000	1547.1	1576.2	1583.9	1584.3	1607.5	1537.0	1475.2	1499.7	1564.4	1583.7	1592.4	1591.8	1561.9
2001	1565.7	1594.7	1600.0	1601.2	1602.0	1559.7	1494.2	1522.8	1603.1	1624.1	1636.3	1630.8	1586.2
2002	1605.4	1638.0	1645.1	1644.7	1647.4	1599.6	1530.3	1550.8	1632.5	1668.1	1677.9	1671.6	1626.0
2003	1642.8	1677.8	1676.1	1677.4	1677.2	1632.1	1555.4	1570.5	1642.2	1664.1	1673.3	1663.7	1646.1
2004	1640.2	1674.4	1676.1	1676.7	1678.7	1636.7	1568.0	1586.2	1661.9	1684.8	1693.9	1688.5	1655.5
2005	1666.5	1700.7	1703.1	1705.2	1707.0	1660.4	1597.5	1618.4	1690.3	1715.9	1727.8	1715.4	1684.0
2006	1696.4	1728.9	1730.0	1726.5	1727.2	1683.9	1609.0	1634.8	1711.3	1741.2	1750.0	1742.5	1706.8
2007	1716.3	1748.1	1754.5	1753.7	1756.7	1717.4	1646.5	1655.6	1731.5	1771.0	1786.0	1781.6	1734.9
2008	1761.8	1793.7	1801.9	1795.2	1799.2	1763.9	1694.1	1701.5	1773.8	1809.5	1828.6	1823.1	1778.9
2009	1804.1	1832.4	1839.2	1845.0	1843.1	1809.1	1731.9	1729.3	1806.8	1862.0	1873.7	1861.5	1819.8

Average Weekly Hours by Selected Industry: Texas, 2007–2009

(Numbers in thousands, not seasonally adjusted.)

Industry and year	January	February	March	April	May	June	July	August	September	October	November	December	Annual average
Total Private													
2007	35.5	36.3	36.2	36.7	36.2	36.7	36.6	36.6	36.8	36.4	36.5	37.0	36.5
2008	36.0	36.4	36.7	36.4	36.2	36.9	36.3	36.2	35.3	36.2	36.4	36.1	36.3
2009	35.4	35.5	35.3	35.0	35.0	35.1	35.0	35.5	34.8	35.1	35.8	35.4	35.3
Goods-Producing													
2007	41.2	41.7	41.4	43.0	42.4	42.3	42.2	42.9	42.8	43.2	43.6	42.6	42.4
2008	42.6	42.9	42.5	42.7	42.1	43.0	43.1	42.5	41.2	43.1	42.3	42.2	42.5
2009	41.1	40.0	39.1	39.6	40.5	40.6	40.7	40.8	39.9	40.5	41.8	41.0	40.5
Construction													
2007	44.7	45.2	44.3	45.9	44.7	44.6	44.7	44.6	43.1	44.9	45.2	42.7	44.5
2008	43.2	43.3	42.1	42.9	41.9	43.0	42.8	41.3	39.4	41.4	41.7	41.5	42.0
2009	41.7	40.1	38.3	39.3	40.9	41.3	42.1	41.5	41.0	42.0	42.0	41.0	40.9
Manufacturing													
2007	39.8	40.9	40.5	40.7	41.3	41.3	40.8	42.1	42.4	42.2	42.7	42.2	41.4
2008	41.8	42.3	42.0	42.0	41.9	42.8	42.3	42.3	41.5	42.6	41.3	41.9	42.1
2009	40.5	38.9	38.9	39.2	39.7	39.7	39.1	39.7	39.4	39.6	40.3	39.9	39.6
Trade, Transportation, and Utilities													
2007	38.6	40.3	38.5	42.5	42.6	45.0	43.4	42.5	42.9	41.4	41.0	40.8	41.6
2008	39.8	39.7	40.7	40.6	40.1	40.0	39.2	39.5	40.4	39.9	41.2	39.6	40.1
2009	38.4	38.5	38.0	37.5	37.3	37.3	37.0	37.0	36.9	36.3	36.8	36.8	37.3
Financial Activities													
2007	37.5	37.9	37.7	39.1	38.1	38.1	39.3	38.4	39.1	38.0	37.8	39.2	38.4
2008	37.4	37.4	38.0	37.2	37.5	38.3	37.3	37.5	37.0	37.6	38.5	37.5	37.6
2009	37.8	38.3	37.8	37.9	36.8	36.9	37.2	38.0	37.1	37.9	38.4	37.7	37.7
Professional and Business Services													
2007	36.1	37.5	37.0	37.3	36.3	36.8	36.4	36.6	36.7	36.0	36.3	37.3	36.7
2008	35.6	36.4	37.1	36.0	35.7	36.8	35.7	35.8	34.9	35.9	36.5	35.5	36.0
2009	34.6	35.1	35.0	34.7	34.6	35.2	34.5	35.2	34.2	34.5	35.5	34.7	34.8
Education and Health Services													
2007	33.0	33.5	33.5	34.2	33.8	35.2	34.7	34.2	34.7	34.3	34.1	35.5	34.2
2008	34.5	34.6	34.9	34.4	34.7	35.4	35.1	34.5	34.7	35.2	35.5	35.0	34.9
2009	34.8	35.4	35.8	35.0	35.0	34.8	34.9	35.0	34.8	34.5	35.2	34.6	35.0
Leisure and Hospitality													
2007	27.8	28.9	28.4	28.0	28.1	28.3	27.8	27.7	27.0	26.8	26.5	27.0	27.7
2008	26.0	26.9	26.9	26.8	26.8	27.2	26.6	27.0	26.0	26.7	27.1	26.9	26.8
2009	26.3	27.2	27.3	26.5	26.3	26.6	26.3	27.0	25.9	26.8	26.5	26.8	26.6
Other Services													
2007	28.1	31.1	30.3	30.5	30.7	30.1	30.1	30.4	31.5	31.6	32.7	33.2	30.9
2008	31.6	32.7	33.4	32.8	32.6	33.6	32.8	32.8	32.0	32.9	33.9	33.5	32.9
2009	32.7	33.5	33.2	32.9	33.1	33.4	33.9	34.1	33.6	34.5	34.9	34.3	33.7

Average Hourly Earnings by Selected Industry: Texas, 2007–2009

(Dollars, not seasonally adjusted.)

Industry and year	January	February	March	April	May	June	July	August	September	October	November	December	Annual average
Total Private													
2007	21.30	20.96	21.07	21.30	21.05	20.94	21.20	21.05	21.08	20.84	20.76	21.34	21.07
2008	20.97	21.12	21.47	21.46	21.39	21.47	21.18	21.15	21.27	21.29	21.41	21.36	21.30
2009	21.32	21.37	21.26	21.22	21.30	21.26	21.40	21.47	21.50	21.47	21.76	21.41	21.40
Goods-Producing													
2007	23.08	22.48	22.74	22.68	21.92	22.29	22.44	21.86	22.05	21.72	21.64	23.64	22.37
2008	22.71	22.61	23.79	22.75	22.89	22.81	22.62	22.70	22.62	22.79	22.60	22.72	22.80
2009	22.68	22.63	22.65	22.60	22.70	22.74	22.85	22.88	22.80	23.04	23.12	23.06	22.81
Construction													
2007	22.33	21.11	22.13	21.18	21.15	21.22	21.17	21.10	21.13	21.12	21.08	21.03	21.30
2008	20.27	19.99	19.89	19.80	19.77	19.70	19.63	19.53	19.43	19.45	19.38	19.35	19.69
2009	19.19	19.36	19.72	19.60	19.48	19.50	19.48	19.52	19.77	19.86	19.63	19.66	19.56
Manufacturing													
2007	22.64	22.54	22.21	22.57	22.57	22.50	22.45	22.40	22.41	22.31	22.21	22.11	22.41
2008	22.21	22.43	22.73	22.98	23.40	23.45	23.40	23.37	23.35	23.25	23.15	23.05	23.06
2009	22.92	22.96	23.14	23.21	23.28	23.40	23.30	23.40	23.45	23.51	23.54	23.57	23.30
Trade, Transportation, and Utilities													
2007	28.56	28.52	28.41	28.66	28.77	28.72	28.79	28.68	28.73	28.48	28.66	28.70	28.64
2008	27.72	27.74	27.49	27.53	27.37	27.54	27.49	27.54	27.61	27.54	27.44	27.52	27.54
2009	27.65	27.60	27.55	27.58	27.64	27.60	27.73	27.68	27.60	27.64	27.41	27.47	27.60
Financial Activities													
2007	25.78	25.71	25.60	25.32	25.26	25.65	25.98	25.53	25.52	25.43	25.77	25.43	25.58
2008	25.24	25.15	25.20	25.48	25.20	25.24	25.20	25.14	25.17	25.25	25.33	25.42	25.25
2009	25.32	25.54	25.37	25.24	25.47	25.48	25.59	25.42	25.47	25.20	25.34	25.20	25.39
Professional and Business Services													
2007	25.22	25.46	25.63	25.54	25.51	25.29	25.57	25.41	25.43	25.30	25.16	25.23	25.40
2008	24.95	25.08	25.16	25.21	25.25	25.37	25.11	25.33	25.21	25.37	25.44	25.65	25.26
2009	25.86	26.18	26.32	26.53	26.21	26.00	26.25	26.39	26.45	25.97	26.22	26.14	26.21
Education and Health Services													
2007	24.55	24.47	24.04	23.77	23.69	23.56	23.81	23.70	23.30	23.04	22.89	22.67	23.61
2008	22.54	22.59	22.45	22.32	22.25	22.15	22.06	22.02	22.13	22.03	22.09	21.95	22.21
2009	21.81	21.64	21.60	21.74	21.74	21.62	21.76	21.82	21.85	21.95	21.85	21.97	21.78
Leisure and Hospitality													
2007	10.95	11.05	11.01	11.10	11.13	11.17	11.16	11.01	11.27	11.30	11.52	11.74	11.20
2008	11.44	11.41	11.35	11.31	11.33	11.34	11.22	11.27	11.40	11.52	11.62	11.69	11.41
2009	11.60	11.69	11.71	11.65	11.58	11.40	11.58	11.50	11.69	11.73	11.88	11.93	11.67
Other Services													
2007	16.51	16.59	16.62	16.64	16.51	16.40	16.13	16.27	16.04	16.09	15.95	16.30	16.33
2008	15.71	15.68	15.80	15.92	15.77	15.76	15.91	16.03	16.12	16.30	16.41	16.52	16.00
2009	16.65	16.78	16.90	16.84	16.70	16.71	16.76	16.74	16.82	16.89	16.75	16.84	16.78

Average Weekly Earnings by Selected Industry: Texas, 2007–2009

(Dollars, not seasonally adjusted.)

Industry and year	January	February	March	April	May	June	July	August	September	October	November	December	Annual average
Total Private													
2007	756.15	760.85	762.73	781.71	762.01	768.50	775.92	770.43	775.74	758.58	757.74	789.58	769.06
2008	754.92	768.77	787.95	781.14	774.32	792.24	768.83	765.63	750.83	770.70	779.32	771.10	773.19
2009	754.73	758.64	750.48	742.70	745.50	746.23	749.00	762.19	748.20	753.60	779.01	757.91	755.42
Goods-Producing													
2007	950.90	937.42	941.44	975.24	929.41	942.87	946.97	937.79	943.74	938.30	943.50	1007.06	948.49
2008	967.45	969.97	1011.08	971.43	963.67	980.83	974.92	964.75	931.94	982.25	955.98	958.78	969.00
2009	932.15	905.20	885.62	894.96	919.35	923.24	930.00	933.50	909.72	933.12	966.42	945.46	923.81
Construction													
2007	998.15	954.17	980.36	972.16	945.41	946.41	946.30	941.06	910.70	948.29	952.82	897.98	947.85
2008	875.66	865.57	837.37	849.42	828.36	847.10	840.16	806.59	765.54	805.23	808.15	803.03	826.98
2009	800.22	776.34	755.28	770.28	796.73	805.35	820.11	810.08	810.57	834.12	824.46	806.06	800.00
Manufacturing													
2007	901.07	921.89	899.51	918.60	932.14	929.25	915.96	943.04	950.18	941.48	948.37	933.04	927.77
2008	928.38	948.79	954.66	965.16	980.46	1003.66	989.82	988.55	969.03	990.45	956.10	965.80	970.83
2009	928.26	893.14	900.15	909.83	924.22	928.98	911.03	928.98	923.93	931.00	948.66	940.44	922.68
Trade, Transportation, and Utilities													
2007	1102.42	1149.36	1093.79	1218.05	1225.60	1292.40	1249.49	1218.90	1232.52	1179.07	1175.06	1170.96	1191.42
2008	1103.26	1101.28	1118.84	1117.72	1097.54	1101.60	1077.61	1087.83	1115.44	1098.85	1130.53	1089.79	1104.35
2009	1061.76	1062.60	1046.90	1034.25	1030.97	1029.48	1026.01	1024.16	1018.44	1003.33	1008.69	1010.90	1029.48
Financial Activities													
2007	966.75	974.41	965.12	990.01	962.41	977.27	1021.01	980.35	997.83	966.34	974.11	996.86	982.27
2008	943.98	940.61	957.60	947.86	945.00	966.69	939.96	942.75	931.29	949.40	975.21	953.25	949.40
2009	957.10	978.18	958.99	956.60	937.30	940.21	951.95	965.96	944.94	955.08	973.06	950.04	957.20
Professional and Business Services													
2007	910.44	954.75	948.31	952.64	926.01	930.67	930.75	930.01	933.28	910.80	913.31	941.08	932.18
2008	888.22	912.91	933.44	907.56	901.43	933.62	896.43	906.81	879.83	910.78	928.56	910.58	909.36
2009	894.76	918.92	921.20	920.59	906.87	915.20	905.63	928.93	904.59	895.97	930.81	907.06	912.11
Education and Health Services													
2007	810.15	819.75	805.34	812.93	800.72	829.31	826.21	810.54	808.51	790.27	780.55	804.79	807.46
2008	777.63	781.61	783.51	767.81	772.08	784.11	774.31	759.69	767.91	775.46	784.20	768.25	775.13
2009	758.99	766.06	773.28	760.90	760.90	752.38	759.42	763.70	760.38	757.28	769.12	760.16	762.30
Leisure and Hospitality													
2007	304.41	319.35	312.68	310.80	312.75	316.11	310.25	304.98	304.29	302.84	305.28	316.98	310.24
2008	297.44	306.93	305.32	303.11	303.64	308.45	298.45	304.29	296.40	307.58	314.90	314.46	305.79
2009	305.08	317.97	319.68	308.73	304.55	305.37	304.55	310.50	302.77	314.36	314.82	319.72	310.42
Other Services													
2007	463.93	515.95	503.59	507.52	506.86	493.64	485.51	494.61	505.26	508.44	521.57	541.16	504.60
2008	496.44	512.74	527.72	522.18	514.10	529.54	521.85	525.78	515.84	536.27	556.30	553.42	526.40
2009	544.46	562.13	561.08	554.04	552.77	558.11	568.16	570.83	565.15	582.71	584.58	577.61	565.49

UTAH
At a Glance

Population:
    1990 census: 1,722,850
    2000 census: 2,233,169
    2009 estimate: 2,784,572

Percent change in population:
    1990–2000: 29.6%
    2000–2009: 24.7%

Percent change in total nonfarm employment:
    1990–2009: 64.7%
    2008–2009: -4.8%

Industry with the largest growth in employment, 1990–2009 (thousands):
    Education and Health Services, 83.6

Industry with the largest decline or smallest growth in employment, 1990–2009 (thousands):
    Mining and logging, 2.9

Civilian labor force:
    1990: 820,436
    2000: 1,136,036
    2009: 1,364,494

Unemployment rate and rank among states (lowest to highest):
    1990: 4.4%, 9th
    2000: 3.4%, 17th
    2009: 6.6%, 9th

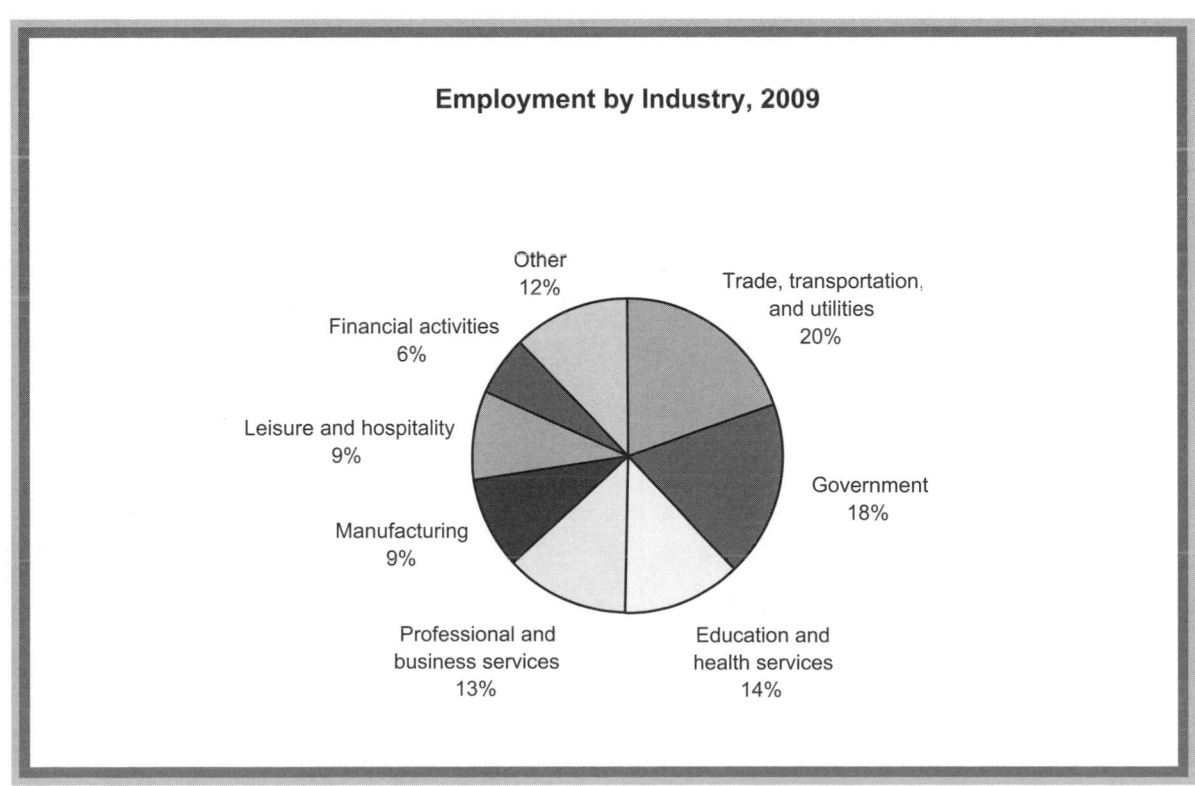

Employment by Industry, 2009

Other 12%

Trade, transportation, and utilities 20%

Financial activities 6%

Leisure and hospitality 9%

Government 18%

Manufacturing 9%

Professional and business services 13%

Education and health services 14%

Employment by Industry: Utah, Selected Years, 1990–2009

(Numbers in thousands, not seasonally adjusted.)

Industry and year	January	February	March	April	May	June	July	August	September	October	November	December	Annual average
Total Nonfarm													
1990	697.9	700.7	707.6	716.1	720.6	729.6	717.7	724.3	737.0	739.4	745.4	747.3	723.6
2000	1044.9	1053.3	1063.1	1071.1	1074.0	1083.5	1067.3	1073.8	1088.4	1089.0	1094.5	1101.7	1075.4
2001	1069.2	1072.9	1080.2	1083.5	1084.3	1091.3	1073.4	1078.4	1088.4	1083.5	1085.3	1085.7	1081.3
2002	1062.8	1069.6	1065.7	1073.4	1072.0	1077.1	1063.3	1066.5	1079.1	1080.3	1084.4	1087.1	1073.4
2003	1058.2	1059.0	1062.3	1069.2	1069.9	1076.0	1062.8	1070.0	1082.4	1087.8	1092.2	1099.2	1074.1
2004	1072.3	1077.7	1086.2	1098.8	1100.1	1109.8	1096.9	1102.9	1117.1	1123.1	1130.3	1136.4	1104.3
2005	1110.8	1118.0	1126.8	1138.4	1139.7	1149.0	1140.1	1152.1	1168.0	1170.0	1177.9	1185.3	1148.0
2006	1162.9	1171.5	1182.5	1192.9	1196.1	1211.1	1196.1	1208.2	1222.5	1222.8	1234.6	1243.3	1203.7
2007	1219.2	1226.7	1238.5	1247.0	1250.3	1261.9	1244.6	1256.2	1266.5	1270.5	1276.6	1281.0	1253.3
2008	1244.5	1248.0	1253.3	1259.1	1256.6	1261.4	1242.8	1252.3	1261.4	1254.9	1249.1	1246.7	1252.5
2009	1203.3	1197.0	1195.9	1194.1	1189.5	1190.1	1172.9	1178.8	1194.4	1197.2	1196.1	1192.6	1191.8
Total Private													
1990	547.9	549.3	555.6	562.2	564.9	576.3	575.9	583.5	588.0	586.2	591.9	595.5	573.1
2000	863.7	866.4	874.6	880.7	882.2	895.7	894.7	901.7	902.7	900.5	905.2	912.1	890.0
2001	882.6	881.0	887.5	889.5	890.1	898.0	896.4	901.3	897.1	890.1	890.4	890.7	891.2
2002	868.5	874.6	867.7	874.5	874.4	879.3	878.9	883.6	883.3	882.5	885.9	888.7	878.5
2003	860.1	859.3	862.4	868.1	870.1	878.0	879.3	886.3	885.7	888.4	892.8	899.9	877.5
2004	873.9	877.7	885.1	895.8	898.6	909.4	911.4	915.8	916.8	920.1	926.9	933.5	905.4
2005	908.5	914.0	922.1	932.4	934.7	944.7	951.3	960.4	964.3	964.5	971.8	979.8	945.7
2006	958.9	965.3	975.6	985.2	989.5	1004.0	1004.8	1014.0	1016.5	1015.3	1026.2	1035.7	999.3
2007	1013.2	1018.7	1029.8	1037.0	1040.8	1052.3	1052.3	1060.2	1057.9	1059.5	1064.7	1070.0	1046.4
2008	1034.4	1035.9	1040.3	1044.7	1042.3	1047.8	1046.5	1051.3	1046.7	1038.0	1031.6	1030.1	1040.8
2009	988.9	980.7	979.4	974.8	971.0	973.5	976.9	978.5	977.7	978.4	977.1	975.2	977.7
Goods-Producing													
1990	131.2	131.2	132.6	136.4	138.2	142.0	143.1	145.3	146.1	145.0	144.5	143.6	139.9
2000	200.2	199.7	200.9	203.6	205.4	209.6	208.8	210.2	209.4	207.3	206.0	204.5	205.5
2001	198.4	197.1	198.5	198.5	201.3	204.2	204.9	206.5	204.1	202.0	199.6	194.7	200.8
2002	185.4	182.0	183.2	185.6	188.6	190.8	191.9	192.8	192.5	192.3	191.2	188.9	188.8
2003	181.3	179.8	180.4	182.8	186.2	188.7	189.4	191.0	190.2	191.2	190.1	189.0	186.7
2004	182.4	182.5	185.3	190.1	194.1	197.6	199.9	200.9	200.6	200.3	200.0	199.5	194.4
2005	194.0	195.4	196.9	202.8	206.4	210.4	213.3	215.6	216.4	215.3	216.4	216.0	208.2
2006	212.0	214.5	218.1	222.0	227.1	232.0	233.0	235.6	236.3	236.1	237.1	237.2	228.4
2007	231.6	232.8	236.7	239.8	243.9	248.6	248.5	250.3	248.2	247.9	244.7	241.6	242.9
2008	231.0	228.9	229.8	230.1	231.7	233.6	233.1	233.0	230.5	226.7	221.5	215.8	228.8
2009	202.1	196.4	194.8	192.2	194.2	195.3	196.3	196.1	194.7	192.4	190.7	187.1	194.4
Mining and Logging													
1990	7.5	7.5	7.4	7.7	7.9	7.9	8.0	8.2	8.4	8.2	8.1	8.1	7.9
2000	7.2	7.2	7.3	7.5	7.6	7.7	7.7	7.7	7.7	7.4	7.3	7.3	7.5
2001	7.2	7.2	7.3	7.3	7.5	7.5	7.4	7.5	7.3	7.1	7.1	7.0	7.3
2002	6.7	6.7	6.7	6.9	7.0	7.1	7.1	7.1	7.2	7.1	7.1	7.0	7.0
2003	6.6	6.5	6.6	6.7	6.8	6.9	6.9	6.8	6.8	6.9	6.8	6.8	6.8
2004	6.7	6.6	6.6	6.9	7.1	7.3	7.4	7.4	7.5	7.6	7.6	7.7	7.2
2005	7.6	7.8	7.8	8.2	8.4	8.6	8.8	8.9	9.0	9.0	9.2	9.2	8.5
2006	9.0	9.2	9.4	9.7	9.9	10.2	10.4	10.5	10.5	10.6	10.7	10.8	10.1
2007	10.6	10.6	10.8	10.9	11.1	11.2	11.3	11.4	11.1	11.4	11.4	11.4	11.1
2008	11.4	11.4	11.5	11.8	12.3	12.6	12.8	13.4	13.5	13.6	13.5	13.2	12.6
2009	12.1	11.8	11.5	10.9	10.7	10.6	10.6	10.5	10.4	10.4	10.2	10.3	10.8
Construction													
1990	23.6	23.4	24.3	26.5	27.8	29.6	31.0	31.9	32.0	31.5	30.8	29.5	28.4
2000	68.0	67.9	68.9	71.0	72.8	75.8	75.5	76.5	75.4	74.1	72.7	71.3	72.5
2001	65.9	65.4	66.8	68.3	71.2	74.1	75.2	77.0	75.7	75.0	73.7	70.5	71.6
2002	63.9	61.5	62.9	65.1	67.6	69.5	70.8	71.6	71.4	71.3	70.4	68.3	67.9
2003	62.6	62.0	62.5	64.4	67.2	69.1	70.2	71.7	71.1	71.4	70.1	68.8	67.6
2004	63.9	63.8	66.1	69.8	72.5	75.2	77.1	77.9	77.6	77.1	76.1	75.2	72.7
2005	71.1	72.1	73.7	78.1	80.5	83.3	85.5	86.9	87.5	86.8	86.9	86.0	81.5
2006	83.0	84.5	87.3	90.4	94.6	98.4	99.1	101.1	101.6	100.9	100.9	100.3	95.2
2007	96.0	96.5	99.3	102.1	105.2	108.6	108.3	109.7	108.0	107.2	103.2	99.7	103.7
2008	91.2	89.3	90.3	91.1	92.6	94.0	93.6	93.9	92.0	89.1	85.3	81.7	90.3
2009	72.1	69.3	69.1	68.4	70.9	72.0	73.3	73.3	72.7	72.0	71.4	67.9	71.0
Manufacturing													
1990	100.1	100.3	100.9	102.2	102.5	104.5	104.1	105.2	105.7	105.3	105.6	106.0	103.5
2000	125.0	124.6	124.7	125.1	125.0	126.1	125.6	126.0	126.3	125.8	126.0	125.9	125.5
2001	125.3	124.5	124.4	122.9	122.6	122.6	122.3	122.0	121.1	119.9	118.8	117.2	122.0
2002	114.8	113.8	113.6	113.6	114.0	114.2	114.0	114.1	113.9	113.9	113.7	113.6	113.9
2003	112.1	111.3	111.3	111.7	112.2	112.7	112.3	112.5	112.3	112.9	113.2	113.4	112.3
2004	111.8	112.1	112.6	113.4	114.5	115.1	115.4	115.6	115.5	115.6	116.3	116.6	114.5
2005	115.3	115.5	115.4	116.5	117.5	118.5	119.0	119.8	119.9	119.5	120.3	120.8	118.2
2006	120.0	120.8	121.4	121.9	122.6	123.4	123.5	124.0	124.2	124.6	125.5	126.1	123.2
2007	125.0	125.7	126.6	126.8	127.6	128.8	128.9	129.2	129.1	129.3	130.1	130.5	128.1
2008	128.4	128.2	128.0	127.2	126.8	127.0	126.7	125.7	125.0	124.0	122.7	120.9	125.9
2009	117.9	115.3	114.2	112.9	112.6	112.7	112.4	112.3	111.6	110.0	109.1	108.9	112.5

Employment by Industry: Utah, Selected Years, 1990–2009—*Continued*

(Numbers in thousands, not seasonally adjusted.)

Industry and year	January	February	March	April	May	June	July	August	September	October	November	December	Annual average
Service-Providing													
1990	566.7	569.5	575.0	579.7	582.4	587.6	574.6	579.0	590.9	594.4	600.9	603.7	583.7
2000	844.7	853.6	862.2	867.5	868.6	873.9	858.5	863.6	879.0	881.7	888.5	897.2	869.9
2001	870.8	875.8	881.7	885.0	883.0	887.1	868.5	871.9	884.3	881.5	885.7	891.0	880.5
2002	877.4	887.6	882.5	887.8	883.4	886.3	871.4	873.7	886.6	888.0	893.2	898.2	884.7
2003	876.9	879.2	881.9	886.4	883.7	887.3	873.4	879.0	892.2	896.6	902.1	910.2	887.4
2004	889.9	895.2	900.9	908.7	906.0	912.2	897.0	902.0	916.5	922.8	930.3	936.9	909.9
2005	916.8	922.6	929.9	935.6	933.3	938.6	926.8	936.5	951.6	954.7	961.5	969.3	939.8
2006	950.9	957.0	964.4	970.9	969.0	979.1	963.1	972.6	986.2	986.7	997.5	1006.1	975.3
2007	987.6	993.9	1001.8	1007.2	1006.4	1013.3	996.1	1005.9	1018.3	1022.6	1031.9	1039.4	1010.4
2008	1013.5	1019.1	1023.5	1029.0	1024.9	1027.8	1009.7	1019.3	1030.9	1028.2	1027.6	1030.9	1023.7
2009	1001.2	1000.6	1001.1	1001.9	995.3	994.8	976.6	982.7	999.7	1004.8	1005.4	1005.5	997.5
Trade, Transportation, and Utilities													
1990	150.5	148.9	149.8	148.9	150.1	152.9	152.7	154.5	156.1	156.6	160.8	163.0	153.7
2000	216.9	214.7	215.7	216.4	216.5	219.1	219.3	220.9	221.6	223.4	228.1	231.4	220.3
2001	219.8	218.1	218.6	219.0	218.7	218.9	218.4	218.8	217.6	217.1	220.7	222.4	219.0
2002	214.2	212.5	211.7	213.5	215.2	215.5	215.3	216.1	215.1	216.2	220.0	221.8	215.6
2003	211.1	209.6	210.0	210.6	212.1	212.8	212.9	214.5	213.9	215.8	220.5	223.4	213.9
2004	214.6	213.1	213.6	215.5	217.5	218.5	218.5	219.4	219.3	221.3	226.3	228.7	218.9
2005	219.7	218.8	221.2	221.8	223.0	223.8	225.1	227.5	227.6	229.7	234.2	237.3	225.8
2006	228.6	228.1	229.6	230.0	231.7	234.2	234.8	237.2	237.6	238.3	244.8	248.6	235.3
2007	240.4	239.9	241.8	241.8	243.4	244.3	245.2	246.8	247.0	248.1	253.5	256.4	245.7
2008	246.9	245.5	246.3	247.0	247.8	248.8	248.2	249.1	248.0	247.5	250.1	251.0	248.0
2009	238.6	236.0	235.1	233.2	233.9	233.6	233.2	233.3	233.1	234.8	238.7	240.1	235.3
Wholesale Trade													
1990	28.0	28.0	28.2	28.7	28.7	29.0	29.3	29.6	29.7	29.7	30.0	29.9	29.0
2000	39.5	39.7	39.9	39.9	40.1	40.5	40.7	40.8	40.9	41.1	41.0	41.3	40.5
2001	40.9	41.1	41.3	41.2	41.4	41.5	41.5	41.4	41.1	40.9	40.9	40.9	41.2
2002	39.9	40.0	40.0	40.1	40.6	40.5	40.5	40.6	40.4	40.5	40.4	40.5	40.3
2003	39.8	39.8	39.9	40.1	40.4	40.5	40.2	40.3	40.2	40.3	40.4	40.5	40.2
2004	40.1	40.2	40.4	40.8	41.1	41.5	41.4	41.4	41.5	41.7	42.0	42.2	41.2
2005	41.8	42.0	42.2	42.4	42.9	43.1	43.1	43.3	43.3	43.5	43.7	43.8	42.9
2006	43.3	43.6	43.8	44.1	44.6	45.2	45.1	45.3	45.5	45.7	46.0	46.4	44.9
2007	46.2	46.4	46.6	46.6	47.2	47.5	47.6	47.9	47.8	48.0	48.2	48.5	47.4
2008	47.7	47.8	48.0	48.2	48.5	48.6	48.5	48.6	48.5	48.2	47.9	48.0	48.2
2009	46.6	46.4	46.0	45.3	45.2	45.1	45.7	45.6	45.4	45.6	45.2	45.6	45.6
Retail Trade													
1990	86.5	84.7	85.2	85.8	87.0	89.1	88.6	89.7	91.1	91.2	95.2	97.0	89.2
2000	129.3	127.0	127.5	128.2	128.6	130.1	129.7	130.9	131.3	132.7	137.1	139.5	131.0
2001	131.6	129.8	130.0	130.6	130.8	131.0	130.4	130.8	129.9	129.7	133.9	135.5	131.2
2002	129.6	127.5	127.5	129.0	130.1	130.6	130.3	131.0	130.5	130.9	135.0	137.1	130.8
2003	127.7	126.3	126.7	127.1	128.1	128.8	128.9	130.2	129.8	131.1	135.8	138.5	129.9
2004	130.1	128.5	128.8	130.2	131.7	132.2	132.3	133.1	132.9	134.2	138.7	140.6	132.8
2005	132.4	130.8	132.8	132.4	133.0	133.5	134.6	136.6	136.4	137.9	142.0	144.3	135.6
2006	137.0	135.9	137.1	137.1	138.3	139.9	140.5	142.3	142.2	142.9	148.6	151.2	141.1
2007	144.3	143.4	144.7	144.8	145.6	145.9	146.5	147.5	147.3	147.8	152.7	154.5	147.1
2008	148.3	146.7	147.2	147.5	148.1	149.1	148.6	149.2	148.3	148.2	151.1	151.8	148.7
2009	142.0	140.2	140.2	139.5	140.5	140.7	139.5	140.1	140.2	141.8	146.6	147.4	141.6
Transportation and Utilities													
1990	36.0	36.2	36.4	34.4	34.4	34.8	34.8	35.2	35.3	35.7	35.6	36.1	35.4
2000	48.1	48.0	48.3	48.3	47.8	48.5	48.9	49.2	49.4	49.6	50.0	50.6	48.9
2001	47.3	47.2	47.3	47.2	46.5	46.4	46.5	46.6	46.6	46.5	45.9	46.0	46.7
2002	44.7	45.0	44.2	44.4	44.5	44.4	44.5	44.5	44.2	44.8	44.6	44.2	44.5
2003	43.6	43.5	43.4	43.4	43.6	43.5	43.8	44.0	43.9	44.4	44.3	44.4	43.8
2004	44.4	44.4	44.4	44.5	44.7	44.8	44.8	44.9	44.9	45.4	45.6	45.9	44.9
2005	45.5	46.0	46.2	47.0	47.1	47.2	47.4	47.6	47.9	48.3	48.5	49.2	47.3
2006	48.3	48.6	48.7	48.8	48.8	49.1	49.2	49.6	49.9	49.7	50.2	51.0	49.3
2007	49.9	50.1	50.5	50.4	50.6	50.9	51.1	51.4	51.9	52.3	52.6	53.4	51.3
2008	50.9	51.0	51.1	51.3	51.2	51.1	51.1	51.3	51.2	51.1	51.1	51.2	51.1
2009	50.0	49.4	48.9	48.4	48.2	47.8	48.0	47.6	47.5	47.4	46.9	47.1	48.1
Information													
1990	12.3	12.8	12.8	13.1	13.0	13.5	13.7	13.8	13.8	13.8	14.0	14.1	13.3
2000	34.2	34.3	34.6	34.5	35.3	35.8	35.7	36.2	36.3	35.9	36.2	36.1	35.4
2001	34.5	33.9	33.8	33.8	34.1	34.2	33.7	33.4	33.0	32.5	32.9	32.5	33.5
2002	31.8	31.7	31.1	30.9	31.3	31.1	31.0	30.7	30.5	30.5	30.8	30.7	31.0
2003	30.1	30.0	29.9	29.4	30.1	30.2	29.8	30.0	29.8	30.2	30.1	30.6	30.0
2004	29.4	30.0	30.1	30.3	30.2	30.7	30.1	30.3	30.2	30.5	31.3	31.3	30.4
2005	31.0	31.5	31.8	31.6	31.7	31.7	32.4	33.0	32.7	32.2	32.5	32.3	32.0
2006	31.7	31.5	31.5	31.9	32.8	33.0	32.1	32.5	32.2	32.0	32.5	32.0	32.1
2007	32.0	32.0	32.2	30.9	31.1	31.0	30.9	31.0	30.4	30.4	30.5	30.5	31.1
2008	29.8	30.5	30.6	30.9	31.4	31.5	31.1	31.1	30.8	30.5	30.7	30.8	30.8
2009	29.9	30.0	29.9	29.5	29.8	29.9	29.5	29.3	29.1	29.8	29.8	30.1	29.7

Employment by Industry: Utah, Selected Years, 1990–2009—*Continued*

(Numbers in thousands, not seasonally adjusted.)

Industry and year	January	February	March	April	May	June	July	August	September	October	November	December	Annual average
Financial Activities													
1990	34.1	34.3	34.5	34.6	34.3	34.8	34.8	35.2	35.3	34.9	35.1	35.4	34.7
2000	58.6	58.4	58.7	58.5	58.3	58.6	58.9	59.2	59.2	59.3	59.8	60.6	59.0
2001	61.2	61.5	61.8	61.6	61.7	62.2	62.6	63.1	63.0	62.7	63.3	63.9	62.4
2002	63.4	63.4	62.9	63.0	63.3	63.4	63.0	63.3	62.9	63.7	63.8	64.6	63.4
2003	64.1	64.8	64.4	64.6	64.9	64.6	65.1	65.2	64.6	64.4	64.3	64.9	64.7
2004	63.7	64.2	64.2	64.7	64.7	64.7	65.0	64.9	65.0	65.3	65.7	66.6	64.9
2005	65.5	66.0	65.5	66.8	66.7	67.2	67.9	68.1	68.1	68.7	69.0	70.3	67.5
2006	69.2	69.9	70.1	70.7	70.9	71.4	71.8	72.1	72.0	72.9	73.5	74.6	71.6
2007	73.7	74.4	74.6	75.0	75.2	75.6	75.6	75.7	75.2	75.7	75.9	76.6	75.3
2008	74.2	74.9	74.6	74.5	74.3	74.2	74.1	74.1	73.4	73.1	72.9	73.8	74.0
2009	72.5	72.5	72.4	71.8	71.4	71.2	71.5	71.5	71.1	72.8	72.7	73.0	72.0
Professional and Business Services													
1990	70.6	70.5	71.8	72.7	73.4	75.4	75.0	76.6	77.0	77.9	78.9	78.8	74.8
2000	131.1	132.4	134.8	136.8	137.0	140.0	139.1	140.7	141.6	142.0	141.6	142.7	138.3
2001	136.8	135.9	137.0	137.3	137.9	138.1	137.4	138.3	136.3	134.7	132.9	131.8	136.2
2002	129.5	132.7	129.6	131.2	132.4	132.6	132.1	133.4	133.3	132.9	133.1	132.0	132.1
2003	126.5	126.4	127.0	129.3	131.0	132.0	132.8	134.6	134.2	135.7	136.1	136.4	131.8
2004	132.2	133.6	134.7	137.1	138.5	139.9	139.5	140.6	139.3	142.1	142.1	142.8	138.5
2005	138.2	139.5	140.9	143.4	145.3	146.1	147.4	149.0	149.1	150.1	150.5	151.1	145.9
2006	147.1	148.5	149.8	152.2	153.8	156.2	156.6	157.5	157.1	156.9	158.1	158.6	154.4
2007	153.5	154.5	156.4	160.0	163.0	164.7	164.1	165.8	165.0	167.0	168.2	167.8	162.5
2008	159.0	159.8	160.6	162.2	164.2	164.4	164.4	165.8	164.6	162.6	160.0	158.9	162.2
2009	150.5	149.6	148.8	149.1	149.7	149.5	151.2	151.3	151.3	152.6	150.0	151.0	150.4
Education and Health Services													
1990	65.5	67.0	67.5	68.0	67.2	66.6	65.5	65.8	68.2	69.6	70.1	70.2	67.6
2000	99.9	102.6	103.1	103.8	103.4	102.5	101.7	102.4	105.1	106.2	107.4	108.2	103.9
2001	107.6	109.0	109.6	109.9	106.8	107.5	105.6	106.4	111.0	112.1	113.1	113.9	109.4
2002	111.7	112.9	113.4	114.5	110.8	110.7	110.0	111.6	116.3	117.6	118.1	119.2	113.9
2003	117.4	118.4	119.1	119.0	115.0	115.6	114.6	115.5	120.1	121.6	122.1	123.3	118.5
2004	121.4	122.9	123.8	123.7	120.2	121.0	120.0	120.9	125.5	126.8	127.8	128.3	123.5
2005	126.8	128.0	128.7	129.0	125.0	125.9	124.5	125.9	130.7	132.0	133.1	133.6	128.6
2006	132.6	133.5	134.6	134.8	131.2	131.6	130.2	131.9	136.5	137.6	138.6	139.1	134.4
2007	137.7	139.1	139.8	140.5	136.7	136.6	135.7	137.7	142.6	144.1	145.2	146.1	140.2
2008	145.0	146.3	146.8	147.2	143.1	142.6	141.7	143.4	148.7	150.4	151.7	152.1	146.6
2009	150.4	150.9	151.7	151.5	147.3	146.6	146.6	147.9	152.8	155.7	157.9	154.6	151.2
Leisure and Hospitality													
1990	59.3	60.0	61.8	63.2	63.4	65.3	64.8	65.9	65.5	62.7	62.8	64.5	63.2
2000	92.5	94.2	96.7	96.8	95.9	99.2	100.0	100.9	98.8	96.4	95.9	98.4	97.1
2001	94.9	96.0	98.5	99.2	98.9	101.4	101.5	102.1	100.2	97.1	95.7	99.1	98.7
2002	100.5	106.3	103.3	103.1	100.0	102.1	102.1	102.2	99.9	96.8	96.1	99.0	101.0
2003	97.7	98.4	99.5	100.1	98.4	101.3	101.7	102.3	100.6	97.6	97.6	100.2	99.6
2004	98.4	99.4	100.9	101.8	100.5	103.9	104.4	104.9	103.9	101.0	100.9	103.5	102.0
2005	100.9	102.2	104.0	103.7	103.2	106.0	106.1	106.8	105.8	103.1	102.5	105.4	104.1
2006	104.5	105.8	107.8	109.5	107.4	110.4	110.8	111.6	109.6	106.9	107.0	110.6	108.5
2007	109.9	111.2	113.3	113.8	111.6	115.2	115.7	116.0	113.6	110.6	111.1	115.4	113.1
2008	113.7	114.9	116.3	117.4	114.2	116.8	117.3	117.7	114.9	112.2	109.9	112.9	114.9
2009	111.0	111.3	112.6	113.5	110.5	112.9	113.3	113.9	111.5	106.4	103.2	105.8	110.5
Other Services													
1990	24.4	24.6	24.8	25.3	25.3	25.8	26.3	26.4	26.0	25.7	25.7	25.9	25.5
2000	30.3	30.1	30.1	30.3	30.4	30.9	31.2	31.2	30.7	30.0	30.2	30.2	30.5
2001	29.4	29.5	29.7	30.2	30.7	31.5	32.3	32.7	31.9	31.9	32.2	32.4	31.2
2002	32.0	33.1	32.5	32.7	32.8	33.1	33.5	33.5	32.8	32.5	32.8	32.5	32.8
2003	31.9	31.9	32.1	32.3	32.4	32.8	33.0	33.2	32.3	31.9	32.0	32.1	32.3
2004	31.8	32.0	32.5	32.6	32.9	33.1	34.0	33.9	33.0	32.8	32.8	32.8	32.9
2005	32.4	32.6	33.1	33.3	33.4	33.6	34.6	34.5	33.9	33.4	33.6	33.8	33.5
2006	33.2	33.5	34.1	34.1	34.6	35.2	35.5	35.6	35.2	34.6	34.6	35.0	34.6
2007	34.4	34.8	35.0	35.2	35.9	36.3	36.6	36.9	35.9	35.7	35.6	35.6	35.7
2008	34.8	35.1	35.3	35.4	35.6	35.9	36.6	37.1	35.8	35.0	34.8	34.8	35.5
2009	33.9	34.0	34.1	34.0	34.2	34.5	35.3	35.2	34.1	33.9	34.1	33.5	34.2
Government													
1990	150.0	151.4	152.0	153.9	155.7	153.3	141.8	140.8	149.0	153.2	153.5	151.8	150.5
2000	181.2	186.9	188.5	190.4	191.8	187.8	172.6	172.1	185.7	188.5	189.3	189.6	185.4
2001	186.6	191.9	192.7	194.0	194.2	193.3	177.0	177.1	191.3	193.4	194.9	195.0	190.1
2002	194.3	195.0	198.0	198.9	197.6	197.8	184.4	182.9	195.8	197.8	198.5	198.4	195.0
2003	198.1	199.7	199.9	201.1	199.8	198.0	183.5	183.7	196.7	199.4	199.4	199.3	196.6
2004	198.4	200.0	201.1	203.0	201.5	200.4	185.5	187.1	200.3	203.0	203.4	202.9	198.9
2005	202.3	204.0	204.7	206.0	205.0	204.3	188.8	191.7	203.7	205.5	206.1	205.5	202.3
2006	204.0	206.2	206.9	207.7	206.6	207.1	191.3	194.2	206.0	207.5	208.4	207.6	204.5
2007	206.0	208.0	208.7	210.0	209.5	209.6	192.3	196.0	208.6	211.0	211.9	211.0	206.9
2008	210.1	212.1	213.0	214.4	214.3	213.6	196.3	201.0	214.7	216.9	217.5	216.6	211.7
2009	214.4	216.3	216.5	219.3	218.5	216.6	196.0	200.3	216.7	218.8	219.0	217.4	214.2

Average Weekly Hours by Selected Industry: Utah, 2007–2009

(Numbers in thousands, not seasonally adjusted.)

Industry and year	January	February	March	April	May	June	July	August	September	October	November	December	Annual average
Total Private													
2007	34.6	34.6	35.1	35.5	35.1	35.1	35.5	34.6	35.3	34.7	34.3	34.7	34.9
2008	33.7	34.3	34.6	33.9	34.4	35.0	34.8	35.2	35.0	34.8	35.0	34.5	34.6
2009	34.1	34.9	34.9	35.9	36.0	36.1	36.2	36.7	36.1	36.1	36.6	36.1	35.8
Goods-Producing													
2007	38.2	38.0	39.2	39.4	39.6	39.5	39.8	39.5	39.1	38.7	38.5	38.6	39.0
2008	37.3	37.4	37.9	37.6	37.7	37.8	38.4	39.7	38.5	38.5	37.6	37.7	38.0
2009	36.8	37.1	37.5	37.0	37.8	37.3	37.9	38.5	37.1	39.1	39.4	38.5	37.8
Construction													
2007	36.2	37.5	38.1	38.2	38.9	38.1	38.8	38.5	37.4	37.4	37.3	36.2	37.7
2008	34.6	35.6	35.5	34.0	34.1	35.2	36.2	36.7	35.4	35.7	34.5	35.3	35.2
2009	35.2	34.6	35.0	35.1	36.9	36.4	36.9	37.5	35.2	38.5	38.0	35.4	36.2
Manufacturing													
2007	39.8	38.4	40.3	40.2	40.3	40.1	40.8	40.5	40.4	40.0	39.2	40.4	40.0
2008	39.4	38.3	39.6	39.3	39.4	39.3	38.8	39.5	39.1	38.9	38.1	37.8	39.0
2009	36.6	37.9	38.1	37.3	37.6	37.1	37.8	38.4	37.8	39.1	39.8	39.9	38.1
Trade, Transportation, and Utilities													
2007	31.1	31.2	31.8	31.9	30.5	30.7	31.0	30.0	31.0	30.7	30.0	31.3	30.9
2008	29.9	30.3	29.7	28.7	29.4	30.5	30.2	30.5	30.1	30.2	30.8	30.9	30.1
2009	30.5	31.3	31.8	31.1	31.4	31.5	31.9	32.6	31.8	31.8	31.9	32.2	31.7
Information													
2007	35.7	35.3	35.4	36.8	35.8	36.2	36.1	35.3	36.2	35.7	34.8	35.7	35.7
2008	33.8	33.5	34.2	33.4	33.9	35.7	34.0	34.0	34.0	34.2	35.3	33.7	34.2
2009	33.3	36.3	35.9	34.2	34.5	34.5	34.4	35.4	33.7	33.6	34.5	32.8	34.4
Financial Activities													
2007	35.6	35.8	36.0	36.6	36.0	35.8	36.3	36.0	35.6	36.1	35.0	36.5	35.9
2008	35.7	36.7	37.4	36.9	36.5	37.2	36.4	36.5	35.6	36.2	36.7	36.1	36.5
2009	34.1	34.6	34.0	33.8	34.1	35.8	34.1	34.9	34.5	34.6	36.6	35.3	34.7
Professional and Business Services													
2007	32.8	32.8	34.0	34.1	33.5	33.6	34.2	33.3	34.2	33.9	33.4	33.2	33.6
2008	31.7	32.3	33.9	33.5	33.5	34.1	33.4	33.8	33.7	33.6	34.3	34.1	33.5
2009	33.4	35.3	34.9	45.0	43.2	42.7	43.2	41.9	39.7	40.0	40.3	40.2	40.0
Education and Health Services													
2007	40.0	40.4	39.8	39.9	40.5	40.1	40.5	40.0	40.6	39.8	40.3	39.7	40.1
2008	39.2	39.6	39.2	38.5	38.9	39.7	39.6	39.1	40.4	39.8	40.4	39.5	39.5
2009	39.7	40.0	39.6	39.3	39.1	39.0	39.3	39.6	41.0	39.5	39.8	39.9	39.7
Leisure and Hospitality													
2007	24.3	24.3	24.6	25.0	23.6	24.3	25.0	24.1	24.6	23.5	22.0	23.9	24.1
2008	23.2	24.2	24.4	23.3	24.2	24.0	24.5	24.9	24.0	23.7	23.4	22.5	23.9
2009	23.9	24.4	24.7	22.8	23.6	24.3	24.5	26.4	24.5	24.5	24.3	23.4	24.3

Average Hourly Earnings by Selected Industry: Utah, 2007–2009

(Dollars, not seasonally adjusted.)

Industry and year	January	February	March	April	May	June	July	August	September	October	November	December	Annual average
Total Private													
2007	21.74	22.84	21.89	22.20	21.77	21.72	20.97	21.05	20.44	20.26	20.73	21.37	21.41
2008	20.95	21.28	20.84	20.65	20.75	20.91	20.96	21.15	21.25	21.23	21.44	21.75	21.10
2009	21.48	22.01	22.14	22.69	22.46	22.44	22.09	22.16	22.20	21.94	22.11	25.96	22.48
Goods-Producing													
2007	20.72	21.72	20.74	21.20	21.03	20.64	20.80	20.78	21.35	21.27	22.19	23.12	21.29
2008	21.89	21.81	22.05	21.83	22.21	22.34	22.85	23.77	23.43	23.01	23.27	24.52	22.75
2009	23.61	23.95	23.94	24.06	23.80	23.72	23.39	23.64	24.01	23.61	23.47	23.68	23.74
Construction													
2007	21.69	21.26	21.19	22.44	22.10	21.71	22.23	22.04	22.79	22.62	23.80	24.03	22.32
2008	22.55	22.02	22.58	22.24	23.32	22.29	22.17	22.93	22.21	22.26	22.62	24.36	22.61
2009	24.01	24.09	24.09	24.48	24.29	24.21	23.32	23.62	23.81	23.95	23.47	24.75	23.99
Manufacturing													
2007	19.73	20.36	19.15	19.30	19.37	19.52	19.58	19.61	20.02	19.94	20.58	20.56	19.81
2008	20.90	21.12	21.12	20.85	20.80	21.50	20.32	21.16	21.61	21.08	21.42	21.72	21.13
2009	20.80	20.28	21.55	21.76	21.69	21.84	21.91	22.30	22.94	22.31	22.50	21.98	21.82
Trade, Transportation, and Utilities													
2007	18.41	19.42	18.32	19.00	18.61	18.90	18.91	18.94	19.18	18.88	19.43	19.37	18.95
2008	19.75	20.75	19.71	19.72	19.43	19.69	19.72	19.81	19.74	19.55	20.02	19.61	19.79
2009	18.85	20.31	19.41	20.24	19.42	19.43	18.55	19.13	18.91	19.09	19.46	19.29	19.34
Information													
2007	27.13	28.25	27.91	26.04	25.61	25.13	26.66	26.64	27.78	27.18	27.11	27.51	26.91
2008	27.05	26.50	26.30	25.41	25.22	25.41	25.42	25.56	25.71	25.77	26.20	26.31	25.90
2009	26.62	26.78	26.63	26.78	26.32	26.26	26.68	28.11	27.31	27.69	28.15	27.60	27.07
Financial Activities													
2007	22.31	21.95	22.36	21.80	21.95	22.09	22.41	22.51	22.86	22.58	22.67	23.31	22.40
2008	21.85	22.07	22.24	22.08	22.26	22.39	22.57	23.15	23.07	23.89	23.71	23.59	22.73
2009	25.58	25.30	25.77	26.06	25.77	25.87	28.09	26.55	26.20	25.95	25.38	25.48	25.99
Professional and Business Services													
2007	41.92	42.46	41.25	42.70	41.50	42.54	42.25	41.75	42.16	41.20	40.94	40.52	41.76
2008	40.47	40.19	39.43	37.46	36.69	36.18	35.56	33.95	33.71	33.40	33.00	32.00	35.95
2009	32.25	31.54	31.33	31.44	31.33	31.12	29.43	30.50	30.02	29.04	29.57	27.93	30.42
Education and Health Services													
2007	17.76	18.80	16.65	16.73	16.47	16.50	16.81	16.82	17.55	17.06	17.15	18.04	17.20
2008	17.72	17.62	18.11	17.96	18.06	18.29	18.40	18.37	18.74	18.60	18.76	19.47	18.35
2009	18.85	19.01	19.16	19.33	19.22	19.39	19.25	19.22	19.65	19.23	19.31	36.11	20.69
Leisure and Hospitality													
2007	11.32	11.47	11.38	11.28	10.93	11.06	11.03	11.28	11.35	11.45	11.49	11.66	11.31
2008	11.75	11.74	11.83	11.60	11.42	11.54	11.38	11.49	11.91	11.87	11.91	12.26	11.72
2009	12.26	11.64	11.92	11.47	11.47	11.49	11.43	11.75	12.01	12.07	12.32	12.63	11.86

Average Weekly Earnings by Selected Industry: Utah, 2007–2009

(Dollars, not seasonally adjusted.)

Industry and year	January	February	March	April	May	June	July	August	September	October	November	December	Annual average
Total Private													
2007	752.20	790.26	768.34	788.10	764.13	762.37	744.44	728.33	721.53	703.02	711.04	741.54	747.21
2008	706.02	729.90	721.06	700.04	713.80	731.85	729.41	744.48	743.75	738.80	750.40	750.38	730.06
2009	732.47	768.15	772.69	814.57	808.56	810.08	799.66	813.27	801.42	792.03	809.23	937.16	804.78
Goods-Producing													
2007	791.50	825.36	813.01	835.28	832.79	815.28	827.84	820.81	834.79	823.15	854.32	892.43	830.31
2008	816.50	815.69	835.70	820.81	837.32	844.45	877.44	943.67	902.06	885.89	874.95	924.40	864.50
2009	868.85	888.55	897.75	890.22	899.64	884.76	886.48	910.14	890.77	923.15	924.72	911.68	897.37
Construction													
2007	785.18	797.25	807.34	857.21	859.69	827.15	862.52	848.54	852.35	845.99	887.74	869.89	841.46
2008	780.23	783.91	801.59	756.16	795.21	784.61	802.55	841.53	786.23	794.68	780.39	859.91	795.87
2009	845.15	833.51	843.15	859.25	896.30	881.24	860.51	885.75	838.11	922.08	891.86	876.15	868.44
Manufacturing													
2007	785.25	781.82	771.75	775.86	780.61	782.75	798.86	794.21	808.81	797.60	806.74	830.62	792.40
2008	823.46	808.90	836.35	819.41	819.52	844.95	788.42	835.82	844.95	820.01	816.10	821.02	824.07
2009	761.28	768.61	821.06	811.65	815.54	810.26	828.20	856.32	867.13	872.32	895.50	877.00	831.34
Trade, Transportation, and Utilities													
2007	572.55	605.90	582.58	606.10	567.61	580.23	586.21	568.20	594.58	579.62	582.90	606.28	585.56
2008	590.53	628.73	585.39	565.96	571.24	600.55	595.54	604.21	594.17	590.41	616.62	605.95	595.68
2009	574.93	635.70	617.24	629.46	609.79	612.05	591.75	623.64	601.34	607.06	620.77	621.14	613.08
Information													
2007	968.54	997.23	988.01	958.27	916.84	909.71	962.43	940.39	1005.64	970.33	943.43	982.11	960.69
2008	914.29	887.75	899.46	848.69	854.96	907.14	864.28	869.04	874.14	881.33	924.86	886.65	885.78
2009	886.45	972.11	956.02	915.88	908.04	905.97	917.79	995.09	920.35	930.38	971.18	905.28	931.21
Financial Activities													
2007	794.24	785.81	804.96	797.88	790.20	790.82	813.48	810.36	813.82	815.14	793.45	850.82	804.16
2008	780.05	809.97	831.78	814.75	812.49	832.91	821.55	844.98	821.29	864.82	870.16	851.60	829.65
2009	872.28	875.38	876.18	880.83	878.76	926.15	957.87	926.60	903.90	897.87	928.91	899.44	901.85
Professional and Business Services													
2007	1374.98	1392.69	1402.50	1456.07	1390.25	1429.34	1444.95	1390.28	1441.87	1396.68	1367.40	1345.26	1403.14
2008	1282.90	1298.14	1336.68	1254.91	1229.12	1233.74	1187.70	1147.51	1136.03	1122.24	1131.90	1091.20	1204.33
2009	1077.15	1113.36	1093.42	1414.80	1353.46	1328.82	1271.38	1277.95	1191.79	1161.60	1191.67	1122.79	1216.80
Education and Health Services													
2007	710.40	759.52	662.67	667.53	667.04	661.65	680.81	672.80	712.53	678.99	691.15	716.19	689.72
2008	694.62	697.75	709.91	691.46	702.53	726.11	728.64	718.27	757.10	740.28	757.90	769.07	724.83
2009	748.35	760.40	758.74	759.67	751.50	756.21	756.53	761.11	805.65	759.59	768.54	1440.79	821.39
Leisure and Hospitality													
2007	275.08	278.72	279.95	282.00	257.95	268.76	275.75	271.85	279.21	269.08	252.78	278.67	272.57
2008	272.60	284.11	288.65	270.28	276.36	287.35	278.81	286.10	285.84	281.32	278.69	275.85	280.11
2009	293.01	284.02	294.42	261.52	270.69	279.21	280.04	310.20	294.25	295.72	299.38	295.54	288.20

VERMONT
At a Glance

Population:
  1990 census: 562,758
  2000 census: 608,827
  2009 estimate: 621,760

Percent change in population:
  1990–2000: 8.2%
  2000–2009: 2.1%

Percent change in total nonfarm employment:
  1990–2009: 15.2%
  2008–2009: -3.4%

Industry with the largest growth in employment, 1990–2009 (thousands):
  Education and Health Services, 25.1

Industry with the largest decline or smallest growth in employment, 1990–2009 (thousands):
  Manufacturing, -11.5

Civilian labor force:
  1990: 309,280
  2000: 335,798
  2009: 359,759

Unemployment rate and rank among states (lowest to highest):
  1990: 4.9%, 16th
  2000: 2.7%, 3rd
  2009: 6.9%, 14th

Employment by Industry, 2009

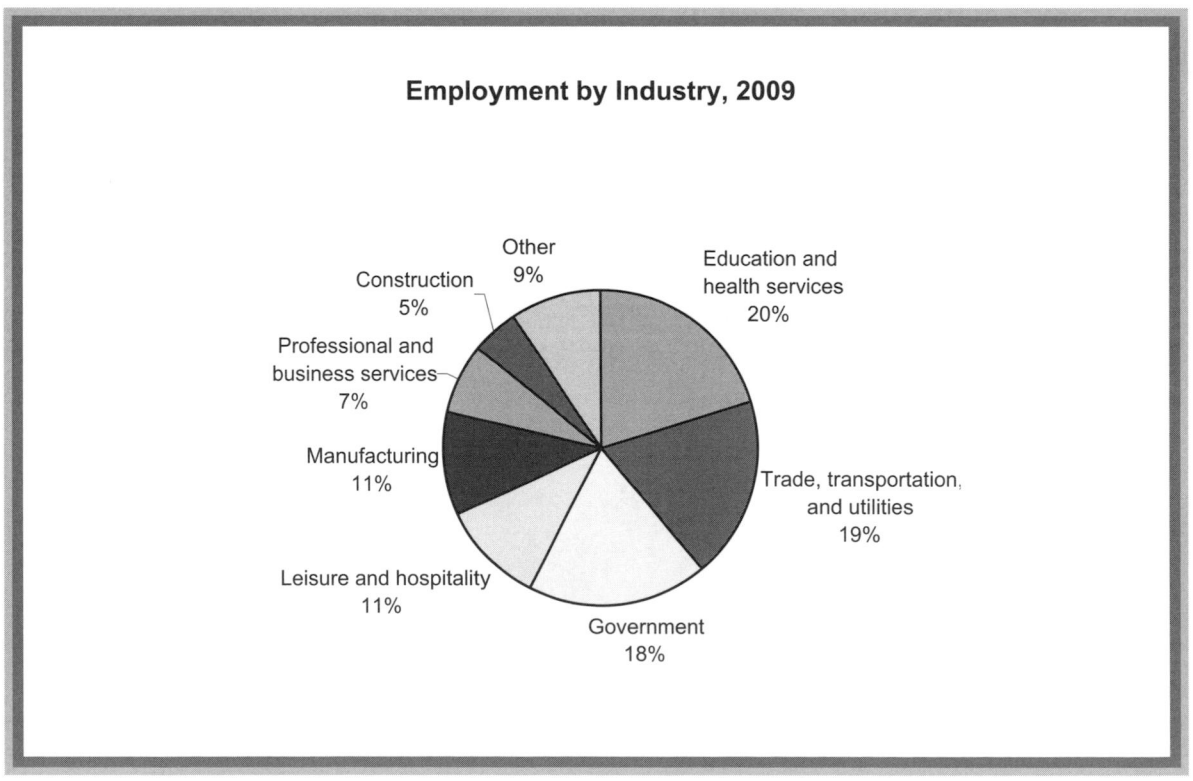

- Other 9%
- Construction 5%
- Professional and business services 7%
- Manufacturing 11%
- Leisure and hospitality 11%
- Government 18%
- Education and health services 20%
- Trade, transportation, and utilities 19%

Employment by Industry: Vermont, Selected Years, 1990–2009

(Numbers in thousands, not seasonally adjusted.)

Industry and year	January	February	March	April	May	June	July	August	September	October	November	December	Annual average
Total Nonfarm													
1990	258.7	258.2	257.8	255.6	257.1	259.9	256.3	257.1	259.3	259.5	255.5	257.2	257.7
2000	293.7	296.9	299.0	293.6	297.2	300.0	293.6	293.8	301.3	304.2	302.4	308.7	298.7
2001	301.7	302.6	302.0	299.6	301.2	304.6	297.8	297.5	303.7	305.3	303.1	306.0	302.1
2002	299.4	299.4	299.1	297.1	299.4	302.1	294.0	293.9	300.8	302.6	300.2	304.1	299.3
2003	297.2	297.8	296.9	293.6	298.0	301.1	294.2	294.9	301.7	304.4	302.5	307.9	299.2
2004	298.7	300.6	300.1	298.8	302.8	305.2	298.8	298.9	306.9	308.2	306.3	310.3	303.0
2005	302.9	304.0	303.5	302.4	305.1	307.1	300.7	301.1	308.4	309.5	308.1	313.6	305.5
2006	305.3	306.4	306.1	303.5	306.8	310.5	301.9	302.6	310.6	312.6	311.5	314.9	307.7
2007	306.2	307.2	306.8	303.3	308.2	311.6	303.7	303.5	310.8	312.1	311.3	315.5	308.4
2008	307.0	308.4	306.6	304.5	308.6	309.0	301.7	301.5	309.2	311.9	307.9	310.3	307.2
2009	299.1	300.9	297.2	293.6	297.7	297.0	289.6	290.2	297.3	299.9	298.3	302.0	296.9
Total Private													
1990	216.5	214.4	213.2	208.8	210.8	215.9	218.7	219.7	216.3	214.3	210.2	211.5	214.2
2000	244.8	246.1	246.7	242.1	244.8	251.1	252.4	252.8	251.4	252.5	250.2	256.4	249.3
2001	251.6	251.0	250.3	247.9	249.4	254.7	256.1	255.8	252.6	251.9	249.6	252.4	251.9
2002	248.1	246.8	246.4	244.2	246.7	251.1	252.2	251.8	249.6	248.6	245.8	250.7	248.5
2003	245.1	243.9	243.1	239.7	244.1	249.2	250.9	252.0	248.9	249.5	247.3	252.8	247.2
2004	246.2	246.3	245.8	244.3	248.5	254.1	255.6	255.6	253.4	252.8	250.3	254.7	250.6
2005	249.5	248.9	248.3	247.3	250.1	255.2	257.3	256.9	254.3	253.3	251.6	257.3	252.5
2006	250.9	250.4	250.1	247.5	251.1	257.3	258.1	258.6	256.1	255.9	254.5	258.1	254.1
2007	251.4	250.8	250.4	247.3	252.0	257.9	259.4	259.4	256.2	255.6	254.7	258.7	254.5
2008	251.5	252.0	250.3	248.2	252.4	255.6	257.1	256.9	254.3	254.6	250.3	252.9	253.0
2009	244.1	243.9	240.6	236.1	240.0	242.9	244.6	245.2	242.6	242.6	240.9	244.5	242.3
Goods-Producing													
1990	57.9	56.6	56.3	57.1	58.4	60.1	60.4	60.9	59.6	58.8	57.0	55.6	58.2
2000	58.8	58.6	59.2	60.7	62.1	64.1	64.2	64.5	63.8	64.0	63.6	63.0	62.2
2001	60.9	60.1	60.2	61.1	62.6	64.1	64.4	63.8	62.6	61.8	60.6	60.1	61.9
2002	56.5	55.3	55.1	56.2	57.6	58.4	58.1	57.0	56.4	56.2	55.3	54.0	56.3
2003	51.7	51.0	51.1	52.2	54.4	55.5	55.9	56.1	54.6	55.0	54.5	53.7	53.8
2004	51.1	51.1	51.0	53.1	55.2	56.6	57.0	57.0	56.3	56.0	55.3	54.5	54.5
2005	51.6	51.1	51.0	52.9	54.9	56.4	57.1	57.1	56.2	56.1	55.4	54.3	54.5
2006	51.7	51.1	51.1	53.3	54.9	56.2	56.8	56.8	56.0	55.9	55.4	54.6	54.5
2007	51.7	50.8	50.9	51.9	54.6	55.7	55.9	55.7	54.7	54.4	53.6	52.7	53.6
2008	50.0	49.6	49.2	50.1	52.2	53.4	53.9	53.5	52.9	52.7	51.4	49.2	51.5
2009	45.6	44.7	43.7	44.2	45.7	46.4	46.7	47.2	46.8	46.4	45.2	43.0	45.5
Mining and Logging													
1990	1.1	1.1	1.1	1.1	1.1	1.2	1.3	1.2	1.2	1.2	1.2	1.1	1.2
2000	1.0	0.9	1.0	1.1	1.1	1.1	1.1	1.2	1.1	1.1	1.1	1.1	1.1
2001	1.0	1.0	1.1	1.0	1.1	1.1	1.2	1.2	1.2	1.2	1.1	1.1	1.1
2002	0.9	0.9	0.9	1.0	1.0	1.1	1.1	1.1	1.1	1.0	1.0	0.9	1.0
2003	0.8	0.8	0.9	0.9	1.0	1.0	1.0	1.0	1.0	1.0	1.0	0.9	0.9
2004	0.8	0.8	0.8	0.9	1.0	1.0	0.9	0.9	0.9	0.9	0.9	0.9	0.9
2005	0.7	0.7	0.8	0.8	0.8	0.9	0.9	0.9	0.9	0.9	0.9	0.8	0.8
2006	0.8	0.7	0.8	0.9	0.9	0.9	0.9	0.9	0.9	0.9	0.9	0.9	0.9
2007	0.8	0.8	0.8	0.8	0.9	0.9	0.9	0.9	0.9	0.8	0.8	0.8	0.8
2008	0.8	0.8	0.8	0.8	0.9	0.9	0.9	0.9	0.9	0.9	0.9	0.8	0.9
2009	0.7	0.7	0.7	0.8	0.8	0.8	0.8	0.8	0.8	0.8	0.8	0.8	0.8
Construction													
1990	13.5	12.5	12.3	13.3	14.7	15.8	16.1	16.4	16.0	15.1	13.7	12.5	14.3
2000	12.7	12.3	12.5	13.9	15.2	16.3	16.7	16.6	16.1	16.0	15.3	14.6	14.9
2001	13.2	12.7	12.8	13.8	15.5	16.6	17.2	17.2	16.5	16.1	15.6	15.1	15.2
2002	13.4	12.9	12.8	13.9	15.3	15.8	16.3	16.3	15.8	15.8	15.3	14.3	14.8
2003	13.0	12.4	12.5	13.7	15.6	16.6	17.2	17.4	16.9	17.0	16.5	15.8	15.4
2004	14.1	13.8	13.9	15.7	17.3	18.3	18.8	18.7	18.2	17.9	17.3	16.2	16.7
2005	14.4	13.8	13.8	15.4	17.3	18.3	19.2	19.1	18.5	18.3	17.6	16.6	16.9
2006	14.9	14.5	14.7	16.4	17.8	18.8	19.4	19.4	18.9	18.6	18.0	17.1	17.4
2007	15.1	14.2	14.4	15.3	17.7	18.5	18.8	18.7	18.1	17.8	17.0	16.0	16.8
2008	14.1	13.5	13.3	14.2	16.2	17.1	17.5	17.3	16.9	16.9	15.9	14.3	15.6
2009	12.3	11.6	11.4	12.4	14.0	14.8	15.2	15.4	15.1	14.7	13.4	11.3	13.5
Manufacturing													
1990	43.3	43.0	42.9	42.7	42.6	43.1	43.0	43.3	42.4	42.5	42.1	42.0	42.7
2000	45.1	45.4	45.7	45.7	45.8	46.7	46.4	46.7	46.6	46.9	47.2	47.3	46.3
2001	46.7	46.4	46.3	46.3	46.0	46.4	46.0	45.4	44.9	44.5	43.9	43.9	45.6
2002	42.2	41.5	41.4	41.3	41.3	41.5	40.7	39.6	39.5	39.4	39.0	38.8	40.5
2003	37.9	37.8	37.7	37.6	37.8	37.9	37.7	37.7	36.7	37.0	37.0	37.0	37.5
2004	36.2	36.5	36.3	36.5	36.9	37.3	37.3	37.4	37.2	37.2	37.1	37.4	36.9
2005	36.5	36.6	36.4	36.7	36.8	37.2	37.0	37.1	36.8	36.9	36.9	36.9	36.8
2006	36.0	35.9	35.6	36.0	36.2	36.5	36.5	36.5	36.2	36.4	36.5	36.6	36.2
2007	35.8	35.8	35.7	35.8	36.0	36.3	36.2	36.1	35.7	35.8	35.8	35.9	35.9
2008	35.1	35.3	35.1	35.1	35.1	35.4	35.5	35.3	35.1	34.9	34.6	34.1	35.1
2009	32.6	32.4	31.6	31.0	30.9	30.8	30.7	31.0	30.9	30.9	31.0	30.9	31.2

Employment by Industry: Vermont, Selected Years, 1990–2009—*Continued*

(Numbers in thousands, not seasonally adjusted.)

Industry and year	January	February	March	April	May	June	July	August	September	October	November	December	Annual average
Service-Providing													
1990	200.8	201.6	201.5	198.5	198.7	199.8	195.9	196.2	199.7	200.7	198.5	201.6	199.5
2000	234.9	238.3	239.8	232.9	235.1	235.9	229.4	229.3	237.5	240.2	238.8	245.7	236.5
2001	240.8	242.5	241.8	238.5	238.6	240.5	233.4	233.7	241.1	243.5	242.5	245.9	240.2
2002	242.9	244.1	244.0	240.9	241.8	243.7	235.9	236.9	244.4	246.4	244.9	250.1	243.0
2003	245.5	246.8	245.8	241.4	243.6	245.6	238.3	238.8	247.1	249.4	248.0	254.2	245.4
2004	247.6	249.5	249.1	245.7	247.6	248.6	241.8	241.9	250.6	252.2	251.0	255.8	248.5
2005	251.3	252.9	252.5	249.5	250.2	250.7	243.6	244.0	252.2	253.4	252.7	259.3	251.0
2006	253.6	255.3	255.0	250.2	251.9	254.3	245.1	245.8	254.6	256.7	256.1	260.3	253.2
2007	254.5	256.4	255.9	251.4	253.6	255.9	247.8	247.8	256.1	257.7	257.7	262.8	254.8
2008	257.0	258.8	257.4	254.4	256.4	255.6	247.8	248.0	256.3	259.2	256.5	261.1	255.7
2009	253.5	256.2	253.5	249.4	252.0	250.6	242.9	243.0	250.5	253.5	253.1	259.0	251.4
Trade, Transportation, and Utilities													
1990	51.4	50.7	50.6	50.3	50.6	51.4	51.6	51.9	51.1	50.9	51.1	51.7	51.1
2000	57.2	57.0	56.9	56.9	57.2	57.9	58.0	58.1	58.0	58.7	59.5	60.5	58.0
2001	58.1	57.6	57.5	57.7	58.4	58.9	58.4	58.5	58.3	59.2	60.1	61.1	58.7
2002	58.3	57.7	57.9	57.9	58.7	59.2	59.1	59.2	58.7	59.1	59.7	60.5	58.8
2003	57.9	57.4	56.8	57.0	57.6	58.4	57.9	58.1	57.8	59.1	59.9	61.1	58.3
2004	57.9	57.4	57.5	57.8	58.7	59.3	59.1	59.0	58.6	59.8	60.8	61.4	58.9
2005	59.0	58.6	58.1	58.6	59.1	59.7	59.4	59.4	59.2	59.8	60.6	61.6	59.4
2006	58.9	58.3	58.2	58.4	59.4	59.9	59.4	59.5	59.4	60.1	61.1	61.9	59.5
2007	59.2	58.4	58.0	57.8	58.9	59.7	59.3	59.0	58.9	59.9	61.2	61.8	59.3
2008	59.0	58.7	58.1	58.2	59.1	59.6	58.8	58.9	58.3	58.9	59.3	59.8	58.9
2009	56.5	56.1	55.1	55.0	56.1	56.6	55.9	56.2	55.8	55.7	56.6	56.3	56.0
Wholesale Trade													
1990	9.4	9.3	9.3	9.5	9.4	9.4	9.6	9.5	9.4	9.3	9.3	9.3	9.4
2000	9.7	9.7	9.8	9.9	9.8	9.8	9.9	9.9	9.8	9.8	9.9	9.9	9.8
2001	9.9	10.0	10.0	10.1	10.0	10.1	10.1	10.1	10.1	10.1	10.1	10.3	10.1
2002	9.9	9.9	10.0	10.0	10.1	10.1	10.2	10.2	10.3	10.2	10.3	10.4	10.1
2003	10.1	10.1	10.1	10.1	10.2	10.3	10.3	10.3	10.3	10.5	10.4	10.4	10.3
2004	10.1	10.1	10.2	10.2	10.3	10.2	10.4	10.1	10.0	10.1	10.2	9.9	10.2
2005	9.9	9.9	9.8	10.0	10.0	10.1	10.2	10.3	10.2	10.2	10.3	10.3	10.1
2006	10.2	10.1	10.2	10.2	10.3	10.2	10.4	10.5	10.5	10.5	10.5	10.6	10.4
2007	10.4	10.3	10.3	10.3	10.4	10.4	10.4	10.4	10.4	10.4	10.5	10.5	10.4
2008	10.2	10.2	10.3	10.3	10.3	10.3	10.2	10.2	10.1	10.0	10.0	9.9	10.2
2009	9.8	9.7	9.7	9.7	9.7	9.7	9.7	9.8	9.7	9.8	10.1	10.0	9.8
Retail Trade													
1990	34.4	33.8	33.6	33.2	33.6	34.1	34.2	34.5	33.8	33.7	34.0	34.5	34.0
2000	38.9	38.7	38.5	38.5	38.9	39.5	39.6	39.8	39.4	40.0	40.7	41.8	39.5
2001	39.6	39.0	39.0	39.0	39.8	40.0	39.9	40.0	39.4	40.2	41.1	41.9	39.9
2002	39.7	39.2	39.3	39.2	39.8	40.3	40.5	40.5	39.7	40.0	40.5	41.2	40.0
2003	39.2	38.8	38.3	38.4	38.9	39.4	39.6	39.7	39.0	39.9	40.9	42.0	39.5
2004	39.2	38.7	38.8	39.1	39.8	40.3	40.3	40.4	39.8	40.6	41.5	42.4	40.1
2005	40.1	39.8	39.4	39.8	40.3	40.7	40.8	40.7	40.2	40.6	41.2	42.1	40.5
2006	39.9	39.5	39.3	39.5	40.3	40.9	40.7	40.7	40.1	40.7	41.6	42.2	40.5
2007	40.0	39.4	39.1	39.0	39.7	40.4	40.5	40.2	39.6	40.4	41.5	42.0	40.2
2008	40.1	39.9	39.3	39.4	40.0	40.4	40.2	40.2	39.4	40.1	40.4	40.8	40.0
2009	38.3	38.0	37.2	37.2	38.1	38.6	38.2	38.3	37.6	37.5	38.1	37.8	37.9
Transportation and Utilities													
1990	7.6	7.6	7.7	7.6	7.6	7.9	7.8	7.9	7.9	7.9	7.8	7.9	7.8
2000	8.6	8.6	8.6	8.5	8.5	8.6	8.5	8.4	8.8	8.9	8.9	8.8	8.6
2001	8.6	8.6	8.5	8.6	8.6	8.8	8.4	8.4	8.8	8.9	8.9	8.9	8.7
2002	8.7	8.6	8.6	8.7	8.8	8.8	8.4	8.5	8.7	8.9	8.9	8.9	8.7
2003	8.6	8.5	8.4	8.5	8.5	8.7	8.0	8.1	8.5	8.7	8.6	8.7	8.5
2004	8.6	8.6	8.5	8.5	8.6	8.8	8.4	8.5	8.8	9.1	9.1	9.1	8.7
2005	9.0	8.9	8.9	8.8	8.8	8.9	8.4	8.4	8.8	9.0	9.1	9.2	8.9
2006	8.8	8.7	8.7	8.7	8.8	8.8	8.3	8.3	8.8	8.9	9.0	9.1	8.7
2007	8.8	8.7	8.6	8.5	8.8	8.9	8.4	8.4	8.9	9.1	9.2	9.3	8.8
2008	8.7	8.6	8.5	8.5	8.8	8.9	8.4	8.5	8.8	8.8	8.9	9.1	8.7
2009	8.4	8.4	8.2	8.1	8.3	8.3	8.0	8.1	8.5	8.4	8.4	8.5	8.3
Information													
1990	5.5	5.5	5.5	5.5	5.5	5.5	5.5	5.5	5.5	5.4	5.4	5.5	5.5
2000	6.7	6.8	6.8	6.8	6.8	6.9	6.9	6.3	6.9	6.9	7.0	7.0	6.8
2001	6.9	7.0	6.8	6.8	6.8	6.9	6.7	6.7	6.6	6.7	6.8	6.8	6.8
2002	6.7	6.7	6.7	6.8	6.7	6.7	6.7	6.7	6.6	6.5	6.6	6.6	6.7
2003	6.5	6.4	6.5	6.4	6.5	6.6	6.5	6.5	6.5	6.5	6.5	6.5	6.5
2004	6.4	6.4	6.4	6.4	6.4	6.4	6.4	6.4	6.2	6.3	6.3	6.3	6.4
2005	6.3	6.2	6.2	6.2	6.2	6.2	6.3	6.2	6.2	6.2	6.2	6.3	6.2
2006	6.1	6.1	6.2	6.0	6.0	6.0	6.0	6.0	6.0	5.9	6.0	6.0	6.0
2007	6.0	5.9	5.9	5.9	5.9	5.9	6.0	6.0	5.9	5.8	5.8	5.8	5.9
2008	5.8	5.8	5.8	5.8	5.8	5.7	5.8	5.8	5.8	5.7	5.7	5.7	5.8
2009	5.6	5.6	5.6	5.5	5.5	5.6	5.4	5.5	5.4	5.4	5.4	5.4	5.5

Employment by Industry: Vermont, Selected Years, 1990–2009—*Continued*

(Numbers in thousands, not seasonally adjusted.)

Industry and year	January	February	March	April	May	June	July	August	September	October	November	December	Annual average
Financial Activities													
1990	13.9	13.7	13.6	13.4	13.5	13.6	13.6	13.5	13.3	13.3	13.2	13.4	13.5
2000	13.0	12.9	13.0	12.8	13.0	13.1	12.9	13.0	12.7	13.0	12.9	13.2	13.0
2001	12.9	13.0	13.1	12.9	13.1	13.4	13.4	13.4	13.3	13.2	13.2	13.3	13.2
2002	13.0	13.0	13.0	12.9	13.1	13.3	13.5	13.5	13.2	13.2	13.0	13.2	13.2
2003	13.0	13.0	13.0	13.0	13.2	13.4	13.5	13.5	13.3	13.3	13.2	13.5	13.2
2004	13.3	13.1	13.1	13.1	13.3	13.4	13.5	13.5	13.3	13.1	13.1	13.4	13.3
2005	13.1	13.1	13.1	13.0	13.1	13.4	13.4	13.4	13.2	13.2	13.1	13.3	13.2
2006	13.2	13.2	13.2	13.1	13.2	13.4	13.4	13.4	13.2	13.1	13.1	13.2	13.2
2007	13.2	13.1	13.2	13.1	13.2	13.4	13.4	13.3	13.1	13.0	13.0	13.0	13.2
2008	12.8	12.8	12.8	12.8	12.9	13.0	13.1	13.0	12.8	12.7	12.6	12.7	12.8
2009	12.5	12.4	12.4	12.2	12.3	12.5	12.6	12.6	12.3	12.3	12.4	12.6	12.4
Professional and Business Services													
1990	14.0	14.1	14.0	14.2	14.3	14.5	14.4	14.4	14.2	14.1	14.0	13.9	14.2
2000	19.5	19.8	20.3	20.7	21.0	21.5	21.4	21.3	20.9	21.0	20.7	20.9	20.8
2001	20.1	20.3	20.4	20.7	21.3	21.4	21.4	21.3	20.8	20.5	20.2	20.0	20.7
2002	19.2	19.2	19.3	20.0	20.5	20.6	20.7	20.9	21.0	20.9	20.4	20.3	20.3
2003	19.3	19.4	19.3	20.0	20.6	21.0	21.0	21.0	20.7	20.7	20.6	20.7	20.4
2004	20.0	20.0	20.3	21.4	21.2	21.7	21.8	21.9	21.8	21.8	21.6	21.8	21.3
2005	20.8	20.9	21.2	21.7	22.0	22.3	22.4	22.4	22.1	22.2	22.1	22.2	21.9
2006	21.5	21.5	21.6	22.0	22.3	22.8	22.8	22.9	22.5	22.4	21.9	22.0	22.2
2007	21.2	21.3	21.6	22.1	22.6	23.1	23.1	23.2	22.9	22.8	22.5	22.7	22.4
2008	21.8	21.9	21.7	22.4	23.3	23.5	23.5	23.3	23.1	23.3	22.7	22.4	22.7
2009	21.3	21.3	21.1	21.8	22.3	22.6	22.6	22.5	22.0	22.3	22.4	22.0	22.0
Education and Health Services													
1990	35.2	35.4	35.6	34.8	34.7	34.3	34.0	34.0	34.5	35.0	35.1	35.1	34.8
2000	45.1	46.2	46.2	46.0	45.5	44.7	44.9	44.8	46.3	47.1	47.3	47.4	46.0
2001	46.8	47.5	47.7	47.7	47.7	47.2	47.1	46.8	48.6	49.0	49.2	49.7	47.9
2002	49.0	49.7	50.0	50.1	50.3	49.5	49.5	49.2	50.7	50.9	51.3	51.5	50.1
2003	50.9	51.4	51.8	52.0	52.2	51.7	51.8	51.7	53.0	53.0	52.9	53.3	52.1
2004	51.9	52.7	53.1	53.1	53.5	52.9	52.5	52.1	53.8	53.4	53.7	53.8	53.0
2005	53.3	53.9	54.2	54.5	54.6	53.7	53.5	53.2	54.7	54.3	54.6	55.2	54.1
2006	54.2	55.1	55.3	55.0	55.1	55.0	55.0	54.8	56.1	56.1	56.3	56.8	55.4
2007	55.7	56.7	56.8	57.1	57.0	57.1	57.1	56.8	58.1	58.0	58.6	58.4	57.3
2008	57.3	58.2	58.6	58.7	59.1	58.0	58.3	58.2	59.3	59.6	59.5	59.6	58.7
2009	58.1	59.5	59.7	59.6	60.2	59.1	59.7	59.1	59.8	61.2	61.4	61.3	59.9
Leisure and Hospitality													
1990	31.0	30.8	29.9	25.7	25.8	28.5	31.1	31.4	30.0	28.7	26.5	28.4	29.0
2000	35.1	35.3	34.7	28.6	29.5	33.0	34.2	34.9	33.1	32.1	29.6	34.7	32.9
2001	36.1	35.8	34.9	31.2	29.6	32.6	34.3	35.1	32.5	31.5	29.5	31.4	32.9
2002	35.6	35.5	34.6	30.4	29.8	33.0	34.1	34.9	32.7	31.7	29.5	34.4	33.0
2003	35.9	35.4	34.6	29.1	29.5	32.2	34.0	34.8	32.8	31.7	29.6	33.7	32.8
2004	35.5	35.5	34.4	29.3	30.0	33.4	35.0	35.5	33.3	32.3	29.6	33.5	33.1
2005	35.6	35.3	34.7	30.4	30.1	33.2	35.0	35.1	32.8	31.7	29.8	34.5	33.2
2006	35.6	35.4	34.8	29.9	30.3	33.9	34.5	35.1	32.9	32.4	30.8	33.7	33.3
2007	34.6	34.8	34.2	29.7	29.9	32.9	34.5	35.3	32.7	31.7	30.1	34.3	32.9
2008	35.1	35.3	34.4	30.4	30.1	32.4	33.8	34.4	32.3	31.9	29.4	33.8	32.8
2009	35.0	34.8	33.6	28.4	28.4	30.4	32.1	32.6	31.1	29.8	28.1	34.3	31.6
Other Services													
1990	7.6	7.6	7.7	7.8	8.0	8.0	8.1	8.1	8.1	8.1	7.9	7.9	7.9
2000	9.4	9.5	9.6	9.6	9.7	9.9	9.9	9.9	9.7	9.7	9.6	9.7	9.7
2001	9.8	9.7	9.7	9.8	9.9	10.2	10.4	10.2	9.9	10.0	10.0	10.0	10.0
2002	9.8	9.7	9.8	9.9	10.0	10.4	10.5	10.4	10.3	10.1	10.0	10.2	10.1
2003	9.9	9.9	10.0	10.0	10.1	10.4	10.3	10.3	10.2	10.2	10.1	10.3	10.1
2004	10.1	10.1	10.0	10.1	10.2	10.4	10.3	10.2	10.1	10.1	9.9	10.0	10.1
2005	9.8	9.8	9.8	10.0	10.1	10.3	10.2	10.1	9.9	9.8	9.8	9.9	10.0
2006	9.7	9.7	9.7	9.8	9.9	10.1	10.2	10.1	10.0	10.0	9.9	9.9	9.9
2007	9.8	9.8	9.8	9.7	9.9	10.1	10.1	10.1	9.9	10.0	9.9	10.0	9.9
2008	9.7	9.7	9.7	9.8	9.9	10.0	9.9	9.8	9.8	9.8	9.7	9.7	9.8
2009	9.5	9.5	9.4	9.4	9.5	9.7	9.6	9.5	9.4	9.5	9.4	9.6	9.5
Government													
1990	42.2	43.8	44.6	46.8	46.3	44.0	37.6	37.4	43.0	45.2	45.3	45.7	43.5
2000	48.9	50.8	52.3	51.5	52.4	48.9	41.2	41.0	49.9	51.7	52.2	52.3	49.4
2001	50.1	51.6	51.7	51.7	51.8	49.9	41.7	41.7	51.1	53.4	53.5	53.6	50.2
2002	51.3	52.6	52.7	52.9	52.7	51.0	41.8	42.1	51.2	54.0	54.4	53.4	50.8
2003	52.1	53.9	53.8	53.9	53.9	51.9	43.3	42.9	52.8	54.9	55.2	55.1	52.0
2004	52.5	54.3	54.3	54.5	54.3	51.1	43.2	43.3	53.5	55.4	56.0	55.6	52.3
2005	53.4	55.1	55.2	55.1	55.0	51.9	43.4	44.2	54.1	56.2	56.5	56.3	53.0
2006	54.4	56.0	56.0	56.0	55.7	53.2	43.8	44.0	54.5	56.7	57.0	56.8	53.7
2007	54.8	56.4	56.4	56.0	56.2	53.7	44.3	44.1	54.6	56.5	56.6	56.8	53.9
2008	55.5	56.4	56.3	56.3	56.2	53.4	44.6	44.6	54.9	57.3	57.6	57.4	54.2
2009	55.0	57.0	56.6	57.5	57.7	54.1	45.0	45.0	54.7	57.3	57.4	57.5	54.6

Average Weekly Hours by Selected Industry: Vermont, 2007–2009

(Not seasonally adjusted.)

Industry and year	January	February	March	April	May	June	July	August	September	October	November	December	Annual average
Total Private													
2007	33.20	33.00	33.20	33.70	34.10	34.70	34.60	34.70	34.90	34.50	34.30	34.20	34.10
2008	33.90	33.80	33.90	34.20	34.60	35.20	34.90	35.00	34.70	34.40	34.10	33.50	34.40
2009	34.10	33.80	33.50	33.70	34.10	34.20	34.30	34.90	34.30	34.50	34.40	33.40	34.10
Goods-Producing													
2007	38.80	36.20	37.40	38.00	38.90	39.40	37.50	38.70	38.40	38.10	37.90	38.30	38.10
2008	38.10	38.00	37.90	38.40	39.00	39.00	38.90	39.50	39.40	38.50	37.50	37.30	38.50
2009	37.40	36.90	36.70	35.80	36.80	37.40	37.50	38.40	37.70	38.40	37.60	36.60	37.30
Construction													
2007	40.00	35.60	35.80	37.00	40.10	39.80	39.70	40.50	39.50	39.70	39.10	39.30	39.00
2008	37.80	36.80	37.30	38.00	39.60	40.10	40.00	41.30	41.00	40.40	38.90	37.70	39.20
2009	36.90	36.90	36.10	36.60	39.80	40.20	40.40	41.00	40.20	41.20	40.40	39.80	39.30
Manufacturing													
2007	38.40	36.60	38.20	38.60	38.40	39.40	36.40	37.90	38.00	37.40	37.50	38.00	37.90
2008	38.30	38.40	38.10	38.60	38.80	38.60	38.50	38.60	38.60	37.50	36.80	37.00	38.20
2009	37.90	37.00	37.00	35.60	35.80	36.50	36.10	36.90	36.30	37.20	36.90	36.40	36.60
Trade, Transportation, and Utilities													
2007	32.10	31.90	32.40	32.40	32.20	33.90	35.00	35.20	35.00	34.30	34.00	34.60	33.60
2008	34.20	33.70	34.10	33.90	34.00	34.10	34.00	33.70	33.30	33.00	33.00	33.10	33.70
2009	32.90	31.50	31.60	32.20	32.60	32.90	32.90	33.60	33.30	33.30	33.20	33.40	32.80
Professional and Business Services													
2007	35.00	35.30	35.70	35.60	36.00	36.30	36.40	36.00	37.70	35.90	36.60	36.50	36.10
2008	36.20	35.80	36.00	36.40	36.20	37.00	36.50	36.80	37.40	37.00	37.10	37.00	36.60
2009	37.40	39.50	39.20	39.20	37.70	37.90	37.10	37.60	36.90	36.90	36.90	36.20	37.70
Education and Health Services													
2007	32.00	31.50	31.40	31.30	31.50	31.60	31.50	32.00	32.10	32.20	32.00	32.60	31.80
2008	32.50	32.60	32.80	32.90	33.00	32.90	33.00	33.00	33.20	33.20	33.10	33.10	32.90
2009	33.70	33.30	32.80	32.80	33.10	32.70	32.90	32.80	32.80	32.60	32.80	33.10	33.00
Leisure and Hospitality													
2007	25.70	28.20	26.40	25.60	26.70	27.30	28.40	27.70	26.40	27.10	26.30	23.80	26.60
2008	24.60	26.20	25.40	24.40	26.90	27.00	26.90	27.20	25.50	26.00	24.20	21.50	25.50
2009	24.70	25.00	23.70	23.80	25.30	25.80	26.70	27.10	26.20	27.00	26.20	25.20	25.50

Average Hourly Earnings by Selected Industry: Vermont, 2007–2009

(Dollars, not seasonally adjusted.)

Industry and year	January	February	March	April	May	June	July	August	September	October	November	December	Annual average
Total Private													
2007	20.01	20.15	20.88	20.43	20.22	19.89	20.16	20.12	20.74	20.63	20.90	20.95	20.42
2008	20.89	21.22	21.27	21.24	20.85	21.05	21.22	21.09	21.51	21.62	22.13	22.16	21.35
2009	21.54	22.11	22.49	22.32	22.23	22.37	22.34	22.29	22.51	22.93	23.17	22.66	22.41
Goods-Producing													
2007	20.48	20.59	20.36	20.23	19.91	19.94	20.43	20.08	20.46	20.23	20.38	21.06	20.34
2008	21.15	21.27	21.22	21.05	20.56	20.68	20.68	20.75	20.96	21.28	21.77	21.87	21.09
2009	21.40	21.83	21.87	21.48	22.23	21.39	21.42	21.33	21.30	21.59	21.60	22.14	21.62
Construction													
2007	21.18	20.41	20.44	20.16	20.02	20.52	20.44	20.96	20.71	20.20	20.46	21.21	20.56
2008	21.88	22.08	21.80	21.64	20.57	20.94	20.88	21.02	21.35	21.50	21.97	22.72	21.47
2009	23.29	23.00	23.22	22.41	21.81	21.95	21.93	21.40	20.83	21.24	21.48	22.16	21.96
Manufacturing													
2007	20.21	20.79	20.45	20.34	19.89	19.61	20.48	19.59	20.35	20.28	20.34	20.97	20.27
2008	20.81	20.94	20.95	20.76	20.28	20.25	20.34	20.38	20.55	20.99	21.49	21.34	20.75
2009	20.69	21.28	21.23	21.12	21.69	21.53	21.58	21.67	21.95	22.11	21.88	22.22	21.57
Trade, Transportation, and Utilities													
2007	16.51	16.95	17.07	16.85	17.37	17.01	17.46	17.19	17.35	17.40	17.63	17.41	17.19
2008	17.69	18.33	18.07	18.12	18.06	18.22	17.97	17.84	17.89	18.01	18.11	19.07	18.11
2009	18.61	19.50	19.56	18.94	18.95	18.90	18.78	18.92	19.01	19.07	18.99	19.40	19.05
Professional and Business Services													
2007	23.02	24.08	23.57	23.65	23.47	22.95	22.75	23.33	23.52	23.78	23.86	24.80	23.56
2008	23.96	24.45	24.62	24.98	24.23	22.97	23.45	23.65	23.52	23.41	24.42	24.08	23.96
2009	21.82	22.92	23.76	23.80	24.21	25.03	25.48	25.43	26.04	26.56	26.57	26.34	24.83
Education and Health Services													
2007	23.51	23.54	23.83	23.93	23.78	23.70	24.02	23.91	24.59	24.53	25.30	25.14	24.16
2008	25.19	25.06	25.01	24.83	24.62	25.03	25.46	25.12	25.75	25.94	26.33	26.28	25.39
2009	25.93	26.12	26.17	25.88	25.37	25.63	25.39	25.63	25.96	25.77	26.60	25.66	25.84
Leisure and Hospitality													
2007	14.37	14.40	14.42	15.87	15.35	14.35	14.85	15.11	15.71	16.00	16.10	14.67	15.07
2008	14.70	14.60	14.54	15.37	15.20	14.86	14.64	14.83	15.65	16.00	16.32	14.87	15.10
2009	14.51	14.63	14.59	15.23	14.80	15.67	15.24	14.96	15.38	15.40	15.21	14.51	15.00

Average Weekly Earnings by Selected Industry: Vermont, 2007–2009

(Dollars, not seasonally adjusted.)

Industry and year	January	February	March	April	May	June	July	August	September	October	November	December	Annual average
Total Private													
2007	664.33	664.95	693.22	688.49	689.50	690.18	697.54	698.16	723.83	711.74	716.87	716.49	696.32
2008	708.17	717.24	721.05	726.41	721.41	740.96	740.58	738.15	746.40	743.73	754.63	742.36	734.44
2009	734.51	747.32	753.42	752.18	758.04	765.05	766.26	777.92	772.09	791.09	797.05	756.84	764.18
Goods-Producing													
2007	794.62	745.36	761.46	768.74	774.50	785.64	766.13	777.10	785.66	770.76	772.40	806.60	774.95
2008	805.82	808.26	804.24	808.32	801.84	806.52	804.45	819.63	825.82	819.28	816.38	815.75	811.97
2009	800.36	805.53	802.63	768.98	818.06	799.99	803.25	819.07	803.01	829.06	812.16	810.32	806.43
Construction													
2007	847.20	726.60	731.75	745.92	802.80	816.70	811.47	848.88	818.05	801.94	799.99	833.55	801.84
2008	827.06	812.54	813.14	822.32	814.57	839.69	835.20	868.13	875.35	868.60	854.63	856.54	841.62
2009	859.40	848.70	838.24	820.21	868.04	882.39	885.97	877.40	837.37	875.09	867.79	881.97	863.03
Manufacturing													
2007	776.06	760.91	781.19	785.12	763.78	772.63	745.47	742.46	773.30	758.47	762.75	796.86	768.23
2008	797.02	804.10	798.20	801.34	786.86	781.65	783.09	786.67	793.23	787.13	790.83	789.58	792.65
2009	784.15	787.36	785.51	751.87	776.50	785.85	779.04	799.62	796.79	822.49	807.37	808.81	789.46
Trade, Transportation, and Utilities													
2007	529.97	540.71	553.07	545.94	559.31	576.64	611.10	605.09	607.25	596.82	599.42	602.39	577.58
2008	605.00	617.72	616.19	614.27	614.04	621.30	610.98	601.21	595.74	594.33	597.63	631.22	610.31
2009	612.27	614.25	618.10	609.87	617.77	621.81	617.86	635.71	633.03	635.03	630.47	647.96	624.84
Professional and Business Services													
2007	805.70	850.02	841.45	841.94	844.92	833.09	828.10	839.88	886.70	853.70	873.28	905.20	850.52
2008	867.35	875.31	886.32	909.27	877.13	849.89	855.93	870.32	879.65	866.17	905.98	890.96	876.94
2009	816.07	905.34	931.39	932.96	912.72	948.64	945.31	956.17	960.88	980.06	980.43	953.51	936.09
Education and Health Services													
2007	752.32	741.51	748.26	749.01	749.07	748.92	756.63	765.12	789.34	789.87	809.60	819.56	768.29
2008	818.68	816.96	820.33	816.91	812.46	823.49	840.18	828.96	854.90	861.21	871.52	869.87	835.33
2009	873.84	869.80	858.38	848.86	839.75	838.10	835.33	840.66	851.49	840.10	872.48	849.35	852.72
Leisure and Hospitality													
2007	369.31	406.08	380.69	406.27	409.85	391.76	421.74	418.55	414.74	433.60	423.43	349.15	400.86
2008	361.62	382.52	369.32	375.03	408.88	401.22	393.82	403.38	399.08	416.00	394.94	319.71	385.05
2009	358.40	365.75	345.78	362.47	374.44	404.29	406.91	405.42	402.96	415.80	398.50	365.65	382.50

VIRGINIA
At a Glance

Population:
  1990 census: 6,189,197
  2000 census: 7,078,515
  2009 estimate: 7,882,590

Percent change in population:
  1990–2000: 14.4%
  2000–2009: 11.4%

Percent change in total nonfarm employment:
  1990–2009: 25.7%
  2008–2009: -3.4%

Industry with the largest growth in employment, 1990–2009 (thousands):
  Professional and Business Services, 291.1

Industry with the largest decline or smallest growth in employment, 1990–2009 (thousands):
  Manufacturing, -148.2

Civilian labor force:
  1990: 3,220,117
  2000: 3,584,037
  2009: 4,173,723

Unemployment rate and rank among states (lowest to highest):
  1990: 4.4%, 9th
  2000: 2.3%, 1st
  2009: 6.7%, 10th

Employment by Industry, 2009

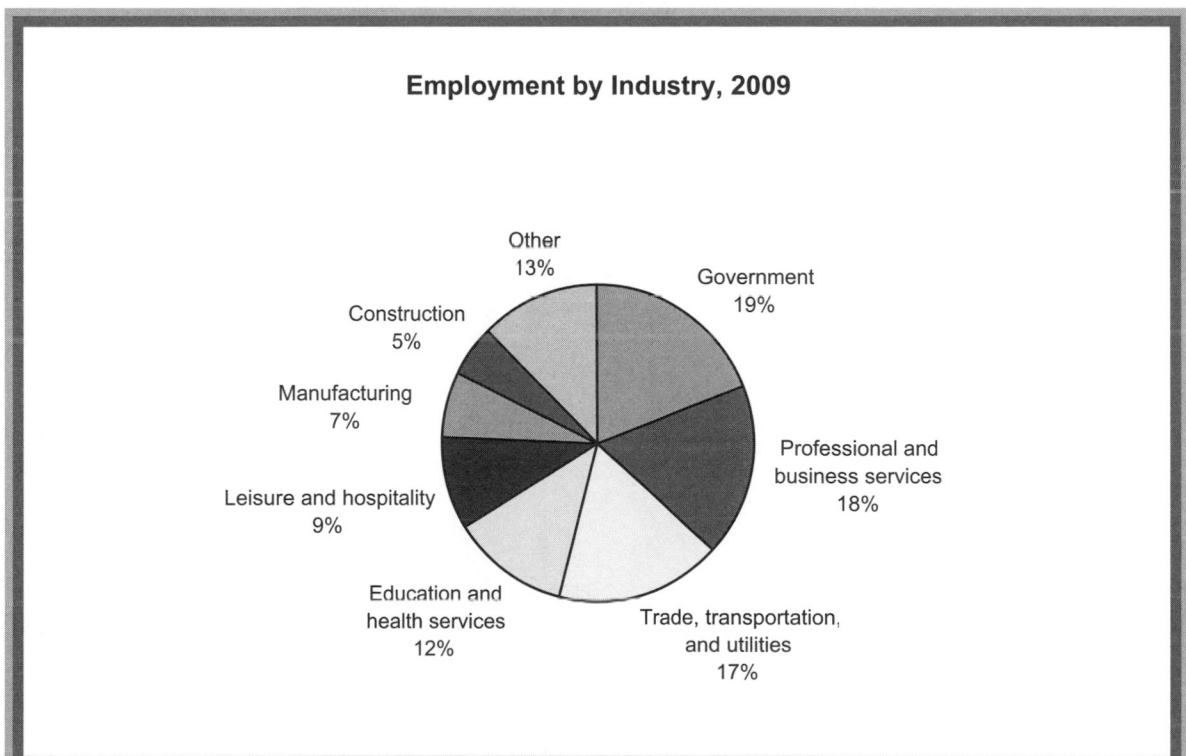

Other 13%
Government 19%
Construction 5%
Manufacturing 7%
Professional and business services 18%
Leisure and hospitality 9%
Education and health services 12%
Trade, transportation, and utilities 17%

Employment by Industry: Virginia, Selected Years, 1990–2009

(Numbers in thousands, not seasonally adjusted.)

Industry and year	January	February	March	April	May	June	July	August	September	October	November	December	Annual average
Total Nonfarm													
1990	2844.7	2856.1	2879.9	2888.0	2915.9	2938.5	2896.1	2898.7	2913.9	2896.6	2901.6	2901.1	2894.3
2000	3408.5	3423.7	3469.9	3492.2	3520.4	3557.4	3517.3	3521.3	3545.7	3560.5	3584.5	3596.9	3516.5
2001	3472.6	3484.7	3514.3	3519.6	3537.9	3568.1	3516.5	3515.6	3520.7	3507.4	3522.0	3524.9	3517.0
2002	3433.6	3444.5	3472.7	3490.6	3510.2	3538.4	3484.7	3487.0	3504.9	3509.3	3524.1	3529.5	3494.1
2003	3439.0	3435.7	3460.8	3476.6	3502.5	3529.0	3485.9	3492.6	3512.8	3527.5	3548.8	3558.4	3497.5
2004	3483.3	3495.8	3535.3	3565.7	3588.0	3621.2	3586.7	3585.8	3607.1	3627.7	3647.5	3660.0	3583.7
2005	3573.4	3588.8	3614.4	3651.0	3671.6	3701.3	3667.3	3668.2	3698.5	3695.0	3717.0	3725.8	3664.4
2006	3654.1	3664.7	3700.7	3714.0	3743.3	3777.6	3724.7	3720.5	3734.8	3744.6	3763.4	3775.2	3726.5
2007	3699.8	3705.7	3737.1	3753.1	3777.8	3808.8	3760.0	3752.5	3770.2	3776.9	3795.3	3799.5	3761.4
2008	3719.8	3728.1	3749.0	3772.8	3790.1	3811.1	3765.0	3759.9	3767.3	3770.5	3764.7	3756.1	3762.9
2009	3643.0	3631.6	3638.3	3647.7	3665.7	3678.0	3620.4	3610.8	3620.5	3626.8	3630.2	3628.2	3636.8
Total Private													
1990	2270.3	2272.5	2294.1	2303.1	2325.7	2355.8	2339.1	2347.3	2339.0	2313.4	2315.4	2315.0	2315.9
2000	2794.5	2802.8	2841.7	2857.5	2883.8	2925.4	2912.5	2919.7	2927.7	2929.3	2946.6	2960.4	2891.8
2001	2847.3	2849.4	2877.9	2882.5	2904.7	2933.8	2907.0	2911.7	2898.9	2874.6	2880.4	2885.6	2887.8
2002	2803.3	2807.2	2832.3	2849.1	2870.5	2898.5	2870.3	2877.0	2875.5	2865.1	2876.7	2885.2	2859.2
2003	2805.1	2795.6	2819.1	2833.5	2861.3	2886.6	2870.6	2881.3	2876.4	2884.0	2896.8	2909.2	2860.0
2004	2840.8	2845.1	2879.9	2907.2	2933.6	2966.7	2958.1	2961.6	2959.9	2967.2	2979.1	2993.8	2932.8
2005	2919.5	2927.5	2950.3	2980.6	3003.4	3033.8	3027.1	3033.1	3037.2	3025.3	3040.1	3052.1	3002.5
2006	2988.1	2989.9	3020.4	3031.9	3061.6	3096.4	3070.0	3071.2	3065.6	3062.0	3075.0	3088.2	3051.7
2007	3020.7	3017.9	3047.8	3061.5	3089.2	3121.8	3098.0	3097.6	3092.9	3088.9	3098.5	3106.2	3078.4
2008	3033.4	3031.3	3047.9	3073.3	3091.5	3114.7	3094.7	3090.6	3077.8	3065.8	3053.8	3047.1	3068.5
2009	2946.8	2927.7	2930.1	2937.3	2956.9	2971.7	2949.5	2941.8	2933.3	2927.1	2925.4	2925.9	2939.5
Goods-Producing													
1990	585.9	587.0	590.6	588.9	591.7	597.1	591.2	590.9	586.9	579.1	574.1	567.0	585.8
2000	574.0	573.8	581.4	582.2	585.7	591.0	585.6	589.4	591.8	588.7	589.1	588.9	585.1
2001	571.2	569.7	573.6	572.5	573.1	576.6	572.3	575.4	570.4	562.4	560.2	556.8	569.5
2002	539.1	538.5	542.5	544.4	547.9	551.4	546.9	550.1	547.5	545.6	543.4	541.2	544.9
2003	528.3	525.1	529.1	528.9	534.0	535.5	534.9	537.8	535.4	534.9	534.3	532.4	532.6
2004	522.6	522.4	529.6	536.0	539.8	545.8	546.4	547.5	546.9	547.5	546.9	547.0	539.9
2005	538.0	537.4	539.8	546.3	549.4	555.3	557.8	560.2	557.3	553.9	553.6	552.8	550.2
2006	543.1	543.0	547.4	549.9	553.7	558.6	554.9	554.9	548.8	543.6	540.4	539.2	548.1
2007	526.8	525.1	529.8	531.2	532.9	537.0	534.0	533.2	529.3	524.1	521.0	518.3	528.6
2008	504.5	500.1	500.4	505.0	504.4	506.5	504.8	503.2	498.7	493.7	486.3	478.9	498.9
2009	456.4	446.7	443.8	441.1	439.8	440.5	439.9	438.1	435.0	433.2	432.6	429.1	439.7
Mining and Logging													
1990	17.4	17.6	16.9	16.8	17.0	17.1	16.8	16.7	16.5	16.1	16.1	16.1	16.7
2000	11.4	11.3	11.4	11.4	11.4	11.5	11.5	11.5	11.5	11.5	11.5	11.6	11.4
2001	11.2	11.3	11.3	11.4	11.5	11.6	11.5	11.6	11.5	11.4	11.4	11.3	11.4
2002	11.0	10.9	11.0	10.7	10.8	10.7	10.5	10.4	10.4	10.2	10.2	10.2	10.6
2003	10.0	9.9	10.1	9.9	10.1	10.2	10.2	10.2	10.1	10.2	10.2	10.3	10.1
2004	10.0	10.1	10.2	10.2	10.3	10.4	10.3	10.3	10.3	10.3	10.4	10.4	10.3
2005	10.4	10.4	10.1	10.3	10.4	10.8	10.9	10.9	10.9	10.9	11.0	11.1	10.7
2006	11.0	11.0	11.2	11.0	11.2	11.5	11.5	11.5	11.3	11.2	11.3	11.3	11.3
2007	11.3	11.2	11.4	10.7	10.8	10.8	11.0	11.0	10.6	10.7	10.6	10.8	10.9
2008	10.6	10.9	10.8	10.9	11.0	11.1	11.2	11.2	11.3	11.5	11.5	11.4	11.1
2009	10.8	10.5	10.4	10.2	10.1	10.1	10.0	10.1	10.1	10.1	10.1	10.0	10.2
Construction													
1990	180.5	182.0	185.9	184.7	187.1	190.0	186.5	185.5	181.7	176.8	173.9	168.2	181.9
2000	196.0	196.9	204.4	207.4	210.3	214.6	214.7	216.4	216.1	215.2	215.1	214.4	210.1
2001	205.9	207.7	213.1	215.9	219.8	223.4	223.3	224.3	221.5	217.7	216.1	214.5	216.9
2002	205.0	206.0	210.0	213.0	216.4	218.9	219.7	220.5	217.7	216.5	214.5	212.9	214.3
2003	204.4	202.6	208.1	211.6	218.3	220.2	224.2	225.7	223.7	225.0	223.5	222.8	217.5
2004	215.3	215.4	221.4	227.3	231.4	235.6	238.6	238.0	236.7	237.6	237.0	236.6	230.9
2005	230.5	230.1	232.9	239.6	242.7	247.5	252.5	253.1	250.9	248.5	248.2	247.1	243.6
2006	240.8	241.7	246.8	248.5	252.1	256.0	254.8	254.0	251.1	247.9	246.0	245.3	248.8
2007	236.1	233.3	237.6	240.9	243.3	246.0	244.9	245.2	242.6	238.7	236.1	233.6	239.9
2008	223.7	222.0	223.9	226.2	226.8	228.6	228.3	227.1	223.8	220.4	214.9	209.6	222.9
2009	195.4	190.8	190.2	190.5	191.0	192.1	192.8	192.0	189.4	188.4	187.6	185.5	190.5
Manufacturing													
1990	388.0	387.4	387.8	387.4	387.6	390.0	387.9	388.7	388.7	386.2	384.1	382.7	387.2
2000	366.6	365.6	365.6	363.4	364.0	364.9	359.4	361.5	364.2	362.0	362.5	362.9	363.5
2001	354.1	350.7	349.2	345.2	341.8	341.6	337.5	339.5	337.4	333.3	332.7	331.0	341.2
2002	323.1	321.6	321.5	320.7	320.7	321.8	316.7	319.2	319.4	318.9	318.7	318.1	320.0
2003	313.9	312.6	310.9	307.4	305.6	305.1	300.5	301.9	301.6	299.7	300.6	299.3	304.9
2004	297.3	296.9	298.0	298.5	298.1	299.8	297.5	299.2	299.9	299.6	299.5	300.0	298.7
2005	297.1	296.9	296.8	296.4	296.3	297.0	294.4	296.2	295.5	294.5	294.4	294.6	295.8
2006	291.3	290.3	289.4	290.4	290.4	291.1	288.6	289.4	286.4	284.5	283.1	282.6	288.1
2007	279.4	280.6	280.8	279.6	278.8	280.2	278.1	277.0	276.1	274.7	274.3	273.9	277.8
2008	270.2	267.2	265.7	267.9	266.6	266.8	265.3	264.9	263.6	261.8	259.9	257.9	264.8
2009	250.2	245.4	243.2	240.4	238.7	238.3	237.1	236.0	235.5	234.7	234.9	233.6	239.0

Employment by Industry: Virginia, Selected Years, 1990–2009—*Continued*

(Numbers in thousands, not seasonally adjusted.)

Industry and year	January	February	March	April	May	June	July	August	September	October	November	December	Annual average
Service-Providing													
1990	2258.8	2269.1	2289.3	2299.1	2324.2	2341.4	2304.9	2307.8	2327.0	2317.5	2327.5	2334.1	2308.4
2000	2834.5	2849.9	2888.5	2910.0	2934.7	2966.4	2931.7	2931.9	2953.9	2971.8	2995.4	3008.0	2931.4
2001	2901.4	2915.0	2940.7	2947.1	2964.8	2991.5	2944.2	2940.2	2950.3	2945.0	2961.8	2968.1	2947.5
2002	2894.5	2906.0	2930.2	2946.2	2962.3	2987.0	2937.8	2936.9	2957.4	2963.7	2980.7	2988.3	2949.3
2003	2910.7	2910.6	2931.7	2947.7	2968.5	2993.5	2951.0	2954.8	2977.4	2992.6	3014.5	3026.0	2964.9
2004	2960.7	2973.4	3005.7	3029.7	3048.2	3075.4	3040.3	3038.3	3060.2	3080.2	3100.6	3113.0	3043.8
2005	3035.4	3051.4	3074.6	3104.7	3122.2	3146.0	3109.5	3108.0	3141.2	3141.1	3163.4	3173.0	3114.2
2006	3111.0	3121.7	3153.3	3164.1	3189.6	3219.0	3169.8	3165.6	3186.0	3201.0	3223.0	3236.0	3178.3
2007	3173.0	3180.6	3207.3	3221.9	3244.9	3271.8	3226.0	3219.3	3240.9	3252.8	3274.3	3281.2	3232.8
2008	3215.3	3228.0	3248.6	3267.8	3285.7	3304.6	3260.2	3256.7	3268.6	3276.8	3278.4	3277.2	3264.0
2009	3186.6	3184.9	3194.5	3206.6	3225.9	3237.5	3180.5	3172.7	3185.5	3193.6	3197.6	3199.1	3197.1
Trade, Transportation, and Utilities													
1990	574.6	563.9	567.5	565.9	571.1	576.4	572.1	576.2	574.0	576.0	585.1	591.5	574.5
2000	637.7	633.8	638.1	637.3	642.8	648.1	645.3	649.2	651.3	661.3	676.8	686.8	650.7
2001	644.0	634.8	638.3	635.0	640.7	645.2	642.9	643.8	641.6	646.0	658.7	664.9	644.7
2002	632.9	623.7	625.5	626.3	630.8	636.2	634.6	636.3	634.8	639.2	652.9	663.7	636.4
2003	625.3	618.4	621.0	622.9	628.5	632.7	632.8	636.0	634.0	643.7	657.8	669.2	635.2
2004	635.8	630.2	633.3	636.0	641.4	646.4	646.3	647.6	644.4	652.5	666.4	676.5	646.4
2005	646.9	640.6	643.6	648.1	651.6	655.1	656.1	657.2	655.6	662.7	678.4	689.4	657.1
2006	659.2	648.1	653.4	652.9	659.0	663.6	660.3	661.0	658.1	665.9	682.0	692.1	663.0
2007	663.5	654.2	658.5	657.6	664.4	668.4	668.2	667.2	665.7	669.1	686.2	694.4	668.1
2008	663.4	653.3	655.3	654.2	658.0	661.5	660.0	659.4	655.7	654.8	663.8	669.7	659.1
2009	633.3	622.3	619.7	618.0	623.7	625.2	621.4	620.4	618.5	619.2	627.9	631.2	623.4
Wholesale Trade													
1990	107.5	107.8	108.5	107.7	108.1	109.0	109.4	109.6	109.3	109.7	109.5	109.2	108.7
2000	111.2	111.8	112.7	113.5	114.0	114.9	113.9	114.4	114.5	116.3	116.7	117.4	114.2
2001	113.9	114.1	115.1	115.2	115.1	115.9	115.2	115.0	114.4	114.1	114.3	114.4	114.7
2002	112.4	112.2	112.6	112.8	113.0	113.4	112.8	113.0	112.6	112.7	113.1	113.5	112.8
2003	112.3	112.3	112.6	112.5	113.3	113.5	113.5	113.7	113.1	113.6	113.8	114.5	113.2
2004	113.0	113.1	113.9	114.1	114.4	115.1	115.5	115.2	114.5	115.2	115.4	115.9	114.6
2005	114.7	115.0	115.6	116.8	117.2	117.4	117.9	118.2	117.8	118.1	118.7	119.1	117.2
2006	117.4	117.8	118.5	119.1	119.7	120.5	119.9	120.1	119.8	120.5	120.8	121.2	119.6
2007	120.0	120.4	121.1	120.7	121.2	121.8	121.2	121.4	120.9	120.7	120.6	121.0	120.9
2008	119.6	119.7	119.7	120.0	120.4	120.6	120.3	120.1	119.2	119.0	118.1	117.6	119.5
2009	115.4	114.7	114.2	113.9	113.9	113.5	112.7	112.6	111.8	112.0	110.6	109.8	112.9
Retail Trade													
1990	365.8	358.0	359.7	359.0	363.8	366.7	362.8	366.1	364.1	365.6	374.7	380.9	365.6
2000	401.9	397.4	400.5	398.9	403.6	407.3	404.6	407.9	410.2	415.8	431.2	440.8	410.0
2001	405.2	395.9	398.2	395.6	400.6	404.0	402.3	404.0	402.9	407.9	421.9	429.1	405.6
2002	402.8	394.7	396.1	396.4	400.1	403.6	401.6	402.8	402.2	405.3	418.1	428.6	404.4
2003	395.8	389.6	391.3	392.0	397.1	400.4	398.9	402.1	401.6	409.4	424.2	434.5	403.1
2004	407.6	401.7	403.5	405.1	409.3	412.6	410.7	411.5	409.2	415.5	428.9	437.0	412.7
2005	412.3	405.9	407.3	410.4	413.3	416.1	416.8	417.7	417.1	422.6	436.5	445.5	418.5
2006	422.2	412.9	416.6	415.8	420.6	423.1	421.2	421.5	418.6	425.3	440.7	447.6	423.8
2007	425.5	416.2	419.2	418.7	424.3	426.4	426.5	425.4	424.4	428.1	444.5	450.3	427.5
2008	425.9	415.8	418.1	415.8	418.5	421.0	420.0	419.2	417.1	417.4	426.7	431.5	420.6
2009	403.5	394.4	392.8	392.3	397.3	399.0	396.4	395.8	394.6	396.7	405.4	411.0	398.3
Transportation and Utilities													
1990	101.3	98.1	99.3	99.2	99.2	100.7	99.9	100.5	100.6	100.7	100.9	101.4	100.1
2000	124.6	124.6	124.9	124.9	125.2	125.9	126.8	126.9	126.6	129.2	128.9	128.6	126.4
2001	124.9	124.8	125.0	124.2	125.0	125.3	125.4	124.8	124.3	124.0	122.5	121.4	124.3
2002	117.7	116.8	116.8	117.1	117.7	119.2	120.2	120.5	120.0	121.2	121.7	121.6	119.2
2003	117.2	116.5	117.1	117.6	118.1	118.8	120.4	120.2	119.3	120.7	119.8	120.2	118.8
2004	115.2	115.4	115.9	116.8	117.7	118.7	120.1	120.9	120.7	121.8	122.1	123.6	119.1
2005	119.9	119.7	120.7	120.9	121.1	121.6	121.4	121.3	120.7	122.0	123.2	124.8	121.4
2006	119.6	117.4	118.3	118.0	118.7	120.0	119.2	119.4	119.7	120.1	120.5	123.3	119.5
2007	118.0	117.6	118.2	118.2	118.9	120.2	120.5	120.4	120.4	120.3	121.1	123.1	119.7
2008	117.9	117.8	117.5	118.4	119.1	119.9	119.7	120.1	119.4	118.4	119.0	120.6	119.0
2009	114.4	113.2	112.7	111.8	112.5	112.7	112.3	112.0	112.1	110.5	111.9	110.4	112.2
Information													
1990	72.2	72.5	72.9	73.9	74.1	75.2	75.7	75.5	75.4	74.4	74.4	74.4	74.2
2000	112.6	113.5	114.7	115.5	117.7	120.0	121.2	116.4	123.3	123.4	124.3	125.3	118.9
2001	123.9	124.2	124.0	121.3	121.2	119.7	119.2	118.0	116.6	114.4	113.4	112.8	119.1
2002	109.9	109.4	108.8	107.4	107.5	107.3	104.9	104.4	102.6	102.2	102.9	102.6	105.8
2003	101.3	101.6	101.5	100.7	101.2	102.2	102.2	101.8	100.9	100.5	101.3	101.5	101.4
2004	101.1	100.7	101.2	99.4	99.1	99.1	98.8	97.7	96.2	95.4	95.5	95.0	98.3
2005	93.5	93.4	93.4	93.0	93.0	93.3	92.9	92.6	91.8	91.6	91.9	92.0	92.7
2006	91.3	91.7	91.8	91.1	93.4	91.8	92.9	91.8	91.3	90.4	90.8	90.8	91.6
2007	91.9	91.3	90.7	90.5	91.0	90.9	90.3	89.8	89.7	89.6	89.7	89.5	90.4
2008	88.7	88.7	88.5	88.1	88.2	88.4	88.0	87.5	86.4	85.6	85.4	84.9	87.4
2009	84.0	83.8	83.1	82.1	81.9	81.8	81.1	80.1	79.1	78.8	78.2	78.0	81.0

Employment by Industry: Virginia, Selected Years, 1990–2009—*Continued*

(Numbers in thousands, not seasonally adjusted.)

Industry and year	January	February	March	April	May	June	July	August	September	October	November	December	Annual average
Financial Activities													
1990	140.7	141.5	142.6	143.2	144.5	146.9	145.8	145.9	144.8	142.8	142.7	143.1	143.7
2000	173.8	174.3	175.3	176.4	178.0	180.7	180.1	181.0	180.4	181.3	181.8	183.4	178.8
2001	176.9	177.8	178.9	179.0	180.2	182.6	182.5	183.0	181.1	178.2	178.9	179.9	179.9
2002	179.0	179.7	180.4	180.3	181.6	184.0	183.9	183.9	182.6	182.4	183.4	184.4	182.1
2003	182.6	183.3	184.2	184.9	186.4	188.9	190.0	190.3	188.1	186.3	185.6	186.7	186.4
2004	184.8	185.0	186.0	188.2	189.0	191.1	191.9	191.9	190.0	189.5	189.8	190.8	189.0
2005	188.7	189.4	189.9	191.2	192.2	194.5	195.9	195.9	194.2	192.3	192.1	193.5	192.5
2006	191.9	192.6	193.6	193.6	195.0	197.6	197.0	197.1	194.8	194.4	194.3	195.5	194.8
2007	193.7	193.9	194.7	194.0	195.1	196.6	196.0	195.1	193.0	191.3	190.2	190.3	193.7
2008	189.3	189.5	189.6	189.1	189.1	190.5	191.1	190.1	187.7	186.7	185.5	185.6	188.7
2009	182.1	181.1	181.1	181.1	180.8	181.8	181.6	181.4	179.0	178.4	177.5	177.7	180.3
Professional and Business Services													
1990	338.4	342.9	347.3	348.4	350.0	354.4	350.3	352.8	352.5	346.7	345.3	344.5	347.7
2000	542.0	548.4	558.0	563.1	564.1	575.2	572.9	575.6	576.1	578.1	579.3	583.4	568.0
2001	554.8	557.8	563.1	561.2	561.2	567.0	563.5	565.2	559.6	554.4	552.2	554.3	559.5
2002	537.1	541.5	547.3	548.4	548.5	552.0	550.3	551.7	548.1	545.7	546.1	546.9	547.0
2003	535.9	535.9	541.4	544.3	545.7	549.9	550.4	554.8	552.8	557.9	560.5	562.6	549.3
2004	551.7	556.7	563.7	570.0	573.5	581.0	586.0	590.5	587.7	592.1	592.9	596.4	578.5
2005	584.8	590.4	595.1	599.4	600.7	607.0	612.8	615.8	616.5	616.1	616.3	618.7	606.1
2006	610.5	615.0	621.1	622.3	625.4	632.4	633.2	636.0	634.3	636.1	637.2	639.0	628.5
2007	628.4	631.9	638.2	642.1	643.6	650.6	650.9	653.7	649.9	655.0	655.3	656.4	646.3
2008	644.9	647.3	650.3	656.4	657.0	662.5	663.2	665.6	661.1	662.0	658.3	655.8	657.0
2009	640.3	639.0	639.2	638.0	636.4	639.3	639.1	639.9	635.7	641.1	638.6	638.6	638.8
Education and Health Services													
1990	231.2	233.6	235.6	236.5	237.9	238.7	236.2	237.6	243.0	245.0	247.0	247.6	239.1
2000	326.2	329.1	331.9	329.1	330.7	330.7	330.3	330.6	335.0	336.7	338.1	339.2	332.3
2001	339.5	342.8	344.6	345.2	346.5	346.7	331.6	332.0	350.1	353.7	355.1	356.5	345.4
2002	355.9	360.2	362.1	363.8	363.5	363.0	343.9	345.4	367.4	370.8	373.0	372.9	361.8
2003	370.2	370.3	370.0	372.7	372.3	371.7	352.9	354.5	373.5	375.6	377.5	378.5	370.0
2004	376.4	379.1	383.0	382.6	383.0	381.6	364.4	365.1	385.7	389.7	391.7	393.0	381.3
2005	387.3	391.3	393.0	395.3	396.9	395.4	377.0	377.9	401.7	400.6	402.8	403.1	393.5
2006	400.4	403.8	406.1	406.0	407.8	408.5	387.7	387.6	410.7	412.9	415.7	416.8	405.3
2007	412.0	414.9	417.7	420.3	422.8	423.9	403.9	405.7	426.7	430.4	432.9	435.0	420.5
2008	430.3	436.1	437.4	441.9	442.7	441.6	423.7	424.5	445.2	448.7	449.8	450.4	439.4
2009	445.5	447.5	448.9	451.0	452.7	450.7	434.3	433.9	452.8	457.3	459.8	460.5	449.6
Leisure and Hospitality													
1990	213.3	216.4	221.9	230.6	239.6	248.8	249.8	250.5	245.2	232.9	230.0	228.4	233.9
2000	272.2	273.1	283.9	294.2	304.6	317.7	314.8	315.2	307.7	297.3	294.5	290.4	297.1
2001	275.1	279.5	289.9	299.8	311.9	324.4	324.0	323.2	309.9	296.9	291.1	289.1	301.2
2002	275.8	279.2	289.3	301.5	312.3	324.5	326.4	326.2	314.4	302.7	298.5	296.2	303.9
2003	283.5	282.7	292.0	303.2	316.9	328.4	330.4	329.7	316.7	310.2	304.8	303.0	308.5
2004	292.4	294.4	304.8	316.3	328.3	340.4	341.9	340.4	329.6	321.0	316.2	314.9	320.1
2005	302.3	305.9	315.6	326.2	337.6	349.9	350.8	350.6	338.4	328.1	324.9	322.2	329.4
2006	313.2	316.7	326.7	335.3	345.4	360.2	360.4	359.4	345.7	336.8	332.7	332.3	338.7
2007	322.3	323.9	333.7	341.0	353.3	367.0	367.2	366.3	353.1	343.2	337.0	335.4	345.3
2008	327.2	329.7	339.2	349.7	362.1	372.7	372.9	369.6	354.3	344.6	336.2	333.6	349.3
2009	320.2	321.9	328.4	339.7	354.6	364.0	363.7	360.6	347.8	333.1	324.9	321.3	340.0
Other Services													
1990	114.0	114.7	115.7	115.7	116.8	118.3	118.0	117.9	117.2	116.5	116.8	118.5	116.7
2000	156.0	156.8	158.4	159.7	160.2	162.0	162.3	162.3	162.1	162.5	162.7	163.0	160.7
2001	161.9	162.8	165.5	168.5	169.9	171.6	171.0	171.1	169.6	168.6	170.8	171.3	168.6
2002	173.6	175.0	176.4	177.0	178.4	180.1	179.4	179.0	178.1	176.5	176.5	177.3	177.3
2003	178.0	178.3	179.9	175.9	176.3	177.3	177.0	176.4	175.0	174.9	175.0	175.3	176.6
2004	176.0	176.6	178.3	178.7	179.5	181.3	182.4	180.9	179.4	179.5	179.7	180.2	179.4
2005	178.0	179.1	179.9	181.1	182.0	183.3	183.8	182.9	181.7	180.0	180.1	180.4	181.0
2006	178.5	179.0	180.3	180.8	181.9	183.7	183.6	183.4	181.9	181.9	181.9	182.5	181.6
2007	182.1	182.7	184.5	184.8	186.1	187.4	187.5	186.6	185.5	186.2	186.2	186.9	185.5
2008	185.1	186.6	187.2	188.9	190.0	191.0	191.0	190.7	188.7	189.7	188.5	188.2	188.8
2009	185.0	185.4	185.9	186.3	187.0	188.4	188.4	187.4	185.4	186.0	185.9	189.5	186.7
Government													
1990	574.4	583.6	585.8	584.9	590.2	582.7	557.0	551.4	574.9	583.2	586.2	586.1	578.3
2000	614.0	620.9	628.2	634.7	636.6	632.0	604.8	601.6	618.0	631.2	637.9	636.5	624.7
2001	625.3	635.3	636.4	637.1	633.2	634.3	609.5	603.9	621.8	632.8	641.6	639.3	629.2
2002	630.3	637.3	640.4	641.5	639.7	639.9	614.4	610.0	629.4	644.2	647.4	644.3	634.9
2003	633.9	640.1	641.7	643.1	641.2	642.4	615.3	611.3	636.4	643.5	652.0	649.2	637.5
2004	642.5	650.7	655.4	658.5	654.4	654.5	628.6	624.2	647.2	660.5	668.4	666.2	650.9
2005	653.9	661.3	664.1	670.4	668.2	667.5	640.2	635.1	661.3	669.7	676.9	673.7	661.9
2006	666.0	674.8	680.3	682.1	681.7	681.2	654.7	649.3	669.2	682.6	688.4	687.0	674.8
2007	679.1	687.8	689.3	691.6	688.6	687.0	662.0	654.9	677.3	688.0	696.8	693.3	683.0
2008	686.4	696.8	701.1	699.5	698.6	696.4	670.3	669.3	689.5	704.7	710.9	709.0	694.4
2009	696.2	703.9	708.2	710.4	708.8	706.3	670.9	669.0	687.2	699.7	704.8	702.3	697.3

Average Weekly Hours by Selected Industry: Virginia, 2007–2009

(Not seasonally adjusted.)

Industry and year	January	February	March	April	May	June	July	August	September	October	November	December	Annual average
Total Private													
2007	34.7	34.7	34.9	35.3	35.1	35.3	35.5	35.4	35.7	35.6	35.2	35.5	35.2
2008	34.4	34.6	35.4	35.1	34.8	35.3	35.0	35.1	35.0	35.2	34.7	34.8	35.0
2009	34.6	34.7	34.6	34.3	34.5	34.3	34.5	35.1	34.3	34.8	35.0	34.6	34.6
Goods-Producing													
2007	38.7	38.3	40.1	39.5	40.5	41.2	39.9	39.6	39.9	41.1	40.3	39.9	39.9
2008	38.9	38.8	40.5	39.9	39.2	40.3	40.0	40.4	40.4	41.1	39.9	40.1	40.0
2009	38.3	38.7	37.9	38.5	38.5	39.1	39.6	39.5	38.6	39.7	39.5	39.4	38.9
Construction													
2007	38.4	37.5	39.3	39.2	39.9	40.8	39.7	40.1	40.6	40.2	39.1	39.8	39.6
2008	38.9	37.8	39.1	39.1	38.8	41.0	40.1	40.8	40.4	40.8	38.6	38.4	39.5
2009	37.5	37.6	37.1	37.5	37.5	37.9	38.6	38.7	37.2	37.7	36.4	37.4	37.6
Manufacturing													
2007	39.0	39.2	41.0	39.8	41.1	41.5	40.0	39.1	39.3	40.7	40.3	38.8	40.0
2008	37.8	38.6	40.7	39.8	40.0	39.9	40.1	40.0	40.4	40.9	40.6	40.6	39.9
2009	37.8	38.6	38.0	38.8	38.9	39.8	40.3	40.0	39.4	40.2	40.3	40.8	39.4
Trade, Transportation, and Utilities													
2007	34.3	34.5	34.2	34.3	34.7	34.9	35.3	35.5	35.6	35.3	35.2	35.6	35.0
2008	34.2	34.5	35.2	35.0	34.9	35.0	34.8	35.0	34.8	34.4	34.6	34.0	34.7
2009	33.9	34.7	34.7	34.4	34.5	34.2	34.4	34.8	34.9	35.1	34.9	34.8	34.6
Financial Activities													
2007	35.3	35.2	35.3	35.6	35.2	35.6	35.8	35.4	35.7	35.4	35.2	35.5	35.4
2008	35.1	35.4	35.5	35.2	35.2	35.5	35.3	35.6	35.9	35.5	35.8	35.4	35.5
2009	35.5	35.9	35.9	34.6	34.8	35.5	35.9	36.9	36.2	36.3	37.2	36.0	35.9
Professional and Business Services													
2007	35.2	35.5	35.4	36.6	35.7	36.1	36.5	36.5	37.1	36.8	36.7	37.0	36.3
2008	36.2	36.9	37.2	36.8	36.7	36.9	36.7	37.0	37.4	37.2	36.6	37.4	36.9
2009	37.5	38.2	38.1	37.8	37.8	36.8	36.7	37.7	36.7	37.2	37.6	36.9	37.4
Education and Health Services													
2007	35.8	35.2	35.5	35.8	35.8	34.9	35.3	35.0	35.2	34.7	34.3	34.8	35.2
2008	34.0	33.9	34.4	34.3	34.5	34.4	34.1	33.9	33.7	33.7	34.7	33.7	34.1
2009	33.6	33.6	33.8	33.6	33.7	33.6	33.2	33.6	33.3	33.5	33.8	33.9	33.6
Leisure and Hospitality													
2007	25.2	25.6	25.9	25.8	25.5	25.5	25.8	25.7	25.8	25.7	25.5	25.8	25.7
2008	25.6	25.7	25.8	25.9	25.8	25.9	25.6	25.4	25.2	25.9	25.5	25.4	25.6
2009	25.4	26.3	26.1	25.9	25.9	25.8	26.3	26.1	25.6	25.8	26.1	25.5	25.9
Other Services													
2007	33.3	32.9	33.7	33.9	33.9	33.9	34.5	34.2	34.0	33.9	33.6	33.8	33.8
2008	32.6	32.2	32.7	33.2	32.7	33.3	33.2	33.0	33.4	32.5	32.6	32.7	32.8
2009	33.2	33.1	32.7	32.4	32.5	32.8	33.5	33.8	33.4	33.5	33.4	32.4	33.1

Average Hourly Earnings by Selected Industry: Virginia, 2007–2009

(Dollars, not seasonally adjusted.)

Industry and year	January	February	March	April	May	June	July	August	September	October	November	December	Annual average
Total Private													
2007	22.43	22.45	22.32	22.70	22.33	22.25	22.57	22.36	22.49	22.37	22.58	22.65	22.46
2008	22.29	22.56	22.56	22.13	22.11	22.26	22.21	22.24	22.31	22.35	22.38	22.37	22.31
2009	22.19	22.24	22.45	22.17	22.20	22.38	22.42	22.72	22.62	22.86	23.30	23.39	22.58
Goods-Producing													
2007	21.35	20.74	20.98	21.17	20.78	20.96	21.03	20.92	20.85	20.80	21.31	21.46	21.03
2008	20.67	20.91	21.03	20.67	20.42	20.70	20.55	20.80	20.86	20.99	21.02	21.05	20.80
2009	20.54	20.53	20.97	20.78	20.79	20.94	20.82	21.01	20.90	20.91	21.12	21.08	20.86
Construction													
2007	22.56	21.99	21.97	22.20	21.75	22.02	22.30	21.78	21.55	21.35	21.29	21.49	21.85
2008	20.99	21.46	21.22	21.18	21.40	21.37	21.16	21.48	21.53	21.65	21.57	21.69	21.39
2009	20.94	20.89	21.33	21.30	21.30	21.29	21.11	21.54	21.60	21.64	21.81	21.98	21.39
Manufacturing													
2007	20.15	19.49	20.00	20.14	19.80	19.88	19.73	20.05	20.13	20.19	20.20	20.08	19.99
2008	19.79	19.81	20.10	19.81	19.72	20.25	20.04	20.16	20.12	20.02	20.20	20.29	20.03
2009	19.91	20.02	20.26	20.03	20.11	20.32	20.46	20.38	20.37	20.35	20.68	20.92	20.32
Trade, Transportation, and Utilities													
2007	18.76	18.67	18.53	18.98	19.08	18.87	18.73	18.61	18.81	18.84	18.94	18.75	18.80
2008	18.45	18.34	18.41	18.55	18.60	18.59	18.57	18.72	18.64	18.46	18.83	19.09	18.60
2009	19.24	19.67	19.53	18.64	18.81	18.87	19.03	19.34	19.61	19.08	19.45	19.32	19.22
Financial Activities													
2007	20.45	20.61	20.66	20.72	20.48	20.22	20.64	20.47	20.57	20.39	20.58	20.77	20.55
2008	20.40	20.65	20.84	20.93	20.97	20.92	20.83	20.96	20.97	21.12	21.15	21.33	20.92
2009	21.03	21.44	21.32	21.65	21.71	21.91	21.76	21.96	21.42	22.63	22.45	22.97	21.85
Professional and Business Services													
2007	32.99	33.09	33.08	33.78	33.16	32.75	33.68	33.05	33.61	33.18	33.55	33.54	33.29
2008	32.85	33.36	33.46	33.23	32.89	33.08	32.82	32.95	33.40	33.21	33.32	33.40	33.17
2009	33.03	33.74	33.70	33.68	33.38	33.69	33.73	33.44	33.49	33.51	33.78	33.62	33.57
Education and Health Services													
2007	18.37	18.61	18.71	18.89	18.83	19.38	19.33	19.15	19.48	19.52	19.67	19.61	19.13
2008	19.55	19.41	19.63	19.47	19.55	20.01	20.27	20.22	20.34	20.36	20.47	20.47	19.98
2009	20.35	20.58	20.65	20.62	20.43	20.25	20.48	20.57	20.87	20.93	21.14	21.14	20.67
Leisure and Hospitality													
2007	11.42	11.58	11.29	11.28	11.37	11.37	11.46	11.39	11.66	11.81	11.89	11.81	11.53
2008	11.72	11.85	11.97	11.96	12.07	12.08	12.04	12.14	12.17	12.21	12.03	12.14	12.03
2009	12.04	11.86	11.95	12.09	12.17	12.15	11.83	12.14	12.40	12.55	12.66	12.70	12.21
Other Services													
2007	21.23	21.87	21.21	21.29	21.37	21.51	21.36	21.57	21.55	21.34	21.58	21.84	21.48
2008	22.18	21.79	21.63	21.42	21.83	21.84	21.56	21.70	21.65	21.79	21.61	21.81	21.73
2009	21.51	21.41	21.60	21.66	21.66	21.50	21.60	21.67	21.66	21.47	21.69	21.60	21.59

Average Weekly Earnings by Selected Industry: Virginia, 2007–2009

(Dollars, not seasonally adjusted.)

Industry and year	January	February	March	April	May	June	July	August	September	October	November	December	Annual average
Total Private													
2007	778.32	779.02	778.97	801.31	783.78	785.43	801.24	791.54	802.89	796.37	794.82	804.08	790.59
2008	766.78	780.58	798.62	776.76	769.43	785.78	777.35	780.62	780.85	786.72	776.59	778.48	780.85
2009	767.77	771.73	776.77	760.43	765.90	767.63	773.49	797.47	775.87	795.53	815.50	809.29	781.27
Goods-Producing													
2007	826.25	794.34	841.30	836.22	841.59	863.55	839.10	828.43	831.92	854.88	858.79	856.25	839.10
2008	804.06	811.31	851.72	824.73	800.46	834.21	822.00	840.32	842.74	862.69	838.70	844.11	832.00
2009	786.68	794.51	794.76	800.03	800.42	818.75	824.47	829.90	806.74	830.13	834.24	830.55	811.45
Construction													
2007	866.30	824.63	863.42	870.24	867.83	898.42	885.31	873.38	874.93	858.27	832.44	855.30	865.26
2008	816.51	811.19	829.70	828.14	830.32	876.17	848.52	876.38	869.81	883.32	832.60	832.90	844.91
2009	785.25	785.46	791.34	798.75	798.75	806.89	814.85	833.60	803.52	815.83	793.88	822.05	804.26
Manufacturing													
2007	785.85	764.01	820.00	801.57	813.78	825.02	789.20	783.96	791.11	821.73	814.06	779.10	799.60
2008	748.06	764.67	818.07	788.44	788.80	807.98	803.60	806.40	812.85	818.82	820.12	823.77	799.20
2009	752.60	772.77	769.88	777.16	782.28	808.74	824.54	815.20	802.58	818.07	833.40	853.54	800.61
Trade, Transportation, and Utilities													
2007	643.47	644.12	633.73	651.01	662.08	658.56	661.17	660.66	669.64	665.05	666.69	667.50	658.00
2008	630.99	632.73	648.03	649.25	649.14	650.65	646.24	655.20	648.67	635.02	651.52	649.06	645.42
2009	652.24	682.55	677.69	641.22	648.95	645.35	654.63	673.03	684.39	669.71	678.81	672.34	665.01
Financial Activities													
2007	721.89	725.47	729.30	737.63	720.90	719.83	738.91	724.64	734.35	721.81	724.42	737.34	727.47
2008	716.04	731.01	739.82	736.74	738.14	742.66	735.30	746.18	752.82	749.76	757.17	755.08	742.66
2009	746.57	769.70	765.39	749.09	755.51	777.81	781.18	810.32	775.40	821.47	835.14	826.92	784.42
Professional and Business Services													
2007	1161.25	1174.70	1171.03	1236.35	1183.81	1182.28	1229.32	1206.33	1246.93	1221.02	1231.29	1240.98	1208.43
2008	1189.17	1230.98	1244.71	1222.86	1207.06	1220.65	1204.49	1219.15	1249.16	1235.41	1219.51	1249.16	1223.97
2009	1238.63	1288.87	1283.97	1273.10	1261.76	1239.79	1237.89	1260.69	1229.08	1246.57	1270.13	1240.58	1255.52
Education and Health Services													
2007	657.65	655.07	664.21	676.26	674.11	676.36	682.35	670.25	685.70	677.34	674.68	682.43	673.38
2008	664.70	658.00	675.27	667.82	674.48	688.34	691.21	685.46	685.46	686.13	710.31	689.84	681.32
2009	683.76	691.49	697.97	692.83	688.49	680.40	679.94	691.15	694.97	701.16	714.53	716.65	694.51
Leisure and Hospitality													
2007	287.78	296.45	292.41	291.02	289.94	289.94	295.67	292.72	300.83	303.52	303.20	304.70	296.32
2008	300.03	304.55	308.83	309.76	311.41	312.87	308.22	308.36	306.68	316.24	306.77	308.36	307.97
2009	305.82	311.92	311.90	313.13	315.20	313.47	311.13	316.85	317.44	323.79	330.43	323.85	316.24
Other Services													
2007	706.96	719.52	714.78	721.73	724.44	720.19	736.92	737.69	732.70	723.43	725.09	738.19	726.02
2008	723.07	701.64	707.30	711.14	713.84	727.27	715.79	716.10	723.11	708.18	704.49	713.19	712.74
2009	714.13	708.67	706.32	701.78	703.95	705.20	723.60	732.45	723.44	719.25	724.45	699.84	714.63

WASHINGTON
At a Glance

Population:
  1990 census: 4,866,669
  2000 census: 5,894,121
  2009 estimate: 6,664,195

Percent change in population:
  1990–2000: 21.1%
  2000–2009: 13.1%

Percent change in total nonfarm employment:
  1990–2009: 31.8%
  2008–2009: -4.5%

Industry with the largest growth in employment, 1990–2009 (thousands):
  Education and Health Services, 166.7

Industry with the largest decline or smallest growth in employment, 1990–2009 (thousands):
  Manufacturing, -70.2

Civilian labor force:
  1990: 2,537,038
  2000: 3,050,021
  2009: 3,528,707

Unemployment rate and rank among states (lowest to highest):
  1990: 5.1%, 18th
  2000: 5.0%, 44th
  2009: 8.9%, 31st

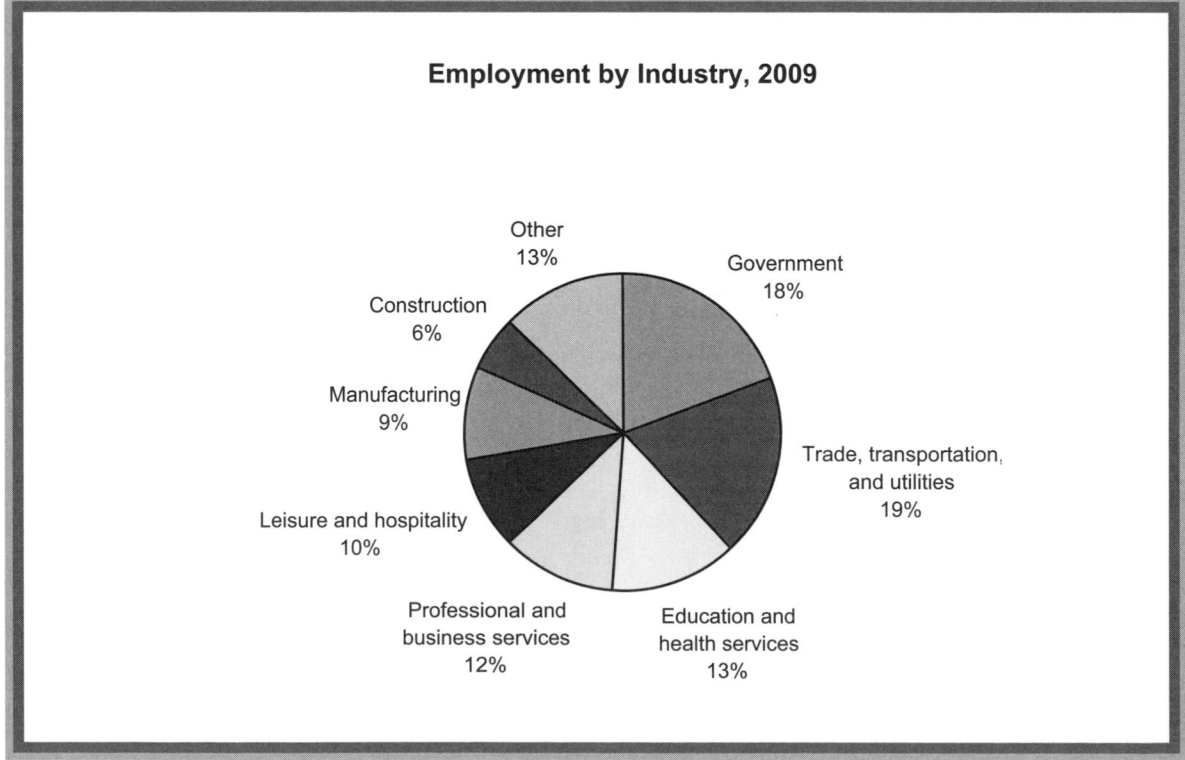

Employment by Industry, 2009

- Other 13%
- Government 18%
- Construction 6%
- Manufacturing 9%
- Trade, transportation, and utilities 19%
- Leisure and hospitality 10%
- Professional and business services 12%
- Education and health services 13%

Employment by Industry: Washington, Selected Years, 1990–2009

(Numbers in thousands, not seasonally adjusted.)

Industry and year	January	February	March	April	May	June	July	August	September	October	November	December	Annual average
Total Nonfarm													
1990	2065.6	2076.5	2100.6	2122.7	2149.8	2177.4	2152.2	2167.3	2190.2	2169.9	2177.8	2166.3	2143.0
2000	2638.8	2645.3	2688.2	2687.0	2721.2	2744.6	2709.3	2721.1	2739.6	2741.7	2749.6	2749.0	2711.3
2001	2670.9	2677.0	2694.5	2699.1	2718.3	2736.6	2700.7	2697.1	2705.5	2697.8	2691.5	2674.9	2697.0
2002	2606.2	2611.2	2623.0	2637.6	2663.7	2679.4	2661.3	2660.3	2674.8	2678.5	2683.4	2669.4	2654.1
2003	2608.9	2617.9	2624.1	2637.8	2663.3	2679.1	2659.9	2659.9	2677.7	2686.4	2689.4	2685.5	2657.5
2004	2613.8	2633.5	2659.6	2682.5	2705.0	2727.5	2710.8	2705.9	2725.9	2744.6	2753.6	2749.6	2701.0
2005	2688.2	2704.2	2729.8	2755.2	2780.3	2800.7	2787.5	2787.7	2800.7	2820.8	2834.5	2835.2	2777.1
2006	2775.7	2796.2	2816.9	2832.6	2862.7	2893.8	2863.5	2867.7	2894.5	2897.4	2906.6	2903.0	2859.2
2007	2843.3	2873.7	2891.4	2909.7	2939.3	2965.7	2944.1	2945.1	2960.5	2970.7	2984.4	2975.1	2933.6
2008	2916.9	2936.9	2949.4	2960.3	2981.3	2993.4	2977.9	2973.6	2979.1	2954.3	2958.2	2925.2	2958.9
2009	2851.2	2843.3	2834.0	2835.6	2848.1	2852.4	2822.3	2799.7	2812.9	2814.6	2805.6	2786.5	2825.5
Total Private													
1990	1676.5	1676.4	1702.9	1722.2	1745.1	1772.2	1771.6	1792.4	1797.2	1765.8	1764.2	1758.8	1745.4
2000	2159.5	2158.1	2198.6	2198.9	2221.6	2249.7	2245.5	2266.0	2268.7	2255.1	2255.9	2258.0	2228.0
2001	2170.6	2170.9	2183.8	2188.3	2204.4	2221.0	2212.9	2222.2	2211.9	2185.0	2169.9	2158.0	2191.6
2002	2093.9	2092.1	2102.0	2115.9	2139.2	2154.7	2163.1	2175.3	2170.7	2154.9	2150.5	2142.8	2137.9
2003	2088.2	2091.6	2096.8	2110.5	2130.4	2148.7	2158.8	2170.3	2170.7	2161.8	2157.2	2157.9	2136.9
2004	2092.1	2105.9	2129.3	2152.2	2172.8	2193.8	2204.4	2213.4	2214.1	2215.9	2216.0	2218.7	2177.4
2005	2161.9	2173.4	2195.9	2220.7	2244.4	2263.1	2278.9	2293.1	2286.6	2288.8	2294.7	2302.6	2250.3
2006	2246.1	2259.7	2278.7	2295.8	2323.6	2351.9	2354.2	2370.9	2376.6	2362.3	2364.0	2366.7	2329.2
2007	2312.6	2336.1	2354.6	2370.0	2397.3	2424.2	2426.6	2440.6	2438.7	2429.5	2435.0	2432.6	2399.8
2008	2375.6	2387.2	2400.2	2410.4	2428.5	2440.2	2446.9	2454.1	2445.3	2398.4	2394.0	2369.9	2412.6
2009	2299.0	2287.2	2275.5	2270.8	2283.2	2291.4	2289.6	2286.3	2282.6	2263.7	2250.4	2237.7	2276.5
Goods-Producing													
1990	446.7	444.9	453.7	459.9	466.7	473.8	476.8	484.6	484.4	472.1	465.6	456.1	465.4
2000	489.2	476.7	496.0	498.4	503.2	510.1	511.7	516.3	514.8	511.9	504.7	496.6	502.4
2001	483.6	480.5	483.5	483.9	488.4	493.6	494.7	498.3	494.1	484.1	471.6	459.7	484.7
2002	443.7	440.2	440.6	443.5	450.4	454.1	458.8	462.7	457.4	452.3	443.4	435.5	448.6
2003	422.4	421.7	421.3	424.8	430.2	436.0	440.5	444.2	442.8	439.0	432.1	427.7	431.9
2004	413.0	416.8	422.7	428.5	434.3	440.0	448.5	450.7	450.5	451.1	445.7	442.0	437.0
2005	431.1	435.0	442.1	448.8	455.7	462.6	472.4	476.2	464.1	477.3	472.0	470.2	459.0
2006	461.8	467.9	472.7	476.9	485.6	496.5	502.2	506.3	508.3	504.7	498.1	493.6	489.6
2007	484.5	490.4	494.5	499.8	508.0	518.5	522.5	526.8	525.9	521.8	515.4	508.1	509.7
2008	496.9	498.7	500.4	500.6	505.4	509.3	513.6	515.6	511.2	479.7	487.0	471.7	499.2
2009	451.0	444.4	436.5	432.8	433.7	435.8	436.5	436.3	433.7	426.7	411.6	399.8	431.6
Mining and Logging													
1990	11.9	11.7	11.6	12.3	12.9	13.2	12.6	13.5	13.4	13.1	12.6	11.8	12.5
2000	10.0	10.1	9.8	9.7	10.1	10.4	10.3	10.4	10.2	9.9	9.7	9.5	10.0
2001	9.9	9.7	9.2	9.0	9.5	9.9	10.4	10.4	10.3	10.1	9.8	9.4	9.8
2002	9.0	9.1	8.9	8.9	9.3	9.5	9.7	9.7	9.8	9.7	9.4	9.3	9.4
2003	8.7	8.7	8.5	8.3	8.5	8.7	8.8	8.8	8.7	8.7	8.5	8.6	8.6
2004	8.5	8.7	8.6	8.8	9.0	9.2	9.5	9.6	9.7	9.5	9.3	9.2	9.1
2005	8.8	8.9	8.8	8.8	9.1	9.2	9.2	9.1	9.1	8.9	8.8	8.8	9.0
2006	8.4	8.5	8.5	8.4	8.8	9.0	9.0	8.9	8.8	8.7	8.6	8.6	8.7
2007	8.4	7.9	7.6	7.9	8.2	8.5	8.5	8.4	8.3	8.3	8.0	7.9	8.2
2008	7.4	7.4	7.3	7.3	7.5	7.6	7.9	7.9	7.8	7.8	7.4	7.2	7.5
2009	6.5	6.4	5.8	5.7	5.8	6.2	6.4	6.4	6.4	6.3	6.0	5.6	6.1
Construction													
1990	103.4	102.3	108.8	113.4	117.8	121.9	123.8	128.8	128.1	122.1	118.2	113.2	116.8
2000	146.7	149.2	153.1	155.8	159.3	163.8	166.6	169.7	170.1	168.1	164.7	159.7	160.5
2001	152.0	150.9	155.4	155.5	159.4	163.3	165.4	168.6	166.5	162.5	155.6	149.8	158.7
2002	143.2	143.5	144.6	148.4	153.6	156.6	161.3	166.0	163.9	161.2	156.5	151.6	154.2
2003	144.9	145.2	145.8	149.8	154.6	158.6	163.0	166.6	165.4	164.2	160.1	156.4	156.2
2004	147.3	151.0	155.5	158.8	163.1	166.5	172.0	174.0	172.7	172.9	170.2	166.6	164.2
2005	158.4	162.0	167.0	170.8	175.0	178.7	184.5	188.2	189.3	187.7	184.5	182.8	177.4
2006	175.6	179.5	184.2	187.7	193.8	200.1	203.3	206.9	207.1	204.6	200.0	196.4	194.9
2007	190.3	194.4	199.6	203.5	210.2	215.3	216.5	220.4	218.0	214.6	210.3	205.2	208.2
2008	196.6	197.3	200.3	201.6	204.6	206.9	209.1	210.1	206.5	200.9	190.6	181.1	200.5
2009	168.4	163.7	162.4	161.4	163.3	164.3	163.7	163.5	161.7	158.0	146.9	137.4	159.6
Manufacturing													
1990	331.4	330.9	333.3	334.2	336.0	338.7	340.4	342.3	342.9	336.9	334.8	331.1	336.1
2000	332.5	317.4	333.1	332.9	333.8	335.9	334.8	336.2	334.5	333.9	330.3	327.4	331.9
2001	321.7	319.9	318.9	319.4	319.5	320.4	318.9	319.3	317.3	311.5	306.2	300.5	316.1
2002	291.5	287.6	287.1	286.2	287.5	288.0	287.8	287.0	283.7	281.4	277.5	274.6	285.0
2003	268.8	267.8	267.0	266.7	267.1	268.7	268.7	268.8	268.7	266.1	263.5	262.7	267.1
2004	257.2	257.1	258.6	260.9	262.2	264.3	267.0	267.1	268.1	268.7	266.2	266.2	263.6
2005	263.9	264.1	266.3	269.2	271.6	274.7	278.7	278.9	265.7	280.7	278.7	278.6	272.6
2006	277.8	279.9	280.0	280.8	283.0	287.4	289.9	290.5	292.4	291.4	289.5	288.6	285.9
2007	285.8	288.1	287.3	288.4	289.6	294.7	297.5	298.0	299.6	298.9	297.1	295.0	293.3
2008	292.9	294.0	292.8	291.7	293.3	294.8	296.6	297.6	296.9	271.0	289.0	283.4	291.2
2009	276.1	274.3	268.3	265.7	264.6	265.3	266.4	266.4	265.6	262.4	258.7	256.8	265.9

Employment by Industry: Washington, Selected Years, 1990–2009—*Continued*

(Numbers in thousands, not seasonally adjusted.)

Industry and year	January	February	March	April	May	June	July	August	September	October	November	December	Annual average
Service-Providing													
1990	1618.9	1631.6	1646.9	1662.8	1683.1	1703.6	1675.4	1682.7	1705.8	1697.8	1712.2	1710.2	1677.6
2000	2149.6	2168.6	2192.2	2188.6	2218.0	2234.5	2197.6	2204.8	2224.8	2229.8	2244.9	2252.4	2208.8
2001	2187.3	2196.5	2211.0	2215.2	2229.9	2243.0	2206.0	2198.8	2211.4	2213.7	2219.9	2215.2	2212.3
2002	2162.5	2171.0	2182.4	2194.1	2213.3	2225.3	2202.5	2197.6	2217.4	2226.2	2240.0	2233.9	2205.5
2003	2186.5	2196.2	2202.8	2213.0	2233.1	2243.1	2219.4	2215.7	2234.9	2247.4	2257.3	2257.8	2225.6
2004	2200.8	2216.7	2236.9	2254.0	2270.7	2287.5	2262.3	2255.2	2275.4	2293.5	2307.9	2307.6	2264.0
2005	2257.1	2269.2	2287.7	2306.4	2324.6	2338.1	2315.1	2311.5	2336.6	2343.5	2362.5	2365.0	2318.1
2006	2313.9	2328.3	2344.2	2355.7	2377.1	2397.3	2361.3	2361.4	2386.2	2392.7	2408.5	2409.4	2369.7
2007	2358.8	2383.3	2396.9	2409.9	2431.3	2447.2	2421.6	2418.3	2434.6	2448.9	2469.0	2467.0	2423.9
2008	2420.0	2438.2	2449.0	2459.7	2475.9	2484.1	2464.3	2458.0	2467.9	2474.6	2471.2	2453.5	2459.7
2009	2400.2	2398.9	2397.5	2402.8	2414.4	2416.6	2385.8	2363.4	2379.2	2387.9	2394.0	2386.7	2394.0
Trade, Transportation, and Utilities													
1990	419.2	415.1	421.0	424.4	430.8	438.9	436.4	440.0	441.8	436.9	444.7	448.9	433.1
2000	520.6	518.8	523.6	522.5	527.1	533.5	530.2	533.0	533.3	539.2	548.2	552.5	531.8
2001	523.5	518.3	520.9	520.4	522.0	527.2	526.3	526.0	523.5	522.2	526.1	527.8	523.7
2002	505.1	498.9	500.1	501.3	505.7	509.9	512.5	512.0	512.8	512.6	518.3	522.2	509.3
2003	502.2	498.0	498.3	499.8	504.2	509.3	513.2	513.5	514.3	515.7	522.0	527.0	509.8
2004	501.9	500.9	504.1	509.1	513.7	519.4	521.1	524.0	523.7	527.4	535.4	540.6	518.4
2005	517.2	515.2	517.9	520.5	525.8	530.4	531.7	535.3	535.7	536.0	546.3	553.4	530.5
2006	530.4	527.2	530.4	531.4	537.4	543.5	543.0	546.0	546.0	546.2	556.2	561.5	541.6
2007	540.5	539.1	541.9	544.0	549.0	554.2	555.8	557.5	556.2	558.3	570.5	573.5	553.4
2008	552.4	548.2	549.7	549.6	552.6	554.6	557.1	557.5	554.3	553.7	555.1	555.7	553.4
2009	531.2	523.0	518.9	517.0	521.2	522.5	524.9	524.3	523.8	520.3	529.5	534.8	524.3
Wholesale Trade													
1990	97.2	97.6	99.1	99.8	100.8	104.2	103.5	103.2	103.7	103.1	102.5	101.7	101.3
2000	118.0	118.8	120.2	120.0	120.6	123.3	121.7	122.4	122.0	123.2	122.6	122.1	121.2
2001	119.3	119.4	120.1	120.1	120.6	122.0	121.5	120.7	119.6	119.0	118.1	116.4	119.7
2002	114.8	115.0	115.3	115.0	115.8	116.3	116.4	116.5	116.4	116.2	115.6	114.5	115.7
2003	113.6	113.8	114.3	115.0	115.4	116.4	117.3	117.2	117.4	117.8	117.5	116.5	116.0
2004	114.9	115.7	116.9	118.7	118.9	119.8	120.8	120.8	120.9	121.7	121.4	121.1	119.3
2005	119.2	119.8	120.6	120.2	121.2	122.7	122.8	123.3	123.5	124.0	124.5	124.4	122.2
2006	123.7	124.2	125.0	124.8	126.0	127.9	128.1	127.8	127.9	128.3	128.1	127.1	126.6
2007	125.9	126.6	127.3	128.0	128.9	130.3	130.7	130.6	130.2	131.2	131.4	130.9	129.3
2008	129.0	129.6	130.0	130.1	130.7	130.7	131.4	130.8	130.7	131.3	129.4	127.7	130.1
2009	125.6	124.7	123.8	123.1	123.1	123.2	123.4	122.4	122.1	122.6	121.1	121.1	123.0
Retail Trade													
1990	240.5	236.6	239.7	242.4	245.8	249.2	248.0	250.4	250.9	248.9	258.4	262.6	247.7
2000	310.0	307.1	309.5	308.9	312.9	315.4	312.6	314.4	314.8	316.7	327.3	332.9	315.2
2001	312.3	307.4	308.9	307.9	308.7	311.1	311.6	312.4	310.9	309.6	317.1	321.2	311.6
2002	303.2	297.2	298.3	299.3	302.1	304.8	306.6	306.3	306.4	306.1	314.1	319.5	305.3
2003	301.7	297.8	298.0	298.7	302.1	305.2	307.4	307.7	307.0	308.0	316.1	321.1	305.9
2004	300.9	299.2	300.5	302.9	306.6	309.0	309.8	312.5	310.7	312.2	321.6	326.7	309.4
2005	308.7	305.5	307.1	309.1	312.4	314.6	316.5	319.2	318.3	319.1	328.6	334.2	316.1
2006	315.4	311.5	313.3	314.2	317.9	320.4	320.6	323.2	322.0	322.7	333.6	337.8	321.1
2007	321.2	318.9	320.3	321.1	324.4	326.8	328.8	329.7	328.3	329.6	341.9	344.4	328.0
2008	328.7	323.5	324.8	324.3	325.7	327.2	328.8	329.7	326.6	326.3	330.6	332.2	327.4
2009	312.3	307.1	305.0	304.1	307.4	308.5	310.0	310.9	309.9	307.9	317.1	322.9	310.3
Transportation and Utilities													
1990	81.5	80.9	82.2	82.2	84.2	85.5	84.9	86.4	87.2	84.9	83.8	84.6	84.0
2000	92.6	92.9	93.9	93.6	93.6	94.8	95.9	96.2	96.5	99.3	98.3	97.5	95.4
2001	91.9	91.5	91.9	92.4	92.7	94.1	93.2	92.9	93.0	93.6	90.9	90.2	92.4
2002	87.1	86.7	86.5	87.0	87.8	88.8	89.5	89.2	90.0	90.3	88.6	88.2	88.3
2003	86.9	86.4	86.0	86.1	86.7	87.7	88.5	88.6	89.9	89.9	88.4	89.4	87.9
2004	86.1	86.0	86.7	87.5	88.2	90.6	90.5	90.7	92.1	93.5	92.4	92.8	89.8
2005	89.3	89.9	90.2	91.2	92.2	93.1	92.4	92.8	93.9	92.9	93.2	94.8	92.2
2006	91.3	91.5	92.1	92.4	93.5	95.2	94.3	95.0	96.1	95.2	94.5	96.6	94.0
2007	93.4	93.6	94.3	94.9	95.7	97.1	96.3	97.2	97.7	97.5	97.2	98.2	96.1
2008	94.7	95.1	94.9	95.2	96.2	96.7	96.9	97.0	97.0	96.1	95.1	95.8	95.9
2009	93.3	91.2	90.1	89.8	90.7	90.8	91.5	91.0	91.8	89.8	91.3	90.8	91.0
Information													
1990	48.7	49.0	48.7	48.8	49.2	50.0	50.1	50.9	50.6	49.5	49.5	49.7	49.5
2000	90.5	92.0	93.5	94.1	95.9	98.7	99.9	101.0	102.0	100.9	101.6	101.9	97.6
2001	101.6	101.8	101.0	99.4	99.6	100.3	99.3	99.1	97.0	96.3	96.1	96.7	99.0
2002	94.2	93.9	93.5	93.2	93.3	93.8	93.9	94.0	93.1	93.3	93.4	93.3	93.6
2003	92.2	92.0	91.5	91.0	91.6	92.1	92.2	93.1	92.4	92.6	93.0	93.6	92.3
2004	91.7	91.7	92.1	92.1	92.8	93.2	93.4	93.7	92.7	93.0	93.7	94.2	92.9
2005	92.7	93.5	93.4	94.1	94.5	94.9	95.7	96.4	95.4	94.6	95.5	96.1	94.7
2006	94.8	95.2	95.9	96.2	96.9	99.5	100.0	100.7	100.6	99.7	100.6	101.1	98.4
2007	100.4	101.3	101.0	101.5	102.4	103.5	103.7	104.0	103.3	102.0	103.1	103.3	102.5
2008	102.7	103.8	104.0	104.2	104.9	106.0	107.2	107.9	106.8	105.9	107.0	107.0	105.6
2009	104.9	105.4	105.0	103.7	104.1	104.3	104.5	103.8	102.5	101.8	101.9	101.5	103.6

Employment by Industry: Washington, Selected Years, 1990–2009—*Continued*

(Numbers in thousands, not seasonally adjusted.)

Industry and year	January	February	March	April	May	June	July	August	September	October	November	December	Annual average
Financial Activities													
1990	109.8	110.4	111.5	112.5	113.6	114.8	114.8	115.1	114.8	113.6	113.3	113.3	113.1
2000	141.9	142.6	142.5	141.7	142.2	142.6	142.6	143.0	142.9	141.3	141.6	142.7	142.3
2001	142.4	143.3	143.1	143.4	144.3	145.2	147.2	147.7	147.9	145.9	145.7	146.1	145.2
2002	143.0	143.6	144.0	144.7	145.6	146.2	147.1	148.1	147.8	147.1	148.1	148.7	146.2
2003	148.2	148.9	149.7	150.8	152.0	152.9	154.2	154.8	153.9	153.0	152.3	152.1	151.9
2004	149.9	150.2	151.4	151.0	151.6	152.3	152.8	153.0	152.3	152.2	151.9	153.3	151.8
2005	150.5	151.2	151.4	152.5	153.6	154.6	156.4	157.5	157.0	156.4	156.4	157.2	154.6
2006	155.2	155.4	155.8	156.0	156.7	157.5	157.7	157.5	156.6	155.6	155.1	155.5	156.2
2007	153.9	154.5	155.2	155.7	156.1	157.1	157.1	157.1	155.2	154.6	154.8	154.7	155.5
2008	153.3	153.5	153.5	153.2	154.2	154.0	153.2	153.4	151.8	150.3	149.4	148.5	152.4
2009	145.6	145.2	143.4	143.7	143.6	144.0	142.9	142.2	141.1	141.2	140.6	139.8	142.8
Professional and Business Services													
1990	187.3	187.9	191.8	194.4	196.0	199.6	201.7	204.8	205.1	201.1	200.8	200.2	197.5
2000	290.3	293.1	298.3	298.6	300.7	305.2	305.9	311.6	312.8	309.8	309.0	310.6	303.8
2001	296.8	296.9	299.6	300.7	300.6	301.3	297.8	299.0	296.5	293.9	290.3	287.5	296.7
2002	279.8	282.3	284.6	287.1	288.6	291.5	293.2	297.2	297.1	295.3	294.9	291.3	290.2
2003	282.2	284.5	285.4	287.8	288.3	289.7	292.1	295.6	295.5	295.4	294.3	293.2	290.3
2004	286.0	289.8	294.2	298.8	299.9	303.0	306.2	308.6	308.1	309.6	309.3	307.4	301.7
2005	300.0	304.7	308.3	312.4	314.9	317.0	320.8	323.0	324.8	322.7	322.5	321.8	316.1
2006	313.6	317.4	320.6	325.6	328.5	333.3	335.1	338.8	339.2	338.3	338.6	338.0	330.6
2007	329.4	335.6	339.9	340.8	343.4	347.2	348.5	351.2	350.8	349.3	349.2	349.7	344.6
2008	340.5	344.2	346.9	351.0	352.4	353.6	354.9	355.5	353.6	349.5	342.8	337.7	348.6
2009	330.0	327.5	325.6	324.3	323.7	325.5	324.8	324.1	323.8	325.5	326.5	324.4	325.5
Education and Health Services													
1990	199.1	202.0	203.8	204.5	205.8	205.9	203.3	205.1	209.4	211.0	212.5	213.4	206.3
2000	285.4	289.8	292.8	290.1	291.2	291.0	289.5	291.3	293.3	294.9	296.3	297.1	291.9
2001	292.4	296.8	298.0	298.6	299.7	298.1	291.6	292.9	299.2	302.5	305.1	305.0	298.3
2002	301.7	305.6	307.3	307.7	309.4	306.2	300.8	301.5	306.7	311.1	312.8	312.0	306.9
2003	307.8	311.4	312.6	314.0	314.7	312.1	308.1	307.8	312.6	316.8	318.3	318.3	312.9
2004	312.9	316.9	318.7	320.9	321.9	320.3	313.9	313.8	319.4	325.0	326.4	326.0	319.7
2005	322.1	325.5	328.2	331.1	332.1	328.3	322.9	323.7	331.2	334.8	336.3	335.5	329.3
2006	331.3	335.4	337.8	338.8	340.2	336.3	329.2	330.7	338.1	342.4	343.4	342.8	337.2
2007	338.9	344.7	346.9	347.7	350.4	347.1	340.9	342.2	349.3	355.9	358.0	357.5	348.3
2008	353.0	358.7	359.9	361.7	363.5	359.8	355.2	356.7	363.4	370.3	371.8	371.0	362.1
2009	369.0	373.1	374.8	374.9	376.2	372.1	365.6	365.0	371.1	376.8	380.2	376.7	373.0
Leisure and Hospitality													
1990	178.3	179.5	183.7	188.7	193.4	198.4	197.3	200.4	199.9	192.1	188.5	187.8	190.6
2000	237.8	240.6	246.4	249.2	254.7	261.2	258.5	261.7	261.9	250.4	248.1	250.1	251.7
2001	235.0	237.7	241.2	245.4	252.4	256.7	257.6	260.6	256.6	243.7	238.9	239.1	247.1
2002	231.4	232.2	236.0	241.2	248.1	253.7	256.7	259.7	257.0	245.4	241.8	242.1	245.4
2003	235.7	237.2	239.6	243.7	249.9	256.2	258.4	261.3	259.8	250.7	247.1	247.6	248.9
2004	239.6	241.6	247.0	252.1	257.9	263.8	266.2	267.5	266.0	256.9	253.5	254.8	255.6
2005	248.1	247.2	252.4	259.2	265.1	271.2	274.7	276.7	274.9	264.4	263.1	265.4	263.5
2006	257.6	258.9	262.3	267.4	273.9	279.7	281.5	285.4	282.7	271.7	268.4	270.3	271.7
2007	262.9	266.7	270.5	275.9	282.5	289.8	291.5	294.8	292.0	282.1	278.3	280.1	280.6
2008	271.8	274.0	278.5	282.7	287.2	293.7	295.6	297.5	295.2	281.4	274.0	272.3	283.7
2009	261.7	262.5	264.5	267.2	273.2	279.0	281.6	282.1	279.3	263.5	253.4	253.7	268.5
Other Services													
1990	87.4	87.6	88.7	89.0	89.6	90.8	91.2	91.5	91.2	89.5	89.3	89.4	89.6
2000	103.8	104.5	105.5	104.3	106.6	107.4	107.2	108.1	107.7	106.7	106.4	106.5	106.2
2001	95.3	95.6	96.5	96.5	97.4	98.6	98.4	98.6	97.1	96.4	96.1	96.1	96.9
2002	95.0	95.4	95.9	97.2	98.1	99.3	100.1	100.1	98.8	97.8	97.8	97.7	97.8
2003	97.5	97.9	98.4	98.6	99.5	100.4	100.1	100.0	99.4	98.6	98.1	98.4	98.9
2004	97.1	98.0	99.1	99.7	100.7	101.8	102.3	102.1	101.4	100.7	100.1	100.4	100.3
2005	100.2	101.1	102.2	102.1	102.7	104.1	104.3	104.3	103.5	102.6	102.6	103.0	102.7
2006	101.4	102.3	103.2	103.5	104.4	105.6	105.5	105.5	105.1	103.7	103.6	103.9	104.0
2007	102.1	103.8	104.7	104.6	105.5	106.8	106.6	107.0	106.0	105.5	105.7	105.7	105.3
2008	105.0	106.1	107.3	107.4	108.3	109.2	110.1	110.0	109.0	107.6	106.9	106.0	107.7
2009	105.6	106.1	106.8	107.2	107.5	108.2	108.8	108.5	107.3	107.9	106.7	107.0	107.3
Government													
1990	389.1	400.1	397.7	400.5	404.7	405.2	380.6	374.9	393.0	404.1	413.6	407.5	397.5
2000	479.3	487.2	489.6	488.1	499.6	494.9	463.8	455.1	470.9	486.6	493.7	491.0	483.3
2001	500.3	506.1	510.7	510.8	513.9	515.6	487.8	474.9	493.6	512.8	521.6	516.9	505.4
2002	512.3	519.1	521.0	521.7	524.5	524.7	498.2	485.0	504.1	523.6	532.9	526.6	516.1
2003	520.7	526.3	527.3	527.3	532.9	530.4	501.1	489.6	507.0	524.6	532.2	527.6	520.6
2004	521.7	527.6	530.3	530.3	532.2	533.7	506.4	492.5	511.8	528.7	537.6	530.9	523.6
2005	526.3	530.8	533.9	534.5	535.9	537.6	508.6	494.6	514.1	532.0	539.8	532.6	526.7
2006	529.6	536.5	538.2	536.8	539.1	541.9	509.3	496.8	517.9	535.1	542.6	536.3	530.0
2007	530.7	537.6	536.8	539.7	542.0	541.5	517.5	504.5	521.8	541.2	549.4	542.5	533.8
2008	541.3	549.7	549.2	549.9	552.8	553.2	531.0	519.5	533.8	555.9	564.2	555.3	546.3
2009	552.2	556.1	558.5	564.8	564.9	561.0	532.7	513.4	530.3	550.9	555.2	548.8	549.1

Average Weekly Hours by Selected Industry: Washington, 2007–2009

(Not seasonally adjusted.)

Industry and year	January	February	March	April	May	June	July	August	September	October	November	December	Annual average
Total Private													
2007	34.1	35.3	34.9	35.8	35.1	35.1	36.0	35.4	36.2	34.9	34.7	35.5	35.3
2008	34.2	34.7	35.3	34.6	34.5	35.5	34.7	35.0	34.2	33.8	35.2	33.8	34.6
2009	33.8	34.9	34.9	34.2	34.2	34.3	34.2	35.3	34.0	34.0	34.7	33.6	34.4
Goods-Producing													
2007	39.0	40.4	40.3	40.7	40.7	40.9	40.8	41.0	41.5	41.2	40.4	41.0	40.7
2008	39.8	40.6	40.9	40.8	40.7	41.1	40.5	40.9	38.8	38.2	40.8	40.7	40.3
2009	40.3	40.6	39.3	39.5	39.4	39.8	39.5	40.1	39.1	39.7	39.7	38.6	39.7
Construction													
2007	35.3	36.9	36.5	37.8	37.9	37.8	38.7	38.7	39.1	38.8	37.1	37.4	37.7
2008	36.1	36.6	37.4	38.0	38.3	38.0	38.1	38.8	39.0	38.3	38.1	36.6	37.8
2009	36.8	37.2	35.8	36.0	36.2	36.5	36.1	37.3	35.0	35.5	34.8	32.3	35.9
Manufacturing													
2007	40.7	42.0	42.1	42.0	42.0	42.4	41.8	42.0	42.6	42.3	41.9	42.6	42.0
2008	41.4	42.4	42.5	42.0	41.7	42.4	41.6	41.9	38.3	37.8	41.9	42.6	41.4
2009	41.9	42.0	40.8	41.1	41.0	41.3	41.1	41.5	41.2	41.8	41.6	41.7	41.4
Trade, Transportation, and Utilities													
2007	33.6	35.3	35.0	36.1	35.3	35.4	36.5	36.2	36.7	35.1	35.1	35.9	35.5
2008	34.6	34.7	35.2	35.0	34.7	35.4	34.9	35.6	35.0	34.4	35.4	34.0	34.9
2009	33.9	35.4	37.2	36.4	36.4	36.4	36.1	37.4	36.7	35.8	35.8	35.0	36.0
Information													
2007	39.0	38.9	38.7	41.9	38.6	38.8	41.6	38.8	41.9	38.4	41.4	41.7	40.0
2008	40.9	40.7	41.4	38.3	38.0	41.6	41.2	38.4	38.2	38.4	41.3	37.7	39.7
2009	38.4	41.7	41.7	38.4	38.3	38.3	39.0	41.6	38.3	38.4	41.9	38.5	39.6
Financial Activities													
2007	36.4	35.7	35.4	37.2	34.9	35.0	36.9	35.1	37.5	35.1	35.2	36.8	35.9
2008	35.0	35.9	37.4	35.9	35.7	37.6	35.7	36.9	36.6	36.6	38.2	36.0	36.5
2009	36.7	38.1	38.0	36.3	36.3	35.6	35.7	37.5	34.9	35.6	37.5	35.5	36.5
Professional and Business Services													
2007	35.0	35.4	35.3	36.2	35.2	35.6	35.8	35.2	35.7	35.0	34.6	35.7	35.4
2008	34.1	35.0	35.7	34.8	35.0	35.9	34.8	35.2	34.7	34.4	35.5	33.9	34.9
2009	34.0	34.8	34.5	34.1	34.2	34.5	34.2	35.0	33.6	33.8	34.5	33.5	34.2
Education and Health Services													
2007	32.1	33.7	32.3	33.2	33.1	32.7	34.0	33.0	34.0	32.1	31.8	32.7	32.9
2008	31.9	31.9	32.6	32.4	31.9	33.2	32.0	32.0	32.2	31.4	32.3	31.0	32.1
2009	31.1	31.9	31.9	31.3	31.3	31.5	31.6	32.8	31.8	31.6	32.6	31.9	31.8
Leisure and Hospitality													
2007	25.0	26.1	26.2	27.1	26.3	26.3	27.7	27.2	27.2	26.1	25.8	26.4	26.5
2008	24.3	25.2	26.0	24.9	25.1	26.6	25.8	26.3	25.5	25.2	25.5	23.9	25.4
2009	23.9	25.2	24.8	24.0	24.6	24.6	24.7	26.1	24.5	24.4	25.3	24.1	24.7
Other Services													
2007	32.1	35.4	34.2	33.6	33.0	32.2	32.5	32.5	32.6	31.7	31.8	32.8	32.9
2008	31.0	31.7	32.7	30.8	31.0	31.8	31.7	31.4	30.6	30.7	31.9	30.0	31.3
2009	31.0	32.3	32.2	30.9	30.8	31.0	31.5	31.0	29.0	28.4	30.1	29.0	30.6

Average Hourly Earnings by Selected Industry: Washington, 2007–2009

(Dollars, not seasonally adjusted.)

Industry and year	January	February	March	April	May	June	July	August	September	October	November	December	Annual average
Total Private													
2007	24.69	24.13	24.10	24.24	23.67	23.73	24.02	23.75	24.20	24.41	24.53	24.87	24.19
2008	24.91	25.01	25.37	25.07	24.85	25.02	25.12	25.01	25.17	25.24	25.74	26.23	25.23
2009	26.23	26.48	26.48	26.25	26.10	25.94	26.49	26.06	26.05	26.26	26.66	26.82	26.33
Goods-Producing													
2007	27.68	26.76	27.16	27.10	27.13	27.13	27.78	27.17	27.34	27.41	27.59	28.08	27.36
2008	28.11	28.01	28.28	28.62	28.27	28.54	28.69	28.82	28.56	28.39	28.79	29.89	28.58
2009	29.69	30.09	30.99	30.69	30.55	30.27	30.14	30.00	30.43	30.20	31.48	31.67	30.50
Construction													
2007	26.73	25.89	26.34	26.12	26.21	26.45	28.29	26.96	27.40	27.62	27.64	28.47	27.03
2008	28.05	28.18	27.74	27.91	28.11	28.56	28.80	28.95	29.09	28.83	29.02	30.69	28.65
2009	30.08	30.10	31.73	30.90	30.38	30.31	30.28	30.20	30.88	30.53	30.65	31.09	30.56
Manufacturing													
2007	27.98	27.18	27.57	27.60	27.61	27.50	27.62	27.34	27.38	27.40	27.63	27.97	27.56
2008	28.23	28.00	28.59	29.04	28.44	28.64	28.74	28.86	28.27	28.19	28.76	29.64	28.62
2009	29.59	30.19	30.80	30.72	30.77	30.42	30.33	30.15	30.48	30.26	32.16	32.23	30.66
Trade, Transportation, and Utilities													
2007	21.33	20.21	20.33	20.13	18.76	18.97	19.12	18.85	19.17	19.23	19.27	19.76	19.58
2008	19.58	19.86	21.19	20.09	20.06	20.46	20.49	20.22	20.44	20.34	20.81	20.92	20.37
2009	21.16	21.62	20.93	20.70	20.58	20.46	20.71	20.79	20.53	20.57	20.80	21.15	20.83
Information													
2007	41.99	42.64	41.71	42.26	42.60	41.53	42.47	43.74	44.36	44.04	43.90	44.09	42.96
2008	43.98	44.06	44.68	43.94	43.95	44.64	44.69	44.23	46.49	46.08	48.31	48.72	45.32
2009	47.78	48.51	47.79	47.33	47.17	47.17	52.18	47.31	46.88	46.95	47.23	46.75	47.77
Financial Activities													
2007	24.50	24.53	24.33	24.85	23.17	23.33	23.56	23.41	23.84	23.64	23.97	24.99	24.02
2008	24.56	25.10	25.43	26.56	24.98	24.17	23.58	24.48	24.29	24.78	24.63	24.61	24.76
2009	24.69	25.55	26.55	25.80	26.11	25.88	26.14	26.69	26.15	26.81	26.63	26.63	26.13
Professional and Business Services													
2007	28.86	28.26	27.46	28.12	27.51	27.64	28.11	27.76	28.64	29.22	28.80	29.02	28.28
2008	29.23	29.77	29.67	29.25	28.95	29.09	28.88	28.98	29.39	29.05	29.81	30.23	29.35
2009	29.94	30.66	30.94	30.55	30.38	29.87	30.11	30.90	30.79	30.34	30.72	31.14	30.53
Education and Health Services													
2007	22.39	23.22	23.38	23.15	23.23	23.37	23.48	23.38	22.51	23.60	24.02	24.03	23.32
2008	23.97	23.60	23.68	23.30	23.54	23.41	24.35	24.03	24.21	25.09	24.47	24.86	24.04
2009	25.76	24.55	24.35	25.14	25.03	25.07	25.97	24.63	25.03	25.84	25.60	25.90	25.24
Leisure and Hospitality													
2007	14.11	14.17	13.93	14.02	13.81	13.72	13.53	13.57	15.40	15.30	15.24	15.58	14.36
2008	15.72	15.48	15.10	14.82	14.79	14.77	14.53	14.75	14.65	14.85	15.05	15.67	15.00
2009	15.12	15.01	15.09	14.96	14.87	14.79	14.60	14.62	14.52	14.73	14.80	15.29	14.86
Other Services													
2007	19.82	18.16	18.54	19.55	18.82	19.03	18.95	18.69	19.30	19.10	19.38	19.55	19.06
2008	19.27	19.25	19.30	19.45	19.44	19.90	19.73	19.23	19.48	20.04	20.90	22.10	19.83
2009	21.13	22.04	22.47	21.76	21.59	22.16	24.22	21.76	22.60	22.91	22.92	23.28	22.40

Average Weekly Earnings by Selected Industry: Washington, 2007–2009

(Dollars, not seasonally adjusted.)

Industry and year	January	February	March	April	May	June	July	August	September	October	November	December	Annual average
Total Private													
2007	841.93	851.79	841.09	867.79	830.82	832.92	864.72	840.75	876.04	851.91	851.19	882.89	853.91
2008	851.92	867.85	895.56	867.42	857.33	888.21	871.66	875.35	860.81	853.11	906.05	886.57	872.96
2009	886.57	924.15	924.15	897.75	892.62	889.74	905.96	919.92	885.70	892.84	925.10	901.15	905.75
Goods-Producing													
2007	1079.52	1081.10	1094.55	1102.97	1104.19	1109.62	1133.42	1113.97	1134.61	1129.29	1114.64	1151.28	1113.55
2008	1118.78	1137.21	1156.65	1167.70	1150.59	1172.99	1161.95	1178.74	1108.13	1084.50	1174.63	1216.52	1151.77
2009	1196.51	1221.65	1217.91	1212.26	1203.67	1204.75	1190.53	1203.00	1189.81	1198.94	1249.76	1222.46	1210.85
Construction													
2007	943.57	955.34	961.41	987.34	993.36	999.81	1094.82	1043.35	1071.34	1071.66	1025.44	1064.78	1019.03
2008	1012.61	1031.39	1037.48	1060.58	1076.61	1085.28	1097.28	1123.26	1134.51	1104.19	1105.66	1123.25	1082.97
2009	1106.94	1119.72	1135.93	1112.40	1099.76	1106.32	1093.11	1126.46	1080.80	1083.82	1066.62	1004.21	1097.10
Manufacturing													
2007	1138.79	1141.56	1160.70	1159.20	1159.62	1166.00	1154.52	1148.28	1166.39	1159.02	1157.70	1191.52	1157.52
2008	1168.72	1187.20	1215.08	1219.68	1185.95	1214.34	1195.58	1209.23	1082.74	1065.58	1205.04	1262.66	1184.87
2009	1239.82	1267.98	1256.64	1262.59	1261.57	1256.35	1246.56	1251.23	1255.78	1264.87	1337.86	1343.99	1269.32
Trade, Transportation, and Utilities													
2007	716.69	713.41	711.55	726.69	662.23	671.54	697.88	682.37	703.54	674.97	676.38	709.38	695.09
2008	677.47	689.14	745.89	703.15	696.08	724.28	715.10	719.83	715.40	699.70	736.67	711.28	710.91
2009	717.32	765.35	778.60	753.48	749.11	744.74	747.63	777.55	753.45	736.41	744.64	740.25	749.88
Information													
2007	1637.61	1658.70	1614.18	1770.69	1644.36	1611.36	1766.75	1697.11	1858.68	1691.14	1817.46	1838.55	1718.40
2008	1798.78	1793.24	1849.75	1682.90	1670.10	1857.02	1841.23	1698.43	1775.92	1769.47	1995.20	1836.74	1799.20
2009	1834.75	2022.87	1992.84	1817.47	1806.61	1806.61	2035.02	1968.10	1795.50	1802.88	1978.94	1799.88	1891.69
Financial Activities													
2007	891.80	875.72	861.28	924.42	808.63	816.55	869.36	821.69	894.00	829.76	843.74	919.63	862.32
2008	859.60	901.09	951.08	953.50	891.79	908.79	841.81	903.31	889.01	906.95	940.87	885.96	903.74
2009	906.12	973.46	1008.90	936.54	947.79	921.33	933.20	1000.88	912.64	954.44	998.63	945.37	953.75
Professional and Business Services													
2007	1010.10	1000.40	969.34	1017.94	968.35	983.98	1006.34	977.15	1022.45	1022.70	996.48	1036.01	1001.11
2008	996.74	1041.95	1059.22	1017.90	1013.25	1044.33	1005.02	1020.10	1019.83	999.32	1058.26	1024.80	1024.32
2009	1017.96	1066.97	1067.43	1041.76	1039.00	1030.52	1029.76	1081.50	1034.54	1025.49	1059.84	1043.19	1044.13
Education and Health Services													
2007	718.72	782.51	755.17	768.58	768.91	764.20	798.32	771.54	765.34	757.56	763.84	785.78	767.23
2008	764.64	752.84	771.97	754.92	750.93	777.21	779.20	768.96	779.56	787.83	790.38	770.66	771.68
2009	801.14	783.15	776.77	786.88	783.44	789.71	820.65	807.86	795.95	816.54	834.56	826.21	802.63
Leisure and Hospitality													
2007	352.75	369.84	364.97	379.94	363.20	360.84	374.78	369.10	418.88	399.33	393.19	411.31	380.54
2008	382.00	390.10	392.60	369.02	371.23	392.88	374.87	387.93	373.58	374.22	383.78	374.51	381.00
2009	361.37	378.25	374.23	359.04	365.80	363.83	360.62	381.58	355.74	359.41	374.44	368.49	367.04
Other Services													
2007	636.22	642.86	634.07	656.88	621.06	612.77	615.88	607.43	629.18	605.47	616.28	641.24	627.07
2008	597.37	610.23	631.11	599.06	602.64	632.82	625.44	603.82	596.09	615.23	666.71	663.00	620.68
2009	655.03	711.89	723.53	672.38	664.97	686.96	762.93	674.56	655.40	650.64	689.89	675.12	685.44

WEST VIRGINIA
At a Glance

Population:
 1990 census: 1,793,477
 2000 census: 1,808,344
 2009 estimate: 1,819,777

Percent change in population:
 1990–2000: 0.8%
 2000–2009: 0.6%

Percent change in total nonfarm employment:
 1990–2009: 18.1%
 2008–2009: -2.3%

Industry with the largest growth in employment, 1990–2009 (thousands):
 Education and Health Services, 48.5

Industry with the largest decline or smallest growth in employment, 1990–2009 (thousands):
 Manufacturing, -31.3

Civilian labor force:
 1990: 756,306
 2000: 808,861
 2009: 797,943

Unemployment rate and rank among states (lowest to highest):
 1990: 8.6%, 51st
 2000: 5.5%, 48th
 2009: 7.9%, 20th

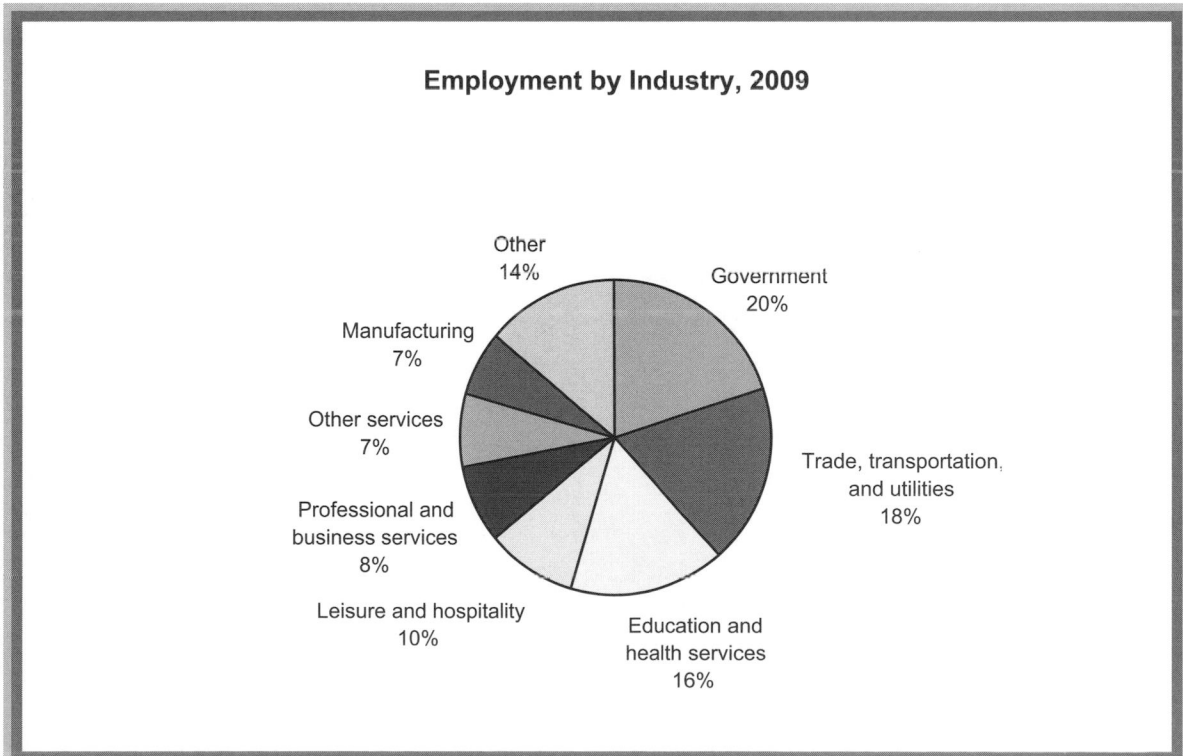

Employment by Industry, 2009

Other 14%
Government 20%
Manufacturing 7%
Other services 7%
Professional and business services 8%
Leisure and hospitality 10%
Education and health services 16%
Trade, transportation, and utilities 18%

Employment by Industry: West Virginia, Selected Years, 1990–2009

(Numbers in thousands, not seasonally adjusted.)

Industry and year	January	February	March	April	May	June	July	August	September	October	November	December	Annual average
Total Nonfarm													
1990	610.5	611.6	620.9	626.4	645.4	637.6	638.2	630.7	633.9	636.3	634.4	634.2	630.0
2000	714.1	714.1	728.6	733.1	751.5	741.1	742.1	733.8	739.8	741.7	744.9	744.8	735.8
2001	719.0	721.9	730.5	735.2	739.6	742.1	734.8	737.8	737.8	740.3	742.2	741.9	735.2
2002	717.2	719.9	727.5	731.5	747.3	737.1	733.8	735.4	735.6	735.9	738.2	737.2	733.1
2003	714.4	711.1	719.6	726.9	731.8	732.7	728.5	730.1	730.5	734.7	733.2	737.3	727.6
2004	716.2	717.4	728.0	736.8	742.1	741.2	739.3	739.9	742.1	746.2	745.9	747.3	736.9
2005	727.1	728.5	734.9	745.1	751.4	752.7	748.5	750.5	753.7	751.0	756.2	758.4	746.5
2006	738.2	741.3	750.4	754.3	759.3	762.5	752.8	756.8	761.6	762.1	766.4	766.1	756.0
2007	740.5	741.5	752.0	755.9	761.8	764.0	755.7	760.2	764.3	765.9	769.2	768.6	758.3
2008	746.7	750.6	754.9	760.4	766.7	763.3	761.4	763.3	768.7	770.4	770.0	767.7	762.0
2009	740.4	740.8	744.8	746.3	751.1	753.1	739.4	741.1	743.2	744.6	744.6	739.7	744.1
Total Private													
1990	485.7	485.5	493.6	499.3	505.3	509.9	507.9	511.4	511.4	508.5	506.2	506.2	502.6
2000	574.9	574.0	583.7	589.6	594.1	599.1	597.1	595.6	600.7	599.9	601.7	601.7	592.7
2001	581.0	581.3	587.7	592.6	597.3	601.2	596.6	599.4	598.8	597.9	598.5	598.2	594.2
2002	578.1	578.9	583.8	588.1	592.8	594.9	596.0	597.0	595.0	592.6	593.1	592.3	590.2
2003	573.6	568.8	575.6	581.9	586.7	590.5	589.7	591.0	590.8	591.2	588.5	592.5	585.1
2004	575.8	575.4	583.3	591.6	597.1	597.9	599.3	600.0	600.3	600.4	600.5	602.2	593.7
2005	584.6	584.9	589.7	599.5	605.6	609.4	609.0	611.0	611.1	607.5	609.9	611.8	602.8
2006	596.9	596.5	603.9	607.9	612.8	618.9	613.6	615.8	617.5	615.1	618.5	618.1	611.3
2007	598.1	595.7	604.6	608.7	613.7	619.6	615.8	619.1	619.7	618.9	621.3	620.9	613.0
2008	603.4	604.1	607.0	612.3	616.3	618.8	619.2	620.1	621.4	620.6	619.6	617.2	615.0
2009	595.1	591.9	593.8	595.8	598.4	598.0	593.8	594.7	594.7	593.8	593.0	588.6	594.3
Goods-Producing													
1990	138.2	138.3	142.0	143.2	145.5	147.3	146.9	148.2	148.0	146.8	144.0	142.4	144.2
2000	127.2	125.6	129.1	130.9	132.2	132.9	133.0	132.5	134.0	133.8	133.3	130.4	131.2
2001	125.0	125.1	127.6	129.9	131.2	132.4	132.0	132.9	133.2	133.8	133.0	131.1	130.6
2002	123.8	123.5	123.9	126.0	126.2	127.0	126.7	127.2	127.0	125.6	124.4	121.3	125.2
2003	116.0	113.6	116.3	118.4	119.8	121.1	121.5	121.1	121.4	121.3	120.6	118.9	119.2
2004	114.5	114.2	117.0	121.6	123.7	123.3	124.1	124.3	124.2	124.2	123.3	122.3	121.4
2005	118.3	118.8	119.9	123.4	125.6	127.3	127.1	127.9	129.0	128.7	128.1	126.8	125.1
2006	122.7	122.7	125.5	128.1	129.9	131.6	130.1	130.5	130.5	130.2	130.0	129.2	128.4
2007	123.4	121.0	124.3	125.9	127.3	129.4	128.6	128.7	128.2	128.4	127.8	125.5	126.5
2008	120.9	119.8	121.1	124.9	126.3	127.7	128.5	129.4	130.4	132.0	130.4	127.4	126.6
2009	118.9	116.8	116.8	116.4	116.0	114.3	112.7	112.9	112.2	112.7	112.9	110.8	114.5
Mining and Logging													
1990	33.7	33.6	33.8	33.7	34.0	34.5	34.2	34.1	34.1	34.0	34.3	34.2	34.0
2000	21.4	21.0	21.0	21.1	21.3	21.0	21.2	21.4	21.7	21.8	21.8	21.8	21.4
2001	21.8	21.8	22.1	22.6	23.0	23.8	24.2	24.2	24.3	24.6	24.8	24.9	23.5
2002	24.4	24.1	23.6	23.3	22.9	22.9	22.6	22.8	22.8	22.7	22.9	22.5	23.1
2003	22.1	21.6	22.1	22.1	22.0	22.1	22.1	21.7	21.8	21.8	22.0	22.2	22.0
2004	22.4	22.1	22.5	23.4	23.9	24.1	24.2	24.2	24.5	24.6	24.6	24.7	23.8
2005	24.4	24.7	25.0	25.4	26.0	26.2	26.2	26.4	26.7	26.8	27.2	27.4	26.0
2006	27.2	27.4	27.7	27.8	27.9	28.3	28.3	28.2	28.3	28.0	28.3	28.4	28.0
2007	28.1	27.9	27.9	28.2	28.2	28.9	28.9	29.2	28.9	28.9	29.1	29.1	28.6
2008	28.7	28.8	29.2	29.8	30.5	31.1	31.3	31.7	32.5	33.3	33.4	33.4	31.1
2009	32.7	32.0	31.8	30.9	29.9	29.3	28.4	28.4	28.3	28.0	27.8	28.1	29.6
Construction													
1990	23.3	23.3	26.1	27.1	28.8	29.2	29.9	31.4	31.5	30.8	29.5	27.4	28.2
2000	28.9	28.1	31.6	33.9	35.2	35.5	35.7	35.5	36.8	36.8	36.4	33.7	34.0
2001	29.3	29.7	32.1	34.1	35.1	35.6	35.6	37.0	37.8	38.7	37.9	35.8	34.8
2002	29.7	30.0	31.0	33.4	34.0	34.9	35.4	35.8	35.7	35.2	34.3	31.8	33.4
2003	28.4	27.1	29.3	31.3	32.9	34.1	34.6	34.9	35.3	35.5	34.9	33.6	32.7
2004	29.1	29.2	31.7	34.7	36.0	36.2	36.8	37.0	36.6	36.9	36.2	34.9	34.6
2005	31.9	32.2	33.0	35.9	37.2	38.3	38.3	38.9	39.6	39.8	39.1	37.5	36.8
2006	34.3	34.0	36.2	39.1	40.8	42.0	40.8	41.3	41.2	41.8	41.3	40.3	39.4
2007	36.2	34.2	37.2	38.7	39.9	40.8	40.2	40.3	40.2	40.9	40.3	38.3	38.9
2008	34.9	34.2	35.3	38.2	39.0	39.6	40.4	41.0	41.6	42.5	41.5	38.7	38.9
2009	32.6	32.6	33.9	33.8	35.1	34.6	34.8	34.5	34.2	35.1	35.2	33.3	34.1
Manufacturing													
1990	81.2	81.4	82.1	82.4	82.7	83.6	82.8	82.7	82.4	82.0	80.2	80.8	82.0
2000	76.9	76.5	76.5	75.9	75.7	76.4	76.1	75.6	75.5	75.2	75.1	74.9	75.9
2001	73.9	73.6	73.4	73.2	73.1	73.0	72.2	71.7	71.1	70.5	70.3	70.4	72.2
2002	69.7	69.4	69.3	69.3	69.3	69.2	68.7	68.6	68.5	67.7	67.2	67.0	68.7
2003	65.5	64.9	64.9	65.0	64.9	64.9	64.8	64.5	64.3	64.0	63.7	63.1	64.5
2004	63.0	62.9	62.8	63.5	63.8	63.0	63.1	63.1	63.1	62.7	62.5	62.7	63.0
2005	62.0	61.9	61.9	62.1	62.4	62.8	62.6	62.6	62.7	62.1	61.8	61.9	62.2
2006	61.2	61.3	61.6	61.2	61.2	61.3	61.0	61.0	61.0	60.4	60.4	60.5	61.0
2007	59.1	58.9	59.2	59.0	59.2	59.7	59.5	59.2	59.1	58.6	58.4	58.1	59.0
2008	57.3	56.8	56.6	56.9	56.8	57.0	56.8	56.7	56.3	56.2	55.5	55.3	56.5
2009	53.6	52.2	51.1	51.7	51.0	50.4	49.5	50.0	49.7	49.6	49.9	49.4	50.7

Employment by Industry: West Virginia, Selected Years, 1990–2009—*Continued*

(Numbers in thousands, not seasonally adjusted.)

Industry and year	January	February	March	April	May	June	July	August	September	October	November	December	Annual average
Service-Providing													
1990	472.3	473.3	478.9	483.2	499.9	490.3	491.3	482.5	485.9	489.5	490.4	491.8	485.8
2000	586.9	588.5	599.5	602.2	619.3	608.2	609.1	601.3	605.8	607.9	611.6	614.4	604.6
2001	594.0	596.8	602.9	605.3	608.4	609.7	602.8	604.9	604.6	606.5	609.2	610.8	604.6
2002	593.4	596.4	603.6	605.5	621.1	610.1	607.1	608.2	608.6	610.3	613.8	615.9	607.8
2003	598.4	597.5	603.3	608.5	612.0	611.6	607.0	609.0	609.1	613.4	612.6	618.4	608.4
2004	601.7	603.2	611.0	615.2	618.4	617.9	615.2	615.6	617.9	622.0	622.6	625.0	615.5
2005	608.8	609.7	615.0	621.7	625.8	625.4	621.4	622.6	624.7	622.3	628.1	621.4	621.4
2006	615.5	618.6	624.9	626.2	629.4	630.9	622.7	626.3	631.1	631.9	636.4	636.9	627.6
2007	617.1	620.5	627.7	630.0	634.5	634.6	627.1	631.5	636.1	637.5	641.4	643.1	631.8
2008	625.8	630.8	633.8	635.5	640.4	635.6	632.9	633.9	638.3	638.4	639.6	640.3	635.4
2009	621.5	624.0	628.0	629.9	635.1	638.8	626.7	628.2	631.0	631.9	631.7	628.9	629.6
Trade, Transportation, and Utilities													
1990	133.4	132.0	133.0	134.0	135.3	136.3	135.9	136.8	136.8	136.3	138.0	139.1	135.6
2000	142.6	141.3	142.6	142.9	144.3	145.5	144.9	145.4	145.1	145.0	147.9	148.8	144.7
2001	140.1	138.4	139.0	139.5	140.5	141.3	139.6	140.0	139.5	139.1	141.3	142.1	140.0
2002	136.1	134.9	135.9	136.2	137.4	137.7	137.1	136.9	136.2	136.6	138.6	139.7	136.9
2003	133.5	131.7	132.9	134.3	135.5	136.1	135.8	136.3	136.2	136.8	136.7	140.2	135.5
2004	134.7	133.3	134.2	135.3	136.5	137.0	137.4	137.9	138.0	139.0	141.4	142.3	137.3
2005	136.9	136.1	136.7	138.1	139.6	139.7	139.6	139.8	139.9	140.3	143.2	144.6	139.5
2006	139.0	138.1	139.6	140.3	141.1	142.1	141.2	141.6	142.2	143.2	146.5	147.2	141.8
2007	141.3	140.1	141.6	141.4	142.6	143.3	142.7	143.4	143.6	144.4	147.2	147.8	143.3
2008	141.7	140.8	141.5	140.9	141.4	141.9	141.7	141.5	141.5	141.0	142.6	143.3	141.7
2009	136.5	134.6	134.6	135.0	135.9	136.4	135.6	135.8	136.1	136.1	137.5	137.2	135.9
Wholesale Trade													
1990	23.6	23.6	23.8	23.9	23.9	24.1	24.2	24.2	24.1	24.2	24.1	24.0	24.0
2000	23.7	23.8	24.0	24.0	24.1	24.1	24.1	24.2	24.3	24.0	24.2	24.1	24.1
2001	23.7	23.8	24.0	24.2	24.2	24.5	24.1	23.9	23.9	23.7	23.6	23.7	23.9
2002	23.0	23.2	23.4	23.5	23.5	23.4	23.3	23.2	23.1	23.0	23.0	23.0	23.2
2003	22.4	22.3	22.6	22.7	22.9	23.0	22.9	22.9	22.8	22.8	22.8	22.8	22.7
2004	22.7	22.8	23.0	23.2	23.2	23.2	23.2	23.1	23.3	23.5	23.6	23.7	23.2
2005	23.6	23.6	23.8	24.1	24.3	24.4	24.4	24.3	24.3	24.3	24.4	24.6	24.2
2006	24.3	24.3	24.5	24.7	24.8	25.3	24.9	25.0	25.1	25.2	25.5	25.6	24.9
2007	24.8	24.7	24.9	24.8	24.8	24.9	25.0	25.1	25.2	25.5	25.6	25.7	25.1
2008	24.5	24.5	24.6	24.6	24.8	24.8	24.6	24.6	24.7	24.5	24.4	24.4	24.6
2009	23.8	23.5	23.5	23.4	23.5	23.4	23.3	23.2	23.1	23.2	23.1	23.3	23.4
Retail Trade													
1990	81.5	80.1	80.5	81.1	82.0	82.5	82.0	82.8	83.0	82.2	84.1	85.4	82.3
2000	91.7	90.4	91.2	91.7	92.8	93.7	93.2	93.7	93.2	93.6	96.5	97.7	93.3
2001	90.3	88.4	88.8	88.9	89.7	90.0	89.0	89.6	89.2	89.0	91.4	92.1	89.7
2002	87.2	86.0	86.9	87.1	88.1	88.3	88.2	88.1	87.8	88.2	90.4	91.5	88.2
2003	86.0	84.5	85.3	86.6	87.4	87.9	87.8	88.2	88.2	89.0	89.0	92.5	87.7
2004	87.4	85.9	86.4	87.0	88.1	88.4	88.7	89.1	88.9	89.6	92.0	92.7	88.7
2005	88.0	87.0	87.3	88.3	89.4	89.2	89.2	89.3	89.3	89.7	92.5	93.5	89.4
2006	88.8	87.9	89.0	89.2	89.7	90.0	89.7	89.9	90.4	91.3	94.2	94.6	90.4
2007	90.0	89.0	90.2	89.9	90.8	91.2	90.7	91.2	91.2	91.9	94.5	94.9	91.3
2008	90.4	89.4	90.1	89.1	89.3	89.6	89.6	89.4	89.3	89.1	90.9	91.5	89.8
2009	86.4	84.8	85.0	85.6	86.4	87.0	86.5	86.8	87.1	87.0	88.5	88.6	86.6
Transportation and Utilities													
1990	28.3	28.3	28.7	29.0	29.4	29.7	29.7	29.8	29.7	29.9	29.8	29.7	29.3
2000	27.2	27.1	27.4	27.2	27.4	27.7	27.6	27.5	27.6	27.4	27.2	27.0	27.4
2001	26.1	26.2	26.2	26.4	26.6	26.8	26.5	26.5	26.4	26.4	26.3	26.3	26.3
2002	25.9	25.7	25.6	25.6	25.8	26.0	25.6	25.6	25.3	25.4	25.2	25.2	25.6
2003	25.1	24.9	25.0	25.0	25.2	25.2	25.1	25.2	25.2	25.0	24.9	24.9	25.1
2004	24.6	24.6	24.8	25.1	25.2	25.4	25.5	25.7	25.8	25.9	25.8	25.9	25.4
2005	25.3	25.5	25.6	25.7	25.9	26.1	26.0	26.2	26.3	26.3	26.3	26.5	26.0
2006	25.9	25.9	26.1	26.4	26.6	26.8	26.6	26.7	26.7	26.7	26.8	27.0	26.5
2007	26.5	26.4	26.5	26.7	27.0	27.2	27.0	27.1	27.2	27.0	27.1	27.2	26.9
2008	26.8	26.9	26.8	27.2	27.3	27.5	27.5	27.5	27.5	27.4	27.3	27.4	27.3
2009	26.3	26.3	26.1	26.0	26.0	26.0	25.8	25.8	25.9	25.9	25.9	25.3	25.9
Information													
1990	11.7	11.8	11.8	12.1	12.0	12.1	12.1	12.0	12.0	12.0	12.0	12.2	12.0
2000	14.0	14.1	14.1	14.2	14.2	14.3	14.4	11.7	14.3	14.3	14.5	14.7	14.1
2001	14.2	14.3	14.3	14.2	14.2	14.3	14.1	14.1	13.9	13.8	13.8	13.8	14.0
2002	13.4	13.4	13.4	13.2	13.3	13.3	13.3	13.3	13.2	13.2	13.4	13.4	13.3
2003	12.9	12.8	12.8	12.7	12.6	12.6	12.6	12.5	12.3	12.2	12.2	12.0	12.5
2004	11.8	11.7	12.0	11.9	11.9	12.0	12.0	12.0	11.8	11.7	11.8	11.8	11.9
2005	11.6	11.4	11.5	11.5	11.7	11.8	11.9	12.0	11.8	11.8	11.9	12.0	11.7
2006	11.7	11.5	11.5	11.4	11.5	11.6	11.5	11.6	11.5	11.5	11.4	11.4	11.5
2007	11.3	11.3	11.2	11.3	11.4	11.5	11.6	11.5	11.5	11.4	11.4	11.5	11.4
2008	11.3	11.3	11.2	11.2	11.2	11.2	11.2	11.2	11.1	11.1	11.0	10.9	11.2
2009	10.9	10.7	10.7	10.6	10.5	10.4	10.3	10.2	10.3	10.2	10.1	10.2	10.4

Employment by Industry: West Virginia, Selected Years, 1990–2009—*Continued*

(Numbers in thousands, not seasonally adjusted.)

Industry and year	January	February	March	April	May	June	July	August	September	October	November	December	Annual average
Financial Activities													
1990	26.0	25.9	26.0	26.0	26.2	26.4	26.2	26.3	26.4	26.2	26.1	26.2	26.2
2000	30.7	30.8	31.2	31.1	31.3	31.6	31.3	31.4	31.1	31.1	31.2	31.6	31.2
2001	30.6	30.5	30.6	30.7	30.8	30.9	30.8	30.6	30.5	30.6	30.5	30.7	30.6
2002	30.2	30.4	30.7	30.8	31.0	31.3	31.5	31.7	31.5	31.6	31.6	31.8	31.2
2003	30.8	30.8	30.8	30.9	30.7	31.0	30.6	30.6	30.7	30.7	30.7	30.8	30.8
2004	30.3	30.1	30.4	30.5	30.5	30.7	30.7	30.4	30.1	30.1	29.9	30.0	30.3
2005	29.6	29.5	29.5	29.7	29.7	29.8	29.8	29.8	29.7	29.6	29.7	29.7	29.7
2006	29.9	29.9	30.0	30.1	30.3	30.7	30.1	30.1	30.0	30.0	29.9	30.0	30.1
2007	29.5	29.5	29.6	29.8	30.0	30.2	30.0	30.1	30.0	29.9	29.9	30.1	29.9
2008	29.8	29.8	29.7	29.9	29.8	29.9	29.9	29.7	29.6	29.6	29.6	29.6	29.7
2009	28.9	28.7	28.7	28.4	28.5	28.7	28.3	28.3	28.0	27.9	27.9	28.0	28.4
Professional and Business Services													
1990	31.0	31.3	32.2	32.9	33.2	33.7	32.9	33.1	33.1	33.0	33.0	33.0	32.7
2000	52.9	53.6	54.8	56.5	56.1	57.2	56.6	56.5	56.8	56.3	56.6	57.0	55.9
2001	56.1	56.7	57.4	57.4	57.6	58.3	57.7	57.9	57.2	57.3	57.2	57.4	57.3
2002	54.5	54.8	55.6	56.5	56.6	57.4	57.8	58.4	57.7	56.8	57.0	57.5	56.7
2003	55.5	55.4	55.8	56.3	56.3	57.0	56.7	57.1	57.0	57.5	57.4	58.7	56.7
2004	57.3	57.2	57.6	57.7	57.6	58.4	59.0	59.2	59.0	59.1	58.5	60.1	58.4
2005	57.6	57.1	57.5	58.6	58.4	59.1	59.2	59.7	59.2	59.3	59.8	60.8	58.9
2006	59.4	59.5	59.7	60.0	59.5	60.6	60.2	60.3	60.2	59.4	59.8	59.6	59.9
2007	59.1	58.8	59.7	60.7	60.7	61.1	60.9	61.4	61.2	61.1	61.4	62.4	60.7
2008	60.2	60.4	60.4	61.4	61.3	61.5	61.4	61.3	60.8	61.1	61.1	61.3	61.0
2009	60.0	59.9	59.6	59.9	59.6	59.6	59.1	59.2	59.1	59.9	59.9	58.8	59.6
Education and Health Services													
1990	67.4	68.3	69.3	69.5	69.8	69.4	69.5	69.7	70.6	71.7	72.1	72.5	70.0
2000	97.5	98.6	99.6	100.1	99.9	99.1	98.1	98.6	100.1	101.7	102.0	102.6	99.8
2001	100.8	101.8	102.7	102.8	102.9	102.4	101.5	102.3	103.9	105.1	105.9	106.7	103.2
2002	105.4	106.7	107.4	106.9	107.3	106.0	106.3	105.9	107.0	108.5	109.3	109.7	107.2
2003	108.4	108.2	108.7	108.6	109.0	107.9	107.0	107.6	108.6	110.3	110.5	110.8	108.8
2004	108.5	110.0	111.0	110.9	111.0	109.9	109.5	109.7	111.2	112.4	112.8	112.7	110.8
2005	110.9	112.1	112.6	113.0	113.1	113.1	112.8	113.2	114.1	113.3	113.9	114.3	113.0
2006	112.7	113.1	113.6	113.4	113.3	112.1	111.1	111.5	113.2	113.6	114.1	114.1	113.0
2007	111.3	112.7	113.5	113.1	113.6	113.5	112.6	113.5	115.5	116.2	116.8	116.4	114.1
2008	114.9	116.6	116.5	116.4	116.4	115.8	115.3	115.6	117.4	117.1	117.6	117.4	116.4
2009	115.5	117.0	117.7	118.3	118.5	118.1	117.5	118.1	119.8	120.5	120.9	120.3	118.5
Leisure and Hospitality													
1990	44.2	44.3	45.5	47.8	49.2	50.5	50.2	51.0	50.0	48.1	46.6	46.3	47.8
2000	58.3	57.8	59.4	61.0	62.8	64.7	64.8	65.4	64.8	62.9	61.2	61.2	62.0
2001	59.2	59.4	60.8	62.6	64.4	65.8	65.6	66.4	65.3	63.1	61.8	61.2	62.9
2002	59.8	60.2	61.7	63.0	65.3	66.6	67.9	68.2	67.1	65.2	63.8	63.7	64.4
2003	61.8	61.7	63.3	65.4	67.6	69.3	70.0	70.4	68.9	66.9	65.4	66.0	66.4
2004	64.1	64.3	65.8	67.8	69.6	70.8	71.2	71.5	70.3	68.3	67.1	67.4	68.2
2005	65.1	65.3	66.6	68.5	70.6	72.0	72.7	73.0	71.7	69.2	68.1	68.3	69.3
2006	66.9	67.0	68.7	69.3	71.7	74.1	73.8	74.4	73.7	70.9	70.5	70.5	71.0
2007	67.0	66.9	69.0	70.9	72.6	74.6	74.0	75.3	74.3	72.1	71.3	71.9	71.7
2008	69.3	69.9	70.9	72.2	74.1	75.0	75.6	76.0	75.2	73.2	71.6	71.6	72.9
2009	68.8	68.7	70.3	71.3	73.4	74.5	74.6	74.9	73.7	71.3	68.9	68.5	71.6
Other Services													
1990	33.8	33.6	33.8	33.8	34.1	34.2	34.2	34.3	34.5	34.4	34.4	34.5	34.1
2000	51.7	52.2	52.9	52.9	53.3	53.8	54.0	54.1	54.5	54.8	55.0	55.4	53.7
2001	55.0	55.1	55.3	55.5	55.7	55.8	55.3	55.2	55.3	55.1	55.0	55.2	55.2
2002	54.9	55.0	55.2	55.5	55.7	55.6	55.4	55.4	55.3	55.1	55.0	55.2	55.3
2003	54.7	54.6	55.0	55.3	55.2	55.5	55.5	55.4	55.7	55.5	55.0	55.1	55.2
2004	54.6	54.6	55.3	55.9	56.3	55.8	55.4	55.0	55.7	55.6	55.7	55.6	55.5
2005	54.6	54.6	55.4	56.7	56.9	56.6	55.9	55.6	55.7	55.3	55.2	55.3	55.7
2006	54.6	54.7	55.3	55.3	55.5	56.1	55.6	55.8	56.2	56.3	56.3	56.1	55.7
2007	55.2	55.4	55.7	55.6	55.5	56.0	55.4	55.2	55.4	55.4	55.5	55.3	55.5
2008	55.3	55.5	55.7	55.4	55.8	55.8	55.6	55.4	55.4	55.5	55.7	55.7	55.6
2009	55.6	55.5	55.4	55.9	56.0	56.0	55.7	55.3	55.5	55.2	54.9	54.8	55.5
Government													
1990	124.8	126.1	127.3	127.1	140.1	127.7	130.3	119.3	122.5	127.8	128.2	128.0	127.4
2000	139.2	140.1	144.9	143.5	157.4	142.0	145.0	138.2	139.1	141.8	143.2	143.1	143.1
2001	138.0	140.6	142.8	142.6	142.3	140.9	138.2	138.4	139.0	142.4	143.7	143.7	141.0
2002	139.1	141.0	143.7	143.4	154.5	142.2	137.8	138.4	140.6	143.3	145.1	144.9	142.8
2003	140.8	142.3	144.0	145.0	145.1	142.2	138.8	139.1	139.7	143.5	144.7	144.8	142.5
2004	140.4	142.0	144.7	145.2	145.0	143.3	140.0	139.9	141.8	145.8	145.4	145.1	143.2
2005	142.5	143.6	145.2	145.6	145.8	143.3	139.5	139.5	142.6	143.5	146.3	143.7	143.7
2006	141.3	144.8	146.5	146.4	146.5	143.6	139.2	141.0	144.1	147.0	147.9	148.0	144.7
2007	142.4	145.8	147.4	147.2	148.1	144.4	139.9	141.1	144.6	147.0	147.9	147.7	145.3
2008	143.3	146.5	147.9	148.1	150.4	144.5	142.2	143.2	147.3	149.8	150.4	150.5	147.0
2009	145.3	148.9	151.0	150.5	152.7	155.1	145.6	146.4	148.5	150.8	151.6	151.1	149.8

Average Weekly Hours by Selected Industry: West Virginia, 2007–2009

(Not seasonally adjusted.)

Industry and year	January	February	March	April	May	June	July	August	September	October	November	December	Annual average
Total Private													
2007	35.1	34.5	35.1	35.5	35.4	35.2	35.6	35.3	35.4	35.2	34.7	35.4	35.2
2008	35.0	34.8	35.2	35.0	35.1	35.9	35.6	35.7	35.2	35.5	35.0	34.5	35.2
2009	34.0	34.1	34.1	34.0	34.3	34.3	34.4	34.6	34.6	34.6	35.1	35.1	34.4
Goods-Producing													
2007	40.9	40.6	41.3	41.2	41.3	41.2	41.4	41.2	41.3	41.5	40.3	41.5	41.1
2008	40.9	40.3	40.8	41.2	40.3	42.1	41.7	42.1	41.7	41.8	41.5	40.8	41.3
2009	40.6	40.3	40.1	40.0	40.3	40.9	40.6	41.5	41.0	41.0	41.5	41.4	40.8
Mining and Logging													
2007	45.9	46.3	46.9	46.3	46.8	45.9	44.8	45.7	45.3	46.1	43.6	44.8	45.7
2008	45.6	45.9	46.2	46.9	45.5	46.5	44.9	45.3	45.6	46.5	46.7	46.1	46.0
2009	45.7	45.1	44.9	45.0	44.2	45.8	45.3	46.1	45.3	45.1	46.0	45.9	45.4
Construction													
2007	36.6	36.5	37.6	38.8	38.9	39.4	39.8	40.1	39.3	40.9	37.4	38.4	38.7
2008	36.6	34.8	36.7	37.6	36.6	38.9	39.1	40.1	40.5	40.4	38.8	36.3	38.1
2009	36.5	36.7	36.4	36.5	38.2	38.5	39.1	39.8	39.1	39.5	40.0	39.7	38.4
Manufacturing													
2007	41.1	40.2	40.9	40.3	40.3	40.2	40.8	39.8	40.7	39.6	40.7	41.8	40.5
2008	41.2	40.8	40.6	40.6	40.1	41.8	41.9	41.8	40.4	40.0	40.4	40.8	40.9
2009	40.1	39.7	39.5	39.5	39.6	39.7	39.0	40.2	39.9	39.7	39.9	39.9	39.7
Trade, Transportation, and Utilities													
2007	35.2	34.8	35.3	35.5	35.7	35.6	35.8	35.7	35.8	35.6	35.1	36.0	35.5
2008	35.2	34.0	34.4	34.3	34.0	34.8	34.5	34.6	34.8	34.6	35.1	34.8	34.6
2009	34.8	34.5	34.5	34.4	34.8	34.6	34.4	34.2	34.1	34.6	34.6	35.0	34.5
Financial Activities													
2007	35.6	35.3	35.0	35.6	35.7	35.1	35.5	34.3	35.5	33.7	32.9	34.8	34.9
2008	34.5	34.5	34.1	34.7	35.5	37.6	35.2	34.9	34.4	36.9	36.7	36.9	35.5
2009	35.3	35.4	35.3	35.4	35.9	35.9	35.9	36.0	35.9	36.0	36.1	35.3	35.7
Professional and Business Services													
2007	35.9	34.4	35.2	35.8	35.0	34.9	35.5	34.9	35.2	35.1	34.8	35.2	35.2
2008	34.2	34.8	35.5	34.8	34.2	35.4	35.2	35.8	35.2	36.2	35.5	35.1	35.2
2009	34.8	35.0	35.4	35.5	35.8	35.3	35.2	36.0	35.6	35.4	36.5	36.5	35.6
Education and Health Services													
2007	34.5	33.6	33.9	34.5	34.3	33.9	34.4	34.0	34.4	34.1	34.1	34.2	34.2
2008	34.6	34.7	34.8	34.5	34.9	34.9	34.7	34.5	34.2	34.5	34.6	34.1	34.6
2009	34.4	34.7	34.7	34.5	34.4	34.2	34.2	34.2	34.5	34.5	34.7	34.4	34.5
Leisure and Hospitality													
2007	26.8	26.9	27.8	27.8	27.7	28.2	28.3	27.7	27.1	26.6	26.1	26.0	27.3
2008	26.5	26.8	27.2	27.7	28.9	29.5	29.6	29.7	28.1	27.9	27.5	27.1	28.1
2009	26.7	27.1	27.0	27.3	27.8	28.2	28.5	27.9	27.6	27.2	27.2	26.7	27.5
Other Services													
2007	30.3	30.4	31.3	31.0	31.3	30.5	30.3	31.0	31.0	30.5	30.1	31.3	30.8
2008	30.6	31.3	31.8	31.4	32.5	32.6	33.1	34.0	32.1	33.4	33.2	32.2	32.4
2009	31.4	31.5	31.8	31.6	31.6	31.6	31.3	32.1	32.1	32.2	32.5	32.4	31.8

Average Hourly Earnings by Selected Industry: West Virginia, 2007–2009

(Dollars, not seasonally adjusted.)

Industry and year	January	February	March	April	May	June	July	August	September	October	November	December	Annual average
Total Private													
2007	17.15	16.80	16.73	16.95	16.84	16.82	16.98	16.96	17.00	17.07	17.37	17.83	17.04
2008	17.43	17.55	17.59	17.63	17.57	17.60	17.64	17.69	17.90	17.84	18.09	17.91	17.70
2009	18.19	18.10	18.13	18.17	17.90	17.86	17.96	18.01	18.12	18.14	18.23	18.28	18.09
Goods-Producing													
2007	21.37	21.26	21.15	21.39	21.18	21.30	21.36	21.43	21.35	21.39	21.99	21.98	21.43
2008	21.85	22.15	22.05	21.97	21.90	22.27	22.04	22.12	22.65	22.64	23.24	22.97	22.33
2009	22.96	22.83	23.02	23.07	22.75	22.81	22.88	22.93	22.85	22.81	23.00	22.86	22.90
Mining and Logging													
2007	23.15	22.97	23.01	22.84	22.68	23.10	23.13	23.98	23.37	23.65	24.93	24.44	23.43
2008	23.57	23.85	24.21	24.19	24.52	25.27	24.79	25.06	25.93	26.12	26.96	26.43	25.13
2009	26.10	26.01	26.26	26.41	26.47	26.26	26.16	27.00	27.03	26.90	26.99	26.59	26.50
Construction													
2007	19.83	19.98	20.03	20.38	20.19	20.57	20.67	19.76	20.12	20.14	20.50	20.55	20.23
2008	20.63	21.69	20.61	20.96	20.99	20.95	21.25	21.40	22.20	22.03	22.08	22.07	21.44
2009	22.18	22.21	23.02	23.10	22.55	22.49	22.89	22.97	22.76	22.93	23.15	22.71	22.76
Manufacturing													
2007	21.27	20.99	20.79	21.24	21.00	20.80	20.86	21.14	21.06	21.00	21.37	21.53	21.09
2008	21.56	21.42	21.60	21.26	20.87	21.31	20.95	20.83	20.85	20.71	21.48	21.16	21.17
2009	21.21	20.98	20.74	20.78	20.44	20.71	20.68	20.25	20.22	20.09	20.32	20.51	20.58
Trade, Transportation, and Utilities													
2007	14.27	13.96	14.04	14.35	14.00	13.88	14.15	14.09	14.09	13.95	14.18	14.18	14.10
2008	14.28	14.93	15.12	14.94	15.40	15.12	15.09	15.04	15.26	15.90	15.37	15.31	15.15
2009	15.40	15.36	15.45	15.43	15.12	15.11	15.09	15.24	15.30	15.37	15.28	15.29	15.29
Financial Activities													
2007	16.09	16.36	16.53	16.48	16.44	16.56	16.59	16.64	16.66	16.59	16.92	16.28	16.51
2008	16.66	16.69	16.68	17.07	16.82	16.62	17.23	16.86	16.71	16.35	16.72	16.92	16.78
2009	17.15	17.13	17.16	17.23	17.08	17.07	17.03	16.81	16.74	16.90	17.00	17.00	17.03
Professional and Business Services													
2007	19.62	20.06	19.50	19.88	20.17	19.81	20.18	20.10	20.64	20.44	20.64	21.66	20.23
2008	21.12	21.00	21.25	20.92	20.48	20.18	20.00	20.01	19.76	20.40	20.42	20.09	20.46
2009	19.89	20.08	20.04	20.18	19.99	19.90	19.92	19.76	19.58	19.49	19.40	19.44	19.80
Education and Health Services													
2007	16.78	17.02	17.07	17.17	17.21	17.30	17.46	17.25	17.15	17.30	17.48	18.27	17.29
2008	17.62	17.39	17.28	17.50	17.42	17.48	17.80	17.90	18.11	17.41	18.38	18.12	17.70
2009	18.22	18.52	18.41	18.39	18.44	18.37	18.42	18.21	18.48	18.59	18.66	18.87	18.47
Leisure and Hospitality													
2007	9.30	9.33	9.31	9.20	9.07	9.09	9.09	9.14	9.26	9.49	9.46	10.74	9.36
2008	9.63	9.67	9.72	9.59	9.56	9.45	9.52	9.65	9.88	10.02	10.12	10.30	9.75
2009	10.34	10.34	10.54	10.66	10.47	10.51	10.45	10.71	10.57	10.43	10.36	10.62	10.50
Other Services													
2007	14.89	14.95	14.70	14.85	14.58	14.98	14.68	14.88	15.18	15.31	16.12	15.83	15.08
2008	15.44	15.78	15.68	15.20	15.07	15.72	15.51	15.67	15.92	15.90	16.97	17.28	15.85
2009	16.84	16.88	17.00	16.93	16.54	16.54	16.36	16.58	16.54	16.54	16.69	16.64	16.67

Average Weekly Earnings by Selected Industry: West Virginia, 2007–2009

(Dollars, not seasonally adjusted.)

Industry and year	January	February	March	April	May	June	July	August	September	October	November	December	Annual average
Total Private													
2007	601.97	579.60	587.22	601.73	596.14	592.06	604.49	598.69	601.80	600.86	602.74	631.18	599.81
2008	610.05	610.74	619.17	617.05	616.71	631.84	627.98	631.53	630.08	633.32	633.15	617.90	623.04
2009	618.46	617.21	618.23	617.78	613.97	612.60	617.82	623.15	626.95	627.64	639.87	641.63	622.30
Goods-Producing													
2007	874.03	863.16	873.50	881.27	874.73	877.56	884.30	882.92	881.76	887.69	886.20	912.17	880.77
2008	893.67	892.65	899.64	905.16	882.57	937.57	919.07	931.25	944.51	946.35	964.46	937.18	922.23
2009	932.18	920.05	923.10	922.80	916.83	932.93	928.93	951.60	936.85	935.21	954.50	946.40	934.32
Mining and Logging													
2007	1062.59	1063.51	1079.17	1057.49	1061.42	1060.29	1036.22	1095.89	1058.66	1090.27	1086.95	1094.91	1070.75
2008	1074.79	1094.72	1118.50	1134.51	1115.66	1175.06	1113.07	1135.22	1182.41	1214.58	1259.03	1218.42	1155.98
2009	1192.77	1173.05	1179.07	1188.45	1169.97	1202.71	1185.05	1244.70	1224.46	1213.19	1241.54	1220.48	1203.10
Construction													
2007	725.78	729.27	753.13	790.74	785.39	810.46	822.67	792.38	790.72	823.73	766.70	789.12	782.90
2008	755.06	754.81	756.39	788.10	768.23	814.96	830.88	858.14	899.10	890.01	856.70	801.14	816.86
2009	809.57	815.11	837.93	843.15	861.41	865.87	895.00	914.21	889.92	905.74	926.00	901.59	873.98
Manufacturing													
2007	874.20	843.80	850.31	855.97	846.30	836.16	851.09	841.37	857.14	831.60	869.76	899.95	854.15
2008	888.27	873.94	876.96	863.16	836.89	890.76	877.81	870.69	842.34	828.40	867.79	863.33	865.85
2009	850.52	832.91	819.23	820.81	809.42	822.19	806.52	814.05	806.78	797.57	810.77	818.35	817.03
Trade, Transportation, and Utilities													
2007	502.30	485.81	495.61	509.43	499.80	494.13	506.57	503.01	504.42	496.62	497.72	510.48	500.55
2008	502.66	507.62	520.13	512.44	523.60	526.18	520.61	520.38	531.05	550.14	539.49	532.79	524.19
2009	535.92	529.92	533.03	530.79	526.18	522.81	519.10	521.21	521.73	531.80	528.69	535.15	527.51
Financial Activities													
2007	572.80	577.51	578.55	586.69	586.91	581.26	588.95	570.75	591.43	559.08	556.67	566.54	576.20
2008	574.77	575.81	568.79	592.33	597.11	624.91	606.50	588.41	574.82	603.32	613.62	624.35	595.69
2009	605.40	606.40	605.75	609.94	613.17	612.81	611.38	605.16	600.97	608.40	613.70	600.10	607.97
Professional and Business Services													
2007	704.36	690.06	686.40	711.70	705.95	691.37	716.39	701.49	726.53	717.44	718.27	762.43	712.10
2008	722.30	730.80	754.38	728.02	700.42	714.37	704.00	716.36	695.55	738.48	724.91	705.16	720.19
2009	692.17	702.80	709.42	716.39	715.64	702.47	701.18	711.36	697.05	689.95	708.10	709.56	704.88
Education and Health Services													
2007	578.91	571.87	578.67	592.37	590.30	586.47	600.62	586.50	589.96	589.93	596.07	624.83	591.32
2008	609.65	603.43	601.34	603.75	607.96	610.05	617.66	617.55	619.36	600.65	635.95	617.89	612.42
2009	626.77	642.64	638.83	634.46	634.34	628.25	629.96	622.78	637.56	641.36	647.50	649.13	637.22
Leisure and Hospitality													
2007	249.24	250.98	258.82	255.76	251.24	256.34	257.25	253.10	250.95	252.43	246.91	279.24	255.53
2008	255.20	259.16	264.38	265.64	276.28	278.78	281.79	286.61	277.63	279.56	278.30	279.13	273.98
2009	276.08	280.21	284.58	291.02	291.07	296.38	297.83	298.81	291.73	283.70	281.79	283.55	288.75
Other Services													
2007	451.17	454.48	460.11	460.35	456.35	456.89	444.80	461.28	470.58	466.96	485.21	495.48	464.46
2008	472.46	493.91	498.62	477.28	489.78	512.47	513.38	532.78	511.03	531.06	563.40	556.42	513.54
2009	528.78	531.72	540.60	534.99	522.66	522.66	512.07	532.22	530.93	532.59	542.43	539.14	530.11

WISCONSIN

At a Glance

Population:
  1990 census: 4,891,954
  2000 census: 5,363,675
  2009 estimate: 5,654,774

Percent change in population:
  1990–2000: 9.6%
  2000–2009: 5.4%

Percent change in total nonfarm employment:
  1990–2009: 19.9%
  2008–2009: -4.5%

Industry with the largest growth in employment, 1990–2009 (thousands):
  Education and Health Services, 176.6

Industry with the largest decline or smallest growth in employment, 1990–2009 (thousands):
  Manufacturing, -87.4

Civilian labor force:
  1990: 2,598,898
  2000: 2,996,091
  2009: 3,081,476

Unemployment rate and rank among states (lowest to highest):
  1990: 4.3%, 7th
  2000: 3.4%, 17th
  2009: 8.5%, 30th

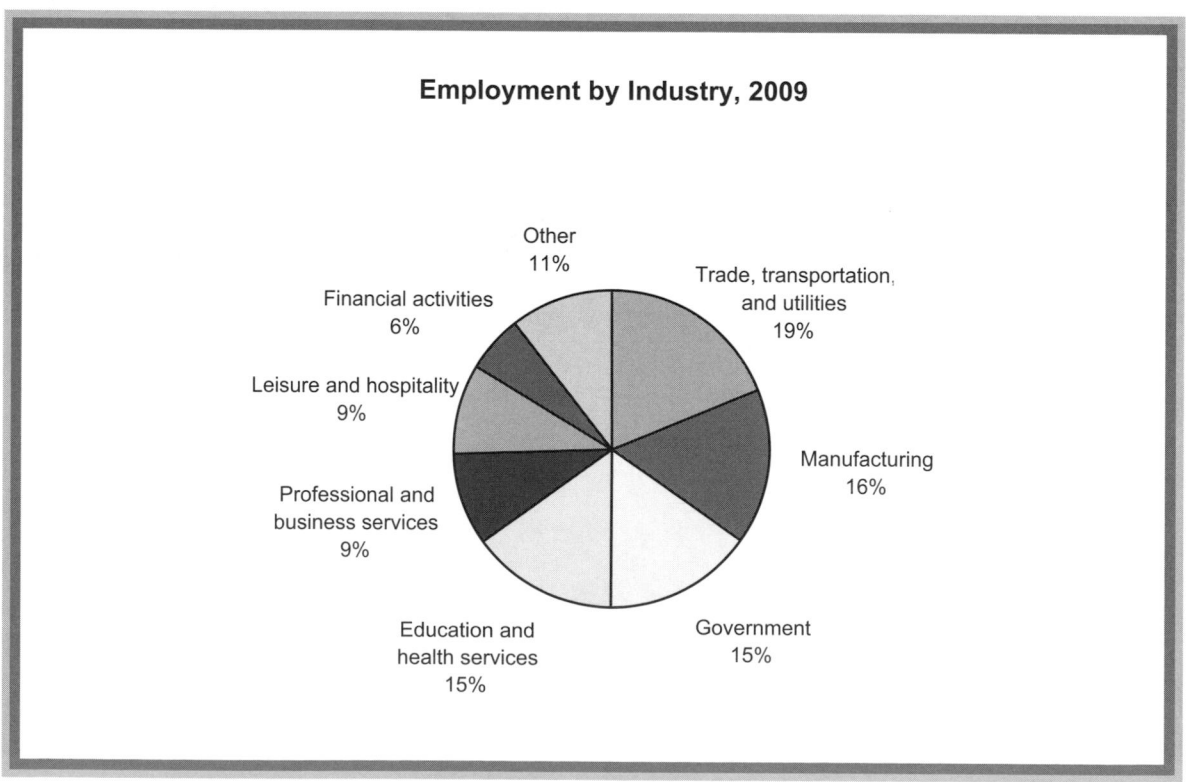

Employment by Industry, 2009

- Other 11%
- Trade, transportation, and utilities 19%
- Financial activities 6%
- Leisure and hospitality 9%
- Manufacturing 16%
- Professional and business services 9%
- Government 15%
- Education and health services 15%

Employment by Industry: Wisconsin, Selected Years, 1990–2009

(Numbers in thousands, not seasonally adjusted.)

Industry and year	January	February	March	April	May	June	July	August	September	October	November	December	Annual average
Total Nonfarm													
1990	2206.7	2220.8	2236.0	2268.6	2298.0	2333.7	2309.7	2315.8	2331.7	2329.5	2329.5	2317.9	2291.5
2000	2748.9	2759.7	2785.1	2820.3	2846.9	2885.5	2852.5	2858.5	2859.3	2864.1	2869.9	2854.7	2833.8
2001	2770.7	2776.5	2788.9	2813.6	2840.1	2861.6	2829.3	2829.1	2825.0	2820.8	2812.6	2798.4	2813.9
2002	2719.4	2717.6	2735.9	2766.1	2799.4	2823.1	2795.4	2800.5	2798.5	2814.2	2816.5	2801.8	2782.4
2003	2710.5	2718.4	2726.6	2761.5	2795.8	2818.2	2781.8	2783.9	2793.0	2810.3	2803.4	2800.1	2775.3
2004	2718.1	2727.3	2744.3	2783.9	2817.3	2847.8	2834.5	2838.9	2836.8	2847.6	2847.1	2841.5	2807.1
2005	2757.2	2768.8	2783.5	2830.7	2854.9	2880.4	2861.8	2864.1	2877.0	2874.1	2876.0	2876.3	2842.1
2006	2790.0	2793.9	2811.8	2851.6	2880.6	2917.0	2885.8	2887.0	2896.1	2895.1	2895.2	2893.1	2866.4
2007	2814.4	2810.0	2830.0	2862.4	2904.3	2942.8	2906.3	2907.7	2908.0	2909.2	2910.5	2906.9	2884.4
2008	2828.3	2824.0	2836.9	2865.5	2907.8	2929.0	2897.5	2896.4	2899.7	2899.9	2887.5	2865.1	2878.1
2009	2755.1	2742.1	2734.4	2748.4	2777.4	2787.3	2742.3	2737.0	2745.2	2754.0	2742.7	2712.9	2748.2
Total Private													
1990	1877.1	1876.0	1888.5	1913.4	1945.5	1988.9	1989.4	2001.1	1987.8	1978.2	1972.6	1964.8	1948.6
2000	2349.3	2350.9	2373.0	2401.6	2429.5	2472.2	2471.4	2480.1	2461.6	2454.1	2452.2	2442.6	2428.2
2001	2368.4	2358.8	2367.9	2388.5	2415.6	2445.5	2441.9	2445.1	2413.4	2396.8	2386.0	2374.1	2400.2
2002	2310.8	2296.1	2309.7	2337.9	2373.3	2409.8	2411.7	2420.4	2394.5	2387.5	2383.7	2375.6	2367.6
2003	2306.2	2293.5	2300.4	2332.6	2370.8	2397.9	2398.8	2404.0	2393.8	2389.9	2381.1	2379.9	2362.4
2004	2314.9	2307.0	2322.3	2361.2	2395.1	2433.2	2449.9	2457.1	2430.8	2426.9	2420.9	2420.0	2394.9
2005	2346.3	2344.2	2359.7	2403.5	2428.9	2466.1	2476.1	2482.6	2462.7	2451.0	2450.6	2449.3	2426.8
2006	2379.9	2374.2	2387.2	2424.1	2454.6	2498.4	2498.5	2503.7	2482.2	2473.7	2470.3	2467.6	2451.2
2007	2404.2	2393.2	2407.5	2435.4	2477.2	2520.7	2518.0	2522.9	2494.0	2485.4	2484.2	2478.1	2468.4
2008	2411.6	2401.8	2409.7	2435.9	2475.3	2506.8	2505.1	2509.4	2476.7	2467.4	2446.1	2429.1	2456.2
2009	2336.5	2310.8	2301.7	2308.4	2336.6	2360.4	2350.9	2352.3	2327.3	2317.3	2301.5	2277.1	2323.4
Goods-Producing													
1990	591.5	590.8	594.6	603.4	614.8	630.5	633.0	638.0	631.0	625.8	617.3	606.7	614.8
2000	701.3	700.7	708.0	716.5	724.4	742.7	741.7	742.5	734.2	729.5	722.6	711.8	723.0
2001	689.5	682.5	683.2	687.1	694.4	706.8	706.1	705.6	694.6	685.4	674.5	664.8	689.5
2002	643.5	634.9	638.6	646.8	658.0	671.8	673.1	675.7	667.4	662.4	657.0	645.7	656.2
2003	621.1	613.0	614.0	623.2	635.8	646.3	647.7	648.2	640.8	637.2	631.1	623.9	631.9
2004	607.0	603.4	608.7	623.3	634.0	646.1	651.4	655.8	648.5	644.1	640.0	634.3	633.3
2005	612.0	611.3	615.0	628.4	637.1	652.2	656.4	657.0	649.0	644.4	640.5	633.2	636.4
2006	618.8	613.9	617.2	629.7	638.8	656.0	656.7	656.9	648.4	642.9	636.5	630.2	637.2
2007	614.4	607.4	612.2	620.8	633.6	649.2	650.1	650.0	640.9	636.2	632.3	623.2	630.9
2008	606.8	601.7	603.6	610.3	621.3	633.8	633.5	632.1	621.9	616.0	605.5	590.1	614.7
2009	561.4	546.8	538.3	536.6	540.8	547.0	545.2	545.6	541.7	538.1	530.4	514.8	540.6
Mining and Logging													
1990	3.5	3.5	3.6	3.8	4.1	4.3	4.2	4.2	4.2	4.2	4.0	3.5	3.9
2000	3.5	3.6	3.7	3.9	4.3	4.4	4.4	4.4	4.3	4.2	4.1	3.6	4.0
2001	3.2	3.3	3.4	3.6	4.1	4.3	4.3	4.3	4.2	4.2	4.0	3.7	3.9
2002	3.2	3.2	3.3	3.6	4.1	4.2	4.2	4.2	4.2	4.1	3.9	3.6	3.8
2003	3.2	3.1	3.2	3.5	4.0	4.1	4.1	4.1	4.1	4.0	3.9	3.7	3.8
2004	3.1	3.2	3.3	3.7	4.0	4.1	4.2	4.2	4.1	4.2	4.1	3.9	3.8
2005	3.3	3.3	3.5	3.8	4.1	4.3	4.4	4.4	4.3	4.2	4.1	3.8	4.0
2006	3.4	3.4	3.5	3.8	4.2	4.3	4.3	4.3	4.2	4.1	3.9	3.7	3.9
2007	3.2	3.2	3.3	3.5	3.9	3.9	4.0	4.0	3.9	3.8	3.7	3.3	3.6
2008	3.0	2.9	3.0	3.1	3.5	3.7	3.7	3.8	3.7	3.6	3.5	3.1	3.4
2009	2.6	2.6	2.6	2.7	3.1	3.2	3.3	3.3	3.3	3.3	3.1	2.8	3.0
Construction													
1990	74.3	72.9	74.4	83.0	90.6	96.2	98.0	98.5	95.7	94.5	91.5	85.0	87.9
2000	107.6	106.1	111.2	121.3	128.7	135.3	137.3	137.5	133.6	131.7	127.7	119.9	124.8
2001	109.3	108.0	110.1	118.1	128.0	134.6	138.1	138.8	134.8	133.3	129.0	122.3	125.4
2002	108.7	105.7	108.0	117.9	127.2	133.4	136.7	136.7	133.1	132.0	129.2	120.9	124.1
2003	108.6	105.0	106.6	116.2	127.8	133.6	136.0	136.5	133.3	132.8	129.1	123.4	124.1
2004	110.4	107.6	110.9	122.2	129.6	135.4	139.7	138.7	135.7	134.0	131.4	125.4	126.8
2005	112.1	109.5	111.8	123.2	130.5	136.5	139.5	138.9	136.2	134.6	132.2	125.2	127.5
2006	114.3	111.9	113.4	124.0	131.1	137.8	138.5	138.1	134.9	132.9	129.3	123.6	127.5
2007	112.5	107.9	113.0	120.0	130.2	135.7	137.0	136.9	133.8	132.8	130.0	121.2	125.9
2008	108.0	104.9	106.8	113.8	123.9	127.9	129.4	129.0	125.6	124.1	118.4	108.9	118.4
2009	93.9	91.4	91.0	98.1	105.8	109.6	110.5	109.4	107.5	109.9	105.1	91.4	102.0
Manufacturing													
1990	513.7	514.4	516.6	516.6	520.1	530.0	530.8	535.3	531.1	527.1	521.8	518.2	523.0
2000	590.2	591.0	593.1	591.3	591.4	603.0	600.0	600.6	596.3	593.6	590.8	588.3	594.1
2001	577.0	571.2	569.7	565.4	562.3	567.9	563.7	562.5	555.6	547.9	541.5	538.8	560.3
2002	531.6	526.0	527.3	525.3	526.7	534.2	532.2	534.8	530.1	526.3	523.9	521.2	528.3
2003	509.3	504.9	504.2	503.5	504.0	508.6	507.6	507.6	503.4	500.4	498.1	496.8	504.0
2004	493.5	492.6	494.5	497.4	500.4	506.6	510.7	512.9	508.7	505.9	504.5	505.0	502.7
2005	496.6	498.5	499.7	501.4	502.5	511.4	512.5	513.7	508.5	505.6	504.2	504.2	504.9
2006	501.1	498.6	500.3	501.9	503.5	513.9	513.9	514.5	509.3	505.9	503.3	502.9	505.8
2007	498.7	496.3	495.9	497.3	499.5	509.6	509.1	509.1	503.2	499.6	498.6	498.7	501.3
2008	495.8	493.9	493.8	493.4	493.9	502.2	500.4	499.3	492.6	488.3	483.6	478.1	492.9
2009	464.9	452.8	444.7	435.8	431.9	434.2	431.4	432.9	430.9	424.9	422.2	420.6	435.6

Employment by Industry: Wisconsin, Selected Years, 1990–2009—*Continued*

(Numbers in thousands, not seasonally adjusted.)

Industry and year	January	February	March	April	May	June	July	August	September	October	November	December	Annual average
Service-Providing													
1990	1615.2	1630.0	1641.4	1665.2	1683.2	1703.2	1676.7	1677.8	1700.7	1703.7	1712.2	1711.2	1676.7
2000	2047.6	2059.0	2077.1	2103.8	2122.5	2142.8	2110.8	2116.0	2125.1	2134.6	2147.3	2142.9	2110.8
2001	2081.2	2094.0	2105.7	2126.5	2145.7	2154.8	2123.2	2123.5	2130.4	2135.4	2138.1	2133.6	2124.3
2002	2075.9	2082.7	2097.3	2119.3	2141.4	2151.3	2122.3	2124.8	2131.1	2151.8	2159.5	2156.1	2126.1
2003	2089.4	2105.4	2112.6	2138.3	2160.0	2171.9	2134.1	2135.7	2152.2	2173.1	2172.3	2176.2	2143.4
2004	2111.1	2123.9	2135.6	2160.6	2183.3	2201.7	2179.9	2183.1	2188.3	2203.5	2207.1	2207.2	2173.8
2005	2145.2	2157.5	2168.5	2202.3	2217.8	2228.2	2205.4	2207.1	2228.0	2229.7	2235.5	2243.1	2205.7
2006	2171.2	2180.0	2194.6	2221.9	2241.8	2261.0	2229.1	2230.1	2247.7	2252.2	2258.7	2262.9	2229.3
2007	2200.0	2202.6	2217.8	2241.6	2270.7	2293.6	2256.2	2257.7	2267.1	2273.0	2278.2	2283.7	2253.5
2008	2221.5	2222.3	2233.3	2255.2	2286.5	2295.2	2264.0	2264.3	2277.8	2283.9	2282.0	2275.0	2263.4
2009	2193.7	2195.3	2196.1	2211.8	2236.6	2240.3	2197.1	2191.4	2203.5	2215.9	2212.3	2198.1	2207.7
Trade, Transportation, and Utilities													
1990	448.0	441.2	443.5	447.6	454.3	462.6	459.0	463.7	464.8	467.4	474.5	477.8	458.7
2000	541.4	535.8	539.4	543.9	548.4	550.6	549.2	552.0	555.7	564.7	574.9	578.7	552.9
2001	549.2	540.0	541.7	544.1	549.2	549.8	543.5	546.2	544.2	548.0	557.2	558.8	547.7
2002	533.0	524.7	527.4	528.9	535.8	538.2	533.5	534.9	535.4	540.8	552.4	555.9	536.7
2003	528.3	521.9	521.8	528.4	535.8	540.1	533.3	535.6	537.7	543.7	551.8	557.7	536.3
2004	529.5	522.5	524.7	529.2	537.1	543.0	539.9	540.6	540.0	545.7	555.6	559.5	538.9
2005	532.0	526.7	529.0	535.4	541.3	543.8	542.1	543.9	544.1	551.7	561.4	566.8	543.2
2006	536.0	529.6	532.7	536.8	542.9	548.0	542.9	544.3	544.4	549.3	561.4	565.8	544.5
2007	541.3	533.5	536.3	538.3	547.7	552.3	547.5	547.2	546.5	550.0	561.0	563.0	547.1
2008	539.9	531.4	533.2	536.6	543.2	546.3	541.6	542.1	538.8	541.5	546.4	547.7	540.7
2009	520.6	511.9	510.2	510.8	517.6	521.7	515.3	515.2	512.4	515.1	519.4	517.0	515.6
Wholesale Trade													
1990	91.0	90.7	91.5	92.6	93.5	96.1	96.5	97.0	96.2	96.2	94.5	95.1	94.2
2000	114.1	114.2	114.9	115.2	115.7	117.1	117.5	117.4	116.3	116.4	116.6	117.0	116.0
2001	115.4	115.2	115.5	115.4	116.4	117.5	117.2	116.8	115.4	115.3	114.8	114.9	115.8
2002	113.2	112.7	113.2	113.9	114.8	115.5	116.1	115.6	114.4	113.6	113.7	113.6	114.2
2003	111.3	111.1	111.3	112.5	113.2	114.4	114.1	114.1	113.2	113.7	113.2	113.9	113.0
2004	112.3	111.8	112.4	112.9	113.6	114.9	116.6	117.0	115.0	115.7	116.0	116.5	114.6
2005	115.0	114.7	114.9	116.9	117.8	119.3	119.8	119.6	118.4	118.9	119.1	119.8	117.9
2006	118.5	118.1	118.8	119.9	120.6	122.6	122.8	122.5	121.2	121.3	121.4	121.9	120.8
2007	120.0	119.7	120.0	121.1	122.2	124.1	124.3	123.5	122.3	122.2	122.6	122.9	122.1
2008	121.1	120.4	120.9	122.0	123.2	124.3	124.2	123.6	121.5	121.1	120.7	120.1	121.9
2009	117.6	116.5	116.0	115.7	116.4	117.3	116.5	115.7	113.9	114.7	114.6	114.2	115.8
Retail Trade													
1990	273.7	266.6	267.3	269.6	273.6	279.4	278.0	281.4	280.1	283.0	292.2	294.5	278.3
2000	325.0	319.2	321.3	323.5	326.2	328.5	328.3	330.5	331.6	338.2	349.1	353.2	331.2
2001	326.4	317.7	318.8	319.6	322.4	323.6	320.4	323.0	319.6	323.1	333.6	336.3	323.7
2002	317.1	309.9	311.3	310.5	314.5	317.6	315.8	317.4	315.0	319.8	331.5	336.4	318.1
2003	314.2	308.0	307.2	310.7	315.6	318.3	315.9	318.3	316.7	321.2	330.6	336.6	317.8
2004	313.8	307.3	308.1	310.4	315.6	319.7	317.9	318.5	316.1	318.9	329.1	333.4	317.4
2005	311.7	306.2	307.4	310.2	314.0	315.4	315.7	317.7	315.1	321.9	331.5	336.1	316.9
2006	310.4	303.9	305.5	307.6	311.4	314.4	312.5	314.0	311.2	315.5	328.0	331.4	313.8
2007	313.5	305.6	307.6	307.9	314.0	316.1	315.7	315.0	311.9	314.9	325.6	327.4	314.6
2008	310.3	302.5	303.8	305.9	309.9	312.0	311.2	312.0	307.9	310.7	316.8	319.1	310.2
2009	299.4	292.4	291.4	292.4	296.8	299.6	297.8	298.3	294.6	297.4	303.9	303.8	297.3
Transportation and Utilities													
1990	83.3	83.9	84.7	85.4	87.2	87.1	84.5	85.3	88.5	88.2	87.8	88.2	86.2
2000	102.3	102.4	103.2	105.2	106.5	105.0	103.4	104.1	107.8	110.1	109.2	108.5	105.6
2001	107.4	107.1	107.4	109.1	110.4	108.7	105.9	106.4	109.2	109.6	108.8	107.6	108.1
2002	102.7	102.1	102.9	104.5	106.5	105.1	101.6	101.9	106.0	107.4	107.2	105.9	104.5
2003	102.8	102.8	103.3	105.2	107.0	107.4	103.3	103.2	107.8	108.8	108.0	107.2	105.6
2004	103.4	103.4	104.2	105.9	107.9	108.4	105.4	105.1	108.9	111.1	110.5	109.6	107.0
2005	105.3	105.8	106.7	108.3	109.5	109.1	106.6	106.6	110.6	110.9	110.8	110.9	108.4
2006	107.1	107.6	108.4	109.3	110.9	111.0	107.6	107.8	112.0	112.5	112.0	112.5	109.9
2007	107.8	108.2	108.7	109.3	111.5	112.1	107.5	108.7	112.3	112.9	112.8	112.7	110.4
2008	108.5	108.5	108.5	108.7	110.1	110.0	106.2	106.5	109.4	109.7	108.9	108.5	108.6
2009	103.6	103.0	102.8	102.7	104.4	104.8	101.0	101.2	103.9	103.0	100.9	99.0	102.5
Information													
1990	43.4	43.5	43.6	43.9	44.2	44.6	44.6	44.7	44.7	44.7	45.3	45.5	44.4
2000	52.5	52.4	52.5	52.6	52.9	53.4	53.8	53.9	53.8	54.6	55.6	55.6	53.6
2001	53.8	53.6	53.8	54.0	53.4	53.7	53.3	53.1	52.6	52.5	52.8	52.5	53.3
2002	51.8	51.3	51.2	51.1	51.0	51.1	51.1	51.2	50.6	50.8	51.2	51.4	51.2
2003	50.7	50.1	50.1	49.9	49.9	50.2	50.2	50.4	50.4	50.3	50.8	51.0	50.3
2004	50.2	49.8	49.9	49.6	49.6	49.7	50.2	50.3	49.7	49.6	50.0	50.1	49.9
2005	49.6	49.4	49.3	49.6	49.7	50.1	49.8	50.0	49.6	49.6	50.0	50.1	49.7
2006	49.6	49.3	49.1	48.9	48.9	49.1	49.2	49.4	48.9	49.3	49.8	50.0	49.3
2007	49.8	49.5	49.4	49.7	49.9	50.4	50.6	50.8	50.3	50.6	50.8	50.9	50.2
2008	50.3	50.0	49.9	50.1	50.9	50.7	50.5	50.5	49.8	49.7	49.9	49.9	50.2
2009	49.1	48.9	48.3	47.9	48.0	48.0	47.9	47.8	47.3	47.2	47.4	47.5	47.9

Employment by Industry: Wisconsin, Selected Years, 1990–2009—*Continued*

(Numbers in thousands, not seasonally adjusted.)

Industry and year	January	February	March	April	May	June	July	August	September	October	November	December	Annual average
Financial Activities													
1990	120.6	121.0	121.6	122.5	123.9	125.6	125.7	125.4	124.4	125.0	124.9	126.0	123.9
2000	146.7	146.6	146.8	148.1	148.6	150.6	151.0	150.8	149.8	149.7	150.0	150.9	149.1
2001	150.0	150.0	151.0	150.6	151.5	153.4	153.8	153.6	152.2	151.4	151.7	151.8	151.8
2002	151.4	151.7	151.7	152.4	153.1	154.8	155.6	156.0	154.5	154.2	154.8	155.5	153.8
2003	154.3	154.9	155.0	155.9	157.1	158.7	158.7	158.8	157.2	156.9	156.9	157.8	156.9
2004	156.7	156.5	156.7	157.7	158.3	159.9	160.8	161.0	158.9	159.1	159.1	160.4	158.8
2005	158.3	157.7	158.1	158.8	159.3	161.0	161.8	161.8	160.4	159.9	159.9	161.0	159.8
2006	159.5	159.2	159.2	160.6	161.7	163.2	164.2	163.9	162.6	162.3	162.3	163.3	161.8
2007	162.1	161.9	161.5	162.3	162.7	164.6	164.5	164.0	162.3	163.5	163.4	164.3	163.1
2008	163.1	163.4	163.0	163.8	164.9	165.7	166.4	166.0	163.5	163.0	162.8	163.3	164.1
2009	162.1	161.5	160.8	160.7	161.0	161.7	161.7	161.5	158.6	157.3	157.1	157.6	160.1
Professional and Business Services													
1990	145.0	146.8	148.7	152.9	152.7	156.8	156.3	157.6	157.0	157.7	156.1	155.2	153.6
2000	236.5	238.7	242.0	245.5	248.8	252.4	250.0	253.0	252.1	250.4	249.4	245.0	247.0
2001	235.3	235.4	235.1	239.0	240.5	242.4	242.3	244.1	240.2	238.5	235.7	233.1	238.5
2002	228.8	229.5	233.1	239.8	241.5	244.2	245.1	247.1	244.6	244.5	240.8	238.7	239.8
2003	234.9	236.4	238.3	243.1	243.6	245.9	247.6	248.8	249.3	249.5	247.3	247.1	244.3
2004	240.0	241.0	243.3	249.5	250.8	256.3	258.4	262.6	258.7	260.7	257.8	257.2	253.0
2005	249.6	251.6	254.7	262.3	261.4	265.3	268.5	271.2	270.2	267.7	267.1	267.5	263.1
2006	257.2	260.2	261.6	270.1	270.7	275.4	275.1	277.5	276.6	276.9	275.4	273.6	270.9
2007	265.5	267.2	269.2	275.8	278.1	284.0	283.8	286.8	284.1	284.0	283.6	284.5	278.9
2008	274.4	276.8	276.0	280.6	282.4	285.9	286.6	289.7	286.5	283.6	278.5	276.0	281.4
2009	260.0	255.6	252.7	254.9	255.3	256.9	257.9	258.9	256.5	254.1	253.5	247.0	255.3
Education and Health Services													
1990	232.3	234.4	235.8	234.5	235.6	236.6	235.9	236.6	239.1	241.1	243.2	243.3	237.4
2000	331.2	334.3	336.6	338.8	338.0	340.2	339.7	340.7	341.3	342.6	345.2	346.3	339.6
2001	341.9	347.6	349.0	349.5	349.3	349.0	347.9	347.9	350.0	352.6	355.2	355.3	349.6
2002	350.3	352.3	353.0	355.6	356.1	358.7	356.5	357.9	358.1	360.9	363.5	363.0	357.2
2003	359.8	361.6	361.9	363.9	363.9	359.5	360.3	360.6	368.0	371.9	372.0	371.5	364.6
2004	368.6	371.3	372.0	374.8	374.4	375.2	374.9	374.8	375.6	377.6	379.6	380.1	374.9
2005	377.1	379.1	380.3	382.7	382.4	384.0	382.5	382.9	385.1	386.4	388.6	388.7	383.3
2006	385.9	388.4	388.8	390.0	391.2	392.2	391.2	391.7	393.6	396.0	397.6	397.5	392.0
2007	393.1	395.4	396.4	397.0	398.6	399.5	398.4	399.7	401.0	400.9	401.7	402.8	398.7
2008	399.0	401.0	402.5	403.4	405.1	405.6	405.0	406.8	408.2	412.8	414.1	416.1	406.6
2009	411.5	413.5	415.4	413.0	413.4	413.3	411.4	412.0	412.2	415.8	417.8	418.9	414.0
Leisure and Hospitality													
1990	181.0	182.4	184.7	192.4	203.2	214.8	217.7	218.3	210.2	200.0	194.0	192.8	199.3
2000	215.5	216.9	221.6	230.1	242.4	254.8	259.6	261.3	248.3	235.9	228.0	226.4	236.7
2001	219.4	220.1	223.0	233.9	246.7	257.7	263.0	262.4	247.8	236.8	227.6	224.7	238.6
2002	221.0	220.7	222.5	231.4	245.8	256.9	264.2	265.0	251.9	241.7	232.0	232.1	240.4
2003	225.6	224.0	226.6	235.8	252.2	262.6	267.5	268.2	257.5	248.3	239.5	237.9	245.5
2004	230.3	229.4	232.6	242.7	256.7	265.9	275.0	275.6	263.4	252.9	243.4	242.6	250.8
2005	233.8	233.9	237.7	250.3	261.5	271.9	278.0	278.8	267.7	255.2	247.7	245.6	255.2
2006	239.0	239.6	243.4	252.6	264.4	276.5	282.1	283.1	271.0	260.6	251.4	250.2	259.5
2007	242.9	242.8	246.0	254.2	268.6	281.0	284.1	286.1	271.4	261.9	253.6	251.0	262.0
2008	242.2	241.1	244.2	252.7	268.3	277.9	281.2	282.2	268.7	259.6	249.2	246.1	259.5
2009	235.1	235.6	237.9	246.3	261.9	271.8	272.5	272.7	260.9	251.4	239.6	237.0	251.9
Other Services													
1990	115.3	115.9	116.0	116.2	116.8	117.4	117.2	116.8	116.6	116.5	117.3	117.5	116.6
2000	124.2	125.5	126.1	126.1	126.0	127.5	126.4	125.9	126.4	126.7	126.5	127.9	126.3
2001	129.3	129.6	131.1	130.3	130.6	132.7	132.0	132.2	131.8	131.6	131.3	133.1	131.3
2002	131.0	131.0	132.2	131.9	132.0	134.1	132.6	132.6	132.0	132.2	132.0	133.3	132.2
2003	131.5	131.6	132.7	132.4	132.5	134.6	133.5	133.4	132.9	132.1	131.7	133.0	132.7
2004	132.6	133.1	134.4	134.4	134.7	137.1	136.1	136.4	136.0	137.2	135.4	135.8	135.3
2005	133.9	134.5	135.6	136.0	136.2	137.8	137.0	137.0	136.6	136.1	135.4	136.4	136.0
2006	133.9	134.0	135.2	135.4	136.0	138.0	137.1	136.9	136.7	136.4	135.9	137.0	136.0
2007	135.1	135.5	136.5	137.3	138.0	139.7	139.0	138.3	137.5	138.3	137.8	138.4	137.6
2008	135.9	136.4	137.3	138.4	139.2	140.9	140.3	140.0	139.3	141.2	139.7	139.9	139.0
2009	136.7	137.0	138.1	138.2	138.6	140.0	139.0	138.6	137.7	138.3	136.3	137.3	138.0
Government													
1990	329.6	344.8	347.5	355.2	352.5	344.8	320.3	314.7	343.9	351.3	356.9	353.1	342.9
2000	399.6	408.8	412.1	418.7	417.4	413.3	381.1	378.4	397.7	410.0	417.7	412.1	405.6
2001	402.3	417.7	421.0	425.1	424.5	416.1	387.4	384.0	411.6	424.0	426.6	424.3	413.7
2002	408.6	421.5	426.2	428.2	426.1	413.3	383.7	380.1	404.0	426.7	432.8	426.2	414.8
2003	404.3	424.9	426.2	428.9	425.0	420.3	383.0	379.9	399.2	420.4	422.3	420.2	412.9
2004	403.2	420.3	422.0	422.7	422.2	414.6	384.6	381.8	406.0	420.7	426.2	421.5	412.2
2005	410.9	424.6	423.8	427.2	426.0	414.3	385.7	381.5	414.3	423.1	425.4	427.0	415.3
2006	410.1	419.7	424.6	427.5	426.0	418.6	387.3	383.3	413.9	421.4	424.9	425.5	415.2
2007	410.2	416.8	422.5	427.0	427.1	422.1	388.3	384.8	414.0	423.8	426.3	428.8	416.0
2008	416.7	422.2	427.2	429.6	432.5	422.2	392.4	387.0	423.0	432.5	441.4	436.0	421.9
2009	418.6	431.3	432.7	440.0	440.8	426.9	391.4	384.7	417.9	436.7	441.2	435.8	424.8

Average Weekly Hours by Selected Industry: Wisconsin, 2007–2009

(Not seasonally adjusted.)

Industry and year	January	February	March	April	May	June	July	August	September	October	November	December	Annual average
Total Private													
2007	32.2	32.1	32.5	32.6	32.6	33.1	33.4	33.2	33.4	33.0	33.1	33.4	32.9
2008	32.8	32.7	33.1	32.8	33.0	33.3	33.1	33.4	33.4	33.0	32.7	33.1	32.4	33.0
2009	31.8	32.2	31.9	31.6	31.8	32.0	32.3	32.8	32.2	32.4	33.3	32.4	32.2
Goods-Producing													
2007	37.7	37.5	37.7	38.0	38.7	38.7	38.8	38.8	39.0	38.8	38.5	39.0	38.4
2008	38.3	38.0	38.3	37.9	38.4	38.2	38.3	38.7	39.1	38.6	38.7	38.0	38.4
2009	36.8	37.3	36.9	37.0	37.6	37.7	37.8	38.0	37.6	38.6	39.4	38.3	37.8
Construction													
2007	35.9	35.0	36.6	36.9	39.3	39.8	39.9	39.2	38.6	39.5	38.7	38.4	38.3
2008	35.9	36.1	36.6	35.7	38.6	38.2	38.7	40.1	39.5	39.0	38.9	35.8	37.9
2009	34.4	35.6	34.7	36.2	37.6	36.7	38.2	38.3	37.8	38.0	38.4	35.0	36.9
Manufacturing													
2007	38.1	38.1	38.0	38.2	38.4	38.3	38.4	38.6	39.0	38.4	38.3	39.0	38.4
2008	38.8	38.4	38.7	38.5	38.3	38.1	38.1	38.2	38.9	38.4	38.5	38.4	38.4
2009	37.3	37.2	36.8	36.6	37.0	37.5	37.3	37.6	37.2	38.2	38.8	38.8	37.5
Trade, Transportation, and Utilities													
2007	32.6	33.1	33.4	33.3	33.5	34.6	34.8	34.5	34.5	34.1	34.0	34.4	33.9
2008	32.9	32.9	33.3	33.3	33.3	33.9	33.6	33.6	33.2	33.2	33.2	32.8	33.3
2009	31.6	32.4	32.3	31.7	31.9	32.5	32.7	33.1	32.5	32.7	33.8	32.6	32.5
Financial Activities													
2007	36.8	35.0	35.2	35.9	34.8	35.1	35.8	35.3	36.2	35.4	35.7	36.2	35.6
2008	36.0	35.6	36.3	35.2	35.2	36.5	35.6	35.8	35.6	35.6	37.5	35.5	35.9
2009	36.6	37.3	36.8	35.9	35.7	35.8	35.6	37.5	35.5	35.9	37.0	36.0	36.3
Professional and Business Services													
2007	33.3	33.6	34.6	34.3	33.8	34.2	33.7	34.1	34.7	34.3	34.5	34.1	34.1
2008	34.3	34.7	35.0	34.5	35.1	35.5	34.0	34.8	34.2	33.4	33.5	32.1	34.3
2009	31.9	32.2	32.1	31.7	31.6	31.5	31.0	32.3	31.0	31.9	32.5	31.6	31.8
Education and Health Services													
2007	28.9	28.6	28.8	29.3	29.0	29.6	30.2	30.4	30.7	30.3	30.5	30.6	29.7
2008	31.0	30.3	30.6	30.7	30.9	31.2	31.1	31.3	30.6	30.9	31.5	30.8	30.9
2009	31.0	31.3	31.1	30.9	31.3	31.3	31.3	31.6	31.4	31.1	31.6	31.0	31.2
Leisure and Hospitality													
2007	20.7	20.9	21.2	21.0	21.0	22.4	23.3	22.4	21.9	21.1	21.3	20.9	21.5
2008	20.7	21.0	21.1	21.7	21.8	22.4	22.9	23.5	22.2	21.2	21.5	21.5	21.8
2009	20.4	21.2	20.6	20.1	20.4	20.8	22.6	22.8	21.4	20.6	21.1	20.8	21.1
Other Services													
2007	25.7	25.6	26.0	25.9	27.1	26.8	27.2	26.7	26.7	26.0	26.4	26.3	26.4
2008	25.8	26.0	27.0	26.6	26.8	27.6	27.6	28.0	27.3	27.0	26.9	26.6	26.9
2009	26.1	26.0	26.2	25.9	25.3	25.7	27.0	26.6	25.0	25.5	26.2	25.3	25.9

Average Hourly Earnings by Selected Industry: Wisconsin, 2007–2009

(Dollars, not seasonally adjusted.)

Industry and year	January	February	March	April	May	June	July	August	September	October	November	December	Annual average
Total Private													
2007	20.27	20.44	20.56	20.99	20.44	20.22	20.25	20.03	20.62	20.58	20.44	20.61	20.45
2008	20.64	20.76	20.86	20.57	20.50	20.45	20.61	20.52	20.84	20.59	20.80	20.94	20.67
2009	21.04	21.37	21.22	21.17	20.99	20.90	21.02	20.95	20.96	21.23	21.17	21.48	21.12
Goods-Producing													
2007	23.18	22.95	23.17	22.94	22.89	22.87	22.88	22.61	22.73	22.87	22.68	22.85	22.88
2008	22.16	22.52	22.43	22.40	22.80	23.09	22.83	22.93	23.13	23.00	23.02	22.95	22.78
2009	22.99	23.34	23.20	22.97	23.07	22.83	22.89	22.60	22.82	22.78	22.86	23.08	22.95
Construction													
2007	31.74	31.45	30.65	30.55	29.73	29.71	29.54	28.98	29.30	28.71	28.20	28.26	29.64
2008	27.41	27.74	27.53	27.14	27.81	27.64	27.96	28.00	28.75	28.31	27.86	28.04	27.87
2009	27.63	28.33	28.34	28.37	28.50	28.19	28.25	28.21	27.81	28.61	27.92	28.86	28.25
Manufacturing													
2007	21.04	20.96	21.33	21.00	20.98	20.88	20.92	20.74	20.80	21.12	21.07	21.40	21.02
2008	20.91	21.29	21.21	21.21	21.25	21.68	21.16	21.18	21.29	21.25	21.49	21.59	21.29
2009	21.78	22.05	21.85	21.52	21.49	21.28	21.28	20.92	21.38	21.08	21.45	21.78	21.49
Trade, Transportation, and Utilities													
2007	18.75	18.44	19.03	20.59	18.86	18.89	18.45	18.53	18.85	18.77	18.15	17.46	18.72
2008	18.80	18.84	19.55	18.94	18.37	18.33	19.50	18.84	18.87	18.21	18.31	18.63	18.76
2009	19.00	18.81	18.93	18.97	18.77	18.63	18.51	18.55	18.45	18.39	18.26	18.59	18.65
Financial Activities													
2007	21.37	23.75	22.10	22.95	22.69	22.40	22.79	22.60	23.25	23.31	23.15	24.37	22.85
2008	23.72	24.91	24.52	24.52	24.93	23.95	23.51	24.72	24.63	24.63	24.48	24.43	24.41
2009	24.02	26.44	25.21	24.62	24.72	25.21	25.75	26.75	25.55	26.01	25.99	26.17	25.54
Professional and Business Services													
2007	24.01	24.16	25.07	24.93	24.29	23.79	23.71	22.42	24.43	23.54	23.78	23.98	24.00
2008	23.26	23.08	23.13	22.71	22.52	23.02	22.51	22.29	22.76	22.73	23.20	23.57	22.89
2009	23.62	24.45	24.64	24.25	24.36	24.10	23.54	23.06	23.69	24.01	24.43	25.82	24.16
Education and Health Services													
2007	19.08	19.32	19.33	19.49	19.45	19.11	19.85	19.31	19.90	19.69	19.78	20.00	19.53
2008	20.27	19.93	20.14	19.89	19.62	19.59	19.91	19.79	20.24	20.03	20.53	20.63	20.05
2009	20.59	20.67	20.67	21.29	20.81	21.24	22.27	21.65	21.40	21.88	21.54	21.66	21.31
Leisure and Hospitality													
2007	11.52	10.94	11.19	11.19	11.10	10.85	11.00	10.96	11.23	11.33	11.25	11.65	11.17
2008	11.65	11.44	11.34	11.24	11.26	10.98	11.22	11.63	11.76	11.28	11.51	11.44	11.39
2009	11.36	11.37	11.66	11.60	11.52	11.18	11.27	11.16	11.32	11.82	11.82	11.85	11.48
Other Services													
2007	16.90	17.06	17.00	17.55	17.36	17.58	17.57	17.73	17.78	17.52	17.51	17.70	17.44
2008	17.96	17.97	17.88	17.62	17.59	17.49	17.40	17.06	17.88	17.47	17.63	17.73	17.63
2009	17.52	17.57	17.45	17.60	17.56	17.10	16.68	17.09	17.60	17.46	17.60	17.90	17.42

Average Weekly Earnings by Selected Industry: Wisconsin, 2007–2009

(Dollars, not seasonally adjusted.)

Industry and year	January	February	March	April	May	June	July	August	September	October	November	December	Annual average
Total Private													
2007	652.69	656.12	668.20	684.27	666.34	669.28	676.35	665.00	688.71	679.14	676.56	688.37	672.81
2008	676.99	678.85	690.47	674.70	676.50	680.99	682.19	685.37	687.72	673.29	688.48	678.46	682.11
2009	669.07	688.11	676.92	668.97	667.48	668.80	678.95	687.16	674.91	687.85	704.96	695.95	680.06
Goods-Producing													
2007	873.89	860.63	873.51	871.72	885.84	885.07	887.74	877.27	886.47	887.36	873.18	891.15	878.59
2008	848.73	855.76	859.07	848.96	875.52	882.04	874.39	887.39	904.38	887.80	890.87	872.10	874.75
2009	846.03	870.58	856.08	849.89	867.43	860.69	865.24	858.80	858.03	879.31	900.68	883.96	867.51
Construction													
2007	1139.47	1100.75	1121.79	1127.30	1168.39	1182.46	1178.65	1136.02	1130.98	1134.05	1091.34	1085.18	1135.21
2008	984.02	1001.41	1007.60	968.90	1073.47	1055.85	1082.05	1122.80	1135.63	1104.09	1083.75	1003.83	1056.27
2009	950.47	1008.55	983.40	1026.99	1071.60	1034.57	1079.15	1080.44	1051.22	1087.18	1072.13	1010.10	1042.43
Manufacturing													
2007	801.62	798.58	810.54	802.20	805.63	799.70	803.33	800.56	811.20	811.01	806.98	834.60	807.17
2008	811.31	817.54	820.83	816.59	813.88	826.01	806.20	809.08	828.18	816.00	827.37	829.06	817.54
2009	812.39	820.26	804.08	787.63	795.13	798.00	793.74	786.59	795.34	805.26	832.26	845.06	805.88
Trade, Transportation, and Utilities													
2007	611.25	610.36	635.60	685.65	631.81	653.59	642.06	639.29	650.33	640.06	617.10	600.62	634.61
2008	618.52	619.84	651.02	630.70	611.72	621.39	655.20	633.02	626.48	604.57	607.89	611.06	624.71
2009	600.40	609.44	611.44	601.35	598.76	605.48	605.28	614.01	599.63	601.35	617.19	606.03	606.13
Financial Activities													
2007	786.42	813.75	777.92	823.91	789.61	786.24	815.88	797.78	841.65	825.17	826.46	882.19	813.46
2008	853.92	886.80	890.08	863.10	877.54	874.18	836.96	884.98	876.83	876.83	918.00	867.27	876.32
2009	879.13	986.21	927.73	883.86	882.50	902.52	916.70	1003.13	907.03	933.76	961.63	942.12	927.10
Professional and Business Services													
2007	799.53	811.78	867.42	855.10	821.00	813.62	799.03	764.52	847.72	807.42	820.41	817.72	818.40
2008	797.82	800.88	809.55	783.50	790.45	817.21	765.34	775.69	778.39	759.18	777.20	756.60	785.13
2009	753.48	787.29	790.94	768.73	769.78	759.15	729.74	744.84	734.39	765.92	793.98	815.91	768.29
Education and Health Services													
2007	551.41	552.55	556.70	571.06	564.05	565.66	599.47	587.02	610.93	596.61	603.29	612.00	580.04
2008	628.37	603.88	616.28	610.62	606.26	611.21	619.20	619.43	619.34	618.93	646.70	635.40	619.55
2009	638.29	646.97	642.84	657.86	651.35	664.81	697.05	684.14	671.96	680.47	680.66	671.46	664.87
Leisure and Hospitality													
2007	238.46	228.65	237.23	234.99	233.10	243.04	256.30	245.50	245.94	239.06	239.63	243.49	240.16
2008	241.16	240.24	239.27	243.91	245.47	245.95	256.94	273.31	261.07	239.14	247.47	245.96	248.30
2009	231.74	241.04	240.20	233.16	235.01	232.54	254.70	254.45	242.25	243.49	249.40	246.48	242.23
Other Services													
2007	434.33	436.74	442.00	454.55	470.46	471.14	477.90	473.39	474.73	455.52	462.26	465.51	460.42
2008	463.37	467.22	482.76	468.69	471.41	482.72	480.24	477.68	488.12	471.69	474.25	471.62	474.25
2009	457.27	456.82	457.19	455.84	444.27	439.47	450.36	454.59	440.00	445.23	461.12	452.87	451.18

WYOMING
At a Glance

Population:
  1990 census: 453,589
  2000 census: 493,782
  2009 estimate: 544,270

Percent change in population:
  1990–2000: 8.9%
  2000–2009: 10.2%

Percent change in total nonfarm employment:
  1990–2009: 44.3%
  2008–2009: -4.0%

Industry with the largest growth in employment, 1990–2009 (thousands):
  Government, 16.4

Industry with the largest decline or smallest growth in employment, 1990–2009 (thousands):
  Manufacturing, 0.1

Civilian labor force:
  1990: 236,043
  2000: 266,882
  2009: 293,927

Unemployment rate and rank among states (lowest to highest):
  1990: 5.3%, 23rd
  2000: 3.8%, 25th
  2009: 6.4%, 7th

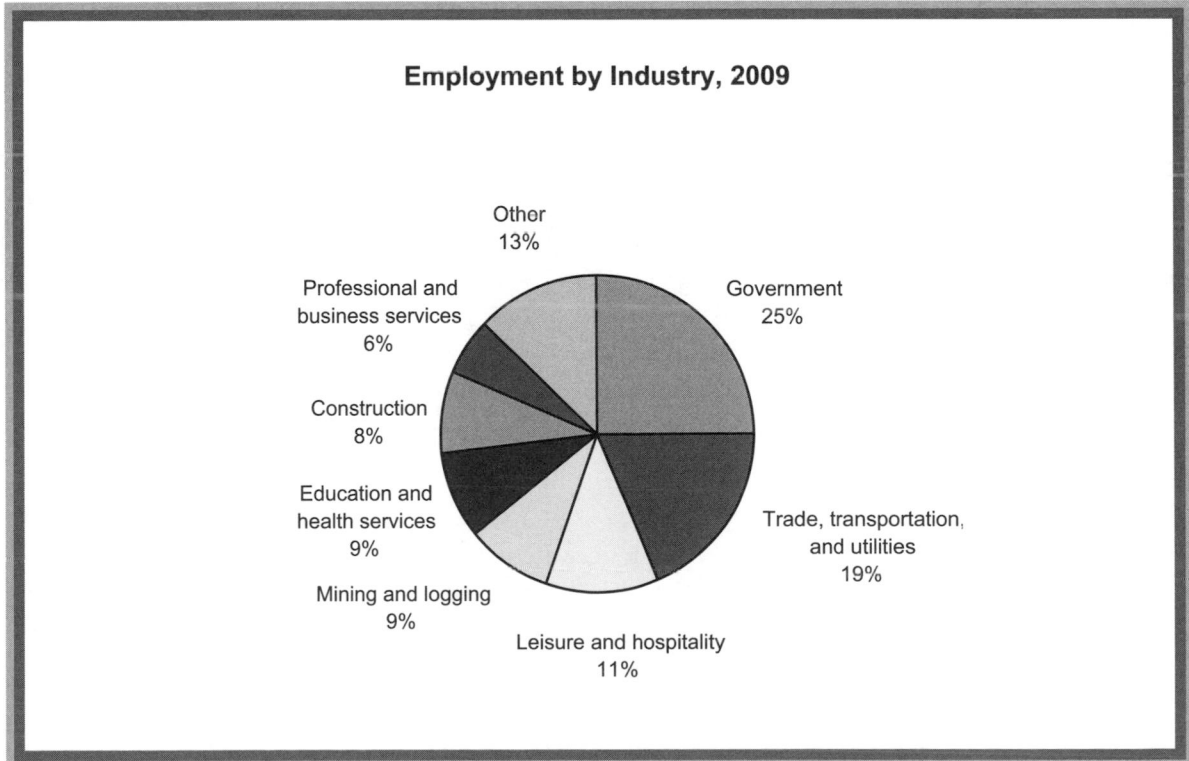

Employment by Industry, 2009

Other 13%

Government 25%

Professional and business services 6%

Construction 8%

Education and health services 9%

Mining and logging 9%

Trade, transportation, and utilities 19%

Leisure and hospitality 11%

Employment by Industry: Wyoming, Selected Years, 1990–2009

(Numbers in thousands, not seasonally adjusted.)

Industry and year	January	February	March	April	May	June	July	August	September	October	November	December	Annual average
Total Nonfarm													
1990	186.8	187.2	190.2	194.4	200.3	208.7	203.0	203.9	206.3	202.0	200.1	199.2	198.5
2000	227.8	228.5	232.2	234.1	241.7	248.8	246.4	247.1	245.0	242.9	238.2	239.3	239.3
2001	233.1	233.5	236.8	239.4	247.2	256.6	252.8	254.5	251.4	248.8	245.5	245.3	245.4
2002	237.9	237.7	240.2	242.4	250.2	258.2	255.7	255.4	254.2	250.5	246.5	246.1	247.9
2003	238.9	238.4	240.0	243.2	250.8	260.3	257.5	258.7	257.2	255.0	249.9	250.4	250.0
2004	243.9	244.3	246.9	250.8	256.4	266.0	263.2	262.8	260.1	258.4	255.4	256.0	255.4
2005	249.6	250.7	254.0	257.1	264.0	273.5	271.6	272.2	271.5	269.4	266.0	267.4	263.9
2006	262.4	264.3	267.5	269.8	277.8	288.7	284.3	284.6	284.7	281.9	279.3	281.9	277.3
2007	275.1	276.9	280.3	280.6	289.3	299.0	295.4	295.8	295.9	293.7	291.6	292.4	288.9
2008	286.1	287.9	289.7	290.4	299.1	308.1	305.8	305.3	306.4	304.0	298.5	297.1	298.2
2009	286.8	285.0	284.9	283.2	290.5	294.6	289.5	288.0	290.3	285.0	280.1	278.9	286.4
Total Private													
1990	131.8	131.4	133.9	137.4	142.2	152.1	154.5	155.1	150.5	145.4	142.6	142.0	143.2
2000	167.7	167.9	169.9	172.1	178.1	187.5	190.1	190.6	184.8	180.8	176.2	177.3	178.5
2001	172.3	172.1	174.6	177.4	184.1	193.3	195.4	196.6	190.2	186.1	182.8	181.9	183.9
2002	176.0	175.4	176.8	179.4	186.1	194.1	197.2	197.0	191.5	186.3	182.2	181.0	185.3
2003	175.6	174.7	175.5	179.0	185.6	195.1	198.3	199.6	194.3	190.1	185.4	185.3	186.5
2004	179.7	179.7	181.6	185.3	189.9	199.6	202.4	202.4	196.4	192.8	189.9	190.3	190.8
2005	184.9	185.5	188.2	191.3	196.9	206.9	210.6	211.1	206.4	202.9	199.8	201.0	198.8
2006	197.6	198.7	201.3	203.7	210.7	221.3	223.0	223.7	219.2	215.0	212.8	214.9	211.8
2007	209.0	210.0	212.9	213.2	220.5	230.3	232.9	233.3	227.9	224.6	222.5	223.4	221.7
2008	218.7	219.2	220.4	220.9	227.7	236.8	240.9	241.0	235.7	232.1	226.7	225.2	228.8
2009	216.7	213.2	212.4	210.3	216.0	221.4	223.5	222.2	217.6	212.0	207.2	205.7	214.9
Goods-Producing													
1990	34.3	33.6	34.6	36.2	37.6	39.7	40.2	40.5	40.2	39.9	39.0	37.6	37.7
2000	42.1	42.0	42.7	43.7	45.2	46.6	47.3	48.0	47.4	47.4	45.6	45.2	45.2
2001	43.0	43.0	43.9	45.6	47.7	49.9	50.6	51.3	50.4	51.2	50.3	48.1	47.9
2002	45.5	44.2	44.7	45.9	48.2	49.0	49.4	50.2	49.4	48.7	47.0	45.1	47.3
2003	42.9	42.3	42.6	44.5	46.8	48.3	49.4	50.9	50.5	50.4	48.8	47.6	47.1
2004	44.6	44.6	45.4	47.1	48.9	50.7	51.4	51.5	50.6	51.0	50.5	49.5	48.8
2005	47.6	47.8	49.0	50.8	52.6	54.4	55.6	56.2	56.0	56.5	56.1	55.3	53.2
2006	54.6	54.8	55.7	58.2	60.8	62.8	62.8	64.1	63.8	63.9	63.3	62.9	60.6
2007	59.7	59.4	60.6	61.7	63.8	65.8	66.3	67.0	65.9	66.5	66.9	65.6	64.1
2008	63.9	63.6	63.9	64.6	66.9	68.7	70.3	71.1	70.2	70.4	69.0	66.2	67.4
2009	61.6	59.3	58.3	57.9	59.3	59.2	59.5	59.2	58.5	58.1	57.6	54.7	58.6
Mining and Logging													
1990	15.8	15.5	15.3	15.4	15.7	16.1	16.6	16.8	16.6	16.7	16.8	16.6	16.1
2000	16.1	16.1	16.0	15.5	15.8	16.1	16.4	16.8	16.7	16.7	16.7	16.9	16.3
2001	16.6	16.8	17.3	17.4	18.0	18.8	19.0	19.3	19.3	19.5	19.3	19.1	18.4
2002	18.4	18.1	17.9	17.4	17.7	18.0	18.3	18.4	18.0	17.8	17.5	17.3	17.9
2003	17.1	17.2	17.2	17.4	17.8	18.3	18.9	19.1	18.9	19.1	19.0	19.2	18.3
2004	18.9	19.0	19.1	19.2	19.4	20.2	20.6	20.9	20.9	21.0	21.3	21.3	20.2
2005	21.0	21.3	21.6	21.8	22.1	22.9	23.2	23.4	23.5	23.6	23.9	24.3	22.7
2006	24.6	25.0	25.4	25.8	26.2	27.0	27.3	27.6	27.5	27.5	27.4	27.6	26.6
2007	27.0	26.9	26.8	26.8	27.2	27.7	27.6	27.7	27.5	27.6	27.8	27.9	27.4
2008	28.1	28.1	28.1	28.0	28.6	29.3	29.8	30.2	30.2	30.5	30.5	30.3	29.3
2009	29.2	28.1	27.2	25.8	25.2	24.8	24.6	24.4	24.2	24.2	24.4	24.4	25.5
Construction													
1990	9.7	9.6	10.6	12.1	13.1	14.4	14.3	14.5	14.1	13.4	12.6	11.6	12.5
2000	15.9	15.8	16.7	18.0	19.1	20.0	20.3	20.7	20.3	19.8	18.1	17.5	18.5
2001	16.1	16.0	16.5	18.2	19.9	21.2	21.6	22.0	21.2	21.4	20.9	19.3	19.5
2002	17.6	17.0	17.5	19.2	21.1	21.5	21.6	22.2	21.9	21.2	19.8	18.2	19.9
2003	16.6	16.2	16.6	18.1	19.9	20.7	21.1	22.3	22.2	21.6	20.1	18.7	19.5
2004	16.5	16.6	17.2	18.7	20.3	20.9	21.2	21.0	20.2	20.2	19.5	18.5	19.2
2005	17.0	17.2	18.0	19.5	21.0	21.8	22.7	23.0	22.7	22.8	22.1	21.0	20.7
2006	20.2	20.1	20.6	22.6	24.6	25.5	25.1	26.2	26.0	25.9	25.4	24.8	23.9
2007	22.4	22.4	23.6	24.9	26.5	28.0	28.6	29.2	28.3	28.6	28.7	27.4	26.6
2008	25.8	25.6	26.2	26.8	28.5	29.4	30.5	30.9	30.1	29.6	28.2	25.9	28.1
2009	22.8	22.0	22.1	23.2	25.1	25.4	25.8	25.8	25.1	24.5	23.9	21.1	23.9
Manufacturing													
1990	8.8	8.5	8.7	8.7	8.8	9.2	9.3	9.2	9.5	9.8	9.6	9.4	9.1
2000	10.1	10.1	10.0	10.2	10.3	10.5	10.6	10.5	10.4	10.9	10.8	10.8	10.4
2001	10.3	10.2	10.1	10.0	9.8	9.9	10.0	10.0	9.9	10.3	10.1	9.7	10.0
2002	9.5	9.1	9.3	9.3	9.4	9.5	9.5	9.6	9.5	9.7	9.7	9.6	9.5
2003	9.2	8.9	8.8	9.0	9.1	9.3	9.4	9.5	9.4	9.7	9.7	9.7	9.3
2004	9.2	9.0	9.1	9.2	9.2	9.6	9.6	9.6	9.5	9.8	9.7	9.7	9.4
2005	9.6	9.3	9.4	9.5	9.5	9.7	9.7	9.8	9.8	10.1	10.1	10.0	9.7
2006	9.8	9.7	9.7	9.8	10.0	10.3	10.4	10.3	10.3	10.5	10.5	10.5	10.2
2007	10.3	10.1	10.2	10.0	10.1	10.1	10.1	10.1	10.1	10.3	10.4	10.3	10.2
2008	10.0	9.9	9.6	9.8	9.8	10.0	10.0	10.0	9.9	10.3	10.3	10.0	10.0
2009	9.6	9.2	9.0	8.9	9.0	9.0	9.1	9.0	9.2	9.4	9.3	9.2	9.2

Employment by Industry: Wyoming, Selected Years, 1990–2009—*Continued*

(Numbers in thousands, not seasonally adjusted.)

Industry and year	January	February	March	April	May	June	July	August	September	October	November	December	Annual average
Service-Providing													
1990	152.5	153.6	155.6	158.2	162.7	169.0	162.8	163.4	166.1	162.1	161.1	161.6	160.7
2000	185.7	186.5	189.5	190.4	196.5	202.2	199.1	199.1	197.6	195.5	192.6	194.1	194.0
2001	190.1	190.5	192.9	193.8	199.5	206.7	202.2	203.2	201.0	197.6	195.2	197.2	197.5
2002	192.4	193.5	195.5	196.5	202.0	209.2	206.3	205.2	204.8	201.8	199.5	201.0	200.6
2003	196.0	196.1	197.4	198.7	204.0	212.0	208.1	207.8	206.7	204.6	201.1	202.8	202.9
2004	199.3	199.7	201.5	203.7	207.5	215.3	211.8	211.3	209.5	207.4	204.9	206.5	206.5
2005	202.0	202.9	205.0	206.3	211.4	219.1	216.0	216.0	215.5	212.9	209.9	212.1	210.8
2006	207.8	209.5	211.8	211.6	217.0	225.9	221.5	220.5	220.9	218.0	216.0	219.0	216.6
2007	215.4	217.5	219.7	218.9	225.5	233.2	229.1	228.8	230.0	227.2	224.7	226.8	224.7
2008	222.2	224.3	225.8	225.8	232.2	239.4	235.5	234.2	236.2	233.6	229.5	230.9	230.8
2009	225.2	225.7	226.6	225.3	231.2	235.4	230.0	228.8	231.8	226.9	222.5	224.2	227.8
Trade, Transportation, and Utilities													
1990	39.5	39.4	39.8	40.3	41.5	42.8	43.2	43.4	42.8	42.0	42.3	42.7	41.6
2000	46.3	46.0	45.9	46.6	47.7	48.9	49.7	50.0	49.1	48.7	49.1	49.4	48.1
2001	47.5	46.9	47.3	47.8	49.0	50.2	50.2	50.1	49.1	48.1	48.1	48.6	48.6
2002	47.0	46.4	46.7	47.2	48.5	49.7	50.0	50.0	49.1	48.7	49.0	49.2	48.5
2003	47.1	46.5	46.5	47.2	48.2	49.5	50.1	50.2	49.4	48.9	48.6	49.1	48.4
2004	47.5	47.4	47.6	48.3	49.1	50.5	51.0	50.8	49.9	49.4	49.5	50.0	49.3
2005	48.2	48.2	48.7	49.3	50.4	52.0	52.4	52.5	51.8	51.5	51.5	52.2	50.7
2006	50.7	50.6	51.1	51.0	52.1	53.9	54.2	54.0	53.3	52.8	53.4	54.0	52.6
2007	53.0	53.2	53.8	53.4	54.7	56.3	56.8	56.9	56.1	55.7	56.0	56.7	55.2
2008	55.0	54.7	54.8	54.8	55.8	56.9	57.4	57.3	56.7	56.0	56.0	56.4	56.0
2009	54.1	53.5	53.3	52.8	53.5	54.5	54.5	54.3	53.6	52.4	52.4	53.4	53.5
Wholesale Trade													
1990	5.0	5.1	5.1	5.1	5.2	5.3	5.4	5.3	5.3	5.3	5.3	5.3	5.2
2000	6.1	6.2	6.2	6.3	6.3	6.5	6.5	6.5	6.5	6.4	6.4	6.5	6.3
2001	6.5	6.5	6.6	6.8	6.9	7.0	7.0	7.1	7.0	7.0	7.0	7.1	6.9
2002	7.0	7.0	7.0	7.0	7.0	7.1	7.1	7.1	7.0	7.0	7.0	7.0	7.0
2003	6.9	6.8	6.8	6.9	6.9	7.0	7.1	7.1	7.0	7.0	7.1	7.1	7.0
2004	7.1	7.2	7.2	7.3	7.4	7.4	7.5	7.4	7.4	7.3	7.4	7.4	7.3
2005	7.3	7.4	7.5	7.6	7.8	7.9	7.9	7.9	7.9	7.9	7.9	8.0	7.8
2006	7.8	7.9	8.0	8.0	8.2	8.4	8.3	8.3	8.3	8.3	8.4	8.4	8.2
2007	8.4	8.5	8.6	8.7	8.8	9.0	8.8	8.9	8.8	8.7	8.8	8.9	8.7
2008	8.8	8.8	8.9	9.0	9.2	9.2	9.2	9.2	9.2	9.2	9.2	9.2	9.1
2009	9.0	9.0	8.9	8.8	8.8	8.9	8.7	8.6	8.5	8.5	8.5	8.6	8.7
Retail Trade													
1990	23.4	23.1	23.4	23.8	24.8	25.8	26.0	26.3	25.7	25.0	25.3	25.8	24.9
2000	28.7	28.4	28.3	28.8	29.9	30.7	31.5	31.7	31.0	30.5	30.8	31.0	30.1
2001	29.5	29.2	29.5	29.7	30.8	31.7	31.6	31.4	30.6	29.7	29.8	30.2	30.3
2002	28.9	28.4	28.7	29.1	30.3	31.2	31.5	31.4	30.7	30.1	30.4	30.6	30.1
2003	28.8	28.3	28.3	28.9	29.7	30.7	31.2	31.2	30.6	30.1	30.1	30.4	29.9
2004	28.8	28.6	28.8	29.2	29.9	31.0	31.3	31.2	30.4	30.0	30.1	30.4	30.0
2005	28.9	28.7	29.0	29.2	30.1	31.4	31.7	31.7	31.1	30.7	30.7	31.0	30.4
2006	29.8	29.5	29.8	29.7	30.5	31.8	32.2	32.0	31.3	30.9	31.4	31.7	30.9
2007	30.8	30.8	31.2	30.7	31.7	32.6	33.3	33.1	32.4	32.2	32.4	32.8	32.0
2008	31.6	31.3	31.3	31.2	31.8	32.8	33.3	33.1	32.7	32.2	32.2	32.4	32.2
2009	30.7	30.1	30.1	30.0	30.7	31.4	31.7	31.5	31.0	30.4	30.5	30.8	30.7
Transportation and Utilities													
1990	11.1	11.2	11.3	11.4	11.5	11.7	11.8	11.8	11.8	11.7	11.7	11.6	11.5
2000	11.5	11.4	11.4	11.5	11.5	11.7	11.7	11.8	11.6	11.8	11.9	11.9	11.6
2001	11.5	11.2	11.2	11.3	11.3	11.5	11.6	11.6	11.5	11.4	11.3	11.3	11.4
2002	11.1	11.0	11.0	11.1	11.2	11.4	11.4	11.5	11.4	11.6	11.6	11.6	11.3
2003	11.4	11.4	11.4	11.4	11.6	11.8	11.8	11.9	11.8	11.8	11.5	11.6	11.6
2004	11.6	11.6	11.6	11.8	11.8	12.1	12.2	12.2	12.1	12.1	12.0	12.2	11.9
2005	12.0	12.1	12.2	12.5	12.5	12.7	12.8	12.9	12.8	12.9	12.9	13.2	12.6
2006	13.1	13.2	13.3	13.3	13.4	13.7	13.7	13.7	13.7	13.6	13.6	13.9	13.5
2007	13.8	13.9	14.0	14.0	14.2	14.7	14.7	14.9	14.9	14.8	14.8	15.0	14.5
2008	14.6	14.6	14.6	14.6	14.8	14.9	14.9	15.0	14.8	14.6	14.6	14.8	14.7
2009	14.4	14.4	14.3	14.0	14.0	14.2	14.1	14.2	14.1	13.5	13.4	14.0	14.1
Information													
1990	3.6	3.6	3.6	3.6	3.6	3.7	3.8	3.8	3.7	3.6	3.7	3.7	3.6
2000	4.0	3.9	3.9	4.0	4.0	4.1	4.1	4.0	4.0	3.9	4.0	4.0	3.9
2001	4.0	3.9	3.9	3.9	4.0	4.1	4.1	4.2	4.2	4.1	4.2	4.2	4.1
2002	4.2	4.2	4.2	4.2	4.1	4.2	4.2	4.1	4.1	4.0	4.1	4.1	4.1
2003	4.1	4.1	4.2	4.1	4.2	4.3	4.3	4.3	4.2	4.3	4.3	4.3	4.2
2004	4.3	4.3	4.3	4.2	4.2	4.3	4.4	4.4	4.4	4.2	4.3	4.3	4.3
2005	4.3	4.3	4.3	4.3	4.3	4.4	4.3	4.3	4.3	4.2	4.3	4.3	4.3
2006	4.3	4.3	4.2	4.1	4.1	4.2	4.1	4.1	4.1	4.0	4.0	4.1	4.1
2007	4.0	4.0	4.0	4.0	4.0	4.1	4.1	4.1	4.0	4.0	4.0	4.1	4.0
2008	4.0	4.0	4.0	4.0	4.0	4.0	4.1	4.1	4.0	4.0	4.0	4.0	4.0
2009	4.0	4.0	4.0	3.9	4.0	4.0	4.0	4.0	3.9	3.9	3.9	3.9	4.0

Employment by Industry: Wyoming, Selected Years, 1990–2009—*Continued*
(Numbers in thousands, not seasonally adjusted.)

Industry and year	January	February	March	April	May	June	July	August	September	October	November	December	Annual average
Financial Activities													
1990	7.7	7.7	7.9	7.9	7.9	8.1	8.1	8.2	7.9	7.9	7.9	7.9	7.9
2000	9.0	8.9	9.1	9.1	9.2	9.4	9.3	9.4	9.2	9.2	9.1	9.3	9.1
2001	9.0	9.0	9.1	9.3	9.4	9.7	9.7	9.9	9.7	9.6	9.6	9.6	9.5
2002	9.6	9.7	9.7	9.8	10.0	10.3	10.4	10.4	10.3	10.0	9.9	9.9	10.0
2003	9.8	9.8	10.0	10.0	10.1	10.4	10.3	10.4	10.3	10.3	10.2	10.2	10.2
2004	10.2	10.2	10.3	10.3	10.5	10.6	10.6	10.7	10.5	10.4	10.5	10.6	10.5
2005	10.5	10.4	10.6	10.6	10.8	11.0	11.0	11.0	10.9	10.8	10.8	11.0	10.8
2006	10.9	10.9	11.0	11.0	11.1	11.3	11.3	11.3	11.2	11.1	11.2	11.3	11.1
2007	11.0	11.0	11.1	11.2	11.3	11.6	11.6	11.6	11.5	11.5	11.4	11.5	11.4
2008	11.4	11.4	11.4	11.5	11.6	11.8	11.9	11.9	11.7	11.7	11.6	11.6	11.6
2009	11.3	11.3	11.2	11.2	11.3	11.4	11.3	11.3	11.1	11.1	10.9	11.0	11.2
Professional and Business Services													
1990	7.9	8.0	8.3	8.8	9.0	9.4	9.6	9.6	9.3	9.1	8.8	8.7	8.8
2000	13.6	13.8	14.2	14.6	15.0	15.5	15.5	15.4	15.0	14.8	14.6	14.4	14.7
2001	14.9	15.0	15.3	15.8	16.0	16.3	16.4	16.5	15.9	15.6	15.4	15.1	15.7
2002	14.5	14.8	15.0	15.5	15.7	16.2	16.6	16.4	15.7	15.8	15.5	15.2	15.6
2003	14.3	14.5	14.5	15.3	15.7	16.5	16.7	16.8	16.0	16.1	15.2	14.9	15.5
2004	14.3	14.3	14.4	15.2	15.4	16.2	16.4	16.5	15.7	15.6	15.1	14.8	15.3
2005	14.5	14.6	14.9	15.5	15.8	16.6	16.8	17.0	16.4	16.3	15.9	15.6	15.8
2006	15.4	15.7	15.9	16.7	17.3	17.9	18.0	18.1	17.8	17.4	17.2	17.3	17.1
2007	16.8	17.1	17.5	17.9	18.8	19.6	19.5	19.5	19.0	18.8	18.0	17.8	18.4
2008	17.3	17.5	17.7	18.2	18.9	19.7	19.8	19.8	19.2	19.0	18.3	18.0	18.6
2009	17.3	17.0	17.0	17.1	17.5	17.8	18.0	17.9	17.4	17.2	16.9	16.4	17.3
Education and Health Services													
1990	12.7	12.6	12.6	12.9	13.1	12.8	12.6	12.8	13.1	13.2	13.1	13.3	12.9
2000	17.6	17.9	18.1	18.0	18.2	18.3	18.2	18.4	18.3	18.7	18.5	18.7	18.2
2001	18.8	18.9	19.2	19.1	19.2	19.2	19.3	19.6	19.3	19.5	19.8	19.6	19.3
2002	19.3	19.7	19.8	19.7	19.9	20.0	20.0	20.1	20.0	19.9	20.1	20.2	19.9
2003	20.4	20.5	20.4	20.7	20.7	20.9	20.9	20.8	20.9	20.8	21.1	21.1	20.8
2004	21.2	21.1	21.2	21.3	21.2	21.5	21.5	21.7	21.6	21.5	22.0	22.0	21.5
2005	21.7	21.7	21.9	21.8	21.9	22.0	22.1	22.2	22.1	22.2	22.5	22.4	22.0
2006	22.1	22.2	22.5	22.3	22.6	22.8	22.7	22.8	22.7	22.7	23.0	22.8	22.6
2007	22.7	22.9	23.0	22.9	23.2	23.4	23.4	23.5	23.5	23.6	24.0	23.8	23.3
2008	23.7	24.1	24.1	24.2	24.2	24.6	24.7	24.7	24.8	25.1	25.1	25.0	24.5
2009	25.2	25.3	25.4	25.4	25.7	25.5	25.6	25.6	25.6	25.7	25.6	25.7	25.5
Leisure and Hospitality													
1990	19.8	20.2	20.7	21.2	22.8	28.8	30.1	29.9	26.7	22.8	20.9	21.2	23.7
2000	26.2	26.4	26.9	27.0	29.6	35.4	36.7	36.1	32.7	29.0	26.2	27.2	29.9
2001	26.3	26.5	26.9	26.8	29.5	34.5	35.7	35.5	32.2	28.6	26.0	27.2	29.6
2002	26.6	27.0	27.2	27.5	29.9	34.9	36.7	35.9	33.2	29.6	27.1	27.7	30.3
2003	27.5	27.5	27.7	27.8	30.3	35.5	36.8	36.4	33.5	29.8	27.7	28.5	30.8
2004	28.1	28.2	28.8	29.2	30.8	36.0	37.1	36.8	34.0	31.1	28.4	29.4	31.5
2005	28.7	28.9	29.2	29.3	31.3	36.5	38.1	37.6	34.8	31.4	28.7	30.0	32.0
2006	29.3	29.8	30.2	29.6	31.6	37.0	38.4	37.8	35.0	31.8	29.4	31.0	32.6
2007	30.5	31.0	31.3	30.5	32.6	37.4	39.1	38.6	36.0	32.6	30.4	31.9	33.5
2008	31.6	32.0	32.5	31.6	34.1	38.8	40.3	39.7	36.9	33.8	30.6	31.9	34.5
2009	31.1	30.8	31.2	30.1	32.5	36.8	38.5	38.0	35.8	32.1	28.7	29.6	32.9
Other Services													
1990	6.3	6.3	6.4	6.5	6.7	6.8	6.9	6.9	6.8	6.9	6.9	6.9	6.6
2000	8.9	9.0	9.1	9.1	9.2	9.3	9.3	9.3	9.1	9.1	9.1	9.1	9.1
2001	8.8	8.9	9.0	9.1	9.3	9.4	9.4	9.5	9.4	9.4	9.4	9.5	9.3
2002	9.3	9.4	9.5	9.6	9.8	9.8	9.9	9.9	9.7	9.6	9.5	9.6	9.6
2003	9.5	9.5	9.6	9.4	9.6	9.7	9.8	9.8	9.5	9.5	9.5	9.6	9.6
2004	9.5	9.6	9.6	9.7	9.8	9.8	10.0	10.0	9.7	9.6	9.6	9.7	9.7
2005	9.4	9.6	9.6	9.7	9.8	10.0	10.3	10.3	10.1	10.0	10.0	10.2	9.9
2006	10.3	10.4	10.7	10.8	11.1	11.4	11.5	11.5	11.3	11.3	11.3	11.5	11.1
2007	11.3	11.4	11.6	11.6	12.1	12.1	12.1	12.1	11.9	11.9	11.8	12.0	11.8
2008	11.8	11.9	12.0	12.0	12.2	12.3	12.4	12.4	12.2	12.1	12.1	12.1	12.1
2009	12.1	12.0	12.0	11.9	12.2	12.2	12.1	11.9	11.7	11.5	11.2	11.0	11.8
Government													
1990	55.0	55.8	56.3	57.0	58.1	56.6	48.5	48.8	55.8	56.6	57.5	57.2	55.2
2000	60.1	60.6	62.3	62.0	63.6	61.3	56.3	56.5	60.2	62.1	62.0	62.0	60.7
2001	60.8	61.4	62.2	62.0	63.1	63.3	57.4	57.9	61.2	62.7	62.7	63.4	61.5
2002	61.9	62.3	63.4	63.0	64.1	64.1	58.5	58.4	62.7	64.2	64.3	65.1	62.7
2003	63.3	63.7	64.5	64.2	65.2	65.2	59.2	59.1	62.9	64.9	64.5	65.1	63.5
2004	64.2	64.6	65.3	65.5	66.5	66.4	60.8	60.4	63.7	65.6	65.5	65.7	64.5
2005	64.7	65.2	65.8	65.8	67.1	66.6	61.0	61.1	65.1	66.5	66.2	66.4	65.1
2006	64.8	65.6	66.2	66.1	67.1	67.4	61.3	60.9	65.5	66.9	66.5	67.0	65.4
2007	66.1	66.9	67.4	67.4	68.8	68.7	62.5	62.5	68.0	69.1	69.1	69.0	67.1
2008	67.4	68.7	69.3	69.5	71.4	71.3	64.9	64.3	70.7	71.9	71.8	71.9	69.4
2009	70.1	71.8	72.5	72.9	74.5	73.2	66.0	65.8	72.7	73.0	72.9	73.2	71.6

Average Weekly Hours by Selected Industry: Wyoming, 2007–2009

(Not seasonally adjusted.)

Industry and year	January	February	March	April	May	June	July	August	September	October	November	December	Annual average
Total Private													
2007	34.7	36.0	35.8	36.1	36.0	36.8	37.4	37.5	36.1	35.6	35.7	36.5	36.2
2008	36.1	36.1	36.5	36.3	36.3	37.3	37.1	37.4	37.1	36.7	37.0	36.2	36.7
2009	35.8	36.3	35.5	35.1	35.3	35.2	35.5	36.7	35.2	35.1	36.1	34.9	35.6
Goods-Producing													
2007	39.3	42.2	41.5	40.9	42.2	42.6	43.4	44.0	43.1	43.5	42.7	43.3	42.4
2008	42.6	42.9	43.3	43.2	43.6	44.2	43.8	43.9	44.0	43.5	43.5	42.9	43.5
2009	41.9	41.9	41.0	40.8	41.2	39.8	41.3	42.9	40.9	40.8	41.8	41.1	41.3
Mining and Logging													
2007	42.4	45.8	44.1	44.5	45.1	45.5	46.0	46.4	46.1	45.2	46.0	47.1	45.4
2008	46.7	47.2	47.1	46.6	45.3	46.2	46.6	46.0	46.8	45.9	46.6	45.3	46.4
2009	44.4	43.5	42.8	42.6	41.6	41.4	42.6	43.7	44.2	44.2	44.7	44.8	43.4
Construction													
2007	37.6	40.9	40.5	39.1	41.6	41.9	43.0	44.0	42.7	43.7	42.1	41.8	41.6
2008	41.0	41.5	42.1	42.3	43.3	43.7	43.0	43.4	43.0	42.6	42.0	41.6	42.5
2009	41.0	41.6	39.9	40.0	41.2	38.8	41.0	42.9	39.8	39.5	40.8	39.2	40.5
Trade, Transportation, and Utilities													
2007	34.9	35.7	36.6	36.9	36.4	36.6	36.4	37.2	35.7	34.0	34.8	36.3	36.0
2008	35.5	35.1	35.8	35.6	35.0	36.3	36.5	36.4	36.0	36.1	36.5	35.7	35.9
2009	35.7	36.6	36.7	37.1	36.5	36.6	36.0	37.3	36.0	36.0	37.2	35.7	36.5
Professional and Business Services													
2007	32.7	32.6	31.2	31.6	31.1	32.2	34.8	35.7	36.8	35.8	35.4	35.7	33.8
2008	34.5	34.9	34.3	33.8	33.4	34.6	34.2	33.8	34.6	34.1	35.1	34.1	34.3
2009	34.9	34.7	33.9	34.1	34.5	34.9	35.2	35.8	34.8	34.4	35.1	33.9	34.7
Education and Health Services													
2007	31.4	33.3	33.8	34.1	33.8	35.1	35.8	34.4	32.6	31.7	31.8	32.5	33.4
2008	32.2	31.9	32.9	31.8	32.4	33.4	33.0	33.4	33.0	32.4	33.1	32.7	32.7
2009	32.4	33.1	32.9	31.9	33.2	33.9	33.5	34.6	33.8	33.7	34.5	33.5	33.4
Leisure and Hospitality													
2007	25.1	26.2	24.8	25.7	25.0	27.0	28.1	27.3	26.1	24.8	24.9	25.4	25.9
2008	25.8	26.4	26.9	26.8	26.5	27.5	27.9	28.3	27.3	25.8	25.6	25.2	26.7
2009	25.5	25.8	25.0	24.7	25.5	27.4	27.7	29.2	27.3	26.7	26.6	25.9	26.5
Other Services													
2007	31.1	33.2	33.1	32.5	32.6	32.8	32.7	33.8	32.3	31.1	30.8	31.0	32.3
2008	31.1	31.1	31.0	30.4	30.1	31.3	30.4	30.1	28.7	29.0	29.7	28.1	30.1
2009	29.9	29.5	29.8	30.2	30.4	29.5	28.9	29.8	27.3	27.8	29.1	28.0	29.2

Average Hourly Earnings by Selected Industry: Wyoming, 2007–2009

(Dollars, not seasonally adjusted.)

Industry and year	January	February	March	April	May	June	July	August	September	October	November	December	Annual average
Total Private													
2007	19.61	19.59	19.69	19.95	19.69	19.92	20.06	20.14	19.93	20.33	20.59	20.91	20.03
2008	20.40	20.46	20.82	20.67	20.86	20.55	20.51	20.68	21.03	21.14	21.38	21.50	20.83
2009	21.27	21.26	21.25	21.26	21.10	20.51	20.46	20.69	20.84	21.23	21.38	21.69	21.07
Goods-Producing													
2007	23.09	22.63	22.82	22.90	22.80	23.43	23.69	23.82	23.64	24.25	24.94	25.39	23.64
2008	24.77	24.53	24.47	24.56	24.68	24.49	24.66	24.66	24.86	24.74	24.87	25.31	24.72
2009	25.17	25.14	25.72	25.89	25.55	25.32	24.96	25.39	25.29	25.57	25.66	26.03	25.47
Mining and Logging													
2007	27.61	26.61	27.16	27.72	27.60	28.28	29.04	28.71	26.28	26.50	27.43	27.35	27.42
2008	27.68	27.13	27.52	27.71	28.20	28.11	27.91	27.92	28.18	28.41	27.98	28.28	27.92
2009	28.04	28.26	28.46	29.10	28.96	28.99	28.83	29.00	29.02	28.77	28.96	28.64	28.73
Construction													
2007	21.11	20.93	21.07	20.92	20.69	21.31	21.25	21.70	23.09	24.10	24.75	25.64	22.38
2008	24.60	24.55	23.88	23.99	24.03	23.47	23.47	23.51	23.71	23.75	24.05	24.69	23.94
2009	24.29	24.07	24.44	24.56	24.26	23.84	23.22	23.84	23.54	24.10	24.01	24.23	24.02
Trade, Transportation, and Utilities													
2007	19.01	19.23	19.53	20.11	19.62	19.30	19.55	19.34	20.06	20.20	20.18	20.86	19.79
2008	19.87	20.47	21.22	21.07	21.55	20.71	20.34	20.42	20.62	20.57	20.61	20.98	20.70
2009	20.39	20.38	20.41	21.07	20.64	19.64	19.79	20.29	20.12	20.84	20.29	20.55	20.36
Professional and Business Services													
2007	24.65	24.71	23.84	24.47	24.14	24.19	24.65	24.71	22.39	22.34	22.04	22.26	23.55
2008	21.98	22.04	22.72	22.23	22.26	22.38	22.37	22.84	22.95	23.47	24.07	24.10	22.79
2009	24.37	24.74	24.87	24.42	23.92	23.84	23.41	23.81	23.79	24.33	24.45	24.58	24.20
Education and Health Services													
2007	17.22	17.16	16.76	17.07	16.58	17.69	17.40	17.49	16.74	16.66	16.87	17.52	17.07
2008	17.76	17.94	18.03	17.61	17.83	18.11	17.96	18.23	18.71	19.07	19.00	19.08	18.29
2009	19.36	19.11	18.83	18.97	19.09	18.83	18.98	19.37	19.48	19.59	19.67	20.08	19.28
Leisure and Hospitality													
2007	11.30	10.98	11.29	11.47	11.14	11.14	11.21	11.27	11.29	11.52	11.26	11.51	11.28
2008	11.17	10.92	10.98	10.94	11.13	11.12	11.34	11.52	11.52	11.56	11.53	11.54	11.28
2009	12.18	12.47	12.42	12.48	12.34	11.92	12.11	12.37	12.92	12.73	12.91	13.24	12.49
Other Services													
2007	17.09	17.80	18.52	18.65	18.50	18.44	18.11	18.64	19.50	18.98	18.68	19.46	18.53
2008	18.48	18.44	18.68	18.70	18.77	18.35	18.77	18.83	19.04	18.75	19.39	19.48	18.80
2009	19.03	18.80	19.26	19.28	19.41	19.40	18.85	18.81	18.50	18.98	19.52	19.99	19.15

Average Weekly Earnings by Selected Industry: Wyoming, 2007–2009

(Dollars, not seasonally adjusted.)

Industry and year	January	February	March	April	May	June	July	August	September	October	November	December	Annual average
Total Private													
2007	680.47	705.24	704.90	720.20	708.84	733.06	750.24	755.25	719.47	723.75	735.06	763.22	725.09
2008	736.44	738.61	759.93	750.32	757.22	766.52	760.92	773.43	780.21	775.84	791.06	778.30	764.46
2009	761.47	771.74	754.38	746.23	744.83	721.95	726.33	759.32	733.57	745.17	771.82	756.98	750.09
Goods-Producing													
2007	907.44	954.99	947.03	936.61	962.16	998.12	1028.15	1048.08	1018.88	1054.88	1064.94	1099.39	1002.34
2008	1055.20	1052.34	1059.55	1060.99	1076.05	1082.46	1080.11	1082.57	1093.84	1076.19	1081.85	1085.80	1075.32
2009	1054.62	1053.37	1054.52	1056.31	1052.66	1007.74	1030.85	1089.23	1034.36	1043.26	1072.59	1069.83	1051.91
Mining and Logging													
2007	1170.66	1218.74	1197.76	1233.54	1244.76	1286.74	1335.84	1332.14	1211.51	1197.80	1261.78	1288.19	1244.87
2008	1292.66	1280.54	1296.19	1291.29	1277.46	1298.68	1300.61	1284.32	1318.82	1304.02	1303.87	1281.08	1295.49
2009	1244.98	1229.31	1218.09	1239.66	1204.74	1200.19	1228.16	1267.30	1282.68	1271.63	1294.51	1283.07	1246.88
Construction													
2007	793.74	856.04	853.34	817.97	860.70	892.89	913.75	954.80	985.94	1053.17	1041.98	1071.75	931.01
2008	1008.60	1018.83	1005.35	1014.78	1040.50	1025.64	1009.21	1020.33	1019.53	1011.75	1010.10	1027.10	1017.45
2009	995.89	1001.31	975.16	982.40	999.51	924.99	952.02	1022.74	936.89	951.95	979.61	949.82	972.81
Trade, Transportation, and Utilities													
2007	663.45	686.51	714.80	742.06	714.17	706.38	711.62	719.45	716.14	686.80	702.26	757.22	712.44
2008	705.39	718.50	759.68	750.09	754.25	751.77	742.41	743.29	742.32	742.58	752.27	748.99	743.13
2009	727.92	745.91	749.05	781.70	753.36	718.82	712.44	756.82	724.32	750.24	754.79	733.64	743.14
Professional and Business Services													
2007	806.06	805.55	743.81	773.25	750.75	778.92	857.82	882.15	823.95	799.77	780.22	794.68	795.99
2008	758.31	769.20	779.30	751.37	743.48	774.35	765.05	771.99	794.07	800.33	844.86	821.81	781.70
2009	850.51	858.48	843.09	832.72	825.24	832.02	824.03	852.40	827.89	836.95	858.20	833.26	839.74
Education and Health Services													
2007	540.71	571.43	566.49	582.09	560.40	620.92	622.92	601.66	545.72	528.12	536.47	569.40	570.14
2008	571.87	572.29	593.19	560.00	577.69	604.87	592.68	608.88	617.43	617.87	628.90	623.92	598.08
2009	627.26	632.54	619.51	605.14	633.79	638.34	635.83	670.20	658.42	660.18	678.62	672.68	643.95
Leisure and Hospitality													
2007	283.63	287.68	279.99	294.78	278.50	300.78	315.00	307.67	294.67	285.70	280.37	292.35	292.15
2008	288.19	288.29	295.36	293.19	294.95	305.80	316.39	326.02	314.50	298.25	295.17	290.81	301.18
2009	310.59	321.73	310.50	308.26	314.67	326.61	335.45	361.20	352.72	339.89	343.41	342.92	330.99
Other Services													
2007	531.50	590.96	613.01	606.13	603.10	604.83	592.20	630.03	629.85	590.28	575.34	603.26	598.52
2008	574.73	573.48	579.08	568.48	564.98	574.36	570.61	566.78	546.45	543.75	575.88	547.39	565.88
2009	569.00	554.60	573.95	582.26	590.06	572.30	544.77	560.54	505.05	527.64	568.03	559.72	559.18

PART B

METROPOLITAN STATISTICAL AREA (MSA) DATA

METROPOLITAN STATISTICAL AREA (MSA) NOTES

Part B provides employment data for the 75 largest metropolitan statistical areas (MSAs) and New England city and town areas (NECTAs) in the United States for 1990 and 2000 to 2009. As mentioned in the technical notes, all employment data are for MSAs unless otherwise noted. NECTAs are similar to MSAs but are defined by cities and towns rather than counties in the New England region.

According to the 2009 estimates from the Census Bureau, New York-Northern New Jersey-Long Island, NY-NJ-PA, was the largest MSA in the United States with a population of 19,069,796—larger than the population of all but three states. Although it was the biggest MSA, it was not among the fastest growing. Many of the MSAs that experienced rapid growth were in the south and the west. From 2000 to 2009, Raleigh-Cary, NC, grew the most quickly, increasing by 41.2 percent, followed by Las Vegas-Paradise, NV, which grew at a rate of 38.3 percent. From 2008 to 2009, Las Vegas-Paradise, NV, experienced a slow down in growth, dropping to 27th of the top 75 MSAs in regards to growth.

Total nonfarm employment also increased rapidly in the south and west from 1990 to 2009. Employment nearly tripled in Las Vegas-Paradise, NV, from 1990 to 2009. However, for the second year in a row, total nonfarm employment experienced a decline (-9.7 percent between 2008 and 2009) after increasing an average of 5.5 percent per year from 1990 to 2007. New for 2009, Orlando-Kissimmee-Sanford, FL, experienced one of the top five largest growths in total nonfarm employment at 74.6 percent from 1990 to 2009.

While employment increased in the vast majority of MSAs from 1990 to 2009, it declined most significantly in the following areas: Detroit-Warren-Livonia, MI; Dayton, OH; Hartford-West Hartford-East Hartford, CT NECTA; New Orleans-Metairie-Kenner, LA; and Cleveland-Elyria-Mentor, OH. Although there has been a steady increase in employment since 1990, last year saw a drastic decrease, in part due to the economic state of the country. In Detroit, total nonfarm employment decreased by more than 160,000 people.

Similar to the state data, manufacturing employment declined in most MSAs from 1990 to 2009. From 2008 to 2009, every MSAs experienced a decrease in manufacturing employment. Employment in education and health services, professional and business services, and leisure and hospitality grew rapidly in many MSAs from 1990 to 2009, but these figures mostly dropped from last year. Only MSAs (and not states) had any sort of growth in employment from 2008 to 2009.

In 2009, unemployment rates increased substantially. Unemployment figures ranged from 4.9 percent in Omaha-Council Bluffs, NE-IA, to a high of 15.1 percent in Fresno, CA, and Detroit-Warren-Livonia, MI. Oklahoma City, OK, and Washington-Arlington-Alexandria, DC-VA-MD-WV, had the lowest unemployment rates at 5.9 and 6.0 percent, respectively, among all MSAs with a population of 1,000,000 or more according to the 2009 unemployment ratings from the Bureau of Labor Statistics.

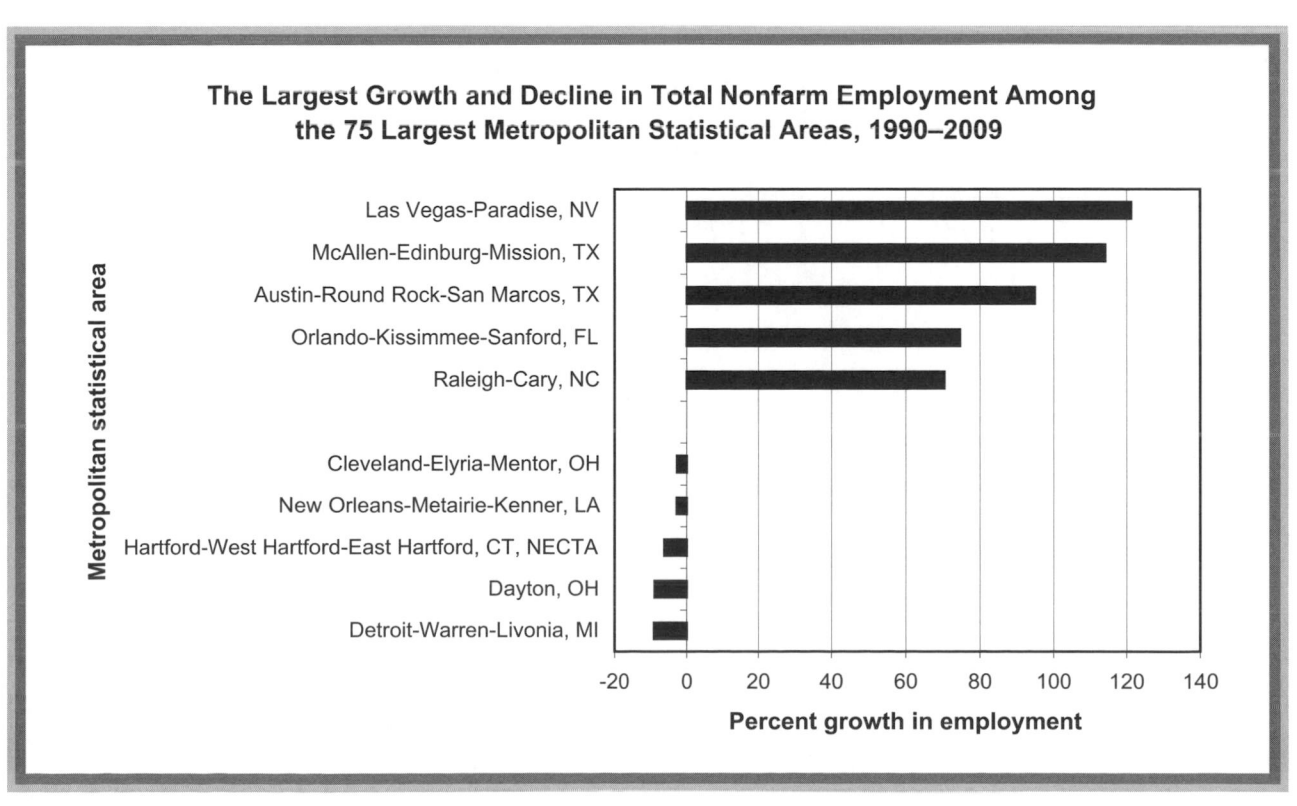

The Largest Growth and Decline in Total Nonfarm Employment Among the 75 Largest Metropolitan Statistical Areas, 1990–2009

Rank	Metropolitan statistical area	2009 Estimated population	1990 Total nonfarm employment	2009 Total nonfarm employment	Percent change in total nonfarm employment, 1990–2009	2009 Unemployment rate
1	New York-Northern New Jersey-Long Island, NY-NJ-PA	19,069,796	7892.9	8304.5	5.2	8.8
2	Los Angeles-Long Beach-Santa Ana, CA................................	12,874,797	5308.1	5200.9	-2.0	10.9
3	Chicago-Naperville-Joliet, IL-IN-WI....................................	9,580,567	4011.2	4291.0	7.0	10.0
4	Dallas-Fort Worth-Arlington, TX..	6,447,615	2001.3	2864.3	43.1	7.8
5	Philadelphia-Camden-Wilmington, PA-NJ-DE-MD	5,968,252	2498.8	2,713.6	8.6	8.3
6	Houston-Sugar Land-Baytown, TX......................................	5,867,489	1764.8	2539.0	43.9	7.6
7	Miami-Fort Lauderdale-Pompano Beach, FL........................	5,547,051	1687.8	2201.9	30.5	10.2
8	Washington-Arlington-Alexandria, DC-VA-MD-WV	5,476,241	2250.1	2950.2	31.1	6.0
9	Atlanta-Sandy Springs-Marietta, GA..................................	5,475,213	1606.2	2290.3	42.6	9.6
10	Boston-Cambridge-Quincy, MA-NH, NECTA	4,588,680	2225.5	2408.8	8.2	7.8
11	Detroit-Warren-Livonia, MI..	4,403,437	1912.1	1740.0	-9.0	15.1
12	Phoenix-Mesa-Scottsdale, AZ..	4,364,094	1013.3	1719.6	69.7	8.5
13	San Francisco-Oakland-Fremont, CA	4,317,853	1826.5	1908.8	4.5	9.7
14	Riverside-San Bernardino-Ontario, CA	4,143,113	712.6	1131.9	58.8	13.3
15	Seattle-Tacoma-Bellevue, WA...	3,407,848	1301.8	1668.7	28.2	8.7
16	Minneapolis-St. Paul-Bloomington, MN-WI........................	3,269,814	1390.9	1702.2	22.4	7.8
17	San Diego-Carlsbad-San Marcos, CA..................................	3,053,793	966.6	1229.6	27.2	9.7
18	St. Louis, MO-IL..	2,828,990	1187.6	1299.3	9.4	9.9
19	Tampa-St. Petersburg-Clearwater, FL................................	2,747,272	869.5	1135.8	30.6	11.0
20	Baltimore-Towson, MD...	2,690,886	1152.8	1271.7	10.3	7.4
21	Denver-Aurora-Broomfield, CO	2,552,195	855.8	1198.5	40.0	7.9
22	Pittsburgh, PA..	2,354,957	1039.9	1120.3	7.7	7.4
23	Portland-Vancouver-Hillsboro, OR-WA	2,241,841	730.4	972.4	33.1	10.6
24	Cincinnati-Middletown, OH-KY-IN.....................................	2,171,896	864.9	995.1	15.1	9.3
25	Sacramento–Arden-Arcade–Roseville, CA...........................	2,127,355	618.5	833.4	34.7	11.2
26	Cleveland-Elyria-Mentor, OH..	2,091,286	1028.5	1001.1	-2.7	9.1
27	Orlando-Kissimmee-Sanford, FL..	2,082,421	578.3	1009.5	74.6	10.5
28	San Antonio-New Braunfels, TX	2,072,128	543.3	834.6	53.6	6.7
29	Kansas City, MO-KS...	2,067,585	828.5	981.5	18.5	8.6
30	Las Vegas-Paradise, NV..	1,902,834	373.6	826.3	121.2	12.0
31	San Jose-Sunnyvale-Santa Clara, CA..................................	1,839,700	824.2	855.6	3.8	11.1
32	Columbus, OH...	1,801,848	730.9	907.7	24.2	8.4
33	Charlotte-Gastonia-Concord, NC-SC	1,745,524	550.2	810.2	47.3	11.7
34	Indianapolis-Carmel, IN...	1,743,658	671.6	872.6	29.9	8.4
35	Austin-Round Rock-San Marcos, TX	1,705,075	389.0	758.2	94.9	6.9
36	Virginia Beach-Norfolk-Newport News, VA-NC	1,674,498	607.5	739.4	21.7	6.8
37	Providence-Fall River-Warwick, RI-MA, NECTA	1,600,642	525.0	540.1	2.9	11.4
38	Nashville-Davidson–Murfreesboro–Franklin, TN.................	1,582,264	526.6	723.7	37.4	9.3
39	Milwaukee-Waukesha-West Allis, WI.................................	1,559,667	756.6	810.0	7.1	8.7
40	Jacksonville, FL...	1,328,144	415.6	585.8	41.0	10.0
41	Memphis, TN-MS-AR..	1,304,926	493.9	600.8	21.6	10.0
42	Louisville-Jefferson County, KY-IN.....................................	1,258,577	512.1	595.8	16.3	10.1
43	Richmond, VA..	1,238,187	493.5	604.1	22.4	7.5
44	Oklahoma City, OK...	1,227,278	426.6	559.8	31.2	5.9
45	Hartford-West Hartford-East Hartford, CT, NECTA	1,195,998	575.7	540.3	-6.1	8.3
46	New Orleans-Metairie-Kenner, LA.....................................	1,189,981	533.8	518.7	-2.8	6.7
47	Birmingham-Hoover, AL	1,131,070	430.5	496.2	15.3	9.4
48	Salt Lake City, UT..	1,130,293	377.2	610.8	61.9	6.4
49	Raleigh-Cary, NC...	1,125,827	293.3	499.7	70.4	8.8
50	Buffalo-Niagara Falls, NY..	1,123,804	547.5	537.9	-1.8	8.4
51	Rochester, NY...	1,035,566	491.1	503.2	2.5	7.9
52	Tucson, AZ...	1,020,200	248.9	361.9	45.4	8.3
53	Tulsa, OK...	929,015	323.1	413.1	27.9	6.9
54	Fresno, CA...	915,267	224.5	286.6	27.7	15.1
55	Honolulu, HI...	907,574	410.7	437.6	6.5	5.7
56	Bridgeport-Stamford-Norwalk, CT, NECTA.........................	901,208	401.3	399.6	-0.4	7.8
57	Albuquerque, NM..	857,903	271.4	379.1	39.7	7.4
58	Albany-Schenectady-Troy, NY	857,592	409.4	442.7	8.1	6.9
59	Omaha-Council Bluffs, NE-IA..	849,517	355.2	459.1	29.3	4.9
60	New Haven-Milford, CT..	848,006	275.1	266.0	-3.3	8.2
61	Dayton, OH..	835,063	408.4	372.6	-8.8	11.2
62	Allentown-Bethlehem-Easton, PA-NJ	816,012	286.6	332.5	16.0	8.8
63	Bakersfield-Delano, CA	807,407	170.7	227.9	33.5	14.4
64	Worcester, MA-CT, NECTA	803,701	221.4	237.8	7.4	9
65	Oxnard-Thousand Oaks-Ventura, CA.................................	802,983	230.3	275.0	19.4	10
66	Baton Rouge, LA...	786,947	259.6	369.9	42.5	6.4
67	Grand Rapids-Wyoming, MI..	778,009	304.7	361.6	18.7	11.2
68	El Paso, TX	751,296	208.8	272.1	30.3	9
69	Columbia, SC..	744,730	284.6	347.2	22.0	9.5
70	McAllen-Edinburg-Mission, TX	741,152	101.4	217.2	114.2	10.6
71	Greensboro-High Point, NC	714,765	298.1	343.8	15.3	11.3
72	Akron, OH	699,935	283.0	319.8	13.0	9.8
73	Knoxville, TN..	699,247	242.8	321.5	32.4	8.7
74	Springfield, MA-CT, NECTA	698,903	290.4	285.7	-1.6	8.9
75	North Port-Bradenton-Sarasota, FL	688,126	170.5	249.1	46.1	11.3

Employment by Industry: Akron, OH, Selected Years, 1990–2009

(Numbers in thousands, not seasonally adjusted.)

Industry and year	January	February	March	April	May	June	July	August	September	October	November	December	Annual average
Total Nonfarm													
1990	272.1	276.8	280.1	282.3	286.7	283.1	280.5	282.6	288.2	287.8	288.4	287.2	283.0
2000	322.2	325.8	328.8	331.8	335.8	332.4	330.1	328.5	331.9	334.0	334.6	333.2	330.8
2001	321.6	323.4	325.5	328.2	329.9	330.2	324.8	325.3	328.5	329.9	330.8	330.0	327.3
2002	316.4	317.4	320.0	320.5	321.7	323.2	321.7	321.2	326.1	326.9	326.0	325.6	322.2
2003	317.3	318.6	320.8	326.5	329.0	326.7	326.3	327.0	331.2	332.2	332.5	333.3	326.7
2004	320.8	323.2	326.2	330.5	332.4	331.6	330.9	331.0	335.2	337.1	338.1	338.5	331.3
2005	328.0	330.8	332.9	337.8	340.7	336.4	336.7	337.3	341.1	341.9	342.7	342.2	337.4
2006	330.4	332.4	334.6	338.6	342.4	338.8	338.1	339.3	342.9	342.1	343.3	342.7	338.8
2007	332.0	333.1	334.8	338.5	340.5	341.6	340.6	341.3	344.1	344.6	346.3	346.6	340.3
2008	335.8	337.9	337.9	340.1	340.9	339.8	339.2	339.6	341.6	340.8	339.8	338.0	339.3
2009	323.7	322.3	321.7	321.9	323.8	317.4	316.9	316.4	319.2	319.9	317.4	316.9	319.8
Total Private													
1990	230.4	230.3	233.1	235.7	239.3	242.2	241.3	243.1	242.3	240.8	240.8	240.2	238.3
2000	275.7	275.4	278.4	281.2	284.1	288.3	287.1	287.1	284.3	284.2	284.5	284.8	282.9
2001	273.8	273.3	274.4	277.3	282.0	285.3	281.3	283.2	280.0	279.7	280.0	280.7	279.3
2002	268.7	267.4	269.1	269.7	273.8	277.4	278.1	279.0	276.9	275.8	274.4	274.8	273.8
2003	269.0	268.1	269.3	273.9	278.0	280.2	281.0	282.2	280.6	280.1	280.0	280.7	276.9
2004	271.2	270.9	273.6	278.1	282.0	285.6	285.8	286.8	285.2	285.2	285.8	286.4	281.4
2005	277.7	278.7	280.7	285.8	288.7	291.1	292.2	292.6	290.9	290.7	290.8	290.7	287.6
2006	280.8	280.9	283.1	287.3	290.7	294.4	294.3	295.4	292.6	291.0	292.1	292.6	289.6
2007	283.8	281.9	283.6	287.4	291.9	295.9	295.8	295.6	293.8	293.3	294.8	295.4	291.1
2008	287.3	286.4	286.3	288.7	292.4	293.8	293.6	293.5	291.0	289.1	288.1	286.7	289.7
2009	274.4	271.1	270.4	269.9	271.4	271.5	270.9	270.7	268.9	268.0	265.5	265.1	269.8
Goods-Producing													
1990	67.1	67.5	68.7	69.4	70.6	71.4	70.9	71.9	71.5	70.9	70.0	68.9	69.9
2000	72.1	72.1	72.5	73.8	74.7	75.6	74.8	74.5	73.5	73.6	73.2	72.1	73.5
2001	68.5	68.1	68.2	68.7	69.1	69.6	67.8	68.7	67.5	66.9	66.2	65.9	67.9
2002	62.1	61.6	62.0	62.2	63.7	64.4	65.2	65.4	64.8	64.3	63.7	63.1	63.5
2003	61.5	61.4	61.8	63.4	64.0	64.3	64.5	64.8	64.4	64.5	63.8	63.4	63.4
2004	60.7	60.6	61.5	62.7	63.8	64.5	64.6	65.3	64.8	64.6	64.2	63.7	63.4
2005	60.9	61.4	61.8	63.2	64.0	64.4	64.5	64.5	64.1	63.6	63.7	62.7	63.2
2006	60.4	60.6	61.7	62.8	63.5	64.2	63.4	63.8	63.6	63.2	62.8	62.4	62.7
2007	60.1	59.1	59.6	60.3	61.4	62.1	62.3	61.8	61.4	60.9	61.0	60.2	60.9
2008	57.4	57.0	56.8	57.4	58.6	59.1	59.2	59.0	58.5	58.2	57.4	55.8	57.9
2009	52.5	51.3	50.4	50.1	49.6	49.3	49.6	49.8	49.4	49.3	48.8	47.8	49.8
Mining, Logging, and Construction													
1990	9.2	9.2	9.7	10.5	11.1	11.5	11.6	11.7	11.4	11.3	11.0	10.1	10.7
2000	13.1	13.1	13.9	14.9	15.7	16.2	16.1	16.0	15.9	15.7	15.2	14.3	15.0
2001	12.7	12.7	13.3	14.1	15.1	15.8	16.1	16.1	15.5	15.4	14.9	14.3	14.7
2002	12.3	12.1	12.5	12.7	13.9	14.6	15.2	15.4	15.0	14.6	14.2	13.5	13.8
2003	12.1	11.7	12.2	13.5	14.3	14.7	14.9	15.2	15.0	14.9	14.4	13.8	13.8
2004	11.8	11.6	12.3	13.3	14.2	14.8	15.4	15.4	15.1	15.0	14.5	13.8	13.9
2005	12.0	12.0	12.2	13.7	14.7	15.3	15.6	15.7	15.6	15.3	15.3	14.4	14.3
2006	12.7	12.6	13.5	14.7	15.5	16.0	16.0	16.1	16.0	15.8	15.3	14.7	14.9
2007	12.9	12.3	13.0	13.8	14.7	15.3	15.5	15.3	15.1	15.0	14.8	13.8	14.3
2008	12.1	11.8	11.8	12.6	13.7	14.2	14.4	14.4	14.3	14.2	13.7	12.5	13.3
2009	11.0	10.9	11.1	11.7	12.5	12.6	13.0	12.7	12.4	12.4	12.1	11.2	12.0
Manufacturing													
1990	57.9	58.3	59.0	58.9	59.5	59.9	59.3	60.2	60.1	59.6	59.0	58.8	59.2
2000	59.0	59.0	58.6	58.9	59.0	59.4	58.7	58.5	57.6	57.9	58.0	57.8	58.5
2001	55.8	55.4	54.9	54.6	54.0	53.8	51.7	52.6	52.0	51.5	51.3	51.6	53.3
2002	49.8	49.5	49.5	49.5	49.8	49.8	50.0	50.0	49.8	49.7	49.5	49.6	49.7
2003	49.4	49.7	49.6	49.9	49.7	49.6	49.6	49.6	49.4	49.6	49.4	49.6	49.5
2004	48.9	49.0	49.2	49.4	49.6	49.7	49.2	49.9	49.7	49.6	49.7	49.9	49.5
2005	48.9	49.4	49.6	49.5	49.3	49.1	48.9	48.8	48.5	48.3	48.4	48.3	48.9
2006	47.7	48.0	48.2	48.1	48.0	48.2	47.4	47.7	47.6	47.4	47.5	47.7	47.8
2007	47.2	46.8	46.6	46.5	46.7	46.8	46.8	46.5	46.3	45.9	46.2	46.4	46.6
2008	45.3	45.2	45.0	44.8	44.9	44.9	44.8	44.6	44.2	44.0	43.7	43.3	44.6
2009	41.5	40.4	39.3	38.4	37.1	36.7	36.6	37.1	37.0	36.9	36.7	36.6	37.9
Service-Providing													
1990	205.0	209.3	211.4	212.9	216.1	211.7	209.6	210.7	216.7	216.9	218.4	218.3	213.1
2000	250.1	253.7	256.3	258.0	261.1	256.8	255.3	254.0	258.4	260.4	261.4	261.1	257.2
2001	253.1	255.3	257.3	259.5	260.8	260.6	257.0	256.6	261.0	263.0	264.6	264.1	259.4
2002	254.3	255.8	258.0	258.3	258.0	258.8	256.5	255.8	261.3	262.6	262.3	262.5	258.7
2003	255.8	257.2	259.0	263.1	265.0	262.4	261.8	262.2	266.8	267.7	268.7	269.9	263.3
2004	260.1	262.6	264.7	267.8	268.6	267.1	266.3	265.7	270.4	272.5	273.9	274.8	267.9
2005	267.1	269.4	271.1	274.6	276.7	272.0	272.2	272.8	277.0	278.3	279.0	279.5	274.1
2006	270.0	271.8	272.9	275.8	278.9	274.6	274.7	275.5	279.3	278.9	280.5	280.3	276.1
2007	271.9	274.0	275.2	278.2	279.1	279.5	278.3	279.5	282.7	283.7	285.3	286.4	279.5
2008	278.4	280.9	281.1	282.7	282.3	280.7	280.0	280.6	283.1	282.6	282.4	282.2	281.4
2009	271.2	271.0	271.3	271.8	274.2	268.1	267.3	266.6	269.8	270.6	268.6	269.1	270.0

Employment by Industry: Akron, OH, Selected Years, 1990–2009—*Continued*

(Numbers in thousands, not seasonally adjusted.)

Industry and year	January	February	March	April	May	June	July	August	September	October	November	December	Annual average
Trade, Transportation, and Utilities													
1990	56.4	55.4	55.4	56.0	56.5	56.7	56.4	57.1	57.0	56.7	57.7	58.6	56.7
2000	65.5	65.0	65.4	65.7	66.0	66.5	66.1	66.4	66.4	67.3	68.8	69.7	66.6
2001	68.6	67.4	67.5	67.9	68.6	68.9	67.6	67.4	66.9	67.0	67.7	68.4	67.8
2002	65.5	64.5	64.7	64.7	65.0	65.3	64.9	65.1	64.6	64.9	65.9	66.4	65.1
2003	64.5	63.7	64.1	64.5	65.0	65.4	65.1	65.4	65.6	66.3	67.4	68.1	65.4
2004	64.8	64.5	64.7	65.3	65.8	66.1	66.0	66.4	66.6	67.6	68.7	69.4	66.3
2005	66.7	66.7	67.1	68.0	68.0	68.1	67.9	67.6	67.3	67.6	68.8	69.5	67.8
2006	67.0	66.3	66.3	66.4	66.8	67.6	67.5	67.8	67.4	68.1	69.7	70.4	67.6
2007	67.7	66.6	66.8	66.9	67.7	67.9	67.8	67.9	67.9	68.8	70.3	71.3	68.1
2008	68.5	67.0	66.8	67.1	67.2	67.3	67.2	67.2	66.8	66.7	67.3	67.5	67.2
2009	63.9	62.5	62.4	61.9	62.1	62.4	62.3	62.2	62.1	61.8	62.1	62.5	62.4
Wholesale Trade													
1990	12.5	12.5	12.6	12.7	12.7	12.7	12.7	12.8	12.7	12.7	12.8	12.9	12.7
2000	16.6	16.6	16.7	16.7	16.8	16.9	16.9	16.9	16.8	16.8	16.8	16.8	16.8
2001	17.5	17.4	17.4	17.3	17.6	17.6	17.3	17.3	17.1	17.0	16.9	17.0	17.3
2002	16.5	16.3	16.4	16.3	16.1	16.0	15.9	15.8	15.7	15.6	15.5	15.6	16.0
2003	16.1	16.1	16.2	16.1	16.1	16.2	16.1	16.2	16.2	16.2	16.3	16.3	16.1
2004	15.9	16.0	16.1	16.1	16.2	16.3	16.4	16.5	16.6	16.7	16.8	17.0	16.4
2005	17.0	17.1	17.2	17.3	17.3	17.4	17.4	17.3	17.3	17.5	17.6	17.7	17.3
2006	17.6	17.7	17.7	17.7	17.8	18.1	18.0	18.2	18.1	18.3	18.4	18.4	18.0
2007	18.4	18.3	18.4	18.3	18.4	18.4	18.3	18.3	18.2	18.4	18.3	18.4	18.3
2008	18.2	18.1	18.1	18.2	18.1	18.1	18.1	18.1	17.9	17.9	17.7	17.6	18.0
2009	17.3	17.1	16.9	16.9	16.8	16.9	17.0	16.9	16.8	16.8	16.8	16.9	16.9
Retail Trade													
1990	35.8	34.8	34.6	35.0	35.5	35.5	35.3	35.7	35.7	35.7	36.5	37.3	35.6
2000	40.5	39.9	40.0	39.8	40.3	40.7	40.1	40.5	40.4	40.7	42.1	43.0	40.7
2001	40.7	40.1	40.0	40.4	40.6	40.8	40.0	39.7	39.4	39.9	40.9	41.5	40.3
2002	38.5	37.9	38.0	38.0	38.3	38.6	38.3	38.5	38.3	38.8	39.9	40.5	38.6
2003	37.9	37.5	37.7	37.9	38.3	38.5	38.4	38.5	38.7	39.2	40.3	41.0	38.6
2004	38.6	38.2	38.3	38.5	38.7	38.8	38.5	38.6	38.7	39.3	40.2	40.7	38.9
2005	38.3	38.1	38.3	38.9	39.0	38.9	38.6	38.5	38.2	38.6	39.6	40.2	38.8
2006	38.3	37.6	37.7	37.7	37.9	38.3	38.3	38.4	38.1	38.5	40.0	40.6	38.5
2007	38.5	37.6	37.7	37.6	38.3	38.4	38.5	38.5	38.7	39.3	41.0	41.8	38.8
2008	39.7	38.4	38.3	38.3	38.3	38.3	38.2	38.1	37.9	37.8	38.6	39.0	38.4
2009	36.2	35.3	35.4	35.0	35.3	35.5	35.4	35.4	35.4	35.0	35.3	35.7	35.4
Transportation and Utilities													
1990	8.3	8.3	8.4	8.4	8.4	8.5	8.4	8.6	8.6	8.5	8.5	8.4	8.4
2000	8.5	8.4	8.4	8.9	9.0	8.9	9.2	9.2	9.3	9.7	9.7	9.8	9.1
2001	10.3	10.0	10.1	10.3	10.3	10.4	10.4	10.2	10.2	10.1	10.0	10.0	10.2
2002	10.5	10.3	10.3	10.4	10.6	10.7	10.7	10.8	10.6	10.5	10.5	10.3	10.5
2003	10.5	10.1	10.2	10.5	10.6	10.7	10.6	10.7	10.7	10.9	10.8	10.8	10.5
2004	10.3	10.3	10.3	10.7	10.9	11.0	11.1	11.3	11.3	11.6	11.7	11.7	11.0
2005	11.4	11.5	11.6	11.8	11.7	11.8	11.9	11.8	11.8	11.5	11.6	11.6	11.7
2006	11.1	11.0	10.9	11.0	11.1	11.2	11.2	11.2	11.2	11.3	11.3	11.4	11.2
2007	10.8	10.7	10.7	11.0	11.0	11.1	11.0	11.1	11.0	11.1	11.0	11.1	11.0
2008	10.6	10.5	10.4	10.6	10.8	10.9	10.9	11.0	11.0	11.0	11.0	10.9	10.8
2009	10.4	10.1	10.1	10.0	10.0	10.0	9.9	9.9	9.9	10.0	10.0	9.9	10.0
Information													
1990	4.9	4.9	4.9	4.9	4.9	5.0	5.1	5.0	5.0	5.0	5.0	5.0	5.0
2000	5.0	5.1	5.1	5.2	5.1	5.2	5.3	5.3	5.4	5.4	5.4	5.4	5.2
2001	5.1	5.2	5.1	5.0	5.0	5.0	5.0	5.1	5.0	5.1	5.1	5.1	5.1
2002	5.5	5.5	5.4	5.3	5.3	5.4	5.5	5.5	5.5	5.5	5.5	5.6	5.5
2003	5.5	5.5	5.5	5.5	5.5	5.4	5.2	5.2	5.0	4.8	4.8	4.7	5.2
2004	4.8	4.7	4.6	4.6	4.6	4.6	4.5	4.4	4.3	4.3	4.3	4.4	4.5
2005	4.4	4.4	4.4	4.4	4.5	4.5	4.5	4.5	4.5	4.5	4.5	4.5	4.5
2006	4.5	4.5	4.5	4.6	4.6	4.6	4.7	4.6	4.5	4.4	4.5	4.5	4.5
2007	4.5	4.5	4.5	4.6	4.6	4.6	4.6	4.6	4.5	4.5	4.5	4.5	4.5
2008	4.5	4.5	4.4	4.4	4.4	4.5	4.5	4.5	4.4	4.3	4.4	4.4	4.4
2009	4.4	4.3	4.3	4.2	4.2	4.2	4.2	4.2	4.1	4.1	4.1	4.1	4.2
Financial Activities													
1990	11.5	11.6	11.6	11.7	11.7	11.8	11.7	11.8	11.7	11.8	11.7	11.8	11.7
2000	14.5	14.4	14.6	14.3	14.6	14.9	14.7	14.8	14.8	14.6	14.6	14.7	14.6
2001	14.1	14.5	14.5	14.4	14.5	14.8	14.7	14.8	14.7	14.6	14.6	14.6	14.6
2002	14.1	14.2	14.2	13.9	14.1	14.2	14.2	14.3	14.3	14.3	14.3	14.4	14.2
2003	14.2	14.2	14.3	14.6	14.7	14.7	14.7	14.7	14.6	14.5	14.5	14.6	14.5
2004	14.5	14.4	14.6	14.6	14.8	14.9	14.9	14.9	14.8	14.7	14.9	15.0	14.8
2005	14.9	14.9	14.9	14.8	14.8	14.8	14.8	14.8	14.8	14.6	14.6	14.5	14.8
2006	14.5	14.4	14.4	14.6	14.5	14.6	14.5	14.5	14.3	14.4	14.4	14.4	14.5
2007	14.2	14.2	14.0	14.1	14.1	14.0	13.9	14.0	13.9	13.8	13.7	13.8	14.0
2008	13.9	13.9	13.9	13.9	14.0	14.1	14.0	14.0	13.9	13.9	13.8	13.9	13.9
2009	13.6	13.4	13.4	13.3	13.4	13.4	13.4	13.4	13.3	13.2	13.1	13.1	13.3

Employment by Industry: Akron, OH, Selected Years, 1990–2009—*Continued*

(Numbers in thousands, not seasonally adjusted.)

Industry and year	January	February	March	April	May	June	July	August	September	October	November	December	Annual average
Professional and Business Services													
1990	25.4	25.5	26.1	26.7	27.1	27.5	27.3	27.4	27.4	27.7	27.6	27.2	26.9
2000	37.3	37.1	38.0	39.2	38.8	39.6	39.4	39.5	39.4	39.3	38.7	38.3	38.7
2001	36.2	36.1	36.5	37.4	38.7	39.4	38.9	39.5	39.9	40.8	41.4	41.3	38.8
2002	38.7	38.7	39.2	39.0	39.1	39.6	40.0	40.5	40.8	41.0	40.1	40.1	39.7
2003	40.1	40.5	40.2	40.9	41.7	42.0	42.5	43.0	43.0	42.7	43.0	43.0	41.8
2004	41.9	42.0	42.8	43.8	43.9	44.9	45.1	45.1	45.2	45.1	45.4	45.5	44.2
2005	44.4	44.8	44.9	46.3	46.8	47.3	48.1	48.6	48.5	49.5	49.1	49.2	47.3
2006	47.0	47.4	47.8	49.4	50.0	50.7	51.3	51.8	51.3	50.6	50.4	50.4	49.8
2007	48.4	48.6	48.6	50.7	51.4	52.3	52.3	52.5	52.7	52.5	52.7	52.9	51.3
2008	52.2	52.9	52.9	53.7	53.8	53.6	53.5	53.5	53.1	52.4	52.0	51.6	52.9
2009	49.2	48.9	48.4	48.7	48.5	48.1	47.6	47.4	47.0	47.9	46.6	46.9	47.9
Education and Health Services													
1990	29.1	29.2	29.4	29.2	29.4	29.5	29.2	29.4	29.9	30.3	30.5	30.6	29.6
2000	38.3	38.6	38.9	38.1	38.3	38.2	38.4	38.6	38.9	39.3	39.5	39.7	38.7
2001	39.0	39.3	39.6	39.8	40.0	39.9	39.5	39.9	40.3	40.6	40.9	41.3	40.0
2002	40.3	40.6	40.8	40.6	40.7	40.5	40.5	40.6	41.0	41.2	41.5	41.6	40.8
2003	41.2	41.2	41.2	41.2	41.3	41.2	41.2	41.3	42.0	42.1	42.3	42.5	41.5
2004	41.8	42.1	42.3	42.8	43.0	43.0	42.8	43.0	43.1	43.6	43.8	44.0	42.9
2005	43.3	43.4	43.7	43.9	44.0	43.8	44.1	44.2	44.6	45.3	45.3	45.5	44.3
2006	44.6	44.7	44.9	45.2	45.4	45.3	44.8	44.9	45.4	45.9	46.1	46.2	45.3
2007	45.9	46.0	46.3	46.5	46.9	47.1	47.2	47.3	47.6	48.0	48.3	48.3	47.1
2008	48.1	48.1	48.3	48.3	48.6	48.7	48.7	48.8	49.1	49.5	49.8	49.8	48.8
Leisure and Hospitality													
1990	25.1	25.3	26.0	26.6	27.7	28.7	29.1	28.8	28.2	26.8	26.5	26.3	27.1
2000	29.3	29.3	30.0	31.3	32.9	34.3	34.5	34.3	32.2	31.1	30.7	31.1	31.8
2001	28.2	28.4	28.8	29.8	31.7	33.2	33.3	33.3	31.4	30.4	29.9	29.8	30.7
2002	28.6	28.4	28.8	29.9	31.7	33.6	33.6	33.5	31.9	30.6	29.5	29.6	30.8
2003	28.1	27.7	28.2	29.8	31.7	33.0	33.7	33.8	32.2	31.4	30.4	30.6	30.8
2004	29.1	29.0	29.4	30.6	32.3	33.6	34.0	33.9	32.6	31.4	30.6	30.3	31.4
2005	29.3	29.1	29.8	31.1	32.4	33.9	34.1	34.2	33.1	31.6	30.8	30.7	31.7
2006	29.2	29.3	29.7	30.6	32.1	33.4	34.3	34.1	32.3	30.7	30.5	30.5	31.4
2007	29.4	29.4	30.1	30.7	32.1	34.1	33.9	33.7	32.2	30.9	30.4	30.4	31.4
2008	28.9	29.1	29.3	30.0	31.8	32.4	32.4	32.4	31.3	30.3	29.6	29.9	30.6
2009	28.2	28.1	28.5	28.9	30.5	31.2	31.0	30.8	30.1	28.5	27.3	27.2	29.2
Other Services													
1990	10.9	10.9	11.0	11.2	11.4	11.6	11.6	11.7	11.6	11.6	11.8	11.8	11.4
2000	13.7	13.8	13.9	13.6	13.7	14.0	13.9	13.7	13.7	13.6	13.6	13.8	13.8
2001	14.1	14.3	14.2	14.3	14.4	14.5	14.5	14.5	14.3	14.3	14.2	14.3	14.3
2002	13.9	13.9	14.0	14.1	14.2	14.4	14.2	14.1	14.0	14.0	13.9	14.0	14.1
2003	13.9	13.9	14.0	14.0	14.1	14.2	14.1	14.0	13.8	13.8	13.8	13.8	13.9
2004	13.6	13.6	13.7	13.7	13.8	14.0	13.9	13.8	13.8	13.9	13.9	14.1	13.8
2005	13.8	14.0	14.1	14.1	14.2	14.3	14.2	14.2	14.0	14.0	14.0	14.1	14.1
2006	13.6	13.7	13.8	13.7	13.8	14.0	13.8	13.9	13.8	13.7	13.8	13.8	13.8
2007	13.6	13.5	13.7	13.6	13.7	13.8	13.8	13.8	13.6	13.9	13.9	14.0	13.7
2008	13.8	13.9	13.9	13.9	14.0	14.1	14.1	14.1	13.9	13.8	13.8	13.8	13.9
2009	13.6	13.5	13.6	13.5	13.5	13.6	13.6	13.5	13.4	13.4	13.5	13.5	13.5
Government													
1990	41.7	46.5	47.0	46.6	47.4	40.9	39.2	39.5	45.9	47.0	47.6	47.0	44.7
2000	46.5	50.4	50.4	50.6	51.7	44.1	43.0	41.4	47.6	49.8	50.1	48.4	47.8
2001	47.8	50.1	51.1	50.9	47.9	44.9	43.5	42.1	48.5	50.2	50.8	49.3	48.1
2002	47.7	50.0	50.9	50.8	47.9	45.8	43.6	42.2	49.2	51.1	51.6	50.8	48.5
2003	48.3	50.5	51.5	52.6	51.0	46.5	45.3	44.8	50.6	52.1	52.5	52.6	49.8
2004	49.6	52.3	52.6	52.4	50.4	46.0	45.1	44.2	50.0	51.9	52.3	52.1	49.9
2005	50.3	52.1	52.2	52.0	52.0	45.3	44.5	44.7	50.2	51.2	51.9	51.5	49.8
2006	49.6	51.5	51.5	51.3	51.7	44.4	43.8	43.9	50.3	51.1	51.2	50.1	49.2
2007	48.2	51.2	51.2	51.1	48.6	45.7	44.8	45.7	50.3	51.3	51.5	51.2	49.2
2008	48.5	51.5	51.6	51.4	48.5	46.0	45.6	46.1	50.6	51.7	51.7	51.3	49.5
2009	49.3	51.2	51.3	52.0	52.4	45.9	46.0	45.7	50.3	51.9	51.9	51.8	50.0

Employment by Industry: Albany-Schenectady-Troy, NY, Selected Years, 1990–2009

(Numbers in thousands, not seasonally adjusted.)

Industry and year	January	February	March	April	May	June	July	August	September	October	November	December	Annual average
Total Nonfarm													
1990	399.2	401.7	405.1	408.4	414.0	417.0	408.2	410.1	411.3	413.1	412.6	411.5	409.4
2000	425.3	428.5	430.9	436.1	439.8	443.1	434.7	435.0	439.4	443.7	446.9	448.0	437.6
2001	433.5	435.7	438.2	440.7	445.3	446.7	439.8	442.9	440.7	443.3	446.4	445.4	441.6
2002	428.6	433.3	436.8	440.7	442.8	443.8	437.1	439.8	442.0	444.3	445.7	444.7	440.0
2003	429.4	433.0	434.0	437.1	441.4	441.7	436.8	439.3	440.3	444.1	446.7	446.4	439.2
2004	432.2	435.7	438.5	441.7	448.8	447.7	442.7	443.2	444.7	448.0	449.5	450.5	443.6
2005	436.2	439.0	439.4	446.2	447.7	449.0	444.5	445.5	447.1	449.9	451.6	451.1	445.6
2006	436.0	440.4	443.5	447.6	449.8	450.7	443.9	444.5	446.7	451.6	453.7	454.8	446.9
2007	438.7	441.5	444.2	445.6	451.5	453.9	445.9	447.0	449.9	455.0	457.3	457.5	449.0
2008	442.2	445.9	446.8	452.1	457.4	458.6	451.7	451.5	452.2	456.7	457.0	454.6	452.2
2009	437.7	441.9	442.0	444.9	447.8	447.1	439.1	438.4	439.2	444.8	445.7	443.4	442.7
Total Private													
1990	290.6	291.1	292.8	295.2	298.9	303.0	300.7	303.8	302.5	302.3	301.9	300.9	298.6
2000	320.2	321.0	323.4	327.9	330.9	334.6	332.2	333.3	333.1	336.0	338.1	340.1	330.9
2001	327.1	326.6	329.3	331.3	335.9	338.5	335.8	338.4	333.7	334.3	336.1	336.1	333.6
2002	321.4	323.0	326.5	330.0	332.2	333.9	333.3	336.6	333.4	334.4	335.2	334.4	331.2
2003	321.4	322.8	324.4	328.1	332.4	333.5	333.9	337.1	333.5	335.6	338.0	337.6	331.5
2004	326.1	327.4	330.1	332.6	339.3	338.4	339.2	340.5	338.5	339.8	340.9	342.0	336.2
2005	329.0	330.5	330.8	337.1	338.6	340.6	341.7	343.4	341.2	341.6	343.1	342.5	338.3
2006	329.9	332.3	335.4	339.0	341.3	343.1	341.6	343.2	341.8	343.7	345.2	345.6	340.2
2007	331.8	332.6	335.6	336.8	342.1	344.7	343.4	344.3	343.8	345.6	347.5	346.6	341.2
2008	335.1	336.7	337.8	341.6	346.1	347.8	346.5	347.4	345.0	346.3	346.5	343.6	343.4
2009	330.4	331.8	332.4	333.8	336.7	336.8	334.8	335.6	333.4	335.7	336.4	334.4	334.4
Goods-Producing													
1990	51.7	51.2	51.7	53.7	55.5	57.0	56.3	56.6	56.1	55.5	54.1	52.5	54.3
2000	43.8	43.1	43.9	45.4	47.0	47.8	47.3	47.8	47.3	47.3	46.9	46.2	46.2
2001	43.8	43.4	43.6	44.9	46.4	47.3	47.0	47.2	46.4	45.9	45.0	43.4	45.4
2002	40.4	39.7	40.3	41.5	42.7	43.4	43.9	44.1	43.6	43.0	42.4	40.8	42.2
2003	38.6	37.8	37.9	38.9	40.5	41.4	41.8	42.4	41.9	42.0	41.3	40.2	40.3
2004	38.0	37.5	37.9	39.6	41.1	41.8	42.7	42.9	42.3	42.0	41.7	40.4	40.7
2005	38.8	38.1	38.3	40.5	41.8	42.6	43.3	43.4	42.8	42.4	42.3	40.9	41.3
2006	39.1	38.5	39.1	40.9	42.1	42.9	43.0	43.3	42.7	42.7	42.0	40.8	41.4
2007	38.8	37.8	38.6	39.9	41.9	42.8	43.4	43.4	42.9	43.0	42.2	40.9	41.3
2008	38.7	37.8	38.1	39.5	41.3	42.3	42.7	42.9	42.4	42.3	41.3	39.6	40.7
2009	36.7	35.8	35.7	36.8	37.9	38.7	39.2	39.4	38.7	38.6	38.1	37.2	37.7
Mining, Logging, and Construction													
1990	16.9	16.3	16.4	17.9	19.5	20.4	20.7	20.9	20.3	19.7	18.5	17.1	18.7
2000	15.4	14.9	15.5	16.7	18.1	18.8	19.1	19.4	19.0	18.7	18.5	17.4	17.6
2001	15.8	15.4	15.6	17.0	18.5	19.2	19.6	19.9	19.4	19.1	18.5	17.3	17.9
2002	15.3	14.8	15.3	16.7	17.9	18.4	19.1	19.3	18.9	18.5	18.3	17.1	17.5
2003	15.5	14.9	15.0	16.1	17.7	18.6	19.5	19.8	19.3	19.3	18.6	17.6	17.6
2004	15.8	15.4	15.7	17.1	18.5	19.0	19.6	19.5	19.2	19.0	18.6	17.4	17.9
2005	16.0	15.4	15.5	17.4	18.6	19.3	20.0	20.0	19.6	19.4	19.2	17.9	18.2
2006	16.1	15.6	16.1	17.6	18.7	19.4	19.6	19.8	19.4	19.4	18.6	17.6	18.2
2007	16.0	15.1	15.7	16.8	18.8	19.4	20.0	20.1	19.8	19.9	19.2	17.9	18.2
2008	16.1	15.5	15.7	17.2	18.7	19.4	20.0	20.2	19.9	19.9	19.0	17.5	18.3
2009	15.3	14.7	14.9	16.1	17.3	18.0	18.7	19.0	18.3	18.3	17.9	17.1	17.1
Manufacturing													
1990	34.8	34.9	35.3	35.8	36.0	36.6	35.6	35.7	35.8	35.8	35.6	35.4	35.6
2000	28.4	28.2	28.4	28.7	28.9	29.0	28.2	28.4	28.3	28.6	28.4	28.8	28.5
2001	28.0	28.0	28.0	27.9	27.9	28.1	27.4	27.3	27.0	26.8	26.5	26.1	27.4
2002	25.1	24.9	25.0	24.8	24.8	25.0	24.8	24.8	24.7	24.5	24.1	23.7	24.7
2003	23.1	22.9	22.9	22.8	22.8	22.8	22.3	22.6	22.6	22.7	22.7	22.6	22.7
2004	22.2	22.1	22.2	22.5	22.6	22.8	23.1	23.4	23.1	23.0	23.1	23.0	22.8
2005	22.8	22.7	22.8	23.1	23.2	23.3	23.3	23.4	23.2	23.0	23.1	23.0	23.1
2006	23.0	22.9	23.0	23.3	23.4	23.5	23.4	23.5	23.3	23.3	23.4	23.2	23.3
2007	22.8	22.7	22.9	23.1	23.1	23.4	23.4	23.3	23.1	23.1	23.0	23.0	23.1
2008	22.6	22.3	22.4	22.3	22.6	22.9	22.7	22.7	22.5	22.4	22.3	22.1	22.5
2009	21.4	21.1	20.8	20.7	20.6	20.7	20.5	20.4	20.4	20.3	20.2	20.1	20.6
Service-Providing													
1990	347.5	350.5	353.4	354.7	358.5	360.0	351.9	353.5	355.2	357.6	358.5	359.0	355.0
2000	381.5	385.4	387.0	390.7	392.8	395.3	387.4	387.2	392.1	396.4	400.0	401.8	391.5
2001	389.7	392.3	394.6	395.8	398.9	399.4	392.8	395.7	394.3	397.4	401.4	402.0	396.2
2002	388.2	393.6	396.5	399.2	400.1	400.4	393.2	395.7	398.4	401.3	403.3	403.9	397.8
2003	390.8	395.2	396.1	398.2	400.9	400.3	395.0	396.9	398.4	402.1	405.4	406.2	398.8
2004	394.2	398.2	400.6	402.1	407.7	405.9	400.0	400.3	402.4	406.0	407.8	410.1	402.9
2005	397.4	400.9	401.1	405.7	405.9	406.4	401.2	402.1	404.3	407.5	409.3	410.2	404.3
2006	396.9	401.9	404.4	406.7	407.7	407.8	400.9	401.2	404.0	408.9	411.7	414.0	405.5
2007	399.9	403.7	405.6	405.7	409.6	411.1	402.5	403.6	407.0	412.0	415.1	416.6	407.7
2008	403.5	408.1	408.7	412.6	416.1	416.3	409.0	408.6	409.8	414.4	415.7	415.0	411.5
2009	401.0	406.1	406.3	408.1	409.9	408.4	399.9	399.0	400.5	406.2	407.6	406.2	404.9

Employment by Industry: Albany-Schenectady-Troy, NY, Selected Years, 1990–2009—*Continued*

(Numbers in thousands, not seasonally adjusted.)

Industry and year	January	February	March	April	May	June	July	August	September	October	November	December	Annual average
Trade, Transportation, and Utilities													
1990	74.5	73.3	73.2	72.3	73.2	74.3	73.2	73.6	73.8	74.3	76.0	76.9	74.1
2000	77.3	76.3	76.6	76.8	77.7	78.5	78.3	79.4	79.3	80.6	82.8	84.6	79.0
2001	78.8	77.6	77.4	76.8	77.6	78.5	77.3	77.5	76.7	77.9	80.5	81.5	78.2
2002	76.8	75.6	76.0	76.4	76.8	77.7	77.1	77.2	77.0	77.4	79.3	80.9	77.4
2003	77.4	76.4	76.5	76.4	77.3	78.4	77.5	78.0	78.1	79.5	81.8	83.2	78.3
2004	78.7	78.0	78.2	77.8	79.0	79.8	78.8	79.0	79.0	80.4	82.3	83.7	79.6
2005	79.4	78.0	77.9	78.6	79.1	79.7	79.8	80.1	79.6	80.2	82.0	83.5	79.8
2006	78.8	77.4	77.7	78.0	79.0	79.6	78.4	78.5	77.8	78.9	81.1	82.4	79.0
2007	77.9	76.1	76.8	75.9	77.2	77.8	77.1	76.8	76.7	77.6	79.4	80.3	77.5
2008	76.4	74.9	75.0	75.2	76.1	76.8	76.1	76.2	75.8	76.5	77.4	78.5	76.2
2009	74.1	72.9	72.5	72.4	73.4	74.1	73.2	73.4	72.7	73.5	74.1	74.3	73.4
Wholesale Trade													
1990	15.5	15.6	15.6	15.8	15.8	16.1	15.9	16.0	15.9	15.8	15.8	15.8	15.8
2000	16.2	16.2	16.4	16.5	16.5	16.5	16.5	16.6	16.5	16.5	16.6	16.7	16.5
2001	16.3	16.3	16.2	16.4	16.4	16.6	16.8	16.6	16.5	16.3	16.2	16.3	16.4
2002	16.3	16.2	16.2	16.2	16.3	16.3	16.4	16.3	16.2	16.1	16.2	16.2	16.2
2003	16.5	16.5	16.5	16.4	16.5	16.6	16.6	16.6	16.6	16.6	16.8	17.0	16.6
2004	16.7	16.9	16.9	16.9	16.8	16.7	16.4	16.4	16.3	16.2	16.2	16.2	16.6
2005	15.9	15.7	15.7	15.7	15.6	15.6	15.9	15.8	15.6	15.6	15.7	15.7	15.7
2006	15.3	15.2	15.2	14.9	14.9	15.0	14.9	14.9	14.7	14.7	14.6	14.8	14.9
2007	14.7	14.6	14.8	14.7	14.7	14.8	14.6	14.5	14.2	14.2	14.1	14.1	14.5
2008	13.7	13.7	13.7	13.7	13.8	13.9	14.0	14.0	13.9	13.9	13.9	14.0	13.9
2009	13.6	13.6	13.5	13.5	13.4	13.4	13.5	13.5	13.3	13.3	13.3	13.2	13.4
Retail Trade													
1990	48.8	47.4	47.3	46.4	47.1	47.8	47.1	47.2	47.4	48.1	49.6	50.6	47.9
2000	49.2	48.1	48.1	48.1	48.5	49.2	49.2	50.0	49.9	50.9	52.9	54.5	49.9
2001	49.3	48.2	48.1	47.2	47.7	48.4	47.5	47.7	46.9	48.1	50.8	51.7	48.5
2002	47.8	46.8	47.2	47.5	47.7	48.5	48.2	48.3	47.9	48.2	50.0	51.6	48.3
2003	48.1	47.0	47.1	47.3	48.0	49.0	48.6	49.0	48.8	50.1	52.2	53.5	49.0
2004	49.9	48.8	48.9	48.5	49.4	50.2	49.8	50.1	49.8	51.0	52.9	54.3	50.3
2005	50.6	49.3	49.2	49.5	49.9	50.3	50.3	50.5	49.8	50.5	52.0	53.5	50.5
2006	49.8	48.5	48.7	49.4	50.2	50.7	50.1	50.0	49.2	50.2	52.6	53.6	50.3
2007	50.0	48.4	48.7	48.1	49.1	49.6	49.3	49.2	49.0	49.8	51.6	52.4	49.6
2008	49.6	48.2	48.2	48.3	48.8	49.3	48.8	48.9	48.3	48.8	49.7	50.6	49.0
2009	47.3	46.2	45.9	45.8	46.7	47.4	46.7	46.8	46.2	46.9	47.4	47.7	46.8
Transportation and Utilities													
1990	10.2	10.3	10.3	10.1	10.3	10.4	10.2	10.4	10.5	10.4	10.6	10.5	10.4
2000	11.9	12.0	12.1	12.2	12.7	12.8	12.6	12.8	12.9	13.2	13.3	13.4	12.7
2001	13.2	13.1	13.1	13.2	13.5	13.5	13.0	13.2	13.3	13.5	13.5	13.5	13.3
2002	12.7	12.6	12.6	12.7	12.8	12.9	12.5	12.6	12.9	13.1	13.1	13.1	12.8
2003	12.8	12.9	12.9	12.7	12.8	12.8	12.3	12.4	12.7	12.8	12.8	12.7	12.7
2004	12.1	12.3	12.4	12.4	12.8	12.9	12.6	12.5	12.9	13.2	13.2	13.2	12.7
2005	12.9	13.0	13.0	13.4	13.6	13.8	13.6	13.8	14.2	14.1	14.3	14.3	13.7
2006	13.7	13.7	13.8	13.7	13.9	13.9	13.4	13.6	13.9	14.0	13.9	14.0	13.8
2007	13.2	13.1	13.3	13.1	13.4	13.4	13.2	13.1	13.5	13.6	13.7	13.8	13.4
2008	13.1	13.0	13.1	13.2	13.5	13.6	13.3	13.3	13.6	13.8	13.8	13.9	13.4
2009	13.2	13.1	13.1	13.1	13.3	13.3	13.0	13.1	13.2	13.3	13.4	13.4	13.2
Information													
1990	10.8	10.9	10.9	10.7	10.6	10.5	10.4	10.5	10.6	10.5	10.6	10.6	10.6
2000	11.8	11.9	12.0	12.3	12.3	12.5	12.3	10.7	12.3	12.0	12.1	12.2	12.0
2001	12.2	12.1	12.2	12.2	12.3	12.4	12.1	12.1	12.1	12.0	12.0	12.0	12.1
2002	11.9	11.9	12.0	12.0	12.1	12.1	11.9	11.9	11.8	11.9	12.0	12.0	12.0
2003	11.6	11.7	12.0	12.0	11.8	11.5	11.2	11.1	10.8	10.6	10.4	10.2	11.2
2004	11.1	11.1	11.5	11.0	10.7	10.7	10.8	10.8	10.8	10.6	10.7	10.5	10.9
2005	10.5	10.6	10.8	11.1	11.0	11.1	11.0	11.1	10.9	10.9	10.8	10.9	10.9
2006	10.8	10.7	10.7	10.6	10.6	10.6	10.5	10.4	10.1	10.2	10.2	10.2	10.5
2007	10.1	10.0	10.0	9.9	10.0	10.0	10.0	10.0	9.8	9.7	9.7	9.8	9.9
2008	9.4	9.4	9.4	9.5	9.8	9.9	9.9	9.9	9.7	9.8	9.8	9.8	9.7
2009	9.8	9.7	9.6	9.5	9.5	9.6	9.5	9.6	9.3	9.1	9.1	9.2	9.5
Financial Activities													
1990	23.3	23.4	23.5	23.6	23.6	24.1	23.7	23.7	23.5	23.3	23.2	23.3	23.5
2000	24.6	24.7	24.7	24.9	25.0	25.3	25.2	25.3	24.9	24.8	24.9	25.3	25.0
2001	24.5	24.6	24.7	24.4	24.6	25.1	25.0	25.0	24.7	24.8	24.8	24.9	24.8
2002	24.4	24.7	24.9	24.8	25.1	25.4	25.0	25.3	24.8	25.2	25.3	25.4	25.0
2003	25.3	25.3	25.4	25.5	25.8	26.3	26.3	26.3	25.9	26.0	26.1	26.1	25.8
2004	25.8	25.6	25.9	25.7	25.8	26.5	26.6	26.5	26.4	26.3	26.1	26.3	26.1
2005	25.9	25.9	26.0	26.1	26.2	26.6	26.8	26.8	26.5	26.5	26.4	26.6	26.4
2006	26.2	26.3	26.5	26.7	26.6	27.0	27.1	27.0	26.6	26.7	26.7	26.7	26.7
2007	26.3	26.0	26.0	26.1	26.2	26.7	26.5	26.4	26.0	26.0	26.1	26.1	26.2
2008	25.9	25.8	25.9	25.9	26.0	26.4	26.4	26.3	25.8	25.6	25.5	25.4	25.9
2009	25.3	25.2	25.2	25.1	25.1	25.5	25.3	25.3	24.8	24.8	24.8	25.0	25.1

Employment by Industry: Albany-Schenectady-Troy, NY, Selected Years, 1990–2009—*Continued*

(Numbers in thousands, not seasonally adjusted.)

Industry and year	January	February	March	April	May	June	July	August	September	October	November	December	Annual average
Professional and Business Services													
1990	38.4	38.4	38.9	40.6	40.9	41.5	41.7	42.4	41.9	41.5	41.2	41.0	40.7
2000	50.0	50.0	50.3	51.3	51.6	52.4	52.1	52.5	51.7	52.2	52.5	52.7	51.6
2001	51.9	52.2	52.1	52.7	53.4	53.8	53.5	53.7	52.4	51.8	51.5	51.9	52.6
2002	49.2	49.0	49.5	50.2	49.9	50.7	50.5	50.8	50.2	50.1	49.5	49.2	49.9
2003	47.5	47.4	47.7	48.8	49.5	50.3	50.5	50.8	50.0	50.0	50.4	50.7	49.5
2004	49.1	49.2	49.6	50.6	51.2	52.2	52.2	52.3	51.6	50.9	51.1	51.2	50.9
2005	50.7	50.9	50.8	51.8	51.7	52.9	53.4	53.1	53.1	52.5	52.7	52.1	52.1
2006	51.8	52.1	52.7	53.6	53.0	53.8	54.3	54.3	54.0	53.5	54.0	54.1	53.4
2007	52.4	52.9	53.4	53.7	53.8	55.3	55.5	55.5	54.9	54.8	55.3	55.4	54.4
2008	55.3	55.4	55.7	56.4	56.2	57.4	57.2	57.3	56.2	56.0	55.7	55.2	56.2
2009	54.0	53.4	53.7	53.7	53.1	53.2	52.7	52.4	52.0	52.0	52.3	52.3	52.9
Education and Health Services													
1990	52.5	53.6	53.8	53.2	52.8	52.9	52.3	52.4	53.9	54.7	55.1	55.1	53.5
2000	68.7	70.5	70.8	70.7	70.1	69.3	68.7	68.8	70.1	72.7	72.9	73.0	70.5
2001	71.3	72.2	74.1	74.0	73.2	71.2	71.2	71.1	73.6	74.8	75.3	75.3	73.1
2002	72.9	75.8	76.5	76.7	75.4	73.5	73.7	73.7	76.2	77.4	77.6	77.6	75.6
2003	74.8	77.6	77.8	78.2	77.6	75.1	74.4	74.1	76.6	77.9	78.7	78.3	76.7
2004	75.9	78.4	78.5	79.0	80.3	75.3	75.5	74.9	77.8	79.4	79.5	80.2	77.9
2005	76.3	79.2	78.8	79.5	78.2	75.9	75.6	75.0	77.4	79.0	79.2	78.8	77.7
2006	76.3	79.4	79.5	79.9	79.0	76.7	75.9	75.6	79.4	80.8	81.1	81.2	78.7
2007	77.9	81.0	81.1	81.2	80.6	78.4	77.3	77.0	81.1	82.4	83.4	83.2	80.4
2008	80.3	83.7	83.3	83.6	83.3	80.8	79.1	78.5	82.2	83.5	84.9	84.2	82.3
2009	81.5	85.3	85.6	85.5	84.4	81.7	80.3	80.0	83.8	85.9	86.6	85.7	83.9
Leisure and Hospitality													
1990	26.0	26.7	27.1	27.5	28.6	28.9	29.2	30.6	29.0	28.6	27.9	27.7	28.2
2000	27.3	27.7	28.2	29.3	30.0	31.4	31.1	31.5	30.4	29.0	28.4	28.4	29.4
2001	27.3	27.2	27.8	29.1	31.0	32.6	32.5	34.6	30.6	29.8	29.4	29.4	30.1
2002	28.5	28.8	29.6	30.5	32.3	33.2	33.4	35.8	32.0	31.3	30.7	30.2	31.4
2003	28.0	28.4	28.9	30.1	31.7	32.3	33.8	36.0	32.0	31.2	30.8	30.5	31.1
2004	29.2	29.2	30.0	30.4	32.6	33.7	34.2	35.8	32.5	31.6	30.9	31.2	31.8
2005	29.1	29.3	29.8	31.1	32.3	33.6	33.8	35.9	32.9	31.9	31.4	31.5	31.9
2006	29.2	29.9	30.9	31.1	32.7	34.2	34.2	36.0	33.1	32.5	31.7	31.7	32.3
2007	30.2	30.4	31.2	31.8	33.9	35.2	35.6	37.2	34.4	33.8	33.0	32.4	33.3
2008	30.7	31.2	31.9	33.1	34.9	35.7	36.5	37.7	34.6	33.9	33.1	32.2	33.8
2009	30.4	30.7	31.2	32.2	34.5	35.3	35.9	37.1	34.3	33.6	33.2	32.5	33.4
Other Services													
1990	13.4	13.6	13.7	13.6	13.7	13.8	13.9	14.0	13.7	13.9	13.8	13.8	13.7
2000	16.7	16.8	16.9	17.2	17.2	17.4	17.2	17.3	17.1	17.4	17.6	17.7	17.2
2001	17.3	17.3	17.4	17.2	17.4	17.6	17.2	17.2	17.2	17.3	17.6	17.7	17.4
2002	17.3	17.5	17.7	17.9	17.9	17.9	17.8	17.8	17.8	18.1	18.4	18.3	17.9
2003	18.2	18.2	18.2	18.2	18.2	18.2	18.4	18.4	18.2	18.4	18.5	18.4	18.2
2004	18.3	18.4	18.5	18.5	18.6	18.4	18.4	18.3	18.1	18.6	18.6	18.5	18.4
2005	18.3	18.5	18.4	18.4	18.3	18.2	18.0	18.0	18.0	18.2	18.3	18.2	18.2
2006	17.7	18.0	18.3	18.2	18.3	18.3	18.2	18.1	18.1	18.4	18.4	18.5	18.2
2007	18.2	18.4	18.5	18.3	18.5	18.5	18.0	18.0	18.0	18.3	18.4	18.5	18.3
2008	18.4	18.5	18.5	18.4	18.5	18.5	18.6	18.6	18.3	18.7	18.8	18.7	18.5
2009	18.6	18.8	18.9	18.6	18.8	18.7	18.7	18.4	17.8	18.2	18.2	18.2	18.5
Government													
1990	108.6	110.6	112.3	113.2	115.1	114.0	107.5	106.3	108.8	110.8	110.7	110.6	110.7
2000	105.1	107.5	107.5	108.2	108.9	108.5	102.5	101.7	106.3	107.7	108.8	107.9	106.7
2001	106.4	109.1	108.9	109.4	109.4	108.2	104.0	104.5	107.0	109.0	110.3	109.3	108.0
2002	107.2	110.3	110.3	110.7	110.6	109.9	103.8	103.2	108.6	109.9	110.5	110.3	108.8
2003	108.0	110.2	109.6	109.0	109.0	108.2	102.9	102.2	106.8	108.5	108.7	108.8	107.7
2004	106.1	108.3	108.4	109.1	109.5	109.3	103.5	102.7	106.2	108.2	108.6	108.5	107.4
2005	107.2	108.5	108.6	109.1	109.1	108.4	102.8	102.1	105.9	108.3	108.5	108.6	107.3
2006	106.1	108.1	108.1	108.6	108.5	107.6	102.3	101.3	104.9	107.9	108.5	109.2	106.8
2007	106.9	108.9	108.6	108.8	109.4	109.2	102.5	102.7	106.1	109.4	109.8	110.9	107.8
2008	107.1	109.2	109.0	110.5	111.3	110.8	105.2	104.1	107.2	110.4	110.5	111.0	108.9
2009	107.3	110.1	109.6	111.1	111.1	110.3	104.3	102.8	105.8	109.1	109.3	109.0	108.3

Employment by Industry: Albuquerque, NM, Selected Years, 1990–2009

(Numbers in thousands, not seasonally adjusted.)

Industry and year	January	February	March	April	May	June	July	August	September	October	November	December	Annual average
Total Nonfarm													
1990	263.7	266.1	269.4	271.9	274.8	274.3	271.6	272.5	275.4	273.6	272.0	271.5	271.4
2000	346.2	349.2	352.8	355.0	358.4	357.9	356.3	357.7	362.6	361.9	364.4	365.9	357.4
2001	356.5	359.8	362.3	363.3	365.0	365.7	361.0	361.3	361.7	361.6	363.2	364.4	362.2
2002	355.5	357.2	359.9	360.7	363.3	364.0	361.4	361.7	364.7	362.1	364.0	366.1	361.7
2003	356.6	359.5	362.0	362.5	364.0	364.4	361.9	363.5	365.0	364.5	365.6	368.0	363.1
2004	360.2	364.5	367.5	369.6	371.3	371.1	369.1	369.4	371.4	375.1	376.0	376.9	370.2
2005	367.5	370.5	373.0	376.4	377.9	378.4	376.5	378.4	381.6	382.2	385.0	387.0	377.9
2006	381.5	385.2	389.6	389.8	391.8	393.8	390.1	391.2	394.8	395.2	397.2	397.8	391.5
2007	388.0	391.6	395.9	395.4	397.7	397.5	393.9	396.0	397.2	398.0	399.1	399.5	395.8
2008	390.1	392.8	394.6	396.7	398.0	396.3	394.0	396.7	398.3	396.9	393.2	390.7	394.9
2009	380.5	379.5	379.3	379.9	380.1	377.5	375.0	377.6	379.3	379.1	380.7	380.5	379.1
Total Private													
1990	210.7	210.8	213.8	215.8	218.7	220.3	218.3	219.2	219.1	217.1	216.1	215.9	216.3
2000	279.2	279.9	282.8	285.0	287.6	290.0	289.2	291.1	292.9	292.4	294.6	296.1	288.4
2001	289.4	289.9	292.0	292.6	294.1	295.4	292.8	293.4	290.7	290.5	291.5	291.7	292.0
2002	285.6	284.7	287.1	287.9	290.5	290.8	290.2	290.9	291.3	289.3	290.8	292.3	289.3
2003	285.8	286.1	288.1	288.7	290.4	290.9	290.0	291.6	291.0	290.5	291.3	292.9	289.8
2004	288.6	289.5	292.0	294.3	296.1	296.6	296.7	297.0	296.3	298.9	299.4	300.0	295.5
2005	293.7	294.1	296.4	300.0	301.7	302.7	302.8	304.4	304.8	304.4	307.1	308.5	301.7
2006	305.1	306.7	310.7	311.2	313.3	316.0	314.2	314.1	315.4	315.4	317.1	317.4	313.1
2007	310.6	312.1	315.4	315.7	318.1	319.0	317.4	318.2	316.8	316.9	317.6	318.0	316.3
2008	311.4	311.8	313.1	315.2	315.9	315.9	315.5	316.9	315.9	313.8	310.2	307.7	313.6
2009	299.3	296.3	295.6	296.1	296.9	296.0	295.9	297.4	296.6	295.3	296.5	296.4	296.5
Goods-Producing													
1990	36.6	36.6	37.2	37.4	38.2	38.6	38.2	38.5	38.4	38.1	37.0	36.4	37.6
2000	47.5	48.0	48.7	49.2	50.5	51.3	52.4	53.1	53.4	53.1	53.2	53.3	51.1
2001	52.4	52.5	52.9	52.7	52.9	53.3	52.2	52.2	51.1	50.5	50.1	49.6	51.9
2002	48.4	47.9	48.2	48.2	48.3	48.8	49.1	49.1	48.4	47.7	47.2	47.3	48.2
2003	46.8	46.7	46.9	47.0	47.5	47.9	48.3	48.6	48.0	47.5	47.1	47.1	47.5
2004	46.2	46.4	46.9	47.5	48.1	49.1	50.1	50.0	49.6	49.8	49.6	49.6	48.6
2005	48.9	49.1	49.6	50.5	51.0	51.5	52.2	52.3	52.4	52.8	53.3	53.6	51.4
2006	53.5	54.3	55.0	54.9	55.5	56.4	56.4	56.4	56.2	56.2	55.4	55.5	55.5
2007	53.6	54.0	54.6	54.6	55.1	55.4	54.9	54.8	53.9	53.6	53.1	52.2	54.2
2008	50.9	50.9	51.1	51.3	51.4	51.9	51.3	51.0	50.5	49.2	48.1	46.9	50.4
2009	44.6	43.3	42.5	42.4	42.2	42.2	42.1	42.3	41.6	41.4	41.5	41.5	42.3
Mining, Logging, and Construction													
1990	14.4	14.4	14.8	14.8	15.3	15.6	15.1	15.1	14.9	14.8	14.1	13.8	14.8
2000	20.9	21.2	21.8	22.2	23.2	23.8	24.3	24.9	25.2	25.0	25.2	25.1	23.6
2001	24.3	24.3	24.6	24.8	25.1	25.7	25.3	25.4	24.7	24.4	24.5	24.1	24.8
2002	23.4	23.1	23.4	23.3	23.4	23.7	23.8	23.9	23.4	23.2	23.1	23.2	23.4
2003	23.1	23.0	23.2	23.5	24.1	24.5	24.8	25.0	24.6	24.4	24.4	24.5	24.1
2004	24.0	24.3	24.7	25.0	25.4	26.3	27.1	27.0	26.7	27.0	26.9	26.9	25.9
2005	26.3	26.6	27.1	27.8	28.2	28.8	29.5	29.5	29.5	29.6	30.0	30.2	28.6
2006	30.2	30.5	31.2	31.0	31.6	32.2	32.0	32.0	31.7	31.7	31.3	31.4	31.4
2007	29.8	29.9	30.6	30.8	31.2	31.4	30.9	30.8	30.3	30.5	30.1	29.4	30.5
2008	28.6	28.6	28.8	29.0	29.0	29.4	28.9	28.5	28.1	27.8	27.1	26.2	28.3
2009	24.7	24.0	23.8	24.0	24.0	24.1	24.1	24.4	24.0	23.9	24.1	24.2	24.1
Manufacturing													
1990	22.2	22.2	22.4	22.6	22.9	23.0	23.1	23.4	23.5	23.3	22.9	22.6	22.8
2000	26.6	26.8	26.9	27.0	27.3	27.5	28.1	28.2	28.2	28.1	28.0	28.2	27.6
2001	28.1	28.2	28.3	27.9	27.8	27.6	26.9	26.8	26.4	26.1	25.6	25.5	27.1
2002	25.0	24.8	24.8	24.9	24.9	25.1	25.3	25.2	25.0	24.5	24.1	24.1	24.8
2003	23.7	23.7	23.7	23.5	23.4	23.4	23.5	23.6	23.4	23.1	22.7	22.6	23.4
2004	22.2	22.1	22.2	22.5	22.7	22.8	23.0	23.0	22.9	22.8	22.7	22.7	22.6
2005	22.6	22.5	22.5	22.7	22.8	22.7	22.7	22.8	22.9	23.2	23.3	23.4	22.8
2006	23.3	23.8	23.8	23.9	23.9	24.2	24.4	24.4	24.5	24.5	24.1	24.1	24.1
2007	23.8	24.1	24.0	23.8	23.9	24.0	24.0	24.0	23.6	23.1	23.0	22.8	23.7
2008	22.3	22.3	22.3	22.3	22.4	22.5	22.4	22.5	22.4	21.4	21.0	20.7	22.0
2009	19.9	19.3	18.7	18.4	18.2	18.1	18.0	17.9	17.6	17.5	17.4	17.3	18.2
Service-Providing													
1990	227.1	229.5	232.2	234.5	236.6	235.7	233.4	234.0	237.0	235.5	235.0	235.1	233.8
2000	298.7	301.2	304.1	305.8	307.9	306.6	303.9	304.6	309.2	308.8	311.2	312.6	306.2
2001	304.1	307.3	309.4	310.6	312.1	312.4	308.8	309.1	310.6	311.1	313.1	314.8	310.3
2002	307.1	309.3	311.7	312.5	315.0	315.2	312.3	312.6	316.3	314.4	316.8	318.8	313.5
2003	309.8	312.8	315.1	315.5	316.5	316.5	313.6	314.9	317.0	317.0	318.5	320.9	315.7
2004	314.0	318.1	320.6	322.1	323.2	322.0	319.0	319.4	321.8	325.3	326.4	327.3	321.6
2005	318.6	321.4	323.4	325.9	326.9	326.9	324.3	326.1	329.2	329.4	331.7	333.4	326.4
2006	328.0	330.9	334.6	334.9	336.3	337.4	333.7	334.8	338.6	339.0	341.8	342.3	336.0
2007	334.4	337.6	341.3	340.8	342.6	342.1	339.0	341.2	343.3	344.4	346.0	347.3	341.7
2008	339.2	341.9	343.5	345.4	346.6	344.4	342.7	345.7	347.8	347.7	345.1	343.8	344.5
2009	335.9	336.2	336.8	337.5	337.9	335.3	332.9	335.3	337.7	337.7	339.2	339.0	336.8

Employment by Industry: Albuquerque, NM, Selected Years, 1990–2009—*Continued*

(Numbers in thousands, not seasonally adjusted.)

Industry and year	January	February	March	April	May	June	July	August	September	October	November	December	Annual average
Trade, Transportation, and Utilities													
1990	53.5	53.1	53.6	53.6	54.1	54.1	53.2	53.3	53.6	53.4	54.6	54.8	53.7
2000	65.2	64.6	64.8	65.3	66.0	65.9	65.2	66.0	66.2	66.7	69.1	69.6	66.2
2001	66.7	65.9	65.8	65.4	65.8	65.6	65.2	65.8	65.4	65.5	67.1	67.9	66.0
2002	65.6	64.5	64.5	64.9	65.8	65.5	65.3	65.7	65.9	66.1	67.8	68.9	65.9
2003	65.6	64.8	65.4	65.2	65.4	65.0	64.7	65.3	65.2	65.7	67.2	68.3	65.7
2004	65.8	65.4	65.6	65.8	65.8	65.5	65.6	65.8	65.6	66.6	68.1	68.8	66.2
2005	66.2	65.9	65.9	66.0	66.6	66.0	66.4	67.1	66.9	67.4	68.8	69.7	66.9
2006	66.7	66.0	66.5	66.6	67.2	66.9	67.1	67.5	67.6	67.8	69.5	70.2	67.5
2007	68.2	67.7	67.9	67.7	68.5	68.4	68.4	68.8	68.7	69.2	70.9	72.0	68.9
2008	69.5	68.6	68.6	68.4	68.3	67.9	68.0	68.2	68.0	67.8	67.9	68.2	68.3
2009	64.9	63.5	63.2	62.5	62.8	62.6	62.7	62.9	62.9	63.1	64.0	64.5	63.3
Wholesale Trade													
1990	13.2	13.3	13.3	13.4	13.4	13.4	13.1	13.0	13.0	12.9	13.0	12.9	13.2
2000	13.9	14.0	14.1	14.2	14.3	14.2	14.1	14.3	14.3	14.1	14.2	14.1	14.2
2001	14.0	14.0	14.0	13.9	14.0	13.9	13.8	13.8	13.8	13.6	13.6	13.6	13.8
2002	13.6	13.5	13.5	13.4	13.5	13.4	13.5	13.4	13.4	13.4	13.4	13.3	13.4
2003	13.0	12.9	13.3	13.2	13.0	13.0	12.9	13.0	13.0	12.8	12.8	12.9	13.0
2004	12.8	12.8	13.0	13.2	12.9	12.8	12.9	12.7	12.7	12.7	12.7	12.7	12.8
2005	12.7	12.9	12.9	12.9	13.0	12.9	13.0	13.0	13.0	13.0	13.1	13.1	13.0
2006	12.9	13.0	13.1	13.2	13.3	13.3	13.3	13.3	13.4	13.4	13.3	13.4	13.2
2007	13.3	13.2	13.2	13.2	13.2	13.3	13.4	13.4	13.4	13.5	13.4	13.6	13.3
2008	13.5	13.3	13.2	13.2	13.2	13.1	13.2	13.1	12.9	12.8	12.6	12.5	13.1
2009	12.2	12.1	12.0	11.8	11.8	11.7	11.9	11.9	11.9	11.9	11.9	11.9	11.9
Retail Trade													
1990	32.3	31.8	32.1	32.3	32.8	32.9	32.4	32.5	32.5	32.5	33.6	33.9	32.6
2000	40.6	40.0	40.1	40.3	40.8	41.1	40.7	41.1	41.2	41.8	44.0	44.7	41.4
2001	42.1	41.2	41.2	40.9	41.2	41.5	41.2	41.3	40.9	41.1	42.8	43.6	41.6
2002	41.4	40.4	40.6	41.0	41.8	41.8	41.5	41.6	41.8	41.9	43.5	44.6	41.8
2003	42.0	41.4	41.6	41.5	41.9	41.7	41.6	41.8	41.7	42.3	43.8	44.8	42.2
2004	42.4	41.9	42.0	42.0	42.3	42.5	42.5	42.6	42.4	43.3	44.9	45.5	42.9
2005	43.1	42.6	42.6	42.8	43.2	43.2	43.4	43.7	43.4	43.9	45.3	45.9	43.6
2006	43.3	42.6	43.0	43.0	43.4	43.3	43.5	43.6	43.6	43.8	45.5	45.8	43.7
2007	44.1	43.6	43.9	43.7	44.4	44.5	44.5	44.5	44.3	44.6	46.4	47.0	44.6
2008	44.9	44.3	44.5	44.3	44.2	44.4	44.4	44.4	44.4	44.6	44.9	45.2	44.5
2009	42.4	41.2	41.2	41.0	41.2	41.4	41.5	41.6	41.7	41.8	42.7	43.0	41.7
Transportation and Utilities													
1990	8.0	8.0	8.2	7.9	7.9	7.8	7.7	7.8	8.1	8.0	8.0	8.0	8.0
2000	10.7	10.6	10.6	10.8	10.9	10.6	10.4	10.6	10.7	10.8	10.9	10.8	10.7
2001	10.6	10.7	10.6	10.6	10.6	10.2	10.2	10.7	10.7	10.8	10.7	10.7	10.6
2002	10.6	10.6	10.4	10.5	10.5	10.3	10.3	10.7	10.7	10.8	10.9	11.0	10.6
2003	10.6	10.5	10.5	10.5	10.5	10.3	10.2	10.5	10.5	10.6	10.6	10.6	10.5
2004	10.6	10.7	10.6	10.6	10.6	10.2	10.2	10.5	10.5	10.6	10.5	10.6	10.5
2005	10.4	10.4	10.4	10.3	10.4	9.9	10.0	10.4	10.5	10.5	10.4	10.7	10.4
2006	10.5	10.4	10.4	10.4	10.5	10.3	10.3	10.6	10.6	10.6	10.7	11.0	10.5
2007	10.8	10.9	10.8	10.8	10.9	10.6	10.5	10.9	11.0	11.1	11.1	11.4	10.9
2008	11.1	11.0	10.9	10.9	10.9	10.4	10.4	10.7	10.7	10.4	10.4	10.5	10.7
2009	10.3	10.2	10.0	9.7	9.8	9.5	9.3	9.4	9.3	9.4	9.4	9.6	9.7
Information													
1990	6.8	6.9	6.8	6.7	6.7	6.7	6.8	6.8	6.7	6.4	6.4	6.4	6.7
2000	11.1	10.9	11.1	11.0	11.0	11.1	10.9	11.0	11.1	11.0	11.0	11.4	11.1
2001	11.5	11.7	11.6	11.2	11.2	11.2	11.4	11.5	11.6	11.4	11.5	11.5	11.4
2002	11.2	11.4	11.5	11.3	11.4	11.1	10.9	10.7	10.4	10.5	10.8	10.8	11.0
2003	10.5	10.5	10.5	10.3	10.3	10.3	10.2	10.0	10.1	9.9	9.9	10.0	10.2
2004	9.9	9.9	9.9	9.6	9.8	9.6	9.4	9.3	9.0	9.4	9.5	9.5	9.6
2005	8.5	8.5	8.6	8.7	8.8	8.7	8.7	8.7	8.5	8.7	8.8	9.0	8.7
2006	8.7	9.3	9.5	9.1	9.2	9.9	9.2	9.3	9.7	9.4	9.9	10.0	9.4
2007	8.7	8.9	9.2	9.1	9.3	9.8	9.1	9.1	9.1	9.3	9.3	9.3	9.2
2008	9.4	9.4	9.3	9.1	9.0	9.0	9.7	9.6	9.6	9.4	9.4	9.3	9.4
2009	8.8	8.7	8.7	8.9	8.8	8.9	9.1	9.3	9.4	8.9	9.1	9.1	9.0
Financial Activities													
1990	16.6	16.4	16.5	16.6	16.7	17.0	17.0	16.9	16.9	17.0	17.0	16.9	16.8
2000	19.2	19.2	19.2	19.4	19.4	19.4	19.5	19.4	19.5	19.6	19.7	19.8	19.4
2001	19.5	19.5	19.7	19.8	19.7	19.8	19.7	19.7	19.4	19.4	19.3	19.5	19.6
2002	18.7	18.6	18.7	18.7	18.8	18.9	19.0	19.1	19.0	19.0	18.9	19.0	18.9
2003	18.5	18.6	18.7	18.7	18.8	18.9	19.0	19.2	19.0	18.8	18.8	18.9	18.8
2004	18.8	18.8	19.0	19.0	19.0	19.1	19.1	19.1	19.1	19.1	19.2	19.3	19.1
2005	19.1	19.1	19.2	19.2	19.3	19.5	19.5	19.4	19.3	19.4	19.4	19.6	19.3
2006	19.3	19.3	19.3	19.3	19.3	19.4	19.3	19.2	19.1	19.1	19.1	19.2	19.2
2007	19.0	19.1	19.2	19.2	19.2	19.3	19.3	19.3	19.2	19.3	19.1	19.1	19.2
2008	18.8	18.8	18.7	18.8	18.7	18.7	18.9	18.9	18.8	18.6	18.4	18.4	18.7
2009	18.0	18.0	17.9	18.0	18.1	18.2	18.2	18.1	18.1	18.0	18.0	18.0	18.1

Employment by Industry: Albuquerque, NM, Selected Years, 1990–2009—*Continued*

(Numbers in thousands, not seasonally adjusted.)

Industry and year	January	February	March	April	May	June	July	August	September	October	November	December	Annual average
Professional and Business Services													
1990	40.9	41.0	41.9	42.5	42.5	43.8	43.1	42.9	43.1	42.5	41.9	43.1	42.4
2000	56.6	56.8	57.4	58.6	58.8	59.6	59.1	59.5	60.0	59.4	59.3	59.8	58.7
2001	57.6	58.2	58.7	58.8	59.0	59.6	59.0	59.0	57.7	58.5	58.4	58.1	58.6
2002	57.2	57.1	57.8	57.1	57.7	57.9	58.0	58.0	58.5	57.8	57.9	58.4	57.8
2003	56.8	57.3	57.6	57.0	57.1	57.5	57.4	57.7	57.6	57.8	57.8	57.9	57.5
2004	57.4	57.8	58.5	58.6	59.0	59.3	59.4	59.6	59.7	60.8	60.1	60.1	59.2
2005	59.3	59.3	59.5	60.6	60.3	61.2	61.1	61.4	61.6	60.8	61.5	61.4	60.7
2006	61.7	62.2	62.7	62.9	62.8	63.8	62.8	62.8	62.9	63.3	63.3	63.6	62.9
2007	62.8	63.6	64.0	63.8	64.2	64.8	64.9	65.6	64.7	64.3	64.2	64.4	64.3
2008	63.5	63.9	63.8	64.0	64.3	64.4	64.8	66.1	65.4	65.1	63.6	63.2	64.3
2009	61.9	61.2	60.6	60.7	60.5	60.6	60.9	61.4	60.8	59.7	59.9	59.5	60.6
Education and Health Services													
1990	23.5	23.6	24.0	24.0	24.2	23.6	23.9	24.2	24.6	24.8	24.9	24.7	24.2
2000	37.5	37.8	38.0	37.5	37.4	36.7	36.2	36.0	37.3	37.6	37.8	37.9	37.3
2001	38.3	38.6	39.0	39.2	39.4	39.0	38.7	38.6	39.7	40.0	40.2	40.4	39.3
2002	40.8	41.1	41.4	41.4	41.6	40.8	40.2	40.5	41.8	41.8	42.1	41.9	41.3
2003	42.4	42.7	42.9	43.0	43.0	42.2	41.5	41.9	43.2	43.2	43.4	43.5	42.7
2004	44.2	44.4	44.7	45.3	45.3	44.5	43.9	44.4	45.4	45.7	46.1	45.9	45.0
2005	45.7	45.9	46.5	46.5	46.7	45.8	45.2	45.6	46.7	46.9	47.1	47.1	46.3
2006	47.2	47.2	48.4	48.0	48.3	47.6	47.2	47.0	48.5	48.3	48.5	48.4	47.9
2007	48.5	48.8	49.5	49.6	49.7	48.5	48.1	47.9	48.8	49.4	49.7	49.8	49.0
2008	49.4	50.0	50.7	51.5	51.8	51.0	50.3	50.6	51.7	52.3	52.5	52.6	51.2
2009	53.0	53.5	54.1	54.1	54.3	53.1	52.6	53.0	54.1	54.3	54.4	54.5	53.8
Leisure and Hospitality													
1990	24.1	24.4	25.0	26.2	27.3	27.2	27.0	27.4	26.9	26.0	25.5	24.9	26.0
2000	31.4	31.8	32.8	33.3	33.7	34.8	34.7	35.0	34.6	34.1	33.5	33.3	33.6
2001	32.5	32.7	33.3	34.4	34.9	35.3	35.1	35.2	34.7	34.2	33.9	33.6	34.2
2002	32.8	33.0	33.8	34.9	35.5	36.0	35.9	36.0	35.7	34.9	34.6	34.5	34.8
2003	33.7	34.0	34.5	36.0	36.7	37.2	36.9	37.0	36.2	35.9	35.5	35.6	35.8
2004	34.7	35.2	35.8	36.9	37.3	37.4	37.0	36.7	36.1	35.8	35.1	35.2	36.1
2005	34.4	34.7	35.4	36.8	37.2	37.8	37.4	37.7	37.5	36.6	36.4	36.3	36.5
2006	36.3	36.6	37.4	38.3	38.9	39.5	39.7	39.6	39.3	39.0	39.2	38.6	38.5
2007	37.9	38.0	38.8	39.6	39.9	40.3	40.2	40.5	40.3	39.6	39.1	39.0	39.4
2008	37.8	37.9	38.6	39.8	40.0	40.1	39.7	39.9	39.4	38.7	37.8	37.1	38.9
2009	36.2	36.1	36.6	37.6	38.2	38.1	38.2	38.5	38.0	38.2	37.9	37.7	37.6
Other Services													
1990	8.7	8.8	8.8	8.8	9.0	9.3	9.1	9.2	8.9	8.9	8.8	8.7	8.9
2000	10.7	10.8	10.8	10.7	10.8	11.2	11.2	11.1	10.8	10.9	11.0	11.0	10.9
2001	10.9	10.8	11.0	11.1	11.2	11.6	11.5	11.4	11.1	11.0	11.0	11.1	11.1
2002	10.9	11.1	11.2	11.4	11.4	11.8	11.8	11.8	11.6	11.5	11.5	11.5	11.5
2003	11.5	11.5	11.6	11.5	11.6	11.9	12.0	11.9	11.7	11.7	11.6	11.6	11.7
2004	11.6	11.6	11.6	11.6	11.8	12.1	12.2	12.1	11.8	11.7	11.7	11.6	11.8
2005	11.6	11.6	11.7	11.7	11.8	12.2	12.3	12.2	11.9	11.8	11.8	11.8	11.9
2006	11.7	11.8	11.9	12.1	12.1	12.5	12.5	12.3	12.1	12.3	12.2	11.9	12.1
2007	11.9	12.0	12.2	12.1	12.2	12.5	12.5	12.2	12.1	12.2	12.2	12.2	12.2
2008	12.1	12.3	12.3	12.3	12.4	12.9	12.8	12.6	12.5	12.7	12.5	12.0	12.5
2009	11.9	12.0	12.0	11.9	12.0	12.3	12.1	11.9	11.7	11.7	11.7	11.6	11.9
Government													
1990	53.0	55.3	55.6	56.1	56.1	54.0	53.3	53.3	56.3	56.5	55.9	55.6	55.1
2000	67.0	69.3	70.0	70.0	70.8	67.9	67.1	66.6	69.7	69.5	69.8	69.8	69.0
2001	67.1	69.9	70.3	70.7	70.9	70.3	68.2	67.9	71.0	71.1	71.7	72.7	70.2
2002	69.9	72.5	72.8	72.8	72.8	73.2	71.2	70.8	73.4	72.8	73.2	73.8	72.4
2003	70.8	73.4	73.9	73.8	73.6	73.5	71.9	71.9	74.0	74.0	74.3	75.1	73.4
2004	71.6	75.0	75.5	75.3	75.2	74.5	72.4	72.4	75.1	76.2	76.6	76.9	74.7
2005	73.8	76.4	76.6	76.4	76.2	75.7	73.7	74.0	76.8	77.8	77.9	78.5	76.2
2006	76.4	78.5	78.9	78.6	78.5	77.8	75.9	77.1	79.4	79.8	80.1	80.4	78.5
2007	77.4	79.5	80.5	79.7	79.6	78.5	76.5	77.8	80.4	81.1	81.5	81.5	79.5
2008	78.7	81.0	81.5	81.5	82.1	80.4	78.5	79.8	82.4	83.1	83.0	83.0	81.3
2009	81.2	83.2	83.7	83.8	83.2	81.5	79.1	80.2	82.7	83.8	84.2	84.1	82.6

Employment by Industry: Allentown-Bethlehem-Easton, PA-NJ, Selected Years, 1990–2009

(Numbers in thousands, not seasonally adjusted.)

Industry and year	January	February	March	April	May	June	July	August	September	October	November	December	Annual average
Total Nonfarm													
1990	281.4	281.3	284.4	285.9	288.8	291.0	284.7	286.5	288.2	289.8	289.0	288.7	286.6
2000	314.4	315.7	319.2	321.1	325.4	328.6	324.2	324.1	324.3	326.2	328.3	329.8	323.4
2001	322.8	323.3	326.7	326.0	329.2	331.3	324.9	326.2	325.8	325.6	325.4	325.6	326.1
2002	318.9	319.2	323.1	322.7	326.4	327.4	323.0	324.1	327.1	327.4	327.1	327.4	324.5
2003	320.7	319.8	322.8	324.9	329.0	329.9	321.4	322.1	328.4	330.3	330.9	330.8	325.9
2004	321.6	323.1	327.2	329.6	333.1	334.9	326.5	326.5	331.1	335.0	334.9	334.2	329.8
2005	325.8	328.1	331.1	336.7	339.5	340.7	334.9	334.1	339.1	340.6	341.4	341.1	336.1
2006	332.7	334.4	339.3	341.6	344.2	346.0	338.4	340.2	344.9	347.0	346.4	346.7	341.8
2007	336.7	337.0	341.8	343.3	348.0	350.2	342.5	342.4	346.5	350.0	349.5	349.4	344.8
2008	338.6	339.3	342.5	344.8	348.7	349.7	342.6	342.4	344.8	346.7	343.7	343.6	344.0
2009	330.9	330.9	332.5	332.3	336.5	335.6	330.1	329.8	332.4	334.2	332.5	332.4	332.5
Total Private													
1990	249.3	248.7	251.5	253.0	255.2	257.6	254.0	256.0	256.7	257.4	256.1	255.6	254.3
2000	276.7	277.3	280.3	282.2	285.3	288.9	287.4	287.5	287.5	287.3	289.1	290.4	285.0
2001	284.9	284.4	287.5	286.9	289.8	292.4	289.2	290.0	287.9	286.2	285.9	285.8	287.6
2002	280.2	279.7	283.3	283.0	286.3	288.2	287.4	288.9	288.6	287.6	287.2	287.4	285.7
2003	281.3	279.2	281.9	284.0	287.7	289.0	286.7	287.9	288.5	289.4	289.3	289.5	286.2
2004	281.6	281.8	285.6	288.1	291.0	293.2	290.9	291.2	290.9	293.4	293.2	292.6	289.5
2005	285.5	286.3	289.2	293.9	297.0	299.2	299.2	299.2	298.5	299.0	299.4	299.0	295.5
2006	291.5	292.3	296.9	299.2	301.5	304.1	302.6	304.1	303.8	304.8	303.5	303.9	300.7
2007	295.2	294.3	298.9	300.3	304.3	307.0	305.2	305.3	304.4	306.8	305.8	305.6	302.8
2008	296.6	296.0	299.0	301.3	304.9	305.6	304.2	304.0	302.2	302.7	299.3	299.3	301.3
2009	288.7	287.0	288.2	287.7	291.7	292.0	291.4	291.0	290.0	290.9	288.9	288.7	289.7
Goods-Producing													
1990	79.0	78.2	79.1	78.9	79.3	80.7	78.6	80.3	80.2	79.0	78.8	78.0	79.2
2000	67.9	67.2	68.4	68.3	68.8	70.2	69.7	70.9	70.5	69.8	70.3	70.4	69.4
2001	69.4	69.2	69.6	70.2	70.3	70.8	69.3	69.8	68.7	67.1	66.0	65.5	68.8
2002	64.5	64.2	64.7	64.6	65.1	65.5	64.6	64.6	63.7	62.6	61.9	61.1	63.9
2003	59.2	58.2	58.4	58.7	59.2	59.7	58.8	58.8	58.3	58.2	57.7	57.1	58.5
2004	56.0	55.7	56.5	57.0	57.7	58.7	58.6	59.1	58.7	58.5	58.6	58.3	57.8
2005	56.8	56.4	56.8	58.1	58.7	59.6	59.2	59.3	59.0	58.6	58.4	57.8	58.2
2006	56.1	56.1	56.8	57.2	57.2	58.4	57.6	58.2	57.5	57.4	56.8	56.6	57.2
2007	55.5	54.9	55.7	56.2	57.0	57.8	57.4	57.5	57.3	57.0	56.6	55.7	56.6
2008	54.4	54.1	54.8	55.4	56.2	56.8	56.1	56.2	55.9	55.4	54.1	53.0	55.2
2009	50.9	49.8	49.6	49.6	49.6	49.6	49.6	49.2	48.7	48.3	48.0	47.4	49.2
Mining, Logging, and Construction													
1990	12.8	12.3	12.9	13.5	13.8	14.5	14.6	14.6	14.5	14.3	13.8	13.1	13.7
2000	13.5	12.9	13.6	14.0	14.4	14.9	15.4	15.5	15.3	15.0	15.0	14.6	14.5
2001	13.9	13.6	13.8	14.4	14.8	15.3	15.6	15.7	15.4	15.0	14.7	14.5	14.7
2002	13.5	13.5	14.0	14.9	15.3	15.8	16.0	15.7	15.3	15.0	15.0	14.6	14.9
2003	13.4	13.0	13.4	14.3	15.0	15.6	15.9	16.0	15.7	15.7	15.5	15.1	14.8
2004	14.5	14.3	15.0	15.5	16.2	16.7	16.9	17.0	16.8	16.6	16.5	16.4	16.0
2005	15.3	15.1	15.3	16.6	17.1	17.8	18.0	17.9	17.6	17.3	17.4	16.9	16.9
2006	15.8	15.8	16.2	16.9	17.1	17.7	17.7	17.9	17.5	17.3	16.9	16.7	17.0
2007	15.6	14.9	15.4	16.2	17.0	17.5	17.7	17.8	17.4	17.0	16.6	15.8	16.6
2008	14.9	14.6	15.0	15.6	16.4	16.9	16.8	16.5	16.2	15.9	15.1	14.3	15.7
2009	13.0	12.6	12.8	13.3	13.6	13.6	13.7	13.5	13.2	13.0	12.8	12.3	13.1
Manufacturing													
1990	66.2	65.9	66.2	65.4	65.5	66.2	64.0	65.7	65.7	64.7	65.0	64.9	65.5
2000	54.4	54.3	54.8	54.3	54.4	55.3	54.3	55.4	55.2	54.8	55.3	55.8	54.9
2001	55.5	55.6	55.8	55.8	55.5	55.5	53.7	54.1	53.3	52.1	51.3	51.0	54.1
2002	51.0	50.7	50.7	49.7	49.8	49.7	48.6	48.9	48.4	47.6	46.9	46.5	49.0
2003	45.8	45.2	45.0	44.4	44.2	44.1	42.9	42.8	42.6	42.5	42.2	42.0	43.6
2004	41.5	41.4	41.5	41.5	41.5	42.0	41.7	42.1	41.9	41.9	42.1	41.9	41.8
2005	41.5	41.3	41.5	41.5	41.6	41.8	41.2	41.4	41.4	41.3	41.0	40.9	41.4
2006	40.3	40.3	40.6	40.3	40.1	40.7	39.9	40.3	40.0	40.1	39.9	39.9	40.2
2007	39.9	40.0	40.3	40.0	40.0	40.3	39.7	39.7	39.9	40.0	40.0	39.9	40.0
2008	39.5	39.5	39.8	39.8	39.8	39.9	39.3	39.7	39.7	39.5	39.0	38.7	39.5
2009	37.9	37.2	36.8	36.3	36.0	36.0	35.9	35.7	35.5	35.3	35.2	35.1	36.1
Service-Providing													
1990	202.4	203.1	205.3	207.0	209.5	210.3	206.1	206.2	208.0	210.8	210.2	210.7	207.5
2000	246.5	248.5	250.8	252.8	256.6	258.4	254.5	253.2	253.8	256.4	258.0	259.4	254.1
2001	253.4	254.1	257.1	255.8	258.9	260.5	255.6	256.4	257.1	258.5	259.4	260.1	257.2
2002	254.4	255.0	258.4	258.1	261.3	261.9	258.4	259.5	263.4	264.8	265.2	266.3	260.6
2003	261.5	261.6	264.4	266.2	269.8	270.2	262.6	263.3	270.1	272.1	273.2	273.7	267.4
2004	265.6	267.4	270.7	272.6	275.4	276.2	267.9	267.4	272.4	276.5	276.3	275.9	272.0
2005	269.0	271.7	274.3	278.6	280.8	281.1	275.7	274.8	280.1	282.0	283.0	283.3	277.9
2006	276.6	278.3	282.5	284.4	287.0	287.6	280.8	282.0	287.4	289.6	289.6	290.1	284.7
2007	281.2	282.1	286.1	287.1	291.0	292.4	285.1	284.9	289.2	293.0	292.9	293.7	288.2
2008	284.2	285.2	287.7	289.4	292.5	292.9	286.5	286.2	288.9	291.3	289.6	290.6	288.8
2009	280.0	281.1	282.9	282.7	286.9	286.0	280.5	280.6	283.7	285.9	284.5	285.0	283.3

Employment by Industry: Allentown-Bethlehem-Easton, PA-NJ, Selected Years, 1990–2009—*Continued*

(Numbers in thousands, not seasonally adjusted.)

Industry and year	January	February	March	April	May	June	July	August	September	October	November	December	Annual average
Trade, Transportation, and Utilities													
1990	54.8	53.9	54.0	53.9	54.1	54.7	54.2	54.4	54.3	54.7	55.6	55.7	54.5
2000	60.5	60.1	60.7	60.8	61.0	61.5	60.8	61.1	61.4	62.5	63.9	64.8	61.6
2001	62.5	61.3	61.9	61.5	61.9	63.1	62.4	62.9	62.4	63.2	64.7	65.5	62.8
2002	63.2	62.2	62.9	62.2	63.0	63.1	63.3	63.9	64.8	64.9	66.3	67.4	63.9
2003	65.0	63.7	64.1	64.4	65.1	65.6	64.3	64.5	64.9	65.8	66.7	67.7	65.2
2004	64.5	63.6	64.5	64.6	64.9	65.2	64.1	64.2	64.4	65.2	66.5	68.1	65.0
2005	66.1	65.5	65.9	66.7	67.5	68.0	67.6	67.7	67.6	68.3	70.0	70.9	67.7
2006	68.9	68.0	68.5	69.3	69.7	70.3	69.9	70.3	70.5	71.1	72.4	73.2	70.2
2007	70.3	68.9	69.3	69.3	70.2	70.7	70.2	70.1	69.9	71.0	72.8	73.5	70.5
2008	70.9	69.3	69.5	69.4	70.1	70.4	69.6	69.5	69.5	70.0	70.7	71.2	70.0
2009	67.9	66.8	66.5	65.9	66.8	67.1	66.5	66.2	66.3	66.5	67.2	67.6	66.8
Wholesale Trade													
1990	9.1	9.1	9.1	9.2	9.2	9.4	9.3	9.3	9.2	9.2	9.2	9.2	9.2
2000	10.7	10.8	11.0	11.2	11.1	11.1	11.3	11.3	11.2	11.6	11.6	11.6	11.2
2001	11.6	11.4	11.6	11.3	11.3	11.6	11.4	11.6	11.3	11.2	11.4	11.4	11.4
2002	11.3	11.1	11.2	11.1	11.2	11.3	11.3	11.2	11.1	11.0	11.1	11.2	11.2
2003	11.2	11.1	11.2	11.1	11.2	11.3	11.3	11.4	11.3	11.4	11.5	11.6	11.3
2004	11.3	11.2	11.4	11.6	11.6	11.8	11.7	11.6	11.7	11.8	11.9	12.1	11.6
2005	12.1	12.1	12.3	12.6	12.6	12.6	12.6	12.5	12.3	12.3	12.3	12.3	12.4
2006	12.5	12.7	12.9	13.3	13.5	13.7	13.7	13.8	13.7	13.8	13.8	13.9	13.4
2007	13.4	13.4	13.5	13.6	13.8	14.0	14.1	14.0	13.9	14.1	14.1	14.1	13.8
2008	13.8	13.8	13.8	14.0	14.1	14.2	14.3	14.2	14.0	14.0	13.9	13.8	14.0
2009	13.4	13.3	13.3	13.4	13.4	13.5	13.4	13.3	13.3	13.3	13.3	13.3	13.4
Retail Trade													
1990	37.0	36.1	36.2	35.8	35.9	36.1	36.0	36.1	36.0	36.5	37.4	37.7	36.4
2000	37.9	37.4	37.6	37.6	37.8	38.2	38.1	38.3	38.0	38.6	40.0	41.0	38.4
2001	38.6	37.6	37.8	37.6	38.0	39.0	38.9	39.2	38.4	39.2	40.6	41.4	38.9
2002	39.6	38.8	39.1	38.7	39.3	39.5	40.0	40.5	40.4	40.4	41.7	42.7	40.1
2003	40.4	39.4	39.6	39.8	40.3	40.7	40.3	40.5	40.4	41.0	41.9	42.9	40.6
2004	40.4	39.6	40.1	40.1	40.8	41.0	40.3	40.5	40.0	40.7	41.8	43.1	40.7
2005	41.2	40.6	40.6	40.8	41.4	41.8	41.6	41.6	40.9	41.2	42.5	43.3	41.5
2006	41.3	40.1	40.4	40.5	40.8	41.3	41.3	41.5	41.2	41.7	43.0	43.7	41.4
2007	41.5	40.2	40.4	40.2	40.8	41.2	41.1	41.1	40.5	41.2	42.9	43.6	41.2
2008	41.8	40.4	40.5	40.3	40.8	41.0	40.5	40.4	40.1	40.5	41.3	42.0	40.8
2009	39.5	38.8	38.6	38.3	39.0	39.4	39.3	39.3	38.8	38.9	39.5	39.8	39.1
Transportation and Utilities													
1990	8.7	8.7	8.7	8.9	9.0	9.2	8.9	9.0	9.1	9.0	9.0	8.8	8.9
2000	11.9	11.9	12.1	12.0	12.1	12.2	11.4	11.5	12.2	12.3	12.3	12.2	12.0
2001	12.3	12.3	12.5	12.6	12.6	12.5	12.1	12.1	12.7	12.8	12.7	12.7	12.5
2002	12.3	12.3	12.6	12.4	12.5	12.3	12.0	12.2	13.3	13.5	13.5	13.5	12.7
2003	13.4	13.2	13.3	13.5	13.6	13.6	12.7	12.6	13.2	13.4	13.3	13.2	13.3
2004	12.8	12.8	13.0	12.9	12.5	12.4	12.1	12.1	12.7	12.7	12.8	12.9	12.6
2005	12.8	12.8	13.0	13.3	13.5	13.6	13.4	13.6	14.4	14.8	15.2	15.3	13.8
2006	15.1	15.2	15.2	15.5	15.4	15.3	14.9	15.0	15.6	15.6	15.6	15.6	15.3
2007	15.4	15.3	15.4	15.5	15.6	15.5	15.0	15.0	15.5	15.7	15.8	15.8	15.5
2008	15.3	15.1	15.2	15.1	15.2	15.2	14.8	14.9	15.4	15.5	15.5	15.4	15.2
2009	15.0	14.7	14.6	14.2	14.4	14.2	13.8	13.6	14.2	14.3	14.4	14.5	14.3
Information													
1990	6.5	6.5	6.5	6.6	6.6	6.7	6.6	6.6	6.6	6.5	6.5	6.5	6.6
2000	8.7	8.7	8.9	8.9	9.0	9.3	9.3	9.0	8.9	9.0	9.1	9.3	9.0
2001	9.4	9.3	9.2	9.1	9.1	9.0	9.0	8.7	8.4	8.4	8.2	8.2	8.8
2002	7.8	7.8	7.8	7.8	7.8	7.9	7.8	7.7	7.6	7.6	7.6	7.7	7.7
2003	7.6	7.7	7.8	7.8	7.8	7.9	7.7	7.7	7.6	7.6	7.7	7.8	7.7
2004	7.6	7.6	7.6	7.7	7.7	7.8	7.8	7.7	7.6	7.7	7.7	7.8	7.7
2005	7.6	7.6	7.6	7.6	7.6	7.6	7.6	7.6	7.4	7.4	7.4	7.4	7.5
2006	7.4	7.4	7.4	7.4	7.5	7.6	7.5	7.5	7.5	7.4	7.4	7.5	7.5
2007	7.4	7.3	7.3	7.3	7.4	7.5	7.5	7.5	7.4	7.4	7.4	7.5	7.4
2008	7.4	7.4	7.4	7.5	7.6	7.5	7.5	7.4	7.3	7.3	7.1	7.2	7.4
2009	7.1	7.1	7.1	7.0	7.1	7.1	7.0	6.9	6.8	6.8	6.7	6.8	7.0
Financial Activities													
1990	13.2	13.0	13.1	12.9	13.1	13.2	13.2	13.2	13.3	13.3	13.2	13.3	13.2
2000	15.7	15.7	15.9	15.9	16.0	16.2	16.2	16.2	16.1	16.2	16.3	16.5	16.1
2001	16.9	16.8	17.0	16.5	16.4	16.8	16.9	17.0	16.9	16.8	16.8	16.9	16.8
2002	16.6	16.6	16.6	16.6	16.5	16.8	16.9	17.0	16.8	16.5	16.5	16.8	16.7
2003	16.7	16.7	16.7	16.6	16.7	16.8	16.8	16.8	16.5	16.5	16.5	16.6	16.6
2004	16.3	16.1	16.2	16.3	16.5	16.5	16.4	16.4	16.2	16.4	16.4	16.5	16.4
2005	16.3	16.3	16.3	16.5	16.6	16.7	16.7	16.8	16.6	16.5	16.6	16.6	16.5
2006	16.4	16.5	16.6	16.6	16.6	16.8	16.7	16.7	16.6	16.4	16.4	16.5	16.6
2007	16.3	16.4	16.4	16.2	16.2	16.3	16.2	16.2	16.0	16.0	15.9	15.8	16.2
2008	15.7	15.8	15.8	15.9	15.9	15.9	16.0	15.9	15.7	15.6	15.7	15.7	15.8
2009	15.5	15.6	15.5	15.6	15.6	15.8	15.8	15.7	15.6	15.5	15.4	15.4	15.6

Employment by Industry: Allentown-Bethlehem-Easton, PA-NJ, Selected Years, 1990–2009—*Continued*

(Numbers in thousands, not seasonally adjusted.)

Industry and year	January	February	March	April	May	June	July	August	September	October	November	December	Annual average
Professional and Business Services													
1990	27.6	27.5	27.8	28.3	28.6	29.4	28.3	28.4	28.4	28.4	28.3	27.9	28.2
2000	35.9	35.9	36.5	37.4	37.5	38.0	38.4	37.7	37.7	37.6	37.5	37.4	37.3
2001	36.8	36.7	37.1	37.7	37.9	38.1	37.2	37.0	36.8	37.0	36.8	36.8	37.2
2002	36.1	35.9	36.6	37.0	36.8	37.3	37.5	38.0	37.7	38.1	37.9	37.9	37.2
2003	36.7	36.6	37.1	38.0	38.6	39.1	39.4	40.4	40.9	41.0	41.3	41.5	39.2
2004	40.1	39.9	40.4	41.1	41.1	41.4	41.4	41.6	41.3	42.2	41.9	41.5	41.2
2005	40.0	40.4	40.4	41.3	41.4	42.0	42.5	42.7	42.6	43.3	43.5	43.1	41.9
2006	41.4	41.6	42.3	42.6	43.0	43.7	44.0	44.5	44.3	44.9	44.4	44.1	43.4
2007	42.7	42.6	43.1	43.6	43.7	44.3	44.0	43.6	43.8	44.6	44.2	44.0	43.7
2008	42.2	41.5	41.9	42.6	42.7	42.7	43.2	43.2	42.7	42.9	42.4	42.7	42.6
2009	40.4	39.7	39.8	39.7	39.9	40.4	39.8	40.4	40.6	41.0	40.8	40.7	40.3
Education and Health Services													
1990	36.4	37.8	38.8	39.2	39.2	37.0	37.0	37.1	39.1	40.3	40.4	40.6	38.6
2000	48.8	50.3	50.6	51.1	51.4	50.3	49.7	49.7	51.6	52.1	52.8	52.3	50.9
2001	50.5	51.8	52.7	52.3	52.1	50.9	50.8	51.3	53.2	53.4	54.0	53.7	52.2
2002	51.9	52.8	53.7	53.4	53.5	52.1	52.2	52.2	54.5	55.6	56.1	55.0	53.6
2003	54.5	55.0	55.9	56.0	55.8	54.3	54.1	54.2	56.3	57.4	57.9	57.5	55.7
2004	55.6	57.3	58.3	58.0	57.9	56.7	56.2	56.0	57.6	59.3	59.4	58.1	57.5
2005	57.4	58.1	59.3	59.6	59.2	57.8	58.1	57.7	59.5	60.8	60.9	60.5	59.1
2006	59.2	60.2	61.8	61.5	60.9	59.2	59.2	59.3	61.4	62.9	62.6	62.3	60.9
2007	60.6	61.6	63.3	63.2	63.0	61.3	61.2	62.0	63.5	65.0	64.7	64.5	62.8
2008	62.6	64.3	65.3	65.3	64.0	62.9	62.9	63.4	64.6	65.8	66.1	65.9	64.4
2009	64.6	65.6	66.6	66.0	65.1	63.5	63.8	64.1	65.4	67.0	67.0	66.7	65.5
Leisure and Hospitality													
1990	19.5	19.5	19.7	20.9	21.8	23.0	23.2	23.2	22.3	22.6	20.6	20.8	21.4
2000	24.9	24.9	24.9	25.5	27.2	28.7	28.7	28.3	27.0	25.8	24.7	25.2	26.3
2001	25.0	24.9	25.3	24.9	27.2	28.5	28.3	28.2	26.8	25.7	24.6	24.4	26.2
2002	25.4	25.5	26.2	26.5	28.6	30.3	29.8	30.3	28.7	27.6	26.2	26.6	27.6
2003	27.0	26.7	27.1	27.7	29.5	30.4	30.3	30.4	29.1	28.0	26.6	26.4	28.2
2004	26.8	26.8	27.2	28.3	30.0	31.4	30.9	30.9	30.0	28.9	27.5	27.0	28.8
2005	26.2	26.7	27.5	28.9	30.6	31.9	31.9	32.0	30.6	29.2	27.7	27.7	29.2
2006	27.4	27.7	28.6	29.5	31.3	32.7	32.3	32.3	30.9	29.8	28.6	28.6	30.0
2007	27.6	27.8	28.7	29.4	31.5	33.7	33.2	33.0	31.3	30.8	29.2	29.4	30.5
2008	28.5	28.6	29.3	30.1	33.2	33.9	33.5	33.2	31.5	30.8	28.4	28.7	30.8
2009	27.8	27.8	28.5	29.7	33.2	34.0	33.9	33.6	32.1	31.3	29.4	29.6	30.9
Other Services													
1990	12.3	12.3	12.5	12.3	12.5	12.9	12.9	12.8	12.5	12.6	12.7	12.8	12.6
2000	14.3	14.5	14.4	14.3	14.4	14.7	14.6	14.6	14.3	14.3	14.5	14.5	14.5
2001	14.4	14.4	14.7	14.7	14.9	15.2	15.3	15.1	14.7	14.6	14.8	14.8	14.8
2002	14.7	14.7	14.8	14.9	15.0	15.2	15.3	15.2	14.8	14.7	14.7	14.9	14.9
2003	14.6	14.6	14.8	14.8	15.0	15.2	15.3	15.1	14.9	14.9	14.9	14.9	14.9
2004	14.7	14.8	14.9	15.1	15.2	15.5	15.5	15.3	15.1	15.2	15.2	15.3	15.2
2005	15.1	15.3	15.4	15.2	15.4	15.6	15.6	15.4	15.2	14.9	14.9	15.0	15.3
2006	14.7	14.8	14.9	15.1	15.3	15.4	15.4	15.3	15.1	14.9	14.9	15.1	15.1
2007	14.8	14.8	15.1	15.1	15.3	15.4	15.5	15.4	15.2	15.0	15.0	15.2	15.2
2008	14.9	15.0	15.0	15.1	15.2	15.5	15.4	15.2	15.0	14.9	14.8	14.9	15.1
2009	14.5	14.6	14.6	14.2	14.4	14.5	15.0	14.9	14.5	14.5	14.4	14.5	14.6
Government													
1990	32.1	32.6	32.9	32.9	33.6	33.4	30.7	30.5	31.5	32.4	32.9	33.1	32.4
2000	37.7	38.4	38.9	38.9	40.1	39.7	36.8	36.6	36.8	38.9	39.2	39.4	38.5
2001	37.9	38.9	39.2	39.1	39.4	38.9	35.7	36.2	37.9	39.4	39.5	39.8	38.5
2002	38.7	39.5	39.8	39.7	40.1	39.2	35.6	35.2	38.5	39.8	39.9	40.0	38.8
2003	39.4	40.6	40.9	40.9	41.3	40.9	34.7	34.2	39.9	40.9	41.6	41.3	39.7
2004	40.0	41.3	41.6	41.5	42.1	41.7	35.6	35.3	40.2	41.6	41.7	41.6	40.4
2005	40.3	41.8	41.9	42.8	42.5	41.5	35.7	34.9	40.6	41.6	42.0	42.1	40.6
2006	41.2	42.1	42.4	42.4	42.7	41.9	35.8	36.1	41.1	42.2	42.9	42.8	41.1
2007	41.5	42.7	42.9	43.0	43.7	43.2	37.3	37.1	42.1	43.2	43.7	43.8	42.0
2008	42.0	43.3	43.5	43.5	43.8	44.1	38.4	38.4	42.6	44.0	44.4	44.3	42.7
2009	42.2	43.9	44.3	44.6	44.8	43.6	38.7	38.8	42.4	43.3	43.6	43.7	42.8

Employment by Industry: Atlanta-Sandy Springs-Marietta, GA, Selected Years, 1990–2009

(Numbers in thousands, not seasonally adjusted.)

Industry and year	January	February	March	April	May	June	July	August	September	October	November	December	Annual average
Total Nonfarm													
1990	1572.1	1580.6	1596.1	1593.6	1603.2	1618.4	1614.0	1622.4	1619.9	1613.8	1620.2	1620.6	1606.2
2000	2235.7	2250.0	2272.3	2272.4	2286.5	2304.3	2285.1	2298.0	2303.4	2311.5	2320.7	2330.7	2289.2
2001	2275.5	2284.7	2301.3	2307.2	2309.9	2313.5	2299.6	2312.4	2310.6	2297.7	2299.3	2299.0	2300.9
2002	2232.6	2235.1	2254.2	2265.7	2272.9	2275.2	2242.1	2263.1	2262.2	2256.6	2267.6	2271.6	2258.2
2003	2206.9	2217.1	2230.6	2227.3	2234.7	2230.6	2219.2	2243.6	2246.4	2246.1	2259.0	2267.3	2235.7
2004	2215.8	2228.3	2245.6	2256.4	2262.0	2257.8	2260.3	2280.7	2273.0	2294.0	2305.7	2312.4	2266.0
2005	2277.4	2289.2	2296.2	2326.5	2338.4	2328.7	2327.2	2351.8	2353.4	2366.7	2384.3	2389.1	2335.7
2006	2352.5	2362.4	2375.8	2387.6	2399.6	2400.7	2385.7	2408.9	2412.2	2437.1	2451.7	2458.3	2402.7
2007	2419.4	2432.3	2444.3	2442.6	2454.2	2447.7	2443.0	2466.6	2462.5	2463.2	2475.7	2477.6	2452.4
2008	2432.5	2444.1	2445.6	2445.8	2453.3	2437.9	2414.2	2427.8	2413.1	2409.1	2402.7	2390.3	2426.4
2009	2329.9	2324.4	2314.3	2310.9	2309.3	2291.6	2264.5	2268.3	2262.4	2266.8	2276.3	2264.8	2290.3
Total Private													
1990	1356.5	1363.8	1377.8	1374.0	1382.4	1395.9	1397.2	1404.3	1401.8	1392.1	1396.3	1397.8	1386.7
2000	1966.0	1977.6	1998.5	1998.8	2012.8	2031.9	2022.9	2030.2	2030.1	2035.3	2043.2	2052.3	2016.6
2001	1996.8	2002.6	2017.8	2025.0	2026.2	2032.9	2027.9	2028.4	2022.4	2007.2	2006.8	2007.7	2016.8
2002	1943.5	1946.2	1960.7	1969.6	1976.7	1984.2	1963.3	1970.8	1962.9	1958.3	1967.5	1974.0	1964.8
2003	1909.3	1917.9	1929.7	1927.5	1936.9	1942.2	1940.3	1953.7	1949.0	1947.2	1959.9	1968.7	1940.2
2004	1917.4	1924.5	1941.2	1952.6	1960.1	1966.6	1976.7	1981.6	1968.1	1989.9	1999.9	2009.3	1965.7
2005	1974.8	1982.2	1988.6	2018.3	2030.6	2031.6	2038.6	2046.2	2044.6	2054.8	2071.5	2077.0	2029.9
2006	2041.1	2047.4	2059.1	2072.6	2085.4	2091.8	2089.5	2096.3	2093.3	2115.3	2127.5	2134.6	2087.8
2007	2097.8	2106.4	2117.2	2116.7	2129.0	2130.9	2132.6	2142.2	2133.2	2134.5	2145.3	2147.3	2127.8
2008	2102.1	2108.4	2108.2	2109.1	2117.3	2109.3	2097.4	2097.9	2082.2	2071.5	2061.9	2052.1	2093.1
2009	1992.3	1983.4	1972.4	1969.8	1972.2	1964.3	1951.2	1946.7	1932.3	1931.3	1941.6	1934.6	1957.7
Goods-Producing													
1990	263.3	265.3	269.0	267.9	268.9	271.6	271.2	271.1	269.1	265.8	262.7	259.6	267.1
2000	331.3	333.3	336.9	336.4	337.9	341.6	340.3	340.5	340.6	339.7	338.0	337.6	337.8
2001	329.7	330.1	331.0	331.9	331.0	333.2	331.7	330.2	328.2	323.8	320.3	318.1	328.3
2002	311.0	311.0	313.4	314.3	314.0	315.4	314.4	314.5	312.4	308.7	307.7	305.3	311.8
2003	299.1	301.7	303.0	300.1	302.1	302.9	302.2	303.8	303.4	304.2	303.0	303.8	302.4
2004	297.6	300.7	302.3	303.2	303.4	306.0	308.1	308.6	307.1	308.2	308.5	308.7	305.2
2005	304.5	306.0	305.8	310.3	312.6	312.9	312.9	314.0	315.8	314.0	316.3	315.5	311.7
2006	312.3	314.1	314.5	314.7	316.9	319.5	319.3	322.1	321.2	322.5	319.3	317.8	317.9
2007	316.0	317.6	318.3	317.1	317.9	318.6	317.2	318.1	315.7	315.3	314.4	312.5	316.6
2008	306.9	307.2	305.7	302.3	302.1	301.1	298.2	296.0	292.8	289.2	284.3	278.6	297.0
2009	266.9	263.7	259.5	255.2	253.2	250.1	244.0	242.1	240.3	237.8	237.3	235.2	248.8
Mining and Logging													
1990	2.8	2.7	2.8	2.7	2.7	2.7	2.7	2.7	2.7	2.7	2.6	2.6	2.7
2000	2.1	2.2	2.2	2.1	2.1	2.1	2.1	2.2	2.1	2.3	2.3	2.2	2.2
2001	2.2	2.2	2.2	2.2	2.2	2.2	2.2	2.1	2.2	2.2	2.2	2.1	2.2
2002	2.2	2.1	2.1	2.1	2.1	2.1	2.1	2.2	2.2	2.1	2.1	2.0	2.1
2003	2.0	2.0	2.0	2.0	2.0	2.0	2.0	2.0	2.0	2.1	2.0	2.0	2.0
2004	2.0	2.0	2.0	2.0	2.0	2.1	2.1	2.1	2.1	2.0	2.1	2.1	2.1
2005	1.9	1.9	1.9	2.1	2.1	2.1	2.1	2.1	2.1	2.1	2.1	2.1	2.1
2006	2.2	2.1	2.1	2.1	2.1	2.1	2.1	2.1	2.0	2.1	2.1	2.1	2.1
2007	2.1	2.0	2.1	2.0	2.0	2.0	2.0	2.0	2.0	2.0	2.0	1.9	2.0
2008	1.8	1.8	1.8	1.7	1.6	1.6	1.5	1.5	1.5	1.5	1.5	1.5	1.6
2009	1.3	1.4	1.3	1.3	1.3	1.3	1.3	1.3	1.3	1.3	1.3	1.3	1.3
Construction													
1990	74.8	76.1	78.0	77.0	77.7	79.2	79.3	79.6	78.9	78.3	76.5	74.7	77.5
2000	121.1	122.7	125.9	127.0	128.6	131.0	131.4	131.4	132.0	131.5	130.1	129.5	128.5
2001	124.9	126.3	127.3	129.6	130.2	131.8	132.5	131.7	130.5	129.2	127.8	126.0	129.0
2002	122.7	123.7	125.0	125.1	124.8	125.1	124.7	124.7	123.8	122.7	122.1	120.6	123.8
2003	117.4	118.0	119.3	119.1	120.1	121.2	122.1	123.2	123.6	123.6	123.4	123.8	121.2
2004	121.0	121.2	122.6	124.1	124.1	126.5	129.0	128.2	127.2	127.9	128.1	128.2	125.7
2005	125.9	127.1	127.0	130.1	132.1	132.5	133.3	134.1	135.0	134.5	135.0	133.8	131.7
2006	131.2	132.8	133.5	134.7	136.5	138.4	140.5	141.4	141.2	141.7	141.2	139.7	137.7
2007	137.0	138.7	139.6	139.1	139.9	140.4	139.8	140.5	139.1	139.1	138.4	136.7	139.0
2008	132.7	133.3	132.2	130.4	130.6	130.0	128.9	127.5	125.7	123.3	120.2	116.9	127.6
2009	110.5	109.3	106.9	104.9	104.2	102.6	99.7	97.8	96.5	96.5	96.8	94.7	101.7
Manufacturing													
1990	185.7	186.5	188.2	188.2	188.5	189.7	189.2	188.8	187.5	184.8	183.6	182.3	186.9
2000	208.1	208.4	208.8	207.3	207.2	208.5	206.8	206.9	206.5	205.9	205.6	205.9	207.2
2001	202.6	201.6	201.5	200.1	198.6	199.2	197.0	196.4	195.5	192.4	190.3	190.0	197.1
2002	186.1	185.2	186.3	187.1	187.1	188.2	187.6	187.6	186.4	183.9	183.5	182.7	186.0
2003	179.7	181.7	181.7	179.0	180.0	179.7	178.1	178.6	177.8	178.5	177.6	178.0	179.2
2004	174.6	177.5	177.7	177.1	177.3	177.4	177.0	178.3	177.8	178.3	178.3	178.4	177.5
2005	176.7	177.0	176.9	178.1	178.4	178.3	177.5	177.8	178.7	177.4	179.2	179.6	178.0
2006	178.9	179.2	178.9	177.9	178.3	179.0	176.7	178.6	178.0	178.7	176.0	176.0	178.0
2007	176.9	176.9	176.6	176.0	176.0	176.2	175.4	175.6	174.6	174.1	174.0	173.9	175.5
2008	172.4	172.1	171.7	170.2	169.9	169.5	167.8	167.0	165.6	164.4	162.6	160.2	167.8
2009	155.1	153.0	151.3	149.0	147.7	146.2	143.0	143.0	142.5	140.0	139.2	139.2	145.8

Employment by Industry: Atlanta-Sandy Springs-Marietta, GA, Selected Years, 1990–2009—*Continued*

(Numbers in thousands, not seasonally adjusted.)

Industry and year	January	February	March	April	May	June	July	August	September	October	November	December	Annual average
Service-Providing													
1990	1308.8	1315.3	1327.1	1325.7	1334.3	1346.8	1342.8	1351.3	1350.8	1348.0	1357.5	1361.0	1339.1
2000	1904.4	1916.7	1935.4	1936.0	1948.6	1962.7	1944.8	1957.5	1962.8	1971.8	1982.7	1993.1	1951.4
2001	1945.8	1954.6	1970.3	1975.3	1978.9	1980.3	1967.9	1982.2	1982.4	1973.9	1979.0	1980.9	1972.6
2002	1921.6	1924.1	1940.8	1951.4	1958.9	1959.8	1927.7	1948.6	1949.8	1947.9	1959.9	1966.3	1946.4
2003	1907.8	1915.4	1927.6	1927.2	1932.6	1927.7	1917.0	1939.8	1943.0	1941.9	1956.0	1963.5	1933.3
2004	1918.2	1927.6	1943.3	1953.2	1958.6	1951.8	1952.2	1972.1	1965.9	1985.8	1997.2	2003.7	1960.8
2005	1972.9	1983.2	1990.4	2016.2	2025.8	2015.8	2014.3	2037.8	2037.6	2052.7	2068.0	2073.6	2024.0
2006	2040.2	2048.3	2061.3	2072.9	2082.7	2081.2	2066.4	2086.8	2091.0	2114.6	2132.4	2140.5	2084.9
2007	2103.4	2114.7	2126.0	2125.5	2136.3	2129.1	2125.8	2148.5	2146.8	2148.0	2161.3	2165.1	2135.9
2008	2125.6	2136.9	2139.9	2143.5	2151.2	2136.8	2116.0	2131.8	2120.3	2119.9	2118.4	2111.7	2129.3
2009	2063.0	2060.7	2054.8	2055.7	2056.1	2041.5	2020.5	2026.2	2022.1	2029.0	2039.0	2029.6	2041.5
Trade, Transportation, and Utilities													
1990	398.3	397.5	400.3	400.2	401.8	404.8	407.0	409.1	410.0	410.1	416.3	421.7	406.4
2000	541.1	541.4	546.0	546.7	548.9	551.3	547.0	550.3	549.6	556.7	566.4	574.1	551.6
2001	551.9	548.9	552.2	547.7	547.9	549.3	547.5	546.5	546.3	546.1	552.0	557.1	549.5
2002	530.8	525.8	528.1	528.9	530.8	533.1	525.1	526.5	526.0	529.2	538.3	546.1	530.7
2003	516.7	513.6	514.9	511.7	514.0	514.1	514.2	516.8	516.1	518.2	528.2	533.5	517.7
2004	513.1	509.8	512.6	511.4	513.6	514.9	517.7	518.5	515.3	522.1	531.9	538.3	518.3
2005	522.1	521.0	522.7	529.7	532.3	532.6	533.3	537.0	535.1	541.2	553.0	559.8	535.4
2006	540.4	537.8	540.9	545.2	548.5	549.5	547.7	548.9	550.5	559.7	572.4	580.1	551.8
2007	560.4	556.4	557.1	557.4	560.8	561.0	561.4	561.2	561.2	563.4	573.8	578.4	562.7
2008	560.2	557.9	558.1	554.5	555.7	553.6	553.2	552.0	549.6	546.8	549.8	551.4	553.6
2009	529.7	523.8	520.2	516.1	516.7	515.3	513.9	514.2	511.6	510.5	519.7	523.3	517.9
Wholesale Trade													
1990	112.0	112.4	113.3	113.3	113.4	114.3	114.6	115.0	115.1	115.3	115.0	115.4	114.1
2000	157.9	159.3	160.3	160.0	160.7	161.4	161.6	162.0	161.3	161.8	162.0	162.1	160.9
2001	161.0	161.2	161.8	162.3	162.1	163.3	163.0	161.8	160.8	159.2	158.2	158.2	161.1
2002	155.0	154.7	155.5	155.0	154.7	154.5	151.9	151.8	150.9	152.4	152.1	152.1	153.4
2003	151.1	151.4	151.9	150.9	151.3	151.3	151.3	151.1	150.5	150.1	151.0	151.7	151.1
2004	149.9	150.1	150.8	151.4	151.2	151.5	152.7	152.6	151.3	152.0	152.3	152.8	151.6
2005	153.2	154.0	154.4	155.3	155.2	155.2	155.8	156.2	155.9	155.4	155.5	156.1	155.2
2006	154.6	155.3	155.6	157.2	158.1	158.3	159.3	159.2	159.3	160.7	160.0	161.2	158.2
2007	159.2	159.6	159.6	160.1	159.9	159.7	160.6	160.6	160.1	160.1	160.0	160.4	160.0
2008	159.7	160.2	159.9	159.6	159.7	159.1	159.4	159.2	158.6	157.6	156.2	155.0	158.7
2009	152.3	150.7	148.9	147.7	146.6	145.2	145.1	144.6	143.7	140.4	141.0	140.8	145.6
Retail Trade													
1990	195.8	193.6	194.4	192.1	193.7	194.7	195.0	195.6	196.1	196.2	202.6	206.9	196.4
2000	258.5	257.6	260.6	260.0	261.6	263.2	258.5	260.7	260.3	264.8	274.0	281.4	263.4
2001	264.2	261.3	264.1	260.3	260.7	260.8	257.1	257.7	258.9	260.1	269.4	274.6	262.4
2002	256.8	252.7	254.3	253.9	255.4	256.3	252.8	253.5	254.3	254.8	263.7	271.6	256.7
2003	246.8	243.8	244.8	244.2	246.1	246.3	245.7	248.0	248.0	250.1	258.7	263.5	248.8
2004	245.9	242.6	244.0	241.6	243.5	244.7	245.2	245.9	244.7	250.0	259.0	264.7	247.7
2005	249.3	246.2	247.3	253.9	256.2	256.8	259.3	258.2	256.3	262.5	272.1	277.3	258.0
2006	263.2	259.8	261.7	263.7	265.3	265.6	262.2	263.0	263.3	271.2	283.8	288.0	267.6
2007	275.2	270.4	270.6	270.3	271.6	270.8	271.5	271.0	270.9	273.3	283.4	286.3	273.8
2008	271.6	268.4	268.7	265.7	266.2	264.8	264.7	263.8	262.4	261.6	266.3	267.7	266.0
2009	251.9	248.6	247.1	246.1	247.3	247.1	245.8	246.7	245.0	247.6	255.9	257.3	248.9
Transportation and Utilities													
1990	90.5	91.5	92.6	94.8	94.7	95.8	97.4	98.5	98.8	98.6	98.7	99.4	95.9
2000	124.7	124.5	125.1	126.7	126.6	126.7	126.9	127.6	128.0	130.1	130.4	130.6	127.3
2001	126.7	126.4	126.3	125.1	125.1	125.2	127.4	127.0	126.6	126.8	124.4	124.3	125.9
2002	119.0	118.4	118.3	120.0	120.7	122.3	120.4	121.2	120.8	122.0	122.5	122.4	120.7
2003	118.8	118.4	118.2	116.6	116.6	116.5	117.2	117.7	117.6	118.0	118.5	118.3	117.7
2004	117.3	117.1	117.8	118.4	118.9	118.7	119.8	120.0	119.3	120.1	120.6	120.8	119.1
2005	119.6	120.8	121.0	120.5	120.9	120.6	123.2	122.6	122.9	123.3	125.4	126.4	122.3
2006	122.6	122.7	123.6	124.3	125.1	125.6	126.2	126.7	127.9	127.8	128.6	130.9	126.0
2007	126.0	126.4	126.9	127.0	129.3	130.5	129.3	129.6	130.2	130.0	130.4	131.7	128.9
2008	128.9	129.3	129.5	129.2	129.8	129.7	129.1	129.0	128.6	127.6	127.3	128.7	128.9
2009	125.5	124.5	124.2	122.3	122.8	123.0	123.0	122.9	122.9	122.5	122.8	125.2	123.5
Information													
1990	70.4	70.3	70.7	71.3	71.1	72.3	71.8	72.0	71.7	70.8	71.5	71.6	71.3
2000	103.7	103.7	105.2	104.5	105.5	107.3	107.2	107.7	107.9	108.8	109.4	110.9	106.8
2001	108.8	109.0	109.6	109.0	108.8	108.9	107.3	106.6	105.8	105.1	104.7	104.8	107.4
2002	104.4	103.5	104.6	101.2	100.2	100.1	99.6	99.1	98.0	98.0	97.5	97.4	100.3
2003	92.5	92.6	92.8	91.2	90.7	91.1	90.5	91.1	90.0	90.2	91.2	91.2	91.3
2004	88.9	88.4	88.9	88.4	88.1	88.5	88.0	87.6	87.0	86.5	87.2	87.1	87.9
2005	85.3	85.3	85.8	85.8	84.8	86.3	85.7	84.4	85.0	85.4	86.2	86.6	85.6
2006	85.0	85.4	85.8	85.4	85.9	85.5	85.0	84.7	84.6	84.8	85.7	85.9	85.3
2007	86.3	86.1	86.1	85.3	85.8	85.8	85.5	85.6	85.7	84.7	85.1	85.2	85.6
2008	83.2	83.7	84.0	84.0	84.5	84.7	83.9	83.7	83.1	82.3	82.5	82.4	83.5
2009	82.3	82.2	81.7	81.4	81.2	80.9	80.2	79.9	79.4	79.3	78.7	78.8	80.5

Employment by Industry: Atlanta-Sandy Springs-Marietta, GA, Selected Years, 1990–2009—*Continued*

(Numbers in thousands, not seasonally adjusted.)

Industry and year	January	February	March	April	May	June	July	August	September	October	November	December	Annual average
Financial Activities													
1990	106.4	106.7	107.4	106.1	106.4	106.7	107.1	107.3	106.9	106.7	106.9	107.4	106.8
2000	146.0	146.5	146.7	149.1	149.5	150.4	149.2	149.3	147.8	148.3	148.4	149.4	148.4
2001	147.4	147.6	148.4	150.9	150.8	151.4	152.5	152.6	152.2	152.1	152.5	152.5	150.9
2002	149.9	150.1	149.8	150.5	150.9	151.2	151.0	151.7	150.7	150.4	150.8	151.3	150.7
2003	149.1	149.7	150.3	150.4	151.5	152.3	152.6	153.3	152.9	150.1	150.4	150.8	151.1
2004	149.1	149.7	150.1	151.7	152.0	151.6	152.6	152.8	152.2	154.1	154.1	154.8	152.1
2005	155.0	155.4	155.4	156.1	157.0	157.3	156.7	157.7	157.7	159.9	160.1	161.4	157.5
2006	158.2	159.1	159.6	161.5	162.1	162.5	162.4	163.2	163.1	164.6	164.4	165.1	162.2
2007	162.1	163.6	163.9	163.2	163.1	162.9	163.0	162.9	161.6	161.4	161.3	161.0	162.5
2008	157.3	157.8	157.3	157.0	157.0	156.3	156.3	155.3	153.5	154.0	152.4	151.7	155.5
2009	148.4	147.7	146.4	147.0	147.2	147.0	146.3	145.4	144.1	140.3	139.7	141.1	145.1
Professional and Business Services													
1990	201.0	204.4	205.9	202.5	204.4	206.6	206.6	207.7	207.9	207.5	207.5	206.1	205.7
2000	385.6	389.6	393.0	389.8	392.9	399.6	396.9	400.1	401.8	400.2	399.4	401.1	395.8
2001	385.6	387.4	390.2	392.8	390.3	389.5	389.5	391.8	388.6	382.7	379.3	379.1	387.2
2002	362.8	366.4	367.4	371.5	372.9	373.6	370.5	372.8	370.8	369.6	369.4	368.7	369.7
2003	357.6	361.3	361.9	363.6	361.4	362.6	362.5	365.9	365.1	366.8	367.7	368.8	363.8
2004	358.1	361.7	366.1	370.4	370.7	371.0	376.5	376.3	373.3	383.0	382.3	383.1	372.7
2005	377.8	381.3	382.0	385.6	386.2	386.7	391.4	394.7	396.1	397.9	399.0	397.4	389.7
2006	393.0	394.4	396.8	399.5	399.7	402.8	403.2	402.8	401.7	405.6	405.9	407.1	401.0
2007	401.3	404.8	408.5	405.2	407.4	408.9	412.7	416.1	415.3	415.5	416.8	417.7	410.9
2008	409.5	410.2	407.9	412.4	411.5	412.4	407.3	408.3	405.0	405.1	401.0	398.4	407.4
2009	381.0	378.4	375.4	374.4	373.0	374.2	372.3	368.5	365.2	370.6	372.3	368.0	372.8
Education and Health Services													
1990	116.9	117.6	118.7	119.7	120.4	120.8	120.8	121.7	122.6	124.0	124.8	125.4	121.1
2000	186.9	188.8	189.7	191.1	191.7	191.4	188.6	189.4	192.1	195.5	196.5	195.7	191.5
2001	193.7	196.2	197.8	198.7	199.4	199.3	200.8	202.2	204.4	205.1	206.4	206.8	200.9
2002	202.6	205.6	208.1	207.8	208.5	208.3	207.5	210.6	211.8	213.0	214.8	214.8	209.5
2003	211.7	214.1	215.6	215.4	216.7	215.3	214.4	217.2	218.1	219.2	220.6	221.4	216.6
2004	219.8	221.3	222.3	223.4	224.3	222.7	223.5	226.1	226.2	230.1	231.0	231.6	225.2
2005	230.4	231.7	229.6	234.6	236.0	233.0	234.2	237.0	238.1	240.8	241.6	241.7	235.7
2006	242.3	244.0	244.1	244.5	245.2	242.3	242.9	245.4	247.5	252.8	253.5	253.4	246.5
2007	251.0	253.6	253.8	255.3	255.3	252.9	253.5	257.8	259.5	262.3	263.3	263.3	256.8
2008	259.9	263.5	263.6	264.5	265.9	260.9	261.4	266.0	266.5	268.6	269.6	269.9	265.0
2009	268.0	269.7	268.7	269.4	270.7	265.7	264.3	268.0	267.8	269.6	270.5	269.2	268.5
Leisure and Hospitality													
1990	135.8	137.1	140.4	140.6	143.5	146.3	146.4	148.6	147.1	141.8	141.2	140.9	142.5
2000	184.9	187.1	193.0	193.2	197.6	200.7	203.7	203.2	200.9	198.4	197.5	195.6	196.3
2001	188.5	191.6	196.2	201.4	204.9	207.4	203.4	203.9	199.6	199.1	198.0	195.9	199.2
2002	189.7	191.7	196.8	203.1	207.2	209.6	203.4	203.8	201.7	199.5	199.4	201.0	200.6
2003	191.7	193.7	199.3	203.6	208.1	210.8	210.7	212.2	210.5	206.1	206.3	206.9	205.0
2004	199.3	201.5	206.1	211.6	215.1	218.4	216.6	218.0	214.5	213.9	212.8	213.7	211.8
2005	206.4	207.5	212.9	220.7	225.6	226.8	223.0	223.8	221.1	220.2	219.9	219.1	218.9
2006	214.6	217.1	221.8	224.8	229.4	231.7	230.6	231.4	228.1	228.7	229.7	229.1	226.4
2007	224.5	227.8	232.6	235.2	240.0	241.7	240.0	241.3	236.6	234.1	233.0	232.2	234.9
2008	227.8	229.8	233.4	236.3	241.4	241.2	238.6	238.1	234.3	228.8	226.1	224.2	233.3
2009	217.4	219.0	222.3	226.3	229.5	230.2	228.3	227.2	223.7	221.8	221.7	218.5	223.8
Other Services													
1990	64.4	64.9	65.4	65.7	65.9	66.8	66.3	66.8	66.5	65.4	65.4	65.1	65.7
2000	86.5	87.2	88.0	88.0	88.8	89.6	90.0	89.7	89.4	87.7	87.6	87.9	88.4
2001	91.2	91.8	92.4	92.6	93.1	93.9	95.2	94.6	97.3	93.2	93.6	93.4	93.5
2002	92.3	92.1	92.5	92.3	92.2	92.9	91.8	91.8	91.5	89.9	89.6	89.4	91.5
2003	90.9	91.2	91.9	91.5	92.4	93.1	93.2	93.4	92.9	92.4	92.5	92.3	92.3
2004	91.5	91.4	92.8	92.5	92.9	93.5	93.7	93.7	92.5	92.0	92.1	92.0	92.6
2005	93.3	94.0	94.4	95.5	96.1	96.0	96.4	97.6	95.7	95.4	95.4	95.5	95.4
2006	95.3	95.5	95.6	97.0	97.7	98.0	98.4	97.8	96.6	96.6	96.6	96.1	96.8
2007	96.2	96.5	96.9	98.0	98.7	99.1	99.3	99.2	97.6	97.9	97.6	97.0	97.8
2008	97.3	98.3	98.2	98.1	99.2	99.1	98.5	98.5	97.4	96.7	96.2	95.5	97.8
2009	98.6	98.9	98.2	100.0	100.7	100.9	101.9	101.4	101.4	100.2	101.4	101.7	100.4
Government													
1990	215.6	216.8	218.3	219.6	220.8	222.5	216.8	218.1	218.1	221.7	223.9	222.8	219.6
2000	269.7	272.4	273.8	273.6	273.7	272.4	262.2	267.8	273.3	276.2	277.5	278.4	272.6
2001	278.7	282.1	283.5	282.2	283.7	280.6	271.7	284.0	288.2	290.5	292.5	291.3	284.1
2002	289.1	288.9	293.5	296.1	296.2	291.0	278.8	292.3	299.3	298.3	300.1	297.6	293.4
2003	297.6	299.2	300.9	299.8	297.8	288.4	278.9	289.9	297.4	298.9	299.1	298.6	295.5
2004	298.4	303.8	304.4	303.8	301.9	291.2	283.6	299.1	304.9	304.1	305.8	303.1	300.3
2005	302.6	307.0	307.6	308.2	307.8	297.1	288.6	305.6	308.8	311.9	312.8	312.1	305.8
2006	311.4	315.0	316.7	315.0	314.2	308.9	296.2	312.6	318.9	321.8	324.2	323.7	314.9
2007	321.6	325.9	327.1	325.9	325.2	316.8	310.4	324.4	329.3	328.7	330.4	330.3	324.7
2008	330.4	335.7	337.4	336.7	336.0	328.6	316.8	329.9	330.9	337.6	340.8	338.2	333.3
2009	337.6	341.0	341.9	341.1	337.1	327.3	313.3	321.6	330.1	335.5	334.7	330.2	332.6

Employment by Industry: Austin-Round Rock, TX, Selected Years, 1990–2009

(Numbers in thousands, not seasonally adjusted.)

Industry and year	January	February	March	April	May	June	July	August	September	October	November	December	Annual average
Total Nonfarm													
1990	378.6	381.3	384.1	387.5	388.5	386.9	382.0	384.0	394.1	397.9	401.8	401.3	389.0
2000	646.2	655.5	662.7	663.8	670.4	674.8	670.2	679.9	682.3	685.9	690.3	690.1	672.7
2001	675.2	679.8	682.8	679.2	678.3	677.7	666.7	672.6	671.5	669.6	669.2	666.2	674.1
2002	652.4	656.5	659.8	661.0	662.5	656.9	652.2	658.1	659.1	658.9	662.7	660.4	658.4
2003	646.5	648.7	649.4	653.6	654.8	653.2	649.3	652.8	654.3	656.3	658.0	659.1	653.0
2004	648.5	655.5	661.0	665.5	667.1	666.9	664.2	669.3	671.5	676.9	680.8	681.8	667.4
2005	672.2	679.2	684.4	690.3	692.8	693.4	690.1	693.7	698.4	699.1	705.7	706.9	692.2
2006	696.4	704.2	710.8	717.0	720.8	723.5	715.9	724.1	734.8	737.7	744.6	748.6	723.2
2007	731.7	743.5	751.5	754.7	758.8	761.6	753.8	757.9	762.7	767.8	773.1	773.4	757.5
2008	763.9	771.8	773.9	776.5	779.2	778.7	770.0	774.3	778.3	780.7	783.4	779.0	775.8
2009	760.2	760.6	760.8	762.4	763.7	761.2	747.2	750.5	753.9	757.2	761.5	758.8	758.2
Total Private													
1990	268.9	269.5	271.5	273.4	274.9	278.1	279.6	282.1	281.4	282.9	285.8	286.4	277.9
2000	511.2	517.0	523.6	525.1	531.0	540.4	540.5	544.9	545.2	547.2	550.5	553.4	535.8
2001	538.6	540.0	541.9	538.4	537.9	540.5	533.8	533.8	528.2	525.1	522.8	523.1	533.7
2002	509.7	510.9	513.0	513.9	516.4	517.8	514.4	516.7	514.1	510.7	512.9	512.8	513.6
2003	499.9	499.6	500.8	503.8	506.2	508.5	508.2	510.7	510.4	511.7	513.1	515.6	507.3
2004	504.8	508.5	512.9	516.7	519.0	523.1	525.8	528.0	526.8	528.6	531.1	534.5	521.7
2005	525.3	528.5	533.5	538.6	541.1	545.8	546.9	549.3	550.6	548.6	553.5	557.2	543.2
2006	547.0	551.1	557.1	562.6	566.9	573.3	573.9	578.2	580.2	581.6	588.6	594.2	571.2
2007	577.7	586.1	592.9	595.8	600.0	606.0	604.7	607.0	606.6	607.7	611.9	614.5	600.9
2008	603.9	608.4	608.1	613.3	616.2	617.6	615.5	618.5	615.6	616.4	616.8	614.4	613.7
2009	595.6	592.7	592.0	592.1	593.7	593.5	590.7	591.6	587.4	588.7	591.3	591.5	591.7
Goods-Producing													
1990	58.3	58.3	58.9	58.8	59.3	60.5	61.3	62.2	61.8	62.5	62.8	62.6	60.6
2000	117.6	119.2	121.8	121.9	122.9	125.9	126.1	126.8	126.7	126.6	126.8	126.8	124.1
2001	125.0	124.8	124.5	120.9	120.0	120.4	117.6	116.6	113.7	111.9	109.8	108.8	117.8
2002	105.4	104.7	104.7	103.0	103.0	103.7	102.1	101.4	99.5	98.6	97.5	96.8	101.7
2003	96.0	95.2	95.2	95.2	95.4	96.0	95.7	95.4	94.8	94.5	94.1	94.0	95.1
2004	92.4	92.6	93.2	94.1	94.4	95.6	96.6	96.7	96.3	96.7	96.4	96.1	95.1
2005	95.1	95.4	96.0	96.4	96.7	98.0	98.7	98.6	98.4	98.1	98.5	99.0	97.4
2006	98.5	99.5	101.0	101.5	102.4	104.5	105.2	105.5	105.3	105.3	105.9	106.9	103.5
2007	104.9	106.2	107.2	108.2	108.9	110.3	110.0	110.2	109.3	109.6	109.7	109.0	108.6
2008	106.8	107.4	107.0	106.6	106.7	106.8	105.9	105.2	103.5	101.4	99.7	98.0	104.6
2009	93.1	91.5	89.6	90.4	89.8	89.9	89.2	88.4	87.7	86.7	86.6	86.5	89.1
Mining, Logging, and Construction													
1990	12.3	12.3	12.5	12.5	12.9	13.5	13.7	14.0	13.6	13.5	13.5	13.4	13.1
2000	38.3	39.2	40.5	40.9	41.4	42.6	42.3	42.6	42.7	42.1	41.7	41.5	41.3
2001	40.4	41.4	42.0	42.0	42.6	43.3	42.7	42.6	41.8	40.8	39.7	39.2	41.5
2002	37.6	38.0	38.7	38.5	38.8	39.4	39.2	39.0	37.9	37.6	37.1	36.5	38.2
2003	36.6	36.5	36.6	37.3	37.8	38.3	38.3	38.3	37.9	37.5	37.1	36.9	37.4
2004	35.9	36.1	36.4	37.2	37.2	37.9	38.8	38.7	38.5	38.9	38.5	38.2	37.7
2005	37.8	38.2	38.8	39.3	39.8	40.5	41.2	41.1	41.3	41.0	41.3	41.5	40.2
2006	41.2	41.9	42.9	43.5	44.1	45.3	45.7	45.9	46.0	45.7	46.1	46.8	44.6
2007	45.7	46.7	47.5	48.2	48.9	49.9	49.8	50.2	49.9	50.3	50.7	49.9	49.0
2008	48.0	48.4	48.3	48.3	48.5	48.6	48.1	48.0	47.2	46.0	44.9	44.0	47.4
2009	42.4	42.0	41.4	40.8	40.8	41.4	41.2	40.6	40.2	39.4	39.5	39.6	40.8
Manufacturing													
1990	46.0	46.0	46.4	46.3	46.4	47.0	47.6	48.2	48.2	49.0	49.3	49.2	47.5
2000	79.3	80.0	81.3	81.0	81.5	83.3	83.8	84.2	84.0	84.5	85.1	85.3	82.8
2001	84.6	83.4	82.5	78.9	77.4	77.1	74.9	74.0	71.9	71.1	70.1	69.6	76.3
2002	67.8	66.7	66.0	64.5	64.2	64.3	62.9	62.4	61.6	61.0	60.4	60.3	63.5
2003	59.4	58.7	58.6	57.9	57.6	57.7	57.4	57.1	56.9	57.0	57.0	57.1	57.7
2004	56.5	56.5	56.8	56.9	57.2	57.7	57.8	58.0	57.8	57.8	57.9	57.9	57.4
2005	57.3	57.2	57.2	57.1	56.9	57.5	57.5	57.5	57.1	57.1	57.2	57.5	57.3
2006	57.3	57.6	58.1	58.0	58.3	59.2	59.5	59.6	59.3	59.6	59.8	60.1	58.9
2007	59.2	59.5	59.7	60.0	60.0	60.4	60.2	60.0	59.4	59.3	59.0	59.1	59.7
2008	58.8	59.0	58.7	58.3	58.2	58.2	57.8	57.2	56.3	55.4	54.8	54.0	57.2
2009	50.7	49.5	48.2	49.6	49.0	48.5	48.0	47.8	47.5	47.3	47.1	46.9	48.3
Service-Providing													
1990	320.3	323.0	325.2	328.7	329.2	326.4	320.7	321.8	332.3	335.4	339.0	338.7	328.4
2000	528.6	536.3	540.9	541.9	547.5	548.9	544.1	553.1	555.6	559.3	563.5	563.3	548.6
2001	550.2	555.0	558.3	558.3	558.3	557.3	549.1	556.0	557.8	557.7	559.4	557.4	556.2
2002	547.0	551.8	555.1	558.0	559.5	553.2	550.1	556.7	559.6	560.3	565.2	563.6	556.7
2003	550.5	553.5	554.2	558.4	559.4	557.2	553.6	557.4	559.5	561.8	563.9	565.1	557.8
2004	556.1	562.9	567.8	571.4	572.7	571.3	567.6	572.6	575.2	580.2	584.4	585.7	572.3
2005	577.1	583.8	588.4	593.9	596.1	595.4	591.4	595.1	600.0	601.0	607.2	607.9	594.8
2006	597.9	604.7	609.8	615.5	618.4	619.0	610.7	618.6	629.5	632.4	638.7	641.7	619.7
2007	626.8	637.3	644.3	646.5	649.9	651.3	643.8	647.7	653.4	658.2	663.4	664.4	648.9
2008	657.1	664.4	666.9	669.9	672.5	671.9	664.1	669.1	674.8	679.3	683.7	681.0	671.2
2009	667.1	669.1	671.2	672.0	673.9	671.3	658.0	662.1	666.2	670.5	674.9	672.3	669.1

Employment by Industry: Austin-Round Rock, TX, Selected Years, 1990–2009—*Continued*

(Numbers in thousands, not seasonally adjusted.)

Industry and year	January	February	March	April	May	June	July	August	September	October	November	December	Annual average
Trade, Transportation, and Utilities													
1990	61.9	60.8	60.7	59.4	59.5	59.6	60.0	59.9	60.4	60.7	62.2	63.2	60.7
2000	111.4	111.6	111.9	111.9	112.8	114.0	114.6	116.2	116.0	117.6	120.5	122.5	115.1
2001	118.6	116.8	116.4	116.6	116.7	116.2	115.5	115.7	115.3	115.9	116.9	118.6	116.6
2002	113.8	112.7	112.7	112.9	113.0	113.1	112.6	113.0	112.2	112.4	114.7	116.6	113.3
2003	110.9	109.7	109.6	109.7	109.9	110.4	111.6	112.7	112.8	113.8	116.1	117.9	112.0
2004	113.5	113.1	113.5	113.0	113.3	113.8	115.1	116.1	115.9	117.0	119.6	121.9	115.5
2005	117.8	117.7	118.6	119.1	120.2	121.4	122.4	123.4	123.1	123.0	126.1	128.3	121.8
2006	123.2	122.7	123.4	124.4	125.2	126.5	127.3	128.4	128.2	129.4	133.4	136.5	127.4
2007	131.9	132.2	133.3	134.0	134.5	136.1	136.4	136.6	136.4	137.8	140.0	143.0	136.0
2008	138.4	137.8	137.5	137.8	137.7	138.3	138.5	139.7	138.9	140.0	141.7	142.5	139.1
2009	136.9	133.0	133.0	131.1	131.4	131.3	131.4	132.6	131.8	132.7	134.2	134.1	132.8
Wholesale Trade													
1990	12.5	12.4	12.4	12.3	12.1	12.3	12.3	12.2	12.4	12.3	12.4	12.4	12.3
2000	33.0	33.5	33.5	33.8	34.1	35.0	35.1	35.4	35.7	36.2	36.6	36.9	34.9
2001	37.0	36.5	36.1	36.5	36.3	35.4	35.5	35.1	34.6	34.5	34.3	34.5	35.5
2002	33.9	33.9	34.0	33.9	33.9	34.2	34.2	34.1	34.0	33.8	33.7	33.7	33.9
2003	33.4	33.4	33.3	33.3	33.5	33.7	33.9	33.9	33.8	33.8	34.1	34.5	33.7
2004	34.4	34.7	34.8	34.8	34.9	35.3	35.7	35.8	35.8	35.9	36.1	36.5	35.4
2005	36.5	36.8	36.8	37.0	37.3	37.5	38.0	38.1	38.0	37.5	37.4	37.4	37.4
2006	37.1	37.3	37.5	37.6	37.8	38.3	38.6	38.7	38.8	39.1	40.0	40.8	38.5
2007	40.4	40.7	40.9	41.0	41.4	42.4	42.1	41.8	41.4	41.5	40.4	41.6	41.3
2008	41.3	41.3	41.2	41.1	41.1	41.5	41.6	41.7	41.6	41.7	41.7	41.6	41.5
2009	41.7	38.2	38.2	37.3	37.3	37.2	37.8	37.9	37.6	37.9	37.9	37.6	38.0
Retail Trade													
1990	43.5	42.5	42.4	41.5	41.7	41.6	41.8	41.9	42.0	42.4	43.7	44.7	42.5
2000	67.6	67.3	67.6	67.7	68.2	68.7	69.0	70.0	69.4	70.5	72.9	74.4	69.4
2001	70.3	69.1	69.1	68.9	69.1	69.6	68.8	69.3	69.3	69.9	71.2	72.7	69.8
2002	68.7	67.7	67.6	67.9	68.0	67.9	67.3	67.7	67.2	67.5	69.9	71.8	68.3
2003	67.0	65.9	65.9	66.0	66.0	66.3	67.2	68.2	68.4	69.2	71.7	72.6	67.8
2004	68.6	67.8	68.1	67.5	67.7	67.8	68.4	69.1	68.8	69.7	72.0	73.7	69.1
2005	69.9	69.5	70.2	70.6	71.3	72.3	72.9	73.6	73.2	73.7	76.7	78.5	72.7
2006	74.2	73.4	73.7	74.5	74.9	75.8	76.2	77.0	76.5	77.3	80.3	82.2	76.3
2007	78.6	78.5	79.1	79.9	79.9	80.5	81.2	81.4	81.5	82.7	85.9	87.5	81.4
2008	83.7	83.0	82.8	83.4	83.3	83.5	83.9	84.7	83.9	85.0	86.6	87.4	84.3
2009	82.8	82.0	82.1	81.1	81.4	81.4	81.2	82.1	81.4	82.0	83.4	83.4	82.0
Transportation and Utilities													
1990	5.9	5.9	5.9	5.6	5.7	5.7	5.9	5.8	6.0	6.0	6.1	6.1	5.9
2000	10.8	10.8	10.8	10.4	10.5	10.3	10.5	10.8	10.9	10.9	11.0	11.2	10.7
2001	11.3	11.2	11.2	11.2	11.3	11.2	11.2	11.3	11.4	11.5	11.4	11.4	11.3
2002	11.2	11.1	11.1	11.1	11.1	11.0	11.1	11.2	11.0	11.1	11.1	11.1	11.1
2003	10.5	10.4	10.4	10.4	10.4	10.4	10.5	10.6	10.6	10.8	10.8	10.8	10.5
2004	10.5	10.6	10.6	10.7	10.7	10.7	11.0	11.2	11.3	11.4	11.5	11.7	11.0
2005	11.4	11.4	11.6	11.5	11.6	11.6	11.5	11.7	11.9	11.8	12.0	12.4	11.7
2006	11.9	12.0	12.2	12.3	12.5	12.4	12.5	12.7	12.9	13.0	13.1	13.5	12.6
2007	12.9	13.0	13.3	13.1	13.2	13.2	13.1	13.4	13.5	13.6	13.7	13.9	13.3
2008	13.4	13.5	13.5	13.3	13.3	13.3	13.0	13.3	13.4	13.3	13.4	13.5	13.4
2009	12.9	12.8	12.7	12.7	12.7	12.7	12.4	12.6	12.8	12.8	12.9	13.1	12.8
Information													
1990	10.1	10.2	10.2	10.4	10.4	10.5	10.5	10.5	10.5	10.6	10.6	10.6	10.4
2000	21.9	22.3	22.7	23.5	24.1	25.0	25.5	25.7	25.5	25.0	25.1	25.3	24.3
2001	24.1	23.8	23.2	23.0	23.0	23.0	23.3	23.3	23.2	23.0	23.1	23.0	23.3
2002	23.0	22.9	23.0	22.9	22.8	23.0	22.7	22.5	22.3	22.1	22.0	21.8	22.6
2003	21.5	21.4	21.3	20.9	20.9	21.1	20.8	20.7	20.5	20.4	20.2	20.2	20.8
2004	20.1	20.1	20.3	20.2	20.4	20.7	20.6	20.7	20.6	20.6	20.9	21.0	20.5
2005	21.0	21.1	21.3	21.2	21.4	21.6	21.7	21.5	22.1	21.5	21.7	21.9	21.5
2006	21.8	21.8	21.8	21.8	21.7	21.7	21.5	21.6	21.6	21.8	22.1	22.2	21.8
2007	21.9	22.1	22.1	22.2	22.3	22.3	21.7	21.6	21.6	21.5	21.8	21.6	21.9
2008	21.3	21.0	20.9	20.8	21.0	21.1	21.1	21.1	20.8	20.8	21.0	20.9	21.0
2009	20.4	20.3	20.2	19.9	19.9	19.6	19.6	19.6	19.4	19.5	19.5	19.5	19.8
Financial Activities													
1990	22.1	22.3	22.2	23.1	23.2	23.2	23.2	23.3	23.1	22.9	23.0	23.2	22.9
2000	34.6	34.9	34.9	35.0	35.0	35.4	35.4	35.6	35.4	35.6	35.5	35.8	35.3
2001	35.5	35.9	36.1	36.3	36.5	36.9	37.0	36.8	36.4	36.6	36.4	36.9	36.4
2002	36.7	36.9	37.0	37.4	37.7	38.1	38.2	38.4	38.5	38.7	38.9	39.1	38.0
2003	38.5	38.6	38.7	39.1	39.4	39.6	39.8	40.0	39.9	40.0	40.1	40.2	39.4
2004	39.3	39.4	39.5	39.7	39.7	40.0	40.0	40.1	40.1	40.4	40.5	40.8	40.0
2005	40.0	40.3	40.5	40.6	40.8	41.1	41.4	41.7	41.7	41.9	41.9	42.4	41.2
2006	41.9	42.2	42.5	42.6	42.9	43.3	43.4	43.7	43.9	44.1	44.1	44.6	43.3
2007	43.8	44.1	44.5	44.5	44.9	45.1	45.0	45.0	44.8	44.6	44.9	45.2	44.7
2008	44.5	44.9	44.8	45.1	45.2	45.4	45.4	45.4	45.2	44.9	45.0	45.2	45.1
2009	43.8	43.9	43.7	43.8	43.8	44.0	43.9	43.7	43.5	43.6	43.5	43.6	43.7

Employment by Industry: Austin-Round Rock, TX, Selected Years, 1990–2009—*Continued*

(Numbers in thousands, not seasonally adjusted.)

Industry and year	January	February	March	April	May	June	July	August	September	October	November	December	Annual average
Professional and Business Services													
1990	34.0	34.1	34.6	35.9	36.4	36.8	37.0	37.5	37.6	38.0	38.2	38.6	36.6
2000	86.5	87.0	88.6	88.9	90.3	92.7	93.5	94.2	94.4	95.0	95.4	95.8	91.9
2001	92.7	93.0	93.7	92.6	91.8	91.5	91.4	91.6	90.3	89.6	89.1	88.8	91.3
2002	86.3	86.4	86.7	87.0	87.4	88.0	87.6	88.8	87.7	86.9	87.1	86.6	87.2
2003	84.6	84.6	84.8	85.4	86.0	86.1	86.1	86.0	86.0	86.2	85.6	86.0	85.6
2004	84.9	86.1	87.1	88.0	88.5	89.4	90.4	91.2	90.9	90.9	90.8	91.4	89.1
2005	90.3	91.2	92.1	93.1	93.2	94.4	95.2	95.8	95.8	95.4	96.2	96.6	94.1
2006	94.7	95.6	96.9	97.5	98.6	99.7	100.2	101.1	101.4	102.1	103.5	103.7	99.6
2007	100.8	102.9	104.4	103.9	104.8	106.3	106.8	108.0	108.0	108.3	108.8	108.7	106.0
2008	108.7	109.5	109.1	111.0	111.8	112.0	111.4	112.3	111.7	112.3	111.6	110.7	111.0
2009	108.2	107.8	107.7	107.3	107.5	107.7	106.0	106.1	105.0	104.8	105.6	104.5	106.5
Education and Health Services													
1990	34.8	35.1	35.6	35.7	35.6	36.0	35.9	36.6	36.5	36.9	37.5	37.5	36.1
2000	60.3	61.2	61.5	61.8	62.6	62.6	61.4	62.3	63.5	63.6	63.5	63.5	62.3
2001	61.5	62.7	63.3	63.5	63.3	64.5	62.5	62.8	63.7	63.8	63.7	63.8	63.3
2002	62.7	63.9	64.0	64.7	64.9	64.1	64.0	64.7	65.7	65.7	66.1	65.8	64.7
2003	64.6	65.4	65.1	65.9	65.9	65.2	65.0	65.8	66.9	67.3	67.3	67.2	65.9
2004	66.2	67.3	67.5	68.5	68.4	67.9	67.7	68.0	68.8	70.0	70.4	70.3	68.4
2005	69.4	70.3	70.8	71.2	71.3	70.5	69.9	70.4	72.1	72.1	72.2	72.5	71.1
2006	71.5	72.5	72.8	73.3	73.4	73.0	72.8	73.8	75.0	75.8	75.7	75.6	73.8
2007	73.6	75.5	76.3	76.2	76.9	76.5	76.7	77.2	78.7	79.1	79.5	79.7	77.2
2008	78.7	80.1	80.0	80.6	81.0	80.0	79.7	80.6	81.5	82.2	82.5	82.7	80.8
2009	80.6	81.9	82.5	83.5	83.9	83.1	83.1	83.7	83.9	84.5	84.6	84.7	83.3
Leisure and Hospitality													
1990	32.7	33.5	34.0	35.0	35.3	35.9	35.9	36.2	36.0	35.8	36.0	35.4	35.1
2000	57.1	58.9	60.1	59.9	60.9	62.1	61.5	61.7	61.3	61.4	61.3	61.1	60.6
2001	58.6	60.2	61.7	62.1	63.0	64.0	63.0	63.5	62.5	61.3	60.7	60.4	61.8
2002	58.8	60.1	61.4	62.4	63.5	63.6	63.1	63.6	63.6	62.3	62.4	62.3	62.3
2003	60.3	61.0	62.2	63.7	64.6	65.4	64.7	65.3	64.8	64.3	64.3	64.6	63.7
2004	62.8	63.9	65.4	67.1	68.2	69.4	69.4	69.1	68.4	67.5	66.8	67.1	67.1
2005	65.8	66.5	68.0	70.3	70.9	71.7	70.9	71.1	70.6	70.4	70.6	70.1	69.7
2006	69.3	70.4	72.0	74.0	74.9	76.4	75.3	75.9	76.4	75.1	75.7	76.3	74.3
2007	73.7	75.3	77.0	78.6	79.2	80.5	79.8	80.2	79.6	78.6	78.7	78.7	78.3
2008	77.3	78.8	79.9	81.6	82.5	83.2	82.2	82.5	82.0	82.7	82.9	81.7	81.4
2009	79.9	80.9	81.9	83.1	84.1	84.2	84.1	84.2	83.1	84.0	84.3	85.6	83.3
Other Services													
1990	15.0	15.2	15.3	15.1	15.2	15.6	15.8	15.9	15.5	15.5	15.5	15.3	15.4
2000	21.8	21.9	22.1	22.2	22.4	22.7	22.5	22.4	22.4	22.4	22.4	22.6	22.3
2001	22.6	22.8	23.0	23.4	23.6	24.0	23.5	23.5	23.1	23.0	23.0	22.9	23.2
2002	23.0	23.3	23.5	23.6	24.1	24.2	24.1	24.3	24.6	24.0	24.2	23.8	23.9
2003	23.5	23.7	23.9	23.9	24.1	24.7	24.5	24.8	24.7	25.2	25.4	25.5	24.4
2004	25.6	26.0	26.4	26.1	26.1	26.3	26.0	26.1	25.8	25.5	25.7	25.9	26.0
2005	25.9	26.0	26.2	26.7	26.6	27.1	26.7	26.8	26.8	26.2	26.3	26.4	26.5
2006	26.1	26.4	26.7	27.5	27.8	28.2	28.2	28.2	28.4	28.0	28.2	28.4	27.7
2007	27.1	27.8	28.1	28.2	28.5	28.9	28.3	28.2	28.2	28.2	28.5	28.6	28.2
2008	28.2	28.9	28.9	29.8	30.3	30.8	31.3	31.7	32.0	32.1	32.4	32.7	30.8
2009	32.7	33.4	33.4	33.0	33.3	33.7	33.4	33.3	33.0	32.9	33.0	33.0	33.2
Government													
1990	109.7	111.8	112.6	114.1	113.6	108.8	102.4	101.9	112.7	115.0	116.0	114.9	111.1
2000	135.0	138.5	139.1	138.7	139.4	134.4	129.7	135.0	137.1	138.7	139.8	136.7	136.8
2001	136.6	139.8	140.9	140.8	140.4	137.2	132.9	138.8	143.3	144.5	146.4	143.1	140.4
2002	142.7	145.6	146.8	147.1	146.1	139.1	137.8	141.4	145.0	148.2	149.8	147.6	144.8
2003	146.6	149.1	148.6	149.8	148.6	144.7	141.1	142.1	143.9	144.6	144.9	143.5	145.6
2004	143.7	147.0	148.1	148.8	148.1	143.8	138.4	141.3	144.7	148.3	149.7	147.3	145.8
2005	146.9	150.7	150.9	151.7	151.7	147.6	143.2	144.4	147.8	150.5	152.2	149.7	148.9
2006	149.4	153.1	153.7	154.4	153.9	150.2	142.0	145.9	154.6	156.1	156.0	154.4	152.0
2007	154.0	157.4	158.6	158.9	158.8	155.6	149.1	150.9	156.1	160.1	161.2	158.9	156.6
2008	160.0	163.4	165.8	163.2	163.0	161.1	154.5	155.8	162.7	164.3	166.6	164.6	162.1
2009	164.6	167.9	168.8	170.3	170.0	167.7	156.5	158.9	166.5	168.5	170.2	167.3	166.4

Employment by Industry: Bakersfield-Delano, CA, Selected Years, 1990–2009

(Numbers in thousands, not seasonally adjusted.)

Industry and year	January	February	March	April	May	June	July	August	September	October	November	December	Annual average
Total Nonfarm													
1990	164.7	165.6	166.8	169.5	170.9	171.8	171.0	169.3	172.7	174.3	175.0	176.9	170.7
2000	189.8	190.8	192.7	193.0	195.1	196.0	191.3	191.0	195.0	196.9	198.4	199.2	194.1
2001	199.3	200.1	201.5	202.2	202.9	205.3	197.9	200.1	201.8	204.2	205.8	205.8	202.2
2002	202.2	202.8	205.3	205.8	206.7	208.2	201.8	202.4	203.2	206.2	208.0	208.5	205.1
2003	204.9	205.2	207.8	207.0	208.0	208.1	205.0	205.4	206.4	208.4	209.3	209.8	207.1
2004	205.1	206.2	208.3	211.7	212.5	215.9	210.3	210.2	212.0	215.0	216.6	217.2	211.8
2005	214.6	215.9	217.4	220.1	222.3	223.8	220.6	221.8	224.6	226.5	228.1	229.0	222.1
2006	227.1	228.6	229.9	230.9	233.6	235.1	230.8	233.1	235.5	237.8	238.7	238.9	233.3
2007	235.3	236.3	237.7	239.9	240.6	240.9	235.1	237.0	239.3	240.0	240.8	241.0	238.7
2008	235.7	237.2	238.0	239.4	240.3	241.1	235.4	235.0	236.8	239.0	239.8	238.2	238.0
2009	232.2	231.4	231.4	230.9	230.7	230.6	223.9	222.0	222.7	225.7	226.8	226.1	227.9
Total Private													
1990	121.3	121.6	122.3	124.3	125.2	126.6	129.1	129.2	129.7	129.5	130.0	131.2	126.7
2000	137.9	138.9	139.9	140.3	141.8	143.0	144.6	145.0	144.4	143.7	144.5	145.7	142.5
2001	146.1	146.2	147.3	147.6	148.3	149.7	149.5	149.8	149.3	149.4	150.2	150.1	148.6
2002	147.1	147.5	148.8	149.2	150.4	151.1	150.0	150.7	150.3	150.5	151.1	151.7	149.9
2003	148.4	149.1	151.0	151.0	152.4	152.8	153.6	154.0	154.2	154.7	154.5	155.2	152.5
2004	151.4	152.2	154.0	157.0	157.9	158.9	159.0	159.9	159.6	160.2	161.1	161.7	157.7
2005	159.3	159.9	161.1	163.9	165.9	167.1	168.6	168.5	170.0	169.1	170.6	171.7	166.3
2006	169.6	170.9	172.0	172.9	175.8	177.0	176.9	178.0	178.5	178.1	178.9	179.3	175.7
2007	175.8	176.7	178.0	178.1	179.0	179.2	179.6	180.6	180.7	178.7	179.0	179.1	178.7
2008	174.2	175.0	175.5	177.0	178.0	178.4	177.2	177.7	177.2	176.3	176.2	175.3	176.5
2009	169.9	168.5	168.2	167.6	167.9	167.7	165.4	166.0	165.7	165.4	165.2	165.0	166.9
Goods-Producing													
1990	32.1	32.3	32.8	33.2	33.4	33.9	34.4	34.7	34.7	34.1	34.2	34.5	33.7
2000	28.5	28.9	29.5	29.8	30.4	30.9	31.4	31.5	31.6	31.5	31.5	31.9	30.6
2001	31.6	31.8	32.2	32.6	32.8	33.1	33.2	33.5	33.3	32.9	32.6	32.3	32.7
2002	31.9	31.9	32.2	32.2	32.4	32.8	33.0	33.2	33.3	33.5	33.5	33.6	32.8
2003	33.5	33.7	33.8	33.6	33.8	33.9	34.5	34.7	34.9	34.7	34.3	34.6	34.1
2004	34.5	34.7	35.3	36.1	36.2	36.8	36.8	36.9	37.2	37.2	36.7	37.2	36.3
2005	36.6	37.0	37.4	38.1	38.5	39.2	40.0	39.7	40.7	40.5	40.6	40.7	39.1
2006	40.6	41.2	41.5	41.5	42.3	42.8	43.2	43.2	43.5	43.1	42.6	42.5	42.3
2007	41.0	41.3	41.6	41.6	41.2	41.4	42.0	42.3	42.2	41.7	41.2	40.9	41.5
2008	40.0	40.0	39.9	40.5	40.7	41.4	41.5	41.5	41.7	41.5	41.1	41.2	40.9
2009	39.0	37.8	37.5	36.6	36.1	36.0	35.7	35.7	35.4	34.9	34.5	34.1	36.1
Mining and Logging													
1990	11.5	11.7	11.7	11.7	11.8	12.0	12.2	12.1	12.1	12.3	12.1	11.8	11.9
2000	7.6	7.8	8.0	7.8	7.9	8.0	8.4	8.6	8.6	8.5	8.6	8.7	8.2
2001	8.5	8.5	8.6	8.6	8.6	8.7	8.7	8.8	8.7	8.7	8.6	8.5	8.6
2002	8.2	8.0	7.9	7.8	7.7	7.8	7.9	7.9	7.9	7.9	7.9	7.9	7.9
2003	7.8	7.9	7.9	7.9	8.0	7.9	8.1	8.1	8.0	8.1	8.0	8.2	7.9
2004	8.0	8.1	8.2	8.1	8.2	8.3	8.1	8.2	8.1	8.1	8.1	8.2	8.1
2005	8.1	8.2	8.3	8.4	8.4	8.4	8.5	8.6	8.7	8.7	8.7	8.8	8.5
2006	8.9	8.9	9.0	9.1	9.2	9.4	9.4	9.6	9.6	9.7	9.7	9.7	9.4
2007	9.5	9.6	9.6	9.6	9.6	9.6	9.9	10.0	9.9	9.9	9.9	10.0	9.8
2008	10.1	10.2	10.3	10.3	10.4	10.5	10.9	10.9	10.9	11.2	11.3	11.2	10.7
2009	10.7	10.4	10.2	10.0	9.9	9.9	9.9	9.7	9.6	9.5	9.6	9.6	9.9
Construction													
1990	10.9	10.8	11.3	11.6	11.7	11.9	12.5	12.9	13.1	12.1	12.4	12.9	12.0
2000	10.6	10.7	10.8	11.1	11.5	11.8	12.0	12.0	12.1	12.1	12.1	12.3	11.5
2001	12.1	12.3	12.7	13.0	13.1	13.2	13.3	13.6	13.4	13.1	13.0	12.9	12.9
2002	12.9	13.1	13.4	13.3	13.4	13.5	13.4	13.5	13.3	13.3	13.5	13.4	13.3
2003	13.2	13.2	13.3	13.2	13.3	13.4	13.7	13.9	13.9	13.9	14.0	13.5	13.5
2004	14.0	14.1	14.6	15.2	15.2	15.8	15.9	16.0	15.8	16.1	16.0	16.3	15.4
2005	15.9	16.3	16.8	17.4	17.8	18.5	19.0	18.7	19.2	19.3	19.5	19.5	18.2
2006	19.0	19.5	19.7	19.8	20.4	20.7	20.8	20.4	20.4	20.0	19.8	19.7	20.0
2007	18.8	18.9	19.1	18.5	18.7	18.7	18.5	18.6	18.2	18.2	17.7	17.4	18.4
2008	16.5	16.4	16.2	16.6	16.6	16.9	16.9	16.8	16.7	16.5	16.0	16.1	16.5
2009	14.8	14.0	14.0	13.4	13.1	13.1	12.7	12.6	12.4	12.2	12.0	11.6	13.0
Manufacturing													
1990	9.7	9.8	9.8	9.9	9.9	10.0	9.7	9.7	9.5	9.7	9.7	9.8	9.8
2000	10.3	10.4	10.7	10.9	11.0	11.1	11.0	10.9	10.9	10.9	10.8	10.9	10.8
2001	11.0	11.0	10.9	11.0	11.1	11.2	11.2	11.1	11.2	11.1	11.0	10.9	11.1
2002	10.8	10.8	10.9	11.1	11.3	11.5	11.7	11.8	12.1	12.3	12.1	12.3	11.6
2003	12.5	12.6	12.6	12.5	12.5	12.6	12.7	12.7	13.0	12.7	12.4	12.4	12.6
2004	12.5	12.5	12.5	12.8	12.8	12.7	12.8	12.7	13.3	13.0	12.6	12.7	12.7
2005	12.6	12.5	12.3	12.3	12.3	12.3	12.5	12.4	12.8	12.5	12.4	12.4	12.4
2006	12.7	12.8	12.8	12.6	12.7	12.7	13.0	13.2	13.5	13.4	13.1	13.1	13.0
2007	12.7	12.8	12.9	12.9	12.9	13.1	13.6	13.7	14.1	13.6	13.6	13.5	13.3
2008	13.4	13.4	13.4	13.6	13.7	14.0	13.7	13.8	14.1	13.8	13.8	13.9	13.7
2009	13.5	13.4	13.3	13.2	13.1	13.0	13.1	13.4	13.4	13.2	12.9	12.9	13.2

Employment by Industry: Bakersfield-Delano, CA, Selected Years, 1990–2009—*Continued*

(Numbers in thousands, not seasonally adjusted.)

Industry and year	January	February	March	April	May	June	July	August	September	October	November	December	Annual average
Service-Providing													
1990	132.6	133.3	134.0	136.3	137.5	137.9	136.6	134.6	138.0	140.2	140.8	142.4	137.0
2000	161.3	161.9	163.2	163.2	164.7	165.1	159.9	159.5	163.4	165.4	166.9	167.3	163.5
2001	167.7	168.3	169.3	169.6	170.1	172.2	164.7	166.6	168.5	171.3	173.2	173.5	169.6
2002	170.3	170.9	173.1	173.6	174.3	175.4	168.8	169.2	169.9	172.7	174.5	174.9	172.3
2003	171.4	171.5	174.0	173.4	174.2	174.2	170.5	170.7	171.5	173.7	175.0	175.2	172.9
2004	170.6	171.5	173.0	175.6	176.3	179.1	173.5	173.3	174.8	177.8	179.9	180.0	175.5
2005	178.0	178.9	180.0	182.0	183.8	184.6	180.6	182.1	183.9	186.0	187.5	188.3	183.0
2006	186.5	187.4	188.4	189.4	191.3	192.3	187.6	189.9	192.0	194.7	196.1	196.4	191.0
2007	194.3	195.0	196.1	198.9	199.4	199.5	193.1	194.7	197.1	198.3	199.6	200.1	197.2
2008	195.7	197.2	198.1	198.9	199.6	199.7	193.9	193.5	195.1	197.5	198.7	197.0	197.1
2009	193.2	193.6	193.9	194.3	194.6	194.6	188.2	186.3	187.3	190.8	192.3	192.0	191.8
Trade, Transportation, and Utilities													
1990	34.2	33.8	34.0	33.7	34.0	34.1	34.9	35.0	35.2	35.4	35.9	36.3	34.7
2000	36.2	36.2	36.3	36.5	36.9	37.0	37.6	37.8	37.6	37.6	38.3	38.8	37.2
2001	38.3	37.8	38.0	38.1	38.2	38.6	38.4	38.2	38.1	38.6	39.2	39.3	38.4
2002	38.0	37.8	38.1	38.5	38.8	39.1	39.3	39.3	39.4	39.3	39.9	40.4	39.0
2003	38.6	38.7	39.2	39.3	39.5	39.7	39.9	39.7	39.6	40.3	40.5	41.0	39.6
2004	39.2	38.9	39.4	40.4	40.8	41.2	41.6	42.0	41.6	42.1	42.8	42.7	41.1
2005	41.5	41.6	41.9	42.4	43.3	43.3	43.7	43.9	44.3	44.6	45.6	46.5	43.6
2006	45.1	44.8	45.1	45.0	46.2	46.3	46.3	46.6	46.7	46.6	47.8	48.2	46.2
2007	46.0	45.6	46.1	46.2	46.8	46.6	46.5	46.6	46.5	46.4	47.2	47.4	46.5
2008	45.2	44.7	44.8	44.8	45.5	45.2	44.6	44.6	44.4	43.9	44.3	44.1	44.7
2009	42.2	42.0	41.6	41.8	42.3	42.1	41.5	41.6	41.9	42.0	42.3	42.6	42.0
Wholesale Trade													
1990	6.2	6.0	6.1	6.0	6.1	6.1	6.3	6.3	6.4	6.6	6.6	6.7	6.3
2000	5.5	5.5	5.5	5.6	5.7	5.7	5.8	5.8	5.7	5.8	5.8	5.8	5.7
2001	5.7	5.7	5.7	5.9	5.9	6.0	5.9	5.9	5.9	6.0	6.0	6.0	5.9
2002	6.0	6.0	6.0	6.0	6.0	6.1	6.3	6.3	6.3	6.2	6.0	6.1	6.1
2003	5.9	5.9	6.0	6.1	6.2	6.2	6.3	6.2	6.2	6.3	6.4	6.5	6.1
2004	6.2	6.2	6.2	6.3	6.4	6.5	6.7	6.7	6.6	6.6	6.6	6.6	6.5
2005	6.6	6.6	6.6	6.8	6.8	6.9	6.9	6.9	6.9	7.0	7.0	7.1	6.8
2006	7.2	7.3	7.4	7.4	7.6	7.7	7.7	7.7	7.8	7.8	7.9	7.9	7.6
2007	7.8	7.8	7.9	8.0	8.0	8.1	8.1	8.0	8.0	8.0	7.9	7.8	8.0
2008	7.7	7.7	7.7	7.7	7.8	7.8	7.8	7.8	7.8	7.6	7.6	7.3	7.7
2009	7.4	7.6	7.3	7.3	7.3	7.2	7.2	7.2	7.1	7.2	7.1	7.1	7.3
Retail Trade													
1990	22.8	22.5	22.6	22.4	22.5	22.6	23.0	22.9	23.1	23.1	23.7	24.1	22.9
2000	22.7	22.6	22.7	22.6	22.9	23.0	23.1	23.2	23.2	23.3	24.1	24.6	23.2
2001	24.3	23.9	24.0	24.0	24.0	24.3	24.0	23.8	23.8	24.2	24.8	25.1	24.2
2002	24.0	23.7	24.0	24.4	24.6	24.8	24.5	24.5	24.6	24.6	25.4	25.9	24.6
2003	24.4	24.4	24.5	24.3	24.5	24.6	24.6	24.5	24.5	25.2	25.5	26.0	24.7
2004	24.8	24.5	24.9	25.6	25.7	25.9	25.8	26.0	25.9	26.3	27.2	27.2	25.8
2005	26.3	26.2	26.5	26.8	27.0	27.2	27.5	27.7	28.0	28.1	29.3	30.1	27.6
2006	28.9	28.4	28.6	28.5	28.9	29.1	29.1	29.4	29.4	29.4	30.5	30.8	29.3
2007	29.1	28.6	28.8	28.8	28.9	28.8	28.7	28.8	28.7	28.5	29.6	29.9	28.9
2008	28.2	27.7	27.8	27.6	27.7	27.7	27.3	27.2	26.9	26.6	27.1	27.3	27.4
2009	25.6	25.3	25.3	25.5	25.7	25.7	25.1	25.1	25.5	25.5	26.0	26.3	25.6
Transportation and Utilities													
1990	5.2	5.3	5.3	5.3	5.4	5.4	5.6	5.8	5.7	5.7	5.6	5.5	5.5
2000	8.0	8.1	8.1	8.3	8.3	8.3	8.7	8.8	8.7	8.5	8.4	8.4	8.4
2001	8.3	8.2	8.3	8.2	8.3	8.3	8.5	8.5	8.4	8.4	8.4	8.2	8.3
2002	8.0	8.1	8.1	8.1	8.2	8.2	8.5	8.5	8.5	8.5	8.5	8.4	8.3
2003	8.3	8.4	8.7	8.9	8.8	8.9	9.0	9.0	8.9	8.8	8.6	8.5	8.7
2004	8.2	8.2	8.3	8.5	8.7	8.8	9.1	9.3	9.1	9.2	9.0	8.9	8.8
2005	8.6	8.8	8.8	8.8	9.5	9.2	9.3	9.3	9.4	9.5	9.3	9.3	9.2
2006	9.0	9.1	9.1	9.1	9.7	9.5	9.5	9.5	9.5	9.4	9.4	9.5	9.4
2007	9.1	9.2	9.4	9.4	9.9	9.7	9.7	9.8	9.8	9.9	9.7	9.7	9.6
2008	9.3	9.3	9.3	9.5	10.0	9.7	9.5	9.6	9.7	9.7	9.6	9.5	9.6
2009	9.2	9.1	9.0	9.0	9.3	9.2	9.2	9.3	9.3	9.3	9.2	9.2	9.2
Information													
1990	3.1	3.2	3.2	3.3	3.4	3.5	3.6	3.5	3.4	3.6	3.6	3.6	3.4
2000	2.5	2.5	2.5	2.5	2.5	2.5	2.6	2.5	2.5	2.5	2.5	2.5	2.5
2001	2.5	2.5	2.5	2.6	2.6	2.7	2.6	2.5	2.5	2.5	2.5	2.5	2.5
2002	2.6	2.6	2.6	2.6	2.6	2.6	2.5	2.4	2.4	2.5	2.5	2.5	2.5
2003	2.6	2.6	2.6	2.6	2.6	2.5	2.5	2.5	2.5	2.5	2.5	2.5	2.5
2004	2.5	2.5	2.5	2.5	2.5	2.6	2.6	2.5	2.5	2.5	2.5	2.6	2.5
2005	2.5	2.5	2.5	2.5	2.5	2.5	2.6	2.5	2.6	2.5	2.6	2.6	2.5
2006	2.6	2.7	2.6	2.6	2.7	2.7	2.7	2.7	2.6	2.6	2.7	2.7	2.7
2007	2.8	2.8	2.7	2.8	2.8	2.9	2.8	2.9	2.8	2.8	2.9	2.9	2.8
2008	2.9	3.0	3.0	3.1	3.1	3.1	3.0	3.0	3.0	3.0	3.0	2.9	3.0
2009	2.8	2.8	2.8	2.8	2.8	2.8	2.8	2.7	2.7	2.7	2.7	2.7	2.8

Employment by Industry: Bakersfield-Delano, CA, Selected Years, 1990–2009—*Continued*

(Numbers in thousands, not seasonally adjusted.)

Industry and year	January	February	March	April	May	June	July	August	September	October	November	December	Annual average
Financial Activities													
1990	6.7	6.8	6.7	6.6	6.6	6.7	6.8	6.8	6.8	6.7	6.7	6.7	6.7
2000	7.6	7.7	7.7	7.5	7.6	7.5	7.6	7.5	7.5	7.5	7.5	7.6	7.6
2001	7.6	7.6	7.6	7.7	7.7	7.9	7.8	7.8	7.8	7.8	7.8	7.9	7.8
2002	7.7	7.8	7.9	8.0	8.0	8.0	8.0	8.0	8.0	8.0	8.1	8.2	8.0
2003	8.1	8.1	8.2	8.2	8.3	8.4	8.4	8.5	8.4	8.4	8.4	8.4	8.3
2004	8.4	8.4	8.5	8.7	8.6	8.6	8.7	8.7	8.7	8.6	8.6	8.6	8.6
2005	8.6	8.5	8.6	8.6	8.7	8.8	8.9	8.9	8.8	8.7	8.8	8.8	8.7
2006	8.9	8.9	8.9	8.9	9.1	9.1	9.0	9.0	8.9	9.0	9.0	9.0	9.0
2007	9.1	9.2	9.2	9.1	9.1	9.2	9.1	9.1	9.0	9.0	8.9	8.9	9.1
2008	8.8	8.8	8.9	9.0	9.0	8.9	8.9	8.9	8.9	8.9	8.8	8.8	8.9
2009	8.6	8.6	8.6	8.6	8.5	8.5	8.5	8.4	8.4	8.4	8.5	8.5	8.5
Professional and Business Services													
1990	15.4	15.7	15.5	16.7	16.9	17.1	17.5	17.6	17.7	17.7	17.3	17.8	16.9
2000	22.1	22.1	22.1	21.9	21.9	22.2	22.2	22.5	22.2	22.0	22.4	22.5	22.2
2001	23.1	23.1	23.2	22.7	22.7	23.0	22.6	23.0	22.7	23.2	23.5	23.5	23.0
2002	23.2	23.3	23.4	22.8	22.6	22.6	21.9	22.3	21.9	21.6	21.4	21.3	22.4
2003	20.7	20.7	21.2	21.3	21.5	21.8	21.8	22.1	22.3	22.1	22.3	22.3	21.6
2004	21.1	21.5	21.6	21.8	21.8	21.7	21.5	21.9	21.6	21.9	22.1	22.2	21.7
2005	22.1	22.1	22.0	22.8	22.8	23.0	23.4	23.6	23.9	23.4	23.8	23.6	23.0
2006	23.7	24.0	24.1	24.3	24.8	25.0	25.3	25.6	25.9	26.0	25.8	25.7	25.0
2007	26.0	26.3	26.2	26.5	26.5	26.3	26.2	26.5	26.7	25.3	25.3	25.4	26.1
2008	24.7	25.2	25.2	25.4	25.1	25.1	25.0	25.1	25.1	25.0	24.9	24.5	25.0
2009	24.6	24.0	24.0	23.8	23.8	23.8	23.7	24.0	24.0	24.2	24.2	24.3	24.0
Education and Health Services													
1990	12.4	12.5	12.5	12.6	12.6	12.9	13.3	13.1	13.2	13.6	13.6	13.7	13.0
2000	18.6	18.9	19.0	19.1	19.2	19.4	19.5	19.4	19.5	19.2	19.2	19.3	19.2
2001	20.1	20.3	20.3	19.9	19.9	20.0	20.3	20.3	20.3	20.3	20.4	20.5	20.2
2002	20.1	20.3	20.4	20.7	20.9	21.0	20.6	20.8	20.8	20.9	21.0	21.1	20.7
2003	20.9	21.1	21.2	21.2	21.4	21.3	21.3	21.4	21.4	21.4	21.4	21.5	21.2
2004	21.2	21.2	21.4	21.5	21.6	21.7	21.7	21.8	21.7	21.6	21.7	21.9	21.6
2005	21.7	21.9	22.0	22.2	22.3	22.2	22.4	22.4	22.2	22.3	22.3	22.4	22.2
2006	22.4	22.6	22.7	22.7	22.7	23.0	22.7	23.0	23.1	23.5	23.7	23.8	23.0
2007	23.9	24.3	24.3	24.2	24.1	24.2	24.6	24.7	24.8	24.8	24.9	25.0	24.5
2008	25.0	25.2	25.4	25.4	25.4	25.4	25.4	25.7	25.6	25.7	25.8	25.8	25.5
2009	25.4	25.7	25.9	25.8	25.9	26.1	25.7	26.1	25.9	25.9	25.9	25.9	25.9
Leisure and Hospitality													
1990	12.4	12.3	12.5	13.2	13.3	13.2	13.4	13.4	13.6	13.3	13.6	13.6	13.2
2000	15.9	16.1	16.2	16.4	16.7	16.9	17.1	16.9	16.7	16.6	16.4	16.4	16.5
2001	16.4	16.5	16.9	17.2	17.5	17.6	17.7	17.6	17.5	17.2	17.3	17.3	17.2
2002	16.8	16.9	17.3	17.6	18.1	18.2	17.9	17.9	17.8	17.7	17.6	17.7	17.6
2003	17.3	17.4	17.9	17.9	18.3	18.3	18.4	18.3	18.1	18.3	18.2	18.0	18.0
2004	17.6	18.1	18.4	19.0	19.4	19.4	19.3	19.3	19.3	19.1	19.3	19.4	19.0
2005	19.3	19.3	19.6	20.1	20.5	20.9	20.6	20.5	20.3	20.0	20.1	20.3	20.1
2006	19.6	19.9	20.2	20.9	21.0	21.3	21.0	20.9	20.9	20.6	20.7	20.9	20.7
2007	20.5	20.7	21.2	21.7	21.9	22.1	21.7	21.7	21.8	21.7	21.6	21.6	21.5
2008	20.9	21.2	21.4	21.8	22.0	22.1	22.0	21.9	21.5	21.2	21.2	21.0	21.5
2009	20.6	20.8	21.1	21.4	21.7	21.7	21.0	20.8	20.8	20.7	20.5	20.4	21.0
Other Services													
1990	5.0	5.0	5.1	5.0	5.0	5.2	5.2	5.1	5.1	5.1	5.1	5.0	5.1
2000	6.5	6.5	6.6	6.6	6.6	6.6	6.6	6.9	6.8	6.8	6.7	6.7	6.7
2001	6.5	6.6	6.6	6.8	6.9	6.8	6.9	6.9	7.1	6.9	6.9	6.8	6.8
2002	6.8	6.9	6.9	6.8	7.0	6.8	6.8	6.8	6.7	7.0	7.1	6.9	6.9
2003	6.7	6.8	6.9	6.9	7.0	6.9	6.8	6.8	7.0	7.0	6.9	6.9	6.8
2004	6.9	6.9	6.9	7.0	7.0	6.9	6.8	6.8	7.0	7.2	7.4	7.1	7.0
2005	7.0	7.0	7.1	7.2	7.3	7.2	7.0	7.0	7.2	7.1	6.8	6.8	7.1
2006	6.7	6.8	6.9	7.0	7.0	6.8	6.7	7.0	6.9	6.7	6.6	6.5	6.8
2007	6.5	6.5	6.7	6.6	6.6	6.5	6.7	6.8	6.9	7.0	7.0	7.0	6.7
2008	6.7	6.9	6.9	7.0	7.2	7.2	6.8	7.0	7.0	7.2	7.1	7.0	7.0
2009	6.7	6.8	6.7	6.8	6.8	6.7	6.5	6.7	6.6	6.6	6.6	6.5	6.7
Government													
1990	43.4	44.0	44.5	45.2	45.7	45.2	41.9	40.1	43.0	44.8	45.0	45.7	44.0
2000	51.9	51.9	52.8	52.7	53.3	53.0	46.7	46.0	50.6	53.2	53.9	53.5	51.6
2001	53.2	53.9	54.2	54.6	54.6	55.6	48.4	50.3	52.5	54.8	55.6	55.7	53.6
2002	55.1	55.3	56.5	56.6	56.3	57.1	51.8	51.7	52.9	55.7	56.9	56.8	55.2
2003	56.5	56.1	56.8	56.0	55.6	55.3	51.4	51.4	52.2	53.7	54.8	54.6	54.5
2004	53.7	54.0	54.3	54.7	54.6	57.0	51.3	50.3	52.4	54.8	55.5	55.5	54.0
2005	55.3	56.0	56.3	56.2	56.4	56.7	52.0	53.3	54.6	57.4	57.5	57.3	55.8
2006	57.5	57.7	57.9	58.0	57.8	58.1	53.9	55.1	57.0	59.7	59.8	59.6	57.7
2007	59.5	59.6	59.7	61.8	61.6	61.7	55.5	56.4	58.6	61.3	61.8	61.9	60.0
2008	61.5	62.2	62.5	62.4	62.3	62.7	58.2	57.3	59.6	62.7	63.6	62.9	61.5
2009	62.3	62.9	63.2	63.3	62.8	62.9	58.5	56.0	57.0	60.3	61.6	61.1	61.0

Employment by Industry: Baltimore-Towson, MD, Selected Years, 1990–2009

(Numbers in thousands, not seasonally adjusted.)

Industry and year	January	February	March	April	May	June	July	August	September	October	November	December	Annual average
Total Nonfarm													
1990	1127.7	1139.2	1153.3	1154.4	1161.9	1168.9	1159.7	1157.3	1161.2	1148.6	1151.5	1149.5	1152.8
2000	1209.6	1212.9	1230.9	1243.3	1254.6	1264.2	1253.1	1251.4	1259.4	1266.8	1275.4	1284.1	1250.5
2001	1231.6	1238.3	1249.6	1255.3	1262.8	1271.9	1260.7	1257.4	1257.6	1260.1	1268.0	1271.2	1257.0
2002	1227.4	1234.2	1246.4	1248.7	1259.1	1265.6	1253.2	1250.3	1251.9	1254.3	1260.2	1261.2	1251.0
2003	1225.9	1223.0	1235.3	1247.4	1256.9	1252.5	1241.7	1253.1	1255.8	1260.2	1266.1	1269.4	1248.9
2004	1234.5	1234.9	1250.8	1258.2	1266.8	1277.3	1269.6	1267.0	1267.0	1275.7	1281.6	1284.8	1264.0
2005	1248.8	1255.2	1263.3	1278.5	1287.6	1294.7	1292.7	1288.1	1300.3	1300.3	1306.5	1311.1	1285.6
2006	1275.3	1280.3	1295.2	1303.9	1312.6	1318.6	1307.7	1306.5	1310.0	1316.9	1323.0	1329.9	1306.6
2007	1292.7	1293.0	1309.0	1315.3	1325.8	1330.6	1321.0	1321.0	1321.1	1324.1	1330.4	1334.0	1318.2
2008	1298.9	1302.0	1311.5	1320.6	1326.6	1327.5	1319.1	1315.9	1312.5	1316.1	1312.4	1310.7	1314.5
2009	1265.7	1263.3	1268.0	1276.5	1283.2	1285.8	1271.6	1267.4	1266.9	1271.9	1270.9	1269.3	1271.7
Total Private													
1990	914.1	921.3	933.2	932.5	938.8	947.9	943.3	946.9	946.5	935.4	938.3	937.3	936.3
2000	993.7	994.7	1008.8	1021.8	1030.2	1043.8	1040.8	1042.9	1045.2	1044.7	1053.4	1061.7	1031.8
2001	1014.3	1016.9	1026.7	1032.3	1040.9	1053.1	1047.2	1046.8	1040.2	1038.1	1044.2	1047.8	1037.4
2002	1006.9	1010.0	1020.1	1025.4	1035.3	1044.6	1037.9	1038.4	1031.9	1029.7	1035.1	1037.6	1029.4
2003	1007.5	1000.8	1011.2	1024.0	1034.3	1037.1	1031.9	1036.4	1038.4	1039.5	1044.7	1049.3	1029.6
2004	1019.7	1018.6	1031.6	1038.2	1047.7	1060.3	1059.9	1059.7	1054.2	1057.7	1061.4	1065.4	1047.9
2005	1035.2	1037.1	1045.2	1058.6	1066.8	1076.6	1082.6	1082.3	1083.2	1078.3	1082.5	1087.7	1068.0
2006	1060.1	1060.2	1073.1	1080.5	1089.0	1099.2	1094.4	1094.0	1091.3	1092.1	1096.3	1102.8	1086.1
2007	1073.6	1069.1	1082.6	1090.0	1099.8	1109.1	1106.4	1106.7	1101.7	1098.8	1103.3	1107.4	1095.7
2008	1079.7	1077.3	1085.3	1092.4	1098.3	1104.0	1100.9	1098.9	1090.3	1087.0	1082.7	1081.1	1089.8
2009	1043.6	1036.1	1039.1	1045.6	1052.5	1059.4	1050.9	1048.7	1045.7	1042.7	1041.8	1041.0	1045.6
Goods-Producing													
1990	196.5	200.0	203.7	202.6	203.7	205.5	202.4	202.8	201.4	196.4	195.0	192.1	200.2
2000	163.6	162.2	165.9	166.9	168.4	170.8	170.4	171.3	171.6	170.4	170.6	170.4	168.5
2001	162.6	163.9	165.8	166.4	166.3	169.1	168.8	169.0	167.7	165.9	165.1	164.7	166.3
2002	156.2	157.2	158.4	159.6	160.4	162.1	160.3	160.8	159.3	157.8	157.5	156.4	158.8
2003	152.9	150.9	151.9	153.2	154.3	155.9	155.4	156.1	155.4	154.9	154.8	154.6	154.2
2004	150.0	149.0	152.0	154.1	155.4	157.4	158.5	159.1	158.2	158.1	158.1	158.6	155.7
2005	154.2	153.6	154.9	158.0	159.1	160.9	161.1	161.7	161.7	160.3	160.8	160.9	158.9
2006	157.0	156.5	158.6	159.3	159.9	161.9	161.8	161.8	160.9	159.1	158.4	158.1	159.4
2007	154.4	152.5	155.0	155.9	157.4	159.3	159.8	159.9	158.5	156.8	156.2	155.3	156.8
2008	152.4	151.3	151.9	151.8	151.9	153.3	153.8	153.5	151.7	149.6	147.8	145.6	151.2
2009	138.7	136.6	135.9	135.1	135.4	136.8	136.1	135.4	133.9	127.7	128.1	125.5	133.8
Mining, Logging, and Construction													
1990	69.6	69.9	72.8	73.6	74.4	75.5	73.4	73.7	72.6	70.4	68.6	66.2	71.7
2000	68.6	67.3	70.6	72.0	73.4	74.9	75.5	76.3	76.2	75.2	75.2	74.6	73.3
2001	70.4	71.2	73.3	74.2	75.1	76.9	76.5	77.0	76.0	75.0	74.6	74.1	74.5
2002	69.6	70.1	71.7	73.1	74.1	75.5	76.0	76.4	75.5	75.2	75.0	74.1	73.9
2003	71.3	69.6	70.6	72.2	73.9	75.4	76.6	77.5	77.3	77.3	77.4	77.4	74.7
2004	74.0	73.1	76.0	77.9	79.1	80.9	81.8	82.4	81.9	81.9	81.9	82.2	79.4
2005	78.9	78.1	79.4	82.3	83.6	85.3	85.9	86.3	86.3	85.6	86.0	85.9	83.6
2006	83.2	82.9	84.7	85.8	86.7	88.4	88.4	88.6	88.0	87.1	86.6	86.3	86.4
2007	83.2	81.5	83.9	84.9	86.2	87.7	88.2	88.4	87.4	86.0	85.5	84.3	85.6
2008	82.1	81.1	81.9	82.4	82.5	83.6	84.4	84.2	83.0	81.8	80.5	78.5	82.2
2009	73.2	72.0	71.6	71.5	72.0	73.2	73.3	72.6	71.2	65.5	65.8	63.3	70.4
Manufacturing													
1990	126.9	130.1	130.9	129.0	129.3	130.0	129.0	129.1	128.8	126.0	126.4	125.9	128.5
2000	95.0	94.9	95.3	94.9	95.0	95.9	94.9	95.0	95.4	95.2	95.4	95.8	95.2
2001	92.2	92.7	92.5	92.2	91.2	92.2	92.3	92.0	91.7	90.9	90.5	90.6	91.8
2002	86.6	87.1	86.7	86.5	86.3	86.6	84.3	84.4	83.8	82.6	82.5	82.3	85.0
2003	81.6	81.3	81.3	81.0	80.4	80.5	78.8	78.6	78.1	77.6	77.4	77.2	79.5
2004	76.0	75.9	76.0	76.2	76.3	76.5	76.7	76.7	76.3	76.2	76.2	76.4	76.3
2005	75.3	75.5	75.5	75.7	75.5	75.6	75.2	75.4	75.4	74.7	74.8	75.0	75.3
2006	73.8	73.6	73.9	73.5	73.2	73.5	73.4	73.2	72.9	72.0	71.8	71.8	73.1
2007	71.2	71.0	71.1	71.0	71.2	71.6	71.6	71.5	71.1	70.8	70.7	71.0	71.2
2008	70.3	70.2	70.0	69.4	69.4	69.7	69.4	69.3	68.7	67.8	67.3	67.1	69.1
2009	65.5	64.6	64.3	63.6	63.4	63.6	62.8	62.8	62.7	62.2	62.3	62.2	63.3
Service-Providing													
1990	931.2	939.2	949.6	951.8	958.2	963.4	957.3	954.5	959.8	952.2	956.5	957.4	952.6
2000	1046.0	1050.7	1065.0	1076.4	1086.2	1093.4	1082.7	1080.1	1087.8	1096.4	1104.8	1113.7	1081.9
2001	1069.0	1074.4	1083.8	1088.9	1096.5	1102.8	1091.9	1088.2	1089.9	1094.2	1102.9	1106.5	1090.8
2002	1071.2	1077.0	1088.0	1089.1	1098.7	1103.5	1092.9	1089.5	1092.6	1096.5	1102.7	1104.8	1092.2
2003	1073.0	1072.1	1083.4	1094.2	1102.6	1096.6	1086.3	1097.0	1100.4	1105.3	1111.3	1114.8	1094.8
2004	1084.5	1085.9	1098.8	1104.1	1111.4	1119.9	1111.1	1107.9	1108.8	1117.6	1123.5	1126.2	1108.3
2005	1094.6	1101.6	1108.4	1120.5	1128.5	1133.8	1131.6	1126.4	1138.6	1140.0	1145.7	1150.2	1126.7
2006	1118.3	1123.8	1136.6	1144.6	1152.7	1156.7	1145.9	1144.7	1149.1	1157.8	1164.6	1171.8	1147.2
2007	1138.3	1140.5	1154.0	1159.4	1168.4	1171.3	1161.2	1161.1	1162.6	1167.3	1174.2	1178.7	1161.4
2008	1146.5	1150.7	1159.6	1168.8	1174.7	1174.2	1165.3	1162.4	1160.8	1166.5	1164.6	1165.1	1163.3
2009	1127.0	1126.7	1132.1	1141.4	1147.8	1149.0	1135.5	1132.0	1133.0	1144.2	1142.8	1143.8	1137.9

Employment by Industry: Baltimore-Towson, MD, Selected Years, 1990–2009—*Continued*

(Numbers in thousands, not seasonally adjusted.)

Industry and year	January	February	March	April	May	June	July	August	September	October	November	December	Annual average
Trade, Transportation, and Utilities													
1990	237.4	234.4	236.0	233.3	233.7	235.0	232.6	234.2	234.7	234.4	238.0	240.5	235.4
2000	238.2	236.4	237.8	239.9	242.0	244.0	243.0	245.1	245.7	248.6	254.6	259.8	244.6
2001	243.6	240.2	241.1	240.7	242.3	243.6	239.9	240.1	240.8	241.7	245.9	249.5	242.5
2002	236.5	233.4	235.4	236.2	238.1	239.9	236.4	236.3	237.3	237.8	241.3	245.6	237.9
2003	234.2	231.2	233.0	234.0	236.5	238.3	236.1	237.8	238.9	241.1	246.2	250.1	238.1
2004	239.5	237.6	239.2	239.0	240.4	242.8	239.8	239.8	239.9	242.0	246.2	249.9	241.3
2005	239.1	237.1	238.1	239.2	240.9	242.7	242.8	242.2	243.4	244.4	248.4	253.1	242.6
2006	243.7	241.4	243.3	243.6	245.2	246.8	244.2	244.0	243.8	246.6	251.9	256.5	245.9
2007	246.3	242.3	244.4	243.7	246.9	247.9	246.2	245.3	244.8	246.1	251.2	255.7	246.7
2008	244.1	240.4	241.4	240.2	241.2	242.4	240.5	239.9	238.6	238.8	240.4	242.7	240.9
2009	231.5	227.5	226.8	226.9	227.9	229.3	226.0	226.0	226.8	227.7	230.8	234.6	228.5
Wholesale Trade													
1990	56.6	56.8	57.2	56.8	56.5	56.8	56.8	56.9	56.7	56.0	56.0	55.8	56.6
2000	52.4	52.7	53.4	53.8	54.1	54.9	55.3	55.7	55.6	55.6	55.9	56.4	54.7
2001	55.4	55.6	56.1	56.4	56.5	56.5	56.2	56.1	56.0	55.7	55.5	55.7	56.0
2002	54.6	54.6	54.6	54.2	54.3	54.4	54.3	54.5	54.4	54.2	54.1	54.3	54.4
2003	53.3	52.9	53.3	53.2	53.4	53.6	53.3	53.3	53.3	53.1	53.1	53.2	53.3
2004	52.6	52.9	53.3	53.5	53.6	53.9	53.9	53.9	53.8	54.1	54.0	54.2	53.6
2005	54.3	54.4	54.5	54.8	55.1	55.6	55.9	55.7	55.8	56.0	56.1	56.5	55.4
2006	56.0	56.3	56.4	56.7	56.7	57.0	56.8	56.8	56.7	56.7	56.6	56.9	56.6
2007	55.9	56.0	56.0	56.2	56.4	56.5	56.4	56.3	56.1	55.8	55.8	56.1	56.1
2008	55.5	55.3	55.7	55.7	55.9	56.0	55.5	55.3	55.0	54.8	54.4	54.2	55.3
2009	53.6	53.3	52.9	52.9	52.8	52.8	52.4	52.4	52.4	52.8	52.1	53.3	52.8
Retail Trade													
1990	144.7	142.6	142.9	140.4	141.2	142.1	140.8	142.3	141.8	141.6	145.9	149.2	143.0
2000	143.6	141.6	142.2	143.2	144.8	145.8	145.1	146.1	145.5	147.9	153.6	157.8	146.4
2001	144.9	141.5	141.9	140.8	142.1	143.3	142.0	142.4	142.0	142.9	147.7	150.9	143.5
2002	141.0	138.2	140.1	139.7	140.8	142.6	141.3	140.9	141.0	141.3	145.3	148.9	141.8
2003	140.1	137.7	138.4	139.8	141.2	142.8	142.2	143.7	143.5	144.8	149.9	153.3	143.1
2004	144.4	142.3	143.4	142.3	143.2	145.1	143.0	143.2	142.2	143.9	148.2	151.3	144.4
2005	140.7	138.7	139.3	140.6	141.6	142.5	143.2	143.2	142.9	143.7	147.7	151.2	142.9
2006	143.6	140.6	142.1	141.9	143.1	144.0	142.8	142.6	141.6	144.4	149.8	153.1	144.1
2007	145.1	141.2	142.8	142.1	144.4	144.9	144.4	144.1	143.0	144.6	149.7	153.2	145.0
2008	143.8	140.3	141.1	140.6	141.0	141.8	141.0	140.7	139.0	139.6	141.7	143.4	141.2
2009	135.0	131.8	131.7	131.9	133.0	133.9	132.7	132.7	132.2	132.6	136.4	138.4	133.5
Transportation and Utilities													
1990	36.2	35.7	36.4	37.1	37.0	37.5	36.0	36.1	36.9	37.0	36.4	36.1	36.5
2000	42.2	42.1	42.2	42.9	43.1	43.3	42.6	43.3	44.6	45.1	45.1	45.6	43.5
2001	43.3	43.1	43.1	43.5	43.7	43.8	41.7	41.6	42.8	43.1	42.7	42.9	42.9
2002	40.9	40.6	40.7	42.3	43.0	42.9	40.8	40.9	41.9	42.3	41.9	42.4	41.7
2003	40.8	40.6	41.3	41.0	41.9	41.9	40.6	40.8	42.1	43.2	43.2	43.6	41.8
2004	42.5	42.4	42.5	43.2	43.6	43.8	42.9	42.7	43.9	44.0	44.0	44.4	43.3
2005	44.1	44.0	44.3	43.8	44.2	44.6	43.7	43.3	44.7	44.7	44.6	45.4	44.3
2006	44.1	44.5	44.8	45.0	45.4	45.8	44.6	44.6	45.5	45.5	45.5	46.5	45.2
2007	45.3	45.1	45.6	45.4	46.1	46.5	45.4	44.9	45.7	45.7	45.7	46.4	45.7
2008	44.8	44.8	44.6	43.9	44.3	44.6	44.0	43.9	44.6	44.4	44.3	45.1	44.4
2009	42.9	42.4	42.2	42.1	42.1	42.6	40.9	40.9	42.2	42.3	42.3	42.9	42.2
Information													
1990	20.8	21.3	21.4	20.9	20.9	21.0	21.1	21.0	20.9	21.0	21.0	20.9	21.0
2000	24.5	24.3	24.5	24.1	24.4	25.0	25.0	22.5	25.3	25.3	25.8	26.5	24.8
2001	25.8	26.1	26.0	25.1	25.2	25.2	24.3	24.3	23.7	23.5	23.6	23.4	24.7
2002	22.5	22.5	22.4	22.3	22.3	22.2	21.7	21.8	21.2	20.6	21.1	20.8	21.8
2003	20.8	20.8	20.8	21.1	21.4	21.2	21.2	21.0	20.7	20.7	21.2	21.3	21.0
2004	21.2	20.8	21.1	21.0	21.2	21.5	21.0	21.3	21.0	21.0	21.2	21.0	21.1
2005	20.8	20.9	21.0	21.2	21.3	21.6	22.2	22.6	22.2	22.2	22.2	22.2	21.7
2006	21.6	21.8	21.9	21.9	22.1	22.3	22.1	22.2	22.3	22.2	22.7	22.9	22.2
2007	22.4	22.6	23.1	23.3	23.5	24.2	23.9	24.3	24.3	23.4	23.9	23.9	23.6
2008	23.4	23.5	23.8	23.6	23.7	23.4	23.2	23.1	23.0	22.4	22.8	22.9	23.2
2009	21.9	22.1	22.4	21.6	21.6	22.0	21.2	21.5	21.2	21.0	21.1	21.2	21.6
Financial Activities													
1990	72.9	73.1	73.2	73.1	73.7	74.2	74.4	74.8	74.7	76.4	76.8	76.8	74.5
2000	76.7	77.1	77.6	77.0	77.5	78.7	79.0	79.1	78.7	78.7	79.2	79.9	78.3
2001	77.4	77.9	78.5	78.5	78.9	80.0	80.3	80.4	80.1	80.0	80.8	81.1	79.5
2002	79.0	79.1	79.3	79.5	79.8	80.6	80.6	80.7	80.8	80.5	81.0	81.3	80.2
2003	81.0	81.0	81.5	81.8	82.3	83.2	83.4	83.7	83.1	82.0	82.3	82.5	82.3
2004	81.4	81.6	82.1	82.1	82.2	82.4	82.2	82.3	81.7	82.0	81.9	82.0	82.0
2005	81.0	81.7	81.7	82.3	82.4	83.0	83.7	84.1	83.7	83.0	83.2	83.6	82.8
2006	82.8	82.9	83.2	82.9	82.7	83.3	83.1	82.8	82.4	82.0	81.8	82.4	82.7
2007	81.6	81.6	81.7	81.7	81.8	82.2	82.1	81.7	80.8	80.4	80.2	80.5	81.4
2008	79.2	79.5	79.7	79.2	79.3	79.7	79.1	78.8	78.1	78.2	77.5	77.7	78.8
2009	75.9	75.7	75.4	75.2	74.9	74.9	74.2	74.0	73.3	73.3	72.3	71.0	74.2

Employment by Industry: Baltimore-Towson, MD, Selected Years, 1990–2009—*Continued*

(Numbers in thousands, not seasonally adjusted.)

Industry and year	January	February	March	April	May	June	July	August	September	October	November	December	Annual average
Professional and Business Services													
1990	117.5	118.8	121.0	123.8	124.4	126.1	126.5	126.8	127.4	122.0	121.8	121.3	123.1
2000	161.0	162.1	166.1	173.0	174.0	176.6	175.8	177.3	175.7	176.5	176.1	175.9	172.5
2001	173.5	174.4	175.9	177.6	179.5	179.7	181.9	182.0	179.2	177.5	178.9	178.0	178.2
2002	171.2	171.8	174.0	174.4	176.5	177.5	177.2	178.7	176.1	175.1	175.3	175.0	175.2
2003	168.8	166.8	169.5	173.9	175.2	176.1	174.1	175.9	174.9	177.1	176.5	177.0	173.8
2004	171.4	172.0	174.9	175.8	178.3	180.4	181.8	181.9	180.0	181.8	181.8	181.7	178.5
2005	177.3	178.5	181.2	183.0	184.6	185.7	189.8	190.4	190.5	189.5	188.8	188.3	185.6
2006	182.0	183.5	186.6	188.9	190.1	191.5	191.6	192.0	191.4	191.3	190.8	191.3	189.3
2007	185.5	185.5	188.1	191.1	191.7	193.5	193.1	194.9	194.5	194.6	195.1	195.1	191.9
2008	190.4	190.6	192.4	194.7	195.6	195.9	196.1	196.8	194.7	193.5	191.0	188.9	193.4
2009	182.0	180.0	180.4	183.1	182.9	184.7	184.7	185.3	183.7	185.6	183.3	182.2	183.2
Education and Health Services													
1990	140.4	144.1	145.7	143.9	144.0	142.7	143.7	144.7	147.3	150.1	151.3	151.3	145.8
2000	182.6	184.9	185.7	188.0	187.5	187.2	187.3	187.4	190.4	191.1	192.5	194.1	188.2
2001	185.6	188.2	189.2	190.3	191.0	191.9	189.8	189.1	190.4	193.1	194.9	195.9	190.8
2002	192.1	195.7	196.5	195.3	195.6	195.0	194.1	193.1	194.9	198.0	200.1	200.2	195.9
2003	196.0	197.7	198.8	199.4	199.8	193.0	192.8	193.0	200.1	201.8	202.9	203.5	198.2
2004	201.7	202.2	203.2	203.2	203.8	204.4	205.2	203.8	205.1	206.9	208.1	207.8	204.6
2005	204.6	206.8	207.0	208.4	209.0	208.2	208.6	208.1	211.0	213.5	214.9	215.8	209.7
2006	212.6	214.4	215.8	216.2	216.8	215.7	214.3	214.1	216.8	220.0	221.0	222.1	216.7
2007	218.6	220.6	222.1	222.8	223.0	222.1	221.5	220.9	223.1	225.2	225.6	226.3	222.7
2008	224.4	226.2	227.4	229.1	229.0	228.2	227.8	227.5	230.5	232.7	233.8	234.6	229.3
2009	232.1	233.4	234.3	235.3	235.1	234.4	232.5	231.6	234.3	237.0	238.1	238.5	234.7
Leisure and Hospitality													
1990	84.5	85.4	87.2	90.0	92.9	97.3	96.1	95.7	93.6	90.0	89.4	89.1	90.9
2000	96.7	96.9	99.9	102.0	104.9	109.1	108.2	108.0	105.5	102.5	102.9	103.2	103.3
2001	94.2	94.3	97.2	100.9	104.1	109.0	107.7	107.5	105.1	103.0	101.5	101.4	102.2
2002	97.0	97.2	100.5	103.8	107.8	111.9	111.9	112.1	107.5	105.2	103.9	103.3	105.2
2003	99.7	98.2	100.7	106.1	109.9	113.7	113.7	114.4	111.2	107.9	106.9	106.3	107.4
2004	101.7	101.9	105.1	108.3	111.4	115.8	115.9	116.5	113.5	111.5	109.6	109.6	110.1
2005	104.4	104.3	106.6	111.4	114.2	118.6	118.9	117.9	115.8	110.8	109.5	108.8	111.8
2006	105.9	105.0	108.5	111.7	115.8	120.8	120.5	120.4	117.1	114.6	113.2	112.9	113.9
2007	108.7	108.0	111.5	115.4	119.0	122.7	122.4	123.0	119.3	115.9	114.5	113.9	116.2
2008	110.0	109.7	112.2	117.1	120.8	123.7	123.4	122.6	117.3	115.5	113.2	112.7	116.5
2009	106.4	105.8	108.5	112.7	118.6	121.0	119.9	118.9	116.6	115.1	112.6	112.2	114.0
Other Services													
1990	44.1	44.2	45.0	44.9	45.5	46.1	46.5	46.9	46.5	45.1	45.0	45.3	45.4
2000	49.8	50.2	50.8	50.9	51.5	52.4	52.1	52.2	52.3	51.6	51.7	51.9	51.5
2001	51.9	52.5	53.2	52.8	53.6	54.6	54.5	54.4	53.4	53.5	53.6	53.9	53.5
2002	52.8	53.2	53.9	54.3	54.8	55.4	55.7	54.9	54.7	54.6	54.8	54.9	54.5
2003	53.8	53.9	54.8	54.5	54.9	55.7	55.2	54.5	54.0	54.0	53.9	54.0	54.4
2004	52.8	53.5	54.0	54.7	55.0	55.6	55.5	55.0	54.8	54.4	54.5	54.8	54.6
2005	53.8	54.2	54.7	55.1	55.3	55.9	55.5	55.3	54.9	54.6	54.7	55.0	54.9
2006	54.5	54.7	55.2	56.0	56.4	56.9	56.8	56.7	56.6	56.3	56.5	56.6	56.1
2007	56.1	56.0	56.7	56.1	56.5	57.2	57.4	56.7	56.4	56.4	56.6	56.7	56.6
2008	55.8	56.1	56.5	56.7	56.8	57.4	57.0	56.7	56.4	56.3	56.2	56.0	56.5
2009	55.1	55.0	55.4	55.7	56.1	56.3	56.3	56.0	55.9	55.3	55.5	55.8	55.7
Government													
1990	213.6	217.9	220.1	221.9	223.1	221.0	216.4	210.4	214.7	213.2	213.2	212.2	216.5
2000	215.9	218.2	222.1	221.5	224.4	220.4	212.3	208.5	214.2	222.1	222.0	222.4	218.7
2001	217.3	221.4	222.9	223.0	221.9	218.8	213.5	210.6	217.4	222.0	223.8	223.4	219.7
2002	220.5	224.2	226.3	223.3	223.8	221.0	215.3	211.9	220.0	224.6	225.1	223.6	221.6
2003	218.4	222.2	224.1	223.4	222.6	215.4	209.8	216.7	217.4	220.7	221.4	220.1	219.4
2004	214.8	216.3	219.2	220.0	219.1	217.0	209.7	207.3	212.8	218.0	220.2	219.4	216.2
2005	213.6	218.1	218.1	219.9	220.8	218.1	210.1	205.8	217.1	222.0	224.0	223.4	217.6
2006	215.2	220.1	222.1	223.4	223.6	219.4	213.3	212.5	218.7	224.8	226.7	227.1	220.5
2007	219.1	223.9	226.4	225.3	226.0	221.5	214.6	214.3	219.4	225.3	227.1	226.6	222.5
2008	219.2	224.7	226.2	228.2	228.3	223.5	218.2	217.0	222.2	229.1	229.7	229.6	224.7
2009	222.1	227.2	228.9	230.9	230.7	226.4	220.7	218.7	221.2	229.2	229.1	228.3	226.1

Employment by Industry: Baton Rouge, LA, Selected Years, 1990–2009

(Numbers in thousands, not seasonally adjusted.)

Industry and year	January	February	March	April	May	June	July	August	September	October	November	December	Annual average
Total Nonfarm													
1990	252.6	253.8	254.7	258.0	261.4	262.2	256.2	259.1	260.2	265.1	266.4	266.0	259.6
2000	335.0	337.6	339.9	344.0	344.5	346.6	332.9	334.6	339.8	337.3	338.6	339.3	339.2
2001	333.6	332.9	334.5	336.3	339.4	339.4	328.6	331.4	334.2	337.1	338.0	337.7	335.3
2002	332.4	333.4	334.3	336.3	337.9	337.0	329.5	331.8	336.4	338.5	339.3	338.2	335.4
2003	331.5	335.3	336.2	339.6	340.7	339.1	336.3	336.5	340.2	343.5	342.7	340.9	338.5
2004	336.6	340.6	344.5	344.9	342.4	343.6	339.9	338.8	341.1	342.3	345.7	344.5	342.1
2005	337.7	343.0	346.1	352.6	350.8	350.4	350.2	351.7	358.1	360.2	364.7	364.0	352.5
2006	356.1	361.5	364.7	363.1	363.2	358.9	349.9	356.5	361.4	362.2	363.9	366.2	360.6
2007	360.1	365.5	369.5	370.6	371.5	372.3	370.7	373.9	378.3	378.9	380.9	382.3	372.9
2008	369.7	374.7	376.1	374.2	374.0	374.6	369.8	372.6	369.5	377.3	380.3	380.9	374.5
2009	368.7	372.1	373.6	373.0	372.5	369.0	365.5	365.7	368.3	370.2	371.0	369.3	369.9
Total Private													
1990	190.4	191.4	192.3	193.6	196.9	198.0	196.6	199.7	200.6	201.6	203.0	202.6	197.2
2000	268.6	271.1	273.5	276.6	277.1	278.7	272.2	274.1	274.1	270.8	272.2	273.1	273.5
2001	267.1	266.4	268.0	269.4	271.9	271.5	267.9	270.4	267.9	269.6	269.8	269.9	269.2
2002	264.0	263.9	264.5	266.5	267.5	266.9	266.8	268.5	267.5	268.5	268.4	267.7	266.7
2003	260.2	261.2	261.9	265.8	266.8	266.3	265.4	266.2	266.5	269.0	268.2	268.4	265.5
2004	265.5	266.5	270.2	270.2	268.9	270.1	267.3	266.5	266.2	266.6	269.9	270.3	268.2
2005	265.1	267.8	270.7	277.3	277.1	276.9	278.7	279.1	282.6	283.3	287.3	287.9	277.8
2006	283.6	286.3	289.3	289.2	289.8	290.5	283.2	284.8	287.4	288.0	289.3	292.6	287.8
2007	287.6	290.3	293.6	293.8	295.5	296.7	297.5	298.0	299.1	300.5	301.9	303.9	296.5
2008	294.2	296.2	297.9	296.1	296.8	298.0	294.9	297.3	293.5	298.1	300.6	302.1	297.1
2009	292.4	293.0	294.4	294.3	294.9	292.4	289.9	290.0	288.5	289.5	290.2	289.4	291.6
Goods-Producing													
1990	56.5	57.2	56.7	55.8	57.7	57.1	56.2	58.3	58.3	59.8	60.2	58.8	57.7
2000	70.7	71.6	72.8	72.9	73.2	72.2	68.2	69.4	68.3	67.6	67.2	66.7	70.1
2001	65.1	65.1	65.9	66.9	68.6	67.2	66.6	67.5	65.0	67.0	66.7	65.9	66.5
2002	64.1	63.2	62.4	63.4	63.5	62.3	62.6	63.3	63.2	65.4	63.3	61.8	63.2
2003	61.0	61.4	61.2	61.8	62.8	62.1	62.0	61.9	62.4	63.4	61.6	61.0	61.9
2004	62.7	62.7	64.9	62.3	61.2	61.1	58.9	58.2	58.9	59.9	61.0	60.7	61.0
2005	58.4	60.5	61.5	65.1	65.1	64.3	63.7	63.8	64.2	63.5	64.8	64.5	63.3
2006	65.6	66.1	67.0	67.4	66.9	66.7	62.6	63.2	64.4	65.4	65.4	66.8	65.6
2007	65.5	66.7	67.5	68.3	69.2	69.2	69.2	68.6	68.8	70.6	70.7	71.3	68.8
2008	66.2	67.0	67.5	67.3	67.7	68.2	67.1	68.3	67.8	69.0	69.5	69.9	68.0
2009	67.6	68.0	68.5	68.1	68.4	67.3	67.5	67.2	66.6	67.0	66.7	65.6	67.4
Mining and Logging													
2005	1.5	1.5	1.5	1.6	1.5	1.6	1.5	1.5	1.6	1.8	1.8	1.8	1.6
2006	1.6	1.6	1.6	1.5	1.5	1.5	1.5	1.4	1.5	1.4	1.4	1.4	1.5
2007	1.6	1.7	1.7	1.8	1.9	1.9	1.8	1.9	1.9	1.9	1.9	1.9	1.8
2008	1.6	1.6	1.7	1.7	1.7	1.7	1.6	1.6	1.6	1.6	1.6	1.6	1.6
2009	1.6	1.5	1.5	1.4	1.4	1.4	1.4	1.4	1.4	1.4	1.4	1.4	1.4
Construction													
2005	31.4	33.4	34.2	37.5	37.6	36.9	36.2	36.4	36.8	36.0	37.3	36.9	35.9
2006	38.5	39.0	39.7	40.4	39.9	39.5	36.0	36.6	37.5	38.5	38.4	39.7	38.6
2007	38.1	39.1	39.8	40.4	41.0	40.6	40.6	40.6	40.8	42.1	42.0	42.5	40.6
2008	38.8	39.4	39.8	39.6	39.9	40.4	39.5	40.7	40.4	41.3	41.8	42.0	40.3
2009	40.4	40.9	41.5	41.1	41.4	40.6	41.1	40.9	40.5	40.8	40.5	39.9	40.8
Manufacturing													
1990	26.1	26.3	26.4	26.6	26.8	27.1	27.3	27.5	27.4	27.5	27.7	27.5	27.0
2000	29.4	29.5	29.4	29.7	29.8	29.8	29.6	29.7	29.7	30.2	30.3	30.4	29.8
2001	30.2	30.1	30.2	29.9	30.1	30.3	29.9	30.0	29.9	29.9	29.7	29.6	30.0
2002	28.5	28.1	28.2	27.9	27.9	28.1	27.8	27.9	27.8	28.0	27.8	27.7	28.0
2003	27.5	27.4	27.5	27.4	27.5	27.5	26.9	26.8	26.8	27.1	27.0	27.0	27.2
2004	26.8	26.8	26.8	26.6	26.5	26.6	26.2	26.1	26.1	26.0	26.0	26.1	26.4
2005	25.5	25.6	25.8	26.0	26.0	25.8	26.0	25.9	25.8	25.7	25.7	25.8	25.8
2006	25.5	25.5	25.7	25.5	25.5	25.7	25.1	25.2	25.4	25.5	25.6	25.7	25.5
2007	25.8	25.9	26.0	26.1	26.3	26.7	26.8	26.1	26.1	26.6	26.8	26.9	26.3
2008	25.8	26.0	26.0	26.0	26.1	26.1	26.0	26.0	25.8	26.1	26.1	26.3	26.0
2009	25.6	25.6	25.5	25.6	25.6	25.3	25.0	24.9	24.7	24.8	24.8	24.3	25.1
Service-Providing													
1990	196.1	196.6	198.0	202.2	203.7	205.1	200.0	200.8	201.9	205.3	206.2	207.2	201.9
2000	264.3	266.0	267.1	271.1	271.3	274.4	264.7	265.2	271.5	269.7	271.4	272.6	269.1
2001	268.5	267.8	268.6	269.4	270.8	272.2	262.0	263.9	269.2	270.1	271.3	271.8	268.8
2002	268.3	270.2	271.9	272.9	274.4	274.7	266.9	268.5	273.2	273.1	276.0	276.4	272.2
2003	270.5	273.9	275.0	277.8	277.9	277.0	274.3	274.6	277.8	280.1	281.1	279.9	276.7
2004	273.9	277.9	279.6	282.6	281.2	282.5	281.0	280.6	282.2	282.4	284.7	283.8	281.0
2005	279.3	282.5	284.6	287.5	285.7	286.1	286.5	287.9	293.9	296.7	299.9	299.5	289.2
2006	290.5	295.4	297.7	295.7	296.3	292.2	287.3	293.3	297.0	296.8	298.5	299.4	295.0
2007	294.6	298.8	302.0	302.3	302.3	303.1	301.5	305.3	309.5	308.3	310.2	311.0	304.1
2008	303.5	307.7	308.6	306.9	306.3	306.4	302.7	304.3	301.7	308.3	310.8	311.0	306.5
2009	301.1	304.1	305.1	304.9	304.1	301.7	298.0	298.5	301.7	303.2	304.3	303.7	302.5

Employment by Industry: Baton Rouge, LA, Selected Years, 1990–2009—*Continued*

(Numbers in thousands, not seasonally adjusted.)

Industry and year	January	February	March	April	May	June	July	August	September	October	November	December	Annual average
Trade, Transportation, and Utilities													
1990	49.9	49.6	50.1	50.6	51.0	51.4	50.8	51.1	51.3	50.9	51.7	52.4	50.9
2000	65.1	65.2	65.7	66.0	66.1	66.9	66.7	66.8	67.2	66.7	68.3	69.1	66.7
2001	66.8	66.0	66.2	65.9	66.0	66.1	65.1	65.7	65.6	65.7	66.7	67.4	66.1
2002	65.1	65.1	65.3	65.8	65.9	66.0	65.5	65.9	65.8	65.4	67.1	67.9	65.9
2003	63.1	62.9	63.1	64.0	63.9	64.0	63.5	63.7	63.7	64.1	65.1	65.9	63.9
2004	63.3	63.2	63.5	63.6	63.7	64.0	63.3	63.4	63.2	63.2	64.3	64.9	63.6
2005	62.3	62.3	62.8	63.1	63.6	63.7	64.7	64.9	65.7	66.5	68.6	69.4	64.8
2006	66.4	66.2	67.0	66.1	66.5	66.3	65.6	65.6	65.8	65.9	67.2	68.2	66.4
2007	65.7	65.5	66.3	65.4	65.9	66.1	66.7	67.2	67.6	67.7	69.4	70.2	67.0
2008	67.7	67.1	67.7	66.7	66.8	66.9	66.8	67.3	66.4	66.8	67.9	68.8	67.2
2009	66.1	65.5	65.6	65.4	65.3	64.7	64.3	64.3	64.1	64.1	65.3	65.6	65.0
Wholesale Trade													
1990	10.8	10.8	10.9	11.0	11.0	11.0	11.1	11.1	11.1	10.9	11.0	11.0	11.0
2000	13.9	13.9	14.0	14.2	14.2	14.4	14.2	14.2	14.1	14.0	14.0	14.1	14.1
2001	14.1	14.2	14.3	14.2	14.2	14.3	14.1	14.0	14.1	14.0	14.0	14.0	14.1
2002	13.7	13.7	13.7	13.6	13.7	13.8	13.7	13.7	13.7	13.5	13.6	13.6	13.7
2003	13.5	13.4	13.5	13.4	13.4	13.5	13.4	13.4	13.4	13.3	13.3	13.2	13.4
2004	13.2	13.2	13.3	13.3	13.2	13.2	12.9	13.0	12.9	12.6	12.7	12.8	13.0
2005	12.6	12.5	12.6	12.7	12.8	12.8	13.1	13.1	13.1	12.9	12.9	13.0	12.8
2006	12.7	12.7	12.8	12.8	12.9	13.0	12.9	12.8	12.9	12.9	13.0	13.0	12.9
2007	13.2	13.2	13.3	13.2	13.3	13.5	13.7	13.8	13.8	13.8	13.9	14.0	13.6
2008	13.6	13.6	13.7	13.4	13.5	13.4	13.4	13.4	13.5	13.5	13.4	13.4	13.5
2009	13.2	13.2	13.1	13.1	13.0	12.8	12.7	12.7	12.7	12.6	12.6	12.6	12.9
Retail Trade													
1990	32.4	32.0	32.2	32.7	33.1	33.4	32.6	32.8	32.9	32.7	33.4	34.1	32.9
2000	39.4	39.4	40.0	39.8	39.9	40.2	40.0	40.2	40.7	40.2	41.7	42.4	40.3
2001	40.1	39.2	39.3	38.9	39.0	38.9	38.5	39.1	38.9	39.0	40.1	40.7	39.3
2002	38.7	38.4	38.4	38.5	38.4	38.3	38.0	38.2	38.2	38.0	39.5	40.3	38.6
2003	36.4	36.2	36.3	37.1	36.9	37.0	36.7	36.8	36.7	37.2	38.1	39.0	37.0
2004	37.0	36.8	37.0	37.2	37.4	37.8	37.5	37.5	37.5	37.8	38.9	39.5	37.7
2005	37.5	37.5	37.9	37.9	38.2	38.4	39.1	39.3	40.1	41.1	43.0	43.6	39.5
2006	41.5	41.2	41.9	41.1	41.2	40.9	40.2	40.3	40.3	40.5	41.6	42.4	41.1
2007	40.3	40.0	40.8	40.0	40.3	40.3	40.6	40.7	41.0	41.4	42.9	43.6	41.0
2008	41.5	40.9	41.4	40.8	40.7	41.0	40.9	41.1	40.2	40.9	42.1	42.9	41.2
2009	40.6	40.3	40.5	40.6	40.6	40.5	40.1	39.9	39.7	39.9	41.1	41.3	40.4
Transportation and Utilities													
1990	6.7	6.8	7.0	6.9	6.9	7.0	7.1	7.2	7.3	7.3	7.3	7.3	7.1
2000	11.8	11.9	11.7	12.0	12.0	12.3	12.5	12.4	12.4	12.5	12.6	12.6	12.2
2001	12.6	12.6	12.6	12.8	12.8	12.9	12.5	12.6	12.6	12.7	12.6	12.7	12.7
2002	12.7	13.0	13.2	13.7	13.8	13.9	13.8	14.0	13.9	13.9	14.0	14.0	13.7
2003	13.2	13.3	13.3	13.5	13.6	13.5	13.4	13.5	13.6	13.6	13.7	13.7	13.5
2004	13.1	13.2	13.2	13.1	13.1	13.0	12.9	12.9	12.8	12.8	12.7	12.6	13.0
2005	12.2	12.3	12.3	12.5	12.6	12.5	12.5	12.5	12.5	12.5	12.7	12.8	12.5
2006	12.2	12.3	12.3	12.2	12.4	12.4	12.5	12.5	12.6	12.5	12.6	12.8	12.4
2007	12.2	12.3	12.2	12.2	12.3	12.3	12.4	12.7	12.8	12.5	12.6	12.6	12.4
2008	12.6	12.6	12.6	12.5	12.6	12.5	12.5	12.8	12.7	12.4	12.4	12.5	12.6
2009	12.3	12.0	12.0	11.7	11.7	11.4	11.5	11.7	11.7	11.6	11.6	11.7	11.7
Information													
1990	4.1	4.2	4.1	4.0	4.1	4.1	4.1	4.1	4.1	4.0	4.0	4.0	4.1
2000	4.8	4.8	5.0	5.3	5.2	5.3	5.5	5.6	5.6	5.6	5.6	5.6	5.3
2001	5.2	5.2	5.3	5.7	5.7	5.7	5.5	5.5	5.4	5.3	5.2	5.2	5.4
2002	5.2	5.2	5.3	5.0	5.1	5.1	5.2	5.2	5.2	5.0	5.0	5.0	5.1
2003	4.9	4.9	5.0	5.2	5.3	5.3	5.4	5.6	5.6	5.6	5.6	5.7	5.3
2004	5.6	5.6	5.6	5.6	5.6	5.6	5.5	5.5	5.4	5.4	5.5	5.5	5.5
2005	5.8	5.7	5.7	5.9	5.6	5.5	5.6	5.5	5.4	5.4	5.6	5.5	5.6
2006	5.6	5.6	5.7	5.7	5.6	5.5	5.4	5.3	5.2	5.4	5.5	5.4	5.5
2007	5.5	5.5	5.5	5.7	5.8	5.6	6.0	5.9	5.8	6.6	5.9	5.8	5.8
2008	5.6	6.0	5.8	6.4	6.2	6.4	5.8	5.8	5.6	5.6	6.0	6.0	5.9
2009	5.5	5.4	5.3	5.1	5.1	4.9	4.9	4.8	4.7	4.7	4.7	4.7	5.0
Financial Activities													
1990	11.1	11.0	11.1	11.3	11.3	11.5	11.3	11.3	11.3	11.3	11.3	11.3	11.3
2000	15.8	15.9	16.0	16.2	16.2	16.4	16.0	16.0	16.0	15.8	15.8	16.0	16.0
2001	16.0	16.1	16.1	16.4	16.3	16.5	16.4	16.5	16.4	16.3	16.5	16.5	16.3
2002	16.7	16.7	16.5	17.0	17.0	17.0	17.1	17.2	17.0	17.3	17.2	17.4	17.0
2003	16.7	16.8	16.8	17.4	17.3	17.4	17.5	17.6	17.6	17.9	17.9	18.0	17.4
2004	17.9	17.9	18.0	18.2	18.2	18.2	18.1	18.1	17.9	17.8	17.8	18.0	18.0
2005	17.9	18.0	18.0	18.1	18.2	18.2	18.5	18.5	18.5	18.5	18.6	18.7	18.3
2006	18.5	18.5	18.6	18.6	18.6	18.6	18.4	18.5	18.5	18.7	18.7	18.8	18.6
2007	19.1	19.2	18.9	18.9	18.8	18.8	18.7	18.7	18.5	18.4	18.5	18.6	18.8
2008	18.3	18.3	18.4	18.2	18.2	18.3	18.1	18.1	17.9	18.0	17.9	17.9	18.1
2009	17.5	17.4	17.4	17.3	17.4	17.3	17.1	17.1	16.9	16.9	16.9	16.8	17.2

Employment by Industry: Baton Rouge, LA, Selected Years, 1990–2009—*Continued*

(Numbers in thousands, not seasonally adjusted.)

Industry and year	January	February	March	April	May	June	July	August	September	October	November	December	Annual average
Professional and Business Services													
1990	24.1	24.1	24.5	24.9	25.2	25.4	26.0	26.4	26.4	26.2	26.4	26.6	25.5
2000	38.9	39.6	39.6	40.2	40.2	40.7	40.0	40.3	40.7	40.5	40.5	40.4	40.1
2001	40.3	39.6	39.5	39.1	39.0	39.6	38.8	39.2	39.0	39.3	39.1	39.6	39.3
2002	39.0	39.0	39.2	39.1	38.9	38.9	38.7	38.8	38.4	38.6	38.6	38.7	38.8
2003	37.6	37.2	37.6	38.3	37.9	37.9	37.2	37.3	36.7	36.8	36.9	37.0	37.4
2004	36.8	37.2	37.5	38.1	37.3	37.6	37.6	37.4	36.9	36.6	36.8	36.8	37.2
2005	37.6	37.7	38.1	39.7	38.5	38.4	38.8	39.1	40.5	41.3	42.0	42.4	39.5
2006	41.1	41.8	42.3	42.7	42.7	43.0	42.5	42.6	43.1	43.4	43.0	43.8	42.7
2007	43.8	44.2	44.9	45.1	44.4	45.0	45.4	45.8	46.3	46.7	47.0	47.3	45.5
2008	47.0	46.7	46.7	45.9	45.8	45.8	44.9	45.2	45.6	46.3	46.3	46.4	46.1
2009	44.8	44.7	44.7	44.0	43.9	43.6	42.3	42.4	41.8	42.4	42.0	42.2	43.2
Education and Health Services													
1990	20.6	20.8	21.0	21.7	21.9	21.9	21.9	22.2	22.9	23.5	23.7	23.7	22.2
2000	34.9	35.0	35.0	35.6	35.4	35.6	34.9	35.1	35.5	35.2	35.2	35.4	35.2
2001	34.8	34.9	35.0	34.9	35.0	35.0	34.8	35.1	35.5	35.4	35.6	35.5	35.1
2002	34.9	35.1	35.5	35.2	35.4	35.6	35.5	36.0	36.4	36.0	36.3	36.4	35.7
2003	35.8	36.1	36.1	36.2	36.4	36.5	37.2	37.4	37.7	38.1	38.1	38.2	37.0
2004	37.7	38.0	38.0	38.5	38.5	38.5	38.9	39.0	39.2	39.4	39.5	39.5	38.7
2005	39.4	39.6	39.7	40.1	40.4	40.4	41.3	41.2	41.6	42.4	42.4	42.0	40.9
2006	41.7	42.1	42.4	42.8	43.0	43.2	42.8	43.3	43.7	43.9	43.8	43.7	43.0
2007	42.9	43.3	43.5	44.0	44.6	44.5	44.3	44.8	44.7	44.3	44.4	44.8	44.2
2008	44.2	44.8	45.0	45.2	45.3	45.6	45.6	46.2	45.3	46.0	46.1	46.3	45.5
2009	45.7	46.2	46.4	48.0	47.7	47.5	46.9	47.1	47.4	47.8	47.9	47.9	47.2
Leisure and Hospitality													
1990	16.7	16.9	17.1	17.6	17.9	18.7	18.4	18.5	18.4	18.0	17.8	17.9	17.8
2000	26.8	27.3	27.6	28.5	28.7	29.5	28.8	28.8	28.7	27.7	27.9	28.2	28.2
2001	27.1	27.6	28.1	28.3	29.1	29.0	28.6	28.8	28.8	28.4	28.1	27.9	28.3
2002	26.8	27.3	27.9	28.3	28.8	29.0	29.0	29.1	28.6	27.9	28.0	27.7	28.2
2003	28.3	29.1	29.3	29.9	30.1	30.0	29.8	29.9	30.0	30.0	30.0	29.7	29.7
2004	28.9	29.2	29.9	30.2	30.7	31.1	30.9	30.9	30.7	30.6	31.2	31.2	30.5
2005	30.2	30.5	31.1	31.5	31.9	32.4	32.0	32.0	32.6	32.0	31.7	31.7	31.6
2006	31.3	32.4	32.7	32.3	32.8	33.2	32.1	32.5	32.7	31.7	32.0	32.1	32.3
2007	31.3	32.0	33.0	32.5	33.0	33.4	32.9	32.8	33.2	32.3	32.3	32.1	32.6
2008	31.7	32.5	32.9	33.3	33.6	33.5	33.2	33.3	32.1	32.9	33.4	33.4	33.0
2009	32.0	32.6	33.3	33.2	33.8	33.6	33.2	33.5	33.2	33.1	33.2	33.3	33.2
Other Services													
1990	7.4	7.6	7.7	7.7	7.8	7.9	7.9	7.8	7.9	7.9	7.9	7.9	7.8
2000	11.6	11.7	11.8	11.9	12.1	12.1	12.1	12.1	12.1	11.7	11.7	11.7	11.9
2001	11.8	11.9	11.9	12.2	12.2	12.4	12.1	12.1	12.2	12.2	11.9	11.9	12.1
2002	12.2	12.3	12.4	12.7	12.9	13.0	13.2	13.0	12.9	12.9	12.9	12.8	12.8
2003	12.8	12.8	12.8	13.0	13.1	13.1	12.8	12.8	12.8	13.1	13.0	12.9	12.9
2004	12.6	12.7	12.8	13.7	13.7	14.0	14.1	14.0	14.0	13.7	13.8	13.7	13.6
2005	13.5	13.5	13.8	13.8	13.8	14.0	14.1	14.1	14.1	13.7	13.6	13.7	13.8
2006	13.4	13.6	13.6	13.6	13.7	14.0	13.8	13.8	14.0	13.6	13.7	13.8	13.7
2007	13.8	13.9	14.0	13.9	13.8	14.1	14.3	14.2	14.2	13.9	13.7	13.8	14.0
2008	13.5	13.8	13.9	13.1	13.2	13.3	13.4	13.1	12.8	13.5	13.5	13.4	13.4
2009	13.2	13.2	13.2	13.2	13.3	13.5	13.7	13.6	13.8	13.5	13.5	13.3	13.4
Government													
1990	62.2	62.4	62.4	64.4	64.5	64.2	59.6	59.4	59.6	63.5	63.4	63.4	62.4
2000	66.4	66.5	66.4	67.4	67.4	67.9	60.7	60.5	65.7	66.5	66.4	66.2	65.7
2001	66.5	66.5	66.5	66.9	67.5	67.9	60.7	61.0	66.3	67.5	68.2	67.8	66.1
2002	68.4	69.5	69.8	69.8	70.4	70.1	62.7	63.3	68.9	70.0	70.9	70.5	68.7
2003	71.3	74.1	74.3	73.8	73.9	72.8	70.9	70.3	73.7	74.5	74.5	72.5	73.1
2004	71.1	74.1	74.3	74.7	73.5	73.5	72.6	72.3	74.9	75.7	75.8	74.2	73.9
2005	72.6	75.2	75.4	75.3	73.7	73.5	71.5	72.6	75.5	76.9	77.4	76.1	74.6
2006	72.5	75.2	75.4	73.9	73.4	68.4	66.7	71.7	74.0	74.2	74.6	73.6	72.8
2007	72.5	75.2	75.9	76.8	76.0	75.6	73.2	75.9	79.2	78.4	79.0	78.4	76.3
2008	75.5	78.5	78.2	78.1	77.2	76.6	74.9	75.3	76.0	79.2	79.7	78.8	77.3
2009	76.3	79.1	79.2	78.7	77.6	76.6	75.6	75.7	79.8	80.7	80.8	79.9	78.3

Employment by Industry: Birmingham-Hoover, AL, Selected Years, 1990–2009

(Numbers in thousands, not seasonally adjusted.)

Industry and year	January	February	March	April	May	June	July	August	September	October	November	December	Annual average
Total Nonfarm													
1990	422.7	424.3	426.3	429.7	431.5	432.7	431.7	429.6	433.0	434.1	434.1	435.9	430.5
2000	509.4	511.3	514.8	514.8	518.3	518.3	516.3	515.4	519.6	520.2	522.0	522.7	516.9
2001	513.4	514.1	517.4	517.6	518.8	520.2	513.8	513.0	513.2	514.5	516.1	517.2	515.8
2002	506.5	507.1	510.2	509.7	510.2	509.4	507.5	506.4	508.1	508.6	511.5	511.1	508.9
2003	498.9	501.0	503.5	504.5	505.3	504.8	503.4	504.8	506.0	508.3	511.1	513.1	505.4
2004	503.5	505.4	508.2	509.9	510.6	511.6	510.2	509.8	510.3	513.2	516.5	517.7	510.6
2005	509.1	511.1	514.0	517.7	518.3	519.1	517.7	518.2	520.3	521.5	524.4	525.3	518.1
2006	517.8	520.0	523.1	525.6	527.6	531.8	526.9	528.3	530.3	530.2	533.1	534.1	527.4
2007	526.4	528.9	532.2	529.1	532.1	534.5	529.5	531.2	532.2	532.5	535.6	536.9	531.8
2008	525.4	526.9	527.7	529.5	531.8	533.0	527.5	527.5	526.1	525.7	524.2	523.3	527.4
2009	505.7	504.0	502.4	500.5	500.9	499.5	493.1	490.9	490.2	489.7	489.8	487.1	496.2
Total Private													
1990	355.8	357.1	358.9	361.6	362.9	367.3	364.9	366.1	364.5	364.6	364.4	365.9	362.8
2000	434.3	436.0	438.9	438.9	440.9	444.3	443.4	444.0	444.5	444.0	446.0	446.5	441.8
2001	437.6	437.8	441.1	441.5	442.4	444.9	440.7	440.3	437.9	437.9	439.4	440.6	440.2
2002	430.5	430.8	433.6	433.0	433.1	433.5	434.2	433.5	431.7	430.9	433.3	432.9	432.6
2003	421.4	422.9	425.1	425.5	426.2	427.6	428.0	429.3	427.7	429.5	432.0	433.7	427.4
2004	424.5	426.3	429.3	430.4	431.5	433.3	433.7	433.3	431.6	434.1	436.9	438.2	431.9
2005	430.3	431.8	434.5	437.9	438.4	439.7	440.8	440.7	440.6	440.8	443.5	444.6	438.6
2006	436.4	438.4	441.4	443.4	445.2	449.5	447.8	448.7	448.0	447.2	449.9	450.8	445.6
2007	443.5	445.6	448.7	445.6	448.3	450.9	449.5	450.5	448.9	448.6	451.5	452.9	448.7
2008	441.8	442.9	443.5	445.1	447.1	448.3	446.4	445.9	442.5	440.7	439.3	438.1	443.5
2009	421.2	419.4	417.8	415.5	416.1	414.7	412.7	410.3	407.6	406.4	406.4	404.0	412.7
Goods-Producing													
1990	85.1	86.5	85.9	87.9	88.5	89.6	88.2	88.5	87.9	87.0	85.6	85.1	87.2
2000	86.5	86.9	87.6	88.6	89.1	90.1	89.6	89.6	89.7	89.2	89.0	88.5	88.7
2001	87.2	86.4	87.2	86.8	86.6	86.6	84.8	84.5	83.9	83.5	82.9	82.8	85.3
2002	80.1	79.4	80.1	80.7	80.4	80.4	80.2	80.3	79.9	80.4	80.0	79.2	80.1
2003	77.7	77.7	78.4	78.4	78.3	78.2	78.2	78.7	78.5	79.9	80.1	80.0	78.7
2004	78.4	79.0	79.5	79.3	79.1	78.9	79.0	78.9	79.0	80.0	80.0	79.8	79.2
2005	78.4	78.4	78.7	79.7	79.4	79.3	80.1	80.4	80.5	80.9	81.1	80.6	79.8
2006	79.7	79.9	80.6	81.3	82.0	82.9	82.8	82.5	82.9	82.5	82.1	81.8	81.8
2007	81.1	81.7	82.2	81.4	81.5	82.2	81.5	81.8	81.7	81.2	80.7	80.5	81.5
2008	79.0	79.0	78.6	78.9	79.2	79.3	79.4	78.6	78.2	76.6	75.5	74.5	78.1
2009	70.4	69.3	68.6	67.1	66.8	66.1	65.7	65.2	64.6	64.3	63.3	63.3	66.2
Mining and Logging													
1990	2.9	2.9	2.9	2.9	3.1	3.2	3.0	3.0	2.9	2.9	2.8	2.8	2.9
2000	3.0	3.0	3.1	3.2	3.2	3.4	3.3	3.3	3.4	3.3	3.3	3.2	3.2
2001	3.1	3.2	3.2	3.3	3.3	3.3	3.3	3.3	3.3	3.3	3.2	3.2	3.3
2002	3.0	3.0	3.1	3.2	3.2	3.2	3.1	3.2	3.2	3.4	3.4	3.2	3.2
2003	3.1	3.0	3.0	3.0	3.0	3.0	2.9	2.8	2.8	2.8	2.8	2.8	2.9
2004	2.7	2.7	2.7	2.8	2.8	2.9	2.9	3.0	3.0	3.0	3.0	3.1	2.9
2005	3.0	3.0	3.1	3.1	3.2	3.2	3.3	3.3	3.3	3.3	3.3	3.3	3.2
2006	3.1	3.1	3.1	3.0	3.1	3.1	3.2	3.1	3.2	3.1	3.1	3.2	3.1
2007	3.1	3.1	3.1	3.0	3.0	3.0	2.9	3.0	3.0	3.0	3.0	3.1	3.0
2008	3.0	3.0	3.0	3.0	3.0	3.0	3.1	3.1	3.1	3.1	3.1	3.1	3.1
2009	2.9	2.9	2.9	2.9	2.9	2.9	2.8	2.7	2.8	2.8	2.8	2.9	2.9
Construction													
1990	26.9	27.0	27.3	27.4	27.6	28.0	27.7	27.9	27.4	27.2	26.9	26.9	27.4
2000	31.0	31.2	31.6	31.9	32.2	32.9	33.0	33.0	33.1	32.6	32.6	32.5	32.3
2001	31.9	31.9	32.5	32.6	32.8	33.0	32.4	32.3	32.1	32.0	31.8	31.9	32.3
2002	30.3	30.6	31.0	31.7	31.6	31.4	31.8	31.8	31.7	32.2	32.0	31.5	31.5
2003	31.1	31.3	32.0	32.1	31.9	31.9	32.6	33.3	33.3	34.8	34.8	34.5	32.8
2004	34.0	34.5	34.9	34.3	33.8	33.3	33.3	33.1	33.2	33.9	33.6	33.1	33.8
2005	32.4	32.6	32.6	33.6	32.9	32.7	33.3	33.3	33.3	34.1	34.0	33.4	33.2
2006	33.0	33.0	33.7	34.3	34.6	35.2	34.8	34.9	35.0	34.9	34.7	34.2	34.4
2007	33.8	34.3	34.8	34.1	34.1	34.4	34.2	34.4	34.7	34.7	34.2	33.9	34.3
2008	33.2	33.0	32.9	33.4	33.8	33.5	33.7	33.2	32.8	31.7	31.0	30.6	32.7
2009	28.5	28.0	28.0	27.0	27.1	27.2	27.1	26.6	26.1	26.0	25.1	25.0	26.8
Manufacturing													
1990	55.3	56.6	55.7	57.6	57.8	58.4	57.5	57.6	57.6	56.9	55.9	55.4	56.9
2000	52.5	52.7	52.9	53.5	53.7	53.8	53.3	53.3	53.2	53.3	53.1	52.8	53.2
2001	52.3	51.3	51.5	50.8	50.4	50.3	49.2	48.9	48.5	48.2	47.8	47.7	49.7
2002	46.8	45.8	46.0	45.8	45.6	45.8	45.2	45.3	45.0	44.7	44.7	44.5	45.4
2003	43.5	43.4	43.4	43.3	43.4	43.3	42.7	42.6	42.4	42.3	42.5	42.7	43.0
2004	41.7	41.8	41.9	42.2	42.5	42.7	42.8	42.8	42.8	43.1	43.4	43.6	42.6
2005	43.0	42.8	43.0	43.0	43.3	43.4	43.5	43.8	43.9	43.5	43.8	43.9	43.4
2006	43.6	43.8	43.8	44.0	44.3	44.6	44.8	44.5	44.7	44.5	44.3	44.4	44.3
2007	44.2	44.3	44.3	44.3	44.4	44.9	44.4	44.4	44.0	43.5	43.5	43.5	44.1
2008	42.8	43.0	42.7	42.5	42.4	42.8	42.6	42.3	42.3	41.8	41.4	40.8	42.3
2009	39.0	38.4	37.7	37.2	36.8	36.0	35.8	35.9	35.7	35.5	35.4	35.4	36.6

Employment by Industry: Birmingham-Hoover, AL, Selected Years, 1990–2009—*Continued*

(Numbers in thousands, not seasonally adjusted.)

Industry and year	January	February	March	April	May	June	July	August	September	October	November	December	Annual average
Service-Providing													
1990	337.6	337.8	340.4	341.8	343.0	343.1	343.5	341.1	345.1	347.1	348.5	350.8	343.3
2000	422.9	424.4	427.2	426.2	429.2	428.2	426.7	425.8	429.9	431.0	433.0	434.2	428.2
2001	426.2	427.7	430.2	430.8	432.2	433.6	429.0	428.5	429.3	431.0	433.2	434.4	430.5
2002	426.4	427.7	430.1	429.0	429.8	429.0	427.3	426.1	428.2	428.2	431.5	431.9	428.8
2003	421.2	423.3	425.1	426.1	427.0	426.6	425.2	426.1	427.5	428.4	431.0	433.1	426.7
2004	425.1	426.4	428.7	430.6	431.5	432.7	431.2	430.9	431.3	433.2	436.5	437.9	431.3
2005	430.7	432.7	435.3	438.0	438.9	439.8	437.6	437.8	439.8	440.6	443.3	444.7	438.3
2006	438.1	440.1	442.5	444.3	445.6	448.9	444.1	445.8	447.4	447.7	451.0	452.3	445.7
2007	445.3	447.2	450.0	447.7	450.6	452.3	448.0	449.4	450.5	451.3	454.9	456.4	450.3
2008	446.4	447.9	449.1	450.6	452.6	453.7	448.1	448.9	447.9	449.1	448.7	448.8	449.3
2009	435.3	434.7	433.8	433.4	434.1	433.4	427.4	425.7	425.6	425.4	426.5	423.8	429.9
Trade, Transportation, and Utilities													
1990	98.5	97.2	97.6	96.8	97.1	98.0	97.6	97.9	97.9	98.2	99.5	101.0	98.1
2000	114.1	113.3	113.6	112.4	113.3	113.4	112.9	112.9	114.0	114.4	116.4	117.4	114.0
2001	113.6	112.4	113.0	112.0	112.7	113.2	112.0	111.8	111.1	111.5	113.6	114.9	112.7
2002	110.9	110.2	110.7	109.3	109.7	109.6	109.9	109.8	108.9	109.6	112.0	113.5	110.3
2003	108.9	108.5	109.0	108.8	109.2	109.8	110.4	110.5	110.3	111.0	112.9	114.4	110.3
2004	110.9	110.8	111.5	111.3	111.6	111.6	111.2	111.1	110.7	111.3	113.4	115.3	111.7
2005	110.5	110.2	110.6	111.0	111.3	111.7	111.4	111.8	111.6	112.2	114.0	115.7	111.8
2006	112.4	112.1	112.9	112.9	113.3	114.0	113.5	114.0	113.8	115.0	117.2	118.7	114.2
2007	114.7	114.4	115.5	114.5	115.5	116.4	116.2	115.8	115.9	116.1	118.4	119.7	116.1
2008	115.7	115.1	115.5	115.2	115.2	115.3	114.9	115.0	114.4	114.2	115.2	115.9	115.1
2009	110.4	109.4	108.8	107.9	107.9	107.4	106.6	106.2	105.6	106.0	106.8	106.9	107.5
Wholesale Trade													
1990	27.3	27.2	27.2	26.9	26.8	26.9	26.7	26.8	26.8	27.0	26.9	26.9	27.0
2000	31.1	31.2	31.3	30.6	30.7	30.8	30.8	30.8	31.0	30.9	31.0	31.0	30.9
2001	31.0	31.1	31.2	30.9	30.9	30.9	30.6	30.4	30.4	30.1	30.0	29.9	30.6
2002	29.9	29.8	29.8	29.6	29.5	29.5	29.5	29.6	29.3	29.2	29.3	29.3	29.5
2003	29.0	29.0	29.0	29.0	29.1	29.2	29.4	29.3	29.4	29.6	29.8	30.0	29.3
2004	29.7	29.8	29.9	29.9	30.1	30.1	30.2	30.3	30.1	30.2	30.3	30.4	30.1
2005	30.1	30.2	30.2	30.3	30.2	30.3	30.4	30.5	30.6	30.4	30.4	30.6	30.4
2006	30.6	30.8	31.0	31.1	31.2	31.5	31.5	31.6	31.5	31.5	31.6	31.7	31.3
2007	31.4	31.6	31.8	31.4	31.4	31.7	31.5	31.5	31.6	31.6	31.7	31.8	31.6
2008	31.5	31.6	31.6	31.6	31.6	31.5	31.4	31.5	31.5	31.5	31.2	31.2	31.5
2009	30.4	30.2	30.0	29.7	29.6	29.4	29.2	29.2	28.9	29.0	28.7	28.5	29.4
Retail Trade													
1990	50.1	49.0	49.4	49.1	49.3	49.9	49.8	50.1	50.2	50.2	51.7	53.2	50.2
2000	61.5	60.8	61.0	60.9	61.4	61.7	61.0	61.2	62.0	62.5	64.3	65.4	62.0
2001	61.6	60.3	60.8	60.2	60.8	61.3	60.5	60.5	60.0	60.6	62.9	64.1	61.1
2002	61.1	60.6	61.0	60.1	60.3	60.3	60.6	60.3	59.8	60.7	62.9	64.3	61.0
2003	60.4	60.0	60.5	60.5	60.7	61.1	61.5	61.9	61.8	62.1	63.8	65.1	61.6
2004	62.0	61.8	62.3	62.1	62.2	62.1	61.5	61.3	61.2	61.7	63.7	65.3	62.3
2005	61.5	61.0	61.2	61.5	61.8	62.0	61.7	62.0	61.6	62.2	64.1	65.5	62.2
2006	62.3	61.8	62.3	62.0	62.2	62.3	61.7	62.0	61.8	62.7	64.8	66.0	62.7
2007	62.8	62.2	62.9	62.4	63.2	63.6	63.4	62.9	62.8	63.1	65.2	66.2	63.4
2008	63.0	62.4	62.8	62.3	62.3	62.5	62.1	61.9	61.4	61.5	62.9	63.6	62.4
2009	59.3	58.6	58.4	58.0	58.2	57.9	57.6	57.1	56.8	57.0	58.2	58.4	58.0
Transportation and Utilities													
1990	20.6	20.5	20.5	20.3	20.5	20.7	20.6	20.5	20.4	20.5	20.4	20.4	20.5
2000	21.0	20.8	20.8	20.4	20.7	20.4	20.6	20.4	20.5	20.5	20.6	20.5	20.6
2001	20.5	20.5	20.5	20.4	20.5	20.5	20.4	20.4	20.2	20.3	20.2	20.4	20.4
2002	19.4	19.3	19.4	19.1	19.4	19.3	19.3	19.4	19.3	19.2	19.3	19.4	19.3
2003	19.0	19.0	19.0	18.8	18.9	19.0	19.0	18.8	18.6	18.8	18.8	18.8	18.8
2004	18.7	18.7	18.8	18.8	18.8	18.9	19.0	19.0	18.9	18.9	18.9	19.1	18.9
2005	18.9	19.0	19.2	19.2	19.3	19.4	19.3	19.3	19.4	19.6	19.5	19.6	19.3
2006	19.5	19.5	19.6	19.8	19.9	20.2	20.3	20.4	20.5	20.8	20.8	21.0	20.2
2007	20.5	20.6	20.8	20.7	20.9	21.1	21.3	21.4	21.5	21.4	21.5	21.7	21.1
2008	21.2	21.1	21.1	21.3	21.3	21.3	21.4	21.6	21.5	21.2	21.1	21.1	21.3
2009	20.7	20.6	20.4	20.2	20.1	20.1	19.8	19.9	19.9	20.0	19.9	20.0	20.1
Information													
1990	14.2	14.1	14.2	14.3	14.4	14.5	14.5	14.6	14.4	14.3	14.3	14.2	14.3
2000	14.3	14.3	14.4	14.1	14.1	14.3	14.7	14.8	14.7	15.0	15.1	15.2	14.6
2001	15.1	15.2	15.4	15.3	15.4	15.4	15.3	15.3	15.1	15.2	15.2	15.1	15.3
2002	15.1	15.0	15.2	15.0	14.9	14.9	15.0	14.8	14.6	14.8	14.7	14.5	14.9
2003	14.1	14.1	14.0	13.2	13.1	13.2	13.2	13.1	13.1	13.1	13.2	13.2	13.4
2004	13.2	13.0	13.1	13.1	13.1	13.2	13.2	13.0	12.8	12.9	13.0	12.9	13.0
2005	12.9	12.8	12.8	12.8	12.7	12.7	12.7	12.6	12.7	12.6	12.5	12.5	12.7
2006	12.2	12.1	12.2	12.0	12.0	12.0	11.9	11.8	11.7	11.7	11.7	11.7	11.9
2007	11.6	11.6	11.6	11.5	11.5	11.5	11.4	11.5	11.4	11.3	11.4	11.4	11.5
2008	11.1	11.1	11.2	11.2	11.2	11.1	11.0	11.1	10.9	10.9	10.8	10.8	11.0
2009	10.5	10.4	10.4	10.2	10.2	10.1	10.0	9.9	9.8	9.8	9.7	9.7	10.1

Employment by Industry: Birmingham-Hoover, AL, Selected Years, 1990–2009—*Continued*

(Numbers in thousands, not seasonally adjusted.)

Industry and year	January	February	March	April	May	June	July	August	September	October	November	December	Annual average
Financial Activities													
1990	32.8	32.9	33.1	33.1	33.1	33.4	33.3	33.1	33.0	32.5	32.2	32.5	32.9
2000	40.3	40.4	40.5	40.7	40.7	40.9	41.4	41.4	41.2	40.9	40.9	41.0	40.9
2001	40.5	40.7	40.7	41.1	41.2	41.5	41.4	41.5	41.2	41.2	41.1	41.2	41.1
2002	41.0	40.8	40.7	40.8	41.0	41.0	41.0	41.0	40.8	40.9	41.0	41.2	40.9
2003	40.1	40.0	39.9	40.2	40.2	40.4	40.5	40.3	40.2	40.2	40.3	40.4	40.2
2004	40.0	40.1	40.1	40.1	40.2	40.4	40.3	40.3	40.1	40.4	40.4	40.5	40.2
2005	39.9	40.1	40.3	40.4	40.3	40.4	40.4	40.2	40.2	40.4	40.5	40.7	40.3
2006	39.9	40.0	40.0	40.0	40.0	40.1	40.1	40.0	39.8	40.0	40.2	40.4	40.0
2007	40.1	40.2	40.4	39.4	39.6	39.8	39.7	39.7	39.8	39.8	40.0	40.1	39.9
2008	39.5	39.6	39.7	39.7	39.6	39.6	39.8	39.9	39.4	39.3	39.2	39.2	39.5
2009	38.8	38.9	38.7	38.5	38.5	38.4	38.1	37.9	37.7	37.7	37.7	37.8	38.2
Professional and Business Services													
1990	38.7	39.0	40.2	40.0	40.1	41.1	41.0	41.3	40.9	41.7	41.5	41.8	40.6
2000	61.6	62.1	62.6	62.9	62.7	63.6	63.3	63.8	64.0	63.5	63.5	63.2	63.1
2001	62.4	62.7	63.4	63.9	64.0	64.8	64.5	64.6	64.2	64.2	64.0	64.0	63.9
2002	62.8	63.0	63.8	63.6	63.2	63.4	62.4	62.6	62.1	61.5	61.3	61.0	62.6
2003	59.6	60.2	60.5	60.3	60.4	60.7	60.8	61.3	60.8	61.0	60.8	61.0	60.6
2004	59.7	59.9	60.1	60.8	61.2	61.8	62.7	62.8	62.6	63.4	63.5	63.6	61.8
2005	63.7	64.5	64.8	65.2	65.2	65.4	66.4	66.2	66.7	67.1	67.5	67.5	65.9
2006	66.8	67.2	67.7	67.9	67.7	69.0	68.6	69.1	69.2	68.9	69.0	69.1	68.4
2007	68.1	68.8	68.7	68.0	68.1	68.3	67.5	67.9	67.7	67.8	68.5	68.1	68.1
2008	66.3	66.6	66.2	66.5	66.7	67.0	65.9	65.9	65.6	65.6	65.4	64.9	66.1
2009	62.0	61.6	61.0	60.6	60.2	60.0	59.2	58.8	58.4	58.6	59.1	58.7	59.9
Education and Health Services													
1990	42.2	42.6	42.7	43.0	42.9	43.1	43.0	43.0	43.6	44.2	44.6	44.6	43.3
2000	54.5	55.1	55.2	55.4	55.4	55.3	56.1	56.2	56.4	56.6	56.8	56.6	55.8
2001	55.6	56.5	56.6	57.0	56.8	56.6	56.5	56.3	57.0	57.5	58.1	58.0	56.9
2002	57.1	58.3	58.5	58.7	58.4	58.2	59.6	59.1	60.2	59.9	60.2	59.7	59.0
2003	59.0	59.8	60.1	60.1	59.8	59.4	59.4	59.5	59.7	60.1	60.7	60.5	59.8
2004	59.8	60.4	60.7	60.8	60.6	60.5	60.5	60.6	61.0	61.1	61.5	61.4	60.7
2005	60.9	61.4	61.7	62.0	62.1	61.9	62.2	62.1	62.1	62.4	62.5	62.5	62.0
2006	61.2	61.9	61.9	62.2	62.2	62.1	62.1	62.3	62.5	62.8	63.5	63.0	62.3
2007	62.2	62.7	62.8	63.3	63.6	63.7	64.0	64.5	64.3	64.6	64.7	64.9	63.8
2008	64.0	64.5	64.7	64.6	65.1	65.0	65.0	65.1	65.2	65.8	65.2	65.1	64.9
2009	63.9	64.1	64.1	64.3	64.5	64.2	64.8	65.0	64.8	64.2	64.4	62.8	64.3
Leisure and Hospitality													
1990	25.3	25.7	26.0	27.3	27.5	28.0	27.7	28.0	27.4	27.2	27.1	27.2	27.0
2000	38.2	38.9	39.6	39.5	40.4	41.0	39.7	39.8	39.3	39.1	39.1	39.2	39.5
2001	38.2	38.9	39.8	40.2	40.6	41.5	40.7	40.8	40.0	39.4	39.2	39.3	39.9
2002	38.0	38.4	38.9	39.4	39.9	40.3	40.2	40.1	39.7	38.5	38.7	38.6	39.2
2003	37.4	38.0	38.6	39.7	40.3	40.8	40.5	40.9	40.5	39.8	39.8	40.1	39.7
2004	38.7	39.2	40.3	41.1	41.8	42.7	42.5	42.4	41.6	41.3	41.3	40.9	41.2
2005	40.5	40.9	42.1	43.2	43.8	44.5	43.8	43.8	43.5	42.0	42.2	42.0	42.7
2006	41.2	42.1	42.9	43.8	44.7	45.5	45.1	45.4	44.7	43.2	42.9	42.8	43.7
2007	42.4	42.9	43.9	43.8	44.7	45.1	45.1	45.3	44.4	44.0	43.9	44.2	44.1
2008	42.2	42.8	43.4	44.7	45.8	46.3	45.6	45.7	44.6	44.2	44.0	43.8	44.4
2009	41.4	41.9	42.4	43.3	44.2	44.2	43.8	43.2	43.0	42.2	42.1	41.4	42.8
Other Services													
1990	19.0	19.1	19.2	19.2	19.3	19.6	19.6	19.7	19.4	19.5	19.6	19.5	19.4
2000	24.8	25.0	25.4	25.3	25.2	25.7	25.7	25.5	25.2	25.3	25.2	25.4	25.3
2001	25.0	25.0	25.0	25.2	25.1	25.3	25.5	25.5	25.4	25.4	25.3	25.3	25.3
2002	25.5	25.7	25.7	25.5	25.6	25.7	25.9	25.8	25.5	25.3	25.4	25.2	25.6
2003	24.6	24.6	24.6	24.8	24.9	25.1	25.0	25.0	24.6	24.4	24.2	24.1	24.6
2004	23.8	23.9	24.0	23.9	23.9	24.2	24.3	24.2	23.8	23.7	23.8	23.8	23.9
2005	23.5	23.5	23.5	23.6	23.6	23.8	23.8	23.6	23.3	23.2	23.2	23.1	23.5
2006	23.0	23.1	23.2	23.3	23.3	23.9	23.7	23.6	23.4	23.1	23.3	23.3	23.4
2007	23.3	23.3	23.6	23.7	23.8	23.9	24.1	24.0	23.7	23.8	23.9	24.0	23.8
2008	24.0	24.2	24.2	24.3	24.3	24.7	24.8	24.6	24.2	24.1	24.0	23.9	24.3
2009	23.8	23.8	23.8	23.6	23.8	24.3	24.5	24.1	23.7	23.6	23.3	23.4	23.8
Government													
1990	66.9	67.2	67.4	68.1	68.6	65.4	66.8	63.5	68.5	69.5	69.7	70.0	67.6
2000	75.1	75.3	75.9	75.9	77.4	74.0	72.9	71.4	75.1	76.2	76.0	76.2	75.1
2001	75.8	76.3	76.3	76.1	76.4	75.3	73.1	72.7	75.3	76.6	76.7	76.6	75.6
2002	76.0	76.3	76.6	76.7	77.1	75.9	73.3	72.9	76.4	77.7	78.2	78.2	76.3
2003	77.5	78.1	78.4	79.0	79.1	77.2	75.4	75.5	78.3	78.8	79.1	79.4	77.9
2004	79.0	79.1	78.9	79.5	79.1	78.3	76.5	76.5	78.7	79.1	79.6	79.5	78.7
2005	78.8	79.3	79.5	79.8	79.9	79.4	76.9	77.5	79.7	80.7	80.9	80.7	79.4
2006	81.4	81.6	81.7	82.2	82.4	82.3	79.1	79.6	82.3	83.0	83.2	83.3	81.8
2007	82.9	83.3	83.5	83.5	83.8	83.6	80.0	80.7	83.3	83.9	84.1	84.0	83.1
2008	83.6	84.0	84.2	84.4	84.7	84.7	81.1	81.6	83.6	85.0	84.9	85.2	83.9
2009	84.5	84.6	84.6	85.0	84.8	84.8	80.4	80.6	82.6	83.3	83.4	83.1	83.5

Employment by Industry: Boston-Cambridge-Quincy, MA-NH, NECTA, Selected Years, 1990–2009

(Numbers in thousands, not seasonally adjusted.)

Industry and year	January	February	March	April	May	June	July	August	September	October	November	December	Annual average
Total Nonfarm													
1990	2236.3	2231.4	2236.5	2234.6	2244.4	2244.4	2212.2	2207.0	2218.4	2214.7	2214.4	2211.7	2225.5
2000	2469.0	2480.9	2499.9	2523.4	2535.3	2559.3	2531.5	2525.8	2558.7	2578.2	2595.4	2608.4	2538.8
2001	2531.3	2535.2	2539.7	2553.7	2557.2	2565.7	2523.3	2515.2	2521.8	2524.1	2524.7	2526.4	2534.9
2002	2451.2	2444.9	2457.0	2472.1	2480.6	2487.1	2450.7	2443.9	2464.3	2472.6	2480.8	2482.4	2465.6
2003	2394.3	2384.3	2392.5	2413.6	2423.7	2430.4	2401.9	2391.6	2414.1	2419.9	2429.6	2426.5	2410.2
2004	2353.9	2359.2	2373.7	2401.3	2412.9	2423.8	2405.6	2395.0	2417.0	2430.1	2438.3	2443.9	2404.6
2005	2370.7	2379.7	2385.6	2421.4	2431.1	2443.3	2422.7	2415.8	2439.2	2447.9	2462.1	2468.4	2424.0
2006	2398.5	2403.8	2417.9	2442.0	2451.9	2471.9	2448.9	2443.0	2468.5	2480.3	2490.6	2498.2	2451.3
2007	2435.2	2436.4	2446.3	2474.5	2493.4	2510.1	2483.9	2478.1	2497.2	2511.9	2524.1	2524.8	2484.7
2008	2463.8	2467.0	2476.0	2499.6	2513.0	2523.7	2496.8	2487.5	2503.6	2516.1	2509.4	2499.3	2496.3
2009	2413.0	2407.0	2402.2	2418.2	2422.3	2422.2	2395.4	2382.5	2402.0	2414.2	2415.0	2411.0	2408.8
Total Private													
1990	1951.3	1942.9	1948.3	1945.6	1949.6	1953.1	1934.2	1935.5	1937.6	1929.5	1927.1	1924.5	1939.9
2000	2168.6	2177.1	2194.1	2216.6	2223.7	2251.5	2245.9	2245.6	2257.3	2274.4	2289.9	2303.0	2237.3
2001	2227.2	2228.2	2232.6	2245.9	2248.9	2259.6	2236.9	2231.0	2217.0	2218.3	2217.9	2218.8	2231.9
2002	2146.7	2138.0	2149.7	2165.7	2173.9	2181.9	2167.3	2164.1	2159.2	2170.0	2175.6	2177.5	2164.1
2003	2093.5	2081.1	2089.6	2110.3	2120.8	2128.9	2119.1	2115.3	2114.4	2122.0	2130.6	2128.1	2112.8
2004	2059.5	2060.8	2075.0	2101.9	2114.3	2127.4	2131.3	2126.9	2122.1	2133.3	2139.8	2145.7	2111.5
2005	2075.3	2079.5	2085.5	2120.6	2130.1	2145.9	2146.7	2145.7	2143.2	2148.3	2160.4	2167.9	2129.1
2006	2101.0	2101.8	2115.6	2139.4	2148.9	2171.9	2169.9	2170.7	2169.7	2178.3	2186.9	2195.2	2154.1
2007	2134.7	2132.5	2141.9	2169.2	2187.1	2207.8	2205.1	2205.5	2196.4	2207.0	2217.2	2218.6	2185.3
2008	2160.1	2159.1	2167.8	2190.1	2203.0	2216.4	2213.7	2210.5	2198.7	2206.9	2198.8	2189.2	2192.9
2009	2107.2	2095.8	2091.5	2105.1	2111.6	2116.2	2110.3	2104.1	2099.3	2105.6	2105.3	2100.2	2104.4
Goods-Producing													
1990	435.0	429.5	428.7	429.1	431.1	433.6	427.9	430.2	427.2	421.1	417.0	412.1	426.9
2000	380.9	379.9	384.4	390.4	394.0	401.6	397.6	401.2	401.1	401.8	402.8	402.2	394.8
2001	392.1	390.6	390.7	396.4	397.9	399.4	393.9	392.6	388.4	384.8	379.2	374.8	390.1
2002	362.4	356.6	357.9	362.0	365.7	367.2	362.6	363.0	360.5	360.1	358.0	352.8	360.7
2003	340.7	333.4	334.0	339.6	343.4	345.7	342.4	342.9	340.4	337.9	337.0	332.5	339.2
2004	319.9	318.2	322.2	329.7	335.3	340.0	339.7	340.9	338.3	335.2	334.1	331.6	332.1
2005	320.1	317.7	318.3	326.2	330.3	335.1	335.6	336.7	334.7	332.3	332.0	329.2	329.0
2006	318.9	316.5	317.8	324.2	327.3	331.7	332.1	333.4	331.6	329.6	327.2	325.1	326.3
2007	315.8	311.9	313.5	317.8	323.8	328.9	329.2	329.6	327.2	325.2	323.6	319.7	322.2
2008	309.7	306.9	308.4	312.7	316.7	320.1	320.6	320.4	317.0	314.0	309.6	302.9	313.3
2009	286.3	280.1	277.1	279.3	280.1	282.0	281.5	280.9	278.2	276.8	275.4	272.6	279.2
Mining and Logging													
1990	1.2	1.2	1.2	1.3	1.2	1.2	1.2	1.2	1.2	1.2	1.1	1.0	1.2
2000	0.8	0.7	0.8	1.0	1.0	1.1	0.9	1.0	1.0	1.0	1.0	0.9	0.9
2001	0.8	0.8	0.8	0.9	1.0	1.0	1.0	1.0	1.0	1.0	1.0	1.0	0.9
2002	0.8	0.8	0.9	1.0	1.1	1.1	1.1	1.1	1.1	1.1	1.1	1.1	1.0
2003	1.0	0.9	0.9	1.1	1.2	1.2	1.3	1.2	1.3	1.3	1.3	1.2	1.2
2004	1.0	1.0	1.0	1.2	1.3	1.3	1.3	1.3	1.3	1.3	1.3	1.3	1.2
2005	1.1	1.0	1.0	1.3	1.3	1.4	1.4	1.3	1.3	1.3	1.3	1.1	1.2
2006	1.0	1.0	1.0	1.1	1.2	1.2	1.3	1.2	1.2	1.2	1.2	1.1	1.1
2007	0.9	0.8	0.9	1.0	1.1	1.1	1.1	1.1	1.1	1.0	1.0	0.9	1.0
2008	0.7	0.7	0.7	0.8	0.9	0.9	0.9	0.8	0.8	0.8	0.8	0.7	0.8
2009	0.7	0.6	0.6	0.7	0.8	0.8	0.8	0.8	0.8	0.8	0.8	0.7	0.7
Construction													
1990	72.3	69.3	69.3	70.3	73.2	75.2	74.7	75.6	74.4	71.0	68.9	65.2	71.6
2000	84.7	83.3	86.9	93.0	96.2	100.2	103.0	104.0	102.7	103.1	102.7	100.8	96.7
2001	93.7	92.6	94.0	100.7	104.7	107.6	109.7	109.7	107.4	107.8	106.3	103.5	103.1
2002	96.7	93.9	95.9	102.6	106.8	108.1	109.1	109.3	107.6	108.9	107.8	102.9	104.1
2003	95.0	90.5	91.6	98.6	103.0	104.8	105.8	106.0	104.5	103.2	102.4	98.9	100.4
2004	90.0	88.6	91.6	97.9	103.0	106.0	107.5	107.6	105.9	104.4	103.7	101.1	100.6
2005	91.5	89.2	90.3	98.5	102.4	105.7	108.2	108.6	107.7	105.5	105.4	102.5	101.3
2006	94.4	92.5	94.0	100.9	103.6	106.3	107.7	108.1	106.6	105.2	102.9	100.2	101.9
2007	92.4	88.9	90.5	95.5	100.8	104.3	106.1	106.1	106.3	105.1	104.1	98.9	99.7
2008	90.8	88.7	90.5	95.3	98.9	100.9	102.7	102.3	100.3	98.7	95.6	91.0	96.3
2009	80.1	76.6	75.9	79.8	82.1	83.7	84.9	84.7	83.3	82.9	80.8	77.3	81.0
Manufacturing													
1990	361.5	359.0	358.2	357.5	356.7	357.2	352.0	353.4	351.6	348.9	347.0	345.9	354.1
2000	295.4	295.9	296.7	296.4	296.8	300.3	293.7	296.2	297.4	297.7	299.1	300.5	297.2
2001	297.6	297.2	295.9	294.8	292.2	290.8	283.2	281.9	280.0	276.0	271.9	270.3	286.0
2002	264.9	261.9	261.1	258.4	257.8	258.0	252.4	252.6	251.8	250.1	249.1	248.8	255.6
2003	244.7	242.0	241.5	239.9	239.2	239.7	235.3	235.7	234.6	233.4	233.3	232.4	237.6
2004	228.9	228.6	229.6	230.6	231.0	232.7	230.9	232.0	231.1	229.5	229.1	229.2	230.3
2005	227.5	227.5	227.0	226.4	226.6	228.0	226.0	226.8	225.7	225.5	225.3	225.6	226.5
2006	223.5	223.0	222.8	222.2	222.5	224.2	223.1	224.1	223.8	223.2	223.1	223.8	223.3
2007	222.5	222.2	222.1	221.3	221.9	223.5	222.0	222.2	221.0	220.1	219.7	219.9	221.5
2008	218.2	217.5	217.2	216.6	216.9	218.3	217.0	217.3	215.9	214.5	213.2	211.2	216.2
2009	205.5	202.9	200.6	198.8	197.2	197.5	195.8	195.4	194.1	193.1	193.8	194.6	197.4

Employment by Industry: Boston-Cambridge-Quincy, MA-NH, NECTA, Selected Years, 1990–2009—*Continued*

(Numbers in thousands, not seasonally adjusted.)

Industry and year	January	February	March	April	May	June	July	August	September	October	November	December	Annual average
Service-Providing													
1990	1801.3	1801.9	1807.8	1805.5	1813.3	1810.8	1784.3	1776.8	1791.2	1793.6	1797.4	1799.6	1798.6
2000	2088.1	2101.0	2115.5	2133.0	2141.3	2157.7	2133.9	2124.6	2157.6	2176.4	2192.6	2206.2	2144.0
2001	2139.2	2144.6	2149.0	2157.3	2159.3	2166.3	2129.4	2122.6	2133.4	2139.3	2145.5	2151.6	2144.8
2002	2088.8	2088.3	2099.1	2110.1	2114.9	2119.9	2088.1	2080.9	2103.8	2112.5	2122.8	2129.6	2104.9
2003	2053.6	2050.9	2058.5	2074.0	2080.3	2084.7	2059.5	2048.7	2073.7	2082.0	2092.6	2094.0	2071.0
2004	2034.0	2041.0	2051.5	2071.6	2077.6	2083.8	2065.9	2054.1	2078.7	2094.9	2104.2	2112.3	2072.5
2005	2050.6	2062.0	2067.3	2095.2	2100.8	2108.2	2087.1	2079.1	2104.5	2115.6	2130.1	2139.2	2095.0
2006	2079.6	2087.3	2100.1	2117.8	2124.6	2140.2	2116.8	2109.6	2136.9	2150.7	2163.4	2173.1	2125.0
2007	2119.4	2124.5	2132.8	2156.7	2169.6	2181.2	2154.7	2148.5	2170.0	2186.7	2200.5	2205.1	2162.5
2008	2154.1	2160.1	2167.6	2186.9	2196.3	2203.6	2176.2	2167.1	2186.6	2202.1	2199.8	2196.4	2183.1
2009	2126.7	2126.9	2125.1	2138.9	2142.2	2140.2	2113.9	2101.6	2123.8	2137.4	2139.6	2138.4	2129.6
Trade, Transportation, and Utilities													
1990	429.2	418.1	418.0	413.2	414.9	417.2	408.5	408.5	411.4	409.2	414.3	419.3	415.2
2000	446.1	441.2	441.7	443.6	445.2	450.3	443.6	443.6	446.7	454.0	464.2	474.4	449.6
2001	450.4	442.5	442.2	442.4	443.5	448.4	440.4	439.2	438.8	441.7	449.9	455.9	444.6
2002	434.4	426.5	427.5	428.5	431.2	436.0	430.0	428.5	430.6	433.3	441.0	449.4	433.1
2003	426.0	419.3	420.7	421.5	423.9	428.5	422.7	422.2	424.3	428.5	436.7	442.0	426.4
2004	422.9	417.4	417.9	417.8	420.4	424.8	419.8	418.4	417.9	425.5	433.0	440.5	423.0
2005	420.1	415.8	414.8	417.6	420.2	423.8	418.8	418.5	417.7	420.9	428.5	437.5	421.2
2006	419.6	411.2	413.1	414.5	416.7	421.8	416.1	416.2	417.3	421.4	430.1	438.4	419.7
2007	419.3	411.1	411.9	412.0	417.1	422.4	416.8	415.9	415.7	420.3	430.1	435.9	419.0
2008	421.1	411.6	412.0	413.2	416.6	420.9	416.4	415.9	414.4	417.3	421.1	425.9	417.2
2009	404.2	395.8	392.7	391.9	395.6	400.0	394.5	393.2	395.0	396.9	401.1	404.5	397.1
Wholesale Trade													
1990	116.9	116.5	116.3	115.9	115.7	116.6	115.3	114.9	114.0	113.8	113.4	113.3	115.2
2000	109.3	109.3	109.8	109.9	110.6	112.1	111.0	111.1	111.3	112.4	113.0	114.2	111.2
2001	111.9	112.0	112.1	111.8	111.4	111.8	111.5	110.8	109.5	109.2	108.7	108.7	110.8
2002	107.1	106.6	106.9	105.9	106.0	106.7	105.7	105.2	104.4	104.7	104.7	105.2	105.8
2003	104.7	104.2	104.1	103.7	103.9	104.4	104.5	104.4	103.6	103.8	104.2	104.7	104.2
2004	102.8	102.6	103.2	102.9	102.6	103.2	102.8	102.5	101.3	101.3	101.2	101.3	102.3
2005	100.8	100.6	100.2	100.9	101.5	102.1	102.8	102.8	102.3	103.1	103.4	104.1	102.1
2006	103.0	102.6	102.8	103.4	103.5	104.7	104.9	105.2	104.5	104.8	104.9	105.4	104.1
2007	104.3	103.9	104.2	103.8	104.1	105.1	104.9	104.6	103.7	103.8	103.5	103.6	104.1
2008	102.6	101.6	101.5	101.9	101.9	102.6	102.5	101.9	100.8	100.3	99.7	99.4	101.4
2009	97.0	95.6	94.9	94.3	94.2	94.7	94.4	94.0	93.2	92.9	92.6	92.1	94.2
Retail Trade													
1990	252.1	241.4	240.9	237.6	238.6	239.5	234.0	234.0	235.5	234.8	240.3	245.2	239.5
2000	263.7	258.7	259.0	259.1	260.0	262.8	259.5	259.4	260.1	265.3	275.5	284.9	264.0
2001	265.5	257.4	257.5	257.0	258.2	262.2	257.5	257.5	256.2	259.6	269.9	277.0	261.3
2002	259.7	252.6	253.5	255.1	257.0	260.6	258.3	257.8	257.8	259.5	267.5	276.0	259.6
2003	255.0	249.2	250.5	251.7	253.2	257.1	254.3	254.4	254.2	258.5	266.3	271.5	256.3
2004	256.6	251.8	251.7	251.1	253.4	257.1	254.9	254.5	253.2	259.6	267.5	275.3	257.2
2005	257.2	253.1	252.6	254.3	255.7	258.3	254.8	255.0	252.9	254.4	263.8	271.4	257.1
2006	256.7	248.8	250.2	250.7	252.0	254.8	251.0	251.3	249.5	253.8	262.5	269.3	254.2
2007	253.2	245.9	246.1	246.5	250.4	253.6	251.1	250.8	248.5	253.2	263.7	268.6	252.6
2008	256.7	248.7	248.8	249.2	251.4	254.3	252.6	253.4	249.9	253.9	258.9	263.1	253.4
2009	246.9	240.3	238.1	238.0	241.2	244.7	242.6	242.9	241.5	244.0	248.3	251.7	243.4
Transportation and Utilities													
1990	60.2	60.2	60.8	59.7	60.6	61.1	59.2	59.6	61.9	60.6	60.6	60.8	60.4
2000	73.1	73.2	72.9	74.6	74.6	75.4	73.1	73.1	75.3	76.3	75.7	75.3	74.4
2001	73.0	73.1	72.6	73.6	73.9	74.4	71.4	70.9	73.1	72.9	71.3	70.2	72.5
2002	67.6	67.3	67.1	67.5	68.2	68.7	66.0	65.5	68.4	69.1	68.8	68.2	67.7
2003	66.3	65.9	66.1	66.1	66.8	67.0	63.9	63.4	66.5	66.2	66.2	65.8	65.9
2004	63.5	63.0	63.0	63.8	64.4	64.5	62.1	61.4	63.4	64.6	64.3	63.9	63.5
2005	62.1	62.1	62.0	62.4	63.0	63.4	61.2	60.7	62.5	61.4	61.3	62.0	62.0
2006	59.9	59.8	60.1	60.4	61.2	62.3	60.2	59.7	63.3	62.8	62.7	63.7	61.3
2007	61.8	61.3	61.6	61.7	62.6	63.7	60.8	60.5	63.5	63.3	62.9	63.7	62.3
2008	61.8	61.3	61.7	62.1	63.3	64.0	61.3	60.6	63.7	63.1	62.5	63.4	62.4
2009	60.3	59.9	59.7	59.6	60.2	60.6	57.5	56.3	60.3	60.0	60.2	60.7	59.6
Information													
1990	69.7	68.9	68.7	68.3	67.9	68.1	68.2	68.4	67.9	67.1	67.2	67.0	68.1
2000	89.5	90.4	92.1	93.5	95.0	97.4	99.3	93.6	99.5	99.7	100.3	100.9	95.9
2001	99.8	99.7	99.0	99.4	98.0	97.9	96.2	95.2	93.3	91.3	90.5	89.8	95.8
2002	88.2	87.5	87.2	85.6	84.9	84.7	84.1	84.3	82.0	82.0	81.8	81.9	84.5
2003	79.5	79.1	79.0	78.0	77.6	78.0	76.9	76.5	75.7	75.4	75.2	75.2	77.2
2004	73.8	73.4	74.0	73.3	73.5	73.7	73.9	73.9	73.5	73.4	73.8	74.1	73.7
2005	73.4	73.6	73.6	73.7	73.8	74.4	74.6	74.3	73.7	73.8	74.0	74.3	73.9
2006	74.0	74.1	74.1	73.7	74.0	74.6	74.4	74.5	73.6	74.5	74.6	74.9	74.3
2007	73.6	73.8	74.0	74.2	74.5	75.3	75.5	75.5	75.0	74.5	74.7	74.9	74.6
2008	74.8	75.2	75.4	75.1	75.1	76.0	76.4	76.5	75.7	75.3	75.0	75.0	75.5
2009	74.8	73.6	73.3	72.4	72.0	72.0	71.7	71.6	71.0	70.7	70.8	70.5	72.0

Employment by Industry: Boston-Cambridge-Quincy, MA-NH, NECTA, Selected Years, 1990–2009—*Continued*

(Numbers in thousands, not seasonally adjusted.)

Industry and year	January	February	March	April	May	June	July	August	September	October	November	December	Annual average
Financial Activities													
1990	166.5	166.2	166.4	165.5	165.4	165.1	164.3	164.0	162.4	162.1	161.1	161.3	164.2
2000	189.0	188.4	188.9	189.1	189.1	192.7	193.0	193.6	192.4	193.6	194.2	196.3	191.7
2001	195.9	196.0	197.1	194.2	193.9	196.4	197.4	197.4	194.7	193.8	194.3	195.3	195.5
2002	195.0	193.7	193.1	190.6	190.9	192.7	193.1	192.6	189.8	190.4	189.8	190.5	191.9
2003	188.5	187.3	187.2	187.1	187.3	188.4	188.3	188.2	184.9	183.7	184.0	184.4	186.6
2004	181.8	182.1	182.3	182.5	182.7	184.9	186.1	185.5	183.4	182.1	182.1	183.1	183.2
2005	182.5	182.4	182.6	183.2	184.1	186.9	189.7	189.9	188.6	187.0	187.8	189.4	186.2
2006	185.7	185.6	185.9	186.1	186.8	189.3	191.6	191.1	189.4	188.9	189.4	190.9	188.4
2007	188.5	188.5	188.5	188.5	189.0	191.3	191.8	191.8	188.7	187.5	187.2	188.2	189.1
2008	186.0	185.6	185.8	185.6	185.9	187.7	188.7	188.4	185.6	184.9	184.3	184.4	186.1
2009	181.8	180.6	179.9	178.6	178.4	179.3	179.2	178.2	175.5	174.2	174.1	174.7	177.9
Professional and Business Services													
1990	279.3	280.0	281.7	280.2	280.2	282.4	280.7	281.4	278.5	275.0	273.8	272.2	278.8
2000	395.0	398.2	403.5	409.9	411.5	422.0	425.3	427.9	427.3	426.7	428.6	429.9	417.2
2001	416.7	414.9	415.6	417.6	416.7	418.7	410.8	409.2	403.3	399.6	396.3	395.2	409.6
2002	382.0	378.7	380.0	385.3	384.9	387.5	385.2	384.4	381.1	381.2	380.2	379.0	382.5
2003	363.4	359.4	359.7	367.0	367.7	370.5	371.8	371.6	369.9	371.2	372.4	371.9	368.0
2004	361.4	361.4	364.1	373.5	374.7	380.0	383.2	383.9	382.8	383.4	383.7	385.0	376.4
2005	372.6	373.1	374.8	384.2	384.9	390.2	391.4	392.2	390.9	390.9	393.3	393.4	386.0
2006	382.5	383.8	386.3	393.5	395.2	402.6	402.1	403.1	401.2	402.4	403.4	403.9	396.7
2007	393.5	395.3	397.6	406.9	409.8	415.4	415.2	417.2	412.9	415.0	416.5	417.0	409.4
2008	408.1	408.9	409.8	415.9	417.9	422.1	421.2	419.9	416.6	416.9	413.3	409.0	415.0
2009	395.4	391.0	389.3	393.6	392.1	394.5	393.3	392.3	389.0	391.2	392.6	389.8	392.0
Education and Health Services													
1990	339.5	347.8	348.8	350.4	345.0	335.7	334.4	333.2	343.9	353.1	355.8	356.5	345.3
2000	404.1	413.1	414.2	412.9	406.2	395.9	393.3	392.9	403.9	413.2	417.3	417.7	407.1
2001	402.8	413.6	413.8	415.7	410.2	400.7	400.2	399.8	410.2	421.5	425.1	426.1	411.6
2002	413.5	423.2	426.2	427.2	421.0	410.3	408.9	407.8	420.1	430.0	435.1	434.9	421.5
2003	419.3	427.6	430.5	431.7	425.1	414.8	413.3	411.0	424.0	432.9	436.7	436.2	425.3
2004	423.9	433.3	435.5	437.1	430.6	420.3	420.8	418.0	429.0	439.0	442.1	441.7	430.9
2005	429.0	438.9	440.1	443.8	437.0	426.4	426.5	424.9	436.6	447.2	451.2	451.4	437.8
2006	439.2	449.7	453.0	453.8	448.3	440.4	438.5	437.1	450.2	458.9	462.6	462.8	449.5
2007	455.5	463.8	464.9	470.8	464.6	454.0	454.8	452.9	463.9	474.7	478.0	478.3	464.7
2008	466.4	476.5	478.9	481.4	474.9	465.0	465.2	463.4	473.9	485.2	488.1	488.5	475.6
2009	476.6	486.3	488.5	489.8	482.6	471.1	472.3	470.6	481.4	490.1	492.8	493.6	483.0
Leisure and Hospitality													
1990	159.0	159.5	162.2	165.8	171.7	176.5	175.6	175.3	172.9	168.7	164.9	162.9	167.9
2000	181.8	183.2	186.1	193.6	198.5	206.0	207.7	207.0	202.4	200.6	197.4	196.1	196.7
2001	185.5	186.6	189.3	194.9	202.6	210.7	210.1	209.8	202.4	199.5	196.1	194.8	198.5
2002	185.9	186.4	191.4	200.0	207.9	215.2	214.7	215.0	208.7	206.1	202.6	201.6	203.0
2003	190.5	189.6	192.2	199.3	209.1	215.5	215.8	215.7	209.4	206.9	202.5	199.9	203.9
2004	190.8	190.2	193.3	202.3	210.8	217.3	220.5	219.3	212.2	209.7	205.6	203.9	206.3
2005	193.2	193.5	196.1	205.6	213.3	221.4	221.7	221.2	214.4	210.4	207.4	205.7	208.7
2006	195.4	195.7	199.1	207.0	213.7	223.2	226.0	226.1	219.3	215.4	212.5	211.7	212.1
2007	202.3	201.5	204.2	211.3	219.3	229.6	230.1	230.9	223.7	220.9	217.5	215.0	217.2
2008	206.1	206.4	209.0	217.2	226.2	233.4	232.7	233.6	225.8	223.8	218.0	214.4	220.6
2009	200.7	201.2	202.8	211.1	221.5	226.4	226.4	226.1	220.8	217.7	211.3	207.2	214.4
Other Services													
1990	73.1	72.9	73.8	73.1	73.4	74.5	74.6	74.5	73.4	73.2	73.0	73.2	73.6
2000	82.2	82.7	83.2	83.6	84.2	85.6	86.1	85.8	84.0	84.8	85.1	85.5	84.4
2001	84.0	84.3	84.9	85.3	86.1	87.4	87.9	87.8	85.9	86.1	86.5	86.9	86.1
2002	85.3	85.4	86.4	86.5	87.4	88.3	88.7	88.5	86.4	86.9	87.1	87.4	87.0
2003	85.6	85.4	86.3	86.1	86.7	87.5	87.9	87.2	85.8	85.5	86.1	86.0	86.3
2004	85.0	84.8	85.7	85.7	86.3	86.4	87.3	87.0	85.0	85.0	85.4	85.8	85.8
2005	84.4	84.5	85.2	86.3	86.5	87.7	88.4	88.0	86.6	85.8	86.2	87.0	86.4
2006	85.7	85.2	86.3	86.6	86.9	88.3	89.1	89.2	87.1	87.2	87.1	87.5	87.2
2007	86.2	86.6	87.3	87.7	89.0	90.9	91.7	91.7	89.3	88.9	89.6	89.6	89.0
2008	87.9	88.0	88.5	89.0	89.7	91.2	92.5	92.4	89.7	89.5	89.4	89.1	89.7
2009	87.4	87.2	87.9	88.4	89.3	90.9	91.4	91.2	88.4	88.0	87.2	87.3	88.7
Government													
1990	285.0	288.5	288.2	289.0	294.8	291.3	278.0	271.5	280.8	285.2	287.3	287.2	285.6
2000	300.4	303.8	305.8	306.8	311.6	307.8	285.6	280.2	301.4	303.8	305.5	305.4	301.5
2001	304.1	307.0	307.1	307.8	308.3	306.1	286.4	284.2	304.8	305.8	306.8	307.6	303.0
2002	304.5	306.9	307.3	306.4	306.7	305.2	283.4	279.8	305.1	302.6	305.2	304.9	301.5
2003	300.8	303.2	302.9	303.3	302.9	301.5	282.8	276.3	299.7	297.9	299.0	298.4	297.4
2004	294.4	298.4	298.7	299.4	298.6	296.4	274.3	268.1	294.9	296.8	298.5	298.2	293.1
2005	295.4	300.2	300.1	300.8	301.0	297.4	276.0	270.1	296.0	299.6	301.7	300.5	294.9
2006	297.5	302.0	302.3	302.6	303.0	300.0	279.0	272.3	298.8	302.0	303.7	303.0	297.2
2007	300.5	303.9	304.4	305.3	306.3	302.3	278.8	272.6	300.8	304.9	306.9	306.2	299.4
2008	303.7	307.9	308.2	309.5	310.0	307.3	283.1	277.0	304.9	309.2	310.6	310.1	303.5
2009	305.8	311.2	310.7	313.1	310.7	306.0	285.1	278.4	302.7	308.6	309.7	310.8	304.4

Employment by Industry: Bridgeport-Stamford-Norwalk, CT, NECTA, Selected Years, 1990–2009

(Numbers in thousands, not seasonally adjusted.)

Industry and year	January	February	March	April	May	June	July	August	September	October	November	December	Annual average
Total Nonfarm													
1990	402.9	399.7	402.0	401.3	404.9	409.1	401.1	398.5	399.8	397.5	398.9	400.1	401.3
2001	420.2	418.8	420.2	422.4	426.0	429.4	420.8	417.4	420.3	422.5	424.4	423.8	422.2
2002	410.6	409.5	412.5	416.8	418.9	421.5	410.7	408.9	412.0	414.7	417.8	418.9	414.4
2003	406.0	404.8	407.1	409.8	413.0	415.5	411.6	406.7	409.7	412.5	413.6	414.1	410.4
2004	402.5	402.1	405.8	407.2	411.4	415.2	412.1	408.2	410.5	412.9	415.1	416.3	409.9
2005	402.0	402.9	404.7	411.0	413.8	417.2	414.2	410.1	411.8	413.1	415.8	418.4	411.3
2006	408.4	408.9	408.8	415.6	418.9	422.1	417.8	414.3	416.0	418.1	421.4	425.2	416.3
2007	412.1	411.7	413.3	417.1	422.0	425.7	424.1	419.6	419.2	421.5	424.0	426.8	419.8
2008	414.3	413.1	415.6	418.0	421.4	424.6	419.2	415.1	415.6	416.3	417.1	416.9	417.3
2009	402.0	399.3	399.2	396.8	400.9	403.3	398.7	395.0	396.8	400.5	401.1	401.5	399.6
Total Private													
1990	359.5	355.2	357.3	356.7	359.9	363.7	361.2	359.2	357.3	354.0	354.5	356.0	357.9
2000	370.6	370.0	373.3	377.5	380.6	386.5	385.5	383.2	383.4	383.7	384.8	387.7	380.6
2001	373.6	371.8	373.4	375.3	378.6	382.2	378.9	376.3	372.0	374.2	375.3	374.8	375.5
2002	362.9	361.4	364.2	368.0	369.9	372.4	369.8	367.5	365.1	366.3	368.6	369.9	367.2
2003	357.9	356.5	358.6	361.8	364.7	367.1	366.5	364.1	363.5	365.4	365.9	366.6	363.2
2004	355.0	354.1	357.3	359.7	363.8	367.7	367.6	365.2	363.8	365.1	366.9	368.8	362.9
2005	355.4	355.9	357.6	363.0	365.5	368.8	368.7	366.1	364.9	365.7	368.3	370.6	364.2
2006	361.1	361.1	360.8	367.8	370.9	375.2	373.5	371.4	369.5	370.9	373.7	377.7	369.5
2007	365.2	364.1	365.7	369.6	373.5	378.4	377.8	374.9	372.4	373.5	375.6	378.7	372.5
2008	366.5	364.5	367.2	370.0	372.6	376.9	374.2	371.5	368.4	368.1	368.0	368.4	369.7
2009	354.5	351.4	351.1	349.9	352.5	355.2	354.0	351.4	349.9	352.4	352.7	353.2	352.4
Goods-Producing													
1990	90.1	88.9	89.0	88.0	88.5	88.4	88.9	87.6	87.4	85.0	84.8	84.1	87.6
2000	64.1	63.8	64.6	65.0	65.6	66.5	65.9	65.9	66.1	65.4	65.3	65.1	65.3
2001	63.1	62.7	63.0	64.1	64.7	64.9	63.3	63.3	63.0	62.1	61.7	61.4	63.1
2002	59.6	59.2	59.5	60.4	60.5	60.9	59.9	60.0	59.7	59.2	58.9	58.3	59.7
2003	56.7	56.2	56.3	56.9	57.5	57.8	56.8	57.2	56.9	57.0	56.8	56.4	56.9
2004	54.8	54.4	55.0	56.2	56.6	57.2	56.8	56.8	56.9	57.2	56.9	56.8	56.3
2005	55.2	54.9	54.9	56.3	56.7	57.2	57.1	56.7	56.3	56.4	56.4	55.9	56.2
2006	54.9	55.1	52.3	56.4	56.6	57.2	57.2	57.1	56.8	56.7	56.5	56.3	56.1
2007	55.0	54.7	55.1	55.7	56.1	57.0	57.0	56.8	56.5	56.1	55.9	55.7	56.0
2008	54.1	53.5	54.0	54.7	55.4	55.7	55.3	55.1	54.9	54.2	53.7	52.8	54.5
2009	50.8	49.8	49.5	49.6	49.5	49.8	49.3	48.8	48.5	48.6	48.3	47.9	49.2
Mining, Logging, and Construction													
1990	14.4	13.9	14.0	14.2	14.9	15.3	15.2	15.2	14.8	14.0	13.6	12.9	14.4
2000	13.1	12.8	13.6	14.2	14.7	15.1	15.3	15.3	15.2	15.1	15.0	14.6	14.5
2001	13.1	12.8	13.2	14.7	15.3	15.6	15.7	15.7	15.3	15.0	14.8	14.6	14.7
2002	13.6	13.4	13.8	14.5	14.8	15.2	15.2	15.2	15.0	14.7	14.6	14.0	14.5
2003	13.0	12.7	12.9	13.9	14.6	14.7	15.0	15.1	14.9	14.9	14.7	14.2	14.2
2004	12.9	12.5	12.9	14.2	14.7	15.0	15.3	15.4	15.2	15.3	15.1	14.8	14.4
2005	13.6	13.4	13.5	15.1	15.5	15.7	16.0	15.9	15.6	15.6	15.6	15.0	15.0
2006	14.3	14.2	14.6	15.5	15.8	16.0	16.4	16.3	16.1	16.0	15.8	15.5	15.5
2007	14.6	14.1	14.4	15.6	16.0	16.4	16.6	16.6	16.3	16.2	16.0	15.7	15.7
2008	14.3	14.1	14.3	15.2	15.7	15.8	15.8	15.8	15.6	15.1	14.7	14.0	15.0
2009	12.6	12.2	12.0	12.3	12.5	12.6	12.7	12.4	12.2	12.2	12.0	11.5	12.3
Manufacturing													
1990	75.7	75.0	75.0	73.8	73.6	73.1	73.7	72.4	72.6	71.0	71.2	71.2	73.2
2000	51.0	51.0	51.0	50.8	50.9	51.4	50.6	50.6	50.9	50.3	50.3	50.5	50.8
2001	50.0	49.9	49.8	49.4	49.4	49.3	47.6	47.6	47.7	47.1	46.9	46.8	48.5
2002	46.0	45.8	45.7	45.9	45.7	45.7	44.7	44.8	44.7	44.5	44.3	44.3	45.2
2003	43.7	43.5	43.4	43.0	42.9	43.1	41.8	42.1	42.0	42.1	42.1	42.2	42.7
2004	41.9	41.9	42.1	42.0	41.9	42.2	41.5	41.4	41.7	41.9	41.8	42.0	41.9
2005	41.6	41.5	41.4	41.2	41.2	41.5	41.1	40.8	40.7	40.8	40.8	40.9	41.1
2006	40.6	40.9	37.7	40.9	40.8	41.2	40.8	40.8	40.7	40.7	40.7	40.8	40.6
2007	40.4	40.6	40.7	40.1	40.1	40.6	40.4	40.2	40.2	39.9	39.9	40.0	40.3
2008	39.8	39.4	39.7	39.5	39.7	39.9	39.5	39.3	39.3	39.1	39.0	38.8	39.4
2009	38.2	37.6	37.5	37.3	37.0	37.2	36.6	36.4	36.3	36.4	36.3	36.4	36.9
Service-Providing													
1990	312.8	310.8	313.0	313.3	316.4	320.7	312.2	310.9	312.4	312.5	314.1	316.0	313.8
2000	352.2	352.8	355.4	358.9	361.8	366.8	361.3	358.7	364.1	364.7	366.5	369.8	361.1
2001	357.1	356.1	357.2	358.3	361.3	364.5	357.5	354.1	357.3	360.4	362.7	362.4	359.1
2002	351.0	350.3	353.0	356.4	358.4	360.6	350.8	348.9	352.3	355.5	358.9	360.6	354.7
2003	349.3	348.6	350.8	352.9	355.5	357.7	354.8	349.5	352.8	355.5	356.8	357.7	353.5
2004	347.7	347.7	350.8	351.0	354.8	358.0	355.3	351.4	353.6	355.7	358.2	359.5	353.6
2005	346.8	348.0	349.8	354.7	357.1	360.0	357.1	353.4	355.5	356.7	359.4	362.5	355.1
2006	353.5	353.8	356.5	359.2	362.3	364.9	360.6	357.2	359.2	361.4	364.9	368.9	360.2
2007	357.1	357.0	358.2	361.4	365.9	368.7	367.1	362.8	362.7	365.4	368.1	371.1	363.8
2008	360.2	359.6	361.6	363.3	366.0	368.9	363.9	360.0	360.7	362.1	363.4	364.1	362.8
2009	351.2	349.5	349.7	347.2	351.4	353.5	349.4	346.2	348.3	351.9	352.8	353.6	350.4

Employment by Industry: Bridgeport-Stamford-Norwalk, CT, NECTA, Selected Years, 1990–2009—*Continued*

(Numbers in thousands, not seasonally adjusted.)

Industry and year	January	February	March	April	May	June	July	August	September	October	November	December	Annual average
Trade, Transportation, and Utilities													
1990	81.9	79.2	79.3	78.5	79.0	79.6	78.8	78.7	79.1	78.3	79.5	80.7	79.4
2000	79.2	78.7	79.1	79.5	79.9	80.5	79.2	78.4	79.6	80.3	82.0	84.0	80.0
2001	80.2	77.8	77.6	77.9	78.4	79.2	77.9	77.2	77.2	78.4	78.9	80.6	78.4
2002	77.4	75.9	76.4	76.9	77.3	78.3	76.4	75.7	76.4	75.5	78.1	79.6	77.0
2003	75.5	74.1	74.5	74.1	74.7	75.3	74.2	73.4	74.4	75.1	76.5	78.0	75.0
2004	74.8	73.6	73.7	73.6	74.5	75.3	74.3	73.5	74.4	75.2	77.1	78.5	74.9
2005	75.3	74.1	74.2	74.2	74.7	75.3	74.1	73.8	74.7	75.5	77.4	79.5	75.2
2006	76.4	75.1	75.3	75.3	75.7	76.6	75.1	74.6	74.9	75.8	78.1	80.0	76.1
2007	76.1	74.3	74.6	74.6	75.8	77.0	75.6	75.3	75.6	76.1	78.6	80.8	76.2
2008	77.1	75.3	75.5	75.1	75.7	76.5	74.9	74.6	74.9	74.7	76.1	77.4	75.7
2009	73.2	71.5	71.2	70.0	70.9	71.6	70.0	69.7	70.2	70.8	72.9	74.0	71.3
Wholesale Trade													
1990	19.8	19.6	19.6	19.3	19.3	19.4	19.3	19.3	19.2	18.8	18.8	18.8	19.3
2000	16.4	16.4	16.4	16.3	16.4	16.5	16.3	16.2	16.2	15.9	16.0	16.2	16.3
2001	15.7	15.7	15.8	15.9	15.9	15.9	15.9	15.8	15.7	15.8	15.9	15.9	15.8
2002	15.8	15.6	15.7	15.6	15.6	15.5	15.5	15.5	15.4	15.4	15.4	15.5	15.5
2003	15.1	15.0	15.0	14.9	14.9	15.0	15.0	14.9	14.9	14.8	14.9	15.0	15.0
2004	14.9	14.8	14.8	14.7	14.8	15.0	14.9	14.9	14.7	14.7	14.8	14.8	14.8
2005	14.7	14.7	14.7	14.6	14.7	14.8	14.7	14.7	14.6	14.7	14.6	14.8	14.7
2006	14.6	14.7	14.7	14.6	14.6	14.6	14.6	14.4	14.4	14.5	14.5	14.6	14.6
2007	14.4	14.4	14.5	14.4	14.4	14.6	14.6	14.7	14.6	14.6	14.7	14.9	14.6
2008	14.8	14.7	14.8	14.8	14.8	14.9	14.8	14.8	14.7	14.7	14.7	14.8	14.8
2009	14.4	14.3	14.2	14.0	13.9	14.0	14.0	13.9	13.9	13.9	13.9	14.0	14.0
Retail Trade													
1990	53.8	51.4	51.3	50.8	51.1	51.5	51.5	51.4	51.3	51.0	52.2	53.2	51.7
2000	52.0	51.4	51.8	52.0	52.2	52.7	52.1	51.7	52.0	52.7	54.3	56.0	52.6
2001	53.0	50.7	50.5	50.6	51.0	51.8	51.1	50.9	50.4	51.2	51.8	53.4	51.4
2002	50.7	49.4	49.8	50.2	50.6	51.6	50.5	50.1	50.0	49.9	51.5	52.9	50.6
2003	49.6	48.3	48.6	48.8	49.3	49.7	49.4	49.0	49.0	49.6	50.9	52.3	49.5
2004	49.5	48.5	48.6	48.5	49.2	49.7	49.5	49.1	49.3	49.8	51.6	53.0	49.7
2005	50.1	49.0	49.0	49.1	49.5	50.0	49.6	49.6	49.6	50.1	52.0	53.7	50.1
2006	51.1	49.7	49.9	49.9	50.1	50.9	50.2	50.0	49.4	50.0	52.2	53.6	50.6
2007	50.3	48.6	48.8	48.8	49.9	50.7	50.2	50.0	49.6	50.1	52.3	54.0	50.3
2008	51.0	49.3	49.4	48.9	49.4	50.0	49.4	49.4	49.1	49.1	50.4	51.4	49.7
2009	47.9	46.4	46.2	45.7	46.4	47.0	46.2	46.2	45.9	46.5	48.4	49.1	46.8
Transportation and Utilities													
1990	8.3	8.2	8.4	8.4	8.6	8.7	8.0	8.0	8.6	8.5	8.5	8.7	8.4
2000	10.8	10.9	10.9	11.2	11.3	11.3	10.8	10.5	11.4	11.7	11.7	11.8	11.2
2001	11.5	11.4	11.3	11.4	11.5	11.5	10.9	10.5	11.1	11.4	11.3	11.3	11.3
2002	10.9	10.9	10.9	11.1	11.1	11.2	10.4	10.1	11.0	10.2	11.2	11.2	10.9
2003	10.8	10.8	10.9	10.4	10.5	10.6	9.8	9.5	10.5	10.7	10.7	10.7	10.5
2004	10.4	10.3	10.3	10.4	10.5	10.6	9.9	9.5	10.4	10.7	10.7	10.7	10.4
2005	10.5	10.4	10.5	10.5	10.5	10.5	9.8	9.5	10.5	10.7	10.8	11.0	10.4
2006	10.7	10.7	10.7	10.8	11.0	11.1	10.3	10.2	11.1	11.3	11.4	11.8	10.9
2007	11.4	11.3	11.3	11.4	11.5	11.7	10.8	10.6	11.4	11.4	11.6	11.9	11.4
2008	11.3	11.3	11.3	11.4	11.5	11.6	10.7	10.4	11.1	10.9	11.0	11.2	11.1
2009	10.9	10.8	10.8	10.3	10.6	10.6	9.8	9.6	10.4	10.4	10.6	10.9	10.5
Information													
1990	12.0	12.0	12.0	11.7	11.7	11.9	11.8	11.7	11.5	11.5	11.4	11.5	11.7
2000	14.8	14.8	14.8	14.8	14.9	15.2	15.3	15.1	15.0	15.0	15.1	15.2	15.0
2001	14.8	14.8	14.8	14.7	14.5	14.5	13.9	13.9	13.6	13.5	13.4	13.4	14.2
2002	13.2	13.0	13.0	12.8	12.7	12.7	12.7	12.6	12.4	12.4	12.4	12.4	12.7
2003	12.3	12.2	12.3	12.2	12.2	12.2	12.2	12.2	12.0	12.0	12.1	12.1	12.2
2004	12.2	12.1	12.0	12.0	12.1	12.2	12.1	12.1	11.9	11.7	11.8	11.7	12.0
2005	11.6	11.6	11.6	11.6	11.6	11.6	11.5	11.5	11.3	11.4	11.4	11.4	11.5
2006	11.3	11.2	11.4	11.3	11.4	11.4	11.3	11.2	11.1	11.1	11.2	11.4	11.3
2007	11.3	11.4	11.5	11.3	11.5	11.5	11.8	11.8	12.1	11.8	11.2	11.3	11.5
2008	11.3	11.3	11.4	11.3	11.3	11.5	11.5	11.6	11.5	11.5	11.6	11.7	11.5
2009	11.8	11.7	11.6	11.5	11.4	11.4	11.4	11.3	11.2	11.2	11.2	11.2	11.4
Financial Activities													
1990	34.4	34.4	34.5	34.4	34.4	34.6	34.2	34.2	33.8	33.6	33.6	33.7	34.2
2000	40.2	40.2	40.3	40.4	40.7	41.4	41.5	41.6	41.2	41.3	41.4	41.8	41.0
2001	40.6	40.7	40.7	40.8	40.9	41.3	41.1	41.1	40.5	40.5	40.5	40.6	40.8
2002	40.0	40.1	39.8	40.3	40.4	40.8	41.0	41.1	40.7	41.0	41.2	41.7	40.7
2003	41.1	41.1	41.3	41.3	41.5	41.8	42.0	41.9	41.3	41.2	41.2	41.4	41.4
2004	40.9	41.0	41.2	41.0	41.3	41.8	42.2	42.2	41.9	42.0	42.1	42.3	41.7
2005	42.1	42.3	42.6	42.7	42.7	43.1	43.4	43.3	42.8	42.9	43.0	43.2	42.8
2006	43.1	43.1	43.4	43.3	43.7	44.2	44.4	44.8	44.4	44.6	45.0	45.2	44.1
2007	45.0	45.0	45.1	45.0	45.3	45.9	46.3	46.1	45.4	45.6	45.6	45.8	45.5
2008	45.2	45.3	45.5	45.4	45.4	46.0	45.8	45.9	45.1	45.0	44.9	45.0	45.4
2009	44.0	44.0	44.0	43.0	42.9	43.3	43.5	43.3	42.9	43.1	43.1	43.3	43.4

Employment by Industry: Bridgeport-Stamford-Norwalk, CT, NECTA, Selected Years, 1990–2009—*Continued*

(Numbers in thousands, not seasonally adjusted.)

Industry and year	January	February	March	April	May	June	July	August	September	October	November	December	Annual average
Professional and Business Services													
1990	60.1	60.0	60.4	60.8	61.3	62.6	61.0	60.7	60.2	60.9	60.8	61.0	60.8
2000	75.7	75.8	77.1	78.0	78.4	79.9	79.9	79.5	79.9	79.5	79.1	79.1	78.5
2001	76.2	76.0	76.6	75.8	77.0	77.6	76.8	76.4	75.3	75.5	74.3	73.3	75.9
2002	70.4	70.3	71.1	71.8	71.7	72.2	70.9	71.0	70.5	71.1	70.8	70.5	71.0
2003	68.8	68.8	68.9	70.7	70.6	71.0	70.6	71.0	71.4	71.2	70.8	70.5	70.4
2004	67.7	67.8	68.8	69.3	70.1	71.1	70.5	70.4	69.9	69.6	69.8	70.2	69.6
2005	66.6	67.1	67.9	69.4	69.6	70.4	70.2	70.3	71.0	70.7	71.2	71.4	69.7
2006	68.6	69.3	70.5	71.5	71.7	72.6	71.1	71.2	71.2	70.9	71.1	72.0	71.0
2007	68.6	68.5	68.7	70.6	71.0	71.7	70.4	70.2	69.9	70.4	70.3	70.4	70.1
2008	67.5	66.8	67.4	68.8	68.7	69.2	68.5	68.2	67.3	67.1	66.5	66.1	67.7
2009	63.7	63.0	63.0	63.2	63.0	63.4	62.8	62.7	62.2	62.4	61.3	61.1	62.7
Education and Health Services													
1990	38.6	38.7	39.1	39.9	40.2	40.1	39.9	39.6	40.1	40.8	41.0	41.5	40.0
2000	53.1	53.5	53.5	53.8	53.8	53.6	53.6	53.2	54.1	55.0	55.3	55.5	54.0
2001	54.1	55.2	55.4	55.7	54.8	54.8	55.1	54.5	55.2	57.1	59.6	58.0	55.8
2002	56.6	57.6	58.3	58.3	58.3	57.2	57.2	56.4	57.4	59.4	59.8	59.7	58.0
2003	58.0	58.7	59.1	58.9	58.8	57.9	58.3	57.2	58.5	60.1	60.2	60.0	58.8
2004	58.4	59.1	59.8	59.4	59.2	58.5	58.7	58.2	58.9	60.2	60.5	60.1	59.3
2005	58.4	59.6	59.4	59.8	59.8	58.7	59.1	58.2	59.0	59.9	60.3	60.3	59.4
2006	59.6	60.3	60.2	60.6	60.8	59.9	60.0	59.1	60.0	61.2	61.8	62.2	60.5
2007	60.6	62.0	61.9	62.3	61.9	61.5	61.3	60.4	61.5	62.8	63.3	63.7	61.9
2008	62.3	63.6	64.0	64.0	63.5	63.5	63.1	62.1	63.4	64.7	65.2	65.4	63.7
2009	63.8	64.6	64.6	64.4	64.6	63.7	63.8	63.2	64.3	66.2	66.8	66.9	64.7
Leisure and Hospitality													
1990	26.1	25.6	26.5	27.2	28.4	29.9	29.6	29.7	28.9	27.8	27.4	27.4	27.9
2000	27.5	27.3	27.9	29.6	30.8	32.6	32.8	32.4	30.9	30.4	29.9	30.1	30.2
2001	28.3	28.2	28.8	29.6	31.5	32.9	33.3	32.6	30.5	30.2	30.0	30.5	30.5
2002	28.8	28.4	29.2	30.5	31.8	33.0	34.2	33.4	31.3	30.9	30.5	30.7	31.1
2003	29.0	28.9	29.6	31.0	32.7	34.3	35.2	34.3	32.5	32.2	31.8	31.7	31.9
2004	29.8	29.7	30.3	31.6	33.3	34.7	35.6	34.8	33.3	32.6	32.1	32.5	32.5
2005	29.8	29.8	30.3	32.1	33.4	35.3	35.8	35.2	33.1	32.2	31.8	31.9	32.6
2006	30.4	30.3	30.9	32.5	34.0	36.1	36.6	36.0	34.1	33.5	32.9	33.4	33.4
2007	31.5	31.2	31.7	33.0	34.7	36.4	37.5	36.8	34.4	33.9	33.9	34.2	34.1
2008	32.3	32.2	32.8	34.0	35.8	37.3	37.6	36.7	34.6	34.2	33.3	33.3	34.5
2009	31.0	30.7	31.0	32.1	33.9	35.3	36.2	35.6	34.4	33.9	32.9	32.6	33.3
Other Services													
1990	16.3	16.4	16.5	16.2	16.4	16.6	17.0	17.0	16.3	16.1	16.0	16.1	16.4
2000	16.0	15.9	16.0	16.4	16.5	16.8	17.3	17.1	16.6	16.8	16.7	16.9	16.6
2001	16.3	16.4	16.5	16.7	16.8	17.0	17.5	17.3	16.7	16.9	16.9	17.0	16.8
2002	16.9	16.9	16.9	17.0	17.2	17.3	17.5	17.3	16.7	16.8	16.9	17.0	17.0
2003	16.5	16.5	16.6	16.7	16.7	16.8	17.2	16.9	16.5	16.6	16.5	16.5	16.7
2004	16.4	16.4	16.5	16.6	16.7	16.9	17.4	17.2	16.6	16.6	16.6	16.7	16.7
2005	16.4	16.5	16.7	16.9	17.0	17.2	17.5	17.1	16.7	16.7	16.8	17.0	16.9
2006	16.8	16.7	16.8	16.9	17.0	17.2	17.8	17.4	16.9	17.1	17.1	17.2	17.1
2007	17.1	17.0	17.1	17.1	17.2	17.4	17.9	17.5	17.0	16.8	16.8	16.8	17.1
2008	16.7	16.5	16.6	16.7	16.8	17.2	17.5	17.3	16.7	16.7	16.7	16.7	16.8
2009	16.2	16.1	16.2	16.1	16.3	16.7	17.0	16.8	16.2	16.2	16.2	16.2	16.4
Government													
1990	43.4	44.5	44.7	44.6	45.0	45.4	39.9	39.3	42.5	43.5	44.4	44.1	43.4
2000	45.7	46.6	46.7	46.4	46.8	46.8	41.7	41.4	46.8	46.4	47.0	47.2	45.8
2001	46.6	47.0	46.8	47.1	47.4	47.2	41.9	41.1	48.3	48.3	49.1	49.0	46.7
2002	47.7	48.1	48.3	48.8	49.0	49.1	40.9	41.4	46.9	48.4	49.2	49.0	47.2
2003	48.1	48.3	48.5	48.0	48.3	48.4	45.1	42.6	46.2	47.1	47.7	47.5	47.2
2004	47.5	48.0	48.5	47.5	47.6	47.5	44.5	43.0	46.7	47.8	48.2	47.5	47.0
2005	46.6	47.0	47.1	48.0	48.3	48.4	45.5	44.0	46.9	47.4	47.5	47.8	47.0
2006	47.3	47.8	48.0	47.8	48.0	46.9	44.3	42.9	46.5	47.2	47.7	47.5	46.8
2007	46.9	47.6	47.6	47.5	48.5	47.3	46.3	44.7	46.8	48.0	48.4	48.1	47.3
2008	47.8	48.6	48.4	48.0	48.8	47.7	45.0	43.6	47.2	48.2	49.1	48.5	47.6
2009	47.5	47.9	48.1	46.9	48.4	48.1	44.7	43.6	46.9	48.1	48.4	48.3	47.2

Employment by Industry: Buffalo-Niagara Falls, NY, Selected Years, 1990–2009

(Numbers in thousands, not seasonally adjusted.)

Industry and year	January	February	March	April	May	June	July	August	September	October	November	December	Annual average
Total Nonfarm													
1990	527.9	537.2	542.0	543.7	552.7	557.0	546.8	549.0	552.0	554.3	554.5	552.5	547.5
2000	545.9	548.9	551.4	555.6	562.1	563.9	558.1	559.1	561.7	567.6	568.7	565.9	559.1
2001	546.9	548.3	550.0	546.6	556.3	558.8	546.6	546.6	547.4	551.1	551.7	550.2	550.0
2002	537.2	539.2	541.2	543.1	550.9	553.4	546.2	548.1	549.2	554.5	554.8	555.7	547.8
2003	535.7	537.5	540.2	542.1	547.6	550.3	541.0	541.8	548.0	551.7	555.1	555.4	545.5
2004	535.2	539.1	543.8	542.6	551.7	551.9	543.6	545.4	551.5	556.4	557.1	558.4	548.1
2005	535.0	538.0	538.9	545.2	550.1	551.1	540.8	544.0	552.1	555.6	556.2	555.5	546.9
2006	534.3	537.5	540.3	544.8	551.0	552.2	541.6	544.8	548.1	548.7	554.9	556.4	546.2
2007	534.7	537.6	541.3	540.9	550.9	552.1	542.6	545.5	550.5	557.4	558.9	559.0	547.6
2008	539.1	541.4	542.9	549.5	556.4	559.1	551.1	552.4	556.3	562.1	559.1	556.2	552.1
2009	531.7	532.1	533.1	535.9	540.9	541.3	536.4	536.5	538.7	543.2	543.7	541.2	537.9
Total Private													
1990	439.7	447.8	451.8	453.7	461.8	466.1	459.1	462.2	466.3	464.0	463.6	461.4	458.1
2000	456.7	457.8	459.5	463.5	469.0	473.5	471.0	472.7	473.3	474.2	475.1	474.6	468.4
2001	456.5	455.7	457.3	454.2	463.1	467.2	459.9	460.1	457.4	458.0	458.1	457.3	458.7
2002	445.4	445.2	446.7	450.3	457.0	460.8	457.0	458.8	458.8	460.2	460.3	461.0	455.1
2003	442.6	441.9	443.2	446.2	451.4	454.9	450.7	451.9	455.0	456.8	457.0	457.2	450.7
2004	439.6	441.2	445.2	446.8	453.9	457.3	454.0	456.0	459.1	460.5	459.8	461.7	452.9
2005	440.4	441.3	443.5	449.9	454.4	457.8	452.8	456.2	459.5	460.3	460.5	460.0	453.1
2006	441.7	443.0	445.9	450.2	456.0	458.2	452.8	456.2	455.9	453.9	459.5	460.8	452.8
2007	441.1	442.4	445.8	446.0	455.3	457.3	453.8	455.4	457.5	461.7	462.2	462.4	453.4
2008	445.3	445.5	446.7	452.9	459.7	463.1	460.4	461.2	462.0	464.4	461.2	458.7	456.8
2009	436.9	435.9	436.6	439.2	443.5	445.5	444.2	444.3	444.7	445.7	446.2	444.2	442.2
Goods-Producing													
1990	110.6	111.6	112.7	113.6	116.3	118.0	117.2	118.2	119.5	117.2	114.7	111.0	115.1
2000	100.5	100.0	100.6	102.5	104.4	105.9	105.5	106.5	105.9	105.7	104.9	103.0	103.8
2001	98.3	97.3	97.3	98.0	98.6	100.7	100.5	99.6	99.1	98.2	97.1	95.6	98.4
2002	89.2	88.7	89.2	91.4	93.4	94.4	94.4	94.2	93.3	93.6	93.1	90.8	92.1
2003	87.0	85.6	86.4	86.2	88.0	89.2	88.3	89.0	89.2	88.7	87.7	86.3	87.6
2004	82.5	82.2	83.7	84.9	86.8	88.0	87.4	88.6	88.5	87.9	87.4	86.3	86.2
2005	81.8	80.9	81.0	82.3	83.9	84.8	83.8	85.4	84.8	84.5	84.3	82.3	83.3
2006	79.8	79.0	79.5	81.5	83.1	84.3	83.3	84.3	83.5	82.1	82.2	80.8	82.0
2007	77.7	76.5	77.3	78.2	81.0	82.4	81.6	82.3	81.6	81.1	80.5	79.0	79.9
2008	75.2	74.7	74.3	76.4	79.3	80.8	80.9	81.6	80.8	80.3	78.3	76.1	78.2
2009	70.6	69.0	68.4	69.6	70.8	70.6	70.7	70.5	70.3	69.7	69.0	67.2	69.7
Mining, Logging, and Construction													
1990	18.7	18.4	19.4	20.3	23.0	24.2	25.2	25.5	25.5	24.4	23.1	21.2	22.4
2000	17.7	17.2	17.9	19.7	21.4	22.2	23.0	23.4	22.9	22.4	21.7	19.6	20.8
2001	17.6	17.3	17.8	19.5	21.5	22.5	23.2	23.3	22.7	22.3	21.6	20.6	20.8
2002	17.1	16.7	17.4	19.4	21.2	22.0	22.9	23.1	22.4	22.4	21.7	20.2	20.5
2003	17.3	16.6	16.9	18.2	20.1	20.9	21.9	22.5	22.0	22.0	20.8	19.8	19.9
2004	16.7	16.6	17.4	19.1	21.0	21.9	22.7	22.9	22.6	22.8	22.1	20.6	20.5
2005	17.4	17.0	16.7	18.7	20.2	21.2	21.7	22.3	21.7	21.6	21.3	19.6	20.0
2006	17.2	16.7	17.1	19.2	20.8	21.8	21.9	22.3	21.7	21.3	21.1	19.9	20.1
2007	17.6	16.3	17.2	18.3	20.8	21.9	22.1	22.4	21.7	21.6	20.8	19.6	20.0
2008	17.3	16.5	16.9	19.0	21.4	22.3	23.5	23.8	23.3	23.1	21.6	20.0	20.7
2009	17.1	16.6	17.0	18.3	20.0	20.6	21.2	21.5	20.8	20.5	20.0	18.8	19.4
Manufacturing													
1990	91.9	93.2	93.3	93.3	93.3	93.8	92.0	92.7	94.0	92.8	91.6	89.8	92.6
2000	82.8	82.8	82.7	82.8	83.0	83.7	82.5	83.1	83.0	83.3	83.2	83.4	83.0
2001	80.7	80.0	79.5	78.5	77.1	78.2	77.3	76.3	76.4	75.9	75.5	75.0	77.5
2002	72.1	72.0	71.8	72.0	72.2	72.4	71.5	71.1	70.9	71.2	71.4	70.6	71.6
2003	69.7	69.0	69.5	68.0	67.9	68.3	66.4	66.5	67.2	66.7	66.9	66.5	67.7
2004	65.8	65.6	66.3	65.8	65.8	66.1	64.7	65.7	65.9	65.1	65.3	65.7	65.7
2005	64.4	63.9	64.3	63.6	63.7	63.6	62.1	63.1	63.1	62.9	63.0	62.7	63.4
2006	62.6	62.3	62.4	62.3	62.3	62.5	61.4	62.0	61.8	60.8	61.1	60.9	61.9
2007	60.1	60.2	60.1	59.9	60.2	60.5	59.5	59.9	59.9	59.5	59.7	59.4	59.9
2008	57.9	58.2	57.4	57.4	57.9	58.5	57.4	57.8	57.5	57.2	56.7	56.1	57.5
2009	53.5	52.4	51.4	51.3	50.8	50.0	49.5	49.0	49.5	49.2	49.0	48.4	50.3
Service-Providing													
1990	417.3	425.6	429.3	430.1	436.4	439.0	429.6	430.8	432.5	437.1	439.8	441.5	432.4
2000	445.4	448.9	450.8	453.1	457.7	458.0	452.6	452.6	455.8	461.9	463.8	462.9	455.3
2001	448.6	451.0	452.7	448.6	457.7	457.8	446.1	447.0	448.3	452.9	454.6	454.6	451.7
2002	448.0	450.5	452.0	451.7	457.5	459.0	451.8	453.9	455.9	460.9	461.7	464.9	455.7
2003	448.7	451.9	453.8	455.9	459.6	461.1	452.7	452.8	458.8	463.0	467.4	469.1	457.9
2004	452.7	456.9	460.1	457.7	464.9	463.9	456.2	456.8	463.0	468.5	469.7	472.1	461.9
2005	453.2	457.1	457.9	462.9	466.2	466.3	457.0	458.6	467.3	471.1	471.9	473.2	463.6
2006	454.5	458.5	460.8	463.3	467.9	467.9	458.3	460.5	464.6	466.6	472.7	475.6	464.3
2007	457.0	461.1	464.0	462.7	469.9	469.7	461.0	463.2	468.9	476.3	478.4	480.0	467.7
2008	463.9	466.7	468.6	473.1	477.1	478.3	470.2	470.8	475.5	481.8	480.8	480.1	473.9
2009	461.1	463.1	464.7	466.3	470.1	470.7	465.7	466.0	468.4	473.5	474.7	474.0	468.2

Employment by Industry: Buffalo-Niagara Falls, NY, Selected Years, 1990–2009—*Continued*

(Numbers in thousands, not seasonally adjusted.)

Industry and year	January	February	March	April	May	June	July	August	September	October	November	December	Annual average
Trade, Transportation, and Utilities													
1990	112.0	112.6	113.1	112.9	114.3	115.4	112.5	113.3	114.2	114.6	117.4	119.2	114.3
2000	108.6	107.4	107.4	106.7	108.1	109.7	108.2	109.3	109.5	109.9	112.6	114.2	109.3
2001	110.1	108.1	108.2	105.9	107.7	108.6	106.0	105.8	105.6	106.2	108.2	109.5	107.5
2002	105.2	103.1	103.2	103.1	104.3	105.9	103.9	104.0	104.4	105.2	106.6	108.0	104.7
2003	102.4	100.4	100.5	100.7	102.1	103.2	102.1	102.3	102.9	103.7	105.4	106.7	102.7
2004	100.8	99.4	99.7	99.9	102.0	102.9	101.9	102.5	103.1	103.9	105.8	107.5	102.5
2005	102.0	100.7	101.8	102.4	103.3	104.3	103.1	103.3	103.6	103.9	105.2	107.1	103.4
2006	102.1	99.5	100.0	100.9	102.2	103.7	102.2	102.7	102.8	103.7	106.1	107.5	102.8
2007	102.7	100.9	101.2	100.8	102.9	104.1	102.9	103.0	104.3	104.9	107.0	108.9	103.6
2008	103.4	101.1	101.2	101.8	103.1	104.4	102.5	102.5	103.3	103.7	104.3	105.0	103.0
2009	98.4	96.9	96.6	96.3	97.5	98.4	97.5	97.7	98.0	99.8	102.1	103.0	98.5
Wholesale Trade													
1990	23.1	23.5	23.6	23.6	23.6	24.1	23.9	24.1	23.8	23.7	23.9	23.9	23.7
2000	24.1	24.3	24.1	23.6	23.7	23.9	23.9	24.0	23.7	23.7	23.9	23.9	23.9
2001	24.0	24.0	24.0	23.8	23.9	24.1	23.9	23.7	23.5	23.6	23.5	23.5	23.8
2002	23.2	23.2	23.1	23.0	23.1	23.3	23.2	23.1	23.1	23.3	23.3	23.3	23.2
2003	22.5	22.4	22.5	22.4	22.8	22.7	23.0	23.0	22.9	22.9	23.0	23.1	22.8
2004	22.8	22.7	22.8	22.9	23.1	23.2	23.3	23.4	23.2	23.4	23.6	23.8	23.2
2005	23.4	23.4	23.5	23.6	23.6	23.7	23.8	23.6	23.5	23.3	23.5	23.5	23.5
2006	23.3	23.2	23.3	23.3	23.4	23.6	23.3	23.3	23.1	23.3	23.4	23.6	23.3
2007	23.6	23.5	23.5	23.5	23.6	23.9	23.9	23.8	23.7	23.8	23.8	24.0	23.7
2008	23.4	23.2	23.2	23.1	23.1	23.2	23.2	23.0	22.7	22.6	22.5	22.4	23.0
2009	22.1	21.8	21.7	21.7	21.5	21.5	21.4	21.3	21.2	21.3	21.4	21.5	21.5
Retail Trade													
1990	70.5	70.3	70.4	70.2	71.2	71.5	70.2	70.9	70.8	71.1	73.8	75.5	71.4
2000	65.3	64.0	64.2	63.8	64.7	65.8	65.4	66.2	65.9	65.9	68.5	70.1	65.8
2001	65.8	64.1	64.1	62.7	63.8	64.4	63.1	63.2	62.5	63.0	65.2	66.5	64.0
2002	62.9	61.2	61.6	61.3	62.0	63.1	62.2	62.3	61.9	62.5	64.0	65.4	62.5
2003	61.2	59.6	59.6	60.0	60.8	61.9	61.4	61.7	61.5	62.3	64.1	65.5	61.6
2004	60.8	59.5	59.7	59.6	61.1	62.0	61.6	62.1	61.9	62.6	64.4	65.8	61.8
2005	61.4	60.2	61.1	61.5	62.0	62.7	62.3	62.6	62.4	62.8	64.2	65.8	62.4
2006	61.8	59.6	59.8	60.5	61.2	62.1	61.6	61.9	61.2	62.0	64.3	65.2	61.8
2007	61.2	59.6	59.8	59.2	60.8	61.5	61.3	61.6	61.7	62.3	64.5	65.9	61.6
2008	62.0	60.1	60.2	60.4	61.4	62.3	62.1	62.2	62.1	62.8	63.6	64.3	62.0
2009	59.7	58.6	58.6	58.4	59.5	60.4	60.0	60.4	60.5	62.1	64.2	65.1	60.6
Transportation and Utilities													
1990	18.4	18.8	19.1	19.1	19.5	19.8	18.4	18.3	19.6	19.8	19.7	19.8	19.2
2000	19.2	19.1	19.1	19.3	19.7	20.0	18.9	19.1	19.9	20.3	20.2	20.2	19.6
2001	20.3	20.0	20.1	19.4	20.0	20.1	19.0	18.9	19.6	19.6	19.5	19.5	19.7
2002	19.1	18.7	18.5	18.8	19.2	19.5	18.5	18.6	19.4	19.4	19.3	19.3	19.0
2003	18.7	18.4	18.4	18.3	18.5	18.6	17.7	17.6	18.5	18.5	18.3	18.1	18.3
2004	17.2	17.2	17.2	17.4	17.8	17.7	17.0	17.0	18.0	17.9	17.8	17.9	17.5
2005	17.2	17.1	17.2	17.3	17.7	17.9	17.0	17.1	17.7	17.8	17.5	17.8	17.4
2006	17.0	16.7	16.9	17.1	17.6	18.0	17.3	17.5	18.5	18.4	18.4	18.7	17.7
2007	17.9	17.8	17.9	18.1	18.5	18.7	17.7	17.6	18.9	18.8	18.7	19.0	18.3
2008	18.0	17.8	17.8	18.3	18.6	18.9	17.2	17.3	18.5	18.3	18.2	18.3	18.1
2009	16.6	16.5	16.3	16.2	16.5	16.5	16.1	16.0	16.3	16.4	16.5	16.4	16.4
Information													
1990	10.6	10.7	10.7	10.6	10.7	10.7	10.8	10.7	10.8	10.9	10.9	10.9	10.8
2000	9.7	9.8	9.7	10.0	10.1	10.1	10.2	9.0	10.3	10.1	10.1	10.2	9.9
2001	11.0	11.0	11.1	11.0	11.2	11.3	11.0	10.8	10.7	10.4	10.4	10.5	10.9
2002	10.4	10.5	10.6	10.6	10.9	10.9	10.7	10.9	10.9	10.8	10.2	10.3	10.6
2003	9.8	9.9	9.9	9.9	9.9	9.8	9.8	10.1	9.8	9.9	9.9	10.0	9.8
2004	9.8	9.8	9.9	9.9	9.9	9.9	9.8	9.9	9.7	9.7	9.6	9.6	9.8
2005	9.5	9.4	9.4	9.5	9.5	9.5	9.7	9.7	9.6	9.6	9.6	9.7	9.6
2006	9.4	9.3	9.3	9.2	9.3	9.3	9.2	9.1	8.9	8.6	8.6	8.6	9.1
2007	8.5	8.5	8.5	8.4	8.6	8.6	8.6	8.5	8.4	8.3	8.4	8.4	8.5
2008	8.3	8.3	8.3	8.3	8.6	8.6	8.6	8.7	8.5	8.4	8.4	8.5	8.5
2009	8.3	8.2	8.3	8.3	8.3	8.4	8.3	8.3	8.1	7.9	7.9	8.0	8.2
Financial Activities													
1990	30.1	30.6	30.8	30.7	30.8	31.0	30.6	30.6	30.3	29.8	29.7	29.8	30.4
2000	29.3	29.3	29.5	29.4	29.8	30.3	30.3	30.3	30.1	30.0	30.2	30.3	29.9
2001	30.2	30.2	30.5	30.3	30.8	30.9	31.5	31.6	31.6	32.1	31.9	32.5	31.2
2002	33.1	33.1	32.9	32.8	32.9	33.3	33.4	33.3	32.9	33.4	33.7	33.8	33.2
2003	33.2	32.8	32.4	33.7	33.8	34.2	34.2	34.4	34.3	34.4	34.5	34.6	33.8
2004	34.4	34.4	34.7	34.1	34.1	34.2	34.5	34.3	34.0	34.0	34.0	34.1	34.2
2005	33.4	33.3	33.3	34.0	34.1	34.7	34.8	34.9	34.8	34.8	35.0	35.2	34.4
2006	35.0	35.1	35.2	34.9	35.1	35.2	35.1	35.0	34.5	34.0	34.0	34.3	34.8
2007	33.3	33.4	33.6	32.9	33.0	33.5	33.5	33.4	33.0	33.3	33.4	33.9	33.4
2008	32.8	32.7	32.6	32.7	32.9	33.1	33.0	32.9	32.5	32.5	32.5	32.8	32.8
2009	31.4	31.3	31.3	31.5	31.6	31.9	32.0	31.7	31.3	31.3	31.3	31.4	31.5

Employment by Industry: Buffalo-Niagara Falls, NY, Selected Years, 1990–2009—*Continued*

(Numbers in thousands, not seasonally adjusted.)

Industry and year	January	February	March	April	May	June	July	August	September	October	November	December	Annual average
Professional and Business Services													
1990	45.9	46.9	47.4	47.7	48.7	49.0	49.3	49.7	49.5	49.5	49.5	49.1	48.5
2000	60.2	60.8	60.9	61.5	62.3	62.9	63.6	63.7	63.0	63.0	62.4	61.5	62.2
2001	60.3	60.5	60.7	61.3	62.7	62.9	62.7	63.2	62.1	61.7	60.9	60.1	61.6
2002	60.3	60.4	60.3	60.9	61.9	63.0	63.4	64.2	64.3	64.0	63.9	63.7	62.5
2003	61.3	62.0	61.9	62.9	63.0	64.0	64.6	64.4	64.4	64.4	64.2	64.2	63.4
2004	62.0	62.5	63.1	64.3	65.0	66.6	66.4	66.6	66.2	66.3	66.0	65.9	65.1
2005	63.4	63.7	63.8	65.7	66.0	67.8	67.5	68.2	68.9	68.8	68.1	67.8	66.6
2006	65.7	66.1	66.4	67.9	68.2	69.4	68.8	69.9	68.9	69.1	70.5	70.4	68.4
2007	67.1	67.6	68.3	68.9	69.6	70.9	70.8	71.5	71.0	71.4	71.5	71.3	70.0
2008	69.4	70.0	70.4	72.9	73.3	74.6	74.8	74.6	73.7	73.2	72.4	71.6	72.6
2009	69.4	69.3	69.7	70.2	70.8	72.5	72.4	72.2	71.4	70.7	70.4	70.0	70.8
Education and Health Services													
1990	69.6	72.2	72.9	73.2	73.5	73.3	70.1	70.0	73.2	74.4	74.7	74.9	72.7
2000	82.7	83.3	83.4	83.9	83.8	82.7	81.7	81.3	83.5	85.6	85.1	85.4	83.5
2001	80.3	80.7	80.4	80.3	80.8	79.7	78.1	78.0	80.2	81.4	81.8	81.5	80.3
2002	80.5	81.7	82.0	81.9	81.8	80.5	79.0	79.0	82.1	83.4	83.7	83.9	81.6
2003	81.5	83.2	83.8	83.5	83.2	81.8	79.9	79.8	83.7	85.2	85.6	85.7	83.0
2004	83.0	84.9	85.2	84.8	84.5	83.3	82.2	81.4	85.0	87.3	87.4	87.6	84.7
2005	83.4	86.2	86.1	86.6	86.1	83.9	81.6	81.2	85.4	86.8	87.2	86.8	85.1
2006	82.9	86.0	86.5	86.2	86.1	83.7	82.2	82.3	85.8	86.8	87.4	87.5	85.3
2007	83.6	86.1	86.9	86.5	86.4	83.8	82.2	82.0	85.9	88.0	88.1	88.1	85.6
2008	85.8	87.7	88.3	88.6	87.6	85.7	84.6	84.3	87.9	90.2	90.5	90.6	87.7
2009	87.9	90.1	90.7	90.0	89.5	87.4	86.1	85.6	88.9	91.4	91.5	92.1	89.3
Leisure and Hospitality													
1990	42.6	44.2	44.9	46.0	48.4	49.8	49.7	50.7	49.7	48.1	47.4	47.4	47.4
2000	43.4	44.5	44.9	46.2	47.3	48.7	48.1	49.1	48.0	46.8	46.8	46.7	46.7
2001	43.0	44.4	45.3	43.9	47.5	48.9	46.9	47.8	45.1	44.7	44.4	43.9	45.5
2002	43.9	44.6	45.1	46.3	48.5	49.5	49.1	50.1	48.2	47.1	46.2	47.5	47.2
2003	44.7	45.1	45.2	45.9	48.0	49.2	48.5	49.0	47.8	47.6	46.8	46.7	47.0
2004	44.7	45.2	45.7	45.8	48.1	49.3	49.0	49.8	49.5	48.3	46.4	47.3	47.4
2005	44.2	44.4	44.8	46.4	48.3	49.7	49.5	50.7	49.6	49.0	48.2	48.0	47.7
2006	44.5	45.6	46.1	46.8	48.9	49.6	49.2	49.9	48.6	46.6	47.6	48.3	47.6
2007	45.6	46.5	46.8	47.2	50.5	50.6	50.8	51.2	50.1	50.6	49.8	49.2	49.1
2008	47.1	47.6	47.9	48.5	51.0	52.0	51.9	52.4	51.5	51.8	50.8	50.1	50.2
2009	47.5	47.5	47.8	49.1	50.8	52.1	53.1	54.1	52.7	50.5	49.4	47.9	50.2
Other Services													
1990	18.3	19.0	19.3	19.0	19.1	18.9	18.9	19.0	19.1	19.5	19.3	19.1	19.0
2000	22.3	22.7	23.1	23.3	23.2	23.2	23.4	23.5	23.0	23.1	23.0	23.3	23.1
2001	23.3	23.5	23.8	23.5	23.8	24.2	23.2	23.3	23.0	23.3	23.4	23.7	23.5
2002	22.8	23.1	23.4	23.3	23.3	23.3	23.1	23.1	22.7	22.7	22.9	23.0	23.1
2003	22.7	22.9	23.1	23.4	23.4	23.5	23.3	22.9	22.9	22.9	22.9	23.0	23.0
2004	22.4	22.8	23.2	23.1	23.5	23.1	22.8	22.9	23.1	23.1	23.2	23.4	23.1
2005	22.7	22.7	23.3	23.0	23.2	23.1	22.8	22.8	22.8	22.9	22.9	23.1	22.9
2006	22.3	22.4	22.9	22.8	23.1	23.0	22.8	23.0	22.9	23.0	23.1	23.4	22.9
2007	22.6	22.9	23.2	23.1	23.3	23.4	23.4	23.5	23.2	23.6	23.5	23.6	23.3
2008	23.3	23.4	23.7	23.7	23.9	23.9	24.1	24.2	23.8	24.3	24.0	24.0	23.9
2009	23.4	23.6	23.8	24.2	24.2	24.2	24.1	24.2	24.0	24.4	24.6	24.6	24.1
Government													
1990	88.2	89.4	90.2	90.0	90.9	90.9	87.7	86.8	85.7	90.3	90.9	91.1	89.3
2000	89.2	91.1	91.9	92.1	93.1	90.4	87.1	86.4	88.4	93.4	93.6	91.3	90.7
2001	90.4	92.6	92.7	92.4	93.2	91.3	86.7	86.5	90.0	93.1	93.6	92.9	91.3
2002	91.8	94.0	94.5	92.8	93.9	92.6	89.2	89.3	90.4	94.3	94.5	94.7	92.7
2003	93.1	95.6	97.0	95.9	96.2	95.4	90.3	89.9	93.0	94.9	98.1	98.2	94.8
2004	95.6	97.9	98.6	95.8	97.8	94.6	89.6	89.4	92.4	95.9	97.3	96.7	95.1
2005	94.6	96.7	95.4	95.3	95.7	93.3	88.0	87.8	92.6	95.3	95.7	95.5	93.8
2006	92.6	94.5	94.4	94.6	95.0	94.0	88.8	88.6	92.2	94.8	95.4	95.6	93.4
2007	93.6	95.2	95.5	94.9	95.6	94.8	88.8	90.1	93.0	96.2	96.7	96.6	94.3
2008	93.8	95.9	96.2	96.6	96.7	96.0	90.7	91.2	94.3	97.7	97.9	97.5	95.4
2009	94.8	96.2	96.5	96.7	97.4	95.8	92.2	92.2	94.0	97.5	97.5	97.0	95.7

Employment by Industry: Charlotte-Gastonia-Concord, NC-SC, Selected Years, 1990–2009

(Numbers in thousands, not seasonally adjusted.)

Industry and year	January	February	March	April	May	June	July	August	September	October	November	December	Annual average
Total Nonfarm													
1990	540.3	545.7	550.7	551.4	553.6	555.9	544.7	547.2	553.5	554.0	553.0	552.8	550.2
2000	748.5	750.3	758.7	766.0	769.8	774.6	759.9	767.2	771.4	778.5	778.0	779.0	766.8
2001	763.0	766.7	771.5	775.7	777.7	777.4	761.1	769.4	771.3	774.6	773.8	771.5	771.1
2002	757.4	761.1	767.3	768.2	771.5	773.8	761.3	770.8	775.2	777.0	777.9	776.3	769.8
2003	758.7	759.2	765.5	767.3	773.6	771.0	744.2	756.3	766.4	772.6	773.7	774.2	765.2
2004	756.0	757.9	764.1	766.2	772.6	771.7	755.6	770.1	778.8	786.4	788.1	787.4	771.2
2005	772.5	776.5	782.5	787.1	791.6	788.4	773.8	790.8	799.9	808.9	810.7	811.1	791.2
2006	801.7	805.1	813.1	821.3	827.0	822.0	808.8	828.8	837.7	844.0	850.2	851.2	825.9
2007	838.8	844.1	853.3	856.9	863.7	858.4	840.9	862.7	867.6	875.3	877.7	879.4	859.9
2008	858.2	863.0	868.3	866.2	870.8	863.7	840.7	862.0	865.0	863.1	857.4	855.4	861.2
2009	824.5	821.8	820.5	814.7	816.2	808.1	786.1	805.4	805.1	805.6	808.3	805.9	810.2
Total Private													
1990	479.3	483.8	488.3	488.2	490.5	492.9	489.3	490.0	491.2	489.4	488.0	487.5	488.2
2000	660.1	661.6	668.8	676.1	680.2	687.2	681.8	683.8	683.3	686.3	686.4	687.5	678.6
2001	673.2	675.4	679.9	683.5	685.6	688.4	681.3	683.0	679.5	679.5	676.5	675.6	680.1
2002	663.4	665.6	671.0	672.7	676.1	681.2	678.5	682.3	680.7	678.5	679.0	678.9	675.7
2003	663.0	662.6	668.2	670.1	675.8	677.2	667.3	670.5	670.1	670.4	671.9	673.5	670.1
2004	657.2	658.1	664.2	666.2	672.4	675.6	677.5	681.9	678.8	683.2	684.4	684.9	673.7
2005	671.9	675.0	680.5	684.3	689.1	690.6	694.4	696.9	697.0	703.3	705.0	705.9	691.2
2006	697.4	700.2	707.8	715.7	721.3	724.9	728.8	732.5	731.5	736.5	740.9	741.9	723.3
2007	730.6	734.4	743.5	747.9	754.0	758.2	757.1	759.3	757.5	763.2	764.2	765.6	753.0
2008	744.8	748.4	753.2	751.1	755.3	755.9	750.7	751.8	747.0	745.4	738.4	735.7	748.1
2009	706.4	703.2	701.5	695.6	697.9	695.9	692.9	692.3	689.2	687.1	688.8	686.8	694.8
Goods-Producing													
1990	158.2	159.2	159.8	160.1	160.9	161.6	160.5	159.9	159.3	158.6	157.8	156.2	159.3
2000	157.5	157.1	158.3	159.7	160.3	161.6	160.0	160.2	160.8	159.1	158.9	158.4	159.3
2001	155.4	155.8	156.4	156.3	156.3	156.6	154.8	154.7	154.5	152.7	150.9	150.1	154.5
2002	149.5	149.1	149.5	148.9	149.7	150.5	149.4	149.7	148.9	147.6	146.6	144.6	148.7
2003	142.5	141.8	142.5	140.7	140.8	140.6	136.3	135.9	135.4	135.6	135.0	134.5	138.5
2004	131.7	131.8	132.9	133.8	135.0	135.9	136.3	136.8	136.3	136.4	135.9	135.5	134.9
2005	133.9	134.6	135.3	134.8	135.7	136.5	136.9	137.1	137.0	136.8	136.6	136.6	136.0
2006	135.4	135.6	137.1	138.7	139.3	140.2	140.9	141.9	141.3	141.5	141.1	141.7	139.6
2007	139.9	140.3	140.7	141.4	141.4	142.2	142.3	142.5	142.0	141.4	140.7	140.2	141.3
2008	137.1	136.8	136.8	135.6	135.7	135.3	134.6	134.1	132.9	130.7	128.0	125.3	133.6
2009	118.9	117.1	115.6	112.7	111.8	111.0	110.4	109.2	108.3	105.3	104.5	103.4	110.7
Mining, Logging, and Construction													
1990	33.9	34.2	34.7	34.8	35.6	36.0	35.7	35.8	35.4	35.2	34.8	34.2	35.0
2000	48.3	48.3	49.6	50.3	51.0	51.7	51.6	51.8	51.8	51.5	51.4	51.2	50.7
2001	49.5	49.8	50.9	51.2	51.7	52.3	52.4	52.4	52.4	51.3	50.5	49.9	51.2
2002	50.0	49.8	50.7	50.9	51.6	51.9	52.1	52.2	51.2	50.2	49.7	49.4	50.8
2003	47.8	47.5	47.9	47.1	47.9	48.3	48.4	48.6	48.6	49.1	49.1	49.0	48.3
2004	47.4	47.3	48.1	48.9	49.8	50.3	50.7	51.0	50.5	51.4	51.3	51.3	49.8
2005	50.5	50.7	51.3	51.1	51.7	52.6	54.0	54.4	54.5	53.9	54.1	54.0	52.7
2006	53.3	53.6	54.8	56.0	56.5	57.4	58.1	58.8	58.5	58.7	58.5	58.7	56.9
2007	57.6	58.1	58.9	59.6	59.7	60.6	60.7	60.8	60.4	60.0	59.3	58.6	59.5
2008	56.3	56.1	56.0	55.6	55.8	55.6	55.1	54.6	53.8	52.3	50.7	49.3	54.3
2009	45.9	45.1	44.3	43.0	43.0	43.1	42.9	42.3	41.4	39.1	38.6	37.8	42.2
Manufacturing													
1990	124.3	125.0	125.1	125.3	125.3	125.6	124.8	124.1	123.9	123.4	123.0	122.0	124.3
2000	109.2	108.8	108.7	109.4	109.3	109.9	108.4	108.4	109.0	107.6	107.5	107.2	108.6
2001	105.9	106.0	105.5	105.1	104.6	104.3	102.4	102.3	102.1	101.4	100.4	100.2	103.4
2002	99.5	99.3	98.8	98.0	98.1	98.6	97.3	97.5	97.7	97.4	96.9	95.2	97.9
2003	94.7	94.3	94.6	93.6	92.9	92.3	87.9	87.3	86.8	86.5	85.9	85.5	90.2
2004	84.3	84.5	84.8	84.9	85.2	85.6	85.6	85.8	85.8	85.0	84.6	84.2	85.0
2005	83.4	83.9	84.0	83.7	84.0	83.9	82.9	82.7	82.5	82.9	82.7	82.6	83.3
2006	82.1	82.0	82.3	82.7	82.8	82.8	82.8	83.1	82.8	82.8	82.6	83.0	82.7
2007	82.3	82.2	81.8	81.8	81.7	81.6	81.6	81.7	81.6	81.4	81.4	81.6	81.7
2008	80.8	80.7	80.8	80.0	79.9	79.7	79.5	79.5	79.1	78.4	77.3	76.0	79.3
2009	73.0	72.0	71.3	69.7	68.8	67.9	67.5	66.9	66.9	66.2	65.9	65.6	68.5
Service-Providing													
1990	382.1	386.5	390.9	391.3	392.7	394.3	384.2	387.3	394.2	395.4	395.2	396.6	390.9
2000	591.0	593.2	600.4	606.3	609.5	613.0	599.9	607.0	610.6	619.4	619.1	620.6	607.5
2001	607.6	610.9	615.1	619.4	621.4	620.8	606.3	614.7	616.8	621.9	622.9	621.4	616.6
2002	607.9	612.0	617.8	619.3	621.8	623.3	611.9	621.1	626.3	629.4	631.3	631.7	621.2
2003	616.2	617.4	623.0	626.6	632.8	630.4	607.9	620.4	631.0	637.0	638.7	639.7	626.8
2004	624.3	626.1	631.2	632.4	637.6	635.8	619.3	633.3	642.5	650.0	652.2	651.9	636.4
2005	638.6	641.9	647.2	652.3	655.9	651.9	636.9	653.7	662.9	672.1	673.9	674.5	655.2
2006	666.3	669.5	676.0	682.6	687.7	681.8	667.9	686.9	696.4	702.5	709.1	709.5	686.4
2007	698.9	703.8	712.6	715.5	722.3	716.2	698.6	720.2	725.6	733.9	737.0	739.2	718.7
2008	721.1	726.2	731.5	730.6	735.1	728.4	706.1	727.9	732.1	732.4	729.4	730.1	727.6
2009	705.6	704.7	704.9	702.0	704.4	697.1	675.7	696.2	696.8	700.3	703.8	702.5	699.5

Employment by Industry: Charlotte-Gastonia-Concord, NC-SC, Selected Years, 1990–2009—*Continued*

(Numbers in thousands, not seasonally adjusted.)

Industry and year	January	February	March	April	May	June	July	August	September	October	November	December	Annual average
Trade, Transportation, and Utilities													
1990	129.5	129.6	130.4	128.9	128.9	128.5	128.0	128.3	128.7	128.7	130.1	131.2	129.2
2000	163.0	163.0	164.3	165.3	166.3	167.9	166.2	166.5	166.5	167.7	170.2	171.7	166.6
2001	167.5	166.7	167.3	169.0	169.3	169.9	167.8	167.8	167.7	168.4	169.7	170.6	168.5
2002	164.4	163.2	164.3	163.3	163.3	164.0	163.6	164.4	163.8	163.8	167.1	168.8	164.5
2003	161.2	160.8	160.9	161.1	161.4	162.1	160.5	161.3	161.8	163.0	165.9	167.7	162.3
2004	162.0	161.8	161.9	163.6	165.0	165.0	164.7	166.0	165.4	166.2	168.6	170.4	165.1
2005	165.5	166.0	167.0	167.4	167.4	166.8	166.7	166.8	166.1	169.5	172.2	174.5	168.0
2006	168.8	167.7	168.8	171.1	172.2	172.1	172.4	172.8	172.5	175.1	179.5	180.9	172.8
2007	176.2	175.4	177.5	178.1	179.2	179.4	180.0	180.2	180.1	181.8	185.7	187.2	180.1
2008	180.6	179.5	180.4	178.8	179.1	178.9	177.4	177.4	176.1	176.7	177.8	178.2	178.4
2009	172.5	170.3	169.6	167.1	167.9	167.6	166.5	166.8	165.9	166.1	170.4	171.9	168.6
Wholesale Trade													
1990	34.6	35.0	35.4	34.8	34.7	34.7	34.9	34.7	34.7	34.8	34.8	34.8	34.8
2000	46.2	46.4	46.8	47.1	47.4	47.8	47.6	47.7	47.8	47.8	48.0	48.1	47.4
2001	48.6	48.6	48.9	49.2	48.9	49.0	48.8	48.6	48.5	48.1	47.9	47.6	48.6
2002	46.8	46.7	46.9	46.8	46.5	46.4	46.5	46.5	46.5	46.4	46.5	46.4	46.6
2003	46.0	46.0	45.9	46.2	46.1	46.1	45.8	45.7	45.6	46.5	46.6	46.7	46.1
2004	47.3	47.4	47.5	46.9	46.9	46.8	47.1	47.1	46.9	46.0	45.7	45.6	46.8
2005	46.0	46.0	46.1	46.7	46.8	46.4	46.5	46.5	46.4	47.0	47.3	47.3	46.6
2006	47.5	47.6	47.8	48.2	48.3	48.2	47.5	47.5	47.3	47.3	47.4	47.5	47.7
2007	47.7	48.0	48.5	49.0	48.9	49.1	49.4	49.3	49.2	49.8	49.7	49.7	49.0
2008	49.2	49.5	50.0	49.2	49.2	49.0	48.3	48.5	48.2	48.3	48.0	48.0	48.8
2009	47.2	47.1	46.6	45.5	45.3	45.0	44.7	44.7	44.4	44.0	44.2	44.2	45.2
Retail Trade													
1990	64.9	64.4	64.8	64.1	64.1	63.9	64.0	64.5	64.7	64.4	65.9	67.2	64.7
2000	83.7	83.3	83.7	84.2	84.9	86.0	84.2	84.1	83.9	84.3	86.9	88.4	84.8
2001	84.2	82.8	83.5	83.7	84.2	84.8	82.9	83.0	83.0	83.3	85.4	86.7	84.0
2002	82.1	81.2	82.1	81.7	81.8	82.2	81.4	81.8	81.5	81.8	85.0	86.6	82.4
2003	80.5	79.8	80.5	80.7	80.9	81.5	80.7	81.2	81.2	81.8	84.6	85.7	81.6
2004	81.0	80.3	80.7	81.7	82.8	82.9	81.8	82.8	82.6	84.3	86.8	88.4	83.0
2005	83.8	84.2	85.0	84.8	84.6	84.1	84.6	84.7	84.3	86.7	89.0	90.7	85.5
2006	85.9	84.7	85.4	87.2	88.1	87.9	88.7	88.9	89.0	91.5	95.7	96.8	89.2
2007	92.8	91.8	93.1	93.2	94.3	94.3	94.6	95.0	95.0	96.2	100.3	101.5	95.2
2008	95.9	94.7	95.4	94.1	94.2	94.3	93.7	93.4	92.7	93.2	94.7	94.9	94.3
2009	91.3	89.8	89.4	88.5	89.6	89.5	89.0	89.4	88.8	89.7	93.5	94.8	90.3
Transportation and Utilities													
1990	30.0	30.2	30.2	30.0	30.1	29.9	29.1	29.1	29.3	29.5	29.4	29.2	29.7
2000	33.1	33.3	33.8	34.0	34.0	34.1	34.4	34.7	34.8	35.6	35.3	35.2	34.4
2001	34.7	35.3	34.9	36.1	36.2	36.1	36.1	36.2	36.2	37.0	36.4	36.3	36.0
2002	35.5	35.3	35.3	34.8	35.0	35.4	35.7	36.1	35.8	35.6	35.6	35.0	35.5
2003	34.7	35.0	34.5	34.2	34.4	34.5	34.0	34.4	35.0	34.7	34.7	35.3	34.6
2004	33.7	34.1	33.7	35.0	35.3	35.3	35.8	36.1	35.9	35.9	36.1	36.4	35.3
2005	35.7	35.8	35.9	35.9	36.0	36.3	35.6	35.6	35.4	35.8	35.9	36.5	35.9
2006	35.4	35.4	35.6	35.7	35.8	36.0	36.2	36.4	36.2	36.3	36.4	36.6	36.0
2007	35.7	35.6	35.9	35.9	36.0	36.0	36.0	35.9	35.9	35.8	35.7	36.0	35.9
2008	35.5	35.3	35.0	35.5	35.7	35.6	35.4	35.5	35.2	35.2	35.1	35.3	35.4
2009	34.0	33.4	33.6	33.1	33.0	33.1	32.8	32.7	32.7	32.4	32.7	32.9	33.0
Information													
1990	15.6	15.7	15.8	15.8	15.8	15.8	15.9	15.8	16.2	16.6	16.6	16.6	16.0
2000	23.8	23.9	24.0	24.1	23.8	24.0	24.0	24.1	24.2	24.3	24.7	24.4	24.1
2001	24.0	24.1	24.2	23.4	23.3	23.5	23.5	23.2	22.6	23.2	23.2	22.9	23.4
2002	23.1	23.0	23.2	22.8	22.8	23.0	22.9	22.8	22.7	23.0	23.0	23.2	23.0
2003	22.5	22.3	22.4	22.1	22.0	22.3	22.0	21.9	21.8	21.9	21.9	22.0	22.1
2004	22.0	21.9	22.0	21.8	21.6	21.8	21.1	20.9	20.6	21.0	21.1	20.8	21.4
2005	20.5	20.4	20.5	20.8	21.0	21.1	21.2	21.2	21.2	21.3	21.7	22.1	21.1
2006	22.2	22.2	22.2	21.9	22.0	22.1	21.7	22.1	22.0	21.9	22.1	22.3	22.1
2007	22.0	22.0	21.9	21.9	22.0	22.4	22.3	22.3	22.2	22.1	22.3	22.4	22.2
2008	21.8	22.0	22.1	22.0	22.1	22.2	22.1	22.0	22.0	22.3	22.3	22.4	22.1
2009	21.6	21.5	21.5	21.5	21.4	21.3	21.1	21.0	20.9	21.0	21.1	21.1	21.3
Financial Activities													
1990	31.0	31.4	31.4	31.4	31.4	31.7	31.7	31.5	31.4	31.4	31.6	31.6	31.5
2000	54.5	54.8	54.8	56.1	56.6	57.5	57.2	57.4	57.2	57.4	57.5	57.8	56.6
2001	57.7	58.1	58.4	58.8	59.0	59.3	59.9	60.3	60.3	60.2	60.8	61.0	59.5
2002	61.5	61.8	62.3	62.8	63.1	63.8	64.7	65.2	65.1	65.8	66.2	66.4	64.1
2003	66.4	66.7	66.9	67.0	67.1	67.6	66.3	66.7	66.7	66.7	66.6	67.0	66.8
2004	66.8	67.0	67.1	67.1	67.1	67.5	68.7	69.0	68.9	69.1	69.3	69.3	68.1
2005	69.4	69.8	69.8	70.3	70.8	71.5	72.6	72.4	72.3	72.7	73.0	73.7	71.5
2006	73.8	74.7	75.2	76.1	76.2	76.6	78.2	78.1	77.7	77.2	77.1	77.2	76.5
2007	76.7	77.3	77.5	77.9	78.0	78.1	77.5	77.3	76.8	77.2	77.0	77.1	77.4
2008	75.8	76.1	76.1	76.5	75.8	75.9	74.8	74.8	74.1	73.9	73.4	73.8	75.1
2009	71.9	71.0	71.5	70.9	71.1	70.7	70.4	70.0	69.2	68.1	67.9	67.8	70.1

Employment by Industry: Charlotte-Gastonia-Concord, NC-SC, Selected Years, 1990–2009—*Continued*
(Numbers in thousands, not seasonally adjusted.)

Industry and year	January	February	March	April	May	June	July	August	September	October	November	December	Annual average
Professional and Business Services													
1990	58.5	59.5	60.6	60.6	61.4	61.9	61.0	61.4	62.1	61.0	60.1	60.1	60.7
2000	113.5	114.2	116.5	120.4	120.4	121.1	121.3	122.2	122.3	123.6	122.2	122.2	120.0
2001	119.4	119.7	120.7	119.5	119.1	117.9	116.3	116.4	115.2	115.3	113.1	113.4	117.2
2002	110.2	112.2	112.9	113.3	114.4	114.9	114.0	116.1	116.2	114.9	113.7	112.8	113.8
2003	111.9	111.5	113.0	114.0	114.9	114.4	113.9	115.9	116.2	115.4	114.9	114.1	114.2
2004	110.1	111.9	113.5	111.3	111.5	113.1	113.8	115.3	115.1	117.5	117.1	115.2	113.8
2005	112.9	113.5	114.2	115.7	116.3	115.8	117.8	118.5	120.4	121.9	121.0	119.3	117.3
2006	117.5	118.7	120.1	122.5	123.9	124.5	125.9	127.3	128.4	129.8	130.2	128.1	124.7
2007	125.5	127.2	129.9	131.7	133.2	134.3	134.1	135.7	136.4	138.2	137.3	136.8	133.4
2008	133.5	136.0	137.1	137.2	138.6	138.9	137.2	137.7	137.2	136.1	133.0	131.6	136.2
2009	126.5	126.3	125.8	124.9	123.9	123.4	123.1	123.4	124.0	124.5	126.0	124.1	124.7
Education and Health Services													
1990	28.4	28.7	28.9	28.7	28.8	28.8	28.8	29.4	29.9	30.6	30.7	30.8	29.4
2000	53.1	53.7	53.9	53.7	53.6	53.6	53.2	53.5	54.4	55.4	55.7	55.8	54.1
2001	54.4	55.2	55.9	55.5	55.8	56.6	55.8	56.6	57.1	57.7	58.2	58.2	56.4
2002	57.2	58.1	58.2	57.8	58.4	58.9	59.2	60.1	60.8	61.4	61.8	62.8	59.6
2003	62.0	62.7	63.2	63.3	63.8	63.9	63.4	64.2	64.2	65.0	65.2	65.9	63.9
2004	64.6	63.0	63.3	64.0	64.1	63.7	64.4	64.9	65.0	65.7	66.0	67.1	64.7
2005	65.7	65.8	66.5	67.0	67.0	66.8	67.2	67.9	68.3	69.1	69.3	69.3	67.5
2006	70.6	71.2	71.5	70.9	70.9	71.6	71.8	72.5	73.1	74.4	74.8	75.4	72.4
2007	74.7	75.7	76.1	76.7	76.9	77.1	77.1	77.7	77.9	79.3	79.2	79.7	77.3
2008	77.6	78.3	78.5	78.2	78.3	78.3	78.1	79.0	79.4	81.2	81.8	82.4	79.3
2009	80.3	80.9	80.7	80.8	81.1	80.7	80.5	81.4	81.4	83.4	83.5	83.8	81.5
Leisure and Hospitality													
1990	40.8	42.0	43.6	44.9	45.4	46.4	45.6	45.9	45.7	44.7	43.3	43.0	44.3
2000	65.6	65.5	67.3	67.0	69.4	71.2	69.6	69.8	67.8	68.1	66.5	66.3	67.8
2001	64.3	64.8	65.5	69.2	70.3	71.6	70.1	70.6	68.5	68.2	66.5	65.0	67.9
2002	62.9	63.5	65.6	68.8	69.8	71.2	70.7	70.5	69.7	68.5	67.2	67.6	68.0
2003	64.8	65.3	67.7	69.7	73.3	73.8	72.3	72.2	71.3	71.2	70.8	70.7	70.3
2004	68.0	68.7	71.0	72.5	75.5	75.6	75.7	76.4	75.2	74.3	73.4	73.3	73.3
2005	71.1	71.9	73.9	75.3	77.3	78.2	78.2	79.3	78.0	78.2	77.3	76.7	76.3
2006	75.3	75.8	78.3	80.6	82.3	82.7	83.7	83.6	82.5	82.4	81.9	81.9	80.9
2007	81.3	81.9	84.7	86.1	88.8	89.9	89.0	88.8	87.5	87.8	86.6	86.7	86.6
2008	84.4	85.7	88.3	89.6	91.9	92.6	92.9	93.2	92.4	91.8	89.6	89.7	90.2
2009	83.5	83.9	85.5	86.6	89.3	89.8	89.2	88.7	88.1	87.9	84.8	84.3	86.8
Other Services													
1990	17.3	17.7	17.8	17.8	17.9	18.2	17.8	17.8	17.9	17.8	17.8	18.0	17.8
2000	29.1	29.4	29.7	29.8	29.8	30.3	30.3	30.1	30.1	30.7	30.7	30.9	30.1
2001	30.5	31.0	31.5	31.8	32.5	33.0	33.1	33.4	33.6	33.8	34.1	34.4	32.7
2002	34.6	34.7	35.0	35.0	34.6	34.9	34.0	33.5	33.5	33.5	33.4	32.7	34.1
2003	31.7	31.5	31.6	32.2	32.5	32.5	32.6	32.4	32.7	31.6	31.6	31.6	32.0
2004	32.0	32.0	32.5	32.1	32.6	33.0	32.8	32.6	32.3	33.0	33.0	33.3	32.6
2005	32.9	33.0	33.3	33.0	33.6	33.9	33.8	33.7	33.7	33.8	33.7	33.7	33.5
2006	33.8	34.3	34.6	33.9	34.5	35.1	34.2	34.2	34.0	34.2	34.2	34.4	34.3
2007	34.3	34.6	35.2	34.1	34.5	34.8	34.8	34.8	34.6	35.4	35.4	35.5	34.8
2008	34.0	34.0	33.9	33.2	33.8	33.8	33.6	33.6	32.9	32.7	32.5	32.3	33.4
2009	31.2	31.4	31.3	31.1	31.4	31.4	31.7	31.8	31.4	30.8	30.6	30.4	31.2
Government													
1990	61.0	61.9	62.4	63.2	63.1	63.0	55.4	57.2	62.3	64.6	65.0	65.3	62.0
2000	88.4	88.7	89.9	89.9	89.6	87.4	78.1	83.4	88.1	92.2	91.6	91.5	88.2
2001	89.8	91.3	91.6	92.2	92.1	89.0	79.8	86.4	91.8	95.1	97.3	95.9	91.0
2002	94.0	95.5	96.3	95.5	95.4	92.6	82.8	88.5	94.5	98.5	98.9	97.4	94.2
2003	95.7	96.6	97.3	97.2	97.8	93.8	76.9	85.8	96.3	102.2	101.8	100.7	95.2
2004	98.8	99.8	99.9	100.0	100.2	96.1	78.1	88.2	100.0	103.2	103.7	102.5	97.5
2005	100.6	101.5	102.0	102.8	102.5	97.8	79.4	93.9	102.9	105.6	105.7	105.2	100.0
2006	104.3	104.9	105.3	105.6	105.7	97.1	80.0	96.3	106.2	107.5	109.3	109.3	102.6
2007	108.2	109.7	109.8	109.0	109.7	100.2	83.8	103.4	110.1	112.1	113.5	113.8	106.9
2008	113.4	114.6	115.1	115.1	115.5	107.8	90.0	110.2	118.0	117.7	119.0	119.7	113.0
2009	118.1	118.6	119.0	119.1	118.3	112.2	93.2	113.1	115.9	118.5	119.5	119.1	115.4

Employment by Industry: Chicago-Naperville-Joliet, IL-IN-WI, Selected Years, 1990–2009

(Numbers in thousands, not seasonally adjusted.)

Industry and year	January	February	March	April	May	June	July	August	September	October	November	December	Annual average
Total Nonfarm													
1990	3938.7	3943.6	3972.8	3978.2	4022.8	4059.1	4042.3	4043.1	4059.0	4021.1	4024.4	4028.9	4011.2
2000	4445.7	4464.9	4509.8	4543.2	4586.9	4626.3	4585.9	4606.9	4608.4	4613.6	4631.5	4633.8	4571.4
2001	4491.0	4498.8	4529.9	4552.3	4590.7	4625.9	4568.8	4571.4	4555.9	4528.8	4527.6	4529.0	4547.5
2002	4377.2	4372.5	4395.3	4436.4	4471.8	4501.6	4477.9	4489.7	4475.4	4476.2	4487.2	4484.5	4453.8
2003	4341.1	4337.1	4358.1	4391.0	4432.2	4461.2	4446.9	4451.3	4436.4	4428.2	4426.7	4436.6	4412.2
2004	4296.5	4299.2	4334.5	4383.3	4431.5	4465.8	4450.2	4450.7	4447.1	4464.7	4475.0	4479.5	4414.8
2005	4339.5	4347.2	4372.8	4440.5	4474.7	4496.9	4498.1	4497.4	4505.1	4510.7	4526.5	4527.0	4461.4
2006	4401.0	4413.7	4446.4	4495.0	4533.4	4577.3	4549.4	4554.0	4557.2	4560.5	4574.5	4576.1	4519.9
2007	4451.8	4450.3	4490.0	4531.2	4580.0	4614.5	4588.7	4590.8	4583.8	4591.6	4606.7	4605.0	4557.0
2008	4472.0	4468.8	4489.0	4535.4	4575.2	4593.1	4567.1	4564.1	4539.9	4535.9	4513.3	4483.5	4528.1
2009	4317.1	4293.5	4286.2	4298.7	4324.9	4332.8	4290.1	4281.3	4274.8	4280.5	4272.5	4239.4	4291.0
Total Private													
1990	3446.9	3444.7	3468.3	3475.9	3511.3	3552.2	3557.4	3571.3	3566.5	3520.5	3519.4	3523.1	3513.1
2000	3910.7	3916.9	3956.5	3992.6	4019.7	4061.1	4042.2	4061.0	4056.6	4057.3	4073.4	4075.0	4018.6
2001	3946.8	3940.8	3969.6	3994.9	4025.3	4062.5	4018.4	4024.7	4002.3	3965.2	3962.3	3961.7	3989.5
2002	3821.9	3806.5	3826.7	3864.6	3895.8	3927.7	3915.4	3930.1	3915.2	3903.1	3911.8	3908.9	3885.6
2003	3778.6	3764.2	3782.7	3818.5	3855.5	3886.2	3875.1	3888.1	3875.0	3862.7	3861.2	3873.6	3843.5
2004	3742.5	3736.5	3769.5	3816.9	3861.1	3897.7	3897.9	3903.6	3892.5	3896.7	3904.4	3914.7	3852.8
2005	3783.2	3780.6	3802.0	3868.9	3900.1	3927.7	3927.7	3941.2	3947.2	3943.9	3943.4	3956.0	3961.3	3896.3
2006	3844.8	3847.2	3877.7	3923.7	3958.4	4003.8	3995.6	4004.9	3992.0	3991.7	4002.9	4008.8	3954.3
2007	3894.0	3881.7	3918.8	3958.6	4005.0	4042.6	4033.9	4038.5	4018.6	4022.5	4035.5	4037.5	3990.6
2008	3912.3	3898.8	3916.3	3961.1	3995.4	4017.4	4007.0	4007.8	3970.4	3959.3	3936.4	3910.0	3957.7
2009	3754.6	3723.9	3713.5	3721.6	3744.2	3758.1	3733.7	3730.1	3706.6	3701.6	3692.2	3666.7	3720.6
Goods-Producing													
1990	859.5	860.4	865.4	867.7	878.8	888.7	887.4	890.9	886.9	871.1	863.3	854.3	872.9
2000	827.6	828.9	841.2	851.5	856.4	862.3	858.0	863.7	862.0	861.1	859.1	847.8	851.6
2001	811.7	811.1	815.9	821.9	826.9	831.3	816.9	819.6	815.9	808.4	802.0	792.4	814.5
2002	754.9	750.8	755.5	765.6	771.1	778.3	773.0	777.0	775.8	772.5	768.7	758.9	766.8
2003	725.3	720.6	725.1	735.8	744.2	749.5	743.8	748.3	745.6	737.2	730.8	723.8	735.8
2004	691.4	687.1	696.5	709.1	719.0	726.5	727.3	728.8	728.6	727.2	724.4	717.9	715.3
2005	686.9	686.6	691.8	708.6	715.2	721.8	721.9	723.8	723.9	723.3	721.1	711.4	711.4
2006	688.8	688.7	692.6	709.1	715.1	724.5	720.1	721.9	721.0	719.9	715.6	708.8	710.5
2007	682.3	673.7	686.0	697.8	706.9	716.3	712.7	712.4	710.5	708.9	704.5	696.0	700.7
2008	667.2	660.6	666.3	677.3	685.2	690.0	688.2	688.1	682.3	676.4	663.3	643.7	674.1
2009	603.0	594.7	590.7	588.9	588.2	591.1	585.6	584.9	581.8	579.2	569.7	553.0	584.2
Mining and Logging													
1990	2.7	2.6	2.6	2.9	3.0	3.0	3.1	3.2	3.1	3.1	3.1	2.9	2.9
2000	2.2	2.1	2.2	2.4	2.4	2.5	2.5	2.6	2.5	2.7	2.6	2.5	2.4
2001	2.2	2.2	2.3	2.5	2.5	2.6	2.5	2.6	2.5	2.6	2.4	2.5	2.5
2002	2.2	2.2	2.4	2.4	2.4	2.6	2.5	2.6	2.5	2.5	2.4	2.5	2.4
2003	2.1	2.1	2.2	2.4	2.4	2.4	2.4	2.5	2.4	2.5	2.5	2.3	2.4
2004	2.0	2.1	2.3	2.4	2.4	2.4	2.4	2.5	2.5	2.4	2.5	2.4	2.4
2005	2.2	2.2	2.3	2.5	2.5	2.6	2.7	2.6	2.6	2.7	2.6	2.5	2.5
2006	2.2	2.2	2.3	2.6	2.7	2.8	2.8	2.8	2.8	2.7	2.8	2.6	2.6
2007	2.3	2.1	2.4	2.3	2.4	2.4	2.4	2.4	2.3	2.3	2.3	2.1	2.3
2008	1.9	1.8	1.9	2.1	2.1	2.2	2.2	2.2	2.1	2.0	1.9	1.8	2.0
2009	1.4	1.5	1.6	1.8	1.8	1.8	1.8	1.8	1.9	1.8	1.8	1.7	1.7
Construction													
1990	163.9	164.2	168.6	175.3	183.3	188.0	192.3	193.1	191.4	185.0	181.1	174.4	180.1
2000	188.4	188.4	197.8	209.3	215.0	219.7	222.3	224.0	222.9	222.7	220.9	211.7	211.9
2001	189.6	191.5	198.1	211.5	220.3	225.4	226.9	228.9	227.1	226.7	226.2	220.5	216.1
2002	194.1	192.8	198.0	209.7	217.1	223.0	227.3	229.2	228.5	227.8	225.7	216.9	215.8
2003	196.0	192.7	198.0	210.4	220.9	226.5	229.6	232.6	231.0	225.6	220.6	214.4	216.5
2004	189.5	186.1	193.6	206.8	214.6	220.1	224.7	224.5	223.8	223.9	221.6	215.2	212.0
2005	189.3	188.8	192.9	209.0	215.2	220.3	224.3	225.5	226.0	226.2	223.8	214.1	213.0
2006	197.9	197.5	203.2	216.6	223.9	229.7	229.0	230.9	228.2	227.8	223.9	216.6	218.8
2007	196.3	188.3	199.4	211.9	220.9	227.1	227.2	227.2	225.6	224.1	221.1	210.7	215.0
2008	188.1	184.6	189.7	201.2	209.3	212.7	215.2	216.0	212.5	209.8	200.6	186.5	202.2
2009	158.6	157.0	159.2	165.6	169.7	173.4	174.1	174.1	171.3	170.5	161.8	147.2	165.2
Manufacturing													
1990	692.9	693.6	694.2	689.5	692.5	697.7	692.0	694.6	692.4	683.0	679.1	677.0	689.9
2000	637.0	638.4	641.2	639.8	639.0	640.1	633.2	637.1	636.6	635.7	635.6	633.6	637.3
2001	619.9	617.4	615.5	607.9	604.1	603.3	587.5	588.1	586.3	579.1	573.4	569.4	596.0
2002	558.6	555.8	555.1	553.5	551.6	552.7	543.2	545.2	544.8	542.2	540.6	539.5	548.6
2003	527.2	525.8	524.9	523.0	520.9	520.6	511.8	513.2	512.2	509.1	507.7	507.1	517.0
2004	499.9	498.9	500.6	499.9	502.0	504.0	500.2	501.8	502.3	500.9	500.3	500.3	500.9
2005	495.4	495.6	496.6	497.1	497.5	498.9	494.9	495.7	495.3	494.4	494.7	494.8	495.9
2006	488.7	489.0	487.1	489.9	488.5	492.0	488.3	488.2	490.0	489.4	488.9	489.6	489.1
2007	483.7	483.3	484.2	483.6	483.6	486.8	483.1	482.8	482.6	482.5	481.1	483.2	483.4
2008	477.2	474.2	474.7	474.0	473.8	475.1	470.8	469.9	467.7	464.6	460.8	455.4	469.9
2009	443.0	436.2	429.9	421.5	416.7	415.9	409.7	409.0	408.6	406.9	406.1	404.1	417.3

Employment by Industry: Chicago-Naperville-Joliet, IL-IN-WI, Selected Years, 1990–2009—*Continued*

(Numbers in thousands, not seasonally adjusted.)

Industry and year	January	February	March	April	May	June	July	August	September	October	November	December	Annual average
Service-Providing													
1990	3079.2	3083.2	3107.4	3110.5	3144.0	3170.4	3154.9	3152.2	3172.1	3150.0	3161.1	3174.6	3138.3
2000	3618.1	3636.0	3668.6	3691.7	3730.5	3764.0	3727.9	3743.2	3746.4	3752.5	3772.4	3786.0	3719.8
2001	3679.3	3687.7	3714.0	3730.4	3763.8	3794.6	3751.9	3751.8	3740.0	3720.4	3725.6	3736.6	3733.0
2002	3622.3	3621.7	3639.8	3670.8	3700.7	3723.3	3704.9	3712.7	3699.6	3703.7	3718.5	3725.6	3687.0
2003	3615.8	3616.5	3633.0	3655.2	3688.0	3711.7	3703.1	3703.0	3690.8	3691.0	3695.9	3712.8	3676.4
2004	3605.1	3612.1	3638.0	3674.2	3712.5	3739.3	3722.9	3721.9	3718.5	3737.5	3750.6	3761.6	3699.5
2005	3652.6	3660.6	3681.0	3731.9	3759.5	3775.1	3776.2	3773.6	3781.2	3787.4	3805.4	3815.6	3750.0
2006	3712.2	3725.0	3753.8	3785.9	3818.3	3852.8	3829.3	3832.1	3836.2	3840.6	3858.9	3867.3	3809.4
2007	3769.5	3776.6	3804.0	3833.4	3873.1	3898.2	3876.0	3878.4	3873.3	3882.7	3902.2	3909.0	3856.4
2008	3804.8	3808.2	3822.7	3858.1	3890.0	3903.1	3878.9	3876.0	3857.6	3859.5	3850.0	3839.8	3854.1
2009	3714.1	3698.8	3695.5	3709.8	3736.7	3741.7	3704.5	3696.4	3693.0	3701.3	3702.8	3686.4	3706.8
Trade, Transportation, and Utilities													
1990	885.6	874.9	877.4	869.9	875.9	883.5	882.2	883.9	879.3	878.3	888.7	900.7	881.7
2000	940.8	933.7	937.5	938.0	943.4	950.3	949.5	955.0	954.3	961.6	980.8	993.8	953.2
2001	957.5	944.4	947.0	950.5	954.7	961.2	950.2	949.2	947.1	939.4	952.7	963.6	951.5
2002	921.2	907.3	910.3	913.1	918.1	922.1	916.8	918.8	918.3	921.6	938.0	949.5	921.3
2003	904.0	895.2	897.0	897.0	903.4	907.8	899.9	902.2	903.8	907.6	921.5	935.1	906.2
2004	895.3	886.8	891.3	895.7	905.8	911.8	907.0	908.4	909.4	915.7	930.8	944.8	908.6
2005	902.6	892.9	896.2	902.3	909.3	913.9	911.6	913.8	915.0	918.9	934.5	949.5	913.4
2006	911.6	903.0	908.2	911.1	918.3	925.1	919.3	920.1	919.0	922.8	942.0	954.7	921.3
2007	923.9	912.0	918.3	916.4	926.9	934.1	928.5	928.4	927.4	931.8	954.1	965.9	930.6
2008	931.4	918.0	920.5	920.7	927.3	930.4	923.4	922.4	917.2	918.6	926.8	931.6	924.0
2009	889.9	875.4	870.0	865.4	870.6	872.3	861.3	861.5	858.0	858.7	870.6	879.2	869.4
Wholesale Trade													
1990	243.0	243.2	244.0	242.4	243.6	244.8	246.0	246.6	243.0	241.8	241.1	240.7	243.4
2000	251.1	252.3	253.0	251.6	252.9	255.1	254.7	255.3	254.4	255.3	255.9	256.9	254.0
2001	255.5	255.1	255.2	258.2	259.6	261.5	261.4	260.9	260.1	255.9	254.7	255.5	257.8
2002	250.8	250.7	251.0	251.2	251.4	252.9	251.2	251.1	250.1	250.0	250.6	250.6	251.0
2003	248.5	248.4	248.9	247.4	247.9	248.6	247.1	246.2	245.1	243.2	243.9	244.6	246.7
2004	240.9	240.4	241.5	242.4	243.9	245.3	244.7	244.6	243.8	244.5	245.1	246.3	243.6
2005	241.1	240.9	241.7	243.4	244.5	246.2	246.4	245.9	246.0	246.3	247.5	249.1	244.9
2006	246.0	246.0	247.2	247.7	248.8	250.8	249.7	249.3	248.4	248.5	248.6	250.1	248.4
2007	247.7	247.7	248.8	248.9	250.2	252.4	252.0	251.3	250.5	251.7	252.0	253.4	250.6
2008	250.3	249.7	250.4	250.8	251.9	252.9	251.0	250.4	249.1	248.6	247.6	247.0	250.0
2009	241.3	239.2	237.7	235.5	234.7	234.2	231.7	231.3	229.5	226.9	225.6	225.2	232.7
Retail Trade													
1990	461.9	450.5	450.6	445.7	449.4	454.6	453.6	454.9	452.2	452.6	463.2	474.7	455.3
2000	475.2	467.3	470.4	470.3	473.3	477.8	477.5	481.1	479.8	484.5	501.9	512.9	481.0
2001	484.3	473.1	475.1	477.2	479.2	485.3	477.0	477.0	474.5	472.4	489.2	501.2	480.5
2002	469.7	457.6	461.1	461.3	466.1	470.6	466.9	467.9	466.8	469.2	485.8	497.6	470.1
2003	459.4	452.1	453.6	454.5	459.0	463.8	459.1	461.1	460.4	464.6	477.6	490.1	462.9
2004	458.7	451.4	454.1	455.5	462.2	468.5	463.9	465.0	463.6	467.3	481.8	494.2	465.5
2005	462.9	453.2	454.8	458.1	463.3	467.2	467.9	469.7	467.5	470.0	483.5	495.2	467.8
2006	466.8	457.6	460.1	461.7	466.0	471.6	469.2	469.9	465.1	469.8	487.8	496.6	470.2
2007	474.5	462.6	466.7	465.6	472.5	478.0	475.8	475.3	471.3	474.2	495.0	502.9	476.2
2008	477.9	465.2	466.3	466.4	470.2	474.2	471.8	469.7	463.6	465.8	475.3	479.7	470.5
2009	452.6	441.8	439.1	438.8	444.0	447.4	443.0	443.0	438.6	440.0	453.3	459.5	445.1
Transportation and Utilities													
1990	180.7	181.2	182.8	181.8	182.9	184.1	182.6	182.4	184.1	183.9	184.4	185.3	183.0
2000	214.5	214.1	214.1	216.1	217.2	217.4	217.3	218.6	220.1	221.8	223.0	224.0	218.2
2001	217.7	216.2	216.7	215.1	215.9	214.4	211.8	211.3	212.5	211.1	208.8	206.9	213.2
2002	200.7	199.0	198.2	200.6	200.6	198.6	198.7	199.8	201.4	202.4	201.6	201.3	200.2
2003	196.2	194.7	194.6	195.2	196.5	195.5	193.7	194.9	198.4	199.9	200.1	200.5	196.7
2004	195.7	195.0	195.7	197.8	199.7	198.0	198.4	198.8	202.0	203.9	203.9	204.3	199.4
2005	198.6	198.8	199.7	200.8	201.5	200.5	197.3	198.2	201.5	202.6	203.5	205.2	200.7
2006	198.8	199.4	200.9	201.7	203.5	202.7	200.4	200.9	205.5	204.5	205.6	208.0	202.7
2007	201.7	201.7	202.8	201.9	204.2	203.7	200.7	201.8	205.6	205.9	207.1	209.6	203.9
2008	203.2	203.1	203.8	203.5	205.2	203.3	200.6	202.3	204.6	204.2	203.9	204.9	203.6
2009	196.0	194.4	193.2	191.1	191.9	190.7	186.6	187.2	189.9	191.8	191.7	194.5	191.6
Information													
1990	101.4	101.5	101.6	100.0	100.9	102.1	101.5	102.5	102.1	101.0	101.2	101.3	101.4
2000	114.4	115.1	116.3	115.2	115.9	117.5	117.3	117.5	117.0	117.6	118.2	118.8	116.7
2001	117.9	118.1	118.4	117.4	118.0	119.1	117.7	117.7	116.1	114.0	114.0	114.1	116.9
2002	111.3	110.7	110.5	110.0	110.1	110.1	107.9	107.6	105.9	105.5	105.0	104.7	108.3
2003	102.1	102.2	101.2	100.3	100.2	100.4	99.8	98.9	97.8	97.5	97.1	96.9	99.6
2004	96.1	96.0	95.8	95.4	95.4	95.7	95.2	94.7	93.5	93.9	93.8	94.5	95.0
2005	93.4	93.1	93.1	93.4	93.1	93.4	93.6	92.8	92.0	91.8	91.7	91.7	92.8
2006	91.4	91.2	91.2	91.3	91.6	92.0	91.7	91.4	90.6	90.8	90.7	91.0	91.3
2007	90.4	90.8	90.5	90.5	90.8	91.3	91.6	91.7	91.0	91.0	91.0	91.1	91.0
2008	90.7	90.9	90.9	90.8	91.1	91.0	90.9	90.7	89.0	88.4	88.0	87.9	90.0
2009	86.6	85.8	84.8	84.1	83.7	83.8	83.3	83.2	82.5	81.5	80.8	81.7	83.5

Employment by Industry: Chicago-Naperville-Joliet, IL-IN-WI, Selected Years, 1990–2009—*Continued*

(Numbers in thousands, not seasonally adjusted.)

Industry and year	January	February	March	April	May	June	July	August	September	October	November	December	Annual average
Financial Activities													
1990	293.9	293.9	294.6	296.4	298.0	302.1	304.8	304.4	301.8	297.4	297.2	298.2	298.6
2000	318.0	318.2	317.9	318.2	318.3	321.7	320.5	320.6	317.2	318.5	318.9	321.9	319.2
2001	321.6	322.3	324.6	325.0	326.1	329.4	328.6	328.0	324.2	322.8	323.7	325.4	325.1
2002	320.5	319.9	320.6	319.8	320.9	324.4	323.9	324.2	322.0	322.5	323.7	325.7	322.3
2003	323.8	323.6	324.6	325.2	326.6	330.4	330.6	330.9	328.2	324.9	325.1	326.6	326.7
2004	321.8	321.5	323.0	322.3	323.5	326.7	327.5	327.5	324.1	323.7	323.5	325.7	324.2
2005	323.1	322.8	323.4	325.2	326.2	329.1	331.4	331.4	329.6	329.7	330.0	332.1	327.8
2006	327.6	327.9	328.9	329.8	330.7	333.8	334.7	334.7	333.1	332.1	331.8	333.2	331.5
2007	329.8	329.5	329.3	329.4	330.0	332.2	331.2	329.8	325.7	324.8	323.9	324.2	328.3
2008	318.7	318.6	318.6	318.0	318.5	320.0	318.4	317.8	313.6	312.4	310.7	310.6	316.3
2009	304.5	302.6	301.0	299.9	299.5	300.0	298.2	297.1	294.0	291.8	291.3	292.8	297.7
Professional and Business Services													
1990	492.7	495.4	502.1	507.7	511.3	520.1	524.2	528.4	527.8	515.4	512.2	508.5	512.2
2000	698.9	702.9	713.4	725.2	730.5	742.4	740.3	746.7	746.5	743.5	741.9	738.2	730.9
2001	704.4	701.8	705.5	709.0	714.2	721.9	711.1	714.1	708.6	703.1	694.3	690.9	706.6
2002	662.1	660.9	662.9	676.0	678.9	684.9	685.5	692.3	690.0	683.8	680.7	673.5	677.6
2003	647.0	644.9	646.9	659.1	663.4	668.0	667.7	673.2	675.7	676.4	671.0	671.8	663.8
2004	645.8	648.7	655.3	671.8	680.2	691.8	690.9	695.9	696.6	703.1	700.8	696.9	681.5
2005	672.0	675.2	680.8	698.7	702.5	711.7	714.5	719.5	721.8	728.2	727.7	723.5	706.3
2006	695.2	698.7	707.9	722.2	726.7	738.8	739.0	745.8	744.2	747.8	745.2	740.0	729.3
2007	711.4	713.9	721.1	739.0	744.9	753.1	754.2	760.1	755.0	757.7	755.2	752.7	743.2
2008	723.1	724.8	724.4	738.8	742.5	745.6	743.6	746.9	738.3	735.8	726.1	716.2	733.8
2009	680.5	672.8	665.3	670.5	673.2	674.4	671.8	672.5	667.4	668.6	664.0	653.8	669.6
Education and Health Services													
1990	381.0	383.3	386.4	384.8	385.5	382.4	379.3	381.6	393.5	397.1	399.0	401.8	388.0
2000	486.9	491.1	493.1	496.0	497.0	496.1	486.9	487.2	495.6	500.5	503.9	504.9	494.9
2001	504.3	509.5	514.9	516.3	516.8	517.1	511.8	514.6	521.0	521.9	525.3	525.5	516.6
2002	518.9	524.0	526.9	528.3	530.3	527.1	521.5	523.0	529.9	533.9	537.0	537.4	528.2
2003	529.7	532.6	535.5	536.6	538.4	534.9	533.2	534.0	540.1	545.0	547.2	548.5	538.0
2004	539.9	543.7	545.9	549.5	549.6	545.1	542.4	542.2	548.6	554.1	556.9	560.1	548.2
2005	552.9	556.2	556.6	562.1	562.7	556.2	555.9	554.7	561.9	566.3	569.0	570.1	560.4
2006	563.0	569.8	572.3	573.1	574.8	571.7	568.6	569.9	578.1	581.9	585.3	585.3	574.5
2007	578.7	586.2	588.8	589.1	591.9	588.8	585.1	584.1	592.7	599.5	603.0	603.8	591.0
2008	596.8	602.4	603.2	608.0	609.0	606.6	604.1	604.7	612.3	618.4	622.6	623.3	609.3
2009	614.8	620.1	622.3	622.1	623.4	620.2	617.0	616.6	622.6	632.1	635.1	630.7	623.1
Leisure and Hospitality													
1990	276.0	278.2	282.2	291.3	300.9	310.1	312.9	313.7	310.2	296.9	293.7	293.4	296.6
2000	340.9	342.9	351.5	361.8	371.3	380.7	379.5	380.1	374.2	367.0	363.0	361.6	364.5
2001	342.7	346.0	354.0	365.0	378.0	388.3	387.0	387.4	377.5	366.5	360.4	359.4	367.7
2002	345.8	345.7	351.6	363.0	376.9	387.9	389.8	389.9	382.4	373.0	367.9	367.8	370.1
2003	351.6	350.1	355.5	368.9	382.7	395.4	394.6	394.6	387.4	377.7	372.7	374.2	375.5
2004	358.1	357.8	365.3	377.3	390.8	400.8	403.3	402.8	395.3	382.9	378.1	377.1	382.5
2005	360.6	361.6	367.0	384.2	396.4	404.7	408.7	408.0	402.6	389.7	385.6	385.1	387.9
2006	370.8	372.6	379.4	392.3	405.1	418.9	419.7	418.5	409.6	399.9	395.6	397.1	398.3
2007	382.9	381.1	387.8	400.4	415.6	426.0	425.5	426.9	417.8	410.8	405.4	404.4	407.1
2008	387.9	386.3	394.0	409.1	421.8	431.5	430.5	429.5	417.9	409.7	399.9	397.4	409.6
2009	380.9	378.0	383.8	395.6	409.2	417.8	415.2	413.7	406.7	396.6	388.9	383.9	397.5
Other Services													
1990	156.8	157.1	158.6	158.1	160.0	163.2	165.1	165.9	164.9	163.3	164.1	164.9	161.8
2000	183.2	184.1	185.6	186.7	186.9	190.1	190.2	190.2	189.8	187.5	187.6	188.0	187.5
2001	186.7	187.6	189.3	189.8	190.6	194.2	195.1	194.1	191.9	189.1	189.9	190.4	190.7
2002	187.2	187.2	188.4	188.8	189.5	192.9	197.0	197.3	190.9	190.3	190.8	191.4	191.0
2003	194.7	194.8	196.7	195.1	196.4	199.6	205.2	205.9	196.1	196.1	195.5	196.4	197.7
2004	194.1	194.9	196.4	195.8	196.8	199.3	204.3	203.3	196.4	196.1	196.1	197.7	197.6
2005	191.7	192.2	193.1	194.4	194.7	196.9	203.6	203.2	197.1	195.5	196.4	197.9	196.4
2006	196.4	195.3	197.2	194.8	196.1	199.0	202.5	202.6	196.4	196.5	196.7	198.7	197.7
2007	194.6	194.5	197.0	196.0	198.0	200.8	205.1	205.1	198.5	198.0	198.4	199.4	198.8
2008	196.5	197.2	198.4	198.4	200.0	202.3	207.9	207.7	199.8	199.6	199.0	199.3	200.5
2009	194.4	194.5	195.6	195.1	196.4	198.5	201.3	200.6	193.6	193.1	191.8	191.6	195.5
Government													
1990	491.8	498.9	504.5	502.3	511.5	506.9	484.9	471.8	492.5	500.6	505.0	505.8	498.0
2000	535.0	548.0	553.3	550.6	567.2	565.2	543.7	545.9	551.8	556.3	558.1	558.8	552.8
2001	544.2	558.0	560.3	557.4	565.4	563.4	550.4	546.7	553.6	563.6	565.3	567.3	558.0
2002	555.3	566.0	568.6	571.8	576.0	573.9	562.5	559.6	560.2	573.1	575.4	575.6	568.2
2003	563.1	573.4	575.9	573.1	577.1	575.3	572.4	563.5	561.9	565.9	565.9	563.4	569.2
2004	554.0	562.7	565.0	566.4	570.4	568.1	552.3	547.1	554.6	568.0	570.6	564.8	562.0
2005	556.3	566.6	570.8	571.6	574.6	569.2	556.9	550.2	561.2	567.3	570.5	565.7	565.1
2006	556.2	566.5	568.7	571.3	575.0	573.5	553.8	549.1	565.2	568.8	571.6	567.3	565.6
2007	557.8	568.6	571.2	572.6	575.0	571.9	554.8	552.3	565.2	569.1	571.2	567.5	566.4
2008	559.7	570.0	572.7	574.3	579.8	575.7	560.1	556.3	569.5	576.6	576.9	573.5	570.4
2009	562.5	569.6	572.7	577.1	580.7	574.7	556.4	551.2	568.2	578.9	580.3	572.7	570.4

Employment by Industry: Cincinnati-Middletown, OH-KY-IN, Selected Years, 1990–2009

(Numbers in thousands, not seasonally adjusted.)

Industry and year	January	February	March	April	May	June	July	August	September	October	November	December	Annual average
Total Nonfarm													
1990	841.4	845.2	854.3	859.6	869.2	869.5	864.8	868.2	874.1	875.4	877.3	880.0	864.9
2000	995.4	1001.6	1011.7	1015.2	1025.2	1027.4	1016.7	1017.9	1020.3	1022.1	1025.2	1029.9	1017.4
2001	998.1	1001.5	1008.7	1010.2	1017.5	1020.2	1010.4	1013.0	1013.0	1014.8	1015.1	1016.0	1011.5
2002	988.2	991.4	998.7	1004.3	1013.3	1014.3	1009.0	1012.8	1014.4	1015.6	1019.8	1021.9	1008.6
2003	998.9	998.0	1007.4	1017.6	1023.6	1024.0	1013.9	1020.9	1019.1	1020.8	1022.9	1026.0	1016.0
2004	997.8	999.8	1012.1	1022.3	1029.9	1034.2	1029.4	1033.7	1033.1	1034.4	1037.7	1039.4	1025.3
2005	1004.3	1010.2	1021.1	1033.7	1041.7	1044.5	1037.1	1039.2	1044.3	1041.0	1045.8	1048.7	1034.3
2006	1017.3	1020.9	1028.1	1036.5	1043.9	1046.8	1036.4	1041.7	1043.1	1040.5	1044.4	1047.1	1037.2
2007	1022.8	1023.1	1036.3	1045.6	1057.9	1059.8	1045.9	1050.0	1050.9	1055.3	1058.4	1060.4	1047.2
2008	1032.9	1034.4	1037.1	1051.2	1059.6	1055.1	1046.7	1048.1	1041.6	1042.1	1037.3	1034.7	1043.4
2009	997.2	993.4	993.1	997.7	1004.9	1002.3	990.7	994.2	989.6	988.4	993.0	996.8	995.1
Total Private													
1990	726.8	727.1	735.4	740.9	748.5	757.6	758.4	762.6	760.8	759.0	758.0	760.6	749.6
2000	872.1	873.8	882.8	885.7	893.4	901.1	898.7	900.6	896.5	895.0	897.0	901.4	891.5
2001	871.9	871.8	878.2	878.9	885.6	892.9	891.1	892.7	885.6	884.7	883.9	884.6	883.5
2002	858.9	858.6	864.7	870.5	878.8	885.6	886.9	888.7	885.2	882.9	886.5	889.2	878.0
2003	866.9	863.4	871.5	881.1	886.9	892.8	890.3	894.2	886.9	884.9	886.6	890.0	882.9
2004	865.7	864.4	875.3	885.2	892.4	901.6	905.9	907.9	901.5	899.2	902.0	904.6	892.4
2005	873.2	876.2	886.1	898.3	905.8	912.8	913.8	914.1	912.7	906.1	910.4	914.0	902.0
2006	886.0	886.4	892.3	900.5	907.1	915.4	913.4	916.6	911.1	905.5	909.1	912.0	904.6
2007	890.6	887.9	899.8	909.4	920.6	926.7	921.9	924.1	919.4	920.8	921.9	924.7	914.0
2008	901.5	898.8	901.6	915.5	922.5	923.9	922.8	922.2	910.4	907.4	900.8	899.1	910.5
2009	865.0	858.7	858.6	862.2	869.0	870.0	866.8	867.1	859.2	854.8	858.2	862.9	862.7
Goods-Producing													
1990	190.5	190.8	192.3	192.6	194.5	196.7	197.3	198.1	197.6	195.4	195.0	193.1	194.5
2000	194.8	195.3	197.8	197.8	199.9	200.8	200.6	200.2	199.2	198.4	197.7	196.8	198.3
2001	190.6	190.7	192.0	191.3	192.4	193.3	191.9	192.6	190.5	188.8	186.8	185.2	190.5
2002	178.2	177.3	177.7	177.8	178.7	180.2	180.5	181.4	180.7	180.2	179.6	177.7	179.2
2003	174.2	172.8	174.9	177.4	178.4	179.3	178.0	178.8	177.5	176.6	175.8	175.5	176.6
2004	171.3	170.9	173.4	176.2	177.8	180.1	179.6	179.4	178.6	177.8	177.2	176.2	176.5
2005	169.7	170.1	172.3	174.6	176.8	178.0	178.5	178.6	178.5	177.4	177.1	175.7	175.6
2006	170.4	170.5	169.4	173.3	174.8	176.5	175.7	176.7	175.2	172.9	172.3	172.1	173.3
2007	167.8	166.8	170.0	172.1	174.0	174.8	174.0	174.3	173.2	172.3	171.2	169.9	171.7
2008	165.5	164.7	165.0	167.9	169.2	169.9	169.3	169.0	166.8	165.5	162.9	160.1	166.3
2009	151.8	149.2	148.2	146.7	147.2	147.0	145.8	146.3	144.8	144.9	146.4	146.1	147.0
Mining, Logging, and Construction													
1990	35.9	36.1	37.5	38.1	39.8	40.6	41.0	41.1	40.5	39.4	38.9	37.2	38.8
2000	47.5	47.3	49.4	49.9	51.4	52.8	53.0	52.9	51.8	51.2	50.6	49.6	50.6
2001	46.6	46.9	48.4	50.2	51.7	53.3	53.7	54.0	53.1	52.7	51.9	50.8	51.1
2002	46.1	46.0	46.8	47.7	48.9	50.6	51.2	51.6	51.0	50.8	50.4	48.7	49.2
2003	45.3	44.4	46.1	49.0	50.2	51.5	51.4	52.3	51.6	51.6	50.9	50.4	49.5
2004	48.3	48.0	49.9	51.7	53.0	54.8	55.2	55.1	54.4	53.6	52.9	51.8	52.4
2005	47.4	48.1	49.6	51.6	53.2	54.3	55.1	55.1	54.9	54.1	53.7	52.1	52.4
2006	48.5	48.8	49.9	52.0	53.0	54.1	54.2	54.8	53.6	52.1	51.4	50.5	51.9
2007	47.3	45.8	48.0	50.4	52.0	52.7	53.0	53.0	52.4	52.2	51.2	49.6	50.6
2008	45.4	44.6	45.1	47.3	48.7	49.4	49.7	49.5	48.2	47.9	46.6	44.7	47.3
2009	40.0	39.1	39.4	39.4	40.9	41.1	41.1	41.2	40.3	40.1	40.5	40.6	40.3
Manufacturing													
1990	154.6	154.7	154.8	154.5	154.7	156.1	156.3	157.0	157.1	156.0	156.1	155.9	155.7
2000	147.3	148.0	148.4	147.9	148.5	148.0	147.6	147.3	147.4	147.2	147.1	147.2	147.7
2001	144.0	143.8	143.6	141.1	140.7	140.0	138.2	138.6	137.4	136.1	134.9	134.4	139.4
2002	132.1	131.3	130.9	130.1	129.8	129.6	129.3	129.8	129.7	129.4	129.2	129.0	130.0
2003	128.9	128.4	128.8	128.4	128.2	127.8	126.6	126.5	125.9	125.0	124.9	125.1	127.0
2004	123.0	122.9	123.5	124.5	124.8	125.3	124.4	124.3	124.2	124.2	124.3	124.4	124.2
2005	122.3	122.0	122.7	123.0	123.6	123.7	123.4	123.5	123.6	123.3	123.4	123.6	123.2
2006	121.9	121.7	119.5	121.3	121.8	122.4	121.5	121.9	121.6	120.8	120.9	121.6	121.4
2007	120.5	121.0	122.0	121.7	122.0	122.1	121.0	121.3	120.8	120.1	120.0	120.3	121.1
2008	120.1	120.1	119.9	120.6	120.5	120.5	119.6	119.5	118.6	117.6	116.3	115.4	119.1
2009	111.8	110.1	108.8	107.3	106.3	105.9	104.7	105.1	104.5	104.8	105.9	105.5	106.7
Service-Providing													
1990	650.9	654.4	662.0	667.0	674.7	672.8	667.5	670.1	676.5	680.0	682.3	686.9	670.4
2000	800.6	806.3	813.9	817.4	825.3	826.6	816.1	817.7	821.1	823.7	827.5	833.1	819.1
2001	807.5	810.8	816.7	818.9	825.1	826.9	818.5	820.4	822.5	826.0	828.3	830.8	821.0
2002	810.0	814.1	821.0	826.5	834.6	834.1	828.5	831.4	833.7	835.4	840.2	844.2	829.5
2003	824.7	825.2	832.5	840.2	845.2	844.7	835.9	842.1	841.6	844.2	847.1	850.5	839.4
2004	826.5	828.9	838.7	846.1	852.1	854.1	849.8	854.3	854.5	856.6	860.5	863.2	848.8
2005	834.6	840.1	848.8	859.1	864.9	866.5	858.6	860.6	865.8	863.6	868.7	873.0	858.7
2006	846.9	850.4	858.7	863.2	869.1	870.3	860.7	865.0	867.9	867.6	872.1	875.0	863.9
2007	855.0	856.3	866.3	873.5	883.9	885.0	871.9	875.7	877.7	883.0	887.2	890.5	875.5
2008	867.4	869.7	872.1	883.3	890.4	885.2	877.4	879.1	874.8	876.6	874.4	874.6	877.1
2009	845.4	844.2	844.9	851.0	857.7	855.3	844.9	847.9	844.8	843.5	846.6	850.7	848.1

Employment by Industry: Cincinnati-Middletown, OH-KY-IN, Selected Years, 1990–2009—*Continued*

(Numbers in thousands, not seasonally adjusted.)

Industry and year	January	February	March	April	May	June	July	August	September	October	November	December	Annual average
Trade, Transportation, and Utilities													
1990	183.4	181.4	183.2	183.0	183.4	184.1	184.7	186.6	186.6	186.9	188.8	192.1	185.4
2000	216.8	215.3	216.5	215.9	217.3	217.5	215.6	215.9	215.7	219.6	223.4	227.4	218.1
2001	217.6	214.8	215.4	212.6	213.5	214.3	215.2	215.1	215.0	216.9	220.3	222.8	216.1
2002	212.5	210.9	211.7	212.1	213.1	213.6	213.0	212.9	213.0	212.5	217.3	221.2	213.7
2003	210.3	208.6	209.5	209.7	210.5	210.6	209.1	210.2	209.4	211.1	214.7	217.4	210.9
2004	207.3	205.3	206.5	207.2	208.3	209.4	210.5	212.2	210.5	211.9	216.1	218.8	210.3
2005	208.2	206.7	208.1	209.1	210.4	210.5	211.5	210.6	210.9	209.9	213.5	217.0	210.5
2006	208.6	206.3	207.0	207.2	209.0	209.5	208.7	209.2	209.6	210.5	214.9	217.5	209.8
2007	210.3	208.3	210.1	210.5	212.9	213.3	212.8	212.6	212.9	214.3	218.5	221.2	213.1
2008	212.2	209.9	210.2	210.9	212.4	211.8	210.9	211.3	209.5	209.4	211.2	212.8	211.0
2009	202.2	199.5	198.2	197.3	198.6	198.0	197.2	198.3	197.6	197.0	199.3	201.0	198.7
Wholesale Trade													
1990	48.9	48.7	48.9	48.8	48.7	49.1	49.2	49.7	49.5	49.6	49.7	50.0	49.2
2000	58.6	58.9	59.1	59.4	59.6	59.4	59.3	59.2	59.4	59.6	59.6	59.8	59.3
2001	58.6	58.6	58.6	58.9	58.9	58.9	59.0	58.8	58.5	58.8	58.8	58.9	58.8
2002	57.6	57.7	57.7	57.9	58.0	58.2	58.7	58.4	58.5	58.7	58.8	59.0	58.3
2003	57.8	57.7	57.9	57.5	57.6	57.9	56.9	56.9	56.3	56.4	56.6	56.8	57.1
2004	55.6	55.5	55.6	55.6	55.8	56.2	57.8	57.9	57.7	57.1	57.4	57.9	56.7
2005	56.7	56.6	56.8	57.2	57.5	58.0	58.6	58.9	59.4	58.6	58.9	59.2	58.0
2006	58.9	58.9	59.0	59.1	59.3	59.8	59.6	59.8	59.5	59.4	59.5	59.9	59.4
2007	60.5	60.4	60.6	60.7	60.8	61.3	61.1	61.1	61.2	61.3	61.3	61.7	61.0
2008	61.3	61.4	61.5	61.3	61.5	61.8	61.6	61.3	60.7	60.8	60.6	60.4	61.2
2009	59.1	58.6	58.0	57.4	57.4	56.9	56.9	56.7	56.4	54.5	54.3	54.9	56.8
Retail Trade													
1990	102.2	100.3	101.5	101.8	101.9	101.9	102.1	103.0	103.4	103.2	105.4	108.4	102.9
2000	114.6	113.2	113.9	113.7	114.5	115.3	114.0	114.2	113.5	116.4	120.1	123.9	115.6
2001	115.8	113.2	114.0	113.5	114.4	115.6	113.9	113.9	113.4	114.3	118.0	120.5	115.0
2002	111.9	110.5	111.2	111.4	112.2	113.2	112.1	112.1	111.7	111.1	115.3	118.6	112.6
2003	109.4	107.7	108.2	109.0	109.8	110.4	110.0	110.6	110.3	111.0	114.4	116.7	110.6
2004	109.5	107.9	108.9	109.3	109.9	110.9	110.3	111.3	109.7	111.0	114.6	116.7	110.8
2005	108.8	107.0	107.9	108.5	109.3	109.1	109.7	108.6	108.1	108.4	111.6	114.9	109.3
2006	108.1	106.2	106.9	107.4	108.7	108.8	108.6	108.8	108.4	109.2	112.8	114.4	109.0
2007	108.1	106.4	108.0	108.5	110.0	109.9	109.9	109.3	108.7	109.5	113.0	114.5	109.7
2008	108.5	106.4	106.7	107.6	108.6	108.4	108.2	108.3	107.1	107.0	108.9	110.3	108.0
2009	103.3	101.7	101.5	101.5	102.8	102.9	102.0	102.1	101.7	102.1	105.0	105.7	102.7
Transportation and Utilities													
1990	32.3	32.4	32.8	32.4	32.8	33.1	33.4	33.9	33.7	34.1	33.7	33.7	33.2
2000	43.6	43.2	43.5	42.8	43.2	42.8	42.3	42.5	42.8	43.6	43.7	43.7	43.1
2001	43.2	43.0	42.8	40.2	40.2	39.8	42.3	42.4	43.1	43.8	43.5	43.4	42.3
2002	43.0	42.7	42.8	42.8	42.9	42.2	42.2	42.4	42.8	42.7	43.2	43.6	42.8
2003	43.1	43.2	43.4	43.2	43.1	42.3	42.2	42.7	42.8	43.7	43.7	43.9	43.1
2004	42.2	41.9	42.0	42.3	42.6	42.3	42.4	43.0	43.1	43.8	44.1	44.2	42.8
2005	42.7	43.1	43.4	43.4	43.6	43.4	43.2	43.1	43.4	42.9	43.0	42.9	43.2
2006	41.6	41.2	41.1	40.7	41.0	40.9	40.5	40.6	41.7	41.9	42.6	43.2	41.4
2007	41.7	41.5	41.5	41.3	42.1	42.1	41.8	42.2	43.0	43.5	44.2	45.0	42.5
2008	42.4	42.1	42.0	42.0	42.3	41.6	41.1	41.7	41.7	41.6	41.7	42.1	41.9
2009	39.8	39.2	38.7	38.4	38.4	38.2	38.3	39.5	39.5	40.4	40.0	40.4	39.2
Information													
1990	18.4	18.4	18.4	18.5	18.6	18.7	18.8	18.8	18.8	18.6	18.5	18.5	18.6
2000	20.3	20.1	20.7	20.5	20.6	20.7	20.1	20.3	20.0	20.0	19.8	19.9	20.3
2001	20.1	19.9	20.0	19.5	19.6	19.7	19.4	19.3	18.9	18.8	18.6	18.5	19.4
2002	18.4	18.1	18.1	17.9	17.9	18.2	18.1	17.8	17.4	16.9	17.1	17.1	17.8
2003	16.4	16.2	16.3	16.3	16.5	16.4	16.5	16.3	16.0	15.7	15.9	16.0	16.2
2004	15.9	15.7	15.7	16.0	16.1	16.2	16.2	16.2	16.0	16.1	16.1	16.1	16.0
2005	15.9	15.9	15.9	15.8	16.0	15.9	15.9	15.8	15.7	15.8	15.9	16.1	15.9
2006	15.7	15.6	15.7	15.8	15.7	15.8	15.8	15.8	15.5	15.5	15.6	15.6	15.7
2007	15.3	15.4	15.3	15.5	15.6	15.7	15.7	15.7	15.3	15.2	15.2	15.2	15.4
2008	15.1	15.1	15.2	15.1	15.1	15.2	15.3	15.3	15.1	15.2	15.1	15.1	15.2
2009	15.0	14.9	14.9	14.8	14.9	14.8	14.8	14.7	14.5	14.4	14.3	14.4	14.7
Financial Activities													
1990	48.3	48.4	48.7	48.9	49.2	50.1	50.1	50.4	49.8	49.2	49.1	49.4	49.3
2000	58.8	58.9	58.8	58.9	59.1	59.5	59.1	59.2	58.6	58.9	59.2	59.8	59.1
2001	59.5	59.8	59.6	60.4	60.6	61.3	61.2	61.6	61.3	61.5	61.7	62.3	60.9
2002	62.4	62.9	62.9	63.3	63.9	64.4	64.5	64.7	64.3	64.7	65.1	65.7	64.1
2003	65.6	65.9	65.9	65.6	65.9	66.2	66.3	66.6	66.1	65.9	65.8	66.0	65.9
2004	64.8	64.9	65.0	65.0	65.0	65.5	65.5	65.5	64.8	64.5	64.6	65.0	65.0
2005	64.7	64.8	64.8	65.0	65.2	65.8	65.6	65.6	65.0	64.9	65.0	65.5	65.2
2006	64.6	64.7	64.9	65.2	65.5	65.7	65.4	65.4	64.9	64.9	64.9	65.2	65.1
2007	65.0	65.2	65.3	65.4	65.7	66.0	66.3	66.0	65.5	65.3	65.1	65.6	65.5
2008	65.2	65.1	65.2	65.7	65.9	66.1	66.2	66.0	65.3	65.1	65.1	64.9	65.5
2009	64.1	63.8	63.7	63.6	63.9	63.9	63.8	63.2	62.6	61.3	61.2	61.7	63.1

Employment by Industry: Cincinnati-Middletown, OH-KY-IN, Selected Years, 1990–2009—*Continued*

(Numbers in thousands, not seasonally adjusted.)

Industry and year	January	February	March	April	May	June	July	August	September	October	November	December	Annual average
Professional and Business Services													
1990	92.0	91.8	94.1	94.6	95.4	96.3	95.5	96.2	96.0	98.9	97.9	97.3	95.5
2000	134.4	135.2	137.3	137.6	138.1	141.1	140.7	141.8	141.2	141.2	140.7	140.1	139.1
2001	136.1	136.6	137.8	139.4	139.4	140.5	138.9	139.5	139.6	141.3	139.9	137.9	138.9
2002	134.9	134.3	135.4	137.0	137.9	139.6	140.5	142.1	142.5	144.2	144.1	143.1	139.6
2003	141.7	141.3	142.7	144.3	144.0	144.7	143.8	144.8	144.5	146.3	145.6	145.2	144.0
2004	142.6	141.3	143.3	144.1	144.2	146.7	149.2	150.3	150.6	150.2	150.6	150.8	147.0
2005	145.0	146.3	148.3	150.5	150.9	153.5	153.9	155.7	157.2	156.8	157.3	158.0	152.8
2006	151.3	151.8	153.8	154.3	153.5	154.6	155.9	156.6	156.3	154.9	154.9	154.7	154.4
2007	150.8	151.0	153.8	155.7	155.8	157.7	156.6	157.7	157.7	160.5	161.3	161.3	156.7
2008	157.8	157.1	157.2	159.3	158.5	159.2	160.3	160.5	159.0	159.6	157.6	156.5	158.6
2009	149.9	148.7	147.9	148.2	147.5	147.5	147.3	147.9	146.6	147.3	149.0	150.6	148.2
Education and Health Services													
1990	95.4	96.4	97.0	97.3	98.2	98.7	98.6	99.4	100.5	101.0	101.6	101.8	98.8
2000	116.9	118.2	118.5	119.3	119.9	119.3	119.6	119.9	121.1	120.1	120.9	121.3	119.6
2001	118.1	119.6	120.1	120.1	120.3	119.4	120.5	120.9	122.2	123.2	123.7	124.3	121.0
2002	121.4	122.6	122.8	123.9	124.4	123.5	123.4	124.4	126.0	127.2	127.8	128.4	124.7
2003	125.5	125.7	125.8	126.2	126.2	125.5	126.4	127.2	128.4	128.9	130.0	130.3	127.1
2004	128.8	129.7	130.3	131.0	130.9	130.4	130.8	130.6	131.6	132.5	133.4	133.6	131.1
2005	131.5	132.8	133.3	135.1	134.8	134.2	133.3	134.1	134.9	135.7	136.3	136.5	134.4
2006	135.1	136.2	137.0	138.1	138.1	137.7	136.6	137.6	138.9	140.1	140.8	141.0	138.1
2007	139.3	139.9	140.9	141.6	142.2	141.0	139.7	140.3	142.9	144.0	145.0	144.9	141.8
2008	143.3	144.2	144.9	146.1	146.5	144.0	144.4	144.6	145.4	146.2	146.8	146.6	145.3
2009	144.2	144.7	145.3	146.7	147.1	145.4	146.1	145.9	146.4	147.2	148.2	148.4	146.3
Leisure and Hospitality													
1990	69.2	70.1	71.5	75.9	78.7	82.0	82.6	82.2	80.7	78.1	76.0	77.1	77.0
2000	88.9	89.5	91.8	94.2	96.8	100.7	101.7	102.2	99.7	96.0	94.6	95.5	96.0
2001	90.0	90.3	92.9	95.1	98.8	103.1	103.2	102.6	97.9	93.9	92.6	93.3	96.1
2002	90.7	91.8	95.1	97.4	101.5	104.2	105.3	104.0	100.7	96.8	95.1	95.6	98.2
2003	92.1	91.5	94.4	99.4	102.8	107.3	107.6	107.8	103.0	98.4	96.9	97.5	99.8
2004	93.4	94.7	98.6	102.7	106.8	109.7	110.7	110.2	106.1	103.2	101.2	101.2	103.2
2005	96.2	97.3	100.7	105.0	108.4	111.5	111.9	110.7	107.8	102.9	102.7	102.5	104.8
2006	98.5	99.5	102.3	104.3	107.8	112.5	112.1	112.1	107.7	104.0	103.1	103.1	105.6
2007	99.8	99.0	101.4	105.4	110.8	113.9	112.9	113.4	108.6	105.5	101.9	102.9	106.3
2008	99.1	99.4	100.3	106.7	110.9	113.3	112.4	111.7	106.3	103.1	99.1	100.0	105.2
2009	95.4	95.5	97.7	102.4	107.0	110.5	109.0	108.3	104.7	100.9	97.9	99.1	102.4
Other Services													
1990	29.6	29.8	30.2	30.1	30.5	31.0	30.8	30.9	30.8	30.9	31.1	31.3	30.6
2000	41.2	41.3	41.4	41.5	41.7	41.5	41.3	41.1	41.0	40.8	40.7	40.6	41.2
2001	39.9	40.1	40.4	40.5	41.0	41.3	40.8	41.1	40.2	40.3	40.3	40.3	40.5
2002	40.4	40.7	41.0	41.1	41.4	41.9	41.6	41.4	40.6	40.4	40.4	40.4	40.9
2003	41.1	41.4	42.0	42.2	42.6	42.8	42.6	42.5	42.0	42.0	41.9	42.1	42.1
2004	41.6	41.9	42.5	43.0	43.3	43.6	43.4	43.5	43.3	43.0	42.8	42.9	42.9
2005	42.0	42.3	42.7	43.2	43.3	43.4	43.2	43.0	42.7	42.7	42.6	42.7	42.8
2006	41.8	41.8	42.2	42.3	42.7	43.1	43.2	43.2	43.0	42.7	42.6	42.8	42.6
2007	42.3	42.3	43.0	43.2	43.6	44.3	43.9	44.1	43.3	43.7	43.7	43.7	43.4
2008	43.3	43.3	43.6	43.8	44.0	44.4	44.0	43.8	43.0	43.3	43.0	43.1	43.6
2009	42.4	42.4	42.7	42.5	42.8	42.9	42.8	42.5	42.0	41.8	41.9	41.6	42.4
Government													
1990	114.6	118.1	118.9	118.7	120.7	111.9	106.4	105.6	113.3	116.4	119.3	119.4	115.3
2000	123.3	127.8	128.9	129.5	131.8	126.3	118.0	117.3	123.8	127.1	128.2	128.5	125.9
2001	126.2	129.7	130.5	131.3	131.9	127.3	119.3	120.3	127.4	130.1	131.2	131.4	128.1
2002	129.3	132.8	134.0	133.8	134.5	128.7	122.1	124.1	129.2	132.7	133.3	132.7	130.6
2003	132.0	134.6	135.9	136.5	136.7	131.2	123.6	126.7	132.2	135.9	136.3	136.0	133.1
2004	132.1	135.4	136.8	137.1	137.5	132.6	123.5	125.8	131.6	135.2	135.7	134.8	133.2
2005	131.1	134.0	135.0	135.4	135.9	131.7	123.3	125.1	131.6	134.9	135.4	134.7	132.3
2006	131.3	134.5	135.8	136.0	136.8	131.4	123.0	125.1	132.0	135.0	135.3	135.1	132.6
2007	132.2	135.2	136.5	136.2	137.3	133.1	124.0	125.9	131.5	134.5	136.5	135.7	133.2
2008	131.4	135.6	135.5	135.7	137.1	131.2	123.9	125.9	131.2	134.7	136.5	135.6	132.9
2009	132.2	134.7	134.5	135.5	135.9	132.3	123.9	127.1	130.4	133.6	134.8	133.9	132.4

Employment by Industry: Cleveland-Elyria-Mentor, OH, Selected Years, 1990–2009

(Numbers in thousands, not seasonally adjusted.)

Industry and year	January	February	March	April	May	June	July	August	September	October	November	December	Annual average
Total Nonfarm													
1990	1005.5	1008.2	1018.9	1024.2	1036.6	1049.3	1034.8	1034.1	1036.7	1032.7	1030.5	1030.3	1028.5
2000	1113.8	1118.2	1126.4	1132.1	1144.5	1149.7	1138.4	1139.9	1140.5	1140.0	1143.4	1145.2	1136.0
2001	1112.7	1114.3	1121.1	1121.6	1129.4	1133.6	1120.0	1119.0	1110.3	1109.3	1110.0	1108.3	1117.5
2002	1069.6	1072.2	1078.5	1078.7	1087.5	1091.2	1081.7	1084.1	1084.5	1087.0	1086.8	1085.9	1082.3
2003	1057.1	1058.1	1063.8	1072.1	1083.4	1085.0	1076.1	1076.3	1077.1	1079.8	1080.4	1081.1	1074.1
2004	1047.3	1050.5	1059.9	1067.7	1076.8	1082.6	1076.2	1076.4	1077.1	1082.0	1084.8	1084.0	1072.1
2005	1044.9	1051.2	1058.1	1068.6	1075.5	1082.0	1075.4	1077.2	1079.8	1082.7	1085.3	1085.3	1072.2
2006	1053.6	1057.6	1065.4	1074.8	1082.1	1088.9	1076.9	1078.4	1079.1	1080.2	1081.1	1081.3	1075.0
2007	1052.8	1052.6	1061.5	1070.4	1080.2	1090.1	1075.6	1076.9	1073.8	1076.6	1079.4	1077.4	1072.3
2008	1049.9	1050.4	1048.2	1060.9	1072.8	1075.8	1064.3	1062.6	1060.8	1058.9	1052.6	1044.9	1058.5
2009	1009.2	1006.2	1003.5	1005.1	1009.4	1007.5	999.1	994.6	994.7	996.6	998.2	989.6	1001.1
Total Private													
1990	876.2	877.1	886.4	892.5	903.2	915.3	911.3	912.6	909.5	903.3	900.4	900.4	899.0
2000	975.4	977.3	984.4	990.9	999.0	1008.5	1002.9	1003.7	999.5	996.8	999.5	1000.7	994.9
2001	971.7	970.6	976.0	977.1	984.2	990.6	982.5	981.1	966.4	963.4	963.5	961.3	974.0
2002	927.5	926.0	931.4	932.8	940.4	946.4	945.3	946.6	940.7	940.6	940.0	939.6	938.1
2003	914.7	912.8	917.4	926.2	937.4	941.5	939.8	942.5	935.9	935.1	934.9	935.3	931.1
2004	906.0	905.8	914.1	922.0	930.4	938.6	941.0	942.6	937.7	939.0	940.9	940.6	929.9
2005	905.8	908.4	914.7	924.9	931.1	938.8	940.7	943.7	940.9	940.5	943.0	942.7	931.3
2006	914.8	915.8	922.3	931.7	938.1	946.6	943.0	945.3	940.3	938.2	937.9	938.2	934.4
2007	913.0	909.3	916.8	925.2	934.3	942.8	936.1	938.6	933.7	932.9	935.1	934.1	929.3
2008	908.6	906.2	904.8	916.9	926.3	928.6	924.8	924.7	920.6	915.3	909.0	902.6	915.7
2009	868.8	863.5	860.8	862.0	865.2	864.7	860.3	858.7	856.5	855.3	856.3	848.3	860.0
Goods-Producing													
1990	244.8	246.4	248.7	250.4	252.6	256.6	256.3	255.7	254.5	252.8	248.2	246.2	251.1
2000	237.4	238.8	241.1	241.3	243.2	246.1	243.6	243.8	241.6	240.7	240.3	237.3	241.3
2001	229.6	228.1	228.2	226.4	227.3	227.8	225.3	224.7	219.6	217.0	216.4	213.8	223.7
2002	203.0	201.5	202.4	202.4	204.4	206.7	206.8	207.2	205.4	204.8	203.4	200.8	204.1
2003	195.1	194.0	195.0	195.8	199.5	200.5	198.5	199.0	197.4	197.5	196.7	194.5	196.9
2004	187.3	187.5	189.9	193.0	195.7	198.0	198.0	198.1	197.4	197.4	196.4	194.2	194.4
2005	185.8	185.4	187.1	191.6	193.4	195.9	195.3	195.8	195.4	194.7	194.1	191.2	192.1
2006	185.5	184.3	185.3	189.0	190.1	193.0	192.6	192.8	191.9	190.9	188.7	184.7	189.1
2007	180.8	178.8	181.1	182.9	186.4	188.5	184.2	186.8	185.5	184.8	184.4	181.9	183.8
2008	176.1	175.3	174.9	177.8	180.3	181.7	181.5	179.6	179.4	178.1	173.4	167.8	177.2
2009	158.6	156.9	154.6	153.0	152.1	151.8	150.0	150.0	150.0	145.5	145.9	142.6	150.9
Mining, Logging, and Construction													
1990	33.8	34.1	35.6	37.4	39.4	42.0	42.8	43.5	42.4	41.8	41.1	38.5	39.4
2000	40.5	40.3	42.6	44.4	46.7	49.0	49.3	49.3	47.6	47.0	46.3	43.7	45.6
2001	39.1	38.8	40.0	42.0	44.6	46.2	47.2	47.8	46.2	46.0	44.9	42.9	43.8
2002	37.8	37.2	38.3	40.3	42.6	44.5	45.0	46.3	45.5	45.5	44.3	42.0	42.5
2003	38.0	37.1	38.4	41.4	44.1	45.9	46.3	46.9	46.1	46.5	45.4	43.3	43.2
2004	38.3	38.4	40.1	42.4	44.8	46.4	47.3	47.0	46.6	46.7	45.6	43.5	43.9
2005	37.1	37.0	37.8	42.2	44.0	45.9	46.4	46.5	45.9	45.7	44.5	41.5	42.9
2006	37.0	36.5	37.5	40.7	42.5	43.7	44.7	44.8	44.3	44.0	43.0	40.7	41.6
2007	36.6	34.9	36.6	39.6	43.0	44.4	43.9	44.2	43.5	43.3	42.4	39.9	41.0
2008	35.1	34.4	34.5	37.1	39.7	40.9	42.0	41.9	40.9	40.6	38.5	35.6	38.4
2009	30.6	29.9	30.6	31.9	34.0	35.3	35.8	35.6	35.0	34.4	32.8	27.2	32.8
Manufacturing													
1990	211.0	212.3	213.1	213.0	213.2	214.6	213.5	212.2	212.1	211.0	207.1	207.7	211.7
2000	196.9	198.5	198.5	196.9	196.5	197.1	194.3	194.5	194.0	193.7	194.0	193.6	195.7
2001	190.5	189.3	188.2	184.4	182.7	181.6	178.1	176.9	173.4	171.0	171.5	170.9	179.9
2002	165.2	164.3	164.1	162.1	161.8	162.2	160.9	160.9	159.9	159.3	159.1	158.8	161.6
2003	157.1	156.9	156.6	154.4	155.4	154.6	152.2	152.1	151.3	151.0	151.3	151.2	153.6
2004	149.0	149.1	149.8	150.6	150.9	151.6	150.7	151.1	150.8	150.7	150.8	150.7	150.5
2005	148.7	148.4	149.3	149.4	149.4	150.0	148.9	149.3	149.5	149.0	149.6	149.7	149.3
2006	148.5	147.8	147.8	148.3	147.6	149.3	147.9	148.0	147.6	146.9	145.7	144.0	147.5
2007	144.2	143.9	144.5	143.3	143.4	144.1	140.3	142.6	142.0	141.5	142.0	142.0	142.8
2008	141.0	140.9	140.4	140.7	140.6	140.8	139.5	137.7	138.5	137.5	134.9	132.2	138.7
2009	128.0	127.0	124.0	121.1	118.1	116.5	114.2	114.4	115.0	111.1	113.1	115.4	118.2
Service-Providing													
1990	760.7	761.8	770.2	773.8	784.0	792.7	778.5	778.4	782.2	779.9	782.3	784.1	777.4
2000	876.4	879.4	885.3	890.8	901.3	903.6	894.8	896.1	898.9	899.3	903.1	907.9	894.7
2001	883.1	886.2	892.9	895.2	902.1	905.8	894.7	894.3	890.7	892.3	893.6	894.5	893.8
2002	866.6	870.7	876.1	876.3	883.1	884.5	874.9	876.9	879.1	882.2	883.4	885.1	878.2
2003	862.0	864.1	868.8	876.3	883.9	884.5	877.6	877.3	879.7	882.3	883.7	886.6	877.2
2004	860.0	863.0	870.0	874.7	881.1	884.6	878.2	878.3	879.7	884.6	888.4	889.8	877.7
2005	859.1	865.8	871.0	877.0	882.1	886.1	880.1	881.4	884.4	888.0	891.2	894.1	880.0
2006	868.1	873.3	880.1	885.8	892.0	895.9	884.3	885.6	887.2	889.3	892.4	896.6	885.9
2007	872.0	873.8	880.4	887.5	893.8	901.6	891.4	890.1	888.3	891.8	895.0	895.5	888.4
2008	873.8	875.1	873.3	883.1	892.5	894.1	882.8	883.0	881.4	880.8	879.2	877.1	881.4

Employment by Industry: Cleveland-Elyria-Mentor, OH, Selected Years, 1990–2009—*Continued*

(Numbers in thousands, not seasonally adjusted.)

Industry and year	January	February	March	April	May	June	July	August	September	October	November	December	Annual average
Trade, Transportation, and Utilities													
1990	208.5	205.5	207.2	208.0	210.2	212.2	210.4	211.1	210.0	209.1	211.9	215.0	209.9
2000	219.1	216.7	217.2	217.5	219.0	220.3	219.0	219.2	218.5	221.3	225.3	229.1	220.2
2001	216.9	213.9	214.5	214.3	214.8	215.5	212.3	211.5	209.4	210.3	213.1	214.2	213.4
2002	204.6	201.3	202.6	200.9	202.5	203.3	202.9	202.9	200.9	202.6	204.9	207.5	203.1
2003	200.4	197.9	197.4	200.2	201.9	202.7	202.1	201.9	200.6	202.8	205.5	208.7	201.8
2004	199.3	197.2	198.0	197.8	199.0	200.4	199.6	199.6	197.5	199.8	203.7	206.1	199.8
2005	197.0	195.5	196.3	196.5	198.0	198.8	199.1	199.0	197.7	198.7	202.0	205.2	198.7
2006	197.6	196.0	197.1	198.5	199.6	200.4	198.9	199.3	198.2	199.3	203.1	206.5	199.5
2007	198.2	195.4	196.9	197.5	198.8	200.0	199.3	198.5	197.0	198.1	201.8	204.6	198.8
2008	197.1	193.9	193.3	194.7	196.2	196.3	195.9	196.2	194.0	193.8	195.1	196.9	195.3
2009	186.9	184.3	183.6	182.4	183.1	183.4	182.2	181.6	179.8	181.3	183.3	185.2	183.1
Wholesale Trade													
1990	53.7	53.7	54.1	54.4	54.3	54.8	55.0	55.2	54.8	54.2	53.9	53.9	54.3
2000	56.8	56.9	57.0	57.2	57.5	57.7	57.8	57.9	58.2	58.5	58.7	58.9	57.8
2001	58.6	58.8	59.2	58.6	58.3	58.5	57.7	57.4	56.6	56.4	56.2	55.6	57.7
2002	55.5	55.1	55.4	54.9	54.9	54.6	54.6	54.3	53.6	53.5	53.2	53.5	54.4
2003	54.6	54.5	54.4	54.7	55.1	55.1	55.1	55.0	54.6	54.7	54.8	55.0	54.8
2004	54.1	54.1	54.3	54.2	54.5	54.9	54.9	54.9	54.3	54.9	55.1	55.4	54.6
2005	54.6	54.6	54.8	54.9	55.0	55.5	55.7	55.8	55.6	55.3	55.4	55.8	55.3
2006	55.5	55.6	55.9	56.2	56.3	56.6	56.5	56.3	56.1	55.8	55.9	56.2	56.1
2007	55.4	55.4	55.6	55.4	55.5	55.6	55.5	55.2	54.5	54.4	54.3	54.4	55.1
2008	54.3	54.2	54.0	54.5	54.7	54.7	54.5	54.3	53.8	53.6	53.2	52.7	54.0
2009	51.8	51.4	50.9	50.3	50.2	50.0	49.7	49.5	49.1	48.4	47.5	47.7	49.7
Retail Trade													
1990	119.7	117.0	117.7	118.0	119.6	121.3	119.2	119.9	119.2	119.1	122.3	125.3	119.9
2000	124.5	122.3	122.6	121.9	123.0	124.1	122.8	123.1	122.1	123.9	127.8	131.5	124.1
2001	122.0	119.2	119.3	118.9	119.3	119.8	118.0	117.6	116.6	117.7	121.6	123.9	119.5
2002	115.9	112.9	114.0	112.4	113.6	114.5	114.1	114.2	113.0	114.0	116.8	119.5	114.6
2003	113.4	111.5	111.5	113.4	114.3	115.1	114.6	114.7	114.0	115.1	117.8	120.9	114.6
2004	113.5	111.5	111.9	111.8	112.6	113.3	112.4	112.2	110.6	111.6	115.1	117.4	112.8
2005	110.2	108.5	108.9	109.2	110.3	110.7	110.5	110.3	109.2	110.1	113.1	115.5	110.5
2006	109.0	107.4	108.0	108.7	109.6	109.9	108.9	109.1	107.8	109.3	112.8	115.4	109.7
2007	108.9	106.3	107.3	107.5	109.0	110.0	109.8	109.2	108.1	109.1	112.8	115.2	109.4
2008	108.9	106.1	105.9	106.4	107.4	107.9	107.8	108.1	106.6	106.8	108.7	110.6	107.6
2009	103.1	100.9	101.1	101.1	102.1	102.7	102.3	102.0	100.8	102.7	105.6	107.4	102.7
Transportation and Utilities													
1990	35.1	34.8	35.4	35.6	36.3	36.1	36.2	36.0	36.0	35.8	35.7	35.8	35.7
2000	37.8	37.5	37.6	38.4	38.5	38.5	38.4	38.2	38.2	38.9	38.8	38.7	38.3
2001	36.3	35.9	36.0	36.8	37.2	37.2	36.6	36.5	36.2	36.2	35.3	34.7	36.2
2002	33.2	33.3	33.2	33.6	34.0	34.2	34.2	34.4	34.3	35.1	34.9	34.5	34.1
2003	32.4	31.9	31.5	32.1	32.5	32.5	32.4	32.2	32.0	33.0	32.9	32.8	32.3
2004	31.7	31.6	31.8	31.8	31.9	32.2	32.3	32.5	32.6	33.3	33.5	33.3	32.4
2005	32.2	32.4	32.6	32.4	32.7	32.6	32.9	32.9	32.9	33.3	33.5	33.9	32.9
2006	33.1	33.0	33.2	33.6	33.7	33.9	33.5	33.9	34.3	34.2	34.4	34.9	33.8
2007	33.9	33.7	34.0	34.6	34.3	34.4	34.0	34.1	34.4	34.6	34.7	35.0	34.3
2008	33.9	33.6	33.4	33.8	34.1	33.7	33.6	33.8	33.6	33.4	33.2	33.6	33.6
2009	32.0	32.0	31.6	31.0	30.8	30.7	30.2	30.1	29.9	30.2	30.2	30.1	30.7
Information													
1990	26.1	26.0	26.2	26.3	26.5	27.0	26.9	26.8	26.7	27.0	27.2	27.2	26.7
2000	23.9	24.0	24.0	24.1	24.1	24.2	24.1	24.2	24.3	24.4	24.5	24.5	24.2
2001	24.5	24.5	24.6	24.3	24.2	24.3	24.2	23.9	23.5	23.3	23.3	23.3	24.0
2002	23.3	23.0	22.9	22.1	21.9	21.9	21.6	21.4	21.2	21.1	21.1	21.0	21.9
2003	21.3	21.2	21.2	21.0	21.0	20.9	20.7	20.5	20.2	20.2	20.2	20.4	20.7
2004	20.1	20.0	20.1	20.0	20.0	20.1	20.1	20.0	19.7	19.7	19.8	19.6	19.9
2005	19.5	19.5	19.4	19.7	19.7	19.6	19.5	19.5	19.2	19.2	19.3	19.2	19.4
2006	19.2	19.1	19.1	18.8	18.9	18.9	18.9	18.9	18.7	18.6	18.7	18.7	18.9
2007	18.4	18.5	18.3	18.5	18.6	18.6	18.7	18.5	18.4	18.3	18.4	18.4	18.5
2008	18.2	18.0	18.0	18.0	18.0	17.9	17.8	17.7	17.2	17.2	17.3	17.3	17.7
2009	17.1	17.0	16.7	16.5	16.5	16.5	16.3	16.2	15.9	15.8	15.9	15.9	16.4
Financial Activities													
1990	60.7	60.9	61.6	61.3	61.9	62.7	63.2	63.3	62.8	62.1	62.0	62.0	62.0
2000	75.6	75.2	75.6	74.8	74.5	75.3	74.8	75.0	74.9	74.2	74.9	75.5	75.0
2001	75.5	75.9	76.1	76.1	76.0	77.1	77.1	77.1	76.0	75.8	76.5	76.9	76.3
2002	75.7	76.0	76.0	75.9	75.8	75.7	75.6	75.4	74.6	74.4	75.1	75.5	75.5
2003	75.8	75.9	76.2	76.0	76.5	77.5	77.7	77.9	77.2	76.6	76.9	77.6	76.8
2004	76.7	76.9	77.1	76.6	76.8	77.8	77.7	77.7	76.7	76.3	76.3	76.4	76.9
2005	75.5	75.4	75.2	74.4	74.3	75.3	75.1	75.0	74.2	74.9	74.7	74.6	74.9
2006	73.6	73.7	73.8	73.5	73.5	74.0	74.4	74.2	73.7	73.5	73.7	73.8	73.8
2007	73.1	73.0	72.9	72.8	72.9	72.8	72.7	72.3	71.3	71.0	70.7	70.5	72.2
2008	69.7	69.3	69.3	69.1	69.2	69.2	69.4	69.2	68.2	67.9	67.9	67.7	68.8
2009	66.9	66.5	66.2	65.8	65.9	66.1	65.7	65.3	64.7	64.0	62.9	63.0	65.3

Employment by Industry: Cleveland-Elyria-Mentor, OH, Selected Years, 1990–2009—*Continued*

(Numbers in thousands, not seasonally adjusted.)

Industry and year	January	February	March	April	May	June	July	August	September	October	November	December	Annual average
Professional and Business Services													
1990	107.1	108.5	110.0	111.7	113.3	115.0	114.6	115.0	114.9	114.3	113.4	111.6	112.5
2000	140.2	140.8	141.9	146.5	147.1	149.3	148.8	149.2	148.3	147.4	146.6	145.8	146.0
2001	143.6	143.7	145.2	145.4	145.9	146.7	145.6	145.1	141.3	140.3	138.6	137.4	143.2
2002	132.5	132.8	134.1	134.3	134.3	135.7	135.2	136.0	134.1	135.7	134.3	133.6	134.4
2003	131.5	131.6	132.9	134.5	135.3	136.6	137.1	138.7	136.5	135.5	134.6	133.1	134.8
2004	129.3	129.8	131.3	135.8	136.9	139.1	140.1	141.7	141.1	140.9	139.8	139.0	137.1
2005	133.2	134.9	136.2	139.4	139.5	141.3	143.0	144.3	144.2	144.6	144.3	143.1	140.7
2006	138.6	139.4	140.8	143.4	143.8	145.8	145.8	147.2	146.4	146.1	145.3	145.3	144.0
2007	140.2	140.4	140.9	143.2	143.9	146.1	145.9	146.6	145.6	145.6	145.5	144.7	144.1
2008	141.5	141.5	140.8	143.5	144.8	145.6	145.6	146.5	144.8	142.2	140.5	137.8	142.9
2009	132.8	131.0	129.9	129.9	130.0	130.3	129.8	129.9	129.3	132.0	131.6	125.9	130.2
Education and Health Services													
1990	120.0	120.5	121.3	121.6	121.3	121.3	120.2	120.5	122.1	122.9	123.4	123.7	121.6
2000	147.4	149.5	150.2	149.9	150.0	149.4	147.7	147.9	150.7	150.8	151.4	152.0	149.7
2001	150.5	153.0	153.7	154.8	155.2	154.5	152.9	153.4	157.0	159.5	160.5	161.0	155.5
2002	158.8	162.2	162.5	162.6	162.4	161.1	160.3	160.7	164.3	165.9	166.8	167.1	162.9
2003	161.5	163.6	164.1	164.1	163.9	161.5	161.5	161.1	164.4	166.0	166.4	165.5	163.6
2004	163.0	165.1	165.7	164.2	163.5	161.5	162.9	161.8	166.0	168.2	168.7	169.3	165.0
2005	164.9	167.5	167.8	166.6	166.2	165.4	164.6	164.9	169.2	170.1	171.3	172.0	167.5
2006	168.5	171.7	172.2	171.3	170.7	169.9	168.0	167.7	170.8	172.5	173.4	173.3	170.8
2007	171.3	172.8	173.9	174.7	174.0	173.2	172.1	172.3	176.6	178.4	179.2	179.5	174.8
2008	176.9	179.2	179.0	179.8	179.0	177.3	174.7	175.4	180.6	183.4	184.1	184.3	179.5
2009	182.1	184.1	184.5	184.8	183.9	181.6	180.8	181.1	185.5	187.1	188.2	188.9	184.4
Leisure and Hospitality													
1990	72.2	72.2	73.8	75.4	79.2	81.5	81.2	81.3	79.7	76.3	75.2	75.3	76.9
2000	86.9	87.1	88.9	91.7	95.7	98.4	99.5	99.1	95.8	92.6	91.1	90.9	93.1
2001	86.2	86.5	88.6	90.3	95.0	98.2	98.6	98.6	93.3	91.3	89.1	88.5	92.0
2002	84.1	83.6	85.0	88.8	93.0	95.4	96.4	96.7	94.2	90.7	89.1	88.8	90.5
2003	85.0	84.5	86.2	90.2	94.7	96.8	97.7	98.8	95.4	92.5	90.8	91.5	92.0
2004	86.6	85.6	87.6	90.1	93.8	96.6	97.5	98.9	94.9	92.3	91.8	91.7	92.3
2005	86.3	86.4	88.6	92.3	95.6	97.8	99.3	100.6	96.8	94.2	93.1	93.0	93.7
2006	88.1	87.9	90.2	93.5	97.4	99.7	99.8	101.0	96.7	93.5	91.3	91.8	94.2
2007	87.6	87.0	89.0	91.6	95.5	98.7	98.3	99.0	95.2	92.8	91.2	90.5	93.0
2008	85.7	85.4	86.0	90.6	95.1	96.7	96.2	96.5	93.2	89.7	87.8	87.8	90.9
2009	82.1	81.4	82.9	87.1	91.1	92.5	92.8	92.2	89.4	87.8	86.7	84.8	87.6
Other Services													
1990	36.8	37.1	37.6	37.8	38.2	39.0	38.5	38.9	38.8	38.8	39.1	39.4	38.3
2000	44.9	45.2	45.5	45.1	45.4	45.5	45.4	45.3	45.4	45.4	45.4	45.6	45.3
2001	44.9	45.0	45.1	45.5	45.8	46.5	46.5	46.8	46.3	45.9	46.0	46.2	45.9
2002	45.5	45.6	45.9	45.8	46.1	46.6	46.5	46.3	46.0	45.4	45.3	45.3	45.9
2003	44.1	44.1	44.4	44.4	44.6	45.0	44.5	44.6	44.2	44.0	43.8	44.0	44.3
2004	43.7	43.7	44.4	44.5	44.7	45.1	45.1	44.8	44.4	44.4	44.4	44.3	44.5
2005	43.6	43.8	44.1	44.4	44.4	44.7	44.8	44.6	44.2	44.1	44.2	44.4	44.3
2006	43.7	43.7	43.8	43.7	44.1	44.9	44.6	44.2	43.9	43.8	43.7	44.1	44.0
2007	43.4	43.4	43.8	44.0	44.2	44.9	44.9	44.6	44.1	43.9	43.9	44.0	44.1
2008	43.4	43.6	43.5	43.4	43.7	43.9	43.7	43.6	43.2	43.0	42.9	43.0	43.4
2009	42.3	42.3	42.4	42.5	42.6	42.5	42.7	42.4	41.9	41.8	41.8	42.0	42.3
Government													
1990	129.3	131.1	132.5	131.7	133.4	134.0	123.5	121.5	127.2	129.4	130.1	129.9	129.5
2000	138.4	140.9	142.0	141.2	145.5	141.2	135.5	136.2	141.0	143.2	143.9	144.5	141.1
2001	141.0	143.7	145.1	144.5	145.2	143.0	137.5	137.9	143.9	145.9	146.5	147.0	143.4
2002	142.1	146.2	147.1	145.9	147.1	144.8	136.4	137.5	143.8	146.4	146.8	146.3	144.2
2003	142.4	145.3	146.4	145.9	146.0	143.5	136.3	133.8	141.2	144.7	145.5	145.8	143.0
2004	141.3	144.7	145.8	145.7	146.4	144.0	135.2	133.8	139.4	143.0	143.9	143.4	142.2
2005	139.1	142.8	143.4	143.7	144.4	143.2	134.7	133.5	138.9	142.2	142.3	142.6	140.9
2006	138.8	141.8	143.1	143.1	144.0	142.3	133.9	133.1	138.8	142.0	143.2	143.1	140.6
2007	139.8	143.3	144.7	145.2	145.9	147.3	139.5	138.3	140.1	143.7	144.3	143.3	143.0
2008	141.3	144.2	143.4	144.0	146.5	147.2	139.5	137.9	140.2	143.6	143.6	142.3	142.8
2009	140.4	142.7	142.7	143.1	144.2	142.8	138.8	135.9	138.2	141.3	141.9	141.3	141.1

Employment by Industry: Columbia, SC, Selected Years, 1990–2009

(Numbers in thousands, not seasonally adjusted.)

Industry and year	January	February	March	April	May	June	July	August	September	October	November	December	Annual average
Total Nonfarm													
1990	279.1	280.8	282.9	284.5	285.6	285.0	281.0	283.4	287.2	287.6	288.5	289.7	284.6
2000	335.3	337.1	341.3	342.4	344.3	345.2	336.2	340.1	343.2	345.8	346.9	348.1	342.2
2001	337.2	338.8	341.0	340.1	341.6	341.7	333.8	338.0	338.9	338.6	340.3	340.7	339.2
2002	331.1	332.7	335.3	337.1	338.8	338.4	333.1	338.1	339.5	342.1	342.4	343.8	337.7
2003	334.9	336.1	337.0	337.2	339.1	337.7	331.3	337.4	338.9	341.9	342.5	344.5	338.2
2004	337.7	338.3	341.2	344.5	345.9	346.2	342.6	345.8	347.9	350.3	350.3	352.3	345.3
2005	347.8	350.5	350.7	351.9	351.8	348.9	349.1	353.9	353.6	355.9	358.6	359.2	352.7
2006	354.9	357.0	358.5	360.0	361.8	358.0	354.2	358.8	360.6	361.5	364.0	366.4	359.6
2007	359.4	361.8	363.7	365.6	368.4	368.9	364.4	366.3	368.2	368.9	369.4	370.1	366.3
2008	364.6	366.1	366.6	367.0	368.6	366.0	360.5	363.9	363.4	362.1	362.3	361.4	364.4
2009	349.8	349.2	349.3	348.1	348.1	345.8	343.3	344.0	345.5	348.2	348.1	346.6	347.2
Total Private													
1990	209.5	210.6	212.0	212.9	214.4	216.7	215.3	217.3	216.6	216.3	217.1	217.4	214.7
2000	259.9	260.5	263.8	265.3	266.8	269.4	264.6	264.4	265.6	267.6	268.6	269.6	265.5
2001	259.8	260.6	262.3	262.0	263.6	265.6	262.1	262.4	261.8	261.8	263.0	263.0	262.3
2002	254.4	255.6	257.9	260.3	261.8	263.7	262.6	263.3	262.8	265.2	265.0	266.2	261.6
2003	257.7	258.3	259.0	260.0	262.0	262.8	261.3	263.4	262.8	265.6	265.7	267.4	262.2
2004	260.7	261.6	264.0	267.4	268.7	270.9	270.0	271.0	271.2	273.8	273.6	275.3	269.0
2005	271.8	273.9	273.8	274.6	274.7	274.0	276.7	278.2	276.3	278.3	280.6	281.3	276.2
2006	277.6	279.0	280.0	282.3	284.2	282.6	281.4	283.6	283.8	284.6	286.5	288.8	282.9
2007	282.4	283.9	285.5	287.7	290.2	291.9	289.5	290.2	290.1	289.9	289.7	290.4	288.5
2008	284.7	285.8	286.2	286.1	287.6	286.9	284.8	285.5	282.5	280.9	280.5	279.7	284.3
2009	269.2	268.0	268.1	266.7	267.1	266.6	266.9	266.5	266.6	268.4	267.6	266.2	267.3
Goods-Producing													
1990	53.1	53.6	53.8	54.6	54.8	55.2	54.2	54.4	53.9	52.8	52.4	52.5	53.8
2000	56.4	56.4	56.9	57.2	57.4	58.0	57.8	57.6	57.6	57.5	57.2	57.4	57.3
2001	56.1	56.3	56.4	56.0	56.3	56.3	55.7	55.3	55.3	54.6	54.7	54.1	55.6
2002	53.3	53.3	53.3	53.7	54.5	54.5	54.4	54.7	54.2	54.0	53.5	53.4	53.9
2003	53.0	52.7	53.1	52.7	53.1	53.1	52.9	52.9	52.4	52.5	52.1	51.9	52.7
2004	50.9	50.9	51.2	51.8	51.8	52.2	52.2	52.3	52.4	52.3	52.2	52.4	51.9
2005	52.0	52.1	52.0	52.2	52.8	52.1	52.1	52.1	51.6	51.7	51.9	51.6	52.0
2006	51.6	51.9	52.1	53.2	53.6	53.8	53.3	53.4	53.1	52.8	52.9	52.5	52.9
2007	52.0	52.3	52.5	52.8	53.3	53.7	53.6	53.7	53.1	52.8	52.7	52.6	52.9
2008	51.5	51.1	50.9	50.3	50.3	50.7	50.4	50.3	49.7	48.9	48.7	48.2	50.1
2009	46.2	45.5	44.9	44.4	44.1	44.1	43.8	43.7	43.3	43.0	43.0	42.9	44.1
Mining, Logging, and Construction													
1990	16.4	16.7	16.9	17.5	17.8	18.1	18.2	18.1	17.7	17.1	16.9	16.8	17.4
2000	19.2	19.1	19.5	19.7	19.9	20.3	20.4	20.4	20.3	20.1	19.9	20.1	19.9
2001	19.6	19.6	19.9	19.9	20.3	20.5	20.1	20.1	20.2	19.7	19.7	19.2	19.9
2002	18.8	18.9	19.1	19.5	19.8	20.0	19.8	19.9	19.7	19.6	19.7	19.7	19.5
2003	20.0	20.0	20.2	19.7	20.1	20.3	20.5	20.6	20.6	20.8	20.5	20.5	20.3
2004	20.1	20.1	20.3	20.6	20.8	21.0	20.7	20.7	20.9	20.8	20.7	20.7	20.6
2005	20.2	20.2	20.0	20.6	21.1	20.5	20.7	20.7	20.4	20.6	20.8	20.6	20.5
2006	20.7	20.9	21.1	22.1	22.4	22.4	22.4	22.5	22.3	22.1	22.2	21.7	21.9
2007	21.0	21.2	21.4	21.6	21.9	22.1	22.1	22.0	21.7	21.4	21.3	21.2	21.6
2008	20.3	20.3	20.2	19.6	19.6	19.9	19.7	19.7	19.4	18.9	18.7	18.4	19.6
2009	17.6	17.2	17.1	17.1	17.0	16.9	16.9	16.8	16.6	16.5	16.4	16.3	16.9
Manufacturing													
1990	36.7	36.9	36.9	37.1	37.0	37.1	36.0	36.3	36.2	35.7	35.5	35.7	36.4
2000	37.2	37.3	37.4	37.5	37.5	37.7	37.4	37.2	37.3	37.4	37.3	37.3	37.4
2001	36.5	36.7	36.5	36.1	36.0	35.8	35.6	35.2	35.1	34.9	35.0	34.9	35.7
2002	34.5	34.4	34.2	34.2	34.7	34.5	34.6	34.8	34.5	34.4	33.8	33.7	34.4
2003	33.0	32.7	32.9	33.0	33.0	32.8	32.4	32.3	31.8	31.7	31.6	31.4	32.4
2004	30.8	30.8	30.9	31.2	31.0	31.2	31.5	31.6	31.5	31.5	31.5	31.7	31.3
2005	31.8	31.9	32.0	31.6	31.7	31.6	31.4	31.4	31.2	31.1	31.1	31.0	31.5
2006	30.9	31.0	31.0	31.1	31.2	31.4	30.9	30.9	30.8	30.7	30.7	30.8	31.0
2007	31.0	31.1	31.1	31.2	31.4	31.6	31.5	31.7	31.4	31.4	31.4	31.4	31.4
2008	31.2	30.8	30.7	30.7	30.7	30.8	30.7	30.6	30.3	30.0	30.0	29.8	30.5
2009	28.6	28.3	27.8	27.3	27.1	27.2	26.9	26.9	26.7	26.5	26.6	26.6	27.2
Service-Providing													
1990	226.0	227.2	229.1	229.9	230.8	229.8	226.8	229.0	233.3	234.8	236.1	237.2	230.8
2000	278.9	280.7	284.4	285.2	286.9	287.2	278.4	282.5	285.6	288.3	289.7	290.7	284.9
2001	281.1	282.5	284.6	284.1	285.3	285.4	278.1	282.7	283.6	284.0	285.6	286.6	283.6
2002	277.8	279.4	282.0	283.4	284.3	283.9	278.7	283.4	285.3	288.1	288.9	290.4	283.8
2003	281.9	283.4	283.9	284.5	286.0	284.6	278.4	284.5	286.5	289.4	290.4	292.6	285.5
2004	286.8	287.4	290.0	292.7	294.1	294.0	290.4	293.5	295.5	298.0	298.1	299.9	293.4
2005	295.8	298.4	298.7	299.7	299.0	296.8	297.0	301.8	302.0	304.2	306.7	307.6	300.6
2006	303.3	305.1	306.4	306.8	308.2	304.2	300.9	305.4	307.5	308.7	311.1	313.9	306.8
2007	307.4	309.5	311.2	312.8	315.1	315.2	310.8	312.6	315.1	316.1	316.7	317.5	313.3
2008	313.1	315.0	315.7	316.7	318.3	315.3	310.1	313.6	313.7	313.2	313.6	313.2	314.3
2009	303.6	303.7	304.4	303.7	304.0	301.7	299.5	300.3	302.2	305.2	305.1	303.7	303.1

Employment by Industry: Columbia, SC, Selected Years, 1990–2009—*Continued*

(Numbers in thousands, not seasonally adjusted.)

Industry and year	January	February	March	April	May	June	July	August	September	October	November	December	Annual average
Trade, Transportation, and Utilities													
1990	54.5	54.1	54.2	53.5	53.9	54.7	54.4	55.0	54.9	54.9	55.8	56.7	54.7
2000	65.7	65.5	66.2	66.5	66.8	67.2	65.6	66.1	66.1	67.3	68.5	69.2	66.7
2001	65.7	64.9	65.2	64.7	65.2	65.7	64.1	63.8	63.6	63.8	64.7	65.6	64.8
2002	61.6	61.8	62.3	63.1	63.5	64.1	63.5	63.3	63.4	63.7	65.1	66.1	63.5
2003	60.9	61.4	61.8	62.2	62.6	63.4	62.3	62.7	63.1	63.9	65.1	66.2	63.0
2004	63.3	62.9	63.3	63.3	64.0	63.9	64.6	64.8	64.4	65.0	66.0	67.3	64.4
2005	65.2	65.0	65.3	65.7	65.6	65.2	65.9	66.0	66.5	66.6	68.0	68.9	66.1
2006	66.6	66.6	67.2	66.9	67.3	66.9	66.6	67.0	67.4	68.0	69.6	71.0	67.6
2007	68.6	68.7	68.9	69.1	69.6	69.7	69.3	69.4	69.2	69.6	70.6	71.2	69.5
2008	69.4	69.4	69.4	69.5	69.2	69.1	68.7	68.3	67.7	66.5	67.0	67.8	68.5
2009	64.3	63.4	62.9	62.7	63.0	62.9	62.6	63.0	62.8	62.5	62.2	62.5	62.9
Wholesale Trade													
1990	11.9	12.1	12.2	11.8	11.9	12.1	12.1	12.1	12.2	12.1	12.1	12.1	12.1
2000	14.7	14.8	14.9	15.0	15.1	15.1	14.9	15.0	15.0	15.0	15.0	15.0	15.0
2001	15.1	15.0	15.1	15.0	15.1	15.2	14.9	14.8	14.8	14.7	14.5	14.7	14.9
2002	14.3	14.7	14.8	15.0	15.0	15.1	14.9	14.8	14.7	14.5	14.5	14.5	14.7
2003	13.5	13.5	13.5	13.8	13.9	14.1	13.8	13.9	14.0	14.0	14.1	14.2	13.9
2004	14.3	14.3	14.4	14.4	14.6	14.6	14.9	15.0	14.8	14.8	14.9	15.0	14.7
2005	15.8	15.7	15.8	15.7	15.8	15.7	16.0	16.0	15.9	16.0	16.0	16.1	15.9
2006	16.3	16.4	16.6	16.7	16.7	16.6	16.7	16.7	16.9	16.8	16.8	16.9	16.7
2007	17.2	17.7	17.5	17.1	16.9	16.9	16.7	16.6	16.5	16.5	16.4	16.4	16.9
2008	16.6	16.7	16.5	16.6	16.6	16.5	16.4	16.0	15.7	15.6	15.5	15.6	16.2
2009	14.9	14.8	14.6	14.5	14.6	14.5	14.5	14.4	14.5	14.5	14.5	14.4	14.6
Retail Trade													
1990	32.4	31.9	31.8	31.8	32.0	32.5	32.5	32.9	32.6	32.6	33.4	34.4	32.6
2000	39.3	39.0	39.5	39.6	39.8	40.0	38.9	39.2	39.3	40.3	41.5	42.2	39.9
2001	39.1	38.4	38.6	38.4	38.8	39.1	38.0	38.0	37.9	38.0	39.1	39.8	38.6
2002	37.2	36.9	37.2	37.7	38.1	38.4	37.8	37.8	38.0	38.3	39.7	40.7	38.2
2003	37.3	37.8	38.1	38.1	38.3	38.8	38.1	38.3	38.5	39.0	40.1	40.9	38.6
2004	38.3	37.8	38.1	38.2	38.5	38.2	38.4	38.4	38.2	38.9	39.6	40.6	38.6
2005	38.2	38.1	38.1	38.7	38.4	38.1	38.4	38.4	38.0	38.8	40.0	40.6	38.7
2006	38.7	38.5	38.8	38.5	38.8	38.5	38.2	38.4	38.5	39.5	40.8	41.7	39.1
2007	39.7	39.3	39.7	40.2	40.7	40.6	40.5	40.7	40.5	40.9	41.8	42.1	40.6
2008	41.2	41.0	41.2	41.2	40.9	40.9	40.5	40.7	40.6	39.8	40.3	40.7	40.8
2009	38.7	37.9	37.8	37.9	38.1	38.1	37.9	38.2	38.0	37.9	37.5	37.7	38.0
Transportation and Utilities													
1990	10.2	10.1	10.2	9.9	10.0	10.1	9.8	10.0	10.1	10.2	10.3	10.2	10.1
2000	11.7	11.7	11.8	11.9	11.9	12.1	11.8	11.9	11.8	12.0	12.0	12.0	11.9
2001	11.5	11.5	11.5	11.3	11.3	11.4	11.2	11.0	10.9	11.1	11.1	11.1	11.2
2002	10.1	10.2	10.3	10.4	10.4	10.6	10.8	10.7	10.7	10.9	10.9	10.9	10.6
2003	10.1	10.1	10.2	10.3	10.4	10.5	10.4	10.5	10.6	10.9	10.9	11.1	10.5
2004	10.7	10.8	10.8	10.7	10.9	11.1	11.3	11.4	11.4	11.3	11.5	11.7	11.1
2005	11.2	11.2	11.4	11.3	11.4	11.4	11.5	11.6	11.6	11.8	12.0	12.2	11.6
2006	11.6	11.7	11.8	11.7	11.8	11.8	11.7	11.9	12.0	11.7	12.0	12.4	11.8
2007	11.7	11.7	11.7	11.8	12.0	12.2	12.1	12.1	12.2	12.2	12.4	12.7	12.1
2008	11.6	11.7	11.7	11.7	11.7	11.7	11.8	11.6	11.4	11.1	11.2	11.5	11.6
2009	10.7	10.7	10.5	10.3	10.3	10.3	10.1	10.1	10.2	10.1	10.2	10.4	10.4
Information													
1990	7.8	7.9	7.9	8.0	8.0	8.0	8.2	8.3	8.2	8.5	8.6	8.5	8.2
2000	7.6	7.6	7.6	7.6	7.5	7.7	7.4	7.4	7.4	7.2	7.2	7.2	7.5
2001	6.9	6.7	6.7	6.6	6.6	6.7	6.3	6.3	6.2	6.3	6.3	6.4	6.5
2002	6.4	6.3	6.4	6.3	6.4	6.5	6.4	6.5	6.3	6.5	6.6	6.6	6.4
2003	6.2	6.1	6.2	6.1	6.3	6.2	6.4	6.3	6.3	6.2	6.2	6.3	6.2
2004	6.1	6.1	6.1	6.0	6.0	6.0	6.1	6.0	6.0	6.0	5.9	6.0	6.0
2005	6.0	6.1	6.0	6.1	6.1	6.2	6.2	6.1	6.0	6.1	6.1	6.1	6.1
2006	6.2	6.2	6.2	6.2	6.2	6.2	6.2	6.1	6.1	6.1	6.3	6.4	6.2
2007	6.1	6.1	6.1	6.1	6.2	6.2	6.1	6.0	6.0	6.2	6.1	6.2	6.1
2008	5.8	5.9	5.9	5.9	5.9	6.0	6.0	6.0	5.9	5.9	5.9	5.9	5.9
2009	5.9	5.8	5.9	5.9	5.8	5.9	5.9	5.9	5.9	5.9	6.0	6.1	5.9
Financial Activities													
1990	20.6	20.5	20.6	20.1	20.2	20.5	20.7	20.7	20.4	20.4	20.5	20.6	20.5
2000	23.6	23.8	23.9	23.6	23.9	24.2	24.4	24.5	24.4	25.0	25.2	25.3	24.3
2001	24.6	24.6	24.6	25.2	25.3	25.9	25.6	25.6	25.5	25.7	26.2	25.9	25.4
2002	25.4	25.6	25.7	25.2	25.3	25.5	25.8	25.8	26.0	26.6	26.7	26.7	25.9
2003	26.3	26.0	26.6	26.2	26.5	26.6	26.2	26.6	26.3	26.5	26.6	26.7	26.4
2004	26.3	26.5	26.6	26.7	26.8	27.1	26.9	27.0	27.3	27.8	27.8	28.1	27.1
2005	28.5	28.9	28.7	28.5	28.9	29.0	29.2	29.2	29.2	29.1	29.3	29.7	29.0
2006	29.4	29.5	29.5	29.3	29.6	29.6	29.7	29.7	29.8	29.9	30.0	30.5	29.7
2007	30.4	30.4	30.3	30.4	30.5	30.6	30.2	29.8	30.0	30.0	30.2	30.3	30.3
2008	30.0	30.1	30.2	30.1	30.1	30.2	29.8	29.8	29.7	29.8	29.9	30.0	30.0
2009	29.3	29.5	29.5	29.7	29.3	29.2	29.2	29.1	29.4	29.5	29.5	29.6	29.4

Employment by Industry: Columbia, SC, Selected Years, 1990–2009—*Continued*

(Numbers in thousands, not seasonally adjusted.)

Industry and year	January	February	March	April	May	June	July	August	September	October	November	December	Annual average
Professional and Business Services													
1990	24.8	25.4	25.8	26.6	27.0	27.5	27.1	27.7	27.8	27.8	28.2	27.8	27.0
2000	36.1	36.2	36.8	38.5	38.8	39.5	38.3	38.3	38.7	38.6	38.2	38.1	38.0
2001	36.3	37.0	37.4	37.8	37.9	37.9	37.7	38.1	37.8	36.6	36.3	36.2	37.3
2002	34.3	34.3	35.0	36.3	36.0	36.5	36.1	36.6	36.3	36.5	36.0	36.1	35.8
2003	35.0	35.2	33.6	35.6	35.6	35.7	35.6	36.1	35.8	36.8	36.8	36.9	35.7
2004	35.9	36.4	37.0	39.3	39.1	40.7	39.8	40.1	40.2	40.5	40.0	39.7	39.1
2005	39.2	39.9	39.2	39.7	39.0	40.2	40.6	41.8	42.0	42.2	42.9	43.0	40.8
2006	42.3	42.1	41.9	43.1	43.6	42.5	42.6	43.9	43.5	42.6	42.6	43.0	42.8
2007	42.1	42.4	42.6	42.8	43.0	43.4	43.0	43.7	44.0	43.8	43.1	43.0	43.1
2008	41.5	41.9	41.5	41.2	42.4	41.0	40.8	42.0	40.5	40.8	40.7	39.7	41.2
2009	37.8	37.3	37.5	37.2	37.1	36.9	37.2	36.4	37.1	39.7	40.3	39.2	37.8
Education and Health Services													
1990	19.3	19.5	19.6	19.8	19.8	19.6	19.4	19.6	19.9	20.7	20.7	20.8	19.9
2000	31.9	31.9	32.2	32.4	32.4	32.5	32.1	32.0	32.4	32.6	32.9	33.1	32.4
2001	32.5	32.9	33.1	32.5	32.6	33.0	33.1	33.2	33.8	34.5	34.7	34.9	33.4
2002	34.8	35.1	35.4	35.6	35.7	35.7	36.1	36.2	36.5	36.4	36.7	37.1	35.9
2003	37.1	37.2	37.5	37.2	37.2	37.2	37.2	37.5	37.9	38.1	38.2	38.5	37.6
2004	37.7	37.9	38.2	38.2	38.2	38.0	38.0	38.1	38.3	38.3	38.6	38.6	38.2
2005	39.0	39.3	39.6	38.8	38.8	37.9	38.7	38.7	38.6	39.3	39.4	39.3	39.0
2006	39.2	39.9	39.8	39.5	39.5	39.3	39.3	39.4	39.7	41.0	41.0	41.1	39.9
2007	40.4	40.8	41.0	41.7	42.1	42.5	42.1	41.9	42.4	42.2	42.2	42.1	41.8
2008	42.7	43.1	43.3	43.2	43.3	43.3	43.1	43.0	43.3	43.2	43.3	43.3	43.2
2009	42.1	42.4	42.5	42.2	42.3	42.0	41.8	41.9	42.2	42.2	42.4	42.4	42.2
Leisure and Hospitality													
1990	19.4	19.6	19.9	20.4	20.8	21.0	21.3	21.6	21.5	21.3	21.1	20.9	20.7
2000	26.7	27.1	27.9	27.4	27.6	27.7	27.0	26.8	27.0	27.4	27.4	27.6	27.3
2001	26.0	26.5	27.0	27.2	27.6	27.8	27.6	28.0	27.5	28.2	27.8	27.6	27.4
2002	26.5	27.1	27.5	27.5	27.8	28.1	28.0	27.9	27.8	28.8	27.8	27.6	27.7
2003	27.0	27.5	27.8	27.7	28.2	28.1	28.4	28.9	28.6	29.1	28.3	28.4	28.2
2004	28.2	28.5	29.1	29.4	29.9	29.9	29.3	29.5	29.4	30.5	29.7	29.7	29.4
2005	28.8	29.2	29.4	30.1	30.0	29.8	30.2	30.3	29.6	30.0	29.6	29.3	29.7
2006	28.8	29.2	29.8	30.4	30.5	30.4	30.2	30.4	30.3	30.7	30.5	30.7	30.2
2007	29.3	29.7	30.3	31.2	31.7	32.0	31.5	31.9	31.8	31.7	31.2	31.1	31.1
2008	30.0	30.5	31.0	31.9	32.3	32.6	31.9	32.0	31.8	31.8	31.1	31.0	31.5
2009	29.8	30.4	31.1	31.5	31.8	31.9	32.8	32.9	32.4	32.0	30.7	30.0	31.4
Other Services													
1990	10.0	10.0	10.2	9.9	9.9	10.2	10.0	10.0	10.0	9.9	9.8	9.6	10.0
2000	11.9	12.0	12.3	12.1	12.4	12.6	12.0	11.7	12.0	12.0	12.0	11.7	12.1
2001	11.7	11.7	11.9	12.0	12.1	12.3	12.0	12.1	12.1	12.1	12.3	12.3	12.1
2002	12.1	12.1	12.3	12.6	12.6	12.8	12.3	12.3	12.3	12.7	12.6	12.6	12.4
2003	12.2	12.2	12.4	12.3	12.5	12.5	12.3	12.4	12.4	12.5	12.4	12.5	12.4
2004	12.3	12.4	12.5	12.7	12.9	13.1	13.1	13.2	13.2	13.4	13.4	13.5	13.0
2005	13.1	13.4	13.6	13.5	13.5	13.6	13.8	14.0	13.8	13.3	13.4	13.4	13.5
2006	13.5	13.6	13.5	13.7	13.9	13.9	13.5	13.7	13.9	13.5	13.6	13.6	13.7
2007	13.5	13.5	13.8	13.6	13.8	13.8	13.7	13.8	13.6	13.6	13.6	13.9	13.7
2008	13.8	13.8	14.0	14.0	14.1	14.0	14.1	14.1	13.9	14.0	13.9	13.8	14.0
2009	13.8	13.7	13.8	13.6	13.7	13.7	13.6	13.6	13.5	13.6	13.5	13.5	13.6
Government													
1990	69.6	70.2	70.9	71.6	71.2	68.3	65.7	66.1	70.6	71.3	71.4	72.3	69.9
2000	75.4	76.6	77.5	77.1	77.5	75.8	71.6	75.7	77.6	78.2	78.3	78.5	76.7
2001	77.4	78.2	78.7	78.1	78.0	76.1	71.7	75.6	77.1	76.8	77.3	77.7	76.9
2002	76.7	77.1	77.4	76.8	77.0	74.7	70.5	74.8	76.7	76.9	77.4	77.6	76.1
2003	77.2	77.8	78.0	77.2	77.1	74.9	70.0	74.0	76.1	76.3	76.8	77.1	76.0
2004	77.0	76.7	77.2	77.1	77.2	75.3	72.6	74.8	76.7	76.5	76.7	77.0	76.2
2005	76.0	76.6	76.9	77.3	77.1	74.9	72.4	75.7	77.3	77.6	78.0	77.9	76.5
2006	77.3	78.0	78.5	77.7	77.6	75.4	72.8	75.2	76.8	76.9	77.5	77.6	76.8
2007	77.0	77.9	78.2	77.9	78.2	77.0	74.9	76.1	78.1	79.0	79.7	79.7	77.8
2008	79.9	80.3	80.4	80.9	81.0	79.1	75.7	78.4	80.9	81.2	81.8	81.7	80.1
2009	80.6	81.2	81.2	81.4	81.0	79.2	76.4	77.5	78.9	79.8	80.5	80.4	79.8

Employment by Industry: Columbus, OH, Selected Years, 1990–2009

(Numbers in thousands, not seasonally adjusted.)

Industry and year	January	February	March	April	May	June	July	August	September	October	November	December	Annual average
Total Nonfarm													
1990	711.3	713.6	718.9	725.7	732.4	741.5	730.8	733.2	734.9	740.9	743.1	744.8	730.9
2000	892.8	896.5	902.1	908.6	914.2	922.2	919.0	920.3	916.4	924.7	931.9	935.6	915.4
2001	912.4	914.3	918.3	921.1	924.3	927.6	919.2	917.7	912.6	919.7	924.6	926.6	919.9
2002	903.9	904.7	909.3	911.3	916.3	919.8	913.4	913.4	911.7	917.0	921.5	921.1	913.6
2003	901.3	898.8	902.2	907.5	912.0	914.3	910.8	911.8	908.0	916.8	921.8	922.6	910.6
2004	894.5	895.1	902.8	909.5	916.8	921.5	917.4	920.0	917.0	928.8	934.2	934.8	916.0
2005	902.7	903.7	909.3	917.7	923.4	926.9	923.2	925.2	925.8	933.9	939.8	940.5	922.7
2006	911.9	915.2	921.8	927.8	934.0	937.8	931.5	933.1	932.5	940.5	946.9	949.5	931.9
2007	926.1	922.5	929.5	938.4	947.0	951.9	943.9	943.8	943.1	950.6	957.2	956.2	942.5
2008	932.1	931.8	931.0	939.9	946.1	946.7	942.5	942.1	938.4	945.0	943.0	939.3	939.8
2009	911.2	906.2	905.7	908.7	913.0	912.5	906.6	906.3	900.1	907.4	911.2	903.7	907.7
Total Private													
1990	579.9	581.3	584.6	590.7	596.3	604.3	604.7	608.5	607.0	606.0	606.8	607.7	598.2
2000	749.7	752.3	757.4	763.7	769.0	775.4	776.0	778.1	772.4	777.9	784.1	786.7	770.2
2001	766.8	766.8	770.0	773.1	775.4	778.3	773.2	773.0	765.7	769.3	773.1	774.5	771.6
2002	753.4	753.6	758.1	760.6	765.2	767.7	766.1	767.0	763.7	766.2	768.9	768.1	763.2
2003	749.3	746.2	749.6	755.2	759.0	760.9	761.2	763.6	759.1	764.7	768.5	768.8	758.8
2004	741.9	741.8	749.0	756.3	762.6	766.3	766.2	768.9	765.6	773.4	777.6	778.4	762.3
2005	748.2	747.5	752.8	761.4	766.4	769.1	769.4	771.4	772.8	776.6	781.8	782.8	766.7
2006	755.8	757.7	763.9	770.5	775.6	780.3	777.9	779.2	779.2	782.9	788.5	791.0	775.2
2007	769.1	765.0	771.6	780.5	788.1	792.5	790.6	791.5	788.1	791.4	797.0	796.5	785.2
2008	773.5	771.9	771.6	780.9	785.5	786.6	787.5	787.8	783.0	784.7	782.8	780.0	781.3
2009	753.2	747.3	746.7	748.9	752.5	751.8	749.5	750.2	744.6	746.3	749.0	742.0	748.5
Goods-Producing													
1990	121.2	121.4	123.3	124.6	125.8	128.1	129.2	129.8	129.1	127.7	126.7	125.1	126.0
2000	138.7	138.7	141.1	142.2	143.9	146.2	146.2	146.1	144.8	144.2	143.3	141.9	143.1
2001	136.6	136.4	137.2	138.3	138.7	139.8	139.9	139.7	137.4	136.2	134.8	133.0	137.3
2002	128.2	127.8	128.5	129.2	130.9	132.6	131.9	133.1	132.5	131.2	129.7	127.9	130.3
2003	123.1	121.5	122.0	124.2	125.1	126.2	126.4	126.8	126.1	125.9	125.0	124.2	124.7
2004	118.6	118.0	119.2	121.8	123.5	123.8	123.7	123.8	123.1	122.1	121.5	120.7	121.7
2005	114.5	114.0	114.8	117.7	119.3	121.0	121.8	121.9	121.7	120.8	120.6	119.3	119.0
2006	114.2	114.3	115.3	117.4	118.3	119.9	119.6	119.9	119.6	118.5	117.2	116.6	117.6
2007	113.0	111.1	112.5	114.1	115.9	117.6	117.5	117.6	116.8	115.2	114.6	113.2	114.9
2008	109.4	108.5	108.1	109.5	111.0	112.2	112.1	111.7	111.1	109.6	107.8	105.4	109.7
2009	99.8	97.4	96.7	96.7	97.1	97.5	96.2	96.1	94.8	94.6	93.8	91.8	96.0
Mining, Logging, and Construction													
1990	26.4	26.3	27.4	28.2	29.6	31.0	32.1	32.5	31.9	31.0	30.4	28.9	29.6
2000	37.8	37.7	39.7	41.9	43.3	44.8	45.0	44.9	44.1	43.0	42.3	40.8	42.1
2001	37.0	38.2	39.5	41.6	42.7	44.4	45.2	45.5	44.4	43.2	42.6	41.3	42.2
2002	37.7	37.4	38.4	39.8	41.2	42.4	43.3	43.5	43.0	42.5	41.9	40.5	41.0
2003	37.1	36.1	36.8	39.6	40.8	42.0	42.7	43.0	42.6	42.5	41.9	41.1	40.5
2004	37.1	36.5	37.5	40.1	41.7	42.4	43.1	42.9	42.5	41.8	41.3	40.3	40.6
2005	35.7	35.3	36.2	39.1	40.7	41.8	42.9	43.0	42.6	41.8	41.5	40.1	40.1
2006	36.6	36.5	37.4	39.3	40.3	41.2	41.6	41.6	41.3	40.7	39.8	38.9	39.6
2007	35.9	34.4	35.8	37.2	38.9	40.3	40.5	40.4	39.8	39.2	38.3	36.7	38.1
2008	33.8	32.9	33.0	35.2	36.6	37.3	36.9	36.7	36.2	35.7	34.2	32.3	35.1
2009	28.9	28.2	28.7	29.1	30.2	31.2	31.5	31.4	30.4	30.7	30.6	28.8	30.0
Manufacturing													
1990	94.8	95.1	95.9	96.4	96.2	97.1	97.1	97.3	97.2	96.7	96.3	96.2	96.4
2000	100.9	101.0	101.4	100.3	100.6	101.4	101.2	101.2	100.7	101.2	101.0	101.1	101.0
2001	98.8	98.2	97.7	96.7	96.0	95.4	94.7	94.2	93.0	93.0	92.2	91.7	95.1
2002	90.5	90.4	90.1	89.4	89.7	90.2	88.6	89.6	89.5	88.7	87.8	87.4	89.3
2003	86.0	85.4	85.2	84.6	84.3	84.2	83.7	83.8	83.5	83.4	83.1	83.1	84.1
2004	81.5	81.5	81.7	81.7	81.8	81.4	80.6	80.9	80.6	80.3	80.2	80.4	81.1
2005	78.8	78.7	78.6	78.6	78.6	79.2	78.9	78.9	79.1	79.0	79.1	79.2	78.9
2006	77.6	77.8	77.9	78.1	78.0	78.7	78.0	78.3	78.3	77.8	77.4	77.7	78.0
2007	77.1	76.7	76.7	76.9	77.0	77.3	77.0	77.2	77.0	76.0	76.3	76.5	76.8
2008	75.6	75.6	75.1	74.3	74.4	74.9	75.2	75.0	74.9	73.9	73.6	73.1	74.6
2009	70.9	69.2	68.0	67.6	66.9	66.3	64.7	64.7	64.4	63.9	63.2	63.0	66.1
Service-Providing													
1990	590.1	592.2	595.6	601.1	606.6	613.4	601.6	603.4	605.8	613.2	616.4	619.7	604.9
2000	754.1	757.8	761.0	766.4	770.3	776.0	772.8	774.2	771.6	780.5	788.6	793.7	772.3
2001	775.8	777.9	781.1	782.8	785.6	787.8	779.3	778.0	775.2	783.5	789.8	793.6	782.5
2002	775.7	776.9	780.8	782.1	785.4	787.2	781.5	780.3	779.2	785.8	791.8	793.2	783.3
2003	778.2	777.3	780.2	783.3	786.9	788.1	784.4	785.0	781.9	790.9	796.8	798.4	785.9
2004	775.9	777.1	783.6	787.7	793.3	797.7	793.7	796.2	793.9	806.7	812.7	814.1	794.4
2005	788.2	789.7	794.5	800.0	804.1	805.9	801.4	803.3	804.1	813.1	819.2	821.2	803.7
2006	797.7	800.9	806.5	810.4	815.7	817.9	811.9	813.2	812.9	822.0	829.7	832.9	814.3
2007	813.1	811.4	817.0	824.3	831.1	834.3	826.4	826.2	826.3	835.4	842.6	843.0	827.6
2008	822.7	823.3	822.9	830.4	835.1	834.5	830.4	830.4	827.3	835.4	835.2	833.9	830.1
2009	811.4	808.8	809.0	812.0	815.9	815.0	810.4	810.2	805.3	812.8	817.4	811.9	811.7

Employment by Industry: Columbus, OH, Selected Years, 1990–2009—*Continued*

(Numbers in thousands, not seasonally adjusted.)

Industry and year	January	February	March	April	May	June	July	August	September	October	November	December	Annual average
Trade, Transportation, and Utilities													
1990	149.9	148.7	148.5	149.4	150.6	151.8	150.8	151.9	151.6	153.2	154.8	157.0	151.5
2000	193.3	191.7	191.5	193.4	193.8	194.5	194.8	195.1	193.9	199.1	206.3	210.9	196.5
2001	198.6	194.5	194.5	194.6	194.5	194.3	191.7	191.2	191.2	194.6	199.9	203.4	195.3
2002	191.0	189.0	189.9	189.5	190.0	189.5	189.2	188.9	188.0	189.2	192.1	194.4	190.1
2003	185.1	182.8	183.4	184.2	184.6	184.6	184.3	185.2	184.5	187.1	191.1	193.6	185.8
2004	182.4	179.9	181.4	180.4	181.7	183.6	184.2	184.6	184.2	188.6	193.9	197.3	185.2
2005	185.8	183.2	184.1	184.2	184.8	184.3	184.1	184.2	184.7	187.8	193.3	197.2	186.5
2006	185.8	183.8	184.1	184.4	186.1	186.0	185.9	185.7	185.8	189.1	196.1	199.3	187.7
2007	189.2	185.9	187.1	187.7	189.7	189.9	190.5	190.6	190.8	193.6	199.7	201.7	191.4
2008	190.8	187.6	187.4	188.7	189.7	189.1	190.0	190.6	189.7	191.5	194.2	196.0	190.4
2009	183.5	179.7	178.4	178.8	179.5	178.7	178.3	178.8	177.7	180.6	184.2	184.5	180.2
Wholesale Trade													
1990	31.2	32.0	32.0	32.1	32.3	32.4	31.9	31.9	32.0	31.9	31.2	31.5	31.9
2000	38.1	38.5	38.6	39.1	39.2	39.7	39.7	39.9	40.0	39.7	39.8	39.8	39.3
2001	39.4	39.5	39.8	40.0	40.0	40.0	39.8	39.7	39.3	39.5	39.2	39.7	39.7
2002	39.1	39.1	39.3	38.8	38.8	38.7	38.8	38.8	38.6	38.6	38.6	38.7	38.8
2003	38.1	38.1	38.3	38.2	38.1	37.8	37.8	37.8	37.8	37.4	37.3	37.3	37.7
2004	36.8	36.6	36.4	36.5	36.8	36.9	37.3	37.5	37.2	37.4	37.5	37.4	37.0
2005	37.0	37.0	37.0	37.3	37.3	37.2	37.7	37.5	37.5	37.4	37.7	37.7	37.4
2006	37.4	37.6	37.5	37.6	37.8	37.8	37.8	37.7	37.6	37.7	38.1	38.1	37.7
2007	37.8	37.8	38.0	38.2	38.7	38.8	38.8	38.8	38.7	38.8	38.8	38.8	38.5
2008	38.9	38.9	38.9	39.2	39.4	39.4	39.5	39.6	39.3	39.0	38.8	38.6	39.1
2009	38.4	38.2	38.2	37.8	37.7	37.7	37.7	37.6	37.1	36.9	36.6	36.6	37.5
Retail Trade													
1990	97.4	95.4	95.7	96.1	97.0	97.8	97.2	97.9	97.7	99.2	101.4	103.6	98.0
2000	120.8	118.9	119.0	119.5	120.0	120.4	120.2	120.4	119.2	123.3	130.4	135.2	122.3
2001	123.5	119.6	119.8	119.1	119.2	119.3	116.4	116.0	116.6	119.0	124.6	127.9	120.1
2002	116.5	114.8	115.6	115.8	116.3	115.7	114.4	113.7	113.2	113.8	116.5	118.8	115.4
2003	110.7	108.4	108.9	109.4	109.7	109.9	109.4	109.9	109.5	111.2	115.0	117.4	110.7
2004	108.0	106.1	107.3	105.9	106.7	108.0	107.6	107.8	107.6	109.6	114.3	117.6	108.9
2005	108.4	106.1	106.8	106.6	107.0	106.5	105.4	105.4	105.4	106.7	110.5	114.3	107.4
2006	104.7	102.7	103.0	102.8	103.9	103.5	103.1	102.6	101.8	103.4	108.3	110.7	104.2
2007	102.2	99.9	100.9	101.2	102.1	101.8	102.4	102.2	101.8	103.0	107.2	108.9	102.8
2008	101.4	99.2	98.9	100.2	101.4	101.3	102.5	102.9	101.8	103.3	105.5	107.7	102.2
2009	98.9	96.6	95.9	96.7	97.6	97.2	96.9	97.2	96.7	98.8	102.3	104.6	98.3
Transportation and Utilities													
1990	21.3	21.3	20.8	21.2	21.3	21.6	21.7	22.1	21.9	22.1	22.2	21.9	21.6
2000	34.4	34.3	33.9	34.8	34.6	34.4	34.9	34.8	34.7	36.1	36.1	35.9	34.9
2001	35.7	35.4	34.9	35.5	35.3	35.0	35.5	35.5	35.3	36.1	36.1	35.8	35.5
2002	35.4	35.1	35.0	34.9	34.9	35.1	36.0	36.4	36.2	36.8	37.0	36.9	35.8
2003	36.3	36.3	36.2	36.6	36.8	36.9	37.1	37.5	37.8	38.5	38.8	38.9	37.3
2004	37.6	37.2	37.7	38.0	38.2	38.7	39.3	39.3	39.4	41.6	42.1	42.3	39.3
2005	40.4	40.1	40.3	40.3	40.5	40.6	41.0	41.3	41.8	43.7	45.1	45.2	41.7
2006	43.7	43.5	43.6	44.0	44.4	44.7	45.0	45.4	46.4	48.0	49.7	50.5	45.7
2007	49.2	48.2	48.2	48.3	48.9	49.3	49.3	49.6	50.3	51.8	53.7	54.0	50.1
2008	50.5	49.5	49.6	49.3	48.9	48.4	48.0	48.1	48.6	49.2	49.9	49.7	49.1
2009	46.2	44.9	44.3	44.3	44.2	43.8	43.7	44.0	43.9	44.9	45.3	43.3	44.4
Information													
1990	18.3	18.4	18.4	18.5	18.5	18.6	18.8	18.9	18.9	18.8	19.0	19.0	18.7
2000	22.0	22.2	22.3	22.0	22.2	22.4	22.5	22.7	22.6	23.1	23.1	23.1	22.5
2001	23.4	23.3	23.0	22.7	22.8	22.9	22.5	22.5	22.0	21.7	21.7	21.5	22.5
2002	21.8	21.5	21.5	21.1	21.1	21.2	21.3	21.4	21.3	21.1	21.2	21.2	21.3
2003	21.1	21.1	20.8	20.7	20.6	20.6	20.4	20.4	20.1	20.2	20.2	20.1	20.5
2004	19.8	19.8	19.6	19.5	19.6	19.8	19.9	19.7	19.7	19.6	19.6	19.5	19.7
2005	19.4	19.2	19.3	19.3	19.4	19.4	19.4	19.5	19.6	19.2	19.2	19.2	19.3
2006	19.1	19.0	19.0	18.8	18.9	18.9	18.8	18.7	18.5	18.4	18.5	18.5	18.8
2007	18.7	18.8	18.7	18.8	18.8	18.8	18.8	18.6	18.3	18.0	18.0	18.0	18.5
2008	17.6	17.7	17.7	17.8	17.7	17.7	17.7	17.7	17.5	17.5	17.6	17.6	17.7
2009	17.6	17.5	17.3	17.1	17.1	17.1	17.1	17.0	16.7	16.5	16.5	16.6	17.0
Financial Activities													
1990	59.8	59.9	60.0	60.5	60.8	61.5	61.7	61.7	61.6	61.1	61.0	61.1	60.9
2000	75.8	75.9	75.6	75.3	75.5	75.9	75.8	75.6	75.5	75.6	76.1	76.7	75.8
2001	76.0	76.4	77.0	77.1	77.2	77.9	77.4	77.3	77.1	76.4	76.8	77.2	77.0
2002	76.7	77.1	77.3	77.3	77.1	76.9	77.0	77.0	76.8	77.4	77.9	78.1	77.2
2003	76.1	76.6	76.6	75.9	75.9	76.1	75.8	75.9	75.4	74.9	75.0	75.1	75.7
2004	74.3	74.4	74.4	74.3	74.1	74.3	74.1	73.9	73.2	73.3	73.2	73.1	73.9
2005	72.3	72.3	72.3	72.3	72.5	72.8	73.1	73.2	73.3	73.3	73.5	73.8	72.9
2006	73.1	73.0	73.1	73.2	73.3	73.8	74.3	73.9	74.0	74.6	74.7	74.5	73.8
2007	74.1	74.0	73.4	74.2	73.7	73.0	72.9	72.9	72.2	72.2	71.8	71.8	73.0
2008	71.2	71.4	71.2	71.0	71.1	71.0	70.6	70.7	70.3	70.5	70.2	70.3	70.8
2009	69.6	69.5	69.5	69.1	69.1	68.9	69.5	69.3	68.8	68.5	69.1	68.6	69.1

Employment by Industry: Columbus, OH, Selected Years, 1990–2009—*Continued*

(Numbers in thousands, not seasonally adjusted.)

Industry and year	January	February	March	April	May	June	July	August	September	October	November	December	Annual average
Professional and Business Services													
1990	80.9	81.7	82.4	83.4	84.4	85.4	86.3	87.6	87.2	87.5	87.2	87.2	85.1
2000	125.2	126.4	127.7	128.4	128.8	130.1	130.8	131.2	131.1	131.6	131.4	131.1	129.5
2001	133.0	133.4	133.8	133.8	132.6	132.3	132.3	132.0	130.5	131.3	130.5	130.5	132.2
2002	129.1	129.2	129.5	129.4	128.4	128.8	128.8	129.0	128.5	129.5	130.1	129.6	129.2
2003	131.4	130.6	131.3	130.9	130.4	129.7	130.5	131.1	130.3	132.2	133.1	132.0	131.1
2004	129.1	129.9	131.4	133.5	133.6	134.5	134.2	136.3	136.2	139.1	138.9	139.1	134.7
2005	134.3	135.0	136.0	136.9	137.0	137.4	137.8	139.6	140.4	142.0	141.7	141.9	138.3
2006	137.5	138.4	140.0	142.2	142.2	144.1	143.7	145.2	145.1	146.1	146.6	147.7	143.2
2007	143.9	144.1	145.9	148.5	149.1	151.0	151.0	151.5	151.2	152.9	153.7	154.2	149.8
2008	151.3	151.6	151.8	154.3	153.6	153.9	155.3	155.0	153.6	153.9	152.9	152.1	153.3
2009	149.0	147.3	146.5	146.9	146.6	146.0	146.1	147.0	145.4	146.2	147.8	145.0	146.7
Education and Health Services													
1990	68.0	68.8	69.0	69.4	69.1	69.6	69.5	69.8	70.7	71.8	72.6	73.2	70.1
2000	86.6	87.7	87.7	88.1	88.0	87.6	87.3	88.4	88.4	89.2	89.4	89.9	88.2
2001	87.9	89.8	90.4	90.4	90.7	90.7	89.5	89.8	90.0	92.6	93.5	93.7	90.8
2002	92.4	93.7	94.1	94.3	94.5	93.7	93.2	93.2	94.4	96.7	97.2	97.3	94.6
2003	95.6	96.7	97.0	97.9	98.0	96.9	96.5	96.7	98.1	100.2	101.0	100.9	97.9
2004	98.4	100.0	100.7	102.1	102.2	100.8	100.6	100.4	101.9	104.0	104.4	104.5	101.7
2005	102.0	103.4	103.9	105.4	104.8	103.5	103.5	103.5	105.5	107.2	107.9	107.7	104.9
2006	105.7	107.6	108.4	108.8	108.1	106.4	105.4	105.6	108.4	109.6	110.1	109.8	107.8
2007	108.5	109.4	110.2	111.2	111.4	110.5	109.8	110.1	111.7	113.0	113.9	113.5	111.1
2008	112.6	114.3	114.1	114.5	114.3	113.2	112.9	113.2	115.0	116.4	117.2	117.2	114.6
2009	116.4	117.8	118.0	118.3	118.2	117.2	117.0	117.3	119.1	119.9	120.1	119.9	118.3
Leisure and Hospitality													
1990	57.5	58.0	58.6	60.0	62.0	63.9	63.2	63.4	62.4	60.4	59.9	59.5	60.7
2000	74.8	76.0	77.6	80.0	82.3	84.0	83.9	84.2	81.7	80.8	80.2	78.9	80.4
2001	77.3	78.5	79.4	80.9	83.3	84.6	84.2	84.6	82.1	81.0	80.0	79.4	81.3
2002	78.8	79.4	81.2	83.2	86.1	87.6	87.4	87.0	85.1	84.1	83.5	82.3	83.8
2003	79.7	79.5	80.9	83.7	86.5	88.5	89.1	89.3	86.9	86.5	85.4	85.0	85.0
2004	81.6	81.8	83.7	86.1	89.3	90.6	90.5	91.3	88.9	88.0	87.0	86.5	87.1
2005	82.8	83.0	84.7	88.0	90.8	92.8	92.2	91.8	90.4	88.7	87.5	86.5	88.3
2006	83.4	84.4	86.5	88.1	91.0	92.9	92.3	92.3	90.3	89.0	87.8	87.3	88.8
2007	84.7	84.6	86.5	89.0	92.1	94.1	92.7	93.0	90.6	89.8	88.7	87.7	89.5
2008	84.7	84.8	85.2	88.7	91.5	92.6	91.8	91.7	89.0	87.8	86.1	85.4	88.3
2009	81.8	82.2	84.3	86.0	88.5	90.0	89.2	88.8	86.8	84.5	82.0	80.6	85.4
Other Services													
1990	24.3	24.4	24.4	24.9	25.1	25.4	25.2	25.4	25.5	25.5	25.6	25.6	25.1
2000	33.3	33.7	33.9	34.3	34.5	34.7	34.7	34.8	34.4	34.3	34.3	34.2	34.3
2001	34.0	34.5	34.7	35.3	35.6	35.8	35.7	35.9	35.4	35.5	35.9	35.8	35.3
2002	35.4	35.9	36.1	36.6	37.1	37.4	37.3	37.4	37.1	37.0	37.2	37.3	36.8
2003	37.2	37.4	37.6	37.7	37.9	38.3	38.2	38.2	37.7	37.7	37.7	37.9	37.7
2004	37.7	38.0	38.6	38.6	38.6	38.9	39.0	38.9	38.4	38.7	39.1	37.7	38.5
2005	37.1	37.4	37.7	37.6	37.8	37.9	37.5	37.7	37.2	37.6	38.1	37.2	37.6
2006	37.0	37.2	37.5	37.6	37.7	38.3	37.9	37.9	37.5	37.6	37.5	37.3	37.6
2007	37.0	37.1	37.3	37.0	37.4	37.6	37.4	37.2	36.5	36.7	36.6	36.4	37.0
2008	35.9	36.0	36.1	36.4	36.6	36.9	37.1	37.2	36.8	37.5	36.8	36.0	36.6
2009	35.5	35.9	36.0	36.0	36.4	36.4	36.1	35.9	35.3	35.5	35.5	35.0	35.8
Government													
1990	131.4	132.3	134.3	135.0	136.1	137.2	126.1	124.7	127.9	134.9	136.3	137.1	132.8
2000	143.1	144.2	144.7	144.9	145.2	146.8	143.0	142.2	144.0	146.8	147.8	148.9	145.1
2001	145.6	147.5	148.3	148.0	148.9	149.3	146.0	144.7	146.9	150.4	151.5	152.1	148.3
2002	150.5	151.1	151.2	150.7	151.1	152.1	147.3	146.4	148.0	150.8	152.6	153.0	150.4
2003	152.0	152.6	152.6	152.3	153.0	153.4	149.6	148.2	148.9	152.1	153.3	153.8	151.8
2004	152.6	153.3	153.8	153.2	154.2	155.2	151.2	151.1	151.4	155.4	156.6	156.4	153.7
2005	154.5	156.2	156.5	156.3	157.0	157.8	153.8	153.8	153.0	157.3	158.0	157.7	156.0
2006	156.1	157.5	157.9	157.3	158.4	157.5	153.6	153.9	153.3	157.6	158.4	158.5	156.7
2007	157.0	157.5	157.9	157.9	158.9	159.4	153.3	152.3	155.0	159.2	160.2	159.7	157.4
2008	158.6	159.9	159.4	159.0	160.6	160.1	155.0	154.3	155.4	160.3	160.2	159.3	158.5
2009	158.0	158.9	159.0	159.8	160.5	160.7	157.1	156.1	155.5	161.1	162.2	161.7	159.2

Employment by Industry: Dallas-Fort Worth-Arlington, TX, Selected Years, 1990–2009

(Numbers in thousands, not seasonally adjusted.)

Industry and year	January	February	March	April	May	June	July	August	September	October	November	December	Annual average
Total Nonfarm													
1990	1949.6	1962.3	1972.0	1981.8	1995.0	2012.7	2006.5	2017.4	2022.4	2024.6	2032.2	2038.9	2001.3
2000	2683.7	2701.1	2725.7	2740.0	2761.6	2784.9	2765.8	2779.8	2792.8	2796.4	2806.2	2820.7	2763.2
2001	2764.0	2777.0	2792.7	2795.1	2797.4	2805.5	2770.3	2780.5	2773.2	2752.8	2747.1	2744.1	2775.0
2002	2689.7	2696.4	2710.9	2711.2	2720.6	2720.7	2691.9	2703.0	2706.2	2698.4	2705.4	2706.3	2705.1
2003	2646.6	2654.2	2660.1	2665.3	2670.4	2668.6	2646.7	2658.3	2668.6	2676.1	2684.1	2687.9	2665.6
2004	2640.7	2654.5	2672.7	2690.5	2697.5	2696.8	2690.7	2704.9	2714.2	2729.8	2737.8	2747.7	2698.2
2005	2689.1	2707.0	2725.5	2751.0	2760.1	2765.7	2763.9	2779.3	2796.9	2804.7	2824.2	2830.1	2766.5
2006	2782.6	2802.3	2823.5	2839.9	2854.9	2868.2	2845.5	2869.5	2883.9	2888.8	2912.3	2925.3	2858.1
2007	2861.8	2889.5	2917.2	2923.7	2939.3	2952.6	2927.6	2947.6	2958.1	2973.1	2992.3	3001.3	2940.3
2008	2941.5	2963.2	2973.6	2979.3	2996.0	2994.4	2971.1	2977.6	2973.7	2975.0	2969.7	2967.3	2973.5
2009	2888.1	2882.3	2880.5	2872.8	2874.6	2865.5	2838.2	2840.2	2839.5	2855.1	2862.4	2872.3	2864.3
Total Private													
1990	1711.5	1721.5	1730.1	1737.9	1748.7	1772.4	1776.0	1788.1	1780.8	1780.0	1784.1	1790.7	1760.2
2000	2371.3	2385.4	2409.1	2422.4	2438.3	2469.2	2465.7	2475.9	2476.5	2475.9	2483.1	2494.5	2447.3
2001	2443.4	2451.1	2466.4	2470.1	2472.2	2484.2	2465.5	2470.4	2449.2	2421.7	2413.1	2410.9	2451.5
2002	2362.1	2360.4	2374.0	2376.4	2384.2	2389.8	2379.4	2383.8	2371.2	2355.5	2358.7	2360.6	2371.3
2003	2309.7	2308.0	2314.7	2319.3	2323.0	2326.4	2324.3	2334.9	2326.5	2330.1	2335.3	2342.2	2324.5
2004	2299.6	2306.4	2326.3	2342.1	2347.1	2353.5	2362.4	2368.8	2360.6	2375.2	2380.0	2390.6	2351.1
2005	2337.2	2347.8	2367.2	2391.7	2399.7	2414.1	2428.2	2435.1	2436.5	2440.7	2456.9	2468.9	2410.3
2006	2423.6	2436.2	2458.7	2474.2	2488.3	2509.7	2500.3	2517.5	2519.0	2517.8	2539.0	2554.6	2494.9
2007	2495.1	2516.0	2542.9	2551.2	2564.8	2585.7	2577.8	2593.6	2587.5	2594.2	2610.2	2620.5	2570.0
2008	2565.3	2579.5	2588.7	2594.7	2609.5	2615.3	2606.0	2610.3	2592.5	2584.9	2576.1	2573.5	2591.4
2009	2501.5	2488.8	2486.1	2478.0	2480.2	2480.6	2469.1	2471.2	2455.5	2459.3	2463.9	2475.7	2475.8
Goods-Producing													
1990	429.8	431.3	431.9	432.1	432.3	437.5	438.2	440.6	439.1	438.1	435.2	431.8	434.8
2000	507.1	511.2	516.5	516.2	519.6	526.1	524.5	524.0	523.1	520.3	518.0	516.4	518.6
2001	512.3	513.7	515.6	513.0	513.4	516.2	509.2	509.2	502.7	493.0	487.5	482.6	505.7
2002	473.5	472.4	474.0	472.7	474.0	477.3	475.0	474.0	469.4	461.9	459.7	456.2	470.0
2003	448.0	448.2	448.0	448.6	450.3	452.5	451.3	451.9	449.9	447.4	446.0	445.2	448.9
2004	441.2	442.6	446.0	448.7	449.9	452.2	455.1	454.6	453.3	451.4	449.4	449.4	449.5
2005	443.0	446.8	450.4	453.8	456.4	461.9	465.6	466.0	465.4	464.4	464.3	465.1	458.6
2006	459.2	463.4	468.0	469.5	474.2	480.7	477.7	480.5	482.1	478.8	480.5	480.9	474.6
2007	473.3	478.1	483.1	481.7	483.9	490.2	486.6	488.8	489.2	485.8	486.0	486.6	484.4
2008	479.4	483.7	484.9	482.7	484.7	487.0	484.6	485.1	482.2	477.8	472.1	468.1	481.0
2009	453.8	449.1	443.8	437.5	433.9	430.5	424.3	425.1	420.2	413.2	413.9	413.7	429.9
Mining, Logging, and Construction													
1990	89.4	89.7	89.5	90.6	92.0	94.7	94.0	95.0	95.2	93.9	93.4	92.7	92.5
2000	154.6	158.0	162.6	162.7	165.4	170.3	171.4	171.7	171.1	168.8	167.4	167.2	165.9
2001	164.8	166.4	169.0	169.7	171.9	174.7	172.6	173.5	170.1	166.1	163.8	162.0	168.7
2002	157.7	158.2	160.2	160.4	161.9	164.5	163.5	163.9	160.7	156.9	156.3	154.3	159.9
2003	150.0	150.2	151.0	152.2	154.2	156.2	157.4	157.8	156.4	154.8	153.9	153.2	153.9
2004	150.8	151.0	153.7	155.6	156.6	158.2	160.6	160.9	160.3	158.9	157.7	157.6	156.8
2005	155.8	157.4	160.1	163.1	165.0	168.4	169.6	169.9	170.5	169.6	168.8	169.0	165.6
2006	165.6	167.8	171.2	171.6	174.9	179.0	177.2	178.9	180.4	179.4	180.4	181.4	175.7
2007	176.9	179.9	184.3	184.7	186.4	191.1	188.9	191.9	192.9	192.0	192.9	192.9	187.9
2008	189.0	192.9	195.2	194.6	196.2	198.7	197.0	197.5	195.9	193.2	189.7	187.2	193.9
2009	179.0	177.6	175.5	172.3	171.0	171.1	168.9	167.0	163.0	157.1	157.3	155.7	168.0
Manufacturing													
1990	340.4	341.6	342.4	341.5	340.3	342.8	344.2	345.6	343.9	344.2	341.8	339.1	342.3
2000	352.5	353.2	353.9	353.5	354.2	355.8	353.1	352.3	352.0	351.5	350.6	349.2	352.7
2001	347.5	347.3	346.6	343.3	341.5	341.5	336.6	335.7	332.6	326.9	323.7	320.6	337.0
2002	315.8	314.2	313.8	312.3	312.1	312.8	311.5	310.1	308.7	305.0	303.4	301.9	310.1
2003	298.0	298.0	297.0	296.4	296.1	296.3	293.9	294.1	293.5	292.6	292.1	292.0	295.0
2004	290.4	291.6	292.3	293.1	293.3	294.0	294.5	293.7	293.0	292.5	291.7	291.8	292.7
2005	287.2	289.4	290.3	290.7	291.4	293.5	296.0	296.1	294.9	294.8	295.5	296.1	293.0
2006	293.6	295.6	296.8	297.9	299.3	301.7	300.5	301.6	301.7	299.4	300.1	299.5	299.0
2007	296.4	298.2	298.8	297.0	297.5	299.1	297.7	296.9	296.3	293.8	293.1	293.7	296.5
2008	290.4	290.8	289.7	288.1	288.5	288.3	287.6	287.6	286.3	284.6	282.4	280.9	287.1
2009	274.8	271.5	268.3	265.2	262.9	259.4	255.4	258.1	257.2	256.1	256.6	258.0	262.0
Service-Providing													
1990	1519.8	1531.0	1540.1	1549.7	1562.7	1575.2	1568.3	1576.8	1583.3	1586.5	1597.0	1607.1	1566.5
2000	2176.6	2189.9	2209.2	2223.8	2242.0	2258.8	2241.3	2255.8	2269.7	2276.1	2288.2	2304.3	2244.6
2001	2251.7	2263.3	2277.1	2282.1	2284.0	2289.3	2261.1	2271.3	2270.5	2259.8	2259.6	2261.5	2269.3
2002	2216.2	2224.0	2236.9	2238.5	2246.6	2243.4	2216.9	2229.0	2236.8	2236.5	2245.7	2250.1	2235.1
2003	2198.6	2206.0	2212.1	2216.7	2220.1	2216.1	2195.4	2206.4	2218.7	2228.7	2238.1	2242.7	2216.6
2004	2199.5	2211.9	2226.7	2241.8	2247.6	2244.6	2235.6	2250.3	2260.9	2278.4	2288.4	2298.3	2248.7
2005	2246.1	2260.2	2275.1	2297.2	2303.7	2303.8	2298.3	2313.3	2331.5	2340.3	2359.9	2365.0	2307.9
2006	2323.4	2338.9	2355.5	2370.4	2380.7	2387.5	2367.8	2389.0	2401.8	2410.0	2431.8	2444.4	2383.4
2007	2388.5	2411.4	2434.1	2442.0	2455.4	2462.4	2441.0	2458.8	2468.9	2487.3	2506.3	2514.7	2455.9
2008	2462.1	2479.5	2488.7	2496.6	2511.3	2507.4	2486.5	2492.5	2491.5	2497.2	2497.6	2499.2	2492.5
2009	2434.3	2433.2	2436.7	2435.3	2440.7	2435.0	2413.9	2415.1	2419.3	2441.9	2448.5	2458.6	2434.4

Employment by Industry: Dallas-Fort Worth-Arlington, TX, Selected Years, 1990–2009—*Continued*

(Numbers in thousands, not seasonally adjusted.)

Industry and year	January	February	March	April	May	June	July	August	September	October	November	December	Annual average
Trade, Transportation, and Utilities													
1990	467.0	465.1	467.5	466.3	468.9	474.4	475.5	478.3	478.3	478.8	485.8	492.1	474.8
2000	612.4	611.5	614.4	615.4	619.6	627.3	626.1	631.9	631.4	637.0	649.5	660.2	628.1
2001	637.9	634.0	636.7	634.2	634.0	636.8	634.5	637.2	634.8	631.2	633.2	637.7	635.2
2002	618.2	613.7	615.4	613.6	614.1	614.9	615.3	615.7	612.3	610.4	616.8	624.0	615.4
2003	598.5	592.7	592.3	588.8	587.0	585.8	583.2	588.1	586.0	588.8	596.1	601.2	590.7
2004	582.5	580.1	583.3	583.8	586.5	587.2	590.0	594.8	591.6	595.2	604.7	611.5	590.9
2005	591.7	586.6	590.7	591.6	593.8	596.9	600.1	604.3	604.1	605.0	618.8	626.6	600.9
2006	604.4	601.1	605.2	606.5	608.9	611.0	609.6	614.0	611.7	613.8	626.6	635.3	612.3
2007	614.5	612.1	617.3	616.4	618.4	621.8	622.0	624.0	622.7	628.0	640.2	647.2	623.7
2008	627.3	624.6	626.4	623.9	625.6	626.9	626.2	629.2	624.1	623.9	628.1	632.6	626.6
2009	609.2	601.3	599.9	594.5	594.4	592.9	592.2	593.1	590.6	592.2	599.1	605.0	597.0
Wholesale Trade													
1990	126.5	127.1	127.3	128.2	128.6	129.6	130.1	130.9	130.5	130.4	130.7	130.9	129.2
2000	166.8	167.1	169.1	170.9	171.4	172.9	171.5	171.8	171.8	172.2	172.7	173.2	171.0
2001	173.3	174.2	175.0	173.9	173.2	173.9	172.8	172.6	171.2	170.2	168.9	168.6	172.3
2002	166.3	166.1	167.1	166.0	166.0	166.5	166.6	166.5	166.2	165.2	165.3	165.7	166.1
2003	162.6	162.1	162.6	161.9	161.3	161.5	160.9	160.6	159.9	159.6	159.1	159.3	161.0
2004	157.7	157.7	158.5	158.1	158.3	158.4	159.1	159.0	158.4	159.2	159.0	159.3	158.6
2005	157.2	157.5	158.2	159.3	159.7	160.2	161.6	162.0	162.4	161.8	162.4	163.5	160.5
2006	162.3	162.8	163.7	164.3	165.0	166.0	166.1	166.9	167.3	167.6	168.5	169.2	165.8
2007	166.9	168.0	168.9	168.8	169.5	171.0	170.8	171.1	171.0	173.1	174.0	174.3	170.6
2008	172.5	173.0	172.8	172.6	172.7	172.7	171.9	171.9	170.9	170.3	169.6	169.0	171.7
2009	165.8	164.9	163.2	161.3	160.8	159.9	159.4	158.8	158.1	157.4	156.8	156.4	160.2
Retail Trade													
1990	247.9	244.5	246.2	245.4	246.5	249.7	249.3	249.8	248.9	250.4	257.1	262.7	249.9
2000	309.9	308.3	308.9	307.5	310.2	315.0	315.1	319.2	318.0	322.1	332.9	341.5	317.4
2001	323.6	319.3	321.1	319.9	319.7	321.1	319.8	321.5	321.2	320.6	327.0	332.2	322.3
2002	316.7	313.1	313.2	312.2	312.0	311.9	312.0	312.0	309.5	307.9	315.1	322.4	313.2
2003	302.2	297.6	296.9	294.3	293.7	293.3	292.2	296.3	295.1	297.1	304.7	309.5	297.7
2004	293.4	290.9	292.9	293.6	295.9	296.3	297.3	301.6	298.9	301.5	311.7	317.4	299.3
2005	300.8	297.1	299.0	300.1	301.3	303.8	304.8	307.4	306.0	307.5	319.7	325.7	306.1
2006	308.0	303.9	306.4	306.6	307.5	307.9	306.3	308.7	305.2	306.4	317.6	323.1	309.0
2007	307.8	303.9	307.4	306.7	307.3	308.4	309.6	310.4	308.5	311.6	322.7	328.1	311.0
2008	313.1	309.8	311.9	308.9	309.9	311.3	311.9	313.5	309.2	310.5	315.5	319.4	312.1
2009	303.1	298.0	298.2	296.4	297.2	297.0	296.9	298.6	296.7	299.0	306.1	311.3	299.9
Transportation and Utilities													
1990	92.6	93.5	94.0	92.7	93.8	95.1	96.1	97.6	98.9	98.0	98.0	98.5	95.7
2000	135.7	136.1	136.4	137.0	138.0	139.4	139.5	140.9	141.6	142.7	143.9	145.5	139.7
2001	141.0	140.5	140.6	140.4	141.1	141.8	141.9	143.1	142.4	140.4	137.3	136.9	140.6
2002	135.2	134.5	135.1	135.4	136.1	136.5	136.7	137.2	136.6	137.3	136.4	135.9	136.1
2003	133.7	133.0	132.8	132.6	132.0	131.0	130.1	131.2	131.0	132.1	132.3	132.4	132.0
2004	131.4	131.5	131.9	132.1	132.3	132.5	133.6	134.2	134.3	134.5	134.0	134.8	133.1
2005	133.7	132.0	133.5	132.2	132.8	132.9	133.7	134.9	135.7	135.7	136.7	137.4	134.3
2006	134.1	134.4	135.1	135.6	136.4	137.1	137.2	138.4	139.2	139.8	140.5	143.0	137.6
2007	139.8	140.2	141.0	140.9	141.6	142.4	141.6	142.5	143.2	143.3	143.5	144.8	142.1
2008	141.7	141.8	141.7	142.4	143.0	142.9	142.4	143.8	144.0	143.1	143.0	144.2	142.8
2009	140.3	138.4	138.5	136.8	136.4	136.0	135.9	135.7	135.8	135.8	136.2	137.3	136.9
Information													
1990	71.6	71.4	71.9	71.8	72.1	72.8	74.6	74.3	73.5	74.3	74.7	75.2	73.2
2000	116.1	117.7	118.8	119.9	120.7	123.0	123.5	124.2	124.7	125.1	126.2	126.2	122.2
2001	122.8	122.9	124.0	123.1	122.6	122.2	120.4	119.8	118.3	117.5	116.7	115.5	120.5
2002	114.2	113.0	112.6	110.1	109.3	108.6	106.2	105.3	104.1	103.5	103.0	102.4	107.7
2003	100.6	100.4	100.1	98.9	98.5	98.2	98.0	97.5	96.4	96.7	96.3	96.3	98.2
2004	96.1	94.7	96.1	94.8	94.9	94.7	94.0	93.4	92.7	92.9	92.8	93.0	94.2
2005	92.5	92.5	92.7	92.4	92.2	92.5	92.8	92.5	92.7	92.2	92.4	92.2	92.5
2006	91.5	92.4	92.3	91.0	90.3	90.3	89.4	88.5	87.9	86.6	86.1	85.8	89.3
2007	87.8	88.4	88.5	88.2	88.8	88.9	89.4	90.0	89.5	89.9	90.3	89.8	89.1
2008	89.1	89.2	89.2	88.9	88.8	88.6	88.2	87.8	86.4	86.0	86.1	86.0	87.9
2009	85.4	84.8	84.1	83.5	83.4	83.2	82.4	81.8	80.9	80.9	80.6	80.9	82.7
Financial Activities													
1990	158.7	160.1	160.4	161.5	161.7	163.0	162.9	163.5	161.9	161.6	161.3	162.2	161.6
2000	204.8	205.0	206.3	208.1	208.3	209.2	209.6	209.2	208.6	208.8	208.7	210.0	208.1
2001	207.2	208.3	209.0	209.7	210.3	212.4	212.3	212.8	211.9	212.4	212.9	213.9	211.1
2002	212.3	212.4	212.8	212.2	212.8	213.3	213.2	213.4	212.4	211.7	212.3	212.1	212.6
2003	210.4	211.2	210.7	211.1	211.9	212.7	213.4	214.2	213.4	213.0	212.9	213.7	212.4
2004	212.0	212.0	212.7	213.6	213.7	214.6	216.2	216.8	216.1	217.5	217.6	218.7	215.1
2005	216.5	217.0	217.3	218.3	218.8	220.4	222.5	223.6	224.2	224.3	225.2	226.4	221.2
2006	224.3	225.4	227.4	229.0	229.4	230.7	229.5	230.6	230.3	230.4	231.1	232.5	229.2
2007	229.3	230.3	231.6	232.4	233.2	235.1	234.3	235.4	234.3	233.7	233.9	234.3	233.2
2008	231.7	232.8	233.0	234.5	235.5	236.1	234.7	234.5	232.6	231.4	230.3	229.9	233.1
2009	227.0	226.8	226.6	225.8	226.6	227.0	226.6	226.7	225.9	225.2	225.9	226.3	226.4

Employment by Industry: Dallas-Fort Worth-Arlington, TX, Selected Years, 1990–2009—*Continued*

(Numbers in thousands, not seasonally adjusted.)

Industry and year	January	February	March	April	May	June	July	August	September	October	November	December	Annual average
Professional and Business Services													
1990	188.7	190.4	193.2	195.0	196.6	201.8	202.9	205.6	206.8	205.9	207.3	208.9	200.3
2000	367.1	370.8	376.3	380.8	382.7	392.3	390.5	393.7	396.9	393.5	392.8	393.4	385.9
2001	380.3	381.2	382.6	384.0	382.8	383.5	379.4	379.8	375.4	366.5	364.0	362.3	376.8
2002	352.2	351.7	354.0	355.4	356.6	357.3	356.1	359.6	357.8	355.4	355.2	353.8	355.4
2003	344.0	343.5	345.4	349.3	349.8	351.5	353.7	356.6	357.3	358.5	361.0	364.5	352.9
2004	354.8	357.3	360.5	366.3	366.3	368.3	371.5	373.1	371.2	376.6	376.4	377.3	368.3
2005	366.4	370.4	373.7	383.0	382.2	385.1	389.7	392.3	395.5	400.1	402.9	405.3	387.2
2006	395.9	399.9	404.4	409.4	411.3	415.3	416.3	421.9	424.1	426.2	431.4	433.9	415.8
2007	422.3	428.3	433.2	435.2	436.2	441.5	440.7	446.8	447.7	451.8	453.8	456.6	441.2
2008	444.1	446.4	448.5	449.9	451.8	453.9	452.2	454.3	450.5	449.2	445.1	440.0	448.8
2009	422.9	418.3	416.3	412.5	412.2	413.9	413.0	413.5	410.2	419.0	417.8	422.6	416.0
Education and Health Services													
1990	160.4	164.2	165.1	165.7	167.3	167.5	169.4	171.8	172.6	174.0	175.0	175.3	169.0
2000	239.0	240.1	242.0	242.3	243.5	242.7	243.2	244.5	246.9	246.5	246.9	247.5	243.8
2001	245.7	248.3	249.8	250.9	252.3	253.9	254.4	255.8	257.0	257.0	257.6	258.0	253.4
2002	256.0	258.5	259.3	260.7	262.2	260.8	260.9	263.7	265.4	265.1	266.5	266.8	262.2
2003	266.4	268.2	268.9	269.5	270.0	267.9	269.6	270.7	272.2	274.2	274.4	272.6	270.4
2004	268.5	272.2	273.1	274.4	274.4	271.5	274.0	274.9	277.3	283.0	283.2	284.1	275.9
2005	277.6	280.8	281.9	285.0	285.4	284.7	288.6	289.1	291.0	293.8	294.3	294.8	287.3
2006	293.0	295.2	295.8	296.7	297.3	298.3	298.1	302.4	305.0	306.6	307.9	310.3	300.6
2007	303.6	308.7	311.7	312.7	314.1	314.0	313.6	316.7	319.0	320.5	322.2	322.7	315.0
2008	318.9	323.8	324.6	325.1	327.8	325.6	326.5	328.6	330.7	331.9	333.3	335.7	327.7
2009	331.0	333.7	336.6	338.4	340.3	339.7	341.8	343.6	346.4	351.2	350.9	352.0	342.1
Leisure and Hospitality													
1990	161.6	164.9	165.5	169.6	173.2	177.5	174.8	176.2	171.6	170.9	168.5	168.9	170.3
2000	225.0	228.4	232.7	236.9	240.8	244.3	244.5	244.8	242.0	241.9	238.5	238.3	238.2
2001	234.1	238.7	243.2	249.9	251.6	252.3	251.0	251.6	246.2	242.7	239.4	239.0	245.0
2002	234.7	236.8	241.9	246.8	250.0	251.5	248.2	247.8	245.8	244.1	241.4	241.5	244.2
2003	237.1	238.3	241.3	245.9	248.4	249.8	247.5	248.7	245.0	246.8	243.9	243.2	244.7
2004	239.3	241.2	245.6	252.8	254.5	257.2	255.7	256.4	254.9	256.3	253.7	253.7	251.8
2005	247.1	250.2	254.1	260.8	263.3	264.4	263.5	262.4	259.4	258.5	256.3	255.3	257.9
2006	252.6	255.3	259.6	264.7	269.4	274.2	270.9	271.1	269.4	267.9	267.0	267.2	265.8
2007	260.9	264.9	270.9	279.0	283.6	285.7	285.0	285.8	280.1	281.2	280.5	280.2	278.2
2008	272.1	275.6	278.8	285.8	290.4	291.3	289.2	286.4	282.0	282.0	278.5	278.6	282.6
2009	271.2	273.1	277.1	282.5	286.1	289.3	285.8	284.8	280.0	278.2	276.5	276.1	280.1
Other Services													
1990	73.7	74.1	74.6	75.9	76.6	77.9	77.7	77.8	77.0	76.4	76.3	76.3	76.2
2000	99.8	100.7	102.1	102.8	103.1	104.3	103.8	103.6	102.9	102.8	102.5	102.5	102.6
2001	103.1	104.0	105.5	105.3	105.2	106.9	104.3	104.2	102.9	101.4	101.8	101.9	103.9
2002	101.0	101.9	104.0	104.9	105.2	106.1	104.5	104.3	104.0	103.4	103.8	103.8	103.9
2003	104.7	105.5	108.0	107.2	107.1	108.0	107.6	107.2	106.3	104.7	104.7	105.5	106.4
2004	105.2	106.3	109.0	107.7	106.9	107.8	105.9	104.8	103.5	102.3	102.2	102.9	105.4
2005	102.4	103.5	106.4	106.8	107.6	108.2	105.4	104.9	104.2	102.4	102.7	103.2	104.8
2006	102.7	103.5	106.0	107.4	107.5	109.2	108.8	108.5	108.5	107.5	108.4	108.7	107.2
2007	103.4	105.2	106.6	105.6	106.6	108.5	106.2	106.1	105.0	103.3	103.3	103.1	105.2
2008	102.7	103.4	103.3	103.9	104.9	105.9	104.4	104.4	104.0	102.7	102.6	102.6	103.7
2009	101.0	101.7	101.7	103.3	103.3	104.1	103.0	102.6	101.3	99.4	99.2	99.1	101.6
Government													
1990	238.1	240.8	241.9	243.9	246.3	240.3	230.5	229.3	241.6	244.6	248.1	248.2	241.1
2000	312.4	315.7	316.6	317.6	323.3	315.7	300.1	303.9	316.3	320.5	323.1	326.2	316.0
2001	320.6	325.9	326.3	325.0	325.2	321.3	304.8	310.1	324.0	331.1	334.0	333.2	323.5
2002	327.6	336.0	336.9	334.8	336.4	330.9	312.5	319.2	335.0	342.9	346.7	345.7	333.7
2003	336.9	346.2	345.4	346.0	347.4	342.2	322.4	323.4	342.1	346.0	348.8	345.7	341.0
2004	341.1	348.1	346.4	348.4	350.4	343.3	328.3	336.1	353.6	354.6	357.8	357.1	347.1
2005	351.9	359.2	358.3	359.3	360.4	351.6	335.7	344.2	360.4	364.0	367.3	361.2	356.1
2006	359.0	366.1	364.8	365.7	366.6	358.5	345.2	352.0	364.9	371.0	373.3	370.7	363.2
2007	366.7	373.5	374.3	372.5	374.5	366.9	349.8	354.0	370.6	378.9	382.1	380.8	370.4
2008	376.2	383.7	384.9	384.6	386.5	379.1	365.1	367.3	381.2	390.1	393.6	393.8	382.2
2009	386.6	393.5	394.4	394.8	394.4	384.9	369.1	369.0	384.0	395.8	398.5	396.6	388.5

Employment by Industry: Dayton, OH, Selected Years, 1990–2009

(Numbers in thousands, not seasonally adjusted.)

Industry and year	January	February	March	April	May	June	July	August	September	October	November	December	Annual average
Total Nonfarm													
1990	402.6	403.2	406.3	407.8	411.2	412.0	405.2	406.5	412.8	410.8	411.2	410.6	408.4
2000	426.4	429.3	432.1	434.5	439.6	437.7	430.5	433.0	435.7	439.6	441.8	443.1	435.3
2001	426.6	429.6	431.9	432.9	433.1	432.3	424.2	425.1	426.0	427.6	428.4	427.4	428.8
2002	418.1	420.4	421.8	421.4	422.2	422.1	417.3	418.3	421.2	420.6	422.3	421.4	420.6
2003	411.5	410.6	413.2	416.8	417.2	418.0	412.8	414.1	416.1	418.1	418.8	418.9	415.5
2004	406.0	406.8	409.1	413.3	413.5	414.6	410.2	411.8	413.8	414.2	414.2	414.4	411.8
2005	404.1	405.6	408.0	412.1	412.3	411.5	407.0	408.9	412.7	412.3	413.0	413.0	410.0
2006	401.9	404.4	407.9	410.1	412.2	412.0	404.5	406.2	408.3	408.5	410.1	411.2	408.1
2007	396.6	399.3	402.4	404.9	406.4	407.0	400.4	402.2	404.7	405.7	406.1	404.7	403.4
2008	394.7	395.4	393.7	395.8	397.3	397.9	392.7	394.2	395.3	394.3	392.3	390.1	394.5
2009	375.5	374.5	374.4	373.5	375.0	373.0	368.7	369.6	372.0	372.3	372.2	370.5	372.6
Total Private													
1990	327.9	328.8	331.6	333.5	335.6	339.1	336.9	337.6	339.8	336.3	336.8	336.4	335.0
2000	362.3	363.0	365.4	367.4	371.0	369.6	365.9	368.9	369.1	371.4	373.3	374.2	368.5
2001	360.5	361.8	363.7	365.1	364.5	364.0	359.8	361.3	359.5	359.6	360.1	358.9	361.6
2002	351.3	352.2	353.7	353.9	353.8	354.3	352.3	353.8	354.5	352.7	354.0	353.4	353.3
2003	346.3	344.3	347.1	350.9	350.5	351.7	349.6	351.5	351.7	352.2	352.8	352.8	350.1
2004	341.3	341.2	343.3	347.6	347.0	348.7	347.3	349.2	349.4	348.6	348.4	348.8	346.7
2005	339.8	339.9	342.5	346.6	346.1	346.8	344.4	346.6	348.1	347.1	347.7	348.4	345.3
2006	337.9	338.9	342.4	344.7	345.8	346.2	341.6	343.6	344.5	343.1	344.7	345.8	343.3
2007	332.5	334.5	337.4	340.1	340.8	342.1	338.7	340.5	340.8	340.7	342.0	341.6	339.3
2008	331.9	330.9	329.1	331.1	331.5	333.7	331.1	332.6	331.1	329.0	326.6	325.5	330.3
2009	311.0	309.4	308.9	307.7	307.7	306.4	304.8	305.6	306.5	305.5	305.7	304.5	307.0
Goods-Producing													
1990	93.8	94.6	95.4	95.9	96.7	97.9	97.4	97.2	97.8	96.5	95.7	94.5	96.1
2000	94.5	93.6	94.4	95.0	95.9	96.2	94.2	95.7	95.8	95.8	95.4	94.8	95.1
2001	88.4	88.6	88.1	86.9	86.6	87.0	85.6	85.9	84.5	84.3	83.5	82.8	86.0
2002	81.4	81.6	81.1	81.7	81.9	82.7	81.6	82.3	81.4	80.8	80.3	79.9	81.4
2003	77.9	76.5	76.6	77.7	78.3	78.8	76.6	77.8	76.9	76.7	76.4	76.0	77.2
2004	73.7	73.2	73.6	74.2	74.6	75.4	74.8	75.5	74.9	74.5	73.8	73.8	74.3
2005	71.4	71.1	71.3	72.7	72.9	74.1	73.4	74.1	73.8	73.2	72.5	71.9	72.7
2006	69.4	69.7	70.5	71.1	71.4	72.3	70.1	71.0	70.4	69.7	69.2	69.3	70.3
2007	63.8	65.6	66.2	66.9	67.3	68.3	67.0	68.0	67.4	66.5	66.6	65.9	66.6
2008	63.5	62.9	60.5	60.5	61.1	63.9	63.3	64.0	62.5	61.8	60.0	58.5	61.9
2009	53.3	52.4	51.7	51.0	50.7	50.2	50.1	50.5	50.1	49.9	49.3	48.3	50.6
Mining, Logging, and Construction													
1990	13.6	13.4	13.9	14.2	14.8	15.2	15.3	15.3	15.0	14.6	14.3	13.6	14.4
2000	14.8	14.6	15.5	16.0	16.7	17.3	17.4	17.2	16.7	16.4	16.0	15.5	16.2
2001	13.8	13.7	14.2	14.6	15.0	15.7	16.0	16.1	15.7	15.8	15.7	15.3	15.1
2002	14.1	14.1	14.4	14.9	15.3	15.8	16.2	16.2	15.8	15.9	15.4	15.0	15.3
2003	13.8	13.3	13.7	14.7	15.3	15.8	16.1	16.3	15.9	16.1	15.9	15.6	15.2
2004	14.5	14.1	14.5	15.2	15.7	16.3	16.8	16.5	16.2	16.0	15.7	15.5	15.6
2005	14.0	13.7	14.2	15.2	15.7	16.3	16.6	16.3	16.1	15.7	15.6	15.0	15.4
2006	14.1	14.0	14.4	15.0	15.4	16.1	16.2	16.2	15.7	15.1	14.8	14.5	15.1
2007	13.4	12.8	13.5	14.5	15.2	15.9	15.9	15.7	15.2	14.9	15.0	14.3	14.7
2008	13.0	12.8	12.9	13.6	14.3	14.5	14.7	14.5	14.0	13.7	13.1	12.5	13.6
2009	11.2	11.1	11.3	11.4	11.9	12.2	12.5	12.2	11.8	11.7	11.6	10.8	11.6
Manufacturing													
1990	80.2	81.2	81.5	81.7	81.9	82.7	82.1	81.9	82.8	81.9	81.4	80.9	81.7
2000	79.7	79.0	78.9	79.0	79.2	78.9	76.8	78.5	79.1	79.4	79.4	79.3	78.9
2001	74.6	74.9	73.9	72.3	71.6	71.3	69.6	69.8	68.8	68.5	67.8	67.5	70.9
2002	67.3	67.5	66.7	66.8	66.6	66.9	65.4	66.1	65.6	64.9	64.9	64.9	66.1
2003	64.1	63.2	62.9	63.0	63.0	63.0	60.5	61.5	61.0	60.6	60.5	60.4	62.0
2004	59.2	59.1	59.1	59.0	58.9	59.1	58.0	59.0	58.7	58.5	58.1	58.3	58.8
2005	57.4	57.4	57.1	57.5	57.2	57.8	56.8	57.8	57.7	57.5	56.9	56.9	57.3
2006	55.3	55.7	56.1	56.1	56.0	56.2	53.9	54.8	54.7	54.6	54.4	54.8	55.2
2007	50.4	52.8	52.7	52.4	52.1	52.4	51.1	52.3	52.2	51.6	51.6	51.6	51.9
2008	50.5	50.1	47.6	46.9	46.8	49.4	48.6	49.5	48.5	48.1	46.9	46.0	48.2
2009	42.1	41.3	40.4	39.6	38.8	38.0	37.6	38.3	38.3	38.2	37.7	37.5	39.0
Service-Providing													
1990	308.8	308.6	310.9	311.9	314.5	314.1	307.8	309.3	315.0	314.3	315.5	316.1	312.2
2000	331.9	335.7	337.7	339.5	343.7	341.5	336.3	337.3	339.9	343.8	346.4	348.3	340.2
2001	338.2	341.0	343.8	346.0	346.5	345.3	338.6	339.2	341.5	343.3	344.9	344.6	342.7
2002	336.7	338.8	340.7	339.7	340.3	339.4	335.7	336.0	339.8	339.8	342.0	341.5	339.2
2003	333.6	334.1	336.6	339.1	338.9	339.2	336.2	336.3	339.2	341.4	342.4	342.9	338.3
2004	332.3	333.6	335.5	339.1	338.9	339.2	335.4	336.3	338.9	339.7	340.4	340.6	337.5
2005	332.7	334.5	336.7	339.4	339.4	337.4	333.6	334.8	338.9	339.1	340.5	341.1	337.3
2006	332.5	334.7	337.4	339.0	340.8	339.7	334.4	335.2	337.9	338.8	340.9	341.9	337.8
2007	332.8	333.7	336.2	338.0	339.1	338.7	333.4	334.2	337.3	339.2	339.5	338.8	336.7
2008	331.2	332.5	333.2	335.3	336.2	334.0	329.4	330.2	332.8	332.5	332.3	331.6	332.6
2009	322.2	322.1	322.7	322.5	324.3	322.8	318.6	319.1	321.9	322.4	322.9	322.2	322.0

Employment by Industry: Dayton, OH, Selected Years, 1990–2009—*Continued*

(Numbers in thousands, not seasonally adjusted.)

Industry and year	January	February	March	April	May	June	July	August	September	October	November	December	Annual average
Trade, Transportation, and Utilities													
1990	69.8	69.1	70.0	70.2	70.5	70.7	70.4	70.7	70.7	70.0	71.2	72.1	70.5
2000	81.0	80.4	80.6	80.9	81.7	81.2	80.3	80.3	80.2	82.2	84.1	85.6	81.5
2001	80.6	79.5	79.4	79.9	79.6	79.4	78.2	77.8	77.3	77.7	79.4	79.6	79.0
2002	75.9	75.2	75.4	74.8	75.1	75.5	74.8	74.2	74.0	73.6	75.2	76.0	75.0
2003	72.7	71.5	71.9	72.6	72.8	72.4	72.0	72.1	72.2	72.7	74.1	74.7	72.6
2004	70.4	69.9	70.4	71.3	71.6	72.0	71.5	71.4	71.5	72.2	73.3	73.9	71.6
2005	70.3	70.2	70.8	71.5	71.5	71.5	71.0	70.9	70.7	70.8	72.2	73.1	71.2
2006	69.6	69.1	69.8	69.9	70.6	70.4	69.7	69.9	69.0	69.2	70.7	71.5	70.0
2007	68.1	67.3	68.1	68.7	69.0	69.0	68.9	68.5	68.4	68.6	70.0	70.6	68.8
2008	67.3	66.4	66.6	67.0	67.2	67.5	66.7	66.9	66.5	66.1	66.7	67.5	66.9
2009	63.9	63.1	63.2	63.1	63.7	63.5	62.8	62.7	62.5	62.1	63.3	63.8	63.1
Wholesale Trade													
1990	13.4	13.4	13.6	13.6	13.6	13.6	13.5	13.3	13.4	13.2	13.2	13.1	13.4
2000	14.8	14.8	14.9	15.0	15.1	15.1	14.8	14.8	14.9	15.0	15.0	15.0	14.9
2001	15.2	15.0	15.0	15.3	15.3	15.0	15.0	15.1	15.2	15.3	15.3	15.3	15.2
2002	15.3	15.4	15.3	15.3	15.2	15.1	15.2	15.0	15.1	15.3	15.2	15.2	15.2
2003	14.8	14.7	14.7	14.6	14.6	14.6	14.6	14.5	14.4	14.5	14.5	14.4	14.5
2004	14.1	14.0	14.1	14.2	14.3	14.4	14.5	14.4	14.4	14.5	14.4	14.4	14.3
2005	14.0	14.1	14.1	14.2	14.2	14.3	14.3	14.2	14.1	14.1	14.0	14.1	14.1
2006	13.8	13.8	13.9	13.9	14.1	14.1	14.1	14.0	14.0	14.0	14.0	14.1	14.0
2007	13.9	13.9	14.0	14.0	14.0	14.1	14.2	14.1	14.0	14.1	14.0	14.1	14.0
2008	14.0	13.9	14.0	14.0	14.0	13.9	13.8	13.7	13.6	13.4	13.3	13.2	13.7
2009	13.1	13.0	12.9	12.8	12.7	12.7	12.6	12.4	12.3	12.2	12.2	12.2	12.6
Retail Trade													
1990	45.9	45.2	45.8	46.0	46.3	46.4	46.2	46.7	46.6	46.1	47.3	48.4	46.4
2000	51.2	50.4	50.6	50.7	51.3	50.9	50.5	50.5	50.1	51.5	53.5	55.0	51.4
2001	50.2	49.3	49.3	49.5	49.5	49.6	48.4	48.0	47.8	48.2	50.0	50.4	49.2
2002	47.1	46.4	46.8	46.3	46.6	47.0	46.3	46.0	45.8	45.5	47.0	47.9	46.6
2003	45.4	44.4	45.0	45.7	45.8	45.5	45.2	45.4	45.6	45.8	47.1	47.7	45.7
2004	44.6	44.0	44.4	45.1	45.2	45.3	44.8	44.7	44.8	45.2	46.3	46.9	45.1
2005	44.1	43.8	44.3	45.0	44.9	44.7	44.0	43.9	43.8	44.0	45.3	46.0	44.5
2006	43.3	42.6	43.1	43.0	43.4	43.1	42.7	42.9	42.8	43.1	44.6	45.2	43.3
2007	42.6	41.8	42.4	43.0	43.2	43.0	42.8	42.5	42.5	42.7	44.2	44.6	42.9
2008	42.0	41.2	41.5	41.9	41.9	42.0	41.4	41.5	41.3	41.2	41.9	42.7	41.7
2009	39.9	39.2	39.5	39.8	40.4	40.3	39.7	39.7	39.6	39.2	40.4	41.0	39.9
Transportation and Utilities													
1990	10.5	10.5	10.6	10.6	10.6	10.7	10.7	10.7	10.7	10.7	10.7	10.6	10.6
2000	15.0	15.2	15.1	15.2	15.3	15.2	15.0	15.0	15.2	15.7	15.6	15.6	15.3
2001	15.2	15.2	15.1	15.1	14.8	14.8	14.8	14.7	14.3	14.2	14.1	13.9	14.7
2002	13.5	13.4	13.3	13.2	13.3	13.4	13.3	13.2	13.1	12.8	13.0	12.9	13.2
2003	12.5	12.4	12.2	12.3	12.4	12.3	12.2	12.2	12.2	12.4	12.5	12.6	12.3
2004	11.7	11.9	11.9	12.0	12.1	12.3	12.2	12.3	12.3	12.5	12.6	12.6	12.2
2005	12.2	12.3	12.4	12.3	12.4	12.5	12.7	12.8	12.8	12.7	12.9	13.0	12.6
2006	12.5	12.7	12.8	13.0	13.1	13.2	12.9	13.0	12.2	12.1	12.1	12.2	12.7
2007	11.6	11.6	11.7	11.7	11.8	11.9	11.9	11.9	11.9	11.8	11.8	11.9	11.8
2008	11.3	11.3	11.1	11.1	11.3	11.6	11.5	11.7	11.6	11.5	11.5	11.6	11.4
2009	10.9	10.9	10.8	10.5	10.6	10.5	10.5	10.6	10.6	10.7	10.7	10.6	10.7
Information													
1990	9.9	9.9	9.9	10.1	10.1	10.1	10.2	10.2	10.2	10.1	10.1	10.2	10.1
2000	11.4	11.4	11.4	11.2	11.3	11.2	11.2	11.2	11.4	11.6	11.9	12.1	11.4
2001	12.5	12.6	12.7	12.5	12.5	12.7	12.8	12.6	12.5	12.5	12.5	12.7	12.6
2002	12.8	12.7	12.7	12.6	12.6	12.6	12.6	12.7	12.7	12.7	12.6	12.6	12.7
2003	12.8	12.7	12.7	12.6	12.5	12.6	12.6	12.5	12.3	12.4	12.4	12.4	12.5
2004	12.2	12.0	12.0	12.1	12.0	12.3	12.4	12.5	12.3	12.3	12.4	12.4	12.2
2005	12.3	12.2	12.2	12.2	12.2	12.3	12.2	12.0	11.8	11.7	11.7	11.8	12.1
2006	11.7	11.7	11.7	11.7	11.7	11.8	11.9	12.0	11.9	12.0	12.0	12.1	11.9
2007	12.1	12.1	12.0	12.1	12.2	12.2	12.1	12.1	12.0	12.0	12.1	12.1	12.1
2008	12.2	12.1	12.1	12.1	12.0	11.9	12.2	12.1	11.7	11.6	11.6	11.5	11.9
2009	11.4	11.4	11.2	11.1	11.1	11.0	10.9	10.9	10.8	10.7	10.7	10.8	11.0
Financial Activities													
1990	16.5	16.7	16.7	16.6	16.7	17.0	16.8	16.9	17.0	16.8	16.9	16.8	16.8
2000	17.2	17.1	17.1	17.3	17.4	17.3	17.3	17.2	17.0	17.2	17.4	17.6	17.3
2001	17.4	17.5	17.8	17.9	18.1	18.1	18.2	18.2	18.2	18.3	18.2	18.2	18.0
2002	18.0	18.1	18.2	18.3	18.3	18.4	18.5	18.6	18.5	18.4	18.4	18.4	18.3
2003	18.4	18.5	18.6	18.7	18.9	19.1	19.1	19.1	18.9	18.8	18.8	18.8	18.8
2004	18.6	18.6	18.8	18.9	19.1	19.2	19.3	19.3	19.1	19.2	19.1	19.2	19.0
2005	18.8	18.9	18.8	19.1	19.2	19.4	19.5	19.6	19.6	19.7	19.7	19.8	19.3
2006	19.7	19.9	20.0	20.1	20.1	20.2	20.2	20.2	20.1	20.2	20.2	20.2	20.1
2007	19.9	20.0	20.0	20.1	20.1	19.9	19.8	19.7	19.4	19.3	19.2	19.1	19.7
2008	19.0	18.7	18.6	18.5	18.4	18.3	18.1	18.0	17.7	17.5	17.4	17.4	18.1
2009	17.3	17.1	16.9	16.9	16.9	16.9	16.9	16.8	16.6	16.5	16.5	16.5	16.8

Employment by Industry: Dayton, OH, Selected Years, 1990–2009—*Continued*

(Numbers in thousands, not seasonally adjusted.)

Industry and year	January	February	March	April	May	June	July	August	September	October	November	December	Annual average
Professional and Business Services													
1990	44.6	44.9	45.0	46.0	46.1	46.6	46.2	46.4	46.8	46.3	46.1	45.7	45.9
2000	50.3	51.2	51.6	52.7	53.0	52.8	52.2	52.6	53.0	53.6	53.2	53.0	52.4
2001	54.2	54.7	55.7	55.8	55.7	55.6	54.6	55.1	54.7	54.4	53.9	53.4	54.8
2002	53.1	53.1	53.6	53.3	53.0	52.9	52.7	52.6	52.7	51.8	52.0	51.3	52.7
2003	52.7	52.3	52.9	54.0	53.9	54.2	54.6	54.8	54.3	54.7	54.4	54.3	53.9
2004	52.5	52.4	52.5	53.6	53.7	54.0	53.4	53.5	54.1	53.3	52.9	52.8	53.2
2005	52.0	51.6	52.0	52.2	52.1	52.0	51.8	52.4	52.4	53.0	52.7	52.9	52.3
2006	51.2	51.1	51.6	52.3	52.7	53.1	52.7	52.9	52.6	52.4	52.4	52.6	52.3
2007	51.6	51.8	52.0	52.2	52.1	52.7	52.3	52.5	52.4	52.9	52.6	52.6	52.3
2008	51.2	51.5	51.6	51.8	51.5	51.7	51.1	50.9	50.4	49.9	48.9	48.8	50.8
2009	46.7	45.9	45.5	45.4	45.0	45.3	45.0	45.3	45.2	45.7	45.5	45.0	45.5
Education and Health Services													
1990	47.3	47.4	47.6	47.0	46.5	46.7	46.4	46.3	47.7	48.3	48.4	48.4	47.3
2000	57.7	58.6	58.5	58.1	58.1	57.4	57.5	58.1	58.5	58.8	59.3	59.4	58.3
2001	58.6	59.7	59.5	60.4	59.0	57.4	56.7	57.1	59.4	60.8	61.4	61.1	59.3
2002	60.2	61.2	61.4	61.3	59.9	58.6	58.3	58.8	61.9	63.0	63.4	63.2	60.9
2003	61.2	62.0	62.4	62.5	60.1	59.4	59.2	59.4	62.8	63.8	64.1	63.6	61.7
2004	62.3	63.1	63.0	63.7	61.1	60.7	60.5	60.9	62.6	64.0	63.9	64.0	62.5
2005	63.4	64.1	64.5	64.8	63.3	61.9	61.7	61.9	65.2	65.7	66.1	66.1	64.1
2006	64.7	65.5	65.8	65.7	64.5	62.7	61.9	62.5	65.8	66.6	67.1	66.9	65.0
2007	65.5	66.2	66.5	66.5	65.6	64.7	64.0	64.8	67.5	68.4	68.7	68.9	66.4
2008	67.8	68.5	68.6	68.5	67.5	66.4	66.0	66.7	69.3	69.9	70.2	70.3	68.3
2009	68.7	69.7	69.8	69.1	68.1	66.9	66.5	66.8	69.6	69.8	69.6	70.2	68.7
Leisure and Hospitality													
1990	32.5	32.7	33.4	34.0	35.1	36.0	35.4	35.4	35.6	34.2	34.1	34.4	34.4
2000	34.4	34.6	35.5	35.8	37.1	37.3	37.1	37.3	36.8	35.9	35.6	35.5	36.1
2001	33.1	33.5	34.6	35.4	36.6	37.3	37.4	37.5	36.5	35.1	34.7	34.7	35.5
2002	33.7	33.8	34.6	35.4	36.4	37.0	37.0	37.2	36.6	35.8	35.4	35.3	35.7
2003	34.2	34.3	35.2	36.0	37.2	38.1	38.4	38.3	37.4	36.3	36.0	36.3	36.4
2004	35.3	35.5	36.3	37.0	38.0	38.2	38.5	38.8	38.1	36.5	36.4	36.2	37.1
2005	35.2	35.4	36.3	37.4	38.1	38.7	38.2	38.6	38.0	36.7	36.6	36.6	37.2
2006	35.6	35.8	36.8	37.4	38.3	39.0	38.7	38.8	38.3	36.9	37.0	37.1	37.5
2007	35.7	35.7	36.5	37.5	38.4	39.0	38.6	38.9	37.8	37.1	36.9	36.6	37.4
2008	35.4	35.3	35.6	37.2	38.2	38.5	38.2	38.5	37.6	36.9	36.5	36.2	37.0
2009	34.8	34.9	35.7	36.3	37.2	37.8	37.8	37.7	36.9	36.0	35.9	35.1	36.3
Other Services													
1990	13.5	13.5	13.6	13.7	13.9	14.1	14.1	14.5	14.0	14.1	14.3	14.3	14.0
2000	15.8	16.1	16.3	16.4	16.5	16.2	16.1	16.5	16.4	16.3	16.4	16.2	16.3
2001	15.7	15.7	15.9	16.3	16.4	16.5	16.3	17.1	16.4	16.5	16.5	16.4	16.3
2002	16.2	16.5	16.7	16.5	16.6	16.6	16.8	17.4	16.7	16.6	16.7	16.7	16.7
2003	16.4	16.5	16.8	16.8	16.8	17.1	17.1	17.5	16.9	16.8	16.6	16.7	16.8
2004	16.3	16.5	16.7	16.8	16.9	16.9	16.9	17.3	16.8	16.6	16.6	16.5	16.7
2005	16.4	16.4	16.6	16.7	16.8	16.9	16.6	17.1	16.6	16.3	16.2	16.2	16.6
2006	16.0	16.1	16.2	16.5	16.5	16.7	16.4	16.3	16.4	16.1	16.1	16.1	16.3
2007	15.8	15.8	16.1	16.1	16.1	16.3	16.0	16.0	15.9	15.9	15.9	15.8	16.0
2008	15.5	15.5	15.5	15.5	15.6	15.5	15.5	15.5	15.4	15.3	15.3	15.3	15.5
2009	14.9	14.9	14.9	14.8	15.0	14.8	14.8	14.9	14.8	14.8	14.9	14.8	14.9
Government													
1990	74.7	74.4	74.7	74.3	75.6	72.9	68.3	68.9	73.0	74.5	74.4	74.2	73.3
2000	64.1	66.3	66.7	67.1	68.6	68.1	64.6	64.1	66.6	68.2	68.5	68.9	66.8
2001	66.1	67.8	68.2	67.8	68.6	68.3	64.4	63.8	66.5	68.0	68.3	68.5	67.2
2002	66.8	68.2	68.1	67.5	68.4	67.8	65.0	64.5	66.7	67.9	68.3	68.0	67.3
2003	65.2	66.3	66.1	65.9	66.7	66.3	63.2	62.6	64.4	65.9	66.0	66.1	65.3
2004	64.7	65.6	65.8	65.7	66.5	65.9	62.9	62.6	64.4	65.6	65.8	65.6	65.1
2005	64.3	65.7	65.5	65.5	66.2	64.7	62.6	62.3	64.6	65.2	65.3	64.6	64.7
2006	64.0	65.5	65.5	65.4	66.4	65.8	62.9	62.6	63.8	65.4	65.4	65.4	64.8
2007	64.1	64.8	65.0	64.8	65.6	64.9	61.7	61.7	63.9	65.0	64.1	63.1	64.1
2008	62.8	64.5	64.6	64.7	65.8	64.2	61.6	61.6	64.2	65.3	65.7	64.6	64.1
2009	64.5	65.1	65.5	65.8	67.3	66.6	63.9	64.0	65.5	66.8	66.5	66.0	65.6

Employment by Industry: Denver-Aurora, CO, Selected Years, 1990–2009

(Numbers in thousands, not seasonally adjusted.)

Industry and year	January	February	March	April	May	June	July	August	September	October	November	December	Annual average
Total Nonfarm													
1990	828.5	834.0	839.5	845.2	859.9	868.9	857.0	863.7	867.3	864.2	869.4	871.6	855.8
2000	1168.0	1177.6	1188.3	1196.6	1210.5	1223.8	1221.1	1225.8	1227.2	1224.1	1231.3	1239.7	1211.2
2001	1204.6	1207.2	1211.2	1212.1	1219.0	1230.0	1216.8	1216.3	1207.7	1196.7	1194.2	1192.4	1209.0
2002	1152.5	1155.8	1159.9	1170.2	1181.1	1188.8	1177.7	1182.1	1175.0	1172.1	1175.3	1177.4	1172.3
2003	1148.6	1148.1	1147.2	1151.4	1160.4	1168.5	1160.7	1164.9	1159.6	1161.1	1161.6	1165.0	1158.1
2004	1135.2	1138.3	1148.1	1162.3	1170.2	1180.8	1175.3	1177.3	1176.0	1177.6	1180.8	1186.1	1167.3
2005	1154.5	1161.8	1170.6	1180.2	1190.2	1201.5	1198.9	1199.0	1203.6	1202.6	1206.2	1212.1	1190.1
2006	1182.1	1187.7	1196.4	1204.2	1217.1	1231.8	1222.3	1225.8	1225.3	1225.3	1229.6	1234.1	1215.1
2007	1202.6	1209.0	1221.4	1230.3	1244.0	1257.7	1249.5	1252.7	1252.9	1254.2	1258.6	1261.1	1241.2
2008	1231.3	1237.2	1244.5	1252.2	1261.9	1271.6	1261.7	1265.9	1259.4	1256.2	1251.2	1244.5	1253.1
2009	1206.6	1198.3	1197.5	1198.3	1206.2	1210.3	1199.2	1197.5	1194.3	1194.3	1192.0	1187.4	1198.5
Total Private													
1990	702.8	703.1	708.1	711.8	724.2	734.3	733.6	740.7	734.8	730.1	733.7	737.0	724.5
2000	1018.4	1024.1	1033.2	1040.8	1051.5	1067.8	1071.3	1074.9	1070.3	1067.5	1073.5	1081.0	1056.2
2001	1050.2	1049.0	1053.5	1053.8	1059.8	1070.9	1062.9	1061.5	1047.0	1035.6	1031.3	1029.6	1050.4
2002	993.0	993.1	995.8	1005.8	1015.4	1024.2	1018.8	1021.7	1010.7	1006.0	1008.4	1010.9	1008.7
2003	986.8	983.1	981.7	986.0	993.0	1002.6	1001.7	1005.0	995.4	996.8	997.0	1001.3	994.2
2004	976.1	975.7	984.2	997.0	1004.3	1016.0	1017.4	1019.1	1011.8	1012.1	1014.6	1020.1	1004.0
2005	994.1	997.3	1005.7	1013.7	1023.0	1035.9	1039.3	1040.3	1037.4	1035.9	1039.1	1045.1	1025.6
2006	1019.5	1021.2	1028.8	1037.1	1048.4	1063.5	1061.2	1063.9	1057.5	1057.3	1060.7	1064.9	1048.7
2007	1038.7	1040.0	1051.1	1059.6	1072.2	1086.9	1086.1	1088.4	1081.2	1081.7	1085.2	1088.1	1071.6
2008	1063.4	1064.9	1070.9	1078.0	1085.6	1097.1	1094.0	1095.4	1084.0	1078.8	1072.9	1067.2	1079.4
2009	1033.8	1022.4	1020.2	1020.0	1025.9	1032.5	1030.2	1027.4	1017.2	1015.3	1012.8	1009.8	1022.3
Goods-Producing													
1990	124.0	123.3	123.7	125.1	127.8	129.9	130.3	131.4	130.2	129.3	128.5	127.2	127.6
2000	173.5	176.0	179.1	179.5	182.0	185.6	186.0	186.6	186.1	185.7	183.9	183.3	182.3
2001	178.6	178.8	180.2	180.0	181.5	183.3	181.9	181.6	179.4	175.9	172.3	169.0	178.5
2002	163.3	164.0	165.9	167.5	169.9	171.4	171.0	170.6	167.7	166.4	163.6	161.1	166.9
2003	157.9	156.7	156.1	156.5	158.4	160.6	160.0	159.5	157.5	157.4	155.7	154.1	157.5
2004	151.0	150.7	153.2	155.6	157.2	160.1	161.1	161.2	160.1	160.8	159.7	158.5	157.4
2005	154.3	155.7	158.1	158.9	160.8	164.6	166.8	167.3	166.8	166.2	165.6	164.3	162.5
2006	161.4	162.6	164.8	165.8	167.9	171.0	170.1	169.8	169.0	167.6	165.8	163.9	166.6
2007	157.3	158.0	161.1	162.5	164.7	168.0	168.6	168.7	167.2	167.6	166.2	163.3	164.4
2008	159.7	159.7	160.9	161.5	163.0	165.6	164.9	165.0	162.8	161.7	158.1	153.9	161.4
2009	146.7	143.2	141.4	139.9	139.9	141.4	141.1	139.5	137.8	136.7	135.7	132.4	139.6
Mining, Logging, and Construction													
1990	39.3	38.7	38.9	40.3	42.3	44.1	44.9	46.1	45.4	45.2	44.8	43.6	42.8
2000	86.4	88.7	91.5	92.9	95.5	98.5	98.9	99.6	99.4	99.1	97.6	96.9	95.4
2001	94.2	94.5	96.3	97.4	99.0	101.3	100.9	101.2	100.1	97.8	95.0	92.3	97.5
2002	88.3	89.2	91.1	93.2	95.5	96.9	96.8	96.6	94.1	92.9	90.8	88.5	92.8
2003	85.4	84.4	84.3	84.9	86.9	89.0	88.8	88.5	86.8	86.8	85.0	83.4	86.1
2004	80.6	80.1	82.3	84.3	85.8	88.1	88.7	88.5	87.9	88.4	87.3	86.2	85.7
2005	82.8	83.9	86.1	87.0	88.8	92.3	94.1	94.7	94.4	93.6	93.2	91.9	90.2
2006	89.7	90.8	92.7	93.7	95.7	98.4	97.4	97.1	96.5	95.3	93.6	92.0	94.4
2007	86.1	87.1	90.1	91.7	93.4	96.1	96.7	96.8	95.4	95.7	94.3	91.5	92.9
2008	88.7	89.3	90.5	91.4	92.9	95.1	94.5	94.8	93.0	92.3	89.7	86.2	91.5
2009	80.7	78.5	77.3	76.3	76.8	78.3	78.2	76.9	75.7	75.1	74.4	71.0	76.6
Manufacturing													
1990	84.7	84.6	84.8	84.8	85.5	85.8	85.4	85.3	84.8	84.1	83.7	83.6	84.8
2000	87.1	87.3	87.6	86.6	86.5	87.1	87.1	87.0	86.7	86.6	86.3	86.4	86.9
2001	84.4	84.3	83.9	82.6	82.5	82.0	81.0	80.4	79.3	78.1	77.3	76.7	81.0
2002	75.0	74.8	74.8	74.3	74.4	74.5	74.2	74.0	73.6	73.5	72.8	72.6	74.0
2003	72.5	72.3	71.8	71.6	71.5	71.6	71.2	71.0	70.7	70.6	70.7	70.7	71.3
2004	70.4	70.6	70.9	71.3	71.4	72.0	72.4	72.7	72.2	72.4	72.4	72.3	71.8
2005	71.5	71.8	72.0	71.9	72.0	72.3	72.7	72.6	72.4	72.6	72.4	72.4	72.2
2006	71.7	71.8	72.1	72.1	72.2	72.6	72.7	72.7	72.5	72.3	72.2	71.9	72.2
2007	71.2	70.9	71.0	70.8	71.3	71.9	71.9	71.9	71.8	71.9	71.9	71.8	71.5
2008	71.0	70.4	70.4	70.1	70.1	70.5	70.4	70.2	69.8	69.4	68.4	67.7	69.9
2009	66.0	64.7	64.1	63.6	63.1	63.1	62.9	62.6	62.1	61.6	61.3	61.4	63.0
Service-Providing													
1990	704.5	710.7	715.8	720.1	732.1	739.0	726.7	732.3	737.1	734.9	740.9	744.4	728.2
2000	994.5	1001.6	1009.2	1017.1	1028.5	1038.2	1035.1	1039.2	1041.1	1038.4	1047.4	1056.4	1028.9
2001	1026.0	1028.4	1031.0	1032.1	1037.5	1046.7	1034.9	1034.7	1028.3	1020.8	1021.9	1023.4	1030.5
2002	989.2	991.8	994.0	1002.7	1011.2	1017.4	1006.7	1011.5	1007.3	1005.7	1011.7	1016.3	1005.5
2003	990.7	991.4	991.1	994.9	1002.0	1007.9	1000.7	1005.4	1002.1	1003.7	1005.9	1010.9	1000.6
2004	984.2	987.6	994.9	1006.7	1013.0	1020.7	1014.2	1016.1	1015.9	1016.8	1021.1	1027.6	1009.9
2005	1000.2	1006.1	1012.5	1021.3	1029.4	1036.9	1032.1	1031.7	1036.8	1036.4	1040.6	1047.8	1027.7
2006	1020.7	1025.1	1031.6	1038.4	1049.2	1060.8	1052.2	1056.0	1056.3	1057.7	1063.8	1070.2	1048.5
2007	1045.3	1051.0	1060.3	1067.8	1079.3	1089.7	1080.9	1084.0	1085.7	1086.6	1092.4	1097.8	1076.7
2008	1071.6	1077.5	1083.6	1090.7	1098.9	1106.0	1096.8	1100.9	1096.6	1094.5	1093.1	1090.6	1091.7
2009	1059.9	1055.1	1056.1	1058.4	1066.3	1068.9	1058.1	1058.0	1056.5	1057.6	1056.3	1055.0	1058.9

Employment by Industry: Denver-Aurora, CO, Selected Years, 1990–2009—*Continued*

(Numbers in thousands, not seasonally adjusted.)

Industry and year	January	February	March	April	May	June	July	August	September	October	November	December	Annual average
Trade, Transportation, and Utilities													
1990	182.1	179.5	179.9	180.2	182.6	183.7	183.0	184.6	184.6	185.2	189.1	192.9	184.0
2000	240.3	240.4	239.2	241.2	243.4	245.3	245.9	246.7	246.1	248.1	256.2	261.1	246.2
2001	249.6	246.2	246.3	245.3	246.8	248.9	247.6	247.1	245.4	244.8	247.2	247.5	246.9
2002	233.5	231.1	230.7	232.5	235.5	237.6	236.7	236.8	235.0	235.7	241.6	245.2	236.0
2003	235.2	232.9	231.6	229.8	230.0	230.7	230.5	231.2	230.5	232.2	236.6	239.6	232.5
2004	229.6	227.3	228.3	229.7	231.3	232.7	233.0	233.2	231.8	233.8	238.6	242.4	232.6
2005	232.4	231.3	232.2	232.5	234.3	236.1	236.6	236.3	237.8	239.6	244.2	247.2	236.7
2006	236.6	233.5	234.3	235.3	236.8	238.8	238.4	239.0	238.6	241.4	246.8	250.8	239.2
2007	242.2	239.4	240.1	241.0	242.8	244.3	244.5	244.5	243.8	245.6	251.2	253.8	244.4
2008	245.8	243.0	244.1	244.3	245.0	246.2	245.9	245.5	243.5	243.0	244.7	246.3	244.8
2009	235.7	231.7	229.8	228.9	230.0	231.0	229.6	229.5	228.1	228.7	231.2	232.9	230.6
Wholesale Trade													
1990	52.3	52.4	52.5	52.3	53.1	53.2	52.6	52.8	52.8	53.1	53.3	53.0	52.8
2000	65.4	66.8	67.3	68.1	68.6	69.0	68.4	67.8	67.6	68.3	68.6	69.0	67.9
2001	68.9	69.5	69.7	69.2	68.9	69.0	68.6	68.3	67.6	67.2	66.9	66.8	68.4
2002	65.4	65.3	65.3	65.1	65.2	65.2	64.9	64.5	64.0	63.9	63.7	63.8	64.7
2003	63.7	63.4	63.3	63.0	62.9	62.9	62.6	62.3	61.9	62.1	61.9	62.0	62.6
2004	61.3	61.5	61.9	62.0	62.1	62.4	62.2	62.2	61.9	62.0	62.1	62.3	62.0
2005	61.6	61.9	62.2	62.4	62.6	63.0	63.1	63.2	63.3	63.3	63.5	63.8	62.8
2006	63.3	63.6	64.0	64.3	64.7	65.4	65.3	65.5	65.3	65.6	65.9	66.4	64.9
2007	65.0	65.4	65.8	65.8	66.3	66.7	66.6	66.7	66.4	66.8	66.9	66.8	66.3
2008	66.5	66.7	66.8	67.0	67.2	67.4	67.4	67.1	66.8	66.4	66.1	66.0	66.8
2009	64.8	64.2	63.5	62.8	62.7	62.6	62.1	61.9	61.3	61.0	60.7	60.5	62.3
Retail Trade													
1990	91.2	88.4	88.3	88.8	90.1	90.8	90.5	91.9	91.9	92.3	95.3	97.9	91.5
2000	123.3	121.9	121.2	120.9	122.2	123.7	123.6	125.1	124.4	125.7	130.9	135.2	124.8
2001	125.4	122.2	122.2	121.8	122.9	124.4	123.2	122.8	122.5	123.3	127.6	129.4	124.0
2002	121.1	118.5	118.7	119.9	121.5	123.2	122.4	122.5	121.3	121.8	127.0	129.8	122.3
2003	121.3	119.3	118.3	118.1	119.0	120.0	119.7	120.6	120.4	121.4	125.3	127.8	120.9
2004	119.8	117.3	117.7	118.5	119.7	120.5	120.7	121.2	120.3	122.3	126.9	129.7	121.2
2005	121.9	120.3	121.0	121.2	122.9	123.9	124.1	123.7	125.2	126.7	131.0	133.2	124.6
2006	124.4	121.1	121.3	122.3	123.2	123.9	123.9	124.3	124.0	126.4	131.3	133.4	125.0
2007	127.0	124.2	124.5	125.1	126.3	127.2	127.5	127.2	126.8	127.7	132.4	134.0	127.5
2008	127.7	125.3	126.2	126.3	126.7	127.6	127.3	127.7	126.7	127.1	128.8	129.6	127.3
2009	122.5	119.8	118.9	118.3	119.6	120.6	119.9	120.0	119.5	120.8	123.4	124.2	120.6
Transportation and Utilities													
1990	38.6	38.7	39.1	39.1	39.4	39.7	39.9	39.9	39.9	39.8	40.5	42.0	39.7
2000	51.6	51.7	50.7	52.2	52.6	52.6	53.9	53.8	54.1	54.1	56.7	56.9	53.4
2001	55.3	54.5	54.4	54.3	55.0	55.5	55.8	56.0	55.3	54.3	52.7	51.3	54.5
2002	47.0	47.3	46.7	47.5	48.8	49.2	49.4	49.8	49.7	50.0	50.9	51.6	49.0
2003	50.2	50.2	50.0	48.7	48.1	47.8	48.2	48.3	48.2	48.7	49.4	49.8	48.9
2004	48.5	48.5	48.7	49.2	49.5	49.8	50.1	49.8	49.6	49.5	49.6	50.4	49.4
2005	48.9	49.1	49.0	48.9	48.8	49.2	49.4	49.4	49.3	49.6	49.7	50.2	49.3
2006	48.9	48.8	49.0	48.7	48.9	49.5	49.2	49.2	49.3	49.4	49.6	51.0	49.3
2007	50.2	49.8	49.8	50.1	50.2	50.4	50.4	50.6	50.6	51.1	51.9	53.0	50.7
2008	51.6	51.0	51.1	51.0	51.1	51.2	51.2	50.7	50.0	49.5	49.8	50.7	50.7
2009	48.4	47.7	47.4	47.8	47.7	47.8	47.6	47.6	47.3	46.9	47.1	48.2	47.6
Information													
1990	35.6	35.8	35.3	34.7	34.9	35.1	35.5	35.4	35.3	34.3	34.6	34.5	35.1
2000	68.6	69.3	70.1	70.9	71.1	71.9	72.8	73.0	72.9	72.9	72.8	73.2	71.6
2001	72.9	72.8	72.4	71.3	70.8	70.5	68.5	67.8	66.6	65.2	64.8	64.0	69.0
2002	62.3	62.0	61.3	60.6	59.6	59.3	58.2	57.9	57.2	56.9	56.9	56.6	59.1
2003	56.1	55.9	55.4	54.7	54.5	54.2	54.0	53.8	53.5	53.2	53.3	53.2	54.3
2004	52.5	52.6	52.3	51.9	52.0	51.9	51.3	51.1	50.4	50.1	50.2	50.0	51.4
2005	49.2	49.0	48.9	48.4	48.4	48.2	47.9	47.7	47.5	47.4	47.7	47.9	48.2
2006	47.7	47.8	48.0	47.7	47.9	48.0	47.8	47.4	47.1	47.2	47.5	47.4	47.6
2007	47.0	47.2	47.2	47.9	48.1	48.5	48.3	48.3	48.0	48.3	48.7	48.9	48.0
2008	48.5	48.7	48.6	48.6	48.5	48.7	48.7	48.5	48.0	48.0	48.2	48.2	48.4
2009	47.5	47.2	47.1	46.7	46.5	46.4	46.3	46.0	45.6	45.5	45.4	45.2	46.3
Financial Activities													
1990	64.4	64.9	65.7	66.2	66.7	67.0	66.7	66.9	66.5	66.1	66.1	66.3	66.1
2000	95.0	95.4	96.0	95.5	95.8	96.6	96.8	96.9	96.6	96.5	96.8	97.7	96.3
2001	96.1	96.3	96.2	96.1	96.1	96.6	95.8	95.4	94.6	94.6	94.6	95.0	95.6
2002	93.5	93.9	93.9	93.5	93.8	94.6	94.5	95.1	95.0	95.8	96.7	97.4	94.8
2003	96.5	96.8	96.9	97.5	98.0	98.7	99.1	99.5	98.9	98.5	98.1	98.6	98.0
2004	97.1	97.4	97.5	97.7	97.9	98.5	98.5	98.4	98.2	98.1	98.0	98.6	98.0
2005	97.3	97.9	98.5	98.8	99.2	99.7	100.3	100.5	100.7	100.6	101.0	101.8	99.7
2006	99.6	99.8	100.0	100.1	100.8	101.4	101.3	101.3	100.9	100.5	100.5	101.1	100.6
2007	99.4	99.9	99.9	100.0	100.1	100.5	100.4	100.0	99.1	98.8	98.7	98.8	99.6
2008	97.5	97.7	98.1	97.8	97.6	98.0	97.9	97.3	96.4	96.0	95.5	95.6	97.1
2009	93.7	93.5	93.0	92.7	92.7	92.6	92.4	92.2	91.6	91.4	91.4	92.5	92.5

Employment by Industry: Denver-Aurora, CO, Selected Years, 1990–2009—*Continued*

(Numbers in thousands, not seasonally adjusted.)

Industry and year	January	February	March	April	May	June	July	August	September	October	November	December	Annual average
Professional and Business Services													
1990	122.8	124.3	126.2	126.1	128.8	131.1	131.7	133.8	133.0	132.0	132.3	132.0	129.5
2000	189.7	190.1	192.6	195.6	197.6	200.6	201.1	202.3	202.5	201.5	201.1	202.1	198.1
2001	193.9	194.9	195.6	197.3	197.2	198.4	197.4	196.8	192.9	189.6	187.0	187.5	194.0
2002	178.9	179.8	180.3	183.5	184.6	185.3	183.6	185.4	183.3	181.2	180.1	180.3	182.2
2003	175.3	175.2	175.5	177.6	178.8	181.1	181.1	182.8	180.7	181.6	180.2	182.1	179.3
2004	176.1	177.8	179.8	184.7	184.9	187.7	188.9	189.2	188.3	187.7	187.0	188.8	185.1
2005	184.3	184.8	186.7	191.1	191.8	194.5	195.9	196.5	195.8	195.1	194.8	196.9	192.4
2006	190.2	192.2	193.8	197.0	199.6	203.5	203.4	204.7	203.9	203.8	203.3	204.6	200.0
2007	201.6	202.7	205.5	208.3	211.1	215.3	215.3	216.6	216.5	215.3	214.3	215.5	211.5
2008	209.7	211.5	212.3	216.3	216.3	218.7	218.0	219.8	217.8	216.2	214.2	212.8	215.3
2009	205.7	202.8	202.7	203.4	203.4	204.1	203.3	202.5	200.9	201.0	199.2	197.4	202.2
Education and Health Services													
1990	70.2	70.8	71.2	71.0	71.7	71.8	71.3	72.2	73.0	73.2	73.9	74.1	72.0
2000	99.8	100.5	100.6	101.4	101.7	102.7	102.4	103.1	103.7	103.7	104.5	105.2	102.4
2001	104.3	105.2	105.7	105.8	106.2	106.3	106.0	106.7	106.4	108.2	108.8	109.1	106.6
2002	108.0	108.6	109.0	109.8	110.0	109.7	109.6	110.2	110.4	111.0	111.4	111.8	110.0
2003	111.3	112.2	112.3	113.1	113.1	113.1	113.0	113.1	113.4	114.1	114.4	114.6	113.1
2004	114.2	115.2	115.7	115.9	116.2	116.1	115.6	116.2	117.0	117.9	118.3	118.5	116.4
2005	117.0	118.6	119.1	119.2	119.8	119.6	118.8	119.3	119.7	119.9	120.6	120.9	119.4
2006	120.3	121.7	122.0	122.7	123.1	123.0	122.3	122.9	123.5	124.7	125.1	125.5	123.1
2007	124.5	126.0	126.8	127.2	127.9	127.8	127.3	127.9	128.5	129.6	130.7	131.5	128.0
2008	130.0	131.8	132.0	132.5	133.4	133.3	132.8	133.8	134.5	136.1	137.1	136.8	133.7
2009	135.7	136.8	136.9	137.1	137.6	137.5	137.3	137.7	137.9	138.6	139.7	139.3	137.7
Leisure and Hospitality													
1990	72.3	73.0	74.4	76.3	79.2	82.6	82.0	83.1	79.5	77.2	76.4	77.2	77.8
2000	108.1	109.3	112.0	113.8	116.7	120.9	121.9	122.0	118.6	115.5	114.6	114.5	115.7
2001	111.4	111.9	113.7	114.7	117.6	122.6	121.7	122.0	118.1	113.9	113.1	113.9	116.2
2002	109.8	110.0	110.8	114.3	117.8	121.6	120.4	120.9	118.0	115.2	114.2	114.6	115.6
2003	110.4	109.7	110.3	112.9	116.1	119.4	119.4	120.6	117.2	116.0	114.8	115.0	115.1
2004	111.4	110.8	113.2	117.1	120.0	123.5	123.4	124.0	120.5	118.2	117.5	117.9	118.1
2005	114.2	114.9	116.9	119.5	123.3	127.3	127.4	127.1	123.9	122.1	120.5	121.1	121.5
2006	118.0	118.1	120.0	122.4	126.0	130.7	131.2	132.0	128.1	125.9	125.5	125.2	125.3
2007	120.4	120.5	123.7	125.8	130.4	134.8	134.3	134.9	130.9	129.2	128.2	128.8	128.5
2008	124.4	124.6	126.7	129.1	133.5	137.9	136.8	136.4	132.1	129.1	126.8	125.8	130.3
2009	120.9	119.9	121.9	124.2	128.2	131.6	132.2	132.2	127.9	126.1	122.9	122.4	125.9
Other Services													
1990	31.4	31.5	31.7	32.2	32.5	33.1	33.1	33.3	32.7	32.8	32.8	32.8	32.5
2000	43.4	43.1	43.6	42.9	43.2	44.2	44.4	44.3	43.8	43.6	43.6	43.9	43.7
2001	43.4	42.9	43.4	43.3	43.6	44.3	44.0	44.1	43.6	43.4	43.5	43.6	43.6
2002	43.7	43.7	43.9	44.1	44.2	44.7	44.8	44.8	44.1	43.8	43.9	43.9	44.1
2003	44.1	43.7	43.6	43.9	44.1	44.8	44.6	44.5	43.7	43.8	43.9	44.1	44.0
2004	44.2	43.9	44.2	44.4	44.8	45.5	45.6	45.8	45.5	45.5	45.3	45.4	45.0
2005	45.4	45.1	45.3	45.3	45.4	45.9	45.6	45.6	45.2	45.0	44.7	45.0	45.3
2006	45.7	45.5	45.9	46.1	46.3	47.1	46.7	46.8	46.4	46.2	46.2	46.4	46.3
2007	46.3	46.3	46.8	46.9	47.1	47.7	47.4	47.5	47.2	47.3	47.2	47.5	47.1
2008	47.8	47.9	48.2	47.9	48.3	48.7	49.0	49.1	48.9	48.7	48.3	47.8	48.4
2009	47.9	47.3	47.4	47.1	47.6	47.9	48.0	47.8	47.4	47.3	47.3	47.7	47.6
Government													
1990	125.7	130.9	131.4	133.4	135.7	134.6	123.4	123.0	132.5	134.1	135.7	134.6	131.3
2000	149.6	153.5	155.1	155.8	159.0	156.0	149.8	150.9	156.9	156.6	157.8	158.7	155.0
2001	154.4	158.2	157.7	158.3	159.2	159.1	153.9	154.8	160.7	161.1	162.9	162.8	158.6
2002	159.5	162.7	164.1	164.4	165.7	164.6	158.9	160.4	164.3	166.1	166.9	166.5	163.7
2003	161.8	165.0	165.5	165.4	167.4	165.9	159.0	159.9	164.2	164.3	164.6	163.7	163.8
2004	159.1	162.6	163.9	165.3	165.9	164.8	157.9	158.2	164.2	165.5	166.2	166.0	163.3
2005	160.4	164.5	164.9	166.5	167.2	165.6	159.6	158.7	166.2	166.7	167.1	167.0	164.5
2006	162.6	166.5	167.6	167.1	168.7	168.3	161.1	161.9	167.8	168.0	168.9	169.2	166.5
2007	163.9	169.0	170.3	170.7	171.8	170.8	163.4	164.3	171.7	172.5	173.4	173.0	169.6
2008	167.9	172.3	173.6	174.2	176.3	174.5	167.7	170.5	175.4	177.4	178.3	177.3	173.8
2009	172.8	175.9	177.3	178.3	180.3	177.8	169.0	170.1	177.1	179.0	179.2	177.6	176.2

Employment by Industry: Detroit-Warren-Livonia, MI, Selected Years, 1990–2009

(Numbers in thousands, not seasonally adjusted.)

Industry and year	January	February	March	April	May	June	July	August	September	October	November	December	Annual average
Total Nonfarm													
1990	1871.9	1883.8	1895.0	1907.8	1934.0	1942.0	1890.7	1896.8	1927.5	1934.3	1927.6	1933.4	1912.1
2000	2160.8	2163.1	2177.3	2210.9	2238.2	2250.0	2171.6	2192.4	2203.1	2225.4	2234.4	2235.9	2205.3
2001	2125.1	2142.0	2151.4	2157.0	2176.1	2182.3	2097.0	2110.4	2122.2	2129.6	2132.6	2139.9	2138.8
2002	2049.3	2059.1	2071.2	2088.6	2114.2	2121.5	2060.5	2080.7	2093.9	2105.5	2114.3	2117.0	2089.7
2003	2052.7	2052.4	2062.2	2067.8	2094.7	2103.4	2019.3	2048.0	2063.1	2073.8	2081.1	2083.2	2066.8
2004	2011.5	2012.7	2024.9	2048.5	2071.9	2074.8	1993.5	2036.0	2061.1	2072.3	2082.9	2081.5	2047.6
2005	2007.5	2022.6	2023.1	2049.0	2073.4	2074.8	2002.9	2032.0	2062.3	2061.2	2074.9	2068.6	2046.0
2006	1990.3	1993.6	2001.6	2013.8	2032.2	2037.6	1955.8	1984.3	2003.4	1997.2	2012.2	2009.2	2002.6
2007	1938.2	1950.9	1954.8	1967.9	1992.9	1996.5	1931.0	1959.5	1969.4	1962.7	1980.1	1972.8	1964.7
2008	1908.8	1910.3	1906.1	1909.9	1930.0	1938.5	1868.1	1888.3	1895.5	1895.2	1886.9	1867.8	1900.5
2009	1752.9	1762.0	1758.6	1758.0	1750.8	1740.1	1706.0	1715.4	1736.0	1743.8	1735.0	1720.8	1740.0
Total Private													
1990	1638.3	1646.2	1656.6	1669.3	1692.1	1712.6	1695.8	1709.3	1708.8	1696.6	1686.9	1693.0	1683.8
2000	1926.5	1926.7	1938.2	1970.4	1994.9	2011.9	1970.0	1995.2	1978.3	1985.4	1992.2	1994.5	1973.7
2001	1889.3	1902.3	1910.6	1915.4	1934.1	1945.0	1892.9	1909.4	1894.2	1888.6	1889.6	1896.3	1905.6
2002	1815.1	1820.0	1830.4	1849.1	1872.6	1884.4	1855.0	1878.4	1865.8	1863.0	1870.9	1874.2	1856.6
2003	1813.2	1808.4	1818.2	1822.6	1848.9	1859.7	1804.5	1836.5	1834.1	1824.6	1832.0	1834.9	1828.1
2004	1772.2	1769.4	1780.3	1805.0	1826.9	1834.7	1782.7	1828.3	1826.7	1830.3	1838.6	1839.9	1811.3
2005	1772.5	1781.7	1782.1	1807.5	1830.1	1836.8	1795.8	1826.4	1829.0	1823.1	1834.3	1831.1	1812.5
2006	1759.0	1756.7	1763.5	1776.2	1793.5	1803.3	1748.4	1780.6	1776.6	1763.5	1776.7	1776.5	1772.9
2007	1709.7	1719.1	1720.7	1735.2	1757.5	1765.3	1726.1	1755.8	1749.2	1736.7	1753.6	1747.7	1739.7
2008	1688.9	1686.4	1681.7	1685.9	1704.3	1715.8	1665.7	1684.8	1678.1	1672.0	1662.8	1646.8	1681.1
2009	1536.3	1541.6	1537.2	1534.6	1528.8	1520.5	1507.8	1520.0	1523.9	1525.2	1517.5	1507.1	1525.0
Goods-Producing													
1990	407.3	417.2	418.0	423.0	430.3	435.7	426.7	435.0	435.4	433.7	417.1	418.0	424.8
2000	473.0	474.9	477.7	491.5	498.8	502.6	485.5	497.6	491.5	491.5	489.1	483.7	488.1
2001	446.5	457.9	457.7	459.1	462.5	464.4	445.1	452.5	452.3	448.0	443.9	444.3	452.9
2002	409.5	415.4	416.5	422.0	426.5	431.3	420.1	430.3	426.7	424.9	424.1	420.9	422.4
2003	400.0	396.1	398.2	395.2	403.9	409.2	378.9	403.4	402.5	395.9	397.9	395.3	398.0
2004	377.2	375.8	380.8	386.5	391.9	392.0	357.3	393.1	393.2	392.0	391.9	386.1	384.8
2005	363.8	369.9	365.1	369.1	379.9	381.7	353.8	375.5	379.5	377.0	379.5	371.7	372.2
2006	345.9	346.3	349.9	356.2	362.0	362.0	326.5	350.9	350.2	342.2	347.4	341.3	348.4
2007	316.6	328.1	328.3	331.0	336.1	338.5	317.7	337.6	335.1	322.3	328.8	323.5	328.6
2008	306.4	307.7	301.8	298.7	302.5	314.1	283.6	300.6	299.8	296.7	293.5	282.0	299.0
2009	233.9	243.6	243.7	241.0	228.8	226.2	227.0	236.7	240.4	237.6	231.2	223.9	234.5
Mining, Logging, and Construction													
1990	63.1	60.9	61.0	63.4	69.9	72.7	74.5	75.0	73.9	71.8	69.8	64.7	68.4
2000	85.5	85.2	88.5	95.5	99.6	102.5	103.9	102.8	101.8	100.5	98.4	93.7	96.5
2001	84.7	84.0	86.1	90.3	95.8	98.3	99.3	99.2	97.9	97.0	95.7	93.3	93.5
2002	83.5	81.8	82.7	87.0	92.3	94.9	95.8	95.4	93.1	92.0	89.9	86.2	89.6
2003	76.0	73.8	74.3	79.5	87.8	91.9	93.0	91.9	90.8	90.3	88.4	85.3	85.3
2004	75.2	74.0	75.8	82.0	87.2	90.8	93.2	92.3	91.0	90.7	89.5	85.7	85.6
2005	76.6	74.8	75.8	81.2	86.5	89.9	92.0	90.4	88.9	87.6	85.9	80.7	84.2
2006	71.5	70.1	70.9	74.6	80.0	82.6	82.8	81.8	79.8	78.5	76.8	72.8	76.9
2007	64.9	62.4	64.4	67.1	72.7	75.5	77.9	77.7	76.4	74.0	71.8	68.1	71.1
2008	61.0	58.6	58.6	61.6	66.8	68.9	69.2	68.9	67.4	66.5	63.3	57.8	64.1
2009	49.8	48.4	48.1	49.8	53.7	54.9	55.2	54.7	53.6	53.7	50.8	47.0	51.6
Manufacturing													
1990	344.2	356.3	357.0	359.6	360.4	363.0	352.2	360.0	361.5	361.9	347.3	353.3	356.4
2000	387.5	389.7	389.2	396.0	399.2	400.1	381.6	394.8	389.7	391.0	390.7	390.0	391.6
2001	361.8	373.9	371.6	368.8	366.7	366.1	345.8	353.3	354.4	351.0	348.2	351.0	359.4
2002	326.0	333.6	333.8	335.0	334.2	336.4	324.3	334.9	333.6	332.9	334.2	334.7	332.8
2003	324.0	322.3	323.9	315.7	316.1	317.3	285.9	311.5	311.7	305.6	309.5	310.0	312.8
2004	302.0	301.8	305.0	304.5	304.7	301.2	264.1	300.8	302.2	301.3	302.4	300.4	299.2
2005	287.2	295.1	289.3	287.9	293.4	291.8	261.8	285.1	290.6	289.4	293.6	291.0	288.0
2006	274.4	276.2	279.0	281.6	282.0	279.4	243.7	269.1	270.4	263.7	270.6	268.5	271.6
2007	251.7	265.7	263.9	263.9	263.4	263.0	239.8	259.9	258.7	248.3	257.0	255.4	257.6
2008	245.4	249.1	243.2	237.1	235.7	245.2	214.4	231.7	232.4	230.2	230.2	224.2	234.9
2009	184.1	195.2	195.6	191.2	175.1	171.3	171.8	182.0	186.8	183.9	180.4	176.9	182.9
Service-Providing													
1990	1464.6	1466.6	1477.0	1484.8	1503.7	1506.3	1464.0	1461.8	1492.1	1500.6	1510.5	1515.4	1487.3
2000	1687.8	1688.2	1699.6	1719.4	1739.4	1747.4	1686.1	1694.8	1711.6	1733.9	1745.3	1752.2	1717.1
2001	1678.6	1684.1	1693.7	1697.9	1713.6	1717.9	1651.9	1657.9	1669.9	1681.6	1688.7	1695.6	1686.0
2002	1639.8	1643.7	1654.7	1666.6	1687.7	1690.2	1640.4	1650.4	1667.2	1680.6	1690.2	1696.1	1667.3
2003	1652.7	1656.3	1664.0	1672.6	1690.8	1694.2	1640.4	1644.6	1660.6	1677.9	1683.2	1687.9	1668.8
2004	1634.3	1636.9	1644.1	1662.0	1680.0	1682.8	1636.2	1642.9	1667.9	1680.3	1691.0	1695.4	1662.8
2005	1643.7	1652.7	1658.0	1679.9	1693.5	1693.1	1649.1	1656.5	1682.8	1684.2	1695.4	1696.9	1673.8
2006	1644.4	1647.3	1651.7	1657.6	1670.2	1675.6	1629.3	1633.4	1653.2	1655.0	1664.8	1667.9	1654.2
2007	1621.6	1622.8	1626.5	1636.9	1656.8	1658.0	1613.3	1621.9	1634.3	1640.4	1651.3	1649.3	1636.1
2008	1602.4	1602.6	1604.3	1611.2	1627.5	1624.4	1584.5	1587.7	1595.7	1598.5	1593.4	1585.8	1601.5
2009	1519.0	1518.4	1514.9	1517.0	1522.0	1513.9	1479.0	1478.7	1495.6	1506.2	1503.8	1496.9	1505.5

Employment by Industry: Detroit-Warren-Livonia, MI, Selected Years, 1990–2009—*Continued*

(Numbers in thousands, not seasonally adjusted.)

Industry and year	January	February	March	April	May	June	July	August	September	October	November	December	Annual average
Trade, Transportation, and Utilities													
1990	389.7	384.8	386.3	386.9	391.1	393.3	391.5	393.1	391.5	388.8	395.2	403.8	391.3
2000	412.6	408.7	409.7	412.3	416.2	420.1	410.6	414.2	413.1	421.5	431.6	440.9	417.6
2001	415.7	411.0	411.6	409.5	411.5	412.7	405.0	406.2	403.8	403.9	411.4	417.4	410.0
2002	394.6	389.4	392.0	390.9	396.3	398.2	393.0	394.8	395.3	394.2	402.6	408.2	395.8
2003	388.7	385.1	385.4	384.3	387.4	388.8	381.6	384.3	384.8	388.4	394.2	399.5	387.7
2004	379.9	376.8	376.9	378.9	383.7	385.1	378.8	380.8	378.7	383.2	391.4	396.9	382.6
2005	376.0	373.5	374.8	376.4	380.0	380.8	378.2	379.5	376.9	379.3	387.1	391.1	379.5
2006	371.8	367.6	368.7	369.7	372.8	374.4	368.8	370.9	369.4	371.5	379.6	384.1	372.4
2007	366.2	361.7	361.5	362.2	366.6	366.8	362.1	365.2	364.4	366.5	375.2	378.7	366.4
2008	363.3	358.3	358.9	357.0	359.7	360.5	356.2	356.4	355.5	354.4	357.2	358.3	358.0
2009	336.6	332.5	330.1	326.1	328.2	327.2	322.8	323.2	322.7	324.0	326.0	328.3	327.3
Wholesale Trade													
1990	89.0	88.8	89.2	89.2	89.6	90.0	90.4	90.8	90.6	89.1	89.1	89.4	89.6
2000	101.4	101.6	101.8	103.0	103.8	104.6	103.3	103.2	102.5	103.1	102.9	103.7	102.9
2001	101.9	102.8	102.6	102.9	103.2	102.7	101.3	100.9	99.8	99.3	99.2	99.6	101.4
2002	98.1	98.5	98.6	98.5	99.1	99.6	98.5	98.8	98.4	97.4	97.7	98.3	98.5
2003	97.3	97.4	97.6	97.6	97.1	97.7	96.1	96.2	95.7	96.0	95.5	95.9	96.7
2004	93.5	93.5	93.9	94.3	94.7	95.0	94.7	94.4	93.7	93.9	93.9	94.1	94.1
2005	93.2	93.2	93.5	93.7	94.2	94.1	93.8	93.5	93.0	93.7	93.4	93.7	93.6
2006	92.4	92.5	92.7	93.0	93.3	93.8	93.0	92.7	91.9	91.8	91.7	91.9	92.6
2007	90.5	90.0	89.8	89.9	90.5	90.4	90.2	89.9	89.4	89.9	89.3	89.7	90.0
2008	89.2	88.8	88.9	89.0	89.3	89.2	88.7	88.5	88.2	87.7	86.7	86.0	88.4
2009	84.1	83.0	81.9	80.9	80.2	78.8	77.7	77.8	77.2	77.1	76.5	76.5	79.3
Retail Trade													
1990	240.6	235.2	235.4	235.1	237.6	238.3	236.9	239.1	237.1	238.0	245.0	252.4	239.2
2000	240.9	237.0	237.9	237.9	241.1	243.8	238.5	241.0	240.9	246.6	256.9	265.6	244.0
2001	244.6	239.8	240.6	236.9	238.7	239.9	235.3	236.3	235.3	236.1	244.6	249.9	239.8
2002	230.8	225.3	226.9	225.9	229.9	231.0	228.0	228.5	229.4	228.9	237.2	242.9	230.4
2003	223.4	220.0	220.2	219.5	223.1	224.0	220.2	221.9	222.8	225.8	232.3	237.1	224.2
2004	221.9	218.6	218.7	219.9	224.3	225.1	220.3	221.6	220.1	223.1	231.3	236.3	223.4
2005	218.7	215.5	216.3	218.7	221.3	222.1	219.8	219.7	218.2	219.9	227.2	230.8	220.7
2006	215.1	210.9	211.5	212.3	214.7	215.7	213.8	214.4	213.5	216.2	223.8	226.6	215.7
2007	212.2	207.0	207.3	207.7	210.7	210.6	209.1	210.2	209.9	212.2	220.7	223.0	211.7
2008	211.3	206.4	206.6	205.6	208.0	207.8	206.6	206.7	205.7	206.3	210.0	211.4	207.7
2009	197.5	193.3	192.3	190.8	194.4	195.6	192.5	192.3	191.4	193.3	195.7	197.2	193.9
Transportation and Utilities													
1990	60.1	60.8	61.7	62.6	63.9	65.0	64.2	63.2	63.8	61.7	61.1	62.0	62.5
2000	70.3	70.1	70.0	71.4	71.3	71.7	68.8	70.0	69.7	71.8	71.8	71.6	70.7
2001	69.2	68.4	68.4	69.7	69.6	70.1	68.4	69.0	68.7	68.5	67.6	67.9	68.8
2002	65.7	65.6	66.5	66.5	67.3	67.6	66.5	67.5	67.5	67.9	67.7	67.0	66.9
2003	68.0	67.7	67.6	67.2	67.2	67.1	65.3	66.2	66.3	66.6	66.4	66.5	66.8
2004	64.5	64.7	64.3	64.7	64.7	65.0	63.8	64.8	64.9	66.2	66.2	66.5	65.0
2005	64.1	64.8	65.0	64.0	64.5	64.6	64.6	66.3	65.7	65.7	66.5	66.6	65.2
2006	64.3	64.2	64.5	64.4	64.8	64.9	62.0	63.8	64.0	63.5	64.1	65.6	64.2
2007	63.5	64.7	64.4	64.6	65.4	65.8	62.8	65.1	65.1	64.4	65.2	66.0	64.8
2008	62.8	63.1	63.4	62.4	62.4	63.5	60.9	61.2	61.6	60.4	60.5	60.9	61.9
2009	55.0	56.2	55.9	54.4	53.6	52.8	52.6	53.1	54.1	53.6	53.8	54.6	54.1
Information													
1990	38.9	38.7	38.9	38.0	38.1	38.6	38.1	38.1	37.9	37.9	37.7	37.8	38.2
2000	41.2	41.2	41.7	41.4	41.9	42.2	42.4	42.5	42.1	42.0	42.6	43.0	42.0
2001	41.8	41.9	42.0	41.8	42.0	42.1	42.1	41.1	40.4	39.5	40.0	39.4	41.2
2002	38.8	38.6	38.6	37.9	38.0	37.9	38.1	37.8	37.2	36.7	36.8	37.5	37.8
2003	37.2	37.3	37.4	36.7	36.9	37.2	36.6	36.4	36.0	36.1	36.4	36.3	36.7
2004	35.8	35.6	35.6	35.7	35.9	36.2	36.0	35.8	35.4	35.4	35.7	35.7	35.7
2005	35.3	34.9	34.9	34.8	35.0	35.1	34.9	34.7	34.3	33.8	34.1	34.2	34.7
2006	33.8	34.0	33.6	33.5	33.8	33.8	33.6	33.5	33.0	33.1	33.2	33.3	33.5
2007	33.5	33.4	33.2	33.4	33.7	33.6	33.4	33.2	32.8	32.8	32.9	32.9	33.2
2008	30.1	30.1	29.7	29.6	29.8	29.9	29.6	29.9	30.2	29.5	29.7	29.3	29.8
2009	28.7	28.7	28.1	27.9	28.0	28.0	27.6	27.3	26.8	26.6	26.6	26.6	27.6
Financial Activities													
1990	113.0	113.4	114.1	112.2	113.6	115.4	116.5	116.9	117.2	114.2	116.0	116.6	114.9
2000	116.4	116.1	116.2	115.5	116.1	117.8	117.7	116.9	115.6	113.9	113.6	114.7	115.9
2001	113.6	115.0	115.5	114.8	116.2	117.3	116.6	116.6	114.9	113.8	114.0	116.4	115.4
2002	116.7	116.7	116.3	116.6	117.2	117.4	117.6	118.3	116.7	116.2	116.8	117.4	117.0
2003	117.8	117.8	117.8	119.8	120.9	121.8	121.4	121.3	119.3	118.1	117.5	118.1	119.3
2004	115.9	115.7	116.2	117.5	118.2	119.2	119.0	118.7	117.6	117.0	117.1	118.0	117.5
2005	117.4	117.5	117.5	118.0	118.2	119.4	118.7	118.7	117.4	117.0	117.0	117.0	117.8
2006	115.3	115.3	114.8	114.6	115.3	116.2	115.5	115.4	113.8	113.1	112.9	113.6	114.7
2007	112.4	112.2	111.9	112.5	112.9	113.7	113.6	112.6	110.5	109.5	109.1	109.0	111.7
2008	106.8	106.7	106.2	105.8	106.7	106.7	105.9	105.0	103.5	102.7	101.9	101.6	105.0
2009	99.7	99.2	98.5	98.7	99.0	99.1	98.2	97.7	96.3	95.6	95.5	94.6	97.7

Employment by Industry: Detroit-Warren-Livonia, MI, Selected Years, 1990–2009—*Continued*

(Numbers in thousands, not seasonally adjusted.)

Industry and year	January	February	March	April	May	June	July	August	September	October	November	December	Annual average
Professional and Business Services													
1990	275.9	276.6	279.2	281.6	285.1	290.0	289.5	290.6	290.9	289.2	286.9	284.6	285.0
2000	392.1	389.8	392.4	401.0	407.6	410.0	402.4	411.3	407.5	405.3	403.0	401.1	402.0
2001	379.6	380.7	382.0	382.1	383.9	385.8	372.6	380.3	375.4	373.3	370.0	368.7	377.9
2002	358.7	359.7	361.1	364.8	368.6	370.4	361.3	369.9	367.5	368.9	368.9	367.9	365.6
2003	359.0	357.6	358.7	363.3	367.6	369.5	359.3	365.6	364.4	357.8	359.4	359.2	361.8
2004	347.9	347.0	347.4	356.0	361.3	364.6	359.4	366.4	366.8	370.5	370.9	371.4	360.8
2005	361.2	361.7	361.0	369.2	371.7	373.7	368.2	373.8	375.5	372.0	372.5	371.8	369.4
2006	359.4	355.9	354.8	357.0	358.6	362.8	356.3	362.1	360.6	359.5	361.1	360.2	359.0
2007	347.0	347.0	344.4	351.3	353.0	355.1	349.7	356.0	353.8	354.2	357.0	353.0	351.8
2008	344.7	344.4	343.0	348.0	349.9	348.1	338.4	339.7	337.1	339.6	334.8	330.3	341.5
2009	308.2	306.7	303.0	301.5	298.3	293.9	290.6	293.0	298.2	300.4	300.5	297.1	299.3
Education and Health Services													
1990	186.0	186.8	187.8	189.5	189.7	191.8	188.8	189.6	191.9	192.4	193.5	193.6	190.1
2000	232.7	235.3	236.4	238.0	237.7	238.7	236.0	236.3	237.3	238.9	241.7	240.5	237.5
2001	235.4	237.8	239.3	241.3	242.8	244.5	240.7	241.4	241.9	244.3	246.6	246.2	241.9
2002	243.4	245.4	246.3	250.0	250.5	252.2	247.9	248.1	247.6	251.1	252.8	252.3	249.0
2003	250.9	253.5	253.7	252.0	252.1	250.7	249.5	249.0	251.9	254.5	256.3	255.7	252.5
2004	252.6	255.0	255.8	258.0	258.1	255.9	256.5	256.0	258.9	261.7	263.4	263.8	258.0
2005	259.5	262.7	263.8	265.5	265.5	263.4	262.2	262.9	267.1	270.8	272.7	273.3	265.8
2006	269.0	271.0	272.8	270.7	272.0	271.0	268.2	267.9	273.1	272.9	274.5	275.4	271.5
2007	272.7	275.4	276.6	276.1	277.5	278.0	273.5	273.4	277.8	279.5	281.4	281.4	276.9
2008	277.8	279.9	280.2	280.5	282.2	280.8	278.3	278.1	281.0	283.3	284.1	284.1	280.9
2009	279.8	283.0	284.0	282.7	284.3	283.7	281.4	281.8	283.0	286.5	287.4	287.4	283.8
Leisure and Hospitality													
1990	141.6	142.1	144.0	148.6	153.4	156.7	155.6	156.0	154.0	151.4	151.2	149.4	150.3
2000	169.6	170.8	172.5	177.6	183.2	186.1	182.0	182.4	178.3	179.9	177.6	177.3	178.1
2001	167.5	167.7	170.7	175.1	182.1	184.9	179.3	179.1	175.5	176.8	174.0	173.3	175.5
2002	165.5	166.3	169.6	175.3	182.3	182.9	183.5	184.7	181.3	180.4	178.5	178.4	177.4
2003	171.6	171.2	174.5	180.0	187.9	190.5	185.2	183.8	183.3	182.7	179.6	179.9	180.9
2004	172.7	172.9	175.8	181.3	187.5	189.9	187.6	188.6	186.1	182.2	178.9	178.5	181.8
2005	171.6	173.1	176.0	183.8	189.4	191.0	188.3	189.7	186.9	182.1	180.1	180.1	182.7
2006	174.3	176.9	178.7	184.3	188.3	191.8	189.5	189.8	186.8	182.3	179.0	179.4	183.4
2007	174.0	173.7	176.8	181.1	189.3	190.6	187.8	189.2	186.7	184.1	181.6	181.3	183.0
2008	174.0	173.3	175.7	179.7	186.0	188.0	186.0	187.5	183.9	179.4	176.1	175.9	180.5
2009	166.0	164.4	166.3	173.0	177.8	177.5	176.1	176.4	172.9	171.1	166.8	165.3	171.1
Other Services													
1990	85.9	86.6	88.3	89.5	90.8	91.1	89.1	90.0	90.0	89.0	89.3	89.2	89.1
2000	88.9	89.9	91.6	93.1	93.4	94.4	93.4	94.0	92.9	92.4	93.0	93.3	92.5
2001	89.2	90.3	91.8	91.7	93.1	93.3	91.5	92.2	90.0	89.0	89.7	90.6	91.0
2002	87.9	88.5	90.0	91.6	93.2	94.1	93.5	94.5	93.5	90.6	90.4	91.6	91.6
2003	88.0	89.8	92.5	91.3	92.2	92.0	92.0	92.7	91.9	91.1	90.7	90.9	91.3
2004	90.2	90.6	91.8	91.1	90.3	91.8	88.1	88.9	90.0	88.3	89.3	89.5	90.0
2005	87.7	88.4	89.0	90.7	90.4	91.7	91.5	91.6	91.4	91.1	91.3	91.0	90.6
2006	89.5	89.7	90.2	90.2	90.7	91.3	90.0	90.1	89.7	88.9	89.0	89.2	89.9
2007	87.3	87.6	88.0	87.6	88.4	89.0	88.3	88.6	88.1	87.8	87.6	87.9	88.0
2008	85.8	86.0	86.2	86.6	87.5	87.7	87.7	87.6	87.1	86.4	85.5	85.3	86.6
2009	83.4	83.5	83.5	83.7	84.4	84.9	84.1	83.9	83.6	83.4	83.5	83.9	83.8
Government													
1990	233.6	237.6	238.4	238.5	241.9	229.4	194.9	187.5	218.7	237.7	240.7	240.4	228.3
2000	234.3	236.4	239.1	240.5	243.3	238.1	201.6	197.2	224.8	240.0	242.2	241.4	231.6
2001	235.8	239.7	240.8	241.6	242.0	237.3	204.1	201.0	228.0	241.0	243.0	243.6	233.2
2002	234.2	239.1	240.8	239.5	241.6	237.1	205.5	202.3	228.1	242.5	243.4	242.8	233.1
2003	239.5	244.0	244.0	245.2	245.8	243.7	214.8	211.5	229.0	249.2	249.1	248.3	238.7
2004	239.3	243.3	244.6	243.5	245.0	240.1	210.8	207.7	234.4	242.0	244.3	241.6	236.4
2005	235.0	240.9	241.0	241.5	243.3	238.0	207.1	205.6	233.3	238.1	240.6	237.5	233.5
2006	231.3	236.9	238.1	237.6	238.7	234.3	207.4	203.7	226.8	233.7	235.5	232.7	229.7
2007	228.5	231.8	234.1	232.7	235.4	231.2	204.9	203.7	220.2	226.0	226.5	225.1	225.0
2008	219.9	223.9	224.4	224.0	225.7	222.7	202.4	203.5	217.4	223.2	224.1	221.0	219.4
2009	216.6	220.4	221.4	223.4	222.0	219.6	198.2	195.4	212.1	218.6	217.5	213.7	214.9

Employment by Industry: El Paso, TX, Selected Years, 1990–2009

(Numbers in thousands, not seasonally adjusted.)

Industry and year	January	February	March	April	May	June	July	August	September	October	November	December	Annual average
Total Nonfarm													
1990	204.8	206.1	206.3	207.2	209.2	209.8	209.3	210.0	210.4	210.7	211.0	210.9	208.8
2000	252.0	253.6	255.4	255.0	256.3	255.9	254.3	256.7	259.1	257.9	259.5	260.7	256.4
2001	254.9	255.6	257.6	255.1	256.3	255.5	251.4	254.7	257.0	253.9	254.8	254.7	255.1
2002	251.6	251.9	254.7	255.3	255.7	254.7	251.7	256.1	261.0	258.6	260.2	261.1	256.1
2003	254.3	255.1	255.4	255.7	254.8	251.2	249.9	253.4	257.4	257.0	258.0	258.3	255.0
2004	254.3	255.8	256.0	256.1	257.3	255.5	255.3	255.7	258.9	259.8	260.7	260.5	257.2
2005	255.2	256.6	258.3	260.1	260.9	260.5	257.3	259.5	264.2	264.2	265.4	266.0	260.7
2006	261.2	262.9	265.4	263.9	264.8	263.5	259.8	262.6	267.7	267.7	269.4	271.3	265.0
2007	265.5	267.0	269.0	270.1	271.5	269.7	266.9	269.0	274.5	277.5	279.0	281.2	271.7
2008	277.4	279.2	279.8	278.3	279.8	276.8	272.5	274.9	277.5	280.5	280.5	280.3	278.1
2009	274.9	274.1	273.8	273.6	272.9	272.3	266.1	267.6	271.2	272.2	273.0	273.0	272.1
Total Private													
1990	161.0	161.8	162.0	162.7	164.4	165.9	166.3	168.0	166.6	165.3	165.4	165.7	164.6
2000	196.0	196.5	198.2	197.5	198.7	200.6	198.9	201.1	202.8	200.8	202.3	203.3	199.7
2001	197.4	197.2	199.1	196.5	197.6	198.4	197.0	198.8	198.3	195.3	195.7	196.5	197.3
2002	193.2	192.5	195.5	196.6	197.9	199.0	198.3	201.1	201.6	198.4	199.8	201.7	198.0
2003	195.0	194.4	194.8	195.2	195.3	194.6	194.4	196.4	196.9	196.6	197.4	198.8	195.8
2004	194.2	194.7	195.0	195.2	195.9	197.0	197.8	198.8	198.3	197.9	198.9	199.6	196.9
2005	194.0	194.6	196.3	198.3	199.0	201.2	200.8	202.5	203.6	202.5	203.9	205.3	200.2
2006	200.2	200.9	203.3	202.2	203.0	205.1	203.8	206.1	206.3	204.9	206.4	208.2	204.2
2007	202.4	203.3	205.2	205.2	206.4	207.6	207.4	209.4	209.6	211.1	212.4	214.7	207.9
2008	211.4	211.8	212.5	213.1	213.8	213.4	213.2	215.5	213.2	213.7	213.7	213.5	213.2
2009	207.9	206.6	206.4	205.6	205.1	205.9	205.4	206.7	204.0	203.9	204.5	204.8	205.6
Goods-Producing													
1990	48.8	49.1	49.1	49.1	49.3	50.3	50.4	51.8	50.8	49.9	49.5	48.9	49.8
2000	51.5	51.5	51.4	50.2	50.5	50.7	49.4	50.7	51.0	49.6	49.5	49.2	50.4
2001	47.7	47.7	47.7	46.0	46.1	46.2	45.7	46.3	46.3	44.9	44.2	44.1	46.1
2002	42.9	41.6	42.4	42.1	41.7	42.0	41.6	43.1	43.2	41.5	40.9	40.8	42.0
2003	39.7	39.6	39.4	39.0	38.3	37.8	37.3	37.7	37.8	36.8	36.4	36.1	37.9
2004	35.3	35.5	35.4	35.4	35.6	35.7	35.6	36.0	36.1	36.3	36.0	35.3	35.7
2005	34.2	34.3	34.6	34.7	35.2	35.3	34.7	35.0	35.6	34.8	34.8	34.7	34.8
2006	34.3	34.2	34.4	34.4	34.7	35.5	34.8	34.8	34.7	34.3	34.1	34.4	34.6
2007	33.7	33.9	34.2	34.4	34.5	34.8	34.7	35.4	35.5	35.7	35.8	35.8	34.9
2008	35.3	35.3	35.2	35.6	35.7	35.5	35.4	35.6	35.4	35.0	34.8	34.3	35.3
2009	33.7	33.2	32.6	32.7	32.6	32.2	32.4	33.0	32.5	32.3	32.1	32.0	32.6
Mining, Logging, and Construction													
1990	8.3	8.2	8.2	8.5	8.6	9.1	9.0	9.1	9.0	9.0	8.8	8.5	8.7
2000	12.9	12.8	12.9	12.6	12.8	12.9	12.5	12.6	12.7	12.5	12.5	12.6	12.7
2001	12.5	12.5	12.7	11.6	11.8	11.8	11.9	12.0	12.3	11.9	11.8	11.8	12.1
2002	11.7	11.7	12.0	11.6	11.5	11.8	11.7	12.0	12.0	11.7	11.7	11.6	11.8
2003	11.9	11.9	11.9	11.8	11.8	11.8	11.6	11.7	11.7	11.6	11.5	11.5	11.7
2004	11.1	11.2	11.3	11.3	11.4	11.6	11.7	11.6	11.6	11.9	11.8	11.8	11.5
2005	11.5	11.6	11.6	11.7	12.0	12.1	12.0	12.1	12.5	12.3	12.3	12.2	12.0
2006	12.2	12.2	12.4	12.5	12.6	12.9	12.8	12.8	12.9	12.9	13.0	13.2	12.7
2007	13.3	13.6	14.0	14.2	14.3	14.6	14.5	15.0	15.1	15.5	15.6	15.6	14.6
2008	15.2	15.2	15.3	15.7	15.8	15.6	15.7	15.9	15.9	15.8	15.7	15.6	15.6
2009	15.3	15.2	15.4	15.3	15.4	15.1	15.4	15.6	15.3	15.2	15.1	15.1	15.3
Manufacturing													
1990	40.5	40.9	40.9	40.6	40.7	41.2	41.4	42.7	41.8	40.9	40.7	40.4	41.1
2000	38.6	38.7	38.5	37.6	37.7	37.8	36.9	38.1	38.3	37.1	37.0	36.6	37.7
2001	35.2	35.2	35.0	34.4	34.3	34.4	33.8	34.3	34.0	33.0	32.4	32.3	34.0
2002	31.2	29.9	30.4	30.5	30.2	30.2	29.9	31.1	31.2	29.8	29.2	29.2	30.2
2003	27.8	27.7	27.5	27.2	26.5	26.0	25.7	26.0	26.1	25.2	24.9	24.6	26.2
2004	24.2	24.3	24.1	24.1	24.2	24.1	23.9	24.4	24.5	24.4	24.2	23.5	24.2
2005	22.7	22.7	23.0	23.0	23.2	23.2	22.7	22.9	23.1	22.5	22.5	22.5	22.8
2006	22.1	22.0	22.0	21.9	22.1	22.6	22.0	22.0	21.8	21.4	21.1	21.2	21.9
2007	20.4	20.3	20.2	20.2	20.2	20.2	20.2	20.4	20.4	20.2	20.2	20.2	20.3
2008	20.1	20.1	19.9	19.9	19.9	19.9	19.7	19.7	19.5	19.2	19.1	18.7	19.6
2009	18.4	18.0	17.2	17.4	17.2	17.1	17.0	17.4	17.2	17.1	17.0	16.9	17.3
Service-Providing													
1990	156.0	157.0	157.2	158.1	159.9	159.5	158.9	158.2	159.6	160.8	161.5	162.0	159.1
2000	200.5	202.1	204.0	204.8	205.8	205.2	204.9	206.0	208.1	208.3	210.0	211.5	205.9
2001	207.2	207.9	209.9	209.1	210.2	209.3	205.7	208.4	210.7	209.0	210.6	210.6	209.1
2002	208.7	210.3	212.3	213.2	214.0	212.7	210.1	213.0	217.8	217.1	219.3	220.3	214.1
2003	214.6	215.5	216.0	216.7	216.5	213.4	212.6	215.7	219.6	220.2	221.6	222.2	217.0
2004	219.0	220.3	220.6	220.7	221.7	219.8	219.7	219.7	222.8	223.5	224.7	225.2	221.5
2005	221.0	222.3	223.7	225.4	225.7	225.2	222.6	224.5	228.6	229.4	230.6	231.3	225.9
2006	226.9	228.7	231.0	229.5	230.1	228.0	225.0	227.8	233.0	233.4	235.3	236.9	230.5
2007	231.8	233.1	234.8	235.7	237.0	234.9	232.2	233.6	239.0	241.8	243.2	245.4	236.9
2008	242.1	243.9	244.6	242.7	244.1	241.3	237.1	239.3	242.1	245.5	245.7	246.0	242.9
2009	241.2	240.9	241.2	240.9	240.3	240.1	233.7	234.6	238.7	239.9	240.9	241.0	239.5

Employment by Industry: El Paso, TX, Selected Years, 1990–2009—*Continued*

(Numbers in thousands, not seasonally adjusted.)

Industry and year	January	February	March	April	May	June	July	August	September	October	November	December	Annual average
Trade, Transportation, and Utilities													
1990	46.2	46.0	45.7	45.6	46.2	46.5	46.6	46.9	47.0	47.2	47.9	48.4	46.7
2000	53.4	52.7	53.2	53.2	53.8	54.2	53.9	54.3	54.7	55.0	56.3	57.0	54.3
2001	54.6	53.6	54.2	53.7	53.8	53.7	53.7	53.8	53.1	52.9	54.1	54.8	53.8
2002	53.0	52.2	53.0	53.2	53.8	54.1	53.7	54.1	54.4	54.6	55.6	56.7	54.0
2003	54.3	53.4	53.9	54.5	54.6	54.6	54.8	55.6	55.6	56.0	57.3	58.1	55.2
2004	55.7	55.4	55.6	54.8	54.9	55.1	55.1	55.3	54.9	55.5	56.8	57.5	55.6
2005	54.9	54.5	54.9	55.3	55.4	55.8	56.1	56.7	56.9	57.0	58.7	59.2	56.3
2006	56.9	56.8	57.6	57.3	57.5	57.7	57.7	58.4	58.5	58.3	59.7	60.4	58.1
2007	58.0	57.6	58.2	58.4	58.6	58.7	58.7	59.2	59.6	60.3	61.4	62.2	59.2
2008	59.9	59.2	59.3	58.9	58.8	58.8	58.9	59.5	58.7	59.0	59.4	59.6	59.2
2009	56.5	55.4	55.4	54.5	54.3	54.5	54.3	54.7	54.5	54.6	55.4	55.9	55.0
Wholesale Trade													
1990	10.3	10.3	10.2	10.2	10.3	10.4	10.4	10.5	10.5	10.4	10.4	10.4	10.4
2000	10.4	10.3	10.4	10.4	10.5	10.5	10.3	10.3	10.3	10.2	10.2	10.3	10.3
2001	10.1	10.1	10.2	10.1	10.1	10.1	10.1	10.1	10.1	9.9	9.9	9.9	10.1
2002	9.7	9.7	9.8	9.8	9.9	9.9	9.8	9.9	9.8	9.7	9.6	9.7	9.8
2003	9.6	9.5	9.6	9.7	9.8	9.8	9.9	10.0	10.0	10.1	10.2	10.3	9.8
2004	10.4	10.3	10.4	10.2	10.2	10.3	10.4	10.4	10.3	10.5	10.5	10.4	10.4
2005	10.1	10.1	10.2	10.2	10.3	10.3	10.3	10.4	10.5	10.4	10.5	10.6	10.3
2006	10.5	10.5	10.6	10.5	10.6	10.6	10.6	10.6	10.6	10.5	10.5	10.5	10.6
2007	10.5	10.5	10.6	10.8	10.8	10.9	10.8	10.9	10.9	11.0	11.0	11.1	10.8
2008	10.8	10.8	10.6	10.9	10.7	10.6	10.8	10.8	10.6	10.6	10.2	10.1	10.6
2009	9.8	9.7	9.6	9.4	9.3	9.3	9.3	9.3	9.2	9.3	9.3	9.3	9.4
Retail Trade													
1990	27.8	27.5	27.4	27.5	27.9	28.0	28.2	28.4	28.4	28.6	29.4	29.7	28.2
2000	30.8	30.1	30.5	30.6	30.9	31.1	31.1	31.4	31.7	32.3	33.5	34.0	31.5
2001	32.3	31.5	32.0	31.6	31.6	31.5	31.7	32.0	31.2	31.3	32.5	33.1	31.9
2002	31.7	30.9	31.5	31.6	32.0	32.3	31.8	32.1	32.5	32.6	33.6	34.5	32.3
2003	32.6	31.9	32.2	32.6	32.6	32.6	32.7	33.4	33.3	33.6	34.8	35.5	33.1
2004	33.1	32.8	32.8	32.2	32.2	32.2	32.0	32.3	31.9	32.1	33.2	34.0	32.6
2005	31.9	31.4	31.6	31.9	31.9	32.2	32.4	32.8	32.8	33.2	34.6	35.1	32.7
2006	33.1	32.9	33.5	33.4	33.4	33.4	33.4	34.0	34.1	34.0	35.4	36.0	33.9
2007	34.0	33.5	34.0	33.9	34.1	34.1	34.2	34.6	35.0	35.8	36.8	37.4	34.8
2008	35.7	35.0	35.3	34.6	34.6	34.8	34.8	35.2	34.9	35.1	35.9	36.2	35.2
2009	33.9	33.0	33.1	32.6	32.5	32.7	32.5	32.9	32.9	32.9	33.6	33.9	33.0
Transportation and Utilities													
1990	8.1	8.2	8.1	7.9	8.0	8.1	8.0	8.0	8.1	8.2	8.1	8.3	8.1
2000	12.2	12.3	12.3	12.2	12.4	12.6	12.5	12.6	12.7	12.5	12.6	12.7	12.5
2001	12.2	12.0	12.0	12.0	12.1	12.1	11.9	11.7	11.8	11.7	11.7	11.8	11.9
2002	11.6	11.6	11.7	11.8	11.9	11.9	12.1	12.1	12.1	12.3	12.4	12.5	12.0
2003	12.1	12.0	12.1	12.2	12.2	12.2	12.2	12.2	12.3	12.3	12.3	12.3	12.2
2004	12.2	12.3	12.4	12.4	12.5	12.6	12.7	12.6	12.7	12.9	13.1	13.1	12.6
2005	12.9	13.0	13.1	13.2	13.2	13.3	13.4	13.5	13.6	13.4	13.6	13.5	13.3
2006	13.3	13.4	13.5	13.4	13.5	13.7	13.7	13.8	13.8	13.8	13.8	13.9	13.6
2007	13.5	13.6	13.6	13.7	13.7	13.7	13.7	13.7	13.7	13.5	13.6	13.7	13.6
2008	13.4	13.4	13.4	13.4	13.5	13.4	13.3	13.5	13.2	13.3	13.3	13.3	13.4
2009	12.8	12.7	12.7	12.5	12.5	12.5	12.5	12.5	12.4	12.4	12.5	12.7	12.6
Information													
1990	3.4	3.5	3.5	3.5	3.6	3.6	3.6	3.5	3.5	3.5	3.5	3.6	3.5
2000	4.9	4.8	4.9	4.9	4.9	4.9	4.9	4.9	4.9	4.8	4.9	5.0	4.9
2001	4.8	4.8	4.8	4.9	5.0	5.1	4.9	4.9	5.0	4.9	5.0	4.9	4.9
2002	5.0	4.9	4.9	5.0	5.0	5.0	5.1	5.2	5.2	5.2	5.3	5.5	5.1
2003	5.5	5.5	5.4	5.5	5.5	5.4	5.4	5.4	5.3	5.5	5.6	5.3	5.4
2004	5.1	5.1	5.0	4.9	4.9	4.9	4.9	4.9	4.8	4.9	4.8	4.9	4.9
2005	4.7	4.7	4.7	4.8	4.8	4.9	4.8	4.8	4.7	4.7	4.8	4.7	4.8
2006	4.7	4.7	4.9	4.6	4.7	4.9	4.6	4.6	4.7	4.8	4.8	5.0	4.8
2007	4.9	5.0	5.0	5.0	5.0	5.0	5.3	5.3	5.2	5.5	5.5	5.5	5.2
2008	5.7	5.7	5.7	5.6	5.8	5.8	5.5	5.5	5.4	5.4	5.4	5.4	5.6
2009	5.3	5.4	5.3	5.3	5.2	5.2	5.1	5.0	5.0	5.0	5.0	4.9	5.1
Financial Activities													
1990	9.4	9.3	9.3	9.3	9.4	9.5	9.3	9.3	9.2	9.0	8.9	9.0	9.2
2000	10.2	10.1	10.1	10.1	10.1	10.3	10.3	10.3	10.3	10.3	10.3	10.4	10.2
2001	10.9	10.9	11.2	11.0	11.1	11.3	11.6	11.7	11.7	11.7	11.7	11.8	11.4
2002	11.8	11.9	12.0	11.8	11.8	11.8	11.8	11.7	11.7	11.8	12.0	12.0	11.8
2003	12.0	12.0	12.1	11.9	11.9	11.9	12.0	11.9	11.8	11.7	11.7	11.6	11.8
2004	11.5	11.6	11.6	11.4	11.3	11.4	11.4	11.4	11.4	11.4	11.3	11.4	11.4
2005	11.2	11.2	11.3	11.4	11.4	11.4	11.5	11.5	11.5	11.5	11.4	11.5	11.4
2006	11.2	11.3	11.3	11.0	11.0	11.1	11.1	11.2	11.3	11.3	11.4	11.5	11.2
2007	11.3	11.3	11.4	11.5	11.6	11.6	11.6	11.7	11.7	11.7	11.8	12.1	11.6
2008	12.1	12.2	12.2	11.9	12.0	12.1	12.2	12.3	12.2	12.3	12.2	12.2	12.2
2009	12.1	12.1	12.1	12.1	12.0	11.9	11.9	12.0	12.0	12.0	12.0	12.0	12.0

Employment by Industry: El Paso, TX, Selected Years, 1990–2009—*Continued*

(Numbers in thousands, not seasonally adjusted.)

Industry and year	January	February	March	April	May	June	July	August	September	October	November	December	Annual average
Professional and Business Services													
1990	13.4	13.7	13.9	13.9	14.0	14.1	14.3	14.0	13.9	13.9	14.0	14.1	13.9
2000	23.8	24.6	25.4	25.2	25.2	25.6	25.0	25.3	25.8	26.0	26.3	26.5	25.4
2001	25.3	25.5	25.7	25.3	25.1	25.2	24.4	24.9	24.9	25.1	24.6	24.7	25.1
2002	24.9	25.5	25.8	26.1	26.1	26.3	26.5	26.8	27.1	27.4	27.3	27.9	26.5
2003	25.6	25.5	24.8	25.0	25.0	24.5	24.8	25.3	26.0	26.6	26.5	27.4	25.5
2004	26.6	26.5	26.1	27.2	27.1	27.4	28.0	28.1	27.8	26.9	26.9	26.9	27.1
2005	25.6	25.8	25.9	26.2	25.8	26.4	26.8	27.3	27.8	27.9	28.1	28.7	26.9
2006	28.2	28.3	28.6	28.6	28.7	29.2	29.3	30.7	30.9	31.0	31.4	31.6	29.7
2007	30.5	30.9	30.8	30.1	29.9	29.8	29.8	30.3	30.2	30.9	30.8	31.4	30.5
2008	30.7	31.0	31.0	31.1	30.8	30.7	31.2	32.4	31.6	32.1	31.8	31.8	31.4
2009	31.2	30.7	30.7	30.8	29.7	29.8	29.5	29.9	29.2	29.5	29.4	29.4	30.0
Education and Health Services													
1990	15.6	15.9	16.0	16.0	16.1	15.9	16.2	16.4	16.4	16.6	16.7	16.6	16.2
2000	23.6	24.0	24.0	23.8	24.0	24.1	24.4	24.7	25.1	25.1	25.3	25.5	24.5
2001	25.1	25.3	25.6	25.6	25.8	26.2	26.1	26.3	26.5	26.0	26.2	26.4	25.9
2002	26.3	26.6	26.8	27.2	27.6	27.7	28.1	28.5	28.5	27.6	27.8	28.0	27.6
2003	27.7	28.0	28.3	28.5	28.6	28.7	28.7	29.0	29.2	29.1	29.2	29.3	28.6
2004	28.8	29.1	29.4	29.6	29.9	30.0	30.4	30.6	31.0	31.5	31.7	32.0	30.3
2005	31.8	32.1	32.3	32.4	32.5	32.9	33.0	33.1	33.2	33.2	33.3	33.5	32.8
2006	33.3	33.5	33.6	32.9	32.4	32.2	32.0	32.4	32.0	31.3	31.5	31.4	32.4
2007	31.0	31.3	31.5	31.5	31.8	32.2	32.1	32.4	32.3	32.1	32.3	32.7	31.9
2008	32.3	32.7	32.9	32.6	32.9	32.9	32.7	33.0	33.1	33.2	33.5	33.7	33.0
2009	33.5	33.9	33.9	33.9	34.2	35.3	35.8	35.8	35.0	35.2	35.3	35.4	34.8
Leisure and Hospitality													
1990	16.9	16.9	17.1	17.9	18.4	18.6	18.4	18.6	18.3	17.7	17.4	17.6	17.8
2000	21.3	21.4	21.7	22.6	22.8	23.2	23.3	23.2	23.3	22.3	22.1	22.2	22.5
2001	21.5	21.8	22.2	22.3	22.9	22.9	22.9	23.0	23.0	22.0	22.1	22.0	22.4
2002	21.6	22.0	22.6	23.2	23.8	24.0	23.6	23.8	23.7	22.6	23.1	23.1	23.1
2003	22.7	22.8	23.3	23.3	23.9	24.1	23.9	24.0	23.8	23.2	23.2	23.5	23.4
2004	23.6	23.7	24.0	24.6	24.8	25.0	25.0	25.0	24.9	24.0	24.0	24.1	24.4
2005	24.2	24.6	25.0	25.7	26.0	26.5	26.2	26.3	26.1	25.6	25.2	25.5	25.6
2006	24.5	24.9	25.6	25.8	26.3	26.7	26.4	26.2	26.4	25.9	25.6	26.0	25.9
2007	25.6	25.8	26.5	26.6	27.1	27.4	27.1	26.9	26.8	26.6	26.4	26.5	26.6
2008	26.8	26.8	27.2	27.9	28.2	28.0	27.8	27.7	27.3	27.3	27.2	27.1	27.4
2009	26.4	26.7	27.1	27.1	28.0	27.9	27.4	27.5	27.0	26.6	26.5	26.5	27.1
Other Services													
1990	7.3	7.4	7.4	7.4	7.4	7.4	7.5	7.5	7.5	7.5	7.5	7.5	7.4
2000	7.3	7.4	7.5	7.5	7.4	7.6	7.7	7.7	7.7	7.7	7.6	7.5	7.6
2001	7.5	7.6	7.7	7.7	7.8	7.8	7.7	7.9	7.8	7.8	7.8	7.8	7.7
2002	7.7	7.8	8.0	8.0	8.1	8.1	7.9	7.9	7.8	7.7	7.8	7.7	7.9
2003	7.5	7.6	7.6	7.5	7.5	7.6	7.5	7.5	7.4	7.7	7.5	7.5	7.5
2004	7.6	7.8	7.9	7.3	7.4	7.5	7.4	7.5	7.4	7.4	7.4	7.5	7.5
2005	7.4	7.4	7.6	7.8	7.9	8.0	7.7	7.8	7.8	7.8	7.6	7.5	7.7
2006	7.1	7.2	7.3	7.6	7.7	7.8	7.9	7.8	7.8	8.0	7.9	7.9	7.7
2007	7.4	7.5	7.6	7.7	7.9	8.1	8.1	8.2	8.3	8.3	8.4	8.5	8.0
2008	8.6	8.9	9.0	9.5	9.6	9.6	9.5	9.5	9.5	9.4	9.4	9.4	9.3
2009	9.2	9.2	9.3	9.2	9.1	9.1	9.0	8.8	8.8	8.7	8.8	8.7	9.0
Government													
1990	43.8	44.3	44.3	44.5	44.8	43.9	43.0	42.0	43.8	45.4	45.6	45.2	44.2
2000	56.0	57.1	57.2	57.5	57.6	55.3	55.4	55.6	56.3	57.1	57.2	57.4	56.6
2001	57.5	58.4	58.5	58.6	58.7	57.1	54.4	55.9	58.7	58.6	59.1	58.2	57.8
2002	58.4	59.4	59.2	58.7	57.8	55.7	53.4	55.0	59.4	60.2	60.4	59.4	58.1
2003	59.3	60.7	60.6	60.5	59.5	56.6	55.5	57.0	60.5	60.4	60.6	59.5	59.2
2004	60.1	61.1	61.0	60.9	61.4	58.5	57.5	56.9	60.6	61.9	61.8	60.9	60.2
2005	61.2	62.0	62.0	61.8	61.9	59.3	56.5	57.0	60.6	61.7	61.5	60.7	60.5
2006	61.0	62.0	62.1	61.7	61.8	58.4	56.0	56.5	61.4	62.8	63.0	63.1	60.8
2007	63.1	63.7	63.8	64.9	65.1	62.1	59.5	59.6	64.9	66.4	66.6	66.5	63.9
2008	66.0	67.4	67.3	65.2	66.0	63.4	59.3	59.4	64.3	66.8	66.8	66.8	64.9
2009	67.0	67.5	67.4	68.0	67.8	66.4	60.7	60.9	67.2	68.3	68.5	68.2	66.5

Employment by Industry: Fresno, CA, Selected Years, 1990–2009

(Numbers in thousands, not seasonally adjusted.)

Industry and year	January	February	March	April	May	June	July	August	September	October	November	December	Annual average
Total Nonfarm													
1990	213.2	215.5	217.8	222.4	224.4	226.4	226.2	228.0	233.7	230.3	228.4	228.0	224.5
2000	261.7	264.7	267.0	268.4	271.2	271.8	272.1	272.1	274.3	274.3	274.8	275.2	270.6
2001	268.0	270.4	273.1	274.3	276.0	277.3	277.5	279.7	278.1	278.3	279.2	278.9	275.9
2002	271.8	275.0	277.7	280.3	283.6	284.2	282.9	285.4	286.1	285.2	286.6	284.8	282.0
2003	276.3	277.6	280.2	280.5	284.4	286.9	282.5	283.3	285.1	285.7	285.2	284.1	282.6
2004	277.9	281.2	282.0	285.6	288.9	287.6	286.8	289.2	291.2	291.5	291.3	289.9	286.9
2005	284.3	287.5	289.6	294.1	295.2	295.3	293.2	295.5	296.5	299.2	299.8	301.6	294.3
2006	293.7	297.7	301.1	301.7	304.8	303.7	300.7	302.9	306.2	306.1	306.4	306.2	302.6
2007	299.4	302.8	306.0	308.1	309.0	308.7	307.0	308.6	308.5	307.0	306.2	305.4	306.4
2008	298.5	302.1	303.7	305.9	308.4	306.6	300.5	301.8	303.7	303.8	301.6	299.4	303.0
2009	289.2	290.1	290.7	290.5	291.7	287.3	282.1	282.6	283.4	284.9	284.2	282.4	286.6
Total Private													
1990	163.5	165.7	167.0	170.0	172.1	175.1	178.9	180.4	182.5	178.1	176.1	176.0	173.8
2000	198.1	199.5	201.1	202.2	204.0	207.0	209.0	210.4	210.4	207.8	208.0	208.7	205.5
2001	201.6	203.3	205.0	205.7	207.9	208.9	211.7	214.5	212.2	210.1	210.0	210.3	208.4
2002	203.6	205.4	207.2	209.2	211.9	213.6	216.0	219.2	219.2	216.0	216.6	216.1	212.8
2003	208.0	208.3	210.7	210.6	214.7	217.1	216.6	219.9	220.6	218.5	217.9	217.9	215.0
2004	211.5	213.2	213.8	216.7	221.1	220.8	223.3	225.8	226.0	224.3	223.9	223.3	220.3
2005	217.8	219.5	220.5	224.7	225.9	227.0	229.3	232.0	231.5	232.1	232.5	234.9	227.3
2006	227.2	229.5	231.1	231.8	234.5	235.9	237.0	239.3	240.2	237.6	237.9	238.3	235.0
2007	231.8	233.0	234.8	236.1	237.5	238.7	241.2	243.1	241.2	237.2	236.3	235.9	237.2
2008	229.5	230.4	231.0	232.6	235.8	234.9	235.5	236.5	235.6	233.5	231.3	230.0	233.1
2009	221.0	219.9	219.4	218.5	220.5	218.7	217.2	218.2	217.0	215.9	216.0	215.2	218.1
Goods-Producing													
1990	35.2	36.2	37.3	39.0	40.0	40.8	41.7	42.7	43.5	42.4	39.6	38.9	39.8
2000	40.7	40.6	40.8	41.2	41.7	43.0	46.2	46.5	45.8	44.0	43.6	43.0	43.1
2001	41.2	41.4	41.9	42.1	43.0	43.4	45.5	47.3	46.5	44.3	42.5	42.4	43.5
2002	40.9	41.2	41.8	42.0	43.5	44.1	45.5	48.0	48.2	45.2	44.3	43.4	44.0
2003	42.0	42.0	42.8	42.6	44.9	46.6	46.5	49.1	49.5	47.6	45.8	45.2	45.4
2004	43.7	43.9	44.2	45.8	48.4	47.4	50.5	52.0	51.5	49.2	48.0	47.3	47.7
2005	45.3	46.0	46.1	47.1	47.6	48.4	51.5	52.7	51.6	50.7	50.0	50.5	49.0
2006	48.7	49.3	49.3	49.3	50.6	51.2	52.6	53.8	53.6	51.6	50.4	49.8	50.9
2007	48.2	48.1	48.6	48.7	49.3	49.7	52.9	53.6	51.7	48.3	46.7	45.9	49.3
2008	44.1	44.2	44.3	44.7	46.4	46.2	47.1	47.3	46.7	45.0	42.9	41.8	45.1
2009	39.8	38.8	38.8	38.5	40.0	39.1	40.1	40.5	39.8	38.9	38.2	37.4	39.2
Mining and Logging													
1990	0.6	0.6	0.6	0.7	0.7	0.8	0.8	0.7	0.8	0.8	0.8	0.7	0.7
2000	0.3	0.3	0.3	0.3	0.4	0.4	0.4	0.4	0.4	0.4	0.4	0.3	0.4
2001	0.3	0.3	0.3	0.3	0.3	0.4	0.4	0.4	0.4	0.4	0.3	0.3	0.3
2002	0.3	0.3	0.2	0.3	0.3	0.3	0.2	0.3	0.3	0.2	0.3	0.2	0.3
2003	0.2	0.2	0.2	0.2	0.2	0.2	0.2	0.2	0.2	0.2	0.2	0.2	0.2
2004	0.2	0.2	0.2	0.2	0.2	0.2	0.2	0.2	0.2	0.2	0.2	0.2	0.2
2005	0.2	0.2	0.2	0.2	0.2	0.2	0.2	0.2	0.2	0.2	0.2	0.2	0.2
2006	0.2	0.2	0.2	0.2	0.2	0.2	0.2	0.2	0.2	0.2	0.2	0.1	0.2
2007	0.1	0.1	0.1	0.1	0.1	0.1	0.2	0.2	0.2	0.2	0.2	0.1	0.1
2008	0.1	0.1	0.1	0.1	0.1	0.1	0.2	0.1	0.1	0.2	0.2	0.1	0.1
2009	0.2	0.2	0.2	0.2	0.2	0.2	0.2	0.2	0.2	0.2	0.2	0.2	0.2
Construction													
1990	12.8	13.0	13.8	14.4	14.7	15.3	15.8	15.7	15.6	15.6	15.1	14.9	14.7
2000	14.1	14.0	14.1	14.6	14.9	15.5	15.6	15.8	16.1	15.5	15.7	15.7	15.1
2001	14.6	14.8	15.1	15.5	16.0	16.6	16.4	16.8	16.5	16.6	16.2	16.2	15.9
2002	16.0	16.2	16.6	16.7	17.1	17.1	17.2	17.4	17.1	17.1	17.2	17.0	16.9
2003	16.5	16.5	17.2	17.6	18.1	18.8	18.6	18.8	18.8	18.8	18.5	18.4	18.1
2004	18.4	18.7	19.0	19.7	19.8	20.1	20.5	20.8	20.8	20.7	20.3	20.3	19.9
2005	19.3	19.8	20.2	20.7	20.9	21.6	22.4	22.7	22.7	22.7	22.9	23.1	21.6
2006	22.3	22.6	22.6	22.8	23.4	23.7	23.8	24.0	23.6	23.3	23.0	22.9	23.2
2007	21.7	21.5	21.9	21.8	21.7	21.9	21.7	21.4	20.4	20.0	19.7	19.0	21.1
2008	17.9	18.1	18.1	18.6	18.6	18.4	18.5	18.3	17.7	17.4	16.7	16.0	17.9
2009	14.6	14.1	14.3	14.1	14.2	14.0	13.9	13.7	13.3	13.0	12.8	12.3	13.7
Manufacturing													
1990	21.8	22.6	22.9	23.9	24.6	24.7	25.1	26.3	27.1	26.0	23.7	23.3	24.3
2000	26.3	26.3	26.4	26.3	26.4	27.1	30.2	30.3	29.3	28.1	27.5	27.0	27.6
2001	26.3	26.3	26.5	26.3	26.7	26.4	28.7	30.1	29.6	27.3	26.0	25.9	27.2
2002	24.6	24.7	25.0	25.0	26.1	26.7	28.1	30.3	30.8	27.9	26.8	26.2	26.9
2003	25.3	25.3	25.4	24.8	26.6	27.6	27.7	30.1	30.5	28.6	27.1	26.6	27.1
2004	25.1	25.0	25.0	25.9	28.4	27.1	29.8	31.0	30.5	28.3	27.5	26.8	27.5
2005	25.8	26.0	25.7	26.2	26.5	26.6	28.9	29.8	28.7	27.8	26.9	27.2	27.2
2006	26.2	26.5	26.5	26.3	27.0	27.3	28.6	29.6	29.8	28.1	27.2	26.8	27.5
2007	26.4	26.5	26.6	26.8	27.5	27.7	31.0	32.0	31.1	28.1	26.8	26.8	28.1
2008	26.1	26.0	26.1	26.0	27.7	27.7	28.4	28.9	28.9	27.4	26.0	25.7	27.1
2009	25.0	24.5	24.3	24.2	25.6	24.9	26.0	26.6	26.3	25.7	25.2	24.9	25.3

Employment by Industry: Fresno, CA, Selected Years, 1990–2009—*Continued*
(Numbers in thousands, not seasonally adjusted.)

Industry and year	January	February	March	April	May	June	July	August	September	October	November	December	Annual average
Service-Providing													
1990	178.0	179.3	180.5	183.4	184.4	185.6	184.5	185.3	190.2	187.9	188.8	189.1	184.8
2000	221.0	224.1	226.2	227.2	229.5	228.8	225.9	225.6	228.5	230.3	231.2	232.2	227.5
2001	226.8	229.0	231.2	232.2	233.0	233.9	232.0	232.4	231.6	234.0	236.7	236.5	232.4
2002	230.9	233.8	235.9	238.3	240.1	240.1	237.4	237.4	237.9	240.0	242.3	241.4	238.0
2003	234.3	235.6	237.4	237.9	239.5	240.3	236.0	234.2	235.6	238.1	239.4	238.9	237.3
2004	234.2	237.3	237.8	239.8	240.5	240.2	236.3	237.2	239.7	242.3	243.3	242.6	239.3
2005	239.0	241.5	243.5	247.0	247.6	246.9	241.7	242.8	244.9	248.5	249.8	251.1	245.4
2006	245.0	248.4	251.8	252.4	254.2	252.5	248.1	249.1	252.6	254.5	256.0	256.4	251.8
2007	251.2	254.7	257.4	259.4	259.7	259.0	254.1	255.0	256.8	258.7	259.5	259.5	257.1
2008	254.4	257.9	259.4	261.2	262.0	260.4	253.4	254.5	257.0	258.8	258.7	257.6	257.9
2009	249.4	251.3	251.9	252.0	251.7	248.2	242.0	242.1	243.6	246.0	246.0	245.0	247.4
Trade, Transportation, and Utilities													
1990	47.0	47.0	46.7	47.9	48.5	49.1	49.5	49.3	49.2	48.8	50.1	50.4	48.6
2000	51.3	51.3	51.7	51.5	52.2	52.9	53.1	53.5	53.9	53.7	54.9	55.3	52.9
2001	52.3	52.2	52.6	53.1	53.5	53.9	54.2	54.6	54.5	54.6	55.6	55.7	53.9
2002	53.0	52.7	52.7	53.5	53.5	54.6	55.2	55.7	55.8	56.1	57.5	57.9	54.9
2003	54.3	53.9	54.3	55.1	55.6	56.5	56.4	56.5	56.5	56.5	57.3	57.9	55.9
2004	54.5	54.3	54.0	54.6	55.4	56.2	56.0	56.1	56.4	56.5	57.3	57.6	55.7
2005	55.7	55.1	55.3	55.8	56.2	56.9	57.3	57.9	58.0	58.4	59.1	60.0	57.1
2006	56.8	56.4	57.0	56.9	57.5	58.4	58.7	59.0	59.5	59.6	60.8	60.9	58.5
2007	58.7	58.2	58.8	59.1	59.9	60.6	61.1	61.4	61.3	61.1	62.0	62.6	60.4
2008	58.8	58.0	58.0	57.8	59.2	59.3	59.4	59.7	60.0	59.8	60.1	60.0	59.2
2009	56.4	55.6	55.1	54.7	55.3	55.4	54.8	55.2	55.5	55.5	56.5	56.8	55.6
Wholesale Trade													
1990	11.4	11.5	11.4	11.7	12.0	12.1	12.2	12.1	12.1	11.8	11.9	11.9	11.8
2000	11.7	11.8	12.0	12.0	12.1	12.2	12.3	12.4	12.2	12.0	12.0	12.0	12.1
2001	11.6	11.7	11.8	12.0	12.0	12.1	12.4	12.6	12.3	12.1	12.0	11.8	12.0
2002	11.8	11.8	11.9	12.3	12.3	12.7	12.8	12.9	12.8	13.0	12.9	12.9	12.5
2003	12.2	12.2	12.3	12.6	12.7	12.9	12.7	12.7	12.6	12.6	12.3	12.2	12.5
2004	11.6	11.8	11.7	11.9	12.2	12.4	12.6	12.7	12.7	12.6	12.3	12.2	12.2
2005	12.0	12.0	12.1	12.3	12.4	12.8	13.0	13.1	13.2	13.1	13.0	12.9	12.7
2006	12.7	12.8	12.9	12.9	13.1	13.7	13.6	13.6	13.6	13.6	13.3	13.0	13.2
2007	12.9	13.0	13.3	13.3	13.6	14.0	14.0	14.0	13.8	13.5	13.3	13.0	13.5
2008	12.5	12.5	12.6	12.9	13.1	13.4	13.3	13.2	13.1	12.8	12.6	12.3	12.9
2009	11.9	11.8	11.7	11.7	11.8	12.1	12.0	12.0	12.0	12.0	11.9	11.8	11.9
Retail Trade													
1990	27.0	26.7	26.8	27.4	27.8	28.1	28.3	28.1	28.1	28.4	29.5	29.9	28.0
2000	31.0	30.9	31.1	30.8	31.2	31.7	31.5	31.6	32.1	32.3	33.6	34.1	31.8
2001	32.0	31.8	32.0	32.1	32.4	32.6	32.3	32.4	32.6	32.8	34.0	34.5	32.6
2002	32.4	32.1	32.0	32.1	32.2	32.7	32.7	32.9	33.0	33.2	34.6	35.2	32.9
2003	33.0	32.6	32.7	33.0	33.2	33.7	33.8	33.8	34.0	34.0	35.4	36.1	33.8
2004	33.6	33.2	32.9	33.2	33.6	34.0	33.7	33.7	34.0	34.2	35.4	35.8	33.9
2005	34.6	34.0	34.0	34.4	34.5	34.6	34.7	35.1	35.1	35.6	36.6	37.7	35.1
2006	35.0	34.5	34.8	34.6	34.7	34.7	34.8	35.1	35.2	35.5	36.7	37.3	35.2
2007	35.7	35.1	35.3	35.5	35.9	36.0	36.2	36.4	36.4	36.6	37.7	38.5	36.3
2008	35.8	35.1	35.0	35.0	35.0	34.8	34.9	35.0	35.2	35.6	36.3	36.6	35.4
2009	33.8	33.2	32.9	32.5	32.8	32.6	32.3	32.5	32.6	32.6	33.8	34.2	33.0
Transportation and Utilities													
1990	8.6	8.8	8.5	8.8	8.7	8.9	9.0	9.1	9.0	8.6	8.7	8.6	8.8
2000	8.6	8.6	8.6	8.7	8.9	9.0	9.3	9.5	9.6	9.4	9.3	9.2	9.1
2001	8.7	8.7	8.8	9.0	9.1	9.2	9.5	9.6	9.6	9.7	9.6	9.4	9.2
2002	8.8	8.8	8.8	9.1	9.0	9.2	9.7	9.9	10.0	9.9	10.0	9.8	9.4
2003	9.1	9.1	9.3	9.5	9.7	9.9	9.9	10.0	9.9	9.9	9.6	9.6	9.6
2004	9.3	9.3	9.4	9.5	9.6	9.8	9.7	9.7	9.7	9.7	9.6	9.6	9.6
2005	9.1	9.1	9.2	9.1	9.3	9.5	9.6	9.7	9.7	9.7	9.5	9.4	9.4
2006	9.1	9.1	9.3	9.4	9.7	10.0	10.3	10.3	10.7	10.5	10.8	10.6	10.0
2007	10.1	10.1	10.2	10.3	10.4	10.6	10.9	11.0	11.1	11.0	11.0	11.1	10.7
2008	10.5	10.4	10.4	9.9	11.1	11.1	11.2	11.5	11.7	11.4	11.2	11.1	11.0
2009	10.7	10.6	10.5	10.5	10.7	10.7	10.5	10.7	10.9	10.9	10.8	10.8	10.7
Information													
1990	4.5	4.5	4.4	4.3	4.4	4.4	4.4	4.4	4.4	4.5	4.5	4.6	4.4
2001	5.5	5.4	5.4	5.1	5.1	5.0	5.1	5.0	4.9	4.7	4.8	4.8	5.1
2002	4.9	4.8	4.9	4.8	4.7	4.7	4.6	4.6	4.5	4.6	4.6	4.5	4.7
2003	4.0	4.1	4.0	4.0	4.0	4.1	4.2	4.3	4.2	4.4	4.5	4.6	4.2
2004	4.5	4.5	4.5	4.5	4.6	4.6	4.6	4.6	4.6	4.7	4.5	4.5	4.6
2005	4.4	4.5	4.4	4.4	4.4	4.4	4.3	4.3	4.3	4.2	4.3	4.2	4.3
2006	4.2	4.2	4.2	4.2	4.2	4.2	4.2	4.2	4.2	4.2	4.2	4.2	4.2
2007	4.1	4.2	4.1	4.1	4.2	4.2	4.2	4.2	4.2	4.2	4.2	4.2	4.2
2008	4.5	4.5	4.4	4.8	4.8	4.8	4.9	4.9	4.8	4.8	4.8	4.8	4.7
2009	4.6	4.6	4.5	4.4	4.4	4.4	4.3	4.4	4.3	4.3	4.3	4.3	4.4

Employment by Industry: Fresno, CA, Selected Years, 1990–2009—*Continued*

(Numbers in thousands, not seasonally adjusted.)

Industry and year	January	February	March	April	May	June	July	August	September	October	November	December	Annual average
Financial Activities													
1990	12.2	12.3	12.3	12.6	12.5	12.6	12.6	12.7	12.8	12.9	12.8	12.8	12.6
2000	13.4	13.6	13.6	13.2	13.2	13.5	13.4	13.4	13.5	13.4	13.4	13.6	13.4
2001	13.8	14.0	14.1	14.1	14.2	14.3	14.4	14.3	14.2	13.9	13.9	14.0	14.1
2002	13.7	13.7	13.8	14.1	14.2	14.2	14.5	14.5	14.4	14.1	14.2	14.2	14.1
2003	13.7	13.7	13.8	13.8	13.9	13.9	13.7	13.7	13.6	13.6	13.5	13.5	13.7
2004	13.5	13.6	13.7	13.7	13.9	14.0	14.0	14.0	14.1	14.2	14.2	14.3	13.9
2005	14.3	14.2	14.3	14.5	14.5	14.6	14.8	14.8	15.0	15.1	15.2	15.3	14.7
2006	15.2	15.3	15.3	15.5	15.6	15.6	15.7	15.7	15.7	15.5	15.5	15.6	15.5
2007	15.3	15.4	15.4	15.5	15.5	15.6	15.4	15.3	15.3	14.9	15.0	15.0	15.3
2008	14.9	14.9	14.9	14.8	14.9	14.9	14.7	14.8	14.6	14.6	14.6	14.5	14.8
2009	14.2	14.1	14.0	14.0	14.0	13.9	13.8	13.7	13.7	13.7	13.7	13.8	13.9
Professional and Business Services													
1990	16.1	16.1	16.1	16.2	16.3	16.5	17.2	17.3	17.3	17.2	17.4	17.3	16.8
2000	24.7	24.7	24.8	26.2	26.0	26.3	25.4	25.6	25.7	25.9	25.4	25.8	25.5
2001	23.4	23.5	23.4	23.4	23.5	24.0	23.2	23.4	23.1	23.7	23.8	24.0	23.5
2002	23.8	24.3	24.2	25.0	25.2	25.3	25.2	25.6	25.5	26.1	26.1	26.1	25.2
2003	26.2	26.0	26.3	25.8	26.2	26.0	26.2	26.6	26.8	26.6	26.9	26.8	26.4
2004	26.7	27.1	27.2	27.4	27.4	27.4	27.6	28.1	28.1	28.3	28.6	28.2	27.7
2005	27.7	28.4	28.6	29.2	29.3	29.0	28.6	28.9	28.6	29.0	29.0	29.3	28.8
2006	28.7	29.1	29.4	29.8	29.5	29.4	29.3	29.9	29.8	29.9	29.7	29.7	29.5
2007	29.3	29.6	29.9	30.0	29.8	30.0	30.2	30.2	30.3	30.6	30.1	29.9	30.0
2008	30.3	30.6	30.4	30.8	30.4	30.3	31.2	31.2	31.1	30.7	30.3	30.5	30.7
2009	29.6	29.4	29.3	28.8	28.3	28.0	27.8	27.5	27.3	27.4	27.2	26.9	28.1
Education and Health Services													
1990	23.1	23.7	23.9	23.8	23.7	24.8	25.9	26.7	27.4	25.3	25.0	25.1	24.9
2000	30.2	30.8	31.0	30.7	30.8	30.9	30.4	30.6	31.0	31.2	31.3	31.5	30.9
2001	31.2	31.6	31.9	32.5	32.3	32.1	32.4	32.7	33.1	33.1	33.5	33.4	32.5
2002	32.6	33.2	33.7	33.9	33.9	33.8	34.0	33.7	34.3	34.2	34.6	34.6	33.9
2003	34.0	34.3	34.7	34.8	34.7	34.7	34.5	34.6	35.2	35.7	35.9	35.9	34.9
2004	35.2	35.8	35.9	35.9	35.6	35.2	35.2	35.3	35.7	36.4	36.4	36.5	35.8
2005	35.7	36.0	36.2	36.9	36.6	36.4	36.1	36.2	37.0	37.4	37.4	37.5	36.6
2006	36.7	37.3	37.4	37.3	37.3	37.2	37.0	37.0	37.7	37.9	38.4	38.6	37.5
2007	38.1	38.7	38.8	39.0	38.6	38.6	38.3	38.7	39.1	39.6	39.6	39.7	38.9
2008	39.1	39.8	40.2	40.8	40.6	40.1	39.3	39.6	39.7	40.4	40.6	40.8	40.1
2009	40.0	40.6	40.7	40.9	40.6	40.1	39.3	39.6	39.9	40.1	40.3	40.4	40.2
Leisure and Hospitality													
1990	16.6	16.7	17.0	17.2	17.5	17.9	18.1	18.0	18.3	17.5	17.3	17.4	17.5
2000	23.2	23.4	23.8	24.0	24.7	25.1	25.3	25.3	24.7	24.1	23.9	23.9	24.3
2001	23.4	23.9	24.4	24.1	24.7	25.0	25.6	25.3	24.4	24.4	24.4	24.5	24.5
2002	23.7	23.9	24.3	23.8	24.6	25.0	25.0	24.7	24.2	23.9	23.6	23.5	24.2
2003	22.6	23.0	23.3	23.2	24.0	24.3	24.5	24.3	23.8	23.3	23.4	23.2	23.6
2004	23.0	23.3	23.5	23.8	24.7	25.2	24.9	24.9	24.7	24.6	24.6	24.5	24.3
2005	24.4	24.8	25.1	25.8	26.3	26.3	26.1	26.1	26.0	26.3	26.5	27.0	25.9
2006	26.5	27.1	27.5	27.8	28.5	28.9	28.7	28.7	28.7	28.1	28.2	28.6	28.1
2007	27.5	27.9	28.3	28.6	28.9	29.1	28.3	28.5	28.2	27.6	27.7	27.7	28.2
2008	27.3	27.7	28.0	28.1	28.7	28.5	28.5	28.4	28.1	27.6	27.5	27.1	28.0
2009	26.2	26.5	26.6	26.9	27.4	27.4	27.1	27.0	26.3	25.9	25.7	25.7	26.6
Other Services													
1990	8.8	9.2	9.3	9.0	9.2	9.0	9.5	9.3	9.6	9.5	9.4	9.5	9.3
2000	9.8	10.2	10.5	10.5	10.5	10.3	10.1	10.4	10.7	10.4	10.4	10.5	10.4
2001	10.4	10.9	10.9	11.3	11.6	11.2	11.3	11.9	11.5	11.4	11.5	11.5	11.3
2002	11.0	11.6	11.8	12.1	12.3	11.9	12.0	12.4	12.3	11.8	11.7	11.9	11.9
2003	11.2	11.3	11.5	11.3	11.4	11.0	10.6	10.8	11.0	10.8	10.6	10.8	11.0
2004	10.4	10.7	10.8	11.0	11.1	10.8	10.5	10.8	10.9	10.4	10.3	10.4	10.7
2005	10.3	10.5	10.5	11.0	11.0	11.0	10.6	11.1	11.0	11.0	11.0	11.1	10.8
2006	10.4	10.8	11.0	11.0	11.3	11.0	10.8	11.0	11.0	10.8	10.7	10.9	10.9
2007	10.6	10.9	10.9	11.1	11.3	10.9	10.8	11.2	11.1	10.9	11.0	10.9	11.0
2008	10.5	10.7	10.8	10.8	10.8	10.8	10.4	10.6	10.6	10.6	10.5	10.5	10.6
2009	10.2	10.3	10.4	10.3	10.5	10.4	10.0	10.3	10.2	10.1	10.1	9.9	10.2
Government													
1990	49.7	49.8	50.8	52.4	52.3	51.3	47.3	47.6	51.2	52.2	52.3	52.0	50.7
2000	63.6	65.2	65.9	66.2	67.2	64.8	63.1	61.7	63.9	66.5	66.8	66.5	65.1
2001	66.8	67.5	68.5	68.6	68.1	68.4	65.8	65.2	65.9	68.2	69.2	68.6	67.6
2002	68.2	69.6	70.5	71.1	71.7	70.6	66.9	66.2	66.9	69.2	70.0	68.7	69.1
2003	68.3	69.3	69.5	69.9	69.7	69.8	65.9	63.4	64.5	67.2	67.3	66.2	67.5
2004	66.4	68.0	68.2	68.9	67.8	66.8	63.5	63.4	65.2	67.2	67.4	66.6	66.6
2005	66.5	68.0	69.1	69.4	69.3	68.3	63.9	63.5	65.0	67.1	67.3	66.7	67.0
2006	66.5	68.2	70.0	69.9	70.3	67.8	63.7	63.6	66.0	68.5	68.5	67.9	67.6
2007	67.6	69.8	71.2	72.0	71.5	70.0	65.8	65.5	67.3	69.8	69.9	69.5	69.2
2008	69.0	71.7	72.7	73.3	72.6	71.7	65.0	65.3	68.1	70.3	70.3	69.4	70.0
2009	68.2	70.2	71.3	72.0	71.2	68.6	64.9	64.4	66.4	69.0	68.2	67.2	68.5

Employment by Industry: Grand Rapids-Wyoming, MI, Selected Years, 1990–2009

(Numbers in thousands, not seasonally adjusted.)

Industry and year	January	February	March	April	May	June	July	August	September	October	November	December	Annual average
Total Nonfarm													
1990	294.2	299.7	302.2	303.7	307.0	307.1	298.8	300.6	307.5	312.2	312.2	311.5	304.7
2000	396.7	400.8	404.0	401.2	405.0	404.4	397.2	398.4	405.9	409.8	410.3	411.0	403.7
2001	396.8	396.0	397.1	402.3	406.5	404.3	392.5	395.2	399.6	400.1	399.0	398.9	399.0
2002	385.1	386.1	388.2	391.3	397.1	396.0	387.3	390.1	395.5	397.4	398.2	398.0	392.5
2003	376.4	376.9	376.6	377.2	386.7	384.0	375.1	379.9	384.7	389.2	391.7	392.9	382.6
2004	378.6	379.1	379.8	386.2	390.9	388.4	379.6	382.7	388.4	390.6	392.2	391.6	385.7
2005	378.5	381.0	383.8	388.1	392.9	390.1	385.1	388.0	394.0	394.2	395.5	395.0	388.9
2006	379.9	382.0	384.3	389.0	394.2	391.9	381.2	384.9	391.1	390.5	392.1	392.3	387.8
2007	379.5	381.7	383.4	385.9	391.8	391.5	382.9	386.0	391.3	391.8	393.8	394.6	387.9
2008	382.7	383.5	383.9	386.3	392.3	390.0	377.3	381.2	384.0	383.5	382.2	379.4	383.9
2009	359.8	360.7	360.0	365.1	369.4	363.0	351.3	353.7	361.9	364.4	365.2	364.2	361.6
Total Private													
1990	262.2	267.3	269.2	270.0	273.1	275.3	269.8	272.2	274.8	278.0	277.6	277.0	272.2
2000	359.7	362.2	365.2	362.8	365.4	367.1	364.9	366.9	368.3	370.8	371.3	372.2	366.4
2001	358.3	356.5	357.3	363.3	366.7	367.2	360.4	363.4	362.1	361.2	360.1	359.8	361.4
2002	346.7	347.0	348.9	352.9	357.8	359.4	355.6	358.6	358.2	357.6	358.0	357.6	354.9
2003	337.2	337.1	336.8	338.1	346.5	346.2	342.1	346.2	346.9	349.6	351.9	353.0	344.3
2004	339.4	339.6	340.0	346.9	350.9	351.9	347.8	350.5	350.9	351.4	352.9	352.2	347.9
2005	340.5	341.7	344.4	348.8	352.8	352.3	352.9	355.5	357.0	355.2	356.4	356.3	351.2
2006	342.1	342.9	345.1	350.0	354.4	354.4	349.2	352.5	354.8	352.3	354.1	354.3	350.5
2007	343.1	344.5	346.1	348.8	354.3	355.1	351.1	353.5	355.3	355.1	357.2	357.9	351.8
2008	347.0	347.1	347.3	349.7	355.5	353.8	345.7	348.4	348.1	346.5	345.5	342.9	348.1
2009	323.5	324.1	323.2	328.1	332.3	327.5	319.1	321.8	326.6	328.1	329.0	328.3	326.0
Goods-Producing													
1990	86.2	88.0	88.4	90.2	91.3	92.2	89.9	90.6	91.1	92.9	91.7	90.5	90.3
2000	109.0	109.6	110.4	109.3	109.9	111.6	110.8	111.5	111.4	112.8	112.0	111.5	110.8
2001	108.0	106.6	106.1	106.6	107.3	108.0	106.8	108.0	107.5	105.5	104.3	103.6	106.5
2002	98.5	97.8	97.7	98.7	100.2	100.7	99.4	99.9	99.2	99.2	98.4	97.8	99.0
2003	93.7	92.8	92.5	91.3	94.9	95.0	92.9	95.0	94.5	94.4	94.2	94.2	93.8
2004	92.1	91.1	91.2	92.8	93.6	94.5	92.9	94.4	94.1	94.0	93.2	93.2	93.1
2005	91.2	90.5	91.5	91.6	92.5	93.4	92.6	93.7	93.3	93.4	93.1	92.7	92.5
2006	90.1	89.5	89.8	91.5	92.6	93.4	91.1	92.7	92.1	90.8	90.0	89.7	91.1
2007	86.8	86.5	86.5	87.8	88.9	90.0	88.6	90.0	89.4	88.8	88.8	88.4	88.4
2008	86.2	85.3	84.8	84.7	86.0	87.4	84.2	86.0	85.0	83.1	81.6	79.7	84.5
2009	72.0	71.5	70.7	70.8	70.8	70.8	69.6	71.5	72.0	71.5	70.8	70.2	71.0
Mining, Logging, and Construction													
1990	13.5	13.5	13.8	14.7	15.4	15.8	15.6	15.7	15.6	15.5	14.7	14.2	14.8
2000	18.6	18.4	19.2	20.4	21.1	22.1	21.7	21.7	21.5	21.3	20.8	20.2	20.6
2001	18.2	18.1	18.6	19.9	20.9	21.7	22.3	22.4	22.2	21.6	21.2	20.5	20.6
2002	19.0	18.8	19.1	20.0	21.2	21.5	21.8	21.7	21.1	20.9	20.3	19.6	20.4
2003	17.2	16.8	16.8	18.1	19.0	19.7	20.3	20.4	19.9	19.6	19.3	19.1	18.9
2004	17.4	16.9	17.2	19.0	19.6	20.2	20.4	20.2	19.9	19.5	19.0	18.7	19.0
2005	17.1	16.6	16.9	18.3	19.0	19.5	19.8	19.8	19.5	19.1	18.7	18.0	18.5
2006	16.5	16.2	16.5	17.9	18.8	19.5	19.3	19.3	18.9	18.4	17.9	17.4	18.1
2007	15.9	15.5	15.7	16.7	17.6	18.2	18.3	18.3	18.0	17.6	17.2	16.7	17.1
2008	15.6	15.3	15.5	16.1	17.1	17.6	17.5	17.6	17.1	16.4	15.7	14.9	16.4
2009	13.2	12.9	12.9	13.6	14.2	14.4	14.6	14.5	14.2	13.8	13.3	12.8	13.7
Manufacturing													
1990	72.7	74.5	74.6	75.5	75.9	76.4	74.3	74.9	75.5	77.4	77.0	76.3	75.4
2000	90.4	91.2	91.2	88.9	88.8	89.5	89.1	89.8	89.9	91.5	91.2	91.3	90.2
2001	89.8	88.5	87.5	86.7	86.4	86.3	84.5	85.6	85.3	83.9	83.1	83.1	85.9
2002	79.5	79.0	78.6	78.7	79.0	79.2	77.6	78.2	78.1	78.3	78.1	78.2	78.5
2003	76.5	76.0	75.7	73.2	75.9	75.3	72.6	74.6	74.6	74.8	74.9	75.1	74.9
2004	74.7	74.2	74.0	73.8	74.0	74.3	72.5	74.2	74.2	74.5	74.2	74.5	74.1
2005	74.1	73.9	74.6	73.3	73.5	73.9	72.8	73.9	73.8	74.3	74.4	74.7	73.9
2006	73.6	73.3	73.3	73.6	73.8	73.9	71.8	73.4	73.2	72.4	72.1	72.3	73.1
2007	70.9	71.0	70.8	71.1	71.3	71.8	70.3	71.7	71.4	71.2	71.6	71.7	71.2
2008	70.6	70.0	69.3	68.6	68.9	69.8	66.7	68.4	67.9	66.7	65.9	64.8	68.1
2009	58.8	58.6	57.8	57.2	56.6	56.4	55.0	57.0	57.8	57.7	57.5	57.4	57.3
Service-Providing													
1990	208.0	211.7	213.8	213.5	215.7	214.9	208.9	210.0	216.4	219.3	220.5	221.0	214.5
2000	287.7	291.2	293.6	291.9	295.1	292.8	286.4	286.9	294.5	297.0	298.3	299.5	292.9
2001	288.8	289.4	291.0	295.7	299.2	296.3	285.7	287.2	292.1	294.6	294.7	295.3	292.5
2002	286.6	288.3	290.5	292.6	296.9	295.3	287.9	290.2	296.3	298.2	299.8	300.2	293.6
2003	282.7	284.1	284.1	285.9	291.8	289.0	282.2	284.9	290.2	294.8	297.5	298.7	288.8
2004	286.5	288.0	288.6	293.4	297.3	293.9	286.7	288.3	294.3	296.6	299.0	298.4	292.6
2005	287.3	290.5	292.3	296.5	300.4	296.7	292.5	294.3	300.7	300.8	302.4	302.3	296.4
2006	289.8	292.5	294.5	297.5	301.6	298.5	290.1	292.2	299.0	299.7	302.1	302.6	296.7
2007	292.7	295.2	296.9	298.1	302.9	301.5	294.3	296.0	301.9	303.0	305.0	306.2	299.5
2008	296.5	298.2	299.1	301.6	306.3	302.6	293.1	295.2	299.0	300.4	300.6	299.7	299.4
2009	287.8	289.2	289.3	294.3	298.6	292.2	281.7	282.2	289.9	292.9	294.4	294.0	290.5

Employment by Industry: Grand Rapids-Wyoming, MI, Selected Years, 1990–2009—*Continued*

(Numbers in thousands, not seasonally adjusted.)

Industry and year	January	February	March	April	May	June	July	August	September	October	November	December	Annual average
Trade, Transportation, and Utilities													
1990	63.5	64.0	64.4	63.9	64.9	64.9	63.9	65.0	65.5	66.1	66.8	67.3	65.0
2000	81.0	81.0	81.6	81.4	81.7	81.0	79.5	79.8	80.6	82.0	83.2	84.4	81.4
2001	82.1	81.1	80.9	81.6	81.9	81.1	78.9	78.9	78.4	79.1	79.9	80.2	80.3
2002	76.9	76.3	76.4	76.5	77.1	77.5	77.0	77.5	77.3	77.4	78.2	79.3	77.3
2003	75.5	74.4	74.3	74.8	75.8	76.3	75.5	75.4	75.4	76.1	77.4	78.1	75.8
2004	74.3	73.3	73.1	74.6	75.1	75.3	74.9	74.9	74.6	75.2	76.6	77.0	74.9
2005	73.7	73.2	73.5	74.6	75.5	75.8	75.8	75.8	75.4	75.4	76.5	76.9	75.2
2006	73.2	72.6	72.7	73.2	73.8	73.9	73.6	73.4	73.3	73.7	75.1	75.7	73.7
2007	73.4	72.4	72.6	73.0	73.9	74.2	73.8	73.6	73.6	73.9	75.1	75.4	73.7
2008	72.8	72.0	72.1	71.9	72.8	73.0	72.0	72.0	71.3	71.1	71.6	71.6	72.0
2009	68.5	67.5	67.1	68.3	68.8	68.7	67.6	67.3	67.1	67.4	68.2	68.6	67.9
Wholesale Trade													
1990	18.6	18.8	19.0	19.0	19.4	19.4	19.2	19.3	19.5	19.4	19.3	19.3	19.2
2000	23.7	24.0	23.9	24.1	24.0	24.1	24.0	23.8	24.0	24.0	23.8	24.2	24.0
2001	24.3	23.9	24.1	24.3	24.0	23.8	23.3	23.2	23.0	23.0	22.9	22.8	23.6
2002	23.2	22.9	22.9	22.9	23.1	23.2	23.0	23.0	22.7	22.9	22.8	22.9	23.0
2003	22.6	22.4	22.3	22.4	22.6	22.5	22.2	22.1	22.0	22.3	22.3	22.3	22.3
2004	21.7	21.7	21.6	22.1	22.2	22.4	22.3	22.1	22.1	22.1	22.2	22.2	22.1
2005	21.7	21.7	21.8	22.0	22.3	22.4	22.4	22.4	22.3	22.4	22.3	22.4	22.2
2006	22.0	22.0	22.0	22.2	22.4	22.5	22.5	22.4	22.4	22.5	22.4	22.4	22.3
2007	22.2	22.1	22.2	22.5	22.6	22.7	22.8	22.7	22.7	22.7	22.6	22.6	22.5
2008	22.2	22.2	22.3	22.3	22.4	22.5	22.3	22.4	22.3	22.0	21.8	21.6	22.2
2009	21.0	20.8	20.6	20.7	20.8	20.6	20.5	20.4	20.3	20.4	20.3	20.3	20.6
Retail Trade													
1990	36.6	36.7	37.0	36.4	36.9	36.7	36.1	36.8	37.2	37.7	38.4	38.9	37.1
2000	46.2	45.9	46.7	46.1	46.6	45.6	44.2	44.6	45.2	46.3	47.7	48.5	46.1
2001	46.3	45.8	45.4	45.6	46.1	45.6	44.0	44.0	43.8	44.3	45.5	46.0	45.2
2002	42.5	42.2	42.2	42.4	42.8	43.1	42.9	43.3	43.5	43.2	44.2	45.2	43.1
2003	42.7	42.0	42.0	42.1	42.8	43.3	43.1	43.2	43.3	43.6	45.0	45.6	43.2
2004	42.6	41.7	41.5	42.0	42.4	42.4	42.2	42.3	41.8	42.1	43.5	44.0	42.4
2005	41.6	41.1	41.2	41.9	42.4	42.4	42.4	42.3	42.0	42.0	43.2	43.4	42.2
2006	40.5	40.0	40.1	40.4	40.7	40.6	40.3	40.3	40.1	40.4	41.9	42.4	40.6
2007	40.6	39.8	39.8	39.9	40.5	40.5	40.1	40.1	40.1	40.5	41.7	42.0	40.5
2008	40.2	39.5	39.6	39.2	39.8	39.8	39.2	39.1	38.6	38.7	39.6	39.8	39.4
2009	37.7	37.1	37.0	37.7	38.0	38.1	37.4	37.2	37.1	37.4	38.3	38.6	37.6
Transportation and Utilities													
1990	8.3	8.5	8.4	8.5	8.6	8.8	8.6	8.9	8.8	9.0	9.1	9.1	8.7
2000	11.1	11.1	11.0	11.2	11.1	11.3	11.3	11.4	11.4	11.7	11.7	11.7	11.3
2001	11.5	11.4	11.4	11.7	11.8	11.7	11.6	11.7	11.6	11.8	11.5	11.4	11.6
2002	11.2	11.2	11.3	11.2	11.2	11.2	11.1	11.2	11.1	11.3	11.2	11.2	11.2
2003	10.2	10.0	10.0	10.3	10.4	10.5	10.2	10.1	10.1	10.2	10.1	10.2	10.2
2004	10.0	9.9	10.0	10.5	10.5	10.5	10.4	10.5	10.7	11.0	10.9	10.8	10.5
2005	10.4	10.4	10.5	10.7	10.8	11.0	11.0	11.1	11.1	11.0	11.0	11.1	10.8
2006	10.7	10.6	10.6	10.6	10.7	10.8	10.8	10.7	10.8	10.8	10.8	10.9	10.7
2007	10.6	10.5	10.6	10.6	10.8	11.0	10.9	10.8	10.8	10.7	10.8	10.8	10.7
2008	10.4	10.3	10.2	10.4	10.6	10.7	10.5	10.5	10.4	10.4	10.2	10.2	10.4
2009	9.8	9.6	9.5	9.9	10.0	10.0	9.7	9.7	9.7	9.6	9.6	9.7	9.7
Information													
1990	5.1	5.1	5.1	5.1	5.1	5.2	5.1	5.1	5.1	5.2	5.2	5.4	5.2
2000	6.1	6.0	6.0	6.0	6.1	6.1	6.2	6.3	6.2	6.1	6.1	6.2	6.1
2001	5.8	5.9	5.9	6.1	6.1	6.3	6.1	6.0	6.0	6.2	6.5	6.5	6.1
2002	6.5	6.5	6.6	6.1	6.1	6.1	6.0	6.0	5.9	6.1	6.1	6.2	6.2
2003	6.1	6.0	6.0	5.9	6.0	5.9	5.5	5.5	5.4	5.5	5.5	5.5	5.7
2004	5.6	5.6	5.6	5.6	5.5	5.6	5.6	5.5	5.4	5.3	5.4	5.4	5.5
2005	5.5	5.6	5.6	5.7	5.6	5.7	5.6	5.6	5.5	5.7	5.9	5.9	5.7
2006	5.7	5.7	5.7	5.6	5.6	5.7	5.5	5.5	5.4	5.4	5.4	5.4	5.6
2007	5.3	5.3	5.2	5.2	5.3	5.3	5.2	5.2	5.0	5.0	5.1	5.1	5.2
2008	5.0	4.9	4.8	4.8	4.9	4.9	4.9	4.9	4.8	4.8	4.8	4.8	4.9
2009	4.7	4.7	4.6	4.6	4.6	4.6	4.6	4.4	4.4	4.4	4.4	4.4	4.5
Financial Activities													
1990	15.0	15.2	15.4	15.0	15.1	15.3	14.7	14.7	14.8	14.8	14.8	14.9	15.0
2000	20.8	20.9	20.8	19.4	19.4	19.4	19.2	19.2	19.3	19.6	19.7	19.8	19.8
2001	19.1	19.1	19.2	19.1	19.4	19.4	19.3	19.3	19.2	19.9	19.7	19.9	19.4
2002	19.7	19.9	20.1	19.7	19.7	19.5	19.4	19.5	19.3	19.7	19.5	19.6	19.6
2003	19.6	19.5	19.5	19.7	19.7	19.7	19.8	19.8	19.8	20.0	19.9	20.1	19.8
2004	20.1	20.0	20.2	20.3	20.4	20.4	20.3	20.3	20.2	19.9	20.0	20.1	20.2
2005	20.1	20.4	20.1	20.3	20.4	20.5	20.6	20.6	20.5	20.6	20.6	20.7	20.5
2006	20.9	20.9	20.8	20.9	20.9	20.9	20.8	20.8	20.7	20.5	20.5	20.4	20.8
2007	20.1	20.1	20.0	20.5	20.6	20.4	20.5	20.1	19.9	20.4	20.2	20.3	20.3
2008	20.3	20.4	20.2	20.3	20.4	20.0	19.9	20.0	19.8	19.9	19.9	19.7	20.1
2009	19.4	19.4	19.2	19.5	19.5	19.5	19.3	19.3	18.8	18.8	18.7	18.7	19.2

Employment by Industry: Grand Rapids-Wyoming, MI, Selected Years, 1990–2009—*Continued*

(Numbers in thousands, not seasonally adjusted.)

Industry and year	January	February	March	April	May	June	July	August	September	October	November	December	Annual average
Professional and Business Services													
1990	24.9	25.9	26.1	26.1	26.4	27.6	27.3	27.2	27.2	27.2	27.2	27.2	26.7
2000	52.1	52.4	52.9	53.3	53.6	54.9	56.2	56.9	56.6	56.1	56.0	55.9	54.7
2001	51.4	50.7	50.7	53.4	54.6	55.3	53.4	54.8	54.2	52.6	51.9	51.1	52.8
2002	49.7	50.0	50.4	52.6	54.0	54.5	54.5	55.7	54.8	54.2	54.4	53.8	53.2
2003	46.6	46.3	45.9	47.5	49.0	49.3	50.4	52.1	51.4	52.1	52.9	52.8	49.7
2004	47.9	48.7	48.5	51.0	52.3	52.6	52.1	53.6	52.7	52.2	52.0	51.3	51.2
2005	48.2	48.3	49.0	51.0	52.1	52.6	54.8	55.8	55.9	54.5	54.6	53.8	52.6
2006	50.1	50.9	50.7	52.6	53.9	55.2	54.7	56.1	56.5	55.5	56.2	56.6	54.1
2007	53.3	54.6	55.4	55.3	57.1	57.7	57.1	58.3	59.5	58.6	59.4	59.6	57.2
2008	57.6	58.1	58.3	58.5	59.7	57.7	55.9	56.5	57.7	58.3	58.0	57.6	57.8
2009	52.7	53.4	53.6	55.0	56.9	53.7	48.6	49.7	53.4	54.5	55.3	54.9	53.5
Education and Health Services													
1990	33.0	33.9	34.1	34.0	33.9	32.9	32.6	32.9	34.3	35.2	35.4	35.3	34.0
2000	43.9	44.8	45.5	45.7	45.7	44.8	43.9	44.3	45.4	46.0	46.4	46.6	45.3
2001	46.3	47.0	47.8	48.4	48.3	48.0	47.1	46.9	48.0	49.3	49.8	50.0	48.1
2002	49.2	50.1	50.8	51.0	51.1	50.9	49.4	49.7	50.7	51.1	52.0	51.4	50.6
2003	49.1	51.5	51.4	51.3	51.9	50.2	49.2	49.3	50.9	52.8	53.7	53.7	51.3
2004	52.4	53.6	53.7	54.3	54.2	53.3	51.9	52.0	54.4	55.6	56.7	56.3	54.0
2005	54.0	55.5	56.0	56.5	56.2	53.4	53.4	53.4	55.7	56.4	56.7	56.7	55.3
2006	54.8	55.4	56.8	57.0	56.9	54.6	53.3	53.7	56.6	57.1	58.1	58.0	56.0
2007	57.0	58.2	58.5	58.9	58.8	57.3	56.3	56.6	58.4	59.3	59.9	60.0	58.3
2008	58.5	59.7	60.0	60.6	61.0	59.7	58.9	59.0	60.2	61.1	62.1	61.7	60.2
2009	60.1	61.1	61.1	62.4	62.5	60.4	59.6	60.0	61.3	62.3	62.8	62.8	61.4
Leisure and Hospitality													
1990	23.5	24.1	24.4	24.5	25.1	25.7	25.1	25.4	25.5	25.2	25.2	25.0	24.9
2000	30.8	31.5	31.8	31.6	32.9	33.1	32.8	32.7	32.8	32.0	31.7	31.5	32.1
2001	29.6	30.0	30.4	31.5	32.5	32.4	32.2	32.9	32.4	32.0	31.4	31.7	31.6
2002	29.9	30.0	30.4	31.6	32.8	33.2	32.7	33.2	33.8	32.7	32.3	32.3	32.1
2003	29.7	29.6	29.9	30.8	32.2	32.6	31.7	31.9	32.1	31.6	31.2	31.2	31.2
2004	30.0	30.1	30.3	31.3	32.7	33.0	32.8	32.7	32.5	32.1	32.0	31.9	31.8
2005	30.6	30.8	31.2	32.4	33.7	33.9	33.2	33.8	34.1	33.0	32.7	33.3	32.7
2006	31.2	31.6	32.2	32.4	33.8	33.6	33.4	33.6	33.7	32.8	32.4	32.0	32.7
2007	31.1	31.3	31.6	31.7	33.2	33.5	33.0	33.2	33.2	32.7	32.3	32.6	32.5
2008	30.4	30.5	30.8	32.1	33.8	33.9	32.9	33.0	32.5	31.2	30.5	30.7	31.9
2009	29.1	29.4	29.6	30.1	31.8	32.1	32.2	32.1	32.1	31.6	31.2	31.1	31.0
Other Services													
1990	11.0	11.1	11.3	11.2	11.3	11.5	11.2	11.3	11.3	11.4	11.3	11.4	11.3
2000	16.0	16.0	16.2	16.1	16.1	16.2	16.3	16.2	16.0	16.2	16.2	16.3	16.2
2001	16.0	16.1	16.3	16.6	16.6	16.7	16.6	16.6	16.4	16.6	16.6	16.8	16.5
2002	16.3	16.4	16.5	16.7	16.8	17.0	17.2	17.1	17.2	17.2	17.1	17.2	16.9
2003	16.9	17.0	17.3	16.8	17.0	17.2	17.1	17.2	17.4	17.1	17.1	17.4	17.1
2004	17.0	17.2	17.4	17.0	17.1	17.2	17.3	17.1	17.0	17.1	17.0	17.0	17.1
2005	17.2	17.4	17.5	16.7	16.8	17.0	16.9	16.8	16.6	16.2	16.3	16.3	16.8
2006	16.1	16.3	16.4	16.8	16.9	17.1	16.8	16.7	16.5	16.5	16.4	16.5	16.6
2007	16.1	16.1	16.3	16.4	16.5	16.7	16.6	16.5	16.3	16.4	16.4	16.5	16.4
2008	16.2	16.2	16.3	16.8	16.9	17.2	17.0	17.0	16.8	17.0	17.0	17.1	16.8
2009	17.0	17.1	17.3	17.4	17.4	17.7	17.6	17.5	17.5	17.6	17.6	17.6	17.4
Government													
1990	32.0	32.4	33.0	33.7	33.9	31.8	29.0	28.4	32.7	34.2	34.6	34.5	32.5
2000	37.0	38.6	38.8	38.4	39.6	37.3	32.3	31.5	37.6	39.0	39.0	38.8	37.3
2001	38.5	39.5	39.8	39.0	39.8	37.1	32.1	31.8	37.5	38.9	38.9	39.1	37.7
2002	38.4	39.1	39.3	38.4	39.3	36.6	31.7	31.5	37.3	39.8	40.2	40.4	37.7
2003	39.2	39.8	39.8	39.1	40.2	37.8	33.0	33.7	37.8	39.6	39.8	39.9	38.3
2004	39.2	39.5	39.8	39.3	40.0	36.5	31.8	32.2	37.5	39.2	39.3	39.4	37.8
2005	38.0	39.3	39.4	39.3	40.1	37.8	32.2	32.5	37.0	39.0	39.1	38.7	37.7
2006	37.8	39.1	39.2	39.0	39.8	37.5	32.0	32.4	36.3	38.2	38.0	38.0	37.3
2007	36.4	37.2	37.3	37.1	37.5	36.4	31.8	32.5	36.0	36.7	36.6	36.7	36.0
2008	35.7	36.4	36.6	36.6	36.8	36.2	31.6	32.8	35.9	37.0	36.7	36.5	35.7
2009	36.3	36.6	36.8	37.0	37.1	35.5	32.2	31.9	35.3	36.3	36.2	35.9	35.6

Employment by Industry: Greensboro-High Point, NC, Selected Years, 1990–2009

(Numbers in thousands, not seasonally adjusted.)

Industry and year	January	February	March	April	May	June	July	August	September	October	November	December	Annual average
Total Nonfarm													
1990	293.7	294.8	296.0	298.1	299.0	300.7	297.5	299.9	299.9	299.7	299.6	298.5	298.1
2000	359.6	361.3	365.0	366.2	367.7	369.3	363.0	367.8	369.0	370.4	372.2	372.7	367.0
2001	363.4	364.7	364.9	365.9	366.6	366.5	357.3	360.6	361.0	360.6	361.0	360.4	362.7
2002	351.4	352.6	354.6	359.7	360.8	361.4	355.5	360.1	361.8	363.8	365.2	364.7	359.3
2003	356.4	356.9	358.9	358.8	358.2	357.2	346.5	350.1	352.2	355.3	354.4	353.8	354.9
2004	347.6	348.7	352.1	358.1	359.8	359.9	352.8	356.8	359.5	361.5	362.0	363.3	356.8
2005	357.0	359.6	362.3	364.5	364.4	363.8	357.5	362.7	363.9	365.3	366.2	366.8	362.8
2006	362.0	363.5	366.7	370.4	373.2	370.3	364.7	370.2	370.6	374.3	376.1	377.5	370.0
2007	367.8	369.0	372.6	373.3	374.8	373.3	366.2	371.9	372.9	375.7	376.1	376.5	372.5
2008	369.7	370.2	371.6	370.1	370.3	367.5	360.6	366.6	368.5	368.6	366.8	361.8	367.7
2009	350.2	349.1	346.1	345.4	344.9	343.2	335.4	339.9	342.3	343.6	343.3	342.2	343.8
Total Private													
1990	264.8	265.7	266.7	268.3	269.0	271.1	269.5	271.7	271.1	269.7	269.5	268.5	268.8
2000	321.4	322.9	325.9	327.0	328.5	330.1	329.3	330.5	330.4	330.6	331.4	331.6	328.3
2001	323.7	324.7	324.7	325.7	326.1	326.5	323.6	323.6	322.1	320.2	319.4	319.4	323.3
2002	311.1	312.0	313.5	318.1	319.3	321.0	321.0	322.5	321.5	322.2	322.6	322.6	319.0
2003	315.4	315.4	317.2	316.7	315.8	316.6	311.4	312.2	311.3	312.2	312.1	311.5	314.0
2004	306.3	307.2	310.1	315.7	317.3	318.8	317.6	318.4	318.3	318.9	319.6	320.5	315.7
2005	315.0	317.2	319.6	321.6	321.3	322.5	321.8	322.7	321.7	321.4	322.8	323.2	320.9
2006	319.3	320.4	323.0	326.3	328.9	328.5	328.2	329.5	327.7	330.2	331.5	332.5	327.2
2007	324.2	325.2	328.3	328.8	330.1	331.0	329.0	330.5	329.3	330.7	330.7	331.5	329.1
2008	324.7	324.8	325.8	324.1	323.9	323.7	322.1	324.0	322.5	322.3	320.3	315.8	322.8
2009	304.5	303.0	299.7	298.5	298.2	297.8	296.0	296.6	295.3	295.0	294.2	294.4	297.8
Goods-Producing													
1990	104.6	104.7	104.8	104.6	104.4	104.7	104.2	104.1	103.6	102.2	101.4	100.8	103.7
2000	99.6	99.7	100.1	99.4	100.1	100.1	100.8	100.8	100.6	99.5	99.2	98.8	99.9
2001	97.1	96.4	96.0	95.6	95.1	95.1	93.8	93.4	92.8	91.7	91.0	90.4	94.0
2002	89.4	88.9	89.2	89.9	90.2	90.8	91.0	91.5	91.2	90.4	89.6	89.0	90.1
2003	88.8	88.6	88.4	87.5	87.4	87.4	85.1	85.2	85.0	84.3	84.1	84.3	86.3
2004	83.0	82.7	83.3	84.1	84.6	85.4	84.9	85.4	85.7	85.2	85.4	85.5	84.6
2005	85.3	85.4	85.5	86.0	86.1	86.4	85.6	85.4	84.9	84.1	84.0	84.1	85.2
2006	82.8	83.0	83.3	83.9	84.0	83.8	83.1	83.6	83.2	83.3	83.2	83.4	83.4
2007	82.4	82.1	82.5	82.6	82.6	82.6	81.9	81.9	81.5	81.8	81.7	82.1	82.1
2008	80.6	80.4	80.4	79.2	79.3	79.0	78.4	78.3	78.0	77.0	76.3	74.8	78.5
2009	71.4	70.2	68.5	68.0	67.0	66.7	65.8	65.8	65.6	64.8	64.6	64.5	66.9
Mining, Logging, and Construction													
1990	15.9	16.1	16.3	16.2	16.2	16.5	16.5	16.5	16.2	15.9	15.6	15.4	16.1
2000	18.8	18.7	19.0	18.7	18.9	19.0	19.2	19.6	19.8	19.7	19.5	19.3	19.2
2001	18.7	18.6	18.9	19.0	19.1	19.4	19.5	19.3	19.2	18.9	18.6	18.4	19.0
2002	17.4	17.4	17.6	17.7	17.7	17.9	18.1	18.1	17.9	17.5	17.3	17.1	17.6
2003	17.3	17.3	17.5	17.7	18.0	18.1	17.9	18.0	18.2	18.4	18.4	18.6	18.0
2004	17.8	17.5	17.9	18.3	18.5	18.9	18.8	19.0	19.0	18.9	18.9	18.9	18.5
2005	18.6	18.5	18.6	19.1	19.3	19.5	19.5	19.5	19.5	19.2	19.2	19.1	19.1
2006	18.6	18.6	18.9	19.2	19.3	19.5	19.6	19.7	19.6	19.5	19.5	19.5	19.3
2007	19.0	18.9	19.3	19.3	19.3	19.5	19.5	19.4	19.2	19.3	19.3	19.3	19.3
2008	18.5	18.5	18.7	18.3	18.3	18.3	18.3	18.1	18.1	17.9	17.7	17.1	18.2
2009	15.9	15.6	15.3	15.2	14.9	14.9	14.7	14.7	14.5	14.1	14.1	14.0	14.8
Manufacturing													
1990	88.7	88.6	88.5	88.4	88.2	88.2	87.7	87.6	87.4	86.3	85.8	85.4	87.6
2000	80.8	81.0	81.1	80.7	81.2	81.1	81.6	81.2	80.8	79.8	79.7	79.5	80.7
2001	78.4	77.8	77.1	76.6	76.0	75.7	74.3	74.1	73.6	72.8	72.4	72.0	75.1
2002	72.0	71.5	71.6	72.2	72.5	72.9	72.9	73.4	73.3	72.9	72.3	71.9	72.5
2003	71.5	71.3	70.9	69.8	69.4	69.3	67.2	67.2	66.8	65.9	65.7	65.7	68.4
2004	65.2	65.2	65.4	65.8	66.1	66.5	66.1	66.4	66.7	66.3	66.5	66.6	66.1
2005	66.7	66.9	66.9	66.9	66.8	66.9	66.1	65.9	65.4	64.9	64.8	65.0	66.1
2006	64.2	64.4	64.4	64.7	64.7	64.3	63.5	63.9	63.6	63.8	63.7	63.9	64.1
2007	63.4	63.2	63.2	63.3	63.0	63.1	62.4	62.5	62.3	62.5	62.4	62.8	62.8
2008	62.1	61.9	61.7	60.9	61.0	60.7	60.1	60.2	59.9	59.1	58.6	57.7	60.3
2009	55.5	54.6	53.2	52.8	52.1	51.8	51.1	51.1	51.1	50.7	50.5	50.5	52.1
Service-Providing													
1990	189.1	190.1	191.2	193.5	194.6	196.0	193.3	195.8	196.3	197.5	198.2	197.7	194.4
2000	260.0	261.6	264.9	266.8	267.6	269.2	262.2	267.0	268.4	270.9	273.0	273.9	267.1
2001	266.3	268.3	268.9	270.3	271.5	271.4	263.5	267.2	268.2	268.9	270.0	270.0	268.7
2002	262.0	263.7	265.4	269.8	270.6	270.6	264.5	268.6	270.6	273.4	275.6	275.7	269.2
2003	267.6	268.3	270.5	271.3	270.8	269.8	261.4	264.9	267.2	271.0	270.3	269.5	268.6
2004	264.6	266.0	268.8	274.0	275.2	274.5	267.9	271.4	273.8	276.3	276.6	277.8	272.2
2005	271.7	274.2	276.8	278.5	278.3	277.4	271.9	277.3	279.0	281.2	282.2	282.7	277.6
2006	279.2	280.5	283.4	286.5	289.2	286.5	281.6	286.6	287.4	291.0	292.9	294.1	286.6
2007	285.4	286.9	290.1	290.7	292.5	290.7	284.3	290.0	291.4	293.9	294.4	294.4	290.4
2008	289.1	289.8	291.2	290.9	291.0	288.5	282.2	288.3	290.5	291.6	290.5	287.0	289.2
2009	278.8	278.9	277.6	277.4	277.9	276.5	269.6	274.1	276.7	278.8	278.7	277.7	276.9

Employment by Industry: Greensboro-High Point, NC, Selected Years, 1990–2009—*Continued*

(Numbers in thousands, not seasonally adjusted.)

Industry and year	January	February	March	April	May	June	July	August	September	October	November	December	Annual average
Trade, Transportation, and Utilities													
1990	65.0	64.5	64.7	65.3	65.4	65.7	65.0	65.9	65.8	66.2	67.1	67.6	65.7
2000	79.0	79.1	79.7	80.3	80.4	80.6	80.0	80.3	80.2	81.1	82.0	82.7	80.5
2001	79.6	79.1	79.1	80.2	80.3	80.1	79.2	78.9	78.4	78.3	78.5	78.9	79.2
2002	74.9	74.3	74.5	75.0	75.1	75.1	74.2	74.4	73.9	74.3	75.7	76.4	74.8
2003	73.5	73.3	73.7	73.5	73.0	73.4	72.1	72.1	72.0	72.4	73.5	73.8	73.0
2004	71.8	71.2	71.8	72.0	72.3	72.3	72.5	72.6	72.3	72.9	74.3	75.4	72.6
2005	72.1	72.2	72.6	73.0	73.1	73.2	73.5	73.7	73.3	74.8	76.1	76.9	73.7
2006	75.4	75.0	75.1	75.8	76.2	75.4	75.6	75.7	75.7	76.3	78.1	78.9	76.1
2007	76.1	75.7	76.5	76.3	76.8	76.6	76.5	76.9	76.7	77.0	78.0	78.9	76.8
2008	75.3	74.8	74.8	74.6	74.8	74.7	73.8	73.8	73.7	74.0	74.2	74.4	74.4
2009	70.9	70.2	70.0	69.1	69.2	68.9	68.4	68.4	68.4	68.0	68.2	68.8	69.0
Wholesale Trade													
1990	15.9	15.9	16.0	16.1	16.2	16.3	16.3	16.5	16.4	16.4	16.3	16.3	16.2
2000	19.0	19.2	19.3	19.6	19.7	19.7	19.8	19.8	19.8	19.8	19.7	19.8	19.6
2001	19.6	19.8	19.8	19.7	19.6	19.6	19.5	19.5	19.2	19.2	19.0	19.0	19.5
2002	18.8	19.0	18.9	19.2	19.1	19.2	19.3	19.3	19.3	19.3	19.4	19.4	19.2
2003	18.9	19.0	19.1	19.0	18.8	18.9	18.5	18.5	18.4	18.5	18.5	18.5	18.7
2004	18.6	18.5	18.6	18.9	18.8	18.8	18.5	18.5	18.3	18.3	18.3	18.3	18.5
2005	18.5	18.5	18.5	18.5	18.6	18.5	18.8	18.9	18.8	18.8	18.8	18.8	18.7
2006	18.9	19.1	19.1	19.4	19.6	19.5	19.5	19.6	19.7	19.8	19.9	20.0	19.5
2007	20.1	20.1	20.3	20.3	20.4	20.5	20.6	20.6	20.6	20.6	20.6	20.7	20.5
2008	20.4	20.4	20.4	20.2	20.3	20.2	20.0	19.9	19.9	19.8	19.6	19.3	20.0
2009	18.8	18.7	18.5	18.5	18.5	18.3	18.2	18.3	18.1	18.1	18.2	18.2	18.4
Retail Trade													
1990	33.5	33.0	33.0	32.7	32.8	33.0	32.7	33.1	33.2	33.5	34.4	34.9	33.3
2000	39.4	39.3	39.8	39.7	39.8	39.9	38.9	39.1	39.1	39.3	40.3	41.0	39.6
2001	39.2	38.7	38.8	38.9	39.2	39.2	39.0	39.0	39.0	39.1	39.8	40.3	39.2
2002	38.2	37.7	38.0	38.1	38.3	38.3	37.7	37.9	37.5	37.6	38.8	39.5	38.1
2003	37.3	36.8	37.0	36.8	36.7	36.6	36.1	36.1	35.9	36.3	37.4	37.7	36.7
2004	35.9	35.5	35.8	36.2	36.6	36.5	36.4	36.6	36.5	37.0	38.3	39.2	36.7
2005	36.6	36.7	37.0	37.3	37.2	37.3	37.4	37.3	36.9	38.4	39.5	40.4	37.7
2006	39.4	38.9	38.9	39.2	39.4	38.8	38.9	39.1	38.9	39.5	41.2	41.8	39.5
2007	39.6	39.3	39.7	39.6	39.9	39.7	39.5	39.6	39.4	39.7	40.6	40.9	39.8
2008	38.7	38.2	38.1	38.1	38.0	37.9	37.7	37.7	37.5	37.9	38.2	38.5	38.0
2009	36.5	36.1	36.2	35.6	35.8	35.7	35.5	35.5	35.5	35.2	35.1	35.8	35.7
Transportation and Utilities													
1990	15.6	15.6	15.7	16.5	16.4	16.4	16.0	16.3	16.2	16.3	16.4	16.4	16.2
2000	20.6	20.6	20.6	21.0	20.9	21.0	21.3	21.4	21.3	22.0	22.0	21.9	21.2
2001	20.8	20.6	20.5	21.6	21.5	21.3	20.7	20.4	20.2	20.0	19.7	19.6	20.6
2002	17.9	17.6	17.6	17.7	17.7	17.6	17.2	17.2	17.1	17.4	17.5	17.5	17.5
2003	17.3	17.5	17.6	17.7	17.5	17.9	17.5	17.5	17.7	17.6	17.6	17.6	17.6
2004	17.3	17.2	17.4	16.9	16.9	17.0	17.6	17.5	17.5	17.6	17.7	17.9	17.4
2005	17.0	17.0	17.1	17.2	17.3	17.4	17.3	17.5	17.6	17.6	17.8	17.7	17.4
2006	17.1	17.0	17.1	17.2	17.2	17.1	17.2	17.0	17.1	17.0	17.0	17.1	17.1
2007	16.4	16.3	16.5	16.4	16.5	16.4	16.4	16.7	16.7	16.7	16.8	17.3	16.6
2008	16.2	16.2	16.3	16.3	16.5	16.6	16.1	16.2	16.3	16.3	16.4	16.6	16.3
2009	15.6	15.4	15.3	15.0	14.9	14.9	14.7	14.6	14.8	14.7	14.9	14.8	15.0
Information													
1990	4.2	4.3	4.3	4.4	4.5	4.6	4.5	4.6	4.7	4.7	4.8	4.8	4.5
2000	7.6	7.6	7.6	7.8	7.9	8.0	8.3	8.3	8.3	8.3	8.3	8.3	8.0
2001	8.4	8.3	8.4	8.3	8.4	8.5	8.6	8.4	8.4	8.0	8.0	8.1	8.3
2002	7.8	7.7	7.6	7.7	7.9	7.8	7.8	7.7	7.6	7.6	7.7	7.7	7.7
2003	7.5	7.4	7.4	7.4	7.6	7.5	7.5	7.6	7.5	7.4	7.5	7.5	7.5
2004	7.1	6.9	6.9	6.8	6.8	6.7	6.7	6.6	6.5	6.5	6.5	6.5	6.7
2005	6.5	6.4	6.5	6.6	6.6	6.6	6.6	6.6	6.6	6.5	6.5	6.6	6.6
2006	6.6	6.5	6.5	6.3	6.4	6.3	6.3	6.3	6.3	6.4	6.4	6.5	6.4
2007	6.3	6.3	6.2	6.3	6.2	6.2	6.2	6.2	6.2	6.2	6.3	6.3	6.2
2008	6.2	6.1	6.2	6.2	6.2	6.3	6.2	6.1	6.0	6.0	6.2	6.2	6.2
2009	5.9	5.8	5.8	5.8	5.8	5.7	5.6	5.6	5.5	5.5	5.5	5.5	5.7
Financial Activities													
1990	16.4	16.5	16.6	16.8	16.8	17.1	17.3	17.2	17.0	17.0	16.8	16.8	16.9
2000	20.6	20.7	20.9	20.9	20.9	21.1	21.0	20.9	20.9	21.0	20.9	21.1	20.9
2001	20.8	20.8	20.9	20.9	20.9	21.1	21.3	21.5	21.4	21.3	21.3	21.4	21.1
2002	21.0	21.0	20.9	21.0	20.9	21.0	21.2	21.2	21.1	21.4	21.1	21.2	21.1
2003	21.6	21.6	21.8	21.4	21.1	20.9	20.7	20.5	20.3	20.1	19.8	19.7	20.8
2004	19.8	19.9	19.9	20.9	20.7	20.8	21.2	21.1	21.1	21.2	21.2	21.3	20.8
2005	21.1	21.2	21.3	21.4	21.4	21.5	21.7	21.7	21.7	21.4	21.5	21.5	21.5
2006	21.5	21.6	21.8	21.8	22.0	22.1	22.3	22.4	22.4	22.5	22.5	22.6	22.1
2007	22.3	22.5	22.5	22.5	22.4	22.6	22.4	22.3	22.4	22.4	22.4	22.2	22.4
2008	21.9	22.0	22.0	22.1	22.2	22.3	22.2	22.2	22.1	22.1	22.2	22.1	22.1
2009	21.6	21.6	21.4	21.4	21.4	21.4	21.3	21.3	21.3	21.3	21.3	21.2	21.4

Employment by Industry: Greensboro-High Point, NC, Selected Years, 1990–2009—*Continued*

(Numbers in thousands, not seasonally adjusted.)

Industry and year	January	February	March	April	May	June	July	August	September	October	November	December	Annual average
Professional and Business Services													
1990	25.9	26.4	26.7	26.8	27.3	27.7	27.7	28.1	28.1	28.0	28.0	27.3	27.3
2000	44.5	45.4	46.2	46.4	46.2	46.3	45.4	45.9	46.0	45.9	45.8	45.5	45.8
2001	43.8	44.1	44.2	43.5	43.4	43.3	42.1	42.6	42.8	42.1	41.6	40.9	42.9
2002	39.2	40.2	40.4	41.1	41.3	41.2	41.0	41.8	42.0	42.0	42.1	42.0	41.2
2003	39.9	40.3	41.2	41.4	41.3	41.4	40.8	41.4	41.8	42.9	42.5	41.7	41.4
2004	41.3	42.0	42.6	43.9	44.2	44.1	44.1	44.4	44.8	45.0	44.6	44.5	43.8
2005	44.7	45.8	46.2	45.9	45.0	45.1	45.2	45.6	46.0	45.3	45.4	45.2	45.5
2006	44.2	44.5	45.6	47.4	48.2	47.9	48.1	48.5	47.8	49.0	48.7	48.3	47.4
2007	45.3	46.2	47.0	47.0	47.2	47.4	47.0	48.2	48.5	48.7	48.1	47.8	47.4
2008	47.2	47.3	47.7	47.6	46.8	46.5	47.1	48.6	48.6	49.1	47.1	44.9	47.4
2009	42.9	42.6	41.7	41.2	40.7	41.3	41.3	42.1	42.7	43.0	42.9	43.0	42.1
Education and Health Services													
1990	23.1	23.4	23.5	23.6	23.7	23.7	23.6	23.9	24.2	24.1	24.1	24.2	23.8
2000	36.1	36.2	36.4	36.0	36.2	36.5	36.7	37.1	37.3	37.6	38.1	37.9	36.8
2001	37.5	38.1	38.1	38.4	38.4	38.6	38.4	38.6	38.8	39.8	40.1	40.5	38.8
2002	39.8	40.2	40.5	40.7	40.7	40.9	40.8	40.9	41.1	41.8	41.9	41.8	40.9
2003	41.2	41.6	41.7	41.5	41.4	41.3	41.1	41.3	41.5	42.0	41.9	41.8	41.5
2004	41.6	42.1	42.1	42.6	42.6	42.6	42.3	42.7	42.9	43.6	43.7	43.8	42.7
2005	43.3	43.8	44.2	44.4	44.4	44.3	44.5	44.8	45.1	45.3	45.5	45.4	44.6
2006	45.6	46.0	46.1	46.0	45.9	45.9	45.8	46.1	46.1	46.4	46.5	46.6	46.1
2007	46.6	47.0	47.1	46.8	47.0	46.7	46.3	46.4	46.1	46.9	46.7	46.7	46.7
2008	46.3	46.5	46.5	47.0	46.9	46.9	46.5	47.0	47.0	47.9	48.4	48.0	47.1
2009	47.7	48.1	47.5	47.9	47.8	47.4	47.3	47.4	46.7	47.3	47.2	47.0	47.4
Leisure and Hospitality													
1990	18.7	19.0	19.1	19.6	19.8	20.2	19.9	20.5	20.4	20.2	19.9	19.6	19.7
2000	25.1	25.0	25.5	26.5	26.8	27.3	26.8	26.7	26.4	26.4	26.1	26.1	26.2
2001	25.2	26.3	26.1	26.8	27.3	27.4	27.5	27.5	26.7	26.1	25.8	25.8	26.5
2002	25.5	25.9	26.4	28.3	28.7	29.3	29.7	29.6	29.4	29.3	29.1	29.2	28.4
2003	27.8	27.5	28.0	28.8	29.0	29.6	29.1	29.4	28.5	28.6	28.3	28.2	28.6
2004	27.2	27.8	28.7	29.9	30.5	31.2	30.8	30.9	30.4	29.7	29.4	29.0	29.6
2005	27.7	27.9	28.8	29.7	30.2	30.8	30.2	30.5	29.8	29.6	29.4	29.0	29.5
2006	28.9	29.4	30.0	30.8	31.6	32.6	32.8	32.9	32.3	32.0	31.9	31.9	31.4
2007	31.0	31.2	32.1	32.6	33.4	34.0	33.6	33.7	33.1	32.6	32.6	32.5	32.7
2008	32.3	32.7	33.2	32.5	33.0	33.2	32.9	33.1	32.4	31.5	31.2	30.7	32.4
2009	29.6	29.9	30.2	30.5	31.5	31.6	31.5	31.3	30.6	30.7	30.2	30.2	30.7
Other Services													
1990	6.9	6.9	7.0	7.2	7.1	7.4	7.3	7.4	7.3	7.3	7.4	7.4	7.2
2000	8.9	9.2	9.5	9.7	10.0	10.2	10.3	10.5	10.7	10.8	11.0	11.2	10.2
2001	11.3	11.6	11.9	12.0	12.3	12.4	12.7	12.7	12.8	12.9	13.1	13.4	12.4
2002	13.5	13.8	14.0	14.4	14.5	14.9	15.3	15.4	15.2	15.4	15.4	15.3	14.8
2003	15.1	15.1	15.0	15.2	15.0	15.1	15.0	14.7	14.7	14.5	14.5	14.5	14.9
2004	14.5	14.6	14.8	15.5	15.6	15.7	15.1	14.7	14.6	14.8	14.5	14.5	14.9
2005	14.3	14.5	14.5	14.6	14.5	14.6	14.5	14.4	14.3	14.4	14.4	14.5	14.5
2006	14.3	14.4	14.6	14.3	14.6	14.5	14.2	14.0	13.9	14.3	14.2	14.3	14.3
2007	14.2	14.2	14.4	14.7	14.8	14.9	15.1	14.9	14.8	15.1	14.9	15.0	14.8
2008	14.9	15.0	15.0	14.9	14.7	14.8	15.0	14.9	14.7	14.7	14.7	14.7	14.8
2009	14.5	14.6	14.6	14.6	14.8	14.8	14.8	14.7	14.5	14.4	14.3	14.2	14.6
Government													
1990	28.9	29.1	29.3	29.8	30.0	29.6	28.0	28.2	28.8	30.0	30.1	30.0	29.3
2000	38.2	38.4	39.1	39.2	39.2	39.2	33.7	37.3	38.6	39.8	40.8	41.1	38.7
2001	39.7	40.0	40.2	40.2	40.5	40.0	33.7	37.0	38.9	40.4	41.6	41.0	39.4
2002	40.3	40.6	41.1	41.6	41.5	40.4	34.5	37.6	40.3	41.6	42.6	42.1	40.4
2003	41.0	41.5	41.7	42.1	42.4	40.6	35.1	37.9	40.9	43.1	42.3	42.3	40.9
2004	41.3	41.5	42.0	42.4	42.5	41.1	35.2	38.4	41.2	42.6	42.4	42.8	41.1
2005	42.0	42.4	42.7	42.9	43.1	41.3	35.7	40.0	42.2	43.9	43.4	43.6	41.9
2006	42.7	43.1	43.7	44.1	44.3	41.8	36.5	40.7	42.9	44.1	44.6	45.0	42.8
2007	43.6	43.8	44.3	44.5	44.7	42.3	37.2	41.4	43.6	45.0	45.4	45.0	43.4
2008	45.0	45.4	45.8	46.0	46.4	43.8	38.5	42.6	46.0	46.3	46.5	46.0	44.9
2009	45.7	46.1	46.4	46.9	46.7	45.4	39.4	43.3	47.0	48.6	49.1	47.8	46.0

Employment by Industry: Hartford-West Hartford-East Hartford, CT, NECTA, Selected Years, 1990–2009

(Numbers in thousands, not seasonally adjusted.)

Industry and year	January	February	March	April	May	June	July	August	September	October	November	December	Annual average
Total Nonfarm													
1990	576.9	576.8	579.2	578.5	581.5	582.9	570.2	566.3	575.9	574.1	573.5	572.8	575.7
2000	547.6	550.9	554.5	555.4	557.4	559.5	554.4	548.8	558.0	561.6	564.5	568.2	556.7
2001	552.4	552.5	554.1	554.9	555.8	557.7	550.2	547.5	552.4	554.2	556.4	557.5	553.8
2002	542.7	544.0	545.8	546.3	549.3	549.6	539.2	536.3	543.2	544.3	546.9	547.9	544.6
2003	534.3	533.2	533.3	536.5	539.0	538.1	529.2	526.4	533.5	539.0	540.9	541.3	535.4
2004	528.3	529.2	531.3	537.5	540.0	541.0	534.0	531.0	539.8	543.3	546.4	548.6	537.5
2005	535.0	536.2	537.3	545.0	546.6	548.8	539.9	538.0	546.8	547.7	552.4	553.2	543.9
2006	541.2	541.8	543.7	549.7	551.8	553.0	547.5	545.4	552.6	557.2	559.5	560.4	550.3
2007	547.0	548.7	550.2	554.8	558.5	561.9	553.3	551.0	558.2	561.2	565.1	564.5	556.2
2008	552.2	555.1	557.1	560.7	562.2	565.1	555.7	551.9	559.9	561.8	560.4	556.7	558.2
2009	541.3	543.1	540.9	541.2	542.9	542.3	533.7	529.6	538.4	544.0	545.4	541.0	540.3
Total Private													
1990	495.0	491.8	493.8	492.8	495.3	498.6	491.4	488.8	493.1	489.2	487.0	486.7	492.0
2000	461.5	461.5	464.6	465.5	467.5	472.9	474.3	470.6	471.7	473.2	475.2	479.5	469.8
2001	465.8	462.9	464.4	465.1	466.7	471.6	469.4	467.3	465.0	464.3	465.0	466.4	466.2
2002	454.8	452.8	454.4	455.5	458.9	462.0	458.2	455.4	454.7	454.6	456.0	457.2	456.2
2003	447.3	443.2	443.8	447.5	451.1	452.7	450.6	448.6	449.9	452.2	453.7	454.2	449.6
2004	444.5	442.2	444.2	449.7	453.4	456.8	455.9	453.8	455.7	456.3	458.4	461.0	452.7
2005	450.6	449.0	450.5	456.8	459.3	464.0	460.4	459.4	460.0	459.3	462.1	464.6	458.0
2006	455.8	454.0	456.0	460.5	463.3	467.6	466.7	465.5	464.9	466.7	467.8	470.2	463.3
2007	459.6	458.6	460.2	464.3	470.6	476.3	472.5	471.1	470.7	470.9	473.9	475.2	468.7
2008	465.8	464.9	466.9	469.9	474.0	479.0	474.3	471.5	472.2	471.6	470.2	468.8	470.8
2009	456.0	452.7	450.8	450.1	454.8	456.6	453.4	450.9	450.8	453.1	453.5	450.9	452.8
Goods-Producing													
1990	119.1	117.5	118.2	119.9	120.2	120.8	118.5	117.2	119.0	117.0	115.7	114.0	118.1
2000	93.7	93.3	94.5	96.0	96.5	97.7	98.6	98.4	99.1	99.2	99.2	99.3	97.1
2001	96.1	95.0	95.2	95.9	96.2	96.6	95.3	95.2	94.5	93.4	92.5	92.3	94.9
2002	89.6	88.7	89.2	90.2	90.8	91.2	90.0	89.7	89.4	88.8	88.1	87.3	89.4
2003	84.5	83.0	83.2	84.5	85.1	85.6	85.6	85.6	85.6	85.5	85.6	85.1	84.9
2004	82.4	81.8	82.6	84.5	85.4	86.6	86.9	86.8	86.9	86.6	86.7	86.3	85.3
2005	83.8	83.1	83.5	85.4	86.2	87.7	87.1	86.9	86.6	86.3	86.4	85.9	85.7
2006	84.1	83.8	84.2	86.1	86.8	88.1	88.6	88.6	88.1	88.0	87.8	87.6	86.8
2007	85.2	84.5	84.9	86.5	87.9	88.9	88.9	88.9	88.0	87.8	87.7	86.9	87.2
2008	84.4	84.0	83.9	85.6	86.1	87.2	86.8	86.5	86.1	85.2	83.9	82.5	85.2
2009	79.7	78.2	77.3	77.1	77.5	77.7	77.3	76.8	76.8	76.5	75.7	74.6	77.1
Mining, Logging, and Construction													
1990	22.3	21.5	22.0	22.8	23.6	24.2	24.4	24.3	24.0	22.8	22.1	20.8	22.9
2000	19.3	19.0	19.9	21.0	21.6	22.3	22.8	23.0	22.8	22.5	22.5	22.2	21.6
2001	20.1	19.8	20.2	21.5	22.4	22.9	22.8	22.9	22.4	21.8	21.2	20.7	21.6
2002	19.6	19.3	19.7	20.9	21.6	21.9	21.8	21.8	21.4	21.2	20.9	20.1	20.9
2003	18.5	17.7	17.9	19.2	20.1	20.6	21.5	21.6	21.4	21.3	21.4	20.7	20.2
2004	18.5	18.1	18.6	20.5	21.3	22.0	22.6	23.0	22.8	22.7	22.6	22.1	21.2
2005	20.1	19.5	19.8	21.3	22.0	23.0	23.1	23.2	22.8	22.4	22.4	21.7	21.8
2006	20.3	19.9	20.2	21.6	22.3	22.9	23.5	23.8	23.3	23.2	23.0	22.5	22.2
2007	20.8	20.1	20.5	22.1	23.4	23.9	24.1	24.2	23.8	23.6	23.3	22.4	22.7
2008	20.4	20.1	20.2	21.4	21.9	22.4	22.5	22.3	21.9	21.4	20.6	19.6	21.2
2009	17.7	17.1	17.1	17.9	18.7	19.1	19.2	19.3	19.1	19.4	18.8	17.4	18.4
Manufacturing													
1990	96.8	96.0	96.2	97.1	96.6	96.6	94.1	92.9	95.0	94.2	93.6	93.2	95.2
2000	74.4	74.3	74.6	75.0	74.9	75.4	75.8	75.4	76.3	76.7	76.7	77.1	75.6
2001	76.0	75.2	75.0	74.4	73.8	73.7	72.5	72.3	72.1	71.6	71.3	71.6	73.3
2002	70.0	69.4	69.5	69.3	69.2	69.3	68.2	67.9	68.0	67.6	67.2	67.2	68.6
2003	66.0	65.3	65.3	65.3	65.0	65.0	64.1	64.0	64.2	64.2	64.2	64.4	64.8
2004	63.9	63.7	64.0	64.0	64.1	64.6	64.3	63.8	64.1	63.9	64.1	64.2	64.1
2005	63.7	63.6	63.7	64.1	64.2	64.7	64.0	63.7	63.8	63.9	64.0	64.2	64.0
2006	63.8	63.9	64.0	64.5	64.5	65.2	65.1	64.8	64.8	64.8	64.8	65.1	64.6
2007	64.4	64.4	64.4	64.4	64.5	65.0	64.8	64.7	64.2	64.2	64.4	64.5	64.5
2008	64.0	63.9	63.7	64.2	64.2	64.8	64.3	64.2	64.2	63.8	63.3	62.9	64.0
2009	62.0	61.1	60.2	59.2	58.8	58.6	58.1	57.5	57.7	57.1	56.9	57.2	58.7
Service-Providing													
1990	457.8	459.3	461.0	458.6	461.3	462.1	451.7	449.1	456.9	457.1	457.8	458.8	457.6
2000	453.9	457.6	460.0	459.4	460.9	461.8	455.8	450.4	458.9	462.4	465.3	468.9	459.6
2001	456.3	457.5	458.9	459.0	459.6	461.1	454.9	452.3	457.9	460.8	463.9	465.2	459.0
2002	453.1	455.3	456.6	456.1	458.5	458.4	449.2	446.6	453.8	455.5	458.8	460.6	455.2
2003	449.8	450.2	450.1	452.0	453.9	452.5	443.6	440.8	447.9	453.5	455.3	456.2	450.5
2004	445.9	447.4	448.7	453.0	454.6	454.4	447.1	444.2	452.9	456.7	459.7	462.3	452.2
2005	451.2	453.1	453.8	459.6	460.4	461.1	452.8	451.1	460.2	461.4	466.0	467.3	458.2
2006	457.1	458.0	459.5	463.6	465.0	464.9	458.9	456.8	464.5	469.2	471.7	472.8	463.5
2007	461.8	464.2	465.3	468.3	470.6	473.0	464.4	462.1	470.2	473.4	477.4	477.6	469.0
2008	467.8	471.1	473.2	475.1	476.1	477.9	468.9	465.4	473.8	476.6	476.5	474.2	473.1
2009	461.6	464.9	463.6	464.1	465.4	464.6	456.4	452.8	461.6	467.5	469.7	466.4	463.2

Employment by Industry: Hartford-West Hartford-East Hartford, CT, NECTA, Selected Years, 1990–2009—*Continued*

(Numbers in thousands, not seasonally adjusted.)

Industry and year	January	February	March	April	May	June	July	August	September	October	November	December	Annual average
Trade, Transportation, and Utilities													
1990	102.8	100.6	101.3	99.8	100.2	100.8	98.0	97.8	99.2	99.9	100.8	101.9	100.3
2000	93.7	92.5	92.9	91.7	92.0	92.5	91.2	90.6	92.0	92.7	94.8	96.2	92.7
2001	91.8	89.9	90.3	91.1	91.5	91.9	90.6	90.0	91.1	91.7	93.4	94.3	91.5
2002	91.0	89.6	89.8	89.1	89.4	90.6	88.2	87.7	88.6	88.3	89.8	91.3	89.5
2003	88.1	86.7	87.0	86.8	87.3	87.7	86.3	86.0	87.5	88.7	90.0	90.8	87.7
2004	88.0	87.1	87.3	88.0	88.6	89.2	88.0	87.5	89.1	90.0	92.3	94.0	89.1
2005	90.2	89.1	89.3	90.1	90.2	90.8	88.4	88.2	89.8	89.7	92.0	93.6	90.1
2006	90.1	88.1	88.6	89.4	89.7	89.9	87.8	87.6	89.0	89.6	91.4	93.0	89.5
2007	89.1	87.6	88.1	87.9	89.6	90.6	88.8	88.3	89.8	90.9	93.1	94.8	89.9
2008	91.3	89.9	90.2	90.1	90.9	91.6	89.3	88.8	90.2	90.5	91.4	92.4	90.6
2009	88.2	86.4	85.8	84.6	86.1	86.6	84.7	84.5	85.7	86.5	87.2	88.8	86.3
Wholesale Trade													
1990	23.2	23.0	23.0	22.4	22.3	22.3	22.2	22.1	21.8	21.7	21.6	21.4	22.3
2000	20.3	20.2	20.3	20.1	20.1	20.1	20.2	20.1	20.1	20.0	20.2	20.3	20.2
2001	20.1	20.1	20.1	20.2	20.1	20.2	20.2	20.1	19.9	20.1	19.9	20.0	20.1
2002	19.7	19.6	19.6	19.4	19.3	19.3	19.4	19.3	19.2	19.1	19.0	19.1	19.3
2003	19.5	19.4	19.6	19.5	19.5	19.6	19.4	19.4	19.3	19.2	19.2	18.9	19.4
2004	18.7	18.6	18.7	18.9	18.9	19.1	19.2	19.2	19.1	19.0	19.1	19.2	19.0
2005	19.1	19.0	19.1	19.4	19.5	19.7	19.5	19.5	19.6	19.5	19.6	19.6	19.4
2006	19.6	19.5	19.6	19.8	19.7	19.9	19.7	19.7	19.6	19.6	19.5	19.5	19.6
2007	19.5	19.5	19.6	19.6	19.8	19.9	20.1	20.0	20.0	20.0	20.0	20.7	19.9
2008	20.0	20.0	20.2	20.1	20.3	20.4	20.2	20.1	20.0	19.9	19.7	19.5	20.0
2009	19.4	19.1	19.0	18.8	18.8	18.8	18.8	18.7	18.5	18.5	18.4	18.4	18.8
Retail Trade													
1990	63.4	61.8	62.0	61.5	61.8	62.2	60.8	60.7	61.6	62.4	63.4	64.6	62.2
2000	57.3	56.2	56.5	55.5	55.8	56.3	55.4	55.3	55.3	55.8	57.7	59.2	56.4
2001	55.7	54.3	54.7	55.5	56.1	56.5	56.0	56.0	55.9	56.1	58.0	58.9	56.1
2002	56.4	55.2	55.6	55.5	55.8	57.0	55.7	55.7	55.4	54.8	56.4	57.8	55.9
2003	54.6	53.4	53.5	53.6	54.0	54.3	53.9	54.0	54.2	55.0	56.2	57.4	54.5
2004	55.2	54.4	54.5	54.7	55.2	55.5	55.2	55.0	55.3	55.7	57.8	59.4	55.7
2005	56.2	55.4	55.4	55.8	55.8	56.0	55.0	55.1	55.3	55.3	57.2	58.5	55.9
2006	55.8	54.0	54.5	55.1	55.3	55.3	54.5	54.4	54.6	55.1	56.9	58.1	55.3
2007	54.9	53.5	53.9	54.0	55.3	56.0	55.1	55.2	55.1	55.9	58.0	59.2	55.5
2008	56.4	54.9	55.0	55.0	55.4	55.9	54.8	54.9	54.6	54.8	55.8	56.7	55.4
2009	53.4	52.0	51.6	51.3	52.1	52.6	52.0	52.1	52.1	52.8	53.5	54.7	52.5
Transportation and Utilities													
1990	16.2	15.8	16.3	15.9	16.1	16.3	15.0	15.0	15.8	15.8	15.8	15.9	15.8
2000	16.1	16.1	16.1	16.1	16.1	16.1	15.6	15.2	16.6	16.9	16.9	16.7	16.2
2001	16.0	15.5	15.5	15.4	15.3	15.2	14.4	13.9	15.3	15.5	15.5	15.4	15.2
2002	14.9	14.8	14.6	14.2	14.3	14.3	13.1	12.7	14.0	14.4	14.4	14.4	14.2
2003	14.0	13.9	13.9	13.7	13.8	13.8	13.0	12.6	14.0	14.5	14.6	14.5	13.9
2004	14.1	14.1	14.1	14.4	14.5	14.6	13.6	13.3	14.7	15.3	15.4	15.4	14.5
2005	14.9	14.7	14.8	14.9	14.9	15.1	13.9	13.6	14.9	14.9	15.2	15.5	14.8
2006	14.7	14.6	14.5	14.5	14.7	14.7	13.6	13.5	14.8	14.9	15.0	15.4	14.6
2007	14.7	14.6	14.6	14.3	14.5	14.7	13.6	13.1	14.7	15.0	15.1	15.4	14.5
2008	14.9	15.0	15.0	15.0	15.2	15.3	14.3	13.8	15.6	15.8	15.9	16.2	15.2
2009	15.4	15.3	15.3	14.5	15.2	15.2	13.9	13.7	15.1	15.2	15.3	15.7	15.0
Information													
1990	9.5	9.5	9.6	9.4	9.5	9.4	9.6	9.5	9.5	9.5	9.4	9.3	9.5
2000	12.5	12.6	12.7	12.8	12.9	13.0	13.2	13.2	13.2	13.3	13.4	13.4	13.0
2001	13.0	13.1	12.8	11.9	11.8	11.7	12.2	12.2	12.0	11.9	12.0	11.8	12.2
2002	11.4	11.3	11.3	11.4	11.4	11.5	11.4	11.3	11.2	11.2	11.2	11.2	11.3
2003	11.3	11.3	11.3	11.1	11.1	11.3	11.2	11.2	11.0	11.0	11.0	11.0	11.2
2004	11.3	11.2	11.3	11.3	11.3	11.4	11.4	11.4	11.3	11.3	11.4	11.4	11.3
2005	11.5	11.4	11.4	11.4	11.5	11.6	11.6	11.6	11.5	11.6	11.7	11.8	11.6
2006	12.0	12.0	12.0	11.9	11.9	12.1	12.1	12.0	11.8	11.9	11.9	11.9	12.0
2007	11.9	12.0	12.0	12.1	12.1	12.3	12.4	12.3	12.2	12.1	12.2	12.3	12.2
2008	12.4	12.4	12.4	12.4	12.4	12.6	12.6	12.4	12.1	12.1	12.2	12.1	12.3
2009	12.0	12.0	11.8	11.8	11.7	11.8	11.7	11.7	11.6	11.5	11.6	11.5	11.7
Financial Activities													
1990	85.9	86.1	86.4	86.2	87.2	88.0	88.5	88.3	86.9	86.0	84.9	85.7	86.7
2000	69.3	69.2	69.6	69.1	69.2	70.2	70.5	70.5	69.8	69.7	69.8	70.2	69.8
2001	70.0	69.7	69.9	70.1	70.4	71.4	71.5	71.4	70.7	70.2	70.2	70.5	70.5
2002	70.2	69.7	69.7	69.3	69.6	70.3	70.6	70.5	69.9	69.5	69.7	69.7	69.9
2003	69.4	68.9	68.6	69.7	69.9	70.6	70.1	69.7	69.1	68.7	68.7	68.8	69.4
2004	68.2	67.6	67.4	67.4	67.3	68.2	68.8	68.7	68.2	67.8	68.0	68.2	68.0
2005	68.1	67.8	67.0	67.9	67.6	68.4	68.4	68.4	67.8	67.5	67.4	67.7	67.8
2006	67.8	67.6	67.5	67.1	67.2	67.9	68.2	68.0	67.4	67.3	67.4	67.6	67.6
2007	67.6	67.1	66.9	66.6	66.7	67.5	67.2	67.1	66.4	66.1	66.1	66.2	66.8
2008	65.9	66.0	66.6	65.9	66.0	66.8	66.8	66.7	65.7	65.3	65.4	65.2	66.0
2009	64.7	64.5	64.4	63.8	63.8	64.1	63.7	63.3	62.5	62.1	62.5	62.0	63.5

Employment by Industry: Hartford-West Hartford-East Hartford, CT, NECTA, Selected Years, 1990–2009—*Continued*
(Numbers in thousands, not seasonally adjusted.)

Industry and year	January	February	March	April	May	June	July	August	September	October	November	December	Annual average
Professional and Business Services													
1990	56.5	56.7	57.6	55.7	55.6	56.1	55.4	55.6	55.8	54.5	54.1	53.4	55.6
2000	58.7	58.7	59.0	59.9	59.6	61.0	61.2	61.1	60.6	60.7	60.7	61.1	60.2
2001	59.2	59.0	59.5	60.0	59.6	60.3	59.3	59.0	58.4	58.4	57.9	57.4	59.0
2002	56.5	56.6	57.5	57.7	57.6	57.9	57.1	57.0	56.7	56.9	57.0	56.8	57.1
2003	55.5	55.1	55.2	56.0	55.9	56.1	55.9	56.0	56.2	56.3	56.7	56.3	55.9
2004	55.7	55.4	55.8	57.1	56.9	57.5	57.5	57.7	57.8	57.8	58.0	58.1	57.1
2005	56.8	56.8	57.5	58.2	58.1	59.3	59.5	59.5	59.6	59.0	59.3	59.6	58.6
2006	58.3	58.6	58.9	60.0	59.8	60.7	60.7	60.8	60.6	60.7	60.5	60.6	60.0
2007	58.8	59.1	59.4	61.0	61.3	62.4	61.7	61.9	61.4	61.0	61.4	62.1	61.0
2008	61.3	61.5	61.8	62.1	62.4	63.3	62.9	62.6	62.1	61.6	61.3	60.5	62.0
2009	59.3	58.6	58.2	58.4	58.7	58.6	58.1	58.3	57.6	58.6	58.9	57.9	58.4
Education and Health Services													
1990	65.2	65.6	64.7	65.9	65.8	65.9	64.3	64.2	65.9	66.6	67.1	67.3	65.7
2000	77.6	78.8	79.2	78.1	77.8	77.7	78.6	77.0	78.1	79.0	79.4	80.5	78.5
2001	79.3	80.0	79.9	79.5	78.4	79.8	80.4	79.9	80.4	81.4	82.4	83.1	80.4
2002	81.3	82.0	82.0	81.6	82.2	81.5	81.1	80.4	81.7	82.8	83.6	83.9	82.0
2003	82.6	82.7	82.5	82.5	82.7	81.7	81.5	80.5	82.3	83.7	84.2	84.3	82.6
2004	82.9	83.2	83.5	83.6	84.3	83.2	82.4	81.6	83.4	84.4	84.7	85.0	83.5
2005	83.6	84.1	84.2	84.6	84.8	83.9	83.3	83.0	84.4	85.9	86.1	86.3	84.5
2006	85.3	85.8	85.8	86.2	86.4	85.7	86.1	85.7	86.7	88.1	88.6	88.7	86.6
2007	88.2	89.2	89.6	89.8	89.9	89.6	88.9	88.1	90.1	91.0	91.8	91.5	89.8
2008	91.1	91.6	91.9	92.4	92.2	92.3	91.9	91.1	93.2	94.3	94.9	94.9	92.7
2009	93.8	94.5	94.8	95.1	94.6	94.3	95.1	94.3	95.3	96.3	97.1	96.2	95.1
Leisure and Hospitality													
1990	34.1	34.5	34.6	34.7	35.6	36.0	35.5	34.7	35.7	34.8	34.1	34.2	34.9
2000	34.7	35.1	35.2	36.3	37.8	38.9	39.0	38.1	37.3	36.8	36.2	37.0	36.9
2001	35.1	34.9	35.3	35.0	37.2	38.0	38.1	37.8	36.5	35.6	34.8	35.1	36.1
2002	33.5	33.6	33.4	34.7	36.3	37.3	38.1	37.5	36.2	35.9	35.3	35.6	35.6
2003	35.2	34.8	35.1	36.0	38.1	38.5	38.8	38.7	37.5	37.6	36.9	37.2	37.0
2004	35.5	35.4	35.7	37.1	38.9	39.7	39.9	39.3	38.4	37.7	36.6	37.3	37.6
2005	36.2	36.3	37.1	38.4	40.2	41.2	41.2	41.1	39.8	38.7	38.6	39.0	39.0
2006	37.7	37.6	38.4	39.0	40.6	42.1	42.1	41.9	40.5	40.2	39.4	40.0	40.0
2007	38.1	38.4	38.6	39.5	42.2	43.7	43.6	43.6	42.0	41.1	40.8	40.6	41.0
2008	38.8	38.8	39.3	40.5	43.0	44.0	43.4	42.9	42.1	41.9	40.4	40.7	41.3
2009	37.9	38.4	38.4	39.1	42.1	43.1	42.7	42.0	41.3	41.4	40.4	39.9	40.6
Other Services													
1990	21.9	21.3	21.4	21.2	21.2	21.6	21.6	21.5	21.1	20.9	20.9	20.9	21.3
2000	21.3	21.3	21.5	21.6	21.7	21.9	22.0	21.7	21.6	21.8	21.7	21.8	21.7
2001	21.3	21.3	21.5	21.6	21.6	21.9	22.0	21.8	21.4	21.7	21.8	21.9	21.7
2002	21.3	21.3	21.5	21.5	21.6	21.7	21.7	21.3	21.0	21.2	21.3	21.4	21.4
2003	20.7	20.7	20.9	20.9	21.0	21.2	21.2	20.9	20.7	20.7	20.6	20.7	20.9
2004	20.5	20.5	20.6	20.7	20.7	21.0	21.0	20.8	20.6	20.7	20.7	20.7	20.7
2005	20.4	20.4	20.5	20.8	20.7	21.1	20.9	20.7	20.5	20.6	20.6	20.7	20.7
2006	20.5	20.5	20.6	20.8	20.9	21.1	21.1	20.9	20.8	20.9	20.8	20.8	20.8
2007	20.7	20.7	20.7	20.9	20.9	21.3	21.0	20.9	20.8	20.9	20.8	20.8	20.9
2008	20.6	20.7	20.8	20.9	21.0	21.2	20.6	20.5	20.7	20.7	20.7	20.5	20.7
2009	20.4	20.1	20.1	20.2	20.3	20.4	20.1	20.0	20.0	20.2	20.1	20.0	20.2
Government													
1990	81.9	85.0	85.4	85.7	86.2	84.3	78.8	77.5	82.8	84.9	86.5	86.1	83.8
2000	86.1	89.4	89.9	89.9	89.9	86.6	80.1	78.2	86.3	88.4	89.3	88.7	86.9
2001	86.6	89.6	89.7	89.8	89.1	86.1	80.8	80.2	87.4	89.9	91.4	91.1	87.6
2002	87.9	91.2	91.4	90.8	90.4	87.6	81.0	80.9	88.5	89.7	90.9	90.7	88.4
2003	87.0	90.0	89.5	89.0	87.9	85.4	78.6	77.8	83.6	86.8	87.2	87.1	85.8
2004	83.8	87.0	87.1	87.8	86.6	84.2	78.1	77.2	84.1	87.0	88.0	87.6	84.9
2005	84.4	87.2	86.8	88.2	87.3	84.8	79.5	78.6	86.8	88.4	90.3	88.6	85.9
2006	85.4	87.8	87.7	89.2	88.5	85.4	80.8	79.9	87.7	90.5	91.7	90.2	87.1
2007	87.4	90.1	90.0	90.5	87.9	85.6	80.8	79.9	87.5	90.3	91.2	89.3	87.5
2008	86.4	90.2	90.2	90.8	88.2	86.1	81.4	80.4	87.7	90.2	90.2	87.9	87.5
2009	85.3	90.4	90.1	91.1	88.1	85.7	80.3	78.7	87.6	90.9	91.9	90.1	87.5

Employment by Industry: Honolulu, HI, Selected Years, 1990–2009

(Numbers in thousands, not seasonally adjusted.)

Industry and year	January	February	March	April	May	June	July	August	September	October	November	December	Annual average
Total Nonfarm													
1990	399.5	406.1	408.3	409.3	412.0	413.4	410.1	409.6	404.9	413.7	419.7	422.3	410.7
2000	404.5	406.5	407.6	409.8	410.6	413.4	412.9	413.1	416.6	415.5	416.2	416.5	411.7
2001	405.9	415.2	417.9	413.0	414.3	419.1	409.3	410.6	412.3	408.3	410.7	413.4	412.5
2002	401.8	408.3	411.0	405.0	414.7	419.6	408.0	409.0	413.0	416.5	421.3	426.2	412.9
2003	414.2	418.8	421.0	416.6	421.2	420.8	414.1	414.6	417.2	420.9	426.4	429.8	419.6
2004	419.0	423.2	425.9	426.3	429.8	430.3	424.7	425.9	429.3	435.2	442.5	444.1	429.7
2005	429.9	437.3	440.0	440.4	443.5	444.3	437.6	441.0	444.2	446.2	451.1	456.3	442.7
2006	440.0	449.6	452.7	448.9	453.5	454.9	445.5	448.7	453.9	451.8	460.1	461.4	451.8
2007	447.2	454.2	457.2	449.9	457.3	458.9	448.3	449.7	456.2	458.0	462.3	465.8	455.4
2008	450.9	456.6	459.0	451.6	457.3	455.5	445.7	447.2	449.4	450.1	455.7	454.3	452.8
2009	440.4	443.4	444.5	439.2	440.3	438.9	428.5	426.7	431.1	436.6	439.4	442.5	437.6
Total Private													
1990	315.2	318.3	317.9	318.0	319.2	323.3	325.3	325.2	324.7	326.3	328.5	330.2	322.7
2000	310.5	313.6	315.6	315.5	317.0	321.6	320.1	322.1	324.6	323.7	326.4	329.3	320.0
2001	320.4	322.2	324.1	321.0	322.7	325.2	323.3	323.7	323.1	316.2	315.6	317.3	321.2
2002	310.7	313.0	314.5	314.6	317.4	319.9	319.9	320.3	322.2	321.6	324.8	328.2	318.9
2003	319.5	321.5	323.2	322.1	323.5	324.1	324.3	325.5	326.7	325.5	329.4	332.4	324.8
2004	324.7	326.6	327.9	329.0	331.1	333.5	334.5	335.4	336.4	339.2	343.4	346.0	334.0
2005	337.8	340.5	342.4	343.6	345.4	347.6	348.0	349.8	351.7	350.7	354.1	358.3	347.5
2006	348.8	352.5	354.7	351.8	354.6	357.5	355.7	357.6	358.7	354.6	358.7	361.7	355.6
2007	352.6	355.4	357.7	355.4	357.7	360.9	358.2	359.8	360.6	360.2	362.9	365.5	358.9
2008	355.4	357.4	358.6	356.1	356.2	356.2	353.6	353.4	352.4	349.8	351.3	352.5	354.4
2009	342.1	343.1	342.7	337.7	337.5	338.1	335.0	334.5	335.4	338.1	340.1	342.5	338.9
Goods-Producing													
1990	41.2	41.6	41.8	41.1	41.3	42.1	42.3	42.4	42.4	42.7	42.8	42.7	42.0
2000	28.7	28.8	29.4	29.5	29.9	30.3	30.6	31.0	31.2	31.0	30.8	31.0	30.2
2001	30.1	30.1	30.0	29.8	29.9	30.1	30.0	30.1	29.9	29.2	29.1	29.2	29.8
2002	28.7	28.6	29.1	28.9	29.2	30.0	30.1	30.3	30.0	29.9	30.1	30.2	29.6
2003	29.6	29.7	30.2	30.3	30.7	30.9	31.2	31.4	31.4	31.7	31.8	31.7	30.9
2004	31.2	31.3	30.7	31.7	32.3	32.9	33.1	33.2	33.4	33.4	33.4	33.7	32.5
2005	33.1	33.5	34.0	34.4	34.8	35.2	35.4	35.9	36.3	36.1	36.2	36.5	35.1
2006	35.5	35.7	35.7	35.5	36.2	36.7	36.9	37.3	37.7	37.3	37.8	38.1	36.7
2007	37.0	37.3	37.4	37.4	37.9	38.6	38.7	39.0	39.2	39.0	39.3	39.3	38.3
2008	38.4	38.6	38.7	38.2	38.0	37.8	38.0	37.9	37.7	36.9	36.9	36.5	37.8
2009	34.8	34.5	34.3	33.6	33.6	33.6	33.3	32.9	32.7	33.0	32.8	33.2	33.5
Mining, Logging, and Construction													
1990	25.7	26.1	26.5	25.7	26.2	26.7	26.9	27.2	27.1	27.7	27.7	27.9	26.8
2000	16.4	16.5	16.8	17.0	17.3	17.6	17.9	18.1	18.2	18.0	17.9	18.1	17.5
2001	17.3	17.2	17.2	16.9	17.0	17.1	17.1	17.2	17.0	16.7	16.6	16.7	17.0
2002	16.5	16.5	16.9	17.1	17.4	18.1	18.4	18.7	18.5	18.5	18.7	18.7	17.8
2003	18.3	18.4	18.8	19.0	19.3	19.4	19.7	19.8	19.8	19.9	19.9	19.7	19.3
2004	19.3	19.4	18.9	19.7	20.3	20.7	21.1	21.2	21.4	21.5	21.5	21.8	20.6
2005	21.4	21.6	22.1	22.6	23.0	23.4	23.7	24.0	24.4	24.3	24.4	24.6	23.3
2006	23.9	24.0	24.0	23.9	24.5	24.8	25.0	25.3	25.7	25.5	25.8	26.1	24.9
2007	25.2	25.4	25.6	25.7	26.1	26.7	26.9	27.1	27.3	27.3	27.4	27.3	26.5
2008	26.6	26.8	26.8	26.4	26.1	26.0	26.2	26.1	26.0	25.5	25.4	25.0	26.1
2009	23.7	23.4	23.2	22.7	22.7	22.7	22.6	22.2	22.0	22.3	22.0	22.4	22.7
Manufacturing													
1990	15.5	15.5	15.3	15.4	15.1	15.4	15.4	15.2	15.3	15.0	15.1	14.8	15.3
2000	12.3	12.3	12.6	12.5	12.6	12.7	12.7	12.9	13.0	13.0	12.9	12.9	12.7
2001	12.8	12.9	12.8	12.9	12.9	13.0	12.9	12.9	12.9	12.5	12.5	12.5	12.8
2002	12.2	12.1	12.2	11.8	11.8	11.9	11.7	11.6	11.5	11.4	11.4	11.5	11.8
2003	11.3	11.3	11.4	11.3	11.4	11.5	11.5	11.6	11.6	11.8	11.9	12.0	11.6
2004	11.9	11.9	11.8	12.0	12.0	12.2	12.0	12.0	12.0	11.9	11.9	11.9	12.0
2005	11.7	11.9	11.9	11.8	11.8	11.8	11.7	11.9	11.9	11.8	11.8	11.9	11.8
2006	11.6	11.7	11.7	11.6	11.7	11.9	11.9	12.0	12.0	11.8	12.0	12.0	11.8
2007	11.8	11.9	11.8	11.7	11.8	11.9	11.8	11.9	11.9	11.7	11.9	12.0	11.8
2008	11.8	11.8	11.9	11.8	11.9	11.8	11.8	11.8	11.7	11.4	11.5	11.5	11.7
2009	11.1	11.1	11.1	10.9	10.9	10.9	10.7	10.7	10.7	10.7	10.8	10.8	10.9
Service-Providing													
1990	358.2	364.5	366.5	368.2	370.6	371.3	367.6	367.2	362.2	371.0	376.6	379.7	368.6
2000	370.1	377.3	380.1	379.9	382.7	385.6	376.4	377.6	381.6	384.0	389.1	393.2	381.5
2001	375.8	385.1	387.9	383.2	384.4	389.0	379.3	380.5	382.4	379.1	381.6	384.2	382.7
2002	373.1	379.7	381.9	376.1	385.5	389.6	377.9	378.7	383.0	386.6	391.2	396.0	383.3
2003	384.6	389.1	390.8	386.3	390.5	389.9	382.9	383.2	385.8	389.2	394.6	398.1	388.8
2004	387.8	391.9	395.2	394.6	397.5	397.4	391.6	392.7	395.9	401.8	409.1	410.4	397.2
2005	396.8	403.8	406.0	406.0	408.7	409.1	402.2	405.1	407.9	410.1	414.9	419.8	407.5
2006	404.5	413.9	417.0	413.4	417.3	418.2	408.6	411.4	416.2	414.5	422.3	423.3	415.1
2007	410.2	416.9	419.8	412.5	419.4	420.3	409.6	410.7	417.0	419.0	423.0	426.5	417.1
2008	412.5	418.0	420.3	413.4	419.3	417.7	407.7	409.3	411.7	413.2	418.8	417.8	415.0
2009	405.6	408.9	410.2	405.6	406.7	405.3	395.2	393.8	398.4	403.6	406.6	409.3	404.1

Employment by Industry: Honolulu, HI, Selected Years, 1990–2009—*Continued*

(Numbers in thousands, not seasonally adjusted.)

Industry and year	January	February	March	April	May	June	July	August	September	October	November	December	Annual average
Trade, Transportation, and Utilities													
1990	85.4	85.9	86.0	85.7	85.9	87.0	87.8	87.2	87.0	88.0	89.3	90.7	87.2
2000	80.5	80.4	80.1	79.7	79.9	81.0	81.1	81.6	81.8	81.8	84.1	85.0	81.4
2001	82.3	81.7	81.8	81.1	81.3	81.8	81.7	81.7	81.5	79.1	77.9	79.0	80.9
2002	75.9	75.3	75.1	75.3	75.8	76.3	76.6	76.8	76.7	76.9	78.2	79.6	76.5
2003	76.6	76.3	76.1	75.7	75.6	76.0	76.3	76.5	76.5	76.6	78.1	79.6	76.7
2004	77.2	76.7	76.9	77.7	78.2	79.0	79.2	79.6	80.0	81.5	83.3	84.3	79.5
2005	81.8	81.7	81.9	82.3	83.1	83.9	84.6	85.1	85.4	85.3	86.7	88.1	84.2
2006	85.3	85.0	85.7	85.2	85.5	86.4	86.0	86.7	86.7	85.7	87.7	88.9	86.2
2007	86.3	85.3	85.8	85.0	85.3	85.5	85.5	85.6	85.4	85.9	88.0	89.7	86.1
2008	86.2	84.9	84.9	83.7	83.7	83.4	82.7	82.9	82.4	81.7	82.6	83.2	83.5
2009	80.6	80.0	79.4	78.3	78.3	78.4	78.2	78.0	78.0	78.1	79.4	80.8	79.0
Wholesale Trade													
1990	14.6	14.7	14.8	14.7	14.8	14.9	15.0	14.8	14.9	15.0	14.9	15.1	14.9
2000	13.1	13.2	13.2	13.2	13.2	13.4	13.5	13.6	13.5	13.5	13.6	13.6	13.4
2001	13.5	13.6	13.6	13.5	13.6	13.7	13.6	13.7	13.6	13.4	13.4	13.5	13.6
2002	13.3	13.3	13.3	13.3	13.5	13.5	13.5	13.5	13.6	13.6	13.7	13.8	13.5
2003	13.5	13.6	13.6	13.7	13.7	13.7	13.7	13.7	13.7	13.6	13.7	13.7	13.7
2004	13.6	13.6	13.7	13.7	13.8	13.9	13.9	13.8	13.8	13.9	14.0	14.0	13.8
2005	13.8	13.9	14.0	14.0	14.1	14.1	14.2	14.3	14.4	14.4	14.4	14.5	14.2
2006	14.2	14.2	14.2	14.3	14.3	14.5	14.4	14.6	14.5	14.6	14.7	14.9	14.5
2007	14.6	14.6	14.7	14.7	14.8	14.9	14.9	15.0	15.0	15.0	15.1	15.3	14.9
2008	15.0	15.0	15.1	15.1	15.1	15.1	15.1	15.1	15.1	15.0	15.0	15.0	15.1
2009	14.7	14.6	14.5	14.4	14.4	14.3	14.3	14.3	14.2	14.3	14.4	14.4	14.4
Retail Trade													
1990	49.7	49.5	49.6	49.4	49.5	50.1	50.3	50.0	49.7	50.5	51.6	52.6	50.2
2000	46.2	45.8	45.4	45.1	45.3	45.8	46.0	46.3	46.4	46.4	48.3	49.0	46.3
2001	46.7	46.0	46.0	45.5	45.4	45.6	45.6	45.6	45.6	44.6	45.0	46.0	45.6
2002	43.7	43.0	42.7	42.7	42.9	43.2	43.6	43.6	43.5	43.6	44.6	46.0	43.6
2003	43.4	42.9	42.7	42.4	42.5	43.0	43.3	43.4	43.3	43.6	44.9	46.4	43.5
2004	44.2	43.7	43.7	43.5	43.8	44.3	44.5	44.9	45.1	46.1	47.6	48.8	45.0
2005	46.3	45.9	45.9	45.7	45.8	46.1	46.7	46.9	46.9	47.3	48.6	49.9	46.8
2006	47.5	47.1	47.2	46.6	46.5	46.9	46.6	46.7	46.5	46.5	48.2	49.0	47.1
2007	47.0	46.3	46.5	45.9	46.0	46.2	46.1	46.1	46.0	46.3	48.2	49.3	46.7
2008	46.7	46.3	46.9	46.1	46.0	46.3	46.4	46.5	46.3	45.9	46.8	47.5	46.5
2009	45.7	45.2	44.8	44.1	44.0	44.2	44.1	43.9	44.3	44.1	45.2	46.6	44.7
Transportation and Utilities													
1990	21.2	21.7	21.6	21.6	21.6	22.0	22.5	22.4	22.3	22.5	22.8	23.0	22.1
2000	21.2	21.4	21.5	21.4	21.4	21.8	21.6	21.7	21.9	21.9	22.2	22.4	21.7
2001	22.1	22.1	22.2	22.1	22.3	22.5	22.5	22.4	22.3	21.1	19.5	19.5	21.7
2002	18.9	19.0	19.1	19.3	19.4	19.6	19.5	19.7	19.6	19.7	19.9	19.8	19.5
2003	19.7	19.8	19.8	19.6	19.4	19.3	19.3	19.4	19.5	19.4	19.5	19.5	19.5
2004	19.4	19.4	19.5	20.5	20.6	20.8	20.8	20.9	21.1	21.5	21.7	21.5	20.6
2005	21.7	21.9	22.0	22.6	23.2	23.7	23.7	23.9	24.1	23.6	23.7	23.7	23.2
2006	23.6	23.7	24.3	24.3	24.7	25.0	25.0	25.4	25.7	24.6	24.8	25.0	24.7
2007	24.7	24.4	24.6	24.4	24.5	24.4	24.5	24.5	24.4	24.6	24.7	25.1	24.6
2008	24.5	23.6	22.9	22.5	22.6	22.0	21.2	21.3	21.0	20.8	20.8	20.7	22.0
2009	20.2	20.2	20.1	19.8	19.9	19.9	19.8	19.8	19.5	19.7	19.8	19.8	19.9
Information													
1990	7.9	8.0	8.1	8.2	8.2	8.2	8.2	8.1	8.3	8.2	8.2	8.3	8.2
2000	9.2	9.2	9.3	10.1	10.1	10.9	10.1	10.7	11.4	11.0	10.5	10.3	10.2
2001	10.2	10.2	10.4	9.8	10.2	10.0	9.8	10.0	9.7	9.7	9.8	9.7	10.0
2002	9.8	9.7	9.7	9.5	9.5	9.3	9.1	9.2	9.9	9.1	9.1	9.7	9.5
2003	8.9	9.0	9.0	8.8	9.4	9.2	8.3	8.2	8.2	8.1	8.3	8.2	8.6
2004	8.4	8.4	8.7	8.5	9.0	8.8	9.2	9.2	9.2	9.3	9.8	9.7	9.0
2005	8.6	8.8	8.6	8.9	9.0	8.7	8.7	9.1	9.1	9.1	9.3	9.8	9.0
2006	9.0	9.3	9.2	8.4	9.2	8.9	8.5	8.7	9.2	8.4	8.8	9.0	8.9
2007	8.4	8.9	8.9	8.6	9.3	9.2	8.5	9.0	8.6	8.4	8.5	8.6	8.7
2008	7.8	8.3	8.6	8.7	9.0	9.4	8.0	7.8	7.8	7.6	8.1	8.3	8.3
2009	7.4	7.9	7.7	7.6	7.3	7.4	6.9	7.1	7.3	7.1	7.3	7.4	7.4
Financial Activities													
1990	24.5	24.5	24.5	24.5	24.9	25.1	25.5	25.6	25.7	25.7	25.7	25.8	25.2
2000	22.9	22.9	22.9	22.7	22.7	22.8	22.8	22.8	22.6	22.5	22.4	22.5	22.7
2001	22.0	22.1	22.2	22.0	22.0	22.1	21.8	21.8	21.7	21.6	21.5	21.6	21.9
2002	21.1	21.2	21.4	21.3	21.5	21.6	21.6	21.5	21.5	21.6	21.7	21.8	21.5
2003	21.3	21.5	21.6	21.5	21.7	21.9	22.0	22.1	22.1	22.1	22.1	22.2	21.8
2004	22.0	22.0	22.1	22.1	22.2	22.2	22.2	22.1	22.0	22.3	22.3	22.4	22.2
2005	22.1	22.3	22.3	22.2	22.4	22.5	22.5	22.6	22.7	22.6	22.8	22.9	22.5
2006	22.5	22.7	22.9	22.8	22.9	23.2	23.0	23.0	22.8	22.9	22.9	23.0	22.9
2007	22.8	22.7	23.0	22.8	22.9	23.1	23.1	23.0	22.9	23.1	23.0	23.1	23.0
2008	22.6	22.7	22.9	22.9	22.9	22.8	22.7	22.7	22.5	22.3	22.3	22.3	22.6
2009	21.7	21.6	21.5	21.4	21.5	21.4	21.3	21.1	21.0	21.5	21.5	21.7	21.4

Employment by Industry: Honolulu, HI, Selected Years, 1990–2009—*Continued*

(Numbers in thousands, not seasonally adjusted.)

Industry and year	January	February	March	April	May	June	July	August	September	October	November	December	Annual average
Professional and Business Services													
1990	41.6	42.4	42.9	42.5	42.4	43.2	43.4	43.8	43.4	43.5	43.3	43.8	43.0
2000	48.1	48.6	49.3	49.5	49.5	50.1	50.3	50.5	51.0	51.2	51.6	52.1	50.2
2001	51.3	51.8	52.5	51.9	52.2	52.8	52.8	53.0	53.0	52.1	52.8	52.8	52.4
2002	52.4	53.5	53.7	54.0	54.5	55.3	55.7	56.3	56.4	56.4	56.5	58.1	55.2
2003	56.6	56.5	56.8	56.5	56.4	56.8	56.9	57.6	57.9	56.5	57.4	58.0	57.0
2004	56.6	57.2	57.5	57.1	56.3	56.9	57.2	57.6	57.2	57.7	58.3	59.1	57.4
2005	58.0	58.5	59.0	59.2	58.7	59.4	59.9	60.4	60.3	60.9	61.7	62.5	59.9
2006	61.0	62.5	62.8	62.0	61.7	62.5	62.2	62.3	61.6	60.2	60.4	61.1	61.7
2007	59.3	59.8	60.2	59.4	59.4	60.9	60.5	60.8	61.1	61.3	61.2	61.8	60.5
2008	60.2	60.6	60.8	60.6	60.1	60.2	60.4	60.6	60.2	60.1	60.0	60.9	60.4
2009	59.3	59.3	59.4	57.9	57.4	57.6	57.0	57.0	57.2	57.4	57.1	56.7	57.8
Education and Health Services													
1990	38.2	38.7	38.9	38.7	39.0	39.3	39.4	39.3	39.7	40.3	41.0	41.1	39.5
2000	46.8	47.9	48.4	47.9	48.1	48.2	47.7	47.5	48.3	48.2	48.9	49.4	48.1
2001	47.8	48.7	49.1	48.9	49.3	49.4	49.0	48.7	49.2	49.2	49.9	50.0	49.1
2002	48.6	49.7	49.8	50.0	50.4	50.2	50.1	49.6	50.6	50.9	52.0	51.2	50.3
2003	50.3	51.6	51.9	51.9	52.1	51.7	51.9	51.7	52.6	52.7	53.4	53.6	52.1
2004	52.0	52.8	53.2	53.2	53.9	53.7	53.3	53.1	54.0	54.3	55.1	55.4	53.7
2005	54.4	55.1	55.5	55.3	55.7	55.5	54.9	54.6	55.5	55.3	55.7	56.1	55.3
2006	54.4	55.2	55.7	55.7	56.3	56.6	55.8	55.9	56.7	56.7	57.2	57.6	56.2
2007	56.3	57.3	57.6	57.6	57.8	58.2	57.2	57.0	57.8	57.8	58.1	58.1	57.6
2008	56.9	57.9	58.2	58.0	58.3	58.5	58.0	57.8	58.3	58.5	59.0	59.3	58.2
2009	58.0	58.7	59.0	58.4	58.5	58.5	57.7	57.5	58.3	58.9	60.2	60.5	58.7
Leisure and Hospitality													
1990	60.6	61.3	59.6	61.3	61.4	61.9	61.8	62.2	61.6	61.5	61.4	61.5	61.3
2000	57.3	58.1	58.4	58.2	58.9	60.0	59.7	59.9	60.0	59.5	59.5	60.4	59.2
2001	58.2	58.9	59.3	58.6	58.9	59.8	59.1	59.5	59.2	56.7	56.0	56.3	58.4
2002	55.7	56.4	56.9	56.8	57.6	58.3	57.8	57.8	58.1	57.9	58.1	58.5	57.5
2003	57.5	57.9	58.5	58.1	58.3	58.3	58.5	58.8	58.8	58.6	59.0	59.8	58.5
2004	58.6	59.3	59.6	59.7	60.0	60.7	61.2	61.5	61.7	61.4	61.9	62.1	60.6
2005	60.8	61.5	61.9	61.8	61.9	62.7	62.4	62.4	62.6	61.7	61.8	62.3	62.0
2006	61.2	62.0	62.4	62.0	62.4	62.8	63.0	63.2	63.5	62.9	63.2	63.4	62.7
2007	62.5	63.7	64.2	64.2	64.6	64.9	64.2	64.8	64.8	63.8	63.9	64.0	64.1
2008	62.8	63.4	63.3	62.8	62.9	63.1	63.0	62.9	62.5	61.7	61.4	61.1	62.6
2009	60.2	60.7	61.0	60.4	60.7	61.1	60.6	60.7	60.6	61.0	61.1	61.4	60.8
Other Services													
1990	15.7	15.9	16.1	16.0	16.0	16.5	16.7	16.6	16.4	16.5	16.5	16.4	16.3
2000	17.3	17.9	18.1	18.1	18.2	18.5	18.4	18.5	18.6	18.8	19.0	18.9	18.4
2001	18.5	18.7	18.8	18.9	18.9	19.2	19.1	18.9	18.9	18.6	18.6	18.7	18.8
2002	18.5	18.6	18.8	18.8	18.9	18.9	18.9	18.8	19.0	18.9	19.1	19.1	18.9
2003	18.7	19.0	19.1	19.3	19.3	19.3	19.2	19.2	19.2	19.2	19.3	19.3	19.2
2004	18.7	18.9	19.2	19.0	19.2	19.3	19.1	19.1	18.9	19.3	19.3	19.3	19.1
2005	19.0	19.1	19.2	19.5	19.8	19.7	19.6	19.7	19.8	19.7	19.9	20.1	19.6
2006	19.9	20.1	20.3	20.2	20.4	20.4	20.3	20.5	20.5	20.5	20.7	20.6	20.4
2007	20.0	20.4	20.6	20.4	20.5	20.5	20.5	20.6	20.8	20.9	20.9	20.9	20.6
2008	20.5	21.0	21.2	21.2	21.3	21.0	20.8	20.8	21.0	21.0	21.0	20.9	21.0
2009	20.1	20.4	20.4	20.1	20.2	20.1	20.0	20.2	20.3	21.1	20.7	20.8	20.4
Government													
1990	84.3	87.8	90.4	91.3	92.8	90.1	84.8	84.4	80.2	87.4	91.2	92.1	88.1
2000	88.3	92.5	93.9	93.9	95.6	94.3	86.9	86.5	88.2	91.3	93.5	94.9	91.7
2001	85.5	93.0	93.8	92.0	91.6	93.9	86.0	86.9	89.2	92.1	95.1	96.1	91.3
2002	91.1	95.3	96.5	90.4	97.3	99.7	88.1	88.7	90.8	94.9	96.5	98.0	93.9
2003	94.7	97.3	97.8	94.5	97.7	96.7	89.8	89.1	90.5	95.4	97.0	97.4	94.8
2004	94.3	96.6	98.0	97.3	98.7	96.8	90.2	90.5	92.9	96.0	99.1	98.1	95.7
2005	92.1	96.8	97.6	96.8	98.1	96.7	89.6	91.2	92.5	95.5	97.0	98.0	95.2
2006	91.2	97.1	98.0	97.1	98.9	97.4	89.8	91.1	95.2	97.2	101.4	99.7	96.2
2007	94.6	98.8	99.5	94.5	99.6	98.0	90.1	89.9	95.6	97.8	99.4	100.3	96.5
2008	95.5	99.2	100.4	95.5	101.1	99.3	92.1	93.8	97.0	100.3	104.4	101.8	98.4
2009	98.3	100.3	101.8	101.5	102.8	100.8	93.5	92.2	95.7	98.5	99.3	100.0	98.7

Employment by Industry: Houston-Sugar Land-Baytown, TX, Selected Years, 1990–2009

(Numbers in thousands, not seasonally adjusted.)

Industry and year	January	February	March	April	May	June	July	August	September	October	November	December	Annual average
Total Nonfarm													
1990	1692.2	1709.2	1724.4	1739.6	1763.9	1782.8	1777.3	1784.1	1790.5	1793.4	1802.2	1818.3	1764.8
2001	2256.6	2277.6	2290.1	2293.0	2302.8	2304.4	2285.3	2298.5	2304.2	2298.7	2305.5	2306.1	2293.6
2002	2263.3	2278.7	2288.6	2286.1	2298.5	2298.4	2276.8	2287.0	2294.0	2291.1	2296.6	2302.9	2288.5
2003	2261.1	2270.6	2278.2	2275.0	2281.0	2281.8	2254.1	2266.5	2277.0	2275.4	2278.6	2291.5	2274.2
2004	2256.9	2268.4	2279.6	2283.7	2287.5	2293.2	2279.8	2287.2	2294.8	2303.8	2314.1	2329.0	2289.8
2005	2296.7	2309.1	2328.1	2339.1	2346.5	2350.7	2345.3	2358.6	2373.8	2380.0	2401.5	2418.2	2354.0
2006	2379.0	2399.9	2424.2	2424.1	2441.7	2453.4	2443.3	2460.5	2478.2	2484.9	2505.3	2524.0	2451.5
2007	2478.8	2502.2	2526.1	2531.4	2550.2	2566.9	2549.4	2558.1	2566.4	2580.3	2599.2	2612.8	2551.8
2008	2560.9	2582.9	2594.2	2600.2	2611.9	2619.3	2607.2	2614.9	2596.0	2615.6	2630.5	2632.3	2605.5
2009	2569.1	2569.8	2566.9	2548.8	2549.1	2544.0	2520.8	2512.1	2511.3	2519.6	2527.0	2529.5	2539.0
Total Private													
1990	1453.0	1464.1	1478.9	1493.0	1513.2	1538.5	1540.0	1549.6	1547.9	1544.6	1551.4	1566.7	1520.1
2000	1892.2	1906.6	1922.8	1923.8	1934.1	1957.9	1954.6	1965.2	1962.7	1963.3	1972.9	1988.9	1945.4
2001	1949.3	1964.3	1975.5	1976.8	1986.5	1998.4	1988.2	1995.2	1983.0	1975.6	1980.4	1981.7	1979.6
2002	1943.0	1951.2	1960.0	1957.6	1969.0	1977.7	1967.4	1974.7	1964.1	1953.6	1958.9	1965.6	1961.9
2003	1929.5	1932.2	1939.4	1936.5	1942.7	1951.7	1939.4	1947.6	1943.5	1937.2	1939.3	1953.4	1941.0
2004	1921.7	1928.4	1939.2	1944.3	1948.4	1960.8	1962.0	1966.8	1958.6	1964.4	1973.9	1988.8	1954.8
2005	1961.4	1967.8	1985.5	1995.9	2003.4	2018.9	2020.9	2031.2	2032.9	2034.2	2052.5	2070.1	2014.6
2006	2035.6	2050.4	2074.0	2076.7	2093.9	2115.4	2117.6	2129.7	2131.5	2132.4	2151.0	2171.0	2106.6
2007	2132.2	2148.3	2170.7	2174.7	2193.3	2220.2	2215.6	2222.3	2214.1	2219.8	2234.9	2248.8	2199.6
2008	2199.7	2217.3	2227.0	2234.1	2246.2	2262.8	2259.8	2268.5	2233.4	2249.4	2259.4	2262.1	2243.3
2009	2202.8	2197.9	2193.4	2175.2	2176.7	2180.0	2167.4	2161.9	2144.1	2142.7	2148.4	2152.8	2170.3
Goods-Producing													
1990	374.8	381.6	386.5	389.3	397.3	403.3	403.6	406.9	406.7	405.7	407.2	408.4	397.6
2000	452.9	459.1	463.5	461.2	463.8	468.7	467.0	469.5	470.3	469.3	470.1	472.1	465.6
2001	469.5	476.5	479.3	480.5	482.0	481.5	477.9	480.0	478.4	477.0	476.7	472.8	477.7
2002	466.1	468.8	470.3	467.5	468.1	468.6	465.4	466.3	464.0	462.8	459.4	457.2	465.4
2003	453.0	452.9	452.1	450.1	450.8	452.0	446.9	447.4	448.3	445.8	441.4	442.0	448.5
2004	439.4	439.7	440.7	440.7	438.8	441.0	440.3	440.7	439.0	441.8	442.9	444.1	440.8
2005	446.5	448.8	452.9	453.7	453.1	457.2	458.2	460.0	462.2	462.4	465.2	468.3	457.4
2006	467.7	473.8	479.6	478.6	484.3	491.2	490.6	494.0	497.3	500.5	503.9	506.5	489.0
2007	504.5	510.3	514.3	513.7	519.4	526.6	525.1	525.0	524.6	530.4	533.3	534.4	521.8
2008	524.6	531.6	532.5	535.6	538.5	540.9	541.0	542.7	539.3	545.8	545.1	540.7	538.2
2009	527.4	523.0	513.9	502.3	498.9	495.4	492.0	487.5	483.5	482.4	480.1	478.1	497.0
Mining and Logging													
1990	59.0	59.5	59.7	60.9	61.4	62.8	62.8	63.2	62.8	63.8	64.6	65.7	62.2
2000	59.7	59.7	60.3	60.4	60.9	61.3	62.4	62.6	62.7	63.4	63.6	65.6	61.9
2001	63.0	63.8	64.3	64.4	64.8	65.5	66.2	66.5	66.0	66.1	66.5	66.2	65.3
2002	63.1	62.7	62.3	62.5	62.7	63.4	63.7	63.8	63.4	63.6	63.8	63.8	63.3
2003	63.5	63.5	63.8	64.0	64.4	64.9	65.7	65.9	65.5	65.4	65.3	66.4	64.8
2004	66.0	65.8	66.3	66.7	66.9	67.2	68.2	68.3	68.0	68.9	69.2	69.5	67.6
2005	69.5	69.9	70.2	69.3	69.7	71.0	71.6	71.8	72.0	72.7	72.9	72.9	71.1
2006	73.6	74.2	74.2	75.2	75.8	77.4	78.6	79.5	80.2	81.6	81.9	82.7	77.9
2007	82.6	83.0	83.3	82.9	83.6	84.8	85.0	85.0	84.3	85.3	85.8	86.1	84.3
2008	86.0	87.0	87.2	87.7	88.5	90.4	91.3	91.8	91.4	92.6	92.5	92.3	89.9
2009	91.0	89.9	89.0	87.3	86.6	86.7	87.7	87.4	86.8	87.3	87.4	87.7	87.9
Construction													
1990	122.8	126.7	129.5	130.8	136.9	138.3	136.2	138.1	138.2	137.1	136.9	135.6	133.9
2000	166.0	170.3	173.0	170.8	172.3	175.2	172.4	173.9	174.6	173.1	172.3	171.6	172.1
2001	172.4	177.0	179.0	180.4	181.2	179.4	177.0	179.3	179.1	179.7	180.6	178.4	178.6
2002	177.6	180.8	183.4	181.8	182.9	182.2	180.2	181.1	180.7	180.9	178.4	176.4	180.5
2003	175.4	176.4	176.1	174.8	176.3	175.7	171.8	173.0	173.9	173.4	168.6	168.2	173.6
2004	166.0	166.5	166.7	166.9	164.8	165.3	163.3	163.5	163.6	165.8	165.2	165.7	165.3
2005	169.4	170.8	173.7	174.6	172.7	172.9	172.9	174.2	176.0	176.0	177.0	179.0	174.1
2006	178.2	183.0	187.3	183.1	185.8	188.6	187.0	188.3	191.0	192.5	193.8	194.3	187.7
2007	193.5	198.5	200.9	200.5	203.6	207.1	204.9	204.9	205.3	209.3	210.1	210.0	204.1
2008	201.4	206.6	207.0	207.9	208.3	206.8	205.1	206.3	203.8	208.7	207.3	203.3	206.0
2009	196.3	194.9	191.2	186.0	185.6	183.7	182.2	179.6	177.5	175.9	173.9	172.3	183.3
Manufacturing													
1990	193.0	195.4	197.3	197.6	199.0	202.2	204.6	205.6	205.7	204.8	205.7	207.1	201.5
2000	227.2	229.1	230.2	230.0	230.6	232.2	232.2	233.0	233.0	232.8	234.2	234.9	231.6
2001	234.1	235.7	236.0	235.7	236.0	236.6	234.7	234.2	233.3	231.2	229.6	228.2	233.8
2002	225.4	225.3	224.6	223.2	222.5	223.0	221.5	221.4	219.9	218.3	217.2	217.0	221.6
2003	214.1	213.0	212.2	211.3	210.1	211.4	209.4	208.5	208.9	207.0	207.5	207.4	210.0
2004	207.4	207.4	207.7	207.1	207.1	208.5	208.8	208.9	207.4	207.1	208.5	208.9	207.9
2005	207.6	208.1	209.0	209.8	210.7	213.3	213.7	214.0	214.2	213.7	215.3	216.4	212.2
2006	215.9	216.6	218.1	220.3	222.7	225.2	225.0	226.2	226.1	226.4	228.2	229.5	223.4
2007	228.4	228.8	230.1	230.3	232.2	234.7	235.2	235.1	235.0	235.8	237.4	238.3	233.4
2008	237.2	238.0	238.3	240.0	241.7	243.7	244.6	244.6	244.1	244.5	245.3	245.1	242.3
2009	240.1	238.2	233.7	229.0	226.7	225.0	222.1	220.5	219.2	219.2	218.8	218.1	225.9

Employment by Industry: Houston-Sugar Land-Baytown, TX, Selected Years, 1990–2009—*Continued*

(Numbers in thousands, not seasonally adjusted.)

Industry and year	January	February	March	April	May	June	July	August	September	October	November	December	Annual average
Service-Providing													
1990	1317.4	1327.6	1337.9	1350.3	1366.6	1379.5	1373.7	1377.2	1383.8	1387.7	1395.0	1409.9	1367.2
2000	1745.3	1759.5	1772.1	1776.3	1790.1	1794.0	1780.0	1788.9	1806.1	1807.9	1816.5	1830.4	1788.9
2001	1787.1	1801.1	1810.8	1812.5	1820.8	1822.9	1807.4	1818.5	1825.8	1821.7	1828.8	1833.3	1815.9
2002	1797.2	1809.9	1818.3	1818.6	1830.4	1829.8	1811.4	1820.7	1830.0	1828.3	1837.2	1845.7	1823.1
2003	1808.1	1817.7	1826.1	1824.9	1830.2	1829.8	1807.2	1819.1	1828.7	1829.6	1837.2	1849.5	1825.7
2004	1817.5	1828.7	1838.9	1843.0	1848.7	1852.2	1839.5	1846.5	1855.8	1862.0	1871.2	1884.9	1849.1
2005	1850.2	1860.3	1875.2	1885.4	1893.4	1893.5	1887.1	1898.6	1911.6	1917.6	1936.3	1949.9	1896.6
2006	1911.3	1926.1	1944.6	1945.5	1957.4	1962.2	1952.7	1966.5	1980.9	1984.4	2001.4	2017.5	1962.5
2007	1974.3	1991.9	2011.8	2017.7	2030.8	2040.3	2024.3	2033.1	2041.8	2049.9	2065.9	2078.4	2030.0
2008	2036.3	2051.3	2061.7	2064.6	2073.4	2078.4	2066.2	2072.2	2056.7	2069.8	2085.4	2091.6	2067.3
2009	2041.7	2046.8	2053.0	2046.5	2050.2	2048.6	2028.8	2024.6	2027.8	2037.2	2046.9	2051.4	2042.0
Trade, Transportation, and Utilities													
1990	394.7	394.2	396.7	397.1	399.4	403.9	404.0	405.8	407.6	407.6	412.2	420.0	403.6
2000	480.7	479.2	481.0	479.8	481.7	486.0	485.1	488.9	485.5	489.5	497.4	507.6	486.9
2001	487.7	485.9	486.6	485.4	487.9	491.1	490.8	493.0	489.7	491.4	495.9	500.2	490.5
2002	484.0	482.3	483.4	481.2	482.9	484.2	482.3	483.5	481.0	480.2	487.2	494.7	483.9
2003	473.2	468.1	468.2	467.2	466.0	468.9	468.4	470.7	469.0	469.3	476.4	484.8	470.9
2004	466.6	464.5	467.0	469.9	469.9	472.1	472.5	475.2	471.6	474.1	482.5	491.8	473.1
2005	473.6	470.7	472.5	476.6	478.8	482.0	483.9	487.4	485.8	488.0	500.0	511.2	484.2
2006	491.0	489.2	493.5	493.5	495.0	498.4	499.1	502.5	501.9	504.1	513.0	522.8	500.3
2007	506.2	504.4	509.7	510.1	513.7	519.6	520.4	523.3	522.5	525.6	535.6	544.3	519.6
2008	525.9	525.5	528.1	526.8	528.7	532.8	533.7	536.9	529.3	530.7	540.8	548.2	532.3
2009	525.7	521.3	521.0	517.4	516.5	517.0	514.7	515.3	512.0	514.0	522.5	529.6	519.0
Wholesale Trade													
1990	99.5	100.8	101.9	102.1	102.5	102.5	102.3	102.7	102.8	103.1	102.8	103.1	102.2
2000	116.8	117.3	117.8	118.0	118.1	118.9	118.9	118.9	118.9	117.9	118.0	118.6	118.2
2001	118.1	118.8	119.7	118.8	119.1	119.8	120.2	120.5	120.1	119.7	119.4	119.4	119.5
2002	117.6	118.0	118.6	117.8	118.2	118.4	118.2	118.5	118.5	118.1	118.5	118.4	118.2
2003	117.1	116.9	117.1	116.4	117.0	117.7	117.8	118.0	118.5	118.1	118.3	118.0	117.6
2004	116.8	117.0	117.8	118.2	118.6	119.4	119.4	119.4	119.6	120.0	120.2	120.8	118.9
2005	119.9	120.1	120.8	121.8	122.2	123.2	123.3	123.6	124.4	124.7	124.9	126.0	122.9
2006	125.3	126.5	127.8	127.5	128.1	129.3	129.3	129.8	130.5	130.7	131.0	131.6	129.0
2007	130.0	131.3	132.3	132.5	133.3	134.8	134.9	135.6	135.7	136.2	136.4	137.1	134.2
2008	136.2	137.5	137.8	138.2	138.9	139.9	139.5	139.9	139.2	139.0	138.9	138.9	138.7
2009	135.5	135.4	134.6	132.8	132.0	131.7	130.5	130.2	129.6	130.0	129.7	129.5	131.8
Retail Trade													
1990	201.2	198.7	199.3	199.6	200.8	203.9	204.1	205.7	206.3	207.3	212.1	217.7	204.7
2000	247.0	243.4	245.0	243.0	244.4	246.6	245.6	248.4	245.4	249.3	256.7	263.8	248.2
2001	247.6	245.0	245.6	245.5	246.5	248.4	247.6	249.0	246.4	247.4	254.1	260.2	248.6
2002	247.4	245.7	247.5	246.4	247.4	247.8	245.3	245.9	244.4	244.0	250.9	257.2	247.5
2003	240.0	236.9	237.5	237.3	237.4	239.1	238.0	240.0	239.1	240.1	247.0	252.4	240.4
2004	239.7	236.8	238.6	241.3	240.1	241.2	240.4	243.6	240.9	241.9	248.7	254.8	242.3
2005	240.7	237.0	238.3	240.8	241.9	244.0	245.1	247.4	245.6	246.0	257.1	263.6	245.7
2006	248.8	245.8	247.9	248.4	248.6	249.9	250.6	252.8	251.2	252.4	260.8	265.6	251.9
2007	255.4	251.6	255.2	255.4	257.6	260.7	261.2	262.6	261.4	264.0	273.5	278.1	261.4
2008	264.2	261.8	264.2	262.8	263.1	265.1	265.6	268.0	262.5	263.9	273.6	278.3	266.1
2009	264.8	261.2	261.7	260.8	261.3	262.2	261.6	263.5	261.9	262.8	271.1	275.7	264.1
Transportation and Utilities													
1990	94.0	94.7	95.5	95.4	96.1	97.5	97.6	97.4	98.5	97.2	97.3	99.2	96.7
2000	116.9	118.5	118.2	118.8	119.2	120.5	120.6	121.6	121.2	122.3	122.7	125.2	120.5
2001	122.0	122.1	121.3	121.1	122.3	122.9	123.0	123.5	123.2	124.3	122.4	120.6	122.4
2002	119.0	118.6	117.3	117.0	117.3	118.0	118.8	119.1	118.1	118.1	117.8	119.1	118.2
2003	116.1	114.3	113.6	113.5	111.6	112.1	112.6	112.7	111.4	111.1	111.1	113.5	112.8
2004	110.1	110.7	110.6	110.4	111.2	111.5	112.7	112.2	111.1	112.2	113.6	116.2	111.9
2005	113.0	113.6	113.4	114.0	114.7	114.8	115.5	116.4	115.8	116.4	118.0	121.6	115.6
2006	116.9	116.9	117.8	117.6	118.3	119.2	119.2	119.9	120.2	121.0	121.2	125.6	119.5
2007	120.8	121.5	122.2	122.2	122.8	124.1	124.3	125.1	125.4	125.4	125.7	129.1	124.1
2008	125.5	126.2	126.1	125.8	126.7	127.8	128.6	129.0	127.6	127.8	128.3	131.0	127.5
2009	125.4	124.7	124.7	123.8	123.2	123.1	122.6	121.6	121.1	121.2	121.7	124.4	123.1
Information													
1990	35.1	35.6	35.6	35.4	35.8	36.3	36.3	36.3	35.9	35.6	35.8	36.2	35.8
2000	45.7	46.0	46.2	46.7	47.1	47.6	47.8	48.0	48.1	48.2	48.5	48.7	47.4
2001	47.8	48.1	48.2	48.0	47.5	47.4	45.8	45.6	44.7	44.4	44.3	43.8	46.3
2002	42.6	42.2	42.0	41.1	41.1	41.3	40.8	40.5	40.1	39.9	39.6	39.5	40.9
2003	39.3	39.2	39.2	38.9	38.8	38.8	38.9	38.6	38.2	37.8	37.8	37.8	38.6
2004	37.7	37.7	37.6	37.5	37.6	38.0	37.4	37.3	36.9	36.5	36.5	36.5	37.3
2005	36.9	36.9	37.1	36.2	36.2	36.5	36.1	36.2	35.8	35.4	35.6	35.7	36.2
2006	35.4	35.5	35.5	35.9	36.2	36.5	36.5	36.5	36.2	36.3	36.5	36.6	36.1
2007	36.6	36.8	36.7	36.5	36.9	37.2	37.1	37.2	36.9	36.7	36.8	36.8	36.9
2008	36.6	36.8	36.7	36.5	36.7	36.7	36.8	36.5	35.9	35.8	35.8	35.9	36.4
2009	35.2	35.2	35.2	34.8	34.8	34.9	34.5	34.4	33.9	33.8	33.8	33.8	34.5

Employment by Industry: Houston-Sugar Land-Baytown, TX, Selected Years, 1990–2009—*Continued*

(Numbers in thousands, not seasonally adjusted.)

Industry and year	January	February	March	April	May	June	July	August	September	October	November	December	Annual average
Financial Activities													
1990	110.8	112.1	112.5	113.8	114.3	116.3	114.8	114.8	114.9	113.7	114.0	115.8	114.0
2000	130.3	130.6	130.9	131.4	131.6	132.9	134.2	134.1	134.2	134.1	134.5	135.1	132.8
2001	133.7	134.3	134.7	134.6	134.8	135.4	135.3	135.0	134.2	133.2	132.7	132.9	134.2
2002	132.1	132.3	132.3	132.2	132.7	133.4	133.2	133.2	132.2	132.6	132.6	132.7	132.6
2003	131.0	131.4	132.0	132.9	133.7	134.4	134.5	135.4	134.6	135.7	135.5	135.9	133.9
2004	134.8	135.2	135.5	136.2	136.5	137.3	137.9	137.9	137.4	137.7	137.0	137.9	136.8
2005	136.3	136.7	137.1	137.3	137.4	138.4	139.8	140.4	140.3	139.5	139.9	139.9	138.6
2006	138.4	138.7	139.5	139.2	139.7	140.9	141.2	141.8	141.6	141.8	141.6	142.5	140.6
2007	141.4	142.3	143.0	142.3	143.1	144.6	145.0	145.5	144.8	145.0	145.1	145.3	144.0
2008	143.3	144.5	144.2	144.0	144.6	145.2	145.1	145.3	143.8	143.0	142.9	143.0	144.1
2009	140.5	140.4	140.1	139.6	139.6	140.0	139.6	139.0	138.1	138.3	137.6	137.7	139.2
Professional and Business Services													
1990	191.1	195.7	198.9	204.2	207.8	212.8	212.4	214.0	213.8	215.0	215.7	218.6	208.3
2000	300.7	304.2	307.8	308.8	310.2	317.5	318.5	321.9	323.1	322.4	322.1	324.1	315.1
2001	316.2	319.1	320.6	320.8	320.3	323.3	321.4	321.4	318.8	316.1	316.5	315.9	319.2
2002	308.5	309.5	311.7	311.9	312.9	313.9	312.2	314.7	312.2	309.6	309.4	309.1	311.3
2003	305.2	306.4	307.3	307.9	306.5	306.9	304.8	306.7	306.8	306.0	306.0	309.2	306.6
2004	303.2	306.1	307.7	311.4	312.0	315.3	317.7	319.0	319.0	321.1	322.9	324.3	315.0
2005	321.1	324.9	328.4	330.8	331.3	333.8	335.7	337.8	341.0	345.1	346.7	348.2	335.4
2006	342.3	346.8	351.7	351.2	354.4	359.5	361.2	363.4	363.9	363.9	367.8	370.1	358.0
2007	362.6	366.6	370.7	374.0	376.1	381.3	382.1	382.5	380.5	380.9	380.7	381.8	376.7
2008	374.8	379.4	381.4	382.9	383.2	387.2	386.5	388.1	381.4	387.2	384.4	381.4	383.2
2009	368.8	366.2	364.6	360.1	358.6	359.0	356.7	355.1	352.7	352.9	351.6	350.0	358.0
Education and Health Services													
1990	164.1	156.8	158.4	158.4	158.9	159.8	160.3	161.6	164.4	163.5	164.6	164.9	161.3
2000	219.0	220.5	222.3	222.9	223.3	222.8	222.5	223.4	225.3	224.6	225.3	226.2	223.2
2001	223.9	226.1	227.4	227.8	229.9	229.9	229.9	233.1	235.4	236.2	237.5	238.4	231.3
2002	237.1	239.4	240.2	241.0	241.9	242.2	241.7	244.3	245.4	243.8	245.3	245.5	242.3
2003	243.6	246.4	248.0	247.7	249.1	247.7	247.3	249.6	251.9	251.9	252.0	252.5	248.9
2004	250.2	252.1	252.8	251.8	252.7	251.9	251.8	254.1	256.0	258.4	258.8	259.9	254.2
2005	256.5	257.9	259.6	260.0	261.0	260.3	260.4	263.2	265.2	265.3	266.7	267.6	262.0
2006	264.6	266.6	267.8	269.0	270.2	269.8	269.4	271.7	273.6	273.8	274.4	276.1	270.6
2007	274.2	276.6	278.0	279.0	280.4	280.0	279.4	281.3	282.3	283.2	283.8	284.2	280.2
2008	279.8	281.7	281.0	283.0	284.0	284.6	284.0	286.8	284.3	287.7	289.3	290.5	284.7
2009	287.4	290.2	291.4	293.2	295.1	296.2	296.7	299.0	299.5	300.7	302.3	303.2	296.2
Leisure and Hospitality													
1990	123.6	128.3	130.1	134.0	138.0	142.3	144.1	145.2	140.6	139.2	137.7	138.3	136.8
2000	174.2	177.5	181.2	183.0	186.2	190.8	187.7	188.0	184.7	183.6	183.1	182.9	183.6
2001	179.0	182.4	185.9	186.9	190.9	195.9	194.4	194.6	189.8	185.5	185.0	185.8	188.0
2002	181.4	184.7	187.5	190.5	196.1	199.8	198.0	198.5	195.8	191.7	192.1	193.3	192.5
2003	188.6	191.9	195.6	196.3	201.6	205.5	202.5	203.2	199.1	197.0	196.6	197.1	197.9
2004	195.5	198.1	201.5	202.3	206.3	209.7	210.0	209.5	206.0	203.7	202.4	203.0	204.0
2005	198.8	199.9	204.8	208.0	212.1	215.8	213.7	214.0	211.0	208.1	207.9	208.7	208.6
2006	206.4	209.3	215.1	216.6	220.7	223.7	224.8	225.2	222.6	217.9	219.3	221.2	218.6
2007	215.4	218.9	224.8	226.9	230.8	236.5	233.7	234.8	230.5	226.9	228.3	230.4	228.2
2008	224.5	227.1	232.2	233.8	238.1	241.6	239.0	238.4	228.4	227.2	228.9	230.5	232.5
2009	226.3	229.6	235.0	235.4	240.4	243.8	239.8	239.3	232.3	229.9	229.8	229.8	234.3
Other Services													
1990	58.8	59.8	60.2	60.8	61.7	63.8	64.5	65.0	64.0	64.3	64.2	64.5	62.6
2000	88.7	89.5	89.9	90.0	90.2	91.6	91.8	91.4	91.5	91.6	91.9	92.2	90.9
2001	91.5	91.9	92.8	92.8	93.2	93.9	92.7	92.5	92.0	91.8	91.8	91.9	92.4
2002	91.2	92.0	92.6	92.2	93.3	94.3	93.8	93.7	93.4	93.0	93.3	93.6	93.0
2003	95.6	95.9	97.0	95.5	96.2	97.5	96.1	96.0	95.6	93.7	93.6	94.1	95.5
2004	94.3	95.0	96.4	94.5	94.6	95.5	94.4	93.1	92.7	91.1	90.9	91.3	93.7
2005	91.7	92.0	93.1	93.3	93.5	94.9	93.1	92.2	91.6	90.4	90.5	90.5	92.2
2006	89.8	90.5	91.3	92.7	93.4	95.4	94.8	94.6	94.4	94.1	94.5	95.2	93.4
2007	91.3	92.4	93.5	92.2	92.9	94.4	92.8	92.7	92.0	91.1	91.3	91.6	92.4
2008	90.2	90.7	90.9	91.5	92.4	93.8	93.7	93.8	91.0	92.0	92.2	91.9	92.0
2009	91.5	92.0	92.2	92.4	92.8	93.7	93.4	92.3	91.5	90.7	90.7	90.6	92.0
Government													
1990	239.2	245.1	245.5	246.6	250.7	244.3	237.3	234.5	242.6	248.8	250.8	251.6	244.8
2000	306.0	312.0	312.8	313.7	319.8	304.8	292.4	293.2	313.7	313.9	313.7	313.6	309.1
2001	307.3	313.3	314.6	316.2	316.3	306.0	297.1	303.3	321.2	323.1	325.1	324.4	314.0
2002	320.3	327.5	328.6	328.5	329.5	320.7	309.4	312.3	329.9	337.5	337.7	337.3	326.6
2003	331.6	338.4	338.8	338.5	338.3	330.1	314.7	318.9	333.5	338.2	339.3	338.1	333.2
2004	335.2	340.0	340.4	339.4	339.1	332.4	317.8	320.4	336.2	339.4	340.2	340.2	335.1
2005	335.3	341.3	342.6	343.2	343.1	331.8	324.4	327.4	340.9	345.8	349.0	348.1	339.4
2006	343.4	349.5	350.2	347.4	347.8	338.0	325.7	330.8	346.7	352.5	354.3	353.0	344.9
2007	346.6	353.9	355.4	356.7	356.9	346.7	333.8	335.8	352.3	360.5	364.3	364.0	352.2
2008	361.2	365.6	367.2	366.1	365.7	356.5	347.4	346.4	362.6	366.2	371.1	370.2	362.2
2009	366.3	371.9	373.5	373.6	372.4	364.0	353.4	350.2	367.2	376.9	378.6	376.7	368.7

Employment by Industry: Indianapolis-Carmel, IN, Selected Years, 1990–2009

(Numbers in thousands, not seasonally adjusted.)

Industry and year	January	February	March	April	May	June	July	August	September	October	November	December	Annual average
Total Nonfarm													
1990	657.0	657.0	662.3	663.8	675.2	672.7	670.1	676.7	682.1	681.1	681.7	679.3	671.6
2000	832.9	839.3	849.3	850.3	860.2	862.7	848.9	857.1	861.6	861.1	858.3	859.4	853.4
2001	842.7	845.1	854.1	861.6	869.7	870.7	857.0	868.0	867.1	865.6	864.9	864.6	860.9
2002	838.6	841.4	847.1	854.1	865.0	864.9	852.6	861.9	863.1	865.8	868.3	868.0	857.6
2003	845.0	843.9	849.2	863.8	873.4	869.4	860.5	869.2	871.5	879.7	881.3	878.9	865.5
2004	851.5	851.2	862.3	874.5	883.7	882.2	879.0	882.4	887.2	891.6	894.2	892.7	877.7
2005	862.8	868.2	875.5	886.2	896.6	892.9	886.9	891.3	899.6	896.7	901.0	897.3	887.9
2006	875.1	881.0	890.2	898.8	911.6	908.2	896.6	903.9	911.7	914.5	919.1	918.2	902.4
2007	891.6	890.3	905.0	912.5	925.0	923.9	909.7	919.4	925.2	929.2	932.6	930.9	916.3
2008	897.8	901.4	907.7	913.7	927.3	922.2	914.4	923.5	921.0	920.8	915.5	907.0	914.4
2009	874.4	871.4	872.0	874.2	879.7	875.6	864.0	874.3	874.8	872.6	871.4	867.0	872.6
Total Private													
1990	553.8	552.7	557.4	558.6	567.7	570.6	573.2	576.5	577.4	576.0	576.1	574.1	567.8
2000	725.3	728.4	737.6	739.9	748.9	756.7	750.9	753.8	749.3	749.6	746.1	747.1	744.5
2001	734.0	734.1	742.3	750.1	757.1	763.4	757.8	764.0	754.5	752.9	752.3	752.0	751.2
2002	729.5	728.4	733.8	740.7	750.6	756.1	751.7	756.1	749.1	750.0	751.7	751.4	745.8
2003	731.4	728.3	733.0	748.1	757.2	759.2	755.6	759.4	756.2	763.7	765.6	763.2	751.7
2004	736.9	735.0	745.7	758.7	767.4	772.6	777.1	776.2	771.0	774.1	776.7	775.2	763.9
2005	747.1	749.5	757.4	769.6	779.7	784.5	784.8	785.2	783.0	780.6	784.6	781.1	773.9
2006	759.9	762.2	771.0	779.6	791.3	797.9	792.4	795.0	792.8	793.7	798.0	796.6	785.9
2007	774.0	769.2	783.0	791.2	802.5	808.7	802.2	804.6	802.3	805.4	808.0	806.0	796.4
2008	776.8	776.0	781.4	788.3	800.4	802.3	798.6	800.9	794.9	793.5	788.0	779.6	790.1
2009	749.9	744.2	744.4	746.9	751.7	756.2	749.8	750.6	748.6	744.8	744.0	740.0	747.6
Goods-Producing													
1990	142.7	142.3	143.7	144.5	146.3	147.7	148.7	149.4	150.0	148.7	146.8	145.0	146.3
2000	155.9	156.4	158.2	159.5	161.2	163.6	163.2	163.8	162.6	160.5	158.8	157.5	160.1
2001	154.8	154.7	156.1	157.9	159.5	161.4	160.4	161.9	159.9	158.1	156.6	155.3	158.1
2002	150.5	149.6	150.6	151.9	154.1	156.3	156.6	157.4	155.9	154.1	153.4	152.0	153.5
2003	148.0	146.9	147.6	150.0	152.0	153.6	153.3	153.7	152.6	153.5	153.1	151.6	151.3
2004	147.1	146.4	148.7	151.6	154.8	156.6	155.4	156.3	155.5	155.4	154.3	153.2	152.9
2005	148.1	147.7	149.4	151.9	153.1	155.3	154.4	155.7	155.0	154.4	154.5	152.8	152.7
2006	148.7	148.8	150.5	153.5	154.7	157.6	155.6	157.1	155.6	154.9	154.3	152.6	153.7
2007	147.6	144.7	148.0	150.4	152.4	154.3	153.9	154.7	153.8	152.0	151.0	149.5	151.0
2008	145.2	145.0	145.7	146.2	148.2	149.2	148.4	148.0	145.2	143.8	141.1	137.2	145.3
2009	130.4	127.5	126.4	126.1	125.6	126.2	125.6	125.8	124.5	122.7	120.8	118.5	125.0
Mining and Logging													
2005	0.8	0.8	0.8	0.8	0.8	0.8	0.8	0.8	0.8	0.8	0.8	0.8	0.8
2006	0.8	0.8	0.8	0.8	0.8	0.8	0.8	0.8	0.8	0.8	0.8	0.8	0.8
2007	0.8	0.7	0.8	0.8	0.8	0.8	0.8	0.8	0.8	0.8	0.8	0.8	0.8
2008	0.7	0.7	0.8	0.8	0.8	0.8	0.8	0.8	0.8	0.8	0.8	0.8	0.8
2009	0.7	0.7	0.7	0.7	0.7	0.7	0.8	0.8	0.8	0.7	0.7	0.7	0.7
Construction													
2005	46.3	46.1	47.7	50.1	51.0	52.5	53.2	53.3	53.1	53.2	52.9	51.4	50.9
2006	47.7	48.0	49.4	52.0	53.2	54.9	54.8	55.0	54.5	54.2	53.5	52.5	52.5
2007	48.6	46.5	49.4	51.9	53.9	55.2	55.5	55.9	55.1	54.6	53.8	51.4	52.7
2008	47.7	47.4	48.3	49.8	51.1	51.4	52.0	51.2	50.1	48.8	47.6	44.9	49.2
Manufacturing													
1990	112.2	111.9	112.2	111.9	112.7	112.8	112.6	112.6	114.0	113.4	111.9	111.2	112.5
2000	111.1	111.5	111.3	111.1	111.8	113.2	112.8	113.6	113.1	112.6	111.8	112.0	112.2
2001	111.1	110.3	110.0	109.6	109.9	110.2	108.6	109.6	108.4	107.6	106.6	106.3	109.0
2002	104.5	104.0	104.2	103.5	104.2	105.4	104.6	105.4	104.8	103.9	103.8	103.5	104.3
2003	102.5	102.4	102.2	102.0	102.4	102.8	101.7	101.8	101.0	101.5	101.4	101.1	101.9
2004	100.1	100.0	100.3	100.3	101.2	102.2	101.2	102.4	102.0	101.9	102.0	102.1	101.3
2005	101.0	100.8	100.9	101.0	101.3	102.0	100.4	101.6	101.1	100.4	100.8	100.6	101.0
2006	100.2	100.0	100.3	100.7	100.7	101.9	100.0	101.3	100.3	99.9	100.0	99.3	100.4
2007	98.2	97.5	97.8	97.7	97.7	98.3	97.6	98.0	97.9	96.6	96.4	97.3	97.6
2008	96.8	96.9	96.6	95.6	96.3	97.0	95.6	96.0	94.3	94.2	92.7	91.5	95.3
2009	89.5	87.4	85.9	84.8	83.8	83.7	82.9	83.5	82.9	81.7	81.1	81.0	84.0
Service-Providing													
1990	514.3	514.7	518.6	519.3	528.9	525.0	521.4	527.3	532.1	532.4	534.9	534.3	525.3
2000	677.0	682.9	691.1	690.8	699.0	699.1	685.7	693.3	699.0	700.6	699.5	701.9	693.3
2001	687.9	690.4	698.0	703.7	710.2	709.3	696.6	706.1	707.2	707.5	708.3	709.3	702.9
2002	688.1	691.8	696.5	702.2	710.9	708.6	696.0	704.5	707.2	711.7	714.9	716.0	704.0
2003	697.0	697.0	701.6	713.8	721.4	715.8	707.2	715.5	718.9	726.2	728.2	727.3	714.2
2004	704.4	704.8	713.6	722.9	728.9	725.6	723.6	726.1	731.7	736.2	739.9	739.5	724.8
2005	714.7	720.5	726.1	734.3	743.5	737.6	732.5	735.6	744.6	742.3	746.5	744.5	735.2
2006	726.4	732.2	739.7	745.3	756.9	750.6	741.0	746.8	756.1	759.6	764.8	765.6	748.8
2007	744.0	745.6	757.0	762.1	772.6	769.6	755.8	764.7	771.4	777.2	781.6	781.4	765.3
2008	752.6	756.4	762.0	767.5	779.1	773.0	766.0	775.5	775.8	777.0	774.4	769.8	769.1
2009	744.0	743.9	745.6	748.1	754.1	749.4	738.4	748.5	750.3	749.9	750.6	748.5	747.6

Employment by Industry: Indianapolis-Carmel, IN, Selected Years, 1990–2009—*Continued*

(Numbers in thousands, not seasonally adjusted.)

Industry and year	January	February	March	April	May	June	July	August	September	October	November	December	Annual average
Trade, Transportation, and Utilities													
1990	141.8	140.0	140.7	139.7	141.4	141.3	142.7	143.6	143.5	143.4	145.8	146.7	142.6
2000	188.9	188.4	190.0	188.3	189.6	190.6	191.6	191.1	190.3	193.3	195.8	199.4	191.4
2001	194.7	191.6	192.3	194.0	194.1	194.3	194.7	195.0	193.8	195.2	198.2	200.8	194.9
2002	191.4	189.5	190.0	190.5	191.7	192.4	191.1	191.6	190.6	190.7	194.7	196.9	191.8
2003	189.6	186.6	188.1	189.2	189.3	189.5	188.6	189.1	188.4	190.1	193.9	195.4	189.8
2004	185.7	183.7	185.2	186.7	188.3	189.4	190.4	190.9	188.9	192.3	196.2	198.2	189.7
2005	189.1	189.0	190.4	192.3	193.6	193.9	194.6	195.2	194.6	196.3	199.9	201.0	194.2
2006	192.8	191.4	193.0	192.7	194.3	195.2	195.0	194.8	194.3	195.7	200.2	202.1	195.1
2007	193.5	190.9	193.9	193.8	196.3	197.8	196.8	196.1	195.7	196.3	200.9	202.6	196.2
2008	193.7	192.2	193.4	193.5	196.4	196.7	195.7	196.3	194.9	195.8	196.9	197.3	195.2
2009	187.9	185.4	185.1	184.4	186.1	186.5	185.0	184.9	183.6	183.7	185.5	185.8	185.3
Wholesale Trade													
1990	34.2	34.3	34.3	34.1	34.3	34.3	34.6	34.7	34.6	34.7	34.7	34.5	34.4
2000	47.6	47.9	48.3	48.1	48.4	48.8	48.8	48.8	48.6	48.8	48.6	48.7	48.5
2001	49.0	49.0	49.0	49.0	49.0	49.1	49.0	48.9	48.6	48.5	48.3	48.4	48.8
2002	47.4	47.7	47.5	47.4	47.7	47.7	47.3	47.2	46.8	46.8	46.7	46.8	47.3
2003	46.3	46.2	46.2	45.8	45.9	46.0	45.7	45.6	45.4	45.6	45.7	45.8	45.9
2004	45.4	45.6	46.0	46.0	46.2	46.6	46.9	46.7	46.3	46.6	46.6	46.5	46.3
2005	46.2	46.4	46.6	46.8	46.8	47.0	47.2	47.2	47.0	47.1	47.1	47.3	46.9
2006	46.9	46.9	47.0	47.1	47.4	47.7	47.5	47.3	47.2	47.5	47.4	47.6	47.3
2007	47.2	47.2	47.6	47.5	47.7	48.1	48.5	48.0	47.8	47.8	48.1	48.2	47.8
2008	47.8	47.9	48.2	48.2	48.5	48.5	48.4	48.1	47.9	47.9	47.8	47.6	48.1
2009	46.4	46.0	45.7	45.2	45.2	45.1	45.2	44.7	44.3	44.1	43.9	44.1	45.0
Retail Trade													
1990	80.3	78.3	78.8	78.4	79.6	79.5	80.5	81.1	81.2	80.8	83.2	84.4	80.5
2000	96.0	94.9	95.8	94.9	96.0	96.8	96.0	96.1	95.6	98.0	101.0	103.4	97.0
2001	99.7	97.4	97.5	97.7	98.2	98.7	97.8	97.6	97.3	98.2	101.9	103.2	98.8
2002	97.8	96.2	96.9	96.4	97.4	98.1	96.8	96.8	96.4	96.0	99.3	101.4	97.5
2003	96.1	94.2	95.4	95.5	96.6	97.0	95.8	96.4	95.8	96.6	100.2	101.8	96.8
2004	95.2	93.0	93.6	94.2	95.4	96.0	95.9	96.2	95.0	97.1	100.9	102.5	96.3
2005	95.2	94.5	95.4	96.4	97.6	97.4	97.5	97.4	96.8	98.1	101.0	102.4	97.5
2006	96.1	94.7	95.8	95.4	96.2	96.5	96.6	96.3	95.6	96.4	100.1	101.6	96.8
2007	95.3	93.1	94.7	94.6	96.3	97.0	96.2	95.7	95.1	95.6	98.9	100.3	96.1
2008	93.9	92.4	92.7	92.6	94.7	94.9	94.9	95.1	94.3	95.1	96.1	96.5	94.4
2009	90.4	88.7	88.9	89.3	90.7	91.3	90.3	90.2	89.2	89.0	90.7	90.9	90.0
Transportation and Utilities													
1990	27.3	27.4	27.6	27.2	27.5	27.5	27.6	27.8	27.7	27.9	27.9	27.8	27.6
2000	45.3	45.6	45.9	45.3	45.2	45.0	46.8	46.2	46.1	46.5	46.2	47.3	46.0
2001	46.0	45.2	45.8	47.3	46.9	46.5	47.9	48.5	47.9	48.5	48.0	49.2	47.3
2002	46.2	45.6	45.6	46.7	46.6	46.6	47.0	47.6	47.4	47.9	48.7	48.7	47.1
2003	47.2	46.2	46.5	47.9	46.8	46.5	47.1	47.1	47.2	47.9	48.0	47.8	47.2
2004	45.1	45.1	45.6	46.5	46.7	46.8	47.6	48.0	47.6	48.6	48.7	49.2	47.1
2005	47.7	48.1	48.4	49.1	49.2	49.5	49.9	50.6	50.8	51.1	51.8	51.3	49.8
2006	49.8	49.8	50.2	50.2	50.7	51.0	50.9	51.2	51.5	51.8	52.7	52.9	51.1
2007	51.0	50.6	51.6	51.7	52.3	52.7	52.1	52.4	52.8	52.9	53.9	54.1	52.3
2008	52.0	51.9	52.5	52.7	53.2	53.3	52.4	53.1	52.7	52.8	53.0	53.2	52.7
2009	51.1	50.7	50.5	49.9	50.2	50.1	49.5	50.0	50.1	50.6	50.9	50.8	50.4
Information													
1990	15.7	15.6	15.6	15.6	15.9	16.0	16.1	16.0	15.9	15.8	15.8	15.8	15.8
2000	17.0	17.1	17.4	16.9	17.0	17.4	17.5	17.7	17.4	17.5	17.6	17.7	17.4
2001	17.6	17.4	17.6	17.0	17.2	17.4	17.2	17.0	16.8	16.7	16.7	16.7	17.1
2002	16.5	16.4	16.6	16.4	16.6	16.7	16.6	16.6	16.4	16.3	16.2	16.2	16.5
2003	16.0	15.9	16.1	15.9	16.2	16.6	16.6	16.8	16.5	16.3	16.4	16.4	16.3
2004	16.3	16.3	16.3	16.2	16.5	16.8	16.8	16.8	16.4	16.6	16.5	16.6	16.5
2005	16.1	16.3	16.3	16.3	16.5	16.7	16.6	16.6	16.2	16.1	16.2	16.4	16.4
2006	15.8	16.0	16.0	16.2	16.3	16.4	16.4	16.3	16.1	16.0	16.1	16.1	16.1
2007	16.1	16.2	16.1	16.2	16.4	16.6	16.7	16.7	16.6	16.5	16.5	16.7	16.4
2008	16.7	16.7	16.7	16.7	16.9	17.0	17.0	16.9	16.6	16.4	16.3	16.3	16.7
2009	16.1	16.1	15.9	15.7	15.9	16.0	15.8	15.8	15.5	15.2	15.2	15.1	15.7
Financial Activities													
1990	47.3	47.6	47.8	47.7	48.1	48.6	48.8	48.8	48.6	48.6	48.6	48.5	48.3
2000	63.1	63.1	62.9	63.0	63.5	64.1	63.5	63.2	62.7	62.6	62.2	62.4	63.0
2001	61.9	62.1	62.3	62.9	63.2	63.9	63.2	62.9	62.2	61.2	61.5	61.8	62.4
2002	62.0	62.0	61.8	61.9	62.2	62.8	62.5	62.6	62.2	62.6	62.8	62.9	62.4
2003	62.7	62.8	62.9	63.2	63.6	64.2	64.2	64.2	63.9	63.9	63.7	63.7	63.6
2004	62.9	63.2	63.2	63.1	63.5	63.9	63.8	63.8	63.1	63.1	63.0	63.4	63.3
2005	62.4	62.5	62.4	62.8	62.8	63.3	63.8	63.8	63.4	63.3	63.2	63.4	63.1
2006	62.5	62.6	62.6	62.7	63.1	63.5	63.4	63.5	62.9	62.7	62.5	62.7	62.9
2007	61.5	61.9	62.0	62.3	62.4	63.0	63.3	63.1	62.7	62.4	62.2	62.3	62.4
2008	60.6	60.7	60.6	60.5	60.7	61.1	61.3	60.8	60.0	59.9	59.3	59.4	60.4
2009	58.8	58.8	58.6	58.4	58.4	58.5	58.4	58.3	57.5	58.0	57.1	58.1	58.2

Employment by Industry: Indianapolis-Carmel, IN, Selected Years, 1990–2009—*Continued*

(Numbers in thousands, not seasonally adjusted.)

Industry and year	January	February	March	April	May	June	July	August	September	October	November	December	Annual average
Professional and Business Services													
1990	59.6	59.7	60.3	60.9	61.7	62.6	62.8	62.9	63.5	64.1	63.4	62.8	62.0
2000	104.1	104.7	106.9	108.0	110.0	111.4	109.0	109.5	109.8	108.5	107.6	106.5	108.0
2001	103.4	104.1	106.3	108.3	108.5	109.3	108.6	109.8	107.3	106.9	106.1	104.6	106.9
2002	104.1	104.4	105.4	107.3	108.2	108.8	108.9	109.2	108.2	109.3	108.5	107.6	107.5
2003	105.0	105.1	105.2	107.8	110.2	110.7	111.2	111.9	111.5	113.7	114.6	113.1	110.0
2004	106.9	107.3	110.4	115.2	116.4	117.5	122.3	121.5	120.5	119.8	120.5	119.3	116.5
2005	115.4	115.8	117.2	118.9	119.5	120.1	121.8	121.2	121.1	122.2	122.2	120.3	119.6
2006	116.8	117.6	119.5	122.1	124.1	125.0	124.7	127.0	126.4	126.6	127.5	126.0	123.6
2007	123.9	123.3	126.5	129.2	131.1	130.7	130.1	131.8	131.8	134.3	134.1	132.0	129.9
2008	127.2	126.3	127.3	129.5	130.4	130.6	129.9	131.9	130.7	132.2	129.6	125.9	129.3
2009	118.3	117.1	116.8	117.4	117.2	118.9	117.0	118.9	119.9	121.3	122.0	121.1	118.8
Education and Health Services													
1990	63.0	63.2	63.4	64.4	64.6	64.4	64.4	64.9	66.0	67.0	67.3	66.9	65.0
2000	90.5	91.8	92.6	91.4	91.3	90.8	90.7	91.1	92.3	92.4	92.3	92.6	91.7
2001	92.3	93.4	93.8	94.2	94.6	93.7	93.5	94.8	97.3	97.0	97.9	98.3	95.1
2002	96.4	96.9	97.5	97.5	97.8	96.8	96.0	96.8	98.8	100.0	100.8	101.0	98.0
2003	99.5	100.1	100.4	105.7	104.8	101.5	101.0	100.8	105.0	107.5	107.5	107.4	103.4
2004	107.1	107.1	107.9	107.6	105.6	103.9	104.6	102.0	105.5	107.3	107.3	106.4	106.0
2005	102.8	104.1	104.9	105.8	108.7	107.2	106.8	104.3	109.1	106.5	107.0	106.2	106.1
2006	106.1	107.6	108.6	108.3	111.1	110.2	109.3	107.0	111.6	113.5	113.7	113.5	110.0
2007	112.2	113.3	114.2	115.1	115.0	115.0	113.6	112.2	116.3	118.3	118.9	119.3	115.3
2008	113.8	115.1	115.7	116.7	117.3	116.8	116.9	115.6	119.2	120.6	121.2	121.5	117.5
2009	120.7	121.5	121.4	122.8	122.6	122.6	122.2	121.0	124.5	124.5	124.9	125.0	122.8
Leisure and Hospitality													
1990	56.9	57.4	58.8	58.9	62.7	62.8	62.5	63.5	62.7	60.8	60.6	60.8	60.7
2000	73.5	74.3	76.6	79.9	83.2	85.3	82.2	84.2	81.7	82.0	79.2	78.4	80.0
2001	76.9	78.1	80.7	82.7	86.4	89.1	86.0	88.6	84.3	84.9	82.3	81.5	83.5
2002	76.2	76.9	78.8	81.6	85.7	87.4	85.3	87.4	83.4	83.4	81.6	81.2	82.4
2003	77.4	77.4	79.0	82.5	86.9	88.4	86.1	88.5	84.6	85.0	82.8	82.2	83.4
2004	77.6	77.5	80.1	84.0	87.6	89.5	88.6	89.7	86.5	85.2	84.7	84.0	84.6
2005	79.3	79.9	82.2	86.8	90.3	92.5	91.2	92.7	88.7	86.9	86.8	86.2	87.0
2006	82.8	83.5	85.8	88.7	92.0	93.6	92.0	93.3	90.4	89.0	88.4	88.3	89.0
2007	84.2	83.8	86.8	88.4	92.6	94.4	91.0	93.7	89.6	89.8	88.8	88.0	89.3
2008	84.5	84.6	86.6	89.2	94.0	94.1	92.5	94.9	92.3	89.1	88.0	86.8	89.7
2009	82.9	83.2	85.4	87.4	90.8	92.0	90.5	91.1	88.9	85.3	84.7	82.8	87.1
Other Services													
1990	26.8	26.9	27.1	26.9	27.0	27.2	27.2	27.4	27.2	27.6	27.8	27.6	27.2
2000	32.3	32.6	33.0	32.9	33.1	33.5	33.2	33.2	32.5	32.8	32.6	32.6	32.9
2001	32.4	32.7	33.2	33.1	33.8	34.3	34.2	34.0	32.9	32.9	33.0	33.0	33.3
2002	32.4	32.7	33.1	33.6	34.3	34.9	34.7	34.5	33.6	33.6	33.7	33.6	33.7
2003	33.2	33.5	33.7	33.8	34.2	34.7	34.6	34.4	33.7	33.7	33.6	33.4	33.9
2004	33.3	33.5	33.9	34.3	34.7	35.0	35.2	35.2	34.6	34.4	34.2	34.1	34.4
2005	33.9	34.2	34.6	34.8	35.2	35.5	35.6	35.7	34.9	34.9	34.8	34.8	34.9
2006	34.4	34.7	35.0	35.4	35.7	36.4	36.0	36.0	35.5	35.3	35.3	35.3	35.4
2007	35.0	35.1	35.5	35.8	36.3	36.9	36.8	36.3	35.8	35.8	35.6	35.6	35.9
2008	35.1	35.4	35.4	36.0	36.5	36.8	36.9	36.5	36.0	35.7	35.6	35.2	35.9
2009	34.8	34.6	34.8	34.7	35.1	35.5	35.3	34.8	34.2	34.1	33.8	33.6	34.6
Government													
1990	103.2	104.3	104.9	105.2	107.5	102.1	96.9	100.2	104.7	105.1	105.6	105.2	103.7
2000	107.6	110.9	111.7	110.4	111.3	106.0	98.0	103.3	112.3	111.5	112.2	112.3	109.0
2001	108.7	111.0	111.8	111.5	112.6	107.3	99.2	104.0	112.6	112.7	112.6	112.6	109.7
2002	109.1	113.0	113.3	113.4	114.4	108.8	100.9	105.8	114.0	115.8	116.6	116.6	111.8
2003	113.6	115.6	116.2	115.7	116.2	110.2	104.9	109.8	115.3	116.0	115.7	115.7	113.7
2004	114.6	116.2	116.6	115.8	116.3	109.6	101.9	106.2	116.2	117.5	117.5	117.5	113.8
2005	115.7	118.7	118.1	116.6	116.9	108.4	102.1	106.1	116.6	116.1	116.4	116.2	114.0
2006	115.2	118.8	119.2	119.2	120.3	110.3	104.2	108.9	118.9	120.8	121.1	121.6	116.5
2007	117.6	121.1	122.0	121.3	122.5	115.2	107.5	114.8	122.9	123.8	124.6	124.9	119.9
2008	121.0	125.4	126.3	125.4	126.9	119.9	115.8	122.6	126.1	127.3	127.5	127.4	124.3
2009	124.5	127.2	127.6	127.3	128.0	119.4	114.2	123.7	126.2	127.8	127.4	127.0	125.0

Employment by Industry: Jacksonville, FL, Selected Years, 1990–2009

(Numbers in thousands, not seasonally adjusted.)

Industry and year	January	February	March	April	May	June	July	August	September	October	November	December	Annual average
Total Nonfarm													
1990	407.5	409.7	413.7	416.3	420.2	419.4	414.8	414.4	417.1	417.6	418.2	418.7	415.6
2000	553.6	556.5	561.6	564.5	568.5	565.5	560.1	567.5	567.3	569.3	570.5	574.0	564.9
2001	553.5	560.2	566.7	567.8	568.6	565.4	560.1	571.1	569.3	565.3	566.5	567.7	565.2
2002	555.8	557.9	563.4	563.3	565.3	559.6	552.5	560.7	558.6	559.8	563.6	566.4	560.6
2003	555.9	558.6	565.1	564.3	566.9	560.9	555.7	563.4	562.3	565.3	568.1	572.1	563.2
2004	564.3	567.2	573.0	577.2	579.0	576.4	573.4	580.1	579.3	583.3	591.1	597.9	578.5
2005	589.9	594.9	598.0	599.6	602.0	598.4	598.1	607.9	610.1	609.3	616.4	620.3	603.7
2006	611.9	617.6	623.6	621.4	625.5	620.7	617.8	626.0	627.1	629.6	636.9	638.9	624.8
2007	628.2	631.6	637.5	636.8	639.0	633.8	626.3	632.7	631.7	632.5	637.5	637.7	633.8
2008	626.4	629.5	630.8	630.1	630.6	621.9	613.7	616.2	615.5	614.2	615.6	613.0	621.5
2009	595.5	595.1	594.5	590.5	590.2	582.5	576.8	578.1	577.2	579.0	584.3	585.7	585.8
Total Private													
1990	342.1	343.9	346.9	348.8	351.1	353.8	350.6	351.2	350.7	349.6	349.7	350.6	349.1
2000	484.9	486.9	491.6	494.2	496.4	499.8	495.6	497.6	497.6	498.8	500.1	503.3	495.6
2001	484.3	489.6	495.8	496.5	497.1	499.1	495.1	499.6	498.0	494.1	494.8	495.6	495.0
2002	485.6	487.0	492.5	491.8	493.6	493.1	487.5	489.3	487.4	488.1	491.3	493.7	490.1
2003	484.1	486.8	493.1	492.0	493.9	492.6	488.8	491.5	490.3	492.4	494.8	498.6	491.6
2004	491.7	494.0	499.5	503.5	505.1	507.0	505.4	506.7	505.5	508.4	515.6	521.7	505.3
2005	514.9	519.0	521.9	524.2	526.2	527.4	529.0	533.2	535.0	534.4	541.3	545.1	529.3
2006	537.5	542.4	548.3	547.0	551.3	550.9	549.5	552.4	552.8	554.2	560.5	562.4	550.8
2007	552.6	555.0	560.7	559.8	561.8	560.8	555.6	556.2	554.8	555.1	559.3	559.6	557.6
2008	549.4	551.6	552.8	552.6	552.9	548.9	542.1	540.3	538.5	536.8	536.9	534.9	544.8
2009	519.2	517.7	517.0	512.9	512.3	509.4	505.0	502.2	500.7	501.2	506.7	508.7	509.4
Goods-Producing													
1990	63.6	64.2	64.5	64.0	63.7	64.6	63.8	63.1	62.7	61.3	60.1	59.6	62.9
2000	70.3	70.9	71.8	71.7	72.1	72.9	73.0	72.9	72.9	72.5	71.7	72.2	72.1
2001	68.6	69.3	69.4	69.3	69.0	69.7	69.8	69.4	68.8	68.8	68.7	68.5	69.1
2002	67.7	67.7	68.3	67.6	68.4	68.9	68.3	68.5	68.3	69.0	69.7	69.8	68.5
2003	69.5	70.1	70.9	69.3	69.9	70.7	69.5	69.7	69.7	69.7	70.2	70.8	70.0
2004	70.4	71.4	72.5	72.9	73.4	74.4	74.9	75.1	75.3	75.7	76.5	77.4	74.2
2005	76.2	76.5	77.3	77.7	78.0	79.0	79.5	80.0	80.6	80.0	80.9	81.5	78.9
2006	80.7	81.9	82.8	83.1	83.9	84.9	84.1	84.5	84.3	83.4	83.4	83.2	83.4
2007	81.6	81.5	82.4	81.4	82.5	83.4	82.8	82.9	82.0	80.5	80.4	80.1	81.8
2008	77.7	78.0	77.8	76.3	76.3	76.2	74.8	74.2	74.0	72.4	71.3	70.1	74.9
2009	67.2	66.2	65.3	62.8	61.8	61.7	60.5	59.9	59.4	58.4	57.9	57.9	61.6
Mining and Logging													
1990	0.4	0.4	0.4	0.4	0.4	0.4	0.4	0.4	0.4	0.4	0.3	0.3	0.4
2000	0.4	0.4	0.4	0.4	0.4	0.5	0.5	0.5	0.5	0.5	0.5	0.5	0.5
2001	0.4	0.5	0.5	0.4	0.4	0.5	0.5	0.5	0.5	0.5	0.5	0.5	0.5
2002	0.5	0.5	0.5	0.4	0.5	0.5	0.5	0.5	0.5	0.5	0.5	0.5	0.5
2003	0.5	0.5	0.5	0.5	0.5	0.5	0.5	0.5	0.5	0.5	0.5	0.5	0.5
2004	0.5	0.4	0.4	0.4	0.4	0.4	0.4	0.4	0.4	0.4	0.4	0.4	0.4
2005	0.4	0.4	0.4	0.4	0.4	0.4	0.4	0.4	0.4	0.4	0.4	0.4	0.4
2006	0.4	0.4	0.4	0.4	0.4	0.4	0.4	0.4	0.4	0.4	0.4	0.4	0.4
2007	0.4	0.4	0.4	0.4	0.4	0.4	0.4	0.4	0.4	0.4	0.4	0.4	0.4
2008	0.4	0.4	0.4	0.4	0.4	0.4	0.4	0.4	0.4	0.4	0.4	0.4	0.4
2009	0.4	0.4	0.4	0.4	0.4	0.4	0.3	0.4	0.4	0.4	0.4	0.4	0.4
Construction													
1990	27.0	27.6	28.0	27.6	27.3	27.7	27.1	26.9	26.6	25.9	24.6	24.4	26.7
2000	30.9	31.2	31.9	31.7	32.0	32.4	32.5	32.6	32.8	32.7	32.5	32.8	32.2
2001	31.6	32.0	31.9	31.9	31.9	32.5	32.8	32.9	32.8	33.1	33.1	33.0	32.5
2002	32.3	32.2	32.9	32.8	33.6	34.0	33.5	33.8	33.8	34.4	35.0	35.2	33.6
2003	35.0	35.4	36.2	35.7	36.0	36.5	36.0	36.4	36.3	36.3	36.8	37.2	36.1
2004	37.3	38.2	39.1	39.4	39.7	40.4	41.0	41.3	41.6	41.9	42.6	43.3	40.5
2005	42.5	42.5	43.2	43.8	44.2	45.0	45.4	46.0	46.5	46.2	47.0	47.5	45.0
2006	46.9	48.1	48.9	49.5	50.1	50.9	50.3	50.8	50.6	50.0	50.1	49.9	49.7
2007	48.4	48.2	49.1	48.8	49.8	50.5	49.9	49.9	49.0	47.7	47.6	47.2	48.8
2008	44.9	45.2	45.1	43.7	43.7	43.7	42.4	42.0	41.8	40.6	39.6	38.5	42.6
2009	36.0	35.7	35.1	33.3	32.8	32.8	31.9	31.4	31.0	30.3	30.0	30.0	32.5
Manufacturing													
1990	36.2	36.2	36.1	36.0	36.0	36.5	36.3	35.8	35.7	35.0	35.2	34.9	35.8
2000	39.0	39.3	39.5	39.6	39.7	40.0	40.0	39.8	39.6	39.3	38.7	38.9	39.5
2001	36.6	36.8	37.0	37.0	36.7	36.7	36.5	36.0	35.5	35.2	35.1	35.0	36.2
2002	34.9	35.0	34.9	34.4	34.3	34.4	34.3	34.2	34.0	34.1	34.2	34.1	34.4
2003	34.0	34.2	34.2	33.1	33.4	33.7	33.0	32.8	32.9	32.9	32.9	33.1	33.3
2004	32.6	32.8	33.0	33.1	33.3	33.6	33.5	33.4	33.3	33.4	33.5	33.7	33.3
2005	33.3	33.6	33.7	33.5	33.4	33.6	33.7	33.6	33.7	33.4	33.5	33.6	33.6
2006	33.4	33.4	33.5	33.2	33.4	33.6	33.4	33.3	33.3	33.0	32.9	32.9	33.3
2007	32.8	32.9	32.9	32.2	32.3	32.5	32.5	32.6	32.6	32.4	32.4	32.5	32.6
2008	32.4	32.4	32.3	32.2	32.2	32.1	32.0	31.8	31.8	31.4	31.3	31.2	31.9
2009	30.8	30.1	29.8	29.1	28.6	28.5	28.3	28.1	28.0	27.7	27.5	27.5	28.7

Employment by Industry: Jacksonville, FL, Selected Years, 1990–2009—*Continued*

(Numbers in thousands, not seasonally adjusted.)

Industry and year	January	February	March	April	May	June	July	August	September	October	November	December	Annual average
Service-Providing													
1990	343.9	345.5	349.2	352.3	356.5	354.8	351.0	351.3	354.4	356.3	358.1	359.1	352.7
2000	483.3	485.6	489.8	492.8	496.4	492.6	487.1	494.6	494.4	496.8	498.8	501.8	492.8
2001	484.9	490.9	497.3	498.5	499.6	495.7	490.3	501.7	500.5	496.5	497.8	499.2	496.1
2002	488.1	490.2	495.1	495.7	496.9	490.7	484.2	492.2	490.3	490.8	493.9	496.6	492.1
2003	486.4	488.5	494.2	495.0	497.0	490.2	486.2	493.7	492.6	495.6	497.9	501.3	493.2
2004	493.9	495.8	500.5	504.3	505.6	502.0	498.5	505.0	504.0	507.6	514.6	520.5	504.4
2005	513.7	518.4	520.7	521.9	524.0	519.4	518.6	527.9	529.5	529.3	535.5	538.8	524.8
2006	531.2	535.7	540.8	538.3	541.6	535.8	533.7	541.5	542.8	546.2	553.5	555.7	541.4
2007	546.6	550.1	555.1	555.4	556.5	550.4	543.5	549.8	549.7	552.0	557.1	557.6	552.0
2008	548.7	551.5	553.0	553.8	554.3	545.7	538.9	542.0	541.5	541.8	544.3	542.9	546.5
2009	528.3	528.9	529.2	527.7	528.4	520.8	516.3	518.2	517.8	520.6	526.4	527.8	524.2
Trade, Transportation, and Utilities													
1990	103.9	102.7	103.1	104.7	105.4	106.8	105.7	106.8	107.2	107.5	109.0	111.0	106.2
2000	128.4	128.6	130.2	129.7	130.1	131.6	127.7	129.0	129.1	129.1	131.1	131.8	129.7
2001	125.9	124.9	126.1	125.3	125.3	125.3	124.3	125.5	125.3	124.5	126.0	128.0	125.5
2002	122.9	122.7	124.1	124.0	124.2	124.0	123.2	124.1	124.1	124.3	126.5	128.9	124.4
2003	124.7	123.9	124.7	124.1	124.2	123.1	123.4	124.4	124.1	125.4	127.8	129.9	124.9
2004	125.5	125.5	126.4	127.5	127.4	126.7	127.0	127.9	127.3	128.9	132.3	134.5	128.1
2005	130.0	130.6	131.5	131.8	132.3	131.8	132.0	132.8	132.9	133.0	135.9	138.0	132.7
2006	133.8	133.6	135.1	135.1	135.8	135.8	135.8	137.1	137.4	138.7	141.2	143.1	136.9
2007	138.0	137.6	139.1	138.9	139.3	138.7	137.9	138.1	138.1	139.1	142.4	143.3	139.2
2008	138.5	138.0	138.3	137.2	137.1	136.0	135.3	135.5	134.2	134.2	135.5	136.0	136.3
2009	130.3	128.9	128.3	126.5	126.7	126.0	125.3	125.0	124.8	125.4	129.8	130.9	127.3
Wholesale Trade													
1990	21.7	21.8	22.0	21.8	21.8	22.0	22.4	22.3	22.2	21.9	21.8	21.7	22.0
2000	26.1	26.3	26.7	26.2	26.3	26.3	26.4	26.3	26.1	26.3	26.5	26.6	26.3
2001	26.1	26.2	26.4	26.1	26.1	26.3	26.4	26.5	26.5	26.1	26.0	25.9	26.2
2002	25.1	25.3	25.4	25.5	25.6	25.9	25.9	26.1	26.2	26.3	26.6	26.9	25.9
2003	27.1	27.1	27.1	26.8	26.7	26.7	26.7	26.7	26.6	26.6	26.7	26.8	26.8
2004	26.4	26.7	26.8	26.7	26.7	26.9	27.0	26.9	26.7	27.1	27.2	27.2	26.9
2005	27.0	27.3	27.2	27.3	27.5	27.7	27.9	28.0	28.1	28.3	28.4	28.7	27.8
2006	29.0	29.1	29.3	29.4	29.6	29.9	29.8	30.1	30.3	30.6	30.7	30.9	29.9
2007	30.2	30.4	30.6	30.4	30.3	30.4	30.3	30.2	30.0	30.1	29.8	29.7	30.2
2008	29.0	29.0	29.0	28.8	28.7	28.8	28.8	28.7	28.5	28.2	28.0	27.9	28.6
2009	27.7	27.4	27.1	27.0	26.8	26.8	26.6	26.4	26.2	26.2	26.6	26.6	26.8
Retail Trade													
1990	57.9	57.2	57.2	58.2	59.1	59.5	58.9	59.6	59.6	59.8	61.5	63.2	59.3
2000	69.3	69.4	70.6	70.3	70.6	71.4	68.7	69.8	69.8	70.1	72.0	73.3	70.4
2001	68.0	67.2	67.9	67.2	67.5	67.4	66.8	67.2	67.0	66.9	68.6	69.7	67.6
2002	67.0	66.5	67.4	67.5	68.0	68.2	67.6	68.0	67.9	68.0	69.7	71.2	68.1
2003	68.6	67.9	68.2	67.8	68.2	68.3	68.2	68.4	68.3	68.9	70.8	72.2	68.8
2004	69.4	69.0	69.7	70.5	70.8	70.7	70.9	70.8	70.3	71.5	74.5	75.8	71.2
2005	72.2	72.4	73.3	73.4	73.6	73.8	73.9	73.9	73.7	73.6	75.8	77.0	73.9
2006	72.9	72.8	73.7	73.7	74.0	74.6	74.7	74.9	74.7	75.5	77.7	78.6	74.8
2007	75.5	75.0	76.2	75.7	76.2	76.0	75.7	76.0	75.7	76.2	79.2	80.2	76.5
2008	77.1	76.5	76.8	75.9	76.0	75.5	74.7	74.5	74.0	73.8	75.2	75.3	75.4
2009	70.8	70.0	70.0	69.1	69.6	69.5	69.2	69.2	68.9	68.9	72.8	73.3	70.1
Transportation and Utilities													
1990	24.3	23.7	23.9	24.7	24.5	25.3	24.4	24.9	25.4	25.8	25.7	26.1	24.9
2000	33.0	32.9	32.9	33.2	33.2	33.9	32.6	32.9	33.2	32.7	32.6	31.9	32.9
2001	31.8	31.5	31.8	32.0	31.7	31.6	31.1	31.8	31.8	31.5	31.4	32.4	31.7
2002	30.8	30.9	31.3	31.0	30.6	29.9	29.7	30.0	30.0	30.0	30.2	30.8	30.4
2003	29.0	28.9	29.4	29.5	29.3	28.1	28.5	29.3	29.2	29.9	30.3	30.9	29.3
2004	29.7	29.8	29.9	30.3	29.9	29.1	29.1	30.2	30.3	30.3	30.6	31.5	30.1
2005	30.8	30.9	31.0	31.1	31.2	30.3	30.2	30.9	31.1	31.1	31.7	32.3	31.1
2006	31.9	31.7	32.1	32.0	32.2	31.3	31.3	32.1	32.4	32.6	32.8	33.6	32.2
2007	32.3	32.2	32.3	32.8	32.8	32.3	31.9	31.9	32.4	32.8	33.4	33.4	32.5
2008	32.4	32.5	32.5	32.5	32.4	31.7	31.8	32.3	31.7	32.2	32.3	32.8	32.3
2009	31.8	31.5	31.2	30.4	30.3	29.7	29.5	29.4	29.7	30.3	30.4	31.0	30.4
Information													
1990	10.3	10.5	10.5	10.9	10.8	10.7	10.8	10.9	10.9	10.7	10.8	10.8	10.7
2000	15.3	15.3	15.3	15.0	15.2	15.2	15.3	15.2	15.3	15.0	15.3	15.6	15.3
2001	15.0	15.0	15.0	14.9	14.7	14.6	14.5	14.2	14.1	13.7	13.6	13.5	14.4
2002	13.8	13.6	13.7	13.6	13.4	13.2	13.2	13.0	12.9	12.9	12.8	12.8	13.2
2003	12.7	12.8	12.8	12.5	12.8	12.3	12.4	12.3	12.2	12.1	12.1	12.2	12.4
2004	12.0	11.5	11.5	11.3	11.4	11.6	11.5	11.6	11.5	11.7	11.9	12.1	11.6
2005	12.0	12.0	11.9	11.8	12.0	12.0	12.1	12.2	12.0	11.7	11.8	11.4	11.9
2006	11.5	11.5	11.5	11.4	11.3	11.4	11.4	11.1	10.6	10.5	10.4	10.5	11.1
2007	10.1	10.1	10.2	10.2	10.2	10.3	10.2	10.2	10.2	10.1	10.0	10.0	10.2
2008	9.9	9.9	10.0	10.1	10.1	10.2	10.4	10.3	10.4	10.4	10.5	10.5	10.2
2009	10.4	10.4	10.4	10.5	10.4	10.5	10.4	10.4	10.2	10.3	10.3	10.2	10.4

Employment by Industry: Jacksonville, FL, Selected Years, 1990–2009—*Continued*

(Numbers in thousands, not seasonally adjusted.)

Industry and year	January	February	March	April	May	June	July	August	September	October	November	December	Annual average
Financial Activities													
1990	39.7	39.6	39.9	39.8	40.1	40.6	40.9	41.2	41.4	41.2	41.5	41.5	40.6
2000	55.8	55.8	55.9	56.5	56.8	57.1	57.1	56.7	56.4	56.4	56.6	57.0	56.5
2001	56.3	56.6	57.0	57.2	57.4	57.9	58.3	58.4	58.5	58.7	58.9	59.1	57.9
2002	58.6	58.0	57.9	57.9	57.8	57.7	57.6	57.5	57.2	57.3	57.4	57.4	57.7
2003	57.1	56.7	56.9	57.1	57.4	57.6	57.9	58.2	58.2	58.0	58.0	58.4	57.6
2004	57.9	57.8	57.8	58.4	58.5	58.6	58.5	58.7	58.6	58.5	58.7	59.1	58.4
2005	58.8	58.9	59.2	59.1	59.0	59.0	58.9	59.0	58.9	59.5	60.1	60.9	59.3
2006	59.7	60.1	60.3	60.4	60.4	60.2	59.9	59.6	59.4	59.1	59.3	59.6	59.8
2007	58.9	59.1	59.4	59.5	59.8	60.1	60.5	60.8	60.7	60.7	61.1	61.1	60.1
2008	60.7	60.7	60.8	60.7	60.5	60.3	60.0	59.6	59.1	58.6	58.0	57.9	59.7
2009	56.9	56.7	56.5	55.7	55.7	55.6	55.4	55.0	54.5	54.7	54.4	54.7	55.5
Professional and Business Services													
1990	23.9	24.5	24.9	25.8	27.7	28.6	27.6	27.2	26.9	27.7	26.9	26.9	26.6
2000	83.9	84.2	85.2	86.9	86.7	87.2	89.4	90.1	90.3	93.0	92.2	92.6	88.5
2001	88.9	92.3	94.6	94.7	94.5	93.6	91.5	93.4	93.1	90.7	89.4	87.8	92.0
2002	86.1	87.5	88.8	88.2	87.9	86.5	84.2	83.9	83.5	82.9	82.1	81.6	85.3
2003	81.0	83.1	85.7	86.4	85.6	84.0	81.9	81.9	81.0	81.7	81.0	80.4	82.8
2004	80.2	81.1	82.9	83.5	83.6	84.6	83.0	82.1	81.7	81.3	82.5	83.7	82.5
2005	83.8	85.5	85.0	85.6	85.9	86.6	88.0	89.5	90.4	91.1	92.4	93.0	88.1
2006	92.3	94.1	95.5	94.1	95.4	94.0	94.1	94.8	95.4	96.9	99.2	99.0	95.4
2007	97.5	97.7	98.3	97.9	96.4	94.7	92.5	91.6	91.1	91.9	91.3	90.5	94.3
2008	88.7	89.9	90.3	90.7	91.3	89.5	85.7	85.6	86.4	86.3	86.0	85.8	88.0
2009	83.1	83.7	83.4	83.0	82.9	82.2	80.5	80.4	81.0	81.2	82.2	83.2	82.2
Education and Health Services													
1990	42.4	43.1	43.4	42.9	42.8	42.9	42.5	42.6	43.2	44.2	44.4	44.1	43.2
2000	59.9	60.1	60.3	59.8	60.1	60.2	58.8	59.2	59.5	59.0	59.2	59.6	59.6
2001	59.0	59.6	60.1	60.1	60.5	61.1	60.8	61.4	61.9	62.6	62.8	63.1	61.1
2002	62.6	62.9	63.3	63.3	63.6	63.7	63.2	63.6	63.7	63.9	64.1	64.3	63.5
2003	63.5	64.0	64.4	64.0	64.4	64.3	64.2	64.6	65.2	66.0	65.9	66.2	64.7
2004	65.8	66.4	66.5	67.4	67.8	67.8	67.5	68.0	68.5	69.3	69.9	70.4	67.9
2005	70.1	70.4	70.6	70.7	71.2	70.8	70.8	71.3	72.3	72.1	72.3	72.7	71.3
2006	72.9	73.5	73.9	73.8	74.0	73.6	73.6	74.5	75.1	76.0	76.4	76.4	74.5
2007	76.2	77.1	77.5	77.4	77.6	77.3	77.0	77.6	78.6	78.9	79.4	79.9	77.9
2008	80.6	81.0	80.9	81.8	81.5	80.9	80.8	80.9	81.5	82.8	83.9	83.8	81.7
2009	82.5	83.2	83.5	83.5	83.5	83.0	82.7	82.9	83.8	84.5	85.0	84.6	83.6
Leisure and Hospitality													
1990	39.0	39.8	41.0	41.3	41.1	40.0	39.8	39.9	39.2	37.8	38.0	37.8	39.6
2000	48.7	49.1	49.8	50.4	51.3	51.2	50.0	50.3	50.2	50.1	50.2	50.6	50.2
2001	47.7	48.6	50.1	51.5	52.2	52.7	51.6	52.8	52.1	50.9	51.2	51.6	51.1
2002	49.8	50.4	51.7	52.7	53.6	54.1	52.5	53.1	52.5	52.6	53.3	53.5	52.5
2003	50.7	51.1	52.4	53.1	53.9	54.4	53.6	54.6	54.1	53.6	53.9	54.5	53.3
2004	53.6	54.1	55.4	56.1	56.5	56.5	56.4	56.7	56.4	57.0	57.8	58.3	56.2
2005	57.8	58.7	59.9	60.7	60.9	61.0	60.5	61.4	60.8	60.4	61.2	61.0	60.4
2006	60.0	60.7	61.9	61.9	63.0	63.2	62.7	63.0	62.7	61.7	62.5	62.3	62.1
2007	62.0	63.4	64.9	66.1	67.5	67.5	66.4	67.0	66.4	66.1	66.8	66.8	65.9
2008	65.6	66.2	66.8	68.2	68.6	68.5	68.5	67.9	67.2	66.8	66.8	66.4	67.3
2009	64.7	64.5	65.5	66.7	67.1	66.3	66.2	64.7	63.2	63.0	63.3	63.4	64.9
Other Services													
1990	19.3	19.5	19.6	19.4	19.5	19.6	19.5	19.5	19.2	19.2	19.0	18.9	19.4
2000	22.6	22.9	23.1	24.2	24.1	24.4	24.3	24.2	23.9	23.7	23.8	23.9	23.8
2001	22.9	23.3	23.5	23.5	23.5	24.2	24.3	24.5	24.2	24.2	24.2	24.0	23.9
2002	24.1	24.2	24.7	24.5	24.7	25.0	25.3	25.6	25.2	25.2	25.4	25.4	24.9
2003	24.9	25.1	25.3	25.5	25.7	26.2	25.9	25.8	25.8	25.9	25.9	26.2	25.6
2004	26.3	26.2	26.5	26.4	26.5	26.8	26.6	26.6	26.2	26.0	26.0	26.2	26.4
2005	26.2	26.4	26.5	26.8	26.9	27.2	27.2	27.0	27.1	26.6	26.7	26.6	26.8
2006	26.6	27.0	27.3	27.2	27.5	27.8	27.9	27.8	27.9	27.9	28.1	28.3	27.6
2007	28.3	28.5	28.9	28.4	28.5	28.8	28.3	28.0	27.7	27.8	27.9	27.9	28.3
2008	27.7	27.9	27.9	27.6	27.5	27.3	26.6	26.3	25.7	25.3	24.9	24.4	26.6
2009	24.1	24.1	24.1	24.2	24.2	24.1	24.0	23.9	23.8	23.7	23.8	23.8	24.0
Government													
1990	65.4	65.8	66.8	67.5	69.1	65.6	64.2	63.2	66.4	68.0	68.5	68.1	66.6
2000	68.7	69.6	70.0	70.3	72.1	65.7	64.5	69.9	69.7	70.5	70.4	70.7	69.3
2001	69.2	70.6	70.9	71.3	71.5	66.3	65.0	71.5	71.3	71.2	71.7	72.1	70.2
2002	70.2	70.9	70.9	71.5	71.7	66.5	65.0	71.4	71.2	71.7	72.3	72.7	70.5
2003	71.8	71.8	72.0	72.3	73.0	68.3	66.9	71.9	72.0	72.9	73.3	73.5	71.6
2004	72.6	73.2	73.5	73.7	73.9	69.4	68.0	73.4	73.8	74.9	75.5	76.2	73.2
2005	75.0	75.9	76.1	75.4	75.8	71.0	69.1	74.7	75.1	74.9	75.1	75.2	74.4
2006	74.4	75.2	75.3	74.4	74.2	69.8	68.3	73.6	74.3	75.4	76.4	76.5	74.0
2007	75.6	76.6	76.8	77.0	77.2	73.0	70.7	76.5	76.9	77.4	78.2	78.1	76.2
2008	77.0	77.9	78.0	77.5	77.7	73.0	71.6	75.9	77.0	77.4	78.7	78.1	76.7
2009	76.3	77.4	77.5	77.6	77.9	73.1	71.8	75.9	76.5	77.8	77.6	77.0	76.4

Employment by Industry: Kansas City, MO-KS, Selected Years, 1990–2009

(Numbers in thousands, not seasonally adjusted.)

Industry and year	January	February	March	April	May	June	July	August	September	October	November	December	Annual average
Total Nonfarm													
1990	811.4	815.2	822.4	828.3	832.1	840.8	817.2	826.8	836.5	835.4	838.9	837.5	828.5
2000	963.9	966.8	977.1	984.5	988.2	996.9	965.7	973.7	987.2	988.5	986.3	987.9	980.6
2001	970.0	971.6	980.8	983.1	987.2	992.7	960.2	967.1	976.5	975.7	973.0	973.5	976.0
2002	955.9	954.9	964.8	973.7	977.2	979.4	944.0	949.4	960.3	959.7	964.5	966.6	962.5
2003	945.9	946.0	951.4	959.3	963.6	969.4	948.7	953.4	963.7	966.3	967.3	968.3	958.6
2004	944.7	942.8	955.7	969.5	973.0	979.8	964.4	964.1	974.3	978.6	979.8	981.5	967.4
2005	955.0	960.8	972.6	983.0	986.0	990.7	972.9	974.1	984.1	986.1	990.2	992.3	979.0
2006	970.8	975.7	985.1	994.9	999.7	1004.7	986.3	990.5	1002.0	1001.7	1007.1	1011.0	994.1
2007	988.3	991.6	1007.1	1013.0	1019.2	1023.7	1014.2	1017.7	1020.5	1018.8	1024.4	1021.2	1013.3
2008	1001.5	1004.3	1013.7	1025.4	1024.9	1027.9	1016.5	1015.4	1018.0	1019.2	1013.9	1008.6	1015.8
2009	982.4	980.2	982.6	988.1	988.9	990.4	976.9	975.4	978.1	979.5	980.9	974.5	981.5
Total Private													
1990	690.7	690.6	698.3	702.8	708.0	718.3	715.1	720.5	715.2	711.3	713.2	712.8	708.1
2000	828.4	828.0	836.9	844.2	848.3	856.7	846.5	851.1	849.8	849.7	846.2	847.7	844.5
2001	829.3	828.7	836.9	839.5	843.3	850.3	837.8	842.2	837.5	834.4	830.8	830.1	836.7
2002	813.6	811.7	820.2	829.4	832.6	836.3	820.9	824.1	821.0	817.9	821.9	822.8	822.7
2003	803.4	801.0	805.3	812.5	816.9	824.0	816.7	823.4	821.3	822.3	823.1	824.0	816.2
2004	802.4	798.1	810.1	822.4	826.4	833.8	827.3	830.3	829.7	833.8	834.2	835.9	823.7
2005	811.8	814.7	824.9	834.0	838.7	845.3	837.7	841.6	839.7	840.8	843.8	845.9	834.9
2006	826.7	827.2	835.5	846.0	850.3	857.8	851.5	857.3	854.5	853.2	857.6	862.5	848.3
2007	841.0	840.6	854.6	859.0	865.9	871.7	869.3	873.7	869.9	867.1	871.3	869.8	862.8
2008	851.4	850.9	858.5	869.3	868.4	872.7	872.1	870.1	864.7	864.5	859.1	853.9	863.0
2009	829.7	823.4	825.6	830.2	830.3	834.0	831.3	830.8	823.6	823.4	824.8	819.4	827.2
Goods-Producing													
1990	123.1	123.1	123.9	124.4	125.3	127.6	127.8	128.8	127.8	127.7	126.9	126.0	126.0
2000	142.4	142.1	143.2	145.0	146.0	148.7	143.2	147.1	145.9	145.4	143.8	142.3	144.6
2001	138.2	138.0	140.4	142.3	143.5	145.8	140.8	144.4	142.9	140.2	139.3	138.1	141.2
2002	133.0	131.9	133.5	135.2	135.9	137.7	133.6	137.5	135.6	134.6	133.7	133.0	134.6
2003	130.2	130.3	132.2	132.5	134.7	135.7	131.0	136.0	135.4	135.6	134.8	132.7	133.4
2004	129.5	126.9	131.3	134.6	135.3	138.0	134.5	137.7	137.4	137.5	136.9	136.2	134.7
2005	129.3	130.5	134.2	135.9	137.4	139.1	135.4	138.7	137.8	137.7	137.7	136.7	135.9
2006	133.4	133.8	136.7	137.9	138.8	141.8	137.4	140.7	137.7	136.8	138.3	138.2	137.6
2007	133.0	130.4	135.2	135.4	136.7	138.2	136.1	138.2	137.7	134.8	135.9	133.2	135.4
2008	129.2	128.5	131.4	133.0	131.3	133.3	134.4	133.2	132.3	131.6	129.6	126.2	131.2
2009	119.6	117.0	117.9	118.4	117.3	119.0	119.1	117.9	116.5	115.8	116.1	113.5	117.3
Mining, Logging, and Construction													
1990	32.7	32.6	33.5	34.3	35.2	36.8	37.2	37.7	37.0	37.1	36.4	35.7	35.5
2000	48.2	48.1	49.0	50.6	51.5	53.4	53.3	53.5	52.4	52.2	50.8	48.8	51.0
2001	46.4	45.9	48.2	50.6	51.8	53.6	53.8	53.4	52.1	50.8	50.6	49.8	50.6
2002	46.8	46.1	48.1	49.3	50.1	51.9	52.6	52.6	51.4	51.0	50.4	49.9	50.0
2003	47.6	47.5	48.8	50.9	51.6	52.6	52.9	52.9	52.3	52.5	51.5	49.3	50.9
2004	46.3	44.3	48.0	50.7	51.3	52.9	53.8	53.6	53.2	53.4	52.2	51.5	50.9
2005	46.1	47.2	50.3	52.0	53.6	55.1	55.9	55.7	55.1	54.8	54.2	53.0	52.8
2006	51.3	51.8	53.4	54.5	55.1	56.9	56.0	56.0	55.7	54.5	53.9	53.3	54.4
2007	50.3	47.8	51.9	52.6	53.9	55.0	55.6	55.1	54.9	54.1	53.6	51.2	53.0
2008	47.7	46.9	49.4	50.7	52.0	52.6	52.5	52.2	51.2	51.1	49.9	47.1	50.3
2009	42.9	42.6	43.3	44.0	45.2	45.7	46.0	44.7	43.5	43.7	43.5	41.4	43.9
Manufacturing													
1990	90.4	90.5	90.4	90.1	90.1	90.8	90.6	91.1	90.8	90.6	90.5	90.3	90.5
2000	94.2	94.0	94.2	94.4	94.5	95.3	89.9	93.6	93.5	93.2	93.0	93.5	93.6
2001	91.8	92.1	92.2	91.7	91.7	92.2	87.0	91.0	90.8	89.4	88.7	88.3	90.6
2002	86.2	85.8	85.4	85.9	85.8	85.8	81.0	84.9	84.2	83.6	83.3	83.1	84.6
2003	82.6	82.8	83.4	81.6	83.1	83.1	78.1	83.1	83.1	83.1	83.3	83.4	82.6
2004	83.2	82.6	83.3	83.9	84.0	85.1	80.7	84.1	84.2	84.1	84.7	84.7	83.7
2005	83.2	83.3	83.9	83.9	83.8	84.0	79.5	83.0	82.7	82.9	83.5	83.7	83.1
2006	82.1	82.0	83.3	83.4	83.7	84.9	81.4	84.7	82.0	82.3	84.4	84.9	83.3
2007	82.7	82.6	83.3	82.8	82.8	83.2	80.5	83.1	82.8	80.7	82.3	82.0	82.4
2008	81.5	81.6	82.0	82.3	79.3	80.7	81.9	81.0	81.1	80.5	79.7	79.1	80.9
2009	76.7	74.4	74.6	74.4	72.1	73.3	73.1	73.2	73.0	72.1	72.6	72.1	73.5
Service-Providing													
1990	688.3	692.1	698.5	703.9	706.8	713.2	689.4	698.0	708.7	707.7	712.0	711.5	702.5
2000	821.5	824.7	833.9	839.5	842.2	848.2	822.5	826.6	841.3	843.1	842.5	845.6	836.0
2001	831.8	833.6	840.4	840.8	843.7	846.9	819.4	822.7	833.6	835.5	833.7	835.4	834.8
2002	822.9	823.0	831.3	838.5	841.3	841.7	810.4	811.9	824.7	825.1	830.8	833.6	827.9
2003	815.7	815.7	819.2	826.8	828.9	833.6	817.6	817.4	828.3	830.7	832.5	835.6	825.1
2004	815.2	815.9	824.4	834.9	837.7	841.8	829.9	826.4	836.9	841.1	842.9	845.3	832.7
2005	825.7	830.3	838.4	847.1	848.6	851.6	837.5	835.4	846.3	848.4	852.5	855.6	843.1
2006	837.4	841.9	848.4	857.0	860.9	862.9	848.9	849.8	864.3	864.9	868.8	872.8	856.5
2007	855.3	861.2	871.9	877.6	882.5	885.5	878.1	879.5	882.8	884.0	888.5	888.0	877.9
2008	872.3	875.8	882.3	892.4	893.6	894.6	882.1	882.2	885.7	887.6	884.3	882.4	884.6
2009	862.8	863.2	864.7	869.7	871.6	871.4	857.8	857.5	861.6	863.7	864.8	861.0	864.2

Employment by Industry: Kansas City, MO-KS, Selected Years, 1990–2009—*Continued*

(Numbers in thousands, not seasonally adjusted.)

Industry and year	January	February	March	April	May	June	July	August	September	October	November	December	Annual average
Trade, Transportation, and Utilities													
1990	185.0	182.6	183.8	183.5	185.5	186.9	184.7	186.5	187.1	186.4	189.9	190.7	186.1
2000	206.8	204.8	205.5	208.3	209.5	208.0	206.0	206.1	208.7	209.8	213.4	214.9	208.5
2001	207.7	205.3	205.4	205.8	207.2	206.2	204.8	205.3	206.5	207.1	209.2	210.0	206.7
2002	204.4	201.7	203.5	204.2	205.0	203.6	200.4	200.3	201.2	202.6	206.5	207.7	203.4
2003	200.4	198.8	199.1	199.0	199.1	199.9	199.3	201.1	201.9	203.9	207.4	209.2	201.6
2004	200.6	198.5	199.6	201.0	202.4	202.5	200.8	200.6	201.8	204.7	208.5	211.2	202.7
2005	202.5	201.1	202.2	202.5	203.6	203.6	201.5	201.8	202.2	204.3	208.3	210.5	203.7
2006	203.5	201.9	203.1	203.6	204.6	204.6	202.8	203.9	205.1	205.7	209.4	212.2	205.0
2007	204.9	204.0	206.0	206.4	207.3	207.3	207.0	207.6	208.0	208.7	212.9	214.3	207.9
2008	206.2	204.6	204.8	205.9	206.2	205.7	205.4	204.9	204.2	206.7	208.0	208.3	205.9
2009	200.0	197.4	196.8	196.2	196.2	196.7	195.8	196.0	195.3	195.3	198.7	199.2	197.0
Wholesale Trade													
1990	44.0	43.6	43.6	43.7	43.9	44.4	44.4	44.4	44.1	43.9	44.0	44.0	44.0
2000	48.9	48.7	48.9	50.0	50.0	50.2	50.1	49.7	50.1	49.5	49.7	49.8	49.6
2001	49.5	49.3	49.3	49.5	49.4	49.5	49.0	48.5	48.6	48.7	48.2	48.2	49.0
2002	48.8	48.6	48.7	48.9	48.5	48.6	47.5	47.6	47.2	47.2	47.2	47.3	48.0
2003	47.3	47.5	47.4	47.2	47.1	47.3	47.0	47.0	46.5	46.6	46.5	46.5	47.0
2004	45.4	45.5	46.0	46.3	46.5	46.8	47.1	47.0	46.8	47.5	47.6	47.9	46.7
2005	48.1	48.2	48.5	49.3	49.4	49.6	49.3	49.4	49.2	49.0	49.3	49.4	49.1
2006	48.8	48.8	49.1	48.7	49.1	49.4	49.2	49.5	49.5	49.9	50.0	50.7	49.4
2007	50.2	50.4	51.1	50.7	50.7	51.2	51.3	51.5	51.5	51.8	51.8	51.9	51.2
2008	51.5	51.5	51.3	51.7	51.6	51.6	51.9	51.8	51.4	52.5	52.2	51.9	51.7
2009	51.1	50.6	50.2	49.7	49.2	49.3	49.1	48.7	48.5	48.7	49.0	49.1	49.4
Retail Trade													
1990	100.3	98.4	98.7	99.0	99.9	101.0	99.5	100.8	100.2	100.6	103.7	104.4	100.5
2000	110.0	108.4	108.8	109.5	110.1	110.4	109.1	109.5	109.3	110.6	114.3	116.0	110.5
2001	110.5	108.8	108.7	108.7	109.6	110.2	109.7	110.4	109.9	110.7	113.5	114.9	110.5
2002	109.1	107.2	108.8	108.7	109.6	110.0	109.0	109.0	109.1	109.5	113.4	115.1	109.9
2003	108.2	106.5	107.0	106.8	107.2	107.9	108.3	109.4	110.0	111.5	115.0	116.6	109.6
2004	110.7	108.4	109.0	109.1	110.0	110.4	109.7	109.2	109.9	110.9	114.6	116.9	110.7
2005	110.2	108.5	109.0	108.8	109.3	109.4	108.9	108.2	107.9	109.5	113.0	114.6	109.8
2006	108.8	107.4	108.2	108.5	109.0	109.2	108.3	108.2	108.3	108.4	111.8	113.2	109.1
2007	107.4	106.5	107.6	108.0	108.7	108.9	108.5	108.2	107.6	108.5	112.2	113.4	108.8
2008	107.5	105.4	106.1	106.4	106.9	107.2	106.9	106.4	105.3	106.3	107.9	108.5	106.7
2009	103.2	101.4	101.9	102.1	102.7	103.4	102.9	102.9	102.5	102.5	105.6	105.4	103.0
Transportation and Utilities													
1990	40.7	40.6	41.5	40.8	41.7	41.5	40.8	41.3	42.8	41.9	42.2	42.3	41.5
2000	47.9	47.7	47.8	48.8	49.4	47.4	46.8	46.9	49.3	49.7	49.4	49.1	48.4
2001	47.7	47.2	47.4	47.6	48.2	46.5	46.1	46.4	48.0	47.7	47.5	46.9	47.3
2002	46.5	45.9	46.0	46.6	46.9	45.0	43.9	43.7	44.9	45.9	45.9	45.3	45.5
2003	44.9	44.8	44.7	45.0	44.8	44.7	44.0	44.7	45.4	45.8	45.9	46.1	45.0
2004	44.5	44.6	44.6	45.6	45.9	45.3	44.0	44.4	45.1	46.3	46.3	46.4	45.3
2005	44.2	44.4	44.7	44.4	44.9	44.6	43.3	44.2	45.1	45.8	46.0	46.5	44.8
2006	45.9	45.7	45.8	46.4	46.5	46.0	45.3	46.2	47.3	47.4	47.6	48.3	46.5
2007	47.3	47.1	47.3	47.7	47.9	47.2	47.2	47.9	48.9	48.4	48.9	49.0	47.9
2008	47.2	47.7	47.4	47.8	47.7	46.9	46.6	46.7	47.5	47.9	47.9	47.9	47.4
2009	45.7	45.4	44.7	44.4	44.3	44.0	43.8	44.4	44.3	44.1	44.1	44.7	44.5
Information													
1990	47.5	47.3	47.8	47.5	47.1	47.2	48.8	48.2	47.6	46.6	46.2	46.3	47.3
2000	53.4	55.2	55.3	55.6	55.7	56.4	57.4	57.4	57.3	56.3	56.3	56.1	56.0
2001	55.1	54.6	54.1	54.0	53.3	55.0	53.9	54.0	53.6	52.6	52.9	51.5	53.7
2002	51.0	51.3	51.6	50.8	51.7	52.0	51.3	50.9	50.1	48.6	49.8	50.3	50.8
2003	49.1	48.5	48.3	48.5	48.2	48.5	47.7	47.6	46.9	46.8	46.6	46.7	47.8
2004	46.5	46.1	45.8	45.8	45.7	45.8	45.4	45.3	44.7	43.6	43.8	43.3	45.2
2005	43.2	43.1	43.1	43.0	42.9	43.1	42.8	42.3	42.0	41.1	40.9	40.8	42.4
2006	40.9	40.8	41.1	42.4	42.4	42.8	42.6	42.6	42.6	41.6	41.8	42.2	42.0
2007	42.2	42.1	42.0	42.0	42.3	42.4	42.8	42.6	42.4	42.8	42.9	43.0	42.5
2008	43.0	42.8	42.8	42.2	42.3	42.4	42.4	42.1	41.5	41.0	40.7	40.5	42.0
2009	40.4	40.1	40.0	40.0	39.6	39.4	39.2	38.7	38.1	37.8	37.8	37.8	39.1
Financial Activities													
1990	62.8	62.8	63.1	63.6	63.6	64.3	64.5	64.6	64.1	63.8	63.4	63.2	63.7
2000	69.8	69.6	70.2	69.4	69.7	70.5	70.4	70.3	69.8	70.4	70.6	71.1	70.2
2001	70.4	70.6	71.1	71.0	71.3	71.7	71.7	71.7	71.1	71.2	71.6	71.6	71.2
2002	71.7	71.5	71.7	72.4	72.6	72.6	72.8	72.3	71.8	71.8	72.0	72.3	72.1
2003	70.9	70.9	70.9	71.1	71.0	71.3	71.3	71.5	70.8	70.5	70.2	70.3	70.9
2004	68.7	68.6	69.2	68.9	68.9	69.9	70.1	69.9	69.6	69.8	69.8	70.3	69.5
2005	70.0	70.1	70.3	70.8	71.0	71.4	71.8	71.6	71.4	71.6	71.7	72.2	71.2
2006	72.0	72.2	72.2	72.5	73.0	73.4	74.1	73.9	73.6	73.1	73.4	73.9	73.1
2007	73.5	73.8	74.5	73.7	73.8	74.4	75.1	74.9	74.3	74.0	74.2	74.2	74.2
2008	73.2	73.5	73.4	73.8	73.8	73.5	73.7	73.3	72.3	71.9	71.3	70.8	72.9
2009	70.3	70.0	70.3	71.1	71.1	71.4	71.3	71.1	70.0	70.2	70.4	70.6	70.7

Employment by Industry: Kansas City, MO-KS, Selected Years, 1990–2009—*Continued*

(Numbers in thousands, not seasonally adjusted.)

Industry and year	January	February	March	April	May	June	July	August	September	October	November	December	Annual average
Professional and Business Services													
1990	87.2	88.6	90.3	90.2	90.4	91.8	92.1	92.6	91.8	91.2	90.8	90.9	90.7
2000	135.0	133.9	137.4	136.8	136.4	138.4	135.7	136.6	136.3	136.6	134.2	135.2	136.0
2001	133.5	134.2	136.2	133.2	133.1	133.4	129.6	130.1	130.0	128.8	126.6	127.2	131.3
2002	124.6	126.0	127.2	127.9	127.1	126.8	122.2	121.8	121.8	121.4	121.6	122.0	124.2
2003	119.9	119.5	119.5	122.0	122.0	124.3	123.2	123.6	123.5	123.3	124.2	126.5	122.6
2004	124.1	124.7	127.6	130.1	129.7	131.5	130.8	131.5	131.9	133.0	133.3	133.7	130.2
2005	131.1	132.9	135.2	137.3	137.0	138.8	138.8	139.6	139.8	139.8	140.8	142.0	137.8
2006	135.9	137.6	139.2	141.1	140.4	141.9	141.6	142.6	143.0	144.8	145.3	146.3	141.6
2007	142.7	143.7	145.7	146.0	147.3	148.6	148.5	149.9	149.8	150.2	151.0	151.2	147.9
2008	147.3	147.9	149.4	151.8	149.4	150.6	150.5	150.2	150.3	148.4	147.8	147.1	149.2
2009	144.1	143.2	142.9	143.2	141.8	141.6	140.9	140.8	139.5	139.2	138.2	137.3	141.1
Education and Health Services													
1990	82.6	83.4	83.7	84.2	84.5	85.3	84.5	85.8	84.9	86.0	86.3	86.5	84.8
2000	98.7	99.7	99.6	100.2	100.1	100.2	100.7	100.2	101.1	101.2	101.5	101.7	100.4
2001	100.5	101.9	102.4	103.0	103.0	103.4	102.6	102.8	103.3	103.3	104.2	104.4	102.9
2002	103.5	104.1	104.5	105.8	106.2	106.4	105.7	106.1	106.7	107.2	107.6	107.7	106.0
2003	106.5	106.7	106.7	108.0	108.4	107.3	107.6	107.1	108.3	108.6	108.8	108.5	107.7
2004	107.0	107.8	108.0	109.0	109.1	108.6	109.1	108.8	109.8	111.2	111.1	110.7	109.2
2005	109.6	110.4	110.4	111.5	111.8	111.5	110.7	110.7	111.8	112.9	113.1	113.2	111.5
2006	111.6	112.7	112.7	114.0	114.3	114.1	114.1	114.2	115.8	116.4	116.8	117.3	114.5
2007	115.4	116.7	117.4	118.1	118.4	118.3	118.6	118.8	119.5	120.6	120.9	120.8	118.6
2008	120.5	121.9	122.1	123.7	123.7	123.7	123.5	123.4	123.8	125.8	126.1	126.1	123.7
2009	124.2	125.0	125.3	126.6	126.7	126.4	127.1	126.7	127.8	129.6	130.1	129.0	127.0
Leisure and Hospitality													
1990	69.7	69.9	72.3	75.7	77.4	80.1	77.5	79.0	77.1	74.7	75.2	75.0	75.3
2000	84.3	84.5	86.4	89.6	91.6	93.7	92.7	93.2	91.4	90.7	87.6	86.6	89.4
2001	84.5	84.5	87.1	89.9	91.4	93.1	92.9	93.3	90.7	90.7	87.7	86.8	89.3
2002	85.1	85.0	87.3	91.2	92.3	93.7	92.4	92.9	91.3	90.1	89.0	87.6	89.8
2003	85.0	85.1	87.1	90.0	91.9	94.8	94.2	94.5	93.3	92.6	90.3	89.4	90.7
2004	86.1	85.7	88.5	92.6	95.0	96.7	95.9	96.1	94.4	93.7	90.8	90.5	92.2
2005	86.4	86.7	89.3	93.3	95.4	97.7	96.3	96.6	94.8	93.9	91.9	91.1	92.8
2006	88.7	88.7	91.0	94.8	96.9	98.9	98.6	99.2	96.9	95.2	93.0	92.8	94.6
2007	89.8	90.2	93.8	96.1	98.6	100.4	98.9	99.6	96.7	94.8	92.7	92.2	95.3
2008	90.6	90.3	93.0	97.2	99.8	101.4	100.1	101.1	98.6	97.4	94.0	93.6	96.4
2009	89.8	89.4	91.4	93.3	96.3	97.9	96.4	98.3	95.8	94.9	93.1	91.8	94.0
Other Services													
1990	32.8	32.9	33.4	33.7	34.2	35.1	35.2	35.0	34.8	34.9	34.5	34.2	34.2
2000	38.0	38.2	39.3	39.3	39.3	40.8	40.4	40.2	39.3	39.3	38.8	39.8	39.4
2001	39.4	39.6	40.2	40.3	40.5	41.7	41.5	40.6	39.9	40.5	39.7	40.5	40.4
2002	40.3	40.2	40.9	41.9	41.8	43.5	42.5	42.3	42.5	41.6	41.7	42.2	41.8
2003	41.4	41.2	41.5	41.4	41.6	42.2	42.4	42.0	41.2	41.0	40.8	40.7	41.4
2004	39.9	39.8	40.1	40.4	40.3	40.8	40.7	40.4	40.1	40.3	40.0	40.0	40.2
2005	39.7	39.9	40.2	39.7	39.6	40.1	40.4	40.3	39.9	39.5	39.4	39.4	39.8
2006	40.7	39.5	39.5	39.7	39.9	40.3	40.3	40.2	39.8	39.6	39.6	39.6	39.9
2007	39.5	39.7	40.0	41.3	41.5	42.1	42.3	42.1	41.5	41.2	41.0	40.9	41.1
2008	41.4	41.4	41.6	41.7	41.9	42.1	42.1	41.9	41.7	41.7	41.6	41.3	41.7
2009	41.3	41.3	41.0	41.4	41.3	41.6	41.5	41.3	40.6	40.6	40.4	40.2	41.0
Government													
1990	120.7	124.6	124.1	125.5	124.1	122.5	102.1	106.3	121.3	124.1	125.7	124.7	120.5
2000	135.5	138.8	140.2	140.3	139.9	140.2	119.2	122.6	137.4	138.8	140.1	140.2	136.1
2001	140.7	142.9	143.9	143.6	143.9	142.4	122.4	124.9	139.0	141.3	142.2	143.4	139.2
2002	142.3	143.2	144.6	144.3	144.6	143.1	123.1	125.3	139.3	141.8	142.6	143.8	139.8
2003	142.5	145.0	146.1	146.8	146.8	145.4	132.0	130.2	142.4	144.0	144.2	144.3	142.5
2004	142.3	144.7	145.6	147.1	146.6	146.0	137.1	133.8	144.6	144.8	145.6	145.6	143.7
2005	143.2	146.1	147.7	149.0	147.3	145.4	135.2	132.5	144.4	145.3	146.4	146.4	144.1
2006	144.1	148.5	149.6	148.9	149.4	146.9	134.8	133.2	147.5	148.5	149.5	148.5	145.8
2007	147.3	151.0	152.5	154.0	153.3	152.0	144.9	144.0	150.6	151.7	153.1	151.4	150.5
2008	150.1	153.4	155.2	156.1	156.5	155.2	144.4	145.3	153.3	154.7	154.8	154.7	152.8
2009	152.7	156.8	157.0	157.9	158.6	156.4	145.6	144.6	154.5	156.1	156.1	155.1	154.3

Employment by Industry: Knoxville, TN, Selected Years, 1990–2009

(Numbers in thousands, not seasonally adjusted.)

Industry and year	January	February	March	April	May	June	July	August	September	October	November	December	Annual average
Total Nonfarm													
1990	238.4	237.4	239.4	240.9	243.1	245.2	241.7	243.8	245.3	244.9	246.1	246.8	242.8
2000	294.9	296.9	300.7	302.3	305.2	306.5	301.7	302.7	305.7	304.9	305.8	307.0	302.9
2001	302.4	303.8	306.8	308.4	309.3	310.7	306.2	305.8	308.1	307.9	309.0	310.2	307.4
2002	303.5	304.2	307.2	312.0	313.9	315.7	312.8	314.0	315.8	318.8	319.2	321.5	313.2
2003	311.2	311.4	313.7	316.8	318.2	318.9	314.0	316.1	316.8	319.0	320.3	320.8	316.4
2004	315.1	317.9	319.8	321.8	322.8	322.8	323.1	324.3	325.2	325.2	327.6	327.5	322.8
2005	321.7	321.9	324.7	325.4	326.5	327.1	325.0	326.5	329.3	328.3	329.7	330.9	326.4
2006	325.3	326.9	329.9	331.4	332.3	332.0	331.1	334.5	337.6	335.3	336.4	338.2	332.6
2007	331.6	332.5	335.4	336.2	336.7	335.4	334.1	337.6	339.1	337.9	340.0	338.7	336.3
2008	333.5	334.6	335.2	336.8	338.5	336.7	333.1	336.5	338.2	339.1	337.6	335.6	336.3
2009	324.9	323.6	321.8	321.7	321.3	318.6	317.9	319.1	321.2	322.3	323.3	322.1	321.5
Total Private													
1990	190.4	189.3	191.2	192.3	193.9	196.5	194.7	196.2	196.4	195.4	196.7	197.4	194.2
2000	244.2	245.4	248.9	249.9	252.0	254.4	252.1	252.4	253.5	252.6	253.5	254.5	251.1
2001	251.2	251.7	254.6	256.2	257.2	258.9	256.2	255.8	256.1	254.8	255.9	257.0	255.5
2002	251.4	251.8	254.7	258.0	259.8	262.0	262.0	263.0	263.4	265.2	265.6	267.4	260.4
2003	259.0	258.9	260.9	263.6	265.0	266.3	263.9	265.7	266.1	265.8	267.1	268.0	264.2
2004	262.1	262.9	265.9	269.0	270.6	270.8	272.1	272.9	273.0	271.5	273.8	274.1	269.9
2005	269.3	268.9	271.9	272.6	274.2	275.6	275.0	276.4	277.3	275.4	276.7	277.6	274.2
2006	273.4	274.1	277.3	278.9	280.2	281.8	280.8	283.5	284.5	281.7	282.9	284.2	280.3
2007	279.2	279.3	282.2	283.3	284.5	285.5	284.9	287.3	286.9	285.5	287.5	287.8	284.5
2008	282.8	283.4	284.5	285.7	287.9	288.5	285.4	286.9	286.4	286.2	285.2	284.1	285.6
2009	274.2	272.2	270.6	269.9	270.0	269.6	269.6	270.4	270.1	270.2	271.2	271.1	270.8
Goods-Producing													
1990	54.0	53.1	53.3	53.2	53.6	53.8	53.1	53.4	53.7	53.8	53.4	53.5	53.5
2000	59.4	59.6	60.4	59.8	59.8	60.1	59.4	59.6	59.6	58.9	58.7	58.9	59.5
2001	58.1	57.7	58.3	57.7	57.4	57.7	56.5	56.4	56.1	55.5	55.4	55.4	56.9
2002	54.5	54.4	55.0	55.3	55.7	56.2	56.6	56.6	56.4	57.0	56.6	56.7	55.9
2003	55.7	55.3	55.9	56.0	56.1	55.7	55.1	55.1	55.0	55.1	55.0	54.9	55.4
2004	54.2	54.3	54.8	55.2	55.3	55.1	55.6	55.6	55.6	55.2	55.4	55.1	55.1
2005	55.2	54.7	55.1	54.9	55.0	55.2	55.5	55.7	55.7	55.4	55.3	55.5	55.3
2006	55.6	55.5	56.2	56.6	56.7	57.3	56.8	57.3	57.5	56.4	56.1	55.8	56.5
2007	55.5	55.2	55.8	55.9	56.0	56.3	56.1	56.4	56.6	56.0	55.7	55.4	55.9
2008	53.9	54.0	54.2	54.0	54.5	55.0	54.1	54.2	53.7	53.3	51.9	50.5	53.6
2009	48.6	47.8	47.3	45.9	45.7	45.5	45.3	45.3	45.3	45.6	45.2	44.3	46.0
Mining, Logging, and Construction													
1990	11.1	10.4	10.5	10.8	10.8	10.8	10.7	10.8	10.9	11.1	10.9	10.6	10.8
2000	15.0	15.2	15.9	15.5	15.4	15.6	15.6	15.7	15.8	15.4	15.3	15.4	15.5
2001	14.4	14.6	15.1	15.2	15.3	15.7	15.2	15.1	15.1	15.0	15.1	15.2	15.1
2002	14.0	14.1	14.5	14.8	15.1	15.3	15.6	15.6	15.5	16.0	15.6	15.6	15.1
2003	15.1	14.7	15.4	15.7	16.0	15.9	15.6	15.7	15.8	16.1	16.0	16.2	15.7
2004	15.6	15.6	16.0	16.4	16.6	16.4	16.7	16.8	16.9	16.9	17.0	16.6	16.5
2005	16.6	16.4	16.6	16.5	16.5	16.7	16.8	17.0	17.1	16.9	16.8	16.7	16.7
2006	16.7	16.8	17.5	17.8	18.0	18.6	18.5	18.9	19.3	19.0	18.8	18.4	18.2
2007	18.0	18.0	18.6	18.8	19.0	19.2	19.1	19.4	19.5	19.3	19.1	18.8	18.9
2008	17.6	17.7	18.2	18.4	18.8	19.0	18.8	18.9	18.9	19.0	18.6	17.7	18.5
2009	16.2	16.0	16.1	15.8	16.1	16.4	16.4	16.3	16.3	16.2	16.0	15.4	16.1
Manufacturing													
1990	42.9	42.7	42.8	42.4	42.8	43.0	42.4	42.6	42.8	42.7	42.5	42.9	42.7
2000	44.4	44.4	44.5	44.3	44.4	44.5	43.8	43.9	43.8	43.5	43.4	43.5	44.0
2001	43.7	43.1	43.2	42.5	42.1	42.0	41.3	41.3	41.0	40.5	40.3	40.2	41.8
2002	40.5	40.3	40.5	40.5	40.6	40.9	41.0	41.0	40.9	41.0	41.0	41.1	40.8
2003	40.6	40.6	40.5	40.3	40.1	39.8	39.5	39.4	39.2	39.0	39.0	38.7	39.7
2004	38.6	38.7	38.8	38.8	38.7	38.7	38.9	38.8	38.7	38.3	38.4	38.5	38.7
2005	38.6	38.3	38.5	38.4	38.5	38.5	38.7	38.7	38.6	38.5	38.5	38.8	38.6
2006	38.9	38.7	38.7	38.8	38.7	38.7	38.3	38.4	38.2	37.4	37.3	37.4	38.3
2007	37.5	37.2	37.2	37.1	37.0	37.1	37.0	37.0	37.1	36.7	36.6	36.6	37.0
2008	36.3	36.3	36.0	35.6	35.7	36.0	35.3	35.3	34.8	34.3	33.3	32.8	35.1
2009	32.4	31.8	31.2	30.1	29.6	29.1	28.9	29.0	29.0	29.4	29.2	28.9	29.9
Service-Providing													
1990	184.4	184.3	186.1	187.7	189.5	191.4	188.6	190.4	191.6	191.1	192.7	193.3	189.3
2000	235.5	237.3	240.3	242.5	245.4	246.4	242.3	243.1	246.1	246.0	247.1	248.1	243.3
2001	244.3	246.1	248.5	250.7	251.9	253.0	249.7	249.4	252.0	252.4	253.6	254.8	250.5
2002	249.0	249.8	252.2	256.7	258.2	259.5	256.2	257.4	259.4	261.8	262.6	264.8	257.3
2003	255.5	256.1	257.8	260.8	262.1	263.2	258.9	261.0	261.8	263.9	265.3	265.9	261.0
2004	260.9	263.6	265.0	266.6	267.5	267.7	267.5	268.7	269.6	270.0	272.2	272.4	267.6
2005	266.5	267.2	269.6	270.5	271.5	271.9	269.5	270.8	273.6	272.9	274.4	275.4	271.2
2006	269.7	271.4	273.7	274.8	275.6	274.7	274.3	277.2	280.1	278.9	280.3	282.4	276.1
2007	276.1	277.3	279.6	280.3	280.7	279.1	278.0	281.2	282.5	281.9	284.3	283.3	280.4
2008	279.6	280.6	281.0	282.8	284.0	281.7	279.0	282.3	284.5	285.8	285.7	285.1	282.7
2009	276.3	275.8	274.5	275.8	275.6	273.1	272.6	273.8	275.9	276.7	278.1	277.8	275.5

Employment by Industry: Knoxville, TN, Selected Years, 1990–2009—*Continued*

(Numbers in thousands, not seasonally adjusted.)

Industry and year	January	February	March	April	May	June	July	August	September	October	November	December	Annual average
Trade, Transportation, and Utilities													
1990	53.5	52.8	53.1	52.5	52.7	53.7	53.0	52.9	52.8	52.8	53.8	54.5	53.2
2000	61.6	61.8	62.3	63.2	63.3	63.8	63.9	63.7	64.1	64.4	65.3	66.3	63.6
2001	64.5	64.3	64.6	65.1	65.2	65.3	64.5	64.5	64.7	65.3	66.0	66.8	65.1
2002	64.7	64.5	65.3	65.4	65.2	65.2	65.7	65.9	66.0	66.9	67.7	68.9	66.0
2003	65.4	65.1	65.2	65.4	65.8	66.4	66.0	66.6	66.6	67.1	68.3	69.2	66.4
2004	66.8	66.9	67.7	67.6	68.1	68.0	68.0	68.4	68.5	69.0	70.3	70.9	68.4
2005	69.0	68.7	69.4	68.9	69.4	69.3	69.4	69.8	69.7	69.2	70.5	71.3	69.6
2006	69.5	69.4	70.2	70.2	70.6	70.8	70.6	71.5	72.0	71.5	72.8	74.2	71.1
2007	72.0	71.5	72.3	72.6	73.0	72.8	72.5	73.1	73.1	73.2	74.9	75.2	73.0
2008	73.4	72.7	72.8	72.6	72.3	72.2	71.7	72.0	71.7	72.5	72.9	72.9	72.5
2009	69.3	68.0	67.1	66.5	66.3	66.2	66.8	66.8	66.6	67.3	68.4	68.7	67.3
Wholesale Trade													
1990	13.1	13.1	13.2	12.9	12.9	13.0	12.9	12.9	12.7	12.8	12.9	12.9	12.9
2000	13.3	13.4	13.5	13.6	13.6	13.9	13.8	13.6	13.8	13.8	13.7	13.9	13.7
2001	14.0	14.1	14.1	13.9	14.0	14.0	13.9	13.8	13.9	14.0	13.9	13.9	14.0
2002	13.8	13.9	14.0	14.0	14.1	14.2	14.6	14.7	14.7	15.0	15.1	15.3	14.5
2003	14.9	14.9	14.9	14.9	14.9	15.1	15.2	15.3	15.3	15.4	15.5	15.6	15.2
2004	15.4	15.5	15.8	15.8	15.9	15.8	16.2	16.2	16.0	16.1	16.2	16.2	15.9
2005	16.0	16.0	16.0	15.8	15.7	15.8	15.8	15.8	15.7	15.5	15.4	15.4	15.7
2006	15.5	15.6	15.7	15.8	15.9	15.9	16.0	16.0	16.1	16.1	16.0	16.2	15.9
2007	16.3	16.2	16.2	16.2	16.4	16.4	16.5	16.7	16.6	16.7	16.7	16.7	16.5
2008	16.6	16.6	16.6	16.8	17.0	17.0	16.9	17.0	17.1	17.2	17.1	17.1	16.9
2009	16.8	16.6	16.3	16.2	16.1	15.9	15.9	15.7	15.6	15.7	15.7	15.7	16.0
Retail Trade													
1990	33.1	32.4	32.6	32.3	32.5	33.5	32.9	32.7	32.8	32.8	33.7	34.4	33.0
2000	38.9	38.9	39.1	39.5	39.7	40.0	40.4	40.3	40.4	40.8	41.8	42.7	40.2
2001	40.6	40.2	40.4	40.7	40.7	40.8	40.2	40.2	40.4	40.5	41.5	42.3	40.7
2002	40.6	40.3	40.9	40.9	40.8	40.7	40.6	40.6	40.8	41.1	41.9	42.9	41.0
2003	40.5	40.0	40.2	40.4	40.7	41.0	40.7	41.0	41.0	41.2	42.3	43.1	41.0
2004	41.2	41.2	41.6	41.5	41.8	41.8	41.6	41.8	42.0	42.4	43.6	44.0	42.0
2005	42.6	42.3	42.8	42.8	43.2	43.1	42.9	43.1	43.0	42.9	44.2	44.8	43.1
2006	43.2	43.0	43.4	43.5	43.6	43.8	43.7	44.3	44.6	44.3	45.6	46.5	44.1
2007	44.8	44.3	44.9	45.3	45.4	45.2	45.0	45.2	45.3	45.4	47.0	47.3	45.4
2008	45.7	45.0	45.2	44.7	44.2	44.1	43.8	43.8	43.4	44.1	44.5	44.5	44.4
2009	42.1	41.2	40.7	40.6	40.5	40.6	41.3	41.3	41.2	41.9	43.0	43.3	41.5
Transportation and Utilities													
1990	7.3	7.3	7.3	7.3	7.3	7.2	7.2	7.3	7.3	7.7	7.2	7.2	7.3
2000	9.4	9.5	9.7	10.1	10.0	9.9	9.7	9.8	9.9	9.8	9.8	9.7	9.8
2001	9.9	10.0	10.1	10.5	10.5	10.5	10.4	10.5	10.4	10.8	10.6	10.6	10.4
2002	10.3	10.3	10.4	10.5	10.3	10.3	10.5	10.6	10.5	10.8	10.7	10.7	10.5
2003	10.0	10.2	10.1	10.1	10.2	10.3	10.1	10.3	10.3	10.5	10.5	10.5	10.3
2004	10.2	10.2	10.3	10.3	10.4	10.4	10.2	10.4	10.5	10.5	10.5	10.7	10.4
2005	10.4	10.4	10.6	10.3	10.5	10.4	10.7	10.9	11.0	10.8	10.9	11.1	10.7
2006	10.8	10.8	11.1	10.9	11.1	11.1	10.9	11.2	11.3	11.1	11.2	11.5	11.1
2007	10.9	11.0	11.2	11.1	11.2	11.2	11.0	11.2	11.2	11.1	11.2	11.2	11.1
2008	11.1	11.1	11.0	11.1	11.1	11.1	11.0	11.2	11.2	11.2	11.3	11.3	11.1
2009	10.4	10.2	10.1	9.7	9.7	9.7	9.6	9.8	9.8	9.7	9.7	9.7	9.8
Information													
1990	5.4	5.4	5.5	5.5	5.4	5.4	5.5	5.5	5.4	5.3	5.3	5.3	5.4
2000	6.1	6.1	6.2	6.0	6.0	6.0	6.0	5.9	5.9	5.9	5.9	5.9	6.0
2001	5.8	5.8	5.8	5.7	5.6	5.7	5.7	5.6	5.6	5.8	5.8	5.8	5.7
2002	5.8	5.8	5.8	5.9	5.9	5.8	5.9	5.9	5.8	6.0	6.0	6.1	5.9
2003	5.9	5.9	5.9	5.9	5.9	6.0	6.0	6.0	6.0	6.0	6.2	6.2	6.0
2004	6.2	6.1	6.2	6.2	6.2	6.1	6.2	6.0	5.9	5.9	5.9	5.8	6.1
2005	5.8	5.8	5.9	5.9	5.9	5.9	6.0	5.9	5.9	5.9	5.9	5.9	5.9
2006	6.0	6.1	6.1	6.1	6.0	6.0	6.0	5.9	5.8	5.8	5.9	5.8	6.0
2007	5.6	5.6	5.6	5.6	5.7	5.7	5.7	5.7	5.6	5.5	5.6	5.6	5.6
2008	5.6	5.6	5.6	5.6	5.7	5.7	5.6	5.5	5.5	5.6	5.6	5.6	5.6
2009	5.6	5.5	5.5	5.5	5.5	5.5	5.5	5.4	5.4	5.3	5.4	5.4	5.5
Financial Activities													
1990	10.7	10.7	10.8	10.7	10.8	10.9	10.8	10.9	10.9	10.7	10.8	10.8	10.8
2000	13.9	13.9	14.0	13.9	14.0	14.1	13.9	13.9	13.8	13.9	14.0	14.1	14.0
2001	13.9	14.0	14.0	14.1	14.2	14.3	14.4	14.3	14.2	14.3	14.4	14.4	14.2
2002	14.3	14.4	14.4	14.5	14.7	14.9	14.9	14.9	15.1	15.3	15.6	15.8	14.9
2003	15.6	15.7	15.8	15.9	16.1	16.3	16.3	16.5	16.5	16.4	16.4	16.5	16.2
2004	16.4	16.4	16.5	16.6	16.7	16.7	16.8	16.8	16.8	16.8	16.9	17.0	16.7
2005	16.9	16.9	17.0	17.1	17.2	17.4	17.2	17.3	17.2	17.2	17.2	17.3	17.2
2006	17.2	17.2	17.3	17.2	17.3	17.3	17.4	17.6	17.5	17.4	17.5	17.5	17.4
2007	17.3	17.3	17.4	17.4	17.5	17.6	17.6	17.6	17.6	17.6	17.7	17.7	17.5
2008	17.4	17.5	17.6	17.6	17.7	17.9	17.9	18.0	17.9	18.0	18.0	18.0	17.8
2009	17.5	17.6	17.4	17.5	17.4	17.3	17.2	17.2	17.2	17.2	17.2	17.2	17.3

Employment by Industry: Knoxville, TN, Selected Years, 1990–2009—*Continued*

(Numbers in thousands, not seasonally adjusted.)

Industry and year	January	February	March	April	May	June	July	August	September	October	November	December	Annual average
Professional and Business Services													
1990	19.8	20.1	20.6	21.5	22.0	22.6	22.3	22.8	22.9	22.8	23.0	23.0	22.0
2000	35.1	35.7	36.8	36.7	37.0	37.9	36.8	37.3	37.6	37.1	37.1	37.0	36.8
2001	37.1	37.2	37.7	38.2	38.0	37.9	38.0	37.7	38.0	37.1	37.4	37.9	37.7
2002	37.4	37.2	37.9	38.2	38.3	38.5	38.5	38.8	38.8	38.6	37.9	37.8	38.2
2003	37.5	37.6	37.9	39.1	38.9	38.8	38.1	38.8	39.0	38.8	38.4	38.4	38.4
2004	37.3	37.4	38.0	39.2	39.0	39.4	39.4	39.8	39.9	39.4	39.4	39.6	39.0
2005	38.0	38.2	38.8	39.2	39.1	39.1	38.7	39.4	40.0	39.5	39.3	39.3	39.1
2006	38.5	38.8	39.3	39.8	40.0	39.8	39.6	40.3	40.8	40.5	40.5	40.6	39.9
2007	39.7	40.2	40.4	40.8	40.5	40.2	40.2	41.2	41.0	41.0	41.1	41.4	40.6
2008	41.1	41.4	41.3	42.2	42.2	42.0	42.0	42.8	43.4	43.6	43.7	44.0	42.5
2009	42.6	42.2	41.5	41.3	41.1	40.7	40.8	41.6	42.0	42.2	42.4	42.8	41.8
Education and Health Services													
1990	21.4	21.5	21.6	21.5	21.6	21.7	21.6	21.9	22.2	22.1	22.3	22.3	21.8
2000	30.8	31.3	31.4	31.5	31.8	31.8	31.5	31.7	31.9	32.2	32.5	32.5	31.7
2001	32.0	32.4	32.8	33.1	33.3	33.6	33.1	33.3	33.4	33.7	34.0	34.1	33.2
2002	33.8	34.1	34.2	34.8	35.0	35.5	35.1	35.4	35.7	36.0	36.3	36.3	35.2
2003	35.5	35.6	35.8	36.0	36.2	36.5	36.5	36.6	37.2	37.4	37.6	37.7	36.6
2004	36.7	36.9	37.1	37.3	37.5	37.7	37.9	38.1	38.2	38.2	38.4	38.5	37.7
2005	38.2	38.1	38.5	38.7	39.0	39.3	39.3	39.5	39.7	40.1	40.2	40.3	39.2
2006	39.9	39.8	40.3	40.2	40.4	40.8	40.8	41.0	41.0	41.1	41.1	41.3	40.6
2007	40.9	40.9	41.1	41.3	41.4	41.7	41.9	42.2	42.4	42.6	42.7	42.8	41.8
2008	42.8	43.0	42.9	43.4	43.7	43.8	43.4	43.5	43.4	43.9	44.0	44.2	43.5
2009	43.3	43.4	43.3	44.0	44.4	44.4	44.6	44.7	44.5	44.4	44.6	44.8	44.2
Leisure and Hospitality													
1990	17.7	17.8	18.3	19.1	19.4	19.8	19.8	20.3	20.1	19.6	19.5	19.4	19.2
2000	25.8	26.0	26.7	27.2	28.5	28.7	28.5	28.3	28.9	28.2	28.1	27.9	27.7
2001	27.8	28.2	28.8	30.2	31.3	31.9	31.4	31.5	31.5	30.8	30.5	30.2	30.3
2002	28.4	28.8	29.3	31.0	31.9	32.6	32.1	32.3	32.2	32.1	32.2	32.3	31.3
2003	29.8	30.0	30.7	31.6	32.2	32.5	31.8	32.2	31.9	31.2	31.4	31.2	31.4
2004	30.7	31.1	31.7	33.0	33.9	33.8	34.3	34.4	34.3	33.4	33.9	33.6	33.2
2005	32.7	33.0	33.6	34.2	34.9	35.5	35.0	35.0	35.3	34.4	34.6	34.2	34.4
2006	33.1	33.6	34.1	35.0	35.3	35.6	35.4	35.8	35.8	35.1	35.0	35.0	34.9
2007	34.1	34.4	35.3	35.6	36.1	36.6	36.4	36.7	36.2	35.2	35.4	35.3	35.6
2008	34.3	34.6	35.4	35.7	36.6	36.9	36.0	36.2	36.1	34.7	34.6	34.4	35.5
2009	32.9	33.3	33.9	34.2	35.0	35.2	34.6	34.7	34.6	33.8	33.6	33.5	34.1
Other Services													
1990	7.9	7.9	8.0	8.3	8.4	8.6	8.6	8.5	8.4	8.3	8.6	8.6	8.3
2000	11.5	11.0	11.1	11.6	11.6	12.0	12.1	12.0	11.7	12.0	11.9	11.9	11.7
2001	12.0	12.1	12.6	12.1	12.2	12.5	12.6	12.5	12.6	12.3	12.4	12.4	12.4
2002	12.5	12.6	12.8	12.9	13.1	13.3	13.2	13.2	13.4	13.3	13.3	13.5	13.1
2003	13.6	13.7	13.7	13.7	13.8	14.1	14.1	13.9	13.9	13.8	13.8	13.9	13.8
2004	13.8	13.8	13.9	13.9	13.9	14.0	13.9	13.8	13.8	13.6	13.6	13.6	13.8
2005	13.5	13.5	13.6	13.7	13.7	13.9	13.9	13.8	13.8	13.7	13.7	13.8	13.7
2006	13.6	13.7	13.8	13.8	13.9	14.2	14.2	14.1	14.1	13.9	14.0	14.0	13.9
2007	14.1	14.2	14.3	14.1	14.3	14.6	14.5	14.4	14.4	14.4	14.4	14.4	14.3
2008	14.3	14.6	14.7	14.6	15.2	15.0	14.7	14.7	14.7	14.6	14.5	14.5	14.7
2009	14.4	14.4	14.6	15.0	14.6	14.8	14.8	14.7	14.5	14.4	14.4	14.4	14.6
Government													
1990	48.0	48.1	48.2	48.6	49.2	48.7	47.0	47.6	48.9	49.5	49.4	49.4	48.6
2000	50.7	51.5	51.8	52.4	53.2	52.1	49.6	50.3	52.2	52.3	52.3	52.5	51.7
2001	51.2	52.1	52.2	52.2	52.1	51.8	50.0	50.0	52.0	53.1	53.1	53.2	51.9
2002	52.1	52.4	52.5	54.0	54.1	53.7	50.8	51.0	52.4	53.6	53.6	54.1	52.9
2003	52.2	52.5	52.8	53.2	53.2	52.6	50.1	50.4	50.7	53.2	53.2	52.8	52.2
2004	53.0	55.0	53.9	52.8	52.2	52.0	51.0	51.4	52.2	53.7	53.8	53.4	52.9
2005	52.4	53.0	52.8	52.8	52.3	51.5	50.0	50.1	52.0	52.9	53.0	53.3	52.2
2006	51.9	52.8	52.6	52.5	52.1	50.2	50.3	51.0	53.1	53.6	53.5	54.0	52.3
2007	52.4	53.2	53.2	52.9	52.2	49.9	49.2	50.3	52.2	52.4	52.5	50.9	51.8
2008	50.7	51.2	50.7	51.1	50.6	48.2	47.7	49.6	51.8	52.9	52.4	51.5	50.7
2009	50.7	51.4	51.2	51.8	51.3	49.0	48.3	48.7	51.1	52.1	52.1	51.0	50.7

Employment by Industry: Los Angeles-Long Beach-Santa Ana, CA, Selected Years, 1990–2009

(Numbers in thousands, not seasonally adjusted.)

Industry and year	January	February	March	April	May	June	July	August	September	October	November	December	Annual average
Total Nonfarm													
1990	5289.7	5325.2	5356.0	5331.4	5335.4	5338.4	5286.1	5258.7	5270.9	5294.7	5301.5	5309.7	5308.1
2000	5343.5	5395.6	5437.4	5446.6	5475.9	5477.2	5425.2	5440.1	5490.0	5499.1	5534.6	5566.3	5461.0
2001	5471.1	5503.6	5546.2	5518.1	5515.8	5522.8	5430.9	5438.0	5459.8	5471.6	5474.8	5494.6	5487.3
2002	5364.4	5393.5	5442.0	5436.3	5453.6	5456.5	5374.3	5389.1	5427.0	5455.5	5481.4	5492.1	5430.5
2003	5366.4	5390.2	5419.1	5410.3	5425.1	5425.1	5366.6	5376.4	5392.4	5442.0	5454.0	5473.3	5411.7
2004	5378.2	5408.8	5443.7	5447.4	5469.7	5467.5	5429.9	5415.9	5439.9	5493.3	5522.7	5528.8	5453.8
2005	5417.9	5452.7	5481.9	5498.8	5510.0	5523.8	5477.6	5487.7	5531.4	5566.2	5603.0	5630.6	5515.1
2006	5519.6	5566.8	5597.4	5597.5	5613.8	5635.0	5576.8	5581.3	5619.9	5652.9	5675.2	5700.9	5611.4
2007	5578.4	5615.7	5649.4	5626.8	5638.7	5655.9	5611.5	5600.4	5633.0	5657.1	5679.4	5705.4	5637.6
2008	5548.8	5583.3	5603.7	5605.1	5605.8	5600.1	5534.3	5504.2	5521.9	5528.7	5503.1	5488.9	5552.3
2009	5313.8	5293.8	5286.9	5251.3	5243.6	5223.0	5119.8	5097.0	5114.1	5154.8	5158.6	5153.5	5200.9
Total Private													
1990	4630.0	4659.6	4684.1	4656.7	4652.3	4656.6	4631.9	4627.5	4621.0	4624.0	4626.2	4637.0	4642.2
2000	4625.3	4667.5	4700.9	4707.1	4716.9	4743.3	4727.4	4751.7	4772.4	4767.8	4792.4	4824.8	4733.1
2001	4730.8	4755.7	4787.5	4758.2	4753.9	4758.8	4713.5	4723.9	4721.8	4713.0	4711.6	4728.7	4738.1
2002	4605.3	4630.1	4667.9	4662.9	4677.1	4682.9	4644.1	4667.4	4677.5	4687.5	4708.3	4720.6	4669.3
2003	4603.6	4623.7	4645.3	4641.7	4657.0	4658.0	4632.6	4660.0	4660.6	4693.0	4700.8	4723.0	4658.2
2004	4631.2	4660.5	4688.9	4693.8	4714.9	4714.8	4711.8	4715.1	4716.0	4752.0	4775.6	4785.2	4713.3
2005	4679.6	4707.2	4731.7	4751.0	4759.8	4773.7	4762.5	4781.7	4806.8	4824.4	4853.3	4882.2	4776.2
2006	4778.2	4818.1	4842.7	4843.5	4857.3	4878.7	4852.1	4869.3	4886.5	4899.9	4914.9	4942.4	4865.3
2007	4826.8	4857.9	4885.5	4864.0	4873.7	4890.7	4878.9	4880.6	4891.1	4895.4	4909.8	4936.6	4882.6
2008	4786.1	4812.6	4828.3	4828.9	4825.8	4821.8	4794.2	4776.0	4774.7	4760.2	4728.2	4717.4	4787.9
2009	4548.5	4523.3	4511.3	4471.6	4466.6	4447.5	4387.2	4377.1	4386.6	4402.5	4403.6	4403.6	4444.1
Goods-Producing													
1990	1280.9	1290.6	1297.6	1281.7	1278.2	1277.7	1272.3	1263.1	1257.6	1252.8	1239.5	1228.8	1268.4
2000	1024.7	1032.4	1041.7	1039.4	1041.8	1052.9	1043.0	1044.0	1048.7	1038.3	1037.9	1043.5	1040.7
2001	1023.2	1025.1	1030.5	1023.7	1022.0	1022.6	1007.6	1007.5	1001.1	988.0	977.5	971.3	1008.3
2002	945.4	950.0	956.4	950.1	952.0	953.0	937.7	941.4	940.9	934.7	931.6	929.0	943.5
2003	910.7	909.9	913.4	907.6	910.0	912.6	901.8	905.3	904.2	900.5	899.7	901.9	906.4
2004	892.2	895.9	902.7	903.4	905.8	910.8	909.2	908.6	909.3	906.8	901.4	899.2	903.8
2005	884.9	893.2	898.1	904.2	908.0	912.4	913.9	916.4	918.2	915.1	913.9	913.2	907.6
2006	902.2	910.3	914.2	913.2	915.5	921.0	916.5	918.3	919.4	912.4	908.7	905.8	913.1
2007	892.2	897.9	902.2	898.3	899.7	906.0	901.8	899.5	895.2	889.5	882.5	878.3	895.3
2008	863.0	864.6	863.9	861.5	860.1	859.2	855.3	852.2	847.0	836.6	823.4	812.2	849.9
2009	787.0	772.9	766.0	752.8	748.9	744.7	730.2	724.5	718.0	711.1	705.2	699.0	738.4
Mining and Logging													
1990	9.7	9.8	9.7	9.7	9.7	9.7	9.7	9.5	9.4	9.4	9.1	8.7	9.5
2000	4.0	4.0	4.0	3.9	4.0	4.0	3.9	3.9	4.0	4.0	3.9	4.3	4.0
2001	4.5	4.4	4.4	4.4	4.4	4.4	4.4	4.4	4.4	4.4	4.4	4.4	4.4
2002	4.4	4.4	4.4	4.1	4.2	4.2	4.2	4.2	4.2	4.2	4.4	4.4	4.3
2003	4.3	4.4	4.4	4.3	4.3	4.3	4.3	4.4	4.2	4.4	4.4	4.4	4.3
2004	4.3	4.3	4.4	4.4	4.3	4.4	4.3	4.3	4.3	4.6	4.6	4.6	4.4
2005	4.5	4.5	4.5	4.3	4.3	4.3	4.4	4.4	4.4	4.3	4.4	4.4	4.4
2006	4.5	4.5	4.5	4.5	4.6	4.7	4.7	4.7	4.7	4.7	4.7	4.7	4.6
2007	4.9	5.0	5.0	4.9	4.9	5.0	5.0	4.9	5.0	5.0	5.1	5.0	5.0
2008	5.0	5.0	5.0	4.9	4.9	5.0	5.0	5.0	5.0	5.1	5.0	5.0	5.0
2009	4.9	4.8	4.8	4.7	4.7	4.7	4.7	4.6	4.4	4.4	4.4	4.4	4.6
Construction													
1990	220.1	222.0	224.8	216.6	217.0	219.0	217.5	216.0	216.4	211.6	206.6	205.0	216.1
2000	198.3	199.1	202.1	203.3	206.6	211.6	208.8	212.9	215.2	214.4	215.0	216.5	208.7
2001	208.7	209.3	212.1	213.5	216.9	220.3	221.2	225.3	223.9	221.9	219.2	217.8	217.4
2002	208.8	209.5	211.8	209.7	211.7	213.2	212.5	217.9	218.2	217.3	216.6	216.5	213.7
2003	210.3	208.2	211.3	212.3	216.3	219.8	220.0	223.6	223.9	224.1	224.2	225.2	218.2
2004	221.9	222.1	224.7	228.2	230.4	234.1	236.6	239.2	240.5	238.7	236.2	235.3	232.3
2005	226.2	232.9	236.3	241.8	246.4	250.7	254.9	258.5	259.4	259.2	258.8	258.3	248.6
2006	253.9	257.0	259.1	260.0	263.5	267.3	267.9	271.0	272.0	267.9	265.6	264.2	264.1
2007	255.1	257.9	261.6	260.1	261.9	265.8	266.7	266.1	263.8	260.6	255.6	252.7	260.7
2008	242.9	243.3	243.6	241.4	240.6	239.3	237.9	237.9	234.7	230.5	224.9	220.1	236.4
2009	209.1	202.1	201.3	195.8	194.9	193.3	187.6	186.4	182.6	178.8	176.4	172.2	190.0
Manufacturing													
1990	1051.1	1058.8	1063.1	1055.4	1051.5	1049.0	1045.1	1037.6	1031.8	1031.8	1023.8	1015.1	1042.8
2000	822.4	829.3	835.6	832.2	831.2	837.3	830.3	827.2	829.5	819.9	819.0	822.7	828.1
2001	810.0	811.4	814.0	805.8	800.7	797.9	782.0	777.8	772.8	761.7	753.9	749.1	786.4
2002	732.2	736.1	740.2	736.3	736.1	735.6	721.0	719.3	718.5	713.2	710.6	708.1	725.6
2003	696.1	697.3	697.7	691.0	689.4	688.5	677.5	677.3	676.1	672.0	671.1	672.3	683.8
2004	666.0	669.5	673.6	670.8	671.1	672.3	668.3	665.1	664.5	663.5	660.6	659.3	667.1
2005	654.2	655.8	657.3	658.1	657.3	657.4	654.6	653.5	654.4	651.6	650.7	650.5	654.6
2006	643.8	648.8	650.6	648.7	647.4	649.0	643.9	642.6	642.7	639.8	638.4	636.9	644.4
2007	632.2	635.0	635.6	633.3	632.9	635.2	630.1	628.5	626.4	623.9	621.8	620.6	629.6
2008	615.1	616.3	615.3	615.2	614.6	614.9	612.4	609.3	607.3	601.0	593.5	587.1	608.5
2009	573.0	566.0	559.9	552.3	549.3	546.7	537.9	533.5	531.0	527.9	524.4	522.4	543.7

Employment by Industry: Los Angeles-Long Beach-Santa Ana, CA, Selected Years, 1990–2009—*Continued*
(Numbers in thousands, not seasonally adjusted.)

Industry and year	January	February	March	April	May	June	July	August	September	October	November	December	Annual average
Service-Providing													
1990	4008.8	4034.6	4058.4	4049.7	4057.2	4060.7	4013.8	3995.6	4013.3	4041.9	4062.0	4080.9	4039.7
2000	4318.8	4363.2	4395.7	4407.2	4434.1	4424.3	4382.2	4396.1	4441.3	4460.8	4496.7	4522.8	4420.3
2001	4447.9	4478.5	4515.7	4494.4	4493.8	4500.2	4423.3	4430.5	4458.7	4483.6	4497.3	4523.3	4478.9
2002	4419.0	4443.5	4485.6	4486.2	4501.6	4503.5	4436.6	4447.7	4486.1	4520.8	4549.8	4563.1	4487.0
2003	4455.7	4480.3	4505.7	4502.7	4515.1	4512.5	4464.8	4471.1	4488.2	4541.5	4554.3	4571.4	4505.2
2004	4486.0	4512.9	4541.0	4544.0	4563.9	4556.7	4520.7	4507.3	4530.6	4586.5	4621.3	4629.6	4550.0
2005	4533.0	4559.5	4583.8	4594.6	4602.0	4611.4	4563.7	4571.3	4613.2	4651.1	4689.1	4717.4	4607.5
2006	4617.4	4656.5	4683.2	4684.3	4698.3	4714.0	4660.3	4663.0	4700.5	4740.5	4766.5	4795.1	4698.3
2007	4686.2	4717.8	4747.2	4728.5	4739.0	4749.9	4709.7	4700.9	4737.8	4767.6	4796.9	4827.1	4742.4
2008	4685.8	4718.7	4739.8	4743.6	4745.7	4740.9	4679.0	4652.0	4674.9	4692.1	4679.7	4676.7	4702.4
2009	4526.8	4520.9	4520.9	4498.5	4494.7	4478.3	4389.6	4372.5	4396.1	4443.7	4453.4	4454.5	4462.5
Trade, Transportation, and Utilities													
1990	1014.4	1009.2	1009.0	997.0	995.9	998.9	1001.0	998.1	998.2	996.4	1015.0	1034.9	1005.7
2000	1032.7	1030.6	1032.3	1028.6	1030.7	1037.3	1036.0	1040.6	1044.5	1052.7	1070.3	1089.7	1043.8
2001	1060.1	1052.3	1055.5	1050.5	1049.7	1054.1	1046.4	1046.8	1048.5	1049.0	1060.0	1076.6	1054.1
2002	1035.6	1030.0	1032.4	1034.2	1038.3	1044.1	1039.1	1042.4	1046.3	1047.8	1065.6	1086.5	1045.2
2003	1039.4	1033.5	1033.8	1029.6	1031.9	1035.7	1029.7	1030.6	1035.2	1050.6	1056.6	1072.1	1039.8
2004	1030.3	1026.3	1031.6	1034.5	1039.2	1045.2	1042.1	1043.2	1044.9	1055.4	1076.3	1088.3	1046.4
2005	1054.3	1048.0	1047.6	1048.1	1051.3	1056.3	1059.7	1062.6	1066.3	1075.7	1096.0	1116.6	1065.2
2006	1074.5	1069.6	1073.4	1070.9	1073.9	1079.3	1080.1	1084.5	1088.6	1095.7	1117.4	1134.8	1086.9
2007	1092.0	1083.1	1081.0	1080.6	1082.5	1086.8	1092.2	1091.5	1092.6	1100.6	1122.1	1141.4	1095.5
2008	1093.6	1085.0	1080.7	1076.9	1076.1	1076.6	1072.8	1067.3	1062.9	1064.5	1068.5	1073.5	1074.9
2009	1027.2	1010.1	1002.0	990.2	990.8	988.0	975.3	975.5	978.1	983.3	991.8	997.0	992.4
Wholesale Trade													
1990	292.9	293.8	294.1	291.9	291.7	291.6	290.7	289.3	289.6	288.9	286.8	287.1	290.7
2000	298.3	299.7	300.4	298.3	298.3	299.5	299.9	300.5	300.8	300.9	301.1	302.0	300.0
2001	302.7	304.9	305.3	304.9	303.7	305.8	303.4	302.0	301.7	302.6	300.8	301.4	303.3
2002	296.1	297.5	299.5	299.2	299.5	300.5	300.0	300.5	301.1	300.1	300.7	302.0	299.7
2003	297.8	298.4	299.1	297.9	297.9	298.7	296.7	296.5	296.5	295.8	295.1	296.7	297.2
2004	294.3	295.3	297.1	297.0	297.7	299.5	298.0	297.1	296.7	299.0	299.3	299.2	297.5
2005	297.9	298.8	299.9	301.7	302.6	303.4	302.6	302.6	302.8	303.9	304.1	306.7	302.3
2006	303.5	305.7	307.0	307.5	308.5	309.9	310.3	310.3	311.4	311.9	312.2	314.5	309.4
2007	311.0	312.5	313.9	313.4	313.3	313.8	314.0	313.6	314.0	315.3	315.0	316.8	313.9
2008	313.9	314.6	315.0	314.6	313.0	312.8	310.6	308.7	307.9	306.7	303.7	302.4	310.3
2009	295.4	292.9	290.7	287.1	285.8	285.0	279.8	278.8	277.7	280.3	279.2	278.0	284.2
Retail Trade													
1990	541.3	533.4	531.4	523.4	522.2	524.6	526.9	525.8	523.8	521.6	542.8	560.5	531.5
2000	532.9	528.6	529.5	526.4	528.2	533.3	533.0	536.1	539.0	543.4	560.5	578.3	539.1
2001	549.5	540.5	541.3	536.5	537.7	540.8	537.2	539.6	540.7	541.8	558.3	575.1	544.9
2002	545.3	536.9	540.0	539.1	541.9	546.5	543.5	545.1	548.6	551.4	569.0	587.4	549.6
2003	549.1	542.9	543.0	540.9	543.1	546.3	543.5	545.5	547.9	564.6	571.3	587.2	552.1
2004	548.9	544.2	546.2	548.6	552.3	556.1	554.0	556.1	556.4	561.7	581.9	596.7	558.6
2005	566.7	558.9	558.6	556.1	559.0	563.2	566.8	570.2	573.3	579.7	600.4	617.4	572.5
2006	580.6	572.7	574.5	571.9	573.5	576.6	576.6	580.8	581.9	588.2	608.6	622.7	584.1
2007	587.4	576.9	576.5	573.4	575.5	579.2	583.0	585.1	583.0	589.1	610.6	626.3	587.2
2008	588.6	577.0	575.6	571.2	569.7	570.5	567.8	564.5	563.3	564.7	573.4	579.4	572.1
2009	546.5	534.3	529.0	523.0	524.4	523.6	518.8	520.2	522.7	524.7	534.9	540.6	528.6
Transportation and Utilities													
1990	180.2	182.0	183.5	181.7	182.0	182.7	183.4	183.0	184.8	185.9	185.4	187.3	183.5
2000	201.5	202.3	202.4	203.9	204.2	204.5	203.1	204.0	204.7	208.4	208.7	209.4	204.8
2001	207.9	206.9	208.9	209.1	208.3	207.5	205.8	205.2	206.1	204.6	200.9	200.1	205.9
2002	194.2	195.6	192.9	195.9	196.9	197.1	195.6	196.8	196.6	196.3	195.9	197.1	195.9
2003	192.5	192.2	191.7	190.8	190.9	190.7	189.5	188.6	190.8	190.2	190.2	188.2	190.5
2004	187.1	186.8	188.3	188.9	189.2	189.6	190.1	190.0	191.8	194.7	195.1	192.4	190.3
2005	189.7	190.3	189.1	190.3	189.7	189.7	190.3	189.8	190.2	192.1	191.5	192.5	190.4
2006	190.4	191.2	191.9	191.5	191.9	192.8	193.2	193.4	195.3	195.6	196.6	197.6	193.5
2007	193.6	193.7	190.6	193.8	193.7	193.8	195.2	192.8	195.6	196.2	196.5	198.3	194.5
2008	191.1	193.4	190.1	191.1	193.4	193.3	194.4	194.1	191.7	193.1	191.4	191.7	192.4
2009	185.3	182.9	182.3	180.1	180.6	179.4	176.7	176.5	177.7	178.3	177.7	178.4	179.7
Information													
1990	206.8	212.0	210.5	224.4	223.6	223.7	206.6	210.0	209.4	216.0	216.9	216.4	214.7
2000	271.8	277.4	279.7	278.6	281.2	280.9	282.4	289.0	287.2	290.2	298.0	292.7	284.1
2001	282.1	285.8	287.3	277.0	265.3	264.8	256.9	256.3	257.3	253.3	255.4	255.9	266.5
2002	247.2	249.4	257.3	245.3	244.6	245.1	235.2	242.3	235.5	242.6	250.0	234.3	244.1
2003	237.1	241.5	239.6	233.7	237.1	229.3	230.1	241.8	230.9	241.9	246.8	240.9	237.5
2004	246.6	249.6	245.5	244.1	249.4	238.3	241.4	243.1	235.2	249.2	257.1	248.1	245.6
2005	238.6	240.3	245.0	237.9	236.7	236.7	234.5	240.5	240.8	241.0	247.8	244.3	240.3
2006	238.9	245.8	245.1	239.0	239.5	240.9	234.5	235.3	232.2	230.4	230.9	236.8	237.4
2007	234.7	241.2	248.9	237.6	241.1	243.4	240.2	244.2	244.5	233.5	238.0	244.6	241.0
2008	226.6	234.8	243.4	242.6	246.6	248.9	240.1	241.4	245.3	240.5	236.5	237.7	240.4
2009	218.5	221.8	225.4	217.1	216.1	219.0	216.6	219.1	223.4	224.7	225.3	226.3	221.1

Employment by Industry: Los Angeles-Long Beach-Santa Ana, CA, Selected Years, 1990–2009—*Continued*

(Numbers in thousands, not seasonally adjusted.)

Industry and year	January	February	March	April	May	June	July	August	September	October	November	December	Annual average
Financial Activities													
1990	373.5	375.0	377.1	371.9	371.2	371.9	368.0	374.8	370.2	366.5	363.4	367.6	370.9
2000	317.3	319.4	319.7	319.4	319.6	321.1	317.9	319.9	319.4	319.6	319.1	322.4	319.6
2001	329.6	332.5	334.9	333.0	333.3	335.2	332.8	335.8	335.4	337.3	337.8	340.6	334.9
2002	336.0	338.3	339.4	339.6	340.5	342.3	342.5	344.1	344.7	346.1	348.5	351.2	342.8
2003	350.3	352.5	354.9	358.4	360.8	362.8	364.0	366.7	366.6	367.4	367.6	369.7	361.8
2004	369.3	370.7	372.6	372.6	372.4	373.5	374.9	375.2	374.3	376.0	376.9	378.6	373.9
2005	374.9	376.5	378.3	380.0	380.9	381.7	382.6	384.0	384.7	386.9	387.5	390.3	382.4
2006	386.5	387.5	388.5	387.8	388.6	387.6	386.5	386.7	386.0	385.9	385.2	387.0	387.0
2007	382.2	383.3	383.6	379.8	377.5	375.3	373.7	371.6	367.0	365.8	363.2	361.3	373.7
2008	356.2	356.1	355.2	353.1	351.9	350.8	349.3	347.3	343.9	341.8	340.0	339.9	348.8
2009	333.2	331.1	330.3	328.0	326.0	326.3	325.3	324.0	321.8	322.0	320.1	321.5	325.8
Professional and Business Services													
1990	698.9	707.7	715.4	706.4	705.4	705.1	707.2	705.0	705.8	709.5	708.1	708.9	707.0
2000	818.9	828.0	835.1	842.6	839.6	846.9	850.1	857.3	860.4	860.0	861.4	863.7	847.0
2001	836.5	841.7	848.1	835.6	841.1	838.5	833.6	839.5	835.8	830.7	826.9	829.1	836.4
2002	812.1	815.5	824.2	823.0	823.9	824.3	820.3	826.7	827.7	829.3	828.3	830.6	823.8
2003	806.4	808.9	816.0	812.7	811.7	812.2	808.7	815.7	813.0	813.8	813.8	817.1	812.5
2004	794.8	801.0	808.3	810.0	814.5	818.9	820.8	823.9	821.4	828.9	831.5	834.1	817.3
2005	820.8	827.2	829.6	835.1	834.9	838.7	838.4	845.0	849.0	852.5	855.4	859.0	840.5
2006	846.1	856.3	862.1	865.2	866.4	875.7	875.8	882.6	883.5	889.4	889.0	888.8	873.4
2007	866.5	875.9	881.5	871.5	872.0	878.8	876.4	881.1	882.8	885.4	884.8	887.9	878.7
2008	851.0	859.8	862.1	859.9	855.2	854.8	851.6	850.4	845.9	842.7	831.4	825.6	849.2
2009	793.5	788.9	783.2	771.2	767.2	764.4	751.3	752.8	750.8	759.8	761.7	761.0	767.2
Education and Health Services													
1990	465.6	474.0	476.4	477.4	475.4	471.3	463.0	464.8	469.9	477.3	478.3	480.0	472.8
2000	517.3	527.9	532.6	535.1	533.0	525.9	518.2	519.7	531.2	534.3	535.5	538.1	529.1
2001	529.4	541.6	547.1	546.7	546.7	539.9	535.5	537.9	549.3	559.9	562.6	564.8	546.8
2002	552.8	563.2	567.1	572.4	572.0	564.3	556.8	558.2	571.3	580.3	583.3	584.5	568.9
2003	570.2	581.2	585.9	590.4	589.4	581.9	575.2	576.4	589.8	598.6	599.8	601.8	586.7
2004	588.4	599.7	604.1	604.7	602.0	592.7	584.2	585.0	597.9	604.8	605.5	606.7	598.0
2005	594.8	604.0	606.4	610.3	608.9	601.2	588.7	590.4	606.8	613.8	615.5	616.9	604.8
2006	603.8	615.7	618.7	620.5	619.0	611.4	599.7	601.8	618.8	627.6	629.1	630.4	616.4
2007	618.6	630.6	634.3	634.1	633.5	624.3	618.4	618.3	637.3	646.8	649.8	651.0	633.1
2008	640.6	652.7	655.3	658.2	655.6	645.7	639.5	638.6	657.2	665.9	669.3	670.6	654.1
2009	655.0	666.5	669.5	675.4	674.1	660.9	647.8	645.9	662.4	672.7	674.7	675.3	665.0
Leisure and Hospitality													
1990	419.4	419.9	425.3	426.5	430.5	436.0	440.6	438.9	437.2	432.3	431.9	429.5	430.7
2000	463.3	471.1	476.6	479.8	486.5	491.3	494.9	496.6	495.3	488.5	486.1	490.2	485.0
2001	484.9	490.1	495.3	502.9	506.1	512.4	512.3	512.4	506.4	505.5	503.0	502.4	502.8
2002	490.7	495.7	501.5	507.9	513.4	516.5	519.9	520.1	517.7	513.0	508.2	511.2	509.7
2003	499.7	505.0	509.3	516.9	522.7	528.8	531.6	532.2	528.1	527.5	524.7	527.5	521.1
2004	520.5	526.8	531.7	531.9	538.0	541.1	546.6	544.9	540.3	539.0	535.4	538.2	536.2
2005	527.0	526.6	533.5	541.5	544.9	551.2	552.9	551.3	548.0	546.7	544.9	549.3	542.7
2006	536.4	541.3	547.8	554.7	560.5	567.3	567.0	568.1	563.8	564.8	560.8	565.1	558.1
2007	550.4	553.3	560.0	568.0	572.7	579.6	581.7	580.2	575.9	577.4	573.8	576.6	570.8
2008	562.8	566.3	573.2	581.5	585.0	590.6	592.2	588.0	581.1	576.5	569.4	569.3	578.0
2009	550.6	548.8	551.2	554.2	560.5	561.3	560.8	556.6	553.3	550.2	546.8	548.1	553.5
Other Services													
1990	170.5	171.2	172.8	171.4	172.1	172.0	173.2	172.8	172.7	173.2	173.1	170.9	172.2
2000	179.3	180.7	183.2	183.6	184.5	187.0	184.9	184.6	185.7	184.2	184.1	184.5	183.9
2001	185.0	186.6	188.8	188.8	189.7	191.3	188.4	187.7	188.0	189.3	188.4	188.0	188.3
2002	185.5	188.0	189.6	190.4	192.4	193.3	192.6	192.2	193.4	193.7	192.8	193.3	191.4
2003	189.8	191.2	192.4	192.4	193.4	194.7	191.5	191.3	192.8	192.7	191.8	192.0	192.1
2004	189.1	190.5	192.4	192.6	193.6	194.3	192.6	191.2	192.7	191.9	191.5	192.0	192.0
2005	189.3	191.4	193.2	193.9	194.2	195.5	191.8	191.5	193.0	192.7	192.3	192.6	192.6
2006	189.8	191.6	192.9	192.2	193.9	195.5	192.0	192.0	194.2	193.7	193.8	193.7	192.9
2007	190.2	192.6	194.0	194.1	194.7	196.5	194.5	194.2	195.8	196.4	195.6	195.5	194.5
2008	192.3	193.3	194.5	195.2	195.3	195.2	193.4	190.8	191.4	191.7	189.7	188.6	192.6
2009	183.5	183.2	183.7	182.7	183.0	182.9	179.9	178.7	178.8	178.7	178.0	175.4	180.7
Government													
1990	659.7	665.6	671.9	674.7	683.1	681.8	654.2	631.2	649.9	670.7	675.3	672.7	665.9
2000	718.2	728.1	736.5	739.5	759.0	733.9	697.8	688.4	717.6	731.3	742.2	741.5	727.8
2001	740.3	747.9	758.7	759.9	761.9	764.0	717.4	714.1	738.0	758.6	763.2	765.9	749.2
2002	759.1	763.4	774.1	773.4	776.5	773.6	730.2	721.7	749.5	768.0	773.1	771.5	761.2
2003	762.8	766.5	773.8	768.6	768.1	767.1	734.0	716.4	731.8	749.0	753.2	750.3	753.4
2004	747.0	748.3	754.8	753.6	754.8	752.7	718.1	700.8	723.9	741.3	747.1	743.6	740.5
2005	738.3	745.5	750.2	747.8	750.2	750.1	715.1	706.0	724.6	741.8	749.7	748.4	739.0
2006	741.4	748.7	754.7	754.0	756.5	756.3	724.7	712.0	733.4	753.0	760.3	758.5	746.1
2007	751.6	757.8	763.9	762.8	765.0	765.2	732.6	719.8	741.9	761.7	769.6	768.8	755.1
2008	762.7	770.7	775.4	776.2	780.0	778.3	740.1	728.2	747.2	768.5	774.9	771.5	764.5
2009	765.3	770.5	775.6	779.7	777.0	775.5	732.6	719.9	727.5	752.3	755.0	749.9	756.7

Employment by Industry: Las Vegas-Paradise, NV, Selected Years, 1990–2009

(Numbers in thousands, not seasonally adjusted.)

Industry and year	January	February	March	April	May	June	July	August	September	October	November	December	Annual average
Total Nonfarm													
1990	358.6	359.5	364.8	367.4	371.6	374.0	374.9	378.9	381.5	382.8	386.4	383.2	373.6
2000	675.1	678.0	685.1	688.8	698.4	694.9	692.5	705.3	708.1	711.4	717.0	716.8	697.6
2001	716.5	723.5	728.8	728.8	732.6	731.9	725.3	731.1	735.5	722.3	722.9	720.9	726.7
2002	709.9	714.3	722.6	727.9	734.2	730.4	726.8	731.6	736.8	743.4	746.0	746.6	730.9
2003	738.2	743.4	749.5	750.0	756.4	754.2	754.0	761.8	770.3	778.8	780.9	785.0	760.2
2004	777.9	781.8	790.7	803.5	808.2	810.4	811.2	815.2	827.4	840.5	841.3	843.9	812.7
2005	832.4	840.6	850.5	867.3	869.9	872.4	870.3	873.4	887.4	892.6	899.2	903.3	871.6
2006	891.4	900.9	910.7	916.0	922.3	923.8	915.7	917.5	925.3	926.7	929.3	927.9	917.3
2007	913.2	923.9	927.9	930.4	936.7	933.3	921.2	921.1	924.6	932.2	935.3	936.3	928.0
2008	919.5	921.4	923.6	926.2	929.6	923.0	910.2	906.7	910.0	903.5	893.5	880.6	912.3
2009	855.7	850.0	842.6	836.1	832.0	823.9	810.3	806.1	814.0	819.8	814.7	810.7	826.3
Total Private													
1990	320.5	321.6	326.1	328.5	332.7	335.8	338.9	343.5	342.3	342.1	345.3	341.9	334.9
2000	606.5	608.5	614.5	617.9	624.1	628.6	626.6	635.6	637.6	638.3	642.9	642.6	627.0
2001	644.8	649.6	654.6	653.0	658.2	659.6	656.7	662.2	659.7	645.8	646.1	644.1	652.9
2002	635.8	637.2	645.0	650.7	656.5	655.1	655.1	659.7	659.8	662.3	664.2	664.7	653.8
2003	659.9	662.2	667.9	668.5	674.5	675.5	678.9	687.1	689.8	695.9	697.6	701.4	679.9
2004	697.7	699.2	706.6	719.4	723.4	729.4	733.8	738.5	742.8	753.3	753.7	756.2	729.5
2005	748.4	753.5	761.9	778.5	780.8	786.9	788.5	792.6	799.9	801.3	806.9	810.7	784.2
2006	802.8	809.0	818.4	822.5	828.6	833.8	829.8	832.1	833.1	830.2	831.8	830.4	825.2
2007	819.4	826.1	829.6	830.5	836.6	837.3	829.6	831.0	827.5	831.0	833.3	833.9	830.5
2008	820.9	819.1	820.6	822.1	825.6	823.6	814.3	812.1	808.3	797.9	787.8	775.0	810.6
2009	755.1	747.5	740.2	734.3	731.2	727.4	717.3	714.4	715.9	720.6	716.2	712.6	727.7
Goods-Producing													
1990	44.6	45.4	46.8	46.6	47.5	48.1	47.3	48.0	47.4	46.7	45.3	44.2	46.5
2000	83.6	84.0	86.1	86.5	87.4	89.2	88.9	89.3	88.1	87.3	87.7	87.8	87.2
2001	86.2	87.1	88.1	88.5	89.9	91.7	91.9	93.3	92.5	91.6	90.3	88.4	90.0
2002	85.4	85.8	87.5	89.5	91.0	91.1	92.2	93.6	92.9	93.1	92.4	91.8	90.5
2003	90.8	91.3	93.0	94.0	95.6	97.0	98.1	100.0	100.5	102.3	101.8	102.2	97.2
2004	100.5	102.6	104.1	108.4	109.7	112.1	115.1	116.6	118.5	120.8	119.7	120.5	112.4
2005	117.7	120.5	122.3	124.6	124.6	126.0	128.4	129.9	131.9	131.6	131.8	132.9	126.9
2006	130.8	133.6	135.8	137.3	138.5	139.9	138.8	139.3	138.2	135.6	133.7	132.3	136.2
2007	128.1	129.6	131.9	131.0	132.7	132.1	131.5	132.0	129.5	127.9	126.5	125.5	129.9
2008	121.3	121.4	120.9	120.7	121.7	122.0	121.9	120.6	118.0	114.7	109.7	104.8	118.1
2009	99.3	96.8	94.0	90.6	86.2	84.3	82.4	81.6	80.3	79.5	79.5	75.2	85.8
Mining and Logging													
1990	0.3	0.3	0.3	0.3	0.3	0.3	0.3	0.4	0.3	0.3	0.3	0.4	0.3
2000	0.5	0.5	0.6	0.6	0.6	0.6	0.6	0.6	0.6	0.6	0.5	0.5	0.6
2001	0.6	0.5	0.5	0.5	0.5	0.5	0.5	0.5	0.5	0.4	0.3	0.3	0.5
2002	0.4	0.3	0.4	0.3	0.3	0.3	0.3	0.3	0.3	0.3	0.3	0.3	0.3
2003	0.3	0.3	0.3	0.3	0.4	0.4	0.4	0.4	0.4	0.4	0.4	0.4	0.3
2004	0.4	0.4	0.4	0.4	0.4	0.4	0.4	0.4	0.4	0.4	0.4	0.4	0.4
2005	0.4	0.4	0.4	0.4	0.4	0.4	0.4	0.4	0.4	0.4	0.4	0.4	0.4
2006	0.4	0.4	0.4	0.4	0.4	0.5	0.5	0.5	0.5	0.5	0.5	0.5	0.5
2007	0.5	0.5	0.5	0.5	0.5	0.5	0.5	0.5	0.5	0.5	0.4	0.4	0.5
2008	0.4	0.4	0.4	0.4	0.4	0.4	0.4	0.4	0.4	0.3	0.3	0.3	0.4
2009	0.3	0.3	0.3	0.3	0.3	0.3	0.3	0.3	0.3	0.3	0.3	0.2	0.3
Construction													
1990	34.6	35.1	36.4	36.1	36.8	37.3	36.5	37.1	36.5	35.8	34.4	33.4	35.8
2000	63.3	63.6	65.3	65.9	66.7	68.4	68.2	68.6	67.3	66.3	66.8	66.7	66.4
2001	65.0	65.8	66.9	67.2	68.4	70.0	70.3	71.5	70.8	70.2	69.0	67.2	68.5
2002	64.5	64.9	66.5	68.5	69.8	69.7	70.6	71.9	71.3	71.0	70.3	69.6	69.1
2003	69.1	69.6	71.3	72.2	73.6	74.8	75.7	77.4	77.9	79.4	78.7	79.1	74.9
2004	77.8	79.7	80.9	85.1	86.1	88.3	91.1	92.4	94.3	96.4	95.2	96.1	88.6
2005	93.2	96.0	97.5	99.5	99.4	100.6	102.9	104.3	105.9	105.6	105.7	106.8	101.5
2006	104.6	107.1	108.9	110.0	110.9	112.0	110.8	111.3	110.0	107.7	105.9	104.4	108.6
2007	100.9	102.4	104.5	103.6	105.2	104.4	104.0	104.6	102.3	101.1	99.8	99.0	102.7
2008	95.0	95.2	94.7	94.5	95.4	95.6	95.7	94.6	92.3	89.5	85.2	80.8	92.4
2009	76.2	74.2	71.8	68.8	64.9	63.3	61.5	60.6	59.3	58.6	58.9	54.8	64.4
Manufacturing													
1990	9.7	10.0	10.1	10.2	10.4	10.5	10.5	10.5	10.6	10.6	10.6	10.4	10.3
2000	19.8	19.9	20.2	20.0	20.1	20.2	20.1	20.1	20.2	20.4	20.4	20.6	20.2
2001	20.6	20.8	20.7	20.8	21.0	21.2	21.1	21.3	21.2	21.0	21.0	20.9	21.0
2002	20.5	20.6	20.6	20.7	20.9	21.1	21.3	21.4	21.3	21.8	21.8	21.9	21.2
2003	21.4	21.4	21.4	21.5	21.6	21.8	22.0	22.2	22.2	22.5	22.7	22.7	21.9
2004	22.3	22.5	22.8	22.9	23.2	23.4	23.6	23.8	23.8	24.0	24.1	24.0	23.4
2005	24.1	24.1	24.4	24.7	24.8	25.0	25.1	25.2	25.6	25.6	25.7	25.7	25.0
2006	25.8	26.1	26.5	26.9	27.2	27.4	27.5	27.5	27.7	27.4	27.3	27.4	27.1
2007	26.7	26.7	26.9	26.9	27.0	27.2	27.0	26.9	26.7	26.3	26.3	26.1	26.7
2008	25.9	25.8	25.8	25.8	25.9	26.0	25.8	25.6	25.3	24.9	24.2	23.7	25.4
2009	22.8	22.3	21.9	21.5	21.0	20.7	20.6	20.7	20.7	20.6	20.3	20.2	21.1

Employment by Industry: Las Vegas-Paradise, NV, Selected Years, 1990–2009—*Continued*

(Numbers in thousands, not seasonally adjusted.)

Industry and year	January	February	March	April	May	June	July	August	September	October	November	December	Annual average
Service-Providing													
1990	314.0	314.1	318.0	320.8	324.1	325.9	327.6	330.9	334.1	336.1	341.1	339.0	327.1
2000	591.5	594.0	599.0	602.3	611.0	605.7	603.6	616.0	620.0	624.1	629.3	629.0	610.5
2001	630.3	636.4	640.7	640.3	642.7	640.2	633.4	637.8	643.0	630.7	632.6	632.5	636.7
2002	624.5	628.5	635.1	638.4	643.2	639.3	634.6	638.0	643.9	650.3	653.6	654.8	640.4
2003	647.4	652.1	656.5	656.0	660.8	657.2	655.9	661.8	669.8	676.5	679.1	682.8	662.9
2004	677.4	679.2	686.6	695.1	698.5	698.3	696.1	698.6	708.9	719.7	721.6	723.4	700.3
2005	714.7	720.1	728.2	742.7	745.3	746.4	741.9	743.5	755.5	761.0	767.4	770.4	744.8
2006	760.6	767.3	774.9	778.7	783.8	783.9	776.9	778.2	787.1	791.1	795.6	795.6	781.1
2007	785.1	794.3	796.0	799.4	804.0	801.2	789.7	789.1	795.1	804.3	808.8	810.8	798.2
2008	798.2	800.0	802.7	805.5	807.9	801.0	788.3	786.1	792.0	788.8	783.8	775.8	794.2
2009	756.4	753.2	748.6	745.5	745.8	739.6	727.9	724.5	733.7	740.3	735.2	735.5	740.5
Trade, Transportation, and Utilities													
1990	63.9	63.4	64.6	65.2	65.6	65.9	66.4	67.1	67.5	68.1	70.0	71.4	66.6
2000	117.1	116.6	116.2	117.2	118.1	118.7	118.9	121.1	122.2	123.8	126.4	128.9	120.4
2001	126.0	125.0	125.2	126.3	127.1	128.0	128.1	128.3	128.1	128.0	129.9	130.9	127.6
2002	126.4	125.3	125.9	128.0	128.2	128.4	128.5	128.6	129.3	131.4	133.1	135.2	129.0
2003	129.3	129.1	130.3	129.4	130.0	130.6	130.9	132.7	134.0	136.9	139.8	142.2	132.9
2004	135.2	135.0	136.4	137.1	137.9	139.6	139.8	140.5	141.1	143.7	146.8	149.0	140.2
2005	143.7	143.2	144.0	145.6	146.2	147.3	148.2	149.0	150.6	151.8	155.2	157.2	148.5
2006	152.6	152.1	153.7	153.8	154.8	155.3	155.3	155.9	156.8	158.0	161.4	163.3	156.1
2007	158.4	157.7	158.4	158.8	160.0	160.7	160.0	161.0	161.0	162.1	166.6	168.9	161.1
2008	163.2	161.2	161.6	161.0	160.9	160.9	161.1	161.1	160.3	159.5	160.4	160.0	160.9
2009	152.8	150.0	149.0	147.5	147.5	147.4	146.5	146.4	147.1	149.9	146.8	146.1	148.1
Wholesale Trade													
1990	10.3	10.3	10.6	10.6	10.6	10.8	10.7	10.8	10.8	10.9	10.9	11.0	10.7
2000	17.1	17.1	17.3	17.7	17.8	17.9	17.8	18.0	18.0	17.9	18.1	18.2	17.7
2001	19.0	19.1	19.3	19.6	19.7	20.0	19.8	19.9	19.9	19.8	19.8	19.9	19.7
2002	19.5	19.7	19.9	20.0	20.0	20.1	19.9	20.0	20.0	20.1	20.1	20.2	20.0
2003	19.7	19.8	19.8	19.7	19.7	19.8	19.9	19.8	19.8	20.0	20.1	20.2	19.8
2004	19.9	20.0	20.1	20.2	20.2	20.4	20.7	20.7	20.8	21.1	21.1	21.2	20.5
2005	21.2	21.4	21.6	21.9	22.0	22.2	22.4	22.5	22.7	22.6	22.7	22.9	22.2
2006	22.8	23.0	23.2	23.4	23.6	23.6	23.7	23.8	24.0	23.9	23.9	24.1	23.6
2007	23.8	23.9	24.0	24.0	24.2	24.3	24.2	24.3	24.3	24.2	24.2	24.2	24.1
2008	24.0	24.0	24.1	23.9	24.0	24.0	24.1	24.1	24.0	23.7	23.4	23.1	23.9
2009	22.5	22.2	21.9	21.6	21.4	21.2	21.1	21.0	21.0	21.0	21.2	21.4	21.5
Retail Trade													
1990	40.0	39.4	40.1	40.6	41.0	41.0	41.5	42.1	42.3	42.8	44.3	45.5	41.7
2000	73.0	72.4	71.5	72.4	73.2	73.5	73.5	75.3	76.0	77.2	79.3	81.7	74.9
2001	78.5	77.3	77.2	77.8	78.2	78.9	79.1	79.3	79.5	79.6	81.7	82.8	79.2
2002	79.0	77.9	78.3	79.4	79.8	80.2	80.0	79.9	80.4	82.1	85.0	87.3	80.8
2003	81.9	81.3	82.3	81.6	82.3	82.7	83.0	84.6	85.5	87.8	90.4	92.4	84.6
2004	85.9	85.4	86.3	87.2	87.9	89.1	88.7	89.3	89.7	91.3	94.5	96.7	89.3
2005	91.6	90.7	91.1	91.7	91.9	92.6	93.5	93.9	94.9	96.1	99.0	100.5	94.0
2006	96.1	95.4	96.3	96.1	96.6	97.0	96.7	97.1	97.4	98.7	101.6	103.1	97.7
2007	98.7	97.8	98.1	98.5	99.2	99.5	99.4	99.9	99.6	100.2	104.1	106.2	100.1
2008	101.6	99.9	100.0	99.6	99.2	99.4	99.4	99.3	98.8	98.5	99.8	100.0	99.6
2009	94.5	92.2	91.6	90.6	90.8	90.9	90.5	90.6	91.5	91.0	90.5	90.0	91.5
Transportation and Utilities													
1990	13.7	13.6	13.9	14.0	14.0	14.0	14.1	14.2	14.5	14.5	14.8	15.0	14.2
2000	27.0	27.1	27.4	27.2	27.1	27.3	27.6	27.9	28.3	28.8	29.1	29.0	27.8
2001	28.4	28.6	28.7	28.9	29.1	29.1	29.2	29.1	28.9	28.6	28.3	28.1	28.8
2002	27.8	27.6	27.7	28.6	28.4	28.2	28.6	28.7	28.9	29.2	28.1	27.8	28.3
2003	27.7	28.0	28.2	28.1	28.0	28.1	28.0	28.3	28.7	29.1	29.3	29.6	28.4
2004	29.4	29.6	30.0	29.7	29.8	30.1	30.4	30.5	30.6	31.3	31.2	31.1	30.3
2005	30.9	31.1	31.3	32.0	32.3	32.5	32.3	32.6	33.0	33.1	33.5	33.8	32.4
2006	33.7	33.7	34.2	34.3	34.6	34.7	34.9	35.0	35.4	35.4	35.9	36.1	34.8
2007	35.9	36.0	36.3	36.3	36.6	36.9	36.4	36.8	37.1	37.7	38.3	38.5	36.9
2008	37.6	37.3	37.5	37.5	37.7	37.5	37.6	37.7	37.5	37.3	37.2	36.9	37.4
2009	35.8	35.6	35.5	35.3	35.3	35.3	34.9	34.8	34.6	34.9	35.1	34.7	35.2
Information													
1990	5.8	5.9	6.4	6.1	6.2	6.3	6.2	6.3	6.2	6.2	6.2	6.2	6.2
2000	13.1	12.7	13.1	12.9	13.7	13.4	13.1	13.4	13.2	13.6	13.8	13.1	13.3
2001	14.0	15.6	15.4	14.1	14.0	13.3	12.4	12.2	11.8	12.2	12.6	12.1	13.3
2002	12.1	11.9	11.6	11.7	11.8	11.4	11.2	11.2	11.2	11.0	11.1	11.0	11.4
2003	10.6	10.4	10.3	10.4	10.6	10.5	10.2	10.0	10.0	10.1	10.2	10.3	10.3
2004	10.2	10.0	10.0	11.1	10.5	10.4	10.4	10.2	10.1	10.5	10.4	10.1	10.3
2005	10.5	10.1	10.1	10.6	11.0	10.4	10.1	10.2	10.2	10.6	10.5	10.3	10.4
2006	10.8	10.8	10.5	10.9	10.9	11.0	11.5	11.5	11.1	11.1	11.0	10.8	11.0
2007	11.3	11.6	11.3	11.4	11.6	11.5	10.9	11.3	10.9	11.4	11.4	11.1	11.3
2008	11.0	11.1	11.1	11.3	11.8	11.2	10.8	10.8	10.7	11.0	10.6	10.2	11.0
2009	9.8	9.9	10.0	9.5	9.5	9.6	9.6	9.7	9.4	9.6	9.4	9.3	9.6

Employment by Industry: Las Vegas-Paradise, NV, Selected Years, 1990–2009—*Continued*

(Numbers in thousands, not seasonally adjusted.)

Industry and year	January	February	March	April	May	June	July	August	September	October	November	December	Annual average
Financial Activities													
1990	19.7	20.0	20.0	20.3	20.5	20.8	21.1	21.0	21.0	20.7	21.1	21.2	20.6
2000	36.9	37.0	37.4	37.4	37.5	37.9	38.3	38.5	38.6	38.3	38.9	39.2	38.0
2001	40.0	40.2	40.7	40.5	40.7	41.0	41.1	41.7	41.8	41.3	41.0	41.6	41.0
2002	40.5	41.0	41.2	41.3	41.3	41.5	41.6	41.5	41.4	41.8	42.3	42.3	41.5
2003	42.1	42.3	42.5	42.8	43.5	43.5	43.9	44.1	44.3	44.4	44.3	44.5	43.5
2004	44.6	44.8	44.9	45.3	45.4	45.8	46.5	46.6	46.7	47.6	47.7	48.4	46.2
2005	47.7	47.6	48.3	48.2	48.4	48.9	48.9	49.1	49.7	49.4	49.6	49.9	48.8
2006	49.0	49.0	49.6	49.6	50.0	50.4	50.5	50.6	50.9	50.6	50.8	51.3	50.2
2007	50.4	50.4	50.7	50.2	50.5	50.6	50.0	49.8	49.7	49.4	48.9	49.0	50.0
2008	48.0	48.1	48.2	48.0	47.9	48.0	47.5	47.1	47.0	46.9	46.4	45.9	47.4
2009	44.1	43.9	43.5	43.2	43.0	43.0	41.8	41.7	41.4	41.8	41.5	41.4	42.5
Professional and Business Services													
1990	34.4	33.2	33.9	33.9	34.8	35.0	34.8	35.9	35.7	36.0	37.9	36.0	35.1
2000	70.9	71.9	72.5	73.7	74.8	74.9	72.5	75.1	77.9	77.1	78.1	76.0	74.6
2001	80.8	82.4	82.6	80.6	81.6	80.5	78.3	80.6	79.9	78.3	78.7	76.8	80.1
2002	80.0	79.7	81.2	80.5	81.3	80.0	79.7	82.3	82.9	82.4	83.2	81.9	81.3
2003	85.4	85.7	85.4	84.8	85.1	83.5	85.1	87.8	88.0	89.5	88.7	88.3	86.4
2004	93.6	92.2	92.6	94.4	95.1	95.0	95.2	97.0	97.6	101.5	99.3	97.8	95.9
2005	101.5	102.4	103.6	104.9	104.6	105.0	104.4	106.3	107.0	109.7	112.2	112.1	106.1
2006	113.0	114.2	115.3	115.5	116.3	116.6	114.4	115.6	115.2	115.6	116.2	114.0	115.2
2007	116.9	119.5	117.5	117.9	117.9	116.9	113.6	115.3	113.8	116.3	115.3	113.1	116.2
2008	115.9	115.1	115.0	115.0	116.0	113.6	109.8	110.0	110.8	107.9	106.7	103.0	111.6
2009	105.5	103.6	101.4	99.3	99.6	98.5	94.6	95.3	97.3	99.9	101.0	102.4	99.9
Education and Health Services													
1990	19.4	19.7	19.8	20.0	20.3	20.4	20.3	20.6	20.9	21.2	21.6	21.9	20.5
2000	39.1	39.5	39.9	39.9	40.2	40.4	40.6	40.8	41.5	42.1	42.5	43.0	40.8
2001	43.3	43.8	44.2	44.5	44.9	45.2	45.0	45.8	46.0	46.0	46.2	46.6	45.1
2002	46.0	46.6	47.1	47.4	48.0	47.8	47.8	48.0	48.2	48.8	49.1	49.2	47.8
2003	48.7	49.5	49.7	50.0	50.4	50.3	50.1	50.6	51.2	51.4	52.0	52.2	50.5
2004	51.9	52.6	53.2	53.6	53.5	53.6	54.0	54.3	55.2	55.6	55.7	56.0	54.1
2005	55.8	56.4	57.0	57.7	57.9	58.1	57.6	57.7	58.1	58.0	58.4	59.0	57.6
2006	58.5	59.1	59.8	59.4	59.6	60.2	59.3	59.8	60.7	61.2	61.7	62.1	60.1
2007	61.5	62.4	62.7	62.6	63.2	63.4	63.3	63.5	64.0	64.6	64.9	64.7	63.4
2008	64.6	65.3	65.6	66.3	66.5	66.6	66.2	66.5	67.0	67.2	67.5	67.6	66.4
2009	66.4	66.9	66.9	66.9	67.3	67.5	67.3	67.6	67.7	68.4	68.7	69.2	67.6
Leisure and Hospitality													
1990	122.1	123.4	123.9	125.7	127.0	128.3	131.8	133.4	132.5	132.0	132.1	130.0	128.5
2000	228.1	228.8	230.9	232.0	233.8	235.2	235.5	238.5	237.2	237.2	236.6	235.7	234.1
2001	235.7	236.4	238.9	238.7	239.8	239.3	239.8	239.8	239.1	228.5	227.8	228.1	236.0
2002	225.6	226.8	230.0	232.0	234.3	234.2	233.7	234.0	233.6	233.6	233.0	233.3	232.0
2003	233.3	234.0	236.5	237.2	239.2	239.6	240.1	241.3	241.2	240.9	240.2	240.9	238.7
2004	240.8	240.5	243.2	247.1	248.4	249.4	249.9	250.4	250.5	250.1	250.8	251.0	247.7
2005	249.2	250.7	253.7	263.9	264.8	267.5	267.2	266.6	268.3	266.2	265.0	264.8	262.3
2006	264.4	266.3	269.4	271.7	273.8	275.3	274.9	274.1	274.7	272.8	271.8	271.5	271.7
2007	268.3	270.4	272.1	273.4	275.1	276.1	274.4	272.1	272.6	273.5	273.8	275.4	273.1
2008	271.1	271.3	272.4	274.1	274.7	275.1	271.1	269.9	268.4	265.0	261.4	258.9	269.5
2009	253.7	253.0	251.9	253.6	254.2	253.1	251.5	248.4	249.0	247.9	245.9	245.7	250.7
Other Services													
1990	10.6	10.6	10.7	10.7	10.8	11.0	11.0	11.2	11.1	11.2	11.1	11.0	10.9
2000	17.7	18.0	18.4	18.3	18.6	18.9	18.8	18.9	18.9	18.9	18.9	18.9	18.6
2001	18.8	19.1	19.5	19.8	20.2	20.6	20.1	20.5	20.5	19.9	19.6	19.6	19.9
2002	19.8	20.1	20.5	20.3	20.6	20.7	20.4	20.5	20.3	20.2	20.0	20.0	20.3
2003	19.7	19.9	20.2	19.9	20.1	20.5	20.5	20.6	20.6	20.4	20.6	20.8	20.3
2004	20.9	21.5	22.2	22.4	22.9	23.5	22.9	22.9	23.1	23.5	23.3	23.4	22.7
2005	22.3	22.6	22.9	23.0	23.3	23.7	23.7	23.8	24.1	24.0	24.2	24.5	23.5
2006	23.7	23.9	24.3	24.3	24.7	25.1	25.1	25.3	25.5	25.3	25.2	25.1	24.8
2007	24.5	24.5	25.0	25.2	25.6	26.0	25.9	26.0	26.0	25.8	25.9	26.2	25.6
2008	25.8	25.6	25.8	25.7	26.1	26.2	25.9	26.1	26.1	25.7	25.1	24.6	25.7
2009	23.5	23.4	23.5	23.7	23.9	24.0	23.6	23.7	23.7	23.6	23.4	23.3	23.6
Government													
1990	38.1	37.9	38.7	38.9	38.9	38.2	36.0	35.4	39.2	40.7	41.1	41.3	38.7
2000	68.6	69.5	70.6	70.9	74.3	66.3	65.9	69.7	70.5	73.1	74.1	74.2	70.6
2001	71.7	73.9	74.2	75.8	74.4	72.3	68.6	68.9	75.8	76.5	76.8	76.8	73.8
2002	74.1	77.1	77.6	77.2	77.7	75.3	71.7	71.9	77.0	81.1	81.8	81.9	77.0
2003	78.3	81.2	81.6	81.5	81.9	78.7	75.1	74.7	80.5	82.9	83.3	83.6	80.2
2004	80.2	82.6	84.1	84.1	84.8	81.0	77.4	76.7	84.6	87.2	87.6	87.7	83.2
2005	84.0	87.1	88.6	88.8	89.1	85.5	81.8	80.8	87.5	91.3	92.3	92.6	87.5
2006	88.6	91.9	92.3	93.5	93.7	90.0	85.9	85.4	92.2	96.5	97.5	97.5	92.1
2007	93.8	97.8	98.3	99.9	100.1	96.0	91.6	90.1	97.1	101.2	102.0	102.4	97.5
2008	98.6	102.3	103.0	104.1	104.0	99.4	95.9	94.6	101.7	105.6	105.7	105.6	101.7
2009	100.6	102.5	102.4	101.8	100.8	96.5	93.0	91.7	98.1	99.2	98.5	98.1	98.6

Employment by Industry: Louisville-Jefferson County, KY-IN, Selected Years, 1990–2009

(Numbers in thousands, not seasonally adjusted.)

Industry and year	January	February	March	April	May	June	July	August	September	October	November	December	Annual average
Total Nonfarm													
1990	496.9	498.2	502.7	506.9	513.9	518.1	513.8	518.0	519.7	518.6	519.1	518.8	512.1
2000	609.9	612.0	617.4	619.6	624.7	629.6	620.7	623.6	622.3	621.1	622.3	621.7	620.4
2001	605.0	606.0	608.3	611.5	615.9	615.1	606.3	609.6	607.0	605.5	605.7	602.4	608.2
2002	586.1	587.1	591.2	596.0	601.4	601.9	594.6	600.6	599.9	600.6	602.5	602.7	597.1
2003	585.5	585.5	590.9	594.2	599.0	601.7	591.3	596.9	598.1	599.3	601.4	603.5	595.6
2004	586.4	587.7	593.2	597.5	599.5	602.9	593.2	603.1	604.2	606.2	609.6	609.3	599.4
2005	591.4	594.4	598.1	604.2	608.2	613.2	601.9	609.7	612.5	613.6	617.2	615.9	606.7
2006	600.9	603.3	611.4	615.7	621.8	625.3	611.1	620.3	622.7	616.5	619.5	626.4	616.2
2007	611.6	611.7	615.0	623.4	631.6	635.8	623.1	626.3	628.8	627.2	633.0	630.7	624.9
2008	615.2	615.6	617.8	623.2	633.0	631.7	619.5	624.4	619.5	618.4	621.5	615.5	621.3
2009	592.0	591.4	593.0	597.3	599.9	599.5	592.8	595.3	595.2	596.7	600.8	595.5	595.8
Total Private													
1990	428.8	429.6	433.6	438.2	444.6	450.3	449.6	453.6	452.4	450.5	450.8	450.3	444.4
2000	534.7	534.9	539.6	540.6	543.9	549.0	547.0	547.6	545.7	544.3	545.5	545.1	543.2
2001	528.9	528.9	530.9	533.4	537.5	538.4	533.9	534.1	529.0	527.8	527.3	524.8	531.2
2002	510.3	510.1	514.1	518.3	524.1	525.8	523.6	526.5	523.6	523.6	525.4	525.7	520.9
2003	509.9	509.0	513.8	515.6	520.4	523.3	520.1	522.8	521.4	522.1	523.9	526.7	519.1
2004	511.1	510.9	516.0	519.8	522.1	525.7	520.6	528.4	526.7	528.9	531.9	532.4	522.9
2005	514.8	517.0	520.3	526.1	529.7	535.1	527.8	533.6	533.9	534.9	538.2	537.2	529.1
2006	523.1	524.5	532.3	536.2	541.9	546.0	535.6	542.1	541.6	536.5	539.3	546.6	537.1
2007	533.2	532.5	535.4	542.4	550.3	554.8	546.5	547.4	548.2	547.2	552.6	550.2	545.1
2008	535.1	534.5	536.4	541.9	551.3	550.5	542.8	545.6	538.7	537.1	540.0	534.4	540.7
2009	512.0	511.3	512.4	515.7	517.8	518.3	514.8	514.9	512.4	513.6	518.0	513.2	514.5
Goods-Producing													
1990	111.2	111.6	112.5	113.7	114.9	116.5	116.8	117.2	116.8	115.6	114.9	114.4	114.7
2001	126.6	126.9	127.2	128.1	128.4	128.6	126.7	126.0	124.8	124.5	123.0	121.5	126.0
2002	117.5	117.2	117.5	118.6	118.5	119.6	119.6	120.6	120.4	119.8	119.1	118.8	118.9
2003	114.3	113.7	114.3	114.4	114.8	115.5	115.3	115.8	115.7	116.7	115.7	116.5	115.2
2004	113.9	112.7	113.7	115.6	115.9	116.6	110.6	117.2	117.3	116.8	117.0	116.2	115.3
2005	112.8	112.9	113.7	114.9	115.2	116.9	111.3	116.0	115.5	115.4	115.7	114.5	114.6
2006	112.1	111.8	112.5	113.3	114.3	115.6	109.4	115.2	114.7	109.6	109.3	113.3	112.6
2007	110.2	109.4	107.8	112.1	113.7	115.3	109.5	110.6	113.6	109.2	112.7	109.7	111.2
2008	108.0	108.2	108.5	108.2	111.6	110.5	105.8	108.4	106.1	105.0	107.3	102.7	107.5
2009	97.0	97.1	95.9	96.9	96.0	95.9	94.3	95.2	94.8	94.8	94.3	92.2	95.4
Mining, Logging, and Construction													
1990	22.5	22.8	23.7	24.4	25.3	26.2	26.8	27.2	26.6	26.1	25.5	24.9	25.2
2000	31.8	31.9	33.4	34.0	34.5	35.1	35.5	35.0	34.9	34.4	34.0	33.8	34.0
2001	31.0	31.6	32.2	33.9	34.7	35.5	35.5	35.0	34.1	33.8	33.1	32.2	33.6
2002	30.4	30.7	31.1	31.9	32.0	33.6	33.9	34.2	34.3	33.8	33.6	33.1	32.8
2003	30.8	30.3	31.2	32.1	32.4	32.9	33.4	33.4	33.2	34.2	33.6	33.6	32.6
2004	31.6	31.0	32.1	33.7	34.1	35.0	36.0	35.6	35.7	35.3	35.0	34.4	34.1
2005	31.5	32.1	32.8	34.1	34.7	36.2	37.1	36.2	35.8	35.9	35.5	34.8	34.7
2006	32.5	32.2	32.9	33.4	34.1	34.6	34.7	34.4	34.1	33.6	33.2	33.0	33.6
2007	30.7	30.2	31.8	33.2	34.3	35.2	35.8	35.6	35.5	35.2	35.0	34.3	33.9
2008	32.2	31.9	32.4	34.0	35.2	35.8	35.8	35.8	35.5	35.3	34.6	33.8	34.4
2009	31.3	30.6	30.5	30.9	30.8	31.1	31.2	31.0	30.9	31.4	30.7	28.5	30.7
Manufacturing													
1990	88.7	88.8	88.8	89.3	89.0	90.3	90.0	90.0	90.2	89.5	89.4	89.5	89.5
2000	96.8	96.5	96.5	96.0	95.8	96.2	96.6	96.7	96.7	97.2	97.4	97.5	96.7
2001	95.6	95.3	95.0	94.2	93.7	93.1	91.2	91.0	90.7	90.7	89.9	89.3	92.5
2002	87.1	86.5	86.4	86.7	85.9	86.0	85.7	86.4	86.1	86.0	85.5	85.7	86.2
2003	83.5	83.4	83.1	82.3	82.4	82.6	81.9	82.4	82.5	82.5	82.1	82.9	82.6
2004	82.3	81.7	81.6	81.9	81.8	81.6	74.6	81.6	81.6	81.5	82.0	81.8	81.2
2005	81.3	80.8	80.9	80.8	80.5	80.7	74.2	79.8	79.7	79.5	80.2	79.7	79.8
2006	79.6	79.6	79.6	79.9	80.2	81.0	74.7	80.8	80.6	76.0	76.1	80.3	79.0
2007	79.5	79.2	76.0	78.9	79.4	80.1	73.7	75.0	78.1	74.0	77.7	75.4	77.3
2008	75.8	76.3	76.1	74.2	76.4	74.7	70.0	72.6	70.6	69.7	72.7	68.9	73.2
2009	65.7	66.5	65.4	66.0	65.2	64.8	63.1	64.2	63.9	63.4	63.6	63.7	64.6
Service-Providing													
1990	385.7	386.6	390.2	393.2	399.0	401.6	397.0	400.8	402.9	403.0	404.2	404.4	397.4
2000	481.3	483.6	487.5	489.6	494.4	498.3	488.6	491.9	490.7	489.5	490.9	490.4	489.7
2001	478.4	479.1	481.1	483.4	487.5	486.5	479.6	483.6	482.2	481.0	482.7	480.9	482.2
2002	468.6	469.9	473.7	477.4	482.9	482.3	475.0	480.0	479.5	480.8	483.4	483.9	478.1
2003	471.2	471.8	476.6	479.8	484.2	486.2	476.0	481.1	482.4	482.6	485.7	487.0	480.4
2004	472.5	475.0	479.5	481.9	483.6	486.3	482.6	485.9	486.9	489.4	492.6	493.1	484.1
2005	478.6	481.5	484.4	489.3	493.0	496.3	490.6	493.7	497.0	498.2	501.5	501.4	492.1
2006	488.8	491.5	498.9	502.4	507.5	509.7	501.7	505.1	508.0	506.9	510.2	513.1	503.7
2007	501.4	502.3	507.2	511.3	517.9	520.5	513.6	515.7	515.2	518.0	520.3	521.0	513.7
2008	507.2	507.4	509.3	515.0	521.4	521.2	513.7	516.0	513.4	513.4	514.2	512.8	513.8
2009	495.0	494.3	497.1	500.4	503.9	503.6	498.5	500.1	500.4	501.9	506.5	503.3	500.4

Employment by Industry: Louisville-Jefferson County, KY-IN, Selected Years, 1990–2009—*Continued*

(Numbers in thousands, not seasonally adjusted.)

Industry and year	January	February	March	April	May	June	July	August	September	October	November	December	Annual average
Trade, Transportation, and Utilities													
1990	118.2	117.2	117.7	117.6	118.6	119.9	120.4	121.7	121.3	122.2	122.7	123.7	120.1
2000	143.1	141.6	142.1	142.4	143.0	143.8	143.7	143.9	142.7	143.1	145.2	146.3	143.4
2001	142.3	140.6	139.9	139.3	139.7	139.3	139.1	139.1	138.0	139.2	140.4	140.7	139.8
2002	135.1	133.8	134.6	134.6	135.4	136.0	135.5	135.9	135.1	134.9	137.3	138.4	135.6
2003	131.2	130.3	130.7	130.1	131.0	131.1	130.5	131.4	131.3	132.3	134.3	136.1	131.7
2004	130.5	129.5	130.2	129.6	130.4	131.2	131.3	131.7	131.4	132.6	134.2	135.4	131.5
2005	130.9	130.0	130.9	131.6	132.4	132.8	132.8	133.0	133.5	134.7	137.8	139.4	133.3
2006	133.9	133.0	135.0	135.5	137.1	138.0	136.4	136.9	137.0	137.5	140.6	142.9	137.0
2007	138.1	136.9	137.8	137.9	139.2	140.7	139.3	139.6	139.8	141.5	143.5	145.2	140.0
2008	138.5	136.6	136.4	136.9	138.4	138.1	136.9	137.4	135.4	135.3	137.6	139.8	137.3
2009	131.1	129.3	129.3	128.7	129.5	129.7	128.4	128.2	127.9	128.3	130.0	130.8	129.3
Wholesale Trade													
1990	25.1	25.2	25.3	25.2	25.3	25.6	25.4	25.6	25.5	25.6	25.5	25.6	25.4
2000	31.4	31.5	31.6	31.4	31.5	31.5	31.2	31.3	31.2	31.4	31.4	31.3	31.4
2001	31.1	31.1	31.0	30.7	30.8	30.6	30.6	30.4	30.3	30.3	29.6	29.5	30.5
2002	29.3	29.3	29.2	29.2	29.3	29.1	29.1	29.6	28.9	29.0	28.9	28.9	29.2
2003	28.5	28.7	28.7	28.5	28.7	28.8	28.7	28.8	29.0	28.9	29.1	29.5	28.8
2004	29.1	29.1	29.2	29.2	29.2	29.3	29.5	29.5	29.3	29.4	29.4	29.5	29.3
2005	29.3	29.4	29.5	29.4	29.5	29.6	29.7	29.6	29.6	29.6	29.7	29.8	29.6
2006	29.9	29.9	30.1	30.0	30.2	30.4	30.1	30.2	30.1	30.2	30.3	30.4	30.2
2007	30.3	30.4	30.5	30.3	30.3	30.4	30.2	30.2	30.2	30.3	30.1	30.2	30.3
2008	29.9	30.0	29.9	30.0	30.1	30.1	30.0	30.0	29.9	29.8	29.6	29.5	29.9
2009	28.7	28.5	28.3	28.2	28.2	28.0	27.8	27.9	27.9	28.2	28.2	27.9	28.2
Retail Trade													
1990	65.3	64.4	64.6	64.5	65.0	65.6	66.0	67.0	66.9	67.3	68.4	69.7	66.2
2000	70.5	69.5	70.0	69.3	70.1	71.2	69.8	70.2	69.7	68.8	71.3	72.8	70.3
2001	69.0	67.8	67.8	67.6	68.4	68.7	67.8	68.1	67.6	68.4	70.3	71.2	68.6
2002	66.7	65.8	66.7	66.7	67.4	68.2	67.5	67.3	67.1	66.7	69.4	70.7	67.5
2003	65.4	64.4	64.8	64.7	65.5	65.7	65.2	65.6	65.4	65.9	68.0	69.3	65.8
2004	64.9	64.0	64.5	64.2	64.8	65.3	65.2	65.4	65.3	65.7	67.5	68.7	65.5
2005	65.0	63.9	64.4	64.8	65.3	65.5	65.2	65.0	64.9	65.7	67.9	69.2	65.6
2006	65.2	64.3	65.2	65.3	65.7	65.4	64.7	64.3	63.8	64.4	66.7	67.7	65.2
2007	64.7	63.7	64.4	64.3	65.1	65.7	65.6	65.3	65.0	65.2	67.3	67.9	65.4
2008	64.6	63.7	64.2	63.8	64.6	64.6	64.4	64.4	63.3	63.5	65.0	65.6	64.3
2009	61.6	60.4	60.7	60.8	61.3	61.5	61.0	60.7	60.3	60.5	61.9	61.9	61.1
Transportation and Utilities													
1990	27.8	27.6	27.8	27.9	28.3	28.7	29.0	29.1	28.9	29.3	28.8	28.4	28.5
2000	41.2	40.6	40.5	41.7	41.4	41.1	42.7	42.4	41.8	42.9	42.5	42.2	41.8
2001	42.2	41.7	41.1	41.0	40.5	40.0	40.7	40.6	40.1	40.5	40.5	40.0	40.7
2002	39.1	38.7	38.7	38.7	38.7	38.7	38.9	39.0	39.1	39.2	39.0	38.8	38.9
2003	37.3	37.2	37.2	36.9	36.8	36.6	36.6	37.0	36.9	37.5	37.2	37.3	37.0
2004	36.5	36.4	36.5	36.2	36.4	36.6	36.6	36.8	36.8	37.5	37.3	37.2	36.7
2005	36.6	36.7	37.0	37.4	37.6	37.7	37.9	38.4	39.0	39.4	40.2	40.4	38.2
2006	38.8	38.8	39.7	40.2	41.2	42.2	41.6	42.4	43.1	42.9	43.6	44.8	41.6
2007	43.1	42.8	42.9	43.3	43.8	44.6	43.5	44.1	44.6	46.0	46.1	47.1	44.3
2008	44.0	42.9	42.3	43.1	43.7	43.4	42.5	43.0	42.2	42.0	43.0	44.7	43.1
2009	40.8	40.4	40.3	39.7	40.0	40.2	39.6	39.6	39.7	39.6	39.9	41.0	40.1
Information													
1990	9.8	9.9	10.0	10.0	10.2	10.2	10.1	10.3	10.2	10.2	10.3	10.5	10.1
2000	12.1	12.0	12.0	12.0	12.0	12.1	12.0	12.0	12.0	12.0	12.0	12.0	12.0
2001	11.9	11.9	12.0	11.9	11.9	11.9	11.9	11.9	11.9	11.9	11.9	11.9	11.9
2002	11.9	11.9	12.0	11.5	11.3	11.4	11.4	11.2	11.2	11.1	11.2	11.3	11.5
2003	11.2	11.2	11.4	10.9	11.0	11.0	11.0	10.8	10.6	10.6	10.5	10.6	10.9
2004	10.4	10.4	10.3	10.2	10.2	10.3	10.3	10.2	10.1	10.0	10.1	10.2	10.2
2005	9.8	9.8	9.8	9.9	10.0	10.1	10.2	10.2	10.1	10.0	10.1	10.2	10.0
2006	9.9	10.0	10.0	10.0	10.1	10.2	10.2	10.2	10.1	10.3	10.3	10.5	10.2
2007	10.5	10.5	10.5	10.5	10.6	10.6	10.7	10.6	10.5	10.4	10.4	10.4	10.5
2008	10.4	10.3	10.4	10.4	10.6	10.9	10.8	10.7	10.5	10.3	10.3	10.2	10.5
2009	10.1	10.0	10.0	9.8	9.9	9.9	9.9	9.9	9.6	9.6	9.7	9.7	9.8
Financial Activities													
1990	31.4	31.3	31.4	31.8	32.0	32.3	32.3	32.3	31.9	31.7	31.7	31.7	31.8
2000	38.0	38.2	37.8	37.8	37.8	38.8	37.3	37.5	37.2	36.9	37.0	37.0	37.6
2001	37.1	37.0	37.3	37.4	37.6	38.0	37.9	38.0	37.7	37.7	37.7	37.9	37.6
2002	38.0	38.2	38.2	38.4	38.6	38.6	37.8	37.9	38.3	38.1	38.2	38.3	38.2
2003	37.7	37.7	38.0	38.2	38.6	39.1	39.2	39.4	39.5	39.3	39.3	39.5	38.8
2004	39.2	39.2	39.3	39.1	39.0	39.1	39.3	39.2	38.8	38.7	39.0	39.4	39.1
2005	39.1	39.1	39.0	39.2	39.2	39.9	39.7	40.1	40.1	40.3	40.4	40.6	39.7
2006	40.8	41.1	41.4	41.5	41.8	42.2	41.9	42.0	42.2	42.1	42.5	43.1	41.9
2007	43.0	43.0	43.1	43.3	43.3	43.6	43.7	43.6	43.3	43.5	43.5	43.5	43.4
2008	43.2	43.4	43.3	43.3	43.5	43.4	43.5	43.6	43.4	43.2	43.3	43.2	43.4
2009	42.9	42.7	42.6	42.6	42.6	42.6	42.6	42.3	41.9	41.6	42.0	42.4	42.4

Employment by Industry: Louisville-Jefferson County, KY-IN, Selected Years, 1990–2009—*Continued*

(Numbers in thousands, not seasonally adjusted.)

Industry and year	January	February	March	April	May	June	July	August	September	October	November	December	Annual average
Professional and Business Services													
1990	40.6	41.1	42.0	43.9	44.6	45.5	45.7	46.4	46.8	45.9	45.7	45.4	44.5
2000	62.6	63.2	64.8	63.5	63.9	64.5	65.5	66.0	66.4	66.8	66.7	66.3	65.0
2001	62.4	62.6	63.2	62.6	62.7	62.8	62.2	63.5	62.9	62.8	62.9	61.8	62.7
2002	60.4	60.5	61.4	61.8	63.4	63.1	62.5	63.9	63.0	63.5	63.8	63.3	62.6
2003	62.6	62.6	63.6	63.8	64.9	64.5	63.2	64.5	64.7	64.7	65.5	65.4	64.2
2004	61.2	62.0	63.2	63.2	63.8	63.8	64.9	66.4	66.9	68.2	69.3	68.9	65.2
2005	65.3	65.9	66.7	67.7	68.0	68.8	68.2	69.0	70.0	70.8	71.8	71.2	68.6
2006	68.0	68.7	71.6	71.2	71.5	72.3	71.5	72.2	73.1	73.0	73.0	73.2	71.6
2007	70.5	71.2	72.6	72.7	74.4	74.6	73.9	74.2	73.9	75.2	75.8	75.2	73.7
2008	72.1	72.2	72.5	74.0	75.3	76.1	74.9	74.9	74.7	74.8	74.5	72.9	74.1
2009	68.6	69.4	69.4	69.6	69.5	69.6	70.1	70.2	70.5	72.1	74.6	72.3	70.5
Education and Health Services													
1990	50.9	51.2	51.6	51.9	52.2	52.8	52.5	53.3	53.4	53.7	54.0	54.1	52.6
2000	65.9	66.4	66.2	65.7	65.8	65.8	66.2	66.7	67.0	66.6	66.5	66.5	66.3
2001	66.9	67.1	67.5	67.4	67.4	67.6	67.2	67.2	67.4	68.1	68.1	68.3	67.5
2002	68.3	68.7	68.8	69.6	69.6	69.9	70.6	70.9	71.0	72.1	72.5	72.7	70.4
2003	72.6	72.9	73.4	73.5	73.3	73.3	73.0	73.3	73.8	73.8	73.9	74.2	73.4
2004	74.1	74.3	74.5	74.6	74.5	74.8	75.1	75.0	75.2	76.5	76.6	77.0	75.2
2005	75.5	76.9	76.3	76.4	76.7	76.7	76.7	76.7	76.8	77.0	76.6	76.6	76.6
2006	75.9	76.2	76.5	77.1	76.9	77.0	76.8	76.6	76.8	77.0	76.9	77.4	76.8
2007	76.7	77.1	77.4	77.7	78.3	78.6	79.2	78.8	78.8	79.6	79.4	79.6	78.4
2008	79.2	79.1	79.3	80.3	80.4	80.4	80.3	80.5	80.4	80.9	80.8	80.9	80.2
2009	80.6	80.5	81.0	81.5	81.6	81.8	81.3	82.3	82.5	83.8	83.2	83.2	81.9
Leisure and Hospitality													
1990	42.3	42.8	43.3	44.5	47.2	47.8	46.8	47.3	47.0	46.4	46.7	45.9	45.7
2000	55.1	55.4	57.0	59.7	61.6	62.7	61.3	60.9	60.0	58.2	57.5	56.4	58.8
2001	52.8	53.8	54.6	57.6	60.6	60.6	59.4	59.1	57.2	55.1	54.8	53.7	56.6
2002	50.7	51.3	52.9	54.8	58.2	57.5	56.9	56.9	55.6	55.0	54.2	53.6	54.8
2003	51.6	51.9	53.4	55.7	57.6	58.9	58.5	58.3	56.9	55.8	55.9	55.3	55.8
2004	53.3	54.0	55.6	58.1	58.8	60.0	59.8	59.4	58.2	57.5	57.3	56.6	57.4
2005	53.2	54.0	55.3	58.2	59.6	61.1	60.6	60.3	59.7	58.4	57.5	56.3	57.9
2006	54.6	55.6	56.9	59.4	61.9	61.9	61.1	60.9	59.9	59.2	59.0	58.2	59.1
2007	56.5	56.7	58.3	60.1	62.4	62.7	62.1	61.9	60.4	60.0	59.5	58.6	59.9
2008	56.4	57.3	58.5	61.1	63.4	62.9	63.0	62.5	61.2	60.2	59.1	57.8	60.3
2009	55.4	56.0	57.8	60.5	62.6	62.4	62.0	60.7	59.4	57.9	58.9	57.1	59.2
Other Services													
1990	24.4	24.5	24.8	24.8	24.9	25.3	25.0	25.1	25.0	24.8	24.8	24.6	24.8
2000	29.3	29.7	29.8	29.5	29.5	30.0	28.9	28.9	28.8	29.1	29.2	29.3	29.3
2001	28.9	29.0	29.2	29.1	29.2	29.6	29.5	29.3	29.1	28.5	28.5	29.0	29.1
2002	28.4	28.5	28.7	29.0	29.1	29.7	29.3	29.2	29.0	29.1	29.1	29.3	29.0
2003	28.7	28.7	29.0	29.0	29.2	29.9	29.4	29.3	28.9	28.9	28.8	29.1	29.1
2004	28.5	28.8	29.2	29.4	29.5	29.9	29.3	29.3	28.8	28.6	28.4	28.7	29.0
2005	28.2	28.4	28.6	28.2	28.6	28.8	28.3	28.3	28.2	28.3	28.3	28.4	28.4
2006	27.9	28.1	28.4	28.2	28.3	28.8	28.3	28.1	27.8	27.8	27.7	28.0	28.1
2007	27.7	27.7	27.9	28.1	28.4	28.7	28.1	28.1	27.9	27.8	27.8	28.0	28.0
2008	27.3	27.4	27.5	27.7	28.1	28.2	27.6	27.6	27.0	27.4	27.1	26.9	27.5
2009	26.3	26.3	26.4	26.1	26.1	26.4	26.2	26.1	25.8	25.5	25.3	25.5	26.0
Government													
1990	68.1	68.6	69.1	68.7	69.3	67.8	64.2	64.4	67.3	68.1	68.3	68.5	67.7
2000	75.2	77.1	77.8	79.0	80.8	80.6	73.7	76.0	76.6	76.8	76.8	76.6	77.3
2001	76.1	77.1	77.4	78.1	78.4	76.7	72.4	75.5	78.0	77.7	78.4	77.6	77.0
2002	75.8	77.0	77.1	77.7	77.3	76.1	71.0	74.1	76.3	77.0	77.1	77.0	76.1
2003	75.6	76.5	77.1	78.6	78.6	78.4	71.2	74.1	76.7	77.2	77.5	76.8	76.5
2004	75.3	76.8	77.2	77.7	77.4	77.2	72.6	74.7	77.5	77.3	77.7	76.9	76.5
2005	76.6	77.4	77.8	78.1	78.5	78.1	74.1	76.1	78.6	78.7	79.0	78.7	77.6
2006	77.8	78.8	79.1	79.5	79.9	79.3	75.5	78.2	81.1	80.0	80.2	79.8	79.1
2007	78.4	79.2	79.6	81.0	81.3	81.0	76.6	78.9	80.6	80.0	80.4	80.5	79.8
2008	80.1	81.1	81.4	81.3	81.7	81.2	76.7	78.8	80.8	81.3	81.5	81.1	80.6
2009	80.0	80.1	80.6	81.6	82.1	81.2	78.0	80.4	82.8	83.1	82.8	82.3	81.3

Employment by Industry: McAllen-Edinburg-Mission, TX, Selected Years, 1990–2009

(Numbers in thousands, not seasonally adjusted.)

Industry and year	January	February	March	April	May	June	July	August	September	October	November	December	Annual average
Total Nonfarm													
1990	100.7	100.0	101.5	102.6	103.6	102.6	97.8	97.9	100.1	102.1	103.4	104.4	101.4
2000	152.9	155.2	157.3	157.1	157.5	157.2	153.0	154.5	157.2	158.2	160.7	162.4	156.9
2001	160.1	161.2	163.0	163.5	163.7	162.9	156.4	158.8	161.6	163.6	165.4	167.3	162.3
2002	165.1	166.1	168.1	168.1	168.1	168.0	161.3	165.6	168.4	170.2	172.9	173.7	168.0
2003	172.1	173.8	174.6	174.9	175.6	175.0	170.0	172.7	176.0	178.0	180.9	183.0	175.6
2004	181.4	182.6	184.0	184.9	186.1	184.7	179.3	183.0	185.2	188.0	191.0	192.6	185.2
2005	189.7	191.9	193.3	196.0	195.4	194.8	187.5	192.3	195.1	198.0	199.9	201.8	194.6
2006	200.8	201.7	202.7	202.2	201.6	201.6	192.8	198.2	201.5	205.4	208.4	209.8	202.2
2007	208.1	208.7	209.9	211.8	211.5	210.6	206.3	210.3	211.9	215.8	218.0	219.4	211.9
2008	218.9	219.9	220.3	221.2	220.9	218.4	212.8	215.4	216.3	221.4	222.1	222.9	219.2
2009	218.7	217.9	217.9	218.9	219.2	216.4	211.4	213.4	214.7	218.0	219.2	220.1	217.2
Total Private													
1990	74.0	73.4	74.5	75.1	76.1	75.8	73.6	73.6	73.6	74.7	75.4	76.0	74.7
2000	113.1	114.5	115.4	115.8	116.3	116.9	115.5	116.1	116.6	116.5	118.4	119.9	116.3
2001	118.4	118.4	120.2	121.0	121.0	121.1	118.6	119.9	119.8	120.3	121.7	123.5	120.3
2002	122.0	122.4	124.0	124.2	124.1	124.5	123.7	125.7	125.6	125.4	127.5	128.4	124.8
2003	127.0	128.5	129.3	129.3	129.8	130.2	130.2	131.4	131.6	132.1	134.1	136.1	130.8
2004	134.9	135.6	136.8	137.6	138.5	138.3	138.0	139.1	138.8	140.3	142.7	144.5	138.8
2005	142.0	143.3	144.6	147.3	146.7	146.7	146.5	147.0	147.5	148.7	150.2	152.1	146.9
2006	150.8	151.0	152.1	152.5	152.0	151.9	151.7	152.4	153.5	154.9	157.4	158.9	153.3
2007	157.9	157.9	158.8	161.2	160.8	160.2	161.3	162.5	161.9	163.9	165.5	166.6	161.5
2008	166.6	167.0	167.1	168.1	167.1	165.9	165.6	166.2	164.4	167.4	167.2	167.8	166.7
2009	164.4	163.1	163.0	164.4	164.1	162.5	162.7	162.4	161.5	162.7	163.3	164.0	163.2
Goods-Producing													
1990	18.1	17.8	17.6	18.1	18.1	18.4	18.2	17.9	17.9	17.8	17.6	17.5	17.9
2000	21.8	22.0	21.9	21.9	22.0	21.9	21.6	21.7	21.9	22.1	22.2	22.3	21.9
2001	22.4	22.6	22.5	22.2	22.2	22.2	21.2	21.1	20.9	21.3	21.4	21.5	21.8
2002	21.0	21.0	21.2	20.6	20.3	20.5	20.4	20.8	20.4	20.1	20.2	20.2	20.6
2003	20.2	20.3	20.3	20.5	20.6	20.4	20.3	20.5	20.5	19.9	20.2	20.3	20.3
2004	19.9	19.9	20.1	19.8	20.0	19.6	19.4	19.4	19.3	19.4	19.4	19.6	19.7
2005	18.8	18.9	19.0	18.8	18.9	19.0	18.6	18.6	18.8	18.9	19.0	19.1	18.9
2006	18.9	19.0	19.2	19.0	18.9	18.9	18.6	18.8	18.9	18.6	19.0	19.2	18.9
2007	19.0	18.9	19.0	19.3	19.3	19.2	18.9	19.5	19.5	19.4	19.4	19.4	19.2
2008	19.3	19.1	19.0	18.7	18.4	18.2	17.6	17.8	17.4	17.9	17.5	17.6	18.2
2009	16.9	16.6	16.3	15.7	15.6	15.4	15.1	15.1	14.9	15.0	14.8	14.8	15.5
Mining, Logging, and Construction													
1990	4.9	5.0	5.1	5.3	5.4	5.5	5.4	5.4	5.3	5.1	5.0	5.0	5.2
2000	9.3	9.4	9.6	9.9	9.9	9.9	9.9	9.9	9.9	9.9	9.9	10.0	9.8
2001	10.1	10.3	10.2	10.2	10.3	10.5	10.5	10.4	10.1	10.3	10.3	10.5	10.3
2002	10.2	10.2	10.4	10.4	10.5	10.8	10.8	11.0	11.0	10.8	10.9	11.0	10.7
2003	10.9	10.9	11.0	11.2	11.3	11.4	11.3	11.4	11.3	11.1	11.1	11.2	11.1
2004	10.8	10.8	11.0	10.9	10.9	10.8	10.8	10.8	10.9	10.7	10.5	10.6	10.8
2005	10.3	10.5	10.5	10.6	10.7	10.9	10.6	10.6	10.7	10.5	10.6	10.6	10.6
2006	10.4	10.6	10.9	10.7	10.8	10.9	11.0	11.1	11.0	10.9	10.9	11.0	10.9
2007	10.9	10.9	11.0	11.1	11.1	11.3	11.4	11.7	11.6	11.3	11.3	11.3	11.2
2008	11.3	11.2	11.1	11.1	10.9	10.8	10.7	10.8	10.6	10.7	10.5	10.5	10.9
2009	10.2	10.0	9.7	9.6	9.4	9.2	9.1	8.9	8.7	8.7	8.6	8.6	9.2
Manufacturing													
1990	13.2	12.8	12.5	12.8	12.7	12.9	12.8	12.5	12.6	12.7	12.6	12.5	12.7
2000	12.5	12.6	12.3	12.0	12.1	12.0	11.7	11.8	12.0	12.2	12.3	12.3	12.2
2001	12.3	12.3	12.3	12.0	11.9	11.7	10.7	10.7	10.8	11.0	11.1	11.0	11.5
2002	10.8	10.8	10.8	10.2	9.8	9.7	9.6	9.8	9.4	9.3	9.3	9.2	9.9
2003	9.3	9.4	9.3	9.3	9.3	9.0	9.0	9.1	9.2	8.8	9.1	9.1	9.1
2004	9.1	9.1	9.1	8.9	9.1	8.8	8.6	8.6	8.4	8.7	8.9	9.0	8.9
2005	8.5	8.4	8.5	8.2	8.2	8.1	8.0	8.0	8.1	8.4	8.4	8.5	8.3
2006	8.5	8.4	8.3	8.3	8.1	8.0	7.6	7.7	7.9	7.7	8.1	8.2	8.1
2007	8.1	8.0	8.0	8.2	8.2	7.9	7.5	7.8	7.9	8.1	8.1	8.1	8.0
2008	8.0	7.9	7.9	7.6	7.5	7.4	6.9	7.0	6.8	7.2	7.0	7.1	7.4
2009	6.7	6.6	6.6	6.1	6.2	6.2	6.0	6.2	6.2	6.3	6.2	6.2	6.3
Service-Providing													
1990	82.6	82.2	83.9	84.5	85.5	84.2	79.6	80.0	82.2	84.3	85.8	86.9	83.5
2000	131.1	133.2	135.4	135.2	135.5	135.3	131.4	132.8	135.3	136.1	138.5	140.1	135.0
2001	137.7	138.6	140.5	141.3	141.5	140.7	135.2	137.7	140.7	142.3	144.0	145.8	140.5
2002	144.1	145.1	146.9	147.5	147.8	147.5	140.9	144.8	148.0	150.1	152.7	153.5	147.4
2003	151.9	153.5	154.3	154.4	155.0	154.6	149.7	152.2	155.5	158.1	160.7	162.7	155.2
2004	161.5	162.7	163.9	165.1	166.1	165.1	159.9	163.6	165.9	168.6	171.6	173.0	165.6
2005	170.9	173.0	174.3	177.2	176.5	175.8	168.9	173.7	176.3	179.1	180.9	182.7	175.8
2006	181.9	182.7	183.5	183.2	182.7	182.7	174.2	179.4	182.6	186.8	189.4	190.6	183.3
2007	189.1	189.8	190.9	192.5	192.2	191.4	187.4	190.8	192.4	196.4	198.6	200.0	192.6
2008	199.6	200.8	201.3	202.5	202.5	200.2	195.2	197.6	198.9	203.5	204.6	205.3	201.0
2009	201.8	201.3	201.6	203.2	203.6	201.0	196.3	198.3	199.8	203.0	204.4	205.3	201.6

Employment by Industry: McAllen-Edinburg-Mission, TX, Selected Years, 1990–2009—*Continued*

(Numbers in thousands, not seasonally adjusted.)

Industry and year	January	February	March	April	May	June	July	August	September	October	November	December	Annual average
Trade, Transportation, and Utilities													
1990	26.3	26.0	26.9	26.9	28.0	27.5	25.5	25.8	25.8	26.5	27.3	27.7	26.7
2000	34.9	34.9	35.4	35.2	35.2	34.9	34.4	34.8	34.8	34.8	35.9	37.0	35.2
2001	35.5	35.0	35.4	35.8	35.4	35.1	34.2	34.3	34.1	34.0	34.7	35.6	34.9
2002	34.5	34.2	34.7	34.8	34.9	34.9	34.7	35.1	35.1	35.0	36.2	37.0	35.1
2003	35.5	35.5	35.8	36.1	36.2	36.3	36.2	36.2	36.2	36.6	37.9	39.2	36.4
2004	38.4	38.3	38.5	39.1	39.1	38.7	38.4	38.7	38.2	38.5	39.7	40.7	38.9
2005	39.4	39.2	39.6	40.8	40.6	40.6	40.7	40.8	40.5	40.8	42.0	42.9	40.7
2006	41.8	41.4	41.9	42.4	42.3	42.1	42.3	42.7	43.2	43.8	45.3	46.0	42.9
2007	44.7	44.3	45.0	45.5	45.2	44.8	45.5	45.8	45.5	46.0	47.3	47.9	45.6
2008	47.0	46.2	46.5	46.7	46.4	46.2	46.3	46.5	45.9	46.5	46.9	47.5	46.6
2009	45.4	44.5	44.6	45.4	45.1	44.9	44.9	45.2	44.9	45.0	45.8	46.3	45.2
Wholesale Trade													
1990	4.3	4.4	4.6	4.8	5.0	4.8	4.2	4.2	4.1	4.3	4.4	4.4	4.5
2000	5.7	5.9	6.1	6.2	6.0	5.8	5.5	5.4	5.4	5.6	5.8	6.0	5.8
2001	5.9	5.9	6.1	6.5	6.3	6.0	5.6	5.5	5.4	5.3	5.4	5.5	5.8
2002	5.6	5.6	5.8	5.8	5.7	5.7	5.6	5.6	5.6	5.6	5.6	5.8	5.7
2003	5.9	6.0	6.1	6.3	6.3	6.3	6.0	5.9	5.9	5.9	6.0	6.3	6.0
2004	6.2	6.2	6.3	6.8	6.9	6.7	6.5	6.5	6.5	6.4	6.6	6.9	6.5
2005	6.8	6.7	6.7	6.9	6.7	6.7	6.6	6.4	6.5	6.6	6.7	6.8	6.7
2006	6.8	6.9	7.0	7.0	6.9	6.8	6.7	6.6	6.6	6.4	6.4	6.5	6.7
2007	6.3	6.4	6.6	6.9	6.8	6.6	6.7	6.6	6.7	7.0	7.0	7.0	6.7
2008	7.1	6.8	6.9	7.2	7.1	6.9	6.7	6.4	6.3	6.8	6.6	6.7	6.8
2009	6.5	6.4	6.3	6.8	6.5	6.3	6.2	6.1	6.0	6.1	6.1	6.1	6.3
Retail Trade													
1990	19.6	19.2	19.8	19.7	20.6	20.2	18.9	19.2	19.3	19.6	20.4	20.8	19.8
2000	24.7	24.4	24.5	24.3	24.3	24.4	24.2	24.7	24.6	24.7	25.6	26.3	24.7
2001	24.9	24.4	24.6	24.6	24.5	24.5	24.1	24.3	24.1	23.9	24.5	25.3	24.5
2002	24.3	24.1	24.3	24.4	24.6	24.6	24.5	24.8	24.9	24.8	25.9	26.5	24.8
2003	25.0	24.8	25.0	24.9	25.0	25.0	25.2	25.2	25.3	25.7	26.8	27.8	25.4
2004	27.0	26.9	26.9	27.0	26.9	26.7	26.5	26.8	26.3	26.7	27.7	28.3	27.0
2005	27.1	27.0	27.3	28.2	28.1	28.0	28.1	28.4	28.0	28.4	29.4	30.1	28.2
2006	28.8	28.3	28.5	29.0	28.9	28.6	29.0	29.4	29.9	30.6	32.0	32.5	29.6
2007	31.6	31.0	31.5	31.7	31.4	31.1	31.7	32.1	31.6	32.1	33.5	34.0	31.9
2008	33.0	32.5	32.6	32.4	32.1	32.1	32.5	33.0	32.5	32.9	33.5	33.9	32.8
2009	32.1	31.4	31.5	31.8	31.7	31.6	31.8	32.2	32.0	32.1	32.8	33.2	32.0
Transportation and Utilities													
1990	2.4	2.4	2.5	2.4	2.4	2.5	2.4	2.4	2.4	2.6	2.5	2.5	2.5
2000	4.5	4.6	4.8	4.7	4.9	4.7	4.7	4.7	4.8	4.5	4.5	4.7	4.7
2001	4.7	4.7	4.7	4.7	4.6	4.6	4.5	4.5	4.6	4.8	4.8	4.8	4.7
2002	4.6	4.5	4.6	4.6	4.6	4.6	4.6	4.7	4.8	4.6	4.7	4.7	4.6
2003	4.6	4.7	4.7	4.9	4.9	5.0	5.0	5.1	5.0	5.0	5.1	5.1	4.9
2004	5.2	5.2	5.3	5.3	5.3	5.3	5.4	5.4	5.4	5.4	5.4	5.5	5.3
2005	5.5	5.5	5.6	5.7	5.8	5.9	6.0	6.0	6.0	5.8	5.9	6.0	5.8
2006	6.2	6.2	6.4	6.4	6.5	6.7	6.6	6.7	6.7	6.8	6.9	7.0	6.6
2007	6.8	6.9	6.9	6.9	7.0	7.1	7.1	7.1	7.2	6.9	6.8	6.9	7.0
2008	6.9	6.9	7.0	7.1	7.2	7.2	7.1	7.1	7.1	6.8	6.8	6.9	7.0
2009	6.8	6.7	6.8	6.8	6.9	7.0	6.9	6.9	6.9	6.8	6.9	7.0	6.9
Information													
1990	0.4	0.4	0.4	0.4	0.4	0.4	0.5	0.4	0.4	0.4	0.4	0.4	0.4
2000	1.3	1.3	1.2	1.3	1.3	1.4	1.4	1.4	1.4	1.3	1.3	1.3	1.3
2001	1.1	1.1	1.1	1.1	1.1	1.2	1.1	1.1	1.1	1.1	1.1	1.1	1.1
2002	1.1	1.1	1.1	1.0	1.1	1.1	1.0	1.0	1.0	0.9	1.0	1.0	1.0
2003	1.0	1.0	1.0	1.0	1.1	1.3	1.4	1.4	1.4	1.5	1.6	1.7	1.3
2004	1.9	1.8	1.8	1.9	1.9	2.0	2.0	2.0	2.0	2.1	2.1	2.1	2.0
2005	2.0	2.0	2.0	2.1	2.1	2.2	2.2	2.2	2.3	2.3	2.3	2.3	2.2
2006	2.2	2.2	2.3	2.2	2.2	2.2	2.1	2.1	2.1	2.3	2.3	2.2	2.2
2007	2.2	2.2	2.2	2.3	2.3	2.3	2.2	2.2	2.1	2.1	2.1	2.2	2.2
2008	2.2	2.2	2.2	2.2	2.2	2.3	2.3	2.3	2.2	2.2	2.3	2.3	2.2
2009	2.2	2.2	2.2	2.2	2.2	2.2	2.2	2.2	2.1	2.1	2.1	2.1	2.2
Financial Activities													
1990	4.6	4.5	4.5	4.6	4.7	4.7	4.5	4.5	4.6	4.5	4.5	4.6	4.6
2000	6.0	5.9	6.0	6.2	6.1	6.1	6.1	6.1	6.1	6.1	6.1	6.2	6.1
2001	6.1	6.1	6.2	6.2	6.2	6.3	6.4	6.4	6.4	6.4	6.5	6.5	6.3
2002	6.5	6.5	6.5	6.6	6.7	6.7	6.7	6.7	6.7	6.8	6.9	7.0	6.7
2003	7.0	7.1	7.1	7.1	7.2	7.3	7.3	7.3	7.3	7.4	7.4	7.4	7.2
2004	7.5	7.5	7.6	7.6	7.5	7.7	7.8	7.7	7.7	7.8	7.9	7.9	7.7
2005	7.9	7.9	8.0	8.1	8.0	8.1	8.2	8.2	8.2	8.3	8.3	8.3	8.1
2006	8.3	8.3	8.4	8.2	8.2	8.3	8.4	8.4	8.4	8.6	8.6	8.7	8.4
2007	8.7	8.7	8.7	8.8	8.8	8.8	8.8	8.8	8.8	8.8	8.9	8.8	8.8
2008	8.9	8.9	8.8	8.9	8.8	8.8	8.8	8.7	8.6	8.5	8.5	8.4	8.7
2009	8.3	8.1	8.1	8.0	8.0	7.9	8.0	7.9	7.8	7.9	7.8	7.9	8.0

Employment by Industry: McAllen-Edinburg-Mission, TX, Selected Years, 1990–2009—*Continued*

(Numbers in thousands, not seasonally adjusted.)

Industry and year	January	February	March	April	May	June	July	August	September	October	November	December	Annual average
Professional and Business Services													
1990	4.5	4.6	4.7	4.9	4.9	5.0	5.3	5.4	5.1	5.3	5.2	5.2	5.0
2000	8.3	8.7	8.9	9.0	9.2	9.6	9.2	9.3	9.2	9.1	9.1	8.9	9.0
2001	9.0	8.9	9.6	10.0	10.1	10.3	10.0	10.4	10.6	10.7	11.0	11.2	10.2
2002	11.1	11.1	11.3	11.3	11.0	11.0	10.7	10.9	10.9	11.3	11.4	11.2	11.1
2003	10.9	11.5	11.2	11.1	11.0	11.1	11.0	11.5	11.6	11.7	11.8	12.0	11.4
2004	11.4	11.5	11.4	11.6	11.8	12.0	12.0	12.3	12.1	12.2	12.4	12.5	11.9
2005	12.3	12.8	13.1	13.4	13.2	13.3	13.3	13.5	13.5	13.5	13.6	13.8	13.3
2006	13.8	14.1	14.3	14.0	13.9	14.1	13.8	13.8	13.9	14.0	14.2	14.6	14.0
2007	14.5	14.6	14.8	14.7	14.7	14.7	14.6	14.6	14.7	14.7	14.8	15.0	14.7
2008	15.2	15.4	15.2	14.8	14.7	14.6	14.6	14.6	14.4	14.9	14.9	14.8	14.8
2009	14.6	14.5	14.3	14.4	14.4	14.2	14.0	13.4	13.3	13.4	13.4	13.4	13.9
Education and Health Services													
1990	8.8	8.8	8.9	8.8	8.8	8.7	8.7	8.8	9.0	9.1	9.2	9.3	8.9
2000	23.3	23.7	23.7	24.0	24.2	24.1	24.3	24.4	24.8	24.8	25.3	25.3	24.3
2001	25.5	25.8	26.1	26.1	26.3	26.4	26.5	27.1	27.4	27.7	27.7	28.0	26.7
2002	28.2	28.4	28.8	29.4	29.7	29.9	30.4	31.0	31.4	31.6	32.1	32.2	30.3
2003	32.4	32.7	33.0	32.9	32.9	32.7	33.1	33.7	34.0	34.3	34.6	34.8	33.4
2004	35.1	35.6	36.0	36.1	36.7	36.8	37.4	37.9	38.7	39.5	40.1	40.5	37.5
2005	40.4	41.0	41.2	41.6	41.7	41.6	41.9	42.3	42.9	43.3	43.5	44.0	42.1
2006	43.6	43.9	43.8	43.9	44.0	44.0	44.0	44.5	44.9	45.0	45.3	45.5	44.4
2007	46.0	46.3	46.3	47.1	47.3	47.1	47.3	47.8	48.2	48.4	48.9	49.0	47.5
2008	49.2	50.1	50.1	50.8	51.0	50.5	50.8	51.0	51.3	52.2	52.5	52.9	51.0
2009	52.4	52.6	52.8	53.7	54.0	53.4	53.9	54.1	54.3	54.9	55.1	55.3	53.9
Leisure and Hospitality													
1990	8.3	8.3	8.4	8.3	8.1	8.1	7.9	7.8	7.8	8.0	8.1	8.2	8.1
2000	13.5	13.9	14.2	14.1	14.2	14.8	14.3	14.3	14.2	14.1	14.3	14.6	14.2
2001	14.5	14.6	15.0	15.1	15.2	15.1	14.8	15.0	14.9	14.8	14.9	15.2	14.9
2002	15.3	15.7	16.0	15.9	15.9	15.9	15.4	15.8	15.8	15.3	15.3	15.4	15.6
2003	15.5	15.9	16.3	16.1	16.2	16.6	16.5	16.4	16.2	16.3	16.2	16.3	16.2
2004	16.2	16.5	16.8	17.0	16.9	16.9	16.4	16.5	16.3	16.3	16.5	16.6	16.6
2005	16.6	16.9	17.0	17.6	17.3	17.0	16.9	16.7	16.6	16.8	16.7	17.0	16.9
2006	17.6	17.5	17.5	17.9	17.6	17.4	17.4	17.1	16.9	17.4	17.4	17.4	17.4
2007	17.9	17.9	17.7	18.3	18.0	18.0	18.6	18.4	17.8	18.9	18.6	18.7	18.2
2008	19.0	19.2	19.3	19.9	19.7	19.4	19.2	19.3	18.8	19.3	18.8	18.7	19.2
2009	19.0	19.0	19.1	19.2	19.0	18.7	19.0	18.9	18.6	18.8	18.7	18.6	18.9
Other Services													
1990	3.0	3.0	3.1	3.1	3.1	3.0	3.0	3.0	3.0	3.1	3.1	3.1	3.1
2000	4.0	4.1	4.1	4.1	4.1	4.1	4.2	4.1	4.2	4.2	4.2	4.3	4.1
2001	4.3	4.3	4.3	4.5	4.5	4.5	4.4	4.5	4.4	4.3	4.4	4.4	4.4
2002	4.3	4.4	4.4	4.6	4.5	4.5	4.4	4.4	4.3	4.4	4.4	4.4	4.4
2003	4.5	4.5	4.6	4.5	4.6	4.5	4.4	4.4	4.4	4.4	4.4	4.4	4.4
2004	4.5	4.5	4.6	4.5	4.6	4.6	4.6	4.6	4.5	4.5	4.6	4.6	4.6
2005	4.6	4.6	4.7	4.9	4.9	4.9	4.7	4.7	4.7	4.8	4.8	4.7	4.8
2006	4.6	4.6	4.7	4.9	4.9	4.9	5.1	5.0	5.2	5.2	5.3	5.3	5.0
2007	4.9	5.0	5.1	5.2	5.2	5.3	5.4	5.4	5.3	5.6	5.5	5.6	5.3
2008	5.8	5.9	6.0	6.1	5.9	5.9	6.0	6.0	5.8	5.9	5.8	5.6	5.9
2009	5.6	5.6	5.6	5.8	5.8	5.8	5.6	5.6	5.6	5.6	5.6	5.6	5.7
Government													
1990	26.7	26.6	27.0	27.5	27.5	26.8	24.2	24.3	26.5	27.4	28.0	28.4	26.7
2000	39.8	40.7	41.9	41.3	41.2	40.3	37.5	38.4	40.6	41.7	42.3	42.5	40.7
2001	41.7	42.8	42.8	42.5	42.7	41.8	37.8	38.9	41.8	43.3	43.7	43.8	42.0
2002	43.1	43.7	44.1	43.9	44.0	43.5	37.6	39.9	42.8	44.8	45.4	45.3	43.2
2003	45.1	45.3	45.3	45.6	45.8	44.8	39.8	41.3	44.4	45.9	46.8	46.9	44.7
2004	46.5	47.0	47.2	47.3	47.6	46.4	41.3	43.9	46.4	47.7	48.3	48.1	46.5
2005	47.7	48.6	48.7	48.7	48.7	48.1	41.0	45.3	47.6	49.3	49.7	49.7	47.8
2006	50.0	50.7	50.6	49.7	49.6	49.7	41.1	45.8	48.0	50.5	51.0	50.9	49.0
2007	50.2	50.8	51.1	50.6	50.7	50.4	45.0	47.8	50.0	51.9	52.5	52.8	50.3
2008	52.3	52.9	53.2	53.1	53.8	52.5	47.2	49.2	51.9	54.0	54.9	55.1	52.5
2009	54.3	54.8	54.9	54.5	55.1	53.9	48.7	51.0	53.2	55.3	55.9	56.1	54.0

Employment by Industry: Memphis, TN-MS-AR, Selected Years, 1990–2009

(Numbers in thousands, not seasonally adjusted.)

Industry and year	January	February	March	April	May	June	July	August	September	October	November	December	Annual average
Total Nonfarm													
1990	483.7	486.6	489.5	494.2	496.9	498.7	493.5	495.4	501.5	496.6	495.5	495.0	493.9
2000	610.6	614.7	623.3	623.5	626.1	627.3	622.3	629.4	628.3	628.7	629.4	629.5	624.4
2001	613.4	615.4	618.7	625.7	623.4	622.7	618.3	621.9	620.0	617.5	616.2	615.2	619.0
2002	603.4	606.9	609.7	613.0	612.6	611.7	610.0	614.2	614.1	618.9	621.5	621.1	613.1
2003	613.0	615.0	618.3	619.6	618.9	614.8	609.0	614.2	616.2	619.9	620.7	620.2	616.7
2004	605.4	610.4	611.5	616.6	614.1	613.3	614.7	620.1	620.9	622.4	624.5	625.3	616.6
2005	610.8	614.7	618.6	625.0	625.6	622.5	626.3	630.9	636.5	632.5	638.0	639.0	626.7
2006	627.8	627.5	632.3	634.2	634.9	633.6	635.5	640.6	643.8	641.2	648.4	649.3	637.4
2007	631.1	632.1	638.1	639.8	641.2	639.8	638.1	643.1	645.3	643.6	648.7	649.2	640.8
2008	632.3	631.3	634.0	636.7	637.6	632.3	631.2	634.2	632.2	630.6	630.9	626.9	632.5
2009	607.9	606.8	605.3	604.0	603.9	601.0	596.8	597.9	596.4	596.3	598.4	595.4	600.8
Total Private													
1990	404.8	405.9	409.2	412.7	416.5	421.1	417.3	420.4	420.8	415.9	414.7	414.2	414.5
2000	528.1	529.8	534.2	537.4	540.6	544.6	543.1	546.3	544.4	542.3	542.8	542.8	539.7
2001	528.7	527.9	530.9	537.4	537.6	540.6	537.1	537.5	533.9	528.6	527.3	527.2	532.9
2002	516.4	516.9	519.4	522.2	523.9	526.9	527.9	528.3	525.6	527.8	529.3	530.3	524.6
2003	522.1	522.0	524.6	527.0	528.7	530.5	526.2	527.8	527.0	528.9	529.6	529.6	527.0
2004	515.3	516.6	519.7	525.4	525.4	528.4	531.7	532.9	530.5	531.3	533.1	535.0	527.1
2005	521.6	524.2	527.9	534.0	536.4	537.8	542.9	543.9	547.2	542.2	547.4	549.2	537.9
2006	539.3	538.4	542.9	545.2	548.0	550.5	552.7	554.7	554.4	550.2	557.9	558.9	549.4
2007	541.3	541.8	548.1	550.5	553.0	556.3	554.8	556.3	556.0	552.9	557.7	559.0	552.3
2008	542.7	540.3	542.9	545.5	547.3	547.4	546.8	546.3	542.6	540.1	540.5	537.7	543.3
2009	519.7	517.7	516.1	514.8	514.4	515.1	511.5	511.7	508.3	507.5	510.0	507.7	512.9
Goods-Producing													
1990	86.6	87.0	87.7	88.5	89.1	89.1	88.3	88.7	88.6	86.7	85.1	84.2	87.5
2000	90.1	90.3	91.2	91.0	91.8	92.4	91.6	91.8	91.2	89.6	88.8	88.2	90.7
2001	85.6	85.4	86.0	86.6	87.0	88.1	86.8	86.7	85.5	83.3	82.5	81.8	85.4
2002	79.0	78.8	79.5	79.9	80.6	81.5	82.0	81.9	81.8	81.0	80.0	79.6	80.5
2003	77.9	78.2	78.5	79.1	79.6	79.9	79.7	79.5	79.5	79.4	78.8	78.4	79.0
2004	76.7	77.1	78.1	78.9	79.3	80.7	80.9	81.0	80.6	79.2	78.9	77.4	79.1
2005	76.5	77.5	78.5	79.6	80.5	81.4	81.8	80.4	82.6	81.6	81.6	79.2	80.1
2006	79.9	80.4	81.3	81.4	82.0	83.0	82.7	82.6	82.5	80.5	79.9	77.5	81.1
2007	77.5	77.9	79.6	79.4	79.8	80.6	80.0	79.4	78.9	78.4	78.0	77.0	78.9
2008	75.6	75.1	75.9	76.5	77.0	77.2	76.4	76.5	75.9	74.5	73.5	72.3	75.5
2009	70.6	69.2	68.8	68.0	68.0	68.3	67.7	67.6	67.5	67.2	66.9	65.2	67.9
Mining, Logging, and Construction													
1990	20.0	20.2	20.4	20.7	21.3	22.0	21.9	21.7	21.4	20.7	20.2	19.9	20.9
2000	26.1	26.4	27.5	27.2	28.0	28.6	27.9	28.1	28.2	27.7	26.8	26.4	27.4
2001	25.6	25.8	26.8	27.0	27.3	27.7	27.6	27.5	27.0	25.6	25.7	25.4	26.6
2002	24.5	24.1	24.6	25.0	25.7	26.2	26.5	26.3	26.6	25.9	25.6	25.5	25.5
2003	24.3	24.2	24.6	25.2	25.7	25.9	26.0	26.1	26.2	26.0	25.8	25.8	25.5
2004	24.9	25.0	25.7	25.9	26.0	26.8	27.2	27.1	27.0	25.7	25.6	25.1	26.0
2005	23.7	24.1	24.7	25.3	26.0	26.7	26.9	27.2	27.6	26.9	26.8	26.7	26.1
2006	25.8	26.0	26.7	27.1	27.7	28.2	28.3	28.2	28.0	27.0	26.5	26.3	27.2
2007	25.5	25.5	26.0	26.3	26.8	27.3	26.9	27.0	26.8	26.5	26.3	26.2	26.4
2008	24.5	24.5	25.0	25.5	25.7	25.8	25.2	25.1	24.7	23.8	23.4	22.9	24.7
2009	21.7	21.4	21.5	21.4	21.5	22.0	21.6	21.6	21.4	21.3	21.2	21.0	21.5
Manufacturing													
1990	66.6	66.8	67.3	67.8	67.8	67.1	66.4	67.0	67.2	66.0	64.9	64.3	66.6
2000	64.0	63.9	63.7	63.8	63.8	63.8	63.7	63.7	63.0	62.4	62.0	61.8	63.3
2001	60.0	59.6	59.2	59.6	59.7	60.4	59.2	59.2	58.5	57.7	56.8	56.4	58.9
2002	54.5	54.7	54.9	54.9	54.9	55.3	55.5	55.6	55.2	55.1	54.4	54.1	54.9
2003	53.6	54.0	53.9	53.9	53.9	54.0	53.7	53.4	53.3	53.4	53.0	52.6	53.6
2004	51.8	52.1	52.4	53.0	53.3	53.9	53.7	53.9	53.6	53.5	53.3	52.3	53.1
2005	52.8	53.4	53.8	54.3	54.5	54.7	54.9	53.2	55.0	54.7	54.8	52.5	54.1
2006	54.1	54.4	54.6	54.3	54.3	54.8	54.4	54.4	54.5	53.5	53.4	51.2	54.0
2007	52.0	52.4	53.6	53.1	53.0	53.3	53.1	52.4	52.1	51.9	51.7	50.8	52.5
2008	51.1	50.6	50.9	51.0	51.3	51.4	51.2	51.4	51.2	50.7	50.1	49.4	50.9
2009	48.9	47.8	47.3	46.6	46.5	46.3	46.1	46.0	46.1	45.9	45.7	44.2	46.5
Service-Providing													
1990	397.1	399.6	401.8	405.7	407.8	409.6	405.2	406.7	412.9	409.9	410.4	410.8	406.5
2000	520.5	524.4	532.1	532.5	534.3	534.9	530.7	537.6	537.1	539.1	540.6	541.3	533.8
2001	527.8	530.0	532.7	539.1	536.4	534.6	531.5	535.2	534.5	534.2	533.7	533.4	533.6
2002	524.4	528.1	530.2	533.1	532.0	530.2	528.0	532.3	532.3	537.9	541.5	541.5	532.6
2003	535.1	536.8	539.8	540.5	539.3	534.9	529.3	534.7	536.7	540.5	541.9	541.8	537.6
2004	528.7	533.3	533.4	537.7	534.8	532.6	533.8	539.1	540.3	543.2	545.6	547.9	537.5
2005	534.3	537.2	540.1	545.4	545.1	541.1	544.5	550.5	553.9	550.9	556.4	559.8	546.6
2006	547.9	547.1	551.0	552.8	552.9	550.6	552.8	558.0	561.3	560.7	568.5	571.8	556.3
2007	553.6	554.2	558.5	560.4	561.4	559.2	558.1	563.7	566.4	565.2	570.7	572.2	562.0
2008	556.7	556.2	558.1	560.2	560.6	555.1	554.8	557.7	556.3	556.1	557.4	554.6	557.0
2009	537.3	537.6	536.5	536.0	535.9	532.7	529.1	530.3	528.9	529.1	531.5	530.2	532.9

Employment by Industry: Memphis, TN-MS-AR, Selected Years, 1990–2009—*Continued*

(Numbers in thousands, not seasonally adjusted.)

Industry and year	January	February	March	April	May	June	July	August	September	October	November	December	Annual average
Trade, Transportation, and Utilities													
1990	136.4	135.9	136.7	136.7	137.8	139.6	138.1	139.8	140.7	139.9	141.6	142.5	138.8
2000	174.3	174.2	175.1	177.2	177.4	178.9	174.8	175.6	175.1	176.9	179.0	180.3	176.6
2001	176.9	174.3	173.9	175.5	175.2	175.3	174.0	174.7	173.9	173.4	174.4	174.7	174.7
2002	169.1	166.8	167.5	168.0	168.3	168.7	169.7	169.5	169.5	170.7	173.8	175.4	169.8
2003	171.4	170.2	170.8	170.9	170.7	170.8	169.8	170.0	170.3	171.1	173.3	174.1	171.1
2004	167.7	167.4	167.8	168.0	168.0	168.5	170.3	170.0	168.9	170.1	172.7	175.3	169.6
2005	169.8	168.7	169.7	170.0	170.5	170.5	173.5	173.2	173.5	172.9	176.2	178.4	172.2
2006	173.6	172.4	173.0	173.3	174.0	173.7	174.7	175.1	174.9	174.7	178.2	179.9	174.8
2007	173.3	172.5	173.8	174.7	175.5	175.6	175.3	175.3	175.6	174.8	178.0	179.1	175.3
2008	172.8	171.4	171.7	171.7	171.6	171.3	170.8	170.2	169.3	168.3	169.9	170.4	170.8
2009	164.4	163.0	162.3	161.0	161.0	160.5	160.2	159.8	159.1	158.6	160.1	160.2	160.9
Wholesale Trade													
1990	33.7	33.7	33.8	33.5	33.7	34.0	34.4	34.2	34.1	33.9	33.8	33.7	33.9
2000	38.2	38.4	38.2	38.1	38.0	38.2	38.2	38.4	38.4	38.3	38.4	38.5	38.3
2001	36.5	36.4	36.5	37.2	37.0	36.9	36.5	36.8	36.7	36.6	36.6	36.1	36.7
2002	36.1	36.0	36.1	36.1	36.2	36.4	36.3	36.2	36.2	36.9	37.1	37.3	36.4
2003	37.9	38.1	38.0	37.7	37.5	37.6	36.7	36.6	36.4	36.2	36.4	36.3	37.1
2004	35.8	35.9	36.2	36.5	36.6	36.9	37.3	37.3	37.1	36.8	36.8	36.8	36.7
2005	36.7	36.8	37.1	37.3	37.4	37.5	37.9	38.0	37.7	37.6	37.6	37.7	37.4
2006	37.3	37.4	37.5	37.5	37.7	37.8	37.8	37.9	37.7	37.3	37.5	37.4	37.6
2007	37.0	37.2	37.3	37.5	37.6	37.6	37.5	37.5	37.6	37.3	37.1	37.0	37.4
2008	36.2	36.0	35.9	36.3	36.1	35.8	35.2	35.2	35.0	34.9	34.7	34.3	35.5
2009	33.6	33.6	33.3	33.4	33.2	33.1	32.7	32.6	32.3	32.1	32.2	32.1	32.9
Retail Trade													
1990	61.9	60.8	61.0	61.9	61.8	62.3	62.4	62.9	63.1	63.6	65.0	65.7	62.7
2000	69.6	68.9	69.6	70.2	70.6	70.8	69.9	69.9	69.6	70.8	72.9	74.2	70.6
2001	73.2	71.7	72.2	72.0	72.0	72.0	71.3	70.5	69.5	70.0	71.8	72.7	71.6
2002	70.4	69.0	69.4	69.6	69.8	70.1	70.4	70.1	70.4	70.4	73.1	74.8	70.6
2003	70.3	69.3	69.8	69.9	69.9	69.8	69.5	69.4	69.9	71.1	73.0	74.3	70.5
2004	69.4	69.3	69.4	69.3	69.4	69.6	70.8	70.3	69.7	70.8	73.0	74.5	70.5
2005	70.5	69.6	69.8	69.8	70.0	70.1	71.5	71.0	71.4	71.4	74.2	75.8	71.3
2006	72.4	71.2	71.8	71.6	71.9	71.8	72.9	72.7	72.6	72.5	75.3	76.3	72.8
2007	72.0	71.0	71.9	72.2	72.5	72.9	72.7	71.8	71.8	71.7	74.8	75.6	72.6
2008	71.6	70.6	71.1	70.5	70.5	70.4	70.5	69.5	68.8	68.4	69.6	69.9	70.1
2009	66.8	65.9	65.8	65.2	65.5	65.7	65.9	65.3	64.9	65.0	66.3	66.4	65.7
Transportation and Utilities													
1990	40.8	41.4	41.9	41.3	42.3	43.3	41.3	42.7	43.5	42.4	42.8	43.1	42.2
2000	66.5	66.9	67.3	68.9	68.8	69.9	66.7	67.3	67.1	67.8	67.7	67.6	67.7
2001	67.2	66.2	65.2	66.3	66.2	66.4	66.2	67.4	67.7	66.8	66.0	65.9	66.5
2002	62.6	61.8	62.0	62.3	62.3	62.2	63.0	63.2	62.9	63.4	63.6	63.3	62.7
2003	63.2	62.8	63.0	63.3	63.3	63.4	63.6	64.0	64.0	63.8	63.9	63.5	63.5
2004	62.5	62.2	62.2	62.2	62.0	62.0	62.2	62.4	62.1	62.5	62.9	64.0	62.4
2005	62.6	62.3	62.8	62.9	63.1	62.9	64.1	64.2	64.4	63.9	64.4	64.9	63.5
2006	63.9	63.8	63.7	64.2	64.4	64.1	64.0	64.5	64.6	64.9	65.4	66.2	64.5
2007	64.3	64.3	64.6	65.0	65.4	65.1	65.1	66.0	66.2	65.8	66.1	66.5	65.4
2008	65.0	64.8	64.7	64.9	65.0	65.1	65.1	65.5	65.5	65.0	65.6	66.2	65.2
2009	64.0	63.5	63.2	62.4	62.3	61.7	61.6	61.9	61.9	61.5	61.6	61.7	62.3
Information													
1990	8.5	8.6	8.6	8.5	8.5	8.6	8.5	8.5	8.5	8.4	8.4	8.4	8.5
2000	10.1	10.1	10.2	10.2	10.3	10.4	10.1	10.4	10.3	10.3	10.5	10.6	10.3
2001	9.4	9.3	9.4	9.6	9.6	9.9	9.6	9.9	9.8	9.9	9.9	9.9	9.7
2002	10.2	10.1	10.2	10.1	10.1	10.0	9.6	10.0	9.8	10.0	10.1	10.0	10.0
2003	9.9	9.8	9.8	9.9	9.7	9.6	9.5	9.5	9.2	9.4	9.3	9.4	9.6
2004	9.0	8.9	8.8	8.8	8.6	8.6	8.5	8.6	8.6	8.6	8.6	8.4	8.7
2005	8.2	8.1	8.2	8.2	8.2	8.0	7.8	7.7	7.6	7.7	7.6	7.4	7.9
2006	7.3	7.3	7.3	7.4	7.5	7.5	7.5	7.5	7.8	7.7	7.8	7.9	7.5
2007	7.4	7.4	7.3	7.4	7.4	7.5	7.5	7.4	7.3	7.3	7.4	7.4	7.4
2008	7.4	7.4	7.4	7.4	7.4	7.4	7.2	7.2	7.2	7.3	7.2	7.3	7.3
2009	7.2	7.1	7.0	7.0	6.9	6.9	6.8	6.8	6.8	6.8	6.8	6.8	6.9
Financial Activities													
1990	26.7	26.7	26.6	26.6	26.6	27.0	26.9	26.9	26.9	26.6	26.4	26.6	26.7
2000	32.6	32.4	32.5	32.8	33.0	33.2	33.7	33.5	33.3	32.6	32.5	32.7	32.9
2001	32.3	32.2	32.2	32.4	32.4	32.5	32.4	32.6	32.5	32.7	32.7	32.4	32.4
2002	32.3	32.4	32.6	32.5	32.6	32.6	32.2	32.3	31.9	32.1	32.3	32.3	32.3
2003	32.5	32.5	32.6	32.7	32.8	32.8	33.0	33.0	32.8	32.8	33.1	33.1	32.8
2004	32.8	32.7	32.6	33.1	33.2	33.2	33.6	33.6	33.4	33.4	33.4	33.5	33.2
2005	32.8	32.7	32.9	32.9	32.9	32.9	32.9	33.0	32.9	32.7	32.8	32.8	32.9
2006	32.7	32.8	32.9	32.7	32.8	33.2	33.1	33.1	33.0	32.5	33.0	33.1	32.9
2007	32.4	32.8	33.0	33.0	33.3	33.6	33.5	33.7	33.5	33.1	33.2	33.2	33.2
2008	32.8	32.7	33.0	32.9	33.0	32.9	32.6	32.5	32.1	32.0	31.9	31.4	32.5
2009	31.2	31.2	31.1	31.1	31.1	31.1	30.9	30.8	30.6	30.6	30.3	30.2	30.9

Employment by Industry: Memphis, TN-MS-AR, Selected Years, 1990–2009—*Continued*

(Numbers in thousands, not seasonally adjusted.)

Industry and year	January	February	March	April	May	June	July	August	September	October	November	December	Annual average
Professional and Business Services													
1990	38.6	39.1	39.8	41.5	42.3	43.1	43.1	43.6	44.0	43.4	43.0	42.7	42.0
2000	70.8	71.2	72.4	70.9	71.8	72.8	76.9	78.5	79.3	78.5	77.6	77.4	74.8
2001	75.3	76.5	77.2	78.5	77.7	77.8	78.4	77.8	78.0	76.4	75.9	76.7	77.2
2002	75.5	77.0	75.8	75.6	74.5	74.9	74.6	74.0	73.6	74.2	74.0	74.2	74.8
2003	72.4	72.3	72.3	73.0	73.6	73.5	71.8	72.9	73.8	74.2	73.8	73.2	73.1
2004	70.2	70.6	70.7	71.9	71.6	72.1	72.9	73.9	73.9	76.1	76.7	77.6	73.2
2005	73.8	75.5	75.2	77.1	77.3	77.2	78.3	80.2	81.3	80.3	81.2	83.8	78.4
2006	79.2	78.9	79.3	79.6	80.0	80.2	81.9	83.5	84.1	83.4	87.2	88.8	82.2
2007	80.4	80.5	81.3	82.0	81.9	81.7	82.7	84.0	85.3	85.4	87.0	87.5	83.3
2008	81.5	81.1	81.0	81.9	81.6	81.5	83.6	84.0	84.1	85.1	85.1	84.0	82.9
2009	77.9	77.8	76.8	75.9	74.9	74.2	73.3	74.4	74.1	74.1	74.8	75.1	75.3
Education and Health Services													
1990	45.7	46.1	46.1	45.6	45.9	45.7	45.8	45.9	46.4	47.1	47.2	47.2	46.2
2000	61.7	62.1	62.4	63.0	63.0	63.1	63.2	63.3	64.0	64.6	65.0	64.8	63.4
2001	63.9	64.4	64.5	64.9	65.1	64.8	65.0	65.4	66.1	65.5	65.6	65.9	65.1
2002	65.8	66.3	66.9	67.3	67.4	66.8	67.2	67.9	68.9	69.5	69.9	69.9	67.8
2003	69.9	70.5	70.6	70.2	70.4	69.9	69.1	69.9	70.4	71.3	71.0	71.2	70.4
2004	70.0	70.8	71.0	71.6	71.5	71.3	71.3	71.6	72.2	72.7	72.6	72.7	71.6
2005	72.4	73.1	73.3	73.7	73.9	73.4	73.4	74.5	75.1	74.5	75.0	74.7	73.9
2006	75.0	74.7	75.4	75.4	75.2	75.2	75.2	75.6	76.1	76.2	76.1	76.2	75.5
2007	76.1	76.3	77.1	76.9	77.4	77.1	77.0	77.8	78.1	78.3	78.4	79.1	77.5
2008	78.6	78.8	79.3	79.2	79.6	79.2	78.5	78.8	79.2	79.7	79.9	79.8	79.2
2009	78.5	79.3	79.5	80.1	80.1	79.9	79.2	79.7	80.1	80.6	81.1	81.1	79.9
Leisure and Hospitality													
1990	43.5	43.7	44.6	46.0	47.1	49.2	47.8	47.9	46.7	44.8	44.2	43.8	45.8
2000	62.2	62.7	63.9	65.4	66.4	68.8	68.8	68.6	66.9	65.3	64.9	64.3	65.7
2001	61.4	61.8	63.4	65.8	66.4	67.8	66.9	66.5	64.4	63.9	62.8	62.3	64.5
2002	61.6	62.6	63.9	65.6	67.0	68.7	68.5	68.8	66.3	66.5	65.4	64.9	65.8
2003	64.2	64.5	65.7	66.8	67.6	69.3	68.8	68.4	66.7	66.5	66.1	66.0	66.7
2004	64.9	65.0	66.3	68.8	68.8	69.1	69.4	69.5	68.1	66.6	65.5	65.3	67.3
2005	63.9	64.2	66.5	67.8	68.4	69.4	70.4	70.3	69.6	68.1	68.6	68.6	67.9
2006	67.5	67.7	69.3	71.0	72.1	72.8	72.9	72.7	71.5	71.2	71.7	71.6	71.0
2007	70.5	70.7	71.9	72.8	73.2	75.3	74.3	74.3	73.1	71.5	71.7	71.7	72.6
2008	70.1	69.8	70.5	71.7	72.5	72.8	72.7	72.1	69.9	68.3	68.1	67.5	70.5
2009	65.1	65.2	65.7	66.8	67.3	68.9	68.1	67.6	65.2	64.8	65.2	64.9	66.2
Other Services													
1990	18.8	18.8	19.1	19.3	19.2	18.8	18.8	19.1	19.0	19.0	18.8	18.8	19.0
2000	26.3	26.8	26.5	26.9	26.9	25.0	24.0	24.6	24.3	24.5	24.5	24.5	25.4
2001	23.9	24.0	24.3	24.1	24.2	24.4	24.0	23.9	23.7	23.5	23.5	23.5	23.9
2002	22.9	22.9	23.0	23.2	23.4	23.7	24.1	23.9	23.8	23.8	23.8	24.0	23.5
2003	23.9	24.0	24.3	24.4	24.3	24.7	24.5	24.6	24.3	24.2	24.2	24.2	24.3
2004	24.0	24.1	24.4	24.3	24.4	24.9	24.8	24.7	24.8	24.6	24.7	24.8	24.5
2005	24.2	24.4	24.6	24.7	24.7	25.0	24.8	24.6	24.6	24.4	24.4	24.3	24.6
2006	24.1	24.2	24.4	24.4	24.4	24.9	24.7	24.6	24.5	24.0	24.0	23.9	24.3
2007	23.7	23.7	24.1	24.3	24.5	24.9	24.5	24.4	24.2	24.1	24.0	24.0	24.2
2008	23.9	24.0	24.1	24.2	24.6	25.1	25.0	25.0	24.9	24.9	24.9	25.0	24.6
2009	24.8	24.9	24.9	24.9	25.1	25.3	25.3	25.0	24.9	24.8	24.8	24.2	24.9
Government													
1990	78.9	80.7	80.3	81.5	80.4	77.6	76.2	75.0	80.7	80.7	80.8	80.8	79.5
2000	82.5	84.9	89.1	86.1	85.5	82.7	79.2	83.1	83.9	86.4	86.6	86.7	84.7
2001	84.7	87.5	87.8	88.3	85.8	82.1	81.2	84.4	86.1	88.9	88.9	88.0	86.1
2002	87.0	90.0	90.3	90.8	88.7	84.8	82.1	85.9	88.5	91.1	92.2	90.8	88.5
2003	90.9	93.0	93.7	92.6	90.2	84.3	82.8	86.4	89.2	91.0	91.1	90.6	89.7
2004	90.1	93.8	91.8	91.2	88.7	84.9	83.0	87.2	90.4	91.1	91.4	90.3	89.5
2005	89.2	90.5	90.7	91.0	89.2	84.7	83.4	87.0	89.3	90.3	90.6	89.8	88.8
2006	88.5	89.1	89.4	89.0	86.9	83.1	82.8	85.9	89.4	91.0	90.5	90.4	88.0
2007	89.8	90.3	90.0	89.3	88.2	83.5	83.3	86.8	89.3	90.7	91.0	90.2	88.5
2008	89.6	91.0	91.1	91.2	90.3	84.9	84.4	87.9	89.6	90.5	90.4	89.2	89.2
2009	88.2	89.1	89.2	89.2	89.5	85.9	85.3	86.2	88.1	88.8	88.4	87.7	88.0

Employment by Industry: Miami-Fort Lauderdale-Pompano Beach, FL, Selected Years, 1990–2009

(Numbers in thousands, not seasonally adjusted.)

Industry and year	January	February	March	April	May	June	July	August	September	October	November	December	Annual average
Total Nonfarm													
1990	1686.3	1700.6	1718.5	1695.5	1699.5	1691.1	1648.0	1650.0	1671.5	1684.4	1697.8	1710.9	1687.8
2000	2116.7	2129.9	2148.8	2147.4	2158.4	2156.1	2117.5	2131.2	2164.6	2167.5	2201.5	2228.1	2155.6
2001	2185.1	2203.3	2220.0	2202.8	2204.0	2199.6	2152.3	2160.2	2187.7	2185.9	2205.0	2224.6	2194.2
2002	2183.5	2192.9	2212.0	2195.9	2201.0	2192.6	2147.1	2156.5	2188.2	2196.1	2220.4	2244.4	2194.2
2003	2197.9	2213.9	2226.2	2208.1	2205.3	2191.1	2145.9	2153.1	2184.0	2201.6	2211.3	2239.1	2198.1
2004	2212.3	2231.9	2249.0	2254.1	2254.5	2245.1	2213.7	2223.8	2239.3	2274.8	2305.8	2334.1	2253.2
2005	2289.6	2313.4	2324.0	2339.1	2341.3	2314.1	2300.5	2340.4	2356.2	2351.4	2370.0	2403.1	2336.9
2006	2359.4	2382.8	2403.7	2390.1	2400.5	2377.1	2346.0	2385.5	2395.2	2398.7	2430.2	2456.4	2393.8
2007	2408.8	2427.3	2443.1	2422.0	2430.1	2401.7	2360.0	2399.8	2407.8	2403.7	2434.7	2456.3	2416.3
2008	2399.6	2413.6	2419.9	2390.7	2384.8	2341.0	2293.8	2319.2	2315.0	2308.2	2320.4	2328.8	2352.9
2009	2258.2	2252.7	2247.4	2225.8	2217.0	2180.5	2145.5	2166.4	2168.3	2174.3	2186.8	2200.1	2201.9
Total Private													
1990	1454.3	1465.4	1477.0	1455.3	1452.4	1451.1	1424.8	1431.7	1432.3	1437.7	1454.8	1467.3	1450.3
2000	1830.0	1842.1	1858.7	1851.4	1856.5	1864.9	1845.7	1858.4	1871.0	1870.1	1902.2	1927.3	1864.9
2001	1886.5	1902.7	1917.7	1899.3	1899.7	1901.0	1873.7	1880.0	1884.0	1878.5	1895.4	1914.1	1894.4
2002	1875.6	1883.8	1899.8	1885.3	1888.4	1887.8	1862.8	1870.1	1877.0	1883.9	1905.6	1927.9	1887.3
2003	1884.2	1898.1	1908.5	1891.7	1886.7	1880.7	1856.0	1861.5	1869.7	1885.0	1894.7	1922.9	1886.6
2004	1897.0	1915.2	1931.5	1935.6	1935.2	1933.0	1921.7	1929.3	1921.7	1953.4	1984.2	2012.1	1939.2
2005	1969.4	1992.0	2001.5	2014.4	2015.9	2017.1	2007.6	2019.6	2032.3	2025.4	2044.7	2077.4	2018.1
2006	2035.1	2057.3	2076.7	2064.7	2074.6	2079.4	2052.5	2063.4	2069.4	2071.5	2099.9	2126.8	2072.6
2007	2082.3	2099.4	2112.9	2091.6	2098.9	2099.6	2062.2	2072.0	2076.2	2073.5	2102.1	2122.8	2091.1
2008	2068.8	2080.3	2086.9	2059.1	2052.2	2037.9	1995.2	1993.8	1987.8	1981.6	1991.8	1999.0	2027.9
2009	1930.3	1926.3	1920.8	1898.8	1891.6	1883.2	1851.9	1848.3	1846.8	1849.4	1861.2	1875.7	1882.0
Goods-Producing													
1990	273.2	273.6	274.5	269.9	269.7	270.0	264.7	265.9	264.4	262.2	260.3	257.2	267.1
2000	249.2	250.9	253.4	251.4	253.3	254.1	250.9	252.2	253.6	253.0	254.2	254.6	252.6
2001	248.9	249.6	249.7	246.2	246.2	246.6	242.3	243.4	243.0	241.7	241.3	241.4	245.0
2002	235.1	235.1	235.4	233.1	233.9	234.2	230.6	231.7	232.3	232.1	232.4	232.6	233.2
2003	227.1	227.3	227.5	224.3	224.8	225.1	222.7	224.8	226.3	226.4	225.3	227.2	225.7
2004	224.3	225.9	228.5	228.8	230.4	232.2	232.2	234.6	234.3	236.9	238.9	240.6	232.3
2005	237.7	239.7	241.4	243.4	245.8	248.4	249.5	251.8	254.8	255.0	256.3	258.7	248.5
2006	254.8	258.3	260.9	262.3	265.4	268.3	266.0	267.5	269.3	267.8	268.7	269.4	264.9
2007	263.7	265.0	266.1	260.7	261.7	264.7	257.5	258.2	258.1	254.0	253.3	252.5	259.6
2008	243.1	242.0	240.6	233.5	232.1	231.1	224.0	222.6	220.7	216.3	212.8	209.6	227.4
2009	197.8	195.0	192.2	186.1	184.6	183.2	179.0	176.8	175.7	172.6	169.9	169.3	181.9
Mining and Logging													
1990	1.1	1.1	1.1	1.0	1.0	1.0	1.0	1.0	1.0	1.0	0.9	0.9	1.0
2000	0.5	0.4	0.5	0.5	0.5	0.5	0.5	0.5	0.5	0.5	0.5	0.5	0.5
2001	0.6	0.5	0.6	0.6	0.6	0.6	0.6	0.6	0.6	0.6	0.6	0.6	0.6
2002	0.6	0.6	0.6	0.6	0.6	0.6	0.6	0.6	0.6	0.6	0.6	0.6	0.6
2003	0.6	0.5	0.5	0.5	0.5	0.5	0.5	0.5	0.5	0.5	0.5	0.5	0.5
2004	0.5	0.5	0.5	0.5	0.6	0.6	0.6	0.6	0.6	0.6	0.6	0.6	0.6
2005	0.6	0.6	0.6	0.6	0.7	0.7	0.7	0.7	0.6	0.6	0.6	0.5	0.6
2006	0.5	0.6	0.6	0.6	0.6	0.7	0.7	0.7	0.7	0.7	0.8	0.8	0.7
2007	0.8	0.8	0.8	0.8	0.8	0.8	0.8	0.8	0.8	0.9	0.9	0.9	0.8
2008	0.7	0.7	0.8	0.8	0.8	0.7	0.6	0.6	0.6	0.6	0.6	0.6	0.7
2009	0.6	0.6	0.5	0.4	0.5	0.5	0.5	0.5	0.5	0.5	0.5	0.5	0.5
Construction													
1990	110.8	110.2	110.7	107.5	106.9	107.7	105.5	106.0	105.2	104.3	102.4	99.4	106.4
2000	113.2	114.1	115.9	116.3	117.7	119.0	118.7	120.1	121.3	121.7	122.4	123.2	118.6
2001	120.3	120.8	121.2	119.7	120.6	122.0	121.2	122.2	122.3	122.9	122.7	122.5	121.5
2002	119.0	118.9	119.5	118.9	119.9	120.6	119.1	120.5	121.0	122.0	121.8	121.8	120.3
2003	118.7	119.2	119.8	119.2	120.5	121.2	121.7	123.1	124.3	124.8	124.3	125.4	121.9
2004	123.8	124.7	126.5	127.0	127.9	130.3	131.5	133.4	133.6	136.0	137.7	138.9	130.9
2005	137.8	139.2	140.3	142.2	143.8	145.9	147.8	149.4	151.9	153.1	154.2	155.7	146.8
2006	153.3	156.3	159.1	161.3	164.0	166.4	165.5	166.6	167.9	167.6	168.0	167.7	163.6
2007	163.2	164.0	165.0	161.0	161.7	164.2	159.7	159.9	159.7	155.9	154.7	153.7	160.2
2008	146.0	144.8	144.1	138.4	137.4	136.8	132.1	130.9	129.2	126.1	123.4	121.1	134.2
2009	111.9	110.1	108.9	104.8	103.9	102.9	100.6	98.7	97.7	95.5	93.1	92.5	101.7
Manufacturing													
1990	161.3	162.3	162.7	161.4	161.8	161.3	158.2	158.9	158.2	156.9	157.0	156.9	159.7
2000	135.5	136.4	137.0	134.6	135.1	134.6	131.7	131.6	131.8	130.8	131.3	130.9	133.4
2001	128.0	128.3	127.9	125.9	125.0	124.0	120.5	120.6	120.1	118.2	118.0	118.3	122.9
2002	115.5	115.6	115.3	113.6	113.4	113.0	110.9	110.6	110.7	109.5	110.0	110.2	112.4
2003	107.8	107.6	107.2	104.6	103.8	103.4	100.5	101.2	101.5	101.1	100.5	101.3	103.4
2004	100.0	100.7	101.5	101.3	101.9	101.3	100.1	100.6	100.1	100.3	100.6	101.1	100.8
2005	99.3	99.9	100.5	100.6	101.3	101.8	101.0	101.7	102.3	101.3	101.5	102.5	101.1
2006	101.0	101.4	101.2	100.4	100.8	101.2	99.8	100.2	100.7	99.5	99.9	100.9	100.6
2007	99.7	100.2	100.3	98.9	99.2	99.7	97.0	97.5	97.6	97.2	97.7	97.9	98.6
2008	96.4	96.5	95.7	94.3	93.9	93.6	91.3	91.1	90.9	89.6	88.8	87.9	92.5
2009	85.3	84.3	82.8	80.9	80.2	79.8	77.9	77.6	77.5	76.6	76.3	76.3	79.6

Employment by Industry: Miami-Fort Lauderdale-Pompano Beach, FL, Selected Years, 1990–2009—*Continued*

(Numbers in thousands, not seasonally adjusted.)

Industry and year	January	February	March	April	May	June	July	August	September	October	November	December	Annual average
Service-Providing													
1990	1413.1	1427.0	1444.0	1425.6	1429.8	1421.1	1383.3	1384.1	1407.1	1422.2	1437.5	1453.7	1420.7
2000	1867.5	1879.0	1895.4	1896.0	1905.1	1902.0	1866.6	1879.0	1911.0	1914.5	1947.3	1973.5	1903.1
2001	1936.2	1953.7	1970.3	1956.6	1957.8	1953.0	1910.0	1916.8	1944.7	1944.2	1963.7	1983.2	1949.2
2002	1948.4	1957.8	1976.6	1962.8	1967.1	1958.4	1916.5	1924.8	1955.9	1964.0	1988.0	2011.8	1961.0
2003	1970.8	1986.6	1998.7	1983.8	1980.5	1966.0	1923.2	1928.3	1957.7	1975.2	1986.0	2011.9	1972.4
2004	1988.0	2006.0	2020.5	2025.3	2024.1	2012.9	1981.5	1989.2	2005.0	2037.9	2066.9	2093.5	2020.9
2005	2051.9	2073.7	2082.6	2095.7	2095.5	2065.7	2051.0	2088.6	2101.4	2096.4	2113.7	2144.4	2088.4
2006	2104.6	2124.5	2142.8	2127.8	2135.1	2108.8	2080.0	2118.0	2125.9	2130.9	2161.5	2187.0	2128.9
2007	2145.1	2162.3	2177.0	2161.3	2168.4	2137.0	2102.5	2141.6	2149.7	2149.7	2181.4	2203.8	2156.7
2008	2156.5	2171.6	2179.3	2157.2	2152.7	2109.9	2069.8	2096.6	2094.3	2091.9	2107.6	2119.2	2125.6
2009	2060.4	2057.7	2055.2	2039.7	2032.4	1997.3	1966.5	1989.6	1992.6	2001.7	2016.9	2030.8	2020.1
Trade, Transportation, and Utilities													
1990	430.5	429.6	431.8	430.3	431.3	432.0	426.8	428.1	428.7	433.1	440.7	449.6	432.7
2000	518.9	517.4	518.1	518.6	519.8	522.0	516.5	519.8	520.4	522.2	535.2	546.6	523.0
2001	526.2	525.7	528.9	524.4	523.5	522.1	518.5	520.1	520.5	520.1	528.8	536.7	524.6
2002	519.4	515.6	518.9	514.0	514.4	513.9	509.9	512.3	513.7	514.1	522.8	532.3	516.8
2003	513.4	511.0	510.4	508.7	507.8	506.8	504.5	505.9	507.5	510.8	519.2	530.0	511.3
2004	511.3	513.4	514.6	514.8	514.6	513.9	512.8	514.5	512.0	518.3	530.5	540.4	517.8
2005	523.7	523.7	524.2	527.0	528.3	527.7	528.7	531.0	531.9	533.5	539.8	552.5	531.0
2006	538.8	539.4	542.1	540.5	542.6	543.0	538.3	540.5	540.7	543.7	555.4	565.7	544.2
2007	547.9	547.1	549.3	546.0	549.5	549.7	543.8	545.7	546.1	547.7	562.1	571.2	550.5
2008	551.8	550.8	550.8	544.9	544.8	541.9	534.9	534.7	533.1	531.5	537.4	542.9	541.6
2009	520.2	516.1	512.9	506.2	505.3	503.3	496.0	496.5	495.5	497.4	503.0	508.4	505.1
Wholesale Trade													
1990	98.4	99.1	99.7	101.2	101.6	101.5	99.9	100.7	101.4	101.7	101.8	102.1	100.8
2000	119.8	120.4	121.3	123.4	124.1	124.9	124.5	125.0	126.0	125.7	126.6	128.2	124.2
2001	129.1	130.5	131.2	131.4	132.0	131.6	130.8	131.0	131.3	131.5	132.3	133.0	131.3
2002	131.6	132.3	133.1	131.8	132.3	132.0	131.5	132.1	132.0	132.5	133.3	134.2	132.4
2003	133.0	133.4	133.3	133.3	133.3	133.3	133.5	134.2	134.6	135.4	136.3	138.2	134.3
2004	136.9	137.8	138.8	138.9	139.3	139.0	137.9	138.0	137.6	138.8	140.1	140.7	138.7
2005	139.5	140.5	140.6	141.4	142.0	141.6	140.9	141.1	141.3	141.2	141.3	142.7	141.2
2006	141.5	142.9	143.6	143.5	144.1	144.7	144.2	145.1	145.3	145.7	146.7	148.2	144.6
2007	146.8	148.4	149.0	147.9	148.6	148.4	146.2	146.5	146.7	146.6	147.4	148.5	147.6
2008	145.9	146.8	146.9	145.9	146.3	145.3	143.2	143.0	143.0	142.2	142.0	142.2	144.4
2009	138.7	138.6	137.3	136.2	136.0	134.6	132.4	132.3	131.7	131.7	132.5	132.4	134.5
Retail Trade													
1990	254.5	252.0	252.2	249.3	249.8	250.3	246.4	246.6	246.7	250.4	257.7	265.4	251.8
2000	296.6	295.1	295.1	293.8	294.8	296.8	291.8	294.9	294.4	297.1	308.2	316.3	297.9
2001	297.6	295.5	297.3	293.4	292.4	291.5	287.9	289.6	290.2	290.5	299.0	305.5	294.2
2002	291.3	286.9	287.9	285.5	285.3	285.1	281.5	283.2	284.7	284.8	291.8	299.4	287.3
2003	284.1	281.3	281.3	280.2	280.5	279.7	278.5	279.5	280.6	283.3	290.8	298.2	283.0
2004	284.6	282.5	282.8	282.9	283.5	283.1	282.7	284.1	282.1	286.0	295.4	302.8	286.0
2005	289.2	288.0	288.4	290.0	290.4	291.1	292.8	295.4	295.8	297.7	302.9	312.6	294.5
2006	301.2	300.2	301.9	301.0	303.1	302.6	299.9	300.4	300.3	303.3	313.1	319.5	303.9
2007	305.5	303.2	304.3	302.4	305.3	305.2	302.1	303.4	303.4	304.5	316.3	322.0	306.5
2008	308.0	305.6	305.5	302.2	302.1	301.2	297.4	297.2	296.2	295.1	300.4	304.2	301.3
2009	288.4	285.0	283.3	279.4	279.4	279.1	275.9	275.9	276.2	276.8	281.8	285.9	280.6
Transportation and Utilities													
1990	77.6	78.5	79.9	79.8	79.9	80.2	80.5	80.8	80.6	81.0	81.2	82.1	80.2
2000	102.5	101.9	101.7	101.4	100.9	100.3	100.2	99.9	100.0	99.4	100.4	102.1	100.9
2001	99.5	99.7	100.4	99.6	99.1	99.0	99.8	99.5	99.0	98.1	97.5	98.2	99.1
2002	96.5	96.4	97.9	96.7	96.8	96.8	96.9	97.0	97.0	96.8	97.7	98.7	97.1
2003	96.3	96.3	95.8	95.2	94.0	93.8	92.5	92.2	92.3	92.1	92.1	93.6	93.9
2004	92.8	93.1	93.0	93.0	91.8	91.8	92.2	92.4	92.3	93.5	95.0	96.9	93.2
2005	95.0	95.2	95.2	95.6	95.9	95.0	95.0	94.5	94.8	94.6	95.6	97.2	95.3
2006	96.1	96.3	96.6	96.0	95.4	95.7	94.2	95.0	95.1	94.7	95.6	98.0	95.7
2007	95.6	95.5	96.0	95.7	95.6	96.1	95.5	95.8	96.0	96.6	98.4	100.7	96.5
2008	97.9	98.4	98.4	96.8	96.4	95.4	94.3	94.5	93.9	94.2	95.0	96.5	96.0
2009	93.1	92.5	92.3	90.6	89.9	89.6	88.5	88.3	87.6	88.9	88.7	90.1	90.0
Information													
1990	43.9	44.0	44.0	43.5	43.7	43.7	43.8	43.7	44.4	43.8	44.2	44.5	43.9
2000	57.2	57.4	58.5	58.4	59.0	60.9	62.3	63.0	63.6	63.0	63.6	64.6	61.0
2001	65.1	65.7	66.4	65.9	66.3	66.2	64.8	64.9	64.1	63.6	63.4	63.9	65.0
2002	62.5	62.6	62.8	61.8	61.7	61.9	60.9	60.3	60.0	59.2	59.0	59.1	61.0
2003	57.3	57.0	57.4	56.3	56.4	56.6	56.6	56.6	56.2	56.5	56.6	57.0	56.7
2004	55.4	55.4	55.6	55.6	55.7	55.9	55.8	55.9	55.5	55.9	56.1	56.6	55.8
2005	55.7	56.1	56.2	55.7	55.6	55.7	55.1	54.9	54.8	53.7	54.0	54.1	55.1
2006	53.0	53.4	53.5	52.7	53.1	53.0	52.5	52.3	51.7	51.3	51.3	51.4	52.4
2007	50.7	51.1	51.4	51.2	51.4	51.7	51.3	51.3	50.7	51.0	51.1	51.3	51.2
2008	50.7	50.7	50.7	50.3	50.4	50.3	49.6	49.3	48.9	48.6	48.7	48.4	49.7
2009	47.1	46.9	46.6	45.9	45.7	45.2	44.3	44.1	43.3	43.4	42.9	42.6	44.8

Employment by Industry: Miami-Fort Lauderdale-Pompano Beach, FL, Selected Years, 1990–2009—*Continued*

(Numbers in thousands, not seasonally adjusted.)

Industry and year	January	February	March	April	May	June	July	August	September	October	November	December	Annual average
Financial Activities													
1990	143.2	144.0	144.7	143.7	143.5	144.2	143.0	143.6	143.4	142.4	142.1	142.6	143.4
2000	156.1	156.8	157.4	157.2	156.9	159.1	157.7	158.3	158.7	158.0	158.6	160.0	157.9
2001	157.2	158.5	159.8	159.4	159.7	160.6	160.0	160.6	160.2	160.3	160.7	161.2	159.9
2002	161.0	161.8	162.6	162.0	162.1	162.2	162.5	163.3	163.1	163.5	164.3	164.8	162.8
2003	162.6	163.2	163.5	163.2	163.5	163.9	164.1	164.8	165.0	165.6	165.4	167.1	164.3
2004	165.1	166.2	167.4	168.9	169.3	169.6	171.1	171.0	170.7	173.0	173.1	174.8	170.0
2005	173.2	174.7	175.4	176.7	177.2	178.3	178.7	179.8	180.0	180.2	181.2	183.2	178.2
2006	179.8	181.9	183.1	183.1	183.8	184.5	183.2	183.9	183.1	183.9	184.6	186.6	183.5
2007	182.2	183.2	183.3	182.1	181.9	182.2	180.9	180.6	179.6	178.8	179.8	181.1	181.3
2008	176.4	176.5	176.6	174.1	173.4	172.2	169.6	168.3	166.8	165.5	164.8	164.9	170.8
2009	159.1	158.6	158.0	156.5	156.1	155.7	153.3	152.7	151.8	151.1	149.7	149.2	154.3
Professional and Business Services													
1990	104.3	107.7	110.5	104.5	104.9	105.8	103.0	105.2	105.2	106.3	108.6	108.5	106.2
2000	285.3	287.8	293.3	292.5	294.3	297.6	295.1	299.4	303.3	300.3	307.1	310.4	297.2
2001	309.6	314.3	317.2	314.5	313.9	317.4	313.3	313.9	315.7	315.4	316.5	318.9	315.1
2002	312.2	314.4	319.8	319.3	321.5	323.4	319.9	319.1	318.6	320.1	324.2	329.0	320.1
2003	319.6	326.8	331.0	326.5	322.8	319.0	312.9	312.1	310.4	317.1	315.2	318.7	319.3
2004	315.5	322.5	327.8	332.3	330.8	329.7	328.4	329.0	327.8	339.3	345.4	352.5	331.8
2005	342.9	350.6	353.2	357.0	356.6	357.2	355.8	358.3	363.1	358.8	363.7	370.0	357.3
2006	357.6	363.2	368.2	365.6	368.8	371.5	366.8	368.4	370.8	370.2	374.0	380.8	368.8
2007	371.0	376.0	378.3	373.1	373.9	373.8	366.3	368.1	368.0	366.2	367.8	370.3	371.1
2008	358.5	363.3	365.2	360.6	357.6	355.3	348.9	348.7	347.7	348.2	348.0	348.7	354.2
2009	332.1	332.1	329.7	325.6	323.8	323.8	319.6	320.0	319.6	322.1	325.9	330.6	325.4
Education and Health Services													
1990	180.8	182.9	184.6	183.7	184.4	185.8	182.4	184.2	186.6	188.3	189.6	191.0	185.4
2000	253.7	256.8	258.3	255.7	256.5	257.4	253.9	255.2	258.0	258.8	260.4	262.6	257.3
2001	255.5	258.9	260.8	260.8	263.0	263.8	261.2	262.9	267.0	268.0	270.0	272.7	263.7
2002	268.6	271.8	274.5	273.1	274.1	274.5	269.7	272.6	276.8	278.1	279.7	281.7	274.6
2003	278.2	281.5	283.2	282.8	283.6	283.9	279.6	282.0	286.2	288.6	287.8	290.5	284.0
2004	287.3	290.8	291.7	293.3	294.4	293.4	290.0	292.0	293.0	297.4	299.1	300.1	293.5
2005	294.2	298.4	298.9	302.0	302.0	300.3	299.4	302.5	305.1	304.1	304.5	306.4	301.5
2006	300.7	303.7	306.1	306.0	307.9	307.3	304.5	307.9	310.4	311.3	313.3	315.6	307.9
2007	312.0	315.4	316.9	317.2	319.0	318.6	314.5	317.8	321.2	322.1	324.0	326.5	318.8
2008	322.6	326.1	328.0	326.3	328.0	326.6	320.9	324.0	326.1	327.3	329.0	330.0	326.2
2009	325.4	327.2	328.7	329.3	331.4	330.5	326.9	328.0	330.9	333.6	334.1	334.7	330.1
Leisure and Hospitality													
1990	199.0	203.2	205.8	198.8	194.4	189.1	181.9	182.2	181.0	183.1	190.5	194.7	192.0
2000	214.9	219.8	223.9	221.8	220.2	216.9	213.5	214.7	216.8	217.9	225.7	230.9	219.8
2001	228.1	233.7	238.1	233.1	232.5	229.9	220.8	222.1	221.5	218.4	223.3	227.5	227.4
2002	224.5	229.1	231.8	229.0	227.5	224.5	216.3	217.5	218.6	221.9	227.0	231.3	224.9
2003	230.2	234.1	237.5	232.9	230.6	227.9	221.2	221.4	223.8	225.7	230.9	236.7	229.4
2004	239.4	244.1	248.0	245.2	242.7	239.9	234.0	234.1	230.2	235.2	242.2	248.1	240.3
2005	243.3	249.1	252.6	252.8	250.7	250.1	242.2	242.9	243.8	242.5	247.0	253.1	247.5
2006	250.9	256.6	260.7	255.3	253.6	251.7	243.4	244.9	245.2	245.5	253.9	257.7	251.6
2007	255.1	260.6	265.2	261.9	261.6	258.6	249.3	251.3	252.8	252.2	260.7	265.0	257.9
2008	261.9	266.4	269.6	265.7	263.0	258.4	247.3	247.0	246.4	246.9	254.2	257.5	257.0
2009	253.7	255.6	257.9	254.7	250.6	247.7	239.7	238.1	238.0	237.3	242.9	247.7	247.0
Other Services													
1990	79.4	80.4	81.1	80.9	80.5	80.5	79.2	78.8	78.6	78.5	78.8	79.2	79.7
2000	94.7	95.2	95.8	95.8	96.5	96.9	95.8	95.8	96.6	96.9	97.4	97.6	96.3
2001	95.9	96.3	96.8	95.0	94.6	94.4	92.8	92.1	92.0	91.0	91.4	91.8	93.7
2002	92.3	93.4	94.0	93.0	93.2	93.2	93.0	93.3	93.9	94.9	96.2	97.1	94.0
2003	95.8	97.2	98.0	97.0	97.2	97.5	94.4	93.9	94.3	94.3	94.3	95.7	95.8
2004	95.7	96.9	97.9	96.7	97.3	98.4	97.4	98.2	98.2	97.4	98.9	99.0	97.7
2005	98.7	99.7	99.6	99.8	99.7	99.4	98.2	98.4	98.8	97.6	98.2	99.4	99.0
2006	99.5	100.8	102.1	99.2	99.4	100.1	97.8	98.0	98.2	97.8	98.7	99.6	99.3
2007	99.7	101.0	102.4	99.4	99.9	100.3	98.6	99.0	99.7	101.5	103.3	104.9	100.8
2008	103.8	104.5	105.4	103.7	102.9	102.1	100.0	99.2	98.1	97.3	96.9	97.0	100.9
2009	94.9	94.8	94.8	94.5	94.1	93.8	92.3	92.1	92.0	91.9	92.8	93.2	93.4
Government													
1990	232.0	235.2	241.5	240.2	247.1	240.0	223.2	218.3	239.2	246.7	243.0	243.6	237.5
2000	286.7	287.8	290.1	296.0	301.9	291.2	271.8	272.8	293.6	297.4	299.3	300.8	290.8
2001	298.6	300.6	302.3	303.5	304.3	298.6	278.6	280.2	303.7	307.4	309.6	310.5	299.8
2002	307.9	309.1	312.2	310.6	312.6	304.8	284.3	286.4	311.2	312.2	314.8	316.5	306.9
2003	313.7	315.8	317.7	316.4	318.6	310.4	289.9	291.6	314.3	316.6	316.6	316.2	311.5
2004	315.3	316.7	317.5	318.5	319.3	312.1	292.0	294.5	317.6	321.4	321.6	322.0	314.0
2005	320.2	321.4	322.5	324.7	325.4	297.0	292.9	320.8	323.9	326.0	325.3	325.7	318.8
2006	324.3	325.5	327.0	325.4	325.9	297.7	293.5	322.1	325.8	327.2	330.3	329.6	321.2
2007	326.5	327.9	330.2	330.4	331.2	302.1	297.8	327.8	331.6	330.2	332.6	333.5	325.2
2008	330.8	333.3	333.0	331.6	332.6	303.1	298.6	325.4	327.2	326.6	328.6	329.8	325.1
2009	327.9	326.4	326.6	327.0	325.4	297.3	293.6	318.1	321.5	324.9	325.6	324.4	319.9

Employment by Industry: Milwaukee-Waukesha-West Allis, WI, Selected Years, 1990–2009

(Numbers in thousands, not seasonally adjusted.)

Industry and year	January	February	March	April	May	June	July	August	September	October	November	December	Annual average
Total Nonfarm													
1990	742.4	744.1	748.4	751.9	758.1	764.9	756.7	758.6	761.7	762.2	764.1	765.7	756.6
2000	850.2	852.8	857.8	865.8	869.4	879.4	869.1	871.7	871.5	874.3	878.0	874.9	867.9
2001	856.5	856.4	858.7	863.1	864.3	866.0	856.1	855.0	853.6	853.7	850.0	849.2	856.9
2002	829.0	828.2	832.4	839.3	843.8	848.7	840.3	840.5	839.0	844.7	845.0	843.6	839.5
2003	820.0	822.8	824.9	830.9	834.0	839.6	826.8	828.8	828.4	837.1	834.8	837.0	830.4
2004	815.1	817.9	822.8	827.1	833.1	842.0	833.9	836.4	834.8	841.0	841.0	840.5	832.1
2005	822.9	825.2	827.8	839.2	842.1	849.0	843.6	844.8	847.5	847.1	849.0	850.4	840.7
2006	830.0	832.5	836.1	845.8	850.7	859.2	851.7	855.1	858.3	861.4	863.0	863.2	850.6
2007	843.3	843.0	846.0	853.0	861.8	870.8	858.9	861.8	860.1	862.3	863.2	863.5	857.3
2008	843.8	842.9	846.1	853.0	860.1	865.0	854.9	854.7	855.7	856.8	852.8	847.8	852.8
2009	820.7	815.1	810.6	813.4	816.7	818.8	802.1	800.8	804.9	810.0	808.2	799.0	810.0
Total Private													
1990	659.0	658.3	661.8	664.3	670.2	677.0	675.8	678.3	675.4	674.3	676.3	677.9	670.7
2000	759.5	760.8	765.3	771.1	775.6	782.5	781.8	784.0	780.9	780.5	783.3	782.2	775.6
2001	763.6	761.0	763.4	766.7	768.9	771.7	770.0	768.5	760.7	757.8	754.4	752.8	763.3
2002	734.8	731.1	734.9	742.6	747.8	752.4	753.0	753.2	747.6	746.6	746.5	745.3	744.7
2003	726.6	725.5	728.1	733.7	739.1	744.1	742.2	743.6	740.3	742.0	740.5	742.3	737.3
2004	725.3	723.0	727.5	733.5	739.5	748.5	750.0	751.5	745.0	748.8	747.5	747.6	740.6
2005	731.3	730.4	734.2	745.5	748.7	755.5	758.5	759.4	755.2	754.1	755.5	757.6	748.8
2006	739.8	739.6	742.7	752.1	757.2	765.3	766.2	769.2	766.1	767.8	769.4	770.0	758.8
2007	753.2	751.3	754.0	760.4	768.8	777.2	773.9	776.9	768.6	770.1	771.0	770.5	766.3
2008	752.6	751.6	752.4	759.7	765.8	770.8	769.0	770.1	762.2	761.7	755.9	752.2	760.3
2009	727.5	720.1	715.7	716.8	720.6	723.7	718.2	717.7	712.8	714.0	712.1	703.3	716.9
Goods-Producing													
1990	188.3	188.3	188.1	188.7	190.6	191.4	191.8	191.8	190.7	189.8	188.6	187.5	189.6
2000	195.5	195.6	196.6	199.0	200.2	202.8	202.1	202.4	200.7	199.5	199.0	197.1	199.2
2001	192.3	190.8	190.8	189.8	189.9	191.6	190.7	190.8	188.8	187.1	184.6	183.2	189.2
2002	176.5	174.9	175.4	176.8	178.1	179.8	178.4	179.4	178.0	177.5	176.7	174.6	177.2
2003	169.1	167.9	167.9	169.5	170.7	172.1	171.2	172.8	171.1	170.7	169.9	168.7	170.1
2004	163.7	163.0	163.9	166.1	167.6	170.2	171.1	171.5	170.2	169.5	169.1	168.2	167.8
2005	164.1	163.8	164.4	166.9	168.3	170.7	171.1	170.9	169.4	168.2	167.7	166.7	167.7
2006	164.1	163.0	163.5	166.3	168.1	171.1	170.9	171.8	170.3	170.3	169.7	169.1	168.2
2007	165.8	163.7	164.8	167.2	169.9	172.4	172.0	172.6	170.6	170.3	169.4	167.8	168.9
2008	164.2	163.1	163.6	165.1	167.0	168.6	167.5	167.7	165.0	164.2	162.2	159.1	164.8
2009	153.2	149.4	146.3	145.3	144.9	145.1	142.9	142.9	141.9	141.3	140.5	135.7	144.1
Mining and Logging													
1990	0.3	0.3	0.3	0.3	0.3	0.3	0.3	0.3	0.3	0.3	0.3	0.3	0.3
2000	0.4	0.4	0.4	0.4	0.5	0.5	0.5	0.5	0.5	0.5	0.5	0.4	0.5
2001	0.4	0.4	0.4	0.4	0.5	0.5	0.5	0.5	0.5	0.5	0.4	0.4	0.5
2002	0.4	0.4	0.4	0.4	0.4	0.5	0.5	0.5	0.5	0.4	0.4	0.4	0.4
2003	0.4	0.4	0.4	0.4	0.4	0.5	0.5	0.5	0.5	0.4	0.4	0.5	0.4
2004	0.4	0.4	0.4	0.4	0.5	0.5	0.5	0.5	0.5	0.5	0.5	0.5	0.5
2005	0.4	0.4	0.4	0.5	0.5	0.5	0.5	0.5	0.5	0.5	0.5	0.5	0.5
2006	0.5	0.5	0.5	0.5	0.5	0.5	0.5	0.5	0.5	0.5	0.5	0.5	0.5
2007	0.5	0.4	0.5	0.5	0.5	0.5	0.5	0.5	0.5	0.5	0.5	0.5	0.5
2008	0.4	0.4	0.4	0.4	0.4	0.4	0.4	0.4	0.4	0.4	0.4	0.4	0.4
2009	0.3	0.3	0.3	0.4	0.4	0.4	0.4	0.4	0.4	0.4	0.4	0.3	0.4
Construction													
1990	25.9	25.6	26.0	27.3	29.1	29.9	30.5	30.6	30.0	29.7	29.3	28.0	28.5
2000	30.3	30.0	31.0	33.2	34.7	36.1	36.3	36.5	35.7	35.1	34.4	32.7	33.8
2001	30.9	30.9	31.4	32.8	34.6	35.9	36.8	36.9	36.0	35.5	34.7	33.6	34.2
2002	29.7	28.9	29.5	32.2	34.0	35.1	35.9	36.1	35.6	35.7	34.9	33.0	33.4
2003	29.9	29.2	29.4	31.5	33.6	34.7	35.7	36.1	35.5	35.4	34.5	33.1	33.2
2004	29.7	29.2	29.9	32.0	33.3	34.7	36.0	36.0	35.4	35.1	34.7	33.5	33.3
2005	30.3	29.9	30.4	32.7	34.4	35.6	36.1	36.0	35.5	35.1	34.8	33.4	33.7
2006	31.2	30.5	31.0	33.5	35.0	36.4	36.7	36.7	36.3	36.1	35.5	34.4	34.4
2007	31.9	30.6	32.3	33.8	36.1	37.5	37.9	37.9	37.1	36.7	36.1	34.0	35.2
2008	31.0	30.2	30.9	32.6	35.0	35.9	36.1	35.9	34.8	35.0	33.6	31.4	33.5
2009	27.6	27.0	26.8	28.4	29.7	30.5	30.6	30.5	29.5	29.7	29.2	24.8	28.7
Manufacturing													
1990	162.1	162.4	161.8	161.1	161.2	161.2	161.0	160.9	160.4	159.8	159.0	159.2	160.8
2000	164.8	165.2	165.2	165.4	165.0	166.2	165.3	165.4	164.5	163.9	164.1	164.0	164.9
2001	161.0	159.5	159.0	156.6	154.8	155.2	153.4	153.4	152.3	151.1	149.5	149.2	154.6
2002	146.4	145.6	145.5	144.2	143.7	144.2	142.0	142.8	141.9	141.4	141.4	141.2	143.4
2003	138.8	138.3	138.1	137.6	136.7	136.9	135.0	136.2	135.1	134.9	135.0	135.1	136.5
2004	133.6	133.4	133.6	133.7	133.8	135.0	134.6	135.0	134.3	133.9	133.9	134.2	134.1
2005	133.4	133.5	133.6	133.7	133.4	134.6	134.5	134.4	133.4	132.6	132.4	132.8	133.5
2006	132.4	132.0	132.0	132.3	132.6	134.2	133.7	134.6	133.5	133.7	133.7	134.2	133.2
2007	133.4	132.7	132.0	132.9	133.3	134.4	133.6	134.2	133.0	133.1	132.8	133.3	133.2
2008	132.8	132.5	132.3	132.1	131.6	132.3	131.0	131.4	129.8	128.8	128.2	127.3	130.8
2009	125.3	122.1	119.2	116.5	114.8	114.2	111.9	112.0	112.0	111.2	110.9	110.6	115.1

Employment by Industry: Milwaukee-Waukesha-West Allis, WI, Selected Years, 1990–2009—*Continued*

(Numbers in thousands, not seasonally adjusted.)

Industry and year	January	February	March	April	May	June	July	August	September	October	November	December	Annual average
Service-Providing													
1990	554.1	555.8	560.3	563.2	567.5	573.5	564.9	566.8	571.0	572.4	575.5	578.2	566.9
2000	654.7	657.2	661.2	666.8	669.2	676.6	667.0	669.3	670.8	674.8	679.0	677.8	668.7
2001	664.2	665.6	667.9	673.3	674.4	674.4	665.4	664.2	664.8	666.6	665.4	666.0	667.7
2002	652.5	653.3	657.0	662.5	665.7	668.9	661.9	661.1	661.0	667.2	668.3	669.0	662.4
2003	650.9	654.9	657.0	661.4	663.3	667.5	655.6	656.0	657.3	666.4	664.9	668.3	660.2
2004	651.4	654.9	658.9	661.0	665.5	671.8	662.8	664.9	664.6	671.5	671.9	672.3	664.3
2005	658.8	661.4	663.4	672.3	673.8	678.3	672.5	673.9	678.1	678.9	681.3	683.7	673.0
2006	665.9	669.5	672.6	679.5	682.6	688.1	680.8	683.3	688.0	691.1	693.3	694.1	682.4
2007	677.5	679.3	681.2	685.8	691.9	698.4	686.9	689.2	689.5	692.0	693.8	695.7	688.4
2008	679.6	679.8	682.5	687.9	693.1	696.4	687.4	687.0	690.7	692.6	690.6	688.7	688.0
2009	667.5	665.7	664.3	668.1	671.8	673.7	659.2	657.9	663.0	668.7	667.7	663.3	665.9
Trade, Transportation, and Utilities													
1990	143.4	141.4	141.9	140.9	142.3	143.7	141.8	143.5	143.7	144.2	148.1	149.8	143.7
2000	159.9	158.0	158.3	158.9	159.5	159.3	160.0	160.8	161.6	162.8	165.2	167.1	161.0
2001	163.5	160.9	161.2	161.0	161.3	160.3	158.0	158.3	157.3	157.9	159.9	160.4	160.0
2002	155.6	152.9	153.7	153.5	154.8	154.6	153.0	152.7	153.4	153.9	157.2	159.1	154.5
2003	152.3	150.4	150.6	151.1	152.3	152.9	149.8	150.7	151.9	153.8	155.6	157.5	152.4
2004	151.4	149.8	150.6	149.7	151.6	153.2	151.3	151.7	152.1	154.1	156.5	157.6	152.5
2005	152.2	150.8	151.3	151.9	153.0	153.6	153.1	153.9	154.2	154.9	157.5	158.9	153.8
2006	153.3	151.5	152.4	152.9	154.2	155.0	153.1	153.6	154.1	155.2	158.2	159.7	154.4
2007	154.2	152.1	152.1	152.0	153.9	154.6	152.7	152.8	152.4	153.2	156.0	156.8	153.6
2008	151.8	149.4	149.5	150.5	151.2	151.8	150.7	150.7	149.8	150.2	150.9	151.4	150.7
2009	145.1	142.6	141.7	140.6	142.4	143.4	141.0	140.7	140.7	141.4	140.9	139.8	141.7
Wholesale Trade													
1990	35.8	35.8	35.9	35.6	35.9	36.3	36.4	36.5	36.1	35.9	35.9	36.1	36.0
2000	42.7	42.9	42.9	43.0	43.2	43.5	43.3	43.3	42.9	42.9	43.0	43.2	43.1
2001	42.9	43.0	43.1	42.7	42.7	42.9	42.5	42.5	41.9	41.7	41.5	41.6	42.4
2002	41.1	41.0	41.0	40.8	40.9	41.0	41.1	40.9	40.5	40.2	40.2	40.2	40.7
2003	40.0	40.0	40.0	39.9	39.9	40.1	40.1	40.0	39.7	39.5	39.3	39.4	39.8
2004	38.9	38.7	38.9	38.9	38.9	39.3	39.7	39.8	39.5	39.9	40.0	40.1	39.4
2005	39.9	39.9	39.8	40.4	40.5	40.9	41.2	41.0	40.7	40.8	40.9	41.0	40.6
2006	40.4	40.5	40.6	40.8	40.9	41.4	41.6	41.5	41.3	41.4	41.4	41.6	41.1
2007	40.9	41.0	41.0	41.1	41.2	41.8	41.8	41.7	41.3	41.3	41.2	41.2	41.3
2008	40.6	40.6	40.6	40.8	40.8	40.9	41.0	40.9	40.3	39.9	39.9	39.6	40.5
2009	38.9	38.6	38.1	37.6	37.6	37.7	37.4	37.2	36.8	36.7	36.1	36.1	37.4
Retail Trade													
1990	80.9	78.7	78.9	78.1	78.9	79.9	79.0	80.1	79.3	80.7	84.5	85.8	80.4
2000	84.1	82.2	82.5	82.4	82.9	83.4	84.2	84.9	84.9	85.1	87.8	89.5	84.5
2001	86.8	84.5	84.9	84.7	85.1	85.0	83.9	84.0	82.7	83.3	85.9	86.8	84.8
2002	84.3	81.9	82.5	82.5	83.5	84.2	83.0	83.0	82.5	82.9	86.3	88.2	83.7
2003	82.3	80.3	80.5	80.6	81.7	82.2	81.2	81.8	81.4	83.2	85.3	87.1	82.3
2004	82.5	81.0	81.4	81.1	82.4	83.3	82.4	82.8	82.1	82.9	85.3	86.8	82.8
2005	82.0	80.6	81.1	81.6	82.3	82.8	82.6	83.5	82.7	83.3	85.4	86.6	82.9
2006	82.5	80.6	81.1	81.4	82.4	83.0	82.1	82.7	81.9	82.9	85.9	86.9	82.8
2007	83.3	81.1	81.1	80.5	81.9	82.0	81.7	81.5	80.1	80.8	83.4	84.2	81.8
2008	81.2	78.9	79.1	79.6	80.2	80.7	80.7	80.6	79.2	79.9	81.0	81.7	80.2
2009	77.6	75.6	75.4	75.2	76.4	77.3	76.6	76.6	76.0	76.8	77.2	76.4	76.4
Transportation and Utilities													
1990	26.7	26.9	27.1	27.2	27.5	27.5	26.4	26.9	28.3	27.6	27.7	27.9	27.3
2000	33.1	32.9	32.9	33.5	33.4	32.4	32.5	32.6	33.8	34.8	34.4	34.4	33.4
2001	33.8	33.4	33.2	33.6	33.5	32.4	31.6	31.8	32.7	32.9	32.5	32.0	32.8
2002	30.2	30.0	30.2	30.2	30.4	29.4	28.9	28.8	30.4	30.8	30.7	30.7	30.1
2003	30.0	30.1	30.1	30.6	30.7	30.6	28.5	28.9	30.8	31.1	31.0	31.0	30.3
2004	30.0	30.1	30.3	29.7	30.3	30.6	29.2	29.1	30.5	31.3	31.2	30.7	30.3
2005	30.3	30.3	30.4	29.9	30.2	29.9	29.3	29.4	30.8	30.8	31.2	31.3	30.3
2006	30.4	30.4	30.7	30.7	30.9	30.6	29.4	29.4	30.9	30.9	30.9	31.2	30.5
2007	30.0	30.0	30.0	30.4	30.8	30.8	29.2	29.6	31.0	31.1	31.4	31.4	30.5
2008	30.0	29.9	29.8	30.1	30.2	30.2	29.0	29.2	30.3	30.4	30.0	30.1	29.9
2009	28.6	28.4	28.2	27.8	28.4	28.4	27.0	26.9	27.9	27.9	27.6	27.3	27.9
Information													
1990	18.9	19.0	19.2	18.8	18.8	19.0	18.9	18.9	18.8	19.0	19.0	18.9	18.9
2000	19.9	20.1	20.2	20.2	20.3	20.4	20.4	20.5	20.6	20.8	20.9	21.0	20.4
2001	19.7	19.7	19.9	20.1	19.9	20.0	20.0	19.9	19.8	20.0	20.0	20.0	19.9
2002	19.7	19.5	19.6	19.5	19.3	19.3	19.2	19.2	18.9	18.8	18.8	18.8	19.2
2003	18.8	18.6	18.6	18.5	18.3	18.3	18.4	18.4	18.3	18.3	18.3	18.3	18.4
2004	18.5	18.5	18.5	18.6	18.5	18.4	18.6	18.6	18.3	18.2	18.3	18.2	18.4
2005	18.2	18.1	18.1	18.2	18.2	18.3	18.1	18.2	18.1	18.1	18.2	18.3	18.2
2006	18.0	18.1	18.0	17.9	17.9	17.7	17.7	17.7	17.5	17.5	17.5	17.5	17.8
2007	17.5	17.5	17.5	17.5	17.5	17.6	17.5	17.5	17.3	17.4	17.5	17.4	17.5
2008	17.1	17.1	17.0	17.5	17.5	17.7	17.5	17.5	17.3	17.3	17.3	17.3	17.3
2009	16.9	16.9	16.8	16.7	16.5	16.5	16.5	16.4	16.2	16.2	16.2	16.3	16.5

Employment by Industry: Milwaukee-Waukesha-West Allis, WI, Selected Years, 1990–2009—*Continued*

(Numbers in thousands, not seasonally adjusted.)

Industry and year	January	February	March	April	May	June	July	August	September	October	November	December	Annual average
Financial Activities													
1990	51.9	52.0	52.2	52.3	52.8	53.2	53.0	52.8	52.5	52.7	52.6	53.0	52.6
2000	56.6	56.7	56.6	57.0	57.2	58.0	58.2	58.1	57.8	58.3	58.8	59.2	57.7
2001	58.5	58.2	58.3	58.4	58.5	59.1	58.8	58.5	57.9	57.4	57.5	57.2	58.2
2002	57.1	57.1	57.0	57.3	57.4	57.9	58.6	58.6	57.9	57.8	58.1	58.1	57.7
2003	57.8	58.0	58.0	58.1	58.3	58.7	58.7	58.4	57.6	57.5	57.2	57.3	57.9
2004	57.4	57.2	57.4	57.6	57.6	58.1	58.5	58.6	57.5	57.9	57.9	58.1	57.8
2005	57.1	56.8	57.1	57.2	57.2	57.4	57.9	57.7	57.1	56.9	57.1	57.3	57.2
2006	57.0	56.8	56.7	57.3	57.5	57.9	58.4	58.3	58.0	58.0	58.1	58.2	57.7
2007	57.8	57.9	57.6	58.0	58.2	58.7	58.7	58.5	57.7	58.2	58.4	58.6	58.2
2008	58.0	58.2	57.9	58.1	58.5	58.5	59.0	58.9	57.9	58.3	58.2	58.2	58.3
2009	57.7	57.5	57.2	57.4	57.4	57.4	57.6	57.5	56.2	56.1	55.8	55.3	56.9
Professional and Business Services													
1990	73.7	74.3	75.7	76.9	77.0	78.9	78.5	79.1	78.4	78.9	78.0	77.7	77.3
2000	108.5	109.7	110.6	110.8	112.0	113.2	111.7	112.2	113.0	111.8	112.3	109.8	111.3
2001	106.2	105.2	105.2	107.0	106.9	106.9	107.1	107.6	105.9	104.0	102.6	102.0	105.6
2002	100.1	100.1	101.6	105.3	105.6	105.7	106.3	106.9	106.0	105.6	103.5	102.8	104.1
2003	100.9	101.3	102.5	103.7	103.2	103.6	104.2	104.0	104.5	105.4	104.4	105.4	103.5
2004	102.0	101.6	103.0	104.4	104.0	106.5	107.0	107.6	106.5	106.9	105.9	105.6	105.1
2005	103.5	103.9	104.8	107.9	107.0	108.8	110.6	110.9	111.2	110.8	110.8	111.6	108.5
2006	106.4	107.3	107.9	110.7	110.3	111.9	112.7	113.7	113.9	114.4	114.1	113.6	111.4
2007	110.4	111.0	111.8	113.2	113.8	116.2	115.9	117.7	116.2	115.9	116.1	116.5	114.6
2008	113.1	113.9	112.8	114.3	114.7	116.0	115.9	116.7	116.0	114.6	112.6	111.5	114.3
2009	105.7	103.4	101.9	102.5	102.5	103.1	103.5	103.0	102.1	101.2	100.8	98.9	102.4
Education and Health Services													
1990	88.9	89.1	89.7	89.8	89.8	89.6	89.9	90.3	91.4	91.9	92.4	92.5	90.4
2000	119.8	120.9	122.0	122.5	122.4	122.1	121.8	122.6	122.7	124.5	125.2	125.9	122.7
2001	121.5	124.2	125.0	124.6	124.7	123.9	124.0	124.1	124.9	126.4	126.6	126.6	124.7
2002	124.4	125.3	125.7	125.9	126.2	125.9	126.0	126.4	126.5	127.9	128.6	128.0	126.4
2003	125.8	128.0	128.1	128.5	128.4	128.0	127.7	127.7	128.1	129.2	129.6	129.4	128.2
2004	129.2	130.0	130.3	130.9	131.2	130.5	130.3	130.5	130.9	132.5	132.8	133.0	131.0
2005	131.1	132.0	132.3	133.2	133.2	132.7	131.7	132.1	133.2	134.8	135.0	135.5	133.1
2006	134.2	135.7	135.6	136.2	136.5	136.1	135.8	136.4	138.2	140.0	140.0	139.9	137.1
2007	137.5	138.9	139.1	139.4	139.8	139.3	138.5	139.4	140.8	141.5	141.9	142.0	139.8
2008	140.0	141.4	141.9	142.3	142.6	141.5	140.6	141.4	142.3	144.6	144.7	145.1	142.4
2009	142.5	143.8	144.2	144.7	144.8	144.3	142.9	143.3	144.2	146.5	147.8	147.5	144.7
Leisure and Hospitality													
1990	55.2	55.2	56.0	58.2	59.7	61.5	62.7	62.8	60.8	58.9	58.6	58.9	59.0
2000	60.1	60.2	61.0	62.5	63.7	66.1	67.3	67.3	64.3	62.4	61.4	61.3	63.1
2001	60.6	60.8	61.5	65.1	66.9	68.5	70.0	68.1	64.0	63.9	62.1	61.8	64.5
2002	60.4	60.3	60.7	63.0	65.2	67.3	70.0	68.6	65.8	63.8	62.5	62.4	64.2
2003	60.9	60.5	61.3	63.2	67.0	68.8	71.0	70.3	68.0	66.3	64.9	64.8	65.5
2004	62.3	61.9	62.7	64.8	67.7	69.5	71.1	70.9	67.7	67.0	65.3	65.2	66.3
2005	63.8	63.6	64.7	68.4	70.1	71.8	73.9	73.6	70.7	69.2	68.2	68.2	68.9
2006	66.2	66.5	67.8	69.6	71.4	73.7	75.6	75.9	72.5	70.9	70.3	70.2	70.9
2007	68.9	68.9	69.7	70.9	73.8	75.8	76.4	76.5	72.3	71.2	69.5	69.1	71.9
2008	66.7	66.5	67.6	69.3	71.6	73.5	74.6	74.2	71.5	69.6	67.4	67.0	70.0
2009	65.0	65.1	66.0	67.6	70.2	71.5	71.7	71.8	69.8	69.4	68.7	68.2	68.8
Other Services													
1990	38.7	39.0	39.0	38.7	39.2	39.7	39.2	39.1	39.1	38.9	39.0	39.6	39.1
2000	39.2	39.6	40.0	40.2	40.3	40.6	40.3	40.1	40.2	40.4	40.5	40.8	40.2
2001	41.3	41.2	41.5	40.7	40.8	41.4	41.4	41.2	41.2	41.1	41.1	41.6	41.2
2002	41.0	41.0	41.2	41.3	41.2	41.9	41.5	41.4	41.1	41.3	41.1	41.5	41.3
2003	41.0	40.8	41.1	41.1	40.9	41.7	41.2	41.3	40.8	40.8	40.6	40.9	41.0
2004	40.8	41.0	41.1	41.4	41.3	42.1	42.1	42.1	41.8	42.7	41.7	41.7	41.7
2005	41.3	41.4	41.5	41.8	41.7	42.2	42.1	42.1	41.3	41.2	41.0	41.1	41.6
2006	40.6	40.7	40.8	41.2	41.3	41.9	42.0	41.8	41.6	41.5	41.5	41.8	41.4
2007	41.1	41.3	41.4	42.2	41.9	42.6	42.2	41.9	41.3	42.4	42.2	42.3	41.9
2008	41.7	42.0	42.1	42.6	42.7	43.2	43.2	43.0	42.4	42.9	42.6	42.6	42.6
2009	41.4	41.4	41.6	42.0	41.9	42.4	42.1	42.1	41.7	41.9	41.4	41.6	41.8
Government													
1990	83.4	85.8	86.6	87.6	87.9	87.9	80.9	80.3	86.3	87.9	87.8	87.8	85.9
2000	90.7	92.0	92.5	94.7	93.8	96.9	87.3	87.7	90.6	93.8	94.7	92.7	92.3
2001	92.9	95.4	95.3	96.4	95.4	94.3	86.1	86.5	92.9	95.9	95.6	96.4	93.6
2002	94.2	97.1	97.5	96.7	96.0	96.3	87.3	87.3	91.4	98.1	98.5	98.3	94.9
2003	93.4	97.3	96.8	97.2	94.9	95.5	84.6	85.2	88.1	95.1	94.3	94.7	93.0
2004	89.8	94.9	95.3	93.6	93.6	93.5	83.9	84.9	89.8	92.2	93.5	92.9	91.5
2005	91.6	94.8	93.6	93.7	93.4	93.5	85.1	85.4	92.3	93.0	93.5	92.8	91.9
2006	90.2	92.9	93.4	93.7	93.5	93.9	85.5	85.9	92.2	93.6	93.6	93.2	91.8
2007	90.1	91.7	92.0	92.6	93.0	93.6	85.0	84.9	91.5	92.2	92.2	93.0	91.0
2008	91.2	91.3	93.7	93.3	94.3	94.2	85.9	84.6	93.5	95.1	96.9	95.6	92.5
2009	93.2	95.0	94.9	96.6	96.1	95.1	83.9	83.1	92.1	96.0	96.1	95.7	93.2

Employment by Industry: Minneapolis-St. Paul-Bloomington, MN-WI, Selected Years, 1990–2009

(Numbers in thousands, not seasonally adjusted.)

Industry and year	January	February	March	April	May	June	July	August	September	October	November	December	Annual average
Total Nonfarm													
1990	1359.6	1364.8	1371.0	1381.9	1396.6	1406.0	1391.0	1395.5	1398.6	1406.5	1410.8	1408.2	1390.9
2000	1698.8	1705.1	1717.7	1736.4	1753.8	1769.8	1747.2	1754.7	1763.2	1771.4	1778.2	1779.5	1748.0
2001	1729.4	1732.2	1737.8	1745.3	1762.6	1770.9	1746.8	1748.3	1753.0	1754.1	1755.4	1750.5	1748.9
2002	1695.9	1694.5	1697.2	1708.2	1729.0	1737.9	1720.9	1719.7	1733.3	1736.2	1742.9	1737.2	1721.1
2003	1691.2	1693.8	1696.3	1714.5	1734.8	1741.9	1721.4	1726.0	1735.5	1742.3	1743.5	1744.2	1723.8
2004	1692.9	1694.9	1700.0	1732.0	1751.3	1765.1	1738.3	1738.3	1750.8	1764.0	1764.0	1767.9	1738.3
2005	1715.0	1716.5	1723.9	1754.0	1775.8	1787.5	1765.6	1768.5	1783.1	1792.5	1796.8	1798.2	1764.8
2006	1754.2	1751.1	1760.2	1777.9	1797.9	1815.8	1787.0	1787.2	1794.5	1801.1	1809.6	1808.1	1787.1
2007	1767.0	1767.1	1772.1	1783.7	1808.4	1822.0	1795.9	1796.1	1801.1	1809.6	1814.5	1808.9	1795.5
2008	1764.4	1766.7	1770.6	1780.0	1802.2	1812.6	1792.9	1791.8	1792.3	1795.3	1786.2	1772.2	1785.6
2009	1713.9	1704.0	1695.9	1707.2	1722.3	1721.3	1700.3	1694.2	1687.1	1698.8	1695.2	1685.6	1702.2
Total Private													
1990	1169.8	1171.2	1178.2	1187.0	1198.8	1211.9	1209.5	1218.6	1214.5	1210.8	1212.0	1210.9	1199.4
2000	1464.8	1467.3	1477.9	1494.8	1509.4	1530.9	1530.0	1538.1	1532.9	1536.3	1539.9	1542.0	1513.7
2001	1498.3	1494.4	1499.4	1506.5	1520.8	1533.5	1526.9	1529.6	1519.2	1514.6	1514.0	1509.2	1513.9
2002	1459.0	1452.5	1454.7	1465.7	1484.4	1498.7	1497.5	1504.2	1495.4	1494.1	1496.0	1492.7	1482.9
2003	1453.4	1449.5	1452.2	1467.5	1487.3	1500.2	1497.2	1503.7	1496.8	1497.4	1497.2	1497.4	1483.3
2004	1452.1	1448.5	1454.3	1485.9	1503.0	1521.3	1517.8	1521.5	1513.2	1520.2	1518.5	1521.6	1498.2
2005	1470.9	1469.4	1476.9	1507.0	1528.6	1543.6	1539.0	1546.6	1542.5	1545.8	1551.1	1551.4	1522.7
2006	1511.1	1506.1	1514.9	1532.8	1551.8	1572.8	1560.5	1566.0	1553.6	1554.8	1561.9	1560.0	1545.5
2007	1526.2	1523.4	1528.9	1541.0	1563.1	1580.4	1572.9	1578.2	1563.5	1566.9	1570.4	1566.0	1556.7
2008	1524.2	1520.8	1525.3	1535.0	1554.2	1567.1	1564.2	1566.0	1549.5	1549.4	1538.6	1526.0	1543.4
2009	1474.7	1458.9	1451.3	1461.4	1475.1	1477.1	1470.5	1469.9	1450.3	1456.7	1450.7	1444.4	1461.8
Goods-Producing													
1990	258.8	258.0	259.3	263.1	267.1	271.9	273.4	275.5	272.6	269.8	267.1	261.4	266.5
2000	300.5	300.4	303.9	310.6	315.9	322.4	323.9	326.5	322.0	322.2	319.8	315.5	315.3
2001	305.1	303.4	303.7	305.7	310.2	314.0	315.2	315.3	313.8	308.7	304.3	298.7	308.2
2002	286.1	283.6	283.7	287.3	293.7	299.3	300.9	303.5	299.4	296.9	293.5	286.8	292.9
2003	277.5	274.2	274.4	279.5	286.5	292.8	292.9	295.1	291.7	289.4	287.1	282.5	285.3
2004	271.8	269.8	271.0	281.1	286.3	293.5	296.0	298.2	295.4	296.0	291.9	288.8	286.7
2005	277.1	275.7	277.3	285.5	293.1	299.8	299.2	301.0	297.8	293.9	292.2	286.5	289.9
2006	277.6	275.0	276.4	283.2	289.4	296.0	294.7	295.8	291.2	289.8	286.4	280.5	286.3
2007	272.0	269.1	269.9	272.7	280.6	286.5	285.7	286.9	281.9	280.8	278.1	272.0	278.0
2008	262.5	259.9	259.6	262.2	270.0	275.2	275.4	275.6	270.7	268.4	261.8	253.1	266.2
2009	240.6	234.1	230.2	232.1	235.9	238.9	238.2	237.1	233.4	229.9	226.3	220.0	233.1
Mining, Logging, and Construction													
1990	43.2	42.2	42.6	47.9	51.7	54.8	56.2	57.1	55.8	54.7	52.2	46.9	50.4
2000	66.4	66.2	68.7	74.6	79.6	84.1	85.6	86.5	84.8	84.0	81.2	77.3	78.3
2001	71.5	70.7	72.1	76.4	82.1	87.8	90.1	91.3	89.0	87.9	85.5	80.7	82.1
2002	72.3	70.9	71.0	75.8	82.6	86.6	89.6	90.7	88.8	87.3	84.6	79.3	81.6
2003	71.5	69.5	69.9	75.2	82.1	87.0	89.3	90.3	88.5	87.6	84.5	79.8	81.3
2004	71.5	70.3	71.9	79.7	85.0	89.0	92.0	92.6	91.1	90.9	88.8	84.3	83.9
2005	74.2	73.3	74.5	81.2	86.6	91.6	93.6	93.7	91.7	89.1	87.4	82.6	85.0
2006	75.0	74.1	74.8	79.7	85.1	89.1	89.4	89.1	87.7	85.3	82.1	77.0	82.4
2007	70.8	68.7	69.9	72.1	78.8	82.7	82.8	83.1	80.7	79.4	76.5	70.8	76.4
2008	64.6	63.2	63.5	65.3	72.0	75.5	76.5	76.5	74.0	71.8	67.0	61.3	69.3
2009	52.6	51.1	50.8	54.0	59.5	61.2	61.8	61.3	59.9	57.3	54.7	48.2	56.0
Manufacturing													
1990	215.6	215.8	216.7	215.2	215.4	217.1	217.2	218.4	216.8	215.1	214.9	214.5	216.1
2000	234.1	234.2	235.2	236.0	236.3	238.3	238.3	240.0	237.2	238.2	238.6	238.2	237.1
2001	233.6	232.7	231.6	229.3	228.1	226.2	225.1	224.0	224.8	220.8	218.8	218.0	226.1
2002	213.8	212.7	212.7	211.5	211.1	212.7	211.3	212.8	210.6	209.6	208.9	207.5	211.3
2003	206.0	204.7	204.5	204.3	204.4	205.8	203.6	204.8	203.2	201.8	202.6	202.7	204.0
2004	200.3	199.5	199.1	201.4	201.3	204.5	204.0	205.6	204.3	205.1	203.1	204.5	202.7
2005	202.9	202.4	202.8	204.3	206.5	208.2	205.6	207.3	206.1	204.8	204.8	203.9	205.0
2006	202.6	200.9	201.6	203.5	204.3	206.9	205.3	206.7	203.5	204.5	204.3	203.5	204.0
2007	201.2	200.4	200.0	200.6	201.8	203.8	202.9	203.8	201.2	201.4	201.6	201.2	201.7
2008	197.9	196.7	196.1	196.9	198.0	199.7	198.9	199.1	196.7	196.6	194.8	191.8	196.9
2009	188.0	183.0	179.4	178.1	176.4	177.7	176.4	175.8	173.5	172.6	171.6	171.8	177.0
Service-Providing													
1990	1100.8	1106.8	1111.7	1118.8	1129.5	1134.1	1117.6	1120.0	1126.0	1136.7	1143.7	1146.8	1124.4
2000	1398.3	1404.7	1413.8	1425.8	1437.9	1447.4	1423.3	1428.2	1441.2	1449.2	1458.4	1464.0	1432.7
2001	1424.3	1428.8	1434.1	1439.6	1452.4	1456.9	1431.6	1433.0	1439.2	1445.4	1451.1	1451.8	1440.7
2002	1409.8	1410.9	1413.5	1420.9	1435.3	1438.6	1420.0	1416.2	1433.9	1439.3	1449.4	1450.4	1428.2
2003	1413.7	1419.6	1421.9	1435.0	1448.3	1449.1	1428.5	1430.9	1443.8	1452.9	1456.4	1461.7	1438.5
2004	1421.1	1425.1	1429.0	1450.9	1465.0	1471.6	1442.3	1440.1	1455.4	1468.0	1472.1	1479.1	1451.6
2005	1437.9	1440.8	1446.6	1468.5	1482.7	1487.7	1466.4	1467.5	1485.3	1498.6	1504.6	1511.7	1474.9
2006	1476.6	1476.1	1483.8	1494.7	1508.5	1519.8	1492.3	1491.4	1503.3	1511.3	1523.2	1527.6	1500.7
2007	1495.0	1498.0	1502.2	1511.0	1527.8	1535.5	1510.2	1509.2	1519.2	1528.8	1536.4	1536.9	1517.5
2008	1501.9	1506.8	1511.0	1517.8	1532.2	1537.4	1517.5	1516.2	1521.6	1526.9	1524.4	1519.1	1519.4
2009	1473.3	1469.9	1465.7	1475.1	1486.4	1482.4	1462.1	1457.1	1453.7	1468.9	1468.9	1465.6	1469.1

Employment by Industry: Minneapolis-St. Paul-Bloomington, MN-WI, Selected Years, 1990–2009—*Continued*

(Numbers in thousands, not seasonally adjusted.)

Industry and year	January	February	March	April	May	June	July	August	September	October	November	December	Annual average
Trade, Transportation, and Utilities													
1990	291.6	288.3	289.6	290.0	292.2	294.6	291.0	293.6	292.9	293.2	299.8	302.7	293.3
2000	345.6	342.0	341.7	341.9	343.9	347.4	346.7	347.9	347.4	352.1	359.3	364.4	348.4
2001	352.2	347.1	346.6	346.7	349.0	350.8	348.6	347.6	344.4	346.9	351.7	353.5	348.8
2002	339.5	332.6	332.6	333.9	336.7	338.2	334.9	335.0	333.4	336.1	343.3	347.0	336.9
2003	335.4	330.5	330.2	331.2	334.2	335.0	330.9	331.8	331.4	335.3	340.2	343.0	334.1
2004	329.6	326.0	326.0	331.4	335.5	338.7	338.1	338.2	336.3	340.8	347.0	350.6	336.5
2005	335.2	331.4	332.4	337.1	340.5	340.5	338.7	339.1	337.7	342.2	348.7	352.1	339.6
2006	338.7	333.8	334.0	335.7	338.7	341.4	337.4	337.5	336.5	338.8	346.9	349.3	339.1
2007	338.1	334.9	334.1	336.3	340.0	342.5	339.2	339.2	337.8	340.6	346.6	349.5	339.9
2008	336.2	331.0	331.9	331.5	334.5	334.7	331.6	330.9	328.3	329.4	332.5	332.8	332.1
2009	318.3	312.4	310.4	309.8	311.9	312.7	309.2	309.0	306.3	304.9	310.3	307.9	310.3
Wholesale Trade													
1990	69.7	69.9	70.5	70.4	70.6	71.6	71.1	71.8	70.5	69.9	70.0	70.2	70.5
2000	84.0	84.0	84.4	84.6	85.2	87.0	85.9	86.0	85.2	85.5	85.7	86.1	85.3
2001	86.9	86.8	86.8	86.5	86.4	86.9	86.8	86.3	85.3	85.2	85.3	85.1	86.2
2002	83.8	83.8	83.6	83.6	83.7	84.2	84.4	84.3	83.3	83.6	83.4	83.4	83.8
2003	83.7	83.7	83.7	82.9	83.3	83.9	84.2	84.0	83.2	83.3	83.2	83.3	83.5
2004	82.4	82.4	82.5	84.1	84.5	85.4	86.2	86.0	84.9	84.9	84.8	84.9	84.4
2005	83.8	83.7	83.6	85.9	86.5	86.8	86.4	86.5	85.7	86.3	86.3	86.6	85.7
2006	85.8	85.9	86.4	86.6	87.1	88.1	88.1	88.2	87.2	87.3	87.2	87.3	87.1
2007	86.5	86.6	86.8	87.0	87.7	88.6	88.5	88.4	87.0	86.9	87.1	87.2	87.4
2008	86.3	86.1	86.4	86.1	86.4	87.1	87.2	86.9	85.5	85.3	84.7	84.2	86.0
2009	82.2	81.3	80.4	80.3	80.2	80.5	80.4	80.2	78.5	79.1	80.0	79.7	80.2
Retail Trade													
1990	160.7	156.7	156.7	156.5	157.6	158.3	157.0	157.9	157.3	159.6	165.5	168.4	159.4
2000	187.2	183.6	183.0	182.3	183.6	185.5	186.1	187.1	186.3	190.2	197.2	202.0	187.8
2001	190.7	186.3	185.7	185.6	187.8	189.4	188.2	188.8	185.8	189.3	195.6	198.6	189.3
2002	187.5	181.7	181.9	182.6	184.9	186.5	185.3	185.6	183.4	185.2	192.7	196.8	186.2
2003	185.8	181.2	181.0	182.8	185.4	186.4	183.2	184.7	183.4	186.0	191.1	194.0	185.4
2004	183.0	179.4	179.2	181.9	185.1	187.4	186.1	186.2	183.7	186.3	192.4	195.9	185.6
2005	184.0	180.1	180.7	184.2	186.4	186.6	185.1	186.1	185.1	188.9	195.2	198.5	186.7
2006	187.2	182.8	182.5	184.3	186.3	188.4	186.0	186.2	183.8	186.1	193.0	195.8	186.9
2007	187.0	183.0	182.9	184.1	186.7	188.6	186.8	186.9	184.6	187.0	192.9	194.7	187.1
2008	184.7	179.6	179.9	180.1	182.3	182.7	181.3	181.1	177.9	179.1	182.8	183.0	181.2
2009	173.7	169.3	167.8	168.1	170.6	172.1	170.4	171.1	167.6	166.5	170.9	169.9	169.8
Transportation and Utilities													
1990	61.2	61.7	62.4	63.1	64.0	64.7	62.9	63.9	65.1	63.7	64.3	64.1	63.4
2000	74.4	74.4	74.3	75.0	75.1	74.9	74.7	74.8	75.9	76.4	76.4	76.3	75.2
2001	74.6	74.0	74.1	74.6	74.8	74.5	73.6	72.5	73.3	72.4	70.8	69.8	73.3
2002	68.2	67.1	67.1	67.7	68.1	67.5	65.2	65.1	66.7	67.3	67.2	66.8	67.0
2003	65.9	65.6	65.5	65.5	65.5	64.7	63.5	63.1	64.8	66.0	65.9	65.7	65.1
2004	64.2	64.2	64.3	65.4	65.9	65.9	65.8	66.0	67.7	69.6	69.8	69.8	66.6
2005	67.4	67.6	68.1	67.0	67.6	67.1	67.2	66.5	66.9	67.0	67.2	67.0	67.2
2006	65.7	65.1	65.1	64.8	65.3	64.9	63.3	63.1	65.5	65.4	66.7	66.2	65.1
2007	64.6	65.3	64.4	65.2	65.6	65.3	63.9	63.9	66.2	66.7	66.6	67.6	65.4
2008	65.2	65.3	65.6	65.3	65.8	64.9	63.1	62.9	64.9	65.0	65.0	65.6	64.9
2009	62.4	61.8	62.2	61.4	61.1	60.1	58.4	57.7	60.2	59.3	59.4	58.3	60.2
Information													
1990	37.2	37.4	37.7	38.0	38.2	38.9	39.0	39.2	39.0	38.2	38.4	38.6	38.3
2000	47.7	48.1	48.3	48.9	49.2	50.5	50.9	50.8	50.2	50.3	50.5	50.7	49.7
2001	50.5	50.4	50.7	50.1	50.1	50.8	50.5	49.7	49.1	49.4	49.5	49.3	50.0
2002	48.0	47.8	47.7	48.2	48.2	48.7	48.3	47.4	46.6	46.6	46.7	47.0	47.6
2003	45.6	45.4	45.3	45.9	45.8	45.4	44.9	44.5	43.9	43.7	43.9	44.3	44.9
2004	43.5	43.3	43.5	44.2	44.3	44.1	43.4	42.7	42.2	42.2	42.7	42.9	43.3
2005	42.1	42.1	41.9	43.6	43.6	43.8	43.0	42.5	42.2	42.0	42.2	42.2	42.6
2006	41.7	41.6	41.7	41.3	41.7	41.9	41.7	41.9	41.3	41.3	41.6	41.9	41.6
2007	42.1	42.2	42.4	42.4	42.5	42.7	42.5	42.6	42.2	42.1	42.0	42.3	42.3
2008	41.9	41.7	41.8	41.7	41.7	42.0	42.2	42.1	41.9	41.4	41.5	41.2	41.8
2009	40.7	40.4	40.3	39.9	39.9	40.0	40.2	39.9	39.5	39.3	39.1	39.1	39.9
Financial Activities													
1990	100.9	101.4	101.8	101.8	101.9	103.0	104.5	104.6	104.2	103.6	102.8	103.2	102.8
2000	130.1	130.1	130.5	131.4	131.9	133.7	134.1	134.4	133.6	134.0	133.9	135.1	132.7
2001	133.1	133.8	134.3	134.8	135.1	136.5	136.9	136.9	135.4	135.0	135.3	135.9	135.3
2002	134.9	135.2	135.2	135.5	135.8	136.4	138.0	138.4	137.6	137.4	138.1	138.6	136.8
2003	135.6	136.2	137.0	138.7	139.4	140.0	142.1	142.4	141.4	140.2	140.1	140.5	139.6
2004	139.9	139.5	139.3	140.1	140.3	141.5	141.5	141.6	140.4	140.7	140.7	141.3	140.6
2005	139.2	139.3	139.6	140.8	141.4	143.6	143.4	143.9	142.9	142.4	142.6	143.3	141.9
2006	142.0	142.1	142.4	141.9	142.6	143.8	143.1	142.8	141.7	141.5	141.7	142.1	142.3
2007	141.2	141.7	141.7	140.8	141.1	142.4	142.2	142.3	141.1	141.0	141.1	141.5	141.5
2008	139.2	139.5	139.6	139.4	139.4	140.2	140.9	140.4	138.9	138.5	138.2	138.8	139.4
2009	136.9	136.5	136.1	135.5	135.8	136.1	136.0	135.6	134.2	134.3	134.0	134.0	135.4

Employment by Industry: Minneapolis-St. Paul-Bloomington, MN-WI, Selected Years, 1990–2009—*Continued*
(Numbers in thousands, not seasonally adjusted.)

Industry and year	January	February	March	April	May	June	July	August	September	October	November	December	Annual average
Professional and Business Services													
1990	178.4	179.9	180.7	180.0	182.3	184.4	182.8	184.9	183.7	185.8	185.0	183.8	182.6
2000	255.9	255.2	258.4	263.0	264.7	270.5	269.3	271.0	269.3	270.1	269.0	267.3	265.3
2001	260.5	258.3	258.4	261.8	261.7	263.5	260.6	260.5	257.6	255.8	253.0	251.8	258.6
2002	241.8	241.0	241.0	242.2	244.2	247.3	247.8	249.2	247.5	248.4	246.7	244.6	245.1
2003	237.2	237.5	237.7	238.8	240.0	242.2	243.1	244.2	244.5	246.2	245.0	245.5	241.8
2004	236.4	237.4	238.7	244.4	245.9	249.2	249.3	249.1	248.0	249.6	248.3	247.3	245.3
2005	238.0	238.4	240.6	247.3	249.4	252.6	251.8	254.0	255.4	259.2	259.4	259.0	250.4
2006	253.2	253.7	255.0	258.3	260.9	265.9	263.4	265.2	263.9	265.4	266.4	266.3	261.5
2007	259.1	259.9	261.5	261.9	263.7	267.9	267.7	270.3	267.0	268.9	269.0	267.7	265.4
2008	260.4	260.9	260.6	262.5	264.2	266.9	268.1	268.2	266.4	267.1	263.9	261.4	264.2
2009	249.1	245.0	242.8	244.1	244.4	244.9	245.0	246.6	242.6	250.1	248.3	250.3	246.1
Education and Health Services													
1990	137.0	139.3	140.0	140.5	141.2	138.1	137.7	138.7	142.1	144.9	145.1	145.9	140.9
2000	180.6	184.8	186.2	186.8	187.3	184.2	182.7	183.1	188.0	190.8	192.2	193.4	186.7
2001	185.9	189.0	190.9	191.0	192.3	189.2	187.9	188.5	193.2	197.0	198.7	199.1	191.9
2002	194.5	197.8	198.9	199.6	201.1	198.2	198.7	199.3	203.1	206.3	207.9	208.1	201.1
2003	205.7	210.0	210.9	211.4	212.5	210.5	208.8	208.7	210.5	213.5	214.7	214.3	211.0
2004	211.2	213.7	214.7	216.3	217.1	215.8	212.6	212.4	214.6	218.5	219.2	220.4	215.5
2005	216.7	220.5	221.5	222.6	224.0	222.0	221.8	223.0	225.9	228.7	230.3	231.9	224.1
2006	229.7	231.8	233.9	237.2	237.8	237.1	237.0	237.4	238.6	241.7	244.0	245.0	237.6
2007	244.7	246.6	248.1	250.7	252.0	250.4	248.7	249.4	250.1	254.1	256.4	255.8	250.6
2008	253.1	256.0	257.5	260.1	259.6	257.7	256.9	257.0	259.3	264.3	265.3	264.8	259.3
2009	262.1	264.8	265.4	268.3	268.4	263.5	261.8	261.4	261.5	266.8	267.7	268.2	265.0
Leisure and Hospitality													
1990	109.5	110.1	112.1	115.7	118.1	121.8	122.5	123.3	122.0	117.4	115.7	116.9	117.1
2000	133.7	135.0	136.6	140.3	144.9	149.8	150.1	151.8	150.6	143.7	142.0	141.9	143.4
2001	138.2	139.5	141.0	143.2	148.7	154.4	153.6	157.3	153.0	147.3	144.9	145.5	147.2
2002	141.3	141.5	142.5	145.3	150.8	156.0	153.9	156.1	153.5	148.0	145.1	145.8	148.3
2003	143.1	142.3	142.8	148.2	154.6	158.1	157.1	159.5	156.6	152.6	149.4	150.5	151.2
2004	144.8	144.3	145.9	152.3	157.8	161.9	160.7	162.5	160.5	156.4	153.0	154.1	154.5
2005	148.3	147.7	149.0	153.7	159.1	164.5	164.4	165.9	163.8	160.8	159.4	159.2	158.0
2006	154.2	154.1	156.1	159.3	164.4	169.3	166.4	168.3	164.2	159.8	157.8	157.8	161.0
2007	154.5	154.6	155.5	160.7	167.2	171.4	170.0	170.7	167.7	163.5	160.4	160.1	163.0
2008	155.0	154.7	156.5	159.6	166.8	171.1	170.2	172.3	166.6	162.8	158.3	157.0	162.6
2009	152.0	150.6	151.1	156.0	163.1	164.6	163.9	164.2	158.0	156.5	149.8	149.4	156.6
Other Services													
1990	56.4	56.8	57.0	57.9	57.8	59.2	58.6	58.8	58.0	57.9	58.1	58.4	57.9
2000	70.7	71.7	72.3	71.9	71.6	72.4	72.3	72.6	71.8	73.1	73.2	73.7	72.3
2001	72.8	72.9	73.8	73.2	73.7	74.3	73.6	73.8	72.7	74.5	76.6	75.4	73.9
2002	72.9	73.0	73.1	73.7	73.9	74.6	75.0	75.3	74.3	74.4	74.7	74.8	74.1
2003	73.3	73.4	73.9	73.8	74.3	75.2	77.4	77.5	76.8	76.5	76.8	76.8	75.5
2004	74.9	74.5	75.2	76.1	75.8	76.6	76.2	76.8	75.8	76.0	75.7	76.2	75.8
2005	74.3	74.3	74.6	76.4	77.5	76.8	76.7	77.2	76.8	76.6	76.5	77.2	76.2
2006	74.0	74.0	75.4	75.9	76.3	77.4	76.8	77.1	76.2	76.5	77.1	77.1	76.2
2007	74.5	74.4	75.7	75.5	76.0	76.6	76.9	76.8	75.7	75.9	76.8	77.1	76.0
2008	75.9	77.1	77.8	78.0	78.0	79.3	78.9	79.5	77.4	77.5	77.1	76.9	77.8
2009	75.0	75.1	75.0	75.7	75.7	76.4	76.2	76.1	74.8	74.9	75.2	75.5	75.5
Government													
1990	189.8	193.6	192.8	194.9	197.8	194.1	181.5	176.9	184.1	195.7	198.8	197.3	191.4
2000	234.0	237.8	239.8	241.6	244.4	238.9	217.2	216.6	230.3	235.1	238.3	237.5	234.3
2001	231.1	237.8	238.4	238.8	241.8	237.4	219.9	218.7	233.8	239.5	241.4	241.3	235.0
2002	236.9	242.0	242.5	242.5	244.6	239.2	223.4	215.5	237.9	242.1	246.9	244.5	238.2
2003	237.8	244.3	244.1	247.0	247.5	241.7	224.2	222.3	238.7	244.9	246.3	246.8	240.5
2004	240.8	246.4	245.7	246.1	248.3	243.8	220.5	216.8	237.6	243.8	245.5	246.3	240.1
2005	244.1	247.1	247.0	247.0	247.2	243.9	226.6	221.9	240.6	246.7	245.7	246.8	242.1
2006	243.1	245.0	245.3	245.1	246.1	243.0	226.5	221.2	240.9	246.3	247.7	248.1	241.5
2007	240.8	243.7	243.2	242.7	245.3	241.6	223.0	217.9	237.6	242.7	244.1	242.9	238.8
2008	240.2	245.9	245.3	245.0	248.0	245.5	228.7	225.8	242.8	245.9	247.6	246.2	242.2
2009	239.2	245.1	244.6	245.8	247.2	244.2	229.8	224.3	236.8	242.1	244.5	241.2	240.4

Employment by Industry: Nashville-Davidson–Murfreesboro–Franklin, TN, Selected Years, 1990–2009

(Numbers in thousands, not seasonally adjusted.)

Industry and year	January	February	March	April	May	June	July	August	September	October	November	December	Annual average
Total Nonfarm													
1990	518.2	520.3	526.0	527.5	531.6	529.2	517.8	526.2	532.2	529.6	530.6	530.2	526.6
2000	683.7	687.8	699.1	696.5	700.0	700.7	693.3	698.0	701.3	703.5	705.7	706.2	698.0
2001	687.2	689.4	693.8	697.1	696.9	695.9	691.1	692.5	696.2	692.6	695.1	694.4	693.5
2002	674.2	677.7	682.5	685.1	688.1	685.6	688.4	692.7	697.1	698.0	701.7	703.0	689.5
2003	687.4	688.6	691.5	696.9	699.2	695.2	691.8	698.5	701.7	703.4	707.0	710.2	697.6
2004	695.8	701.3	705.5	711.1	711.8	709.5	712.4	719.6	721.6	727.9	732.0	735.5	715.3
2005	713.7	719.2	724.5	732.7	734.1	731.1	733.1	740.6	744.8	746.0	751.3	753.2	735.4
2006	736.9	739.4	746.9	748.8	750.0	750.3	749.6	757.5	760.0	756.1	761.7	764.2	751.8
2007	744.2	747.8	755.6	754.6	758.2	759.4	759.0	769.8	773.6	770.5	778.4	778.6	762.5
2008	756.0	758.9	762.1	762.8	767.4	761.1	753.4	760.6	764.1	760.9	760.2	759.1	760.6
2009	731.4	730.0	728.1	726.3	726.3	716.7	711.1	718.2	722.7	723.4	725.8	724.7	723.7
Total Private													
1990	444.7	446.5	451.5	452.6	456.5	460.2	457.7	460.2	458.7	455.4	455.8	455.6	454.6
2000	594.5	597.2	604.5	605.2	607.5	613.0	609.2	610.0	612.4	612.2	613.8	614.4	607.8
2001	596.9	597.1	601.4	603.6	604.2	607.8	603.2	604.7	603.8	599.2	600.9	600.5	601.9
2002	582.0	583.8	587.7	591.0	594.5	597.3	602.2	604.6	604.5	604.3	607.9	608.7	597.4
2003	593.5	593.3	595.7	600.4	603.8	606.1	603.1	606.2	606.1	607.6	611.6	613.9	603.4
2004	599.8	601.2	607.0	613.0	615.2	619.9	623.0	626.5	625.8	630.8	634.6	636.9	619.5
2005	617.4	621.0	626.3	634.1	636.5	639.5	641.5	644.8	646.2	647.5	652.7	654.4	638.5
2006	638.7	639.5	646.7	648.7	651.0	657.7	656.2	660.1	659.8	655.8	660.7	662.8	653.1
2007	644.4	646.7	654.4	655.4	660.7	667.4	665.8	670.7	668.9	667.4	673.4	675.2	662.5
2008	653.6	654.7	657.8	659.0	662.5	666.0	658.5	660.7	658.5	654.4	653.0	651.0	657.5
2009	626.6	622.4	621.1	618.8	619.4	621.6	615.2	617.4	616.6	616.2	618.1	616.6	619.2
Goods-Producing													
1990	109.0	109.1	110.1	110.0	110.7	111.5	110.4	109.9	109.9	109.4	109.3	108.0	109.8
2000	129.9	130.3	131.5	130.6	130.4	131.5	129.5	128.9	127.7	126.4	125.0	124.8	128.9
2001	124.7	123.5	124.0	122.9	123.1	124.1	122.7	122.8	122.2	120.6	119.7	119.5	122.5
2002	115.4	114.7	114.5	115.7	116.9	117.6	117.6	117.9	117.7	116.9	116.5	117.1	116.5
2003	114.9	114.7	114.9	115.4	116.4	117.0	117.0	116.8	117.0	117.2	117.0	116.6	116.7	116.2
2004	115.0	115.0	115.8	117.6	118.4	119.3	119.5	119.3	119.2	118.7	118.9	119.2	118.0
2005	116.5	117.3	118.2	120.1	120.7	121.7	120.7	121.9	121.8	122.0	122.2	122.5	120.5
2006	121.4	121.3	122.4	123.0	123.0	124.9	124.1	124.8	124.5	123.1	123.4	123.4	123.3
2007	120.7	120.3	121.4	121.0	121.1	122.3	121.3	121.4	121.6	120.4	120.3	119.8	121.0
2008	116.7	116.1	115.7	115.4	115.8	116.1	114.1	113.5	111.4	108.1	106.0	104.3	112.8
2009	99.3	97.8	96.6	94.9	93.8	93.6	92.8	92.7	91.9	90.8	90.2	89.3	93.6
Mining, Logging, and Construction													
1990	22.3	22.0	22.6	22.4	22.8	23.2	23.4	23.2	22.6	22.1	21.9	21.5	22.5
2000	34.5	34.5	35.6	36.1	37.0	37.5	36.9	36.8	36.1	35.6	34.9	34.7	35.9
2001	32.3	32.5	33.2	33.4	33.9	34.8	34.9	35.0	34.2	33.6	33.4	33.3	33.7
2002	31.1	31.0	31.2	31.5	32.5	33.0	33.6	34.1	34.0	33.6	33.8	33.8	32.8
2003	32.7	32.6	33.2	33.9	34.7	35.4	35.7	35.6	35.5	34.9	34.5	34.6	34.4
2004	33.1	32.9	33.4	34.0	34.6	35.4	35.5	35.3	35.1	34.6	34.5	34.5	34.4
2005	32.8	33.1	34.0	35.2	36.1	37.1	37.2	37.5	37.5	37.3	37.2	37.2	36.0
2006	37.0	37.3	38.3	38.7	39.2	40.3	40.1	40.3	40.2	39.6	39.5	39.6	39.2
2007	38.8	39.3	40.8	41.1	41.7	42.9	42.8	43.1	43.1	42.7	42.4	41.9	41.7
2008	40.3	40.1	40.1	40.1	40.5	40.7	40.0	40.0	39.3	38.1	36.9	35.9	39.3
2009	33.5	32.7	32.4	31.7	31.6	31.8	31.8	31.6	31.2	30.5	29.8	29.1	31.5
Manufacturing													
1990	86.7	87.1	87.5	87.6	87.9	88.3	87.0	86.7	87.3	87.3	87.4	86.5	87.3
2000	95.4	95.8	95.9	94.6	93.4	94.1	92.6	92.1	91.6	90.8	90.0	90.1	93.0
2001	92.4	91.0	90.8	89.5	89.2	89.3	87.8	87.8	88.0	87.0	86.3	86.2	88.8
2002	84.3	83.7	83.3	84.2	84.4	84.5	83.9	83.9	83.7	83.3	82.7	83.3	83.8
2003	82.2	82.1	81.7	81.5	81.7	81.6	81.1	81.4	81.7	82.1	82.1	82.1	81.8
2004	81.9	82.1	82.4	83.6	83.8	83.9	84.0	84.0	84.1	84.1	84.4	84.7	83.6
2005	83.7	84.2	84.2	84.9	84.6	84.6	83.5	84.4	84.3	84.7	85.0	85.3	84.5
2006	84.4	84.0	84.1	84.3	83.8	84.6	84.0	84.5	84.3	83.5	83.9	83.8	84.1
2007	81.9	81.0	80.6	79.9	79.4	79.4	78.5	78.3	78.5	77.7	77.9	77.9	79.3
2008	76.4	76.0	75.6	75.3	75.3	75.4	74.1	73.5	72.1	70.0	69.1	68.4	73.4
2009	65.8	65.1	64.2	63.2	62.2	61.8	61.0	61.1	60.7	60.3	60.4	60.2	62.2
Service-Providing													
1990	409.2	411.2	415.9	417.5	420.9	417.7	407.4	416.3	422.3	420.2	421.3	422.2	416.8
2000	553.8	557.5	567.6	565.8	569.7	569.2	563.8	569.1	573.6	577.2	580.8	581.4	569.1
2001	562.5	565.9	569.8	574.2	573.8	571.9	568.4	569.7	574.0	572.0	575.4	574.9	571.0
2002	558.8	563.0	568.0	569.3	571.2	568.1	570.8	574.7	579.4	581.1	585.2	585.9	573.0
2003	572.5	573.9	576.6	581.5	582.8	578.2	575.0	581.5	584.5	586.4	590.4	593.5	581.4
2004	580.8	586.3	589.7	593.5	593.4	590.2	592.9	600.3	602.4	609.2	613.1	616.3	597.3
2005	597.2	601.9	606.3	612.6	613.4	609.4	612.4	618.7	623.0	624.0	629.1	630.7	614.9
2006	615.5	618.1	624.5	625.8	627.0	625.4	625.5	632.7	635.5	633.0	638.3	640.8	628.5
2007	623.5	627.5	634.2	633.6	637.1	637.1	637.7	648.4	652.0	650.1	658.1	658.8	641.5
2008	639.3	642.8	646.4	647.4	651.6	645.0	639.3	647.1	652.7	652.8	654.2	654.8	647.8
2009	632.1	632.2	631.5	631.4	632.5	623.1	618.3	625.5	630.8	632.6	635.6	635.4	630.1

Employment by Industry: Nashville-Davidson–Murfreesboro–Franklin, TN, Selected Years, 1990–2009—*Continued*

(Numbers in thousands, not seasonally adjusted.)

Industry and year	January	February	March	April	May	June	July	August	September	October	November	December	Annual average
Trade, Transportation, and Utilities													
1990	113.9	112.7	113.2	113.3	114.0	114.0	114.0	115.3	115.2	114.9	116.4	117.4	114.5
2000	139.6	139.5	140.2	140.4	140.2	141.0	142.0	142.6	143.9	146.3	148.4	149.3	142.8
2001	142.4	141.5	142.0	142.5	142.5	142.5	140.8	140.7	140.5	140.5	142.9	143.4	141.9
2002	135.8	134.7	136.0	134.5	135.2	136.0	137.2	137.6	138.3	140.7	143.1	145.4	137.9
2003	139.3	139.0	139.3	139.7	140.0	141.3	140.6	142.0	141.9	143.9	146.5	148.3	141.8
2004	142.5	141.8	142.9	143.0	143.7	144.8	144.9	146.1	146.6	149.2	152.2	153.7	146.0
2005	146.4	146.1	147.3	148.5	149.1	149.1	150.5	150.9	152.1	153.3	156.8	158.5	150.7
2006	151.9	151.4	152.9	152.5	153.0	153.7	152.7	153.6	153.9	153.3	156.4	158.6	153.7
2007	152.6	152.0	153.6	152.8	153.5	153.7	153.4	154.1	154.6	154.9	158.7	160.7	154.6
2008	154.3	153.9	154.8	153.7	153.9	153.9	154.2	154.4	154.4	154.3	156.1	157.5	154.6
2009	150.5	148.2	147.2	145.8	146.1	146.0	145.5	146.1	145.4	146.4	148.5	148.9	147.1
Wholesale Trade													
1990	28.9	28.6	28.8	28.8	29.0	29.0	29.0	29.3	29.3	29.2	29.6	29.8	29.1
2000	35.5	35.4	35.6	35.7	35.6	35.8	36.1	36.2	36.6	37.2	37.7	37.9	36.3
2001	36.2	35.9	36.1	36.2	36.2	36.2	35.8	35.7	35.7	35.7	36.3	36.4	36.0
2002	34.5	34.2	34.6	34.2	34.3	34.5	34.8	35.0	35.1	35.7	36.3	36.9	35.0
2003	34.8	34.8	34.7	34.7	34.9	34.8	34.5	34.5	34.5	34.2	34.0	33.9	34.5
2004	33.7	33.9	34.1	34.2	34.3	34.6	34.6	35.0	35.1	35.5	35.4	35.5	34.7
2005	35.4	35.7	35.7	36.1	36.3	36.1	36.2	36.3	36.6	36.7	37.0	36.8	36.2
2006	36.4	36.5	36.5	36.4	36.5	36.6	36.5	36.7	36.9	36.3	36.2	36.3	36.5
2007	35.8	36.0	36.3	36.3	36.5	36.7	36.7	36.8	37.2	37.2	37.4	37.4	36.7
2008	37.1	37.3	37.2	37.2	37.6	37.8	38.0	38.2	38.5	38.4	38.4	38.2	37.8
2009	37.2	36.9	36.5	36.3	36.1	35.8	35.7	35.7	35.6	35.7	35.7	35.6	36.1
Retail Trade													
1990	63.6	62.9	63.2	63.2	63.6	63.6	63.6	64.3	64.3	64.1	65.0	65.5	63.9
2000	77.9	77.8	78.2	78.3	78.2	78.7	79.2	79.6	80.3	81.6	82.8	83.3	79.7
2001	79.5	79.0	79.2	79.5	79.5	79.5	78.6	78.5	78.4	78.4	79.8	80.0	79.2
2002	75.8	75.2	75.9	75.0	75.5	75.9	76.6	76.8	77.2	78.5	79.8	81.1	76.9
2003	78.0	77.5	77.7	78.0	78.0	79.1	78.6	79.8	80.3	82.5	85.1	86.8	80.1
2004	81.9	80.9	81.3	81.2	81.5	82.1	81.9	82.4	82.5	84.3	87.0	88.0	82.9
2005	83.2	82.6	83.6	83.9	84.2	84.1	84.3	84.3	84.9	85.5	88.4	89.7	84.9
2006	84.8	84.3	85.3	85.5	85.8	86.0	85.3	85.8	85.6	85.8	89.1	90.6	86.2
2007	86.4	85.6	86.8	86.1	86.7	86.5	86.1	86.5	86.6	87.3	90.7	92.5	87.3
2008	87.6	87.1	88.1	86.8	86.5	86.2	86.1	86.2	85.8	85.7	87.7	88.6	86.9
2009	83.9	82.5	82.1	81.6	82.1	82.2	82.3	82.7	82.0	83.0	85.5	86.2	83.0
Transportation and Utilities													
1990	21.5	21.3	21.4	21.4	21.5	21.5	21.5	21.8	21.8	21.7	22.0	22.2	21.6
2000	26.4	26.4	26.5	26.5	26.5	26.6	26.8	27.0	27.2	27.7	28.1	28.2	27.0
2001	26.9	26.7	26.8	26.9	26.9	26.9	26.6	26.6	26.6	26.5	27.0	27.1	26.8
2002	25.7	25.5	25.7	25.4	25.6	25.7	25.9	26.0	26.1	26.6	27.0	27.5	26.1
2003	26.5	26.7	26.9	27.0	27.1	27.4	27.5	27.7	27.1	27.2	27.4	27.6	27.2
2004	26.9	27.0	27.5	27.6	27.9	28.1	28.4	28.7	29.0	29.4	29.8	30.2	28.4
2005	27.8	27.8	28.0	28.5	28.6	28.9	30.0	30.3	30.6	31.1	31.4	32.0	29.6
2006	30.7	30.6	31.1	30.6	30.7	31.1	30.9	31.1	31.4	31.2	31.1	31.7	31.0
2007	30.4	30.4	30.5	30.4	30.3	30.5	30.6	30.8	30.8	30.4	30.6	30.8	30.5
2008	29.6	29.5	29.5	29.7	29.8	29.9	30.1	30.0	30.1	30.2	30.0	30.7	29.9
2009	29.4	28.8	28.6	27.9	27.9	28.0	27.5	27.7	27.8	27.7	27.3	27.1	28.0
Information													
1990	16.5	16.5	16.7	16.2	16.1	16.3	16.2	16.3	16.2	16.1	16.1	16.2	16.3
2000	21.1	21.0	21.3	21.2	21.2	21.4	21.7	21.7	21.7	21.8	22.3	22.5	21.6
2001	23.9	24.1	24.1	23.4	23.4	23.4	23.0	22.7	22.5	22.8	22.9	22.9	23.3
2002	22.3	22.2	22.4	21.9	21.8	21.5	21.5	21.3	21.0	21.3	21.1	20.9	21.6
2003	20.2	20.1	20.1	19.9	20.0	19.8	19.8	19.8	19.6	19.6	19.8	19.8	19.9
2004	19.5	19.4	19.3	19.3	19.3	19.5	19.5	19.5	18.8	19.1	19.2	19.9	19.4
2005	19.8	19.9	19.8	19.5	19.5	19.7	19.7	19.6	19.6	19.7	19.8	19.8	19.7
2006	19.6	19.6	19.7	19.6	19.7	19.7	19.0	18.9	19.0	19.0	19.1	19.2	19.3
2007	19.0	19.0	19.0	19.2	19.6	19.7	19.9	20.0	20.1	20.3	20.4	20.8	19.8
2008	21.1	21.1	21.2	21.2	21.3	21.3	21.0	21.0	20.9	21.2	21.1	21.2	21.1
2009	20.8	20.7	20.6	20.4	20.3	20.2	20.1	20.3	20.2	20.2	20.2	20.2	20.4
Financial Activities													
1990	37.8	38.0	38.1	38.3	38.6	38.8	38.7	38.6	38.2	37.7	37.6	37.7	38.2
2000	47.2	47.3	47.3	47.0	47.0	47.3	47.2	46.8	46.5	46.1	46.3	46.3	46.9
2001	43.9	44.2	44.4	44.6	44.6	44.8	44.8	44.6	44.1	43.7	43.5	43.2	44.2
2002	42.7	42.8	42.7	43.1	43.3	43.9	43.8	44.0	43.8	44.1	44.3	44.4	43.6
2003	44.4	44.5	44.7	44.8	44.8	45.1	44.8	44.8	44.6	44.6	44.5	44.7	44.7
2004	44.0	44.0	44.2	44.5	44.4	44.4	44.5	44.6	44.5	44.9	45.1	45.2	44.5
2005	44.4	44.5	44.7	45.1	45.3	45.4	45.5	45.6	45.6	45.4	45.6	45.7	45.2
2006	45.3	45.2	45.5	45.7	45.9	45.9	46.0	45.9	45.7	45.8	45.7	45.9	45.7
2007	45.3	45.6	45.8	46.1	46.6	46.8	46.6	46.6	46.3	46.3	46.2	46.4	46.2
2008	45.9	46.2	46.1	46.1	46.2	46.4	46.3	46.1	45.7	45.3	45.1	45.1	45.9
2009	44.8	44.7	44.5	44.5	44.5	44.6	44.3	44.4	44.1	44.1	44.0	44.3	44.4

Employment by Industry: Nashville-Davidson–Murfreesboro–Franklin, TN, Selected Years, 1990–2009—*Continued*

(Numbers in thousands, not seasonally adjusted.)

Industry and year	January	February	March	April	May	June	July	August	September	October	November	December	Annual average
Professional and Business Services													
1990	40.2	40.9	41.4	41.6	42.0	42.5	42.2	43.1	43.1	43.0	43.1	42.9	42.2
2000	85.0	86.4	88.1	88.0	88.7	89.0	88.0	88.9	90.1	90.3	90.2	90.2	88.6
2001	84.9	84.8	85.5	86.4	85.8	86.0	86.8	88.0	88.4	87.1	87.3	87.6	86.6
2002	84.3	85.7	86.8	87.2	87.5	87.2	87.9	88.7	88.0	86.7	87.5	86.3	87.0
2003	82.4	82.2	82.2	82.8	83.6	84.0	83.0	84.0	84.5	85.4	87.1	87.7	84.1
2004	85.7	86.6	87.7	89.4	89.7	91.0	91.5	93.0	94.0	96.5	96.6	96.5	91.5
2005	92.3	93.4	93.9	95.3	95.2	95.7	96.1	97.8	99.3	99.7	100.5	101.0	96.7
2006	95.4	95.4	96.3	96.6	96.9	99.3	98.7	101.1	102.4	100.8	102.1	102.1	98.9
2007	96.5	97.3	98.9	98.9	100.0	102.6	103.3	104.8	104.2	104.4	106.2	105.8	101.9
2008	99.2	98.9	99.3	100.2	101.1	103.5	98.8	100.5	101.8	102.0	101.9	100.0	100.6
2009	93.4	92.9	92.2	91.2	91.6	93.2	89.9	91.5	92.4	92.9	93.1	92.1	92.2
Education and Health Services													
1990	60.6	61.1	61.3	61.8	61.9	62.0	62.0	62.3	63.5	63.4	63.5	63.6	62.3
2000	80.5	81.2	82.0	83.0	82.4	82.4	82.6	82.6	83.5	83.9	84.4	84.3	82.7
2001	83.3	84.3	84.7	86.1	86.0	86.5	86.7	86.7	87.0	86.7	87.1	87.7	86.1
2002	87.2	88.0	88.4	89.5	90.0	90.0	92.0	92.0	92.3	92.6	92.8	92.8	90.6
2003	93.0	93.4	93.7	94.9	94.9	94.9	95.5	95.5	95.5	95.6	95.6	95.8	94.9
2004	96.3	96.6	97.2	98.3	97.9	97.9	99.3	99.2	99.0	99.6	99.7	99.8	98.4
2005	98.7	99.4	99.5	101.2	101.7	101.6	102.5	102.5	102.3	102.2	102.3	102.5	101.4
2006	102.2	102.8	103.5	104.1	104.2	104.5	104.8	105.0	105.1	105.2	105.7	105.6	104.4
2007	104.9	105.8	106.2	107.0	107.5	107.8	108.7	109.5	110.2	109.5	109.7	110.0	108.1
2008	108.9	109.7	109.8	111.3	111.5	111.8	112.2	112.9	113.7	113.8	114.2	114.7	112.0
2009	113.6	114.0	114.0	115.1	114.7	114.3	114.7	114.6	116.3	116.5	116.9	117.0	115.1
Leisure and Hospitality													
1990	46.4	47.7	50.1	50.7	52.4	54.0	53.3	53.8	51.7	50.4	49.4	49.4	50.8
2000	64.6	64.7	66.6	67.6	69.9	72.1	70.9	71.0	71.0	69.7	69.4	69.7	68.9
2001	66.4	66.8	68.4	68.9	69.7	71.0	69.5	70.2	69.4	68.0	67.9	67.4	68.6
2002	65.6	66.3	67.7	69.3	69.5	70.6	71.3	72.4	71.9	70.0	71.0	70.7	69.7
2003	68.1	68.8	70.1	71.9	73.1	73.8	73.0	73.7	73.1	71.8	71.9	71.6	71.7
2004	67.4	68.0	69.5	71.2	72.5	73.5	74.0	74.8	74.2	73.0	72.9	73.3	72.0
2005	70.4	71.3	72.7	74.6	75.4	76.3	76.7	76.8	75.6	75.4	75.4	74.7	74.6
2006	73.2	73.9	75.8	77.1	77.9	78.9	80.4	80.4	78.9	78.2	78.1	78.1	77.6
2007	75.9	76.8	79.0	80.1	81.8	83.8	82.4	83.8	81.6	81.0	81.3	81.2	80.7
2008	77.1	77.9	79.4	80.3	81.6	81.9	80.8	81.4	80.1	78.5	77.8	77.5	79.5
2009	74.4	74.0	75.5	76.8	78.1	79.0	77.5	77.7	76.6	75.1	75.3	74.9	76.2
Other Services													
1990	20.3	20.5	20.6	20.7	20.8	21.1	20.9	20.9	20.9	20.5	20.4	20.4	20.7
2000	26.5	26.9	27.5	27.4	27.7	28.4	27.5	27.7	28.1	27.9	27.9	27.2	27.6
2001	27.4	28.0	28.4	28.9	29.1	29.6	29.0	29.1	29.8	29.9	29.6	28.7	29.0
2002	28.8	29.3	29.2	29.7	30.3	30.6	30.9	30.7	31.4	32.1	31.6	31.3	30.5
2003	31.2	30.6	30.7	31.0	31.0	30.2	29.6	29.4	29.7	29.8	29.6	29.3	30.2
2004	29.4	29.8	30.4	29.7	29.3	29.5	29.8	30.0	29.5	29.8	30.0	29.3	29.7
2005	28.9	29.1	30.2	29.8	29.6	30.0	29.8	29.7	29.9	29.8	30.1	29.7	29.7
2006	29.7	29.9	30.6	30.1	30.4	30.8	30.5	30.4	30.3	30.4	30.2	29.9	30.3
2007	29.5	29.9	30.5	30.3	30.6	30.7	30.2	30.5	30.3	30.6	30.6	30.5	30.4
2008	30.4	30.9	31.5	30.8	31.1	31.1	31.1	30.9	30.5	31.2	30.8	30.7	30.9
2009	29.8	30.1	30.5	30.1	30.3	30.7	30.4	30.1	29.7	30.2	29.9	29.9	30.1
Government													
1990	73.5	73.8	74.5	74.9	75.1	69.0	60.1	66.0	73.5	74.2	74.8	74.6	72.0
2000	89.2	90.6	94.6	91.3	92.6	87.7	84.2	88.0	89.0	91.3	91.9	91.8	90.2
2001	90.3	92.3	92.4	93.6	92.8	88.2	87.9	87.8	92.4	93.4	94.2	93.9	91.6
2002	92.2	93.9	94.7	94.1	93.6	88.3	86.2	88.1	92.6	93.7	93.8	94.2	92.1
2003	93.9	95.3	95.8	96.5	95.4	89.1	88.7	92.3	95.6	95.8	95.4	96.3	94.2
2004	96.0	100.1	98.5	98.1	96.6	89.6	89.4	93.1	95.8	97.1	97.4	98.6	95.9
2005	96.3	98.2	98.2	98.6	97.6	91.6	91.6	95.8	98.6	98.5	98.6	98.8	96.9
2006	98.2	99.9	100.2	100.1	99.0	92.6	93.4	97.4	100.2	100.3	101.0	101.4	98.6
2007	99.8	101.1	101.2	99.2	97.5	92.0	93.2	99.1	104.7	103.1	105.0	103.4	99.9
2008	102.4	104.2	104.3	103.8	104.9	95.1	94.9	99.9	105.6	106.5	107.2	108.1	103.1
2009	104.8	107.6	107.0	107.5	106.9	95.1	95.9	100.8	106.1	107.2	107.7	108.1	104.6

Employment by Industry: New Haven, CT, Selected Years, 1990–2009

(Numbers in thousands, not seasonally adjusted.)

Industry and year	January	February	March	April	May	June	July	August	September	October	November	December	Annual average
Total Nonfarm													
1990	273.0	273.8	276.4	276.7	278.3	279.6	271.4	269.3	276.2	275.4	276.1	274.7	275.1
2000	269.0	272.7	275.0	275.1	276.6	278.9	269.8	269.0	275.5	275.5	277.5	279.2	274.5
2001	268.1	270.3	271.4	273.8	275.7	279.0	269.2	269.4	275.1	275.1	276.8	278.1	273.5
2002	269.0	270.9	272.6	275.2	277.6	281.3	271.0	270.5	276.0	275.0	277.0	278.1	274.5
2003	267.5	269.0	269.0	270.6	271.6	271.7	265.8	265.1	267.7	271.4	274.6	275.5	270.0
2004	266.6	268.0	269.2	271.5	273.4	273.8	269.8	267.6	271.3	275.5	277.0	278.0	271.8
2005	268.2	270.7	269.3	275.1	275.6	277.6	270.2	268.0	274.5	274.8	277.7	278.8	273.4
2006	270.2	273.7	273.4	276.9	278.8	280.3	272.2	270.5	276.6	278.7	280.5	281.9	276.1
2007	272.3	275.0	273.8	277.8	279.7	281.8	273.8	272.6	278.4	280.9	282.5	283.4	277.7
2008	276.0	278.4	276.9	278.6	280.6	280.4	271.6	270.0	276.1	277.2	279.1	278.4	276.9
2009	268.1	269.1	265.7	266.6	268.7	268.4	259.7	258.4	264.7	266.2	268.8	267.9	266.0
Total Private													
1990	236.5	237.0	239.4	239.7	241.3	243.3	238.2	236.6	241.4	239.2	239.0	238.1	239.1
2000	234.3	236.9	239.1	239.1	241.2	243.9	239.2	238.6	240.7	240.1	241.7	243.3	239.8
2001	233.0	234.6	235.8	238.0	240.0	243.7	238.4	238.2	240.9	239.5	240.1	241.5	238.6
2002	233.3	234.6	236.4	239.5	241.8	245.1	240.3	239.5	241.9	239.3	240.2	241.3	239.4
2003	231.7	232.9	232.7	234.4	235.5	237.5	234.6	234.3	233.7	236.1	238.2	239.5	235.1
2004	231.8	232.4	233.3	235.8	237.7	239.8	238.3	237.1	237.8	240.3	241.2	242.3	237.3
2005	233.9	235.5	234.2	239.4	240.2	241.8	239.8	238.2	240.8	240.1	242.3	243.3	239.1
2006	234.9	238.2	238.0	241.5	243.1	244.3	241.4	240.1	242.7	243.8	245.1	246.4	241.6
2007	237.3	239.7	238.5	242.6	244.3	245.6	243.2	242.3	244.4	245.7	246.7	247.7	243.2
2008	240.7	242.6	241.4	243.6	244.8	245.1	241.2	240.1	241.8	241.9	243.2	242.7	242.4
2009	232.9	233.8	230.5	231.7	233.0	233.7	229.9	229.2	231.3	232.6	234.3	233.7	232.2
Goods-Producing													
1990	59.5	58.9	59.1	59.5	59.8	59.9	59.7	59.5	59.8	58.6	58.0	57.0	59.1
2000	50.3	50.3	50.8	50.6	51.0	51.8	51.3	51.3	51.4	51.1	50.9	50.7	51.0
2001	49.3	48.8	49.3	49.6	49.8	50.4	50.6	50.1	50.2	49.8	49.4	48.9	49.7
2002	47.5	46.9	47.2	47.4	47.7	48.1	47.7	47.5	47.3	46.8	46.5	46.1	47.2
2003	44.4	44.0	44.0	44.6	45.1	45.7	45.3	45.4	45.1	45.1	45.1	45.0	44.9
2004	43.9	43.5	44.3	45.1	45.7	46.3	46.4	46.4	46.1	45.7	45.6	45.3	45.4
2005	43.9	43.4	43.7	44.2	44.5	45.3	45.3	45.1	44.5	44.2	44.1	43.8	44.3
2006	43.3	43.1	43.3	44.0	44.4	45.0	44.9	44.7	44.1	44.0	43.9	43.7	44.0
2007	42.9	42.5	42.7	43.4	43.6	44.2	43.9	44.1	43.8	43.6	43.7	43.3	43.5
2008	42.6	42.1	42.1	42.3	42.7	42.9	42.8	42.6	42.2	41.8	41.6	40.8	42.2
2009	38.1	37.2	36.9	37.5	37.9	38.2	37.3	37.2	36.8	36.7	36.6	36.3	37.2
Mining, Logging, and Construction													
1990	14.1	13.9	14.0	14.6	15.0	15.2	15.6	15.6	15.6	14.3	13.8	12.8	14.5
2000	10.1	10.0	10.4	10.7	11.2	11.7	11.7	11.7	11.6	11.4	11.2	10.9	11.1
2001	9.8	9.7	10.1	11.3	11.7	12.0	12.0	12.0	11.8	11.5	11.5	11.1	11.2
2002	10.0	10.0	10.4	11.1	11.5	11.7	11.7	11.7	11.5	11.3	11.2	10.6	11.1
2003	9.6	9.4	9.6	10.2	10.8	11.1	11.3	11.4	11.1	11.1	11.0	10.8	10.6
2004	9.9	9.7	10.3	11.3	11.8	12.1	12.3	12.3	12.0	11.7	11.5	11.1	11.3
2005	10.0	9.7	9.9	10.6	11.0	11.4	11.7	11.8	11.4	11.3	11.2	10.9	10.9
2006	10.1	10.1	10.3	11.1	11.5	11.9	12.1	12.1	12.0	11.7	11.6	11.4	11.3
2007	10.7	10.4	10.7	11.3	11.7	12.1	12.3	12.4	12.2	12.1	12.2	11.8	11.7
2008	11.0	10.8	10.9	11.1	11.5	11.6	11.7	11.7	11.4	11.1	11.0	10.5	11.2
2009	9.3	8.9	8.9	9.4	9.8	10.0	9.9	10.0	9.7	9.7	9.6	9.3	9.5
Manufacturing													
1990	45.4	45.0	45.1	44.9	44.8	44.7	44.1	43.9	44.2	44.3	44.2	44.2	44.6
2000	40.2	40.3	40.4	39.9	39.8	40.1	39.6	39.6	39.8	39.7	39.7	39.8	39.9
2001	39.5	39.1	39.2	38.3	38.1	38.4	38.6	38.1	38.4	38.3	37.9	37.8	38.5
2002	37.5	36.9	36.8	36.3	36.2	36.4	36.0	35.8	35.8	35.5	35.3	35.5	36.2
2003	34.8	34.6	34.4	34.4	34.3	34.6	34.0	34.0	34.0	34.0	34.1	34.2	34.3
2004	34.0	33.8	34.0	33.8	33.9	34.2	34.1	34.1	34.1	34.0	34.1	34.2	34.0
2005	33.9	33.7	33.8	33.6	33.5	33.9	33.6	33.3	33.1	32.9	32.9	32.9	33.4
2006	33.2	33.0	33.0	32.9	32.9	33.1	32.8	32.6	32.1	32.3	32.3	32.3	32.7
2007	32.2	32.1	32.0	32.1	31.9	32.1	31.6	31.7	31.6	31.5	31.5	31.5	31.8
2008	31.6	31.3	31.2	31.2	31.2	31.3	31.1	30.9	30.8	30.7	30.6	30.3	31.0
2009	28.8	28.3	28.0	28.1	28.1	28.2	27.4	27.2	27.1	27.0	27.0	27.0	27.7
Service-Providing													
1990	213.5	214.9	217.3	217.2	218.5	219.7	211.7	209.8	216.4	216.8	218.1	217.7	216.0
2000	218.7	222.4	224.2	224.5	225.6	227.1	218.5	217.7	224.1	224.4	226.6	228.5	223.5
2001	218.8	221.5	222.1	224.2	225.9	228.6	218.6	219.3	224.9	225.3	227.4	229.2	223.8
2002	221.5	224.0	225.4	227.8	229.9	233.2	223.3	223.0	228.7	228.2	230.5	232.0	227.3
2003	223.1	225.0	225.0	226.0	226.5	226.0	220.5	219.7	222.6	226.3	229.5	230.5	225.1
2004	222.7	224.5	224.9	226.4	227.7	227.5	223.4	221.2	225.2	229.8	231.4	232.7	226.5
2005	224.3	227.3	225.6	230.9	231.1	232.3	224.9	222.9	230.0	230.6	233.6	235.0	229.0
2006	226.9	230.6	230.1	232.9	234.4	235.3	227.3	225.8	232.5	234.7	236.6	238.2	232.1
2007	229.4	232.5	231.1	234.4	236.1	237.6	229.9	228.5	234.6	237.3	238.8	240.1	234.2
2008	233.4	236.3	234.8	236.3	237.9	237.5	228.8	227.4	233.9	235.4	237.5	237.6	234.7
2009	230.0	231.9	228.8	229.1	230.8	230.2	222.4	221.2	227.9	229.5	232.2	231.6	228.8

Employment by Industry: New Haven, CT, Selected Years, 1990–2009—*Continued*

(Numbers in thousands, not seasonally adjusted.)

Industry and year	January	February	March	April	May	June	July	August	September	October	November	December	Annual average
Trade, Transportation, and Utilities													
1990	53.5	51.8	52.0	51.4	51.6	52.2	50.8	50.7	51.1	51.0	51.6	51.8	51.6
2000	49.1	48.6	49.1	48.8	49.0	49.3	48.8	48.8	49.4	49.8	50.8	51.7	49.4
2001	48.8	47.9	47.9	48.2	48.8	49.3	48.8	48.8	49.1	49.7	50.5	51.3	49.1
2002	49.5	48.7	49.0	50.2	50.7	51.4	50.1	49.7	50.5	50.5	51.4	52.3	50.3
2003	49.7	48.8	49.2	48.8	49.4	49.8	48.4	48.4	49.0	50.1	51.0	51.7	49.5
2004	49.8	48.9	49.3	49.2	49.7	50.3	49.7	49.6	50.4	51.2	52.1	52.9	50.3
2005	51.0	50.3	50.2	50.8	51.3	51.6	50.6	50.4	51.1	51.3	52.4	53.1	51.2
2006	51.4	50.4	50.8	51.1	51.7	52.1	50.8	50.5	51.0	51.4	52.5	53.3	51.4
2007	51.6	51.0	51.0	50.9	51.7	52.3	51.1	50.8	51.1	51.5	52.3	52.8	51.5
2008	51.7	50.6	50.6	50.5	50.8	51.2	50.3	49.9	50.2	50.1	50.8	51.2	50.7
2009	49.1	48.3	47.9	47.4	48.3	48.7	47.7	47.5	47.9	48.4	49.4	49.7	48.4
Wholesale Trade													
1990	13.4	13.3	13.3	13.2	13.1	13.2	13.1	13.0	12.9	12.5	12.5	12.4	13.0
2000	11.2	11.3	11.4	11.3	11.4	11.5	11.4	11.4	11.5	11.4	11.5	11.6	11.4
2001	11.3	11.4	11.3	11.4	11.4	11.4	11.5	11.4	11.3	11.3	11.2	11.2	11.3
2002	11.1	11.0	11.0	11.3	11.4	11.4	11.1	11.1	11.1	11.0	11.0	11.0	11.1
2003	10.8	10.7	10.8	10.8	11.0	11.1	11.1	11.2	11.2	11.5	11.6	11.7	11.1
2004	11.4	11.3	11.4	11.5	11.5	11.6	11.3	11.3	11.4	11.4	11.4	11.5	11.4
2005	11.4	11.3	11.3	11.4	11.4	11.4	11.4	11.4	11.4	11.5	11.6	11.6	11.4
2006	11.5	11.5	11.5	11.6	11.7	11.8	11.7	11.7	11.6	11.5	11.5	11.5	11.6
2007	11.6	11.6	11.5	11.4	11.5	11.6	11.6	11.6	11.6	11.5	11.5	11.6	11.6
2008	11.9	11.8	11.8	11.9	11.9	12.0	12.0	12.0	12.1	12.0	12.1	12.1	12.0
2009	11.9	11.8	11.7	11.5	11.5	11.6	11.5	11.5	11.5	11.5	11.5	11.6	11.6
Retail Trade													
1990	33.2	32.1	32.0	31.4	31.6	32.1	31.3	31.2	31.1	31.2	31.8	32.1	31.8
2000	30.2	29.6	30.1	29.8	29.9	30.1	30.0	30.1	30.0	30.4	31.3	32.1	30.3
2001	29.9	29.0	29.2	29.2	29.7	30.1	29.9	30.2	30.2	30.7	31.6	32.4	30.2
2002	31.0	30.2	30.6	30.9	31.2	32.0	31.5	31.3	31.4	31.4	32.3	33.2	31.4
2003	31.2	30.4	30.6	30.3	30.6	30.8	30.0	30.0	29.9	30.4	31.2	31.8	30.6
2004	30.4	29.6	29.9	29.7	30.0	30.4	30.6	30.6	30.4	30.8	31.6	32.2	30.5
2005	30.4	29.7	29.5	29.9	30.2	30.5	30.2	30.1	30.1	30.4	31.3	32.0	30.4
2006	30.7	29.8	30.1	30.3	30.8	31.2	30.8	30.7	30.5	31.1	32.2	32.8	30.9
2007	31.2	30.6	30.7	30.7	31.2	31.6	31.0	30.9	30.5	30.8	31.7	32.0	31.1
2008	30.9	29.9	29.9	29.6	29.9	30.1	29.6	29.5	29.1	29.1	29.8	30.2	29.8
2009	28.7	28.0	27.7	27.6	28.2	28.5	28.1	28.1	27.9	28.4	29.4	29.6	28.4
Transportation and Utilities													
1990	6.9	6.4	6.7	6.8	6.9	6.9	6.4	6.5	7.1	7.3	7.3	7.3	6.9
2000	7.7	7.7	7.6	7.7	7.7	7.7	7.4	7.3	7.9	8.0	8.0	8.0	7.7
2001	7.6	7.5	7.4	7.6	7.7	7.8	7.4	7.2	7.6	7.7	7.7	7.7	7.6
2002	7.4	7.5	7.4	8.0	8.1	8.0	7.5	7.3	8.0	8.1	8.1	8.1	7.8
2003	7.7	7.7	7.8	7.7	7.8	7.9	7.3	7.2	7.9	8.2	8.2	8.2	7.8
2004	8.0	8.0	8.0	8.0	8.2	8.3	7.8	7.7	8.6	9.0	9.1	9.2	8.3
2005	9.2	9.3	9.4	9.5	9.7	9.7	9.0	8.9	9.6	9.4	9.5	9.5	9.4
2006	9.2	9.1	9.2	9.2	9.2	9.1	8.3	8.1	8.9	8.8	8.8	9.0	8.9
2007	8.8	8.8	8.8	8.8	9.0	9.1	8.5	8.3	9.0	9.2	9.1	9.2	8.9
2008	8.9	8.9	8.9	9.0	9.0	9.1	8.7	8.4	9.0	9.0	8.9	8.9	8.9
2009	8.5	8.5	8.5	8.3	8.6	8.6	8.1	7.9	8.5	8.5	8.5	8.5	8.4
Information													
1990	11.3	11.1	11.4	11.1	11.1	11.4	11.4	11.4	11.1	11.0	11.0	11.0	11.2
2000	9.7	9.7	9.8	9.6	9.6	9.8	10.1	10.2	10.2	10.5	10.5	10.4	10.0
2001	10.6	10.6	10.5	10.2	10.2	10.2	10.1	10.2	10.1	10.1	10.1	10.3	10.3
2002	10.0	10.0	10.0	9.8	9.8	9.8	9.7	9.6	9.6	9.5	9.4	9.5	9.7
2003	9.2	9.2	9.2	9.1	9.1	9.1	9.1	9.1	9.0	8.9	9.0	9.0	9.1
2004	8.7	8.6	8.6	8.6	8.6	8.7	8.7	8.7	8.6	8.7	8.7	8.7	8.7
2005	8.6	8.8	8.5	8.4	8.4	8.5	8.4	8.3	8.3	8.2	8.3	8.2	8.4
2006	8.3	8.3	8.2	8.2	8.2	8.2	8.1	8.1	8.0	8.1	8.2	8.2	8.2
2007	8.1	8.2	8.1	8.2	8.2	8.1	8.1	8.1	8.1	8.1	8.1	8.2	8.1
2008	8.1	8.3	8.0	7.9	7.8	7.8	7.7	7.8	7.6	7.6	7.6	7.5	7.8
2009	7.3	7.3	7.0	6.9	6.8	6.8	6.9	6.8	6.7	6.6	6.6	6.5	6.9
Financial Activities													
1990	15.6	15.6	15.7	15.6	15.6	15.7	15.7	15.6	15.5	15.3	15.3	15.4	15.6
2000	13.8	13.7	13.7	13.7	13.7	13.9	14.0	13.9	13.7	13.7	13.7	13.9	13.8
2001	13.9	14.0	14.0	13.8	13.9	14.1	14.2	14.2	14.1	14.1	14.2	14.2	14.1
2002	14.0	13.8	13.9	14.1	14.2	14.3	14.6	14.6	14.3	14.2	14.2	14.3	14.2
2003	14.1	14.1	14.1	14.1	14.2	14.4	14.4	14.5	14.4	14.2	14.2	14.3	14.3
2004	14.1	14.1	14.2	14.2	14.2	14.4	14.2	14.1	14.0	14.0	14.0	14.0	14.1
2005	13.8	13.8	13.8	13.9	14.1	14.3	14.3	14.3	14.1	14.0	14.1	14.1	14.1
2006	14.0	14.0	13.9	14.0	14.0	14.1	14.1	14.1	13.9	13.9	14.0	14.0	14.0
2007	13.8	13.8	13.7	13.7	13.8	13.9	13.8	13.7	13.4	13.4	13.3	13.4	13.6
2008	13.3	13.3	13.3	13.0	13.1	13.2	13.1	13.1	12.9	12.7	12.7	12.7	13.0
2009	12.5	12.5	12.5	12.4	12.4	12.6	12.4	12.3	12.2	12.1	12.1	12.2	12.4

Employment by Industry: New Haven, CT, Selected Years, 1990–2009—*Continued*

(Numbers in thousands, not seasonally adjusted.)

Industry and year	January	February	March	April	May	June	July	August	September	October	November	December	Annual average
Professional and Business Services													
1990	25.2	25.4	25.8	26.3	26.6	27.3	28.0	27.9	27.5	27.0	26.9	26.8	26.7
2000	28.5	29.2	29.6	29.1	29.9	30.6	29.7	29.9	29.7	28.9	29.3	29.8	29.5
2001	27.6	27.9	28.5	28.3	29.4	29.5	28.6	28.9	29.5	27.9	27.8	28.3	28.5
2002	27.4	27.4	28.0	27.6	27.9	28.9	28.1	28.8	29.0	27.7	27.9	27.9	28.1
2003	26.5	26.7	26.6	26.4	26.6	26.8	26.4	26.6	26.5	26.5	26.8	26.9	26.6
2004	25.2	25.6	25.5	25.7	25.9	26.3	26.0	26.0	25.8	25.1	25.2	25.6	25.7
2005	24.6	24.7	24.8	25.7	25.5	26.5	26.2	26.1	25.9	25.5	25.6	25.9	25.6
2006	25.0	25.6	25.8	26.1	26.4	27.2	25.9	26.1	26.2	26.0	26.2	26.4	26.1
2007	25.4	25.6	25.8	26.0	26.3	26.8	26.4	26.7	26.7	26.6	26.6	27.1	26.3
2008	26.4	26.8	26.6	27.1	27.1	27.5	26.0	26.1	26.1	25.3	25.1	25.3	26.3
2009	24.4	23.9	23.7	23.7	23.6	23.6	23.0	23.5	23.2	23.7	23.5	23.5	23.6
Education and Health Services													
1990	47.0	49.7	49.9	49.8	49.6	48.7	44.6	43.5	49.5	50.1	50.3	50.2	48.6
2000	56.3	58.4	58.8	59.3	59.3	58.2	54.8	54.3	57.3	57.5	57.8	58.0	57.5
2001	55.9	58.3	58.2	59.9	58.4	59.8	56.0	55.9	59.5	59.8	60.1	60.3	58.5
2002	58.1	60.7	60.3	61.6	61.6	61.5	58.9	58.4	61.8	61.8	62.4	62.6	60.8
2003	60.6	62.6	61.6	62.5	61.5	60.3	59.1	58.7	59.4	61.4	62.4	62.8	61.1
2004	61.5	63.2	62.1	62.8	62.0	60.9	60.2	59.2	61.2	64.7	65.1	64.8	62.3
2005	62.8	65.0	63.5	65.4	64.4	62.3	61.7	60.8	64.8	65.5	66.6	66.8	64.1
2006	62.7	66.7	65.1	66.9	65.9	64.0	63.9	63.1	67.1	68.4	68.9	68.8	66.0
2007	64.9	68.3	66.5	68.7	67.8	66.2	65.8	64.9	68.5	69.9	70.4	70.5	67.7
2008	68.0	70.8	69.4	70.9	70.1	68.4	67.7	67.0	70.1	72.2	73.4	73.0	70.1
2009	71.0	74.0	71.2	72.1	71.3	70.0	69.0	68.6	71.8	72.8	73.8	73.0	71.6
Leisure and Hospitality													
1990	16.1	16.1	16.7	17.4	18.2	19.1	19.0	18.9	17.7	17.1	16.7	16.7	17.5
2000	16.8	17.1	17.4	18.0	18.7	20.2	20.4	20.2	18.9	18.5	18.5	18.6	18.6
2001	17.1	17.3	17.5	18.1	19.3	20.1	19.9	19.9	18.4	18.1	17.9	18.0	18.5
2002	16.6	16.9	17.6	18.5	19.4	20.5	20.7	20.5	19.1	18.6	18.2	18.2	18.7
2003	17.1	17.5	17.8	18.9	19.5	20.9	21.5	21.3	20.2	19.7	19.3	19.3	19.4
2004	18.4	18.4	19.0	19.8	20.8	22.0	22.1	22.0	21.0	20.3	19.8	20.1	20.3
2005	18.5	18.8	18.9	20.2	21.1	22.1	22.2	22.2	21.3	20.6	20.3	20.3	20.5
2006	19.5	19.5	20.2	20.4	21.5	22.6	22.6	22.4	21.5	20.9	20.4	20.8	21.0
2007	19.7	19.6	20.0	20.8	22.0	22.9	23.0	22.9	21.9	21.6	21.4	21.3	21.4
2008	19.9	20.0	20.5	21.1	22.3	23.0	22.7	22.7	22.0	21.5	21.3	21.3	21.5
2009	19.9	20.0	20.6	21.0	22.1	22.9	22.9	22.7	22.1	21.7	21.6	21.7	21.6
Other Services													
1990	8.3	8.4	8.8	8.6	8.8	9.0	9.0	9.1	9.2	9.1	9.2	9.2	8.9
2000	9.8	9.9	9.9	10.0	10.0	10.1	10.1	10.0	10.1	10.1	10.2	10.2	10.0
2001	9.8	9.8	9.9	9.9	10.2	10.3	10.2	10.2	10.0	10.0	10.2	10.2	10.1
2002	10.2	10.2	10.4	10.3	10.5	10.6	10.5	10.4	10.3	10.2	10.2	10.4	10.4
2003	10.1	10.0	10.2	10.0	10.1	10.5	10.4	10.3	10.1	10.2	10.4	10.5	10.2
2004	10.2	10.1	10.3	10.4	10.8	10.9	11.0	11.1	10.7	10.6	10.7	10.9	10.6
2005	10.7	10.7	10.8	10.8	10.9	11.2	11.1	11.0	10.8	10.8	10.9	11.1	10.9
2006	10.7	10.6	10.7	10.8	11.0	11.1	11.1	11.1	10.9	11.1	11.1	11.2	11.0
2007	10.9	10.7	10.7	10.9	10.9	11.2	11.1	11.1	10.9	11.0	10.9	11.1	11.0
2008	10.7	10.7	10.9	10.8	10.9	11.1	10.9	10.9	10.7	10.7	10.7	10.9	10.8
2009	10.6	10.6	10.7	10.7	10.6	10.9	10.7	10.6	10.6	10.6	10.7	10.8	10.7
Government													
1990	36.5	36.8	37.0	37.0	37.0	36.3	33.2	32.7	34.8	36.2	37.1	36.6	35.9
2000	34.7	35.8	35.9	36.0	35.4	35.0	30.6	30.4	34.8	35.4	35.8	35.9	34.6
2001	35.1	35.7	35.6	35.8	35.7	35.3	30.8	31.2	34.2	35.6	36.7	36.6	34.9
2002	35.7	36.3	36.2	35.7	35.8	36.2	30.7	31.0	34.1	35.7	36.8	36.8	35.1
2003	35.8	36.1	36.3	36.2	36.1	34.2	31.2	30.8	34.0	35.3	36.4	36.0	34.9
2004	34.8	35.6	35.9	35.7	35.7	34.0	31.5	30.5	33.5	35.2	35.8	35.7	34.5
2005	34.3	35.2	35.1	35.7	35.4	35.8	30.4	29.8	33.7	34.7	35.4	35.5	34.3
2006	35.3	35.5	35.4	35.4	35.7	36.0	30.8	30.4	33.9	34.9	35.4	35.5	34.5
2007	35.0	35.3	35.3	35.2	35.4	36.2	30.6	30.3	34.0	35.2	35.8	35.7	34.5
2008	35.3	35.8	35.5	35.0	35.8	35.3	30.4	29.9	34.3	35.3	35.9	35.7	34.5
2009	35.2	35.3	35.2	34.9	35.7	34.7	29.8	29.2	33.4	33.6	34.5	34.2	33.8

Employment by Industry: New Orleans-Metairie-Kenner, LA, Selected Years, 1990–2009

(Numbers in thousands, not seasonally adjusted.)

Industry and year	January	February	March	April	May	June	July	August	September	October	November	December	Annual average
Total Nonfarm													
1990	524.8	526.8	529.1	530.9	533.3	534.0	534.8	538.4	537.3	537.8	540.2	538.6	533.8
2000	614.3	616.8	619.6	619.6	622.8	619.7	610.7	611.8	616.9	617.0	619.0	624.5	617.7
2001	616.1	621.0	625.2	622.8	623.9	623.1	611.6	612.5	617.7	614.5	617.1	618.2	618.6
2002	603.3	605.6	608.9	613.1	611.0	614.1	601.5	602.9	607.6	606.4	612.3	612.7	608.3
2003	604.2	607.4	608.8	615.5	614.2	615.5	607.0	604.2	610.1	611.1	616.5	617.6	611.0
2004	608.0	610.2	614.5	620.6	619.7	618.4	610.0	612.0	610.1	613.9	618.1	616.0	614.3
2005	606.5	607.2	613.1	613.0	612.4	616.3	604.5	603.7	473.2	425.8	438.9	450.9	555.5
2006	446.4	456.3	469.0	472.0	477.6	484.7	480.8	485.0	489.3	496.0	503.0	507.5	480.6
2007	503.8	508.5	515.2	508.3	509.6	512.4	506.5	511.0	511.9	522.2	527.2	530.9	514.0
2008	520.9	524.8	528.4	527.4	526.8	526.2	519.0	526.3	519.3	527.6	530.2	532.3	525.8
2009	519.2	521.8	521.7	520.2	521.3	517.7	513.2	515.3	514.2	518.8	520.0	521.5	518.7
Total Private													
1990	446.8	448.8	451.2	452.5	454.3	456.5	454.9	457.6	459.2	459.3	461.3	460.0	455.2
2000	510.8	512.9	515.2	515.3	518.8	516.0	511.5	512.0	513.9	514.2	516.3	520.7	514.8
2001	512.6	516.8	521.1	518.1	519.6	518.9	512.4	511.8	514.8	511.7	514.6	515.0	515.6
2002	500.4	501.6	504.8	509.2	507.5	509.2	502.0	502.1	504.9	503.2	508.0	508.2	505.1
2003	500.4	502.6	503.6	510.7	509.8	510.3	503.8	504.0	505.6	508.0	512.5	513.7	507.1
2004	504.8	506.2	510.0	513.7	512.8	512.5	506.3	509.3	504.3	509.6	513.1	510.8	509.5
2005	501.3	500.9	506.2	507.9	507.8	511.4	503.1	501.5	371.3	345.5	358.9	371.3	457.3
2006	373.7	383.5	395.5	398.6	403.8	411.3	408.8	412.4	413.4	419.9	425.8	429.5	406.4
2007	427.5	431.1	437.1	435.6	436.5	439.0	435.1	438.6	436.2	444.1	448.4	451.9	438.4
2008	443.0	446.1	449.9	446.7	446.0	446.8	440.5	445.6	437.6	445.0	447.1	449.4	445.3
2009	437.4	439.3	439.8	437.4	438.8	436.2	433.1	434.7	431.4	435.7	436.9	438.3	436.6
Goods-Producing													
1990	88.4	88.9	90.3	91.1	91.1	91.3	91.5	92.6	91.5	92.9	92.3	91.9	91.2
2000	88.6	88.4	88.8	87.7	88.8	89.1	88.6	89.2	87.8	86.9	85.9	85.7	88.0
2001	85.3	86.3	88.1	85.9	86.5	86.8	86.1	85.5	85.0	83.8	82.7	81.9	85.3
2002	80.4	79.9	80.6	80.6	81.1	81.3	80.2	80.7	80.4	80.2	80.1	79.9	80.5
2003	79.4	79.4	79.4	80.5	81.2	81.5	80.3	79.9	79.3	79.4	78.5	78.7	79.8
2004	77.8	77.5	78.2	78.8	78.2	78.4	77.7	77.5	76.9	77.2	76.9	76.9	77.7
2005	75.1	75.8	76.6	76.5	76.9	77.6	77.1	77.2	60.5	65.7	68.8	71.2	73.3
2006	71.5	72.5	73.9	74.5	74.8	76.5	74.8	75.9	75.9	76.6	76.7	76.9	75.0
2007	75.1	75.5	75.8	75.8	76.1	76.8	76.7	77.0	77.1	77.2	77.1	77.4	76.5
2008	77.2	76.7	76.6	77.0	77.4	77.8	78.1	78.4	77.8	78.6	77.8	78.1	77.6
2009	76.3	75.9	75.3	75.0	75.1	74.7	74.8	74.1	73.3	73.2	72.7	72.6	74.4
Mining and Logging													
2005	8.3	8.4	8.6	8.3	8.4	8.6	8.4	8.5	8.1	8.3	8.3	8.4	8.4
2006	7.9	8.0	8.1	8.0	8.0	8.1	8.4	8.5	8.7	8.7	8.5	8.3	8.3
2007	7.8	8.0	8.1	8.3	8.3	8.3	8.4	8.3	8.3	8.6	8.6	8.6	8.3
2008	8.9	8.4	8.4	8.5	8.4	8.4	8.6	8.7	8.8	8.9	8.8	8.7	8.6
Construction													
2005	29.2	29.0	29.6	29.8	30.0	30.0	29.8	29.7	21.8	25.8	28.4	29.4	28.5
2006	30.6	31.1	32.2	32.7	32.9	33.7	31.4	32.0	31.8	32.5	32.3	32.3	32.1
2007	31.6	31.6	31.9	31.7	31.9	32.1	32.0	32.4	32.2	32.2	31.9	31.8	31.9
2008	31.8	31.9	31.8	32.4	32.5	32.6	32.9	33.2	33.1	33.5	32.9	33.0	32.6
Manufacturing													
1990	46.2	46.2	46.1	46.0	46.1	47.2	47.2	47.4	47.5	47.6	47.5	47.7	46.9
2000	46.2	45.8	45.7	44.7	45.3	45.3	45.4	45.4	44.7	44.2	44.1	44.0	45.1
2001	44.2	44.1	44.2	43.7	44.0	44.3	43.4	43.1	43.2	42.3	42.2	42.1	43.4
2002	41.3	41.2	41.2	41.4	41.5	41.7	41.1	41.3	40.6	40.3	40.4	40.4	41.0
2003	39.5	39.4	39.3	39.1	39.3	39.4	39.3	39.3	39.1	39.3	39.0	39.4	39.3
2004	38.5	38.5	38.4	38.9	38.9	39.2	38.9	39.1	38.8	38.4	38.1	38.4	38.7
2005	37.6	38.4	38.4	38.4	38.5	39.0	38.9	39.0	30.6	31.6	32.1	33.4	36.3
2006	33.0	33.4	33.6	33.8	33.9	34.7	35.0	35.4	35.4	35.4	35.9	36.3	34.7
2007	35.7	35.9	35.8	35.8	35.9	36.4	36.3	36.3	36.6	36.4	36.6	37.0	36.2
2008	36.5	36.4	36.4	36.1	36.5	36.8	36.6	36.5	35.9	36.2	36.1	36.4	36.4
2009	35.8	35.5	35.2	35.2	35.2	34.8	34.9	34.6	34.3	34.4	34.2	33.8	34.8
Service-Providing													
1990	436.4	437.8	438.8	439.8	442.3	442.8	443.3	445.9	445.8	444.9	447.9	446.7	442.7
2000	525.6	528.4	530.8	532.0	534.0	530.6	522.0	522.6	529.1	530.1	533.1	538.8	529.8
2001	530.9	534.6	537.0	536.9	537.4	536.3	525.5	527.0	532.8	530.6	534.4	536.3	533.3
2002	522.8	525.7	528.4	532.5	529.9	532.8	521.3	522.2	527.2	526.2	532.2	532.8	527.8
2003	524.8	528.0	529.4	535.0	533.0	534.0	526.7	524.3	530.8	531.7	538.0	538.9	531.2
2004	530.2	532.7	536.3	541.8	541.5	540.0	532.3	534.5	533.2	536.7	541.2	539.1	536.6
2005	531.4	531.4	536.5	536.5	535.5	538.7	527.4	526.5	412.7	360.1	370.1	379.7	482.2
2006	374.9	383.8	395.1	397.5	402.8	408.2	406.0	409.1	413.4	419.4	426.3	430.6	405.6
2007	428.7	433.0	439.4	432.5	433.5	435.6	429.8	434.0	434.8	445.0	450.1	453.5	437.5
2008	443.7	448.1	451.8	450.4	449.4	448.4	440.9	447.9	441.5	449.0	452.4	454.2	448.1
2009	442.9	445.9	446.4	445.2	446.2	443.0	438.4	441.2	440.9	445.6	447.3	448.9	444.3

Employment by Industry: New Orleans-Metairie-Kenner, LA, Selected Years, 1990–2009—*Continued*

(Numbers in thousands, not seasonally adjusted.)

Industry and year	January	February	March	April	May	June	July	August	September	October	November	December	Annual average
Trade, Transportation, and Utilities													
1990	130.4	129.6	129.3	129.7	130.0	131.4	130.6	130.9	130.5	130.7	132.4	133.1	130.7
2000	127.5	127.8	128.3	127.3	128.4	129.3	127.0	127.0	126.5	126.6	128.5	131.5	128.0
2001	127.1	127.2	127.8	127.4	127.3	127.8	126.3	126.8	126.5	125.7	127.3	128.8	127.2
2002	123.1	122.3	123.9	123.9	123.9	125.6	123.5	123.4	123.1	122.5	124.1	126.4	123.8
2003	121.0	120.9	121.3	121.0	120.9	121.4	121.4	121.8	121.1	121.9	124.2	125.6	121.9
2004	121.4	121.3	122.3	123.0	123.3	123.2	122.1	122.4	121.1	122.8	124.2	126.4	122.8
2005	121.5	120.7	121.7	121.3	121.6	122.0	121.1	120.6	88.6	84.1	89.9	94.3	110.6
2006	94.7	96.7	99.3	101.0	102.2	104.0	103.9	104.4	104.2	106.0	107.8	110.1	102.9
2007	107.6	107.2	108.4	107.5	107.7	108.0	107.7	107.8	107.1	109.8	112.3	114.0	108.8
2008	110.0	109.1	109.6	108.6	108.8	108.7	108.2	108.6	106.3	108.3	110.2	111.3	109.0
2009	106.4	105.6	105.5	104.3	104.2	104.7	104.1	103.9	103.5	104.1	105.1	106.2	104.8
Wholesale Trade													
1990	27.2	27.2	27.2	27.3	27.5	27.8	27.4	27.3	27.3	27.3	27.3	27.3	27.3
2000	28.0	28.2	28.5	28.6	28.8	29.0	28.8	28.7	28.6	28.3	28.2	28.5	28.5
2001	28.4	28.5	28.6	28.5	28.6	28.8	28.2	28.2	28.1	28.1	27.9	27.9	28.3
2002	27.1	27.1	27.3	27.4	27.5	27.6	27.1	27.2	27.0	26.9	26.8	26.8	27.2
2003	27.0	27.1	27.1	26.6	26.6	26.6	26.6	26.6	26.3	26.8	26.7	26.6	26.7
2004	26.3	26.3	26.4	26.4	26.5	26.5	26.3	26.3	26.2	25.8	25.8	25.8	26.2
2005	25.3	25.3	25.4	25.8	25.9	26.0	26.2	26.1	21.8	21.9	22.2	22.5	24.5
2006	21.8	22.2	22.4	22.6	22.8	23.0	23.0	23.1	23.1	23.1	23.2	23.4	22.8
2007	23.6	23.7	24.0	23.8	24.0	24.2	24.6	24.8	24.5	24.9	24.9	25.0	24.3
2008	24.5	24.6	24.7	24.0	24.0	24.0	23.9	23.9	23.7	23.8	23.9	23.9	24.1
2009	23.3	23.3	23.3	23.0	22.9	22.9	22.8	22.7	22.5	22.4	22.4	22.6	22.8
Retail Trade													
1990	69.7	68.7	68.4	68.9	69.1	69.8	69.5	69.6	68.9	69.4	71.0	71.8	69.6
2000	70.5	70.2	70.4	69.9	70.6	71.1	69.4	69.8	69.3	69.3	71.5	73.6	70.5
2001	69.4	68.8	69.2	68.6	68.6	68.8	68.3	68.7	68.6	68.1	70.3	71.5	69.1
2002	67.5	66.8	68.1	67.4	67.3	68.6	67.0	66.8	66.5	65.7	67.5	69.4	67.4
2003	66.1	65.9	66.5	66.3	66.5	67.0	66.7	67.3	67.0	67.3	69.5	71.0	67.3
2004	67.8	67.4	67.9	68.7	68.7	68.7	67.9	67.6	66.6	68.0	69.5	71.0	68.3
2005	67.6	66.8	67.4	67.5	67.8	68.0	67.2	66.9	44.1	41.0	45.7	48.8	59.9
2006	50.3	51.6	53.2	54.3	55.1	56.2	56.7	56.8	56.8	58.7	60.1	61.3	55.9
2007	59.4	58.9	59.7	59.1	59.4	59.4	59.4	59.0	58.9	60.5	62.8	64.1	60.1
2008	61.4	60.2	60.6	60.1	60.1	60.1	59.8	60.0	58.3	59.5	61.0	62.0	60.3
2009	58.4	58.1	58.0	57.5	57.7	58.0	57.7	57.6	57.4	57.9	58.7	59.2	58.0
Transportation and Utilities													
1990	33.5	33.6	33.6	33.5	33.4	33.9	33.7	34.0	34.3	34.1	34.2	34.1	33.8
2000	28.9	29.3	29.3	28.8	28.9	29.2	28.8	28.5	28.6	29.0	28.8	29.4	29.0
2001	29.3	29.9	30.0	30.2	30.1	30.2	29.7	29.9	29.8	29.5	29.1	29.4	29.8
2002	28.5	28.4	28.5	29.1	29.1	29.5	29.4	29.5	29.6	30.0	29.8	30.3	29.3
2003	27.9	27.9	27.7	28.1	27.8	27.8	28.1	27.9	27.8	27.8	28.0	28.0	27.9
2004	27.3	27.6	28.0	27.9	28.1	28.0	27.9	28.5	28.3	29.0	28.9	29.6	28.3
2005	28.6	28.6	28.9	28.0	27.9	28.0	27.7	27.6	22.7	21.2	22.0	23.0	26.2
2006	22.6	22.9	23.7	24.1	24.3	24.8	24.2	24.5	24.3	24.2	24.5	25.4	24.1
2007	24.6	24.6	24.7	24.6	24.3	24.4	23.7	24.0	23.7	24.4	24.6	24.9	24.4
2008	24.1	24.3	24.3	24.5	24.7	24.6	24.5	24.7	24.3	25.0	25.3	25.4	24.6
2009	24.7	24.2	24.2	23.8	23.6	23.8	23.6	23.6	23.6	23.8	24.0	24.4	23.9
Information													
1990	8.6	8.6	8.6	8.6	8.6	8.7	8.9	8.9	9.2	8.4	8.4	8.4	8.7
2000	10.3	10.3	10.4	10.4	10.5	10.8	11.3	11.3	11.0	10.8	10.9	11.2	10.8
2001	11.0	11.1	11.2	10.7	10.8	10.8	10.6	10.5	10.3	10.3	10.4	10.2	10.7
2002	10.0	10.0	10.0	9.6	9.5	9.7	9.6	9.6	9.5	9.3	9.3	9.4	9.6
2003	9.8	9.7	9.9	10.0	10.4	10.7	9.2	9.5	9.4	9.1	9.2	9.2	9.7
2004	9.4	9.8	9.8	10.7	10.4	10.7	9.7	11.2	10.1	11.0	12.7	10.8	10.5
2005	10.8	10.6	10.5	9.5	9.6	9.8	10.1	10.5	9.0	7.3	7.4	7.7	9.4
2006	7.1	7.3	8.8	8.1	8.4	7.5	6.7	6.8	6.9	6.9	7.4	7.5	7.5
2007	7.4	8.2	10.1	9.5	9.2	9.8	8.7	8.3	7.3	7.1	7.4	7.3	8.4
2008	8.0	9.2	11.2	9.8	10.6	11.2	7.2	8.6	8.9	6.9	7.4	7.9	8.9
2009	6.0	6.4	6.6	6.3	6.6	7.0	6.4	6.4	6.4	6.4	6.5	6.5	6.5
Financial Activities													
1990	37.3	37.6	37.6	37.7	37.6	38.2	37.6	37.8	37.8	37.6	37.8	37.8	37.7
2000	33.5	33.7	33.8	33.8	33.7	33.5	34.0	34.0	33.7	33.4	33.4	33.6	33.7
2001	33.7	33.9	33.7	33.9	34.0	34.0	34.3	34.2	34.0	34.1	34.2	34.1	34.0
2002	33.7	33.9	34.1	34.5	34.6	34.9	34.7	35.2	35.0	35.5	35.6	35.5	34.8
2003	35.1	34.7	34.6	34.4	34.4	34.5	34.6	34.9	34.6	34.6	34.5	34.5	34.6
2004	33.9	33.8	33.8	34.2	34.1	34.2	34.7	34.7	34.3	34.3	34.1	34.2	34.2
2005	33.2	33.2	33.2	32.8	32.7	32.8	32.9	33.0	27.6	26.2	26.1	25.9	30.8
2006	25.7	25.8	26.1	25.7	26.0	26.3	26.4	26.4	26.4	26.6	26.7	26.8	26.2
2007	27.4	27.5	27.3	27.1	27.2	27.4	27.6	27.5	27.3	27.6	27.5	27.5	27.4
2008	27.0	27.2	27.2	26.9	26.9	26.9	26.6	26.4	26.0	26.2	26.1	26.1	26.6
2009	25.7	25.8	25.8	25.6	25.5	25.6	25.7	25.4	25.3	25.4	25.3	25.3	25.5

Employment by Industry: New Orleans-Metairie-Kenner, LA, Selected Years, 1990–2009—*Continued*

(Numbers in thousands, not seasonally adjusted.)

Industry and year	January	February	March	April	May	June	July	August	September	October	November	December	Annual average
Professional and Business Services													
1990	50.2	50.6	51.1	51.2	51.7	52.6	53.7	54.4	54.2	54.1	54.2	53.6	52.6
2000	72.8	72.7	73.3	74.9	74.7	74.2	73.9	74.5	75.0	74.3	75.4	75.6	74.3
2001	74.9	75.5	75.9	74.3	75.2	75.0	73.8	73.8	74.1	73.9	74.1	74.8	74.6
2002	72.8	72.9	73.2	73.5	72.1	72.2	71.5	71.9	71.3	70.4	70.4	70.9	71.9
2003	70.7	71.6	72.3	73.9	72.0	72.5	71.8	71.9	71.6	73.7	74.5	75.1	72.6
2004	72.8	73.4	73.8	75.0	74.6	74.7	71.5	71.7	71.0	73.1	73.7	73.6	73.2
2005	73.2	73.4	74.3	76.9	75.8	75.2	74.1	73.8	54.0	55.6	59.1	61.1	68.9
2006	60.7	62.8	64.4	64.5	65.1	66.3	65.6	66.6	66.2	66.7	67.0	67.4	65.3
2007	67.3	68.4	69.0	68.4	69.0	68.8	66.8	67.9	67.8	69.9	70.1	70.2	68.6
2008	67.1	68.7	69.1	69.5	69.3	68.7	68.3	69.1	67.8	68.8	68.9	69.0	68.7
2009	66.7	67.5	67.3	66.4	66.7	66.3	65.4	65.2	64.8	65.6	66.2	66.1	66.2
Education and Health Services													
1990	58.3	58.6	58.9	58.4	58.8	56.9	56.7	56.8	59.5	60.4	60.8	60.4	58.7
2000	76.9	77.8	77.9	78.1	77.7	73.5	73.1	73.0	78.5	79.5	79.4	79.5	77.1
2001	78.8	79.3	79.2	81.1	80.3	78.3	76.8	76.3	81.3	81.5	83.7	82.9	80.0
2002	79.9	81.2	80.8	82.9	81.2	79.8	78.2	77.9	83.2	83.6	85.6	83.7	81.5
2003	83.0	83.4	82.5	84.0	83.5	81.6	80.9	80.5	85.3	85.3	87.5	85.9	83.6
2004	85.5	85.1	85.2	85.7	84.8	82.3	82.9	83.9	84.3	84.5	84.3	81.2	84.1
2005	81.9	81.5	82.1	82.3	81.5	82.9	79.4	78.4	64.4	51.1	50.2	50.9	72.2
2006	53.0	52.9	54.2	55.4	55.9	55.5	55.4	55.6	57.7	58.9	60.9	60.0	56.3
2007	61.5	62.2	62.8	63.1	61.9	61.7	61.6	63.3	64.5	66.3	66.9	67.1	63.6
2008	66.7	67.5	68.0	68.0	65.9	65.8	65.9	67.6	67.7	70.0	70.5	70.6	67.9
2009	71.1	71.9	72.2	72.7	73.0	70.1	70.3	72.0	72.2	74.2	74.4	74.4	72.4
Leisure and Hospitality													
1990	54.7	56.0	56.4	56.6	57.3	58.0	56.4	57.0	57.2	56.0	56.1	55.6	56.4
2000	79.0	79.9	80.2	80.8	82.7	83.0	81.1	80.6	79.2	80.5	80.8	81.6	80.8
2001	80.0	81.6	82.9	82.8	83.1	83.6	82.3	82.2	81.1	79.8	79.7	79.7	81.6
2002	78.4	79.2	79.9	81.7	82.5	82.9	81.6	80.6	79.7	78.6	79.8	79.1	80.3
2003	78.5	79.8	80.5	83.2	83.5	84.9	83.1	83.0	81.9	81.0	81.1	81.7	81.9
2004	81.3	82.5	83.9	83.7	84.8	86.5	85.1	85.3	84.2	84.3	84.9	85.3	84.3
2005	83.6	83.6	85.5	86.2	87.2	88.6	85.8	85.6	51.7	42.2	44.1	46.3	72.5
2006	47.3	51.2	54.1	54.4	56.1	59.6	60.2	60.7	59.9	61.6	62.7	64.1	57.7
2007	63.5	64.0	65.4	65.1	66.1	67.0	65.9	66.5	64.8	65.5	66.4	67.6	65.7
2008	67.1	67.6	68.1	68.8	68.9	69.4	68.3	69.0	65.4	67.0	66.9	67.2	67.8
2009	66.1	67.0	67.8	67.8	68.3	68.5	67.0	68.1	66.3	67.1	66.9	67.6	67.4
Other Services													
1990	18.8	18.8	18.9	19.2	19.2	19.5	19.6	19.3	19.4	19.1	19.2	19.2	19.2
2000	22.1	22.3	22.5	22.3	22.3	22.6	22.5	22.5	22.2	22.2	22.0	22.0	22.3
2001	21.7	21.9	22.1	22.1	22.3	22.6	22.3	22.3	22.4	22.5	22.6	22.6	22.3
2002	22.0	22.1	22.4	22.4	22.7	22.8	22.8	22.8	22.7	23.0	23.1	23.3	22.7
2003	22.9	23.1	23.1	23.7	23.9	23.2	22.5	22.5	22.4	23.0	23.0	23.0	23.0
2004	22.7	22.8	23.0	22.6	22.6	22.5	22.6	22.6	22.4	22.4	22.3	22.4	22.6
2005	22.0	22.1	22.3	22.4	22.5	22.5	22.6	22.4	15.5	13.3	13.3	13.9	19.6
2006	13.7	14.3	14.7	15.0	15.3	15.6	15.8	16.0	16.2	16.6	16.6	16.7	15.5
2007	17.7	18.1	18.3	19.1	19.3	19.5	20.1	20.3	20.3	20.7	20.7	20.8	19.6
2008	19.9	20.1	20.1	18.1	18.2	18.3	17.9	17.9	17.7	19.2	19.3	19.2	18.8
2009	19.1	19.2	19.3	19.3	19.4	19.3	19.4	19.6	19.6	19.7	19.8	19.6	19.4
Government													
1990	78.0	78.0	77.9	78.3	79.0	77.6	79.9	80.8	78.1	78.6	78.9	78.6	78.6
2000	103.5	103.9	104.4	104.3	104.0	103.8	99.2	99.8	103.0	102.8	102.7	103.8	102.9
2001	103.5	104.1	104.1	104.7	104.3	104.2	99.2	100.7	103.0	102.8	102.5	103.2	103.0
2002	102.9	104.0	104.1	103.9	103.5	104.9	99.4	100.8	102.7	103.2	104.2	104.5	103.2
2003	103.8	104.8	105.2	104.8	104.4	105.2	103.2	100.2	104.5	103.1	104.0	103.9	103.9
2004	103.2	104.0	104.5	106.9	106.9	105.9	103.7	102.7	105.8	104.3	105.0	105.2	104.8
2005	105.2	106.3	106.9	105.1	104.6	104.9	101.4	102.2	101.9	80.3	80.0	79.6	98.2
2006	72.7	72.8	73.5	73.4	73.8	73.4	72.0	72.6	75.9	76.1	77.2	78.0	74.3
2007	76.3	77.4	78.1	72.7	73.1	73.4	71.4	72.4	75.7	78.1	78.8	79.0	75.5
2008	77.9	78.7	78.5	80.7	80.8	79.4	78.5	80.7	81.7	82.6	83.1	82.9	80.5
2009	81.8	82.5	81.9	82.8	82.5	81.5	80.1	80.6	82.8	83.1	83.1	83.2	82.2

Employment by Industry: New York-Northern New Jersey-Long Island, NY-NJ-PA, Selected Years, 1990–2009

(Numbers in thousands, not seasonally adjusted.)

Industry and year	January	February	March	April	May	June	July	August	September	October	November	December	Annual average
Total Nonfarm													
1990	7844.7	7849.5	7913.3	7893.8	7959.1	8023.3	7892.8	7879.6	7882.2	7849.9	7861.7	7864.3	7892.9
2000	8165.3	8197.9	8279.1	8357.8	8417.7	8491.0	8403.0	8353.9	8404.8	8485.3	8545.4	8604.6	8392.2
2001	8321.7	8341.6	8396.7	8415.6	8468.9	8528.3	8446.6	8395.7	8353.5	8341.2	8390.4	8418.7	8401.6
2002	8134.3	8165.3	8222.3	8252.4	8311.8	8356.4	8268.0	8232.9	8239.2	8316.4	8373.5	8407.8	8273.4
2003	8130.5	8137.6	8185.0	8211.9	8268.6	8313.4	8250.8	8210.0	8233.0	8311.6	8362.4	8396.8	8251.0
2004	8092.7	8122.4	8201.5	8239.8	8312.0	8376.6	8323.8	8280.1	8294.3	8366.1	8413.8	8462.5	8290.5
2005	8166.0	8186.5	8239.1	8326.8	8374.1	8448.5	8373.6	8341.4	8373.2	8400.8	8471.3	8502.0	8350.3
2006	8260.0	8281.3	8358.3	8400.6	8474.7	8551.1	8465.2	8428.3	8464.1	8531.4	8600.3	8662.1	8456.5
2007	8393.6	8412.3	8473.9	8519.0	8595.8	8679.1	8589.0	8544.9	8563.7	8653.6	8711.5	8756.8	8574.4
2008	8497.3	8518.2	8568.8	8613.9	8657.0	8710.0	8628.3	8572.9	8573.0	8615.8	8624.8	8625.2	8600.4
2009	8296.7	8283.7	8291.8	8308.3	8361.8	8388.7	8316.1	8246.7	8243.2	8295.7	8320.6	8300.8	8304.5
Total Private													
1990	6615.9	6613.1	6664.2	6638.5	6690.0	6750.1	6667.8	6674.4	6672.4	6612.8	6611.8	6614.2	6652.1
2000	6948.0	6977.0	7045.9	7111.3	7157.8	7244.5	7166.1	7156.5	7207.1	7248.6	7302.3	7358.6	7160.3
2001	7094.2	7111.4	7158.2	7168.4	7227.0	7284.3	7197.3	7172.5	7145.1	7097.0	7129.9	7153.8	7161.6
2002	6882.4	6905.0	6955.1	6987.3	7040.6	7083.8	7018.0	7009.3	7013.0	7057.8	7098.5	7128.3	7014.9
2003	6867.5	6861.2	6904.9	6931.3	6988.3	7031.7	6991.8	6978.3	6999.9	7037.3	7075.2	7106.8	6981.2
2004	6831.1	6846.9	6918.6	6958.2	7027.0	7087.1	7059.3	7042.5	7054.8	7089.0	7124.4	7172.9	7017.7
2005	6893.7	6903.5	6953.2	7033.9	7079.9	7146.8	7096.6	7091.5	7119.0	7119.6	7176.1	7203.8	7068.1
2006	6981.7	6993.1	7066.0	7107.1	7178.8	7252.9	7195.1	7185.1	7208.5	7244.0	7300.4	7355.6	7172.4
2007	7107.0	7113.3	7170.2	7217.3	7288.7	7368.4	7312.7	7288.3	7295.3	7354.5	7401.9	7440.4	7279.8
2008	7204.0	7212.1	7257.8	7297.8	7339.0	7389.5	7326.8	7303.6	7295.3	7302.6	7301.3	7297.5	7293.9
2009	6996.6	6972.7	6975.7	6989.9	7040.0	7070.8	7005.3	6966.0	6978.6	6987.4	7008.0	6993.9	6998.7
Goods-Producing													
1990	1156.5	1162.3	1174.4	1166.5	1177.0	1188.3	1163.4	1171.5	1171.2	1151.7	1133.9	1110.3	1160.6
2000	925.5	929.5	946.6	958.9	967.9	979.9	962.2	970.0	977.6	977.1	976.7	971.1	961.9
2001	912.7	917.5	926.2	933.8	942.5	951.2	931.7	935.4	930.1	926.5	919.9	910.9	928.2
2002	861.0	863.0	870.1	878.9	886.8	891.9	883.4	889.2	888.9	885.5	879.8	871.3	879.2
2003	828.8	824.8	832.5	842.1	852.5	858.6	851.8	855.0	856.8	851.9	849.2	843.1	845.6
2004	801.0	801.8	816.5	823.6	835.1	846.9	843.2	846.8	848.3	843.3	840.2	836.2	831.9
2005	791.4	788.7	796.5	810.4	819.5	828.6	822.7	829.3	831.7	822.9	825.4	821.3	815.7
2006	788.8	788.8	799.0	811.6	821.6	831.2	824.1	829.3	830.8	827.9	825.1	821.2	816.6
2007	787.6	781.0	789.5	803.7	814.9	825.2	821.7	823.6	822.2	822.5	819.6	812.6	810.3
2008	782.6	779.4	786.7	795.7	800.3	805.0	802.4	803.7	799.1	791.9	780.7	762.7	790.9
2009	713.1	704.1	702.8	705.7	709.2	711.0	705.5	704.0	698.5	694.9	689.2	676.2	701.2
Mining, Logging, and Construction													
1990	282.9	281.8	289.3	294.0	300.3	305.0	302.8	302.4	299.9	291.3	286.6	277.6	292.8
2000	292.0	290.4	303.6	314.3	322.1	329.0	328.0	331.7	335.2	336.0	337.5	335.1	321.2
2001	303.9	305.0	312.5	327.0	335.6	341.6	340.3	342.0	338.6	343.7	342.5	339.4	331.0
2002	309.6	310.0	315.3	326.7	332.3	337.3	340.7	343.7	342.6	342.2	339.8	334.9	331.3
2003	306.5	301.6	308.8	321.6	331.4	336.2	339.1	340.3	340.3	338.3	336.6	331.9	327.7
2004	303.5	301.9	313.3	324.8	333.9	342.0	345.2	347.7	347.6	345.0	343.2	340.1	332.4
2005	309.6	305.5	311.6	328.6	337.2	344.0	345.3	350.4	351.9	344.7	348.1	343.9	335.1
2006	320.4	320.2	329.2	342.8	351.1	358.7	359.7	364.6	365.3	363.3	361.6	359.9	349.7
2007	336.4	330.3	338.5	354.9	365.8	374.6	375.3	378.3	377.2	377.8	376.2	370.5	363.0
2008	346.9	344.6	351.0	362.1	367.9	371.2	374.2	376.1	371.8	368.7	361.2	348.4	362.0
2009	314.9	310.9	313.5	320.3	324.3	326.2	326.8	326.1	320.4	318.2	313.2	304.4	318.3
Manufacturing													
1990	873.6	880.5	885.1	872.5	876.7	883.3	860.6	869.1	871.3	860.4	847.3	832.7	867.8
2000	633.5	639.1	643.0	644.6	645.8	650.9	634.2	638.3	642.4	641.1	639.2	636.0	640.7
2001	608.8	612.5	613.7	606.8	606.9	609.6	591.4	593.4	591.5	582.8	577.4	571.5	597.2
2002	551.4	553.0	554.8	552.2	554.5	554.6	542.7	545.5	546.3	543.3	540.0	536.4	547.9
2003	522.3	523.2	523.7	520.5	521.1	522.4	512.7	514.7	516.5	513.6	512.6	511.2	517.9
2004	497.5	499.9	503.2	498.8	501.2	504.9	498.0	499.1	500.7	498.3	497.0	496.1	499.6
2005	481.8	483.2	484.9	481.8	482.3	484.6	477.4	478.9	479.8	478.2	477.3	477.4	480.6
2006	468.4	468.6	469.8	468.8	470.5	472.5	464.4	464.7	465.5	464.6	463.5	461.3	466.9
2007	451.2	450.7	451.0	448.8	449.1	450.6	446.4	445.3	445.0	444.7	443.4	442.1	447.4
2008	435.7	434.8	435.7	433.6	432.4	433.8	428.2	427.6	427.3	423.2	419.5	414.3	428.8
2009	398.2	393.2	389.3	385.4	384.9	384.8	378.7	377.9	378.1	376.7	376.0	371.8	382.9
Service-Providing													
1990	6688.2	6687.2	6738.9	6727.3	6782.1	6835.0	6729.4	6708.1	6711.0	6698.2	6727.8	6754.0	6732.3
2000	7239.8	7268.4	7332.5	7398.9	7449.8	7511.1	7440.8	7383.9	7427.2	7508.2	7568.7	7633.5	7430.2
2001	7409.0	7424.1	7470.5	7481.8	7526.4	7577.1	7514.9	7460.3	7423.4	7414.7	7470.5	7507.8	7473.4
2002	7273.3	7302.3	7352.2	7373.5	7425.0	7464.5	7384.6	7343.7	7350.3	7430.9	7493.7	7536.5	7394.2
2003	7301.7	7312.8	7352.5	7369.8	7416.1	7454.8	7399.0	7355.0	7376.2	7459.7	7513.2	7553.7	7405.4
2004	7291.7	7320.6	7385.0	7416.2	7476.9	7529.7	7480.6	7433.3	7446.0	7522.8	7573.6	7626.3	7458.6
2005	7374.6	7397.8	7442.6	7516.4	7554.6	7619.9	7550.9	7512.1	7541.5	7577.9	7645.9	7680.7	7534.6
2006	7471.2	7492.5	7559.3	7589.0	7653.1	7719.9	7641.1	7599.0	7633.3	7703.5	7775.2	7840.9	7639.8
2007	7606.0	7631.3	7684.4	7715.3	7780.9	7853.9	7767.3	7721.3	7741.5	7831.1	7891.9	7944.2	7764.1
2008	7714.7	7738.8	7782.1	7818.2	7856.7	7905.0	7825.9	7769.2	7773.9	7823.9	7844.1	7862.5	7809.6
2009	7583.6	7579.6	7589.0	7602.6	7652.6	7677.7	7610.6	7542.7	7544.7	7600.8	7631.4	7624.6	7603.3

Employment by Industry: New York-Northern New Jersey-Long Island, NY-NJ-PA, Selected Years, 1990–2009—*Continued*

(Numbers in thousands, not seasonally adjusted.)

Industry and year	January	February	March	April	May	June	July	August	September	October	November	December	Annual average
Trade, Transportation, and Utilities													
1990	1614.7	1591.6	1598.8	1582.7	1595.1	1607.6	1580.9	1582.2	1592.0	1590.0	1602.6	1621.0	1596.6
2000	1609.5	1595.1	1603.6	1610.0	1616.6	1634.0	1605.6	1607.4	1625.8	1643.8	1678.2	1713.3	1628.6
2001	1634.3	1613.7	1615.5	1609.8	1619.4	1631.3	1600.4	1593.2	1601.2	1602.5	1623.9	1648.9	1616.2
2002	1573.2	1557.0	1567.6	1562.8	1570.9	1586.7	1561.1	1557.3	1577.6	1590.1	1618.0	1648.7	1580.9
2003	1574.5	1558.9	1563.2	1557.4	1568.2	1579.9	1557.3	1555.6	1573.3	1589.7	1614.6	1640.8	1577.8
2004	1561.8	1549.9	1558.4	1555.2	1572.2	1588.6	1570.1	1567.7	1582.7	1600.1	1625.2	1653.7	1582.1
2005	1567.5	1552.8	1557.5	1566.9	1578.5	1593.2	1570.5	1568.7	1584.8	1591.6	1622.1	1645.4	1583.3
2006	1582.5	1561.3	1569.9	1572.4	1586.6	1603.5	1580.8	1576.4	1592.8	1610.9	1646.0	1677.2	1596.7
2007	1604.9	1583.8	1589.6	1590.8	1608.7	1628.5	1602.2	1592.4	1608.8	1621.3	1658.4	1687.4	1614.7
2008	1615.0	1593.2	1599.6	1595.7	1605.0	1618.5	1593.5	1588.1	1598.8	1601.8	1619.3	1635.8	1605.4
2009	1549.2	1524.6	1518.0	1507.6	1521.4	1533.5	1505.6	1502.0	1516.6	1518.5	1540.1	1554.7	1524.3
Wholesale Trade													
1990	477.4	477.0	479.8	476.7	478.3	480.8	475.1	475.5	474.8	470.5	469.0	467.9	475.2
2000	440.0	441.5	444.1	443.7	444.6	448.2	443.9	445.2	446.6	447.6	448.6	451.6	445.5
2001	452.4	454.0	454.9	450.2	450.3	451.9	447.7	446.8	446.0	444.3	443.5	443.9	448.8
2002	434.5	435.1	437.5	432.3	432.6	433.5	429.3	430.3	431.1	432.8	433.5	435.0	433.1
2003	431.8	432.1	433.4	430.9	432.2	433.6	431.9	431.2	431.2	431.7	432.7	434.1	432.2
2004	425.4	426.4	428.9	427.9	429.3	432.2	432.1	431.8	431.5	432.9	433.2	435.1	430.6
2005	424.5	425.6	426.5	427.5	428.8	430.9	428.6	429.5	430.6	430.5	431.6	434.9	429.1
2006	425.3	425.6	427.5	429.4	431.7	434.5	432.9	432.6	432.4	434.4	435.4	438.4	431.7
2007	431.4	431.2	432.2	432.4	434.2	437.7	436.1	435.3	434.6	437.5	437.5	439.4	435.0
2008	432.0	432.0	432.0	431.0	431.6	433.1	430.3	428.8	427.6	425.6	423.0	421.2	429.1
2009	411.8	407.8	405.5	402.5	402.1	402.4	397.9	397.1	395.8	397.6	399.5	399.8	401.7
Retail Trade													
1990	805.8	788.1	790.1	778.6	786.1	793.1	783.7	783.4	784.4	786.6	800.2	816.0	791.3
2000	833.7	817.9	822.9	828.1	833.2	845.1	830.7	834.5	837.0	847.1	879.6	910.0	843.3
2001	841.7	819.1	820.1	821.0	826.3	837.0	822.4	822.5	819.1	822.5	850.5	877.1	831.6
2002	819.5	802.6	810.3	810.2	816.8	830.6	820.2	820.3	823.9	830.6	859.0	887.9	827.7
2003	825.2	810.3	811.5	813.3	820.6	830.5	821.6	823.0	825.0	837.0	860.6	883.8	830.2
2004	823.2	810.9	815.5	816.1	827.5	839.5	834.6	834.7	835.6	847.2	872.0	897.6	837.9
2005	836.1	820.4	822.1	829.3	836.8	847.0	840.8	840.6	839.1	845.7	872.2	891.2	843.4
2006	843.8	822.7	828.0	829.3	836.7	848.4	843.6	842.0	839.6	854.6	886.1	907.7	848.5
2007	855.8	835.4	838.9	840.9	851.1	864.2	858.1	852.8	850.2	858.5	893.7	915.0	859.6
2008	863.1	841.5	844.9	842.0	848.7	858.7	854.6	852.1	847.8	854.2	873.1	887.1	855.7
2009	825.6	806.5	803.7	799.7	810.6	821.8	815.1	815.2	816.2	813.2	831.7	842.1	816.8
Transportation and Utilities													
1990	331.4	326.5	328.8	327.3	330.7	333.9	322.1	323.3	332.7	332.8	333.6	337.1	330.0
2000	335.1	335.0	336.0	337.6	338.3	340.2	330.4	327.4	341.6	348.8	349.8	351.2	339.3
2001	340.6	341.0	340.9	338.9	343.1	342.7	330.6	324.2	336.5	336.0	330.2	320.2	336.1
2002	319.4	319.5	320.0	320.5	321.7	322.8	311.8	306.9	322.8	326.9	325.7	326.0	320.3
2003	317.5	316.5	318.3	313.2	315.4	315.8	303.8	301.4	317.1	321.0	321.3	322.9	315.4
2004	313.2	312.6	314.0	311.2	315.4	316.9	303.4	301.2	315.6	320.0	320.0	321.0	313.7
2005	306.9	306.8	308.9	310.1	312.9	315.3	301.1	298.6	315.1	315.4	318.3	319.3	310.7
2006	313.4	313.0	314.4	313.7	318.2	320.6	304.3	301.8	320.8	321.9	324.5	331.1	316.5
2007	317.7	317.2	318.5	317.5	323.4	326.6	308.0	304.3	324.0	325.3	327.2	333.0	320.2
2008	319.9	319.7	321.8	322.7	324.7	326.7	308.6	307.2	323.4	322.0	323.2	327.5	320.6
2009	311.8	310.3	308.8	305.4	308.7	309.3	292.6	289.7	304.6	307.7	308.9	312.8	305.9
Information													
1990	300.4	300.8	299.9	298.8	300.9	301.4	303.3	302.8	302.5	299.8	299.0	301.3	300.9
2000	317.9	321.1	323.8	326.8	330.1	335.1	334.4	316.4	337.1	338.9	342.6	343.3	330.6
2001	348.3	351.4	352.0	349.6	351.8	351.9	348.0	345.0	341.0	338.2	342.2	339.4	346.6
2002	321.0	324.3	319.8	316.7	322.9	320.5	310.2	312.6	307.4	308.1	312.1	310.3	315.5
2003	296.3	299.3	296.3	293.2	297.8	295.0	292.3	296.2	292.6	294.4	298.4	296.7	295.7
2004	286.4	286.2	288.1	286.7	287.6	287.5	286.6	288.4	288.4	288.3	290.8	290.4	288.0
2005	282.4	284.1	284.9	284.1	286.2	291.0	288.6	289.7	289.7	290.1	292.1	292.5	288.0
2006	287.0	287.7	289.3	287.0	289.1	292.2	290.9	291.9	291.0	287.9	289.9	291.7	289.6
2007	283.6	285.5	285.6	284.4	286.3	288.6	287.2	287.4	286.3	284.7	286.3	287.5	286.1
2008	282.1	284.2	284.3	282.4	283.8	286.3	283.0	283.3	282.5	280.5	280.7	281.2	282.9
2009	273.9	272.0	272.6	271.0	271.0	271.0	269.8	268.6	268.7	268.0	267.6	269.2	270.3
Financial Activities													
1990	856.0	855.3	855.7	851.5	851.5	858.1	855.3	854.4	846.4	836.6	835.0	837.0	849.4
2000	809.1	811.3	812.7	812.8	814.7	828.6	825.4	825.7	820.1	817.6	819.4	824.5	818.5
2001	807.3	807.0	808.3	804.7	805.0	815.1	815.0	811.0	801.1	773.0	774.4	777.8	800.0
2002	774.9	774.0	773.1	768.8	768.9	776.2	777.5	775.7	767.5	766.8	766.9	770.1	771.7
2003	764.8	762.8	762.4	760.4	762.7	770.0	773.8	772.6	765.7	764.0	765.4	770.2	766.2
2004	759.5	760.4	762.3	763.0	764.4	773.3	780.5	779.5	771.2	774.8	776.0	781.6	770.5
2005	768.0	767.7	770.3	774.4	774.1	784.3	791.0	791.3	784.1	783.2	785.2	786.7	780.0
2006	776.4	778.3	781.3	783.6	786.7	797.6	801.7	802.4	794.4	793.8	795.8	800.7	791.1
2007	788.5	789.9	791.6	791.7	792.5	804.0	807.5	804.8	795.7	797.9	799.4	801.3	797.1
2008	790.6	791.0	791.3	788.0	787.4	794.5	795.7	794.5	780.3	775.7	771.8	771.3	786.0
2009	754.9	749.9	745.8	742.0	739.7	741.3	740.0	736.5	729.4	727.7	727.2	725.8	738.4

Employment by Industry: New York-Northern New Jersey-Long Island, NY-NJ-PA, Selected Years, 1990–2009—*Continued*

(Numbers in thousands, not seasonally adjusted.)

Industry and year	January	February	March	April	May	June	July	August	September	October	November	December	Annual average
Professional and Business Services													
1990	1000.2	1002.3	1010.5	1010.4	1012.2	1022.3	1014.4	1015.4	1010.4	997.0	995.0	994.5	1007.1
2000	1220.5	1233.7	1250.9	1268.3	1277.5	1300.1	1293.7	1301.6	1299.2	1301.0	1306.9	1315.3	1280.7
2001	1283.0	1290.5	1300.1	1298.4	1300.8	1313.4	1302.0	1297.8	1288.6	1263.5	1262.3	1258.6	1288.3
2002	1211.5	1216.3	1227.4	1238.9	1241.0	1249.2	1240.9	1243.0	1237.9	1243.9	1247.3	1248.2	1237.1
2003	1194.3	1191.5	1204.1	1213.6	1217.2	1228.7	1226.5	1229.7	1229.6	1234.4	1237.7	1242.6	1220.8
2004	1188.2	1192.6	1209.1	1224.1	1229.7	1242.0	1238.5	1239.4	1235.3	1238.6	1244.8	1252.6	1227.9
2005	1204.6	1205.7	1215.0	1239.0	1240.6	1257.6	1254.2	1257.7	1256.7	1255.1	1262.4	1263.0	1242.6
2006	1222.4	1230.3	1247.8	1258.7	1267.5	1287.6	1284.9	1290.2	1284.7	1288.9	1297.6	1304.9	1272.1
2007	1260.1	1264.9	1280.9	1295.2	1304.5	1325.5	1329.2	1333.3	1322.6	1334.8	1339.8	1343.2	1311.2
2008	1300.6	1305.8	1315.4	1329.5	1331.2	1345.4	1345.5	1342.6	1331.0	1325.2	1320.0	1313.8	1325.5
2009	1256.1	1249.8	1248.4	1255.4	1254.5	1264.4	1258.1	1253.2	1246.3	1236.2	1238.0	1227.1	1249.0
Education and Health Services													
1990	935.7	947.3	956.8	954.0	956.2	953.6	940.2	939.6	954.0	964.7	976.8	981.2	955.0
2000	1225.4	1238.1	1246.4	1249.9	1247.8	1236.3	1218.1	1212.4	1238.4	1265.3	1272.9	1281.5	1244.4
2001	1242.3	1258.2	1270.6	1272.7	1279.6	1270.8	1251.0	1245.0	1262.7	1292.6	1303.8	1309.8	1271.6
2002	1278.1	1298.8	1310.4	1314.1	1319.6	1306.0	1291.9	1283.6	1305.2	1334.8	1345.1	1347.0	1311.2
2003	1320.8	1333.0	1344.9	1344.6	1346.1	1333.1	1316.6	1305.0	1329.9	1357.1	1365.3	1366.6	1338.6
2004	1333.9	1350.9	1364.3	1362.1	1367.5	1351.8	1335.4	1324.3	1344.2	1376.7	1383.9	1389.3	1357.0
2005	1352.9	1371.9	1381.6	1387.8	1387.3	1371.1	1353.5	1344.3	1374.0	1401.3	1410.9	1414.1	1379.2
2006	1387.5	1405.6	1417.3	1420.1	1423.1	1408.0	1383.0	1373.7	1406.3	1438.3	1447.9	1456.6	1414.0
2007	1421.6	1440.3	1450.9	1448.1	1448.7	1434.8	1409.5	1399.0	1431.0	1466.7	1472.9	1480.5	1442.0
2008	1448.8	1469.3	1478.1	1480.7	1480.1	1465.4	1434.5	1428.0	1459.7	1491.0	1501.8	1509.5	1470.6
2009	1477.1	1497.7	1504.4	1507.2	1507.8	1493.1	1472.4	1455.5	1483.8	1517.7	1527.5	1529.2	1497.8
Leisure and Hospitality													
1990	470.8	471.5	483.8	490.8	510.7	529.2	523.3	522.2	511.7	491.5	488.0	487.2	498.4
2000	515.5	521.4	532.0	552.3	568.9	593.1	590.5	589.6	575.6	569.9	569.4	571.7	562.5
2001	537.3	542.1	551.7	562.8	587.5	606.4	606.5	604.9	584.2	563.6	564.2	567.5	573.2
2002	527.5	534.5	547.0	567.1	587.0	607.2	607.9	605.6	588.8	584.4	583.1	585.3	577.1
2003	549.5	551.3	559.4	576.8	597.8	617.6	624.6	617.2	605.2	596.6	594.1	594.5	590.4
2004	560.2	563.1	574.8	592.4	615.5	638.4	646.2	639.3	627.5	611.1	606.3	609.5	607.0
2005	570.6	573.8	586.1	606.3	626.2	649.7	651.1	647.2	634.9	614.1	614.5	613.7	615.7
2006	580.6	583.2	599.7	613.9	640.3	664.2	667.6	661.6	647.3	636.0	635.6	637.5	630.6
2007	600.6	605.5	616.9	637.2	662.3	686.8	689.1	684.5	665.7	660.2	657.4	658.5	652.1
2008	622.8	626.5	638.0	660.3	682.7	703.3	704.6	698.0	679.8	671.2	661.8	658.1	667.3
2009	618.4	619.7	628.1	644.2	676.0	693.6	695.2	689.4	681.5	669.1	663.6	657.3	661.3
Other Services													
1990	281.6	282.0	284.3	283.8	286.4	289.6	287.0	286.3	284.2	281.5	281.5	281.7	284.2
2000	324.6	326.8	329.9	332.3	334.3	337.4	336.2	333.4	333.3	335.0	336.2	337.9	333.1
2001	329.0	331.0	333.8	336.6	340.4	344.2	342.7	340.2	336.2	337.1	339.2	340.9	337.6
2002	335.2	337.1	339.7	340.0	343.5	346.1	345.1	342.3	339.7	344.2	346.2	347.4	342.2
2003	338.5	339.6	342.1	343.2	346.0	348.8	348.9	347.0	346.8	349.2	350.5	352.3	346.1
2004	340.1	342.0	345.1	351.1	355.0	358.6	358.8	357.1	357.2	356.1	357.2	359.6	353.2
2005	356.3	358.8	361.3	365.0	367.5	371.3	365.0	363.3	363.1	361.3	363.5	367.1	363.6
2006	356.5	357.9	361.7	359.8	363.9	368.6	362.1	359.6	361.2	360.3	362.5	365.8	361.7
2007	360.1	362.4	365.2	366.2	370.8	375.0	366.3	363.3	363.0	366.4	368.1	369.4	366.4
2008	361.5	362.7	364.4	365.5	368.5	371.1	367.6	365.4	364.1	365.3	365.2	365.1	365.5
2009	353.9	354.9	355.6	356.8	360.4	362.9	358.7	356.8	353.8	355.3	354.8	354.4	356.5
Government													
1990	1228.8	1236.4	1249.1	1255.3	1269.1	1273.2	1225.0	1205.2	1209.8	1237.1	1249.9	1250.1	1240.8
2000	1217.3	1220.9	1233.2	1246.5	1259.9	1246.5	1236.9	1197.4	1197.7	1236.7	1243.1	1246.0	1231.8
2001	1227.5	1230.2	1238.5	1247.2	1241.9	1244.0	1249.3	1223.2	1208.4	1244.2	1260.5	1264.9	1240.0
2002	1251.9	1260.3	1267.2	1265.1	1271.2	1272.6	1250.0	1223.6	1226.2	1258.6	1275.0	1279.5	1258.4
2003	1263.0	1276.4	1280.1	1280.6	1280.3	1281.7	1259.0	1231.7	1233.1	1274.3	1287.2	1290.0	1269.8
2004	1261.6	1275.5	1282.9	1281.6	1285.0	1289.5	1264.5	1237.6	1239.5	1277.1	1289.4	1289.6	1272.8
2005	1272.3	1283.0	1285.9	1292.9	1294.2	1301.7	1277.0	1249.9	1254.2	1281.2	1295.2	1298.2	1282.1
2006	1278.3	1288.2	1292.3	1293.5	1295.9	1298.2	1270.1	1243.2	1255.6	1287.4	1299.9	1306.5	1284.1
2007	1286.6	1299.0	1303.7	1301.7	1307.1	1310.7	1276.3	1256.6	1268.4	1299.1	1309.6	1316.4	1294.6
2008	1293.3	1306.1	1311.0	1316.1	1318.0	1320.5	1301.5	1269.3	1277.7	1313.2	1323.5	1327.7	1306.5
2009	1300.1	1311.0	1316.1	1318.4	1321.8	1317.9	1310.8	1280.7	1264.6	1308.3	1312.6	1306.9	1305.8

Employment by Industry: North Port-Bradenton-Sarasota, FL, Selected Years, Selected Years, 1990–2009

(Numbers in thousands, not seasonally adjusted.)

Industry and year	January	February	March	April	May	June	July	August	September	October	November	December	Annual average
Total Nonfarm													
1990	169.0	172.1	172.4	171.9	171.7	170.6	166.0	165.8	169.7	170.5	173.2	173.4	170.5
2000	236.4	238.8	241.4	242.5	242.2	241.4	237.4	240.5	240.4	242.3	244.9	247.0	241.3
2001	236.0	239.5	241.7	240.6	241.3	238.4	235.3	239.0	238.7	243.4	247.8	250.8	241.0
2002	244.8	248.7	252.5	254.3	252.7	249.4	247.0	250.7	251.0	252.3	254.1	256.2	251.1
2003	251.7	253.5	255.1	253.5	254.5	255.1	248.8	253.7	254.5	257.0	261.4	265.5	255.4
2004	259.3	262.2	265.7	266.5	267.9	266.3	266.3	270.1	270.5	274.5	278.0	282.5	269.2
2005	276.9	280.5	282.7	282.0	283.0	280.1	278.6	282.1	282.8	283.9	287.1	290.8	282.5
2006	284.6	288.7	292.9	291.2	292.1	290.1	285.4	288.6	288.9	286.7	289.8	291.8	289.2
2007	285.4	287.6	289.9	285.6	284.9	281.2	274.9	278.4	277.0	275.8	279.2	282.0	281.8
2008	276.6	279.3	280.7	274.3	273.0	267.8	262.9	265.1	264.1	261.8	262.2	263.0	269.2
2009	256.1	255.5	256.2	253.5	251.7	247.2	242.9	244.5	243.8	244.9	245.9	247.1	249.1
Total Private													
1990	146.7	148.5	149.6	148.6	147.8	146.8	144.1	144.6	144.4	145.6	147.5	149.5	147.0
2000	212.1	214.3	216.8	217.8	216.8	218.9	215.2	216.2	216.3	217.9	220.2	222.1	217.1
2001	211.6	214.8	216.8	215.9	216.4	215.9	213.0	214.4	214.0	218.2	222.2	225.0	216.5
2002	219.5	223.0	226.7	228.6	226.8	226.0	223.8	225.1	225.2	226.4	227.9	230.0	225.8
2003	225.5	227.1	228.6	227.1	227.8	231.0	224.9	227.2	227.9	230.3	234.3	238.2	229.2
2004	232.6	235.2	238.7	239.4	240.6	241.7	242.0	243.1	243.7	247.5	250.8	255.1	242.5
2005	250.0	253.4	255.6	254.7	255.6	255.6	254.2	255.1	255.6	256.1	259.1	262.9	255.7
2006	256.8	260.8	264.8	262.8	263.6	264.5	260.1	260.4	260.3	258.1	260.5	262.5	261.3
2007	256.6	258.5	260.7	256.4	255.8	255.1	249.0	249.6	248.1	247.0	250.1	252.9	253.3
2008	247.6	250.1	251.2	244.8	243.5	241.3	236.6	235.9	234.9	232.8	233.4	234.2	240.5
2009	227.5	226.8	227.3	224.2	222.8	221.4	217.3	216.9	215.7	216.1	216.9	218.4	220.9
Goods-Producing													
1990	35.6	35.3	35.4	34.6	34.5	34.4	33.8	33.9	34.2	33.2	33.3	33.3	34.3
2000	42.7	42.9	43.3	44.1	43.7	43.6	43.0	42.5	42.5	42.2	42.1	42.2	42.9
2001	41.3	41.1	41.2	41.1	41.3	41.7	41.5	41.7	41.9	42.3	42.5	42.6	41.7
2002	42.3	42.6	42.5	42.3	42.5	42.5	42.4	42.9	42.6	42.5	42.5	42.7	42.5
2003	41.9	42.4	42.2	41.6	41.8	42.0	41.9	42.0	41.9	42.4	42.3	42.6	42.1
2004	42.8	43.1	43.6	43.9	44.3	44.5	45.0	45.1	45.3	45.9	46.1	46.6	44.7
2005	45.9	46.6	46.9	46.8	47.5	47.7	48.2	48.5	49.1	49.2	49.6	50.1	48.0
2006	49.8	50.4	50.8	50.6	51.1	51.4	51.0	51.0	50.8	50.2	49.7	49.6	50.5
2007	48.1	47.7	47.6	46.2	46.0	45.6	44.5	44.3	43.4	42.5	42.1	41.8	45.0
2008	40.5	40.4	39.9	38.8	38.6	38.5	37.5	37.2	36.9	35.5	34.9	34.7	37.8
2009	32.3	31.4	31.1	30.5	30.3	30.0	29.4	29.1	28.7	28.3	27.9	27.9	29.7
Mining, Logging, and Construction													
1990	17.4	17.1	17.2	16.6	16.6	16.8	16.6	16.7	16.8	16.4	16.4	16.3	16.7
2000	20.7	21.0	21.2	21.6	21.6	21.7	21.5	21.4	21.3	21.4	21.4	21.6	21.4
2001	20.7	20.8	20.9	20.8	21.0	21.3	21.3	21.6	21.7	22.3	22.5	22.4	21.4
2002	22.4	22.6	22.6	22.5	22.8	22.9	22.9	23.2	23.1	23.4	23.5	23.7	23.0
2003	23.2	23.7	23.7	23.4	23.6	23.7	23.6	23.7	23.7	24.1	24.1	24.3	23.7
2004	24.6	24.8	25.2	25.6	25.8	25.9	26.3	26.2	26.4	27.1	27.2	27.5	26.1
2005	27.2	27.8	28.1	28.1	28.6	28.7	29.1	29.3	29.8	29.9	30.3	30.7	29.0
2006	30.6	31.2	31.6	31.5	31.9	32.1	31.9	32.1	32.1	31.7	31.3	31.1	31.6
2007	29.9	29.7	29.6	28.4	28.2	27.8	26.7	26.6	25.8	25.0	24.6	24.3	27.2
2008	23.1	23.0	22.7	21.9	21.7	21.7	21.1	21.0	20.9	19.9	19.4	19.3	21.3
2009	17.7	17.3	17.1	16.8	16.7	16.6	16.4	16.2	15.9	15.7	15.4	15.5	16.4
Manufacturing													
1990	18.2	18.2	18.2	18.0	17.9	17.6	17.2	17.2	17.4	16.8	16.9	17.0	17.6
2000	22.0	21.9	22.1	22.5	22.1	21.9	21.5	21.1	21.2	20.8	20.7	20.6	21.5
2001	20.6	20.3	20.3	20.3	20.3	20.4	20.2	20.1	20.2	20.0	20.0	20.2	20.2
2002	19.9	20.0	19.9	19.8	19.7	19.6	19.5	19.7	19.5	19.1	19.0	19.0	19.6
2003	18.7	18.7	18.5	18.2	18.2	18.3	18.3	18.3	18.2	18.3	18.2	18.3	18.3
2004	18.2	18.3	18.4	18.3	18.5	18.6	18.7	18.9	18.9	18.8	18.9	19.1	18.6
2005	18.7	18.8	18.8	18.7	18.9	19.0	19.1	19.2	19.3	19.3	19.3	19.4	19.0
2006	19.2	19.2	19.2	19.1	19.2	19.3	19.1	18.9	18.7	18.5	18.4	18.5	18.9
2007	18.2	18.0	18.0	17.8	17.8	17.8	17.8	17.7	17.6	17.5	17.5	17.5	17.8
2008	17.4	17.4	17.2	16.9	16.9	16.8	16.4	16.2	16.0	15.6	15.5	15.4	16.5
2009	14.6	14.1	14.0	13.7	13.6	13.4	13.0	12.9	12.8	12.6	12.5	12.4	13.3
Service-Providing													
1990	133.4	136.8	137.0	137.3	137.2	136.2	132.2	131.9	135.5	137.3	139.9	140.1	136.2
2000	193.7	195.9	198.1	198.4	198.5	197.8	194.4	198.0	197.9	200.1	202.8	204.8	198.4
2001	194.7	198.4	200.5	199.5	200.0	196.7	193.8	197.3	196.8	201.1	205.3	208.2	199.4
2002	202.5	206.1	210.0	212.0	210.2	206.9	204.6	207.8	208.4	209.8	211.6	213.5	208.6
2003	209.8	211.1	212.9	211.9	212.7	213.1	206.9	211.7	212.6	214.6	219.1	222.9	213.3
2004	216.5	219.1	222.1	222.6	223.6	221.8	221.3	225.0	225.2	228.6	231.9	235.9	224.5
2005	231.0	233.9	235.8	235.2	235.5	232.4	230.4	233.6	233.7	234.7	237.5	240.7	234.5
2006	234.8	238.3	242.1	240.6	241.0	238.7	234.4	237.6	238.1	236.5	240.1	242.2	238.7
2007	237.3	239.9	242.3	239.4	238.9	235.6	230.4	234.1	233.6	233.3	237.1	240.2	236.8
2008	236.1	238.9	240.8	235.5	234.4	229.3	225.4	227.9	227.2	226.3	227.3	228.3	231.5
2009	223.8	224.1	225.1	223.0	221.4	217.2	213.5	215.4	215.1	216.6	218.0	219.2	219.4

Employment by Industry: North Port-Bradenton-Sarasota, FL, Selected Years, Selected Years, 1990–2009—*Continued*

(Numbers in thousands, not seasonally adjusted.)

Industry and year	January	February	March	April	May	June	July	August	September	October	November	December	Annual average
Trade, Transportation, and Utilities													
1990	37.6	37.6	37.7	37.7	37.4	36.9	36.3	36.3	36.2	37.0	38.0	38.9	37.3
2000	48.6	48.8	48.8	49.4	49.1	48.8	47.7	48.0	47.9	48.6	50.3	51.1	48.9
2001	47.7	47.8	48.2	48.1	47.7	47.2	46.5	46.5	46.4	47.5	48.9	49.9	47.7
2002	48.3	48.0	48.3	48.0	47.7	47.4	46.8	47.0	47.3	47.5	48.8	49.9	47.9
2003	48.0	47.6	48.0	47.9	47.7	47.3	46.6	47.0	47.2	47.8	49.1	50.7	47.9
2004	49.3	49.5	49.7	49.5	49.4	49.2	49.3	49.3	49.3	50.3	51.9	52.8	50.0
2005	50.8	51.2	51.5	51.6	51.5	51.1	50.6	50.5	50.5	50.6	51.7	52.5	51.2
2006	50.7	50.8	51.3	51.4	51.4	51.2	50.1	50.1	50.1	50.1	51.4	52.5	50.9
2007	51.7	51.3	51.6	50.8	50.8	50.4	49.8	49.5	49.2	49.5	50.7	52.1	50.6
2008	50.6	50.4	50.6	49.4	49.1	48.4	47.6	47.3	47.2	47.0	47.5	48.2	48.6
2009	46.3	46.0	45.7	45.0	44.5	44.1	43.3	43.0	43.0	42.8	43.6	44.2	44.3
Wholesale Trade													
1990	4.4	4.3	4.3	4.5	4.5	4.5	4.5	4.5	4.5	4.5	4.5	4.5	4.5
2000	6.9	6.9	7.0	7.0	7.0	6.8	6.8	6.8	6.8	6.9	7.1	6.9	6.9
2001	6.6	6.6	6.7	7.0	7.0	6.9	6.8	6.9	6.8	7.1	7.2	7.2	6.9
2002	7.1	7.1	7.1	7.2	7.2	7.2	7.2	7.3	7.4	7.5	7.5	7.5	7.3
2003	7.2	7.2	7.4	7.4	7.4	7.3	7.2	7.3	7.4	7.3	7.4	7.5	7.3
2004	7.3	7.4	7.4	7.6	7.6	7.4	7.5	7.5	7.5	7.6	7.9	7.9	7.6
2005	7.8	8.0	8.0	8.2	8.3	8.2	8.1	8.2	8.3	8.3	8.4	8.6	8.2
2006	8.4	8.5	8.6	8.6	8.7	8.8	8.6	8.6	8.7	8.5	8.4	8.6	8.6
2007	8.7	8.7	8.7	8.8	8.9	8.9	8.8	8.8	8.7	8.7	8.7	8.8	8.8
2008	8.5	8.5	8.5	8.4	8.3	8.2	8.1	8.0	8.0	8.0	7.8	7.7	8.2
2009	7.4	7.4	7.3	7.3	7.1	7.3	7.2	7.1	7.2	7.2	7.2	7.2	7.2
Retail Trade													
1990	30.2	30.2	30.3	30.2	29.9	29.4	28.9	28.9	28.7	29.5	30.5	31.2	29.8
2000	38.3	38.5	38.4	39.0	38.8	38.7	37.6	37.8	37.7	38.4	39.9	40.7	38.7
2001	37.9	37.8	38.1	37.7	37.4	37.0	36.4	36.4	36.3	37.1	38.4	39.3	37.5
2002	38.0	37.7	38.0	37.6	37.3	37.0	36.4	36.6	36.7	36.9	38.1	39.1	37.5
2003	37.6	37.3	37.5	37.3	37.1	36.8	36.1	36.4	36.5	37.2	38.3	39.5	37.3
2004	38.5	38.5	38.6	38.3	38.2	38.2	38.1	38.1	38.1	38.8	40.0	40.9	38.7
2005	39.3	39.5	39.7	39.6	39.4	39.1	38.7	38.5	38.4	38.5	39.2	39.7	39.1
2006	38.5	38.5	38.9	38.9	38.8	38.6	37.8	37.8	37.6	37.8	39.1	39.6	38.5
2007	39.1	38.9	39.1	38.3	38.3	37.9	37.5	37.3	37.1	37.4	38.5	39.5	38.2
2008	38.8	38.6	38.7	37.7	37.5	37.0	36.3	36.1	36.0	35.8	36.4	36.9	37.2
2009	35.6	35.4	35.2	34.5	34.2	33.7	33.1	32.9	32.8	32.5	33.3	33.8	33.9
Transportation and Utilities													
1990	3.0	3.1	3.1	3.0	3.0	3.0	2.9	2.9	3.0	3.0	3.0	3.2	3.0
2000	3.4	3.4	3.4	3.4	3.3	3.3	3.3	3.4	3.4	3.3	3.3	3.5	3.4
2001	3.2	3.4	3.4	3.4	3.3	3.3	3.3	3.2	3.3	3.3	3.3	3.4	3.3
2002	3.2	3.2	3.2	3.2	3.2	3.2	3.2	3.1	3.2	3.1	3.2	3.3	3.2
2003	3.2	3.1	3.1	3.2	3.2	3.2	3.3	3.3	3.3	3.3	3.4	3.7	3.2
2004	3.5	3.6	3.7	3.6	3.6	3.6	3.7	3.7	3.7	3.9	4.0	4.0	3.7
2005	3.7	3.7	3.8	3.8	3.8	3.8	3.8	3.8	3.8	3.8	4.1	4.2	3.8
2006	3.8	3.8	3.8	3.8	3.9	3.9	3.8	3.7	3.7	3.8	3.9	4.3	3.9
2007	3.9	3.7	3.8	3.7	3.6	3.6	3.5	3.4	3.4	3.4	3.5	3.8	3.6
2008	3.3	3.3	3.4	3.3	3.3	3.2	3.2	3.2	3.2	3.2	3.3	3.6	3.3
2009	3.3	3.2	3.2	3.2	3.2	3.1	3.0	3.0	3.0	3.1	3.1	3.2	3.1
Information													
1990	3.7	3.7	3.7	3.6	3.6	3.7	3.6	3.6	3.6	3.5	3.5	3.5	3.6
2000	4.3	4.2	4.3	4.4	4.3	4.4	4.6	4.6	4.5	4.5	4.5	4.5	4.4
2001	4.5	4.5	4.4	4.3	4.4	4.5	4.4	4.4	4.3	4.2	4.3	4.3	4.4
2002	4.3	4.3	4.3	4.3	4.3	4.3	4.3	4.2	4.2	4.3	4.3	4.3	4.3
2003	4.3	4.3	4.3	4.2	4.3	4.3	4.3	4.4	4.3	4.2	4.3	4.3	4.2
2004	4.2	4.2	4.2	4.1	4.3	4.3	4.2	4.1	4.1	4.1	4.2	4.2	4.2
2005	4.1	4.2	4.2	4.3	4.3	4.4	4.4	4.4	4.3	4.3	4.4	4.4	4.3
2006	4.2	4.3	4.3	4.3	4.3	4.3	4.4	4.5	4.4	4.6	4.6	4.6	4.4
2007	4.4	4.3	4.3	4.3	4.2	4.2	4.1	4.1	4.1	4.1	4.1	4.0	4.2
2008	4.0	4.0	4.0	3.9	3.9	3.9	3.8	3.8	3.8	3.7	3.6	3.6	3.8
2009	3.6	3.6	3.5	3.5	3.4	3.5	3.4	3.4	3.3	3.4	3.4	3.3	3.4
Financial Activities													
1990	8.8	9.0	8.9	9.0	9.1	9.1	9.2	9.3	9.3	9.3	9.4	9.4	9.2
2000	12.9	12.9	13.0	13.3	13.5	13.6	13.2	13.0	12.9	13.0	13.0	13.0	13.1
2001	12.9	12.9	13.0	13.1	13.1	13.3	13.2	13.3	13.3	13.4	13.6	13.7	13.2
2002	13.7	13.7	13.7	13.6	13.5	13.7	13.7	13.8	13.7	13.7	13.8	14.0	13.7
2003	13.7	13.6	13.6	13.8	13.8	13.8	14.1	14.1	14.0	14.1	14.1	14.3	13.9
2004	14.1	14.3	14.4	14.5	14.5	14.7	15.0	15.0	15.1	15.4	15.7	15.8	14.9
2005	15.4	15.5	15.4	15.6	15.6	15.7	15.7	15.9	15.9	16.2	16.3	16.5	15.8
2006	16.1	16.2	16.3	16.2	16.2	16.3	16.2	16.1	16.1	16.3	16.3	16.5	16.2
2007	16.0	16.0	16.1	16.4	16.4	16.3	16.2	16.2	16.3	16.5	16.4	16.5	16.3
2008	16.3	16.3	16.2	15.8	15.7	15.7	15.4	15.3	15.2	15.1	15.0	15.0	15.6
2009	14.5	14.4	14.3	14.2	14.1	14.2	14.0	14.0	13.9	13.9	13.8	13.9	14.1

Employment by Industry: North Port-Bradenton-Sarasota, FL, Selected Years, Selected Years, 1990–2009—*Continued*

(Numbers in thousands, not seasonally adjusted.)

Industry and year	January	February	March	April	May	June	July	August	September	October	November	December	Annual average
Professional and Business Services													
1990	5.3	5.7	6.2	6.3	6.3	6.4	5.8	5.7	5.9	6.9	7.3	7.6	6.3
2000	27.3	28.1	29.0	26.7	27.1	29.0	30.0	31.4	31.4	31.2	31.2	31.5	29.5
2001	27.9	29.8	30.4	30.0	31.6	31.2	30.6	31.1	30.7	32.6	33.3	33.9	31.1
2002	31.6	34.3	36.8	40.1	39.0	38.0	37.6	37.4	37.5	37.4	35.7	34.8	36.7
2003	35.2	35.4	35.6	36.0	36.9	41.0	37.4	38.8	39.6	40.3	41.5	42.3	38.3
2004	38.4	39.9	40.9	41.8	42.9	44.4	44.7	45.6	46.2	47.1	46.9	48.6	44.0
2005	47.4	48.7	49.3	49.1	49.9	50.5	50.7	50.9	50.9	50.5	50.6	52.0	50.0
2006	49.5	51.1	52.8	51.3	51.8	52.8	51.6	51.4	51.8	49.5	49.4	49.0	51.0
2007	46.9	47.9	48.6	47.1	47.6	48.4	46.1	46.9	46.7	45.2	46.1	46.8	47.0
2008	44.5	45.9	46.6	44.8	45.2	45.3	44.9	45.1	45.1	44.2	44.2	43.7	45.0
2009	41.7	41.8	42.2	41.3	41.5	42.1	41.2	41.3	41.4	41.2	41.0	41.4	41.5
Education and Health Services													
1990	20.8	21.2	21.4	21.3	21.5	21.7	21.2	21.4	21.5	22.0	21.9	22.1	21.5
2000	35.1	35.5	35.8	36.3	36.0	36.5	35.6	35.8	36.3	36.7	37.0	37.1	36.1
2001	35.2	35.6	35.8	35.5	35.4	35.7	35.0	35.2	35.6	35.5	35.7	36.1	35.5
2002	35.4	35.5	35.8	35.8	36.0	36.1	36.0	36.5	36.9	37.3	37.8	38.1	36.4
2003	37.4	37.8	38.1	37.8	38.1	38.0	37.4	37.7	38.1	38.3	38.6	38.6	38.0
2004	38.2	38.5	38.7	38.8	39.1	39.0	38.6	38.9	39.2	39.6	39.9	40.1	39.1
2005	39.1	39.4	39.6	39.3	39.5	39.4	39.1	39.3	39.5	39.6	39.9	40.3	39.5
2006	39.5	40.0	40.3	40.2	40.4	40.4	40.0	40.3	40.5	40.3	40.7	41.1	40.3
2007	40.8	41.6	41.5	41.3	41.3	41.3	41.0	41.3	41.6	41.7	42.0	42.2	41.5
2008	42.5	43.0	43.2	42.7	42.7	42.4	41.9	42.1	42.4	42.7	43.1	43.3	42.7
2009	43.3	43.3	43.4	43.2	43.2	42.9	42.6	43.0	42.8	43.7	43.9	43.6	43.2
Leisure and Hospitality													
1990	24.9	26.0	26.2	26.2	25.5	24.7	23.8	23.8	23.2	23.2	23.5	24.1	24.6
2000	29.0	29.6	30.3	31.1	30.6	30.1	28.6	28.4	28.2	29.0	29.5	29.9	29.5
2001	29.7	30.4	31.1	31.1	30.3	29.5	29.1	29.3	29.0	29.8	30.9	31.4	30.1
2002	30.7	31.2	32.0	31.1	30.5	30.6	30.0	30.2	29.9	30.4	31.7	32.7	30.9
2003	31.7	32.4	33.3	32.6	32.1	31.5	30.4	30.4	30.0	30.3	31.6	32.4	31.6
2004	32.5	32.9	33.8	33.8	33.1	32.4	32.1	31.9	31.5	32.2	33.1	33.9	32.8
2005	34.0	34.5	35.3	34.9	34.3	33.7	32.6	32.7	32.4	32.7	33.7	34.0	33.7
2006	33.8	34.5	35.3	35.2	34.7	34.3	33.5	33.4	32.9	33.3	34.3	35.1	34.2
2007	34.9	35.9	37.0	36.6	35.9	35.0	33.8	33.7	33.1	33.5	34.4	35.0	34.9
2008	34.8	35.5	36.0	35.3	34.3	33.4	32.2	32.0	31.4	31.9	32.7	33.4	33.6
2009	33.7	34.2	34.9	34.5	33.7	32.6	31.5	31.2	30.7	30.9	31.4	32.2	32.6
Other Services													
1990	10.0	10.0	10.1	9.9	9.9	9.9	10.4	10.6	10.5	10.5	10.6	10.6	10.3
2000	12.3	12.3	12.4	12.5	12.6	12.9	12.5	12.5	12.6	12.7	12.7	12.8	12.6
2001	12.5	12.7	12.7	12.7	12.7	12.8	12.8	12.9	12.9	12.9	13.0	13.1	12.8
2002	13.3	13.4	13.3	13.4	13.4	13.4	13.1	13.1	13.2	13.3	13.4	13.5	13.3
2003	13.4	13.6	13.6	13.2	13.2	13.1	12.9	12.8	12.9	12.9	12.9	13.0	13.1
2004	13.2	12.8	13.4	13.0	13.1	13.2	13.2	13.2	13.1	12.9	13.0	13.1	13.1
2005	13.3	13.3	13.4	13.1	13.1	13.1	12.9	12.9	13.1	13.0	13.0	13.1	13.1
2006	13.3	13.5	13.7	13.6	13.7	13.8	13.4	13.6	13.8	13.8	14.1	14.1	13.7
2007	13.8	13.8	14.0	13.7	13.6	13.9	13.5	13.6	13.7	14.0	14.3	14.5	13.9
2008	14.4	14.6	14.7	14.1	14.0	13.7	13.3	13.1	12.9	12.7	12.4	12.3	13.5
2009	12.1	12.1	12.2	12.0	12.1	12.0	11.9	11.9	11.9	11.9	11.9	11.9	12.0
Government													
1990	22.3	23.6	22.8	23.3	23.9	23.8	21.9	21.2	25.3	24.9	25.7	23.9	23.6
2000	24.3	24.5	24.6	24.7	25.4	22.5	22.2	24.3	24.1	24.4	24.7	24.9	24.2
2001	24.4	24.7	24.9	24.7	24.9	22.5	22.3	24.6	24.7	25.2	25.6	25.8	24.5
2002	25.3	25.7	25.8	25.7	25.9	23.4	23.2	25.6	25.8	25.9	26.2	26.2	25.4
2003	26.2	26.4	26.5	26.4	26.7	24.1	23.9	26.5	26.6	26.7	27.1	27.3	26.2
2004	26.7	27.0	27.0	27.1	27.3	24.6	24.3	27.0	26.8	27.0	27.2	27.4	26.6
2005	26.9	27.1	27.1	27.3	27.4	24.5	24.4	27.0	27.2	27.8	28.0	27.9	26.9
2006	27.8	27.9	28.1	28.4	28.5	25.6	25.3	28.2	28.6	28.6	29.3	29.3	28.0
2007	28.8	29.1	29.2	29.2	29.1	26.1	25.9	28.8	28.9	28.8	29.1	29.1	28.5
2008	29.0	29.2	29.5	29.5	29.5	26.5	26.3	29.2	29.2	29.0	28.8	28.8	28.7
2009	28.6	28.7	28.9	29.3	28.9	25.8	25.6	27.6	28.1	28.8	29.0	28.7	28.2

Employment by Industry: Oklahoma City, OK, Selected Years, 1990–2009

(Numbers in thousands, not seasonally adjusted.)

Industry and year	January	February	March	April	May	June	July	August	September	October	November	December	Annual average
Total Nonfarm													
1990	415.9	421.7	426.4	427.7	430.5	431.7	421.6	421.3	431.7	430.2	430.4	430.0	426.6
2000	522.3	525.3	530.2	533.6	538.3	537.1	529.0	534.5	543.7	543.2	546.7	546.1	535.8
2001	532.9	535.5	540.7	544.6	547.7	548.4	534.9	539.0	546.8	544.0	547.8	547.4	542.5
2002	527.4	533.0	537.8	539.9	543.9	541.2	530.9	535.9	542.7	541.0	543.1	542.9	538.3
2003	523.1	526.0	527.3	529.5	532.3	526.2	520.9	525.1	532.7	534.9	535.7	537.2	529.2
2004	524.5	528.7	534.2	538.6	540.5	536.8	532.3	536.8	545.3	546.2	547.6	550.6	538.5
2005	532.6	539.3	545.1	551.3	552.8	550.2	545.3	549.5	557.8	557.6	562.2	564.4	550.7
2006	549.3	554.6	560.0	560.9	563.5	562.5	552.6	557.6	565.2	564.1	565.7	568.5	560.4
2007	554.8	560.4	567.7	567.3	570.0	570.0	559.9	566.1	572.8	575.3	580.3	578.6	568.6
2008	565.2	571.4	575.4	577.4	580.0	575.5	567.7	572.7	580.9	581.4	583.3	581.9	576.1
2009	567.2	565.3	566.9	564.1	563.2	558.7	549.7	550.1	556.1	557.1	559.1	559.8	559.8
Total Private													
1990	314.7	318.6	322.6	324.7	326.8	330.1	328.5	326.4	329.5	326.0	326.8	326.6	325.1
2000	416.6	418.1	421.7	425.3	428.5	431.1	431.6	434.4	435.7	434.0	436.1	436.6	429.1
2001	424.9	425.9	430.3	434.6	437.0	440.7	435.3	436.2	436.0	431.3	433.8	434.0	433.3
2002	417.2	420.8	424.8	427.1	430.9	432.0	430.6	432.8	431.2	427.4	429.2	429.1	427.8
2003	414.3	414.3	416.3	418.7	421.6	419.0	421.2	423.7	423.1	423.8	424.2	425.5	420.5
2004	416.7	417.4	422.5	427.0	428.7	428.4	431.2	431.5	432.0	432.8	433.8	436.2	428.2
2005	421.7	426.1	431.5	437.1	438.2	439.8	441.8	443.8	444.5	442.4	446.3	448.7	438.5
2006	436.8	439.2	444.3	445.1	447.4	450.6	448.1	450.3	451.3	446.9	448.2	451.3	446.6
2007	440.0	443.4	450.0	449.8	452.2	455.7	452.9	456.4	456.5	456.2	460.6	459.8	452.8
2008	451.3	453.5	456.7	458.8	460.8	462.3	460.9	461.7	462.7	461.3	462.2	461.5	459.5
2009	448.4	446.3	446.7	443.4	442.2	442.5	439.2	437.9	437.2	436.3	438.3	439.3	441.5
Goods-Producing													
1990	66.8	69.0	70.5	70.3	70.7	71.1	71.2	68.3	70.8	69.8	68.8	68.3	69.6
2000	79.7	80.0	80.6	80.1	80.6	81.5	81.5	82.2	82.0	81.4	81.8	82.0	81.1
2001	79.4	79.3	80.0	80.0	81.1	81.6	80.3	78.6	79.6	77.0	77.8	77.2	79.3
2002	70.6	71.7	71.9	70.9	72.2	72.4	72.4	72.2	71.5	70.4	70.1	69.9	71.4
2003	68.8	68.6	68.8	69.1	69.4	67.3	70.5	70.7	70.2	70.2	69.7	70.0	69.4
2004	69.3	69.0	69.7	70.8	71.6	70.3	73.1	73.3	73.1	72.9	72.2	73.2	71.5
2005	70.5	72.0	73.2	73.5	73.7	73.1	75.4	75.6	75.5	76.0	76.3	77.3	74.3
2006	76.3	76.7	77.5	77.1	77.5	78.4	77.5	77.9	77.7	77.7	77.3	77.9	77.5
2007	75.4	75.5	76.9	77.1	77.4	78.8	78.6	79.4	79.0	79.2	79.8	79.3	78.0
2008	78.5	79.0	79.6	80.3	81.0	82.1	82.0	82.1	81.6	81.4	80.7	79.7	80.7
2009	77.6	75.9	74.6	72.5	71.8	71.4	71.0	70.1	69.2	69.1	68.6	68.4	71.7
Mining and Logging													
1990	9.0	8.8	8.9	8.9	8.9	8.9	8.9	8.9	8.8	9.0	9.1	9.3	9.0
2000	6.0	6.2	6.2	6.3	6.3	6.5	6.7	6.9	6.9	7.1	7.2	7.5	6.7
2001	7.1	7.3	7.5	7.4	7.5	7.7	7.7	7.7	7.5	7.5	7.4	7.4	7.5
2002	7.4	7.5	7.5	7.3	7.5	7.5	7.6	7.6	7.5	7.4	7.4	7.4	7.5
2003	7.5	7.5	7.5	7.7	7.7	7.8	8.1	8.2	8.2	8.3	8.3	8.4	7.9
2004	8.5	8.5	8.6	8.8	8.9	9.1	9.2	9.2	9.3	9.4	9.5	9.6	9.1
2005	9.7	9.8	10.0	10.1	10.2	10.3	10.6	10.7	10.9	11.0	11.3	11.7	10.5
2006	11.7	12.0	12.2	12.4	12.6	12.8	12.7	13.0	13.1	13.3	13.5	13.8	12.8
2007	13.7	13.7	13.7	13.9	14.0	14.2	14.6	14.9	14.9	15.1	15.3	15.3	14.4
2008	14.9	15.1	15.2	15.6	15.9	16.3	16.4	16.6	16.5	16.8	16.7	16.3	16.0
2009	15.9	15.2	14.5	13.6	13.3	13.1	12.8	12.6	12.4	12.3	12.4	12.4	13.4
Construction													
1990	11.8	11.9	12.1	12.5	12.8	13.4	13.8	13.9	13.6	13.4	13.2	12.9	12.9
2000	21.5	21.4	21.9	22.2	22.7	23.2	23.0	23.3	23.0	23.1	22.8	22.5	22.6
2001	21.7	22.2	22.8	23.4	24.0	24.6	24.3	24.5	23.9	23.2	22.6	22.3	23.3
2002	21.6	21.4	21.7	21.6	22.1	22.5	22.7	22.6	22.2	22.0	21.8	21.8	22.0
2003	21.5	21.4	21.6	22.0	22.8	23.6	23.6	23.7	23.3	23.2	22.8	22.9	22.7
2004	22.3	22.1	22.7	23.1	23.4	24.0	24.5	24.5	24.3	23.9	23.4	23.9	23.5
2005	23.1	23.2	24.1	24.6	24.9	25.7	26.0	26.1	26.0	26.1	26.2	26.4	25.2
2006	25.8	25.9	26.6	26.2	26.5	27.2	26.7	26.9	26.7	26.3	26.1	26.2	26.4
2007	25.3	25.2	26.2	26.3	26.3	27.3	26.9	27.2	27.0	26.9	27.2	26.8	26.6
2008	26.6	26.9	27.4	27.5	27.9	28.4	28.5	28.3	28.1	27.7	27.4	27.1	27.7
2009	26.1	25.8	26.1	25.6	25.7	26.4	26.3	26.1	25.7	25.6	25.3	25.0	25.8
Manufacturing													
1990	46.0	48.3	49.5	48.9	49.0	48.8	48.5	45.5	48.4	47.4	46.5	46.1	47.7
2000	52.2	52.4	52.5	51.6	51.6	51.8	51.8	52.0	52.1	51.2	51.8	52.0	51.9
2001	50.6	49.8	49.7	49.2	49.6	49.3	48.3	46.4	48.2	46.3	47.8	47.5	48.6
2002	41.6	42.8	42.7	42.0	42.6	42.4	42.1	42.0	41.8	41.0	40.9	40.7	41.9
2003	39.8	39.7	39.7	39.4	38.9	35.9	38.8	38.8	38.7	38.7	38.6	38.7	38.8
2004	38.5	38.4	38.4	38.9	39.3	37.2	39.4	39.6	39.5	39.6	39.3	39.7	39.0
2005	37.7	39.0	39.1	38.8	38.6	37.1	38.8	38.8	38.6	38.9	38.8	39.2	38.6
2006	38.8	38.8	38.7	38.5	38.4	38.4	38.1	38.0	37.9	38.1	37.7	37.9	38.3
2007	36.4	36.6	37.0	36.9	37.1	37.3	37.1	37.3	37.1	37.2	37.3	37.2	37.0
2008	37.0	37.0	37.0	37.2	37.2	37.4	37.1	37.2	37.0	36.9	36.6	36.3	37.0
2009	35.6	34.9	34.0	33.3	32.8	31.9	31.9	31.4	31.1	31.2	30.9	31.0	32.5

Employment by Industry: Oklahoma City, OK, Selected Years, 1990–2009—*Continued*

(Numbers in thousands, not seasonally adjusted.)

Industry and year	January	February	March	April	May	June	July	August	September	October	November	December	Annual average
Service-Providing													
1990	349.1	352.7	355.9	357.4	359.8	360.6	350.4	353.0	360.9	360.4	361.6	361.7	357.0
2000	442.6	445.3	449.6	453.5	457.7	455.6	447.5	452.3	461.7	461.8	464.9	464.1	454.7
2001	453.5	456.2	460.7	464.6	466.6	466.8	454.6	460.4	467.2	467.0	470.0	470.2	463.2
2002	456.8	461.3	465.9	469.0	471.7	468.8	458.5	463.7	471.2	470.6	473.0	473.0	467.0
2003	454.3	457.4	458.5	460.4	462.9	458.9	450.4	454.4	462.5	464.7	466.0	467.2	459.8
2004	455.2	459.7	464.5	467.8	468.9	466.5	459.2	463.5	472.2	473.3	475.4	477.4	467.0
2005	462.1	467.3	471.9	477.8	479.1	477.1	469.9	473.9	482.3	481.6	485.9	487.1	476.3
2006	473.0	477.9	482.5	483.8	486.0	484.1	475.1	479.7	487.5	486.4	488.4	490.6	482.9
2007	479.4	484.9	490.8	490.2	492.6	491.2	481.3	486.7	493.8	496.1	500.5	499.3	490.6
2008	486.7	492.4	495.8	497.1	499.0	493.4	485.7	490.6	499.3	500.0	502.6	502.2	495.4
2009	489.6	489.4	492.3	491.6	491.4	487.3	478.7	480.0	486.9	488.0	490.5	491.4	488.1
Trade, Transportation, and Utilities													
1990	83.0	82.1	82.4	82.6	82.7	83.5	83.5	84.0	83.8	83.7	85.1	85.7	83.5
2000	101.3	99.9	99.8	100.6	101.2	101.1	101.2	102.1	102.0	102.6	105.1	106.6	102.0
2001	101.7	100.0	100.1	100.8	100.8	100.9	99.8	99.8	99.5	100.1	101.9	103.0	100.7
2002	99.0	98.3	99.3	98.7	98.9	98.9	98.7	99.1	98.8	98.0	100.3	101.2	99.1
2003	96.6	95.5	95.9	96.0	96.4	96.4	95.8	96.5	96.5	97.5	99.5	101.0	96.9
2004	96.3	95.7	96.3	96.1	96.3	96.5	96.0	95.8	95.7	96.8	99.3	100.9	96.8
2005	96.4	96.4	97.1	97.8	98.0	98.0	98.6	99.3	99.5	100.0	102.6	104.2	99.0
2006	99.1	99.0	99.5	99.3	99.7	100.1	99.4	100.1	100.4	100.4	102.5	104.0	100.3
2007	100.3	100.3	102.0	100.9	101.3	101.2	100.4	100.7	100.3	100.7	102.9	103.3	101.2
2008	100.4	99.8	100.5	99.8	99.9	100.1	100.5	100.4	100.8	100.9	102.5	102.9	100.7
2009	98.9	97.9	98.2	97.5	97.5	97.6	96.4	96.4	96.2	95.6	97.4	97.2	97.2
Wholesale Trade													
1990	18.1	18.1	18.3	18.7	18.6	18.9	19.4	19.6	19.5	19.1	18.9	18.9	18.8
2000	21.9	21.8	21.8	22.0	22.0	22.1	22.1	22.4	22.3	22.0	22.1	22.2	22.1
2001	21.3	21.4	21.5	21.5	21.6	22.0	21.9	22.0	21.9	21.8	21.8	22.0	21.7
2002	21.4	21.3	21.4	21.2	21.4	21.5	21.7	21.6	21.6	21.3	21.3	21.3	21.4
2003	21.2	21.1	21.2	21.0	21.0	21.0	20.9	20.9	21.0	21.0	20.9	21.1	21.0
2004	20.8	20.7	20.6	20.6	20.8	21.2	21.2	21.1	21.0	21.2	21.3	21.4	21.0
2005	21.1	21.2	21.3	21.4	21.4	21.6	22.0	22.0	21.9	22.0	22.2	22.4	21.7
2006	22.2	22.4	22.5	22.4	22.6	22.8	22.8	22.9	23.0	23.0	23.0	23.2	22.7
2007	22.8	22.9	23.0	23.0	23.0	23.1	22.9	22.7	22.6	23.0	22.9	23.1	22.9
2008	22.9	22.8	22.9	22.9	22.9	23.1	23.1	22.9	23.0	23.0	23.0	22.9	23.0
2009	22.5	22.4	22.3	22.0	21.8	21.8	21.6	21.6	21.6	21.5	21.6	21.7	21.9
Retail Trade													
1990	49.5	48.6	48.7	49.2	49.4	49.7	49.3	49.8	49.7	50.1	51.4	52.1	49.8
2000	62.2	61.0	61.0	61.3	61.7	61.7	61.8	62.4	62.4	63.2	65.6	67.0	62.6
2001	62.9	61.4	61.4	61.4	61.5	61.5	60.4	60.3	60.3	61.2	63.1	64.2	61.6
2002	61.4	60.8	61.7	61.7	61.2	61.1	60.5	61.0	60.9	60.6	63.1	64.3	61.5
2003	60.0	59.0	59.2	59.7	60.1	60.2	59.6	60.3	60.3	61.1	63.3	64.7	60.6
2004	60.2	59.8	60.3	60.2	60.2	60.0	59.5	59.4	59.2	59.9	62.3	63.6	60.4
2005	60.0	59.8	60.3	60.7	60.8	60.7	60.6	61.2	61.4	61.9	64.2	65.4	61.4
2006	61.1	60.8	61.1	61.1	61.2	61.4	60.8	61.3	61.3	61.1	63.1	64.2	61.5
2007	61.1	60.9	62.2	61.3	61.7	61.6	61.2	61.7	61.5	61.9	64.3	64.4	62.0
2008	62.5	62.0	62.4	61.5	61.5	61.4	61.8	61.9	62.2	62.3	63.8	64.1	62.3
2009	60.8	60.0	60.2	59.9	60.1	60.1	59.3	59.3	59.2	58.8	60.6	60.1	59.9
Transportation and Utilities													
1990	15.4	15.4	15.4	14.7	14.7	14.9	14.8	14.6	14.6	14.5	14.8	14.7	14.9
2000	17.2	17.1	17.0	17.3	17.5	17.3	17.3	17.3	17.3	17.4	17.4	17.4	17.3
2001	17.5	17.2	17.2	17.9	17.7	17.4	17.5	17.5	17.3	17.1	17.0	16.8	17.3
2002	16.2	16.2	16.2	16.3	16.3	16.3	16.5	16.5	16.3	16.1	15.9	15.6	16.2
2003	15.4	15.4	15.5	15.3	15.3	15.2	15.3	15.3	15.2	15.4	15.3	15.2	15.3
2004	15.3	15.2	15.4	15.3	15.3	15.3	15.3	15.3	15.5	15.7	15.7	15.9	15.4
2005	15.3	15.4	15.5	15.7	15.8	15.7	16.0	16.1	16.2	16.1	16.2	16.4	15.9
2006	15.8	15.8	15.9	15.8	15.9	15.9	15.8	15.9	16.1	16.3	16.4	16.6	16.0
2007	16.4	16.5	16.8	16.6	16.6	16.5	16.3	16.3	16.2	15.8	15.7	15.8	16.3
2008	15.0	15.0	15.2	15.4	15.5	15.6	15.6	15.6	15.6	15.6	15.7	15.9	15.5
2009	15.6	15.5	15.7	15.6	15.6	15.7	15.5	15.5	15.4	15.3	15.2	15.4	15.5
Information													
1990	9.1	9.1	9.1	8.7	8.8	8.9	8.9	8.9	8.9	8.8	8.7	8.7	8.9
2000	12.8	13.2	13.3	13.9	13.8	14.0	14.2	14.2	14.4	14.4	14.4	14.4	13.9
2001	14.6	14.8	14.8	14.5	14.5	14.6	14.4	14.1	14.2	14.4	14.3	14.3	14.5
2002	14.3	14.4	14.2	14.1	14.2	14.1	14.0	14.0	13.8	13.7	13.9	13.8	14.0
2003	13.6	13.5	13.5	13.4	13.5	13.4	13.4	13.4	13.3	13.4	13.5	13.7	13.4
2004	13.5	13.4	13.3	13.5	13.5	13.8	14.0	13.8	13.5	13.8	13.7	13.7	13.6
2005	13.6	13.7	13.6	13.7	13.7	13.5	13.6	13.3	13.0	12.9	13.0	13.0	13.4
2006	12.4	12.5	12.6	13.5	13.4	13.3	13.5	13.5	13.4	13.2	13.2	13.7	13.2
2007	13.1	12.7	12.4	12.4	12.4	12.5	12.4	12.4	12.4	12.4	12.5	12.5	12.5
2000	12.5	12.6	12.5	12.7	12.7	12.7	12.8	12.7	12.5	12.4	12.5	12.4	12.6
2009	12.3	12.2	12.2	12.3	12.3	12.3	12.2	12.1	12.0	12.0	12.1	12.0	12.2

Employment by Industry: Oklahoma City, OK, Selected Years, 1990–2009—*Continued*

(Numbers in thousands, not seasonally adjusted.)

Industry and year	January	February	March	April	May	June	July	August	September	October	November	December	Annual average
Financial Activities													
1990	28.2	28.1	28.2	28.9	29.1	29.1	29.2	29.3	29.2	28.5	28.7	28.7	28.8
2000	33.5	33.7	33.6	33.5	33.6	33.7	33.7	33.9	33.8	33.8	33.9	34.0	33.7
2001	33.4	33.6	33.8	34.1	34.3	34.6	34.6	34.9	34.7	34.8	34.8	34.8	34.4
2002	34.8	34.8	34.9	34.9	35.1	35.6	35.6	35.8	35.6	35.5	35.6	35.8	35.3
2003	34.3	34.4	34.5	34.7	34.8	35.0	35.0	35.3	35.2	35.2	35.0	35.1	34.8
2004	34.8	34.9	35.1	35.8	35.7	35.9	35.6	35.5	35.3	35.3	35.2	35.3	35.4
2005	34.1	34.1	34.3	34.3	34.5	34.8	34.9	34.8	34.7	34.2	34.3	35.0	34.5
2006	34.6	34.5	34.6	34.2	34.4	34.4	34.5	34.6	34.5	34.5	34.4	34.4	34.5
2007	34.7	35.1	34.9	34.4	34.5	34.5	34.3	34.3	33.9	33.9	33.9	33.9	34.4
2008	34.2	34.1	34.1	34.2	34.4	34.4	34.5	34.2	34.0	33.9	34.0	34.1	34.2
2009	33.3	33.2	33.3	32.9	33.0	33.1	32.9	32.9	32.7	32.8	32.8	32.9	33.0
Professional and Business Services													
1990	35.4	35.9	36.5	37.4	37.6	38.8	38.1	38.5	38.3	37.9	38.7	39.1	37.7
2000	62.8	63.5	64.8	65.8	66.5	67.7	68.4	68.3	69.0	67.7	67.4	68.0	66.7
2001	65.7	66.4	67.7	69.1	68.9	70.3	68.7	70.3	70.8	68.3	68.0	68.5	68.6
2002	65.6	67.0	68.1	69.4	69.4	69.5	67.8	68.5	68.5	67.0	66.7	66.8	67.9
2003	63.3	63.5	63.7	64.5	65.2	65.0	65.0	65.5	65.7	65.6	65.3	65.1	64.7
2004	63.1	63.3	64.6	66.5	66.4	66.7	67.6	68.0	67.9	68.0	68.1	68.0	66.5
2005	65.3	66.5	67.5	70.0	69.9	71.2	71.1	72.2	72.2	70.9	71.6	71.0	70.0
2006	69.6	70.1	71.3	71.4	72.1	73.4	73.0	73.6	74.3	72.1	72.5	72.8	72.2
2007	71.3	72.6	73.7	74.0	74.6	75.9	74.6	75.7	76.4	75.6	76.7	76.9	74.8
2008	74.5	75.2	75.4	75.3	75.3	75.4	74.1	74.7	75.1	74.5	74.4	74.3	74.9
2009	71.1	71.2	70.9	69.9	68.8	68.9	68.5	68.3	68.9	69.9	69.6	70.7	69.7
Education and Health Services													
1990	39.4	39.9	40.1	40.0	40.1	40.2	40.2	40.4	41.2	41.4	41.5	41.6	40.5
2000	56.7	57.2	57.5	58.5	59.1	58.6	58.4	58.9	59.8	59.3	59.6	59.3	58.6
2001	58.9	59.5	60.1	59.9	60.6	60.7	60.5	61.3	61.6	62.2	62.1	62.3	60.8
2002	61.2	62.1	62.6	63.8	64.5	64.3	64.6	65.4	65.5	65.7	66.4	66.4	64.4
2003	64.5	65.3	65.8	65.4	65.4	64.9	64.8	65.5	66.3	65.8	66.1	65.9	65.4
2004	66.8	67.4	68.1	67.9	67.7	67.1	66.6	67.1	68.0	68.5	68.5	68.6	67.7
2005	66.6	67.3	67.9	68.8	68.5	68.3	68.7	69.6	70.6	70.5	70.7	71.1	69.1
2006	68.5	69.3	69.6	70.0	70.2	70.7	70.1	70.6	71.2	70.9	70.7	70.9	70.2
2007	70.5	71.2	71.8	72.2	72.4	72.5	72.1	72.8	73.7	74.3	74.6	74.5	72.7
2008	73.4	74.3	74.4	75.4	75.7	75.1	75.3	76.0	76.5	76.8	77.0	77.0	75.6
2009	76.4	76.2	76.4	76.3	76.5	76.7	76.5	76.7	77.5	78.2	78.7	78.5	77.1
Leisure and Hospitality													
1990	36.3	37.9	38.9	39.7	40.4	40.8	39.9	39.5	39.9	38.8	38.3	37.5	39.0
2000	46.3	47.1	48.4	48.9	49.6	50.1	50.0	50.5	50.3	50.6	49.7	48.0	49.1
2001	47.5	48.5	49.6	52.1	52.5	53.1	52.4	52.6	51.3	50.4	50.8	49.9	50.9
2002	48.6	49.3	50.4	51.3	52.5	52.9	53.1	53.4	53.1	53.0	52.2	51.1	51.7
2003	49.7	50.0	50.6	52.2	53.3	53.1	53.0	53.3	52.6	52.9	51.9	51.4	52.0
2004	49.9	50.6	52.0	53.0	54.0	54.4	54.8	54.8	55.4	54.7	54.0	53.6	53.4
2005	52.3	53.1	54.8	55.9	56.8	57.6	56.0	55.7	55.7	54.7	54.6	53.9	55.1
2006	53.5	54.2	56.0	56.7	56.9	56.8	56.9	57.0	56.8	55.3	54.9	54.8	55.8
2007	52.1	53.3	55.4	55.5	56.1	56.5	57.0	57.7	57.5	56.9	57.0	56.4	56.0
2008	54.7	55.1	56.6	57.2	57.8	58.3	57.6	57.5	58.1	57.4	57.2	57.3	57.1
2009	55.2	56.1	57.4	58.2	58.5	58.5	58.1	58.1	57.5	55.7	56.2	56.5	57.2
Other Services													
1990	16.5	16.6	16.9	17.1	17.4	17.7	17.5	17.5	17.4	17.1	17.0	17.0	17.1
2000	23.5	23.5	23.7	24.0	24.1	24.4	24.2	24.3	24.4	24.2	24.2	24.3	24.1
2001	23.7	23.8	24.2	24.1	24.3	24.9	24.6	24.6	24.3	24.1	24.1	24.0	24.2
2002	23.1	23.2	23.4	24.0	24.1	24.3	24.4	24.4	24.4	24.1	24.0	24.1	24.0
2003	23.5	23.5	23.5	23.4	23.6	23.9	23.7	23.5	23.3	23.2	23.2	23.3	23.5
2004	23.0	23.1	23.4	23.4	23.5	23.7	23.5	23.2	23.1	22.8	22.8	22.9	23.2
2005	22.9	23.0	23.1	23.1	23.1	23.3	23.5	23.3	23.3	23.2	23.2	23.2	23.2
2006	22.8	22.9	23.2	22.9	23.2	23.5	23.2	23.0	23.0	22.8	22.7	22.8	23.0
2007	22.6	22.7	22.9	23.3	23.5	23.8	23.5	23.4	23.3	23.2	23.2	23.0	23.2
2008	23.1	23.4	23.6	23.9	24.0	24.2	24.1	24.1	24.1	24.0	23.9	23.8	23.9
2009	23.6	23.6	23.7	23.8	23.8	24.0	23.6	23.3	23.2	23.0	22.9	23.1	23.5
Government													
1990	101.2	103.1	103.8	103.0	103.7	101.6	93.1	94.9	102.2	104.2	103.6	103.4	101.5
2000	105.7	107.2	108.5	108.3	109.8	106.0	97.4	100.1	108.0	109.2	110.6	109.5	106.7
2001	108.0	109.6	110.4	110.0	110.7	107.7	99.6	102.8	110.8	112.7	114.0	113.4	109.1
2002	110.2	112.2	113.0	112.8	113.0	109.2	100.3	103.1	111.5	113.6	113.9	113.8	110.6
2003	108.8	111.7	111.0	110.8	110.7	107.2	99.7	101.4	109.6	111.1	111.5	111.7	108.7
2004	107.8	111.3	111.7	111.6	111.8	108.4	101.1	105.3	113.3	113.4	113.8	114.4	110.3
2005	110.9	113.2	113.6	114.2	114.6	110.4	103.5	105.7	113.3	115.2	115.9	115.7	112.2
2006	112.5	115.4	115.7	115.8	116.1	111.9	104.5	107.3	113.9	117.2	117.5	117.2	113.8
2007	114.8	117.0	117.7	117.5	117.8	114.3	107.0	109.7	116.3	119.1	119.7	118.8	115.8
2008	113.9	117.9	118.7	118.6	119.2	113.2	106.8	111.0	118.2	120.1	121.1	120.4	116.6
2009	118.8	119.0	120.2	120.7	121.0	116.2	110.5	112.2	118.9	120.8	120.8	120.5	118.3

Employment by Industry: Omaha-Council Bluffs, NE-IA, Selected Years, 1990–2009

(Numbers in thousands, not seasonally adjusted.)

Industry and year	January	February	March	April	May	June	July	August	September	October	November	December	Annual average
Total Nonfarm													
1990	344.9	345.8	348.3	352.0	355.5	359.9	356.1	358.2	359.4	359.1	361.9	361.8	355.2
2000	428.5	429.8	432.1	437.5	442.9	449.1	445.0	446.0	446.6	445.7	447.8	448.6	441.6
2001	436.0	435.0	437.2	442.7	446.0	451.7	446.8	448.1	447.1	445.5	449.2	449.0	444.5
2002	432.9	434.1	435.8	440.1	443.1	446.1	440.1	440.6	439.8	438.9	441.3	440.2	439.4
2003	433.9	433.4	435.2	436.1	440.5	443.1	442.8	443.5	443.5	444.8	446.0	445.1	440.7
2004	435.2	432.8	436.9	439.4	444.0	446.8	442.7	443.5	443.3	443.9	446.9	447.2	441.9
2005	437.3	438.1	441.7	447.1	450.3	453.9	449.8	450.1	451.3	452.8	456.4	456.3	448.8
2006	444.8	446.9	450.6	454.3	459.2	462.7	457.3	457.7	460.4	460.9	463.9	463.4	456.8
2007	451.8	452.6	455.1	460.7	465.7	468.6	463.1	465.8	466.9	469.5	472.2	471.3	463.6
2008	461.3	461.7	464.1	469.0	474.8	474.5	469.3	471.3	471.1	474.3	474.1	471.5	469.8
2009	457.6	456.4	456.6	459.8	463.1	462.5	460.2	459.9	458.0	459.8	459.9	455.9	459.1
Total Private													
1990	292.2	292.8	295.0	298.0	301.1	305.4	304.2	306.8	306.6	304.8	307.3	307.8	301.8
2000	373.6	374.8	377.3	381.9	387.1	393.1	391.3	392.6	391.6	389.6	391.4	392.1	386.4
2001	380.1	378.9	381.1	386.0	388.9	394.1	391.8	393.3	390.9	388.4	391.8	391.4	388.1
2002	375.9	376.5	378.4	382.7	385.4	388.3	385.3	386.0	383.4	380.9	383.2	382.4	382.4
2003	376.2	375.3	377.5	377.0	381.2	383.7	387.2	389.4	387.0	385.9	387.1	386.7	382.9
2004	376.6	374.0	377.8	380.1	384.3	387.2	385.8	386.7	384.5	383.9	386.9	387.4	382.9
2005	377.7	378.0	381.7	387.0	389.6	393.4	392.4	393.0	391.7	391.7	395.1	395.4	388.9
2006	384.1	385.9	389.6	392.7	397.2	401.0	399.7	400.0	399.6	399.2	402.0	402.1	396.1
2007	390.6	391.0	393.6	398.5	403.1	406.6	406.4	408.1	406.0	407.1	409.8	409.7	402.5
2008	399.6	399.7	402.4	406.0	411.4	412.6	411.2	412.2	409.1	410.2	409.8	408.0	407.7
2009	394.1	392.5	392.8	394.6	397.3	398.3	396.9	397.2	393.9	394.1	394.0	391.5	394.8
Goods-Producing													
1990	43.1	42.9	43.5	44.7	45.4	46.4	46.6	46.6	46.4	46.0	45.9	44.8	45.2
2000	55.6	55.9	56.8	58.3	59.2	60.8	60.5	60.7	60.5	60.4	59.6	58.5	58.9
2001	56.2	55.8	56.2	58.2	59.0	60.1	60.4	60.0	59.6	58.9	58.4	57.6	58.4
2002	55.4	55.2	55.7	57.1	57.6	58.3	58.0	58.0	57.5	57.3	57.3	56.4	57.0
2003	55.9	55.3	55.6	56.7	58.1	59.2	60.7	60.9	60.2	60.1	59.6	58.8	58.4
2004	56.4	55.4	57.1	58.1	59.1	59.7	59.9	59.5	59.0	58.9	58.7	58.3	58.3
2005	56.0	55.6	57.1	58.5	58.7	60.0	60.3	60.1	59.6	59.4	59.2	58.2	58.6
2006	56.4	56.8	57.7	59.2	60.2	61.4	61.6	61.6	61.7	61.1	60.2	59.2	59.8
2007	56.6	55.7	56.2	57.6	58.7	59.8	60.2	60.6	59.9	60.5	60.2	59.1	58.8
2008	57.5	57.3	57.9	59.4	60.6	61.2	60.9	60.9	60.4	60.2	59.4	58.1	59.5
2009	54.9	54.5	54.5	55.8	56.1	56.5	56.4	56.2	55.7	55.5	55.4	53.5	55.4
Mining, Logging, and Construction													
1990	10.4	10.4	10.8	12.2	12.8	13.5	13.6	13.7	13.4	13.2	13.1	12.2	12.4
2000	20.7	20.7	21.5	22.9	23.6	24.5	24.6	24.8	24.6	24.4	23.4	22.3	23.2
2001	20.4	20.3	20.8	22.8	23.8	24.5	24.8	24.8	24.3	24.2	23.8	23.1	23.1
2002	20.9	20.8	21.7	23.3	23.9	24.7	25.1	25.1	24.7	24.7	24.7	23.8	23.6
2003	23.0	22.4	22.8	24.0	25.1	25.9	27.6	27.8	27.1	27.0	26.6	25.8	25.4
2004	23.6	22.8	24.3	25.4	26.2	26.6	26.7	26.5	26.0	25.9	25.8	25.1	25.4
2005	23.1	23.0	24.3	25.5	25.9	27.0	27.2	27.3	26.8	26.7	26.4	25.3	25.7
2006	24.1	24.4	25.2	26.4	27.3	28.3	28.4	28.5	28.7	27.8	26.8	25.8	26.8
2007	23.7	22.7	23.1	24.4	25.3	26.2	26.3	26.6	26.1	26.5	26.2	25.2	25.2
2008	23.6	23.4	24.0	25.5	26.5	27.0	27.0	27.1	26.8	26.5	25.9	25.1	25.7
2009	22.6	22.4	22.8	24.4	24.8	25.2	25.3	25.1	24.6	24.4	23.9	21.8	23.9
Manufacturing													
1990	32.7	32.5	32.7	32.5	32.6	32.9	33.0	32.9	33.0	32.8	32.8	32.6	32.8
2000	34.9	35.2	35.3	35.4	35.6	36.3	35.9	35.9	35.9	36.0	36.2	36.2	35.7
2001	35.8	35.5	35.4	35.4	35.2	35.6	35.6	35.2	35.3	34.7	34.6	34.5	35.2
2002	34.5	34.4	34.0	33.8	33.7	33.6	32.9	32.9	32.8	32.6	32.6	32.6	33.4
2003	32.9	32.9	32.8	32.7	33.0	33.3	33.1	33.1	33.1	33.1	33.0	33.0	33.0
2004	32.8	32.6	32.8	32.7	32.9	33.1	33.2	33.0	33.0	33.0	32.9	33.2	32.9
2005	32.9	32.6	32.8	33.0	32.8	33.0	33.1	32.8	32.8	32.7	32.8	32.9	32.9
2006	32.3	32.4	32.5	32.8	32.9	33.1	33.2	33.1	33.0	33.3	33.4	33.4	33.0
2007	32.9	33.0	33.1	33.2	33.4	33.6	33.9	34.0	33.8	34.0	34.0	33.9	33.6
2008	33.9	33.9	33.9	33.9	34.1	34.2	33.9	33.8	33.6	33.7	33.5	33.0	33.8
2009	32.3	32.1	31.7	31.4	31.3	31.3	31.1	31.1	31.1	31.1	31.5	31.7	31.5
Service-Providing													
1990	301.8	302.9	304.8	307.3	310.1	313.5	309.5	311.6	313.0	313.1	316.0	317.0	310.1
2000	372.9	373.9	375.3	379.2	383.7	388.3	384.5	385.3	386.1	385.3	388.2	390.1	382.7
2001	379.8	379.2	381.0	384.5	387.0	391.6	386.4	388.1	387.5	386.6	390.8	391.4	386.2
2002	377.5	378.9	380.1	383.0	385.5	387.8	382.1	382.6	382.3	381.6	384.0	383.8	382.4
2003	378.0	378.1	379.6	379.4	382.4	383.9	382.1	382.6	383.3	384.7	386.4	386.3	382.2
2004	378.8	377.4	379.8	381.3	384.9	387.1	382.8	384.0	384.3	385.0	388.2	388.9	383.5
2005	381.3	382.5	384.6	388.6	391.6	393.9	389.5	390.0	391.7	393.4	397.2	398.1	390.2
2006	388.4	390.1	392.9	395.1	399.0	401.3	395.7	396.1	398.7	399.8	403.7	404.2	397.1
2007	395.2	396.9	398.9	403.1	407.0	408.8	402.9	405.2	407.0	409.0	412.0	412.2	404.9
2008	403.8	404.4	406.2	409.6	414.2	413.3	408.4	410.4	410.7	414.1	414.7	413.4	410.3
2009	402.7	401.9	402.1	404.0	407.0	406.0	403.8	403.7	402.3	404.3	404.5	402.4	403.7

Employment by Industry: Omaha-Council Bluffs, NE-IA, Selected Years, 1990–2009—*Continued*

(Numbers in thousands, not seasonally adjusted.)

Industry and year	January	February	March	April	May	June	July	August	September	October	November	December	Annual average
Trade, Transportation, and Utilities													
1990	89.6	89.0	89.2	89.7	90.3	91.2	90.2	90.7	90.9	91.2	92.6	93.1	90.6
2000	105.6	104.9	104.7	106.4	107.4	108.5	107.4	107.6	107.3	108.1	110.0	111.5	107.5
2001	107.2	106.3	106.2	106.7	107.2	107.5	106.6	107.4	107.8	107.7	110.3	111.5	107.7
2002	105.6	104.2	103.9	103.6	103.9	103.7	103.0	102.7	102.9	102.3	103.9	104.4	103.7
2003	99.3	98.2	98.9	97.2	97.8	97.9	97.9	97.9	98.0	97.9	99.2	100.1	98.4
2004	96.3	94.9	94.6	95.6	97.0	97.8	97.3	98.5	98.9	98.2	100.7	102.0	97.7
2005	98.1	97.8	98.2	98.1	99.4	99.4	98.8	99.2	99.3	99.8	101.9	102.8	99.4
2006	97.0	96.6	97.4	97.4	98.5	98.7	98.6	98.9	99.1	100.0	102.7	103.7	99.1
2007	98.6	98.1	98.7	99.2	100.0	100.1	99.8	100.3	100.4	100.6	103.2	103.9	100.2
2008	99.4	98.5	99.0	98.7	99.9	99.6	99.0	99.4	98.9	100.1	101.8	102.6	99.7
2009	96.7	95.3	95.1	94.3	95.2	94.7	94.0	94.4	94.2	94.2	96.3	97.8	95.2
Wholesale Trade													
1990	18.8	19.0	19.1	19.2	19.2	19.4	19.3	19.4	19.3	19.4	19.4	19.5	19.3
2000	22.1	22.2	22.1	22.3	22.2	22.4	22.3	22.3	22.3	22.2	22.1	22.1	22.2
2001	21.6	21.7	21.7	22.0	22.0	22.1	22.0	21.7	21.6	21.6	21.5	21.4	21.7
2002	21.0	21.0	21.1	21.0	21.1	21.2	21.2	21.3	21.2	21.0	21.0	21.0	21.1
2003	20.7	20.7	20.9	20.8	20.6	20.5	20.4	20.3	20.2	19.6	19.7	19.6	20.3
2004	19.2	19.0	19.1	19.1	19.0	19.2	19.2	19.3	19.2	19.2	19.1	19.1	19.1
2005	18.6	18.6	18.8	18.6	18.6	18.6	18.7	18.5	18.3	18.4	18.4	18.4	18.5
2006	18.1	18.2	18.3	18.2	18.3	18.3	18.4	18.2	18.1	18.1	18.1	18.2	18.2
2007	17.7	17.7	17.8	18.0	18.0	18.3	18.3	18.3	18.4	18.4	18.5	18.6	18.2
2008	18.4	18.4	18.5	18.4	18.6	18.6	18.6	18.5	18.4	18.4	18.4	18.3	18.5
2009	18.0	17.9	17.8	17.9	17.9	17.9	17.9	17.8	17.7	17.6	17.6	17.5	17.8
Retail Trade													
1990	47.2	46.0	46.2	46.8	46.9	47.4	47.4	47.4	47.3	47.1	48.7	49.1	47.3
2000	54.0	53.2	53.0	54.0	55.1	56.2	55.0	55.0	55.0	56.3	58.4	59.6	55.4
2001	54.8	53.5	53.7	54.4	54.9	55.1	54.7	55.6	56.1	56.6	59.1	60.0	55.7
2002	54.4	53.2	53.1	53.4	54.0	54.1	53.8	53.9	54.6	54.6	56.6	57.6	54.4
2003	53.2	52.0	52.3	51.3	51.5	51.4	51.2	51.1	51.2	52.1	53.7	54.6	52.1
2004	51.4	50.2	50.0	50.1	50.8	51.1	50.7	50.6	50.5	51.1	53.1	54.3	51.2
2005	50.8	50.1	50.2	50.6	51.2	51.0	50.8	51.0	50.9	51.8	53.6	54.4	51.4
2006	50.5	49.6	50.1	50.3	50.8	50.9	50.7	50.7	50.7	51.7	54.0	54.8	51.2
2007	50.9	50.2	50.6	51.1	51.9	51.9	51.7	51.7	51.5	52.4	54.5	55.3	52.0
2008	52.1	51.1	51.2	50.9	51.3	51.2	50.8	50.7	50.2	51.0	52.6	53.6	51.4
2009	50.1	49.1	49.0	49.1	49.9	49.9	49.5	49.5	49.3	49.4	51.7	53.2	50.0
Transportation and Utilities													
1990	23.6	24.0	23.9	23.7	24.2	24.4	23.5	23.9	24.3	24.7	24.5	24.5	24.1
2000	29.5	29.5	29.6	30.1	30.1	29.9	30.1	30.3	30.0	29.6	29.5	29.8	29.8
2001	30.8	31.1	30.8	30.3	30.3	30.3	29.9	30.1	30.1	29.5	29.7	30.1	30.3
2002	30.2	30.0	29.7	29.2	28.8	28.4	28.0	27.5	27.1	26.7	26.3	25.8	28.1
2003	25.4	25.5	25.7	25.1	25.7	26.0	26.3	26.5	26.6	26.2	25.8	25.9	25.9
2004	25.7	25.7	25.5	26.4	27.2	27.5	27.4	28.6	29.2	27.9	28.5	28.6	27.4
2005	28.7	29.1	29.2	28.9	29.6	29.8	29.3	29.7	30.1	29.6	29.9	30.0	29.5
2006	28.4	28.8	29.0	28.9	29.4	29.5	29.5	30.0	30.3	30.2	30.6	30.7	29.6
2007	30.0	30.2	30.3	30.1	30.1	29.9	29.8	30.3	30.5	29.8	30.2	30.0	30.1
2008	28.9	29.0	29.3	29.4	30.0	29.8	29.6	30.2	30.3	30.7	30.8	30.7	29.9
2009	28.6	28.3	28.3	27.3	27.4	26.9	26.6	27.1	27.2	27.2	27.0	27.1	27.4
Information													
1990	11.0	11.1	10.8	10.6	10.7	10.8	10.8	10.9	11.0	10.7	10.7	10.7	10.8
2000	15.7	15.5	15.3	15.3	15.1	15.0	14.9	14.9	14.8	14.8	14.9	14.9	15.1
2001	14.8	14.7	14.7	14.9	15.0	15.1	14.9	14.9	14.6	14.7	14.7	14.6	14.8
2002	14.4	14.4	14.4	14.3	14.4	14.4	14.4	14.3	14.1	14.0	14.1	14.1	14.3
2003	14.0	14.0	13.9	13.7	13.7	13.8	13.9	13.8	13.7	13.8	13.8	13.9	13.8
2004	13.6	13.6	13.6	13.4	13.5	13.5	13.6	13.5	13.4	13.4	13.4	13.5	13.5
2005	13.3	13.3	13.3	13.2	13.1	13.3	13.3	13.4	13.2	13.3	13.4	13.4	13.3
2006	13.1	13.0	13.0	13.0	13.1	13.1	13.0	12.8	12.7	12.5	12.6	12.6	12.9
2007	12.3	12.4	12.4	12.5	12.6	12.7	12.7	12.7	12.6	12.6	12.6	12.6	12.6
2008	12.3	12.3	12.3	12.4	12.4	12.3	12.3	12.1	12.0	12.0	12.0	11.9	12.2
2009	11.6	11.6	11.6	11.4	11.4	11.5	11.5	11.5	11.4	11.4	11.5	11.4	11.5
Financial Activities													
1990	29.4	29.7	29.8	29.6	29.8	30.0	29.9	30.1	30.1	29.6	29.6	29.8	29.8
2000	35.2	35.2	35.3	35.3	35.6	35.9	35.7	35.8	36.0	36.0	36.0	36.4	35.7
2001	36.0	36.0	36.0	35.9	36.1	36.6	36.6	36.4	36.2	36.4	36.4	36.4	36.3
2002	35.6	35.9	36.1	36.3	36.8	37.1	37.5	37.6	37.4	37.7	38.0	38.2	37.0
2003	38.2	38.3	38.3	37.3	37.3	37.5	38.2	38.2	38.0	37.8	37.8	38.1	37.9
2004	37.6	37.6	38.0	37.3	37.4	37.6	37.5	37.4	37.1	37.5	37.4	37.5	37.5
2005	37.3	37.3	37.3	37.3	37.5	37.6	37.6	37.8	37.7	37.6	37.7	38.0	37.6
2006	37.8	38.1	38.2	38.3	38.6	39.1	39.2	39.4	39.1	39.1	39.3	39.6	38.8
2007	39.3	39.5	39.7	39.8	40.1	40.3	40.2	40.0	39.9	39.9	39.9	40.1	39.9
2008	40.2	40.5	40.7	40.5	40.8	41.0	40.9	40.7	40.6	40.7	40.6	40.8	40.7
2009	40.1	40.4	40.4	40.1	40.0	40.0	39.8	39.8	39.5	39.7	39.6	39.2	39.9

Employment by Industry: Omaha-Council Bluffs, NE-IA, Selected Years, 1990–2009—*Continued*

(Numbers in thousands, not seasonally adjusted.)

Industry and year	January	February	March	April	May	June	July	August	September	October	November	December	Annual average
Professional and Business Services													
1990	38.8	38.6	39.1	39.8	40.0	41.0	40.9	41.4	41.8	41.7	42.5	43.5	40.8
2000	56.4	56.8	57.6	59.3	59.4	60.9	60.8	61.3	60.7	60.0	60.2	61.2	59.6
2001	59.7	59.5	59.7	60.0	60.5	61.5	61.0	61.6	60.5	60.0	60.3	60.5	60.4
2002	58.0	58.6	59.1	59.6	59.5	60.1	58.1	58.3	57.4	57.7	57.9	57.7	58.5
2003	58.0	58.6	59.2	59.0	59.6	59.5	61.3	62.6	62.6	63.0	62.9	62.9	60.8
2004	61.2	61.0	61.7	60.9	61.1	61.3	60.5	60.9	59.7	60.0	60.3	60.2	60.7
2005	59.4	59.7	60.4	61.5	61.7	62.1	61.7	61.9	62.1	62.6	62.9	63.6	61.6
2006	61.8	62.3	63.1	63.4	63.7	64.6	64.4	64.1	63.9	63.3	63.1	63.2	63.4
2007	62.0	62.7	63.2	63.9	64.3	65.1	65.4	65.3	65.3	65.4	65.9	66.6	64.6
2008	64.8	64.8	65.1	66.1	66.3	66.4	65.8	66.1	65.5	65.5	65.2	64.7	65.5
2009	63.1	62.9	62.5	63.0	63.0	63.5	63.2	63.1	62.1	61.8	61.4	61.1	62.6
Education and Health Services													
1990	39.1	40.5	40.6	40.0	39.6	39.6	39.7	41.0	41.6	42.1	42.5	42.4	40.7
2000	52.8	53.9	54.1	52.7	53.9	54.1	53.9	54.4	55.8	55.5	56.5	55.8	54.5
2001	54.3	54.7	55.4	55.8	55.3	56.1	55.4	55.9	57.0	56.9	58.0	57.6	56.0
2002	55.4	56.5	56.6	57.1	57.3	57.4	56.5	57.1	57.7	57.5	58.0	57.9	57.1
2003	58.0	58.2	58.0	58.1	58.0	58.2	57.6	58.1	58.3	58.2	59.3	59.0	58.3
2004	58.2	58.4	58.8	59.3	59.0	58.8	58.6	58.6	59.1	59.5	60.2	59.9	59.0
2005	58.5	59.1	59.3	60.3	59.9	60.0	59.9	59.8	60.5	60.8	62.0	61.9	60.2
2006	60.9	61.7	62.0	61.7	61.9	61.9	61.3	61.8	62.8	62.6	63.9	63.3	62.2
2007	62.7	63.6	63.8	64.0	64.3	64.5	64.3	65.1	65.4	65.9	66.4	66.4	64.7
2008	65.7	66.7	66.9	67.2	67.6	67.3	67.4	68.3	68.7	68.9	69.4	69.3	67.8
2009	68.6	68.9	68.8	68.8	68.8	68.2	68.4	68.8	69.2	69.1	69.4	69.1	68.8
Leisure and Hospitality													
1990	28.3	28.3	29.1	30.5	32.2	33.0	32.6	32.8	31.7	30.5	30.6	30.5	30.8
2000	38.3	38.5	39.3	40.6	42.2	43.5	43.4	43.3	42.3	40.8	40.2	39.8	41.0
2001	37.7	37.9	38.5	39.8	41.0	42.1	42.1	42.4	40.7	39.1	39.0	38.6	39.9
2002	37.2	37.2	38.0	39.6	40.8	42.1	42.4	43.0	41.7	39.7	39.3	39.0	40.0
2003	38.4	38.3	39.0	39.9	41.0	41.8	41.7	42.0	40.5	39.5	38.9	38.4	40.0
2004	37.8	37.6	38.3	39.9	41.5	42.5	42.3	42.3	41.4	40.4	40.2	39.9	40.3
2005	39.2	39.2	40.1	42.1	43.2	44.7	44.4	44.5	43.3	42.1	41.9	41.5	42.2
2006	40.9	41.2	42.0	43.3	44.7	45.6	45.0	44.9	43.9	44.0	43.7	43.9	43.6
2007	42.7	42.6	43.1	44.9	46.5	47.4	47.2	47.6	46.1	45.7	45.0	44.4	45.3
2008	43.2	43.1	43.9	45.1	46.9	48.0	48.1	48.0	46.4	45.8	44.4	43.7	45.6
2009	42.4	42.2	43.2	44.4	46.0	46.9	46.7	46.6	45.1	45.6	43.5	42.7	44.6
Other Services													
1990	12.9	12.7	12.9	13.1	13.1	13.4	13.5	13.3	13.1	13.0	12.9	13.0	13.1
2000	14.0	14.1	14.2	14.0	14.3	14.4	14.7	14.6	14.2	14.0	14.0	14.0	14.2
2001	14.2	14.0	14.4	14.7	14.8	15.1	14.8	14.7	14.5	14.7	14.7	14.6	14.6
2002	14.3	14.5	14.6	15.1	15.1	15.2	15.4	15.0	14.7	14.7	14.7	14.7	14.8
2003	14.4	14.4	14.6	15.1	15.7	15.8	15.9	15.9	15.7	15.6	15.6	15.5	15.4
2004	15.5	15.5	15.7	15.6	15.7	16.0	16.1	16.0	15.9	16.0	16.0	16.1	15.8
2005	15.9	16.0	16.0	16.0	16.1	16.3	16.4	16.3	16.0	16.1	16.1	16.0	16.1
2006	16.2	16.2	16.2	16.4	16.5	16.6	16.6	16.5	16.4	16.6	16.5	16.6	16.4
2007	16.4	16.4	16.5	16.6	16.6	16.7	16.6	16.5	16.4	16.5	16.6	16.6	16.5
2008	16.5	16.5	16.6	16.6	16.9	16.8	16.8	16.7	16.6	17.0	17.0	16.9	16.7
2009	16.7	16.7	16.7	16.8	16.8	17.0	16.9	16.8	16.7	16.8	16.9	16.7	16.8
Government													
1990	52.7	53.0	53.3	54.0	54.4	54.5	51.9	51.4	52.8	54.3	54.6	54.0	53.4
2000	54.9	55.0	54.8	55.6	55.8	56.0	53.7	53.4	55.0	56.1	56.4	56.5	55.3
2001	55.9	56.1	56.1	56.7	57.1	57.6	55.0	54.8	56.2	57.1	57.4	57.6	56.5
2002	57.0	57.6	57.4	57.4	57.7	57.8	54.8	54.6	56.4	58.0	58.1	57.8	57.1
2003	57.7	58.1	57.7	59.1	59.3	59.4	55.6	54.1	56.5	58.9	58.9	58.4	57.8
2004	58.6	58.8	59.1	59.3	59.7	59.6	56.9	56.8	58.8	60.0	60.0	59.8	59.0
2005	59.6	60.1	60.0	60.1	60.7	60.5	57.4	57.1	59.6	61.1	61.3	60.9	59.9
2006	60.7	61.0	61.0	61.6	62.0	61.7	57.6	57.7	60.8	61.7	61.9	61.3	60.8
2007	61.2	61.6	61.5	62.2	62.6	62.0	56.7	57.7	60.9	62.4	62.4	61.6	61.1
2008	61.7	62.0	61.7	63.0	63.4	61.9	58.1	59.1	62.0	64.1	64.3	63.5	62.1
2009	63.5	63.9	63.8	65.2	65.8	64.2	63.3	62.7	64.1	65.7	65.9	64.4	64.4

Employment by Industry: Orlando-Kissimmee, FL, Selected Years, 1990–2009

(Numbers in thousands, not seasonally adjusted.)

Industry and year	January	February	March	April	May	June	July	August	September	October	November	December	Annual average
Total Nonfarm													
1990	562.9	572.9	578.6	578.8	582.8	587.0	577.9	577.4	579.7	577.0	582.0	582.4	578.3
2000	895.4	905.8	913.4	911.3	916.0	912.3	900.0	911.3	917.0	915.1	922.5	928.4	912.4
2001	908.2	917.5	925.4	919.9	921.9	912.2	903.3	914.3	913.9	904.1	903.8	905.1	912.5
2002	888.3	898.3	905.4	901.8	906.1	898.4	892.9	906.2	908.8	913.7	922.9	930.8	906.1
2003	912.9	918.2	922.9	922.9	924.5	915.6	909.9	924.8	925.1	933.2	940.1	945.9	924.7
2004	939.8	947.8	954.1	963.3	966.7	959.5	958.3	969.9	969.8	982.9	994.8	1002.8	967.5
2005	994.3	1002.1	1009.6	1016.7	1023.5	1013.3	1013.2	1028.4	1033.8	1036.4	1047.4	1054.5	1022.8
2006	1044.5	1051.6	1060.5	1065.9	1070.4	1061.1	1052.0	1070.0	1075.1	1075.7	1087.8	1095.6	1067.5
2007	1083.4	1093.4	1099.0	1099.2	1100.6	1087.3	1079.3	1092.4	1091.7	1095.8	1107.1	1107.9	1094.8
2008	1089.1	1099.4	1103.0	1091.7	1089.2	1072.2	1062.7	1070.7	1064.1	1060.1	1058.0	1056.0	1076.4
2009	1029.4	1029.4	1027.0	1021.4	1017.1	999.8	989.4	998.1	995.6	999.6	1001.9	1005.7	1009.5
Total Private													
1990	491.3	499.9	505.0	505.0	507.7	513.5	510.4	511.5	504.8	500.8	505.0	505.8	505.1
2000	803.8	812.5	819.6	817.7	820.2	827.9	817.5	819.6	824.3	821.5	828.4	833.7	820.6
2001	814.6	821.8	828.0	822.3	824.5	824.5	817.7	818.6	816.8	805.0	803.8	804.8	816.9
2002	788.2	797.2	804.2	800.0	803.6	806.7	803.1	804.8	805.8	809.2	817.8	825.3	805.5
2003	808.5	813.1	817.7	817.3	818.4	820.8	817.1	821.1	820.0	826.4	832.7	838.3	821.0
2004	833.1	839.8	845.9	855.2	858.4	862.7	863.5	863.8	861.1	872.2	883.2	891.3	860.9
2005	883.5	890.3	897.4	904.5	910.3	912.4	914.4	917.9	920.6	922.5	932.9	940.2	912.2
2006	930.6	936.3	945.3	949.7	954.4	956.0	949.2	954.7	958.3	958.3	969.7	978.3	953.4
2007	965.6	974.1	979.3	978.8	980.5	978.5	972.7	972.5	971.1	976.0	987.2	989.1	977.1
2008	970.7	980.1	982.6	971.2	968.5	963.7	956.4	952.3	944.6	940.6	937.8	935.9	958.7
2009	910.4	909.4	906.9	901.4	898.8	892.4	884.2	880.5	877.4	880.4	882.2	886.8	892.6
Goods-Producing													
1990	99.1	99.5	99.5	98.0	97.7	97.5	95.7	95.4	93.6	92.8	92.7	91.3	96.1
2000	111.2	112.1	112.3	112.4	112.9	113.6	112.5	112.7	112.9	111.1	111.6	112.0	112.3
2001	110.5	110.3	110.8	110.3	109.7	110.2	109.5	109.8	109.2	108.3	107.6	107.0	109.4
2002	106.2	106.7	107.1	106.2	106.4	106.1	105.7	106.6	106.8	107.7	108.0	108.6	106.8
2003	106.4	107.2	107.8	107.3	108.0	108.9	108.6	109.8	110.5	111.3	111.4	112.7	109.2
2004	112.4	113.5	114.9	116.4	117.1	118.6	119.7	120.0	119.9	121.4	122.7	123.8	118.4
2005	123.9	125.0	126.3	128.0	129.1	130.2	131.4	131.9	132.5	132.1	133.0	133.6	129.8
2006	132.5	133.7	135.5	135.8	136.9	137.6	136.6	136.7	136.4	135.9	135.0	135.1	135.6
2007	131.7	131.4	131.9	130.4	130.4	130.6	129.1	129.4	128.9	127.4	127.0	125.5	129.5
2008	121.3	121.3	120.7	117.9	117.2	116.4	114.8	113.7	113.0	110.2	107.8	105.7	115.0
2009	102.3	100.3	98.9	95.1	94.1	93.4	91.5	90.6	89.3	88.3	86.7	85.3	93.0
Mining and Logging													
1990	0.4	0.4	0.4	0.4	0.5	0.5	0.5	0.5	0.5	0.4	0.4	0.4	0.4
2000	0.5	0.5	0.5	0.5	0.5	0.5	0.5	0.4	0.5	0.5	0.5	0.4	0.5
2001	0.4	0.5	0.5	0.5	0.5	0.5	0.5	0.5	0.5	0.5	0.4	0.5	0.5
2002	0.4	0.5	0.5	0.5	0.5	0.5	0.5	0.5	0.5	0.5	0.5	0.5	0.5
2003	0.5	0.5	0.5	0.5	0.5	0.5	0.5	0.5	0.5	0.4	0.4	0.4	0.4
2004	0.4	0.4	0.4	0.4	0.4	0.4	0.4	0.4	0.4	0.4	0.3	0.4	0.4
2005	0.3	0.3	0.3	0.4	0.4	0.4	0.4	0.3	0.3	0.3	0.3	0.3	0.3
2006	0.3	0.3	0.3	0.3	0.3	0.3	0.3	0.3	0.3	0.3	0.3	0.4	0.3
2007	0.3	0.4	0.4	0.4	0.4	0.4	0.3	0.3	0.3	0.4	0.4	0.4	0.4
2008	0.4	0.4	0.4	0.4	0.4	0.3	0.3	0.3	0.3	0.3	0.2	0.2	0.3
2009	0.2	0.2	0.2	0.2	0.2	0.2	0.3	0.2	0.2	0.2	0.2	0.2	0.2
Construction													
1990	45.2	45.6	46.1	44.8	44.5	44.5	42.9	42.8	41.7	41.4	40.9	39.8	43.4
2000	58.2	59.1	59.1	60.1	60.2	61.0	60.1	60.2	60.5	59.3	59.4	59.7	59.7
2001	59.1	59.0	59.5	59.2	59.1	59.9	60.2	60.7	60.6	60.4	60.3	60.0	59.8
2002	59.2	59.5	59.9	59.6	60.0	60.1	60.4	61.4	61.7	62.6	63.1	63.6	60.9
2003	62.0	62.8	63.3	63.6	64.3	65.2	65.3	66.5	67.1	68.1	68.3	69.4	65.5
2004	69.2	70.1	71.2	72.2	72.7	73.9	74.9	75.3	75.2	76.1	77.2	77.9	73.8
2005	78.4	79.4	80.5	81.7	83.0	84.0	85.4	86.2	87.0	86.9	87.9	88.8	84.1
2006	88.1	89.3	90.6	91.1	92.0	92.4	91.7	91.9	91.7	91.1	90.3	90.2	90.9
2007	87.4	86.9	87.2	85.6	85.7	85.8	84.6	85.0	84.6	83.3	82.7	81.2	85.0
2008	77.7	77.7	77.2	74.5	74.0	73.3	72.1	71.5	70.9	68.4	66.5	64.8	72.4
2009	62.3	60.7	59.6	56.6	55.7	55.0	53.4	52.7	51.7	51.0	49.4	48.1	54.7
Manufacturing													
1990	53.5	53.5	53.0	52.8	52.7	52.5	52.3	52.1	51.4	51.0	51.4	51.1	52.3
2000	52.5	52.5	52.7	51.8	52.2	52.1	51.9	52.1	51.9	51.3	51.7	51.9	52.1
2001	51.0	50.8	50.8	50.6	50.1	49.8	48.8	48.6	48.1	47.4	46.9	46.5	49.1
2002	46.6	46.7	46.7	46.1	45.9	45.5	44.8	44.7	44.6	44.6	44.4	44.5	45.4
2003	43.9	43.9	44.0	43.2	43.2	43.2	42.8	42.8	42.9	42.8	42.7	42.9	43.2
2004	42.8	43.0	43.3	43.8	44.0	44.3	44.4	44.3	44.3	44.9	45.2	45.5	44.2
2005	45.2	45.3	45.5	45.9	45.7	45.8	45.7	45.4	45.2	44.9	44.8	44.5	45.3
2006	44.1	44.1	44.6	44.4	44.6	44.9	44.6	44.5	44.4	44.5	44.4	44.5	44.5
2007	44.0	44.1	44.3	44.4	44.3	44.4	44.2	44.1	44.0	43.7	43.9	43.9	44.1
2008	43.2	43.2	43.1	43.0	42.8	42.8	42.4	41.9	41.8	41.5	41.1	40.7	42.3
2009	39.8	39.4	39.1	38.3	38.2	38.2	37.8	37.7	37.4	37.1	37.1	37.0	38.1

Employment by Industry: Orlando-Kissimmee, FL, Selected Years, 1990–2009—*Continued*

(Numbers in thousands, not seasonally adjusted.)

Industry and year	January	February	March	April	May	June	July	August	September	October	November	December	Annual average
Service-Providing													
1990	463.8	473.4	479.1	480.8	485.1	489.5	482.2	482.0	486.1	484.2	489.3	491.1	482.2
2001	797.7	807.2	814.6	809.6	812.2	802.0	793.8	804.5	804.7	795.8	796.2	798.1	803.0
2002	782.1	791.6	798.3	795.6	799.7	792.3	787.2	799.6	802.0	806.0	814.9	822.2	799.3
2003	806.5	811.0	815.1	815.6	816.5	806.7	801.3	815.0	814.6	821.9	828.7	833.2	815.5
2004	827.4	834.3	839.2	846.9	849.6	840.9	838.6	849.9	849.9	861.5	872.1	879.0	849.1
2005	870.4	877.1	883.3	888.7	894.4	883.1	881.8	896.5	901.3	904.3	914.4	920.9	893.0
2006	912.0	917.9	925.0	930.1	933.5	923.5	915.4	933.3	938.7	939.8	952.8	960.5	931.9
2007	951.7	962.0	967.1	968.8	970.2	956.7	950.2	963.0	962.8	968.4	980.1	982.4	965.3
2008	967.8	978.1	982.3	973.8	972.0	955.8	947.9	957.0	951.1	949.9	950.2	950.3	961.4
2009	927.1	929.1	928.1	926.3	923.0	906.4	897.9	907.5	906.3	911.3	915.2	920.4	916.6
Trade, Transportation, and Utilities													
1990	120.7	121.3	121.5	121.2	121.9	122.2	120.5	121.6	121.1	121.4	123.4	125.1	121.8
2000	176.7	176.7	177.7	178.0	178.3	179.6	177.9	179.3	179.9	180.1	184.4	187.4	179.7
2001	179.1	178.1	178.8	178.6	178.6	178.2	177.8	178.0	177.7	175.8	177.7	179.4	178.2
2002	171.9	170.6	171.0	170.6	170.9	170.3	169.2	170.1	170.6	170.9	174.8	178.2	171.6
2003	172.1	171.0	171.2	170.8	170.6	170.5	171.6	172.8	173.6	175.0	178.8	182.4	173.4
2004	176.9	175.7	176.6	179.0	179.9	180.5	181.3	181.8	181.2	184.5	189.4	193.1	181.7
2005	187.7	187.9	189.2	190.8	191.7	191.8	192.8	193.3	193.2	194.4	198.4	201.8	192.8
2006	196.8	196.3	196.7	197.3	198.3	198.1	197.4	198.0	197.8	198.4	203.5	207.1	198.8
2007	200.7	201.2	200.9	201.2	203.1	202.9	202.4	203.5	204.1	205.1	210.1	212.6	204.0
2008	205.7	205.1	204.7	201.9	201.3	200.4	199.0	198.6	197.5	196.3	198.6	199.9	200.8
2009	191.9	190.1	188.4	186.6	185.9	184.7	183.3	183.2	182.6	183.0	184.9	187.5	186.0
Wholesale Trade													
1990	26.3	26.7	26.6	26.8	26.7	26.8	26.8	26.9	26.8	26.6	26.6	26.4	26.7
2000	38.0	38.4	38.7	40.3	40.6	41.1	41.3	41.5	41.7	41.5	41.6	41.9	40.6
2001	42.0	42.2	42.4	42.2	42.2	42.2	41.9	41.9	42.0	41.7	41.4	40.9	41.9
2002	39.9	39.9	40.0	39.7	39.7	39.4	39.2	39.2	39.3	39.4	39.5	39.4	39.6
2003	39.6	39.6	39.8	39.7	39.8	39.9	40.1	40.2	40.4	40.2	40.4	40.6	40.0
2004	40.8	41.0	41.2	41.9	42.0	42.2	42.3	42.2	42.1	42.3	42.5	42.8	41.9
2005	43.3	43.7	43.7	44.3	44.6	44.8	45.0	45.1	45.3	45.2	45.5	45.9	44.7
2006	45.7	46.1	46.2	46.2	46.8	46.5	46.4	46.0	46.2	46.1	46.1	46.3	46.2
2007	46.6	47.2	47.1	47.1	47.3	47.2	47.2	47.1	47.2	47.6	47.6	47.8	47.3
2008	47.3	48.0	47.5	46.4	46.2	46.0	45.5	45.3	45.0	44.4	44.2	43.9	45.8
2009	42.4	42.5	41.6	41.0	40.7	40.5	40.0	39.7	39.5	40.1	39.8	39.5	40.6
Retail Trade													
1990	75.3	75.3	75.4	74.6	75.3	75.4	74.1	75.2	74.6	75.4	77.2	78.8	75.6
2000	109.9	109.3	109.9	108.1	108.3	109.4	107.3	108.3	108.5	108.9	112.5	114.5	109.6
2001	106.8	105.9	106.4	106.0	106.2	106.2	106.3	106.6	106.3	105.7	108.1	109.7	106.7
2002	104.9	103.7	104.0	103.4	103.8	103.6	102.7	103.6	104.0	104.5	108.1	110.7	104.8
2003	105.8	105.1	105.2	105.0	105.0	105.2	105.8	106.8	107.5	109.3	112.8	115.5	107.4
2004	110.8	109.2	109.8	111.0	111.7	112.2	113.0	113.3	112.9	115.6	119.9	122.3	113.5
2005	117.5	117.4	118.3	119.0	119.2	119.2	120.0	120.1	119.5	120.7	124.0	126.3	120.1
2006	122.1	121.2	121.3	121.6	121.6	121.6	121.0	121.3	120.6	121.3	126.1	128.4	122.3
2007	122.6	121.8	121.7	121.5	123.0	123.2	122.6	123.3	123.2	123.8	128.4	129.8	123.7
2008	124.5	123.2	123.3	121.6	121.3	121.1	120.6	120.7	120.2	120.0	122.6	123.4	121.9
2009	117.8	116.4	115.8	115.1	114.9	114.4	113.7	114.1	113.7	113.3	115.5	117.8	115.2
Transportation and Utilities													
1990	19.1	19.3	19.5	19.8	19.9	20.0	19.6	19.5	19.7	19.4	19.6	19.9	19.6
2000	28.8	29.0	29.1	29.6	29.4	29.1	29.3	29.5	29.7	29.7	30.3	31.0	29.5
2001	30.3	30.0	30.0	30.4	30.2	29.8	29.6	29.5	29.4	28.4	28.2	28.8	29.6
2002	27.1	27.0	27.0	27.5	27.4	27.3	27.3	27.3	27.3	27.0	27.2	28.1	27.3
2003	26.7	26.3	26.2	26.1	25.8	25.4	25.7	25.8	25.7	25.5	25.6	26.3	25.9
2004	25.3	25.5	25.6	26.1	26.2	26.1	26.0	26.3	26.2	26.6	27.0	28.0	26.2
2005	26.9	26.8	27.2	27.5	27.9	27.8	27.8	28.1	28.4	28.5	28.9	29.6	28.0
2006	29.0	29.0	29.2	29.5	29.9	30.0	30.0	30.7	31.0	31.0	31.3	32.4	30.3
2007	31.5	32.2	32.1	32.6	32.8	32.5	32.6	33.1	33.7	33.7	34.1	35.0	33.0
2008	33.9	33.9	33.9	33.9	33.8	33.3	32.9	32.6	32.3	31.9	31.8	32.6	33.1
2009	31.7	31.2	31.0	30.5	30.3	29.8	29.6	29.4	29.4	29.6	29.6	30.2	30.2
Information													
1990	14.7	14.7	14.5	14.2	14.3	14.5	14.6	14.7	14.7	14.5	14.6	14.7	14.6
2000	23.5	23.3	23.6	23.1	23.3	23.5	23.5	23.6	23.9	23.3	23.4	23.6	23.5
2001	23.2	23.3	23.1	22.9	23.1	23.1	23.0	22.9	22.8	22.6	22.8	23.0	23.0
2002	22.6	22.6	22.5	22.2	22.6	22.5	22.4	22.7	22.4	22.4	22.6	22.7	22.5
2003	22.4	22.9	22.8	22.6	23.2	23.3	23.0	23.4	23.1	23.1	23.5	23.6	23.1
2004	23.2	23.4	23.4	23.6	23.9	23.8	24.0	24.0	23.7	23.8	24.3	24.2	23.8
2005	23.8	24.2	24.1	24.2	25.1	24.9	24.8	24.9	24.9	24.9	25.2	25.4	24.7
2006	25.3	25.5	25.8	25.9	26.0	26.0	25.9	25.7	25.9	25.9	26.0	26.0	25.8
2007	26.2	26.4	26.9	27.2	27.4	27.3	27.0	26.8	26.6	26.6	26.5	26.6	26.8
2008	26.6	26.8	26.8	26.5	26.5	26.5	26.4	26.3	25.6	26.0	26.0	25.9	26.3
2009	25.9	26.0	25.8	25.3	25.3	25.2	24.9	24.7	24.3	24.5	24.5	24.3	25.1

Employment by Industry: Orlando-Kissimmee, FL, Selected Years, 1990–2009—*Continued*

(Numbers in thousands, not seasonally adjusted.)

Industry and year	January	February	March	April	May	June	July	August	September	October	November	December	Annual average
Financial Activities													
1990	38.3	39.0	39.2	39.9	39.8	39.9	39.9	40.0	39.9	39.4	39.3	39.5	39.5
2000	54.1	54.5	55.0	54.0	54.4	54.9	54.4	54.5	54.5	54.1	54.3	54.7	54.5
2001	53.3	53.4	53.7	54.4	54.4	54.9	54.7	54.9	54.6	53.9	54.0	54.3	54.2
2002	53.6	53.8	54.3	53.8	54.2	54.6	54.9	55.0	55.2	55.4	55.8	56.4	54.8
2003	56.0	56.4	56.7	56.6	56.7	57.4	57.5	57.9	57.9	58.2	58.4	58.9	57.4
2004	57.4	58.0	58.1	58.7	59.0	59.5	59.9	60.3	59.9	60.6	60.8	61.7	59.5
2005	60.7	61.5	61.9	62.6	63.0	63.4	64.5	64.8	64.9	65.3	65.6	66.2	63.7
2006	65.6	66.1	66.4	66.7	66.9	67.1	66.8	67.2	67.1	67.6	68.1	68.5	67.0
2007	67.3	67.9	68.1	67.6	67.8	68.4	67.9	67.8	67.5	67.5	67.6	67.9	67.8
2008	66.9	67.2	67.3	66.7	67.2	66.8	66.6	66.6	66.0	65.6	65.5	65.6	66.5
2009	64.3	64.1	63.8	63.6	63.4	63.3	62.5	62.3	61.8	62.3	62.6	62.9	63.1
Professional and Business Services													
1990	36.8	37.8	38.8	41.0	41.4	42.3	42.1	42.8	42.3	40.7	41.8	41.4	40.8
2000	141.3	144.6	147.2	145.9	147.6	149.7	146.7	148.1	151.7	152.2	153.9	153.7	148.6
2001	151.7	155.2	157.7	153.7	154.4	152.0	151.1	151.4	150.7	149.5	148.8	148.4	152.1
2002	146.3	149.5	151.5	148.9	149.1	148.4	148.9	148.4	149.7	151.6	153.7	155.2	150.1
2003	150.5	151.3	151.9	152.9	151.1	149.4	145.6	145.7	144.7	148.9	148.1	145.9	148.8
2004	147.4	149.8	150.9	153.9	153.8	153.9	152.0	152.7	152.6	156.5	158.1	158.9	153.4
2005	159.4	160.9	161.8	164.3	165.3	165.5	165.1	166.6	167.9	168.9	171.2	171.9	165.7
2006	171.2	171.4	174.1	177.1	178.2	179.0	176.2	178.8	181.8	181.4	184.6	186.7	178.4
2007	185.7	188.3	188.9	189.1	189.0	185.7	185.0	184.3	184.6	186.9	188.8	187.1	187.0
2008	184.7	188.9	187.8	185.6	184.2	181.8	180.4	180.3	180.5	181.2	179.1	177.5	182.7
2009	172.5	172.3	171.1	169.8	171.2	168.7	166.2	165.8	167.2	167.6	168.6	168.4	169.1
Education and Health Services													
1990	45.9	46.8	46.9	47.4	47.9	48.3	47.9	48.5	48.7	49.9	50.3	50.2	48.2
2000	84.1	84.4	84.9	85.8	86.4	86.0	85.1	85.8	86.4	85.9	85.7	86.1	85.6
2001	84.2	85.0	85.6	86.3	86.7	86.8	86.4	87.6	88.3	88.8	89.1	89.2	87.0
2002	86.9	87.8	88.1	88.9	89.3	88.8	88.6	89.9	90.5	90.9	91.3	91.4	89.4
2003	91.5	92.0	92.1	92.7	93.4	93.3	93.1	94.1	94.9	94.8	95.3	95.5	93.5
2004	95.2	96.1	96.5	96.7	97.3	97.1	97.1	97.4	97.7	98.4	99.1	99.3	97.3
2005	99.6	100.1	100.6	100.8	101.7	100.9	101.3	102.8	103.6	104.2	105.0	105.3	102.2
2006	104.8	105.8	106.3	106.4	107.0	106.8	106.3	107.9	108.9	109.3	109.9	110.3	107.5
2007	109.5	110.6	111.0	111.7	112.5	112.3	111.5	112.7	113.7	114.8	115.8	116.1	112.7
2008	115.5	116.3	116.6	116.6	117.2	116.3	115.3	116.0	116.2	116.9	117.0	117.4	116.4
2009	116.0	116.8	117.8	117.4	117.7	117.4	117.6	117.7	118.1	117.5	119.0	118.8	117.7
Leisure and Hospitality													
1990	112.1	116.8	120.2	118.7	120.1	123.9	124.9	123.6	119.8	117.6	118.4	119.0	119.6
2000	173.6	177.4	179.4	178.6	177.3	180.5	178.0	176.4	175.6	174.8	175.4	176.4	177.0
2001	172.7	175.9	177.1	174.6	175.4	176.6	172.4	171.0	170.0	162.6	159.9	159.2	170.6
2002	156.2	161.3	164.6	164.7	166.0	170.7	168.0	166.4	164.7	164.4	165.5	166.9	165.0
2003	163.9	166.3	169.1	169.0	169.8	172.3	172.2	172.0	169.6	169.5	171.6	173.5	169.9
2004	174.1	176.6	178.4	179.9	180.0	181.3	181.7	180.3	178.4	179.1	180.5	181.8	179.3
2005	180.0	182.1	184.8	184.7	184.7	185.8	184.4	183.4	182.8	182.0	183.6	184.8	183.6
2006	183.0	185.5	188.4	188.5	188.5	188.3	187.0	186.8	185.9	184.7	187.0	188.6	186.9
2007	188.0	191.1	193.9	194.7	193.5	194.8	194.2	193.0	190.8	193.1	197.1	199.3	193.6
2008	196.9	201.2	205.0	203.4	202.5	203.6	202.6	200.3	195.4	194.6	194.6	195.0	199.6
2009	189.1	191.3	192.3	194.6	192.5	191.4	190.0	188.3	186.2	189.3	188.1	191.5	190.4
Other Services													
1990	23.7	24.0	24.4	24.6	24.6	24.9	24.8	24.9	24.7	24.5	24.5	24.6	24.5
2000	39.3	39.5	39.5	39.9	40.0	40.1	39.4	39.2	39.4	40.0	39.7	39.8	39.7
2001	39.9	40.6	41.2	41.5	42.2	42.7	42.8	43.0	43.5	43.5	43.9	44.3	42.4
2002	44.5	44.9	45.1	44.7	45.1	45.3	45.4	45.7	45.9	45.9	46.1	45.9	45.4
2003	45.7	46.0	46.1	45.4	45.6	45.7	45.5	45.4	45.7	45.6	45.6	45.8	45.6
2004	46.5	46.7	47.1	47.0	47.4	48.0	47.8	47.3	47.7	47.9	48.3	48.5	47.5
2005	48.4	48.6	48.7	49.1	49.7	49.9	50.1	50.2	50.8	50.7	50.9	51.2	49.9
2006	51.4	52.0	52.1	52.0	52.6	53.1	53.0	53.6	54.5	55.1	55.6	56.0	53.4
2007	56.5	57.2	57.7	56.9	56.8	56.5	55.6	55.0	54.9	54.6	54.3	54.0	55.8
2008	53.1	53.3	53.7	52.6	52.4	51.9	51.3	50.5	50.4	49.8	49.2	48.9	51.4
2009	48.4	48.5	48.8	49.0	48.7	48.3	48.2	47.9	47.9	47.9	47.8	48.1	48.3
Government													
1990	71.6	73.0	73.6	73.8	75.1	73.5	67.5	65.9	74.9	76.2	77.0	76.6	73.2
2000	91.6	93.3	93.8	93.6	95.8	84.4	82.5	91.7	92.7	93.6	94.1	94.7	91.8
2001	93.6	95.7	97.4	97.6	97.4	87.7	85.6	95.7	97.1	99.1	100.0	100.3	95.6
2002	100.1	101.1	101.2	101.8	102.5	91.7	89.8	101.4	103.0	104.5	105.1	105.5	100.6
2003	104.4	105.1	105.2	105.6	106.1	94.8	92.8	103.7	105.1	106.8	107.4	107.6	103.7
2004	106.7	108.0	108.2	108.1	108.3	96.8	94.8	106.1	108.7	110.7	111.6	111.5	106.6
2005	110.8	111.8	112.2	112.2	113.2	100.9	98.8	110.5	113.2	113.9	114.5	114.3	110.5
2006	113.9	115.3	115.2	116.2	116.0	105.1	102.8	115.3	116.8	117.4	118.1	117.3	114.1
2007	117.8	119.3	119.7	120.4	120.1	108.8	106.6	119.9	120.6	119.8	119.9	118.8	117.6
2008	118.4	119.3	120.4	120.5	120.7	108.5	106.3	118.4	119.5	119.5	120.2	120.1	117.7
2009	119.0	120.0	120.1	120.0	118.3	107.4	105.2	117.6	118.2	119.2	119.7	118.9	117.0

Employment by Industry: Oxnard-Thousand Oaks-Ventura, CA, Selected Years, 1990–2009

(Numbers in thousands, not seasonally adjusted.)

Industry and year	January	February	March	April	May	June	July	August	September	October	November	December	Annual average
Total Nonfarm													
1990	224.7	225.9	227.7	228.1	230.2	231.7	231.1	230.6	230.4	231.7	234.3	236.9	230.3
2000	267.4	267.9	270.3	273.3	275.2	277.2	275.5	274.3	277.4	278.4	279.9	283.1	275.0
2001	277.3	277.1	278.8	279.0	280.6	280.9	279.3	277.8	279.6	281.4	283.0	284.5	279.9
2002	277.7	279.6	280.4	280.2	281.7	283.8	281.1	278.3	282.4	282.9	286.9	286.9	281.8
2003	279.7	280.1	282.4	283.5	285.9	287.5	283.1	281.7	284.3	286.7	287.7	287.9	284.2
2004	280.8	283.3	285.9	286.5	286.9	288.7	285.0	284.1	285.0	288.0	289.3	291.1	286.2
2005	285.7	288.4	290.3	291.5	292.1	293.2	289.1	288.9	291.1	292.3	294.5	296.7	291.2
2006	292.2	294.9	296.5	297.5	300.0	301.1	296.6	296.4	298.2	298.2	300.0	301.3	297.7
2007	293.7	295.4	297.3	295.8	298.3	299.8	295.8	295.7	296.0	296.7	298.2	299.4	296.8
2008	291.1	293.0	293.0	293.5	294.2	294.2	288.9	288.1	289.9	290.2	289.4	290.2	291.3
2009	281.4	279.5	278.2	277.5	277.4	277.0	269.8	270.4	270.9	272.4	272.8	272.8	275.0
Total Private													
1990	182.1	182.5	183.8	184.1	185.2	186.7	186.9	186.6	186.4	187.4	189.6	192.0	186.1
2000	223.3	223.3	225.3	228.0	229.5	232.2	232.3	233.0	234.5	233.8	234.8	237.8	230.7
2001	231.5	231.5	233.4	234.3	235.7	236.7	234.4	235.1	235.4	235.8	236.4	237.7	234.8
2002	231.8	233.1	234.4	234.5	236.1	237.7	237.3	236.6	238.0	237.8	240.2	241.3	236.6
2003	234.2	234.6	236.3	237.7	239.3	241.5	240.1	240.1	240.7	241.9	242.5	244.1	239.4
2004	237.7	239.9	242.2	242.8	243.5	244.9	244.4	244.4	244.2	245.7	246.7	248.4	243.7
2005	243.5	245.7	247.5	248.8	249.0	250.3	248.9	249.0	249.3	250.1	251.6	253.9	249.0
2006	249.7	252.1	253.5	254.5	257.1	257.9	255.7	256.0	255.6	255.7	256.8	258.2	255.2
2007	251.0	252.3	254.0	252.3	254.6	256.0	254.3	254.6	253.0	253.6	254.4	255.6	253.8
2008	247.6	249.1	249.0	249.7	250.1	249.8	247.8	247.9	248.2	247.0	245.7	246.4	248.2
2009	238.3	236.0	234.5	233.4	233.3	232.6	229.7	229.8	229.4	229.2	229.2	229.4	232.1
Goods-Producing													
1990	52.5	52.7	53.3	52.6	52.3	52.9	51.5	50.7	50.2	50.1	50.6	50.8	51.7
2000	55.0	54.8	55.3	56.0	56.7	57.8	58.1	58.4	59.1	58.8	58.3	58.5	57.2
2001	57.1	57.1	57.6	57.5	57.7	58.0	57.3	57.6	57.5	57.1	56.2	55.5	57.2
2002	53.9	54.7	54.7	54.4	54.8	55.2	54.4	54.0	54.2	53.7	54.2	54.0	54.4
2003	52.9	52.7	53.2	53.8	54.4	55.1	55.3	55.2	55.1	54.8	54.7	54.3	54.3
2004	54.0	54.7	55.3	55.8	56.0	56.5	56.7	56.4	56.3	56.4	56.4	56.5	55.9
2005	55.6	56.6	57.3	57.4	57.4	58.1	57.6	57.5	57.5	57.5	57.2	57.5	57.3
2006	57.7	58.8	59.1	59.3	60.2	61.2	61.1	61.2	61.1	60.2	59.8	59.2	59.9
2007	58.0	58.2	58.6	57.9	58.7	59.0	58.3	58.3	57.5	57.3	56.7	56.1	57.9
2008	54.0	54.3	54.2	54.3	54.2	54.3	54.2	53.9	53.8	53.5	52.5	52.0	53.8
2009	50.2	48.9	48.9	48.3	47.7	47.9	46.8	46.3	45.7	45.3	44.9	44.6	47.1
Mining and Logging													
1990	1.7	1.8	2.0	2.0	2.0	2.0	2.0	1.9	1.9	1.8	1.9	1.9	1.9
2000	0.7	0.7	0.7	0.7	0.7	0.7	0.7	0.7	0.7	0.7	0.6	0.6	0.7
2001	0.6	0.6	0.6	0.6	0.6	0.6	0.6	0.6	0.6	0.6	0.6	0.6	0.6
2002	0.6	0.7	0.7	0.7	0.7	0.7	0.7	0.7	0.7	0.7	0.7	0.6	0.7
2003	0.6	0.6	0.6	0.6	0.6	0.6	0.6	0.6	0.6	0.6	0.6	0.6	0.6
2004	0.6	0.6	0.7	0.7	0.7	0.7	0.7	0.7	0.7	0.7	0.7	0.7	0.7
2005	0.7	0.6	0.7	0.7	0.7	0.8	0.8	0.8	0.8	0.9	0.9	0.9	0.8
2006	1.0	1.0	1.0	1.0	1.0	1.0	1.1	1.1	1.1	1.1	1.1	1.1	1.1
2007	1.1	1.1	1.1	1.1	1.1	1.1	1.0	1.0	1.0	1.1	1.1	1.1	1.1
2008	1.0	1.1	1.1	1.1	1.1	1.1	1.2	1.2	1.2	1.3	1.3	1.3	1.2
2009	1.3	1.3	1.3	1.3	1.2	1.3	1.2	1.2	1.2	1.2	1.2	1.2	1.2
Construction													
1990	17.6	17.3	17.5	16.6	16.1	16.4	16.0	15.6	15.2	15.1	15.0	15.1	16.1
2000	14.2	14.0	14.2	14.7	15.2	15.9	16.0	16.2	16.6	16.1	15.8	15.9	15.4
2001	15.1	15.0	15.4	15.7	16.1	16.5	16.4	16.9	16.9	16.6	16.2	16.0	16.1
2002	15.3	15.8	15.5	15.3	15.4	15.6	15.8	15.8	15.9	16.0	16.0	15.9	15.7
2003	15.3	15.1	15.4	16.0	16.9	17.3	17.6	17.7	17.5	17.1	17.0	16.8	16.6
2004	16.4	16.4	16.5	16.5	16.5	16.9	17.3	17.1	17.2	17.4	17.3	17.5	16.9
2005	16.6	17.4	18.0	18.5	18.7	19.2	19.2	19.4	19.5	19.7	19.5	19.8	18.8
2006	19.8	20.4	20.4	20.4	21.0	21.4	21.2	21.2	21.0	20.2	19.6	19.2	20.5
2007	18.3	18.5	18.7	18.5	19.1	19.7	19.5	19.7	19.1	18.8	18.3	17.9	18.8
2008	16.9	17.1	17.0	17.2	17.1	17.2	17.0	16.7	16.6	16.2	15.7	15.4	16.7
2009	14.2	13.6	13.9	13.7	13.6	13.7	13.3	13.2	12.8	12.6	12.4	12.1	13.3
Manufacturing													
1990	33.2	33.6	33.8	34.0	34.2	34.5	33.5	33.2	33.1	33.2	33.7	33.8	33.7
2000	40.1	40.1	40.4	40.6	40.8	41.2	41.4	41.5	41.8	42.0	41.9	42.0	41.2
2001	41.4	41.5	41.6	41.2	41.0	40.9	40.3	40.1	40.0	39.9	39.4	38.9	40.5
2002	38.0	38.2	38.5	38.4	38.7	38.9	37.9	37.5	37.6	37.0	37.5	37.5	38.0
2003	37.0	37.0	37.2	37.2	36.9	37.2	37.1	36.9	37.0	37.1	37.1	36.9	37.1
2004	37.0	37.7	38.1	38.6	38.8	38.9	38.7	38.6	38.4	38.3	38.4	38.3	38.3
2005	38.3	38.6	38.6	38.2	38.0	38.1	37.6	37.3	37.2	36.9	36.8	36.8	37.7
2006	36.9	37.4	37.7	37.9	38.2	38.8	38.8	38.9	39.0	38.9	39.1	38.9	38.4
2007	38.6	38.6	38.8	38.3	38.5	38.2	37.8	37.6	37.4	37.4	37.3	37.1	38.0
2008	36.1	36.1	36.1	36.0	36.0	36.0	36.0	36.0	36.0	36.0	35.5	35.3	35.9
2009	34.7	34.0	33.7	33.3	32.9	32.9	32.3	31.9	31.7	31.5	31.3	31.3	32.6

Employment by Industry: Oxnard-Thousand Oaks-Ventura, CA, Selected Years, 1990–2009—*Continued*

(Numbers in thousands, not seasonally adjusted.)

Industry and year	January	February	March	April	May	June	July	August	September	October	November	December	Annual average
Service-Providing													
1990	172.2	173.2	174.4	175.5	177.9	178.8	179.6	179.9	180.2	181.6	183.7	186.1	178.6
2000	212.4	213.1	215.0	217.3	218.5	219.4	217.4	215.9	218.3	219.6	221.6	224.6	217.8
2001	220.2	220.0	221.2	221.5	222.9	222.9	222.0	220.2	222.1	224.3	226.8	229.0	222.8
2002	223.8	224.9	225.7	225.8	226.9	228.6	226.7	224.3	228.2	229.2	232.7	232.9	227.5
2003	226.8	227.4	229.2	229.7	231.5	232.4	227.8	226.5	229.2	231.9	233.0	233.6	229.9
2004	226.8	228.6	230.6	230.7	230.9	232.2	228.3	227.7	228.7	231.6	232.9	234.6	230.3
2005	230.1	231.8	233.0	234.1	234.7	235.1	231.5	231.4	233.6	234.8	237.3	239.2	233.9
2006	234.5	236.1	237.4	238.2	239.8	239.9	235.5	235.2	237.1	238.0	240.2	242.1	237.8
2007	235.7	237.2	238.7	237.9	239.6	240.8	237.5	237.4	238.5	239.4	241.5	243.3	239.0
2008	237.1	238.7	238.8	239.2	240.0	239.9	234.7	234.2	236.1	236.7	236.9	238.2	237.5
2009	231.2	230.6	229.3	229.2	229.7	229.1	223.0	224.1	225.2	227.1	227.9	228.2	227.9
Trade, Transportation, and Utilities													
1990	41.0	40.3	40.4	39.9	40.7	41.0	41.6	41.7	41.6	42.2	43.2	44.8	41.5
2000	48.4	48.1	48.2	48.6	48.7	49.1	49.1	49.3	49.5	49.8	51.7	53.2	49.5
2001	51.1	50.5	50.7	50.7	50.4	50.4	50.1	50.6	50.4	51.0	52.2	53.3	51.0
2002	51.9	51.5	51.5	50.6	50.9	51.4	50.8	51.0	51.1	51.7	53.0	54.2	51.6
2003	51.5	51.3	51.3	51.0	51.2	51.3	51.3	51.5	51.8	53.1	53.4	54.9	52.0
2004	52.5	52.6	53.0	52.5	52.8	53.0	52.8	52.8	52.9	53.4	54.7	55.6	53.2
2005	53.7	53.5	53.6	54.0	54.2	54.6	54.5	54.7	55.0	55.3	56.8	58.1	54.8
2006	55.4	55.1	55.2	55.8	56.3	56.5	56.4	56.4	56.1	56.6	58.1	59.1	56.4
2007	56.4	55.8	55.9	55.5	55.8	56.5	56.7	57.1	56.7	56.6	58.3	59.8	56.8
2008	56.5	56.4	56.4	56.1	56.1	56.1	55.7	55.5	55.7	55.6	56.2	57.1	56.1
2009	54.0	52.9	52.0	51.7	51.8	51.6	51.5	51.5	51.5	51.5	52.1	52.5	52.1
Wholesale Trade													
1990	7.3	7.5	7.5	7.6	7.9	8.0	8.1	8.2	8.0	8.2	8.1	8.5	7.9
2000	9.6	9.8	9.9	10.2	10.3	10.4	10.5	10.5	10.6	10.6	10.8	10.8	10.3
2001	10.8	11.0	11.2	11.1	11.0	11.0	11.0	11.2	10.9	10.9	11.0	11.1	11.0
2002	11.6	11.9	11.8	11.6	11.7	11.7	11.5	11.6	11.5	11.6	11.8	11.8	11.7
2003	11.7	11.8	12.0	12.0	12.0	12.0	11.9	11.9	11.9	11.5	11.6	11.7	11.8
2004	11.6	12.0	12.2	12.1	12.1	12.3	12.5	12.5	12.5	12.4	12.3	12.3	12.2
2005	12.3	12.4	12.4	12.5	12.5	12.6	12.6	12.7	12.7	12.6	12.5	12.6	12.5
2006	12.4	12.6	12.7	12.8	12.9	12.9	12.8	12.6	12.5	12.6	12.4	12.5	12.6
2007	12.6	12.9	13.0	13.1	13.1	13.2	13.1	13.2	13.1	13.0	13.0	13.0	13.0
2008	12.7	12.9	12.8	12.8	12.9	12.9	12.9	12.9	12.9	12.9	12.7	12.8	12.8
2009	12.6	12.4	12.3	12.2	12.1	12.1	11.9	11.9	11.9	11.8	11.8	11.7	12.1
Retail Trade													
1990	29.0	28.1	27.9	27.3	27.6	27.8	28.3	28.2	28.3	28.7	29.7	30.7	28.5
2000	33.3	32.8	32.8	32.7	32.8	33.1	33.3	33.5	33.5	33.7	35.1	36.3	33.6
2001	34.1	33.3	33.3	33.2	33.2	33.4	33.5	33.7	33.9	34.3	35.5	36.5	34.0
2002	34.4	33.6	33.7	33.3	33.5	33.9	33.6	33.7	34.0	34.4	35.3	36.5	34.2
2003	34.1	33.8	33.7	33.5	33.7	33.8	33.8	34.0	34.2	35.9	36.1	37.5	34.5
2004	35.3	35.0	35.1	34.6	34.9	34.9	34.8	34.8	34.8	35.3	36.6	37.4	35.3
2005	35.7	35.5	35.4	35.6	35.8	36.1	36.2	36.3	36.5	36.9	38.4	39.5	36.5
2006	37.1	36.5	36.5	36.9	37.2	37.3	37.5	37.6	37.4	37.9	39.5	40.3	37.6
2007	37.9	37.0	36.9	36.6	36.7	37.1	37.4	37.7	37.4	37.4	38.9	40.2	37.6
2008	37.5	37.1	37.0	37.0	36.9	37.1	37.0	36.9	37.0	37.1	38.0	38.7	37.3
2009	35.8	35.1	34.4	34.3	34.4	34.2	34.3	34.3	34.3	34.3	35.0	35.4	34.7
Transportation and Utilities													
1990	4.7	4.7	5.0	5.0	5.2	5.2	5.2	5.3	5.3	5.3	5.4	5.6	5.2
2000	5.5	5.5	5.5	5.7	5.6	5.6	5.3	5.3	5.4	5.5	5.8	6.1	5.6
2001	6.2	6.2	6.2	6.4	6.2	6.0	5.6	5.7	5.6	5.8	5.7	5.7	5.9
2002	5.9	6.0	6.0	5.7	5.7	5.8	5.7	5.7	5.6	5.7	5.9	5.9	5.8
2003	5.7	5.7	5.6	5.5	5.5	5.5	5.6	5.6	5.7	5.7	5.7	5.7	5.6
2004	5.6	5.6	5.7	5.8	5.8	5.8	5.5	5.5	5.6	5.7	5.8	5.9	5.7
2005	5.7	5.6	5.8	5.9	5.9	5.9	5.7	5.7	5.8	5.8	5.9	6.0	5.8
2006	5.9	6.0	6.0	6.1	6.2	6.3	6.1	6.2	6.2	6.1	6.2	6.3	6.1
2007	5.9	5.9	6.0	5.8	6.0	6.2	6.2	6.2	6.2	6.2	6.4	6.6	6.1
2008	6.3	6.4	6.6	6.3	6.3	6.1	5.8	5.7	5.8	5.6	5.5	5.6	6.0
2009	5.6	5.4	5.3	5.2	5.3	5.3	5.3	5.3	5.3	5.4	5.3	5.4	5.3
Information													
1990	7.4	7.4	7.4	7.7	7.6	7.8	8.6	8.5	8.5	8.6	8.7	8.1	8.0
2000	7.8	7.8	7.9	7.6	7.7	7.8	7.9	7.9	8.0	8.1	8.1	8.3	7.9
2001	8.3	8.3	8.5	8.3	8.5	8.6	8.5	8.4	8.3	8.2	8.2	8.2	8.4
2002	8.3	8.3	8.4	8.3	8.3	8.2	8.0	7.9	7.8	7.8	7.8	7.8	8.1
2003	7.5	7.4	7.4	7.1	7.1	7.1	7.3	7.2	7.1	7.0	7.0	7.0	7.1
2004	6.9	6.7	7.1	7.0	7.0	7.0	6.9	6.8	6.6	6.5	6.4	6.3	6.8
2005	6.1	6.2	6.1	6.2	6.2	6.2	6.1	6.2	6.2	6.1	6.1	6.2	6.2
2006	6.1	6.1	6.1	6.0	6.1	6.0	6.0	5.9	5.8	5.8	5.7	5.8	6.0
2007	5.7	5.9	5.9	5.8	5.9	5.9	5.8	5.8	5.8	5.7	5.8	5.7	5.8
2008	5.7	5.7	5.7	5.7	5.7	5.7	5.6	5.6	5.5	5.5	5.5	5.4	5.6
2009	5.4	5.4	5.3	5.3	5.3	5.3	5.2	5.2	5.2	5.1	5.1	5.1	5.2

Employment by Industry: Oxnard-Thousand Oaks-Ventura, CA, Selected Years, 1990–2009—*Continued*

(Numbers in thousands, not seasonally adjusted.)

Industry and year	January	February	March	April	May	June	July	August	September	October	November	December	Annual average
Financial Activities													
1990	11.5	12.2	12.3	12.7	12.8	12.5	12.3	12.2	12.2	12.7	12.1	12.2	12.3
2000	17.2	17.1	17.3	17.4	17.6	17.7	17.9	18.0	18.1	18.2	18.1	18.3	17.7
2001	18.5	18.7	19.0	19.1	19.2	19.6	19.7	20.0	20.1	20.5	20.6	20.9	19.7
2002	20.9	21.1	21.4	21.8	22.0	22.2	22.5	22.7	22.8	22.9	23.2	23.3	22.2
2003	22.5	22.7	23.1	23.2	23.5	23.8	23.6	23.9	23.7	23.7	23.7	23.7	23.4
2004	23.5	23.8	23.8	24.1	24.2	24.5	24.3	24.3	24.5	24.3	24.4	24.5	24.2
2005	24.1	24.2	24.3	24.1	24.3	24.5	24.4	24.6	24.6	24.7	24.8	25.1	24.5
2006	25.0	24.8	24.9	24.6	24.5	24.4	23.9	23.6	23.3	23.2	22.9	23.3	24.0
2007	22.7	22.7	22.8	22.8	22.9	23.1	23.0	22.8	22.6	22.7	22.1	22.1	22.7
2008	21.5	21.5	21.3	21.4	21.4	21.4	21.1	20.9	20.8	20.7	20.5	20.5	21.1
2009	20.6	20.7	20.6	20.5	20.4	20.3	20.4	20.3	20.5	20.5	20.4	20.4	20.5
Professional and Business Services													
1990	25.8	25.7	25.5	26.2	26.3	26.1	26.6	27.1	27.2	27.1	27.4	28.0	26.6
2000	38.0	37.9	38.4	40.0	39.9	40.4	40.0	39.8	40.0	39.3	39.1	39.6	39.4
2001	37.1	36.9	37.2	37.3	37.6	37.8	37.2	36.8	37.0	36.8	36.9	37.3	37.2
2002	35.9	36.1	36.3	36.7	36.8	36.9	36.8	36.4	36.7	36.6	36.9	37.0	36.6
2003	35.9	35.9	36.4	36.5	36.7	37.3	37.2	37.1	37.0	37.2	37.4	37.8	36.9
2004	36.4	36.8	37.2	37.1	36.9	37.3	37.2	37.6	37.2	37.9	37.7	38.4	37.3
2005	37.6	38.1	38.3	39.0	38.7	38.7	38.4	38.4	38.0	38.1	38.3	38.4	38.3
2006	38.0	38.8	39.2	39.4	40.0	39.9	39.1	39.6	39.5	39.5	39.4	39.7	39.3
2007	38.8	39.1	39.4	38.6	38.6	38.7	38.2	38.0	37.5	37.5	37.6	37.7	38.3
2008	37.6	38.0	38.0	38.0	38.2	38.3	38.4	38.8	39.0	38.5	38.3	38.5	38.3
2009	37.3	36.9	36.8	36.2	36.0	35.9	35.6	35.7	35.5	35.6	35.7	35.7	36.1
Education and Health Services													
1990	17.1	17.1	17.4	17.9	18.0	18.2	18.3	18.2	18.4	19.0	19.3	19.5	18.2
2000	23.7	24.0	24.2	23.9	24.0	24.1	23.9	24.1	24.4	24.2	24.3	24.4	24.1
2001	24.4	24.7	24.6	25.3	25.6	25.5	25.4	25.3	25.6	25.8	25.9	25.9	25.3
2002	25.4	25.5	25.7	25.9	26.0	25.9	26.3	26.3	27.0	27.3	27.2	27.1	26.3
2003	27.0	27.3	27.5	27.9	28.0	28.2	27.1	27.1	27.7	27.8	27.9	28.0	27.6
2004	27.1	27.4	27.6	27.7	27.7	27.7	27.1	27.0	27.3	27.9	27.8	27.8	27.5
2005	27.7	28.1	28.4	28.5	28.5	28.5	28.1	27.8	28.3	28.6	28.6	28.7	28.3
2006	28.2	28.7	28.7	28.9	29.0	28.9	28.3	28.3	28.8	29.6	29.7	29.9	28.9
2007	29.3	29.9	30.2	30.1	30.3	30.3	29.9	30.3	30.7	31.4	31.5	31.6	30.5
2008	30.9	31.7	31.4	31.9	32.0	31.5	30.8	31.4	32.1	32.6	32.5	32.8	31.8
2009	32.0	32.5	32.3	32.6	32.7	32.1	31.1	31.6	32.1	32.6	32.6	32.7	32.2
Leisure and Hospitality													
1990	19.5	19.9	20.2	19.9	20.2	20.8	20.4	20.6	20.7	20.2	20.7	20.9	20.3
2000	23.7	24.1	24.4	24.7	25.1	25.4	25.6	25.7	25.6	25.7	25.5	25.6	25.1
2001	25.6	25.8	26.1	26.6	27.0	27.1	26.8	27.0	26.8	26.6	26.5	26.7	26.6
2002	25.8	26.1	26.5	26.8	27.2	27.6	28.1	28.0	28.0	27.6	27.5	27.5	27.2
2003	26.7	27.0	27.1	27.5	27.7	27.9	27.8	27.8	28.0	27.9	28.1	28.1	27.6
2004	27.1	27.6	27.8	28.1	28.5	28.6	29.0	29.2	29.2	28.9	29.0	29.0	28.5
2005	28.2	28.4	28.8	29.0	29.2	29.3	29.5	29.6	29.4	29.6	29.6	29.7	29.2
2006	29.2	29.6	30.0	30.2	30.6	30.6	30.9	31.0	30.9	30.0	31.1	31.2	30.5
2007	30.6	31.1	31.4	31.7	32.3	32.5	32.5	32.5	32.2	32.0	32.3	32.5	32.0
2008	31.4	31.4	31.8	32.1	32.3	32.3	31.9	31.8	31.3	30.9	30.7	30.6	31.5
2009	29.5	29.4	29.3	29.4	30.0	30.1	29.8	29.7	29.4	29.2	29.0	29.2	29.5
Other Services													
1990	7.3	7.2	7.3	7.2	7.3	7.4	7.6	7.6	7.6	7.5	7.6	7.7	7.4
2000	9.5	9.5	9.6	9.8	9.8	9.9	9.8	9.8	9.8	9.7	9.7	9.9	9.7
2001	9.4	9.5	9.7	9.5	9.7	9.7	9.4	9.4	9.7	9.8	9.9	9.9	9.6
2002	9.7	9.8	9.9	10.0	10.1	10.3	10.4	10.3	10.4	10.2	10.4	10.4	10.2
2003	10.2	10.3	10.3	10.7	10.7	10.8	10.5	10.3	10.3	10.4	10.3	10.3	10.4
2004	10.2	10.3	10.4	10.5	10.4	10.3	10.4	10.3	10.2	10.4	10.3	10.3	10.3
2005	10.5	10.6	10.7	10.6	10.5	10.4	10.3	10.2	10.3	10.2	10.2	10.2	10.4
2006	10.1	10.2	10.3	10.3	10.4	10.4	10.0	10.0	10.1	10.0	10.1	10.0	10.2
2007	9.5	9.6	9.8	9.9	10.1	10.0	9.9	9.8	10.0	10.4	10.1	10.1	9.9
2008	10.0	10.1	10.2	10.2	10.2	10.2	10.1	10.0	10.0	9.7	9.5	9.5	10.0
2009	9.3	9.3	9.3	9.4	9.4	9.4	9.3	9.5	9.5	9.4	9.4	9.2	9.4
Government													
1990	42.6	43.4	43.9	44.0	45.0	45.0	44.2	44.0	44.0	44.3	44.7	44.9	44.2
2000	44.1	44.6	45.0	45.3	45.7	45.0	43.2	41.3	42.9	44.0	45.1	45.3	44.3
2001	45.8	45.6	45.4	44.7	44.9	44.2	44.9	42.7	44.2	45.6	46.6	46.8	45.1
2002	45.9	46.5	46.0	45.7	45.6	46.1	43.8	41.7	44.4	45.1	46.7	45.6	45.3
2003	45.5	45.5	46.1	45.8	46.6	46.0	43.0	41.6	43.6	44.8	45.2	43.8	44.7
2004	43.1	43.4	43.7	43.7	43.4	43.8	40.6	39.7	40.8	42.3	42.6	42.7	42.5
2005	42.2	42.7	42.8	42.7	43.1	42.9	40.2	39.9	41.8	42.2	42.9	42.8	42.2
2006	42.5	42.8	43.0	43.0	42.9	43.2	40.9	40.4	42.6	42.5	43.2	43.1	42.5
2007	42.7	43.1	43.3	43.5	43.7	43.8	41.5	41.1	43.0	43.1	43.8	43.8	43.0
2008	43.5	43.9	44.0	43.8	44.1	44.4	41.1	40.2	41.7	43.2	43.7	43.8	43.1
2009	43.1	43.5	43.7	44.1	44.1	44.4	40.1	40.6	41.5	43.2	43.6	43.4	42.9

Employment by Industry: Philadelphia-Camden-Wilmington, PA-NJ-DE-MD, Selected Years, 1990–2009

(Numbers in thousands, not seasonally adjusted.)

Industry and year	January	February	March	April	May	June	July	August	September	October	November	December	Annual average
Total Nonfarm													
1990	2474.2	2485.4	2502.9	2498.7	2509.5	2520.9	2492.3	2488.4	2497.8	2499.8	2506.7	2508.8	2498.8
2000	2686.7	2697.1	2725.3	2747.0	2757.8	2767.7	2728.0	2718.5	2748.7	2763.2	2786.6	2806.2	2744.4
2001	2717.3	2728.8	2746.4	2759.1	2768.3	2778.7	2733.1	2728.3	2743.1	2754.8	2772.9	2781.2	2751.0
2002	2704.5	2715.2	2733.1	2741.0	2751.5	2764.6	2716.6	2711.8	2733.6	2753.6	2770.6	2775.6	2739.3
2003	2692.1	2694.4	2714.5	2732.3	2743.9	2751.6	2715.0	2705.6	2727.2	2749.4	2763.4	2768.4	2729.8
2004	2688.1	2699.1	2722.4	2742.0	2754.9	2766.8	2734.9	2727.4	2753.1	2780.0	2793.4	2799.8	2746.8
2005	2717.5	2730.0	2742.8	2778.8	2791.4	2791.7	2767.7	2757.0	2783.1	2801.7	2818.3	2821.0	2775.1
2006	2748.2	2761.6	2779.7	2808.0	2820.3	2821.5	2786.9	2779.5	2799.1	2821.5	2834.2	2838.3	2799.9
2007	2765.6	2771.8	2791.2	2812.3	2826.2	2834.4	2803.8	2793.9	2807.6	2836.6	2852.2	2852.1	2812.3
2008	2781.3	2792.3	2804.6	2833.4	2837.1	2838.4	2798.0	2788.7	2804.0	2824.0	2819.2	2811.8	2811.1
2009	2722.3	2723.7	2719.3	2730.9	2736.5	2732.1	2693.8	2677.3	2691.0	2710.8	2714.6	2710.6	2713.6
Total Private													
1990	2140.6	2147.3	2163.8	2158.7	2169.8	2181.2	2167.0	2168.8	2170.0	2162.8	2166.6	2168.8	2163.8
2000	2346.1	2350.0	2373.3	2392.9	2398.0	2415.6	2399.8	2397.9	2408.6	2415.5	2435.1	2453.5	2398.9
2001	2370.0	2374.6	2390.7	2402.1	2414.0	2428.2	2405.6	2406.2	2400.9	2402.5	2416.1	2422.0	2402.7
2002	2350.6	2355.0	2371.7	2379.0	2390.8	2407.8	2387.1	2390.2	2389.9	2400.1	2412.8	2417.7	2387.7
2003	2341.3	2336.8	2354.7	2372.1	2384.7	2395.3	2383.8	2381.0	2381.2	2391.9	2402.8	2407.8	2377.8
2004	2334.8	2339.4	2360.2	2378.2	2394.3	2410.3	2405.3	2402.2	2404.0	2420.8	2431.7	2439.0	2393.4
2005	2362.6	2368.9	2379.2	2414.9	2429.9	2434.8	2431.9	2426.1	2434.2	2443.1	2458.2	2461.8	2420.5
2006	2394.9	2401.1	2417.0	2444.5	2457.7	2464.7	2453.5	2448.4	2450.2	2463.5	2473.8	2479.4	2445.7
2007	2415.2	2413.6	2430.8	2452.1	2467.2	2478.4	2471.7	2465.8	2460.8	2479.3	2492.8	2494.3	2460.2
2008	2430.4	2434.4	2445.4	2472.9	2478.8	2481.1	2469.6	2460.6	2453.5	2462.0	2455.7	2448.3	2457.7
2009	2366.6	2360.7	2354.6	2365.2	2374.3	2371.5	2360.2	2347.1	2339.3	2349.1	2350.4	2348.2	2357.3
Goods-Producing													
1990	461.5	461.2	465.4	465.7	469.5	472.8	469.2	470.4	467.5	460.6	454.5	448.9	463.9
2000	400.7	397.5	405.2	411.5	413.4	418.1	414.9	416.6	415.5	414.2	412.7	411.7	411.0
2001	399.1	398.4	402.1	403.8	405.5	408.9	406.8	406.6	404.9	399.2	396.4	394.0	402.1
2002	381.6	380.9	382.3	382.6	385.7	388.0	386.1	387.3	385.1	382.5	380.3	377.3	383.3
2003	362.8	359.2	361.8	365.8	369.7	372.0	370.8	370.1	368.2	366.6	364.8	361.0	366.1
2004	351.2	350.1	355.1	357.8	362.0	366.0	366.9	367.0	365.7	364.3	363.3	360.6	360.8
2005	346.8	345.6	349.1	356.8	361.1	363.3	364.1	365.2	363.6	362.2	365.3	360.1	358.6
2006	352.7	351.4	355.2	360.3	363.4	365.1	363.0	362.9	360.1	358.3	354.7	352.7	358.3
2007	343.2	338.6	342.8	346.9	350.4	354.2	354.4	354.8	352.3	351.9	351.3	347.7	349.0
2008	338.1	337.2	340.0	343.8	344.0	347.4	345.5	344.3	339.5	335.6	332.1	324.7	339.4
2009	309.1	303.2	301.7	301.3	301.0	301.7	300.5	299.7	295.9	293.1	289.7	285.0	298.5
Mining, Logging, and Construction													
1990	109.8	109.7	113.4	114.9	118.7	121.2	121.6	121.3	119.3	115.9	111.8	107.0	115.4
2000	110.8	107.9	114.7	120.6	122.6	125.3	123.0	124.0	123.5	123.3	121.4	119.5	119.7
2001	112.3	112.3	116.1	119.9	122.9	125.8	126.9	127.8	127.0	125.7	124.7	122.0	122.0
2002	114.9	114.8	116.6	118.7	121.5	123.5	124.3	125.3	123.1	123.1	121.7	119.5	120.6
2003	113.0	109.8	112.3	118.9	123.0	124.9	127.3	127.4	125.6	125.3	124.6	121.5	121.1
2004	115.1	113.6	118.5	120.9	124.5	127.3	129.0	129.8	129.9	128.9	127.9	125.2	124.2
2005	116.6	114.7	117.6	125.3	129.1	131.5	133.4	133.4	132.7	133.0	134.3	130.1	127.6
2006	122.8	122.2	126.3	131.6	134.8	136.0	135.8	135.8	134.1	133.1	130.5	128.8	131.0
2007	121.7	117.9	121.7	126.1	128.9	131.3	132.5	133.3	132.4	131.8	129.9	125.9	127.8
2008	120.4	118.6	121.2	126.0	127.2	128.5	128.6	128.2	125.3	123.1	120.1	114.9	123.5
2009	104.6	101.9	103.2	104.5	105.2	106.3	107.0	106.9	104.4	103.4	100.9	96.1	103.7
Manufacturing													
1990	351.7	351.5	352.0	350.8	350.8	351.6	347.6	349.1	348.2	344.7	342.7	341.9	348.6
2000	289.9	289.6	290.5	290.9	290.8	292.8	291.9	292.6	292.0	290.9	291.3	292.2	291.3
2001	286.8	286.1	286.0	283.9	282.6	283.1	279.9	278.8	277.9	273.5	271.7	272.0	280.2
2002	266.7	266.1	265.7	263.9	264.2	264.5	261.8	262.0	262.0	259.4	258.6	257.8	262.7
2003	249.8	249.4	249.5	246.9	246.7	247.1	243.5	242.7	242.6	241.3	240.2	239.5	244.9
2004	236.1	236.5	236.6	236.9	237.5	238.7	237.9	237.2	235.8	235.4	235.4	235.4	236.6
2005	230.2	230.9	231.5	231.5	232.0	231.8	230.7	231.8	230.9	229.2	231.0	230.0	231.0
2006	229.9	229.2	228.9	228.7	228.6	229.1	227.2	227.1	226.0	225.2	224.2	223.9	227.3
2007	221.5	220.7	221.1	220.8	221.5	222.9	221.9	221.5	219.9	220.1	221.4	221.8	221.3
2008	217.7	218.6	218.8	217.8	216.8	218.9	216.9	216.1	214.2	212.5	212.0	209.8	215.8
2009	204.5	201.3	198.5	196.8	195.8	195.4	193.5	192.8	191.5	189.7	188.8	188.9	194.8
Service-Providing													
1990	2012.7	2024.2	2037.5	2033.0	2040.0	2048.1	2023.1	2018.0	2030.3	2039.2	2052.2	2059.9	2034.9
2000	2286.0	2299.6	2320.1	2335.5	2344.4	2349.6	2313.1	2301.9	2333.2	2349.0	2373.9	2394.5	2333.4
2001	2318.2	2330.4	2344.3	2355.3	2362.8	2369.8	2326.3	2321.7	2338.2	2355.6	2376.5	2387.2	2348.9
2002	2322.9	2334.3	2350.8	2358.4	2365.8	2376.6	2330.5	2324.5	2348.5	2371.1	2390.3	2398.3	2356.0
2003	2329.3	2335.2	2352.7	2366.5	2374.2	2379.6	2344.2	2335.5	2359.0	2382.8	2398.6	2407.4	2363.8
2004	2336.9	2349.0	2367.3	2384.2	2392.9	2400.8	2368.0	2360.4	2387.4	2415.7	2430.1	2439.2	2386.0
2005	2370.7	2384.4	2393.7	2422.0	2430.3	2428.4	2403.6	2391.8	2419.5	2439.5	2453.0	2460.9	2416.5
2006	2395.5	2410.2	2424.5	2447.7	2456.9	2456.4	2423.9	2416.6	2439.0	2463.2	2479.5	2485.6	2441.6
2007	2422.4	2433.2	2448.4	2465.4	2475.8	2480.2	2449.4	2439.1	2455.3	2484.7	2500.9	2504.4	2463.3
2008	2443.2	2455.1	2464.6	2489.6	2493.1	2491.0	2452.5	2444.4	2464.5	2488.4	2487.1	2487.1	2471.7
2009	2413.2	2420.5	2417.6	2429.6	2435.5	2430.4	2393.3	2377.6	2395.1	2417.7	2424.9	2425.6	2415.1

Employment by Industry: Philadelphia-Camden-Wilmington, PA-NJ-DE-MD, Selected Years, 1990–2009—*Continued*

(Numbers in thousands, not seasonally adjusted.)

Industry and year	January	February	March	April	May	June	July	August	September	October	November	December	Annual average
Trade, Transportation, and Utilities													
1990	521.0	513.1	514.0	509.2	510.1	511.4	506.4	507.9	509.3	511.2	520.3	527.2	513.4
2000	531.3	525.0	526.9	532.0	534.7	537.2	531.0	533.4	536.7	543.4	557.0	568.5	538.1
2001	542.4	533.2	534.8	532.0	533.6	536.0	527.6	527.9	529.4	533.9	546.5	554.7	536.0
2002	529.8	521.1	525.3	523.8	527.5	531.3	524.6	526.3	528.6	535.3	545.6	557.0	531.4
2003	528.4	520.6	523.4	525.7	528.7	532.2	525.5	525.5	528.4	534.9	545.0	553.4	531.0
2004	524.9	521.1	522.9	523.2	527.7	531.1	526.4	526.0	527.2	534.1	544.0	552.7	530.1
2005	529.0	523.3	525.0	527.4	531.1	532.1	529.8	528.9	529.8	534.3	544.8	554.6	532.5
2006	531.2	523.3	527.2	527.7	531.0	532.5	527.7	526.3	527.1	533.0	544.4	551.9	531.9
2007	530.8	521.3	523.3	524.2	529.2	532.5	529.3	527.2	527.0	531.5	544.0	551.8	531.0
2008	532.0	522.2	523.9	525.3	528.5	529.1	523.5	521.8	522.4	526.6	530.0	536.0	526.8
2009	509.8	501.5	498.5	496.2	500.2	502.2	495.1	493.5	495.1	498.3	505.8	511.8	500.7
Wholesale Trade													
1990	133.2	133.1	133.4	132.4	132.2	132.5	132.1	131.9	131.4	129.8	130.2	129.9	131.8
2000	125.0	125.3	126.3	128.1	128.2	129.2	128.6	128.7	128.3	128.2	128.7	129.5	127.8
2001	130.0	130.2	130.7	131.1	131.0	131.3	131.2	130.7	130.4	130.0	130.2	130.9	130.6
2002	129.5	129.1	130.1	130.1	130.4	130.6	129.9	129.9	129.2	130.6	130.5	131.3	130.1
2003	129.1	129.0	129.9	129.8	130.0	130.3	129.5	129.5	129.4	129.4	130.0	130.5	129.7
2004	127.9	128.1	128.9	129.3	129.8	130.3	130.5	130.3	129.6	130.1	129.9	130.2	129.6
2005	129.8	129.1	129.7	130.1	130.4	130.6	130.5	130.5	129.8	129.9	130.1	130.7	130.1
2006	128.6	128.7	129.6	129.9	130.3	131.3	131.3	131.2	130.3	129.9	129.8	130.1	130.1
2007	128.7	128.2	129.0	130.0	130.2	131.4	131.8	131.3	130.4	130.5	131.0	131.4	130.3
2008	130.0	129.8	130.2	130.4	131.0	131.4	131.5	131.0	130.0	130.1	129.1	128.8	130.3
2009	127.2	126.2	125.8	124.9	124.7	124.7	124.2	123.6	122.6	122.2	121.9	122.7	124.2
Retail Trade													
1990	309.8	301.6	301.2	297.4	298.0	298.7	296.9	298.3	298.1	300.6	309.1	316.1	302.2
2000	312.7	306.6	307.2	310.0	312.4	315.0	311.6	314.3	314.2	319.2	332.6	342.4	316.5
2001	317.8	308.9	310.3	305.7	307.4	310.0	304.7	306.9	305.6	308.6	321.5	329.4	311.4
2002	308.6	300.9	303.5	300.8	303.4	306.9	303.5	305.4	304.7	307.4	318.2	328.6	307.7
2003	304.4	297.0	299.2	300.7	303.6	307.3	304.6	305.7	305.2	310.3	320.2	328.2	307.2
2004	305.1	300.9	301.9	301.7	305.5	308.1	306.6	307.3	305.7	311.8	321.3	328.8	308.7
2005	308.4	303.4	304.0	305.5	308.5	309.0	309.0	308.7	306.6	310.6	319.7	327.5	310.1
2006	309.4	301.1	303.3	303.6	305.1	306.1	304.2	302.8	301.3	307.0	317.7	323.1	307.1
2007	307.5	299.0	299.8	300.2	304.1	305.9	305.1	304.2	302.0	307.3	318.4	324.3	306.5
2008	308.0	298.7	300.0	300.4	302.7	303.9	301.0	300.6	298.8	302.6	307.2	312.0	303.0
2009	291.7	285.0	282.9	281.8	286.0	287.8	285.7	285.5	283.9	286.9	294.0	297.5	287.4
Transportation and Utilities													
1990	78.0	78.4	79.4	79.4	79.9	80.2	77.4	77.7	79.8	80.8	81.0	81.2	79.4
2000	93.6	93.1	93.4	93.9	94.1	93.0	90.8	90.4	94.2	96.0	95.7	96.6	93.7
2001	94.6	94.1	93.8	95.2	95.2	94.7	91.7	90.3	93.4	95.3	94.8	94.4	94.0
2002	91.7	91.1	91.7	92.9	93.7	93.8	91.2	91.0	94.7	97.3	96.9	97.1	93.6
2003	94.9	94.6	94.3	95.2	95.1	94.6	91.4	90.3	93.8	95.2	94.8	94.7	94.1
2004	91.9	92.1	92.1	92.2	92.4	92.7	89.3	88.4	91.9	92.2	92.8	93.7	91.8
2005	90.8	90.8	91.3	91.8	92.2	92.5	90.3	89.7	93.4	93.8	95.0	96.4	92.3
2006	93.2	93.5	94.3	94.2	95.6	95.1	92.2	92.3	95.5	96.1	96.9	98.7	94.8
2007	94.6	94.1	94.5	94.0	94.9	95.2	92.4	91.7	94.6	93.7	94.6	96.1	94.2
2008	94.0	93.7	93.7	94.5	94.8	93.8	91.0	90.2	93.6	93.9	93.7	95.2	93.5
2009	90.9	90.3	89.8	89.5	89.5	89.7	85.2	84.4	88.6	89.2	89.9	91.6	89.1
Information													
1990	62.5	62.9	62.9	62.6	63.2	64.0	63.3	63.3	63.1	62.9	63.2	63.5	63.1
2000	69.6	70.0	70.9	70.6	71.0	71.7	73.1	67.7	73.2	72.7	73.5	74.1	71.5
2001	72.4	72.4	72.3	71.4	71.8	72.4	71.8	70.8	70.0	69.5	70.0	70.2	71.3
2002	69.5	69.4	69.9	68.0	68.6	68.5	67.8	67.4	67.0	66.3	66.7	66.4	68.0
2003	65.2	64.9	65.3	64.1	63.6	63.0	62.0	61.1	60.1	58.9	58.6	57.6	62.0
2004	56.7	56.2	56.3	56.2	56.3	56.5	56.5	56.3	55.5	55.3	55.5	55.5	56.1
2005	54.7	54.7	54.9	55.4	55.5	56.1	55.7	55.7	58.6	55.7	56.0	56.3	55.8
2006	55.4	56.1	55.4	55.4	55.7	55.9	55.8	55.9	56.4	56.4	56.3	56.8	56.0
2007	56.4	56.4	56.5	57.1	57.3	58.1	57.8	58.1	58.9	58.2	58.3	58.8	57.7
2008	57.8	57.8	57.6	57.9	57.9	57.6	57.3	57.1	56.5	56.3	56.2	56.1	57.2
2009	55.4	55.1	54.8	54.5	54.3	54.2	54.0	53.6	53.2	53.0	52.9	53.1	54.0
Financial Activities													
1990	198.4	199.3	199.7	199.3	200.7	201.5	201.6	200.8	198.7	196.3	196.3	197.2	199.2
2000	217.4	218.0	217.7	217.8	217.7	219.6	219.4	219.2	217.1	217.6	218.7	220.6	218.4
2001	218.2	218.5	219.2	220.1	220.3	221.4	220.9	221.0	217.8	217.6	217.4	218.6	219.3
2002	217.9	217.7	218.1	217.9	217.8	219.4	220.1	220.4	218.8	218.7	219.3	220.1	218.9
2003	219.0	219.2	219.7	220.1	220.7	222.2	223.1	222.9	220.5	219.2	219.2	219.5	220.4
2004	218.4	217.7	218.1	218.8	219.5	220.7	221.1	220.4	217.7	217.3	217.8	218.9	218.9
2005	217.9	218.0	218.1	218.4	219.3	221.1	221.9	222.1	220.2	219.8	220.3	221.3	219.9
2006	219.6	219.2	219.2	220.2	220.4	222.0	222.6	222.3	220.5	220.4	220.6	221.1	220.7
2007	219.6	219.6	219.6	219.9	220.0	221.7	222.8	222.1	219.7	220.0	220.0	220.4	220.5
2008	217.8	218.0	218.2	218.1	217.9	218.9	219.4	218.2	215.3	214.1	213.6	212.7	216.9
2009	210.1	209.1	208.4	208.2	208.0	208.7	208.2	206.6	204.5	202.9	202.3	201.9	206.6

Employment by Industry: Philadelphia-Camden-Wilmington, PA-NJ-DE-MD, Selected Years, 1990–2009—*Continued*

(Numbers in thousands, not seasonally adjusted.)

Industry and year	January	February	March	April	May	June	July	August	September	October	November	December	Annual average
Professional and Business Services													
1990	300.8	303.4	307.9	309.5	311.0	314.1	312.9	312.5	310.7	307.6	306.9	305.7	308.6
2000	387.3	388.0	395.1	395.1	395.0	399.1	397.9	397.5	397.0	394.6	396.3	397.2	395.0
2001	386.1	387.2	391.6	394.3	395.7	397.2	392.0	394.3	392.4	391.2	390.9	388.9	391.8
2002	377.4	377.4	382.4	386.3	386.6	389.3	384.7	385.8	383.2	385.4	386.9	387.0	384.4
2003	378.6	377.0	381.3	387.3	388.6	390.4	390.2	391.0	392.6	394.7	396.5	398.3	388.9
2004	388.4	389.5	395.9	398.6	400.8	406.0	405.7	406.0	405.7	410.1	411.1	411.6	402.5
2005	395.7	396.8	399.1	410.7	410.8	413.2	414.7	413.2	413.0	415.3	416.4	417.2	409.7
2006	404.3	407.0	411.8	420.2	421.4	424.6	424.5	425.3	425.2	428.5	430.9	432.2	421.3
2007	417.6	418.3	422.6	430.6	432.6	435.8	434.2	434.7	431.8	435.5	438.5	438.2	430.9
2008	425.4	424.7	428.7	435.4	435.7	437.0	434.4	434.0	430.8	430.9	428.3	425.2	430.9
2009	411.5	408.9	408.3	412.3	410.7	410.3	407.7	406.9	403.2	405.2	405.1	404.8	407.9
Education and Health Services													
1990	344.0	352.8	355.3	353.1	350.0	347.4	346.6	346.8	357.2	364.5	366.3	366.6	354.2
2000	448.9	460.0	458.6	460.4	455.5	452.3	446.2	447.5	457.2	462.7	466.3	470.3	457.2
2001	457.7	468.9	469.3	469.9	467.9	466.0	460.3	461.1	468.5	475.1	479.1	478.0	468.5
2002	471.1	482.8	483.0	480.8	476.8	475.3	470.3	470.2	479.4	486.2	489.5	486.4	479.3
2003	475.6	485.1	485.9	486.3	482.1	478.3	473.5	471.6	480.6	489.6	492.1	490.8	482.6
2004	479.5	490.0	491.8	493.5	490.2	484.2	482.3	480.2	491.5	501.2	503.5	502.1	490.8
2005	492.1	505.2	502.3	506.9	504.3	493.6	492.5	490.1	503.3	515.1	516.5	513.9	503.0
2006	503.8	516.0	513.5	518.6	516.5	507.3	505.4	502.3	514.7	523.8	525.9	523.3	514.3
2007	516.2	528.1	529.2	529.3	526.0	517.5	517.2	514.6	524.0	537.2	537.6	535.2	526.0
2008	527.8	543.0	540.6	546.1	541.4	531.6	530.3	529.6	541.0	552.6	555.3	555.2	541.2
2009	545.9	558.3	554.3	557.0	553.2	543.0	542.6	538.4	547.6	559.9	563.0	560.9	552.0
Leisure and Hospitality													
1990	158.6	159.6	162.8	163.6	168.9	172.4	170.3	170.4	167.9	163.7	163.4	163.8	165.5
2000	182.2	182.0	187.8	194.3	199.0	204.8	204.3	203.4	200.1	197.0	196.7	196.9	195.7
2001	181.8	183.3	186.9	195.9	203.4	209.3	209.0	207.7	202.2	199.3	198.7	200.0	198.1
2002	186.5	188.0	192.3	200.3	206.4	212.6	210.9	210.1	206.3	204.9	203.9	202.8	202.1
2003	192.8	191.9	197.2	202.8	210.4	214.8	217.0	217.4	210.8	207.4	205.6	205.7	206.2
2004	196.2	195.0	198.9	207.8	214.6	221.1	221.1	221.0	216.0	214.4	212.3	213.1	211.0
2005	202.4	200.9	205.5	214.2	222.1	228.5	227.4	225.8	221.4	216.8	214.9	214.2	216.2
2006	205.0	205.0	210.5	218.1	224.6	231.5	229.7	229.5	223.6	220.4	218.5	218.9	219.6
2007	210.1	209.7	214.6	221.2	227.9	233.4	231.7	231.1	224.7	222.5	220.4	219.5	222.2
2008	209.8	209.8	214.8	224.8	230.9	236.2	236.3	233.4	226.6	225.1	219.8	218.1	223.8
2009	206.2	206.0	209.6	216.8	226.7	230.3	231.8	228.9	221.8	218.5	213.5	212.3	218.5
Other Services													
1990	93.8	95.0	95.8	95.7	96.4	97.6	96.7	96.7	95.6	96.0	95.7	95.9	95.9
2000	108.7	109.5	111.1	111.2	111.7	112.8	113.0	112.6	111.8	113.3	113.9	114.2	112.0
2001	112.3	112.7	114.5	114.7	115.8	117.0	117.2	116.8	115.7	116.7	117.1	117.6	115.7
2002	116.8	117.7	118.4	119.3	121.4	123.4	122.6	122.7	121.5	120.8	120.6	120.7	120.5
2003	118.9	118.9	120.1	120.0	120.9	122.4	121.7	121.4	120.0	120.6	121.0	121.5	120.6
2004	119.5	119.8	121.2	122.3	123.2	124.7	125.3	125.3	124.7	124.1	124.2	124.5	123.2
2005	124.0	124.4	125.2	125.1	125.7	126.9	125.8	125.1	124.3	123.9	124.0	124.2	124.9
2006	122.9	123.1	124.2	124.0	124.7	125.8	124.8	123.9	122.6	122.7	122.5	122.5	123.6
2007	121.3	121.6	122.2	122.9	123.8	125.2	124.3	123.2	122.4	122.5	122.7	122.7	122.9
2008	121.7	121.7	121.6	121.5	122.5	123.3	122.9	122.2	121.4	120.8	120.4	120.3	121.7
2009	118.6	118.6	119.0	118.9	120.1	121.0	120.3	119.5	118.0	118.2	118.1	118.4	119.1
Government													
1990	333.6	338.1	339.1	340.0	339.7	339.7	325.3	319.6	327.8	337.0	340.1	340.0	335.0
2000	340.6	347.1	352.0	354.1	359.8	352.1	328.2	320.6	340.1	347.7	351.5	352.7	345.5
2001	347.3	354.2	355.7	357.0	354.3	350.5	327.5	322.1	342.2	352.3	356.8	359.2	348.3
2002	353.9	360.2	361.4	362.0	360.7	356.8	329.5	321.6	343.7	353.5	357.8	357.9	351.6
2003	350.8	357.6	359.8	360.2	359.2	356.3	331.2	324.6	346.0	357.5	360.6	360.6	352.0
2004	353.3	359.7	362.2	363.8	360.6	356.5	329.6	325.2	349.1	359.2	361.7	360.8	353.5
2005	354.9	361.1	363.6	363.9	361.5	356.9	335.8	330.9	348.9	358.6	360.1	359.2	354.6
2006	353.3	360.5	362.7	363.5	362.6	356.8	333.4	331.1	348.9	358.0	360.4	358.9	354.2
2007	350.4	358.2	360.4	360.2	359.0	356.0	332.1	328.1	346.8	357.3	359.4	357.8	352.1
2008	350.9	357.9	359.2	360.5	358.3	357.3	328.4	328.1	350.5	362.0	363.5	363.5	353.3
2009	355.7	363.0	364.7	365.7	362.3	360.7	333.6	330.2	351.7	361.7	364.2	362.4	356.3

Employment by Industry: Phoenix-Mesa-Scottsdale, AZ, Selected Years, 1990–2009

(Numbers in thousands, not seasonally adjusted.)

Industry and year	January	February	March	April	May	June	July	August	September	October	November	December	Annual average
Total Nonfarm													
1990	991.7	1004.6	1012.5	1020.4	1024.1	1012.4	991.8	994.6	1016.6	1023.4	1034.7	1032.8	1013.3
2000	1534.7	1558.7	1570.7	1573.5	1583.7	1564.7	1545.5	1565.2	1592.7	1603.1	1616.9	1631.9	1578.4
2001	1582.2	1606.8	1617.8	1611.9	1607.7	1589.3	1566.4	1583.9	1597.4	1600.4	1602.3	1606.0	1597.7
2002	1566.5	1581.4	1592.8	1605.7	1601.5	1589.6	1562.0	1585.3	1596.9	1608.3	1632.1	1631.3	1596.1
2003	1587.2	1606.3	1614.7	1621.0	1623.1	1604.8	1582.5	1609.3	1621.9	1642.6	1656.6	1667.8	1619.8
2004	1626.4	1648.2	1662.4	1677.0	1678.9	1664.3	1654.6	1675.3	1694.7	1725.0	1740.7	1756.7	1683.7
2005	1714.5	1742.5	1758.4	1783.1	1785.2	1768.3	1761.7	1787.9	1816.5	1825.6	1848.1	1860.5	1787.7
2006	1829.6	1862.2	1879.2	1883.4	1891.3	1871.3	1853.9	1879.0	1899.9	1907.9	1922.2	1929.6	1884.1
2007	1881.9	1908.3	1921.2	1915.3	1919.8	1898.7	1882.0	1910.9	1922.3	1931.3	1942.6	1943.7	1914.8
2008	1897.0	1909.0	1905.6	1896.9	1890.2	1851.2	1818.0	1848.7	1853.5	1848.2	1845.2	1832.6	1866.3
2009	1772.2	1767.2	1760.3	1746.0	1733.4	1689.1	1665.9	1679.6	1689.4	1704.4	1715.3	1712.9	1719.6
Total Private													
1990	851.6	856.7	863.1	868.8	869.5	871.3	859.0	861.6	865.8	868.4	877.6	876.4	865.8
2000	1342.4	1359.2	1370.4	1372.2	1378.0	1384.7	1371.4	1383.6	1392.1	1399.5	1412.7	1426.3	1382.7
2001	1387.3	1400.4	1410.8	1404.4	1401.2	1402.9	1383.8	1389.2	1387.4	1385.8	1386.8	1391.1	1394.3
2002	1359.3	1366.7	1377.6	1388.3	1389.0	1389.5	1373.2	1381.7	1379.7	1385.5	1402.9	1408.0	1383.5
2003	1375.4	1384.3	1392.7	1398.9	1401.7	1399.1	1390.3	1400.6	1403.9	1418.7	1432.1	1442.5	1403.4
2004	1412.7	1424.6	1438.5	1451.8	1454.2	1457.9	1457.0	1463.3	1467.8	1494.0	1509.1	1524.2	1462.9
2005	1493.4	1510.7	1528.3	1552.1	1555.9	1559.3	1560.3	1571.1	1584.7	1592.0	1612.9	1625.6	1562.2
2006	1606.0	1628.0	1645.0	1649.3	1655.4	1661.0	1647.9	1658.5	1664.5	1668.6	1682.4	1692.3	1654.9
2007	1651.1	1667.8	1679.3	1673.7	1677.4	1679.2	1665.6	1675.2	1676.2	1683.0	1691.9	1693.1	1676.1
2008	1647.8	1655.4	1652.1	1643.5	1638.0	1626.8	1605.3	1609.4	1602.0	1594.7	1590.3	1579.3	1620.4
2009	1526.9	1515.5	1509.6	1494.8	1486.1	1472.2	1456.1	1455.9	1447.5	1460.6	1470.3	1470.8	1480.5
Goods-Producing													
1990	195.5	195.7	196.7	196.7	197.6	199.7	199.1	200.2	199.7	199.4	198.2	195.7	197.9
2000	278.8	281.3	283.0	282.9	284.8	288.9	288.4	290.1	290.8	290.8	290.6	291.5	286.8
2001	285.3	286.7	288.3	287.1	287.3	288.3	287.2	287.3	283.5	278.6	274.4	271.4	283.8
2002	265.8	265.5	266.3	266.6	267.1	268.6	268.3	268.7	266.1	263.6	262.5	260.8	265.8
2003	257.3	256.9	257.1	259.6	261.3	263.1	263.1	265.2	265.4	265.5	265.6	266.2	262.1
2004	262.2	264.3	266.6	269.1	271.4	275.0	277.4	279.6	281.1	285.0	286.3	288.6	275.6
2005	283.9	287.3	291.5	297.2	300.1	305.1	306.6	308.5	310.1	310.6	313.5	316.3	302.6
2006	312.8	317.9	321.9	324.1	326.3	329.5	328.3	327.9	325.8	321.6	318.9	317.0	322.7
2007	310.2	311.9	312.4	310.8	311.9	315.1	314.1	314.8	311.1	307.6	301.4	297.1	309.9
2008	288.7	286.5	283.9	281.0	279.8	278.0	274.4	272.7	267.9	261.3	253.3	246.2	272.8
2009	234.9	227.7	223.4	218.4	215.3	213.7	210.4	207.9	204.6	202.2	200.2	197.7	213.0
Mining and Logging													
1990	4.5	4.5	4.5	4.5	4.5	4.5	4.5	4.5	4.6	4.5	4.5	4.5	4.5
2000	2.4	2.4	2.4	2.4	2.4	2.4	2.4	2.4	2.4	2.4	2.4	2.4	2.4
2001	2.5	2.4	2.5	2.4	2.4	2.4	2.3	2.4	2.3	2.3	2.3	2.3	2.4
2002	2.3	2.3	2.3	2.3	2.3	2.3	2.2	2.3	2.1	2.1	2.0	2.0	2.2
2003	2.0	2.0	1.9	2.0	2.0	2.0	2.0	2.0	1.9	1.9	2.0	2.0	1.9
2004	1.9	1.9	1.9	2.0	2.0	2.1	2.1	2.1	2.1	2.2	2.2	2.2	2.1
2005	2.2	2.2	2.2	2.3	2.4	2.4	2.0	1.9	1.9	1.9	2.1	2.4	2.2
2006	2.5	2.4	2.5	2.6	2.6	2.8	2.8	2.9	2.9	2.8	2.9	2.9	2.7
2007	2.9	3.0	3.1	3.0	3.0	3.1	3.4	3.4	3.4	3.5	3.5	3.5	3.2
2008	3.5	3.5	3.6	3.6	3.7	3.9	3.9	4.0	3.9	3.9	3.9	3.8	3.8
2009	3.3	3.3	3.3	3.2	3.0	2.9	2.9	2.9	2.8	2.9	2.9	2.9	3.0
Construction													
1990	55.2	55.3	56.3	56.2	56.6	58.0	57.8	58.9	59.1	58.6	57.7	56.0	57.1
2000	117.0	118.4	119.8	121.1	122.9	124.8	124.5	125.5	126.1	126.8	126.0	126.7	123.3
2001	122.8	124.9	127.1	127.6	128.9	131.3	131.8	133.4	131.3	128.8	126.7	124.5	128.3
2002	122.2	122.2	123.7	124.6	126.1	127.9	128.2	129.5	128.5	127.4	127.1	126.0	126.1
2003	123.7	124.0	124.6	125.8	127.9	129.7	130.4	132.2	132.9	133.4	133.5	133.8	129.3
2004	130.9	132.4	134.1	136.4	138.3	140.9	143.2	144.9	146.2	149.2	150.2	152.0	141.6
2005	149.0	151.8	155.4	159.7	161.4	165.1	166.8	168.4	170.2	170.7	173.2	174.7	163.9
2006	172.2	176.1	179.5	181.1	183.1	185.6	184.3	184.0	182.6	179.4	177.6	175.5	180.1
2007	169.8	171.0	171.4	170.4	171.3	174.4	172.3	173.1	171.1	167.5	162.2	158.2	169.4
2008	151.5	149.9	148.7	146.0	145.0	143.4	140.5	139.1	135.4	130.1	124.0	118.7	139.4
2009	110.2	105.1	102.8	99.5	98.0	97.6	95.2	93.3	90.8	88.7	86.6	84.8	96.1
Manufacturing													
1990	135.8	135.9	135.9	136.0	136.5	137.2	136.8	136.8	136.0	136.3	136.0	135.2	136.2
2000	159.4	160.5	160.8	159.4	159.5	161.7	161.5	162.2	162.3	161.6	162.2	162.4	161.1
2001	160.0	159.4	158.7	157.1	156.0	154.6	153.1	151.5	149.9	147.5	145.4	144.6	153.2
2002	141.3	141.0	140.3	139.7	138.7	138.4	137.9	136.9	135.5	134.1	133.4	132.8	137.5
2003	131.6	130.9	130.6	131.8	131.4	131.4	130.7	131.0	130.6	130.2	130.1	130.4	130.8
2004	129.4	130.0	130.6	130.7	131.1	132.0	132.1	132.6	132.8	133.6	133.9	134.4	131.9
2005	132.7	133.3	133.9	135.2	136.3	137.6	137.8	138.2	138.0	138.0	138.2	139.2	136.5
2006	138.1	139.4	139.9	140.4	140.6	141.1	141.2	141.0	140.3	139.4	138.4	138.6	139.9
2007	137.5	137.9	137.9	137.4	137.6	137.6	138.4	138.3	136.6	136.6	135.7	135.4	137.2
2008	133.7	133.1	131.6	131.4	131.1	130.7	130.0	129.6	128.6	127.3	125.4	123.7	129.7
2009	121.4	119.3	117.3	115.7	114.3	113.2	112.3	111.7	111.0	110.6	110.7	110.0	114.0

Employment by Industry: Phoenix-Mesa-Scottsdale, AZ, Selected Years, 1990–2009—*Continued*

(Numbers in thousands, not seasonally adjusted.)

Industry and year	January	February	March	April	May	June	July	August	September	October	November	December	Annual average
Service-Providing													
1990	796.2	808.9	815.8	823.7	826.5	812.7	792.7	794.4	816.9	824.0	836.5	837.1	815.5
2000	1255.9	1277.4	1287.7	1290.6	1298.9	1275.8	1257.1	1275.1	1301.9	1312.3	1326.3	1340.4	1291.6
2001	1296.9	1320.1	1329.5	1324.8	1320.4	1301.0	1279.2	1296.6	1313.9	1321.8	1327.9	1334.6	1313.9
2002	1300.7	1315.9	1326.5	1339.1	1334.4	1321.0	1293.7	1316.6	1330.8	1344.7	1369.6	1370.5	1330.3
2003	1329.9	1349.4	1357.6	1361.4	1361.8	1341.7	1319.4	1344.1	1356.5	1377.1	1391.0	1401.6	1357.6
2004	1364.2	1383.9	1395.8	1407.9	1407.5	1389.3	1377.2	1395.7	1413.6	1440.0	1454.4	1468.1	1408.1
2005	1430.6	1455.2	1466.9	1485.9	1485.1	1463.2	1455.1	1479.4	1506.4	1515.0	1534.6	1544.2	1485.1
2006	1516.8	1544.3	1557.3	1559.3	1565.0	1541.8	1525.6	1551.1	1574.1	1586.3	1603.3	1612.6	1561.5
2007	1571.7	1596.4	1608.8	1604.5	1607.9	1583.6	1567.9	1596.1	1611.2	1623.7	1641.2	1646.6	1605.0
2008	1608.3	1622.5	1621.7	1615.9	1610.4	1573.2	1543.6	1576.0	1585.6	1586.9	1591.9	1586.4	1593.5
2009	1537.3	1539.5	1536.9	1527.6	1518.1	1475.4	1455.5	1471.7	1484.8	1502.2	1515.1	1515.2	1506.6
Trade, Transportation, and Utilities													
1990	220.1	219.1	220.4	219.9	220.9	221.1	217.4	218.1	220.3	220.9	227.1	228.9	221.2
2000	316.9	317.0	316.3	315.6	316.2	318.7	316.3	318.7	321.1	324.7	334.2	340.7	321.4
2001	326.1	324.3	323.4	323.2	322.7	323.0	320.5	320.8	320.7	324.6	330.0	333.0	324.4
2002	321.6	318.8	320.9	322.7	324.0	325.3	322.2	323.2	324.6	326.9	335.0	340.3	325.5
2003	326.5	325.4	325.5	325.2	325.5	324.8	324.4	325.8	325.9	332.2	340.2	345.0	328.8
2004	333.7	333.8	334.8	336.9	337.4	337.5	338.1	339.1	337.4	345.3	354.1	359.3	340.6
2005	352.1	353.3	354.9	357.4	358.0	358.0	361.0	362.0	364.1	366.7	376.3	381.4	362.1
2006	371.4	371.2	374.1	375.2	375.6	375.6	377.2	378.5	378.7	384.2	393.3	399.3	379.5
2007	386.5	385.9	386.9	387.3	388.3	388.4	389.4	390.6	391.9	394.1	403.2	408.3	391.7
2008	391.7	389.9	388.4	386.1	386.2	385.0	378.9	379.6	377.0	377.7	381.9	381.9	383.7
2009	367.0	360.7	359.0	355.3	354.4	352.1	350.6	350.1	348.1	352.2	357.6	362.4	355.8
Wholesale Trade													
1990	50.8	51.0	51.2	50.8	51.4	51.7	51.1	51.0	50.7	50.7	50.8	50.6	51.0
2000	76.7	77.4	77.9	77.6	77.6	78.4	78.5	78.7	79.0	79.5	80.0	80.7	78.5
2001	80.3	80.9	80.9	80.4	80.4	79.9	79.4	79.3	78.6	78.4	78.2	78.1	79.6
2002	76.9	77.1	77.6	78.0	78.9	79.0	78.8	78.8	78.7	78.9	79.1	79.0	78.4
2003	77.9	78.0	77.8	77.7	78.0	77.8	77.0	77.1	76.9	76.8	77.1	77.5	77.4
2004	77.8	78.1	78.2	78.4	78.6	78.8	79.7	79.8	78.6	80.5	80.7	81.0	79.2
2005	80.4	81.3	81.8	82.5	82.6	82.7	83.3	83.3	83.5	83.9	84.7	85.3	82.9
2006	84.7	85.4	85.7	86.3	86.5	87.0	87.4	87.6	87.9	88.5	88.5	89.1	87.1
2007	88.0	88.5	88.9	89.1	89.3	89.9	90.4	90.4	90.3	90.6	90.7	91.0	89.8
2008	89.5	90.0	89.8	89.6	89.9	89.5	89.0	89.2	89.1	89.3	88.6	88.0	89.3
2009	86.5	85.7	84.9	84.2	83.6	83.1	83.2	83.1	82.3	83.2	84.7	86.4	84.2
Retail Trade													
1990	130.0	128.4	128.9	129.6	129.7	129.7	127.2	127.7	129.3	129.8	135.7	137.6	130.3
2000	182.8	182.5	182.2	181.8	182.3	183.6	181.1	182.7	184.3	187.0	195.2	200.5	185.5
2001	187.8	185.2	184.4	184.3	183.1	183.8	182.2	182.4	183.2	187.5	193.6	197.1	186.2
2002	187.2	184.3	185.3	186.4	186.5	186.8	184.1	184.8	186.3	187.7	195.5	201.0	188.0
2003	189.0	187.9	188.2	188.2	188.3	188.1	188.7	189.9	190.0	195.7	203.3	207.4	192.0
2004	196.4	196.2	196.6	198.2	198.6	198.5	197.9	198.8	198.7	203.0	211.7	216.8	201.0
2005	210.5	210.5	211.8	213.5	213.3	213.2	215.4	215.7	217.0	219.4	227.2	230.9	216.5
2006	223.2	222.3	224.7	224.6	224.6	224.3	225.0	225.4	224.8	229.8	238.5	242.6	227.5
2007	231.9	230.6	231.3	231.2	231.5	230.9	231.8	232.6	233.7	235.6	244.5	247.8	234.5
2008	235.0	232.3	231.2	229.0	228.9	228.4	223.3	223.6	221.4	222.3	226.6	227.0	227.4
2009	215.4	210.6	209.9	208.4	208.2	206.7	205.4	205.1	204.8	208.2	211.9	213.5	209.0
Transportation and Utilities													
1990	39.3	39.7	40.3	39.5	39.8	39.7	39.1	39.4	40.3	40.4	40.6	40.7	39.9
2000	57.4	57.1	56.2	56.2	56.3	56.7	56.7	57.3	57.8	58.2	59.0	59.5	57.4
2001	58.0	58.2	58.1	58.5	59.2	59.3	58.9	59.1	58.9	58.7	58.2	57.8	58.6
2002	57.5	57.4	58.0	58.3	58.6	59.5	59.3	59.6	59.6	60.3	60.4	60.3	59.1
2003	59.6	59.5	59.5	59.3	59.2	58.9	58.7	58.8	59.0	59.7	59.8	60.1	59.3
2004	59.5	59.5	60.0	60.3	60.2	60.2	60.5	60.5	60.1	61.8	61.7	61.5	60.5
2005	61.2	61.5	61.3	61.4	62.1	62.1	62.3	63.0	63.6	63.4	64.4	65.2	62.6
2006	63.5	63.5	63.7	64.3	64.5	64.3	64.8	65.5	66.0	65.9	66.3	67.6	65.0
2007	66.6	66.8	66.7	67.0	67.5	67.6	67.2	67.6	67.9	67.9	68.0	69.5	67.5
2008	67.2	67.6	67.4	67.5	67.4	67.1	66.6	66.8	66.5	66.1	66.7	66.9	67.0
2009	65.1	64.4	64.2	62.7	62.6	62.3	62.0	61.9	61.0	60.8	61.0	62.5	62.5
Information													
1990	23.3	23.5	23.3	23.9	24.0	24.3	24.3	24.1	23.9	23.6	23.9	23.7	23.8
2000	39.3	40.0	42.4	42.8	43.1	43.2	42.8	42.6	42.2	41.3	41.7	42.3	42.0
2001	41.3	42.4	42.1	42.4	41.6	42.1	41.6	41.5	41.1	41.0	41.4	40.8	41.6
2002	40.7	40.5	40.1	40.4	39.9	39.4	39.4	39.1	38.3	37.7	38.3	38.5	39.4
2003	37.5	37.7	38.0	38.1	37.8	37.9	37.2	37.0	36.5	36.5	37.1	36.9	37.3
2004	36.4	36.2	36.6	36.5	35.7	35.5	34.4	33.4	32.6	32.6	32.9	32.5	34.6
2005	32.2	32.9	33.2	34.0	34.1	33.7	33.3	33.0	32.6	32.9	33.5	34.0	33.3
2006	33.1	33.2	33.3	32.8	32.9	32.7	32.1	32.1	31.3	31.1	31.7	32.1	32.4
2007	30.1	31.0	30.9	31.2	31.8	31.8	31.6	31.2	31.0	30.6	31.5	31.1	31.2
2008	30.6	31.6	32.0	31.3	32.3	32.1	30.9	30.6	31.1	30.3	30.7	30.6	31.2
2009	29.7	30.0	29.6	30.7	31.2	30.5	29.0	28.8	28.2	28.4	28.2	27.7	29.3

Employment by Industry: Phoenix-Mesa-Scottsdale, AZ, Selected Years, 1990–2009—*Continued*

(Numbers in thousands, not seasonally adjusted.)

Industry and year	January	February	March	April	May	June	July	August	September	October	November	December	Annual average
Financial Activities													
1990	78.5	78.8	79.5	80.3	80.4	80.6	80.3	80.4	79.5	79.6	79.6	79.2	79.7
2000	122.5	124.7	124.7	124.8	125.6	127.0	126.1	126.7	127.5	127.9	128.6	129.8	126.3
2001	125.9	127.4	128.6	128.2	128.9	129.4	130.1	130.7	131.4	130.9	131.3	132.4	129.6
2002	129.8	131.0	130.4	131.7	130.8	130.9	130.3	130.5	130.3	131.6	133.3	134.0	131.2
2003	132.2	132.8	134.0	133.8	134.5	134.8	135.2	136.0	135.1	134.8	135.3	136.0	134.5
2004	134.6	135.3	136.1	138.1	137.9	138.2	139.1	139.4	139.2	141.3	141.8	142.9	138.7
2005	141.7	143.1	143.3	145.5	145.7	146.1	147.3	148.4	149.1	150.5	151.0	152.0	147.0
2006	150.6	151.8	152.6	152.3	152.9	153.3	153.3	153.9	154.1	154.6	154.9	156.1	153.4
2007	154.0	155.2	155.7	155.8	155.4	154.9	154.0	153.1	152.3	151.1	151.0	151.2	153.6
2008	148.1	149.2	149.0	148.5	148.2	147.9	147.0	146.5	146.1	146.3	145.3	145.0	147.3
2009	141.6	141.6	141.3	140.2	140.3	139.7	139.2	138.8	137.7	136.7	137.1	137.7	139.3
Professional and Business Services													
1990	107.1	108.1	109.6	110.5	110.2	111.2	111.5	112.6	112.2	110.7	111.0	111.3	110.5
2000	248.6	253.8	258.2	262.0	265.3	265.7	264.1	268.3	268.8	270.7	271.1	272.8	264.1
2001	260.1	264.2	267.8	265.4	263.7	263.8	257.3	257.7	257.4	253.9	250.1	251.4	259.4
2002	244.1	247.5	252.3	256.2	256.0	256.4	253.2	256.2	254.7	254.2	255.8	255.9	253.5
2003	248.3	252.8	256.2	258.3	259.4	259.3	256.2	258.6	259.8	263.3	264.1	266.6	258.6
2004	257.2	260.4	264.8	270.9	271.5	273.9	275.0	275.8	278.4	284.3	285.3	288.4	273.8
2005	279.9	284.3	288.5	294.4	294.0	296.7	298.0	300.9	304.6	304.3	307.3	308.6	296.8
2006	302.8	310.0	313.1	315.4	317.8	321.4	319.1	322.7	325.7	326.5	327.3	328.7	319.2
2007	317.9	322.3	326.3	324.3	324.6	326.5	324.6	326.8	325.5	328.2	329.1	327.1	325.3
2008	316.7	319.6	316.8	314.8	312.5	309.2	306.4	307.9	305.4	304.4	301.7	298.8	309.5
2009	285.7	283.3	280.4	277.5	274.3	272.3	270.7	269.4	268.5	274.5	276.0	276.2	275.7
Education and Health Services													
1990	87.9	89.2	90.2	91.8	91.0	91.7	90.2	90.1	91.5	92.2	92.9	92.8	91.0
2000	134.5	136.5	137.6	136.8	137.1	136.9	135.3	137.0	138.5	138.9	139.6	141.1	137.5
2001	139.9	141.5	142.8	142.7	142.5	143.4	140.7	144.1	144.9	146.1	147.1	148.9	143.7
2002	148.5	149.9	151.0	150.8	152.0	152.3	149.5	152.7	154.0	156.9	158.7	159.4	153.0
2003	158.4	160.1	160.8	162.6	162.8	162.6	161.2	163.6	165.4	166.4	167.4	168.2	163.2
2004	167.9	169.6	170.4	172.5	172.8	173.0	171.2	173.6	175.0	178.0	179.0	180.5	173.6
2005	176.4	178.2	181.1	184.0	185.0	183.6	181.8	185.1	186.6	187.9	189.1	189.9	184.1
2006	189.3	192.1	194.0	194.9	195.4	194.7	193.7	197.5	198.8	200.1	201.4	203.5	196.3
2007	199.6	202.9	204.2	203.4	204.1	204.6	202.9	206.7	208.5	211.5	212.1	213.3	206.2
2008	210.7	214.1	214.8	216.5	217.5	216.4	215.5	218.7	220.7	221.9	223.2	224.8	217.9
2009	220.1	221.7	222.5	222.6	222.9	221.2	219.7	223.6	224.8	228.7	231.1	230.7	224.1
Leisure and Hospitality													
1990	103.1	105.8	106.6	107.2	105.8	103.8	98.0	97.9	100.3	103.1	105.9	105.5	103.6
2000	147.8	150.9	152.7	152.8	151.0	148.9	143.7	145.6	148.6	150.3	151.8	152.7	149.7
2001	151.7	155.7	158.7	156.7	155.2	152.3	146.5	147.0	148.3	151.3	152.9	153.6	152.5
2002	148.9	153.1	155.5	158.0	157.1	153.8	148.9	149.6	149.8	152.7	157.3	157.0	153.5
2003	154.2	157.4	159.3	160.3	159.1	155.1	150.4	151.1	152.3	156.1	158.0	159.1	156.0
2004	157.5	160.8	161.7	164.2	163.9	160.9	157.6	158.1	159.8	162.9	165.1	167.0	161.9
2005	163.5	167.3	170.6	174.0	173.0	169.0	166.2	167.1	170.8	172.1	174.8	175.6	170.4
2006	175.5	179.6	182.6	183.5	182.4	180.3	175.1	176.2	179.4	181.2	184.7	185.1	180.5
2007	182.8	186.9	190.5	189.8	189.1	184.6	177.8	181.0	183.4	187.4	190.2	191.1	186.2
2008	188.0	190.4	192.6	191.5	187.7	184.2	178.6	180.0	180.5	180.5	181.6	180.0	184.6
2009	177.9	179.9	182.9	181.2	178.5	173.3	168.2	169.1	167.7	171.2	172.8	172.2	174.6
Other Services													
1990	36.1	36.5	36.8	38.5	38.7	38.9	38.2	38.2	38.4	38.9	39.0	39.3	38.1
2000	54.0	55.0	55.5	54.5	54.9	55.4	54.7	54.6	54.6	54.9	55.1	55.4	54.9
2001	57.0	58.2	59.1	58.7	59.3	60.6	59.9	60.1	60.1	59.4	59.6	59.6	59.3
2002	59.9	60.4	61.1	61.9	62.1	62.8	61.4	61.7	61.9	61.9	62.0	62.1	61.6
2003	61.0	61.2	61.8	61.0	61.3	61.5	62.6	63.3	63.5	63.9	64.4	64.5	62.5
2004	63.2	64.2	64.5	63.6	63.6	63.9	64.2	64.3	64.3	64.6	64.6	65.0	64.2
2005	63.7	64.3	65.2	65.6	66.0	66.2	66.1	66.1	66.8	67.0	67.4	67.8	66.0
2006	70.5	72.2	73.4	71.1	72.1	73.5	69.1	69.7	70.7	69.3	70.2	70.5	71.0
2007	70.0	71.7	72.4	71.1	72.2	73.3	71.2	71.0	72.5	72.5	73.4	73.9	72.1
2008	73.3	74.1	74.6	73.8	73.8	74.0	73.6	73.4	73.3	72.3	72.6	72.0	73.4
2009	70.0	70.6	70.5	68.9	69.2	69.4	68.3	68.2	67.9	66.7	67.3	66.2	68.6
Government													
1990	140.1	147.9	149.4	151.6	154.6	141.1	132.8	133.0	150.8	155.0	157.1	156.4	147.5
2000	192.3	199.5	200.3	201.3	205.7	180.0	174.1	181.6	200.6	203.6	204.2	205.6	195.7
2001	194.9	206.4	207.0	207.5	206.5	186.4	182.6	194.7	210.0	214.6	215.5	214.9	203.4
2002	207.2	214.7	215.2	217.4	212.5	200.1	188.8	203.6	217.2	222.8	229.2	223.3	212.7
2003	211.8	222.0	222.0	222.1	221.4	205.7	192.2	208.7	218.0	223.9	224.5	225.3	216.4
2004	213.7	223.6	223.9	225.2	224.7	206.4	197.6	212.0	226.9	231.0	231.6	232.5	220.8
2005	221.1	231.8	230.1	231.0	229.3	209.0	201.4	216.8	231.8	233.6	235.2	234.9	225.5
2006	223.6	234.2	234.2	234.1	235.9	210.3	206.0	220.5	235.4	239.3	239.8	237.3	229.2
2007	230.8	240.5	241.9	241.6	242.4	219.5	216.4	235.7	246.1	248.3	250.7	250.6	238.7
2008	249.2	253.6	253.5	253.4	252.2	224.4	212.7	239.3	251.5	253.5	254.9	253.3	246.0
2009	245.3	251.7	250.7	251.2	247.3	216.9	209.8	223.7	241.9	243.8	245.0	242.1	239.1

Employment by Industry: Pittsburgh, PA, Selected Years, 1990–2009

(Numbers in thousands, not seasonally adjusted.)

Industry and year	January	February	March	April	May	June	July	August	September	October	November	December	Annual average
Total Nonfarm													
1990	1011.5	1016.4	1025.9	1037.0	1045.1	1052.8	1045.8	1042.2	1049.3	1050.9	1052.6	1049.5	1039.9
2000	1115.3	1120.0	1132.8	1147.4	1156.8	1160.5	1151.4	1142.2	1157.1	1158.2	1162.5	1159.8	1147.0
2001	1137.9	1142.6	1149.7	1158.1	1164.1	1172.1	1154.2	1150.2	1154.2	1154.1	1156.8	1152.8	1153.9
2002	1123.3	1125.7	1134.2	1142.3	1153.6	1158.7	1141.6	1139.5	1146.4	1148.9	1149.3	1141.3	1142.1
2003	1117.8	1113.2	1121.5	1134.2	1141.8	1147.6	1130.0	1128.2	1137.8	1145.6	1146.4	1143.9	1134.0
2004	1110.6	1110.2	1122.3	1133.3	1143.5	1151.8	1134.4	1127.4	1137.7	1143.2	1145.3	1143.3	1133.6
2005	1110.9	1110.8	1118.2	1134.7	1142.6	1147.7	1133.6	1129.6	1138.9	1141.0	1144.3	1141.2	1132.8
2006	1110.3	1115.0	1124.9	1135.7	1145.4	1151.5	1136.1	1130.9	1144.3	1149.1	1151.1	1150.7	1137.1
2007	1120.3	1119.9	1132.3	1142.0	1156.1	1164.4	1147.4	1145.0	1151.8	1157.8	1159.7	1156.7	1146.1
2008	1125.9	1128.0	1135.5	1150.2	1161.9	1165.3	1151.1	1147.6	1154.7	1160.1	1157.0	1149.6	1148.9
2009	1112.5	1111.4	1114.3	1123.4	1132.4	1132.3	1115.9	1111.7	1118.6	1124.8	1125.8	1120.0	1120.3
Total Private													
1990	887.0	888.9	897.3	908.0	916.9	924.4	925.0	925.5	926.0	922.8	923.8	921.3	913.9
2000	988.3	990.7	1001.2	1016.1	1023.2	1031.8	1032.0	1026.8	1030.8	1028.6	1031.6	1030.1	1019.3
2001	1009.4	1012.4	1018.8	1026.9	1033.3	1044.3	1036.4	1034.7	1026.5	1023.1	1024.5	1022.1	1026.0
2002	994.9	994.0	1002.4	1010.3	1021.4	1028.3	1021.4	1022.2	1018.5	1016.5	1015.4	1008.8	1012.8
2003	987.8	980.5	987.9	1001.2	1009.6	1016.7	1011.6	1012.4	1009.3	1012.8	1012.8	1011.7	1004.5
2004	981.4	979.0	990.1	1000.5	1011.2	1020.8	1016.7	1013.8	1010.7	1012.7	1013.5	1012.7	1005.3
2005	983.1	980.8	987.3	1003.7	1012.3	1018.3	1017.6	1017.6	1013.2	1011.7	1013.1	1011.1	1005.8
2006	983.4	984.9	994.2	1005.1	1015.0	1022.3	1018.9	1017.3	1017.6	1019.7	1020.4	1020.7	1010.0
2007	993.6	990.4	1002.0	1012.2	1027.5	1037.1	1029.8	1028.8	1026.4	1029.4	1030.2	1027.6	1019.6
2008	1000.5	999.3	1006.2	1021.1	1033.6	1038.7	1032.7	1030.5	1028.3	1030.3	1026.8	1020.6	1022.4
2009	987.3	982.6	985.1	993.0	1002.8	1005.1	996.7	994.3	992.6	995.5	995.2	990.7	993.4
Goods-Producing													
1990	178.3	178.1	181.0	184.0	187.2	189.4	190.5	191.2	190.7	188.1	186.5	183.0	185.7
2000	183.6	183.0	187.5	191.3	194.1	196.4	198.5	198.0	199.2	195.4	193.8	190.3	192.6
2001	185.0	185.6	186.6	188.9	191.0	192.7	192.5	192.3	189.4	187.7	184.1	180.7	188.0
2002	172.5	173.1	174.9	178.3	181.1	182.6	181.3	182.7	180.8	180.0	176.7	172.2	178.0
2003	166.5	163.5	166.2	169.6	170.8	172.1	171.6	171.2	169.6	168.9	166.5	162.7	168.2
2004	154.4	153.1	156.8	160.8	164.2	166.8	167.0	165.9	164.6	164.0	162.0	159.0	161.6
2005	151.9	150.8	152.6	158.3	160.7	162.0	163.0	164.0	163.5	162.4	161.1	157.3	159.0
2006	152.1	152.5	155.8	159.5	161.5	163.0	164.2	164.9	164.8	163.7	162.7	160.5	160.4
2007	155.7	153.3	157.5	161.1	164.8	166.8	166.3	166.0	165.4	164.9	163.1	159.2	162.0
2008	154.2	152.6	155.3	160.3	163.6	165.3	165.7	165.8	165.0	164.6	160.7	156.1	160.8
2009	148.2	146.2	146.7	148.2	149.0	149.7	148.5	147.5	146.8	146.4	144.6	140.8	146.9
Mining and Logging													
2005	5.1	5.1	4.7	5.1	5.0	5.0	5.0	5.0	5.0	4.9	5.0	5.0	5.0
2006	4.9	4.9	4.9	4.9	4.9	4.9	4.9	4.9	4.8	4.8	4.8	4.8	4.9
2007	4.8	4.7	4.7	4.7	4.8	4.9	5.0	5.0	4.9	4.9	5.0	5.0	4.9
2008	5.0	5.0	5.0	5.1	5.3	5.5	5.5	5.6	5.6	5.7	5.7	5.7	5.4
Construction													
2005	46.0	45.3	47.0	52.3	54.8	55.6	57.0	57.9	57.9	57.3	56.0	52.1	53.3
2006	48.1	48.6	51.4	54.7	56.3	57.2	58.4	59.1	59.6	58.5	57.1	54.7	55.3
2007	50.6	48.7	52.5	55.8	59.2	60.5	60.5	60.6	60.8	60.4	58.3	54.4	56.9
2008	50.6	49.2	51.6	56.7	59.4	60.4	61.0	61.4	61.1	60.9	57.8	53.9	57.0
Manufacturing													
1990	129.5	129.4	129.8	130.0	130.0	131.1	131.9	132.1	132.1	130.6	130.6	129.9	130.6
2000	128.9	129.0	129.5	128.7	128.9	130.2	131.1	130.6	130.3	129.5	129.5	130.0	129.7
2001	127.9	127.4	126.6	125.8	124.5	124.7	123.7	123.1	121.8	120.6	119.5	119.0	123.7
2002	116.5	115.9	115.5	115.3	115.5	116.0	114.9	115.0	114.5	114.4	113.7	113.5	115.1
2003	112.4	110.2	110.0	110.4	109.7	109.6	108.3	107.3	106.3	105.5	104.7	104.5	108.2
2004	102.8	102.2	102.5	103.2	103.0	103.9	103.4	103.1	102.7	102.4	102.4	102.3	102.8
2005	100.8	100.4	100.9	100.9	100.9	101.4	101.0	101.1	100.6	100.2	100.1	100.2	100.7
2006	99.1	99.0	99.5	99.9	100.3	100.9	100.9	100.9	100.4	100.4	100.8	101.0	100.3
2007	100.3	99.9	100.3	100.6	100.8	101.4	100.8	100.4	99.7	99.6	99.8	99.8	100.3
2008	98.6	98.4	98.7	98.5	98.9	99.4	99.2	98.8	98.3	98.0	97.2	96.5	98.4
2009	93.9	91.8	90.6	89.7	88.6	88.3	87.5	86.9	86.3	86.1	86.0	85.9	88.5
Service-Providing													
1990	833.2	838.3	844.9	853.0	857.9	863.4	855.3	851.0	858.6	862.8	866.1	866.5	854.3
2000	931.7	937.0	945.3	956.1	962.7	964.1	952.9	944.2	957.9	962.8	968.7	969.5	954.4
2001	952.9	957.0	963.1	969.2	973.1	979.4	961.7	957.9	964.8	966.4	972.7	972.1	965.9
2002	950.8	952.6	959.3	964.0	972.5	976.1	960.3	956.8	965.6	968.9	972.6	969.1	964.1
2003	951.3	949.7	955.3	964.6	971.0	975.5	958.4	957.0	968.2	976.7	979.9	981.2	965.7
2004	956.2	957.1	965.5	972.5	979.3	985.0	967.4	961.5	973.1	979.2	983.3	984.3	972.0
2005	959.0	960.0	965.6	976.4	981.9	985.7	970.6	965.6	975.4	978.6	983.2	983.9	973.8
2006	958.2	962.5	969.1	976.2	983.9	988.5	971.9	966.0	979.5	985.4	988.4	990.2	976.7
2007	964.6	966.6	974.8	980.9	991.3	997.6	981.1	979.0	986.4	992.9	996.6	997.5	984.1
2008	971.7	975.4	980.2	989.9	998.3	1000.0	985.4	981.8	989.7	995.5	996.3	993.5	988.1
2009	964.3	965.2	967.6	975.2	983.4	982.6	967.4	964.2	971.8	978.4	981.2	979.2	973.4

Employment by Industry: Pittsburgh, PA, Selected Years, 1990–2009—*Continued*

(Numbers in thousands, not seasonally adjusted.)

Industry and year	January	February	March	April	May	June	July	August	September	October	November	December	Annual average
Trade, Transportation, and Utilities													
1990	223.5	222.2	222.9	224.1	226.3	227.1	224.8	224.9	224.8	226.4	229.4	231.0	225.6
2000	239.1	236.6	237.5	241.6	242.8	244.4	241.7	241.6	242.4	245.0	249.0	252.6	242.9
2001	243.9	240.6	241.4	242.0	243.5	244.7	239.9	239.8	240.3	241.0	245.4	246.3	242.4
2002	236.6	233.5	234.6	235.2	236.9	237.6	233.9	234.0	234.5	236.3	239.9	241.6	236.2
2003	231.2	227.9	228.2	230.0	231.9	232.7	229.6	230.6	231.7	235.0	238.5	241.4	232.3
2004	231.9	229.5	230.7	231.3	232.6	232.8	229.3	229.2	229.3	231.2	234.6	237.3	231.6
2005	226.6	224.0	224.8	225.9	227.6	227.9	225.5	225.9	225.7	227.8	231.9	235.3	227.4
2006	226.3	223.2	224.4	224.5	226.3	226.2	222.7	223.0	224.5	226.9	230.7	233.9	226.1
2007	225.9	221.5	223.3	223.4	225.9	226.2	222.8	222.1	222.6	224.2	228.8	231.3	224.8
2008	223.6	220.0	220.9	221.1	223.3	223.2	219.4	218.7	220.3	222.6	225.0	227.6	222.1
2009	217.2	213.8	213.0	213.7	215.8	215.0	210.9	211.0	212.5	213.9	217.1	219.6	214.5
Wholesale Trade													
1990	48.4	48.6	48.7	48.9	49.1	49.5	49.3	49.3	49.1	49.2	49.5	49.0	49.1
2000	45.8	46.0	46.3	46.9	47.1	47.4	47.0	47.2	46.9	47.3	47.3	47.2	46.9
2001	46.7	46.8	46.9	47.2	47.2	47.4	47.3	47.2	46.6	46.2	46.1	45.9	46.8
2002	45.3	45.1	45.2	45.6	46.0	46.3	45.9	45.7	45.4	45.6	45.7	45.4	45.6
2003	45.2	45.1	45.2	45.6	45.8	45.9	46.0	45.9	45.9	46.3	46.4	46.6	45.8
2004	45.8	45.7	45.9	45.8	46.1	46.6	46.7	46.7	46.2	46.3	46.3	46.4	46.2
2005	46.4	46.6	46.7	47.0	47.4	47.7	47.7	47.8	47.6	47.8	48.0	48.1	47.4
2006	48.0	48.0	48.1	48.3	48.7	49.1	49.1	49.2	48.9	49.2	49.1	49.4	48.8
2007	49.1	48.9	49.2	49.1	49.2	49.5	49.5	49.6	49.1	49.0	49.1	49.1	49.2
2008	48.9	48.8	48.9	49.2	49.5	49.7	49.5	49.4	49.0	49.0	48.7	48.6	49.1
2009	47.8	47.4	47.1	47.0	47.0	46.9	46.6	46.5	46.3	46.2	46.2	45.9	46.7
Retail Trade													
1990	130.5	129.0	129.1	129.5	131.0	131.5	130.9	131.0	129.7	130.9	133.9	136.0	131.1
2000	139.5	137.1	137.2	140.3	141.2	142.4	141.6	141.7	141.0	141.6	145.7	149.0	141.5
2001	141.9	138.6	139.2	139.2	140.2	141.5	139.3	139.4	138.2	138.5	143.2	145.6	140.4
2002	138.1	135.5	136.3	136.7	138.0	139.3	138.4	138.5	137.1	138.0	142.1	144.8	138.6
2003	136.6	133.8	134.3	135.7	137.0	138.2	137.5	138.2	136.9	138.8	142.2	145.1	137.8
2004	137.7	135.6	136.4	136.9	137.8	138.4	137.7	137.4	135.5	136.5	140.3	142.5	137.7
2005	133.9	131.5	132.0	132.8	134.0	134.7	135.0	135.0	132.0	133.8	137.5	140.3	134.4
2006	132.6	129.8	130.6	130.6	131.8	132.4	131.2	131.5	129.8	131.8	135.9	138.3	132.2
2007	131.6	127.7	129.0	129.0	131.2	131.9	131.4	130.9	128.7	130.6	135.3	137.4	131.2
2008	130.9	127.6	128.5	128.0	129.3	129.8	129.2	128.7	127.5	129.0	131.6	133.8	129.5
2009	126.1	123.3	123.2	123.8	125.7	126.3	125.5	125.5	123.8	125.0	128.1	130.2	125.5
Transportation and Utilities													
1990	44.6	44.6	45.1	45.7	46.2	46.1	44.6	44.6	46.0	46.3	46.0	46.0	45.5
2000	53.8	53.5	54.0	54.4	54.5	54.6	53.1	52.7	54.5	56.1	56.0	56.4	54.5
2001	55.3	55.2	55.3	55.6	56.1	55.8	53.3	53.2	55.5	56.3	56.1	54.8	55.2
2002	53.2	52.9	53.1	52.9	52.9	52.0	49.6	49.8	52.0	52.7	52.1	51.4	52.1
2003	49.4	49.0	48.7	48.7	49.1	48.6	46.1	46.5	48.9	49.9	49.9	49.7	48.7
2004	48.4	48.2	48.4	48.6	48.7	47.8	44.9	45.1	47.6	48.4	48.0	48.4	47.7
2005	46.3	45.9	46.1	46.1	46.2	45.5	42.8	43.1	46.1	46.2	46.4	46.9	45.6
2006	45.7	45.4	45.7	45.6	45.8	44.7	42.4	47.3	45.0	45.9	45.7	46.2	45.1
2007	45.2	44.9	45.1	45.3	45.5	44.8	41.9	41.6	44.8	44.6	44.4	44.8	44.4
2008	43.8	43.6	43.5	43.9	44.5	43.7	40.7	40.6	43.8	44.6	44.7	45.2	43.6
2009	43.3	43.1	42.7	42.9	43.1	41.8	38.8	39.0	42.4	42.7	42.8	43.5	42.2
Information													
1990	20.8	20.9	21.0	21.2	21.2	21.3	21.5	21.4	21.3	21.1	21.0	21.1	21.2
2000	25.8	25.9	25.9	25.1	25.4	25.7	26.3	23.6	26.3	26.7	26.9	27.1	25.9
2001	27.4	27.5	27.5	27.1	27.4	27.6	27.4	27.3	27.0	26.8	27.0	27.0	27.3
2002	26.7	26.4	26.4	26.1	26.3	26.1	25.9	25.8	25.4	25.2	25.5	25.5	25.9
2003	25.6	25.4	25.6	25.3	25.5	25.5	25.2	25.3	24.9	24.7	24.9	25.1	25.2
2004	24.8	24.5	24.5	24.2	24.3	24.3	24.1	23.8	23.5	23.3	23.2	23.1	24.0
2005	23.2	23.0	23.0	23.0	23.3	23.5	23.3	23.2	22.9	23.0	23.2	23.3	23.2
2006	22.9	22.9	23.0	23.0	23.0	23.1	23.0	22.9	22.6	22.6	22.4	22.7	22.8
2007	22.0	21.9	22.1	21.8	21.9	22.2	21.9	21.8	21.4	21.2	21.2	21.6	21.8
2008	21.3	21.2	21.1	21.3	21.4	21.3	20.8	20.5	20.2	20.1	20.1	20.2	20.8
2009	19.9	19.8	19.8	20.0	19.8	20.0	19.9	19.7	19.5	19.5	19.6	19.7	19.8
Financial Activities													
1990	58.1	58.3	58.6	58.7	59.0	59.3	59.6	59.8	59.5	59.3	59.2	59.2	59.1
2000	67.0	66.9	66.8	67.4	67.5	68.0	67.8	67.5	66.9	66.8	67.1	67.3	67.3
2001	67.5	67.7	67.9	67.3	67.7	68.4	68.6	68.4	67.5	67.4	67.6	67.8	67.8
2002	67.7	68.0	68.3	68.0	68.6	69.1	69.1	69.1	68.5	68.2	68.3	68.6	68.5
2003	69.0	68.9	69.2	69.8	70.3	70.7	71.2	71.2	70.6	70.2	70.2	70.3	70.1
2004	70.0	69.7	69.9	69.5	69.8	70.2	70.3	70.0	69.1	69.0	68.9	69.1	69.6
2005	68.7	68.6	68.9	69.0	69.3	69.5	70.1	70.0	69.2	69.1	69.2	69.2	69.2
2006	68.1	68.3	68.4	68.7	69.0	69.6	69.0	68.8	67.9	67.7	67.7	67.9	68.4
2007	67.6	67.8	68.0	67.8	68.2	68.8	68.9	68.8	68.0	67.7	67.8	67.6	68.1
2008	66.8	67.1	67.5	67.7	68.3	69.0	68.9	68.8	67.6	67.4	67.4	67.4	67.8
2009	66.9	66.9	66.8	67.0	67.4	68.1	68.0	67.9	67.3	67.1	67.0	66.7	67.3

Employment by Industry: Pittsburgh, PA, Selected Years, 1990–2009—*Continued*

(Numbers in thousands, not seasonally adjusted.)

Industry and year	January	February	March	April	May	June	July	August	September	October	November	December	Annual average
Professional and Business Services													
1990	121.9	122.8	124.3	125.6	126.4	128.6	128.9	129.4	129.1	127.4	127.5	127.2	126.6
2000	134.8	135.4	136.4	140.3	139.9	142.1	142.3	141.9	140.4	139.1	139.2	138.5	139.2
2001	138.5	138.9	139.8	142.2	141.7	143.5	141.7	142.3	140.7	140.1	140.1	139.2	140.7
2002	134.6	134.0	134.6	136.3	137.2	138.5	138.8	139.0	137.1	136.5	136.6	136.6	136.7
2003	131.9	130.6	131.3	134.1	135.0	135.5	135.7	136.9	135.5	136.3	136.7	136.7	134.6
2004	133.7	133.8	135.3	138.4	139.6	141.8	142.5	143.7	143.1	144.7	145.2	145.7	140.6
2005	141.4	141.3	142.5	145.8	145.8	146.8	147.4	147.7	146.1	145.9	145.9	145.5	145.2
2006	141.5	142.5	144.2	146.4	147.4	149.7	151.1	151.2	150.7	151.4	151.6	150.8	148.2
2007	148.2	149.4	151.1	154.2	155.7	159.1	158.7	159.7	158.0	158.3	159.2	159.4	155.9
2008	156.2	156.8	157.2	160.6	161.1	162.8	163.2	163.0	161.0	160.7	160.3	158.6	160.1
2009	154.3	153.7	153.3	153.8	154.6	154.9	153.8	153.7	152.6	153.2	153.2	151.8	153.6
Education and Health Services													
1990	157.1	158.5	159.4	160.2	158.5	157.2	156.7	155.6	160.3	165.7	166.6	166.4	160.2
2000	194.9	198.3	198.7	199.0	196.2	194.4	194.8	193.7	199.1	202.1	203.0	202.3	198.0
2001	199.2	202.3	203.6	202.9	199.1	200.1	199.5	197.7	202.4	203.3	204.6	204.9	201.6
2002	205.8	208.3	209.8	208.2	206.5	205.6	203.6	202.2	207.2	209.6	209.9	205.9	206.9
2003	211.2	212.9	213.6	212.4	210.1	209.6	207.5	205.2	210.1	214.0	214.7	214.3	211.3
2004	211.7	213.3	214.4	214.7	212.6	212.3	211.4	208.6	213.6	217.0	218.4	218.2	213.9
2005	217.0	218.8	219.3	219.9	217.2	217.1	217.2	215.4	220.1	222.9	224.1	224.6	219.5
2006	221.0	223.6	223.9	223.8	222.0	220.3	219.5	217.9	223.6	226.0	227.3	227.1	223.0
2007	222.6	225.4	226.5	226.4	225.2	224.0	223.3	221.9	226.9	230.7	231.2	230.4	226.2
2008	226.3	229.9	230.1	231.0	229.4	227.4	226.5	225.8	231.1	234.1	235.3	234.0	230.1
2009	231.1	232.7	233.0	234.0	232.7	231.1	230.2	228.1	232.6	236.1	237.1	236.3	232.9
Leisure and Hospitality													
1990	82.1	82.6	84.3	88.0	91.8	94.5	95.4	95.8	93.3	88.5	87.5	87.3	89.3
1991	82.0	81.8	83.8	86.2	91.0	93.1	93.1	93.9	91.2	87.9	87.3	86.6	88.2
2000	87.8	88.9	91.8	95.3	101.3	104.0	103.9	104.0	100.0	96.6	95.5	94.9	97.0
2001	90.8	92.1	94.1	98.5	104.5	108.3	107.9	108.5	101.7	99.2	98.0	98.6	100.2
2002	94.2	93.8	96.3	100.5	106.6	109.8	109.6	110.6	107.2	102.8	100.6	100.3	102.7
2003	95.3	94.3	96.4	101.8	107.5	111.5	111.0	112.3	108.3	104.8	102.5	102.3	104.0
2004	96.2	96.8	99.2	102.6	108.7	112.2	111.4	112.5	108.6	104.7	102.5	101.7	104.8
2005	96.3	96.3	98.0	103.7	110.4	113.4	113.4	114.7	110.9	106.2	103.7	102.7	105.8
2006	97.2	97.9	100.2	104.4	110.7	114.6	113.6	113.5	109.1	107.5	104.2	104.1	106.4
2007	98.7	98.4	100.2	104.2	112.3	116.0	113.8	114.9	111.2	109.5	105.9	105.4	107.5
2008	100.0	99.9	102.0	106.4	113.4	116.1	114.6	114.9	110.7	108.4	105.7	104.2	108.0
Other Services													
1990	45.2	45.5	45.8	46.2	46.5	47.0	47.6	47.4	47.0	46.3	46.1	46.1	46.4
2000	55.3	55.7	56.6	56.1	56.0	56.8	56.7	56.5	56.5	56.9	57.1	57.1	56.4
2001	57.1	57.7	57.9	58.0	58.4	59.0	58.9	58.4	57.5	57.6	57.7	57.6	58.0
2002	56.8	56.9	57.5	57.7	58.2	59.0	59.2	58.8	57.8	57.9	57.9	58.1	58.0
2003	57.1	57.0	57.4	58.2	58.5	59.1	59.8	59.7	58.6	58.9	58.8	58.9	58.5
2004	58.7	58.3	59.3	59.0	59.4	60.4	60.7	60.1	58.9	58.8	58.7	58.6	59.2
2005	58.0	58.0	58.2	58.1	58.0	58.1	57.7	56.7	54.8	54.4	54.0	53.2	56.6
2006	54.3	54.0	54.3	54.8	55.1	55.8	55.8	55.1	54.4	53.9	53.8	53.7	54.6
2007	52.9	52.7	53.3	53.3	53.5	54.0	54.1	53.6	52.9	52.9	53.0	52.7	53.2
2008	52.1	51.8	52.1	52.7	53.1	53.6	53.6	53.0	52.4	52.4	52.3	52.5	52.6
2009	51.5	51.4	51.8	51.8	52.3	53.0	53.0	52.4	51.3	51.7	51.4	51.6	51.9
Government													
1990	124.5	127.5	128.6	129.0	128.2	128.4	120.8	116.7	123.3	128.1	128.8	128.2	126.0
2000	127.0	129.3	131.6	131.3	133.6	128.7	119.4	115.4	126.3	129.6	130.9	129.7	127.7
2001	128.5	130.2	130.9	131.2	130.8	127.8	117.8	115.5	127.7	131.0	132.3	130.7	127.9
2002	128.4	131.7	131.8	132.0	132.2	130.4	120.2	117.3	127.9	132.4	133.9	132.5	129.2
2003	130.0	132.7	133.6	133.0	132.2	130.9	118.4	115.8	128.5	132.8	133.6	132.2	129.4
2004	129.2	131.2	132.2	132.8	132.3	131.0	117.7	113.6	127.0	130.5	131.8	130.6	128.3
2005	127.8	130.0	130.9	131.0	130.3	129.4	116.0	112.0	125.7	129.3	131.2	130.1	127.0
2006	126.9	130.1	130.7	130.6	130.4	129.2	117.2	113.6	126.7	129.4	130.7	130.0	127.1
2007	126.7	129.5	130.3	129.8	128.6	127.3	117.6	116.2	125.4	128.4	129.5	129.1	126.5
2008	125.4	128.7	129.3	129.1	128.3	126.6	118.4	117.1	126.4	129.8	130.2	129.0	126.5
2009	125.2	128.8	129.2	130.4	129.6	127.2	119.2	117.4	126.0	129.3	130.6	129.3	126.9

Employment by Industry: Portland-Vancouver-Hillsboro, OR-WA, Selected Years, 1990–2009

(Numbers in thousands, not seasonally adjusted.)

Industry and year	January	February	March	April	May	June	July	August	September	October	November	December	Annual average
Total Nonfarm													
1990	706.9	707.6	717.1	724.7	731.1	737.9	731.0	741.4	741.2	740.4	743.3	741.8	730.4
2000	945.6	954.0	957.6	964.3	972.2	978.8	973.7	974.6	981.7	987.1	994.5	995.2	973.3
2001	970.6	973.2	974.0	973.4	974.5	975.9	957.1	954.3	962.2	960.8	960.0	956.6	966.1
2002	935.6	939.3	942.0	945.3	948.8	952.0	934.9	935.1	944.9	951.4	952.0	948.3	944.1
2003	926.7	927.4	928.9	930.8	933.5	934.3	926.6	929.3	936.5	943.8	946.8	947.1	934.3
2004	919.3	929.7	937.6	947.3	953.6	959.1	954.8	955.8	963.6	973.4	976.6	978.2	954.1
2005	954.3	962.8	969.0	975.6	981.0	985.9	980.1	983.7	990.8	1000.6	1007.8	1012.1	983.6
2006	986.1	995.1	1001.8	1008.8	1016.3	1021.3	1012.1	1013.5	1022.4	1031.7	1037.3	1037.6	1015.3
2007	1013.0	1022.3	1029.0	1029.4	1036.6	1038.0	1030.2	1031.1	1037.7	1047.8	1052.5	1051.4	1034.9
2008	1026.5	1033.3	1036.9	1040.4	1043.2	1041.0	1034.9	1032.2	1037.5	1036.3	1030.3	1018.2	1034.2
2009	988.0	984.9	979.3	977.8	978.6	974.4	963.4	958.9	961.9	968.5	967.8	965.2	972.4
Total Private													
1990	604.2	603.6	612.4	618.5	623.0	629.7	632.7	645.1	639.8	634.0	635.7	635.3	626.2
2000	816.5	822.4	825.5	831.7	836.6	844.6	849.1	853.1	856.8	854.6	860.9	861.7	842.8
2001	838.7	839.8	839.8	839.4	838.8	840.8	837.9	838.1	833.4	824.8	822.8	819.8	834.5
2002	801.1	802.2	804.0	807.2	809.5	812.6	814.3	817.6	815.7	814.5	813.6	811.1	810.3
2003	792.6	792.1	793.2	794.5	796.4	798.4	801.9	806.2	806.3	808.1	809.6	810.4	800.8
2004	784.7	792.9	799.5	809.1	814.9	819.7	825.3	828.9	830.3	834.0	836.5	838.4	817.9
2005	816.0	822.5	828.4	835.3	839.9	844.5	851.2	856.4	858.9	861.3	866.4	871.4	846.0
2006	847.8	854.7	860.3	867.3	872.9	878.3	881.5	885.4	888.8	890.6	893.7	895.4	876.4
2007	871.9	879.4	884.9	885.1	890.1	891.5	895.5	899.5	901.6	902.5	905.5	904.5	892.7
2008	880.8	886.2	888.6	891.8	893.1	891.2	893.8	893.9	894.7	886.8	878.5	867.4	887.2
2009	839.2	834.1	827.8	826.1	826.0	823.4	821.8	820.2	821.4	818.3	815.9	814.8	824.1
Goods-Producing													
1990	156.3	157.0	159.9	161.5	163.3	166.3	168.1	171.9	169.4	165.8	164.4	162.9	163.9
2000	191.0	192.3	193.3	194.1	196.1	200.0	202.5	203.0	204.9	201.1	201.7	200.7	198.4
2001	197.0	196.1	194.2	192.9	192.1	193.5	194.8	194.2	191.5	187.8	183.8	180.9	191.6
2002	176.0	175.7	175.6	175.6	176.0	178.1	180.4	182.5	180.0	177.7	175.0	172.4	177.1
2003	169.5	168.0	167.6	166.8	167.8	169.7	171.7	173.5	172.4	171.4	170.2	169.8	169.9
2004	164.5	166.9	169.1	171.8	174.0	176.9	180.8	182.1	182.1	181.7	179.3	179.1	175.7
2005	176.1	177.0	178.6	179.8	181.4	183.9	187.6	188.9	188.0	188.6	187.0	187.4	183.7
2006	184.0	185.4	186.7	188.1	189.8	193.3	196.0	197.2	196.9	195.3	193.0	192.3	191.5
2007	188.9	190.0	191.1	190.2	192.3	193.2	196.5	197.7	196.5	195.5	193.2	191.2	193.0
2008	186.7	186.9	186.8	186.3	187.2	187.9	189.6	189.1	188.0	183.6	179.6	174.3	185.5
2009	168.3	164.4	161.3	159.1	158.5	158.7	159.1	158.6	158.2	156.4	153.3	151.9	159.0
Mining and Logging													
1990	1.8	1.8	1.9	2.0	2.1	2.1	2.2	2.3	2.3	2.2	2.0	1.9	2.1
2000	1.8	1.9	1.8	1.8	1.8	2.0	1.9	2.0	1.9	1.9	1.9	1.8	1.9
2001	1.7	1.7	1.7	1.7	1.7	1.8	1.8	1.8	1.8	1.8	1.7	1.6	1.7
2002	1.5	1.5	1.5	1.6	1.6	1.7	1.8	1.8	1.8	1.8	1.7	1.6	1.7
2003	1.6	1.6	1.6	1.6	1.6	1.7	1.7	1.7	1.8	1.7	1.7	1.7	1.7
2004	1.5	1.5	1.6	1.6	1.7	1.7	1.8	1.8	1.8	1.8	1.7	1.7	1.7
2005	1.7	1.7	1.7	1.7	1.8	1.8	1.9	1.9	1.8	1.8	1.8	1.7	1.8
2006	1.6	1.6	1.6	1.6	1.7	1.8	1.8	1.8	1.8	1.7	1.6	1.6	1.7
2007	1.5	1.6	1.6	1.6	1.7	1.7	1.7	1.7	1.7	1.7	1.6	1.5	1.6
2008	1.5	1.5	1.5	1.5	1.6	1.6	1.6	1.7	1.6	1.6	1.5	1.4	1.6
2009	1.2	1.2	1.2	1.1	1.2	1.2	1.2	1.2	1.2	1.2	1.1	1.1	1.2
Construction													
1990	32.2	33.2	35.3	36.9	37.3	38.0	38.6	40.0	39.8	38.3	37.4	35.9	36.9
2000	48.7	49.3	49.9	50.9	51.8	53.5	55.3	56.6	57.1	56.1	54.9	54.2	53.2
2001	53.5	53.4	53.6	52.8	53.3	54.6	55.8	56.7	55.7	54.3	52.6	51.4	54.0
2002	49.3	49.6	49.9	50.1	50.8	51.8	53.6	55.3	54.2	53.5	51.6	49.6	51.6
2003	48.2	47.6	47.6	47.4	48.6	49.6	51.3	53.2	52.8	52.7	51.4	50.7	50.1
2004	47.4	49.0	50.2	51.8	53.3	55.0	56.8	57.8	57.5	57.1	55.8	55.2	53.9
2005	53.3	53.8	55.1	55.8	57.1	58.4	60.8	62.2	62.2	61.8	60.6	60.8	58.5
2006	58.3	59.4	60.1	61.0	62.2	64.3	65.6	66.7	66.6	65.9	64.5	63.7	63.2
2007	61.4	62.2	63.2	63.4	65.4	65.5	67.8	68.9	68.3	67.4	66.0	64.4	65.3
2008	60.9	61.0	61.0	60.9	61.9	62.5	63.2	63.3	62.7	60.4	57.2	54.4	60.8
2009	51.8	50.4	49.4	48.9	49.1	50.0	50.4	50.4	49.8	48.6	46.7	45.4	49.2
Manufacturing													
1990	122.3	122.0	122.7	122.6	123.9	126.2	127.3	129.6	127.3	125.3	125.0	125.1	124.9
2000	140.5	141.1	141.6	141.4	142.5	144.5	145.3	144.4	145.9	143.1	144.9	144.7	143.3
2001	141.8	141.0	138.9	138.4	137.1	137.1	137.2	135.7	134.0	131.7	129.5	127.9	135.9
2002	125.2	124.6	124.2	123.9	123.6	124.6	125.0	125.4	124.0	122.4	121.7	121.2	123.8
2003	119.7	118.8	118.4	117.8	117.6	118.4	118.7	118.6	117.8	117.0	117.1	117.4	118.1
2004	115.6	116.4	117.3	118.4	119.0	120.2	122.2	122.5	122.8	122.8	121.8	122.2	120.1
2005	121.1	121.5	121.8	122.3	122.5	123.7	124.9	124.8	124.0	125.0	124.6	124.9	123.4
2006	124.1	124.4	125.0	125.5	125.9	127.2	128.6	128.7	128.5	127.7	126.9	127.0	126.6
2007	126.0	126.2	126.3	125.2	125.2	126.0	127.0	127.1	126.5	126.4	125.6	125.3	126.1
2008	124.3	124.4	124.3	123.9	123.7	123.8	124.8	124.1	123.7	121.6	120.9	118.5	123.2
2009	115.3	112.8	110.7	109.1	108.2	107.5	107.5	107.0	107.2	106.6	105.5	105.4	108.6

Employment by Industry: Portland-Vancouver-Hillsboro, OR-WA, Selected Years, 1990–2009—*Continued*
(Numbers in thousands, not seasonally adjusted.)

Industry and year	January	February	March	April	May	June	July	August	September	October	November	December	Annual average
Service-Providing													
1990	550.6	550.6	557.3	563.3	567.9	571.6	563.0	569.5	571.8	574.6	578.9	578.9	566.5
2000	754.6	761.7	764.3	770.2	776.1	778.8	771.2	771.6	776.8	786.0	792.8	794.5	774.9
2001	773.6	777.1	779.8	780.5	782.4	782.4	762.3	760.1	770.7	773.0	776.2	775.7	774.5
2002	759.6	763.6	766.4	769.7	772.8	773.9	754.5	752.6	764.9	773.7	777.0	775.9	767.1
2003	757.2	759.4	761.3	764.0	765.7	764.6	754.9	755.8	764.1	772.4	776.6	777.3	764.4
2004	754.8	762.8	768.5	775.5	779.6	782.2	774.0	773.7	781.5	791.7	797.3	799.1	778.4
2005	778.2	785.8	790.4	795.8	799.6	802.0	792.5	794.8	802.8	812.0	820.8	824.7	800.0
2006	802.1	809.7	815.1	820.7	826.5	828.0	816.1	816.3	825.5	836.4	844.3	845.3	823.8
2007	824.1	832.3	837.9	839.2	844.3	844.8	833.7	833.4	841.2	852.3	859.3	860.2	841.9
2008	839.8	846.4	850.1	854.1	856.0	853.1	845.3	843.1	849.5	852.7	850.7	843.9	848.7
2009	819.7	820.5	818.0	818.7	820.1	815.7	804.3	800.3	803.7	812.1	814.5	813.3	813.4
Trade, Transportation, and Utilities													
1990	152.5	150.0	151.9	153.1	154.1	156.3	156.7	159.5	157.8	157.0	159.9	162.1	155.9
2000	197.3	196.3	196.4	197.8	198.7	201.2	201.6	202.0	201.4	202.7	207.3	209.1	201.0
2001	199.6	198.0	197.9	197.7	197.9	199.6	198.5	198.4	196.6	195.5	198.0	199.3	198.1
2002	191.6	189.9	190.1	190.8	191.9	193.0	193.4	192.6	192.0	191.8	194.8	197.1	·192.4
2003	189.8	188.0	187.8	187.9	189.0	190.3	190.7	191.3	190.6	192.3	195.8	197.3	190.9
2004	189.1	188.4	188.9	190.5	191.5	193.2	194.1	194.5	193.8	195.5	199.7	201.8	193.4
2005	193.9	193.0	193.6	194.3	195.2	196.9	198.3	199.1	199.3	200.1	204.7	207.9	198.0
2006	199.0	198.0	198.5	199.2	200.9	202.3	203.0	203.5	203.2	203.5	208.3	211.2	202.6
2007	202.8	201.8	202.3	202.4	204.0	205.2	205.9	206.2	206.5	206.7	211.6	213.5	205.7
2008	205.1	203.8	203.5	203.5	203.7	203.6	204.8	204.8	204.2	203.1	203.5	203.5	203.9
2009	194.4	191.4	189.0	188.1	189.0	188.8	188.3	188.1	188.1	187.7	190.1	191.8	189.6
Wholesale Trade													
1990	40.4	40.5	41.0	41.3	41.4	41.9	41.9	42.5	41.9	41.9	42.2	42.4	41.6
2000	54.1	54.3	54.4	54.9	55.2	55.5	56.1	56.4	56.1	56.5	56.7	56.8	55.6
2001	56.6	56.8	56.9	56.8	56.7	57.0	56.7	56.7	56.0	55.2	55.2	54.9	56.3
2002	54.4	54.3	54.2	54.5	54.6	54.7	55.0	55.1	54.8	54.6	54.7	54.7	54.6
2003	54.7	54.7	54.7	54.7	54.7	55.0	55.2	55.2	54.9	54.6	54.6	54.5	54.8
2004	54.1	54.5	54.5	54.8	55.0	55.3	55.9	55.9	55.3	55.2	55.4	55.5	55.1
2005	55.2	55.7	55.8	55.8	56.0	56.4	56.8	56.7	56.8	56.6	56.7	57.0	56.3
2006	56.2	56.7	56.7	57.2	57.6	57.8	58.0	58.2	57.7	57.8	57.9	58.0	57.5
2007	57.5	58.0	58.0	58.0	58.4	58.4	58.7	58.3	58.0	58.2	58.1	58.1	58.1
2008	57.5	57.9	57.7	57.6	58.0	58.0	58.6	58.3	58.0	57.9	57.6	57.0	57.8
2009	55.9	55.7	55.0	54.9	55.0	54.6	54.6	54.2	53.7	53.4	53.1	53.1	54.4
Retail Trade													
1990	81.2	78.8	79.6	80.3	80.8	82.1	83.1	84.7	83.8	83.2	85.8	87.3	82.6
2000	105.1	104.1	104.1	104.3	105.1	106.7	107.1	107.0	106.3	107.2	111.1	113.2	106.8
2001	105.3	103.3	103.0	102.7	102.4	103.8	103.2	102.7	101.8	101.5	104.5	106.3	103.4
2002	100.0	98.4	98.6	98.8	99.7	100.6	101.0	100.2	99.9	100.0	103.3	105.5	100.5
2003	98.6	97.3	97.1	97.2	98.1	99.0	99.4	99.7	99.0	100.4	103.9	105.5	99.6
2004	98.4	97.3	97.8	98.9	99.8	101.1	101.6	101.9	101.3	102.3	106.5	108.4	101.3
2005	102.4	100.8	101.1	101.7	102.6	103.7	105.0	105.8	105.4	106.4	110.6	112.7	104.9
2006	105.9	104.1	104.5	105.0	106.1	106.8	107.8	108.1	107.8	107.9	112.4	114.6	107.6
2007	108.1	106.5	106.7	106.9	107.8	108.9	110.1	110.6	110.4	110.3	114.8	116.2	109.8
2008	110.1	108.3	108.2	107.8	107.6	107.8	109.1	109.0	108.4	107.4	109.0	109.4	108.5
2009	102.7	100.7	99.5	99.1	99.8	100.1	100.4	100.4	100.3	100.4	103.0	104.2	100.9
Transportation and Utilities													
1990	30.9	30.7	31.3	31.5	31.9	32.3	31.7	32.3	32.1	31.9	31.9	32.4	31.7
2000	38.1	37.9	37.9	38.6	38.4	39.0	38.4	38.6	39.0	39.0	39.5	39.1	38.6
2001	37.7	37.9	38.0	38.2	38.8	38.8	38.6	39.0	38.8	38.8	38.3	38.1	38.4
2002	37.2	37.2	37.3	37.5	37.6	37.7	37.4	37.3	37.3	37.2	36.8	36.9	37.3
2003	36.5	36.0	36.0	36.0	36.2	36.3	36.1	36.4	36.7	37.3	37.3	37.3	36.5
2004	36.6	36.6	36.6	36.8	36.7	36.8	36.6	36.7	37.2	38.0	37.8	37.9	37.0
2005	36.3	36.5	36.7	36.8	36.6	36.8	36.5	36.6	37.1	37.1	37.4	38.2	36.9
2006	36.9	37.2	37.3	37.0	37.2	37.7	37.2	37.2	37.7	37.8	38.0	38.6	37.5
2007	37.2	37.3	37.6	37.5	37.8	37.9	37.1	37.3	38.1	38.2	38.7	39.2	37.8
2008	37.5	37.6	37.6	38.1	38.1	37.8	37.1	37.5	37.8	37.8	36.9	37.1	37.6
2009	35.8	35.0	34.5	34.1	34.2	34.1	33.3	33.5	34.1	33.9	34.0	34.5	34.3
Information													
1990	16.1	16.2	16.1	15.9	16.1	16.4	15.9	16.3	16.2	16.1	16.2	16.1	16.1
2000	24.7	24.9	25.0	25.3	25.5	25.8	26.4	26.6	26.8	26.7	26.8	27.0	26.0
2001	27.0	27.0	26.8	26.5	26.3	26.1	25.8	25.5	25.3	25.0	24.8	24.8	25.9
2002	24.6	24.5	24.3	24.0	23.9	23.9	23.6	23.6	23.4	23.4	23.4	23.3	23.8
2003	23.0	22.7	22.5	22.3	22.5	22.5	22.4	22.3	22.3	22.4	22.6	22.7	22.5
2004	22.5	22.5	22.6	22.4	22.4	22.5	22.6	22.6	22.4	22.3	22.5	22.6	22.5
2005	22.5	22.6	22.6	22.8	23.0	23.2	23.3	23.3	23.3	23.3	23.5	23.7	23.1
2006	23.5	23.6	23.7	23.6	23.7	23.8	24.5	24.2	24.3	24.5	24.1	24.3	24.0
2007	24.2	24.4	24.6	24.6	24.9	24.8	24.9	25.0	24.8	24.9	25.0	25.1	24.8
2008	24.9	24.9	24.9	24.9	24.9	24.8	24.8	24.7	24.5	24.1	24.0	23.8	24.6
2009	23.6	23.4	23.3	23.1	22.9	23.0	22.8	22.7	22.5	22.4	22.3	22.4	22.9

Employment by Industry: Portland-Vancouver-Hillsboro, OR-WA, Selected Years, 1990–2009—*Continued*

(Numbers in thousands, not seasonally adjusted.)

Industry and year	January	February	March	April	May	June	July	August	September	October	November	December	Annual average
Financial Activities													
1990	48.3	48.7	49.1	49.6	50.0	50.3	50.3	50.9	50.7	50.6	50.5	50.5	50.0
2000	64.6	64.7	64.4	64.7	64.8	65.1	65.4	65.2	64.9	64.6	64.6	65.1	64.8
2001	64.3	64.6	65.0	65.0	65.1	65.3	65.5	65.3	65.1	64.9	65.1	65.3	65.0
2002	64.9	65.0	64.8	64.9	65.0	65.3	65.8	66.0	65.8	66.2	66.4	66.8	65.6
2003	66.8	66.9	67.3	67.4	67.1	67.0	66.6	66.7	66.0	65.5	65.0	64.9	66.4
2004	65.0	65.1	65.3	65.8	65.9	66.3	66.5	66.6	66.4	66.4	66.7	66.9	66.1
2005	66.4	66.6	66.7	67.2	67.7	68.2	68.8	69.1	69.1	69.3	69.7	70.0	68.2
2006	69.3	69.5	69.7	70.1	70.3	70.7	71.3	71.5	71.4	71.2	71.3	71.4	70.6
2007	70.7	70.9	71.0	70.8	70.8	70.8	70.9	70.6	69.7	69.5	69.5	69.3	70.4
2008	68.6	68.7	68.4	68.5	68.5	68.1	68.1	67.9	67.2	66.9	66.4	65.9	67.8
2009	65.2	65.0	64.3	64.5	64.5	64.4	64.4	64.3	63.6	63.5	63.2	63.3	64.2
Professional and Business Services													
1990	73.8	74.0	75.9	76.8	76.9	78.0	78.5	80.2	79.2	79.3	79.1	78.6	77.5
2000	124.0	125.6	126.4	128.1	128.8	130.9	132.4	133.9	133.7	134.2	134.3	133.4	130.5
2001	129.8	130.2	130.9	130.5	129.4	129.3	127.7	127.5	126.3	124.8	123.9	122.4	127.7
2002	120.9	121.1	121.4	121.8	121.4	122.2	123.0	123.6	123.0	122.3	120.6	118.9	121.7
2003	115.4	116.2	116.2	116.8	116.7	117.0	118.9	119.5	120.1	119.9	119.2	119.0	117.9
2004	114.7	116.3	117.8	119.9	121.1	122.9	124.6	125.4	124.5	126.3	126.2	125.9	122.1
2005	121.6	123.4	124.8	126.9	127.1	128.8	130.4	131.6	131.7	131.9	132.0	132.2	128.5
2006	128.3	130.2	131.3	132.9	133.9	135.9	136.2	137.3	137.7	138.3	138.2	136.5	134.7
2007	132.5	133.8	135.4	135.7	135.5	136.7	137.0	138.5	138.4	138.6	137.8	136.9	136.4
2008	133.8	135.4	136.5	137.7	137.5	137.8	138.9	139.7	138.5	136.8	133.9	131.5	136.5
2009	127.3	126.1	125.3	125.2	124.5	124.6	125.0	124.7	123.6	122.7	122.2	121.4	124.4
Education and Health Services													
1990	71.8	72.3	72.9	73.2	73.0	71.6	72.0	72.9	74.3	75.8	76.1	76.0	73.5
2000	101.0	103.1	103.3	103.5	102.9	100.2	98.7	99.4	103.5	106.1	106.7	106.7	102.9
2001	104.4	106.5	106.9	107.3	106.8	105.2	103.1	103.0	106.6	108.6	109.6	109.6	106.5
2002	108.1	110.3	111.2	112.0	111.6	109.2	107.4	107.7	110.8	114.1	114.9	114.4	111.0
2003	112.2	114.2	114.6	114.9	114.3	111.7	109.8	109.8	113.1	115.8	116.4	116.5	113.6
2004	112.5	115.7	116.5	116.9	116.2	113.4	111.7	111.6	116.2	118.6	119.3	119.2	115.7
2005	116.5	119.7	120.4	120.9	120.3	116.9	115.5	116.1	120.6	123.1	123.9	124.1	119.8
2006	120.1	123.5	124.3	124.9	124.1	120.6	118.0	118.5	122.9	126.6	127.6	127.8	123.2
2007	124.1	127.9	128.8	129.0	128.3	125.1	122.9	123.0	127.8	131.6	132.5	132.1	127.8
2008	128.8	132.7	133.4	134.0	133.0	130.1	127.9	127.9	133.2	136.2	136.9	136.5	132.6
2009	132.5	135.7	136.0	136.8	136.0	133.0	130.3	130.2	134.5	137.8	137.9	137.8	134.9
Leisure and Hospitality													
1990	60.6	60.6	61.6	63.1	64.1	65.0	65.1	66.9	66.0	63.5	63.5	63.2	63.6
2000	81.7	82.8	83.5	85.0	86.2	87.8	88.7	89.4	87.7	85.5	85.5	85.8	85.8
2001	83.2	83.5	83.9	85.2	86.7	87.1	88.3	89.3	87.6	84.0	83.5	83.5	85.5
2002	81.3	81.7	82.5	84.0	85.6	87.0	87.0	88.0	87.0	85.0	84.4	84.5	84.8
2003	82.3	82.3	83.3	84.5	84.9	86.4	87.9	89.0	87.5	86.6	86.3	86.1	85.6
2004	82.9	83.8	84.6	87.0	88.8	89.3	89.9	91.1	89.7	88.2	88.0	88.5	87.7
2005	85.4	86.1	87.5	89.0	90.6	92.0	92.5	93.5	92.2	90.3	90.8	91.3	90.1
2006	89.3	89.7	91.0	93.1	94.3	95.5	96.4	97.3	96.5	95.2	95.2	95.7	94.1
2007	93.1	94.3	95.3	96.1	97.7	98.8	100.9	101.8	101.0	98.7	98.8	99.3	98.0
2008	96.2	96.9	98.0	99.6	100.8	101.3	102.3	102.5	101.5	98.9	97.5	95.7	99.3
2009	92.4	92.5	93.1	94.0	95.1	95.6	96.5	96.4	95.8	92.9	92.2	91.5	94.0
Other Services													
1990	24.8	24.8	25.0	25.3	25.5	25.8	26.1	26.5	26.7	25.9	26.0	25.9	25.7
2000	32.2	32.7	33.2	33.2	33.6	33.6	33.4	33.6	33.9	33.7	34.0	33.9	33.4
2001	33.4	33.9	34.2	34.3	34.5	34.7	34.2	34.3	34.4	34.2	34.1	34.0	34.2
2002	33.7	34.0	34.1	34.1	34.1	33.9	33.7	33.6	33.7	34.0	34.1	33.7	33.9
2003	33.6	33.8	33.9	33.9	34.1	33.8	33.9	34.1	34.3	34.2	34.1	34.1	34.0
2004	33.5	34.2	34.7	34.8	35.0	35.2	35.1	35.0	35.2	35.0	34.8	34.4	34.7
2005	33.6	34.1	34.2	34.4	34.6	34.6	34.8	34.8	34.7	34.7	34.8	34.8	34.5
2006	34.3	34.8	35.1	35.4	35.9	36.2	36.1	35.9	35.9	36.0	36.0	36.2	35.7
2007	35.6	36.3	36.4	36.3	36.6	36.9	36.5	36.7	36.9	37.0	37.1	37.1	36.6
2008	36.7	36.9	37.1	37.3	37.5	37.6	37.4	37.3	37.6	37.2	36.7	36.2	37.1
2009	35.5	35.6	35.5	35.3	35.5	35.3	35.4	35.2	35.1	34.9	34.7	34.7	35.2
Government													
1990	102.7	104.0	104.8	106.3	108.2	108.2	98.4	96.3	101.4	106.4	107.6	106.5	104.2
2000	129.1	131.6	132.1	132.6	135.6	134.2	124.6	121.5	124.9	132.5	133.6	133.5	130.5
2001	131.9	133.4	134.2	134.0	135.7	135.1	119.2	116.2	128.8	136.0	137.2	130.0	131.5
2002	134.5	137.1	138.0	138.1	139.3	139.4	120.6	117.5	129.2	136.9	138.4	137.2	133.9
2003	134.1	135.3	135.7	136.3	137.1	135.9	124.7	123.1	130.2	135.7	137.2	136.7	133.5
2004	134.6	136.8	138.1	138.2	138.7	139.4	129.5	126.9	133.3	139.4	140.1	139.8	136.2
2005	138.3	140.3	140.6	140.3	141.1	141.4	128.9	127.3	131.9	139.3	141.4	140.7	137.6
2006	138.3	140.4	141.5	141.5	143.4	143.0	130.6	128.1	133.6	141.1	143.6	142.2	138.9
2007	141.1	142.9	144.1	144.3	146.5	146.5	134.7	131.6	136.1	145.3	147.0	146.9	142.3
2008	145.7	147.1	148.3	148.6	150.1	149.8	141.1	138.3	142.8	149.5	151.8	150.8	147.0
2009	148.8	150.8	151.5	151.7	152.6	151.0	141.6	138.7	140.5	150.2	151.9	150.4	148.3

Employment by Industry: Providence-Fall River-Warwick, RI-MA, NECTA, Selected Years, 1990–2009

(Numbers in thousands, not seasonally adjusted.)

Industry and year	January	February	March	April	May	June	July	August	September	October	November	December	Annual average
Total Nonfarm													
1990	520.8	519.5	522.8	526.0	530.0	531.5	516.2	521.5	531.0	528.0	527.4	525.0	525.0
2000	559.3	559.9	564.2	573.9	580.7	583.1	571.6	573.6	583.6	585.3	588.3	590.4	576.2
2001	565.2	566.5	568.5	574.9	579.0	580.4	566.0	571.7	577.8	576.0	576.1	577.6	573.3
2002	560.5	561.5	566.7	574.2	580.0	580.9	568.7	574.2	581.1	579.6	582.2	580.9	574.2
2003	564.5	563.3	566.8	575.4	583.3	585.3	572.2	574.9	583.5	585.8	587.9	587.5	577.5
2004	566.2	567.6	571.5	580.1	589.4	590.2	577.3	579.0	587.5	589.7	591.0	590.0	581.6
2005	568.3	570.1	571.7	583.8	588.3	591.2	579.9	581.6	588.9	588.6	590.9	589.2	582.7
2006	565.8	568.5	573.1	586.0	589.8	592.9	579.9	582.9	591.3	593.4	595.0	593.9	584.4
2007	571.9	572.4	575.1	583.3	590.0	592.0	580.5	581.1	585.4	585.2	585.4	584.2	582.2
2008	562.0	563.5	565.8	573.7	579.2	579.3	566.1	566.7	572.6	571.3	568.1	563.9	569.4
2009	538.4	538.5	537.7	542.2	548.3	548.0	534.9	534.8	541.0	542.0	539.3	535.8	540.1
Total Private													
1990	454.3	452.5	455.1	456.9	460.1	463.9	456.1	462.1	465.4	461.3	460.0	456.7	458.7
2000	484.7	485.1	488.5	497.8	502.4	508.0	501.1	504.4	508.3	509.1	511.5	513.8	501.2
2001	489.2	490.4	491.8	498.8	502.6	504.5	494.8	501.3	502.3	501.3	500.6	501.8	498.3
2002	483.1	483.7	488.4	496.2	501.9	503.5	496.4	502.5	504.3	503.3	504.8	504.0	497.7
2003	487.4	486.1	489.5	498.3	505.7	507.7	502.2	505.5	508.3	509.5	511.4	510.9	501.9
2004	490.5	491.7	495.0	504.4	512.7	513.7	508.8	510.8	513.1	514.4	515.0	514.7	507.1
2005	493.3	494.9	496.7	508.6	512.6	515.7	511.0	513.4	515.7	513.5	515.4	513.8	508.7
2006	491.1	493.3	498.0	511.1	514.6	517.9	510.8	514.2	517.3	518.3	518.9	518.1	510.3
2007	497.0	497.4	500.0	508.3	514.4	517.2	510.7	511.6	512.2	511.0	511.0	509.5	508.4
2008	488.0	489.2	491.3	499.1	503.8	504.9	498.1	499.4	501.0	498.7	494.6	490.7	496.6
2009	466.1	466.1	465.3	469.5	475.2	475.7	469.1	469.3	471.0	470.5	467.6	464.0	469.1
Goods-Producing													
1990	141.0	140.4	140.5	139.7	140.4	142.3	136.0	141.5	142.1	140.8	139.3	136.7	140.1
2000	114.7	114.9	115.3	117.4	118.6	119.6	115.0	118.7	119.8	120.2	119.6	119.3	117.8
2001	114.2	114.1	113.9	115.5	115.2	115.2	108.6	113.2	113.4	113.0	111.0	110.5	113.2
2002	105.3	105.2	106.2	106.9	108.2	108.4	103.3	108.2	108.3	107.4	107.0	105.8	106.7
2003	101.4	100.1	100.6	103.4	105.0	105.7	101.7	105.3	105.9	105.2	105.1	103.7	103.6
2004	98.4	97.6	98.5	101.0	102.6	104.0	101.9	104.2	104.1	103.9	103.6	102.5	101.9
2005	97.3	96.5	96.3	99.4	100.6	102.1	98.7	101.1	100.9	99.7	100.0	98.6	99.3
2006	93.8	93.7	94.3	97.5	98.3	99.7	96.6	99.0	98.5	98.0	96.9	96.2	96.9
2007	92.3	90.9	91.3	92.5	94.1	95.1	92.7	94.9	94.6	93.0	92.1	90.6	92.8
2008	86.3	85.2	85.7	87.5	88.7	89.2	86.7	88.3	87.7	86.1	84.3	82.2	86.5
2009	76.4	74.2	73.1	73.9	74.3	74.5	72.7	73.3	73.0	72.6	72.0	70.8	73.4
Mining and Logging													
1990	0.2	0.2	0.2	0.2	0.2	0.2	0.2	0.2	0.2	0.2	0.2	0.2	0.2
2000	0.3	0.3	0.3	0.3	0.3	0.3	0.3	0.3	0.3	0.3	0.3	0.3	0.3
2001	0.3	0.3	0.3	0.3	0.3	0.4	0.4	0.4	0.4	0.4	0.4	0.4	0.4
2002	0.3	0.3	0.3	0.3	0.3	0.3	0.3	0.3	0.3	0.3	0.3	0.3	0.3
2003	0.2	0.2	0.2	0.3	0.3	0.3	0.3	0.3	0.3	0.3	0.3	0.3	0.3
2004	0.3	0.2	0.2	0.3	0.3	0.3	0.3	0.3	0.3	0.3	0.3	0.3	0.3
2005	0.3	0.2	0.2	0.3	0.3	0.3	0.3	0.3	0.3	0.3	0.3	0.3	0.3
2006	0.2	0.2	0.2	0.3	0.3	0.3	0.3	0.3	0.3	0.3	0.3	0.3	0.3
2007	0.3	0.2	0.2	0.3	0.3	0.3	0.3	0.3	0.3	0.3	0.3	0.3	0.3
2008	0.2	0.2	0.2	0.2	0.3	0.3	0.3	0.3	0.3	0.3	0.3	0.3	0.3
2009	0.2	0.2	0.2	0.2	0.2	0.2	0.2	0.2	0.2	0.2	0.2	0.2	0.2
Construction													
1990	18.2	18.0	18.5	19.6	20.6	21.5	21.9	21.8	21.5	21.0	20.3	18.9	20.2
2000	19.6	19.0	19.4	21.4	22.1	23.2	23.3	23.5	23.4	23.4	23.3	22.7	22.0
2001	20.2	20.1	20.7	23.0	23.8	24.4	24.5	24.7	24.4	24.5	24.1	23.8	23.2
2002	21.3	21.1	22.0	23.2	24.3	24.8	24.9	25.2	25.1	24.7	24.5	23.7	23.7
2003	21.2	20.3	21.1	23.9	25.8	26.6	27.6	27.9	27.9	27.6	27.3	26.2	25.3
2004	22.6	21.9	22.6	24.9	26.1	27.0	27.7	27.7	27.6	27.7	27.4	26.8	25.8
2005	23.2	22.6	23.0	26.4	27.6	28.8	29.0	29.2	29.0	28.4	28.9	27.7	27.0
2006	24.7	24.2	25.1	28.2	29.1	30.3	30.3	30.6	30.3	29.9	29.3	28.7	28.4
2007	25.9	24.5	25.1	26.6	28.2	29.0	29.5	29.4	28.9	28.3	27.8	26.5	27.5
2008	23.2	22.6	23.1	25.1	26.2	26.9	27.2	27.1	26.8	25.8	24.9	23.3	25.2
2009	20.1	19.5	19.4	20.8	21.7	21.9	22.0	21.8	21.4	21.2	20.6	20.0	20.9
Manufacturing													
1990	122.6	122.2	121.8	119.9	119.6	120.6	113.9	119.5	120.4	119.6	118.8	117.6	119.7
2000	94.8	95.6	95.6	95.7	96.2	96.1	91.4	94.9	96.1	96.5	96.0	96.3	95.4
2001	93.7	93.7	92.9	92.2	91.1	90.4	83.7	88.1	88.6	88.1	86.5	86.3	89.6
2002	83.7	83.8	83.9	83.4	83.6	83.3	78.1	82.7	82.9	82.4	82.2	81.8	82.7
2003	80.0	79.6	79.3	79.2	78.9	78.8	73.8	77.1	77.7	77.3	77.5	77.2	78.0
2004	75.5	75.5	75.7	75.8	76.2	76.7	73.9	76.2	76.2	75.9	75.9	75.4	75.7
2005	73.8	73.7	73.1	72.7	72.7	73.0	69.4	71.6	71.6	71.0	70.8	70.6	72.0
2006	68.9	69.3	69.0	69.0	68.9	69.1	66.0	68.1	67.9	67.8	67.3	67.2	68.2
2007	66.1	66.2	66.0	65.6	65.6	65.8	62.9	65.2	65.4	64.4	64.0	63.8	65.1
2008	62.9	62.4	62.4	62.2	62.2	62.0	59.2	60.9	60.6	60.0	59.1	58.6	61.0
2009	56.1	54.5	53.5	52.9	52.4	52.4	50.5	51.3	51.4	51.2	51.2	50.6	52.3

Employment by Industry: Providence-Fall River-Warwick, RI-MA, NECTA, Selected Years, 1990–2009—*Continued*

(Numbers in thousands, not seasonally adjusted.)

Industry and year	January	February	March	April	May	June	July	August	September	October	November	December	Annual average
Service-Providing													
1990	379.8	379.1	382.3	386.3	389.6	389.2	380.2	380.0	388.9	387.2	388.1	388.3	384.9
2000	444.6	445.0	448.9	456.5	462.1	463.5	456.6	454.9	463.8	465.1	468.7	471.1	458.4
2001	451.0	452.4	454.6	459.4	463.8	465.2	457.4	458.5	464.4	463.0	465.1	467.1	460.2
2002	455.2	456.3	460.5	467.3	471.8	472.5	465.4	466.0	472.8	472.2	475.2	475.1	467.5
2003	463.1	463.2	466.2	472.0	478.3	479.6	470.5	469.6	477.6	480.6	482.8	483.8	473.9
2004	467.8	470.0	473.0	479.1	486.8	486.2	475.4	474.8	483.4	485.8	487.4	487.5	479.8
2005	471.0	473.6	475.4	484.4	487.7	489.1	481.2	480.5	488.0	488.9	490.9	490.6	483.4
2006	472.0	474.8	478.8	488.5	491.5	493.2	483.3	483.9	492.8	495.4	498.1	497.7	487.5
2007	479.6	481.5	483.8	490.8	495.9	496.9	487.8	486.2	490.8	492.2	493.3	493.6	489.4
2008	475.7	478.3	480.1	486.2	490.5	490.1	479.4	478.4	484.9	485.2	483.8	481.7	482.9
2009	462.0	464.3	464.6	468.3	474.0	473.5	462.2	461.5	468.0	469.4	467.3	465.0	466.7
Trade, Transportation, and Utilities													
1990	95.6	93.7	94.0	94.2	94.9	95.8	94.1	95.3	96.1	96.6	98.2	99.1	95.6
2000	99.9	98.3	98.7	100.3	100.2	101.1	99.8	100.6	101.7	103.1	105.7	107.9	101.4
2001	101.4	99.6	99.2	100.1	100.3	101.8	100.6	100.7	101.8	102.2	104.9	106.9	101.6
2002	101.6	100.0	100.6	101.7	102.7	104.0	102.5	102.7	103.2	103.7	106.2	108.0	103.1
2003	102.2	100.7	100.8	101.6	102.8	103.8	102.2	102.5	103.7	104.8	107.1	108.3	103.4
2004	102.3	101.3	101.5	101.3	103.3	103.6	102.0	101.8	102.6	104.0	105.9	107.1	103.1
2005	101.7	100.8	100.7	102.0	102.6	103.5	102.1	102.5	102.9	103.9	106.0	107.8	103.0
2006	102.0	100.3	100.8	102.2	102.6	103.4	101.5	101.7	102.6	103.6	105.9	107.5	102.8
2007	102.2	100.4	100.7	101.4	102.3	103.3	101.7	101.4	101.9	102.1	104.4	105.8	102.3
2008	100.1	98.5	98.5	98.9	99.8	100.5	99.0	99.1	99.4	99.6	100.3	100.8	99.5
2009	95.2	93.7	93.3	92.6	94.2	95.0	92.9	93.0	94.1	93.9	94.5	94.8	93.9
Wholesale Trade													
1990	19.6	19.3	19.4	18.9	18.9	19.0	18.8	19.1	19.0	18.7	18.8	18.5	19.0
2000	18.7	18.8	19.1	19.3	19.4	19.5	19.4	19.5	19.6	19.8	19.9	20.1	19.4
2001	19.6	19.8	19.9	20.2	20.1	20.2	20.5	20.5	20.4	20.7	20.3	20.5	20.2
2002	20.3	20.2	20.4	20.5	20.6	20.7	20.4	20.5	20.4	20.4	20.7	20.6	20.5
2003	20.5	20.3	20.4	20.5	20.8	20.9	20.7	20.6	20.5	20.6	20.8	20.6	20.6
2004	20.2	20.2	20.4	20.7	20.7	20.8	20.7	20.7	20.7	20.8	20.9	20.9	20.6
2005	20.5	20.5	20.6	21.0	21.0	21.2	21.1	21.2	21.1	21.1	21.2	21.5	21.0
2006	21.0	21.0	21.1	21.3	21.4	21.5	21.4	21.4	21.4	21.5	21.4	21.4	21.3
2007	21.3	21.1	21.1	21.4	21.4	21.5	21.5	21.4	21.2	21.2	21.3	21.4	21.3
2008	20.8	20.8	20.8	20.9	21.0	21.1	21.0	20.9	20.9	20.9	20.8	20.6	20.9
2009	20.1	19.9	19.9	19.9	20.0	20.1	19.8	19.8	19.9	20.0	20.0	20.0	20.0
Retail Trade													
1990	64.4	62.7	63.0	63.4	63.9	64.6	64.0	65.1	65.0	65.9	67.4	68.5	64.8
2000	68.6	66.9	67.0	68.0	67.7	68.5	68.1	68.5	68.9	70.0	72.6	74.6	69.1
2001	69.0	67.1	66.6	66.8	67.1	68.4	67.6	67.8	68.1	68.9	71.5	73.4	68.5
2002	68.6	67.3	67.6	68.4	69.0	69.9	69.4	69.4	69.8	70.1	72.4	74.3	69.7
2003	68.9	67.6	67.5	68.1	68.7	69.5	69.0	69.4	69.6	70.7	72.8	74.2	69.7
2004	69.1	68.2	68.2	68.3	69.2	69.6	69.2	69.0	68.6	70.0	71.9	73.1	69.5
2005	68.7	67.8	67.7	68.2	68.6	69.1	68.6	68.8	68.6	69.6	71.6	73.0	69.2
2006	68.4	66.8	67.1	68.0	68.1	68.6	67.9	67.9	67.8	68.7	71.1	72.6	68.6
2007	68.1	66.8	67.0	67.1	67.8	68.4	67.8	67.6	67.2	67.6	69.8	70.8	68.0
2008	66.6	65.1	65.1	65.1	65.6	66.1	65.5	65.5	64.9	65.5	66.5	66.9	65.7
2009	62.8	61.6	61.3	60.7	61.9	62.4	61.8	61.8	61.7	61.5	62.3	62.3	61.8
Transportation and Utilities													
1990	11.6	11.7	11.6	11.9	12.1	12.2	11.3	11.1	12.1	12.0	12.0	12.1	11.8
2000	12.6	12.6	12.6	13.0	13.1	13.1	12.3	12.6	13.2	13.3	13.2	13.2	12.9
2001	12.8	12.7	12.7	13.1	13.1	13.2	12.5	12.4	13.3	13.1	13.1	13.0	12.9
2002	12.7	12.5	12.6	12.8	13.1	13.4	12.7	12.8	13.0	13.2	13.1	13.1	12.9
2003	12.8	12.8	12.9	13.0	13.3	13.4	12.5	12.5	13.6	13.5	13.5	13.5	13.1
2004	13.0	12.9	12.9	12.3	13.4	13.2	12.1	12.1	13.3	13.2	13.1	13.1	12.9
2005	12.5	12.5	12.4	12.8	13.0	13.2	12.4	12.5	13.2	13.2	13.2	13.3	12.9
2006	12.6	12.5	12.6	12.9	13.1	13.3	12.2	12.4	13.4	13.4	13.4	13.5	12.9
2007	12.8	12.5	12.6	12.9	13.1	13.4	12.4	12.4	13.5	13.3	13.3	13.6	13.0
2008	12.7	12.6	12.6	12.9	13.2	13.3	12.5	12.7	13.6	13.2	13.0	13.3	13.0
2009	12.3	12.2	12.1	12.0	12.3	12.5	11.3	11.4	12.5	12.4	12.2	12.5	12.1
Information													
1990	11.1	11.0	10.9	10.9	10.9	10.9	11.0	11.0	11.0	10.7	10.8	10.9	10.9
2000	11.6	11.7	11.5	11.6	11.7	12.0	12.1	10.6	11.9	11.7	11.8	11.8	11.7
2001	11.8	11.8	11.9	11.9	12.0	12.0	11.8	11.7	11.7	11.4	11.4	11.4	11.7
2002	11.9	11.9	11.9	11.9	11.9	12.1	12.0	12.0	11.9	11.6	11.9	11.9	11.9
2003	12.0	12.0	11.9	11.9	11.9	12.1	11.9	11.9	11.7	11.9	11.9	11.8	11.9
2004	11.9	11.9	11.9	11.9	11.8	11.8	11.6	11.5	11.4	11.4	11.5	11.5	11.7
2005	11.7	11.7	11.6	11.6	11.5	11.6	11.6	11.6	11.5	11.6	11.8	11.8	11.6
2006	11.9	11.8	11.8	12.2	12.1	12.2	11.6	11.5	11.5	11.4	11.7	11.7	11.8
2007	11.3	11.2	11.2	11.3	11.4	11.5	11.5	11.6	11.5	11.5	11.7	11.7	11.5
2008	11.6	11.9	11.9	11.7	11.8	12.0	11.8	12.2	11.9	11.9	11.7	11.6	11.8
2009	11.6	11.5	11.4	11.6	11.6	11.6	11.2	11.2	11.1	11.1	11.2	11.3	11.4

Employment by Industry: Providence-Fall River-Warwick, RI-MA, NECTA, Selected Years, 1990–2009—*Continued*

(Numbers in thousands, not seasonally adjusted.)

Industry and year	January	February	March	April	May	June	July	August	September	October	November	December	Annual average
Financial Activities													
1990	32.4	32.4	32.8	32.3	32.3	32.7	32.4	32.2	32.0	31.8	31.5	31.2	32.2
2000	32.7	32.8	32.9	33.3	33.2	34.1	34.6	34.3	34.1	34.0	34.2	34.5	33.7
2001	34.7	34.8	34.9	34.5	34.4	34.9	35.0	34.8	34.6	34.8	34.8	35.1	34.8
2002	35.1	35.0	35.0	35.4	35.3	35.9	36.0	36.0	36.0	36.2	36.4	36.6	35.7
2003	36.4	36.4	36.7	36.3	36.6	37.1	37.1	37.1	37.0	37.0	37.1	37.3	36.8
2004	37.0	37.0	37.0	37.1	37.4	37.4	37.3	37.3	37.1	37.3	37.3	37.3	37.2
2005	36.9	37.1	37.1	37.6	37.5	37.8	37.9	37.9	37.7	37.4	37.5	37.8	37.5
2006	37.3	37.3	37.5	37.7	37.9	38.1	38.3	38.7	38.8	38.7	38.9	39.3	38.2
2007	38.4	38.5	38.4	38.5	38.6	38.4	38.1	37.7	37.6	37.2	37.1	37.1	38.0
2008	36.7	36.8	36.6	36.4	36.5	36.4	36.2	36.0	36.1	35.3	35.1	35.1	36.1
2009	34.6	34.5	34.2	33.9	34.0	34.1	33.8	33.4	33.1	32.9	32.9	33.3	33.7
Professional and Business Services													
1990	40.4	40.4	40.6	41.4	41.9	42.3	42.1	42.2	42.6	41.7	41.4	40.8	41.5
2000	56.7	56.7	57.9	59.2	59.7	60.7	58.6	59.6	59.9	59.9	59.8	60.0	59.1
2001	56.5	56.6	56.8	58.1	58.5	58.9	57.8	59.0	58.7	58.9	57.9	57.2	57.9
2002	55.1	54.6	55.2	56.8	57.1	57.6	56.5	57.0	57.4	57.7	57.2	56.3	56.5
2003	54.6	54.3	54.7	56.6	57.2	58.5	58.3	59.0	58.9	59.4	59.3	59.3	57.5
2004	57.8	57.9	58.4	60.7	61.4	62.2	61.3	62.1	62.5	62.4	62.0	61.5	60.9
2005	59.0	59.0	59.5	62.3	62.2	62.9	62.8	63.5	63.7	62.6	62.5	61.9	61.8
2006	58.8	59.1	59.8	63.0	63.0	64.2	63.1	64.3	65.0	65.0	64.4	63.7	62.8
2007	60.5	60.2	60.6	62.9	63.4	64.5	63.3	63.3	63.0	62.6	62.5	62.2	62.4
2008	59.5	59.0	59.3	61.6	61.4	62.5	61.7	61.9	62.3	61.8	60.8	59.6	61.0
2009	56.9	56.5	56.8	58.1	58.1	58.8	57.8	58.2	58.4	59.0	58.1	56.4	57.8
Education and Health Services													
1990	76.6	77.6	78.2	78.1	77.9	75.4	74.6	74.4	76.8	78.4	78.8	78.9	77.1
2000	96.2	97.6	97.8	98.7	99.0	96.5	96.4	96.3	99.5	100.6	101.7	102.2	98.5
2001	96.6	98.8	99.8	100.4	100.6	96.0	95.3	96.3	99.2	100.7	101.8	102.2	99.0
2002	99.0	101.2	102.5	102.9	102.9	98.4	97.8	98.9	102.4	103.7	104.7	105.1	101.6
2003	102.8	104.7	106.0	106.3	106.2	101.8	100.5	99.9	103.7	106.3	107.1	107.4	104.4
2004	104.6	107.0	108.2	108.9	108.8	104.1	103.2	102.9	106.7	109.0	109.7	110.1	106.9
2005	106.8	109.4	110.4	110.9	110.6	106.7	106.0	105.6	110.1	112.3	112.9	112.0	109.5
2006	108.2	111.8	113.1	113.7	112.8	109.1	107.9	107.6	111.5	114.6	115.7	114.8	111.7
2007	111.5	115.0	115.6	116.0	115.7	111.4	110.2	109.8	113.5	116.2	117.1	116.4	114.0
2008	113.0	116.5	117.3	117.6	116.7	112.6	111.2	111.1	114.8	117.6	118.1	117.8	115.4
2009	114.0	117.6	118.0	117.8	117.2	113.5	112.3	111.8	115.1	118.1	118.7	118.0	116.0
Leisure and Hospitality													
1990	35.6	35.4	36.3	38.5	40.2	42.7	43.7	43.3	42.5	39.2	38.2	37.4	39.4
2000	49.1	49.3	50.3	52.9	55.5	58.9	59.3	58.9	56.8	54.8	54.0	53.2	54.4
2001	49.4	50.1	50.6	53.3	56.5	60.0	59.8	59.6	57.8	55.2	53.5	53.2	54.9
2002	49.8	50.4	51.6	55.1	58.1	60.8	61.6	61.3	59.4	57.0	55.5	54.3	56.2
2003	52.0	51.9	52.6	56.2	59.6	61.9	63.3	62.9	61.1	58.6	57.2	56.5	57.8
2004	52.6	53.1	53.4	57.2	60.8	63.7	64.2	63.9	62.2	59.7	58.2	58.0	58.9
2005	53.8	54.3	54.8	58.4	61.0	64.1	64.6	63.9	62.5	59.7	58.3	57.5	59.4
2006	53.6	53.7	54.9	58.5	61.3	64.0	64.5	64.3	63.0	60.3	58.8	58.3	59.6
2007	54.8	55.2	56.0	59.4	62.3	65.6	65.8	65.7	63.8	62.0	59.7	59.1	60.8
2008	55.0	55.5	56.0	59.3	62.6	65.0	64.5	64.1	62.8	60.3	58.4	57.7	60.1
2009	52.3	52.9	53.3	56.2	60.2	62.3	62.3	62.5	61.2	57.8	54.9	53.9	57.5
Other Services													
1990	21.6	21.6	21.8	21.8	21.6	21.8	22.2	22.2	22.3	22.1	21.8	21.7	21.9
2000	23.8	23.8	24.1	24.4	24.5	25.1	25.3	25.4	24.6	24.8	24.7	24.9	24.6
2001	24.6	24.6	24.7	25.0	25.1	25.7	25.9	26.0	25.1	25.1	25.3	25.3	25.2
2002	25.3	25.4	25.4	25.5	25.7	26.3	26.7	26.4	25.7	26.0	25.9	26.0	25.9
2003	26.0	26.0	26.2	26.0	26.4	26.8	27.2	26.9	26.3	26.3	26.6	26.6	26.4
2004	25.9	25.9	26.1	26.3	26.6	26.9	27.3	27.1	26.5	26.7	26.8	26.7	26.6
2005	26.1	26.1	26.3	26.4	26.6	27.0	27.3	27.3	26.4	26.3	26.4	26.4	26.6
2006	25.5	25.6	25.8	26.3	26.6	27.2	27.3	27.1	26.4	26.7	26.6	26.6	26.5
2007	26.0	26.0	26.2	26.3	26.6	27.4	27.4	27.2	26.3	26.4	26.4	26.6	26.6
2008	25.8	25.8	26.0	26.1	26.3	26.7	27.0	26.7	26.0	26.1	25.9	25.9	26.2
2009	25.1	25.2	25.2	25.4	25.6	25.9	26.1	25.9	25.0	25.1	25.3	25.5	25.4
Government													
1990	66.5	67.0	67.7	69.1	69.9	67.6	60.1	59.4	65.6	66.7	67.4	68.3	66.3
2000	74.6	74.8	75.7	76.1	78.3	75.1	70.5	69.2	75.3	76.2	76.8	76.6	74.9
2001	76.0	76.1	76.7	76.1	76.4	75.9	71.2	70.4	75.5	74.7	75.5	75.8	75.0
2002	77.4	77.8	78.3	78.0	78.1	77.4	72.3	71.7	76.8	76.3	77.4	76.9	76.5
2003	77.1	77.2	77.3	77.1	77.6	77.6	70.0	69.4	75.2	76.3	76.5	76.6	75.7
2004	75.7	75.9	76.5	75.7	76.7	76.5	68.5	68.2	74.4	75.3	76.0	75.3	74.6
2005	75.0	75.2	75.0	75.2	75.7	75.5	68.9	68.2	73.2	75.1	75.5	75.4	74.0
2006	74.7	75.2	75.1	74.9	75.2	75.0	69.1	68.7	74.0	75.1	76.1	75.8	74.1
2007	74.9	75.0	75.1	75.0	75.6	74.8	69.8	69.5	73.2	74.2	74.4	74.7	73.9
2008	74.0	74.3	74.5	74.6	75.4	74.4	68.0	67.3	71.6	72.6	73.5	73.2	72.8
2009	72.3	72.4	72.4	72.7	73.1	72.3	65.8	65.5	70.0	71.5	71.7	71.8	71.0

Employment by Industry: Raleigh-Cary, NC, Selected Years, 1990–2009

(Numbers in thousands, not seasonally adjusted.)

Industry and year	January	February	March	April	May	June	July	August	September	October	November	December	Annual average
Total Nonfarm													
1990	287.3	290.4	291.6	291.5	293.2	296.1	292.5	293.1	295.5	295.6	296.6	296.6	293.3
2000	425.8	428.0	432.6	435.9	438.3	442.5	434.0	436.8	442.8	443.3	446.2	446.9	437.8
2001	437.0	439.3	441.6	443.5	444.9	446.5	435.1	436.3	438.7	439.7	439.3	439.3	440.1
2002	425.5	426.9	428.0	432.0	435.2	436.0	430.3	433.5	438.3	439.4	440.7	441.4	433.9
2003	428.8	429.8	431.4	435.5	438.8	439.9	432.7	436.2	437.9	442.2	443.1	444.1	436.7
2004	436.5	437.6	441.4	442.9	447.3	448.7	447.9	451.1	454.1	456.4	458.3	460.7	448.6
2005	450.9	452.8	456.3	461.3	465.0	466.4	466.3	471.9	474.7	474.0	478.7	479.2	466.5
2006	471.7	473.6	477.4	485.2	489.6	492.5	489.9	496.2	498.1	501.8	507.3	508.8	491.0
2007	500.8	504.2	508.8	510.0	516.4	519.3	513.6	519.9	519.9	524.3	527.4	527.7	516.0
2008	517.5	519.6	520.8	520.8	525.0	522.8	519.4	523.2	523.1	524.1	522.1	519.3	521.5
2009	502.7	501.0	500.0	500.2	503.5	500.6	494.9	496.5	496.1	499.5	501.4	499.4	499.7
Total Private													
1990	240.4	242.5	243.0	242.6	244.1	246.5	247.1	247.9	247.0	246.8	247.1	248.0	245.3
2000	355.6	357.1	361.5	364.7	366.7	370.9	368.5	369.6	369.7	370.8	373.0	373.9	366.8
2001	364.0	365.4	367.6	369.8	371.0	372.7	368.1	368.2	365.0	365.1	364.8	365.4	367.3
2002	352.5	353.0	354.9	358.9	361.8	362.9	363.7	365.3	364.1	364.6	365.8	366.9	361.2
2003	354.8	355.3	356.5	360.3	363.2	364.9	361.2	363.8	362.0	363.9	365.5	366.8	361.5
2004	360.0	360.7	363.9	365.3	369.3	371.3	373.9	375.0	373.3	375.4	377.6	380.3	370.5
2005	371.5	372.7	375.7	380.7	384.2	386.9	389.4	390.6	392.0	393.4	396.4	399.2	386.1
2006	390.5	391.5	394.7	401.2	405.0	408.7	409.5	411.5	412.3	415.2	420.1	422.1	406.9
2007	414.4	416.9	420.9	421.8	427.5	431.9	429.6	432.6	430.6	434.7	437.4	438.0	428.0
2008	428.3	429.6	430.3	430.0	433.9	433.4	432.3	433.7	431.0	429.9	428.8	426.4	430.6
2009	412.6	410.6	408.9	407.5	410.8	410.0	408.4	408.7	406.1	408.8	410.2	408.6	409.3
Goods-Producing													
1990	59.0	59.2	59.5	58.4	58.6	59.2	58.6	58.7	58.0	56.9	57.0	56.5	58.3
2000	70.3	70.3	71.6	72.7	73.3	74.4	74.7	75.0	75.0	74.9	75.1	74.8	73.5
2001	72.2	72.5	73.3	73.6	74.1	74.4	73.8	73.4	72.7	72.1	71.2	70.0	72.8
2002	67.8	68.0	68.1	68.4	68.7	68.5	68.6	68.4	67.7	67.4	66.8	66.4	67.9
2003	63.8	63.7	63.8	63.6	64.5	64.8	64.6	64.9	64.4	65.0	64.9	64.9	64.4
2004	63.2	63.2	64.3	65.0	65.6	65.8	66.5	66.2	65.8	66.8	66.6	66.4	65.5
2005	64.8	65.2	65.8	67.1	67.9	69.0	69.5	69.5	69.8	69.7	69.9	69.9	68.2
2006	69.0	69.2	70.3	71.1	72.2	73.2	73.7	74.0	73.9	73.9	74.1	74.3	72.4
2007	73.1	73.3	74.1	74.0	74.5	75.1	75.3	75.9	75.3	74.7	74.5	73.9	74.5
2008	72.2	72.1	72.2	71.2	71.4	71.3	71.1	70.5	69.9	68.4	67.2	65.6	70.3
2009	62.5	61.4	60.7	59.4	59.1	59.1	58.6	58.5	57.8	56.7	56.0	56.0	58.9
Mining, Logging, and Construction													
1990	19.5	20.1	20.5	20.3	20.5	20.9	20.7	20.7	20.2	19.6	19.5	19.0	20.1
2000	31.0	30.9	31.9	32.9	33.4	34.2	34.1	34.4	34.5	34.1	34.3	34.0	33.3
2001	31.8	32.1	33.1	33.6	34.5	35.0	34.8	34.9	34.5	34.3	33.7	33.0	33.8
2002	31.5	32.0	32.2	32.6	33.3	33.1	33.3	33.5	33.0	32.9	32.4	32.0	32.7
2003	30.1	30.1	30.3	30.2	31.0	31.4	31.8	32.1	31.9	32.2	32.1	32.1	31.3
2004	30.8	30.9	31.7	32.5	33.1	33.2	33.9	33.8	33.5	34.0	33.8	33.6	32.9
2005	32.3	32.5	33.0	33.8	34.6	35.3	35.7	35.8	36.0	36.1	36.1	35.9	34.8
2006	35.2	35.4	36.1	37.2	38.0	38.8	39.5	39.7	39.6	39.5	39.6	39.7	38.2
2007	39.2	39.4	40.1	40.3	40.8	41.3	41.5	41.8	41.5	41.1	40.9	40.4	40.7
2008	39.2	39.2	39.3	38.3	38.6	38.5	38.4	38.0	37.6	36.4	35.3	34.2	37.8
2009	31.7	31.1	30.7	29.9	30.0	30.2	29.9	29.7	29.3	28.3	28.3	28.0	29.8
Manufacturing													
1990	39.5	39.1	39.0	38.1	38.1	38.3	37.9	38.0	37.8	37.3	37.5	37.5	38.2
2000	39.3	39.4	39.7	39.8	39.9	40.2	40.6	40.6	40.5	40.8	40.8	40.8	40.2
2001	40.4	40.4	40.2	40.0	39.6	39.4	39.0	38.5	38.2	37.8	37.5	37.0	39.0
2002	36.3	36.0	35.9	35.8	35.4	35.4	35.3	34.9	34.7	34.5	34.4	34.4	35.3
2003	33.7	33.6	33.5	33.4	33.5	33.4	32.8	32.8	32.5	32.8	32.8	32.8	33.1
2004	32.4	32.3	32.6	32.5	32.5	32.6	32.6	32.4	32.3	32.8	32.8	32.8	32.6
2005	32.5	32.7	32.8	33.3	33.3	33.7	33.8	33.7	33.8	33.6	33.8	34.0	33.4
2006	33.8	33.8	34.2	33.9	34.2	34.4	34.2	34.3	34.3	34.4	34.5	34.6	34.2
2007	33.9	33.9	34.0	33.7	33.7	33.8	33.8	34.1	33.8	33.6	33.6	33.5	33.8
2008	33.0	32.9	32.9	32.9	32.8	32.8	32.7	32.5	32.3	32.0	31.9	31.4	32.5
2009	30.8	30.3	30.0	29.5	29.1	28.9	28.7	28.8	28.5	28.4	28.3	28.0	29.1
Service-Providing													
1990	228.3	231.2	232.1	233.1	234.6	236.9	233.9	234.4	237.5	238.7	239.6	240.1	235.0
2000	355.5	357.7	361.0	363.2	365.0	368.1	359.3	361.8	367.8	368.4	371.1	372.1	364.3
2001	364.8	366.8	368.3	369.9	370.8	372.1	361.3	362.9	366.0	367.6	368.1	369.3	367.3
2002	357.7	358.9	359.9	363.6	366.5	367.5	361.7	365.1	370.6	372.0	373.9	375.0	366.0
2003	365.0	366.1	367.6	371.9	374.3	375.1	368.1	371.3	373.5	377.2	378.2	379.2	372.3
2004	373.3	374.4	377.1	377.9	381.7	382.9	381.4	384.9	388.3	389.6	391.7	394.3	383.1
2005	386.1	387.6	390.5	394.2	397.1	397.4	396.8	402.4	404.9	404.3	408.8	409.3	398.3
2006	402.7	404.4	407.1	414.1	417.4	419.3	416.2	422.2	424.2	427.9	433.2	434.5	418.6
2007	427.7	430.9	434.7	436.0	441.9	444.2	438.3	444.0	444.6	449.6	452.9	453.8	441.6
2008	445.3	447.5	448.6	449.6	453.6	451.5	448.3	452.7	453.2	455.7	454.9	453.7	451.2
2009	440.2	439.6	439.3	440.8	444.4	441.5	436.3	438.0	438.3	442.8	444.8	443.4	440.8

Employment by Industry: Raleigh-Cary, NC, Selected Years, 1990–2009—*Continued*

(Numbers in thousands, not seasonally adjusted.)

Industry and year	January	February	March	April	May	June	July	August	September	October	November	December	Annual average
Trade, Transportation, and Utilities													
1990	57.7	57.6	57.6	57.6	57.8	57.8	57.8	57.8	58.0	58.9	59.4	60.4	58.2
2000	83.8	83.3	84.2	84.6	85.1	85.8	84.1	84.4	84.5	86.0	87.0	88.1	85.1
2001	83.6	82.8	83.2	84.4	84.5	84.0	83.9	83.9	83.8	84.1	84.7	85.6	84.0
2002	80.2	79.6	80.1	80.3	80.6	80.6	80.5	81.0	81.2	81.6	83.2	84.2	81.1
2003	79.9	79.5	79.8	80.9	81.6	82.4	80.5	81.4	81.5	82.8	84.2	85.2	81.6
2004	81.8	81.4	81.5	81.4	81.8	81.9	82.0	82.6	82.8	83.6	85.1	86.2	82.7
2005	83.1	82.4	82.9	83.5	84.1	84.2	84.8	84.9	85.0	86.4	88.0	89.6	84.9
2006	85.7	84.9	85.1	85.8	86.2	86.6	87.7	88.6	88.5	89.7	92.7	94.0	88.0
2007	90.7	89.9	90.9	90.9	91.9	92.1	92.0	91.9	91.8	92.8	95.7	97.1	92.3
2008	92.7	92.3	92.7	92.6	92.6	92.8	92.4	92.5	91.7	92.3	93.1	93.6	92.6
2009	88.9	87.9	87.9	87.2	87.8	87.9	87.5	87.4	87.1	87.8	88.7	88.7	87.9
Wholesale Trade													
1990	14.7	14.9	15.0	15.1	15.1	15.0	14.8	14.7	14.7	15.1	14.9	14.7	14.9
2000	21.6	21.6	21.7	21.6	21.6	21.9	21.8	21.9	21.8	22.1	21.8	21.8	21.8
2001	21.7	21.7	21.8	21.3	21.2	21.2	21.2	21.0	20.9	20.7	20.4	20.3	21.1
2002	20.0	20.0	19.9	19.7	19.9	19.9	20.4	20.4	20.4	20.7	20.6	20.5	20.2
2003	20.1	20.0	20.2	20.1	20.0	20.1	20.0	20.1	20.1	20.2	20.0	20.0	20.1
2004	19.5	19.5	19.7	19.6	19.7	19.8	20.1	20.1	20.1	20.4	20.3	20.4	19.9
2005	19.8	19.8	19.8	19.9	20.1	20.2	20.1	20.3	20.4	20.6	20.5	20.7	20.2
2006	20.4	20.4	20.4	20.5	20.6	20.9	21.1	21.3	21.5	21.4	21.6	21.7	21.0
2007	21.9	22.0	22.2	22.1	22.2	22.2	22.3	22.2	22.2	22.1	22.2	22.2	22.2
2008	22.0	22.2	22.2	22.1	22.2	22.3	22.3	22.4	22.2	22.3	22.0	21.9	22.2
2009	21.4	21.4	21.2	21.0	21.0	20.9	20.6	20.7	20.6	20.6	20.5	20.4	20.9
Retail Trade													
1990	33.8	33.4	33.2	33.3	33.5	33.5	33.8	33.9	34.0	34.2	35.0	36.0	34.0
2000	51.6	51.1	51.8	52.8	53.3	53.6	52.3	52.6	52.8	53.8	55.3	56.4	53.1
2001	52.0	51.3	51.5	53.3	53.5	53.0	52.6	52.9	53.0	53.3	54.9	55.6	53.1
2002	50.6	50.2	50.7	50.8	50.9	50.9	50.1	50.9	51.2	51.3	53.2	54.3	51.3
2003	50.2	49.9	50.0	51.0	51.8	52.4	50.7	51.3	51.4	52.7	54.4	55.3	51.8
2004	52.6	52.1	52.0	51.8	52.2	52.2	52.2	52.7	53.0	53.5	55.1	56.0	53.0
2005	53.3	52.7	53.0	53.5	53.9	53.8	54.3	54.2	54.2	54.8	56.4	57.8	54.3
2006	54.4	53.6	53.7	54.2	54.5	54.5	55.1	55.7	55.4	56.8	59.3	60.4	55.6
2007	57.1	56.3	57.0	57.0	57.8	58.0	57.9	57.9	57.8	59.1	61.9	62.8	58.4
2008	59.3	58.8	59.1	58.9	58.8	58.9	58.6	58.5	58.0	58.5	59.7	59.9	58.9
2009	56.2	55.4	55.7	55.4	56.1	56.3	56.3	56.2	55.9	56.6	57.4	57.6	56.3
Transportation and Utilities													
1990	9.2	9.3	9.4	9.2	9.2	9.3	9.2	9.2	9.3	9.6	9.5	9.7	9.3
2000	10.6	10.6	10.7	10.2	10.2	10.3	10.0	9.9	9.9	10.1	9.9	9.9	10.2
2001	9.9	9.8	9.9	9.8	9.8	9.8	10.1	10.0	9.9	10.1	9.4	9.7	9.9
2002	9.6	9.4	9.5	9.8	9.8	9.8	10.0	9.7	9.6	9.6	9.4	9.4	9.6
2003	9.6	9.6	9.6	9.8	9.8	9.9	9.8	10.0	10.0	9.9	9.8	9.9	9.8
2004	9.7	9.8	9.8	10.0	9.9	9.9	9.7	9.8	9.7	9.7	9.7	9.8	9.8
2005	10.0	9.9	10.1	10.1	10.1	10.2	10.4	10.4	10.4	11.0	11.1	11.1	10.4
2006	10.9	10.9	11.0	11.1	11.1	11.2	11.5	11.6	11.6	11.5	11.8	11.9	11.3
2007	11.7	11.6	11.7	11.8	11.9	11.9	11.8	11.8	11.8	11.6	11.6	12.1	11.8
2008	11.4	11.3	11.4	11.6	11.6	11.6	11.5	11.6	11.5	11.5	11.4	11.8	11.5
2009	11.3	11.1	11.0	10.8	10.7	10.7	10.6	10.5	10.6	10.6	10.8	10.7	10.8
Information													
1990	10.9	11.0	11.0	10.6	10.6	10.8	11.1	11.1	11.0	11.1	11.1	11.2	11.0
2000	17.6	17.7	18.0	17.9	18.0	18.5	18.7	18.7	18.6	18.4	18.5	18.6	18.3
2001	18.8	18.8	18.8	18.5	18.5	18.4	18.0	18.0	18.0	17.8	17.8	18.0	18.3
2002	18.3	18.2	18.4	18.2	18.1	18.2	17.9	17.8	17.7	17.7	17.7	17.7	18.0
2003	17.6	17.7	17.7	17.7	17.8	17.9	17.9	17.8	17.5	17.3	17.3	17.4	17.6
2004	17.5	17.4	17.5	17.1	17.0	17.1	17.0	17.0	16.8	16.5	16.8	16.9	17.1
2005	16.7	16.7	16.9	17.1	17.2	17.3	17.3	17.4	17.2	17.0	17.1	17.2	17.1
2006	17.0	16.9	16.6	16.8	16.8	16.8	16.7	16.6	16.5	16.4	16.4	16.4	16.7
2007	16.3	16.6	16.5	16.4	16.5	16.8	16.9	16.9	16.7	16.9	16.8	16.8	16.7
2008	16.7	16.8	16.7	17.0	17.1	17.2	17.1	17.2	17.1	17.2	17.2	17.3	17.1
2009	17.1	17.0	16.9	16.9	16.8	16.9	16.9	16.8	16.7	16.8	16.8	16.8	16.9
Financial Activities													
1990	14.5	14.6	14.8	14.8	14.9	15.1	15.0	15.0	14.9	15.0	15.0	15.0	14.9
2000	21.4	21.6	21.9	22.0	22.2	22.4	22.0	22.1	22.2	22.4	22.4	22.5	22.1
2001	22.2	22.2	22.3	21.8	21.9	22.2	21.8	21.8	21.7	21.8	21.9	22.0	22.0
2002	22.2	22.3	22.1	21.9	22.1	22.4	22.0	22.4	22.4	22.4	22.5	22.3	22.3
2003	22.1	22.1	22.2	22.3	22.5	22.6	22.3	22.4	22.5	23.1	23.0	23.1	22.5
2004	23.6	23.8	23.9	23.8	23.6	23.6	24.0	23.9	23.7	23.8	23.9	23.9	23.8
2005	23.7	23.7	23.7	23.7	23.8	23.9	24.1	24.3	24.4	24.7	24.8	25.1	24.2
2006	24.7	24.7	24.9	25.2	25.3	25.5	25.6	25.7	25.7	25.9	26.1	26.2	25.5
2007	25.9	26.0	26.1	26.6	26.9	27.2	27.4	27.6	27.4	27.8	27.7	28.0	27.1
2008	27.1	27.3	27.3	27.4	27.5	27.7	27.7	27.8	27.7	27.8	27.6	27.6	27.5
2009	27.2	27.1	27.0	27.0	26.9	27.0	26.9	26.8	26.4	26.9	26.7	26.8	26.9

Employment by Industry: Raleigh-Cary, NC, Selected Years, 1990–2009—*Continued*

(Numbers in thousands, not seasonally adjusted.)

Industry and year	January	February	March	April	May	June	July	August	September	October	November	December	Annual average
Professional and Business Services													
1990	35.1	36.1	36.0	37.0	37.1	37.4	37.9	37.9	38.3	39.4	39.0	38.9	37.5
2000	73.0	73.6	74.3	75.3	75.1	75.7	75.3	76.0	76.2	76.2	76.7	76.8	75.4
2001	74.5	74.9	74.9	75.5	74.7	75.0	72.8	73.2	72.4	72.5	72.4	72.7	73.8
2002	69.6	69.7	70.0	70.6	71.1	71.5	72.7	73.3	73.1	73.2	73.9	73.9	71.8
2003	71.2	71.3	71.4	72.9	72.5	72.7	71.9	72.2	71.3	71.8	71.8	71.9	71.9
2004	70.7	71.2	71.7	72.5	73.4	74.4	75.6	75.8	75.7	76.4	76.5	77.7	74.3
2005	76.0	76.5	77.0	79.1	78.6	79.1	80.8	81.1	81.5	81.2	81.5	81.8	79.5
2006	80.9	81.2	82.0	83.9	83.9	84.9	85.7	86.1	87.3	88.5	88.8	88.8	85.2
2007	87.3	88.3	89.0	89.4	89.7	91.6	89.2	89.7	89.5	92.2	90.8	90.0	89.7
2008	88.5	88.5	88.6	89.1	89.2	88.9	88.1	89.1	88.1	88.1	88.3	87.3	86.0	88.3
2009	84.1	83.3	81.9	81.8	81.9	81.7	81.3	81.3	81.6	83.6	83.4	83.8	82.5
Education and Health Services													
1990	27.3	27.5	27.7	27.8	27.6	27.4	27.7	27.9	28.1	28.5	28.6	28.8	27.9
2000	39.9	40.3	40.5	40.7	40.7	40.9	40.2	40.5	40.6	41.1	41.1	41.2	40.6
2001	41.4	41.8	42.1	42.3	42.6	42.5	42.1	42.7	42.7	43.2	43.5	43.7	42.6
2002	43.3	43.8	44.0	45.2	45.3	45.2	44.8	45.4	46.0	46.4	46.9	46.7	45.3
2003	46.5	47.1	47.2	47.1	47.3	46.8	46.7	47.2	47.8	47.8	48.0	48.1	47.3
2004	47.8	48.1	48.6	48.3	48.8	48.6	48.7	49.3	49.8	50.2	50.6	50.6	49.1
2005	50.1	50.6	50.9	50.8	51.0	50.6	50.7	51.0	52.1	52.7	53.1	53.0	51.4
2006	52.3	52.9	53.3	54.1	54.6	54.2	53.8	54.1	54.8	55.6	56.4	56.5	54.4
2007	55.7	56.6	57.0	57.4	57.8	57.3	56.9	57.7	58.3	59.3	59.5	59.6	57.8
2008	58.9	59.7	59.7	59.7	60.1	59.2	58.7	59.2	60.0	60.8	61.4	61.1	59.9
2009	60.0	60.7	60.8	61.1	61.7	60.6	60.0	60.9	61.0	62.0	63.0	61.8	61.1
Leisure and Hospitality													
1990	25.3	25.8	25.7	25.7	26.6	27.5	27.7	28.1	27.8	26.3	26.2	26.6	26.6
2000	35.0	35.5	36.2	36.4	37.1	37.6	37.9	37.6	37.4	36.4	36.8	36.6	36.7
2001	36.1	36.9	37.5	38.0	38.6	39.7	39.0	38.6	37.5	37.1	36.7	36.9	37.7
2002	34.8	35.1	36.0	37.7	38.9	39.5	40.1	40.1	39.4	39.2	38.8	39.1	38.2
2003	37.2	37.3	37.8	38.8	39.2	39.7	39.0	39.7	38.9	38.4	38.5	38.3	38.6
2004	37.2	37.2	38.0	38.6	40.0	40.6	41.2	41.5	40.3	39.6	39.5	40.0	39.5
2005	38.6	39.0	40.0	40.5	42.0	43.0	42.6	42.7	42.8	42.1	42.3	42.8	41.5
2006	41.3	41.8	42.6	44.0	45.4	46.2	45.6	45.9	45.9	45.1	45.2	45.3	44.5
2007	44.7	45.2	45.8	45.5	48.1	49.1	48.8	49.7	49.0	47.5	48.6	48.8	47.6
2008	47.6	48.0	48.5	48.5	50.9	50.9	51.3	51.5	50.8	49.4	49.5	50.1	49.8
2009	48.4	48.6	49.0	49.2	51.4	51.4	51.5	51.3	50.2	49.6	49.6	49.6	50.0
Other Services													
1990	10.6	10.7	10.7	10.7	10.9	11.3	11.3	11.4	10.9	10.7	10.8	10.6	10.9
2000	14.6	14.8	14.8	15.1	15.2	15.6	15.6	15.3	15.2	15.4	15.4	15.3	15.2
2001	15.2	15.5	15.5	15.7	16.1	16.5	16.7	16.6	16.2	16.5	16.6	16.5	16.1
2002	16.3	16.3	16.2	16.6	17.0	17.0	17.1	16.9	16.6	16.7	16.7	16.6	16.7
2003	16.5	16.6	16.6	17.0	17.8	18.0	18.3	18.2	18.1	17.7	17.8	17.9	17.5
2004	18.2	18.4	18.4	18.6	19.1	19.3	18.9	18.7	18.4	18.5	18.6	18.6	18.6
2005	18.5	18.6	18.5	18.9	19.6	19.8	19.6	19.7	19.2	19.6	19.7	19.8	19.3
2006	19.6	19.9	19.9	20.3	20.6	21.3	20.7	20.5	19.7	20.1	20.4	20.6	20.3
2007	20.7	21.0	21.5	21.6	22.1	22.7	23.1	23.2	22.6	23.5	23.8	23.8	22.5
2008	24.6	24.9	24.6	24.5	25.1	25.4	25.9	25.9	25.7	25.7	25.5	25.1	25.2
2009	24.4	24.6	24.7	24.9	25.2	25.4	25.7	25.7	25.3	25.4	25.4	25.1	25.2
Government													
1990	46.9	47.9	48.6	48.9	49.1	49.6	45.4	45.2	48.5	48.8	49.5	48.6	48.1
2000	70.2	70.9	71.1	71.2	71.6	71.6	65.5	67.2	73.1	72.5	73.2	73.0	70.9
2001	73.0	73.9	74.0	73.7	73.9	73.8	67.0	68.1	73.7	74.6	74.5	73.9	72.8
2002	73.0	73.9	73.1	73.1	73.4	73.1	66.6	68.2	74.2	74.8	74.9	74.5	72.7
2003	74.0	74.5	74.9	75.2	75.6	75.0	71.5	72.4	75.9	78.3	77.6	77.3	75.2
2004	76.5	76.9	77.5	77.6	78.0	77.4	74.0	76.1	80.8	81.0	80.7	80.4	78.1
2005	79.4	80.1	80.6	80.6	80.8	79.5	76.9	81.3	82.7	80.6	82.3	80.0	80.4
2006	81.2	82.1	82.7	84.0	84.6	83.8	80.4	84.7	85.8	86.6	87.2	86.7	84.2
2007	86.4	87.3	87.9	88.2	88.9	87.4	84.0	87.3	89.3	89.6	90.0	89.7	88.0
2008	89.2	90.0	90.5	90.8	91.1	89.4	87.1	89.5	92.1	94.2	93.3	92.9	90.8
2009	90.1	90.4	91.1	92.7	92.7	90.6	86.5	87.8	90.0	90.7	91.2	90.8	90.4

Employment by Industry: Richmond, VA, Selected Years, 1990–2009

(Numbers in thousands, not seasonally adjusted.)

Industry and year	January	February	March	April	May	June	July	August	September	October	November	December	Annual average
Total Nonfarm													
1990	485.7	487.3	490.9	491.3	496.0	500.3	492.1	493.8	498.5	493.9	496.8	495.7	493.5
2000	574.3	576.3	582.3	585.5	589.8	595.2	587.4	587.9	590.5	589.3	593.2	596.2	587.3
2001	584.2	585.1	590.1	589.5	592.4	596.9	589.4	589.0	587.6	585.1	587.8	590.0	588.9
2002	578.5	581.3	586.7	587.3	591.4	594.7	586.2	586.8	586.3	585.6	588.1	589.1	586.8
2003	575.4	575.3	580.1	588.6	592.1	594.4	586.9	587.2	588.3	592.3	595.8	598.8	587.9
2004	589.7	592.1	598.3	601.7	605.8	609.4	601.7	597.7	605.1	610.6	613.4	615.0	603.4
2005	603.1	605.8	609.8	617.8	620.3	623.8	614.5	611.1	617.8	619.1	622.7	623.1	615.7
2006	612.3	612.7	620.7	622.0	627.5	629.9	626.5	625.0	623.8	631.5	635.6	636.5	625.3
2007	624.3	627.8	630.2	631.1	636.2	642.2	633.1	633.2	633.7	634.8	635.8	637.0	633.3
2008	625.9	627.1	629.7	633.2	632.9	636.7	629.2	628.2	629.4	632.7	631.0	628.5	630.4
2009	612.9	608.1	609.3	609.1	610.1	611.4	599.1	596.1	599.0	598.6	597.6	598.1	604.1
Total Private													
1990	392.1	392.5	395.4	397.8	401.1	406.1	402.4	404.4	405.4	401.1	402.6	402.2	400.3
2000	467.8	469.6	474.8	477.7	481.6	486.0	482.5	483.2	483.7	481.4	483.8	486.4	479.9
2001	475.1	475.5	480.2	480.3	483.2	487.1	483.2	482.8	480.1	476.1	477.1	478.9	480.0
2002	468.3	470.2	475.2	476.0	480.1	483.0	478.7	479.2	478.1	475.3	476.9	477.8	476.6
2003	463.5	462.2	467.6	474.7	479.1	481.9	478.6	480.6	479.3	481.6	482.9	485.5	476.5
2004	478.2	478.8	484.1	488.2	492.5	496.8	493.5	493.0	493.3	495.5	497.6	500.0	491.0
2005	489.4	490.2	493.7	500.7	504.1	508.0	504.4	503.9	505.6	507.2	509.5	509.8	502.2
2006	498.5	497.9	505.7	507.6	513.0	515.6	516.5	515.5	512.6	517.5	520.3	521.0	511.8
2007	509.0	511.3	514.7	515.7	521.3	528.0	524.0	525.1	525.1	523.8	524.4	526.3	520.7
2008	515.8	516.0	518.6	519.9	520.6	524.0	522.0	521.7	519.2	519.2	516.6	515.8	519.1
2009	499.5	494.3	495.0	494.2	496.1	497.5	492.1	489.1	488.5	488.4	486.4	486.7	492.3
Goods-Producing													
1990	95.3	95.8	96.1	95.8	96.5	97.0	96.7	96.9	96.6	96.0	95.3	94.3	96.0
2000	94.6	94.9	96.0	96.9	97.1	97.3	97.1	97.5	97.6	96.9	97.1	97.7	96.7
2001	95.3	95.6	96.2	96.1	95.9	96.1	95.1	94.8	94.5	93.2	93.1	92.7	94.9
2002	90.1	90.4	91.4	91.7	92.1	92.5	91.6	92.3	92.3	91.8	91.6	91.3	91.6
2003	88.0	87.5	88.7	89.8	90.3	89.7	89.6	89.8	89.3	88.6	88.2	87.9	88.9
2004	86.3	86.1	87.2	87.5	87.7	88.6	89.3	89.1	90.0	89.7	90.2	90.4	88.5
2005	89.3	88.6	88.6	89.3	89.5	90.2	91.1	91.1	90.5	90.0	90.3	90.2	89.9
2006	88.3	88.7	89.4	89.3	89.7	90.5	90.5	90.1	90.1	89.3	88.9	88.5	89.3
2007	87.4	87.1	87.8	88.7	89.5	90.5	90.0	90.2	89.8	89.0	88.3	88.1	88.9
2008	85.5	85.1	84.9	84.8	84.3	84.0	83.6	83.3	82.1	81.7	79.5	78.2	83.1
2009	74.5	71.6	71.4	70.7	70.0	70.1	69.4	68.6	68.2	68.9	67.9	66.8	69.8
Mining, Logging, and Construction													
1990	33.5	33.8	34.4	34.5	35.0	35.2	35.3	35.2	34.7	34.2	33.6	32.8	34.4
2000	37.5	37.7	39.0	40.3	40.5	40.9	40.7	41.2	41.1	40.9	40.9	40.7	40.1
2001	39.1	39.5	40.7	40.8	41.2	41.5	41.3	41.2	41.1	40.2	40.3	39.8	40.6
2002	38.5	38.7	39.9	40.5	41.0	41.0	40.7	41.3	41.3	41.1	40.9	40.6	40.5
2003	38.3	38.0	39.5	40.6	41.4	41.2	41.7	41.9	41.6	41.0	40.5	40.2	40.4
2004	39.2	39.2	40.3	41.2	41.9	42.6	43.3	43.0	43.7	43.8	44.1	44.1	42.2
2005	43.2	42.9	43.3	44.0	44.3	44.9	46.2	46.0	45.4	45.1	45.2	44.9	44.6
2006	43.7	44.2	45.1	45.0	45.7	46.5	46.6	46.5	46.0	46.0	45.8	45.7	45.6
2007	44.8	44.7	45.3	46.3	47.1	47.8	47.7	47.9	47.8	47.0	46.3	45.9	46.6
2008	43.7	43.4	43.6	43.6	43.3	43.3	43.3	43.3	42.3	42.1	40.6	39.7	42.7
2009	37.3	36.2	36.1	36.2	36.1	36.1	35.9	35.5	35.0	35.9	34.9	33.9	35.8
Manufacturing													
1990	61.8	62.0	61.7	61.3	61.5	61.8	61.4	61.7	61.9	61.8	61.7	61.5	61.7
2000	57.1	57.2	57.0	56.6	56.6	56.4	56.4	56.3	56.5	56.0	56.2	57.0	56.6
2001	56.2	56.1	55.5	55.3	54.7	54.6	53.8	53.6	53.4	53.0	52.8	52.9	54.3
2002	51.6	51.7	51.5	51.2	51.1	51.5	50.9	51.0	51.0	50.7	50.7	50.7	51.1
2003	49.7	49.5	49.2	49.2	48.9	48.5	47.9	47.9	47.7	47.6	47.7	47.7	48.4
2004	47.1	46.9	46.9	46.3	45.8	46.0	46.0	46.1	46.3	45.9	46.1	46.3	46.3
2005	46.1	45.7	45.3	45.3	45.2	45.3	44.9	45.1	45.1	44.9	45.1	45.3	45.3
2006	44.6	44.5	44.3	44.3	44.0	44.0	43.5	43.6	43.3	42.9	42.7	42.8	43.7
2007	42.6	42.4	42.5	42.4	42.4	42.7	42.3	42.3	42.0	42.0	42.0	42.2	42.3
2008	41.8	41.7	41.3	41.2	41.0	40.7	40.3	40.0	39.8	39.6	38.9	38.5	40.4
2009	37.2	35.4	35.3	34.5	33.9	34.0	33.5	33.1	33.2	33.0	33.0	32.9	34.1
Service-Providing													
1990	390.4	391.5	394.8	395.5	399.5	403.3	395.4	396.9	401.9	397.9	401.5	401.4	397.5
2000	479.7	481.4	486.3	488.6	492.7	497.9	490.3	490.4	492.9	492.4	496.1	498.5	490.6
2001	488.9	489.5	493.9	493.4	496.5	500.8	494.3	494.2	493.1	491.9	494.7	497.3	494.0
2002	488.4	490.9	495.3	495.6	499.3	502.2	494.6	494.5	494.0	493.8	496.5	497.8	495.2
2003	487.4	487.8	491.4	498.8	501.8	504.7	497.3	497.4	499.0	503.7	507.6	510.9	499.0
2004	503.4	506.0	511.1	514.2	518.1	520.8	512.4	508.6	515.1	520.9	523.2	524.6	514.9
2005	513.8	517.2	521.2	528.5	530.8	533.6	523.5	520.0	527.3	529.1	532.4	532.9	525.9
2006	524.0	524.0	531.3	532.7	537.8	539.4	536.4	534.9	534.5	542.6	547.1	548.0	536.1
2007	536.9	540.7	542.4	542.4	546.7	551.7	543.1	543.0	543.9	545.8	547.5	548.9	544.4
2008	540.4	542.0	544.8	548.4	548.6	552.7	545.6	544.9	547.3	551.0	551.5	550.3	547.3
2009	538.4	536.5	537.9	538.4	540.1	541.3	529.7	527.5	530.8	529.7	529.7	531.3	534.3

Employment by Industry: Richmond, VA, Selected Years, 1990–2009—*Continued*

(Numbers in thousands, not seasonally adjusted.)

Industry and year	January	February	March	April	May	June	July	August	September	October	November	December	Annual average
Trade, Transportation, and Utilities													
1990	96.9	95.0	95.2	94.4	95.0	95.6	95.4	96.4	95.6	96.2	98.6	99.6	96.2
2000	111.2	110.7	111.4	111.4	112.1	112.3	112.4	113.0	112.8	113.6	115.8	117.5	112.9
2001	112.6	111.5	112.0	110.9	111.5	111.7	111.4	111.6	111.4	112.1	114.1	115.5	112.2
2002	111.1	109.9	110.7	110.6	111.3	111.8	111.6	112.2	111.9	112.6	114.4	116.2	112.0
2003	110.8	109.8	109.9	110.8	111.8	112.1	111.7	112.1	111.7	113.7	115.6	117.2	112.3
2004	112.8	111.9	112.4	112.7	113.2	113.5	113.0	112.7	111.9	113.2	114.8	116.1	113.2
2005	111.4	110.5	111.3	111.9	112.4	112.9	113.1	113.5	113.2	113.9	116.5	118.5	113.3
2006	114.5	113.2	114.2	113.9	115.0	115.3	115.1	115.5	114.8	116.6	119.0	121.1	115.7
2007	117.0	116.0	116.8	116.4	117.6	118.4	118.3	118.4	118.5	119.0	121.4	122.8	118.4
2008	117.9	116.4	116.6	116.2	116.7	117.4	117.0	117.0	117.0	117.7	119.2	120.2	117.4
2009	114.5	112.6	111.9	110.9	111.2	111.2	110.2	110.0	109.4	109.9	109.9	110.5	111.0
Wholesale Trade													
1990	22.9	22.9	22.9	22.8	22.8	22.9	23.3	23.2	23.1	23.2	23.3	23.2	23.0
2000	23.7	23.7	24.0	24.1	24.1	24.3	24.3	24.4	24.4	24.5	24.6	24.7	24.2
2001	24.3	24.3	24.4	24.2	24.0	24.1	24.1	24.0	24.1	24.2	24.3	24.6	24.2
2002	24.3	24.4	24.8	24.7	24.9	25.1	25.3	25.5	25.6	25.6	25.7	25.9	25.2
2003	26.0	26.0	26.1	25.9	26.2	26.2	26.2	26.2	25.9	26.0	26.0	26.1	26.1
2004	25.7	25.8	25.9	26.1	26.2	26.3	26.4	26.2	26.0	26.2	26.1	26.1	26.1
2005	25.8	25.8	25.9	26.2	26.2	26.3	26.5	26.7	26.6	26.6	26.7	26.8	26.3
2006	26.9	27.0	27.1	27.2	27.4	27.6	27.8	27.9	27.8	28.0	28.1	28.1	27.6
2007	28.1	28.3	28.5	28.5	28.6	28.8	28.8	28.8	28.7	28.9	28.7	28.7	28.6
2008	28.5	28.6	28.6	28.6	28.5	28.6	28.7	28.6	28.4	28.3	28.1	27.9	28.5
2009	27.5	27.2	27.0	26.7	26.6	26.4	26.2	26.2	25.9	26.0	25.9	26.0	26.5
Retail Trade													
1990	60.3	58.3	58.3	58.0	58.4	58.6	58.3	59.2	58.5	58.9	61.1	62.1	59.2
2000	66.3	65.7	66.2	66.0	66.8	66.9	66.5	67.1	67.0	67.5	69.6	71.2	67.2
2001	67.3	66.2	66.0	65.7	66.4	66.5	66.4	66.5	66.2	67.0	69.2	70.5	67.0
2002	66.9	65.8	66.3	65.9	66.4	66.8	66.1	66.4	66.1	66.7	68.3	70.0	66.8
2003	65.1	64.1	64.1	64.8	65.5	65.7	65.2	65.6	65.7	67.2	69.2	70.7	66.0
2004	67.2	66.2	66.6	66.3	66.7	66.9	65.9	65.8	65.4	66.6	68.2	69.2	66.8
2005	65.9	65.0	65.4	65.7	66.2	66.5	66.3	66.5	66.2	66.7	69.0	70.6	66.7
2006	67.3	66.1	66.8	66.6	67.4	67.4	67.0	67.0	66.3	67.7	69.9	71.4	67.6
2007	68.1	67.0	67.4	67.1	68.2	68.6	68.6	68.5	68.6	69.2	71.5	72.4	68.8
2008	68.9	67.4	67.6	67.1	67.6	68.1	67.7	67.8	68.1	69.0	70.5	71.2	68.4
2009	67.0	65.6	65.2	64.7	65.1	65.3	64.6	64.5	64.3	64.8	64.8	65.3	65.1
Transportation and Utilities													
1990	13.7	13.8	14.0	13.6	13.8	14.1	13.8	14.0	14.0	14.1	14.2	14.3	14.0
2000	21.2	21.3	21.2	21.3	21.2	21.1	21.6	21.5	21.4	21.6	21.6	21.6	21.4
2001	21.0	21.0	21.0	21.0	21.1	21.1	20.9	21.1	21.1	20.9	20.6	20.4	20.9
2002	19.9	19.7	19.6	20.0	20.0	19.9	20.2	20.3	20.2	20.3	20.4	20.3	20.1
2003	19.7	19.7	19.7	20.1	20.1	20.2	20.3	20.3	20.1	20.5	20.4	20.4	20.1
2004	19.9	19.9	19.9	20.3	20.3	20.3	20.7	20.7	20.5	20.4	20.5	20.8	20.4
2005	19.7	19.7	20.0	20.0	20.0	20.1	20.3	20.3	20.4	20.6	20.8	21.1	20.3
2006	20.3	20.1	20.3	20.1	20.2	20.3	20.3	20.6	20.7	20.9	21.0	21.6	20.5
2007	20.8	20.7	20.9	20.8	20.8	21.0	20.9	21.1	21.2	20.9	21.2	21.7	21.0
2008	20.5	20.4	20.4	20.5	20.6	20.7	20.6	20.6	20.5	20.4	20.6	21.1	20.6
2009	20.0	19.8	19.7	19.5	19.5	19.5	19.4	19.3	19.2	19.1	19.2	19.2	19.5
Information													
1990	11.0	11.0	11.1	11.0	10.9	11.1	11.4	11.4	11.5	11.3	11.3	11.2	11.2
2000	12.5	12.4	12.6	12.6	12.8	13.1	13.2	13.3	13.4	13.1	13.2	13.3	13.0
2001	13.1	13.1	13.1	12.6	12.6	12.5	12.5	12.6	12.4	12.3	12.2	12.3	12.6
2002	12.6	12.6	12.6	12.5	12.6	12.5	12.3	12.4	12.2	11.9	12.2	12.2	12.4
2003	11.7	12.0	12.0	11.9	11.9	12.0	11.9	11.9	11.7	11.5	11.6	11.5	11.8
2004	11.5	11.4	11.5	11.2	11.2	11.2	11.1	11.0	10.9	10.9	11.0	11.0	11.2
2005	11.0	11.0	11.1	11.1	11.1	11.1	11.1	11.1	11.1	11.0	11.1	11.1	11.1
2006	11.0	11.0	11.0	10.8	12.9	10.8	11.8	11.2	11.1	11.1	11.2	11.2	11.3
2007	11.6	11.6	11.5	11.7	11.9	11.6	11.3	11.2	11.0	10.8	10.8	10.6	11.3
2008	10.5	10.5	10.5	10.4	10.3	10.4	10.3	10.2	10.1	10.3	10.4	10.4	10.4
2009	10.5	10.4	10.4	10.4	10.4	10.3	10.2	9.8	9.7	9.7	9.6	9.6	10.1
Financial Activities													
1990	35.8	35.8	35.9	35.9	36.0	36.4	36.4	36.3	36.0	35.9	35.9	35.8	36.0
2000	44.3	44.3	44.5	44.4	44.8	45.1	45.3	45.5	45.3	45.4	45.8	46.5	45.1
2001	46.0	46.3	46.6	46.7	46.8	47.3	47.3	47.6	47.4	47.3	47.5	47.7	47.0
2002	47.0	47.2	47.3	47.2	47.0	47.1	46.8	46.3	46.4	46.1	45.9	45.7	46.7
2003	45.2	45.4	45.6	46.2	46.5	46.7	47.0	47.2	46.9	46.3	46.5	47.0	46.3
2004	46.6	46.9	46.8	47.1	47.0	47.3	47.1	47.2	46.7	46.5	46.6	46.8	46.9
2005	46.6	46.7	46.8	46.5	46.6	46.7	47.3	47.2	46.7	46.4	46.3	46.5	46.7
2006	46.4	46.5	46.8	46.5	46.7	46.9	47.0	47.0	46.4	46.2	46.0	46.1	46.5
2007	45.7	45.6	45.9	45.9	46.0	46.3	46.2	46.4	45.7	45.3	45.1	45.0	45.8
2008	44.6	44.5	44.5	44.0	43.8	44.0	44.3	44.3	43.7	44.1	44.0	44.1	44.2
2009	43.7	43.4	43.6	43.5	43.0	43.0	43.0	43.0	42.5	42.4	42.2	42.3	43.0

Employment by Industry: Richmond, VA, Selected Years, 1990–2009—*Continued*

(Numbers in thousands, not seasonally adjusted.)

Industry and year	January	February	March	April	May	June	July	August	September	October	November	December	Annual average
Professional and Business Services													
1990	63.7	64.4	64.9	66.7	67.4	67.9	66.3	66.9	66.7	65.8	65.9	65.6	66.0
2000	88.3	90.0	91.0	92.2	92.9	93.8	92.8	92.3	93.0	92.2	92.2	92.5	91.9
2001	90.0	90.0	90.6	90.4	90.9	91.6	90.5	90.3	88.7	87.5	87.6	88.1	89.7
2002	86.5	87.6	88.3	88.6	88.9	89.0	88.3	88.0	87.9	86.4	86.8	86.6	87.7
2003	81.7	81.1	82.3	83.8	84.3	84.9	84.5	84.6	84.3	85.0	85.1	85.7	83.9
2004	84.5	84.6	85.0	86.4	87.4	88.4	88.8	89.4	89.1	90.9	91.1	92.3	88.2
2005	89.7	90.3	90.8	92.3	92.7	93.4	93.8	93.5	93.6	95.2	94.9	95.1	92.9
2006	93.2	93.4	94.3	93.7	94.6	95.4	95.3	95.9	96.4	98.5	98.8	99.3	95.7
2007	97.0	97.7	98.8	98.6	98.3	99.8	99.5	99.7	100.0	100.2	99.8	100.2	99.1
2008	99.4	99.9	100.3	100.1	99.9	100.5	99.7	99.8	99.0	99.1	98.2	97.4	99.4
2009	95.2	94.7	95.0	93.1	92.7	92.2	91.9	91.7	91.4	91.7	91.8	91.7	92.8
Education and Health Services													
1990	40.4	40.7	41.0	41.1	41.3	41.8	39.9	40.3	43.1	43.0	43.4	43.3	41.6
2000	52.4	52.4	52.7	51.5	51.6	51.5	49.3	49.5	51.8	52.2	52.5	52.7	51.7
2001	53.0	53.2	53.4	53.5	53.8	54.2	52.5	52.6	54.7	55.2	55.2	55.4	53.9
2002	55.5	55.9	56.0	56.1	57.1	57.3	55.3	55.7	57.3	57.8	58.2	58.2	56.7
2003	59.8	59.9	60.0	60.7	60.5	60.2	57.7	59.4	61.6	62.1	62.4	62.8	60.5
2004	63.7	64.2	64.7	65.1	65.8	65.7	62.1	62.3	65.6	66.7	67.4	67.5	65.1
2005	67.2	68.0	68.0	68.6	69.0	68.5	64.8	64.7	69.6	71.2	71.7	70.9	68.5
2006	69.3	68.6	71.1	73.2	71.6	71.3	70.9	70.0	71.2	73.1	73.5	72.3	71.3
2007	71.9	74.3	72.9	71.6	73.0	73.5	71.0	71.5	75.6	76.9	77.8	78.6	74.1
2008	78.3	79.3	79.6	80.8	80.8	80.7	78.5	78.8	81.5	82.5	83.0	83.1	80.6
2009	82.0	82.4	82.3	82.9	83.8	83.6	80.7	80.7	83.3	84.5	85.3	86.3	83.2
Leisure and Hospitality													
1990	31.8	32.5	33.7	35.5	36.6	38.6	38.6	38.6	38.4	35.6	34.8	35.0	35.8
2000	40.8	41.0	42.3	44.4	45.9	48.2	47.6	47.4	45.4	43.6	42.9	41.8	44.3
2001	41.4	41.8	44.1	45.8	47.0	49.0	49.1	48.7	46.6	44.2	42.9	42.8	45.3
2002	41.1	41.9	44.0	44.4	46.0	47.6	47.7	47.2	45.2	43.9	42.8	42.7	44.5
2003	41.7	41.7	44.1	46.0	47.8	49.6	49.3	48.7	46.7	46.9	45.5	45.2	46.1
2004	44.3	44.5	46.6	48.4	50.2	52.0	52.2	51.4	49.7	48.1	47.0	46.4	48.4
2005	44.8	45.3	47.4	49.3	50.9	52.9	52.9	52.4	50.9	49.4	48.7	47.8	49.4
2006	46.8	47.4	49.6	50.9	52.8	55.4	54.9	54.5	51.8	52.4	51.1	50.9	51.5
2007	48.6	49.1	50.7	51.6	53.8	56.3	56.1	55.7	53.5	52.0	50.6	50.3	52.4
2008	49.0	49.3	51.1	53.1	55.2	57.1	56.7	55.9	53.1	52.0	50.5	50.6	52.8
2009	48.7	48.8	49.9	52.1	54.4	56.2	55.8	54.7	52.8	50.0	48.4	48.2	51.7
Other Services													
1990	17.2	17.3	17.5	17.4	17.4	17.7	17.7	17.6	17.5	17.3	17.4	17.4	17.5
2000	23.7	23.9	24.3	24.3	24.4	24.7	24.8	24.7	24.4	24.4	24.3	24.4	24.4
2001	23.7	24.0	24.2	24.3	24.7	24.7	24.8	24.6	24.4	24.3	24.5	24.4	24.4
2002	24.4	24.7	24.9	24.9	25.1	25.2	25.1	25.1	24.9	24.8	25.0	24.9	24.9
2003	24.6	24.8	25.0	25.5	26.0	26.7	26.9	26.9	27.1	27.5	28.0	28.2	26.4
2004	28.5	29.2	29.9	29.8	30.0	30.1	29.9	29.9	29.4	29.5	29.5	29.5	29.6
2005	29.4	29.8	29.7	31.7	31.9	32.3	30.4	30.4	29.9	30.1	30.0	29.7	30.4
2006	29.0	29.1	29.3	29.3	29.7	30.0	31.4	31.3	31.6	30.7	32.2	31.6	30.4
2007	29.8	29.9	30.3	31.2	31.2	31.6	31.6	32.0	31.0	30.6	30.6	30.7	30.9
2008	30.6	31.0	31.1	30.5	29.6	29.9	31.9	32.4	32.7	31.8	31.8	31.8	31.3
2009	30.4	30.4	30.5	30.6	30.6	30.9	30.9	30.6	31.2	31.3	31.3	31.3	30.8
Government													
1990	93.6	94.8	95.5	93.5	94.9	94.2	89.7	89.4	93.1	92.8	94.2	93.5	93.3
2000	106.5	106.7	107.5	107.8	108.2	109.2	104.9	104.7	106.8	107.9	109.4	109.8	107.5
2001	109.1	109.6	109.9	109.2	109.2	109.8	106.2	106.2	107.5	109.0	110.7	111.1	109.0
2002	110.2	111.1	111.5	111.3	111.3	111.7	107.5	107.6	108.2	110.3	111.2	111.3	110.3
2003	111.9	113.1	112.5	113.9	113.0	112.5	108.3	106.6	109.0	110.7	112.9	113.3	111.4
2004	111.5	113.3	114.2	113.5	113.3	112.6	108.2	104.7	111.8	115.1	115.8	115.0	112.4
2005	113.7	115.6	116.1	117.1	116.2	115.8	110.1	107.2	112.2	111.9	113.2	113.3	113.5
2006	113.8	114.8	115.0	114.4	114.5	114.3	110.0	109.5	111.2	114.0	115.3	115.5	113.5
2007	115.3	116.5	115.5	115.4	114.9	114.2	109.1	108.1	108.6	111.0	111.4	110.7	112.6
2008	110.1	111.1	111.1	113.3	112.3	112.7	107.2	106.5	110.2	113.5	114.4	112.7	111.3
2009	113.4	113.8	114.3	114.9	114.0	113.9	107.0	107.0	110.5	110.2	111.2	111.4	111.8

Employment by Industry: Riverside-San Bernardino-Ontario, CA, Selected Years, 1990–2009

(Numbers in thousands, not seasonally adjusted.)

Industry and year	January	February	March	April	May	June	July	August	September	October	November	December	Annual average
Total Nonfarm													
1990	696.1	702.1	707.8	708.7	713.8	718.2	708.5	702.3	713.4	721.5	726.8	732.1	712.6
2000	964.6	969.5	977.3	980.9	992.2	994.1	980.0	980.5	994.7	998.4	1010.7	1017.9	988.4
2001	1010.1	1011.4	1022.8	1023.1	1029.2	1034.6	1026.4	1023.9	1034.5	1039.8	1049.4	1051.7	1029.7
2002	1035.2	1043.0	1049.1	1061.0	1069.7	1074.0	1054.5	1059.1	1069.7	1074.9	1089.2	1095.0	1064.5
2003	1075.5	1078.6	1088.1	1090.9	1096.8	1101.3	1089.9	1088.3	1102.5	1117.8	1126.9	1133.7	1099.2
2004	1122.8	1128.5	1139.5	1151.9	1159.0	1161.6	1152.0	1152.3	1166.5	1183.7	1197.4	1205.0	1160.0
2005	1184.4	1195.8	1207.7	1220.1	1221.0	1221.8	1210.0	1213.6	1230.1	1240.6	1254.3	1264.4	1222.0
2006	1246.5	1254.7	1264.9	1268.8	1273.4	1278.1	1262.9	1259.5	1268.2	1271.8	1280.5	1282.9	1267.7
2007	1262.7	1267.4	1275.0	1272.9	1279.2	1278.6	1264.5	1259.4	1263.4	1269.5	1278.1	1280.2	1270.9
2008	1247.5	1246.1	1246.3	1244.3	1238.8	1234.3	1208.9	1205.3	1202.6	1206.1	1205.9	1199.6	1223.8
2009	1169.4	1158.9	1157.3	1147.5	1145.0	1138.6	1109.2	1109.7	1105.3	1111.1	1115.5	1114.8	1131.9
Total Private													
1990	549.7	555.2	558.7	557.8	560.1	564.0	561.2	561.5	563.7	567.6	572.7	576.7	562.4
2000	775.3	779.3	783.8	787.3	793.8	799.9	793.4	799.1	805.2	804.3	813.9	819.8	796.3
2001	811.9	814.2	821.8	823.8	828.6	832.9	831.7	835.3	835.0	835.9	840.1	842.9	829.5
2002	827.2	831.4	837.9	842.2	851.5	855.1	847.5	856.1	860.1	861.0	872.8	878.8	851.8
2003	860.3	863.4	870.8	874.3	881.9	887.2	884.3	888.9	895.6	907.8	914.7	922.4	887.6
2004	911.1	916.6	925.7	937.0	944.0	948.2	946.5	950.4	956.5	969.4	979.5	985.6	947.5
2005	964.4	974.3	984.5	995.6	996.5	1001.6	999.2	1003.0	1012.6	1018.1	1030.0	1038.9	1001.6
2006	1025.5	1033.4	1041.5	1042.7	1046.5	1050.8	1046.8	1047.4	1049.6	1046.9	1054.2	1057.3	1045.2
2007	1038.0	1042.2	1047.4	1044.5	1050.0	1049.6	1047.2	1046.2	1044.2	1041.3	1047.7	1048.7	1045.6
2008	1016.7	1014.5	1012.8	1009.7	1003.8	1001.0	987.9	984.6	980.9	975.0	973.5	967.1	994.0
2009	938.0	927.8	924.6	913.3	911.2	907.1	892.8	889.9	888.4	885.3	888.2	888.6	904.6
Goods-Producing													
1990	140.1	142.2	143.1	141.3	142.2	143.9	141.0	141.2	139.2	133.8	130.1	127.9	138.8
2000	191.1	192.7	193.8	197.4	199.5	202.9	203.2	205.6	206.6	205.7	206.0	205.9	200.9
2001	203.5	204.3	206.9	207.4	209.1	209.8	211.1	213.0	211.7	209.9	207.6	205.7	208.3
2002	199.8	201.4	203.1	204.0	206.0	207.8	208.2	212.4	212.1	212.2	212.5	210.8	207.5
2003	207.6	207.5	210.5	211.2	215.3	217.0	216.8	220.0	220.8	222.7	222.6	223.1	216.3
2004	221.3	223.2	224.2	229.0	231.5	234.4	237.0	238.4	240.2	240.8	239.1	238.2	233.1
2005	230.7	235.3	238.3	242.3	243.2	247.0	248.6	250.7	252.7	253.3	253.1	253.1	245.7
2006	250.4	253.4	254.4	253.7	256.5	259.4	257.1	256.7	255.3	247.7	242.2	240.3	252.3
2007	234.2	234.6	235.8	235.0	236.4	237.8	237.2	236.7	233.1	226.6	223.3	218.5	232.4
2008	208.9	207.2	206.8	205.0	203.8	203.5	200.5	199.4	196.0	190.2	184.9	179.5	198.8
2009	169.8	164.2	163.3	160.1	160.5	159.5	156.5	155.0	152.3	149.6	147.9	146.1	157.1
Mining and Logging													
1990	1.4	1.4	1.4	1.3	1.3	1.3	1.3	1.3	1.3	1.4	1.4	1.4	1.3
2000	1.3	1.3	1.3	1.3	1.2	1.2	1.3	1.3	1.2	1.2	1.2	1.2	1.2
2001	1.2	1.2	1.2	1.2	1.2	1.2	1.2	1.1	1.2	1.1	1.1	1.2	1.1
2002	1.1	1.1	1.1	1.2	1.2	1.2	1.3	1.3	1.3	1.2	1.3	1.3	1.2
2003	1.3	1.3	1.3	1.3	1.2	1.2	1.2	1.2	1.2	1.2	1.2	1.2	1.2
2004	1.2	1.2	1.2	1.2	1.2	1.2	1.2	1.2	1.2	1.2	1.3	1.3	1.2
2005	1.3	1.3	1.3	1.3	1.3	1.3	1.4	1.4	1.4	1.4	1.4	1.4	1.4
2006	1.4	1.4	1.4	1.4	1.4	1.4	1.5	1.4	1.4	1.4	1.4	1.4	1.4
2007	1.4	1.3	1.3	1.3	1.3	1.3	1.4	1.4	1.4	1.3	1.3	1.2	1.3
2008	1.3	1.3	1.3	1.2	1.2	1.2	1.2	1.2	1.2	1.2	1.1	1.2	1.2
2009	1.2	1.2	1.2	1.2	1.2	1.2	1.1	1.1	1.1	1.1	1.1	1.1	1.2
Construction													
1990	60.8	62.4	63.0	61.1	61.1	62.5	60.9	61.2	60.0	54.8	51.5	50.4	59.1
2000	73.5	73.9	74.7	77.1	79.2	81.0	81.0	82.7	84.0	83.5	84.0	84.0	79.9
2001	81.6	82.2	84.5	86.5	88.6	89.7	90.9	93.0	92.3	92.1	90.9	89.6	88.5
2002	84.8	85.7	86.7	87.3	88.7	90.2	91.6	95.1	95.0	95.9	95.8	93.9	90.9
2003	92.7	91.9	94.2	94.6	98.6	99.8	99.7	102.2	102.7	104.0	103.7	103.4	99.0
2004	102.4	103.6	104.0	108.4	110.1	112.2	114.5	115.9	117.4	118.6	117.3	116.6	111.8
2005	109.9	113.8	116.1	120.5	121.7	124.9	125.7	127.6	129.3	130.2	130.2	129.9	123.3
2006	126.7	128.6	128.9	128.3	130.2	132.6	131.6	131.5	130.2	123.9	119.6	117.7	127.5
2007	112.2	112.9	114.2	114.4	115.3	116.6	116.5	116.4	113.6	108.8	105.8	103.2	112.5
2008	95.8	94.8	95.3	94.0	93.6	93.8	92.3	92.0	89.5	85.7	82.5	79.5	90.7
2009	73.6	70.0	70.5	68.8	69.8	69.6	68.1	67.6	65.7	63.2	61.8	60.1	67.4
Manufacturing													
1990	77.9	78.4	78.7	78.9	79.8	80.1	78.8	78.7	77.9	77.6	77.2	76.1	78.3
2000	116.3	117.5	117.8	119.0	119.1	120.7	120.9	121.6	121.4	121.0	120.8	120.7	119.7
2001	120.7	120.9	121.2	119.7	119.3	118.9	119.0	118.9	118.2	116.7	115.6	114.9	118.7
2002	113.9	114.6	115.3	115.5	116.1	116.4	115.3	116.0	115.8	115.1	115.4	115.6	115.4
2003	113.6	114.3	115.0	115.3	115.5	116.0	115.9	116.6	116.9	117.5	117.7	118.5	116.1
2004	117.7	118.4	119.0	119.4	120.2	121.0	121.3	121.3	121.6	121.0	120.5	120.3	120.1
2005	119.5	120.2	120.9	120.5	120.2	120.8	121.5	121.7	122.0	121.7	121.5	121.8	121.0
2006	122.3	123.4	124.1	124.0	124.9	125.4	124.0	123.8	123.7	122.4	121.2	121.2	123.4
2007	120.6	120.4	120.3	119.3	119.8	119.9	119.3	118.9	118.1	116.5	115.2	114.1	118.5
2008	111.8	111.1	110.2	109.8	109.0	108.5	107.0	106.2	105.3	103.3	101.3	98.8	106.9
2009	95.0	93.0	91.6	90.1	89.5	88.7	87.3	86.3	85.5	85.3	85.0	84.9	88.5

Employment by Industry: Riverside-San Bernardino-Ontario, CA, Selected Years, 1990–2009—*Continued*

(Numbers in thousands, not seasonally adjusted.)

Industry and year	January	February	March	April	May	June	July	August	September	October	November	December	Annual average
Service-Providing													
1990	556.0	559.9	564.7	567.4	571.6	574.3	567.5	561.1	574.2	587.7	596.7	604.2	573.8
2000	773.5	776.8	783.5	783.5	792.7	791.2	776.8	774.9	788.1	792.7	804.7	812.0	787.5
2001	806.6	807.1	815.9	815.7	820.1	824.8	815.3	810.9	822.8	829.9	841.8	846.0	821.4
2002	835.4	841.6	846.0	857.0	863.7	866.2	846.3	846.7	857.6	862.7	876.7	884.2	857.0
2003	867.9	871.1	877.6	879.7	881.5	884.3	873.1	868.3	881.7	895.1	904.3	910.6	882.9
2004	901.5	905.3	915.3	922.9	927.5	927.2	915.0	913.9	926.3	942.9	958.3	966.8	926.9
2005	953.7	960.5	969.4	977.8	977.8	974.8	961.4	962.9	977.4	987.3	1001.2	1011.3	976.3
2006	996.1	1001.3	1010.5	1015.1	1016.9	1018.7	1005.8	1002.8	1012.9	1024.1	1038.3	1042.6	1015.4
2007	1028.5	1032.8	1039.2	1037.9	1042.8	1040.8	1027.3	1022.7	1030.3	1042.9	1055.8	1061.7	1038.6
2008	1038.6	1038.9	1039.5	1039.3	1035.0	1030.8	1008.4	1005.9	1006.6	1015.9	1021.0	1020.1	1025.0
Trade, Transportation, and Utilities													
1990	143.3	143.1	143.5	144.7	145.6	146.6	148.4	147.8	148.7	152.7	157.3	161.1	148.6
2000	207.5	206.2	206.7	207.7	209.5	210.7	210.8	211.1	212.6	213.1	219.0	222.5	211.5
2001	218.6	215.9	217.4	217.2	217.9	218.9	219.3	219.2	219.6	221.0	225.0	227.7	219.8
2002	220.0	218.5	220.0	222.2	224.8	226.4	225.9	226.9	228.3	229.1	234.8	238.2	226.3
2003	231.0	229.8	230.7	231.9	233.4	234.7	234.4	235.3	236.7	243.3	245.8	250.2	236.4
2004	243.1	242.1	244.2	247.6	249.9	251.7	253.4	255.6	258.0	266.7	274.1	278.4	255.4
2005	269.5	267.8	269.2	270.8	272.2	273.6	274.6	276.3	279.4	281.2	289.9	296.8	276.8
2006	285.2	283.5	286.1	286.8	288.6	290.6	291.3	291.9	293.0	296.8	305.0	309.4	292.4
2007	299.1	296.7	297.9	297.5	298.9	299.0	300.4	300.7	301.9	303.1	311.7	315.7	301.9
2008	302.1	297.3	296.0	294.8	294.5	293.3	290.1	289.3	288.7	287.1	290.5	291.1	292.9
2009	280.3	275.5	273.0	269.2	269.4	268.8	265.2	264.4	265.3	265.0	268.7	271.3	269.7
Wholesale Trade													
1990	23.0	23.3	23.4	24.5	24.6	24.8	25.1	25.2	25.0	25.2	24.9	25.0	24.5
2000	35.8	36.0	36.2	38.4	38.7	39.1	39.3	39.0	39.5	38.8	38.7	38.9	38.2
2001	41.7	41.9	42.7	42.6	42.3	42.0	42.2	41.6	41.2	40.8	40.3	40.1	41.6
2002	40.4	40.7	40.9	41.6	41.8	42.2	42.1	42.5	42.7	42.5	42.8	42.9	41.9
2003	42.9	43.3	43.5	44.0	44.1	44.0	43.4	43.4	43.4	43.4	43.0	43.1	43.5
2004	42.9	43.3	43.7	44.2	44.6	45.1	46.2	46.4	46.6	47.6	47.8	48.2	45.6
2005	47.9	48.0	48.5	49.3	49.6	49.9	50.2	50.4	50.8	51.1	51.4	52.1	49.9
2006	52.6	53.1	53.5	54.0	54.0	54.2	54.6	54.6	54.8	54.6	54.8	55.0	54.2
2007	55.3	55.9	56.2	56.3	56.5	56.9	57.1	57.2	57.4	57.5	57.6	57.7	56.8
2008	56.3	56.0	55.6	55.2	55.1	55.0	53.8	53.6	53.1	52.7	51.9	51.2	54.1
2009	50.4	49.8	49.1	48.7	48.5	48.5	48.1	47.8	47.4	47.2	47.0	46.8	48.3
Retail Trade													
1990	97.2	96.5	96.6	96.9	97.6	98.1	98.6	98.3	98.9	102.5	106.9	109.5	99.8
2000	125.0	123.5	123.6	123.1	124.4	125.1	125.3	126.2	126.7	128.8	134.3	137.4	127.0
2001	131.1	129.4	130.3	130.3	130.9	131.6	131.3	131.7	132.2	133.3	137.6	140.5	132.5
2002	134.3	132.4	133.9	134.8	136.6	137.3	137.1	137.4	138.0	138.6	143.9	146.0	137.5
2003	139.6	138.6	138.9	138.8	139.5	140.4	140.7	141.5	142.0	147.0	150.1	154.2	142.6
2004	147.7	145.8	147.3	148.9	150.5	151.0	151.2	152.6	153.8	158.7	165.8	169.5	153.6
2005	162.3	160.1	160.4	161.0	161.7	162.7	163.4	164.6	166.0	166.9	174.3	179.7	165.3
2006	168.9	166.8	168.1	168.6	169.7	171.0	171.5	171.8	171.7	175.0	182.2	185.1	172.5
2007	176.7	173.2	174.2	173.1	174.1	173.3	173.2	173.5	173.4	174.4	182.4	185.3	175.6
2008	175.2	170.8	170.3	169.2	168.7	168.1	166.7	165.8	165.3	164.7	168.7	169.6	168.6
2009	161.1	157.5	156.0	154.2	154.3	153.6	152.5	152.0	152.2	151.9	155.5	157.5	154.9
Transportation and Utilities													
1990	23.1	23.3	23.5	23.3	23.4	23.7	24.7	24.3	24.8	25.0	25.5	26.6	24.3
2000	46.7	46.7	46.9	46.2	46.4	46.5	46.2	45.9	46.4	45.5	46.0	46.2	46.3
2001	45.8	44.6	44.4	44.3	44.7	45.3	45.8	45.9	46.2	46.9	47.1	47.1	45.7
2002	45.3	45.4	45.2	45.8	46.4	46.9	46.7	47.0	47.6	48.0	48.1	49.3	46.8
2003	48.5	47.9	48.3	49.1	49.8	50.3	50.3	50.4	51.3	52.9	52.7	52.9	50.4
2004	52.5	53.0	53.2	54.5	54.8	55.6	56.0	56.6	57.6	60.4	60.5	60.7	56.3
2005	59.3	59.7	60.3	60.5	60.9	61.0	61.0	61.3	62.6	63.2	64.2	65.0	61.6
2006	63.7	63.6	64.5	64.2	64.9	65.4	65.2	65.5	66.5	67.2	68.0	69.3	65.7
2007	67.1	67.6	67.5	68.1	68.3	68.8	70.1	70.0	71.1	71.2	71.7	72.7	69.5
2008	70.6	70.5	70.1	70.4	70.7	70.2	69.6	69.9	70.3	69.7	69.9	70.3	70.2
2009	68.8	68.2	67.9	66.3	66.6	66.7	64.6	64.6	65.7	65.9	66.2	67.0	66.5
Information													
1990	13.4	13.4	13.5	13.4	13.6	13.7	14.0	13.3	13.2	13.2	13.3	13.4	13.5
2000	13.7	13.8	13.9	14.0	14.1	14.3	14.4	14.5	14.6	14.6	14.6	14.7	14.3
2001	14.7	14.6	14.3	14.3	14.5	14.7	14.8	14.7	14.5	14.4	14.5	14.7	14.6
2002	14.5	14.3	14.2	13.9	14.1	14.2	13.9	14.1	13.8	14.0	14.0	14.0	14.1
2003	13.9	13.9	13.8	13.6	13.7	13.8	14.1	14.0	13.9	13.8	14.0	13.9	13.9
2004	13.9	13.7	13.8	13.9	13.9	14.0	14.3	14.0	13.9	14.2	14.4	14.4	14.0
2005	14.3	14.5	14.5	14.6	14.7	14.6	14.5	14.2	14.4	14.4	14.6	14.7	14.5
2006	14.6	14.9	14.9	15.1	15.2	15.4	15.5	15.5	15.5	15.4	15.6	15.7	15.3
2007	15.7	15.6	15.3	15.3	15.5	15.5	15.5	15.4	15.2	15.1	15.3	15.3	15.4
2008	15.3	15.4	15.2	15.1	15.1	14.9	14.8	14.8	14.6	14.6	14.7	14.6	14.9
2009	14.5	14.6	14.7	14.7	14.8	14.9	14.9	14.9	14.9	14.8	14.8	14.8	14.8

Employment by Industry: Riverside-San Bernardino-Ontario, CA, Selected Years, 1990–2009—*Continued*

(Numbers in thousands, not seasonally adjusted.)

Industry and year	January	February	March	April	May	June	July	August	September	October	November	December	Annual average
Financial Activities													
1990	32.1	32.6	33.0	32.9	33.0	33.2	32.7	33.1	33.6	33.9	34.0	34.0	33.2
2000	35.3	35.2	35.2	35.2	35.4	35.7	35.5	35.7	35.8	36.1	36.3	36.8	35.7
2001	35.9	36.4	36.7	36.8	37.0	37.3	37.3	37.3	37.4	38.3	38.5	38.8	37.3
2002	38.7	38.7	38.7	39.4	39.6	39.9	39.3	39.5	39.5	39.6	40.0	40.6	39.5
2003	40.3	40.7	40.9	41.9	42.3	42.9	43.0	43.5	43.8	43.7	44.1	44.4	42.6
2004	44.4	44.5	45.0	45.1	45.4	45.5	46.0	45.9	45.9	46.4	47.0	47.4	45.7
2005	47.6	47.9	48.1	48.5	48.5	48.5	49.0	49.3	49.6	49.9	50.2	50.4	49.0
2006	51.2	51.3	51.7	52.0	52.3	52.2	51.5	51.6	51.5	51.3	51.5	51.5	51.6
2007	51.4	51.6	51.7	50.9	50.7	50.6	50.0	49.8	49.4	48.7	48.7	48.7	50.2
2008	47.5	47.5	47.5	47.3	47.0	47.1	46.3	46.3	46.0	46.0	46.0	45.7	46.7
2009	45.4	45.2	44.9	44.3	43.5	43.3	42.7	42.7	42.6	42.7	42.7	42.6	43.6
Professional and Business Services													
1990	56.5	57.4	57.9	58.5	58.5	58.8	59.0	59.4	59.7	60.6	61.2	61.5	59.1
1991	61.7	61.9	61.8	61.8	60.4	60.6	61.0	61.4	61.4	62.2	61.6	61.4	61.4
2000	92.4	93.6	94.9	95.8	96.5	98.7	96.0	98.1	99.5	97.8	98.9	98.8	96.8
2001	97.3	98.3	99.2	99.7	100.9	103.5	103.8	104.7	105.7	103.0	102.6	102.5	101.8
2002	101.2	102.7	103.7	103.6	105.4	106.5	106.6	109.2	109.9	109.3	111.7	111.8	106.8
2003	109.4	109.6	111.0	111.1	112.6	113.9	117.0	117.8	119.9	120.3	121.1	121.6	115.4
2004	119.5	121.0	123.3	124.8	125.7	127.0	126.5	127.6	127.4	127.8	127.9	127.5	125.5
2005	125.4	128.4	130.3	132.7	131.4	132.7	133.7	135.1	136.4	137.1	137.8	137.0	133.2
2006	138.2	139.5	140.5	141.1	140.5	141.7	142.9	143.1	144.9	145.2	145.8	144.3	142.3
2007	142.3	144.2	145.7	144.0	145.3	145.1	145.8	145.9	146.1	146.4	145.5	144.1	145.0
2008	139.2	140.0	138.8	137.2	135.6	137.9	137.5	137.5	137.3	137.1	136.3	134.1	137.4
Education and Health Services													
1990	65.8	66.3	66.3	66.5	67.0	67.9	68.0	68.9	70.5	73.2	75.6	75.9	69.3
2000	101.1	101.9	102.1	101.7	102.4	101.5	100.1	100.6	101.4	103.1	102.9	103.4	101.9
2001	103.6	104.3	105.0	105.0	105.8	105.6	105.1	105.8	106.2	108.0	109.2	109.9	106.1
2002	109.7	110.9	111.5	111.1	112.6	112.6	110.1	111.0	113.3	114.2	115.3	116.0	112.4
2003	113.3	115.2	115.5	116.5	116.3	116.6	114.1	114.3	115.4	117.0	117.3	118.1	115.8
2004	116.6	118.2	118.8	119.7	119.4	119.3	117.2	116.7	117.3	118.7	119.1	119.5	118.4
2005	118.1	119.6	120.3	121.0	120.9	120.7	117.9	117.4	118.9	121.3	121.5	121.7	119.9
2006	120.5	122.7	123.1	122.9	122.5	121.7	119.9	120.3	121.2	122.9	123.5	123.6	122.1
2007	123.4	125.0	125.7	125.6	125.9	125.8	126.5	126.9	127.7	130.2	130.6	130.8	127.0
2008	129.2	131.7	132.0	133.3	132.2	130.8	129.1	129.0	130.4	133.1	133.4	133.4	131.5
2009	131.4	133.3	133.6	133.7	132.9	132.3	130.7	131.1	131.3	133.1	133.3	134.0	132.6
Leisure and Hospitality													
1990	75.5	77.0	78.0	76.5	76.2	75.5	73.7	73.3	74.2	75.2	76.1	77.7	75.7
2000	100.3	101.6	102.4	101.1	101.8	101.0	98.5	98.3	99.1	99.0	101.2	102.4	100.6
2001	102.8	104.2	105.2	106.5	106.1	105.6	103.2	103.0	102.5	103.7	104.9	106.0	104.5
2002	106.2	107.3	108.7	109.5	110.1	108.8	105.3	104.8	105.0	104.9	106.6	109.5	107.2
2003	107.4	108.8	110.2	109.8	109.6	109.3	107.0	106.3	106.9	108.5	111.3	113.2	109.0
2004	114.1	115.4	117.1	118.2	119.4	117.6	113.4	113.6	115.0	115.8	119.1	121.3	116.7
2005	119.2	120.9	123.4	125.1	125.0	124.3	121.4	120.8	121.2	121.4	123.4	125.4	122.6
2006	125.3	127.2	129.4	130.0	129.4	128.4	127.0	126.6	126.4	126.4	129.5	131.5	128.1
2007	131.7	133.6	134.6	134.6	135.4	133.8	130.7	129.7	129.4	130.2	132.5	134.7	132.6
2008	133.8	134.4	134.9	134.6	133.0	131.3	128.8	127.5	127.5	127.4	128.8	130.2	131.0
2009	129.2	129.1	129.2	127.3	126.4	124.1	120.1	118.5	118.0	117.1	118.2	119.1	123.0
Other Services													
1990	23.0	23.2	23.4	24.0	24.0	24.4	24.4	24.5	24.6	25.0	25.1	25.2	24.2
2000	33.9	34.3	34.8	34.4	34.6	35.1	34.9	35.2	35.6	34.9	35.0	35.3	34.8
2001	35.5	36.2	37.1	36.9	37.3	37.5	37.1	37.6	37.4	37.6	37.8	37.6	37.1
2002	37.1	37.6	38.0	38.5	38.9	38.9	38.2	38.2	38.2	37.7	37.9	37.9	38.1
2003	37.4	37.9	38.2	38.3	38.7	39.0	37.9	37.7	38.2	38.5	38.5	37.9	38.2
2004	38.2	38.5	39.3	38.7	38.8	38.7	38.7	38.6	38.8	39.0	38.8	38.9	38.8
2005	39.6	39.9	40.4	40.6	40.6	40.2	39.5	39.2	40.0	39.5	39.5	39.8	39.9
2006	40.1	40.9	41.4	41.1	41.5	41.4	41.6	41.7	41.8	41.2	41.1	41.0	41.2
2007	40.2	40.9	40.7	41.6	41.9	42.0	41.1	41.1	41.4	41.0	41.1	40.9	41.2
2008	40.7	41.0	41.6	42.4	42.6	42.2	40.8	40.8	40.4	39.5	38.9	38.5	40.8
2009	37.2	37.1	37.4	37.4	37.5	37.5	36.6	36.4	36.0	35.6	35.7	35.5	36.7
Government													
1990	146.4	146.9	149.1	150.9	153.7	154.2	147.3	140.8	149.7	153.9	154.1	155.4	150.2
2000	189.3	190.2	193.5	193.6	198.4	194.2	186.6	181.4	189.5	194.1	196.8	198.1	192.1
2001	198.2	197.2	201.0	199.3	200.6	201.7	194.7	188.6	199.5	203.9	209.3	208.8	200.2
2002	208.0	211.6	211.2	218.8	218.2	218.9	207.0	203.0	209.6	213.9	216.4	216.2	212.7
2003	215.2	215.2	217.3	216.6	214.9	214.1	205.6	199.4	206.9	210.0	212.2	211.3	211.5
2004	211.7	211.9	213.8	214.9	215.0	213.4	205.5	201.9	210.0	214.3	217.9	219.4	212.5
2005	220.0	221.5	223.2	224.5	224.5	220.2	210.8	210.6	217.5	222.5	224.3	225.5	220.4
2006	221.0	221.3	223.4	226.1	226.9	227.3	216.1	212.1	218.6	224.9	226.3	225.6	222.5
2007	224.7	225.2	227.6	228.4	229.2	229.0	217.3	213.2	219.2	228.2	230.4	231.5	225.3
2008	230.8	231.6	233.5	234.6	235.0	233.3	221.0	220.7	221.7	231.1	232.4	232.5	229.9
2009	231.4	231.1	232.7	234.2	233.8	231.5	216.4	219.8	216.9	225.8	227.3	226.2	227.3

Employment by Industry: Rochester, NY, Selected Years, 1990–2009

(Numbers in thousands, not seasonally adjusted.)

Industry and year	January	February	March	April	May	June	July	August	September	October	November	December	Annual average
Total Nonfarm													
1990	480.1	483.2	485.0	487.0	495.7	497.5	488.4	488.4	494.3	498.2	498.9	496.3	491.1
2000	517.3	521.1	524.1	531.0	535.0	538.6	529.7	529.8	535.1	534.8	536.7	537.8	530.9
2001	521.4	523.6	524.8	526.8	532.7	535.3	522.7	521.5	525.2	526.2	528.0	526.4	526.2
2002	505.4	507.0	508.5	511.8	517.9	518.4	510.3	511.0	513.2	517.0	518.7	518.9	513.2
2003	501.5	502.9	505.0	505.2	514.5	514.8	507.1	507.6	511.7	515.2	515.2	517.1	509.8
2004	499.5	502.3	504.7	507.6	516.1	517.1	508.8	507.8	512.9	520.4	520.2	520.1	511.5
2005	503.9	507.3	509.5	515.9	520.3	520.6	511.7	511.5	514.9	520.5	522.1	523.4	515.1
2006	504.0	506.3	508.6	512.1	516.3	518.1	507.7	507.7	514.1	519.8	520.7	521.3	513.1
2007	505.7	508.1	509.5	511.3	519.6	521.3	511.3	510.4	515.2	521.7	522.1	522.4	514.9
2008	505.4	509.5	510.2	516.0	522.4	522.8	514.1	513.2	518.0	523.4	520.8	519.5	516.3
2009	500.3	501.3	500.7	501.3	506.0	504.1	500.0	498.5	500.1	508.9	509.3	507.9	503.2
Total Private													
1990	412.7	413.7	415.5	416.8	424.6	427.6	426.2	426.3	428.7	427.9	427.2	424.4	422.6
2000	441.1	441.5	443.7	450.3	454.6	459.9	458.3	458.5	458.2	455.9	456.2	457.6	453.0
2001	443.5	442.1	443.1	445.3	451.6	455.4	449.6	448.3	446.2	443.9	444.3	442.3	446.3
2002	426.4	424.1	424.9	429.7	435.4	436.5	436.0	436.9	434.9	434.7	435.3	434.3	432.4
2003	420.9	419.4	421.0	422.5	430.9	432.3	432.6	433.5	433.0	434.0	433.0	433.4	428.9
2004	419.5	422.0	423.7	425.3	432.6	434.6	434.3	433.6	434.5	438.3	437.4	436.0	431.0
2005	423.7	424.2	426.1	432.4	436.5	437.7	436.5	436.6	435.8	438.3	438.9	439.3	433.8
2006	425.0	424.9	426.6	430.6	434.8	438.1	435.4	435.5	435.9	439.3	439.3	439.7	433.8
2007	426.8	427.0	428.2	429.8	437.6	440.0	437.9	437.6	436.5	440.3	440.1	439.6	435.1
2008	426.0	427.9	428.3	433.5	439.7	440.8	439.4	439.2	438.3	440.9	438.0	436.4	435.7
2009	420.5	419.0	418.5	418.5	423.1	422.7	422.3	422.7	421.7	424.6	424.1	423.1	421.7
Goods-Producing													
1990	141.3	140.8	140.6	141.5	144.2	146.1	146.2	145.6	144.6	144.0	142.3	140.2	143.1
2000	120.5	119.2	119.4	119.8	120.9	123.3	123.7	124.2	123.2	122.2	121.5	120.3	121.5
2001	117.4	115.9	115.5	115.9	117.1	117.8	118.1	117.9	115.8	113.4	111.6	109.9	115.5
2002	107.5	105.1	104.7	105.4	106.2	106.7	107.4	108.1	105.9	105.4	104.7	102.8	105.8
2003	99.9	98.0	98.0	97.9	99.9	100.9	102.9	103.3	102.1	101.2	100.2	98.9	100.2
2004	96.0	95.0	95.3	96.3	97.8	98.8	100.4	100.0	98.9	99.0	97.9	96.4	97.7
2005	94.1	93.3	93.3	95.1	96.5	97.8	99.2	99.6	98.6	97.9	97.3	95.6	96.5
2006	93.2	92.4	92.2	93.8	95.3	97.2	97.3	97.6	96.3	95.9	95.2	94.0	95.0
2007	91.3	90.2	90.5	91.4	93.1	94.2	94.0	94.1	92.9	92.2	91.4	90.3	92.1
2008	87.9	86.8	86.5	87.4	89.5	90.9	91.9	91.8	90.8	90.0	88.1	86.1	89.0
2009	82.5	80.8	79.7	79.5	80.6	81.0	81.7	82.4	80.9	80.1	79.2	77.9	80.5
Mining and Logging													
2003	0.4	0.4	0.4	0.5	0.5	0.6	0.6	0.6	0.6	0.6	0.5	0.6	0.5
2004	0.6	0.6	0.6	0.6	0.6	0.6	0.6	0.6	0.6	0.6	0.6	0.6	0.6
2005	0.5	0.5	0.5	0.6	0.6	0.7	0.7	0.7	0.7	0.6	0.6	0.6	0.6
2006	0.5	0.5	0.5	0.6	0.6	0.7	0.7	0.7	0.6	0.6	0.6	0.4	0.6
2007	0.4	0.5	0.5	0.6	0.6	0.6	0.6	0.6	0.6	0.6	0.6	0.6	0.6
2008	0.6	0.5	0.5	0.5	0.6	0.6	0.6	0.6	0.6	0.6	0.6	0.6	0.6
2009	0.5	0.5	0.5	0.5	0.6	0.6	0.6	0.6	0.6	0.6	0.5	0.5	0.6
Construction													
2003	14.8	14.3	14.5	15.3	17.0	17.9	19.3	19.6	19.2	18.5	17.8	16.9	17.0
2004	15.2	14.8	15.1	16.5	17.9	18.9	19.9	20.3	19.8	19.6	19.0	17.9	17.9
2005	16.0	15.5	15.4	17.0	18.7	19.2	19.7	20.1	19.6	19.2	18.8	17.5	18.1
2006	16.0	15.3	15.2	16.5	18.0	19.0	19.4	19.6	19.0	18.9	18.3	17.7	17.7
2007	16.2	15.2	15.7	16.9	18.7	19.7	20.0	20.2	19.7	19.6	19.1	18.1	18.3
2008	16.8	16.0	16.1	17.4	19.1	20.0	20.8	21.0	20.6	20.3	19.1	17.9	18.8
2009	15.6	14.9	14.8	15.8	17.4	18.4	19.1	19.4	18.6	18.3	17.9	17.0	17.3
Manufacturing													
1990	124.7	124.5	124.2	123.6	124.8	125.3	124.8	124.0	123.5	123.9	123.6	122.7	124.1
2000	104.0	103.2	103.1	102.2	102.1	103.2	103.0	103.0	102.9	102.2	101.7	101.4	102.7
2001	99.8	98.8	98.1	97.4	96.8	96.6	96.3	96.1	95.0	93.5	92.6	92.0	96.1
2002	91.4	89.7	89.2	88.6	88.2	87.8	87.7	87.8	86.3	86.2	86.2	85.7	87.9
2003	84.7	83.3	83.1	82.1	82.4	82.4	83.0	83.1	82.3	82.1	81.9	81.4	82.6
2004	80.2	79.6	79.6	79.2	79.3	79.3	79.9	79.1	78.5	78.8	78.3	77.9	79.1
2005	77.6	77.3	77.4	77.5	77.2	77.9	78.8	78.8	78.3	78.1	77.9	77.5	77.9
2006	76.7	76.6	76.5	76.7	76.7	77.5	77.2	77.3	76.7	76.4	76.3	75.9	76.7
2007	74.7	74.5	74.3	73.9	73.8	73.9	73.4	73.3	72.6	72.0	71.7	71.6	73.3
2008	70.5	70.3	69.9	69.5	69.8	70.3	70.5	70.2	69.6	69.1	68.4	67.6	69.6
2009	66.4	65.4	64.4	63.2	62.6	62.0	62.0	62.4	61.7	61.2	60.8	60.4	62.7
Service-Providing													
1990	338.8	342.4	344.4	345.5	351.5	351.4	342.2	342.8	349.7	354.2	356.6	356.1	348.0
2000	396.8	401.9	404.7	411.2	414.1	415.3	406.0	405.6	411.9	412.6	415.2	417.5	409.4
2001	404.0	407.7	409.3	410.9	415.6	417.5	404.6	403.6	409.4	412.8	416.4	416.5	410.7
2002	397.9	401.9	403.8	406.4	411.7	411.7	402.9	402.9	407.3	411.6	414.0	416.1	407.4
2003	401.6	404.9	407.0	407.3	414.6	413.9	404.2	404.3	409.6	414.0	415.0	418.2	409.6
2004	403.5	407.3	409.4	411.3	418.3	418.3	408.4	407.8	414.0	421.4	422.3	423.7	413.8
2005	409.8	414.0	416.2	420.8	423.8	422.8	412.5	411.9	416.3	422.6	424.8	427.8	418.6
2006	410.8	413.9	416.4	418.3	421.0	420.9	410.4	410.1	417.8	423.9	425.5	427.3	418.0
2007	414.4	417.9	419.0	419.9	426.5	427.1	417.3	416.3	422.3	429.5	430.7	432.1	422.8
2008	417.5	422.7	423.7	428.6	432.9	431.9	422.2	421.4	427.2	433.4	432.7	433.4	427.3
2009	417.8	420.5	421.0	421.8	425.4	423.1	418.3	416.1	419.2	428.8	430.1	430.0	422.7

Employment by Industry: Rochester, NY, Selected Years, 1990–2009—*Continued*

(Numbers in thousands, not seasonally adjusted.)

Industry and year	January	February	March	April	May	June	July	August	September	October	November	December	Annual average
Trade, Transportation, and Utilities													
1990	85.3	84.0	84.2	83.2	84.2	85.1	84.4	84.9	84.6	84.7	86.1	87.2	84.8
2000	89.1	87.5	87.6	87.9	89.0	89.8	88.8	89.5	89.0	89.4	91.1	92.9	89.3
2001	89.7	87.3	87.3	88.0	89.1	90.3	88.2	88.2	87.3	88.1	89.9	90.7	88.7
2002	86.9	84.7	84.5	84.7	86.1	87.1	86.0	86.3	85.3	85.5	86.9	87.9	86.0
2003	85.2	83.2	83.3	83.1	84.8	85.6	84.1	84.5	84.3	84.8	86.0	87.1	84.7
2004	83.6	82.5	82.6	82.2	84.9	86.0	85.4	85.3	85.4	86.2	87.3	88.6	85.0
2005	85.2	83.6	83.7	84.3	85.4	86.8	86.0	86.4	85.2	86.0	87.2	89.1	85.7
2006	85.2	82.9	83.2	83.2	84.5	86.2	85.1	85.6	84.8	85.9	87.3	88.5	85.2
2007	85.6	83.4	83.9	83.3	86.3	87.4	86.6	86.2	85.5	86.6	88.0	89.0	86.0
2008	86.0	84.0	83.9	84.5	85.9	86.6	85.4	85.2	84.3	85.3	85.6	86.3	85.3
2009	82.3	80.5	80.2	79.9	81.7	82.6	82.0	82.0	80.7	81.9	83.4	83.5	81.7
Wholesale Trade													
1990	16.8	16.7	16.9	16.8	16.9	17.0	17.0	17.0	16.9	17.1	17.0	16.9	16.9
2000	18.2	18.1	18.2	18.6	18.7	19.0	19.1	19.2	18.9	19.0	19.1	19.2	18.8
2001	19.2	19.1	19.1	19.2	19.4	19.7	19.4	19.2	18.8	18.8	18.8	18.7	19.1
2002	18.6	18.5	18.3	18.6	18.7	18.8	18.8	18.7	18.4	18.1	18.1	18.1	18.5
2003	17.9	17.7	17.8	17.8	18.0	18.1	18.1	18.0	17.7	17.5	17.6	17.7	17.8
2004	17.7	17.8	17.8	17.9	18.1	18.4	18.3	18.3	17.9	18.1	18.0	18.1	18.0
2005	18.2	18.2	18.2	18.2	18.3	18.5	18.6	18.6	18.2	17.9	18.2	18.2	18.3
2006	18.2	18.1	18.2	18.2	18.3	18.7	18.8	19.1	18.6	18.4	18.4	18.5	18.5
2007	18.6	18.6	18.7	18.5	18.8	19.0	19.2	19.1	18.8	18.9	18.7	18.8	18.8
2008	18.4	18.3	18.2	18.5	18.7	18.8	18.8	18.7	18.5	18.8	18.6	18.5	18.6
2009	18.1	18.0	17.8	17.6	17.8	17.8	17.8	17.8	17.5	17.6	17.6	17.5	17.7
Retail Trade													
1990	58.2	57.0	57.0	56.1	56.9	57.6	57.2	57.6	56.9	57.0	58.5	59.9	57.5
2000	60.2	58.7	58.7	58.5	59.5	60.0	59.5	60.1	59.2	59.5	61.1	62.0	59.8
2001	60.2	58.1	58.0	58.6	59.2	60.1	58.8	59.1	58.1	58.6	60.5	61.5	59.2
2002	58.9	56.8	56.9	56.8	58.0	58.8	58.4	58.8	57.6	57.9	59.4	60.4	58.2
2003	57.8	56.2	56.2	55.9	57.4	58.2	57.4	57.8	57.2	57.7	58.8	59.7	57.5
2004	56.4	55.2	55.3	54.4	56.7	57.4	57.3	57.3	57.3	57.8	59.0	60.2	57.0
2005	57.0	55.4	55.4	55.9	56.8	57.9	57.6	57.9	56.5	57.4	58.3	60.0	57.2
2006	56.6	54.4	54.6	54.5	55.6	56.7	56.1	56.3	55.5	56.8	58.2	59.2	56.2
2007	56.6	54.5	54.9	54.6	57.0	57.9	57.4	57.1	56.1	57.0	58.5	59.3	56.7
2008	57.1	55.2	55.2	55.4	56.4	57.0	56.4	56.4	55.5	56.2	56.7	57.3	56.2
2009	54.4	52.7	52.8	52.6	54.0	54.8	54.4	54.4	53.3	54.4	55.7	55.8	54.1
Transportation and Utilities													
1990	10.3	10.3	10.3	10.3	10.4	10.5	10.2	10.3	10.8	10.6	10.6	10.4	10.4
2000	10.7	10.7	10.7	10.8	10.8	10.8	10.2	10.2	10.9	10.9	10.9	11.7	10.8
2001	10.3	10.1	10.2	10.2	10.5	10.5	10.0	9.9	10.4	10.7	10.6	10.5	10.3
2002	9.4	9.4	9.3	9.3	9.4	9.5	8.8	8.8	9.3	9.5	9.4	9.4	9.3
2003	9.5	9.3	9.3	9.4	9.4	9.3	8.6	8.7	9.4	9.6	9.6	9.7	9.3
2004	9.5	9.5	9.5	9.9	10.1	10.2	9.8	9.7	10.2	10.3	10.3	10.3	9.9
2005	10.0	10.0	10.1	10.2	10.3	10.4	9.8	9.9	10.5	10.7	10.7	10.9	10.3
2006	10.4	10.4	10.4	10.5	10.6	10.8	10.2	10.2	10.7	10.7	10.7	10.8	10.5
2007	10.4	10.3	10.3	10.2	10.5	10.5	10.0	10.0	10.6	10.7	10.8	10.9	10.4
2008	10.5	10.5	10.5	10.6	10.8	10.8	10.2	10.1	10.3	10.3	10.3	10.5	10.5
2009	9.8	9.8	9.6	9.7	9.9	10.0	9.8	9.8	9.9	9.9	10.1	10.2	9.9
Information													
1990	9.7	9.7	9.7	9.7	9.7	9.9	10.0	10.0	9.8	9.8	9.9	9.9	9.8
2000	11.3	11.4	11.4	11.5	11.6	11.7	11.8	11.9	11.9	12.0	12.1	12.3	11.7
2001	12.9	13.0	13.1	12.9	13.1	13.2	13.1	13.0	12.9	13.2	13.3	13.4	13.1
2002	13.5	13.1	13.3	13.0	13.1	12.9	12.7	12.6	12.5	12.4	12.4	12.5	12.8
2003	12.3	12.3	12.2	12.2	12.5	12.4	12.3	12.3	12.2	12.3	12.3	12.3	12.3
2004	12.4	12.3	12.3	12.2	12.2	12.2	12.1	12.0	12.0	12.0	12.0	11.9	12.1
2005	11.8	11.6	11.6	11.6	11.7	11.7	11.6	11.6	11.6	11.8	11.7	11.8	11.7
2006	11.7	11.6	11.5	11.1	11.1	11.1	10.9	10.7	10.5	10.6	10.6	10.5	11.0
2007	10.6	10.5	10.5	10.6	10.7	10.7	10.7	10.7	10.6	10.6	10.6	10.7	10.6
2008	10.5	10.5	10.5	10.4	10.4	10.4	10.4	10.4	10.2	10.3	10.4	10.4	10.4
2009	10.2	10.0	10.0	10.0	10.0	10.0	10.0	9.9	9.7	9.6	9.7	9.6	9.9
Financial Activities													
1990	23.3	23.2	23.3	23.5	23.7	23.9	24.2	24.3	23.8	23.6	23.8	23.5	23.7
2000	21.3	21.4	21.3	21.7	21.8	22.3	22.0	21.8	21.2	21.4	21.4	21.4	21.6
2001	21.3	21.5	21.4	21.4	21.6	22.2	22.0	22.0	21.4	21.3	21.4	21.3	21.6
2002	20.7	20.7	20.6	20.6	20.9	21.3	21.7	21.8	21.1	21.2	21.2	21.2	21.1
2003	21.0	20.9	20.9	21.1	21.7	22.0	22.3	22.3	21.8	21.9	21.9	22.2	21.6
2004	21.5	21.5	21.6	21.7	21.8	22.1	22.6	22.7	22.2	21.9	21.9	22.1	22.0
2005	21.7	21.5	21.6	21.5	21.8	22.0	22.2	22.2	21.7	21.7	21.9	22.0	21.8
2006	21.7	21.5	21.5	21.5	21.7	22.1	22.5	22.5	21.6	21.8	21.6	21.6	21.8
2007	21.6	21.5	21.5	21.5	21.5	22.0	22.3	22.3	21.4	21.4	21.4	21.5	21.7
2008	21.0	21.0	21.0	21.1	21.5	21.9	22.1	22.1	21.4	21.3	21.2	21.2	21.4
2009	20.4	20.2	20.1	20.2	20.7	21.1	21.2	21.3	20.8	20.8	20.7	20.7	20.7

Employment by Industry: Rochester, NY, Selected Years, 1990–2009—*Continued*

(Numbers in thousands, not seasonally adjusted.)

Industry and year	January	February	March	April	May	June	July	August	September	October	November	December	Annual average
Professional and Business Services													
1990	40.0	40.3	40.9	40.7	41.3	41.7	41.7	42.2	42.1	41.4	41.4	40.6	41.2
2000	58.5	58.7	59.1	59.8	60.3	62.1	63.0	62.8	62.1	61.5	61.1	60.7	60.8
2001	60.1	59.7	60.4	59.0	59.7	61.0	60.7	60.5	59.7	58.8	58.3	57.6	59.6
2002	54.5	54.5	54.6	56.5	57.4	58.4	58.2	58.1	58.0	57.6	57.9	57.6	56.9
2003	55.2	55.2	55.5	56.7	57.5	58.4	57.7	58.0	57.7	58.3	57.7	57.8	57.1
2004	54.9	55.6	55.7	56.4	57.0	58.6	58.0	58.0	58.1	59.1	58.8	58.2	57.4
2005	56.3	56.5	57.2	59.3	59.6	60.2	60.7	60.2	59.9	60.3	60.6	60.7	59.3
2006	58.3	57.7	58.4	59.7	59.5	60.9	60.6	60.4	61.2	61.4	60.8	61.3	60.0
2007	59.6	60.0	59.9	60.1	60.7	62.0	61.5	61.7	60.8	61.7	61.3	61.2	60.9
2008	60.0	60.4	60.6	62.2	62.4	63.6	63.4	64.0	62.9	63.3	62.7	62.2	62.3
2009	60.1	59.6	59.5	59.0	58.8	59.7	59.5	59.5	59.1	59.0	59.0	59.0	59.3
Education and Health Services													
1990	66.1	68.3	68.6	68.2	68.9	67.3	66.7	66.1	71.4	73.4	73.0	73.0	69.3
2000	87.0	89.3	90.4	93.2	92.0	89.4	88.7	88.0	92.8	92.1	92.6	93.2	90.7
2001	90.5	92.6	92.8	94.1	94.0	91.3	88.1	87.6	92.5	93.5	94.4	94.1	92.1
2002	90.9	93.2	93.9	93.8	93.2	90.5	89.9	89.9	94.3	96.0	96.4	96.6	93.2
2003	93.5	96.1	96.5	96.2	95.4	92.8	92.0	92.0	96.1	97.9	98.2	98.4	95.4
2004	96.9	100.5	101.1	100.0	99.3	95.7	94.1	93.9	98.6	101.5	101.9	101.3	98.7
2005	99.1	102.0	102.4	102.5	100.9	96.9	95.2	95.0	100.0	102.7	103.4	103.2	100.3
2006	100.5	103.8	103.9	104.0	103.1	99.1	96.9	96.9	102.3	105.1	105.8	105.6	102.3
2007	102.3	105.4	105.6	105.8	104.3	100.3	99.2	99.5	105.1	108.0	108.4	108.3	104.4
2008	104.4	108.4	108.7	109.1	107.6	103.7	102.3	102.0	108.2	110.7	111.4	111.6	107.3
2009	108.2	111.5	111.9	111.6	109.4	105.1	103.9	103.8	109.3	112.8	113.5	113.7	109.6
Leisure and Hospitality													
1990	32.0	32.2	33.0	34.5	36.8	37.8	37.3	37.4	36.5	35.1	34.7	34.0	35.1
2000	36.2	36.8	37.2	38.9	41.3	43.3	42.7	42.6	40.7	39.8	38.9	39.2	39.8
2001	34.8	35.1	35.5	36.8	39.7	41.9	41.8	41.5	39.4	38.2	37.7	37.7	38.3
2002	34.8	35.1	35.6	37.6	40.3	41.3	41.7	41.5	39.4	38.1	37.2	37.1	38.3
2003	35.4	35.3	36.0	36.6	40.2	41.3	42.3	42.2	40.1	38.8	37.8	37.7	38.6
2004	35.7	35.9	36.3	37.5	40.4	42.0	42.7	42.8	40.6	39.6	38.7	38.5	39.2
2005	36.6	36.7	37.1	38.6	41.1	42.8	42.4	42.6	40.0	38.9	37.8	37.8	39.4
2006	35.5	36.0	36.8	38.2	40.4	42.5	43.0	43.0	40.5	39.7	38.9	38.8	39.4
2007	36.6	36.8	37.1	37.9	41.5	43.9	44.3	43.8	41.2	40.4	39.6	39.1	40.2
2008	36.9	37.5	37.8	39.2	42.6	43.9	44.0	44.0	41.2	40.5	39.1	39.1	40.5
2009	37.3	36.9	37.5	38.7	42.1	43.5	44.2	44.1	41.9	40.8	39.0	39.0	40.4
Other Services													
1990	15.0	15.2	15.2	15.5	15.8	15.8	15.7	15.8	15.9	15.9	16.0	16.0	15.7
2000	17.2	17.2	17.3	17.5	17.7	18.0	17.6	17.7	17.3	17.5	17.5	17.6	17.5
2001	16.8	17.0	17.1	17.2	17.3	17.7	17.6	17.6	17.2	17.4	17.7	17.6	17.4
2002	17.6	17.7	17.7	18.1	18.2	18.3	18.4	18.6	18.4	18.5	18.6	18.6	18.2
2003	18.4	18.4	18.6	18.7	18.9	18.9	19.0	18.9	18.7	18.8	18.9	19.0	18.7
2004	18.5	18.7	18.8	19.0	19.2	19.2	19.0	18.9	18.7	19.0	18.9	19.0	18.9
2005	18.9	19.0	19.2	19.5	19.5	19.5	19.2	19.0	18.8	19.0	19.0	19.1	19.1
2006	18.9	19.0	19.1	19.1	19.2	19.0	19.1	18.8	18.7	18.9	19.1	19.4	19.0
2007	19.2	19.2	19.2	19.2	19.5	19.5	19.3	19.3	19.0	19.4	19.4	19.5	19.3
2008	19.3	19.3	19.3	19.6	19.8	19.8	19.9	19.7	19.3	19.5	19.5	19.5	19.5
2009	19.5	19.5	19.6	19.6	19.8	19.7	19.8	19.7	19.3	19.6	19.6	19.7	19.6
Government													
1990	67.4	69.5	69.5	70.2	71.1	69.9	62.2	62.1	65.6	70.3	71.7	71.9	68.5
2000	76.2	79.6	80.4	80.7	80.4	78.7	71.4	71.3	76.9	78.9	80.5	80.2	77.9
2001	77.9	81.5	81.7	81.5	81.1	79.9	73.1	73.2	79.0	82.3	83.7	84.1	79.9
2002	79.0	82.9	83.6	82.1	82.5	81.9	74.3	74.1	78.3	82.3	83.4	84.6	80.8
2003	80.6	83.5	84.0	82.7	83.6	82.5	74.5	74.1	78.7	81.2	82.2	83.7	80.9
2004	80.0	80.3	81.0	82.3	83.5	82.5	74.5	74.2	78.4	82.1	82.8	84.1	80.5
2005	80.2	83.1	83.4	83.5	83.8	82.9	75.2	74.9	79.1	82.2	83.2	84.1	81.3
2006	79.0	81.4	82.0	81.5	81.5	80.0	72.3	72.2	78.2	80.5	81.4	81.6	79.3
2007	78.9	81.1	81.3	81.5	82.0	81.3	73.4	72.8	78.7	81.4	82.0	82.8	79.8
2008	79.4	81.6	81.9	82.5	82.7	82.0	74.7	74.0	79.7	82.5	82.8	83.1	80.6
2009	79.8	82.3	82.2	82.8	82.9	81.4	77.7	75.8	78.4	84.3	85.2	84.8	81.5

Employment by Industry: Sacramento–Arden-Arcade–Roseville, CA, Selected Years, 1990–2009

(Numbers in thousands, not seasonally adjusted.)

Industry and year	January	February	March	April	May	June	July	August	September	October	November	December	Annual average
Total Nonfarm													
1990	598.9	601.8	607.0	612.3	618.0	623.5	620.2	621.3	627.2	628.3	630.9	633.0	618.5
2000	773.3	778.7	786.0	789.5	795.9	805.6	795.2	803.6	804.5	804.0	811.8	818.2	797.2
2001	799.6	803.4	813.3	814.7	817.3	824.1	820.2	824.1	822.7	824.1	829.9	832.9	818.9
2002	814.8	817.1	827.6	826.9	833.6	837.7	832.1	834.6	836.7	839.0	842.7	843.5	832.2
2003	831.6	833.0	837.7	842.5	847.7	853.9	847.0	848.7	850.2	847.7	855.6	856.7	846.0
2004	843.3	845.5	850.3	856.4	859.5	866.0	861.1	858.8	864.0	865.2	868.0	870.7	859.1
2005	861.4	865.1	870.6	874.9	879.2	883.5	882.7	883.1	887.8	889.3	894.6	898.6	880.9
2006	888.0	891.7	893.3	890.1	899.8	907.6	900.6	901.5	903.9	901.5	904.3	905.9	899.0
2007	892.7	895.9	902.8	900.5	906.9	910.9	905.1	905.5	905.0	901.6	904.6	905.0	903.0
2008	884.6	888.1	889.7	888.3	891.1	891.9	883.5	878.9	876.3	872.6	870.9	868.9	882.1
2009	849.6	844.4	842.4	841.0	841.8	840.0	829.6	827.7	821.9	822.5	822.7	817.5	833.4
Total Private													
1990	415.5	417.0	421.0	425.1	430.6	436.2	440.0	443.8	445.2	443.6	445.1	447.8	434.2
2000	567.0	569.5	574.1	577.7	580.6	589.8	590.8	596.5	596.1	592.0	598.9	605.5	586.5
2001	588.4	590.2	596.3	596.8	599.0	605.2	605.9	607.7	602.7	602.2	605.9	608.9	600.8
2002	592.8	593.3	598.4	597.6	603.0	608.0	608.5	610.2	610.6	611.4	614.7	616.0	605.4
2003	606.6	606.1	610.0	614.5	617.5	625.0	622.7	626.1	625.6	624.3	627.8	632.3	619.9
2004	620.8	622.4	627.3	632.8	635.1	641.1	643.5	643.6	644.7	643.8	645.3	649.6	637.5
2005	639.6	642.3	646.6	649.8	653.0	657.4	661.7	663.4	663.8	663.9	668.3	672.5	656.9
2006	662.9	664.4	664.7	661.1	670.1	676.8	675.0	678.4	676.7	671.8	672.6	673.2	670.6
2007	661.3	663.0	666.8	664.4	669.3	672.1	673.8	674.7	671.0	665.2	667.1	667.3	668.0
2008	647.6	649.2	648.9	648.3	649.1	650.0	647.4	646.6	641.8	635.1	632.0	630.0	643.8
2009	610.9	603.9	600.2	597.9	598.5	598.4	596.4	594.8	587.5	584.5	584.2	582.4	595.0
Goods-Producing													
1990	76.4	77.4	79.0	80.3	82.6	84.8	85.3	86.2	86.4	83.7	81.3	79.0	81.9
2000	95.5	95.7	97.2	98.2	100.8	103.1	103.6	105.7	104.7	104.1	103.8	103.4	101.3
2001	99.4	99.7	101.9	103.6	106.2	108.5	109.0	109.5	108.5	107.5	105.6	103.5	105.2
2002	99.0	99.0	100.3	101.7	104.1	105.3	105.8	107.7	107.6	107.9	106.3	104.5	104.1
2003	100.8	101.8	103.7	105.3	107.7	111.0	110.8	113.5	113.9	113.5	111.5	109.9	108.6
2004	107.5	107.8	110.6	111.8	113.6	116.5	117.5	119.0	118.7	117.3	114.8	113.8	114.1
2005	110.8	112.0	113.7	114.5	116.1	118.0	119.8	121.7	122.0	121.0	119.1	117.4	117.2
2006	113.0	113.1	111.3	109.3	114.4	117.2	116.8	119.0	119.0	115.1	112.2	109.6	114.2
2007	107.2	107.4	108.5	108.1	110.7	112.0	111.1	112.3	110.5	107.2	104.6	101.6	108.4
2008	95.0	94.9	95.2	95.3	96.9	98.3	98.7	99.4	97.9	95.1	91.4	88.8	95.6
2009	83.2	79.8	79.1	78.4	79.1	79.7	78.4	78.6	77.3	75.7	73.5	71.9	77.9
Mining and Logging													
1990	0.4	0.5	0.5	0.6	0.7	0.8	0.8	0.8	0.8	0.8	0.8	0.7	0.7
2000	0.8	0.8	0.8	0.9	0.9	0.9	0.9	0.9	0.9	0.9	0.9	0.9	0.9
2001	0.8	0.8	0.8	0.9	0.9	0.9	0.9	0.9	0.9	0.9	0.8	0.8	0.9
2002	0.7	0.7	0.8	0.8	0.8	0.8	0.8	0.8	0.8	0.8	0.8	0.8	0.8
2003	0.6	0.6	0.6	0.6	0.6	0.7	0.7	0.7	0.7	0.7	0.7	0.7	0.6
2004	0.6	0.6	0.7	0.7	0.7	0.7	0.8	0.7	0.8	0.8	0.7	0.7	0.7
2005	0.7	0.7	0.7	0.7	0.7	0.7	0.8	0.8	0.7	0.7	0.7	0.7	0.7
2006	0.7	0.7	0.7	0.6	0.8	0.8	0.7	0.8	0.8	0.7	0.7	0.7	0.7
2007	0.6	0.6	0.6	0.6	0.7	0.7	0.7	0.7	0.7	0.8	0.7	0.7	0.7
2008	0.6	0.6	0.6	0.7	0.7	0.7	0.7	0.7	0.7	0.7	0.6	0.6	0.7
2009	0.4	0.4	0.4	0.4	0.4	0.4	0.5	0.5	0.5	0.5	0.5	0.5	0.5
Construction													
1990	37.5	38.3	39.8	41.2	43.2	44.8	44.3	45.1	45.4	42.6	41.0	39.4	41.9
2000	47.7	47.3	48.5	50.9	52.9	55.2	55.1	56.2	56.3	55.7	55.6	55.2	53.1
2001	53.0	53.4	55.5	57.9	60.1	62.2	62.8	64.1	63.2	62.2	60.9	58.9	59.5
2002	55.8	56.5	57.6	58.8	61.0	62.3	63.1	64.9	64.9	64.6	64.1	62.3	61.3
2003	60.1	60.9	62.7	64.2	66.1	68.2	68.3	70.0	70.2	70.4	69.2	67.5	66.5
2004	65.3	65.8	68.5	69.6	70.9	73.2	73.5	74.2	73.5	73.2	71.3	70.3	70.8
2005	67.8	68.9	70.4	71.8	73.1	74.8	76.0	76.5	76.6	76.5	75.2	73.2	73.4
2006	69.5	69.6	67.9	66.1	71.1	73.3	73.4	74.6	74.3	71.4	69.7	67.1	70.7
2007	65.7	65.7	67.0	66.8	69.0	70.0	69.6	69.8	68.2	66.1	63.9	61.1	66.9
2008	55.2	55.3	55.5	55.7	57.2	58.5	59.2	59.0	57.6	56.2	53.6	51.2	56.2
2009	47.0	44.2	43.9	43.5	44.3	44.9	43.8	43.5	42.4	41.3	39.4	38.1	43.0
Manufacturing													
1990	38.5	38.6	38.7	38.5	38.7	39.2	40.2	40.3	40.2	40.3	39.5	38.9	39.3
2000	47.0	47.6	47.9	46.4	47.0	47.0	47.6	48.6	47.5	47.5	47.3	47.3	47.4
2001	45.6	45.5	45.6	44.8	45.2	45.4	45.3	44.5	44.4	44.4	43.9	43.8	44.9
2002	42.5	41.8	41.9	42.1	42.3	42.2	41.9	42.0	41.9	42.5	41.4	41.4	42.0
2003	40.1	40.3	40.4	40.5	41.0	42.1	41.8	42.8	43.0	42.4	41.6	41.7	41.5
2004	41.6	41.4	41.4	41.5	42.0	42.6	43.2	44.1	44.4	43.3	42.8	42.8	42.6
2005	42.3	42.4	42.6	42.0	42.3	42.5	43.0	44.4	44.7	43.8	43.2	43.5	43.1
2006	42.8	42.8	42.7	42.6	42.7	43.1	42.7	43.6	43.9	43.0	41.8	41.8	42.8
2007	40.9	41.1	40.9	40.7	41.0	41.3	40.8	41.8	41.6	40.3	40.0	39.8	40.9
2008	39.2	39.0	39.1	38.9	39.0	39.1	38.8	39.7	39.6	38.2	37.2	37.0	38.7
2009	35.8	35.2	34.8	34.5	34.4	34.4	34.1	34.6	34.4	33.9	33.6	33.3	34.4

Employment by Industry: Sacramento–Arden-Arcade–Roseville, CA, Selected Years, 1990–2009—*Continued*

(Numbers in thousands, not seasonally adjusted.)

Industry and year	January	February	March	April	May	June	July	August	September	October	November	December	Annual average
Service-Providing													
1990	522.5	524.4	528.0	532.0	535.4	538.7	534.9	535.1	540.8	544.6	549.6	554.0	536.7
2000	677.8	683.0	688.8	691.3	695.1	702.5	691.6	697.9	699.8	699.9	708.0	714.8	695.9
2001	700.2	703.7	711.4	711.1	711.1	715.6	711.2	714.6	714.2	716.6	724.3	729.4	713.6
2002	715.8	718.1	727.3	725.2	729.5	732.4	726.3	726.9	729.1	731.1	736.4	739.0	728.1
2003	730.8	731.2	734.0	737.2	740.0	742.9	736.2	735.2	736.3	734.2	741.1	746.8	737.4
2004	735.8	737.7	739.7	744.6	745.9	749.5	743.6	739.8	745.3	747.9	753.2	756.9	745.0
2005	750.6	753.1	756.9	760.4	763.1	765.5	762.9	761.4	765.8	768.3	775.5	781.2	763.7
2006	775.0	778.6	782.0	780.8	785.4	790.4	783.8	782.5	784.9	786.4	792.1	796.3	784.9
2007	785.5	788.5	794.3	792.4	796.2	798.9	794.0	793.2	794.5	794.4	800.0	803.4	794.6
2008	789.6	793.2	794.5	793.0	794.2	793.6	784.8	779.5	778.4	777.5	779.5	780.1	786.5
2009	766.4	764.6	763.3	762.6	762.7	760.3	751.2	749.1	744.6	746.8	749.2	745.6	755.5
Trade, Transportation, and Utilities													
1990	108.8	107.6	108.2	110.9	111.6	113.1	114.2	114.9	115.9	116.9	119.2	121.2	113.5
2000	136.7	135.2	135.3	135.9	135.9	137.0	137.6	139.4	139.8	139.6	144.6	147.3	138.7
2001	139.9	138.0	138.5	138.3	138.6	140.3	139.9	140.2	140.9	141.4	144.7	146.5	140.6
2002	138.5	137.4	138.5	138.6	139.0	140.2	140.3	140.5	140.7	141.8	145.0	146.8	140.6
2003	141.6	139.6	139.6	140.2	140.8	142.3	142.9	143.5	143.3	144.5	148.4	150.9	143.1
2004	144.1	143.1	143.0	143.9	144.8	145.9	145.8	145.7	145.8	147.5	151.0	152.3	146.1
2005	147.0	145.9	146.2	146.2	146.7	147.2	148.4	148.7	149.1	150.1	154.1	157.5	148.9
2006	151.2	149.9	150.8	150.4	151.8	153.1	154.3	155.1	154.4	154.6	157.8	159.9	153.6
2007	153.9	152.2	152.0	151.2	151.7	152.2	152.8	152.7	152.2	152.3	156.3	158.2	153.1
2008	150.5	148.5	148.2	147.3	147.0	147.1	146.4	145.7	144.3	143.7	145.2	145.8	146.6
2009	138.1	135.4	134.0	133.4	134.5	134.5	133.5	133.0	133.1	133.4	135.2	135.8	134.5
Wholesale Trade													
1990	19.1	19.4	19.4	19.4	19.5	19.8	20.1	20.3	20.3	20.4	20.5	20.4	19.9
2000	24.4	24.6	24.8	25.2	25.2	25.5	25.2	25.3	25.3	25.5	25.4	25.2	25.1
2001	25.0	25.3	25.4	25.7	25.7	25.9	25.9	26.1	26.0	26.0	26.1	26.1	25.8
2002	25.3	25.5	25.7	25.5	25.6	25.5	25.5	25.6	25.5	25.7	25.8	25.7	25.6
2003	25.9	26.0	26.0	26.2	26.2	26.3	26.3	26.4	26.4	26.4	26.5	26.6	26.3
2004	26.3	26.4	26.4	26.3	26.4	26.6	26.7	26.8	26.7	26.6	26.5	26.6	26.5
2005	26.4	26.5	26.5	26.7	26.7	26.7	26.9	27.0	27.1	27.4	27.5	27.6	26.9
2006	27.7	28.0	28.3	28.1	28.5	28.7	28.8	28.8	28.6	28.7	28.6	28.4	28.4
2007	28.4	28.2	28.5	28.1	28.0	28.1	27.8	27.7	27.5	27.4	27.3	27.5	27.9
2008	27.0	27.0	26.8	26.8	26.9	26.8	26.6	26.3	26.2	26.0	25.7	25.4	26.5
2009	25.0	24.7	24.4	24.3	24.6	24.6	24.1	23.7	23.5	23.5	23.4	23.2	24.1
Retail Trade													
1990	74.3	72.6	73.0	75.6	76.2	77.2	77.6	78.1	78.9	79.9	82.1	84.1	77.5
2000	88.6	86.9	86.9	87.1	87.3	88.1	88.9	90.2	90.6	90.9	95.5	98.0	89.9
2001	91.3	89.5	89.6	89.7	90.2	91.3	90.9	90.8	91.5	91.9	95.1	96.9	91.6
2002	91.3	89.9	90.7	90.6	90.8	92.0	92.1	92.3	92.8	93.8	96.9	99.0	92.7
2003	94.2	92.2	92.2	92.5	92.9	94.1	94.6	94.8	94.6	95.7	99.5	101.9	94.9
2004	95.2	94.3	94.3	95.1	95.9	96.6	96.4	96.0	95.9	97.3	101.1	102.3	96.7
2005	97.3	96.3	96.4	96.5	96.8	97.2	98.3	98.3	98.5	99.3	103.1	105.8	98.7
2006	100.1	98.7	99.1	98.9	99.7	100.3	100.9	101.0	100.3	100.6	103.7	105.2	100.7
2007	100.4	98.9	98.4	98.2	98.6	98.7	99.5	99.3	98.9	99.3	103.3	104.4	99.8
2008	98.4	96.3	96.1	95.5	95.2	95.2	94.5	94.1	92.9	92.8	94.8	95.4	95.1
2009	89.3	87.0	86.1	85.8	86.8	86.9	86.5	86.2	86.4	86.7	88.7	89.2	87.1
Transportation and Utilities													
1990	15.4	15.6	15.8	15.9	15.9	16.1	16.5	16.5	16.7	16.6	16.6	16.7	16.2
2000	23.7	23.7	23.6	23.6	23.4	23.4	23.5	23.9	23.9	23.2	23.7	24.1	23.6
2001	23.6	23.2	23.5	22.9	22.7	23.1	23.1	23.3	23.4	23.5	23.5	23.5	23.3
2002	21.9	22.0	22.1	22.5	22.6	22.7	22.7	22.6	22.4	22.3	22.3	22.1	22.4
2003	21.5	21.4	21.4	21.5	21.7	21.9	22.0	22.3	22.3	22.4	22.4	22.4	21.9
2004	22.6	22.4	22.3	22.5	22.5	22.7	22.7	22.9	23.2	23.6	23.4	23.4	22.9
2005	23.3	23.1	23.3	23.0	23.2	23.3	23.2	23.4	23.5	23.4	23.5	24.1	23.4
2006	23.4	23.2	23.4	23.4	23.6	24.1	24.6	25.3	25.5	25.3	25.5	26.3	24.5
2007	25.1	25.1	25.1	24.9	25.1	25.4	25.5	25.7	25.8	25.6	25.7	26.3	25.4
2008	25.1	25.2	25.3	25.0	24.9	25.1	25.3	25.3	25.2	24.9	24.7	25.0	25.1
2009	23.8	23.7	23.5	23.3	23.1	23.0	22.9	23.1	23.2	23.2	23.1	23.4	23.3
Information													
1990	14.6	14.7	14.8	14.9	15.0	15.0	15.1	15.1	15.2	15.2	15.1	15.1	15.0
2000	18.6	18.5	18.4	18.4	18.3	18.4	18.6	18.8	18.8	18.8	18.9	19.0	18.6
2001	20.7	20.8	21.2	22.0	22.0	21.9	22.7	23.0	22.9	23.6	23.6	23.7	22.3
2002	24.1	23.8	23.7	23.5	23.7	23.6	23.3	22.7	22.4	22.3	21.9	21.6	23.1
2003	21.8	22.0	21.7	22.2	22.6	22.8	21.7	21.6	21.3	21.4	21.5	21.6	21.9
2004	21.3	21.5	21.3	21.1	21.1	21.1	21.0	20.8	20.5	20.4	20.5	20.6	20.9
2005	20.5	20.6	20.2	20.3	20.1	19.9	19.8	19.8	19.5	19.2	19.4	19.5	19.9
2006	19.6	19.8	19.7	19.9	19.9	19.8	20.4	20.3	20.1	20.0	20.1	20.4	20.0
2007	20.4	20.7	20.4	20.1	20.3	20.0	20.0	20.0	19.8	19.7	19.7	19.7	20.1
2008	19.5	19.7	19.5	19.4	19.4	19.4	19.3	19.3	19.1	18.6	18.8	18.8	19.2
2009	18.9	18.8	18.6	18.1	18.2	18.1	18.4	18.3	18.1	18.0	18.1	18.1	18.3

Employment by Industry: Sacramento–Arden-Arcade–Roseville, CA, Selected Years, 1990–2009—*Continued*

(Numbers in thousands, not seasonally adjusted.)

Industry and year	January	February	March	April	May	June	July	August	September	October	November	December	Annual average
Financial Activities													
1990	39.1	39.6	39.9	39.7	40.3	40.8	41.0	40.9	41.2	41.1	41.1	41.2	40.5
2000	52.3	52.7	53.0	52.6	52.6	52.8	52.1	52.5	52.3	50.8	51.1	52.2	52.3
2001	51.6	52.1	52.5	51.9	52.0	52.5	52.4	52.8	52.4	52.9	53.1	53.5	52.5
2002	53.1	53.4	53.5	54.1	54.0	54.3	55.1	55.6	56.4	57.3	57.8	58.3	55.2
2003	57.9	58.5	58.6	59.5	59.7	59.8	59.9	60.2	59.8	59.4	59.3	59.6	59.3
2004	58.7	59.1	59.1	59.8	60.0	60.2	60.8	61.1	61.1	61.5	61.5	62.0	60.4
2005	61.9	62.2	62.6	62.9	63.4	63.4	63.8	64.0	64.1	64.2	64.4	64.7	63.5
2006	65.2	65.3	65.3	65.1	65.0	65.2	64.8	64.6	64.4	63.5	63.7	63.5	64.6
2007	63.0	63.2	62.8	62.8	62.6	62.4	62.2	61.7	61.0	60.5	59.9	59.9	61.8
2008	58.9	58.9	58.5	58.3	58.0	57.8	57.7	57.2	56.8	56.1	55.9	55.7	57.5
2009	55.5	55.3	55.1	54.5	54.2	54.0	53.6	53.5	52.4	52.0	51.5	51.3	53.6
Professional and Business Services													
1990	52.4	52.7	53.3	53.4	54.0	54.3	55.0	56.0	55.9	56.3	57.2	58.3	54.9
2000	102.7	104.3	106.1	107.4	107.6	110.0	109.4	110.4	110.1	108.8	109.5	110.0	108.0
2001	104.6	105.5	106.3	104.9	105.0	105.3	105.7	105.1	103.3	101.6	101.5	101.7	104.2
2002	98.3	99.4	101.7	100.5	100.4	102.1	102.6	102.5	103.0	100.5	100.7	100.8	101.0
2003	99.5	100.0	100.2	100.3	100.3	101.2	100.5	100.9	101.4	100.2	101.5	101.5	100.6
2004	100.1	100.8	101.6	103.2	103.0	103.6	104.0	104.2	104.0	104.4	104.0	104.4	103.1
2005	103.6	105.0	106.3	107.7	107.9	109.7	109.7	109.7	109.7	110.5	111.3	112.0	108.6
2006	111.0	112.0	112.3	111.7	112.4	113.5	112.9	113.3	112.7	113.1	113.0	112.6	112.5
2007	108.6	110.0	110.8	111.4	111.3	112.3	113.3	113.7	113.2	113.5	113.4	113.9	112.1
2008	110.0	111.2	110.9	111.3	110.8	110.2	110.0	109.9	109.4	109.9	108.8	108.3	110.1
2009	103.8	103.1	102.2	101.2	100.0	100.0	101.9	101.3	99.6	99.0	98.8	97.9	100.7
Education and Health Services													
1990	51.3	51.7	51.9	52.2	52.5	52.6	53.3	53.8	54.3	55.1	55.6	56.2	53.4
2000	68.5	68.9	68.9	69.2	69.0	69.4	70.4	70.5	71.4	73.1	73.3	74.2	70.6
2001	73.5	74.1	74.9	75.8	76.8	76.4	75.6	75.9	76.5	76.8	77.0	76.9	75.9
2002	78.3	77.3	77.6	76.6	78.6	77.4	77.1	76.6	77.7	79.0	80.2	79.2	78.0
2003	80.8	79.2	80.1	81.2	81.3	81.0	80.9	79.7	81.3	81.6	82.2	82.3	81.0
2004	83.1	83.1	83.4	84.4	85.0	84.6	84.8	82.9	85.9	85.5	85.7	86.2	84.6
2005	86.9	86.7	87.2	88.1	88.7	88.1	88.0	87.2	88.6	89.4	89.9	89.7	88.2
2006	91.2	90.7	91.3	91.3	92.4	92.4	91.4	91.0	92.4	94.0	93.6	93.5	92.1
2007	94.9	95.1	96.6	96.4	97.5	96.4	96.5	96.0	97.4	97.5	99.1	98.5	96.8
2008	98.2	99.4	99.2	99.9	100.2	99.1	98.0	98.6	99.5	99.7	100.7	100.1	99.4
2009	99.9	100.1	99.9	100.2	100.7	99.3	98.2	98.5	97.8	98.8	99.5	99.6	99.4
Leisure and Hospitality													
1990	52.2	52.3	52.6	52.2	52.8	53.5	53.9	54.8	54.2	53.4	53.9	55.0	53.4
2000	66.9	67.8	68.5	69.4	69.4	71.8	72.2	72.4	71.7	70.0	71.0	72.5	70.3
2001	72.1	72.9	73.6	72.7	70.5	72.0	72.6	73.3	70.3	70.2	71.5	75.1	72.2
2002	73.9	74.8	75.3	74.9	74.5	76.6	76.0	76.6	74.8	74.2	74.5	76.4	75.2
2003	76.9	77.4	78.5	77.5	76.5	78.1	77.7	78.4	76.6	75.9	75.7	78.7	77.3
2004	78.3	79.1	80.1	80.1	78.8	80.6	80.8	81.2	79.8	78.4	79.3	81.7	79.9
2005	80.6	81.3	81.4	81.0	81.1	82.3	83.7	83.9	82.4	81.4	82.2	84.0	82.1
2006	83.0	85.2	86.6	95.2	95.5	86.0	86.5	87.0	85.2	83.2	83.9	85.6	85.3
2007	85.5	86.2	87.2	85.8	86.1	87.6	88.6	88.8	87.4	85.1	85.0	86.2	86.6
2008	87.0	87.7	88.4	87.1	86.7	88.1	87.1	86.3	84.6	82.2	81.8	83.3	85.9
2009	82.6	82.4	82.5	82.9	82.4	83.6	83.6	83.0	80.8	79.3	79.2	80.1	81.9
Other Services													
1990	20.7	21.0	21.3	21.5	21.8	22.1	22.2	22.1	22.1	21.9	21.7	21.8	21.7
2000	23.8	26.4	26.7	26.6	27.0	27.3	26.0	26.8	27.3	26.8	26.7	26.9	26.8
2001	26.6	27.1	27.4	27.6	27.9	28.3	28.0	27.9	27.9	28.2	28.0	28.0	27.7
2002	27.6	28.2	27.8	27.7	28.7	28.5	28.3	28.0	28.0	28.4	28.3	28.4	28.2
2003	27.3	27.6	27.6	28.3	28.6	28.8	28.3	28.3	28.0	27.8	27.7	27.8	28.0
2004	27.7	27.9	28.2	28.5	28.8	28.6	28.8	28.7	28.9	28.8	28.5	28.6	28.5
2005	28.3	28.6	29.0	29.1	29.0	28.8	28.5	28.4	28.4	28.1	27.9	27.7	28.5
2006	27.9	28.4	28.5	28.2	28.7	28.7	27.9	28.1	28.5	28.3	28.3	28.1	28.3
2007	27.8	28.2	28.5	28.6	29.1	29.2	29.3	29.5	29.5	29.4	29.1	29.3	29.0
2008	28.5	28.9	29.0	29.7	30.1	30.0	30.2	30.2	30.2	29.8	29.4	29.2	29.6
2009	28.9	29.0	28.8	29.2	29.4	29.2	28.8	28.6	28.4	28.3	28.4	27.7	28.7
Government													
1990	183.4	184.8	186.0	187.2	187.4	187.3	180.2	177.5	182.0	184.7	185.8	185.2	184.3
2000	206.3	209.2	211.9	211.8	215.3	215.8	204.4	207.1	208.4	212.0	212.9	212.7	210.7
2001	211.2	213.2	217.0	217.9	218.3	218.9	214.3	216.4	220.0	221.9	224.0	224.0	218.1
2002	222.0	223.8	229.2	229.3	230.6	229.7	223.6	224.4	226.1	227.6	228.0	227.5	226.8
2003	225.0	226.9	227.7	228.0	230.2	228.9	224.3	222.6	224.6	223.4	227.8	224.4	226.1
2004	222.5	223.1	223.0	223.6	224.4	224.9	217.6	215.2	219.3	221.4	222.7	221.1	221.6
2005	221.8	222.8	224.0	225.1	226.2	226.1	221.0	219.7	224.0	225.4	226.3	226.1	224.0
2006	225.1	227.3	228.6	229.0	229.7	230.8	225.6	223.1	227.2	229.7	231.7	232.7	228.4
2007	231.4	232.9	236.0	236.1	237.6	238.8	231.3	230.8	234.0	236.4	237.5	237.7	235.0
2008	237.0	238.9	240.8	240.0	242.0	241.9	236.1	232.3	234.5	237.5	238.9	238.9	238.2
2009	238.7	240.5	242.2	243.1	243.3	241.6	233.2	232.9	234.4	238.0	238.5	235.1	238.5

Employment by Industry: Salt Lake City, UT, Selected Years, 1990–2009

(Numbers in thousands, not seasonally adjusted.)

Industry and year	January	February	March	April	May	June	July	August	September	October	November	December	Annual average
Total Nonfarm													
1990	369.3	369.6	372.9	369.7	372.8	377.9	374.9	379.4	383.0	381.5	386.0	389.2	377.2
2000	552.5	555.9	559.6	561.2	563.0	565.7	560.7	564.7	569.5	571.6	577.1	585.1	565.6
2001	573.9	574.6	576.8	574.6	574.1	576.1	568.4	570.5	572.6	570.5	572.1	576.6	573.4
2002	567.5	572.3	564.2	562.7	560.1	561.9	557.2	558.7	560.6	560.8	565.0	568.0	563.3
2003	553.8	553.5	553.4	553.5	553.4	554.9	552.2	555.5	556.4	558.2	562.0	567.8	556.2
2004	554.2	556.1	558.7	560.9	560.0	564.4	563.3	565.9	567.6	570.3	575.9	583.1	565.0
2005	572.1	574.9	576.4	581.5	580.8	585.2	586.5	591.3	594.3	595.2	601.5	608.9	587.4
2006	597.5	601.4	605.6	608.2	608.4	614.8	612.3	617.9	620.2	620.6	628.5	636.2	614.3
2007	625.8	628.6	632.4	633.9	634.1	639.5	635.2	639.9	639.7	641.0	646.9	653.0	637.5
2008	640.0	641.3	642.5	643.1	640.1	642.7	638.6	642.5	641.6	639.2	637.7	640.6	640.8
2009	620.7	617.1	615.1	611.1	607.4	607.2	602.5	605.1	609.2	609.7	611.9	612.3	610.8
Total Private													
1990	305.3	305.0	308.6	305.7	307.9	312.8	313.4	317.8	318.3	316.3	321.3	325.1	313.1
2000	470.8	472.3	475.9	476.3	476.3	481.8	481.9	486.3	485.3	486.8	492.0	500.1	482.2
2001	489.1	487.9	490.1	487.4	486.3	489.1	487.4	489.6	485.8	483.1	484.2	487.9	487.3
2002	479.5	485.8	475.7	474.0	472.0	473.2	471.8	474.6	472.0	472.1	475.9	478.7	475.4
2003	464.9	464.2	464.4	464.0	464.6	466.1	467.0	470.9	467.9	469.3	473.2	478.9	468.0
2004	465.4	467.1	469.7	470.8	470.6	474.8	476.8	479.1	477.5	480.0	485.6	492.3	475.8
2005	481.6	484.1	485.9	490.4	490.2	494.5	498.4	502.9	503.1	503.7	509.7	516.8	496.8
2006	506.1	509.4	513.7	516.1	516.8	522.5	523.1	528.6	528.1	528.1	535.9	543.2	522.6
2007	533.6	536.2	540.0	541.0	541.4	546.1	545.7	549.8	546.7	547.4	553.0	558.8	545.0
2008	546.1	547.1	547.9	548.4	545.3	547.3	547.2	550.0	545.4	542.7	540.9	543.7	546.0
2009	524.8	520.8	518.8	514.1	510.6	510.4	512.9	514.1	512.1	512.3	513.7	514.8	515.0
Goods-Producing													
1990	65.4	65.7	66.5	67.0	68.4	69.8	70.4	71.7	72.0	71.4	71.1	70.6	69.2
2000	93.7	93.5	93.9	95.3	96.5	98.2	97.3	98.4	97.8	97.4	96.7	96.1	96.2
2001	93.2	92.5	93.2	92.6	93.9	95.4	95.5	96.1	95.4	94.8	93.2	91.0	93.9
2002	86.8	84.8	85.1	85.6	86.8	87.9	88.0	88.3	87.9	87.4	86.6	85.4	86.7
2003	82.3	81.9	82.0	83.1	84.9	85.5	85.8	86.4	86.1	86.3	85.6	84.8	84.6
2004	81.8	81.8	83.0	84.9	86.9	88.0	89.1	89.5	89.4	89.1	88.5	88.5	86.7
2005	86.2	86.5	87.1	89.6	91.2	93.0	94.3	95.4	95.5	94.7	94.9	94.7	91.9
2006	92.8	93.9	95.4	97.0	99.7	102.0	102.4	103.7	104.2	104.3	104.4	103.9	100.3
2007	101.5	101.8	103.4	104.7	106.7	108.9	108.9	110.0	108.8	107.8	106.9	105.4	106.2
2008	102.1	101.0	101.7	102.2	103.0	104.1	104.4	104.6	103.4	102.1	99.4	97.3	102.1
2009	91.0	88.7	88.3	87.2	88.5	89.0	89.9	89.9	89.4	88.0	86.9	84.7	88.5
Mining, Logging, and Construction													
1990	16.2	16.3	16.7	17.5	18.5	19.3	20.1	20.8	20.8	20.3	20.0	19.3	18.8
2000	37.3	37.2	37.5	38.8	39.8	41.2	40.7	41.4	41.0	40.5	39.7	39.0	39.5
2001	36.4	35.9	36.5	36.7	38.1	39.6	39.7	40.5	40.0	39.7	38.8	37.0	38.2
2002	33.7	32.1	32.5	33.4	34.5	35.7	36.1	36.3	36.1	35.8	35.1	34.1	34.6
2003	31.8	31.5	31.7	32.6	34.0	34.5	34.9	35.4	35.1	35.1	34.3	33.4	33.7
2004	31.0	31.1	32.0	33.5	34.8	35.7	36.6	37.0	37.0	36.7	36.0	35.9	34.8
2005	34.0	34.1	35.1	37.0	38.1	39.2	40.4	41.2	41.3	41.0	41.0	40.6	38.6
2006	39.0	39.7	41.0	42.4	44.5	46.2	46.6	47.5	47.9	47.9	47.6	47.1	44.8
2007	45.2	45.2	46.4	47.5	49.2	50.7	50.7	51.4	50.5	49.5	48.4	46.9	48.5
2008	43.6	42.6	43.3	44.2	45.1	46.1	46.4	46.9	46.0	44.9	42.9	41.3	44.4
2009	36.5	35.4	35.4	34.9	36.3	36.7	37.4	37.5	37.3	36.3	35.7	33.8	36.1
Manufacturing													
1990	49.2	49.4	49.8	49.5	49.9	50.5	50.3	50.9	51.2	51.1	51.1	51.3	50.4
2000	56.4	56.3	56.4	56.5	56.7	57.0	56.6	57.0	56.8	56.9	57.0	57.1	56.7
2001	56.8	56.6	56.7	55.9	55.8	55.8	55.8	55.6	55.4	55.1	54.4	54.0	55.7
2002	53.1	52.7	52.6	52.2	52.3	52.2	51.9	52.0	51.8	51.6	51.5	51.3	52.1
2003	50.5	50.4	50.3	50.5	50.9	51.0	50.9	51.0	51.0	51.2	51.3	51.4	50.9
2004	50.8	50.7	51.0	51.4	52.1	52.3	52.5	52.5	52.4	52.4	52.5	52.6	51.9
2005	52.2	52.4	52.0	52.6	53.1	53.8	53.9	54.2	54.2	53.7	53.9	54.1	53.3
2006	53.8	54.2	54.4	54.6	55.2	55.8	55.8	56.2	56.3	56.4	56.8	56.8	55.5
2007	56.3	56.6	57.0	57.2	57.5	58.2	58.2	58.6	58.3	58.3	58.5	58.5	57.8
2008	58.5	58.4	58.4	58.0	57.9	58.0	58.0	57.7	57.4	57.2	56.5	56.0	57.7
2009	54.5	53.3	52.9	52.3	52.2	52.3	52.5	52.4	52.1	51.7	51.2	50.9	52.4
Service-Providing													
1990	303.9	303.9	306.4	302.7	304.4	308.1	304.5	307.7	311.0	310.1	314.9	318.6	308.0
2000	458.8	462.4	465.7	465.9	466.5	467.5	463.4	466.3	471.7	474.2	480.4	489.0	469.3
2001	480.7	482.1	483.6	482.0	480.2	480.7	472.9	474.4	477.2	475.7	478.9	485.6	479.5
2002	480.7	487.5	479.1	477.1	473.3	474.0	469.2	470.4	472.7	473.4	478.4	482.6	476.5
2003	471.5	471.6	471.4	470.4	468.5	469.4	466.4	469.1	470.3	471.9	476.4	483.0	471.7
2004	472.4	474.3	475.7	476.0	473.1	476.4	474.2	476.4	478.2	481.2	487.4	494.6	478.3
2005	485.9	488.4	489.3	491.9	489.6	492.2	492.2	495.9	498.8	500.5	506.6	514.2	495.5
2006	504.7	507.5	510.2	511.2	508.7	512.8	509.9	514.2	516.0	516.3	524.1	532.3	514.0
2007	524.3	526.8	529.0	529.2	527.4	530.6	526.3	529.9	530.9	533.2	540.0	547.6	531.3
2008	537.9	540.3	540.8	540.9	537.1	538.6	534.2	537.9	538.2	537.1	538.3	543.3	538.7
2009	529.7	528.4	526.8	523.9	518.9	518.2	512.6	515.2	519.8	521.7	525.0	527.6	522.3

Employment by Industry: Salt Lake City, UT, Selected Years, 1990–2009—*Continued*

(Numbers in thousands, not seasonally adjusted.)

Industry and year	January	February	March	April	May	June	July	August	September	October	November	December	Annual average
Trade, Transportation, and Utilities													
1990	87.2	86.3	86.9	85.6	86.3	87.5	87.4	88.4	88.8	89.4	92.2	93.4	88.3
2000	120.7	119.6	120.2	120.0	120.5	121.8	122.3	122.9	122.9	124.3	127.0	129.3	122.6
2001	124.9	123.8	123.7	123.5	123.0	123.0	122.9	122.9	122.2	122.4	124.2	125.6	123.5
2002	120.9	120.1	118.6	119.0	119.5	119.6	119.7	119.9	119.3	120.4	122.6	123.7	120.3
2003	116.9	115.8	115.8	115.4	116.0	116.1	116.4	117.2	116.5	117.4	119.8	121.6	117.1
2004	117.0	116.2	116.3	116.5	117.0	118.1	118.4	118.6	118.2	119.4	122.1	123.8	118.5
2005	119.8	119.5	119.9	120.7	121.2	121.4	122.4	123.3	123.0	124.2	126.6	128.5	122.5
2006	124.2	123.9	124.3	124.2	124.7	125.9	126.1	127.5	127.5	127.7	131.2	133.9	126.8
2007	129.9	129.4	130.2	129.9	130.6	131.2	131.6	132.5	132.3	132.9	136.0	138.1	132.1
2008	133.2	132.2	132.2	132.5	132.6	133.3	132.8	133.3	132.4	132.5	133.7	134.4	132.9
2009	128.3	126.5	125.6	124.1	123.9	123.6	123.8	124.0	123.8	124.8	127.3	128.1	125.3
Wholesale Trade													
1990	20.7	20.7	20.9	20.9	21.0	21.1	21.3	21.5	21.5	21.6	21.7	21.6	21.2
2000	27.5	27.6	27.8	27.8	28.0	28.2	28.5	28.5	28.5	28.5	28.6	28.9	28.2
2001	28.7	29.0	29.1	29.0	29.1	29.2	29.2	29.2	28.9	28.8	28.7	28.6	29.0
2002	28.2	28.2	28.1	28.3	28.6	28.5	28.6	28.7	28.6	28.6	28.6	28.5	28.5
2003	27.1	27.0	27.1	27.2	27.4	27.3	27.3	27.4	27.3	27.2	27.2	27.3	27.2
2004	27.0	27.1	27.3	27.5	27.7	28.0	27.9	27.9	27.9	28.1	28.3	28.3	27.8
2005	28.1	28.2	28.4	28.5	28.7	28.6	28.7	28.7	28.6	28.7	28.8	28.8	28.6
2006	28.5	28.8	28.9	29.0	29.3	29.6	29.6	29.7	29.7	29.8	29.9	30.3	29.4
2007	30.0	30.1	30.2	30.2	30.5	30.7	30.8	31.0	30.9	30.9	31.0	31.2	30.6
2008	30.9	30.9	30.9	31.3	31.4	31.5	31.4	31.5	31.3	31.1	31.0	31.0	31.2
2009	30.2	30.1	29.8	29.5	29.4	29.3	29.9	29.8	29.6	29.7	29.6	29.4	29.7
Retail Trade													
1990	46.3	45.2	45.4	44.3	44.8	45.7	45.4	45.8	46.2	46.5	48.9	50.0	46.2
2000	64.0	62.8	62.9	62.7	63.3	64.0	63.9	64.2	64.1	65.3	67.7	69.3	64.5
2001	65.7	64.5	64.3	64.4	64.4	64.4	64.3	64.3	63.9	64.2	66.4	67.8	64.9
2002	64.3	63.3	62.8	62.9	63.3	63.5	63.3	63.5	63.2	63.7	66.0	67.3	63.9
2003	62.9	62.1	62.1	62.0	62.2	62.4	62.5	63.0	62.6	63.5	65.9	67.4	63.2
2004	63.2	62.4	62.3	62.6	62.9	63.4	63.9	64.1	63.8	64.7	66.9	68.3	64.0
2005	64.5	63.5	63.5	63.7	64.0	64.3	65.1	66.0	65.7	66.6	68.6	70.1	65.5
2006	66.4	65.8	66.1	66.0	66.2	66.9	67.1	67.9	67.8	68.0	71.0	72.4	67.6
2007	69.3	68.6	69.2	69.0	69.3	69.5	69.8	70.3	69.9	70.2	72.9	74.3	70.2
2008	71.1	70.1	70.2	70.2	70.3	71.0	70.6	71.0	70.4	70.7	72.1	72.8	70.9
2009	68.1	66.8	66.6	65.9	66.1	66.2	65.7	66.1	66.2	67.2	69.9	70.8	67.1
Transportation and Utilities													
1990	20.2	20.4	20.6	20.4	20.5	20.7	20.7	21.1	21.1	21.3	21.6	21.8	20.9
2000	29.2	29.2	29.5	29.5	29.2	29.6	29.9	30.2	30.3	30.5	30.7	31.1	29.9
2001	30.5	30.3	30.3	30.1	29.5	29.4	29.4	29.4	29.4	29.4	29.1	29.2	29.7
2002	28.4	28.6	27.7	27.8	27.6	27.6	27.8	27.7	27.5	28.1	28.0	27.9	27.9
2003	26.9	26.7	26.6	26.2	26.4	26.4	26.6	26.8	26.6	26.7	26.7	26.9	26.6
2004	26.8	26.7	26.7	26.4	26.4	26.7	26.6	26.6	26.5	26.6	26.9	27.2	26.7
2005	27.2	27.8	28.0	28.5	28.5	28.5	28.6	28.6	28.7	28.9	29.2	29.6	28.5
2006	29.3	29.3	29.3	29.2	29.2	29.4	29.4	29.9	30.0	29.9	30.3	31.2	29.7
2007	30.6	30.7	30.8	30.7	30.8	31.0	31.0	31.2	31.5	31.8	32.1	32.6	31.2
2008	31.2	31.2	31.1	31.0	30.9	30.8	30.8	30.8	30.7	30.7	30.6	30.6	30.9
2009	30.0	29.6	29.2	28.7	28.4	28.1	28.2	28.1	28.0	27.9	27.8	27.9	28.5
Information													
1990	8.2	8.2	8.1	8.2	8.1	8.3	8.5	8.6	8.6	8.6	8.7	8.8	8.4
2000	20.0	20.0	20.1	19.9	20.6	21.2	21.2	21.6	21.7	21.7	22.2	22.0	21.0
2001	21.3	20.7	20.7	20.9	21.3	21.5	21.1	21.0	20.8	20.4	20.8	20.5	20.9
2002	20.0	19.9	19.2	18.9	19.2	19.0	19.0	18.6	18.5	18.6	18.7	18.5	19.0
2003	17.9	17.7	17.6	17.4	18.0	18.1	17.9	18.2	18.0	18.3	18.1	18.4	18.0
2004	17.4	17.9	17.9	17.9	17.8	18.1	17.5	17.5	17.6	17.8	18.3	18.1	17.8
2005	17.9	18.3	18.7	18.2	18.2	18.1	18.6	19.0	18.8	18.4	18.7	18.6	18.5
2006	18.2	18.3	18.3	18.6	19.3	19.4	18.6	18.8	18.7	18.5	18.8	18.7	18.7
2007	18.7	18.6	18.8	17.6	17.8	17.6	17.5	17.7	17.3	17.2	17.3	17.4	17.8
2008	17.0	17.6	17.7	18.0	18.3	18.2	17.9	18.0	17.8	17.5	17.7	17.7	17.8
2009	17.3	17.4	17.2	16.9	17.1	17.2	16.9	16.8	16.6	16.6	16.7	16.7	17.0
Financial Activities													
1990	25.1	25.3	25.5	25.0	24.8	25.0	25.0	25.3	25.4	25.2	25.5	25.7	25.2
2000	42.4	42.2	42.4	42.3	42.0	42.1	42.4	42.5	42.5	42.8	43.2	44.0	42.6
2001	44.9	45.0	45.2	44.7	44.6	45.0	45.2	45.3	45.2	44.9	45.2	45.6	45.1
2002	46.1	46.0	45.5	45.3	45.5	45.6	45.1	45.3	44.9	45.3	45.1	45.6	45.4
2003	45.7	46.1	45.6	45.9	45.9	45.4	45.5	45.6	45.1	44.9	44.8	45.2	45.5
2004	44.5	44.7	44.7	44.8	44.6	44.4	44.6	44.5	44.5	44.7	45.2	45.8	44.8
2005	45.1	45.5	44.9	45.9	45.7	46.0	46.5	46.6	46.7	46.9	47.3	48.1	46.3
2006	47.6	48.2	48.3	48.5	48.5	48.8	49.2	49.4	49.3	50.0	50.4	51.1	49.1
2007	51.0	51.7	51.8	51.9	52.0	52.1	52.1	52.0	51.7	52.1	52.2	52.6	51.9
2008	51.5	52.0	51.8	51.8	51.5	51.3	51.4	51.4	50.9	50.8	50.5	51.1	51.3
2009	50.4	50.6	50.4	49.8	49.5	49.4	49.5	49.5	49.4	50.2	50.2	50.5	50.0

Employment by Industry: Salt Lake City, UT, Selected Years, 1990–2009—*Continued*

(Numbers in thousands, not seasonally adjusted.)

Industry and year	January	February	March	April	May	June	July	August	September	October	November	December	Annual average
Professional and Business Services													
1990	44.0	43.8	44.7	45.1	46.3	47.2	47.0	47.6	47.4	47.1	47.9	48.1	46.4
2000	84.4	85.7	87.3	88.2	88.7	90.0	90.3	91.0	91.1	91.7	91.7	93.0	89.4
2001	89.6	89.4	89.8	89.6	90.0	90.1	89.1	89.8	88.0	87.0	85.6	85.4	88.6
2002	82.8	85.7	82.6	82.8	83.4	83.3	82.9	84.1	83.5	82.9	83.3	82.6	83.3
2003	79.9	79.9	80.7	81.7	82.5	82.7	83.2	84.1	83.3	83.8	84.0	84.7	82.5
2004	81.8	82.5	83.1	83.9	84.5	85.3	85.7	86.7	85.8	87.5	87.7	88.7	85.3
2005	86.0	86.4	87.0	89.3	90.2	91.3	91.9	93.2	93.5	94.2	95.0	95.6	91.1
2006	92.8	93.6	94.8	96.4	97.2	97.9	98.6	99.0	98.7	98.2	99.2	99.3	97.1
2007	96.5	97.3	97.8	100.0	101.4	102.0	101.6	102.3	101.7	103.3	104.0	103.9	101.0
2008	100.5	100.8	100.8	101.3	101.9	101.7	101.9	102.6	101.8	100.9	99.6	99.1	101.1
2009	94.9	94.5	93.7	93.7	93.7	93.5	94.7	94.7	94.2	93.9	93.2	93.2	94.0
Education and Health Services													
1990	28.9	29.1	29.2	28.7	28.9	29.2	28.9	29.0	29.4	29.5	29.8	30.0	29.2
2000	43.0	43.6	43.8	43.8	44.1	44.1	43.5	44.1	44.4	44.3	44.7	45.5	44.1
2001	46.3	46.9	47.0	47.3	47.5	47.7	46.9	47.1	47.8	48.0	48.7	49.4	47.6
2002	48.0	48.5	48.4	48.8	48.8	48.8	48.4	49.2	50.1	50.3	50.5	50.9	49.2
2003	50.4	50.7	51.0	50.7	50.8	50.9	50.7	51.1	51.7	52.1	52.3	52.5	51.2
2004	51.7	52.3	52.7	52.7	52.8	52.9	52.6	52.8	53.5	53.9	54.3	54.4	53.1
2005	53.9	54.5	54.5	55.0	55.0	55.1	54.5	54.7	55.5	55.8	56.3	56.4	55.1
2006	55.4	55.9	56.3	56.2	56.5	56.7	55.8	56.8	57.4	58.1	58.4	58.3	56.8
2007	57.8	58.4	58.8	59.2	59.3	59.2	58.8	59.9	60.8	61.1	61.6	61.8	59.7
2008	61.4	62.4	62.5	62.5	62.5	62.3	62.0	62.6	63.5	64.6	65.4	65.5	63.1
2009	64.5	64.8	65.3	65.3	65.3	64.8	64.4	65.1	66.3	67.3	67.3	66.5	65.6
Leisure and Hospitality													
1990	34.4	34.5	35.4	34.3	33.2	33.7	33.4	34.2	34.1	32.9	34.0	36.2	34.2
2000	49.4	50.4	50.9	49.4	46.3	46.8	47.1	47.9	47.2	47.1	48.9	52.5	48.7
2001	51.9	52.5	53.3	51.5	48.7	48.9	48.8	49.4	48.9	48.1	49.0	52.9	50.3
2002	56.6	61.5	57.7	55.0	50.1	50.3	49.7	50.2	49.2	48.8	50.4	53.6	52.8
2003	53.8	54.1	53.7	51.7	48.5	49.3	49.2	49.9	49.2	48.6	50.6	53.7	51.0
2004	53.5	53.9	54.0	51.9	48.7	49.7	50.0	50.6	50.1	49.5	51.3	54.7	51.5
2005	54.5	55.1	55.3	53.1	50.2	51.0	51.0	51.6	51.2	51.0	52.4	56.2	52.7
2006	56.7	57.1	57.5	56.3	51.8	52.4	52.9	53.9	52.9	52.3	54.5	58.7	54.8
2007	59.2	59.9	59.9	58.4	54.0	55.3	55.1	55.2	54.4	53.5	55.5	60.0	56.7
2008	61.1	61.6	61.6	60.5	55.8	56.6	56.6	56.8	55.6	55.0	55.4	59.3	58.0
2009	59.5	59.4	59.3	58.2	53.5	53.7	54.1	54.5	53.4	52.7	53.3	56.3	55.7
Other Services													
1990	12.1	12.1	12.3	11.8	11.9	12.1	12.8	13.0	12.6	12.2	12.1	12.3	12.3
2000	17.2	17.3	17.3	17.4	17.6	17.6	17.8	17.9	17.7	17.5	17.6	17.7	17.6
2001	17.0	17.1	17.2	17.3	17.3	17.5	17.9	18.0	17.5	17.5	17.5	17.5	17.4
2002	18.3	19.3	18.6	18.6	18.7	18.7	19.0	19.0	18.6	18.4	18.7	18.4	18.7
2003	18.0	18.0	18.0	18.1	18.0	18.1	18.3	18.4	18.0	17.9	18.0	18.0	18.1
2004	17.7	17.8	18.0	18.2	18.3	18.3	18.9	18.9	18.4	18.1	18.2	18.3	18.3
2005	18.2	18.3	18.5	18.6	18.5	18.6	19.2	19.1	18.9	18.5	18.5	18.7	18.6
2006	18.4	18.5	18.8	18.9	19.1	19.4	19.5	19.5	19.4	19.0	19.0	19.3	19.1
2007	19.0	19.1	19.3	19.3	19.6	19.8	20.1	20.2	19.7	19.5	19.5	19.6	19.6
2008	19.3	19.5	19.6	19.6	19.7	19.8	20.2	20.7	20.0	19.3	19.2	19.3	19.7
2009	18.9	18.9	19.0	18.9	19.1	19.2	19.6	19.6	19.0	18.8	18.8	18.8	19.1
Government													
1990	64.0	64.6	64.3	64.0	64.9	65.1	61.5	61.6	64.7	65.2	64.7	64.1	64.1
2000	81.7	83.6	83.7	84.9	86.7	83.9	78.8	78.4	84.2	84.8	85.1	85.0	83.4
2001	84.8	86.7	86.7	87.2	87.8	87.0	81.0	80.9	86.8	87.4	87.9	88.7	86.1
2002	88.0	86.5	88.5	88.7	88.1	88.7	85.4	84.1	88.6	88.7	89.1	89.3	87.8
2003	88.9	89.3	89.0	89.5	88.8	88.8	85.2	84.6	88.5	88.9	88.8	88.9	88.3
2004	88.8	89.0	89.0	90.1	89.4	89.6	86.5	86.8	90.1	90.3	90.3	90.8	89.2
2005	90.5	90.8	90.5	91.1	90.6	90.7	88.1	88.4	91.2	91.5	91.8	92.1	90.6
2006	91.4	92.0	91.9	92.1	91.6	92.3	89.2	89.3	92.1	92.5	92.6	93.0	91.7
2007	92.2	92.4	92.4	92.9	92.7	93.4	89.5	90.1	93.0	93.6	93.9	94.2	92.5
2008	93.9	94.2	94.6	94.7	94.8	95.4	91.4	92.5	96.2	96.5	96.8	96.9	94.8
2009	95.9	96.3	96.3	97.0	96.8	96.8	89.6	91.0	97.1	97.4	98.2	97.5	95.8

Employment by Industry: San Antonio-New Braunfels, TX, Selected Years, 1990–2009

(Numbers in thousands, not seasonally adjusted.)

Industry and year	January	February	March	April	May	June	July	August	September	October	November	December	Annual average
Total Nonfarm													
1990	532.6	535.6	539.1	541.5	545.6	547.6	538.7	540.5	546.8	549.1	551.0	551.7	543.3
2000	727.4	734.8	738.4	744.0	751.2	751.2	744.2	746.3	752.1	748.1	750.3	754.5	745.2
2001	737.7	746.7	753.3	754.3	760.4	764.3	753.5	758.6	757.2	750.5	750.7	752.3	753.3
2002	737.2	745.0	751.6	755.2	760.8	759.5	750.6	756.1	760.0	756.5	758.0	758.2	754.1
2003	739.0	745.3	751.3	752.1	755.0	755.2	747.1	751.0	751.9	754.2	756.9	757.4	751.3
2004	742.0	749.8	756.5	759.8	763.3	765.4	759.5	764.0	764.1	763.8	765.7	766.2	760.0
2005	756.7	765.9	771.9	778.3	783.1	785.5	780.7	784.9	789.9	791.2	796.0	799.3	782.0
2006	786.9	795.0	803.7	809.6	814.4	817.5	809.7	814.1	818.7	819.8	823.2	825.8	811.5
2007	809.2	820.1	826.4	829.6	837.1	840.0	833.7	836.6	840.1	840.6	847.8	851.9	834.4
2008	836.0	845.8	850.7	855.5	859.7	860.8	851.9	853.3	853.2	854.3	856.4	855.1	852.7
2009	832.5	837.1	838.2	838.9	840.7	841.9	830.1	828.9	829.0	832.0	833.7	831.8	834.6
Total Private													
1990	407.7	409.1	412.4	415.4	418.2	423.4	422.3	423.7	423.1	422.9	424.4	425.5	419.0
2000	588.6	593.6	596.8	602.2	607.0	614.0	612.4	613.7	614.0	608.4	610.1	614.5	606.3
2001	598.7	606.2	612.5	613.3	619.2	626.2	622.0	624.0	617.8	610.0	608.7	610.4	614.1
2002	597.0	601.7	607.9	611.9	616.6	620.2	617.6	621.2	618.4	612.3	613.2	613.6	612.6
2003	596.6	600.5	606.6	606.8	609.5	614.1	611.3	613.8	610.7	611.1	612.4	613.4	608.9
2004	600.8	605.3	612.3	615.4	618.4	624.6	623.6	625.5	621.0	619.7	621.3	621.9	617.5
2005	614.2	620.6	626.7	632.7	637.5	642.5	643.6	646.1	646.2	645.3	649.1	652.4	638.1
2006	641.5	647.2	656.1	660.2	665.3	670.7	670.3	673.5	672.4	670.4	672.9	675.8	664.7
2007	660.5	669.0	674.9	678.4	685.7	691.3	690.2	692.6	689.6	689.6	694.7	697.8	684.5
2008	683.0	690.3	694.8	700.0	704.0	705.9	703.8	704.5	700.5	697.0	697.8	696.9	698.2
2009	675.4	677.4	678.3	677.7	680.3	682.6	678.4	676.9	671.8	670.0	671.5	670.4	675.9
Goods-Producing													
1990	71.1	71.2	71.1	71.2	70.8	72.0	70.7	71.3	70.8	71.4	70.9	70.8	71.1
2000	97.2	98.1	98.3	98.4	99.7	101.5	100.7	100.5	100.8	99.9	99.4	100.3	99.6
2001	98.0	98.7	99.8	99.7	100.4	101.6	101.6	101.5	101.3	99.2	97.9	98.0	99.8
2002	95.6	95.4	96.3	96.1	96.4	97.3	96.5	96.0	94.7	93.2	92.9	92.9	95.3
2003	91.0	91.5	91.4	91.8	92.1	92.5	91.9	91.8	91.4	91.1	90.6	90.6	91.4
2004	88.8	89.0	89.4	90.0	90.1	91.0	91.7	91.4	91.4	91.8	91.8	91.8	90.7
2005	90.6	91.2	92.4	93.8	94.0	94.7	95.1	94.9	95.6	95.4	95.7	96.7	94.2
2006	96.0	97.4	98.8	98.2	99.0	100.5	100.2	100.3	100.8	100.0	100.2	100.4	99.3
2007	98.9	100.3	100.7	100.8	102.0	103.7	103.4	103.8	103.5	104.2	104.2	104.8	102.5
2008	103.4	104.2	104.6	104.8	105.3	105.9	104.7	104.8	103.8	103.1	102.2	100.8	104.0
2009	97.9	96.8	96.2	95.6	95.1	94.7	93.6	92.9	92.2	91.5	91.1	90.7	94.0
Mining and Logging													
1990	1.7	1.5	1.6	1.8	1.7	1.5	1.6	1.5	1.6	1.8	1.8	1.7	1.7
2000	2.6	2.8	2.8	2.7	2.7	2.7	2.6	2.5	2.7	2.7	2.6	2.7	2.7
2001	2.7	2.7	2.8	3.0	3.0	3.1	3.1	3.2	3.3	3.5	3.6	3.6	3.1
2002	3.1	3.0	3.1	2.8	2.8	2.7	3.2	3.2	3.1	3.1	3.2	3.1	3.1
2003	2.5	2.7	2.7	2.8	2.7	2.8	2.8	2.8	2.9	2.9	2.9	3.0	2.8
2004	2.9	2.9	2.9	2.8	2.8	2.8	2.7	2.7	2.5	2.4	2.4	2.3	2.7
2005	2.3	2.4	2.4	2.4	2.4	2.5	2.6	2.6	2.6	2.8	2.8	2.8	2.5
2006	2.9	3.0	3.0	3.0	3.1	3.1	3.1	3.2	3.2	3.1	3.2	3.2	3.1
2007	3.1	3.2	3.2	3.2	3.3	3.3	3.4	3.5	3.5	3.6	3.6	3.7	3.4
2008	3.6	3.6	3.6	3.7	3.8	3.9	3.9	3.9	3.8	3.8	3.7	3.6	3.7
2009	3.6	3.5	3.5	3.4	3.4	3.3	3.4	3.3	3.3	3.3	3.3	3.3	3.4
Construction													
1990	24.0	24.1	24.2	24.0	24.4	25.4	25.1	25.2	24.8	24.7	24.2	23.9	24.5
2000	39.7	39.9	40.2	40.0	40.6	41.7	41.7	42.2	42.0	41.3	41.4	41.5	41.0
2001	40.9	41.6	42.5	42.4	43.2	44.6	45.1	45.6	45.1	43.4	43.3	43.1	43.4
2002	42.2	42.5	43.0	43.4	43.9	44.6	43.7	43.9	43.0	42.0	41.6	41.4	42.9
2003	41.3	41.1	41.3	41.5	42.1	42.5	42.4	42.6	42.0	41.9	41.6	41.6	41.8
2004	40.6	40.5	40.8	41.1	41.5	42.4	42.8	43.1	43.1	43.4	43.6	43.8	42.2
2005	43.0	43.3	44.4	45.6	45.9	46.4	46.3	46.3	46.7	46.1	46.1	46.5	45.5
2006	45.9	46.7	47.6	47.4	47.7	48.7	48.3	48.3	48.2	47.6	47.5	47.4	47.6
2007	46.6	47.8	48.7	48.6	49.5	50.8	50.7	51.1	50.9	51.4	51.5	52.1	50.0
2008	51.6	52.7	53.2	53.6	54.0	54.5	53.9	54.2	53.7	53.3	52.6	51.6	53.2
2009	49.6	49.0	48.7	48.5	48.3	48.4	48.0	47.7	46.7	46.1	45.8	45.5	47.7
Manufacturing													
1990	45.4	45.6	45.3	45.4	44.7	45.1	44.0	44.6	44.4	44.9	44.9	45.2	45.0
2000	54.9	55.4	55.3	55.7	56.4	57.1	56.4	55.8	56.1	55.9	55.4	56.1	55.9
2001	54.4	54.4	54.5	54.3	54.2	53.9	53.4	52.7	52.9	52.3	51.0	51.3	53.3
2002	50.3	49.9	50.2	49.9	49.7	50.0	49.6	48.9	48.6	48.1	48.1	48.4	49.3
2003	47.2	47.7	47.4	47.5	47.3	47.2	46.7	46.4	46.5	46.3	46.1	46.0	46.8
2004	45.3	45.6	45.7	46.1	45.8	45.8	46.2	45.6	45.8	46.0	45.8	45.7	45.8
2005	45.3	45.5	45.6	45.8	45.7	45.8	46.2	46.0	46.3	46.5	46.8	47.4	46.1
2006	47.2	47.7	48.2	47.8	48.2	48.7	48.8	48.8	49.4	49.3	49.5	49.8	48.6
2007	49.2	49.3	48.8	49.0	49.2	49.6	49.3	49.2	49.1	49.2	49.1	49.0	49.2
2008	48.2	47.9	47.8	47.5	47.5	47.5	46.9	46.7	46.3	46.0	45.9	45.6	47.0
2009	44.7	44.3	44.0	43.7	43.4	43.0	42.2	41.9	42.2	42.1	42.0	41.9	43.0

Employment by Industry: San Antonio-New Braunfels, TX, Selected Years, 1990–2009—*Continued*

(Numbers in thousands, not seasonally adjusted.)

Industry and year	January	February	March	April	May	June	July	August	September	October	November	December	Annual average
Service-Providing													
1990	461.5	464.4	468.0	470.3	474.8	475.6	468.0	469.2	476.0	477.7	480.1	480.9	472.2
2000	630.2	636.7	640.1	645.6	651.5	649.7	643.5	645.8	651.3	648.2	650.9	654.2	645.6
2001	639.7	648.0	653.5	654.6	660.0	662.7	651.9	657.1	655.9	651.3	652.8	654.3	653.5
2002	641.6	649.6	655.3	659.1	664.4	662.2	654.1	660.1	665.3	663.3	665.1	665.3	658.8
2003	648.0	653.8	659.9	660.3	662.9	662.7	655.2	659.2	660.5	663.1	666.3	666.8	659.8
2004	653.2	660.8	667.1	669.8	673.2	674.4	667.8	672.6	672.7	672.0	673.9	674.4	669.3
2005	666.1	674.7	679.5	684.5	689.1	690.8	685.6	690.0	694.3	695.8	700.3	702.6	687.8
2006	690.9	697.6	704.9	711.4	715.4	717.0	709.5	713.8	717.9	719.8	723.0	725.4	712.2
2007	710.3	719.8	725.7	728.8	735.1	736.3	730.3	732.8	736.6	736.4	743.6	747.1	731.9
2008	732.6	741.6	746.1	750.7	754.4	754.9	747.2	748.5	749.4	751.2	754.2	754.3	748.8
2009	734.6	740.3	742.0	743.3	745.6	747.2	736.5	736.0	736.8	740.5	742.6	741.1	740.5
Trade, Transportation, and Utilities													
1990	106.3	105.5	105.8	105.3	105.3	106.4	106.0	106.4	106.3	107.5	109.5	111.3	106.8
2000	135.2	134.7	134.6	135.5	136.0	137.6	138.0	139.4	139.2	140.5	143.4	145.6	138.3
2001	139.3	139.2	140.3	139.8	140.3	140.4	139.4	140.0	139.1	138.7	140.8	142.1	140.0
2002	136.7	135.3	136.4	137.2	137.8	137.9	137.7	138.3	138.5	137.8	140.2	141.2	137.9
2003	134.0	133.2	134.3	133.6	133.5	133.9	134.0	134.4	134.7	136.7	138.3	139.9	135.0
2004	134.4	133.9	135.0	135.6	135.8	135.9	136.2	137.5	136.9	137.4	139.6	141.2	136.6
2005	136.5	136.1	137.1	137.8	138.3	138.8	139.7	140.5	140.0	140.8	143.9	145.5	139.6
2006	141.0	140.4	142.0	142.0	142.5	142.8	143.1	144.5	144.7	146.8	150.7	152.7	144.4
2007	147.7	146.5	147.5	147.5	148.1	148.3	149.5	150.4	149.6	150.2	153.8	155.6	149.6
2008	149.9	149.4	150.2	149.5	149.4	149.6	150.3	151.5	150.0	150.4	152.1	152.6	150.4
2009	146.1	144.6	143.7	143.5	143.4	143.8	143.3	144.2	143.3	143.6	145.7	146.6	144.3
Wholesale Trade													
1990	21.2	21.1	21.2	20.7	20.7	20.9	20.9	20.9	20.8	20.7	20.9	20.9	20.9
2000	26.2	26.4	26.6	26.5	26.6	26.9	27.2	27.2	27.4	27.4	27.2	27.4	26.9
2001	27.1	27.2	27.3	27.5	27.7	27.8	27.8	27.9	27.8	27.6	27.6	27.8	27.6
2002	27.0	26.9	27.1	27.1	27.2	27.4	27.4	27.4	27.3	27.2	27.3	27.3	27.2
2003	26.6	26.7	26.9	26.9	27.0	27.2	27.4	27.3	27.4	27.5	27.3	27.2	27.1
2004	27.0	27.0	27.0	27.1	27.1	27.1	27.2	27.1	26.8	26.7	26.3	26.2	26.9
2005	26.3	26.4	26.5	26.7	26.9	27.1	27.2	27.3	27.3	27.1	27.4	27.5	27.0
2006	27.5	27.6	27.7	27.8	28.0	28.4	28.4	28.5	28.6	28.7	29.1	29.1	28.3
2007	28.9	29.0	29.2	29.4	29.5	29.6	29.6	29.7	29.6	29.7	29.7	29.8	29.5
2008	29.3	29.4	29.4	29.4	29.4	29.5	29.5	29.7	29.5	29.4	29.3	29.1	29.4
2009	28.8	28.7	28.5	28.5	28.5	28.5	28.1	28.1	28.0	28.0	28.1	28.0	28.3
Retail Trade													
1990	70.9	70.1	70.2	70.3	70.3	71.2	71.0	71.3	71.3	72.7	74.3	76.1	71.6
2000	88.8	88.3	88.2	89.0	89.3	90.4	90.6	91.7	91.3	92.2	95.0	96.8	91.0
2001	91.3	91.3	92.1	91.5	91.7	91.9	91.2	91.7	91.0	91.6	94.0	95.3	92.1
2002	90.9	89.5	90.0	90.7	90.9	90.6	90.5	90.9	91.4	90.7	92.8	93.9	91.1
2003	87.6	86.7	87.4	87.2	86.9	86.9	86.8	87.3	87.3	89.0	90.8	92.3	88.0
2004	87.4	86.7	87.6	88.2	88.2	88.3	88.6	90.0	89.7	90.4	92.9	94.4	89.4
2005	90.0	89.4	90.2	90.6	90.6	90.7	91.3	91.8	91.1	92.2	94.6	95.9	91.5
2006	92.0	91.2	92.4	92.3	92.5	92.3	92.7	93.9	93.9	95.9	99.2	100.8	94.1
2007	96.6	95.1	95.7	95.4	96.0	96.0	97.3	98.0	97.4	98.1	101.7	103.3	97.6
2008	98.8	98.2	98.9	98.3	98.1	98.3	98.8	99.9	98.7	99.3	101.1	101.7	99.2
2009	96.2	95.1	94.4	94.5	94.5	94.9	95.1	96.1	95.4	95.8	97.6	98.0	95.6
Transportation and Utilities													
1990	14.2	14.3	14.4	14.3	14.3	14.3	14.1	14.2	14.2	14.1	14.3	14.3	14.3
2000	20.2	20.0	19.8	20.0	20.1	20.3	20.2	20.5	20.5	20.9	21.2	21.4	20.4
2001	20.9	20.7	20.9	20.8	20.9	20.7	20.4	20.4	20.3	19.5	19.2	19.0	20.3
2002	18.8	18.9	19.3	19.4	19.7	19.9	19.8	20.0	19.8	19.9	20.1	20.0	19.6
2003	19.8	19.8	20.0	19.5	19.6	19.8	19.8	19.8	20.0	20.2	20.2	20.4	19.9
2004	20.0	20.2	20.4	20.3	20.5	20.5	20.4	20.4	20.4	20.3	20.4	20.6	20.4
2005	20.2	20.3	20.4	20.5	20.8	21.0	21.2	21.4	21.6	21.5	21.9	22.1	21.1
2006	21.5	21.6	21.9	21.9	22.0	22.1	22.0	22.1	22.2	22.2	22.4	22.8	22.1
2007	22.2	22.4	22.6	22.7	22.6	22.7	22.6	22.7	22.6	22.4	22.4	22.5	22.5
2008	21.8	21.8	21.9	21.8	21.9	21.8	22.0	21.9	21.8	21.7	21.7	21.8	21.8
2009	21.1	20.8	20.8	20.5	20.4	20.4	20.1	20.0	19.9	19.8	20.0	20.6	20.4
Information													
1990	13.9	14.0	14.0	14.5	14.4	14.6	15.3	15.1	15.1	14.7	14.9	14.9	14.6
2000	22.9	23.1	23.0	24.1	24.6	24.9	25.3	25.5	25.8	25.5	25.6	25.3	24.6
2001	24.4	24.5	24.5	24.7	24.6	25.0	25.0	25.1	24.7	24.9	24.8	24.9	24.8
2002	24.5	24.4	24.1	23.9	23.9	23.8	22.9	22.9	22.5	22.7	22.8	22.4	23.4
2003	22.2	22.0	22.2	22.2	22.3	22.4	22.6	22.5	22.4	22.4	22.7	22.5	22.3
2004	22.0	21.8	21.8	22.2	22.2	22.0	21.9	21.7	21.3	21.4	21.3	21.0	21.7
2005	20.6	20.7	20.5	20.2	20.4	20.8	20.7	20.8	20.7	20.8	21.1	21.1	20.7
2006	20.7	20.5	20.6	20.6	21.0	21.3	21.2	21.3	21.1	21.4	21.7	21.9	21.1
2007	21.7	21.9	21.7	21.6	21.8	21.8	21.8	21.6	21.4	21.4	21.5	21.5	21.6
2008	21.5	21.6	21.7	21.5	21.7	21.5	21.1	21.0	20.7	20.8	20.8	20.6	21.2
2009	20.5	20.5	20.6	20.3	20.1	19.7	19.4	19.3	19.0	19.0	19.0	18.9	19.7

Employment by Industry: San Antonio-New Braunfels, TX, Selected Years, 1990–2009—*Continued*

(Numbers in thousands, not seasonally adjusted.)

Industry and year	January	February	March	April	May	June	July	August	September	October	November	December	Annual average
Financial Activities													
1990	43.4	43.5	43.7	43.8	43.8	44.1	43.2	43.3	43.2	42.3	42.1	42.8	43.3
2000	55.7	56.1	56.2	56.8	56.8	57.3	57.1	56.7	56.7	56.9	57.1	57.6	56.8
2001	57.1	57.7	58.2	58.3	58.9	59.5	59.5	59.8	59.6	58.7	58.9	59.3	58.8
2002	58.7	58.8	59.1	59.4	59.9	60.1	60.1	60.4	60.3	60.6	60.8	61.2	60.0
2003	60.2	60.4	60.7	60.5	60.5	61.0	60.9	61.1	60.7	60.6	60.7	61.1	60.7
2004	60.6	60.7	60.8	61.5	61.6	62.0	62.3	62.3	62.2	61.5	61.7	61.8	61.6
2005	61.2	61.4	61.3	61.5	61.8	62.3	63.3	63.4	63.3	63.4	63.4	63.7	62.5
2006	63.0	63.1	63.2	63.6	63.9	64.2	64.4	64.3	64.4	64.5	64.6	64.9	64.0
2007	64.3	64.9	64.7	65.4	65.9	65.8	65.8	65.6	65.3	65.5	65.6	65.8	65.4
2008	65.1	65.4	65.2	67.0	67.3	67.1	67.5	66.9	66.6	66.3	65.9	66.5	66.4
2009	64.8	65.0	64.4	64.3	64.5	64.9	65.1	65.0	64.9	64.9	64.9	65.1	64.8
Professional and Business Services													
1990	42.3	42.7	43.6	44.2	45.1	45.8	46.8	47.7	48.1	48.5	49.1	48.8	46.1
2000	85.3	85.9	86.3	88.6	90.0	92.0	92.4	92.4	91.5	90.5	89.7	90.3	89.6
2001	88.2	89.0	89.4	89.8	90.2	92.2	90.7	90.7	88.5	85.9	84.7	85.5	88.7
2002	83.3	84.6	85.2	86.7	87.1	88.0	88.7	90.1	90.1	89.0	88.1	87.8	87.4
2003	84.6	85.6	87.0	86.8	87.7	88.2	87.7	89.0	88.1	88.6	89.0	88.4	87.5
2004	87.0	87.6	88.7	88.9	89.2	90.5	89.5	90.4	89.5	89.4	89.3	89.4	89.1
2005	92.2	93.7	94.1	96.7	97.4	97.9	96.7	97.8	99.4	99.9	100.0	101.1	97.2
2006	98.9	100.3	101.9	103.7	104.5	104.8	105.0	105.7	105.6	103.8	103.3	104.0	103.5
2007	101.4	102.6	103.3	104.7	105.6	106.2	105.4	106.1	106.2	106.8	107.4	107.3	105.3
2008	106.6	108.1	108.3	109.1	108.7	108.5	106.2	106.3	106.7	105.3	105.1	104.4	106.9
2009	101.0	100.5	100.6	99.5	99.1	99.8	98.0	98.7	98.1	98.6	98.4	98.0	99.2
Education and Health Services													
1990	56.6	57.5	57.8	58.5	58.3	58.2	58.2	58.1	59.7	60.5	60.9	60.8	58.8
2000	89.7	91.3	91.0	90.4	90.5	89.1	88.6	89.4	92.1	90.7	91.0	90.9	90.4
2001	89.8	92.0	92.6	92.1	92.8	92.3	91.8	93.4	94.5	95.3	95.8	95.7	93.2
2002	94.5	96.1	96.4	96.7	97.0	95.8	95.0	96.7	98.6	98.9	99.4	99.5	97.1
2003	97.9	99.0	99.2	99.5	99.4	99.1	97.9	99.5	101.1	101.6	101.9	101.8	99.8
2004	101.4	102.1	102.9	102.7	102.5	103.1	101.9	103.2	103.7	105.2	105.5	105.6	103.3
2005	103.8	105.6	106.1	105.5	105.6	105.3	105.4	106.7	108.7	109.1	109.7	110.2	106.8
2006	108.4	109.6	110.3	109.4	109.8	109.4	108.4	110.2	112.1	112.0	112.1	112.1	110.3
2007	110.0	112.4	113.1	112.7	113.5	113.3	112.7	113.8	115.1	115.7	116.5	116.9	113.8
2008	113.9	116.0	116.0	116.7	117.7	116.6	116.4	117.5	119.8	120.9	121.4	122.2	117.9
2009	119.2	121.1	121.3	121.9	122.7	122.0	122.4	121.9	123.0	123.8	124.3	124.7	122.4
Leisure and Hospitality													
1990	52.7	53.3	55.0	56.5	58.5	59.9	59.8	59.4	57.6	55.8	54.7	54.0	56.4
2000	75.5	77.1	79.9	80.6	81.4	83.0	81.8	81.4	79.6	76.9	76.3	76.6	79.2
2001	74.5	77.4	79.6	81.0	83.8	86.4	85.4	84.9	81.9	79.6	77.8	77.2	80.8
2002	76.2	79.2	82.3	83.5	85.8	88.1	88.0	88.0	84.9	81.7	80.1	80.0	83.2
2003	78.5	80.5	83.1	84.0	85.6	88.1	88.0	87.2	84.3	82.6	81.3	81.4	83.7
2004	79.2	82.5	85.8	86.8	89.2	91.9	92.5	91.4	88.6	86.2	85.0	84.2	86.9
2005	82.8	85.4	88.4	90.0	92.8	95.1	95.1	94.5	91.0	89.0	88.3	87.2	90.0
2006	86.8	88.9	92.0	94.6	96.2	98.9	99.3	98.5	94.9	93.4	91.5	91.3	93.9
2007	90.0	93.4	95.7	97.3	100.0	102.7	102.3	101.8	98.7	96.1	95.4	95.7	97.3
2008	92.7	95.3	98.1	100.4	102.7	105.2	106.0	105.0	101.7	99.5	99.4	99.1	100.4
2009	95.5	98.2	100.8	101.8	104.0	106.1	105.2	103.7	100.4	98.0	97.4	95.9	100.6
Other Services													
1990	21.4	21.4	21.4	21.4	22.0	22.4	22.3	22.4	22.3	22.2	22.3	22.1	22.0
2000	27.1	27.3	27.5	27.8	28.0	28.6	28.5	28.4	28.3	27.5	27.6	27.9	27.9
2001	27.4	27.7	28.1	27.9	28.2	28.8	28.6	28.6	28.2	27.7	28.0	27.7	28.1
2002	27.5	27.9	28.1	28.4	28.7	29.2	28.7	28.8	28.8	28.4	28.9	28.6	28.5
2003	28.2	28.3	28.7	28.4	28.4	28.9	28.3	28.3	28.0	27.5	27.9	27.7	28.2
2004	27.4	27.7	27.9	27.7	27.8	28.2	27.6	27.6	27.4	26.8	27.1	26.9	27.5
2005	26.5	26.5	26.8	27.2	27.2	27.6	27.6	27.5	27.5	26.9	27.0	26.9	27.1
2006	26.7	27.0	27.3	28.1	28.4	28.8	28.7	28.7	28.8	28.5	28.8	28.5	28.2
2007	27.5	28.0	28.2	28.4	28.8	29.5	29.3	29.5	29.8	29.7	30.3	30.2	29.1
2008	29.9	30.3	30.7	31.0	31.2	31.5	31.6	31.5	31.2	30.7	30.9	30.7	30.9
2009	30.4	30.7	30.7	30.8	31.4	31.6	31.4	31.2	30.9	30.6	30.7	30.5	30.9
Government													
1990	124.9	126.5	126.7	126.1	127.4	124.2	116.4	116.8	123.7	126.2	126.6	126.2	124.3
2000	138.8	141.2	141.6	141.8	144.2	137.2	131.8	132.6	138.1	139.7	140.2	140.0	138.9
2001	139.0	140.5	140.8	141.0	141.2	138.1	131.5	134.6	139.4	140.5	142.0	141.9	139.2
2002	140.2	143.3	143.7	143.3	144.2	139.3	133.0	134.9	141.6	144.2	144.8	144.6	141.4
2003	142.4	144.8	144.7	145.3	145.5	141.1	135.8	137.2	141.2	143.1	144.5	144.0	142.4
2004	141.2	144.5	144.2	144.4	144.9	140.8	135.9	138.5	143.1	144.1	144.4	144.3	142.5
2005	142.5	145.3	145.2	145.6	145.6	143.0	137.1	138.8	143.7	145.9	146.9	146.9	143.9
2006	145.4	147.8	147.6	149.4	149.1	146.8	139.4	140.6	146.3	149.4	150.3	150.0	146.8
2007	148.7	151.1	151.5	151.2	151.4	148.7	143.5	144.0	150.5	151.0	153.1	154.1	149.9
2008	153.0	155.5	155.9	155.5	155.7	154.9	148.1	148.8	152.7	157.3	158.6	158.2	154.5
2009	157.1	159.7	159.9	161.2	160.4	159.3	151.7	152.0	157.2	162.0	162.2	161.4	158.7

Employment by Industry: San Diego-Carlsbad-San Marcos, CA, Selected Years, 1990–2009

(Numbers in thousands, not seasonally adjusted.)

Industry and year	January	February	March	April	May	June	July	August	September	October	November	December	Annual average
Total Nonfarm													
1990	949.2	956.5	962.6	962.8	969.4	970.4	962.5	965.1	972.8	973.4	977.2	977.7	966.6
2000	1164.0	1173.7	1184.2	1184.7	1197.1	1203.0	1185.6	1188.4	1198.8	1206.3	1215.1	1224.9	1193.8
2001	1196.9	1205.6	1214.0	1217.7	1225.6	1229.6	1211.1	1213.2	1216.6	1225.4	1231.0	1234.5	1218.4
2002	1206.9	1217.6	1224.4	1230.8	1237.5	1244.2	1220.8	1225.6	1225.6	1237.5	1245.5	1251.7	1230.7
2003	1221.4	1226.7	1231.8	1236.6	1240.9	1246.5	1234.0	1240.3	1240.5	1249.9	1252.5	1260.5	1240.1
2004	1234.1	1240.9	1248.8	1256.1	1260.4	1267.4	1259.0	1260.7	1263.4	1271.3	1276.8	1285.1	1260.3
2005	1256.1	1264.3	1271.3	1280.8	1285.5	1290.9	1279.3	1282.4	1287.3	1287.0	1296.2	1303.9	1282.1
2006	1277.8	1287.2	1293.9	1295.0	1303.5	1312.3	1297.6	1301.8	1306.3	1306.9	1316.9	1319.5	1301.6
2007	1288.8	1297.3	1304.9	1303.0	1311.6	1320.0	1310.7	1311.3	1310.6	1309.6	1316.1	1322.1	1308.8
2008	1291.2	1299.5	1304.2	1303.5	1307.4	1311.2	1299.3	1298.8	1294.6	1293.5	1292.6	1289.1	1298.7
2009	1251.7	1247.7	1245.4	1235.5	1236.9	1237.0	1216.0	1218.1	1212.9	1215.9	1219.3	1218.8	1229.6
Total Private													
1990	775.1	779.9	783.6	783.0	786.6	789.7	795.4	797.8	796.4	792.9	795.0	795.8	789.3
2000	956.9	965.5	973.6	975.5	983.6	993.5	990.4	996.0	997.4	997.4	1003.6	1013.0	987.2
2001	986.9	993.0	999.3	1000.8	1006.3	1011.6	1008.7	1011.9	1006.9	1006.9	1009.9	1013.8	1004.7
2002	987.0	994.8	1000.7	1007.7	1014.7	1021.0	1010.1	1015.2	1012.7	1016.1	1022.7	1029.2	1011.0
2003	1000.5	1005.2	1009.6	1014.9	1019.9	1025.5	1025.0	1032.0	1028.8	1033.0	1035.8	1044.0	1022.8
2004	1021.0	1025.1	1032.1	1037.5	1043.0	1049.6	1053.1	1056.2	1052.4	1054.4	1059.6	1068.3	1046.0
2005	1041.1	1047.5	1053.7	1062.8	1066.8	1071.8	1071.4	1077.1	1075.8	1071.0	1078.3	1086.4	1067.0
2006	1061.6	1068.4	1074.2	1075.1	1083.5	1091.1	1087.0	1093.6	1091.8	1086.7	1094.0	1096.4	1083.6
2007	1067.3	1073.6	1079.9	1077.9	1086.6	1094.3	1095.8	1099.1	1092.5	1085.2	1090.2	1095.0	1086.5
2008	1067.0	1072.0	1075.5	1075.7	1078.6	1081.1	1082.6	1083.5	1074.5	1066.7	1064.6	1061.7	1073.6
2009	1025.6	1020.6	1016.6	1005.8	1007.9	1007.4	999.2	1002.3	993.7	991.2	993.5	994.7	1004.9
Goods-Producing													
1990	185.5	185.4	186.6	184.7	185.4	185.4	186.1	185.3	184.4	182.2	180.4	178.3	184.1
2000	186.6	187.4	187.8	188.8	190.2	192.8	191.5	192.4	192.3	192.6	193.2	194.7	190.9
2001	193.1	194.0	195.2	195.1	196.2	196.4	196.1	196.6	194.3	194.0	193.0	191.6	194.6
2002	188.2	188.5	189.5	189.5	191.1	191.8	189.3	189.9	188.9	188.0	187.7	186.9	189.1
2003	182.1	180.5	182.9	183.0	185.0	186.9	188.0	189.6	188.5	188.0	186.9	188.3	185.8
2004	185.9	187.0	189.0	190.1	191.6	193.2	195.1	195.8	195.7	195.6	195.0	195.0	192.4
2005	189.0	191.7	193.6	195.0	196.8	197.9	198.8	198.9	198.0	196.2	195.8	196.6	195.7
2006	194.2	196.1	197.4	196.6	198.8	200.3	198.4	198.8	198.1	196.0	195.6	194.6	197.1
2007	189.8	190.4	191.4	189.9	191.6	193.1	192.2	191.6	189.5	187.0	185.9	185.3	189.8
2008	181.0	181.0	181.3	180.3	180.9	181.6	181.2	180.6	179.0	177.0	174.5	172.1	179.2
2009	167.4	164.5	163.2	159.4	158.3	157.2	154.9	154.2	152.0	150.6	150.5	150.4	156.9
Mining and Logging													
1990	0.6	0.6	0.6	0.6	0.7	0.7	0.6	0.6	0.6	0.6	0.6	0.6	0.6
2000	0.3	0.3	0.3	0.3	0.3	0.3	0.3	0.3	0.3	0.3	0.3	0.3	0.3
2001	0.3	0.3	0.3	0.3	0.3	0.3	0.3	0.3	0.3	0.3	0.3	0.3	0.2
2002	0.3	0.3	0.3	0.3	0.3	0.3	0.3	0.3	0.3	0.3	0.3	0.3	0.3
2003	0.3	0.3	0.3	0.3	0.3	0.3	0.3	0.4	0.4	0.4	0.4	0.4	0.3
2004	0.4	0.4	0.4	0.4	0.4	0.4	0.4	0.4	0.4	0.4	0.4	0.4	0.4
2005	0.4	0.4	0.4	0.4	0.4	0.4	0.4	0.4	0.4	0.4	0.4	0.4	0.4
2006	0.5	0.4	0.4	0.4	0.5	0.5	0.5	0.5	0.5	0.5	0.5	0.5	0.5
2007	0.4	0.4	0.4	0.4	0.4	0.4	0.4	0.4	0.4	0.4	0.4	0.4	0.4
2008	0.4	0.4	0.4	0.4	0.4	0.4	0.4	0.4	0.4	0.4	0.4	0.4	0.4
2009	0.4	0.4	0.4	0.4	0.4	0.4	0.4	0.4	0.4	0.4	0.3	0.3	0.4
Construction													
1990	61.7	61.5	62.1	61.1	61.5	61.2	60.6	60.7	60.1	57.8	57.1	56.4	60.2
2000	66.4	67.1	67.2	67.3	68.3	70.1	70.8	71.9	72.2	71.6	71.9	73.0	69.8
2001	72.3	72.5	73.1	73.9	75.5	75.9	76.2	77.4	76.4	77.0	76.4	75.8	75.2
2002	73.6	73.3	74.0	75.3	76.9	77.7	77.0	78.2	77.6	77.9	77.8	78.0	76.4
2003	75.9	74.5	76.2	76.5	78.9	80.7	82.8	84.3	83.5	83.4	82.3	83.2	80.2
2004	82.5	83.4	84.8	85.8	86.8	88.0	89.5	90.4	90.9	90.7	90.0	89.8	87.7
2005	84.1	86.6	88.5	89.9	91.5	92.7	93.4	93.7	93.5	91.9	91.6	92.4	90.8
2006	90.5	91.8	92.5	92.1	94.1	95.1	93.4	94.2	93.7	92.2	91.6	90.7	92.7
2007	86.8	87.6	88.3	87.9	89.5	90.9	89.1	88.8	87.0	83.9	82.4	81.3	87.0
2008	78.0	78.0	77.9	77.0	77.5	77.9	77.7	76.9	75.7	73.8	72.0	70.2	76.1
2009	66.0	64.2	64.0	62.1	62.1	61.5	60.4	60.2	58.5	57.9	57.9	58.1	61.1
Manufacturing													
1990	123.2	123.3	123.9	123.0	123.2	123.5	124.9	124.0	123.7	123.8	122.7	121.3	123.4
2000	119.9	120.0	120.3	121.2	121.6	122.4	120.4	120.2	119.8	120.7	121.0	121.4	120.7
2001	120.5	121.2	121.8	120.9	120.4	120.2	119.6	118.9	117.6	116.7	116.3	115.5	119.1
2002	114.3	114.9	115.2	113.9	113.9	113.8	112.0	111.4	111.0	109.8	109.6	108.6	112.4
2003	105.9	105.7	106.4	106.2	105.8	105.9	104.9	104.9	104.6	104.2	104.2	104.7	105.3
2004	103.0	103.2	103.8	103.9	104.4	104.8	105.2	105.0	104.4	104.5	104.6	104.8	104.3
2005	104.5	104.7	104.7	104.7	104.9	104.8	105.0	104.8	104.1	103.9	103.8	103.8	104.5
2006	103.2	103.9	104.5	104.1	104.2	104.7	104.5	104.1	103.9	103.3	103.5	103.4	103.9
2007	102.6	102.4	102.7	101.6	101.7	101.8	102.7	102.4	102.1	102.7	103.1	103.6	102.5
2008	102.6	102.6	103.0	102.9	103.0	103.3	103.1	103.3	102.9	102.8	102.1	101.5	102.8
2009	101.0	99.9	98.8	96.9	95.8	95.3	94.1	93.6	93.1	92.3	92.3	92.0	95.4

Employment by Industry: San Diego-Carlsbad-San Marcos, CA, Selected Years, 1990–2009—*Continued*

(Numbers in thousands, not seasonally adjusted.)

Industry and year	January	February	March	April	May	June	July	August	September	October	November	December	Annual average
Service-Providing													
1990	763.7	771.1	776.0	778.1	784.0	785.0	776.4	779.8	788.4	791.2	796.8	799.4	782.5
2000	977.4	986.3	996.4	995.9	1006.9	1010.2	994.1	996.0	1006.5	1013.7	1021.9	1030.2	1003.0
2001	1003.8	1011.6	1018.8	1022.6	1029.4	1033.2	1015.0	1016.6	1022.3	1031.4	1038.0	1042.9	1023.8
2002	1018.7	1029.1	1034.9	1041.3	1046.4	1052.4	1031.5	1035.7	1036.7	1049.5	1057.8	1064.8	1041.6
2003	1039.3	1046.2	1048.9	1053.6	1055.9	1059.6	1046.0	1050.7	1052.0	1061.9	1065.6	1072.2	1054.3
2004	1048.2	1053.9	1059.8	1066.0	1068.8	1074.2	1063.9	1064.9	1067.7	1075.7	1081.8	1090.1	1067.9
2005	1067.1	1072.6	1077.7	1085.8	1088.7	1093.0	1080.5	1083.5	1089.3	1090.8	1100.4	1107.3	1086.4
2006	1083.6	1091.1	1096.5	1098.4	1104.7	1112.0	1099.2	1103.0	1108.2	1110.9	1121.3	1124.9	1104.5
2007	1099.0	1106.9	1113.5	1113.1	1120.0	1126.9	1118.5	1119.7	1121.1	1122.6	1130.2	1136.8	1119.0
2008	1110.2	1118.5	1122.9	1123.2	1126.5	1129.6	1118.1	1118.2	1115.6	1116.5	1118.1	1117.0	1119.5
2009	1084.3	1083.2	1082.2	1076.1	1078.6	1079.8	1061.1	1063.9	1060.9	1065.3	1068.8	1068.4	1072.7
Trade, Transportation, and Utilities													
1990	169.6	168.5	168.8	168.1	169.6	171.1	172.3	172.6	172.1	172.9	176.1	178.6	171.7
2000	198.5	198.9	199.0	199.3	201.4	202.9	202.2	202.2	202.6	204.9	210.8	215.6	203.2
2001	207.6	206.1	206.0	206.0	207.1	208.4	207.9	207.9	207.1	209.3	212.6	215.7	208.5
2002	206.0	204.8	205.7	206.6	207.6	209.2	207.1	207.5	207.3	207.8	212.6	217.6	208.3
2003	205.7	204.7	205.0	205.3	206.5	207.2	208.2	209.4	209.9	215.6	217.1	221.7	209.7
2004	211.5	210.8	210.6	211.9	213.4	214.6	213.8	214.3	213.9	217.9	223.5	227.2	215.3
2005	217.6	216.1	215.6	215.4	216.5	216.7	217.7	218.8	220.0	220.3	226.2	231.3	219.4
2006	220.7	219.3	218.9	218.3	219.5	220.0	220.1	221.3	221.4	222.4	229.4	232.8	222.0
2007	222.3	220.4	219.9	218.9	220.3	220.8	221.9	223.1	221.6	221.0	226.8	230.5	222.3
2008	219.5	216.9	215.9	215.9	214.9	215.0	216.3	215.3	214.3	213.4	215.8	217.1	215.9
2009	204.1	200.9	199.0	197.0	198.1	198.3	196.7	196.9	196.4	195.6	197.4	198.7	198.3
Wholesale Trade													
1990	31.3	31.8	32.0	32.1	32.4	32.6	32.7	32.7	32.5	32.5	32.3	31.9	32.2
2000	38.5	38.9	38.7	39.1	39.5	39.9	39.2	39.1	39.1	39.2	39.4	39.8	39.2
2001	40.5	41.0	41.1	41.2	42.3	42.8	41.3	41.4	41.2	41.5	41.5	41.7	41.5
2002	40.4	40.8	40.9	41.4	41.6	41.8	41.4	41.6	41.4	41.5	41.6	41.6	41.3
2003	40.9	41.2	41.4	41.5	41.8	41.9	41.6	41.7	41.6	41.6	41.9	41.9	41.6
2004	41.2	41.7	41.4	42.1	42.2	42.1	41.8	41.9	41.4	42.2	42.4	42.6	41.9
2005	42.3	42.8	42.7	43.3	43.6	43.7	43.8	43.9	44.2	44.2	44.5	44.5	43.6
2006	44.3	44.9	44.8	45.0	45.4	45.3	45.1	45.2	45.1	45.0	45.2	45.3	45.1
2007	44.7	45.2	45.3	45.2	45.7	45.7	46.0	45.9	45.7	45.4	45.6	45.5	45.5
2008	44.8	45.2	45.0	45.5	44.9	44.7	45.3	45.2	44.8	44.6	44.3	44.2	44.9
2009	42.1	42.0	41.4	41.0	41.1	40.6	40.3	40.2	39.8	39.8	39.8	39.7	40.7
Retail Trade													
1990	114.4	113.0	112.9	112.4	113.4	114.3	115.1	115.4	115.2	116.1	119.5	122.1	115.3
2000	131.5	131.4	131.2	130.2	131.4	132.2	132.0	132.7	133.5	136.0	141.4	145.5	134.1
2001	136.9	134.8	134.2	133.7	133.9	134.6	134.8	135.4	135.5	136.2	140.3	143.6	136.2
2002	136.6	134.7	135.4	135.5	136.3	137.5	137.5	136.2	137.1	138.1	138.7	143.6	148.8
2003	138.6	137.3	137.0	136.9	137.6	138.0	139.0	139.9	140.4	145.8	147.2	151.7	140.8
2004	142.5	141.1	141.1	141.7	142.9	144.0	143.6	144.1	144.1	146.5	152.0	155.6	144.9
2005	146.8	144.8	144.4	143.9	144.5	144.8	145.5	146.6	147.4	148.1	153.6	158.1	147.4
2006	148.2	146.2	145.8	145.0	145.7	146.0	146.2	147.3	147.3	148.6	155.1	157.7	148.3
2007	149.5	146.9	146.6	145.8	146.4	146.4	146.7	147.9	146.6	146.7	151.9	155.2	148.1
2008	145.7	142.3	141.7	141.5	141.0	141.3	141.9	141.1	140.5	140.2	143.0	144.2	142.0
2009	134.1	131.6	130.3	128.9	130.0	130.2	129.6	129.9	129.8	128.9	130.9	132.1	130.5
Transportation and Utilities													
1990	23.9	23.7	23.9	23.6	23.8	24.2	24.5	24.5	24.4	24.3	24.3	24.6	24.1
2000	28.5	28.6	29.1	30.0	30.5	30.8	31.0	30.4	30.0	29.7	30.0	30.3	29.9
2001	30.2	30.3	30.7	31.1	30.9	31.0	31.8	31.1	30.4	31.6	30.8	30.4	30.9
2002	29.0	29.3	29.4	29.7	29.7	29.9	29.5	28.8	27.8	27.6	27.4	27.2	28.8
2003	26.2	26.2	26.6	26.9	27.1	27.3	27.6	27.8	27.9	28.2	28.0	28.1	27.3
2004	27.8	28.0	28.1	28.1	28.3	28.5	28.4	28.3	28.4	29.2	29.1	29.0	28.4
2005	28.5	28.5	28.5	28.2	28.4	28.2	28.4	28.3	28.4	28.0	28.1	28.7	28.4
2006	28.2	28.2	28.3	28.3	28.4	28.7	28.8	28.8	29.0	28.8	29.1	29.8	28.7
2007	28.1	28.3	28.0	27.9	28.2	28.7	29.2	29.3	29.3	28.9	29.3	29.8	28.8
2008	29.0	29.4	29.2	28.9	29.0	29.0	29.1	29.0	29.0	28.6	28.5	28.7	29.0
2009	27.9	27.3	27.3	27.1	27.0	27.5	26.8	26.8	26.8	26.9	26.7	26.9	27.1
Information													
1990	21.4	21.5	21.5	21.2	21.4	21.7	22.0	22.1	21.9	22.0	21.9	22.1	21.7
2000	37.2	37.9	38.9	39.5	40.4	41.1	39.7	39.7	39.8	38.9	39.1	39.1	39.3
2001	39.1	39.1	39.3	39.2	39.1	39.3	38.7	38.7	38.1	38.0	38.3	38.3	38.8
2002	38.0	38.0	38.2	38.1	38.0	37.8	37.0	36.7	36.3	38.3	38.3	38.0	37.7
2003	37.6	37.9	37.3	36.9	36.8	36.8	37.0	36.8	36.7	36.6	36.6	36.3	36.9
2004	36.3	36.3	36.2	35.9	36.1	36.5	36.7	36.7	36.5	37.0	37.1	37.4	36.6
2005	37.3	37.5	37.3	37.4	37.5	37.5	37.6	37.4	37.2	37.2	37.4	37.5	37.4
2006	37.2	37.1	36.9	36.7	36.8	37.2	37.7	37.7	37.2	37.6	37.6	37.9	37.3
2007	37.5	37.7	37.6	37.5	37.4	37.4	37.6	37.7	37.4	37.7	38.0	38.2	37.6
2008	38.1	38.3	38.1	38.0	38.4	38.7	39.1	39.1	38.7	38.5	38.6	38.6	38.5
2009	38.1	38.0	37.6	37.3	37.1	37.1	36.9	36.7	36.1	36.1	36.2	36.2	37.0

Employment by Industry: San Diego-Carlsbad-San Marcos, CA, Selected Years, 1990–2009—*Continued*

(Numbers in thousands, not seasonally adjusted.)

Industry and year	January	February	March	April	May	June	July	August	September	October	November	December	Annual average
Financial Activities													
1990	65.8	66.3	66.6	66.0	66.2	66.3	64.5	64.5	64.7	64.1	64.0	65.0	65.3
2000	70.2	70.7	71.0	71.1	71.3	71.7	71.4	71.5	71.3	71.7	72.0	72.2	71.3
2001	70.1	70.9	71.3	71.4	71.7	72.3	72.5	73.0	72.5	72.5	72.9	73.5	72.1
2002	72.2	73.1	73.5	74.0	74.6	75.1	75.0	75.7	75.7	76.3	77.3	77.9	75.0
2003	77.5	78.2	78.6	79.5	80.3	80.7	80.7	81.0	80.7	80.5	80.6	80.6	79.9
2004	80.6	80.9	81.4	81.7	81.8	81.8	82.4	82.4	82.2	82.6	82.5	83.0	81.9
2005	81.7	82.1	82.3	82.8	82.9	83.2	83.6	83.8	83.5	84.1	84.2	84.4	83.2
2006	83.9	84.4	84.4	84.2	84.7	84.5	83.5	83.6	83.2	82.8	82.6	82.6	83.7
2007	80.9	81.9	81.9	81.2	81.5	81.6	80.7	80.2	79.3	78.6	77.9	77.8	80.3
2008	76.3	76.7	76.6	76.6	76.3	75.9	75.4	75.0	74.1	73.7	73.2	72.9	75.2
2009	71.6	72.0	71.7	70.7	70.6	70.6	70.3	70.1	69.3	69.0	68.6	68.5	70.3
Professional and Business Services													
1990	120.0	121.6	123.1	124.4	124.5	124.7	124.0	125.3	125.5	125.0	125.4	126.2	124.1
2000	187.3	189.4	192.8	191.7	192.3	194.6	196.1	199.0	200.5	200.2	200.6	202.2	195.6
2001	196.0	198.4	199.4	198.1	198.2	198.7	196.3	197.7	198.0	198.8	200.5	200.7	198.4
2002	197.7	200.7	201.9	200.8	200.9	202.1	200.7	202.5	202.0	203.0	204.0	204.9	201.8
2003	199.5	201.8	201.8	201.5	200.1	200.7	199.7	200.8	200.1	201.7	203.0	203.7	201.2
2004	200.6	201.9	203.5	203.5	202.7	204.0	205.9	205.5	205.5	206.0	206.6	208.8	204.5
2005	205.9	207.8	208.8	211.6	210.6	212.1	210.2	211.1	211.5	211.3	211.8	212.4	210.4
2006	209.0	211.6	212.7	212.8	213.5	215.3	214.3	215.8	216.1	214.2	214.3	213.9	213.6
2007	212.0	214.3	215.2	215.5	215.7	217.7	218.3	219.2	218.6	218.5	218.2	218.3	216.8
2008	215.2	217.5	218.3	218.1	216.9	216.5	215.2	216.4	214.6	212.7	210.5	209.7	215.1
2009	204.0	202.6	200.1	197.9	196.9	196.0	195.9	195.7	193.5	194.2	195.6	195.7	197.3
Education and Health Services													
1990	80.3	81.9	82.1	83.2	83.4	82.7	83.4	83.6	85.0	87.0	88.2	88.0	84.1
2000	113.8	115.7	116.1	115.1	115.7	115.2	114.4	114.3	115.2	116.4	116.4	116.9	115.4
2001	111.4	112.8	114.4	115.0	116.2	116.1	115.6	115.7	117.4	118.8	119.1	119.4	116.0
2002	117.8	120.2	120.3	120.6	121.0	120.1	117.4	117.2	118.5	120.6	121.1	121.2	119.7
2003	119.8	120.5	121.2	123.0	123.2	122.7	119.9	120.5	121.6	122.2	123.1	124.0	121.8
2004	121.4	121.4	123.0	123.1	122.9	122.3	119.1	119.4	120.1	122.0	122.3	123.0	121.7
2005	121.1	121.5	122.5	123.9	123.6	122.8	120.1	120.3	122.5	122.8	124.5	124.6	122.5
2006	122.7	123.5	124.9	125.1	125.3	125.0	123.3	123.6	125.7	126.7	127.7	127.6	125.1
2007	125.4	126.9	128.7	128.7	129.8	128.8	127.7	129.0	130.9	131.9	132.7	134.0	129.5
2008	132.9	135.0	135.7	135.8	136.5	135.8	135.3	136.6	137.8	140.9	142.4	143.3	137.3
2009	141.5	143.1	144.6	142.5	142.9	142.8	139.7	141.5	142.9	144.9	145.0	144.9	143.0
Leisure and Hospitality													
1990	99.5	101.2	101.3	101.9	102.6	104.0	108.6	110.0	108.5	105.8	105.1	103.5	104.3
2000	122.1	123.8	125.8	127.7	129.9	132.1	132.3	134.5	133.2	130.6	129.4	129.6	129.3
2001	126.8	128.4	129.7	131.7	132.8	134.1	135.6	136.5	133.2	130.6	128.7	129.5	131.5
2002	123.8	125.6	127.1	132.0	134.9	137.3	137.5	140.3	138.3	136.3	135.8	136.6	133.8
2003	132.9	135.9	136.8	138.7	140.5	142.2	144.4	146.7	144.0	142.0	142.1	142.6	140.7
2004	138.3	140.0	141.3	144.3	147.0	149.0	151.1	153.2	149.5	145.2	144.4	145.3	145.7
2005	141.0	142.5	144.9	147.7	149.7	152.2	154.2	157.5	154.4	150.5	149.7	150.7	149.6
2006	147.0	148.7	151.3	153.0	155.9	159.4	161.7	164.8	161.3	158.3	158.0	158.1	156.5
2007	152.1	154.2	157.0	158.5	161.9	165.7	168.5	169.7	166.5	162.5	162.4	162.4	161.8
2008	156.6	158.7	161.1	162.9	166.1	168.2	171.0	171.4	167.7	162.4	161.5	159.9	164.0
2009	152.6	152.5	153.1	154.4	156.8	158.0	158.2	160.0	157.3	153.8	152.8	152.7	155.2
Other Services													
1990	33.0	33.5	33.6	33.5	33.5	33.8	34.5	34.4	34.3	33.9	33.9	34.1	33.8
2000	41.2	41.7	42.2	42.3	42.4	43.1	42.8	42.4	42.5	42.1	42.1	42.7	42.3
2001	42.8	43.3	44.0	44.3	45.0	46.3	46.0	45.8	46.3	44.9	44.8	45.1	44.9
2002	43.3	43.9	44.5	46.1	46.6	47.6	46.1	45.4	45.7	45.8	45.9	46.1	45.6
2003	45.4	45.7	46.0	47.0	47.5	48.3	47.1	47.2	47.3	46.4	46.4	46.8	46.8
2004	46.4	46.8	47.1	47.0	47.5	48.2	49.0	48.9	49.0	48.1	48.2	48.6	47.9
2005	47.5	48.3	48.7	49.0	49.2	49.4	49.2	49.3	48.7	48.6	48.7	48.9	48.8
2006	46.9	47.7	47.7	48.4	49.0	49.4	48.0	48.0	48.8	48.7	48.8	48.9	48.4
2007	47.3	47.8	48.2	47.7	48.4	49.2	48.9	48.6	48.7	48.0	48.3	48.5	48.3
2008	47.4	47.9	48.5	48.1	48.6	49.4	49.1	49.1	48.3	48.1	48.1	48.1	48.4
2009	46.3	47.0	47.3	46.6	47.2	47.4	46.6	47.2	46.2	47.0	47.4	47.6	47.0
Government													
1990	174.1	176.6	179.0	179.8	182.8	180.7	167.1	167.3	176.4	180.5	182.2	181.9	177.4
2000	207.1	208.2	210.6	209.2	213.5	209.5	195.2	192.4	201.4	208.9	211.5	211.9	206.6
2001	210.0	212.6	214.7	216.9	219.3	218.0	202.4	201.3	209.7	218.5	221.1	220.7	213.8
2002	219.9	222.8	223.7	223.1	222.8	223.2	210.7	210.4	212.9	221.4	222.8	222.5	219.7
2003	220.9	221.5	222.2	221.7	221.0	221.0	209.0	208.3	211.7	216.9	216.7	216.5	217.2
2004	213.1	215.8	216.7	218.6	217.4	217.8	205.9	204.5	211.0	216.9	217.2	216.8	214.3
2005	215.0	216.8	217.6	218.0	218.7	219.1	207.9	205.3	211.5	216.0	217.9	217.5	215.1
2006	216.2	218.8	219.7	219.9	220.0	221.2	210.6	208.2	214.5	220.2	222.9	223.1	217.9
2007	221.5	223.7	225.0	225.1	225.0	225.7	214.9	212.2	218.1	224.4	225.9	227.1	222.4
2008	224.2	227.5	228.7	227.8	228.8	230.1	216.7	215.3	220.1	226.8	228.0	227.4	225.1
2009	226.1	227.1	228.8	229.7	229.0	229.6	216.8	215.8	219.2	224.7	225.8	224.1	224.7

Employment by Industry: San Francisco-Oakland-Fremont, CA, Selected Years, 1990–2009

(Numbers in thousands, not seasonally adjusted.)

Industry and year	January	February	March	April	May	June	July	August	September	October	November	December	Annual average
Total Nonfarm													
1990	1793.2	1796.3	1804.5	1811.3	1817.8	1831.0	1829.3	1822.0	1837.7	1848.8	1859.0	1867.0	1826.5
2000	2053.8	2074.5	2095.8	2106.0	2123.4	2143.0	2129.4	2139.0	2150.5	2151.1	2169.4	2184.4	2126.7
2001	2127.4	2137.9	2153.5	2131.0	2129.2	2130.9	2097.8	2092.6	2086.6	2074.7	2069.5	2072.4	2108.6
2002	2013.3	2020.4	2033.0	2026.8	2034.4	2038.5	2014.4	2017.8	2022.5	2027.4	2036.8	2037.7	2026.9
2003	1980.8	1987.7	1990.0	1981.2	1982.6	1986.0	1958.7	1959.8	1963.9	1966.3	1971.8	1979.5	1975.6
2004	1933.8	1943.9	1954.6	1957.7	1965.9	1972.0	1956.5	1951.4	1957.4	1969.2	1978.0	1988.9	1960.8
2005	1941.0	1954.5	1962.2	1968.9	1973.3	1981.3	1968.3	1968.3	1981.1	1986.7	1999.3	2007.0	1974.3
2006	1968.5	1984.9	1993.5	1994.6	2012.0	2022.4	2005.7	2009.5	2019.5	2027.6	2038.2	2041.2	2009.8
2007	1999.6	2015.8	2027.2	2020.8	2036.8	2045.2	2036.1	2038.5	2044.4	2050.5	2063.2	2068.7	2037.2
2008	2018.4	2030.7	2032.6	2034.7	2038.2	2041.9	2031.1	2024.1	2022.0	2023.3	2016.0	2011.5	2027.0
2009	1952.5	1941.9	1934.0	1924.9	1921.1	1916.3	1890.3	1884.2	1879.3	1886.6	1887.4	1886.6	1908.8
Total Private													
1990	1490.3	1489.0	1495.1	1500.1	1503.8	1518.2	1530.3	1530.1	1532.2	1540.6	1547.7	1556.2	1519.5
2000	1753.8	1771.1	1789.0	1793.0	1804.7	1826.5	1830.8	1838.7	1847.9	1842.5	1857.1	1873.2	1819.0
2001	1823.0	1830.2	1842.5	1817.7	1816.7	1820.5	1798.9	1793.6	1779.4	1760.4	1754.3	1757.4	1799.6
2002	1699.6	1703.4	1711.8	1704.3	1711.5	1718.0	1710.0	1714.2	1708.7	1705.5	1713.5	1716.0	1709.7
2003	1662.9	1667.2	1668.1	1660.9	1662.7	1667.9	1656.3	1660.4	1657.2	1654.8	1660.0	1669.0	1662.2
2004	1625.4	1632.8	1641.6	1645.1	1653.3	1660.2	1657.0	1657.3	1656.3	1660.4	1666.9	1679.3	1653.0
2005	1633.9	1643.8	1650.5	1655.9	1659.6	1668.9	1666.9	1671.3	1674.6	1674.8	1685.0	1695.3	1665.0
2006	1654.2	1667.2	1673.5	1675.2	1691.9	1703.9	1696.5	1702.6	1704.6	1705.9	1713.5	1720.1	1692.4
2007	1680.6	1692.4	1702.0	1695.7	1709.1	1718.7	1722.0	1725.3	1722.7	1733.7	1743.8	1750.0	1716.3
2008	1703.5	1713.0	1713.6	1715.1	1719.3	1721.1	1720.7	1717.4	1710.6	1707.9	1699.1	1696.5	1711.5
2009	1639.5	1626.5	1617.2	1606.7	1605.0	1599.9	1588.7	1584.5	1576.0	1579.1	1580.3	1582.7	1598.8
Goods-Producing													
1990	257.5	256.6	258.7	259.4	261.7	264.9	265.0	265.7	266.5	265.3	263.8	261.6	262.2
2000	279.3	281.1	282.9	285.2	287.4	292.4	293.9	296.4	299.4	298.7	300.2	301.9	291.6
2001	293.7	294.3	297.3	293.5	292.3	293.1	289.6	289.4	285.4	280.3	276.1	273.6	288.2
2002	261.9	263.1	264.4	265.5	266.7	270.2	268.8	271.3	269.4	267.8	264.7	261.9	266.3
2003	254.2	253.8	253.9	252.7	252.8	254.4	254.7	257.0	256.9	257.6	256.6	255.2	254.9
2004	249.7	250.1	251.6	253.4	255.1	257.7	259.4	260.6	260.1	258.6	256.0	254.5	255.6
2005	246.4	248.2	250.0	250.5	251.0	254.5	256.7	258.0	258.1	257.7	257.2	255.5	253.7
2006	249.7	251.9	252.0	250.1	256.3	260.3	260.9	263.7	263.0	261.5	259.8	256.5	257.1
2007	251.0	251.6	254.1	253.5	255.4	258.2	259.0	260.8	259.4	258.9	258.2	256.2	256.4
2008	248.9	249.8	248.7	247.4	247.9	248.8	249.2	248.3	246.2	242.9	237.4	233.5	245.8
2009	224.1	217.2	215.3	211.1	209.8	210.0	208.8	208.3	206.6	206.2	204.8	201.4	210.3
Mining and Logging													
1990	9.7	9.7	9.8	9.5	9.5	9.5	8.6	9.4	9.4	9.6	9.5	9.4	9.4
2000	2.4	2.6	2.6	2.6	2.6	2.6	2.6	2.5	2.5	2.5	2.5	2.6	2.5
2001	2.0	2.0	2.0	1.9	1.9	1.8	1.8	1.7	1.7	1.7	1.6	1.6	1.8
2002	1.5	1.5	1.5	1.5	1.5	1.4	1.3	1.3	1.2	1.2	1.2	1.2	1.4
2003	1.0	1.0	1.0	1.0	1.0	1.0	1.0	1.0	1.0	1.4	1.4	1.4	1.1
2004	1.4	1.4	1.4	1.4	1.4	1.4	1.4	1.4	1.4	1.3	1.4	1.4	1.4
2005	1.3	1.4	1.3	1.3	1.3	1.3	1.4	1.3	1.3	1.3	1.3	1.3	1.3
2006	1.3	1.3	1.3	1.3	1.4	1.4	1.4	1.5	1.5	1.5	1.5	1.5	1.4
2007	1.4	1.5	1.4	1.5	1.5	1.5	1.4	1.5	1.4	1.4	1.4	1.4	1.4
2008	1.4	1.4	1.4	1.4	1.4	1.4	1.4	1.4	1.4	1.4	1.4	1.4	1.4
2009	1.4	1.4	1.4	1.4	1.4	1.4	1.4	1.4	1.4	1.4	1.4	1.4	1.4
Construction													
1990	79.5	78.6	80.1	81.7	83.2	84.9	84.1	84.4	84.8	83.3	82.3	80.5	82.3
2000	103.0	102.9	105.1	106.3	108.3	111.6	114.3	116.2	117.6	116.4	115.8	115.6	111.0
2001	112.7	113.5	116.7	116.5	117.9	119.8	120.3	121.5	120.5	118.1	115.9	114.2	117.3
2002	106.5	107.7	108.7	110.1	111.2	114.0	113.8	116.4	115.4	114.7	112.7	110.8	111.8
2003	107.9	108.1	108.6	108.1	108.6	110.5	111.5	113.7	113.6	113.8	112.6	110.8	110.6
2004	106.2	106.1	107.2	109.5	111.1	113.3	115.0	116.3	116.8	116.0	113.4	112.2	111.9
2005	106.3	108.0	110.1	111.4	112.4	115.3	117.3	118.5	118.5	118.5	117.6	115.8	114.1
2006	110.1	112.0	111.0	109.7	115.5	118.4	120.0	122.3	122.1	121.2	118.8	116.2	116.4
2007	112.3	112.3	114.7	114.8	116.5	118.8	120.5	121.7	120.3	119.3	117.7	115.9	117.1
2008	110.3	110.8	109.8	109.5	110.2	110.9	111.6	111.3	109.9	108.9	104.7	102.0	109.2
2009	95.5	90.7	90.3	88.4	88.4	89.0	88.8	88.4	87.0	86.9	85.5	82.9	88.5
Manufacturing													
1990	168.3	168.3	168.8	168.2	169.0	170.5	172.3	171.9	172.3	172.4	172.0	171.7	170.5
2000	173.9	175.6	175.2	176.3	176.5	178.2	177.0	177.7	179.3	179.8	181.9	183.7	177.9
2001	179.2	179.0	178.8	175.3	172.7	171.7	167.7	166.4	163.4	160.7	158.8	158.0	169.3
2002	153.9	153.9	154.2	153.9	154.0	154.8	153.7	153.6	152.8	151.9	150.8	149.9	153.1
2003	145.3	144.7	144.3	143.6	143.2	142.9	142.2	142.3	142.3	142.4	142.6	143.0	143.2
2004	142.1	142.6	143.0	142.5	142.6	143.0	143.0	142.9	141.9	141.3	141.2	140.9	142.3
2005	138.8	138.8	138.6	137.8	137.3	137.9	138.0	138.2	138.3	137.9	138.3	138.4	138.2
2006	138.3	138.6	139.7	139.1	139.4	140.5	139.5	139.9	139.4	138.8	139.5	138.8	139.3
2007	137.3	137.8	138.0	137.2	137.4	137.9	137.1	137.6	137.7	138.2	139.1	138.9	137.9
2008	137.2	137.6	137.5	136.5	136.3	136.5	136.2	135.6	134.9	132.6	131.3	130.1	135.2
2009	127.2	125.1	123.6	121.3	120.0	119.6	118.6	118.5	118.2	117.9	117.9	117.1	120.4

Employment by Industry: San Francisco-Oakland-Fremont, CA, Selected Years, 1990–2009—*Continued*

(Numbers in thousands, not seasonally adjusted.)

Industry and year	January	February	March	April	May	June	July	August	September	October	November	December	Annual average
Service-Providing													
1990	1535.7	1539.7	1545.8	1551.9	1556.1	1566.1	1564.3	1556.3	1571.2	1583.5	1595.2	1605.4	1564.3
2000	1774.5	1793.4	1812.9	1820.8	1836.0	1850.6	1835.5	1842.6	1851.1	1852.4	1869.2	1882.5	1835.1
2001	1833.7	1843.6	1856.2	1837.5	1836.9	1837.8	1808.2	1803.2	1801.2	1794.4	1793.4	1798.8	1820.4
2002	1751.4	1757.3	1768.6	1761.3	1767.7	1768.3	1745.6	1746.5	1753.1	1759.6	1772.1	1775.8	1760.6
2003	1726.6	1733.9	1736.1	1728.5	1729.8	1731.6	1704.0	1702.8	1707.0	1708.7	1715.2	1724.3	1720.7
2004	1684.1	1693.8	1703.0	1704.3	1710.8	1714.3	1697.1	1690.8	1697.3	1710.6	1722.0	1734.4	1705.2
2005	1694.6	1706.3	1712.2	1718.4	1722.3	1726.8	1711.6	1710.3	1723.0	1729.0	1742.1	1751.5	1720.7
2006	1718.8	1733.0	1741.5	1744.5	1755.7	1762.1	1744.8	1745.8	1756.5	1766.1	1778.4	1784.7	1752.7
2007	1748.6	1764.2	1773.1	1767.3	1781.4	1787.0	1777.1	1777.7	1785.0	1791.6	1805.0	1812.5	1780.9
2008	1769.5	1780.9	1783.9	1787.3	1790.3	1793.1	1781.9	1775.8	1775.8	1780.4	1778.6	1778.0	1781.3
2009	1728.4	1724.7	1718.7	1713.8	1711.3	1706.3	1681.5	1675.9	1672.7	1680.4	1682.6	1685.2	1698.5
Trade, Transportation, and Utilities													
1990	369.7	363.4	362.6	363.5	364.0	367.1	372.1	371.1	371.4	376.3	384.2	390.5	371.3
2000	391.5	389.0	391.1	392.7	395.4	398.5	399.8	399.8	400.2	399.0	408.6	417.4	398.6
2001	403.5	400.2	401.2	398.0	397.4	399.2	396.1	394.3	393.5	388.7	392.3	395.5	396.7
2002	381.6	378.5	379.0	374.7	376.2	378.1	377.4	376.3	377.1	378.5	385.5	390.3	379.4
2003	373.6	369.3	367.9	362.5	363.0	363.8	361.4	360.6	359.8	360.8	367.7	373.6	365.3
2004	355.7	353.1	353.5	354.2	356.5	358.0	356.6	356.1	355.6	360.1	368.0	375.1	358.5
2005	359.0	355.2	354.3	354.4	355.1	357.0	356.4	357.1	357.8	356.8	364.2	371.9	358.3
2006	358.8	355.3	355.6	354.1	356.2	358.6	357.6	358.2	358.5	359.7	367.4	373.8	359.5
2007	363.0	359.6	359.4	356.3	357.9	359.4	359.8	360.5	360.1	361.2	369.9	375.9	361.9
2008	361.5	357.2	356.4	353.0	353.6	353.8	353.0	351.8	348.9	348.2	351.4	353.4	353.5
2009	340.8	334.7	331.1	327.2	327.2	326.3	323.5	324.3	323.1	324.1	328.8	332.7	328.7
Wholesale Trade													
1990	78.4	78.1	78.3	79.7	79.9	80.3	81.0	80.9	81.1	82.1	82.2	82.0	80.3
2000	83.1	83.6	84.7	85.1	85.5	86.0	86.7	86.7	87.0	86.6	86.8	87.8	85.8
2001	87.5	88.4	88.5	87.5	87.1	87.0	86.2	85.8	85.8	85.0	84.9	84.7	86.5
2002	83.0	83.4	83.6	82.0	82.3	82.3	81.9	81.8	81.6	81.2	81.1	81.2	82.1
2003	79.5	79.5	79.5	78.9	78.7	78.4	77.6	77.4	77.0	76.9	76.6	76.8	78.0
2004	74.3	74.4	74.8	75.7	75.7	76.2	76.0	75.8	76.0	76.1	76.4	76.6	75.7
2005	74.6	74.3	74.2	74.9	74.7	75.2	74.7	74.6	74.5	74.4	74.5	74.7	74.6
2006	74.1	74.5	74.9	75.2	75.6	76.0	75.4	75.6	75.8	76.1	76.1	76.6	75.5
2007	75.7	76.1	76.6	75.5	76.0	76.2	75.6	75.6	75.4	75.7	75.5	75.6	75.8
2008	75.1	75.3	75.3	75.1	75.2	74.9	74.5	74.1	73.9	73.6	73.0	72.6	74.4
2009	70.6	70.2	69.4	69.1	68.9	68.6	68.2	67.9	67.1	67.4	67.1	66.4	68.4
Retail Trade													
1990	201.1	194.8	193.9	192.4	193.0	194.9	198.4	198.0	197.7	200.5	208.4	214.6	199.0
2000	210.1	207.2	207.6	208.4	210.4	212.5	212.8	212.7	212.6	213.9	222.4	229.1	213.3
2001	217.5	213.4	213.9	212.5	212.3	214.2	213.6	212.5	212.1	209.7	216.4	220.8	214.1
2002	209.2	205.7	206.5	205.4	206.3	207.6	207.5	206.8	208.0	209.3	216.8	221.4	209.2
2003	208.8	205.1	204.0	201.3	201.9	202.9	202.6	202.6	202.5	203.5	211.3	216.5	205.2
2004	202.5	200.0	199.9	199.8	201.5	202.2	202.2	202.5	201.6	204.0	211.4	218.0	203.8
2005	206.4	202.7	202.0	201.9	202.3	203.4	203.6	204.9	205.2	205.6	212.5	219.2	205.8
2006	208.2	203.8	203.6	202.5	203.5	204.8	205.5	206.1	205.2	206.5	214.0	218.7	206.9
2007	210.0	205.9	205.7	203.5	204.4	205.3	206.7	207.1	206.5	207.2	215.8	220.8	208.2
2008	209.6	204.9	204.2	202.6	202.2	203.1	203.1	202.3	200.0	199.8	203.5	205.4	203.4
2009	197.7	192.3	190.1	187.1	187.0	186.5	185.1	185.9	186.3	187.2	192.5	196.1	189.5
Transportation and Utilities													
1990	90.2	90.5	90.4	91.4	91.1	91.9	92.7	92.2	92.6	93.7	93.6	93.9	92.0
2000	98.3	98.2	98.8	99.2	99.5	100.0	100.3	100.4	100.6	98.5	99.4	100.5	99.5
2001	98.5	98.4	98.8	98.0	98.0	98.0	96.3	96.0	95.6	94.0	91.0	90.0	96.1
2002	89.4	89.4	88.9	87.3	87.6	88.2	88.0	87.7	87.5	88.0	87.6	87.7	88.1
2003	85.3	84.7	84.4	82.3	82.4	82.5	81.2	80.6	80.3	80.4	79.8	80.3	82.0
2004	78.9	78.7	78.8	78.7	79.3	79.6	78.4	77.8	78.0	80.0	80.2	80.5	79.1
2005	78.0	78.2	78.1	77.6	78.1	78.4	78.1	77.6	78.1	76.8	77.2	78.0	77.9
2006	76.5	77.0	77.1	76.4	77.1	77.8	76.7	76.5	77.5	77.1	77.3	78.5	77.1
2007	77.3	77.6	77.1	77.3	77.5	77.9	77.5	77.8	78.2	78.3	78.6	79.5	77.9
2008	76.8	77.0	76.9	75.3	76.2	75.8	75.4	75.4	75.0	74.8	74.9	75.4	75.7
2009	72.5	72.2	71.6	71.0	71.3	71.2	70.2	70.5	69.7	69.5	69.2	70.2	70.8
Information													
1990	58.2	57.9	57.9	57.1	57.4	57.7	58.8	58.0	57.9	58.5	58.4	58.7	58.0
2000	92.6	95.1	97.6	99.1	102.2	105.0	104.4	105.7	106.1	105.7	106.4	106.5	102.2
2001	109.7	108.6	107.9	102.3	99.9	98.3	95.3	93.6	91.3	89.9	88.6	87.7	97.8
2002	88.2	87.4	87.3	85.8	86.7	86.8	85.7	85.6	85.0	83.6	84.1	83.9	85.8
2003	81.7	82.1	80.6	79.5	79.5	79.2	78.4	78.0	77.2	76.4	76.9	76.6	78.8
2004	75.5	75.7	75.7	75.3	75.3	75.3	75.3	74.7	74.0	73.5	73.5	73.5	74.8
2005	73.1	73.5	72.5	71.8	71.7	71.7	71.3	71.3	70.6	70.1	70.2	69.9	71.5
2006	69.4	69.6	69.3	68.7	68.8	68.9	68.7	69.1	68.7	68.9	69.3	69.5	69.1
2007	68.2	68.4	68.4	68.3	68.7	68.7	69.0	69.0	68.5	68.2	68.1	68.1	68.5
2008	67.9	68.3	68.0	68.5	68.7	68.7	69.7	69.5	68.8	68.6	68.4	68.2	68.6
2009	67.5	66.6	66.3	64.9	64.7	64.7	64.9	64.5	63.8	63.7	63.8	63.8	64.9

Employment by Industry: San Francisco-Oakland-Fremont, CA, Selected Years, 1990–2009—*Continued*

(Numbers in thousands, not seasonally adjusted.)

Industry and year	January	February	March	April	May	June	July	August	September	October	November	December	Annual average
Financial Activities													
1990	156.2	155.8	156.6	156.1	156.4	156.9	159.8	158.2	157.7	157.9	157.1	157.2	157.2
2000	145.7	146.5	146.9	146.5	147.2	148.9	148.2	147.4	147.9	149.0	148.9	150.5	147.8
2001	158.7	159.9	161.9	161.5	161.0	161.9	160.9	160.4	159.9	159.8	159.9	160.1	160.5
2002	156.4	156.5	156.8	157.0	157.1	158.0	157.8	158.8	157.9	158.5	159.0	159.9	157.8
2003	158.3	159.1	159.7	158.9	159.2	159.2	157.4	157.2	156.6	155.4	155.0	155.5	157.6
2004	154.7	154.7	154.8	154.0	154.5	155.2	155.2	155.3	154.6	155.3	155.5	156.3	155.0
2005	155.9	156.3	156.7	156.7	157.4	158.4	158.0	157.9	157.6	157.0	157.1	157.7	157.2
2006	156.4	157.0	157.3	157.3	157.9	157.8	156.3	156.3	156.0	155.3	154.6	154.2	156.4
2007	152.4	153.0	153.2	152.1	152.5	152.4	151.8	151.6	150.4	148.7	148.8	148.1	151.3
2008	145.9	145.8	145.6	144.9	144.8	145.1	144.2	144.0	142.7	142.4	141.3	141.2	144.0
2009	136.7	136.2	135.3	133.9	133.3	133.2	132.0	131.5	130.1	130.2	129.9	130.1	132.7
Professional and Business Services													
1990	266.9	269.8	271.0	271.0	272.1	276.4	277.9	278.4	279.1	280.9	280.5	284.4	275.7
2000	390.7	397.0	403.5	406.9	406.6	413.1	415.2	420.1	422.1	421.7	423.2	425.1	412.1
2001	394.7	396.2	397.0	386.2	383.7	383.7	375.6	372.7	367.2	362.2	359.2	360.6	378.3
2002	343.5	343.8	345.3	341.5	339.7	339.8	335.9	336.0	333.2	331.1	333.2	333.2	338.0
2003	321.8	323.1	324.0	322.3	320.2	321.4	319.9	321.0	319.5	319.1	320.0	322.6	321.2
2004	317.3	319.6	322.1	322.4	322.5	324.9	323.3	324.2	323.1	326.0	328.0	330.9	323.7
2005	325.6	328.9	331.0	331.2	330.2	332.6	333.3	335.2	335.4	336.7	339.6	342.7	333.5
2006	335.8	339.8	342.4	343.0	344.4	348.3	347.8	349.8	349.9	351.1	352.6	355.0	346.7
2007	349.1	352.7	354.8	353.4	355.9	359.4	362.5	364.6	363.6	374.3	375.5	376.5	361.9
2008	370.1	372.3	373.1	372.8	371.6	373.6	374.7	375.2	373.1	373.1	369.7	368.0	372.3
2009	357.4	354.6	351.8	348.4	345.3	346.1	343.5	342.6	339.6	341.1	340.3	341.1	346.0
Education and Health Services													
1990	168.3	170.6	171.3	173.9	172.5	172.9	172.7	173.8	174.7	176.5	178.7	178.6	173.7
2000	205.3	209.8	210.8	205.2	205.3	204.0	202.8	202.1	204.7	205.5	207.6	208.9	206.0
2001	201.5	205.8	207.7	207.3	208.7	207.8	207.2	207.8	209.9	211.5	213.0	213.9	208.5
2002	209.9	213.5	215.2	211.0	211.6	208.7	209.4	209.3	211.3	213.5	215.4	215.0	212.0
2003	211.3	215.8	216.4	218.6	218.6	216.5	214.2	213.6	215.5	216.1	217.4	218.0	216.0
2004	214.0	218.4	219.4	219.6	219.2	217.3	214.0	213.3	215.5	217.7	218.9	219.5	217.2
2005	213.6	219.5	220.4	220.5	220.9	218.2	216.5	216.1	219.0	221.3	222.4	223.0	219.3
2006	218.1	223.2	224.5	226.5	227.2	225.3	222.1	221.9	225.3	227.5	228.7	229.5	225.0
2007	222.7	229.3	231.4	229.5	230.5	229.7	226.4	225.2	228.5	232.1	233.6	234.0	229.4
2008	228.5	234.6	235.2	237.7	238.1	233.6	232.5	232.0	236.2	240.1	241.4	242.9	236.1
2009	237.0	241.1	242.1	242.0	241.6	236.1	232.9	230.8	233.8	236.7	237.1	237.8	237.4
Leisure and Hospitality													
1990	152.0	153.1	154.6	156.2	156.8	158.6	159.7	160.7	160.8	160.7	160.5	160.8	157.9
2000	179.0	181.9	184.8	185.5	188.3	191.6	193.2	194.3	195.2	190.3	189.3	189.6	188.6
2001	187.4	190.2	193.3	193.5	197.4	199.2	197.5	198.7	195.8	191.5	188.9	189.4	193.6
2002	182.8	184.4	187.2	192.1	196.4	198.8	197.3	199.6	197.5	196.0	194.9	195.0	193.5
2003	187.0	187.9	189.4	190.5	193.3	196.9	195.2	197.9	196.6	195.0	192.4	193.2	192.9
2004	186.2	188.2	190.6	192.1	195.8	197.4	198.9	199.6	199.7	196.3	194.6	196.5	194.7
2005	189.3	190.6	193.1	197.7	200.1	202.6	201.8	203.6	204.0	202.7	202.2	202.0	199.1
2006	195.1	198.6	200.0	202.6	207.1	210.0	209.0	209.9	209.5	208.5	207.9	208.0	205.5
2007	202.0	204.4	206.6	208.5	213.2	215.7	217.8	218.1	216.9	214.8	214.2	215.3	212.3
2008	207.1	210.3	211.5	215.1	218.4	221.1	220.9	220.9	219.4	216.7	214.3	214.2	215.8
2009	203.2	203.5	202.8	205.9	209.8	210.4	210.8	210.7	208.3	207.2	205.9	206.1	207.1
Other Services													
1990	61.5	61.8	62.4	62.9	62.9	63.7	64.3	64.2	64.1	64.5	64.5	64.4	63.4
2000	69.7	70.7	71.4	71.9	72.3	73.0	73.3	72.9	72.3	72.6	72.9	73.3	72.2
2001	73.8	75.0	76.2	75.4	76.3	77.3	76.7	76.7	76.4	76.5	76.3	76.6	76.1
2002	75.3	76.2	76.6	76.7	77.1	77.6	77.7	77.3	77.3	76.5	76.7	76.8	76.8
2003	75.0	76.1	76.2	75.9	76.1	76.5	75.1	75.1	75.1	74.4	74.0	74.3	75.3
2004	72.3	73.0	73.9	74.1	74.4	74.4	74.3	73.5	73.7	72.9	72.4	73.0	73.5
2005	71.0	71.6	72.5	73.1	73.2	73.9	72.9	72.1	72.1	72.5	72.1	72.6	72.5
2006	70.9	71.8	72.4	72.9	74.0	74.7	74.1	73.7	73.7	73.4	73.2	73.6	73.2
2007	72.2	73.4	74.1	74.1	75.0	75.2	75.7	75.5	75.3	75.5	75.5	75.9	74.8
2008	73.6	74.7	75.1	75.7	76.2	76.4	76.5	75.7	75.3	75.9	75.2	75.1	75.5
2009	72.8	72.6	72.5	73.3	73.3	73.1	72.3	71.8	70.7	69.9	69.7	69.7	71.8
Government													
1990	302.9	307.3	309.4	311.2	314.0	312.8	299.0	291.9	305.5	308.2	311.3	310.8	307.0
2000	300.0	303.4	306.8	313.0	318.7	316.5	298.6	300.3	302.6	308.6	312.3	311.2	307.7
2001	304.4	307.7	311.0	313.3	312.5	310.4	298.9	299.0	307.2	314.3	315.2	315.0	309.1
2002	313.7	317.0	321.2	322.5	322.9	320.5	304.4	303.6	313.8	321.9	323.3	321.7	317.2
2003	317.9	320.5	321.9	320.3	319.9	318.1	302.4	299.4	306.7	311.5	311.8	310.5	313.4
2004	308.4	311.1	313.0	312.6	312.6	311.8	299.5	294.1	301.1	308.8	311.1	309.6	307.8
2005	307.1	310.7	311.7	313.0	313.7	312.4	301.4	297.0	306.5	311.9	314.3	311.7	309.3
2006	314.3	317.7	320.0	319.4	320.1	318.5	309.2	306.9	314.9	321.7	324.7	321.1	317.4
2007	319.0	323.4	325.2	325.1	327.7	326.5	314.1	313.2	321.7	316.8	319.4	318.7	320.9
2008	314.9	317.7	319.0	319.6	318.9	320.8	310.4	306.7	311.4	315.4	316.9	315.0	315.6
2009	313.0	315.4	316.8	318.2	316.1	316.4	301.6	299.7	303.3	307.5	307.1	303.9	309.9

Employment by Industry: San Jose-Sunnyvale-Santa Clara, CA, Selected Years, 1990–2009

(Numbers in thousands, not seasonally adjusted.)

Industry and year	January	February	March	April	May	June	July	August	September	October	November	December	Annual average
Total Nonfarm													
1990	812.4	816.7	819.3	821.4	824.9	827.5	829.6	831.7	825.6	828.2	826.8	826.4	824.2
2000	999.6	1008.5	1023.2	1023.4	1036.7	1051.9	1056.7	1058.4	1060.9	1061.9	1070.3	1080.3	1044.3
2001	1054.7	1057.9	1062.7	1044.8	1040.3	1037.1	1014.5	1003.4	987.1	976.6	969.0	967.0	1017.9
2002	933.1	933.7	938.9	929.2	927.8	926.2	915.2	908.9	901.1	900.6	897.2	894.1	917.2
2003	874.0	872.8	874.0	875.6	875.8	877.0	866.7	864.1	862.8	865.2	866.1	869.0	870.3
2004	849.5	854.1	859.3	859.0	864.0	868.6	861.1	860.7	859.4	866.8	869.3	872.1	862.0
2005	855.9	859.4	862.9	863.4	867.1	872.8	870.1	871.6	871.1	877.4	880.6	887.0	869.9
2006	872.2	880.0	883.4	883.6	890.8	896.3	893.3	895.2	895.2	896.9	900.5	906.4	891.2
2007	892.3	898.6	904.6	901.7	909.1	916.9	916.1	914.6	913.6	919.5	923.1	924.5	911.2
2008	911.0	914.2	917.8	915.4	918.6	921.4	915.5	919.5	918.0	913.4	909.1	905.1	914.9
2009	878.8	871.0	866.2	859.6	859.1	858.4	847.4	846.5	842.1	847.6	844.8	846.1	855.6
Total Private													
1990	720.4	724.8	726.6	728.7	730.4	733.1	738.4	739.9	733.8	735.1	733.1	733.5	731.5
2000	901.5	910.7	923.3	923.8	936.0	948.2	957.3	964.2	967.1	963.0	971.0	981.3	945.6
2001	957.3	959.9	963.8	945.6	939.7	937.4	917.5	908.8	890.4	876.2	867.3	865.5	919.1
2002	831.9	831.5	835.5	824.6	823.1	821.8	813.9	810.3	801.4	797.4	793.6	791.0	814.7
2003	771.8	771.8	772.3	773.8	774.4	776.2	769.8	769.5	767.5	766.6	767.6	772.0	771.1
2004	753.6	757.3	761.4	761.1	765.9	771.0	766.3	767.8	765.9	770.6	771.9	776.1	765.7
2005	760.4	763.2	766.0	766.4	769.7	775.8	775.8	777.9	777.3	781.2	784.0	790.8	774.0
2006	776.5	783.5	786.7	786.3	793.0	798.9	798.2	801.5	800.9	799.2	802.9	808.9	794.7
2007	794.6	801.6	806.3	803.6	810.8	819.1	821.0	820.7	818.7	821.2	824.5	826.2	814.0
2008	812.0	816.0	818.7	817.0	819.6	822.8	821.5	825.0	820.0	814.7	810.8	807.3	817.1
2009	781.4	774.1	768.6	761.0	760.5	760.2	751.6	751.0	745.0	746.6	744.6	746.7	757.6
Goods-Producing													
1990	282.1	281.4	280.0	284.3	283.3	284.0	288.5	289.2	286.4	285.1	281.9	279.4	283.8
2000	283.8	286.1	290.3	291.7	295.1	300.8	305.7	309.0	312.0	311.7	313.5	315.8	301.3
2001	307.9	307.9	306.7	301.8	298.4	296.6	289.7	286.4	279.9	273.8	267.7	265.6	290.2
2002	256.9	253.3	254.2	249.8	249.4	249.2	247.3	245.5	241.3	237.4	232.5	228.9	245.5
2003	223.9	221.6	221.0	219.2	217.5	217.9	217.2	216.7	215.6	213.1	211.7	211.6	217.3
2004	206.8	207.6	208.5	208.8	209.9	212.0	212.8	213.5	212.6	211.6	210.2	209.7	210.3
2005	206.3	206.0	206.0	208.3	208.4	210.7	212.4	212.8	212.0	211.7	210.2	210.7	209.6
2006	208.5	209.3	209.1	208.2	210.6	211.6	213.5	214.3	213.4	211.7	209.6	209.8	210.8
2007	208.1	209.8	210.6	210.6	212.4	216.2	218.8	219.4	218.6	217.1	215.2	213.9	214.2
2008	211.8	212.1	211.8	211.6	213.4	214.6	216.1	216.5	214.6	211.8	208.3	206.4	212.4
2009	200.4	196.7	194.5	192.1	190.6	189.8	188.8	188.3	186.8	185.0	182.8	182.3	189.8
Mining and Logging													
1990	0.3	0.3	0.3	0.4	0.3	0.3	0.4	0.3	0.3	0.4	0.4	0.4	0.3
2000	0.4	0.4	0.3	0.3	0.3	0.3	0.4	0.4	0.4	0.4	0.4	0.5	0.4
2001	0.2	0.2	0.2	0.2	0.2	0.2	0.2	0.2	0.2	0.2	0.2	0.2	0.2
2002	0.3	0.3	0.3	0.2	0.2	0.2	0.2	0.2	0.2	0.2	0.2	0.2	0.2
2003	0.2	0.2	0.2	0.2	0.2	0.2	0.2	0.2	0.2	0.2	0.2	0.1	0.1
2004	0.1	0.1	0.1	0.1	0.1	0.2	0.1	0.2	0.2	0.2	0.1	0.1	0.1
2005	0.1	0.1	0.1	0.2	0.2	0.2	0.2	0.2	0.2	0.3	0.3	0.2	0.2
2006	0.3	0.3	0.2	0.2	0.2	0.3	0.3	0.3	0.3	0.3	0.3	0.3	0.3
2007	0.3	0.3	0.3	0.3	0.3	0.3	0.3	0.3	0.3	0.3	0.3	0.3	0.3
2008	0.3	0.3	0.3	0.3	0.3	0.3	0.3	0.3	0.3	0.3	0.3	0.3	0.3
2009	0.3	0.2	0.2	0.2	0.2	0.2	0.2	0.2	0.2	0.3	0.3	0.3	0.2
Construction													
1990	28.2	27.6	27.9	29.2	29.2	29.7	30.4	30.5	30.2	30.1	29.6	29.0	29.3
2000	45.4	45.4	46.7	47.3	48.3	49.7	50.7	51.5	52.5	52.0	52.2	52.0	49.5
2001	51.1	50.9	51.5	51.1	51.0	51.2	50.4	50.7	49.3	48.3	47.4	46.4	49.9
2002	43.7	43.3	44.1	43.6	44.4	45.3	45.6	46.7	45.6	44.5	43.8	42.2	44.4
2003	40.0	39.9	40.2	40.1	40.4	41.2	41.9	43.3	43.5	43.2	42.7	42.3	41.6
2004	40.3	40.8	41.2	41.7	42.4	43.7	44.2	44.6	44.5	44.8	44.2	43.9	43.0
2005	41.6	41.7	42.3	43.0	43.6	45.0	45.7	46.4	46.7	46.3	46.0	45.9	44.5
2006	44.9	45.4	45.1	44.3	46.2	47.4	47.9	48.7	48.9	48.2	47.6	46.9	46.8
2007	45.0	45.5	46.3	46.0	47.0	47.9	48.6	49.2	49.2	48.3	47.3	46.6	47.2
2008	44.3	44.6	44.2	44.0	44.6	45.1	45.5	45.9	45.1	43.7	41.9	40.9	44.2
2009	37.8	36.2	35.9	34.8	34.3	34.1	33.5	33.5	33.1	32.0	31.0	30.4	33.9
Manufacturing													
1990	253.6	253.5	251.8	254.7	253.8	254.0	257.7	258.4	255.9	254.6	251.9	250.0	254.2
2000	238.0	240.3	243.3	244.1	246.5	250.8	254.6	257.1	259.1	259.3	260.9	263.3	251.4
2001	256.6	256.8	255.0	250.5	247.2	245.2	239.1	235.5	230.4	225.3	220.1	219.0	240.1
2002	212.9	209.7	209.8	206.0	204.8	203.7	201.5	198.6	195.5	192.7	188.5	186.5	200.9
2003	183.7	181.5	180.6	178.9	176.9	176.5	175.1	173.2	171.9	169.7	168.8	169.2	175.5
2004	166.4	166.7	167.2	167.0	167.4	168.1	168.5	168.7	167.9	166.6	165.9	165.7	167.2
2005	164.6	164.2	163.6	165.1	164.6	165.5	166.5	166.2	165.1	165.1	163.9	164.6	164.9
2006	163.3	163.6	163.8	163.7	164.2	163.9	165.3	165.3	164.2	163.2	161.7	162.6	163.7
2007	162.8	164.0	164.0	164.3	165.1	168.0	169.9	169.9	169.1	168.5	167.6	167.0	166.7
2008	167.2	167.2	167.3	167.3	168.5	169.2	170.3	170.3	169.2	167.8	166.1	165.2	168.0
2009	162.3	160.3	158.4	157.1	156.1	155.5	155.1	154.6	153.4	152.7	151.5	151.6	155.7

Employment by Industry: San Jose-Sunnyvale-Santa Clara, CA, Selected Years, 1990–2009—*Continued*

(Numbers in thousands, not seasonally adjusted.)

Industry and year	January	February	March	April	May	June	July	August	September	October	November	December	Annual average
Service-Providing													
1990	530.3	535.3	539.3	537.1	541.6	543.5	541.1	542.5	539.2	543.1	544.9	547.0	540.4
2000	715.8	722.4	732.9	731.7	741.6	751.1	751.0	749.4	748.9	750.2	756.8	764.5	743.0
2001	746.8	750.0	756.0	743.0	741.9	740.5	724.8	717.0	707.2	702.8	701.3	701.4	727.7
2002	676.2	680.4	684.7	679.4	678.4	677.0	667.9	663.4	659.8	663.2	664.7	665.2	671.7
2003	650.1	651.2	653.0	656.4	658.3	659.1	649.5	647.4	647.2	652.1	654.4	657.4	653.0
2004	642.7	646.5	650.8	650.2	654.1	656.6	648.3	647.2	646.8	655.2	659.1	662.4	651.7
2005	649.6	653.4	656.9	655.1	658.7	662.1	657.7	658.8	659.1	665.7	670.4	676.3	660.3
2006	663.7	670.7	674.3	675.4	680.2	684.7	679.8	680.9	681.8	685.2	690.9	696.6	680.4
2007	684.2	688.8	694.0	691.1	696.7	700.7	697.3	695.2	695.0	702.4	707.9	710.6	697.0
2008	699.2	702.1	706.0	703.8	705.2	706.8	699.4	703.0	703.4	701.6	700.8	698.7	702.5
2009	678.4	674.3	671.7	667.5	668.5	668.6	658.6	658.2	655.3	662.6	662.0	663.8	665.8
Trade, Transportation, and Utilities													
1990	129.1	128.2	127.6	127.2	127.3	127.9	128.7	128.5	127.9	128.8	131.0	133.6	128.8
2000	152.3	151.3	152.1	151.7	152.5	153.3	154.2	154.7	154.6	153.5	156.8	159.8	153.9
2001	153.5	151.5	152.5	149.8	149.4	149.7	148.4	146.8	145.6	143.9	146.2	147.7	148.8
2002	139.8	138.3	138.8	137.0	137.0	136.8	136.4	136.0	135.8	135.5	137.6	139.5	137.4
2003	133.1	131.2	130.9	131.0	131.0	131.3	130.8	131.1	130.8	131.7	134.3	136.6	132.0
2004	130.7	129.6	129.2	128.8	129.8	130.1	129.8	130.1	129.9	131.4	134.2	136.6	130.9
2005	131.3	130.2	130.3	130.2	130.7	131.2	132.1	132.8	133.5	134.2	137.1	140.0	132.8
2006	135.3	133.8	133.8	133.7	134.4	135.2	136.4	137.6	138.1	138.6	142.6	145.1	137.1
2007	139.3	137.6	137.8	137.2	137.8	138.8	140.0	139.9	139.6	140.0	143.3	145.3	139.7
2008	140.2	138.7	138.9	137.1	137.2	136.9	137.3	137.5	136.3	136.0	137.4	138.1	137.6
2009	130.7	128.5	126.9	125.3	125.9	125.5	124.7	124.9	124.8	125.1	126.4	128.2	126.4
Wholesale Trade													
1990	38.3	38.3	38.5	38.4	38.1	38.0	37.9	37.3	36.9	37.2	36.8	36.2	37.7
2000	42.9	43.1	43.2	43.0	43.1	43.0	42.9	42.8	42.5	42.4	42.1	41.9	42.7
2001	42.7	42.8	43.1	41.8	41.4	41.2	41.3	41.1	40.4	39.8	39.3	39.2	41.2
2002	38.6	38.1	38.2	37.2	37.0	36.5	35.9	35.5	34.9	34.6	34.0	33.6	36.2
2003	33.6	33.6	33.8	34.1	34.2	34.2	34.3	34.5	34.3	34.3	34.2	34.3	34.1
2004	34.0	33.9	33.9	34.3	34.4	34.6	34.5	34.6	34.5	34.9	34.9	34.9	34.5
2005	34.8	35.1	35.1	35.2	35.5	35.8	36.1	36.3	36.5	36.5	36.4	36.7	35.8
2006	37.0	37.3	37.4	37.8	37.9	38.2	38.7	38.8	39.0	39.0	39.1	39.3	38.3
2007	38.9	39.3	39.3	39.0	39.2	39.8	40.0	40.0	40.1	40.4	40.5	40.8	39.8
2008	40.5	40.4	40.9	40.2	40.3	40.1	39.6	39.4	39.3	39.2	38.8	38.4	39.8
2009	37.1	36.7	36.3	36.2	36.0	35.7	35.1	35.1	34.7	34.7	34.6	34.6	35.6
Retail Trade													
1990	77.0	76.1	75.2	74.8	75.1	75.7	76.5	76.9	76.7	77.0	79.7	82.9	77.0
2000	92.2	91.0	91.6	90.8	91.7	92.4	93.4	93.8	94.1	93.1	96.6	99.6	93.4
2001	93.4	91.3	91.9	90.8	90.8	91.3	90.3	89.1	88.9	88.5	91.7	93.4	91.0
2002	86.5	85.4	85.8	84.8	84.6	84.9	85.1	85.2	85.6	85.5	88.3	90.6	86.0
2003	84.9	83.2	82.8	82.3	82.4	82.6	82.3	82.4	82.5	83.3	86.1	88.4	83.6
2004	82.9	81.9	81.5	81.1	81.9	81.9	82.0	82.3	82.0	83.0	85.8	88.2	82.9
2005	83.4	82.0	82.1	81.9	82.1	82.3	82.9	83.5	83.9	84.8	87.8	90.3	83.9
2006	85.8	83.9	83.8	83.4	83.7	84.0	84.8	85.6	85.8	86.5	90.1	92.3	85.8
2007	87.5	85.3	85.4	84.8	85.1	85.2	86.2	86.1	85.6	85.9	89.1	90.6	86.4
2008	86.5	84.9	84.6	83.6	83.3	83.1	84.3	84.6	83.5	83.4	85.2	86.0	84.4
2009	80.9	79.3	78.5	77.3	77.9	78.0	77.9	78.1	78.4	78.7	80.1	81.3	78.9
Transportation and Utilities													
1990	13.8	13.8	13.9	14.0	14.1	14.2	14.3	14.3	14.3	14.6	14.5	14.5	14.2
2000	17.2	17.2	17.3	17.9	17.7	17.9	17.9	18.1	18.0	18.0	18.1	18.3	17.8
2001	17.4	17.4	17.5	17.2	17.2	17.2	16.8	16.6	16.3	15.6	15.2	15.1	16.6
2002	14.7	14.8	14.8	15.0	15.4	15.4	15.4	15.3	15.3	15.4	15.3	15.3	15.2
2003	14.6	14.4	14.3	14.6	14.4	14.5	14.2	14.2	14.0	14.1	14.0	13.9	14.3
2004	13.8	13.8	13.8	13.4	13.5	13.6	13.3	13.2	13.4	13.5	13.5	13.5	13.5
2005	13.1	13.1	13.1	13.1	13.1	13.1	13.1	13.0	13.1	12.9	12.9	13.0	13.1
2006	12.5	12.6	12.6	12.5	12.8	13.0	12.9	13.2	13.3	13.1	13.4	13.5	13.0
2007	12.9	13.0	13.1	13.4	13.5	13.8	13.8	13.8	13.9	13.7	13.7	13.9	13.5
2008	13.2	13.4	13.4	13.3	13.6	13.7	13.4	13.5	13.5	13.4	13.4	13.7	13.5
2009	12.7	12.5	12.1	11.8	12.0	11.8	11.7	11.7	11.7	11.7	11.7	12.3	12.0
Information													
1990	20.6	20.7	20.9	21.0	21.0	21.1	21.4	21.4	21.0	21.3	21.3	21.4	21.1
2000	36.9	37.7	39.2	40.1	41.5	43.1	44.2	45.0	45.6	46.1	46.6	47.1	42.8
2001	46.5	46.2	46.1	43.8	43.4	42.8	41.4	40.7	39.6	38.3	37.6	37.3	42.0
2002	37.0	36.9	36.7	35.7	34.9	34.2	33.5	33.2	32.8	32.4	32.6	32.2	34.3
2003	31.8	32.0	31.6	31.1	31.1	31.2	31.2	31.1	31.0	31.3	31.5	31.7	31.4
2004	31.7	32.0	32.2	32.1	32.2	32.5	32.6	32.6	32.8	33.2	33.7	34.0	32.6
2005	33.8	34.1	34.4	34.0	34.4	35.0	35.5	35.8	35.7	36.2	36.9	37.3	35.3
2006	37.1	37.3	37.4	37.3	37.5	37.6	37.9	37.9	37.5	37.1	37.3	37.6	37.5
2007	37.8	38.2	38.5	38.1	38.9	39.7	40.3	40.5	40.3	40.5	41.1	41.4	39.6
2008	41.3	41.2	41.0	41.5	42.0	42.4	43.6	43.4	42.8	42.5	42.8	42.5	42.3
2009	42.5	41.5	41.1	40.6	40.7	41.0	41.7	41.5	40.6	40.6	40.7	40.7	41.1

Employment by Industry: San Jose-Sunnyvale-Santa Clara, CA, Selected Years, 1990–2009—*Continued*

(Numbers in thousands, not seasonally adjusted.)

Industry and year	January	February	March	April	May	June	July	August	September	October	November	December	Annual average
Financial Activities													
1990	32.8	33.2	33.1	33.0	33.5	33.7	33.5	33.4	33.2	33.0	32.6	33.0	33.2
2000	33.7	34.1	34.3	34.2	34.2	34.6	34.7	34.6	34.5	34.5	34.7	34.9	34.4
2001	34.5	34.8	35.2	35.4	35.6	36.0	35.9	36.3	36.1	35.8	36.0	36.3	35.7
2002	35.6	35.8	35.8	35.3	35.7	35.6	35.6	35.8	35.4	35.4	35.3	35.3	35.6
2003	34.9	34.9	35.1	35.1	35.2	35.1	35.3	35.4	35.2	35.0	34.9	35.1	35.1
2004	34.7	34.8	35.0	35.1	35.4	35.4	35.5	35.5	35.5	36.0	35.9	36.1	35.4
2005	35.9	35.8	36.0	35.9	36.0	36.2	36.3	36.6	36.4	36.7	36.7	37.0	36.3
2006	36.7	36.8	37.0	37.1	37.5	37.2	37.3	37.2	37.1	37.1	37.1	37.1	37.1
2007	37.3	37.4	37.4	37.3	37.5	37.3	37.4	37.2	37.1	36.9	36.5	36.6	37.2
2008	35.6	35.8	35.4	35.2	35.1	34.8	34.6	34.3	34.1	33.7	33.0	33.1	34.6
2009	32.5	32.2	32.1	32.0	32.0	31.8	31.7	31.5	31.1	31.1	31.0	31.0	31.7
Professional and Business Services													
1990	108.6	110.7	112.3	109.8	110.7	111.8	112.6	113.0	112.6	112.0	112.1	112.0	111.5
2000	213.5	217.7	221.2	219.7	224.6	230.1	231.1	234.4	234.4	231.9	234.3	237.4	227.5
2001	229.7	230.8	231.7	223.8	219.6	218.0	210.3	206.1	199.9	195.1	191.1	189.0	212.1
2002	180.6	180.7	180.8	177.6	175.7	175.5	174.1	173.0	171.2	171.0	170.1	169.8	175.0
2003	166.4	166.7	166.9	168.1	168.6	169.3	166.1	167.8	168.4	166.9	167.0	168.4	167.6
2004	164.7	165.8	166.0	165.3	165.1	166.6	163.8	165.0	164.9	166.2	166.4	167.5	165.6
2005	164.3	166.0	166.8	164.9	165.1	166.0	164.4	165.2	165.7	166.2	166.5	168.4	165.8
2006	166.2	168.6	169.3	169.5	169.8	171.6	172.6	173.9	174.8	174.3	175.1	177.8	172.0
2007	176.2	177.7	177.8	177.2	177.6	178.2	178.7	178.3	178.2	178.9	179.8	180.5	178.3
2008	177.4	178.5	179.7	179.8	178.9	180.2	180.1	180.6	179.9	178.2	177.2	176.0	178.9
2009	168.5	166.7	165.2	161.9	160.6	161.1	159.9	159.9	159.1	159.5	159.5	160.5	161.9
Education and Health Services													
1990	70.4	72.6	72.8	72.6	73.1	72.3	70.3	70.6	69.7	72.6	73.0	73.1	71.9
2000	87.0	87.5	87.6	86.5	87.2	84.4	84.0	83.0	83.3	86.1	86.8	87.4	85.9
2001	87.7	89.2	90.4	89.8	90.8	90.7	88.5	89.5	89.4	92.2	93.0	93.8	90.4
2002	89.4	92.1	93.1	93.1	93.1	92.6	89.5	89.7	89.4	91.9	93.0	93.0	91.7
2003	91.4	93.4	94.0	94.8	95.2	94.5	92.8	91.4	91.2	93.8	94.7	95.1	93.5
2004	93.8	94.7	95.7	95.0	95.9	95.9	93.4	93.2	93.2	95.9	96.8	96.9	95.0
2005	95.9	96.7	96.7	96.2	96.4	96.5	95.2	95.2	95.1	98.4	99.7	100.0	96.8
2006	98.2	100.8	101.6	101.0	101.7	102.0	98.8	98.3	98.4	100.5	101.7	101.5	100.4
2007	99.4	102.3	103.5	101.7	103.4	104.1	102.1	101.6	101.8	105.4	106.7	106.4	103.2
2008	106.7	108.9	109.1	108.4	107.8	107.4	104.0	107.4	107.3	108.7	109.9	109.7	107.9
2009	108.5	109.9	109.7	109.3	109.9	109.3	105.3	105.5	104.5	108.4	108.6	108.6	108.1
Leisure and Hospitality													
1990	54.6	55.6	57.1	58.2	58.8	59.4	60.1	60.4	59.6	59.3	58.6	58.6	58.4
2000	68.2	69.8	71.7	72.7	73.7	74.3	75.7	75.8	75.5	72.7	71.8	71.8	72.8
2001	71.0	72.9	74.6	74.8	75.9	76.6	76.4	76.0	73.2	70.5	69.0	69.1	73.3
2002	66.3	67.7	69.2	69.4	70.6	71.2	70.8	70.5	69.3	68.1	66.5	66.5	68.8
2003	65.5	66.9	67.7	68.8	70.1	71.1	70.9	70.9	70.2	69.5	68.1	68.2	69.0
2004	66.9	68.0	69.9	70.8	72.2	73.1	73.2	72.9	72.0	71.3	69.7	70.2	70.9
2005	68.4	69.5	70.9	72.1	73.7	74.8	75.2	75.3	74.5	73.5	72.7	73.1	72.8
2006	70.5	72.4	73.8	74.7	76.2	77.9	76.9	77.4	76.6	75.4	74.9	75.3	75.2
2007	72.6	74.0	75.9	76.7	78.0	79.2	78.6	78.7	77.7	76.9	76.5	76.7	76.8
2008	74.3	75.6	77.3	77.9	79.3	80.6	80.5	80.2	79.5	78.3	76.9	76.3	78.1
2009	73.8	74.0	74.4	75.0	75.9	76.9	75.4	75.5	74.0	72.9	71.7	71.9	74.3
Other Services													
1990	22.2	22.4	22.8	22.6	22.7	22.9	23.3	23.4	23.4	23.0	22.6	22.4	22.8
2000	26.1	26.5	26.9	27.2	27.2	27.6	27.7	27.7	27.2	26.5	26.5	27.1	27.0
2001	26.5	26.6	26.6	26.4	26.6	27.0	26.9	27.0	26.7	26.6	26.7	26.7	26.7
2002	26.3	26.7	26.9	26.7	26.7	26.7	26.7	26.6	26.2	25.7	26.0	25.8	26.4
2003	24.8	25.1	25.1	25.7	25.7	25.8	25.5	25.1	25.1	25.3	25.4	25.3	25.3
2004	24.3	24.8	24.9	25.2	25.4	25.4	25.2	25.0	25.0	25.0	25.0	25.1	25.0
2005	24.5	24.9	24.9	24.8	25.0	25.4	24.7	24.2	24.4	24.3	24.2	24.3	24.6
2006	24.0	24.5	24.7	24.8	25.3	25.8	24.8	24.9	25.0	24.5	24.6	24.7	24.8
2007	23.9	24.6	24.8	24.8	25.2	25.6	25.1	25.1	25.4	25.5	25.4	25.4	25.1
2008	24.7	25.2	25.5	25.5	25.9	25.9	25.3	25.1	25.5	25.5	25.3	25.2	25.4
2009	24.5	24.6	24.7	24.8	24.9	24.8	24.1	23.9	24.1	24.0	23.9	23.5	24.3
Government													
1990	92.0	91.9	92.7	92.7	94.5	94.4	91.2	91.8	91.8	93.1	93.7	92.9	92.7
2000	98.1	97.8	99.9	99.6	100.7	103.7	99.4	94.2	93.8	98.9	99.3	99.0	98.7
2001	97.4	98.0	98.9	99.2	100.6	99.7	97.0	94.6	96.7	100.4	101.7	101.5	98.8
2002	101.2	102.2	103.4	104.6	104.7	104.4	101.3	98.6	99.7	103.2	103.6	103.1	102.5
2003	102.2	101.0	101.7	101.8	101.4	100.8	96.9	94.6	95.3	98.6	98.5	97.0	99.2
2004	95.9	96.8	97.9	97.9	98.1	97.6	94.8	92.9	93.5	96.2	97.4	96.0	96.3
2005	95.5	96.2	96.9	97.0	97.4	97.0	94.3	93.7	93.8	96.2	96.6	96.2	95.9
2006	95.7	96.5	96.7	97.3	97.8	97.4	95.1	93.7	94.3	97.7	97.6	97.5	96.4
2007	97.7	97.0	98.3	98.1	98.3	97.8	95.1	93.9	94.9	98.3	98.6	98.3	97.2
2008	99.0	98.2	99.1	98.4	99.0	98.6	94.0	94.5	98.0	98.7	98.3	97.8	97.8
2009	97.4	96.9	97.6	98.6	98.6	98.2	95.8	95.5	97.1	101.0	100.2	99.4	98.0

Employment by Industry: Seattle-Tacoma-Bellevue, WA, Selected Years, 1990–2009

(Numbers in thousands, not seasonally adjusted.)

Industry and year	January	February	March	April	May	June	July	August	September	October	November	December	Annual average
Total Nonfarm													
1990	1262.0	1268.5	1279.1	1285.9	1300.7	1315.6	1308.6	1317.6	1325.4	1314.2	1324.2	1319.5	1301.8
2000	1609.8	1607.4	1636.8	1630.7	1646.3	1660.8	1643.4	1650.9	1663.0	1661.7	1671.0	1678.3	1646.7
2001	1629.0	1631.1	1636.9	1632.4	1640.2	1646.3	1629.6	1625.5	1629.2	1615.9	1615.8	1610.2	1628.5
2002	1568.6	1569.1	1571.4	1573.0	1584.7	1593.0	1583.3	1582.2	1587.5	1585.0	1594.5	1587.7	1581.7
2003	1552.9	1556.7	1557.6	1559.2	1572.0	1577.0	1568.8	1568.6	1577.6	1579.2	1586.8	1588.6	1570.4
2004	1548.5	1558.9	1569.4	1577.1	1587.9	1599.4	1592.1	1589.4	1601.2	1607.9	1619.8	1620.9	1589.4
2005	1586.3	1593.9	1605.6	1616.2	1630.9	1642.1	1640.2	1641.0	1643.1	1656.9	1671.7	1676.7	1633.7
2006	1641.9	1653.0	1661.7	1668.9	1685.5	1701.4	1688.8	1692.9	1708.4	1706.7	1719.5	1721.8	1687.5
2007	1689.1	1709.1	1716.8	1722.1	1739.0	1754.2	1747.0	1748.8	1752.4	1758.0	1772.5	1772.8	1740.2
2008	1738.9	1751.4	1752.2	1757.4	1767.4	1775.6	1769.6	1769.2	1768.2	1739.2	1756.7	1741.5	1757.3
2009	1698.1	1691.8	1681.5	1675.8	1679.0	1682.3	1664.9	1650.0	1653.5	1650.1	1650.4	1646.6	1668.7
Total Private													
1990	1076.9	1076.5	1090.8	1096.3	1108.6	1122.6	1125.0	1136.4	1136.4	1122.3	1124.8	1124.7	1111.8
2000	1376.5	1368.9	1399.0	1393.6	1404.1	1418.6	1416.2	1427.3	1430.6	1425.0	1430.7	1437.9	1410.7
2001	1388.1	1387.8	1391.8	1387.6	1394.1	1398.6	1392.5	1396.4	1388.7	1370.6	1363.7	1360.8	1385.1
2002	1321.7	1318.8	1321.1	1322.6	1333.5	1341.2	1342.3	1348.7	1342.9	1335.5	1338.0	1336.1	1333.5
2003	1302.4	1302.8	1304.2	1306.1	1314.6	1322.2	1326.9	1332.2	1331.7	1328.5	1330.6	1333.6	1319.7
2004	1298.3	1305.0	1315.2	1323.4	1333.3	1343.2	1347.9	1352.9	1352.5	1355.8	1360.9	1366.1	1337.9
2005	1334.5	1340.1	1350.6	1361.5	1375.3	1385.6	1395.4	1404.0	1394.0	1403.9	1412.6	1422.2	1381.6
2006	1388.9	1396.2	1404.7	1413.0	1428.4	1443.8	1444.0	1455.4	1459.2	1452.8	1459.7	1467.0	1434.4
2007	1436.0	1452.1	1459.7	1465.3	1481.1	1495.2	1497.3	1505.3	1504.5	1501.1	1509.6	1513.9	1485.1
2008	1481.0	1488.3	1490.9	1495.8	1504.2	1511.0	1513.4	1518.1	1512.2	1474.5	1485.4	1475.7	1495.9
2009	1432.9	1425.3	1414.4	1405.7	1408.8	1412.3	1406.2	1402.7	1399.6	1387.1	1384.3	1382.6	1405.2
Goods-Producing													
1990	303.4	301.8	306.4	306.3	308.5	311.5	314.9	317.4	315.6	309.1	306.3	302.6	308.7
2000	312.1	298.2	315.9	315.1	315.9	318.2	317.8	319.4	318.9	317.3	315.2	313.4	314.8
2001	307.6	305.7	306.9	305.7	307.4	309.0	310.0	311.6	308.9	302.6	296.0	290.8	305.2
2002	282.2	280.0	278.9	277.9	280.2	281.2	281.0	282.5	278.8	275.9	272.0	268.2	278.2
2003	260.9	259.8	259.3	259.3	261.5	262.9	264.4	266.1	264.8	262.9	260.3	258.3	261.7
2004	252.9	254.1	256.4	257.5	259.8	261.8	266.0	267.4	266.6	268.1	266.9	266.3	262.0
2005	261.4	263.7	267.6	270.3	273.5	277.3	282.7	285.3	271.6	286.1	285.5	286.3	275.9
2006	283.1	286.9	288.5	290.5	294.3	299.0	301.5	303.9	305.3	304.5	303.1	302.4	296.9
2007	299.3	304.6	305.7	307.4	311.9	317.4	319.8	322.3	322.0	320.0	318.9	316.0	313.8
2008	310.9	312.8	311.8	311.0	312.8	314.0	315.7	316.7	313.4	285.4	301.3	294.5	308.4
2009	283.7	280.8	274.1	270.6	269.5	269.4	268.3	267.3	265.1	260.0	254.2	250.1	267.8
Mining and Logging													
1990	2.2	2.1	2.1	2.4	2.4	2.5	2.5	2.5	2.5	2.5	2.4	2.3	2.4
2000	2.4	2.5	2.6	2.6	2.6	2.7	2.6	2.7	2.7	2.7	2.5	2.4	2.6
2001	2.7	2.6	2.6	2.5	2.5	2.5	2.6	2.6	2.5	2.5	2.3	2.3	2.5
2002	2.1	2.2	2.3	2.2	2.2	2.2	2.2	2.2	2.2	2.2	2.1	2.1	2.2
2003	2.0	2.0	2.1	1.9	1.8	1.8	1.7	1.8	1.7	1.8	1.7	1.7	1.8
2004	1.6	1.6	1.6	1.6	1.7	1.7	1.6	1.6	1.6	1.6	1.6	1.6	1.6
2005	1.5	1.5	1.5	1.5	1.5	1.5	1.5	1.5	1.5	1.5	1.5	1.5	1.5
2006	1.4	1.5	1.5	1.5	1.5	1.5	1.5	1.5	1.5	1.5	1.5	1.5	1.5
2007	1.4	1.5	1.4	1.6	1.6	1.6	1.7	1.6	1.5	1.6	1.5	1.5	1.5
2008	1.3	1.4	1.4	1.4	1.4	1.4	1.4	1.4	1.4	1.4	1.3	1.3	1.4
2009	1.3	1.3	1.2	1.1	1.1	1.1	1.2	1.2	1.2	1.2	1.2	1.1	1.2
Construction													
1990	67.7	67.2	70.7	72.0	74.1	76.1	77.1	79.5	78.5	74.8	72.6	69.8	73.3
2000	91.7	93.4	95.9	96.8	98.4	100.6	102.0	103.7	104.0	103.0	101.8	100.5	99.3
2001	96.7	95.9	97.3	96.2	97.9	99.5	101.1	102.5	101.3	97.9	94.2	91.2	97.6
2002	88.5	89.1	89.0	89.3	91.7	93.1	94.9	97.7	96.5	94.5	92.3	89.9	92.2
2003	86.2	86.4	86.6	88.3	90.9	92.8	94.9	97.0	96.6	95.7	94.0	92.4	91.8
2004	88.8	90.3	91.9	92.7	94.6	96.2	99.2	100.4	99.4	99.9	98.6	97.3	95.8
2005	93.1	94.9	97.1	98.9	101.1	103.2	106.5	108.7	109.9	108.9	107.9	107.9	103.2
2006	104.3	106.8	108.8	110.6	113.4	116.4	117.9	120.1	120.5	119.8	117.6	116.5	114.4
2007	114.4	117.5	119.7	121.6	124.9	128.2	128.8	131.1	130.3	128.3	126.4	124.5	124.6
2008	120.0	120.2	120.7	120.7	121.7	122.5	123.7	124.1	122.2	119.0	113.3	108.4	119.7
2009	101.2	98.8	97.0	95.5	95.7	95.9	95.3	94.7	93.7	90.5	85.0	81.8	93.8
Manufacturing													
1990	222.6	221.6	222.8	221.2	221.4	222.3	224.6	224.6	223.9	221.2	220.7	220.0	222.2
2000	215.1	214.0	214.6	212.9	212.1	212.1	210.4	210.2	209.4	208.9	208.2	207.7	211.3
2001	205.4	204.4	204.3	204.3	204.1	204.2	203.6	203.8	202.4	199.4	196.9	194.6	202.3
2002	191.8	188.9	187.7	186.6	186.6	186.2	184.1	182.9	180.1	179.3	177.8	176.5	184.0
2003	172.7	171.4	170.6	169.1	168.8	168.3	167.8	167.3	166.5	165.4	164.6	164.2	168.1
2004	162.5	162.2	162.9	163.2	163.5	163.9	165.2	165.4	165.6	166.6	166.7	167.4	164.6
2005	166.8	167.3	169.0	169.9	170.9	172.6	174.7	175.1	160.2	175.7	176.1	176.9	171.3
2006	177.4	178.6	178.2	178.4	179.4	181.1	182.1	182.3	183.3	183.2	184.0	184.4	181.0
2007	183.5	185.6	184.6	184.2	185.4	187.6	189.3	189.6	190.2	190.1	191.0	190.0	187.6
2008	189.6	191.2	189.7	188.9	189.7	190.1	190.6	191.2	189.8	165.0	186.7	184.8	187.3
2009	181.2	180.7	175.9	174.0	172.7	172.4	171.8	171.4	170.2	168.3	168.0	167.2	172.8

Employment by Industry: Seattle-Tacoma-Bellevue, WA, Selected Years, 1990–2009—*Continued*

(Numbers in thousands, not seasonally adjusted.)

Industry and year	January	February	March	April	May	June	July	August	September	October	November	December	Annual average
Service-Providing													
1990	958.6	966.7	972.6	979.5	992.3	1004.1	993.6	1000.2	1009.8	1005.1	1017.9	1017.0	993.1
2000	1297.8	1309.2	1320.8	1315.6	1330.4	1342.6	1325.6	1331.5	1344.0	1344.3	1355.8	1364.9	1331.9
2001	1321.4	1325.4	1329.9	1326.7	1332.8	1337.3	1319.6	1313.9	1320.3	1313.4	1319.8	1319.4	1323.3
2002	1286.4	1289.1	1292.5	1295.1	1304.5	1311.8	1302.4	1299.7	1308.7	1309.1	1322.5	1319.4	1303.4
2003	1292.0	1296.9	1298.3	1299.9	1310.5	1314.1	1304.4	1302.5	1312.8	1316.3	1326.5	1330.3	1308.7
2004	1295.6	1304.8	1313.0	1319.6	1328.1	1337.6	1326.1	1322.0	1334.6	1339.8	1352.9	1354.6	1327.4
2005	1324.9	1330.2	1338.0	1345.9	1357.4	1364.8	1357.5	1355.7	1371.5	1370.8	1386.2	1390.4	1357.8
2006	1358.8	1366.1	1373.2	1378.4	1391.2	1402.4	1387.3	1389.0	1403.1	1402.2	1416.4	1419.4	1390.6
2007	1389.8	1404.5	1411.1	1414.7	1427.1	1436.8	1427.2	1426.5	1430.4	1438.0	1453.6	1456.8	1426.4
2008	1428.0	1438.6	1440.4	1446.4	1454.6	1461.6	1453.9	1452.5	1454.8	1453.8	1455.4	1447.0	1448.9
2009	1414.4	1411.0	1407.4	1405.2	1409.5	1412.9	1396.6	1382.7	1388.4	1390.1	1396.2	1396.5	1400.9
Trade, Transportation, and Utilities													
1990	259.1	255.9	258.3	259.2	263.2	266.4	266.0	268.4	268.2	267.4	273.6	276.8	265.2
2000	320.1	318.6	320.6	320.8	323.0	325.5	324.4	326.2	325.9	329.7	335.9	339.9	325.9
2001	324.3	320.6	320.9	319.4	319.2	320.8	320.6	320.3	318.5	316.5	319.5	322.2	320.2
2002	309.0	304.6	304.1	303.8	306.0	308.6	309.6	309.8	308.8	308.8	313.3	316.9	308.6
2003	304.5	301.3	300.9	300.3	302.0	304.0	306.5	306.1	305.2	305.8	311.1	316.1	305.3
2004	301.2	300.2	301.2	303.5	305.6	308.0	308.6	310.1	309.1	310.7	315.9	320.4	307.9
2005	307.0	305.6	306.6	307.1	310.4	312.3	313.6	315.3	315.0	315.7	322.0	327.7	313.2
2006	313.8	311.4	312.5	312.5	315.6	318.9	318.9	320.6	319.8	319.2	326.1	331.3	318.4
2007	319.5	319.0	319.5	320.1	322.9	325.3	326.8	327.4	325.8	326.7	334.3	338.2	325.5
2008	326.5	324.4	324.2	323.7	324.6	326.0	327.4	328.5	325.3	323.9	325.4	327.6	325.6
2009	312.8	307.6	304.8	302.5	304.2	304.8	305.7	305.4	304.9	304.3	310.7	315.1	306.9
Wholesale Trade													
1990	66.8	67.0	67.6	67.4	68.3	69.3	70.1	69.8	69.7	69.5	69.3	69.2	68.7
1991	67.8	67.7	68.1	68.0	68.3	68.5	68.5	68.8	68.8	67.7	68.6	68.0	68.2
2000	80.4	80.9	81.6	81.6	81.9	82.8	82.7	83.0	82.6	83.1	82.7	83.1	82.2
2001	81.3	81.6	81.7	81.7	81.6	82.0	81.7	81.8	81.3	80.1	79.6	79.5	81.2
2002	78.7	78.7	78.9	78.4	78.6	78.8	78.3	78.5	78.0	77.0	76.9	76.9	78.1
2003	76.8	76.9	77.1	76.9	77.0	77.0	77.4	77.3	77.0	76.9	76.8	77.1	77.0
2004	76.5	77.0	77.5	78.0	78.1	78.1	78.6	78.4	78.3	78.1	78.0	78.2	77.9
2005	77.5	77.9	78.3	77.6	78.0	78.4	78.9	79.3	79.4	79.4	79.6	80.2	78.7
2006	80.2	80.4	80.9	80.7	81.3	81.8	82.1	82.2	82.2	81.8	82.1	82.2	81.5
2007	81.6	82.0	82.3	82.4	83.0	83.5	83.7	83.8	83.5	83.6	84.0	84.4	83.2
2008	83.5	83.9	84.0	84.0	84.4	84.6	84.4	84.6	84.1	83.5	83.0	82.6	83.9
Retail Trade													
1990	141.7	138.7	139.6	140.3	141.9	143.8	142.8	144.2	144.0	144.8	151.5	154.4	144.0
2000	177.0	175.0	175.9	175.6	177.8	178.9	177.8	178.8	179.2	180.7	187.0	190.9	179.6
2001	178.8	175.0	175.6	174.3	174.3	175.2	175.8	175.8	175.0	174.5	179.1	182.0	176.3
2002	171.4	167.0	167.1	167.2	168.5	170.1	170.7	170.6	170.3	170.9	176.0	179.7	170.8
2003	168.7	166.1	165.7	165.4	166.6	168.1	169.5	169.3	168.7	169.6	175.2	179.3	169.4
2004	167.2	165.7	166.0	166.7	168.5	169.8	169.6	171.3	170.0	171.2	176.8	180.6	170.3
2005	170.3	168.0	168.3	169.1	171.3	172.3	173.4	174.8	173.9	175.1	180.8	184.8	173.5
2006	172.9	170.3	170.6	170.5	172.3	174.3	174.2	175.6	174.5	175.2	181.8	185.5	174.8
2007	176.2	175.1	175.0	174.9	176.7	177.8	179.3	179.6	178.5	179.4	186.7	189.3	179.0
2008	180.8	177.9	177.8	177.3	177.2	178.1	179.5	180.6	178.5	178.7	181.1	183.0	179.2
2009	170.6	167.7	166.1	164.4	166.0	166.7	167.5	168.0	167.6	167.6	173.5	177.2	168.6
Transportation and Utilities													
1990	54.5	53.9	54.8	55.2	56.7	57.1	56.9	58.3	58.4	57.0	57.0	57.6	56.5
2000	62.4	62.5	62.9	63.4	63.2	63.7	63.8	64.2	64.0	65.8	66.1	65.8	64.0
2001	64.0	63.8	63.5	63.3	63.3	63.4	62.9	62.6	62.1	61.7	60.7	60.5	62.7
2002	58.8	58.7	58.0	58.1	58.9	59.5	60.5	60.5	60.3	60.7	60.2	60.1	59.5
2003	59.0	58.3	58.1	58.0	58.4	58.9	59.6	59.5	59.5	59.3	59.1	59.7	59.0
2004	57.5	57.5	57.7	58.8	59.0	60.1	60.4	60.4	60.8	61.4	61.1	61.6	59.7
2005	59.2	59.7	60.0	60.4	61.1	61.6	61.3	61.2	61.7	61.2	61.6	62.7	61.0
2006	60.7	60.7	61.0	61.3	62.0	62.8	62.6	62.8	63.1	62.2	62.2	63.6	62.1
2007	61.7	61.9	62.2	62.8	63.2	64.0	63.8	64.0	63.8	63.7	63.6	64.5	63.3
2008	62.2	62.6	62.4	62.4	63.0	63.3	63.5	63.3	62.7	61.7	61.3	62.0	62.5
2009	60.4	59.1	58.5	58.5	58.9	58.9	59.0	58.8	59.1	58.5	59.0	60.4	59.1
Information													
1990	34.4	34.6	34.1	34.0	34.4	34.9	35.3	35.9	35.4	34.6	34.5	34.7	34.7
2000	73.2	74.5	75.8	75.9	77.4	79.8	81.3	82.3	83.2	82.7	83.3	83.6	79.4
2001	82.4	82.7	82.1	80.6	80.8	81.3	80.4	80.3	78.6	78.4	78.4	78.8	80.4
2002	76.6	76.4	76.0	75.6	75.7	76.0	76.2	76.2	75.5	75.5	75.8	75.6	75.9
2003	74.6	74.5	74.0	73.6	74.1	74.3	74.7	75.4	75.0	75.1	75.4	75.8	74.7
2004	74.9	74.9	75.2	75.1	75.6	76.0	76.3	76.5	75.8	76.2	76.6	76.9	75.8
2005	76.2	76.8	76.6	76.8	77.1	77.3	78.1	78.8	78.1	77.6	78.4	78.9	77.6
2006	77.9	78.1	78.7	79.2	79.8	82.1	82.5	83.3	83.4	82.8	83.6	84.0	81.3
2007	83.3	84.3	83.9	84.3	85.1	85.9	86.1	86.4	86.0	85.1	86.2	86.4	85.3
2008	85.9	87.0	87.2	87.5	88.0	89.1	90.4	91.2	90.2	89.6	90.6	90.7	89.0
2009	88.9	89.4	89.1	87.9	88.3	88.4	88.6	88.0	87.1	86.5	86.6	86.3	87.9

Employment by Industry: Seattle-Tacoma-Bellevue, WA, Selected Years, 1990–2009—*Continued*

(Numbers in thousands, not seasonally adjusted.)

Industry and year	January	February	March	April	May	June	July	August	September	October	November	December	Annual average
Financial Activities													
1990	82.5	83.0	83.7	84.1	84.9	85.6	85.5	85.8	85.6	84.7	84.8	84.8	84.6
2000	99.8	100.5	100.3	100.0	100.0	100.4	99.7	100.2	100.0	99.4	99.9	101.0	100.1
2001	100.2	100.9	100.8	100.7	101.0	101.4	102.8	102.9	103.2	101.8	101.8	102.3	101.7
2002	99.3	99.9	100.2	100.2	100.7	100.8	101.1	101.6	101.5	101.3	102.2	102.4	100.9
2003	101.9	102.4	102.6	102.9	103.7	104.0	104.9	105.4	104.9	104.7	104.4	104.1	103.8
2004	102.8	102.8	103.6	102.8	103.0	103.3	103.6	103.7	103.2	103.1	103.0	103.8	103.2
2005	101.7	102.1	102.2	102.5	103.1	103.6	105.0	105.7	105.4	105.6	105.8	106.2	104.1
2006	104.9	105.2	105.0	105.1	105.3	105.5	105.8	105.6	104.9	104.6	104.4	104.7	105.1
2007	103.5	103.8	104.2	104.3	104.3	104.6	104.9	104.9	103.7	103.7	104.1	104.0	104.2
2008	102.9	102.9	102.8	102.3	102.9	102.7	102.2	102.2	101.3	99.9	99.5	98.9	101.7
2009	96.9	96.8	95.5	95.4	95.1	95.0	94.0	93.4	92.7	93.1	92.6	92.3	94.4
Professional and Business Services													
1990	130.8	132.3	134.6	136.3	137.3	139.9	141.5	143.7	144.4	141.5	141.7	141.1	138.8
2000	207.8	209.2	212.8	211.3	212.8	216.6	218.0	221.6	222.8	220.4	220.4	222.3	216.3
2001	214.5	214.0	215.4	214.1	214.3	213.9	210.0	210.3	208.3	206.1	203.8	201.7	210.5
2002	194.6	195.8	196.6	197.9	199.0	200.4	201.8	204.5	203.9	203.1	204.1	201.4	200.3
2003	192.8	194.1	194.3	195.1	195.1	195.8	197.1	199.2	199.0	199.5	199.1	198.1	196.6
2004	193.7	196.6	198.3	200.7	201.5	203.3	205.7	207.2	207.1	209.0	209.5	208.3	203.4
2005	203.6	206.2	207.4	210.1	212.0	213.8	216.8	218.9	220.6	220.4	221.3	221.2	214.4
2006	215.2	217.4	219.6	222.6	225.2	228.3	229.9	232.7	233.3	233.6	234.5	234.6	227.2
2007	228.0	232.3	234.7	235.2	237.1	239.7	240.6	242.6	243.0	242.4	243.2	244.1	238.6
2008	237.5	239.5	240.5	243.2	244.4	244.9	245.7	245.5	244.9	242.8	238.3	234.5	241.8
2009	228.3	226.3	224.4	221.9	220.4	221.4	219.8	219.2	219.4	219.2	219.1	218.4	221.5
Education and Health Services													
1990	110.9	111.9	113.3	113.4	114.3	114.7	113.0	114.2	116.6	117.9	118.6	119.0	114.8
2000	158.7	160.9	162.8	162.7	163.1	162.5	161.0	161.5	164.0	165.3	166.3	166.0	162.9
2001	163.6	166.3	166.5	167.4	167.6	166.2	163.0	163.4	166.5	168.9	170.6	170.6	166.7
2002	169.2	171.4	172.1	171.9	172.6	171.3	167.9	168.2	170.3	173.7	175.0	174.5	171.5
2003	171.4	173.1	174.0	174.3	174.3	173.0	170.0	169.7	172.0	175.0	176.3	175.9	173.3
2004	173.4	175.4	176.4	177.0	177.8	176.5	172.5	172.8	175.8	179.2	180.7	180.1	176.5
2005	179.0	180.8	182.2	183.4	184.3	182.1	178.3	178.8	182.7	184.9	186.0	185.2	182.3
2006	183.7	185.7	186.9	187.1	188.2	185.9	181.1	182.1	185.8	188.8	189.6	189.0	186.2
2007	187.7	190.2	191.9	192.2	193.8	191.2	187.5	188.1	191.5	196.6	197.9	197.6	192.2
2008	195.3	198.4	198.6	199.6	200.7	199.4	196.0	196.6	199.9	204.9	205.8	205.8	200.1
2009	205.5	207.5	208.1	208.2	209.1	207.4	202.7	202.3	204.9	208.1	209.6	208.2	206.8
Leisure and Hospitality													
1990	100.7	100.8	103.3	105.4	107.8	110.4	111.2	112.9	112.4	109.4	107.3	107.5	107.4
2000	139.1	140.7	143.7	143.9	146.1	149.3	146.6	148.4	149.2	144.2	143.7	145.8	145.1
2001	139.0	140.9	142.2	142.9	146.4	148.1	148.2	149.3	147.6	141.2	138.5	139.4	143.6
2002	135.5	135.3	137.3	139.1	142.4	145.8	146.9	148.2	147.4	141.3	139.9	141.2	141.7
2003	137.1	138.0	139.3	140.9	143.6	147.3	148.3	149.5	150.4	145.8	144.1	145.1	144.1
2004	140.3	141.4	144.0	146.3	148.9	152.5	153.0	153.0	153.3	148.5	147.3	149.1	148.1
2005	145.1	144.0	146.5	149.9	153.1	156.7	158.2	158.5	158.5	152.1	152.1	154.7	152.5
2006	149.3	150.0	151.6	154.0	157.5	160.8	161.3	164.0	163.7	157.5	156.5	158.7	157.1
2007	153.7	155.9	157.3	159.5	163.0	167.4	168.0	169.6	169.1	163.7	161.9	164.3	162.8
2008	159.3	160.0	161.9	164.3	165.9	169.6	170.2	171.5	171.6	163.6	160.1	159.9	164.8
2009	153.3	153.3	154.4	155.2	158.0	161.4	162.2	162.3	161.5	152.9	148.4	149.0	156.0
Other Services													
1990	47.9	48.2	48.8	48.8	49.4	50.0	50.2	50.6	50.4	49.6	49.4	49.5	49.4
2000	56.8	57.3	57.9	58.0	59.0	59.6	59.8	60.1	59.9	59.2	59.1	59.3	58.8
2001	58.6	58.8	59.2	59.3	59.8	60.9	61.0	61.3	60.3	59.4	59.6	59.8	59.8
2002	58.3	58.5	58.9	59.6	60.2	61.1	61.6	61.9	61.1	60.2	60.4	60.8	60.2
2003	59.2	59.6	59.8	59.7	60.3	60.9	61.0	60.8	60.4	59.7	59.9	60.2	60.1
2004	59.1	59.6	60.1	60.5	61.1	61.8	62.2	62.2	61.6	61.0	61.0	61.2	61.0
2005	60.5	60.9	61.5	61.4	61.8	62.5	62.7	62.7	62.1	61.5	61.5	62.0	61.8
2006	61.0	61.5	61.9	62.0	62.5	63.3	63.0	63.2	63.0	61.8	61.9	62.3	62.3
2007	61.0	62.0	62.5	62.3	63.0	63.7	63.6	64.0	63.4	62.9	63.1	63.3	62.9
2008	62.7	63.3	63.9	64.2	64.9	65.3	65.8	65.9	65.6	64.4	64.4	63.8	64.5
2009	63.5	63.6	64.0	64.0	64.2	64.5	64.9	64.8	64.0	63.0	63.1	63.2	63.9
Government													
1990	185.1	192.1	188.3	189.5	192.2	193.0	183.5	181.2	189.0	191.8	199.5	194.9	190.0
2000	233.4	238.6	237.8	237.1	242.2	242.2	227.2	223.6	232.3	236.7	240.4	240.4	236.0
2001	240.9	243.4	245.1	244.8	246.1	247.7	237.1	229.1	240.5	245.3	252.1	249.4	243.5
2002	247.0	250.4	250.3	250.5	251.3	251.8	241.0	233.5	244.6	249.6	256.5	251.6	248.2
2003	250.5	253.9	253.4	253.1	257.4	254.8	241.9	236.4	245.9	250.7	256.2	255.0	250.8
2004	250.2	253.9	254.2	253.7	254.6	256.2	244.2	236.5	248.7	252.1	258.9	254.8	251.5
2005	251.8	253.8	255.0	254.7	255.6	256.5	244.8	237.0	249.1	253.0	259.1	254.5	252.1
2006	253.0	256.8	257.0	255.9	257.1	257.6	244.8	237.5	249.2	253.9	259.8	254.8	253.1
2007	253.1	257.0	257.1	256.8	257.9	259.0	249.7	243.5	247.9	256.9	262.9	258.9	255.1
2008	257.9	263.1	261.3	261.6	263.2	264.6	256.2	251.1	256.0	264.7	271.3	265.8	261.4
2009	265.2	266.5	267.1	270.1	270.2	270.0	258.7	247.3	253.9	263.0	266.1	264.0	263.5

Employment by Industry: Springfield, MA-CT, NECTA, Selected Years, 1990–2009

(Numbers in thousands, not seasonally adjusted.)

Industry and year	January	February	March	April	May	June	July	August	September	October	November	December	Annual average
Total Nonfarm													
1990	290.8	290.2	291.7	291.8	293.2	294.7	284.0	284.0	290.7	291.5	291.7	290.9	290.4
2000	294.9	295.3	296.8	301.2	303.5	305.5	299.2	298.7	302.3	306.2	307.4	310.1	301.8
2001	300.3	300.0	301.0	303.1	305.5	307.2	299.8	299.9	304.1	304.4	304.8	305.1	302.9
2002	294.6	294.5	296.5	299.0	302.3	303.9	297.6	294.5	301.9	301.0	301.3	301.5	299.1
2003	290.4	289.6	290.8	295.0	297.8	298.9	292.4	292.6	296.4	296.4	296.9	297.4	294.6
2004	287.7	288.2	291.2	295.7	297.8	299.0	293.8	292.5	298.2	299.3	299.5	299.8	295.2
2005	289.2	290.9	292.0	297.2	299.0	299.5	293.6	293.0	299.4	299.7	300.5	300.9	296.2
2006	290.5	292.1	293.8	300.3	300.8	301.6	294.7	293.1	300.2	301.1	301.8	302.4	297.7
2007	292.5	293.1	294.2	298.9	301.6	302.6	295.6	293.5	299.2	300.9	301.7	302.2	298.0
2008	291.5	293.2	295.9	300.9	302.0	301.6	294.4	293.0	299.1	300.5	297.9	297.0	297.3
2009	285.3	285.7	286.7	289.1	289.3	289.9	282.3	280.2	286.0	286.5	284.2	283.6	285.7
Total Private													
1990	247.0	246.3	247.6	248.4	249.5	250.5	245.9	246.5	248.1	248.4	248.3	247.3	247.8
2000	245.2	245.5	246.9	251.0	252.6	254.3	251.1	251.0	252.3	255.7	256.2	258.5	251.7
2001	249.8	249.3	250.2	251.9	254.2	255.1	251.6	252.4	252.8	253.2	253.1	252.9	252.2
2002	243.6	243.6	245.5	248.3	251.4	252.5	249.5	249.4	251.1	250.4	250.1	249.9	248.8
2003	239.5	238.8	240.0	244.7	247.4	247.8	245.7	246.2	246.8	247.4	247.6	247.5	245.0
2004	239.1	239.1	241.7	245.9	247.8	249.0	248.6	247.9	249.4	250.1	250.0	249.8	246.5
2005	240.5	241.2	242.2	247.4	249.1	250.0	248.9	249.0	250.8	250.2	250.8	250.8	247.6
2006	241.8	242.4	243.9	250.2	250.6	251.7	249.9	249.5	250.8	251.0	251.1	251.3	248.7
2007	243.2	242.8	243.8	248.4	251.0	252.5	250.3	249.5	249.5	250.2	251.0	250.7	248.6
2008	241.7	242.1	244.8	249.2	250.7	251.0	248.9	248.7	249.2	249.4	246.7	245.1	247.3
2009	235.7	234.9	235.6	237.9	238.7	239.7	236.9	236.2	237.4	236.9	234.4	233.1	236.5
Goods-Producing													
1990	69.2	68.4	68.6	69.4	69.7	70.9	69.4	69.6	69.5	69.1	68.8	67.8	69.2
2000	56.8	56.3	57.0	57.8	58.1	58.8	58.5	59.1	58.9	59.2	59.2	58.8	58.2
2001	56.3	55.9	55.8	55.8	56.2	56.8	55.7	56.1	55.8	55.5	55.1	54.6	55.8
2002	52.3	51.5	51.8	52.2	52.9	53.4	52.7	53.2	52.8	52.7	52.4	51.8	52.5
2003	49.1	48.6	48.9	50.0	50.9	51.3	50.7	51.3	50.8	50.6	50.5	50.0	50.2
2004	47.8	47.6	48.0	48.9	49.6	50.1	50.0	50.5	50.3	50.2	50.1	49.5	49.4
2005	47.6	47.0	47.2	49.0	49.6	50.2	50.1	50.5	50.3	49.6	49.4	49.0	49.1
2006	47.0	46.8	47.1	48.4	48.7	49.3	49.0	49.2	48.9	48.6	48.4	48.3	48.3
2007	46.5	45.9	46.0	47.0	47.9	48.7	48.3	48.7	48.4	48.1	48.1	47.5	47.6
2008	45.4	44.9	45.5	46.5	47.1	47.5	47.0	47.7	47.2	47.0	46.1	45.2	46.4
2009	42.4	41.3	41.0	41.3	41.7	42.1	42.0	41.9	41.7	41.4	40.8	40.0	41.5
Mining, Logging, and Construction													
1990	9.2	8.5	8.8	9.6	10.0	10.5	10.5	10.6	10.5	10.1	9.7	8.9	9.7
2000	8.7	8.4	9.0	9.9	10.3	10.7	10.9	11.1	10.8	10.7	10.5	10.0	10.1
2001	8.7	8.6	8.9	9.8	10.6	11.1	11.3	11.4	11.1	11.2	11.1	10.7	10.4
2002	9.4	9.0	9.3	10.3	10.9	11.3	11.3	11.3	11.0	10.9	10.7	10.2	10.5
2003	8.9	8.6	8.9	9.9	10.8	11.1	11.5	11.6	11.2	11.0	10.9	10.3	10.4
2004	8.9	8.7	9.1	10.1	10.8	11.1	11.6	11.6	11.4	11.3	11.1	10.7	10.5
2005	9.4	8.9	9.1	10.6	11.3	11.6	12.1	12.2	12.1	11.7	11.6	11.1	11.0
2006	9.8	9.5	9.8	11.1	11.5	11.8	12.0	12.0	11.8	11.5	11.3	10.9	11.1
2007	9.5	9.0	9.1	10.2	11.1	11.5	11.7	11.7	11.4	11.4	11.2	10.5	10.7
2008	9.1	8.9	9.2	10.2	10.9	11.0	11.2	11.3	11.0	10.9	10.6	9.8	10.3
Manufacturing													
1990	60.0	59.9	59.8	59.8	59.7	60.4	58.9	59.0	59.0	59.0	59.1	58.9	59.5
2000	48.1	47.9	48.0	47.9	47.8	48.1	47.6	48.0	48.1	48.5	48.7	48.8	48.1
2001	47.6	47.3	46.9	46.0	45.6	45.7	44.4	44.7	44.7	44.3	44.0	43.9	45.4
2002	42.9	42.5	42.5	41.9	42.0	42.1	41.4	41.9	41.8	41.8	41.7	41.6	42.0
2003	40.2	40.0	40.0	40.1	40.1	40.2	39.2	39.7	39.6	39.6	39.6	39.7	39.8
2004	38.9	38.9	38.9	38.8	38.8	39.0	38.4	38.9	38.9	38.9	39.0	38.8	38.9
2005	38.2	38.1	38.1	38.4	38.3	38.6	38.0	38.3	38.2	37.9	37.8	37.9	38.2
2006	37.2	37.3	37.3	37.3	37.2	37.5	37.0	37.2	37.1	37.1	37.1	37.4	37.2
2007	37.0	36.9	36.9	36.8	36.8	37.2	36.6	37.0	37.0	36.7	36.9	37.0	36.9
2008	36.3	36.0	36.3	36.3	36.2	36.5	35.8	36.4	36.2	36.1	35.5	35.4	36.1
2009	34.1	33.4	33.0	32.5	32.3	32.3	31.9	31.9	31.9	31.8	31.4	31.4	32.3
Service-Providing													
1990	221.6	221.8	223.1	222.4	223.5	223.8	214.6	214.4	221.2	222.4	222.9	223.1	221.2
2000	238.1	239.0	239.8	243.4	245.4	246.7	240.7	239.6	243.4	247.0	248.2	251.3	243.6
2001	244.0	244.1	245.2	247.3	249.3	250.4	244.1	243.8	248.3	248.9	249.7	250.5	247.1
2002	242.3	243.0	244.7	246.8	249.4	250.5	244.9	241.3	249.1	248.3	248.9	249.7	246.6
2003	241.3	241.0	241.9	245.0	246.9	247.6	241.7	241.3	245.6	245.8	246.4	247.4	244.3
2004	239.9	240.6	243.2	246.8	248.2	248.9	243.8	242.0	247.9	249.1	249.4	250.3	245.8
2005	241.6	243.9	244.8	248.2	249.4	249.3	243.5	242.5	249.1	250.1	251.1	251.9	247.1
2006	243.5	245.3	246.7	251.9	252.1	252.3	245.7	243.9	251.3	252.5	253.4	254.1	249.4
2007	246.0	247.2	248.2	251.9	253.7	253.9	247.3	244.8	250.8	252.8	253.6	254.7	250.4
2008	246.1	248.3	250.4	254.4	254.9	254.1	247.4	245.3	251.9	253.5	251.8	251.8	250.8
2009	242.9	244.4	245.7	247.8	247.6	247.8	240.3	238.3	244.3	245.1	243.4	243.6	244.3

Employment by Industry: Springfield, MA-CT, NECTA, Selected Years, 1990–2009—*Continued*

(Numbers in thousands, not seasonally adjusted.)

Industry and year	January	February	March	April	May	June	July	August	September	October	November	December	Annual average
Trade, Transportation, and Utilities													
1990	63.3	62.0	62.1	61.9	61.8	61.8	61.1	61.0	62.1	62.5	63.2	63.4	62.2
2000	61.8	61.3	61.2	61.8	62.1	62.5	61.3	61.5	62.5	63.5	65.1	67.2	62.7
2001	63.7	62.7	62.7	63.0	63.3	63.3	61.8	61.9	62.8	63.1	64.2	64.9	63.1
2002	61.3	60.4	60.6	61.8	62.0	62.7	61.4	61.3	62.4	61.9	62.5	63.3	61.8
2003	60.0	59.3	59.3	60.4	60.6	60.9	59.3	59.3	60.6	61.3	62.4	62.9	60.5
2004	60.4	59.7	60.1	60.0	60.8	61.3	60.6	60.5	61.7	62.3	63.2	64.1	61.2
2005	61.4	60.9	60.8	61.3	61.8	62.1	60.9	60.8	61.6	61.8	63.1	64.0	61.7
2006	61.3	60.0	60.2	61.2	61.5	61.6	60.3	60.3	61.3	61.6	63.1	63.8	61.4
2007	60.9	59.8	59.8	60.1	60.7	60.9	59.4	59.2	60.1	60.5	62.1	62.9	60.5
2008	60.4	59.4	59.4	59.8	60.3	60.5	59.4	59.4	60.0	60.1	60.5	60.7	60.0
2009	58.2	57.1	56.7	56.1	56.5	57.0	55.7	55.8	56.5	56.5	56.9	57.3	56.7
Wholesale Trade													
1990	14.7	14.6	14.7	14.8	14.8	14.8	14.8	14.8	14.8	14.6	14.3	14.3	14.7
2000	12.0	12.1	12.1	12.0	12.0	12.1	12.1	12.1	12.0	12.1	12.2	12.4	12.1
2001	12.3	12.2	12.2	12.0	11.9	12.0	11.8	11.9	11.9	11.7	11.7	11.7	11.9
2002	11.2	11.2	11.2	11.3	11.2	11.3	11.1	11.1	11.1	10.8	10.9	11.0	11.1
2003	10.6	10.6	10.6	10.7	10.7	10.8	10.7	10.6	10.8	10.8	10.9	10.9	10.7
2004	10.6	10.7	10.9	10.8	10.9	11.1	11.5	11.5	11.4	11.6	11.6	11.6	11.2
2005	11.6	11.5	11.5	11.5	11.6	11.6	11.4	11.4	11.3	11.2	11.2	11.2	11.4
2006	11.3	11.1	11.1	11.5	11.5	11.6	11.7	11.7	11.8	11.8	11.9	11.9	11.6
2007	11.7	11.6	11.6	11.7	11.7	11.8	11.7	11.8	11.7	11.8	11.7	11.8	11.7
2008	11.6	11.6	11.7	11.8	12.0	12.0	11.9	11.8	11.8	11.7	11.6	11.5	11.8
2009	11.3	11.0	10.9	10.8	10.8	10.9	10.9	10.8	10.9	10.9	10.9	10.8	10.9
Retail Trade													
1990	37.3	36.2	36.0	36.0	35.8	35.9	35.7	35.6	36.0	36.3	37.3	37.6	36.3
2000	37.3	36.7	36.6	36.7	37.0	37.2	36.9	37.1	37.4	37.9	39.3	40.2	37.5
2001	37.2	36.4	36.4	36.7	37.1	37.1	36.6	36.8	36.8	37.2	38.3	39.0	37.1
2002	36.3	35.5	35.7	36.0	36.3	36.8	36.5	36.6	36.8	36.6	37.4	38.2	36.6
2003	36.0	35.4	35.5	36.3	36.6	36.8	36.2	36.4	36.6	37.1	38.1	38.6	36.6
2004	36.6	35.9	36.1	35.9	36.5	36.7	36.5	36.6	36.9	37.1	38.0	38.8	36.8
2005	36.3	35.9	35.8	36.3	36.6	36.8	36.5	36.6	36.6	36.9	38.0	38.6	36.7
2006	36.1	35.1	35.2	35.8	36.0	36.0	35.6	35.7	35.8	36.2	37.5	37.9	36.1
2007	35.9	35.0	35.0	35.0	35.6	35.6	35.1	35.0	34.9	35.2	36.8	37.1	35.5
2008	35.4	34.4	34.4	34.7	34.9	35.1	34.7	34.9	34.6	35.0	35.5	35.6	34.9
2009	33.8	33.2	33.0	32.8	33.2	33.6	33.0	33.3	33.2	33.3	33.8	34.0	33.4
Transportation and Utilities													
1990	11.3	11.2	11.4	11.1	11.2	11.1	10.6	10.6	11.3	11.6	11.6	11.5	11.2
2000	12.5	12.5	12.5	13.1	13.1	13.2	12.3	12.3	13.1	13.5	13.6	14.6	13.0
2001	14.2	14.1	14.1	14.3	14.3	14.2	13.4	13.2	14.1	14.2	14.2	14.2	14.0
2002	13.8	13.7	13.7	14.5	14.5	14.6	13.8	13.6	14.5	14.5	14.2	14.1	14.1
2003	13.4	13.3	13.2	13.4	13.3	13.3	12.4	12.3	13.2	13.4	13.4	13.4	13.2
2004	13.2	13.1	13.1	13.3	13.4	13.5	12.6	12.4	13.4	13.6	13.6	13.7	13.2
2005	13.5	13.5	13.5	13.5	13.6	13.7	13.0	12.8	13.7	13.7	13.9	14.2	13.6
2006	13.9	13.8	13.9	13.9	14.0	14.0	13.0	12.9	13.7	13.6	13.7	14.0	13.7
2007	13.3	13.2	13.2	13.4	13.4	13.5	12.6	12.4	13.5	13.5	13.6	14.0	13.3
2008	13.4	13.4	13.3	13.3	13.4	13.4	12.8	12.7	13.6	13.4	13.4	13.6	13.3
2009	13.1	12.9	12.8	12.5	12.5	12.5	11.8	11.7	12.4	12.3	12.2	12.5	12.4
Information													
1990	5.8	5.7	5.7	5.8	5.8	5.8	5.7	5.7	5.7	5.8	5.8	5.8	5.8
2000	5.7	5.8	5.7	5.9	5.9	5.9	5.9	5.3	5.9	5.9	6.0	6.1	5.8
2001	6.1	6.0	6.0	6.0	6.0	6.0	5.9	5.8	5.7	5.8	5.8	5.8	5.9
2002	5.7	5.7	5.7	5.5	5.6	5.6	5.5	5.5	5.4	5.4	5.5	5.5	5.6
2003	5.4	5.3	5.3	5.3	5.2	5.2	5.2	5.2	5.1	4.9	4.9	4.9	5.2
2004	4.8	4.8	4.8	4.7	4.7	4.8	4.8	4.7	4.6	4.6	4.7	4.7	4.7
2005	4.6	4.6	4.6	4.6	4.6	4.6	4.6	4.6	4.5	4.4	4.5	4.5	4.6
2006	4.5	4.5	4.4	4.4	4.4	4.6	4.6	4.6	4.5	4.5	4.5	4.5	4.5
2007	4.5	4.5	4.4	4.5	4.5	4.5	4.6	4.5	4.5	4.6	4.6	4.6	4.5
2008	4.5	4.6	4.5	4.5	4.6	4.5	4.4	4.4	4.3	4.3	4.3	4.4	4.4
2009	4.3	4.2	4.2	4.2	4.1	4.1	4.0	4.0	4.0	3.9	3.9	3.9	4.1
Financial Activities													
1990	16.5	16.4	16.5	16.4	16.4	16.5	16.3	16.4	16.2	16.3	16.2	16.3	16.4
2000	16.2	16.2	16.2	16.2	16.2	16.4	16.4	16.5	16.5	16.5	16.6	16.8	16.4
2001	16.7	16.7	16.7	16.8	16.9	17.1	17.1	17.1	16.9	17.0	17.1	17.0	16.9
2002	16.8	16.8	16.8	16.6	16.7	16.8	16.8	16.9	16.7	16.5	16.6	16.7	16.7
2003	16.4	16.3	16.4	16.4	16.5	16.7	16.6	16.6	16.4	16.3	16.1	16.2	16.4
2004	16.3	16.2	16.3	16.3	16.3	16.4	16.3	16.2	16.1	15.8	15.8	15.9	16.2
2005	15.7	15.6	15.8	15.7	15.7	15.8	16.3	16.3	16.2	16.3	16.4	16.5	16.0
2006	16.7	16.7	16.7	17.2	17.2	17.3	17.1	17.1	17.0	17.0	17.0	17.0	17.0
2007	17.2	17.2	17.2	17.2	17.3	17.4	17.4	17.4	17.2	17.2	17.2	17.3	17.3
2008	17.4	17.5	17.6	17.5	17.6	17.7	17.6	17.5	17.4	17.2	17.2	17.2	17.5
2009	17.1	17.1	17.0	17.0	16.8	16.9	16.8	16.8	16.6	16.5	16.5	16.5	16.8

Employment by Industry: Springfield, MA-CT, NECTA, Selected Years, 1990–2009—*Continued*

(Numbers in thousands, not seasonally adjusted.)

Industry and year	January	February	March	April	May	June	July	August	September	October	November	December	Annual average
Professional and Business Services													
1990	19.7	19.9	20.2	20.4	20.4	20.6	20.5	20.9	20.8	19.8	19.9	19.7	20.2
2000	24.0	24.0	24.3	24.7	24.7	25.0	24.8	25.0	25.0	24.8	24.4	24.4	24.6
2001	23.6	23.7	23.9	24.1	24.3	24.3	24.0	24.1	24.0	24.1	23.7	23.4	23.9
2002	22.6	23.0	23.5	23.8	23.8	24.1	23.9	23.8	24.0	23.3	23.1	22.8	23.5
2003	21.6	21.4	21.7	22.8	23.0	23.1	23.1	23.2	23.0	23.4	23.5	23.7	22.8
2004	22.4	22.2	22.7	24.4	24.4	24.7	24.6	24.5	24.9	24.6	24.6	24.5	24.0
2005	23.0	22.9	23.2	24.4	24.2	24.4	24.3	24.2	24.6	25.1	24.8	24.4	24.1
2006	23.6	23.8	23.8	25.1	24.0	24.6	24.1	24.1	24.2	23.9	23.6	23.4	24.0
2007	22.3	22.3	22.5	23.8	23.8	24.5	23.9	24.0	23.5	23.8	23.7	23.3	23.5
2008	22.2	22.2	22.4	24.1	23.4	24.0	23.4	23.4	23.9	23.2	22.5	21.9	23.1
2009	21.3	20.9	21.0	22.4	21.6	21.9	21.6	21.6	22.0	21.8	21.1	20.6	21.5
Education and Health Services													
1990	39.8	41.2	41.2	40.9	41.1	39.9	38.9	39.0	40.0	41.2	41.4	41.4	40.5
2000	47.2	48.2	48.2	48.7	48.9	47.8	46.5	46.2	46.7	49.2	49.4	49.8	48.1
2001	49.0	49.9	49.9	50.1	50.2	49.6	48.8	49.0	49.9	50.9	51.4	51.5	50.0
2002	50.4	51.6	51.7	52.1	52.3	51.5	50.4	50.2	51.6	52.9	53.5	53.5	51.8
2003	52.4	53.2	53.2	53.3	53.0	51.8	51.6	51.6	52.7	53.3	53.6	53.4	52.8
2004	52.2	53.3	53.5	53.8	53.3	52.2	52.1	51.8	53.2	54.4	54.8	54.4	53.3
2005	52.9	54.5	54.6	54.3	54.2	53.0	52.7	52.7	54.5	55.1	55.6	55.4	54.1
2006	53.4	55.1	55.5	55.5	55.2	53.9	54.1	53.6	55.3	56.3	56.7	56.6	55.1
2007	55.5	56.7	56.9	57.2	56.8	55.7	55.5	55.1	56.4	57.4	57.8	57.8	56.6
2008	56.1	57.4	58.4	58.1	58.0	56.6	56.8	56.5	57.7	58.6	58.8	58.6	57.6
2009	57.0	58.3	59.1	58.7	58.6	57.9	56.8	56.5	57.7	58.3	58.5	58.3	58.0
Leisure and Hospitality													
1990	21.9	21.8	22.4	22.7	23.4	23.9	23.0	22.9	23.2	23.0	22.4	22.2	22.7
2000	22.6	22.7	23.1	24.8	25.5	26.5	26.2	26.0	25.7	25.3	24.2	23.9	24.7
2001	23.1	23.1	23.8	24.8	25.8	26.4	26.5	26.6	26.4	25.4	24.4	24.1	25.0
2002	23.1	23.2	23.9	24.9	26.4	26.9	27.0	26.8	26.9	26.3	25.0	24.6	25.4
2003	23.5	23.6	24.1	25.3	26.8	27.5	27.6	27.5	27.2	26.4	25.4	25.1	25.8
2004	24.2	24.3	25.2	26.7	27.5	28.3	28.6	28.1	27.5	26.9	25.6	25.3	26.5
2005	24.2	24.5	24.7	26.5	27.5	28.2	28.1	28.1	27.7	26.4	25.5	25.2	26.4
2006	24.1	24.2	24.8	26.9	28.0	28.7	28.7	28.6	28.1	27.5	26.2	25.9	26.8
2007	24.9	24.9	25.4	27.0	28.3	29.0	29.1	28.7	28.0	27.1	26.0	25.7	27.0
2008	24.2	24.6	25.4	27.1	28.2	28.6	28.5	28.1	27.4	27.6	26.0	25.7	26.8
2009	24.3	24.8	25.4	27.0	28.2	28.5	28.4	28.1	27.8	27.3	25.6	25.3	26.7
Other Services													
1990	10.8	10.9	10.9	10.9	10.9	11.1	11.0	11.0	10.6	10.7	10.6	10.7	10.8
2000	10.9	11.0	11.2	11.1	11.2	11.4	11.5	11.4	11.1	11.3	11.3	11.5	11.2
2001	11.3	11.3	11.4	11.3	11.5	11.6	11.8	11.8	11.3	11.4	11.4	11.6	11.5
2002	11.4	11.4	11.5	11.4	11.7	11.5	11.8	11.7	11.3	11.4	11.5	11.7	11.5
2003	11.1	11.1	11.1	11.2	11.4	11.3	11.6	11.5	11.0	11.2	11.2	11.3	11.3
2004	11.0	11.0	11.1	11.1	11.2	11.2	11.6	11.6	11.1	11.3	11.2	11.4	11.2
2005	11.1	11.2	11.3	11.6	11.5	11.7	11.9	11.8	11.4	11.5	11.5	11.8	11.5
2006	11.2	11.3	11.4	11.5	11.6	11.7	12.0	12.0	11.5	11.6	11.6	11.8	11.6
2007	11.4	11.5	11.6	11.6	11.7	11.8	12.1	11.9	11.4	11.5	11.5	11.6	11.6
2008	11.5	11.5	11.6	11.6	11.5	11.6	11.8	11.7	11.3	11.4	11.3	11.4	11.5
2009	11.1	11.2	11.2	11.2	11.2	11.3	11.6	11.5	11.1	11.2	11.1	11.2	11.2
Government													
1990	43.8	43.9	44.1	43.4	43.7	44.2	38.1	37.5	42.6	43.1	43.4	43.6	42.6
2000	49.7	49.8	49.9	50.2	50.9	51.2	48.1	47.7	50.0	50.5	51.2	51.6	50.1
2001	50.5	50.7	50.8	51.2	51.3	52.1	48.2	47.5	51.3	51.2	51.7	52.2	50.7
2002	51.0	50.9	51.0	50.7	50.9	51.4	48.1	45.1	50.8	50.6	51.2	51.6	50.3
2003	50.9	50.8	50.8	50.3	50.4	51.1	46.7	46.4	49.6	49.0	49.3	49.9	49.6
2004	48.6	49.1	49.5	49.8	50.0	50.0	45.2	44.6	48.8	49.2	49.5	50.0	48.7
2005	48.7	49.7	49.8	49.8	49.9	49.5	44.7	44.0	48.6	49.5	49.7	50.1	48.7
2006	48.7	49.7	49.9	50.1	50.2	49.9	44.8	43.6	49.4	50.1	50.7	51.1	49.0
2007	49.3	50.3	50.4	50.5	50.6	50.1	45.3	44.0	49.7	50.7	50.7	51.5	49.4
2008	49.8	51.1	51.1	51.7	51.3	50.6	45.5	44.3	49.9	51.1	51.2	51.9	50.0
2009	49.6	50.8	51.1	51.2	50.6	50.2	45.4	44.0	48.6	49.6	49.8	50.5	49.3

Employment by Industry: St. Louis, MO-IL, Selected Years, 1990–2009

(Numbers in thousands, not seasonally adjusted.)

Industry and year	January	February	March	April	May	June	July	August	September	October	November	December	Annual average
Total Nonfarm													
1990	1166.5	1167.3	1175.0	1185.9	1194.1	1209.0	1182.2	1185.9	1201.2	1194.9	1194.8	1194.0	1187.6
2000	1311.1	1310.8	1324.1	1340.8	1349.3	1362.1	1331.6	1332.0	1348.6	1350.4	1351.6	1347.4	1338.3
2001	1310.0	1320.6	1335.3	1347.2	1355.0	1364.0	1333.8	1333.2	1341.8	1339.3	1345.0	1346.5	1339.3
2002	1309.0	1311.8	1320.8	1333.2	1341.0	1351.0	1324.7	1329.8	1340.4	1340.3	1342.0	1345.1	1332.4
2003	1307.3	1306.6	1315.2	1324.2	1331.0	1335.7	1312.9	1315.8	1323.8	1328.8	1325.6	1327.4	1321.2
2004	1293.9	1292.4	1307.9	1321.5	1328.8	1333.6	1311.4	1318.1	1329.6	1336.1	1336.9	1339.0	1320.8
2005	1304.4	1310.2	1322.2	1341.6	1345.7	1350.0	1326.8	1337.7	1347.7	1346.1	1348.7	1351.1	1336.0
2006	1319.5	1324.3	1335.7	1351.4	1358.4	1366.0	1343.0	1345.7	1360.6	1362.3	1362.2	1367.3	1349.7
2007	1327.9	1331.2	1348.3	1360.4	1373.6	1374.3	1345.3	1353.6	1366.3	1368.7	1372.5	1374.0	1358.0
2008	1340.5	1346.4	1350.1	1361.9	1374.9	1378.1	1344.5	1352.6	1359.8	1354.1	1346.2	1339.8	1354.1
2009	1299.2	1297.9	1300.2	1306.5	1312.3	1308.3	1284.2	1289.6	1296.2	1299.2	1300.3	1297.2	1299.3
Total Private													
1990	1025.3	1024.5	1030.7	1039.1	1049.3	1063.1	1061.7	1065.7	1061.0	1051.6	1048.1	1049.3	1047.5
2000	1146.2	1143.6	1155.2	1171.7	1179.4	1192.8	1185.8	1184.3	1179.8	1181.6	1181.2	1176.5	1173.2
2001	1142.6	1150.5	1164.5	1176.1	1182.9	1191.7	1185.1	1182.9	1172.6	1168.3	1172.5	1173.4	1171.9
2002	1138.8	1140.3	1148.8	1161.2	1167.2	1180.7	1176.7	1178.6	1171.4	1168.5	1169.0	1172.3	1164.5
2003	1138.3	1136.0	1144.1	1152.1	1157.7	1165.3	1163.6	1164.7	1156.2	1159.0	1154.9	1157.0	1154.1
2004	1125.9	1123.0	1138.0	1151.0	1157.1	1166.3	1162.8	1166.1	1161.4	1166.2	1166.0	1168.1	1154.3
2005	1137.2	1139.9	1152.0	1169.6	1172.8	1181.1	1176.0	1181.5	1178.2	1175.6	1176.7	1179.6	1168.4
2006	1151.6	1153.5	1164.6	1179.1	1185.0	1198.5	1192.0	1190.9	1190.1	1190.0	1188.8	1193.8	1181.5
2007	1158.3	1158.5	1175.5	1187.2	1199.2	1205.9	1198.8	1200.2	1195.2	1194.6	1197.2	1199.0	1189.1
2008	1169.5	1171.0	1175.6	1187.0	1198.0	1207.5	1194.9	1195.6	1185.9	1177.3	1169.3	1163.4	1182.9
2009	1126.1	1122.4	1123.9	1129.6	1134.1	1135.1	1129.2	1126.5	1116.8	1118.1	1118.5	1115.7	1124.7
Goods-Producing													
1990	254.6	254.9	253.9	257.6	259.9	263.8	260.9	262.0	259.5	256.3	251.6	251.1	257.2
2000	245.9	245.8	248.1	250.8	252.9	255.8	252.6	250.2	252.1	252.7	251.6	246.4	250.4
2001	237.4	243.1	246.6	248.8	249.7	251.0	250.8	249.1	247.3	241.2	243.7	241.2	245.8
2002	231.9	232.5	234.5	235.6	236.0	239.6	240.4	239.4	238.1	235.7	234.7	234.3	236.1
2003	224.4	222.4	225.3	226.6	228.4	231.2	229.4	231.7	228.6	228.0	226.4	225.0	227.3
2004	218.5	216.8	221.9	224.1	225.6	228.7	223.5	229.3	228.4	226.5	225.3	224.4	224.4
2005	216.6	217.0	220.4	223.1	224.7	226.7	221.7	226.9	226.3	225.6	224.6	223.0	223.1
2006	217.2	217.3	219.8	221.5	222.1	226.4	225.5	222.9	224.4	222.5	221.2	219.8	221.7
2007	210.9	210.6	216.1	217.6	220.7	222.0	219.1	220.5	219.7	218.8	217.6	215.4	217.4
2008	206.0	206.6	205.7	208.5	211.9	215.9	211.1	211.0	210.2	206.7	201.6	197.1	207.7
2009	184.6	182.9	182.4	179.6	179.4	179.6	180.4	178.1	176.5	176.4	174.8	172.6	178.9
Mining, Logging, and Construction													
1990	49.0	47.9	48.6	49.4	51.0	53.0	54.6	54.7	52.5	52.1	50.9	49.0	51.1
2000	71.3	71.1	73.8	76.3	78.0	80.1	79.9	80.5	80.5	79.8	78.1	75.7	77.1
2001	71.5	72.3	75.7	78.6	80.3	83.9	83.5	83.4	82.1	81.2	80.6	78.4	79.3
2002	73.8	73.5	75.3	77.1	78.0	81.0	82.8	82.3	81.2	80.1	78.8	77.9	78.5
2003	72.8	71.1	73.5	76.4	78.2	80.6	82.9	82.9	81.8	81.7	80.3	78.8	78.4
2004	74.0	72.2	77.0	79.8	81.1	83.1	84.8	84.3	83.6	82.1	81.1	80.0	80.3
2005	74.3	74.8	78.1	80.5	82.2	83.7	85.2	85.2	84.6	83.8	82.8	81.1	81.4
2006	78.2	78.0	79.8	82.4	83.0	86.0	86.1	86.0	85.1	83.8	82.5	80.8	82.6
2007	77.4	74.4	79.9	81.4	84.3	87.2	86.7	86.6	84.7	84.1	83.0	80.4	82.5
2008	76.2	74.1	76.5	78.4	80.4	82.5	82.7	82.6	81.1	78.4	75.4	72.0	78.4
2009	64.3	63.3	64.9	65.1	66.0	67.1	68.0	67.0	66.0	65.3	63.7	61.3	65.2
Manufacturing													
1990	205.6	207.0	205.3	208.2	208.9	210.8	206.3	207.3	207.0	204.2	200.7	202.1	206.1
2000	174.6	174.7	174.3	174.5	174.9	175.7	172.7	169.7	171.6	172.9	173.5	170.7	173.3
2001	165.9	170.8	170.9	170.2	169.4	167.1	167.3	165.7	165.2	160.0	163.1	162.8	166.5
2002	158.1	159.0	159.2	158.5	158.0	158.6	157.6	157.1	156.9	155.6	155.9	156.4	157.6
2003	151.6	151.3	151.8	150.2	150.2	150.6	146.5	148.8	146.8	146.3	146.1	146.2	148.9
2004	144.5	144.6	144.9	144.3	144.5	145.6	138.7	145.0	144.8	144.4	144.2	144.4	144.2
2005	142.3	142.2	142.3	142.6	142.5	143.0	136.5	141.7	141.7	141.8	141.8	141.9	141.7
2006	139.0	139.3	140.0	139.1	139.1	140.4	139.4	136.9	139.3	138.7	138.7	139.0	139.1
2007	133.5	136.2	136.2	136.2	136.4	134.8	132.4	133.9	135.0	134.7	134.6	135.0	134.9
2008	129.8	132.5	129.2	130.1	131.5	133.4	128.4	128.4	129.1	128.3	126.2	125.1	129.3
2009	120.3	119.6	117.5	114.5	113.4	112.5	112.4	111.1	110.5	111.1	111.1	111.3	113.8
Service-Providing													
1990	911.9	912.4	921.1	928.3	934.2	945.2	921.3	923.9	941.7	938.6	943.2	942.9	930.4
2000	1065.2	1065.0	1076.0	1090.0	1096.4	1106.3	1079.0	1081.8	1096.5	1097.7	1100.0	1101.0	1087.9
2001	1072.6	1077.5	1088.7	1098.4	1105.3	1113.0	1083.0	1084.1	1094.5	1098.1	1101.3	1105.3	1093.5
2002	1077.1	1079.3	1086.3	1097.6	1105.0	1111.4	1084.3	1090.4	1102.3	1104.6	1107.3	1110.8	1096.4
2003	1082.9	1084.2	1089.9	1097.6	1102.6	1104.5	1083.5	1084.1	1095.2	1100.8	1099.2	1102.4	1093.9
2004	1075.4	1075.6	1086.0	1097.4	1103.2	1104.9	1087.9	1088.8	1101.2	1109.6	1111.6	1114.6	1096.4
2005	1087.8	1093.2	1101.8	1118.5	1121.0	1123.3	1105.1	1110.8	1121.4	1120.5	1124.1	1128.1	1113.0
2006	1102.3	1107.0	1115.9	1129.9	1136.3	1139.6	1117.5	1122.8	1136.2	1139.8	1141.0	1147.5	1128.0
2007	1117.0	1120.6	1132.2	1142.8	1152.9	1152.3	1126.2	1133.1	1146.6	1149.9	1154.9	1158.6	1140.6
2008	1134.5	1139.8	1144.4	1153.4	1163.0	1162.2	1133.4	1141.6	1149.6	1147.4	1144.6	1142.7	1146.4
2009	1114.6	1115.0	1117.8	1126.9	1132.9	1128.7	1103.8	1111.5	1119.7	1122.8	1125.5	1124.6	1120.3

Employment by Industry: St. Louis, MO-IL, Selected Years, 1990–2009—*Continued*

(Numbers in thousands, not seasonally adjusted.)

Industry and year	January	February	March	April	May	June	July	August	September	October	November	December	Annual average
Trade, Transportation, and Utilities													
1990	252.2	248.5	250.2	249.7	251.9	253.2	252.4	253.3	253.6	254.5	258.1	260.3	253.2
2000	259.0	255.0	256.8	257.9	259.1	259.4	258.7	258.1	259.3	261.2	265.4	269.3	259.9
2001	258.8	255.1	256.1	256.6	256.8	257.6	254.5	253.5	254.5	256.5	261.5	264.7	257.2
2002	256.1	252.2	253.4	254.4	256.1	258.9	256.9	257.5	258.7	258.5	263.5	267.1	257.8
2003	258.8	254.8	255.3	256.0	256.5	256.0	255.7	255.0	254.3	259.1	261.3	264.0	257.2
2004	251.7	248.2	249.8	250.7	252.7	253.3	253.6	252.1	252.1	254.8	259.9	263.2	253.5
2005	253.5	250.4	251.9	253.5	254.5	254.8	254.9	255.4	254.0	254.8	259.7	262.9	255.0
2006	252.9	249.8	251.2	252.4	254.1	255.5	254.3	255.0	254.9	256.6	261.3	265.1	255.3
2007	256.1	253.0	256.1	257.3	259.6	260.3	258.8	258.1	258.4	259.4	265.5	268.2	259.2
2008	260.2	256.7	257.8	258.1	259.6	260.7	258.4	258.8	257.4	256.9	259.5	260.8	258.7
2009	250.5	247.1	246.5	246.7	247.6	247.1	244.7	245.6	245.0	245.6	248.1	249.1	247.0
Wholesale Trade													
1990	62.2	62.2	62.4	62.3	62.7	63.4	63.4	63.7	63.2	62.9	62.8	62.6	62.8
2000	57.7	57.8	58.1	58.5	58.6	59.2	59.1	59.1	59.0	59.0	59.1	59.3	58.7
2001	58.4	58.5	58.5	58.7	58.7	59.0	58.3	58.2	57.7	57.4	57.2	57.4	58.2
2002	56.6	56.5	56.7	56.7	56.9	57.2	56.8	56.8	56.5	56.2	56.0	55.9	56.6
2003	57.1	56.9	56.9	57.5	57.5	57.7	58.5	58.5	57.8	57.9	57.8	57.9	57.7
2004	58.2	58.2	58.6	58.6	58.7	59.1	60.4	59.7	59.5	58.9	58.9	59.1	59.0
2005	59.8	59.2	59.4	59.8	59.8	60.2	60.6	60.8	60.0	59.7	59.8	60.1	59.9
2006	59.5	59.4	59.7	60.5	60.8	61.5	61.6	61.7	61.5	61.5	61.5	62.0	60.9
2007	61.4	61.6	62.0	61.8	62.2	62.7	63.0	62.9	62.7	62.8	62.9	63.1	62.4
2008	62.8	62.8	62.9	63.2	63.4	63.8	63.7	63.7	63.3	62.7	62.2	62.1	63.1
2009	60.9	60.6	60.3	59.9	59.7	59.9	59.8	59.6	59.2	59.0	58.9	59.0	59.7
Retail Trade													
1990	143.1	139.0	139.9	139.3	140.7	141.6	141.8	141.8	141.2	142.6	145.9	148.8	142.1
2000	147.1	143.3	144.6	144.4	145.3	146.1	145.7	145.2	145.1	146.4	151.0	155.0	146.6
2001	146.6	142.7	143.3	143.5	143.7	145.3	143.0	142.1	142.9	144.6	149.8	153.2	145.1
2002	146.1	142.8	143.5	143.9	145.0	146.8	146.0	146.4	147.1	146.6	152.0	156.3	146.9
2003	147.3	143.8	144.9	145.1	146.0	146.5	146.0	146.5	146.0	150.6	154.1	156.8	147.8
2004	145.4	141.9	142.7	143.7	145.2	146.2	145.8	144.6	144.0	147.1	152.1	154.6	146.1
2005	145.9	143.4	144.2	145.2	146.1	146.6	147.1	147.1	145.4	146.9	151.4	153.5	146.9
2006	145.4	142.4	143.4	144.2	145.2	146.2	145.6	145.5	144.7	146.7	151.4	153.9	146.2
2007	146.3	143.3	145.5	146.7	148.0	148.9	147.5	146.4	146.0	146.9	152.6	154.5	147.7
2008	148.0	144.6	145.4	145.5	146.5	147.5	145.8	145.5	143.9	144.2	147.1	148.3	146.0
2009	140.3	137.7	137.6	138.6	139.5	140.1	138.9	139.1	138.3	139.3	142.0	142.4	139.5
Transportation and Utilities													
1990	46.9	47.3	47.9	48.1	48.5	48.2	47.2	47.8	49.2	49.0	49.4	48.9	48.2
2000	54.2	53.9	54.1	55.0	55.2	54.1	53.9	53.8	55.2	55.8	55.3	55.0	54.6
2001	53.8	53.9	54.3	54.4	54.4	53.3	53.2	53.2	53.9	54.5	54.5	54.1	54.0
2002	53.4	52.9	53.2	53.8	54.2	54.9	54.1	54.3	55.1	55.7	55.5	54.9	54.3
2003	54.4	54.1	53.5	53.4	53.0	51.8	51.2	50.0	50.5	50.6	49.4	49.3	51.8
2004	48.1	48.1	48.5	48.4	48.8	48.0	47.4	47.8	48.6	48.8	48.9	49.5	48.4
2005	47.8	47.8	48.3	48.5	48.6	48.0	47.2	47.5	48.6	48.2	48.5	49.3	48.2
2006	48.0	48.0	48.1	47.7	48.1	47.8	47.1	47.8	48.7	48.4	48.4	49.2	48.1
2007	48.4	48.1	48.6	48.8	49.4	48.7	48.3	48.8	49.7	49.7	50.0	50.6	49.1
2008	49.4	49.3	49.5	49.4	49.7	49.4	48.9	49.6	50.2	50.0	50.2	50.4	49.7
2009	49.3	48.8	48.6	48.2	48.4	47.1	46.0	46.9	47.5	47.3	47.2	47.7	47.8
Information													
1990	29.1	28.9	29.1	29.1	28.9	29.3	29.1	28.8	28.6	28.7	28.8	29.0	29.0
2000	31.2	31.2	31.5	31.5	31.7	32.1	32.1	32.1	32.1	32.5	32.9	32.4	31.9
2001	31.7	31.9	32.1	32.0	32.1	32.3	32.2	32.3	31.9	31.5	31.4	31.6	31.9
2002	30.8	30.7	30.5	30.4	30.6	30.5	29.8	29.9	29.4	29.3	29.3	29.4	30.1
2003	30.8	31.1	31.0	29.3	29.0	29.2	29.1	28.9	28.5	28.3	28.3	28.5	29.3
2004	29.5	29.5	29.5	29.5	29.5	29.6	29.5	28.8	28.8	29.4	29.4	29.3	29.4
2005	29.1	29.1	29.1	29.4	29.4	29.7	30.0	29.9	29.9	30.1	30.1	30.3	29.7
2006	30.1	29.9	29.9	29.9	30.0	30.2	30.4	30.3	30.1	30.5	30.5	30.7	30.2
2007	29.8	29.7	29.8	30.1	30.4	30.6	30.4	30.4	30.3	30.7	30.9	30.9	30.3
2008	30.4	30.2	30.3	30.8	31.2	31.3	31.2	31.0	30.8	30.9	31.0	31.1	30.9
2009	30.8	30.7	30.6	30.4	30.3	30.5	30.5	30.4	30.3	30.0	29.9	30.0	30.4
Financial Activities													
1990	69.6	69.8	70.3	70.3	70.8	71.4	71.1	71.2	70.6	69.9	69.6	69.9	70.4
2000	74.4	74.3	74.1	74.8	75.0	76.0	76.0	75.8	75.0	74.8	74.7	75.1	75.0
2001	74.8	74.8	75.4	75.9	76.5	77.3	77.4	77.3	76.4	76.2	76.5	76.9	76.3
2002	76.6	76.7	77.2	77.4	77.9	78.5	78.7	79.0	78.4	78.8	79.2	80.0	78.2
2003	77.8	77.7	78.1	78.5	78.9	79.7	79.7	80.1	79.0	78.9	78.5	78.6	78.8
2004	76.7	76.5	76.7	76.9	77.2	78.0	78.9	78.7	77.9	78.3	78.1	78.5	77.7
2005	76.5	76.9	77.0	78.1	78.0	78.7	79.3	79.2	78.9	78.4	78.2	78.5	78.1
2006	77.5	77.7	77.9	78.6	79.2	79.7	79.6	79.7	79.2	79.0	79.1	79.3	78.9
2007	78.7	78.8	79.0	79.2	80.0	80.5	80.7	80.5	79.8	79.9	79.5	79.8	79.7
2008	80.2	80.4	80.5	80.0	80.1	80.2	79.7	80.0	79.2	78.5	78.3	78.2	79.6
2009	78.3	78.5	78.6	79.1	79.2	79.5	79.5	79.3	78.7	78.9	79.4	79.9	79.1

Employment by Industry: St. Louis, MO-IL, Selected Years, 1990–2009—*Continued*

(Numbers in thousands, not seasonally adjusted.)

Industry and year	January	February	March	April	May	June	July	August	September	October	November	December	Annual average
Professional and Business Services													
1990	144.0	144.5	145.2	146.1	147.2	148.7	150.1	150.9	150.9	148.8	148.4	148.6	147.8
2000	182.4	182.4	185.2	189.7	188.6	192.6	192.2	192.9	189.6	189.4	189.8	189.6	188.7
2001	184.6	185.8	188.9	188.7	188.2	189.6	187.1	188.3	184.7	184.3	183.0	183.2	186.4
2002	177.7	178.6	179.6	180.1	179.2	180.3	179.1	179.8	178.3	178.4	178.7	178.6	179.0
2003	176.1	177.1	178.2	178.4	177.4	178.9	178.9	180.0	178.8	179.9	178.2	178.4	178.4
2004	174.7	175.0	178.7	180.1	179.2	181.5	180.8	181.8	181.0	181.6	181.5	182.0	179.8
2005	180.7	181.8	184.5	188.8	187.4	189.3	188.1	188.9	188.9	188.4	188.6	188.9	187.0
2006	185.7	186.6	189.3	192.4	192.1	195.3	193.5	194.7	194.8	195.7	194.5	196.0	192.6
2007	189.1	189.7	192.3	194.8	194.9	195.7	195.0	195.7	195.3	195.3	194.9	195.2	194.0
2008	193.7	195.2	196.8	200.3	199.1	200.4	198.7	198.7	195.9	194.1	191.5	189.6	196.2
2009	183.9	183.7	182.4	184.3	182.9	182.8	181.2	180.9	179.3	179.5	178.8	178.8	181.5
Education and Health Services													
1990	130.5	132.1	132.6	133.2	133.5	134.2	134.9	135.8	137.3	138.6	139.0	139.3	135.1
2000	176.6	177.6	178.3	179.3	179.2	179.5	179.4	179.3	180.3	180.5	181.3	181.3	179.4
2001	178.8	181.1	181.9	183.8	184.0	184.6	184.7	185.1	185.9	187.0	188.2	188.9	184.5
2002	186.2	188.6	188.9	190.6	191.8	191.9	191.8	192.7	193.9	193.5	194.3	194.8	191.6
2003	190.1	191.5	192.1	191.4	191.0	190.6	191.0	190.9	192.3	192.8	192.9	193.8	191.7
2004	190.1	192.6	193.3	193.8	193.6	193.0	193.3	193.0	194.8	196.7	197.1	196.9	194.0
2005	194.7	197.3	197.6	198.2	197.5	197.0	196.8	196.4	199.2	200.3	201.0	201.6	198.1
2006	198.9	201.8	203.0	203.0	202.7	202.5	201.1	200.9	203.8	206.0	206.6	207.0	203.1
2007	203.3	206.0	207.1	207.9	208.0	207.4	207.2	207.0	209.5	211.1	212.1	212.6	208.3
2008	207.5	210.7	210.5	211.2	211.1	210.3	210.0	210.3	212.8	214.2	214.9	215.2	211.6
2009	211.9	214.1	214.3	213.7	213.8	212.2	211.4	211.3	214.1	216.0	216.9	216.5	213.9
Leisure and Hospitality													
1990	97.3	97.8	100.7	104.3	107.6	111.5	112.1	112.6	110.6	104.8	102.9	101.2	105.3
2000	120.9	120.9	123.6	129.3	133.7	137.4	135.8	136.9	133.1	132.2	127.4	124.3	129.6
2001	119.9	121.0	124.1	130.8	135.3	138.2	138.6	137.3	132.7	132.8	128.6	127.1	130.5
2002	122.0	122.2	125.1	132.5	135.6	140.4	140.0	140.4	135.4	135.2	130.2	129.0	132.3
2003	123.1	123.4	125.6	132.9	137.0	139.7	140.9	139.6	137.0	134.2	131.8	130.9	133.0
2004	128.1	127.3	130.2	137.7	141.3	143.9	144.4	144.1	140.4	140.3	136.4	135.2	137.4
2005	129.1	129.9	133.5	140.6	143.6	146.5	147.3	147.1	144.1	140.6	137.4	137.0	139.7
2006	132.7	133.7	136.4	143.6	147.1	150.4	149.4	149.2	145.0	142.1	138.1	138.2	142.2
2007	133.7	133.8	137.7	142.7	147.7	151.2	149.8	150.2	145.1	142.0	139.2	139.6	142.7
2008	134.7	134.4	136.8	140.6	146.9	150.3	147.7	147.9	142.3	138.4	135.4	134.7	140.8
2009	130.5	129.9	133.3	139.7	144.7	147.4	145.9	145.7	138.4	137.4	136.3	134.8	138.7
Other Services													
1990	48.0	48.0	48.7	48.8	49.5	51.0	51.1	51.1	49.9	50.0	49.7	49.9	49.6
2000	55.8	56.4	57.6	58.4	59.2	60.0	59.0	59.0	58.3	58.3	58.1	58.1	58.2
2001	56.6	57.7	59.4	59.5	60.3	61.1	59.8	60.0	59.2	58.8	59.6	59.8	59.3
2002	57.5	58.8	59.6	60.2	60.0	60.6	60.0	59.9	59.2	59.1	59.1	59.1	59.4
2003	57.2	58.0	58.5	59.0	59.5	60.0	58.9	58.5	57.7	57.8	57.5	57.8	58.4
2004	56.6	57.1	57.9	58.2	58.0	58.3	58.8	58.3	58.0	58.6	58.3	58.6	58.1
2005	57.0	57.5	58.0	57.9	57.7	58.4	57.9	57.7	56.9	57.4	57.1	57.4	57.6
2006	56.6	56.7	57.1	57.7	57.7	58.5	58.2	58.2	57.9	57.6	57.5	57.7	57.6
2007	56.7	56.9	57.4	57.6	57.9	58.2	57.8	57.8	57.1	57.4	57.5	57.3	57.5
2008	56.8	56.8	57.2	57.5	58.1	58.4	58.1	57.9	57.3	57.6	57.1	56.7	57.5
2009	55.6	55.5	55.8	56.1	56.2	56.0	55.6	55.2	54.5	54.3	54.3	54.0	55.2
Government													
1990	141.2	142.8	144.3	146.8	144.8	145.9	120.5	120.2	140.2	143.3	146.7	144.7	140.1
2000	164.9	167.2	168.9	169.1	169.9	169.3	145.8	147.7	168.8	168.8	170.4	170.9	165.1
2001	167.4	170.1	170.8	171.1	172.1	172.3	148.7	150.3	169.2	171.0	172.5	173.1	167.4
2002	170.2	171.5	172.0	172.0	173.8	170.3	148.0	151.2	169.0	171.8	173.0	172.8	168.0
2003	169.0	170.6	171.1	172.1	173.3	170.4	149.3	151.1	167.6	169.8	170.7	170.4	167.1
2004	168.0	169.4	169.9	170.5	171.7	167.3	148.6	152.0	168.2	169.9	170.9	170.9	166.4
2005	167.2	170.3	170.2	172.0	172.9	168.9	150.8	156.2	169.5	170.5	172.0	171.5	167.7
2006	167.9	170.8	171.1	172.3	173.4	167.5	151.0	154.8	170.5	172.3	173.4	173.5	168.2
2007	169.6	172.7	172.8	173.2	174.4	168.4	146.5	153.4	171.1	174.1	175.3	175.0	168.9
2008	171.0	175.4	174.5	174.9	176.9	170.6	149.6	157.0	173.9	176.8	176.9	176.4	171.2
2009	173.1	175.5	176.3	176.9	178.2	173.2	155.0	163.1	179.4	181.1	181.8	181.5	174.6

Employment by Industry: Tampa-St. Petersburg-Clearwater, FL, Selected Years, 1990–2009

(Numbers in thousands, not seasonally adjusted.)

Industry and year	January	February	March	April	May	June	July	August	September	October	November	December	Annual average
Total Nonfarm													
1990	859.0	868.9	876.3	874.4	874.7	874.7	853.9	863.7	869.7	867.3	874.4	876.7	869.5
2000	1136.6	1151.6	1170.8	1167.1	1171.5	1158.5	1141.8	1155.9	1161.1	1158.6	1170.4	1177.2	1160.1
2001	1137.9	1151.2	1161.1	1156.1	1156.2	1145.4	1131.8	1145.1	1143.0	1145.2	1152.6	1157.6	1148.6
2002	1130.1	1142.9	1150.0	1148.0	1149.0	1132.5	1121.6	1134.3	1135.2	1137.8	1150.9	1157.0	1140.8
2003	1130.6	1139.6	1150.1	1146.3	1145.6	1132.5	1123.2	1136.4	1139.5	1146.5	1151.2	1159.5	1141.8
2004	1151.0	1164.6	1176.8	1185.9	1187.5	1177.8	1170.2	1182.1	1183.3	1195.7	1207.6	1216.5	1183.3
2005	1200.4	1214.8	1221.3	1226.7	1229.1	1215.3	1210.1	1222.6	1227.7	1226.7	1236.2	1243.9	1222.9
2006	1227.5	1237.4	1253.9	1252.3	1255.0	1244.3	1233.0	1250.2	1253.0	1249.9	1257.7	1266.4	1248.4
2007	1245.0	1253.5	1265.5	1259.9	1256.7	1247.5	1229.5	1242.3	1238.8	1236.6	1244.6	1249.0	1247.4
2008	1223.6	1231.5	1236.3	1223.0	1217.9	1201.1	1184.8	1195.3	1190.2	1184.6	1183.9	1185.8	1204.9
2009	1155.8	1156.4	1156.8	1149.7	1142.9	1127.1	1113.8	1123.8	1124.3	1123.8	1126.4	1128.2	1135.8
Total Private													
1990	744.5	753.2	759.8	757.4	757.3	758.4	747.2	752.0	751.5	748.2	753.9	758.1	753.5
2000	994.8	1009.2	1027.6	1022.2	1024.2	1025.3	1010.0	1014.6	1017.0	1012.6	1022.6	1029.3	1017.5
2001	992.2	1003.7	1012.8	1008.0	1007.4	1007.6	995.6	998.2	994.9	995.5	1002.9	1007.0	1002.2
2002	983.1	994.1	1000.9	998.9	1000.9	996.0	986.4	988.0	987.2	988.2	1000.3	1005.3	994.1
2003	983.3	990.3	1001.0	998.3	997.2	996.0	987.7	990.4	992.1	997.7	1002.3	1011.1	995.6
2004	1004.8	1015.4	1028.0	1036.9	1038.1	1040.3	1033.4	1034.8	1034.6	1045.4	1056.7	1065.6	1036.2
2005	1051.9	1063.7	1071.0	1077.2	1079.2	1077.2	1072.8	1074.8	1077.9	1075.6	1084.7	1093.2	1074.9
2006	1077.9	1087.0	1103.6	1101.5	1104.7	1105.8	1095.6	1101.0	1100.9	1096.1	1104.2	1113.5	1099.3
2007	1092.7	1100.1	1111.4	1106.1	1104.5	1105.2	1088.2	1091.1	1084.7	1081.2	1089.2	1094.0	1095.7
2008	1070.2	1075.7	1081.1	1068.2	1064.7	1059.4	1043.4	1042.8	1034.5	1028.2	1026.9	1027.8	1051.9
2009	1000.2	998.3	999.3	991.2	987.3	981.6	969.6	969.4	966.7	965.5	968.0	970.3	980.6
Goods-Producing													
1990	140.5	141.1	140.9	139.7	140.3	140.7	138.7	139.5	139.1	137.2	135.5	134.3	139.0
2000	153.7	155.4	157.6	156.6	157.5	160.2	158.3	158.9	159.4	156.9	157.5	157.2	157.4
2001	152.0	152.2	152.6	151.9	152.2	152.8	152.2	152.5	151.6	150.8	151.3	151.2	151.9
2002	148.4	148.3	148.4	148.2	148.6	149.5	149.2	150.5	151.0	151.0	151.2	150.8	149.6
2003	147.1	148.0	147.9	147.4	148.1	148.7	147.4	148.3	148.2	148.0	147.9	149.1	148.0
2004	148.8	150.1	152.1	154.5	154.9	155.9	156.3	157.0	157.8	160.1	160.2	161.0	155.7
2005	159.3	160.8	161.9	162.9	164.1	165.3	167.0	167.7	168.6	168.9	170.2	170.7	165.6
2006	169.4	170.6	172.4	172.6	173.6	174.6	172.8	173.6	173.0	171.6	170.6	170.4	172.1
2007	168.1	168.3	169.0	165.4	165.4	165.5	162.0	161.2	160.3	157.6	156.3	155.9	162.9
2008	152.5	153.2	153.0	150.5	150.2	150.2	147.6	146.4	144.6	141.5	139.0	136.6	147.1
2009	130.3	128.5	126.8	124.6	123.3	122.6	120.4	119.5	118.3	117.4	114.7	114.1	121.7
Mining and Logging													
1990	0.7	0.7	0.7	0.6	0.6	0.6	0.6	0.6	0.6	0.6	0.6	0.6	0.6
2000	0.5	0.5	0.5	0.5	0.5	0.5	0.5	0.5	0.5	0.5	0.5	0.5	0.5
2001	0.5	0.5	0.5	0.5	0.5	0.5	0.5	0.5	0.5	0.5	0.5	0.5	0.5
2002	0.5	0.5	0.5	0.5	0.5	0.5	0.5	0.5	0.5	0.5	0.5	0.5	0.5
2003	0.5	0.5	0.5	0.5	0.5	0.5	0.5	0.5	0.5	0.5	0.6	0.6	0.5
2004	0.6	0.6	0.6	0.6	0.6	0.6	0.6	0.6	0.6	0.6	0.6	0.6	0.6
2005	0.6	0.6	0.6	0.6	0.7	0.7	0.7	0.8	0.8	0.8	0.8	0.8	0.7
2006	0.9	0.9	0.9	0.9	0.9	0.8	0.7	0.6	0.6	0.6	0.6	0.7	0.8
2007	0.6	0.6	0.6	0.7	0.7	0.7	0.7	0.7	0.7	0.7	0.7	0.7	0.7
2008	0.7	0.6	0.7	0.7	0.7	0.7	0.6	0.6	0.6	0.5	0.5	0.5	0.6
2009	0.5	0.5	0.5	0.5	0.5	0.5	0.5	0.5	0.5	0.5	0.5	0.5	0.5
Construction													
1990	54.8	54.8	55.0	54.6	54.8	55.0	54.8	55.4	55.4	54.9	53.8	53.1	54.7
2000	64.4	65.4	66.7	66.8	67.4	69.2	67.9	68.3	68.7	67.8	68.4	68.3	67.4
2001	65.0	65.5	66.0	66.3	67.0	67.7	68.1	68.2	68.2	67.7	68.5	68.6	67.2
2002	67.0	67.4	67.4	67.6	68.4	68.7	68.8	69.9	70.5	71.0	71.4	71.2	69.1
2003	69.1	70.1	70.3	70.4	71.4	72.1	71.5	72.4	72.3	72.5	72.5	73.6	71.5
2004	73.2	74.3	75.8	77.2	77.6	78.1	78.9	79.3	80.2	82.3	82.4	83.1	78.5
2005	82.6	83.9	84.9	85.5	86.5	87.3	88.9	89.2	89.7	90.0	91.2	91.7	87.6
2006	90.5	91.6	92.8	93.5	94.2	94.8	94.0	94.5	94.1	93.2	92.4	92.2	93.2
2007	90.8	90.8	91.7	88.4	88.3	88.5	85.8	85.1	84.4	82.6	81.9	81.7	86.7
2008	78.7	79.5	79.3	77.5	77.3	77.4	75.3	74.6	73.6	71.6	70.0	68.6	75.3
2009	63.9	62.7	61.8	60.8	60.0	59.8	59.0	58.5	57.9	58.0	56.0	55.6	59.5
Manufacturing													
1990	85.0	85.6	85.2	84.5	84.9	85.1	83.3	83.5	83.1	81.7	81.1	80.6	83.6
2000	88.8	89.5	90.4	89.3	89.6	90.5	89.9	90.1	90.2	88.6	88.6	88.4	89.5
2001	86.5	86.2	86.1	85.1	84.7	84.6	83.6	83.8	82.9	82.6	82.3	82.1	84.2
2002	80.9	80.4	80.5	80.1	79.7	80.3	79.9	80.1	80.0	79.5	79.3	79.1	80.0
2003	77.5	77.4	77.1	76.5	76.2	76.1	75.4	75.4	75.4	75.0	74.8	74.9	76.0
2004	75.0	75.2	75.7	76.7	76.7	77.2	76.8	77.1	77.0	77.2	77.2	77.3	76.6
2005	76.1	76.3	76.4	76.8	76.9	77.3	77.4	77.7	78.1	78.1	78.2	78.2	77.3
2006	78.0	78.1	78.7	78.2	78.5	79.0	78.1	78.5	78.3	77.8	77.6	77.5	78.2
2007	76.7	76.9	76.7	76.3	76.4	76.3	75.5	75.4	75.2	74.3	73.7	73.5	75.6
2008	73.1	73.1	73.0	72.3	72.2	72.1	71.7	71.2	70.4	69.4	68.5	67.5	71.2
2009	65.9	65.3	64.5	63.3	62.8	62.3	60.9	60.5	59.9	58.9	58.2	58.0	61.7

Employment by Industry: Tampa-St. Petersburg-Clearwater, FL, Selected Years, 1990–2009—*Continued*

(Numbers in thousands, not seasonally adjusted.)

Industry and year	January	February	March	April	May	June	July	August	September	October	November	December	Annual average
Service-Providing													
1990	718.5	727.8	735.4	734.7	734.4	734.0	715.2	724.2	730.6	730.1	738.9	742.4	730.5
2000	982.9	996.2	1013.2	1010.5	1014.0	998.3	983.5	997.0	1001.7	1001.7	1012.9	1020.0	1002.7
2001	985.9	999.0	1008.5	1004.2	1004.0	992.6	979.6	992.6	991.4	994.4	1001.3	1006.4	996.7
2002	981.7	994.6	1001.6	999.8	1000.4	983.0	972.4	983.8	984.2	986.8	999.7	1006.2	991.2
2003	983.5	991.6	1002.2	998.9	997.5	983.8	975.8	988.1	991.3	998.5	1003.3	1010.4	993.7
2004	1002.2	1014.5	1024.7	1031.4	1032.6	1021.9	1013.9	1025.1	1025.5	1035.6	1047.4	1055.5	1027.5
2005	1041.1	1054.0	1059.4	1063.8	1065.0	1050.0	1043.1	1054.9	1059.1	1057.8	1066.0	1073.2	1057.3
2006	1058.1	1066.8	1081.5	1079.7	1081.4	1069.7	1060.2	1076.6	1080.0	1078.3	1087.1	1096.0	1076.3
2007	1076.9	1085.2	1096.5	1094.5	1091.3	1082.0	1067.5	1081.1	1078.5	1079.0	1088.3	1093.1	1084.5
2008	1071.1	1078.3	1083.3	1072.5	1067.7	1051.9	1037.2	1048.9	1045.6	1043.1	1044.9	1049.2	1057.8
2009	1025.5	1027.9	1030.0	1025.1	1019.6	1004.5	993.4	1004.3	1006.0	1006.4	1011.7	1014.1	1014.0
Trade, Transportation, and Utilities													
1990	204.0	203.8	205.1	204.3	204.6	204.2	201.2	202.2	201.1	201.2	205.0	210.2	203.9
2000	236.7	237.7	240.6	237.9	239.2	240.5	237.3	239.3	239.4	240.0	246.3	249.8	240.4
2001	233.7	233.1	233.9	230.9	230.8	230.4	228.0	228.4	228.6	229.9	234.8	237.8	231.7
2002	231.1	229.4	229.5	228.1	228.3	226.0	224.0	225.5	223.9	225.1	227.9	231.6	227.5
2003	221.1	219.8	219.8	219.3	220.2	219.3	218.5	218.8	219.9	222.6	225.4	228.9	221.1
2004	224.4	224.0	224.4	224.4	225.2	225.1	223.8	223.6	223.5	226.8	232.2	236.0	226.1
2005	230.1	230.2	231.2	233.0	233.7	233.1	232.0	232.1	232.0	233.4	238.0	242.5	233.4
2006	236.0	235.4	237.4	235.2	235.6	234.7	233.1	233.4	233.2	233.4	238.3	242.4	235.7
2007	234.7	233.5	234.7	233.5	234.2	233.7	231.3	232.0	232.0	231.9	237.9	240.4	234.2
2008	232.6	231.7	231.7	228.4	228.2	226.3	223.5	223.0	221.3	221.2	223.7	225.6	226.4
2009	216.3	213.7	212.3	209.9	210.2	208.6	206.1	206.3	206.0	205.4	208.4	210.2	209.5
Wholesale Trade													
1990	45.5	45.9	46.1	45.8	46.1	46.0	45.6	45.8	45.6	45.2	45.3	45.6	45.7
2000	54.4	54.6	55.3	55.5	56.0	56.7	55.5	55.7	56.1	56.4	57.0	57.4	55.9
2001	55.7	55.7	55.8	55.3	55.0	54.6	54.0	54.0	53.8	53.9	53.7	54.1	54.6
2002	54.1	54.1	54.1	53.6	53.9	53.4	52.9	52.9	52.7	52.6	52.6	52.7	53.3
2003	51.0	51.1	50.8	51.0	51.0	50.6	50.1	50.0	50.0	49.8	49.8	50.0	50.4
2004	50.4	50.9	50.7	50.6	50.8	51.1	50.7	50.8	50.8	51.0	51.5	51.8	50.9
2005	52.1	52.1	52.6	52.9	53.3	53.1	52.6	52.6	52.6	52.8	52.9	53.6	52.8
2006	53.3	53.5	53.8	53.8	54.2	54.0	53.7	54.0	54.0	54.1	54.6	55.0	54.0
2007	54.4	54.5	54.6	54.3	54.6	54.5	53.8	54.0	53.8	54.0	54.6	54.8	54.3
2008	54.3	54.3	54.2	53.8	54.0	53.4	52.5	52.2	51.8	51.5	51.4	51.2	52.9
2009	50.0	49.4	49.1	48.5	48.7	48.0	47.1	47.1	47.0	46.3	47.1	47.0	47.9
Retail Trade													
1990	128.1	127.2	127.9	127.0	126.9	126.4	124.4	124.9	124.0	124.6	128.0	131.6	126.8
2000	146.2	146.7	148.1	145.7	146.2	146.6	144.3	146.0	145.8	147.1	152.2	154.9	147.5
2001	143.5	142.8	143.5	141.2	141.3	141.3	139.9	140.4	141.0	142.5	147.6	149.6	142.9
2002	144.0	142.3	142.8	141.7	141.8	140.1	138.7	140.2	139.4	140.7	143.8	147.2	141.9
2003	139.6	138.3	138.5	137.8	138.5	138.2	137.5	137.8	138.6	141.3	144.1	146.6	139.7
2004	142.3	141.3	141.8	141.8	142.2	141.9	141.2	140.9	141.1	143.9	148.7	151.9	143.3
2005	146.2	146.1	146.5	147.9	148.4	148.3	148.0	148.2	148.2	149.5	153.8	156.7	149.0
2006	151.5	150.7	152.3	150.3	150.3	149.8	148.7	148.8	148.9	149.6	153.9	156.5	150.9
2007	151.0	150.0	150.9	150.2	150.8	150.3	148.6	149.0	149.3	149.1	154.3	155.8	150.8
2008	150.1	149.1	149.2	146.4	146.0	144.9	143.6	143.6	142.4	142.5	145.1	146.2	145.8
2009	139.4	137.8	137.0	135.4	135.6	134.9	133.5	133.9	133.8	133.7	135.9	137.0	135.7
Transportation and Utilities													
1990	30.4	30.7	31.1	31.5	31.6	31.8	31.2	31.5	31.5	31.4	31.7	33.0	31.5
2000	36.1	36.4	37.2	36.7	37.0	37.2	37.5	37.6	37.5	36.5	37.1	37.5	37.0
2001	34.5	34.6	34.6	34.4	34.5	34.5	34.1	34.0	33.8	33.3	33.5	34.1	34.2
2002	33.0	33.0	32.6	32.8	32.6	32.5	32.4	32.4	31.8	31.8	31.5	31.7	32.3
2003	30.5	30.4	30.5	30.5	30.7	30.5	30.9	31.0	31.3	31.5	31.5	32.3	31.0
2004	31.7	31.8	31.9	32.0	32.2	32.1	31.9	31.9	31.6	31.9	32.0	32.3	31.9
2005	31.8	32.0	32.1	32.2	32.0	31.7	31.4	31.3	31.2	31.1	31.3	32.2	31.7
2006	31.2	31.2	31.3	31.1	31.1	30.9	30.7	30.6	30.3	29.7	29.8	30.9	30.7
2007	29.3	29.0	29.2	29.0	28.8	28.9	28.9	29.0	28.9	28.8	29.0	29.8	29.1
2008	28.2	28.3	28.3	28.2	28.2	28.0	27.4	27.2	27.1	27.2	27.2	28.2	27.8
2009	26.9	26.5	26.2	26.0	25.9	25.7	25.5	25.3	25.2	25.4	25.4	26.2	25.9
Information													
1990	26.4	26.3	25.9	25.5	25.6	25.9	25.6	25.7	25.7	25.7	25.8	25.5	25.8
2000	37.3	37.6	38.3	37.6	37.9	38.9	38.7	39.0	39.5	40.2	40.7	40.9	38.9
2001	39.7	39.7	39.7	39.3	38.9	38.5	38.2	37.5	36.7	36.7	36.5	35.8	38.1
2002	35.9	35.5	35.7	35.3	35.2	34.8	34.6	34.5	34.6	34.4	34.9	34.8	35.0
2003	34.3	34.1	34.2	34.5	34.4	34.0	33.9	33.6	33.5	32.9	32.9	32.8	33.8
2004	32.6	32.3	32.9	32.0	32.1	32.2	31.6	31.8	31.8	31.8	31.9	32.0	32.1
2005	31.6	31.6	31.8	31.5	31.6	31.6	31.8	32.0	32.4	32.2	32.3	32.2	31.9
2006	32.1	32.2	32.0	31.8	31.9	32.0	31.8	31.7	31.6	31.5	31.6	31.7	31.8
2007	31.6	31.8	31.9	32.1	32.2	32.4	31.9	31.9	31.7	31.4	31.4	31.3	31.8
2008	30.9	31.1	31.0	31.0	30.9	30.7	30.3	30.0	29.5	29.6	29.3	29.0	30.3
2009	28.7	28.6	28.5	28.2	28.0	27.8	27.8	27.4	27.2	27.4	27.3	26.9	27.8

Employment by Industry: Tampa-St. Petersburg-Clearwater, FL, Selected Years, 1990–2009—*Continued*

(Numbers in thousands, not seasonally adjusted.)

Industry and year	January	February	March	April	May	June	July	August	September	October	November	December	Annual average
Financial Activities													
1990	65.2	65.7	65.9	66.4	66.8	66.9	67.2	67.5	67.2	66.5	66.9	67.3	66.6
2000	89.6	90.1	91.0	91.8	91.9	91.8	91.7	91.8	92.0	91.9	92.5	92.8	91.6
2001	91.3	92.1	92.8	93.2	93.1	93.3	92.2	92.4	91.9	91.7	91.8	91.9	92.3
2002	91.3	92.3	92.3	91.9	92.0	92.4	92.7	92.9	92.5	92.8	93.4	93.9	92.5
2003	92.9	93.6	93.7	93.9	94.2	94.4	94.3	94.6	94.0	93.8	93.6	94.1	93.9
2004	93.7	94.2	94.6	95.8	95.9	95.6	95.4	95.5	95.3	96.2	96.6	97.1	95.5
2005	96.7	97.4	97.4	98.6	99.0	99.8	100.1	99.5	100.0	100.8	101.3	102.7	99.4
2006	101.7	102.5	103.1	103.3	103.5	103.4	102.6	102.6	102.2	102.3	102.1	102.8	102.7
2007	101.7	102.7	102.8	102.9	102.7	102.5	102.2	101.3	100.9	100.6	100.5	100.3	101.8
2008	99.0	99.0	98.7	97.8	97.6	97.1	96.8	96.5	95.9	95.7	95.5	95.4	97.1
2009	94.5	93.8	93.5	92.9	92.9	92.5	91.8	91.5	90.7	91.2	90.7	91.7	92.3
Professional and Business Services													
1990	61.1	63.7	65.3	66.2	65.4	67.4	65.8	67.5	67.7	68.9	69.8	66.9	66.3
2000	184.1	189.1	195.2	192.9	193.5	191.0	185.1	187.5	188.4	186.0	186.1	188.0	188.9
2001	180.6	187.4	189.8	188.3	186.8	187.5	182.8	184.3	183.2	181.6	182.4	182.0	184.7
2002	175.1	182.3	183.5	183.6	183.9	181.4	178.8	174.9	174.6	173.7	180.1	179.4	179.3
2003	177.2	181.5	188.0	186.5	183.4	183.2	180.6	180.7	181.1	186.1	187.0	188.7	183.7
2004	188.9	193.4	197.6	203.9	203.1	205.4	203.6	203.4	201.8	205.1	208.0	211.1	202.1
2005	207.3	212.7	213.7	215.6	215.0	213.3	212.4	213.8	215.7	211.6	213.3	214.1	213.2
2006	212.1	214.9	221.7	222.3	223.2	224.4	223.7	226.2	225.5	222.1	223.6	225.4	222.1
2007	221.6	222.9	226.1	226.3	224.1	226.0	221.8	223.3	218.5	217.2	217.7	218.1	222.0
2008	212.6	213.7	215.3	210.6	208.7	209.2	206.6	206.9	204.5	201.5	200.7	201.7	207.7
2009	197.0	197.4	197.5	195.9	194.2	194.8	192.8	193.4	192.9	189.8	192.0	192.1	194.2
Education and Health Services													
1990	107.4	108.8	109.5	109.7	110.1	110.3	109.8	110.4	111.6	111.4	112.1	113.1	110.4
2000	140.0	141.5	142.3	142.2	140.7	139.7	139.0	139.7	140.8	140.4	141.3	141.6	140.8
2001	138.0	139.0	140.1	140.4	140.6	141.1	139.4	140.7	141.8	142.4	143.2	144.4	140.9
2002	140.2	141.3	142.8	143.2	144.0	143.7	142.5	143.8	144.7	145.7	147.1	147.7	143.9
2003	144.5	145.8	147.1	147.9	148.5	148.1	147.5	149.4	150.6	150.1	150.9	151.5	148.5
2004	150.0	151.3	152.1	153.1	153.8	153.3	152.2	153.1	153.7	154.2	155.2	155.6	153.1
2005	153.8	154.7	155.3	156.4	156.0	155.4	154.4	155.3	155.5	156.2	156.7	157.5	155.6
2006	155.9	157.4	158.6	158.9	159.2	158.5	157.1	158.3	160.0	161.1	162.6	164.0	159.3
2007	162.1	163.9	165.8	166.1	166.3	166.1	164.0	166.1	167.1	168.9	170.5	171.3	166.5
2008	169.5	170.8	171.9	171.5	171.8	170.0	168.3	169.6	170.2	171.4	172.8	173.5	170.9
2009	170.0	170.8	172.2	171.9	172.1	170.8	170.1	170.7	171.9	175.0	176.2	176.8	172.4
Leisure and Hospitality													
1990	101.6	105.0	108.0	106.7	105.7	104.2	100.5	100.8	100.7	99.1	100.6	102.4	102.9
2000	109.2	113.1	117.3	118.4	118.3	117.7	114.8	113.6	112.6	112.3	113.2	114.0	114.5
2001	113.0	116.2	119.3	119.2	119.5	117.6	117.1	116.7	115.4	116.6	116.6	117.2	117.0
2002	114.3	117.7	121.1	121.4	121.4	120.1	116.7	117.9	117.9	116.7	116.7	117.8	118.3
2003	117.1	118.5	121.5	120.8	120.4	120.0	117.8	117.8	117.5	117.3	117.6	118.6	118.7
2004	118.6	121.8	125.2	124.6	124.0	122.9	121.2	121.4	121.4	121.6	122.5	122.9	122.3
2005	123.0	125.7	128.9	128.6	129.1	128.0	125.6	125.6	125.1	124.7	125.3	126.1	126.3
2006	124.8	127.5	131.3	130.6	130.2	130.0	127.2	128.2	128.2	126.9	128.1	129.1	128.5
2007	126.0	129.2	132.6	132.7	131.8	130.5	127.7	128.0	127.0	125.7	126.4	127.5	128.8
2008	124.6	127.2	130.3	130.1	128.6	127.1	122.7	123.0	121.8	121.4	120.4	120.7	124.8
2009	118.8	121.0	123.8	123.4	122.0	120.1	116.7	116.6	115.9	115.2	114.9	114.5	118.6
Other Services													
1990	38.3	38.8	39.2	38.9	38.8	38.8	38.4	38.4	38.4	38.2	38.2	38.4	38.6
2000	44.2	44.7	45.3	44.8	45.2	45.5	45.1	44.8	44.9	44.9	45.0	45.0	45.0
2001	43.9	44.0	44.6	44.8	45.5	46.4	45.7	45.7	45.7	45.8	46.3	46.7	45.4
2002	46.8	47.3	47.6	47.2	47.5	48.1	47.9	48.0	48.0	48.8	49.0	49.3	48.0
2003	49.1	49.0	48.8	48.0	48.0	48.3	47.7	47.2	47.3	46.9	47.0	47.4	47.9
2004	47.8	48.3	49.1	48.6	49.1	49.9	49.3	49.0	49.3	49.6	50.1	49.9	49.2
2005	50.1	50.6	50.8	50.6	50.7	50.7	49.5	48.8	48.6	47.8	47.6	47.4	49.4
2006	45.9	46.5	47.1	46.8	47.5	48.2	47.3	47.0	47.2	47.2	47.3	47.7	47.1
2007	46.9	47.8	48.5	47.1	47.8	48.5	47.3	47.3	47.2	47.9	48.5	49.2	47.8
2008	48.5	49.0	49.2	48.3	48.7	48.8	47.6	47.4	46.7	45.9	45.5	45.3	47.6
2009	44.6	44.5	44.7	44.4	44.6	44.4	43.9	44.0	43.8	44.1	43.8	44.0	44.2
Government													
1990	114.5	115.7	116.5	117.0	117.4	116.3	106.7	111.7	118.2	119.1	120.5	118.6	116.0
2000	141.8	142.4	143.2	144.9	147.3	133.2	131.8	141.3	144.1	146.0	147.8	147.9	142.6
2001	145.7	147.5	148.3	148.1	148.8	137.8	136.2	146.9	148.1	149.7	149.7	150.6	146.5
2002	147.0	148.8	149.1	149.1	148.1	136.5	135.2	146.3	148.0	149.6	150.6	151.7	146.7
2003	147.3	149.3	149.1	148.0	148.4	136.5	135.5	146.0	147.4	148.8	148.9	148.4	146.1
2004	146.2	149.2	148.8	149.0	149.4	137.5	136.8	147.3	148.7	150.3	150.9	150.9	147.1
2005	148.5	151.1	150.3	149.5	149.9	138.1	137.3	147.8	149.8	151.1	151.5	150.7	148.0
2006	149.6	150.4	150.3	150.8	150.3	138.5	137.4	149.2	152.1	153.8	153.5	152.9	149.1
2007	152.3	153.4	154.1	153.8	152.2	142.3	141.3	151.2	154.1	155.4	155.4	155.0	151.7
2008	153.4	155.8	155.2	154.8	153.2	142.7	141.4	152.5	155.7	156.4	157.0	158.0	153.0
2009	155.6	158.1	157.5	158.5	155.6	145.5	144.2	154.4	157.6	158.3	158.4	157.9	155.1

Employment by Industry: Tucson, AZ, Selected Years, 1990–2009

(Numbers in thousands, not seasonally adjusted.)

Industry and year	January	February	March	April	May	June	July	August	September	October	November	December	Annual average
Total Nonfarm													
1990	247.1	250.7	253.0	249.5	251.5	242.6	238.6	244.0	249.6	251.6	253.9	255.0	248.9
2000	342.0	347.0	349.9	348.3	349.0	345.0	336.8	340.3	346.0	349.9	353.6	355.5	346.9
2001	341.2	346.9	349.6	349.7	348.1	341.6	333.8	339.3	344.3	343.9	347.3	347.7	344.5
2002	341.1	344.4	345.3	347.0	346.2	338.6	329.2	335.9	341.9	345.7	349.3	350.0	342.9
2003	340.6	343.7	345.8	345.9	346.2	338.6	333.4	340.4	347.0	350.7	353.3	356.8	345.2
2004	350.0	354.0	354.8	359.0	358.8	351.8	345.5	352.0	358.0	363.8	367.6	369.4	357.1
2005	356.3	362.2	364.2	368.5	368.4	361.1	358.7	364.7	370.8	371.4	374.9	378.8	366.7
2006	371.4	378.3	379.0	380.2	380.0	373.5	369.4	375.9	381.6	386.0	388.2	391.8	379.6
2007	380.6	387.5	388.7	387.2	387.2	379.0	375.9	379.3	386.5	388.5	391.5	391.8	385.3
2008	379.2	385.2	385.1	385.6	384.5	376.3	375.4	379.7	382.5	381.7	381.6	380.9	381.5
2009	369.8	369.9	367.5	365.6	363.1	353.2	351.7	356.2	359.5	360.9	362.7	362.1	361.9
Total Private													
1990	195.8	197.1	198.6	194.7	195.9	196.1	193.0	194.6	195.6	196.0	197.2	197.9	196.0
2000	270.2	273.0	274.7	272.8	272.3	273.3	270.2	272.5	273.5	274.7	277.5	279.5	273.7
2001	268.6	271.3	273.2	273.0	271.8	271.0	269.5	270.6	269.6	268.3	269.9	270.5	270.6
2002	266.4	267.5	268.4	268.8	268.8	267.2	264.4	266.4	267.0	268.3	270.9	271.8	268.0
2003	264.9	265.6	267.3	267.7	267.9	267.9	266.7	269.7	271.0	272.6	275.4	277.8	269.5
2004	273.5	275.1	275.9	279.9	279.8	278.2	279.0	280.9	280.1	283.9	287.1	288.6	280.2
2005	280.1	282.7	284.3	288.8	288.8	288.2	288.3	291.3	293.2	293.1	296.0	300.1	289.6
2006	295.7	299.9	300.8	301.6	302.1	302.2	300.9	303.5	305.9	306.8	308.6	311.9	303.3
2007	303.8	307.4	308.9	307.6	308.5	307.5	305.0	305.9	305.9	307.8	310.2	310.7	307.4
2008	302.5	303.8	304.4	303.9	302.7	301.5	300.4	301.7	301.3	299.7	299.0	298.7	301.6
2009	290.2	288.3	286.4	283.7	282.5	280.3	279.3	280.2	279.7	280.8	282.3	282.1	283.0
Goods-Producing													
1990	42.7	42.4	42.6	41.7	42.4	42.6	42.7	43.0	42.6	43.2	42.9	42.7	42.6
2000	56.1	56.2	56.8	56.7	56.6	57.7	57.9	58.5	58.5	58.2	58.5	59.1	57.6
2001	56.9	57.1	57.7	57.5	57.7	58.2	58.4	58.7	58.1	57.3	56.7	56.0	57.5
2002	55.1	54.5	54.6	54.4	54.7	55.0	54.9	55.1	54.7	54.2	54.0	53.9	54.6
2003	53.0	52.3	52.7	52.2	52.6	53.0	52.9	53.1	52.5	53.1	52.9	53.2	52.7
2004	52.9	52.8	52.9	53.2	53.4	53.6	54.2	54.0	54.1	54.4	54.4	54.8	53.7
2005	53.1	53.8	54.2	54.8	55.1	55.8	55.8	56.4	56.5	56.0	56.3	56.9	55.4
2006	56.3	57.3	57.0	57.5	57.8	58.5	58.8	58.6	58.4	58.1	56.6	56.3	57.6
2007	54.9	56.4	56.0	55.5	55.9	56.5	56.4	56.5	55.9	55.2	54.9	54.3	55.7
2008	53.6	53.3	53.2	52.5	52.4	52.8	52.6	52.4	51.6	50.4	49.3	48.3	51.9
2009	46.2	45.1	44.3	43.5	43.3	43.5	43.5	43.0	42.6	42.4	41.9	41.0	43.4
Mining and Logging													
1990	2.2	2.2	2.1	2.1	2.2	2.2	2.2	2.2	2.2	2.2	2.3	2.3	2.2
2000	1.8	1.8	1.8	1.8	1.8	1.8	1.8	1.8	1.8	1.8	1.8	1.8	1.8
2001	1.8	1.8	1.8	1.8	1.8	1.8	1.8	1.8	1.7	1.7	1.7	1.7	1.8
2002	1.7	1.6	1.6	1.6	1.6	1.6	1.4	1.4	1.5	1.4	1.4	1.4	1.5
2003	1.3	1.1	1.2	1.1	1.2	1.2	1.2	1.2	1.2	1.2	1.2	1.2	1.1
2004	1.2	1.2	1.2	1.3	1.3	1.3	1.3	1.3	1.4	1.4	1.4	1.4	1.3
2005	1.4	1.4	1.5	1.5	1.5	1.5	1.2	1.2	1.2	1.2	1.4	1.5	1.4
2006	1.4	1.5	1.5	1.5	1.5	1.6	1.6	1.6	1.6	1.6	1.7	1.7	1.6
2007	1.7	1.7	1.7	1.7	1.8	1.8	1.8	1.8	1.8	1.8	1.8	1.9	1.8
2008	1.9	1.9	1.9	1.9	1.9	2.0	2.0	2.0	2.0	1.9	1.9	1.9	1.9
2009	1.8	1.8	1.7	1.7	1.7	1.7	1.7	1.7	1.7	1.8	1.8	1.8	1.7
Construction													
1990	14.6	14.4	14.6	14.6	15.1	15.4	15.1	15.3	15.1	15.3	15.0	14.7	14.9
2000	22.3	22.3	22.6	22.5	22.5	23.0	23.1	23.5	23.4	23.1	23.0	23.3	22.9
2001	21.9	22.2	22.6	22.3	22.5	22.9	23.3	23.6	23.5	22.9	22.6	22.3	22.7
2002	21.9	21.8	22.0	21.8	22.2	22.6	22.9	23.3	23.0	23.0	23.0	23.0	22.5
2003	22.5	22.3	22.4	22.5	22.8	23.2	23.1	23.2	22.8	23.4	23.3	23.4	22.9
2004	23.3	23.3	23.3	23.6	23.8	23.9	24.3	24.2	24.2	24.6	24.6	24.9	24.0
2005	23.7	24.2	24.6	25.3	25.5	26.0	26.2	26.5	26.8	26.4	26.6	26.8	25.7
2006	26.3	26.7	26.9	27.5	27.9	28.4	28.7	28.7	28.7	28.7	28.5	28.3	27.9
2007	27.1	26.9	26.9	26.5	26.8	27.1	26.9	26.9	26.3	25.8	25.4	24.8	26.5
2008	24.0	23.8	23.8	23.3	23.2	23.3	23.3	23.2	22.6	21.8	20.8	20.0	22.8
2009	18.7	17.8	17.3	16.7	16.6	16.7	16.5	16.2	16.0	15.7	15.2	14.9	16.5
Manufacturing													
1990	25.9	25.8	25.9	25.0	25.1	25.0	25.4	25.5	25.3	25.7	25.6	25.7	25.5
2000	32.0	32.1	32.4	32.4	32.3	32.9	33.0	33.2	33.3	33.3	33.7	34.0	32.9
2001	33.2	33.1	33.3	33.4	33.4	33.5	33.3	33.3	32.9	32.7	32.4	32.0	33.0
2002	31.5	31.1	31.0	31.0	30.9	30.8	30.6	30.4	30.2	29.8	29.6	29.5	30.5
2003	29.2	28.9	29.1	28.6	28.6	28.6	28.6	28.7	28.5	28.5	28.4	28.6	28.6
2004	28.4	28.3	28.4	28.3	28.3	28.4	28.6	28.5	28.5	28.4	28.4	28.5	28.4
2005	28.0	28.2	28.1	28.0	28.1	28.3	28.4	28.7	28.5	28.4	28.3	28.6	28.3
2006	28.6	29.1	28.6	28.5	28.4	28.5	28.5	28.3	28.1	27.8	26.4	26.3	28.1
2007	26.1	27.8	27.4	27.3	27.3	27.6	27.7	27.8	27.8	27.6	27.7	27.6	27.5
2008	27.7	27.6	27.5	27.3	27.3	27.5	27.3	27.2	27.0	26.7	26.6	26.4	27.2
2009	25.7	25.5	25.3	25.1	25.0	25.1	25.3	25.1	24.9	24.9	24.9	24.3	25.1

Employment by Industry: Tucson, AZ, Selected Years, 1990–2009—*Continued*

(Numbers in thousands, not seasonally adjusted.)

Industry and year	January	February	March	April	May	June	July	August	September	October	November	December	Annual average
Service-Providing													
1990	204.4	208.3	210.4	207.8	209.1	200.0	195.9	201.0	207.0	208.4	211.0	212.3	206.3
2000	285.9	290.8	293.1	291.6	292.4	287.3	278.9	281.8	287.5	291.7	295.1	296.4	289.4
2001	284.3	289.8	291.9	292.2	290.4	283.4	275.4	280.6	286.2	286.6	290.6	291.7	286.9
2002	286.0	289.9	290.7	292.6	291.5	283.6	274.3	280.8	287.2	291.5	295.3	296.1	288.3
2003	287.6	291.4	293.1	293.7	293.6	285.6	280.5	287.3	294.5	297.6	300.4	303.6	292.4
2004	297.1	301.2	301.9	305.8	305.4	298.2	291.3	298.0	303.9	309.4	313.2	314.6	303.3
2005	303.2	308.4	310.0	313.7	313.3	305.3	302.9	308.3	314.3	315.4	318.6	321.9	311.3
2006	315.1	321.0	322.0	322.7	322.2	315.0	310.6	317.3	323.2	327.9	331.6	335.5	322.0
2007	325.7	331.1	332.7	331.7	331.3	322.5	319.5	322.8	330.6	333.3	336.6	337.5	329.6
2008	325.6	331.9	331.9	333.1	332.1	323.5	322.8	327.3	330.9	331.3	332.3	332.6	329.6
2009	323.6	324.8	323.2	322.1	319.8	309.7	308.2	313.2	316.9	318.5	320.8	321.1	318.5
Trade, Transportation, and Utilities													
1990	45.6	45.7	46.1	45.1	45.4	45.4	44.5	45.0	45.5	45.3	46.4	46.8	45.6
2000	54.2	54.0	53.8	53.5	53.7	53.8	54.1	54.7	54.9	56.0	57.9	58.9	55.0
2001	55.7	55.2	55.1	55.0	55.0	54.9	54.6	54.6	54.9	54.9	56.5	57.6	55.3
2002	54.1	53.8	53.8	54.0	54.4	54.2	53.5	53.6	53.5	54.4	55.9	57.0	54.4
2003	54.0	54.0	54.4	54.1	54.1	54.2	54.0	54.9	54.9	55.7	57.6	58.8	55.1
2004	56.2	56.1	56.4	57.1	57.8	57.9	57.9	58.0	57.7	58.5	60.3	61.0	57.9
2005	58.0	58.0	58.2	58.3	58.3	58.3	58.8	59.4	59.8	60.8	62.6	64.1	59.6
2006	61.1	61.0	61.2	61.3	61.7	61.5	61.9	62.7	63.1	63.8	65.5	67.0	62.7
2007	63.9	63.3	64.0	63.8	64.1	63.8	63.7	64.0	64.0	64.5	66.1	66.7	64.3
2008	63.6	62.9	63.0	62.2	62.4	62.4	62.2	62.7	62.3	62.5	63.0	63.2	62.7
2009	60.6	59.3	58.6	57.9	57.7	57.1	57.0	57.3	57.2	57.5	58.7	59.2	58.2
Wholesale Trade													
1990	6.2	6.4	6.4	6.2	6.2	6.3	6.2	6.2	6.2	6.1	6.0	6.1	6.2
2000	7.6	7.6	7.6	7.2	7.3	7.4	7.4	7.4	7.4	7.4	7.5	7.6	7.5
2001	7.3	7.3	7.4	7.4	7.4	7.5	7.4	7.4	7.4	7.3	7.4	7.4	7.4
2002	7.5	7.4	7.4	7.2	7.3	7.3	7.2	7.3	7.3	7.4	7.4	7.4	7.3
2003	7.2	7.3	7.3	7.3	7.4	7.4	7.4	7.5	7.5	7.5	7.6	7.6	7.4
2004	7.5	7.5	7.6	8.1	8.4	8.4	8.3	8.2	8.2	8.0	8.1	8.2	8.0
2005	8.0	8.1	8.2	8.3	8.4	8.5	8.6	8.7	8.9	9.0	9.0	9.2	8.6
2006	9.0	9.1	9.2	9.2	9.3	9.4	9.5	9.7	9.8	9.7	9.8	9.9	9.5
2007	9.6	9.6	9.8	9.7	9.8	9.9	9.8	9.9	9.9	9.9	9.9	9.9	9.8
2008	9.7	9.7	9.8	9.7	9.7	9.7	9.7	9.7	9.7	9.6	9.5	9.4	9.7
2009	9.1	8.9	8.6	8.5	8.5	8.4	8.4	8.4	8.4	8.4	8.4	8.5	8.5
Retail Trade													
1990	33.7	33.8	34.1	33.3	33.5	33.4	32.6	33.1	33.6	33.5	34.7	35.0	33.7
2000	38.0	37.9	37.7	37.8	37.9	37.9	37.7	38.3	38.6	39.6	41.3	42.1	38.7
2001	39.0	38.5	38.3	38.3	38.2	38.1	37.9	37.9	38.3	38.6	40.1	41.3	38.7
2002	39.1	38.8	38.8	39.1	39.4	39.2	38.6	38.6	38.7	39.2	40.7	41.8	39.3
2003	39.0	38.9	39.3	39.0	38.9	39.0	38.8	39.2	39.3	40.0	41.8	42.9	39.6
2004	40.6	40.5	40.7	40.8	41.1	41.2	41.3	41.4	41.1	41.7	43.4	43.9	41.5
2005	41.2	41.0	41.0	41.1	41.0	40.8	41.3	41.8	42.0	42.8	44.6	45.8	42.0
2006	43.1	42.9	43.0	43.0	43.2	42.9	43.1	43.7	43.9	44.7	46.2	47.3	43.9
2007	45.1	44.6	45.0	44.9	44.9	44.6	44.6	44.7	44.7	45.3	46.8	47.1	45.2
2008	44.6	43.9	44.0	43.4	43.6	43.6	43.4	43.7	43.3	43.6	44.2	44.2	43.8
2009	42.2	41.1	40.8	40.5	40.4	40.0	39.9	40.2	40.0	40.3	41.5	41.7	40.7
Transportation and Utilities													
1990	5.7	5.5	5.6	5.6	5.7	5.7	5.7	5.7	5.7	5.7	5.7	5.7	5.7
2000	8.6	8.5	8.5	8.5	8.5	8.5	9.0	9.0	8.9	9.0	9.1	9.2	8.8
2001	9.4	9.4	9.4	9.3	9.4	9.3	9.3	9.3	9.2	9.0	9.0	8.9	9.2
2002	7.5	7.6	7.6	7.7	7.7	7.7	7.7	7.7	7.5	7.8	7.8	7.8	7.7
2003	7.8	7.8	7.8	7.8	7.8	7.8	7.8	8.2	8.1	8.2	8.2	8.3	7.9
2004	8.1	8.1	8.1	8.2	8.3	8.3	8.3	8.4	8.4	8.8	8.8	8.9	8.4
2005	8.8	8.9	9.0	8.9	8.9	9.0	8.9	8.9	8.9	9.0	9.0	9.1	8.9
2006	9.0	9.0	9.0	9.1	9.2	9.2	9.3	9.3	9.4	9.4	9.5	9.8	9.3
2007	9.2	9.1	9.2	9.2	9.4	9.3	9.3	9.4	9.4	9.3	9.4	9.7	9.3
2008	9.3	9.3	9.2	9.1	9.1	9.1	9.1	9.3	9.3	9.3	9.3	9.6	9.3
2009	9.3	9.3	9.2	8.9	8.8	8.7	8.7	8.7	8.8	8.8	8.8	9.0	8.9
Information													
1990	5.1	5.1	5.1	5.2	5.4	5.4	5.1	5.1	4.9	4.8	4.8	4.8	5.1
2000	7.9	8.1	8.0	8.0	8.1	8.0	7.9	8.1	7.8	7.8	7.8	7.8	7.9
2001	7.8	7.8	7.8	7.7	7.7	7.6	7.6	7.7	7.7	7.6	7.8	7.9	7.7
2002	7.9	8.0	8.0	7.9	8.0	7.8	7.8	7.9	7.8	7.8	7.9	7.8	7.9
2003	7.6	7.7	7.5	7.5	7.6	7.5	7.5	7.6	7.3	7.4	7.7	7.7	7.5
2004	7.5	7.7	7.5	7.5	7.6	7.5	7.6	7.8	7.3	7.4	7.7	7.6	7.6
2005	7.3	7.2	7.2	7.2	7.2	7.2	7.2	7.2	7.2	7.2	7.2	7.3	7.2
2006	7.5	7.5	7.4	6.9	6.9	6.9	6.7	6.5	6.5	6.3	6.2	6.0	6.8
2007	6.3	6.2	6.2	6.1	6.1	5.8	5.7	5.7	5.7	5.8	5.8	5.7	5.9
2008	5.7	5.5	5.4	5.3	5.3	5.2	5.2	5.1	5.1	5.0	5.1	5.2	5.3
2009	5.1	5.1	4.9	4.9	4.8	4.7	4.7	4.6	4.6	4.6	4.6	4.6	4.8

Employment by Industry: Tucson, AZ, Selected Years, 1990–2009—*Continued*

(Numbers in thousands, not seasonally adjusted.)

Industry and year	January	February	March	April	May	June	July	August	September	October	November	December	Annual average
Financial Activities													
1990	12.2	12.2	12.3	11.8	11.9	11.9	11.9	12.0	12.0	11.7	11.5	11.5	11.9
2000	14.6	14.8	14.9	14.6	14.6	14.7	14.9	15.0	15.0	15.2	14.8	14.8	14.8
2001	14.2	14.4	14.5	14.8	14.7	14.7	14.8	14.5	14.1	14.2	14.3	14.3	14.5
2002	14.0	14.1	14.2	14.2	14.4	14.3	14.2	14.3	14.4	14.7	14.7	14.8	14.4
2003	14.8	14.9	15.1	15.0	15.2	15.2	15.5	15.7	16.2	16.3	16.1	16.2	15.5
2004	16.1	16.2	16.1	16.2	16.1	15.8	16.0	15.9	15.7	15.7	15.7	15.8	15.9
2005	15.5	15.7	15.7	16.0	16.2	16.4	16.6	17.0	17.1	17.1	17.2	17.5	16.5
2006	16.7	16.9	17.0	17.3	17.4	17.5	17.6	17.8	18.0	18.3	18.4	18.7	17.6
2007	18.4	18.5	18.6	18.7	18.8	18.8	18.8	17.7	17.4	17.4	17.4	17.7	18.2
2008	16.9	17.0	17.1	17.3	17.2	17.4	17.4	17.4	17.3	16.9	16.9	17.2	17.2
2009	16.9	17.0	17.0	17.2	17.3	17.3	17.8	17.8	17.6	17.6	17.7	17.7	17.4
Professional and Business Services													
1990	21.1	21.1	21.2	21.3	21.2	21.4	21.5	21.8	21.6	21.5	21.3	21.4	21.4
2000	42.3	43.4	44.6	44.2	44.1	44.5	42.8	43.4	43.3	42.8	43.0	43.3	43.5
2001	41.0	42.2	42.4	42.3	41.5	41.6	41.4	41.4	40.5	40.6	40.5	40.3	41.3
2002	40.4	41.0	41.3	41.5	40.9	41.1	41.2	41.9	42.0	42.0	42.4	42.2	41.5
2003	40.6	40.6	40.7	41.0	40.8	41.5	41.2	41.6	42.1	41.7	41.5	41.5	41.2
2004	41.2	41.7	41.8	43.4	42.7	42.8	43.5	43.9	43.8	45.3	45.3	45.4	43.4
2005	44.1	44.5	44.5	45.8	45.5	45.5	46.3	47.0	47.0	46.5	46.6	47.6	45.9
2006	47.3	48.4	48.5	48.6	48.6	49.1	49.5	50.0	50.9	50.9	52.0	53.1	49.7
2007	51.5	52.1	52.3	52.1	52.0	52.5	52.0	52.9	53.0	53.6	53.9	53.6	52.6
2008	51.8	52.0	52.3	52.3	51.4	51.2	51.7	51.9	51.6	50.6	50.0	50.2	51.4
2009	49.0	48.3	48.0	47.2	46.7	46.7	46.7	46.7	46.7	47.0	47.2	47.6	47.3
Education and Health Services													
1990	29.6	30.1	30.3	29.6	29.7	30.0	29.1	29.1	29.8	30.5	30.9	31.1	30.0
2000	42.4	42.5	42.3	41.8	41.6	41.4	41.0	41.6	42.1	42.2	42.4	42.4	42.0
2001	40.7	41.0	41.6	41.5	41.4	41.3	41.3	41.7	42.2	42.4	42.9	43.2	41.8
2002	42.9	43.4	43.4	43.4	43.7	43.4	42.7	43.5	43.9	44.0	44.3	44.3	43.6
2003	44.3	44.9	45.0	45.4	45.5	45.3	45.3	46.1	46.5	46.1	46.6	46.8	45.6
2004	46.7	46.7	46.9	47.1	47.5	47.2	47.2	48.2	48.5	48.9	49.1	49.2	47.8
2005	49.1	49.5	49.7	50.2	50.5	49.8	49.9	50.8	51.4	51.6	51.7	52.2	50.5
2006	51.6	52.1	52.5	52.0	52.3	52.0	51.7	52.6	53.0	53.3	53.6	54.2	52.6
2007	53.5	54.0	54.3	54.0	54.7	54.1	54.0	54.6	54.9	55.9	55.9	56.2	54.7
2008	55.0	55.6	56.0	57.0	57.1	56.6	56.7	57.6	58.1	58.4	58.8	58.8	57.1
2009	58.4	58.7	58.7	58.3	58.5	57.9	57.8	58.4	58.6	58.9	59.2	59.3	58.6
Leisure and Hospitality													
1990	29.6	30.5	31.0	29.9	29.7	29.2	28.2	28.5	29.2	29.1	29.4	29.6	29.5
2000	39.8	40.9	41.3	41.0	40.6	39.9	38.5	38.4	39.0	39.6	40.1	40.0	39.9
2001	38.5	39.7	40.0	40.0	39.4	38.1	36.9	37.4	37.6	37.0	36.9	36.9	38.2
2002	37.8	38.4	38.8	38.7	37.9	36.7	35.5	35.6	36.2	36.8	37.3	37.4	37.3
2003	36.4	36.9	37.5	37.9	37.5	36.6	35.7	36.1	36.9	37.5	38.2	38.9	37.1
2004	38.6	39.4	39.7	40.5	39.8	38.6	37.7	38.3	38.4	38.8	39.7	40.0	39.1
2005	38.7	39.6	40.2	41.6	41.1	40.4	39.0	38.9	39.6	39.1	39.4	39.6	39.8
2006	39.7	40.9	41.2	41.9	41.1	40.2	39.3	39.9	40.8	40.5	40.7	40.9	40.6
2007	39.8	41.1	41.5	41.5	41.0	39.9	38.6	38.7	39.3	39.6	40.3	40.7	40.2
2008	40.3	41.7	41.6	41.3	41.0	39.9	38.8	39.0	39.7	40.4	40.4	40.6	40.4
2009	39.1	39.9	39.9	39.9	39.5	38.4	37.0	37.6	37.9	38.2	38.4	38.3	38.7
Other Services													
1990	9.9	10.0	10.0	10.1	10.2	10.2	10.0	10.1	10.0	9.9	10.0	10.0	10.0
2000	12.9	13.1	13.0	13.0	13.0	13.3	13.1	12.8	12.9	12.9	13.0	13.2	13.0
2001	13.8	13.9	14.1	14.2	14.4	14.6	14.5	14.6	14.5	14.3	14.3	14.3	14.3
2002	14.2	14.3	14.3	14.7	14.8	14.7	14.6	14.5	14.5	14.4	14.4	14.4	14.5
2003	14.2	14.3	14.4	14.6	14.6	14.6	14.6	14.6	14.6	14.8	14.8	14.7	14.5
2004	14.3	14.5	14.6	14.9	14.9	14.8	14.9	14.8	14.6	14.9	14.9	14.8	14.7
2005	14.3	14.4	14.6	14.9	14.9	14.8	14.7	14.6	14.6	14.8	15.0	14.9	14.7
2006	15.5	15.8	16.0	16.1	16.3	16.5	15.4	15.4	15.2	15.6	15.6	15.7	15.8
2007	15.5	15.8	16.0	15.9	15.9	16.1	15.8	15.8	15.7	15.8	15.9	15.8	15.8
2008	15.6	15.8	15.8	16.0	15.9	16.0	15.8	15.6	15.6	15.5	15.5	15.2	15.7
2009	14.9	14.9	15.0	14.8	14.7	14.7	14.8	14.8	14.5	14.6	14.6	14.4	14.7
Government													
1990	51.3	53.6	54.4	54.8	55.6	46.5	45.6	49.4	54.0	55.6	56.7	57.1	52.9
2000	71.8	74.0	75.2	75.5	76.7	71.7	66.6	67.8	72.5	75.2	76.1	76.0	73.3
2001	72.6	75.6	76.4	76.7	76.3	70.6	64.3	68.7	74.7	75.6	77.4	77.2	73.8
2002	74.7	76.9	76.9	78.2	77.4	71.4	64.8	69.5	74.9	77.4	78.4	78.2	74.9
2003	75.7	78.1	78.5	78.2	78.3	70.7	66.7	70.7	76.0	78.1	77.9	79.0	75.7
2004	76.5	78.9	78.9	79.1	79.0	73.6	66.5	71.1	77.9	79.9	80.5	80.8	76.9
2005	76.2	79.5	79.9	79.7	79.6	72.9	70.4	73.4	77.6	78.3	78.9	78.7	77.1
2006	75.7	78.4	78.2	78.6	77.9	71.3	68.5	72.4	75.7	79.2	79.6	79.9	76.3
2007	76.8	80.1	79.8	79.6	78.7	71.5	70.9	73.4	80.6	80.7	81.3	81.1	77.9
2008	76.7	81.4	80.7	81.7	81.8	74.8	75.0	78.0	81.2	82.0	82.6	82.2	79.8
2009	79.6	81.6	81.1	81.9	80.6	72.9	72.4	76.0	79.8	80.1	80.4	80.0	78.9

Employment by Industry: Tulsa, OK, Selected Years, 1990–2009

(Numbers in thousands, not seasonally adjusted.)

Industry and year	January	February	March	April	May	June	July	August	September	October	November	December	Annual average
Total Nonfarm													
1990	314.5	314.3	316.9	318.5	321.2	325.7	322.1	326.3	328.2	327.9	329.4	331.6	323.1
2000	395.8	396.9	401.7	405.6	409.2	411.3	407.3	410.3	412.5	412.7	414.3	415.3	407.7
2001	400.4	403.9	407.1	411.1	413.2	415.2	410.2	412.8	411.6	410.0	411.7	411.8	409.9
2002	403.1	403.0	404.8	407.2	409.6	405.8	399.0	401.0	400.2	398.5	399.2	399.8	402.6
2003	391.3	390.8	391.2	392.6	394.0	390.6	387.3	388.6	389.1	390.5	391.4	392.7	390.8
2004	387.2	389.2	392.0	392.2	392.6	393.4	391.6	393.1	394.6	395.9	396.1	398.0	393.0
2005	394.3	397.0	400.3	403.3	406.6	408.3	405.1	408.2	411.2	411.4	414.2	416.5	406.4
2006	410.6	412.9	417.5	416.9	421.7	422.9	415.7	418.6	421.3	422.8	424.2	426.4	419.3
2007	416.7	420.7	426.3	426.9	430.0	430.2	425.7	427.5	429.0	432.4	433.7	431.8	427.6
2008	427.6	431.1	434.0	434.0	437.0	434.6	430.6	432.2	434.7	434.4	434.0	433.5	433.1
2009	420.6	419.6	419.8	417.3	417.2	413.5	405.7	405.0	406.8	411.1	410.0	411.0	413.1
Total Private													
1990	274.0	272.9	275.7	278.1	280.3	284.7	284.8	287.5	287.8	286.9	288.3	289.7	282.6
2000	348.7	349.2	353.1	357.2	360.2	363.5	362.9	365.0	365.2	363.6	365.3	365.7	360.0
2001	353.2	355.5	358.5	362.6	364.1	367.0	365.2	367.2	363.6	360.5	362.1	362.0	361.8
2002	354.6	353.6	355.1	357.2	358.7	357.0	353.1	354.4	352.0	348.7	349.5	349.9	353.7
2003	342.9	341.7	342.1	343.7	344.6	342.8	341.7	342.9	340.9	341.6	342.6	343.6	342.6
2004	339.2	340.1	342.7	342.9	343.2	344.9	344.2	345.1	344.2	344.8	345.8	347.3	343.7
2005	343.5	345.3	348.4	351.3	353.8	356.0	357.2	358.9	359.4	357.7	360.6	362.7	354.6
2006	357.5	359.0	363.2	363.5	367.5	370.5	368.2	370.4	369.2	368.9	370.7	373.0	366.8
2007	364.9	367.5	372.6	373.1	375.8	378.9	378.2	379.5	376.4	378.0	379.5	377.9	375.2
2008	375.0	377.1	379.8	379.3	381.7	382.5	381.8	382.7	379.9	377.4	377.1	376.6	379.2
2009	366.6	364.0	363.6	360.6	360.0	361.1	356.8	354.1	350.9	352.5	352.1	353.3	358.0
Goods-Producing													
1990	74.8	74.2	74.7	75.7	76.0	77.4	77.3	77.9	77.6	78.1	78.1	78.3	76.7
2000	79.6	79.5	80.3	79.6	80.0	80.9	81.0	81.5	81.1	80.1	80.4	80.6	80.4
2001	78.4	79.1	79.9	80.3	80.9	82.1	81.4	81.8	80.7	79.7	79.7	79.6	80.3
2002	78.4	77.3	77.1	76.7	76.8	76.6	75.4	75.3	73.9	73.0	72.6	72.7	75.5
2003	71.7	71.0	71.1	71.3	71.4	71.8	72.2	72.1	71.6	70.8	70.5	70.8	71.4
2004	69.4	69.4	69.8	69.8	70.2	70.9	71.4	70.8	70.3	70.0	69.7	69.9	70.1
2005	68.9	69.0	69.9	70.6	71.2	72.0	72.7	73.1	73.3	73.2	73.7	75.0	71.9
2006	74.5	75.0	76.2	75.0	76.3	77.5	77.7	78.4	78.2	78.3	78.7	79.0	77.1
2007	77.8	77.8	79.1	78.6	79.4	80.6	81.4	81.9	81.0	81.8	82.1	81.8	80.3
2008	81.9	82.2	82.9	82.8	83.8	84.2	84.5	84.5	84.0	82.9	82.6	82.9	83.3
2009	81.0	79.1	77.8	75.8	74.4	74.5	72.8	71.6	70.8	71.2	70.6	71.3	74.2
Mining and Logging													
1990	10.2	10.1	10.1	10.1	10.0	10.3	10.3	10.5	10.2	10.0	10.0	10.3	10.2
2000	5.8	5.9	5.7	5.2	5.1	5.2	5.1	5.1	5.0	4.6	4.7	4.6	5.2
2001	4.1	4.2	4.3	4.1	4.2	4.4	4.4	4.4	4.4	4.5	4.5	4.5	4.3
2002	4.3	4.4	4.4	4.3	4.3	4.5	4.2	4.2	4.1	4.0	3.9	3.9	4.2
2003	4.0	3.9	3.9	3.8	3.8	3.8	3.9	3.9	4.0	4.0	4.0	4.0	3.9
2004	4.4	4.4	4.3	4.3	4.3	4.4	4.5	4.4	4.4	4.4	4.3	4.4	4.4
2005	4.8	4.8	4.8	4.9	5.0	5.1	5.3	5.3	5.4	5.3	5.4	5.5	5.1
2006	5.6	5.7	5.8	6.2	6.1	6.2	6.3	6.3	6.3	6.2	6.3	6.3	6.1
2007	6.4	6.4	6.5	6.4	6.5	6.7	6.9	6.9	6.8	7.0	7.0	7.1	6.7
2008	7.0	7.1	7.1	7.0	7.1	7.4	7.5	7.5	7.4	7.2	7.1	7.1	7.2
2009	7.3	7.1	6.9	6.8	6.6	6.7	6.8	6.8	6.7	6.6	6.7	6.7	6.8
Construction													
1990	12.4	12.0	12.2	12.2	12.3	12.7	12.7	12.8	12.7	12.3	12.3	12.1	12.4
2000	18.7	18.7	19.3	19.5	19.6	19.9	20.0	20.1	19.8	19.8	19.8	19.6	19.6
2001	19.1	19.7	20.3	20.7	21.1	21.6	21.5	21.8	21.1	21.2	21.0	21.0	20.8
2002	20.8	20.7	20.6	20.3	20.6	20.7	20.8	21.1	20.4	20.2	19.9	20.0	20.5
2003	19.4	19.1	19.4	20.1	20.4	20.6	20.9	20.8	20.4	19.7	19.4	19.5	19.9
2004	18.6	18.5	18.8	18.9	19.2	19.6	20.3	20.1	19.9	19.6	19.3	19.2	19.3
2005	18.4	18.4	18.9	19.3	19.7	20.1	20.7	20.8	20.8	20.6	20.5	20.9	19.9
2006	20.7	20.7	21.2	21.1	21.3	21.9	21.8	21.9	21.9	22.1	22.0	22.1	21.6
2007	20.6	20.6	21.5	21.3	21.5	22.2	22.2	22.5	22.1	22.4	22.5	22.1	21.8
2008	22.1	22.2	22.7	22.9	23.2	23.3	23.6	23.5	23.3	23.0	22.8	22.7	22.9
2009	21.7	21.5	21.5	21.1	20.8	21.0	20.6	20.2	20.0	20.0	19.8	19.7	20.7
Manufacturing													
1990	52.2	52.1	52.4	53.4	53.7	54.4	54.3	54.6	54.7	55.8	55.8	55.9	54.1
2000	55.1	54.9	55.3	54.9	55.3	55.8	55.9	56.3	56.3	55.7	55.9	56.4	55.7
2001	55.2	55.2	55.3	55.5	55.6	56.1	55.5	55.6	55.2	54.0	54.2	54.1	55.1
2002	53.3	52.2	52.1	52.1	51.9	51.4	50.4	50.0	49.4	48.8	48.8	48.8	50.8
2003	48.3	48.0	47.8	47.4	47.2	47.4	47.4	47.4	47.2	47.1	47.1	47.3	47.4
2004	46.4	46.5	46.7	46.6	46.7	46.9	46.6	46.3	46.0	46.0	46.1	46.3	46.4
2005	45.7	45.8	46.2	46.4	46.5	46.8	46.7	47.0	47.1	47.3	47.8	48.6	46.8
2006	48.2	48.6	49.2	47.7	48.9	49.4	49.6	50.2	50.0	50.0	50.4	50.6	49.4
2007	50.8	50.8	51.1	50.9	51.4	51.7	52.3	52.5	52.1	52.4	52.6	52.6	51.8
2008	52.8	52.9	53.1	52.9	53.5	53.5	53.4	53.5	53.3	52.7	52.7	53.1	53.1
2009	52.0	50.5	49.4	47.9	47.0	46.8	45.4	44.6	44.1	44.6	44.1	44.9	46.8

Employment by Industry: Tulsa, OK, Selected Years, 1990–2009—*Continued*

(Numbers in thousands, not seasonally adjusted.)

Industry and year	January	February	March	April	May	June	July	August	September	October	November	December	Annual average
Service-Providing													
1990	239.7	240.1	242.2	242.8	245.2	248.3	244.8	248.4	250.6	249.8	251.3	253.3	246.4
2000	316.2	317.4	321.4	326.0	329.2	330.4	326.3	328.8	331.4	332.6	333.9	334.7	327.4
2001	322.0	324.8	327.2	330.8	332.3	333.1	328.8	331.0	330.9	330.3	332.0	332.2	329.6
2002	324.7	325.7	327.7	330.5	332.8	329.2	323.6	325.7	326.3	325.5	326.6	327.1	327.1
2003	319.6	319.8	320.1	321.3	322.6	318.8	315.1	316.5	317.5	319.7	320.9	321.9	319.5
2004	317.8	319.8	322.2	322.4	322.4	322.5	320.2	322.3	324.3	325.9	326.4	328.1	322.9
2005	325.4	328.0	330.4	332.7	335.4	336.3	332.4	335.1	337.9	338.2	340.5	341.5	334.5
2006	336.1	337.9	341.3	341.9	345.4	345.4	338.0	340.2	343.1	344.5	345.5	347.4	342.2
2007	338.9	342.9	347.2	348.3	350.6	349.6	344.3	345.6	348.0	350.6	351.6	350.0	347.3
2008	345.7	348.9	351.1	351.2	353.2	350.4	346.1	347.7	350.7	351.5	351.4	350.6	349.9
2009	339.6	340.5	342.0	341.5	342.8	339.0	332.9	333.4	336.0	339.9	339.4	339.7	338.9
Trade, Transportation, and Utilities													
1990	75.5	74.8	75.6	75.1	76.0	77.3	76.9	77.7	77.6	77.9	79.4	80.8	77.1
2000	86.8	86.3	86.9	87.8	88.8	89.7	89.5	90.1	90.6	90.6	92.4	93.1	89.4
2001	88.0	87.1	87.6	87.6	87.9	88.4	86.8	87.0	86.3	85.8	87.3	87.5	87.3
2002	85.0	84.1	84.9	86.1	86.3	85.8	85.1	85.1	85.0	84.4	85.9	86.7	85.4
2003	83.7	82.7	82.7	83.0	82.9	82.1	81.7	81.9	81.3	82.0	83.5	84.6	82.7
2004	80.9	79.8	80.8	80.8	81.2	81.2	79.8	79.7	79.2	79.6	80.8	81.5	80.4
2005	79.9	79.3	79.4	79.7	80.1	80.2	80.8	81.3	81.4	81.7	83.2	84.2	80.9
2006	81.2	80.8	81.7	83.2	84.0	83.9	83.4	83.5	83.6	83.8	85.5	86.7	83.4
2007	83.8	83.9	85.2	84.7	85.0	85.3	84.9	84.3	84.2	85.1	86.7	86.7	85.0
2008	83.6	83.9	84.8	85.3	85.6	85.6	86.2	86.4	85.8	85.7	86.9	87.3	85.6
2009	83.6	82.8	83.1	83.6	84.0	83.9	83.2	82.9	82.5	82.4	83.2	84.1	83.3
Wholesale Trade													
1990	15.0	15.1	15.2	15.3	15.4	15.5	15.6	15.6	15.6	15.3	15.5	15.4	15.4
2000	17.1	17.2	17.4	17.5	17.4	17.7	17.7	17.9	17.9	17.9	17.9	17.9	17.6
2001	17.7	17.7	17.8	18.0	18.1	18.1	17.7	17.6	17.5	17.3	17.5	17.5	17.7
2002	17.6	17.4	17.6	17.7	17.7	17.7	17.7	17.8	17.7	17.4	17.5	17.5	17.6
2003	17.0	16.8	16.9	16.9	16.8	16.8	16.9	16.8	16.8	16.8	16.7	16.8	16.8
2004	16.3	16.0	16.0	16.0	16.2	16.3	16.3	16.3	16.4	16.3	16.4	16.6	16.3
2005	16.7	16.7	16.8	16.9	17.0	17.2	17.5	17.5	17.5	17.5	17.6	17.7	17.2
2006	17.2	17.3	17.4	17.7	17.8	17.9	17.7	17.7	17.7	17.7	17.7	17.7	17.6
2007	17.8	18.0	18.2	18.3	18.2	18.3	18.2	18.0	17.9	18.0	18.0	17.9	18.1
2008	17.7	17.7	17.7	17.5	17.4	17.4	17.5	17.4	17.3	17.1	17.1	17.0	17.4
2009	16.6	16.5	16.4	16.3	16.3	16.2	16.2	16.0	16.0	16.0	16.0	16.0	16.2
Retail Trade													
1990	39.6	38.6	39.1	38.3	38.7	39.2	38.8	39.3	39.2	39.1	40.3	41.5	39.3
2000	47.6	47.1	47.5	48.0	48.8	49.2	48.7	49.1	49.6	49.6	51.5	51.9	49.1
2001	47.7	46.8	47.1	47.3	47.4	47.6	46.5	46.8	46.5	46.7	48.1	48.7	47.3
2002	46.8	46.2	46.6	46.9	47.1	46.6	45.7	45.7	45.5	45.5	46.9	47.6	46.4
2003	45.2	44.5	44.5	44.9	45.0	44.7	44.4	44.6	44.3	44.9	46.5	47.4	45.0
2004	44.7	43.8	44.7	44.8	44.9	44.7	43.4	43.2	42.7	43.5	44.7	45.2	44.2
2005	43.2	42.6	42.6	42.8	43.0	42.8	43.2	43.5	43.8	44.2	45.5	46.3	43.6
2006	43.0	43.4	43.9	44.4	44.9	44.6	44.4	44.2	44.2	44.6	46.1	47.0	44.6
2007	44.1	43.8	44.9	44.7	45.0	45.1	44.5	44.4	44.3	44.9	46.4	46.5	44.9
2008	43.9	44.2	45.1	45.7	45.9	45.8	46.0	46.2	45.6	45.5	46.6	46.9	45.6
2009	44.8	44.3	44.8	44.9	45.5	45.5	44.9	45.0	44.7	44.7	45.6	46.3	45.1
Transportation and Utilities													
1990	20.9	21.1	21.3	21.5	21.9	22.6	22.5	22.8	22.8	23.5	23.6	23.9	22.4
2000	22.1	22.0	22.0	22.3	22.6	22.8	23.1	23.1	23.1	23.1	23.0	23.3	22.7
2001	22.6	22.6	22.7	22.3	22.4	22.7	22.6	22.6	22.3	21.8	21.7	21.3	22.3
2002	20.6	20.5	20.7	21.5	21.5	21.5	21.7	21.6	21.8	21.5	21.5	21.6	21.3
2003	21.5	21.4	21.3	21.2	21.1	20.6	20.4	20.5	20.2	20.3	20.3	20.4	20.8
2004	19.9	20.0	20.1	20.0	20.1	20.2	20.1	20.2	20.1	19.8	19.7	19.7	20.0
2005	20.0	20.0	20.0	20.0	20.1	20.2	20.1	20.3	20.1	20.0	20.1	20.2	20.1
2006	20.3	20.1	20.4	21.1	21.3	21.4	21.3	21.6	21.7	21.5	21.7	22.0	21.2
2007	21.9	22.1	22.1	21.7	21.8	21.9	22.2	21.9	22.0	22.2	22.3	22.3	22.0
2008	22.0	22.0	22.0	22.1	22.3	22.4	22.7	22.8	22.9	23.1	23.2	23.4	22.6
2009	22.2	22.0	21.9	22.4	22.2	22.2	22.1	21.9	21.8	21.7	21.6	21.8	22.0
Information													
1990	7.0	6.9	7.0	7.1	7.2	7.4	7.3	7.3	7.3	7.4	7.5	7.5	7.2
2000	14.3	14.5	14.5	14.3	14.7	14.9	15.1	15.3	15.6	15.5	15.9	15.9	15.0
2001	14.5	14.6	14.3	15.0	14.8	14.4	15.0	16.1	16.1	16.1	15.8	15.6	15.2
2002	15.7	15.8	15.4	14.6	14.4	14.2	14.0	13.9	13.8	13.7	13.6	13.2	14.4
2003	12.9	12.8	12.5	12.6	12.6	12.4	12.0	11.7	11.6	11.8	11.8	12.0	12.2
2004	12.0	12.0	11.9	11.5	11.3	11.2	11.1	10.8	10.5	10.5	10.5	10.5	11.2
2005	10.8	10.7	10.5	10.6	10.6	10.7	10.7	10.7	10.8	10.8	11.0	11.0	10.7
2006	10.5	10.3	10.3	10.0	10.1	10.1	10.0	10.0	9.7	9.8	9.8	10.2	10.1
2007	9.9	10.1	10.0	9.9	10.0	9.9	10.0	9.9	9.9	10.0	10.0	10.0	10.0
2008	9.8	9.9	9.8	10.0	10.0	10.0	10.0	9.8	9.7	9.6	9.7	9.7	9.8
2009	9.4	9.4	9.2	9.1	9.1	9.1	9.1	9.0	8.8	8.9	8.9	8.8	9.1

Employment by Industry: Tulsa, OK, Selected Years, 1990–2009—*Continued*

(Numbers in thousands, not seasonally adjusted.)

Industry and year	January	February	March	April	May	June	July	August	September	October	November	December	Annual average
Financial Activities													
1990	18.8	18.8	18.9	19.0	19.0	19.2	19.2	19.2	19.1	18.6	18.7	18.7	18.9
2000	24.6	24.6	24.6	25.0	25.2	25.7	25.0	25.1	25.1	24.9	24.7	24.9	25.0
2001	24.5	24.8	24.9	25.0	25.2	25.4	25.2	25.4	25.3	25.4	25.4	25.3	25.2
2002	25.0	24.9	24.8	24.9	24.9	25.0	25.0	24.9	24.7	24.5	24.5	24.5	24.8
2003	24.4	24.4	24.4	24.6	24.7	24.7	24.6	24.5	24.4	24.4	24.3	24.2	24.4
2004	24.7	24.8	24.9	24.7	24.7	24.8	24.6	24.7	24.5	24.5	24.6	24.6	24.7
2005	25.1	25.2	25.2	24.9	24.9	25.1	25.2	25.2	25.0	24.9	25.1	25.1	25.1
2006	25.3	25.4	25.5	25.3	25.4	25.7	25.3	25.4	25.3	25.4	25.5	25.7	25.4
2007	24.9	25.1	25.3	25.0	25.0	25.1	25.2	25.1	24.9	25.0	24.8	24.8	25.0
2008	24.6	24.6	24.6	24.6	24.6	24.6	24.9	24.8	24.5	24.5	24.4	24.5	24.6
2009	24.0	23.9	23.9	23.9	24.0	24.0	24.0	23.7	23.5	23.6	23.6	23.5	23.8
Professional and Business Services													
1990	33.9	33.8	34.4	35.4	35.7	35.8	36.5	36.6	37.0	36.0	35.4	35.1	35.5
2000	49.8	50.2	51.5	53.5	54.0	54.3	54.7	55.2	55.0	55.8	55.6	54.7	53.7
2001	53.6	54.7	55.5	56.9	57.1	57.6	57.4	56.3	54.9	54.0	53.9	53.7	55.5
2002	51.5	51.8	52.0	52.6	53.4	52.8	51.6	51.8	51.2	50.7	50.2	50.1	51.6
2003	48.6	48.8	48.7	48.8	49.0	48.6	48.7	49.5	49.5	50.2	50.3	50.0	49.2
2004	50.6	51.8	51.5	52.2	51.8	52.4	53.4	54.1	54.9	56.1	56.2	56.6	53.5
2005	56.2	57.7	58.3	59.3	59.8	59.8	59.9	60.3	61.2	60.5	61.1	61.0	59.6
2006	59.8	60.7	61.1	61.1	61.7	61.8	61.2	62.1	61.9	61.4	61.4	60.5	61.2
2007	60.2	61.0	61.7	62.1	62.8	62.7	62.4	63.6	62.8	63.1	63.0	62.5	62.3
2008	63.3	64.0	64.4	64.2	64.1	63.9	63.3	63.8	63.5	62.7	62.0	60.6	63.3
2009	57.2	57.0	56.4	55.0	54.5	54.4	53.2	52.9	52.2	52.2	52.0	51.9	54.1
Education and Health Services													
1990	31.7	32.2	32.5	32.2	31.7	32.1	32.3	32.8	33.4	33.6	33.8	33.9	32.7
2000	46.6	47.0	47.3	47.9	48.1	47.6	47.5	47.9	48.8	48.0	48.4	48.5	47.8
2001	47.2	47.4	48.0	48.8	48.5	48.4	48.7	49.2	49.9	49.4	50.2	50.4	48.8
2002	50.5	50.9	51.1	51.0	50.7	50.0	50.7	51.8	52.6	52.1	53.0	53.0	51.5
2003	52.7	52.8	52.7	53.0	52.8	51.9	51.7	52.1	52.4	52.2	52.3	52.0	52.3
2004	52.1	52.4	52.7	52.8	52.5	52.0	52.1	52.7	53.4	53.1	53.1	53.3	52.7
2005	52.7	53.1	53.5	53.8	54.0	54.0	53.9	54.2	54.4	54.4	54.6	54.7	53.9
2006	54.3	54.7	54.9	55.0	55.4	56.0	55.5	55.8	56.5	56.7	56.8	57.1	55.7
2007	56.1	56.7	57.2	57.6	57.8	58.4	57.9	58.1	58.2	58.2	58.1	57.8	57.7
2008	58.0	58.4	58.6	57.6	57.9	57.8	57.0	57.2	57.4	57.3	57.4	57.4	57.7
2009	57.7	57.9	58.2	58.2	58.4	58.9	58.9	58.9	58.8	59.4	59.6	59.6	58.7
Leisure and Hospitality													
1990	22.6	22.5	23.0	24.0	24.9	25.4	25.2	26.0	25.7	25.3	25.3	25.3	24.6
2000	33.0	33.2	33.8	34.6	34.8	35.4	35.1	35.1	34.4	34.2	33.5	33.4	34.2
2001	32.6	33.2	33.5	34.1	34.5	35.1	35.1	35.5	34.7	34.4	33.9	34.0	34.2
2002	32.8	33.1	33.9	34.7	35.6	35.6	34.4	35.0	34.3	34.1	33.5	33.5	34.2
2003	32.4	32.6	33.2	33.9	34.5	34.4	34.0	34.4	33.5	33.5	33.3	33.2	33.5
2004	32.7	33.1	34.0	34.2	34.6	35.1	34.8	35.3	34.6	34.2	34.1	34.0	34.2
2005	33.1	33.4	34.5	35.5	36.2	36.9	36.4	36.8	36.1	35.2	34.9	34.6	35.3
2006	34.8	35.0	36.2	36.5	37.2	37.6	37.4	37.6	36.5	36.2	35.6	36.3	36.4
2007	35.0	35.6	36.6	36.9	37.4	37.8	37.6	37.7	36.8	36.4	36.4	36.0	36.7
2008	35.5	35.8	36.4	36.8	37.6	38.0	37.4	37.9	37.0	36.7	36.3	36.4	36.8
2009	36.1	36.4	37.4	37.6	38.1	38.5	37.8	37.6	37.0	37.6	37.0	36.9	37.3
Other Services													
1990	9.7	9.7	9.6	9.6	9.8	10.1	10.1	10.0	10.1	10.0	10.1	10.1	9.9
2000	14.0	13.9	14.2	14.5	14.6	15.0	15.0	14.8	14.6	14.5	14.4	14.6	14.5
2001	14.4	14.6	14.8	14.9	15.2	15.6	15.6	15.9	15.7	15.7	15.9	15.9	15.4
2002	15.7	15.7	15.9	16.6	16.6	17.0	16.9	16.6	16.5	16.2	16.2	16.2	16.3
2003	16.5	16.6	16.8	16.5	16.7	16.9	16.8	16.7	16.6	16.7	16.6	16.8	16.7
2004	16.8	16.8	17.1	16.9	16.9	17.3	17.0	17.0	16.8	16.8	16.9	16.9	16.9
2005	16.8	16.9	17.1	16.9	17.0	17.3	17.6	17.3	17.2	17.0	17.0	17.1	17.1
2006	17.1	17.1	17.3	17.4	17.4	17.9	17.7	17.6	17.5	17.3	17.4	17.5	17.4
2007	17.2	17.3	17.5	18.3	18.4	19.1	18.8	18.9	18.6	18.4	18.4	18.3	18.3
2008	18.3	18.3	18.3	18.0	18.1	18.4	18.5	18.3	18.0	18.0	17.8	17.8	18.2
2009	17.6	17.5	17.6	17.4	17.5	17.8	17.8	17.5	17.3	17.2	17.2	17.2	17.5
Government													
1990	40.5	41.4	41.2	40.4	40.9	41.0	37.3	38.8	40.4	41.0	41.1	41.9	40.5
2000	47.1	47.7	48.6	48.4	49.0	47.8	44.4	45.3	47.3	49.1	49.0	49.6	47.8
2001	47.2	48.4	48.6	48.5	49.1	48.2	45.0	45.6	48.0	49.5	49.6	49.8	48.1
2002	48.5	49.4	49.7	50.0	50.9	48.8	45.9	46.6	48.2	49.8	49.7	49.9	49.0
2003	48.4	49.1	49.1	48.9	49.4	47.8	45.6	45.7	48.2	48.9	48.8	49.1	48.2
2004	48.0	49.1	49.3	49.3	49.4	48.5	47.4	48.0	50.4	51.1	50.3	50.7	49.3
2005	50.8	51.7	51.9	52.0	52.8	52.3	47.9	49.3	51.8	53.7	53.6	53.8	51.8
2006	53.1	53.9	54.3	53.4	54.2	52.4	47.5	48.2	52.1	53.9	53.5	53.4	52.5
2007	51.8	53.2	53.7	53.8	54.2	51.3	47.5	48.0	52.6	54.4	54.2	53.9	52.4
2008	52.6	54.0	54.2	54.7	55.3	52.1	48.8	49.5	54.8	57.0	56.9	56.9	53.9
2009	54.0	55.6	56.2	56.7	57.2	52.4	48.9	50.9	55.9	58.6	57.9	57.7	55.2

Employment by Industry: Virginia Beach-Norfolk-Newport News, VA-NC, Selected Years, 1990–2009

(Numbers in thousands, not seasonally adjusted.)

Industry and year	January	February	March	April	May	June	July	August	September	October	November	December	Annual average
Total Nonfarm													
1990	592.5	593.9	600.2	601.8	610.7	620.0	611.8	612.8	612.6	610.9	611.7	611.1	607.5
2000	699.7	703.7	713.1	714.4	720.6	731.1	722.4	726.0	726.6	726.0	730.6	730.5	720.4
2001	707.3	710.5	718.9	726.4	733.7	743.5	736.4	739.0	737.9	734.9	739.7	739.1	730.6
2002	714.4	719.2	725.6	730.4	737.5	746.5	734.7	738.5	736.1	739.2	742.3	744.2	734.1
2003	721.9	723.9	730.6	731.4	739.6	747.1	740.0	742.0	739.8	741.7	746.8	746.9	737.6
2004	729.4	730.3	738.3	746.1	752.9	761.2	754.6	756.7	755.7	754.4	758.1	759.8	749.8
2005	738.2	741.3	749.2	759.3	766.2	775.9	767.6	770.6	771.0	760.5	764.7	765.0	760.8
2006	747.8	750.0	759.2	766.1	772.7	782.7	772.1	772.4	768.0	768.7	773.2	774.8	767.3
2007	758.1	759.3	767.6	772.9	780.0	788.5	786.6	784.5	781.9	772.8	776.6	775.1	775.3
2008	753.3	756.6	762.9	766.7	775.2	782.8	776.2	775.3	768.6	762.7	760.1	756.7	766.4
2009	736.3	734.8	738.1	741.6	748.2	752.7	741.5	740.5	737.4	734.4	734.4	733.4	739.4
Total Private													
1990	450.6	451.4	456.9	457.9	465.1	474.5	472.7	474.5	469.7	466.7	467.0	466.7	464.5
2000	554.5	557.8	566.1	567.9	573.7	584.6	580.1	584.0	581.3	578.9	582.2	583.4	574.5
2001	561.4	562.9	571.1	578.5	585.9	594.4	591.5	594.6	590.8	586.2	589.6	589.8	583.1
2002	566.7	569.9	575.3	580.3	586.5	595.0	589.5	593.0	587.1	588.1	590.9	593.1	584.6
2003	572.6	573.6	579.6	582.4	590.0	596.5	592.9	595.5	590.7	592.9	596.2	596.3	588.3
2004	579.6	579.2	586.5	594.5	600.7	608.2	606.8	607.8	604.9	602.7	604.6	606.8	598.5
2005	588.6	590.3	597.7	606.9	613.3	621.8	618.3	620.9	619.7	609.3	611.8	613.1	609.3
2006	597.2	598.3	606.9	612.0	618.5	627.6	620.9	621.6	617.0	614.9	617.7	619.7	614.4
2007	604.4	604.2	612.0	617.7	624.8	632.5	633.8	631.8	627.4	617.6	619.1	618.5	620.3
2008	598.5	599.6	605.4	610.4	618.4	624.6	621.9	620.9	612.6	604.8	600.0	598.0	609.6
2009	578.6	576.4	579.0	582.3	589.3	593.0	588.9	586.2	581.4	577.0	576.6	576.6	582.1
Goods-Producing													
1990	102.6	102.3	103.4	103.0	104.2	106.5	105.8	105.6	104.6	103.8	103.3	101.8	103.9
2000	106.6	107.1	108.4	108.4	109.0	110.4	109.9	109.7	109.6	110.0	110.1	110.1	109.1
2001	106.4	106.8	108.1	108.4	109.0	109.6	108.6	110.3	109.4	108.4	108.2	108.2	108.5
2002	104.2	104.1	104.5	104.0	104.7	105.4	104.0	105.7	104.7	105.1	105.1	105.4	104.7
2003	103.9	104.4	105.5	105.0	106.3	107.1	104.6	107.3	106.2	108.5	110.0	108.9	106.5
2004	106.2	105.2	106.4	107.6	108.5	109.7	108.6	110.0	109.7	110.3	110.3	110.0	108.5
2005	108.3	108.3	109.0	110.4	110.6	111.4	110.0	112.0	111.2	109.2	109.0	109.2	109.9
2006	107.2	107.2	108.6	109.0	109.5	110.3	107.9	109.8	107.2	106.7	106.7	108.1	108.2
2007	105.9	104.8	105.7	106.8	107.0	107.6	107.5	107.5	107.0	105.2	105.1	104.5	106.2
2008	102.2	101.9	101.9	102.1	102.5	103.0	102.9	102.8	101.5	100.5	99.7	98.4	101.6
2009	94.2	93.1	92.8	92.1	92.0	92.0	92.0	91.7	91.0	90.9	91.1	91.0	92.0
Mining, Logging, and Construction													
1990	37.7	37.6	38.2	37.9	38.3	39.0	38.6	38.3	37.6	36.8	36.7	35.3	37.7
2000	41.8	42.1	43.2	43.6	44.0	45.0	44.8	44.8	44.6	44.5	44.8	44.8	44.0
2001	43.9	44.3	45.3	45.8	46.5	47.2	47.3	47.5	46.8	45.9	45.6	45.4	46.0
2002	43.6	44.0	44.6	44.3	44.8	45.3	45.7	45.5	44.6	44.7	44.4	44.5	44.7
2003	43.9	44.5	45.2	45.6	47.0	47.5	48.1	48.1	47.1	49.3	50.2	49.5	47.2
2004	46.9	46.3	47.2	48.3	48.9	49.8	50.4	49.9	49.3	49.6	49.2	49.3	48.8
2005	48.1	48.1	48.7	50.0	50.3	50.8	51.5	51.4	51.2	49.7	49.8	50.1	50.0
2006	48.6	48.6	49.8	50.4	50.6	51.1	50.6	50.3	49.8	49.3	49.3	49.3	49.8
2007	48.0	47.9	48.6	48.7	48.8	49.2	49.7	49.7	49.2	47.8	47.5	46.9	48.5
2008	45.5	45.4	45.6	45.8	46.1	46.4	46.4	46.3	45.2	44.6	43.8	42.6	45.3
2009	39.9	39.2	39.0	38.6	38.4	38.4	38.5	38.3	37.6	37.7	38.0	38.1	38.5
Manufacturing													
1990	64.9	64.8	65.2	65.2	66.0	67.4	67.2	67.3	67.0	67.2	66.7	66.5	66.3
2000	64.9	65.0	65.2	64.8	65.1	65.4	65.1	64.8	64.9	65.5	65.2	65.2	65.1
2001	62.5	62.5	62.8	62.6	62.5	62.6	61.2	62.8	62.5	62.4	62.6	62.7	62.5
2002	60.6	60.3	60.0	59.9	60.0	60.1	58.3	60.2	60.3	60.4	60.7	60.8	60.1
2003	60.0	59.9	60.3	59.4	59.3	59.6	56.5	59.2	59.1	59.2	59.8	59.4	59.3
2004	59.3	58.9	59.2	59.3	59.6	59.9	58.2	60.1	60.4	60.7	61.1	60.7	59.8
2005	60.2	60.2	60.3	60.4	60.3	60.6	58.5	60.6	60.0	59.5	59.2	59.1	59.9
2006	58.6	58.6	58.8	58.6	58.9	59.2	57.3	59.5	57.4	57.4	57.4	58.8	58.4
2007	57.9	56.9	57.1	58.1	58.2	58.4	57.8	57.8	57.8	57.4	57.6	57.6	57.7
2008	56.7	56.5	56.3	56.3	56.4	56.6	56.5	56.5	56.3	55.9	55.9	55.8	56.3
2009	54.3	53.9	53.8	53.5	53.6	53.6	53.5	53.4	53.4	53.2	53.1	52.9	53.5
Service-Providing													
1990	489.9	491.6	496.7	498.8	506.5	513.6	505.9	507.2	507.8	507.1	508.3	509.2	503.6
2000	593.1	596.6	604.7	606.0	611.6	620.8	612.5	616.3	617.0	615.9	620.6	620.4	611.3
2001	600.9	603.8	610.9	617.9	624.7	633.7	627.8	628.6	628.5	626.5	631.5	630.9	622.1
2002	610.2	614.9	621.1	626.4	632.8	641.2	630.8	632.9	631.3	634.1	637.3	638.8	629.3
2003	618.0	619.5	625.1	626.4	633.3	640.0	635.4	634.7	633.6	633.2	636.8	638.0	631.2
2004	623.2	625.1	631.9	638.5	644.4	651.5	646.0	646.7	646.0	644.1	647.8	649.8	641.3
2005	629.9	633.0	640.2	648.9	655.6	664.5	657.6	658.6	659.8	651.3	655.7	655.8	650.9
2006	640.6	642.8	650.6	657.1	663.2	672.4	664.2	662.6	660.8	662.0	666.5	666.7	659.1
2007	652.2	654.5	661.9	666.1	673.0	680.9	679.1	677.0	674.9	667.6	671.5	670.6	669.1
2008	651.1	654.7	661.0	664.6	672.7	679.8	673.3	672.5	667.1	662.2	660.4	658.3	664.8
2009	642.1	641.7	645.3	649.5	656.2	660.7	649.5	648.8	646.4	643.5	643.3	642.4	647.5

Employment by Industry: Virginia Beach-Norfolk-Newport News, VA-NC, Selected Years, 1990–2009—Continued

(Numbers in thousands, not seasonally adjusted.)

Industry and year	January	February	March	April	May	June	July	August	September	October	November	December	Annual average
Trade, Transportation, and Utilities													
1990	122.2	120.6	121.6	120.8	121.5	123.3	121.9	123.3	121.7	124.7	126.3	127.8	123.0
2000	134.6	134.4	134.8	134.6	135.9	137.2	136.4	138.0	138.5	141.4	144.9	146.6	138.1
2001	138.0	135.8	136.4	136.7	138.3	139.3	138.3	139.2	139.9	141.2	144.4	145.8	139.4
2002	138.1	136.4	135.5	136.6	138.2	140.1	138.7	139.2	138.9	141.3	145.0	147.3	139.6
2003	138.1	135.9	135.5	133.0	133.6	134.1	134.3	135.2	134.9	137.3	141.8	144.5	136.5
2004	136.8	135.8	135.4	136.8	138.1	139.2	139.6	140.1	139.5	141.2	144.7	146.1	139.4
2005	138.0	136.6	137.6	139.4	140.2	141.0	142.1	142.3	142.2	142.4	146.3	146.9	141.3
2006	139.9	138.3	139.7	140.4	141.6	142.6	142.4	141.9	140.8	143.2	147.9	148.4	142.3
2007	142.3	140.5	141.3	140.8	142.2	143.4	145.4	144.7	143.0	143.2	147.7	147.9	143.5
2008	140.0	138.0	138.3	138.2	138.9	139.9	139.6	139.4	138.0	136.5	139.1	139.8	138.8
2009	130.8	128.2	127.9	128.1	129.7	130.0	129.7	129.2	127.9	128.1	129.2	130.6	129.1
Wholesale Trade													
1990	19.7	19.7	19.8	19.4	19.6	19.6	19.6	19.8	19.6	19.9	19.7	19.8	19.7
2000	23.6	23.9	24.0	24.0	24.1	24.2	24.1	24.3	24.2	24.4	24.5	24.6	24.2
2001	24.7	24.9	25.2	25.0	25.1	25.3	25.3	25.2	25.2	25.1	25.3	25.3	25.1
2002	25.2	25.2	25.2	25.5	25.6	25.7	25.3	25.3	25.2	25.3	25.5	25.5	25.4
2003	25.1	24.8	24.5	24.6	24.3	23.9	23.5	22.9	22.8	23.1	23.1	23.2	23.8
2004	22.8	22.9	23.0	23.1	23.2	23.4	23.6	23.6	23.4	23.5	23.6	23.7	23.3
2005	23.5	23.6	23.6	23.9	24.0	24.1	24.1	24.2	24.1	24.0	24.1	24.3	24.0
2006	23.9	23.9	24.0	24.1	24.1	24.2	24.3	24.1	24.1	24.1	24.2	24.2	24.1
2007	24.1	24.2	24.3	24.2	24.3	24.3	24.4	24.2	24.1	23.7	23.7	23.7	24.1
2008	23.5	23.4	23.4	23.5	23.5	23.5	23.4	23.4	23.1	22.9	22.7	22.6	23.2
2009	22.3	22.1	22.1	22.0	22.1	22.0	22.0	21.9	21.7	21.6	21.6	21.6	21.9
Retail Trade													
1990	79.4	78.0	78.4	78.2	79.5	80.7	79.5	80.5	79.0	81.2	83.1	83.8	80.1
2000	85.6	85.1	85.2	84.8	85.9	87.0	86.0	87.2	88.1	89.8	93.6	95.0	87.8
2001	87.4	85.0	85.0	85.8	87.0	87.5	86.8	88.1	88.6	89.7	93.1	94.3	88.2
2002	87.7	85.8	84.7	85.7	86.9	88.1	87.1	87.8	87.7	89.5	93.0	95.0	88.3
2003	87.9	86.3	85.8	83.7	84.7	85.4	85.3	86.6	86.5	87.8	92.2	94.7	87.2
2004	88.7	87.5	86.9	88.1	89.2	89.9	90.1	90.4	90.2	91.3	94.7	95.8	90.2
2005	88.7	87.2	87.4	89.1	89.8	90.4	91.5	91.7	91.9	92.1	95.4	95.9	90.9
2006	90.6	88.9	89.9	90.5	91.5	92.2	92.1	91.7	90.7	92.8	97.1	97.8	92.2
2007	93.0	91.1	91.6	91.2	92.3	93.1	94.6	94.5	93.1	93.5	97.8	98.1	93.7
2008	92.0	90.0	90.4	89.6	90.2	90.8	90.6	90.4	89.5	88.3	90.8	91.5	90.3
2009	84.7	82.7	82.5	82.9	84.3	84.8	84.3	84.2	83.2	83.5	84.3	85.7	83.9
Transportation and Utilities													
1990	23.2	23.0	23.3	23.2	22.5	23.0	22.9	23.1	23.2	23.8	23.5	24.2	23.2
2000	25.5	25.6	25.7	25.9	26.0	26.1	26.3	26.5	26.2	27.2	26.9	26.9	26.2
2001	26.0	25.9	26.2	26.0	26.3	26.5	26.2	26.0	26.2	26.5	26.2	26.2	26.2
2002	25.2	25.4	25.4	25.4	25.8	26.4	26.3	26.1	26.0	26.5	26.6	26.8	26.0
2003	25.1	24.8	25.2	24.7	24.6	24.8	25.5	25.7	25.6	26.4	26.5	26.6	25.4
2004	25.3	25.4	25.5	25.6	25.7	25.9	25.9	26.1	25.9	26.4	26.4	26.6	25.9
2005	25.8	25.8	26.6	26.4	26.4	26.5	26.5	26.4	26.2	26.3	26.8	26.7	26.4
2006	25.4	25.5	25.8	25.8	26.0	26.2	26.0	26.1	26.0	26.3	26.6	26.4	26.0
2007	25.2	25.2	25.4	25.4	25.6	26.0	26.4	26.0	25.8	26.0	26.2	26.1	25.8
2008	24.5	24.6	24.5	25.1	25.2	25.6	25.6	25.6	25.4	25.3	25.6	25.7	25.2
2009	23.8	23.4	23.3	23.2	23.3	23.2	23.4	23.1	23.0	23.0	23.3	23.3	23.3
Information													
1990	11.9	12.0	12.0	11.7	11.9	12.0	12.1	12.1	12.1	12.4	12.0	12.1	12.0
2000	16.4	16.3	16.3	16.3	16.7	16.8	17.0	17.0	17.0	16.7	16.6	16.7	16.7
2001	15.6	15.5	15.6	15.6	15.8	16.1	16.4	16.5	16.5	16.6	16.9	17.0	16.2
2002	16.4	16.4	16.4	16.4	16.6	16.6	16.4	16.5	16.3	16.3	16.6	16.7	16.5
2003	16.1	16.1	16.1	16.0	16.0	16.3	16.3	15.9	15.9	15.8	15.9	15.9	16.0
2004	15.8	15.8	15.8	15.5	15.6	15.7	15.7	15.6	15.4	15.1	15.1	15.0	15.5
2005	15.0	14.8	14.7	14.9	15.0	15.1	15.3	15.4	15.3	15.2	15.3	15.5	15.1
2006	15.5	15.5	15.5	15.4	15.5	15.6	15.6	15.5	15.3	15.2	15.3	15.4	15.4
2007	15.5	15.6	15.6	15.6	15.7	15.8	15.6	15.6	15.4	15.2	15.2	15.3	15.5
2008	15.3	15.2	15.1	15.0	15.2	15.2	15.0	14.9	14.5	14.2	14.0	13.9	14.8
2009	13.7	13.7	13.6	13.5	13.6	13.5	13.3	13.2	13.0	12.9	12.8	12.8	13.3
Financial Activities													
1990	27.0	27.3	27.7	27.6	28.1	29.1	28.9	29.1	28.6	27.4	27.5	27.5	28.0
2000	35.0	35.3	35.4	36.0	36.3	37.6	37.1	37.4	37.1	36.7	36.6	36.9	36.5
2001	35.5	35.8	36.0	36.5	36.8	37.7	37.7	37.7	37.1	36.3	36.3	36.2	36.6
2002	35.4	35.7	35.9	36.2	36.7	37.9	37.0	37.3	36.6	37.1	37.2	37.5	36.7
2003	36.2	36.5	36.7	36.9	37.5	38.2	38.7	38.7	38.3	37.6	37.5	37.8	37.5
2004	38.3	38.4	38.7	39.4	39.7	40.4	41.1	41.0	40.2	39.5	39.5	39.6	39.7
2005	38.4	38.6	38.7	39.9	40.2	41.4	41.5	41.4	40.7	39.3	39.3	39.8	39.9
2006	39.1	39.3	39.5	40.2	40.6	41.7	41.9	41.9	41.2	40.9	40.9	41.1	40.7
2007	40.9	41.1	41.3	41.6	41.8	42.3	42.5	42.5	41.8	41.1	40.8	40.8	41.5
2008	40.3	40.5	40.5	40.3	40.3	41.0	41.3	41.0	40.2	39.3	38.8	38.7	40.2
2009	38.2	38.1	37.9	38.0	38.0	38.4	38.3	38.3	37.4	36.8	36.6	36.6	37.7

Employment by Industry: Virginia Beach-Norfolk-Newport News, VA-NC, Selected Years, 1990–2009—*Continued*

(Numbers in thousands, not seasonally adjusted.)

Industry and year	January	February	March	April	May	June	July	August	September	October	November	December	Annual average
Professional and Business Services													
1990	58.2	59.4	60.2	59.6	60.0	61.5	60.8	61.1	61.2	61.0	60.9	60.8	60.4
2000	95.9	98.3	100.2	99.1	97.8	100.6	99.1	100.1	99.0	98.4	99.1	99.3	98.9
2001	97.8	98.9	100.3	102.8	102.9	104.3	103.3	104.9	105.3	105.0	105.7	105.9	103.1
2002	101.7	104.0	105.8	105.6	104.8	105.8	104.2	105.9	104.8	104.5	104.8	104.6	104.7
2003	101.8	102.4	104.3	106.2	104.2	105.0	104.6	105.0	104.6	105.9	105.0	103.2	104.4
2004	98.4	98.0	99.3	100.2	99.6	100.8	101.2	101.7	101.1	100.4	101.2	101.6	100.3
2005	99.2	100.2	101.3	101.4	101.7	102.6	102.3	102.6	102.8	101.0	101.2	101.3	101.5
2006	99.7	100.4	101.5	101.6	102.4	102.6	102.0	102.2	102.5	102.7	102.8	103.0	102.0
2007	100.0	100.4	101.7	102.1	102.5	103.0	103.4	104.1	104.3	103.5	104.5	104.9	102.9
2008	101.8	102.6	103.7	105.1	105.3	106.5	106.2	107.1	106.5	105.4	104.2	104.0	104.9
2009	100.7	100.4	100.5	100.2	99.1	99.3	98.3	98.3	98.1	97.7	98.0	97.6	99.0
Education and Health Services													
1990	54.5	55.1	55.6	55.1	55.7	55.9	54.9	55.3	56.6	57.4	58.1	58.4	56.1
2000	71.2	71.9	72.2	71.8	73.1	72.9	72.7	72.7	73.5	73.6	73.9	74.1	72.8
2001	72.8	73.3	73.6	73.3	73.9	74.2	73.4	73.4	75.1	75.2	75.9	76.2	74.2
2002	75.0	75.9	76.6	76.1	76.8	77.0	75.9	76.0	77.5	78.4	78.9	79.2	76.9
2003	76.6	77.0	77.5	78.1	78.7	78.8	76.4	76.4	79.3	79.1	79.7	79.8	78.1
2004	81.2	81.7	82.5	82.4	82.7	81.8	78.7	78.6	82.7	83.4	83.7	84.3	82.0
2005	83.6	83.9	84.2	84.3	85.0	85.3	81.0	81.6	86.6	86.5	86.9	87.4	84.7
2006	86.0	86.7	87.1	86.9	87.6	88.2	84.1	83.7	88.6	88.9	89.1	89.7	87.2
2007	88.5	88.9	89.5	89.8	90.3	90.7	87.4	87.3	91.3	91.4	91.5	92.1	89.9
2008	89.4	90.2	90.7	91.0	91.8	91.8	89.3	89.2	91.7	92.7	92.6	93.0	91.1
2009	92.7	92.9	93.2	93.0	93.4	93.1	90.4	90.0	93.6	93.6	94.1	94.5	92.9
Leisure and Hospitality													
1990	52.9	53.4	55.4	59.0	62.1	64.2	66.5	66.1	63.2	58.5	57.4	56.8	59.6
2000	67.0	66.4	70.4	73.5	76.7	80.6	79.5	80.4	78.0	73.7	72.6	71.3	74.2
2001	67.3	68.7	72.4	76.6	80.1	83.9	84.6	83.2	78.4	74.4	73.3	71.9	76.2
2002	67.7	68.8	71.7	76.6	79.8	83.2	84.0	83.4	79.1	76.2	74.3	73.5	76.5
2003	69.6	70.2	72.5	74.8	79.9	83.0	84.2	83.6	78.6	75.9	72.9	72.4	76.4
2004	69.3	70.6	74.3	78.6	82.4	86.2	87.5	86.4	81.9	78.6	76.0	76.0	79.0
2005	72.1	73.6	77.7	81.7	85.4	89.7	90.8	90.2	85.3	80.5	78.6	77.8	82.0
2006	75.8	76.7	80.4	84.6	87.2	92.3	92.9	92.4	87.2	83.4	81.0	79.8	84.5
2007	77.2	78.5	82.3	85.2	88.7	93.5	95.9	94.7	89.7	84.4	81.0	80.2	85.9
2008	78.1	79.6	83.4	86.4	90.9	94.2	94.7	93.7	87.9	84.1	79.4	78.1	85.9
2009	74.3	75.9	78.8	83.0	88.8	91.8	92.0	90.9	86.1	82.9	80.9	79.6	83.8
Other Services													
1990	21.1	21.1	21.2	21.3	21.6	22.0	21.9	21.9	21.7	21.6	21.6	21.6	21.6
2000	27.5	27.8	28.1	28.1	28.3	28.5	28.5	28.6	28.6	28.5	28.5	28.3	28.3
2001	28.0	28.2	28.7	28.8	29.1	29.4	29.4	29.4	29.2	28.9	28.8	28.5	28.9
2002	28.1	28.4	28.9	28.8	28.9	29.2	29.2	29.0	29.1	29.2	29.0	29.0	28.9
2003	30.3	31.1	31.5	32.4	33.8	34.0	33.8	33.4	32.9	32.8	33.4	33.8	32.8
2004	33.6	33.7	34.1	34.0	34.1	34.4	34.4	34.4	34.4	34.2	34.1	34.2	34.1
2005	34.0	34.3	34.5	34.9	35.2	35.3	35.3	35.4	35.6	35.2	35.2	35.2	35.0
2006	34.0	34.2	34.6	33.9	34.1	34.3	34.1	34.2	34.2	33.9	34.0	34.2	34.1
2007	34.1	34.4	34.6	35.8	36.6	36.2	36.1	35.4	34.9	33.6	33.3	32.8	34.8
2008	31.4	31.6	31.8	32.3	33.5	33.0	32.9	32.8	32.3	32.1	32.2	32.1	32.3
2009	34.0	34.1	34.3	34.4	34.7	34.9	34.9	34.6	34.3	34.1	33.9	33.9	34.3
Government													
1990	141.9	142.4	143.3	143.9	145.6	145.5	139.0	138.3	142.7	144.1	144.5	144.3	143.0
2000	145.3	145.9	147.1	146.5	147.0	146.5	142.2	142.0	145.3	147.0	148.4	147.2	145.9
2001	145.9	147.6	147.9	147.8	147.8	149.0	144.8	144.4	147.1	148.8	150.1	149.3	147.5
2002	147.6	149.2	150.3	150.1	151.0	151.6	145.3	145.5	149.0	151.1	151.4	151.1	149.4
2003	149.3	150.3	151.0	149.0	149.6	150.6	147.1	146.5	149.1	148.8	150.6	150.6	149.3
2004	149.8	151.1	151.8	151.6	152.2	153.0	147.8	148.9	150.8	151.7	153.5	153.0	151.3
2005	149.6	151.0	151.5	152.4	152.9	154.1	149.3	149.7	151.3	151.2	152.9	151.9	151.5
2006	150.6	151.7	152.3	154.1	154.2	155.1	151.2	150.8	151.0	153.8	155.5	155.1	153.0
2007	153.7	155.1	155.6	155.2	155.2	156.0	152.8	152.7	154.5	155.2	157.5	156.6	155.0
2008	154.8	157.0	157.5	156.3	156.8	158.2	154.3	154.4	156.0	157.9	160.1	158.7	156.8
2009	157.7	158.4	159.1	159.3	158.9	159.7	152.6	154.3	156.0	157.4	157.8	156.8	157.3

Employment by Industry: Washington-Arlington-Alexandria, DC-VA-MD-WV, Selected Years, 1990–2009

(Numbers in thousands, not seasonally adjusted.)

Industry and year	January	February	March	April	May	June	July	August	September	October	November	December	Annual average
Total Nonfarm													
1990	2223.5	2227.3	2245.7	2244.8	2265.6	2292.9	2253.6	2251.2	2263.2	2240.2	2243.0	2250.3	2250.1
2000	2583.6	2594.1	2629.4	2656.5	2677.5	2711.9	2691.0	2694.1	2702.8	2714.7	2733.1	2752.5	2678.4
2001	2672.7	2680.8	2702.0	2707.3	2725.9	2755.0	2729.6	2727.8	2719.7	2724.5	2731.7	2749.3	2718.9
2002	2680.9	2688.7	2709.6	2715.4	2733.1	2754.7	2730.5	2730.8	2735.7	2741.1	2752.9	2761.9	2727.9
2003	2721.0	2717.0	2741.5	2768.5	2788.3	2810.9	2807.1	2799.5	2804.4	2806.7	2817.9	2830.6	2784.5
2004	2772.6	2784.5	2819.3	2830.8	2854.3	2875.5	2869.7	2866.6	2872.3	2892.7	2905.1	2915.7	2854.9
2005	2848.3	2860.8	2879.0	2901.2	2919.4	2937.6	2936.5	2930.0	2935.6	2935.7	2956.9	2967.9	2917.4
2006	2908.6	2919.7	2946.7	2953.7	2971.7	2996.1	2979.6	2972.5	2973.9	2980.7	2992.6	3006.9	2966.9
2007	2942.2	2948.1	2971.9	2978.1	2995.9	3013.0	3001.5	2990.9	2987.6	3005.3	3018.3	3029.0	2990.2
2008	2959.2	2968.1	2985.9	3004.4	3021.5	3029.1	3027.4	3015.6	3004.5	3007.1	3008.3	3006.6	3003.1
2009	2934.4	2932.0	2940.6	2949.0	2963.9	2975.1	2971.2	2953.2	2928.6	2951.2	2953.6	2949.7	2950.2
Total Private													
1990	1647.9	1647.9	1664.3	1666.2	1679.5	1700.0	1687.9	1690.7	1681.0	1656.9	1657.8	1660.8	1670.1
2000	2010.8	2020.3	2050.7	2075.0	2089.5	2124.8	2128.3	2132.7	2126.7	2136.6	2150.8	2166.6	2101.1
2001	2093.2	2101.3	2119.5	2124.4	2139.9	2166.0	2157.7	2156.2	2130.0	2134.3	2140.2	2152.1	2134.6
2002	2086.0	2090.9	2108.5	2116.6	2130.8	2150.6	2146.0	2144.8	2131.7	2132.4	2143.1	2149.4	2127.6
2003	2108.1	2103.0	2124.8	2151.4	2168.4	2189.9	2192.6	2190.5	2185.7	2189.7	2199.6	2211.4	2167.9
2004	2156.8	2164.7	2195.0	2209.6	2228.7	2254.3	2257.4	2255.9	2250.8	2259.9	2269.0	2280.1	2231.9
2005	2222.7	2233.1	2249.1	2270.8	2285.6	2306.3	2308.6	2305.1	2304.7	2298.7	2313.9	2325.5	2285.3
2006	2275.8	2281.6	2305.1	2313.5	2328.0	2356.4	2345.4	2341.9	2334.8	2333.8	2344.3	2356.6	2326.4
2007	2306.0	2305.9	2326.9	2333.9	2347.6	2368.7	2359.6	2352.9	2343.0	2350.3	2359.6	2368.4	2343.6
2008	2309.9	2311.1	2325.0	2348.2	2361.7	2371.6	2368.6	2359.6	2348.2	2341.7	2338.7	2335.5	2343.3
2009	2275.2	2264.7	2269.2	2275.0	2287.2	2299.7	2288.8	2280.3	2262.6	2273.1	2272.0	2268.7	2276.4
Goods-Producing													
1990	220.0	215.6	217.9	216.3	217.4	218.8	215.7	214.3	211.5	205.3	201.7	197.0	212.6
2000	221.0	221.8	227.8	229.6	232.2	236.9	239.5	240.6	240.1	239.0	238.9	238.1	233.8
2001	231.2	232.4	236.0	238.0	241.4	244.4	244.1	244.9	242.7	240.2	239.2	237.1	239.3
2002	230.3	231.1	233.9	235.0	237.4	239.6	239.3	239.8	237.6	235.8	234.5	231.8	235.5
2003	226.5	225.7	228.7	231.9	235.5	237.8	240.5	241.4	240.2	239.4	238.6	237.3	235.3
2004	231.6	231.6	236.7	240.2	243.3	246.0	249.4	249.5	248.7	248.4	247.8	247.4	243.4
2005	240.7	240.6	242.9	249.1	251.9	256.0	257.9	259.0	258.7	255.4	256.3	255.6	252.0
2006	248.8	249.1	253.3	254.9	256.9	260.8	261.1	260.5	258.0	254.3	252.3	251.8	255.2
2007	244.2	241.0	245.0	247.4	249.2	252.5	251.8	252.0	249.3	246.6	244.3	241.6	247.1
2008	234.6	233.5	234.8	235.6	235.8	237.3	236.7	236.4	234.2	230.9	226.6	222.1	233.2
2009	210.9	207.8	206.5	206.3	206.0	206.3	206.3	205.2	202.6	201.1	198.0	196.6	204.5
Mining, Logging, and Construction													
1990	145.2	141.4	143.6	142.5	143.5	144.6	141.7	141.0	138.4	133.4	129.8	125.5	139.2
2000	141.4	141.8	147.4	149.6	151.9	155.5	158.0	159.0	158.8	157.9	158.2	157.4	153.1
2001	151.9	153.2	156.9	159.8	163.1	166.2	166.2	167.2	165.5	164.4	163.5	161.9	161.7
2002	156.6	157.8	160.2	161.9	164.5	166.9	167.1	168.0	166.1	165.4	164.6	162.1	163.4
2003	157.6	156.8	160.4	164.7	168.4	170.6	173.3	174.6	173.6	173.3	172.4	171.2	168.1
2004	165.9	166.0	170.7	174.4	177.5	179.8	182.6	182.9	182.3	182.5	181.9	181.4	177.3
2005	175.5	175.4	177.6	183.6	186.2	190.0	192.1	193.1	193.1	190.7	191.3	190.5	186.6
2006	185.4	185.7	189.7	191.1	193.2	196.5	196.4	196.1	194.2	191.3	189.6	188.7	191.5
2007	182.2	178.9	182.9	185.4	187.1	189.6	189.0	189.4	187.1	184.7	182.5	179.7	184.9
2008	173.4	172.3	173.6	174.5	174.7	176.0	175.5	175.2	173.5	170.6	166.7	162.5	172.4
2009	153.3	150.9	150.0	150.3	150.1	150.6	151.3	150.3	148.3	147.0	143.7	142.4	149.0
Manufacturing													
1990	74.8	74.2	74.3	73.8	73.9	74.2	74.0	73.3	73.1	71.9	71.9	71.5	73.4
2000	79.6	80.0	80.4	80.0	80.3	81.4	81.5	81.6	81.3	81.1	80.7	80.7	80.7
2001	79.3	79.2	79.1	78.2	78.3	78.2	77.9	77.7	77.2	75.8	75.7	75.2	77.7
2002	73.7	73.3	73.7	73.1	72.9	72.7	72.2	71.8	71.5	70.4	69.9	69.7	72.1
2003	68.9	68.9	68.3	67.2	67.1	67.2	67.2	66.8	66.6	66.1	66.2	66.1	67.2
2004	65.7	65.6	66.0	65.8	65.8	66.2	66.8	66.6	66.4	65.9	65.9	66.0	66.1
2005	65.2	65.2	65.3	65.5	65.7	66.0	65.8	65.9	65.6	64.7	65.0	65.1	65.4
2006	63.4	63.4	63.6	63.8	63.7	64.3	64.7	64.4	63.8	63.0	62.7	63.1	63.7
2007	62.0	62.1	62.1	62.0	62.1	62.9	62.8	62.6	62.2	61.9	61.8	61.9	62.2
2008	61.2	61.2	61.2	61.1	61.1	61.3	61.2	61.2	60.7	60.3	59.9	59.6	60.8
2009	57.6	56.9	56.5	56.0	55.9	55.7	55.0	54.9	54.3	54.1	54.3	54.2	55.5
Service-Providing													
1990	2003.5	2011.7	2027.8	2028.5	2048.2	2074.1	2037.9	2036.9	2051.7	2034.9	2041.3	2053.3	2037.5
2001	2441.5	2448.4	2466.0	2469.3	2484.5	2510.6	2485.5	2482.9	2477.0	2484.3	2492.5	2512.2	2479.6
2002	2450.6	2457.6	2475.7	2480.4	2495.7	2515.1	2491.2	2491.0	2498.1	2505.3	2518.4	2530.1	2492.4
2003	2494.5	2491.3	2512.8	2536.6	2552.8	2573.1	2566.6	2558.1	2564.2	2567.3	2579.3	2593.3	2549.2
2004	2541.0	2552.9	2582.6	2590.6	2611.0	2629.5	2620.3	2617.1	2623.6	2644.3	2657.3	2668.3	2611.5
2005	2607.6	2620.2	2636.1	2652.1	2667.5	2681.6	2678.6	2671.0	2676.9	2680.3	2700.6	2712.3	2665.4
2006	2659.8	2670.6	2693.4	2698.8	2714.8	2735.3	2718.5	2712.0	2715.9	2726.4	2740.3	2755.1	2711.7
2007	2698.0	2707.1	2726.9	2730.7	2746.7	2760.5	2749.7	2738.9	2738.3	2758.7	2774.0	2787.4	2743.1
2008	2724.6	2734.6	2751.1	2768.8	2785.7	2791.8	2790.7	2779.2	2770.3	2776.2	2781.7	2784.5	2769.9
2009	2723.5	2724.2	2734.1	2742.7	2757.9	2768.8	2764.9	2748.0	2726.0	2750.1	2755.6	2753.1	2745.7

Employment by Industry: Washington-Arlington-Alexandria, DC-VA-MD-WV, Selected Years, 1990–2009—*Continued*

(Numbers in thousands, not seasonally adjusted.)

Industry and year	January	February	March	April	May	June	July	August	September	October	November	December	Annual average
Trade, Transportation, and Utilities													
1990	382.2	376.6	378.7	378.4	381.4	385.1	380.0	381.2	380.1	377.1	382.9	390.2	381.2
2000	386.3	382.6	385.5	385.1	388.3	393.5	391.8	393.2	392.5	397.1	408.6	418.7	393.6
2001	391.4	385.2	386.4	384.0	387.8	392.0	390.6	390.8	387.9	390.1	398.6	406.9	391.0
2002	384.7	379.7	381.1	381.5	384.6	388.7	386.9	386.7	386.2	389.2	397.1	405.4	387.7
2003	385.2	380.5	382.6	385.3	388.3	393.0	391.8	392.6	392.2	395.2	404.6	412.5	392.0
2004	391.8	388.1	391.5	390.6	395.0	402.1	398.8	399.2	397.6	404.9	413.8	422.0	399.6
2005	401.7	398.6	400.1	400.7	403.5	406.6	407.5	406.7	404.1	406.8	415.5	426.2	406.5
2006	405.3	396.7	398.7	397.4	401.8	405.8	403.6	403.3	402.1	404.5	414.4	422.8	404.7
2007	404.3	396.6	398.9	399.5	402.8	406.6	405.1	403.1	401.1	403.2	413.8	422.0	404.8
2008	402.2	395.3	395.7	395.7	397.8	400.5	399.1	397.3	394.3	393.8	399.1	404.2	397.9
2009	383.1	375.7	374.8	372.6	376.1	378.4	376.0	375.4	374.5	377.7	383.8	389.2	378.1
Wholesale Trade													
1990	67.5	67.5	67.8	67.9	68.0	68.2	68.3	68.3	67.9	66.7	66.4	66.4	67.6
2000	66.8	67.3	67.7	67.6	68.0	68.6	68.3	68.3	68.1	68.1	68.5	68.8	68.0
2001	68.1	68.1	68.5	68.5	68.4	68.5	68.2	67.9	67.4	67.3	67.5	67.2	68.0
2002	66.5	66.3	66.4	66.4	66.5	66.6	66.4	66.3	65.7	66.3	66.5	66.8	66.4
2003	67.9	68.0	68.3	68.0	68.3	68.5	67.6	67.5	67.0	67.9	68.3	68.6	68.0
2004	68.6	68.8	69.2	68.3	68.3	68.8	69.0	68.8	68.7	69.8	70.3	70.5	69.1
2005	70.4	70.8	71.0	71.5	71.6	71.4	71.9	71.9	71.3	70.5	70.6	70.9	71.2
2006	69.4	69.6	70.0	70.0	70.5	70.7	70.4	70.3	69.9	70.1	70.1	70.5	70.1
2007	70.2	70.3	70.7	70.7	70.9	71.3	70.6	70.5	70.2	70.4	70.5	70.6	70.6
2008	69.9	70.2	70.1	69.9	69.9	70.1	69.8	69.5	68.9	68.7	68.0	67.6	69.4
2009	67.1	66.6	66.3	65.9	65.8	65.9	65.4	65.3	64.8	65.5	65.1	65.4	65.8
Retail Trade													
1990	255.8	250.9	251.9	251.2	253.5	255.6	251.4	252.4	251.2	250.3	255.8	262.9	253.6
2000	251.2	247.1	249.2	249.2	251.8	255.5	254.3	255.8	256.0	258.6	269.9	279.6	256.5
2001	255.4	249.4	250.4	247.4	250.7	254.3	252.5	253.2	251.9	254.8	264.0	273.5	254.8
2002	253.7	249.0	250.4	250.4	252.9	256.0	254.0	253.8	254.6	256.0	263.4	271.7	255.5
2003	251.4	247.0	248.4	250.6	252.8	256.8	255.5	256.7	257.1	259.1	268.1	275.2	256.6
2004	257.3	253.5	255.7	256.4	260.1	265.6	262.8	263.2	261.5	267.4	275.6	283.2	263.5
2005	265.3	261.4	262.5	263.0	265.4	268.1	268.9	268.3	266.7	269.2	277.2	285.8	268.5
2006	270.5	263.7	264.8	263.8	267.1	270.1	269.0	269.1	267.8	270.5	280.1	285.5	270.2
2007	271.4	263.6	265.1	266.0	268.6	271.1	270.6	268.6	267.0	269.2	279.2	284.8	270.4
2008	269.8	262.5	263.3	263.6	265.2	267.0	266.2	264.5	262.5	262.5	267.5	271.2	265.5
2009	254.2	248.2	247.6	246.1	248.8	250.6	249.3	249.1	248.5	250.7	257.4	261.6	251.0
Transportation and Utilities													
1990	58.9	58.2	59.0	59.3	59.9	61.3	60.3	60.5	61.0	60.1	60.7	60.9	60.0
2000	68.3	68.2	68.6	68.3	68.5	69.4	69.2	69.1	68.4	70.4	70.2	70.3	69.1
2001	67.9	67.7	67.5	68.1	68.7	69.2	69.9	69.7	68.6	68.0	67.1	66.2	68.2
2002	64.5	64.4	64.3	64.7	65.2	66.1	66.5	66.6	65.9	66.9	67.2	66.9	65.8
2003	65.9	65.5	65.9	66.7	67.2	67.7	68.7	68.4	68.1	68.2	68.2	68.7	67.4
2004	65.9	65.8	66.6	65.9	66.6	67.7	67.0	67.2	67.4	67.7	67.9	68.3	67.0
2005	66.0	66.4	66.6	66.2	66.5	67.1	66.7	66.5	66.1	67.1	67.7	69.5	66.9
2006	65.4	63.4	63.9	63.6	64.2	65.0	64.2	63.9	64.4	63.9	64.2	66.8	64.4
2007	62.7	62.7	63.1	62.8	63.3	64.2	63.9	64.0	63.9	63.6	64.1	66.6	63.7
2008	62.5	62.6	62.3	62.2	62.7	63.4	63.1	63.3	62.9	62.6	63.6	65.4	63.1
2009	61.8	60.9	60.9	60.6	61.5	61.9	61.3	61.0	61.2	61.5	61.3	62.2	61.3
Information													
1990	81.3	81.5	82.0	82.2	82.0	82.9	83.5	83.4	82.5	81.9	82.1	82.2	82.3
2000	118.2	119.6	121.1	123.2	125.0	127.8	128.1	129.5	129.8	132.5	133.0	134.2	126.8
2001	134.9	135.4	135.4	133.8	133.5	132.2	131.4	130.3	128.5	126.6	125.3	124.9	131.0
2002	120.8	119.9	119.6	117.8	117.6	117.3	114.6	113.8	112.0	110.0	110.2	109.7	115.3
2003	109.7	109.9	110.0	109.2	109.9	110.4	110.2	110.1	109.2	108.3	109.0	109.1	109.6
2004	108.8	108.1	109.2	107.4	107.3	107.2	107.5	106.6	104.8	102.0	101.8	101.4	106.0
2005	100.0	100.4	100.3	99.6	99.7	100.2	100.4	99.7	99.5	99.4	99.3	99.4	99.8
2006	98.3	98.7	99.4	98.0	97.9	97.9	97.3	96.6	95.8	94.5	94.5	94.2	96.9
2007	94.5	94.6	94.4	93.4	93.7	94.3	94.5	94.2	93.3	92.8	93.1	93.4	93.9
2008	92.0	92.4	92.3	92.1	91.9	91.8	91.5	91.0	90.2	89.0	89.2	88.4	91.0
2009	86.1	86.0	85.4	84.3	84.1	84.6	83.6	83.1	81.7	81.4	80.9	80.3	83.5
Financial Activities													
1990	136.3	137.0	137.9	136.9	137.9	139.6	140.1	141.0	139.2	136.9	136.8	137.2	138.1
2000	142.9	143.3	144.3	144.3	144.7	146.6	147.0	147.1	146.1	145.7	146.6	147.8	145.5
2001	145.0	145.5	146.3	146.9	147.7	149.2	149.6	149.6	147.9	148.1	148.4	149.6	147.8
2002	149.2	149.8	150.2	149.6	150.0	151.4	151.5	151.8	150.8	151.6	152.2	153.3	151.0
2003	152.9	153.0	153.4	155.3	156.2	157.7	159.2	158.8	157.2	155.9	155.3	155.6	155.9
2004	153.7	153.7	154.6	156.9	157.9	158.8	158.8	158.8	158.0	159.0	158.9	159.9	157.4
2005	158.3	158.8	158.6	160.3	161.0	161.9	162.1	161.6	161.0	160.2	159.9	160.8	160.4
2006	159.4	160.2	161.0	160.7	161.7	163.4	162.8	162.6	161.8	161.1	161.1	162.2	161.5
2007	160.2	160.6	160.8	159.7	160.2	161.1	160.9	159.7	158.4	157.4	156.8	156.9	159.4
2008	154.6	154.6	154.5	155.1	155.0	155.9	156.0	155.2	153.8	152.8	152.2	152.0	154.3
2009	149.2	148.3	147.8	147.6	147.8	148.9	148.5	147.9	146.4	145.7	145.9	145.5	147.5

Employment by Industry: Washington-Arlington-Alexandria, DC-VA-MD-WV, Selected Years, 1990–2009—*Continued*

(Numbers in thousands, not seasonally adjusted.)

Industry and year	January	February	March	April	May	June	July	August	September	October	November	December	Annual average
Professional and Business Services													
1990	358.1	361.8	367.3	368.4	370.3	375.5	372.9	373.8	371.1	367.3	365.8	366.0	368.2
2000	530.0	534.2	543.0	549.8	551.5	562.7	563.0	564.7	564.1	566.6	567.5	571.5	555.7
2001	561.4	566.0	570.6	571.1	571.6	578.6	573.4	572.7	564.5	568.3	567.2	569.8	569.6
2002	551.8	554.9	560.0	560.1	560.6	564.4	563.3	562.2	558.7	560.3	561.1	562.3	560.0
2003	565.8	565.7	571.1	583.6	586.5	592.2	594.2	594.9	592.8	596.3	598.0	602.1	586.9
2004	588.9	593.9	603.6	607.7	611.8	620.2	625.0	626.6	624.9	628.4	628.3	632.6	616.0
2005	623.4	629.1	634.9	641.5	643.5	650.6	655.6	655.7	656.3	654.0	655.3	656.6	646.4
2006	645.5	651.2	657.6	661.8	663.9	673.2	672.7	672.8	669.2	667.8	668.6	670.1	664.5
2007	659.9	664.9	670.3	673.7	675.7	682.6	680.0	680.1	673.6	679.2	679.7	681.1	675.1
2008	669.6	672.8	676.4	683.9	684.2	688.5	688.9	687.8	682.9	683.7	682.1	680.3	681.8
2009	671.1	670.5	671.9	673.7	674.2	680.1	678.8	677.0	669.5	671.8	672.4	672.0	673.6
Education and Health Services													
1990	190.9	193.1	194.3	194.5	195.1	194.4	193.2	194.7	198.2	199.2	200.5	200.3	195.7
2000	264.6	269.5	271.9	276.3	274.6	275.1	276.8	276.6	277.9	281.3	284.1	283.8	276.0
2001	274.0	278.0	280.4	281.7	280.3	281.3	282.8	283.0	285.5	289.3	290.9	293.2	283.4
2002	289.1	291.5	292.7	293.4	294.4	293.6	292.9	293.5	295.9	299.9	302.0	301.9	295.1
2003	291.3	293.3	296.5	296.3	294.0	291.8	288.4	287.1	295.2	297.3	298.6	298.6	294.0
2004	296.7	302.3	305.2	305.2	303.4	300.2	296.8	294.7	303.1	308.2	309.8	308.9	302.9
2005	305.7	310.5	311.4	311.2	309.6	305.1	300.0	299.0	308.9	313.5	317.4	316.9	309.1
2006	311.5	317.0	319.3	319.7	317.0	313.7	307.9	307.0	317.3	323.7	327.5	328.1	317.5
2007	324.3	329.3	332.0	330.7	328.1	323.9	318.5	317.2	328.1	335.4	337.1	337.9	328.5
2008	331.2	334.8	336.4	338.8	340.1	335.2	332.7	332.3	341.2	345.2	347.0	348.1	338.6
2009	344.7	347.6	348.8	352.0	351.9	346.1	341.6	340.0	346.0	353.1	354.1	350.4	348.0
Leisure and Hospitality													
1990	169.5	172.4	175.4	178.1	182.9	189.7	189.6	189.4	185.9	177.1	175.5	175.7	180.1
2000	202.7	203.6	209.9	217.7	223.7	231.8	231.1	230.5	225.4	221.5	218.8	218.3	219.6
2001	205.9	208.8	213.8	217.3	224.2	232.3	230.2	229.6	219.7	217.8	216.8	215.8	219.4
2002	207.1	209.7	215.5	222.7	229.4	237.0	237.6	236.9	232.0	227.4	227.6	225.7	225.7
2003	219.1	216.9	222.4	229.1	236.5	243.9	244.2	243.0	237.6	235.3	233.7	232.9	232.9
2004	224.5	225.5	231.3	236.7	244.1	252.2	252.4	252.5	246.8	243.1	242.0	241.8	241.1
2005	229.5	230.9	235.4	242.5	250.0	258.5	257.6	256.3	250.1	244.3	244.4	243.4	245.2
2006	234.8	235.9	241.8	245.8	252.7	263.2	261.1	260.9	253.7	248.8	247.0	247.3	249.4
2007	239.7	239.0	244.7	250.4	257.5	265.5	266.8	266.0	259.3	255.2	253.6	253.3	254.3
2008	245.4	246.5	252.3	262.6	270.6	275.0	275.8	273.2	266.2	261.5	257.6	255.1	261.8
2009	246.3	245.4	250.1	255.7	263.5	269.6	269.6	267.8	259.9	258.8	253.3	250.7	257.6
Other Services													
1990	109.7	110.0	110.8	111.5	112.6	114.0	112.9	112.9	112.5	112.1	112.5	112.2	112.0
2000	145.1	145.7	147.2	149.0	149.5	150.4	151.0	150.5	150.8	152.9	153.3	154.2	150.0
2001	149.4	150.0	150.6	151.6	153.4	156.0	155.6	155.3	153.3	153.9	153.8	154.8	153.1
2002	153.0	154.3	155.5	156.5	156.8	158.6	159.9	160.1	158.5	158.2	158.4	159.3	157.4
2003	157.6	158.0	160.1	160.7	161.5	163.1	164.1	162.6	161.3	162.0	161.8	163.3	161.3
2004	160.8	161.5	162.9	164.9	165.9	167.6	168.7	168.0	166.9	165.9	166.6	166.1	165.5
2005	163.4	164.2	165.5	165.9	166.4	167.4	167.5	167.1	166.1	165.1	165.8	166.6	165.9
2006	172.2	172.8	174.0	175.2	176.1	178.4	178.9	178.2	176.9	179.1	178.9	180.1	176.7
2007	178.9	179.9	180.8	179.1	180.4	182.2	182.0	180.6	179.9	180.5	181.2	182.2	180.6
2008	180.3	181.2	182.6	184.4	186.3	187.4	187.9	186.4	185.4	184.8	184.9	185.3	184.7
2009	183.8	183.4	183.9	182.8	183.6	185.7	184.4	183.9	182.0	183.5	183.6	184.0	183.7
Government													
1990	575.6	579.4	581.4	578.6	586.1	593.2	568.7	561.6	582.2	583.3	585.2	589.5	580.4
2000	572.8	573.8	578.7	581.5	588.0	587.4	565.7	562.5	576.1	578.1	582.3	585.9	577.7
2001	579.5	579.5	582.5	582.9	586.0	589.3	574.9	572.7	589.7	590.2	591.5	597.2	584.7
2002	594.9	597.8	601.1	598.8	602.3	604.5	587.7	587.2	604.0	608.7	609.8	612.5	600.8
2003	612.9	614.0	616.7	617.1	619.9	621.0	614.5	609.0	618.7	617.0	618.3	619.2	616.5
2004	615.8	619.8	624.3	621.2	625.6	621.2	612.3	610.7	621.5	632.8	636.1	635.6	623.1
2005	625.6	627.7	629.9	630.4	633.8	631.3	627.9	624.9	630.9	637.0	643.0	642.4	632.1
2006	632.8	638.1	641.6	640.2	643.7	639.7	634.2	630.6	639.1	646.9	648.3	650.3	640.5
2007	636.2	642.2	645.0	644.2	648.3	644.3	641.9	638.0	644.6	655.0	658.7	660.6	646.6
2008	649.3	657.0	660.9	656.2	659.8	657.5	658.8	656.0	656.3	665.4	669.6	671.1	659.8
2009	659.2	667.3	671.4	674.0	676.7	675.4	682.4	672.9	666.0	678.1	681.6	681.0	673.8

Employment by Industry: Worcester, MA-CT, NECTA, Selected Years, 1990–2009

(Numbers in thousands, not seasonally adjusted.)

Industry and year	January	February	March	April	May	June	July	August	September	October	November	December	Annual average
Total Nonfarm													
1990	224.1	223.5	223.3	223.2	224.1	223.5	217.7	217.8	220.8	220.1	219.8	219.4	221.4
2000	241.1	241.9	243.3	245.2	246.1	247.2	242.5	242.2	246.4	247.5	247.6	250.2	245.1
2001	243.1	243.6	244.2	247.6	249.1	249.4	243.3	241.8	246.8	247.0	246.9	247.5	245.9
2002	240.4	240.2	240.9	244.2	246.2	246.0	240.8	240.6	245.3	246.0	246.7	247.3	243.7
2003	240.9	239.7	240.6	242.4	244.4	244.6	241.1	239.9	244.7	246.5	246.3	246.6	243.1
2004	239.2	239.5	241.1	244.1	245.8	247.0	242.3	242.5	245.8	246.4	246.9	247.5	244.0
2005	239.9	240.7	241.1	244.3	246.3	246.9	242.4	241.5	245.8	246.5	247.8	248.2	244.3
2006	242.7	242.2	243.8	246.9	248.5	249.7	245.6	246.1	249.3	251.1	250.9	251.3	247.3
2007	244.3	245.0	245.9	247.7	250.6	252.1	245.4	245.6	248.8	251.6	252.6	251.7	248.4
2008	245.2	246.2	246.6	247.9	249.3	249.5	244.4	244.2	247.9	249.1	247.5	246.0	247.0
2009	239.4	238.7	238.1	239.2	240.5	240.1	234.1	234.0	237.1	238.4	237.3	236.9	237.8
Total Private													
1990	194.3	193.6	193.5	193.2	193.8	194.0	189.9	189.5	191.9	190.0	189.7	189.3	191.9
2000	206.9	207.4	208.3	210.2	210.3	211.8	209.1	209.6	211.6	211.8	211.8	214.3	210.3
2001	207.8	207.9	208.5	211.7	212.6	213.0	209.0	209.0	211.2	210.9	210.5	210.8	210.2
2002	204.4	203.8	204.6	207.7	209.3	209.5	207.3	207.8	209.4	209.9	210.2	210.8	207.9
2003	205.2	203.7	204.4	206.4	208.2	208.4	207.5	206.9	208.7	210.8	210.8	210.5	207.6
2004	204.1	204.0	205.2	208.0	209.7	211.3	209.0	209.5	209.8	210.0	210.2	210.6	208.5
2005	203.8	204.0	204.7	208.0	209.7	210.5	209.3	209.3	210.2	209.7	210.9	211.3	208.5
2006	206.1	205.6	207.0	209.8	211.1	212.9	212.1	212.6	212.7	213.7	213.1	213.6	210.9
2007	207.3	207.6	208.5	210.1	212.4	214.3	211.3	211.9	211.8	213.9	214.6	213.6	211.4
2008	208.0	208.5	208.8	210.1	211.3	212.3	210.1	210.5	211.0	211.3	209.7	208.4	210.0
2009	202.1	200.8	200.1	201.0	202.4	202.6	199.7	199.9	200.4	201.1	199.8	199.0	200.7
Goods-Producing													
1990	52.8	51.9	51.8	51.6	52.1	52.3	51.9	51.9	51.5	50.8	50.5	49.9	51.6
2000	46.8	46.3	46.7	47.4	47.8	48.7	48.2	48.5	48.6	49.0	48.7	49.0	48.0
2001	47.6	47.2	47.1	47.8	47.8	47.9	46.5	46.3	46.3	45.7	45.4	45.3	46.7
2002	43.2	42.6	42.6	43.1	43.4	43.6	42.7	43.1	43.0	42.7	42.5	42.3	42.9
2003	41.3	40.3	40.1	40.6	40.9	41.2	40.9	40.9	40.9	41.0	40.8	40.4	40.8
2004	39.1	38.5	38.8	39.9	40.4	40.8	40.7	41.2	41.0	40.7	40.7	40.5	40.2
2005	38.7	38.2	38.2	39.2	39.8	40.2	40.0	40.0	39.9	39.7	39.8	39.8	39.5
2006	38.9	38.5	38.4	39.3	39.8	40.4	40.4	40.6	40.2	40.0	39.7	39.6	39.7
2007	38.2	37.6	37.7	38.1	38.7	39.5	39.4	39.4	39.3	39.5	39.5	39.1	38.8
2008	37.9	37.3	37.3	37.6	38.0	38.6	38.3	38.1	38.1	38.0	37.5	36.7	37.8
2009	34.8	33.8	33.2	33.2	33.3	33.7	33.3	33.4	33.2	33.0	32.7	32.5	33.3
Mining, Logging, and Construction													
1990	6.2	5.8	5.8	6.3	6.7	6.9	7.1	7.1	7.0	6.7	6.5	6.1	6.5
2000	8.2	7.8	8.1	8.8	9.1	9.6	10.0	10.0	10.0	9.9	9.8	9.6	9.2
2001	8.9	8.8	8.8	9.7	10.1	10.3	10.6	10.7	10.7	10.1	10.0	9.8	9.9
2002	9.0	8.7	8.8	9.5	9.9	10.1	10.2	10.3	10.1	10.0	10.0	9.7	9.7
2003	8.8	8.2	8.3	9.2	9.9	10.1	10.5	10.7	10.6	10.7	10.6	10.2	9.8
2004	9.1	8.8	9.1	10.0	10.5	10.8	11.2	11.3	11.1	10.9	10.8	10.4	10.3
2005	9.2	8.8	8.9	9.9	10.5	10.8	11.2	11.2	11.1	10.8	10.9	10.6	10.3
2006	9.8	9.5	9.6	10.4	10.8	11.1	11.4	11.5	11.2	11.0	10.6	10.2	10.6
2007	9.1	8.6	8.7	9.2	9.9	10.3	10.5	10.5	10.5	10.3	10.2	9.7	9.8
2008	8.7	8.4	8.5	9.0	9.5	9.9	9.9	9.9	9.8	9.6	9.3	8.7	9.3
2009	7.6	7.2	7.1	7.6	7.9	8.2	8.3	8.4	8.3	8.2	7.9	7.6	7.9
Manufacturing													
1990	46.6	46.1	46.0	45.3	45.4	45.4	44.8	44.8	44.5	44.1	44.0	43.8	45.1
2000	38.6	38.5	38.6	38.6	38.7	39.1	38.2	38.5	38.6	39.1	38.9	39.4	38.7
2001	38.7	38.4	38.3	38.1	37.7	37.6	35.9	35.6	35.6	35.6	35.4	35.5	36.9
2002	34.2	33.9	33.8	33.6	33.5	33.5	32.5	32.8	32.9	32.7	32.5	32.6	33.2
2003	32.5	32.1	31.8	31.4	31.0	31.1	30.4	30.2	30.3	30.3	30.2	30.2	31.0
2004	30.0	29.7	29.7	29.9	29.9	30.0	29.5	29.9	29.9	29.8	29.9	30.1	29.9
2005	29.5	29.4	29.3	29.3	29.3	29.4	28.8	28.8	28.8	28.9	28.9	29.2	29.1
2006	29.1	29.0	28.8	28.9	29.0	29.3	29.0	29.1	29.0	29.0	29.1	29.4	29.1
2007	29.1	29.0	29.0	28.9	28.8	29.2	28.9	28.9	28.8	29.2	29.3	29.4	29.0
2008	29.2	28.9	28.8	28.6	28.5	28.7	28.4	28.2	28.3	28.4	28.2	28.0	28.5
2009	27.2	26.6	26.1	25.6	25.4	25.5	25.0	25.0	24.9	24.8	24.8	24.9	25.5
Service-Providing													
1990	171.3	171.6	171.5	171.6	172.0	171.2	165.8	165.9	169.3	169.3	169.3	169.5	169.9
2000	194.3	195.6	196.6	197.8	198.3	198.5	194.3	193.7	197.8	198.5	198.9	201.2	197.1
2001	195.5	196.4	197.1	199.8	201.3	201.5	196.8	195.5	200.5	201.3	201.5	202.2	199.1
2002	197.2	197.6	198.3	201.1	202.8	202.4	198.1	197.5	202.3	203.3	204.2	205.0	200.8
2003	199.6	199.4	200.5	201.8	203.5	203.4	200.2	199.0	203.8	205.5	205.5	206.2	202.4
2004	200.1	201.0	202.3	204.2	205.4	206.2	201.6	201.3	204.8	205.7	206.2	207.0	203.8
2005	201.2	202.5	202.9	205.1	206.5	206.7	202.4	201.5	205.9	206.8	208.0	208.4	204.8
2006	203.8	203.7	205.4	207.6	208.7	209.3	205.2	205.5	209.1	211.1	211.2	211.7	207.7
2007	206.1	207.4	208.2	209.6	211.9	212.6	206.0	206.2	209.5	212.1	213.1	212.6	209.6
2008	207.3	208.9	209.3	210.3	211.3	210.9	206.1	206.1	209.8	211.1	210.0	209.3	209.2
2009	204.6	204.9	204.9	206.0	207.2	206.4	200.8	200.6	203.9	205.4	204.6	204.4	204.5

Employment by Industry: Worcester, MA-CT, NECTA, Selected Years, 1990–2009—*Continued*

(Numbers in thousands, not seasonally adjusted.)

Industry and year	January	February	March	April	May	June	July	August	September	October	November	December	Annual average
Trade, Transportation, and Utilities													
1990	45.1	43.9	43.8	43.4	43.1	43.5	42.0	42.0	43.0	42.6	43.0	43.2	43.2
2000	47.1	46.4	46.4	46.7	46.4	46.5	45.4	45.5	45.8	46.2	47.0	48.1	46.5
2001	45.8	45.0	45.1	45.8	46.0	46.3	45.3	45.5	45.7	46.5	47.4	48.0	46.0
2002	45.2	44.5	44.9	45.2	45.2	45.6	44.6	44.3	45.0	45.6	46.2	46.8	45.3
2003	45.1	44.2	44.6	45.0	45.3	45.7	45.2	45.2	45.8	46.1	46.6	46.8	45.5
2004	45.0	44.5	44.7	45.0	45.2	45.7	44.5	44.5	44.8	45.5	46.2	46.6	45.2
2005	45.4	44.7	44.8	45.1	45.5	45.6	44.9	45.1	45.3	45.5	46.3	46.7	45.4
2006	45.3	44.6	45.0	45.2	45.3	45.6	45.3	45.7	46.2	46.5	47.0	47.4	45.8
2007	46.1	45.5	45.9	45.9	46.4	46.9	46.0	45.8	46.1	47.0	47.8	48.1	46.5
2008	46.8	45.8	46.1	46.1	46.3	46.4	45.6	45.7	46.0	46.4	46.6	46.7	46.2
2009	44.6	43.6	43.6	43.5	43.8	44.1	43.0	42.8	43.2	43.4	43.6	43.6	43.6
Wholesale Trade													
1990	11.7	11.7	11.7	11.9	11.8	11.9	11.8	11.8	11.8	11.7	11.4	11.3	11.7
2000	10.4	10.4	10.4	10.7	10.5	10.3	10.1	10.2	10.2	10.2	10.2	10.3	10.3
2001	9.9	10.0	10.0	10.0	10.1	10.1	9.9	10.1	9.9	10.1	10.0	9.9	10.0
2002	9.7	9.6	9.6	9.8	9.7	9.9	9.8	9.8	9.8	10.0	10.0	10.0	9.8
2003	10.0	9.9	10.0	10.0	10.0	10.0	10.1	10.0	9.9	9.8	9.8	9.7	9.9
2004	9.5	9.5	9.6	9.7	9.7	9.8	9.5	9.5	9.4	9.4	9.5	9.4	9.5
2005	9.4	9.3	9.4	9.6	9.6	9.7	9.6	9.8	9.7	9.8	9.9	9.9	9.6
2006	9.7	9.8	9.9	9.9	9.9	9.9	10.0	10.1	10.1	10.1	10.1	10.1	10.0
2007	9.9	9.9	10.0	10.0	10.1	10.1	10.1	10.1	10.0	10.4	10.5	10.4	10.1
2008	10.4	10.4	10.6	10.7	10.8	10.8	10.8	10.9	10.8	11.0	10.9	10.9	10.8
2009	10.4	10.2	10.3	10.4	10.3	10.3	10.3	10.3	10.2	10.3	10.2	10.2	10.3
Retail Trade													
1990	27.3	26.1	26.0	25.6	25.4	25.6	24.7	24.5	24.7	24.7	25.4	25.5	25.5
2000	29.2	28.5	28.5	28.1	28.1	28.7	28.2	28.3	28.1	28.2	29.2	30.2	28.6
2001	28.4	27.6	27.6	28.1	28.3	28.7	28.2	28.3	28.2	28.7	29.8	30.5	28.5
2002	27.9	27.4	27.8	27.7	27.8	28.0	27.8	27.6	27.7	27.9	28.5	29.0	27.9
2003	27.6	27.0	27.2	27.5	27.8	28.2	28.0	28.2	28.4	28.6	29.2	29.5	28.1
2004	28.3	27.8	27.9	28.0	28.2	28.5	28.1	28.2	28.1	28.6	29.3	29.8	28.4
2005	28.8	28.2	28.1	28.2	28.5	28.5	28.2	28.3	28.0	28.1	28.7	28.9	28.4
2006	28.1	27.4	27.6	27.7	27.7	27.9	27.9	28.2	28.1	28.3	28.8	29.1	28.1
2007	28.2	27.6	27.9	27.9	28.2	28.6	28.2	28.0	27.8	28.4	29.0	29.2	28.3
2008	28.1	27.2	27.3	27.2	27.3	27.5	27.4	27.5	27.2	27.4	27.7	27.8	27.5
2009	26.6	25.9	25.8	25.8	26.0	26.4	25.8	25.7	25.6	25.7	26.1	26.0	26.0
Transportation and Utilities													
1990	6.1	6.1	6.1	5.9	5.9	6.0	5.5	5.7	6.5	6.2	6.2	6.4	6.1
2000	7.5	7.5	7.5	7.9	7.8	7.5	7.1	7.0	7.5	7.8	7.6	7.6	7.5
2001	7.5	7.4	7.5	7.7	7.6	7.5	7.2	7.1	7.6	7.7	7.6	7.6	7.5
2002	7.6	7.5	7.5	7.7	7.7	7.7	7.0	6.9	7.5	7.7	7.7	7.8	7.5
2003	7.5	7.3	7.4	7.5	7.5	7.5	7.1	7.0	7.5	7.7	7.6	7.6	7.4
2004	7.2	7.2	7.2	7.3	7.3	7.4	6.9	6.8	7.3	7.5	7.4	7.4	7.2
2005	7.2	7.2	7.3	7.3	7.4	7.4	7.1	7.0	7.6	7.6	7.7	7.9	7.4
2006	7.5	7.4	7.5	7.6	7.7	7.8	7.4	7.4	8.0	8.1	8.1	8.2	7.7
2007	8.0	8.0	8.0	8.0	8.1	8.2	7.7	7.7	8.3	8.2	8.3	8.5	8.1
2008	8.3	8.2	8.2	8.2	8.2	8.1	7.4	7.3	8.0	8.0	8.0	8.0	8.0
2009	7.6	7.5	7.5	7.3	7.5	7.4	6.9	6.8	7.4	7.4	7.3	7.4	7.3
Information													
1990	4.1	4.1	4.1	4.2	4.2	4.2	4.1	4.0	4.0	4.0	4.0	3.9	4.1
2000	3.7	3.8	3.8	3.8	3.9	4.0	4.1	3.7	4.2	4.2	4.3	4.4	4.0
2001	4.4	4.4	4.4	4.5	4.5	4.5	4.4	4.4	4.3	4.4	4.3	4.3	4.4
2002	4.5	4.4	4.4	4.3	4.4	4.4	4.4	4.3	4.2	4.2	4.2	4.2	4.3
2003	4.1	4.1	4.0	4.0	4.0	4.0	4.0	3.9	3.8	3.9	3.9	3.9	4.0
2004	3.9	3.9	3.9	3.9	4.0	4.2	4.2	4.1	3.9	3.9	3.9	3.9	4.0
2005	3.9	3.9	3.9	3.7	3.7	3.6	3.6	3.6	3.6	3.6	3.6	3.6	3.7
2006	3.6	3.6	3.6	3.6	3.6	3.7	3.7	3.7	3.7	3.7	3.7	3.7	3.7
2007	3.9	3.9	3.9	3.9	4.0	4.0	4.0	4.0	3.9	4.0	4.0	3.9	4.0
2008	4.0	4.0	4.0	4.1	4.1	4.1	4.0	4.0	3.9	3.6	3.6	3.6	3.9
2009	3.5	3.5	3.4	3.4	3.4	3.5	3.4	3.5	3.4	3.4	3.4	3.4	3.4
Financial Activities													
1990	13.7	13.7	13.7	13.6	13.7	13.9	13.6	13.6	13.5	13.2	13.2	13.2	13.6
2000	14.1	14.0	14.0	13.8	13.8	13.8	13.6	13.5	13.4	13.4	13.5	13.5	13.7
2001	13.5	13.4	13.4	13.8	13.9	14.0	14.1	14.1	14.0	14.2	14.1	14.1	13.9
2002	14.0	14.0	14.0	14.2	14.2	14.2	14.2	14.3	14.1	14.3	14.3	14.3	14.2
2003	13.9	13.9	14.0	14.1	14.1	14.2	14.3	14.3	14.2	14.2	14.2	14.2	14.1
2004	14.2	14.1	14.1	14.1	14.2	14.2	14.3	14.3	14.1	14.0	13.9	14.0	14.1
2005	13.8	13.8	13.9	14.0	14.0	14.2	14.3	14.3	14.2	14.1	14.2	14.3	14.1
2006	14.2	14.2	14.2	14.3	14.3	14.4	14.3	14.2	14.0	14.1	14.0	14.0	14.2
2007	13.9	13.8	13.8	13.8	13.7	13.7	13.7	13.7	13.5	13.6	13.6	13.6	13.7
2008	13.4	13.5	13.4	13.5	13.5	13.6	13.7	13.6	13.5	13.4	13.5	13.4	13.5
2009	13.5	13.4	13.4	13.4	13.4	13.5	13.5	13.4	13.3	13.3	13.4	13.3	13.4

Employment by Industry: Worcester, MA-CT, NECTA, Selected Years, 1990–2009—*Continued*

(Numbers in thousands, not seasonally adjusted.)

Industry and year	January	February	March	April	May	June	July	August	September	October	November	December	Annual average
Professional and Business Services													
1990	24.5	24.8	24.7	24.5	24.3	24.3	24.2	24.4	24.6	23.6	23.5	23.5	24.2
2000	29.0	29.2	29.4	30.1	29.6	30.0	30.1	30.5	30.3	29.5	29.6	29.9	29.8
2001	27.8	27.8	28.0	28.6	28.5	28.8	28.2	28.5	28.3	27.5	27.3	27.3	28.1
2002	26.6	26.6	26.7	27.2	27.3	27.2	28.1	28.1	28.4	27.3	27.6	27.1	27.4
2003	26.6	26.5	26.6	27.1	27.3	27.4	27.6	27.6	27.7	27.9	28.0	28.3	27.4
2004	27.3	27.6	27.8	28.6	28.8	29.2	29.3	29.5	29.5	29.2	29.3	29.4	28.8
2005	27.7	27.9	28.2	29.1	29.5	29.7	29.6	29.7	30.0	29.8	30.1	30.0	29.3
2006	28.7	28.5	29.0	29.4	29.9	30.2	30.5	30.6	30.1	30.2	29.8	29.7	29.7
2007	28.1	28.1	28.1	28.9	29.3	29.7	28.9	28.8	28.5	28.4	28.6	28.6	28.7
2008	27.1	27.1	27.0	27.4	27.6	27.9	27.6	27.9	27.8	27.4	27.2	27.1	27.4
2009	26.2	25.7	25.5	25.6	25.7	25.4	25.1	25.3	25.0	25.1	24.7	24.4	25.3
Education and Health Services													
1990	29.4	30.3	30.4	31.0	31.1	30.5	29.1	28.9	30.5	31.6	31.7	31.9	30.5
2000	40.6	41.8	41.7	41.8	41.6	41.0	40.2	40.2	41.9	41.9	41.9	42.0	41.4
2001	42.1	43.5	43.7	44.1	44.1	42.8	41.8	41.7	44.5	44.4	44.2	44.3	43.4
2002	43.5	44.4	44.6	45.6	45.7	44.9	44.0	43.9	45.4	46.2	46.2	46.5	45.1
2003	45.5	46.3	46.5	46.8	46.2	45.4	44.1	43.8	45.8	46.7	46.8	46.4	45.9
2004	45.5	46.3	46.5	46.3	45.8	45.4	44.4	44.3	45.6	46.2	46.3	46.2	45.7
2005	45.2	46.4	46.4	46.6	46.3	45.9	45.3	45.3	46.5	47.0	47.3	47.0	46.3
2006	46.2	47.3	47.5	47.8	47.4	46.6	46.1	46.0	47.4	48.6	48.6	48.6	47.3
2007	47.3	48.8	48.9	49.1	48.9	48.1	47.5	48.0	49.6	50.6	50.7	50.4	49.0
2008	49.2	51.1	51.2	51.1	50.4	49.9	49.5	49.7	51.2	52.3	52.3	52.1	50.8
2009	51.4	52.6	52.7	52.8	52.4	52.0	51.1	51.5	52.7	53.3	53.4	53.3	52.4
Leisure and Hospitality													
1990	15.5	15.6	15.7	15.7	16.1	16.1	16.0	15.8	16.0	15.4	15.0	14.9	15.7
2000	17.4	17.6	18.0	18.3	18.8	19.2	18.9	19.0	18.9	19.0	18.2	18.7	18.5
2001	18.0	17.9	18.2	18.0	19.2	19.9	19.7	19.6	19.4	19.4	19.0	18.7	19.0
2002	18.6	18.5	18.6	19.4	20.3	20.7	20.6	20.9	20.8	21.0	20.6	20.9	20.1
2003	20.0	19.7	19.9	20.1	21.6	21.5	22.0	21.9	21.7	22.1	21.5	21.5	21.1
2004	20.2	20.1	20.4	21.3	22.3	22.7	22.2	22.2	22.0	21.6	21.0	21.1	21.4
2005	20.2	20.1	20.3	21.2	21.9	22.2	22.1	21.9	21.5	20.9	20.5	20.7	21.1
2006	20.1	19.9	20.2	21.1	21.7	22.7	22.4	22.4	22.0	21.7	21.3	21.5	21.4
2007	20.8	20.9	21.2	21.4	22.3	23.0	22.3	22.7	21.8	21.8	21.3	20.9	21.7
2008	20.7	20.8	20.8	21.5	22.5	22.9	22.3	22.6	22.0	21.7	20.6	20.5	21.6
2009	19.9	19.9	20.0	20.8	21.9	21.9	21.6	21.4	21.2	21.2	20.3	20.2	20.9
Other Services													
1990	9.2	9.3	9.3	9.2	9.2	9.2	9.0	8.9	8.8	8.8	8.8	8.8	9.0
2000	8.2	8.3	8.3	8.3	8.4	8.6	8.6	8.7	8.5	8.6	8.6	8.7	8.5
2001	8.6	8.7	8.6	8.5	8.6	8.8	9.0	8.9	8.7	8.8	8.8	8.8	8.7
2002	8.8	8.8	8.8	8.7	8.8	8.9	8.7	8.9	8.5	8.6	8.6	8.7	8.7
2003	8.7	8.7	8.7	8.7	8.8	9.0	9.4	9.3	8.8	8.9	9.0	9.0	8.9
2004	8.9	9.0	9.0	8.9	9.0	9.1	9.4	9.4	8.9	8.9	8.9	8.9	9.0
2005	8.9	9.0	9.0	9.1	9.0	9.1	9.5	9.4	9.2	9.1	9.1	9.2	9.1
2006	9.1	9.0	9.1	9.1	9.1	9.3	9.4	9.4	9.1	8.9	9.0	9.1	9.1
2007	9.0	9.0	9.0	9.0	9.1	9.4	9.5	9.5	9.1	9.0	9.1	9.0	9.1
2008	8.9	8.9	9.0	8.8	8.9	8.9	9.1	8.9	8.5	8.5	8.4	8.3	8.8
2009	8.2	8.3	8.3	8.3	8.5	8.5	8.7	8.6	8.4	8.4	8.3	8.3	8.4
Government													
1990	29.8	29.9	29.8	30.0	30.3	29.5	27.8	28.3	28.9	30.1	30.1	30.1	29.6
2000	34.2	34.5	35.0	35.0	35.8	35.4	33.4	32.6	34.8	35.7	35.8	35.9	34.8
2001	35.3	35.7	35.7	35.9	36.5	36.4	34.3	32.8	35.6	36.1	36.4	36.7	35.6
2002	36.0	36.4	36.3	36.5	36.9	36.5	33.5	32.8	35.9	36.1	36.5	36.5	35.8
2003	35.7	36.0	36.2	36.0	36.2	36.2	33.6	33.0	36.0	35.7	35.5	36.1	35.5
2004	35.1	35.5	35.9	36.1	36.1	35.7	33.3	33.0	36.0	36.4	36.7	36.9	35.6
2005	36.1	36.7	36.4	36.3	36.6	36.4	33.1	32.2	35.6	36.8	36.9	36.9	35.8
2006	36.6	36.6	36.8	37.1	37.4	36.8	33.5	33.5	36.6	37.4	37.8	37.7	36.5
2007	37.0	37.4	37.4	37.6	38.2	37.8	34.1	33.7	37.0	37.7	38.0	38.1	37.0
2008	37.2	37.7	37.8	37.8	38.0	37.2	34.3	33.7	36.9	37.8	37.8	37.6	37.0
2009	37.3	37.9	38.0	38.2	38.1	37.5	34.4	34.1	36.7	37.3	37.5	37.9	37.1

APPENDIX

METROPOLITAN STATISTICAL AREAS (MSAS) AND COMPONENTS

Akron, OH
Portage County, OH
Summit County, OH

Albany-Schenectady-Troy, NY
Albany County, NY
Rensselaer County, NY
Saratoga County, NY
Schenectady County, NY
Schoharie County, NY

Albuquerque, NM
Bernalillo County, NM
Sandoval County, NM
Torrance County, NM
Valencia County, NM

Allentown-Bethlehem-Easton, PA-NJ
Warren County, NJ
Carbon County, PA
Lehigh County, PA
Northampton County, PA

Atlanta-Sandy Springs-Marietta, GA
Barrow County, GA
Bartow County, GA
Butts County, GA
Carroll County, GA
Cherokee County, GA
Clayton County, GA
Cobb County, GA
Coweta County, GA
Dawson County, GA
DeKalb County, GA
Douglas County, GA
Fayette County, GA
Forsyth County, GA
Fulton County, GA
Gwinnett County, GA
Haralson County, GA
Heard County, GA
Henry County, GA
Jasper County, GA
Lamar County, GA
Meriwether County, GA
Newton County, GA
Paulding County, GA
Pickens County, GA
Pike County, GA
Rockdale County, GA
Spalding County, GA
Walton County, GA

Austin-Round Rock-San Marcos, TX
Bastrop County, TX
Caldwell County, TX
Hays County, TX

Travis County, TX
Williamson County, TX

Bakersfield-Delano, CA
Kern County, CA

Baltimore-Towson, MD
Anne Arundel County, MD
Baltimore County, MD
Carroll County, MD
Harford County, MD

Baton Rouge, LA
Ascension Parish, LA
East Baton Rouge Parish, LA
East Feliciana Parish, LA
Iberville Parish, LA
Livingston Parish, LA
Pointe Coupee Parish, LA
St. Helena Parish, LA
West Baton Rouge Parish, LA
West Feliciana Parish, LA

Birmingham-Hoover, AL
Bibb County, AL
Blount County, AL
Chilton County, AL
Jefferson County, AL
St. Clair County, AL
Shelby County, AL
Walker County, AL

Boston-Cambridge-Quincy, MA-NH, NECTA
Boston-Cambridge-Quincy, MA, NECTA Division
    Acton town, MA
    Andover town, MA
    Arlington town, MA
    Ayer town, MA
    Bedford town, MA
    Belmont town, MA
    Beverly city, MA
    Bolton town, MA
    Boston city, MA
    Boxborough town, MA
    Boxford town, MA
    Braintree town, MA
    Brookline town, MA
    Burlington town, MA
    Cambridge city, MA
    Canton town, MA
    Carlisle town, MA
    Carver town, MA
    Chelsea city, MA
    Cohasset town, MA
    Concord town, MA
    Dedham town, MA
    Dover town, MA

Duxbury town, MA
Essex town, MA
Everett city, MA
Foxborough town, MA
Franklin city, MA
Gloucester city, MA
Groton town, MA
Hamilton town, MA
Hanover town, MA
Harvard town, MA
Hingham town, MA
Holbrook town, MA
Hull town, MA
Ipswich town, MA
Kingston town, MA
Lexington town, MA
Lincoln town, MA
Littleton town, MA
Lynnfield town, MA
Malden city, MA
Manchester-by-the-Sea town, MA
Mansfield town, MA
Marshfield town, MA
Maynard town, MA
Medfield town, MA
Medford city, MA
Medway town, MA
Melrose city, MA
Middleton town, MA
Millis town, MA
Milton town, MA
Needham town, MA
Newbury town, MA
Newburyport city, MA
Newton city, MA
Norfolk town, MA
North Reading town, MA
Norwell town, MA
Norwood town, MA
Pembroke town, MA
Plymouth town, MA
Quincy city, MA
Randolph town, MA
Reading town, MA
Revere city, MA
Rockland town, MA
Rockport town, MA
Rowley town, MA
Saugus town, MA
Scituate town, MA
Sharon town, MA
Sherborn town, MA
Shirley town, MA
Somerville city, MA
Stoneham town, MA
Stoughton town, MA
Stow town, MA
Sudbury town, MA
Topsfield town, MA
Wakefield town, MA
Walpole town, MA
Waltham city, MA

Watertown city, MA
Wayland town, MA
Wellesley town, MA
Wenham town, MA
Weston town, MA
Westwood town, MA
Weymouth town, MA
Wilmington town, MA
Winchester town, MA
Winthrop town, MA
Woburn city, MA
Wrentham town, MA
Brockton-Bridgewater-Easton, MA, NECTA Division
Abington town, MA
Avon town, MA
Bridgewater town, MA
Brockton city, MA
East Bridgewater town, MA
Easton town, MA
Halifax town, MA
Hanson town, MA
Middleborough town, MA
Plympton town, MA
West Bridgewater town, MA
Whitman town, MA
Framingham, MA, NECTA Division
Ashland town, MA
Berlin town, MA
Framingham town, MA
Holliston town, MA
Hopedale town, MA
Hopkinton town, MA
Hudson town, MA
Marlborough city, MA
Mendon town, MA
Milford town, MA
Natick town, MA
Southborough town, MA
Upton town, MA
Haverhill-North Andover-Amesbury, MA-NH, NECTA Division
Amesbury town, MA
Georgetown town, MA
Groveland town, MA
Haverhill city, MA
Merrimac town, MA
North Andover town, MA
Salisbury town, MA
West Newbury town, MA
Atkinson town, NH
Brentwood town, NH
Danville town, NH
East Kingston town, NH
Epping town, NH
Exeter town, NH
Fremont town, NH
Hampstead town, NH
Hampton Falls town, NH
Kensington town, NH
Kingston town, NH
Newfields town, NH
Newton town, NH

Plaistow town, NH
Sandown town, NH
Seabrook town, NH
South Hampton town, NH
Lawrence-Methuen-Salem, MA-NH, NECTA Division
    Lawrence city, MA
    Methuen city, MA
    Salem town, NH
Lowell-Billerica-Chelmsford, MA-NH, NECTA Division
    Billerica town, NH
    Chelmsford town, MA
    Dracut town, MA
    Dunstable town, MA
    Lowell city, MA
    Tewksbury town, MA
    Tyngsborough town, MA
    Westford town, MA
    Pelham town, NH
Nashua, NH-MA, NECTA Division
    Pepperell town, MA
    Townsend town, MA
    Amherst town, NH
    Brookline town, NH
    Chester town, NH
    Derry town, NH
    Greenfield town, NH
    Greenville town, NH
    Hollis town, NH
    Hudson town, NH
    Litchfield town, NH
    Londonderry town, NH
    Lyndeborough town, NH
    Mason town, NH
    Merrimack town, NH
    Milford town, NH
    Mont Vernon town, NH
    Nashua city, NH
    Raymond town, NH
    Wilton town, NH
    Windham town, NH
Peabody, MA, NECTA Division
    Danvers town, MA
    Lynn city, MA
    Marblehead town, MA
    Nahant town, MA
    Peabody city, MA
    Salem city, MA
    Swampscott town, MA
Taunton-Norton-Raynham, MA, NECTA Division
    Berkley town, MA
    Dighton town, MA
    Norton town, MA
    Raynham town, MA
    Taunton city, MA

Bridgeport-Stamford-Norwalk, CT, NECTA
Ansonia city and town, CT
Bridgeport city and town, CT
Darien town, CT
Derby city and town, CT
Easton town, CT
Fairfield town, CT

Greenwich town, CT
Milford city and town, CT
Monroe town, CT
New Canaan town, CT
Newtown town, CT
Norwalk city and town, CT
Oxford town, CT
Redding town, CT
Ridgefield town, CT
Seymour town, CT
Shelton city and town, CT
Southbury town, CT
Stamford city and town, CT
Stratford town, CT
Trumbull town, CT
Weston town, CT
Westport town, CT
Wilton town, CT
Woodbridge town, CT

Buffalo-Niagara Falls, NY
Erie County, NY
Niagara County, NY

Charlotte-Gastonia-Concord, NC-SC
Anson County, NC
Cabarrus County, NC
Gaston County, NC
Mecklenburg County, NC
Union County, NC
York County, SC

Chicago-Naperville-Joliet, IL-IN-WI
Chicago-Naperville-Joliet, IL, Metropolitan Division
    Cook County, IL
    DeKalb County, IL
    DuPage County, IL
    Grundy County, IL
    Kane County, IL
    Kendall County, IL
    McHenry County, IL
    Will County, IL
Gary, IN, Metropolitan Division
    Jasper County, IN
    Lake County, IN
    Newton County, IN
    Porter County, IN
Lake County-Kenosha County, IL-WI, Metropolitan Division
    Lake County, IL
    Kenosha County, WI

Cincinnati-Middletown, OH-KY-IN
Dearborn County, IN
Franklin County, IN
Ohio County, IN
Boone County, KY
Bracken County, KY
Campbell County, KY
Gallatin County, KY
Grant County, KY
Kenton County, KY

Pendleton County, KY
Brown County, OH
Butler County, OH
Clermont County, OH
Hamilton County, OH
Warren County, OH

Cleveland-Elyria-Mentor, OH
Cuyahoga County, OH
Geauga County, OH
Lake County, OH
Lorain County, OH
Medina County, OH

Columbia, SC
Calhoun County, SC
Fairfield County, SC
Kershaw County, SC
Lexington County, SC
Richland County, SC
Saluda County, SC

Columbus, OH
Delaware County, OH
Fairfield County, OH
Franklin County, OH
Licking County, OH
Madison County, OH
Morrow County, OH
Pickaway County, OH
Union County, OH

Dallas-Fort Worth-Arlington, TX
Dallas-Plano-Irving, TX, Metropolitan Division
        Collin County, TX
        Dallas County, TX
        Delta County, TX
        Denton County, TX
        Ellis County, TX
        Hunt County, TX
        Kaufman County, TX
        Rockwall County, TX
Fort Worth-Arlington, TX, Metropolitan Division
        Johnson County, TX
        Parker County, TX
        Tarrant County, TX
        Wise County, TX

Dayton, OH
Greene County, OH
Miami County, OH
Montgomery County, OH
Preble County, OH

Denver-Aurora-Broomfield, CO
Adams County, CO
Arapahoe County, CO
Broomfield County, CO
Clear Creek County, CO
Denver County, CO
Douglas County, CO
Elbert County, CO

Gilpin County, CO
Jefferson County, CO
Park County, CO

Detroit-Warren-Livonia, MI
Detroit-Livonia-Dearborn, MI, Metropolitan Division
        Wayne County, MI
Warren-Troy-Farmington Hills, MI, Metropolitan Division
        Lapeer County, MI
        Livingston County, MI
        Macomb County, MI
        Oakland County, MI
        St. Clair County, MI

El Paso, TX
El Paso County, TX

Fresno, CA
Fresno County, CA

Grand Rapids-Wyoming, MI
Barry County, MI
Ionia County, MI
Kent County, MI
Newaygo County, MI

Greensboro-High Point, NC
Guilford County, NC
Randolph County, NC
Rockingham County, NC

Hartford-West Hartford-East Hartford, CT, NECTA
Andover town, CT
Ashford town, CT
Avon town, CT
Barkhamsted town, CT
Berlin town, CT
Bloomfield town, CT
Bolton town, CT
Bristol city and town, CT
Burlington town, CT
Canton town, CT
Colchester town, CT
Columbia town, CT
Coventry town, CT
Cromwell town, CT
East Granby town, CT
East Haddam town, CT
East Hampton town, CT
East Hartford town, CT
Ellington town, CT
Farmington town, CT
Glastonbury town, CT
Granby town, CT
Haddam town, CT
Hartford city and town, CT
Hartland town, CT
Harwinton town, CT
Hebron town, CT
Lebanon town, CT
Manchester town, CT

Mansfield town, CT
Marlborough town, CT
Middlefield town, CT
Middletown city and town, CT
New Britain city and town, CT
New Hartford town, CT
Newington town, CT
Plainville town, CT
Plymouth town, CT
Portland town, CT
Rocky Hill town, CT
Simsbury town, CT
South Windsor town, CT
Southington town, CT
Stafford town, CT
Thomaston town, CT
Tolland town, CT
Union town, CT
Vernon town, CT
West Hartford town, CT
Wethersfield town, CT
Willington town, CT
Windsor town, CT

Honolulu, HI
Honolulu County, HI

Houston-Sugar Land-Baytown, TX
Austin County, TX
Brazoria County, TX
Chambers County, TX
Fort Bend County, TX
Galveston County, TX
Harris County, TX
Liberty County, TX
Montgomery County, TX
San Jacinto County, TX
Waller County, TX

Indianapolis-Carmel, IN
Boone County, IN
Brown County, IN
Hamilton County, IN
Hancock County, IN
Hendricks County, IN
Johnson County, IN
Marion County, IN
Morgan County, IN
Putnam County, IN
Shelby County, IN

Jacksonville, FL
Baker County, FL
Clay County, FL
Duval County, FL
Nassau County, FL
St. Johns County, FL

Kansas City, MO-KS
Franklin County, KS
Johnson County, KS
Leavenworth County, KS

Linn County, KS
Miami County, KS
Wyandotte County, KS
Bates County, MO
Caldwell County, MO
Cass County, MO
Clay County, MO
Clinton County, MO
Jackson County, MO
Lafayette County, MO
Platte County, MO
Ray County, MO

Knoxville, TN
Anderson County, TN
Blount County, TN
Knox County, TN
Loudon County, TN
Union County, TN

Las Vegas-Paradise, NV
Clark County, NV

Los Angeles-Long Beach-Santa Ana, CA
Los Angeles-Long Beach-Glendale, CA, Metropolitan
Division
Los Angeles County, CA
Santa Ana-Anaheim-Irvine, CA, Metropolitan Division
Orange County, CA

Louisville-Jefferson County, KY-IN
Clark County, IN
Floyd County, IN
Harrison County, IN
Washington County, IN
Bullitt County, KY
Henry County, KY
Jefferson County, KY
Meade County, KY
Nelson County, KY
Oldham County, KY
Shelby County, KY
Spencer County, KY
Trimble County, KY

McAllen-Edinburg-Mission, TX
Hidalgo County, TX

Memphis, TN-MS-AR
Crittenden County, AR
DeSoto County, MS
Marshall County, MS
Tate County, MS
Tunica County, MS
Fayette County, TN
Shelby County, TN
Tipton County, TN

Miami-Fort Lauderdale-Pompano Beach, FL
Fort Lauderdale-Pompano Beach-Deerfield Beach, FL,
Metropolitan Division
Broward County, FL

Miami-Miami Beach-Kendall, FL, Metropolitan Division
        Miami-Dade County, FL
West Palm Beach-Boca Raton-Boynton Beach, FL, Metropolitan Division
        Palm Beach County, FL

Milwaukee-Waukesha-West Allis, WI
Milwaukee County, WI
Ozaukee County, WI
Washington County, WI
Waukesha County, WI

Minneapolis-St. Paul-Bloomington, MN-WI
Anoka County, MN
Carver County, MN
Chisago County, MN
Dakota County, MN
Hennepin County, MN
Isanti County, MN
Ramsey County, MN
Scott County, MN
Sherburne County, MN
Washington County, MN
Wright County, MN
Pierce County, WI
St. Croix County, WI

Nashville-Davidson–Murfreesboro–Franklin, TN
Cannon County, TN
Cheatham County, TN
Davidson County, TN
Dickson County, TN
Hickman County, TN
Macon County, TN
Robertson County, TN
Rutherford County, TN
Smith County, TN
Sumner County, TN
Trousdale County, TN
Williamson County, TN
Wilson County, TN

New Haven, CT, NECTA
Bethany town, CT
Branford town, CT
Cheshire town, CT
Chester town, CT
Clinton town, CT
Deep River town, CT
Durham town, CT
East Haven town, CT
Essex town, CT
Guilford town, CT
Hamden town, CT
Killingworth town, CT
Madison town, CT
Meriden city and town, CT
New Haven city and town, CT
North Branford town, CT
North Haven town, CT
Old Saybrook town, CT
Orange town, CT

Wallingford town, CT
West Haven city and town, CT
Westbrook town, CT

New Orleans-Metairie-Kenner, LA
Jefferson Parish, LA
Orleans Parish, LA
Plaquemines Parish, LA
St. Bernard Parish, LA
St. Charles Parish, LA
St. John the Baptist Parish, LA
St. Tammany Parish, LA

New York-Northern New Jersey-Long Island, NY-NJ-PA
Edison, NJ, Metropolitan Division
        Middlesex County, NJ
        Monmouth County, NJ
        Ocean County, NJ
        Somerset County, NJ
Nassau-Suffolk, NY, Metropolitan Division
        Nassau County, NY
        Suffolk County, NY
New York-White Plains-Wayne, NY-NJ, Metropolitan Division
        Bergen County, NJ
        Hudson County, NJ
        Passaic County, NJ
        Bronx County, NY
        Kings County, NY
        New York County, NY
        Putnam County, NY
        Queens County, NY
        Richmond County, NY
        Rockland County, NY
        Westchester County, NY
Newark-Union, NJ-PA, Metropolitan Division
        Essex County, NJ
        Hunterdon County, NJ
        Morris County, NJ
        Sussex County, NJ
        Union County, NJ
        Pike County, PA

North Port-Bradenton-Sarasota, FL
Manatee County, FL
Sarasota County, FL

Oklahoma City, OK
Canadian County, OK
Cleveland County, OK
Grady County, OK
Lincoln County, OK
Logan County, OK
McClain County, OK
Oklahoma County, OK

Omaha-Council Bluffs, NE-IA
Harrison County, IA
Mills County, IA
Pottawattamie County, IA
Cass County, NE
Douglas County, NE

Sarpy County, NE
Saunders County, NE
Washington County, NE

Orlando-Kissimmee, FL
Lake County, FL
Orange County, FL
Osceola County, FL
Seminole County, FL

Oxnard-Thousand Oaks-Ventura, CA
Ventura County, CA

Philadelphia-Camden-Wilmington, PA-NJ-DE-MD
Camden, NJ, Metropolitan Division
        Burlington County, NJ
        Camden County, NJ
        Gloucester County, NJ
Philadelphia, PA, Metropolitan Division
        Bucks County, PA
        Chester County, PA
        Delaware County, PA
        Montgomery County, PA
        Philadelphia County, PA
Wilmington, DE-MD-NJ, Metropolitan Division
        New Castle County, DE
        Cecil County, MD
        Salem County, NJ

Phoenix-Mesa-Scottsdale, AZ
Maricopa County, AZ
Pinal County, AZ

Pittsburgh, PA
Allegheny County, PA
Armstrong County, PA
Beaver County, PA
Butler County, PA
Fayette County, PA
Washington County, PA
Westmoreland County, PA

Portland-Vancouver-Beaverton, OR-WA
Clackamas County, OR
Columbia County, OR
Multnomah County, OR
Washington County, OR
Yamhill County, OR
Clark County, WA
Skamania County, WA

Providence-Fall River-Warwick, RI-MA, NECTA
Attleboro city, MA
Bellingham town, MA
Blackstone town, MA
Fall River city, MA
Millville town, MA
North Attleborough town, MA
Plainville town, MA
Rehoboth town, MA
Seekonk town, MA
Somerset town, MA

Swansea town, MA
Westport town, MA
Barrington town, RI
Bristol town, RI
Burrillville town, RI
Central Falls city, RI
Charlestown town, RI
Coventry town, RI
Cranston city, RI
Cumberland town, RI
East Greenwich town, RI
East Providence city, RI
Exeter town, RI
Foster town, RI
Glocester town, RI
Hopkinton town, RI
Jamestown town, RI
Johnston town, RI
Lincoln town, RI
Little Compton town, RI
Middletown town, RI
Narragansett town, RI
Newport city, RI
North Kingstown town, RI
North Providence town, RI
North Smithfield town, RI
Pawtucket city, RI
Portsmouth town, RI
Providence city, RI
Richmond town, RI
Scituate town, RI
Smithfield town, RI
South Kingstown town, RI
Tiverton town, RI
Warren town, RI
Warwick city, RI
West Greenwich town, RI
West Warwick town, RI
Woonsocket city, RI

Raleigh-Cary, NC
Franklin County, NC
Johnston County, NC
Wake County, NC

Richmond, VA
Amelia County, VA
Caroline County, VA
Charles City County, VA
Chesterfield County, VA
Cumberland County, VA
Dinwiddie County, VA
Goochland County, VA
Hanover County, VA
Henrico County, VA
King and Queen County, VA
King William County, VA
Louisa County, VA
New Kent County, VA
Powhatan County, VA
Prince George County, VA
Sussex County, VA

Colonial Heights city, VA
Hopewell city, VA
Petersburg city, VA
Richmond city, VA

Riverside-San Bernardino-Ontario, CA
Riverside County, CA
San Bernardino County, CA

Rochester, NY
Livingston County, NY
Monroe County, NY
Ontario County, NY
Orleans County, NY
Wayne County, NY

Sacramento–Arden-Arcade–Roseville, CA
El Dorado County, CA
Placer County, CA
Sacramento County, CA
Yolo County, CA

Salt Lake City, UT
Salt Lake County, UT
Summit County, UT
Tooele County, UT

San Antonio, TX
Atascosa County, TX
Bandera County, TX
Bexar County, TX
Comal County, TX
Guadalupe County, TX
Kendall County, TX
Medina County, TX
Wilson County, TX

San Diego-Carlsbad-San Marcos, CA
San Diego County, CA

San Francisco-Oakland-Fremont, CA
Oakland-Fremont-Hayward, CA, Metropolitan Division
        Alameda County, CA
        Contra Costa County, CA
San Francisco-San Mateo-Redwood City, CA, Metropolitan Division
        Marin County, CA
        San Francisco County, CA
        San Mateo County, CA

San Jose-Sunnyvale-Santa Clara, CA
        San Benito County, CA
        Santa Clara County, CA

Seattle-Tacoma-Bellevue, WA
Seattle-Bellevue-Everett, WA, Metropolitan Division
        King County, WA
        Snohomish County, WA
Tacoma, WA, Metropolitan Division
        Pierce County, WA

Springfield, MA-CT, NECTA
Agawam city, MA
Ashfield town, MA
Belchertown town, MA
Blandford town, MA
Brimfield town, MA
Chester town, MA
Chesterfield town, MA
Chicopee city, MA
Cummington town, MA
Deerfield town, MA
East Longmeadow town, MA
Easthampton city, MA
Goshen town, MA
Granby town, MA
Granville town, MA
Hadley town, MA
Hampden town, MA
Hatfield town, MA
Holyoke city, MA
Huntington town, MA
Longmeadow town, MA
Ludlow town, MA
Middlefield town, MA
Monson town, MA
Montgomery town, MA
Northampton city, MA
Palmer town, MA
Plainfield town, MA
Russell town, MA
South Hadley town, MA
Southampton town, MA
Southwick town, MA
Springfield city, MA
Tolland town, MA
Wales town, MA
Ware town, MA
West Springfield town, MA
Westfield city, MA
Westhampton town, MA
Whately town, MA
Wilbraham town, MA
Williamsburg town, MA
Worthington town, MA
East Windsor town, CT
Enfield town, CT
Somers town, CT
Suffield town, CT
Windsor Locks town, CT

St. Louis, MO-IL
Bond County, IL
Calhoun County, IL
Clinton County, IL
Jersey County, IL
Macoupin County, IL
Madison County, IL
Monroe County, IL
St. Clair County, IL

Crawford County, MO[1]
Franklin County, MO
Jefferson County, MO
Lincoln County, MO
St. Louis County, MO
Warren County, MO
Washington County, MO
St. Louis city, MO

Tampa-St. Petersburg-Clearwater, FL
Hernando County, FL
Hillsborough County, FL
Pasco County, FL
Pinellas County, FL

Tucson, AZ
Pima County, AZ

Tulsa, OK
Creek County, OK
Okmulgee County, OK
Osage County, OK
Pawnee County, OK
Rogers County, OK
Tulsa County, OK
Wagoner County, OK

Virginia Beach-Norfolk-Newport News, VA-NC
Currituck County, NC
Gloucester County, VA
Isle of Wight County, VA
James City County, VA
Mathews County, VA
Surry County, VA
York County, VA
Chesapeake city, VA
Hampton city, VA
Newport News city, VA
Norfolk city, VA
Poquoson city, VA
Portsmouth city, VA
Suffolk city, VA
Virginia Beach city, VA
Williamsburg city, VA

Washington-Arlington-Alexandria, DC-VA-MD-WV
Bethesda-Gaithersburg-Frederick, MD, Metropolitan
Division
    Frederick County, MD
    Montgomery County, MD
Washington-Arlington-Alexandria, DC-VA-MD-WV,
Metropolitan Division
    District of Columbia, DC
    Calvert County, MD
    Charles County, MD
    Prince George's County, MD
    Arlington County, VA

Clarke County, VA
Fairfax County, VA
Fauquier County, VA
Loudoun County, VA
Prince William County, VA
Spotsylvania County, VA
Stafford County, VA
Warren County, VA
Alexandria city, VA
Fairfax city, VA
Falls Church city, VA
Fredericksburg city, VA
Manassas city, VA
Manassas Park city, VA
Jefferson County, WV

Worcester, MA-CT, NECTA
Auburn town, MA
Barre town, MA
Boylston town, MA
Brookfield town, MA
Charlton town, MA
Clinton town, MA
Douglas town, MA
Dudley town, MA
East Brookfield town, MA
Grafton town, MA
Holden town, MA
Holland town, MA
Hubbardston town, MA
Lancaster town, MA
Leicester town, MA
Millbury town, MA
New Braintree town, MA
North Brookfield town, MA
Northborough town, MA
Northbridge town, MA
Oakham town, MA
Oxford town, MA
Paxton town, MA
Princeton town, MA
Putnam town, CT
Rutland town, MA
Shrewsbury town, MA
Southbridge town, MA
Spencer town, MA
Sterling town, MA
Sturbridge town, MA
Sutton town, MA
Thompson town, CT
Uxbridge town, MA
Webster town, MA
West Boylston town, MA
West Brookfield town, MA
Westborough town, MA
Woodstock town, CT
Worcester city, MA

[1]The portion of Sullivan city in Crawford County, Missouri, is legally part of the St. Louis, MO-IL, MSA. Census 2000 tabulations and intercensal estimates for the St. Louis, MO-IL, MSA do not include this area.